rma

ANNUAL STATEMENT STUDIES

1995

fiscal year ends 4/1/94 through 3/31/95

including comparative historical
data and other sources of composite
financial data

ROBERT MORRIS ASSOCIATES

The Association of Lending and Credit Risk Professionals
One Liberty Place, Suite 2300, Philadelphia, PA 19103-7398
(800) 677-7621 • FAX (215) 851-9206

Interpretation of Statement Studies Figures

RMA recommends that Statement Studies data be regarded only as general guidelines and not as absolute industry norms. There are several reasons why the data may not be fully representative of a given industry:

(1) The financial statements used in the *Statement Studies* are not selected by any random or statistically reliable method. RMA member banks voluntarily submit the raw data they have available each year provided that the companies' total assets are less than $250 million, except for contractors' statements which have no upper size limit.

(2) Many companies have varied product lines; however, the *Statement Studies* categorize them by their primary product Standard Industrial Classification (SIC) number only.

(3) Some of our industry samples are rather small in relation to the total number of firms in a given industry. A relatively small sample can increase the chances that some of our composites do not fully represent an industry.

(4) There is the chance that an extreme statement can be present in a sample, causing a disproportionate influence on the industry composite. This is particularly true in a relatively small sample.

(5) Companies within the same industry may differ in their method of operations which in turn can directly influence their financial statements. Since they are included in our sample, too, these statements can significantly affect our composite calculations.

(6) Other considerations that can result in variations among different companies engaged in the same general line of business are different labor markets; geographical location; different accounting methods; quality of products handled; sources and methods of financing; and terms of sale.

For these reasons, RMA does not recommend the Statement Studies *figures be considered as absolute norms for a given industry. Rather the figures should be used only as general guidelines and in addition to the other methods of financial analysis. RMA makes no claim as to the representativeness of the figures printed in this book.*

Robert Morris Associates
One Liberty Place
Philadelphia, PA 19103

© 1995 by Robert Morris Associates

ISBN 1-57070-012-5

CAUTION

Printed in U.S.A.

TABLE OF CONTENTS

ABOUT ROBERT MORRIS ASSOCIATES

Robert Morris Associates (RMA) is the association of lending and credit risk professionals. Founded in 1914, RMA has grown to nearly 3,000 commercial banks and thrift institutions, which account for almost 80% of the C & I lending done by these types of U.S. financial institutions. RMA members are represented in the association by more than 16,000 commercial loan and credit officers and related personnel in all 50 states, Puerto Rico, Canada, and several offshore cities.

RMA was named after the American patriot who signed the Declaration of Independence, was largely responsible for the financing of our Revolutionary War, and helped establish our banking system.

The association's original purpose back in 1914 was to facilitate the flow and interchange of credit information. Today, this purpose has been expanded to include working continuously to improve the principles and practices of commercial lending, loan administration, and other related areas in its members and institutions comprising the financial services industry.

RMA seeks to fulfill its purpose by providing commercial bankers with programs, products, and services they need to increase their proficiency in lending, credit, and related areas. RMA's reason for being, then, is to provide these bankers with the tools they need to make better loans, keep abreast of the continual changes that affect the lending function, and, at the bottom line, help them increase the profitability of their institutions.

INTRODUCTION

Robert Morris Associates, the association of lending and credit risk professionals, is proud to publish this 73rd edition of the *Annual Statement Studies*. This publication is made possible through the voluntary cooperation of RMA's member institutions, and is a product of the commercial lending community.

The *Statement Studies* contains composite financial data on manufacturing, wholesaling, retailing, service, agricultural and contracting lines of business. Financial statements on each industry are shown in common size form, and are accompanied by widely used ratios.

PART I, II and III (pages 51, 379, and 501)

In Parts I through III, data for a particular industry appear on both the right- and left-hand pages. The heading Current Data Sorted By Assets is on the far left. The center section of the double page presentation contains the Comparative Historical Data, with the All Sizes column for the current year shown under the heading 4/1/94–3/31/95. Comparable data from past editions of the *Annual Statement Studies* also appear in this section. To the far right is the display Current Data Sorted By Sales.

Except for the contractor section (Part IV), only companies having less than $250 million in total assets were used in our calculations, regardless of the way the data were sorted. The contractor section contains only Data Sorted By Revenue, the same as it appeared in previous editions.

The information shown at the top of each page includes the identity of the industry group; its Standard Industrial Classification (SIC) number; a breakdown by size categories of the types of financial statements reported; the number of statements in each category; the dates of the statements used; and the size categories. Although abbreviated, the information is understandable. For instance, 16 (4/1-9/30/94) means that 16 statements with fiscal dates between April 1 and September 30, 1994, make up part of the sample. The number of statements with fiscal dates falling between October 1, 1994 and March 31, 1995 are shown in the same manner.

Information appears at the top of each page on the number of statements reflecting postretirement benefit costs. Financial Accounting Standards Board Statement of Financial Accounting Standards (SFAS) No. 106, "Employers' Accounting for Post-retirement Benefits Other Than Pensions," now requires employers' statements effective December 15, 1992, to account for postretirement benefits other than pensions. The effect of SFAS No. 109, "Accounting for Income Taxes," allowing recognition of deferred tax benefits, is immaterial for Statement Studies purposes.

When there are fewer than 10 financial statements in a particular size category, the composite data are not shown because such a small sample is not considered representative and could be misleading. However, all the data for that industry are shown in the All Sizes column. The total number of statements for each size category is shown in bold print at the top of each page.

At the bottom of each page, the sum of the sales (or revenues) and total assets for all the financial statements in each size category are shown. These data are provided to allow recasting the common size statements into dollar amounts. To do this, divide the number at the bottom of the page by the number of statements in that size category. Then multiply the result by the percentages in the common size statement.

Balance sheets and income statements are shown in common size, with each item a percentage of total assets and sales (or revenues), respectively. Common size statements are computed for each individual statement in an industry group, then all the figures are added and averaged. In some cases, the figures to the right of the decimal point do not balance exactly with the totals shown because of computer rounding. Credits and losses are indicated by a minus sign beside the value.

The ratio section is described in detail starting on page 9.

PART IV (page 867)

This section includes only statements on contractors. Size categories are determined only by contract revenues with no upper limit placed on revenue size. Only companies reporting on a percentage-of-completion basis have been included in our sample. Comparative Historical Data are also shown. It includes data for the All Sizes category for the current and the previous four years.

PART V (page 889)

We appreciate the cooperation of the Construction Financial Management Association (CFMA) in permitting us to reproduce excerpts from their *Seventh Annual Construction Industry Financial Survey*. Their data complements our own contractor industry data.

PART VI (page 903)

Comparative ratios on consumer finance companies are provided in this section to assist in the analysis of that industry. These ratios were prepared by The First National Bank of Chicago. RMA is grateful to this bank for its contribution.

PART VII (page 907)

This year once again our bibliography of other sources of data has been expanded to include several new listings.

RMA thanks the Statement Studies chairpersons, analysts, and the many other people who have made this publication possible, not the least of whom are the representatives of our member institutions who submitted more than 120,500 financial statements this year.

<table>
<tr><td>William E. Corcoran
Chairman-National
Statement Studies Committee</td><td>Susan M. Kelsay, Editor
Statement Studies Manager</td></tr>
</table>

September 1995

Explanation of Noncontractor Balance Sheet and Income Data

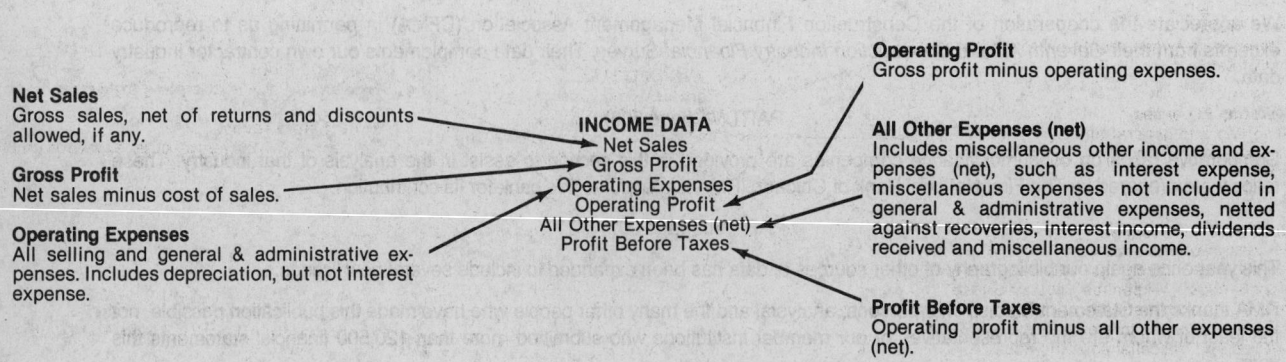

Cash & Equivalents
All cash, marketplace securities, and other near-cash items. Excludes sinking funds.

Trade Receivables—(net)
All accounts from trade, net of allowance for doubtful accounts.

Inventory
Anything constituting inventory for the firm.

All Other Current
Any other current assets. Does not include prepaid items.

Total Current
Total of all current assets listed above.

Fixed Assets (net)
All property, plant, leasehold improvements and equipment, net or accumulated depreciation or depletion.

Intangibles (net)
Intangible assets, including goodwill, trademarks, patents, catalogs, brands, copyrights, formulas, franchises, and mailing lists, net of accumulated amortization.

All Other Non-Current
Prepaid items and any other non-current assets.

Total
Total of all items listed above.

ASSETS
Cash & Equivalents
Trade Receivables (net)
Inventory
All Other Current
Total Current
Fixed Assets (net)
Intangibles (net)
All Other Non-Current
Total

Notes Payable—Short Term
All short term note obligations, including bank and commercial paper. Does not include trade notes payable.

Current Maturities—L/T/D
That portion of long term obligations which is due within the next fiscal year.

Trade Payables
Open accounts due to the trade.

Income Taxes Payable
Income taxes including current portion of deferred taxes.

All Other Current
Any other current liabilities, including bank overdrafts and accrued expenses.

Total Current
Total of all current liabilities listed above.

Long Term Debt
All senior debt, including bonds, debentures, bank debt, mortgages, deferred portions of long term debt, and capital lease obligations.

Deferred Taxes
All deferred taxes.

All Other Non-Current
Any other non-current liabilities, including subordinated debt, and liability reserves.

Net Worth
Difference between Total Liabilities and Total Assets. Minority interest is included here.

Total Liabilities & Net Worth
Total of all items listed above.

LIABILITIES
Notes Payable-Short Term
Cur. Mat.-L/T/D
Trade Payables
Income Taxes Payable
All Other Current
Total Current
Long Term Debt
Deferred Taxes
All Other Non-Current
Net Worth
Total Liabilities & Net Worth

Net Sales
Gross sales, net of returns and discounts allowed, if any.

Gross Profit
Net sales minus cost of sales.

Operating Expenses
All selling and general & administrative expenses. Includes depreciation, but not interest expense.

Operating Profit
Gross profit minus operating expenses.

All Other Expenses (net)
Includes miscellaneous other income and expenses (net), such as interest expense, miscellaneous expenses not included in general & administrative expenses, netted against recoveries, interest income, dividends received and miscellaneous income.

Profit Before Taxes
Operating profit minus all other expenses (net).

INCOME DATA
Net Sales
Gross Profit
Operating Expenses
Operating Profit
All Other Expenses (net)
Profit Before Taxes

Explanation of Contractor Balance Sheet and Income Data

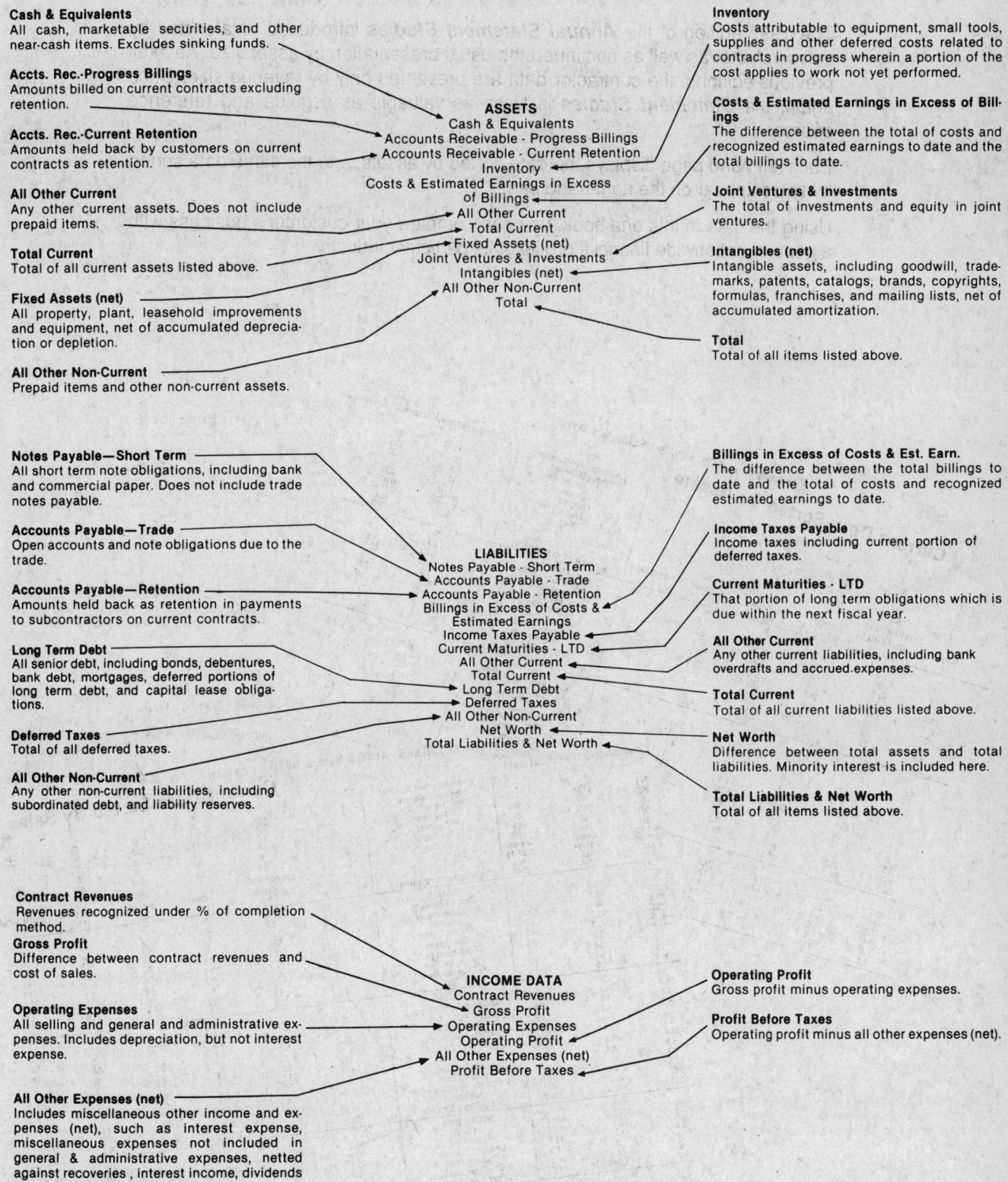

Cash & Equivalents
All cash, marketable securities, and other near-cash items. Excludes sinking funds.

Accts. Rec.-Progress Billings
Amounts billed on current contracts excluding retention.

Accts. Rec.-Current Retention
Amounts held back by customers on current contracts as retention.

All Other Current
Any other current assets. Does not include prepaid items.

Total Current
Total of all current assets listed above.

Fixed Assets (net)
All property, plant, leasehold improvements and equipment, net of accumulated depreciation or depletion.

All Other Non-Current
Prepaid items and other non-current assets.

Inventory
Costs attributable to equipment, small tools, supplies and other deferred costs related to contracts in progress wherein a portion of the cost applies to work not yet performed.

Costs & Estimated Earnings in Excess of Billings
The difference between the total of costs and recognized estimated earnings to date and the total billings to date.

Joint Ventures & Investments
The total of investments and equity in joint ventures.

Intangibles (net)
Intangible assets, including goodwill, trademarks, patents, catalogs, brands, copyrights, formulas, franchises, and mailing lists, net of accumulated amortization.

Total
Total of all items listed above.

ASSETS
Cash & Equivalents
Accounts Receivable - Progress Billings
Accounts Receivable - Current Retention
Inventory
Costs & Estimated Earnings in Excess of Billings
All Other Current
Total Current
Fixed Assets (net)
Joint Ventures & Investments
Intangibles (net)
All Other Non-Current
Total

Notes Payable—Short Term
All short term note obligations, including bank and commercial paper. Does not include trade notes payable.

Accounts Payable—Trade
Open accounts and note obligations due to the trade.

Accounts Payable—Retention
Amounts held back as retention in payments to subcontractors on current contracts.

Long Term Debt
All senior debt, including bonds, debentures, bank debt, mortgages, deferred portions of long term debt, and capital lease obligations.

Deferred Taxes
Total of all deferred taxes.

All Other Non-Current
Any other non-current liabilities, including subordinated debt, and liability reserves.

Billings in Excess of Costs & Est. Earn.
The difference between the total billings to date and the total of costs and recognized estimated earnings to date.

Income Taxes Payable
Income taxes including current portion of deferred taxes.

Current Maturities - LTD
That portion of long term obligations which is due within the next fiscal year.

All Other Current
Any other current liabilities, including bank overdrafts and accrued.expenses.

Total Current
Total of all current liabilities listed above.

Net Worth
Difference between total assets and total liabilities. Minority interest is included here.

Total Liabilities & Net Worth
Total of all items listed above.

LIABILITIES
Notes Payable - Short Term
Accounts Payable - Trade
Accounts Payable - Retention
Billings in Excess of Costs & Estimated Earnings
Income Taxes Payable
Current Maturities - LTD
All Other Current
Total Current
Long Term Debt
Deferred Taxes
All Other Non-Current
Net Worth
Total Liabilities & Net Worth

Contract Revenues
Revenues recognized under % of completion method.

Gross Profit
Difference between contract revenues and cost of sales.

Operating Expenses
All selling and general and administrative expenses. Includes depreciation, but not interest expense.

All Other Expenses (net)
Includes miscellaneous other income and expenses (net), such as interest expense, miscellaneous expenses not included in general & administrative expenses, netted against recoveries , interest income, dividends received and miscellaneous income.

Operating Profit
Gross profit minus operating expenses.

Profit Before Taxes
Operating profit minus all other expenses (net).

INCOME DATA
Contract Revenues
Gross Profit
Operating Expenses
Operating Profit
All Other Expenses (net)
Profit Before Taxes

Data Sorted By Assets *and* Sales

The 1990 edition of the *Annual Statement Studies* introduced data sorted by sales volume, as well as continued the usual presentation by asset size. As in all previous editions, the contractor data are presented only by revenue size. Once again, the *Statement Studies* is twice as valuable as a guide and reference source.

Each left-hand page displays the data sorted by assets, and the same data sorted by sales appear on the right-hand page.

Using the data in this one book, you can compare your customer's business with a general nationwide financial profile of its particular industry.

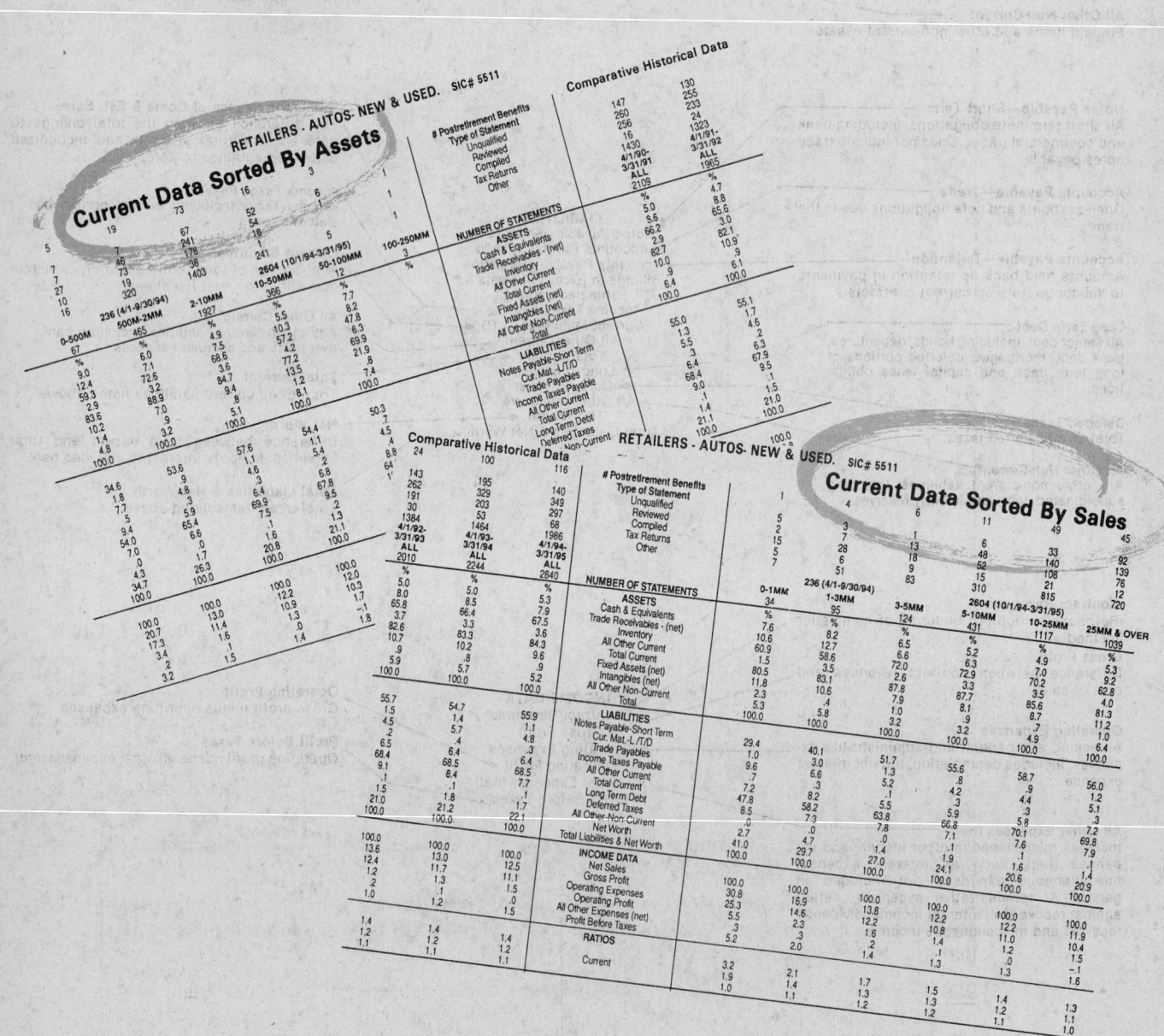

DEFINITION OF RATIOS
INTRODUCTION

Below the common size balance sheet and income statement presented on each data page are series of ratios which have been computed from the financial statement data. Each ratio has three values: the upper quartile, median, and lower quartile. For any given ratio, these figures are calculated by first computing the value of the ratio for *each* financial statement in the sample. These values are then arrayed—"listed"—in an order from the strongest to the weakest. (We acknowledge that, for certain ratios, there may be differences of opinion concerning what is a strong or a weak value. RMA has resolved this problem by following general banking guidelines consistent with sound credit practice in its presentation of data.)

The array of values are then divided into four groups of equal size. The three points that divide the array are called quartiles — upper quartile, second quartile or median, and lower quartile. The upper quartile is that point at which ¼ of the array of ratios falls between the strongest ratio and the upper quartile point. The median is the middle value and the lower quartile is that point at which ¾'s of the array falls between the strongest ratio and the lower quartile point. The median and quartile values will be shown on all *Statement Studies* data pages in the order indicated below. An actual example of the Current Ratio for the SIZE CLASS 500M-2MM SIC #2396, appearing on page 52 is also shown below for illustrative purposes.

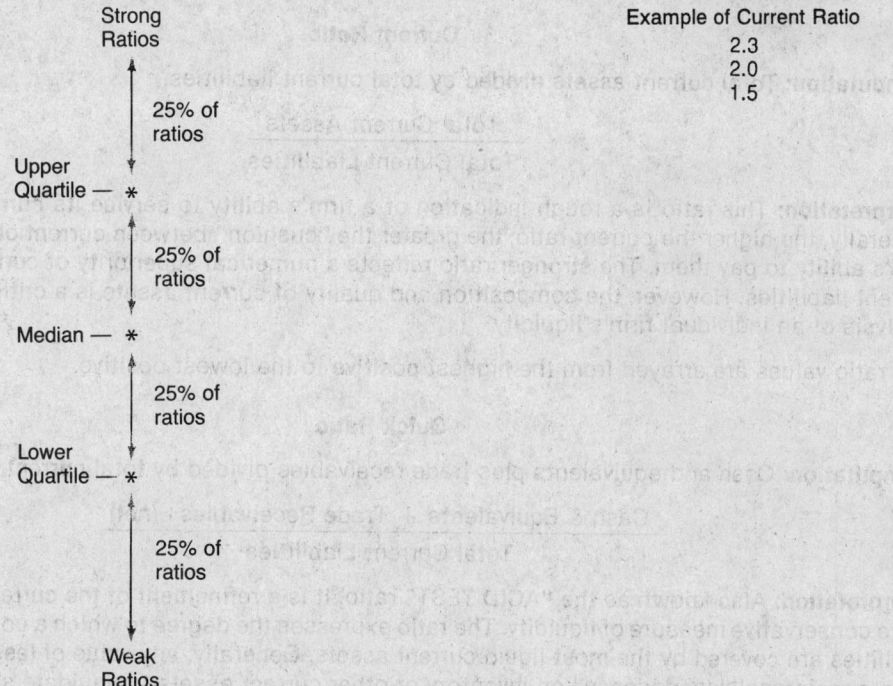

There are several reasons for using medians and quartiles instead of an average. One is to eliminate the influence which values in an "unusual" statement would have on an average. The method used more accurately reflects the ranges of ratio values than would a straight averaging method.

It is important to understand that the spread (range) between the upper and lower quartiles represents the middle 50% of all the companies in a sample. Ratio values greater than the upper or less than the lower quartiles, therefore, begin to approach "unusual" values.

For some ratio values, you will occasionally see an entry that is other than a conventional number. These unusual entries are defined as follows:

(1) *UND*—This stands for "undefined," the result of the denominator in a ratio calculation approaching zero.

(2) *NM*—This may occasionally appear as a quartile or median for the ratios sales/working capital, debt/worth, and fixed/worth. It stands for "no meaning" in cases where the dispersion is so small that any interpretation is meaningless.

(3) *999.8*—When a ratio value equals 1,000 or more, it also becomes an "unusual" value and is given the "999.8" designation. This is considered to be a close enough approximation to the actual unusually large value.

(4) *−.0*—In a few places in this book, we encounter a negative value so minute that, when rounded, it becomes zero. We have used the symbol "−.0" to reflect this, but it is important to recognize that it is the result of rounding a *negative* number.

Throughout the *Statement Studies,* the ratio values have been omitted whenever there were less than ten statements in a sample. Occasionally, the number of statements used in a ratio array will differ from the number of statements in a sample because certain elements of data may not be present in all financial statements. In these cases, the number of statements used is shown in parentheses to the left of the array.

In interpreting ratios, the "strongest" or "best" value is not always the largest numerical value, nor is the "weakest" always the lowest numerical value. The following description of each of the ratios appearing in the *Statement Studies* will provide details regarding the arraying of the values.

The ratios in the *Statement Studies* are grouped into five principal categories: liquidity, coverage, leverage, operating, and specific expense items.

LIQUIDITY RATIOS

Liquidity is a measure of the quality and adequacy of current assets to meet current obligations as they come due.

Current Ratio

Computation: Total current assets divided by total current liabilities.

$$\frac{\text{Total Current Assets}}{\text{Total Current Liabilities}}$$

Interpretation: This ratio is a rough indication of a firm's ability to service its current obligations. Generally, the higher the current ratio, the greater the "cushion" between current obligations and a firm's ability to pay them. The stronger ratio reflects a numerical superiority of current assets over current liabilities. However, the composition and quality of current assets is a critical factor in the analysis of an individual firm's liquidity.

The ratio values are arrayed from the highest positive to the lowest positive.

Quick Ratio

Computation: Cash and equivalents plus trade receivables divided by total current liabilities.

$$\frac{\text{Cash \& Equivalents} + \text{Trade Receivables - (net)}}{\text{Total Current Liabilities}}$$

Interpretation: Also known as the "ACID TEST" ratio, it is a refinement of the current ratio and is a more conservative measure of liquidity. The ratio expresses the degree to which a company's current liabilities are covered by the most liquid current assets. Generally, any value of less than 1 to 1 implies a reciprocal "dependency" on inventory or other current assets to liquidate short-term debt.

The ratio values are arrayed from the highest positive to the lowest positive.

If the number of statements used in the calculation of this ratio differs from the sample size used in the asset category column, the sample size for each ratio will be printed in parentheses to the left of the array.

Sales/Receivables

Computation: Net sales divided by trade receivables.

$$\frac{\text{Net Sales}}{\text{Trade Receivables - (net)}}$$

In the contractor section both Accounts Receivable—Progress Billings and Accounts Receivable—Current Retention are included in the Receivables figure used in calculating the Revenues/Receivables and Receivables/Payables ratios.

Interpretation: This ratio measures the number of times trade receivables turn over during the year. The higher the turnover of receivables, the shorter the time between sale and cash collection. For example, a company with sales of $720,000 and receivables of $120,000 would have a sales/receivables ratio of 6.0, which means receivables turn over six times a year. If a company's receivables appear to be turning slower than the rest of the industry, further research is needed and the quality of the receivables should be examined closely.

A problem with this ratio is that it compares one day's receivables, shown at statement date, to total annual sales and does not take into consideration seasonal fluctuations. An additional problem in interpretation may arise when there is a large proportion of cash sales to total sales.

When the receivables figure is zero, the quotient will be undefined (UND) and represents the best possible ratio. The ratio values are therefore arrayed starting with undefined (UND) and then from the numerically highest to the numerically lowest value. The only time a zero will appear in the array is when the sales figure is low and the quotient rounds off to zero. By definition, this ratio cannot be negative.

Days' Receivables: The sales/receivables ratio will have a figure printed in bold type directly to the left of the array. This figure is the days' receivables.

Computation: The sales/receivables ratio divided into 365 (the number of days in one year).

$$\frac{365}{\text{Sales/Receivable ratio}}$$

Interpretation: This figure expresses the average time in days that receivables are outstanding. Generally, the greater number of days outstanding, the greater the probability of delinquencies in accounts receivable. A comparison of a company's daily receivables may indicate the extent of a company's control over credit and collections. The terms offered by a company to its customers, however, may differ from terms within the industry and should be taken into consideration.

In the example above, $365 \div 6 = 61$—i.e., the average receivable is collected in 61 days.

Cost of Sales/Inventory

Computation: Cost of sales divided by inventory.

$$\frac{\text{Cost of Sales}}{\text{Inventory}}$$

Interpretation: This ratio measures the number of times inventory is turned over during the year. High inventory turnover can indicate better liquidity or superior merchandising. Conversely it can indicate a shortage of needed inventory for sales. Low inventory turnover can indicate poor liquidity; possible overstocking, obsolescence, or in contrast to these negative interpretations a planned inventory buildup in the case of material shortages. A problem with this ratio is that it compares one day's inventory to cost of goods sold and does not take seasonal fluctuations into account. When the inventory figure is zero, the quotient will be undefined (UND) and represents the best possible ratio. The ratio values are arrayed starting with undefined (UND) and then from the numerically highest to the numerically lowest value. The only time a zero will appear in the array is when the cost of sales figure is very low and the quotient rounds off to zero.

Some service industries report data for cost of sales, while others do not. Note that in cases where the sample reporting it was insufficient, we have adjusted the data for cost of sales by putting it into operating expenses.

Please be aware, too, that our data collection process does not provide for differentiating the method of inventory valuation.

Days' Inventory
The cost of sales/inventory ratio will have a figure printed in bold type directly to the left of the array. This figure is the days' inventory.

Computation: The cost of sales/inventory ratio divided into 365 (the number of days in one year).

$$\frac{365}{\text{Cost of Sales/Inventory ratio}}$$

Interpretation: Division of the inventory turnover ratio into 365 days yields the average length of time units are in inventory.

Cost of Sales/Payables

Computation: Cost of sales divided by trade payables.

$$\frac{\text{Cost of Sales}}{\text{Trade Payables}}$$

In the contractor section both Accounts Payable—Trade and Accounts Payable—Retention are included in the Payables figure used in calculating the Cost of Revenues/Payables and Receivables/Payables ratios.

Interpretation: This ratio measures the number of times trade payables turn over during the year. The higher the turnover of payables, the shorter the time between purchase and payment. If a company's payables appear to be turning more slowly than the industry, then the company may be experiencing cash shortages, disputing invoices with suppliers, enjoying extended terms, or deliberately expanding its trade credit. The ratio comparison of company to industry suggests the existence of these possible causes or others. If a firm buys on 30 day terms, it is reasonable to expect this ratio to turn over in approximately 30 days.

A problem with this ratio is that it compares one day's payables to cost of goods sold and does not take seasonal fluctuations into account. When the payables figure is zero, the quotient will be undefined (UND) and represents the best possible ratio. The ratio values are arrayed starting with undefined (UND) and then from the numerically highest to the numerically lowest value. The only time a zero will appear in the array is when the cost of sales figure is very low and the quotient rounds off to zero.

Days' Payables

The cost of sales/payables ratio will have a figure printed in bold type directly to the left of the array. This figure is the days' payables.

Computation: The cost of sales/payables ratio divided into 365 (the number of days in one year).

$$\frac{365}{\text{Cost of Sales/Payables ratio}}$$

Interpretation: Division of the payables turnover ratio into 365 days yields the average length of time trade debt is outstanding.

Sales/Working Capital

Computation: Net sales divided by net working capital (current assets less current liabilities equals net working capital).

$$\frac{\text{Net Sales}}{\text{Net Working Capital}}$$

Interpretation: Working capital is a measure of the margin of protection for current creditors. It reflects the ability to finance current operations. Relating the level of sales arising from operations to the underlying working capital measures how efficiently working capital is employed. A low ratio may indicate an inefficient use of working capital while a very high ratio often signifies over-trading—vulnerable position for creditors.

If working capital is zero, the quotient is undefined (UND). If working capital is negative, the quotient is negative. The ratio values are arrayed from the lowest positive to the highest positive, to undefined (UND), and then from the highest negative to the lowest negative.

NM may occasionally appear as a quartile or median for the ratios sales/working capital, debt/worth, and fixed/worth. It stands for "no meaning" in cases where the dispersion is so small that any interpretation is meaningless.

COVERAGE RATIOS

Coverage ratios measure a firm's ability to service debt.

Earnings Before Interest And Taxes (Ebit)/Interest

Computation: Earnings (profit) before annual interest expense and taxes divided by annual interest expense.

$$\frac{\text{Earnings Before Interest \& Taxes}}{\text{Annual Interest Expense}}$$

Interpretation: This ratio is a measure of a firm's ability to meet interest payments. A high ratio may indicate that a borrower would have little difficulty in meeting the interest obligations of a loan. This ratio also serves as an indicator of a firm's capacity to take on additional debt.

Only those statements which reported annual interest expense were used in the calculation of this ratio. If the number of statements used in the calculation of these ratios differed from the sample size used in the asset category column, the sample size for each ratio will be printed in parentheses to the left of the array. If there were less than 10 ratios in an array, no entry will be shown. The ratio values are arrayed from the highest positive to the lowest positive and then from the lowest negative to the highest negative.

Net Profit + Depreciation, Depletion, Amortization/Current Maturities Long-Term Debt

Computation: Net profit plus depreciation, depletion, and amortization expenses, divided by the current portion of long-term debt.

Net Profit + Depreciation, Depletion, Amortization Expenses
Current Portion of Long-Term Debt

Interpretation: This ratio expresses the coverage of current maturities by cash flow from operations. Since cash flow is the primary source of debt retirement, this ratio measures the ability of a firm to service principal repayment and is an indicator of additional debt capacity. Although it is misleading to think that all cash flow is available for debt service, the ratio is a valid measure of the ability to service long-term debt.

Only data for *corporations* which have the following items were used;

(1) Profit or loss after taxes (positive, negative, or zero)
(2) A positive figure for Depreciation/Depletion/Amortization expenses
(3) A positive figure for current maturities of long-term debt

If the number of ratios used differed with the total number of firms reported in a column, the sample size is printed to the left of the array. If less than 10 ratios were available, the array was not printed. Ratio values are arrayed from the highest to lowest positive and then from the lowest to the highest negative.

LEVERAGE RATIOS

Highly leveraged firms (those with heavy debt in relation to net worth) are more vulnerable to business downturns than those with lower debt to worth positions. While leverage ratios help to measure this vulnerability, it must be remembered that they vary greatly depending on the requirements of particular industry groups.

Fixed/Worth

Computation: Fixed assets (net of accumulated depreciation) divided by tangible net worth.

Net Fixed Assets
Tangible Net Worth

Interpretation: This ratio measures the extent to which owner's equity (capital) has been invested in plant and equipment (fixed assets). A lower ratio indicates a proportionately smaller investment in fixed assets in relation to net worth, and a better "cushion" for creditors in case of liquidation. Similarly, a higher ratio would indicate the opposite situation. The presence of substantial leased fixed assets (not shown on the balance sheet) may deceptively lower this ratio.

Fixed assets may be zero, in which case the quotient is zero. If tangible net worth is zero, the quotient is undefined (UND). If tangible net worth is negative, the quotient is negative. The ratio values are arrayed from the lowest positive to the highest positive, undefined, and then from the highest negative to the lowest negative.

NM may occasionally appear as a quartile or median for the ratios sales/working capital, debt/worth, and fixed/worth. It stands for "no meaning" in cases where the dispersion is so small that any interpretation is meaningless.

Debt/Worth

Computation: Total liabilities divided by tangible net worth.

Total Liabilities
Tangible Net Worth

Interpretation: This ratio expresses the relationship between capital contributed by creditors and that contributed by owners. It expresses the degree of protection provided by the owners for the creditors. The higher the ratio, the greater the risk being assumed by creditors. A lower ratio generally indicates greater long-term financial safety. A firm with a low debt/worth ratio usually has greater flexibility to borrow in the future. A more highly leveraged company has a more limited debt capacity.

Tangible net worth may be zero, in which case the ratio is undefined (UND). Tangible net worth may also be negative which results in the quotient being negative. The ratio values are arrayed from the lowest to highest positive, undefined, and then from the highest to lowest negative.

NM may occasionally appear as a quartile or median for the ratios sales/working capital, debt/worth, and fixed/worth. It stands for "no meaning" in cases where the dispersion is so small that any interpretation is meaningless.

OPERATING RATIOS

Operating ratios are designed to assist in the evaluation of management performance.

% Profits Before Taxes/Tangible Net Worth

Computation: Profit before taxes divided by tangible net worth and multiplied by 100.

$$\frac{\text{Profit Before Taxes}}{\text{Tangible Net Worth}} \times 100$$

Interpretation: This ratio expresses the rate of return on tangible capital employed. While it can serve as an indicator of management performance, the analyst is cautioned to use it in conjunction with other ratios. A high return, normally associated with effective management, could indicate an under-capitalized firm. Whereas, a low return, usually an indicator of inefficient management performance, could reflect a highly capitalized, conservatively operated business.

This ratio has been multiplied by 100 since it is shown as a percentage.

Profit before taxes may be zero, in which case the ratio is zero. Profits before taxes may be negative resulting in negative quotients. Firms with negative tangible net worth have been omitted from the ratio arrays. Negative ratios will therefore only result in the case of negative profit before taxes. If the tangible net worth is zero, the quotient is undefined (UND). If there are less than 10 ratios for a particular size class, the result is not shown. The ratio values are arrayed starting with undefined (UND), and then from the highest to the lowest positive values, and from the lowest to the highest negative values.

% Profit Before Taxes/Total Assets

Computation: Profit before taxes divided by total assets and multiplied by 100.

$$\frac{\text{Profit Before Taxes}}{\text{Total Assets}} \times 100$$

Interpretation: This ratio expresses the pre-tax return on total assets and measures the effectiveness of management in employing the resources available to it. If a specific ratio varies considerably from the ranges found in this book, the analyst will need to examine the makeup of the assets and take a closer look at the earnings figure. A heavily depreciated plant and a large amount of intangible assets or unusual income or expense items will cause distortions of this ratio.

This ratio has been multiplied by 100 since it is shown as a percentage. If profit before taxes is zero, the quotient is zero. If profit before taxes is negative, the quotient is negative. These ratio values are arrayed from the highest to the lowest positive and then from the lowest to the highest negative.

Sales/Net Fixed Assets

Computation: Net sales divided by net fixed assets (net of accumulated depreciation).

$$\frac{\text{Net Sales}}{\text{Net Fixed Assets}}$$

Interpretation: This ratio is a measure of the productive use of a firm's fixed assets. Largely depreciated fixed assets or a labor intensive operation may cause a distortion of this ratio.

If the net fixed figure is zero, the quotient is undefined (UND). The only time a zero will appear in the array will be when the net sales figure is low and the quotient rounds off to zero. These ratio values cannot be negative.

They are arrayed from undefined (UND), and then from the highest to the lowest positive values.

Sales/Total Assets

Computation: Net sales divided by total assets.

$$\frac{\text{Net Sales}}{\text{Total Assets}}$$

Interpretation: This ratio is a general measure of a firm's ability to generate sales in relation to total assets. It should be used only to compare firms within specific industry groups and in conjunction with other operating ratios to determine the effective employment of assets.

The only time a zero will appear in the array will be when the net sales figure is low and the quotient rounds off to zero. The ratio values cannot be negative. They are arrayed from the highest to the lowest positive values.

EXPENSE TO SALES RATIOS

The following two ratios relate specific expense items to net sales and express this relationship as a percentage. Comparisons are convenient because the item, net sales, is used as a constant. Variations in these ratios are most pronounced between capital and labor intensive industries.

% Depreciation, Depletion, Amortization/Sales

Computation: Annual depreciation, amortization, and depletion expenses divided by net sales and multiplied by 100.

$$\frac{\text{Depreciation, Amortization, Depletion Expenses}}{\text{Net Sales}} \times 100$$

% Officers', Directors', Owners' Compensation/Sales

Computation: Annual Officers', Directors', Owners' Compensation divided by net sales and multiplied by 100. Included here are total salaries, bonuses, commissions, and other monetary remuneration to all officers; directors; and/or owners of the firm during the year covered by the statement. This includes drawings of partners and proprietors.

$$\frac{\text{Officers', Directors', Owners' Compensation}}{\text{Net Sales}} \times 100$$

Only statements showing a positive figure for each of the expense categories shown above were used. If the number of statements used in an array differs from the sample population for an asset size category, the number of statements used is shown in parentheses to the left of the array. When there are less than 10 ratios, the array is not printed. The ratios are arrayed from the lowest to highest positive values.

*SIC NUMBERS APPEARING IN THE STATEMENT STUDIES

SIC No.	Page	SIC No.	Page	SIC No.	Page
0161	844-845	2084	82-83	2678	280-281
0174	848-849	2085	82-83	2711	308-309
0175	838-839	2086	78-79	2721	310-311
0181	864-865	2087	80-81	2731	298-299
0191	850-851	2211	340-341	2732	294-295
0211	846-847	2221	340-341	2741	306-307
0212	834-835	2241	352-353	2752	302-303
0241	842-843	2251	348-349	2761	304-305
0252	840-841	2252	346-347	2791	314-315
0723	836-837	2253	350-351	2796	312-313
0741	818-819	2254	350-351	2821	98-99
0742	818-819	2257	350-351	2833	88-89
0781	852-853	2258	350-351	2834	88-89
0782	852-853	2261	344-345	2835	88-89
0783	852-853	2262	344-345	2836	88-89
1221	856-857	2273	342-343	2841	100-101
1222	856-857	2281	354-355	2842	102-103
1311	860-861	2311	68-69	2844	96-97
1381	880	2325	64-65	2851	94-95
1422	854-855	2326	70-71	2861	92-93
1442	862-863	2335	72-73	2865	92-93
1521	874	2337	74-75	2873	90-91
1522	874	2341	76-77	2874	90-91
1541	875	2353	60-61	2891	86-87
1542	875	2391	58-59	2911	292-293
1611	877	2392	62-63	2992	290-291
1622	868	2394	54-55	3021	322-323
1623	887	2396	52-53	3053	316-317
1711	883	2411	146-147	3086	320-321
1721	881	2421	152-153	3143	138-139
1731	871	2426	142-143	3144	138-139
1741	878	2431	148-149	3161	140-141
1742	882	2434	154-155	3171	140-141
1751	869	2435	144-145	3172	140-141
1752	873	2448	156-157	3231	334-335
1761	884	2451	364-365	3251	328-329
1771	870	2452	150-151	3271	330-331
1791	885	2491	158-159	3272	330-331
1793	876	2511	130-131	3273	338-339
1794	872	2512	132-133	3281	332-333
2011	116-117	2515	124-125	3291	326-327
2013	122-123	2521	134-135	3312	222-223
2015	118-119	2522	126-127	3315	240-241
2021	110-111	2541	128-129	3316	224-225
2022	110-111	2542	128-129	3317	238-239
2023	110-111	2621	288-289	3321	228-229
2024	110-111	2631	288-289	3322	228-229
2026	110-111	2652	284-285	3324	228-229
2033	108-109	2653	284-285	3325	228-229
2034	108-109	2655	284-285	3341	236-237
2037	114-115	2656	284-285	3356	234-235
2041	112-113	2671	282-283	3363	232-233
2048	120-121	2672	278-279	3364	232-233
2051	104-105	2673	286-287	3365	232-233
2064	106-107	2677	280-281	3366	232-233

*This list does not include SIC Numbers ending in "9" (Not Elsewhere Classified) although some of them are included in the Studies. Please refer to the full industry descriptions beginning on page 19 to determine which categories of the Not Elsewhere Classified industries are included in the Studies.

*SIC NUMBERS APPEARING IN THE STATEMENT STUDIES

*This list does not include SIC Numbers ending in "9" (Not Elsewhere Classified) although some of them are included in the Studies. Please refer to the full industry descriptions beginning on page 19 to determine which categories of the Not Elsewhere Classified industries are included in the Studies.

*SIC NUMBERS APPEARING IN THE STATEMENT STUDIES

SIC No.	Page	SIC No.	Page	SIC No.	Page
5162	392-393	5944	600-601	7533	642-643
5171	482-483	5945	598-599	7534	802-803
5172	480-481	5946	546-547	7538	644-645
5181	428-429	5947	604-605	7542	658-659
5182	428-429	5948	604-605	7623	768-769
5191	402-403, 864-865	5961	548-549	7692	832-833
5192	388-389	5962	616-617	7812	736-737
5193	404-405	5983	584-585	7832	798-799
5194	426-427	5984	586-587	7841	820-821
5198	440-441	5992	564-565	7922	800-801
5211	536-537, 540-541	5995	608-609	7933	648-649
5231	542-543	6411	712-713	7948	758-759
5251	538-539	6531	764-765	7991	750-751
5261	562-563, 864-865	7011	734-735	7992	704-705
5271	522-523	7211	716-717	7996	634-635
5311	552-553	7213	722-723	7997	668-669
5331	556-557	7216	716-717	8011	740-741, 754-755
5411	570-571, 574-575	7221	748-749	8021	686-687
5441	568-569	7231	706-707	8041	664-665
5461	566-567	7241	706-707	8042	742-743
5511	514-515, 528-529	7261	702-703	8051	738-739
5521	516-517	7311	622-623	8071	730-731
5531	518-519	7312	624-625	8072	684-685
5541	520-521	7322	620-621	8082	708-709
5551	530-531	7331	690-691	8092	714-715
5561	526-527	7334	744-745	8111	720-721
5571	524-525	7335	748-749	8211	782-783
5611	508-509	7336	638-639	8322	788-789
5621	512-513	7342	692-693	8331	806-807
5632	506-507	7352	728-729	8351	682-683
5651	504-505	7353	698-699	8361	660-661
5661	510-511	7361	694-695	8621	732-733
5712	590-591	7363	710-711	8641	640-641
5713	588-589	7371	676-677	8661	772-773
5722	592-593	7372	790-791	8711	696-697
5731	596-597	7373	670-671	8712	696-697
5734	550-551	7374	674-675	8713	696-697
5736	606-607	7377	678-679	8721	618-619
5812	578-579, 580-581, 582-583	7378	672-673	8731	778-779
5813	572-573	7381	688-689	8732	776-777
5912	558-559	7382	784-785	8734	796-797
5921	602-603	7384	746-747	8741	724-725
5932	614-615	7513	810-811	8742	680-681
5941	612-613	7514	774-775	8743	756-757
5942	532-533	7515	718-719		
5943	534-535	7532	646-647		

*This list does not include SIC Numbers ending in "9" (Not Elsewhere Classified) although some of them are included in the Studies. Please refer to the full industry descriptions beginning on page 19 to determine which categories of the Not Elsewhere Classified industries are included in the Studies.

DESCRIPTION OF INDUSTRIES INCLUDED IN THE STATEMENT STUDIES

PART I
MANUFACTURING INDUSTRIES

PART I—MANUFACTURING INDUSTRIES   Page

FURNITURE & FIXTURES.

JEWELRY, PRECIOUS METALS.

LEATHER & LEATHER PRODUCTS.

PART I—MANUFACTURING INDUSTRIES **Page**

PART I—MANUFACTURING INDUSTRIES

MACHINERY & COMPUTER EQUIPMENT.

PART I—MANUFACTURING INDUSTRIES   **Page**

MEASURING, ANALYZING & CONTROLLING INSTRUMENTS: PHOTOGRAPHIC, MEDICAL & OPTICAL GOODS: WATCHES & CLOCKS.

PART I—MANUFACTURING INDUSTRIES

PART I—MANUFACTURING INDUSTRIES   Page

PART I—MANUFACTURING INDUSTRIES   Page

PART II
WHOLESALING INDUSTRIES

PART II—WHOLESALING INDUSTRIES

34

PART III—RETAILING INDUSTRIES (INCLUDING COMBINED WHOLESALE-RETAIL)   Page

PART III
RETAILING INDUSTRIES
(INCLUDING COMBINED WHOLESALE-RETAIL)

AIRCRAFT.

APPAREL & ACCESSORIES.

AUTOMOTIVE DEALERS.

PART III—RETAILING INDUSTRIES (INCLUDING COMBINED WHOLESALE-RETAIL)   Page

DEPARTMENT STORES & GENERAL MERCHANDISE.

PART III—SERVICE INDUSTRIES   Page

PART III
SERVICE INDUSTRIES

40

PART III—SERVICE INDUSTRIES

PART III—SERVICE INDUSTRIES **Page**

PART III—SERVICE INDUSTRIES   **Page**

PART III—SERVICE INDUSTRIES

PART III
AGRICULTURAL INDUSTRIES

PART III—NOT ELSEWHERE CLASSIFIED INDUSTRIES

PART III
NOT ELSEWHERE CLASSIFIED INDUSTRIES

PART IV
CONTRACTOR INDUSTRIES

49

PART IV—CONTRACTOR INDUSTRIES

Page

OIL & GAS FIELD SERVICES. Performing oil and gas field services for others on a contract or fee basis. Included are excavating slush pits and cellars; grading an building of foundations at well locations; well surveying; running, cutting, and pulling casings, tubes and rods; cementing wells; shooting wells, perforating well casings; acidizing and chemically treating wells, and cleaning out, bailing, and swabbing wells. (SIC No. 1389) 879

OIL & GAS WELL DRILLING. Establishments primarily engaged in drilling wells for oil or gas field operations for others on a contract, or fee basis. This industry includes contractors that specialize in "spudding in," "drilling in," redrilling and directional drilling. (SIC No. 1381) . . . 880

PAINTING & PAPER HANGING. Special trade contractors engaged in painting and paper hanging. Those engaged in roof painting are not included. (SIC No. 1721) 881

PLASTERING, DRYWALL, ACOUSTICAL & INSULATION WORK. Special trade contractors engaged in applying plaster, plain or ornamental including the installation of lathing and other appurtenances to receive plaster, or in drywall, acoustical and building insulation work. (SIC No. 1742) 882

PLUMBING, HEATING & AIR CONDITIONING. Special trade contractors primarily engaged in heating, plumbing, air conditioning, and similar work, or any combination of these types of work. Sheet metal work combined with any of the above types of work is included here, but roofing and sheet metal work contractors are not included. Trade contractors primarily engaged in electrical work are not included. (SIC No. 1711) 883

ROOFING, SIDING, & SHEET METAL WORK. Special trade contractors primarily engaged in the installation of roofing, siding, and sheet metal work. This industry does not include contractors engaged in sheet metal in connection with plumbing, heating, or air conditioning. (SIC No. 1761) 884

STRUCTURAL STEEL ERECTION. Special trade contractors primarily engaged in the erection of structural steel and similar products of prestressed or precast concrete. (SIC No. 1791) 885

SWIMMING POOL CONSTRUCTION. Contractors primarily engaged in the construction of swimming pools. (SIC No. 1799) 886

WATER, SEWER, PIPELINE, COMMUNICATION & POWER LINE CONSTRUCTION. General and special trade contractors primarily engaged in the construction of pipelines, communication and power lines, and sewer and water mains. (SIC No. 1623) 887

PART I

MANUFACTURING

INDUSTRIES

Current Data Sorted By Assets | Comparative Historical Data

0-500M	500M-2MM	2-10MM	10-50MM	50-100MM	100-250MM	# Postretirement Benefits / Type of Statement	4/1/90-3/31/91 ALL	4/1/91-3/31/92 ALL
	1	4	3	1	1	Unqualified	7	16
1	4	2	1			Reviewed	11	13
1	9	3				Compiled	9	10
4		1				Tax Returns	2	
		1	1	1	1	Other	5	9
6	14 (4/1-9/30/94) 14	11	26 (10/1/94-3/31/95) 5	2	2	NUMBER OF STATEMENTS	34	48
%	%	%	%	%	%	**ASSETS**	%	%
	2.7	4.9				Cash & Equivalents	5.7	5.7
	30.2	35.6				Trade Receivables - (net)	31.7	29.7
	37.1	28.1				Inventory	30.1	30.1
	2.6	.6				All Other Current	1.4	4.5
	72.7	69.3				Total Current	69.0	69.9
	20.7	20.6				Fixed Assets (net)	24.2	22.2
	.7	3.5				Intangibles (net)	1.4	2.6
	5.9	6.6				All Other Non-Current	5.4	5.3
	100.0	100.0				Total	100.0	100.0
						LIABILITIES		
	11.6	7.7				Notes Payable-Short Term	10.7	14.2
	4.9	3.4				Cur. Mat. -L/T/D	4.1	4.1
	17.9	20.8				Trade Payables	18.0	22.3
	.3	.5				Income Taxes Payable	.3	.5
	5.3	4.5				All Other Current	7.7	10.0
	40.0	36.8				Total Current	40.8	51.2
	12.1	11.1				Long Term Debt	18.6	10.4
	.3	.0				Deferred Taxes	.2	.2
	1.7	12.2				All Other-Non-Current	6.7	3.0
	46.0	40.0				Net Worth	33.8	35.2
	100.0	100.0				Total Liabilities & Net Worth	100.0	100.0
						INCOME DATA		
	100.0	100.0				Net Sales	100.0	100.0
	35.0	27.8				Gross Profit	29.6	28.0
	31.7	24.4				Operating Expenses	23.7	23.8
	3.4	3.4				Operating Profit	5.9	4.3
	.8	1.9				All Other Expenses (net)	1.5	1.9
	2.5	1.5				Profit Before Taxes	4.4	2.4
						RATIOS		
	2.3	3.0				Current	2.9	2.2
	2.0	2.1					1.7	1.4
	1.5	1.4					1.2	1.0
	1.3	1.6				Quick	1.5	1.0
	.8	1.0					.8	.7
	.5	.7					.6	.4
	25 14.5	44 8.3				Sales/Receivables	24 15.2	23 16.2
	35 10.5	45 8.1					47 7.8	46 8.0
	48 7.6	66 5.5					72 5.1	57 6.4
	38 9.6	34 10.7				Cost of Sales/Inventory	26 14.1	28 13.2
	81 4.5	57 6.4					63 5.8	54 6.7
	107 3.4	101 3.6					118 3.1	83 4.4
	13 27.7	33 11.0				Cost of Sales/Payables	19 19.1	21 17.5
	25 14.6	44 8.3					34 10.7	37 10.0
	55 6.6	47 7.8					48 7.6	60 6.1
	5.4	4.4				Sales/Working Capital	4.9	6.9
	9.9	6.4					9.5	14.7
	18.0	14.6					30.9	−147.5
	6.9	5.2				EBIT/Interest	(30) 8.1	(43) 4.7
(13)	2.3	3.7					2.6	1.7
	.9	1.5					1.3	1.0
						Net Profit + Depr., Dep., Amort./Cur. Mat. L./T/D	(18) 5.8	(19) 7.5
							1.4	2.4
							.6	1.0
	.2	.4				Fixed/Worth	.4	.3
	.5	.6					.7	.6
	.9	1.0					2.0	2.1
	.6	.6				Debt/Worth	1.0	.9
	1.3	1.1					2.3	2.3
	2.6	3.7					5.9	6.3
	25.3	32.8				% Profit Before Taxes/Tangible Net Worth	(28) 59.0	(43) 43.2
	13.7	(10) 15.6					30.5	9.6
	.5	10.7					10.1	2.9
	10.4	9.7				% Profit Before Taxes/Total Assets	22.1	6.9
	6.0	5.6					7.5	2.7
	−.2	2.9					2.0	.4
	32.8	35.6				Sales/Net Fixed Assets	23.4	36.5
	16.4	12.4					11.1	19.1
	10.1	6.8					6.4	8.8
	3.6	2.9				Sales/Total Assets	3.4	3.5
	3.0	2.4					2.4	2.8
	2.5	2.0					1.6	2.1
	.8	.3				% Depr., Dep., Amort./Sales	(29) 1.1	(42) .7
	1.3	1.4					2.1	1.3
	2.1	2.1					3.2	2.9
						% Officers', Directors', Owners' Comp/Sales	(12) 3.0	(23) 2.4
							4.5	5.6
							9.0	8.8
5962M	44288M	89715M	298517M	258553M	545952M	Net Sales ($)	781300M	799183M
1636M	14058M	37423M	104326M	128332M	285154M	Total Assets ($)	412334M	381663M

M = $ thousand   MM = $ million
See Pages 1 through 15 for Explanation of Ratios and Data

Comparative Historical Data / Current Data Sorted By Sales

Postretirement Benefits — Type of Statement / Current Data Sorted By Sales

Hist 1	Hist 2	Hist 3	Type of Statement	0-1MM	1-3MM	3-5MM	5-10MM	10-25MM	25MM & OVER
19	8	10	Unqualified				4	2	4
10	9	8	Reviewed		2	3	1		1
6	10	13	Compiled	1	7	2	3	1	1
1		1	Tax Returns		1				
5	4	8	Other	3				1	3
4/1/92-3/31/93 ALL	4/1/93-3/31/94 ALL	4/1/94-3/31/95 ALL		0-1MM	14 (4/1-9/30/94) 1-3MM	3-5MM	26 (10/1/94-3/31/95) 5-10MM	10-25MM	25MM & OVER
41	31	40	NUMBER OF STATEMENTS	4	10	6	8	4	8

%	%	%	ASSETS	%	%	%	%	%	%
6.3	9.4	4.6	Cash & Equivalents		3.0				
29.0	31.6	34.3	Trade Receivables - (net)		27.7				
31.2	28.0	29.5	Inventory		33.1				
4.0	.9	1.4	All Other Current		2.6				
70.6	69.8	69.9	Total Current		66.3				
21.4	23.7	23.0	Fixed Assets (net)		27.2				
3.1	.8	1.3	Intangibles (net)		1.0				
4.9	5.7	5.9	All Other Non-Current		5.5				
100.0	100.0	100.0	Total		100.0				
			LIABILITIES						
12.0	12.2	9.5	Notes Payable-Short Term		6.6				
3.2	4.1	4.3	Cur. Mat.-L/T/D		6.5				
16.7	19.3	19.0	Trade Payables		14.8				
.4	1.9	.5	Income Taxes Payable		.3				
7.0	7.2	4.7	All Other Current		4.4				
39.3	44.8	38.0	Total Current		32.6				
12.0	13.8	15.2	Long Term Debt		19.6				
.3	.1	.3	Deferred Taxes		.0				
1.4	3.5	5.9	All Other-Non-Current		3.8				
47.0	37.7	40.6	Net Worth		44.0				
100.0	100.0	100.0	Total Liabilities & Net Worth		100.0				
			INCOME DATA						
100.0	100.0	100.0	Net Sales		100.0				
28.6	23.3	30.0	Gross Profit		41.0				
25.3	23.8	26.7	Operating Expenses		37.5				
3.3	-.5	3.3	Operating Profit		3.6				
.9	.4	1.0	All Other Expenses (net)		.9				
2.4	-.9	2.3	Profit Before Taxes		2.6				

RATIOS

Hist 1	Hist 2	Hist 3	Ratio	1-3MM
3.9	2.6	3.0	Current	2.4
1.9	1.5	2.0		2.0
1.2	1.2	1.4		1.7
1.7	1.5	1.5	Quick	1.5
1.0	.8	1.0		1.0
.6	.5	.7		.4
30 12.0	29 12.6	37 10.0	Sales/Receivables	21 17.3
46 8.0	42 8.7	44 8.3		26 13.9
57 6.4	60 6.1	54 6.7		41 8.9
30 12.1	26 13.8	28 13.0	Cost of Sales/Inventory	29 12.4
55 6.6	45 8.2	53 6.9		83 4.4
111 3.3	89 4.1	101 3.6		118 3.1
19 18.9	15 23.8	20 18.0	Cost of Sales/Payables	14 25.2
31 11.8	25 14.8	32 11.3		24 15.4
45 8.1	41 9.0	46 7.9		34 10.7
4.6	6.0	4.8	Sales/Working Capital	5.3
9.8	11.1	9.9		10.8
20.0	34.7	18.3		18.0
(36) 6.3	(26) 5.6	(39) 6.0	EBIT/Interest	
3.1	1.9	3.7		
.9	-2.2	1.5		
(18) 15.6	(13) 18.9	(16) 2.7	Net Profit + Depr., Dep., Amort./Cur. Mat. L/T/D	
2.2	1.6	1.8		
.8	.3	1.0		
.3	.2	.3	Fixed/Worth	.5
.5	.5	.6		.8
.8	1.5	1.0		1.0
.5	.7	.9	Debt/Worth	.5
1.4	1.3	1.5		1.5
3.8	3.9	3.4		2.9
(40) 31.9	(28) 20.0	(38) 42.6	% Profit Before Taxes/Tangible Net Worth	53.2
10.9	9.7	17.4		19.8
-1.2	-9.9	10.3		.4
12.2	8.9	14.9	% Profit Before Taxes/Total Assets	14.6
5.1	4.5	6.5		7.5
-.4	-6.8	2.3		.5
29.1	30.0	27.1	Sales/Net Fixed Assets	18.3
14.1	14.1	13.4		12.3
7.7	8.0	7.0		8.7
3.4	3.5	3.3	Sales/Total Assets	3.8
2.4	3.1	2.7		2.8
1.9	2.2	2.2		2.3
(37) .7	(27) .8	(37) .9	% Depr., Dep., Amort./Sales	.9
1.7	1.6	1.9		2.1
2.7	3.5	2.9		3.2
(19) 1.8		(19) 2.9	% Officers', Directors', Owners' Comp/Sales	
2.6		3.4		
8.8		6.3		

1300604M	1302719M	1242987M	Net Sales ($)	3512M	18798M	23634M	57906M	60560M	1078577M
557313M	463955M	570929M	Total Assets ($)	1047M	6522M	10152M	23353M	22478M	507377M

M = $ thousand   MM = $ million
See Pages 1 through 15 for Explanation of Ratios and Data

MANUFACTURERS—CANVAS & RELATED PRODUCTS. SIC# 2394

54

Current Data Sorted By Assets							Comparative Historical Data	
	1		1				# Postretirement Benefits	
							Type of Statement	
			4	4		1	Unqualified	7	6
	2	5	8				Reviewed	13	16
	9	9	3				Compiled	14	15
							Tax Returns		1
	1	1	4	1			Other	10	5
		13 (4/1-9/30/94)		39 (10/1/94-3/31/95)				4/1/90-3/31/91 ALL	4/1/91-3/31/92 ALL
	0-500M	500M-2MM	2-10MM	10-50MM	50-100MM	100-250MM	**NUMBER OF STATEMENTS**	44	43
	12	15	19	5		1			
	%	%	%	%	%	%	**ASSETS**	%	%
	8.8	8.6	9.5				Cash & Equivalents	5.5	9.9
	23.4	26.0	28.1				Trade Receivables - (net)	24.3	21.5
	27.9	34.0	30.9				Inventory	36.2	31.6
	2.9	1.1	.8				All Other Current	1.2	1.1
	63.0	69.8	69.4				Total Current	67.1	64.1
	27.1	22.2	21.8				Fixed Assets (net)	25.2	23.1
	4.4	2.4	2.6				Intangibles (net)	.7	6.6
	5.6	5.6	6.2				All Other Non-Current	6.9	6.2
	100.0	100.0	100.0				Total	100.0	100.0
							LIABILITIES		
	7.1	11.6	11.6				Notes Payable-Short Term	14.4	11.1
	11.2	4.4	3.1				Cur. Mat. -L/T/D	3.9	6.7
	17.8	14.7	14.6				Trade Payables	16.6	14.3
	.2	1.3	.1				Income Taxes Payable	.8	.6
	10.3	9.9	6.9				All Other Current	11.6	8.2
	46.5	41.8	36.3				Total Current	47.3	40.9
	32.1	12.8	13.1				Long Term Debt	17.6	15.6
	.0	.0	.6				Deferred Taxes	.1	.2
	2.5	3.9	2.2				All Other-Non-Current	4.5	2.6
	18.9	41.5	47.8				Net Worth	30.5	40.8
	100.0	100.0	100.0				Total Liabilities & Net Worth	100.0	100.0
							INCOME DATA		
	100.0	100.0	100.0				Net Sales	100.0	100.0
	42.6	36.4	23.2				Gross Profit	32.8	34.9
	40.1	32.4	18.5				Operating Expenses	31.0	29.6
	2.6	4.0	4.7				Operating Profit	1.8	5.3
	1.7	.3	1.0				All Other Expenses (net)	1.3	1.4
	.9	3.7	3.7				Profit Before Taxes	.5	4.0
							RATIOS		
	2.6	2.5	3.1				Current	2.6	2.7
	1.4	1.9	2.0					1.5	1.7
	.9	1.2	1.2					1.0	1.0
	1.2	1.4	2.2				Quick	1.1	1.1
	.5	.9	.9					.6	.7
	.4	.5	.6					.4	.5
	19 19.1	16 22.3	38 9.7				Sales/Receivables	22 16.5	22 16.4
	25 14.8	31 11.6	42 8.6					34 10.7	33 11.1
	33 11.0	45 8.2	51 7.1					47 7.8	43 8.4
	28 13.0	47 7.8	55 6.6				Cost of Sales/Inventory	57 6.4	50 7.3
	47 7.7	64 5.7	72 5.1					81 4.5	76 4.8
	91 4.0	94 3.9	89 4.1					111 3.3	96 3.8
	12 31.1	7 52.2	21 17.7				Cost of Sales/Payables	14 25.8	14 26.9
	29 12.6	23 16.1	28 13.2					29 12.7	29 12.8
	56 6.5	28 13.2	41 9.0					53 6.9	44 8.3
	8.7	7.8	3.1				Sales/Working Capital	5.4	5.6
	20.7	10.0	7.3					10.2	9.7
	-41.6	20.5	22.0					NM	-96.8
	11.0	5.1	10.1				EBIT/Interest	4.0	4.6
	(11) 1.6	(13) 2.9	(16) 4.2					(40) 1.7	(36) 2.4
	1.3	1.8	2.0					-.7	1.1
							Net Profit + Depr., Dep., Amort./Cur. Mat. L/T/D	5.1	5.0
								(20) 1.4	(18) 1.7
								-.0	.2
	.4	.2	.2				Fixed/Worth	.2	.2
	NM	.4	.5					.8	.5
	-1.2	1.5	1.5					2.2	2.0
	.6	.7	.3				Debt/Worth	1.0	.6
	NM	1.6	1.4					2.2	1.8
	-5.6	3.2	2.5					5.4	8.9
		40.3	75.8				% Profit Before Taxes/Tangible Net Worth	26.7	32.9
		(14) 24.3	(18) 16.6					(37) 9.3	(35) 17.3
		11.2	5.1					-7.9	3.8
	11.6	19.6	27.6				% Profit Before Taxes/Total Assets	7.7	16.3
	3.5	7.7	6.6					2.2	6.1
	.8	3.3	2.1					-5.1	.7
	24.9	39.9	24.7				Sales/Net Fixed Assets	28.6	28.9
	11.3	22.4	8.9					11.1	16.3
	7.3	9.7	7.4					6.3	6.7
	4.0	3.4	2.6				Sales/Total Assets	3.5	3.1
	3.2	3.0	2.4					2.4	2.5
	2.5	2.4	1.7					1.7	1.7
	2.2	.7	.7				% Depr., Dep., Amort./Sales	1.0	.7
	(10) 3.1	1.3	(18) 1.6					(38) 1.7	(39) 1.4
	4.5	2.6	2.5					2.9	2.9
		3.2					% Officers', Directors', Owners' Comp/Sales	3.7	3.1
		(11) 5.9						(21) 5.3	(21) 4.6
		12.4						7.6	8.6
	10440M	49747M	155623M	248068M		445772M	Net Sales ($)	323915M	302059M
	3399M	16213M	72419M	137862M		147092M	Total Assets ($)	169532M	162804M

M = $ thousand   MM = $ million
See Pages 1 through 15 for Explanation of Ratios and Data

MANUFACTURERS—CANVAS & RELATED PRODUCTS. SIC# 2394

Comparative Historical Data / Current Data Sorted By Sales

Comparative Historical Data				Current Data Sorted By Sales					
1	1	2	**# Postretirement Benefits**		1		1		
			Type of Statement						
7	7	9	Unqualified			1	1	2	5
25	15	15	Reviewed	1	4	4	4	2	
14	19	21	Compiled	7	8		5	1	
1	1		Tax Returns						
9	12	7	Other	1	1	1	2	1	1
4/1/92-3/31/93	4/1/93-3/31/94	4/1/94-3/31/95		0-1MM	1-3MM	3-5MM	5-10MM	10-25MM	25MM & OVER
ALL	ALL	ALL			13 (4/1-9/30/94)		39 (10/1/94-3/31/95)		
56	54	52	**NUMBER OF STATEMENTS**	9	13	6	12	6	6
%	%	%	**ASSETS**	%	%	%	%	%	%
9.4	7.8	9.2	Cash & Equivalents		10.8		12.5		
23.1	24.0	27.1	Trade Receivables - (net)		21.3		33.5		
36.7	35.7	31.4	Inventory		35.8		29.9		
1.3	1.7	1.4	All Other Current		1.7		.4		
70.4	69.1	69.2	Total Current		69.6		76.3		
20.4	22.6	22.0	Fixed Assets (net)		23.5		16.4		
2.5	1.2	2.7	Intangibles (net)		3.6		1.3		
6.7	7.1	6.1	All Other Non-Current		3.4		5.9		
100.0	100.0	100.0	Total		100.0		100.0		
			LIABILITIES						
11.9	10.7	11.0	Notes Payable-Short Term		9.6		15.4		
3.6	4.5	5.1	Cur. Mat.-L/T/D		9.1		2.1		
14.2	16.3	15.4	Trade Payables		19.8		11.5		
.6	1.4	.5	Income Taxes Payable		1.3		.0		
8.7	9.0	8.5	All Other Current		9.4		10.2		
39.0	41.9	40.4	Total Current		49.1		39.2		
13.9	15.9	16.3	Long Term Debt		18.2		6.1		
.2	.2	.3	Deferred Taxes		.1		.4		
4.1	6.4	2.6	All Other-Non-Current		6.6		3.1		
42.7	35.7	40.4	Net Worth		25.9		51.1		
100.0	100.0	100.0	Total Liabilities & Net Worth		100.0		100.0		
			INCOME DATA						
100.0	100.0	100.0	Net Sales		100.0		100.0		
34.5	33.2	32.3	Gross Profit		33.6		27.8		
30.0	30.9	27.9	Operating Expenses		32.0		20.1		
4.6	2.2	4.3	Operating Profit		1.6		7.7		
.6	.8	.8	All Other Expenses (net)		1.3		1.2		
4.0	1.4	3.5	Profit Before Taxes		.2		6.5		
			RATIOS						
2.8 / 1.8 / 1.4	2.5 / 1.5 / 1.2	2.7 / 1.9 / 1.2	Current		1.9 / 1.4 / 1.1		3.0 / 2.0 / 1.2		
1.1 / .8 / .5	(53) 1.5 / .8 / .5	1.8 / .9 / .5	Quick		1.2 / .5 / .4		2.1 / 1.1 / .6		
21 17.0 / 37 10.0 / 49 7.4	20 18.2 / 39 9.4 / 47 7.7	25 14.7 / 38 9.6 / 48 7.6	Sales/Receivables		14 26.9 / 26 14.0 / 43 8.4		33 10.9 / 42 8.6 / 70 5.2		
49 7.4 / 83 4.4 / 122 3.0	50 7.3 / 66 5.5 / 126 2.9	47 7.7 / 66 5.5 / 94 3.9	Cost of Sales/Inventory		49 7.5 / 83 4.4 / 107 3.4		47 7.8 / 61 6.0 / 85 4.3		
14 26.8 / 27 13.7 / 41 9.0	15 24.1 / 29 12.4 / 51 7.1	15 24.5 / 26 14.1 / 43 8.4	Cost of Sales/Payables		10 37.6 / 28 13.2 / 54 6.7		13 28.0 / 26 14.3 / 36 10.1		
4.2 / 8.3 / 17.0	4.7 / 9.1 / 21.2	5.9 / 9.4 / 21.7	Sales/Working Capital		8.1 / 16.5 / 66.3		3.5 / 8.9 / 19.1		
(49) 6.1 / 3.6 / 1.5	(48) 9.6 / 2.9 / .5	(44) 10.1 / 3.0 / 1.7	EBIT/Interest		4.8 / 2.8 / 1.4				
(22) 6.6 / 3.4 / 1.6	(23) 3.1 / 1.4 / .1	(19) 5.0 / 2.3 / 1.0	Net Profit + Depr., Dep., Amort./Cur. Mat. L/T/D						
.2 / .5 / 1.0	.2 / .6 / 2.2	.2 / .5 / 1.6	Fixed/Worth		.3 / 1.3 / -40.4		.2 / .2 / .7		
.7 / 1.3 / 2.9	.6 / 2.2 / 9.7	.6 / 1.6 / 3.2	Debt/Worth		1.3 / 2.4 / -185.3		.4 / 1.2 / 2.3		
(52) 39.9 / 17.1 / 3.9	(46) 67.9 / 22.0 / 4.9	(44) 46.0 / 21.0 / 8.5	% Profit Before Taxes/Tangible Net Worth				72.2 / 27.8 / 6.2		
17.1 / 6.6 / 1.7	13.7 / 6.3 / -3.7	18.4 / 7.0 / 2.8	% Profit Before Taxes/Total Assets		9.6 / 3.6 / 2.7		29.2 / 10.4 / 2.6		
35.8 / 15.9 / 7.7	27.1 / 12.6 / 6.2	28.2 / 12.3 / 8.3	Sales/Net Fixed Assets		39.6 / 16.4 / 6.3		39.6 / 18.5 / 8.4		
3.2 / 2.3 / 1.8	3.2 / 2.4 / 1.7	3.2 / 2.6 / 2.0	Sales/Total Assets		3.4 / 2.7 / 2.4		3.2 / 2.5 / 1.7		
(51) .9 / 1.7 / 2.7	(51) 1.0 / 1.7 / 2.9	(47) .9 / 1.5 / 2.9	% Depr., Dep., Amort./Sales		(12) 1.1 / 2.1 / 3.6		(11) .7 / .9 / 2.4		
(27) 2.6 / 5.3 / 9.4	(23) 3.0 / 5.3 / 7.1	(26) 3.2 / 5.4 / 9.2	% Officers', Directors', Owners' Comp/Sales						
500825M	438958M	909650M	Net Sales ($)	5801M	27179M	24783M	80110M	77937M	693840M
259095M	218125M	376985M	Total Assets ($)	2465M	10824M	10851M	36442M	31449M	284954M

© Robert Morris Associates 1995

M = $ thousand   MM = $ million

See Pages 1 through 15 for Explanation of Ratios and Data

Current Data Sorted By Assets							Comparative Historical Data	
1	1	1	1		1	# Postretirement Benefits		
						Type of Statement		
		4	6	2	3	Unqualified	18	19
1	6	3	4			Reviewed	8	6
1						Compiled	3	5
						Tax Returns		
1	2	1	1			Other	7	5
	8 (4/1-9/30/94)		27 (10/1/94-3/31/95)				4/1/90-3/31/91	4/1/91-3/31/92
0-500M	500M-2MM	2-10MM	10-50MM	50-100MM	100-250MM		ALL	ALL
3	8	8	11	2	3	NUMBER OF STATEMENTS	36	35
%	%	%	%	%	%	ASSETS	%	%
			3.9			Cash & Equivalents	5.7	3.5
			39.6			Trade Receivables - (net)	22.8	26.2
			37.2			Inventory	45.7	42.8
			2.9			All Other Current	3.1	5.7
			83.7			Total Current	77.3	78.3
			13.4			Fixed Assets (net)	14.6	16.0
			.1			Intangibles (net)	1.6	1.0
			2.8			All Other Non-Current	6.5	4.7
			100.0			Total	100.0	100.0
						LIABILITIES		
			20.7			Notes Payable-Short Term	15.4	17.0
			1.9			Cur. Mat. -L/T/D	3.4	3.5
			15.1			Trade Payables	16.6	15.7
			.1			Income Taxes Payable	.6	.5
			8.3			All Other Current	7.5	9.6
			46.1			Total Current	43.6	46.3
			4.5			Long Term Debt	7.3	13.2
			.2			Deferred Taxes	.4	.3
			5.0			All Other-Non-Current	2.5	3.1
			44.3			Net Worth	46.2	37.1
			100.0			Total Liabilities & Net Worth	100.0	100.0
						INCOME DATA		
			100.0			Net Sales	100.0	100.0
			21.0			Gross Profit	27.7	27.4
			17.3			Operating Expenses	24.0	25.2
			3.7			Operating Profit	3.8	2.2
			.8			All Other Expenses (net)	1.3	1.4
			2.9			Profit Before Taxes	2.4	.8
						RATIOS		
			3.2				2.4	2.1
			1.6			Current	1.8	1.7
			1.3				1.4	1.4
			1.8				1.2	1.0
			.8			Quick	.6	.7
			.7				.3	.4
		43	8.4				13 28.2	20 18.1
		73	5.0			Sales/Receivables	37 9.8	46 8.0
		96	3.8				51 7.2	64 5.7
		65	5.6				65 5.6	73 5.0
		73	5.0			Cost of Sales/Inventory	107 3.4	96 3.8
		104	3.5				130 2.8	135 2.7
		15	24.7				18 19.9	18 20.8
		31	11.9			Cost of Sales/Payables	27 13.5	27 13.7
		47	7.8				44 8.3	40 9.1
			3.6				4.8	4.4
			6.6			Sales/Working Capital	6.7	7.6
			9.7				13.9	17.1
			5.5				4.0	3.6
			2.6			EBIT/Interest	(31) 2.3	(33) 2.0
			1.7				1.3	1.3
						Net Profit + Depr., Dep.,	7.6	7.1
						Amort./Cur. Mat. L/T/D	(17) 2.8	(16) 2.1
							1.2	1.2
			.1				.1	.2
			.3			Fixed/Worth	.2	.3
			.4				.5	.6
			.8				1.0	1.1
			1.5			Debt/Worth	1.3	1.7
			2.5				1.9	2.7
			46.4			% Profit Before Taxes/Tangible	31.3	28.9
			9.1			Net Worth	18.0	(34) 16.0
			3.4				5.5	2.7
			12.0			% Profit Before Taxes/Total	11.0	9.5
			3.4			Assets	6.6	5.1
			1.7				2.5	.8
			73.8				51.6	35.1
			16.6			Sales/Net Fixed Assets	21.7	20.5
			8.6				9.1	9.1
			2.5				2.9	2.8
			2.2			Sales/Total Assets	2.4	2.3
			1.5				1.7	1.7
			.4				.6	.6
		(10)	.8			% Depr., Dep., Amort./Sales	(30) 1.1	(31) 1.1
			1.8				2.0	1.5
						% Officers', Directors',	1.9	
						Owners' Comp/Sales	(13) 3.3	
							5.1	
1197M	18333M	82981M	480935M	191004M	496626M	Net Sales ($)	525483M	539806M
892M	7418M	37574M	249228M	120179M	355625M	Total Assets ($)	235571M	250729M

M = $ thousand   MM = $ million
See Pages 1 through 15 for Explanation of Ratios and Data

Comparative Historical Data | Current Data Sorted By Sales

	4/1/92-3/31/93 ALL	4/1/93-3/31/94 ALL	4/1/94-3/31/95 ALL	0-1MM	1-3MM	3-5MM	5-10MM	10-25MM	25MM & OVER
# Postretirement Benefits				1		1		1	2
Type of Statement									
Unqualified	19	13	15	1		1		1	2
Reviewed	7	14	14			1	1	2	11
Compiled	7	8	1	2	4	1	1	2	4
Tax Returns	1	1							
Other	6	11	5	1		1	1		1
	4/1/92-3/31/93	4/1/93-3/31/94	4/1/94-3/31/95		8 (4/1-9/30/94)			27 (10/1/94-3/31/95)	
	ALL	ALL	ALL	0-1MM	1-3MM	3-5MM	5-10MM	10-25MM	25MM & OVER
NUMBER OF STATEMENTS	40	47	35	4	5	3	3	4	16
	%	%	%	%	%	%	%	%	%
ASSETS									
Cash & Equivalents	5.7	6.3	4.2						3.4
Trade Receivables - (net)	25.7	26.4	26.5						33.8
Inventory	41.5	41.6	47.2						40.7
All Other Current	4.3	2.8	1.6						2.3
Total Current	77.3	77.2	79.5						80.1
Fixed Assets (net)	15.9	15.6	12.2						13.0
Intangibles (net)	1.1	1.8	2.0						3.4
All Other Non-Current	5.7	5.4	6.3						3.4
Total	100.0	100.0	100.0						100.0
LIABILITIES									
Notes Payable-Short Term	15.5	17.7	24.6						22.2
Cur. Mat.-L /T/D	3.0	2.7	2.3						1.8
Trade Payables	17.6	14.0	14.2						12.7
Income Taxes Payable	.6	1.8	.1						.1
All Other Current	11.0	9.1	8.3						9.2
Total Current	47.7	45.3	49.5						46.0
Long Term Debt	12.4	11.0	8.7						5.3
Deferred Taxes	.1	.3	.5						1.1
All Other-Non-Current	3.7	4.6	7.5						7.0
Net Worth	36.0	38.9	33.8						40.6
Total Liabilities & Net Worth	100.0	100.0	100.0						100.0
INCOME DATA									
Net Sales	100.0	100.0	100.0						100.0
Gross Profit	29.2	27.1	29.5						23.3
Operating Expenses	25.0	24.8	26.5						18.7
Operating Profit	4.2	2.3	3.1						4.6
All Other Expenses (net)	1.5	1.7	2.1						1.5
Profit Before Taxes	2.8	.6	1.0						3.1
RATIOS									
Current	2.5	2.6	2.0						2.2
	1.6	1.8	1.6						1.6
	1.3	1.3	1.3						1.4
Quick	1.1	1.4	.9						1.1
	.6	.7	.7						.8
	.5	.4	.4						.4
Sales/Receivables	19 19.5	21 17.1	26 13.9						44 8.3
	39 9.4	46 7.9	47 7.7						66 5.5
	59 6.2	72 5.1	72 5.1						94 3.9
Cost of Sales/Inventory	62 5.9	62 5.9	73 5.0						70 5.2
	89 4.1	79 4.6	122 3.0						96 3.8
	122 3.0	135 2.7	203 1.8						159 2.3
Cost of Sales/Payables	16 22.5	15 24.2	19 18.8						17 22.1
	31 11.9	26 14.2	31 11.8						28 12.9
	48 7.6	34 10.8	42 8.7						40 9.1
Sales/Working Capital	5.0	3.9	5.2						4.0
	8.5	8.1	7.1						6.6
	23.2	17.2	10.4						7.7
EBIT/Interest	(36) 4.8	(43) 4.9	(34) 3.7						4.7
	2.0	2.1	1.9						2.8
	1.3	.7	1.1						1.7
Net Profit + Depr., Dep., Amort./Cur. Mat. L/T/D	(18) 5.3	(15) 3.6	(13) 5.1						
	1.5	.5	1.8						
	.7	-1.3	.5						
Fixed/Worth	.2	.1	.1						.1
	.3	.3	.4						.3
	.7	.8	.5						.5
Debt/Worth	.8	.8	1.3						1.0
	1.8	1.5	2.1						1.6
	3.6	2.6	3.5						2.6
% Profit Before Taxes/Tangible Net Worth	(37) 29.7	(43) 28.2	(31) 24.4					(14)	29.9
	8.9	9.3	8.6						13.3
	1.9	-.8	.8						5.8
% Profit Before Taxes/Total Assets	12.0	11.5	7.3						9.4
	4.6	3.4	2.9						4.3
	.9	-.8	.4						2.0
Sales/Net Fixed Assets	37.7	44.8	61.1						33.9
	19.6	19.6	22.7						16.6
	10.9	10.3	9.5						8.8
Sales/Total Assets	3.6	3.2	2.6						2.5
	2.5	2.3	2.2						1.7
	1.9	1.7	1.5						1.3
% Depr., Dep., Amort./Sales	(36) .6	(39) .4	(32) .6					(15)	.6
	1.0	1.2	1.5						1.5
	1.7	1.8	2.0						2.0
% Officers', Directors', Owners' Comp/Sales	(17) 2.1	(17) 1.2	(13) 1.5						
	3.2	3.6	2.8						
	8.5	9.0	4.4						
Net Sales ($)	865369M	1100517M	1271076M	1977M	10243M	10783M	18065M	61443M	1168565M
Total Assets ($)	474873M	572036M	770916M	1435M	4200M	7071M	8872M	24306M	725032M

© Robert Morris Associates 1995

M = $ thousand   MM = $ million
See Pages 1 through 15 for Explanation of Ratios and Data

Current Data Sorted By Assets

0-500M	500M-2MM	2-10MM	10-50MM	50-100MM	100-250MM
					1
		4	4	3	
	2	3	1		
2	3				
1	1				
1		1	1		
11 (4/1-9/30/94)			17 (10/1/94-3/31/95)		
4	7	8	6	3	
%	%	%	%	%	%

Comparative Historical Data

# Postretirement Benefits Type of Statement		4/1/90-3/31/91 ALL	4/1/91-3/31/92 ALL
Unqualified		7	12
Reviewed		11	8
Compiled		8	7
Tax Returns			
Other		2	3
NUMBER OF STATEMENTS		28	30
ASSETS		%	%
Cash & Equivalents		4.2	5.9
Trade Receivables - (net)		28.8	27.8
Inventory		37.1	39.2
All Other Current		2.6	2.4
Total Current		72.6	75.2
Fixed Assets (net)		18.2	15.5
Intangibles (net)		1.7	1.5
All Other Non-Current		7.5	7.7
Total		100.0	100.0
LIABILITIES			
Notes Payable-Short Term		21.8	16.3
Cur. Mat. -L/T/D		3.7	3.1
Trade Payables		19.5	16.3
Income Taxes Payable		.3	.2
All Other Current		7.9	12.1
Total Current		53.2	48.0
Long Term Debt		10.9	9.2
Deferred Taxes		.2	.1
All Other-Non-Current		2.5	6.0
Net Worth		33.1	36.6
Total Liabilities & Net Worth		100.0	100.0
INCOME DATA			
Net Sales		100.0	100.0
Gross Profit		30.6	31.2
Operating Expenses		30.5	29.8
Operating Profit		.1	1.5
All Other Expenses (net)		1.5	1.2
Profit Before Taxes		-1.4	.3
RATIOS			
Current		1.8 / 1.3 / 1.1	2.4 / 1.6 / 1.2
Quick		.9 / .7 / .4	1.2 / .8 / .4
Sales/Receivables		25 14.7 / 39 9.3 / 50 7.3	32 11.4 / 41 8.8 / 59 6.2
Cost of Sales/Inventory		35 10.3 / 65 5.6 / 104 3.5	56 6.5 / 76 4.8 / 130 2.8
Cost of Sales/Payables		20 18.2 / 35 10.5 / 41 8.8	20 18.0 / 32 11.5 / 58 6.3
Sales/Working Capital		7.7 / 17.5 / 76.9	5.6 / 8.2 / 16.8
EBIT/Interest		(26) 2.9 / 1.7 / -1.5	(27) 2.8 / 1.6 / 1.2
Net Profit + Depr., Dep., Amort./Cur. Mat. L /T/D		(16) 3.9 / 1.4 / -1.8	(21) 6.9 / 3.2 / .5
Fixed/Worth		.2 / .5 / 1.2	.2 / .3 / 1.0
Debt/Worth		1.0 / 2.3 / 4.8	.8 / 1.6 / 4.4
% Profit Before Taxes/Tangible Net Worth		(26) 29.8 / 9.8 / -11.4	(27) 18.7 / 6.1 / 1.2
% Profit Before Taxes/Total Assets		7.6 / 3.6 / -4.6	4.9 / 1.6 / -2.8
Sales/Net Fixed Assets		31.8 / 25.9 / 12.3	45.1 / 18.7 / 11.5
Sales/Total Assets		4.0 / 2.9 / 2.3	3.2 / 2.4 / 2.1
% Depr., Dep., Amort./Sales		(26) .7 / 1.1 / 1.7	(28) .8 / 1.1 / 1.9
% Officers', Directors', Owners' Comp/Sales		(14) 2.6 / 6.8 / 9.9	(15) 1.5 / 6.7 / 9.4

0-500M	500M-2MM	2-10MM	10-50MM	50-100MM			4/1/90-3/31/91	4/1/91-3/31/92
4375M	14452M	102949M	311397M	363564M	Net Sales ($)		262063M	291854M
974M	5891M	48062M	142080M	207612M	Total Assets ($)		113322M	146248M

M = $ thousand   MM = $ million
See Pages 1 through 15 for Explanation of Ratios and Data

Comparative Historical Data | | Current Data Sorted By Sales

4/1/92-3/31/93 ALL	4/1/93-3/31/94 ALL	4/1/94-3/31/95 ALL		0-1MM	1-3MM	3-5MM	5-10MM	10-25MM	25MM & OVER
		1	# Postretirement Benefits						1
			Type of Statement						
10	8	11	Unqualified					5	6
6	3	6	Reviewed		3			2	1
5	9	5	Compiled		4	1			
	1	2	Tax Returns	1	2				
7	4	4	Other		1			1	1
					11 (4/1-9/30/94)			17 (10/1/94-3/31/95)	
28	25	28	**NUMBER OF STATEMENTS**	1	10	1		8	8
%	%	%	**ASSETS**	%	%	%	%	%	%
4.0	8.2	5.5	Cash & Equivalents		4.1				
31.8	26.6	32.5	Trade Receivables - (net)		37.3				
37.7	34.8	34.2	Inventory		32.6				
4.1	1.7	1.3	All Other Current		1.3				
77.6	71.3	73.5	Total Current		75.3				
15.2	21.9	18.6	Fixed Assets (net)		13.4				
1.0	2.4	1.0	Intangibles (net)		.5				
6.2	4.4	6.9	All Other Non-Current		10.8				
100.0	100.0	100.0	Total		100.0				
			LIABILITIES						
20.4	13.8	9.9	Notes Payable-Short Term		10.3				
2.2	5.2	3.0	Cur. Mat.-L /T/D		1.1				
16.7	20.2	17.8	Trade Payables		19.5				
.5	.4	.3	Income Taxes Payable		.3				
8.8	9.2	10.6	All Other Current		15.6				
48.5	48.7	41.6	Total Current		46.9				
7.4	13.3	19.6	Long Term Debt		21.6				
.1	.1	.1	Deferred Taxes		.0				
7.4	8.4	2.8	All Other-Non-Current		1.4				
36.6	29.6	35.9	Net Worth		30.2				
100.0	100.0	100.0	Total Liabilities & Net Worth		100.0				
			INCOME DATA						
100.0	100.0	100.0	Net Sales		100.0				
29.2	32.9	30.1	Gross Profit		36.1				
25.6	30.9	24.3	Operating Expenses		33.1				
3.6	2.0	5.8	Operating Profit		3.0				
1.2	.7	1.6	All Other Expenses (net)		.9				
2.3	1.3	4.1	Profit Before Taxes		2.1				
			RATIOS						
2.2	2.1	2.6	Current		3.0				
1.6	1.6	1.8			1.6				
1.3	1.2	1.4			1.2				
1.1	1.3	1.1	Quick		1.3				
.7	.8	.9			.8				
.5	.4	.6			.5				
37 9.9	28 13.2	35 10.5	Sales/Receivables		33 11.2				
46 8.0	47 7.8	44 8.3			39 9.3				
56 6.5	53 6.9	62 5.9			61 6.0				
37 10.0	32 11.4	41 8.8	Cost of Sales/Inventory		16 22.6				
81 4.5	66 5.5	76 4.8			58 6.3				
146 2.5	101 3.6	114 3.2			159 2.3				
20 18.6	22 16.7	25 14.8	Cost of Sales/Payables		15 23.7				
30 12.1	37 9.8	37 9.8			31 11.7				
50 7.3	57 6.4	49 7.4			60 6.1				
5.2	6.5	4.7	Sales/Working Capital		3.8				
9.3	13.4	7.5			14.0				
14.6	20.4	15.6			41.3				
(25) 6.6	(22) 4.2	(27) 10.7	EBIT/Interest						
2.5	2.0	2.9							
1.4	1.3	1.8							
(18) 6.8	(13) 7.5	(17) 10.3	Net Profit + Depr., Dep., Amort./Cur. Mat. L/T/D						
2.6	1.6	3.1							
.4	.3	1.4							
.1	.4	.2	Fixed/Worth		.1				
.4	.6	.4			.3				
.8	3.3	1.2			5.7				
.8	1.0	.9	Debt/Worth		.8				
2.3	3.0	1.7			3.2				
3.2	22.7	4.2			23.0				
(27) 33.6	(23) 33.0	(27) 52.3	% Profit Before Taxes/Tangible Net Worth						
22.8	9.0	18.7							
4.2	.0	4.5							
10.9	5.6	15.2	% Profit Before Taxes/Total Assets		13.7				
5.1	2.9	6.9			5.0				
1.4	-.2	2.2			.4				
52.9	27.7	44.4	Sales/Net Fixed Assets		71.8				
22.3	18.9	21.9			34.5				
12.6	11.0	8.5			12.4				
3.4	3.6	2.8	Sales/Total Assets		4.4				
2.4	2.8	2.3			2.3				
2.0	2.0	1.9			1.8				
(27) .4	(20) .7	(26) .6	% Depr., Dep., Amort./Sales		.5				
.9	1.0	1.1			.7				
1.5	1.6	1.9			1.6				
(13) 3.7	(16) 1.8	(17) 1.5	% Officers', Directors', Owners' Comp/Sales						
8.1	3.4	3.1							
12.2	7.8	6.7							
384551M	277176M	796737M	Net Sales ($)	599M	17704M	3114M		117571M	657749M
209956M	111671M	404619M	Total Assets ($)	240M	8809M	789M		62099M	332682M

M = $ thousand   MM = $ million
See Pages 1 through 15 for Explanation of Ratios and Data

Current Data Sorted By Assets

Postretirement Benefits — Type of Statement

0-500M	500M-2MM	2-10MM	10-50MM	50-100MM	100-250MM		4/1/90-3/31/91 ALL	4/1/91-3/31/92 ALL
		1		1		Unqualified	9	7
		3	2	3	1	Reviewed	9	12
	5	4				Compiled	7	7
	1	3				Tax Returns		
	1	6				Other	5	5

11 (4/1-9/30/94) spans 0-500M & 500M-2MM · *18 (10/1/94-3/31/95)* spans 2-10MM through 100-250MM

0-500M	500M-2MM	2-10MM	10-50MM	50-100MM	100-250MM	NUMBER OF STATEMENTS	4/1/90-3/31/91 ALL 30	4/1/91-3/31/92 ALL 31
	7	16	2	3	1			
%	%	%	%	%	%	**ASSETS**	%	%
		7.1				Cash & Equivalents	5.5	3.9
		30.8				Trade Receivables - (net)	31.4	33.8
		35.8				Inventory	38.1	37.4
		.6				All Other Current	.6	1.0
		74.4				Total Current	75.6	76.1
		18.4				Fixed Assets (net)	19.1	14.6
		1.3				Intangibles (net)	.9	2.0
		5.9				All Other Non-Current	4.4	7.4
		100.0				Total	100.0	100.0
						LIABILITIES		
		16.4				Notes Payable-Short Term	12.9	14.8
		1.7				Cur. Mat. -L/T/D	4.7	3.3
		8.1				Trade Payables	13.7	16.4
		.2				Income Taxes Payable	.9	.6
		9.9				All Other Current	8.0	11.0
		36.3				Total Current	40.2	46.0
		9.2				Long Term Debt	15.2	15.5
		.1				Deferred Taxes	.3	.2
		4.7				All Other-Non-Current	1.8	2.0
		49.7				Net Worth	42.5	36.3
		100.0				Total Liabilities & Net Worth	100.0	100.0
						INCOME DATA		
		100.0				Net Sales	100.0	100.0
		31.7				Gross Profit	30.8	31.5
		24.9				Operating Expenses	25.6	24.5
		6.8				Operating Profit	5.2	6.9
		1.0				All Other Expenses (net)	1.6	2.4
		5.8				Profit Before Taxes	3.6	4.5
						RATIOS		
		5.1 / 2.3 / 1.3				Current	2.8 / 1.9 / 1.4	2.8 / 1.6 / 1.3
		2.2 / 1.2 / .7				Quick	1.6 / .9 / .7	1.2 / .8 / .6
		38 9.7 / 49 7.5 / 65 5.6				Sales/Receivables	33 11.1 / 49 7.5 / 61 6.0	37 9.8 / 49 7.5 / 68 5.4
		59 6.2 / 85 4.3 / 130 2.8				Cost of Sales/Inventory	55 6.6 / 81 4.5 / 118 3.1	68 5.4 / 85 4.3 / 101 3.6
		12 29.9 / 18 19.9 / 33 11.1				Cost of Sales/Payables	16 23.3 / 29 12.6 / 34 10.6	19 19.5 / 29 12.8 / 45 8.2
		3.1 / 5.4 / 17.6				Sales/Working Capital	3.8 / 7.8 / 10.9	4.7 / 10.7 / 16.6
	(15)	9.0 / 3.0 / 2.2				EBIT/Interest	(29) 6.4 / 3.4 / 1.2	(29) 5.3 / 2.8 / 1.4
						Net Profit + Depr., Dep., Amort./Cur. Mat. L./T/D	(15) 3.1 / 1.8 / .3	(15) 7.8 / 4.3 / .6
		.2 / .4 / 1.0				Fixed/Worth	.2 / .5 / .8	.2 / .4 / 1.0
		.3 / 1.2 / 2.5				Debt/Worth	.5 / 1.5 / 3.6	.8 / 2.2 / 4.8
		45.6 / 20.0 / 10.9				% Profit Before Taxes/Tangible Net Worth	(28) 37.6 / 21.5 / 6.6	(30) 55.5 / 24.5 / 8.7
		15.9 / 10.0 / 4.4				% Profit Before Taxes/Total Assets	15.4 / 9.3 / 1.3	20.9 / 8.7 / 1.7
		38.6 / 11.8 / 7.0				Sales/Net Fixed Assets	31.2 / 17.7 / 8.0	41.2 / 28.1 / 8.5
		2.8 / 2.1 / 1.5				Sales/Total Assets	3.0 / 2.3 / 1.8	2.9 / 2.5 / 1.9
		.4 / 1.0 / 1.5				% Depr., Dep., Amort./Sales	(29) .7 / 1.5 / 2.5	.5 / 1.2 / 2.0
						% Officers', Directors', Owners' Comp/Sales	(10) 2.5 / 4.7 / 6.7	(18) 1.9 / 3.1 / 6.0
	21760M	149721M	114819M	248598M	153577M	Net Sales ($)	246323M	391071M
	8818M	71283M	63664M	174849M	230142M	Total Assets ($)	133504M	218820M

Comparative Historical Data

M = $ thousand   MM = $ million

See Pages 1 through 15 for Explanation of Ratios and Data

Comparative Historical Data

Current Data Sorted By Sales

				# Postretirement Benefits						1			1
		3		**2**	Type of Statement					1	2		6
	5		8	9	Unqualified		3	2		2	2		
	10		11	9	Reviewed				1	2			
	5		6	4	Compiled						1		
	1				Tax Returns								
	5		10	7	Other		1	2	1	3			
	4/1/92-		4/1/93-	4/1/94-		0-1MM	11 (4/1-9/30/94)			18 (10/1/94-3/31/95)			
	3/31/93		3/31/94	3/31/95			1-3MM	3-5MM	5-10MM	10-25MM		25MM & OVER	
	ALL		ALL	ALL									
	26		35	29	**NUMBER OF STATEMENTS**		4	5	5	8		6	
	%		%	%	**ASSETS**	%	%	%	%	%		%	
	3.1		6.7	6.3	Cash & Equivalents								
	37.7		31.1	30.7	Trade Receivables - (net)								
	35.7		39.7	35.4	Inventory								
	1.3		.5	.9	All Other Current								
	77.8		78.1	73.3	Total Current								
	16.1		15.2	17.4	Fixed Assets (net)								
	1.9		2.5	3.7	Intangibles (net)								
	4.3		4.2	5.6	All Other Non-Current								
	100.0		100.0	100.0	Total								
					LIABILITIES								
	16.5		15.2	14.0	Notes Payable-Short Term								
	2.9		2.3	1.9	Cur. Mat.-L /T/D								
	15.7		11.7	8.5	Trade Payables								
	.2		.4	.2	Income Taxes Payable								
	9.2		11.2	9.9	All Other Current								
	44.5		40.9	34.5	Total Current								
	12.9		7.2	15.7	Long Term Debt								
	.2		.2	.5	Deferred Taxes								
	3.0		2.4	3.4	All Other-Non-Current								
	39.5		49.3	45.9	Net Worth								
	100.0		100.0	100.0	Total Liabilities & Net Worth								
					INCOME DATA								
	100.0		100.0	100.0	Net Sales								
	32.9		28.9	31.2	Gross Profit								
	25.9		24.9	24.3	Operating Expenses								
	7.0		4.0	6.8	Operating Profit								
	1.8		1.3	1.5	All Other Expenses (net)								
	5.2		2.7	5.3	Profit Before Taxes								
					RATIOS								
	2.6		3.2	4.1									
	1.7		1.8	2.4	Current								
	1.3		1.3	1.5									
	1.4		1.4	2.0									
	.9		.9	1.2	Quick								
	.6		.6	.7									
41	9.0	35	10.3	42 8.7									
51	7.2	49	7.4	54 6.8	Sales/Receivables								
61	6.0	64	5.7	65 5.6									
49	7.4	68	5.4	61 6.0									
78	4.7	83	4.4	87 4.2	Cost of Sales/Inventory								
104	3.5	130	2.8	130 2.8									
18	20.2	12	29.5	15 24.4									
29	12.8	22	16.4	20 18.6	Cost of Sales/Payables								
43	8.5	36	10.2	34 10.8									
	4.6		3.3	3.2									
	9.6		5.9	4.6	Sales/Working Capital								
	14.5		17.8	12.0									
	12.6		8.8	8.6									
(24)	4.2	(33)	3.4	(28) 3.0	EBIT/Interest								
	2.3		1.7	2.1									
	3.5			8.9	Net Profit + Depr., Dep.,								
(10)	2.0			(10) 4.7	Amort./Cur. Mat. L/T/D								
	1.2			1.5									
	.2		.1	.1									
	.4		.3	.3	Fixed/Worth								
	1.0		.6	1.0									
	.7		.4	.5									
	1.8		1.3	1.2	Debt/Worth								
	3.7		2.3	2.7									
	58.3		38.8	32.0	% Profit Before Taxes/Tangible								
(25)	30.6	(33)	19.1	(26) 21.2	Net Worth								
	16.7		2.9	14.4									
	19.7		17.5	15.7	% Profit Before Taxes/Total								
	12.5		9.2	8.2	Assets								
	6.3		2.0	4.0									
	31.5		36.2	37.3									
	18.6		16.3	10.1	Sales/Net Fixed Assets								
	10.5		9.2	7.0									
	3.4		2.9	2.7									
	2.5		2.2	2.0	Sales/Total Assets								
	1.8		1.7	1.6									
	.7		.8	.6									
(25)	1.0	(31)	1.6	(26) 1.4	% Depr., Dep., Amort./Sales								
	1.7		2.2	2.2									
	2.6		2.9	1.8	% Officers', Directors',								
(12)	4.6	(18)	3.8	(11) 3.1	Owners' Comp/Sales								
	7.4		7.6	7.1									
	296783M		624246M	688475M	Net Sales ($)		8723M	20260M	40169M	102329M		516994M	
	155044M		382922M	548756M	Total Assets ($)		3969M	13154M	19475M	43503M		468655M	

© Robert Morris Associates 1995   M = $ thousand   MM = $ million
See Pages 1 through 15 for Explanation of Ratios and Data

Current Data Sorted By Assets | Comparative Historical Data

 # Postretirement Benefits

Type of Statement

0-500M	500M-2MM	2-10MM	10-50MM	50-100MM	100-250MM	Type of Statement	4/1/90-3/31/91	4/1/91-3/31/92
	2		3	2		(# Postretirement Benefits)		
1	1	1	7	2		Unqualified	18	12
	4	8	1			Reviewed	12	12
	4		1			Compiled	7	10
						Tax Returns		
1	2	4	5			Other		
	8 (4/1-9/30/94)		34 (10/1/94-3/31/95)				6 4/1/90-3/31/91 ALL	7 4/1/91-3/31/92 ALL
2	11	13	14	2		NUMBER OF STATEMENTS	43	41

0-500M %	500M-2MM %	2-10MM %	10-50MM %	50-100MM %	100-250MM %		4/1/90-3/31/91 ALL %	4/1/91-3/31/92 ALL %
						ASSETS		
	8.2	2.1	4.5			Cash & Equivalents	3.6	5.1
	24.8	33.8	21.1			Trade Receivables - (net)	29.8	25.9
	33.4	42.6	36.6			Inventory	40.5	36.4
	.2	.7	5.2			All Other Current	.7	.9
	66.6	79.2	67.3			Total Current	74.6	68.3
	26.0	16.1	23.6			Fixed Assets (net)	18.3	24.6
	1.1	.4	1.2			Intangibles (net)	1.6	2.2
	6.4	4.3	7.9			All Other Non-Current	5.5	4.9
	100.0	100.0	100.0			Total	100.0	100.0
						LIABILITIES		
	5.7	20.9	7.3			Notes Payable-Short Term	14.4	13.2
	4.8	5.3	4.8			Cur. Mat. -L/T/D	2.3	3.6
	18.2	20.1	16.6			Trade Payables	20.5	20.7
	.7	.1	.3			Income Taxes Payable	.6	.3
	4.6	12.4	10.5			All Other Current	8.1	7.3
	33.9	58.8	39.5			Total Current	46.0	45.1
	8.9	10.5	20.7			Long Term Debt	13.7	13.9
	.0	.2	1.3			Deferred Taxes	.2	.2
	.3	3.2	2.1			All Other-Non-Current	3.5	2.3
	56.8	27.3	36.4			Net Worth	36.5	38.5
	100.0	100.0	100.0			Total Liabilities & Net Worth	100.0	100.0
						INCOME DATA		
	100.0	100.0	100.0			Net Sales	100.0	100.0
	29.6	27.2	25.8			Gross Profit	25.2	26.6
	24.0	23.3	19.2			Operating Expenses	21.3	21.7
	5.6	3.9	6.6			Operating Profit	3.9	4.9
	1.2	1.9	1.7			All Other Expenses (net)	2.1	1.6
	4.4	2.1	4.8			Profit Before Taxes	1.7	3.3
						RATIOS		
	3.0	1.7	2.6			Current	2.1	2.1
	2.3	1.2	1.6				1.6	1.6
	1.2	1.1	1.3				1.2	1.1
	1.7	.9	1.1			Quick	1.1	1.0
	.9	.6	.7				.7	.7
	.6	.5	.3				.5	.4
	11 33.5	39 9.3	3 106.8			Sales/Receivables	35 10.5	27 13.5
	33 11.2	58 6.3	46 8.0				47 7.8	41 8.9
	42 8.7	70 5.2	55 6.6				54 6.7	54 6.8
	26 13.9	57 6.4	45 8.1			Cost of Sales/Inventory	53 6.9	51 7.1
	59 6.2	78 4.7	91 4.0				81 4.5	70 5.2
	78 4.7	152 2.4	118 3.1				126 2.9	99 3.7
	11 32.3	22 16.4	28 13.2			Cost of Sales/Payables	23 15.9	17 21.1
	24 15.4	31 11.8	38 9.7				40 9.1	39 9.4
	49 7.5	54 6.7	43 8.5				57 6.4	57 6.4
	6.2	7.2	4.4			Sales/Working Capital	6.0	6.2
	11.2	11.6	10.9				7.9	9.3
	36.1	39.0	12.3				16.2	38.4
	16.5	5.8	6.0			EBIT/Interest	(41) 3.6	(37) 5.2
	5.6	(12) 3.4	2.9				1.8	2.3
	2.0	1.3	1.3				1.1	1.4
						Net Profit + Depr., Dep., Amort./Cur. Mat. L./T/D	(28) 13.3	(24) 3.9
							2.7	1.8
							1.5	1.3
	.1	.4	.3			Fixed/Worth	.2	.4
	.5	.5	.6				.5	.7
	.8	.9	1.3				.9	1.2
	.4	1.7	1.0			Debt/Worth	1.0	.9
	.8	2.9	1.6				2.1	2.0
	2.2	4.5	3.4				3.9	3.5
	35.1	50.6	35.7			% Profit Before Taxes/Tangible Net Worth	(41) 29.9	(39) 40.9
	19.2	28.1	(13) 18.5				10.9	16.8
	8.1	2.9	7.0				2.0	8.4
	23.8	13.8	17.0			% Profit Before Taxes/Total Assets	7.8	11.1
	10.9	10.8	7.6				3.7	6.0
	5.4	1.1	2.7				.4	2.1
	55.3	26.8	17.8			Sales/Net Fixed Assets	30.4	23.2
	12.9	18.1	11.9				18.4	12.7
	8.5	9.7	6.5				7.2	6.5
	4.4	2.7	3.0			Sales/Total Assets	2.9	3.0
	2.9	2.4	2.0				2.4	2.4
	2.4	1.8	1.7				1.6	2.1
	(10) 1.5	.5	(12) .9			% Depr., Dep., Amort./Sales	(40) .9	(39) 1.1
	2.1	1.2	1.5				1.4	1.7
	4.0	1.5	3.0				1.9	2.2
						% Officers', Directors', Owners' Comp/Sales	(17) 2.6	(15) 2.1
							4.1	4.1
							5.7	7.0
29M	37159M	136950M	639581M	202402M		Net Sales ($)	752980M	670166M
12M	11666M	58988M	288114M	124305M		Total Assets ($)	383528M	429984M

M = $ thousand   MM = $ million
See Pages 1 through 15 for Explanation of Ratios and Data

Comparative Historical Data				Current Data Sorted By Sales					
2	2	5	# Postretirement Benefits	2				1	2
			Type of Statement		8 (4/1-9/30/94)		34 (10/1/94-3/31/95)		
14	8	12	Unqualified	1		1		1	9
17	20	13	Reviewed		3	2	4	3	1
7	3	5	Compiled		2	2			1
1			Tax Returns						
9	13	12	Other	1		1		2	4
4/1/92-3/31/93 ALL	4/1/93-3/31/94 ALL	4/1/94-3/31/95 ALL		0-1MM	1-3MM	3-5MM	5-10MM	10-25MM	25MM & OVER
48	44	42	NUMBER OF STATEMENTS	2	5	6	8	6	15
%	%	%	ASSETS	%	%	%	%	%	%
4.6	3.7	4.7	Cash & Equivalents						5.0
25.3	31.4	27.3	Trade Receivables - (net)						22.0
38.2	34.7	37.6	Inventory						38.0
2.4	1.5	2.0	All Other Current						4.9
70.5	71.3	71.7	Total Current						69.8
21.3	22.0	21.3	Fixed Assets (net)						22.0
2.1	2.2	1.2	Intangibles (net)						2.4
6.1	4.5	5.8	All Other Non-Current						5.8
100.0	100.0	100.0	Total						100.0
			LIABILITIES						
14.4	14.9	11.8	Notes Payable-Short Term						9.7
3.9	2.8	4.6	Cur. Mat.-L./T/D						4.5
16.9	17.3	17.2	Trade Payables						16.7
.6	2.4	.3	Income Taxes Payable						.3
8.4	8.5	9.9	All Other Current						8.3
44.1	45.9	43.8	Total Current						39.3
15.2	13.9	13.3	Long Term Debt						19.7
.4	.6	.5	Deferred Taxes						1.0
4.4	1.9	1.9	All Other-Non-Current						2.2
35.9	37.7	40.5	Net Worth						37.8
100.0	100.0	100.0	Total Liabilities & Net Worth						100.0
			INCOME DATA						
100.0	100.0	100.0	Net Sales						100.0
26.1	25.5	27.5	Gross Profit						25.4
20.9	22.6	21.7	Operating Expenses						18.6
5.2	2.9	5.8	Operating Profit						6.7
1.8	1.4	1.5	All Other Expenses (net)						1.5
3.4	1.6	4.3	Profit Before Taxes						5.2
			RATIOS						
2.3	2.2	2.4	Current						3.0
1.6	1.6	1.6							1.6
1.3	1.2	1.2							1.4
1.2	1.2	1.1	Quick						1.5
.8	.8	.7							.7
.5	.5	.5							.4
31 11.7	35 10.3	27 13.6	Sales/Receivables						28 13.2
47 7.8	49 7.4	47 7.8							43 8.5
54 6.8	64 5.7	64 5.7							66 5.5
54 6.7	48 7.6	45 8.1	Cost of Sales/Inventory						45 8.1
81 4.5	68 5.4	76 4.8							94 3.9
104 3.5	104 3.5	118 3.1							114 3.2
21 17.8	22 16.9	20 18.6	Cost of Sales/Payables						29 12.5
33 10.9	38 9.7	31 11.7							36 10.1
46 7.9	46 7.9	45 8.2							42 8.6
6.4	5.5	4.7	Sales/Working Capital						4.5
10.4	7.9	10.9							9.5
14.7	17.9	18.8							12.2
(45) 5.5	(40) 5.0	(38) 6.8	EBIT/Interest					(14)	10.8
3.0	2.6	4.0							3.8
1.6	1.3	1.7							2.2
(27) 4.3	(18) 4.8	(18) 16.0	Net Profit + Depr., Dep., Amort./Cur. Mat. L/T/D						
2.6	2.3	3.0							
1.3	.3	1.7							
.4	.3	.3	Fixed/Worth						.3
.6	.5	.5							.6
1.2	1.0	.9							1.3
1.2	1.0	.9	Debt/Worth						1.2
2.1	1.8	1.6							1.6
3.3	3.6	3.0							3.4
(46) 40.6	(42) 28.0	(41) 38.3	% Profit Before Taxes/Tangible Net Worth					(14)	33.5
15.7	13.7	22.2							25.5
7.8	4.7	7.6							8.7
12.6	9.8	13.8	% Profit Before Taxes/Total Assets						13.7
7.1	6.3	9.1							8.0
2.1	1.1	3.3							4.2
22.1	23.4	28.8	Sales/Net Fixed Assets						13.8
12.2	12.4	12.6							12.1
6.7	7.3	8.5							7.3
3.1	3.0	3.0	Sales/Total Assets						3.0
2.2	2.2	2.4							2.0
1.7	1.8	1.8							1.8
(46) .9	(42) .9	(38) .8	% Depr., Dep., Amort./Sales					(13)	.8
1.7	1.2	1.5							1.4
2.7	1.9	2.2							2.1
(16) 1.8	(16) 2.0	(19) 1.4	% Officers', Directors', Owners' Comp/Sales						
4.4	4.6	3.1							
6.8	6.0	5.3							
1378639M	1336258M	1016121M	Net Sales ($)	29M	9609M	22208M	57026M	92534M	834715M
667868M	645115M	483085M	Total Assets ($)	12M	6151M	6613M	21980M	47921M	400408M

© Robert Morris Associates 1995

M = $ thousand   MM = $ million

See Pages 1 through 15 for Explanation of Ratios and Data

Current Data Sorted By Assets							Comparative Historical Data	
1			1					
2	5		5					
	3					# Postretirement Benefits		
						Type of Statement		
						Unqualified	13	10
						Reviewed	3	3
						Compiled	3	3
						Tax Returns		
1			2	1	1	Other	3	1
	9 (4/1-9/30/94)		11 (10/1/94-3/31/95)				4/1/90- 3/31/91	4/1/91- 3/31/92
0-500M	500M-2MM	2-10MM	10-50MM	50-100MM	100-250MM		ALL	ALL
3		8	7	1	1	NUMBER OF STATEMENTS	22	17
%	%	%	%	%	%	ASSETS	%	%
						Cash & Equivalents	5.2	6.9
						Trade Receivables - (net)	26.0	27.2
						Inventory	36.6	34.5
						All Other Current	3.1	1.1
						Total Current	70.9	69.7
						Fixed Assets (net)	19.3	18.0
						Intangibles (net)	.5	2.5
						All Other Non-Current	9.2	9.8
						Total	100.0	100.0
						LIABILITIES		
						Notes Payable-Short Term	14.1	9.6
						Cur. Mat. -L/T/D	1.9	3.0
						Trade Payables	14.9	12.7
						Income Taxes Payable	.3	.2
						All Other Current	9.6	9.5
						Total Current	40.7	35.1
						Long Term Debt	8.7	9.4
						Deferred Taxes	.6	1.1
						All Other-Non-Current	.7	3.1
						Net Worth	49.2	51.3
						Total Liabilities & Net Worth	100.0	100.0
						INCOME DATA		
						Net Sales	100.0	100.0
						Gross Profit	20.8	19.6
						Operating Expenses	17.8	18.9
						Operating Profit	3.0	.6
						All Other Expenses (net)	1.7	2.1
						Profit Before Taxes	1.4	−1.5
						RATIOS		
						Current	3.3	3.0
							1.6	2.1
							1.3	1.6
						Quick	1.4	1.4
							.8	.9
							.6	.7
						Sales/Receivables	23 15.9	27 13.4
							39 9.4	51 7.2
							64 5.7	61 6.0
						Cost of Sales/Inventory	41 8.9	54 6.8
							69 5.3	89 4.1
							118 3.1	104 3.5
						Cost of Sales/Payables	8 43.3	14 25.8
							21 17.8	23 15.8
							33 11.1	38 9.5
						Sales/Working Capital	4.2	3.6
							7.8	5.2
							20.8	8.5
						EBIT/Interest	12.7	4.5
							(21) 1.2	2.3
							−.1	−1.9
						Net Profit + Depr., Dep., Amort./Cur. Mat. L /T/D	12.0	
							(13) 2.4	
							−.3	
						Fixed/Worth	.2	.1
							.3	.3
							.8	1.1
						Debt/Worth	.3	.5
							1.4	1.1
							2.3	2.1
						% Profit Before Taxes/Tangible Net Worth	18.1	15.3
							5.4	2.3
							−8.2	−14.3
						% Profit Before Taxes/Total Assets	10.1	6.7
							1.6	1.6
							−2.8	−11.0
						Sales/Net Fixed Assets	31.6	44.9
							12.6	12.2
							8.3	8.4
						Sales/Total Assets	2.5	2.7
							2.2	2.0
							1.7	1.6
						% Depr., Dep., Amort./Sales	.7	.7
							1.2	(14) 1.5
							1.8	2.4
						% Officers', Directors', Owners' Comp/Sales		
9227M	154920M	442713M	100359M	400000M		Net Sales ($)	1142207M	460388M
4558M	41077M	214815M	52023M	205718M		Total Assets ($)	642454M	255499M

M = $ thousand   MM = $ million

See Pages 1 through 15 for Explanation of Ratios and Data

Comparative Historical Data				Current Data Sorted By Sales					
3	3	2	# Postretirement Benefits		1				1
			Type of Statement						
14	17	12	Unqualified			3		3	6
5	4	3	Reviewed				2	1	
2		5	Compiled						
			Tax Returns						
			Other		1				4
3 4/1/92-3/31/93 ALL	**4** 4/1/93-3/31/94 ALL	**5** 4/1/94-3/31/95 ALL		0-1MM	1-3MM **9 (4/1-9/30/94)**	3-5MM	5-10MM	10-25MM **11 (10/1/94-3/31/95)**	25MM & OVER **4**
24	30	20	**NUMBER OF STATEMENTS**		1	3	2	4	10
%	%	%	**ASSETS**	%	%	%	%	%	%
6.7	5.4	4.4	Cash & Equivalents						4.0
32.3	24.5	27.1	Trade Receivables - (net)						28.5
35.6	42.7	41.8	Inventory						47.1
2.5	2.9	1.1	All Other Current						1.3
77.0	75.7	74.4	Total Current						80.9
17.7	14.5	14.7	Fixed Assets (net)						16.4
.6	1.4	3.2	Intangibles (net)						.3
4.7	8.3	7.7	All Other Non-Current						2.4
100.0	100.0	100.0	Total						100.0
			LIABILITIES						
17.4	11.1	12.9	Notes Payable-Short Term						12.0
1.6	2.6	1.7	Cur. Mat.-L /T/D						1.8
18.0	20.4	24.2	Trade Payables						28.5
.2	.5	.5	Income Taxes Payable						.2
8.4	9.0	6.6	All Other Current						5.8
45.6	43.7	45.7	Total Current						48.3
10.2	9.9	9.0	Long Term Debt						9.1
.3	.4	.4	Deferred Taxes						.5
4.8	4.5	2.4	All Other-Non-Current						1.3
39.1	41.4	42.5	Net Worth						40.9
100.0	100.0	100.0	Total Liabilities & Net Worth						100.0
			INCOME DATA						
100.0	100.0	100.0	Net Sales						100.0
26.5	20.8	17.4	Gross Profit						16.1
20.5	16.8	13.2	Operating Expenses						10.2
6.0	4.0	4.3	Operating Profit						5.9
.9	.4	.4	All Other Expenses (net)						.8
5.1	3.6	3.8	Profit Before Taxes						5.1
			RATIOS						
3.1 / 1.9 / 1.2	2.4 / 2.1 / 1.3	2.2 / 1.7 / 1.3	Current						2.3 / 1.7 / 1.2
1.4 / 1.0 / .5	1.1 / .6 / .4	1.3 / .6 / .5	Quick						1.3 / .6 / .5
(28) 13.0 / (48) 7.6 / (66) 5.5	(25) 14.8 / (40) 9.1 / (57) 6.4	(35) 10.3 / (45) 8.2 / (62) 5.9	Sales/Receivables						(36) 10.1 / (45) 8.1 / (62) 5.9
(29) 12.5 / (101) 3.6 / (126) 2.9	(40) 9.2 / (89) 4.1 / (146) 2.5	(45) 8.2 / (89) 4.1 / (122) 3.0	Cost of Sales/Inventory						(49) 7.4 / (107) 3.4 / (122) 3.0
(15) 25.1 / (30) 12.1 / (45) 8.2	(23) 16.1 / (33) 11.0 / (47) 7.8	(26) 13.9 / (42) 8.6 / (50) 7.3	Cost of Sales/Payables						(43) 8.5 / (47) 7.7 / (56) 6.5
3.9 / 5.7 / 15.1	3.9 / 6.6 / 18.1	4.9 / 7.3 / 11.7	Sales/Working Capital						4.4 / 6.7 / 17.8
(23) 23.4 / 3.3 / 1.4	(29) 7.8 / 3.8 / 2.0	(19) 6.7 / 4.2 / 1.3	EBIT/Interest						244.6 / 4.5 / 3.2
(11) 11.9 / 6.4 / .9	(12) 12.4 / 3.5 / .9	(11) 7.9 / 2.2 / 1.0	Net Profit + Depr., Dep., Amort./Cur. Mat. L/T/D						
.2 / .4 / .8	.1 / .3 / .5	.1 / .3 / .9	Fixed/Worth						.2 / .3 / .8
.6 / 1.4 / 5.0	.6 / 1.3 / 2.9	.8 / 1.9 / 3.9	Debt/Worth						.8 / 1.7 / 3.9
(22) 52.9 / 21.3 / 12.3	(29) 36.7 / 17.0 / 8.8	40.7 / 24.9 / 4.2	% Profit Before Taxes/Tangible Net Worth						42.8 / 27.3 / 13.7
18.2 / 7.4 / 1.6	13.2 / 4.9 / 2.2	13.5 / 8.8 / 1.5	% Profit Before Taxes/Total Assets						14.5 / 9.9 / 4.7
27.7 / 13.3 / 7.3	59.1 / 18.2 / 12.0	60.7 / 14.5 / 10.1	Sales/Net Fixed Assets						38.7 / 13.9 / 10.0
2.8 / 2.0 / 1.6	3.0 / 2.2 / 1.8	2.9 / 2.2 / 1.8	Sales/Total Assets						2.3 / 2.1 / 1.9
(21) .6 / 1.2 / 1.9	(26) .3 / .6 / 1.2	(17) .9 / 1.2 / 1.5	% Depr., Dep., Amort./Sales						
	(12) .8 / 2.4 / 4.4		% Officers', Directors', Owners' Comp/Sales						
2241127M	1983353M	1107219M	Net Sales ($)		1967M	12232M	14304M	73354M	1005362M
1175457M	942066M	518191M	Total Assets ($)		676M	7218M	6704M	22541M	481052M

M = $ thousand   MM = $ million
See Pages 1 through 15 for Explanation of Ratios and Data

Current Data Sorted By Assets   Comparative Historical Data

0-500M	500M-2MM	2-10MM	10-50MM	50-100MM	100-250MM		4/1/90-3/31/91 ALL	4/1/91-3/31/92 ALL
	3	2	2			# Postretirement Benefits		
						Type of Statement		
	2	10	18	1	4	Unqualified	28	32
	9	16	4		1	Reviewed	21	26
4	4	3				Compiled	14	12
1	2					Tax Returns		
2	8	6	2			Other	14	10
	23 (4/1-9/30/94)		74 (10/1/94-3/31/95)					
7	25	35	24	1	5	**NUMBER OF STATEMENTS**	77	80
%	%	%	%	%	%	**ASSETS**	%	%
	4.6	6.7	5.2			Cash & Equivalents	5.8	7.9
	23.7	25.0	24.1			Trade Receivables - (net)	29.4	31.1
	48.3	44.3	37.3			Inventory	38.3	39.2
	1.2	1.8	2.8			All Other Current	1.7	1.9
	77.9	77.8	69.4			Total Current	75.2	80.1
	17.8	11.5	20.2			Fixed Assets (net)	16.3	13.6
	.8	2.3	1.5			Intangibles (net)	1.9	1.2
	3.5	8.4	8.9			All Other Non-Current	6.6	5.1
	100.0	100.0	100.0			Total	100.0	100.0
						LIABILITIES		
	14.6	15.0	13.5			Notes Payable-Short Term	19.8	17.3
	5.3	2.8	2.8			Cur. Mat. -L/T/D	3.6	2.1
	22.5	20.0	17.0			Trade Payables	13.0	16.9
	.1	.7	1.3			Income Taxes Payable	.4	.6
	9.7	5.7	11.2			All Other Current	6.6	7.5
	52.2	44.2	45.7			Total Current	43.4	44.3
	14.2	9.0	11.8			Long Term Debt	12.6	8.5
	.6	.3	.7			Deferred Taxes	.4	.3
	5.7	1.7	4.1			All Other-Non-Current	5.6	5.2
	27.4	44.7	37.6			Net Worth	38.0	41.7
	100.0	100.0	100.0			Total Liabilities & Net Worth	100.0	100.0
						INCOME DATA		
	100.0	100.0	100.0			Net Sales	100.0	100.0
	31.6	27.0	20.8			Gross Profit	31.4	25.8
	26.9	22.6	18.1			Operating Expenses	26.9	21.6
	4.8	4.5	2.8			Operating Profit	4.5	4.1
	2.0	1.5	1.4			All Other Expenses (net)	1.6	1.7
	2.7	3.0	1.4			Profit Before Taxes	2.9	2.4
						RATIOS		
	2.0 / 1.6 / 1.1	2.8 / 1.7 / 1.4	2.6 / 1.5 / 1.1			Current	3.2 / 1.8 / 1.2	2.8 / 1.8 / 1.4
	.9 / .6 / .3	1.0 / .7 / .6	1.3 / .7 / .2			Quick	1.4 / .8 / .5	1.5 / .8 / .6
	15 24.9 / 29 12.6 / 60 6.1	23 16.0 / 41 9.0 / 59 6.2	8 45.0 / 45 8.2 / 73 5.0			Sales/Receivables	35 10.3 / 49 7.4 / 70 5.2	26 13.8 / 47 7.7 / 64 5.7
	48 7.6 / 114 3.2 / 174 2.1	66 5.5 / 91 4.0 / 146 2.5	54 6.8 / 81 4.5 / 140 2.6			Cost of Sales/Inventory	57 6.4 / 104 3.5 / 166 2.2	41 8.8 / 85 4.3 / 135 2.7
	26 14.3 / 35 10.5 / 68 5.4	25 14.5 / 40 9.2 / 56 6.5	22 16.8 / 32 11.4 / 47 7.7			Cost of Sales/Payables	16 22.6 / 29 12.5 / 49 7.5	19 19.3 / 33 11.2 / 42 8.7
	5.3 / 10.1 / 523.9	4.5 / 6.8 / 11.8	4.4 / 8.2 / 40.8			Sales/Working Capital	3.5 / 6.2 / 16.7	4.2 / 7.0 / 16.9
	(22) 3.6 / 2.5 / 1.1	(31) 4.9 / 3.0 / 1.7	(22) 6.7 / 2.2 / .6			EBIT/Interest	(70) 6.0 / 2.5 / 1.0	(71) 5.7 / 2.4 / .6
		(11) 12.3 / 3.0 / .7	(13) 14.0 / 2.3 / .9			Net Profit + Depr., Dep., Amort./Cur. Mat. L /T/D	(37) 9.5 / 1.5 / .2	(34) 13.3 / 4.0 / 1.2
	.1 / .6 / 1.6	.1 / .2 / .7	.3 / .5 / 1.1			Fixed/Worth	.1 / .3 / 1.0	.1 / .3 / .8
	1.3 / 3.2 / 6.4	.7 / 1.9 / 2.8	.9 / 2.0 / 3.2			Debt/Worth	.9 / 1.7 / 4.3	.6 / 1.5 / 3.2
	(23) 35.3 / 23.1 / 6.7	54.3 / 22.8 / 9.1	31.0 / 10.0 / -2.3			% Profit Before Taxes/Tangible Net Worth	(71) 34.4 / 17.2 / .9	(75) 41.1 / 18.4 / .0
	11.0 / 7.2 / .5	14.9 / 7.3 / 3.7	13.6 / 4.0 / -.5			% Profit Before Taxes/Total Assets	14.9 / 5.7 / .2	14.7 / 6.4 / -.7
	71.5 / 30.1 / 10.2	49.0 / 22.3 / 11.2	30.4 / 11.3 / 5.6			Sales/Net Fixed Assets	53.1 / 18.1 / 8.4	58.9 / 22.2 / 11.6
	3.3 / 2.8 / 1.8	2.9 / 2.1 / 1.6	2.3 / 1.7 / 1.5			Sales/Total Assets	2.6 / 1.8 / 1.4	3.4 / 2.5 / 1.8
	.5 / 1.3 / 2.0	(34) .6 / 1.2 / 2.1	(21) .5 / 1.4 / 2.9			% Depr., Dep., Amort./Sales	(66) .6 / 1.3 / 2.2	(71) .4 / 1.1 / 1.7
	(15) 1.4 / 2.9 / 9.1	(16) 1.5 / 2.9 / 4.2				% Officers', Directors', Owners' Comp/Sales	(31) 2.5 / 4.0 / 5.1	(33) 1.6 / 3.0 / 5.2
8096M	74694M	340163M	1245917M	64239M	1574203M	Net Sales ($)	2863846M	2085730M
2623M	27927M	142919M	623753M	50414M	829961M	Total Assets ($)	1593711M	943329M

M = $ thousand   MM = $ million
See Pages 1 through 15 for Explanation of Ratios and Data

Comparative Historical Data				Current Data Sorted By Sales					
2	9	7	**# Postretirement Benefits**		2	2		1	2
			Type of Statement						
34	35	35	Unqualified		2	1	4	6	22
30	27	30	Reviewed		5	7	7	8	3
15	18	11	Compiled	2	4	2	1	2	
1	1	3	Tax Returns		3				
9	18	18	Other		7	3	4	3	1
4/1/92-3/31/93 ALL	4/1/93-3/31/94 ALL	4/1/94-3/31/95 ALL		0-1MM	23 (4/1-9/30/94) 1-3MM	3-5MM	74 (10/1/94-3/31/95) 5-10MM	10-25MM	25MM & OVER
89	99	97	**NUMBER OF STATEMENTS**	2	21	13	16	19	26
%	%	%	**ASSETS**	%	%	%	%	%	%
4.4	5.8	5.6	Cash & Equivalents		5.7	8.4	5.3	4.2	5.3
26.8	26.7	24.4	Trade Receivables - (net)		23.8	22.1	29.6	26.4	21.9
41.4	40.9	42.8	Inventory		45.4	39.5	40.4	43.6	41.4
2.9	3.6	1.9	All Other Current		.8	2.8	1.5	1.7	3.0
75.5	77.1	74.7	Total Current		75.6	72.8	76.8	75.9	71.6
17.7	15.2	16.5	Fixed Assets (net)		18.8	15.5	14.7	12.8	19.4
.8	1.6	1.9	Intangibles (net)		.6	1.1	3.7	1.0	3.1
6.0	6.2	6.9	All Other Non-Current		5.0	10.6	4.8	10.3	5.9
100.0	100.0	100.0	Total		100.0	100.0	100.0	100.0	100.0
			LIABILITIES						
13.5	13.9	13.8	Notes Payable-Short Term		12.5	16.7	15.7	21.5	7.8
2.8	1.9	3.7	Cur. Mat.-L /T/D		5.2	2.7	3.2	2.7	3.0
15.7	16.3	19.4	Trade Payables		22.7	16.5	20.4	21.6	16.7
1.0	1.0	.6	Income Taxes Payable		.1	.2	.4	1.3	1.0
8.2	10.0	8.4	All Other Current		7.4	5.5	12.1	5.3	10.8
41.2	43.1	45.9	Total Current		47.9	41.6	51.9	52.4	39.4
11.9	10.2	12.3	Long Term Debt		20.6	14.0	10.6	5.9	11.3
.3	.2	.5	Deferred Taxes		.2	.1	1.1	.2	.9
4.1	3.8	3.8	All Other-Non-Current		1.7	3.2	1.5	1.5	6.3
42.5	42.6	37.4	Net Worth		29.7	41.0	34.9	40.1	42.1
100.0	100.0	100.0	Total Liabilities & Net Worth		100.0	100.0	100.0	100.0	100.0
			INCOME DATA						
100.0	100.0	100.0	Net Sales		100.0	100.0	100.0	100.0	100.0
29.9	25.9	26.7	Gross Profit		30.8	27.4	25.6	28.6	21.8
24.1	22.0	22.5	Operating Expenses		25.1	26.9	20.3	22.6	18.6
5.8	3.9	4.3	Operating Profit		5.7	.4	5.3	5.9	3.2
1.6	1.5	1.7	All Other Expenses (net)		2.0	1.9	1.5	1.1	2.0
4.2	2.4	2.5	Profit Before Taxes		3.7	-1.5	3.8	4.9	1.2
			RATIOS						
2.5	2.9	2.5	Current		2.0	3.1	2.4	1.8	3.2
1.8	1.8	1.7			1.6	1.9	1.4	1.5	2.0
1.4	1.3	1.3			1.3	1.3	1.1	1.2	1.4
1.3	1.3	1.1	Quick		1.0	1.0	1.1	.9	1.4
.7	.8	.7			.6	.7	.6	.6	.7
.4	.5	.4			.4	.5	.5	.3	.4
26 14.2	24 15.4	17 21.4	Sales/Receivables	18 20.4	16 23.5	18 20.5	11 33.5	21 17.3	
47 7.8	43 8.4	41 8.8		34 10.7	37 10.0	49 7.5	39 9.4	45 8.2	
59 6.2	61 6.0	60 6.1		61 6.0	54 6.7	63 5.8	58 6.3	64 5.7	
61 6.0	53 6.9	59 6.2	Cost of Sales/Inventory	41 8.9	62 5.9	49 7.5	59 6.2	63 5.8	
99 3.7	89 4.1	91 4.0		114 3.2	87 4.2	89 4.1	74 4.9	91 4.0	
152 2.4	126 2.9	146 2.5		152 2.4	166 2.2	122 3.0	140 2.6	146 2.5	
21 17.7	16 22.5	23 15.7	Cost of Sales/Payables	25 14.5	27 13.3	20 18.4	27 13.6	20 18.3	
35 10.3	31 11.8	34 10.7		37 9.9	37 10.0	35 10.4	38 9.5	31 11.6	
46 7.9	40 9.2	51 7.1		79 4.6	48 7.6	58 6.3	56 6.5	45 8.1	
4.9	4.3	4.8	Sales/Working Capital		6.0	3.6	5.0	6.2	3.4
7.3	7.2	7.4			7.8	5.8	10.0	9.5	6.0
10.5	14.4	21.8			25.1	30.2	50.1	20.7	10.7
(84) 9.0	(86) 8.2	(88) 4.9	EBIT/Interest	(17) 7.0	(12) 3.7	(15) 3.7	(17) 11.1	(25) 10.9	
3.4	3.4	2.6		3.5	2.1	2.6	3.2	2.3	
1.8	1.5	1.4		1.7	1.1	1.4	2.0	.1	
(38) 9.7	(32) 7.3	(36) 16.8	Net Profit + Depr., Dep., Amort./Cur. Mat. L/T/D				(17) 7.5		
4.7	3.5	3.1					2.3		
1.5	1.6	.8					.8		
.1	.1	.1	Fixed/Worth		.1	.1	.1	.1	.3
.4	.3	.4			.6	.6	.3	.3	.4
.9	.7	1.0			1.8	1.1	1.1	.7	.9
.7	.7	.9	Debt/Worth		1.2	.6	1.1	.8	.8
1.6	1.5	1.9			2.3	1.9	2.5	2.1	1.4
2.5	3.0	3.6			4.9	4.8	6.7	3.3	2.4
(84) 43.6	(94) 40.2	(93) 45.0	% Profit Before Taxes/Tangible Net Worth	(19) 52.6	27.8	(15) 72.4	46.0	(25) 36.4	
20.1	17.4	22.7		30.2	14.7	19.3	29.9	8.8	
5.8	5.3	6.3		6.7	1.1	9.1	14.9	-5.0	
15.6	14.4	13.9	% Profit Before Taxes/Total Assets		19.5	7.8	9.7	17.0	16.3
7.4	6.7	5.9			10.1	4.1	5.8	9.8	3.5
2.2	2.4	1.6			3.4	.5	2.2	3.7	-2.5
48.1	46.5	49.5	Sales/Net Fixed Assets		87.8	40.9	54.4	54.0	27.3
19.1	20.8	19.4			31.3	19.4	26.7	17.5	12.3
9.1	11.8	9.1			7.7	8.4	9.5	11.5	6.2
2.9	3.2	3.0	Sales/Total Assets		3.1	3.2	3.3	3.7	2.6
2.3	2.5	2.2			2.7	1.9	2.2	2.1	1.8
1.6	1.6	1.6			1.7	1.6	1.9	1.6	1.5
(83) .6	(96) .6	(90) .6	% Depr., Dep., Amort./Sales	(19) .4	(12) .7	.7	(18) .4	(23) .6	
1.2	1.3	1.4		1.3	1.6	1.5	1.2	1.4	
1.7	1.8	2.4		2.9	2.5	2.0	1.7	2.8	
(38) 2.4	(33) 1.4	(44) 1.5	% Officers', Directors', Owners' Comp/Sales	(13) 2.2					
4.2	2.9	3.3		6.7					
6.6	7.4	6.8		10.8					
2201693M	2292657M	3307312M	Net Sales ($)	1526M	39697M	48932M	104285M	300252M	2812620M
1190111M	1244622M	1677597M	Total Assets ($)	878M	18878M	25840M	45996M	141304M	1444701M

M = $ thousand   MM = $ million
See Pages 1 through 15 for Explanation of Ratios and Data

Current Data Sorted By Assets							Comparative Historical Data	
		1	1			# Postretirement Benefits		
						Type of Statement		
		6	4	1	2	Unqualified	17	14
	5	3	2			Reviewed	8	9
	4	1				Compiled	5	4
						Tax Returns	1	
	2	1	1			Other	5	9
	11 (4/1-9/30/94)		21 (10/1/94-3/31/95)				4/1/90-3/31/91	4/1/91-3/31/92
0-500M	500M-2MM	2-10MM	10-50MM	50-100MM	100-250MM		ALL	ALL
	11	11	7	1	2	NUMBER OF STATEMENTS	36	36
%	%	%	%	%	%	ASSETS	%	%
	4.5	6.4				Cash & Equivalents	5.6	4.5
	26.5	21.0				Trade Receivables - (net)	26.7	31.2
	47.7	43.4				Inventory	40.5	36.5
	3.7	.7				All Other Current	2.4	2.4
	82.4	71.6				Total Current	75.3	74.6
	13.7	18.2				Fixed Assets (net)	16.8	17.5
	.4	.7				Intangibles (net)	1.4	.9
	3.5	9.5				All Other Non-Current	6.5	7.1
	100.0	100.0				Total	100.0	100.0
						LIABILITIES		
	16.3	20.1				Notes Payable-Short Term	13.3	14.4
	3.0	2.5				Cur. Mat. -L/T/D	2.4	1.8
	14.6	11.3				Trade Payables	17.7	12.6
	.8	.1				Income Taxes Payable	.6	.9
	7.8	6.9				All Other Current	7.7	10.7
	42.5	40.9				Total Current	41.7	40.5
	17.9	16.3				Long Term Debt	15.9	13.8
	.1	.0				Deferred Taxes	.5	.5
	6.7	5.2				All Other-Non-Current	3.1	.9
	32.9	37.6				Net Worth	38.8	44.2
	100.0	100.0				Total Liabilities & Net Worth	100.0	100.0
						INCOME DATA		
	100.0	100.0				Net Sales	100.0	100.0
	23.0	24.6				Gross Profit	27.7	25.1
	27.6	22.7				Operating Expenses	24.3	22.4
	−4.6	1.9				Operating Profit	3.4	2.7
	1.3	1.3				All Other Expenses (net)	1.0	1.1
	−5.9	.6				Profit Before Taxes	2.4	1.6
						RATIOS		
	2.6	2.5					3.3	3.0
	1.8	1.8				Current	1.8	2.1
	1.6	1.4					1.3	1.3
	1.0	.8					1.2	1.4
	.7	.7				Quick	.9	.9
	.5	.7					.5	.6
	20 18.6	24 15.0					20 18.3	33 11.0
	37 10.0	31 11.8				Sales/Receivables	51 7.2	46 7.9
	49 7.4	56 6.5					64 5.7	66 5.5
	61 6.0	50 7.3					58 6.3	56 6.5
	99 3.7	101 3.6				Cost of Sales/Inventory	91 4.0	81 4.5
	146 2.5	174 2.1					152 2.4	126 2.9
	23 16.1	7 51.2					20 18.3	14 26.3
	27 13.3	23 15.7				Cost of Sales/Payables	33 11.1	28 13.1
	37 9.8	51 7.1					51 7.2	41 8.9
	4.6	5.0					3.9	4.0
	6.7	7.2				Sales/Working Capital	8.0	6.2
	8.7	11.4					17.4	11.7
	4.4	3.1					4.6	6.4
	2.9	1.7				EBIT/Interest	(34) 2.0	(32) 2.7
	−2.4	1.3					1.0	1.1
						Net Profit + Depr., Dep.,	10.6	4.7
						Amort./Cur. Mat. L./T/D	(23) 3.0	(20) 2.6
							1.0	.2
	.1	.2					.2	.1
	.2	.3				Fixed/Worth	.3	.4
	.9	.6					.9	.7
	1.2	1.0					.9	.7
	1.8	1.7				Debt/Worth	1.9	1.3
	2.5	2.8					4.9	2.7
	29.1	26.3				% Profit Before Taxes/Tangible	39.9	21.6
	(10) 19.7	9.6				Net Worth	12.8	7.9
	−2.3	3.2					1.2	.6
	11.6	8.4				% Profit Before Taxes/Total	12.1	8.2
	5.3	3.5				Assets	4.6	3.3
	−6.5	1.0					.3	.3
	110.0	29.4					55.8	49.3
	40.9	15.6				Sales/Net Fixed Assets	21.7	15.6
	7.1	8.1					9.6	8.2
	2.8	2.8					3.1	3.1
	2.4	1.9				Sales/Total Assets	1.9	2.0
	1.6	1.6					1.6	1.5
		.9					.7	.8
		1.3				% Depr., Dep., Amort./Sales	(33) 1.2	(34) 1.1
		2.4					1.7	2.2
						% Officers', Directors',	1.4	1.4
						Owners' Comp/Sales	(11) 3.4	(10) 2.4
							6.2	4.2
	28386M	127128M	334443M	128449M	867568M	Net Sales ($)	1655761M	1514972M
	12654M	55573M	205750M	57078M	397947M	Total Assets ($)	792455M	768188M

© Robert Morris Associates 1995

M = $ thousand   MM = $ million
See Pages 1 through 15 for Explanation of Ratios and Data

Comparative Historical Data | **Current Data Sorted By Sales**

4/1/92-3/31/93 ALL	4/1/93-3/31/94 ALL	4/1/94-3/31/95 ALL	# Postretirement Benefits / Type of Statement	0-1MM	1-3MM	3-5MM	5-10MM	10-25MM	25MM & OVER
14	10	13	Unqualified		1	1	1	4	7
8	12	10	Reviewed		4	1	2	2	1
4	4	5	Compiled		4	1			
1		1	Tax Returns						
7	6	4	Other			1		2	
					11 (4/1-9/30/94)		21 (10/1/94-3/31/95)		
34	33	32	NUMBER OF STATEMENTS		9	4	3	8	8

4/1/92-3/31/93	4/1/93-3/31/94	4/1/94-3/31/95		0-1MM	1-3MM	3-5MM	5-10MM	10-25MM	25MM & OVER
%	%	%	**ASSETS**	%	%	%	%	%	%
4.7	5.0	4.3	Cash & Equivalents						
27.9	28.6	26.4	Trade Receivables - (net)						
43.6	44.6	44.7	Inventory						
3.1	1.1	1.8	All Other Current						
79.3	79.3	77.2	Total Current						
15.5	14.5	15.5	Fixed Assets (net)						
1.0	1.4	.5	Intangibles (net)						
4.2	4.8	6.8	All Other Non-Current						
100.0	100.0	100.0	Total						
			LIABILITIES						
16.7	18.5	19.1	Notes Payable-Short Term						
2.3	2.1	2.4	Cur. Mat.-L /T/D						
17.7	16.9	12.9	Trade Payables						
.3	.6	.4	Income Taxes Payable						
10.1	7.1	8.4	All Other Current						
47.0	45.2	43.1	Total Current						
12.4	12.3	14.2	Long Term Debt						
.2	.6	.1	Deferred Taxes						
3.1	7.2	4.5	All Other-Non-Current						
37.4	34.7	38.2	Net Worth						
100.0	100.0	100.0	Total Liabilities & Net Worth						
			INCOME DATA						
100.0	100.0	100.0	Net Sales						
24.9	23.1	22.7	Gross Profit						
21.4	22.7	23.8	Operating Expenses						
3.5	.3	-1.1	Operating Profit						
2.0	1.2	1.1	All Other Expenses (net)						
1.5	-.9	-2.3	Profit Before Taxes						
			RATIOS						
2.8 / 1.9 / 1.3	2.7 / 1.9 / 1.3	2.5 / 1.8 / 1.4	Current						
1.2 / .7 / .4	1.3 / .8 / .5	.9 / .7 / .6	Quick						
(24) 15.4 / (49) 7.4 / (64) 5.7	(21) 17.8 / (45) 8.2 / (64) 5.7	(30) 12.1 / (43) 8.4 / (68) 5.4	Sales/Receivables						
(50) 7.3 / (104) 3.5 / (152) 2.4	(63) 5.8 / (91) 4.0 / (135) 2.7	(73) 5.0 / (107) 3.4 / (159) 2.3	Cost of Sales/Inventory						
(21) 17.7 / (35) 10.3 / (50) 7.3	(18) 20.4 / (31) 11.8 / (49) 7.5	(20) 18.0 / (30) 12.3 / (40) 9.1	Cost of Sales/Payables						
4.4 / 6.5 / 14.0	4.6 / 6.9 / 10.2	4.6 / 6.8 / 9.3	Sales/Working Capital						
(33) 7.7 / 2.0 / .9	(32) 4.1 / 2.4 / 1.2	(31) 4.0 / 2.8 / 1.3	EBIT/Interest						
(19) 6.6 / 3.8 / .3	(13) 12.8 / 7.6 / 3.2	(10) 8.7 / 4.1 / 1.6	Net Profit + Depr., Dep., Amort./Cur. Mat. L/T/D						
.1 / .3 / .8	.1 / .3 / 1.6	.2 / .3 / .7	Fixed/Worth						
.8 / 1.8 / 3.4	1.0 / 1.7 / 4.2	1.0 / 1.6 / 2.8	Debt/Worth						
(31) 31.4 / 14.1 / .6	(29) 25.6 / 14.8 / 3.1	(31) 22.8 / 10.0 / 3.2	% Profit Before Taxes/Tangible Net Worth						
11.4 / 3.7 / -.3	11.2 / 4.3 / .9	8.3 / 4.6 / .4	% Profit Before Taxes/Total Assets						
51.2 / 25.7 / 13.7	79.0 / 27.8 / 11.4	63.2 / 18.9 / 7.4	Sales/Net Fixed Assets						
3.1 / 2.1 / 1.5	3.1 / 2.2 / 1.6	2.6 / 2.0 / 1.5	Sales/Total Assets						
(32) .6 / 1.0 / 1.5	(29) .5 / 1.1 / 1.7	(30) .7 / 1.2 / 2.4	% Depr., Dep., Amort./Sales						
(12) 1.1 / 2.4 / 7.2	(13) 1.2 / 3.2 / 5.7	(15) 1.5 / 3.7 / 5.3	% Officers', Directors', Owners' Comp/Sales						
1892627M	1893722M	1485974M	Net Sales ($)		18779M	16292M	17651M	124918M	1308334M
912851M	942614M	729002M	Total Assets ($)		9529M	8359M	9257M	89277M	612580M

M = $ thousand   MM = $ million
See Pages 1 through 15 for Explanation of Ratios and Data

Current Data Sorted By Assets | **Comparative Historical Data**

# Postretirement Benefits / Type of Statement	0-500M	500M-2MM	2-10MM	10-50MM	50-100MM	100-250MM	4/1/90-3/31/91 ALL	4/1/91-3/31/92 ALL
Unqualified		1	1	1		1	12	15
Reviewed		2		5	2	2	4	7
Compiled		2	1				4	3
Tax Returns								
Other			3	3		1	2	4

Periods: 8 (4/1-9/30/94); 15 (10/1/94-3/31/95)

NUMBER OF STATEMENTS	0-500M	500M-2MM	2-10MM	10-50MM	50-100MM	100-250MM	4/1/90-3/31/91 ALL	4/1/91-3/31/92 ALL
		4	6	8	2	3	22	29
	%	%	%	%	%	%	%	%
ASSETS								
Cash & Equivalents							1.8	5.8
Trade Receivables - (net)							28.8	26.0
Inventory							44.1	45.4
All Other Current							2.4	.8
Total Current							77.2	78.1
Fixed Assets (net)							17.5	17.0
Intangibles (net)							1.4	1.5
All Other Non-Current							3.9	3.5
Total							100.0	100.0
LIABILITIES								
Notes Payable-Short Term							11.2	14.0
Cur. Mat. -L/T/D							2.7	2.5
Trade Payables							17.5	16.5
Income Taxes Payable							.6	.5
All Other Current							6.7	6.3
Total Current							38.7	39.7
Long Term Debt							18.0	12.2
Deferred Taxes							.5	.4
All Other-Non-Current							1.6	5.3
Net Worth							41.2	42.4
Total Liabilities & Net Worth							100.0	100.0
INCOME DATA								
Net Sales							100.0	100.0
Gross Profit							21.5	24.0
Operating Expenses							17.8	19.0
Operating Profit							3.7	5.0
All Other Expenses (net)							1.8	2.4
Profit Before Taxes							1.9	2.6

RATIOS

Ratio	4/1/90-3/31/91 ALL	4/1/91-3/31/92 ALL
Current	2.8 / 2.2 / 1.4	3.3 / 2.0 / 1.5
Quick	1.2 / .8 / .5	1.7 / .8 / .5
Sales/Receivables	(33) 10.9 / (53) 6.9 / (65) 5.6	(38) 9.6 / (50) 7.3 / (60) 6.1
Cost of Sales/Inventory	(85) 4.3 / (122) 3.0 / (140) 2.6	(94) 3.9 / (114) 3.2 / (166) 2.2
Cost of Sales/Payables	(26) 13.9 / (34) 10.8 / (54) 6.8	(22) 16.9 / (34) 10.7 / (47) 7.7
Sales/Working Capital	3.5 / 4.8 / 8.1	3.5 / 4.4 / 6.8
EBIT/Interest	5.5 / 2.7 / 1.1	6.0 / (28) 2.6 / 1.9
Net Profit + Depr., Dep., Amort./Cur. Mat. L./T/D	6.0 / (16) 1.7 / 1.1	11.7 / (23) 3.6 / 1.3
Fixed/Worth	.2 / .4 / .9	.2 / .3 / .7
Debt/Worth	.6 / 1.4 / 3.6	.5 / 1.6 / 3.5
% Profit Before Taxes/Tangible Net Worth	26.8 / (20) 20.7 / 3.5	25.4 / (27) 20.1 / 13.9
% Profit Before Taxes/Total Assets	12.4 / 5.5 / .3	10.9 / 7.0 / 3.0
Sales/Net Fixed Assets	29.2 / 16.4 / 8.0	24.5 / 12.3 / 8.7
Sales/Total Assets	2.2 / 1.9 / 1.6	2.5 / 1.8 / 1.5
% Depr., Dep., Amort./Sales	.9 / (20) 1.3 / 1.5	.7 / (27) 1.3 / 2.1
% Officers', Directors', Owners' Comp/Sales		

	0-500M	500M-2MM	2-10MM	10-50MM	50-100MM	100-250MM	4/1/90-3/31/91 ALL	4/1/91-3/31/92 ALL
Net Sales ($)		10080M	62199M	344502M	262047M	480249M	1094529M	1582201M
Total Assets ($)		3599M	30523M	207454M	146335M	404319M	682716M	1021339M

M = $ thousand   MM = $ million
See Pages 1 through 15 for Explanation of Ratios and Data

	Comparative Historical Data			Current Data Sorted By Sales					
# Postretirement Benefits		2	4		1			1	2
Type of Statement				0-1MM	1-3MM	3-5MM	5-10MM	10-25MM	25MM & OVER
Unqualified	11	12	11			1		2	8
Reviewed	4	7	2		2	1			
Compiled	3	1	3		1	1		1	
Tax Returns	1								
Other	2	3	7				1	3	3
	4/1/92-3/31/93 ALL	4/1/93-3/31/94 ALL	4/1/94-3/31/95 ALL		8 (4/1-9/30/94)			15 (10/1/94-3/31/95)	
NUMBER OF STATEMENTS	21	23	23		3	3		6	11
ASSETS	%	%	%	%	%	%	%	%	%
Cash & Equivalents	4.0	5.0	3.0						3.1
Trade Receivables - (net)	27.6	26.0	27.2						26.1
Inventory	45.2	42.3	42.2						39.9
All Other Current	2.3	.9	1.5						2.2
Total Current	79.1	74.2	74.0						71.3
Fixed Assets (net)	15.8	15.6	18.2						21.7
Intangibles (net)	.9	1.5	1.5						1.0
All Other Non-Current	4.2	8.6	6.3						6.0
Total	100.0	100.0	100.0						100.0
LIABILITIES									
Notes Payable-Short Term	12.0	10.4	16.7						10.6
Cur. Mat.-L /T/D	1.9	2.9	3.6						2.3
Trade Payables	19.7	14.6	13.1						10.4
Income Taxes Payable	1.0	.1	.4						.3
All Other Current	8.2	5.0	5.0						6.4
Total Current	42.8	33.0	38.8						30.0
Long Term Debt	9.7	11.2	10.7						14.2
Deferred Taxes	.4	.4	1.0						2.0
All Other-Non-Current	1.1	3.1	3.7						3.6
Net Worth	46.1	52.2	45.9						50.1
Total Liabilities & Net Worth	100.0	100.0	100.0						100.0
INCOME DATA									
Net Sales	100.0	100.0	100.0						100.0
Gross Profit	28.0	26.6	25.3						26.0
Operating Expenses	21.2	20.3	18.8						20.5
Operating Profit	6.8	6.3	6.5						5.5
All Other Expenses (net)	1.6	.8	1.2						1.1
Profit Before Taxes	5.2	5.5	5.3						4.4
RATIOS									
Current	3.6	2.7	2.7						3.2
	2.1	2.0	1.9						2.6
	1.3	1.8	1.5						1.6
Quick	1.4	1.6	1.1						1.1
	.8	.8	.8						1.0
	.6	.7	.6						.7
Sales/Receivables	35 10.3	37 9.9	36 10.2						36 10.2
	53 6.9	49 7.5	47 7.7						46 7.9
	63 5.8	65 5.6	68 5.4						74 4.9
Cost of Sales/Inventory	81 4.5	68 5.4	79 4.6						101 3.6
	107 3.4	114 3.2	118 3.1						126 2.9
	146 2.5	140 2.6	159 2.3						159 2.3
Cost of Sales/Payables	26 13.9	23 15.8	21 17.0						25 14.7
	32 11.3	35 10.3	29 12.6						29 12.6
	64 5.7	46 8.0	38 9.6						38 9.6
Sales/Working Capital	3.1	2.9	3.4						3.2
	5.6	4.8	5.2						3.5
	13.6	9.1	9.0						6.0
EBIT/Interest	33.4	(22) 16.3	(21) 6.8						17.9
	4.4	4.3	2.9						2.9
	1.8	2.6	1.2						2.7
Net Profit + Depr., Dep., Amort./Cur. Mat. L/T/D		(10) 14.2							
		5.5							
		1.3							
Fixed/Worth	.2	.2	.1						.3
	.3	.3	.4						.4
	.7	.4	.9						.9
Debt/Worth	.3	.4	.7						.5
	1.0	1.0	1.3						1.0
	3.7	1.9	2.5						1.7
% Profit Before Taxes/Tangible Net Worth	(19) 40.5	30.1	27.6						23.2
	19.5	14.5	15.7						15.7
	8.4	7.1	2.5						6.7
% Profit Before Taxes/Total Assets	17.2	13.8	13.3						11.4
	11.1	5.5	5.9						5.5
	2.8	3.8	.8						3.5
Sales/Net Fixed Assets	21.9	28.9	24.4						17.3
	15.2	13.2	16.2						6.1
	8.9	8.6	5.6						4.2
Sales/Total Assets	2.4	2.4	2.5						1.8
	2.1	1.9	1.7						1.6
	1.8	1.6	1.4						1.3
% Depr., Dep., Amort./Sales	(17) .5	(21) .8	(20) .7					(10) 1.5	1.5
	1.2	1.6	1.5						1.7
	2.2	2.0	2.1						2.4
% Officers', Directors', Owners' Comp/Sales									
Net Sales ($)	1144157M	867514M	1159077M		6663M	11567M		95602M	1045245M
Total Assets ($)	557040M	525570M	792230M		2601M	5499M		65067M	719063M

M = $ thousand   MM = $ million
See Pages 1 through 15 for Explanation of Ratios and Data

Current Data Sorted By Assets							Comparative Historical Data	

 # Postretirement Benefits — Type of Statement

0-500M	500M-2MM	2-10MM	10-50MM	50-100MM	100-250MM	Type of Statement	4/1/90-3/31/91 ALL	4/1/91-3/31/92 ALL
	1		1					
1	4	3	6	2		Unqualified	12	23
	2	4	2			Reviewed	13	14
2	3					Compiled	8	4
						Tax Returns		
2		2	1			Other	3	3
	7 (4/1-9/30/94)		27 (10/1/94-3/31/95)					
5	9	9	9	2		NUMBER OF STATEMENTS	36	44

0-500M %	500M-2MM %	2-10MM %	10-50MM %	50-100MM %	100-250MM %		%	%
						ASSETS		
						Cash & Equivalents	6.9	6.6
						Trade Receivables - (net)	33.6	38.0
						Inventory	39.8	37.8
						All Other Current	2.8	2.6
						Total Current	83.0	85.0
						Fixed Assets (net)	10.6	7.2
						Intangibles (net)	1.9	1.2
						All Other Non-Current	4.5	6.7
						Total	100.0	100.0
						LIABILITIES		
						Notes Payable-Short Term	15.4	18.0
						Cur. Mat. -L/T/D	3.2	.7
						Trade Payables	14.8	27.2
						Income Taxes Payable	.5	1.2
						All Other Current	12.4	7.2
						Total Current	46.3	54.4
						Long Term Debt	6.6	5.1
						Deferred Taxes	.3	.1
						All Other-Non-Current	3.9	2.4
						Net Worth	43.0	38.0
						Total Liabilities & Net Worth	100.0	100.0
						INCOME DATA		
						Net Sales	100.0	100.0
						Gross Profit	30.6	29.2
						Operating Expenses	26.0	25.0
						Operating Profit	4.6	4.2
						All Other Expenses (net)	1.5	1.9
						Profit Before Taxes	3.1	2.3
						RATIOS		
						Current	3.0 / 1.8 / 1.4	2.0 / 1.6 / 1.3
						Quick	1.7 / 1.0 / .4	1.1 / .8 / .5
						Sales/Receivables	(35) 10.3 / (49) 7.5 / (63) 5.8	(29) 12.5 / (42) 8.7 / (54) 6.7
						Cost of Sales/Inventory	(54) 6.8 / (78) 4.7 / (99) 3.7	(29) 12.8 / (53) 6.9 / (101) 3.6
						Cost of Sales/Payables	(13) 29.0 / (28) 12.9 / (40) 9.2	(24) 15.1 / (35) 10.5 / (48) 7.6
						Sales/Working Capital	4.8 / 7.9 / 15.4	6.9 / 11.3 / 21.3
						EBIT/Interest	(31) 8.2 / 2.3 / 1.2	(39) 7.7 / 3.3 / 1.6
						Net Profit + Depr., Dep., Amort./Cur. Mat. L /T/D	(16) 23.7 / 6.8 / 1.2	(12) 18.3 / 7.3 / 2.1
						Fixed/Worth	.1 / .2 / .5	.1 / .1 / .3
						Debt/Worth	.6 / 1.4 / 2.8	.9 / 1.8 / 3.3
						% Profit Before Taxes/Tangible Net Worth	(33) 33.5 / 16.7 / -.9	(43) 33.0 / 16.8 / 11.3
						% Profit Before Taxes/Total Assets	13.6 / 6.2 / -1.6	11.0 / 7.2 / 3.5
						Sales/Net Fixed Assets	97.2 / 43.2 / 15.3	191.5 / 58.1 / 30.2
						Sales/Total Assets	3.5 / 2.8 / 2.1	4.4 / 3.4 / 2.4
						% Depr., Dep., Amort./Sales	(33) .3 / .5 / 1.0	(40) .2 / .4 / .8
						% Officers', Directors', Owners' Comp/Sales	(17) 2.6 / 4.2 / 9.2	(22) 1.5 / 2.1 / 4.7
3451M	29564M	171726M	508766M	322512M		Net Sales ($)	784602M	1311636M
1071M	9387M	45740M	246191M	130864M		Total Assets ($)	317530M	432954M

M = $ thousand   MM = $ million
See Pages 1 through 15 for Explanation of Ratios and Data

Comparative Historical Data				Current Data Sorted By Sales					
	3	2	# Postretirement Benefits		1				1
			Type of Statement						
19	13	16	Unqualified	2	2	2		1	9
14	15	8	Reviewed		1	1	1	2	3
12	9	5	Compiled	2	3				
			Tax Returns						
			Other	2				2	1
3	7	5			7 (4/1-9/30/94)			27 (10/1/94-3/31/95)	
4/1/92-3/31/93 ALL	4/1/93-3/31/94 ALL	4/1/94-3/31/95 ALL		0-1MM	1-3MM	3-5MM	5-10MM	10-25MM	25MM & OVER
48	44	34	NUMBER OF STATEMENTS	6	6	3	1	5	13
%	%	%	ASSETS	%	%	%	%	%	%
5.6	9.4	7.8	Cash & Equivalents						8.2
35.5	34.2	32.1	Trade Receivables - (net)						33.7
38.3	36.8	32.7	Inventory						30.1
4.2	2.1	2.2	All Other Current						4.8
83.5	82.5	74.8	Total Current						76.8
10.8	12.1	15.8	Fixed Assets (net)						11.0
1.3	.5	1.5	Intangibles (net)						3.1
4.4	4.9	7.9	All Other Non-Current						9.1
100.0	100.0	100.0	Total						100.0
			LIABILITIES						
15.3	17.0	18.9	Notes Payable-Short Term						18.9
2.3	.9	1.9	Cur. Mat.-L /T/D						1.7
18.1	23.2	15.4	Trade Payables						17.4
1.1	.4	.5	Income Taxes Payable						.1
11.4	7.4	7.5	All Other Current						5.6
48.1	48.9	44.2	Total Current						43.7
5.8	11.1	11.3	Long Term Debt						8.1
.2	.1	.0	Deferred Taxes						.0
4.8	4.5	2.9	All Other-Non-Current						3.2
41.1	35.4	41.6	Net Worth						44.9
100.0	100.0	100.0	Total Liabilities & Net Worth						100.0
			INCOME DATA						
100.0	100.0	100.0	Net Sales						100.0
34.0	31.3	33.4	Gross Profit						28.1
29.1	28.3	30.6	Operating Expenses						26.4
4.9	3.1	2.8	Operating Profit						1.7
1.2	1.6	1.2	All Other Expenses (net)						1.1
3.7	1.5	1.6	Profit Before Taxes						.5
			RATIOS						
2.7	2.8	2.8	Current						3.3
1.8	1.8	2.0							2.0
1.4	1.3	1.3							1.3
1.6	1.7	1.9	Quick						1.9
1.0	.9	1.1							1.1
.6	.6	.6							.7
32 11.3	18 20.8	24 14.9	Sales/Receivables						35 10.3
49 7.4	44 8.3	49 7.5							47 7.8
60 6.1	65 5.6	74 4.9							76 4.8
41 8.8	28 12.9	34 10.8	Cost of Sales/Inventory						48 7.6
66 5.5	56 6.5	81 4.5							73 5.0
122 3.0	104 3.5	130 2.8							87 4.2
21 17.3	15 23.7	14 26.0	Cost of Sales/Payables						17 21.8
31 11.6	31 11.9	29 12.4							25 14.4
42 8.7	45 8.1	40 9.2							39 9.3
5.3	5.5	4.7	Sales/Working Capital						4.8
7.7	10.4	7.1							8.4
12.2	16.0	12.1							10.7
12.9	9.1	9.9	EBIT/Interest						
(40) 4.5	(41) 2.8	(24) 3.1							
2.3	1.1	1.1							
15.9			Net Profit + Depr., Dep.,						
(17) 7.7			Amort./Cur. Mat. L/T/D						
2.4									
.1	.1	.1	Fixed/Worth						.1
.2	.2	.2							.2
.4	.5	.5							.4
.6	.9	.5	Debt/Worth						.5
1.3	1.6	1.1							1.9
2.8	3.7	6.0							2.7
42.5	41.5	20.1	% Profit Before Taxes/Tangible						20.4
(45) 22.2	(40) 16.0	(29) 12.3	Net Worth					(12)	13.6
7.5	2.8	3.0							5.2
15.0	15.9	12.8	% Profit Before Taxes/Total						13.6
9.0	4.0	4.0	Assets						6.3
3.1	.7	.9							1.0
100.2	194.6	72.1	Sales/Net Fixed Assets						73.3
43.0	64.8	41.3							37.6
18.9	17.7	9.4							7.8
3.7	4.6	3.3	Sales/Total Assets						3.1
2.9	3.2	2.4							2.3
2.2	2.3	1.6							1.6
.2	.2	.4	% Depr., Dep., Amort./Sales						
(40) .5	(39) .6	(23) .8							
1.0	1.3	2.7							
2.1	2.3	2.3	% Officers', Directors',						
(24) 3.3	(22) 3.9	(10) 3.3	Owners' Comp/Sales						
6.5	6.4	5.8							
1360396M	1092547M	1036019M	Net Sales ($)	3253M	11180M	11528M	9876M	88117M	912065M
520865M	371785M	433253M	Total Assets ($)	2061M	5396M	6298M	5529M	21188M	392781M

M = $ thousand   MM = $ million
See Pages 1 through 15 for Explanation of Ratios and Data

	Current Data Sorted By Assets							Comparative Historical Data	
	1	1	1	4	1	1	# Postretirement Benefits		
							Type of Statement		
	1	1	9	16	4	4	Unqualified	31	53
	4	13	18	3			Reviewed	26	53
	9	6	2				Compiled	26	17
							Tax Returns		
	1	2	5	3	1	1	Other	10	6
	26 (4/1-9/30/94)			77 (10/1/94-3/31/95)				4/1/90-3/31/91	4/1/91-3/31/92
	0-500M	500M-2MM	2-10MM	10-50MM	50-100MM	100-250MM		ALL	ALL
	15	22	34	22	5	5	**NUMBER OF STATEMENTS**	93	129
	%	%	%	%	%	%	**ASSETS**	%	%
	10.1	14.0	9.2	3.8			Cash & Equivalents	7.1	5.0
	17.2	25.4	29.0	24.4			Trade Receivables - (net)	32.0	30.1
	34.5	38.0	37.0	50.6			Inventory	39.2	42.2
	1.5	4.4	5.9	5.0			All Other Current	2.6	4.7
	63.2	81.9	81.1	83.8			Total Current	80.8	82.0
	25.1	10.7	10.9	11.7			Fixed Assets (net)	13.4	11.0
	1.1	.2	1.3	1.0			Intangibles (net)	1.1	1.4
	10.6	7.2	6.7	3.5			All Other Non-Current	4.8	5.5
	100.0	100.0	100.0	100.0			Total	100.0	100.0
							LIABILITIES		
	17.4	12.1	16.0	22.0			Notes Payable-Short Term	21.2	17.4
	2.5	2.6	3.0	2.6			Cur. Mat. -L/T/D	2.2	2.5
	16.0	26.3	19.0	20.4			Trade Payables	17.0	21.3
	.3	.2	.2	.3			Income Taxes Payable	.4	.5
	13.3	7.1	8.7	8.9			All Other Current	9.5	8.9
	49.6	48.3	47.0	54.2			Total Current	50.2	50.6
	10.9	7.3	5.5	5.6			Long Term Debt	9.3	9.1
	.1	.0	.0	.1			Deferred Taxes	.1	.3
	2.6	4.0	2.0	2.7			All Other-Non-Current	2.2	3.4
	36.9	40.3	45.6	37.4			Net Worth	38.2	36.6
	100.0	100.0	100.0	100.0			Total Liabilities & Net Worth	100.0	100.0
							INCOME DATA		
	100.0	100.0	100.0	100.0			Net Sales	100.0	100.0
	30.5	22.1	26.0	27.9			Gross Profit	24.3	26.7
	28.9	17.9	23.3	21.6			Operating Expenses	20.6	22.2
	1.6	4.2	2.7	6.4			Operating Profit	3.7	4.5
	.5	.9	.9	1.8			All Other Expenses (net)	1.7	2.1
	1.2	3.3	1.8	4.6			Profit Before Taxes	2.0	2.4
							RATIOS		
	4.8	2.8	2.5	1.9				2.1	2.0
	1.1	1.6	1.7	1.6			Current	1.5	1.6
	.6	1.3	1.3	1.3				1.3	1.3
	2.0	1.5	1.3	.9				1.1	1.1
	.5	.9	.8	.5			Quick	.8	.7
	.3	.5	.4	.3				.6	.3
	5 71.1	15 24.3	16 22.2	11 32.2				24 15.0	17 21.8
	21 17.3	26 13.8	42 8.6	29 12.6			Sales/Receivables	47 7.8	42 8.7
	30 12.0	52 7.0	54 6.8	61 6.0				64 5.7	58 6.3
	0 837.0	23 16.0	39 9.3	64 5.7				49 7.4	53 6.9
	59 6.2	42 8.7	60 6.1	91 4.0			Cost of Sales/Inventory	72 5.1	74 4.9
	96 3.8	118 3.1	96 3.8	114 3.2				104 3.5	104 3.5
	7 54.4	17 21.6	16 23.2	20 18.2				17 21.5	21 17.6
	23 16.0	34 10.7	33 11.2	39 9.3			Cost of Sales/Payables	28 13.0	35 10.4
	37 9.8	49 7.4	46 7.9	45 8.1				43 8.5	49 7.4
	4.2	7.2	5.7	6.1				6.0	6.1
	88.9	10.6	8.4	8.8			Sales/Working Capital	8.9	9.3
	-12.8	16.6	22.3	15.7				17.1	17.5
	(12) 5.8	(21) 11.0	(28) 7.0	9.1				(82) 4.2	(105) 4.8
	2.1	3.4	3.3	3.0			EBIT/Interest	2.1	2.4
	-2.3	2.3	1.4	1.9				1.3	1.3
				(10) 8.6				(41) 13.5	(50) 10.1
				5.7			Net Profit + Depr., Dep., Amort./Cur. Mat. L /T/D	3.2	2.2
				1.8				.7	.7
	.1	.1	.1	.2				.1	.1
	1.6	.3	.1	.3			Fixed/Worth	.3	.2
	3.9	.5	.3	.5				.6	.5
	.3	.8	.6	1.1				1.0	1.1
	2.3	1.4	1.6	1.7			Debt/Worth	1.8	1.9
	8.6	3.1	2.5	3.1				3.6	3.4
	(13) 37.0	(21) 48.1	(32) 42.2	42.5			% Profit Before Taxes/Tangible Net Worth	(90) 27.9	(124) 34.6
	7.4	32.3	19.3	19.3				14.0	17.3
	5.5	10.5	4.1	8.5				3.5	6.1
	11.1	19.4	17.6	18.2			% Profit Before Taxes/Total Assets	9.0	10.1
	5.0	7.0	7.8	6.6				4.0	5.8
	.6	2.4	.9	3.5				1.4	1.4
	46.7	204.5	81.8	46.7				78.7	125.3
	21.6	35.4	43.0	30.2			Sales/Net Fixed Assets	28.9	38.3
	9.0	19.4	17.7	15.9				14.1	15.9
	4.2	4.5	3.7	3.7				3.3	3.9
	3.0	3.5	2.6	2.9			Sales/Total Assets	2.4	2.8
	2.6	2.4	2.1	2.3				2.0	2.1
	(12) .5	(19) .1	(30) .3	(19) .6			% Depr., Dep., Amort./Sales	(85) .4	(106) .3
	.6	.4	.5	.9				.7	.6
	2.7	.6	1.0	1.4				1.2	1.3
		(13) 1.8	(15) 1.1				% Officers', Directors', Owners' Comp/Sales	(45) 1.6	(53) 2.6
		3.0	1.6					3.7	3.7
		3.8	4.0					6.4	7.8
	13174M	100773M	513278M	1272632M	539111M	1636384M	Net Sales ($)	2535679M	3735052M
	3745M	29184M	176358M	461042M	321544M	892341M	Total Assets ($)	1069158M	1563085M

M = $ thousand   MM = $ million
See Pages 1 through 15 for Explanation of Ratios and Data

Comparative Historical Data				Current Data Sorted By Sales					
7	7	9	# Postretirement Benefits	1	1		2		5
			Type of Statement						
39	35	35	Unqualified	1		1	3	8	22
46	34	38	Reviewed	1	3	4	13	10	7
20	19	17	Compiled	6	8		1	2	
1		1	Tax Returns						
18	15	13	Other	1		2	3	3	4
4/1/92-3/31/93	4/1/93-3/31/94	4/1/94-3/31/95		26 (4/1-9/30/94)			77 (10/1/94-3/31/95)		
ALL	ALL	ALL		0-1MM	1-3MM	3-5MM	5-10MM	10-25MM	25MM & OVER
124	104	103	NUMBER OF STATEMENTS	9	11	7	20	23	33
%	%	%	ASSETS	%	%	%	%	%	%
7.9	7.0	9.3	Cash & Equivalents		8.0		15.1	8.1	5.6
26.2	27.2	24.8	Trade Receivables - (net)		20.6		23.7	31.5	23.1
41.3	41.0	39.2	Inventory		44.9		35.8	36.0	43.9
5.6	2.6	4.3	All Other Current		.6		6.1	4.3	5.4
81.0	77.8	77.6	Total Current		74.0		80.7	79.9	78.0
12.4	15.3	14.3	Fixed Assets (net)		18.3		8.7	12.5	14.6
1.4	.8	1.4	Intangibles (net)		.7		1.6	.7	2.4
5.2	6.1	6.7	All Other Non-Current		7.0		9.0	6.9	5.0
100.0	100.0	100.0	Total		100.0		100.0	100.0	100.0
			LIABILITIES						
15.7	15.4	15.4	Notes Payable-Short Term		17.9		16.2	17.9	12.8
3.0	2.8	2.7	Cur. Mat.-L /T/D		4.9		4.1	2.0	2.0
18.8	18.7	19.7	Trade Payables		19.8		22.0	16.7	20.5
.7	1.2	.3	Income Taxes Payable		.5		.2	.2	.3
10.3	9.1	8.7	All Other Current		12.4		5.0	9.8	8.1
48.5	47.2	46.8	Total Current		55.6		47.5	46.6	43.7
7.5	8.3	8.4	Long Term Debt		11.1		3.6	5.4	11.2
.1	.1	.2	Deferred Taxes		.1		.0	.0	.6
4.1	2.8	2.8	All Other-Non-Current		.0		2.9	2.6	2.4
39.8	41.7	41.7	Net Worth		33.3		45.9	45.5	42.1
100.0	100.0	100.0	Total Liabilities & Net Worth		100.0		100.0	100.0	100.0
			INCOME DATA						
100.0	100.0	100.0	Net Sales		100.0		100.0	100.0	100.0
27.5	28.0	26.1	Gross Profit		25.6		25.6	22.8	27.1
24.0	24.8	22.3	Operating Expenses		22.8		21.7	20.9	21.3
3.5	3.2	3.8	Operating Profit		2.9		3.9	1.9	5.8
1.0	1.3	1.0	All Other Expenses (net)		1.2		1.0	.7	1.3
2.5	1.9	2.8	Profit Before Taxes		1.6		2.9	1.2	4.6
			RATIOS						
2.3 / 1.6 / 1.3	2.4 / 1.7 / 1.3	2.6 / 1.7 / 1.3	Current		4.5 / 1.3 / .7		1.9 / 1.6 / 1.0	2.6 / 1.7 / 1.3	2.5 / 1.8 / 1.5
1.1 / .8 / .3	1.1 / .8 / .4	1.3 / .8 / .4	Quick		2.2 / .5 / .3		1.0 / .8 / .4	1.3 / 1.0 / .6	1.2 / .8 / .3
12 29.7 / 33 11.0 / 57 6.4	14 25.8 / 37 9.8 / 58 6.3	14 27.0 / 31 11.6 / 51 7.1	Sales/Receivables		20 17.9 / 24 15.2 / 38 9.7		13 27.3 / 25 14.7 / 47 7.8	18 19.8 / 42 8.6 / 59 6.2	11 34.7 / 33 11.0 / 57 6.4
47 7.8 / 73 5.0 / 104 3.5	40 9.1 / 76 4.8 / 118 3.1	41 8.8 / 69 5.3 / 107 3.4	Cost of Sales/Inventory		59 6.2 / 78 4.7 / 159 2.3		32 11.3 / 47 7.7 / 107 3.4	38 9.6 / 59 6.2 / 89 4.1	64 5.7 / 76 4.8 / 111 3.3
17 21.6 / 31 11.8 / 41 8.9	18 19.8 / 29 12.4 / 47 7.8	16 22.4 / 31 11.7 / 45 8.2	Cost of Sales/Payables		8 48.5 / 26 13.8 / 57 6.4		19 19.4 / 38 9.5 / 51 7.1	14 25.3 / 23 15.8 / 40 9.2	23 16.1 / 38 9.5 / 44 8.3
5.6 / 9.3 / 19.2	5.9 / 8.3 / 19.3	5.5 / 8.9 / 20.0	Sales/Working Capital		5.4 / 8.0 / -23.9		5.8 / 10.3 / 18.8	5.7 / 7.5 / 15.7	5.3 / 8.2 / 13.7
(106) 5.4 / 2.4 / 1.3	(92) 5.5 / 2.3 / 1.1	(92) 7.0 / 3.4 / 1.9	EBIT/Interest		4.5 / 2.4 / 1.2		(18) 10.7 / 3.6 / 1.5	(19) 6.4 / 4.0 / 1.2	(31) 7.2 / 3.7 / 1.2
(37) 2.7 / 1.3 / .5	(31) 5.7 / 2.6 / .1	(34) 8.5 / 2.5 / .7	Net Profit + Depr., Dep., Amort./Cur. Mat. L/T/D						(15) 17.2 / 6.5 / 2.3
.1 / .2 / .5	.1 / .2 / .5	.1 / .2 / .8	Fixed/Worth		.1 / .5 / 4.6		.0 / .1 / .5	.1 / .2 / .4	.2 / .3 / .8
.9 / 1.6 / 3.1	.7 / 1.5 / 3.0	.9 / 1.6 / 3.0	Debt/Worth		.7 / 3.1 / 7.8		.9 / 1.4 / 2.5	.6 / 1.6 / 2.0	.9 / 1.4 / 2.4
(121) 38.1 / 14.4 / 4.9	(101) 32.8 / 13.9 / 1.7	(98) 43.0 / 19.5 / 6.5	% Profit Before Taxes/Tangible Net Worth				(19) 42.4 / 17.8 / 5.7	(22) 44.2 / 20.4 / -2.7	44.5 / 22.7 / 12.0
12.2 / 4.8 / 1.6	11.8 / 4.3 / .8	16.7 / 7.1 / 2.2	% Profit Before Taxes/Total Assets		11.1 / 5.0 / .8		19.5 / 7.2 / 1.4	17.6 / 7.6 / -.9	18.5 / 10.1 / 3.9
86.3 / 36.7 / 17.5	69.5 / 30.2 / 14.5	70.1 / 31.0 / 14.0	Sales/Net Fixed Assets		70.1 / 28.5 / 16.8		275.3 / 76.4 / 19.2	80.1 / 39.0 / 14.0	39.9 / 29.8 / 11.1
3.9 / 2.8 / 2.2	3.6 / 2.8 / 2.0	3.8 / 2.9 / 2.1	Sales/Total Assets		4.2 / 3.5 / 1.9		4.3 / 2.8 / 1.9	3.8 / 2.8 / 2.2	3.6 / 2.8 / 2.1
(112) .3 / .7 / 1.2	(88) .3 / .8 / 1.3	(87) .4 / .6 / 1.4	% Depr., Dep., Amort./Sales		(10) .4 / .6 / 1.9		(18) .1 / .3 / .9	(22) .4 / .6 / 1.4	(25) .6 / .9 / 1.5
(50) 1.5 / 2.8 / 7.3	(46) 1.8 / 4.0 / 10.3	(43) 1.3 / 3.0 / 5.8	% Officers', Directors', Owners' Comp/Sales				(10) 1.6 / 2.9 / 3.3	(10) 1.0 / 1.5 / 3.5	
4038761M	2763272M	4075352M	Net Sales ($)	4984M	16717M	28546M	139839M	354951M	3530315M
1648452M	1188982M	1884214M	Total Assets ($)	2011M	5925M	9270M	56838M	154362M	1655808M

M = $ thousand   MM = $ million
See Pages 1 through 15 for Explanation of Ratios and Data

Current Data Sorted By Assets

	1		1		1	2
	1	5	2	1	1	
	4	2	2			
	2					
2		2	2	3	1	

Comparative Historical Data

	# Postretirement Benefits Type of Statement	4/1/90- 3/31/91 ALL	4/1/91- 3/31/92 ALL
	Unqualified	11	17
	Reviewed	11	12
	Compiled	3	7
	Tax Returns	1	
	Other	5	1

Current Data Sorted By Assets columns:
- 6 (4/1-9/30/94)
- 24 (10/1/94-3/31/95)

0-500M	500M-2MM	2-10MM	10-50MM	50-100MM	100-250MM		4/1/90-3/31/91 ALL	4/1/91-3/31/92 ALL
2	9	9	7	2	1	**NUMBER OF STATEMENTS**	31	37
%	%	%	%	%	%	**ASSETS**	%	%
						Cash & Equivalents	4.7	5.9
						Trade Receivables - (net)	27.6	27.2
						Inventory	42.7	46.0
						All Other Current	5.8	3.5
						Total Current	80.9	82.6
						Fixed Assets (net)	12.8	12.2
						Intangibles (net)	1.3	.8
						All Other Non-Current	5.1	4.4
						Total	100.0	100.0
						LIABILITIES		
						Notes Payable-Short Term	17.4	19.5
						Cur. Mat. -L/T/D	4.8	1.9
						Trade Payables	13.4	13.2
						Income Taxes Payable	.8	.5
						All Other Current	11.5	9.8
						Total Current	47.7	45.0
						Long Term Debt	10.6	10.5
						Deferred Taxes	.4	.2
						All Other-Non-Current	1.8	3.5
						Net Worth	39.5	40.9
						Total Liabilities & Net Worth	100.0	100.0
						INCOME DATA		
						Net Sales	100.0	100.0
						Gross Profit	22.8	25.6
						Operating Expenses	19.1	21.3
						Operating Profit	3.7	4.3
						All Other Expenses (net)	1.4	1.6
						Profit Before Taxes	2.3	2.8
						RATIOS		
						Current	2.7 / 1.6 / 1.3	2.5 / 1.7 / 1.5
						Quick	1.0 / .7 / .5	1.2 / .7 / .4
						Sales/Receivables	35 10.4 / 45 8.2 / 53 6.9	33 10.9 / 43 8.5 / 60 6.1
						Cost of Sales/Inventory	60 6.1 / 91 4.0 / 118 3.1	74 4.9 / 101 3.6 / 166 2.2
						Cost of Sales/Payables	14 26.0 / 23 16.1 / 31 11.6	17 21.2 / 29 12.5 / 42 8.7
						Sales/Working Capital	4.1 / 7.2 / 15.1	4.2 / 5.6 / 9.9
						EBIT/Interest	(29) 3.8 / 1.7 / 1.2	(35) 4.2 / 2.1 / 1.3
						Net Profit + Depr., Dep., Amort./Cur. Mat. L /T/D	(18) 8.7 / 2.2 / .4	(15) 14.1 / 3.2 / 1.3
						Fixed/Worth	.1 / .3 / .8	.1 / .2 / .4
						Debt/Worth	.8 / 1.8 / 2.7	.8 / 1.7 / 2.8
						% Profit Before Taxes/Tangible Net Worth	36.5 / 15.7 / 1.8	29.8 / 16.8 / 4.7
						% Profit Before Taxes/Total Assets	12.6 / 3.9 / 1.0	10.2 / 5.6 / 1.4
						Sales/Net Fixed Assets	56.9 / 23.0 / 11.0	91.8 / 24.7 / 11.2
						Sales/Total Assets	3.2 / 2.2 / 1.8	2.8 / 2.5 / 1.7
						% Depr., Dep., Amort./Sales	(24) .6 / .9 / 1.3	(32) .4 / .8 / 1.4
						% Officers', Directors', Owners' Comp/Sales	(11) 1.3 / 3.6 / 5.1	(16) 1.0 / 3.5 / 8.1
1839M / 700M	28496M / 11010M	108950M / 43188M	308941M / 168877M	197689M / 133727M	414800M / 224471M	Net Sales ($) / Total Assets ($)	715651M / 367856M	1096517M / 620514M

© Robert Morris Associates 1995

M = $ thousand   MM = $ million
See Pages 1 through 15 for Explanation of Ratios and Data

Comparative Historical Data / Current Data Sorted By Sales

		2	5	# Postretirement Benefits				2		3
				Type of Statement						
	13	18	10	Unqualified	1	1		1	2	5
	16	13	8	Reviewed		1	2	2	1	2
	5	2	2	Compiled		2				
				Tax Returns						
	5	4	10	Other	2			3		3

	4/1/92-3/31/93 ALL	4/1/93-3/31/94 ALL	4/1/94-3/31/95 ALL		6 (4/1-9/30/94) 0-1MM	1-3MM	3-5MM	24 (10/1/94-3/31/95) 5-10MM	10-25MM	25MM & OVER
	39	37	30	**NUMBER OF STATEMENTS**	3	5	2	6	4	10
	%	%	%	**ASSETS**	%	%	%	%	%	%
	5.4	5.2	4.3	Cash & Equivalents						5.8
	23.2	25.8	26.6	Trade Receivables - (net)						29.0
	45.3	48.5	41.8	Inventory						45.4
	3.4	.9	2.0	All Other Current						1.8
	77.2	80.4	74.7	Total Current						82.0
	15.5	12.9	17.7	Fixed Assets (net)						12.8
	1.0	1.2	3.8	Intangibles (net)						1.4
	6.3	5.5	3.9	All Other Non-Current						3.8
	100.0	100.0	100.0	Total						100.0
				LIABILITIES						
	13.1	16.2	14.1	Notes Payable-Short Term						16.4
	2.1	1.1	2.5	Cur. Mat.-L /T/D						1.4
	15.2	12.9	13.4	Trade Payables						11.0
	.2	1.0	.2	Income Taxes Payable						.3
	11.2	8.9	12.3	All Other Current						8.5
	41.9	40.1	42.6	Total Current						37.6
	10.5	9.5	14.1	Long Term Debt						17.6
	.3	.2	.3	Deferred Taxes						.4
	1.4	2.2	3.4	All Other-Non-Current						.8
	45.9	48.0	39.5	Net Worth						43.6
	100.0	100.0	100.0	Total Liabilities & Net Worth						100.0
				INCOME DATA						
	100.0	100.0	100.0	Net Sales						100.0
	22.5	23.4	25.3	Gross Profit						24.1
	18.3	19.4	20.4	Operating Expenses						16.8
	4.2	3.9	5.0	Operating Profit						7.2
	1.3	1.4	1.3	All Other Expenses (net)						2.2
	2.9	2.5	3.6	Profit Before Taxes						5.0
				RATIOS						
	2.2	2.6	2.6							3.3
	1.8	2.1	1.9	Current						2.0
	1.4	1.5	1.3							1.7
	1.2	1.0	1.2							1.9
	.6	.7	.7	Quick						.7
	.3	.5	.4							.5
	15 24.8	33 11.2	30 12.2							41 8.8
	40 9.1	43 8.4	45 8.2	Sales/Receivables						47 7.8
	50 7.3	50 7.3	62 5.9							94 3.9
	53 6.9	69 5.3	68 5.4							76 4.8
	94 3.9	99 3.7	96 3.8	Cost of Sales/Inventory						107 3.4
	126 2.9	135 2.7	135 2.7							140 2.6
	15 24.3	13 28.1	16 23.2							14 26.5
	26 14.3	24 15.4	26 13.9	Cost of Sales/Payables						25 14.8
	40 9.1	43 8.4	49 7.4							44 8.3
	4.3	4.2	3.8							3.2
	7.2	5.7	5.8	Sales/Working Capital						4.3
	17.1	13.1	19.1							10.1
	(35) 5.8	(36) 4.2	6.1							7.2
	3.0	2.4	3.0	EBIT/Interest						4.5
	1.3	1.3	1.3							2.2
	(12) 16.8	(11) 6.6	(10) 9.6	Net Profit + Depr., Dep.,						
	4.2	2.8	4.0	Amort./Cur. Mat. L/T/D						
	1.0	.9	1.0							
	.1	.1	.2							.2
	.3	.2	.3	Fixed/Worth						.3
	.6	.4	.9							.4
	.8	.7	1.0							.9
	1.4	1.0	1.7	Debt/Worth						1.0
	2.5	2.3	2.9							2.5
	(38) 30.9	23.2	(27) 38.7	% Profit Before Taxes/Tangible						
	13.6	10.7	25.2	Net Worth						
	5.2	3.3	4.2							
	14.9	9.4	15.1	% Profit Before Taxes/Total						14.7
	6.4	4.6	6.2	Assets						8.5
	1.4	1.3	1.3							4.0
	47.5	65.6	42.2							43.8
	18.1	20.1	16.1	Sales/Net Fixed Assets						14.5
	11.4	11.5	7.5							10.5
	3.1	3.0	2.9							2.3
	2.3	2.3	2.1	Sales/Total Assets						1.8
	1.9	1.8	1.6							1.4
	(38) .4	(36) .3	(24) .4	% Depr., Dep., Amort./Sales						
	.8	.8	1.0							
	2.0	1.6	1.7							
	(13) 1.1	(13) 1.8	(11) 3.1	% Officers', Directors',						
	3.0	4.2	6.0	Owners' Comp/Sales						
	5.7		14.6							
	965364M	1204194M	1060715M	Net Sales ($)	2556M	8748M	8783M	41562M	76823M	922243M
	499767M	766233M	581973M	Total Assets ($)	1658M	6909M	2909M	18853M	30376M	521268M

M = $ thousand   MM = $ million
See Pages 1 through 15 for Explanation of Ratios and Data

MANUFACTURERS—BOTTLED & CANNED SOFT DRINKS & CARBONATED WATERS. SIC# 2086

Current Data Sorted By Assets / Comparative Historical Data

Type of Statement (counts)

	0-500M	500M-2MM	2-10MM	10-50MM	50-100MM	100-250MM	# Postretirement Benefits / Type of Statement	4/1/90-3/31/91 ALL	4/1/91-3/31/92 ALL
	1	1	6	23	6	6	Unqualified	49	48
		4	6	4			Reviewed	15	8
		6	5	2		1	Compiled	17	14
							Tax Returns		
	2	4	6	13	2	5	Other	23	17
		28 (4/1-9/30/94)		75 (10/1/94-3/31/95)					
	3	15	23	42	8	12	NUMBER OF STATEMENTS	104	87

Main Data

0-500M	500M-2MM	2-10MM	10-50MM	50-100MM	100-250MM		4/1/90-3/31/91 ALL	4/1/91-3/31/92 ALL
%	%	%	%	%	%	ASSETS	%	%
	6.3	7.1	6.1		9.0	Cash & Equivalents	7.5	7.2
	22.0	19.7	16.9		12.9	Trade Receivables - (net)	19.1	17.5
	12.9	17.6	15.1		7.7	Inventory	13.1	10.7
	2.9	2.8	1.6		1.5	All Other Current	2.0	1.4
	44.1	47.2	39.6		31.1	Total Current	41.7	36.8
	38.1	33.7	43.7		23.9	Fixed Assets (net)	38.1	38.0
	8.2	8.0	10.4		42.8	Intangibles (net)	11.4	14.5
	9.6	11.1	6.2		2.2	All Other Non-Current	8.8	10.7
	100.0	100.0	100.0		100.0	Total	100.0	100.0
						LIABILITIES		
	10.4	8.7	5.7		1.0	Notes Payable-Short Term	5.4	4.9
	7.8	2.8	4.0		7.8	Cur. Mat.-L/T/D	3.7	4.5
	13.1	14.0	15.8		10.4	Trade Payables	13.0	11.3
	.5	2.1	.3		.1	Income Taxes Payable	.5	.4
	11.7	4.8	13.4		6.3	All Other Current	7.0	6.0
	43.5	32.5	39.0		25.5	Total Current	29.5	27.2
	16.9	17.4	17.5		54.9	Long Term Debt	26.2	27.2
	2.0	1.3	1.8		1.3	Deferred Taxes	1.5	.7
	3.1	7.0	3.0		10.6	All Other-Non-Current	3.3	5.8
	34.4	41.8	38.7		7.6	Net Worth	39.5	39.1
	100.0	100.0	100.0		100.0	Total Liabilities & Net Worth	100.0	100.0
						INCOME DATA		
	100.0	100.0	100.0		100.0	Net Sales	100.0	100.0
	40.0	34.2	27.5		37.4	Gross Profit	35.2	35.5
	37.6	30.4	22.0		28.1	Operating Expenses	29.6	30.5
	2.4	3.8	5.5		9.3	Operating Profit	5.7	5.0
	1.6	.3	1.2		5.7	All Other Expenses (net)	2.0	2.0
	.8	3.5	4.3		3.6	Profit Before Taxes	3.6	3.0
						RATIOS		
	2.2	2.7	1.9		1.9		2.1	2.2
	1.3	1.4	1.1		1.4	Current	1.5	1.4
	.6	1.0	.8		.8		1.0	1.0
	1.4	1.7	1.2		1.1		1.6	1.4
	.9	.7	.6		1.0	Quick	.9	.9
	.3	.5	.4		.6		.3	.6
19 18.9	21 17.6	18 20.0		25 14.7		Sales/Receivables	20 17.9	22 16.9
30 12.1	27 13.5	26 13.8		29 12.5			28 13.2	27 13.6
65 5.6	31 11.6	33 11.1		34 10.6			35 10.4	33 11.2
16 22.5	21 17.4	19 19.3		19 19.2		Cost of Sales/Inventory	18 20.6	18 20.4
27 13.3	30 12.0	24 14.9		28 13.2			23 15.8	24 15.3
60 6.1	37 9.9	37 10.0		39 9.3			34 10.7	31 11.9
16 22.5	10 37.7	14 25.6		26 14.3		Cost of Sales/Payables	15 24.7	13 27.1
41 9.0	24 15.2	25 14.4		32 11.5			24 15.3	23 15.7
54 6.8	39 9.4	42 8.7		53 6.9			34 10.6	36 10.1
	11.3	8.3	10.5		9.0	Sales/Working Capital	10.1	10.0
	18.5	23.3	105.6		17.3		21.3	24.7
	-14.7	-396.1	-32.1		-30.6		251.2	803.1
	9.8	11.1	12.0		3.0	EBIT/Interest	6.3	6.4
	2.6	(20) 4.9	(38) 5.5		(11) 1.6		(91) 3.0	(78) 2.3
	-1.4	1.6	1.8		1.1		1.2	.8
		6.9	9.3			Net Profit + Depr., Dep., Amort./Cur. Mat. L/T/D	7.0	9.2
		(11) 2.2	(20) 4.3				(67) 3.5	(43) 3.4
		1.6	1.5				1.7	1.2
	.7	.4	.9		2.2	Fixed/Worth	.6	.6
	1.4	1.3	1.3		-.5		1.3	1.6
	4.9	3.6	3.2		-.2		28.6	-40.5
	.6	.4	1.0		4.6	Debt/Worth	.6	.6
	2.0	1.9	2.0		-2.1		2.1	2.5
	17.3	11.6	7.5		-1.5		84.4	-47.7
	26.0	71.2	41.7			% Profit Before Taxes/Tangible Net Worth	33.9	30.6
	(12) 18.5	(20) 50.5	(36) 19.0				(79) 20.0	(65) 18.0
	-.6	15.3	4.3				11.8	6.6
	11.3	25.2	13.9		10.8	% Profit Before Taxes/Total Assets	14.8	14.1
	7.4	9.4	5.7		3.8		7.5	5.5
	-9.2	1.6	1.2		1.7		1.5	-1.0
	12.3	18.6	10.1		7.4	Sales/Net Fixed Assets	10.4	8.3
	7.9	6.6	6.6		6.2		6.8	6.1
	3.9	3.1	3.3		4.6		4.4	4.6
	3.7	3.3	3.7		2.1	Sales/Total Assets	3.4	2.9
	2.0	2.3	2.1		1.5		2.4	2.2
	1.3	1.4	1.7		1.0		1.6	1.6
	1.7	2.0	2.1			% Depr., Dep., Amort./Sales	2.5	2.4
	3.0	(19) 3.4	(40) 2.9				(92) 3.5	(73) 3.5
	5.0	5.0	4.5				5.2	4.5
						% Officers', Directors', Owners' Comp/Sales	2.0	1.2
							(18) 5.1	(21) 2.6
							8.9	6.2
885M	51151M	265962M	2363424M	1084748M	3047668M	Net Sales ($)	4008451M	5576279M
624M	17259M	115861M	916788M	559375M	2014974M	Total Assets ($)	2240755M	3677446M

M = $ thousand   MM = $ million
See Pages 1 through 15 for Explanation of Ratios and Data

Comparative Historical Data | Current Data Sorted By Sales

	8	7	10	# Postretirement Benefits	1		1			8
				Type of Statement						
	56	37	43	Unqualified	2			2	7	32
	14	11	14	Reviewed		2	2	5	1	4
	12	9	14	Compiled	1	4		2	5	2
	4			Tax Returns						
	19	26	32	Other	2	1	1	5	6	17
	4/1/92-3/31/93 ALL	4/1/93-3/31/94 ALL	4/1/94-3/31/95 ALL		0-1MM	1-3MM	3-5MM	5-10MM	10-25MM	25MM & OVER
					28 (4/1-9/30/94)			75 (10/1/94-3/31/95)		
	105	83	103	**NUMBER OF STATEMENTS**	5	7	3	14	19	55
	%	%	%	**ASSETS**	%	%	%	%	%	%
	7.4	6.7	6.6	Cash & Equivalents				5.1	9.3	6.2
	17.5	17.6	17.5	Trade Receivables - (net)				20.4	18.7	16.5
	14.3	11.7	14.2	Inventory				17.6	13.4	14.1
	1.4	1.7	2.1	All Other Current				1.7	1.4	1.8
	40.7	37.6	40.3	Total Current				44.8	42.9	38.7
	38.3	36.0	37.2	Fixed Assets (net)				31.5	42.0	36.0
	13.2	14.7	15.1	Intangibles (net)				11.6	9.5	19.4
	7.8	11.6	7.4	All Other Non-Current				12.1	5.6	6.0
	100.0	100.0	100.0	Total				100.0	100.0	100.0
				LIABILITIES						
	4.8	4.6	6.4	Notes Payable-Short Term				10.6	5.2	5.3
	3.9	3.6	4.5	Cur. Mat.-L/T/D				5.8	2.8	4.6
	12.6	11.1	14.1	Trade Payables				16.0	11.7	14.5
	.2	1.9	.7	Income Taxes Payable				.9	1.9	.3
	7.0	7.3	9.6	All Other Current				6.6	12.5	9.2
	28.3	28.5	35.2	Total Current				39.9	34.1	33.9
	23.9	23.6	24.5	Long Term Debt				16.7	14.5	30.7
	.7	1.3	1.6	Deferred Taxes				2.4	1.0	1.6
	6.1	5.7	4.7	All Other-Non-Current				8.5	3.0	4.6
	41.0	40.9	34.0	Net Worth				32.4	47.4	29.3
	100.0	100.0	100.0	Total Liabilities & Net Worth				100.0	100.0	100.0
				INCOME DATA						
	100.0	100.0	100.0	Net Sales				100.0	100.0	100.0
	32.6	34.0	33.5	Gross Profit				33.6	33.9	29.5
	26.8	27.9	28.2	Operating Expenses				32.2	28.2	23.3
	5.8	6.1	5.3	Operating Profit				1.4	5.7	6.2
	2.0	1.7	1.8	All Other Expenses (net)				1.6	1.6	2.3
	3.8	4.4	3.4	Profit Before Taxes				-.1	4.1	3.8
				RATIOS						
	2.3	2.2	2.0	Current				2.2	2.7	1.6
	1.4	1.4	1.3					1.2	1.9	1.2
	1.1	1.0	.9					.9	.9	.9
	1.4	1.5	1.3	Quick				1.6	2.4	1.1
	1.0	.9	.7					.8	1.2	.7
	.6	.6	.5					.4	.5	.5
	19 19.0	23 15.6	21 17.6	Sales/Receivables				21 17.3	21 17.6	21 17.7
	27 13.5	30 12.3	28 12.9					29 12.7	26 13.8	28 13.1
	34 10.7	35 10.4	35 10.5					32 11.4	30 12.0	33 11.0
	18 20.3	18 20.5	19 19.5	Cost of Sales/Inventory				18 20.3	14 26.2	19 19.5
	24 15.4	24 15.1	27 13.3					28 13.1	27 13.3	24 15.0
	33 10.9	34 10.6	39 9.3					39 9.3	37 10.0	33 11.0
	14 25.9	12 31.6	18 20.2	Cost of Sales/Payables				15 23.6	10 37.7	19 19.1
	26 14.1	24 15.1	28 12.9					22 16.5	22 16.6	27 13.3
	34 10.6	38 9.5	47 7.7					41 9.0	47 7.7	41 8.8
	10.8	9.2	9.7	Sales/Working Capital				13.4	8.3	12.6
	23.6	24.0	28.3					39.0	11.2	45.4
	90.5	262.7	-51.5					-71.8	-43.7	-55.4
	8.6	8.6	10.5	EBIT/Interest				10.0	19.2	9.4
	(91) 3.2	(73) 3.3	(95) 3.0					2.7	(15) 3.4	(51) 2.8
	1.4	1.1	1.5					.5	2.3	1.5
	13.9	8.6	9.0	Net Profit + Depr., Dep., Amort./Cur. Mat. L/T/D						7.0
	(39) 4.5	(35) 3.1	(46) 4.1						(27)	3.2
	1.4	1.5	1.6							1.5
	.7	.7	.9	Fixed/Worth				.8	.7	1.0
	1.4	1.3	1.8					2.1	.9	2.2
	5.6	9.0	43.9					-140.6	3.6	-3.6
	.6	.5	1.0	Debt/Worth				.8	.4	1.3
	2.0	2.0	2.3					7.6	.9	3.3
	10.4	19.3	111.1					-324.8	8.3	-7.7
	36.6	44.4	55.7	% Profit Before Taxes/Tangible Net Worth				69.0	67.7	45.1
	(84) 20.5	(64) 18.9	(78) 21.0			(10)		23.2	(17) 25.8	(38) 19.0
	12.9	8.9	8.3					12.3	15.4	4.7
	13.5	13.3	13.1	% Profit Before Taxes/Total Assets				12.8	21.6	12.2
	6.8	6.4	6.9					5.1	9.4	4.5
	2.5	1.8	1.4					-2.2	2.5	1.4
	10.4	11.4	10.7	Sales/Net Fixed Assets				20.1	9.9	10.5
	6.5	6.2	6.2					8.8	6.1	6.6
	4.5	4.2	3.6					3.7	3.0	4.3
	3.0	2.8	3.1	Sales/Total Assets				3.8	3.3	3.1
	2.4	2.1	2.0					3.0	2.1	2.1
	1.7	1.5	1.4					1.2	1.7	1.6
	2.0	2.0	2.0	% Depr., Dep., Amort./Sales				1.8	2.2	1.9
	(94) 2.9	(72) 3.2	(91) 3.3			(13)		3.1	(16) 3.7	(47) 2.8
	4.2	4.9	4.9					6.0	4.9	4.6
	1.6	.8	1.7	% Officers', Directors', Owners' Comp/Sales						
	(23) 3.6	(19) 2.9	(19) 3.4							
	7.7	4.2	6.7							
	6466330M	5312253M	6813838M	Net Sales ($)	2108M	9605M	11643M	100863M	312664M	6376955M
	3286900M	3058924M	3624881M	Total Assets ($)	2387M	5508M	8922M	55137M	144996M	3407931M

© Robert Morris Associates 1995   M = $ thousand   MM = $ million
See Pages 1 through 15 for Explanation of Ratios and Data

Current Data Sorted By Assets						# Postretirement Benefits Type of Statement	Comparative Historical Data	
	1	3	1				9	7
	1	3	3	3		Unqualified		
1	4	9	2			Reviewed	4	11
2	3	4				Compiled	2	2
	1					Tax Returns		
1		3			1	Other	4	2
0-500M	500M-2MM	2-10MM	10-50MM	50-100MM	100-250MM		4/1/90-3/31/91 ALL	4/1/91-3/31/92 ALL
	11 (4/1-9/30/94)		31 (10/1/94-3/31/95)					
4	10	19	5	3	1	NUMBER OF STATEMENTS	19	22
%	%	%	%	%	%		%	%
						ASSETS		
	4.4	9.6				Cash & Equivalents	5.0	6.1
	19.5	21.6				Trade Receivables - (net)	17.4	20.7
	29.4	27.9				Inventory	27.0	25.7
	.5	3.2				All Other Current	2.3	2.9
	53.7	62.4				Total Current	51.7	55.6
	33.4	24.2				Fixed Assets (net)	37.9	32.2
	6.6	2.7				Intangibles (net)	3.3	8.4
	6.4	10.7				All Other Non-Current	7.1	3.8
	100.0	100.0				Total	100.0	100.0
						LIABILITIES		
	15.5	5.0				Notes Payable-Short Term	10.3	7.6
	4.6	5.6				Cur. Mat. -L/T/D	1.9	2.9
	13.0	12.9				Trade Payables	14.8	13.3
	.0	.3				Income Taxes Payable	.5	.1
	3.8	7.2				All Other Current	6.5	5.8
	36.9	30.9				Total Current	33.9	29.7
	15.4	12.0				Long Term Debt	14.3	19.7
	.3	1.5				Deferred Taxes	2.0	1.3
	1.6	2.5				All Other-Non-Current	2.3	4.5
	45.7	53.1				Net Worth	47.5	44.7
	100.0	100.0				Total Liabilities & Net Worth	100.0	100.0
						INCOME DATA		
	100.0	100.0				Net Sales	100.0	100.0
	36.5	37.1				Gross Profit	28.1	33.7
	29.9	29.3				Operating Expenses	22.1	25.6
	6.7	7.8				Operating Profit	6.0	8.1
	1.9	.8				All Other Expenses (net)	.7	2.3
	4.8	7.0				Profit Before Taxes	5.3	5.8
						RATIOS		
	2.0	6.4					2.4	3.2
	1.5	2.0				Current	1.7	1.8
	1.0	1.4					1.2	1.3
	1.2	2.5					1.3	1.7
	.4	1.0				Quick	.7	.9
	.4	.9					.4	.4
	12 30.1	25 14.8					22 16.6	23 15.9
	29 12.5	31 11.9				Sales/Receivables	34 10.6	33 10.9
	36 10.1	41 9.0					38 9.7	41 9.0
	54 6.8	52 7.0					37 10.0	39 9.4
	76 4.8	70 5.2				Cost of Sales/Inventory	70 5.2	50 7.3
	146 2.5	114 3.2					122 3.0	96 3.8
	14 26.7	12 31.4					22 16.9	14 26.8
	24 15.4	24 15.1				Cost of Sales/Payables	32 11.3	25 14.6
	39 9.3	46 8.0					38 9.7	40 9.1
	7.5	3.3					4.7	5.1
	27.7	7.9				Sales/Working Capital	11.3	9.3
	NM	15.7					42.4	34.6
	12.3	36.7					13.9	14.2
	(18) 2.0	4.3				EBIT/Interest	(17) 3.7	(21) 5.3
	-.0	1.7					1.5	1.8
						Net Profit + Depr., Dep., Amort./Cur. Mat. L./T/D		
	.4	.3					.5	.4
	1.0	.4				Fixed/Worth	.9	.9
	2.4	1.3					1.7	1.9
	.6	.4					.6	.5
	1.2	1.1				Debt/Worth	1.1	1.3
	4.1	2.1					2.8	3.8
		35.9				% Profit Before Taxes/Tangible Net Worth	29.5	44.1
	(18)	18.4					22.1	(18) 22.7
		7.3					4.3	10.0
	29.3	17.5				% Profit Before Taxes/Total Assets	14.1	19.3
	2.5	10.7					8.9	9.6
	-2.9	1.5					2.0	4.6
	35.5	20.4					9.2	16.5
	6.2	8.7				Sales/Net Fixed Assets	4.9	8.4
	2.6	5.0					2.5	4.5
	3.4	3.1					2.6	3.1
	2.2	2.2				Sales/Total Assets	1.6	2.5
	1.2	1.6					1.1	1.6
		1.1					1.2	.8
	(17)	1.4				% Depr., Dep., Amort./Sales	(17) 1.8	(21) 1.5
		4.7					3.0	2.9
						% Officers', Directors', Owners' Comp/Sales		
4084M	37041M	197886M	179912M	227449M	187259M	Net Sales ($)	963826M	1792408M
1463M	12389M	84493M	74732M	177074M	149636M	Total Assets ($)	716603M	692533M

M = $ thousand   MM = $ million
See Pages 1 through 15 for Explanation of Ratios and Data

Comparative Historical Data / Current Data Sorted By Sales

1	2	5		0-1MM	1-3MM	3-5MM	5-10MM	10-25MM	25MM & OVER
			# Postretirement Benefits		1	2	1		1
			Type of Statement						
11	11	10	Unqualified		1	2		1	6
10	13	16	Reviewed	1	2	3	4	5	1
5	5	9	Compiled	1	4	2	1		
1		1	Tax Returns					1	
4	7	6	Other	1	1	1		1	2
4/1/92-3/31/93	4/1/93-3/31/94	4/1/94-3/31/95		11 (4/1-9/30/94)			31 (10/1/94-3/31/95)		
ALL	ALL	ALL							
31	36	42	**NUMBER OF STATEMENTS**	3	8	8	5	9	9
%	%	%	**ASSETS**	%	%	%	%	%	%
9.4	8.7	7.6	Cash & Equivalents						
21.5	21.7	20.3	Trade Receivables - (net)						
26.4	27.9	28.9	Inventory						
1.8	2.7	2.0	All Other Current						
59.0	61.1	58.8	Total Current						
30.8	30.0	28.4	Fixed Assets (net)						
3.3	2.4	4.3	Intangibles (net)						
6.9	6.5	8.4	All Other Non-Current						
100.0	100.0	100.0	Total						
			LIABILITIES						
7.5	10.6	11.3	Notes Payable-Short Term						
2.0	3.7	4.9	Cur. Mat.-L /T/D						
13.1	12.0	13.2	Trade Payables						
.6	.1	.3	Income Taxes Payable						
10.7	4.9	5.9	All Other Current						
34.0	31.4	35.7	Total Current						
11.6	12.7	15.2	Long Term Debt						
1.1	.4	1.0	Deferred Taxes						
4.3	4.1	2.0	All Other-Non-Current						
49.0	51.4	46.1	Net Worth						
100.0	100.0	100.0	Total Liabilities & Net Worth						
			INCOME DATA						
100.0	100.0	100.0	Net Sales						
32.3	34.1	34.8	Gross Profit						
27.4	27.1	28.3	Operating Expenses						
4.9	6.9	6.5	Operating Profit						
.5	1.1	1.1	All Other Expenses (net)						
4.5	5.8	5.4	Profit Before Taxes						
			RATIOS						
3.1	3.4	3.1	Current						
1.7	2.2	1.8							
1.2	1.4	1.2							
1.2	1.7	1.8	Quick						
.8	1.2	.9							
.5	.5	.4							
22 16.4	24 15.1	24 15.0	Sales/Receivables						
26 13.8	33 11.1	30 12.3							
40 9.2	39 9.4	38 9.5							
27 13.5	41 8.8	51 7.1	Cost of Sales/Inventory						
49 7.5	61 6.0	72 5.1							
111 3.3	122 3.0	114 3.2							
15 24.7	14 25.6	15 24.1	Cost of Sales/Payables						
22 16.6	24 15.3	24 15.5							
31 11.7	35 10.5	46 8.0							
5.5	4.8	5.3	Sales/Working Capital						
9.6	7.4	8.8							
28.8	18.0	33.3							
13.5	10.7	12.5	EBIT/Interest						
5.4	(34) 6.3	(41) 3.4							
2.2	2.1	1.6							
8.9		5.5	Net Profit + Depr., Dep., Amort./Cur. Mat. L/T/D						
(13) 4.6		(17) 2.3							
2.0		.9							
.3	.3	.3	Fixed/Worth						
.7	.6	.6							
1.2	1.2	1.4							
.6	.5	.5	Debt/Worth						
1.0	.7	1.2							
2.1	2.7	2.6							
37.8	42.0	32.9	% Profit Before Taxes/Tangible Net Worth						
(29) 16.2	(35) 20.8	(39) 16.6							
5.7	7.1	3.9							
13.8	20.7	15.8	% Profit Before Taxes/Total Assets						
9.1	9.7	5.5							
2.7	2.1	1.3							
18.1	16.7	18.9	Sales/Net Fixed Assets						
9.8	8.3	8.0							
4.0	5.3	3.6							
3.2	3.2	3.0	Sales/Total Assets						
2.5	2.4	2.2							
1.7	1.6	1.4							
.9	.9	1.0	% Depr., Dep., Amort./Sales						
(28) 1.6	(33) 1.6	(36) 1.7							
3.6	3.3	3.4							
1.7	1.3	2.6	% Officers', Directors', Owners' Comp/Sales						
(14) 3.9	(12) 3.6	(13) 5.2							
5.0	6.7	13.6							
1780748M	1870795M	833631M	Net Sales ($)	2094M	14541M	29165M	37013M	139944M	610874M
598918M	588630M	499787M	Total Assets ($)	1725M	9574M	19053M	16326M	54098M	399011M

M = $ thousand   MM = $ million
See Pages 1 through 15 for Explanation of Ratios and Data

MANUFACTURERS—WINES, DISTILLED LIQUOR & LIQUEURS.   SIC# 2084 (85)

Current Data Sorted By Assets | **Comparative Historical Data**

Type of Statement / # Postretirement Benefits

	0-500M	500M-2MM	2-10MM	10-50MM	50-100MM	100-250MM		4/1/90-3/31/91 ALL	4/1/91-3/31/92 ALL
# Postretirement Benefits	1					1			
Unqualified		1	6	7	1	3		15	15
Reviewed		4	5	4				6	11
Compiled	3	4	1					8	6
Tax Returns									
Other		1	5	5	2	2		13	10
	29 (4/1-9/30/94)			25 (10/1/94-3/31/95)				13	10
NUMBER OF STATEMENTS	3	10	17	16	3	5		42	42

Data

	0-500M %	500M-2MM %	2-10MM %	10-50MM %	50-100MM %	100-250MM %		4/1/90-3/31/91 ALL %	4/1/91-3/31/92 ALL %
ASSETS									
Cash & Equivalents		1.1	1.7	3.0				3.1	5.8
Trade Receivables - (net)		10.8	11.8	20.7				14.0	12.3
Inventory		47.8	49.9	36.4				44.4	37.8
All Other Current		.4	4.8	.7				1.2	1.9
Total Current		60.1	68.3	60.8				62.6	57.7
Fixed Assets (net)		34.5	26.5	31.2				28.0	31.4
Intangibles (net)		3.6	.3	1.1				4.5	3.2
All Other Non-Current		1.9	4.9	7.0				4.9	7.7
Total		100.0	100.0	100.0				100.0	100.0
LIABILITIES									
Notes Payable-Short Term		18.3	19.3	13.2				18.1	12.5
Cur. Mat. -L/T/D		3.4	2.3	2.2				2.6	2.1
Trade Payables		10.5	7.8	12.4				9.7	11.3
Income Taxes Payable		.3	.4	.9				.3	1.2
All Other Current		3.6	4.2	7.5				4.9	5.7
Total Current		36.0	33.9	36.2				35.8	32.9
Long Term Debt		22.5	13.3	19.2				18.2	20.9
Deferred Taxes		1.0	.5	.2				.8	.7
All Other-Non-Current		3.6	5.8	3.3				3.6	2.0
Net Worth		36.8	46.4	41.1				41.6	43.5
Total Liabilities & Net Worth		100.0	100.0	100.0				100.0	100.0
INCOME DATA									
Net Sales		100.0	100.0	100.0				100.0	100.0
Gross Profit		43.8	40.3	27.1				38.1	36.1
Operating Expenses		31.9	31.1	18.4				27.5	24.4
Operating Profit		11.9	9.1	8.7				10.6	11.7
All Other Expenses (net)		5.0	3.3	2.3				4.8	5.0
Profit Before Taxes		7.0	5.8	6.4				5.8	6.7
RATIOS									
Current		2.8 1.7 1.1	3.1 1.9 1.5	4.1 1.6 1.2				3.1 1.8 1.4	2.6 1.7 1.3
Quick		1.0 .3 .2	.6 .4 .2	1.5 .7 .4				.7 .5 .2	1.0 .6 .3
Sales/Receivables		29 12.7 41 8.8 54 6.7	24 14.9 36 10.1 73 5.0	33 11.1 44 8.3 61 6.0				24 15.5 36 10.1 45 8.1	11 34.4 36 10.1 53 6.9
Cost of Sales/Inventory		140 2.6 406 .9 608 .6	192 1.9 456 .8 730 .5	47 7.8 118 3.1 365 1.0				81 4.5 261 1.4 608 .6	56 6.5 130 2.8 608 .6
Cost of Sales/Payables		24 15.0 70 5.2 94 3.9	29 12.5 40 9.2 89 4.1	14 26.6 28 12.9 41 8.9				20 18.7 43 8.5 61 6.0	14 26.2 27 13.4 83 4.4
Sales/Working Capital		2.3 4.8 20.7	1.4 2.2 4.0	2.1 11.5 24.7				2.2 4.7 8.4	2.5 5.6 16.4
EBIT/Interest		3.8 2.2 (15) 1.2	6.6 3.2 (15) .5	9.9 4.1 1.1				(38) 4.7 2.2 1.5	(37) 4.6 2.4 1.2
Net Profit + Depr., Dep., Amort./Cur. Mat. L /T/D								(17) 8.6 4.2 1.6	(13) 10.3 4.2 1.6
Fixed/Worth		.6 1.1 1.8	.2 .4 .9	.5 .8 1.3				.3 .6 1.1	.3 .8 1.9
Debt/Worth		1.3 2.5 4.1	.6 1.2 2.0	.7 1.9 5.6				.9 1.7 3.3	.6 1.9 2.9
% Profit Before Taxes/Tangible Net Worth		51.0 15.4 1.6	23.2 4.3 -1.3	33.8 18.0 3.6				(40) 30.5 16.1 8.4	(40) 38.1 16.6 1.9
% Profit Before Taxes/Total Assets		10.2 5.7 .7	12.5 1.4 -.6	12.4 8.8 1.8				11.2 5.4 2.7	13.0 5.5 .4
Sales/Net Fixed Assets		7.9 2.7 1.3	9.6 3.9 2.6	23.5 4.7 1.8				23.9 3.8 2.0	25.5 3.1 1.4
Sales/Total Assets		1.3 .9 .6	1.1 .8 .6	3.0 1.5 .8				2.1 1.2 .6	2.7 1.0 .6
% Depr., Dep., Amort./Sales		1.6 3.8 (16) 6.5	.7 2.7 (15) 6.3	.5 2.2 6.8				(41) .9 2.3 4.8	(40) .9 3.8 6.5
% Officers', Directors', Owners' Comp/Sales			2.8 4.1 (10) 6.9					(10) .6 2.5 8.3	(10) 1.8 2.7 5.4
Net Sales ($)	2171M	11244M	78752M	869363M	98347M	936155M		1597948M	1578300M
Total Assets ($)	1284M	12479M	89582M	338054M	162422M	833146M		925798M	1066259M

M = $ thousand   MM = $ million
See Pages 1 through 15 for Explanation of Ratios and Data

Comparative Historical Data | Current Data Sorted By Sales

Type of Statement

# Postretirement Benefits	13	11	15		1				1	
Unqualified	11	16	18		1	4	1	1		11
Reviewed	18	14	13		3	2	1	4		
Compiled	5	5	8		3					
Tax Returns			1							
Other					3	2	2	2		6

	4/1/92-3/31/93 ALL	4/1/93-3/31/94 ALL	4/1/94-3/31/95 ALL		29 (4/1-9/30/94) 0-1MM	1-3MM	3-5MM	25 (10/1/94-3/31/95) 5-10MM	10-25MM	25MM & OVER
NUMBER OF STATEMENTS	47	47	54		9	9	8	4	7	17
	%	%	%		%	%	%	%	%	%
ASSETS										
Cash & Equivalents	3.8	5.5	2.7							3.6
Trade Receivables - (net)	16.6	11.6	14.2							21.7
Inventory	45.2	46.4	42.0							31.8
All Other Current	.8	1.6	2.0							.7
Total Current	66.4	65.2	61.0							57.8
Fixed Assets (net)	29.5	25.8	31.9							29.9
Intangibles (net)	.9	2.3	1.6							2.2
All Other Non-Current	3.3	6.7	5.5							10.1
Total	100.0	100.0	100.0							100.0
LIABILITIES										
Notes Payable-Short Term	13.4	17.0	15.0							11.5
Cur. Mat.-L /T/D	2.6	2.5	2.6							2.6
Trade Payables	11.6	9.8	9.3							13.2
Income Taxes Payable	.4	.1	.5							.4
All Other Current	7.3	4.4	5.3							6.4
Total Current	35.2	33.8	32.7							34.1
Long Term Debt	19.6	20.2	18.5							20.3
Deferred Taxes	.4	.4	.7							.9
All Other-Non-Current	4.1	1.1	5.2							2.8
Net Worth	40.7	44.6	42.9							41.9
Total Liabilities & Net Worth	100.0	100.0	100.0							100.0
INCOME DATA										
Net Sales	100.0	100.0	100.0							100.0
Gross Profit	37.0	36.7	35.0							19.7
Operating Expenses	26.7	28.2	24.5							13.0
Operating Profit	10.3	8.5	10.5							6.7
All Other Expenses (net)	3.5	4.1	3.1							1.6
Profit Before Taxes	6.8	4.4	7.4							5.1
RATIOS										
Current	2.8 / 1.8 / 1.4	3.2 / 1.9 / 1.4	3.0 / 1.9 / 1.2							2.4 / 1.7 / 1.2
Quick	.9 / .5 / .3	.8 / .4 / .2	1.0 / .5 / .3							1.5 / .6 / .5
Sales/Receivables	29 12.7 / 43 8.4 / 57 6.4	20 18.7 / 37 9.9 / 68 5.4	29 12.6 / 41 9.0 / 61 6.0							33 10.9 / 41 8.9 / 61 6.0
Cost of Sales/Inventory	59 6.2 / 281 1.3 / 730 .5	89 4.1 / 406 .9 / 608 .6	104 3.5 / 281 1.3 / 521 .7							38 9.5 / 78 4.7 / 152 2.4
Cost of Sales/Payables	16 23.1 / 49 7.4 / 85 4.3	20 18.1 / 38 9.5 / 87 4.2	24 15.3 / 34 10.6 / 65 5.6							21 17.3 / 32 11.3 / 57 6.4
Sales/Working Capital	1.9 / 3.6 / 12.6	1.6 / 3.3 / 10.3	2.0 / 3.4 / 12.5							2.6 / 9.0 / 22.4
EBIT/Interest	(46) 7.7 / 2.7 / 1.1	(41) 6.7 / 2.9 / 1.2	(51) 6.6 / 3.6 / 1.3						(16)	5.9 / 4.3 / 3.2
Net Profit + Depr., Dep., Amort./Cur. Mat. L/T/D	(13) 19.9 / 6.1 / 2.8	(17) 6.4 / 3.5 / -.1	(26) 4.6 / 3.0 / .9						(10)	4.6 / 3.2 / 1.9
Fixed/Worth	.3 / .8 / 1.6	.2 / .7 / 1.2	.3 / .8 / 1.3							.4 / .8 / 1.1
Debt/Worth	.7 / 1.9 / 2.7	.6 / 1.4 / 3.6	.7 / 1.4 / 3.5							.8 / 1.8 / 3.4
% Profit Before Taxes/Tangible Net Worth	(45) 44.0 / 13.2 / 2.3	(46) 28.9 / 12.2 / -1.1	(53) 28.7 / 16.4 / 2.1							28.7 / 22.4 / 12.6
% Profit Before Taxes/Total Assets	17.7 / 4.4 / .5	10.8 / 4.5 / -.6	12.5 / 7.3 / 1.0							10.2 / 8.2 / 6.3
Sales/Net Fixed Assets	23.5 / 3.5 / 1.4	21.9 / 3.9 / 1.5	9.1 / 3.2 / 1.7							30.4 / 4.7 / 2.1
Sales/Total Assets	2.5 / 1.0 / .6	1.6 / .9 / .6	1.5 / .9 / .7							2.7 / 1.6 / .8
% Depr., Dep., Amort./Sales	(44) 1.1 / 3.2 / 6.0	1.0 / 2.9 / 5.6	(50) 1.0 / 3.9 / 6.1						(15)	.5 / 2.2 / 4.8
% Officers', Directors', Owners' Comp/Sales	(13) 1.5 / 2.2 / 4.4	(10) 2.4 / 3.1 / 3.4	(19) 2.0 / 3.2 / 4.8							
Net Sales ($)	1446489M	1310626M	1996032M		5837M	16545M	28690M	28931M	97181M	1818848M
Total Assets ($)	1067665M	1125094M	1436967M		17171M	19361M	39368M	45518M	91830M	1223719M

M = $ thousand   MM = $ million
See Pages 1 through 15 for Explanation of Ratios and Data

Current Data Sorted By Assets | Comparative Historical Data

 # Postretirement Benefits

Type of Statement	0-500M	500M-2MM	2-10MM	10-50MM	50-100MM	100-250MM		4/1/90-3/31/91 ALL	4/1/91-3/31/92 ALL
Unqualified			1	1				15	11
Reviewed		2	4	3				7	4
Compiled		4	4					5	9
Tax Returns		5	1						
Other	1		3	3		1		3	4

Date ranges: 500M-2MM = 11 (4/1-9/30/94); 10-50MM = 20 (10/1/94-3/31/95)

0-500M	500M-2MM	2-10MM	10-50MM	50-100MM	100-250MM		4/1/90-3/31/91 ALL	4/1/91-3/31/92 ALL
1	11	12	6		1	**NUMBER OF STATEMENTS**	30	28
%	%	%	%	%	%		%	%
						ASSETS		
	3.1	1.7				Cash & Equivalents	3.4	6.0
	26.5	27.2				Trade Receivables - (net)	22.4	25.7
	34.5	33.5				Inventory	36.3	30.1
	1.1	1.4				All Other Current	.8	1.0
	65.1	63.9				Total Current	62.9	62.7
	29.8	26.3				Fixed Assets (net)	28.6	28.4
	.0	1.4				Intangibles (net)	2.1	1.3
	5.1	8.4				All Other Non-Current	6.4	7.6
	100.0	100.0				Total	100.0	100.0
						LIABILITIES		
	9.5	11.0				Notes Payable-Short Term	15.3	8.0
	4.4	2.5				Cur. Mat. -L/T/D	4.3	3.4
	15.7	14.6				Trade Payables	12.6	11.7
	.3	.1				Income Taxes Payable	.4	.4
	5.7	4.8				All Other Current	5.3	7.0
	35.7	33.1				Total Current	37.9	30.5
	17.4	12.9				Long Term Debt	13.5	15.8
	.4	1.1				Deferred Taxes	.7	.6
	4.4	7.2				All Other-Non-Current	1.1	6.0
	42.1	45.8				Net Worth	46.8	47.1
	100.0	100.0				Total Liabilities & Net Worth	100.0	100.0
						INCOME DATA		
	100.0	100.0				Net Sales	100.0	100.0
	31.2	31.1				Gross Profit	30.2	30.5
	28.0	25.3				Operating Expenses	26.1	26.2
	3.2	5.8				Operating Profit	4.2	4.3
	.7	1.2				All Other Expenses (net)	2.1	1.5
	2.5	4.6				Profit Before Taxes	2.1	2.8
						RATIOS		
	2.6	3.0					2.3	3.2
	1.6	2.3				Current	1.7	2.2
	1.4	1.5					1.3	1.4
	1.1	1.4					1.0	1.6
	.9	1.0				Quick	.7	1.2
	.7	.7					.5	.8
	35 10.4	40 9.2					33 10.9	33 10.9
	43 8.5	46 8.0				Sales/Receivables	41 9.0	40 9.2
	50 7.3	60 6.1					46 8.0	48 7.6
	52 7.0	49 7.5					79 4.6	38 9.6
	69 5.3	96 3.8				Cost of Sales/Inventory	99 3.7	78 4.7
	114 3.2	126 2.9					126 2.9	104 3.5
	10 37.9	20 17.9					17 21.3	19 19.4
	38 9.6	32 11.5				Cost of Sales/Payables	26 13.8	24 15.1
	51 7.1	51 7.2					42 8.7	38 9.5
	6.3	4.5					4.7	4.7
	7.7	6.3				Sales/Working Capital	7.3	7.3
	11.5	10.5					16.0	11.5
	5.4	6.4					3.2	4.9
	3.8	2.5				EBIT/Interest	(28) 1.9	2.4
	1.8	1.7					1.0	1.2
							4.9	4.2
						Net Profit + Depr., Dep., Amort./Cur. Mat. L/T/D	(20) 1.7	(15) 2.5
							.6	.9
	.4	.2					.4	.3
	.8	.4				Fixed/Worth	.7	.5
	1.1	1.4					1.0	1.0
	.9	.4					.6	.7
	1.4	1.4				Debt/Worth	1.1	1.1
	2.0	3.2					3.4	2.1
	27.9	21.1					21.3	23.4
	12.5 (11)	10.7				% Profit Before Taxes/Tangible Net Worth	12.1	12.7
	4.7	8.4					.5	2.8
	12.9	8.0					8.6	10.0
	4.2	4.6				% Profit Before Taxes/Total Assets	3.9	6.2
	2.1	3.1					.2	.6
	18.2	21.8					14.4	16.7
	9.6	12.4				Sales/Net Fixed Assets	7.4	6.6
	4.5	4.6					4.0	4.4
	2.6	2.2					2.4	3.2
	2.3	1.8				Sales/Total Assets	2.1	1.9
	1.8	1.7					1.7	1.7
	1.0	1.2					1.9	1.3
	1.4	2.5				% Depr., Dep., Amort./Sales	(28) 2.3	(25) 2.6
	3.1	3.3					3.7	3.8
								2.1
						% Officers', Directors', Owners' Comp/Sales		(14) 4.5
								8.0
1541M	31972M	111744M	289300M		73467M	Net Sales ($)	371494M	190948M
443M	13761M	57768M	134843M		165799M	Total Assets ($)	235026M	102321M

M = $ thousand   MM = $ million
See Pages 1 through 15 for Explanation of Ratios and Data

Comparative Historical Data | Current Data Sorted By Sales

5 4/1/92-3/31/93 ALL	4 4/1/93-3/31/94 ALL	8 4/1/94-3/31/95 ALL		0-1MM	11 (4/1-9/30/94) 1-3MM	3-5MM	20 (10/1/94-3/31/95) 5-10MM	10-25MM	25MM & OVER
	3	2	# Postretirement Benefits		1				1
			Type of Statement						
13	10	9	Unqualified		2		3	1	3
4	6	8	Reviewed		2	2	3	1	
4	6	6	Compiled		4	1		1	
			Tax Returns						
			Other		1	1	2		4
26	26	31	**NUMBER OF STATEMENTS**		9	4	8	3	7
%	%	%	**ASSETS**	%	%	%	%	%	%
4.1	4.0	2.2	Cash & Equivalents						
25.1	27.4	27.1	Trade Receivables - (net)						
34.9	31.2	32.6	Inventory						
.9	1.5	1.3	All Other Current						
65.0	64.1	63.1	Total Current						
28.3	29.0	26.6	Fixed Assets (net)						
1.9	1.4	3.9	Intangibles (net)						
4.8	5.5	6.4	All Other Non-Current						
100.0	100.0	100.0	Total						
			LIABILITIES						
8.9	10.0	10.6	Notes Payable-Short Term						
4.3	5.1	3.4	Cur. Mat.-L /T/D						
11.3	13.3	16.1	Trade Payables						
.3	1.8	.5	Income Taxes Payable						
5.6	6.1	5.4	All Other Current						
30.4	36.3	36.1	Total Current						
18.3	16.6	15.0	Long Term Debt						
.5	1.9	.7	Deferred Taxes						
3.3	2.7	5.7	All Other-Non-Current						
47.6	42.5	42.5	Net Worth						
100.0	100.0	100.0	Total Liabilities & Net Worth						
			INCOME DATA						
100.0	100.0	100.0	Net Sales						
32.6	28.5	30.6	Gross Profit						
27.9	25.2	26.7	Operating Expenses						
4.8	3.2	3.9	Operating Profit						
1.1	.9	1.3	All Other Expenses (net)						
3.6	2.3	2.6	Profit Before Taxes						
			RATIOS						
3.7	2.6	2.5	Current						
2.5	1.8	1.8							
1.5	1.3	1.4							
1.8	1.2	1.2	Quick						
.9	.9	.9							
.7	.7	.7							
36 10.2	34 10.7	38 9.6	Sales/Receivables						
41 9.0	38 9.7	45 8.2							
53 6.9	57 6.4	52 7.0							
66 5.5	47 7.7	50 7.3	Cost of Sales/Inventory						
96 3.8	66 5.5	73 5.0							
130 2.8	89 4.1	111 3.3							
18 19.9	14 25.8	20 18.2	Cost of Sales/Payables						
30 12.3	23 15.9	35 10.5							
37 9.8	42 8.7	51 7.1							
4.1	5.4	5.8	Sales/Working Capital						
5.4	8.7	7.4							
7.9	17.1	11.6							
4.7	5.5	5.4	EBIT/Interest						
(25) 3.5	(25) 4.3	3.3							
1.4	1.6	1.7							
3.3	5.2	5.6	Net Profit + Depr., Dep., Amort./Cur. Mat. L/T/D						
(14) 1.7	(17) 2.4	(14) 2.7							
.9	.8	.8							
.3	.3	.3	Fixed/Worth						
.6	.8	.5							
1.2	1.3	1.3							
.7	.6	.7	Debt/Worth						
1.0	1.4	1.5							
2.8	3.3	2.5							
26.2	35.6	30.9	% Profit Before Taxes/Tangible Net Worth						
12.9	(25) 20.8	(28) 15.4							
5.9	7.2	5.5							
10.1	10.9	11.3	% Profit Before Taxes/Total Assets						
6.2	6.1	4.3							
1.5	2.3	2.1							
12.5	13.7	22.0	Sales/Net Fixed Assets						
8.3	8.3	9.6							
4.7	4.8	4.6							
2.2	3.0	2.4	Sales/Total Assets						
2.0	2.2	2.0							
1.7	1.8	1.7							
1.8	1.3	1.1	% Depr., Dep., Amort./Sales						
(24) 2.5	(25) 1.9	(29) 2.1							
3.5	3.2	3.0							
1.5	1.5	2.2	% Officers', Directors', Owners' Comp/Sales						
(10) 3.9	(11) 4.3	(13) 4.6							
7.2	5.3	6.3							
221500M	300498M	508024M	Net Sales ($)		20281M	18109M	61419M	45448M	362767M
109165M	143106M	372614M	Total Assets ($)		9528M	7318M	34308M	20818M	300642M

M = $ thousand   MM = $ million
See Pages 1 through 15 for Explanation of Ratios and Data

Current Data Sorted By Assets **Comparative Historical Data**

0-500M	500M-2MM	2-10MM	10-50MM	50-100MM	100-250MM		4/1/90-3/31/91 ALL	4/1/91-3/31/92 ALL
	1	2	1	2		# Postretirement Benefits **Type of Statement**		
	3	16	9	2	1	Unqualified	18	18
	7	7	2			Reviewed	16	19
6	12	2				Compiled	21	11
1						Tax Returns		1
	9	14	7			Other	12	17
	37 (4/1-9/30/94)		62 (10/1/94-3/31/95)					
7	31	39	50	3	1	**NUMBER OF STATEMENTS**	67	66
%	%	%	%	%	%	**ASSETS**	%	%
	8.4	7.0	4.3			Cash & Equivalents	7.5	7.8
	33.2	30.5	25.1			Trade Receivables - (net)	28.5	28.8
	29.2	24.5	21.5			Inventory	25.8	26.5
	2.2	.8	.6			All Other Current	2.1	1.5
	73.0	62.8	51.5			Total Current	64.0	64.6
	19.3	25.1	34.8			Fixed Assets (net)	26.9	24.8
	1.2	4.5	3.9			Intangibles (net)	3.2	3.3
	6.4	7.6	9.8			All Other Non-Current	5.9	7.3
	100.0	100.0	100.0			Total	100.0	100.0
						LIABILITIES		
	9.0	10.1	8.3			Notes Payable-Short Term	9.6	8.8
	2.2	2.6	3.3			Cur. Mat. -L/T/D	3.6	3.1
	16.4	16.1	14.2			Trade Payables	16.2	15.1
	.4	.4	.5			Income Taxes Payable	.8	.7
	7.8	8.9	6.8			All Other Current	7.6	6.3
	35.8	38.1	33.0			Total Current	37.7	34.1
	9.6	9.5	14.2			Long Term Debt	14.1	13.4
	.1	1.1	1.3			Deferred Taxes	.6	.6
	5.0	2.3	1.5			All Other-Non-Current	4.2	6.6
	49.5	49.0	50.0			Net Worth	43.3	45.2
	100.0	100.0	100.0			Total Liabilities & Net Worth	100.0	100.0
						INCOME DATA		
	100.0	100.0	100.0			Net Sales	100.0	100.0
	36.1	29.1	35.7			Gross Profit	30.9	33.2
	30.2	25.4	27.1			Operating Expenses	25.7	28.1
	5.9	3.7	8.5			Operating Profit	5.3	5.1
	.6	1.1	.7			All Other Expenses (net)	1.8	1.5
	5.3	2.6	7.8			Profit Before Taxes	3.4	3.6
						RATIOS		
	3.1	2.5	2.2				2.6	3.4
	2.0	1.4	1.7			Current	1.7	1.9
	1.5	1.3	1.4				1.3	1.4
	1.8	1.5	1.2				1.5	2.0
	1.1	.9	1.0			Quick	1.0	1.0
	.8	.7	.7				.6	.7
	35 10.5	37 9.8	44 8.3				34 10.6	34 10.6
	39 9.4	51 7.2	56 6.5			Sales/Receivables	43 8.4	47 7.8
	51 7.1	65 5.6	69 5.3				52 7.0	56 6.5
	49 7.5	34 10.6	51 7.1				42 8.6	46 7.9
	55 6.6	53 6.9	70 5.2			Cost of Sales/Inventory	60 6.1	59 6.2
	69 5.3	87 4.2	135 2.7				79 4.6	91 4.0
	15 24.2	19 19.3	31 11.9				26 14.3	18 20.0
	34 10.8	34 10.6	45 8.1			Cost of Sales/Payables	35 10.4	30 12.0
	50 7.3	58 6.3	57 6.4				43 8.4	54 6.8
	5.3	6.0	4.2				5.7	5.1
	7.8	10.5	8.4			Sales/Working Capital	8.7	7.8
	11.8	24.1	15.5				21.1	16.3
	19.0	13.8	12.9				6.4	6.0
	(27) 3.5	(36) 5.1	7.3			EBIT/Interest	(57) 2.7	(59) 3.3
	1.8	.4	2.8				1.2	1.6
		(22) 6.5				Net Profit + Depr., Dep.,	5.4	4.3
		3.1				Amort./Cur. Mat. L /T/D	(36) 3.3	(33) 2.4
		1.3					1.3	1.1
	.2	.3	.4				.3	.3
	.2	.5	.8			Fixed/Worth	.5	.6
	.7	1.2	1.2				1.6	1.1
	.6	.6	.5				.6	.4
	.9	1.4	1.5			Debt/Worth	1.4	1.1
	2.3	2.0	2.1				3.6	3.3
	(29) 38.1	(37) 31.1	43.0			% Profit Before Taxes/Tangible	(61) 32.4	(58) 39.8
	16.2	12.9	19.3			Net Worth	14.9	17.4
	4.7	.7	12.1				5.3	4.5
	22.9	15.3	15.5			% Profit Before Taxes/Total	12.2	16.7
	8.9	7.1	9.2			Assets	7.1	7.4
	2.2	–.6	4.2				1.5	2.4
	43.3	17.3	7.4				20.1	22.7
	24.2	10.2	5.3			Sales/Net Fixed Assets	9.2	10.9
	8.1	5.2	3.5				4.9	5.3
	3.7	2.7	2.3				3.1	2.8
	2.7	2.2	1.8			Sales/Total Assets	2.2	2.2
	2.1	1.6	1.1				1.7	1.7
	(30) .7	(37) 1.2	(15) 2.0			% Depr., Dep., Amort./Sales	(61) 1.2	(60) 1.1
	1.5	2.1	2.4				2.0	2.1
	2.5	3.1	5.8				3.5	3.3
	(13) 3.3	(15) 2.8				% Officers', Directors',	(20) 2.1	(26) 2.8
	7.5	4.6				Owners' Comp/Sales	3.6	4.0
	10.9	6.4					7.4	11.4
7689M	102575M	465574M	578287M	315786M	197536M	Net Sales ($)	1281202M	802273M
1778M	36078M	202692M	345984M	196081M	178926M	Total Assets ($)	726002M	446370M

M = $ thousand   MM = $ million
See Pages 1 through 15 for Explanation of Ratios and Data

Comparative Historical Data | # Postretirement Benefits | Current Data Sorted By Sales

4/1/92-3/31/93 ALL	4/1/93-3/31/94 ALL	4/1/94-3/31/95 ALL	Type of Statement	0-1MM	1-3MM	3-5MM	5-10MM	10-25MM	25MM & OVER
24	22	31	Unqualified		1	3	7	11	9
16	18	16	Reviewed	1	2	1	7	4	1
18	14	20	Compiled	3	10	3	4		
4		1	Tax Returns	1					
15	19	31	Other	2	4	3	5	10	7
				37 (4/1-9/30/94)			62 (10/1/94-3/31/95)		
77	73	99	**NUMBER OF STATEMENTS**	7	17	10	23	25	17
%	%	%	**ASSETS**	%	%	%	%	%	%
6.9	5.9	7.8	Cash & Equivalents		5.2	19.0	5.6	5.1	7.0
29.7	30.5	30.7	Trade Receivables - (net)		37.1	30.5	33.0	29.0	24.4
29.4	27.7	25.1	Inventory		26.4	27.5	28.0	25.1	20.7
1.3	1.1	1.2	All Other Current		.9	.7	1.7	.9	.6
67.3	65.3	64.8	Total Current		69.6	77.7	68.3	60.1	52.8
23.7	25.6	25.0	Fixed Assets (net)		18.8	10.4	20.9	29.7	37.0
2.1	3.0	3.1	Intangibles (net)		4.5	1.1	2.1	3.6	4.6
6.8	6.1	7.1	All Other Non-Current		7.1	10.8	8.7	6.6	5.7
100.0	100.0	100.0	Total		100.0	100.0	100.0	100.0	100.0
			LIABILITIES						
13.1	11.5	9.2	Notes Payable-Short Term		11.5	3.0	10.3	13.0	4.0
3.6	3.3	2.4	Cur. Mat.-L./T/D		2.0	2.7	2.0	2.6	3.6
15.6	15.9	16.0	Trade Payables		15.9	17.7	15.4	15.8	16.0
.7	1.4	.4	Income Taxes Payable		.3	1.0	.4	.3	.4
9.6	8.2	8.9	All Other Current		10.3	7.9	6.7	9.4	7.8
42.6	40.3	36.9	Total Current		39.9	32.2	34.8	41.2	31.7
10.9	11.4	10.4	Long Term Debt		9.8	4.2	6.9	13.4	16.1
.6	.8	.8	Deferred Taxes		.0	.2	.8	1.0	1.7
2.7	2.3	4.2	All Other-Non-Current		6.2	6.9	2.8	2.1	4.6
43.3	45.3	47.8	Net Worth		44.1	56.4	54.6	42.4	45.9
100.0	100.0	100.0	Total Liabilities & Net Worth		100.0	100.0	100.0	100.0	100.0
			INCOME DATA						
100.0	100.0	100.0	Net Sales		100.0	100.0	100.0	100.0	100.0
35.3	31.9	33.7	Gross Profit		39.5	33.9	35.0	26.4	31.6
30.4	27.9	27.6	Operating Expenses		33.7	26.5	30.2	23.1	23.7
4.9	3.9	6.1	Operating Profit		5.7	7.4	4.8	3.3	7.8
1.0	1.6	.9	All Other Expenses (net)		1.4	.8	.2	1.4	.7
3.9	2.3	5.3	Profit Before Taxes		4.3	6.6	4.5	1.9	7.1
			RATIOS						
2.2 / 1.6 / 1.3	2.0 / 1.6 / 1.3	2.9 / 1.7 / 1.3	Current		3.1 / 1.8 / 1.2	4.8 / 2.2 / 1.8	3.2 / 1.7 / 1.4	2.3 / 1.4 / 1.1	2.1 / 1.8 / 1.4
1.4 / .9 / .6	1.3 / .9 / .6	1.6 / 1.0 / .7	Quick		1.7 / 1.3 / .8	3.4 / 1.5 / .9	2.6 / 1.0 / .7	1.3 / .8 / .5	1.1 / 1.0 / .7
35 10.4 / 45 8.2 / 55 6.6	37 10.0 / 51 7.2 / 65 5.6	35 10.3 / 47 7.8 / 62 5.9	Sales/Receivables		37 9.9 / 44 8.3 / 51 7.1	35 10.5 / 38 9.7 / 54 6.8	39 9.4 / 53 6.9 / 68 5.4	37 9.8 / 47 7.8 / 63 5.8	41 8.9 / 49 7.4 / 63 5.8
46 8.0 / 65 5.6 / 89 4.1	46 8.0 / 64 5.7 / 87 4.2	40 9.2 / 58 6.3 / 83 4.4	Cost of Sales/Inventory		40 9.2 / 58 6.3 / 70 5.2	46 7.9 / 54 6.7 / 74 4.9	50 7.3 / 61 6.0 / 87 4.2	31 11.9 / 47 7.7 / 126 2.9	39 9.4 / 64 5.7 / 73 5.0
24 15.2 / 35 10.5 / 47 7.8	22 16.6 / 37 9.9 / 54 6.8	20 18.0 / 35 10.4 / 51 7.1	Cost of Sales/Payables		14 26.9 / 34 10.8 / 47 7.8	19 19.4 / 35 10.3 / 48 7.6	13 28.8 / 33 11.0 / 50 7.3	20 17.9 / 37 10.0 / 58 6.3	27 13.3 / 40 9.1 / 51 7.1
6.4 / 9.6 / 16.2	6.4 / 9.4 / 17.3	5.4 / 8.6 / 16.9	Sales/Working Capital		5.9 / 8.7 / 35.1	3.0 / 6.8 / 10.6	4.9 / 8.1 / 11.6	6.3 / 10.5 / 85.6	7.5 / 8.8 / 22.6
10.9 / (71) 3.2 / 1.8	7.7 / (70) 4.1 / 1.5	14.3 / (90) 5.1 / 1.8	EBIT/Interest		(16) 15.6 / 6.1 / 1.8		22.2 / 5.4 / 1.8	(23) 8.4 / 3.4 / .1	14.2 / 6.3 / 2.5
4.4 / (35) 2.5 / 1.1	5.3 / (40) 2.0 / .3	5.9 / (43) 3.1 / 1.4	Net Profit + Depr., Dep., Amort./Cur. Mat. L/T/D					(16) 5.4 / 3.2 / .9	(11) 15.6 / 4.7 / 2.9
.3 / .5 / 1.0	.3 / .5 / 1.0	.2 / .5 / 1.2	Fixed/Worth		.2 / .3 / 1.4	.1 / .2 / .5	.2 / .3 / .6	.4 / .7 / 1.3	.6 / .8 / 1.6
.6 / 1.4 / 3.1	.7 / 1.4 / 2.3	.6 / 1.3 / 2.2	Debt/Worth		.7 / 1.2 / 3.6	.2 / .8 / 2.5	.4 / .7 / 1.7	1.1 / 1.7 / 2.3	.6 / 1.3 / 2.7
39.7 / (71) 21.9 / 5.4	27.8 / (69) 16.8 / 4.6	35.6 / (92) 19.2 / 6.8	% Profit Before Taxes/Tangible Net Worth		(16) 62.7 / 12.8 / 4.3	43.5 / 26.2 / 9.3	(21) 31.0 / 12.9 / 3.9	(24) 26.9 / 12.8 / -7.5	(16) 44.3 / 25.4 / 12.8
18.3 / 7.5 / 1.9	14.4 / 7.1 / 1.5	20.8 / 8.8 / 2.5	% Profit Before Taxes/Total Assets		28.3 / 9.0 / 2.1	21.6 / 10.8 / 5.3	19.7 / 8.8 / 2.0	10.3 / 6.3 / -2.2	18.1 / 12.5 / 3.9
29.7 / 10.8 / 6.7	26.8 / 10.1 / 5.0	27.3 / 11.2 / 5.3	Sales/Net Fixed Assets		60.6 / 27.3 / 6.1	67.2 / 34.8 / 17.6	26.8 / 13.4 / 6.9	13.2 / 7.0 / 4.6	9.1 / 5.4 / 4.2
3.2 / 2.4 / 1.8	2.8 / 2.2 / 1.6	3.1 / 2.3 / 1.6	Sales/Total Assets		3.7 / 2.6 / 1.9	4.1 / 2.5 / 1.9	3.1 / 2.4 / 1.7	2.8 / 2.0 / 1.5	2.5 / 1.8 / 1.3
1.0 / (66) 1.7 / 2.8	1.2 / (69) 1.9 / 3.6	1.2 / (89) 2.0 / 3.2	% Depr., Dep., Amort./Sales		(14) 1.2 / 1.9 / 3.2		.7 / 1.8 / 3.7	(24) 1.4 / 2.3 / 3.6	(14) 1.9 / 2.3 / 4.5
5.0 / (24) 7.4 / 12.0	2.9 / (26) 6.0 / 9.3	3.0 / (31) 5.1 / 10.4	% Officers', Directors', Owners' Comp/Sales						
982272M	1246651M	1667447M	Net Sales ($)	5303M	35656M	37128M	157210M	376675M	1055475M
512691M	745204M	961539M	Total Assets ($)	2666M	16094M	17511M	83031M	204661M	637576M

M = $ thousand   MM = $ million
See Pages 1 through 15 for Explanation of Ratios and Data

MANUFACTURERS—DRUGS & MEDICINES. SIC# 2833 (34–36)

Current Data Sorted By Assets

Comparative Historical Data

						# Postretirement Benefits / Type of Statement		
	2	5	5	3	1			
	3	28	24	14	10	Unqualified	43	64
	2	2	5			Reviewed	17	26
3	7	5	1		1	Compiled	17	12
	1					Tax Returns		
3	9	12	14	7	4	Other	21	22
	58 (4/1-9/30/94)		97 (10/1/94-3/31/95)				4/1/90-3/31/91 ALL	4/1/91-3/31/92 ALL
0-500M	500M-2MM	2-10MM	10-50MM	50-100MM	100-250MM			
6	22	47	44	21	15	NUMBER OF STATEMENTS	98	124
%	%	%	%	%	%	ASSETS	%	%
	12.9	14.9	15.6	9.6	14.3	Cash & Equivalents	9.5	13.6
	26.3	20.5	17.5	18.3	15.6	Trade Receivables - (net)	22.1	21.0
	27.0	23.5	19.3	23.8	19.7	Inventory	26.2	23.6
	2.9	1.5	2.4	2.5	4.7	All Other Current	2.3	1.5
	69.1	60.4	54.9	54.2	54.2	Total Current	60.1	59.8
	23.2	30.5	29.4	27.7	31.4	Fixed Assets (net)	27.5	28.2
	2.0	1.9	8.0	9.0	7.5	Intangibles (net)	3.9	5.0
	5.7	7.2	7.7	9.2	6.9	All Other Non-Current	8.5	7.1
	100.0	100.0	100.0	100.0	100.0	Total	100.0	100.0
						LIABILITIES		
	7.6	5.4	6.4	3.4	2.7	Notes Payable-Short Term	7.9	6.4
	3.0	3.8	3.3	1.2	1.1	Cur. Mat. -L/T/D	3.5	3.4
	19.3	12.7	9.0	8.5	9.8	Trade Payables	12.6	12.0
	.0	.7	.8	.4	2.0	Income Taxes Payable	1.0	.5
	11.5	6.4	8.7	10.4	9.3	All Other Current	8.7	9.5
	41.4	28.9	28.1	23.8	24.9	Total Current	33.5	31.7
	8.6	14.2	17.2	9.4	7.2	Long Term Debt	16.9	13.0
	.2	.6	.7	.7	1.2	Deferred Taxes	1.0	1.1
	8.1	5.5	2.5	5.5	2.2	All Other-Non-Current	2.3	1.6
	41.8	50.7	51.6	60.6	64.5	Net Worth	46.2	52.6
	100.0	100.0	100.0	100.0	100.0	Total Liabilities & Net Worth	100.0	100.0
						INCOME DATA		
	100.0	100.0	100.0	100.0	100.0	Net Sales	100.0	100.0
	42.7	44.3	42.6	41.0	52.4	Gross Profit	44.1	42.9
	36.7	40.5	34.2	33.3	42.1	Operating Expenses	36.8	36.0
	6.0	3.8	8.5	7.7	10.3	Operating Profit	7.3	6.8
	1.6	.3	1.1	1.7	.0	All Other Expenses (net)	1.6	2.0
	4.4	3.5	7.4	6.0	10.3	Profit Before Taxes	5.7	4.9
						RATIOS		
	2.2	4.3	3.7	2.8	3.9		2.7	3.3
	1.9	2.2	2.0	2.4	2.5	Current	1.9	2.1
	1.2	1.4	1.4	1.7	1.4		1.3	1.4
	1.6	2.7	3.0	1.8	2.7		1.4	2.0
	1.0	1.4	1.0	1.0	1.3	Quick	.9	1.1
	.5	.7	.6	.8	.6		.7	.6
	32 11.5	38 9.7	40 9.2	47 7.7	39 9.3		36 10.2	35 10.3
	40 9.2	48 7.6	51 7.1	59 6.2	55 6.6	Sales/Receivables	47 7.7	47 7.7
	49 7.4	61 6.0	73 5.0	69 5.3	73 5.0		60 6.1	68 5.4
	33 11.1	62 5.9	74 4.9	74 4.9	126 2.9		62 5.9	59 6.2
	61 6.0	104 3.5	114 3.2	126 2.9	152 2.4	Cost of Sales/Inventory	104 3.5	96 3.8
	104 3.5	183 2.0	183 2.0	183 2.0	174 2.1		159 2.3	166 2.2
	27 13.3	29 12.7	29 12.6	29 12.4	45 8.2		28 13.2	28 13.0
	38 9.6	59 6.2	45 8.1	49 7.5	76 4.8	Cost of Sales/Payables	43 8.5	43 8.4
	69 5.3	91 4.0	73 5.0	57 6.4	135 2.7		62 5.9	69 5.3
	5.7	2.3	2.5	2.9	2.1		4.0	3.0
	9.3	4.9	4.8	4.3	4.0	Sales/Working Capital	6.2	6.0
	17.3	16.2	12.3	5.9	7.3		13.1	11.8
(19)	33.1	(43) 26.9	(36) 16.7	(18) 28.9	(10) 696.2		(84) 10.0	(113) 11.1
	4.7	5.8	4.2	10.0	17.7	EBIT/Interest	2.8	4.4
	1.6	1.9	2.5	2.7	2.2		1.4	1.8
		(28) 13.2	(27) 17.3	(11) 22.3		Net Profit + Depr., Dep., Amort./Cur. Mat. L /T/D	(55) 8.8	(69) 6.9
		2.2	3.5	4.1			3.2	3.2
		.6	.5	3.1			1.1	1.0
	.1	.3	.3	.3	.3		.3	.3
	.7	.6	.7	.5	.6	Fixed/Worth	.7	.6
	1.1	1.3	1.3	.8	1.1		1.2	1.1
	.7	.4	.5	.3	.3		.7	.4
	1.1	1.0	1.0	.6	.6	Debt/Worth	1.3	.9
	3.2	2.8	3.1	1.4	1.0		2.6	1.9
(20)	90.8	(45) 33.5	(41) 48.0	(20) 38.4	28.3	% Profit Before Taxes/Tangible Net Worth	(94) 37.8	(118) 35.4
	22.9	20.4	21.6	19.2	18.7		20.2	21.7
	5.0	2.5	2.4	8.3	6.9		2.5	4.8
	33.2	16.7	16.8	18.8	18.8	% Profit Before Taxes/Total Assets	16.5	16.6
	7.7	6.1	8.0	8.7	11.7		7.4	9.4
	1.4	.7	1.1	5.3	1.8		1.1	1.8
	55.6	8.6	6.5	8.2	4.9		12.2	12.9
	14.1	5.2	4.0	4.0	3.9	Sales/Net Fixed Assets	6.3	5.6
	5.0	2.9	2.6	2.7	2.1		3.6	3.4
	3.9	2.1	1.6	1.3	1.4		2.1	2.2
	2.4	1.3	1.1	1.1	1.0	Sales/Total Assets	1.6	1.5
	1.8	1.0	.8	.9	.8		1.1	1.0
(19)	.9	(43) 1.9	(41) 2.2	(19) 2.6	(11) 2.6	% Depr., Dep., Amort./Sales	(81) 1.6	(107) 1.9
	1.4	3.0	3.3	3.6	3.0		2.5	3.1
	2.6	5.2	5.8	4.1	3.6		3.8	5.5
		(11) 3.3				% Officers', Directors', Owners' Comp/Sales	(27) 2.8	(32) 2.8
		4.6					6.3	6.7
		9.4					9.9	10.4
5234M	61879M	389298M	1223740M	1743491M	2337076M	Net Sales ($)	2662577M	3673718M
2366M	25262M	255905M	1059069M	1451056M	2221858M	Total Assets ($)	2024282M	3283608M

M = $ thousand   MM = $ million
See Pages 1 through 15 for Explanation of Ratios and Data

Comparative Historical Data — Current Data Sorted By Sales

3	12	16	# Postretirement Benefits	1	2	4	4	5
			Type of Statement					
78	66	79	Unqualified	3	10	13	18	35
16	17	9	Reviewed		2	2	4	2
11	21	17	Compiled	9	4	1	1	1
	1	1	Tax Returns		1			
30	35	49	Other	10	5	1	11	19

Compiled and Other also include 1 and 3 respectively in the 0–1MM column.

Historical periods: 4/1/92–3/31/93 ALL · 4/1/93–3/31/94 ALL · 4/1/94–3/31/95 ALL
Current periods: 58 (4/1–9/30/94) · 97 (10/1/94–3/31/95)

3yr	12	16		0-1MM	1-3MM	3-5MM	5-10MM	10-25MM	25MM & OVER
135	140	155	**NUMBER OF STATEMENTS**	4	22	21	17	34	57
%	%	%	**ASSETS**	%	%	%	%	%	%
13.8	13.5	13.8	Cash & Equivalents		16.3	12.8	20.0	12.2	12.6
22.6	23.1	20.3	Trade Receivables - (net)		24.0	20.5	16.3	21.3	18.4
24.1	24.0	22.2	Inventory		23.1	24.5	17.8	22.1	22.6
1.9	1.9	2.6	All Other Current		2.0	3.4	1.8	1.6	3.1
62.4	62.6	58.9	Total Current		65.4	61.3	55.9	57.1	56.6
26.3	26.6	28.4	Fixed Assets (net)		26.4	27.1	29.9	29.3	29.0
4.7	4.7	5.1	Intangibles (net)		2.1	1.9	6.1	5.5	7.2
6.7	6.2	7.6	All Other Non-Current		6.0	9.7	8.0	8.0	7.2
100.0	100.0	100.0	Total		100.0	100.0	100.0	100.0	100.0
			LIABILITIES						
7.5	5.1	5.7	Notes Payable-Short Term		8.3	4.8	5.0	7.4	4.3
3.1	2.6	2.8	Cur. Mat.-L/T/D		2.2	4.2	2.5	3.4	2.4
13.0	14.2	11.6	Trade Payables		15.6	12.1	11.1	12.2	9.6
.8	.8	.7	Income Taxes Payable		.3	.7	1.0	.6	.9
9.0	9.4	8.9	All Other Current		9.1	7.1	8.5	7.3	9.7
33.4	32.1	29.7	Total Current		35.5	29.0	28.1	30.8	26.9
12.4	14.1	12.6	Long Term Debt		9.7	12.0	14.1	17.7	10.7
.6	.8	.8	Deferred Taxes		1.5	.6	.5	.7	.7
2.0	2.5	4.5	All Other-Non-Current		9.1	2.5	9.5	3.6	3.0
51.6	50.5	52.4	Net Worth		44.2	56.0	47.8	47.1	58.7
100.0	100.0	100.0	Total Liabilities & Net Worth		100.0	100.0	100.0	100.0	100.0
			INCOME DATA						
100.0	100.0	100.0	Net Sales		100.0	100.0	100.0	100.0	100.0
44.7	43.3	43.9	Gross Profit		42.3	47.7	42.7	41.0	45.9
37.7	35.4	37.5	Operating Expenses		41.0	43.6	36.4	34.0	36.5
7.0	7.9	6.4	Operating Profit		1.3	4.1	6.4	7.0	9.4
1.1	1.2	.9	All Other Expenses (net)		.6	.2	.7	1.3	1.1
5.9	6.8	5.5	Profit Before Taxes		.6	3.9	5.7	5.7	8.3
			RATIOS						
3.6	3.7	3.6	Current		3.7	4.6	4.6	3.6	3.0
2.1	2.2	2.1			2.0	2.2	2.1	2.0	2.4
1.3	1.4	1.4			1.3	1.4	1.2	1.2	1.6
2.1	2.1	2.0	Quick		1.9	3.1	2.8	2.1	1.9
1.1	1.1	1.1			1.2	1.2	1.6	1.0	1.1
.7	.8	.6			.6	.5	.6	.6	.7
36 10.1	39 9.4	39 9.3	Sales/Receivables		38 9.5	34 10.6	31 11.6	42 8.6	40 9.2
47 7.7	48 7.6	50 7.3			45 8.2	46 8.0	41 9.0	50 7.3	54 6.8
62 5.9	62 5.9	64 5.7			68 5.4	55 6.6	62 5.9	69 5.3	65 5.6
56 6.5	57 6.4	62 5.9	Cost of Sales/Inventory		19 19.5	59 6.2	45 8.1	49 7.5	81 4.5
104 3.5	94 3.9	111 3.3			68 5.4	166 2.2	104 3.5	99 3.7	126 2.9
166 2.2	159 2.3	166 2.2			135 2.7	215 1.7	183 2.0	159 2.3	166 2.2
31 11.9	29 12.6	29 12.7	Cost of Sales/Payables		26 13.8	28 13.2	24 14.9	32 11.3	31 11.8
43 8.5	50 7.3	51 7.2			46 7.9	60 6.1	49 7.4	53 6.9	51 7.2
69 5.3	68 5.4	74 4.9			107 3.4	107 3.4	85 4.3	74 4.9	70 5.2
2.9	3.0	2.7	Sales/Working Capital		2.7	2.1	2.4	2.9	2.9
5.7	5.1	5.1			6.1	6.2	4.6	5.7	4.3
14.2	11.9	11.1			15.5	14.2	76.8	25.7	7.1
(120) 17.1	(126) 29.1	(130) 23.0	EBIT/Interest	(20) 8.0	(19) 22.7	(12) 34.9	(30) 12.5	(47) 29.8	
6.5	7.1	5.2		4.8	4.7	12.5	4.2	9.6	
1.8	2.3	2.2		-.2	-7.5	1.9	2.2	2.8	
(68) 14.1	(63) 10.1	(77) 15.3	Net Profit + Depr., Dep., Amort./Cur. Mat. L/T/D				(22) 11.4	(31) 22.3	
6.5	3.8	3.1					2.3	4.1	
2.2	1.2	1.2					1.4	1.3	
.3	.3	.3	Fixed/Worth		.1	.3	.3	.4	.4
.5	.6	.6			.6	.7	.7	1.0	.6
1.0	.9	1.1			2.1	1.0	1.7	1.4	.9
.4	.4	.4	Debt/Worth		.5	.3	.5	.5	.4
.9	1.0	.9			.9	.8	1.1	1.7	.7
2.5	2.7	2.5			12.9	1.9	2.5	4.1	1.4
(129) 42.3	(131) 53.1	(147) 41.8	% Profit Before Taxes/Tangible Net Worth	(19) 59.8	36.3	(15) 35.0	(33) 48.6	(55) 41.0	
24.4	24.5	19.7		13.0	15.5	2.0	25.1	20.6	
6.4	7.3	4.0		2.9	.6	-7.5	11.3	6.9	
18.5	22.7	17.4	% Profit Before Taxes/Total Assets		12.9	23.4	14.8	16.5	18.9
10.3	9.9	8.4			3.7	5.5	5.7	8.7	10.4
2.5	2.7	1.4			-.2	-.7	-3.8	3.8	4.6
16.6	13.2	9.6	Sales/Net Fixed Assets		48.2	13.9	8.5	8.4	7.1
6.1	6.9	4.8			10.2	5.0	4.7	5.0	4.3
3.5	3.5	2.8			1.9	3.7	2.0	3.0	2.8
2.4	2.5	2.0	Sales/Total Assets		2.8	2.1	2.1	2.1	1.6
1.5	1.5	1.3			1.8	1.3	1.1	1.4	1.3
1.1	1.2	.9			.8	1.0	.7	.8	.9
(121) 1.8	(123) 1.4	(138) 1.9	% Depr., Dep., Amort./Sales	(19) 1.2	(19) 1.6	(15) 1.5	(31) 1.9	(51) 2.2	
2.8	2.7	2.9		2.9	2.6	3.9	3.3	2.9	
4.4	4.1	4.6		5.4	5.0	5.6	5.7	4.0	
(28) 2.8	(30) 2.5	(24) 2.5	% Officers', Directors', Owners' Comp/Sales						
6.6	6.5	4.8							
14.4	10.4	9.2							
3577511M	4657531M	5760718M	Net Sales ($)	2914M	46259M	83982M	130899M	543389M	4953275M
3064841M	3594841M	5015516M	Total Assets ($)	1550M	38904M	65736M	134330M	502401M	4272595M

M = $ thousand   MM = $ million
See Pages 1 through 15 for Explanation of Ratios and Data

Current Data Sorted By Assets   Comparative Historical Data

						# Postretirement Benefits		
1	3	2	2		1	**Type of Statement**		
1	4	11	10	1	3	Unqualified	24	26
	6	6	1			Reviewed	12	10
4	2	4				Compiled	8	12
	1					Tax Returns		
1	5	4	4		1	Other	9	6
	35 (4/1-9/30/94)			34 (10/1/94-3/31/95)			4/1/90- 3/31/91	4/1/91- 3/31/92
0-500M	500M-2MM	2-10MM	10-50MM	50-100MM	100-250MM		ALL	ALL
6	18	25	15	1	4	**NUMBER OF STATEMENTS**	53	54
%	%	%	%	%	%	**ASSETS**	%	%
	4.7	5.4	5.5			Cash & Equivalents	7.8	6.6
	21.4	22.1	28.9			Trade Receivables - (net)	28.3	30.0
	34.6	23.2	27.2			Inventory	23.8	22.8
	2.2	1.1	2.6			All Other Current	2.8	2.5
	63.0	51.7	64.2			Total Current	62.6	61.9
	29.5	34.4	20.3			Fixed Assets (net)	26.7	28.7
	1.9	3.5	3.3			Intangibles (net)	2.1	.9
	5.6	10.4	12.2			All Other Non-Current	8.6	8.4
	100.0	100.0	100.0			Total	100.0	100.0
						LIABILITIES		
	13.2	18.8	19.4			Notes Payable-Short Term	10.6	12.8
	2.1	4.8	1.9			Cur. Mat. -L/T/D	4.7	4.3
	8.4	13.0	14.1			Trade Payables	15.0	13.3
	.1	.1	.5			Income Taxes Payable	.8	.5
	5.1	7.8	10.5			All Other Current	9.7	11.8
	29.0	44.5	46.4			Total Current	40.9	42.8
	12.7	11.9	6.3			Long Term Debt	12.2	11.9
	.6	.6	.6			Deferred Taxes	.9	.9
	11.6	1.4	3.4			All Other-Non-Current	1.3	1.1
	46.2	41.6	43.4			Net Worth	44.7	43.2
	100.0	100.0	100.0			Total Liabilities & Net Worth	100.0	100.0
						INCOME DATA		
	100.0	100.0	100.0			Net Sales	100.0	100.0
	29.2	21.4	21.9			Gross Profit	25.2	22.9
	26.2	17.2	19.4			Operating Expenses	20.7	19.2
	3.0	4.2	2.5			Operating Profit	4.6	3.8
	.8	.6	-1.0			All Other Expenses (net)	.5	.1
	2.2	3.5	3.5			Profit Before Taxes	4.0	3.6
						RATIOS		
	5.1	1.8	2.0				2.5	2.3
	2.1	1.3	1.3			Current	1.5	1.5
	1.5	.8	1.0				1.1	1.1
	2.1	1.0	1.5				1.7	1.5
	.9	.6	.6			Quick	.8	.8
	.5	.4	.4				.5	.5

14	26.6	28	13.2	33	10.9				Sales/Receivables	27	13.4	27	13.7
22	16.4	43	8.5	42	8.6					39	9.3	47	7.8
55	6.6	66	5.5	70	5.2					55	6.6	70	5.2
30	12.2	37	10.0	33	11.1				Cost of Sales/Inventory	31	11.6	25	14.7
55	6.6	57	6.4	49	7.4					47	7.8	43	8.4
118	3.1	74	4.9	69	5.3					73	5.0	64	5.7
4	84.6	13	27.5	20	18.4				Cost of Sales/Payables	13	27.9	15	24.7
13	27.9	23	15.9	29	12.7					26	13.8	26	14.3
26	14.2	49	7.5	37	7.0					38	9.5	39	9.3
	5.2		9.2		7.4				Sales/Working Capital		6.4		7.0
	8.0		22.3		16.5						10.5		11.4
	15.6		-19.1		275.1						45.9		58.8
	7.4		4.9		10.7				EBIT/Interest		4.8		4.4
(15)	2.6		2.3	(13)	3.4					(47)	2.6	(52)	2.5
	1.5		1.2		1.6						1.4		1.6
			5.1						Net Profit + Depr., Dep.,		10.5		8.1
		(11)	1.4						Amort./Cur. Mat. L./T/D	(26)	2.3	(26)	2.7
			.8								1.8		1.7
	.3		.5		.1				Fixed/Worth		.4		.4
	.5		.8		.6						.6		.6
	2.6		1.9		1.6						1.2		1.1
	.4		.9		.5				Debt/Worth		.5		.8
	1.1		1.6		2.2						1.1		1.4
	10.8		4.4		3.6						3.0		2.7
	34.7		24.3		24.9				% Profit Before Taxes/Tangible		32.2		23.9
(17)	10.1	(24)	11.8		15.9				Net Worth	(51)	16.2	(53)	16.0
	5.1		2.0		5.3						6.1		7.1
	7.4		9.8		12.0				% Profit Before Taxes/Total		13.0		10.6
	4.5		4.6		5.5				Assets		7.7		6.4
	2.6		.7		1.8						2.3		2.5
	18.5		9.6		32.9				Sales/Net Fixed Assets		17.4		17.7
	8.4		5.4		12.2						9.8		9.6
	6.5		3.6		6.6						5.9		5.7
	3.5		2.1		2.5				Sales/Total Assets		2.9		3.0
	2.3		1.8		2.0						2.3		2.3
	1.9		1.3		1.6						1.7		1.8
	1.1		1.7		.9				% Depr., Dep., Amort./Sales		1.2		1.2
(16)	2.5	(22)	3.4	(13)	1.9					(48)	1.9	(52)	1.7
	4.0		4.8		2.6						3.0		3.3
	1.4		1.3						% Officers', Directors',		1.8		.8
(11)	3.8	(10)	2.4						Owners' Comp/Sales	(19)	3.7	(22)	2.7
	6.5		6.1								7.3		5.1

3685M	51696M	217973M	692227M	161466M	885447M	Net Sales ($)	1740075M	1690856M
1926M	21910M	118671M	308671M	82783M	581462M	Total Assets ($)	851474M	808628M

M = $ thousand   MM = $ million
See Pages 1 through 15 for Explanation of Ratios and Data

Comparative Historical Data / Current Data Sorted By Sales

Current Data periods: **35 (4/1-9/30/94)** covers 0-1MM, 1-3MM, 3-5MM; **34 (10/1/94-3/31/95)** covers 5-10MM, 10-25MM, 25MM & Over.

Historical period columns: ALL (4/1/92-3/31/93), ALL (4/1/93-3/31/94), ALL (4/1/94-3/31/95).

Item	92/93 ALL	93/94 ALL	94/95 ALL	0-1MM	1-3MM	3-5MM	5-10MM	10-25MM	25MM & OVER
# Postretirement Benefits	2	5	9	1	2	2	1		3
Type of Statement									
Unqualified	20	29	30	1	2	4	3	8	12
Reviewed	17	17	13		4	5	3		1
Compiled	7	3	10	3	2	1	2	2	
Tax Returns	1		1			1			
Other	13	16	15	1	2	4	2	3	3
NUMBER OF STATEMENTS	58	65	69	5	10	15	10	13	16
ASSETS (%)	%	%	%	%	%	%	%	%	%
Cash & Equivalents	10.5	7.4	5.6		3.2	6.1	4.8	8.2	2.8
Trade Receivables - (net)	26.1	25.5	23.7		17.5	23.6	23.2	23.4	26.9
Inventory	23.8	26.3	26.9		31.2	30.2	16.0	25.0	29.3
All Other Current	1.7	1.0	1.9		3.1	1.1	.9	1.4	2.7
Total Current	62.1	60.3	58.2		55.1	61.0	44.9	58.0	61.8
Fixed Assets (net)	28.0	29.3	30.1		35.4	30.4	36.2	24.2	30.4
Intangibles (net)	.9	1.4	3.1		.2	3.3	4.9	4.6	1.3
All Other Non-Current	8.9	9.0	8.6		9.3	5.2	14.0	13.3	6.5
Total	100.0	100.0	100.0		100.0	100.0	100.0	100.0	100.0
LIABILITIES									
Notes Payable-Short Term	12.8	12.5	15.7		14.7	11.8	17.0	18.2	20.1
Cur. Mat.-L/T/D	2.8	3.1	3.4		1.2	4.1	5.7	2.5	2.9
Trade Payables	11.5	13.3	13.0		8.0	9.9	9.5	14.5	16.9
Income Taxes Payable	.6	1.4	.3		.0	.2	.1	.2	.5
All Other Current	9.1	7.1	7.5		4.5	5.2	4.4	11.3	10.7
Total Current	36.7	37.3	39.9		28.5	31.3	36.6	46.7	51.0
Long Term Debt	11.5	12.3	13.5		9.4	19.8	13.5	4.6	12.0
Deferred Taxes	.9	.7	.5		.8	.2	.3	.9	.6
All Other-Non-Current	3.3	5.2	6.6		19.3	2.5	1.5	.8	7.0
Net Worth	47.5	44.5	39.5		42.0	46.3	48.1	47.0	29.4
Total Liabilities & Net Worth	100.0	100.0	100.0		100.0	100.0	100.0	100.0	100.0
INCOME DATA									
Net Sales	100.0	100.0	100.0		100.0	100.0	100.0	100.0	100.0
Gross Profit	22.1	22.5	25.3		32.5	26.9	20.9	20.1	20.3
Operating Expenses	19.8	20.1	22.1		28.1	22.0	17.6	19.9	14.6
Operating Profit	2.3	2.4	3.3		4.4	4.9	3.3	.2	5.6
All Other Expenses (net)	-.2	.3	.6		1.7	.7	.0	-1.8	1.3
Profit Before Taxes	2.5	2.1	2.6		2.6	4.3	3.3	2.0	4.3

RATIOS (each cell upper / median / lower)

Ratio	92/93	93/94	94/95	0-1MM	1-3MM	3-5MM	5-10MM	10-25MM	25MM & OVER
Current	2.9	2.4	2.1		5.1	3.1	1.9	1.9	1.6
	1.7	1.5	1.5		2.0	2.0	1.3	1.3	1.1
	1.1	1.2	1.1		1.2	1.5	.8	.9	1.1
Quick	1.8	1.6	1.2		2.1	1.3	1.6	1.0	1.0
	1.0	.8	.7		1.2	.8	.7	.6	.5
	.5	.5	.4		.3	.4	.4	.4	.4
Sales/Receivables	19 19.1	24 15.3	22 16.4		11 32.4	12 29.5	33 11.1	25 14.5	24 15.5
	40 9.2	37 9.8	39 9.3		22 16.8	54 6.7	40 9.2	34 10.6	43 8.5
	61 6.0	61 6.0	66 5.5		24 15.2	68 5.4	64 5.7	59 6.2	69 5.3
Cost of Sales/Inventory	29 12.5	33 11.2	34 10.6		23 15.6	57 6.4	20 18.4	31 11.7	39 9.3
	42 8.7	51 7.2	54 6.7		34 10.6	76 4.8	45 8.2	47 7.8	52 7.0
	89 4.1	83 4.4	83 4.4		70 5.2	107 3.4	64 5.7	70 5.2	83 4.4
Cost of Sales/Payables	13 28.5	10 37.7	13 28.5		0 UND	14 26.5	1 297.1	12 31.2	28 13.1
	23 16.1	27 13.7	27 13.4		7 49.1	20 18.5	19 19.7	19 19.6	33 11.1
	37 9.8	39 9.3	47 7.8		28 13.1	42 8.7	48 7.6	54 6.8	47 7.7
Sales/Working Capital	5.1	5.6	5.9		5.6	4.6	10.0	4.7	8.0
	9.3	11.5	15.4		14.7	7.1	15.0	19.7	49.5
	32.0	27.5	74.2		NM	15.5	-22.4	-47.8	NM
EBIT/Interest	(54) 8.8	(62) 5.7	(64) 5.6			(14) 9.1	5.9	(12) 4.2	(15) 5.7
	3.5	2.5	2.7			2.6	2.2	2.2	4.9
	1.4	1.1	1.5			1.4	1.4	.5	2.8
Net Profit + Depr., Dep., Amort./Cur. Mat. L/T/D	(20) 6.4	(27) 3.7	(27) 6.2						
	2.3	2.0	1.8						
	1.2	1.0	1.2						
Fixed/Worth	.3	.3	.3		.2	.3	.4	.3	.4
	.6	.6	.8		.8	.7	1.2	.6	1.2
	1.2	1.3	2.0		2.8	1.9	2.2	1.5	2.1
Debt/Worth	.4	.5	.6		.5	.5	.3	.3	1.8
	1.4	1.4	2.1		1.2	1.3	1.7	1.3	2.6
	2.6	3.5	4.6		8.3	5.0	4.1	-4.4	5.6
% Profit Before Taxes/Tangible Net Worth	31.3	(62) 16.0	(66) 33.0		49.7	(14) 34.9		22.6	74.9
	13.3	9.8	14.7		14.1	16.9		8.3	23.0
	4.0	2.9	4.8		8.1	5.2		-1.7	9.3
% Profit Before Taxes/Total Assets	12.2	7.3	10.8		12.4	10.3	8.4	7.6	11.8
	6.9	3.9	5.2		5.3	5.9	3.5	4.6	8.3
	1.4	.6	1.9		3.0	2.6	1.7	-.9	2.9
Sales/Net Fixed Assets	20.5	16.4	15.7		18.1	9.4	10.1	16.9	19.2
	9.7	9.7	7.6		7.9	8.3	5.3	8.7	7.6
	4.0	4.2	4.5		5.9	3.3	3.7	5.4	4.3
Sales/Total Assets	2.7	2.7	2.5		4.0	2.4	2.0	2.7	2.4
	2.2	2.0	2.0		2.7	2.0	1.7	2.1	2.0
	1.7	1.6	1.5		1.7	1.3	1.3	1.4	1.7
% Depr., Dep., Amort./Sales	(54) 1.1	(62) 1.2	(62) 1.4			(12) 1.5	1.8	(11) 1.5	1.3
	2.0	2.0	2.4			3.1	2.9	1.7	1.9
	4.1	3.2	4.1			6.8	4.8	3.8	3.8
% Officers', Directors', Owners' Comp/Sales	(20) 1.6	(23) 1.0	(26) 1.7						
	2.7	3.1	3.9						
	4.7	7.6	8.5						
Net Sales ($)	1450607M	1693561M	2012494M	2543M	20774M	54558M	71473M	186320M	1676826M
Total Assets ($)	1036791M	893237M	1115423M	1513M	8560M	31829M	50294M	100957M	922270M

M = $ thousand   MM = $ million

See Pages 1 through 15 for Explanation of Ratios and Data

	Current Data Sorted By Assets						# Postretirement Benefits	Comparative Historical Data	
							Type of Statement		
1	4	8	3	4	2				
2	6	13	21	4	8		Unqualified	49	43
1	9	13	4				Reviewed	25	23
2	10	5					Compiled	24	27
1	1	1					Tax Returns	1	2
	7	12	11	6	4		Other	19	18
0-500M	44 (4/1-9/30/94) 500M-2MM	2-10MM	97 (10/1/94-3/31/95) 10-50MM	50-100MM	100-250MM			4/1/90- 3/31/91 ALL	4/1/91- 3/31/92 ALL
6	33	44	36	10	12		**NUMBER OF STATEMENTS**	118	113
%	%	%	%	%	%		**ASSETS**	%	%
	5.4	8.6	5.5	11.9	2.8		Cash & Equivalents	7.9	8.1
	36.9	32.3	25.7	22.4	18.7		Trade Receivables - (net)	26.9	26.2
	22.9	21.1	20.8	21.5	16.6		Inventory	24.4	22.9
	2.1	2.1	1.3	1.6	2.0		All Other Current	2.3	1.6
	67.2	64.1	53.3	57.4	40.2		Total Current	61.5	58.8
	22.1	26.3	34.8	33.8	50.5		Fixed Assets (net)	29.8	32.1
	3.1	2.1	4.0	.3	2.6		Intangibles (net)	2.6	2.6
	7.5	7.5	8.0	8.6	6.8		All Other Non-Current	6.1	6.5
	100.0	100.0	100.0	100.0	100.0		Total	100.0	100.0
							LIABILITIES		
	12.1	8.5	11.3	5.6	1.0		Notes Payable-Short Term	6.9	9.8
	3.1	2.3	4.9	1.4	1.7		Cur. Mat. -L/T/D	2.7	3.8
	20.4	20.4	17.0	14.3	8.7		Trade Payables	18.3	17.0
	.3	.7	.2	.1	1.1		Income Taxes Payable	.4	.5
	11.3	8.6	7.7	11.6	10.5		All Other Current	8.2	8.3
	47.1	40.5	41.1	33.1	23.0		Total Current	36.5	39.5
	11.0	16.1	11.7	15.8	21.2		Long Term Debt	15.9	13.2
	.2	.5	1.5	.5	2.5		Deferred Taxes	1.6	1.3
	5.1	4.5	6.7	3.4	4.4		All Other-Non-Current	2.2	3.6
	36.7	38.4	39.0	47.2	48.9		Net Worth	43.8	42.4
	100.0	100.0	100.0	100.0	100.0		Total Liabilities & Net Worth	100.0	100.0
							INCOME DATA		
	100.0	100.0	100.0	100.0	100.0		Net Sales	100.0	100.0
	37.7	30.7	28.9	27.4	23.8		Gross Profit	32.3	33.9
	33.2	27.2	20.7	19.5	21.2		Operating Expenses	26.2	28.9
	4.5	3.5	8.2	7.8	2.6		Operating Profit	6.1	5.0
	1.3	1.2	1.4	1.9	1.8		All Other Expenses (net)	1.3	1.4
	3.2	2.3	6.8	5.9	.8		Profit Before Taxes	4.9	3.6
							RATIOS		
	2.0	2.2	1.9	3.2	2.9			2.8	2.3
	1.3	1.5	1.3	1.8	1.7		Current	1.7	1.6
	1.1	1.2	1.0	1.2	1.2			1.3	1.2
	1.5	1.4	1.1	1.7	1.3			1.6	1.4
	.9	1.0	.8	1.0	1.0		Quick	1.0	.9
	.7	.7	.5	.7	.7			.6	.6
34 10.6	40 9.1	41 8.8	41 8.8	48 7.6			Sales/Receivables	35 10.4	33 11.0

0-500M	500M-2MM	2-10MM	10-50MM	50-100MM	100-250MM			4/1/90-3/31/91	4/1/91-3/31/92
34 10.6	40 9.1	41 8.8	41 8.8	48 7.6		Sales/Receivables	35 10.4	33 11.0
43 8.4	48 7.6	51 7.2	55 6.6	58 6.3			43 8.4	43 8.4
53 6.9	58 6.3	58 6.3	65 5.6	65 5.6			54 6.8	56 6.5
20 18.1	27 13.6	37 10.0	41 8.8	53 6.9		Cost of Sales/Inventory	37 9.8	35 10.4
45 8.2	51 7.2	58 6.3	79 4.6	63 5.8			58 6.3	54 6.7
68 5.4	69 5.3	91 4.0	101 3.6	89 4.1			89 4.1	99 3.7
19 19.5	27 13.6	29 12.7	26 14.2	23 16.1		Cost of Sales/Payables	24 15.2	25 14.5
41 8.9	41 8.8	45 8.2	35 10.5	34 10.7			38 9.6	40 9.1
57 6.4	59 6.2	69 5.3	51 7.2	66 5.5			56 6.5	56 6.5
8.8	6.9	6.9	3.9	3.7		Sales/Working Capital	4.9	5.7
15.6	11.9	12.7	6.2	7.7			9.0	10.3
48.9	28.1	NM	21.7	24.7			20.8	29.8
10.0	8.2	16.9		13.5		EBIT/Interest	7.6	7.1
(31) 3.3	(40) 3.3	(32) 4.7	(10) 3.4			(103) 3.1	(99) 3.6
1.5	1.3	2.5		-.3			1.4	1.3
8.3	8.0	23.9				Net Profit + Depr., Dep., Amort./Cur. Mat. L /T/D	8.9	6.7
(12) 3.8	(19) 2.7	(17) 2.5					(58) 3.0	(59) 2.6
2.5	1.1	1.6					1.5	1.3
.3	.2	.5	.3	.7		Fixed/Worth	.3	.4
.6	.6	1.0	.6	1.1			.7	.7
2.2	1.8	2.0	1.1	3.1			1.6	1.7
.8	1.0	.9	.6	.5		Debt/Worth	.6	.5
1.6	2.3	2.1	1.0	1.1			1.3	1.6
7.9	3.7	5.7	3.4	3.7			3.4	3.5
59.7	42.5	52.9	31.6	20.4		% Profit Before Taxes/Tangible Net Worth	33.0	35.7
(31) 23.2	(43) 22.4	(33) 27.0	17.0	11.2			(111) 16.4	(106) 17.9
8.9	4.3	14.4	-6.7	6.8			6.2	4.2
21.0	18.5	14.9	15.1	12.1		% Profit Before Taxes/Total Assets	14.2	15.6
6.6	6.4	9.1	7.2	5.0			6.0	7.0
-.1	1.0	4.6	-.6	2.4			2.3	1.5
50.9	43.7	12.4	7.9	3.7		Sales/Net Fixed Assets	20.4	14.7
17.7	9.8	4.7	5.2	2.2			8.1	6.3
7.2	4.1	2.9	2.3	1.6			3.6	3.7
4.3	3.1	2.3	1.9	1.3		Sales/Total Assets	3.0	2.7
3.1	2.2	1.7	1.4	1.1			2.1	1.9
1.9	1.8	1.1	1.1	.9			1.4	1.4
.9	.8	1.2	1.3		% Depr., Dep., Amort./Sales	1.2	1.1
(28) 1.7	(38) 1.7	(35) 2.3	2.5			(104) 2.2	(99) 2.3
3.3	3.4	5.8	5.6			4.5	3.6
2.9	3.1				% Officers', Directors', Owners' Comp/Sales	2.1	2.3
(16) 5.7	(16) 3.7					(39) 5.0	(47) 5.6
8.2	7.8					9.2	8.3
3857M	112261M	456459M	1387094M	954641M	2209070M	Net Sales ($)	3227561M	2889706M
1810M	37823M	190527M	837140M	620580M	1965490M	Total Assets ($)	2309032M	1975783M

© Robert Morris Associates 1995

M = $ thousand   MM = $ million
See Pages 1 through 15 for Explanation of Ratios and Data

	Comparative Historical Data				Current Data Sorted By Sales					
# Postretirement Benefits	8	14	22		1	3	2	5	2	9
Type of Statement										
Unqualified	47	58	54		2	4	3	11	6	28
Reviewed	25	22	27			6	2	7	7	5
Compiled	20	20	17		3	6	4	3		1
Tax Returns	2	1	3		1	1	1			
Other	19	34	40			4	4	7	9	16
	4/1/92-3/31/93	4/1/93-3/31/94	4/1/94-3/31/95			44 (4/1-9/30/94)		97 (10/1/94-3/31/95)		
	ALL	ALL	ALL		0-1MM	1-3MM	3-5MM	5-10MM	10-25MM	25MM & OVER
NUMBER OF STATEMENTS	113	135	141		6	20	14	29	22	50
ASSETS	%	%	%		%	%	%	%	%	%
Cash & Equivalents	7.8	7.4	6.9			6.5	5.3	8.8	6.1	6.2
Trade Receivables - (net)	27.2	26.8	30.1			27.0	40.5	30.4	35.9	25.1
Inventory	24.9	21.8	21.1			17.0	25.0	20.2	21.7	21.2
All Other Current	1.1	1.5	1.8			3.0	.8	2.8	1.0	1.5
Total Current	60.9	57.5	59.9			53.4	71.7	62.2	64.7	54.0
Fixed Assets (net)	29.1	31.5	29.7			32.2	18.2	29.4	21.4	37.0
Intangibles (net)	2.1	3.7	2.7			4.6	.7	2.4	4.0	2.3
All Other Non-Current	8.0	7.4	7.7			9.8	9.3	6.0	9.9	6.7
Total	100.0	100.0	100.0			100.0	100.0	100.0	100.0	100.0
LIABILITIES										
Notes Payable-Short Term	9.0	7.8	9.0			13.7	7.8	8.8	12.2	7.0
Cur. Mat.-L /T/D	3.8	3.0	3.0			4.1	1.4	3.2	5.6	2.2
Trade Payables	16.6	16.5	18.4			15.7	19.2	18.3	24.8	16.3
Income Taxes Payable	.6	.6	.5			.4	.3	.7	.2	.5
All Other Current	7.5	8.7	9.6			10.9	16.0	6.5	7.4	9.3
Total Current	37.5	36.5	40.5			44.7	44.8	37.5	50.2	35.3
Long Term Debt	13.9	15.2	14.0			12.0	13.5	16.3	11.3	14.8
Deferred Taxes	.8	.9	.9			.3	.7	.4	.1	1.7
All Other-Non-Current	4.5	3.6	5.3			8.5	2.7	4.2	6.1	4.6
Net Worth	43.3	43.8	39.3			34.5	38.2	41.6	32.3	43.6
Total Liabilities & Net Worth	100.0	100.0	100.0			100.0	100.0	100.0	100.0	100.0
INCOME DATA										
Net Sales	100.0	100.0	100.0			100.0	100.0	100.0	100.0	100.0
Gross Profit	35.4	31.8	31.4			45.1	28.8	37.5	24.1	26.1
Operating Expenses	29.6	25.9	26.4			38.1	27.1	32.8	19.0	20.3
Operating Profit	5.8	5.9	5.0			6.9	1.7	4.7	5.1	5.9
All Other Expenses (net)	1.2	1.2	1.3			1.8	.6	1.2	2.1	1.2
Profit Before Taxes	4.6	4.7	3.7			5.1	1.1	3.5	3.0	4.7
RATIOS										
Current	2.6	2.4	2.3			1.6	2.9	2.9	1.6	2.5
	1.6	1.6	1.4			1.3	1.5	1.5	1.4	1.6
	1.3	1.2	1.2			.9	1.2	1.2	1.0	1.2
Quick	1.6	1.4	1.3			1.2	1.9	1.7	1.1	1.2
	1.0	1.0	.9			.8	1.0	1.0	.8	.9
	.6	.7	.7			.5	.6	.7	.7	.7
Sales/Receivables	36 10.2	38 9.6	41 9.0			34 10.6	35 10.4	37 9.9	47 7.7	43 8.4
	45 8.2	47 7.8	49 7.5			45 8.1	48 7.6	46 8.0	51 7.2	51 7.2
	57 6.4	56 6.5	59 6.2			56 6.5	60 6.1	55 6.6	64 5.7	63 5.8
Cost of Sales/Inventory	42 8.7	35 10.5	33 10.9			18 19.9	24 15.0	26 14.2	27 13.4	43 8.4
	60 6.1	54 6.8	52 7.0			50 7.3	37 9.9	54 6.7	42 8.6	62 5.9
	91 4.0	81 4.5	83 4.4			85 4.3	55 6.6	81 4.5	68 5.4	85 4.3
Cost of Sales/Payables	26 14.2	25 14.5	26 14.3			21 17.6	11 34.1	27 13.6	38 9.6	26 14.0
	41 9.0	39 9.3	41 8.8			49 7.4	33 11.2	43 8.5	51 7.2	39 9.3
	58 6.3	53 6.9	60 6.1			85 4.3	45 8.2	63 5.8	61 6.0	62 5.9
Sales/Working Capital	5.3	5.6	6.5			9.1	8.0	6.4	8.4	5.6
	9.7	10.5	11.9			26.7	12.7	12.3	14.2	10.2
	18.4	23.7	34.8			-62.4	35.5	37.3	NM	29.0
EBIT/Interest	9.4	10.4	10.7			6.8	10.5	12.0	5.6	16.4
	(98) 3.7	(120) 4.9	(127) 3.6		(18)	4.1	3.3	(28) 5.0	(20) 2.3	(41) 3.6
	1.7	2.2	1.6			1.7	-.3	1.7	.6	2.1
Net Profit + Depr., Dep., Amort./Cur. Mat. L/T/D	8.0	8.1	8.6					6.3		31.5
	(52) 2.7	(64) 3.1	(60) 2.7					(15) 2.7	(24)	3.2
	1.4	1.6	1.3					1.1		1.5
Fixed/Worth	.4	.3	.4			.5	.2	.2	.2	.5
	.7	.7	.7			1.4	.5	.7	.6	.9
	1.4	1.4	1.7			2.5	2.5	1.9	2.0	1.4
Debt/Worth	.7	.7	.8			.8	.7	.7	1.7	.6
	1.3	1.5	1.7			2.0	1.6	1.8	2.9	1.3
	3.4	3.4	4.4			7.5	16.0	3.5	5.9	4.1
% Profit Before Taxes/Tangible Net Worth	36.2	43.6	45.5			54.6	46.7	57.6	44.4	37.4
	(107) 22.9	(129) 21.7	(134) 21.0		(19)	22.0	(13) 23.2	(28) 24.0	(21) 21.2	(48) 18.9
	6.7	9.7	7.3			8.9	-36.4	7.8	-8.5	9.1
% Profit Before Taxes/Total Assets	17.0	14.8	16.3			13.3	17.9	21.5	12.0	14.2
	8.0	8.0	6.6			6.8	4.9	7.1	4.1	8.9
	2.4	3.3	1.9			1.2	-4.0	2.4	-1.0	3.4
Sales/Net Fixed Assets	18.9	18.5	22.1			17.0	57.4	23.9	67.2	9.1
	8.6	6.1	7.5			5.9	25.9	8.9	12.0	4.4
	3.8	3.3	3.7			3.2	11.4	4.0	4.5	2.4
Sales/Total Assets	2.9	2.8	3.0			3.2	4.7	3.2	3.6	2.3
	2.1	2.0	1.9			1.9	3.4	2.1	2.4	1.6
	1.4	1.3	1.3			1.3	2.4	1.6	1.4	1.1
% Depr., Dep., Amort./Sales	1.0	1.0	1.0			1.6	.8	.9	.4	1.2
	(99) 2.1	(124) 2.3	(124) 2.2		(17)	3.4	(11) 1.1	(26) 2.2	(21) 1.5	(44) 2.5
	3.6	4.0	4.0			5.5	1.8	3.8	3.1	4.5
% Officers', Directors', Owners' Comp/Sales	3.2	3.0	2.7					3.3		
	(37) 6.1	(33) 4.5	(44) 4.6					(14) 4.6		
	10.8	7.0	8.1					7.4		
Net Sales ($)	3354896M	4667287M	5123382M		3474M	43913M	55701M	214957M	357073M	4448264M
Total Assets ($)	2356150M	3253956M	3653370M		1931M	25303M	20828M	131935M	197300M	3276073M

M = $ thousand   MM = $ million
See Pages 1 through 15 for Explanation of Ratios and Data

MANUFACTURERS—PAINT, VARNISH, LACQUER, ENAMEL & ALLIED PRODUCTS. SIC# 2851

	Current Data Sorted By Assets							Comparative Historical Data	
		3	3	4		2	# Postretirement Benefits		
							Type of Statement		
	2	7	15	15	1	3	Unqualified	40	38
	1	10	15	1			Reviewed	37	25
	1	10	8	4			Compiled	30	30
	1	3					Tax Returns	1	
	6		17	5		1	Other	11	24
		37 (4/1-9/30/94)		93 (10/1/94-3/31/95)				4/1/90-3/31/91	4/1/91-3/31/92
	0-500M	500M-2MM	2-10MM	10-50MM	50-100MM	100-250MM		ALL	ALL
NUMBER OF STATEMENTS	11	34	55	25	1	4		119	117
	%	%	%	%	%	%	ASSETS	%	%
	8.8	9.8	7.5	6.8			Cash & Equivalents	7.5	7.2
	32.3	29.8	26.4	28.7			Trade Receivables - (net)	27.1	28.6
	29.7	30.9	27.5	25.1			Inventory	31.0	30.0
	.6	.6	2.9	1.7			All Other Current	1.7	2.0
	71.4	71.0	64.3	62.4			Total Current	67.3	67.7
	22.7	18.7	24.6	26.9			Fixed Assets (net)	24.7	23.0
	.8	2.9	2.9	2.8			Intangibles (net)	1.6	3.2
	5.1	7.4	8.1	7.9			All Other Non-Current	6.4	6.1
	100.0	100.0	100.0	100.0			Total	100.0	100.0
							LIABILITIES		
	8.7	7.2	9.8	3.3			Notes Payable-Short Term	8.4	8.8
	4.1	2.6	3.4	3.0			Cur. Mat. -L/T/D	3.2	2.5
	27.2	20.8	15.9	14.6			Trade Payables	17.8	16.4
	.4	.4	.6	1.4			Income Taxes Payable	1.0	.6
	6.2	7.3	7.2	10.6			All Other Current	8.3	7.5
	46.7	38.3	37.0	32.9			Total Current	38.7	35.9
	18.3	12.4	14.3	9.1			Long Term Debt	11.9	12.8
	.5	.1	.3	1.5			Deferred Taxes	.6	.6
	2.3	3.8	4.6	1.9			All Other-Non-Current	2.9	2.2
	32.2	45.4	43.8	54.6			Net Worth	45.9	48.4
	100.0	100.0	100.0	100.0			Total Liabilities & Net Worth	100.0	100.0
							INCOME DATA		
	100.0	100.0	100.0	100.0			Net Sales	100.0	100.0
	35.8	36.7	32.1	33.0			Gross Profit	33.2	31.9
	29.9	32.7	27.6	26.6			Operating Expenses	30.1	28.2
	5.9	4.0	4.5	6.4			Operating Profit	3.1	3.7
	1.0	.4	.9	.4			All Other Expenses (net)	.7	.8
	4.9	3.6	3.6	6.1			Profit Before Taxes	2.3	2.9
							RATIOS		
	4.7	3.6	2.8	2.9				2.8	2.9
	1.9	2.0	1.9	2.0			Current	1.8	2.0
	1.5	1.2	1.3	1.6				1.3	1.4
	2.5	1.7	1.6	1.5				1.7	1.6
	.9	1.0	.9	1.0			Quick	.9	1.0
	.7	.7	.6	.9				.6	.7
	24 15.3	31 11.8	34 10.6	41 8.8				33 11.0	34 10.7
	33 10.9	40 9.2	46 8.0	51 7.2			Sales/Receivables	43 8.4	46 8.0
	70 5.2	48 7.6	55 6.6	57 6.4				54 6.8	57 6.4
	13 27.5	50 7.3	46 8.0	46 7.9				53 6.9	54 6.7
	58 6.3	59 6.2	69 5.3	66 5.5			Cost of Sales/Inventory	68 5.4	73 5.0
	104 3.5	85 4.3	91 4.0	91 4.0				94 3.9	91 4.0
	30 12.2	29 12.6	26 14.3	25 14.5				25 14.7	25 14.6
	38 9.5	45 8.2	41 9.0	37 10.0			Cost of Sales/Payables	36 10.1	35 10.4
	62 5.9	62 5.9	51 7.2	45 8.2				54 6.7	47 7.7
	4.1	6.0	5.1	4.7				5.3	4.6
	9.3	8.5	7.1	6.8			Sales/Working Capital	7.6	6.8
	16.6	21.4	15.3	8.9				16.1	14.3
		7.8	11.8	21.3				6.8	6.3
		(28) 3.7	(49) 2.6	(24) 8.6			EBIT/Interest	(111) 2.4	(107) 2.7
		1.6	1.3	3.3				1.0	.8
		5.4	7.4	18.1			Net Profit + Depr., Dep.,	5.5	9.4
		(11) 2.1	(21) 2.3	(15) 4.7			Amort./Cur. Mat. L /T/D	(79) 2.4	(56) 2.2
		.9	1.5	1.4				.4	.4
	.4	.2	.3	.3				.3	.3
	.7	.4	.5	.5			Fixed/Worth	.5	.5
	1.0	1.2	1.6	.9				.9	.9
	1.3	.5	.7	.6				.5	.6
	1.9	1.5	1.3	.9			Debt/Worth	1.2	1.1
	8.6	3.5	3.6	1.2				2.2	2.4
	73.9	45.1	35.5	29.9			% Profit Before Taxes/Tangible	25.7	27.6
	(10) 16.2	16.0	(51) 12.5	16.6			Net Worth	(114) 11.2	(113) 10.4
	−11.7	6.4	4.6	7.4				1.3	1.2
	15.0	14.7	15.3	15.3			% Profit Before Taxes/Total	11.8	11.4
	7.8	6.4	4.5	8.4			Assets	5.3	4.2
	2.4	2.3	1.1	4.8				.1	.4
	49.4	37.9	21.7	13.8				21.4	22.0
	19.8	21.0	10.2	8.5			Sales/Net Fixed Assets	10.7	10.4
	4.8	7.4	6.1	5.3				6.4	6.2
	4.9	3.4	2.7	2.5				2.7	2.7
	3.8	2.6	2.3	2.2			Sales/Total Assets	2.3	2.3
	1.7	2.2	1.8	1.7				1.9	1.8
	.6	.8	1.0	1.2				1.0	1.0
	(10) 2.1	(32) 1.3	(49) 1.4	(21) 1.7			% Depr., Dep., Amort./Sales	(111) 1.4	(104) 1.5
	3.9	1.8	2.1	2.3				2.3	2.3
		3.7	2.9				% Officers', Directors',	2.8	2.0
		(19) 4.8	(21) 4.0				Owners' Comp/Sales	(41) 4.2	(27) 4.0
		8.4	5.1					6.6	6.7
	10430M	110270M	536147M	1229875M	77457M	1130700M	Net Sales ($)	3189467M	5130278M
	3301M	41113M	252391M	592709M	55480M	695246M	Total Assets ($)	1696701M	2085475M

M = $ thousand   MM = $ million
See Pages 1 through 15 for Explanation of Ratios and Data

Comparative Historical Data | Current Data Sorted By Sales

4	8	12	# Postretirement Benefits / Type of Statement	2	2	3		5
37	30	43	Unqualified	2 / 2	9	8	3	19
29	31	27	Reviewed	1 / 4	5	8	8	1
27	30	23	Compiled	6	7	3	3	4
	4	4	Tax Returns	2		2		
19	26	33	Other	3 / 8	3	8	7	4
4/1/92-3/31/93 ALL	4/1/93-3/31/94 ALL	4/1/94-3/31/95 ALL		37 (4/1-9/30/94)		93 (10/1/94-3/31/95)		
				0-1MM / 1-3MM	3-5MM	5-10MM	10-25MM	25MM & OVER
112	121	130	**NUMBER OF STATEMENTS**	6 / 22	24	29	21	28
%	%	%	**ASSETS**	% / %	%	%	%	%
5.4	7.0	8.3	Cash & Equivalents	5.2	11.1	6.2	11.4	7.1
28.1	28.6	28.1	Trade Receivables - (net)	32.1	25.0	30.6	26.8	28.1
28.8	29.5	27.9	Inventory	31.0	28.4	28.1	28.7	25.2
2.9	2.4	1.9	All Other Current	.5	1.3	2.1	3.6	2.2
65.3	67.4	66.2	Total Current	68.8	65.7	67.0	70.5	62.7
23.6	23.6	23.2	Fixed Assets (net)	19.8	21.3	23.5	21.8	26.2
2.9	2.5	3.1	Intangibles (net)	2.9	4.4	1.7	2.2	4.6
8.2	6.5	7.5	All Other Non-Current	8.5	8.6	7.9	5.5	6.6
100.0	100.0	100.0	Total	100.0	100.0	100.0	100.0	100.0
			LIABILITIES					
8.3	8.1	7.4	Notes Payable-Short Term	7.6	8.0	12.2	5.6	3.0
3.7	3.1	3.1	Cur. Mat.-L /T/D	3.5	3.2	3.4	2.3	2.9
15.8	16.8	17.8	Trade Payables	26.5	15.7	18.6	15.1	15.1
.7	1.2	.7	Income Taxes Payable	.4	.8	.6	.4	1.3
7.8	6.0	7.8	All Other Current	6.2	8.3	6.6	8.1	9.5
36.4	35.3	36.8	Total Current	44.2	36.0	41.5	31.4	31.8
13.3	14.0	13.3	Long Term Debt	14.0	15.3	15.9	7.2	11.2
.9	.9	.5	Deferred Taxes	.0	.0	.3	.6	1.4
3.6	3.7	3.7	All Other-Non-Current	2.1	4.9	5.8	2.3	2.7
45.8	46.1	45.6	Net Worth	39.8	43.9	36.4	58.4	53.0
100.0	100.0	100.0	Total Liabilities & Net Worth	100.0	100.0	100.0	100.0	100.0
			INCOME DATA					
100.0	100.0	100.0	Net Sales	100.0	100.0	100.0	100.0	100.0
33.6	34.2	34.2	Gross Profit	36.4	34.3	32.0	33.9	34.5
29.2	31.5	29.1	Operating Expenses	35.0	28.7	28.0	26.6	28.4
4.4	2.7	5.1	Operating Profit	1.4	5.6	4.0	7.3	6.1
.8	.7	.7	All Other Expenses (net)	.6	.7	.9	.4	.5
3.6	2.0	4.4	Profit Before Taxes	.8	4.8	3.1	6.9	5.6
			RATIOS					
2.7	2.9	2.9	Current	2.3	3.1	2.2	4.6	2.9
1.9	2.0	2.0		1.8	2.0	1.7	2.7	2.1
1.4	1.5	1.3		1.2	1.2	1.3	1.4	1.7
1.4	1.6	1.6	Quick	1.5	2.1	1.6	2.4	1.6
1.0	1.0	1.0		.8	1.1	.9	1.2	1.2
.7	.6	.7		.7	.6	.5	.8	1.0
35 10.5	34 10.8	34 10.7	Sales/Receivables	33 11.2	31 11.6	31 11.6	34 10.7	43 8.5
43 8.4	45 8.2	46 8.0		43 8.4	40 9.1	43 8.5	43 8.5	51 7.1
54 6.8	55 6.6	54 6.7		60 6.1	49 7.4	55 6.6	51 7.2	58 6.3
49 7.4	47 7.8	47 7.8	Cost of Sales/Inventory	46 7.9	51 7.2	46 7.9	46 8.0	47 7.8
70 5.2	72 5.1	66 5.5		70 5.2	64 5.7	66 5.5	65 5.6	66 5.5
89 4.1	96 3.8	89 4.1		107 3.4	99 3.7	79 4.6	85 4.3	94 3.9
22 16.3	26 13.8	28 12.9	Cost of Sales/Payables	43 8.4	25 14.6	26 13.8	21 17.2	29 12.5
35 10.5	35 10.4	40 9.1		57 6.4	35 10.3	40 9.1	31 11.6	39 9.3
48 7.6	51 7.1	53 6.9		73 5.0	49 7.4	46 7.9	51 7.1	53 6.9
5.4	5.2	5.0	Sales/Working Capital	6.4	4.5	6.3	4.2	4.6
7.3	7.2	7.1		10.8	7.2	9.6	7.0	6.8
13.4	13.0	15.3		21.4	28.8	18.5	13.7	8.8
(107) 9.0	(105) 9.2	(115) 13.4	EBIT/Interest	(17) 5.7	(21) 5.3	(28) 11.0	(17) 37.4	21.3
3.5	3.3	4.5		3.3	3.7	2.7	12.5	10.0
1.2	1.6	1.5		1.4	1.5	1.2	1.9	4.3
(63) 9.9	6.2	(54) 7.3	Net Profit + Depr., Dep., Amort./Cur. Mat. L/T/D			(12) 4.8		(19) 18.1
2.7	(57) 2.2	2.6				2.2		5.9
1.4	.8	1.4				1.4		2.5
.3	.2	.3	Fixed/Worth	.2	.2	.3	.2	.3
.5	.4	.5		.4	.5	.7	.3	.5
1.0	1.1	1.1		1.8	1.4	1.6	.6	.9
.7	.6	.6	Debt/Worth	.7	.4	.9	.3	.6
1.2	1.2	1.2		1.8	1.6	2.0	.7	1.0
2.4	2.4	2.8		4.9	4.4	5.1	1.2	1.7
(105) 27.5	(115) 25.7	(125) 37.8	% Profit Before Taxes/Tangible Net Worth	(21) 34.5	(23) 39.5	(27) 35.5	(20) 48.9	36.7
11.8	12.4	16.6		11.2	12.6	12.5	19.6	18.4
2.6	2.7	6.6		1.9	5.5	3.6	5.8	12.0
13.3	11.3	15.2	% Profit Before Taxes/Total Assets	10.2	15.8	12.0	27.3	17.2
5.9	4.6	7.0		4.8	3.9	6.1	11.8	8.5
.8	1.6	2.2		1.8	1.5	1.0	3.1	5.2
22.9	28.9	24.3	Sales/Net Fixed Assets	34.7	32.1	26.1	24.5	12.8
10.0	11.3	10.9		18.3	12.2	10.2	13.0	8.9
6.2	6.5	6.3		6.9	6.2	7.0	5.8	5.7
2.9	2.8	2.9	Sales/Total Assets	3.5	2.9	2.9	3.0	2.5
2.3	2.3	2.3		2.4	2.0	2.5	2.5	2.0
1.8	1.9	1.7		1.6	1.7	1.8	2.0	1.7
(101) .9	(107) 1.0	(117) 1.0	% Depr., Dep., Amort./Sales	(20) .6	(23) .8	(27) 1.0	(17) 1.1	(25) 1.2
1.5	1.4	1.6		1.4	1.2	1.6	1.4	2.0
2.1	2.2	2.2		1.8	1.7	2.1	2.2	2.6
(32) 2.9	(38) 3.7	(47) 2.9	% Officers', Directors', Owners' Comp/Sales	(12) 3.6	(11) 2.4	(15) 2.9		
3.4	4.8	4.2		5.6	3.7	4.0		
6.2	8.8	6.9		9.0	6.0	5.8		
3470902M	3309847M	3094879M	Net Sales ($)	4028M	41596M	91795M	218973M	323055M 2415432M
1793413M	1616196M	1640240M	Total Assets ($)	1744M	23696M	78206M	101494M	139637M 1295463M

M = $ thousand   MM = $ million
See Pages 1 through 15 for Explanation of Ratios and Data

Current Data Sorted By Assets | Comparative Historical Data

Postretirement Benefits — Type of Statement

0-500M	500M-2MM	2-10MM	10-50MM	50-100MM	100-250MM	Type of Statement	4/1/90-3/31/91 ALL	4/1/91-3/31/92 ALL
		2						
		11	16	1	2	Unqualified	22	25
1	6	11	1			Reviewed	10	13
1	5	1				Compiled	7	11
	1					Tax Returns		
2	7	11	9	1	1	Other	12	8
	30 (4/1-9/30/94)		58 (10/1/94-3/31/95)					
4	19	34	26	2	3	NUMBER OF STATEMENTS	51	57

0-500M	500M-2MM	2-10MM	10-50MM	50-100MM	100-250MM		4/1/90-3/31/91 ALL	4/1/91-3/31/92 ALL
%	%	%	%	%	%	**ASSETS**	%	%
	3.3	5.3	9.1			Cash & Equivalents	6.3	6.8
	26.5	28.9	20.8			Trade Receivables - (net)	23.3	28.2
	34.0	33.5	31.8			Inventory	32.1	29.7
	.6	3.5	3.2			All Other Current	3.4	4.0
	64.5	71.2	64.9			Total Current	65.1	68.7
	26.4	21.6	21.9			Fixed Assets (net)	23.2	21.0
	2.6	3.2	4.4			Intangibles (net)	5.8	5.5
	6.5	4.0	8.8			All Other Non-Current	5.8	4.8
	100.0	100.0	100.0			Total	100.0	100.0
						LIABILITIES		
	13.2	12.6	7.2			Notes Payable-Short Term	13.5	11.0
	6.7	3.2	4.7			Cur. Mat. -L/T/D	2.2	2.2
	15.3	18.7	16.9			Trade Payables	15.5	15.0
	1.5	1.2	1.4			Income Taxes Payable	1.2	1.0
	6.1	6.5	9.3			All Other Current	7.0	10.3
	42.8	42.3	39.4			Total Current	39.4	39.5
	18.1	15.8	10.8			Long Term Debt	16.6	13.2
	.4	.2	.5			Deferred Taxes	.6	.4
	7.5	3.4	1.2			All Other-Non-Current	2.3	3.1
	31.3	38.2	48.1			Net Worth	41.1	43.8
	100.0	100.0	100.0			Total Liabilities & Net Worth	100.0	100.0
						INCOME DATA		
	100.0	100.0	100.0			Net Sales	100.0	100.0
	40.5	42.2	48.5			Gross Profit	44.2	44.7
	34.1	35.9	45.3			Operating Expenses	40.1	40.8
	6.4	6.3	3.2			Operating Profit	4.2	3.9
	1.9	.9	.6			All Other Expenses (net)	1.5	1.1
	4.5	5.5	2.5			Profit Before Taxes	2.6	2.8
						RATIOS		
	2.0	2.8	2.4			Current	2.5	2.9
	1.7	1.8	1.9				1.9	1.8
	1.2	1.3	1.2				1.4	1.2
	1.3	1.3	1.1			Quick	1.1	1.6
	.7	.8	.8				.7	1.0
	.6	.6	.6				.5	.6
	33 11.2	41 8.9	37 9.9			Sales/Receivables	33 11.1	37 9.8
	47 7.8	52 7.0	47 7.8				47 7.7	50 7.3
	54 6.7	65 5.6	65 5.6				59 6.2	58 6.3
	38 9.6	74 4.9	89 4.1			Cost of Sales/Inventory	66 5.5	78 4.7
	87 4.2	104 3.5	159 2.3				107 3.4	107 3.4
	203 1.8	166 2.2	215 1.7				166 2.2	140 2.6
	27 13.7	31 11.9	31 11.7			Cost of Sales/Payables	31 11.9	27 13.7
	40 9.2	58 6.3	62 5.9				42 8.7	42 8.6
	69 5.3	91 4.0	152 2.4				66 5.5	68 5.4
	5.3	4.0	3.2			Sales/Working Capital	4.7	4.6
	10.9	7.6	6.8				7.0	6.8
	16.2	10.0	11.8				13.9	17.5
	7.7	9.7	18.2			EBIT/Interest	6.5	8.5
	(18) 4.5	(31) 3.8	(25) 3.3				(46) 2.2	(48) 3.8
	1.6	1.9	-.9				1.1	1.4
		11.8	10.7			Net Profit + Depr., Dep., Amort./Cur. Mat. L /T/D	12.8	7.5
		(15) 2.6	(11) 2.0				(27) 3.6	(31) 3.7
		1.3	-.1				2.1	2.2
	.5	.3	.2			Fixed/Worth	.3	.3
	.7	.6	.5				.6	.5
	1.3	.9	1.0				1.3	1.1
	1.3	.8	.6			Debt/Worth	.6	.7
	1.6	2.2	1.3				2.2	1.5
	4.5	3.8	2.7				3.8	3.1
	55.3	51.0	38.8			% Profit Before Taxes/Tangible Net Worth	46.6	42.6
	(17) 26.3	20.3	(25) 18.8				(46) 19.4	(56) 15.5
	7.9	10.8	-7.1				7.2	4.6
	17.2	16.6	18.5			% Profit Before Taxes/Total Assets	14.1	15.6
	10.2	7.1	8.1				5.4	6.5
	2.4	3.4	-3.4				.6	1.1
	15.6	24.7	14.0			Sales/Net Fixed Assets	22.6	23.6
	12.2	10.5	7.6				10.1	10.3
	3.8	5.1	4.9				4.4	6.6
	2.7	2.4	2.0			Sales/Total Assets	2.8	2.6
	2.2	2.0	1.7				2.0	2.1
	1.4	1.6	1.2				1.4	1.5
	1.5	.8	1.7			% Depr., Dep., Amort./Sales	1.0	1.1
	(17) 2.5	(31) 1.2	(24) 2.5				(46) 2.0	(52) 2.1
	3.5	2.6	3.4				3.2	2.8
	2.3	2.5				% Officers', Directors', Owners' Comp/Sales	2.7	2.9
	(10) 5.6	(13) 4.3					(17) 5.9	(26) 4.5
	9.6	5.1					8.5	6.3
2845M	47911M	307313M	965389M	292023M	727665M	Net Sales ($)	1888386M	1679299M
866M	23152M	159584M	605635M	142342M	470569M	Total Assets ($)	1237376M	1015026M

M = $ thousand   MM = $ million
See Pages 1 through 15 for Explanation of Ratios and Data

	Comparative Historical Data				Current Data Sorted By Sales					
	3	3	2	# Postretirement Benefits			1	1		
				Type of Statement	0-1MM	1-3MM	3-5MM	5-10MM	10-25MM	25MM & OVER
	28	36	30	Unqualified			2	6	10	12
	13	15	19	Reviewed	1	4	3	5	6	
	13	11	7	Compiled		4	1	2		
	2	1	1	Tax Returns			1			
	18	21	31	Other	2	5	4	5	6	9
	4/1/92-3/31/93 ALL	4/1/93-3/31/94 ALL	4/1/94-3/31/95 ALL			30 (4/1-9/30/94)			58 (10/1/94-3/31/95)	
	74	84	88	**NUMBER OF STATEMENTS**	3	13	11	18	22	21
	%	%	%	**ASSETS**	%	%	%	%	%	%
	8.3	7.9	5.8	Cash & Equivalents		4.0	5.3	4.6	9.4	4.6
	26.4	26.6	25.6	Trade Receivables - (net)		24.9	28.1	27.9	26.2	22.6
	30.9	30.9	32.2	Inventory		36.5	30.1	36.0	32.1	30.7
	1.8	1.9	2.7	All Other Current		.6	4.6	2.1	4.3	2.0
	67.4	67.3	66.3	Total Current		66.0	68.2	70.6	72.0	59.9
	23.0	21.7	23.7	Fixed Assets (net)		26.7	21.1	23.4	18.1	24.6
	5.1	3.4	4.1	Intangibles (net)		1.6	3.3	3.1	4.7	6.9
	4.5	7.6	5.8	All Other Non-Current		5.7	7.4	2.9	5.1	8.7
	100.0	100.0	100.0	Total		100.0	100.0	100.0	100.0	100.0
				LIABILITIES						
	8.3	8.0	10.8	Notes Payable-Short Term		14.0	10.5	10.1	13.5	7.2
	2.7	4.7	4.5	Cur. Mat.-L./T/D		3.5	3.0	4.2	3.6	4.2
	15.3	16.9	16.8	Trade Payables		12.9	15.8	18.8	17.8	17.6
	.8	1.7	1.3	Income Taxes Payable		.7	1.8	1.1	1.6	.6
	9.3	9.2	7.5	All Other Current		5.5	6.0	8.0	6.8	10.2
	36.5	40.5	40.9	Total Current		36.6	37.2	42.1	43.2	39.8
	15.6	13.6	15.2	Long Term Debt		15.4	25.1	12.0	15.7	12.6
	.3	.3	.4	Deferred Taxes		.5	.2	.2	.3	.6
	5.4	4.2	3.8	All Other-Non-Current		9.6	6.2	3.3	1.6	.9
	42.2	41.4	39.7	Net Worth		37.9	31.4	42.3	39.3	46.1
	100.0	100.0	100.0	Total Liabilities & Net Worth		100.0	100.0	100.0	100.0	100.0
				INCOME DATA						
	100.0	100.0	100.0	Net Sales		100.0	100.0	100.0	100.0	100.0
	47.4	47.1	44.6	Gross Profit		42.3	46.4	38.0	46.8	48.9
	41.0	40.8	39.4	Operating Expenses		35.8	36.9	34.8	43.9	43.1
	6.4	6.4	5.2	Operating Profit		6.5	9.5	3.3	2.9	5.8
	1.3	1.6	1.0	All Other Expenses (net)		1.8	1.4	.6	1.1	.6
	5.1	4.8	4.1	Profit Before Taxes		4.7	8.1	2.7	1.8	5.2
				RATIOS						
	2.8 / 1.9 / 1.4	2.6 / 1.8 / 1.3	2.3 / 1.8 / 1.3	Current		2.3 / 1.7 / 1.5	2.5 / 2.0 / 1.2	3.0 / 1.9 / 1.4	2.8 / 1.7 / 1.2	2.1 / 1.9 / 1.2
	1.6 / .9 / .6	1.3 / .8 / .6	1.2 / .8 / .6	Quick		1.3 / .9 / .5	1.8 / .8 / .6	1.3 / .8 / .6	1.3 / .7 / .5	1.0 / .7 / .6
	38 9.6 / 47 7.8 / 58 6.3	34 10.7 / 48 7.6 / 60 6.1	40 9.2 / 50 7.3 / 64 5.7	Sales/Receivables		26 14.2 / 45 8.1 / 59 6.2	43 8.5 / 54 6.8 / 72 5.1	37 9.8 / 51 7.1 / 59 6.2	43 8.4 / 51 7.1 / 66 5.5	33 11.2 / 45 8.1 / 58 6.3
	73 5.0 / 101 3.6 / 152 2.4	68 5.4 / 107 3.4 / 146 2.5	72 5.1 / 114 3.2 / 192 1.9	Cost of Sales/Inventory		33 10.9 / 101 3.6 / 215 1.7	65 5.6 / 152 2.4 / 192 1.9	62 5.9 / 94 3.9 / 174 2.1	79 4.6 / 135 2.7 / 215 1.7	85 4.3 / 114 3.2 / 174 2.1
	27 13.5 / 42 8.6 / 68 5.4	31 11.7 / 47 7.8 / 85 4.3	31 11.9 / 57 6.4 / 89 4.1	Cost of Sales/Payables		24 15.0 / 38 9.5 / 74 4.9	27 13.5 / 44 8.3 / 78 4.7	27 13.6 / 55 6.6 / 76 4.8	35 10.4 / 59 6.2 / 111 3.3	38 9.6 / 60 6.1 / 87 4.2
	4.3 / 6.6 / 11.3	4.5 / 7.0 / 15.9	4.1 / 7.9 / 12.3	Sales/Working Capital		4.5 / 8.9 / 13.4	3.2 / 6.4 / 16.2	4.5 / 7.3 / 9.8	3.2 / 7.4 / 11.9	5.4 / 8.9 / 19.0
	9.9 / (67) 3.5 / 1.7	12.8 / (76) 3.9 / 1.8	10.7 / (81) 4.2 / 1.8	EBIT/Interest		17.9 / (12) 4.5 / .8	10.8 / (10) 5.0 / 2.4	5.7 / (17) 2.9 / 2.0	9.1 / (21) 1.8 / -1.8	19.7 / (19) 7.1 / 3.3
	16.7 / (32) 3.3 / 1.6	10.1 / (37) 2.9 / 1.3	11.5 / (36) 2.5 / .6	Net Profit + Depr., Dep., Amort./Cur. Mat. L/T/D				12.1 / (10) 2.9 / 1.9		
	.3 / .6 / 1.4	.2 / .6 / 1.1	.3 / .6 / 1.2	Fixed/Worth		.5 / .7 / 1.3	.2 / .7 / 1.1	.3 / .6 / .9	.2 / .6 / .9	.3 / .5 / 1.3
	.8 / 1.5 / 3.4	.8 / 1.6 / 3.3	.8 / 1.6 / 4.4	Debt/Worth		1.0 / 1.6 / 3.9	1.2 / 2.0 / 5.2	.7 / 1.2 / 3.3	1.1 / 2.3 / 4.5	.6 / 1.3 / 3.4
	46.2 / (67) 30.5 / 8.8	46.8 / (80) 22.6 / 10.7	46.4 / (83) 20.2 / 6.6	% Profit Before Taxes/Tangible Net Worth		49.2 / (12) 14.5 / -.6	63.8 / (10) 34.3 / 24.3	39.6 / 16.4 / 8.5	50.3 / 12.2 / -21.9	41.1 / (18) 24.8 / 14.9
	19.3 / 9.2 / 2.4	16.3 / 7.9 / 4.0	16.0 / 7.8 / 2.4	% Profit Before Taxes/Total Assets		14.1 / 7.8 / -.7	19.3 / 12.5 / 7.4	11.4 / 5.1 / 3.6	22.1 / 2.5 / -6.6	20.5 / 10.9 / 3.1
	20.3 / 9.5 / 5.1	24.8 / 12.3 / 5.5	19.6 / 9.7 / 5.0	Sales/Net Fixed Assets		19.0 / 12.4 / 3.5	32.8 / 11.1 / 6.6	21.0 / 8.3 / 5.0	22.6 / 13.7 / 5.6	11.7 / 7.6 / 5.2
	2.5 / 2.0 / 1.5	2.4 / 2.2 / 1.6	2.4 / 1.9 / 1.4	Sales/Total Assets		3.0 / 2.1 / 1.3	2.3 / 2.1 / 1.4	2.5 / 2.1 / 1.6	2.1 / 1.9 / 1.4	2.4 / 1.8 / 1.6
	1.1 / (66) 1.9 / 2.9	.9 / (76) 1.8 / 2.6	1.2 / (78) 2.2 / 3.3	% Depr., Dep., Amort./Sales		1.7 / (12) 2.9 / 3.7	.9 / (10) 2.0 / 3.3	.7 / (18) 1.5 / 2.7	1.1 / (18) 2.2 / 3.0	1.5 / 2.3 / 3.2
	2.6 / (30) 3.7 / 6.6	2.6 / (25) 3.1 / 7.2	2.4 / (33) 4.4 / 6.5	% Officers', Directors', Owners' Comp/Sales						
	2744475M	3033942M	2343146M	Net Sales ($)	753M	23207M	40980M	126793M	355896M	1795517M
	1775764M	1940857M	1402148M	Total Assets ($)	681M	13021M	24607M	68603M	262579M	1032657M

© Robert Morris Associates 1995

M = $ thousand   MM = $ million

See Pages 1 through 15 for Explanation of Ratios and Data

		Current Data Sorted By Assets						Comparative Historical Data	

Type of Statement counts

	0-500M	500M-2MM	2-10MM	10-50MM	50-100MM	100-250MM	# Postretirement Benefits / Type of Statement	4/1/90-3/31/91	4/1/91-3/31/92
		2	9	2	4	2	Unqualified	49	44
		2	24	29	7	9	Reviewed	38	43
		15	26	2			Compiled	26	14
	2	21	3				Tax Returns		1
	5	10	16	12	8	2	Other	20	25
		58 (4/1-9/30/94)		135 (10/1/94-3/31/95)				ALL	ALL
NUMBER OF STATEMENTS	7	48	69	43	15	11		133	127

Main Data

0-500M	500M-2MM	2-10MM	10-50MM	50-100MM	100-250MM		4/1/90-3/31/91 ALL	4/1/91-3/31/92 ALL
%	%	%	%	%	%	**ASSETS**	%	%
	7.3	5.0	4.2	2.4	8.4	Cash & Equivalents	6.1	5.7
	32.3	29.8	25.8	21.1	21.6	Trade Receivables - (net)	28.7	28.1
	22.3	21.6	20.6	13.8	15.4	Inventory	21.3	21.1
	2.0	1.4	2.0	2.1	1.9	All Other Current	2.0	1.4
	63.9	57.8	52.5	39.2	47.3	Total Current	58.0	56.3
	32.1	36.2	39.4	50.7	40.5	Fixed Assets (net)	34.2	36.5
	.9	1.6	1.4	3.5	4.9	Intangibles (net)	2.2	1.6
	3.0	4.3	6.7	6.6	7.3	All Other Non-Current	5.5	5.6
	100.0	100.0	100.0	100.0	100.0	Total	100.0	100.0
						LIABILITIES		
	10.7	9.4	8.4	5.7	1.4	Notes Payable-Short Term	8.4	10.3
	3.0	5.1	2.6	4.1	1.4	Cur. Mat.-L/T/D	4.3	4.5
	19.3	18.8	17.3	17.1	11.8	Trade Payables	17.8	16.8
	.3	.4	.4	.3	.9	Income Taxes Payable	.6	.3
	9.5	7.6	6.5	7.8	6.8	All Other Current	6.2	6.9
	42.8	41.2	35.2	35.0	22.4	Total Current	37.4	38.6
	11.2	19.5	19.2	36.6	21.0	Long Term Debt	21.1	18.4
	.8	.8	1.7	1.4	3.4	Deferred Taxes	1.1	.9
	7.6	3.3	1.9	8.3	1.5	All Other-Non-Current	3.1	3.4
	37.7	35.1	42.0	18.7	51.7	Net Worth	37.4	38.8
	100.0	100.0	100.0	100.0	100.0	Total Liabilities & Net Worth	100.0	100.0
						INCOME DATA		
	100.0	100.0	100.0	100.0	100.0	Net Sales	100.0	100.0
	28.6	26.6	21.2	22.2	26.1	Gross Profit	25.5	27.7
	24.7	20.9	15.0	13.1	15.7	Operating Expenses	20.8	23.1
	3.9	5.6	6.2	9.1	10.4	Operating Profit	4.7	4.5
	.8	1.3	1.2	2.6	1.5	All Other Expenses (net)	1.4	1.8
	3.1	4.4	5.0	6.5	8.9	Profit Before Taxes	3.3	2.7
						RATIOS		
	2.2	2.0	2.3	1.4	2.6		2.4	2.3
	1.6	1.4	1.6	1.3	1.8	Current	1.6	1.5
	1.2	1.1	1.1	1.0	1.5		1.2	1.0
	1.4	1.3	1.4	1.1	1.5		1.4	1.3
	1.0	.8	.9	.7	1.1	Quick	.9 (126)	.8
	.6	.6	.6	.5	1.0		.6	.6
31	11.9 / 41 9.0	39 9.4	44 8.3	51 7.1			39 9.4	37 9.8
45	8.2 / 50 7.3	51 7.1	47 7.8	58 6.3		Sales/Receivables	47 7.8	49 7.5
58	6.3 / 62 5.9	57 6.4	72 5.1	61 6.0			59 6.2	58 6.3
27	13.6 / 31 11.6	32 11.5	27 13.3	41 9.0			32 11.3	33 10.9
41	9.0 / 51 7.1	46 7.9	33 11.1	50 7.3		Cost of Sales/Inventory	46 8.0	51 7.2
65	5.6 / 70 5.2	60 6.1	64 5.7	79 4.6			63 5.8	73 5.0
23	16.1 / 28 12.9	27 13.3	29 12.5	36 10.1			26 13.8	26 14.2
37	9.8 / 44 8.3	41 9.0	43 8.5	41 8.9		Cost of Sales/Payables	36 10.1	37 9.9
51	7.1 / 61 6.0	54 6.8	54 6.8	55 6.6			52 7.0	51 7.2
	5.7	7.2	6.0	13.1	5.3		6.5	5.5
	9.4	12.8	9.8	17.4	8.6	Sales/Working Capital	11.2	12.1
	32.1	52.3	42.5	-281.2	9.5		28.8	449.9
	9.7	9.5	11.9	4.4			5.7	5.2
	(44) 4.0	(67) 4.0	(39) 4.1	(14) 3.5		EBIT/Interest	(120) 2.9	(116) 2.2
	1.1	1.6	1.6	1.8			1.3	1.2
	4.6	5.6	12.2				6.0	2.9
	(19) 3.1	(35) 2.3	(24) 4.1			Net Profit + Depr., Dep., Amort./Cur. Mat. L./T/D	(82) 2.6	(65) 1.7
	1.6	1.3	2.0				1.1	.9
	.4	.6	.5	1.6	.4		.5	.5
	.8	1.0	.9	2.4	1.1	Fixed/Worth	1.0	.9
	1.7	2.0	1.9	5.5	1.3		1.8	2.0
	.7	1.1	.8	2.4	.5		1.0	.7
	1.5	2.0	1.7	3.5	1.2	Debt/Worth	1.8	1.6
	3.8	4.0	3.0	7.5	1.7		3.8	4.1
	45.1	49.8	53.9	90.1	32.3		38.5	31.6
	(45) 20.4	(65) 27.8	(42) 25.7	(12) 34.4	24.6	% Profit Before Taxes/Tangible Net Worth	(127) 21.4	(115) 12.6
	3.9	7.0	11.9	22.3	20.5		5.3	3.2
	15.5	14.4	20.4	14.9	15.9		12.4	10.4
	8.2	7.6	7.1	7.5	12.9	% Profit Before Taxes/Total Assets	6.9	4.4
	.6	2.2	3.7	3.7	10.1		1.7	.5
	24.8	11.3	8.1	3.9	4.8		12.3	11.1
	6.2	5.8	4.7	2.9	3.5	Sales/Net Fixed Assets	6.2	6.1
	4.6	3.5	3.1	1.9	2.6		3.8	3.5
	3.1	2.5	2.3	1.9	1.7		2.8	2.7
	2.2	2.1	1.9	1.2	1.4	Sales/Total Assets	2.2	2.2
	1.9	1.6	1.4	1.2	1.1		1.5	1.5
	1.0	1.8	1.9	3.1	2.5		1.6	1.6
	(43) 2.7	(65) 2.5	(37) 2.8	(13) 4.3	(10) 4.1	% Depr., Dep., Amort./Sales	(113) 2.6	(116) 2.7
	4.2	3.8	3.9	5.0	5.0		3.6	3.9
	3.5	1.8					2.2	1.9
	(26) 4.6	(23) 3.4				% Officers', Directors', Owners' Comp/Sales	(43) 3.6	(41) 3.7
	8.4	6.6					7.3	7.2
7589M	139352M	659430M	1726763M	1605517M	2197444M	Net Sales ($)	2953696M	3466294M
2449M	57006M	331880M	929117M	1136315M	1622913M	Total Assets ($)	1788723M	2389152M

M = $ thousand   MM = $ million
See Pages 1 through 15 for Explanation of Ratios and Data

Comparative Historical Data | Current Data Sorted By Sales

7	10	19	# Postretirement Benefits / Type of Statement	1	2	4	4	8
40	55	71	Unqualified		2	1	12	16	40
34	29	43	Reviewed		8	11	14	9	1
23	19	26	Compiled	2	13	9	2		
1	3		Tax Returns						
40	31	53	Other	3	5	8		15	14

4/1/92-3/31/93 ALL	4/1/93-3/31/94 ALL	4/1/94-3/31/95 ALL		0-1MM	1-3MM (58, 4/1-9/30/94)	3-5MM	5-10MM (135, 10/1/94-3/31/95)	10-25MM	25MM & OVER
138	137	193	**NUMBER OF STATEMENTS**	5	31	26	36	40	55
%	%	%	**ASSETS**	%	%	%	%	%	%
5.8	5.5	5.3	Cash & Equivalents		7.1	4.3	4.8	6.1	4.2
26.8	27.8	28.7	Trade Receivables - (net)		30.4	29.9	33.6	26.4	25.3
21.0	21.4	20.7	Inventory		25.6	21.2	21.2	21.0	17.7
1.5	2.0	1.8	All Other Current		2.3	1.8	1.8	.8	2.3
55.1	56.7	56.5	Total Current		65.4	57.1	61.4	54.3	49.5
35.1	36.5	37.0	Fixed Assets (net)		30.2	39.0	31.4	40.5	40.9
2.7	2.0	1.8	Intangibles (net)		1.4	.1	2.7	1.5	2.2
7.2	4.8	4.7	All Other Non-Current		3.0	3.8	4.5	3.8	7.4
100.0	100.0	100.0	Total		100.0	100.0	100.0	100.0	100.0
			LIABILITIES						
8.4	7.9	9.0	Notes Payable-Short Term		9.6	13.4	8.7	9.4	6.0
4.2	4.1	3.6	Cur. Mat.-L /T/D		2.9	4.1	4.2	4.8	2.7
17.9	16.5	18.4	Trade Payables		17.4	19.5	23.2	15.6	17.2
.3	1.1	.4	Income Taxes Payable		.3	.3	.2	.6	.4
7.8	7.7	7.9	All Other Current		9.9	7.3	9.2	6.6	7.1
38.6	37.3	39.3	Total Current		40.1	44.6	45.6	36.9	33.4
19.3	20.9	18.3	Long Term Debt		11.7	17.8	18.5	18.1	22.9
1.0	1.0	1.2	Deferred Taxes		1.0	.3	.5	1.3	2.1
4.0	2.9	4.3	All Other-Non-Current		8.7	3.7	3.8	3.7	3.3
37.1	37.8	36.8	Net Worth		38.5	33.6	31.5	40.0	38.4
100.0	100.0	100.0	Total Liabilities & Net Worth		100.0	100.0	100.0	100.0	100.0
			INCOME DATA						
100.0	100.0	100.0	Net Sales		100.0	100.0	100.0	100.0	100.0
27.9	26.5	25.8	Gross Profit		27.4	29.4	26.7	25.4	21.3
22.9	20.1	19.9	Operating Expenses		23.5	26.3	20.9	18.9	14.0
5.0	6.4	5.9	Operating Profit		3.9	3.1	5.7	6.5	7.3
1.2	1.6	1.2	All Other Expenses (net)		1.2	1.2	1.1	1.5	1.3
3.8	4.8	4.7	Profit Before Taxes		2.7	2.0	4.6	5.0	6.0
			RATIOS						
2.4	2.3	2.2	Current		2.3	1.8	1.6	2.2	2.2
1.6	1.6	1.5			1.8	1.4	1.4	1.4	1.5
1.1	1.2	1.1			1.2	1.1	1.1	1.0	1.2
1.5	1.2	1.3	Quick		1.5	1.1	1.4	1.3	1.2
.9	.9	.9			1.1	.7	.9	.8	1.0
.6	.7	.6			.6	.6	.6	.6	.6
33 10.9	38 9.5	40 9.2	Sales/Receivables		31 11.9	32 11.5	45 8.1	40 9.1	42 8.6
46 8.0	47 7.8	49 7.4			43 8.4	46 8.0	51 7.1	47 7.8	51 7.1
55 6.6	55 6.6	60 6.1			59 6.2	58 6.3	64 5.7	58 6.3	61 6.0
31 11.6	33 11.1	30 12.0	Cost of Sales/Inventory		30 12.0	30 12.1	27 13.5	32 11.4	31 11.6
47 7.7	47 7.8	46 8.0			52 7.0	49 7.5	47 7.8	48 7.6	44 8.3
64 5.7	69 5.3	66 5.5			87 4.2	70 5.2	72 5.1	73 5.0	58 6.3
23 15.7	22 16.5	26 13.8	Cost of Sales/Payables		17 21.4	34 10.6	27 13.3	26 14.3	29 12.6
38 9.7	33 11.1	40 9.1			34 10.7	46 7.9	45 8.1	34 10.7	40 9.1
51 7.1	53 6.9	56 6.5			51 7.1	60 6.1	64 5.7	57 6.4	51 7.2
6.1	6.6	6.6	Sales/Working Capital		5.4	7.5	7.6	6.6	7.1
12.1	12.0	11.3			7.5	15.7	17.1	11.3	10.0
69.1	28.5	39.4			32.1	62.9	100.1	94.1	29.1
(124) 8.5	(126) 10.1	(177) 10.1	EBIT/Interest		(29) 9.9	(25) 7.9	(33) 9.0	(37) 10.4	(51) 11.6
3.2	3.8	4.0			3.1	4.1	3.0	4.3	4.3
1.5	1.5	1.6			.6	1.4	1.1	1.9	2.6
(66) 6.3	(66) 4.2	(96) 7.6	Net Profit + Depr., Dep., Amort./Cur. Mat. L/T/D		(14) 3.7	(16) 5.3	(19) 6.7		(37) 22.8
2.6	2.5	2.9			2.5	2.3	2.3		6.4
1.2	1.3	1.8			.4	1.5	1.7		2.2
.5	.5	.6	Fixed/Worth		.3	.6	.6	.6	.6
1.0	1.0	1.1			.8	1.2	.8	1.2	1.1
2.0	2.1	2.0			1.7	3.0	1.7	2.0	2.1
.8	.8	1.0	Debt/Worth		.7	1.1	1.4	.9	.9
1.8	1.8	1.9			1.6	1.6	2.0	1.7	1.9
4.3	4.1	3.7			4.8	4.3	4.2	2.8	3.3
(121) 37.5	(126) 45.6	(180) 47.7	% Profit Before Taxes/Tangible Net Worth		(28) 31.4	(24) 51.0	(32) 50.0	(39) 53.4	(53) 50.7
24.8	25.0	25.1			15.0	28.5	29.0	25.1	25.1
8.6	7.3	10.4			.8	8.9	12.2	4.7	15.6
16.2	14.9	15.8	% Profit Before Taxes/Total Assets		12.5	15.8	12.7	17.4	16.6
8.0	8.7	8.1			5.5	7.9	6.6	9.1	11.2
2.5	1.5	2.5			-1.0	2.1	1.0	2.2	4.2
11.1	10.4	11.0	Sales/Net Fixed Assets		20.9	13.0	12.4	7.7	6.8
6.2	5.6	5.4			6.9	5.2	8.2	4.6	3.9
3.8	3.6	3.4			4.6	3.8	4.0	3.1	2.8
2.7	2.7	2.5	Sales/Total Assets		2.7	2.5	2.9	2.5	2.2
2.1	2.1	1.9			2.1	2.2	2.3	1.9	1.8
1.6	1.5	1.5			1.9	1.6	1.6	1.5	1.2
(128) 1.5	(127) 1.8	(173) 1.9	% Depr., Dep., Amort./Sales		(28) 1.0	(25) 1.2	(32) 1.1	(36) 2.0	(49) 2.1
2.6	2.8	2.8			2.7	2.7	2.5	2.9	3.1
4.1	3.9	4.2			4.6	3.7	4.1	3.8	4.8
(39) 2.6	(38) 2.3	(56) 2.1	% Officers', Directors', Owners' Comp/Sales		(15) 3.6	(14) 2.3	(13) 3.0	(11) .9	
4.7	3.9	4.2			4.6	4.8	4.2	1.8	
6.1	7.3	6.2			8.4	7.4	6.5	2.2	
3435518M	4493968M	6336095M	Net Sales ($)	2569M	65109M	95835M	262545M	614535M	5295502M
2140275M	2778441M	4079680M	Total Assets ($)	2194M	31986M	54248M	182468M	352505M	3456279M

M = $ thousand   MM = $ million
See Pages 1 through 15 for Explanation of Ratios and Data

Current Data Sorted By Assets | Comparative Historical Data

0-500M	500M-2MM	2-10MM	10-50MM	50-100MM	100-250MM	# Postretirement Benefits / Type of Statement	4/1/90-3/31/91 ALL	4/1/91-3/31/92 ALL
	2			2		# Postretirement Benefits		
	3	8	5	2		Unqualified	11	9
2	3	4	1		2	Reviewed	7	4
	3	3				Compiled	6	5
						Tax Returns		
1		3	1		1	Other	3	4
	15 (4/1-9/30/94)		26 (10/1/94-3/31/95)					
3	10	18	7	2	1	**NUMBER OF STATEMENTS**	27	22
%	%	%	%	%	%	**ASSETS**	%	%
	5.1	3.6				Cash & Equivalents	6.1	3.4
	29.4	25.8				Trade Receivables - (net)	28.9	28.7
	29.9	30.3				Inventory	24.7	30.2
	1.5	4.3				All Other Current	1.0	.6
	65.9	64.0				Total Current	60.7	63.0
	23.1	25.3				Fixed Assets (net)	27.6	28.4
	.4	3.6				Intangibles (net)	2.3	1.4
	10.6	7.0				All Other Non-Current	9.4	7.2
	100.0	100.0				Total	100.0	100.0
						LIABILITIES		
	6.3	6.9				Notes Payable-Short Term	9.0	7.6
	5.4	1.8				Cur. Mat. -L/T/D	3.9	2.9
	23.8	18.8				Trade Payables	17.0	17.3
	1.4	.5				Income Taxes Payable	.7	.2
	12.1	8.7				All Other Current	8.4	8.3
	49.1	36.7				Total Current	39.0	36.3
	10.2	14.5				Long Term Debt	14.0	17.2
	.2	.4				Deferred Taxes	1.4	.1
	3.0	4.4				All Other-Non-Current	1.6	1.7
	37.5	44.1				Net Worth	44.1	44.8
	100.0	100.0				Total Liabilities & Net Worth	100.0	100.0
						INCOME DATA		
	100.0	100.0				Net Sales	100.0	100.0
	36.7	30.5				Gross Profit	37.0	39.2
	35.0	23.7				Operating Expenses	32.5	33.6
	1.7	6.8				Operating Profit	4.5	5.6
	.5	.5				All Other Expenses (net)	1.0	1.1
	1.2	6.3				Profit Before Taxes	3.5	4.6
						RATIOS		
	3.5	3.5				Current	2.3	2.7
	1.1	1.8					1.5	1.9
	.8	1.3					1.2	1.3
	2.1	1.4				Quick	1.6	1.6
	.6	.9					.9	1.0
	.4	.6					.6	.6
	29 12.5	31 11.6				Sales/Receivables	35 10.3	37 10.0
	37 9.8	44 8.3					43 8.4	46 8.0
	46 8.0	55 6.6					56 6.5	55 6.6
	36 10.1	46 8.0				Cost of Sales/Inventory	46 7.9	59 6.2
	69 5.3	69 5.3					53 6.9	68 5.4
	87 4.2	99 3.7					72 5.1	99 3.7
	15 25.0	16 22.6				Cost of Sales/Payables	29 12.8	23 15.6
	26 13.8	39 9.4					35 10.5	39 9.3
	99 3.7	70 5.2					51 7.2	60 6.1
	5.2	4.2				Sales/Working Capital	6.7	5.8
	NM	7.0					11.0	7.5
	-26.1	17.1					24.5	13.1
	12.7	12.2				EBIT/Interest	7.4	13.1
	3.4	(16) 3.7					(26) 4.2	(19) 4.2
	-2.3	2.2					1.8	2.4
		33.1				Net Profit + Depr., Dep., Amort./Cur. Mat. L./T/D	7.4	
		(10) 4.2					(17) 3.5	
		1.8					2.1	
	.1	.2				Fixed/Worth	.3	.4
	1.0	.7					.7	.7
	2.4	2.2					1.7	1.5
	.4	.6				Debt/Worth	.9	.6
	2.9	1.4					1.4	1.4
	6.2	6.5					2.3	2.8
	42.0	60.1				% Profit Before Taxes/Tangible Net Worth	36.5	32.0
	14.8	(17) 16.3					(26) 23.6	(21) 22.7
	-22.8	3.0					9.4	9.9
	13.6	11.9				% Profit Before Taxes/Total Assets	14.5	13.5
	6.6	6.9					7.8	8.7
	-4.5	1.1					2.7	3.7
	68.8	16.6				Sales/Net Fixed Assets	21.6	15.3
	12.4	7.4					6.6	8.8
	7.9	4.9					4.6	4.2
	3.3	2.5				Sales/Total Assets	3.1	2.9
	2.6	2.3					2.4	2.3
	2.1	1.4					1.6	1.5
		.9				% Depr., Dep., Amort./Sales	.9	1.1
		(17) 1.7					(25) 1.8	(20) 2.0
		2.7					3.7	2.9
						% Officers', Directors', Owners' Comp/Sales		
3723M	37218M	185055M	366574M	144110M	236699M	Net Sales ($)	743872M	201539M
1063M	13416M	89042M	161663M	123260M	132608M	Total Assets ($)	415475M	97703M

M = $ thousand   MM = $ million
See Pages 1 through 15 for Explanation of Ratios and Data

Comparative Historical Data | Current Data Sorted By Sales

				0-1MM	1-3MM	3-5MM	5-10MM	10-25MM	25MM & OVER
1	1	4	# Postretirement Benefits			2	2		
			Type of Statement						
11	15	18	Unqualified		1	2	5	4	6
11	2	10	Reviewed	1	2	1	3	3	
5	6	6	Compiled		1	2	1	2	
	1		Tax Returns						
			Other		2		1	2	2
7	13	7			15 (4/1-9/30/94)			26 (10/1/94-3/31/95)	
4/1/92-3/31/93 ALL	4/1/93-3/31/94 ALL	4/1/94-3/31/95 ALL		0-1MM	1-3MM	3-5MM	5-10MM	10-25MM	25MM & OVER
34	37	41	**NUMBER OF STATEMENTS**	1	6	5	10	11	8
%	%	%	**ASSETS**	%	%	%	%	%	%
3.9	5.0	4.9	Cash & Equivalents				3.1	6.6	
30.2	28.7	26.5	Trade Receivables - (net)				27.4	25.6	
26.6	29.2	28.1	Inventory				30.3	28.8	
1.8	1.6	2.6	All Other Current				3.5	3.8	
62.5	64.4	62.1	Total Current				64.3	64.8	
29.2	28.2	27.7	Fixed Assets (net)				29.7	29.2	
2.3	.9	2.5	Intangibles (net)				3.4	.6	
6.0	6.5	7.7	All Other Non-Current				2.6	5.3	
100.0	100.0	100.0	Total				100.0	100.0	
			LIABILITIES						
7.0	10.9	8.3	Notes Payable-Short Term				6.2	6.2	
5.4	2.5	3.5	Cur. Mat.-L /T/D				4.0	4.9	
20.2	17.6	19.4	Trade Payables				22.5	18.1	
.3	.9	.6	Income Taxes Payable				.2	.7	
6.1	8.4	8.9	All Other Current				10.2	5.1	
39.0	40.3	40.7	Total Current				43.1	35.1	
14.0	12.5	13.5	Long Term Debt				16.6	12.1	
.9	.6	.5	Deferred Taxes				.5	.2	
2.7	3.9	3.9	All Other-Non-Current				5.3	.7	
43.3	42.7	41.4	Net Worth				34.4	51.8	
100.0	100.0	100.0	Total Liabilities & Net Worth				100.0	100.0	
			INCOME DATA						
100.0	100.0	100.0	Net Sales				100.0	100.0	
37.3	31.5	33.5	Gross Profit				33.8	28.0	
31.4	26.4	28.2	Operating Expenses				28.4	22.5	
5.9	5.1	5.3	Operating Profit				5.4	5.5	
.7	.8	.7	All Other Expenses (net)				.8	.7	
5.2	4.3	4.6	Profit Before Taxes				4.6	4.8	
			RATIOS						
2.9	2.5	3.5					4.0	3.7	
1.8	1.5	1.4	Current				1.4	2.2	
1.1	1.2	1.0					1.0	1.3	
1.8	1.2	1.5					1.4	1.6	
.9	.9	.8	Quick				.8	1.2	
.5	.5	.5					.5	.6	
34 10.6	33 11.1	29 12.4					25 14.7	28 12.9	
50 7.3	44 8.3	41 9.0	Sales/Receivables				37 9.8	42 8.7	
62 5.9	50 7.3	54 6.7					60 6.1	54 6.8	
51 7.2	43 8.5	48 7.6					30 12.1	47 7.7	
68 5.4	55 6.6	66 5.5	Cost of Sales/Inventory				69 5.3	57 6.4	
89 4.1	89 4.1	87 4.2					94 3.9	78 4.7	
27 13.4	21 17.8	20 17.9					20 18.3	23 15.8	
50 7.3	35 10.5	35 10.4	Cost of Sales/Payables				64 5.7	31 11.7	
69 5.3	61 6.0	69 5.3					72 5.1	60 6.1	
5.4	7.2	4.9					8.5	4.0	
9.5	12.0	11.7	Sales/Working Capital				8.1	7.0	
40.7	28.5	NM					NM	18.0	
10.3	8.7	11.4						13.8	
(30) 3.8	(34) 3.0	(39) 3.8	EBIT/Interest					(10) 4.1	
1.3	1.3	1.1						2.1	
4.9	4.8	23.5							
(19) 1.3	(14) 1.7	(21) 4.5	Net Profit + Depr., Dep., Amort./Cur. Mat. L/T/D						
.8	.7	1.8							
.4	.4	.3					.4	.2	
.6	.6	.8	Fixed/Worth				1.6	.7	
1.3	1.5	2.1					6.0	1.2	
.7	.7	.7					.6	.4	
1.5	1.5	1.6	Debt/Worth				3.4	1.1	
2.9	2.8	4.6					16.2	1.6	
42.5	39.9	52.1					84.0	22.0	
17.2	15.0	(40) 17.0	% Profit Before Taxes/Tangible Net Worth				31.6	14.4	
6.8	4.9	1.5					-10.3	2.7	
13.7	16.9	14.6					11.9	10.7	
6.1	6.0	7.2	% Profit Before Taxes/Total Assets				7.3	7.2	
1.9	1.4	.2					-1.3	1.1	
11.8	18.1	18.1					16.0	14.4	
8.7	7.1	7.4	Sales/Net Fixed Assets				6.9	8.5	
4.5	5.1	5.1					4.8	5.1	
3.0	2.9	2.8					2.9	2.6	
2.3	2.4	2.3	Sales/Total Assets				2.5	2.3	
1.6	2.0	1.6					1.5	2.0	
1.0	.9	1.0						1.1	
(32) 2.2	(34) 1.9	(39) 1.7	% Depr., Dep., Amort./Sales					2.0	
3.1	2.7	3.1						2.8	
1.8	2.2	1.8							
(13) 3.1	(10) 4.0	(12) 3.6	% Officers', Directors', Owners' Comp/Sales						
5.6	6.6	5.4							
408851M	783714M	973379M	Net Sales ($)	681M	12204M	17192M	64714M	166282M	712306M
234132M	362138M	521052M	Total Assets ($)	215M	5559M	9826M	31272M	80097M	394083M

© Robert Morris Associates 1995

M = $ thousand   MM = $ million
See Pages 1 through 15 for Explanation of Ratios and Data

Current Data Sorted By Assets   **Comparative Historical Data**

Top annotation (over 2-10MM / 10-50MM / 50-100MM): 4   1   2

Postretirement Benefits — Type of Statement

0-500M	500M-2MM	2-10MM	10-50MM	50-100MM	100-250MM	Type of Statement	4/1/90-3/31/91 ALL	4/1/91-3/31/92 ALL
	2	5	8			Unqualified	20	22
3	6	10	1			Reviewed	15	15
4	8	1				Compiled	20	13
1						Tax Returns		1
2	5	4	5	2		Other	5	10

Period groupings: 28 (4/1-9/30/94) covers the 500M-2MM / 2-10MM range; 39 (10/1/94-3/31/95) covers the 10-50MM range.

0-500M	500M-2MM	2-10MM	10-50MM	50-100MM	100-250MM		5 / 4/1/90-3/31/91 ALL	10 / 4/1/91-3/31/92 ALL
10	21	20	14	2		NUMBER OF STATEMENTS	60	61
%	%	%	%	%	%	**ASSETS**	%	%
8.6	4.1	6.9	4.3			Cash & Equivalents	6.4	6.3
40.2	27.9	29.7	25.7			Trade Receivables - (net)	26.6	27.7
25.9	29.9	27.5	27.6			Inventory	25.5	25.0
.3	1.0	3.3	1.3			All Other Current	.9	3.0
74.9	62.8	67.4	59.0			Total Current	59.4	62.0
15.0	25.6	20.7	26.3			Fixed Assets (net)	28.3	26.5
2.7	2.1	2.5	5.3			Intangibles (net)	2.8	3.2
7.4	9.4	9.4	9.4			All Other Non-Current	9.6	8.3
100.0	100.0	100.0	100.0			Total	100.0	100.0
						LIABILITIES		
3.6	10.2	10.2	7.9			Notes Payable-Short Term	11.9	9.5
3.2	4.7	2.2	2.5			Cur. Mat. -L/T/D	2.7	5.2
24.9	22.7	16.1	10.6			Trade Payables	18.8	16.4
.2	.2	.4	.0			Income Taxes Payable	.5	.2
10.5	8.0	8.7	8.4			All Other Current	7.3	7.9
42.5	45.8	37.6	29.4			Total Current	41.2	39.2
7.8	10.0	7.0	17.2			Long Term Debt	13.0	15.1
.2	.5	.4	.9			Deferred Taxes	.4	.6
4.2	8.3	2.3	6.4			All Other-Non-Current	3.9	3.5
45.3	35.4	52.7	46.2			Net Worth	41.5	41.5
100.0	100.0	100.0	100.0			Total Liabilities & Net Worth	100.0	100.0
						INCOME DATA		
100.0	100.0	100.0	100.0			Net Sales	100.0	100.0
41.1	45.1	39.9	42.7			Gross Profit	37.6	39.1
35.9	42.8	35.3	37.4			Operating Expenses	34.5	34.5
5.2	2.3	4.6	5.2			Operating Profit	3.2	4.6
1.4	.0	-.3	1.5			All Other Expenses (net)	1.4	1.1
3.8	2.2	4.9	3.8			Profit Before Taxes	1.8	3.5
						RATIOS		
4.9 / 2.8 / 1.2	2.1 / 1.6 / 1.0	2.8 / 2.0 / 1.4	3.0 / 2.3 / 1.3			Current	2.1 / 1.6 / 1.0	2.5 / 1.5 / 1.2
3.2 / 1.5 / .7	1.2 / .8 / .5	1.3 / 1.1 / .7	1.7 / 1.2 / .6			Quick	1.3 / .9 / .5	1.5 / .9 / .7
33 10.9 / 42 8.7 / 76 4.8	27 13.7 / 36 10.2 / 43 8.5	34 10.7 / 42 8.6 / 54 6.7	41 8.9 / 55 6.6 / 60 6.1			Sales/Receivables	29 12.7 / 37 9.9 / 47 7.7	34 10.8 / 43 8.5 / 56 6.5
22 16.7 / 43 8.4 / 83 4.4	41 9.0 / 74 4.9 / 111 3.3	40 9.2 / 73 5.0 / 87 4.2	74 4.9 / 107 3.4 / 130 2.8			Cost of Sales/Inventory	33 11.0 / 60 6.1 / 87 4.2	35 10.4 / 70 5.2 / 107 3.4
13 29.1 / 45 8.1 / 96 3.8	28 13.1 / 42 8.6 / 66 5.5	30 12.0 / 40 9.1 / 57 6.4	22 16.8 / 40 9.1 / 59 6.2			Cost of Sales/Payables	26 14.0 / 36 10.2 / 54 6.7	29 12.8 / 41 8.8 / 66 5.5
3.9 / 5.4 / 29.2	8.0 / 13.3 / 505.7	4.0 / 8.2 / 14.0	4.0 / 6.6 / 12.3			Sales/Working Capital	7.4 / 12.8 / 171.2	5.2 / 12.8 / 37.7
	(20) 7.1 / 2.3 / 1.5	(18) 22.3 / 13.5 / 2.4	(12) 17.1 / 2.9 / 2.1			EBIT/Interest	(53) 4.6 / 2.2 / .9	(57) 7.7 / 3.1 / 1.4
	(15) 5.3 / 2.2 / 1.0	(10) 19.9 / 6.5 / .1				Net Profit + Depr., Dep., Amort./Cur. Mat. L./T/D	(29) 3.7 / 1.9 / .7	(28) 4.1 / 2.0 / .4
.1 / .2 / .8	.4 / .6 / 1.5	.1 / .3 / 1.0	.5 / .8 / 1.0			Fixed/Worth	.3 / .6 / 2.0	.3 / .7 / 1.3
.3 / 1.4 / 2.0	1.2 / 2.3 / 4.3	.4 / .7 / 2.0	1.1 / 1.8 / 2.5			Debt/Worth	.6 / 1.7 / 4.6	.7 / 2.1 / 3.4
	39.5 / 14.4 / 7.3	(19) 50.0 / 22.2 / 11.0	24.2 / 17.3 / 8.4			% Profit Before Taxes/Tangible Net Worth	(57) 35.4 / 14.5 / 2.8	(59) 33.4 / 17.1 / 4.9
15.6 / 10.0 / 3.7	10.1 / 4.2 / 2.8	19.8 / 13.2 / 3.5	11.4 / 5.4 / 3.2			% Profit Before Taxes/Total Assets	10.8 / 5.2 / .1	13.5 / 5.6 / 1.6
114.5 / 27.6 / 12.3	25.0 / 13.8 / 8.5	32.8 / 18.9 / 8.5	9.3 / 6.5 / 5.2			Sales/Net Fixed Assets	21.5 / 11.6 / 6.2	19.1 / 11.4 / 5.4
3.4 / 2.8 / 2.1	3.7 / 2.9 / 2.2	3.4 / 2.2 / 1.6	2.2 / 1.7 / 1.4			Sales/Total Assets	3.0 / 2.6 / 1.9	2.9 / 2.2 / 1.6
	1.0 / 1.4 / 2.7	(10) .9 / 1.4 / 2.3	1.4 / 2.0 / 3.7			% Depr., Dep., Amort./Sales	(55) .8 / 1.7 / 2.5	(60) .9 / 1.5 / 3.2
	(10) 2.5 / 5.8 / 10.1	(10) 3.2 / 5.6 / 10.4				% Officers', Directors', Owners' Comp/Sales	(18) 1.5 / 3.6 / 5.8	(25) 1.9 / 3.7 / 7.2
9173M	66005M	222544M	643613M	96097M		Net Sales ($)	749670M	712917M
3103M	23476M	85398M	357667M	122485M		Total Assets ($)	347592M	405715M

M = $ thousand   MM = $ million
See Pages 1 through 15 for Explanation of Ratios and Data

Comparative Historical Data				Current Data Sorted By Sales					
1	4	7	# Postretirement Benefits	1	2	1		2	1
			Type of Statement						
15	13	15	Unqualified		1	2	2	2	8
26	16	20	Reviewed		5	6	4	4	1
17	15	13	Compiled	3	7	3			
4		1	Tax Returns	1					
14	14	18	Other	3	1	3		3	5
4/1/92- 3/31/93 ALL	4/1/93- 3/31/94 ALL	4/1/94- 3/31/95 ALL		0-1MM	28 (4/1-9/30/94) 1-3MM	3-5MM	5-10MM	39 (10/1/94-3/31/95) 10-25MM	25MM & OVER
76	58	67	**NUMBER OF STATEMENTS**	7	14	14	9	9	14
%	%	%	**ASSETS**	%	%	%	%	%	%
6.1	8.2	5.5	Cash & Equivalents		3.6	6.6			2.5
26.4	29.4	29.4	Trade Receivables - (net)		29.6	25.5			28.3
25.4	27.3	27.6	Inventory		30.9	30.3			27.5
1.6	.7	1.6	All Other Current		3.6	.6			1.0
59.4	65.5	64.1	Total Current		67.7	63.0			59.3
25.9	24.5	22.1	Fixed Assets (net)		22.0	23.5			20.9
5.1	1.9	4.0	Intangibles (net)		1.5	3.0			10.0
9.5	8.1	9.8	All Other Non-Current		8.8	10.5			9.8
100.0	100.0	100.0	Total		100.0	100.0			100.0
			LIABILITIES						
7.5	9.6	8.4	Notes Payable-Short Term		9.2	9.4			7.4
4.8	3.6	3.3	Cur. Mat.-L./T/D		3.8	4.4			2.6
16.6	14.7	18.1	Trade Payables		17.7	20.5			12.5
.6	1.3	.2	Income Taxes Payable		.3	.1			.3
8.3	10.6	8.5	All Other Current		7.2	6.9			10.2
37.8	39.8	38.5	Total Current		38.3	41.4			33.0
16.5	12.4	11.4	Long Term Debt		7.5	11.2			19.8
.3	.3	.5	Deferred Taxes		.4	.4			1.1
2.0	4.0	5.6	All Other-Non-Current		4.4	4.8			1.8
43.4	43.4	44.1	Net Worth		49.4	42.3			44.2
100.0	100.0	100.0	Total Liabilities & Net Worth		100.0	100.0			100.0
			INCOME DATA						
100.0	100.0	100.0	Net Sales		100.0	100.0			100.0
36.8	41.4	43.2	Gross Profit		41.8	46.1			46.8
32.4	37.1	38.9	Operating Expenses		40.0	43.4			39.9
4.4	4.3	4.3	Operating Profit		1.8	2.7			6.9
1.2	.4	.6	All Other Expenses (net)		.6	.1			2.0
3.2	4.0	3.7	Profit Before Taxes		1.3	2.6			4.9
			RATIOS						
2.5	2.4	2.8			2.6	2.7			2.6
1.6	1.6	2.0	Current		2.0	1.8			1.9
1.0	1.1	1.3			1.2	1.0			1.5
1.4	1.6	1.4			1.3	1.2			1.4
.9	1.0	1.0	Quick		1.0	.9			1.1
.5	.6	.6			.7	.5			.7
29 12.4	31 11.8	33 10.9			34 10.8	31 11.9			34 10.6
39 9.3	41 8.9	42 8.7	Sales/Receivables		39 9.3	37 10.0			53 6.9
51 7.2	50 7.3	56 6.5			50 7.3	42 8.6			60 6.1
37 9.9	39 9.3	44 8.3			31 11.6	72 5.1			68 5.4
57 6.4	68 5.4	78 4.7	Cost of Sales/Inventory		85 4.3	85 4.3			85 4.3
85 4.3	101 3.6	107 3.4			146 2.5	91 4.0			140 2.6
21 17.6	20 18.6	30 12.1			15 25.0	30 12.1			22 16.5
35 10.3	35 10.3	42 8.6	Cost of Sales/Payables		43 8.5	45 8.1			47 7.8
56 6.5	52 7.0	66 5.5			68 5.4	66 5.5			68 5.4
6.3	5.2	4.8			3.7	6.7			4.8
11.9	11.1	8.9	Sales/Working Capital		9.4	10.8			9.1
228.0	35.5	22.6			29.2	-278.4			12.7
5.1	13.3	13.4			10.6	7.4			19.5
(69) 2.8	(54) 3.4	(61) 3.3	EBIT/Interest		2.8	(11) 2.1		(13) 3.3
1.4	1.8	1.9			.9	1.0			2.2
7.1	4.4	10.3			8.2				
(37) 2.3	(25) 1.7	(35) 2.7	Net Profit + Depr., Dep., Amort./Cur. Mat. L/T/D	(10) 2.6					
1.2	.7	1.2			.7				
.2	.2	.2			.1	.3			.4
.6	.5	.5	Fixed/Worth		.5	.6			.8
1.4	1.2	1.2			.9	1.5			1.1
.7	.7	.6			.5	.7			1.1
1.5	1.5	1.6	Debt/Worth		1.2	2.4			1.8
3.3	2.9	2.9			1.9	3.9			3.0
34.7	31.7	37.9			20.3	38.7			45.4
(70) 15.4	(55) 17.5	(63) 17.7	% Profit Before Taxes/Tangible Net Worth		13.1	13.2		(12) 21.9
3.8	4.3	9.3			-.9	.5			11.1
15.3	16.0	15.1			9.2	11.8			17.1
4.3	5.2	7.3	% Profit Before Taxes/Total Assets		5.1	3.2			7.3
1.0	1.2	3.2			-.3	.6			4.5
32.3	36.9	29.8			47.1	28.8			17.6
15.7	13.7	14.0	Sales/Net Fixed Assets		15.1	13.5			9.4
5.0	6.6	7.1			7.0	8.0			6.2
3.1	3.4	3.2			3.3	3.6			2.9
2.5	2.5	2.4	Sales/Total Assets		2.7	2.8			2.2
1.6	1.9	1.6			1.5	1.7			1.4
.9	.7	.9			.4	1.0			1.1
(68) 1.6	(53) 1.3	(60) 1.5	% Depr., Dep., Amort./Sales		2.2	1.4		(10) 2.0
3.1	2.5	2.6			2.8	2.4			2.2
3.1	3.4	3.3							
(36) 4.0	(26) 5.6	(28) 7.1	% Officers', Directors', Owners' Comp/Sales						
7.7	10.6	10.3							
751710M	620281M	1037432M	Net Sales ($)	4122M	26655M	56896M	65859M	157578M	726322M
405482M	333753M	592129M	Total Assets ($)	1911M	12746M	25232M	28906M	92357M	430977M

M = $ thousand   MM = $ million
See Pages 1 through 15 for Explanation of Ratios and Data

Current Data Sorted By Assets						# Postretirement Benefits / Type of Statement	Comparative Historical Data	
1	2	6	4	1	1			
1	3	27	21	2	1	Unqualified	32	29
2	8	9	3			Reviewed	17	28
7	18	6	3			Compiled	23	27
7	1					Tax Returns	2	1
6	11	5	8	3		Other	22	18
0-500M	500M-2MM 52 (4/1-9/30/94)	2-10MM	10-50MM 100 (10/1/94-3/31/95)	50-100MM	100-250MM		4/1/90-3/31/91 ALL	4/1/91-3/31/92 ALL
23	41	47	35	5	1	NUMBER OF STATEMENTS	96	103
%	%	%	%	%	%	ASSETS	%	%
10.8	7.8	7.5	5.6			Cash & Equivalents	6.5	6.7
19.7	23.2	21.3	17.6			Trade Receivables - (net)	21.1	20.0
10.6	14.2	13.9	9.9			Inventory	12.0	12.7
1.1	1.3	1.5	1.8			All Other Current	2.1	1.4
42.2	46.5	44.2	34.9			Total Current	41.6	40.8
42.3	43.8	50.1	49.3			Fixed Assets (net)	48.3	49.1
2.6	1.2	1.6	5.9			Intangibles (net)	1.9	2.0
13.0	8.4	4.2	9.9			All Other Non-Current	8.1	8.1
100.0	100.0	100.0	100.0			Total	100.0	100.0
						LIABILITIES		
7.0	7.0	4.8	4.7			Notes Payable-Short Term	6.1	5.1
6.6	5.0	4.4	4.4			Cur. Mat. -L/T/D	5.2	5.9
16.9	15.1	16.1	13.3			Trade Payables	14.9	15.7
.6	.4	.3	.3			Income Taxes Payable	.4	.4
13.4	7.3	8.3	7.5			All Other Current	6.5	7.4
44.6	34.8	33.9	30.1			Total Current	33.1	34.5
20.7	23.4	23.7	22.8			Long Term Debt	25.9	26.8
.9	.4	.9	1.2			Deferred Taxes	1.1	.8
4.1	6.5	3.6	6.2			All Other-Non-Current	3.7	3.5
29.7	34.8	37.9	39.7			Net Worth	36.2	34.4
100.0	100.0	100.0	100.0			Total Liabilities & Net Worth	100.0	100.0
						INCOME DATA		
100.0	100.0	100.0	100.0			Net Sales	100.0	100.0
53.7	40.1	31.3	37.4			Gross Profit	38.0	38.1
48.8	36.3	27.4	33.0			Operating Expenses	33.5	33.9
4.9	3.9	3.9	4.4			Operating Profit	4.5	4.3
1.5	1.4	.7	1.4			All Other Expenses (net)	1.7	1.3
3.4	2.5	3.2	3.0			Profit Before Taxes	2.9	2.9
						RATIOS		
2.0	2.3	1.8	1.7			Current	1.9	1.8
1.0	1.5	1.3	1.0				1.4	1.3
.6	.9	1.1	.7				.9	.9
1.4	1.7	1.3	1.1			Quick	1.3	1.2
.8	.9	.8	.7				.8	.8
.4	.5	.6	.4				.6	.6
0 UND	21 17.2	21 17.7	21 17.5			Sales/Receivables	20 18.2	19 19.5
20 18.4	26 13.8	24 14.9	26 13.9				26 13.9	25 14.6
26 13.8	35 10.4	35 10.3	39 9.4				34 10.6	33 11.2
7 50.4	13 27.8	16 22.8	11 33.4			Cost of Sales/Inventory	12 30.4	13 28.1
17 22.0	26 14.1	25 14.6	21 17.4				21 17.0	21 17.4
31 11.9	45 8.2	40 9.2	66 5.5				35 10.4	34 10.7
8 45.0	16 22.8	18 20.2	24 15.3			Cost of Sales/Payables	16 22.8	22 16.4
19 19.7	30 12.1	29 12.7	32 11.5				30 12.1	28 13.2
50 7.3	44 8.3	42 8.7	46 8.0				43 8.4	38 9.6
18.6	12.5	11.1	15.2			Sales/Working Capital	11.7	14.0
-244.0	23.4	25.4	476.2				24.5	39.9
-32.1	-100.3	62.6	-18.9				-96.1	-57.9
(20) 9.0	(40) 7.2	(42) 7.9	(32) 6.0			EBIT/Interest	(89) 6.6	(97) 5.6
3.6	2.9	3.5	3.1				2.3	2.7
1.1	.2	1.0	1.4				.9	1.2
	(16) 3.4	(27) 4.0	(16) 5.6			Net Profit + Depr., Dep., Amort./Cur. Mat. L /T/D	(57) 6.5	(51) 5.0
	1.7	2.2	2.2				2.7	2.3
	.9	1.1	1.4				1.0	1.1
.8	.8	.9	.8			Fixed/Worth	.8	.9
1.4	1.3	1.4	1.7				1.3	1.4
3.5	3.5	2.4	3.8				3.3	3.0
.7	1.0	.8	1.0			Debt/Worth	.9	1.0
2.7	1.8	1.5	1.7				1.7	1.9
15.8	5.9	3.7	4.8				6.3	4.4
(19) 120.3	(35) 47.7	(44) 44.4	(31) 30.6			% Profit Before Taxes/Tangible Net Worth	(88) 35.6	(97) 40.8
20.0	22.4	18.5	17.5				16.9	17.4
9.1	.0	1.5	2.9				5.0	4.8
23.8	14.5	14.3	10.2			% Profit Before Taxes/Total Assets	12.9	12.7
10.6	5.8	5.0	5.9				6.0	5.6
1.7	-1.1	.0	1.9				.1	1.1
15.9	12.1	9.0	5.8			Sales/Net Fixed Assets	8.8	8.1
9.3	7.7	5.5	3.8				5.7	5.8
7.5	3.8	3.0	2.6				3.6	4.0
5.8	3.7	3.5	2.7			Sales/Total Assets	3.6	3.7
4.4	2.8	2.6	2.1				2.6	2.9
2.4	2.0	1.7	1.4				2.0	2.1
(19) 1.9	(39) 1.5	(45) 1.9	(34) 2.5			% Depr., Dep., Amort./Sales	(90) 2.0	(98) 2.2
3.0	2.6	3.0	2.9				3.0	3.1
4.0	4.7	4.6	4.8				4.5	4.5
(15) 4.8	(26) 3.1	(12) 1.7				% Officers', Directors', Owners' Comp/Sales	(42) 1.9	(49) 2.2
7.2	5.6	2.0					4.9	3.6
10.6	6.9	3.6					7.0	6.1
23423M	127453M	546229M	1528509M	676456M	174425M	Net Sales ($)	2576652M	2353694M
5667M	43325M	217786M	693732M	343967M	127366M	Total Assets ($)	1027728M	972051M

M = $ thousand   MM = $ million
See Pages 1 through 15 for Explanation of Ratios and Data

Comparative Historical Data				Current Data Sorted By Sales					
2	6	14	# Postretirement Benefits	1	1		3	4	5
			Type of Statement						
37	37	55	Unqualified	2	2	2	11	22	16
29	26	22	Reviewed	1	5	5	3	6	2
20	21	34	Compiled	1	17	5	7	1	3
1	6	8	Tax Returns	7		1			
32	18	33	Other	3	10	4	3	7	6
4/1/92-3/31/93 ALL	4/1/93-3/31/94 ALL	4/1/94-3/31/95 ALL		52 (4/1-9/30/94)			100 (10/1/94-3/31/95)		
				0-1MM	1-3MM	3-5MM	5-10MM	10-25MM	25MM & OVER
119	108	152	**NUMBER OF STATEMENTS**	14	34	17	24	36	27
%	%	%	**ASSETS**	%	%	%	%	%	%
8.0	8.0	7.6	Cash & Equivalents	9.4	10.0	8.2	7.5	5.4	6.3
20.7	20.9	20.5	Trade Receivables - (net)	16.3	21.0	20.5	24.3	19.7	19.9
11.1	12.2	12.6	Inventory	11.5	11.8	13.2	12.6	14.0	11.9
1.5	.8	1.5	All Other Current	.6	1.9	.8	1.6	.6	2.8
41.2	41.8	42.2	Total Current	37.9	44.7	42.8	46.0	39.8	40.9
49.3	48.2	46.9	Fixed Assets (net)	43.0	45.9	47.2	47.0	48.4	48.0
1.5	3.5	2.7	Intangibles (net)	2.5	1.9	1.1	3.7	3.7	2.5
8.0	6.5	8.2	All Other Non-Current	16.6	7.5	9.0	3.3	8.2	8.7
100.0	100.0	100.0	Total	100.0	100.0	100.0	100.0	100.0	100.0
			LIABILITIES						
3.9	5.5	5.8	Notes Payable-Short Term	10.3	4.4	6.5	5.2	5.9	5.0
5.7	5.9	4.8	Cur. Mat.-L /T/D	3.3	7.7	3.3	4.0	4.9	3.5
14.2	14.4	15.0	Trade Payables	19.8	16.0	11.4	13.0	15.4	14.8
.6	.5	.4	Income Taxes Payable	.8	.3	.1	.7	.1	.5
7.4	7.2	8.6	All Other Current	14.2	7.9	7.8	6.1	9.2	8.6
31.8	33.4	34.6	Total Current	48.4	36.4	29.1	29.0	35.5	32.5
23.8	24.0	22.6	Long Term Debt	21.6	23.8	27.4	16.8	23.9	21.7
.9	1.6	.9	Deferred Taxes	1.3	.4	.5	.8	1.2	1.2
2.9	3.5	5.4	All Other-Non-Current	7.0	5.4	5.9	3.2	4.8	6.8
40.6	37.5	36.6	Net Worth	21.7	34.0	37.0	50.2	34.7	37.9
100.0	100.0	100.0	Total Liabilities & Net Worth	100.0	100.0	100.0	100.0	100.0	100.0
			INCOME DATA						
100.0	100.0	100.0	Net Sales	100.0	100.0	100.0	100.0	100.0	100.0
38.3	36.7	38.8	Gross Profit	54.5	42.1	41.1	34.2	32.4	37.5
33.4	33.6	34.5	Operating Expenses	49.5	38.4	40.0	27.5	28.3	32.9
5.0	3.1	4.2	Operating Profit	4.9	3.7	1.1	6.7	4.1	4.6
1.1	1.1	1.1	All Other Expenses (net)	1.5	1.3	.8	.9	1.5	.6
3.9	1.9	3.1	Profit Before Taxes	3.4	2.4	.3	5.8	2.5	4.0
			RATIOS						
1.9	1.9	1.9	Current	1.4	2.3	2.7	2.3	1.5	1.8
1.3	1.3	1.2		1.0	1.3	1.5	1.6	1.2	1.4
.9	.9	.9		.6	.6	1.1	1.2	.9	.8
1.3	1.3	1.4	Quick	1.1	1.8	1.8	2.0	1.0	1.4
.9	.9	.8		.7	.7	1.0	1.0	.7	.8
.6	.6	.5		.4	.4	.5	.6	.5	.5
20 18.5	19 19.1	20 18.2	Sales/Receivables	0 UND	19 18.9	20 18.2	19 19.0	21 17.5	21 17.5
25 14.5	26 14.2	26 14.1		17 21.7	25 14.4	26 13.8	29 12.8	24 15.0	26 13.9
32 11.5	33 11.0	35 10.5		28 13.0	36 10.2	35 10.4	35 10.5	38 9.7	37 9.8
12 30.9	13 29.2	14 26.6	Cost of Sales/Inventory	4 83.1	14 26.2	12 29.3	14 25.4	17 22.1	11 33.4
19 18.9	20 18.0	24 15.3		16 23.4	24 15.2	29 12.4	28 13.1	24 15.2	20 18.0
28 13.0	30 12.2	42 8.6		54 6.7	34 10.7	54 6.7	42 8.7	35 10.5	51 7.1
17 21.3	14 25.3	18 20.5	Cost of Sales/Payables	0 UND	16 22.5	16 23.5	17 21.7	18 20.3	24 15.4
26 14.1	25 14.8	29 12.5		20 18.4	32 11.4	33 11.2	24 15.4	29 12.5	26 14.1
38 9.5	39 9.3	45 8.1		60 6.1	48 7.6	48 9.6	39 9.4	48 7.6	39 9.3
13.0	12.5	13.5	Sales/Working Capital	38.2	13.8	9.2	7.6	20.7	9.8
32.2	30.0	30.9		-185.5	25.7	15.3	18.6	42.0	27.5
-67.0	-69.2	-69.8		-12.7	-21.3	UND	40.3	-58.2	-31.9
(109) 7.3	(104) 7.8	(139) 8.1	EBIT/Interest	(12) 10.8	(32) 5.0	6.9	(21) 15.8	(33) 6.2	(24) 12.1
3.5	3.2	3.5		2.9	3.1	2.8	4.3	2.3	4.1
1.4	1.2	1.0		.8	.2	1.0	1.9	.8	2.1
(71) 4.2	(52) 3.9	(66) 4.0	Net Profit + Depr., Dep., Amort./Cur. Mat. L/T/D		(11) 1.7		(12) 5.1	(19) 4.2	(14) 4.9
2.4	2.0	1.9			1.6		3.1	1.6	2.8
1.2	1.1	1.2			1.3		1.9	1.1	1.6
.8	1.0	.8	Fixed/Worth	1.0	.9	.9	.6	1.0	.9
1.3	1.4	1.4		1.5	1.8	1.3	1.0	1.5	1.5
2.2	3.4	2.9		-13.3	3.2	4.0	2.4	2.2	3.8
.7	1.0	.9	Debt/Worth	1.6	1.1	.7	.5	1.2	1.0
1.5	1.7	1.7		3.2	2.4	1.5	.9	1.8	1.4
3.0	5.2	4.9		-18.2	6.6	6.4	2.8	4.2	4.8
(115) 48.8	(96) 42.3	(135) 44.8	% Profit Before Taxes/Tangible Net Worth	(10) 145.2	(30) 46.6	(15) 38.5	(23) 63.9	(31) 30.6	(26) 36.5
22.9	23.1	20.3		35.1	20.9	8.5	18.3	16.8	22.1
4.8	3.1	4.8		15.5	-.7	1.2	4.8	.0	14.2
15.1	14.8	13.6	% Profit Before Taxes/Total Assets	24.8	12.7	10.5	23.0	13.2	11.3
8.0	7.0	6.5		11.8	5.7	2.9	9.1	3.9	8.8
1.5	.6	.6		1.1	-.9	-.2	2.3	-.8	3.6
8.7	9.4	9.4	Sales/Net Fixed Assets	16.8	15.0	8.5	9.8	9.0	7.2
6.1	5.5	5.7		8.6	7.6	6.1	5.0	5.0	4.2
3.8	3.8	3.2		3.6	3.1	2.9	2.8	3.0	3.6
3.5	3.5	3.7	Sales/Total Assets	5.7	4.1	3.5	3.6	3.8	2.8
2.8	2.8	2.6		3.4	2.9	2.7	2.4	2.6	2.5
2.2	2.0	1.7		1.6	1.9	1.8	1.5	1.7	1.8
(114) 2.0	(105) 2.1	(141) 1.9	% Depr., Dep., Amort./Sales	(11) 1.9	(32) 1.8	(16) 1.6	(22) 2.5	(35) 1.8	(25) 2.1
2.7	3.1	2.9		4.0	2.6	4.0	3.7	2.7	2.8
4.1	4.6	4.4		4.8	3.4	4.9	5.5	4.1	4.1
(49) 2.1	(41) 1.8	(61) 2.2	% Officers', Directors', Owners' Comp/Sales		(21) 4.5	(10) 3.1		(10) 1.8	
4.7	4.2	4.8			5.7	4.8		2.5	
8.4		7.0			7.2	16.4		4.0	
4075103M	2606261M	3076495M	Net Sales ($)	7375M	67381M	63499M	174661M	579516M	2184063M
1326848M	1062783M	1431843M	Total Assets ($)	2674M	38079M	31404M	98305M	272195M	989186M

M = $ thousand   MM = $ million
See Pages 1 through 15 for Explanation of Ratios and Data

Current Data Sorted By Assets　　　　　　　　　　**Comparative Historical Data**

Type of Statement (# Postretirement Benefits)

0-500M	500M-2MM	2-10MM	10-50MM	50-100MM	100-250MM		4/1/90-3/31/91 ALL	4/1/91-3/31/92 ALL
2	4	2	1			# Postretirement Benefits		
	1	14	14	3	1	Unqualified	32	33
2	6	11	2			Reviewed	20	11
7	10	1	1			Compiled	11	16
1						Tax Returns		2
3		7	3			Other	15	12
	43 (4/1-9/30/94)		48 (10/1/94-3/31/95)					
13	21	33	20	3	1	NUMBER OF STATEMENTS	78	74

Assets

0-500M %	500M-2MM %	2-10MM %	10-50MM %	50-100MM %	100-250MM %	ASSETS	4/1/90-3/31/91 ALL %	4/1/91-3/31/92 ALL %
5.2	-.1	7.2	10.3			Cash & Equivalents	6.3	7.3
18.3	22.0	17.7	11.7			Trade Receivables - (net)	16.4	18.0
34.3	30.5	27.0	23.9			Inventory	30.9	28.2
1.5	5.4	1.2	1.9			All Other Current	1.4	1.5
59.4	57.7	53.2	47.8			Total Current	55.0	54.9
31.3	37.6	39.0	43.8			Fixed Assets (net)	36.2	35.3
4.5	1.2	1.9	1.8			Intangibles (net)	2.5	3.4
4.8	3.5	6.0	6.6			All Other Non-Current	6.4	6.4
100.0	100.0	100.0	100.0			Total	100.0	100.0

Liabilities

0-500M	500M-2MM	2-10MM	10-50MM	50-100MM	100-250MM	LIABILITIES	4/1/90-3/31/91	4/1/91-3/31/92
6.7	14.2	17.0	4.2			Notes Payable-Short Term	13.5	7.9
4.7	6.1	5.4	2.8			Cur. Mat. -L/T/D	3.5	3.9
14.6	20.4	11.6	6.8			Trade Payables	12.9	11.8
.2	.3	.4	.6			Income Taxes Payable	.8	.8
8.1	4.6	4.8	5.6			All Other Current	6.9	6.2
34.3	45.5	39.2	20.0			Total Current	37.6	30.6
23.6	12.3	15.3	16.2			Long Term Debt	17.9	21.0
.2	.6	.8	1.5			Deferred Taxes	1.2	.7
19.4	17.6	4.0	3.9			All Other-Non-Current	2.6	6.0
22.5	24.0	40.6	58.5			Net Worth	40.7	41.7
100.0	100.0	100.0	100.0			Total Liabilities & Net Worth	100.0	100.0

Income Data

0-500M	500M-2MM	2-10MM	10-50MM	50-100MM	100-250MM	INCOME DATA	4/1/90-3/31/91	4/1/91-3/31/92
100.0	100.0	100.0	100.0			Net Sales	100.0	100.0
38.6	33.3	28.5	32.9			Gross Profit	33.3	35.4
34.9	31.1	27.2	26.3			Operating Expenses	28.2	29.4
3.7	2.2	1.4	6.6			Operating Profit	5.1	6.0
2.4	1.5	1.3	1.1			All Other Expenses (net)	1.2	2.4
1.3	.7	.1	5.5			Profit Before Taxes	3.9	3.6

Ratios

0-500M	500M-2MM	2-10MM	10-50MM	50-100MM	100-250MM	RATIOS	4/1/90-3/31/91	4/1/91-3/31/92
2.4	3.2	2.8	4.5			Current	2.4	3.7
1.9	1.2	1.4	2.4				1.4	2.0
1.2	.7	1.1	1.5				1.1	1.2
1.1	1.0	1.4	2.0			Quick	.9	1.7
.9	(20) .6	.6	1.0				.6	.7
.2	.3	.3	.5				.4	.4
7 51.2	7 50.0	18 20.1	16 23.1			Sales/Receivables	12 29.3	15 23.7
33 11.2	24 15.5	27 13.6	22 16.3				21 17.0	23 16.1
40 9.1	38 9.5	31 11.6	31 11.7				35 10.5	34 10.7
50 7.3	33 11.1	31 11.6	54 6.8			Cost of Sales/Inventory	47 7.8	41 8.8
66 5.5	53 6.9	48 7.6	66 5.5				68 5.4	68 5.4
87 4.2	81 4.5	83 4.4	101 3.6				91 4.0	96 3.8
10 37.6	17 21.5	13 28.8	11 32.2			Cost of Sales/Payables	11 34.5	13 27.5
25 14.4	30 12.2	23 15.6	21 17.1				20 17.9	21 17.6
48 7.6	51 7.1	47 7.8	30 12.3				36 10.1	39 9.4
7.9	6.5	6.7	4.7			Sales/Working Capital	6.8	5.1
13.0	31.3	19.8	6.2				14.0	9.2
27.6	-13.3	121.9	18.6				54.4	46.3
3.8	6.0	8.7	16.0			EBIT/Interest	6.9	6.5
(12) 2.1	1.6	(29) 1.7	(19) 3.8				(70) 2.8	(69) 2.6
-1.6	.0	-.0	2.5				1.3	1.3
		6.6	4.2			Net Profit + Depr., Dep., Amort./Cur. Mat. L./T/D	6.3	3.5
		(16) 2.5	(12) 3.1				(44) 3.6	(35) 2.0
		.3	1.8				1.7	.8
.8	.6	.4	.5			Fixed/Worth	.5	.5
1.3	1.6	1.1	.8				1.0	1.0
-9.2	4.0	2.5	1.4				1.8	2.2
1.0	1.4	.7	.2			Debt/Worth	.6	.6
2.7	2.2	1.6	.6				1.7	1.5
-37.4	5.4	3.9	1.4				4.1	4.6
	28.2	37.7	29.7			% Profit Before Taxes/Tangible Net Worth	31.6	34.8
	(18) 8.8	(30) 11.5	(19) 15.0				(71) 19.8	(66) 19.1
	-8.8	-2.5	6.4				5.5	6.7
11.2	10.2	16.3	14.0			% Profit Before Taxes/Total Assets	14.6	14.0
8.3	2.8	1.8	6.9				7.5	6.9
-4.9	-3.0	-5.0	4.0				1.5	1.1
16.1	16.6	13.3	6.0			Sales/Net Fixed Assets	15.0	13.1
12.5	8.5	6.3	3.6				7.4	6.4
7.3	5.2	4.0	2.7				4.2	3.9
4.0	4.1	3.1	2.4			Sales/Total Assets	3.2	3.2
3.0	3.0	2.6	1.6				2.3	2.3
2.7	1.9	1.7	1.3				1.8	1.5
1.1	1.0	1.6	2.2			% Depr., Dep., Amort./Sales	1.5	1.5
2.3	(20) 1.9	2.5	(18) 3.0				(73) 2.3	(69) 2.5
2.7	2.9	3.4	5.4				3.8	3.8
	3.0	1.4				% Officers', Directors', Owners' Comp/Sales	1.5	1.9
	(12) 7.0	(16) 2.2					(37) 2.9	(26) 4.3
	14.2	3.7					7.7	8.0
13619M	63979M	370075M	929113M	408810M	208970M	Net Sales ($)	1720798M	1396402M
4168M	21558M	157546M	504581M	201899M	199714M	Total Assets ($)	881802M	807759M

M = $ thousand　　MM = $ million
See Pages 1 through 15 for Explanation of Ratios and Data

Comparative Historical Data | Current Data Sorted By Sales

H1	H2	H3		0-1MM	1-3MM	3-5MM	5-10MM	10-25MM	25MM & OVER
1	1	9	# Postretirement Benefits	2	2	1	3	1	
			Type of Statement						
31	28	33	Unqualified		1		3	14	15
14	17	21	Reviewed		7	1	7	4	2
19	14	19	Compiled	4	7	4	3		1
		1	Tax Returns						
12	15	17	Other	2	5		5	2	3
4/1/92-3/31/93 ALL	4/1/93-3/31/94 ALL	4/1/94-3/31/95 ALL		43 (4/1-9/30/94)			48 (10/1/94-3/31/95)		
76	75	91	**NUMBER OF STATEMENTS**	6	21	5	18	20	21
%	%	%	**ASSETS**	%	%	%	%	%	%
8.3	9.0	6.0	Cash & Equivalents		2.8		2.5	7.8	8.8
16.9	16.0	17.2	Trade Receivables - (net)		16.5		23.3	15.1	13.1
28.4	28.8	28.4	Inventory		29.0		30.5	26.5	26.8
1.4	1.4	2.4	All Other Current		2.3		2.1	1.0	1.6
55.1	55.1	54.0	Total Current		50.6		58.4	50.5	50.3
36.0	35.9	38.7	Fixed Assets (net)		42.5		34.3	39.9	43.6
3.4	2.5	2.1	Intangibles (net)		1.8		1.9	1.6	1.7
5.6	6.5	5.3	All Other Non-Current		5.1		5.3	8.1	4.3
100.0	100.0	100.0	Total		100.0		100.0	100.0	100.0
			LIABILITIES						
9.5	9.6	12.0	Notes Payable-Short Term		10.6		20.9	14.8	6.5
4.4	4.7	4.7	Cur. Mat.-L /T/D		6.7		6.4	3.7	2.3
10.7	10.6	13.1	Trade Payables		17.1		13.7	10.4	8.8
.6	1.7	.6	Income Taxes Payable		.3		.2	.5	1.5
4.8	6.4	5.4	All Other Current		6.5		4.2	4.5	6.3
30.0	33.1	35.7	Total Current		41.3		45.4	33.9	25.4
18.8	19.8	16.1	Long Term Debt		22.0		15.4	13.5	14.5
.7	.6	.8	Deferred Taxes		.5		.6	.6	1.8
4.7	6.0	9.2	All Other-Non-Current		16.3		5.2	3.7	2.7
45.7	40.6	38.2	Net Worth		20.0		33.3	48.3	55.6
100.0	100.0	100.0	Total Liabilities & Net Worth		100.0		100.0	100.0	100.0
			INCOME DATA						
100.0	100.0	100.0	Net Sales		100.0		100.0	100.0	100.0
36.0	35.0	32.3	Gross Profit		35.4		31.0	26.2	34.1
29.8	31.1	28.9	Operating Expenses		33.0		28.5	25.0	26.8
6.2	3.9	3.4	Operating Profit		2.4		2.5	1.2	7.3
1.2	1.6	1.4	All Other Expenses (net)		1.8		1.8	.4	1.1
4.9	2.3	1.9	Profit Before Taxes		.6		.7	.7	6.2
			RATIOS						
3.5	3.3	2.8			1.9		3.4	2.9	3.5
1.9	1.6	1.5	Current		1.2		1.2	1.6	2.4
1.2	1.1	1.1			.7		.9	1.1	1.2
1.6	1.7	1.3			1.1		1.3	1.5	1.6
.9	.7	(90) .6	Quick		.4	(17)	.6	.8	.8
.4	.4	.3			.2		.4	.2	.4
10 36.4	11 33.5	13 28.9		6 58.9	20 17.9		14 26.5	16 22.8	
22 16.3	21 17.4	25 14.6	Sales/Receivables	15 24.3	29 12.6		26 14.1	24 15.3	
35 10.3	36 10.2	37 9.9		37 9.8	41 8.8		31 11.9	34 10.8	
40 9.2	36 10.2	42 8.7		47 7.8	29 12.5		32 11.4	55 6.6	
66 5.5	69 5.3	62 5.9	Cost of Sales/Inventory	66 5.5	57 6.4		49 7.5	70 5.2	
107 3.4	111 3.3	91 4.0		81 4.5	91 4.0		81 4.5	114 3.2	
11 34.5	10 36.6	13 28.9		15 24.9	13 28.8		12 29.7	10 35.7	
17 21.0	20 17.9	23 15.7	Cost of Sales/Payables	26 14.0	25 14.4		18 19.8	22 16.8	
30 12.0	36 10.2	43 8.5		51 7.1	51 7.2		30 12.2	29 12.8	
5.4	5.3	6.0		10.6	5.7		6.1	4.9	
9.9	14.8	15.4	Sales/Working Capital	34.1	26.1		12.1	9.5	
39.5	81.8	59.1		-16.1	-68.7		43.7	33.4	
16.0	10.4	8.7		3.6	3.8		9.2	26.8	
(73) 4.2	(66) 2.6	(85) 2.7	EBIT/Interest	1.6	(16) 1.2	(18) 4.1	(20) 5.3		
1.4	1.1	.8		.6	-.6		1.2	2.4	
10.0	4.5	4.1		1.8	3.4			5.6	
(40) 3.5	(35) 2.1	(44) 1.9	Net Profit + Depr., Dep., Amort./Cur. Mat. L/T/D	(10) 1.4	(10) 1.7		(11) 3.0		
1.1	.6	.8		1.0	-.1		1.6		
.4	.4	.6		.9	.3		.4	.7	
.9	1.0	1.1	Fixed/Worth	1.6	1.4		.9	.8	
1.9	1.9	2.2		4.1	3.3		2.0	1.3	
.4	.6	.6		1.4	1.3		.5	.4	
1.3	1.5	1.6	Debt/Worth	2.3	2.4		.9	.8	
3.0	3.4	3.9		9.0	4.9		4.8	2.0	
37.6	33.6	30.8		30.8	44.1		36.6	34.6	
(70) 21.0	(68) 16.0	(80) 13.1	% Profit Before Taxes/Tangible Net Worth	(18) 14.2	(16) 1.6	(19) 12.9	(20) 15.1		
7.0	4.3	1.2		-2.9	-15.1		1.5	5.8	
18.9	15.0	13.7		9.7	12.4		16.8	22.2	
11.0	7.0	5.1	% Profit Before Taxes/Total Assets	2.8	.6		6.9	7.7	
1.6	.9	-.5		-1.9	-8.8		.3	2.6	
13.9	14.5	13.0		13.9	14.2		8.6	8.4	
6.4	7.4	6.3	Sales/Net Fixed Assets	7.3	7.9		5.5	4.1	
3.4	3.8	3.6		3.9	3.9		3.7	2.7	
3.4	3.1	3.2		3.6	3.1		3.1	3.0	
2.4	2.3	2.5	Sales/Total Assets	3.0	2.4		2.4	1.8	
1.6	1.6	1.6		1.9	1.8		1.6	1.4	
1.7	1.7	1.6		1.2	1.5		2.1	2.0	
(73) 2.6	(69) 2.6	(85) 2.4	% Depr., Dep., Amort./Sales	1.9	(17) 2.2		2.8	(16) 2.9	
3.9	3.9	3.7		2.8	3.6		3.9	5.2	
2.2	1.3	1.6		2.6			1.1		
(32) 5.0	(31) 3.9	(39) 3.1	% Officers', Directors', Owners' Comp/Sales	(10) 5.3		(11) 1.4			
8.7	10.3	6.2		9.0			2.4		
1587607M	1438079M	1994566M	Net Sales ($)	4244M	38100M	19390M	133035M	284252M	1515545M
993016M	718124M	1089466M	Total Assets ($)	1741M	17686M	5163M	58252M	148087M	858537M

M = $ thousand   MM = $ million
See Pages 1 through 15 for Explanation of Ratios and Data

Current Data Sorted By Assets							Comparative Historical Data	
	1	1	2	1	1	**# Postretirement Benefits**		
						Type of Statement		
	1	10	21	7	5	Unqualified	40	37
	6	10	2			Reviewed	18	22
	5	2	3			Compiled	12	9
1			1			Tax Returns	1	1
	3	10	6	2	2	Other	19	16
	51 (4/1-9/30/94)			46 (10/1/94-3/31/95)			4/1/90-3/31/91	4/1/91-3/31/92
0-500M	500M-2MM	2-10MM	10-50MM	50-100MM	100-250MM		ALL	ALL
1	15	32	33	9	7	**NUMBER OF STATEMENTS**	90	85
%	%	%	%	%	%	**ASSETS**	%	%
	7.4	2.8	5.6			Cash & Equivalents	4.9	5.0
	20.9	22.6	14.2			Trade Receivables - (net)	18.7	17.9
	31.4	28.6	34.2			Inventory	37.3	36.0
	.2	1.6	2.9			All Other Current	1.9	2.2
	59.7	55.8	56.9			Total Current	62.8	61.1
	25.7	34.8	36.1			Fixed Assets (net)	29.9	29.2
	3.1	2.9	2.1			Intangibles (net)	1.5	3.1
	11.5	6.4	4.9			All Other Non-Current	5.8	6.7
	100.0	100.0	100.0			Total	100.0	100.0
						LIABILITIES		
	9.8	12.5	19.4			Notes Payable-Short Term	14.6	14.9
	1.3	3.0	2.2			Cur. Mat. -L/T/D	2.8	2.8
	19.0	18.8	11.6			Trade Payables	17.8	14.8
	.4	.3	.1			Income Taxes Payable	.6	.5
	6.1	5.1	5.6			All Other Current	5.6	7.5
	36.6	39.6	38.9			Total Current	41.4	40.5
	8.5	19.1	13.2			Long Term Debt	14.9	16.7
	.2	.5	.5			Deferred Taxes	1.1	.8
	3.4	5.0	3.6			All Other-Non-Current	2.6	1.8
	51.3	35.8	43.8			Net Worth	40.0	40.2
	100.0	100.0	100.0			Total Liabilities & Net Worth	100.0	100.0
						INCOME DATA		
	100.0	100.0	100.0			Net Sales	100.0	100.0
	25.3	24.1	22.6			Gross Profit	24.1	23.4
	22.2	19.3	16.9			Operating Expenses	18.6	18.2
	3.1	4.8	5.8			Operating Profit	5.5	5.2
	.3	1.0	1.6			All Other Expenses (net)	1.2	1.4
	2.8	3.8	4.2			Profit Before Taxes	4.2	3.8
						RATIOS		
	2.7	1.8	2.2			Current	2.3	2.4
	1.8	1.4	1.4				1.5	1.4
	1.2	1.1	1.1				1.2	1.1
	1.1	.9	1.0			Quick	.9	.9
	.9	.7	.4				.6	.5
	.3	.4	.3				.3	.3
	14 25.9	23 15.6	24 15.4			Sales/Receivables	22 16.8	19 19.1
	28 13.2	29 12.6	30 12.0				26 13.9	27 13.6
	39 9.4	40 9.2	38 9.5				32 11.5	35 10.5
	27 13.7	31 11.7	39 9.4			Cost of Sales/Inventory	44 8.3	39 9.3
	47 7.7	47 7.7	94 3.9				81 4.5	81 4.5
	79 4.6	85 4.3	152 2.4				146 2.5	130 2.8
	7 51.3	21 17.7	22 16.6			Cost of Sales/Payables	17 22.1	12 29.9
	26 13.9	31 11.8	29 12.5				29 12.4	28 13.1
	51 7.1	46 8.0	51 7.1				59 6.2	49 7.4
	4.8	9.4	5.1			Sales/Working Capital	5.7	5.5
	11.3	15.1	7.6				12.9	12.7
	46.4	78.4	21.5				39.3	44.2
	12.6	(28) 7.9	(29) 4.8			EBIT/Interest	5.9	5.2
	(14) 4.5	3.3	2.3				(85) 3.2	(80) 2.6
	1.0	1.3	1.2				1.5	1.5
		(18) 8.7	3.3			Net Profit + Depr., Dep.,	8.1	8.9
		2.5	(12) 2.4			Amort./Cur. Mat. L /T/D	(59) 4.2	(52) 3.4
		1.2	1.4				1.2	1.5
	.3	.5	.6			Fixed/Worth	.4	.3
	.5	1.4	.8				.7	.8
	.6	2.0	1.6				1.4	1.5
	.5	1.3	.8			Debt/Worth	.9	.8
	1.1	2.3	1.4				1.6	1.7
	1.9	4.7	2.9				3.6	3.7
	28.2	54.6	26.3			% Profit Before Taxes/Tangible	36.4	36.1
	20.9	(29) 19.9	13.5			Net Worth	(89) 17.4	(80) 16.1
	.4	4.2	2.7				7.4	8.9
	12.5	14.1	9.1			% Profit Before Taxes/Total	14.0	11.7
	9.7	5.5	4.2			Assets	7.4	6.0
	.4	.5	1.4				2.4	2.6
	17.6	14.2	6.9			Sales/Net Fixed Assets	14.2	17.1
	11.5	7.7	4.5				8.0	7.4
	5.8	3.4	2.8				4.6	4.7
	4.4	3.2	2.0			Sales/Total Assets	3.1	2.7
	3.1	2.5	1.6				2.0	1.9
	1.2	1.8	1.2				1.6	1.4
	.9	1.4	1.8			% Depr., Dep., Amort./Sales	1.2	1.1
	(14) 1.4	(31) 2.1	(28) 2.4				(84) 2.0	(79) 2.0
	3.2	3.7	3.7				2.8	2.9
						% Officers', Directors',	1.2	1.0
						Owners' Comp/Sales	(23) 2.5	(18) 1.9
							5.3	2.7
1482M	59459M	440053M	1171881M	1377506M	1530110M	Net Sales ($)	4118211M	4303987M
165M	20631M	171014M	767794M	644334M	1016744M	Total Assets ($)	2120801M	2223196M

M = $ thousand   MM = $ million
See Pages 1 through 15 for Explanation of Ratios and Data

Comparative Historical Data / Current Data Sorted By Sales

Comp. Hist.				# Postretirement Benefits / Type of Statement	Current Data Sorted By Sales					
					1			1		4
4	4	6								
38	39	44		Unqualified		1		3	12	28
23	18	18		Reviewed			2	8	6	2
5	9	10		Compiled	1	4	1	1	2	1
1	1	2		Tax Returns		1			1	
9	17	23		Other		1	1	6	6	9
4/1/92-3/31/93 ALL	4/1/93-3/31/94 ALL	4/1/94-3/31/95 ALL			51 (4/1-9/30/94)			46 (10/1/94-3/31/95)		
					0-1MM	1-3MM	3-5MM	5-10MM	10-25MM	25MM & OVER
76	84	97		**NUMBER OF STATEMENTS**	1	7	4	18	27	40
%	%	%		**ASSETS**	%	%	%	%	%	%
4.4	6.4	4.6		Cash & Equivalents				4.2	4.6	4.4
19.0	16.9	18.7		Trade Receivables - (net)				20.4	18.8	16.7
38.9	34.4	32.4		Inventory				20.7	31.9	37.8
2.2	1.6	2.1		All Other Current				1.0	1.9	3.3
64.5	59.3	57.9		Total Current				46.4	57.1	62.3
28.6	31.2	33.4		Fixed Assets (net)				38.5	35.1	31.5
1.1	1.9	2.3		Intangibles (net)				4.3	2.2	1.0
5.8	7.7	6.4		All Other Non-Current				10.8	5.5	5.2
100.0	100.0	100.0		Total				100.0	100.0	100.0
				LIABILITIES						
13.6	13.6	14.1		Notes Payable-Short Term				9.0	16.7	15.4
2.1	2.7	2.3		Cur. Mat.-L /T/D				3.3	2.5	2.3
16.6	13.7	15.9		Trade Payables				18.5	16.9	13.9
.5	.3	.4		Income Taxes Payable				.6	.2	.2
7.2	6.1	5.7		All Other Current				9.0	4.5	6.0
39.9	36.4	38.4		Total Current				40.4	40.8	37.9
15.0	17.9	15.0		Long Term Debt				15.7	18.8	13.4
.9	.8	.7		Deferred Taxes				.5	.2	1.4
2.7	3.2	3.6		All Other-Non-Current				4.8	2.3	4.3
41.4	41.8	42.2		Net Worth				38.6	37.8	43.0
100.0	100.0	100.0		Total Liabilities & Net Worth				100.0	100.0	100.0
				INCOME DATA						
100.0	100.0	100.0		Net Sales				100.0	100.0	100.0
21.2	23.8	23.1		Gross Profit				28.4	27.2	18.3
16.5	19.3	18.0		Operating Expenses				23.1	20.3	14.1
4.8	4.4	5.1		Operating Profit				5.3	6.9	4.2
1.2	1.0	1.2		All Other Expenses (net)				.8	1.5	1.4
3.6	3.5	3.9		Profit Before Taxes				4.5	5.4	2.9
				RATIOS						
2.4	2.6	2.2						1.8	2.0	2.7
1.5	1.6	1.5		Current				1.1	1.4	1.6
1.3	1.3	1.2						.9	1.2	1.2
1.1	1.2	1.0						.9	.9	.9
.5	.7	.6		Quick				.6	.5	.5
.4	.4	.4						.4	.3	.3
21 17.3	21 17.3	24 15.4						20 18.1	24 15.3	24 15.2
28 13.0	27 13.3	29 12.6		Sales/Receivables				30 12.1	29 12.6	29 12.4
35 10.4	37 9.9	39 9.3						40 9.2	39 9.3	38 9.5
42 8.6	41 8.8	35 10.5						23 16.2	33 10.9	49 7.5
89 4.1	74 4.9	76 4.8		Cost of Sales/Inventory				43 8.5	60 6.1	94 3.9
126 2.9	140 2.6	114 3.2						76 4.8	159 2.3	130 2.8
14 26.2	15 24.5	20 18.3						24 15.5	21 17.8	20 18.5
25 14.4	26 14.1	29 12.5		Cost of Sales/Payables				38 9.6	33 11.2	26 13.8
51 7.2	42 8.6	49 7.5						48 7.6	70 5.2	47 7.7
5.2	4.6	5.5						11.1	7.2	4.8
10.0	9.0	11.3		Sales/Working Capital				55.3	12.1	7.4
19.8	20.7	39.5						-58.7	26.7	17.5
(69) 5.8	(73) 9.6	(86) 6.1			(17) 12.1				(24) 5.5	(35) 4.6
3.4	4.0	3.0		EBIT/Interest	7.7				2.9	2.5
1.7	1.6	1.4			1.9				1.9	1.4
(40) 11.3	(38) 5.1	(48) 5.4			(10) 11.3				(11) 4.0	(24) 4.8
4.6	3.0	2.5		Net Profit + Depr., Dep., Amort./Cur. Mat. L/T/D	3.3				2.4	2.5
2.5	1.5	1.9			1.5				1.1	2.0
.3	.4	.5						.5	.5	.6
.7	.8	.8		Fixed/Worth				1.2	1.2	.8
1.4	1.7	1.5						1.9	2.1	1.2
.7	.6	.8						1.1	.7	.9
1.6	1.6	1.6		Debt/Worth				1.8	2.3	1.3
3.2	3.0	3.0						3.0	4.8	2.9
(72) 38.4	(78) 36.7	(94) 33.2			(17) 40.4				(26) 46.3	(39) 24.5
19.7	17.1	16.0		% Profit Before Taxes/Tangible Net Worth	28.2				21.2	13.2
8.8	8.0	3.5			8.1				7.3	2.5
14.5	15.2	10.9						16.7	10.6	8.0
7.4	7.0	5.6		% Profit Before Taxes/Total Assets				10.3	6.5	4.1
2.7	2.1	1.5						1.9	3.3	1.1
17.3	11.2	10.7						14.9	10.7	7.2
9.5	6.2	5.8		Sales/Net Fixed Assets				4.9	6.4	5.5
4.1	4.0	3.6						3.2	2.6	3.8
2.9	2.6	2.8						3.6	2.8	2.1
2.1	1.9	1.9		Sales/Total Assets				2.5	2.0	1.8
1.6	1.3	1.4						1.6	1.3	1.5
(68) 1.0	(77) 1.4	(89) 1.4						1.2	(24) 1.6	(36) 1.4
1.9	2.1	2.2		% Depr., Dep., Amort./Sales				1.9	2.1	2.6
2.8	3.5	3.3						3.7	3.5	3.1
(15) 1.4	(16) 1.0	(20) 1.0								
2.3	2.2	2.2		% Officers', Directors', Owners' Comp/Sales						
4.7	4.6	4.0								
4480469M	3988196M	4580491M		Net Sales ($)	840M	13286M	13375M	137278M	464817M	3950895M
2341532M	2456803M	2620682M		Total Assets ($)	1331M	7907M	5370M	60960M	288673M	2256441M

M = $ thousand   MM = $ million
See Pages 1 through 15 for Explanation of Ratios and Data

Current Data Sorted By Assets							Comparative Historical Data	
2	3	3	6		2	# Postretirement Benefits		
						Type of Statement		
1	3	11	23	6	6	Unqualified	68	60
1	7	17	6	1		Reviewed	28	30
1	4	8	3			Compiled	18	26
1						Tax Returns	2	
2	10	13	13	2	3	Other	42	30
	46 (4/1-9/30/94)		96 (10/1/94-3/31/95)				4/1/90-3/31/91	4/1/91-3/31/92
0-500M	500M-2MM	2-10MM	10-50MM	50-100MM	100-250MM		ALL	ALL
6	24	49	45	9	9	**NUMBER OF STATEMENTS**	158	146
%	%	%	%	%	%	**ASSETS**	%	%
	6.8	5.7	8.4			Cash & Equivalents	6.5	6.1
	23.1	27.2	27.0			Trade Receivables - (net)	25.6	24.8
	24.5	18.7	17.0			Inventory	18.1	17.9
	5.1	.7	2.7			All Other Current	1.2	1.4
	59.5	52.3	55.1			Total Current	51.4	50.2
	35.0	39.4	36.1			Fixed Assets (net)	38.4	40.5
	1.4	1.4	1.7			Intangibles (net)	1.7	1.6
	4.1	6.9	7.1			All Other Non-Current	8.5	7.7
	100.0	100.0	100.0			Total	100.0	100.0
						LIABILITIES		
	15.6	9.3	5.9			Notes Payable-Short Term	10.0	8.7
	4.0	3.2	3.6			Cur. Mat. -L/T/D	4.5	4.5
	20.0	21.8	20.3			Trade Payables	19.8	19.0
	.4	.3	.1			Income Taxes Payable	.4	.4
	12.4	6.1	9.5			All Other Current	7.6	6.9
	52.4	40.6	39.3			Total Current	42.3	39.5
	13.3	15.7	13.3			Long Term Debt	18.9	18.9
	.4	.9	.9			Deferred Taxes	.9	.8
	1.1	2.1	4.2			All Other-Non-Current	2.3	3.2
	32.9	40.7	42.3			Net Worth	35.5	37.7
	100.0	100.0	100.0			Total Liabilities & Net Worth	100.0	100.0
						INCOME DATA		
	100.0	100.0	100.0			Net Sales	100.0	100.0
	22.6	23.2	18.7			Gross Profit	21.1	25.1
	20.3	20.5	15.4			Operating Expenses	18.6	21.7
	2.3	2.7	3.2			Operating Profit	2.5	3.4
	.6	1.0	.4			All Other Expenses (net)	.8	.9
	1.7	1.7	2.8			Profit Before Taxes	1.7	2.5
						RATIOS		
	1.3	1.9	2.1				1.7	2.1
	1.1	1.3	1.5			Current	1.2	1.3
	1.0	1.0	1.1				.9	.9
	1.0	1.1	1.4				1.1	1.3
	.6	.9	1.0			Quick	(144) .7	.8
	.3	.6	.7				.5	.5
	(12) 30.6	(25) 14.8	(22) 16.5				(19) 19.2	(20) 18.5
	18 20.0	28 13.1	27 13.4			Sales/Receivables	25 14.5	26 14.1
	26 14.2	35 10.3	35 10.5				32 11.5	33 11.1
	13 28.2	12 29.8	8 45.4				11 32.1	15 24.7
	16 22.4	23 16.0	21 17.8			Cost of Sales/Inventory	22 16.3	24 15.4
	32 11.4	43 8.4	37 9.9				34 10.8	43 8.4
	10 34.9	21 17.0	18 20.8				16 23.1	16 22.3
	17 21.5	27 13.3	23 15.9			Cost of Sales/Payables	22 16.3	26 14.3
	25 14.4	37 10.0	31 11.7				30 12.0	34 10.7
	23.7	12.4	9.3				13.6	11.9
	64.8	25.7	18.8			Sales/Working Capital	39.1	29.3
	NM	-649.2	94.3				-87.6	-95.2
	3.0	6.1	16.7				5.8	8.2
	(21) 1.9	(48) 2.8	(41) 4.5			EBIT/Interest	(145) 2.1	(134) 2.4
	-.1	.6	2.1				.6	1.2
		3.8	17.6				5.8	7.1
	(20)	2.8	(18) 4.3			Net Profit + Depr., Dep., Amort./Cur. Mat. L./T/D	(89) 1.8	(74) 2.5
		.8	1.6				.7	1.1
	.5	.5	.5				.5	.6
	.9	1.0	.8			Fixed/Worth	1.1	1.2
	1.7	1.9	1.4				2.3	2.3
	1.4	.9	.7				1.1	.9
	2.1	1.5	1.5			Debt/Worth	2.0	1.8
	2.9	3.3	3.7				4.4	4.2
	33.5	22.0	46.0				32.5	32.8
	(23) 7.1	(47) 7.4	(44) 13.9			% Profit Before Taxes/Tangible Net Worth	(142) 16.3	(134) 18.8
	-3.6	1.7	6.1				.6	6.7
	8.9	9.5	12.4				12.2	12.2
	3.1	3.4	6.3			% Profit Before Taxes/Total Assets	4.3	5.7
	-1.5	-1.0	2.3				-1.2	1.2
	29.7	16.0	15.5				19.1	15.6
	17.0	9.0	8.0			Sales/Net Fixed Assets	9.6	8.3
	6.9	4.7	5.1				5.8	4.8
	6.9	4.4	4.2				4.5	4.2
	4.7	3.2	2.9			Sales/Total Assets	3.4	3.3
	3.2	2.1	2.3				2.6	2.2
	1.0	.9	1.2				1.0	1.1
	(22) 1.4	(47) 1.9	(42) 1.9			% Depr., Dep., Amort./Sales	(143) 1.7	(134) 1.8
	2.4	2.6	2.8				2.9	2.9
		2.0					.8	.8
	(13)	2.4				% Officers', Directors', Owners' Comp/Sales	(38) 1.7	(40) 1.8
		6.2					4.0	3.3
5931M	168944M	912349M	3906862M	2515585M	3240575M	Net Sales ($)	9654271M	11313693M
1520M	28567M	272575M	1021452M	658875M	1296451M	Total Assets ($)	2857887M	3542889M

M = $ thousand   MM = $ million
See Pages 1 through 15 for Explanation of Ratios and Data

Comparative Historical Data				Current Data Sorted By Sales					
2	6	16	# Postretirement Benefits	1	1	1	1	4	8
			Type of Statement						
59	58	50	Unqualified	1			2	10	37
33	23	32	Reviewed	2	3	2	4	11	10
25	13	16	Compiled		2	2	4	4	4
	2	1	Tax Returns	1					
40	40	43	Other	1	3	4	6	9	20
4/1/92- 3/31/93	4/1/93- 3/31/94	4/1/94- 3/31/95		46 (4/1-9/30/94)			96 (10/1/94-3/31/95)		
ALL	ALL	ALL		0-1MM	1-3MM	3-5MM	5-10MM	10-25MM	25MM & OVER
157	136	142	**NUMBER OF STATEMENTS**	5	8	8	16	34	71
%	%	%	**ASSETS**	%	%	%	%	%	%
7.4	7.6	6.9	Cash & Equivalents				7.9	7.1	6.7
25.1	27.8	25.5	Trade Receivables - (net)				25.2	24.0	27.9
17.9	15.9	18.3	Inventory				24.7	21.0	15.6
2.8	2.3	2.3	All Other Current				4.0	2.0	2.3
53.1	53.6	53.0	Total Current				61.9	54.0	52.5
38.2	36.7	38.3	Fixed Assets (net)				27.7	38.0	37.8
1.4	2.1	2.0	Intangibles (net)				.6	1.7	2.6
7.3	7.6	6.7	All Other Non-Current				9.9	6.3	7.1
100.0	100.0	100.0	Total				100.0	100.0	100.0
			LIABILITIES						
8.4	8.5	8.3	Notes Payable-Short Term				11.2	9.9	5.9
4.5	3.4	3.2	Cur. Mat.-L /T/D				3.4	2.9	3.2
21.1	21.3	20.4	Trade Payables				19.4	21.1	21.9
.3	1.6	.2	Income Taxes Payable				.4	.2	.1
7.9	9.1	8.9	All Other Current				7.2	7.7	10.4
42.2	44.0	41.0	Total Current				41.6	41.8	41.5
17.9	15.7	14.9	Long Term Debt				14.5	14.5	12.6
.7	.8	.7	Deferred Taxes				.6	1.0	.8
1.7	3.3	2.5	All Other-Non-Current				2.0	1.7	3.1
37.4	36.2	41.0	Net Worth				41.3	41.0	41.9
100.0	100.0	100.0	Total Liabilities & Net Worth				100.0	100.0	100.0
			INCOME DATA						
100.0	100.0	100.0	Net Sales				100.0	100.0	100.0
22.5	21.4	21.9	Gross Profit				22.3	23.0	18.0
19.2	18.9	19.0	Operating Expenses				20.2	19.4	15.5
3.3	2.5	3.0	Operating Profit				2.1	3.5	2.5
.5	1.0	.7	All Other Expenses (net)				.7	.6	.4
2.8	1.5	2.2	Profit Before Taxes				1.4	3.0	2.0
			RATIOS						
1.9	1.7	1.9	Current				2.8	1.9	1.8
1.2	1.3	1.3					1.3	1.2	1.3
1.0	1.0	1.1					1.2	1.0	1.1
1.1	1.2	1.2	Quick				1.2	1.1	1.2
.8	.8	.8					.7	.8	.9
.5	.6	.6					.6	.5	.6
19 18.9	22 16.8	21 17.4	Sales/Receivables				17 21.1	18 20.1	22 16.7
26 13.9	27 13.7	26 13.8					23 16.1	26 14.0	27 13.7
32 11.3	33 10.9	34 10.8					38 9.6	33 11.2	33 11.2
12 30.2	9 41.0	12 30.3	Cost of Sales/Inventory				18 20.4	13 27.6	8 44.8
24 15.1	17 22.0	20 17.9					28 12.9	23 16.1	17 21.0
41 8.9	31 11.9	36 10.2					46 7.9	46 8.0	26 13.8
19 19.7	17 20.9	17 21.4	Cost of Sales/Payables				13 28.5	18 20.5	17 21.3
24 15.0	24 15.0	23 15.8					19 18.8	26 14.0	23 16.0
35 10.5	33 11.1	33 11.0					37 9.9	35 10.4	30 12.0
12.8	14.3	12.8	Sales/Working Capital				8.0	14.6	13.9
37.2	33.6	27.9					20.4	42.6	31.5
-546.2	-158.0	156.8					71.0	-285.2	156.7
(147) 10.5	(122) 7.8	(127) 8.1	EBIT/Interest		(15) 3.1	(32) 9.0	(63) 14.0		
3.0	3.0	3.1				2.0	4.0	4.3	
1.4	1.2	1.1				.4	1.1	2.0	
(67) 5.3	(61) 5.0	(58) 8.0	Net Profit + Depr., Dep., Amort./Cur. Mat. L/T/D				(14) 3.6	(31) 15.9	
2.4	2.7	3.2					1.8	5.3	
.9	.9	1.3					.7	2.8	
.6	.6	.6	Fixed/Worth				.3	.5	.6
1.0	1.1	.9					.8	1.0	.9
2.1	1.9	1.7					1.3	1.8	1.4
1.0	1.0	.8	Debt/Worth				1.0	.8	.7
1.7	1.9	1.6					1.7	1.6	1.5
4.1	3.9	3.1					2.8	3.7	3.1
(149) 33.1	(125) 29.1	(137) 28.6	% Profit Before Taxes/Tangible Net Worth				22.9	(33) 31.3	(68) 31.0
18.0	13.7	11.6					5.9	15.0	12.8
5.7	2.6	2.5					-1.9	4.1	5.5
12.8	9.4	10.0	% Profit Before Taxes/Total Assets				7.9	13.7	10.3
6.3	5.0	5.3					3.1	5.7	6.2
1.3	.5	.7					-1.2	.8	1.3
16.5	17.1	17.0	Sales/Net Fixed Assets				29.7	18.0	15.8
8.4	9.5	8.4					15.9	8.9	9.0
5.2	5.6	5.1					7.0	4.6	5.5
4.3	4.5	4.8	Sales/Total Assets				5.5	5.2	4.8
3.2	3.4	3.3					3.4	3.2	3.3
2.4	2.6	2.4					2.6	2.1	2.6
(137) 1.1	(123) 1.1	(130) 1.0	% Depr., Dep., Amort./Sales				(15) .9	(31) .9	(64) .8
1.9	1.6	1.9					1.4	1.9	1.7
3.0	2.5	2.7					2.3	3.4	2.5
(38) .9	(32) 1.0	(31) 1.5	% Officers', Directors', Owners' Comp/Sales					(10) 2.3	
2.4	1.6	2.4						3.3	
5.3	3.2	5.1						7.2	
11318047M	11720039M	10750246M	Net Sales ($)	2478M	17179M	32949M	114740M	544386M	10038514M
3329360M	3355099M	3279440M	Total Assets ($)	2385M	10399M	11881M	44608M	213745M	2996422M

M = $ thousand   MM = $ million
See Pages 1 through 15 for Explanation of Ratios and Data

MANUFACTURERS—FLOUR & OTHER GRAIN MILL PRODUCTS. SIC# 2041

Current Data Sorted By Assets / Comparative Historical Data

 # Postretirement Benefits — Type of Statement

0-500M	500M-2MM	2-10MM	10-50MM	50-100MM	100-250MM		4/1/90-3/31/91 ALL	4/1/91-3/31/92 ALL
	2	1	1			# Postretirement Benefits		
	1	12	8	5		Unqualified	13	17
	7	3	1			Reviewed	7	6
1	6	3	1			Compiled	7	3
		1				Tax Returns		
3	3	1	2	4		Other	3	8
	34 (4/1-9/30/94)		28 (10/1/94-3/31/95)					

0-500M	500M-2MM	2-10MM	10-50MM	50-100MM	100-250MM		4/1/90-3/31/91 ALL	4/1/91-3/31/92 ALL
4	17	20	12	9		**NUMBER OF STATEMENTS**	30	34
%	%	%	%	%	%	**ASSETS**	%	%
	10.2	6.6	7.7			Cash & Equivalents	7.4	5.4
	27.6	16.0	19.6			Trade Receivables - (net)	21.5	17.3
	20.0	19.8	29.3			Inventory	23.7	23.9
	1.1	1.2	1.8			All Other Current	1.5	1.7
	58.9	43.6	58.4			Total Current	54.1	48.3
	37.6	46.7	34.1			Fixed Assets (net)	36.1	38.9
	.1	2.7	3.6			Intangibles (net)	1.2	4.0
	3.4	6.9	4.0			All Other Non-Current	8.6	8.8
	100.0	100.0	100.0			Total	100.0	100.0
						LIABILITIES		
	9.8	6.6	7.9			Notes Payable-Short Term	12.8	7.4
	5.0	5.3	1.1			Cur. Mat. -L/T/D	4.5	3.3
	20.4	11.3	15.2			Trade Payables	9.3	13.0
	.5	.2	.3			Income Taxes Payable	.1	.3
	5.6	7.1	6.2			All Other Current	3.8	6.0
	41.4	30.7	30.7			Total Current	30.5	30.0
	19.0	23.0	10.5			Long Term Debt	23.1	20.6
	.6	2.2	3.7			Deferred Taxes	2.1	2.5
	2.3	2.4	5.1			All Other-Non-Current	3.6	3.5
	36.8	41.8	50.0			Net Worth	40.7	43.4
	100.0	100.0	100.0			Total Liabilities & Net Worth	100.0	100.0
						INCOME DATA		
	100.0	100.0	100.0			Net Sales	100.0	100.0
	26.1	25.5	21.9			Gross Profit	21.2	22.7
	23.7	19.1	16.7			Operating Expenses	17.3	17.5
	2.3	6.4	5.2			Operating Profit	3.9	5.2
	1.1	1.8	.3			All Other Expenses (net)	.8	.9
	1.2	4.6	4.8			Profit Before Taxes	3.1	4.3
						RATIOS		
	1.9	2.0	3.2			Current	3.3	3.0
	1.5	1.6	2.0				1.7	1.6
	1.1	.8	1.2				1.2	1.1
	1.1	1.1	1.4			Quick	1.8	1.3
	1.0	.8	.7				.8	.7
	.8	.4	.5				.5	.4
	28 13.1	17 22.0	24 15.3			Sales/Receivables	20 18.2	17 21.4
	32 11.4	27 13.7	29 12.4				23 16.1	26 13.9
	37 9.9	33 11.1	38 9.6				32 11.3	31 11.9
	15 24.4	20 18.6	30 12.0			Cost of Sales/Inventory	25 14.4	24 15.1
	29 12.8	37 10.0	51 7.1				37 9.8	43 8.5
	46 8.0	62 5.9	101 3.6				51 7.2	68 5.4
	9 42.6	16 22.8	9 40.7			Cost of Sales/Payables	7 49.0	10 36.9
	30 12.1	24 15.5	31 11.7				14 25.3	21 17.6
	45 8.2	33 10.9	42 8.7				25 14.8	37 10.0
	11.5	7.3	3.6			Sales/Working Capital	6.6	5.3
	21.0	13.4	7.4				12.0	16.4
	60.9	-32.1	40.0				44.0	46.0
	8.6	7.2	21.6			EBIT/Interest	5.9	9.1
	(19) 2.7	(11) 4.0	8.7				(26) 2.2	(31) 2.4
	1.5	1.7	3.8				.8	1.8
		7.5				Net Profit + Depr., Dep.,	7.0	7.1
	(11) 3.6					Amort./Cur. Mat. L/T/D	(15) 2.3	(17) 2.3
	1.0						.7	1.3
	.5	.6	.3			Fixed/Worth	.6	.5
	.9	1.2	.7				1.0	1.1
	1.9	2.7	1.6				1.8	2.0
	1.0	.8	.5			Debt/Worth	.7	.7
	1.7	1.3	1.1				1.9	1.4
	2.4	4.3	2.2				2.8	3.0
	22.7	42.3	26.7			% Profit Before Taxes/Tangible	35.3	28.0
(16)	11.5	(19) 15.4	(11) 22.9			Net Worth	16.5	(32) 17.7
	1.8	9.3	9.7				-1.8	6.4
	11.5	12.5	14.9			% Profit Before Taxes/Total	14.7	14.0
	5.6	7.0	8.6			Assets	7.0	5.5
	1.5	2.2	6.8				-.4	3.0
	13.9	10.5	10.5			Sales/Net Fixed Assets	12.9	12.8
	9.3	4.4	5.8				6.4	6.3
	4.4	2.0	4.2				4.1	3.6
	4.3	3.5	2.6			Sales/Total Assets	3.7	3.4
	3.5	1.7	2.2				2.4	2.4
	2.5	1.2	1.5				1.9	1.6
	1.2	1.2	1.4			% Depr., Dep., Amort./Sales	1.1	1.5
(15)	2.2	(19) 2.3	2.2				(25) 2.1	(29) 2.1
	3.0	3.8	2.8				2.5	3.2
						% Officers', Directors', Owners' Comp/Sales		
2722M	60509M	194968M	636908M	2250483M		Net Sales ($)	964148M	1812592M
677M	17822M	93915M	268660M	642522M		Total Assets ($)	418317M	710293M

M = $ thousand   MM = $ million
See Pages 1 through 15 for Explanation of Ratios and Data

Type of Statement

Comparative Historical Data			# Postretirement Benefits	Current Data Sorted By Sales					
	1	4	Type of Statement	1		2			1
18	15	26	Unqualified		1		6	9	9
5		11	Reviewed	1	1	3	2	3	1
6	7	11	Compiled	1	6	2	1		1
		1	Tax Returns		1				
8	6	13	Other	2	1	1	2	1	6

Data Periods

	8	6	13							
	4/1/92-3/31/93	4/1/93-3/31/94	4/1/94-3/31/95		34 (4/1-9/30/94)			28 (10/1/94-3/31/95)		
	ALL	ALL	ALL		0-1MM	1-3MM	3-5MM	5-10MM	10-25MM	25MM & OVER
NUMBER OF STATEMENTS	37	28	62		4	10	7	11	13	17

ASSETS (%)

	H1	H2	H3	0-1MM	1-3MM	3-5MM	5-10MM	10-25MM	25MM & OVER
Cash & Equivalents	8.3	5.7	7.2		4.7		8.8	7.7	4.4
Trade Receivables - (net)	17.8	16.9	20.9		16.7		21.2	19.0	20.2
Inventory	21.6	23.2	22.3		16.2		21.4	27.6	22.6
All Other Current	1.1	2.1	1.5		.4		1.6	1.4	2.5
Total Current	48.7	47.8	51.9		38.0		53.1	55.6	49.8
Fixed Assets (net)	39.6	40.2	39.0		53.1		38.5	36.6	35.9
Intangibles (net)	3.6	4.7	4.3		3.6		.3	3.4	10.6
All Other Non-Current	8.1	7.3	4.8		5.4		8.1	4.4	3.7
Total	100.0	100.0	100.0		100.0		100.0	100.0	100.0

LIABILITIES

	H1	H2	H3	0-1MM	1-3MM	3-5MM	5-10MM	10-25MM	25MM & OVER
Notes Payable-Short Term	8.4	6.7	9.3		9.5		10.7	6.9	7.6
Cur. Mat.-L /T/D	5.3	4.8	3.8		9.4		3.0	1.8	1.6
Trade Payables	10.9	10.7	15.7		12.5		16.3	11.8	14.9
Income Taxes Payable	.4	.5	.4		.1		.0	.3	.4
All Other Current	4.6	5.7	6.4		7.2		7.4	7.2	5.8
Total Current	29.6	28.5	35.6		38.7		37.3	28.1	30.3
Long Term Debt	21.4	24.1	19.6		24.6		22.6	12.5	18.6
Deferred Taxes	2.1	3.1	2.1		3.4		2.1	1.6	2.6
All Other-Non-Current	3.8	5.5	4.4		.6		3.4	4.1	9.2
Net Worth	43.1	38.8	38.3		32.8		34.6	53.8	39.4
Total Liabilities & Net Worth	100.0	100.0	100.0		100.0		100.0	100.0	100.0

INCOME DATA

	H1	H2	H3	0-1MM	1-3MM	3-5MM	5-10MM	10-25MM	25MM & OVER
Net Sales	100.0	100.0	100.0		100.0		100.0	100.0	100.0
Gross Profit	22.1	22.3	23.7		29.5		26.5	17.5	18.8
Operating Expenses	18.1	17.4	18.8		21.7		22.3	13.4	12.4
Operating Profit	3.9	4.9	4.8		7.8		4.2	4.1	6.5
All Other Expenses (net)	.9	1.2	1.5		2.6		1.2	.5	2.3
Profit Before Taxes	3.0	3.7	3.3		5.2		3.0	3.6	4.1

RATIOS

	H1	H2	H3	0-1MM	1-3MM	3-5MM	5-10MM	10-25MM	25MM & OVER
Current	2.7 / 1.7 / 1.2	2.4 / 1.5 / 1.0	2.3 / 1.6 / 1.0		1.7 / 1.0 / .5		2.0 / 1.7 / 1.0	3.4 / 1.9 / 1.4	3.0 / 1.6 / 1.1
Quick	1.4 / .9 / .5	1.1 / .7 / .4	1.2 / .9 / .6		1.0 / .6 / .3		1.3 / .9 / .4	1.2 / 1.0 / .6	1.4 / .9 / .5
Sales/Receivables	(17) 21.4 / (30) 12.1 / (36) 10.2	(18) 19.8 / (29) 12.8 / (34) 10.6	(23) 16.2 / (29) 12.4 / (34) 10.7		(11) 32.1 / (32) 11.4 / (37) 9.8		(26) 14.0 / (29) 12.4 / (34) 10.8	(21) 17.1 / (25) 14.6 / (33) 11.1	(19) 19.0 / (29) 12.4 / (35) 10.4
Cost of Sales/Inventory	(27) 13.7 / (36) 10.2 / (56) 6.5	(24) 15.1 / (41) 8.9 / (60) 6.1	(22) 16.3 / (34) 10.6 / (59) 6.2		(16) 23.2 / (21) 17.3 / (51) 7.1		(29) 12.8 / (40) 9.1 / (89) 4.1	(25) 14.5 / (45) 8.2 / (78) 4.7	(24) 15.2 / (28) 12.9 / (54) 6.8
Cost of Sales/Payables	(12) 30.4 / (19) 19.6 / (33) 11.2	(12) 31.5 / (19) 19.3 / (27) 13.5	(13) 27.3 / (24) 15.1 / (38) 9.7		(9) 38.5 / (22) 16.9 / (34) 10.6		(23) 16.0 / (39) 9.4 / (62) 5.9	(14) 26.2 / (20) 18.7 / (24) 14.9	(13) 29.2 / (15) 24.5 / (39) 9.4
Sales/Working Capital	6.5 / 11.3 / 24.4	7.3 / 15.5 / NM	7.4 / 15.4 / 149.6		10.0 / NM / -9.1		8.7 / 12.9 / 102.1	4.7 / 9.7 / 24.4	7.4 / 15.5 / 153.6
EBIT/Interest	(35) 6.4 / 3.2 / 1.0	(27) 9.4 / 3.4 / 1.5	(60) 7.1 / 3.4 / 1.9		5.9 / 2.9 / 2.0		(12) 8.7 / 2.8 / 1.6	19.3 / 4.8 / 2.2	(16) 15.0 / 3.3 / 2.1
Net Profit + Depr., Dep., Amort./Cur. Mat. L/T/D	(22) 5.1 / 2.2 / .7	(17) 2.2 / 1.3 / .8	(31) 6.7 / 3.5 / 1.1					(11) 13.2 / 3.9 / 2.3	
Fixed/Worth	.4 / .8 / 2.0	.5 / 1.4 / 2.7	.6 / 1.1 / 2.5		.8 / 1.9 / NM		.6 / 1.0 / 1.8	.4 / .7 / 1.4	.6 / 1.5 / 3.9
Debt/Worth	.7 / 1.6 / 2.8	.6 / 2.3 / 3.5	.8 / 1.8 / 4.2		.8 / 2.2 / NM		1.3 / 2.1 / 3.1	.5 / .9 / 1.2	1.1 / 2.7 / 7.2
% Profit Before Taxes/Tangible Net Worth	(35) 19.7 / 13.2 / 2.3	(26) 27.9 / 13.9 / 10.0	(55) 28.2 / 15.4 / 9.0				22.9 / 9.9 / 8.1	30.3 / 14.1 / 4.0	(14) 29.4 / 22.8 / 9.7
% Profit Before Taxes/Total Assets	11.0 / 6.7 / .6	13.7 / 5.4 / 2.2	11.3 / 6.8 / 3.1		9.8 / 6.1 / 4.8		7.1 / 4.0 / 1.9	10.8 / 7.7 / 2.2	12.5 / 7.7 / 4.2
Sales/Net Fixed Assets	8.6 / 5.6 / 3.2	10.6 / 4.9 / 2.9	12.8 / 6.2 / 3.1		11.4 / 3.6 / 1.5		13.2 / 6.4 / 2.8	11.3 / 9.1 / 3.6	12.9 / 5.3 / 3.0
Sales/Total Assets	3.2 / 2.2 / 1.5	3.0 / 2.2 / 1.0	3.7 / 2.6 / 1.5		3.4 / 2.0 / .8		3.5 / 2.1 / 1.6	3.6 / 2.7 / 1.4	3.0 / 2.4 / 1.4
% Depr., Dep., Amort./Sales	(34) 1.4 / 2.5 / 3.2	(27) 1.6 / 2.4 / 3.2	(59) 1.2 / 2.2 / 2.8		1.8 / 2.2 / 4.8		1.2 / 2.3 / 2.7	(12) 1.2 / 2.1 / 2.9	1.1 / 2.0 / 2.6
% Officers', Directors', Owners' Comp/Sales	(10) 1.2 / 4.4 / 9.1	(11) 1.0 / 2.2 / 3.9	(14) 2.1 / 3.0 / 8.1						
Net Sales ($)	1380641M	1031826M	3145590M	2201M	18192M	28391M	81986M	199131M	2815689M
Total Assets ($)	574455M	412827M	1023596M	1514M	14732M	6931M	46591M	95971M	857857M

M = $ thousand   MM = $ million
See Pages 1 through 15 for Explanation of Ratios and Data

MANUFACTURERS—FROZEN FRUITS, FRUIT JUICES & VEGETABLES. SIC# 2037

Current Data Sorted By Assets						# Postretirement Benefits	Comparative Historical Data		
		1				**Type of Statement**			
	1	5	8	2	2	Unqualified		8	8
		5	1			Reviewed		7	8
1	4					Compiled		4	3
	1					Tax Returns			
	1	6	1	1	1	Other		8	7
	24 (4/1-9/30/94)			16 (10/1/94-3/31/95)				4/1/90-3/31/91	4/1/91-3/31/92
0-500M	500M-2MM	2-10MM	10-50MM	50-100MM	100-250MM		ALL	ALL
1	7	16	10	3	3	**NUMBER OF STATEMENTS**	27	26
%	%	%	%	%	%	**ASSETS**	%	%
		6.9	1.6			Cash & Equivalents	3.4	8.3
		26.1	13.2			Trade Receivables - (net)	17.9	16.1
		26.4	35.1			Inventory	28.5	24.6
		1.7	3.2			All Other Current	1.5	2.2
		61.1	53.1			Total Current	51.4	51.2
		35.1	43.4			Fixed Assets (net)	39.9	41.1
		.4	.3			Intangibles (net)	4.0	.3
		3.4	3.2			All Other Non-Current	4.7	7.3
		100.0	100.0			Total	100.0	100.0
						LIABILITIES		
		14.1	19.3			Notes Payable-Short Term	16.1	16.4
		3.3	3.0			Cur. Mat. -L/T/D	4.7	5.6
		20.4	10.4			Trade Payables	15.3	16.3
		.1	.2			Income Taxes Payable	.2	.3
		10.7	4.6			All Other Current	6.2	9.4
		48.6	37.4			Total Current	42.5	48.0
		17.5	21.0			Long Term Debt	29.0	19.5
		.3	1.1			Deferred Taxes	1.2	1.0
		6.4	5.4			All Other-Non-Current	2.6	2.6
		27.1	35.1			Net Worth	24.7	28.9
		100.0	100.0			Total Liabilities & Net Worth	100.0	100.0
						INCOME DATA		
		100.0	100.0			Net Sales	100.0	100.0
		23.7	17.8			Gross Profit	25.4	22.2
		20.2	11.3			Operating Expenses	19.8	18.3
		3.5	6.5			Operating Profit	5.6	3.9
		.6	2.0			All Other Expenses (net)	3.7	1.0
		3.0	4.5			Profit Before Taxes	2.0	2.9
						RATIOS		
		2.4	1.6				1.6	2.2
		1.2	1.4			Current	1.3	1.0
		.7	1.3				1.0	.9
		1.4	.5				.7	.8
		.6	.3			Quick	.5 (25)	.6
		.3	.2				.4	.3
	23	15.6	20 18.2				25 14.6	17 21.7
	36	10.2	26 13.8			Sales/Receivables	33 10.9	31 11.6
	59	6.2	37 9.8				41 8.8	37 9.8
	29	12.4	81 4.5				34 10.6	27 13.3
	51	7.1	99 3.7			Cost of Sales/Inventory	78 4.7	58 6.3
	114	3.2	122 3.0				114 3.2	91 4.0
	14	25.6	11 32.3				17 21.9	17 21.7
	35	10.4	25 14.4			Cost of Sales/Payables	34 10.6	36 10.1
	62	5.9	37 9.8				51 7.1	59 6.2
		6.1	9.9				9.2	5.7
		26.8	11.9			Sales/Working Capital	13.9	130.8
		−14.4	12.7				353.9	−17.9
		4.6	5.7				2.8	3.6
	(12)	2.4	3.9			EBIT/Interest	(26) 1.6	(25) 2.5
		−1.2	2.4				1.3	.8
						Net Profit + Depr., Dep.,	3.5	4.0
						Amort./Cur. Mat. L /T/D	(16) 2.0	(17) 2.2
							.9	.5
		.5	.8				1.0	.7
		1.2	1.0			Fixed/Worth	1.4	1.4
		3.0	2.3				3.9	2.6
		1.1	1.0				1.7	1.7
		3.2	1.8			Debt/Worth	3.6	2.4
		9.9	4.3				5.0	8.1
		52.8	43.9			% Profit Before Taxes/Tangible	54.2	31.6
	(15)	13.7	22.6			Net Worth	(24) 18.2	(24) 18.5
		4.4	9.8				3.4	9.8
		10.6	14.7			% Profit Before Taxes/Total	9.5	8.5
		5.2	8.6			Assets	4.3	4.9
		.7	3.2				1.0	−.4
		12.5	6.6				8.2	9.6
		4.8	3.2			Sales/Net Fixed Assets	4.8	5.0
		2.5	2.7				2.9	2.9
		3.2	2.2				2.1	2.5
		1.7	1.6			Sales/Total Assets	1.9	2.0
		1.2	1.3				1.6	1.3
		1.7					1.7	1.3
	(15)	3.5				% Depr., Dep., Amort./Sales	(23) 3.5	(25) 3.5
		6.0					4.7	4.5
						% Officers', Directors', Owners' Comp/Sales		
2800M	26902M	225624M	354273M	430953M	587105M	Net Sales ($)	784232M	1274031M
415M	8913M	85220M	223906M	213027M	431235M	Total Assets ($)	511627M	778376M

M = $ thousand   MM = $ million
See Pages 1 through 15 for Explanation of Ratios and Data

Comparative Historical Data / Current Data Sorted By Sales

Type of Statement

		2	1	# Postretirement Benefits / Type of Statement	0-1MM	1-3MM	3-5MM	5-10MM	10-25MM	25MM & OVER
										1
	22	16	18	Unqualified		1		2	5	10
	12	12	6	Reviewed			1	1	2	2
	5	2	5	Compiled	3	2				
			1	Tax Returns					1	
				Other		3		3		4
	8	9	10			24 (4/1-9/30/94)		16 (10/1/94-3/31/95)		
	4/1/92-3/31/93 ALL	4/1/93-3/31/94 ALL	4/1/94-3/31/95 ALL	NUMBER OF STATEMENTS						
	47	39	40			4	6	6	8	16

Main Data

8 (4/1/92-3/31/93) ALL	9 (4/1/93-3/31/94) ALL	10 (4/1/94-3/31/95) ALL		0-1MM	1-3MM	3-5MM	5-10MM	10-25MM	25MM & OVER
%	%	%	**ASSETS**	%	%	%	%	%	%
5.2	4.6	4.6	Cash & Equivalents						4.4
20.5	17.3	20.4	Trade Receivables - (net)						20.0
28.9	29.8	27.3	Inventory						31.6
3.0	2.1	2.4	All Other Current						2.7
57.6	53.9	54.7	Total Current						58.6
34.5	35.7	39.9	Fixed Assets (net)						34.8
1.2	3.3	1.4	Intangibles (net)						1.2
6.7	7.1	4.0	All Other Non-Current						5.4
100.0	100.0	100.0	Total						100.0
			LIABILITIES						
16.3	14.4	16.2	Notes Payable-Short Term						16.4
3.7	2.7	3.4	Cur. Mat.-L /T/D						2.4
16.7	12.8	15.6	Trade Payables						15.9
.4	.6	.3	Income Taxes Payable						.0
7.8	9.9	9.7	All Other Current						12.5
44.9	40.4	45.1	Total Current						47.3
15.6	17.7	17.5	Long Term Debt						14.3
1.4	1.1	1.3	Deferred Taxes						1.7
3.6	6.3	6.1	All Other-Non-Current						3.0
34.5	34.5	30.0	Net Worth						33.7
100.0	100.0	100.0	Total Liabilities & Net Worth						100.0
			INCOME DATA						
100.0	100.0	100.0	Net Sales						100.0
23.1	21.6	23.8	Gross Profit						17.5
17.6	17.3	19.0	Operating Expenses						12.3
5.5	4.3	4.8	Operating Profit						5.2
1.5	1.6	1.2	All Other Expenses (net)						1.3
4.0	2.7	3.6	Profit Before Taxes						3.9
			RATIOS						
1.7	1.9	1.5	Current						1.5
1.3	1.5	1.2							1.2
1.0	1.2	1.0							1.1
.8	.7	.9	Quick						.8
.5	.6	.4							.5
.4	.3	.2							.2
24 15.5	25 14.5	21 17.2	Sales/Receivables						23 15.6
31 11.8	31 11.8	31 11.8							27 13.6
40 9.1	41 9.0	42 8.7							37 9.8
27 13.4	38 9.5	35 10.4	Cost of Sales/Inventory						26 14.2
46 7.9	68 5.4	62 5.9							73 5.0
111 3.3	99 3.7	114 3.2							118 3.1
16 22.3	13 28.8	14 25.6	Cost of Sales/Payables						13 28.9
26 14.2	23 16.0	29 12.5							24 14.9
48 7.6	46 8.0	46 8.0							33 11.2
9.0	7.3	10.3	Sales/Working Capital						10.3
25.2	9.6	16.3							12.4
221.0	21.9	NM							89.3
(42) 6.7	(33) 4.2	(35) 5.5	EBIT/Interest					(15)	6.3
3.1	2.0	2.7							4.3
1.2	1.3	.9							2.7
(25) 4.5	(20) 5.9	(15) 8.1	Net Profit + Depr., Dep., Amort./Cur. Mat. L/T/D						
2.8	2.9	2.1							
1.9	1.0	1.2							
.6	.7	.6	Fixed/Worth						.5
1.1	1.2	1.3							.9
1.8	2.0	3.3							1.9
1.2	1.0	1.1	Debt/Worth						.9
2.0	2.0	2.7							2.3
4.5	5.4	5.4							4.5
(45) 43.8	(35) 31.2	(39) 43.4	% Profit Before Taxes/Tangible Net Worth						61.9
25.6	12.0	14.9							40.5
3.2	4.1	4.4							7.9
12.8	6.6	14.0	% Profit Before Taxes/Total Assets						15.2
6.3	3.7	5.2							11.5
1.1	1.3	.7							3.2
11.1	7.4	9.9	Sales/Net Fixed Assets						32.6
5.7	5.4	4.5							5.3
3.5	3.3	2.7							2.9
2.9	2.4	2.5	Sales/Total Assets						2.5
1.9	1.8	1.7							1.8
1.4	1.3	1.3							1.4
(43) 1.1	(37) 1.6	(34) 1.7	% Depr., Dep., Amort./Sales					(12)	.7
2.0	3.0	3.6							3.0
3.7	4.1	5.1							4.5
		(10) 2.0	% Officers', Directors', Owners' Comp/Sales						
		3.5							
		5.4							
1776372M	1587917M	1627657M	Net Sales ($)		9257M	22112M	46244M	126396M	1423648M
1055925M	961268M	962716M	Total Assets ($)		4365M	14070M	32476M	73780M	838025M

M = $ thousand   MM = $ million
See Pages 1 through 15 for Explanation of Ratios and Data

MANUFACTURERS—MEAT PACKING. SIC# 2011

Current Data Sorted By Assets							Comparative Historical Data	
		3	2		2	# Postretirement Benefits		
						Type of Statement		
1	2	16	12	4	3	Unqualified	34	28
2	5	15	2		2	Reviewed	15	21
3	10	6	1			Compiled	26	24
1	1					Tax Returns	2	2
	5	4	7		2	Other	14	17
	45 (4/1-9/30/94)		59 (10/1/94-3/31/95)				4/1/90-3/31/91	4/1/91-3/31/92
0-500M	500M-2MM	2-10MM	10-50MM	50-100MM	100-250MM		ALL	ALL
7	23	41	22	4	7	NUMBER OF STATEMENTS	91	92
%	%	%	%	%	%	**ASSETS**	%	%
	7.1	7.0	4.1			Cash & Equivalents	7.8	5.4
	29.0	34.1	24.1			Trade Receivables - (net)	30.5	28.6
	23.7	18.3	19.0			Inventory	21.5	22.8
	2.5	1.0	.8			All Other Current	2.5	2.5
	62.4	60.4	48.1			Total Current	62.3	59.3
	29.0	30.7	37.6			Fixed Assets (net)	30.4	31.7
	.7	1.7	4.6			Intangibles (net)	1.5	1.7
	7.9	7.2	9.7			All Other Non-Current	5.8	7.3
	100.0	100.0	100.0			Total	100.0	100.0
						LIABILITIES		
	9.8	16.4	11.7			Notes Payable-Short Term	17.8	14.3
	4.6	2.2	1.7			Cur. Mat. -L/T/D	3.3	4.0
	18.4	15.4	12.7			Trade Payables	14.6	14.6
	1.1	.3	.2			Income Taxes Payable	.5	.4
	5.4	6.5	5.2			All Other Current	5.2	5.7
	39.3	40.7	31.5			Total Current	41.4	39.0
	14.2	10.9	14.9			Long Term Debt	16.4	16.4
	.2	.4	1.3			Deferred Taxes	.6	.6
	4.6	3.1	4.7			All Other-Non-Current	3.8	2.5
	41.7	44.9	47.6			Net Worth	37.8	41.6
	100.0	100.0	100.0			Total Liabilities & Net Worth	100.0	100.0
						INCOME DATA		
	100.0	100.0	100.0			Net Sales	100.0	100.0
	21.8	13.8	13.1			Gross Profit	15.6	15.4
	21.8	11.1	9.6			Operating Expenses	13.3	13.8
	.0	2.6	3.6			Operating Profit	2.2	1.6
	.0	.4	.6			All Other Expenses (net)	.6	1.0
	.0	2.2	3.0			Profit Before Taxes	1.7	.7
						RATIOS		
	2.4	2.3	2.1			Current	2.5	2.3
	1.5	1.5	1.5				1.4	1.5
	1.2	1.1	1.1				1.2	1.1
	1.2	1.5	1.3			Quick	1.5	1.3
	.9	1.0	.9				.9	.9
	.7	.6	.6				.7	.6
	12 30.5	14 26.2	15 24.5			Sales/Receivables	13 28.9	12 30.1
	17 21.4	16 22.4	20 18.1				17 21.8	16 22.6
	21 17.6	21 17.2	29 12.7				21 17.2	22 16.8
	15 25.1	6 61.9	12 30.0			Cost of Sales/Inventory	7 49.2	8 43.0
	17 21.0	10 35.3	17 21.3				15 24.1	15 25.1
	33 11.1	22 16.8	29 12.6				24 15.4	25 14.7
	3 119.9	5 74.1	7 51.7			Cost of Sales/Payables	4 84.6	4 87.8
	13 28.7	7 49.3	12 29.6				8 44.1	10 36.6
	31 11.9	14 25.6	18 20.3				18 20.1	17 21.2
	16.5	20.3	13.2			Sales/Working Capital	15.2	16.0
	22.3	39.0	26.5				29.1	30.3
	57.7	197.2	148.8				95.9	94.0
	7.6	8.8	13.9			EBIT/Interest	(84) 4.9	(85) 4.6
	(22) 2.5	(39) 4.2	4.0				2.3	2.3
	.8	1.4	1.8				1.0	1.2
	5.5	8.7	50.9			Net Profit + Depr., Dep.,	(52) 5.8	(48) 6.0
	(11) 2.1	(19) 3.8	(12) 4.3			Amort./Cur. Mat. L./T/D	3.2	2.7
	.7	2.8	2.2				1.2	.9
	.4	.4	.4			Fixed/Worth	.5	.5
	.7	.7	.9				.8	.7
	1.1	1.2	2.2				1.5	1.4
	.7	.6	.6			Debt/Worth	.8	.8
	1.1	1.4	1.2				1.9	1.5
	2.9	2.6	2.4				3.2	3.8
	29.0	43.4	40.0			% Profit Before Taxes/Tangible	(86) 32.0	(88) 30.3
	(21) 10.5	(40) 14.3	(21) 15.1			Net Worth	14.9	10.8
	-2.3	2.7	3.7				4.0	3.8
	9.2	14.8	17.2			% Profit Before Taxes/Total	12.7	12.0
	5.4	7.2	6.1			Assets	4.5	4.3
	-.7	1.5	2.0				.1	.7
	41.6	54.1	39.2			Sales/Net Fixed Assets	39.2	42.1
	27.4	22.1	10.1				21.8	20.8
	8.2	10.9	3.9				12.0	9.4
	10.0	10.4	8.6			Sales/Total Assets	9.1	9.4
	4.3	6.7	2.9				6.4	6.3
	3.2	4.2	2.1				3.6	3.1
	.5	.4	.4			% Depr., Dep., Amort./Sales	(83) .4	(88) .3
	(20) 1.0	.6	(20) 1.0				.8	.9
	2.3	1.2	2.3				1.5	1.9
	1.6	.2				% Officers', Directors',	(25) .8	(31) .5
	(14) 2.6	(15) 1.5				Owners' Comp/Sales	1.7	1.4
	4.4	2.4					3.9	2.6
12456M	151543M	1303848M	2072309M	1881799M	4325810M	Net Sales ($)	7179562M	7481576M
1806M	25906M	195570M	437416M	249473M	1162893M	Total Assets ($)	1201892M	1309769M

M = $ thousand   MM = $ million
See Pages 1 through 15 for Explanation of Ratios and Data

Comparative Historical Data						Current Data Sorted By Sales				
1	4	7	# Postretirement Benefits / Type of Statement						1	6
30	25	38	Unqualified	1	1	1		9	26
16	20	26	Reviewed		2	2	3	6	13
24	26	20	Compiled	1	3	4	3	4	5
1	1	2	Tax Returns		1	1			
14	28	18	Other		2	2		6	8

4/1/92-3/31/93 ALL	4/1/93-3/31/94 ALL	4/1/94-3/31/95 ALL		0-1MM	1-3MM	3-5MM	5-10MM	10-25MM	25MM & OVER
					45 (4/1-9/30/94)			59 (10/1/94-3/31/95)	
85	100	104	NUMBER OF STATEMENTS	2	9	10	6	25	52
%	%	%	**ASSETS**	%	%	%	%	%	%
5.8	5.1	6.4	Cash & Equivalents			8.5		8.2	5.1
29.7	30.7	29.2	Trade Receivables - (net)			23.5		24.1	33.9
20.8	21.7	19.8	Inventory			22.5		19.3	17.8
2.1	1.6	1.4	All Other Current			4.4		.5	1.2
58.4	59.2	56.8	Total Current			59.0		52.2	57.9
31.7	32.4	33.2	Fixed Assets (net)			31.8		36.9	31.8
2.9	1.8	2.4	Intangibles (net)			1.3		3.5	2.2
7.0	6.7	7.5	All Other Non-Current			8.0		7.3	8.1
100.0	100.0	100.0	Total			100.0		100.0	100.0
			LIABILITIES						
16.1	17.9	13.7	Notes Payable-Short Term			8.6		9.5	15.7
3.3	2.9	2.9	Cur. Mat.-L /T/D			3.8		3.2	1.9
14.2	15.0	15.4	Trade Payables			22.0		11.6	15.9
.6	.9	.4	Income Taxes Payable			1.1		.4	.3
6.6	7.7	7.2	All Other Current			3.8		7.7	7.0
40.8	44.3	39.7	Total Current			39.4		32.4	40.8
16.5	16.8	14.7	Long Term Debt			14.6		20.0	10.6
.6	.5	.7	Deferred Taxes			.1		.6	.9
3.4	5.2	4.3	All Other-Non-Current			4.6		6.0	4.3
38.7	33.2	40.6	Net Worth			41.4		41.0	43.3
100.0	100.0	100.0	Total Liabilities & Net Worth			100.0		100.0	100.0
			INCOME DATA						
100.0	100.0	100.0	Net Sales			100.0		100.0	100.0
16.2	15.5	16.5	Gross Profit			25.8		18.2	12.7
13.7	12.8	13.8	Operating Expenses			24.7		15.1	9.8
2.5	2.7	2.7	Operating Profit			1.1		3.1	2.9
.3	.6	.5	All Other Expenses (net)			−.2		.2	.7
2.2	2.2	2.2	Profit Before Taxes			1.3		3.0	2.2
			RATIOS						
2.0	2.1	2.3	Current			2.6		2.1	2.3
1.5	1.5	1.5				1.6		1.5	1.5
1.1	1.0	1.0				1.0		1.1	1.0
1.3	1.3	1.4	Quick			1.9		1.4	1.4
.9	.8	.9				.7		1.1	1.0
.6	.6	.6				.4		.6	.6
14 26.8	14 25.2	13 27.3	Sales/Receivables			16 23.3		13 27.7	14 26.0
17 22.1	18 20.5	17 21.4				18 20.7		18 20.5	17 21.6
23 16.0	23 15.9	23 16.2				28 13.0		23 16.2	21 17.1
7 49.1	9 42.1	8 43.6	Cost of Sales/Inventory			17 21.8		12 31.6	7 51.5
15 24.0	15 24.7	16 22.5				27 13.4		17 21.0	10 34.9
27 13.4	26 14.3	27 13.7				36 10.2		27 13.3	21 17.5
5 71.9	5 75.2	6 65.5	Cost of Sales/Payables			12 31.7		4 83.3	6 62.2
11 34.1	11 34.0	10 38.0				30 12.1		9 40.3	9 42.3
18 20.3	18 20.0	17 21.0				45 8.2		19 19.2	16 23.4
15.7	16.1	16.7	Sales/Working Capital			8.2		19.2	18.6
31.3	33.3	28.8				16.2		24.3	35.0
125.2	377.4	188.3				−393.6		84.4	−495.5
(81) 6.7	(94) 6.1	(100) 8.9	EBIT/Interest			35.9		(24) 6.9	(51) 12.0
3.2	2.5	3.5				1.4		2.9	4.9
1.3	1.0	1.3				.3		1.8	2.1
(43) 7.7	(41) 6.3	(51) 8.7	Net Profit + Depr., Dep., Amort./Cur. Mat. L/T/D					(10) 6.1	(30) 11.8
3.1	2.4	3.8						3.8	4.6
1.3	1.3	2.1						1.6	2.4
.6	.6	.5	Fixed/Worth			.5		.6	.4
.8	.9	.7				.8		.9	.7
1.6	1.7	1.5				1.5		1.8	1.2
.8	.8	.7	Debt/Worth			.7		.9	.6
1.8	1.8	1.4				1.7		1.4	1.2
4.1	5.4	3.6				3.2		2.9	3.6
(83) 35.4	(94) 41.4	(95) 42.2	% Profit Before Taxes/Tangible Net Worth					(23) 66.9	(48) 39.9
16.6	14.5	15.2						17.8	16.2
2.0	.7	2.9						7.6	3.4
13.1	11.3	13.9	% Profit Before Taxes/Total Assets			11.1		16.6	13.9
4.4	4.0	6.9				1.6		6.7	7.3
1.0	−.1	1.5				−3.4		2.3	1.9
35.4	35.1	41.3	Sales/Net Fixed Assets			35.5		28.1	55.0
20.1	19.7	19.1				9.2		11.5	25.9
9.1	9.0	8.1				6.9		5.4	10.8
8.6	8.4	9.2	Sales/Total Assets			4.1		8.2	10.4
5.5	5.8	5.2				3.6		4.3	7.3
3.2	3.4	2.9				3.1		2.0	3.9
(77) .5	(89) .5	(96) .4	% Depr., Dep., Amort./Sales					.6	(48) .4
1.0	.9	1.0						1.0	.6
1.5	1.6	1.8						2.0	1.1
(33) .6	(32) .5	(36) .6	% Officers', Directors', Owners' Comp/Sales				(10)	.9	(12) .2
1.5	1.3	2.1						2.7	.5
3.1	3.9	3.6						4.3	.7
7636755M	9561662M	9747765M	Net Sales ($)	1008M	17554M	44683M	40344M	421736M	9222440M
1262074M	1846824M	2073064M	Total Assets ($)	409M	7096M	13326M	4802M	139100M	1908331M

M = $ thousand   MM = $ million
See Pages 1 through 15 for Explanation of Ratios and Data

Current Data Sorted By Assets　　　　　　　　　　　　　**Comparative Historical Data**

0-500M	500M-2MM	2-10MM	10-50MM	50-100MM	100-250MM	# Postretirement Benefits	4/1/90-3/31/91 ALL	4/1/91-3/31/92 ALL
		2	2	1	3	# Postretirement Benefits		
						Type of Statement		
		8	12	8	8	Unqualified	32	31
	2	1	1			Reviewed	7	4
	2	2		1		Compiled	1	2
	1					Tax Returns		
		7	1	3	4	Other	11	7
							51	44

0-500M	500M-2MM	2-10MM	10-50MM	50-100MM	100-250MM	NUMBER OF STATEMENTS	ALL 51	ALL 44
	5	18	14	12	12	NUMBER OF STATEMENTS	51	44

20 (4/1-9/30/94)　　41 (10/1/94-3/31/95)

%	%	%	%	%	%	ASSETS	%	%
		6.2	2.8	2.8	2.8	Cash & Equivalents	5.4	5.4
		27.1	18.7	17.6	12.9	Trade Receivables - (net)	20.0	14.9
		19.1	26.0	20.3	29.0	Inventory	23.3	23.3
		2.1	1.6	1.3	1.1	All Other Current	1.6	2.4
		54.4	49.0	41.9	45.8	Total Current	50.2	45.9
		38.6	38.6	45.2	47.9	Fixed Assets (net)	41.6	46.5
		1.1	1.7	2.8	1.3	Intangibles (net)	2.0	2.1
		5.9	10.6	10.1	5.0	All Other Non-Current	6.1	5.4
		100.0	100.0	100.0	100.0	Total	100.0	100.0
						LIABILITIES		
		8.1	13.6	7.3	6.2	Notes Payable-Short Term	9.3	5.8
		5.1	3.0	3.8	3.6	Cur. Mat.-L/T/D	3.6	3.1
		24.3	13.6	11.3	10.4	Trade Payables	13.0	14.0
		.4	.1	.5	.5	Income Taxes Payable	.6	.7
		6.3	7.5	7.0	5.0	All Other Current	5.3	6.0
		44.3	37.8	29.9	25.7	Total Current	31.9	29.7
		15.3	21.6	21.5	22.3	Long Term Debt	18.6	24.0
		1.2	1.1	7.1	7.7	Deferred Taxes	4.9	3.8
		5.4	2.6	3.9	2.0	All Other-Non-Current	2.1	3.6
		33.8	37.0	37.6	42.2	Net Worth	42.5	39.0
		100.0	100.0	100.0	100.0	Total Liabilities & Net Worth	100.0	100.0
						INCOME DATA		
		100.0	100.0	100.0	100.0	Net Sales	100.0	100.0
		18.0	19.8	8.9	9.8	Gross Profit	17.8	13.8
		13.7	16.4	8.3	6.9	Operating Expenses	12.9	10.8
		4.3	3.4	.6	2.9	Operating Profit	4.9	2.9
		.8	1.3	2.2	.8	All Other Expenses (net)	1.1	1.2
		3.5	2.1	-1.6	2.1	Profit Before Taxes	3.8	1.8
						RATIOS		
		2.2	2.3	2.6	2.9	Current	2.6	2.2
		1.2	1.2	1.5	1.9		1.6	1.7
		1.0	1.0	.9	1.4		1.1	1.1
		1.4	.9	1.3	1.3	Quick	1.1	1.0
		1.0	.6	.7	.7		.8	.7
		.4	.3	.4	.4		.4	.5
		16 23.0	13 29.2	21 17.4	15 24.1	Sales/Receivables	19 19.5	15 23.7
		20 17.9	23 16.1	23 15.8	20 18.6		21 17.0	20 18.4
		25 14.7	33 11.2	26 14.1	23 16.2		31 11.8	22 16.3
		5 67.9	21 17.5	30 12.3	33 11.2	Cost of Sales/Inventory	23 15.9	19 19.0
		19 19.3	42 8.6	37 9.8	45 8.2		40 9.1	33 10.9
		42 8.7	74 4.9	41 8.8	62 5.9		56 6.5	45 8.1
		13 27.6	9 41.3	12 29.5	10 36.8	Cost of Sales/Payables	10 35.3	11 32.1
		18 20.8	21 17.1	15 25.0	15 23.7		17 20.9	17 21.4
		29 12.4	31 11.6	32 11.3	21 17.5		25 14.4	26 14.1
		14.0	11.5	10.6	7.8	Sales/Working Capital	7.0	9.0
		31.9	24.7	15.1	10.8		16.6	15.2
		NM	NM	-43.2	18.4		80.9	131.0
		14.7	10.5	9.7	7.2	EBIT/Interest	(47) 10.0	4.8
		4.5	2.8	4.4	2.9		2.8	2.1
		1.3	1.0	-.5	2.2		1.3	1.2
				(10) 6.6		Net Profit + Depr., Dep.,	(33) 10.2	(30) 6.7
				2.6		Amort./Cur. Mat. L/T/D	3.5	2.6
				-2.7			1.5	.8
		.6	.5	.9	1.0	Fixed/Worth	.7	.9
		1.1	1.2	1.2	1.3		1.0	1.3
		3.8	1.7	4.9	1.8		1.8	1.8
		1.0	1.2	1.0	.7	Debt/Worth	.7	1.0
		2.5	1.9	1.5	1.4		1.7	1.5
		5.7	3.1	7.2	3.3		2.9	3.2
		47.3	36.6	31.5	21.3	% Profit Before Taxes/Tangible	29.4	22.6
		27.5	(13) 23.8	(10) 20.8	12.7	Net Worth	(49) 12.2	(41) 9.8
		5.1	1.9	10.2	4.0		2.9	2.6
		16.6	10.6	16.6	7.3	% Profit Before Taxes/Total	10.5	9.7
		7.6	5.9	7.2	4.3	Assets	4.8	3.1
		1.5	.0	-4.2	1.7		1.2	.5
		19.4	15.3	8.6	7.2	Sales/Net Fixed Assets	10.7	9.5
		10.8	6.2	4.8	4.9		5.2	5.3
		6.7	3.9	3.6	3.8		4.3	3.8
		5.9	4.4	2.8	2.9	Sales/Total Assets	3.4	2.9
		3.6	2.9	2.5	2.1		2.4	2.4
		2.4	1.9	1.7	2.0		2.0	2.1
		(14) .8	(13) 1.1	(11) 1.7		% Depr., Dep., Amort./Sales	(45) 1.3	(40) 2.0
		2.0	1.8	2.4			2.2	2.7
		3.4	3.3	3.0			3.3	3.5
						% Officers', Directors', Owners' Comp/Sales		
	18847M	501256M	941020M	2005973M	4814773M	Net Sales ($)	3552348M	4678471M
	7112M	99121M	327142M	824992M	1763122M	Total Assets ($)	1458604M	2009063M

M = $ thousand　　MM = $ million
See Pages 1 through 15 for Explanation of Ratios and Data

Comparative Historical Data / **Current Data Sorted By Sales**

Type of Statement

2	5	8	# Postretirement Benefits / Type of Statement	0-1MM	1-3MM	3-5MM	5-10MM	10-25MM	25MM & OVER
			# Postretirement Benefits				1	1	6
35	36	36	Unqualified				3	4	29
4	8	4	Reviewed		1		2		1
5	5	5	Compiled		1	1			3
	1	1	Tax Returns		1	1			
7	12	15	Other			1		3	11
7 4/1/92-3/31/93 ALL	12 4/1/93-3/31/94 ALL	15 4/1/94-3/31/95 ALL		20 (4/1-9/30/94)			41 (10/1/94-3/31/95)		
51	62	61	**NUMBER OF STATEMENTS**		2	3	5	7	44

ASSETS

%	%	%			%	%	%	%	%
4.2	4.7	4.9	Cash & Equivalents						3.5
19.8	18.9	20.2	Trade Receivables - (net)						20.4
22.0	22.4	22.4	Inventory						23.3
2.5	1.1	1.5	All Other Current						1.2
48.5	47.2	48.9	Total Current						48.4
44.0	42.7	42.1	Fixed Assets (net)						42.7
1.5	2.1	1.7	Intangibles (net)						1.8
6.0	8.1	7.2	All Other Non-Current						7.1
100.0	100.0	100.0	Total						100.0

LIABILITIES

10.5	12.0	8.4	Notes Payable-Short Term						8.8
3.8	3.6	3.9	Cur. Mat.-L /T/D						3.4
15.2	15.4	15.9	Trade Payables						15.1
.1	1.0	.4	Income Taxes Payable						.3
6.7	5.5	6.6	All Other Current						7.0
36.4	37.5	35.0	Total Current						34.7
20.9	21.9	20.9	Long Term Debt						18.3
3.9	4.3	3.5	Deferred Taxes						4.5
2.7	3.1	3.4	All Other-Non-Current						3.4
36.1	33.2	37.1	Net Worth						39.1
100.0	100.0	100.0	Total Liabilities & Net Worth						100.0

INCOME DATA

100.0	100.0	100.0	Net Sales						100.0
14.7	14.3	15.2	Gross Profit						12.4
13.2	12.4	12.0	Operating Expenses						10.1
1.6	1.9	3.2	Operating Profit						2.2
.6	1.4	1.2	All Other Expenses (net)						1.1
1.0	.6	2.0	Profit Before Taxes						1.1

RATIOS

1.9	2.1	2.3	Current						2.2
1.5	1.4	1.6							1.6
.9	.9	1.1							1.1
.9	1.1	1.3	Quick						1.2
.7	.5	.7							.7
.4	.4	.4							.5
18 / 20.6	18 / 20.3	18 / 20.7	Sales/Receivables						18 / 20.5
21 / 17.6	22 / 16.9	22 / 16.6							21 / 17.0
25 / 14.8	27 / 13.4	27 / 13.3							24 / 15.2
18 / 20.2	18 / 20.6	17 / 21.5	Cost of Sales/Inventory						17 / 20.9
31 / 11.6	35 / 10.5	34 / 10.7							34 / 10.6
50 / 7.3	56 / 6.5	61 / 6.0							61 / 6.0
10 / 35.9	11 / 32.9	12 / 29.3	Cost of Sales/Payables						13 / 28.7
15 / 23.7	18 / 20.4	17 / 21.5							15 / 24.2
23 / 16.2	27 / 13.7	29 / 12.6							25 / 14.5
10.2	10.0	9.4	Sales/Working Capital						10.7
22.2	23.6	16.7							16.7
-208.9	-49.9	92.1							122.0
(50) 9.7	(60) 8.4	9.8	EBIT/Interest						9.8
1.9	2.7	3.3							3.7
.1	1.6	1.2							1.2
(30) 5.6	(36) 5.6	(30) 11.0	Net Profit + Depr., Dep., Amort./Cur. Mat. L/T/D					(25)	11.1
2.5	2.4	3.4							3.6
1.3	1.1	1.0							.9
.8	.9	.7	Fixed/Worth						.7
1.3	1.5	1.2							1.2
2.6	2.4	2.2							1.8
.9	.9	1.0	Debt/Worth						.9
1.5	2.1	1.8							1.6
6.0	6.1	3.1							3.4
(48) 29.1	(55) 31.7	(58) 37.1	% Profit Before Taxes/Tangible Net Worth					(41)	31.2
8.7	18.4	16.0							16.0
-6.5	9.0	3.6							2.8
7.9	11.5	10.8	% Profit Before Taxes/Total Assets						10.3
2.2	5.0	6.2							6.3
-3.6	1.9	.9							.6
12.6	15.8	12.6	Sales/Net Fixed Assets						11.8
5.5	5.7	5.9							5.5
4.2	3.5	4.0							4.2
4.1	3.7	4.1	Sales/Total Assets						4.4
2.8	2.7	2.7							2.7
2.1	1.8	1.9							2.0
(45) 1.4	(56) 1.3	(49) 1.5	% Depr., Dep., Amort./Sales					(36)	1.5
2.1	2.3	2.0							2.0
3.2	3.1	3.2							3.0
(11) .8	(14) .8	.8	% Officers', Directors', Owners' Comp/Sales						
2.4	1.6								
3.3	3.3	3.3							
5272670M	6785801M	8281869M	Net Sales ($)		4041M	11004M	37836M	122802M	8106186M
2193826M	2957413M	3021489M	Total Assets ($)		1888M	8026M	26513M	37059M	2948003M

M = $ thousand   MM = $ million
See Pages 1 through 15 for Explanation of Ratios and Data

Current Data Sorted By Assets / Comparative Historical Data

1	3	3	3			# Postretirement Benefits		
	4	10	20	2	2	Type of Statement		
	4	10	20	2	2	Unqualified	30	29
	10	5	2			Reviewed	12	12
4	17	5	2			Compiled	14	11
2	1					Tax Returns		1
4	8	6	4	1		Other	19	16
	51 (4/1-9/30/94)		58 (10/1/94-3/31/95)				4/1/90-3/31/91	4/1/91-3/31/92
0-500M	500M-2MM	2-10MM	10-50MM	50-100MM	100-250MM		ALL	ALL
10	40	26	28	3	2	NUMBER OF STATEMENTS	75	69

0-500M	500M-2MM	2-10MM	10-50MM	50-100MM	100-250MM		ALL 91	ALL 92
%	%	%	%	%	%	**ASSETS**	%	%
13.2	7.5	7.6	3.9			Cash & Equivalents	7.2	7.9
31.1	32.6	27.0	28.0			Trade Receivables - (net)	22.4	25.1
23.7	23.5	24.1	25.8			Inventory	25.2	22.2
.6	1.3	3.8	1.2			All Other Current	2.6	2.6
68.6	64.9	62.5	58.9			Total Current	57.3	57.8
21.2	28.6	30.0	31.4			Fixed Assets (net)	32.2	30.7
1.1	1.0	.5	3.1			Intangibles (net)	1.5	3.0
9.1	5.5	7.0	6.7			All Other Non-Current	8.9	8.5
100.0	100.0	100.0	100.0			Total	100.0	100.0
						LIABILITIES		
18.8	10.1	12.6	13.4			Notes Payable-Short Term	14.5	13.5
2.5	7.7	2.3	3.2			Cur. Mat. -L/T/D	3.7	4.9
18.5	21.3	18.0	20.3			Trade Payables	14.4	15.2
.3	.2	.2	.4			Income Taxes Payable	.3	.3
1.2	6.7	11.1	7.7			All Other Current	9.4	9.6
41.3	45.9	44.1	45.1			Total Current	42.2	43.5
19.8	18.3	12.0	11.4			Long Term Debt	16.4	15.5
.0	.3	.7	.4			Deferred Taxes	1.1	1.3
4.8	1.6	6.0	3.2			All Other-Non-Current	3.0	2.9
34.1	34.0	37.2	40.0			Net Worth	37.3	36.8
100.0	100.0	100.0	100.0			Total Liabilities & Net Worth	100.0	100.0
						INCOME DATA		
100.0	100.0	100.0	100.0			Net Sales	100.0	100.0
31.2	23.9	20.8	22.4			Gross Profit	21.3	23.3
29.6	20.1	18.0	14.1			Operating Expenses	17.6	18.9
1.5	3.7	2.8	8.3			Operating Profit	3.7	4.4
-.2	.5	.2	1.1			All Other Expenses (net)	.7	.2
1.7	3.2	2.6	7.2			Profit Before Taxes	2.9	4.2
						RATIOS		
5.9 / 1.9 / 1.0	2.5 / 1.4 / 1.1	2.2 / 1.3 / 1.1	1.6 / 1.3 / 1.1			Current	2.0 / 1.5 / 1.0	1.8 / 1.4 / 1.1
3.2 / 1.2 / .7	1.6 / 1.1 / .6	1.2 / .8 / .5	1.0 / .6 / .5			Quick	1.3 / .7 / .4	1.2 / .7 / .5
7 50.4 / 15 24.4 / 37 10.0	22 16.7 / 29 12.5 / 58 6.3	16 23.3 / 24 15.5 / 42 8.6	26 14.1 / 34 10.8 / 41 8.8			Sales/Receivables	14 25.5 / 23 15.8 / 34 10.6	20 18.5 / 29 12.8 / 40 9.2
18 20.3 / 38 9.5 / 52 7.0	17 21.4 / 26 13.9 / 64 5.7	18 20.0 / 37 9.8 / 47 7.7	23 16.2 / 36 10.1 / 56 6.5			Cost of Sales/Inventory	17 21.2 / 31 11.6 / 54 6.8	17 21.3 / 30 12.3 / 49 7.4
4 84.7 / 12 30.0 / 47 7.7	12 29.3 / 22 16.3 / 35 10.4	10 37.2 / 18 19.8 / 29 12.4	18 20.7 / 28 13.1 / 42 8.7			Cost of Sales/Payables	9 41.7 / 19 19.6 / 30 12.0	9 38.8 / 21 17.1 / 37 10.0
9.5 / 13.5 / NM	7.3 / 19.4 / 63.2	14.4 / 23.4 / 183.3	9.9 / 22.9 / 67.6			Sales/Working Capital	8.3 / 16.3 / 383.0	9.7 / 17.1 / 92.0
	(39) 9.2 / 2.8 / 1.0	(23) 11.6 / 2.9 / 1.3	(24) 18.0 / 2.1 / -.1			EBIT/Interest	(70) 7.4 / 2.6 / 1.1	(64) 6.7 / 2.5 / 1.4
	(15) 3.3 / 1.4 / .6	(12) 10.1 / 6.0 / 4.2	(15) 3.2 / 2.3 / .1			Net Profit + Depr., Dep., Amort./Cur. Mat. L /T/D	(35) 6.4 / 2.2 / .8	(38) 5.0 / 1.9 / .9
.1 / .5 / NM	.5 / .8 / 1.7	.5 / .8 / 1.4	.5 / .8 / 1.0			Fixed/Worth	.4 / .9 / 2.8	.4 / .9 / 1.6
.7 / 1.5 / NM	.8 / 2.4 / 5.1	.8 / 1.6 / 6.8	.9 / 1.9 / 3.9			Debt/Worth	.7 / 1.6 / 5.8	.8 / 2.2 / 4.3
	(37) 46.6 / 25.2 / 4.6	30.7 / 14.3 / 4.9	27.7 / 15.0 / -7.7			% Profit Before Taxes/Tangible Net Worth	(68) 31.9 / 14.2 / 1.7	(63) 33.1 / 15.2 / 6.9
22.2 / 9.3 / .0	15.1 / 6.9 / .1	12.5 / 5.0 / .7	13.4 / 3.9 / -2.1			% Profit Before Taxes/Total Assets	15.6 / 4.7 / .4	14.6 / 5.5 / 1.8
207.9 / 26.3 / 9.6	35.4 / 11.2 / 6.7	20.7 / 13.5 / 7.6	21.0 / 10.9 / 5.4			Sales/Net Fixed Assets	20.9 / 10.8 / 6.1	26.5 / 10.4 / 5.3
7.0 / 3.6 / 2.7	4.4 / 3.5 / 2.3	4.2 / 3.4 / 2.3	3.8 / 2.9 / 2.3			Sales/Total Assets	4.0 / 3.1 / 2.2	3.5 / 3.0 / 2.1
	(39) 1.0 / 1.8 / 3.1	(22) 1.4 / 1.5 / 2.1	(26) .6 / 1.3 / 3.1			% Depr., Dep., Amort./Sales	(73) 1.1 / 1.7 / 2.9	(64) 1.2 / 1.7 / 2.7
(18) .8 / 1.2 / 2.8						% Officers', Directors', Owners' Comp/Sales	(22) 1.2 / 1.7 / 2.4	(23) 1.5 / 2.7 / 4.2
11930M	168752M	462783M	1706711M	400412M	600326M	Net Sales ($)	1412758M	1587388M
2236M	45689M	127954M	539392M	219019M	249928M	Total Assets ($)	491180M	600059M

M = $ thousand   MM = $ million
See Pages 1 through 15 for Explanation of Ratios and Data

Comparative Historical Data   **Current Data Sorted By Sales**

Type of Statement

3	8	10	# Postretirement Benefits / Type of Statement	1	2	1	3	3
30	37	38	Unqualified		1	2		12	23
14	14	17	Reviewed		4	4	3	4	2
17	19	28	Compiled	2	7	7	7	2	3
		3	Tax Returns	2	1				
26	18	23	Other	3	5	2	4	2	7

Historical periods: 4/1/92-3/31/93 ALL (87); 4/1/93-3/31/94 ALL (88); 4/1/94-3/31/95 ALL (109)
Current: 51 (4/1-9/30/94); 58 (10/1/94-3/31/95)

Data

3	8	10		0-1MM	1-3MM	3-5MM	5-10MM	10-25MM	25MM & OVER
87	88	109	NUMBER OF STATEMENTS	7	18	15	14	20	35
%	%	%	**ASSETS**	%	%	%	%	%	%
6.3	7.9	7.0	Cash & Equivalents		7.7	8.2	9.9	7.7	3.0
27.0	27.4	29.1	Trade Receivables - (net)		27.7	36.9	37.7	23.1	27.3
22.5	22.0	24.5	Inventory		23.9	20.2	25.9	23.5	27.0
3.3	2.1	1.8	All Other Current		.5	3.2	1.5	2.9	1.5
59.1	59.4	62.4	Total Current		59.8	68.5	75.0	57.3	58.9
32.4	30.3	28.8	Fixed Assets (net)		33.5	24.2	19.5	35.1	29.9
2.3	3.3	2.3	Intangibles (net)		2.2	.5	.3	1.0	5.2
6.3	7.0	6.4	All Other Non-Current		4.6	6.8	5.1	6.7	6.1
100.0	100.0	100.0	Total		100.0	100.0	100.0	100.0	100.0
			LIABILITIES						
10.6	9.9	12.6	Notes Payable-Short Term		8.7	9.7	15.0	10.6	14.4
4.5	3.5	4.5	Cur. Mat.-L /T/D		10.0	4.7	4.7	2.2	2.7
16.3	18.3	19.6	Trade Payables		14.3	23.3	24.0	16.2	20.9
.3	.4	.3	Income Taxes Payable		.2	.2	.1	.2	.4
6.7	8.1	7.6	All Other Current		2.7	9.3	10.1	11.1	7.6
38.6	40.1	44.5	Total Current		35.9	47.2	53.9	40.2	46.0
16.0	14.1	15.3	Long Term Debt		25.4	15.1	10.2	14.2	12.5
.7	.7	.5	Deferred Taxes		.1	.3	.2	.2	1.1
3.3	3.8	3.7	All Other-Non-Current		3.7	1.4	6.2	3.2	4.4
41.5	41.4	36.0	Net Worth		34.8	36.0	29.4	42.2	36.0
100.0	100.0	100.0	Total Liabilities & Net Worth		100.0	100.0	100.0	100.0	100.0
			INCOME DATA						
100.0	100.0	100.0	Net Sales		100.0	100.0	100.0	100.0	100.0
22.6	23.4	23.0	Gross Profit		29.8	14.9	18.8	25.4	19.6
17.8	19.4	18.5	Operating Expenses		25.3	14.3	15.7	19.4	13.1
4.8	4.0	4.6	Operating Profit		4.6	.5	3.1	5.9	6.5
.6	.6	.6	All Other Expenses (net)		1.0	-.1	.3	.5	1.1
4.2	3.4	4.0	Profit Before Taxes		3.6	.6	2.7	5.5	5.3
			RATIOS						
2.3	2.2	2.1			5.4	2.4	2.7	2.2	1.6
1.7	1.5	1.4	Current		1.7	1.6	1.3	1.3	1.3
1.2	1.1	1.1			1.1	1.2	1.1	1.1	1.1
1.4	1.3	1.3			2.7	1.9	1.5	1.3	1.0
1.0	.9	.8	Quick		1.1	1.1	.9	.8	.7
.6	.6	.6			.7	.6	.6	.5	.5
19 19.6	19 19.2	19 19.2			23 15.9	18 20.5	17 21.8	16 23.1	23 16.1
27 13.5	28 13.0	28 13.0	Sales/Receivables		31 11.6	31 11.9	29 12.8	22 16.6	29 12.6
41 8.9	40 9.1	43 8.4			57 6.4	72 5.1	49 7.5	34 10.8	41 9.0
16 22.7	17 21.2	20 18.1			16 22.3	16 22.9	12 29.8	20 18.6	22 16.6
28 12.9	28 13.1	35 10.5	Cost of Sales/Inventory		43 8.4	22 16.7	22 16.4	35 10.5	35 10.5
44 8.3	53 6.9	56 6.5			68 5.4	46 7.9	76 4.8	49 7.5	51 7.1
11 32.0	14 25.8	13 28.8			7 52.9	12 29.5	11 33.8	10 37.6	18 20.8
19 19.5	21 17.3	22 16.5	Cost of Sales/Payables		15 23.9	24 15.4	20 18.3	18 20.0	26 14.0
30 12.0	33 10.9	37 10.0			33 10.9	47 7.7	33 11.2	26 14.2	38 9.5
9.6	8.9	9.9			7.2	7.2	11.4	10.4	13.8
15.8	19.9	21.5	Sales/Working Capital		15.0	16.7	31.0	24.6	22.6
43.3	52.6	70.4			54.5	50.8	117.9	155.0	69.2
(78) 12.0	(81) 12.2	(97) 10.4			(17) 10.2	(12) 17.1	(13) 6.3	(18) 22.6	(32) 9.2
3.8	4.6	2.9	EBIT/Interest		2.8	2.4	2.6	5.1	2.7
1.6	2.2	1.1			.7	1.2	1.2	1.1	1.2
(38) 4.9	(38) 6.6	(45) 5.8						(10) 8.9	(19) 5.9
2.6	3.3	3.2	Net Profit + Depr., Dep., Amort./Cur. Mat. L/T/D					5.4	3.2
1.6	1.9	1.1						2.6	1.2
.4	.4	.5			.6	.1	.4	.5	.6
.8	.8	.8	Fixed/Worth		.9	.7	.6	.8	.8
1.3	1.2	1.5			1.8	2.1	1.3	1.6	1.4
.8	.6	.8			.7	.7	1.1	.6	1.0
1.7	1.4	1.9	Debt/Worth		1.9	3.1	2.1	1.4	2.7
2.7	3.4	5.0			4.7	4.3	15.0	6.5	4.0
(85) 38.6	(82) 36.7	(102) 37.3			(16) 69.8	(14) 38.5	(13) 31.7	37.8	(33) 26.6
23.5	19.5	19.2	% Profit Before Taxes/Tangible Net Worth		40.7	20.1	17.9	18.2	14.8
7.5	6.4	2.1			.7	4.6	4.6	5.0	.6
16.0	12.9	13.6			22.9	14.4	13.0	14.6	11.6
8.0	7.0	5.7	% Profit Before Taxes/Total Assets		9.6	5.7	4.6	5.4	4.1
2.7	1.6	.2			-.5	.4	.6	1.2	.3
18.4	20.3	26.8			19.6	39.3	56.2	19.2	20.2
10.9	12.3	11.3	Sales/Net Fixed Assets		10.1	14.7	23.9	10.9	10.8
6.6	6.8	7.0			5.5	7.9	14.4	5.6	6.0
4.7	4.2	4.3			3.9	4.3	5.9	5.5	3.9
3.1	3.2	3.2	Sales/Total Assets		3.3	3.4	3.8	3.1	3.1
2.4	2.3	2.3			2.1	2.3	2.9	2.1	2.6
(84) .7	(84) .9	(99) 1.0			(17) 1.1	(13) .5	(13) .9	(18) 1.0	(32) .7
1.4	1.7	1.6	% Depr., Dep., Amort./Sales		2.2	1.6	1.4	1.6	1.3
2.3	2.7	2.5			3.4	2.4	2.6	2.2	2.2
(25) 1.1	(26) 1.1	(30) .8							
1.6	1.7	1.5	% Officers', Directors', Owners' Comp/Sales						
2.7	4.0	4.4							
2420032M	2765589M	3350914M	Net Sales ($)	3440M	33124M	60012M	102820M	318217M	2833301M
817004M	980855M	1184218M	Total Assets ($)	2302M	12895M	19372M	27299M	110120M	1012230M

M = $ thousand   MM = $ million
See Pages 1 through 15 for Explanation of Ratios and Data

Current Data Sorted By Assets | **Comparative Historical Data**

Type of Statement

# Postretirement Benefits / Type of Statement	0-500M	500M-2MM	2-10MM	10-50MM	50-100MM	100-250MM		4/1/90-3/31/91 ALL	4/1/91-3/31/92 ALL
# Postretirement Benefits	1	1	2	4		1			
Unqualified	1	1	15	17	5	2		33	29
Reviewed	2	7	13	1				17	19
Compiled		8	8					17	19
Tax Returns								1	
Other	2	7	9	6	3	1		16	20
		36 (4/1-9/30/94)		72 (10/1/94-3/31/95)					
NUMBER OF STATEMENTS	5	23	45	24	8	3		84	87

Financial Data

	0-500M %	500M-2MM %	2-10MM %	10-50MM %	50-100MM %	100-250MM %		4/1/90-3/31/91 ALL %	4/1/91-3/31/92 ALL %
ASSETS									
Cash & Equivalents		7.3	9.2	6.6				6.9	8.8
Trade Receivables - (net)		23.4	21.2	21.0				24.8	21.6
Inventory		25.7	21.3	21.9				22.9	21.2
All Other Current		.3	.5	1.6				1.0	.8
Total Current		56.7	52.2	51.1				55.5	52.4
Fixed Assets (net)		35.9	38.5	37.6				35.7	39.5
Intangibles (net)		.8	2.4	4.2				1.4	2.6
All Other Non-Current		6.6	6.9	7.1				7.4	5.5
Total		100.0	100.0	100.0				100.0	100.0
LIABILITIES									
Notes Payable-Short Term		16.1	7.7	8.8				11.5	9.9
Cur. Mat. -L/T/D		5.2	3.3	2.8				3.7	4.6
Trade Payables		16.1	12.8	11.5				15.8	14.8
Income Taxes Payable		.1	.4	.4				.5	.8
All Other Current		5.6	5.7	7.4				6.0	7.8
Total Current		43.1	30.0	30.8				37.6	37.9
Long Term Debt		22.7	16.2	15.4				19.5	20.6
Deferred Taxes		.2	.6	1.4				.8	.6
All Other-Non-Current		4.3	5.1	2.5				2.3	2.1
Net Worth		29.6	48.1	49.9				39.8	38.8
Total Liabilities & Net Worth		100.0	100.0	100.0				100.0	100.0
INCOME DATA									
Net Sales		100.0	100.0	100.0				100.0	100.0
Gross Profit		24.1	23.7	23.8				20.3	20.4
Operating Expenses		21.4	20.1	17.5				17.6	17.5
Operating Profit		2.7	3.6	6.2				2.7	2.8
All Other Expenses (net)		1.4	.5	.8				.9	1.0
Profit Before Taxes		1.3	3.2	5.5				1.8	1.8

RATIOS

	0-500M	500M-2MM	2-10MM	10-50MM	50-100MM	100-250MM		4/1/90-3/31/91 ALL	4/1/91-3/31/92 ALL
Current		2.0	2.8	2.8				2.2	2.2
		1.5	1.7	1.5				1.5	1.4
		1.1	1.3	1.1				1.1	1.0
Quick		1.0	1.7	1.4				1.3	1.3
		.8	.9	.8			(83)	.8	.8
		.4	.6	.6				.6	.6
Sales/Receivables	16	23.4	14 · 26.7	19 · 19.1			17	21.7	14 · 25.5
	18	20.7	18 · 20.5	22 · 16.6			20	18.3	19 · 19.3
	33	11.2	24 · 15.1	34 · 10.6			29	12.6	25 · 14.8
Cost of Sales/Inventory	22	16.5	20 · 18.7	18 · 20.6			15	25.1	14 · 25.5
	27	13.4	24 · 14.9	30 · 12.3			24	15.1	21 · 17.5
	35	10.3	42 · 8.7	68 · 5.4			39	9.3	34 · 10.8
Cost of Sales/Payables	12	29.7	8 · 48.6	11 · 33.6			11	33.5	11 · 33.5
	20	18.0	14 · 26.5	18 · 20.7			18	20.7	16 · 22.5
	29	12.7	20 · 18.0	23 · 16.1			22	16.6	23 · 16.2
Sales/Working Capital		13.6	8.7	5.8				11.3	10.9
		26.8	21.5	26.8				22.3	27.2
		207.0	46.2	150.8				93.6	206.4
EBIT/Interest		5.6	26.1	12.1				5.5	4.7
		2.2	(41) 6.2	(21) 6.4			(76)	2.3	(79) 2.6
		1.0	1.7	2.0				1.2	1.4
Net Profit + Depr., Dep., Amort./Cur. Mat. L./T/D			8.5	15.5				4.7	3.1
			(18) 3.9	(12) 5.0			(47)	2.4	(45) 2.0
			2.4	2.3				1.4	1.0
Fixed/Worth		.5	.4	.5				.5	.5
		1.2	.8	.9				.9	1.0
		5.9	1.9	1.5				1.8	2.6
Debt/Worth		1.0	.4	.5				.7	.8
		2.5	1.2	1.1				1.6	1.7
		12.9	2.9	3.4				3.9	4.1
% Profit Before Taxes/Tangible Net Worth		37.4	50.7	44.0				35.8	37.8
	(18)	13.5	(43) 24.1	18.6			(81)	15.6	(79) 16.5
		3.8	14.3	11.3				3.6	6.1
% Profit Before Taxes/Total Assets		8.8	21.7	19.7				12.4	13.1
		4.8	11.2	8.1				5.7	5.4
		.0	4.9	4.6				1.2	2.6
Sales/Net Fixed Assets		21.1	21.3	13.0				21.2	17.1
		12.0	8.9	7.6				10.7	10.4
		6.2	5.3	5.3				7.0	6.4
Sales/Total Assets		5.7	5.3	3.6				5.2	5.0
		3.5	3.6	2.7				3.7	3.9
		2.6	2.6	2.1				2.8	2.7
% Depr., Dep., Amort./Sales		.8	.7	1.0				1.0	1.0
	(21)	1.2	(43) 1.7	(20) 1.9			(81)	1.6	(80) 1.4
		2.3	2.4	2.3				2.3	2.0
% Officers', Directors', Owners' Comp/Sales		1.4	.5					1.8	1.3
	(11)	2.5	(18) 2.0				(26)	2.8	(31) 3.1
		5.1	4.5					4.7	5.2
Net Sales ($)	5971M	110405M	1067257M	1677408M	1545632M	3070317M		5715324M	5002061M
Total Assets ($)	1206M	28398M	253027M	543722M	480528M	559399M		1405141M	1263383M

M = $ thousand   MM = $ million
See Pages 1 through 15 for Explanation of Ratios and Data

Comparative Historical Data				Current Data Sorted By Sales					
3	4	8	**# Postretirement Benefits**				1	2	5
			Type of Statement						
37	40	41	Unqualified	1	1		2	9	28
12	16	21	Reviewed			4	5	9	3
20	15	16	Compiled	1	1	2	7	2	3
	3	2	Tax Returns	1	1				
15	16	28	Other		3	4	5	4	12
4/1/92-3/31/93	4/1/93-3/31/94	4/1/94-3/31/95		36 (4/1-9/30/94)			72 (10/1/94-3/31/95)		
ALL	ALL	ALL		0-1MM	1-3MM	3-5MM	5-10MM	10-25MM	25MM & OVER
84	90	108	**NUMBER OF STATEMENTS**	3	6	10	19	24	46
%	%	%	**ASSETS**	%	%	%	%	%	%
8.6	6.3	8.1	Cash & Equivalents			5.1	9.4	5.2	8.7
22.8	23.1	21.3	Trade Receivables - (net)			23.3	19.2	20.1	22.5
23.8	21.6	21.9	Inventory			22.3	20.9	24.0	21.1
1.1	2.4	.9	All Other Current			.3	.3	1.3	1.0
56.4	53.4	52.3	Total Current			51.0	49.7	50.6	53.2
36.1	37.7	37.2	Fixed Assets (net)			38.4	44.4	35.8	36.9
1.9	1.8	3.5	Intangibles (net)			.3	.7	6.4	3.6
5.7	7.1	7.0	All Other Non-Current			10.3	5.2	7.2	6.4
100.0	100.0	100.0	Total			100.0	100.0	100.0	100.0
			LIABILITIES						
10.6	9.7	9.7	Notes Payable-Short Term			17.3	9.0	7.7	7.8
3.8	2.5	3.6	Cur. Mat.-L/T/D			4.6	3.6	3.5	3.0
12.6	14.7	14.1	Trade Payables			14.3	12.1	12.3	15.4
.8	1.1	.3	Income Taxes Payable			.5	.3	.4	.3
7.6	6.9	6.7	All Other Current			3.8	6.1	7.6	7.5
35.3	35.0	34.4	Total Current			40.6	31.1	31.6	33.9
18.7	17.8	17.2	Long Term Debt			29.7	24.9	15.3	14.0
.5	.6	.7	Deferred Taxes			.3	.4	.9	.9
1.6	3.1	4.1	All Other-Non-Current			4.6	8.8	4.8	1.9
43.9	43.4	43.6	Net Worth			24.9	34.8	47.5	49.3
100.0	100.0	100.0	Total Liabilities & Net Worth			100.0	100.0	100.0	100.0
			INCOME DATA						
100.0	100.0	100.0	Net Sales			100.0	100.0	100.0	100.0
23.7	21.4	23.8	Gross Profit			27.7	27.9	23.7	19.9
19.5	18.6	19.9	Operating Expenses			24.9	23.6	20.0	15.0
4.2	2.8	3.9	Operating Profit			2.8	4.3	3.7	4.9
.9	.9	.8	All Other Expenses (net)			1.3	1.4	.4	.7
3.3	1.9	3.1	Profit Before Taxes			1.5	2.9	3.3	4.2
			RATIOS						
2.5	2.3	2.3				2.0	2.0	2.5	2.4
1.6	1.5	1.5	Current			1.5	1.9	1.4	1.5
1.2	1.1	1.1				1.0	1.2	1.1	1.0
1.4	1.3	1.4				1.0	1.4	1.1	1.4
1.0	.9	.8	Quick			.9	.9	.8	.8
.6	.5	.6				.4	.7	.6	.6
18 20.7	**17** 21.8	**15** 24.3				**14** 25.4	**16** 23.3	**13** 28.2	**16** 23.5
20 17.9	**21** 17.5	**19** 18.8	Sales/Receivables			**17** 21.1	**21** 17.3	**18** 20.2	**20** 18.5
27 13.3	**28** 12.9	**27** 13.7				**40** 9.2	**27** 13.7	**27** 13.3	**23** 15.6
17 21.6	**16** 22.3	**20** 18.7				**24** 15.0	**22** 16.3	**20** 17.9	**15** 23.7
27 13.3	**26** 14.3	**26** 14.0	Cost of Sales/Inventory			**29** 12.4	**27** 13.4	**25** 14.8	**23** 15.7
54 6.8	**44** 8.3	**42** 8.7				**66** 5.5	**42** 8.6	**64** 5.7	**37** 10.0
9 39.2	**9** 41.2	**10** 37.5				**8** 46.5	**12** 31.3	**8** 43.5	**10** 38.1
12 29.4	**16** 23.3	**18** 20.3	Cost of Sales/Payables			**22** 16.9	**17** 21.0	**17** 21.2	**17** 21.7
23 15.8	**22** 16.3	**23** 15.8				**30** 12.3	**23** 15.8	**22** 16.4	**21** 17.0
9.8	9.5	10.2				11.5	11.2	10.6	9.7
17.2	19.7	26.6	Sales/Working Capital			27.1	18.8	28.7	29.4
51.4	67.3	137.2				NM	35.0	171.6	205.2
8.5	7.6	14.3				10.0	7.7	15.8	26.1
(72) 4.4	(78) 4.0	(100) 5.1	EBIT/Interest			1.2	(18) 3.1	(23) 5.9	(41) 8.2
1.8	1.8	1.7				.7	1.5	1.4	2.9
5.8	12.1	6.8						7.1	14.5
(38) 2.2	(33) 3.0	(47) 3.8	Net Profit + Depr., Dep., Amort./Cur. Mat. L/T/D					(10) 3.6	(24) 4.5
1.5	1.0	1.8						1.7	2.1
.5	.5	.5				.9	.6	.6	.4
.7	.8	1.0	Fixed/Worth			1.9	1.2	.9	.9
1.7	1.9	2.3				-31.0	2.9	1.8	1.5
.7	.6	.5				1.2	.8	.5	.5
1.2	1.4	1.5	Debt/Worth			4.4	1.7	1.5	1.0
2.8	3.3	3.7				-64.1	3.7	5.0	3.0
41.2	31.6	40.9					39.9	56.4	45.3
(80) 23.7	(84) 17.0	(97) 20.6	% Profit Before Taxes/Tangible Net Worth				(17) 24.1	(23) 20.3	(44) 21.3
7.5	4.4	12.1					15.8	8.3	15.7
15.5	14.2	15.8				8.9	14.4	20.6	19.6
8.6	5.7	8.6	% Profit Before Taxes/Total Assets			1.5	7.9	9.4	9.0
2.5	1.4	4.0				-1.4	3.6	4.1	5.7
18.4	18.1	16.9				12.3	16.0	16.3	23.0
11.1	9.7	9.5	Sales/Net Fixed Assets			7.9	6.2	9.2	10.0
5.6	5.4	5.5				5.3	3.7	5.9	6.3
4.8	4.8	5.0				4.3	4.2	5.0	5.5
3.5	3.3	3.2	Sales/Total Assets			3.1	2.9	3.3	3.6
2.4	2.4	2.5				2.4	2.3	2.3	2.7
1.0	.9	.8					.9	1.1	.7
(75) 1.4	(83) 1.7	(97) 1.7	% Depr., Dep., Amort./Sales				2.1	(22) 1.6	(40) 1.5
2.0	2.2	2.3					2.9	2.3	2.0
1.5	1.8	1.3						.5	
(26) 2.7	(30) 2.9	(35) 2.1	% Officers', Directors', Owners' Comp/Sales					(11) 1.7	
5.0	4.2	4.4						2.2	
4847888M	8088607M	7476990M	Net Sales ($)	1562M	11256M	39571M	134481M	435631M	6854489M
1163411M	1794220M	1866280M	Total Assets ($)	1109M	3412M	13731M	47025M	161881M	1639122M

M = $ thousand MM = $ million

See Pages 1 through 15 for Explanation of Ratios and Data

Current Data Sorted By Assets | Comparative Historical Data

						# Postretirement Benefits Type of Statement		
1	1	7	7		2	Unqualified	11	12
	4	8	1			Reviewed	12	8
4	4	1				Compiled	15	12
1						Tax Returns		3
5	2	7	3		1	Other	8	8
	12 (4/1-9/30/94)		47 (10/1/94-3/31/95)				4/1/90-3/31/91 ALL	4/1/91-3/31/92 ALL
0-500M	500M-2MM	2-10MM	10-50MM	50-100MM	100-250MM	NUMBER OF STATEMENTS	46	43
11	11	23	11		3			
%	%	%	%	%	%	ASSETS	%	%
7.7	8.8	5.6	10.8			Cash & Equivalents	5.0	6.3
27.4	22.2	32.6	21.1			Trade Receivables - (net)	29.6	29.4
33.8	30.4	31.3	22.4			Inventory	30.4	29.5
3.1	1.9	.8	2.1			All Other Current	1.6	1.1
72.2	63.3	70.2	56.5			Total Current	66.6	66.3
19.3	28.5	21.4	23.2			Fixed Assets (net)	25.3	22.8
1.5	5.0	2.5	15.2			Intangibles (net)	2.7	5.3
7.1	3.2	5.8	5.1			All Other Non-Current	5.5	5.6
100.0	100.0	100.0	100.0			Total	100.0	100.0
						LIABILITIES		
15.3	1.3	9.4	1.6			Notes Payable-Short Term	6.9	5.0
2.9	5.2	3.6	2.3			Cur. Mat. -L/T/D	3.9	6.2
22.8	22.5	22.7	14.4			Trade Payables	23.4	21.3
.1	.1	.2	.8			Income Taxes Payable	.8	.9
14.7	12.0	5.2	9.2			All Other Current	7.4	10.1
55.8	41.1	41.2	28.3			Total Current	42.5	43.3
8.5	16.1	7.6	15.1			Long Term Debt	19.1	16.6
.1	.0	.2	.7			Deferred Taxes	.4	.1
3.7	4.0	8.6	8.0			All Other-Non-Current	1.2	4.7
31.8	38.8	42.6	48.0			Net Worth	36.8	35.2
100.0	100.0	100.0	100.0			Total Liabilities & Net Worth	100.0	100.0
						INCOME DATA		
100.0	100.0	100.0	100.0			Net Sales	100.0	100.0
36.6	33.1	26.8	31.0			Gross Profit	28.9	31.2
37.2	33.1	25.5	23.7			Operating Expenses	25.9	26.7
-.6	.0	1.3	7.3			Operating Profit	2.9	4.5
.0	.6	1.2	1.1			All Other Expenses (net)	.8	1.0
-.6	-.6	.1	6.1			Profit Before Taxes	2.1	3.5
						RATIOS		
2.6	2.3	2.7	2.6			Current	2.3	2.2
1.6	1.3	1.7	2.1				1.6	1.7
.9	1.1	1.3	1.6				1.4	1.3
1.3	1.1	1.3	1.9			Quick	1.2	1.4
(10) .9	.8	1.0	1.1				.9	.9
.5	.5	.7	.6				.6	.6
12 31.5	2 212.1	27 13.3	31 11.9			Sales/Receivables	22 16.4	18 19.9
22 16.3	26 13.8	47 7.8	45 8.1				35 10.3	32 11.3
36 10.1	48 7.6	54 6.8	47 7.8				45 8.1	43 8.4
32 11.5	26 14.2	32 11.5	38 9.6			Cost of Sales/Inventory	35 10.3	26 13.8
47 7.7	44 8.3	45 8.2	43 8.4				46 8.0	38 9.5
66 5.5	63 5.8	69 5.3	91 4.0				54 6.7	51 7.1
3 127.0	26 14.0	22 16.8	26 14.3			Cost of Sales/Payables	19 18.9	16 23.0
31 11.8	36 10.2	32 11.3	27 13.4				32 11.4	26 13.8
47 7.7	45 8.2	57 6.4	38 9.5				45 8.2	44 8.3
7.7	7.2	6.7	5.8			Sales/Working Capital	8.1	8.8
10.3	28.5	10.7	7.2				13.9	12.8
-56.2	64.6	19.5	8.9				21.4	66.4
	25.8	9.6	15.1			EBIT/Interest	5.6	8.5
	(10) 3.4	(19) 2.4	8.7				(42) 3.1	(38) 3.6
	-2.2	1.2	2.7				1.1	1.3
						Net Profit + Depr., Dep., Amort./Cur. Mat. L./T/D	6.9	5.7
							(23) 2.4	(19) 2.3
							1.4	1.2
.1	.3	.2	.4			Fixed/Worth	.3	.4
.3	.8	.6	.6				.6	.6
15.3	2.2	1.0	1.5				2.1	1.4
.7	.9	.5	1.0			Debt/Worth	1.0	1.0
1.6	2.5	1.2	1.3				1.8	2.1
36.6	2.9	6.3	3.1				4.7	5.7
	60.9	41.8	59.1			% Profit Before Taxes/Tangible Net Worth	26.9	49.8
	30.7	(22) 12.6	(10) 49.3				(38) 11.5	(37) 27.9
	-35.5	2.7	22.8				.5	1.1
34.9	27.0	9.5	25.4			% Profit Before Taxes/Total Assets	12.0	17.4
3.6	7.9	3.9	10.7				6.8	8.1
-43.1	-3.9	.7	9.5				.3	.6
52.1	52.4	28.6	19.2			Sales/Net Fixed Assets	31.6	42.0
24.7	16.3	21.2	10.8				19.1	17.8
12.6	5.3	11.2	6.8				8.2	8.8
5.1	5.3	3.7	2.5			Sales/Total Assets	4.2	4.9
3.9	3.6	3.0	2.2				3.4	3.4
3.4	2.5	2.5	1.7				2.5	2.7
.8		.8	.8			% Depr., Dep., Amort./Sales	.8	.7
(10) 1.3		(22) 1.1	(10) 1.7				(42) 1.3	(39) 1.1
1.8		2.0	2.3				2.0	1.9
						% Officers', Directors', Owners' Comp/Sales	2.6	2.4
							(16) 3.8	(15) 4.1
							7.0	5.8
11719M	56005M	301101M	359778M		955306M	Net Sales ($)	973442M	608806M
2940M	15043M	100514M	180639M		523921M	Total Assets ($)	369036M	360819M

M = $ thousand   MM = $ million
See Pages 1 through 15 for Explanation of Ratios and Data

Comparative Historical Data   **Current Data Sorted By Sales**

Comparative Historical Data			# Postretirement Benefits / Type of Statement	Current Data Sorted By Sales					
2	1	1					1		
14	11	18	Unqualified		2	1	1	6	8
17	14	13	Reviewed			2	6	4	1
15	16	9	Compiled	2	3	2	1	1	
	4	1	Tax Returns		1				
8	12	18	Other	3	3	1	3	4	4
4/1/92-3/31/93 ALL	4/1/93-3/31/94 ALL	4/1/94-3/31/95 ALL		0-1MM (12 4/1-9/30/94)	1-3MM	3-5MM	5-10MM (47 10/1/94-3/31/95)	10-25MM	25MM & OVER
54	57	59	**NUMBER OF STATEMENTS**	5	9	6	11	15	13
%	%	%	**ASSETS**	%	%	%	%	%	%
8.9	8.4	7.4	Cash & Equivalents				9.2	3.7	9.9
30.4	29.6	27.0	Trade Receivables - (net)				27.6	31.8	23.7
30.9	29.1	29.4	Inventory				28.4	30.4	24.7
1.1	1.0	1.7	All Other Current				1.4	1.7	1.4
71.3	68.1	65.5	Total Current				66.6	67.6	59.7
20.1	22.4	22.6	Fixed Assets (net)				28.4	14.2	24.8
4.0	3.3	6.5	Intangibles (net)				.3	11.7	10.1
4.6	6.2	5.4	All Other Non-Current				4.7	6.6	5.3
100.0	100.0	100.0	Total				100.0	100.0	100.0
			LIABILITIES						
8.5	7.3	7.2	Notes Payable-Short Term				3.7	12.2	1.7
3.8	2.9	3.4	Cur. Mat.-L /T/D				5.3	3.0	2.6
20.4	23.1	20.5	Trade Payables				27.8	20.3	17.3
.4	1.1	.3	Income Taxes Payable				.1	.3	.6
8.1	9.5	9.1	All Other Current				7.7	5.6	7.9
41.2	43.9	40.5	Total Current				44.6	41.4	30.2
15.1	14.5	11.8	Long Term Debt				14.5	7.2	17.9
.2	.2	.3	Deferred Taxes				.0	.4	.7
4.1	2.8	6.6	All Other-Non-Current				2.6	14.5	4.1
39.4	38.6	40.8	Net Worth				38.3	36.5	47.1
100.0	100.0	100.0	Total Liabilities & Net Worth				100.0	100.0	100.0
			INCOME DATA						
100.0	100.0	100.0	Net Sales				100.0	100.0	100.0
28.8	30.6	30.6	Gross Profit				22.8	32.2	28.5
26.0	27.3	28.5	Operating Expenses				23.2	28.4	22.6
2.9	3.3	2.1	Operating Profit				−.4	3.8	5.9
.9	.8	.9	All Other Expenses (net)				1.0	1.1	.9
1.9	2.5	1.2	Profit Before Taxes				−1.5	2.7	5.0
			RATIOS						
2.7 1.8 1.3	2.5 1.7 1.2	2.6 1.7 1.3	Current				2.1 1.3 1.3	2.2 1.7 1.3	2.9 2.0 1.5
1.7 .9 .6	1.5 .9 .6	1.4 (58) .9 .6	Quick				1.1 .8 .6	1.3 .8 .6	2.1 1.0 .7
26 13.8 40 9.2 48 7.6	17 21.2 33 11.2 48 7.6	18 20.1 37 9.9 48 7.6	Sales/Receivables				17 22.1 37 9.9 47 7.8	31 11.9 47 7.8 54 6.8	23 15.8 35 10.3 46 7.9
33 11.0 42 8.6 61 6.0	26 14.3 41 8.9 63 5.8	32 11.5 45 8.2 66 5.5	Cost of Sales/Inventory				26 14.0 43 8.5 54 6.8	32 11.5 45 8.2 99 3.7	33 11.0 41 8.8 74 4.9
15 24.3 28 13.2 43 8.5	15 24.0 27 13.4 53 6.9	24 14.9 29 12.5 51 7.2	Cost of Sales/Payables				29 12.8 36 10.2 51 7.2	23 15.9 27 13.3 60 6.1	25 14.6 27 13.7 35 10.3
6.7 10.4 25.6	7.6 12.6 29.6	6.7 9.7 28.5	Sales/Working Capital				7.7 19.5 37.0	6.9 9.0 15.2	5.7 7.7 20.5
(44) 7.2 2.3 1.2	10.6 (52) 4.8 1.0	(52) 9.5 3.3 1.2	EBIT/Interest					(13) 9.7 2.7 1.4	13.6 8.6 2.7
(24) 5.9 2.8 .7	(26) 4.6 2.8 1.7	(22) 8.6 2.5 .7	Net Profit + Depr., Dep., Amort./Cur. Mat. L/T/D						
.3 .5 2.0	.3 .6 1.4	.3 .6 1.5	Fixed/Worth				.3 1.0 2.2	.3 .6 1.5	.4 .6 1.2
.8 1.5 5.9	.7 1.2 3.4	.7 1.5 4.9	Debt/Worth				.9 2.5 4.9	1.0 2.3 10.6	.8 1.3 2.5
(49) 43.8 16.8 7.4	(51) 53.0 24.2 7.9	(54) 48.9 17.9 2.9	% Profit Before Taxes/Tangible Net Worth				48.8 17.6 −4.8	(13) 46.3 38.1 7.5	(12) 50.9 30.6 13.5
11.9 7.6 1.1	16.1 8.1 .2	12.2 6.1 .7	% Profit Before Taxes/Total Assets				8.7 7.8 −3.9	13.8 4.6 1.7	18.8 10.4 5.4
26.9 17.9 11.1	34.3 19.0 11.3	31.1 19.8 6.8	Sales/Net Fixed Assets				37.2 11.6 6.2	27.3 21.2 15.4	15.8 8.9 6.8
4.0 3.2 2.6	4.5 3.4 2.6	4.1 3.0 2.2	Sales/Total Assets				4.4 3.6 3.0	3.4 3.0 2.5	2.7 2.4 1.9
(52) .8 1.3 2.1	(53) .7 1.2 1.7	(53) .8 1.2 2.0	% Depr., Dep., Amort./Sales				.8 1.1 1.9	(13) .9 1.1 2.1	(12) .8 1.3 2.2
(20) 2.1 3.4 4.7	(23) 2.6 3.9 6.6	(21) 2.6 4.2 8.3	% Officers', Directors', Owners' Comp/Sales						
1084027M 559790M	825276M 311649M	1683909M 823057M	Net Sales ($) Total Assets ($)	2879M 700M	15743M 5977M	24697M 11818M	90809M 30786M	233400M 106801M	1316381M 666975M

© Robert Morris Associates 1995   M = $ thousand   MM = $ million
See Pages 1 through 15 for Explanation of Ratios and Data

Current Data Sorted By Assets   Comparative Historical Data

	0-500M	500M-2MM	2-10MM	10-50MM	50-100MM	100-250MM		4/1/90-3/31/91 ALL	4/1/91-3/31/92 ALL
		11 (4/1-9/30/94)		34 (10/1/94-3/31/95)			# Postretirement Benefits / Type of Statement		
Unqualified			2	3	1			6	18
Reviewed		1	7	5	1	1		9	4
Compiled	2	3						6	4
Tax Returns	4		3						
Other	1	6	5					11	8
NUMBER OF STATEMENTS	7	10	17	8	2	1		32	34
	%	%	%	%	%	%	**ASSETS**	%	%
		2.9	5.5				Cash & Equivalents	7.0	9.2
		38.7	31.8				Trade Receivables - (net)	29.8	29.2
		29.4	26.9				Inventory	27.1	26.6
		2.3	2.5				All Other Current	1.3	1.3
		73.3	66.7				Total Current	65.2	66.3
		22.3	24.5				Fixed Assets (net)	29.1	25.3
		2.6	2.1				Intangibles (net)	1.1	2.3
		1.8	6.6				All Other Non-Current	4.6	6.0
		100.0	100.0				Total	100.0	100.0
							LIABILITIES		
		10.7	15.0				Notes Payable-Short Term	11.9	6.6
		2.8	3.5				Cur. Mat. -L/T/D	3.2	4.2
		29.6	15.8				Trade Payables	12.7	15.6
		1.3	.5				Income Taxes Payable	.8	.1
		6.8	11.6				All Other Current	11.6	11.2
		51.2	46.4				Total Current	40.1	37.6
		17.7	12.9				Long Term Debt	15.1	16.9
		.9	.3				Deferred Taxes	.5	.8
		8.2	3.0				All Other-Non-Current	2.7	4.2
		22.0	37.4				Net Worth	41.5	40.5
		100.0	100.0				Total Liabilities & Net Worth	100.0	100.0
							INCOME DATA		
		100.0	100.0				Net Sales	100.0	100.0
		30.7	31.4				Gross Profit	31.5	27.7
		25.8	26.0				Operating Expenses	28.2	25.8
		5.0	5.4				Operating Profit	3.2	1.9
		1.9	.7				All Other Expenses (net)	1.4	.8
		3.1	4.7				Profit Before Taxes	1.9	1.1
							RATIOS		
		1.7	2.6				Current	2.8	3.3
		1.4	1.6					1.8	2.1
		1.1	1.1					1.3	1.4
		1.0	1.5				Quick	1.5	2.3
		.9	1.0					1.0	1.1
		.6	.5					.6	.6
	30	12.2	38 9.5				Sales/Receivables	35 10.5	38 9.5
	43	8.4	50 7.3					41 9.0	48 7.6
	57	6.4	64 5.7					49 7.5	57 6.4
	20	18.2	39 9.3				Cost of Sales/Inventory	33 10.9	41 9.0
	43	8.5	65 5.6					63 5.8	60 6.1
	91	4.0	101 3.6					91 4.0	91 4.0
	35	10.5	19 19.4				Cost of Sales/Payables	18 20.0	21 17.7
	39	9.3	33 10.9					23 15.7	30 12.1
	56	6.5	51 7.1					32 11.3	43 8.5
		8.8	5.5				Sales/Working Capital	5.1	4.0
		16.7	8.8					8.1	7.3
		63.8	46.5					17.7	14.2
		11.7	157.9				EBIT/Interest	(30) 7.2	(29) 5.5
		4.8	(14) 4.9					2.5	1.9
		1.7	1.3					1.0	-.2
							Net Profit + Depr., Dep., Amort./Cur. Mat. L/T/D	(20) 7.5	(15) 4.5
								2.9	1.3
								1.1	.4
		.5	.2				Fixed/Worth	.4	.3
		.7	.6					.7	.7
		1.3	1.4					1.2	2.3
		1.7	.5				Debt/Worth	.6	.3
		2.5	1.4					1.3	1.7
		3.6	3.3					3.7	6.4
			53.5				% Profit Before Taxes/Tangible Net Worth	(31) 37.7	(30) 25.2
		(15)	30.9					15.9	8.1
			13.3					.7	2.5
		20.4	17.6				% Profit Before Taxes/Total Assets	13.4	7.7
		9.3	10.4					5.7	4.4
		3.2	4.5					-.5	-1.4
		25.4	20.1				Sales/Net Fixed Assets	22.2	20.5
		16.0	8.6					7.4	7.1
		13.2	5.8					4.7	6.0
		3.9	2.7				Sales/Total Assets	3.1	2.6
		3.2	2.3					2.3	1.9
		2.8	1.5					1.7	1.6
		.7	1.0				% Depr., Dep., Amort./Sales	(28) 1.4	(29) 1.3
		1.0	(16) 2.4					2.0	2.5
		1.8	3.4					2.9	3.3
							% Officers', Directors', Owners' Comp/Sales	(16) 1.8	
								4.0	
								7.7	
	9968M	38695M	203090M	318593M	201231M	284535M	Net Sales ($)	307438M	714102M
	2389M	11612M	90712M	150427M	148815M	163333M	Total Assets ($)	148561M	365809M

M = $ thousand   MM = $ million
See Pages 1 through 15 for Explanation of Ratios and Data

Comparative Historical Data   Current Data Sorted By Sales

Type of Statement (# Postretirement Benefits)

	CHD 1	CHD 4	CHD 6	Type of Statement	0-1MM	1-3MM	3-5MM	5-10MM	10-25MM	25MM & OVER
								1	2	3
	17	14	15	Unqualified		1	1	2	5	6
	5	3	7	Reviewed	1	2	2	2	5	
	12	2	7	Compiled	1	2	1	1	2	
		1		Tax Returns						
	8	11	16	Other		3	2	4	4	3
	4/1/92-3/31/93	4/1/93-3/31/94	4/1/94-3/31/95		11 (4/1-9/30/94)			34 (10/1/94-3/31/95)		
	ALL	ALL	ALL							
	42	31	45	**NUMBER OF STATEMENTS**	2	8	6	9	11	9

ASSETS

	CHD 1 %	CHD 4 %	CHD 6 %	ASSETS	0-1MM %	1-3MM %	3-5MM %	5-10MM %	10-25MM %	25MM & OVER %
	7.2	4.7	5.9	Cash & Equivalents					6.8	
	31.8	32.1	33.7	Trade Receivables - (net)					29.6	
	26.5	26.7	26.5	Inventory					32.6	
	1.6	3.6	1.8	All Other Current					1.8	
	67.1	67.2	68.0	Total Current					70.8	
	22.5	23.9	23.3	Fixed Assets (net)					19.5	
	3.7	1.4	2.7	Intangibles (net)					.7	
	6.7	7.5	6.0	All Other Non-Current					9.1	
	100.0	100.0	100.0	Total					100.0	

LIABILITIES

	CHD 1	CHD 4	CHD 6	LIABILITIES	0-1MM	1-3MM	3-5MM	5-10MM	10-25MM	25MM & OVER
	6.8	10.0	14.6	Notes Payable-Short Term					14.2	
	4.9	2.1	3.5	Cur. Mat.-L./T/D					1.7	
	16.9	13.3	18.7	Trade Payables					13.7	
	.4	1.0	.5	Income Taxes Payable					.0	
	9.1	8.4	10.1	All Other Current					8.2	
	38.0	34.8	47.4	Total Current					37.8	
	14.7	11.4	14.3	Long Term Debt					5.7	
	.4	.2	.4	Deferred Taxes					.1	
	3.2	4.1	4.3	All Other-Non-Current					.7	
	43.7	49.5	33.6	Net Worth					55.6	
	100.0	100.0	100.0	Total Liabilities & Net Worth					100.0	

INCOME DATA

	CHD 1	CHD 4	CHD 6	INCOME DATA	0-1MM	1-3MM	3-5MM	5-10MM	10-25MM	25MM & OVER
	100.0	100.0	100.0	Net Sales					100.0	
	29.7	28.0	30.6	Gross Profit					26.2	
	25.3	23.9	25.2	Operating Expenses					24.5	
	4.4	4.1	5.3	Operating Profit					1.7	
	1.0	.8	1.1	All Other Expenses (net)					.3	
	3.4	3.3	4.2	Profit Before Taxes					1.4	

RATIOS

	CHD 1	CHD 4	CHD 6	RATIOS	5-10MM	10-25MM
	3.8	3.2	2.4	Current		2.7
	2.1	2.1	1.4			1.9
	1.2	1.3	1.1			1.5
	2.1	1.5	1.2	Quick		1.6
	1.1	1.0	.9			1.1
	.7	.7	.6			.5
35	10.4	43 8.5	35 10.5	Sales/Receivables		35 10.5
45	8.1	49 7.5	50 7.3			47 7.7
57	6.4	56 6.5	61 6.0			58 6.3
41	8.8	37 10.0	34 10.8	Cost of Sales/Inventory		47 7.8
56	6.5	58 6.3	51 7.1			99 3.7
78	4.7	94 3.9	91 4.0			122 3.0
16	22.9	20 18.1	21 17.7	Cost of Sales/Payables		19 18.8
29	12.8	25 14.4	33 10.9			23 15.9
46	8.0	39 9.4	50 7.3			35 10.4
	4.3	4.4	6.1	Sales/Working Capital		3.6
	8.0	7.7	11.5			7.0
	18.3	15.6	56.9			11.5
(38)	11.6	(28) 11.0	(42) 14.0	EBIT/Interest		14.0
	4.4	4.3	4.4			4.4
	1.2	1.1	1.5			1.5
(17)	5.8	(15) 9.5	(21) 4.8	Net Profit + Depr., Dep., Amort./Cur. Mat. L/T/D		4.8
	2.2	3.8	2.5			2.5
	.3	-1.1	.6			.6
	.2	.3	.4	Fixed/Worth		.1
	.5	.6	.7			.4
	1.7	.9	1.3			.5
	.4	.4	.9	Debt/Worth		.4
	1.3	1.1	2.1			.8
	5.1	2.5	3.8			1.4
(37)	49.6	35.5	(40) 61.0	% Profit Before Taxes/Tangible Net Worth		30.9
	13.8	11.8	33.0			9.7
	7.0	2.3	11.9			-.9
	12.8	16.3	19.2	% Profit Before Taxes/Total Assets		11.9
	5.8	6.2	8.2			7.4
	1.1	.2	3.5			-.6
	25.0	14.4	23.6	Sales/Net Fixed Assets		25.5
	12.5	10.0	12.7			9.0
	6.6	5.5	6.9			6.4
	2.8	2.6	3.3	Sales/Total Assets		2.7
	2.4	2.2	2.5			2.5
	1.9	1.8	1.8			1.3
(35)	.9	(29) 1.4	(42) .8	% Depr., Dep., Amort./Sales	(10)	.5
	2.2	2.2	2.1			1.9
	3.0	2.5	2.9			3.2
(13)	3.1	(13) .8	(15) 2.6	% Officers', Directors', Owners' Comp/Sales		
	5.8	3.4	4.4			
	7.7	5.5	6.4			

	CHD 1	CHD 4	CHD 6		0-1MM	1-3MM	3-5MM	5-10MM	10-25MM	25MM & OVER
	1007236M	999735M	1056112M	Net Sales ($)	1178M	15590M	23226M	66255M	171355M	778508M
	499295M	532495M	567288M	Total Assets ($)	438M	6449M	7375M	30904M	90095M	432027M

M = $ thousand   MM = $ million
See Pages 1 through 15 for Explanation of Ratios and Data

Current Data Sorted By Assets | | | | | | **Comparative Historical Data**

	0-500M	500M-2MM	2-10MM	10-50MM	50-100MM	100-250MM	# Postretirement Benefits / Type of Statement	4/1/90-3/31/91 ALL	4/1/91-3/31/92 ALL
	3	2	5	3	3				
	1	3	20	13	5		Unqualified	42	33
	2	21	29	3			Reviewed	50	58
	16	35	9	1			Compiled	44	44
	4	1	1				Tax Returns	3	2
	8	16	16	1	2		Other	41	33
		51 (4/1-9/30/94)		155 (10/1/94-3/31/95)					
	31	76	75	17	7		NUMBER OF STATEMENTS	180	170
	%	%	%	%	%	%	**ASSETS**	%	%
	12.2	7.8	10.0	8.1			Cash & Equivalents	8.1	7.4
	41.0	35.9	28.5	31.4			Trade Receivables - (net)	33.3	32.3
	21.9	22.0	27.0	29.6			Inventory	25.0	25.5
	.5	3.2	2.5	2.5			All Other Current	1.7	1.7
	75.7	68.8	68.1	71.6			Total Current	68.0	66.9
	19.6	24.4	24.0	22.5			Fixed Assets (net)	23.9	24.5
	.2	2.8	.8	.7			Intangibles (net)	1.2	1.1
	4.5	4.0	7.1	5.2			All Other Non-Current	6.8	7.5
	100.0	100.0	100.0	100.0			Total	100.0	100.0
							LIABILITIES		
	9.7	11.0	8.9	12.6			Notes Payable-Short Term	11.8	10.4
	4.3	3.2	2.6	4.6			Cur. Mat. -L/T/D	3.7	3.1
	18.3	18.2	13.8	17.9			Trade Payables	14.5	14.9
	.2	.6	.8	.3			Income Taxes Payable	.7	.4
	11.0	11.7	11.0	10.9			All Other Current	11.8	11.7
	43.5	44.8	37.1	46.2			Total Current	42.3	40.6
	17.4	12.4	10.0	13.0			Long Term Debt	13.9	14.8
	.0	.4	.4	.3			Deferred Taxes	.7	.3
	2.1	4.4	5.5	2.0			All Other-Non-Current	3.5	2.2
	37.0	38.1	47.1	38.5			Net Worth	39.6	42.1
	100.0	100.0	100.0	100.0			Total Liabilities & Net Worth	100.0	100.0
							INCOME DATA		
	100.0	100.0	100.0	100.0			Net Sales	100.0	100.0
	35.4	31.0	26.9	24.4			Gross Profit	28.5	29.4
	28.2	26.8	20.7	18.5			Operating Expenses	24.7	25.7
	7.3	4.2	6.2	5.9			Operating Profit	3.8	3.8
	1.1	.9	.8	1.0			All Other Expenses (net)	1.3	1.1
	6.2	3.2	5.4	4.9			Profit Before Taxes	2.5	2.6
							RATIOS		
	3.8	2.1	3.2	2.9			Current	2.7	2.8
	1.5	1.6	2.1	1.4				1.7	1.8
	1.2	1.2	1.2	1.1				1.2	1.2
	2.5	1.6	1.9	1.3			Quick	1.7	1.6
	1.3	.9	1.1	.8				1.0	1.0
	.9	.7	.6	.5				.6	.6
	30 12.3	32 11.3	32 11.4	36 10.1			Sales/Receivables	34 10.8	33 11.2
	43 8.5	47 7.8	43 8.4	53 6.9				46 7.9	46 8.0
	56 6.5	65 5.6	53 6.9	74 4.9				61 6.0	58 6.3
	7 53.7	17 21.1	36 10.2	43 8.5			Cost of Sales/Inventory	25 14.6	24 14.9
	28 13.0	37 9.8	54 6.7	61 6.0				46 7.9	54 6.8
	60 6.1	65 5.6	87 4.2	94 3.9				81 4.5	79 4.6
	11 34.4	17 21.4	15 24.2	16 23.0			Cost of Sales/Payables	14 26.4	16 23.1
	24 15.1	31 11.7	22 16.3	35 10.5				25 14.4	24 15.0
	41 8.8	55 6.6	38 9.7	54 6.8				40 9.2	40 9.1
	6.3	7.3	4.5	4.1			Sales/Working Capital	5.9	5.3
	15.0	10.4	7.6	8.4				10.0	9.3
	26.7	26.2	18.0	41.9				27.1	25.3
	14.8	10.9	19.2	15.2			EBIT/Interest	6.7	9.5
	(28) 6.2	(74) 2.9	(66) 5.4	5.0				(162) 2.9	(154) 2.1
	2.1	1.1	2.1	2.1				1.1	.7
		5.2	6.6				Net Profit + Depr., Dep., Amort./Cur. Mat. L /T/D	6.2	5.7
		(37) 2.0	(24) 2.9					(96) 2.2	(86) 2.2
		.9	1.6					1.0	.8
	.2	.3	.2	.4			Fixed/Worth	.3	.3
	.4	.6	.5	.7				.5	.6
	1.3	1.3	1.2	.9				1.0	1.0
	1.0	.9	.4	.8			Debt/Worth	.7	.7
	2.2	1.6	1.1	2.1				1.4	1.4
	3.1	4.5	2.9	3.9				3.5	3.3
	109.1	52.3	48.9	34.1			% Profit Before Taxes/Tangible Net Worth	36.5	31.1
	(30) 46.5	(72) 18.4	(72) 24.3	25.9				(164) 18.5	(159) 12.0
	15.7	.6	9.3	13.0				5.9	.0
	30.0	15.8	24.7	15.4			% Profit Before Taxes/Total Assets	13.8	14.8
	18.0	7.2	11.8	8.6				6.2	4.1
	3.2	.2	4.0	4.1				.7	-.7
	40.4	23.9	20.3	14.9			Sales/Net Fixed Assets	25.5	23.1
	29.0	11.4	11.3	8.7				12.4	11.7
	18.1	7.6	6.6	6.8				7.2	7.4
	4.4	3.3	2.8	2.8			Sales/Total Assets	3.4	3.3
	3.7	2.7	2.3	2.1				2.5	2.4
	2.9	2.1	1.9	1.6				1.9	1.9
	.8	.9	.9	1.5			% Depr., Dep., Amort./Sales	1.0	1.1
	(29) 1.2	(69) 1.9	(71) 1.5	(15) 1.9				(167) 1.7	(161) 1.7
	2.0	3.0	2.3	2.5				2.4	2.6
	4.5	2.8	1.6				% Officers', Directors', Owners' Comp/Sales	2.5	2.6
	(20) 6.6	(45) 3.8	(32) 3.8					(81) 5.8	(70) 5.0
	9.2	6.9	5.8					11.4	8.7
	31525M	243223M	764498M	725755M	956706M		Net Sales ($)	1988804M	1806472M
	8123M	90104M	321044M	359965M	547506M		Total Assets ($)	1011731M	874147M

M = $ thousand   MM = $ million
See Pages 1 through 15 for Explanation of Ratios and Data

MANUFACTURERS—PARTITIONS, SHELVING, LOCKERS & OFFICE & STORE FIXTURES. SIC# 2541 (42,99)

Comparative Historical Data				Current Data Sorted By Sales					
8	5	16	# Postretirement Benefits	1	2	3	3	1	6
			Type of Statement						
29	31	42	Unqualified	1	2	1	13	8	17
65	49	55	Reviewed	1	13	12	12	12	5
45	43	60	Compiled	8	29	8	14	1	
	4	6	Tax Returns	2	3		1		
33	39	43	Other	5	9	10	9	7	3
4/1/92-3/31/93 ALL	4/1/93-3/31/94 ALL	4/1/94-3/31/95 ALL		0-1MM	51 (4/1-9/30/94) 1-3MM	3-5MM	5-10MM	155 (10/1/94-3/31/95) 10-25MM	25MM & OVER
172	166	206	**NUMBER OF STATEMENTS**	17	56	31	49	28	25
%	%	%	**ASSETS**	%	%	%	%	%	%
7.2	8.3	9.2	Cash & Equivalents	11.7	9.2	6.6	11.3	7.6	8.5
33.7	33.6	33.1	Trade Receivables - (net)	38.9	35.7	33.3	31.7	31.7	27.6
24.4	22.0	24.6	Inventory	20.2	21.5	26.4	25.5	26.1	29.4
2.4	2.5	2.5	All Other Current	.2	3.4	1.8	1.6	4.2	2.3
67.7	66.4	69.4	Total Current	71.0	69.8	68.1	70.1	69.6	67.8
25.1	24.6	23.7	Fixed Assets (net)	22.3	24.4	23.5	22.4	23.2	26.1
1.6	1.8	1.4	Intangibles (net)	1.5	2.1	1.9	.7	1.4	.7
5.7	7.2	5.4	All Other Non-Current	5.2	3.7	6.5	6.8	5.8	5.4
100.0	100.0	100.0	Total	100.0	100.0	100.0	100.0	100.0	100.0
			LIABILITIES						
10.8	10.4	10.1	Notes Payable-Short Term	8.4	10.6	12.6	7.5	11.2	10.9
3.6	3.8	3.2	Cur. Mat.-L/T/D	2.2	4.6	3.6	2.5	1.6	3.9
14.7	12.9	16.3	Trade Payables	11.3	18.3	16.1	17.2	16.0	13.9
.6	1.5	.6	Income Taxes Payable	.0	.6	.6	.8	.8	.3
12.3	9.9	11.2	All Other Current	13.1	11.2	12.2	10.7	10.4	10.3
42.1	38.5	41.4	Total Current	35.1	45.3	45.1	38.7	39.9	39.3
13.0	12.7	12.6	Long Term Debt	20.6	13.9	10.7	9.3	10.4	15.5
.5	.3	.4	Deferred Taxes	.0	.2	.5	.4	.5	.4
2.6	3.5	4.2	All Other-Non-Current	.7	4.6	3.7	4.1	5.0	5.9
41.8	44.9	41.4	Net Worth	43.6	36.0	40.0	47.6	44.1	38.9
100.0	100.0	100.0	Total Liabilities & Net Worth	100.0	100.0	100.0	100.0	100.0	100.0
			INCOME DATA						
100.0	100.0	100.0	Net Sales	100.0	100.0	100.0	100.0	100.0	100.0
29.4	29.1	29.5	Gross Profit	42.6	31.0	27.8	28.5	26.8	24.4
25.6	25.0	23.9	Operating Expenses	32.4	27.5	24.3	22.0	19.2	18.2
3.8	4.2	5.7	Operating Profit	10.3	3.6	3.4	6.5	7.6	6.2
1.0	1.2	.9	All Other Expenses (net)	1.4	.9	1.1	.8	.7	1.0
2.8	3.0	4.7	Profit Before Taxes	8.8	2.7	2.3	5.7	6.8	5.2
			RATIOS						
2.7	3.2	2.9	Current	4.0	2.2	2.0	3.4	3.0	3.0
1.7	1.7	1.7		2.3	1.5	1.7	2.0	2.0	1.6
1.2	1.2	1.2		1.4	1.2	1.2	1.2	1.2	1.3
1.7	2.1	1.7	Quick	2.6	1.7	1.6	1.9	1.8	1.4
1.0	1.1	1.0		1.7	1.0	.9	1.1	.9	.8
.7	.7	.6		.8	.7	.6	.6	.6	.6
37 9.8	33 10.9	32 11.3	Sales/Receivables	31 11.9	30 12.3	31 11.6	34 10.8	34 10.7	34 10.8
47 7.8	45 8.1	44 8.3		45 8.1	46 8.0	47 7.7	42 8.6	44 8.3	42 8.6
61 6.0	60 6.1	57 6.4		72 5.1	57 6.4	65 5.6	53 6.9	54 6.7	63 5.8
27 13.7	22 16.5	24 15.3	Cost of Sales/Inventory	6 60.0	17 21.6	22 16.9	25 14.6	24 15.1	41 8.9
50 7.3	42 8.6	50 7.3		43 8.5	31 11.6	54 6.7	51 7.1	51 7.1	61 6.0
68 5.4	68 5.4	79 4.6		83 4.4	63 5.8	81 4.5	73 5.0	87 4.2	94 3.9
16 22.2	14 27.0	16 23.0	Cost of Sales/Payables	8 44.4	16 22.8	17 21.2	17 21.4	14 26.2	14 25.4
23 16.1	23 15.7	27 13.4		21 17.5	29 12.4	33 11.0	28 13.0	26 13.8	29 12.6
39 9.3	37 9.8	41 8.8		36 10.1	54 6.7	46 8.0	41 9.0	40 9.1	35 10.4
5.8	5.6	5.4	Sales/Working Capital	5.2	7.3	6.8	4.7	5.5	4.2
9.6	9.5	9.4		7.1	12.0	9.5	8.6	8.0	8.4
27.6	30.5	23.7		18.7	26.8	22.1	24.0	18.5	21.5
(159) 12.9	(148) 10.0	(192) 13.7	EBIT/Interest	(14) 19.0	(54) 11.1	(28) 9.0	(45) 27.2	(26) 20.0	14.9
3.0	4.3	4.9		7.3	2.8	2.7	5.8	9.3	5.5
1.4	1.5	1.7		3.4	.5	1.1	2.4	2.9	2.1
(86) 5.0	(65) 8.9	(82) 5.4	Net Profit + Depr., Dep., Amort./Cur. Mat. L/T/D		(28) 6.3	(15) 2.8	(17) 6.2		(14) 7.2
2.2	2.9	2.5			2.0	1.7	2.7		2.9
1.3	.8	1.1			.6	.8	1.8		1.0
.3	.3	.3	Fixed/Worth	.1	.3	.2	.2	.3	.5
.6	.5	.6		.3	.6	.5	.5	.5	.7
1.0	1.0	1.2		2.2	1.2	1.0	1.2	1.4	1.1
.7	.5	.7	Debt/Worth	.5	1.1	.8	.4	.5	1.0
1.4	1.3	1.4		1.4	1.8	1.8	1.2	1.2	1.8
2.9	3.3	3.2		2.7	4.0	4.4	2.4	3.6	3.2
(162) 36.1	(157) 34.4	(198) 54.3	% Profit Before Taxes/Tangible Net Worth	(16) 112.1	(53) 62.6	43.9	(47) 49.0	(26) 61.9	41.0
17.4	18.0	25.6		43.2	14.9	17.4	24.2	34.0	26.4
3.5	4.6	7.7		26.3	-3.4	.7	9.7	12.1	12.9
13.5	13.9	20.6	% Profit Before Taxes/Total Assets	32.1	16.9	12.6	24.5	29.0	15.4
6.1	6.6	10.1		20.2	7.4	5.3	12.4	15.2	9.6
1.0	1.1	2.6		10.1	-1.2	.3	3.9	5.2	5.0
24.7	23.9	26.4	Sales/Net Fixed Assets	43.3	23.9	28.6	27.0	26.2	14.9
11.9	12.3	11.7		22.6	13.1	11.1	12.9	11.2	8.0
6.8	7.0	7.1		11.1	8.0	7.9	8.3	6.0	5.5
3.4	3.5	3.3	Sales/Total Assets	4.3	3.5	3.0	3.2	3.2	3.1
2.6	2.6	2.6		3.2	2.8	2.5	2.4	2.5	2.1
1.9	1.9	2.0		2.7	2.2	2.0	2.1	1.9	1.7
(163) 1.1	(151) 1.0	(191) 1.0	% Depr., Dep., Amort./Sales	(15) .7	(51) 1.0	(30) .7	(47) .9	(25) .8	(23) 1.4
1.8	1.8	1.8		1.4	2.0	1.7	1.3	1.5	1.8
2.6	2.7	2.4		2.0	3.6	2.5	2.0	2.2	2.4
(79) 3.0	(76) 2.3	(105) 2.5	% Officers', Directors', Owners' Comp/Sales	(11) 5.7	(29) 2.8	(20) 2.8	(27) 2.9	(10) 1.4	
5.3	4.9	4.1		7.5	4.9	3.9	4.0	2.4	
9.1	8.6	6.8		11.8	7.3	6.8	5.6	3.8	
2072196M	2023742M	2721707M	Net Sales ($)	10295M	111272M	120856M	341856M	404304M	1733124M
1055443M	1089096M	1326742M	Total Assets ($)	4871M	43623M	56086M	143769M	176946M	901447M

M = $ thousand   MM = $ million
See Pages 1 through 15 for Explanation of Ratios and Data

Current Data Sorted By Assets / Comparative Historical Data

0-500M	500M-2MM	2-10MM	10-50MM	50-100MM	100-250MM		4/1/90-3/31/91 ALL	4/1/91-3/31/92 ALL
2	2	2	4		3	**# Postretirement Benefits**		
						Type of Statement		
1	3	17	23	4	4	Unqualified	41	42
3	10	13	4		4	Reviewed	34	36
8	11	4	2			Compiled	31	34
2	1					Tax Returns	1	3
11	8	11	6	3	4	Other	33	23
45 (4/1-9/30/94)			108 (10/1/94-3/31/95)					
25	33	45	35	7	8	**NUMBER OF STATEMENTS**	140	138
%	%	%	%	%	%	**ASSETS**	%	%
9.3	4.5	4.2	1.4			Cash & Equivalents	4.7	6.1
21.2	25.8	25.4	26.6			Trade Receivables - (net)	23.2	22.3
32.1	33.5	35.3	34.0			Inventory	32.0	33.2
2.1	1.3	1.5	1.6			All Other Current	2.0	1.2
64.8	65.1	66.4	63.6			Total Current	61.9	62.8
30.6	27.0	25.1	26.8			Fixed Assets (net)	29.7	30.4
.4	1.8	2.2	1.1			Intangibles (net)	2.1	1.6
4.2	6.1	6.3	8.5			All Other Non-Current	6.3	5.2
100.0	100.0	100.0	100.0			Total	100.0	100.0
						LIABILITIES		
10.8	13.7	13.5	13.8			Notes Payable-Short Term	13.1	12.7
4.0	2.3	3.2	4.3			Cur. Mat. -L/T/D	4.2	4.5
16.5	15.8	15.4	11.8			Trade Payables	13.0	12.9
.5	.3	.3	.5			Income Taxes Payable	.8	.5
9.6	6.7	9.9	9.2			All Other Current	8.5	7.5
41.3	38.8	42.4	39.6			Total Current	39.6	38.1
19.6	16.1	16.0	17.7			Long Term Debt	19.6	19.0
.2	.4	.6	.6			Deferred Taxes	.8	.8
3.2	4.1	5.3	2.7			All Other-Non-Current	2.4	1.9
35.7	40.6	35.8	39.4			Net Worth	37.7	40.3
100.0	100.0	100.0	100.0			Total Liabilities & Net Worth	100.0	100.0
						INCOME DATA		
100.0	100.0	100.0	100.0			Net Sales	100.0	100.0
41.2	29.3	24.3	20.4			Gross Profit	27.1	27.7
34.7	25.3	20.8	16.0			Operating Expenses	23.7	25.1
6.5	4.1	3.6	4.4			Operating Profit	3.4	2.6
2.9	1.4	1.1	.8			All Other Expenses (net)	1.8	1.6
3.7	2.7	2.4	3.6			Profit Before Taxes	1.6	1.0
						RATIOS		
3.4	3.2	2.1	2.6				3.0	2.9
1.8	1.6	1.6	1.6			Current	1.9	1.9
1.3	1.2	1.3	1.2				1.1	1.2
1.5	1.8	1.0	1.2				1.2	1.4
.9	.8	.6	.7			Quick	.8	.8
.4	.5	.5	.4				.5	.5
2 190.1	21 17.7	24 15.4	44 8.3				22 16.8	20 18.5
20 17.9	33 11.1	41 8.9	50 7.3			Sales/Receivables	38 9.6	39 9.4
32 11.3	50 7.3	51 7.2	55 6.6				50 7.3	51 7.1
31 11.9	36 10.1	39 9.3	47 7.8				43 8.5	42 8.6
53 6.9	55 6.6	73 5.0	74 4.9			Cost of Sales/Inventory	73 5.0	73 5.0
94 3.9	122 3.0	114 3.2	111 3.3				111 3.3	111 3.3
7 54.1	11 34.5	11 32.1	14 26.4				13 27.8	12 29.3
21 17.8	28 13.1	24 15.2	24 15.1			Cost of Sales/Payables	23 16.2	23 15.7
37 9.8	47 7.7	45 8.1	35 10.3				40 9.1	37 9.8
6.6	5.5	7.4	5.6				5.2	5.0
12.4	10.6	9.6	8.4			Sales/Working Capital	8.8	9.4
26.7	26.3	20.6	17.2				37.6	34.3
13.8	7.4	9.0	12.9				4.2	4.1
(20) 5.9	(30) 3.2	(39) 2.9	(34) 3.3			EBIT/Interest	(127) 2.0	(128) 2.0
2.0	1.6	1.4	1.9				.5	.5
	7.6	6.6	7.9				5.0	3.4
(11) 3.0	(20) 2.9	(20) 2.9				Net Profit + Depr., Dep., Amort./Cur. Mat. L./T/D	(79) 2.1	(67) 1.7
1.4	1.4	1.8					.7	.9
.5	.3	.4	.4				.4	.4
.8	.7	.7	.7			Fixed/Worth	.8	.8
2.5	1.5	1.4	1.3				1.6	1.6
.6	.7	1.1	.8				.7	.7
1.8	1.3	1.9	1.5			Debt/Worth	1.8	1.5
5.9	4.4	4.1	3.2				4.8	3.3
94.5	42.9	34.6	28.5				27.7	27.1
(22) 38.4	(30) 21.6	(42) 13.6	(33) 18.4			% Profit Before Taxes/Tangible Net Worth	(123) 14.8	(125) 7.8
8.0	1.1	4.5	11.1				-1.1	-2.3
25.5	17.5	9.9	13.5				10.8	10.5
13.9	8.6	5.2	7.4			% Profit Before Taxes/Total Assets	5.1	2.9
4.0	2.1	.6	3.1				-1.5	-2.1
42.0	20.3	18.2	12.5				16.5	16.6
11.2	10.6	11.2	7.5			Sales/Net Fixed Assets	7.2	7.3
7.2	6.4	6.5	5.0				5.0	4.5
4.6	3.7	3.1	2.5				2.9	3.0
3.2	2.5	2.5	2.0			Sales/Total Assets	2.2	2.2
2.3	2.0	1.7	1.5				1.6	1.6
.7	.8	.8	1.3				1.2	1.4
(18) 2.4	(31) 1.3	(41) 1.6	(31) 1.7			% Depr., Dep., Amort./Sales	(127) 1.9	(127) 2.2
2.8	2.4	2.5	2.6				2.9	2.9
5.0	1.7	1.2					2.0	1.9
(12) 8.9	(16) 3.8	(21) 1.6				% Officers', Directors', Owners' Comp/Sales	(55) 3.7	(56) 3.9
13.2	6.0	2.8					8.5	7.2
20076M	103002M	520001M	1732326M	722634M	1997505M	Net Sales ($)	2901162M	2565917M
5717M	37173M	218745M	873636M	455010M	1125240M	Total Assets ($)	1666716M	1458303M

M = $ thousand   MM = $ million
See Pages 1 through 15 for Explanation of Ratios and Data

Comparative Historical Data — 5 / 12 / 13
Current Data Sorted By Sales — 4 / 2 / 7

4/1/92-3/31/93 ALL	4/1/93-3/31/94 ALL	4/1/94-3/31/95 ALL		0-1MM	1-3MM	3-5MM	5-10MM	10-25MM	25MM & OVER
5	12	13	# Postretirement Benefits			4	2		7
			Type of Statement						
48	51	52	Unqualified	1	1	3	5	12	30
25	30	30	Reviewed	3	6	6	7	5	3
19	19	25	Compiled	6	9	2	3	3	2
4	3	3	Tax Returns	2			1		
26	34	43	Other	8	11	1	3	9	11
				45 (4/1-9/30/94)			108 (10/1/94-3/31/95)		
122	137	153	**NUMBER OF STATEMENTS**	20	27	12	19	29	46
%	%	%	**ASSETS**	%	%	%	%	%	%
5.5	5.0	4.2	Cash & Equivalents	7.4	6.3	1.4	7.5	3.1	1.8
23.9	24.3	25.0	Trade Receivables - (net)	20.5	23.3	23.8	26.2	27.3	26.3
32.9	33.9	33.5	Inventory	30.3	33.8	40.4	33.7	35.0	31.7
2.1	1.3	1.5	All Other Current	1.9	1.4	.5	1.6	2.0	1.4
64.4	64.4	64.2	Total Current	60.1	64.7	66.1	69.0	67.3	61.3
28.8	27.0	27.1	Fixed Assets (net)	33.7	26.8	22.8	27.1	24.4	27.4
1.6	2.8	2.2	Intangibles (net)	.5	2.6	1.7	.4	3.1	2.9
5.1	5.7	6.5	All Other Non-Current	5.7	5.8	9.4	3.6	5.2	8.4
100.0	100.0	100.0	Total	100.0	100.0	100.0	100.0	100.0	100.0
			LIABILITIES						
10.5	10.2	12.0	Notes Payable-Short Term	13.3	13.2	11.7	10.3	16.1	8.8
3.8	3.1	3.2	Cur. Mat.-L./T/D	4.3	2.2	2.8	2.8	5.1	2.4
13.4	12.8	14.1	Trade Payables	17.0	12.4	14.1	20.2	13.9	11.5
.6	1.1	.4	Income Taxes Payable	.5	.2	.3	.2	.4	.5
8.5	10.5	8.9	All Other Current	8.4	7.5	8.0	10.6	9.7	9.1
36.8	37.8	38.6	Total Current	43.6	35.6	36.9	44.0	45.3	32.3
18.9	17.2	17.8	Long Term Debt	25.3	15.8	12.9	13.7	16.7	19.4
.7	.7	.6	Deferred Taxes	.5	.2	.4	.6	.5	1.1
2.6	2.3	3.8	All Other-Non-Current	4.1	4.8	.2	2.8	7.1	2.5
41.1	42.0	39.1	Net Worth	26.6	43.6	49.6	38.8	30.5	44.7
100.0	100.0	100.0	Total Liabilities & Net Worth	100.0	100.0	100.0	100.0	100.0	100.0
			INCOME DATA						
100.0	100.0	100.0	Net Sales	100.0	100.0	100.0	100.0	100.0	100.0
26.1	26.2	27.1	Gross Profit	44.6	29.4	27.5	25.2	23.7	21.0
22.2	22.1	22.5	Operating Expenses	38.0	25.9	23.4	20.7	19.8	16.1
3.9	4.1	4.6	Operating Profit	6.6	3.5	4.1	4.6	4.0	4.9
1.2	1.1	1.3	All Other Expenses (net)	3.9	1.0	1.7	1.1	1.1	.5
2.8	3.0	3.3	Profit Before Taxes	2.7	2.5	2.4	3.4	2.8	4.4
			RATIOS						
3.0 / 1.8 / 1.3	2.9 / 1.7 / 1.3	2.9 / 1.7 / 1.3	Current	3.2 / 1.7 / .9	3.3 / 1.7 / 1.3	3.6 / 1.7 / 1.3	2.1 / 1.6 / 1.2	1.8 / 1.6 / 1.2	3.0 / 2.2 / 1.4
1.5 / .9 / .5	1.3 / .8 / .5	1.3 / .8 / .5	Quick	1.6 / .8 / .2	1.8 / .9 / .5	1.6 / .6 / .3	1.2 / .7 / .4	.9 / .6 / .5	1.4 / 1.1 / .7
23 15.9 / 42 8.6 / 54 6.8	26 14.1 / 40 9.2 / 52 7.0	24 15.1 / 41 8.8 / 51 7.1	Sales/Receivables	2 154.1 / 21 17.5 / 41 8.8	23 16.2 / 32 11.4 / 41 8.9	16 23.0 / 32 11.3 / 48 7.6	14 26.0 / 30 12.2 / 58 6.3	34 10.7 / 42 8.6 / 49 7.5	42 8.7 / 50 7.3 / 56 6.5
47 7.7 / 78 4.7 / 101 3.6	41 8.8 / 66 5.5 / 104 3.5	43 8.4 / 70 5.2 / 107 3.4	Cost of Sales/Inventory	38 9.7 / 72 5.1 / 135 2.7	42 8.7 / 55 6.6 / 118 3.1	53 6.9 / 96 3.8 / 174 2.1	37 9.9 / 51 7.1 / 96 3.8	46 8.0 / 73 5.0 / 104 3.5	49 7.4 / 72 5.1 / 99 3.7
14 26.8 / 22 16.9 / 38 9.5	11 33.0 / 22 16.3 / 34 10.7	12 30.8 / 24 15.5 / 40 9.1	Cost of Sales/Payables	7 54.8 / 27 13.6 / 53 9.5	11 32.8 / 19 18.9 / 32 11.3	9 42.1 / 13 28.1 / 52 7.0	17 21.5 / 37 9.8 / 48 7.6	11 33.8 / 22 16.7 / 38 9.7	15 24.9 / 24 15.5 / 32 11.4
4.6 / 8.4 / 16.9	5.4 / 9.7 / 21.1	5.6 / 8.8 / 19.7	Sales/Working Capital	6.6 / 11.5 / NM	5.3 / 9.4 / 27.2	4.5 / 10.9 / 19.8	7.5 / 9.6 / 38.7	7.8 / 9.9 / 19.3	4.4 / 6.5 / 13.9
(116) 5.9 / 2.6 / 1.1	(128) 10.3 / 3.8 / 1.4	(137) 10.4 / 3.4 / 1.8	EBIT/Interest	(15) 9.5 / 3.2 / .0	(23) 8.1 / 3.6 / 1.8	(11) 5.5 / 2.9 / 1.8	(25) 9.0 / 3.4 / 1.8	(44) 12.1 / 2.8 / 1.0	20.5 / 4.2 / 2.3
(65) 4.9 / 2.5 / 1.2	(55) 6.6 / 2.3 / 1.0	(67) 7.6 / 3.0 / 1.8	Net Profit + Depr., Dep., Amort./Cur. Mat. L/T/D		(11) 8.2 / 4.1 / 2.5		(13) 9.4 / 3.3 / .9		(24) 9.2 / 4.5 / 2.1
.4 / .7 / 1.3	.4 / .7 / 1.2	.4 / .7 / 1.3	Fixed/Worth	.5 / 1.2 / 2.8	.3 / .7 / 1.5	.2 / .4 / 1.0	.4 / .7 / 1.2	.4 / .7 / 1.9	.4 / .7 / 1.0
.8 / 1.4 / 3.5	.7 / 1.7 / 3.1	.9 / 1.5 / 3.9	Debt/Worth	1.1 / 2.6 / 6.9	.3 / 1.2 / 4.8	.6 / 1.1 / 3.4	1.0 / 1.6 / 2.6	1.2 / 2.3 / 6.3	.7 / 1.1 / 2.1
(114) 27.0 / 16.7 / 2.3	(128) 34.9 / 13.8 / 3.1	(141) 38.9 / 19.9 / 6.9	% Profit Before Taxes/Tangible Net Worth	(17) 97.5 / 62.3 / 3.5	(24) 39.3 / 21.1 / 2.1	32.4 / 11.1 / 5.3	(18) 47.3 / 15.9 / 10.3	(26) 44.8 / 22.1 / .2	(44) 30.5 / 20.1 / 12.9
12.8 / 5.5 / 1.0	14.0 / 6.3 / 1.5	15.6 / 7.4 / 2.9	% Profit Before Taxes/Total Assets	26.7 / 11.5 / .4	16.3 / 5.8 / 3.4	10.2 / 4.6 / 2.3	13.3 / 7.3 / .4	16.6 / 6.4 / .0	14.7 / 7.8 / 4.3
17.5 / 7.3 / 5.4	20.9 / 8.6 / 5.7	16.8 / 8.9 / 6.0	Sales/Net Fixed Assets	12.2 / 10.3 / 5.4	17.6 / 10.6 / 6.3	40.6 / 12.5 / 5.6	21.0 / 13.6 / 6.5	17.7 / 11.7 / 6.3	9.7 / 7.6 / 5.2
2.8 / 2.1 / 1.7	3.2 / 2.3 / 1.7	3.1 / 2.3 / 1.7	Sales/Total Assets	3.4 / 2.5 / 1.8	3.8 / 2.5 / 2.0	3.5 / 2.0 / 1.2	3.6 / 3.0 / 1.7	3.0 / 2.5 / 1.7	2.5 / 2.0 / 1.5
(112) 1.1 / 2.1 / 2.9	(126) 1.1 / 1.9 / 2.8	(135) .9 / 1.7 / 2.7	% Depr., Dep., Amort./Sales	(14) 1.6 / 2.4 / 3.3	(25) .7 / 1.6 / 2.8	(11) .9 / 2.2 / 3.2	(18) .3 / 1.1 / 1.8	(26) 1.1 / 1.6 / 2.4	(41) 1.3 / 1.9 / 2.6
(42) 1.6 / 2.8 / 6.7	(39) 1.4 / 3.2 / 6.7	(55) 1.6 / 3.1 / 6.0	% Officers', Directors', Owners' Comp/Sales		(13) 3.4 / 5.1 / 12.2		(12) 1.2 / 1.7 / 2.3		
3737201M	4790188M	5095544M	Net Sales ($)	10272M	55189M	46353M	133531M	462961M	4387238M
2037437M	2611566M	2715521M	Total Assets ($)	4274M	23802M	25102M	57337M	219888M	2385118M

M = $ thousand   MM = $ million
See Pages 1 through 15 for Explanation of Ratios and Data

Current Data Sorted By Assets / Comparative Historical Data

Type of Statement

0-500M	500M-2MM	2-10MM	10-50MM	50-100MM	100-250MM	# Postretirement Benefits / Type of Statement	4/1/90-3/31/91 ALL	4/1/91-3/31/92 ALL
	1	1	1			# Postretirement Benefits		
	2	8	8	4	1	Unqualified	36	28
	4	2				Reviewed	16	16
4	12		2			Compiled	22	27
	2					Tax Returns		
3	11	3	5	1	1	Other	16	15
	26 (4/1-9/30/94)		47 (10/1/94-3/31/95)					
7	31	13	15	5	2	NUMBER OF STATEMENTS	90	86

ASSETS

0-500M	500M-2MM	2-10MM	10-50MM	50-100MM	100-250MM	ASSETS	4/1/90-3/31/91 ALL	4/1/91-3/31/92 ALL
%	%	%	%	%	%		%	%
	3.8	12.4	2.8			Cash & Equivalents	5.1	6.9
	28.2	30.0	21.3			Trade Receivables - (net)	26.0	24.7
	44.2	28.0	29.9			Inventory	34.1	35.2
	1.5	2.1	3.0			All Other Current	1.7	1.7
	77.7	72.5	57.0			Total Current	66.8	68.6
	18.3	23.1	32.8			Fixed Assets (net)	25.6	23.6
	.2	.6	3.4			Intangibles (net)	1.1	.7
	3.8	3.9	6.8			All Other Non-Current	6.6	7.2
	100.0	100.0	100.0			Total	100.0	100.0

LIABILITIES

0-500M	500M-2MM	2-10MM	10-50MM	50-100MM	100-250MM	LIABILITIES	4/1/90-3/31/91 ALL	4/1/91-3/31/92 ALL
	10.7	4.9	8.3			Notes Payable-Short Term	9.3	12.4
	5.0	4.4	3.3			Cur. Mat. -L/T/D	2.9	2.9
	24.1	19.5	15.4			Trade Payables	17.6	21.0
	.1	.7	.5			Income Taxes Payable	.5	.5
	10.4	11.0	8.6			All Other Current	9.8	9.8
	50.2	40.6	36.0			Total Current	40.1	46.6
	16.4	16.2	23.2			Long Term Debt	14.5	13.6
	.2	.1	1.6			Deferred Taxes	.7	.4
	3.9	1.9	3.0			All Other-Non-Current	1.3	2.7
	29.3	41.3	36.2			Net Worth	43.4	36.7
	100.0	100.0	100.0			Total Liabilities & Net Worth	100.0	100.0

INCOME DATA

0-500M	500M-2MM	2-10MM	10-50MM	50-100MM	100-250MM	INCOME DATA	4/1/90-3/31/91 ALL	4/1/91-3/31/92 ALL
	100.0	100.0	100.0			Net Sales	100.0	100.0
	29.7	25.5	22.4			Gross Profit	25.4	24.7
	26.8	20.6	19.9			Operating Expenses	21.5	22.0
	2.9	4.9	2.5			Operating Profit	3.8	2.8
	.7	–.3	1.3			All Other Expenses (net)	1.2	.9
	2.3	5.2	1.2			Profit Before Taxes	2.6	1.9

RATIOS

0-500M	500M-2MM	2-10MM	10-50MM	50-100MM	100-250MM	RATIOS	4/1/90-3/31/91 ALL	4/1/91-3/31/92 ALL
	2.0	2.6	2.6			Current	2.9	2.5
	1.5	1.7	1.5				1.7	1.6
	1.3	1.2	1.4				1.2	1.1
	1.0	1.5	1.0			Quick	1.4	1.2
	.6	1.0	.6				.9	.7
	.3	.5	.5				.4	.4
	13 28.8	24 15.0	17 21.1			Sales/Receivables	14 25.3	16 22.8
	32 11.4	43 8.5	37 10.0				37 10.0	31 11.8
	55 6.6	49 7.4	45 8.1				49 7.4	46 8.0
	38 9.7	23 15.8	37 10.0			Cost of Sales/Inventory	38 9.6	38 9.7
	69 5.3	56 6.5	51 7.2				50 7.3	54 6.8
	135 2.7	96 3.8	107 3.4				76 4.8	83 4.4
	19 19.3	17 21.6	14 26.5			Cost of Sales/Payables	14 25.8	19 19.6
	27 13.6	33 11.2	26 14.2				21 17.1	29 12.7
	41 8.9	51 7.2	46 8.0				35 10.3	42 8.7
	6.4	6.0	7.7			Sales/Working Capital	5.9	7.1
	11.2	9.1	11.3				9.5	13.0
	28.7	33.5	37.1				30.4	70.8
	(28) 4.8	(11) 57.4	5.0			EBIT/Interest	(84) 7.6	(75) 5.3
	2.1	5.3	1.6				2.3	1.7
	1.0	1.6	.0				.9	.8
		(10)	4.7			Net Profit + Depr., Dep., Amort./Cur. Mat. L /T/D	(45) 7.2	(38) 5.0
			3.1				2.6	2.0
			1.0				.7	.7
	.2	.2	.6			Fixed/Worth	.3	.3
	.3	.7	.9				.5	.5
	1.0	1.8	1.7				1.3	1.2
	1.2	.8	1.0			Debt/Worth	.7	.8
	2.2	1.8	1.7				1.3	2.0
	4.4	3.4	4.3				2.9	3.7
	(29) 35.3	34.7	(13) 30.7			% Profit Before Taxes/Tangible Net Worth	(87) 32.0	(79) 29.6
	8.1	29.0	17.9				16.3	11.0
	.0	9.5	1.7				.0	.8
	9.5	16.4	15.4			% Profit Before Taxes/Total Assets	14.3	10.1
	2.0	11.4	2.2				5.9	3.8
	.0	2.9	-5.6				–.6	-1.2
	59.6	24.9	11.5			Sales/Net Fixed Assets	29.5	47.6
	27.2	18.0	7.9				11.7	13.4
	11.9	8.9	5.1				6.9	7.8
	4.0	3.3	3.1			Sales/Total Assets	3.9	3.7
	3.6	3.2	2.3				2.9	2.9
	2.0	2.1	1.9				2.2	2.1
	(27) .3	.7	1.2			% Depr., Dep., Amort./Sales	(77) .6	(76) .5
	.8	.8	1.7				.9	1.0
	1.5	1.4	1.9				2.0	1.9
	(13) 1.5					% Officers', Directors', Owners' Comp/Sales	(30) 1.4	(29) 2.0
	3.9						2.8	2.9
	6.0						5.2	4.3
7169M	123202M	214304M	826067M	680264M	718632M	Net Sales ($)	2528644M	1792790M
1984M	34703M	70501M	315790M	365166M	378704M	Total Assets ($)	1155755M	765345M

M = $ thousand   MM = $ million
See Pages 1 through 15 for Explanation of Ratios and Data

Comparative Historical Data				Current Data Sorted By Sales					
4	4	3	# Postretirement Benefits			1		1	1
			Type of Statement						
28	24	23	Unqualified		2		1	5	15
17	9	6	Reviewed		1	4		1	
26	19	18	Compiled	4	2	9	1	1	1
	2	2	Tax Returns		1		1		
10	22	24	Other	1	7	2	5	2	7
4/1/92-3/31/93 ALL	4/1/93-3/31/94 ALL	4/1/94-3/31/95 ALL		0-1MM	26 (4/1-9/30/94) 1-3MM	3-5MM	47 (10/1/94-3/31/95) 5-10MM	10-25MM	25MM & OVER
81	76	73	NUMBER OF STATEMENTS	5	13	15	8	9	23
%	**%**	**%**	**ASSETS**	**%**	**%**	**%**	**%**	**%**	**%**
6.1	7.5	6.5	Cash & Equivalents		10.8	3.0			4.5
25.6	23.0	26.9	Trade Receivables - (net)		19.7	32.4			26.2
34.6	35.0	35.7	Inventory		45.8	41.7			28.0
1.9	2.8	1.9	All Other Current		.6	2.5			2.7
68.2	68.4	70.9	Total Current		77.0	79.7			61.4
24.6	24.7	23.1	Fixed Assets (net)		20.3	15.8			28.9
1.6	.8	1.2	Intangibles (net)		.0	.7			2.7
5.6	6.1	4.7	All Other Non-Current		2.7	3.8			7.0
100.0	100.0	100.0	Total		100.0	100.0			100.0
			LIABILITIES						
8.3	9.7	8.4	Notes Payable-Short Term		9.3	13.7			5.9
3.9	5.5	4.1	Cur. Mat.-L./T/D		4.5	4.8			2.5
18.7	17.0	19.7	Trade Payables		19.9	21.4			15.7
.4	2.1	.4	Income Taxes Payable		.0	.1			.3
8.7	8.8	9.7	All Other Current		7.5	12.1			8.4
40.0	43.1	42.3	Total Current		41.3	52.1			32.8
16.3	12.4	17.6	Long Term Debt		21.6	13.5			19.4
.4	.4	.5	Deferred Taxes		.0	.4			1.0
3.0	4.4	3.7	All Other-Non-Current		7.5	3.4			4.5
40.3	39.6	35.9	Net Worth		29.6	30.6			42.3
100.0	100.0	100.0	Total Liabilities & Net Worth		100.0	100.0			100.0
			INCOME DATA						
100.0	100.0	100.0	Net Sales		100.0	100.0			100.0
24.5	24.8	27.7	Gross Profit		32.6	28.8			21.6
20.3	21.5	24.0	Operating Expenses		26.7	26.6			18.3
4.2	3.3	3.8	Operating Profit		5.9	2.2			3.3
1.3	.8	.7	All Other Expenses (net)		.1	.8			1.0
2.9	2.5	3.1	Profit Before Taxes		5.9	1.5			2.3
			RATIOS						
2.8	3.0	2.9			3.9	1.7			3.1
1.7	1.6	1.6	Current		1.7	1.5			2.0
1.2	1.1	1.3			1.1	1.3			1.4
1.5	1.3	1.3			1.3	1.0			1.4
.8	.7	.7	Quick		.6	.7			1.0
.4	.5	.4			.1	.4			.6
16 23.5	13 28.4	17 21.7		4 91.4	21 17.5				26 13.8
34 10.7	28 13.2	37 10.0	Sales/Receivables	23 16.1	40 9.2				42 8.7
49 7.4	49 7.5	51 7.1		85 4.3	55 6.6				49 7.4
41 8.9	38 9.6	37 9.8		58 6.3	38 9.5				37 10.0
51 7.1	52 7.0	63 5.8	Cost of Sales/Inventory	96 3.8	69 5.3				59 6.2
76 4.8	78 4.7	111 3.3		166 2.2	118 3.1				89 4.1
16 23.4	15 24.3	16 22.2		23 15.7	18 19.9				14 26.5
28 13.2	24 15.3	27 13.6	Cost of Sales/Payables	37 9.8	29 12.5				25 14.4
38 9.6	35 10.4	41 8.9		68 5.4	41 8.8				39 9.3
5.8	5.4	5.2		1.8	6.4				4.4
12.1	12.0	10.6	Sales/Working Capital	10.6	11.4				8.3
41.0	69.4	28.6		NM	20.7				28.5
9.4	7.4	8.7		14.6	4.8				8.7
(74) 2.9	(69) 3.4	(67) 2.7	EBIT/Interest	(12) 3.4	(14) 1.5				3.5
1.5	1.3	1.2		1.5	.8				1.4
5.7	5.6	4.5							6.0
(41) 2.6	(35) 2.4	(29) 2.7	Net Profit + Depr., Dep., Amort./Cur. Mat. L/T/D					(14)	3.2
.6	1.3	.7							2.2
.4	.3	.3		.1	.2				.5
.5	.6	.6	Fixed/Worth	.3	.6				.7
1.3	1.2	1.1		2.8	.7				1.1
.8	.5	1.0		1.1	1.7				.6
1.6	1.7	2.0	Debt/Worth	2.2	2.4				1.4
3.3	3.4	4.1		8.3	3.7				2.7
40.7	36.8	33.1		52.4	39.5				25.6
(76) 17.4	(68) 16.5	(67) 18.1	% Profit Before Taxes/Tangible Net Worth	(11) 13.0	9.2			(21)	18.7
4.0	6.4	3.9		4.2	.0				4.6
14.2	14.4	15.3		20.1	11.5				15.0
6.2	6.9	5.0	% Profit Before Taxes/Total Assets	6.3	2.5				6.0
1.0	1.5	1.0		1.7	.0				1.2
29.0	29.0	27.5		47.4	59.6				11.5
13.8	11.5	12.5	Sales/Net Fixed Assets	26.8	21.3				8.3
7.3	8.1	7.6		8.1	12.6				5.9
3.9	3.9	3.6		3.6	3.6				3.1
2.9	2.7	3.0	Sales/Total Assets	3.0	3.2				2.2
2.0	2.2	2.0		1.4	2.1				1.8
.5	.6	.7			.2				.9
(75) 1.0	(69) .8	(66) 1.2	% Depr., Dep., Amort./Sales		(14) .8				1.6
2.0	1.8	1.7			1.6				1.8
2.0	1.9	1.5							
(35) 3.9	(29) 3.8	(22) 2.7	% Officers', Directors', Owners' Comp/Sales						
5.7	7.9	4.6							
2246845M	3370497M	2569638M	Net Sales ($)	2233M	22573M	61519M	59667M	142367M	2281279M
1037979M	1449978M	1166848M	Total Assets ($)	1146M	11409M	21207M	15313M	52162M	1065611M

M = $ thousand   MM = $ million
See Pages 1 through 15 for Explanation of Ratios and Data

	Current Data Sorted By Assets							Comparative Historical Data	
			1			1	# Postretirement Benefits		
							Type of Statement		
		4	3		2		Unqualified	12	6
	2	6	1				Reviewed	8	8
6	3						Compiled	7	11
2							Tax Returns		
	2	3	2				Other	3	4
	11 (4/1-9/30/94)		25 (10/1/94-3/31/95)					4/1/90-3/31/91 ALL	4/1/91-3/31/92 ALL
0-500M	500M-2MM	2-10MM	10-50MM	50-100MM	100-250MM		NUMBER OF STATEMENTS	30	29
8	7	13	6		2				
%	%	%	%	%	%		ASSETS	%	%
		2.1					Cash & Equivalents	4.2	8.5
		40.0					Trade Receivables - (net)	25.7	31.1
		26.9					Inventory	31.3	27.9
		.6					All Other Current	1.4	3.4
		69.6					Total Current	62.7	70.9
		21.9					Fixed Assets (net)	29.1	22.3
		3.7					Intangibles (net)	2.0	1.6
		4.8					All Other Non-Current	6.2	5.3
		100.0					Total	100.0	100.0
							LIABILITIES		
		15.2					Notes Payable-Short Term	9.7	18.1
		3.0					Cur. Mat. -L/T/D	4.6	3.4
		18.7					Trade Payables	17.0	18.2
		.1					Income Taxes Payable	.7	.3
		9.8					All Other Current	9.7	7.4
		46.8					Total Current	41.7	47.4
		14.2					Long Term Debt	19.0	12.2
		.5					Deferred Taxes	.5	.2
		5.7					All Other-Non-Current	5.0	3.6
		32.8					Net Worth	33.8	36.7
		100.0					Total Liabilities & Net Worth	100.0	100.0
							INCOME DATA		
		100.0					Net Sales	100.0	100.0
		29.9					Gross Profit	28.2	29.6
		27.3					Operating Expenses	22.8	27.1
		2.6					Operating Profit	5.4	2.5
		.5					All Other Expenses (net)	1.8	1.4
		2.1					Profit Before Taxes	3.6	1.1
							RATIOS		
		2.5						2.2	2.6
		1.5					Current	1.7	1.6
		1.2						1.3	1.2
		1.6						1.2	1.5
		.7					Quick	.7	.9
		.6						.6	.5
		39 9.4						26 13.8	19 19.1
		57 6.4					Sales/Receivables	38 9.7	37 9.8
		94 3.9						50 7.3	49 7.4
		38 9.5						39 9.3	16 23.4
		68 5.4					Cost of Sales/Inventory	61 6.0	53 6.9
		83 4.4						107 3.4	74 4.9
		20 18.0						19 18.8	17 22.1
		31 11.7					Cost of Sales/Payables	26 13.9	27 13.6
		59 6.2						38 9.6	37 9.9
		5.9						6.6	6.9
		11.2					Sales/Working Capital	10.3	13.2
		48.6						18.3	37.2
		4.0						7.4	5.5
		2.0					EBIT/Interest	(29) 2.7	(27) 2.7
		.5						2.2	1.0
							Net Profit + Depr., Dep.,	10.4	
							Amort./Cur. Mat. L /T/D	(15) 1.8	
								.3	
		.5						.5	.4
		.7					Fixed/Worth	.8	.6
		2.8						1.1	1.4
		1.1						.9	.9
		1.8					Debt/Worth	1.6	2.0
		27.9						2.8	7.2
		79.8					% Profit Before Taxes/Tangible	48.7	44.8
	(11)	14.1					Net Worth	(28) 19.1	(27) 18.1
		-3.6						10.5	2.4
		11.5					% Profit Before Taxes/Total	11.9	11.8
		3.9					Assets	7.3	5.9
		-1.0						5.3	.4
		26.8						19.5	35.1
		18.6					Sales/Net Fixed Assets	12.0	17.9
		6.0						4.9	9.5
		2.7						3.7	4.0
		2.3					Sales/Total Assets	2.2	3.2
		1.9						1.6	2.1
		.6						.9	.8
		1.2					% Depr., Dep., Amort./Sales	(26) 2.0	(28) 1.5
		2.5						3.0	2.0
							% Officers', Directors',		3.0
							Owners' Comp/Sales		(13) 4.9
									6.8
11463M	23980M	148847M	232228M		642442M		Net Sales ($)	504698M	193655M
2315M	9834M	66835M	92632M		392405M		Total Assets ($)	252268M	86468M

M = $ thousand   MM = $ million
See Pages 1 through 15 for Explanation of Ratios and Data

Comparative Historical Data / Current Data Sorted By Sales

2	5	3		1					2
14	11	9	# Postretirement Benefits						
			Type of Statement						
14	11	9	Unqualified				1	3	5
14	15	9	Reviewed		2		3	3	1
11	16	9	Compiled	2	6	1			
	1	2	Tax Returns	1	1				
6	13	7	Other			1	3	1	2

				0-1MM	1-3MM	3-5MM	5-10MM	10-25MM	25MM & OVER
4/1/92-3/31/93	4/1/93-3/31/94	4/1/94-3/31/95			11 (4/1-9/30/94)			25 (10/1/94-3/31/95)	
ALL	ALL	ALL							
45	56	36	**NUMBER OF STATEMENTS**	3	9	1	8	7	8
%	%	%	**ASSETS**	%	%	%	%	%	%
6.1	6.1	5.1	Cash & Equivalents						
33.8	34.4	39.1	Trade Receivables - (net)						
27.5	24.8	25.7	Inventory						
1.7	2.7	1.5	All Other Current						
69.1	68.0	71.4	Total Current						
23.5	24.2	21.7	Fixed Assets (net)						
1.7	2.6	1.9	Intangibles (net)						
5.8	5.2	5.0	All Other Non-Current						
100.0	100.0	100.0	Total						
			LIABILITIES						
16.1	14.4	12.5	Notes Payable-Short Term						
4.3	3.9	2.2	Cur. Mat.-L /T/D						
15.0	17.8	16.4	Trade Payables						
.4	1.8	.3	Income Taxes Payable						
10.4	8.6	9.2	All Other Current						
46.2	46.5	40.5	Total Current						
17.1	12.7	11.4	Long Term Debt						
.3	.5	.5	Deferred Taxes						
5.7	4.3	3.3	All Other-Non-Current						
30.7	35.9	44.2	Net Worth						
100.0	100.0	100.0	Total Liabilities & Net Worth						
			INCOME DATA						
100.0	100.0	100.0	Net Sales						
28.0	29.0	30.6	Gross Profit						
24.6	26.2	27.8	Operating Expenses						
3.3	2.8	2.8	Operating Profit						
1.3	1.0	.5	All Other Expenses (net)						
2.0	1.8	2.2	Profit Before Taxes						
			RATIOS						
2.0 / 1.5 / 1.2	2.0 / 1.4 / 1.2	2.8 / 1.8 / 1.4	Current						
1.1 / .8 / .6	1.3 / .9 / .5	1.9 / 1.2 / .7	Quick						
33 11.2 / 44 8.3 / 59 6.2	33 10.9 / 53 6.9 / 70 5.2	34 10.7 / 52 7.0 / 72 5.1	Sales/Receivables						
34 10.6 / 62 5.9 / 81 4.5	29 12.6 / 48 7.6 / 68 5.4	26 14.0 / 46 7.9 / 76 4.8	Cost of Sales/Inventory						
19 19.3 / 26 14.2 / 39 9.3	22 16.6 / 33 10.9 / 51 7.2	18 20.3 / 28 12.9 / 46 7.9	Cost of Sales/Payables						
6.8 / 10.9 / 23.4	7.3 / 12.0 / 23.3	5.7 / 9.3 / 17.0	Sales/Working Capital						
(39) 4.2 / 2.0 / 1.2	(49) 4.2 / 2.3 / 1.3	(32) 7.7 / 2.4 / .7	EBIT/Interest						
(21) 4.1 / 2.4 / 1.1	(23) 5.1 / 1.7 / .8	(17) 7.2 / 3.3 / 1.5	Net Profit + Depr., Dep., Amort./Cur. Mat. L/T/D						
.4 / .9 / 2.7	.4 / .8 / 1.5	.2 / .6 / 1.0	Fixed/Worth						
.9 / 2.3 / 9.0	.8 / 2.1 / 5.8	.6 / 1.1 / 2.1	Debt/Worth						
(39) 41.7 / 14.3 / 1.0	(51) 33.3 / 15.3 / 3.4	(32) 32.9 / 14.4 / 6.4	% Profit Before Taxes/Tangible Net Worth						
13.6 / 4.3 / -.8	10.6 / 3.4 / 1.1	14.2 / 4.6 / .5	% Profit Before Taxes/Total Assets						
24.2 / 16.6 / 7.3	27.3 / 13.7 / 5.8	30.7 / 19.2 / 7.1	Sales/Net Fixed Assets						
3.2 / 2.5 / 1.9	3.1 / 2.5 / 1.9	3.8 / 2.5 / 1.9	Sales/Total Assets						
(41) .8 / 1.4 / 2.6	(48) .9 / 1.9 / 3.0	(34) .5 / 1.4 / 2.5	% Depr., Dep., Amort./Sales						
(22) 1.6 / 2.9 / 5.7	(22) 1.8 / 3.2 / 4.5	(18) 1.6 / 3.5 / 6.1	% Officers', Directors', Owners' Comp/Sales						
520482M	485862M	1058960M	Net Sales ($)	1827M	19622M	3231M	50537M	109073M	874670M
247496M	204940M	564021M	Total Assets ($)	433M	6196M	1943M	21239M	49173M	485037M

M = $ thousand   MM = $ million
See Pages 1 through 15 for Explanation of Ratios and Data

Current Data Sorted By Assets   Comparative Historical Data

Type of Statement / # Postretirement Benefits

0-500M	500M-2MM	2-10MM	10-50MM	50-100MM	100-250MM	Type of Statement	4/1/90-3/31/91 ALL	4/1/91-3/31/92 ALL
			1			# Postretirement Benefits		
1	2	14	15	4	2	Unqualified	26	26
	20	21	1	1		Reviewed	39	35
5	6	3				Compiled	23	22
		1				Tax Returns	1	1
4	10	7	13	4		Other	24	23
	45 (4/1-9/30/94)		89 (10/1/94-3/31/95)					
10	38	46	29	9	2	NUMBER OF STATEMENTS	113	107

Common Size Statements & Ratios

0-500M	500M-2MM	2-10MM	10-50MM	50-100MM	100-250MM		4/1/90-3/31/91 ALL	4/1/91-3/31/92 ALL
%	%	%	%	%	%	**ASSETS**	%	%
5.9	9.0	2.6	2.6			Cash & Equivalents	4.9	7.0
34.3	32.4	34.2	29.5			Trade Receivables - (net)	31.8	31.6
41.3	38.8	44.5	44.8			Inventory	43.4	44.1
.9	.6	.5	1.8			All Other Current	.9	.7
82.3	80.8	81.8	78.6			Total Current	81.0	83.4
6.9	13.9	13.3	12.8			Fixed Assets (net)	10.6	10.1
1.7	1.8	.3	1.7			Intangibles (net)	1.4	1.0
9.1	3.4	4.6	6.9			All Other Non-Current	6.9	5.4
100.0	100.0	100.0	100.0			Total	100.0	100.0
						LIABILITIES		
17.4	14.2	28.1	30.7			Notes Payable-Short Term	18.1	17.8
1.5	3.0	2.0	1.9			Cur. Mat. -L/T/D	2.6	2.6
16.3	16.0	11.5	11.2			Trade Payables	17.5	15.1
.4	.1	.5	.3			Income Taxes Payable	.5	.3
5.2	7.2	7.7	9.1			All Other Current	9.6	9.0
40.8	40.5	49.8	53.1			Total Current	48.3	44.3
7.7	9.5	6.2	5.8			Long Term Debt	8.4	8.9
.0	.1	.0	.4			Deferred Taxes	.3	.4
.3	8.2	5.3	2.8			All Other-Non-Current	3.4	3.0
51.1	41.7	38.8	37.9			Net Worth	39.7	43.5
100.0	100.0	100.0	100.0			Total Liabilities & Net Worth	100.0	100.0
						INCOME DATA		
100.0	100.0	100.0	100.0			Net Sales	100.0	100.0
38.0	31.7	28.2	28.4			Gross Profit	31.2	34.0
34.8	27.8	22.4	24.0			Operating Expenses	25.4	29.2
3.2	3.9	5.8	4.4			Operating Profit	5.8	4.8
-.6	.8	1.6	1.7			All Other Expenses (net)	1.4	1.5
3.8	3.1	4.1	2.8			Profit Before Taxes	4.4	3.3
						RATIOS		
3.9	2.9	2.2	1.8			Current	2.5	2.9
2.0	1.8	1.5	1.5				1.7	1.9
1.6	1.6	1.3	1.1				1.3	1.4
1.8	1.5	1.1	.8			Quick	1.2	1.5
.9	1.0	.7	.7				.7	.8
.7	.5	.5	.5				.6	.6
32 11.3	33 11.2	37 9.9	40 9.1			Sales/Receivables	33 10.9	39 9.4
38 9.5	43 8.4	54 6.8	68 5.4				54 6.8	57 6.4
60 6.1	63 5.8	81 4.5	89 4.1				81 4.5	79 4.6
56 6.5	49 7.4	49 7.4	107 3.4			Cost of Sales/Inventory	59 6.2	66 5.5
107 3.4	81 4.5	99 3.7	146 2.5				118 3.1	140 2.6
140 2.6	152 2.4	203 1.8	192 1.9				192 1.9	215 1.7
6 62.4	17 20.9	6 58.6	16 22.2			Cost of Sales/Payables	14 25.9	15 25.0
21 17.8	33 11.1	20 18.7	35 10.4				31 11.7	31 11.9
51 7.1	47 7.7	47 7.8	57 6.4				76 4.8	60 6.1
3.7	4.1	4.1	4.1			Sales/Working Capital	3.6	3.3
7.8	7.1	7.1	7.3				5.8	5.3
12.0	11.2	11.9	15.4				13.9	9.5
	4.9	4.6	5.1			EBIT/Interest	5.2	5.2
	(34) 2.8	2.5	2.1				(101) 2.4	(98) 2.3
	1.5	1.7	1.3				1.3	1.1
	11.5	6.5	5.8			Net Profit + Depr., Dep.,	6.5	10.2
	(12) 2.0	(16) 3.0	(11) 4.3			Amort./Cur. Mat. L /T/D	(49) 2.2	(41) 3.2
	.7	1.7	.5				1.1	.7
.1	.1	.2	.2			Fixed/Worth	.1	.1
.1	.3	.3	.3				.2	.2
.3	.9	.6	.6				.5	.4
.6	.7	1.3	1.1			Debt/Worth	.8	.7
1.1	1.6	1.8	1.6				1.7	1.3
2.2	5.2	2.9	6.3				3.2	2.7
39.0	39.5	33.3	34.3			% Profit Before Taxes/Tangible	(108) 31.9	25.0
13.9	(36) 17.3	17.1	17.0			Net Worth	13.5	(103) 12.9
2.6	4.4	6.8	2.3				3.3	1.0
17.7	11.9	10.4	11.4			% Profit Before Taxes/Total	12.7	11.4
7.0	4.0	5.2	4.7			Assets	4.5	4.7
.5	1.6	2.2	.9				1.0	.4
80.3	93.5	54.2	33.5			Sales/Net Fixed Assets	70.3	91.1
62.1	20.8	23.1	12.8				33.2	34.1
25.7	9.9	10.2	9.2				13.9	13.6
3.4	3.1	3.0	1.9			Sales/Total Assets	2.9	2.7
2.9	2.4	2.1	1.6				2.0	1.9
2.4	1.8	1.4	1.3				1.5	1.3
	.5	.5	.9			% Depr., Dep., Amort./Sales	.4	.4
	(33) 1.1	(45) 1.0	(25) 1.1				(94) .8	(93) 1.1
	1.5	1.7	1.9				1.5	1.7
	2.6	1.9	1.3			% Officers', Directors',	2.0	2.1
	(20) 4.3	(32) 3.4	(10) 1.5			Owners' Comp/Sales	(60) 4.4	(69) 3.7
	8.3	5.9	2.1				8.5	7.2
8839M	104938M	495539M	983205M	1332392M	309448M	Net Sales ($)	1951939M	1825296M
3136M	42335M	212385M	618146M	662070M	286720M	Total Assets ($)	1137655M	1194608M

M = $ thousand   MM = $ million
See Pages 1 through 15 for Explanation of Ratios and Data

Comparative Historical Data | **Current Data Sorted By Sales**

4/1/92-3/31/93 ALL	4/1/93-3/31/94 ALL	4/1/94-3/31/95 ALL		0-1MM	1-3MM	3-5MM	5-10MM	10-25MM	25MM & OVER
1	1	1	# Postretirement Benefits **Type of Statement**						1
24	35	38	Unqualified		1	5	4	7	21
49	43	43	Reviewed		13	14	8	5	3
18	17	14	Compiled	4	6	2	1	1	
2	3	1	Tax Returns					1	
15	25	38	Other	4	7	5	3	10	9
					45 (4/1-9/30/94)		89 (10/1/94-3/31/95)		
108	123	134	**NUMBER OF STATEMENTS**	8	27	26	16	24	33
%	%	%	**ASSETS**	%	%	%	%	%	%
5.6	4.9	5.1	Cash & Equivalents		9.7	4.9	3.5	2.5	4.7
33.3	30.7	32.0	Trade Receivables - (net)		31.1	31.1	36.8	35.6	28.6
41.0	45.0	42.6	Inventory		40.7	45.7	36.2	42.7	43.3
1.0	1.5	1.0	All Other Current		.8	.5	.2	.7	2.5
80.9	82.1	80.8	Total Current		82.2	82.1	76.7	81.4	79.0
12.8	11.8	12.7	Fixed Assets (net)		11.2	13.6	18.8	11.6	12.9
1.4	1.3	1.5	Intangibles (net)		3.1	.1	.5	.4	2.8
4.9	4.7	5.0	All Other Non-Current		3.6	4.2	3.9	6.6	5.2
100.0	100.0	100.0	Total		100.0	100.0	100.0	100.0	100.0
			LIABILITIES						
20.5	23.6	23.5	Notes Payable-Short Term		13.6	25.0	17.2	29.2	28.7
2.5	2.2	2.1	Cur. Mat.-L /T/D		2.7	2.5	2.2	1.7	1.9
18.9	14.4	13.3	Trade Payables		13.7	16.7	13.1	10.9	12.2
.3	.4	.4	Income Taxes Payable		.1	.0	.6	.5	.9
8.6	7.6	7.5	All Other Current		6.4	7.4	7.9	9.3	6.9
50.7	48.2	46.8	Total Current		36.5	51.6	41.1	51.5	50.7
7.7	6.9	7.1	Long Term Debt		7.7	8.8	8.7	5.4	5.1
.2	.3	.2	Deferred Taxes		.0	.2	.0	.0	.5
5.6	5.6	4.9	All Other-Non-Current		5.9	7.9	5.4	4.2	3.2
35.9	39.0	41.0	Net Worth		49.8	31.5	44.7	38.8	40.4
100.0	100.0	100.0	Total Liabilities & Net Worth		100.0	100.0	100.0	100.0	100.0
			INCOME DATA						
100.0	100.0	100.0	Net Sales		100.0	100.0	100.0	100.0	100.0
31.8	27.9	29.5	Gross Profit		33.4	30.2	29.5	26.8	25.5
27.1	23.7	24.7	Operating Expenses		30.7	25.1	23.9	21.6	20.3
4.7	4.2	4.8	Operating Profit		2.7	5.1	5.6	5.3	5.2
1.0	1.3	1.2	All Other Expenses (net)		.8	1.5	1.4	1.3	1.5
3.7	3.0	3.7	Profit Before Taxes		1.9	3.6	4.2	4.0	3.7
			RATIOS						
2.3 / 1.6 / 1.2	2.9 / 1.6 / 1.3	2.4 / 1.7 / 1.3	Current		3.3 / 2.2 / 1.7	1.8 / 1.6 / 1.3	2.8 / 1.7 / 1.4	1.9 / 1.5 / 1.3	2.5 / 1.5 / 1.3
1.2 / .8 / .6	1.1 / .7 / .5	1.2 / .7 / .5	Quick		1.9 / 1.0 / .6	1.1 / .6 / .4	1.4 / 1.0 / .7	1.1 / .7 / .5	.8 / .6 / .4
36 10.2 / 51 7.1 / 79 4.6	30 12.0 / 49 7.5 / 74 4.9	35 10.4 / 53 6.9 / 78 4.7	Sales/Receivables		34 10.6 / 48 7.1 / 70 5.2	33 11.2 / 41 8.8 / 59 6.2	51 7.2 / 68 5.4 / 101 3.6	33 11.1 / 54 6.8 / 83 4.4	33 11.0 / 53 6.9 / 89 4.1
61 6.0 / 107 3.4 / 159 2.3	62 5.9 / 126 2.9 / 203 1.8	60 6.1 / 118 3.1 / 183 2.0	Cost of Sales/Inventory		60 6.1 / 107 3.4 / 174 2.1	57 6.4 / 96 3.8 / 192 1.9	43 8.5 / 81 4.5 / 215 1.7	48 7.6 / 122 3.0 / 183 2.0	68 5.4 / 118 3.1 / 174 2.1
16 23.3 / 38 9.7 / 74 4.9	9 39.2 / 29 12.5 / 54 6.7	11 33.5 / 25 14.6 / 50 7.3	Cost of Sales/Payables		12 31.4 / 27 13.6 / 42 8.6	11 32.0 / 24 14.9 / 48 7.6	12 31.4 / 24 15.2 / 62 5.9	7 52.0 / 25 14.7 / 53 6.9	9 42.4 / 24 15.5 / 50 7.3
4.4 / 7.7 / 13.8	3.6 / 6.3 / 12.8	4.1 / 7.1 / 11.7	Sales/Working Capital		3.4 / 4.7 / 7.9	5.9 / 7.7 / 11.9	3.4 / 6.2 / 11.0	4.3 / 10.3 / 15.8	4.8 / 7.4 / 12.6
(103) 5.7 / 3.1 / 1.4	(111) 5.5 / 2.4 / 1.3	(126) 4.7 / 2.5 / 1.5	EBIT/Interest		(24) 4.5 / 1.8 / 1.2	(24) 4.0 / 2.4 / 1.6	5.7 / 2.4 / 1.7	4.6 / 3.3 / 1.6	(31) 5.9 / 2.4 / 1.4
(31) 4.1 / 2.0 / .8	(39) 4.8 / 2.1 / .6	(43) 6.8 / 3.0 / 1.2	Net Profit + Depr., Dep., Amort./Cur. Mat. L/T/D					(10) 11.5 / 5.0 / 1.5	(11) 6.6 / 4.3 / 1.2
.1 / .2 / .6	.1 / .3 / .5	.1 / .3 / .6	Fixed/Worth		.1 / .2 / .5	.1 / .3 / 1.0	.2 / .5 / .6	.2 / .3 / .5	.2 / .3 / .6
1.1 / 2.1 / 4.7	.8 / 1.7 / 3.9	.9 / 1.6 / 3.7	Debt/Worth		.6 / 1.1 / 2.8	1.4 / 2.0 / 5.8	.7 / 1.4 / 2.6	1.3 / 1.6 / 3.8	.9 / 1.7 / 4.1
(106) 35.3 / 15.1 / 6.3	(118) 32.6 / 14.9 / 3.9	(132) 34.0 / 17.0 / 5.1	% Profit Before Taxes/Tangible Net Worth		(26) 27.9 / 7.0 / 2.2	(25) 48.0 / 22.9 / 9.5	33.2 / 15.8 / 3.7	46.5 / 25.2 / 4.2	33.3 / 17.0 / 5.4
11.5 / 4.9 / 1.5	11.2 / 4.0 / 1.0	11.3 / 5.0 / 1.8	% Profit Before Taxes/Total Assets		11.8 / 2.4 / .6	9.2 / 5.0 / 1.8	11.4 / 3.9 / 2.2	10.8 / 6.5 / 1.8	12.8 / 5.9 / 1.9
84.6 / 31.4 / 10.7	84.1 / 23.0 / 10.9	50.0 / 21.3 / 10.7	Sales/Net Fixed Assets		76.3 / 28.9 / 11.1	78.5 / 22.4 / 9.7	30.2 / 13.7 / 5.0	52.8 / 19.3 / 11.3	40.5 / 20.3 / 9.6
2.8 / 2.1 / 1.6	2.8 / 2.0 / 1.3	2.7 / 2.1 / 1.5	Sales/Total Assets		2.8 / 2.2 / 1.7	2.9 / 2.4 / 1.6	2.5 / 2.3 / 1.1	3.3 / 1.9 / 1.4	2.4 / 1.9 / 1.4
(99) .4 / 1.0 / 1.6	(110) .4 / .9 / 1.6	(121) .5 / 1.0 / 1.6	% Depr., Dep., Amort./Sales		(23) .5 / .7 / 1.3	.4 / 1.2 / 1.7	(15) .6 / 1.2 / 2.8	.6 / 1.0 / 1.5	(27) .8 / 1.1 / 2.0
(66) 2.3 / 3.9 / 7.6	(72) 2.1 / 3.2 / 6.3	(73) 1.8 / 3.2 / 6.4	% Officers', Directors', Owners' Comp/Sales		(18) 2.9 / 5.5 / 10.4	(16) 2.3 / 5.5 / 11.8	(15) 2.6 / 3.5 / 5.3		(12) 1.1 / 1.4 / 1.9
1740314M	2956261M	3234361M	Net Sales ($)	5445M	53612M	106313M	112585M	438058M	2518348M
927944M	1978902M	1824792M	Total Assets ($)	3461M	27876M	56892M	69153M	229794M	1437616M

M = $ thousand   MM = $ million
See Pages 1 through 15 for Explanation of Ratios and Data

Current Data Sorted By Assets | Comparative Historical Data

						# Postretirement Benefits / Type of Statement		
			1		1	# Postretirement Benefits		
1		3	9	1	1	Unqualified	16	20
	2	3				Reviewed	7	3
	1		1			Compiled	1	2
						Tax Returns		
1	4	2	5		2	Other	4	8
0-500M	9 (4/1-9/30/94) 500M-2MM	2-10MM	28 (10/1/94-3/31/95) 10-50MM	50-100MM	100-250MM		4 / 4/1/90-3/31/91 ALL	8 / 4/1/91-3/31/92 ALL
2	7	8	15	2	3	NUMBER OF STATEMENTS	28	33
%	%	%	%	%	%		%	%

ASSETS

Item	0-500M	500M-2MM	2-10MM	10-50MM	50-100MM	100-250MM	ALL 4/1/90-3/31/91	ALL 4/1/91-3/31/92
Cash & Equivalents				7.0			8.1	9.0
Trade Receivables - (net)				31.7			28.2	25.9
Inventory				32.5			38.2	38.7
All Other Current				3.0			2.9	1.8
Total Current				74.2			77.4	75.5
Fixed Assets (net)				12.1			12.8	13.7
Intangibles (net)				7.8			2.2	2.9
All Other Non-Current				5.9			7.5	8.0
Total				100.0			100.0	100.0

LIABILITIES

Item	0-500M	500M-2MM	2-10MM	10-50MM	50-100MM	100-250MM	ALL 4/1/90-3/31/91	ALL 4/1/91-3/31/92
Notes Payable-Short Term				22.4			16.4	13.9
Cur. Mat. -L/T/D				1.6			1.4	1.7
Trade Payables				14.2			16.5	15.5
Income Taxes Payable				.2			.3	.6
All Other Current				6.8			8.6	7.0
Total Current				45.1			43.3	38.6
Long Term Debt				6.7			12.6	11.2
Deferred Taxes				.1			.8	.6
All Other-Non-Current				6.2			1.2	2.8
Net Worth				41.9			42.1	46.7
Total Liabilities & Net Worth				100.0			100.0	100.0

INCOME DATA

Item	0-500M	500M-2MM	2-10MM	10-50MM	50-100MM	100-250MM	ALL 4/1/90-3/31/91	ALL 4/1/91-3/31/92
Net Sales				100.0			100.0	100.0
Gross Profit				26.5			26.5	29.5
Operating Expenses				20.4			23.9	26.0
Operating Profit				6.1			2.6	3.5
All Other Expenses (net)				1.5			2.1	1.6
Profit Before Taxes				4.7			.6	1.9

RATIOS

Item	2-10MM	10-50MM	ALL 4/1/90-3/31/91	ALL 4/1/91-3/31/92
Current		4.0 / 1.4 / 1.3	3.6 / 1.6 / 1.2	3.6 / 1.8 / 1.4
Quick		1.2 / .7 / .5	1.6 / .7 / .5	1.8 / .8 / .5
Sales/Receivables	40 / 76 / 96	9.1 / 4.8 / 3.8	32 11.3 / 54 6.7 / 73 5.0	37 9.8 / 47 7.7 / 70 5.2
Cost of Sales/Inventory	74 / 94 / 135	4.9 / 3.9 / 2.7	68 5.4 / 96 3.8 / 118 3.1	74 4.9 / 104 3.5 / 135 2.7
Cost of Sales/Payables	20 / 45 / 54	18.0 / 8.2 / 6.8	19 19.1 / 29 12.5 / 53 6.9	22 16.5 / 33 11.0 / 57 6.4
Sales/Working Capital		5.3 / 7.5 / 12.7	3.1 / 7.2 / 20.7	3.4 / 6.1 / 9.7
EBIT/Interest		71.5 / (14) 3.5 / 1.6	(26) 4.1 / 2.3 / -.6	(32) 4.0 / 2.4 / .9
Net Profit + Depr., Dep., Amort./Cur. Mat. L./T/D			(15) 9.8 / 2.9 / -.4	(19) 5.3 / 1.3 / .1
Fixed/Worth		.1 / .5 / .6	.2 / .3 / .6	.2 / .3 / .6
Debt/Worth		.4 / 2.5 / 6.6	.6 / 1.4 / 3.6	.6 / 1.1 / 2.1
% Profit Before Taxes/Tangible Net Worth		202.2 / 24.3 / 8.4	(26) 25.9 / 16.0 / -9.9	(31) 24.7 / 9.9 / .4
% Profit Before Taxes/Total Assets		17.7 / 7.6 / 2.4	9.1 / 5.9 / -5.8	9.6 / 4.0 / -.2
Sales/Net Fixed Assets		27.1 / 14.3 / 13.0	35.3 / 16.4 / 9.5	28.0 / 15.2 / 9.5
Sales/Total Assets		2.1 / 1.9 / 1.3	2.4 / 1.9 / 1.5	2.4 / 1.9 / 1.5
% Depr., Dep., Amort./Sales		(13) .6 / 1.2 / 1.6	(26) .5 / 1.2 / 1.7	(31) .6 / 1.3 / 2.1
% Officers', Directors', Owners' Comp/Sales				

	0-500M	500M-2MM	2-10MM	10-50MM	50-100MM	100-250MM	1922129M	1955596M
Net Sales ($)	939M	25001M	112250M	596017M	173310M	863986M	1922129M	1955596M
Total Assets ($)	530M	8234M	52707M	355669M	101453M	507450M	1142080M	1096257M

M = $ thousand   MM = $ million
See Pages 1 through 15 for Explanation of Ratios and Data

Comparative Historical Data | Current Data Sorted By Sales

Postretirement Benefits — Type of Statement

	4/1/92-3/31/93 ALL	4/1/93-3/31/94 ALL	4/1/94-3/31/95 ALL		0-1MM	1-3MM	3-5MM	5-10MM	10-25MM	25MM & OVER
# Postretirement Benefits	1	2	2						1	1
Unqualified	18	12	15		1				5	9
Reviewed	7	7	5			1	1		3	
Compiled	3	2	2				1			1
Tax Returns		2								
Other	3	7	15		1	2	1	2	3	6
					9 (4/1-9/30/94)			28 (10/1/94-3/31/95)		
NUMBER OF STATEMENTS	31	30	37		2	3	2	3	11	16

4/1/92-3/31/93 ALL	4/1/93-3/31/94 ALL	4/1/94-3/31/95 ALL		0-1MM	1-3MM	3-5MM	5-10MM	10-25MM	25MM & OVER
%	%	%	**ASSETS**	%	%	%	%	%	%
6.7	8.1	6.3	Cash & Equivalents					10.3	3.2
26.5	30.1	27.5	Trade Receivables - (net)					32.6	29.8
34.3	35.7	39.6	Inventory					30.9	39.5
2.5	2.5	2.7	All Other Current					.7	4.5
70.0	76.3	76.2	Total Current					74.4	77.0
15.9	14.1	14.6	Fixed Assets (net)					11.1	15.1
2.1	1.7	4.4	Intangibles (net)					8.6	3.3
12.0	7.8	4.8	All Other Non-Current					5.8	4.6
100.0	100.0	100.0	Total					100.0	100.0
			LIABILITIES						
17.7	14.1	16.5	Notes Payable-Short Term					18.5	20.2
2.8	1.9	1.5	Cur. Mat.-L /T/D					.9	1.8
11.6	12.1	18.7	Trade Payables					11.6	15.9
.7	.9	.2	Income Taxes Payable					.4	.3
7.3	10.6	8.8	All Other Current					6.4	8.6
40.1	39.6	45.6	Total Current					37.8	46.8
10.3	6.0	11.1	Long Term Debt					5.3	12.3
.2	.3	.6	Deferred Taxes					1.5	.2
2.6	3.5	4.0	All Other-Non-Current					2.5	6.8
46.8	50.6	38.7	Net Worth					53.0	33.8
100.0	100.0	100.0	Total Liabilities & Net Worth					100.0	100.0
			INCOME DATA						
100.0	100.0	100.0	Net Sales					100.0	100.0
28.9	26.0	27.1	Gross Profit					25.5	29.4
22.8	21.0	22.2	Operating Expenses					19.8	23.1
6.1	5.0	4.9	Operating Profit					5.7	6.3
.9	.8	1.3	All Other Expenses (net)					.9	1.9
5.2	4.2	3.6	Profit Before Taxes					4.8	4.4
			RATIOS						
3.1 / 1.7 / 1.3	3.1 / 1.9 / 1.3	3.4 / 1.4 / 1.2	Current					4.2 / 2.1 / 1.4	2.4 / 1.4 / 1.3
1.3 / .8 / .5	1.5 / 1.0 / .5	1.1 / .7 / .4	Quick					2.9 / .9 / .6	1.1 / .7 / .4
32 11.3 51 7.1 66 5.5	34 10.6 49 7.5 63 5.8	34 10.6 51 7.2 78 4.7	Sales/Receivables					42 8.6 70 5.2 91 4.0	41 8.8 59 6.2 87 4.2
58 6.3 96 3.8 135 2.7	50 7.3 99 3.7 111 3.3	73 5.0 96 3.8 135 2.7	Cost of Sales/Inventory					72 5.1 83 4.4 96 3.8	78 4.7 122 3.0 152 2.4
14 25.4 25 14.7 48 7.6	15 24.8 29 12.8 35 10.4	22 16.3 42 8.6 54 6.7	Cost of Sales/Payables					16 22.3 20 18.0 48 7.6	26 13.9 45 8.2 54 6.8
3.8 / 9.0 / 13.5	3.6 / 6.2 / 10.8	4.3 / 7.5 / 13.3	Sales/Working Capital					3.1 / 6.0 / 8.4	4.5 / 7.4 / 12.8
15.1 (27) 4.4 1.2	10.6 (28) 4.8 3.3	15.2 (31) 3.4 1.3	EBIT/Interest					56.4 (10) 10.4 2.0	12.5 (14) 2.5 1.2
8.2 (13) 1.0 .5	5.3 (14) 3.7 1.9		Net Profit + Depr., Dep., Amort./Cur. Mat. L/T/D						
.2 / .4 / .9	.1 / .3 / .5	.2 / .5 / .9	Fixed/Worth					.1 / .2 / .6	.3 / .6 / .9
.6 / 1.0 / 3.8	.6 / 1.1 / 1.9	.9 / 2.3 / 4.7	Debt/Worth					.3 / 1.7 / 3.3	1.3 / 2.3 / 7.1
35.3 (30) 18.4 6.8	33.4 18.1 11.7	41.3 (36) 16.8 4.4	% Profit Before Taxes/Tangible Net Worth					36.4 16.8 8.4	162.2 29.0 8.3
16.6 / 9.4 / 2.0	13.6 / 9.2 / 5.2	11.7 / 6.6 / .8	% Profit Before Taxes/Total Assets					12.6 / 7.6 / 2.5	21.4 / 7.5 / 2.4
28.9 / 12.7 / 8.9	36.1 / 14.6 / 8.9	24.3 / 16.5 / 11.6	Sales/Net Fixed Assets					23.0 / 18.5 / 13.0	22.6 / 14.3 / 7.8
2.3 / 1.9 / 1.5	2.5 / 2.0 / 1.8	2.2 / 1.9 / 1.6	Sales/Total Assets					2.1 / 2.0 / 1.3	2.1 / 1.9 / 1.5
.7 (26) 1.2 1.9	.5 (27) 1.2 1.9	.7 (30) 1.2 1.5	% Depr., Dep., Amort./Sales					.9 1.1 1.4	.5 (12) 1.2 2.0
		1.2 (11) 3.7 4.6	% Officers', Directors', Owners' Comp/Sales						
1331910M 765918M	1514043M 802619M	1771503M 1026043M	Net Sales ($) Total Assets ($)	939M 530M	4451M 2360M	7789M 2855M	21098M 5796M	173847M 108006M	1563379M 906496M

M = $ thousand   MM = $ million
See Pages 1 through 15 for Explanation of Ratios and Data

	Current Data Sorted By Assets							Comparative Historical Data	
	1	2	1	1			# Postretirement Benefits Type of Statement		
		1	3	2	2	1	Unqualified	7	6
	1	5	5	2			Reviewed	9	13
	3	8	1				Compiled	10	6
			1				Tax Returns	1	1
			7	2			Other	7	5
		12 (4/1-9/30/94)		32 (10/1/94-3/31/95)				4/1/90-3/31/91	4/1/91-3/31/92
	0-500M	500M-2MM	2-10MM	10-50MM	50-100MM	100-250MM		ALL	ALL
	4	14	17	6	2	1	NUMBER OF STATEMENTS	34	31
	%	%	%	%	%	%		%	%
							ASSETS		
		8.1	2.3				Cash & Equivalents	6.0	6.8
		30.8	31.3				Trade Receivables - (net)	32.0	32.6
		40.0	45.6				Inventory	36.9	40.4
		1.0	.8				All Other Current	1.2	1.0
		79.9	80.0				Total Current	76.1	80.8
		14.8	10.1				Fixed Assets (net)	19.0	14.6
		1.4	2.2				Intangibles (net)	.2	.6
		3.8	7.7				All Other Non-Current	4.7	4.0
		100.0	100.0				Total	100.0	100.0
							LIABILITIES		
		18.8	23.0				Notes Payable-Short Term	12.9	19.2
		1.7	4.5				Cur. Mat. -L/T/D	4.5	2.8
		15.0	18.3				Trade Payables	16.0	12.3
		1.0	.6				Income Taxes Payable	1.2	1.1
		8.4	10.2				All Other Current	10.4	10.7
		45.0	56.5				Total Current	45.0	46.1
		8.4	6.8				Long Term Debt	14.9	10.6
		.0	.0				Deferred Taxes	.4	.2
		6.5	6.8				All Other-Non-Current	3.0	2.1
		40.1	29.9				Net Worth	36.7	41.0
		100.0	100.0				Total Liabilities & Net Worth	100.0	100.0
							INCOME DATA		
		100.0	100.0				Net Sales	100.0	100.0
		28.3	32.3				Gross Profit	33.9	32.2
		26.3	27.9				Operating Expenses	29.8	26.9
		2.0	4.3				Operating Profit	4.1	5.3
		1.1	2.0				All Other Expenses (net)	1.3	2.0
		.9	2.3				Profit Before Taxes	2.8	3.2
							RATIOS		
		2.6	1.7					2.2	2.9
		1.8	1.5				Current	1.6	1.7
		1.3	1.2					1.3	1.3
		1.3	.9					1.3	1.2
		.9	.6				Quick	.8	.9
		.5	.5					.5	.6
		28 13.0	41 8.8					31 11.8 / 31 11.6	
		43 8.5	51 7.2				Sales/Receivables	46 8.0 / 48 7.6	
		55 6.6	68 5.4					64 5.7 / 72 5.1	
		39 9.3	73 5.0					40 9.2 / 53 6.9	
		66 5.5	111 3.3				Cost of Sales/Inventory	99 3.7 / 89 4.1	
		91 4.0	146 2.5					135 2.7 / 122 3.0	
		11 33.3	29 12.6					16 22.7 / 14 25.2	
		28 13.1	34 10.8				Cost of Sales/Payables	25 14.8 / 27 13.6	
		45 8.2	51 7.1					46 7.9 / 36 10.1	
		4.9	6.9					5.6	4.3
		8.8	7.8				Sales/Working Capital	9.0	7.3
		16.2	14.9					15.1	14.5
		9.1	4.0					(29) 8.0	(28) 5.5
	(13)	2.7	2.7				EBIT/Interest	3.3	2.8
		1.2	1.2					1.2	1.1
								(16) 4.7	(11) 4.9
							Net Profit + Depr., Dep., Amort./Cur. Mat. L./T/D	1.6	2.3
								-.7	1.6
		.1	.2					.2	.2
		.4	.4				Fixed/Worth	.5	.4
		.9	.5					.8	.7
		.6	1.4					1.1	.9
		1.1	2.4				Debt/Worth	2.0	1.8
		2.9	7.7					3.4	3.0
		39.2	32.4					56.4	30.1
	(13)	26.1	(16) 12.3				% Profit Before Taxes/Tangible Net Worth	(32) 23.3	(30) 15.6
		2.2	5.3					9.7	1.2
		18.3	9.4					19.3	13.9
		5.1	3.1				% Profit Before Taxes/Total Assets	11.7	6.1
		-4.3	1.0					1.7	.2
		62.5	48.2					29.6	35.2
		29.2	23.3				Sales/Net Fixed Assets	21.5	22.1
		16.1	17.0					9.8	12.6
		3.2	2.6					3.2	3.0
		2.8	2.2				Sales/Total Assets	2.4	2.4
		2.1	1.7					2.0	1.9
		.9	.7					(32) .7	(27) .9
	(11)	1.6	(16) 1.1				% Depr., Dep., Amort./Sales	1.1	1.3
		2.0	1.7					1.8	1.7
								2.7	3.3
							% Officers', Directors', Owners' Comp/Sales	(16) 4.8	(20) 4.7
								8.6	6.8
	5907M	39404M	176300M	234607M	255349M	127378M	Net Sales ($)	560078M	517036M
	1587M	14818M	82044M	128200M	152398M	102498M	Total Assets ($)	293581M	277116M

© Robert Morris Associates 1995

M = $ thousand   MM = $ million
See Pages 1 through 15 for Explanation of Ratios and Data

Comparative Historical Data | Current Data Sorted By Sales

				0-1MM	1-3MM	3-5MM	5-10MM	10-25MM	25MM & OVER
			# Postretirement Benefits	2	1			1	1
			Type of Statement						
	3	5							
8	8	9	Unqualified			1	2	2	4
16	11	13	Reviewed	1	2	4	2	2	2
12	12	12	Compiled	3	6	2	1		
1		1	Tax Returns				1		
9	11	9	Other			1	2	5	1
4/1/92-3/31/93 ALL	4/1/93-3/31/94 ALL	4/1/94-3/31/95 ALL		12 (4/1-9/30/94)			32 (10/1/94-3/31/95)		
46	42	44	**NUMBER OF STATEMENTS**	4	8	8	8	9	7
%	%	%	**ASSETS**	%	%	%	%	%	%
7.5	6.6	5.6	Cash & Equivalents						
29.7	31.0	31.1	Trade Receivables - (net)						
36.7	38.9	40.6	Inventory						
1.3	1.0	1.1	All Other Current						
75.2	77.4	78.4	Total Current						
15.3	12.7	12.5	Fixed Assets (net)						
2.3	2.5	2.3	Intangibles (net)						
7.2	7.4	6.9	All Other Non-Current						
100.0	100.0	100.0	Total						
			LIABILITIES						
14.1	13.5	19.7	Notes Payable-Short Term						
4.4	2.3	3.1	Cur. Mat.-L/T/D						
18.0	14.9	15.5	Trade Payables						
.4	2.1	.7	Income Taxes Payable						
7.9	8.1	9.0	All Other Current						
44.9	40.9	47.9	Total Current						
12.4	6.9	8.8	Long Term Debt						
.1	.2	.2	Deferred Taxes						
4.1	5.0	5.9	All Other-Non-Current						
38.5	47.1	37.2	Net Worth						
100.0	100.0	100.0	Total Liabilities & Net Worth						
			INCOME DATA						
100.0	100.0	100.0	Net Sales						
31.1	30.9	32.3	Gross Profit						
27.5	26.8	28.4	Operating Expenses						
3.6	4.0	3.9	Operating Profit						
1.3	.9	1.4	All Other Expenses (net)						
2.4	3.2	2.5	Profit Before Taxes						
			RATIOS						
2.7	3.1	2.2	Current						
1.5	1.9	1.6							
1.2	1.3	1.3							
1.5	1.7	1.0	Quick						
.8	.8	.6							
.5	.6	.6							
26 13.9	26 14.2	37 9.9	Sales/Receivables						
44 8.3	45 8.2	50 7.3							
55 6.6	57 6.4	68 5.4							
41 9.0	51 7.2	66 5.5	Cost of Sales/Inventory						
76 4.8	74 4.9	81 4.5							
104 3.5	118 3.1	159 2.3							
15 23.9	13 27.9	20 18.3	Cost of Sales/Payables						
32 11.3	24 15.3	33 10.9							
51 7.1	43 8.5	43 8.5							
4.7	4.3	5.2	Sales/Working Capital						
11.0	8.6	7.8							
18.8	15.6	15.1							
7.6	7.5	6.4	EBIT/Interest						
(42) 3.3	(36) 3.5	(40) 2.7							
1.5	1.6	1.4							
8.9	5.2	3.9	Net Profit + Depr., Dep., Amort./Cur. Mat. L/T/D						
(20) 2.8	(17) 1.8	(17) 2.3							
1.2	.9	1.6							
.1	.1	.1	Fixed/Worth						
.3	.2	.3							
.7	.6	.7							
.9	.6	1.0	Debt/Worth						
1.8	1.2	2.1							
3.3	2.7	4.0							
37.5	30.1	38.1	% Profit Before Taxes/Tangible Net Worth						
(43) 20.1	(40) 17.5	(42) 19.0							
9.1	5.9	7.9							
11.9	14.7	11.3	% Profit Before Taxes/Total Assets						
6.2	5.5	6.1							
1.7	1.1	1.3							
59.7	52.7	49.7	Sales/Net Fixed Assets						
25.2	27.2	22.8							
14.7	14.7	14.2							
3.3	3.1	2.8	Sales/Total Assets						
2.6	2.6	2.2							
2.2	2.1	1.7							
.4	.5	.8	% Depr., Dep., Amort./Sales						
(39) .9	(36) 1.0	(35) 1.2							
1.5	1.7	2.0							
2.6	3.1	2.4	% Officers', Directors', Owners' Comp/Sales						
(25) 4.0	(24) 5.1	(19) 4.0							
6.4	7.5	8.6							
542863M	412189M	838945M	Net Sales ($)	3391M	18796M	31738M	58358M	148290M	578372M
206135M	186973M	481545M	Total Assets ($)	2151M	5795M	13905M	24747M	76423M	358524M

MANUFACTURERS—HARDWOOD DIMENSION & FLOORING MILLS. SIC# 2426

Current Data Sorted By Assets   **Comparative Historical Data**

Type of Statement

# Postretirement Benefits / Type of Statement	4/1/90-3/31/91 ALL	4/1/91-3/31/92 ALL
Unqualified	17	13
Reviewed	11	15
Compiled	10	16
Tax Returns		
Other	13	10

Current statement-type distribution (as positioned in source):

```
                1       2
                        5      6
         4      7       1
3        3     11
         3
4        2             1
```

16 (4/1-9/30/94)   36 (10/1/94-3/31/95)

0-500M	500M-2MM	2-10MM	10-50MM	50-100MM	100-250MM	NUMBER OF STATEMENTS	51	54
7	12	25	8				51	54

ASSETS (%)

500M-2MM	2-10MM		ASSETS	90-91	91-92
9.8	5.5		Cash & Equivalents	4.2	4.7
22.0	19.9		Trade Receivables - (net)	20.4	20.0
28.0	31.5		Inventory	33.0	33.2
3.5	.8		All Other Current	2.2	.8
63.2	57.6		Total Current	59.8	58.7
30.2	36.9		Fixed Assets (net)	32.7	32.4
1.1	.4		Intangibles (net)	.5	.5
5.5	5.1		All Other Non-Current	7.0	8.4
100.0	100.0		Total	100.0	100.0

LIABILITIES

500M-2MM	2-10MM		LIABILITIES	90-91	91-92
4.9	12.5		Notes Payable-Short Term	14.4	12.5
4.0	5.7		Cur. Mat. -L/T/D	3.9	4.3
11.5	8.5		Trade Payables	8.7	11.6
.1	.5		Income Taxes Payable	.6	.3
4.3	6.4		All Other Current	6.0	6.7
24.7	33.5		Total Current	33.5	35.4
12.9	19.7		Long Term Debt	19.4	19.5
.0	1.0		Deferred Taxes	.9	.8
5.3	2.7		All Other-Non-Current	1.8	1.1
57.1	43.0		Net Worth	44.3	43.2
100.0	100.0		Total Liabilities & Net Worth	100.0	100.0

INCOME DATA

500M-2MM	2-10MM		INCOME DATA	90-91	91-92
100.0	100.0		Net Sales	100.0	100.0
24.8	18.8		Gross Profit	23.2	22.3
18.5	13.6		Operating Expenses	18.3	19.6
6.4	5.2		Operating Profit	4.9	2.7
.5	1.2		All Other Expenses (net)	2.3	1.9
5.9	4.0		Profit Before Taxes	2.6	.9

RATIOS

500M-2MM	2-10MM		RATIOS	90-91	91-92
7.8	2.6		Current	3.0	2.8
3.5	1.7			1.8	1.7
1.4	1.3			1.2	1.3
3.1	1.2		Quick	1.2	1.4
1.2	.7			.7	.7
.8	.5			.4	.4
16 22.7	15 24.8		Sales/Receivables	20 18.6	20 18.2
26 14.1	26 14.1			28 13.0	30 12.3
45 8.2	40 9.1			43 8.4	42 8.7
24 15.4	35 10.3		Cost of Sales/Inventory	38 9.5	35 10.3
41 8.8	56 6.5			91 4.0	73 5.0
91 4.0	85 4.3			118 3.1	126 2.9
8 48.1	7 52.1		Cost of Sales/Payables	7 50.1	9 41.7
12 29.7	15 24.8			13 29.1	16 22.4
24 15.0	22 16.4			21 17.6	35 10.3
3.5	6.4		Sales/Working Capital	4.6	5.1
5.9	10.5			9.1	11.3
17.3	16.3			21.1	20.6
	(24) 12.1		EBIT/Interest	(47) 4.6	(51) 5.1
	4.5			2.3	2.1
	1.8			1.3	1.0
	(15) 3.5		Net Profit + Depr., Dep.,	(31) 2.8	(31) 3.7
	1.8		Amort./Cur. Mat. L./T/D	1.6	1.9
	.9			.9	.6
.3	.5		Fixed/Worth	.5	.4
.5	.8			.7	.8
1.3	1.1			1.3	1.2
.2	.5		Debt/Worth	.8	.6
1.0	1.4			1.5	1.5
2.6	3.1			2.3	2.5
43.1	39.0		% Profit Before Taxes/Tangible	(50) 23.7	(51) 20.4
24.3	20.9		Net Worth	10.9	10.7
18.7	12.8			3.3	2.6
22.6	15.1		% Profit Before Taxes/Total	10.5	8.4
15.0	11.3		Assets	5.4	4.5
6.2	2.8			1.1	-.2
16.1	11.0		Sales/Net Fixed Assets	12.2	14.1
10.4	6.4			6.9	7.1
4.5	4.5			3.9	3.9
3.7	2.9		Sales/Total Assets	2.8	3.0
2.6	2.4			1.9	2.1
2.0	2.0			1.5	1.3
.9	1.0		% Depr., Dep., Amort./Sales	(45) 1.8	(49) .9
1.9	1.9			2.3	2.2
4.5	2.7			3.8	4.0
	(12) 1.3		% Officers', Directors',	(16) 2.5	(23) 1.5
	2.1		Owners' Comp/Sales	4.5	4.0
	4.2			7.3	6.4

0-500M	500M-2MM	2-10MM	10-50MM				90-91	91-92
4373M	38810M	241041M	303208M			Net Sales ($)	470667M	662413M
2443M	14808M	95680M	129205M			Total Assets ($)	231742M	345459M

M = $ thousand   MM = $ million
See Pages 1 through 15 for Explanation of Ratios and Data

Comparative Historical Data | Current Data Sorted By Sales

Hist 1	Hist 2	Hist 3	# Postretirement Benefits / Type of Statement	0-1MM	1-3MM	3-5MM	5-10MM	10-25MM	25MM & OVER
			# Postretirement Benefits				1	1	1
14	13	11	Unqualified				1	4	6
17	10	12	Reviewed	1	2	3	6		
16	17	17	Compiled	3	1	5	4	4	
2	3	3	Tax Returns		1	2			
11	5	9	Other	3	2	1	1	1	1
4/1/92-3/31/93 ALL	4/1/93-3/31/94 ALL	4/1/94-3/31/95 ALL		16 (4/1-9/30/94)			36 (10/1/94-3/31/95)		
60	48	52	NUMBER OF STATEMENTS	7	6	11	12	9	7
%	%	%	**ASSETS**	%	%	%	%	%	%
3.8	4.3	6.6	Cash & Equivalents			9.6	4.9		
20.8	19.1	19.8	Trade Receivables - (net)			18.9	19.0		
29.6	30.1	29.2	Inventory			26.7	31.6		
1.1	1.5	1.3	All Other Current			3.6	.5		
55.3	55.0	56.8	Total Current			58.8	56.0		
35.2	36.9	36.8	Fixed Assets (net)			34.9	37.4		
.7	.5	.6	Intangibles (net)			.6	.4		
8.8	7.5	5.8	All Other Non-Current			5.6	6.2		
100.0	100.0	100.0	Total			100.0	100.0		
			LIABILITIES						
13.6	11.6	10.5	Notes Payable-Short Term			5.2	13.1		
5.6	5.2	4.7	Cur. Mat.-L./T/D			3.6	4.9		
10.3	10.0	9.2	Trade Payables			11.3	8.9		
.8	.9	.3	Income Taxes Payable			.4	.8		
7.8	5.6	7.1	All Other Current			6.9	4.1		
38.0	33.3	31.8	Total Current			27.4	31.7		
22.1	20.8	20.3	Long Term Debt			15.6	20.6		
1.0	.4	.5	Deferred Taxes			.0	1.2		
1.5	3.9	3.0	All Other-Non-Current			4.8	3.9		
37.4	41.6	44.3	Net Worth			52.3	42.5		
100.0	100.0	100.0	Total Liabilities & Net Worth			100.0	100.0		
			INCOME DATA						
100.0	100.0	100.0	Net Sales			100.0	100.0		
22.5	25.5	23.8	Gross Profit			23.7	22.3		
17.2	18.7	16.9	Operating Expenses			17.3	14.9		
5.3	6.8	6.9	Operating Profit			6.4	7.4		
1.6	1.8	1.3	All Other Expenses (net)			1.2	1.6		
3.7	5.0	5.6	Profit Before Taxes			5.2	5.8		
			RATIOS						
2.1 1.6 1.2	2.4 1.8 1.3	3.1 1.7 1.3	Current			6.9 1.8 1.3	2.8 1.7 1.4		
1.2 .6 .5	1.3 .6 .4	1.5 .8 .5	Quick			1.9 .9 .6	1.1 .6 .5		
21 17.3 32 11.3 46 7.9	22 16.3 30 12.2 38 9.5	18 20.4 29 12.5 39 9.4	Sales/Receivables			15 23.6 19 19.5 34 10.7	13 27.4 26 14.2 43 8.5		
32 11.4 68 5.4 101 3.6	31 11.6 62 5.9 104 3.5	30 12.0 58 6.3 94 3.9	Cost of Sales/Inventory			27 13.7 56 6.5 62 5.9	28 13.2 76 4.8 96 3.8		
9 42.7 15 24.2 29 12.7	8 45.5 15 24.1 27 13.3	7 54.9 12 29.3 24 15.5	Cost of Sales/Payables			9 42.6 17 21.3 25 14.8	7 54.3 16 22.8 22 16.8		
6.4 13.1 43.9	5.7 10.0 18.7	5.0 9.5 25.6	Sales/Working Capital			4.7 11.8 35.3	5.9 9.5 15.1		
(57) 7.8 2.7 1.4	(47) 10.4 6.0 1.8	(46) 8.1 4.5 2.4	EBIT/Interest				11.8 4.5 1.9		
(39) 3.2 1.9 .7	(21) 3.9 2.1 1.0	(25) 4.3 2.0 1.0	Net Profit + Depr., Dep., Amort./Cur. Mat. L/T/D				(10) 5.6 2.3 1.1		
.4 1.0 1.7	.5 .9 1.4	.5 .9 1.5	Fixed/Worth			.3 .8 1.4	.5 .8 1.2		
.8 1.7 4.2	.6 1.4 3.9	.4 1.4 3.2	Debt/Worth			.2 1.1 2.8	.5 1.5 4.0		
(53) 29.6 15.4 6.6	(45) 37.0 18.7 5.7	(49) 39.0 23.1 14.7	% Profit Before Taxes/Tangible Net Worth			26.9 20.9 14.7	42.1 21.2 12.3		
14.2 5.8 2.3	17.5 9.3 2.1	19.9 11.1 4.9	% Profit Before Taxes/Total Assets			21.2 10.9 3.9	17.5 11.1 5.1		
11.8 6.0 4.6	9.9 6.5 4.2	11.5 6.6 4.0	Sales/Net Fixed Assets			16.2 6.3 4.0	11.2 7.8 4.4		
2.7 2.1 1.6	3.1 2.1 1.4	2.9 2.4 1.9	Sales/Total Assets			3.0 2.5 1.9	2.7 2.4 1.9		
(59) 1.8 2.5 3.4	1.9 2.5 4.0	(51) 1.1 2.1 3.9	% Depr., Dep., Amort./Sales			.8 2.0 4.8	.7 1.7 2.3		
(26) 1.9 3.6 6.4	(26) 2.1 4.3 6.7	(23) 1.7 3.2 4.9	% Officers', Directors', Owners' Comp/Sales						
619083M 326332M	586435M 329223M	587432M 242136M	Net Sales ($) Total Assets ($)	3862M 3534M	12356M 7230M	45074M 19112M	93805M 48020M	138511M 46594M	293824M 117646M

M = $ thousand   MM = $ million
See Pages 1 through 15 for Explanation of Ratios and Data

Current Data Sorted By Assets

0-500M	500M-2MM	2-10MM	10-50MM	50-100MM	100-250MM	Type of Statement	4/1/90-3/31/91 ALL	4/1/91-3/31/92 ALL
	1	3	2	1	2	# Postretirement Benefits		
		10	14	1	2	Unqualified	25	24
5	5	10	2			Reviewed	15	19
	9	4				Compiled	16	19
1	1					Tax Returns	1	1
	5	11	4			Other	12	16

Period headers for Comparative Historical Data: 4/1/90-3/31/91 ALL (69 statements); 4/1/91-3/31/92 ALL (79 statements).

Current Data periods: 29 (4/1-9/30/94); 55 (10/1/94-3/31/95).

0-500M	500M-2MM	2-10MM	10-50MM	50-100MM	100-250MM		4/1/90-3/31/91 ALL	4/1/91-3/31/92 ALL
6	20	35	20	1	2	NUMBER OF STATEMENTS	69	79
%	%	%	%	%	%	**ASSETS**	%	%
	10.5	3.4	3.9			Cash & Equivalents	4.2	4.7
	30.8	20.5	20.0			Trade Receivables - (net)	24.5	20.9
	24.9	31.5	31.9			Inventory	28.1	31.2
	.9	2.4	2.7			All Other Current	4.0	1.4
	67.1	57.8	58.6			Total Current	60.8	58.2
	26.9	35.3	29.2			Fixed Assets (net)	30.9	33.4
	.2	.6	4.1			Intangibles (net)	.6	1.1
	5.7	6.3	8.1			All Other Non-Current	7.8	7.2
	100.0	100.0	100.0			Total	100.0	100.0
						LIABILITIES		
	6.1	15.2	18.5			Notes Payable-Short Term	15.2	13.3
	3.3	6.5	3.6			Cur. Mat. -L/T/D	4.4	4.3
	14.1	12.0	10.2			Trade Payables	14.1	12.7
	.8	.4	.8			Income Taxes Payable	.4	.2
	8.7	7.2	4.6			All Other Current	9.1	9.5
	33.0	41.1	37.6			Total Current	43.3	40.0
	14.2	17.0	16.4			Long Term Debt	15.5	17.5
	.0	.8	.9			Deferred Taxes	.7	.9
	7.5	1.1	2.8			All Other-Non-Current	1.7	4.5
	45.4	40.0	42.2			Net Worth	38.9	37.1
	100.0	100.0	100.0			Total Liabilities & Net Worth	100.0	100.0
						INCOME DATA		
	100.0	100.0	100.0			Net Sales	100.0	100.0
	27.6	20.5	19.8			Gross Profit	18.0	18.9
	19.0	15.4	12.9			Operating Expenses	14.7	15.7
	8.6	5.1	6.9			Operating Profit	3.3	3.2
	.7	1.3	1.0			All Other Expenses (net)	1.1	1.8
	7.9	3.8	5.9			Profit Before Taxes	2.3	1.4
						RATIOS		
	3.8	2.5	2.2				1.9	2.4
	2.5	1.6	1.5			Current	1.5	1.6
	1.5	1.1	1.2				1.0	1.0
	2.6	1.1	1.1				1.1	1.1
	1.6	.6	.8			Quick	.6	.6
	.6	.4	.3				.4	.4
	17 21.6	21 17.7	26 14.1				24 15.5	21 17.1
	38 9.6	35 10.4	45 8.1			Sales/Receivables	34 10.8	34 10.6
	49 7.5	45 8.1	64 5.7				57 6.4	52 7.0
	19 19.6	35 10.4	61 6.0				31 11.6	36 10.1
	37 9.8	60 6.1	99 3.7			Cost of Sales/Inventory	56 6.5	60 6.1
	70 5.2	87 4.2	118 3.1				91 4.0	94 3.9
	3 109.1	12 29.3	13 27.9				12 31.6	8 43.4
	15 23.8	21 17.7	26 14.0			Cost of Sales/Payables	19 18.9	16 23.2
	35 10.4	42 8.7	47 7.7				34 10.8	33 11.1
	5.0	5.7	4.1				6.8	5.8
	11.4	10.2	7.1			Sales/Working Capital	13.0	9.2
	26.2	55.8	21.3				61.3	246.4
	19.7	6.6	5.4				5.6	3.5
	(18) 5.6	(34) 3.4	2.9			EBIT/Interest	(65) 2.5	(72) 1.7
	2.0	2.1	2.1				1.0	.3
		4.4	3.4				6.0	3.0
		(19) 2.1	(14) 2.1			Net Profit + Depr., Dep., Amort./Cur. Mat. L/T/D	(39) 2.0	(45) 1.5
		1.3	1.7				1.0	.4
	.2	.5	.5				.4	.4
	.4	.7	.8			Fixed/Worth	.7	.9
	1.4	1.6	1.5				1.4	2.2
	.3	.8	1.0				.8	.9
	1.0	1.7	2.0			Debt/Worth	1.6	1.7
	3.0	3.9	3.1				3.3	4.3
	55.1	41.0	38.8				30.8	25.9
	(18) 26.5	(33) 20.7	(19) 15.4			% Profit Before Taxes/Tangible Net Worth	(64) 14.9	(70) 12.9
	5.7	10.1	11.0				-1.0	-3.8
	35.7	13.7	14.9				10.7	9.4
	13.2	7.7	5.2			% Profit Before Taxes/Total Assets	6.7	4.2
	2.8	3.0	2.9				.1	-3.5
	37.0	12.7	10.5				13.3	15.5
	13.4	6.6	5.4			Sales/Net Fixed Assets	7.6	7.1
	8.1	4.4	3.2				4.5	3.6
	5.2	2.8	1.9				3.1	3.1
	3.1	2.1	1.4			Sales/Total Assets	2.2	2.2
	2.2	1.7	1.1				1.4	1.2
	.8	1.2	1.7				1.3	1.0
	(19) 1.6	2.2	(18) 2.2			% Depr., Dep., Amort./Sales	(63) 2.5	(70) 2.1
	3.3	4.7	5.1				3.3	3.6
	1.1	1.5					1.5	1.6
	(11) 3.4	(11) 2.2				% Officers', Directors', Owners' Comp/Sales	(19) 2.5	(25) 2.7
	5.9	5.0					5.6	7.6
5832M	83830M	469653M	673295M	105658M	533733M	Net Sales ($)	1042041M	1361913M
1951M	23143M	180844M	427866M	97874M	282295M	Total Assets ($)	627312M	915601M

M = $ thousand   MM = $ million
See Pages 1 through 15 for Explanation of Ratios and Data

Comparative Historical Data / Current Data Sorted By Sales

3	6	9	# Postretirement Benefits	1				5	3
			Type of Statement						
24	23	27	Unqualified		2	3	9		13
13	15	17	Reviewed		5	4	5		3
11	11	18	Compiled	3	5	5	4	1	
2	1	2	Tax Returns	2					
12	9	20	Other	1	2	4	3	8	2
4/1/92-3/31/93 ALL	4/1/93-3/31/94 ALL	4/1/94-3/31/95 ALL		0-1MM	1-3MM	3-5MM	5-10MM	10-25MM	25MM & OVER
				29 (4/1-9/30/94)		55 (10/1/94-3/31/95)			
62	59	84	**NUMBER OF STATEMENTS**	6	7	16	14	23	18

ASSETS (%)

4/1/92-3/31/93	4/1/93-3/31/94	4/1/94-3/31/95	Item	0-1MM	1-3MM	3-5MM	5-10MM	10-25MM	25MM & OVER
4.5	3.9	5.9	Cash & Equivalents			9.0	6.5	3.0	3.2
21.9	21.6	22.9	Trade Receivables - (net)			26.0	22.3	22.4	21.1
29.7	28.0	29.3	Inventory			22.4	29.3	33.5	32.7
1.8	2.6	2.1	All Other Current			.7	1.2	2.2	3.8
57.9	56.1	60.2	Total Current			58.1	59.3	61.8	60.9
33.7	33.5	31.4	Fixed Assets (net)			37.1	31.6	28.4	30.9
.9	2.5	1.3	Intangibles (net)			.5	.7	3.3	.6
7.5	7.8	7.2	All Other Non-Current			4.3	8.4	6.5	7.6
100.0	100.0	100.0	Total			100.0	100.0	100.0	100.0

LIABILITIES

4/1/92-3/31/93	4/1/93-3/31/94	4/1/94-3/31/95	Item	0-1MM	1-3MM	3-5MM	5-10MM	10-25MM	25MM & OVER
13.9	14.1	12.5	Notes Payable-Short Term			3.9	11.8	21.1	15.5
3.6	4.4	4.6	Cur. Mat.-L./T/D			5.1	4.8	6.4	3.6
10.1	10.0	11.3	Trade Payables			10.5	13.4	11.3	10.0
.4	.6	.5	Income Taxes Payable			1.0	.5	.6	.5
8.4	5.6	7.2	All Other Current			10.1	3.8	6.1	4.4
36.4	34.6	36.1	Total Current			30.6	34.3	45.5	34.0
19.8	18.6	16.8	Long Term Debt			18.8	16.3	15.9	13.6
.4	.7	.6	Deferred Taxes			.1	.4	1.2	.7
4.6	5.1	3.1	All Other-Non-Current			6.5	1.1	2.9	1.2
38.8	40.9	43.5	Net Worth			44.1	48.0	34.5	50.4
100.0	100.0	100.0	Total Liabilities & Net Worth			100.0	100.0	100.0	100.0

INCOME DATA

4/1/92-3/31/93	4/1/93-3/31/94	4/1/94-3/31/95	Item	0-1MM	1-3MM	3-5MM	5-10MM	10-25MM	25MM & OVER
100.0	100.0	100.0	Net Sales			100.0	100.0	100.0	100.0
20.0	20.1	23.3	Gross Profit			30.7	19.6	18.0	15.7
14.6	13.6	16.7	Operating Expenses			25.7	13.0	12.9	9.6
5.4	6.5	6.6	Operating Profit			5.0	6.6	5.1	6.1
1.8	1.3	1.0	All Other Expenses (net)			1.4	1.0	1.1	.4
3.6	5.2	5.6	Profit Before Taxes			3.6	5.6	4.0	5.7

RATIOS

4/1/92-3/31/93	4/1/93-3/31/94	4/1/94-3/31/95	Item	0-1MM	1-3MM	3-5MM	5-10MM	10-25MM	25MM & OVER
3.1	2.3	3.0				4.2	3.1	1.8	3.7
1.6	1.6	1.9	Current			2.1	2.3	1.3	1.9
1.1	1.2	1.2				1.3	1.6	1.1	1.2
1.6	1.2	1.6				2.1	1.7	.8	1.3
.7	.7	.8	Quick			1.4	.8	.5	.8
.4	.4	.4				.7	.5	.4	.4
26 14.3	20 17.9	21 17.8				25 14.7	19 18.8	26 14.2	23 16.2
34 10.8	33 11.0	37 10.0	Sales/Receivables			40 9.1	29 12.5	39 9.3	28 12.9
51 7.2	54 6.8	49 7.4				60 6.1	43 8.5	47 7.7	56 6.5
44 8.3	38 9.6	35 10.4				29 12.7	34 10.8	40 9.2	37 10.0
63 5.8	58 6.3	61 6.0	Cost of Sales/Inventory			51 7.2	61 6.0	83 4.4	61 6.0
89 4.1	89 4.1	99 3.7				70 5.2	83 4.4	114 3.2	101 3.6
8 48.1	10 37.4	10 35.7				9 40.9	14 26.6	13 28.3	11 34.3
18 20.5	20 18.4	18 20.6	Cost of Sales/Payables			17 21.5	20 18.0	22 16.7	15 24.1
31 11.9	29 12.8	38 9.5				41 8.9	42 8.6	42 8.6	26 13.8
4.6	5.9	5.1				3.9	5.1	6.8	4.2
8.9	10.3	9.7	Sales/Working Capital			9.3	8.4	12.6	10.3
38.4	26.2	28.5				23.4	21.5	41.4	26.1
(57) 5.9	(56) 7.4	(79) 7.4		(15) 20.0			19.7	5.0	(17) 12.1
2.9	3.0	3.8	EBIT/Interest	2.5			6.7	2.9	3.4
1.6	1.8	2.2		1.2			3.7	1.8	2.3
(30) 4.5	(23) 3.9	(39) 4.0						(13) 2.9	(11) 4.0
2.5	2.4	2.0	Net Profit + Depr., Dep., Amort./Cur. Mat. L/T/D					1.9	1.9
1.7	1.6	1.3						1.3	1.3
.3	.4	.4				.3	.5	.5	.4
.9	.9	.6	Fixed/Worth			.6	.7	.7	.7
2.1	1.6	1.5				1.5	1.0	2.3	1.0
.8	1.0	.6				.3	.4	1.5	.4
1.8	1.8	1.6	Debt/Worth			1.2	.8	2.2	1.4
4.0	2.7	2.6				3.0	3.5	4.1	2.2
(58) 41.1	(57) 49.8	(79) 44.4		(14) 46.5		(13) 72.2		(22) 39.6	40.9
19.9	24.7	20.7	% Profit Before Taxes/Tangible Net Worth	17.5		35.3		20.9	14.3
7.7	12.0	10.5		2.7		18.9		9.7	9.8
14.1	18.7	15.8				15.3	21.0	13.3	17.0
7.4	6.2	8.1	% Profit Before Taxes/Total Assets			5.9	14.7	7.1	8.9
2.5	3.4	3.0				-.3	9.3	2.9	3.3
15.0	12.5	13.5				20.7	14.4	10.8	12.4
6.8	6.1	7.8	Sales/Net Fixed Assets			6.3	7.0	8.5	7.7
3.7	3.6	4.2				3.3	5.2	4.1	4.2
2.8	2.8	3.0				3.2	3.1	2.8	3.0
1.9	2.0	2.1	Sales/Total Assets			2.3	2.1	2.0	2.1
1.3	1.2	1.4				1.3	2.0	1.3	1.4
(55) 1.6	(51) 1.0	(79) 1.2				.8	1.1	(22) 1.2	(16) 1.0
2.7	2.5	2.0	% Depr., Dep., Amort./Sales			2.5	1.9	2.3	1.7
4.5	4.4	4.5				5.2	4.7	4.3	3.0
(20) 2.0	(14) 1.3	(27) 1.5							
2.9	1.7	2.7	% Officers', Directors', Owners' Comp/Sales						
4.8	3.9	5.0							
1241398M	1444519M	1872001M	Net Sales ($)	3817M	12724M	62070M	101781M	384256M	1307353M
807610M	928446M	1013973M	Total Assets ($)	3700M	5240M	33974M	42449M	217579M	711031M

M = $ thousand   MM = $ million
See Pages 1 through 15 for Explanation of Ratios and Data

Current Data Sorted By Assets

Comparative Historical Data

							# Postretirement Benefits		
1		1	2	1		1	Type of Statement		
			5	3	1	2	Unqualified	11	5
1		10	13	2			Reviewed	14	23
10		18	9			1	Compiled	24	35
9		4					Tax Returns	2	5
2		7	4	1		1	Other	6	9
		42 (4/1-9/30/94)		61 (10/1/94-3/31/95)				4/1/90-3/31/91	4/1/91-3/31/92
0-500M		500M-2MM	2-10MM	10-50MM	50-100MM	100-250MM		ALL	ALL
22		39	31	6	1	4	NUMBER OF STATEMENTS	57	77
%		%	%	%	%	%	ASSETS	%	%
15.2		10.0	5.9				Cash & Equivalents	12.1	8.9
6.2		9.0	11.8				Trade Receivables - (net)	12.0	11.2
9.4		12.8	25.4				Inventory	18.5	19.8
4.1		4.4	3.0				All Other Current	5.2	2.4
34.9		36.3	46.0				Total Current	47.7	42.3
53.3		54.8	39.5				Fixed Assets (net)	40.9	46.5
.3		1.3	.0				Intangibles (net)	.7	.7
11.5		7.7	14.5				All Other Non-Current	10.7	10.5
100.0		100.0	100.0				Total	100.0	100.0
							LIABILITIES		
14.4		12.9	18.8				Notes Payable-Short Term	17.1	15.9
11.3		11.8	9.3				Cur. Mat. -L/T/D	9.2	11.8
6.2		4.6	5.8				Trade Payables	7.3	6.6
.9		.3	.2				Income Taxes Payable	.5	.6
5.5		5.8	4.8				All Other Current	8.1	7.1
38.3		35.5	39.0				Total Current	42.1	42.0
26.2		23.8	14.9				Long Term Debt	21.9	21.3
.1		.8	1.3				Deferred Taxes	.7	.7
5.4		.5	1.1				All Other-Non-Current	2.3	5.7
30.0		39.4	43.7				Net Worth	33.0	30.2
100.0		100.0	100.0				Total Liabilities & Net Worth	100.0	100.0
							INCOME DATA		
100.0		100.0	100.0				Net Sales	100.0	100.0
47.5		39.3	19.1				Gross Profit	21.9	28.7
41.9		36.8	13.6				Operating Expenses	18.5	26.0
5.6		2.6	5.5				Operating Profit	3.4	2.6
.9		-.1	.8				All Other Expenses (net)	.5	1.3
4.8		2.7	4.6				Profit Before Taxes	2.9	1.3
							RATIOS		
2.2		1.8	1.7					1.9	1.9
.9		.8	1.1				Current	1.2	1.2
.4		.5	.7					.7	.6
1.4		.9	.6					1.1	1.0
.4		.4	.3				Quick	.5	.4
.1		.2	.2					.3	.3
0 UND	0	UND	10 35.2					5 78.2	3 142.1
0 UND	6	59.7	18 20.0				Sales/Receivables	12 29.9	16 23.2
8 48.2	19	19.3	24 15.3					23 16.0	28 13.0
0 UND	0	UND	12 29.5					0 UND	0 UND
0 UND	6	65.1	33 11.0				Cost of Sales/Inventory	19 19.0	26 14.1
33 10.9	61	6.0	91 4.0					64 5.7	76 4.8
0 UND	0	UND	2 209.9					1 326.4	2 167.4
1 400.8	4	87.4	9 38.9				Cost of Sales/Payables	11 33.3	11 32.0
16 22.6	19	19.0	18 20.1					19 19.3	22 16.8
18.7		14.5	7.9					10.1	14.3
NM		-30.3	64.0				Sales/Working Capital	57.7	45.3
-12.6		-12.5	-8.0					-14.1	-11.9
10.4		6.3	6.3					5.0	3.7
(21) 4.3	(38)	2.8	(29) 3.6				EBIT/Interest	(55) 1.9	(73) 1.8
1.9		1.8	1.7					1.1	.3
		2.9	2.0					4.9	2.9
	(20)	1.7	(15) 1.7				Net Profit + Depr., Dep., Amort./Cur. Mat. L /T/D	(32) 1.5	(38) 1.4
		1.1	1.1					.4	.3
.6		.6	.4					.5	.8
1.9		1.7	1.0				Fixed/Worth	1.1	1.3
6.9		3.1	2.0					2.3	3.5
.7		.8	.9					.9	1.1
2.7		1.6	1.4				Debt/Worth	1.9	2.2
16.4		5.1	2.9					5.0	6.8
93.3		46.2	33.7					37.9	38.4
(19) 39.6	(36)	16.7	20.6				% Profit Before Taxes/Tangible Net Worth	(51) 16.2	(68) 13.7
7.1		9.1	9.0					5.6	-6.1
26.3		10.6	14.3					11.9	11.6
9.8		5.8	6.7				% Profit Before Taxes/Total Assets	4.3	3.9
4.7		1.1	3.3					.7	-4.9
15.4		8.5	9.4					16.5	10.2
5.1		4.5	5.8				Sales/Net Fixed Assets	6.9	4.6
2.8		2.6	2.8					3.2	3.1
6.8		3.3	2.8					3.8	3.1
2.6		2.3	2.0				Sales/Total Assets	2.4	2.4
1.9		1.6	1.7					1.7	1.7
3.7		3.7	2.3					1.1	1.9
(20) 6.4	(38)	6.8	(30) 3.8				% Depr., Dep., Amort./Sales	(55) 3.8	(75) 4.2
12.8		12.3	5.9					6.5	7.6
2.1		1.7	.7					1.7	1.9
(15) 4.5	(22)	4.0	(17) 1.6				% Officers', Directors', Owners' Comp/Sales	(23) 2.9	(39) 3.7
8.1		6.6	3.9					4.3	5.7
27830M		121558M	359419M	161098M	24472M	637308M	Net Sales ($)	1156314M	708746M
6805M		43050M	148156M	107933M	61739M	514781M	Total Assets ($)	641047M	457120M

M = $ thousand   MM = $ million
See Pages 1 through 15 for Explanation of Ratios and Data

Comparative Historical Data   Current Data Sorted By Sales

Hist 1	Hist 7	Hist 6	# Postretirement Benefits / Type of Statement	0-1MM	1-3MM	3-5MM	5-10MM	10-25MM	25MM & OVER
1	7	6	# Postretirement Benefits	1		1	1	1	2
			Type of Statement						
6	13	11	Unqualified		1			7	3
20	19	26	Reviewed		7	6	6	6	1
27	41	38	Compiled	7	13	9	5	1	3
4	14	13	Tax Returns	5	6	2			
11	19	15	Other	1	5	2	3	2	2
4/1/92-3/31/93 ALL	4/1/93-3/31/94 ALL	4/1/94-3/31/95 ALL		42 (4/1-9/30/94)			61 (10/1/94-3/31/95)		
68	106	103	**NUMBER OF STATEMENTS**	13	31	20	14	16	9
%	%	%	**ASSETS**	%	%	%	%	%	%
10.1	8.7	9.6	Cash & Equivalents	22.3	10.1	6.8	6.4	6.2	
10.7	11.5	9.2	Trade Receivables - (net)	3.4	3.6	14.5	14.1	13.1	
29.0	22.2	16.7	Inventory	8.0	10.3	17.4	23.0	26.4	
1.8	4.2	3.7	All Other Current	.4	6.7	3.1	1.5	3.4	
51.6	46.6	39.2	Total Current	34.2	30.8	41.9	44.9	49.1	
38.7	39.8	49.2	Fixed Assets (net)	51.9	56.6	47.8	43.6	41.9	
1.0	.9	.8	Intangibles (net)	.3	1.6	.3	.0	.9	
8.8	12.6	10.8	All Other Non-Current	13.6	11.1	10.0	11.5	8.2	
100.0	100.0	100.0	Total	100.0	100.0	100.0	100.0	100.0	
			LIABILITIES						
17.5	16.6	14.5	Notes Payable-Short Term	9.3	15.1	17.1	19.4	13.3	
11.3	9.0	10.1	Cur. Mat.-L./T/D	7.9	13.7	10.6	7.6	7.7	
7.7	5.6	5.6	Trade Payables	2.3	4.1	6.3	8.2	7.3	
.5	.7	.4	Income Taxes Payable	1.3	.2	.5	.3	.1	
7.3	6.2	5.2	All Other Current	4.2	5.6	4.1	8.9	4.9	
44.3	38.1	35.8	Total Current	24.9	38.7	38.5	44.5	33.3	
18.2	19.0	21.9	Long Term Debt	28.0	27.7	17.0	15.1	16.9	
.8	.4	.9	Deferred Taxes	.0	.2	2.4	1.1	1.1	
2.8	2.8	2.0	All Other-Non-Current	6.3	.5	2.4	.5	1.8	
33.8	39.6	39.4	Net Worth	40.8	33.0	39.7	38.9	46.9	
100.0	100.0	100.0	Total Liabilities & Net Worth	100.0	100.0	100.0	100.0	100.0	
			INCOME DATA						
100.0	100.0	100.0	Net Sales	100.0	100.0	100.0	100.0	100.0	
25.2	27.5	33.8	Gross Profit	64.8	43.3	26.0	17.9	17.9	
21.2	20.7	29.1	Operating Expenses	60.2	38.5	23.1	14.6	10.3	
4.0	6.8	4.7	Operating Profit	4.6	4.8	3.0	3.2	7.6	
.7	.8	.7	All Other Expenses (net)	.9	.4	.4	.5	1.1	
3.3	6.0	4.0	Profit Before Taxes	3.7	4.5	2.5	2.8	6.5	
			RATIOS						
1.8	2.2	1.8	Current	3.8	1.5	1.3	1.7	1.9	
1.2	1.3	1.0		1.4	.8	.9	1.0	1.4	
.8	.7	.6		.4	.3	.7	.5	1.0	
(67) .9	(104) 1.1	.9	Quick	3.8	.7	.8	.7	.9	
.4	.5	.4		.6	.2	.6	.4	.5	
.3	.2	.2		.2	.1	.2	.1	.3	
2 146.5	2 212.2	0 UND	Sales/Receivables	0 UND	0 UND	6 61.2	5 68.5	13 27.4	
12 31.3	14 25.7	11 34.1		2 201.3	0 UND	16 23.4	14 25.3	20 18.1	
22 16.4	30 12.1	21 17.6		14 26.8	8 43.0	23 15.7	22 16.8	27 13.4	
4 83.9	2 187.2	0 UND	Cost of Sales/Inventory	0 UND	0 UND	0 UND	0 UND	31 11.9	
34 10.8	29 12.5	16 22.7		0 UND	3 113.0	0 UND	14 27.0	39 9.4	
85 4.3	74 4.9	65 5.6		37 10.0	65 5.6	61 6.0	91 4.0	85 4.3	
3 105.4	1 552.8	0 UND	Cost of Sales/Payables	0 UND	0 UND	0 UND	2 196.3	5 76.2	
10 37.7	10 36.7	7 55.9		0 UND	1 488.0	8 47.4	7 56.0	12 30.2	
19 19.5	17 21.4	19 18.8		17 22.1	20 18.1	22 16.8	15 24.8	33 11.2	
15.4	8.3	9.8	Sales/Working Capital	8.7	19.5	29.6	8.0	6.5	
41.7	34.1	753.5		20.6	-14.4	-144.9	NM	13.2	
-26.2	-25.0	-13.9		-12.8	-9.8	-19.8	-7.9	NM	
(65) 5.4	(103) 10.5	(99) 7.0	EBIT/Interest	(12) 7.8	(30) 8.1	(19) 6.1	3.6	(15) 8.0	
2.7	4.1	3.4		3.6	3.2	2.9	3.2	4.6	
1.8	1.5	1.7		1.8	1.9	1.4	1.3	1.8	
(26) 2.7	(22) 4.8	(45) 3.6	Net Profit + Depr., Dep., Amort./Cur. Mat. L/T/D		(16) 3.9	(12) 3.5			
1.5	2.0	2.0			2.1	1.3			
.9	.8	1.2			1.4	.8			
.5	.4	.5	Fixed/Worth	.3	.6	.7	.4	.4	
1.2	.9	1.3		.9	1.9	1.3	1.0	1.1	
2.4	2.3	2.4		9.4	4.4	2.3	2.3	1.7	
.8	.6	.8	Debt/Worth	.4	1.0	.8	.9	.7	
2.5	1.5	1.6		1.4	1.6	1.6	1.8	1.4	
4.7	6.0	3.7		16.7	5.3	3.6	3.1	2.0	
(62) 46.7	(100) 54.9	(97) 43.9	% Profit Before Taxes/Tangible Net Worth	(12) 92.0	(26) 54.1	45.6	33.5	38.1	
24.8	29.2	19.5		24.5	21.4	20.6	17.8	22.1	
9.5	13.6	8.7		4.5	10.4	-.1	2.1	12.3	
12.8	23.0	12.5	% Profit Before Taxes/Total Assets	10.7	23.1	15.1	10.4	15.3	
7.3	10.3	6.6		5.1	7.2	6.1	4.5	7.2	
2.7	2.2	3.6		2.4	4.4	-1.6	1.8	5.1	
24.0	16.1	9.3	Sales/Net Fixed Assets	11.2	6.6	16.2	9.6	10.3	
8.3	6.1	4.7		3.2	4.4	5.4	7.6	3.9	
3.4	3.3	2.6		2.2	2.2	4.3	4.4	2.3	
4.4	3.3	3.1	Sales/Total Assets	2.6	2.9	4.1	4.8	2.7	
2.7	2.3	2.1		2.0	2.1	2.7	2.3	2.0	
1.6	1.5	1.5		1.4	1.5	2.0	1.9	1.2	
(65) 1.0	(93) 1.5	(97) 3.1	% Depr., Dep., Amort./Sales	(11) 7.3	(30) 3.9	2.6	(13) 1.3	2.2	
2.5	3.8	5.0		12.5	7.5	4.9	3.7	3.9	
7.4	7.9	8.5		19.4	13.4	7.2	5.9	5.5	
(39) 2.3	(49) 2.0	(55) 1.5	% Officers', Directors', Owners' Comp/Sales	(10) 4.1	(16) 1.8	(11) 1.0	(11) 1.1		
3.6	3.0	3.1		4.8	4.2	2.7	1.7		
6.4	5.4	5.7		8.8	6.3	8.4	3.2		
881616M	1656251M	1331685M	Net Sales ($)	7771M	54464M	80815M	108021M	236488M	844126M
533404M	1143134M	882464M	Total Assets ($)	4039M	30020M	33377M	44475M	174432M	596121M

© Robert Morris Associates 1995   M = $ thousand   MM = $ million

See Pages 1 through 15 for Explanation of Ratios and Data

Current Data Sorted By Assets / Comparative Historical Data

	0-500M	500M-2MM	2-10MM	10-50MM	50-100MM	100-250MM	# Postretirement Benefits / Type of Statement	4/1/90-3/31/91 ALL	4/1/91-3/31/92 ALL
	2	3	10	3					
	1	5	17	15	2	1	Unqualified	35	41
	4	28	29	6			Reviewed	52	49
	28	38	10				Compiled	57	48
	3	2		1			Tax Returns		1
	11	17	16	3	2	2	Other	30	35
	56 (4/1-9/30/94)			185 (10/1/94-3/31/95)					
	47	90	72	25	4	3	NUMBER OF STATEMENTS	174	174

	0-500M %	500M-2MM %	2-10MM %	10-50MM %	50-100MM %	100-250MM %		4/1/90-3/31/91 ALL %	4/1/91-3/31/92 ALL %
							ASSETS		
	10.0	5.4	5.1	3.7			Cash & Equivalents	5.9	6.9
	30.5	33.7	27.1	23.0			Trade Receivables - (net)	27.3	26.6
	22.5	26.4	32.5	30.1			Inventory	29.0	27.3
	.5	1.5	2.0	3.5			All Other Current	3.2	2.0
	63.5	67.1	66.8	60.3			Total Current	65.4	62.7
	31.0	25.1	26.0	26.8			Fixed Assets (net)	27.6	29.0
	2.2	.7	1.1	2.8			Intangibles (net)	1.3	1.2
	3.2	7.1	6.1	10.1			All Other Non-Current	5.6	7.0
	100.0	100.0	100.0	100.0			Total	100.0	100.0
							LIABILITIES		
	15.9	13.1	15.4	8.8			Notes Payable-Short Term	13.7	15.0
	2.9	3.5	5.1	3.4			Cur. Mat. -L/T/D	4.8	4.9
	15.6	16.9	14.9	9.3			Trade Payables	14.1	12.8
	.6	.6	.6	.8			Income Taxes Payable	.6	.3
	11.4	9.0	8.7	10.7			All Other Current	7.4	8.6
	46.4	43.1	44.7	33.1			Total Current	40.6	41.6
	16.9	14.4	14.0	8.1			Long Term Debt	19.9	18.2
	.0	.4	.3	.3			Deferred Taxes	.3	.4
	4.9	7.3	4.7	3.5			All Other-Non-Current	3.1	3.7
	31.6	34.9	36.2	55.0			Net Worth	36.1	36.1
	100.0	100.0	100.0	100.0			Total Liabilities & Net Worth	100.0	100.0
							INCOME DATA		
	100.0	100.0	100.0	100.0			Net Sales	100.0	100.0
	32.7	25.0	21.7	22.1			Gross Profit	25.6	24.3
	28.8	20.6	17.1	14.4			Operating Expenses	23.1	22.6
	3.9	4.3	4.7	7.7			Operating Profit	2.5	1.7
	.6	1.8	1.0	.7			All Other Expenses (net)	1.4	1.6
	3.3	2.5	3.7	7.0			Profit Before Taxes	1.1	.0
							RATIOS		
	2.2	2.3	2.0	3.2				2.5	2.1
	1.4	1.7	1.5	2.0			Current	1.7	1.5
	1.0	1.1	1.1	1.3				1.2	1.1
	1.5	1.3	1.1	1.7				1.3	1.3
	.8	1.0	.7	.9			Quick	.8	.7
	.6	.6	.5	.4				.5	.5
	16 22.5	27 13.3	23 16.1	22 16.6				21 17.0	26 14.2
	34 10.7	38 9.7	35 10.3	30 12.0			Sales/Receivables	36 10.2	37 9.9
	43 8.4	55 6.6	55 6.6	38 9.7				51 7.2	53 6.9
	12 29.4	25 14.8	38 9.5	47 7.8				32 11.3	35 10.5
	26 14.0	44 8.3	57 6.4	70 5.2			Cost of Sales/Inventory	49 7.4	51 7.1
	56 6.5	69 5.3	79 4.6	89 4.1				78 4.7	78 4.7
	10 38.1	15 24.6	15 25.1	8 46.4				11 32.8	10 35.1
	19 18.8	24 15.2	28 13.2	15 25.1			Cost of Sales/Payables	21 17.7	20 18.3
	42 8.7	41 8.9	39 9.4	28 13.0				38 9.5	33 10.9
	14.6	6.9	6.7	5.1				5.8	6.5
	22.9	12.3	13.1	8.7			Sales/Working Capital	10.6	12.9
	UND	35.4	32.4	22.7				42.2	38.0
	14.0	7.8	7.3	54.4				4.7	4.0
	(43) 3.3	(89) 3.2	(71) 3.6	(23) 9.6			EBIT/Interest	(160) 1.9	(162) 1.8
	1.0	1.6	1.7	3.7				.7	.0
		6.0	6.2	15.0				4.0	2.9
		(36) 2.3	(37) 2.6	(12) 6.8			Net Profit + Depr., Dep., Amort./Cur. Mat. L./T/D	(87) 1.9	(88) 1.0
		.9	1.1	4.6				.7	-.2
	.4	.3	.4	.4				.3	.4
	.9	.8	.8	.5			Fixed/Worth	.8	.8
	7.7	1.5	1.5	.7				1.8	1.9
	.8	.9	.8	.3				.9	.8
	2.1	2.0	2.3	.6			Debt/Worth	2.0	2.2
	14.4	4.7	4.1	2.5				4.6	5.6
	72.5	62.7	48.3	47.6				29.6	25.4
	(38) 37.8	(83) 24.2	(68) 20.0	29.0			% Profit Before Taxes/Tangible Net Worth	(155) 10.9	(155) 9.0
	8.6	10.1	10.7	11.3				-.7	-5.8
	24.5	15.8	14.7	21.7				12.5	8.3
	9.2	6.9	6.5	16.0			% Profit Before Taxes/Total Assets	4.0	2.9
	.0	2.0	2.0	7.9				-1.3	-4.5
	24.6	29.6	23.3	10.2				22.2	19.3
	14.4	14.8	13.3	7.8			Sales/Net Fixed Assets	12.0	10.4
	9.2	7.0	6.9	5.2				5.9	5.5
	5.1	3.7	3.2	2.5				3.4	3.2
	3.8	2.9	2.5	2.0			Sales/Total Assets	2.6	2.4
	2.9	2.2	2.0	1.5				1.9	1.8
	1.4	.8	.9	1.4				1.1	1.1
	(39) 2.1	(86) 1.4	(69) 1.4	(23) 1.9			% Depr., Dep., Amort./Sales	(153) 1.8	(165) 1.8
	3.5	2.3	2.3	2.5				2.8	3.0
	3.1	1.7	1.2					2.6	2.4
	(23) 5.4	(51) 3.3	(28) 2.5				% Officers', Directors', Owners' Comp/Sales	(66) 4.6	(73) 4.7
	10.0	5.0	4.7					8.0	9.2
	49633M	328990M	766430M	1151799M	614380M	851012M	Net Sales ($)	2066166M	2526207M
	12121M	110804M	305842M	515240M	263030M	560730M	Total Assets ($)	872257M	1090147M

M = $ thousand   MM = $ million
See Pages 1 through 15 for Explanation of Ratios and Data

Comparative Historical Data / Current Data Sorted By Sales

1	11	18		2	2	5	5	4
			# Postretirement Benefits					
			Type of Statement					
41	40	41	Unqualified	3	2	8	12	16
58	62	67	Reviewed	2	14	12 / 20	12	7
33	58	76	Compiled	21	25	15 / 12	3	
2	6	6	Tax Returns	1	3	1		1
24	51	51	Other	9	10	8 / 11	5	8

4/1/92-3/31/93 ALL	4/1/93-3/31/94 ALL	4/1/94-3/31/95 ALL		56 (4/1-9/30/94)		185 (10/1/94-3/31/95)			
				0-1MM	1-3MM	3-5MM	5-10MM	10-25MM	25MM & OVER
158	217	241	**NUMBER OF STATEMENTS**	33	55	38	51	32	32

1 (%)	11 (%)	18 (%)		0-1MM (%)	1-3MM (%)	3-5MM (%)	5-10MM (%)	10-25MM (%)	25MM & OVER (%)
			ASSETS						
5.0	5.8	6.5	Cash & Equivalents	8.3	6.5	4.6	8.2	3.6	7.1
31.2	29.2	29.5	Trade Receivables - (net)	28.7	31.3	32.3	32.5	25.7	23.2
28.3	28.6	27.8	Inventory	20.8	26.5	25.5	28.5	37.4	29.4
3.1	1.8	1.7	All Other Current	.7	1.2	1.6	2.2	2.4	2.1
67.7	65.3	65.5	Total Current	58.5	65.5	64.0	71.4	69.1	61.8
26.5	27.1	26.7	Fixed Assets (net)	35.2	28.3	26.9	21.4	22.3	27.8
1.0	1.1	1.4	Intangibles (net)	2.3	1.3	.6	.7	2.2	1.9
4.8	6.5	6.4	All Other Non-Current	4.0	5.0	8.5	6.5	6.3	8.4
100.0	100.0	100.0	Total	100.0	100.0	100.0	100.0	100.0	100.0
			LIABILITIES						
17.5	15.6	13.6	Notes Payable-Short Term	22.3	9.6	13.8	13.7	16.3	8.6
4.7	3.5	3.8	Cur. Mat.-L /T/D	2.9	3.8	3.9	4.7	4.0	2.8
15.5	14.7	15.0	Trade Payables	13.1	14.9	17.4	17.1	14.9	10.8
.6	.9	.6	Income Taxes Payable	.6	.4	.6	.9	.4	.3
7.7	9.3	9.8	All Other Current	10.3	10.7	7.4	9.5	8.6	12.3
45.9	44.1	42.8	Total Current	49.1	39.4	43.1	45.9	44.1	35.3
15.7	14.9	13.9	Long Term Debt	16.5	19.6	10.9	13.9	11.0	8.3
.3	.3	.3	Deferred Taxes	.0	.4	.8	.1	.0	.3
3.0	3.9	5.5	All Other-Non-Current	4.0	7.8	8.5	6.0	1.0	3.2
35.0	36.8	37.5	Net Worth	30.4	32.9	36.7	34.1	43.9	52.9
100.0	100.0	100.0	Total Liabilities & Net Worth	100.0	100.0	100.0	100.0	100.0	100.0
			INCOME DATA						
100.0	100.0	100.0	Net Sales	100.0	100.0	100.0	100.0	100.0	100.0
22.4	24.9	25.4	Gross Profit	33.8	28.3	23.8	23.9	18.2	23.2
19.6	20.8	20.5	Operating Expenses	30.5	25.3	17.5	18.6	14.2	15.2
2.9	4.0	4.9	Operating Profit	3.3	3.0	6.3	5.3	4.0	8.1
1.4	.9	1.1	All Other Expenses (net)	1.1	1.2	2.4	.8	.8	.5
1.4	3.2	3.7	Profit Before Taxes	2.3	1.7	3.9	4.5	3.2	7.6
			RATIOS						
2.1	2.3	2.2	Current	1.9	2.5	2.2	2.1	2.2	3.0
1.5	1.6	1.6		1.2	1.7	1.7	1.6	1.6	1.9
1.1	1.1	1.1		.9	1.2	1.0	1.2	1.1	1.3
1.2	1.4	1.3	Quick	1.4	1.5	1.3	1.4	.9	1.5
.8	.8	.9		.8	1.0	.9	.9	.6	1.0
.5	.5	.5		.5	.5	.5	.6	.4	.5
29 12.8	26 14.1	23 15.6	Sales/Receivables	18 20.7	24 15.0	28 13.0	32 11.4	18 19.8	23 16.1
41 9.0	37 9.8	35 10.5		37 10.0	34 10.6	40 9.1	38 9.5	28 13.2	30 12.3
60 6.1	51 7.1	54 6.8		54 6.8	64 5.7	50 7.3	55 6.6	47 7.7	38 9.7
29 12.6	31 11.6	26 13.9	Cost of Sales/Inventory	15 24.5	20 18.4	24 15.2	26 13.9	32 11.3	43 8.5
46 8.0	53 6.9	49 7.5		33 11.0	44 8.3	41 8.9	50 7.3	60 6.1	68 5.4
74 4.9	74 4.9	73 5.0		74 4.9	73 5.0	59 6.2	73 5.0	79 4.6	83 4.4
12 31.3	12 31.5	13 27.2	Cost of Sales/Payables	10 38.0	15 24.5	15 24.8	15 23.8	9 39.0	10 36.3
22 16.7	21 17.7	24 15.4		24 15.2	24 15.2	24 14.9	28 13.1	17 21.2	16 22.8
37 9.9	35 10.4	38 9.5		46 7.9	42 8.7	43 8.5	41 8.9	34 10.7	28 12.9
6.7	7.1	6.9	Sales/Working Capital	12.5	6.6	8.8	6.7	7.1	5.2
12.2	11.6	13.9		26.6	13.5	13.5	13.0	15.3	8.8
39.9	54.5	38.0		−41.3	24.1	108.6	30.4	34.4	16.5
(149) 6.0	(203) 7.5	(231) 10.7	EBIT/Interest	(30) 13.4	(54) 5.0	(37) 10.1	(50) 12.7	(31) 5.9	(29) 57.9
2.6	3.7	3.7		2.8	3.0	3.7	3.8	3.9	15.0
.9	1.6	1.7		.5	1.5	2.0	1.6	1.8	3.7
(67) 3.3	(81) 5.8	(95) 7.2	Net Profit + Depr., Dep., Amort./Cur. Mat. L/T/D		(20) 2.8	(15) 3.0	(29) 8.0	(11) 7.5	(15) 22.9
1.6	2.5	2.8			1.5	2.0	3.9	3.4	8.4
.4	1.3	1.1			.4	1.1	1.3	1.2	4.5
.3	.4	.4	Fixed/Worth	.4	.4	.3	.3	.2	.4
.8	.7	.7		1.0	.9	.8	.8	.7	.5
1.8	1.4	1.5		NM	2.4	1.3	1.3	1.1	.8
.9	.9	.8	Debt/Worth	.9	1.0	.8	.8	.5	.3
2.0	1.5	1.9		1.9	2.1	2.0	2.1	1.6	.8
5.0	4.1	4.2		NM	5.6	3.7	4.2	3.3	2.3
(144) 37.6	(195) 43.8	(221) 54.0	% Profit Before Taxes/Tangible Net Worth	(25) 67.2	(49) 57.5	(35) 53.2	(48) 69.7	30.6	49.0
16.3	21.9	27.0		29.4	21.5	27.1	38.4	17.8	31.1
.3	5.0	11.1		1.4	4.9	11.2	11.4	11.1	19.5
12.1	15.4	18.6	% Profit Before Taxes/Total Assets	22.5	10.3	20.1	24.2	11.7	22.6
4.9	7.4	8.1		6.7	6.6	8.4	7.8	7.4	17.7
−.4	1.4	2.9		−2.1	1.0	2.5	2.1	3.6	9.0
23.7	22.9	25.9	Sales/Net Fixed Assets	20.8	24.0	29.3	27.9	32.1	10.3
12.5	10.6	11.7		10.7	11.1	12.8	15.1	16.9	8.6
6.1	6.5	7.0		4.4	6.5	6.8	9.3	6.7	5.7
3.3	3.4	3.6	Sales/Total Assets	4.3	3.8	3.4	3.4	3.8	2.8
2.7	2.7	2.8		3.1	2.9	2.9	2.8	2.8	2.2
2.0	2.1	2.1		2.0	2.1	2.2	2.1	2.1	1.6
(149) .8	(201) .9	(221) 1.0	% Depr., Dep., Amort./Sales	(27) 1.6	(53) 1.1	(36) .9	(46) .9	.6	(27) 1.3
1.6	1.6	1.7		2.5	1.9	1.6	1.3	1.2	1.9
2.7	2.5	2.5		4.0	2.5	2.5	2.1	2.0	2.5
(57) 2.7	(90) 1.9	(106) 1.7	% Officers', Directors', Owners' Comp/Sales	(16) 3.3	(29) 2.4	(25) 2.1	(20) 1.3	(11) .5	
4.3	3.5	3.4		5.9	3.4	3.6	3.2	1.8	
8.6	7.1	5.9		11.0	7.0	4.7	4.8	6.4	
2779266M	4368847M	3762244M	Net Sales ($)	18733M	110195M	154890M	366550M	457978M	2653898M
1273824M	2034464M	1767767M	Total Assets ($)	8060M	46453M	57670M	151007M	181029M	1323548M

M = $ thousand   MM = $ million
See Pages 1 through 15 for Explanation of Ratios and Data

Current Data Sorted By Assets   Comparative Historical Data

0-500M	500M-2MM	2-10MM	10-50MM	50-100MM	100-250MM		4/1/90-3/31/91 ALL	4/1/91-3/31/92 ALL
		2	1			# Postretirement Benefits		
						Type of Statement		
2	1	11	7		1	Unqualified	21	22
	9	8				Reviewed	16	19
3	12	2				Compiled	18	13
						Tax Returns		1
2	5	6	1	1	1	Other	10	12
	20 (4/1-9/30/94)			52 (10/1/94-3/31/95)				
7	27	27	8	1	2	**NUMBER OF STATEMENTS**	65	67
%	%	%	%	%	%		%	%
						ASSETS		
	8.5	10.5				Cash & Equivalents	8.2	8.6
	25.2	23.2				Trade Receivables - (net)	25.5	22.3
	27.2	26.5				Inventory	27.2	26.7
	1.2	2.1				All Other Current	2.5	2.6
	62.1	62.3				Total Current	63.3	60.2
	31.4	30.5				Fixed Assets (net)	29.3	30.1
	1.4	.3				Intangibles (net)	.5	1.2
	5.1	6.9				All Other Non-Current	6.9	8.6
	100.0	100.0				Total	100.0	100.0
						LIABILITIES		
	10.8	7.7				Notes Payable-Short Term	12.2	9.9
	4.9	3.2				Cur. Mat. -L/T/D	5.7	5.2
	14.5	13.6				Trade Payables	14.3	13.3
	.3	.6				Income Taxes Payable	.8	.8
	15.1	17.0				All Other Current	12.2	10.1
	45.6	42.2				Total Current	45.2	39.4
	18.5	14.7				Long Term Debt	17.3	19.4
	.2	.4				Deferred Taxes	.4	.8
	3.7	2.8				All Other-Non-Current	1.8	2.9
	31.9	39.9				Net Worth	35.3	37.5
	100.0	100.0				Total Liabilities & Net Worth	100.0	100.0
						INCOME DATA		
	100.0	100.0				Net Sales	100.0	100.0
	29.1	21.0				Gross Profit	25.0	24.8
	24.0	15.0				Operating Expenses	21.8	22.7
	5.1	6.0				Operating Profit	3.2	2.1
	.9	.4				All Other Expenses (net)	1.0	.6
	4.3	5.6				Profit Before Taxes	2.2	1.5
						RATIOS		
	2.0	2.1					1.9	2.5
	1.6	1.4				Current	1.4	1.6
	1.2	1.1					1.1	1.0
	1.2	1.4					1.1	1.3
	.8	.8				Quick	.7	.7
	.5	.5					.5	.5
	15 24.5	12 31.7					15 24.2	15 24.9
	26 14.0	27 13.6				Sales/Receivables	30 12.1	27 13.6
	35 10.4	47 7.7					41 8.8	40 9.1
	27 13.7	22 16.9					23 15.9	28 12.9
	34 10.6	33 10.9				Cost of Sales/Inventory	42 8.6	46 7.9
	51 7.1	60 6.1					64 5.7	72 5.1
	6 56.7	13 28.3					10 35.3	13 29.2
	18 20.4	18 20.4				Cost of Sales/Payables	20 18.7	21 17.6
	33 10.9	25 14.5					29 12.6	29 12.7
	9.1	8.3					9.3	6.1
	13.8	16.6				Sales/Working Capital	18.9	10.9
	33.4	62.1					45.2	142.7
	12.2	(22) 25.8					(63) 6.6	7.0
	5.0	6.1				EBIT/Interest	2.6	(58) 2.0
	2.7	3.4					.9	1.0
		(11) 13.1					(47) 6.4	(33) 6.7
		4.0				Net Profit + Depr., Dep., Amort./Cur. Mat. L./T/D	2.6	1.8
		3.6					.5	.4
	.5	.3					.4	.4
	.8	.6				Fixed/Worth	.7	.8
	2.0	1.6					1.6	2.0
	.9	.8					.9	.7
	1.8	1.7				Debt/Worth	1.8	1.5
	3.2	2.7					3.5	4.2
	(25) 102.6	(26) 72.9					(60) 39.8	(63) 40.9
	39.2	45.7				% Profit Before Taxes/Tangible Net Worth	15.7	11.8
	25.1	18.0					2.1	.0
	29.3	27.0					14.5	12.1
	14.8	13.6				% Profit Before Taxes/Total Assets	5.2	4.4
	6.8	5.7					-.2	-.5
	22.6	25.0					21.3	17.8
	12.9	11.1				Sales/Net Fixed Assets	10.7	8.4
	7.3	5.5					7.7	6.1
	4.7	3.9					3.8	3.6
	3.5	3.1				Sales/Total Assets	3.1	2.8
	2.6	2.1					2.3	1.6
	1.2	(24) .7					(64) 1.0	(61) 1.2
	(26) 1.8	1.3				% Depr., Dep., Amort./Sales	1.6	1.8
	2.6	1.7					2.2	2.4
	1.0						(23) 2.5	(20) 1.8
	(22) 2.7					% Officers', Directors', Owners' Comp/Sales	4.5	4.1
	4.6						7.3	6.0
13560M	114714M	352344M	305709M	119251M	1058724M	Net Sales ($)	893983M	704462M
2927M	32067M	120267M	162787M	50986M	289644M	Total Assets ($)	319612M	348887M

M = $ thousand   MM = $ million
See Pages 1 through 15 for Explanation of Ratios and Data

Comparative Historical Data					Current Data Sorted By Sales					
2	2	3	# Postretirement Benefits						2	1
			Type of Statement							
21	20	22	Unqualified		3		4	9		6
18	19	17	Reviewed	1	1	3	6	6		
13	17	17	Compiled	1	6	4	4	2		
1	1		Tax Returns							
12	12	16	Other		4	1	4	4		3
4/1/92-	4/1/93-	4/1/94-		20 (4/1-9/30/94)			52 (10/1/94-3/31/95)			
3/31/93	3/31/94	3/31/95		0-1MM	1-3MM	3-5MM	5-10MM	10-25MM		25MM & OVER
ALL	ALL	ALL								
65	69	72	NUMBER OF STATEMENTS	2	14	8	18	21		9
%	%	%	ASSETS	%	%	%	%	%		%
8.3	7.3	9.9	Cash & Equivalents		11.4		11.9	6.9		
24.4	25.0	21.9	Trade Receivables - (net)		19.5		20.6	25.1		
28.0	27.3	26.9	Inventory		31.9		22.0	29.0		
2.6	3.4	2.2	All Other Current		2.1		.6	3.1		
63.3	63.1	61.0	Total Current		64.9		55.1	64.1		
26.6	24.5	28.5	Fixed Assets (net)		26.1		32.0	24.6		
1.9	1.3	1.7	Intangibles (net)		3.9		.1	.3		
8.2	11.2	8.8	All Other Non-Current		5.1		12.8	11.0		
100.0	100.0	100.0	Total		100.0		100.0	100.0		
			LIABILITIES							
12.4	10.4	9.8	Notes Payable-Short Term		8.8		6.2	8.5		
2.6	3.0	4.2	Cur. Mat.-L./T/D		6.9		4.7	2.2		
15.6	12.0	13.8	Trade Payables		12.7		14.3	14.2		
.3	2.1	.5	Income Taxes Payable		.5		.3	.7		
11.0	12.3	15.6	All Other Current		19.1		15.5	17.1		
41.8	39.8	43.9	Total Current		48.0		41.1	42.7		
14.7	17.5	16.4	Long Term Debt		20.2		19.5	13.0		
.7	.8	.5	Deferred Taxes		.1		.4	.4		
2.2	4.8	4.2	All Other-Non-Current		3.0		4.5	1.8		
40.7	37.1	35.0	Net Worth		28.7		34.5	42.1		
100.0	100.0	100.0	Total Liabilities & Net Worth		100.0		100.0	100.0		
			INCOME DATA							
100.0	100.0	100.0	Net Sales		100.0		100.0	100.0		
23.0	22.6	24.2	Gross Profit		26.8		27.3	18.8		
20.7	18.6	18.9	Operating Expenses		20.9		21.8	13.3		
2.3	3.9	5.3	Operating Profit		6.0		5.6	5.5		
.3	.1	.5	All Other Expenses (net)		1.3		.1	.2		
2.0	3.9	4.8	Profit Before Taxes		4.6		5.5	5.3		
			RATIOS							
2.5	2.2	2.1			2.1		2.4	2.1		
1.4	1.5	1.4	Current		1.5		1.6	1.4		
1.0	1.2	1.1			1.1		.8	1.2		
1.2	1.4	1.2			1.2		1.7	1.2		
.7	.8	.7	Quick		.6		.8	.8		
.5	.5	.5			.4		.4	.5		
15 23.7	14 26.6	11 31.8		7 55.3		5 68.7	17 21.3			
27 13.4	27 13.5	23 15.9	Sales/Receivables	18 19.8		22 16.6	27 13.6			
42 8.7	45 8.2	35 10.3		31 11.6		33 11.0	48 7.6			
27 13.3	24 15.4	24 15.2		27 13.5		21 17.5	22 16.7			
43 8.5	42 8.7	35 10.4	Cost of Sales/Inventory	46 7.9		31 11.6	38 9.6			
72 5.1	66 5.5	59 6.2		52 7.0		40 9.1	64 5.7			
14 26.8	10 36.8	12 31.3		4 93.4		9 40.8	12 29.3			
22 16.8	20 18.7	18 20.2	Cost of Sales/Payables	17 21.6		18 20.4	16 23.4			
31 11.8	25 14.6	28 13.0		30 12.1		29 12.7	26 13.8			
6.4	6.6	9.3		8.9		8.2	11.9			
15.9	13.4	16.6	Sales/Working Capital	15.5		22.0	14.9			
197.1	34.0	61.9		NM		-22.8	28.3			
9.8	10.0	18.3		19.8		19.5	21.0			
(59) 3.5	(63) 5.7	(65) 5.5	EBIT/Interest	(13) 4.3		(14) 7.4	(20) 7.4			
1.4	2.2	3.3		1.2		3.4	3.6			
7.5	15.0	13.1	Net Profit + Depr., Dep.,							
(31) 3.6	(27) 2.7	(27) 4.8	Amort./Cur. Mat. L/T/D							
1.8	1.4	2.4								
.3	.4	.3		.3		.4	.3			
.6	.7	.7	Fixed/Worth	.8		.8	.5			
1.4	1.2	1.8		NM		22.5	1.0			
.7	.9	.8		1.1		.8	.8			
1.6	1.6	1.7	Debt/Worth	1.7		1.6	1.4			
4.2	3.7	3.9		NM		35.4	2.3			
41.9	58.2	83.1	% Profit Before Taxes/Tangible	103.2		85.4	68.1			
(62) 15.5	(63) 23.7	(65) 45.7	Net Worth	(11) 38.3		(15) 45.5	46.0			
4.4	9.7	16.1		2.4		28.4	17.6			
12.2	17.1	27.1	% Profit Before Taxes/Total	32.6		30.0	27.1			
5.2	7.4	13.7	Assets	18.0		15.9	13.6			
1.3	3.6	5.4		.4		5.1	7.6			
24.1	21.5	23.2		28.9		17.1	31.8			
10.5	12.8	13.3	Sales/Net Fixed Assets	20.1		11.3	13.0			
5.9	6.9	7.3		7.1		6.8	7.6			
3.9	3.5	4.4		4.3		4.8	4.0			
2.7	2.8	3.3	Sales/Total Assets	3.3		3.3	3.3			
1.9	1.8	2.3		2.5		2.0	2.0			
1.1	.9	.9		1.7		1.0	.6			
(59) 1.6	(66) 1.4	(67) 1.5	% Depr., Dep., Amort./Sales	(13) 2.2		1.6	(19) 1.1			
2.2	2.0	2.2		2.9		1.9	1.5			
2.1	1.3	1.0	% Officers', Directors',							
(16) 4.7	(19) 2.3	(29) 2.6	Owners' Comp/Sales							
8.0	4.0	5.0								
1480183M	842534M	1964302M	Net Sales ($)	1167M	25903M	32065M	128358M	311720M		1465089M
666013M	442175M	658678M	Total Assets ($)	1480M	9590M	8640M	58663M	129000M		451305M

© Robert Morris Associates 1995

M = $ thousand   MM = $ million
See Pages 1 through 15 for Explanation of Ratios and Data

MANUFACTURERS—SAWMILLS & PLANING MILLS. SIC# 2421

	Current Data Sorted By Assets							Comparative Historical Data	
	2	1	15	6	2	1	# Postretirement Benefits		
							Type of Statement		
	2	3	21	36	5	6	Unqualified	56	55
		17	31	16	2	2	Reviewed	51	61
	9	47	29	4			Compiled	87	90
	4	3	2				Tax Returns	4	9
	3	13	24	9	2	1	Other	41	35
	96 (4/1-9/30/94)			195 (10/1/94-3/31/95)				4/1/90-3/31/91	4/1/91-3/31/92
	0-500M	500M-2MM	2-10MM	10-50MM	50-100MM	100-250MM		ALL	ALL
	18	83	107	65	9	9	NUMBER OF STATEMENTS	239	250
	%	%	%	%	%	%	**ASSETS**	%	%
	10.0	7.9	6.0	3.7			Cash & Equivalents	4.9	4.8
	11.2	13.9	11.6	10.6			Trade Receivables - (net)	13.4	13.6
	29.9	28.9	30.6	29.9			Inventory	28.0	27.4
	2.0	2.6	1.7	7.6			All Other Current	3.8	3.2
	53.0	53.4	49.8	51.7			Total Current	50.2	49.0
	39.0	39.0	41.3	33.4			Fixed Assets (net)	39.8	41.7
	.0	.2	.7	.4			Intangibles (net)	.7	.6
	7.9	7.5	8.2	14.4			All Other Non-Current	9.3	8.7
	100.0	100.0	100.0	100.0			Total	100.0	100.0
							LIABILITIES		
	20.8	14.0	12.6	14.0			Notes Payable-Short Term	13.2	16.1
	5.6	6.0	5.3	4.2			Cur. Mat. -L/T/D	6.4	6.4
	6.8	6.5	7.2	7.0			Trade Payables	7.4	7.5
	.2	.5	.5	.2			Income Taxes Payable	.3	.3
	5.2	4.1	6.1	6.3			All Other Current	5.7	6.7
	38.5	31.1	31.8	31.7			Total Current	33.1	37.1
	17.6	16.3	20.7	17.8			Long Term Debt	20.9	20.2
	.4	.2	.6	.6			Deferred Taxes	.5	.5
	2.0	2.9	2.1	3.4			All Other-Non-Current	2.5	2.9
	41.4	49.5	44.7	46.5			Net Worth	43.0	39.2
	100.0	100.0	100.0	100.0			Total Liabilities & Net Worth	100.0	100.0
							INCOME DATA		
	100.0	100.0	100.0	100.0			Net Sales	100.0	100.0
	33.2	26.5	23.5	16.7			Gross Profit	21.3	23.2
	29.3	21.4	15.7	8.4			Operating Expenses	18.4	20.8
	3.8	5.1	7.8	8.4			Operating Profit	2.9	2.3
	.7	.4	1.3	1.1			All Other Expenses (net)	1.1	1.6
	3.1	4.7	6.5	7.3			Profit Before Taxes	1.8	.7
							RATIOS		
	2.8	2.9	2.6	2.7			Current	2.7	2.3
	1.2	1.8	1.5	1.8				1.6	1.3
	1.0	1.1	1.1	1.2				1.0	.9
	1.2	1.3	.9	.9			Quick	1.0	.8
	.6	.8	.6	.4				.6	.5
	.2	.4	.3	.2				.3	.3
	0 UND	9 38.9	12 30.2	14 25.8			Sales/Receivables	12 30.1	12 31.1
	13 28.0	17 21.6	17 21.4	17 21.1				19 19.0	20 17.9
	25 14.8	26 13.9	24 15.2	23 15.7				29 12.7	33 11.2
	21 17.6	22 16.5	33 11.0	43 8.5			Cost of Sales/Inventory	30 12.0	31 11.8
	47 7.8	46 7.9	68 5.4	69 5.3				52 7.0	58 6.3
	140 2.6	78 4.7	104 3.5	104 3.5				94 3.9	96 3.8
	0 UND	2 156.2	6 65.5	10 36.7			Cost of Sales/Payables	6 57.9	5 69.1
	3 125.4	8 43.0	11 34.5	15 25.1				13 27.9	13 28.1
	21 17.0	16 22.5	23 16.0	21 17.2				21 17.7	22 16.3
	8.4	5.8	6.4	5.6			Sales/Working Capital	5.8	6.6
	33.7	12.7	15.2	8.9				13.0	16.6
	NM	81.3	39.3	31.1				324.5	-48.0
	5.9	9.8	10.2	13.2			EBIT/Interest	3.8	3.3
(16)	2.6	(80) 4.8	(101) 4.7	(63) 4.4				(224) 1.8	(234) 1.4
	-.9	2.2	2.2	2.0				.9	-.1
		4.3	5.1	6.7			Net Profit + Depr., Dep.,	4.3	2.6
		(31) 1.6	(46) 2.6	(29) 2.7			Amort./Cur. Mat. L./T/D	(126) 1.8	(110) 1.2
		.8	1.6	1.7				.6	.4
	.5	.4	.5	.4			Fixed/Worth	.5	.6
	.9	.8	.9	.7				.9	1.1
	1.9	1.5	1.6	1.2				1.6	2.4
	1.0	.5	.6	.5			Debt/Worth	.6	.7
	1.2	1.0	1.3	1.2				1.3	1.6
	4.1	2.0	2.9	2.9				3.2	3.6
	65.8	40.5	49.4	40.0			% Profit Before Taxes/Tangible	23.2	22.5
(17)	29.3	(80) 23.8	(104) 29.2	(64) 28.5			Net Worth	(226) 9.9	(226) 5.0
	.0	10.6	15.7	10.3				-1.0	-9.8
	25.3	17.7	19.1	20.7			% Profit Before Taxes/Total	9.7	8.5
	8.9	10.3	11.3	11.1			Assets	3.9	1.8
	-2.1	4.3	5.4	3.0				-.7	-5.3
	16.7	14.5	9.0	9.0			Sales/Net Fixed Assets	11.1	9.3
	7.0	7.2	5.7	5.5				6.1	5.4
	4.7	4.4	3.4	3.3				3.2	3.0
	3.6	3.5	2.7	2.6			Sales/Total Assets	3.1	2.9
	2.6	2.8	2.1	1.6				2.1	2.0
	2.0	1.8	1.6	1.2				1.4	1.4
	3.5	1.1	1.9	1.5			% Depr., Dep., Amort./Sales	1.8	2.2
(15)	3.9	(81) 2.6	(101) 3.2	(63) 2.9				(216) 3.1	(237) 3.7
	5.4	4.6	4.5	3.9				5.1	5.7
		1.4	1.7	.2			% Officers', Directors',	1.5	1.5
		(44) 2.7	(40) 3.9	(11) .7			Owners' Comp/Sales	(82) 3.2	(98) 2.8
		5.3						5.3	4.8
	15381M	295582M	1158593M	2834598M	1313486M	2201398M	Net Sales ($)	3821897M	2917768M
	4976M	103374M	511270M	1560297M	666645M	1182239M	Total Assets ($)	2170518M	1760494M

© Robert Morris Associates 1995

M = $ thousand   MM = $ million
See Pages 1 through 15 for Explanation of Ratios and Data

Comparative Historical Data				Current Data Sorted By Sales					
2	9	27	# Postretirement Benefits	2	1	1	6	7	10
			Type of Statement						
62	73	73	Unqualified	2	2	2	5	18	44
67	69	68	Reviewed		9	10	15	17	17
90	72	89	Compiled	7	27	22	18	13	2
4	6	9	Tax Returns	2	4	1	2		
39	49	52	Other	1	9	6	10	16	10
4/1/92-3/31/93 ALL	4/1/93-3/31/94 ALL	4/1/94-3/31/95 ALL		96 (4/1-9/30/94) 0-1MM	1-3MM	3-5MM	195 (10/1/94-3/31/95) 5-10MM	10-25MM	25MM & OVER
262	269	291	**NUMBER OF STATEMENTS**	12	51	41	50	64	73
%	%	%	**ASSETS**	%	%	%	%	%	%
5.7	5.3	6.1	Cash & Equivalents	8.7	9.0	7.8	4.2	6.5	3.9
14.0	13.6	11.8	Trade Receivables - (net)	11.6	11.2	13.1	11.8	11.4	11.8
27.4	29.3	29.4	Inventory	32.0	24.7	31.7	33.4	30.7	27.3
2.9	3.5	3.8	All Other Current	3.8	1.8	1.3	2.1	2.8	8.5
50.0	51.7	51.2	Total Current	56.2	46.7	53.9	51.6	51.3	51.5
40.2	37.9	38.3	Fixed Assets (net)	35.7	44.2	39.2	40.5	36.2	34.4
.7	.3	.4	Intangibles (net)	.0	.2	.4	1.0	.5	.2
9.1	10.1	10.1	All Other Non-Current	8.1	8.9	6.5	6.9	12.0	14.0
100.0	100.0	100.0	Total	100.0	100.0	100.0	100.0	100.0	100.0
			LIABILITIES						
14.4	14.3	13.6	Notes Payable-Short Term	26.7	9.6	18.4	14.3	12.5	12.1
5.8	5.3	5.2	Cur. Mat.-L.-/T/D	6.0	6.1	5.0	4.9	4.6	5.4
7.4	7.1	6.8	Trade Payables	7.3	3.8	6.8	8.6	7.4	7.2
.7	.9	.4	Income Taxes Payable	.2	.3	.4	.7	.6	.1
5.6	6.7	5.6	All Other Current	4.7	3.4	5.4	4.6	7.3	6.4
33.9	34.3	31.6	Total Current	44.9	23.2	36.0	33.0	32.4	31.2
20.7	19.3	19.4	Long Term Debt	16.8	18.1	20.2	21.9	15.0	22.6
.5	.4	.5	Deferred Taxes	.6	.2	.2	.3	.8	.8
2.6	2.3	2.6	All Other-Non-Current	.3	1.9	2.4	3.5	2.2	3.3
42.3	43.7	45.9	Net Worth	37.4	56.6	41.2	41.3	49.6	42.2
100.0	100.0	100.0	Total Liabilities & Net Worth	100.0	100.0	100.0	100.0	100.0	100.0
			INCOME DATA						
100.0	100.0	100.0	Net Sales	100.0	100.0	100.0	100.0	100.0	100.0
23.4	24.8	23.1	Gross Profit	31.2	31.8	21.9	26.0	21.5	15.8
17.2	17.2	16.0	Operating Expenses	28.0	25.4	16.6	18.9	13.9	7.1
6.3	7.6	7.1	Operating Profit	3.2	6.4	5.4	7.1	7.6	8.8
1.2	.8	1.0	All Other Expenses (net)	1.2	.4	1.0	1.6	.7	1.4
5.1	6.8	6.0	Profit Before Taxes	2.1	5.9	4.4	5.5	6.9	7.3
			RATIOS						
2.3	2.5	2.8	Current	2.1	3.6	3.4	2.4	2.8	2.6
1.5	1.6	1.7		1.3	2.0	1.5	1.4	1.7	1.7
1.0	1.1	1.1		.6	1.2	.7	1.1	1.2	1.2
1.0	1.0	1.1	Quick	.7	1.9	1.2	.8	1.0	.8
.5	(267) .6	.5		.3	.8	.6	.5	.6	.4
.3	.3	.3		.2	.5	.2	.3	.3	.2
13 28.3	13 27.5	12 31.1	Sales/Receivables	8 44.8	10 35.2	8 43.7	10 35.0	11 32.3	14 25.8
20 18.7	18 20.1	17 21.9		15 24.8	18 20.8	16 23.5	18 19.8	17 21.0	17 21.3
30 12.0	26 14.1	24 15.3		34 10.8	28 13.2	23 15.7	23 15.7	24 15.0	22 16.3
31 11.8	31 11.7	33 11.2	Cost of Sales/Inventory	29 12.4	22 16.5	27 13.4	39 9.4	29 12.5	37 9.8
56 6.5	62 5.9	58 6.3		73 5.0	47 7.7	57 6.4	70 5.2	60 6.1	55 6.6
96 3.8	104 3.5	101 3.6		146 2.5	118 3.1	83 4.4	114 3.2	104 3.5	78 4.7
6 61.3	7 55.1	6 66.1	Cost of Sales/Payables	0 UND	1 347.7	3 111.1	7 54.3	6 66.0	8 43.5
13 28.7	13 27.1	11 33.4		4 93.5	6 60.4	10 37.2	14 27.0	11 32.6	12 29.6
21 17.2	21 17.6	21 17.7		25 14.8	15 24.3	19 19.6	24 14.9	22 16.7	21 17.7
6.6	6.4	5.9	Sales/Working Capital	7.5	5.5	6.0	6.3	6.9	5.6
12.9	12.9	12.7		19.8	11.7	15.0	17.3	13.1	10.1
197.2	69.3	42.1		-13.0	42.4	-27.5	40.8	38.9	29.0
7.4	13.6	9.9	EBIT/Interest	4.1	9.0	6.7	6.7	15.8	11.2
(248) 3.9	(259) 4.9	(278) 4.4		(11) 2.0	(49) 4.7	(37) 3.4	(49) 3.3	(60) 6.1	(72) 4.3
1.7	2.2	2.1		-1.9	1.9	2.0	2.0	2.9	2.2
4.0	5.6	5.6	Net Profit + Depr., Dep., Amort./Cur. Mat. L/T/D		3.9	6.1	4.3	5.3	11.9
(111) 2.2	(101) 2.4	(119) 2.4			(24) 1.6	(10) 3.7	(23) 2.0	(25) 2.7	(33) 4.3
1.0	1.2	1.4			.8	1.4	.9	1.8	1.8
.5	.5	.5	Fixed/Worth	.3	.5	.3	.6	.4	.5
.9	.8	.8		.9	.8	.8	1.2	.7	.7
1.8	1.6	1.5		2.1	1.2	2.5	2.0	1.2	1.3
.7	.6	.6	Debt/Worth	1.0	.4	.7	.9	.4	.7
1.4	1.3	1.3		1.4	.8	1.4	1.6	1.1	1.6
2.8	2.9	2.5		4.4	1.3	5.0	4.2	2.2	2.7
39.4	46.7	45.0	% Profit Before Taxes/Tangible Net Worth	43.0	38.0	37.5	47.0	49.4	44.2
(241) 20.0	(258) 27.9	(283) 27.6		(11) 13.3	16.3	(37) 28.4	(49) 22.5	(63) 32.4	(72) 29.6
8.9	11.3	12.3		-31.4	5.9	14.1	11.5	16.0	14.3
16.4	20.6	19.1	% Profit Before Taxes/Total Assets	19.0	22.5	15.1	16.2	22.4	19.0
9.0	10.3	10.6		3.6	10.5	9.6	9.2	15.1	10.2
2.8	4.2	4.2		-9.1	3.3	2.7	3.1	6.3	5.1
10.7	10.4	10.3	Sales/Net Fixed Assets	54.1	8.4	17.8	9.2	10.2	10.8
5.8	5.9	5.8		5.1	5.2	6.9	5.5	5.9	6.6
3.4	3.8	3.6		4.5	2.8	3.9	3.6	4.4	3.4
3.0	2.9	3.0	Sales/Total Assets	2.7	3.0	3.5	3.1	2.9	2.8
2.0	2.1	2.1		2.2	2.0	2.7	2.2	2.1	1.9
1.4	1.5	1.6		1.7	1.5	1.7	1.6	1.6	1.2
1.8	1.7	1.7	% Depr., Dep., Amort./Sales	3.3	2.3	.9	1.9	1.7	1.4
(251) 3.0	(265) 3.0	(274) 2.9		(10) 3.8	(49) 3.6	(39) 2.8	(48) 3.0	(61) 2.6	(67) 2.7
4.8	4.6	4.5		5.5	5.4	4.6	4.6	3.6	3.8
1.9	1.7	1.3	% Officers', Directors', Owners' Comp/Sales		2.0	2.0	1.4	1.0	.2
(117) 3.5	(93) 3.8	(106) 2.8			(24) 3.4	(19) 3.7	(21) 4.9	(24) 1.9	(13) .7
5.7	5.2	5.6			6.2	4.8	7.5	6.1	3.8
4461661M	6223856M	7819038M	Net Sales ($)	6246M	103694M	164074M	355631M	955184M	6234209M
2760087M	3501369M	4028801M	Total Assets ($)	2919M	54751M	76631M	176610M	503270M	3214620M

M = $ thousand   MM = $ million
See Pages 1 through 15 for Explanation of Ratios and Data

Current Data Sorted By Assets   **Comparative Historical Data**

Type of Statement / # Postretirement Benefits

	0-500M	500M-2MM	2-10MM	10-50MM	50-100MM	100-250MM		4/1/90-3/31/91 ALL	4/1/91-3/31/92 ALL
# Postretirement Benefits	3	3	2	1					
Unqualified		3	8	4	1		Unqualified	20	13
Reviewed	2	14	12	1			Reviewed	23	28
Compiled	15	16	5				Compiled	64	43
Tax Returns	6	3	1				Tax Returns	2	1
Other	15	9	7		4		Other	25	25

Periods: 51 (4/1-9/30/94) · 75 (10/1/94-3/31/95) · Historical: 4/1/90-3/31/91 ALL · 4/1/91-3/31/92 ALL

	0-500M	500M-2MM	2-10MM	10-50MM	50-100MM	100-250MM		4/1/90-3/31/91 ALL	4/1/91-3/31/92 ALL
NUMBER OF STATEMENTS	38	45	33	9	1		NUMBER OF STATEMENTS	134	110
	%	%	%	%	%	%	**ASSETS**	%	%
	9.3	5.5	6.8				Cash & Equivalents	6.2	6.2
	27.9	32.5	30.9				Trade Receivables - (net)	28.8	30.4
	22.1	21.7	22.6				Inventory	23.7	22.7
	.3	.8	2.4				All Other Current	2.5	2.1
	59.7	60.6	62.7				Total Current	61.2	61.4
	32.4	33.7	29.5				Fixed Assets (net)	31.8	32.0
	2.0	1.6	2.5				Intangibles (net)	1.6	1.5
	5.8	4.1	5.3				All Other Non-Current	5.4	5.2
	100.0	100.0	100.0				Total	100.0	100.0
							LIABILITIES		
	10.6	14.0	12.5				Notes Payable-Short Term	12.0	15.1
	5.8	4.3	2.1				Cur. Mat. -L/T/D	5.2	4.9
	19.7	17.4	11.2				Trade Payables	14.8	17.1
	.4	.6	.7				Income Taxes Payable	.6	.5
	12.7	8.3	8.5				All Other Current	9.1	11.2
	49.1	44.6	35.1				Total Current	41.7	48.9
	18.4	21.3	13.4				Long Term Debt	21.4	18.5
	.4	.2	.4				Deferred Taxes	.2	.2
	2.6	4.0	6.2				All Other-Non-Current	2.9	3.6
	29.5	29.9	44.9				Net Worth	33.8	28.8
	100.0	100.0	100.0				Total Liabilities & Net Worth	100.0	100.0
							INCOME DATA		
	100.0	100.0	100.0				Net Sales	100.0	100.0
	36.9	24.6	26.9				Gross Profit	30.8	30.1
	32.0	21.6	21.6				Operating Expenses	27.3	27.2
	5.0	3.0	5.2				Operating Profit	3.5	2.9
	.8	1.0	.0				All Other Expenses (net)	1.2	1.4
	4.2	1.9	5.2				Profit Before Taxes	2.3	1.5
							RATIOS		
	2.5	2.0	2.7					2.5	2.1
	1.5	1.4	1.9				Current	1.5	1.4
	.8	1.0	1.3					1.1	.9
	1.8	1.3	1.9					1.4	1.4
	.7	.8	1.2				Quick	.8	.8
	.5	.6	.6					.6	.5
	14 25.6	28 12.9	28 13.0					24 15.0	29 12.7
	25 14.4	38 9.6	43 8.5				Sales/Receivables	36 10.2	36 10.1
	41 9.0	57 6.4	53 6.9					47 7.7	51 7.1
	14 26.5	23 15.9	30 12.1					23 16.1	25 14.8
	30 12.2	35 10.3	42 8.7				Cost of Sales/Inventory	43 8.4	42 8.7
	46 8.0	59 6.2	60 6.1					66 5.5	60 6.1
	15 24.3	18 20.3	9 41.1					15 24.6	16 23.3
	29 12.8	28 13.0	16 23.3				Cost of Sales/Payables	23 16.2	27 13.7
	44 8.3	41 9.0	33 11.0					37 10.0	45 8.2
	9.9	9.4	6.1					7.1	8.5
	27.7	19.8	9.0				Sales/Working Capital	15.3	19.0
	−19.5	545.6	24.0					50.7	−90.2
	9.9	5.4	14.3					4.7	4.9
	4.0	(43) 2.4	(31) 7.3				EBIT/Interest	(129) 2.2	(107) 1.7
	1.0	.6	2.1					.6	.1
		5.7	10.0					4.4	3.0
	(18) 1.9	(15) 3.6					Net Profit + Depr., Dep., Amort./Cur. Mat. L /T/D	(71) 1.8	(56) 1.1
	.9	1.6						.1	.1
	.4	.6	.3					.4	.5
	1.0	1.2	.6				Fixed/Worth	1.0	1.1
	UND	2.8	1.8					2.8	3.4
	.7	1.3	.6					.9	.9
	1.7	2.8	1.1				Debt/Worth	2.0	2.1
	UND	6.3	3.3					5.4	10.2
	82.9	56.0	50.6					45.6	29.0
	(30) 43.7	(40) 22.6	(31) 28.3				% Profit Before Taxes/Tangible Net Worth	(115) 20.2	(89) 11.1
	9.8	.7	15.6					1.1	−3.0
	22.7	14.8	21.0					15.1	13.3
	8.7	6.4	12.4				% Profit Before Taxes/Total Assets	4.9	3.6
	.2	−1.7	4.8					−2.6	−3.6
	23.0	16.8	24.9					19.3	19.5
	12.6	8.3	8.4				Sales/Net Fixed Assets	9.2	10.0
	6.8	5.3	5.4					5.6	5.4
	5.2	3.2	3.5					3.7	3.7
	3.5	2.6	2.6				Sales/Total Assets	2.8	2.8
	2.5	2.2	1.7					2.1	2.1
	1.2	1.2	.8					1.5	1.3
	(34) 1.8	(42) 1.9	(32) 1.8				% Depr., Dep., Amort./Sales	(124) 2.3	(101) 2.2
	3.3	3.2	2.7					3.4	3.6
	5.0	1.9	1.3					2.6	3.2
	(22) 9.7	(22) 4.0	(13) 2.8				% Officers', Directors', Owners' Comp/Sales	(69) 4.7	(46) 5.1
	12.7	7.5	5.4					6.9	6.3
	31627M	137796M	374353M	438877M	171343M		Net Sales ($)	895574M	684211M
	9084M	50536M	137082M	205678M	72321M		Total Assets ($)	390239M	294955M

M = $ thousand   MM = $ million
See Pages 1 through 15 for Explanation of Ratios and Data

Comparative Historical Data | **Current Data Sorted By Sales**

Current Data groupings: 51 (4/1-9/30/94) covers 0-1MM, 1-3MM, 3-5MM · 75 (10/1/94-3/31/95) covers 5-10MM, 10-25MM, 25MM & OVER

4/1/92-3/31/93 ALL	4/1/93-3/31/94 ALL	4/1/94-3/31/95 ALL	Item	0-1MM	1-3MM	3-5MM	5-10MM	10-25MM	25MM & OVER
2	2	9	# Postretirement Benefits		6		1	1	1
			Type of Statement						
17	15	16	Unqualified			3	2	7	4
30	34	29	Reviewed		8	8	4	8	1
53	46	36	Compiled	10	16	7	1	2	
		2	Tax Returns	4	2	2	2		
17	25	35	Other	12	9	3	3	3	5
117	122	126	**NUMBER OF STATEMENTS**	26	35	23	12	20	10
%	%	%	**ASSETS**	%	%	%	%	%	%
6.6	6.6	6.8	Cash & Equivalents	10.5	5.5	5.3	9.5	4.9	6.5
28.6	30.1	29.9	Trade Receivables - (net)	23.9	33.5	29.5	33.0	34.3	20.9
22.3	24.3	22.6	Inventory	20.7	22.6	22.0	22.5	23.6	26.5
1.8	1.2	1.1	All Other Current	.3	.8	.9	1.2	2.8	.9
59.4	62.2	60.3	Total Current	55.4	62.4	57.7	66.2	65.7	54.7
33.7	32.0	32.7	Fixed Assets (net)	38.3	30.1	36.8	26.3	26.9	36.9
1.5	.9	2.0	Intangibles (net)	2.1	.7	1.9	4.2	2.6	2.3
5.3	5.0	5.0	All Other Non-Current	4.3	6.8	3.6	3.3	4.9	6.1
100.0	100.0	100.0	Total	100.0	100.0	100.0	100.0	100.0	100.0
			LIABILITIES						
14.1	12.7	11.7	Notes Payable-Short Term	11.6	13.2	12.8	9.4	13.8	2.8
4.7	4.4	4.1	Cur. Mat.-L /T/D	4.7	5.1	4.1	3.1	2.4	3.4
16.2	16.1	15.7	Trade Payables	14.2	22.7	15.3	9.8	13.4	8.7
.5	1.0	.6	Income Taxes Payable	.1	1.0	.6	.2	.7	.8
9.7	11.6	9.7	All Other Current	12.2	10.1	7.4	7.7	9.4	10.5
45.2	45.8	41.9	Total Current	42.9	52.1	40.1	30.2	39.7	26.0
19.2	19.1	18.0	Long Term Debt	25.7	15.8	19.7	19.3	9.8	17.2
.3	.2	.4	Deferred Taxes	.0	.6	.6	.4	.1	1.1
2.3	3.9	4.0	All Other-Non-Current	3.3	2.8	4.4	3.4	8.5	1.0
33.0	31.1	35.7	Net Worth	28.1	28.7	35.2	46.7	42.0	54.6
100.0	100.0	100.0	Total Liabilities & Net Worth	100.0	100.0	100.0	100.0	100.0	100.0
			INCOME DATA						
100.0	100.0	100.0	Net Sales	100.0	100.0	100.0	100.0	100.0	100.0
29.6	30.7	28.9	Gross Profit	41.3	25.6	24.9	28.8	23.4	28.4
25.8	27.3	24.4	Operating Expenses	33.4	24.3	20.4	23.7	19.6	21.5
3.8	3.4	4.5	Operating Profit	7.9	1.3	4.5	5.1	3.9	6.9
1.1	.9	.7	All Other Expenses (net)	1.6	.6	.7	.4	-.1	.5
2.7	2.5	3.8	Profit Before Taxes	6.3	.7	3.8	4.7	4.0	6.4

RATIOS (quartile values: upper / median / lower)

4/1/92-3/31/93	4/1/93-3/31/94	4/1/94-3/31/95	Ratio	0-1MM	1-3MM	3-5MM	5-10MM	10-25MM	25MM & OVER
2.0 / 1.4 / .9	2.2 / 1.4 / 1.0	2.4 / 1.6 / 1.0	Current	2.5 / 1.6 / .8	2.1 / 1.4 / .9	2.2 / 1.4 / 1.0	5.1 / 1.9 / 1.6	2.5 / 1.7 / 1.2	3.2 / 2.2 / 1.2
1.2 / .7 / .5	1.3 / .8 / .5	1.6 / .8 / .5	Quick	1.8 / .8 / .5	1.4 / .7 / .5	1.5 / .7 / .5	3.9 / 1.3 / .7	1.6 / 1.1 / .6	1.8 / 1.0 / .8
(26) 14.3 / (37) 9.9 / (47) 7.7	(26) 13.9 / (38) 9.7 / (49) 7.4	(22) 16.4 / (35) 10.5 / (51) 7.1	Sales/Receivables	(9) 39.2 / (22) 16.7 / (44) 8.3	(24) 15.2 / (39) 9.3 / (55) 6.6	(27) 13.3 / (37) 9.9 / (51) 7.2	(24) 15.2 / (38) 9.6 / (83) 4.4	(30) 12.3 / (42) 8.6 / (52) 7.0	(23) 15.7 / (30) 12.3 / (41) 8.9
(20) 18.0 / (39) 9.3 / (65) 5.6	(24) 14.9 / (43) 8.5 / (70) 5.2	(22) 16.5 / (36) 10.1 / (58) 6.3	Cost of Sales/Inventory	(14) 27.0 / (33) 10.9 / (54) 6.8	(17) 21.1 / (35) 10.3 / (49) 7.4	(22) 16.9 / (35) 10.3 / (61) 6.0	(33) 11.0 / (51) 7.1 / (62) 5.9	(25) 14.8 / (37) 10.0 / (46) 8.0	(34) 10.8 / (54) 6.7 / (74) 4.9
(16) 23.1 / (26) 13.8 / (46) 8.0	(15) 24.9 / (27) 13.5 / (43) 8.5	(15) 25.0 / (23) 15.8 / (39) 9.3	Cost of Sales/Payables	(14) 25.8 / (29) 12.4 / (44) 8.3	(21) 17.1 / (30) 12.0 / (51) 7.1	(15) 24.7 / (23) 16.2 / (41) 9.0	(9) 41.3 / (14) 25.7 / (26) 14.0	(13) 29.0 / (18) 20.5 / (35) 10.3	(8) 44.9 / (20) 18.7 / (28) 13.0
7.2 / 18.9 / -67.2	7.4 / 16.6 / -285.3	7.4 / 14.2 / 341.2	Sales/Working Capital	8.9 / 25.3 / -18.9	9.4 / 20.1 / -101.1	6.8 / 16.4 / 95.5	3.8 / 7.1 / 11.9	7.5 / 10.0 / 28.4	4.6 / 8.7 / 33.9
(107) 5.4 / 2.4 / 1.1	(116) 8.0 / 2.3 / 1.1	(121) 9.8 / 4.0 / 1.5	EBIT/Interest	10.8 / 4.0 / 1.0	(34) 6.3 / 3.0 / -.7	(22) 8.3 / 3.1 / 2.0	(11) 11.3 / 2.4 / 1.6	(19) 14.6 / 7.6 / 2.4	
(39) 4.3 / 2.2 / .8	(42) 3.9 / 1.8 / .3	(46) 5.5 / 2.9 / 1.1	Net Profit + Depr., Dep., Amort./Cur. Mat. L/T/D			(12) 7.5 / 3.2 / 1.1			
.5 / 1.0 / 3.4	.5 / 1.0 / 3.1	.4 / .9 / 2.6	Fixed/Worth	.4 / 1.4 / NM	.4 / 1.2 / 2.6	.6 / 1.1 / 2.4	.2 / .6 / 2.8	.2 / .5 / 2.2	.4 / .7 / 1.3
.8 / 2.1 / 7.1	.9 / 2.2 / 8.2	.8 / 1.8 / 6.0	Debt/Worth	.8 / 2.2 / NM	1.0 / 2.4 / 6.3	1.3 / 2.3 / 4.1	.4 / 1.4 / 5.9	.6 / 1.0 / 3.7	.7 / 1.1 / 1.5
(101) 34.1 / 18.9 / 2.0	(107) 52.7 / 17.4 / 3.7	(111) 54.1 / 26.4 / 11.3	% Profit Before Taxes/Tangible Net Worth	(20) 78.4 / 47.0 / 16.5	(30) 73.7 / 31.4 / -2.9	(21) 53.1 / 21.5 / 13.6	34.8 / 23.1 / 3.8	(18) 49.7 / 31.9 / 15.2	37.8 / 26.7 / 20.6
13.2 / 4.2 / .4	15.7 / 4.8 / .3	19.1 / 8.7 / 2.2	% Profit Before Taxes/Total Assets	20.3 / 8.7 / .2	20.5 / 6.7 / -4.7	17.0 / 6.4 / 4.5	16.4 / 7.1 / 2.1	21.4 / 10.6 / 2.9	26.0 / 12.8 / 8.1
15.0 / 8.1 / 4.9	23.0 / 10.4 / 5.3	19.5 / 9.0 / 5.3	Sales/Net Fixed Assets	17.5 / 10.0 / 4.5	20.4 / 12.2 / 6.6	15.6 / 5.6 / 5.1	21.7 / 8.7 / 7.9	28.2 / 16.6 / 6.5	12.6 / 7.7 / 4.3
3.4 / 2.7 / 1.9	3.6 / 2.8 / 2.2	3.5 / 2.7 / 2.2	Sales/Total Assets	5.0 / 2.9 / 2.1	4.1 / 3.1 / 2.2	3.3 / 2.5 / 2.2	3.0 / 2.5 / 1.6	3.7 / 3.1 / 2.6	2.8 / 2.3 / 2.2
(109) 1.2 / 2.0 / 3.1	(112) 1.0 / 2.0 / 2.7	(118) 1.2 / 1.9 / 3.2	% Depr., Dep., Amort./Sales	(23) 1.6 / 3.2 / 4.1	(33) 1.1 / 1.7 / 2.0	(21) 1.3 / 1.9 / 3.2	1.8 / 2.7 / 3.8	(19) .6 / 1.3 / 2.0	1.6 / 2.3 / 3.4
(46) 3.6 / 5.2 / 7.3	(53) 3.5 / 5.8 / 8.5	(58) 2.5 / 5.3 / 10.0	% Officers', Directors', Owners' Comp/Sales	(14) 4.3 / 11.0 / 13.7	(19) 3.8 / 6.4 / 9.3	(11) 1.5 / 2.6 / 4.4		(10) 1.6 / 2.7 / 5.1	
876869M	787708M	1153996M	Net Sales ($)	13833M	60133M	93890M	75771M	288938M	621431M
398992M	311661M	474701M	Total Assets ($)	6418M	21664M	37475M	34300M	113116M	261728M

M = $ thousand   MM = $ million
See Pages 1 through 15 for Explanation of Ratios and Data

Current Data Sorted By Assets / Comparative Historical Data

						# Postretirement Benefits / Type of Statement	4/1/90-3/31/91 ALL	4/1/91-3/31/92 ALL
	2	5	3			Unqualified	7	5
3	8	8				Reviewed	18	11
13	27	9				Compiled	36	24
1	1					Tax Returns	2	4
5	9	6	4			Other	12	12
0-500M	500M-2MM	2-10MM	10-50MM	50-100MM	100-250MM			
	34 (4/1-9/30/94)		70 (10/1/94-3/31/95)					
22	47	28	7			NUMBER OF STATEMENTS	75	56
%	%	%	%	%	%	ASSETS	%	%
3.5	5.9	6.0				Cash & Equivalents	5.7	6.8
31.0	28.4	23.4				Trade Receivables - (net)	26.2	24.7
20.5	22.8	23.6				Inventory	19.8	16.6
.6	1.6	1.4				All Other Current	1.2	2.4
55.6	58.8	54.5				Total Current	53.0	50.6
40.7	34.9	39.2				Fixed Assets (net)	39.0	39.0
.6	1.3	.7				Intangibles (net)	1.6	1.4
3.2	5.0	5.6				All Other Non-Current	6.4	9.0
100.0	100.0	100.0				Total	100.0	100.0
						LIABILITIES		
19.0	9.3	9.8				Notes Payable-Short Term	10.7	9.7
6.4	5.7	5.6				Cur. Mat. -L/T/D	4.9	5.9
8.9	12.2	9.8				Trade Payables	11.4	10.4
.4	1.6	.2				Income Taxes Payable	.5	.2
6.0	5.9	7.7				All Other Current	6.5	9.5
40.6	34.7	33.1				Total Current	33.9	35.7
30.0	22.5	18.1				Long Term Debt	19.6	18.8
.6	.5	.4				Deferred Taxes	.3	.2
3.7	1.6	3.4				All Other-Non-Current	1.7	2.7
25.2	40.7	44.9				Net Worth	44.6	42.5
100.0	100.0	100.0				Total Liabilities & Net Worth	100.0	100.0
						INCOME DATA		
100.0	100.0	100.0				Net Sales	100.0	100.0
39.8	28.4	24.2				Gross Profit	27.5	25.8
32.9	24.1	17.1				Operating Expenses	23.0	22.3
6.9	4.3	7.1				Operating Profit	4.5	3.5
1.7	.7	1.1				All Other Expenses (net)	.9	.6
5.3	3.6	6.0				Profit Before Taxes	3.6	2.9
						RATIOS		
2.3	3.2	2.3					2.5	3.3
1.4	1.7	1.5				Current	1.5	1.6
.8	1.2	1.2					1.1	1.1
1.1	2.1	1.3					1.5	1.9
.8	1.0	.8				Quick	.9	.9
.4	.6	.5					.6	.6
18 20.2	26 14.1	23 15.9					25 14.8	24 15.5
30 12.3	33 11.1	30 12.0				Sales/Receivables	30 12.1	29 12.6
40 9.1	40 9.1	41 8.8					39 9.3	38 9.5
5 71.1	18 19.9	24 15.3					20 18.1	12 29.3
27 13.6	33 11.2	41 8.8				Cost of Sales/Inventory	33 10.9	28 13.2
51 7.2	60 6.1	83 4.4					55 6.6	44 8.3
0 UND	8 45.1	9 38.9					7 51.2	8 46.8
11 32.0	18 20.4	17 21.2				Cost of Sales/Payables	16 22.3	14 25.2
33 11.2	29 12.5	20 18.2					31 11.6	30 12.1
12.8	6.5	9.6					9.4	8.7
26.6	13.0	14.3				Sales/Working Capital	16.1	17.4
−40.7	39.5	29.2					66.6	116.7
(21) 12.6	9.8	(26) 6.9					(69) 7.5	(49) 6.8
8.3	(46) 3.8	5.4				EBIT/Interest	3.4	3.0
.7	1.7	3.3					1.5	1.0
	(19) 3.4	(13) 4.9					(33) 7.1	(20) 4.6
	1.9	2.3				Net Profit + Depr., Dep., Amort./Cur. Mat. L /T/D	3.1	2.0
	1.1	.6					2.0	1.2
.8	.4	.5					.4	.6
1.5	1.1	.9				Fixed/Worth	.9	.9
11.5	2.5	1.4					1.7	1.7
1.1	.6	.8					.6	.5
2.7	2.1	1.3				Debt/Worth	1.2	1.2
13.9	4.3	2.1					3.0	2.9
(18) 106.6	(46) 55.7	48.3					(69) 44.0	(53) 34.8
41.5	19.6	21.0				% Profit Before Taxes/Tangible Net Worth	20.3	13.7
14.3	8.1	11.1					7.8	.6
38.3	18.7	16.8					19.4	16.1
24.5	7.2	8.9				% Profit Before Taxes/Total Assets	7.3	7.2
−1.0	3.1	5.5					2.9	.0
18.6	16.6	12.7					15.2	12.1
8.4	9.8	7.2				Sales/Net Fixed Assets	8.0	7.1
6.3	5.6	3.7					4.8	4.6
5.3	4.3	3.2					3.8	3.7
3.4	3.0	2.3				Sales/Total Assets	2.9	2.6
2.8	2.3	1.7					2.1	2.1
(21) 1.5	(46) 1.5	(26) 1.0					(70) 1.4	(53) 1.4
2.8	2.0	2.5				% Depr., Dep., Amort./Sales	2.3	2.8
4.7	3.0	3.9					3.8	4.3
(10) 3.0	(26) 1.5	(13) 1.5					(33) 2.1	(23) 2.0
6.2	3.5	2.7				% Officers', Directors', Owners' Comp/Sales	3.3	4.2
12.6	5.3	4.1					7.0	7.8
25342M	160012M	319130M	277763M			Net Sales ($)	392112M	291257M
6243M	50874M	125121M	122554M			Total Assets ($)	149783M	123158M

M = $ thousand   MM = $ million
See Pages 1 through 15 for Explanation of Ratios and Data

Comparative Historical Data / Current Data Sorted By Sales

Hist 1	Hist 2	Hist 3		0-1MM	1-3MM	3-5MM	5-10MM	10-25MM	25MM & OVER
	2	6	# Postretirement Benefits			2	1	2	1
			Type of Statement						
7	7	10	Unqualified		1	2	2	3	2
16	19	19	Reviewed	2	7	3	4	3	
26	42	49	Compiled	8	17	9	10	4	1
1	4	2	Tax Returns	1	1				
16	17	24	Other	3	7	4	2	5	3
4/1/92-3/31/93 ALL	4/1/93-3/31/94 ALL	4/1/94-3/31/95 ALL		34 (4/1-9/30/94)			70 (10/1/94-3/31/95)		
66	89	104	**NUMBER OF STATEMENTS**	14	33	18	18	15	6
%	%	%	**ASSETS**	%	%	%	%	%	%
7.8	5.0	5.1	Cash & Equivalents	2.4	8.8	4.5	4.3	2.8	
24.4	27.5	27.2	Trade Receivables - (net)	27.2	24.1	32.0	26.3	25.1	
16.7	20.9	22.4	Inventory	21.7	23.4	16.9	24.8	26.1	
1.7	1.9	1.5	All Other Current	1.0	1.3	1.8	1.2	1.9	
50.5	55.3	56.1	Total Current	52.3	57.7	55.3	56.7	55.8	
42.2	37.2	38.0	Fixed Assets (net)	43.0	37.8	38.6	35.8	38.3	
.4	1.4	.9	Intangibles (net)	.7	.4	1.6	1.9	.7	
6.9	6.1	5.0	All Other Non-Current	3.9	4.2	4.6	5.7	5.2	
100.0	100.0	100.0	Total	100.0	100.0	100.0	100.0	100.0	
			LIABILITIES						
7.6	9.0	12.1	Notes Payable-Short Term	24.3	6.7	14.8	9.5	12.6	
4.8	6.9	5.9	Cur. Mat.-L /T/D	5.7	6.7	4.7	4.6	7.5	
9.7	10.5	10.8	Trade Payables	10.0	9.0	10.3	14.2	10.3	
.3	1.8	.8	Income Taxes Payable	.2	.4	2.6	1.1	.1	
5.8	8.6	7.0	All Other Current	6.0	5.7	3.8	11.1	9.3	
28.3	36.8	36.6	Total Current	46.2	28.6	36.2	40.5	39.9	
17.1	17.4	22.3	Long Term Debt	26.0	27.9	23.3	13.3	14.9	
.3	.5	.5	Deferred Taxes	.1	.5	.8	.6	.5	
2.5	2.3	2.5	All Other-Non-Current	4.2	1.3	2.7	3.5	2.6	
51.8	42.9	38.1	Net Worth	23.5	41.7	37.0	42.0	42.1	
100.0	100.0	100.0	Total Liabilities & Net Worth	100.0	100.0	100.0	100.0	100.0	
			INCOME DATA						
100.0	100.0	100.0	Net Sales	100.0	100.0	100.0	100.0	100.0	
28.1	25.2	28.7	Gross Profit	41.0	34.8	24.5	20.5	24.7	
24.7	21.6	23.3	Operating Expenses	31.8	28.5	21.1	16.3	20.6	
3.4	3.7	5.4	Operating Profit	9.3	6.3	3.4	4.2	4.1	
.4	.7	1.0	All Other Expenses (net)	2.1	.9	1.3	.9	.7	
3.0	2.9	4.4	Profit Before Taxes	7.2	5.4	2.1	3.3	3.4	
			RATIOS						
3.2	2.4	2.6	Current	1.6	3.5	3.2	1.8	1.8	
2.0	1.5	1.5		1.1	2.0	1.4	1.4	1.3	
1.3	1.1	1.1		.7	1.4	1.0	1.1	1.1	
2.0	1.6	1.4	Quick	.9	2.8	2.2	1.2	1.1	
1.4	.9	.8		.7	1.1	.9	.9	.7	
.7	.5	.5		.4	.6	.6	.3	.4	
21 17.4	24 15.2	24 14.9	Sales/Receivables	18 20.2	21 17.0	25 14.4	18 20.5	25 14.8	
29 12.8	32 11.4	33 11.2		33 11.2	33 11.1	29 12.4	30 12.1	33 10.9	
35 10.4	39 9.4	40 9.1		42 8.6	43 8.4	37 9.9	35 10.4	43 8.5	
15 24.1	17 21.0	18 20.8	Cost of Sales/Inventory	11 33.9	19 19.3	14 25.9	19 19.6	26 14.3	
24 14.9	30 12.2	33 10.9		33 11.2	37 9.8	29 12.7	44 12.6	44 8.3	
41 8.9	42 8.6	58 6.3		73 5.0	69 5.3	40 9.1	46 7.9	91 4.0	
5 73.1	7 52.0	9 40.6	Cost of Sales/Payables	9 41.5	7 50.4	1 370.8	13 27.8	9 38.9	
13 29.0	13 29.1	17 22.0		13 28.7	14 26.8	13 28.9	19 19.5	17 21.3	
26 14.1	23 15.8	27 13.7		36 10.2	37 10.0	26 14.0	27 13.6	20 18.6	
8.3	9.5	8.6	Sales/Working Capital	12.3	4.4	8.1	12.9	13.0	
12.5	15.9	16.7		NM	10.0	20.3	22.3	19.9	
21.9	75.6	46.5		−29.9	23.2	NM	NM	32.4	
7.6	9.4	9.5	EBIT/Interest	13.0	12.2	7.8	7.0	6.8	
(56) 3.2	(78) 4.1	(99) 4.8		9.6	(32) 3.8	(17) 2.9	(16) 5.2	5.1	
1.2	1.3	2.0		2.2	.8	.8	3.4	2.9	
3.9	4.7	3.6	Net Profit + Depr., Dep., Amort./Cur. Mat. L/T/D		3.6				
(31) 2.4	(34) 2.3	(40) 2.0			(14) 1.4				
1.1	1.0	1.0			.3				
.5	.5	.5	Fixed/Worth	1.1	.4	.6	.4	.6	
.7	.8	1.1		1.5	1.1	1.2	.9	.9	
1.1	1.6	2.1		NM	2.4	2.6	2.4	1.4	
.4	.6	.7	Debt/Worth	1.4	.4	.8	1.1	.8	
.8	1.4	1.9		2.7	1.7	2.2	1.6	1.2	
1.7	2.9	4.1		NM	4.5	5.2	3.1	3.0	
27.3	44.9	55.7	% Profit Before Taxes/Tangible Net Worth	106.1	47.8	57.8	74.4	41.2	
(64) 14.6	(84) 24.0	(99) 24.0		(11) 41.0	(31) 17.0	21.8	29.8	17.3	
3.9	5.6	9.2		24.0	6.2	−3.7	15.0	10.9	
13.5	18.6	21.0	% Profit Before Taxes/Total Assets	41.8	21.5	25.7	20.1	10.1	
7.2	9.3	9.4		23.3	7.1	5.6	10.0	7.9	
1.7	2.2	3.4		3.9	3.0	−.6	5.6	5.0	
11.4	13.2	13.8	Sales/Net Fixed Assets	14.5	14.2	16.0	23.2	12.8	
6.5	8.7	8.2		7.5	7.8	6.7	11.5	6.9	
4.1	5.2	4.9		4.3	4.6	5.2	6.6	3.9	
3.6	3.9	4.1	Sales/Total Assets	4.6	3.6	4.1	4.4	2.9	
2.7	3.0	2.9		3.0	3.0	3.3	3.9	2.3	
2.1	2.1	2.2		2.3	2.1	2.3	2.5	1.7	
2.2	1.7	1.4	% Depr., Dep., Amort./Sales	1.8	1.6	2.0	1.2	.5	
(59) 3.3	(84) 2.4	(100) 2.2		(13) 2.9	(32) 2.1	2.5	(17) 1.7	2.1	
4.2	3.7	3.5		4.8	4.0	5.1	2.9	3.2	
2.4	1.7	1.6	% Officers', Directors', Owners' Comp/Sales		1.6	1.7			
(26) 3.6	(39) 3.4	(50) 3.3			(17) 3.8	(10) 3.1			
5.5	5.3	5.0			6.1	3.9			
395200M	550173M	782247M	Net Sales ($)	9473M	64493M	67229M	125457M	221179M	294416M
161873M	212780M	304792M	Total Assets ($)	4045M	32014M	23139M	49095M	97294M	99205M

158 MANUFACTURERS—WOOD PRESERVING. SIC# 2491

Current Data Sorted By Assets						# Postretirement Benefits	Comparative Historical Data	
		2	3			Type of Statement		
1	1	6	6		1	Unqualified	15	13
	4	11	4			Reviewed	11	15
1	6	4				Compiled	11	14
	1					Tax Returns		
1	3	4	5			Other	13	9
	14 (4/1-9/30/94)		45 (10/1/94-3/31/95)				4/1/90-3/31/91	4/1/91-3/31/92
0-500M	500M-2MM	2-10MM	10-50MM	50-100MM	100-250MM		ALL	ALL
3	15	25	15		1	NUMBER OF STATEMENTS	50	51
%	%	%	%	%	%	ASSETS	%	%
	3.6	4.2	2.0			Cash & Equivalents	4.5	3.9
	20.1	19.2	16.4			Trade Receivables - (net)	18.9	18.9
	41.3	37.8	42.0			Inventory	33.6	33.7
	.9	.8	.3			All Other Current	.7	2.1
	66.0	62.0	60.7			Total Current	57.7	58.6
	27.8	28.9	30.6			Fixed Assets (net)	33.8	33.2
	1.3	.4	.2			Intangibles (net)	.7	.7
	4.9	8.7	8.4			All Other Non-Current	7.8	7.6
	100.0	100.0	100.0			Total	100.0	100.0
						LIABILITIES		
	13.3	10.6	22.8			Notes Payable-Short Term	15.1	16.8
	5.0	3.6	5.3			Cur. Mat. -L/T/D	6.2	6.1
	10.2	11.1	9.1			Trade Payables	10.8	12.3
	.1	.2	.1			Income Taxes Payable	.7	.3
	7.2	7.1	6.7			All Other Current	5.5	6.2
	35.8	32.7	43.9			Total Current	38.3	41.7
	23.3	14.4	14.2			Long Term Debt	23.8	22.1
	.3	.3	.7			Deferred Taxes	.7	.4
	4.8	5.2	.7			All Other-Non-Current	1.3	3.4
	35.8	47.5	40.6			Net Worth	35.9	32.4
	100.0	100.0	100.0			Total Liabilities & Net Worth	100.0	100.0
						INCOME DATA		
	100.0	100.0	100.0			Net Sales	100.0	100.0
	23.3	15.2	11.3			Gross Profit	18.9	20.3
	19.7	11.3	9.4			Operating Expenses	13.9	16.9
	3.6	3.9	1.9			Operating Profit	5.0	3.4
	.8	.8	.8			All Other Expenses (net)	2.1	2.2
	2.8	3.0	1.1			Profit Before Taxes	2.9	1.2
						RATIOS		
	3.2	3.2	1.8				2.2	2.3
	1.9	1.9	1.4			Current	1.5	1.4
	1.4	1.3	1.1				1.1	1.0
	1.0	1.2	.7				1.0	.9
	.7	.8	.3			Quick	.6	.5
	.4	.5	.3				.4	.3
	15 24.9	12 30.1	9 40.3				12 29.7	13 28.5
	27 13.5	21 17.1	17 21.4			Sales/Receivables	20 18.4	23 16.1
	37 9.9	27 13.3	30 12.0				34 10.7	33 11.1
	35 10.3	33 11.2	38 9.6				24 15.2	26 13.8
	89 4.1	38 9.6	52 7.0			Cost of Sales/Inventory	51 7.2	49 7.4
	130 2.8	62 5.9	81 4.5				85 4.3	94 3.9
	9 40.7	8 48.2	8 47.8				7 50.0	9 41.9
	11 34.0	17 21.4	11 32.3			Cost of Sales/Payables	13 28.5	14 26.7
	28 13.0	22 16.9	17 21.0				29 12.8	34 10.8
	5.1	7.5	12.7				8.8	6.9
	8.4	14.3	29.3			Sales/Working Capital	13.9	24.0
	16.6	20.8	66.6				113.8	-199.9
	4.2	7.4	3.4				3.4	2.6
(14)	2.6	(21) 4.4	(13) 2.7			EBIT/Interest	(45) 2.1	2.0
	1.7	2.4	1.4				1.2	.7
		7.6					3.0	2.7
	(10)	2.6				Net Profit + Depr., Dep.,	(30) 1.1	(25) 1.1
		1.5				Amort./Cur. Mat. L /T/D	.7	.2
	.3	.4	.4				.6	.6
	.7	.5	.6			Fixed/Worth	1.0	1.1
	4.6	1.2	1.8				2.2	2.5
	.9	.7	.8				1.0	1.4
	1.4	1.5	1.4			Debt/Worth	1.7	2.1
	9.7	2.4	4.8				4.7	6.0
	42.2	25.9	21.1				35.9	24.5
(12)	13.3	18.2	13.8			% Profit Before Taxes/Tangible Net Worth	(48) 15.0	(45) 12.3
	2.6	13.6	3.6				7.1	-3.5
	9.3	15.1	8.9				11.0	8.1
	4.8	7.7	5.8			% Profit Before Taxes/Total Assets	6.1	3.9
	1.3	5.5	1.8				1.2	-1.2
	18.2	25.4	17.1				18.1	14.1
	9.0	15.2	13.5			Sales/Net Fixed Assets	9.3	9.0
	5.5	6.9	6.8				5.2	5.1
	4.3	4.3	4.6				3.9	3.7
	2.3	3.6	3.1			Sales/Total Assets	2.7	2.7
	1.6	2.6	2.6				2.0	1.8
	1.1	.8	.9				1.0	1.2
	1.6	1.2	(13) 1.2			% Depr., Dep., Amort./Sales	(45) 1.4	(48) 1.7
	3.0	2.8	1.9				3.0	2.9
							1.0	2.0
						% Officers', Directors', Owners' Comp/Sales	(19) 2.5	(14) 3.1
							5.9	8.1
1691M	53647M	335717M	955831M		865972M	Net Sales ($)	708809M	1334036M
536M	17971M	106203M	287464M		169076M	Total Assets ($)	263352M	398822M

© Robert Morris Associates 1995

M = $ thousand   MM = $ million
See Pages 1 through 15 for Explanation of Ratios and Data

Comparative Historical Data				Current Data Sorted By Sales					
3	2	5	# Postretirement Benefits					2	3
			Type of Statement						
15	21	15	Unqualified	1	1	1	3	1	8
20	15	19	Reviewed	1	1	2	4	8	4
12	8	11	Compiled	2	3	1	2	1	2
		1	Tax Returns			1			
13	11	13	Other		2		4	2	4
4/1/92-3/31/93 ALL	4/1/93-3/31/94 ALL	4/1/94-3/31/95 ALL		14 (4/1-9/30/94)			45 (10/1/94-3/31/95)		
				0-1MM	1-3MM	3-5MM	5-10MM	10-25MM	25MM & OVER
60	55	59	**NUMBER OF STATEMENTS**	4	7	5	13	12	18
%	%	%	**ASSETS**	%	%	%	%	%	%
3.0	5.0	3.6	Cash & Equivalents				3.1	2.8	2.6
20.0	18.9	19.0	Trade Receivables - (net)				21.7	18.5	19.0
35.5	35.3	39.3	Inventory				38.3	38.5	41.1
1.5	2.3	.7	All Other Current				.4	.9	.5
60.0	61.5	62.7	Total Current				63.5	60.8	63.1
32.9	30.4	29.6	Fixed Assets (net)				26.2	33.6	28.1
.3	.8	.6	Intangibles (net)				.8	.0	.4
6.8	7.2	7.2	All Other Non-Current				9.6	5.6	8.4
100.0	100.0	100.0	Total				100.0	100.0	100.0
			LIABILITIES						
16.6	16.5	14.8	Notes Payable-Short Term				7.3	14.7	21.2
4.0	5.0	4.2	Cur. Mat.-L./T/D				2.3	5.6	4.7
13.4	12.2	10.1	Trade Payables				9.3	12.7	10.6
.3	.8	.1	Income Taxes Payable				.2	.1	.1
7.4	5.6	8.3	All Other Current				11.0	3.3	6.9
41.6	39.9	37.5	Total Current				30.1	36.5	43.4
15.4	18.7	16.5	Long Term Debt				14.7	20.5	11.5
.6	.5	.4	Deferred Taxes				.1	.3	.7
4.3	4.4	3.6	All Other-Non-Current				.7	4.5	.6
38.2	36.5	41.9	Net Worth				54.4	38.2	43.7
100.0	100.0	100.0	Total Liabilities & Net Worth				100.0	100.0	100.0
			INCOME DATA						
100.0	100.0	100.0	Net Sales				100.0	100.0	100.0
20.5	17.7	16.3	Gross Profit				16.8	14.4	11.0
15.3	14.5	13.0	Operating Expenses				12.5	11.7	8.5
5.2	3.2	3.3	Operating Profit				4.4	2.8	2.5
1.2	1.1	.8	All Other Expenses (net)				1.0	.9	.7
4.0	2.1	2.5	Profit Before Taxes				3.4	1.8	1.8
			RATIOS						
1.9 / 1.4 / 1.0	2.4 / 1.5 / 1.2	3.1 / 1.7 / 1.3	Current				4.2 / 2.3 / 1.3	2.2 / 1.8 / 1.2	1.8 / 1.4 / 1.2
.9 / .5 / .3	1.1 / .5 / .3	1.0 / .6 / .3	Quick				1.4 / .8 / .6	1.0 / .6 / .3	.8 / .5 / .3
11 32.1 / 19 18.9 / 37 9.9	12 29.4 / 19 19.5 / 32 11.5	11 34.2 / 22 16.3 / 33 11.0	Sales/Receivables				18 19.9 / 23 16.1 / 27 13.5	9 38.9 / 19 19.4 / 27 13.3	9 39.4 / 19 19.2 / 32 11.3
26 14.2 / 47 7.8 / 76 4.8	29 12.6 / 46 7.9 / 79 4.6	33 10.9 / 52 7.0 / 87 4.2	Cost of Sales/Inventory				26 14.2 / 35 10.3 / 72 5.1	32 11.3 / 38 9.6 / 51 7.2	35 10.4 / 51 7.2 / 78 4.7
7 50.7 / 14 25.2 / 29 12.7	8 43.0 / 13 27.3 / 20 18.2	7 48.8 / 11 32.3 / 21 17.1	Cost of Sales/Payables				2 162.3 / 10 37.4 / 22 16.5	8 48.5 / 17 21.0 / 20 18.1	7 49.0 / 12 31.3 / 20 17.9
9.7 / 21.0 / 165.6	9.1 / 17.3 / 35.7	7.3 / 14.3 / 31.4	Sales/Working Capital				5.9 / 11.1 / 30.6	9.8 / 15.5 / 52.4	12.5 / 18.9 / 40.3
(51) 4.4 / 2.9 / 1.3	5.5 / 3.1 / 1.2	(52) 5.6 / 3.0 / 2.0	EBIT/Interest	(10)			8.5 / 4.3 / 2.4	(11) 7.1 / 3.4 / 1.7	(16) 4.2 / 3.2 / 1.7
(24) 3.1 / 2.2 / 1.1	(29) 4.4 / 2.4 / .7	(22) 5.1 / 2.4 / 1.4	Net Profit + Depr., Dep., Amort./Cur. Mat. L/T/D						
.5 / .9 / 1.8	.5 / .8 / 1.5	.4 / .7 / 1.6	Fixed/Worth				.3 / .4 / .8	.3 / .9 / 1.9	.4 / .6 / 1.2
.8 / 2.0 / 4.2	1.0 / 1.7 / 3.4	.8 / 1.5 / 2.5	Debt/Worth				.5 / 1.0 / 1.8	.9 / 2.0 / 2.5	.8 / 1.4 / 2.8
(57) 42.1 / 18.3 / 5.6	(52) 34.2 / 21.0 / 5.5	(56) 26.5 / 16.1 / 10.8	% Profit Before Taxes/Tangible Net Worth				22.7 / 16.6 / 13.6	41.8 / 21.7 / 10.3	22.2 / 15.6 / 9.5
12.9 / 6.3 / 1.5	11.7 / 7.6 / .7	12.2 / 6.2 / 2.8	% Profit Before Taxes/Total Assets				15.1 / 8.1 / 6.0	17.0 / 9.3 / 3.6	9.7 / 6.2 / 2.6
18.9 / 9.2 / 6.0	16.6 / 11.7 / 6.1	22.1 / 11.4 / 6.7	Sales/Net Fixed Assets				25.6 / 16.5 / 7.8	46.1 / 18.4 / 3.5	17.1 / 14.1 / 7.9
4.4 / 3.0 / 2.1	4.3 / 2.9 / 2.2	4.5 / 3.1 / 2.2	Sales/Total Assets				4.2 / 3.9 / 2.6	5.0 / 4.2 / 1.9	4.6 / 3.1 / 2.8
.9 / 1.5 / 2.9	(52) .9 / 1.5 / 2.7	(57) .9 / 1.3 / 2.2	% Depr., Dep., Amort./Sales				1.0 / 1.2 / 2.1	.6 / 1.1 / 3.8	(16) .8 / 1.0 / 1.6
(17) .9 / 2.0 / 5.7	(18) 1.5 / 2.9 / 4.0	(17) 1.0 / 3.1 / 4.1	% Officers', Directors', Owners' Comp/Sales						
932999M / 321722M	1891054M / 629890M	2212858M / 581250M	Net Sales ($) / Total Assets ($)	2044M / 1405M	13964M / 8316M	20684M / 6751M	103733M / 33646M	182032M / 58525M	1890401M / 472607M

M = $ thousand   MM = $ million
See Pages 1 through 15 for Explanation of Ratios and Data

Current Data Sorted By Assets							Comparative Historical Data	
	2	2				# Postretirement Benefits		
						Type of Statement		
1	2	7	6		1	Unqualified	19	25
1		7				Reviewed	14	12
	6	2				Compiled	12	8
						Tax Returns		
3	4	10	2			Other	7	10
	10 (4/1-9/30/94)		42 (10/1/94-3/31/95)				4/1/90-3/31/91	4/1/91-3/31/92
0-500M	500M-2MM	2-10MM	10-50MM	50-100MM	100-250MM		ALL	ALL
5	12	26	8		1	**NUMBER OF STATEMENTS**	52	55
%	%	%	%	%	%	**ASSETS**	%	%
	8.5	3.9				Cash & Equivalents	5.1	5.1
	35.8	29.8				Trade Receivables - (net)	29.1	28.0
	27.1	25.9				Inventory	31.4	28.8
	1.4	.9				All Other Current	1.3	1.6
	72.7	60.6				Total Current	66.9	63.5
	12.9	29.4				Fixed Assets (net)	24.0	25.6
	11.0	4.0				Intangibles (net)	.6	4.9
	3.4	6.1				All Other Non-Current	8.6	6.0
	100.0	100.0				Total	100.0	100.0
						LIABILITIES		
	7.9	13.0				Notes Payable-Short Term	12.5	10.4
	1.0	3.1				Cur. Mat. -L/T/D	2.8	2.7
	30.3	15.9				Trade Payables	16.9	14.4
	.3	.4				Income Taxes Payable	1.5	1.2
	13.9	7.9				All Other Current	7.0	8.9
	53.5	40.3				Total Current	40.7	37.6
	9.4	12.9				Long Term Debt	15.0	14.3
	.1	.1				Deferred Taxes	.5	.3
	2.9	2.6				All Other-Non-Current	2.5	4.9
	34.1	44.1				Net Worth	41.3	42.9
	100.0	100.0				Total Liabilities & Net Worth	100.0	100.0
						INCOME DATA		
	100.0	100.0				Net Sales	100.0	100.0
	32.2	30.8				Gross Profit	27.7	30.1
	30.4	22.3				Operating Expenses	22.6	25.6
	1.8	8.5				Operating Profit	5.2	4.5
	.3	1.8				All Other Expenses (net)	1.4	2.1
	1.5	6.7				Profit Before Taxes	3.8	2.5
						RATIOS		
	1.8	2.3					2.5	2.8
	1.4	1.6				Current	1.8	1.7
	1.2	1.1					1.2	1.3
	1.3	1.3					1.2	1.3
	.9	.8				Quick	.8	.9
	.6	.6					.6	.6
	(40) 9.2	(37) 10.0					(38) 9.6	(39) 9.4
	(48) 7.6	(47) 7.8				Sales/Receivables	(46) 7.9	(49) 7.4
	(56) 6.5	(55) 6.6					(52) 7.0	(59) 6.2
	(32) 11.5	(39) 9.3					(39) 9.4	(39) 9.3
	(43) 8.4	(52) 7.0				Cost of Sales/Inventory	(62) 5.9	(81) 4.5
	(83) 4.4	(104) 3.5					(99) 3.7	(114) 3.2
	(40) 9.2	(16) 22.2					(20) 18.4	(18) 20.5
	(53) 6.9	(36) 10.2				Cost of Sales/Payables	(28) 12.9	(29) 12.8
	(70) 5.2	(49) 7.4					(43) 8.4	(51) 7.1
	7.7	6.4					5.3	4.2
	15.1	10.6				Sales/Working Capital	8.7	7.3
	34.3	98.2					24.6	26.2
	13.8	16.8					8.1	7.5
	(11) 3.9	(24) 5.8				EBIT/Interest	(49) 3.4	(52) 2.3
	.7	2.4					1.6	.8
		3.7					10.0	14.6
	(11)	2.3				Net Profit + Depr., Dep., Amort./Cur. Mat. L/T/D	(32) 3.2	(25) 4.3
		1.6					1.7	.8
	.2	.4					.3	.3
	.7	.8				Fixed/Worth	.6	.7
	1.2	1.2					1.0	1.2
	1.4	.7					.7	.7
	3.0	1.5				Debt/Worth	1.4	1.4
	7.8	3.5					2.7	3.1
	58.5	54.3					40.5	34.4
	(25) 32.9	30.7				% Profit Before Taxes/Tangible Net Worth	(51) 20.6	(52) 11.5
	-10.6	14.5					8.7	-6.7
	11.0	20.3					20.7	11.2
	5.0	10.1				% Profit Before Taxes/Total Assets	7.7	4.5
	-.3	5.3					2.7	-2.0
	69.2	12.8					24.0	18.1
	29.8	8.0				Sales/Net Fixed Assets	9.4	9.3
	8.6	4.8					5.5	4.2
	3.9	3.0					2.9	2.8
	2.7	2.4				Sales/Total Assets	2.1	1.7
	1.6	1.6					1.6	1.5
	.5	1.1					.8	.9
	(11) 1.2	(24) 1.8				% Depr., Dep., Amort./Sales	(47) 2.0	(51) 2.4
	2.5	3.4					2.8	3.8
		3.4					1.6	2.3
		(10) 3.8				% Officers', Directors', Owners' Comp/Sales	(20) 3.8	(23) 4.0
		7.3					6.3	6.2
7770M	32728M	307830M	334487M		439699M	Net Sales ($)	1674046M	1935765M
1946M	12534M	127850M	180020M		203809M	Total Assets ($)	963356M	1237446M

M = $ thousand   MM = $ million
See Pages 1 through 15 for Explanation of Ratios and Data

Comparative Historical Data / **Current Data Sorted By Sales**

4/1/92-3/31/93 ALL	4/1/93-3/31/94 ALL	4/1/94-3/31/95 ALL		0-1MM	1-3MM	3-5MM	5-10MM	10-25MM	25MM & OVER
			# Postretirement Benefits		2		2		
			Type of Statement						
18	18	17	Unqualified	1	2	1	3	4	6
8	10	8	Reviewed		1		3	4	
9	8	8	Compiled		3	3	2		
	1		Tax Returns						
7	16	19	Other		6	2	4	6	1
					10 (4/1-9/30/94)		42 (10/1/94-3/31/95)		
42	53	52	**NUMBER OF STATEMENTS**	1	12	6	12	14	7
%	%	%	**ASSETS**	%	%	%	%	%	%
9.0	7.2	5.6	Cash & Equivalents		7.6		5.1	5.6	
27.5	25.6	32.5	Trade Receivables - (net)		33.0		27.8	32.8	
29.6	28.7	27.1	Inventory		24.1		26.8	27.0	
1.1	2.2	2.4	All Other Current		6.9		1.3	.7	
67.2	63.8	67.5	Total Current		71.7		61.1	66.1	
25.0	25.5	22.1	Fixed Assets (net)		14.3		28.7	27.8	
1.7	4.0	5.4	Intangibles (net)		11.0		4.5	3.5	
6.1	6.8	4.9	All Other Non-Current		3.0		5.7	2.7	
100.0	100.0	100.0	Total		100.0		100.0	100.0	
			LIABILITIES						
10.7	8.8	10.0	Notes Payable-Short Term		7.0		7.3	17.5	
1.7	1.5	2.3	Cur. Mat.-L /T/D		1.4		3.4	2.4	
14.0	12.0	19.4	Trade Payables		24.9		16.7	14.6	
.4	1.0	.5	Income Taxes Payable		.2		.2	.6	
9.4	8.2	11.3	All Other Current		14.7		7.1	13.7	
36.1	31.4	43.5	Total Current		48.1		34.7	48.8	
11.4	13.6	10.5	Long Term Debt		11.8		14.7	9.4	
.3	.7	.3	Deferred Taxes		.1		.2	.1	
3.6	3.1	2.3	All Other-Non-Current		.9		3.4	2.1	
48.6	51.2	43.4	Net Worth		39.0		47.0	39.6	
100.0	100.0	100.0	Total Liabilities & Net Worth		100.0		100.0	100.0	
			INCOME DATA						
100.0	100.0	100.0	Net Sales		100.0		100.0	100.0	
30.5	30.7	31.7	Gross Profit		38.2		34.3	27.4	
24.6	25.3	24.6	Operating Expenses		34.4		25.4	18.1	
5.9	5.5	7.0	Operating Profit		3.8		8.9	9.3	
.8	.4	1.2	All Other Expenses (net)		.5		2.2	1.1	
5.0	5.0	5.8	Profit Before Taxes		3.2		6.7	8.2	
			RATIOS						
3.2	3.6	2.3	Current		1.8		2.3	1.8	
2.2	2.1	1.6			1.6		1.9	1.3	
1.5	1.4	1.2			1.2		1.3	1.1	
1.6	1.7	1.4	Quick		1.5		1.4	1.1	
1.3	1.1	.9			.9		.9	.7	
.7	.7	.6			.5		.6	.6	
37 9.8	38 9.6	40 9.2	Sales/Receivables		31 11.7		36 10.1	40 9.1	
47 7.8	45 8.1	47 7.7			44 8.3		48 7.6	45 8.1	
54 6.8	54 6.8	58 6.3			62 5.9		57 6.4	56 6.5	
37 10.0	45 8.2	37 9.9	Cost of Sales/Inventory		26 14.2		45 8.2	36 10.2	
70 5.2	59 6.2	49 7.4			42 8.7		64 5.7	43 8.5	
114 3.2	91 4.0	104 3.5			83 4.4		118 3.1	60 6.1	
18 20.1	16 22.3	29 12.8	Cost of Sales/Payables		28 13.1		29 12.8	13 28.9	
28 13.0	26 13.8	39 9.4			54 6.7		46 7.9	22 16.6	
39 9.3	35 10.3	54 6.8			83 4.4		54 6.7	42 8.6	
4.3	4.5	6.3	Sales/Working Capital		7.6		5.4	7.4	
7.0	6.6	11.2			13.9		7.6	17.6	
12.2	12.5	27.4			25.2		25.5	NM	
14.2	16.6	17.3	EBIT/Interest				19.9	19.3	
(37) 4.5	(48) 5.3	(46) 5.9					10.4	(12) 5.4	
2.1	2.5	2.6					3.6	2.7	
43.9	25.2	4.4	Net Profit + Depr., Dep., Amort./Cur. Mat. L/T/D						
(19) 5.7	(17) 3.8	(21) 2.8							
2.4	1.9	2.1							
.3	.3	.3	Fixed/Worth		.3		.3	.4	
.4	.6	.6			.6		.6	.9	
1.0	1.0	1.0			.9		1.2	1.3	
.6	.5	.8	Debt/Worth		1.4		.7	1.0	
.9	1.0	1.6			2.9		1.0	2.1	
2.8	2.1	3.2			3.8		4.0	3.5	
34.4	45.1	62.1	% Profit Before Taxes/Tangible Net Worth		80.6		47.5	74.5	
(41) 19.5	(52) 14.7	(51) 30.7			40.6		(11) 33.6	36.4	
11.8	5.9	11.4			.7		14.3	24.0	
17.0	17.8	18.9	% Profit Before Taxes/Total Assets		17.9		20.9	29.1	
10.0	8.5	10.1			8.0		14.0	10.1	
5.3	2.6	4.4			.2		6.5	7.0	
26.9	24.4	32.7	Sales/Net Fixed Assets		55.1		10.4	23.1	
10.2	9.1	11.2			25.7		5.8	11.3	
4.6	4.1	6.1			8.6		4.6	6.2	
2.6	2.8	3.2	Sales/Total Assets		4.5		3.1	3.3	
2.0	2.1	2.3			2.7		2.0	2.5	
1.7	1.5	1.6			1.6		1.5	2.3	
.9	1.0	1.0	% Depr., Dep., Amort./Sales		(11) .5		1.3	1.0	
(40) 2.5	(50) 2.3	(46) 1.8			1.5		2.5	(11) 1.6	
3.6	3.6	3.0			2.5		3.9	2.3	
2.8	2.7	3.5	% Officers', Directors', Owners' Comp/Sales						
(23) 4.3	(19) 4.9	(22) 5.1							
10.1	12.9	6.7							
749613M	1286763M	1122514M	Net Sales ($)	249M	23482M	24790M	86458M	246242M	741293M
476109M	778007M	526159M	Total Assets ($)	282M	10105M	10215M	50827M	94725M	360005M

M = $ thousand   MM = $ million
See Pages 1 through 15 for Explanation of Ratios and Data

Current Data Sorted By Assets							Comparative Historical Data	
4	6	14	11	2	1	**# Postretirement Benefits**		
						Type of Statement		
4	21	90	88	29	29	Unqualified	180	227
6	47	54	7			Reviewed	93	100
17	47	19				Compiled	87	80
4	6		1			Tax Returns	5	3
14	36	48	26	6	9	Other	110	115
240 (4/1-9/30/94)		368 (10/1/94-3/31/95)					4/1/90- 3/31/91	4/1/91- 3/31/92
0-500M	500M-2MM	2-10MM	10-50MM	50-100MM	100-250MM		ALL	ALL
45	157	211	122	35	38	**NUMBER OF STATEMENTS**	475	525
%	%	%	%	%	%	**ASSETS**	%	%
8.5	8.8	6.9	10.6	20.1	13.4	Cash & Equivalents	8.6	9.3
32.8	32.5	29.0	24.8	24.4	22.6	Trade Receivables - (net)	29.4	28.0
23.8	28.4	28.3	26.8	20.7	22.4	Inventory	27.8	28.1
3.5	2.0	2.0	1.8	3.4	3.3	All Other Current	2.5	2.2
68.6	71.7	66.2	64.0	68.7	61.7	Total Current	68.2	67.6
24.5	21.0	27.0	26.6	23.5	25.9	Fixed Assets (net)	24.7	25.0
.8	1.7	2.0	2.7	3.0	5.0	Intangibles (net)	1.9	2.1
6.0	5.7	4.8	6.7	4.9	7.4	All Other Non-Current	5.2	5.4
100.0	100.0	100.0	100.0	100.0	100.0	Total	100.0	100.0
						LIABILITIES		
7.6	9.0	9.8	7.1	2.0	5.1	Notes Payable-Short Term	9.8	9.4
3.0	4.7	5.1	3.1	2.0	1.9	Cur. Mat. -L/T/D	4.3	4.3
15.8	17.9	14.9	12.0	13.1	12.1	Trade Payables	14.9	14.7
.4	.6	.7	.8	.6	1.1	Income Taxes Payable	1.1	.7
11.6	8.2	8.7	10.4	10.0	9.8	All Other Current	9.0	9.2
38.3	40.4	39.2	33.4	27.7	30.0	Total Current	39.0	38.3
13.2	14.2	13.7	10.9	8.1	12.1	Long Term Debt	15.4	15.0
.1	.3	.7	1.3	1.0	.9	Deferred Taxes	.9	.6
3.2	3.7	2.3	2.2	2.0	2.7	All Other-Non-Current	2.9	3.1
45.2	41.4	44.2	52.2	61.3	54.3	Net Worth	41.8	43.0
100.0	100.0	100.0	100.0	100.0	100.0	Total Liabilities & Net Worth	100.0	100.0
						INCOME DATA		
100.0	100.0	100.0	100.0	100.0	100.0	Net Sales	100.0	100.0
40.0	34.1	28.9	31.5	34.5	31.2	Gross Profit	33.3	32.7
36.7	29.0	23.4	24.5	26.8	23.3	Operating Expenses	28.3	27.7
3.3	5.1	5.5	7.0	7.6	8.0	Operating Profit	5.0	5.0
1.1	.9	1.4	1.0	.8	.7	All Other Expenses (net)	1.7	1.5
2.2	4.2	4.1	6.1	6.8	7.2	Profit Before Taxes	3.3	3.5
						RATIOS		
2.9	2.8	2.7	2.9	3.7	2.8	Current	2.9	2.8
2.0	1.9	1.7	2.1	2.6	2.3		1.9	1.8
1.2	1.4	1.2	1.4	1.7	1.6		1.2	1.3
1.9	1.9	1.4	1.7	2.4	2.0	Quick	1.6	1.6
1.1	1.1	.9	1.2	1.6	1.2		1.0	1.0
.7	.7	.6	.7	1.1	.7		.6	.6
35 10.4	34 10.6	40 9.2	46 7.9	46 8.0	52 7.0	Sales/Receivables	41 9.0	39 9.4
51 7.2	47 7.7	48 7.6	57 6.4	58 6.3	61 6.0		51 7.2	49 7.5
62 5.9	57 6.4	61 6.0	72 5.1	78 4.7	69 5.3		66 5.5	62 5.9
23 16.1	31 11.8	42 8.6	57 6.4	60 6.1	66 5.5	Cost of Sales/Inventory	41 8.8	43 8.5
54 6.7	55 6.6	72 5.1	76 4.8	87 4.2	94 3.9		74 4.9	76 4.8
107 3.4	96 3.8	107 3.4	130 2.8	114 3.2	118 3.1		122 3.0	122 3.0
15 24.8	20 17.9	21 17.5	22 16.8	32 11.4	32 11.5	Cost of Sales/Payables	20 18.4	20 18.0
30 12.2	33 11.0	31 11.9	34 10.6	40 9.1	42 8.7		33 11.2	34 10.8
62 5.9	51 7.2	44 8.3	51 7.2	62 5.9	62 5.9		54 6.8	51 7.2
5.0	4.8	4.6	3.4	2.3	2.9	Sales/Working Capital	3.9	3.9
8.4	7.8	7.6	5.3	3.5	4.0		7.2	7.4
21.7	15.9	19.3	9.5	5.9	8.0		18.9	16.7
17.0	14.7	10.0	22.5	29.9	74.5	EBIT/Interest	6.5	6.4
(31) 3.2	(146) 5.0	(189) 4.3	(114) 7.3	(31) 10.3	(36) 7.1		(427) 2.8	(479) 3.1
.9	1.6	1.9	2.4	4.8	2.8		1.1	1.1
3.0	6.4	6.0	14.2	43.6	20.7	Net Profit + Depr., Dep.,	4.9	5.8
(14) 1.9	(59) 2.7	(109) 3.2	(81) 3.7	(22) 10.7	(22) 8.1	Amort./Cur. Mat. L /T/D	(252) 2.1	(276) 2.4
1.1	.9	1.6	1.7	3.5	2.3		1.0	.9
.2	.2	.3	.3	.2	.3	Fixed/Worth	.3	.3
.5	.5	.6	.5	.5	.6		.6	.6
1.0	1.1	1.2	.8	.6	1.0		1.3	1.2
.4	.7	.7	.5	.3	.5	Debt/Worth	.6	.6
1.5	1.5	1.3	1.0	.8	.7		1.4	1.4
3.5	2.9	2.7	1.8	1.1	2.2		3.4	2.9
46.6	45.9	36.4	35.3	35.8	31.6	% Profit Before Taxes/Tangible	35.7	36.6
(44) 22.8	(148) 23.8	(205) 21.3	(118) 20.4	24.0	20.4	Net Worth	(439) 16.5	(493) 16.2
-.6	7.6	7.0	10.1	7.7	8.4		2.1	2.7
18.0	20.7	14.8	18.2	18.2	14.5	% Profit Before Taxes/Total	14.9	14.4
7.5	10.1	7.5	10.8	11.7	8.3	Assets	6.1	6.2
-.1	2.2	2.4	4.4	4.7	3.3		.4	.6
37.8	36.2	17.3	11.4	9.6	8.4	Sales/Net Fixed Assets	19.4	18.3
13.4	15.3	8.5	5.9	6.7	5.2		8.9	8.5
6.4	7.3	5.0	4.2	4.3	3.7		4.7	4.8
3.7	3.2	2.7	2.0	1.7	1.5	Sales/Total Assets	2.6	2.6
2.8	2.5	2.0	1.6	1.4	1.3		1.9	2.0
1.6	1.9	1.5	1.2	1.0	1.1		1.4	1.4
1.3	1.0	1.2	2.5	1.9	2.0	% Depr., Dep., Amort./Sales	1.4	1.5
(36) 2.5	(140) 1.9	(187) 2.3	(112) 3.5	(32) 3.7	(28) 3.4		(410) 2.7	(464) 2.6
3.7	3.4	3.8	5.1	5.0	4.1		4.6	4.4
4.6	3.1	2.1				% Officers', Directors',	3.0	2.8
(21) 7.9	(82) 4.2	(58) 3.3				Owners' Comp/Sales	(135) 5.1	(143) 5.3
12.3	6.3	5.2					10.6	9.7
37500M	482722M	1979238M	4832771M	3468567M	7359975M	Net Sales ($)	9480200M	13090939M
13823M	177813M	958641M	2716935M	2422062M	5689801M	Total Assets ($)	6674078M	9170171M

M = $ thousand   MM = $ million
See Pages 1 through 15 for Explanation of Ratios and Data

Comparative Historical Data				Current Data Sorted By Sales					
9	27	38	**# Postretirement Benefits / Type of Statement**	2	7	3	6	10	10
222	230	261	Unqualified	5	14	19	44	69	110
124	122	114	Reviewed	3	29	20	39	18	5
88	92	83	Compiled	11	37	16	13	6	
11	11	11	Tax Returns	3	5	1	1		1
102	155	139	Other	10	26	21	24	24	34
4/1/92-3/31/93	4/1/93-3/31/94	4/1/94-3/31/95		240 (4/1-9/30/94)			368 (10/1/94-3/31/95)		
ALL	ALL	ALL		0-1MM	1-3MM	3-5MM	5-10MM	10-25MM	25MM & OVER
547	610	608	**NUMBER OF STATEMENTS**	32	111	77	121	117	150
%	%	%	**ASSETS**	%	%	%	%	%	%
9.5	9.2	9.4	Cash & Equivalents	8.2	9.6	8.4	7.5	8.7	12.2
28.9	27.8	28.6	Trade Receivables - (net)	26.6	29.9	30.8	30.7	28.4	25.6
27.2	27.3	26.9	Inventory	27.5	25.9	27.7	28.7	27.8	24.8
1.9	2.3	2.2	All Other Current	4.8	2.8	1.3	1.7	2.2	2.3
67.6	66.6	67.2	Total Current	67.1	68.3	68.1	68.6	67.2	64.9
25.6	26.0	24.9	Fixed Assets (net)	24.5	23.9	24.2	25.2	25.1	25.8
1.7	2.0	2.2	Intangibles (net)	1.4	1.3	2.5	2.0	2.2	3.0
5.1	5.4	5.7	All Other Non-Current	7.0	6.5	5.2	4.2	5.5	6.3
100.0	100.0	100.0	Total	100.0	100.0	100.0	100.0	100.0	100.0
			LIABILITIES						
9.0	9.0	8.1	Notes Payable-Short Term	10.7	7.0	8.7	9.3	10.8	5.1
4.3	4.1	4.1	Cur. Mat.-L /T/D	3.7	5.2	3.9	4.4	4.3	2.8
14.9	13.8	14.9	Trade Payables	14.0	14.9	14.9	16.4	14.9	13.7
.5	1.2	.7	Income Taxes Payable	.6	.5	.9	.8	.7	.8
9.6	9.8	9.3	All Other Current	10.4	8.5	8.6	9.0	8.6	10.8
38.3	38.0	37.0	Total Current	39.2	36.1	37.0	39.9	39.3	33.3
13.5	13.7	12.8	Long Term Debt	16.6	14.7	15.5	12.7	11.1	10.6
.7	.6	.7	Deferred Taxes	.1	.2	.5	.6	1.0	1.1
3.0	2.9	2.7	All Other-Non-Current	2.3	3.1	3.0	3.6	2.0	2.1
44.5	44.8	46.8	Net Worth	41.7	45.8	44.1	43.1	46.6	53.0
100.0	100.0	100.0	Total Liabilities & Net Worth	100.0	100.0	100.0	100.0	100.0	100.0
			INCOME DATA						
100.0	100.0	100.0	Net Sales	100.0	100.0	100.0	100.0	100.0	100.0
32.9	33.0	32.0	Gross Profit	43.4	37.7	31.7	28.9	29.4	30.1
28.3	28.3	26.2	Operating Expenses	40.6	31.5	26.5	23.4	25.2	22.1
4.6	4.7	5.8	Operating Profit	2.8	6.3	5.2	5.5	4.2	8.0
1.3	1.3	1.1	All Other Expenses (net)	1.6	1.1	1.3	1.2	.9	.9
3.2	3.5	4.7	Profit Before Taxes	1.2	5.2	3.8	4.3	3.3	7.1
			RATIOS						
2.9	2.8	2.9	Current	2.6	2.9	2.9	2.7	2.7	3.0
1.8	1.8	2.0		2.0	2.0	2.0	1.8	1.7	2.2
1.3	1.3	1.4		1.2	1.4	1.3	1.3	1.3	1.6
1.7	1.6	1.7	Quick	1.7	2.1	1.9	1.4	1.5	1.9
1.0	.9	1.1		.9	1.1	1.0	1.0	1.0	1.2
.7	.7	.7		.5	.7	.7	.7	.7	.7
40 9.1	39 9.3	40 9.2	Sales/Receivables	40 9.1	35 10.3	38 9.6	38 9.5	41 8.9	46 8.0
51 7.2	49 7.4	51 7.1		59 6.2	49 7.4	47 7.7	49 7.5	52 7.0	57 6.4
62 5.9	60 6.1	63 5.8		81 4.5	59 6.2	56 6.5	61 6.0	66 5.5	66 5.5
39 9.4	41 9.0	41 8.9	Cost of Sales/Inventory	41 9.0	30 12.2	39 9.4	41 8.9	43 8.4	55 6.6
74 4.9	74 4.9	72 5.1		96 3.8	65 5.6	66 5.5	62 5.9	70 5.2	79 4.6
114 3.2	118 3.1	107 3.4		192 1.9	107 3.4	104 3.5	101 3.6	111 3.3	111 3.3
22 16.5	20 18.6	22 16.8	Cost of Sales/Payables	18 20.5	19 18.9	19 18.8	20 18.2	23 15.7	26 14.0
35 10.4	32 11.4	34 10.8		41 8.9	32 11.4	29 12.4	31 11.8	33 10.9	38 9.5
52 7.0	50 7.3	50 7.3		107 3.4	56 6.5	41 8.8	46 8.0	49 7.4	52 7.0
3.8	4.2	4.1	Sales/Working Capital	4.1	4.3	4.4	4.9	4.1	3.4
7.0	7.4	6.6		6.7	7.5	6.9	8.1	7.1	5.0
18.6	18.6	13.7		13.1	15.0	15.6	16.6	19.0	8.6
(506) 8.6	(548) 11.1	(547) 14.9	EBIT/Interest	(23) 9.6	(95) 14.8	(74) 10.6	(111) 10.9	(104) 11.5	(140) 27.9
3.5	4.0	5.2		1.9	4.8	4.6	5.0	4.0	9.2
1.3	1.5	2.0		-1.7	1.7	1.6	2.0	1.9	3.3
(270) 7.5	(288) 7.3	(307) 10.7	Net Profit + Depr., Dep., Amort./Cur. Mat. L/T/D	(13) 2.3	(33) 5.7	(41) 7.3	(59) 8.2	(61) 6.0	(100) 16.3
3.0	2.7	3.4		1.6	2.9	3.3	3.2	2.9	5.2
1.2	1.0	1.5		.7	1.1	.8	1.7	1.4	2.4
.3	.3	.3	Fixed/Worth	.3	.2	.3	.3	.3	.3
.5	.6	.5		.6	.5	.5	.5	.5	.5
1.2	1.2	1.0		1.0	1.1	1.1	1.1	.9	.8
.6	.6	.6	Debt/Worth	.6	.4	.8	.8	.5	.5
1.3	1.3	1.1		1.5	1.1	1.4	1.3	1.2	.9
3.1	3.1	2.6		2.8	3.7	2.6	2.8	2.2	2.0
(519) 33.1	(581) 38.1	(588) 38.8	% Profit Before Taxes/Tangible Net Worth	27.4	47.4	36.6	54.4	28.3	36.4
14.7	18.3	21.3		(104) 12.2	(74) 25.4	(117) 24.3	(113) 21.3	(148) 17.4	21.1
3.4	4.8	7.7		-13.6	7.4	7.6	6.4	8.1	12.0
12.9	15.5	17.3	% Profit Before Taxes/Total Assets	12.4	21.3	16.3	18.9	14.9	18.3
6.0	7.0	9.1		3.1	10.1	9.9	10.3	6.9	10.9
1.0	1.4	2.7		-3.0	3.1	2.2	2.1	2.3	4.8
18.3	18.6	18.6	Sales/Net Fixed Assets	23.3	29.5	18.6	31.4	14.4	11.5
8.2	8.6	8.4		6.9	13.1	11.6	9.2	8.4	6.3
4.6	4.6	4.8		3.3	5.9	6.2	4.7	5.0	4.3
2.7	2.7	2.7	Sales/Total Assets	2.3	2.9	2.8	3.1	2.7	2.0
2.0	2.0	1.9		1.6	2.3	2.3	2.2	2.0	1.5
1.4	1.4	1.4		1.0	1.6	1.7	1.6	1.3	1.2
(485) 1.4	(529) 1.4	(535) 1.4	% Depr., Dep., Amort./Sales	(25) 2.3	(93) 1.4	(72) 1.2	(109) 1.0	(103) 1.6	(133) 1.9
2.6	2.6	2.6		2.9	2.6	2.1	2.2	3.0	3.3
4.1	4.2	4.2		5.7	4.4	3.3	3.5	4.3	4.5
(164) 2.9	(186) 2.7	(171) 2.5	% Officers', Directors', Owners' Comp/Sales	(13) 4.7	(53) 3.6	(36) 2.0	(36) 2.3	(23) 1.6	(10) .6
5.7	4.8	4.0		7.9	5.1	3.6	3.8	2.4	1.1
10.2	9.1	6.4		11.3	8.9	5.6	4.9	4.6	2.4
13051668M	16203158M	18160773M	Net Sales ($)	16890M	205690M	299370M	854813M	1899632M	14884378M
9063909M	10674400M	11979075M	Total Assets ($)	11313M	113045M	148836M	468675M	1190419M	10046787M

M = $ thousand   MM = $ million
See Pages 1 through 15 for Explanation of Ratios and Data

Current Data Sorted By Assets | **Comparative Historical Data**

Type of Statement

# Postretirement Benefits / Type of Statement	0-500M	500M-2MM	2-10MM	10-50MM	50-100MM	100-250MM	4/1/90-3/31/91 ALL	4/1/91-3/31/92 ALL
Unqualified		2	21	12	5	4	60	57
Reviewed	6	12	21	1	1	1	38	28
Compiled	7	19	3		1	1	29	22
Tax Returns							1	2
Other		7	22	5	4	4	29	27

Current year timing: 55 (4/1-9/30/94) covers 0-500M & 500M-2MM; 102 (10/1/94-3/31/95) covers 2-10MM through 100-250MM.

	0-500M	500M-2MM	2-10MM	10-50MM	50-100MM	100-250MM	ALL 4/1/90-3/31/91	ALL 4/1/91-3/31/92
NUMBER OF STATEMENTS	13	40	67	18	11	8	157	136
ASSETS	%	%	%	%	%	%	%	%
Cash & Equivalents	9.7	8.6	4.2	7.3	10.9		6.4	5.8
Trade Receivables - (net)	32.0	36.7	36.3	30.3	20.0		33.7	28.7
Inventory	26.0	30.6	29.4	27.1	26.3		29.3	29.8
All Other Current	.3	1.4	3.9	1.6	1.7		3.0	3.7
Total Current	68.1	77.2	73.8	66.4	59.0		72.3	67.9
Fixed Assets (net)	19.5	17.8	20.3	19.2	19.0		20.1	22.0
Intangibles (net)	6.0	1.0	1.6	4.8	15.7		2.0	2.8
All Other Non-Current	6.4	3.9	4.3	9.7	6.3		5.5	7.3
Total	100.0	100.0	100.0	100.0	100.0		100.0	100.0
LIABILITIES								
Notes Payable-Short Term	9.3	13.2	14.0	7.0	6.6		14.9	13.0
Cur. Mat.-L/T/D	3.2	2.7	2.4	2.0	1.6		3.9	4.1
Trade Payables	12.3	20.6	18.5	11.2	9.1		17.3	14.8
Income Taxes Payable	.6	.5	.5	.3	.3		1.0	.5
All Other Current	10.4	8.9	10.0	10.3	10.5		9.3	8.9
Total Current	35.8	45.9	45.5	31.7	28.1		46.3	41.3
Long Term Debt	6.8	11.9	12.0	13.8	27.0		12.0	13.9
Deferred Taxes	.1	.3	.3	1.8	.1		.7	.7
All Other-Non-Current	5.0	4.0	2.8	1.5	3.2		2.6	2.8
Net Worth	52.3	38.0	39.4	51.1	41.5		38.4	41.3
Total Liabilities & Net Worth	100.0	100.0	100.0	100.0	100.0		100.0	100.0
INCOME DATA								
Net Sales	100.0	100.0	100.0	100.0	100.0		100.0	100.0
Gross Profit	37.3	32.7	27.4	28.7	34.0		29.4	29.7
Operating Expenses	33.2	28.5	21.4	23.3	22.6		24.1	24.9
Operating Profit	4.0	4.2	6.0	5.3	11.5		5.3	4.7
All Other Expenses (net)	.4	1.2	1.1	1.3	1.8		1.2	1.7
Profit Before Taxes	3.6	3.1	4.9	4.0	9.6		4.1	3.0
RATIOS								
Current	2.9 / 2.4 / 1.8	2.7 / 1.7 / 1.3	2.2 / 1.6 / 1.3	2.9 / 2.1 / 1.5	2.9 / 2.4 / 1.6		2.3 / 1.5 / 1.2	2.7 / 1.7 / 1.2
Quick	2.3 / 1.4 / .5	1.7 / 1.0 / .6	1.1 / .8 / .7	2.1 / 1.0 / .8	1.9 / 1.0 / .5		(156) 1.4 / .8 / .6	1.4 / .8 / .6
Sales/Receivables	34 10.7 / 52 7.0 / 59 6.2	38 9.7 / 49 7.5 / 65 5.6	44 8.3 / 54 6.7 / 63 5.8	45 8.2 / 59 6.2 / 72 5.1	49 7.4 / 51 7.1 / 65 5.6		43 8.4 / 53 6.9 / 65 5.6	41 9.0 / 52 7.0 / 63 5.8
Cost of Sales/Inventory	15 23.8 / 66 5.5 / 104 3.5	23 16.2 / 59 6.2 / 101 3.6	46 7.9 / 70 5.2 / 89 4.1	48 7.6 / 81 4.5 / 130 2.8	91 4.0 / 107 3.4 / 140 2.6		46 7.9 / 70 5.2 / 104 3.5	49 7.4 / 79 4.6 / 118 3.1
Cost of Sales/Payables	8 43.9 / 19 18.8 / 51 7.2	23 15.9 / 38 9.5 / 56 6.5	27 13.6 / 36 10.1 / 47 7.7	20 18.1 / 29 12.4 / 41 8.8	22 16.8 / 29 12.4 / 41 8.8		23 15.8 / 35 10.3 / 54 6.8	19 19.2 / 32 11.5 / 53 6.9
Sales/Working Capital	5.1 / 9.1 / 95.7	4.8 / 9.2 / 15.8	5.5 / 9.2 / 13.0	3.2 / 5.8 / 8.4	3.9 / 4.4 / 6.0		5.3 / 8.8 / 20.2	4.2 / 6.5 / 19.0
EBIT/Interest	(11) 12.0 / 2.3 / .6	(37) 8.2 / 2.9 / 1.4	(65) 14.0 / 4.1 / 2.0	(15) 24.0 / 4.4 / 1.8	(10) 7.6 / 5.6 / 2.9		(142) 7.6 / 2.7 / 1.5	(121) 7.6 / 2.1 / .9
Net Profit + Depr., Dep., Amort./Cur. Mat. L/T/D			(33) 7.8 / 4.1 / 2.5				(90) 9.6 / 3.0 / 1.5	(68) 5.2 / 1.8 / .3
Fixed/Worth	.1 / .5 / .9	.1 / .4 / 1.5	.2 / .4 / 1.0	.2 / .4 / .7	.4 / .8 / 4.4		.2 / .5 / 1.0	.2 / .5 / 1.3
Debt/Worth	.3 / 1.3 / 2.9	.6 / 1.8 / 4.8	.9 / 1.9 / 3.2	.4 / .9 / 2.0	.8 / 1.7 / 12.6		.8 / 1.8 / 3.3	.7 / 1.5 / 3.5
% Profit Before Taxes/Tangible Net Worth	(11) 72.8 / 6.9 / -1.5	(36) 32.4 / 12.3 / 1.7	(66) 47.5 / 25.0 / 8.0	(16) 25.6 / 14.3 / 8.8			(145) 36.5 / 20.7 / 7.5	(125) 33.6 / 13.9 / .3
% Profit Before Taxes/Total Assets	26.3 / 6.1 / -.7	11.2 / 6.6 / .9	17.6 / 7.8 / 2.6	10.8 / 7.5 / 2.5	17.0 / 8.8 / 5.9		15.1 / 7.1 / 2.2	13.5 / 4.8 / -.1
Sales/Net Fixed Assets	185.4 / 14.5 / 7.4	32.1 / 15.5 / 10.6	27.9 / 13.6 / 6.5	18.2 / 9.7 / 5.5	10.2 / 6.6 / 4.9		29.9 / 11.4 / 6.6	21.3 / 9.6 / 5.3
Sales/Total Assets	3.5 / 2.8 / 2.0	3.2 / 2.6 / 2.0	2.9 / 2.3 / 1.9	2.4 / 2.0 / 1.4	1.6 / 1.3 / 1.1		2.8 / 2.1 / 1.7	2.5 / 1.9 / 1.5
% Depr., Dep., Amort./Sales	(10) 1.1 / 3.0 / 5.2	(35) .7 / 1.4 / 2.3	(64) .8 / 1.3 / 2.4	(16) 1.2 / 2.3 / 3.5			(140) .9 / 1.7 / 2.8	(122) 1.2 / 1.9 / 3.2
% Officers', Directors', Owners' Comp/Sales		(20) 4.3 / 6.2 / 14.0	(29) 1.8 / 3.6 / 7.4				(49) 3.3 / 5.0 / 9.5	(39) 3.7 / 5.4 / 9.8
Net Sales ($)	11176M	107689M	738205M	729054M	942018M	1530305M	3483341M	3194468M
Total Assets ($)	3657M	39498M	318652M	380253M	722552M	1054033M	1958419M	2203908M

M = $ thousand   MM = $ million
See Pages 1 through 15 for Explanation of Ratios and Data

Comparative Historical Data | **Current Data Sorted By Sales**

Type of Statement	5	15	13	0-1MM	1-3MM	2	5-10MM	4	7
# Postretirement Benefits						2		4	7
Unqualified	63	48	44		2	1	7	15	19
Reviewed	32	32	41	4	8	9	9	9	2
Compiled	24	21	30	5	14	6	3	1	1
Tax Returns	1								
Other	30	24	42		7	5	6	12	12
	4/1/92-3/31/93	4/1/93-3/31/94	4/1/94-3/31/95	0-1MM	1-3MM	3-5MM	5-10MM	10-25MM	25MM & OVER
	ALL	ALL	ALL	55 (4/1-9/30/94)		102 (10/1/94-3/31/95)			

	150	125	157	9	31	21	25	37	34
NUMBER OF STATEMENTS	%	%	%	%	%	%	%	%	%
ASSETS									
Cash & Equivalents	7.7	9.6	6.7		10.0	6.7	5.7	5.8	5.8
Trade Receivables - (net)	30.1	30.6	33.4		32.4	40.6	35.2	37.4	26.5
Inventory	28.1	25.8	28.5		30.8	24.7	30.3	26.4	27.4
All Other Current	3.1	3.8	2.5		1.5	.7	3.2	5.1	1.6
Total Current	69.1	69.8	71.1		74.7	72.8	74.4	74.7	61.4
Fixed Assets (net)	22.3	21.3	20.2		18.1	24.1	17.7	18.7	23.3
Intangibles (net)	2.4	2.8	3.3		1.8	.7	2.7	1.6	7.9
All Other Non-Current	6.2	6.1	5.3		5.4	2.4	5.2	5.0	7.4
Total	100.0	100.0	100.0		100.0	100.0	100.0	100.0	100.0
LIABILITIES									
Notes Payable-Short Term	13.5	10.7	11.6		14.4	12.2	12.6	13.0	7.0
Cur. Mat.-L.T/D	3.4	2.9	2.6		2.9	3.3	2.3	1.6	2.9
Trade Payables	13.9	14.2	16.6		16.5	18.9	21.9	17.0	11.6
Income Taxes Payable	.6	.8	.5		.2	.9	.4	.5	.3
All Other Current	10.0	8.7	10.0		12.3	9.5	7.5	10.8	11.1
Total Current	41.4	37.3	41.2		46.4	44.8	44.7	43.0	32.9
Long Term Debt	12.6	14.6	13.7		12.0	12.7	14.3	11.2	19.6
Deferred Taxes	.7	1.0	.5		.3	.2	.0	1.3	.3
All Other-Non-Current	2.5	3.0	3.1		3.2	4.2	2.1	3.2	2.6
Net Worth	42.8	44.1	41.5		38.2	38.1	38.8	41.3	44.5
Total Liabilities & Net Worth	100.0	100.0	100.0		100.0	100.0	100.0	100.0	100.0
INCOME DATA									
Net Sales	100.0	100.0	100.0		100.0	100.0	100.0	100.0	100.0
Gross Profit	29.7	29.5	30.3		33.8	32.9	27.6	27.3	29.1
Operating Expenses	25.1	24.6	24.5		29.6	27.9	21.1	21.6	21.2
Operating Profit	4.6	4.9	5.8		4.3	4.9	6.5	5.7	8.0
All Other Expenses (net)	1.0	1.0	1.1		.8	1.7	1.1	.9	1.4
Profit Before Taxes	3.6	3.9	4.7		3.4	3.2	5.4	4.8	6.5

RATIOS

	4/1/92-3/31/93	4/1/93-3/31/94	4/1/94-3/31/95	0-1MM	1-3MM	3-5MM	5-10MM	10-25MM	25MM & OVER
Current	2.7	3.2	2.5		2.6	2.4	2.1	2.5	2.4
	1.6	1.9	1.8		1.7	1.6	1.5	1.8	1.9
	1.2	1.3	1.4		1.0	1.3	1.3	1.4	1.4
Quick	1.5	1.9	1.4		1.9	1.4	1.1	1.4	1.1
	.9	1.0	.9		1.0	1.0	.8	.9	.9
	.6	.7	.7		.5	.9	.6	.7	.8
Sales/Receivables	42 8.6	44 8.3	43 8.5		36 10.2	45 8.3	41 8.9	46 7.9	46 7.9
	53 6.9	54 6.8	53 6.9		46 7.9	60 6.1	52 7.0	58 6.3	53 6.9
	68 5.4	63 5.8	64 5.7		64 5.7	70 5.2	65 5.6	63 5.8	65 5.6
Cost of Sales/Inventory	47 7.8	41 8.9	43 8.4		21 17.4	31 11.7	54 6.8	38 9.6	59 6.2
	73 5.0	70 5.2	70 5.2		76 4.8	58 6.3	73 5.0	63 5.8	91 4.0
	107 3.4	104 3.5	99 3.7		118 3.1	96 3.8	94 3.9	79 4.6	118 3.1
Cost of Sales/Payables	20 18.5	19 19.7	24 15.5		18 20.2	26 14.3	25 14.5	27 13.5	24 15.2
	32 11.4	30 12.2	35 10.3		35 10.4	40 9.1	37 9.8	33 11.2	30 12.3
	47 7.8	48 7.6	48 7.6		63 5.8	49 7.4	54 6.8	46 7.9	41 9.0
Sales/Working Capital	4.4	3.9	4.9		4.7	5.4	6.5	5.2	4.2
	7.9	6.2	8.3		9.3	11.5	9.2	7.1	6.0
	18.2	13.3	13.0		107.4	15.8	11.8	13.0	10.3
EBIT/Interest	(133) 9.5	(112) 9.1	(146) 11.9	(29) 9.9	(20) 7.8	(24) 9.0	(33) 19.0	(32) 11.9	
	3.5	3.6	4.1	2.9	3.3	3.4	4.3	5.2	
	1.3	1.3	1.8	1.4	1.4	1.8	2.0	3.2	
Net Profit + Depr., Dep., Amort./Cur. Mat. L/T/D	(76) 6.0	(57) 9.5	(63) 7.5			(11) 7.7	(19) 8.9	(16) 6.7	
	2.7	2.3	3.1			3.1	6.0	3.1	
	1.0	.8	1.9			2.1	2.5	1.5	
Fixed/Worth	.3	.2	.2		.2	.2	.2	.2	.3
	.6	.4	.4		.4	.6	.4	.4	.6
	1.2	1.2	1.0		3.1	1.6	.9	.9	1.2
Debt/Worth	.6	.5	.8		.5	1.1	1.3	.8	.9
	1.6	1.4	1.7		1.7	2.1	1.9	1.8	1.6
	3.1	4.0	3.3		6.4	3.5	3.7	3.2	2.7
% Profit Before Taxes/Tangible Net Worth	(141) 37.8	(116) 35.4	(146) 39.7	(26) 67.5	(20) 26.0	(24) 46.2	(36) 45.7	(32) 42.7	
	17.2	16.0	18.7	17.5	13.1	28.4	17.9	28.3	
	5.4	2.4	6.9	1.7	4.6	6.0	8.2	12.6	
% Profit Before Taxes/Total Assets	13.5	13.3	13.5		23.0	11.7	19.1	14.1	13.6
	7.3	6.6	7.6		7.4	5.9	9.4	6.6	9.0
	1.1	1.2	2.2		1.0	1.5	1.7	2.5	5.3
Sales/Net Fixed Assets	19.8	22.4	26.0		29.9	31.7	42.6	27.4	14.8
	9.8	10.6	12.5		15.9	13.6	17.7	13.6	7.1
	5.7	5.1	6.2		9.0	5.2	8.0	7.6	5.0
Sales/Total Assets	2.6	2.6	2.9		3.2	3.4	3.1	2.9	2.2
	2.0	2.0	2.2		2.6	2.5	2.3	2.4	1.6
	1.5	1.4	1.7		1.7	1.6	1.9	1.9	1.4
% Depr., Dep., Amort./Sales	(130) .9	(110) .9	(140) 1.0	(28) .9	(19) 1.1	(24) .6	(35) .8	(28) 1.5	
	1.9	1.7	1.6	1.4	1.7	1.2	1.4	2.4	
	3.1	2.7	2.6	2.3	3.0	2.0	2.6	3.3	
% Officers', Directors', Owners' Comp/Sales	(45) 3.4	(43) 3.2	(59) 2.9	(16) 4.6	(13) 3.6	(11) 1.0	(12) 2.4		
	6.7	5.9	4.9	6.2	5.8	2.4	4.1		
	10.5	10.7	9.7	9.4	13.4	3.8	12.2		
Net Sales ($)	3809208M	3319161M	4058447M	4230M	57037M	88602M	182063M	562388M	3164127M
Total Assets ($)	2530262M	2306586M	2518645M	2471M	24491M	40565M	86292M	307748M	2057078M

M = $ thousand   MM = $ million
See Pages 1 through 15 for Explanation of Ratios and Data

Current Data Sorted By Assets   Comparative Historical Data

0-500M	500M-2MM	2-10MM	10-50MM	50-100MM	100-250MM		4/1/90-3/31/91 ALL	4/1/91-3/31/92 ALL
1		1	1		2	**# Postretirement Benefits** / **Type of Statement**		
	1	5	10	1	1	Unqualified	11	19
		4				Reviewed	11	7
2	2	4				Compiled	2	4
1						Tax Returns		
	1	7	2		1	Other	7	7
	18 (4/1-9/30/94)		24 (10/1/94-3/31/95)					
3	4	20	12	1	2	**NUMBER OF STATEMENTS**	31	37
%	%	%	%	%	%	**ASSETS**	%	%
		5.0	9.3			Cash & Equivalents	9.6	9.7
		34.9	35.7			Trade Receivables - (net)	28.3	26.4
		37.0	32.7			Inventory	37.7	36.6
		1.3	1.1			All Other Current	.9	1.3
		78.2	78.7			Total Current	76.6	73.9
		14.1	13.4			Fixed Assets (net)	16.0	19.8
		1.4	2.8			Intangibles (net)	3.2	3.0
		6.3	5.1			All Other Non-Current	4.2	3.2
		100.0	100.0			Total	100.0	100.0
						LIABILITIES		
		8.2	15.7			Notes Payable-Short Term	12.6	8.4
		3.0	2.0			Cur. Mat. -L/T/D	2.8	5.0
		21.0	15.6			Trade Payables	14.9	12.2
		.3	.3			Income Taxes Payable	.6	.6
		9.3	6.7			All Other Current	13.2	12.1
		41.8	40.3			Total Current	44.1	38.2
		7.8	5.7			Long Term Debt	11.4	13.2
		1.0	.5			Deferred Taxes	.5	.3
		3.1	2.3			All Other-Non-Current	2.1	2.4
		46.4	51.2			Net Worth	41.9	45.9
		100.0	100.0			Total Liabilities & Net Worth	100.0	100.0
						INCOME DATA		
		100.0	100.0			Net Sales	100.0	100.0
		35.9	33.5			Gross Profit	36.3	35.5
		29.5	27.8			Operating Expenses	30.3	32.0
		6.5	5.7			Operating Profit	6.0	3.5
		1.1	.9			All Other Expenses (net)	1.2	1.6
		5.3	4.8			Profit Before Taxes	4.8	1.9
						RATIOS		
		2.4	3.9			Current	2.4	3.3
		2.1	2.1				1.9	2.0
		1.6	1.4				1.2	1.6
		1.2	2.9			Quick	1.2	1.7
		1.0	1.0				.8	.9
		.6	.6				.6	.6
		40 9.2	54 6.8			Sales/Receivables	31 11.7	31 11.6
		54 6.7	65 5.6				43 8.4	45 8.2
		69 5.3	78 4.7				53 6.9	57 6.4
		60 6.1	58 6.3			Cost of Sales/Inventory	60 6.1	65 5.6
		101 3.6	81 4.5				89 4.1	107 3.4
		140 2.6	140 2.6				118 3.1	135 2.7
		37 10.0	20 18.3			Cost of Sales/Payables	23 15.7	22 16.6
		54 6.7	45 8.1				34 10.7	31 11.6
		70 5.2	78 4.7				44 8.3	45 8.1
		4.2	2.9			Sales/Working Capital	5.8	4.4
		5.2	7.2				7.7	6.3
		9.4	13.6				19.6	10.4
		23.5	11.0			EBIT/Interest	13.5	7.3
		(19) 9.0	4.8				(29) 4.7	(34) 3.4
		3.5	1.6				2.3	1.0
						Net Profit + Depr., Dep., Amort./Cur. Mat. L /T/D	29.5	15.1
							(22) 6.6	(16) 2.2
							1.9	.4
		.1	.1			Fixed/Worth	.1	.1
		.3	.2				.3	.4
		.5	.8				.6	.8
		.6	.4			Debt/Worth	.8	.4
		1.0	.7				1.2	1.0
		2.3	2.7				3.2	2.1
		37.0	24.4			% Profit Before Taxes/Tangible Net Worth	70.8	45.7
		(19) 24.9	(11) 15.6				(28) 40.9	(34) 18.5
		9.2	1.5				15.1	3.0
		16.9	15.8			% Profit Before Taxes/Total Assets	29.8	18.8
		10.5	7.7				13.2	6.9
		4.2	2.1				5.4	.5
		48.4	29.8			Sales/Net Fixed Assets	39.0	39.4
		22.8	18.8				24.8	11.9
		9.5	9.0				10.4	5.6
		2.6	2.7			Sales/Total Assets	3.3	2.9
		2.3	1.9				2.4	2.0
		1.9	1.6				1.8	1.7
		.5	1.2			% Depr., Dep., Amort./Sales	.7	.7
		(18) 1.7	(10) 2.1				(29) 1.2	(36) 1.6
		2.4	2.6				2.1	2.7
						% Officers', Directors', Owners' Comp/Sales	1.5	2.6
							(13) 3.0	(10) 3.8
							4.2	6.5
1227M	21492M	195443M	453352M	89001M	340346M	Net Sales ($)	308522M	760791M
430M	4939M	85536M	226692M	74863M	222431M	Total Assets ($)	144435M	404693M

M = $ thousand   MM = $ million
See Pages 1 through 15 for Explanation of Ratios and Data

Comparative Historical Data

Current Data Sorted By Sales

	8 4/1/92-3/31/93 ALL	10 4/1/93-3/31/94 ALL	11 4/1/94-3/31/95 ALL	# Postretirement Benefits Type of Statement	0-1MM	1-3MM	3-5MM	5-10MM	10-25MM	25MM & OVER
	19	14	18	Unqualified				1	7	10
	9	5	4	Reviewed			2	1	1	
	7	5	8	Compiled	2	1		3	2	
			1	Tax Returns	1					
				Other		2		4	3	2
	43	34	42	**NUMBER OF STATEMENTS**	3	3	2	9	13	12
	%	%	%	**ASSETS**	%	%	%	%	%	%
	4.8	8.0	6.7	Cash & Equivalents					9.1	5.7
	29.5	32.5	33.7	Trade Receivables - (net)					41.2	34.4
	37.3	36.8	36.5	Inventory					30.2	37.3
	1.2	2.1	1.2	All Other Current					2.1	1.7
	72.8	79.4	78.1	Total Current					82.6	79.1
	16.9	14.3	15.0	Fixed Assets (net)					11.5	15.3
	5.7	1.8	2.1	Intangibles (net)					2.1	1.2
	4.6	4.4	4.8	All Other Non-Current					3.8	4.4
	100.0	100.0	100.0	Total					100.0	100.0
				LIABILITIES						
	11.6	15.4	9.6	Notes Payable-Short Term					12.6	8.9
	2.5	2.5	2.5	Cur. Mat.-L /T/D					2.9	1.5
	17.1	21.5	20.2	Trade Payables					20.6	15.1
	.9	.2	.5	Income Taxes Payable					.2	.6
	8.6	7.5	7.2	All Other Current					7.4	5.5
	40.8	47.1	40.1	Total Current					43.7	31.6
	10.0	5.8	7.3	Long Term Debt					6.0	5.9
	.3	.2	.6	Deferred Taxes					.0	.5
	5.9	4.5	2.3	All Other-Non-Current					1.4	1.9
	43.1	42.4	49.7	Net Worth					48.9	60.0
	100.0	100.0	100.0	Total Liabilities & Net Worth					100.0	100.0
				INCOME DATA						
	100.0	100.0	100.0	Net Sales					100.0	100.0
	33.7	33.9	37.1	Gross Profit					30.3	34.3
	28.4	30.5	31.4	Operating Expenses					25.9	27.2
	5.4	3.4	5.7	Operating Profit					4.3	7.1
	1.3	.8	.9	All Other Expenses (net)					.5	.6
	4.0	2.6	4.8	Profit Before Taxes					3.8	6.5
				RATIOS						
	2.8 / 1.7 / 1.5	2.9 / 1.7 / 1.2	2.9 / 2.1 / 1.4	Current					2.7 / 2.1 / 1.4	6.2 / 2.6 / 1.6
	1.4 / .9 / .7	1.6 / .8 / .5	1.8 / 1.0 / .6	Quick					2.2 / 1.0 / .7	3.3 / 1.4 / .9
	36 10.1 / 48 7.6 / 68 5.4	36 10.1 / 49 7.4 / 70 5.2	41 9.0 / 56 6.5 / 73 5.0	Sales/Receivables					55 6.6 / 65 5.6 / 72 5.1	46 7.9 / 66 5.5 / 78 4.7
	59 6.2 / 101 3.6 / 130 2.8	63 5.8 / 101 3.6 / 126 2.9	59 6.2 / 94 3.9 / 146 2.5	Cost of Sales/Inventory					30 12.3 / 81 4.5 / 111 3.3	58 6.3 / 96 3.8 / 159 2.3
	24 14.9 / 40 9.1 / 63 5.8	28 13.0 / 46 8.0 / 72 5.1	22 16.6 / 49 7.5 / 65 5.6	Cost of Sales/Payables					20 17.9 / 38 9.5 / 65 5.6	18 20.0 / 39 9.4 / 60 6.1
	4.2 / 7.3 / 11.4	4.4 / 7.4 / 19.7	3.6 / 6.3 / 13.2	Sales/Working Capital					4.7 / 6.3 / 13.4	2.6 / 5.0 / 8.3
	(41) 9.4 / 3.6 / 1.9	(30) 11.4 / 3.1 / 1.2	(39) 19.6 / 9.0 / 3.2	EBIT/Interest				(12)	34.5 / 9.1 / 3.5	(11) 19.6 / 9.9 / 3.2
	(20) 11.9 / 7.1 / 1.4	(13) 9.5 / 3.0 / .7	(18) 24.2 / 5.4 / 1.6	Net Profit + Depr., Dep., Amort./Cur. Mat. L/T/D						
	.2 / .3 / .9	.1 / .2 / .7	.1 / .3 / .6	Fixed/Worth					.2 / .2 / .4	.1 / .2 / .6
	.8 / 1.6 / 2.4	.5 / 1.3 / 4.0	.5 / .9 / 2.4	Debt/Worth					.6 / 1.1 / 2.3	.3 / .5 / 1.6
	(38) 33.0 / 20.6 / 8.0	(31) 40.5 / 16.5 / 3.1	(40) 33.7 / 18.8 / 9.4	% Profit Before Taxes/Tangible Net Worth					31.6 / 17.2 / 8.0	(11) 24.4 / 17.6 / 12.6
	12.9 / 5.7 / 1.2	18.1 / 7.8 / 1.0	16.2 / 10.1 / 4.3	% Profit Before Taxes/Total Assets					15.1 / 8.4 / 4.3	16.1 / 12.4 / 6.1
	34.5 / 17.2 / 7.8	42.3 / 26.5 / 10.0	41.2 / 22.2 / 9.0	Sales/Net Fixed Assets					44.9 / 22.3 / 13.5	23.7 / 14.5 / 8.0
	2.6 / 2.1 / 1.6	2.9 / 2.3 / 1.7	2.8 / 2.2 / 1.7	Sales/Total Assets					3.3 / 2.3 / 2.0	2.7 / 1.8 / 1.6
	(39) 1.0 / 1.5 / 3.1	(31) .5 / 1.0 / 2.1	(37) .9 / 1.7 / 2.3	% Depr., Dep., Amort./Sales				(11)	.3 / 1.4 / 1.8	(11) 1.1 / 2.1 / 2.6
	(13) 1.7 / 3.6 / 4.6	(11) 2.3 / 2.8 / 8.0	(15) 1.9 / 2.7 / 4.7	% Officers', Directors', Owners' Comp/Sales						
	843512M	559275M	1100861M	Net Sales ($)	1227M	6083M	7969M	61505M	196671M	827406M
	576545M	307454M	614891M	Total Assets ($)	430M	5724M	4949M	26024M	103521M	474243M

© Robert Morris Associates 1995

M = $ thousand   MM = $ million

See Pages 1 through 15 for Explanation of Ratios and Data

Current Data Sorted By Assets | Comparative Historical Data

Sample period notes: 27 (4/1-9/30/94) for the 500M-2MM group; 50 (10/1/94-3/31/95) for the 10-50MM group.

Statement type breakdown

Type of Statement	0-500M	500M-2MM	2-10MM	10-50MM	50-100MM	100-250MM	4/1/90-3/31/91 ALL	4/1/91-3/31/92 ALL
# Postretirement Benefits				5	1	3		
Unqualified		1	9	11	5	5	17	29
Reviewed		2	10	2	1		14	16
Compiled	1	4	2				10	6
Tax Returns	1							
Other	4	4	8	3		2	10	10
NUMBER OF STATEMENTS	6	11	29	16	8	7	51	61

Main data

	0-500M	500M-2MM %	2-10MM %	10-50MM %	50-100MM	100-250MM	4/1/90-3/31/91 ALL %	4/1/91-3/31/92 ALL %
ASSETS								
Cash & Equivalents		2.7	7.0	4.5			8.5	9.0
Trade Receivables - (net)		33.2	30.5	28.4			28.7	29.7
Inventory		35.3	28.0	33.5			34.6	29.8
All Other Current		.6	2.2	1.8			2.6	2.3
Total Current		71.7	67.8	68.1			74.4	70.8
Fixed Assets (net)		17.3	22.5	20.6			16.0	19.1
Intangibles (net)		1.6	3.6	5.6			1.4	3.4
All Other Non-Current		9.5	6.1	5.6			8.2	6.7
Total		100.0	100.0	100.0			100.0	100.0
LIABILITIES								
Notes Payable-Short Term		18.9	8.6	11.2			12.1	9.2
Cur. Mat. -L/T/D		4.4	3.1	2.0			3.2	4.8
Trade Payables		14.9	20.4	18.7			15.6	13.4
Income Taxes Payable		1.2	.5	1.0			.9	1.3
All Other Current		4.3	9.7	12.0			10.2	9.1
Total Current		43.7	42.3	45.0			41.9	37.8
Long Term Debt		14.9	13.5	12.1			11.4	15.3
Deferred Taxes		.6	.2	.7			.5	.3
All Other-Non-Current		2.4	7.1	.9			4.0	5.4
Net Worth		38.4	36.8	41.3			42.2	41.2
Total Liabilities & Net Worth		100.0	100.0	100.0			100.0	100.0
INCOME DATA								
Net Sales		100.0	100.0	100.0			100.0	100.0
Gross Profit		33.5	26.4	32.1			27.3	29.7
Operating Expenses		27.2	24.4	25.3			24.1	24.4
Operating Profit		6.4	2.1	6.9			3.2	5.4
All Other Expenses (net)		.8	1.0	1.7			1.3	1.7
Profit Before Taxes		5.6	1.1	5.2			1.9	3.7
RATIOS								
Current		1.9 1.7 1.3	2.2 1.6 1.3	2.2 1.4 1.2			2.9 1.8 1.3	3.4 2.0 1.3
Quick		1.0 .9 .7	1.5 .8 .7	1.0 .6 .5			1.3 1.0 .6	1.8 1.0 .7
Sales/Receivables		40 9.1 49 7.4 85 4.3	32 11.3 54 6.8 63 5.8	37 9.9 60 6.1 79 4.6			32 11.3 53 6.9 74 4.9	41 8.9 50 7.3 73 5.0
Cost of Sales/Inventory		51 7.2 69 5.3 140 2.6	35 10.4 54 6.8 85 4.3	76 4.8 96 3.8 126 2.9			47 7.7 79 4.6 126 2.9	50 7.3 73 5.0 114 3.2
Cost of Sales/Payables		24 15.3 29 12.4 54 6.7	18 20.1 36 10.1 62 5.9	22 16.5 51 7.1 74 4.9			23 15.6 32 11.3 46 8.0	20 18.3 32 11.4 45 8.2
Sales/Working Capital		5.9 7.1 12.4	5.5 9.0 21.5	4.9 10.3 18.9			4.2 7.4 19.8	3.9 7.3 14.1
EBIT/Interest		10.5 4.7 1.9	(25) 6.2 3.0 1.4	8.2 5.1 1.8			(47) 6.9 2.4 .4	(55) 10.6 1.8 .9
Net Profit + Depr., Dep., Amort./Cur. Mat. L /T/D			(10) 20.1 5.4 .9				(26) 9.5 2.4 .6	(37) 10.4 3.4 1.0
Fixed/Worth		.1 .5 1.9	.2 .6 1.6	.2 .6 1.1			.2 .3 1.2	.2 .6 1.8
Debt/Worth		.8 1.4 5.2	.9 1.6 4.7	.9 2.2 3.5			.5 1.7 4.3	.6 1.6 6.2
% Profit Before Taxes/Tangible Net Worth		(10) 53.0 21.5 5.7	(28) 43.4 17.1 4.3	47.1 31.8 5.4			(48) 28.1 14.9 -1.0	(52) 32.3 15.6 2.1
% Profit Before Taxes/Total Assets		19.3 8.3 4.2	10.3 5.8 .9	21.6 7.1 2.2			10.5 5.3 -.8	13.0 6.8 .4
Sales/Net Fixed Assets		57.5 16.2 6.9	28.7 12.2 6.2	19.5 10.4 5.6			29.3 16.2 6.9	26.0 12.0 7.6
Sales/Total Assets		2.8 2.5 1.7	2.7 2.3 1.8	2.6 1.8 1.2			2.8 2.0 1.6	2.6 2.1 1.4
% Depr., Dep., Amort./Sales			(26) .7 1.8 3.0	.7 1.8 3.2			(43) .8 1.6 2.7	(51) 1.0 1.8 2.7
% Officers', Directors', Owners' Comp/Sales		(13) 1.9 5.6 11.7					(13) .7 3.8 7.7	
Net Sales ($)	4982M	35511M	342848M	692112M	1267938M	2208652M	2253093M	3595372M
Total Assets ($)	1676M	14966M	142042M	357381M	541513M	1203137M	1413258M	1976161M

M = $ thousand   MM = $ million

See Pages 1 through 15 for Explanation of Ratios and Data

Comparative Historical Data / Current Data Sorted By Sales

1	6	9	# Postretirement Benefits	0-1MM	1-3MM	3-5MM	5-10MM	10-25MM	25MM & OVER
			(Postretirement Benefits counts)			2	2	1	4
			Type of Statement						
28	18	31	Unqualified			2	5	5	19
9	10	15	Reviewed		2	1	5	3	4
7	12	7	Compiled		2	1	2	2	
1		1	Tax Returns	1					
14	16	23	Other	3	3	2	2	6	7
4/1/92-3/31/93 ALL	4/1/93-3/31/94 ALL	4/1/94-3/31/95 ALL		27 (4/1-9/30/94)			50 (10/1/94-3/31/95)		
59	56	77	**NUMBER OF STATEMENTS**	4	7	6	14	16	30
%	%	%	**ASSETS**	%	%	%	%	%	%
5.3	8.4	5.7	Cash & Equivalents				7.6	7.2	5.6
31.0	30.4	30.7	Trade Receivables - (net)				30.3	28.8	29.7
30.2	29.3	30.0	Inventory				26.9	30.0	30.5
1.6	2.9	1.8	All Other Current				1.5	2.4	2.3
68.0	71.0	68.3	Total Current				66.4	68.4	68.0
20.5	19.0	20.7	Fixed Assets (net)				23.8	23.4	18.5
5.1	3.5	4.3	Intangibles (net)				3.1	2.9	6.6
6.4	6.5	6.7	All Other Non-Current				6.7	5.2	6.8
100.0	100.0	100.0	Total				100.0	100.0	100.0
			LIABILITIES						
10.9	10.2	9.5	Notes Payable-Short Term				8.2	9.4	9.3
2.8	2.9	3.3	Cur. Mat.-L /T/D				4.0	3.2	2.0
15.6	13.3	16.6	Trade Payables				19.0	12.6	18.2
.7	2.2	.7	Income Taxes Payable				.4	.4	1.0
9.2	10.1	10.8	All Other Current				9.7	11.2	14.2
39.2	38.6	41.0	Total Current				41.4	36.8	44.6
8.8	11.9	15.7	Long Term Debt				18.3	11.2	15.3
.5	.3	.4	Deferred Taxes				.1	.5	.5
6.0	3.6	4.3	All Other-Non-Current				8.3	4.2	3.0
45.5	45.6	38.5	Net Worth				31.9	47.4	36.5
100.0	100.0	100.0	Total Liabilities & Net Worth				100.0	100.0	100.0
			INCOME DATA						
100.0	100.0	100.0	Net Sales				100.0	100.0	100.0
29.1	27.9	29.9	Gross Profit				29.1	25.9	30.0
23.4	23.8	25.1	Operating Expenses				28.4	21.8	24.3
5.6	4.1	4.8	Operating Profit				.7	4.1	5.7
1.3	1.3	1.5	All Other Expenses (net)				1.0	1.0	1.6
4.3	2.8	3.3	Profit Before Taxes				-.3	3.1	4.1
			RATIOS						
3.2 / 1.9 / 1.4	3.1 / 1.9 / 1.3	2.2 / 1.8 / 1.3	Current				2.2 / 1.5 / 1.3	2.6 / 1.9 / 1.6	2.4 / 1.7 / 1.2
1.6 / 1.0 / .6	1.5 / 1.1 / .7	1.3 / .9 / .6	Quick				1.4 / .8 / .7	1.6 / 1.1 / .7	1.3 / .8 / .5
39 9.3 / 54 6.8 / 65 5.6	40 9.1 / 52 7.0 / 63 5.8	35 10.5 / 51 7.1 / 65 5.6	Sales/Receivables				34 10.7 / 49 7.5 / 58 6.3	31 11.7 / 54 6.8 / 68 5.4	38 9.7 / 57 6.4 / 69 5.3
44 8.3 / 83 4.4 / 107 3.4	48 7.6 / 68 5.4 / 91 4.0	46 7.9 / 68 5.4 / 111 3.3	Cost of Sales/Inventory				44 8.3 / 56 6.5 / 68 5.4	38 9.7 / 79 4.6 / 126 2.9	50 7.3 / 72 5.1 / 104 3.5
22 16.8 / 30 12.0 / 47 7.8	16 22.3 / 25 14.4 / 46 8.0	20 18.5 / 31 11.9 / 55 6.6	Cost of Sales/Payables				18 20.0 / 48 7.6 / 63 5.8	15 24.0 / 22 16.4 / 50 7.3	20 18.4 / 31 11.8 / 47 7.7
4.2 / 6.8 / 14.5	3.4 / 6.3 / 18.8	5.4 / 7.4 / 16.5	Sales/Working Capital				5.2 / 10.8 / 21.1	4.4 / 6.9 / 9.4	5.6 / 8.2 / 18.4
(57) 9.8 / 3.4 / 1.2	(50) 10.9 / 4.2 / 1.1	(71) 6.6 / 3.9 / 1.5	EBIT/Interest				(13) 5.4 / 2.1 / 1.2	(14) 5.9 / 4.5 / 1.4	(28) 9.4 / 4.1 / 1.6
(28) 12.0 / 4.9 / 2.1	(22) 9.2 / 2.9 / .3	(31) 11.0 / 2.5 / 1.0	Net Profit + Depr., Dep., Amort./Cur. Mat. L/T/D						(16) 17.5 / 3.3 / .5
.2 / .5 / 1.0	.2 / .5 / 1.1	.2 / .6 / 1.3	Fixed/Worth				.2 / .8 / 1.8	.2 / .4 / 1.2	.3 / .6 / 1.1
.6 / 1.6 / 2.7	.6 / 1.4 / 2.9	.9 / 1.6 / 4.2	Debt/Worth				1.2 / 3.3 / 4.6	.7 / 1.2 / 2.0	1.3 / 2.0 / 4.6
(56) 38.9 / 14.0 / 2.5	(54) 27.7 / 14.4 / 4.3	(73) 48.1 / 18.1 / 4.1	% Profit Before Taxes/Tangible Net Worth				26.6 / 17.1 / 2.1	40.1 / 15.0 / 5.1	(27) 50.6 / 28.1 / 13.9
14.7 / 5.7 / 1.1	13.3 / 6.1 / 1.3	14.5 / 7.3 / 1.9	% Profit Before Taxes/Total Assets				8.7 / 3.1 / .3	12.8 / 7.1 / 1.8	16.2 / 7.6 / 1.7
25.2 / 11.3 / 5.9	25.5 / 11.6 / 6.7	26.5 / 11.4 / 6.5	Sales/Net Fixed Assets				41.0 / 11.8 / 5.1	27.4 / 8.9 / 6.3	26.1 / 12.1 / 7.6
2.7 / 2.0 / 1.3	2.9 / 2.0 / 1.4	2.7 / 2.3 / 1.5	Sales/Total Assets				2.8 / 2.3 / 1.9	2.6 / 2.1 / 1.2	2.8 / 2.1 / 1.5
(54) .9 / 1.7 / 2.7	(50) 1.0 / 1.7 / 3.1	(66) .7 / 1.8 / 3.1	% Depr., Dep., Amort./Sales				(13) 1.5 / 2.2 / 3.4	(13) .8 / 2.2 / 3.0	(25) .6 / 1.4 / 2.7
(17) 2.4 / 4.7 / 7.4	(15) 2.3 / 4.9 / 9.1	(21) 1.4 / 4.5 / 6.8	% Officers', Directors', Owners' Comp/Sales						
2211763M	2974621M	4552043M	Net Sales ($)	2576M	12272M	22490M	101190M	230134M	4183381M
1340238M	1796986M	2260715M	Total Assets ($)	887M	6410M	11504M	48823M	132336M	2060755M

M = $ thousand   MM = $ million
See Pages 1 through 15 for Explanation of Ratios and Data

0-500M	500M-2MM	2-10MM	10-50MM	50-100MM	100-250MM		4/1/90-3/31/91 ALL	4/1/91-3/31/92 ALL
Current Data Sorted By Assets							**Comparative Historical Data**	
1	3	4	3			**# Postretirement Benefits**		
						Type of Statement		
1	4	25	22	8	1	Unqualified	31	57
1	8	9	1			Reviewed	4	12
1	5	3				Compiled	8	7
2						Tax Returns		
1	6	8	10	2	3	Other	15	17
	52 (4/1-9/30/94)		69 (10/1/94-3/31/95)					
6	23	45	33	10	4	**NUMBER OF STATEMENTS**	58	93
%	%	%	%	%	%	**ASSETS**	%	%
	8.9	9.0	18.7	20.6		Cash & Equivalents	8.9	12.1
	29.6	27.8	27.2	23.1		Trade Receivables - (net)	28.1	27.1
	31.4	29.4	25.3	20.1		Inventory	33.9	30.5
	2.4	3.0	3.2	2.4		All Other Current	2.8	1.8
	72.3	69.2	74.5	66.2		Total Current	73.7	71.5
	22.8	20.3	17.3	15.4		Fixed Assets (net)	18.7	21.6
	1.1	3.7	2.3	11.2		Intangibles (net)	2.1	3.4
	3.8	6.8	5.9	7.2		All Other Non-Current	5.5	3.5
	100.0	100.0	100.0	100.0		Total	100.0	100.0
						LIABILITIES		
	8.9	8.6	7.1	1.6		Notes Payable-Short Term	11.8	8.2
	4.6	3.4	1.1	1.7		Cur. Mat. -L/T/D	3.8	3.8
	20.3	14.2	11.6	9.4		Trade Payables	15.0	14.1
	.6	.4	1.7	.6		Income Taxes Payable	.7	.7
	11.4	11.6	12.0	11.6		All Other Current	10.0	13.1
	45.9	38.3	33.4	24.9		Total Current	41.4	39.9
	10.8	10.0	6.4	11.7		Long Term Debt	11.5	11.1
	1.5	.7	.8	.7		Deferred Taxes	.5	.5
	4.8	2.1	2.6	2.7		All Other-Non-Current	3.0	2.2
	36.9	48.9	56.7	60.0		Net Worth	43.6	46.2
	100.0	100.0	100.0	100.0		Total Liabilities & Net Worth	100.0	100.0
						INCOME DATA		
	100.0	100.0	100.0	100.0		Net Sales	100.0	100.0
	38.7	41.1	40.7	43.7		Gross Profit	38.0	38.9
	32.9	35.6	33.3	32.0		Operating Expenses	31.8	33.4
	5.8	5.5	7.4	11.6		Operating Profit	6.2	5.5
	.4	.8	.5	.9		All Other Expenses (net)	1.3	1.0
	5.3	4.7	6.9	10.7		Profit Before Taxes	4.9	4.5
						RATIOS		
	2.1	3.2	4.0	4.6			3.0	3.2
	1.7	1.8	2.4	2.5	Current	2.0	2.1
	1.3	1.3	1.4	1.7		1.3	1.4
	1.2	1.9	2.8	3.8		1.4	1.7
	.8	1.0	1.2	1.3	Quick	.9	1.2
	.6	.6	.8	.8		.6	.6
	24 15.2	37 10.0	47 7.7	35 10.5			38 9.6	38 9.7
	40 9.1	55 6.6	65 5.6	68 5.4		Sales/Receivables	52 7.0	52 7.0
	50 7.3	62 5.9	87 4.2	83 4.4			70 5.2	69 5.3
	38 9.7	59 6.2	66 5.5	73 5.0			81 4.5	64 5.7
	64 5.7	107 3.4	111 3.3	101 3.6		Cost of Sales/Inventory	107 3.4	111 3.3
	135 2.7	166 2.2	152 2.4	140 2.6			146 2.5	152 2.4
	17 21.4	21 17.1	36 10.2	24 15.3			25 14.5	24 15.3
	43 8.4	38 9.6	43 8.5	43 8.5		Cost of Sales/Payables	33 11.2	37 9.8
	68 5.4	65 5.6	63 5.8	63 5.8			55 6.6	57 6.4
	5.8	3.1	1.7	1.4			3.5	2.9
	10.1	5.7	3.5	3.8	Sales/Working Capital	5.4	5.8
	17.1	13.4	8.8	7.5		12.0	9.6
	15.5	19.1	84.6				11.5	10.7
	(22) 7.2	(38) 4.5	(28) 7.5			EBIT/Interest	(55) 4.0	(82) 3.0
	2.2	1.7	1.1				1.4	1.3
	11.8	14.4	19.4			Net Profit + Depr., Dep.,	9.7	6.7
	(12) 3.2	(21) 2.1	(15) 5.6			Amort./Cur. Mat. L./T/D	(35) 3.4	(47) 2.9
	1.6	.8	1.7				1.2	.1
	.2	.2	.2	.1			.2	.2
	.4	.4	.3	.2	Fixed/Worth	.4	.3
	1.0	.7	.5	1.5		.8	.9
	1.2	.5	.3	.2		.5	.5
	2.2	1.2	.7	.7	Debt/Worth	1.4	1.1
	3.4	2.1	1.5	3.1		2.9	2.5
	69.5	48.3	42.9	38.3		% Profit Before Taxes/Tangible	39.6	35.7
	39.2	(43) 22.1	14.4	22.5		Net Worth	(56) 21.6	(86) 17.1
	17.4	5.8	.1	12.1			4.0	2.1
	19.7	16.1	23.9	16.1		% Profit Before Taxes/Total	16.7	15.4
	12.4	7.8	7.6	11.9		Assets	8.6	6.5
	4.4	1.3	.1	5.6			1.9	1.0
	69.8	29.6	13.5	18.7			19.0	17.0
	17.6	11.1	10.5	9.1	Sales/Net Fixed Assets	11.9	9.8
	7.8	4.5	4.3	5.0		7.4	5.3
	3.1	2.2	1.9	1.8			2.7	2.2
	2.5	1.6	1.4	1.2	Sales/Total Assets	1.9	1.7
	1.7	1.2	1.0	.9		1.5	1.3
	.8	.9	2.6	1.5			1.4	1.6
	(20) 2.6	(41) 1.8	(29) 3.5	2.1		% Depr., Dep., Amort./Sales	(52) 2.1	(81) 2.5
	4.1	3.6	4.4	4.2			3.2	4.7
	4.3	2.6				% Officers', Directors',		2.9
	(11) 6.9	(10) 5.1				Owners' Comp/Sales		(13) 5.0
	8.8	9.7						13.2
5237M	78323M	404710M	1007423M	825964M	886963M	Net Sales ($)	1384092M	2396917M
1649M	28472M	223445M	709493M	643245M	691788M	Total Assets ($)	995653M	1736276M

M = $ thousand   MM = $ million
See Pages 1 through 15 for Explanation of Ratios and Data

Comparative Historical Data						Current Data Sorted By Sales				
2	2	11	# Postretirement Benefits	2	1	3	2	1	2
			Type of Statement						
51	49	61	Unqualified	1	3	3	14	18	22
12	13	19	Reviewed	1	4	5	6	2	1
4	7	9	Compiled	1	3	3	2		
3	2	2	Tax Returns	1	1				
24	23	30	Other	2	5	3	5	5	10
4/1/92-3/31/93	4/1/93-3/31/94	4/1/94-3/31/95			52 (4/1-9/30/94)			69 (10/1/94-3/31/95)	
ALL	ALL	ALL		0-1MM	1-3MM	3-5MM	5-10MM	10-25MM	25MM & OVER
94	94	121	**NUMBER OF STATEMENTS**	6	16	14	27	25	33
%	%	%	**ASSETS**	%	%	%	%	%	%
10.0	9.0	12.3	Cash & Equivalents		7.4	5.9	12.8	12.2	18.2
27.4	27.8	27.6	Trade Receivables - (net)		23.2	24.3	31.0	28.0	29.0
33.6	33.1	28.3	Inventory		27.8	37.7	29.2	27.7	23.7
2.6	3.2	2.9	All Other Current		1.3	3.4	1.5	5.1	3.3
73.7	73.0	71.1	Total Current		59.6	71.3	74.5	73.0	74.2
18.9	18.0	19.9	Fixed Assets (net)		30.9	19.0	16.9	18.6	15.4
2.4	3.5	3.3	Intangibles (net)		3.0	1.8	2.6	3.6	4.8
5.0	5.5	5.7	All Other Non-Current		6.4	7.9	6.0	4.8	5.6
100.0	100.0	100.0	Total		100.0	100.0	100.0	100.0	100.0
			LIABILITIES						
7.9	7.0	7.6	Notes Payable-Short Term		5.5	5.9	10.9	9.3	5.7
3.7	3.4	2.8	Cur. Mat.-L./T/D		4.2	2.7	2.1	2.8	1.0
13.2	14.0	14.7	Trade Payables		13.8	15.7	15.3	16.0	11.2
.6	1.2	.9	Income Taxes Payable		.4	.5	.3	1.8	1.0
10.9	10.8	11.6	All Other Current		9.3	11.3	12.5	12.0	12.8
36.2	36.4	37.6	Total Current		33.2	36.1	42.2	41.9	31.7
9.4	9.8	9.3	Long Term Debt		16.4	7.7	8.7	9.3	7.1
1.0	.7	.9	Deferred Taxes		.6	1.3	.9	.6	.9
1.8	1.8	2.7	All Other-Non-Current		6.2	1.1	2.8	2.6	1.9
51.6	51.3	49.5	Net Worth		43.7	53.8	45.3	45.6	58.4
100.0	100.0	100.0	Total Liabilities & Net Worth		100.0	100.0	100.0	100.0	100.0
			INCOME DATA						
100.0	100.0	100.0	Net Sales		100.0	100.0	100.0	100.0	100.0
37.3	37.5	40.6	Gross Profit		41.7	43.5	44.8	35.2	40.9
32.0	33.6	33.9	Operating Expenses		39.9	35.3	38.7	27.9	32.5
5.3	3.9	6.7	Operating Profit		1.8	8.2	6.1	7.3	8.4
1.4	1.1	.6	All Other Expenses (net)		.5	.8	.5	.9	.6
3.9	2.8	6.1	Profit Before Taxes		1.3	7.4	5.6	6.4	7.8
			RATIOS						
3.3	3.7	3.1			2.7	3.4	2.9	2.4	4.3
2.2	2.1	2.0	Current		1.5	2.1	2.0	1.6	2.4
1.5	1.6	1.3			1.3	1.5	1.4	1.3	1.5
1.7	2.0	2.1			1.7	1.5	1.5	1.8	3.3
1.0	1.0	1.0	Quick		.8	.9	1.0	.8	1.3
.6	.6	.6			.4	.6	.8	.6	.9
36 10.1	38 9.5	35 10.3		25 14.8	23 16.1	40 9.1	42 8.7	44 8.3	
49 7.5	54 6.7	53 6.9	Sales/Receivables	41 8.9	38 9.7	56 6.5	59 6.2	66 5.5	
69 5.3	76 4.8	73 5.0		58 6.3	50 7.3	83 4.4	72 5.1	89 4.1	
62 5.9	72 5.1	59 6.2		36 10.1	59 6.2	70 5.2	47 7.7	66 5.5	
101 3.6	104 3.5	99 3.7	Cost of Sales/Inventory	130 2.8	89 4.1	114 3.2	99 3.7	104 3.5	
146 2.5	152 2.4	146 2.5		152 2.4	174 2.1	159 2.3	152 2.4	140 2.6	
20 18.3	28 13.2	24 15.5		14 26.4	17 21.9	18 19.8	34 10.6	31 11.7	
36 10.2	40 9.1	41 8.8	Cost of Sales/Payables	52 7.0	40 9.1	39 9.4	43 8.5	42 8.7	
54 6.8	60 6.1	65 5.6		74 4.9	64 5.7	68 5.4	65 5.6	61 6.0	
3.1	3.0	2.9			2.9	4.0	3.0	3.4	1.8
5.1	5.0	5.8	Sales/Working Capital		9.2	5.7	5.7	6.8	3.3
10.6	8.4	13.1			16.5	14.2	13.5	12.9	9.4
17.1	14.2	26.1			6.0	16.4	45.7	15.6	120.9
(86) 5.3	(80) 5.0	(102) 5.7	EBIT/Interest	(14) 1.4	(13) 6.1	(23) 7.5	(22) 5.3	(25) 16.1	
1.1	1.6	1.7			-.3	2.6	1.9	2.7	1.7
8.5	7.5	14.8				17.5	17.1	29.8	
(52) 3.0	(47) 2.0	(54) 3.1	Net Profit + Depr., Dep., Amort./Cur. Mat. L/T/D		(12) 1.9	(15) 3.6	(10) 11.1	
.9	.3	1.4				1.0	1.6	3.2	
.2	.2	.2			.1	.2	.2	.2	.2
.3	.3	.3	Fixed/Worth		.6	.4	.3	.4	.2
.6	.8	.7			4.7	.6	.5	1.0	.4
.5	.5	.5			.3	.5	.7	.8	.3
1.0	1.0	1.3	Debt/Worth		2.1	.9	1.5	1.9	.6
2.1	2.2	2.5			6.6	1.8	2.2	2.6	1.7
36.1	36.3	52.8			34.8	54.5	69.5	64.8	38.8
(92) 16.8	(92) 19.2	(119) 21.7	% Profit Before Taxes/Tangible Net Worth	(14) 10.6	35.8	21.7	22.1	18.6	
1.3	4.3	3.7			-3.6	16.2	6.4	8.7	4.7
15.1	16.8	18.1			11.8	20.2	18.9	23.2	15.1
9.0	8.3	10.3	% Profit Before Taxes/Total Assets		2.3	13.6	8.9	8.2	10.9
.4	1.1	1.6			-3.9	9.5	2.1	2.6	2.1
21.8	22.3	21.3			13.9	21.7	65.8	26.3	18.1
11.4	10.8	11.0	Sales/Net Fixed Assets		6.9	17.8	12.8	11.8	10.5
6.2	5.8	5.3			2.6	10.0	5.2	4.3	6.7
2.5	2.4	2.4			2.7	3.0	2.8	2.0	1.9
1.9	1.8	1.7	Sales/Total Assets		1.5	2.4	1.8	1.6	1.5
1.3	1.2	1.2			1.0	1.6	1.2	1.4	.9
1.4	1.3	1.4			3.2	1.3	.6	1.2	1.7
(85) 2.5	(84) 2.6	(106) 2.7	% Depr., Dep., Amort./Sales	(14) 4.2	(13) 2.2	(23) 1.7	(24) 2.6	(27) 2.9	
3.5	3.8	4.0			5.3	2.9	3.1	4.1	4.0
4.2	2.9	3.8							
(14) 6.2	(13) 4.2	(25) 6.0	% Officers', Directors', Owners' Comp/Sales						
10.3	8.5	8.8							
2436703M 1695208M	3084152M 2322676M	3208620M 2298092M	Net Sales ($) / Total Assets ($)	3148M 2337M	32951M 34899M	55259M 25718M	203942M 131320M	406257M 251382M	2507063M 1852436M

© Robert Morris Associates 1995   M = $ thousand   MM = $ million
See Pages 1 through 15 for Explanation of Ratios and Data

Current Data Sorted By Assets						Comparative Historical Data		
1	3	2				# Postretirement Benefits		
						Type of Statement		
1	3	14	16	2	7	Unqualified	19	28
1	12	11	1			Reviewed	21	19
4	3					Compiled	6	12
						Tax Returns		1
3	6	10	3		1	Other	8	16
	35 (4/1-9/30/94)		63 (10/1/94-3/31/95)				4/1/90-3/31/91	4/1/91-3/31/92
0-500M	500M-2MM	2-10MM	10-50MM	50-100MM	100-250MM		ALL	ALL
9	24	35	20	2	8	NUMBER OF STATEMENTS	54	76
%	%	%	%	%	%	**ASSETS**	%	%
	3.6	3.8	8.7			Cash & Equivalents	7.6	9.2
	36.2	31.1	30.1			Trade Receivables - (net)	32.3	30.8
	25.7	32.1	25.6			Inventory	31.5	27.8
	7.8	3.3	2.4			All Other Current	1.6	4.1
	73.3	70.3	66.8			Total Current	73.0	71.8
	18.5	19.8	24.6			Fixed Assets (net)	19.4	21.1
	2.6	3.8	4.1			Intangibles (net)	1.7	1.8
	5.6	6.2	4.5			All Other Non-Current	5.9	5.2
	100.0	100.0	100.0			Total	100.0	100.0
						LIABILITIES		
	11.8	13.8	9.9			Notes Payable-Short Term	12.3	11.1
	2.1	2.8	3.1			Cur. Mat. -L/T/D	3.0	2.1
	18.8	15.8	14.7			Trade Payables	15.0	13.2
	.6	.5	1.2			Income Taxes Payable	.8	.4
	12.1	11.6	8.3			All Other Current	12.6	11.9
	45.4	44.5	37.1			Total Current	43.7	38.7
	12.5	9.5	11.1			Long Term Debt	9.1	12.2
	1.5	.1	.6			Deferred Taxes	.9	.5
	3.9	8.1	6.6			All Other-Non-Current	4.1	3.4
	36.7	37.9	44.6			Net Worth	42.2	45.1
	100.0	100.0	100.0			Total Liabilities & Net Worth	100.0	100.0
						INCOME DATA		
	100.0	100.0	100.0			Net Sales	100.0	100.0
	33.1	34.9	35.2			Gross Profit	34.9	37.8
	29.2	29.2	28.1			Operating Expenses	29.2	32.0
	3.9	5.7	7.1			Operating Profit	5.7	5.8
	1.5	1.8	1.5			All Other Expenses (net)	2.0	1.4
	2.4	3.9	5.6			Profit Before Taxes	3.8	4.4
						RATIOS		
	2.0 1.6 1.2	2.3 1.5 1.2	2.5 2.0 1.3			Current	2.2 1.7 1.3	3.3 1.8 1.5
	1.1 1.0 .6	1.0 .7 .5	1.5 1.0 .7			Quick	1.3 .9 .7	1.7 1.0 .8
	40 9.2 51 7.1 62 5.9	47 7.7 56 6.5 62 5.9	56 6.5 62 5.9 76 4.8			Sales/Receivables	41 9.0 56 6.5 68 5.4	46 7.9 54 6.8 63 5.8
	9 40.6 51 7.1 91 4.0	65 5.6 91 4.0 152 2.4	61 6.0 78 4.7 130 2.8			Cost of Sales/Inventory	59 6.2 99 3.7 126 2.9	55 6.6 79 4.6 130 2.8
	21 17.8 38 9.5 52 7.0	28 12.9 41 8.8 58 6.3	33 11.2 38 9.5 76 4.8			Cost of Sales/Payables	26 14.3 39 9.3 54 6.8	20 18.0 35 10.4 46 8.0
	6.5 11.1 18.4	5.1 7.9 26.1	4.1 5.2 10.3			Sales/Working Capital	4.7 6.9 13.9	4.0 6.8 11.2
	(23) 9.8 4.2 1.5	(31) 5.4 3.9 1.4	13.7 6.4 2.5			EBIT/Interest	(50) 7.1 3.4 1.4	(71) 10.8 3.1 1.1
		(12) 7.3 4.1 2.2	(10) 15.1 3.4 2.0			Net Profit + Depr., Dep., Amort./Cur. Mat. L/T/D	(29) 6.9 3.7 1.5	(32) 12.2 2.9 1.4
	.3 .5 .7	.4 .5 1.0	.3 .6 1.0			Fixed/Worth	.2 .4 .7	.2 .5 1.0
	1.4 2.2 4.0	1.3 2.1 4.6	.7 1.2 2.6			Debt/Worth	.8 1.4 3.0	.6 1.3 2.7
	35.6 (34) 17.3 5.4	45.1 25.8 9.1	45.8 27.2 9.4			% Profit Before Taxes/Tangible Net Worth	40.8 (52) 19.6 2.4	48.7 (74) 20.1 2.3
	12.6 6.6 1.7	13.6 7.3 1.3	19.9 8.3 3.0			% Profit Before Taxes/Total Assets	14.9 7.5 1.5	19.7 7.6 .9
	42.8 19.9 11.1	20.4 12.3 7.0	10.8 7.9 4.9			Sales/Net Fixed Assets	34.6 13.7 5.8	29.7 13.8 5.2
	3.1 2.7 2.2	2.3 1.9 1.5	2.1 1.7 1.1			Sales/Total Assets	2.5 2.0 1.4	2.7 1.9 1.5
	.7 (23) 1.0 1.4	1.3 (27) 2.1 2.9	1.8 (14) 3.1 4.4			% Depr., Dep., Amort./Sales	1.0 (47) 1.8 3.5	1.1 (62) 1.7 3.5
						% Officers', Directors', Owners' Comp/Sales		3.2 (16) 7.9 14.7
7199M	69561M	306006M	659445M	245971M	1353763M	Net Sales ($)	1494167M	2062634M
2650M	25003M	151734M	399905M	118098M	1174396M	Total Assets ($)	1035209M	1458977M

M = $ thousand   MM = $ million
See Pages 1 through 15 for Explanation of Ratios and Data

Comparative Historical Data (top counts: 4 | 2 | 6) — **Current Data Sorted By Sales** (# Postretirement Benefits: 3 | 1 | 2)

Current data grouping: 35 (4/1-9/30/94) and 63 (10/1/94-3/31/95)

Type of Statement

Type of Statement	4/1/92-3/31/93 ALL	4/1/93-3/31/94 ALL	4/1/94-3/31/95 ALL	0-1MM	1-3MM	3-5MM	5-10MM	10-25MM	25MM & OVER
Unqualified	30	31	43	2	2	3	7	9	20
Reviewed	12	23	25		10	2	10	3	
Compiled	12	16	7	4	3				
Tax Returns									
Other	17	13	23	2	5	5	4	4	3
NUMBER OF STATEMENTS	**71**	**83**	**98**	**8**	**20**	**10**	**21**	**16**	**23**

ASSETS (%)

	4/1/92-3/31/93	4/1/93-3/31/94	4/1/94-3/31/95	0-1MM	1-3MM	3-5MM	5-10MM	10-25MM	25MM & OVER
Cash & Equivalents	8.7	8.3	6.5		2.8	5.1	3.9	3.5	13.3
Trade Receivables - (net)	32.1	33.4	32.7		39.2	26.2	34.7	30.1	27.9
Inventory	26.3	26.6	27.2		24.1	30.2	29.3	31.0	24.2
All Other Current	2.9	3.4	3.9		8.4	2.4	3.7	4.4	1.4
Total Current	70.0	71.6	70.3		74.4	63.9	71.6	68.9	66.8
Fixed Assets (net)	20.3	20.3	20.3		19.0	19.7	17.5	24.6	23.0
Intangibles (net)	4.2	3.4	3.9		1.6	7.6	4.5	2.3	5.6
All Other Non-Current	5.5	4.7	5.5		5.0	8.8	6.4	4.1	4.6
Total	100.0	100.0	100.0		100.0	100.0	100.0	100.0	100.0

LIABILITIES

	4/1/92-3/31/93	4/1/93-3/31/94	4/1/94-3/31/95	0-1MM	1-3MM	3-5MM	5-10MM	10-25MM	25MM & OVER
Notes Payable-Short Term	11.4	7.8	11.4		13.5	6.9	14.7	11.6	10.1
Cur. Mat.-L/T/D	3.3	2.7	2.7		4.2	2.3	2.0	2.7	2.3
Trade Payables	14.0	13.1	16.1		19.1	9.4	19.2	14.9	14.1
Income Taxes Payable	.4	1.4	.8		.4	.5	.8	.0	2.0
All Other Current	12.2	12.0	11.3		12.3	11.7	11.7	11.3	9.0
Total Current	41.3	37.0	42.3		49.5	30.8	48.3	40.5	37.5
Long Term Debt	12.1	11.9	10.9		15.9	14.8	8.0	8.3	11.3
Deferred Taxes	1.0	1.2	.7		.7	.9	.1	.2	1.3
All Other-Non-Current	2.7	4.5	5.4		4.5	3.1	7.3	9.5	4.0
Net Worth	42.9	45.4	40.6		29.4	50.3	36.2	41.4	45.9
Total Liabilities & Net Worth	100.0	100.0	100.0		100.0	100.0	100.0	100.0	100.0

INCOME DATA

	4/1/92-3/31/93	4/1/93-3/31/94	4/1/94-3/31/95	0-1MM	1-3MM	3-5MM	5-10MM	10-25MM	25MM & OVER
Net Sales	100.0	100.0	100.0		100.0	100.0	100.0	100.0	100.0
Gross Profit	36.3	35.3	36.1		32.1	48.6	34.2	30.4	36.5
Operating Expenses	30.7	29.3	30.0		29.3	40.9	28.0	24.5	28.9
Operating Profit	5.6	5.9	6.1		2.8	7.6	6.2	5.8	7.6
All Other Expenses (net)	1.3	1.3	1.4		.8	1.6	1.6	1.6	1.4
Profit Before Taxes	4.4	4.6	4.7		2.0	6.1	4.6	4.2	6.1

RATIOS

	4/1/92-3/31/93	4/1/93-3/31/94	4/1/94-3/31/95	0-1MM	1-3MM	3-5MM	5-10MM	10-25MM	25MM & OVER
Current	2.4 / 1.6 / 1.3	3.1 / 2.0 / 1.5	2.3 / 1.6 / 1.2		1.9 / 1.5 / 1.2	3.6 / 1.8 / 1.5	1.8 / 1.3 / 1.1	2.5 / 1.7 / 1.3	2.4 / 1.7 / 1.4
Quick	1.5 / .9 / .7	1.8 / 1.1 / .7	1.4 / .9 / .6		1.1 / .9 / .5	2.1 / 1.0 / .6	1.0 / .9 / .5	1.3 / .7 / .5	1.5 / 1.0 / .8
Sales/Receivables	45 8.2 / 54 6.7 / 70 5.2	45 8.1 / 55 6.6 / 64 5.7	47 7.7 / 58 6.3 / 70 5.2		41 8.8 / 59 6.2 / 70 5.2	31 11.8 / 52 7.0 / 58 6.3	52 7.0 / 61 6.0 / 72 5.1	40 9.1 / 54 6.8 / 58 6.3	55 6.6 / 60 6.1 / 72 5.1
Cost of Sales/Inventory	43 8.5 / 81 4.5 / 118 3.1	51 7.2 / 76 4.8 / 104 3.5	47 7.8 / 87 4.2 / 135 2.7		4 82.4 / 45 8.1 / 107 3.4	52 7.0 / 135 2.7 / 166 2.2	45 8.1 / 91 4.0 / 174 2.1	45 8.2 / 87 4.2 / 130 2.8	65 5.6 / 81 4.5 / 101 3.6
Cost of Sales/Payables	22 16.8 / 33 11.2 / 58 6.3	20 18.4 / 33 10.9 / 49 7.5	31 11.9 / 41 8.8 / 54 6.7		32 11.4 / 41 9.0 / 53 6.9	13 28.6 / 32 11.4 / 62 5.9	41 9.0 / 51 7.2 / 59 6.2	23 15.9 / 36 10.2 / 45 8.2	32 11.3 / 38 9.5 / 59 6.2
Sales/Working Capital	4.2 / 7.2 / 13.4	4.5 / 6.6 / 10.2	5.1 / 7.8 / 17.7		6.5 / 10.5 / 20.4	3.5 / 8.4 / 14.7	5.5 / 11.0 / 26.4	4.9 / 6.9 / 27.9	4.5 / 5.9 / 11.9
EBIT/Interest	(64) 7.8 / 3.4 / 1.4	(72) 10.7 / 4.1 / 1.7	(89) 9.7 / 4.4 / 1.9		6.2 / 2.7 / 1.4		(18) 9.3 / 4.4 / 1.3	(15) 10.6 / 4.1 / 2.3	(22) 10.6 / 6.3 / 3.0
Net Profit + Depr., Dep., Amort./Cur. Mat. L/T/D	(33) 12.3 / 2.2 / .9	(33) 8.0 / 2.5 / .9	(36) 7.5 / 3.3 / 1.2					(10) 53.3 / 7.5 / 2.3	
Fixed/Worth	.3 / .4 / .9	.2 / .5 / 1.0	.3 / .5 / .9		.3 / .5 / 1.5	.3 / .5 / .7	.3 / .6 / 1.5	.3 / .5 / .9	.4 / .6 / 1.0
Debt/Worth	.7 / 1.5 / 3.2	.6 / 1.3 / 2.8	.9 / 1.7 / 3.8		1.6 / 2.9 / 5.9	.8 / 1.4 / 2.2	1.3 / 2.1 / 6.0	.7 / 1.9 / 3.7	.8 / 1.2 / 4.3
% Profit Before Taxes/Tangible Net Worth	(66) 35.7 / 12.9 / .7	(78) 35.2 / 16.1 / 4.3	(95) 43.0 / 25.0 / 9.3		(19) 35.6 / 16.4 / 5.1	47.5 / 24.1 / 9.2	(20) 43.2 / 24.9 / 8.7	41.0 / 29.8 / 17.1	(22) 50.5 / 30.0 / 12.3
% Profit Before Taxes/Total Assets	13.6 / 4.5 / .4	13.8 / 7.2 / 1.4	17.8 / 7.7 / 2.5		12.5 / 5.0 / 1.4	24.8 / 8.8 / 3.6	12.6 / 6.9 / .9	18.0 / 10.5 / 4.5	20.4 / 9.4 / 4.1
Sales/Net Fixed Assets	25.1 / 11.9 / 5.7	29.5 / 11.4 / 7.0	21.5 / 11.0 / 6.1		28.4 / 19.2 / 9.8	29.9 / 12.9 / 6.8	23.2 / 13.4 / 5.6	19.4 / 8.8 / 6.4	10.9 / 7.1 / 4.8
Sales/Total Assets	2.6 / 2.0 / 1.4	2.5 / 2.1 / 1.6	2.7 / 2.0 / 1.4		3.0 / 2.6 / 2.0	3.0 / 1.9 / 1.4	2.6 / 1.9 / 1.3	2.7 / 2.0 / 1.6	2.1 / 1.7 / 1.1
% Depr., Dep., Amort./Sales	(54) 1.0 / 2.1 / 3.2	(65) 1.0 / 1.6 / 3.3	(77) 1.0 / 1.7 / 3.0		.6 / 1.1 / 1.6		(17) 1.2 / 1.6 / 2.9	(12) 1.3 / 2.2 / 3.6	(13) 2.0 / 2.8 / 3.5
% Officers', Directors', Owners' Comp/Sales	(17) 3.9 / 6.1 / 7.8	(16) 3.6 / 6.7 / 15.9	(22) 2.0 / 4.3 / 10.3						
Net Sales ($)	1907963M	2900520M	2641945M	4770M	44275M	37570M	153480M	241629M	2160221M
Total Assets ($)	1378987M	2098460M	1871786M	2356M	20337M	19123M	95737M	131511M	1602722M

M = $ thousand   MM = $ million
See Pages 1 through 15 for Explanation of Ratios and Data

Current Data Sorted By Assets							Comparative Historical Data	
	2	2	3			# Postretirement Benefits		
						Type of Statement	25	22
1		13	7	3	2	Unqualified	25	22
3	10	8				Reviewed	16	23
5	11	7	1			Compiled	28	12
						Tax Returns	3	1
3	9	4	4	1	1	Other	10	14
	33 (4/1-9/30/94)		60 (10/1/94-3/31/95)				4/1/90-3/31/91	4/1/91-3/31/92
0-500M	500M-2MM	2-10MM	10-50MM	50-100MM	100-250MM		ALL	ALL
12	30	32	12	4	3	**NUMBER OF STATEMENTS**	82	72
%	%	%	%	%	%	**ASSETS**	%	%
3.9	7.2	5.9	7.1			Cash & Equivalents	6.3	5.9
32.4	28.7	34.8	28.4			Trade Receivables - (net)	30.9	25.8
43.5	34.6	33.7	37.2			Inventory	36.5	41.3
1.5	2.2	2.7	1.0			All Other Current	1.8	1.8
81.3	72.8	77.2	73.8			Total Current	75.5	74.7
13.2	17.8	13.8	18.9			Fixed Assets (net)	16.1	17.4
.5	.9	4.3	2.8			Intangibles (net)	2.1	1.6
5.0	8.5	4.8	4.5			All Other Non-Current	6.3	6.3
100.0	100.0	100.0	100.0			Total	100.0	100.0
						LIABILITIES		
5.1	8.3	20.0	6.4			Notes Payable-Short Term	13.7	14.2
5.0	2.5	1.9	1.5			Cur. Mat. -L/T/D	2.5	3.0
26.2	23.3	16.9	15.6			Trade Payables	18.0	15.9
.4	1.1	.3	.1			Income Taxes Payable	.7	.2
8.8	10.6	8.7	7.2			All Other Current	9.4	8.8
45.4	45.8	47.7	30.8			Total Current	44.3	42.1
19.8	10.0	7.3	10.9			Long Term Debt	13.4	11.6
.0	.6	.7	.3			Deferred Taxes	.3	.4
7.0	2.8	4.2	4.0			All Other-Non-Current	2.2	2.7
27.9	40.8	40.1	53.9			Net Worth	39.7	43.2
100.0	100.0	100.0	100.0			Total Liabilities & Net Worth	100.0	100.0
						INCOME DATA		
100.0	100.0	100.0	100.0			Net Sales	100.0	100.0
35.5	36.3	35.3	36.4			Gross Profit	32.7	31.7
31.1	31.6	28.9	34.0			Operating Expenses	28.6	28.3
4.4	4.6	6.4	2.4			Operating Profit	4.1	3.5
.3	.7	1.9	.6			All Other Expenses (net)	1.3	1.5
4.1	4.0	4.6	1.8			Profit Before Taxes	2.8	2.0
						RATIOS		
3.9	2.5	2.6	4.6			Current	2.4	3.1
1.7	1.7	1.6	2.6				1.7	1.8
1.1	1.1	1.2	1.7				1.3	1.4
1.2	1.5	1.2	2.2			Quick	1.3	1.4
.6	.8	.8	1.0				.8	.8
.5	.3	.5	.8				.6	.5
26 13.8	15 24.3	46 7.9	43 8.5			Sales/Receivables	36 10.2	32 11.3
38 9.5	45 8.2	55 6.6	55 6.6				47 7.7	47 7.7
55 6.6	59 6.2	63 5.8	69 5.3				65 5.6	56 6.5
36 10.1	36 10.1	56 6.5	74 4.9			Cost of Sales/Inventory	58 6.3	64 5.7
70 5.2	78 4.7	76 4.8	111 3.3				79 4.6	101 3.6
146 2.5	111 3.3	114 3.2	183 2.0				152 2.4	146 2.5
20 18.5	26 14.0	23 15.7	22 16.5			Cost of Sales/Payables	21 17.5	22 16.3
41 9.0	46 7.9	38 9.7	24 15.3				42 8.6	33 10.9
72 5.1	78 4.7	58 6.3	47 7.8				59 6.2	46 8.0
5.1	5.4	5.1	3.1			Sales/Working Capital	4.2	4.6
7.5	9.1	8.8	4.4				7.4	6.8
186.2	66.5	21.6	7.8				17.2	13.0
	14.0	16.7	275.8			EBIT/Interest	5.9	5.3
	(23) 4.1	(29) 2.5	(10) 4.4				(76) 2.8	(66) 2.0
	1.6	1.5	-1.0				1.5	1.2
	7.0	7.5				Net Profit + Depr., Dep., Amort./Cur. Mat. L /T/D	9.5	5.0
	(13) 4.9	(13) 4.0					(37) 3.0	(35) 2.6
	1.9	2.2					1.2	.6
.0	.1	.2	.1			Fixed/Worth	.2	.2
.2	.4	.4	.3				.3	.3
NM	.9	.7	.8				.9	.8
.7	.7	.8	.3			Debt/Worth	.6	.5
4.0	1.3	1.8	1.0				1.7	1.4
NM	2.9	4.8	3.0				4.2	3.4
	37.3	60.4	58.7			% Profit Before Taxes/Tangible Net Worth	32.0	21.6
	(29) 24.1	(29) 22.6	(10) 12.7				(76) 14.2	(68) 12.3
	7.1	8.4	-9.6				1.3	1.0
17.5	16.2	27.6	14.1			% Profit Before Taxes/Total Assets	12.0	7.5
8.1	9.5	7.5	7.8				4.8	3.9
1.1	2.9	1.7	.1				.5	.3
535.4	55.2	44.4	17.1			Sales/Net Fixed Assets	50.6	38.4
34.6	26.7	20.9	8.5				19.1	16.6
10.4	12.0	11.9	6.5				10.3	6.9
4.2	3.7	2.8	2.2			Sales/Total Assets	2.8	2.8
3.2	2.8	2.4	1.8				2.2	2.2
2.2	2.0	1.9	1.3				1.6	1.6
	.5	.6	.8			% Depr., Dep., Amort./Sales	.6	.6
	(27) .8	(28) 1.2	(11) 1.8				(72) 1.3	(63) 1.3
	1.9	2.0	2.6				2.1	2.5
	2.4	2.4				% Officers', Directors', Owners' Comp/Sales	3.2	3.0
	(21) 3.7	(15) 5.2					(39) 3.9	(33) 4.2
	6.3	6.3					8.8	6.5
9501M	98528M	309331M	555382M	435055M	741981M	Net Sales ($)	1041121M	1137764M
3321M	35362M	141286M	294104M	297629M	469185M	Total Assets ($)	702916M	725041M

M = $ thousand   MM = $ million
See Pages 1 through 15 for Explanation of Ratios and Data

Comparative Historical Data			# Postretirement Benefits	Current Data Sorted By Sales					
3	2	7		2	1		4		
			Type of Statement						
13	17	26	Unqualified	1		1	7	7	10
25	17	21	Reviewed	3	4	4	6	4	
20	18	24	Compiled	4	6	7	6		1
	2		Tax Returns						
17	17	22	Other	3	5	3	2	4	5
4/1/92-3/31/93 ALL	4/1/93-3/31/94 ALL	4/1/94-3/31/95 ALL		**33 (4/1-9/30/94)**		**60 (10/1/94-3/31/95)**			
				0-1MM	1-3MM	3-5MM	5-10MM	10-25MM	25MM & OVER
75	71	93	**NUMBER OF STATEMENTS**	11	15	15	21	15	16
%	%	%	**ASSETS**	%	%	%	%	%	%
4.8	5.8	6.1	Cash & Equivalents	4.8	3.8	12.3	5.7	5.1	4.7
31.7	33.1	31.1	Trade Receivables - (net)	31.8	26.0	32.9	31.8	36.8	27.6
38.3	36.2	34.8	Inventory	41.0	35.7	31.3	37.0	33.2	31.8
1.7	1.6	2.2	All Other Current	.9	4.8	.6	.7	4.9	1.9
76.5	76.7	74.3	Total Current	78.5	70.3	77.1	75.2	79.9	66.1
15.5	15.9	16.8	Fixed Assets (net)	16.4	21.0	12.2	13.5	16.1	22.4
1.8	2.5	2.8	Intangibles (net)	.5	1.5	1.6	5.4	.4	5.4
6.2	4.9	6.1	All Other Non-Current	4.6	7.2	9.0	5.9	3.5	6.1
100.0	100.0	100.0	Total	100.0	100.0	100.0	100.0	100.0	100.0
			LIABILITIES						
14.8	14.6	11.7	Notes Payable-Short Term	5.2	10.3	7.1	14.1	24.0	7.3
2.0	2.3	2.5	Cur. Mat.-L /T/D	5.4	3.9	.9	1.9	1.7	2.0
16.7	16.3	19.8	Trade Payables	25.2	22.3	23.8	16.0	22.5	12.3
.5	1.4	.6	Income Taxes Payable	.9	.5	.8	.7	.3	.3
11.2	11.7	9.1	All Other Current	9.1	7.5	13.3	9.5	7.3	7.8
45.1	46.3	43.6	Total Current	45.9	44.4	45.9	42.2	55.7	29.7
8.1	10.1	11.2	Long Term Debt	25.3	10.2	6.6	8.7	5.7	15.2
.2	.5	.6	Deferred Taxes	.2	.1	1.0	.5	.7	.9
4.6	2.7	4.3	All Other-Non-Current	5.5	6.6	.5	4.1	3.6	5.5
42.0	40.3	40.3	Net Worth	23.0	38.6	46.0	44.5	34.3	48.7
100.0	100.0	100.0	Total Liabilities & Net Worth	100.0	100.0	100.0	100.0	100.0	100.0
			INCOME DATA						
100.0	100.0	100.0	Net Sales	100.0	100.0	100.0	100.0	100.0	100.0
33.4	36.3	35.7	Gross Profit	35.4	35.8	37.0	37.5	33.7	34.0
28.6	32.0	30.4	Operating Expenses	29.8	33.6	31.4	30.1	29.5	28.4
4.8	4.3	5.3	Operating Profit	5.7	2.3	5.6	7.4	4.2	5.6
.9	1.1	1.2	All Other Expenses (net)	.6	1.1	.4	2.1	1.1	1.1
3.9	3.2	4.1	Profit Before Taxes	5.1	1.2	5.1	5.3	3.0	4.5
			RATIOS						
2.5 / 1.7 / 1.4	2.6 / 1.7 / 1.2	2.8 / 1.7 / 1.2	Current	4.1 / 1.7 / 1.0	2.5 / 1.8 / 1.0	2.8 / 1.8 / 1.1	3.1 / 1.6 / 1.2	1.7 / 1.3 / 1.1	3.3 / 2.3 / 1.6
1.1 / .9 / .5	1.4 / .8 / .5	1.3 / .8 / .6	Quick	1.2 / .6 / .4	1.2 / .6 / .3	2.0 / 1.2 / .6	1.8 / .9 / .5	.9 / .7 / .5	1.6 / 1.0 / .8
38 9.7 / 48 7.6 / 61 6.0	41 8.8 / 53 6.9 / 66 5.5	38 9.5 / 52 7.0 / 61 6.0	Sales/Receivables	30 12.3 / 40 9.1 / 64 5.7	22 16.9 / 41 9.0 / 59 6.2	30 12.2 / 51 7.2 / 60 6.1	42 8.6 / 55 6.6 / 59 6.2	45 8.1 / 54 6.8 / 83 4.4	43 8.5 / 55 6.6 / 72 5.1
59 6.2 / 89 4.1 / 126 2.9	57 6.4 / 83 4.4 / 122 3.0	53 6.9 / 78 4.7 / 118 3.1	Cost of Sales/Inventory	33 11.0 / 85 4.3 / 192 1.9	41 8.9 / 76 4.8 / 130 2.8	30 12.3 / 70 5.2 / 94 3.9	66 5.5 / 78 4.7 / 101 3.6	42 8.6 / 91 4.0 / 146 2.5	58 6.3 / 89 4.1 / 104 3.5
23 15.7 / 36 10.1 / 52 7.0	20 17.9 / 33 11.1 / 52 7.0	24 15.3 / 39 9.3 / 63 5.8	Cost of Sales/Payables	23 15.9 / 47 7.7 / 78 4.7	24 15.0 / 49 7.5 / 81 4.5	26 13.8 / 45 8.1 / 70 5.2	20 18.2 / 37 9.8 / 51 7.1	30 12.3 / 40 9.2 / 60 6.1	23 15.9 / 32 11.4 / 52 6.1
4.6 / 7.9 / 13.9	5.0 / 7.9 / 22.2	4.9 / 8.3 / 20.7	Sales/Working Capital	4.6 / 5.7 / 243.0	5.3 / 9.3 / 171.7	5.4 / 7.4 / 31.5	4.8 / 6.6 / 20.3	5.1 / 11.6 / 31.5	3.7 / 5.3 / 9.3
(70) 8.9 / 4.2 / 1.9	(63) 10.7 / 3.0 / 1.4	(78) 12.7 / 3.4 / 1.6	EBIT/Interest		(13) 5.8 / 1.9 / -.4	(11) 19.9 / 4.5 / 1.9	(18) 22.7 / 2.7 / 1.2	(14) 11.4 / 2.9 / 1.4	(14) 7.3 / 5.6 / 3.1
(27) 5.7 / 2.6 / 1.4	(22) 8.1 / 2.9 / .9	(38) 7.7 / 3.6 / 1.6	Net Profit + Depr., Dep., Amort./Cur. Mat. L/T/D				(11) 10.3 / 4.9 / 1.6		
.2 / .3 / .6	.2 / .4 / .8	.1 / .4 / .9	Fixed/Worth	.0 / .3 / -11.8	.2 / .6 / .9	.1 / .1 / .8	.2 / .3 / .6	.3 / .4 / .8	.2 / .5 / 1.3
.6 / 1.3 / 3.2	.6 / 1.9 / 5.2	.7 / 1.7 / 4.2	Debt/Worth	1.4 / 7.2 / -39.0	.6 / 2.3 / 5.4	.6 / 1.1 / 2.0	.6 / 1.4 / 3.9	1.4 / 2.3 / 5.2	.5 / 1.5 / 3.2
(72) 46.2 / 20.6 / 5.5	(67) 53.2 / 18.4 / 7.7	(84) 56.4 / 24.0 / 8.4	% Profit Before Taxes/Tangible Net Worth		(14) 34.7 / 10.7 / -33.9	35.9 / 24.7 / 7.3	(18) 64.7 / 47.9 / 8.6	(14) 32.1 / 17.2 / 7.8	(15) 57.8 / 29.4 / 10.0
15.0 / 6.8 / 1.7	12.7 / 6.8 / 1.2	16.5 / 8.0 / 2.3	% Profit Before Taxes/Total Assets	12.7 / 9.1 / .0	12.5 / 4.5 / -4.8	16.5 / 11.1 / 3.6	30.0 / 11.5 / 2.0	14.4 / 5.8 / 1.4	14.1 / 8.2 / 4.1
37.8 / 21.8 / 8.6	36.7 / 19.5 / 9.3	47.7 / 18.0 / 9.1	Sales/Net Fixed Assets	615.0 / 23.5 / 8.6	48.3 / 21.0 / 11.1	66.7 / 30.1 / 16.3	45.9 / 22.3 / 11.7	44.6 / 16.0 / 8.1	17.1 / 10.4 / 5.8
2.9 / 2.2 / 1.8	2.8 / 2.2 / 1.9	3.0 / 2.3 / 1.8	Sales/Total Assets	4.2 / 2.5 / 1.8	3.2 / 2.2 / 1.9	4.0 / 2.8 / 2.3	3.0 / 2.8 / 2.0	2.8 / 2.3 / 1.4	2.0 / 1.7 / 1.4
(65) .6 / 1.1 / 2.0	(62) .6 / 1.2 / 2.2	(76) .6 / .9 / 1.9	% Depr., Dep., Amort./Sales	(12)	(12) .6 / 1.2 / 2.8	(12) .4 / .8 / .9	(20) .6 / .8 / 1.6	(13) .5 / 1.9 / 2.5	(12) .8 / 1.5 / 2.1
(39) 3.2 / 5.3 / 7.5	(39) 3.1 / 5.6 / 10.0	(50) 2.5 / 4.8 / 6.8	% Officers', Directors', Owners' Comp/Sales	(11)	(11) 2.8 / 5.1 / 8.5	(11) 2.3 / 3.5 / 6.3	2.5 / 5.0 / 7.3		
693748M / 338490M	811649M / 415325M	2149778M / 1240887M	Net Sales ($) / Total Assets ($)	7334M / 3483M	29765M / 13324M	58314M / 23736M	142991M / 64259M	227557M / 114887M	1683817M / 1021198M

M = $ thousand   MM = $ million
See Pages 1 through 15 for Explanation of Ratios and Data

Current Data Sorted By Assets **Comparative Historical Data**

	0-500M	500M-2MM	2-10MM	10-50MM	50-100MM	100-250MM		90-91 ALL	91-92 ALL
# Postretirement Benefits				1					
Type of Statement									
Unqualified	1	3	11	10	10	8		22	44
Reviewed	1	3	4	1				9	4
Compiled	1	1	2					4	1
Tax Returns									
Other		2	6	4	2	3		10	14
		25 (4/1-9/30/94)		48 (10/1/94-3/31/95)				4/1/90-3/31/91	4/1/91-3/31/92
NUMBER OF STATEMENTS	3	9	23	15	12	11		45	63
	%	%	%	%	%	%	**ASSETS**	%	%
			11.6	15.5	19.4	29.1	Cash & Equivalents	8.7	17.6
			33.4	29.6	21.9	21.1	Trade Receivables - (net)	30.1	26.5
			28.3	20.1	25.2	18.8	Inventory	29.5	25.7
			2.4	1.1	12.4	5.8	All Other Current	2.8	2.8
			75.7	66.3	78.9	74.8	Total Current	71.0	72.6
			13.4	22.5	12.7	12.6	Fixed Assets (net)	17.4	16.7
			4.1	.1	2.6	5.2	Intangibles (net)	2.4	3.9
			6.8	11.0	5.9	7.4	All Other Non-Current	9.2	6.8
			100.0	100.0	100.0	100.0	Total	100.0	100.0
							LIABILITIES		
			8.2	5.7	1.7	.8	Notes Payable-Short Term	10.3	5.5
			3.5	3.6	2.8	1.5	Cur. Mat. -L/T/D	4.2	2.8
			13.9	11.1	8.9	11.2	Trade Payables	11.9	9.6
			1.0	.8	.6	.6	Income Taxes Payable	.6	.6
			11.9	13.1	9.6	16.5	All Other Current	15.9	14.0
			38.5	34.3	23.6	30.5	Total Current	42.9	32.4
			6.7	7.7	2.4	13.0	Long Term Debt	12.8	9.1
			.3	.1	1.1	.5	Deferred Taxes	.6	.5
			2.1	2.4	1.2	7.6	All Other-Non-Current	2.5	2.0
			52.4	55.6	71.7	48.4	Net Worth	41.2	55.9
			100.0	100.0	100.0	100.0	Total Liabilities & Net Worth	100.0	100.0
							INCOME DATA		
			100.0	100.0	100.0	100.0	Net Sales	100.0	100.0
			45.1	42.8	37.8	47.4	Gross Profit	39.9	44.4
			42.0	34.0	27.7	39.8	Operating Expenses	35.8	41.5
			3.1	8.8	10.1	7.6	Operating Profit	4.0	2.9
			.3	3.4	-.4	-.2	All Other Expenses (net)	1.3	1.5
			2.9	5.4	10.4	7.9	Profit Before Taxes	2.8	1.4
							RATIOS		
			2.3	4.5	5.8	4.7		2.9	4.3
			2.0	2.4	3.8	2.6	Current	1.9	2.5
			1.5	1.3	2.5	1.4		1.2	1.5
			1.7	2.9	3.1	4.3		1.7	2.9
			1.4	1.5	2.4	1.5	Quick	1.0	1.3
			.8	.8	.8	.7		.6	.8
			50 7.3	54 6.8	49 7.4	58 6.3		50 7.3	42 8.7
			62 5.9	79 4.6	58 6.3	66 5.5	Sales/Receivables	61 6.0	63 5.8
			91 4.0	101 3.6	72 5.1	87 4.2		76 4.8	87 4.2
			63 5.8	45 8.2	81 4.5	79 4.6		73 5.0	83 4.4
			76 4.8	73 5.0	111 3.3	91 4.0	Cost of Sales/Inventory	104 3.5	104 3.5
			174 2.1	118 3.1	159 2.3	122 3.0		146 2.5	159 2.3
			33 11.2	28 13.2	31 11.9	47 7.8		27 13.5	25 14.8
			45 8.1	39 9.4	38 9.7	55 6.6	Cost of Sales/Payables	39 9.4	37 9.8
			62 5.9	68 5.4	61 6.0	85 4.3		57 6.4	64 5.7
			3.5	2.2	1.7	1.3		3.4	2.1
			4.7	3.2	2.4	2.5	Sales/Working Capital	6.1	4.1
			9.0	16.6	2.9	5.9		22.9	8.1
			8.9	(10) 42.1	(11) 152.0			(42) 7.0	(55) 13.1
			(20) 5.2	2.8	25.3		EBIT/Interest	2.6	2.7
			2.5	.9	4.9			1.3	-.5
			5.7					(24) 6.9	(34) 7.4
			(17) 3.5				Net Profit + Depr., Dep., Amort./Cur. Mat. L /T/D	3.4	2.5
			2.8					.4	.2
			.1	.1	.1	.1		.2	.2
			.2	.3	.2	.3	Fixed/Worth	.4	.3
			.4	.7	.2	.5		.8	.6
			.7	.3	.2	.8		.7	.4
			.9	.9	.4	1.4	Debt/Worth	1.5	.8
			2.3	1.6	.6	2.2		2.7	1.9
			37.8	20.1	21.8	24.7	% Profit Before Taxes/Tangible Net Worth	(40) 37.1	(62) 23.7
			15.6	15.9	18.2	17.6		14.0	8.7
			6.6	.2	10.0	8.8		6.7	-5.5
			17.1	13.3	15.3	14.2	% Profit Before Taxes/Total Assets	14.0	10.7
			6.9	6.9	11.7	7.2		5.4	4.2
			3.4	.1	7.0	4.0		1.9	-3.5
			43.5	18.1	18.3	15.4	Sales/Net Fixed Assets	31.4	25.1
			16.9	7.1	10.2	8.8		12.0	9.2
			10.9	5.6	6.4	6.8		5.9	5.7
			2.3	2.0	1.5	1.5	Sales/Total Assets	2.4	2.1
			2.0	1.4	1.3	1.2		1.7	1.4
			1.2	.9	1.0	.8		1.2	1.1
			1.0	2.7	1.5		% Depr., Dep., Amort./Sales	(38) 1.1	(51) 1.9
			(11) 1.5	(10) 2.9	2.8			1.9	3.5
			3.2	4.6	3.5			3.5	4.5
							% Officers', Directors', Owners' Comp/Sales	(10) 1.6	
								5.3	
								15.9	
	1653M	37865M	203354M	461027M	1101225M	2041763M	Net Sales ($)	1617995M	2756008M
	638M	11930M	112346M	334403M	862849M	1807726M	Total Assets ($)	1245923M	2396738M

M = $ thousand   MM = $ million
See Pages 1 through 15 for Explanation of Ratios and Data

Comparative Historical Data   **Current Data Sorted By Sales**

	1	5	# Postretirement Benefits / Type of Statement				1	1	3
49	32	43	Unqualified	1	1	2	9	6	24
10	8	9	Reviewed		4	1	2	2	
4	2	4	Compiled	1	1			2	
			Tax Returns					2	
			Other	1		1	4	4	7

20 4/1/92-3/31/93 ALL	20 4/1/93-3/31/94 ALL	17 4/1/94-3/31/95 ALL		25 (4/1-9/30/94) 0-1MM	1-3MM	3-5MM	48 (10/1/94-3/31/95) 5-10MM	10-25MM	25MM & OVER
83	62	73	**NUMBER OF STATEMENTS**	2	7	4	15	14	31
%	%	%	**ASSETS**	%	%	%	%	%	%
15.3	12.7	17.1	Cash & Equivalents				15.6	7.8	23.5
27.7	29.2	28.8	Trade Receivables - (net)				34.5	31.1	25.0
24.9	26.7	23.6	Inventory				26.1	24.8	21.4
2.0	2.5	4.2	All Other Current				3.2	3.0	6.1
69.9	71.2	73.7	Total Current				79.4	66.6	76.1
18.7	18.0	15.8	Fixed Assets (net)				10.8	24.4	13.7
3.3	4.5	2.7	Intangibles (net)				2.2	1.8	2.7
8.0	6.2	7.8	All Other Non-Current				7.6	7.2	7.6
100.0	100.0	100.0	Total				100.0	100.0	100.0
			LIABILITIES						
7.6	7.0	5.1	Notes Payable-Short Term				5.8	8.5	2.5
3.2	3.1	3.2	Cur. Mat.-L /T/D				2.5	7.6	1.7
12.2	14.4	12.2	Trade Payables				11.4	18.2	10.1
1.2	1.6	.9	Income Taxes Payable				2.7	.0	.8
12.8	11.8	12.8	All Other Current				14.3	9.5	13.5
36.9	37.9	34.3	Total Current				36.7	43.8	28.6
8.7	8.5	7.9	Long Term Debt				6.3	10.3	6.5
.5	.5	.5	Deferred Taxes				.6	.0	.7
3.3	3.8	3.0	All Other-Non-Current				2.7	.7	4.2
50.6	49.3	54.3	Net Worth				53.7	45.2	60.0
100.0	100.0	100.0	Total Liabilities & Net Worth				100.0	100.0	100.0
			INCOME DATA						
100.0	100.0	100.0	Net Sales				100.0	100.0	100.0
46.1	42.7	43.1	Gross Profit				50.1	27.7	45.3
41.8	36.9	36.5	Operating Expenses				44.2	26.7	34.9
4.4	5.8	6.6	Operating Profit				6.0	1.0	10.4
.7	.5	.9	All Other Expenses (net)				.3	1.2	1.0
3.6	5.3	5.8	Profit Before Taxes				5.7	-.2	9.4
			RATIOS						
3.4	3.1	4.0	Current				2.3	2.8	4.6
2.1	2.2	2.3					2.0	1.3	3.0
1.4	1.4	1.5					1.9	1.2	1.9
2.7	2.1	2.5	Quick				1.7	1.5	3.3
1.2	1.2	1.4					1.4	.8	2.1
.7	.7	.8					.9	.7	1.1
40 9.2	40 9.1	50 7.3	Sales/Receivables				50 7.3	39 9.4	53 6.9
54 6.7	62 5.9	62 5.9					81 4.5	59 6.2	65 5.6
79 4.6	79 4.6	89 4.1					107 3.4	91 4.0	87 4.2
65 5.6	65 5.6	62 5.9	Cost of Sales/Inventory				68 5.4	29 12.6	73 5.0
99 3.7	99 3.7	81 4.5					76 4.8	57 6.4	91 4.0
140 2.6	130 2.8	146 2.5					166 2.2	85 4.3	122 3.0
30 12.3	29 12.8	32 11.5	Cost of Sales/Payables				32 11.4	24 15.3	37 10.0
44 8.3	42 8.7	45 8.1					45 8.1	39 9.3	47 7.8
69 5.3	65 5.6	69 5.3					60 6.1	64 5.7	74 4.9
2.4	2.8	2.3	Sales/Working Capital				3.5	2.7	1.6
4.9	4.9	4.5					4.6	13.8	2.6
13.2	12.1	8.6					5.8	94.4	4.5
(74) 26.2	(56) 22.7	(58) 28.6	EBIT/Interest			(12)	40.9	(13) 7.2	(24) 71.4
5.0	10.4	5.2					4.9	3.5	12.7
1.5	2.3	2.1					3.8	1.5	3.7
(35) 21.8	(29) 36.9	(32) 33.2	Net Profit + Depr., Dep., Amort./Cur. Mat. L/T/D			(10)	5.4		(12) 81.6
3.4	4.3	5.1					3.4		23.7
.9	.8	2.8					2.8		7.3
.2	.2	.1	Fixed/Worth				.1	.1	.1
.3	.3	.2					.2	.5	.2
.8	.6	.5					.3	1.2	.4
.4	.5	.4	Debt/Worth				.7	.6	.3
.9	.9	.9					.9	1.4	.7
2.5	1.8	1.6					1.2	2.7	1.4
(79) 38.0	(59) 38.8	32.2	% Profit Before Taxes/Tangible Net Worth				45.7	21.5	24.7
13.8	23.8	17.6					25.0	9.0	17.6
.9	8.4	6.8					11.5	-6.4	13.1
15.3	17.8	15.3	% Profit Before Taxes/Total Assets				21.7	7.5	15.2
8.3	13.2	8.1					8.1	3.4	10.8
.2	3.3	3.3					6.5	-.4	5.3
22.0	26.5	22.5	Sales/Net Fixed Assets				34.0	28.5	18.4
10.1	11.9	12.1					16.9	6.9	10.8
5.6	6.3	6.8					11.5	5.4	6.6
2.4	2.3	2.2	Sales/Total Assets				2.3	2.9	1.6
1.7	1.7	1.6					1.9	2.2	1.3
1.1	1.3	1.1					1.1	.9	1.0
(72) 1.3	(54) 1.2	(58) 1.3	% Depr., Dep., Amort./Sales			(14)	1.2	(13) .6	(22) 1.8
3.0	2.4	2.9					2.9	1.1	2.9
5.0	3.9	4.5					3.3	4.6	4.7
(14) 1.9	(15) 3.7		% Officers', Directors', Owners' Comp/Sales						
4.2	4.8								
9.5	8.4								
3534802M	3282650M	3846887M	Net Sales ($)	623M	14110M	15931M	113091M	222594M	3480538M
2725565M	2366232M	3129892M	Total Assets ($)	479M	7922M	8940M	71093M	196413M	2845045M

M = $ thousand   MM = $ million
See Pages 1 through 15 for Explanation of Ratios and Data

Current Data Sorted By Assets | Comparative Historical Data

Type of Statement

# Postretirement Benefits / Type of Statement	0-500M	500M-2MM	2-10MM	10-50MM	50-100MM	100-250MM	4/1/90-3/31/91 ALL	4/1/91-3/31/92 ALL
# Postretirement Benefits	1	2	4	3		4		
Unqualified	1	4	15	10	5	3	42	40
Reviewed	7	16	10	2	1		28	31
Compiled	1	12	2	1			18	28
Tax Returns			1				1	1
Other	4	5	10	11	1	3	19	19

Date ranges: **35 (4/1-9/30/94)** · **89 (10/1/94-3/31/95)**

	0-500M	500M-2MM	2-10MM	10-50MM	50-100MM	100-250MM		4/1/90-3/31/91 ALL	4/1/91-3/31/92 ALL
NUMBER OF STATEMENTS	13	37	38	24	6	6		108	119
ASSETS	%	%	%	%	%	%		%	%
Cash & Equivalents	10.5	6.4	5.9	4.4				7.2	6.9
Trade Receivables - (net)	34.6	34.4	35.0	24.4				32.5	29.9
Inventory	24.7	38.1	29.0	32.2				27.7	29.6
All Other Current	4.2	1.1	2.4	1.4				2.6	2.6
Total Current	74.0	80.0	72.3	62.5				70.0	69.0
Fixed Assets (net)	21.7	12.5	18.7	31.0				20.9	22.6
Intangibles (net)	.5	2.2	2.4	1.7				3.0	2.6
All Other Non-Current	3.8	5.3	6.6	4.8				6.1	5.8
Total	100.0	100.0	100.0	100.0				100.0	100.0
LIABILITIES									
Notes Payable-Short Term	5.7	10.7	9.5	6.4				13.0	8.5
Cur. Mat. -L/T/D	3.2	3.7	2.6	3.0				3.1	3.1
Trade Payables	13.1	22.6	17.5	15.0				16.1	15.3
Income Taxes Payable	.2	.3	.5	.2				.5	.5
All Other Current	18.0	15.3	13.3	12.4				11.3	11.9
Total Current	40.2	52.7	43.5	37.0				43.9	39.3
Long Term Debt	9.3	9.3	13.4	16.8				11.4	13.7
Deferred Taxes	1.5	.2	.6	.8				.5	.7
All Other-Non-Current	2.3	3.9	2.6	.9				5.1	3.8
Net Worth	46.8	34.0	39.9	44.6				39.1	42.6
Total Liabilities & Net Worth	100.0	100.0	100.0	100.0				100.0	100.0
INCOME DATA									
Net Sales	100.0	100.0	100.0	100.0				100.0	100.0
Gross Profit	39.3	30.5	25.3	26.9				30.3	29.5
Operating Expenses	34.5	27.1	22.2	19.8				25.4	25.4
Operating Profit	4.8	3.4	3.2	7.1				4.9	4.1
All Other Expenses (net)	2.3	.7	.4	1.1				1.7	1.4
Profit Before Taxes	2.6	2.7	2.7	6.0				3.2	2.7
RATIOS									
Current	3.6	1.8	2.3	2.3				2.6	2.7
	2.0	1.5	1.7	1.9				1.7	1.9
	1.4	1.2	1.3	1.3				1.3	1.3
Quick	2.2	1.0	1.6	1.2				1.5	1.4
	1.3	.8	1.0	.8				.9	1.0
	1.0	.5	.6	.5				.6	.6
Sales/Receivables	28 12.9	31 11.8	33 11.0	41 9.0				35 10.3	37 9.8
	39 9.4	42 8.6	49 7.4	49 7.5				48 7.6	47 7.7
	62 5.9	60 6.1	61 6.0	54 6.7				63 5.8	58 6.3
Cost of Sales/Inventory	9 41.2	35 10.4	32 11.4	68 5.4				34 10.7	41 8.9
	48 7.6	63 5.8	60 6.1	76 4.8				60 6.1	69 5.3
	96 3.8	126 2.9	83 4.4	104 3.5				101 3.6	96 3.8
Cost of Sales/Payables	6 64.3	17 22.1	18 20.7	22 16.6				19 19.2	20 18.7
	19 18.8	41 8.8	28 13.1	32 11.3				29 12.7	30 12.1
	41 8.9	58 6.3	39 9.3	61 6.0				49 7.5	42 8.6
Sales/Working Capital	4.5	6.2	5.8	4.9				4.7	4.7
	8.5	13.8	10.7	6.2				7.4	7.5
	19.9	26.4	20.6	22.0				18.9	15.5
EBIT/Interest	(11) 19.8	(32) 9.1	(34) 14.7	(23) 10.9				(100) 6.8	(116) 7.6
	6.2	4.0	6.0	6.7				3.9	2.9
	2.3	1.9	1.5	2.8				1.4	1.3
Net Profit + Depr., Dep., Amort./Cur. Mat. L./T/D		(16) 7.3	(15) 4.4	(17) 9.3				(57) 10.0	(67) 11.2
		2.4	2.3	3.4				2.8	2.7
		.3	1.1	1.8				1.4	1.3
Fixed/Worth	.1	.2	.2	.3				.3	.2
	.3	.4	.4	.6				.5	.5
	.8	.8	1.3	1.3				1.1	1.1
Debt/Worth	.6	1.1	.5	.6				.7	.7
	1.2	2.2	1.6	1.5				1.5	1.3
	1.8	4.5	4.2	2.3				3.7	3.1
% Profit Before Taxes/Tangible Net Worth	(12) 101.7	(32) 53.8	(35) 62.3	59.2				(99) 39.7	(112) 30.0
	19.0	18.0	24.1	21.1				16.2	11.5
	6.0	5.4	9.9	10.7				4.8	3.2
% Profit Before Taxes/Total Assets	28.8	12.6	18.7	16.0				14.7	13.3
	16.7	7.7	9.5	9.7				6.3	4.4
	2.4	1.6	3.8	4.1				1.2	1.2
Sales/Net Fixed Assets	76.6	57.9	38.1	10.2				28.5	29.0
	19.5	30.0	16.8	6.2				14.7	11.4
	12.3	13.1	7.8	3.7				6.8	5.8
Sales/Total Assets	4.3	3.6	3.1	2.2				3.2	3.1
	3.1	2.9	2.5	1.8				2.2	2.2
	2.4	1.9	2.2	1.5				1.7	1.7
% Depr., Dep., Amort./Sales	(11) 1.3	(32) .5	(35) .8	(20) 1.2				(94) .8	(110) 1.0
	2.2	1.1	1.2	1.9				1.4	1.8
	3.8	1.8	2.2	2.6				2.2	2.7
% Officers', Directors', Owners' Comp/Sales		(19) 2.9	(11) .9					(36) 2.4	(39) 2.5
		4.0	2.3					4.3	4.0
		9.6	6.5					8.4	5.6
Net Sales ($)	13777M	131021M	466652M	1087717M	750243M	1406568M		2730358M	2989011M
Total Assets ($)	4111M	43926M	179505M	570129M	487422M	953410M		1790627M	1841041M

M = $ thousand   MM = $ million
See Pages 1 through 15 for Explanation of Ratios and Data

Comparative Historical Data — Current Data Sorted By Sales

	3	11	14	# Postretirement Benefits / Type of Statement		2	2	1	2	7
	42	45	37	Unqualified		4	1	4	10	18
	25	35	29	Reviewed	2	7	6	8	5	1
	27	25	22	Compiled	4	9	3	5	1	
	4	3	2	Tax Returns	1		1			
	24	31	34	Other	2	4	3	2	11	12
	4/1/92-3/31/93 ALL	4/1/93-3/31/94 ALL	4/1/94-3/31/95 ALL		35 (4/1-9/30/94) 0-1MM	1-3MM	3-5MM	89 (10/1/94-3/31/95) 5-10MM	10-25MM	25MM & OVER
	122	139	124	NUMBER OF STATEMENTS	9	24	14	19	27	31
	%	%	%	ASSETS	%	%	%	%	%	%
	7.3	5.8	6.8	Cash & Equivalents		6.8	8.8	5.1	7.2	6.1
	30.5	28.3	31.3	Trade Receivables - (net)		28.0	32.0	40.5	33.5	24.6
	28.3	30.2	31.2	Inventory		35.7	33.7	28.5	29.0	29.3
	3.6	3.2	2.1	All Other Current		1.3	.9	3.0	1.7	1.9
	69.7	67.5	71.4	Total Current		71.8	75.4	77.2	71.4	62.0
	20.9	24.3	19.9	Fixed Assets (net)		19.6	13.6	15.9	22.5	25.6
	1.8	2.7	2.8	Intangibles (net)		2.1	2.5	2.1	1.9	5.1
	7.5	5.5	5.9	All Other Non-Current		6.5	8.4	4.8	4.2	7.3
	100.0	100.0	100.0	Total		100.0	100.0	100.0	100.0	100.0
				LIABILITIES						
	10.6	12.2	8.1	Notes Payable-Short Term		9.8	9.9	11.0	6.5	5.5
	3.6	3.9	3.0	Cur. Mat.-L /T/D		3.2	5.4	2.5	2.8	2.7
	16.6	15.8	17.5	Trade Payables		17.3	18.4	21.6	17.8	15.7
	.3	1.1	.4	Income Taxes Payable		.3	.4	.6	.3	.6
	11.0	12.7	14.2	All Other Current		13.7	21.4	13.4	15.0	11.3
	42.1	45.7	43.1	Total Current		44.3	55.5	49.1	42.4	35.8
	12.1	13.9	12.3	Long Term Debt		15.0	5.3	9.4	15.3	14.4
	1.0	.7	.6	Deferred Taxes		.2	.7	.1	.6	1.0
	2.7	3.0	2.9	All Other-Non-Current		4.7	1.4	3.4	1.4	2.4
	42.1	36.7	41.1	Net Worth		35.8	37.1	37.9	40.3	46.4
	100.0	100.0	100.0	Total Liabilities & Net Worth		100.0	100.0	100.0	100.0	100.0
				INCOME DATA						
	100.0	100.0	100.0	Net Sales		100.0	100.0	100.0	100.0	100.0
	29.1	27.6	28.7	Gross Profit		32.1	30.8	25.3	26.2	26.0
	24.7	23.6	24.2	Operating Expenses		28.4	28.8	25.0	20.4	19.2
	4.4	3.9	4.5	Operating Profit		3.7	2.0	.3	5.8	6.8
	.8	1.2	.9	All Other Expenses (net)		1.4	-.6	.4	.6	1.0
	3.6	2.7	3.7	Profit Before Taxes		2.3	2.6	-.1	5.2	5.8
				RATIOS						
	2.4 / 1.8 / 1.3	2.3 / 1.6 / 1.2	2.3 / 1.7 / 1.3	Current		2.4 / 1.6 / 1.3	1.7 / 1.4 / 1.1	1.9 / 1.4 / 1.2	2.8 / 1.9 / 1.3	2.3 / 1.9 / 1.5
	1.3 / 1.0 / .6	1.1 / .8 / .5	1.3 / 1.0 / .6	Quick		1.2 / .8 / .7	1.0 / .6 / .5	1.5 / .8 / .7	1.6 / 1.0 / .7	1.1 / 1.0 / .6
	37 10.0 / 49 7.5 / 61 6.0	31 11.6 / 46 8.0 / 60 6.1	33 10.9 / 48 7.6 / 58 6.3	Sales/Receivables	29 12.6 / 41 8.9 / 49 7.4	26 13.8 / 36 10.1 / 60 6.1	37 9.9 / 45 8.1 / 59 6.2	41 9.0 / 49 7.4 / 54 6.8	38 9.6 / 54 6.8 / 58 6.3	
	30 12.1 / 66 5.5 / 107 3.4	38 9.6 / 68 5.4 / 96 3.8	40 9.2 / 64 5.7 / 96 3.8	Cost of Sales/Inventory	30 12.3 / 54 6.8 / 130 2.8	37 9.9 / 63 5.8 / 118 3.1	33 11.1 / 46 8.0 / 68 5.4	40 9.2 / 60 6.1 / 87 4.2	61 6.0 / 74 4.9 / 99 3.7	
	21 17.0 / 31 11.8 / 49 7.5	18 20.4 / 31 11.7 / 44 8.3	18 20.2 / 31 11.7 / 51 7.2	Cost of Sales/Payables	14 26.1 / 29 12.6 / 54 6.7	14 25.7 / 28 13.2 / 73 5.0	16 23.4 / 28 13.0 / 47 7.8	19 19.4 / 28 12.9 / 38 9.7	24 14.9 / 35 10.4 / 60 6.1	
	4.7 / 7.0 / 17.6	5.4 / 9.8 / 26.5	5.2 / 9.2 / 20.4	Sales/Working Capital		7.4 / 10.4 / 21.7	6.3 / 16.0 / 67.2	6.1 / 13.1 / 24.9	5.3 / 8.4 / 16.2	4.9 / 6.0 / 13.8
	(110) 8.3 / 3.8 / 1.8	(125) 7.3 / 2.7 / 1.2	(110) 12.6 / 5.6 / 2.3	EBIT/Interest	(21) 9.3 / 3.8 / 1.5	(12) 15.7 / 3.9 / 2.9	(16) 13.4 / 3.2 / -.9	(25) 15.8 / 6.2 / 2.6	(29) 11.8 / 6.7 / 2.8	
	(71) 7.9 / 2.9 / 1.6	(60) 5.5 / 2.3 / 1.2	(58) 7.3 / 3.2 / 1.6	Net Profit + Depr., Dep., Amort./Cur. Mat. L/T/D					(24) 13.4 / 3.6 / 1.9	
	.2 / .4 / .8	.3 / .7 / 2.0	.2 / .5 / .9	Fixed/Worth		.2 / .4 / 1.9	.1 / .6 / 1.6	.2 / .4 / .7	.2 / .4 / 1.2	.3 / .7 / .9
	.7 / 1.2 / 2.7	.8 / 2.0 / 4.5	.7 / 1.6 / 3.3	Debt/Worth		.9 / 1.7 / 4.7	.9 / 1.6 / 11.4	1.0 / 2.2 / 3.5	.6 / 1.3 / 4.0	.7 / 1.4 / 2.1
	(114) 32.6 / 16.9 / 5.8	(126) 40.0 / 16.0 / 4.6	(115) 55.0 / 21.5 / 9.6	% Profit Before Taxes/Tangible Net Worth	(20) 59.4 / 19.1 / 5.4	(12) 20.9 / 13.2 / 9.8	(18) 65.3 / 28.7 / -1.7	(25) 47.4 / 24.1 / 14.6	65.6 / 25.4 / 11.0	
	13.9 / 6.7 / 1.9	13.1 / 4.6 / .8	16.0 / 8.9 / 2.7	% Profit Before Taxes/Total Assets		18.9 / 8.3 / 1.3	8.4 / 5.8 / 2.1	18.6 / 8.2 / .3	15.2 / 11.3 / 7.3	19.7 / 9.7 / 4.6
	32.7 / 14.1 / 6.4	24.2 / 11.3 / 5.4	42.1 / 14.2 / 6.9	Sales/Net Fixed Assets		53.3 / 19.1 / 9.4	78.9 / 26.6 / 12.4	45.5 / 24.1 / 8.0	40.4 / 14.9 / 6.6	11.6 / 7.3 / 5.4
	3.0 / 2.3 / 1.6	3.0 / 2.3 / 1.7	3.2 / 2.4 / 1.7	Sales/Total Assets		3.7 / 2.8 / 1.6	3.3 / 2.8 / 1.8	4.0 / 3.0 / 2.3	3.1 / 2.6 / 2.0	2.3 / 1.8 / 1.5
	(111) .9 / 1.4 / 2.6	(125) 1.0 / 1.8 / 2.8	(108) .8 / 1.5 / 2.3	% Depr., Dep., Amort./Sales	(20) .8 / 1.5 / 3.7	(15) .5 / 1.1 / 1.9	(22) .8 / 1.2 / 2.1	(29) .7 / 1.2 / 2.2	1.5 / 2.1 / 2.5	
	(39) 2.7 / 5.4 / 8.9	(40) 2.0 / 3.7 / 7.1	(41) 2.5 / 4.0 / 8.2	% Officers', Directors', Owners' Comp/Sales	(12) 3.4 / 7.0 / 10.9					
	2560011M / 1380636M	3814127M / 2095337M	3855978M / 2238503M	Net Sales ($) / Total Assets ($)	6500M / 4101M	50111M / 21249M	53347M / 25415M	142154M / 50208M	438328M / 203569M	3165538M / 1933961M

M = $ thousand   MM = $ million
See Pages 1 through 15 for Explanation of Ratios and Data

Current Data Sorted By Assets | **Comparative Historical Data**

	0-500M	500M-2MM	2-10MM	10-50MM	50-100MM	100-250MM		4/1/90-3/31/91 ALL	4/1/91-3/31/92 ALL
	1	6	7	4	1	4	# Postretirement Benefits		
							Type of Statement		
		7	32	17	6	14	Unqualified	61	46
1		14	12	2		1	Reviewed	26	26
6		5	2	1			Compiled	21	25
		1	1				Tax Returns		
2		18	21	12	3	1	Other	28	34
	57 (4/1-9/30/94)			122 (10/1/94-3/31/95)					
	9	45	68	32	9	16	NUMBER OF STATEMENTS	136	131
	%	%	%	%	%	%	ASSETS	%	%
		6.2	5.6	4.7		5.6	Cash & Equivalents	7.7	7.3
		30.5	23.5	24.1		25.0	Trade Receivables - (net)	26.4	25.0
		34.2	35.2	35.8		27.5	Inventory	33.4	34.3
		2.1	2.8	3.0		5.2	All Other Current	2.8	2.3
		73.0	67.1	67.6		63.3	Total Current	70.3	68.8
		19.0	21.0	22.5		19.8	Fixed Assets (net)	22.8	23.1
		1.8	2.3	3.5		4.2	Intangibles (net)	1.4	1.9
		6.2	9.6	6.4		12.8	All Other Non-Current	5.5	6.2
		100.0	100.0	100.0		100.0	Total	100.0	100.0
							LIABILITIES		
		9.0	10.7	10.1		10.8	Notes Payable-Short Term	14.3	13.9
		3.8	3.5	3.2			Cur. Mat. -L/T/D	3.8	4.3
		16.8	15.0	14.9		12.0	Trade Payables	14.1	14.2
		.5	.3	1.5		.4	Income Taxes Payable	.7	.7
		10.8	10.5	9.3		16.2	All Other Current	9.3	10.5
		40.9	39.9	39.0		40.4	Total Current	42.1	43.5
		14.7	13.0	14.5		10.7	Long Term Debt	15.9	14.6
		.6	.7	1.1		1.6	Deferred Taxes	.8	.5
		3.2	4.8	3.2		7.3	All Other-Non-Current	2.6	2.5
		40.6	41.6	42.2		40.1	Net Worth	38.6	38.9
		100.0	100.0	100.0		100.0	Total Liabilities & Net Worth	100.0	100.0
							INCOME DATA		
		100.0	100.0	100.0		100.0	Net Sales	100.0	100.0
		31.0	27.0	25.6		23.7	Gross Profit	26.6	27.4
		27.3	24.4	20.4		16.9	Operating Expenses	22.0	24.5
		3.7	2.6	5.2		6.8	Operating Profit	4.7	2.9
		.6	1.0	1.3		1.4	All Other Expenses (net)	1.8	1.5
		3.1	1.6	3.9		5.5	Profit Before Taxes	2.9	1.4
							RATIOS		
		2.8	2.8	2.5		2.1		2.6	2.3
		1.8	1.6	1.7		1.6	Current	1.6	1.7
		1.3	1.2	1.3		1.2		1.2	1.3
		1.4	1.3	1.3		1.1		1.3	1.3
		.9	.7	.9		.8	Quick	.7	.7
		.6	.4	.4		.6		.5	.5

0-500M		500M-2MM		2-10MM		10-50MM		50-100MM	100-250MM		Comparative		
	25	14.7	34	10.8	36	10.2		47	7.8	Sales/Receivables	33	11.0	34	10.6
	41	8.9	45	8.1	50	7.3		54	6.8		46	8.0	48	7.6
	60	6.1	65	5.6	60	6.1		74	4.9		64	5.7	64	5.7
	29	12.6	60	6.1	70	5.2		55	6.6	Cost of Sales/Inventory	43	8.4	51	7.1
	91	4.0	91	4.0	99	3.7		79	4.6		94	3.9	101	3.6
	130	2.8	130	2.8	159	2.3		122	3.0		130	2.8	146	2.5
	13	27.4	21	17.2	26	14.2		21	17.6	Cost of Sales/Payables	18	20.4	20	18.1
	35	10.4	40	9.1	41	9.0		32	11.5		30	12.3	33	11.0
	52	7.0	56	6.5	55	6.6		51	7.2		44	8.3	48	7.6

	0-500M	500M-2MM	2-10MM	10-50MM	50-100MM	100-250MM		Comp 90-91	Comp 91-92
		4.2	4.4	3.6		3.8	Sales/Working Capital	4.2	4.1
		8.8	7.7	7.0		8.2		7.2	7.2
		22.9	14.7	11.5		12.8		20.4	16.2
		7.2	13.6	7.0		26.1	EBIT/Interest	5.7	5.1
	(41)	3.5	(60) 2.7	(30) 4.2		(15) 4.4		(123) 1.9	(118) 2.0
		1.8	1.3	1.8		1.8		.9	1.0
		8.9	6.0	10.5			Net Profit + Depr., Dep.,	4.0	5.4
	(23)	2.3	(24) 2.0	(20) 3.7			Amort./Cur. Mat. L /T/D	(82) 1.8	(72) 1.6
		1.0	.9	1.0				.5	.9
		.2	.3	.3		.3	Fixed/Worth	.3	.3
		.4	.6	.5		.4		.6	.6
		1.1	1.1	1.4		1.1		1.1	1.2
		.8	.6	.7		.7	Debt/Worth	.9	.8
		1.4	1.6	1.3		1.4		1.9	1.8
		6.3	3.9	3.8		7.6		3.7	3.4
		49.6	29.2	31.9		31.4	% Profit Before Taxes/Tangible	31.4	23.1
	(42)	22.4	(60) 15.0	(31) 20.9		(15) 20.3	Net Worth	(128) 12.6	(122) 8.4
		3.9	4.5	4.8		13.4		.6	.5
		18.5	13.9	10.5		12.0	% Profit Before Taxes/Total	12.1	8.8
		6.7	5.4	6.5		7.5	Assets	4.1	3.6
		1.2	.6	2.1		3.6		.1	.1
		41.1	24.0	13.7		11.6	Sales/Net Fixed Assets	21.2	19.8
		15.3	11.9	7.9		7.9		9.2	8.3
		6.4	5.8	5.6		4.7		5.2	4.8
		3.1	2.3	2.2		1.7	Sales/Total Assets	2.6	2.4
		2.3	1.8	1.7		1.4		1.9	1.7
		1.9	1.2	1.3		1.2		1.4	1.4
		.7	1.0	1.2		1.6	% Depr., Dep., Amort./Sales	1.1	1.2
	(43)	1.4	(63) 1.7	(29) 2.2		(14) 1.9		(125) 2.0	(118) 2.4
		3.0		3.4	3.1		2.5		3.3	4.0
		3.9	1.5				% Officers', Directors',	2.1	2.3
	(19)	5.6	(16) 3.0				Owners' Comp/Sales	(35) 4.1	(35) 3.6
		10.1	7.2					7.5	6.0
	8218M	149007M	627991M	1249193M	936009M	3362755M	Net Sales ($)	2596486M	3337942M
	2191M	58794M	347401M	713557M	616509M	2366418M	Total Assets ($)	1794269M	2578098M

M = $ thousand   MM = $ million
See Pages 1 through 15 for Explanation of Ratios and Data

Comparative Historical Data				Current Data Sorted By Sales					
2	8	23	# Postretirement Benefits / Type of Statement	2	2	3	4	3	9
55	49	76	Unqualified	1	2	8	15	17	33
30	28	30	Reviewed	1	7	5	11	4	2
30	16	14	Compiled	5	3	2	1	3	
		2	Tax Returns		1	1			
38	28	57	Other	1	14	9	12	8	13
4/1/92-3/31/93 ALL	4/1/93-3/31/94 ALL	4/1/94-3/31/95 ALL		57 (4/1-9/30/94)			122 (10/1/94-3/31/95)		
153	121	179	NUMBER OF STATEMENTS	0-1MM 8	1-3MM 27	3-5MM 25	5-10MM 39	10-25MM 32	25MM & OVER 48
%	%	%	**ASSETS**	%	%	%	%	%	%
7.7	6.6	5.7	Cash & Equivalents		6.4	10.2	4.0	4.9	5.2
22.5	24.3	25.5	Trade Receivables - (net)		24.5	27.4	25.4	23.9	25.1
34.3	34.1	34.8	Inventory		39.8	28.7	32.4	39.0	34.2
2.7	3.8	2.9	All Other Current		1.0	2.1	3.2	4.7	3.4
67.3	68.9	68.9	Total Current		71.6	68.3	65.0	72.5	67.9
23.2	23.2	20.7	Fixed Assets (net)		19.6	21.7	20.1	20.8	21.0
2.1	1.8	2.6	Intangibles (net)		1.2	2.7	2.7	2.5	3.2
7.4	6.1	7.8	All Other Non-Current		7.6	7.3	12.3	4.2	7.9
100.0	100.0	100.0	Total		100.0	100.0	100.0	100.0	100.0
			LIABILITIES						
10.1	9.4	10.2	Notes Payable-Short Term		10.3	7.4	8.3	11.6	11.4
3.8	3.3	3.4	Cur. Mat.-L /T/D		3.8	2.2	5.1	2.2	2.7
11.6	13.3	14.9	Trade Payables		12.5	16.4	16.1	16.5	13.5
.5	1.0	.6	Income Taxes Payable		.3	.1	.6	.3	1.2
8.8	11.5	11.7	All Other Current		11.7	12.4	10.0	9.6	12.2
34.7	38.5	40.8	Total Current		38.6	38.5	40.2	40.2	41.0
13.5	14.2	13.1	Long Term Debt		13.6	10.9	17.8	10.2	11.7
.5	.9	.7	Deferred Taxes		.5	.6	.9	.9	.9
3.8	3.3	4.0	All Other-Non-Current		3.8	2.1	3.1	6.3	3.5
47.4	43.1	41.4	Net Worth		41.5	47.9	38.0	42.5	42.9
100.0	100.0	100.0	Total Liabilities & Net Worth		100.0	100.0	100.0	100.0	100.0
			INCOME DATA						
100.0	100.0	100.0	Net Sales		100.0	100.0	100.0	100.0	100.0
28.9	27.1	27.7	Gross Profit		31.3	33.8	26.3	24.0	24.6
25.5	23.0	23.7	Operating Expenses		28.3	30.8	23.3	20.9	18.5
3.4	4.1	4.0	Operating Profit		3.0	3.0	3.0	3.0	6.1
.7	.9	.9	All Other Expenses (net)		1.1	.6	1.2	.6	1.0
2.7	3.2	3.1	Profit Before Taxes		1.9	2.5	1.8	2.4	5.0
			RATIOS						
3.1	2.9	2.7	Current		3.4	3.6	2.7	2.8	2.5
2.1	1.9	1.7			1.8	1.9	1.6	1.9	1.6
1.4	1.3	1.2			1.2	1.2	1.2	1.3	1.4
1.5	1.4	1.3	Quick		1.4	2.4	1.2	1.3	1.2
.8	.8	.8			.7	1.2	.8	.8	.8
.5	.5	.5			.4	.6	.4	.4	.5
30 12.2	31 11.9	34 10.7	Sales/Receivables	20 18.6	37 9.8	34 10.8	30 12.0	42 8.6	
46 7.9	44 8.3	46 8.0		38 9.7	46 8.0	45 8.1	41 9.0	51 7.2	
59 6.2	60 6.1	60 6.1		54 6.8	60 6.1	66 5.5	53 6.9	60 6.1	
51 7.2	53 6.9	56 6.5	Cost of Sales/Inventory	24 15.2	40 9.1	56 6.5	50 7.3	65 5.6	
96 3.8	91 4.0	96 3.8		94 3.9	99 3.7	81 4.5	114 3.2	94 3.9	
146 2.5	135 2.7	140 2.6		166 2.2	130 2.8	111 3.3	152 2.4	122 3.0	
18 20.8	16 22.7	20 18.2	Cost of Sales/Payables	12 29.3	19 19.7	19 19.1	21 17.2	25 14.7	
29 12.8	29 12.6	38 9.7		31 11.6	42 8.7	38 9.7	41 8.9	33 10.9	
41 8.9	43 8.4	54 6.7		49 7.5	57 6.4	58 6.3	59 6.2	51 7.1	
3.4	3.9	4.2	Sales/Working Capital		3.6	3.9	6.2	4.4	4.0
5.2	6.0	7.5			6.6	7.8	9.1	6.9	7.3
11.4	15.6	13.7			33.5	19.3	15.0	11.2	10.1
(130) 7.4	(106) 9.3	(163) 8.9	EBIT/Interest	(24) 7.3	(22) 6.8	(37) 12.4	(29) 15.3	(45) 8.2	
2.3	3.3	3.6		3.5	3.0	2.6	4.4	5.0	
1.0	1.6	1.6		1.4	.2	1.6	1.8	2.1	
(78) 4.9	(57) 4.6	(84) 7.7	Net Profit + Depr., Dep., Amort./Cur. Mat. L/T/D	(10) 16.2	(10) 10.0	(18) 5.2	(14) 8.6	(29) 13.6	
1.8	2.1	2.8		1.3	2.4	1.5	5.8	4.3	
.8	.7	1.0		-.7	.7	.9	2.4	1.6	
.3	.3	.2	Fixed/Worth		.2	.2	.1	.3	.3
.5	.5	.5			.4	.5	.5	.5	.5
.8	1.0	1.0			2.1	1.0	1.1	.9	.8
.5	.7	.7	Debt/Worth		.5	.3	.7	.7	.8
1.2	1.3	1.5			1.3	1.1	1.7	1.8	1.3
2.6	3.7	4.0			11.3	3.2	3.3	4.6	3.8
(146) 21.7	(112) 28.4	(164) 34.0	% Profit Before Taxes/Tangible Net Worth	(24) 46.4	(23) 23.8	(34) 34.1	(30) 29.9	(47) 34.1	
11.3	15.0	20.7		23.7	12.7	18.0	20.2	23.0	
.2	5.2	6.8		2.2	.5	6.5	8.1	10.3	
10.8	11.1	13.0	% Profit Before Taxes/Total Assets		12.2	16.5	14.3	14.4	12.7
4.8	5.8	6.3			5.1	5.8	5.4	6.0	8.4
.1	1.5	1.6			.3	-.1	1.4	3.2	3.6
17.6	17.6	24.4	Sales/Net Fixed Assets		43.7	40.9	28.1	21.8	12.4
8.6	9.5	10.7			12.6	10.7	12.6	12.8	9.2
4.8	5.6	5.6			6.4	4.8	6.7	6.1	5.8
2.2	2.5	2.4	Sales/Total Assets		2.5	2.4	2.6	2.8	2.0
1.8	1.9	1.9			2.2	1.7	2.1	1.9	1.7
1.3	1.4	1.3			1.4	1.1	1.2	1.4	1.4
(139) 1.1	(114) 1.2	(163) 1.0	% Depr., Dep., Amort./Sales	(23) 1.2	(24) .9	(38) .8	(28) .7	(43) 1.2	
2.0	1.9	1.9		2.2	1.6	1.6	1.8	1.9	
3.4	3.0	3.2		3.2	4.4	3.1	3.2	2.6	
(46) 2.1	(41) 2.9	(43) 2.3	% Officers', Directors', Owners' Comp/Sales	(11) 4.1	(15) 2.3				
4.0	3.8	4.1		6.1	3.8				
6.4	7.9	8.0		10.1	7.8				
3763273M	3787954M	6333173M	Net Sales ($)	4045M	55393M	98151M	274820M	488636M	5412128M
2656910M	2434325M	4104870M	Total Assets ($)	3240M	29184M	61467M	167684M	283513M	3559782M

M = $ thousand   MM = $ million
See Pages 1 through 15 for Explanation of Ratios and Data

Current Data Sorted By Assets   **Comparative Historical Data**

Postretirement Benefits — Type of Statement

0-500M	500M-2MM	2-10MM	10-50MM	50-100MM	100-250MM		ALL 4/1/90-3/31/91	ALL 4/1/91-3/31/92
1	2	7	1			Unqualified	27	30
	3	17	11			Reviewed	24	30
	11	22	3			Compiled	30	28
3	11	7				Tax Returns	1	1
3 / 2	8	9	6			Other	13	11

Time-period statement counts: 36 (4/1-9/30/94); 80 (10/1/94-3/31/95)

0-500M	500M-2MM	2-10MM	10-50MM	50-100MM	100-250MM		ALL 4/1/90-3/31/91	ALL 4/1/91-3/31/92
8	33	55	20			**NUMBER OF STATEMENTS**	95	100
%	%	%	%	%	%	**ASSETS**	%	%
	9.3	8.8	8.6			Cash & Equivalents	8.6	10.3
	36.0	34.3	36.6			Trade Receivables - (net)	34.1	31.2
	25.3	24.7	20.3			Inventory	22.3	22.0
	5.0	5.8	4.6			All Other Current	5.3	4.4
	75.5	73.5	70.1			Total Current	70.3	67.9
	18.2	21.1	18.7			Fixed Assets (net)	20.6	22.6
	1.7	.6	1.2			Intangibles (net)	1.7	1.3
	4.5	4.8	9.9			All Other Non-Current	7.3	8.2
	100.0	100.0	100.0			Total	100.0	100.0
						LIABILITIES		
	9.0	8.9	7.5			Notes Payable-Short Term	11.2	10.2
	2.1	4.5	1.9			Cur. Mat. -L/T/D	2.6	2.4
	25.4	19.1	17.4			Trade Payables	18.1	17.9
	.6	.6	1.1			Income Taxes Payable	.8	.8
	15.5	17.1	15.2			All Other Current	15.9	13.2
	52.6	50.1	43.1			Total Current	48.6	44.4
	9.7	9.4	10.7			Long Term Debt	12.7	10.6
	.3	.3	1.2			Deferred Taxes	.4	.5
	6.5	2.3	4.6			All Other-Non-Current	1.3	3.2
	30.9	37.9	40.4			Net Worth	37.0	41.4
	100.0	100.0	100.0			Total Liabilities & Net Worth	100.0	100.0
						INCOME DATA		
	100.0	100.0	100.0			Net Sales	100.0	100.0
	32.1	29.5	24.9			Gross Profit	29.7	30.0
	28.6	22.9	20.5			Operating Expenses	25.6	26.0
	3.5	6.6	4.4			Operating Profit	4.1	3.9
	.4	1.0	.8			All Other Expenses (net)	.9	.9
	3.1	5.6	3.5			Profit Before Taxes	3.3	3.0
						RATIOS		
	2.6	2.1	2.6				2.2	2.6
	1.6	1.4	1.9			Current	1.5	1.5
	1.1	1.2	1.2				1.1	1.2
	1.2	1.4	1.5				1.5	1.8
	1.0	.8	1.3			Quick	.9	.9
	.7	.6	.8				.6	.5
	35 10.3	42 8.6	54 6.8				38 9.7	35 10.5
	47 7.8	58 6.3	63 5.8			Sales/Receivables	51 7.1	47 7.7
	60 6.1	73 5.0	85 4.3				65 5.6	64 5.7
	26 14.0	30 12.2	14 25.8				19 18.9	23 16.0
	45 8.2	55 6.6	60 6.1			Cost of Sales/Inventory	47 7.7	49 7.4
	89 4.1	85 4.3	89 4.1				79 4.6	81 4.5
	26 14.0	24 15.4	29 12.7				21 17.2	21 17.8
	35 10.4	39 9.4	37 9.9			Cost of Sales/Payables	31 11.7	34 10.6
	79 4.6	55 6.6	51 7.1				53 6.9	55 6.6
	4.8	4.9	4.3				5.8	4.8
	10.4	10.5	6.7			Sales/Working Capital	11.7	9.9
	38.6	21.7	16.7				32.9	34.3
	12.5	12.3	13.3				7.0	8.2
	(30) 3.6	(46) 7.6	(17) 9.3			EBIT/Interest	(84) 3.2	(88) 3.1
	1.9	3.4	1.2				1.2	1.3
	8.3	7.9	11.2				5.5	8.1
	(16) 2.7	(26) 3.4	(15) 2.7			Net Profit + Depr., Dep., Amort./Cur. Mat. L /T/D	(54) 2.4	(45) 2.6
	1.1	2.5	.1				1.2	1.2
	.2	.2	.2				.3	.2
	.4	.5	.6			Fixed/Worth	.6	.6
	1.8	.8	.9				1.1	1.1
	1.0	.8	.5				.8	.6
	2.7	1.8	1.3			Debt/Worth	1.8	1.6
	9.1	4.0	5.1				3.5	3.4
	49.2	41.2	32.9				38.1	38.0
	(29) 27.4	(52) 20.5	(19) 20.6			% Profit Before Taxes/Tangible Net Worth	(88) 16.1	(94) 15.1
	7.5	12.5	1.0				3.0	4.5
	11.0	20.8	16.4				14.8	14.6
	5.6	8.4	10.5			% Profit Before Taxes/Total Assets	6.6	6.0
	2.4	4.8	.3				.6	1.3
	44.8	26.7	16.6				23.9	25.8
	16.7	11.7	9.4			Sales/Net Fixed Assets	13.7	11.9
	9.9	6.6	6.4				7.5	6.6
	3.2	2.7	2.4				3.0	3.1
	2.9	2.1	1.9			Sales/Total Assets	2.3	2.2
	2.1	1.6	1.2				1.8	1.6
	.8	.9	1.5				.9	.9
	1.4	(50) 1.5	(19) 1.9			% Depr., Dep., Amort./Sales	(88) 1.5	(89) 1.5
	2.2	2.5	2.6				2.3	2.7
	2.4	2.0					4.5	3.5
	(18) 4.7	(21) 2.8				% Officers', Directors', Owners' Comp/Sales	(35) 5.5	(41) 5.5
	9.5	8.5					7.3	8.0
6494M	108814M	557295M	907235M			Net Sales ($)	960913M	1016512M
1568M	40911M	268394M	463814M			Total Assets ($)	472204M	515356M

© Robert Morris Associates 1995

M = $ thousand   MM = $ million
See Pages 1 through 15 for Explanation of Ratios and Data

MANUFACTURERS—CONVEYORS & CONVEYING EQUIPMENT. SIC# 3535

	Comparative Historical Data				Current Data Sorted By Sales					
	1		11	# Postretirement Benefits	1	3	3	3		1
				Type of Statement						
	22	25	31	Unqualified			4	11	7	9
	24	17	36	Reviewed	1	4	8	7	13	3
	26	21	21	Compiled	3	5	7	5	1	
		1	3	Tax Returns	1	2				
	17	20	25	Other	3	6	1	5	6	4
	4/1/92-3/31/93 ALL	4/1/93-3/31/94 ALL	4/1/94-3/31/95 ALL		0-1MM	36 (4/1-9/30/94) 1-3MM	3-5MM	80 (10/1/94-3/31/95) 5-10MM	10-25MM	25MM & OVER
	89	84	116	**NUMBER OF STATEMENTS**	8	17	20	28	27	16
	%	%	%	**ASSETS**	%	%	%	%	%	%
	8.3	10.6	8.9	Cash & Equivalents		10.6	7.0	10.9	7.7	8.7
	34.5	33.3	35.0	Trade Receivables - (net)		37.4	35.2	32.3	39.0	38.7
	22.9	24.6	23.1	Inventory		26.7	32.3	20.9	22.8	19.5
	4.6	3.6	5.1	All Other Current		2.3	4.8	9.9	2.9	5.5
	70.3	72.1	72.1	Total Current		77.0	79.4	73.9	72.5	72.4
	21.1	20.8	21.1	Fixed Assets (net)		18.0	14.7	20.9	19.8	17.8
	1.7	1.1	1.0	Intangibles (net)		1.5	1.6	.6	.6	1.5
	6.9	6.1	5.8	All Other Non-Current		3.5	4.2	4.6	7.1	8.2
	100.0	100.0	100.0	Total		100.0	100.0	100.0	100.0	100.0
				LIABILITIES						
	8.3	8.4	9.3	Notes Payable-Short Term		8.0	11.4	8.3	12.2	3.6
	3.2	4.4	3.4	Cur. Mat.-L /T/D		1.2	2.6	5.5	2.8	1.9
	18.8	17.2	20.3	Trade Payables		23.5	24.8	20.3	18.2	18.8
	.5	2.8	.6	Income Taxes Payable		.7	.4	.6	.7	1.1
	13.6	13.5	16.6	All Other Current		15.8	20.1	16.4	14.8	17.0
	44.4	46.4	50.2	Total Current		49.2	59.2	51.1	48.8	42.5
	9.8	11.0	10.5	Long Term Debt		7.3	7.1	7.9	8.2	11.5
	.3	.3	.4	Deferred Taxes		.3	.2	.4	.5	1.0
	3.1	3.4	3.7	All Other-Non-Current		3.6	6.7	4.2	1.0	5.7
	42.4	38.9	35.1	Net Worth		39.7	26.8	36.4	41.5	39.3
	100.0	100.0	100.0	Total Liabilities & Net Worth		100.0	100.0	100.0	100.0	100.0
				INCOME DATA						
	100.0	100.0	100.0	Net Sales		100.0	100.0	100.0	100.0	100.0
	28.7	33.0	29.6	Gross Profit		34.7	29.0	29.2	26.4	26.1
	25.4	27.1	24.7	Operating Expenses		30.1	24.5	23.7	22.1	20.3
	3.3	5.9	4.9	Operating Profit		4.6	4.5	5.6	4.3	5.7
	.6	.8	.9	All Other Expenses (net)		.1	1.2	.8	.0	.9
	2.7	5.1	4.1	Profit Before Taxes		4.5	3.3	4.8	4.2	4.9
				RATIOS						
	2.5	2.6	2.4	Current		2.8	1.6	2.2	1.9	2.6
	1.5	1.6	1.5			1.7	1.3	1.5	1.4	2.2
	1.2	1.2	1.1			1.2	1.1	1.1	1.3	1.2
	1.7	1.5	1.4	Quick		1.8	1.1	1.5	1.4	1.5
	1.0	1.0	1.0			1.1	.7	.9	.8	1.3
	.7	.7	.7			.7	.5	.6	.7	.9
	40 9.2	37 9.9	39 9.4	Sales/Receivables	35 10.4	38 9.6	35 10.5	49 7.4	53 6.9	
	49 7.4	46 7.9	53 6.9		41 8.8	50 7.3	51 7.1	65 5.6	57 6.4	
	65 5.6	57 6.4	70 5.2		50 7.3	65 5.6	65 5.6	81 4.5	74 4.9	
	22 16.9	32 11.4	25 14.4	Cost of Sales/Inventory	15 24.2	32 11.4	20 18.4	33 11.1	14 25.8	
	54 6.7	57 6.4	49 7.5		56 6.5	63 5.8	38 9.6	60 6.1	53 6.9	
	83 4.4	83 4.4	87 4.2		96 3.8	140 2.6	81 4.5	79 4.6	85 4.3	
	17 21.9	17 21.8	24 15.3	Cost of Sales/Payables	17 21.9	28 12.9	21 17.2	29 12.4	26 13.9	
	32 11.5	28 13.1	37 9.9		30 12.1	37 10.0	36 10.1	43 8.5	37 9.9	
	57 6.4	49 7.4	54 6.7		62 5.9	68 5.4	60 6.1	54 6.8	46 7.9	
	5.5	5.3	4.9	Sales/Working Capital		4.5	5.7	4.9	5.0	4.9
	12.1	9.9	10.4			8.0	13.0	9.5	10.5	6.8
	22.2	23.6	27.8			32.2	33.1	42.0	18.2	19.1
	(76) 10.3	(71) 12.8	(99) 12.3	EBIT/Interest	(13) 34.5	(17) 7.0	(25) 12.0	(24) 11.7	(14) 23.4	
	4.2	5.8	6.4		5.0	3.4	5.0	8.1	10.0	
	1.5	2.1	2.2		.7	2.2	2.4	3.0	2.3	
	(41) 6.7	(39) 7.1	(59) 8.4	Net Profit + Depr., Dep., Amort./Cur. Mat. L/T/D		(10) 2.7	(16) 38.7	(13) 5.5	(11) 13.5	
	3.1	4.7	3.1			1.7	3.3	3.5	3.6	
	.9	1.1	1.6			.6	2.7	2.0	1.9	
	.3	.2	.2	Fixed/Worth		.2	.3	.3	.2	.2
	.5	.6	.5			.3	.4	.5	.5	.6
	1.0	1.1	1.1			1.5	1.6	1.4	.8	1.0
	.5	.7	.8	Debt/Worth		.7	1.2	.8	.7	.6
	1.7	1.9	2.1			1.7	4.1	1.8	1.7	1.2
	3.5	3.5	4.9			5.0	8.5	4.1	3.9	6.0
	(86) 30.1	(78) 45.6	(106) 40.6	% Profit Before Taxes/Tangible Net Worth	(16) 70.7	(18) 42.3	(25) 36.3	(26) 39.0	(15) 33.3	
	16.4	23.5	20.5		26.1	27.6	19.3	19.3	26.5	
	5.2	12.4	8.7		4.7	10.0	9.3	6.2	9.8	
	13.4	20.1	16.0	% Profit Before Taxes/Total Assets		21.2	9.3	18.4	16.5	18.2
	4.8	10.2	6.4			5.8	4.1	9.5	6.5	11.6
	1.5	4.2	3.3			1.9	3.0	2.9	3.9	5.9
	27.9	25.7	31.1	Sales/Net Fixed Assets		38.0	44.8	25.7	32.3	32.8
	15.2	12.8	13.4			15.7	18.8	10.0	11.7	12.4
	7.0	8.1	6.8			10.2	10.2	6.9	5.9	6.9
	3.1	2.9	3.0	Sales/Total Assets		4.0	2.9	3.0	2.7	2.5
	2.3	2.4	2.2			3.0	2.3	2.2	2.1	2.3
	1.8	2.0	1.6			1.7	1.8	1.6	1.7	1.8
	(77) .8	(77) .9	(108) .9	% Depr., Dep., Amort./Sales	(16) .6	1.0	(27) .9	(22) .7	.6	
	1.3	1.6	1.7		1.3	1.6	1.4	2.1	1.8	
	2.4	2.5	2.5		2.3	2.3	2.5	2.9	2.5	
	(33) 3.8	(35) 2.9	(45) 2.2	% Officers', Directors', Owners' Comp/Sales		(14) 2.7				
	6.0	4.3	4.3			4.3				
	12.1	8.2	9.0			8.3				
	1057190M	1088410M	1579838M	Net Sales ($)	3778M	34532M	78742M	195059M	417060M	850667M
	501366M	500384M	774687M	Total Assets ($)	4800M	14672M	39441M	100937M	217357M	397480M

© Robert Morris Associates 1995

M = $ thousand   MM = $ million
See Pages 1 through 15 for Explanation of Ratios and Data

Current Data Sorted By Assets   **Comparative Historical Data**

0-500M	500M-2MM	2-10MM	10-50MM	50-100MM	100-250MM	# Postretirement Benefits / Type of Statement	4/1/90-3/31/91 ALL	4/1/91-3/31/92 ALL
2			1	1	1	1		
2	3	16	18	2	8	Unqualified	43	43
1	5	4				Reviewed	13	18
2	8	2				Compiled	9	16
						Tax Returns		4
9	9	10	5		4	Other	13	18
	48 (4/1-9/30/94)		60 (10/1/94-3/31/95)					
14	25	32	23	2	12	NUMBER OF STATEMENTS	78	99
%	%	%	%	%	%	ASSETS	%	%
9.2	8.5	12.5	15.5		25.9	Cash & Equivalents	12.3	10.4
36.1	37.5	31.2	25.5		24.4	Trade Receivables - (net)	31.5	33.9
28.4	26.2	29.0	18.9		19.4	Inventory	25.1	27.4
4.7	.6	3.1	5.6		2.8	All Other Current	3.1	3.1
78.5	72.8	75.7	65.4		72.5	Total Current	71.9	74.8
12.4	19.4	15.6	16.6		17.1	Fixed Assets (net)	17.7	14.5
1.6	3.1	3.2	9.7		1.7	Intangibles (net)	4.0	4.5
7.5	4.7	5.5	8.3		8.6	All Other Non-Current	6.3	6.2
100.0	100.0	100.0	100.0		100.0	Total	100.0	100.0
						LIABILITIES		
8.6	13.2	11.6	4.4		.6	Notes Payable-Short Term	8.7	10.9
2.7	2.6	3.4	2.0		2.2	Cur. Mat. -L/T/D	2.7	3.1
20.6	24.3	17.7	11.5		9.9	Trade Payables	15.8	16.8
.1	.4	1.2	.2		.8	Income Taxes Payable	1.2	.8
20.7	10.7	12.1	13.9		14.2	All Other Current	12.0	12.2
52.7	51.2	46.0	31.8		27.6	Total Current	40.4	43.8
14.9	12.2	6.6	13.1		9.1	Long Term Debt	11.7	9.0
.0	.4	.2	1.2		.4	Deferred Taxes	1.5	.4
3.3	5.5	3.6	3.1		7.5	All Other-Non-Current	4.2	5.1
29.1	30.6	43.6	50.7		55.4	Net Worth	42.3	41.7
100.0	100.0	100.0	100.0		100.0	Total Liabilities & Net Worth	100.0	100.0
						INCOME DATA		
100.0	100.0	100.0	100.0		100.0	Net Sales	100.0	100.0
38.8	37.3	35.8	42.2		39.2	Gross Profit	39.5	42.8
39.1	33.7	34.2	38.6		37.3	Operating Expenses	36.5	39.5
-.3	3.6	1.6	3.6		1.9	Operating Profit	2.9	3.3
1.6	.4	.7	.6		2.4	All Other Expenses (net)	.8	1.5
-1.9	3.2	.9	3.0		-.5	Profit Before Taxes	2.1	1.7
						RATIOS		
2.2	2.5	2.5	3.5		4.4	Current	2.7	2.5
1.6	1.5	1.7	2.0		2.6		1.8	1.7
1.4	1.2	1.3	1.3		1.9		1.2	1.4
1.4	1.4	1.3	1.9		3.4	Quick	1.8	1.7
.9	.9	1.0	1.0		2.0		1.2	1.0
.6	.8	.7	.7		1.0		.8	.7
21 17.8	32 11.4	41 8.8	53 6.9		60 6.1	Sales/Receivables	41 9.0	42 8.6
45 8.2	42 8.6	50 7.3	72 5.1		65 5.6		54 6.7	56 6.5
61 6.0	60 6.1	74 4.9	79 4.6		76 4.8		76 4.8	79 4.6
16 23.4	15 25.0	38 9.5	46 7.9		73 5.0	Cost of Sales/Inventory	36 10.1	45 8.2
45 8.1	53 6.9	89 4.1	85 4.3		99 3.7		69 5.3	83 4.4
140 2.6	83 4.4	140 2.6	118 3.1		130 2.8		107 3.4	114 3.2
20 18.4	15 24.3	27 13.3	34 10.6		29 12.6	Cost of Sales/Payables	23 15.6	28 13.0
29 12.5	48 7.6	41 8.9	49 7.4		49 7.4		42 8.7	41 8.9
63 5.8	69 5.3	65 5.6	96 3.8		54 6.7		63 5.8	69 5.3
6.6	7.1	4.9	2.6		1.9	Sales/Working Capital	3.6	4.1
12.8	15.5	7.7	4.3		2.7		6.0	7.1
NM	40.5	14.9	10.8		4.6		16.5	15.1
(13) 8.7	(20) 18.6	(28) 10.9	(18) 9.4		(10) 25.9	EBIT/Interest	(65) 10.4	(87) 8.2
2.3	10.2	2.0	2.6		.6		2.2	2.0
-3.5	2.1	-5.3	.5		-6.0		.8	-.2
		(10) 34.0	(13) 11.3			Net Profit + Depr., Dep., Amort./Cur. Mat. L/T/D	(36) 11.1	(38) 13.0
		2.8	1.8				3.6	3.3
		-.1	1.0				1.3	.9
.1	.2	.1	.1		.1	Fixed/Worth	.2	.2
.3	.7	.4	.2		.3		.4	.3
NM	3.1	.8	1.2		.8		1.0	.7
.8	1.0	.6	.3		.3	Debt/Worth	.7	.6
1.6	2.6	1.5	1.2		.7		1.5	1.5
NM	11.1	2.2	3.9		2.1		4.0	4.7
(11) 32.5	(21) 77.5	(30) 44.5	(21) 26.9		17.6	% Profit Before Taxes/Tangible Net Worth	(70) 40.6	(90) 36.7
22.2	43.6	16.6	14.9		-2.8		20.6	15.8
2.5	24.8	-32.0	-3.3		-27.8		6.4	.6
12.5	25.0	18.3	11.6		13.5	% Profit Before Taxes/Total Assets	13.4	13.4
6.9	12.2	6.9	5.5		-2.5		7.7	5.0
-14.1	4.8	-10.4	.0		-9.3		1.1	-2.9
83.0	49.9	41.2	16.4		12.6	Sales/Net Fixed Assets	25.0	36.8
36.0	25.7	16.4	8.2		8.3		12.9	17.1
13.0	11.2	8.0	5.2		4.7		6.2	7.4
4.3	4.2	2.7	1.6		1.5	Sales/Total Assets	2.6	2.9
3.5	2.8	1.9	1.3		1.4		2.0	1.9
2.1	2.1	1.5	1.0		1.0		1.3	1.4
(10) .5	(20) .3	(25) 1.0	(17) 2.4			% Depr., Dep., Amort./Sales	(53) .9	(68) .9
1.5	1.4	1.7	4.1				2.6	2.1
2.6	2.4	3.7	5.2				4.0	3.7
	(10) 1.3					% Officers', Directors', Owners' Comp/Sales		(20) 2.2
	3.5							5.6
	6.5							9.9
16477M	89137M	357872M	753269M	247439M	2233652M	Net Sales ($)	3910447M	5701101M
4648M	27642M	158445M	581185M	179020M	1813571M	Total Assets ($)	2639217M	3885095M

M = $ thousand   MM = $ million
See Pages 1 through 15 for Explanation of Ratios and Data

Comparative Historical Data | **Current Data Sorted By Sales**

92-93 ALL	93-94 ALL	94-95 ALL	Item	0-1MM	1-3MM	3-5MM	5-10MM	10-25MM	25MM & OVER
6	3	6	# Postretirement Benefits	1	1		1		3
			Type of Statement						
56	36	49	Unqualified	1	5	1	4	15	23
8	14	10	Reviewed	1	3	2	2	2	
8	10	12	Compiled		5	4	2	1	
1		1	Tax Returns						
27	26	37	Other	5	11	3	6	6	6
4/1/92-3/31/93 ALL	4/1/93-3/31/94 ALL	4/1/94-3/31/95 ALL		48 (4/1-9/30/94)			60 (10/1/94-3/31/95)		
100	87	108	**NUMBER OF STATEMENTS**	7	24	10	14	24	29
%	%	%	**ASSETS**	%	%	%	%	%	%
13.1	13.1	13.6	Cash & Equivalents		11.3	6.9	12.0	11.4	22.4
32.3	31.6	31.1	Trade Receivables - (net)		34.6	41.5	30.1	30.3	25.6
21.9	28.5	24.8	Inventory		22.4	31.6	29.4	27.4	19.5
4.8	2.8	3.3	All Other Current		1.4	.6	3.8	4.0	4.1
72.1	76.0	72.8	Total Current		69.8	80.6	75.3	73.1	71.5
17.4	15.8	16.4	Fixed Assets (net)		19.4	14.6	16.6	15.3	15.9
4.7	3.1	4.2	Intangibles (net)		4.8	1.6	2.3	7.1	3.3
5.8	5.1	6.7	All Other Non-Current		6.1	3.2	5.8	4.5	9.4
100.0	100.0	100.0	Total		100.0	100.0	100.0	100.0	100.0
			LIABILITIES						
7.6	11.8	8.7	Notes Payable-Short Term		12.0	12.0	17.1	8.1	1.9
3.2	2.3	2.7	Cur. Mat.-L./T/D		2.4	3.2	3.5	2.7	2.1
14.1	16.3	17.2	Trade Payables		20.1	27.1	15.1	15.9	12.0
1.5	1.7	.6	Income Taxes Payable		.3	.4	.7	1.3	.5
13.0	11.8	13.5	All Other Current		14.6	10.0	10.4	13.0	14.0
39.4	43.8	42.7	Total Current		49.4	52.7	46.7	41.1	30.4
10.2	7.4	10.7	Long Term Debt		11.7	10.1	8.2	8.7	10.5
.9	.7	.5	Deferred Taxes		.4	.2	.0	.7	.8
6.3	4.0	4.5	All Other-Non-Current		6.7	2.2	7.2	1.8	5.4
43.2	44.0	41.7	Net Worth		31.8	34.7	37.9	47.7	52.9
100.0	100.0	100.0	Total Liabilities & Net Worth		100.0	100.0	100.0	100.0	100.0
			INCOME DATA						
100.0	100.0	100.0	Net Sales		100.0	100.0	100.0	100.0	100.0
42.1	37.0	38.1	Gross Profit		39.9	38.1	39.7	38.5	36.2
38.1	34.7	35.8	Operating Expenses		41.4	36.5	36.0	32.5	34.3
4.0	2.3	2.3	Operating Profit		-1.5	1.6	3.7	6.0	1.9
1.2	.7	.9	All Other Expenses (net)		.5	.6	1.8	.0	1.2
2.9	1.6	1.4	Profit Before Taxes		-2.0	1.0	1.8	6.1	.7
			RATIOS						
3.0	3.0	2.7	Current		2.8	2.2	2.5	2.5	3.8
1.9	1.9	1.8			1.5	1.6	1.9	1.6	2.4
1.2	1.3	1.3			1.0	1.4	1.2	1.3	1.6
1.9	1.9	1.6	Quick		1.6	1.1	1.3	1.4	2.7
1.2	1.0	1.0			1.0	.8	1.2	.9	1.5
.8	.7	.8			.6	.8	.5	.7	.9
44 8.3	40 9.1	41 8.9	Sales/Receivables		36 10.2	33 10.9	41 8.9	41 8.8	51 7.2
60 6.1	51 7.2	54 6.7			49 7.4	38 9.6	53 6.9	57 6.4	64 5.7
76 4.8	66 5.5	73 5.0			76 4.8	48 7.6	66 5.5	74 4.9	76 4.8
33 11.1	37 9.8	37 9.9	Cost of Sales/Inventory		21 17.4	29 12.4	15 25.1	44 8.3	49 7.5
83 4.4	78 4.7	79 4.6			61 6.0	60 6.1	66 5.5	96 3.8	81 4.5
111 3.3	135 2.7	126 2.9			122 3.0	83 4.4	135 2.7	135 2.7	122 3.0
26 14.1	23 16.2	26 14.3	Cost of Sales/Payables		23 16.2	17 21.2	15 25.1	30 12.3	26 14.0
38 9.6	37 9.9	44 8.3			49 7.4	41 9.0	38 9.7	42 8.6	43 8.4
73 5.0	58 6.3	65 5.6			70 5.2	70 5.2	85 4.3	66 5.5	54 6.8
3.5	3.7	3.7	Sales/Working Capital		5.5	8.8	4.9	4.3	2.3
7.0	8.4	7.5			11.6	14.3	7.7	7.7	3.0
15.1	18.2	16.1			NM	23.3	18.1	10.6	5.7
(88) 13.7	(70) 12.3	(91) 12.7	EBIT/Interest		(21) 15.9		(12) 10.1	(19) 16.6	(24) 16.5
3.3	3.0	3.0			2.3		1.1	5.7	1.9
1.4	-.3	-1.6			-9.2		-5.0	1.9	-3.7
(36) 21.0	(31) 17.1	(38) 15.3	Net Profit + Depr., Dep., Amort./Cur. Mat. L/T/D						(14) 50.5
3.2	2.5	3.0							7.2
1.9	.8	1.0							1.6
.2	.1	.1	Fixed/Worth			.2	.1	.2	.1
.4	.3	.4				.6	.4	.4	.2
1.1	.9	1.0				3.1	1.2	1.3	.8
.5	.4	.7	Debt/Worth			.8	.9	.6	.3
1.3	1.5	1.5				1.9	2.0	1.3	1.1
5.1	4.4	3.7				10.4	9.3	7.0	2.2
(91) 47.9	(81) 47.2	(97) 38.9	% Profit Before Taxes/Tangible Net Worth		(19) 37.8	92.2	(12) 44.5	(23) 46.5	(28) 20.1
18.0	15.6	19.0			24.3	37.6	16.1	24.4	6.6
2.6	.7	-.3			-46.7	12.0	-26.1	12.1	-13.3
15.4	15.3	14.9	% Profit Before Taxes/Total Assets		21.0	15.3	17.1	18.3	8.9
5.7	5.0	6.6			7.1	7.9	3.3	10.5	2.5
1.0	-2.2	-5.1			-12.1	4.7	-11.8	3.8	-6.7
29.4	32.7	37.3	Sales/Net Fixed Assets		37.1	98.0	51.0	41.2	17.4
10.0	15.1	14.0			14.4	30.7	22.0	14.0	9.5
6.1	8.2	7.3			8.9	11.4	7.7	6.2	4.7
2.4	3.1	2.9	Sales/Total Assets		3.2	4.4	2.9	2.6	1.6
1.6	2.1	1.8			2.2	3.7	2.3	1.8	1.4
1.2	1.4	1.3			1.5	2.9	1.4	1.3	1.1
(65) 1.2	(65) 1.0	(79) 1.2	% Depr., Dep., Amort./Sales		(18) 1.1		(12) .5	(20) 1.4	(17) 1.7
2.5	2.1	2.0			2.1		1.7	2.1	4.1
4.6	3.9	4.0			3.1		3.5	4.0	5.4
(14) 2.8	(12) 1.3	(20) 1.7	% Officers', Directors', Owners' Comp/Sales						
6.0	2.4	3.5							
9.7	5.5	5.8							
5359438M	4195764M	3697846M	Net Sales ($)	4724M	50086M	37296M	96108M	392530M	3117102M
3639799M	2718450M	2764511M	Total Assets ($)	1967M	26976M	10803M	50329M	254238M	2420198M

M = $ thousand   MM = $ million
See Pages 1 through 15 for Explanation of Ratios and Data

MANUFACTURERS—FARM MACHINERY & EQUIPMENT. SIC# 3523

Current Data Sorted By Assets | **Comparative Historical Data**

0-500M	500M-2MM	2-10MM	10-50MM	50-100MM	100-250MM		4/1/90-3/31/91 ALL	4/1/91-3/31/92 ALL
	5	3	4	1	1	# Postretirement Benefits		
						Type of Statement		
	4	23	16	3	1	Unqualified	42	50
1	12	15	3			Reviewed	21	31
8	17	9	1			Compiled	22	25
1	2					Tax Returns	1	2
2	11	14	7	2	3	Other	25	24
	51 (4/1-9/30/94)		104 (10/1/94-3/31/95)					
12	46	61	27	5	4	**NUMBER OF STATEMENTS**	111	132
%	%	%	%	%	%	**ASSETS**	%	%
11.6	10.1	5.0	6.5			Cash & Equivalents	5.8	6.1
15.4	19.5	22.3	27.6			Trade Receivables - (net)	21.9	21.5
46.7	47.7	43.6	30.3			Inventory	42.2	42.7
.9	.9	2.4	3.6			All Other Current	1.6	2.0
74.6	78.2	73.2	68.1			Total Current	71.5	72.3
18.5	15.2	19.5	23.7			Fixed Assets (net)	21.2	18.6
2.1	1.3	.8	.5			Intangibles (net)	.9	1.4
4.7	5.3	6.4	7.7			All Other Non-Current	6.4	7.7
100.0	100.0	100.0	100.0			Total	100.0	100.0
						LIABILITIES		
15.0	15.1	12.5	8.2			Notes Payable-Short Term	13.1	13.7
1.7	1.8	3.2	2.1			Cur. Mat. -L/T/D	3.2	3.4
18.4	14.1	13.8	10.3			Trade Payables	12.8	11.6
.2	.6	.5	.7			Income Taxes Payable	.8	.6
7.4	8.1	11.6	11.6			All Other Current	9.2	11.5
42.6	39.7	41.5	32.9			Total Current	39.1	40.9
8.8	10.5	13.4	12.7			Long Term Debt	16.2	12.9
.1	.2	.5	.7			Deferred Taxes	.5	.4
4.2	4.7	3.9	3.4			All Other-Non-Current	2.8	1.6
44.3	44.9	40.8	50.2			Net Worth	41.4	44.2
100.0	100.0	100.0	100.0			Total Liabilities & Net Worth	100.0	100.0
						INCOME DATA		
100.0	100.0	100.0	100.0			Net Sales	100.0	100.0
36.1	31.0	28.5	28.8			Gross Profit	29.1	29.1
30.2	25.9	21.6	22.1			Operating Expenses	22.4	25.4
5.8	5.1	6.9	6.8			Operating Profit	6.7	3.7
.1	.1	1.2	.1			All Other Expenses (net)	2.2	1.4
5.7	5.0	5.7	6.7			Profit Before Taxes	4.4	2.3
						RATIOS		
4.5	3.5	2.6	2.9				2.6	2.9
1.7	2.3	1.8	2.5			Current	1.8	1.9
1.4	1.4	1.4	1.7				1.5	1.3
1.3	1.4	.9	1.6				1.2	1.2
.6	.7	.7	1.1			Quick	.6	.6
.4	.4	.4	.6				.4	.4
5 79.4	18 20.8	27 13.7	41 8.9				22 16.4	22 16.4
18 20.6	30 12.2	42 8.7	64 5.7			Sales/Receivables	36 10.2	34 10.8
25 14.7	44 8.3	61 6.0	111 3.3				63 5.8	57 6.4
53 6.9	64 5.7	81 4.5	52 7.0				69 5.3	66 5.5
65 5.6	118 3.1	122 3.0	96 3.8			Cost of Sales/Inventory	107 3.4	114 3.2
111 3.3	192 1.9	174 2.1	174 2.1				159 2.3	174 2.1
5 66.8	10 36.4	20 18.1	19 19.7				16 22.4	14 26.7
28 12.9	25 14.8	31 11.9	26 13.9			Cost of Sales/Payables	27 13.5	24 15.0
44 8.3	47 7.7	52 7.0	49 7.4				45 8.2	43 8.5
4.8	3.6	3.7	2.2				3.4	3.2
8.8	5.4	5.9	3.6			Sales/Working Capital	6.1	6.2
18.3	9.9	11.7	6.8				11.1	12.9
	(40) 9.1	(57) 7.7	(26) 14.5				(106) 4.8	(124) 5.7
	5.0	4.3	6.2			EBIT/Interest	2.5	2.6
	2.5	1.7	2.8				1.6	.8
	(15) 8.6	(23) 5.2	(17) 7.8				(73) 7.5	(74) 4.7
	4.8	1.7	3.5			Net Profit + Depr., Dep., Amort./Cur. Mat. L./T/D	2.8	1.6
	1.9	1.3	1.7				1.2	.6
.1	.2	.2	.3				.2	.2
.2	.3	.5	.5			Fixed/Worth	.4	.4
1.0	.6	.7	.7				1.0	.8
.3	.5	.7	.4				.8	.7
1.7	1.0	1.6	.7			Debt/Worth	1.5	1.3
2.7	2.6	2.8	2.3				2.8	2.6
(10) 64.0	(43) 44.0	(60) 42.1	41.2				(108) 35.4	(127) 25.9
35.4	22.2	21.5	16.8			% Profit Before Taxes/Tangible Net Worth	20.4	12.5
13.4	7.7	10.8	6.9				6.9	-.9
23.9	16.1	16.6	14.7				14.4	10.9
17.8	8.2	9.1	9.1			% Profit Before Taxes/Total Assets	7.2	5.6
5.3	4.5	2.9	4.5				2.0	-.9
177.4	33.2	17.1	12.3				20.0	23.3
24.5	18.7	10.8	6.8			Sales/Net Fixed Assets	10.0	11.3
10.3	11.0	6.8	4.9				6.5	6.9
5.3	2.7	2.4	2.0				2.6	2.4
2.9	2.1	1.9	1.4			Sales/Total Assets	1.8	1.7
2.3	1.5	1.4	1.0				1.3	1.4
(10) .7	(41) .7	(57) 1.1	(25) 1.2				(104) 1.0	(117) 1.1
1.2	1.6	1.6	2.1			% Depr., Dep., Amort./Sales	1.6	1.9
1.9	2.8	2.7	3.4				2.6	2.8
	(26) 2.0	(20) 1.4					(29) 1.6	(48) 1.4
	4.4	1.6				% Officers', Directors', Owners' Comp/Sales	2.6	3.1
	9.1	3.6					10.2	6.0
14462M	114547M	546901M	737101M	675548M	441658M	Net Sales ($)	2227589M	1793077M
4105M	53210M	282593M	522844M	442865M	607261M	Total Assets ($)	1546077M	1167740M

M = $ thousand   MM = $ million
See Pages 1 through 15 for Explanation of Ratios and Data

Comparative Historical Data | Current Data Sorted By Sales

2	9	14		0-1MM	1-3MM	3-5MM	5-10MM	10-25MM	25MM & OVER
2	9	14	# Postretirement Benefits		3	4	2	2	3
			Type of Statement						
49	57	47	Unqualified	1	3	4	10	19	10
23	26	31	Reviewed	2	9	7	4	8	1
22	30	35	Compiled	4	17	6	4	3	1
5	3	3	Tax Returns	1	2				
34	32	39	Other		12	7	4	6	10
4/1/92- 3/31/93 ALL	4/1/93- 3/31/94 ALL	4/1/94- 3/31/95 ALL		51 (4/1-9/30/94)		104 (10/1/94-3/31/95)			
133	148	155	**NUMBER OF STATEMENTS**	8	43	24	22	36	22

2	9	14		0-1MM	1-3MM	3-5MM	5-10MM	10-25MM	25MM & OVER
%	%	%	**ASSETS**	%	%	%	%	%	%
6.8	6.2	7.2	Cash & Equivalents		8.1	10.8	3.3	5.5	5.8
19.5	21.8	22.0	Trade Receivables - (net)		17.5	20.6	27.4	23.2	27.7
42.4	44.1	41.5	Inventory		51.2	39.2	40.4	37.8	30.3
2.4	1.4	2.3	All Other Current		1.0	.9	4.5	2.3	4.7
71.0	73.4	73.1	Total Current		77.9	71.5	75.6	68.9	68.5
21.9	20.3	18.8	Fixed Assets (net)		15.8	19.2	16.7	23.6	19.0
.7	.9	1.2	Intangibles (net)		2.1	.6	.6	.5	2.4
6.4	5.3	6.9	All Other Non-Current		4.2	8.7	7.1	7.0	10.0
100.0	100.0	100.0	Total		100.0	100.0	100.0	100.0	100.0
			LIABILITIES						
13.2	12.4	12.6	Notes Payable-Short Term		15.3	14.8	12.9	12.1	6.3
3.8	3.6	2.4	Cur. Mat.-L/T/D		2.6	2.3	2.3	2.5	2.3
11.0	12.8	13.3	Trade Payables		15.1	10.8	20.4	11.8	11.1
.5	1.0	.5	Income Taxes Payable		.5	.3	.6	.6	.7
8.2	9.7	10.1	All Other Current		7.6	11.3	12.2	9.9	12.5
36.7	39.5	39.0	Total Current		41.1	39.6	48.4	37.0	32.8
15.0	13.7	12.9	Long Term Debt		10.4	15.1	12.2	13.2	16.3
.5	.4	.4	Deferred Taxes		.2	.4	.3	.9	.3
2.1	2.7	4.0	All Other-Non-Current		4.3	5.3	3.8	1.8	3.3
45.8	43.8	43.7	Net Worth		43.9	39.5	35.3	47.2	47.4
100.0	100.0	100.0	Total Liabilities & Net Worth		100.0	100.0	100.0	100.0	100.0
			INCOME DATA						
100.0	100.0	100.0	Net Sales		100.0	100.0	100.0	100.0	100.0
30.3	28.6	29.7	Gross Profit		32.9	31.7	28.5	26.6	26.0
25.7	23.6	23.3	Operating Expenses		27.5	24.0	21.7	21.4	16.6
4.6	5.0	6.5	Operating Profit		5.4	7.7	6.8	5.2	9.4
1.3	1.0	.6	All Other Expenses (net)		.6	.9	.6	.5	1.1
3.3	4.0	5.9	Profit Before Taxes		4.8	6.8	6.2	4.7	8.3
			RATIOS						
3.5 / 2.0 / 1.4	3.0 / 1.9 / 1.4	2.9 / 2.0 / 1.4	Current		3.2 / 2.1 / 1.4	2.8 / 1.9 / 1.3	2.4 / 1.7 / 1.3	2.8 / 2.0 / 1.4	2.8 / 2.5 / 1.5
1.1 / .7 / .4	(147) 1.2 / .8 / .4	1.3 / .7 / .5	Quick		1.1 / .6 / .3	1.3 / .7 / .4	1.2 / .6 / .4	1.2 / .7 / .5	1.6 / 1.2 / .6
20 18.7 / 32 11.4 / 54 6.8	20 18.5 / 35 10.5 / 57 6.4	22 16.6 / 38 9.5 / 60 6.1	Sales/Receivables		16 23.0 / 26 14.3 / 43 8.4	18 20.6 / 36 10.2 / 59 6.2	26 14.2 / 39 9.3 / 64 5.7	35 10.5 / 47 7.7 / 64 5.7	29 12.7 / 45 8.1 / 114 3.2
74 4.9 / 118 3.1 / 192 1.9	69 5.3 / 107 3.4 / 166 2.2	63 5.8 / 111 3.3 / 174 2.1	Cost of Sales/Inventory		73 5.0 / 122 3.0 / 203 1.8	60 6.1 / 122 3.0 / 174 2.1	47 7.7 / 99 3.7 / 159 2.3	66 5.5 / 101 3.6 / 130 2.8	50 7.3 / 81 4.5 / 146 2.5
15 23.6 / 24 15.2 / 38 9.6	16 22.2 / 27 13.6 / 41 8.9	17 21.8 / 28 13.2 / 47 7.7	Cost of Sales/Payables		16 22.8 / 27 13.4 / 52 7.0	9 41.9 / 25 14.5 / 58 6.3	24 15.2 / 39 9.3 / 57 6.4	17 21.3 / 26 14.3 / 37 9.9	18 19.8 / 27 13.4 / 48 7.6
3.2 / 5.2 / 12.4	3.5 / 6.3 / 10.6	3.4 / 5.6 / 11.3	Sales/Working Capital		3.1 / 5.8 / 13.0	4.8 / 6.1 / 10.3	3.7 / 6.5 / 12.5	3.6 / 5.4 / 10.2	2.4 / 4.1 / 13.1
(121) 6.4 / 2.0 / .8	(140) 8.8 / 3.4 / 1.5	(139) 9.4 / 4.9 / 2.3	EBIT/Interest		(38) 7.0 / 4.3 / 2.2	(21) 9.2 / 5.9 / 1.7	(21) 7.9 / 4.4 / 3.4	(33) 11.7 / 3.4 / 1.5	(20) 14.3 / 7.9 / 3.9
(65) 4.0 / 1.7 / .7	(69) 4.0 / 1.9 / .9	(64) 7.8 / 3.3 / 1.5	Net Profit + Depr., Dep., Amort./Cur. Mat. L/T/D		(16) 7.1 / 2.8 / 1.3			(20) 8.5 / 3.3 / 1.2	(13) 25.4 / 3.5 / 1.9
.2 / .4 / .9	.2 / .4 / .8	.2 / .4 / .7	Fixed/Worth		.1 / .3 / .6	.2 / .5 / .9	.3 / .4 / .6	.3 / .5 / .7	.2 / .5 / .8
.6 / 1.4 / 2.9	.7 / 1.4 / 2.6	.6 / 1.4 / 2.6	Debt/Worth		.8 / 1.3 / 2.4	.6 / 1.7 / 4.3	.6 / 1.9 / 4.7	.5 / 1.3 / 1.8	.5 / 1.3 / 2.9
(129) 32.0 / 12.8 / 1.1	(140) 31.3 / 16.8 / 5.1	(149) 42.1 / 22.9 / 10.9	% Profit Before Taxes/Tangible Net Worth		(41) 53.6 / 21.5 / 9.6	(23) 45.0 / 22.4 / 12.1	(20) 41.8 / 35.3 / 18.0	34.9 / 14.0 / 3.8	44.2 / 27.8 / 16.6
13.9 / 4.2 / -.1	13.8 / 6.8 / 1.4	16.6 / 9.1 / 4.0	% Profit Before Taxes/Total Assets		16.4 / 9.2 / 2.9	20.8 / 7.2 / 3.6	16.6 / 10.7 / 5.3	14.4 / 5.8 / 1.6	16.6 / 10.6 / 7.4
19.8 / 9.2 / 6.1	22.5 / 11.2 / 6.7	22.0 / 11.5 / 6.8	Sales/Net Fixed Assets		32.0 / 14.7 / 9.9	27.2 / 15.0 / 4.7	31.8 / 13.6 / 7.7	13.4 / 9.1 / 5.7	20.2 / 8.0 / 6.3
2.3 / 1.8 / 1.3	2.6 / 1.9 / 1.4	2.6 / 1.9 / 1.4	Sales/Total Assets		3.0 / 2.0 / 1.5	2.6 / 2.1 / 1.4	2.6 / 2.1 / 1.5	2.4 / 1.9 / 1.3	2.2 / 1.4 / 1.1
(121) 1.0 / 2.0 / 2.8	(135) 1.2 / 1.8 / 2.8	(142) 1.0 / 1.7 / 2.8	% Depr., Dep., Amort./Sales		(38) 1.1 / 1.6 / 2.9	(22) .6 / 2.1 / 3.0	(20) 1.0 / 1.5 / 2.8	(33) 1.1 / 1.6 / 2.6	(21) 1.1 / 2.0 / 2.7
(36) 1.6 / 3.7 / 6.5	(53) 1.1 / 3.5 / 7.5	(52) 1.6 / 3.5 / 7.6	% Officers', Directors', Owners' Comp/Sales		(21) 1.6 / 4.4 / 9.8	(11) 1.6 / 3.7 / 9.2		(10) 1.4 / 2.4 / 4.0		
1989722M	2537436M	2530217M	Net Sales ($)	5718M	84121M	94956M	155330M	567459M	1622633M
1327531M	1512759M	1912878M	Total Assets ($)	4364M	48486M	59275M	91028M	373927M	1335798M

M = $ thousand   MM = $ million
See Pages 1 through 15 for Explanation of Ratios and Data

MANUFACTURERS—GENERAL INDUSTRIAL MACHINERY & EQUIPMENT.
SIC# 3561 (64,66,67,69)

Current Data Sorted By Assets   **Comparative Historical Data**

	3	12	13	4	2	7	# Postretirement Benefits		
							Type of Statement		
	3	8	58	36	5	9	Unqualified	125	160
	5	42	48	4			Reviewed	90	102
	20	59	22	3			Compiled	86	81
	9	3	2				Tax Returns	1	2
	13	22	41	10	5	12	Other	101	81
		139 (4/1-9/30/94)		300 (10/1/94-3/31/95)				4/1/90-3/31/91	4/1/91-3/31/92
	0-500M	500M-2MM	2-10MM	10-50MM	50-100MM	100-250MM		ALL	ALL
	50	134	171	53	10	21	**NUMBER OF STATEMENTS**	403	426
	%	%	%	%	%	%	**ASSETS**	%	%
	9.1	9.8	6.3	7.3	10.1	10.5	Cash & Equivalents	7.0	7.6
	30.6	31.5	30.0	27.1	24.0	22.4	Trade Receivables - (net)	30.5	29.4
	26.9	26.5	31.0	23.6	20.6	19.0	Inventory	27.4	25.8
	1.8	2.2	2.7	4.2	4.5	2.9	All Other Current	3.1	2.6
	68.4	70.0	69.9	62.1	59.3	54.8	Total Current	68.1	65.5
	23.7	21.4	22.6	26.9	24.6	28.5	Fixed Assets (net)	23.5	25.5
	1.5	1.6	1.8	3.6	7.6	6.3	Intangibles (net)	1.8	2.7
	6.4	7.0	5.7	7.3	8.6	10.4	All Other Non-Current	6.6	6.3
	100.0	100.0	100.0	100.0	100.0	100.0	Total	100.0	100.0
							LIABILITIES		
	10.0	9.7	11.6	7.4	4.6	4.2	Notes Payable-Short Term	9.9	11.7
	6.6	4.7	3.1	2.2	4.6	1.6	Cur. Mat. -L/T/D	3.6	3.9
	18.4	17.0	16.0	11.6	10.1	8.2	Trade Payables	15.3	15.2
	.8	.5	.4	.6	.5	.7	Income Taxes Payable	.7	.6
	11.3	11.1	12.3	11.9	9.0	13.2	All Other Current	12.7	12.2
	47.1	42.9	43.3	33.8	28.6	27.9	Total Current	42.2	43.6
	14.6	11.7	12.1	12.3	14.6	11.8	Long Term Debt	12.9	12.7
	.1	.2	.4	1.0	1.9	1.9	Deferred Taxes	.8	.7
	7.7	2.2	4.7	3.6	4.0	7.4	All Other-Non-Current	3.0	2.9
	30.5	42.9	39.4	49.4	50.9	51.1	Net Worth	41.0	40.1
	100.0	100.0	100.0	100.0	100.0	100.0	Total Liabilities & Net Worth	100.0	100.0
							INCOME DATA		
	100.0	100.0	100.0	100.0	100.0	100.0	Net Sales	100.0	100.0
	40.6	36.6	30.5	29.9	32.1	31.2	Gross Profit	32.1	32.7
	36.7	31.5	25.7	22.6	23.1	22.2	Operating Expenses	27.0	28.6
	3.9	5.0	4.8	7.3	8.9	9.1	Operating Profit	5.1	4.1
	1.3	.7	1.2	.7	.4	.7	All Other Expenses (net)	1.3	1.2
	2.6	4.3	3.5	6.6	8.5	8.4	Profit Before Taxes	3.8	2.9
							RATIOS		
	2.5	2.5	2.2	2.9	3.0	3.1	Current	2.4	2.3
	1.5	1.6	1.6	1.8	1.9	2.6		1.7	1.6
	1.1	1.2	1.3	1.3	1.4	1.6		1.2	1.2
	1.3	1.7	1.3	1.6	1.8	1.8	Quick	1.5	1.4
	1.0	.9	.8	1.0	.9	1.2		.9 (425)	.9
	.6	.7	.6	.7	.8	.9		.6	.6
	31 11.8	35 10.3	42 8.7	48 7.6	50 7.3	46 7.9	Sales/Receivables	38 9.6	37 9.8
	41 9.0	47 7.8	51 7.2	59 6.2	74 4.9	66 5.5		51 7.1	52 7.0
	52 7.0	61 6.0	65 5.6	74 4.9	85 4.3	79 4.6		68 5.4	65 5.6
	18 20.5	27 13.7	49 7.5	48 7.6	61 6.0	64 5.7	Cost of Sales/Inventory	38 9.6	35 10.4
	51 7.1	56 6.5	76 4.8	78 4.7	94 3.9	101 3.6		70 5.2	68 5.4
	101 3.6	99 3.7	122 3.0	107 3.4	146 2.5	126 2.9		114 3.2	111 3.3
	20 18.7	18 19.8	23 15.6	22 16.6	29 12.4	24 14.9	Cost of Sales/Payables	19 19.2	21 17.0
	31 11.6	36 10.1	39 9.4	37 9.8	40 9.2	39 9.4		32 11.4	34 10.6
	47 7.7	57 6.4	55 6.6	52 7.0	55 6.6	46 8.0		51 7.2	51 7.1
	6.1	5.4	4.8	3.2	3.3	2.9	Sales/Working Capital	4.7	5.2
	13.5	9.4	8.3	6.1	3.9	4.3		8.0	9.0
	105.7	22.2	15.1	12.6	9.8	6.2		18.9	28.1
	(45) 7.4	(116) 9.1	(158) 8.2	(43) 14.0	82.0	21.3	EBIT/Interest	(368) 7.3	(398) 6.6
	3.4	4.0	3.2	4.8	4.9	12.9		3.0	2.5
	1.1	1.8	1.6	2.0	3.2	4.1		1.3	1.0
	(12) 4.5	(55) 5.1	(77) 5.9	(30) 15.0		(15) 45.6	Net Profit + Depr., Dep., Amort./Cur. Mat. L /T/D	(238) 5.8	(225) 5.3
	2.1	2.2	2.5	3.4		9.3		2.1	2.3
	.3	.8	1.1	2.0		2.9		.9	.8
	.2	.2	.3	.3	.4	.5	Fixed/Worth	.3	.3
	.8	.4	.6	.6	.6	.6		.6	.6
	2.8	1.1	1.2	1.1	1.6	.7		1.2	1.3
	1.0	.7	1.0	.5	.5	.7	Debt/Worth	.8	.7
	2.0	1.5	1.7	1.1	1.1	1.1		1.5	1.6
	27.9	3.4	3.2	2.6	3.4	1.5		3.3	4.1
	(42) 80.6	(128) 39.2	(160) 34.2	43.7	51.4	(20) 28.2	% Profit Before Taxes/Tangible Net Worth	(384) 34.0	(393) 32.5
	27.3	19.6	17.6	19.7	25.1	21.9		17.6	14.5
	5.0	7.5	7.5	9.4	13.8	11.2		5.2	1.8
	23.4	15.3	12.2	15.4	14.3	14.3	% Profit Before Taxes/Total Assets	14.1	13.1
	6.9	6.5	5.8	7.1	10.1	10.0		6.2	4.7
	1.2	2.5	1.8	3.2	6.3	5.1		1.7	.1
	52.9	27.3	23.2	10.0	6.0	5.9	Sales/Net Fixed Assets	21.3	18.6
	14.4	16.8	10.9	6.1	5.6	4.3		10.4	8.8
	6.9	6.8	5.7	4.2	4.4	3.3		5.2	4.9
	3.8	3.2	2.4	1.9	1.5	1.6	Sales/Total Assets	2.7	2.7
	2.7	2.4	2.1	1.7	1.1	1.3		2.0	1.9
	2.0	1.8	1.5	1.2	1.0	.8		1.5	1.5
	(43) .8	(126) .8	(159) 1.1	(46) 1.7		(19) 2.3	% Depr., Dep., Amort./Sales	(364) 1.0	(390) 1.2
	1.8	1.6	1.7	2.0		3.3		1.9	2.2
	3.9	2.8	3.1	3.6		4.6		3.3	3.6
	(32) 5.4	(73) 3.3	(56) 2.0				% Officers', Directors', Owners' Comp/Sales	(131) 3.0	(139) 3.3
	7.1	5.4	5.1					4.9	5.5
	11.6	10.9	7.3					7.3	9.3
	43831M	384443M	1577940M	1916265M	1029116M	4084612M	Net Sales ($)	6728330M	8025201M
	14653M	157645M	766749M	1174019M	776053M	3280841M	Total Assets ($)	4570445M	5552579M

© Robert Morris Associates 1995

M = $ thousand   MM = $ million
See Pages 1 through 15 for Explanation of Ratios and Data

Comparative Historical Data				Current Data Sorted By Sales					
9	28	41	# Postretirement Benefits	3	8	4	8	5	13
			Type of Statement						
123	134	119	Unqualified	3	7	6	33	34	36
107	112	99	Reviewed	5	22	28	31	9	4
75	86	104	Compiled	18	41	18	18	8	1
6	4	14	Tax Returns	9	2		3		
92	108	103	Other	11	20	12	19	15	26
4/1/92-3/31/93	4/1/93-3/31/94	4/1/94-3/31/95		139 (4/1-9/30/94)		300 (10/1/94-3/31/95)			
ALL	ALL	ALL		0-1MM	1-3MM	3-5MM	5-10MM	10-25MM	25MM & OVER
403	444	439	**NUMBER OF STATEMENTS**	46	92	64	104	66	67
%	%	%	**ASSETS**	%	%	%	%	%	%
7.9	8.5	8.1	Cash & Equivalents	8.9	9.5	9.1	6.7	7.1	7.7
30.6	29.8	29.7	Trade Receivables - (net)	26.9	30.5	30.8	29.0	32.4	27.7
24.7	24.4	27.5	Inventory	25.3	24.2	30.0	30.7	31.5	22.0
3.0	2.5	2.7	All Other Current	1.8	3.4	1.9	1.9	3.1	3.9
66.2	65.3	67.9	Total Current	62.8	67.6	71.7	68.4	74.1	61.2
24.8	25.1	23.2	Fixed Assets (net)	26.7	24.1	20.3	22.3	19.5	27.4
2.4	2.9	2.3	Intangibles (net)	1.5	1.6	2.3	2.8	1.3	4.0
6.6	6.7	6.6	All Other Non-Current	9.0	6.7	5.7	6.5	5.2	7.4
100.0	100.0	100.0	Total	100.0	100.0	100.0	100.0	100.0	100.0
			LIABILITIES						
9.3	9.4	9.8	Notes Payable-Short Term	9.5	10.0	9.4	10.8	11.6	6.7
3.7	4.1	3.8	Cur. Mat.-L /T/D	7.3	4.6	4.9	3.1	2.0	2.4
14.3	13.3	15.5	Trade Payables	16.3	15.5	16.5	15.5	17.6	12.1
.6	1.5	.5	Income Taxes Payable	.9	.5	.3	.6	.4	.6
12.4	11.8	11.7	All Other Current	10.0	9.4	14.6	11.1	13.3	13.0
40.3	40.2	41.4	Total Current	44.0	40.0	45.6	41.1	44.8	34.7
13.0	12.7	12.3	Long Term Debt	18.6	13.7	10.4	12.2	6.4	14.0
.7	.6	.5	Deferred Taxes	.2	.2	.2	.5	.4	1.3
3.3	3.3	4.3	All Other-Non-Current	6.8	3.1	3.2	5.1	4.1	4.2
42.7	43.2	41.5	Net Worth	30.4	43.1	40.6	41.1	44.2	45.8
100.0	100.0	100.0	Total Liabilities & Net Worth	100.0	100.0	100.0	100.0	100.0	100.0
			INCOME DATA						
100.0	100.0	100.0	Net Sales	100.0	100.0	100.0	100.0	100.0	100.0
32.7	31.7	33.5	Gross Profit	43.9	39.0	29.5	32.8	27.6	29.5
28.6	27.6	28.2	Operating Expenses	39.4	32.3	26.5	27.6	23.3	21.9
4.1	4.2	5.3	Operating Profit	4.5	6.6	3.1	5.2	4.3	7.6
1.1	.9	1.0	All Other Expenses (net)	1.4	1.0	.8	1.1	.6	.8
3.0	3.3	4.4	Profit Before Taxes	3.1	5.6	2.3	4.1	3.7	6.9
			RATIOS						
2.6	2.6	2.5	Current	2.5	2.7	2.3	2.2	2.4	2.7
1.7	1.6	1.6		1.5	1.7	1.6	1.6	1.7	1.9
1.2	1.2	1.3		1.1	1.2	1.2	1.3	1.3	1.4
1.5	1.5	1.5	Quick	1.4	1.8	1.3	1.5	1.3	1.7
.9	1.0	.9		.9	.9	.9	.8	.9	1.0
.7	.6	.6		.6	.6	.6	.6	.7	.8
39 9.4	41 8.9	40 9.1	Sales/Receivables	37 10.0	39 9.4	33 11.0	43 8.5	41 8.8	46 8.0
51 7.1	52 7.0	51 7.2		43 8.4	49 7.5	47 7.8	49 7.4	53 6.9	57 6.4
64 5.7	66 5.5	65 5.6		59 6.2	64 5.7	59 6.2	64 5.7	69 5.3	74 4.9
37 10.0	34 10.6	41 8.8	Cost of Sales/Inventory	25 14.7	26 14.1	35 10.4	54 6.7	49 7.4	48 7.6
64 5.7	63 5.8	70 5.2		73 5.0	56 6.5	62 5.9	76 4.8	78 4.7	74 4.9
104 3.5	101 3.6	111 3.3		118 3.1	101 3.6	130 2.8	122 3.0	101 3.6	104 3.5
20 17.9	18 19.9	22 16.8	Cost of Sales/Payables	21 17.1	18 20.1	21 17.2	23 16.1	27 13.4	24 15.0
33 10.9	29 12.5	37 10.0		38 9.5	33 11.1	37 9.9	37 9.8	42 8.7	35 10.5
48 7.6	47 7.8	54 6.7		66 5.5	57 6.4	51 7.1	56 6.5	54 6.8	46 8.0
4.5	4.7	4.6	Sales/Working Capital	5.8	4.7	5.7	4.5	3.6	3.7
8.4	8.5	8.3		13.1	8.3	9.9	7.8	8.8	5.5
22.6	17.8	17.4		105.7	24.5	20.3	13.6	17.3	12.8
(366) 9.1	(395) 9.1	(393) 9.8	EBIT/Interest	(40) 6.0	(80) 8.4	(58) 9.5	(96) 8.0	(55) 17.6	(64) 19.0
3.1	3.6	3.9		3.1	3.9	3.2	3.8	3.0	6.3
1.3	1.4	1.8		1.5	1.5	2.0	1.6	1.6	2.9
(224) 7.9	(205) 4.6	(197) 7.5	Net Profit + Depr., Dep., Amort./Cur. Mat. L/T/D	(13) 7.4	(37) 4.2	(25) 5.5	(50) 5.9	(28) 8.6	(44) 17.8
2.6	2.1	2.9		2.2	2.1	3.0	2.6	2.3	3.8
.9	1.0	1.2		.4	.7	1.3	1.3	.6	2.3
.3	.3	.3	Fixed/Worth	.3	.2	.2	.3	.3	.4
.5	.6	.6		.8	.5	.5	.6	.4	.6
1.1	1.1	1.1		2.8	1.6	1.1	1.1	.8	1.1
.7	.7	.7	Debt/Worth	1.0	.7	1.0	.8	.6	.6
1.3	1.4	1.6		2.3	1.6	1.5	1.7	1.4	1.4
3.2	2.8	3.2		29.5	3.6	3.4	3.0	2.6	2.6
(379) 30.9	(420) 37.6	(413) 38.2	% Profit Before Taxes/Tangible Net Worth	(39) 78.2	(87) 44.8	(59) 31.2	(99) 35.4	(63) 26.4	(66) 37.4
15.4	14.8	19.5		20.5	21.4	18.4	19.0	16.0	23.0
3.0	4.1	7.9		4.5	6.3	9.7	7.6	5.1	12.3
11.4	13.4	14.7	% Profit Before Taxes/Total Assets	18.9	18.0	12.4	12.0	13.2	14.7
5.7	5.6	6.6		6.2	7.8	6.5	6.1	5.0	8.1
.9	1.2	2.4		1.3	2.4	3.3	2.4	1.6	4.9
20.9	18.7	22.4	Sales/Net Fixed Assets	28.5	23.5	28.7	21.5	26.1	9.3
9.1	8.4	10.4		9.3	12.5	14.9	10.2	12.6	5.7
5.0	4.8	5.2		3.8	5.2	6.6	6.1	7.1	4.3
2.7	2.6	2.7	Sales/Total Assets	3.0	3.0	3.1	2.5	2.7	1.9
2.0	1.9	2.1		2.2	2.1	2.3	2.1	2.2	1.6
1.5	1.5	1.5		1.3	1.6	1.6	1.7	1.7	1.3
(373) 1.2	(410) 1.3	(401) 1.1	% Depr., Dep., Amort./Sales	(40) 1.0	(86) .8	(60) .9	(98) 1.1	(56) .9	(61) 1.7
2.0	2.2	1.8		2.2	1.7	1.7	1.9	1.5	2.6
3.5	3.6	3.3		4.3	3.4	3.4	2.9	1.9	3.6
(158) 2.7	(148) 2.8	(164) 3.1	% Officers', Directors', Owners' Comp/Sales	(24) 4.8	(54) 5.0	(32) 2.4	(37) 2.6	(12) 1.4	
5.3	5.0	5.7		7.6	7.2	4.0	5.5	2.7	
8.3	8.9	9.5		11.6	12.2	5.9	7.9	6.3	
7800060M	8218152M	9036207M	Net Sales ($)	29897M	187253M	249148M	741690M	1045166M	6783053M
5286496M	6121795M	6169960M	Total Assets ($)	16455M	98954M	121462M	428349M	615140M	4889600M

M = $ thousand   MM = $ million
See Pages 1 through 15 for Explanation of Ratios and Data

Current Data Sorted By Assets   **Comparative Historical Data**

Postretirement Benefits — Type of Statement

0-500M	500M-2MM	2-10MM	10-50MM	50-100MM	100-250MM	Type of Statement =	4/1/90-3/31/91 ALL	4/1/91-3/31/92 ALL
		1			1			
	1	7	3	3	3	Unqualified	14	9
	3	1	1			Reviewed	6	4
1	3	3				Compiled	7	3
	1					Tax Returns		
	2	4	1	1	2	Other	12	6
	20 (4/1-9/30/94)			20 (10/1/94-3/31/95)				
1	10	15	5	4	5	**NUMBER OF STATEMENTS**	39	22

ASSETS

0-500M %	500M-2MM %	2-10MM %	10-50MM %	50-100MM %	100-250MM %		ALL %	ALL %
	3.1	7.3				Cash & Equivalents	4.9	1.9
	21.0	29.7				Trade Receivables - (net)	24.1	21.8
	41.8	39.2				Inventory	38.7	39.3
	1.1	1.2				All Other Current	3.1	7.7
	67.0	77.3				Total Current	70.7	70.7
	23.5	18.6				Fixed Assets (net)	19.7	19.9
	2.2	.9				Intangibles (net)	4.7	2.6
	7.2	3.2				All Other Non-Current	4.9	6.8
	100.0	100.0				Total	100.0	100.0

LIABILITIES

0-500M	500M-2MM	2-10MM	10-50MM	50-100MM	100-250MM		ALL	ALL
	21.7	13.9				Notes Payable-Short Term	18.2	24.3
	2.4	1.6				Cur. Mat. -L/T/D	4.6	3.1
	9.9	14.0				Trade Payables	12.2	7.2
	.4	.3				Income Taxes Payable	.8	1.0
	11.7	9.7				All Other Current	10.4	11.2
	46.1	39.5				Total Current	46.3	46.9
	8.4	9.6				Long Term Debt	16.5	19.6
	.1	.7				Deferred Taxes	.4	.2
	9.7	1.1				All Other-Non-Current	3.9	3.0
	35.7	49.1				Net Worth	32.9	30.3
	100.0	100.0				Total Liabilities & Net Worth	100.0	100.0

INCOME DATA

0-500M	500M-2MM	2-10MM	10-50MM	50-100MM	100-250MM		ALL	ALL
	100.0	100.0				Net Sales	100.0	100.0
	29.7	28.9				Gross Profit	30.8	29.0
	29.5	22.6				Operating Expenses	27.2	22.9
	.1	6.4				Operating Profit	3.6	6.1
	1.6	1.3				All Other Expenses (net)	2.8	3.0
	-1.5	5.0				Profit Before Taxes	.8	3.1

RATIOS

0-500M	500M-2MM	2-10MM	10-50MM	50-100MM	100-250MM		ALL	ALL
	2.5	3.3				Current	2.1	2.3
	1.8	2.1					1.6	1.6
	.9	1.6					1.3	1.2
	1.0	1.8				Quick	1.3	.8
	.5	.9					.7	.6
	.3	.5					.3	.3
	14 25.9	35 10.3				Sales/Receivables	26 14.0	28 13.0
	31 11.9	50 7.3					42 8.6	48 7.6
	49 7.5	66 5.5					60 6.1	55 6.6
	79 4.6	61 6.0				Cost of Sales/Inventory	64 5.7	81 4.5
	94 3.9	101 3.6					107 3.4	111 3.3
	130 2.8	140 2.6					159 2.3	159 2.3
	2 153.1	16 23.3				Cost of Sales/Payables	12 31.2	9 40.3
	18 20.5	33 11.2					22 16.6	13 28.0
	40 9.2	47 7.7					40 9.2	29 12.7
	6.2	3.4				Sales/Working Capital	5.4	4.0
	10.5	5.9					7.9	6.9
	-41.9	8.0					14.0	17.8
	4.5	21.1				EBIT/Interest	(35) 2.4	(21) 4.6
	2.2	3.4					1.5	1.5
	1.5	1.8					.7	.8
						Net Profit + Depr., Dep., Amort./Cur. Mat. L /T/D	(22) 5.2	(12) 4.8
							1.2	1.4
							.3	.5
	.3	.3				Fixed/Worth	.4	.3
	.7	.4					.5	.7
	31.2	.5					1.9	1.2
	.6	.6				Debt/Worth	1.5	1.8
	1.4	1.0					2.9	2.9
	82.6	2.3					6.3	4.6
		35.4				% Profit Before Taxes/Tangible Net Worth	(35) 32.8	(20) 46.2
		20.8					14.8	14.2
		9.5					-9.6	-.3
	15.1	22.0				% Profit Before Taxes/Total Assets	7.9	15.8
	3.7	8.8					2.9	2.9
	2.0	3.7					-1.9	-.9
	19.5	26.3				Sales/Net Fixed Assets	26.8	48.3
	11.2	10.0					12.3	8.7
	6.8	7.2					5.3	5.4
	3.1	2.8				Sales/Total Assets	2.6	2.4
	2.8	2.1					1.9	1.9
	1.8	1.4					1.5	1.3
		.8				% Depr., Dep., Amort./Sales	(34) .8	.5
		(13) 1.3					1.8	1.5
		2.2					2.7	2.3
						% Officers', Directors', Owners' Comp/Sales	(14) 2.1	
							3.8	
							4.3	
294M	27356M	149896M	275059M	437040M	1220096M	Net Sales ($)	1081283M	832000M
37M	11358M	79190M	134757M	263785M	743577M	Total Assets ($)	689831M	473123M

M = $ thousand   MM = $ million
See Pages 1 through 15 for Explanation of Ratios and Data

Comparative Historical Data   **Current Data Sorted By Sales**

	4/1/92-3/31/93 ALL	4/1/93-3/31/94 ALL	4/1/94-3/31/95 ALL		20 (4/1-9/30/94) 0-1MM	1-3MM	3-5MM	20 (10/1/94-3/31/95) 5-10MM	10-25MM	25MM & OVER
# Postretirement Benefits	2	1	2							2
Type of Statement										
Unqualified	16	14	17			1		4	3	9
Reviewed	4	5	5			1	2		1	1
Compiled	3	6	7		1	2	1	2	1	1
Tax Returns	1	2	1			1				
Other	6	7	10		1		1	1	3	4
NUMBER OF STATEMENTS	30	34	40		2	4	5	7	8	14
ASSETS	%	%	%		%	%	%	%	%	%
Cash & Equivalents	2.9	6.2	5.9							3.1
Trade Receivables - (net)	21.7	23.1	25.6							26.2
Inventory	36.6	37.8	36.8							33.2
All Other Current	2.1	1.9	1.7							2.8
Total Current	63.3	69.0	70.0							65.2
Fixed Assets (net)	26.1	23.7	21.5							21.8
Intangibles (net)	3.6	2.5	1.9							2.9
All Other Non-Current	7.0	4.8	6.6							10.0
Total	100.0	100.0	100.0							100.0
LIABILITIES										
Notes Payable-Short Term	14.5	9.7	18.3							22.0
Cur. Mat.-L /T/D	4.4	4.7	1.7							1.5
Trade Payables	11.5	16.4	12.3							13.0
Income Taxes Payable	.5	.9	.4							.3
All Other Current	7.9	7.0	9.9							9.6
Total Current	38.8	38.7	42.7							46.4
Long Term Debt	14.2	17.7	11.5							13.2
Deferred Taxes	.3	.5	.5							.6
All Other-Non-Current	3.9	4.4	3.7							2.3
Net Worth	42.8	38.8	41.6							37.5
Total Liabilities & Net Worth	100.0	100.0	100.0							100.0
INCOME DATA										
Net Sales	100.0	100.0	100.0							100.0
Gross Profit	30.6	25.8	30.4							30.6
Operating Expenses	27.1	21.4	24.7							23.3
Operating Profit	3.6	4.4	5.7							7.3
All Other Expenses (net)	2.2	2.1	1.4							1.3
Profit Before Taxes	1.4	2.4	4.3							6.0
RATIOS										
Current	3.3	2.9	2.4							1.7
	1.8	1.8	1.6							1.4
	1.1	1.3	1.2							1.2
Quick	1.1	1.3	1.0							.8
	.6	.7	.7							.6
	.4	.5	.5							.5
Sales/Receivables	27 13.7	29 12.6	27 13.3							33 11.2
	38 9.7	38 9.5	44 8.3							49 7.5
	54 6.8	53 6.9	63 5.8							69 5.3
Cost of Sales/Inventory	58 6.3	53 6.9	68 5.4							68 5.4
	107 3.4	89 4.1	99 3.7							78 4.7
	146 2.5	135 2.7	140 2.6							166 2.2
Cost of Sales/Payables	15 23.6	18 19.8	16 22.8							26 13.9
	21 17.4	29 12.7	32 11.5							33 11.0
	43 8.5	53 6.9	46 8.0							50 7.3
Sales/Working Capital	4.4	4.8	5.5							6.6
	7.2	6.3	8.0							11.7
	40.7	16.6	20.8							19.7
EBIT/Interest	5.8	7.6	9.1							6.6
	1.3	(33) 3.4	(39) 3.3							(13) 3.6
	.5	1.6	1.9							2.1
Net Profit + Depr., Dep., Amort./Cur. Mat. L/T/D	3.8	3.6	39.3							
	(15) 1.3	(18) 2.3	(16) 2.7							
	.3	.5	1.7							
Fixed/Worth	.4	.4	.3							.4
	.7	.7	.5							.7
	.9	1.1	.9							1.0
Debt/Worth	.9	.9	.8							1.3
	1.4	1.6	1.4							1.7
	2.5	3.1	2.9							3.3
% Profit Before Taxes/Tangible Net Worth	24.4	29.6	35.4							37.6
	(28) 6.1	(32) 14.2	(39) 24.5							28.6
	-3.3	9.6	11.2							15.6
% Profit Before Taxes/Total Assets	10.5	12.7	16.1							14.0
	2.3	6.5	7.3							7.9
	-1.3	3.3	3.2							3.6
Sales/Net Fixed Assets	23.5	18.6	18.9							11.8
	7.3	8.5	10.5							9.6
	5.1	5.7	7.1							6.9
Sales/Total Assets	2.6	2.7	2.8							2.1
	1.9	2.0	2.1							1.8
	1.5	1.6	1.6							1.6
% Depr., Dep., Amort./Sales	1.2	1.2	1.2							1.7
	(29) 1.9	(33) 1.9	(36) 1.9							(13) 2.0
	4.2	3.5	2.8							2.8
% Officers', Directors', Owners' Comp/Sales	3.1	2.7	1.8							
	(12) 4.2	(14) 4.2	(17) 2.9							
	7.0	7.9	6.0							
Net Sales ($)	749364M	1017452M	2109741M		1212M	7612M	18826M	48608M	101288M	1932195M
Total Assets ($)	453608M	549105M	1232704M		909M	3918M	6568M	25010M	54180M	1142119M

M = $ thousand   MM = $ million
See Pages 1 through 15 for Explanation of Ratios and Data

	Current Data Sorted By Assets							Comparative Historical Data	
	10	9	15	3		1	# Postretirement Benefits		
							Type of Statement		
	1	5	27	15	3	3	Unqualified	56	46
	15	79	76	4			Reviewed	185	196
	90	130	32	1			Compiled	254	206
	11	5	1				Tax Returns	10	11
	27	53	43	11	1		Other	102	108
		233 (4/1-9/30/94)		400 (10/1/94-3/31/95)				4/1/90-3/31/91	4/1/91-3/31/92
	0-500M	500M-2MM	2-10MM	10-50MM	50-100MM	100-250MM		ALL	ALL
NUMBER OF STATEMENTS	144	272	179	31	4	3		607	567
	%	%	%	%	%	%	ASSETS	%	%
	12.0	8.0	6.9	9.8			Cash & Equivalents	7.4	7.8
	27.3	26.5	26.5	25.3			Trade Receivables - (net)	25.6	25.4
	14.1	15.7	20.0	22.2			Inventory	17.8	17.4
	2.1	1.8	1.8	4.8			All Other Current	2.4	2.2
	55.6	52.0	55.2	62.1			Total Current	53.2	52.9
	38.5	41.3	39.2	29.9			Fixed Assets (net)	39.6	40.0
	1.0	1.1	.9	.6			Intangibles (net)	1.1	1.0
	4.9	5.6	4.7	7.3			All Other Non-Current	6.1	6.1
	100.0	100.0	100.0	100.0			Total	100.0	100.0
							LIABILITIES		
	7.3	7.5	9.2	9.6			Notes Payable-Short Term	8.9	9.2
	6.3	7.0	4.7	2.9			Cur. Mat. -L/T/D	7.3	7.6
	11.0	11.4	12.6	12.6			Trade Payables	10.8	10.8
	.4	.5	.6	1.2			Income Taxes Payable	.9	.6
	7.6	7.6	8.8	7.8			All Other Current	7.0	7.3
	32.7	33.9	35.8	34.1			Total Current	34.9	35.5
	25.0	22.9	20.7	15.0			Long Term Debt	23.0	23.0
	.1	.5	.7	.6			Deferred Taxes	.8	.7
	3.7	3.0	3.3	1.6			All Other-Non-Current	2.8	2.8
	38.4	39.7	39.5	48.6			Net Worth	38.5	38.0
	100.0	100.0	100.0	100.0			Total Liabilities & Net Worth	100.0	100.0
							INCOME DATA		
	100.0	100.0	100.0	100.0			Net Sales	100.0	100.0
	40.3	34.3	26.4	26.1			Gross Profit	32.8	33.2
	34.4	27.8	20.5	18.2			Operating Expenses	27.2	28.8
	5.9	6.5	5.9	7.9			Operating Profit	5.6	4.5
	1.3	1.5	1.3	.5			All Other Expenses (net)	1.9	1.8
	4.6	4.9	4.6	7.4			Profit Before Taxes	3.8	2.6
							RATIOS		
	2.9	2.4	2.3	3.0				2.5	2.4
	1.8	1.6	1.6	1.7			Current	1.5	1.6
	1.0	1.1	1.1	1.2				1.1	1.1
	2.4	1.7	1.6	2.3				1.6	1.6
(143)	1.2	1.0	.9	.9			Quick	1.0	.9
	.7	.7	.6	.6				.6	.6
	25 14.5	36 10.1	40 9.2	45 8.2				33 11.2	33 11.1
	39 9.4	47 7.7	48 7.6	56 6.5			Sales/Receivables	43 8.5	44 8.3
	54 6.8	60 6.1	62 5.9	73 5.0				56 6.5	57 6.4
	2 172.8	17 21.3	28 13.2	28 13.0				16 23.5	14 26.0
	21 17.8	33 11.1	52 7.0	62 5.9			Cost of Sales/Inventory	38 9.7	38 9.6
	48 7.6	69 5.3	79 4.6	96 3.8				72 5.1	72 5.1
	10 37.8	15 24.4	16 22.5	19 19.6				13 27.1	13 28.7
	18 20.4	25 14.8	29 12.7	32 11.3			Cost of Sales/Payables	23 16.1	24 15.3
	36 10.1	43 8.4	46 7.9	50 7.3				39 9.4	40 9.1
	6.5	6.4	5.3	2.5				6.1	5.9
	12.0	11.3	10.1	6.3			Sales/Working Capital	11.5	11.7
	129.0	44.1	29.9	19.7				38.0	103.7
	11.5	7.3	7.9	15.4				5.3	4.8
(130)	3.9	(261) 3.4	(171) 3.3	(29) 7.8			EBIT/Interest	(573) 2.6	(536) 2.0
	1.6	1.4	1.6	2.8				1.2	.9
	4.1	3.8	4.3	6.9			Net Profit + Depr., Dep.,	3.1	2.7
(46)	2.5	(138) 2.0	(100) 2.0	(19) 4.0			Amort./Cur. Mat. L /T/D	(367) 1.8	(321) 1.5
	1.2	1.0	1.0	1.2				1.0	.8
	.4	.6	.6	.3				.6	.6
	1.1	1.1	1.1	.5			Fixed/Worth	1.0	1.1
	2.7	2.1	1.8	1.1				2.0	2.1
	.6	.9	.8	.4				.8	.8
	1.7	1.6	1.7	1.1			Debt/Worth	1.6	1.7
	4.0	3.4	3.6	3.4				3.3	3.7
	58.1	44.3	33.4	48.2			% Profit Before Taxes/Tangible	34.9	32.0
(126)	24.2	(259) 20.4	(174) 19.0	23.3			Net Worth	(562) 17.5	(518) 13.9
	7.5	5.4	4.0	10.8				4.6	1.1
	19.9	15.7	13.6	18.6			% Profit Before Taxes/Total	13.9	12.3
	9.2	7.6	5.8	12.6			Assets	6.8	4.8
	1.5	1.4	1.3	4.1				.9	-.6
	15.6	7.5	8.8	10.6				9.8	9.3
	7.8	4.6	4.5	5.9			Sales/Net Fixed Assets	5.1	5.1
	4.4	3.2	2.7	3.7				3.2	3.1
	3.6	2.4	2.3	1.9				2.6	2.6
	2.5	1.9	1.8	1.5			Sales/Total Assets	2.0	1.9
	1.8	1.6	1.4	1.2				1.5	1.4
	2.6	2.9	2.0	1.7				2.3	2.2
(128)	4.3	(264) 4.3	(174) 3.5	(30) 2.8			% Depr., Dep., Amort./Sales	(569) 4.3	(537) 4.1
	6.2	6.4	5.3	4.6				6.6	6.9
	5.9	4.0	2.1	.8			% Officers', Directors',	3.1	4.0
(78)	9.5	(163) 6.4	(99) 4.0	(13) 2.6			Owners' Comp/Sales	(328) 6.2	(318) 6.9
	14.0	10.6	6.7	3.1				9.9	10.9
	113369M	606671M	1360324M	785627M	349244M	821590M	Net Sales ($)	2255787M	2263491M
	43043M	305674M	740373M	536628M	249063M	599989M	Total Assets ($)	1309949M	1330088M

M = $ thousand   MM = $ million
See Pages 1 through 15 for Explanation of Ratios and Data

Comparative Historical Data				Current Data Sorted By Sales					
12	20	38	# Postretirement Benefits	9	10	6	6	5	2
			Type of Statement						
46	30	54	Unqualified	1	5	8	11	14	15
167	145	174	Reviewed	18	52	43	46	14	1
264	203	253	Compiled	82	117	34	13	7	
15	22	17	Tax Returns	10	4	2	1		
90	91	135	Other	21	57	16	19	17	5
4/1/92-3/31/93 ALL	4/1/93-3/31/94 ALL	4/1/94-3/31/95 ALL		233 (4/1-9/30/94) 0-1MM	1-3MM	3-5MM	400 (10/1/94-3/31/95) 5-10MM	10-25MM	25MM & OVER
582	491	633	**NUMBER OF STATEMENTS**	132	235	103	90	52	21
%	%	%	**ASSETS**	%	%	%	%	%	%
8.0	9.0	8.7	Cash & Equivalents	11.3	8.3	8.2	7.7	6.6	7.5
24.9	25.4	26.6	Trade Receivables - (net)	25.2	26.2	26.0	28.2	30.9	26.1
16.9	16.3	16.9	Inventory	13.8	15.5	16.7	21.2	22.2	20.7
2.0	2.0	2.0	All Other Current	1.9	1.6	2.6	1.7	3.8	1.4
51.8	52.7	54.2	Total Current	52.2	51.6	53.5	58.9	63.4	55.6
41.2	40.3	39.5	Fixed Assets (net)	41.3	42.1	40.7	34.8	30.4	36.9
1.1	1.5	1.0	Intangibles (net)	1.2	.9	1.1	.7	1.0	2.6
5.8	5.5	5.2	All Other Non-Current	5.3	5.4	4.6	5.7	5.2	4.9
100.0	100.0	100.0	Total	100.0	100.0	100.0	100.0	100.0	100.0
			LIABILITIES						
8.0	7.9	8.0	Notes Payable-Short Term	7.5	7.6	8.0	8.4	10.4	7.1
6.9	6.3	6.0	Cur. Mat.-L./T/D	6.3	6.9	6.4	4.6	3.4	3.6
10.7	9.7	11.7	Trade Payables	9.6	11.1	11.9	13.2	16.8	11.4
.6	1.3	.5	Income Taxes Payable	.4	.4	.6	.6	.8	1.3
7.0	7.8	7.9	All Other Current	7.6	7.5	7.2	9.6	9.1	8.6
33.2	33.0	34.1	Total Current	31.4	33.5	34.2	36.5	40.4	32.1
23.0	21.7	22.3	Long Term Debt	27.2	24.6	19.7	16.9	16.4	17.5
.7	.7	.5	Deferred Taxes	.2	.4	.7	.7	.4	1.5
3.3	3.3	3.2	All Other-Non-Current	3.5	3.1	3.5	3.3	2.4	3.0
39.9	41.2	39.9	Net Worth	37.8	38.4	41.9	42.7	40.4	45.8
100.0	100.0	100.0	Total Liabilities & Net Worth	100.0	100.0	100.0	100.0	100.0	100.0
			INCOME DATA						
100.0	100.0	100.0	Net Sales	100.0	100.0	100.0	100.0	100.0	100.0
34.2	33.4	33.0	Gross Profit	41.9	34.7	28.7	27.1	24.5	26.8
29.6	28.8	26.8	Operating Expenses	34.2	28.9	22.7	21.9	17.7	19.2
4.6	4.6	6.3	Operating Profit	7.7	5.7	6.0	5.2	6.8	7.6
1.8	1.2	1.3	All Other Expenses (net)	1.9	1.4	1.5	.8	.5	1.0
2.8	3.4	4.9	Profit Before Taxes	5.8	4.3	4.5	4.4	6.3	6.6
			RATIOS						
2.5	2.4	2.5	Current	2.9	2.5	2.3	2.5	2.3	2.2
1.6	1.6	1.6		1.7	1.6	1.6	1.6	1.6	1.6
1.1	1.2	1.1		1.0	1.1	1.2	1.2	1.1	1.3
1.7	1.7	1.7	Quick	2.1	1.7	1.7	1.7	1.6	1.5
(581) 1.0	1.0	(632) 1.0		(131) 1.1	1.0	1.0	.9	.9	.9
.6	.6	.7		.7	.7	.6	.7	.6	.7
31 11.7	33 10.9	36 10.1	Sales/Receivables	28 13.0	36 10.2	34 10.7	39 9.4	44 8.3	43 8.4
44 8.3	43 8.4	47 7.8		44 8.3	46 7.9	46 7.9	48 7.6	55 6.6	49 7.5
56 6.5	56 6.5	60 6.1		62 5.9	58 6.2	59 6.2	61 6.0	68 5.4	70 5.2
14 26.4	15 24.6	17 22.0	Cost of Sales/Inventory	5 76.9	13 28.6	17 20.9	27 13.5	27 13.5	28 13.2
37 9.8	37 9.9	38 9.6		28 13.0	32 11.3	40 9.2	47 7.8	48 7.6	51 7.2
73 5.0	65 5.6	72 5.1		63 5.8	69 5.3	72 5.1	74 4.9	78 4.7	83 4.4
13 28.3	12 31.0	15 24.7	Cost of Sales/Payables	10 37.8	14 26.5	16 22.8	16 22.7	19 19.2	24 15.2
24 15.2	21 17.0	25 14.6		22 16.6	24 15.3	24 15.5	29 12.5	32 11.5	33 11.1
39 9.4	35 10.5	42 8.6		43 8.4	42 8.7	38 9.5	45 8.2	53 6.9	43 8.5
5.8	6.1	5.7	Sales/Working Capital	4.5	6.4	6.1	5.5	5.2	4.6
11.4	11.4	10.5		9.6	11.9	10.6	10.0	10.6	8.6
63.7	42.6	40.1		129.8	54.0	29.9	25.8	29.4	18.7
5.1	5.9	8.9	EBIT/Interest	12.0	7.0	7.8	8.3	12.3	15.8
(544) 2.1	(457) 2.9	(597) 3.6		(119) 4.2	(223) 3.1	(85) 3.0	(48) 3.8	(19) 4.0	9.0
1.0	1.3	1.5		1.3	1.5	1.5	1.8	2.2	3.7
2.5	3.4	4.1	Net Profit + Depr., Dep., Amort./Cur. Mat. L/T/D	3.2	3.5	3.7	6.8	6.6	5.6
(282) 1.6	(207) 1.7	(307) 2.2		(43) 2.3	(115) 1.9	(48) 1.8	(57) 2.3	(30) 3.1	(14) 2.7
.8	.9	1.0		1.0	1.0	1.1	1.0	1.2	1.5
.6	.5	.5	Fixed/Worth	.5	.6	.7	.5	.3	.5
1.1	1.0	1.0		1.1	1.2	1.0	.9	.8	1.0
2.1	2.1	2.1		2.8	2.3	1.7	1.4	2.2	1.4
.8	.8	.8	Debt/Worth	.7	.9	.8	.6	.7	.6
1.6	1.4	1.6		1.6	1.7	1.5	1.5	1.7	1.2
3.2	3.2	3.6		4.2	3.5	2.9	2.9	4.4	3.6
30.2	34.2	42.4	% Profit Before Taxes/Tangible Net Worth	64.9	42.1	39.6	31.8	48.5	53.0
(548) 13.5	(458) 14.8	(597) 21.1		(115) 25.9	(222) 18.6	(101) 16.4	(88) 19.7	(50) 24.8	(19) 26.5
.6	3.2	6.4		5.0	6.5	3.7	5.1	8.7	16.8
11.2	13.4	16.3	% Profit Before Taxes/Total Assets	20.6	15.2	14.4	14.3	19.9	18.5
4.6	5.9	7.6		10.1	7.5	6.0	7.0	8.9	11.8
.1	.8	1.6		.7	1.3	1.3	1.9	3.4	6.7
9.2	9.2	9.3	Sales/Net Fixed Assets	10.4	8.1	7.8	11.4	11.1	9.0
5.0	5.4	5.1		5.5	4.6	4.8	6.1	6.9	4.8
3.1	3.4	3.3		3.1	3.2	2.9	3.7	4.5	3.3
2.6	2.7	2.6	Sales/Total Assets	2.9	2.5	2.7	2.6	2.6	2.1
2.0	2.0	1.9		1.9	2.0	1.9	2.0	1.9	1.8
1.4	1.5	1.5		1.3	1.6	1.5	1.5	1.5	1.2
2.3	2.5	2.5	% Depr., Dep., Amort./Sales	3.0	2.7	2.5	1.9	1.2	1.4
(555) 4.1	(476) 4.0	(601) 3.9		(120) 4.6	(223) 4.3	(100) 3.9	(88) 3.1	(51) 2.7	(19) 3.1
6.5	6.4	6.0		7.0	6.4	5.3	5.1	4.2	5.6
3.9	3.7	3.3	% Officers', Directors', Owners' Comp/Sales	5.6	4.4	2.4	2.2	1.6	
(330) 6.7	(292) 6.7	(353) 6.0		(68) 9.5	(139) 7.0	(63) 4.8	(56) 4.2	(22) 3.0	
11.2	12.4	10.7		14.3	11.4	6.8	7.6	5.3	
3135241M	2594507M	4036825M	Net Sales ($)	79165M	430316M	392141M	641159M	807916M	1686128M
1880103M	1642490M	2474770M	Total Assets ($)	49072M	241004M	229260M	359836M	448506M	1147092M

M = $ thousand   MM = $ million
See Pages 1 through 15 for Explanation of Ratios and Data

Current Data Sorted By Assets   Comparative Historical Data

	5	9	5		2	# Postretirement Benefits		
						Type of Statement		
4	10	31	19	5	4	Unqualified	83	85
3	52	50	6			Reviewed	105	102
47	55	24	3		1	Compiled	107	106
8	3					Tax Returns		4
21	30	25	17	4	2	Other	69	73

	0-500M	500M-2MM	2-10MM	10-50MM	50-100MM	100-250MM		4/1/90-3/31/91 ALL	4/1/91-3/31/92 ALL
		146 (4/1-9/30/94)		278 (10/1/94-3/31/95)					
NUMBER OF STATEMENTS	83	150	130	45	9	7		364	370
	%	%	%	%	%	%		%	%
ASSETS									
Cash & Equivalents	9.8	6.8	5.8	4.7				8.1	7.0
Trade Receivables - (net)	32.5	31.0	26.4	27.8				26.6	25.1
Inventory	18.2	23.7	27.5	27.7				24.0	24.9
All Other Current	2.9	1.7	3.2	5.2				3.1	2.4
Total Current	63.4	63.2	63.0	65.4				61.8	59.3
Fixed Assets (net)	31.6	30.3	29.5	25.8				30.6	32.2
Intangibles (net)	.3	1.4	1.0	2.1				1.1	1.5
All Other Non-Current	4.7	5.1	6.6	6.6				6.5	7.0
Total	100.0	100.0	100.0	100.0				100.0	100.0
LIABILITIES									
Notes Payable-Short Term	9.5	8.5	10.9	10.8				10.7	10.3
Cur. Mat. -L/T/D	5.8	6.8	4.3	3.5				5.0	5.3
Trade Payables	14.3	15.1	12.5	11.9				11.4	10.7
Income Taxes Payable	1.4	.5	.7	.7				.7	.6
All Other Current	10.9	9.8	10.8	12.7				10.7	9.7
Total Current	42.0	40.7	39.1	39.6				38.4	36.6
Long Term Debt	20.1	15.7	13.2	15.4				16.3	17.4
Deferred Taxes	.1	.5	1.0	.6				.6	.6
All Other-Non-Current	4.2	5.9	3.2	3.8				2.6	2.6
Net Worth	33.6	37.1	43.5	40.6				42.1	42.7
Total Liabilities & Net Worth	100.0	100.0	100.0	100.0				100.0	100.0
INCOME DATA									
Net Sales	100.0	100.0	100.0	100.0				100.0	100.0
Gross Profit	42.0	32.0	28.9	26.6				32.4	31.6
Operating Expenses	36.8	27.2	23.1	20.1				27.2	27.8
Operating Profit	5.2	4.8	5.8	6.5				5.3	3.8
All Other Expenses (net)	1.4	1.3	1.3	1.0				1.5	1.6
Profit Before Taxes	3.8	3.5	4.5	5.5				3.7	2.2
RATIOS									
Current	2.4	2.4	2.4	2.3				2.7	2.6
	1.5	1.6	1.6	1.6				1.7	1.7
	1.1	1.1	1.2	1.2				1.2	1.2
Quick	1.8	1.5	1.3	1.1				1.5	1.5
	1.1	.9	.9	.8				1.0	.9
	.7	.7	.6	.6				.6	.6
Sales/Receivables	30 12.0	40 9.1	43 8.5	46 8.0				39 9.4	38 9.5
	45 8.2	51 7.2	54 6.7	58 6.3				50 7.3	49 7.4
	60 6.1	63 5.8	65 5.6	74 4.9				64 5.7	63 5.8
Cost of Sales/Inventory	4 100.0	20 18.0	45 8.1	54 6.8				26 14.0	29 12.4
	29 12.8	51 7.1	73 5.0	78 4.7				63 5.8	65 5.6
	68 5.4	87 4.2	135 2.7	140 2.6				118 3.1	118 3.1
Cost of Sales/Payables	13 27.3	18 20.6	19 19.6	25 14.4				14 27.0	14 25.6
	25 14.8	32 11.3	32 11.3	37 9.8				27 13.5	27 13.4
	48 7.6	47 7.8	56 6.5	52 7.0				43 8.5	41 8.8
Sales/Working Capital	5.7	6.0	4.1	3.5				4.4	4.1
	14.0	9.5	8.3	7.0				7.9	8.0
	38.9	30.1	21.7	11.8				26.0	21.8
EBIT/Interest	7.2	6.6	9.7	10.6				6.1	4.5
	(72) 3.0	(141) 3.4	(118) 3.6	(43) 5.0				(333) 2.4	(338) 1.9
	1.0	1.2	1.9	2.0				1.2	.6
Net Profit + Depr., Dep., Amort./Cur. Mat. L /T/D	4.6	4.6	4.1	3.8				4.6	3.6
	(25) 2.1	(77) 2.2	(76) 2.0	(27) 2.7				(212) 2.2	(198) 1.6
	1.1	.9	1.2	1.9				.9	.7
Fixed/Worth	.3	.4	.3	.4				.3	.4
	.9	.8	.7	.7				.7	.7
	3.0	1.7	1.5	1.1				1.3	1.4
Debt/Worth	.8	.9	.6	1.0				.7	.7
	1.8	1.7	1.5	1.6				1.4	1.3
	5.2	4.8	2.9	2.9				3.2	2.8
% Profit Before Taxes/Tangible Net Worth	62.5	45.2	29.4	39.0				32.3	25.3
	(72) 26.7	(142) 18.9	(124) 18.7	(44) 21.6				(342) 14.7	(350) 9.4
	2.5	5.6	7.1	8.7				3.1	-2.2
% Profit Before Taxes/Total Assets	20.2	13.0	14.4	13.6				14.0	9.7
	9.6	5.5	6.2	9.4				5.1	3.4
	.0	1.1	2.6	2.6				.9	-1.6
Sales/Net Fixed Assets	21.9	17.3	12.7	11.0				13.3	13.1
	9.1	7.6	6.0	6.0				6.7	6.0
	4.6	3.7	3.1	3.9				4.1	3.3
Sales/Total Assets	3.4	2.7	2.1	1.9				2.4	2.2
	2.4	2.1	1.7	1.6				1.8	1.7
	1.9	1.5	1.3	1.2				1.4	1.3
% Depr., Dep., Amort./Sales	1.3	1.8	1.5	1.7				1.8	1.8
	(70) 2.6	(138) 3.1	(122) 2.8	(39) 2.7				(332) 3.0	(342) 3.3
	6.5	5.6	4.6	3.8				4.6	5.2
% Officers', Directors', Owners' Comp/Sales	6.4	4.3	3.4					3.3	3.7
	(50) 8.9	(75) 6.6	(57) 4.5					(174) 6.3	(160) 6.7
	17.9	9.3	7.6					11.5	11.6
Net Sales ($)	64689M	375768M	988280M	1489344M	895206M	1067437M		4504148M	4938421M
Total Assets ($)	23525M	173328M	585496M	982524M	638294M	1080561M		3160854M	3813860M

M = $ thousand   MM = $ million
See Pages 1 through 15 for Explanation of Ratios and Data

Comparative Historical Data				Current Data Sorted By Sales					
11	13	21	# Postretirement Benefits	1	3	3	3	6	5
			Type of Statement						
74	63	73	Unqualified	8	4	8	12	19	22
99	101	111	Reviewed	3	38	29	25	12	4
101	92	130	Compiled	37	59	20	6	5	3
6	5	11	Tax Returns	8	2	1			
72	85	99	Other	19	23	14	14	14	15
4/1/92-3/31/93 ALL	4/1/93-3/31/94 ALL	4/1/94-3/31/95 ALL		146 (4/1-9/30/94)			278 (10/1/94-3/31/95)		
				0-1MM	1-3MM	3-5MM	5-10MM	10-25MM	25MM & OVER
352	346	424	**NUMBER OF STATEMENTS**	75	126	72	57	50	44
%	%	%	**ASSETS**	%	%	%	%	%	%
6.4	7.2	6.9	Cash & Equivalents	10.3	6.9	6.6	5.1	5.0	5.9
27.1	28.1	29.5	Trade Receivables - (net)	28.9	30.4	28.9	29.3	28.5	30.0
25.3	23.3	24.2	Inventory	17.2	23.3	25.1	31.0	26.5	26.1
2.1	2.0	3.0	All Other Current	4.2	2.0	1.7	2.0	5.2	4.6
60.8	60.7	63.6	Total Current	60.5	62.7	62.3	67.3	65.3	66.6
32.2	31.1	29.5	Fixed Assets (net)	33.0	31.7	30.8	24.9	26.9	24.3
1.1	1.6	1.2	Intangibles (net)	.6	.9	1.7	1.2	1.1	2.3
5.8	6.6	5.7	All Other Non-Current	5.9	4.7	5.2	6.6	6.8	6.9
100.0	100.0	100.0	Total	100.0	100.0	100.0	100.0	100.0	100.0
			LIABILITIES						
10.8	11.3	9.7	Notes Payable-Short Term	7.3	9.7	9.9	11.2	11.3	10.1
6.0	4.5	5.2	Cur. Mat.-L /T/D	6.4	6.7	5.1	4.2	3.1	3.0
13.0	11.3	13.6	Trade Payables	11.1	14.7	14.4	14.6	13.4	12.5
.4	1.6	.8	Income Taxes Payable	.5	1.0	.8	.6	.8	.5
9.3	9.4	10.9	All Other Current	9.0	11.0	10.3	10.8	12.3	13.3
39.6	38.1	40.3	Total Current	34.3	43.2	40.6	41.4	40.9	39.4
18.4	16.5	15.6	Long Term Debt	21.4	16.6	13.5	11.4	12.0	15.6
.5	.6	.6	Deferred Taxes	.1	.5	1.0	.5	.8	.9
3.4	3.6	4.5	All Other-Non-Current	5.0	4.9	5.3	2.3	3.3	5.7
38.1	41.2	39.0	Net Worth	39.2	34.7	39.6	44.5	43.0	38.4
100.0	100.0	100.0	Total Liabilities & Net Worth	100.0	100.0	100.0	100.0	100.0	100.0
			INCOME DATA						
100.0	100.0	100.0	Net Sales	100.0	100.0	100.0	100.0	100.0	100.0
32.1	31.9	32.1	Gross Profit	42.9	33.1	29.2	29.0	28.0	24.2
28.6	27.2	26.8	Operating Expenses	37.0	28.5	23.8	23.9	21.3	19.0
3.5	4.7	5.3	Operating Profit	5.9	4.6	5.4	5.1	6.7	5.2
1.5	1.6	1.3	All Other Expenses (net)	1.7	1.3	1.1	1.1	1.2	1.3
2.1	3.1	4.0	Profit Before Taxes	4.2	3.3	4.2	4.0	5.5	3.9
			RATIOS						
2.4	2.6	2.4	Current	3.0	2.1	2.4	2.7	2.3	2.6
1.6	1.7	1.6		1.8	1.5	1.6	1.6	1.6	1.7
1.2	1.2	1.2		1.3	1.1	1.1	1.2	1.2	1.3
1.4	1.5	1.4	Quick	2.0	1.4	1.3	1.3	1.2	1.4
.9	1.0	.9		1.2	.9	.9	.8	.9	.8
.6	.6	.6		.7	.6	.6	.6	.6	.7
40 9.2	41 9.0	41 9.0	Sales/Receivables	31 11.7	39 9.3	41 9.0	41 8.8	41 8.8	48 7.6
52 7.0	50 7.3	52 7.0		50 7.3	51 7.1	50 7.3	54 6.7	54 6.8	59 6.2
66 5.5	66 5.5	65 5.6		69 5.3	63 5.6	58 6.3	65 5.6	65 5.6	89 4.1
28 13.1	29 12.7	27 13.6	Cost of Sales/Inventory	4 100.0	22 16.7	24 15.2	52 7.0	43 8.5	53 6.9
68 5.4	63 5.8	60 6.1		30 12.0	51 7.2	51 7.2	79 4.6	73 5.0	74 4.9
126 2.9	118 3.1	107 3.4		85 4.3	111 3.3	91 4.0	135 2.7	122 3.0	107 3.4
18 20.7	14 26.5	18 20.5	Cost of Sales/Payables	13 27.3	17 21.0	17 21.6	23 15.7	19 19.1	23 15.6
30 12.1	27 13.4	32 11.4		27 13.3	30 12.2	31 11.6	36 10.1	33 11.0	37 9.9
47 7.7	45 8.2	49 7.4		58 6.3	55 6.6	43 8.4	56 6.5	51 7.1	47 7.7
4.6	4.7	4.6	Sales/Working Capital	4.3	5.3	6.0	3.7	6.1	3.5
9.0	8.5	8.8		9.0	9.6	10.6	6.7	8.8	5.9
23.1	23.4	24.5		21.3	38.3	40.1	22.0	17.1	10.3
(328) 5.1	(318) 5.8	(390) 8.4	EBIT/Interest	(65) 7.0	(118) 6.6	(69) 10.3	(50) 8.6	(46) 12.4	(42) 12.5
2.3	2.6	3.6		2.9	3.3	4.1	3.5	5.2	3.7
1.1	1.1	1.6		.9	1.2	1.3	2.2	2.8	1.7
(182) 3.6	(156) 3.1	(213) 4.2	Net Profit + Depr., Dep., Amort./Cur. Mat. L/T/D	(25) 5.2	(65) 3.6	(36) 5.0	(29) 4.2	(31) 5.1	(27) 4.1
1.6	1.7	2.2		2.1	1.9	1.9	1.9	2.8	2.7
.7	.9	1.1		.9	.9	.9	1.5	1.7	1.5
.4	.4	.4	Fixed/Worth	.3	.4	.4	.3	.3	.4
.8	.7	.8		.8	.9	.7	.6	.7	.7
1.8	1.6	1.5		2.2	2.1	1.5	1.2	1.2	1.2
.8	.7	.8	Debt/Worth	.6	1.0	.6	.8	.7	1.1
1.5	1.4	1.6		1.4	2.1	1.5	1.3	1.4	2.1
3.6	4.2	3.9		4.2	5.0	3.3	2.5	3.0	3.8
(327) 29.4	(325) 28.9	(398) 37.4	% Profit Before Taxes/Tangible Net Worth	(67) 55.9	(119) 41.1	(67) 35.6	(54) 29.7	(49) 34.6	(42) 32.7
10.5	10.7	19.6		23.7	18.5	19.7	16.4	22.0	19.6
2.3	1.6	5.8		1.9	2.9	5.7	8.3	11.1	8.3
9.8	10.7	14.0	% Profit Before Taxes/Total Assets	18.8	12.2	16.3	12.5	16.6	13.3
3.9	4.2	6.5		8.4	5.9	5.7	5.8	9.7	6.3
.4	.2	1.5		.0	1.1	.6	3.1	3.6	2.2
13.3	13.3	14.7	Sales/Net Fixed Assets	16.0	16.1	14.8	16.3	13.3	11.5
6.3	6.6	6.7		6.2	6.6	7.6	7.6	6.6	6.0
3.5	3.5	3.7		3.3	3.6	3.7	3.8	4.4	4.7
2.4	2.3	2.5	Sales/Total Assets	2.8	2.9	2.6	2.2	2.5	1.9
1.8	1.8	1.9		2.0	2.0	2.1	1.9	1.8	1.6
1.3	1.3	1.4		1.3	1.4	1.6	1.4	1.4	1.2
(323) 1.8	(312) 1.8	(384) 1.6	% Depr., Dep., Amort./Sales	(62) 1.6	(119) 1.7	(65) 1.9	(51) 1.3	(48) 1.2	(39) 1.8
3.2	3.1	2.8		4.6	3.4	2.6	2.4	2.4	2.4
5.1	5.2	5.3		8.5	5.6	5.8	4.1	3.4	3.7
(157) 3.8	(176) 3.0	(190) 3.8	% Officers', Directors', Owners' Comp/Sales	(39) 6.9	(71) 4.1	(36) 4.1	(22) 3.3	(15) 1.7	
6.0	5.9	6.5		8.9	6.7	5.5	4.6	3.7	
10.2	10.6	10.1		17.9	10.4	8.8	7.6	5.2	
4094946M	4263626M	4880724M	Net Sales ($)	44458M	234418M	283995M	389327M	771237M	3157289M
3164630M	3341334M	3483728M	Total Assets ($)	30319M	149030M	152941M	254545M	493419M	2403474M

M = $ thousand   MM = $ million
See Pages 1 through 15 for Explanation of Ratios and Data

Current Data Sorted By Assets   Comparative Historical Data

0-500M	500M-2MM	2-10MM	10-50MM	50-100MM	100-250MM		4/1/90-3/31/91 ALL	4/1/91-3/31/92 ALL
		5	2		1	**# Postretirement Benefits**		
						Type of Statement		
	1	5	2	2	2	Unqualified	16	17
	3	2				Reviewed	7	5
1	4	3	1			Compiled	12	14
1						Tax Returns	1	
1	4	4	5			Other	8	10
	19 (4/1-9/30/94)		**22 (10/1/94-3/31/95)**					
3	12	14	8	2	2	**NUMBER OF STATEMENTS**	44	46
%	%	%	%	%	%	**ASSETS**	%	%
	5.1	2.0				Cash & Equivalents	6.4	5.7
	32.7	33.1				Trade Receivables - (net)	24.9	27.0
	33.0	33.9				Inventory	32.7	27.1
	1.4	2.4				All Other Current	.9	2.4
	72.2	71.4				Total Current	64.8	62.2
	22.6	21.0				Fixed Assets (net)	26.8	28.1
	.6	2.0				Intangibles (net)	1.0	3.3
	4.7	5.6				All Other Non-Current	7.4	6.5
	100.0	100.0				Total	100.0	100.0
						LIABILITIES		
	14.6	15.0				Notes Payable-Short Term	14.2	12.5
	2.7	3.0				Cur. Mat. -L/T/D	4.6	5.1
	21.9	15.9				Trade Payables	12.3	13.7
	.9	.8				Income Taxes Payable	.8	.8
	5.3	17.4				All Other Current	8.0	9.3
	45.5	52.0				Total Current	40.0	41.4
	13.8	10.7				Long Term Debt	13.6	12.0
	.2	.5				Deferred Taxes	.9	.5
	.9	.4				All Other-Non-Current	.7	2.5
	39.6	36.4				Net Worth	44.8	43.6
	100.0	100.0				Total Liabilities & Net Worth	100.0	100.0
						INCOME DATA		
	100.0	100.0				Net Sales	100.0	100.0
	32.0	29.0				Gross Profit	36.6	37.5
	27.8	25.4				Operating Expenses	30.3	31.6
	4.2	3.6				Operating Profit	6.3	5.9
	1.6	.8				All Other Expenses (net)	2.2	.6
	2.6	2.9				Profit Before Taxes	4.1	5.3
						RATIOS		
	2.6	2.4					2.3	2.8
	1.6	1.4				Current	1.7	1.8
	1.3	1.1					1.3	1.1
	1.3	1.0					1.3	1.5
	.8	.7				Quick	.9	.8
	.6	.5					.5	.6
49	7.5	49 7.5					39 9.3	41 8.9
61	6.0	64 5.7				Sales/Receivables	58 6.3	60 6.1
87	4.2	79 4.6					68 5.4	72 5.1
27	13.3	52 7.0					57 6.4	42 8.7
91	4.0	101 3.6				Cost of Sales/Inventory	104 3.5	87 4.2
122	3.0	146 2.5					166 2.2	159 2.3
20	18.4	30 12.2					19 19.0	24 15.1
54	6.8	37 10.0				Cost of Sales/Payables	41 9.0	39 9.4
81	4.5	64 5.7					56 6.5	61 6.0
	5.1	5.2					4.0	3.5
	6.2	14.6				Sales/Working Capital	6.7	7.5
	11.2	38.0					13.0	NM
	5.8	7.6					5.5	8.8
	2.4 (13)	3.6				EBIT/Interest	(42) 3.2	(42) 4.1
	.9	−.6					1.6	1.8
							7.0	8.2
						Net Profit + Depr., Dep., Amort./Cur. Mat. L./T/D	(30) 2.5	(27) 2.9
							1.0	1.5
	.1	.3					.3	.3
	.5	.6				Fixed/Worth	.6	.7
	1.0	1.1					1.0	1.2
	.9	.8					.8	.6
	1.8	1.6				Debt/Worth	1.5	1.4
	3.6	4.0					2.3	2.7
	24.2	36.5					22.8	36.1
	7.3 (12)	19.2				% Profit Before Taxes/Tangible Net Worth	(43) 14.8	15.6
	−2.8	2.8					5.7	8.1
	9.7	10.1					10.0	17.5
	4.2	4.1				% Profit Before Taxes/Total Assets	6.0	5.9
	−.5	−2.7					1.9	2.9
	50.2	18.1					16.9	10.6
	10.9	10.3				Sales/Net Fixed Assets	6.6	6.2
	5.1	5.3					3.4	3.9
	2.7	2.3					2.4	2.2
	1.8	2.1				Sales/Total Assets	1.7	1.7
	1.4	1.6					1.2	1.2
	.5	1.0					1.0	1.5
(11)	1.7 (13)	1.6				% Depr., Dep., Amort./Sales	(39) 2.4	(42) 2.7
	2.5	2.7					4.4	4.0
							2.0	6.5
						% Officers', Directors', Owners' Comp/Sales	(11) 5.3	(12) 11.5
							6.6	21.3
3144M	29346M	123173M	292439M	173760M	197929M	Net Sales ($)	961648M	2005881M
552M	15997M	62002M	178962M	148768M	262532M	Total Assets ($)	795702M	1380170M

M = $ thousand   MM = $ million
See Pages 1 through 15 for Explanation of Ratios and Data

Comparative Historical Data / Current Data Sorted By Sales

Current data date groups: columns 0-1MM and 1-3MM = **19 (4/1-9/30/94)**; columns 3-5MM, 5-10MM, 10-25MM, 25MM & OVER = **22 (10/1/94-3/31/95)**

	4/1/92-3/31/93 ALL	4/1/93-3/31/94 ALL	4/1/94-3/31/95 ALL	Item	0-1MM	1-3MM	3-5MM	5-10MM	10-25MM	25MM & OVER
Column #	1	5	8	# Postretirement Benefits	1	2		2		3
	17	15	12	Type of Statement — Unqualified		2		2	3	5
	5	7	6	Reviewed	1	3		2		
	10	12	9	Compiled		3			2	1
				Tax Returns						
	16	9	14	Other	1	4	3	3	3	3
	48	43	41	**NUMBER OF STATEMENTS**	2	12	3	7	8	9
	%	%	%	**ASSETS**	%	%	%	%	%	%
	7.5	6.4	5.7	Cash & Equivalents		4.9				
	23.8	28.1	32.7	Trade Receivables - (net)		35.4				
	27.1	26.6	27.7	Inventory		28.9				
	1.3	1.5	1.8	All Other Current		1.6				
	59.6	62.5	67.9	Total Current		70.7				
	32.1	29.2	25.2	Fixed Assets (net)		21.6				
	.9	2.6	1.9	Intangibles (net)		2.8				
	7.3	5.7	4.9	All Other Non-Current		4.9				
	100.0	100.0	100.0	Total		100.0				
				LIABILITIES						
	9.2	9.3	10.5	Notes Payable-Short Term		10.8				
	4.4	4.0	2.8	Cur. Mat.-L./T/D		2.5				
	13.9	12.7	18.8	Trade Payables		25.4				
	.5	1.8	1.0	Income Taxes Payable		.9				
	6.8	11.1	13.3	All Other Current		5.9				
	34.8	38.9	46.4	Total Current		45.5				
	13.3	11.3	14.2	Long Term Debt		15.1				
	1.4	1.1	1.1	Deferred Taxes		.4				
	2.8	2.4	1.0	All Other-Non-Current		1.1				
	47.7	46.3	37.4	Net Worth		37.9				
	100.0	100.0	100.0	Total Liabilities & Net Worth		100.0				
				INCOME DATA						
	100.0	100.0	100.0	Net Sales		100.0				
	32.0	31.8	30.2	Gross Profit		32.2				
	27.1	28.7	27.2	Operating Expenses		28.1				
	4.9	3.0	2.9	Operating Profit		4.0				
	1.8	.3	1.1	All Other Expenses (net)		1.3				
	3.2	2.8	1.8	Profit Before Taxes		2.8				
				RATIOS						
	2.7 / 1.8 / 1.2	2.6 / 1.7 / 1.2	2.4 / 1.5 / 1.1	Current		2.6 / 1.6 / 1.3				
	1.6 / .8 / .5	1.6 / .8 / .5	1.3 / .9 / .6	Quick		1.3 / 1.0 / .6				
	36 / 10.1 ; 52 / 7.0 ; 74 / 4.9	42 / 8.7 ; 58 / 6.3 ; 76 / 4.8	48 / 7.6 ; 64 / 5.7 ; 79 / 4.6	Sales/Receivables		49 / 7.5 ; 61 / 6.0 ; 89 / 4.1				
	45 / 8.2 ; 87 / 4.2 ; 166 / 2.2	37 / 9.9 ; 70 / 5.2 ; 152 / 2.4	40 / 9.1 ; 81 / 4.5 ; 104 / 3.5	Cost of Sales/Inventory		27 / 13.3 ; 91 / 4.0 ; 192 / 1.9				
	21 / 17.3 ; 38 / 9.5 ; 65 / 5.6	21 / 17.0 ; 36 / 10.2 ; 60 / 6.1	27 / 13.3 ; 41 / 8.9 ; 64 / 5.7	Cost of Sales/Payables		27 / 13.4 ; 54 / 6.8 ; 81 / 4.5				
	3.2 / 6.1 / 28.1	3.0 / 7.1 / 18.2	4.6 / 6.8 / 22.1	Sales/Working Capital		3.9 / 6.2 / 11.2				
	(44) 10.4 / 3.4 / 1.1	(39) 6.1 / 2.3 / .6	(38) 6.9 / 2.6 / -.2	EBIT/Interest		(11) 4.9 / 2.1 / .7				
	(21) 3.4 / 2.2 / .6	(23) 3.6 / 1.5 / .4	(23) 4.9 / 3.6 / .5	Net Profit + Depr., Dep., Amort./Cur. Mat. L/T/D						
	.3 / .7 / 1.2	.4 / .6 / 1.1	.3 / .5 / 1.2	Fixed/Worth		.1 / .5 / .8				
	.6 / 1.0 / 2.2	.6 / 1.2 / 3.1	.8 / 1.7 / 3.9	Debt/Worth		1.0 / 1.8 / 3.6				
	33.8 / 13.6 / .5	(42) 32.4 / 4.0 / -2.4	(36) 32.7 / 10.4 / 1.7	% Profit Before Taxes/Tangible Net Worth		25.6 / 7.3 / -2.8				
	11.5 / 6.1 / .2	10.8 / 2.4 / -1.2	8.6 / 3.7 / -1.7	% Profit Before Taxes/Total Assets		6.9 / 3.6 / -.5				
	9.8 / 5.2 / 3.1	13.9 / 5.8 / 3.2	17.0 / 7.1 / 4.5	Sales/Net Fixed Assets		50.2 / 7.6 / 4.6				
	2.0 / 1.7 / 1.0	2.3 / 1.7 / .9	2.4 / 1.8 / 1.3	Sales/Total Assets		2.7 / 1.6 / 1.0				
	(41) 1.9 / 3.0 / 5.1	(37) 1.5 / 3.4 / 5.0	(36) 1.0 / 2.2 / 4.9	% Depr., Dep., Amort./Sales		(10) .6 / 2.1 / 4.7				
	(10) 1.9 / 11.6 / 19.2	(10) 4.0 / 8.2 / 10.4	(10) 3.0 / 4.2 / 6.4	% Officers', Directors', Owners' Comp/Sales						
	1457289M	1383337M	819791M	Net Sales ($)	947M	25845M	11528M	42650M	129546M	609275M
	1317945M	1300426M	668813M	Total Assets ($)	379M	16526M	6636M	22159M	68883M	554230M

M = $ thousand   MM = $ million
See Pages 1 through 15 for Explanation of Ratios and Data

Current Data Sorted By Assets — **Comparative Historical Data**

0-500M	500M-2MM	2-10MM	10-50MM	50-100MM	100-250MM	# Postretirement Benefits / Type of Statement	4/1/90-3/31/91 ALL	4/1/91-3/31/92 ALL
3	6	7	1					
2	4	28	12	1		Unqualified	64	61
22	95	75	12	2		Reviewed	194	180
75	110	47	2			Compiled	203	211
13	3	1				Tax Returns	3	8
37	42	45	8		1	Other	89	74

229 (4/1-9/30/94)   406 (10/1/94-3/31/95)

0-500M	500M-2MM	2-10MM	10-50MM	50-100MM	100-250MM		4/1/90-3/31/91 ALL	4/1/91-3/31/92 ALL
149	254	196	34	1	1	**NUMBER OF STATEMENTS**	553	534
%	%	%	%	%	%	**ASSETS**	%	%
10.7	7.8	5.5	5.0			Cash & Equivalents	7.7	7.4
29.9	30.9	28.7	27.9			Trade Receivables - (net)	27.2	27.9
12.1	14.4	20.4	16.9			Inventory	17.4	17.1
1.8	1.9	2.8	4.9			All Other Current	2.3	1.9
54.4	55.1	57.3	54.8			Total Current	54.6	54.3
38.9	38.2	37.0	35.7			Fixed Assets (net)	38.1	38.3
1.4	1.0	.8	2.8			Intangibles (net)	1.0	1.0
5.2	5.7	4.9	6.7			All Other Non-Current	6.3	6.4
100.0	100.0	100.0	100.0			Total	100.0	100.0
						LIABILITIES		
10.4	9.1	11.5	9.3			Notes Payable-Short Term	10.6	10.8
7.2	6.3	5.1	4.6			Cur. Mat.-L/T/D	5.8	6.1
12.4	10.1	10.8	13.9			Trade Payables	10.4	10.6
.6	.5	.6	.4			Income Taxes Payable	.5	.5
8.7	10.8	10.4	9.2			All Other Current	9.8	10.0
39.3	36.8	38.4	37.5			Total Current	37.1	38.1
21.6	20.0	16.9	21.2			Long Term Debt	20.9	19.6
1.0	.6	.9	1.1			Deferred Taxes	.9	.7
2.0	2.8	2.8	3.1			All Other-Non-Current	2.1	2.7
36.1	39.8	40.9	37.1			Net Worth	39.0	38.9
100.0	100.0	100.0	100.0			Total Liabilities & Net Worth	100.0	100.0
						INCOME DATA		
100.0	100.0	100.0	100.0			Net Sales	100.0	100.0
38.9	31.7	26.1	26.2			Gross Profit	30.8	29.6
31.9	25.6	17.7	16.4			Operating Expenses	25.2	25.6
7.0	6.1	8.4	9.8			Operating Profit	5.5	4.0
1.9	1.4	1.5	1.9			All Other Expenses (net)	2.0	1.7
5.1	4.7	6.8	7.9			Profit Before Taxes	3.5	2.3
						RATIOS		
2.6 / 1.5 / .9	2.3 / 1.5 / 1.1	2.1 / 1.4 / 1.1	2.2 / 1.3 / 1.2			Current	2.5 / 1.5 / 1.1	2.3 / 1.5 / 1.0
2.0 / 1.1 / .6	1.6 / 1.1 / .8	1.3 / .9 / .6	1.4 / .9 / .6			Quick	1.6 / .9 / .6	1.6 / .9 / .6
28 13.0 / 46 8.0 / 60 6.1	40 9.1 / 54 6.8 / 70 5.2	45 8.1 / 57 6.4 / 83 4.4	48 7.6 / 72 5.1 / 94 3.9			Sales/Receivables	36 10.1 / 49 7.5 / 64 5.7	37 9.8 / 50 7.3 / 66 5.5
6 61.4 / 21 17.1 / 46 7.9	15 23.6 / 32 11.5 / 56 6.5	33 11.1 / 56 6.5 / 91 4.0	34 10.8 / 41 8.8 / 89 4.1			Cost of Sales/Inventory	21 17.5 / 40 9.1 / 69 5.3	20 18.5 / 38 9.6 / 68 5.4
9 41.7 / 20 18.0 / 42 8.6	12 30.3 / 22 16.3 / 36 10.1	17 21.1 / 28 13.2 / 46 7.9	21 17.6 / 39 9.3 / 60 6.1			Cost of Sales/Payables	12 30.8 / 22 16.3 / 38 9.6	11 32.1 / 23 15.9 / 40 9.1
6.9 / 15.4 / -72.0	5.9 / 11.1 / 35.1	4.7 / 10.0 / 28.9	4.5 / 9.6 / 16.4			Sales/Working Capital	5.7 / 11.1 / 50.4	5.8 / 11.0 / 120.5
(136) 9.1 / 3.9 / 1.5	(243) 8.0 / 3.2 / 1.7	(184) 9.3 / 3.8 / 2.1	(32) 7.2 / 3.9 / 2.3			EBIT/Interest	(509) 5.0 / 2.3 / 1.0	(503) 5.2 / 2.2 / .6
(48) 4.3 / 2.2 / 1.1	(134) 3.2 / 1.9 / 1.2	(106) 4.1 / 2.1 / 1.2	(17) 3.1 / 2.3 / 1.3			Net Profit + Depr., Dep., Amort./Cur. Mat. L /T/D	(314) 3.9 / 2.1 / .9	(295) 3.3 / 1.7 / .6
.6 / 1.1 / 3.3	.6 / 1.0 / 1.7	.5 / 1.0 / 1.7	.5 / 1.0 / 1.7			Fixed/Worth	.6 / 1.0 / 1.9	.5 / 1.0 / 2.0
.7 / 1.8 / 9.1	.8 / 1.5 / 2.9	.8 / 1.7 / 3.3	1.2 / 1.9 / 3.7			Debt/Worth	.8 / 1.6 / 3.5	.7 / 1.5 / 3.7
(127) 62.8 / 28.3 / 6.7	(241) 39.4 / 19.2 / 3.9	(189) 39.2 / 22.0 / 11.3	(33) 36.0 / 24.2 / 10.3			% Profit Before Taxes/Tangible Net Worth	(519) 37.0 / 17.5 / 1.8	(495) 32.1 / 12.3 / -.8
21.0 / 10.8 / 2.4	14.3 / 7.1 / 1.7	14.8 / 8.0 / 3.3	12.5 / 8.4 / 4.5			% Profit Before Taxes/Total Assets	13.2 / 5.6 / .3	11.5 / 4.7 / -1.4
14.4 / 7.1 / 4.0	8.8 / 5.4 / 3.5	6.9 / 4.4 / 3.0	6.4 / 4.8 / 2.5			Sales/Net Fixed Assets	8.9 / 5.2 / 3.2	9.2 / 5.1 / 3.2
3.4 / 2.4 / 1.8	2.5 / 2.0 / 1.5	2.0 / 1.6 / 1.3	1.9 / 1.4 / 1.0			Sales/Total Assets	2.4 / 1.9 / 1.5	2.4 / 1.9 / 1.4
(136) 2.4 / 3.9 / 6.3	(248) 2.6 / 4.0 / 6.1	(186) 2.5 / 3.6 / 5.4	(32) 1.9 / 3.5 / 5.5			% Depr., Dep., Amort./Sales	(533) 2.5 / 4.0 / 5.9	(517) 2.3 / 4.0 / 5.9
(81) 6.2 / 9.5 / 15.9	(165) 4.1 / 6.6 / 10.1	(104) 2.2 / 4.4 / 6.9	(13) 1.9 / 3.1 / 5.5			% Officers', Directors', Owners' Comp/Sales	(303) 3.9 / 6.6 / 11.7	(315) 3.7 / 6.5 / 11.5
111192M	553893M	1433271M	970642M	97732M	210019M	Net Sales ($)	2314008M	2311811M
42977M	278065M	881604M	670628M	50027M	155733M	Total Assets ($)	1518206M	1489014M

M = $ thousand   MM = $ million
See Pages 1 through 15 for Explanation of Ratios and Data

Comparative Historical Data				Current Data Sorted By Sales					
11	29	17	**# Postretirement Benefits**	3	5	1	3	5	
			Type of Statement						
52	58	47	Unqualified	1	8	1	15	14	8
178	182	204	Reviewed	21	78	44	34	24	3
202	221	234	Compiled	77	103	22	23	9	
10	14	17	Tax Returns	12	3	1		1	
81	83	133	Other	33	44	19	17	5	5
4/1/92-3/31/93 ALL	4/1/93-3/31/94 ALL	4/1/94-3/31/95 ALL		229 (4/1-9/30/94)			406 (10/1/94-3/31/95)		
				0-1MM	1-3MM	3-5MM	5-10MM	10-25MM	25MM & OVER
523	558	635	**NUMBER OF STATEMENTS**	144	236	87	89	63	16
%	%	%	**ASSETS**	%	%	%	%	%	%
6.9	7.5	7.6	Cash & Equivalents	10.1	8.0	5.9	6.1	5.2	6.3
27.8	29.0	29.8	Trade Receivables - (net)	26.8	31.1	31.1	30.6	28.7	32.2
16.1	16.8	15.9	Inventory	11.1	15.2	18.0	20.9	18.0	20.2
1.8	1.7	2.3	All Other Current	1.7	2.3	2.7	2.0	4.2	.9
52.6	55.1	55.6	Total Current	49.7	56.5	57.6	59.6	56.1	59.7
40.1	38.3	37.9	Fixed Assets (net)	43.0	37.3	36.0	34.9	36.6	32.9
1.3	1.2	1.1	Intangibles (net)	1.6	.9	1.1	.6	1.9	1.3
6.0	5.5	5.4	All Other Non-Current	5.7	5.3	5.3	4.9	5.4	6.1
100.0	100.0	100.0	Total	100.0	100.0	100.0	100.0	100.0	100.0
			LIABILITIES						
10.3	10.4	10.1	Notes Payable-Short Term	10.7	8.9	11.0	11.6	10.1	10.2
7.3	5.6	6.0	Cur. Mat.-L./T/D	8.1	5.8	5.5	5.3	4.5	2.9
10.3	10.3	11.1	Trade Payables	10.6	10.5	11.6	11.9	10.9	17.0
.7	1.7	.6	Income Taxes Payable	.6	.5	.6	.6	.6	.3
10.2	9.8	10.1	All Other Current	8.7	10.3	11.4	10.9	10.0	9.6
38.8	37.8	37.9	Total Current	38.6	36.1	40.1	40.2	36.1	39.9
20.3	19.0	19.5	Long Term Debt	24.3	19.7	18.5	14.6	16.7	16.2
.8	.7	.8	Deferred Taxes	1.2	.4	1.1	.6	1.2	1.3
2.6	2.7	2.6	All Other-Non-Current	2.3	2.4	3.3	3.1	3.0	.3
37.6	39.9	39.2	Net Worth	33.5	41.3	37.0	41.6	43.0	42.3
100.0	100.0	100.0	Total Liabilities & Net Worth	100.0	100.0	100.0	100.0	100.0	100.0
			INCOME DATA						
100.0	100.0	100.0	Net Sales	100.0	100.0	100.0	100.0	100.0	100.0
30.0	31.1	31.3	Gross Profit	39.4	32.6	26.0	26.4	24.5	21.8
25.0	25.6	24.1	Operating Expenses	31.8	25.9	20.5	18.3	15.1	15.5
5.1	5.5	7.2	Operating Profit	7.6	6.7	5.5	8.1	9.4	6.4
1.9	1.5	1.6	All Other Expenses (net)	2.2	1.3	1.3	1.5	1.5	.8
3.2	4.1	5.7	Profit Before Taxes	5.4	5.4	4.2	6.6	7.9	5.6
			RATIOS						
2.1	2.2	2.3	Current	2.4	2.4	2.1	2.0	2.2	2.4
1.4	1.5	1.5		1.4	1.6	1.4	1.5	1.4	1.4
1.0	1.1	1.1		.9	1.2	1.0	1.1	1.2	1.2
1.4	1.6	1.6	Quick	1.8	1.7	1.4	1.3	1.4	1.4
.9	1.0	1.0		1.0	1.1	1.0	.9	.9	1.0
.6	.6	.7		.6	.7	.6	.6	.6	.7
37 10.0	38 9.7	40 9.1	Sales/Receivables	30 12.0	40 9.1	43 8.4	41 8.9	45 8.1	45 8.1
49 7.5	50 7.3	53 6.9		48 7.6	51 7.1	58 6.3	53 6.9	55 6.6	51 7.1
64 5.7	68 5.4	72 5.1		70 5.2	72 5.1	72 5.1	74 4.9	81 4.5	81 4.5
18 19.9	20 18.6	17 21.9	Cost of Sales/Inventory	6 65.7	14 25.4	23 16.0	28 13.0	28 13.1	35 10.4
35 9.5	38 9.5	38 9.7		26 14.2	32 11.3	43 8.5	53 6.9	49 7.5	39 9.3
64 5.7	66 5.5	64 5.7		51 7.1	65 5.6	64 5.7	85 4.3	64 5.7	50 7.3
12 30.5	12 30.8	14 27.0	Cost of Sales/Payables	9 42.6	13 27.7	15 24.3	15 23.8	15 24.3	23 15.6
23 15.9	22 16.4	24 15.1		20 17.9	24 15.3	25 14.6	26 14.1	24 15.0	39 9.3
39 9.3	38 9.6	41 8.9		52 7.0	40 9.2	41 8.9	39 9.3	40 9.2	58 6.3
6.5	6.2	5.7	Sales/Working Capital	5.9	5.3	6.8	5.4	5.5	6.1
14.0	11.5	11.2		13.9	10.7	11.5	10.2	9.6	13.1
-277.8	66.4	40.9		-47.3	28.2	67.7	29.1	22.1	23.4
(497) 5.4	(517) 6.8	(597) 8.2	EBIT/Interest	(133) 7.6	(224) 9.2	(84) 3.0	(85) 8.1	(55) 12.2	10.0
2.6	3.0	3.7		3.7	3.5	3.0	5.0	4.2	6.4
1.1	1.6	1.8		1.4	1.8	1.7	2.2	2.2	3.2
(282) 3.0	(261) 3.6	(306) 4.0	Net Profit + Depr., Dep., Amort./Cur. Mat. L/T/D	(56) 3.7	(113) 3.2	(47) 3.1	(51) 4.7	(31) 4.8	
1.7	2.0	2.1		1.9	1.9	1.8	2.5	2.4	
.9	1.2	1.2		.5	1.3	1.0	1.4	1.5	
.6	.6	.6	Fixed/Worth	.7	.5	.5	.5	.5	.5
1.1	1.0	1.0		1.4	1.0	1.0	.9	1.0	.9
2.3	1.9	1.9		5.5	1.6	2.3	1.5	1.6	1.1
.8	.8	.8	Debt/Worth	.9	.7	.9	.9	.6	.7
1.7	1.6	1.6		1.9	1.5	1.9	1.5	1.5	1.6
3.8	3.3	3.4		9.7	2.7	3.9	3.1	3.3	2.2
(476) 31.9	(529) 37.8	(592) 42.2	% Profit Before Taxes/Tangible Net Worth	(122) 61.1	(223) 38.2	(81) 43.0	(88) 39.4	(62) 47.2	29.9
15.0	18.6	21.5		23.7	20.2	16.6	23.8	28.7	23.0
2.4	5.7	8.1		3.8	4.6	7.9	13.0	13.0	15.4
11.6	13.8	16.0	% Profit Before Taxes/Total Assets	18.8	16.2	12.2	15.7	17.6	11.9
5.3	6.4	8.0		8.3	7.1	7.1	8.8	9.0	9.0
.3	1.9	2.6		1.3	1.9	2.1	4.6	4.6	5.1
8.3	9.4	8.7	Sales/Net Fixed Assets	9.6	10.0	9.5	8.6	6.9	8.5
5.0	5.4	5.2		4.9	5.5	5.9	5.0	5.0	5.7
3.3	3.5	3.3		2.5	3.5	3.4	3.8	3.3	4.8
2.5	2.5	2.5	Sales/Total Assets	2.6	2.6	2.4	2.2	2.1	2.2
1.9	2.0	1.9		1.9	2.0	1.9	1.9	1.8	1.9
1.5	1.5	1.4		1.4	1.5	1.4	1.4	1.3	1.6
(500) 2.6	(536) 2.4	(604) 2.4	% Depr., Dep., Amort./Sales	(137) 2.7	(224) 2.7	(82) 2.2	(86) 2.3	(59) 2.4	1.6
4.1	4.2	3.8		5.1	4.1	3.5	3.6	3.3	2.8
5.9	6.1	5.9		7.9	5.8	4.9	4.9	5.0	3.5
(312) 3.6	(318) 3.8	(363) 3.8	% Officers', Directors', Owners' Comp/Sales	(78) 6.5	(146) 4.4	(55) 3.0	(50) 2.7	(28) 1.7	
6.4	6.1	6.3		9.6	6.6	5.2	4.9	2.3	
10.1	10.8	10.4		15.2	10.5	8.2	7.1	5.3	
2243157M	2887322M	3376749M	Net Sales ($)	88064M	438039M	337516M	632544M	910853M	969733M
1355548M	1642723M	2079034M	Total Assets ($)	62853M	278887M	195823M	368421M	625799M	547251M

M = $ thousand   MM = $ million
See Pages 1 through 15 for Explanation of Ratios and Data

Current Data Sorted By Assets | **Comparative Historical Data**

0-500M	500M-2MM	2-10MM	10-50MM	50-100MM	100-250MM		4/1/90-3/31/91 ALL	4/1/91-3/31/92 ALL
2	7	8	9	7	3	**# Postretirement Benefits**		
						Type of Statement		
3	9	40	58	16	9	Unqualified	116	122
4	42	42	6			Reviewed	113	106
21	32	19			1	Compiled	77	86
2		1				Tax Returns		2
8	28	24	27	4	4	Other	59	84
	136 (4/1-9/30/94)		264 (10/1/94-3/31/95)					
38	111	126	91	21	13	**NUMBER OF STATEMENTS**	365	400
%	%	%	%	%	%	**ASSETS**	%	%
7.4	9.0	7.7	11.0	9.2	16.7	Cash & Equivalents	8.2	8.8
36.0	27.4	27.5	25.1	25.3	23.0	Trade Receivables - (net)	27.0	26.2
28.6	29.2	30.8	30.6	23.3	26.0	Inventory	29.7	28.8
4.7	2.9	3.0	4.0	2.6	2.5	All Other Current	2.7	3.6
76.6	68.4	69.0	70.7	60.4	68.2	Total Current	67.6	67.5
17.2	24.2	22.0	20.2	25.0	15.4	Fixed Assets (net)	24.0	24.1
2.3	1.8	2.3	2.2	3.8	9.6	Intangibles (net)	2.0	1.8
3.9	5.6	6.7	6.9	10.8	6.8	All Other Non-Current	6.4	6.6
100.0	100.0	100.0	100.0	100.0	100.0	Total	100.0	100.0
						LIABILITIES		
12.5	10.1	9.0	8.6	2.0	1.0	Notes Payable-Short Term	9.7	10.2
7.1	3.2	3.1	2.3	1.7	2.8	Cur. Mat. -L/T/D	3.8	3.7
19.4	15.8	14.9	11.6	10.3	11.9	Trade Payables	14.0	14.2
.2	.7	.7	.9	.8	.9	Income Taxes Payable	1.2	.6
11.0	14.4	16.0	15.9	16.1	17.0	All Other Current	13.9	15.2
50.2	44.2	43.8	39.3	30.9	33.6	Total Current	42.6	43.9
14.3	10.7	13.3	11.3	11.7	9.1	Long Term Debt	12.5	13.2
.2	.4	.4	.9	1.7	.8	Deferred Taxes	.6	.6
8.1	3.1	2.1	2.7	2.4	4.4	All Other-Non-Current	2.4	2.4
27.1	41.5	40.4	45.7	53.2	52.1	Net Worth	41.9	39.8
100.0	100.0	100.0	100.0	100.0	100.0	Total Liabilities & Net Worth	100.0	100.0
						INCOME DATA		
100.0	100.0	100.0	100.0	100.0	100.0	Net Sales	100.0	100.0
35.8	33.3	32.4	30.8	29.0	35.9	Gross Profit	31.5	31.9
32.9	29.5	28.2	25.4	22.2	26.9	Operating Expenses	26.6	28.1
3.0	3.8	4.2	5.4	6.9	9.0	Operating Profit	4.9	3.8
.7	.8	1.1	.8	.8	-.1	All Other Expenses (net)	1.2	1.1
2.2	3.0	3.2	4.6	6.1	9.1	Profit Before Taxes	3.7	2.7
						RATIOS		
2.9	2.3	2.2	2.9	2.8	2.9	Current	2.3	2.5
1.6	1.6	1.6	1.8	2.0	2.6		1.6	1.6
1.1	1.2	1.2	1.3	1.6	1.6		1.2	1.1
1.5	1.2	1.3	1.5	1.4	1.8	Quick	1.3	1.3
.9	.8	.7	.9	1.1	1.2		.8	.8
.6	.6	.5	.6	.9	.9		.6	.5
27 13.4	28 13.0	37 10.0	45 8.2	48 7.6	50 7.3	Sales/Receivables	35 10.5	34 10.8
37 10.0	42 8.7	47 7.7	55 6.6	68 5.4	72 5.1		49 7.5	49 7.5
56 6.5	54 6.8	68 5.4	79 4.6	85 4.3	85 4.3		64 5.7	62 5.9
15 23.8	33 11.0	51 7.1	65 5.6	62 5.9	94 3.9	Cost of Sales/Inventory	46 8.0	40 9.2
55 6.6	64 5.7	85 4.3	111 3.3	85 4.3	101 3.6		76 4.8	76 4.8
94 3.9	111 3.3	140 2.6	159 2.3	107 3.4	159 2.3		126 2.9	130 2.8
21 17.4	16 23.0	23 15.9	21 17.2	25 14.6	24 15.5	Cost of Sales/Payables	18 20.1	21 17.8
31 11.6	32 11.4	37 9.9	35 10.3	40 9.1	62 5.9		33 11.2	33 11.2
58 6.3	51 7.2	56 6.5	49 7.5	51 7.1	74 4.9		49 7.5	49 7.4
5.7	5.2	4.6	2.7	3.2	2.1	Sales/Working Capital	4.7	4.3
14.1	10.6	8.0	5.6	5.3	4.2		8.0	9.1
52.5	22.6	17.6	11.2	6.6	8.2		17.9	28.4
(33) 13.2	(100) 10.5	(114) 8.3	(82) 12.3	(20) 24.1		EBIT/Interest	(327) 7.8	(362) 7.2
4.6	3.7	3.4	5.4	5.9			2.8	2.7
-.7	1.6	1.3	2.3	4.2			1.2	1.0
	(35) 3.8	(58) 4.4	(56) 11.3	(16) 40.0		Net Profit + Depr., Dep., Amort./Cur. Mat. L./T/D	(222) 5.0	(217) 6.2
	2.2	2.1	4.3	7.8			2.5	2.0
	1.1	1.1	2.4	2.8			1.0	.6
.2	.3	.2	.3	.3	.3	Fixed/Worth	.3	.3
.4	.5	.4	.4	.5	.4		.5	.6
2.0	1.2	1.3	.8	.8	.7		1.2	1.3
.8	.8	.9	.6	.5	.6	Debt/Worth	.8	.8
2.9	1.5	1.9	1.5	1.0	.9		1.5	1.7
7.9	3.1	3.2	2.5	1.3	4.6		3.4	3.5
(32) 76.0	(108) 33.6	(120) 33.7	(88) 38.2	28.4	41.6	% Profit Before Taxes/Tangible Net Worth	(351) 38.2	(378) 32.4
29.0	15.9	17.5	18.6	16.7	21.0		17.4	14.7
-1.7	4.0	2.6	7.7	9.3	11.4		1.9	1.9
22.5	11.0	12.1	13.8	11.3	15.8	% Profit Before Taxes/Total Assets	14.4	12.3
9.7	6.0	5.9	7.0	8.0	9.6		6.0	5.1
-6.6	1.6	.8	3.2	4.7	3.3		.5	.2
76.4	26.1	22.5	15.0	7.9	20.5	Sales/Net Fixed Assets	18.3	19.8
29.5	13.8	10.6	8.1	5.5	8.4		8.3	8.9
12.2	5.8	5.6	5.4	3.9	5.9		5.1	4.6
3.9	3.1	2.4	1.8	1.6	1.5	Sales/Total Assets	2.5	2.6
3.1	2.4	1.9	1.5	1.4	1.2		1.9	1.9
2.3	1.8	1.4	1.2	1.1	.9		1.4	1.4
(30) .9	(103) 1.0	(113) 1.0	(83) 1.4	(18) 1.5	(10) 1.4	% Depr., Dep., Amort./Sales	(329) 1.3	(364) 1.2
1.2	1.8	1.9	2.4	2.4	2.3		2.2	2.1
2.1	3.1	3.3	3.3	3.5	3.2		3.5	3.6
(14) 4.8	(59) 3.5	(40) 2.6				% Officers', Directors', Owners' Comp/Sales	(118) 2.7	(130) 3.1
7.0	5.2	5.1					4.4	5.2
11.9	8.3	7.9					7.4	9.0
34084M	306685M	1059476M	3093143M	2306082M	2592460M	Net Sales ($)	6327010M	7738142M
10899M	131044M	552537M	2068891M	1634924M	1990437M	Total Assets ($)	4516915M	5654563M

M = $ thousand   MM = $ million
See Pages 1 through 15 for Explanation of Ratios and Data

Comparative Historical Data				Current Data Sorted By Sales					
10	24	36	# Postretirement Benefits	2	5	2	5	6	16
			Type of Statement						
136	144	135	Unqualified	2	9	6	18	39	61
112	115	94	Reviewed	2	28	27	23	11	3
76	80	73	Compiled	16	32	9	13	2	1
4	7	3	Tax Returns	1	1			1	
90	92	95	Other	6	23	12	10	17	27
4/1/92-3/31/93	4/1/93-3/31/94	4/1/94-3/31/95		136 (4/1-9/30/94)			264 (10/1/94-3/31/95)		
ALL	ALL	ALL		0-1MM	1-3MM	3-5MM	5-10MM	10-25MM	25MM & OVER
418	438	400	**NUMBER OF STATEMENTS**	27	93	54	64	70	92
%	%	%	**ASSETS**	%	%	%	%	%	%
8.7	9.5	9.1	Cash & Equivalents	7.6	8.8	8.5	8.1	9.5	10.7
27.7	28.3	27.5	Trade Receivables - (net)	34.8	26.9	26.4	26.5	28.0	26.8
28.3	27.7	29.5	Inventory	26.6	29.2	28.6	32.4	31.6	27.8
3.1	3.7	3.3	All Other Current	4.6	3.4	2.6	3.0	3.3	3.6
67.8	69.2	69.5	Total Current	73.7	68.3	66.0	70.0	72.5	68.9
23.2	22.5	21.7	Fixed Assets (net)	17.9	24.6	25.2	20.9	19.8	19.7
2.1	2.0	2.5	Intangibles (net)	3.9	1.5	1.2	2.5	2.7	3.5
6.9	6.2	6.4	All Other Non-Current	4.6	5.6	7.5	6.6	5.0	7.9
100.0	100.0	100.0	Total	100.0	100.0	100.0	100.0	100.0	100.0
			LIABILITIES						
9.0	8.5	8.9	Notes Payable-Short Term	9.5	10.9	8.0	11.4	9.1	5.5
3.3	3.4	3.2	Cur. Mat.-L./T/D	8.3	3.3	3.4	2.6	3.0	2.2
14.1	13.7	14.5	Trade Payables	16.4	15.1	14.9	15.4	14.5	12.5
.6	1.6	.7	Income Taxes Payable	.4	.4	.8	.7	1.0	.8
15.7	15.4	15.1	All Other Current	12.0	13.0	13.6	16.8	16.5	16.9
42.9	42.6	42.5	Total Current	46.6	42.7	40.6	47.0	44.0	38.0
13.0	12.8	12.0	Long Term Debt	10.7	13.7	14.0	11.0	11.9	10.3
.6	.5	.6	Deferred Taxes	.2	.5	.7	.1	.6	1.1
2.8	2.3	3.2	All Other-Non-Current	9.3	3.6	1.2	2.7	1.9	3.3
40.7	41.8	41.7	Net Worth	33.2	39.5	43.4	39.2	41.5	47.2
100.0	100.0	100.0	Total Liabilities & Net Worth	100.0	100.0	100.0	100.0	100.0	100.0
			INCOME DATA						
100.0	100.0	100.0	Net Sales	100.0	100.0	100.0	100.0	100.0	100.0
32.6	32.9	32.6	Gross Profit	39.8	32.8	33.2	31.8	31.9	30.9
28.9	28.3	28.0	Operating Expenses	34.9	29.5	30.6	28.0	26.3	24.3
3.8	4.6	4.5	Operating Profit	4.9	3.3	2.6	3.8	5.6	6.6
1.1	.7	.8	All Other Expenses (net)	.9	.8	.7	1.0	.7	.9
2.7	3.9	3.7	Profit Before Taxes	4.0	2.5	1.9	2.8	4.9	5.7
			RATIOS						
2.4	2.5	2.5		3.3	2.2	2.5	2.1	2.6	2.8
1.6	1.6	1.7	Current	1.9	1.7	1.6	1.5	1.5	1.9
1.2	1.2	1.2		1.2	1.2	1.1	1.2	1.2	1.4
1.4	1.4	1.3		1.9	1.2	1.3	1.2	1.3	1.5
.9	.9	.8	Quick	.9	.8	.8	.7	.8	1.0
.6	.6	.5		.5	.5	.5	.5	.5	.7
35 10.3	37 10.0	36 10.2		33 10.9	28 13.2	33 10.9	31 11.6	42 8.6	46 8.0
50 7.3	51 7.2	49 7.4	Sales/Receivables	42 8.6	42 8.7	43 8.4	46 8.0	56 6.5	58 6.3
64 5.7	65 5.6	66 5.5		69 5.3	54 6.8	59 6.2	57 6.4	76 4.8	81 4.5
40 9.1	40 9.1	46 7.9		18 20.0	34 10.8	42 8.6	39 9.4	55 6.6	66 5.5
78 4.7	73 5.0	85 4.3	Cost of Sales/Inventory	65 5.6	66 5.5	69 5.3	83 4.4	104 3.5	96 3.8
118 3.1	130 2.8	130 2.8		104 3.5	130 2.8	122 3.0	114 3.2	159 2.3	130 2.8
20 18.6	17 21.5	21 17.3		24 14.9	16 23.3	18 19.9	21 17.7	24 15.3	21 17.2
32 11.5	30 12.0	35 10.3	Cost of Sales/Payables	33 11.2	35 10.3	34 10.8	32 11.4	38 9.5	37 9.8
51 7.2	52 7.0	54 6.7		59 6.2	49 7.4	53 6.9	55 6.6	55 6.6	60 6.1
4.6	4.2	4.2		4.7	4.9	4.6	5.0	3.5	3.2
8.1	7.7	7.5	Sales/Working Capital	9.6	8.9	9.2	9.8	7.2	5.4
19.1	21.7	17.1		32.6	19.3	27.9	20.5	17.7	10.1
8.6	9.4	10.7		24.0	9.6	10.2	7.5	12.0	18.6
(387) 3.1	(381) 3.8	(358) 4.4	EBIT/Interest	(24) 3.9	(82) 3.3	(48) 2.9	(60) 4.1	(63) 5.1	(81) 5.2
1.3	1.7	1.6		1.1	1.2	1.2	1.4	1.9	2.6
5.6	7.0	7.6			4.4	3.5	5.2	7.1	23.8
(202) 2.3	(191) 2.7	(179) 2.8	Net Profit + Depr., Dep., Amort./Cur. Mat. L/T/D		(28) 1.6	(25) 1.4	(24) 2.8	(38) 2.9	(59) 6.2
1.0	1.0	1.2			.8	.5	1.9	1.5	2.7
.3	.3	.2		.1	.2	.3	.2	.2	.3
.5	.5	.5	Fixed/Worth	.2	.5	.6	.4	.5	.4
1.2	1.1	1.1		1.0	1.5	1.2	1.2	1.0	.8
.7	.7	.7		.7	.8	.8	.8	.7	.6
1.5	1.6	1.6	Debt/Worth	1.9	1.6	1.7	1.8	2.0	1.1
3.6	3.2	3.0		3.5	3.3	2.5	3.6	3.0	2.4
34.4	35.8	36.1		61.4	34.9	34.0	34.0	33.2	39.7
(395) 15.8	(411) 15.7	(382) 18.6	% Profit Before Taxes/Tangible Net Worth	(24) 24.6	(88) 15.2	(62) 12.3	(64) 19.6	(90) 19.0	20.1
3.8	5.6	5.4		4.0	2.8	-.4	4.3	7.7	10.9
12.3	13.1	13.2		18.0	12.0	11.1	11.4	13.5	16.0
5.8	6.3	6.7	% Profit Before Taxes/Total Assets	9.2	5.8	5.2	6.4	7.9	7.3
.9	1.9	1.6		.3	.4	-.1	1.1	2.8	4.2
21.4	20.5	22.1		76.2	26.2	20.9	23.2	20.7	16.0
10.2	10.3	10.1	Sales/Net Fixed Assets	26.2	12.3	10.5	10.9	10.2	8.1
5.3	5.6	5.6		9.0	5.4	4.7	7.0	5.7	5.5
2.6	2.6	2.6		3.3	3.1	2.7	2.7	2.3	1.9
1.9	1.9	1.9	Sales/Total Assets	2.4	2.4	2.0	2.1	1.6	1.5
1.4	1.4	1.4		1.4	1.4	1.6	1.7	1.3	1.2
1.2	1.2	1.1		.9	1.0	1.1	1.1	1.0	1.4
(377) 2.0	(402) 2.1	(357) 1.9	% Depr., Dep., Amort./Sales	(21) 1.3	(83) 1.9	(50) 1.7	(59) 1.9	(63) 1.9	(81) 2.3
3.2	3.3	3.2		3.6	3.1	3.6	2.9	3.3	3.1
2.5	2.7	3.1		5.1	3.3	2.9	2.9	2.0	
(150) 4.9	(154) 4.7	(122) 5.5	% Officers', Directors', Owners' Comp/Sales	(10) 7.6	(43) 5.9	(27) 5.0	(27) 5.8	(11) 3.2	
9.2	9.1	8.2		12.8	10.2	7.2	7.0	6.6	
8553977M	8873485M	9391930M	Net Sales ($)	17282M	186451M	214655M	442602M	1127282M	7403658M
6066310M	6422747M	6388732M	Total Assets ($)	8822M	108045M	116019M	226698M	777192M	5151956M

M = $ thousand   MM = $ million
See Pages 1 through 15 for Explanation of Ratios and Data

Current Data Sorted By Assets							Comparative Historical Data	

			1			# Postretirement Benefits		
						Type of Statement		
1	3	21	15	1	6	Unqualified		
	2					Reviewed		
1		1				Compiled		
						Tax Returns		
	1	4	6	4	3	Other		

	40 (4/1-9/30/94)		29 (10/1/94-3/31/95)				4/1/90-3/31/91 ALL	4/1/91-3/31/92 ALL
0-500M	500M-2MM	2-10MM	10-50MM	50-100MM	100-250MM	**NUMBER OF STATEMENTS**		
2	6	26	21	5	9			
%	%	%	%	%	%	**ASSETS**	%	%
		12.4	18.5			Cash & Equivalents	D	D
		26.5	27.2			Trade Receivables - (net)	A	A
		29.9	21.5			Inventory	T	T
		2.9	3.2			All Other Current	A	A
		71.7	70.5			Total Current		
		13.5	14.6			Fixed Assets (net)	N	N
		3.2	2.3			Intangibles (net)	O	O
		11.6	12.7			All Other Non-Current	T	T
		100.0	100.0			Total		
						LIABILITIES	A	A
		6.1	1.9			Notes Payable-Short Term	V	V
		3.0	3.1			Cur. Mat. -L/T/D	A	A
		9.7	8.9			Trade Payables	I	I
		.4	.5			Income Taxes Payable	L	L
		14.0	16.3			All Other Current	A	A
		33.0	30.7			Total Current	B	B
		8.1	4.7			Long Term Debt	L	L
		.2	.7			Deferred Taxes	E	E
		2.9	2.7			All Other-Non-Current		
		55.8	61.3			Net Worth		
		100.0	100.0			Total Liabilities & Net Worth		
						INCOME DATA		
		100.0	100.0			Net Sales		
		50.4	53.5			Gross Profit		
		47.9	49.1			Operating Expenses		
		2.5	4.4			Operating Profit		
		.8	-.8			All Other Expenses (net)		
		1.6	5.2			Profit Before Taxes		
						RATIOS		
		4.9	4.7			Current		
		2.2	2.9					
		1.4	1.5					
		2.0	3.4			Quick		
		1.2	2.3					
		.7	.7					
		47 7.7	57 6.4			Sales/Receivables		
		63 5.8	72 5.1					
		78 4.7	114 3.2					
		114 3.2	99 3.7			Cost of Sales/Inventory		
		174 2.1	126 2.9					
		243 1.5	166 2.2					
		29 12.5	31 11.8			Cost of Sales/Payables		
		48 7.6	48 7.6					
		79 4.6	74 4.9					
		2.2	1.8			Sales/Working Capital		
		5.4	2.3					
		8.0	8.9					
		7.2	26.3			EBIT/Interest		
		(23) 3.4	(14) 11.1					
		-.0	1.1					
		9.3	14.5			Net Profit + Depr., Dep., Amort./Cur. Mat. L./T/D		
		(12) 1.3	(12) 6.7					
		-1.1	.9					
		.1	.1			Fixed/Worth		
		.2	.2					
		.5	.4					
		.3	.3			Debt/Worth		
		.9	.5					
		1.6	1.4					
		18.7	25.2			% Profit Before Taxes/Tangible Net Worth		
		(24) 7.6	9.6					
		-2.0	-8.9					
		9.9	19.2			% Profit Before Taxes/Total Assets		
		4.1	5.1					
		-1.9	-4.1					
		20.4	17.2			Sales/Net Fixed Assets		
		13.7	10.4					
		10.3	5.4					
		1.9	1.5			Sales/Total Assets		
		1.4	1.3					
		1.1	.8					
		1.5	1.9			% Depr., Dep., Amort./Sales		
		(24) 2.2	(19) 2.9					
		3.5	4.5					
						% Officers', Directors', Owners' Comp/Sales		
102M	18203M	223349M	528373M	350721M	1546352M	Net Sales ($)		
98M	6953M	149412M	478666M	362492M	1544833M	Total Assets ($)		

M = $ thousand   MM = $ million
See Pages 1 through 15 for Explanation of Ratios and Data

Comparative Historical Data   **Current Data Sorted By Sales**

Type of Statement

# Postretirement Benefits		2	1	0-1MM	1-3MM	3-5MM	5-10MM	10-25MM	1 (25MM & OVER)
Unqualified	18	37	47	1	2	6	9	13	16
Reviewed		3	2		1		1		
Compiled	2	2	2	1			1		
Tax Returns									
Other	10	13	18		2	2		6	8

	4/1/92-3/31/93 ALL	4/1/93-3/31/94 ALL	4/1/94-3/31/95 ALL	0-1MM	1-3MM	3-5MM	5-10MM	10-25MM	25MM & OVER
					40 (4/1-9/30/94)			**29 (10/1/94-3/31/95)**	
NUMBER OF STATEMENTS	30	55	69	2	5	8	11	19	24
ASSETS	%	%	%	%	%	%	%	%	%
Cash & Equivalents	22.2	20.0	15.7				10.6	16.4	20.0
Trade Receivables - (net)	28.0	27.5	26.0				31.5	25.4	25.9
Inventory	25.2	25.0	24.7				33.9	24.3	20.8
All Other Current	1.8	2.4	2.9				4.1	3.2	2.9
Total Current	77.1	74.9	69.3				80.1	69.3	69.6
Fixed Assets (net)	9.0	15.8	16.2				10.3	14.1	20.1
Intangibles (net)	3.7	4.2	3.3				2.0	3.7	3.0
All Other Non-Current	10.2	5.0	11.2				7.6	12.8	7.3
Total	100.0	100.0	100.0				100.0	100.0	100.0
LIABILITIES									
Notes Payable-Short Term	7.3	2.7	4.4				6.5	5.3	1.4
Cur. Mat.-L /T/D	2.0	1.7	3.2				1.9	3.5	1.2
Trade Payables	11.8	10.8	8.6				12.0	10.7	6.2
Income Taxes Payable	.3	.4	.4				.4	.3	.7
All Other Current	17.0	12.3	13.8				13.7	15.0	14.0
Total Current	38.4	27.9	30.4				34.5	34.8	23.4
Long Term Debt	5.9	10.9	7.7				6.0	6.0	6.2
Deferred Taxes	.2	.1	.6				.2	.2	1.0
All Other-Non-Current	3.6	2.3	3.0				1.8	4.4	3.0
Net Worth	52.0	58.8	58.4				57.6	54.5	66.4
Total Liabilities & Net Worth	100.0	100.0	100.0				100.0	100.0	100.0
INCOME DATA									
Net Sales	100.0	100.0	100.0				100.0	100.0	100.0
Gross Profit	54.3	50.9	50.5				48.9	50.9	52.5
Operating Expenses	50.8	46.6	45.8				46.1	47.7	43.4
Operating Profit	3.6	4.3	4.7				2.8	3.3	9.1
All Other Expenses (net)	1.6	.1	.4				.3	-.4	.0
Profit Before Taxes	2.0	4.2	4.3				2.5	3.7	9.1
RATIOS									
Current	6.6 / 2.2 / 1.3	5.2 / 3.0 / 2.1	5.2 / 2.8 / 1.5				5.6 / 2.2 / 1.7	3.4 / 1.9 / 1.4	5.5 / 4.1 / 2.1
Quick	5.3 / 1.3 / .7	3.7 / 1.9 / 1.1	3.4 / 1.7 / .7				2.0 / 1.3 / .9	3.0 / 1.1 / .6	3.7 / 2.8 / 1.2
Sales/Receivables	54 6.7 / 65 5.6 / 94 3.9	54 6.7 / 73 5.0 / 91 4.0	49 7.4 / 68 5.4 / 94 3.9				41 8.9 / 65 5.6 / 81 4.5	49 7.5 / 68 5.4 / 81 4.5	58 6.3 / 72 5.1 / 101 3.6
Cost of Sales/Inventory	101 3.6 / 152 2.4 / 215 1.7	87 4.2 / 130 2.8 / 174 2.1	96 3.8 / 130 2.8 / 192 1.9				111 3.3 / 174 2.1 / 243 1.5	94 3.9 / 140 2.6 / 192 1.9	111 3.3 / 126 2.9 / 174 2.1
Cost of Sales/Payables	43 8.5 / 58 6.3 / 104 3.5	31 11.6 / 47 7.8 / 65 5.6	27 13.4 / 43 8.5 / 68 5.4				32 11.3 / 45 8.2 / 85 4.3	35 10.3 / 56 6.5 / 79 4.6	27 13.5 / 34 10.8 / 54 6.8
Sales/Working Capital	1.8 / 3.1 / 11.5	1.9 / 2.8 / 5.2	1.9 / 3.3 / 8.2				2.3 / 4.2 / 6.2	1.9 / 5.5 / 9.0	1.7 / 2.3 / 4.2
EBIT/Interest	(21) 57.0 / 1.3 / -2.3	(43) 14.8 / 5.4 / -2.7	(55) 31.5 / 5.1 / 1.3				31.8 / 4.6 / 1.7	(15) 17.2 / 5.7 / .7	(19) 88.6 / 22.6 / 2.2
Net Profit + Depr., Dep., Amort./Cur. Mat. L/T/D	(12) 14.2 / 6.1 / .6	(25) 16.0 / 4.2 / -.8	(33) 13.9 / 4.6 / .8						(14) 38.1 / 11.4 / 3.8
Fixed/Worth	.1 / .2 / .4	.1 / .3 / .5	.1 / .2 / .5				.1 / .1 / .2	.1 / .2 / .5	.2 / .3 / .5
Debt/Worth	.2 / .7 / 2.5	.3 / .6 / 1.1	.2 / .7 / 1.5				.2 / .8 / 2.6	.4 / 1.0 / 1.8	.2 / .3 / 1.0
% Profit Before Taxes/Tangible Net Worth	(27) 23.7 / 13.3 / -1.5	(51) 22.2 / 9.7 / -3.1	(66) 20.1 / 10.0 / -.1				12.9 / 8.3 / 2.6	(18) 23.8 / 10.7 / -14.7	20.1 / 15.8 / 7.3
% Profit Before Taxes/Total Assets	12.7 / 4.4 / -2.6	13.9 / 4.7 / -2.6	13.6 / 6.6 / -.4				9.6 / 4.4 / .5	16.8 / 6.6 / -7.5	15.4 / 11.8 / 2.9
Sales/Net Fixed Assets	29.9 / 20.6 / 9.5	26.1 / 11.3 / 5.2	17.9 / 10.9 / 5.1				23.8 / 17.3 / 14.0	16.1 / 9.0 / 5.7	11.4 / 5.3 / 4.4
Sales/Total Assets	1.7 / 1.2 / 1.0	2.0 / 1.3 / 1.0	1.8 / 1.3 / 1.0				2.0 / 1.7 / 1.2	1.9 / 1.4 / .9	1.3 / 1.2 / 1.0
% Depr., Dep., Amort./Sales	(24) 1.4 / 2.3 / 3.1	(50) 1.7 / 2.6 / 3.5	(59) 1.6 / 2.6 / 4.1					(18) 1.9 / 3.0 / 4.2	(19) 2.4 / 3.5 / 5.7
% Officers', Directors', Owners' Comp/Sales									
Net Sales ($)	1076748M	1795236M	2667100M	102M	11985M	30324M	79674M	309265M	2235750M
Total Assets ($)	985390M	1674335M	2542454M	98M	6842M	29317M	52884M	297889M	2155424M

Current Data Sorted By Assets							Comparative Historical Data	
	2	4	1	2	1	**# Postretirement Benefits**		
						Type of Statement		
	6	27	21	3	10	Unqualified	46	54
3	27	27	1			Reviewed	43	44
2	16	5				Compiled	25	16
	1	1				Tax Returns		1
5	16	18	11	3	1	Other	37	37
	86 (4/1-9/30/94)		118 (10/1/94-3/31/95)				4/1/90-3/31/91	4/1/91-3/31/92
0-500M	500M-2MM	2-10MM	10-50MM	50-100MM	100-250MM		ALL	ALL
10	66	78	33	6	11	**NUMBER OF STATEMENTS**	151	152
%	%	%	%	%	%	**ASSETS**	%	%
10.2	10.1	9.0	12.7		14.6	Cash & Equivalents	7.5	10.9
32.2	35.2	34.2	26.4		21.0	Trade Receivables - (net)	31.2	31.5
35.3	30.8	28.4	27.5		17.6	Inventory	30.1	27.0
.9	2.4	3.0	2.7		5.1	All Other Current	3.5	3.6
78.5	78.5	74.6	69.3		58.3	Total Current	72.3	73.0
17.8	15.1	18.1	19.9		27.6	Fixed Assets (net)	19.0	18.4
.9	1.3	3.2	2.9		7.0	Intangibles (net)	2.6	2.6
2.8	5.2	4.0	7.9		7.1	All Other Non-Current	6.1	6.0
100.0	100.0	100.0	100.0		100.0	Total	100.0	100.0
						LIABILITIES		
26.1	10.2	10.0	2.0		4.0	Notes Payable-Short Term	11.5	10.1
5.0	3.3	3.0	1.7		1.6	Cur. Mat. -L/T/D	3.3	2.5
19.9	15.5	15.3	9.2		7.7	Trade Payables	13.4	12.0
.1	.5	.5	.7		.8	Income Taxes Payable	.7	.6
4.8	13.6	10.7	12.7		12.6	All Other Current	9.6	13.1
55.8	43.2	39.5	26.2		26.8	Total Current	38.7	38.4
4.2	8.5	9.7	9.7		8.2	Long Term Debt	13.1	11.0
.0	.5	.6	1.1		1.7	Deferred Taxes	1.1	.7
13.6	5.1	3.9	3.2		1.0	All Other-Non-Current	4.3	2.4
26.4	42.7	46.4	59.8		62.4	Net Worth	42.8	47.4
100.0	100.0	100.0	100.0		100.0	Total Liabilities & Net Worth	100.0	100.0
						INCOME DATA		
100.0	100.0	100.0	100.0		100.0	Net Sales	100.0	100.0
40.1	38.0	41.3	41.8		42.9	Gross Profit	39.5	42.0
35.2	34.5	35.2	34.5		32.1	Operating Expenses	34.3	37.3
4.9	3.5	6.1	7.3		10.8	Operating Profit	5.2	4.8
1.1	1.1	1.4	.5		-.3	All Other Expenses (net)	1.8	1.5
3.8	2.4	4.7	6.8		11.1	Profit Before Taxes	3.4	3.3
						RATIOS		
2.1	2.8	3.6	4.5		3.0		3.0	3.1
1.7	1.7	1.7	2.7		2.3	Current	2.0	2.1
1.1	1.4	1.3	1.9		1.5		1.4	1.4
1.2	1.6	2.2	2.4		1.6		1.6	1.9
.8	1.1	1.0	1.5		1.2	Quick	1.1	1.2
.4	.7	.8	1.0		.8		.7	.7
35 10.3	41 9.0	51 7.1	51 7.1		54 6.8		46 8.0	47 7.8
44 8.3	51 7.1	60 6.1	61 6.0		79 4.6	Sales/Receivables	58 6.3	57 6.4
60 6.1	62 5.9	73 5.0	76 4.8		96 3.8		74 4.9	73 5.0
13 27.1	35 10.4	61 6.0	87 4.2		91 4.0		63 5.8	53 6.9
76 4.8	73 5.0	94 3.9	126 2.9		107 3.4	Cost of Sales/Inventory	104 3.5	99 3.7
166 2.2	140 2.6	140 2.6	152 2.4		130 2.8		152 2.4	140 2.6
16 23.4	21 17.2	24 15.3	17 22.1		31 11.8		21 17.5	20 18.2
29 12.6	32 11.4	43 8.5	29 12.6		38 9.5	Cost of Sales/Payables	37 9.8	32 11.4
78 4.7	49 7.4	59 6.2	43 8.4		46 8.0		59 6.2	51 7.2
6.7	4.8	3.4	1.9		1.5		3.4	3.2
8.6	7.4	6.9	4.1		3.5	Sales/Working Capital	5.1	5.5
28.2	13.4	12.3	5.5		9.5		10.8	12.2
	7.6	11.8	34.8				8.0	10.8
(60) 3.5	(66) 4.0	(26) 16.8				EBIT/Interest	(131) 2.5	(130) 3.1
1.1	1.5	3.3					1.2	.8
	6.1	7.0	10.6			Net Profit + Depr., Dep.,		6.1	7.0
(26) 2.9	(31) 2.9	(17) 3.8				Amort./Cur. Mat. L /T/D	(76) 2.1	(75) 2.3
1.6	.9	1.4					.8	.3
.1	.2	.2	.2		.4		.2	.2
.4	.3	.4	.3		.6	Fixed/Worth	.4	.3
NM	.7	.9	.5		.8		1.0	.7
.9	.8	.5	.5		.5		.7	.5
1.9	1.4	1.4	.7		.8	Debt/Worth	1.4	1.0
NM	2.3	3.3	1.5		1.2		3.5	2.5
	29.9	49.8	37.6		22.5	% Profit Before Taxes/Tangible	34.0	35.2
(62) 13.3	(73) 18.7	16.3			18.3	Net Worth	(139) 16.1	(142) 15.7
1.9	7.9	2.9			13.3		4.1	.7
16.0	10.9	18.6	19.7		19.6	% Profit Before Taxes/Total	14.4	16.2
8.6	5.9	8.1	11.5		9.4	Assets	5.3	6.9
3.2	.3	1.8	2.1		2.8		1.2	-.6
237.4	48.6	23.8	16.3		4.7		24.7	25.8
37.0	22.1	14.0	9.8		4.2	Sales/Net Fixed Assets	11.5	13.3
7.3	10.3	7.8	4.9		3.3		5.3	6.4
3.1	3.3	2.4	2.0		1.4		2.4	2.6
2.8	2.4	2.0	1.6		1.1	Sales/Total Assets	1.8	1.8
1.9	1.8	1.5	1.0		.8		1.3	1.4
	.9	1.3	1.4				1.2	1.0
(59) 1.3	(69) 1.8	(27) 1.9				% Depr., Dep., Amort./Sales	(133) 2.1	(135) 2.1
2.0	2.9	3.1					3.6	3.4
	2.3	1.8				% Officers', Directors',	3.1	2.3
(30) 4.8	(23) 4.0					Owners' Comp/Sales	(42) 5.4	(38) 5.8
	8.2	8.3					8.6	10.0
7363M	209907M	650345M	962812M	494430M	1985843M	Net Sales ($)	2299599M	3170447M
2637M	82527M	333471M	712299M	405363M	1551884M	Total Assets ($)	1653479M	2521578M

M = $ thousand   MM = $ million
See Pages 1 through 15 for Explanation of Ratios and Data

Comparative Historical Data | **Current Data Sorted By Sales**

Hist	Hist	Hist	Item	0-1MM	1-3MM	3-5MM	5-10MM	10-25MM	25MM & OVER
9	9	10	# Postretirement Benefits		1	2	1	2	4
			Type of Statement						
60	76	67	Unqualified	1	6	5	10	22	23
48	51	58	Reviewed	1	17	16	16	7	1
28	30	23	Compiled	3	5	10	3	2	
1	1	2	Tax Returns				2		
45	41	54	Other	4	9	10	10	9	12
4/1/92-3/31/93 ALL	4/1/93-3/31/94 ALL	4/1/94-3/31/95 ALL			86 (4/1-9/30/94)		118 (10/1/94-3/31/95)			
182	199	204	**NUMBER OF STATEMENTS**	9	37	41	41	40	36
%	%	%	**ASSETS**	%	%	%	%	%	%
9.5	9.5	10.3	Cash & Equivalents		11.9	7.3	10.9	11.5	11.3
32.3	30.4	32.2	Trade Receivables - (net)		29.4	37.3	35.7	30.5	26.4
28.9	29.6	28.7	Inventory		32.4	28.5	28.3	28.0	25.5
2.2	2.7	2.8	All Other Current		1.7	2.2	3.3	3.4	3.1
72.9	72.3	73.9	Total Current		75.3	75.4	78.2	73.4	66.3
18.5	19.5	18.2	Fixed Assets (net)		17.9	17.3	14.9	18.0	22.8
2.8	2.6	2.7	Intangibles (net)		2.8	2.6	2.6	2.4	3.7
5.7	5.6	5.2	All Other Non-Current		4.0	4.7	4.3	6.1	7.2
100.0	100.0	100.0	Total		100.0	100.0	100.0	100.0	100.0
			LIABILITIES						
9.7	7.6	9.1	Notes Payable-Short Term		10.6	12.4	8.6	5.2	3.7
3.3	2.8	2.8	Cur. Mat.-L /T/D		4.1	3.2	2.7	2.1	1.7
12.9	12.7	14.0	Trade Payables		14.0	17.1	16.0	13.7	8.8
.6	1.4	.5	Income Taxes Payable		.8	.3	.4	.6	.7
13.5	12.5	11.7	All Other Current		12.6	13.7	10.1	11.4	12.7
40.1	37.1	38.2	Total Current		42.1	46.7	37.8	33.0	27.6
9.7	10.7	9.1	Long Term Debt		10.8	9.8	7.6	8.9	9.4
.7	.7	.7	Deferred Taxes		.8	.6	.5	.8	.9
2.9	3.0	4.5	All Other-Non-Current		7.1	2.7	5.9	3.0	2.3
46.7	48.5	47.5	Net Worth		39.1	40.2	48.3	54.3	59.8
100.0	100.0	100.0	Total Liabilities & Net Worth		100.0	100.0	100.0	100.0	100.0
			INCOME DATA						
100.0	100.0	100.0	Net Sales		100.0	100.0	100.0	100.0	100.0
42.4	39.6	40.2	Gross Profit		42.0	38.3	38.0	42.4	41.3
37.0	36.9	34.6	Operating Expenses		39.2	33.9	32.3	34.9	33.3
5.4	2.6	5.7	Operating Profit		2.8	4.4	5.7	7.5	8.0
1.1	.9	1.1	All Other Expenses (net)		1.7	1.6	1.0	.4	.5
4.3	1.7	4.6	Profit Before Taxes		1.1	2.8	4.6	7.1	7.5
			RATIOS						
3.1	3.4	3.4	Current		2.7	2.1	4.0	4.0	4.0
1.9	2.0	1.9			1.7	1.6	2.5	2.3	2.5
1.4	1.5	1.5			1.5	1.3	1.4	1.6	1.8
1.7	1.8	1.8	Quick		1.5	1.4	2.5	2.0	2.1
1.0	1.1	1.1			.9	1.0	1.1	1.3	1.3
.7	.7	.8			.6	.7	.8	1.0	.8
47 7.8	46 7.9	47 7.8	Sales/Receivables	41 9.0	47 7.8	43 8.4	49 7.5	54 6.8	
59 6.2	55 6.6	58 6.3		54 6.7	57 6.4	54 6.7	58 6.3	64 5.7	
74 4.9	70 5.2	70 5.2		64 5.7	72 5.1	66 5.5	73 5.0	78 4.7	
61 6.0	63 5.8	56 6.5	Cost of Sales/Inventory	51 7.1	35 10.4	38 9.7	76 4.8	89 4.1	
99 3.7	94 3.9	96 3.8		118 3.1	73 5.0	79 4.6	107 3.4	111 3.3	
146 2.5	140 2.6	140 2.6		183 2.0	126 2.9	135 2.7	146 2.5	135 2.7	
20 18.1	18 19.8	22 16.5	Cost of Sales/Payables	23 15.7	24 15.2	20 17.9	19 19.0	23 15.6	
33 10.9	34 10.6	35 10.3		38 9.6	35 10.3	35 10.4	39 9.3	31 11.6	
59 6.2	55 6.6	57 6.4		64 5.7	61 6.0	59 6.2	51 7.1	44 8.3	
3.4	3.4	3.4	Sales/Working Capital		4.2	5.5	3.1	3.1	3.1
5.8	5.6	6.0			7.3	9.4	6.5	4.4	3.9
11.5	11.3	11.0			10.1	16.5	13.8	8.2	6.3
8.3	9.0	14.1	EBIT/Interest	5.3	6.2	13.5	41.6	29.8	
(153) 3.1	(167) 3.5	(174) 4.5		(33) 1.8	(38) 3.2	(34) 5.2	(30) 10.8	(31) 9.1	
1.3	1.2	1.6		-.6	1.4	2.7	2.1	2.5	
7.8	7.7	7.3	Net Profit + Depr., Dep., Amort./Cur. Mat. L/T/D	4.3	8.3	7.7	4.5	11.3	
(86) 3.1	(80) 2.9	(83) 3.1		(18) 1.9	(20) 2.1	(10) 5.5	(16) 2.5	(19) 5.5	
1.0	1.1	1.5		.3	1.2	2.0	1.1	3.1	
.2	.2	.2	Fixed/Worth		.2	.2	.2	.2	.3
.4	.4	.4			.4	.4	.3	.3	.5
.8	.8	.7			1.0	1.0	.6	.6	.6
.6	.5	.5	Debt/Worth		.9	1.0	.4	.3	.4
1.4	1.1	1.2			1.5	1.8	1.2	1.0	.7
2.4	2.5	2.4			3.0	3.3	3.9	1.9	1.4
29.3	22.4	37.2	% Profit Before Taxes/Tangible Net Worth	33.8	27.4	50.6	49.1	33.4	
(175) 14.3	(192) 11.2	(193) 16.8		(33) 12.9	(39) 16.2	(38) 14.3	18.6	15.5	
3.8	2.8	5.9		-2.2	10.3	8.4	4.0	5.6	
13.4	11.1	16.2	% Profit Before Taxes/Total Assets		11.3	10.5	17.1	23.4	17.3
5.8	5.1	7.3			5.3	6.7	7.4	13.7	9.5
1.3	.5	1.7			-1.2	1.6	2.9	2.1	2.5
28.8	27.2	25.7	Sales/Net Fixed Assets		42.3	33.9	35.8	22.5	12.4
13.0	11.2	13.0			13.0	19.2	21.2	13.0	5.8
5.8	5.7	6.4			7.1	9.5	10.1	6.8	4.3
2.5	2.5	2.6	Sales/Total Assets		2.7	2.7	3.0	2.4	2.0
1.9	1.9	2.0			2.0	2.2	2.2	1.9	1.5
1.4	1.4	1.5			1.5	1.8	1.6	1.2	1.1
1.1	1.2	1.2	% Depr., Dep., Amort./Sales		.9	1.1	1.2	1.1	1.6
(161) 1.8	(166) 2.1	(173) 1.7		(32) 1.6	(38) 1.5	(35) 1.5	(35) 1.9	(28) 2.9	
3.1	3.3	2.9			3.0	2.3	2.2	3.0	3.7
2.9	3.0	2.0	% Officers', Directors', Owners' Comp/Sales		2.5	2.1	1.8		
(49) 6.0	(57) 4.9	(55) 4.8		(12) 4.7	(17) 4.1	(16) 4.0			
10.8	9.2	8.3			9.7	7.2	7.0		
4063148M	4176066M	4310700M	Net Sales ($)	5572M	73506M	162055M	278119M	567425M	3224023M
3101371M	3272994M	3088181M	Total Assets ($)	3104M	43244M	77151M	141038M	493038M	2330606M

M = $ thousand   MM = $ million
See Pages 1 through 15 for Explanation of Ratios and Data

Current Data Sorted By Assets							Comparative Historical Data	
1	3	2	1	2	2	# Postretirement Benefits		
						Type of Statement		
	3	11	16	6	4	Unqualified	23	41
	9	2				Reviewed	10	15
3	9	1				Compiled	8	15
		1				Tax Returns		
4	4	6	5	4	2	Other	9	16
	37 (4/1-9/30/94)		53 (10/1/94-3/31/95)				4/1/90-3/31/91	4/1/91-3/31/92
0-500M	500M-2MM	2-10MM	10-50MM	50-100MM	100-250MM		ALL	ALL
7	25	21	21	10	6	NUMBER OF STATEMENTS	50	87
%	%	%	%	%	%	ASSETS	%	%
	10.4	9.9	18.2	23.1		Cash & Equivalents	8.9	10.4
	32.0	30.0	25.7	26.4		Trade Receivables - (net)	31.6	27.8
	34.6	32.5	23.4	21.5		Inventory	29.6	31.7
	2.6	3.1	4.1	2.3		All Other Current	1.8	1.4
	79.6	75.5	71.4	73.4		Total Current	71.8	71.3
	11.1	18.9	19.1	14.3		Fixed Assets (net)	19.9	22.2
	3.2	.6	1.9	4.8		Intangibles (net)	3.9	2.8
	6.1	5.0	7.6	7.6		All Other Non-Current	4.4	3.7
	100.0	100.0	100.0	100.0		Total	100.0	100.0
						LIABILITIES		
	6.5	10.7	3.5	1.7		Notes Payable-Short Term	6.9	7.4
	3.0	5.5	2.9	1.3		Cur. Mat. -L/T/D	3.0	3.0
	9.8	11.2	9.6	6.8		Trade Payables	10.2	9.9
	.8	.4	1.0	1.6		Income Taxes Payable	.7	1.0
	17.6	10.7	12.5	13.8		All Other Current	11.4	11.4
	37.6	38.4	29.5	25.3		Total Current	32.2	32.7
	9.2	12.0	7.6	11.5		Long Term Debt	9.7	10.4
	.5	.6	.7	.3		Deferred Taxes	1.4	1.0
	4.5	3.0	2.0	10.1		All Other-Non-Current	3.6	3.4
	48.2	46.0	60.2	52.8		Net Worth	53.0	52.5
	100.0	100.0	100.0	100.0		Total Liabilities & Net Worth	100.0	100.0
						INCOME DATA		
	100.0	100.0	100.0	100.0		Net Sales	100.0	100.0
	50.5	40.8	47.3	49.9		Gross Profit	43.9	42.9
	47.1	34.7	39.9	41.9		Operating Expenses	38.4	38.9
	3.4	6.1	7.4	8.0		Operating Profit	5.5	4.0
	.0	.4	1.2	.1		All Other Expenses (net)	1.6	1.3
	3.4	5.7	6.2	7.8		Profit Before Taxes	3.9	2.6
						RATIOS		
	3.8	3.1	5.3	4.4		Current	3.5	3.7
	2.5	2.3	3.5	3.2			2.3	2.4
	1.6	1.2	1.6	2.3			1.7	1.6
	2.3	2.0	3.7	3.6		Quick	2.1	2.0
	1.1	1.1	1.9	2.0			1.3	1.1
	.7	.6	.8	1.1			.9	.7
	40 9.2	46 8.0	53 6.9	69 5.3		Sales/Receivables	49 7.4	45 8.1
	55 6.6	54 6.8	63 5.8	81 4.5			59 6.2	60 6.1
	76 4.8	69 5.3	79 4.6	101 3.6			78 4.7	74 4.9
	56 6.5	76 4.8	76 4.8	114 3.2		Cost of Sales/Inventory	70 5.2	85 4.3
	135 2.7	118 3.1	107 3.4	152 2.4			114 3.2	126 2.9
	261 1.4	183 2.0	166 2.2	174 2.1			166 2.2	159 2.3
	13 27.8	21 17.2	15 24.3	29 12.8		Cost of Sales/Payables	19 19.1	24 15.3
	36 10.2	35 10.3	39 9.3	40 9.1			33 11.0	31 11.6
	58 6.3	55 6.6	61 6.0	70 5.2			47 7.7	54 6.7
	2.8	2.6	1.9	1.4		Sales/Working Capital	2.8	2.9
	5.2	4.2	3.0	2.3			4.5	4.6
	7.5	18.4	5.7	4.1			7.8	8.0
	12.2	20.1	73.3	71.6		EBIT/Interest	10.5	9.7
	(22) 3.8	(17) 1.8	(18) 11.3	8.1			(38) 3.6	(70) 3.6
	1.8	.7	1.6	1.5			1.8	-.0
			80.0			Net Profit + Depr., Dep.,		6.0	8.9
			(13) 4.9			Amort./Cur. Mat. L /T/D	(26) 2.4	(46) 2.8
			.2				1.2	.1
	.1	.1	.1	.2		Fixed/Worth	.2	.2
	.2	.4	.2	.3			.3	.4
	.5	.9	.7	NM			.6	.8
	.4	.5	.2	.3		Debt/Worth	.4	.5
	1.2	.7	.6	.5			.8	.9
	3.6	2.5	1.7	NM			1.9	1.8
	41.4	35.9	25.2			% Profit Before Taxes/Tangible	31.0	28.8
	13.8	(19) 13.5	12.0			Net Worth	(48) 19.0	(84) 11.4
	4.9	-9.1	5.0				4.8	-6.9
	13.0	17.4	19.9	22.0		% Profit Before Taxes/Total	14.0	13.0
	4.9	2.8	8.5	7.3		Assets	7.3	5.2
	1.9	-1.7	3.6	1.8			1.7	-4.6
	51.0	22.6	13.8	10.9		Sales/Net Fixed Assets	20.9	14.5
	21.2	11.7	8.9	8.9			9.8	8.4
	11.7	6.4	4.9	6.6			5.2	5.1
	2.5	2.2	1.8	1.6		Sales/Total Assets	2.3	2.2
	1.9	1.8	1.4	1.2			1.7	1.7
	1.5	1.3	1.1	.7			1.2	1.3
	.9	.9	2.3	1.1		% Depr., Dep., Amort./Sales	.9	1.6
	(23) 1.4	(20) 2.1	(20) 3.3	4.0			(39) 1.9	(77) 2.6
	2.9	5.0	4.6	5.2			3.2	4.2
	6.8					% Officers', Directors',	3.1	1.8
	(11) 10.5					Owners' Comp/Sales	(12) 6.5	(19) 5.8
	16.8						11.2	11.5
5421M	58669M	203349M	716183M	787460M	1155751M	Net Sales ($)	1351776M	2701369M
2487M	30307M	110415M	522998M	691717M	992443M	Total Assets ($)	1034780M	2161872M

M = $ thousand   MM = $ million
See Pages 1 through 15 for Explanation of Ratios and Data

Comparative Historical Data				Current Data Sorted By Sales					
1	2	11			2	2		2	5
			# Postretirement Benefits						
			Type of Statement						
37	29	40	Unqualified		1	5	4	11	19
11	14	11	Reviewed		7	3		1	
10	8	13	Compiled	3	7	3			
1	1	1	Tax Returns				1		
16	13	25	Other	2	5	1	2	8	7
4/1/92-3/31/93	4/1/93-3/31/94	4/1/94-3/31/95			37 (4/1-9/30/94)			53 (10/1/94-3/31/95)	
ALL	ALL	ALL		0-1MM	1-3MM	3-5MM	5-10MM	10-25MM	25MM & OVER
75	65	90	**NUMBER OF STATEMENTS**	5	20	12	7	20	26
%	%	%	**ASSETS**	%	%	%	%	%	%
9.0	11.3	14.0	Cash & Equivalents		9.9	6.1		17.6	17.1
28.4	27.8	28.8	Trade Receivables - (net)		30.9	36.0		28.0	27.0
32.2	30.4	29.1	Inventory		36.4	29.2		25.4	25.2
2.1	3.0	3.0	All Other Current		3.1	2.4		3.0	3.2
71.7	72.4	74.8	Total Current		80.2	73.7		74.0	72.6
19.1	20.3	16.5	Fixed Assets (net)		10.3	19.5		18.8	16.9
3.9	3.6	2.8	Intangibles (net)		3.5	1.7		2.0	3.1
5.4	3.7	5.8	All Other Non-Current		6.0	5.1		5.2	7.5
100.0	100.0	100.0	Total		100.0	100.0		100.0	100.0
			LIABILITIES						
9.3	7.0	6.6	Notes Payable-Short Term		9.3	4.6		9.7	2.9
2.4	3.6	3.1	Cur. Mat.-L /T/D		3.1	5.7		3.0	2.7
9.6	10.0	10.0	Trade Payables		10.2	12.4		10.4	9.0
.6	.6	.8	Income Taxes Payable		.4	1.1		.5	1.3
12.4	12.3	13.8	All Other Current		14.1	20.5		9.4	14.1
34.4	33.5	34.3	Total Current		37.1	44.3		33.0	30.1
12.2	14.0	10.0	Long Term Debt		7.7	11.1		17.0	6.5
.6	.7	.5	Deferred Taxes		.5	.9		.2	.8
3.8	5.1	4.0	All Other-Non-Current		3.9	5.0		2.3	4.7
49.0	46.7	51.2	Net Worth		50.9	38.7		47.5	57.9
100.0	100.0	100.0	Total Liabilities & Net Worth		100.0	100.0		100.0	100.0
			INCOME DATA						
100.0	100.0	100.0	Net Sales		100.0	100.0		100.0	100.0
45.0	42.9	46.2	Gross Profit		48.8	48.3		43.6	48.1
42.2	41.4	40.6	Operating Expenses		45.6	42.8		35.5	40.7
2.8	1.4	5.6	Operating Profit		3.2	5.6		8.1	7.4
1.2	1.3	.4	All Other Expenses (net)		.6	–.7		1.2	1.2
1.6	.1	5.2	Profit Before Taxes		2.6	6.3		6.9	6.2
			RATIOS						
3.1	3.9	3.9			4.0	2.6		6.2	3.7
2.3	2.7	2.6	Current		2.6	1.7		3.2	2.9
1.5	1.6	1.6			1.5	1.2		1.2	1.8
1.8	2.1	2.8			2.5	1.7		4.5	2.8
1.1	1.3	1.3	Quick		1.0	1.0		2.2	1.5
.7	.6	.7			.7	.7		.7	1.1
46 7.9	48 7.6	49 7.4		40 9.2	38 9.7		52 7.0	59 6.2	
57 6.4	58 6.3	61 6.0	Sales/Receivables	50 7.3	68 5.4		58 6.3	73 5.0	
76 4.8	70 5.2	79 4.6		68 5.4	81 4.5		81 4.5	85 4.3	
81 4.5	72 5.1	76 4.8		51 7.1	59 6.2		69 5.3	104 3.5	
130 2.8	118 3.1	126 2.9	Cost of Sales/Inventory	203 1.8	122 3.0		94 3.9	135 2.7	
192 1.9	174 2.1	183 2.0		281 1.3	159 2.3		152 2.4	166 2.2	
22 16.7	17 21.9	23 15.7		16 23.2	26 13.9		14 25.9	28 13.0	
33 11.0	29 12.8	39 9.4	Cost of Sales/Payables	34 10.7	40 9.2		37 9.8	44 8.3	
54 6.8	55 6.6	56 6.5		47 7.8	89 4.1		54 6.7	60 6.1	
2.9	2.9	2.3			2.7	2.8		1.9	1.9
4.4	4.3	3.7	Sales/Working Capital		4.7	5.8		3.0	3.0
9.7	8.9	7.5			7.5	21.9		16.8	6.2
13.2	8.8	27.7		10.9	27.5		76.5	70.1	
(67) 3.7	(53) 2.7	(79) 4.5	EBIT/Interest	(18) 3.3	(10) 6.8	(18) 3.5	(23) 10.2	
.1	1.0	1.4		1.5	2.0		1.3	2.4	
22.0	18.7	15.7	Net Profit + Depr., Dep.,					50.7	
(31) 7.1	(28) 2.8	(43) 3.3	Amort./Cur. Mat. L/T/D				(19) 5.8	
2.1	1.0	.9					.6	
.2	.2	.1		.1	.1		.2	.2	
.4	.4	.3	Fixed/Worth	.2	.4		.6	.3	
.6	.8	.8		.6	1.5		1.0	.5	
.6	.5	.3		.4	.7		.2	.3	
1.2	1.1	.7	Debt/Worth	1.0	1.9		1.2	.6	
2.0	2.9	2.2		3.0	4.2		2.8	1.2	
29.0	24.1	31.2	% Profit Before Taxes/Tangible	39.3	71.8		27.6	26.5	
(70) 14.9	(59) 11.1	(85) 13.5	Net Worth	7.1	21.0	(17) 15.5	(25) 15.0	
.8	.2	3.4		2.7	12.4		5.0	7.2	
12.7	9.3	13.2	% Profit Before Taxes/Total	12.3	16.5		12.6	19.8	
5.8	4.9	7.2	Assets	3.3	8.3		8.0	8.3	
–.7	–2.1	1.9		1.2	3.0		2.6	4.0	
19.0	18.3	22.3		44.9	62.6		13.2	10.3	
9.3	8.9	11.0	Sales/Net Fixed Assets	23.1	16.0		10.4	8.4	
5.4	5.4	6.4		14.4	5.2		6.3	5.7	
2.1	2.1	2.0		2.6	2.4		1.9	1.6	
1.6	1.6	1.6	Sales/Total Assets	1.8	1.9		1.7	1.4	
1.3	1.3	1.2		1.4	1.4		1.1	1.0	
1.7	1.5	1.2		.9	.8		1.8	2.1	
(63) 2.8	(57) 2.7	(85) 2.5	% Depr., Dep., Amort./Sales	(10) 1.7	2.0	(19) 3.1	(25) 3.5	
4.1	4.7	4.2		2.8	3.8		4.6	5.0	
1.5	1.7	2.5	% Officers', Directors',						
(18) 7.2	(11) 2.9	(18) 7.0	Owners' Comp/Sales						
10.5	11.6	15.4							
2768812M	1596897M	2926833M	Net Sales ($)	3099M	34661M	44616M	50409M	328628M	2465420M
1999112M	1239472M	2350367M	Total Assets ($)	2174M	19067M	27094M	33552M	273721M	1994759M

M = $ thousand   MM = $ million
See Pages 1 through 15 for Explanation of Ratios and Data

Current Data Sorted By Assets   **Comparative Historical Data**

Postretirement Benefits

Type of Statement

	0-500M	500M-2MM	2-10MM	10-50MM	50-100MM	100-250MM
# Postretirement Benefits				1		
Unqualified			6	4	1	1
Reviewed			3			
Compiled		4				
Tax Returns		1				
Other	2	2	1	3	1	3

	0-500M	500M-2MM	2-10MM	10-50MM	50-100MM	100-250MM		4/1/90-3/31/91 ALL	4/1/91-3/31/92 ALL
	16 (4/1-9/30/94)			16 (10/1/94-3/31/95)					
NUMBER OF STATEMENTS	2	7	10	7	2	4			
	%	%	%	%	%	%		%	%
ASSETS									
Cash & Equivalents			10.0					D	D
Trade Receivables - (net)			27.5					A	A
Inventory			27.9					T	T
All Other Current			1.4					A	A
Total Current			66.8						
Fixed Assets (net)			22.8					N	N
Intangibles (net)			1.8					O	O
All Other Non-Current			8.6					T	T
Total			100.0						
LIABILITIES								A	A
Notes Payable-Short Term			8.3					V	V
Cur. Mat. -L/T/D			1.6					A	A
Trade Payables			12.9					I	I
Income Taxes Payable			.6					L	L
All Other Current			8.6					A	A
Total Current			32.1					B	B
Long Term Debt			11.5					L	L
Deferred Taxes			.6					E	E
All Other-Non-Current			.7						
Net Worth			55.1						
Total Liabilities & Net Worth			100.0						
INCOME DATA									
Net Sales			100.0						
Gross Profit			50.9						
Operating Expenses			44.5						
Operating Profit			6.4						
All Other Expenses (net)			1.2						
Profit Before Taxes			5.2						
RATIOS									
Current			3.2						
			2.5						
			1.3						
Quick			2.0						
			1.2						
			.7						
Sales/Receivables			47 7.7						
			54 6.7						
			72 5.1						
Cost of Sales/Inventory			96 3.8						
			114 3.2						
			135 2.7						
Cost of Sales/Payables			31 11.7						
			41 9.0						
			61 6.0						
Sales/Working Capital			3.7						
			5.0						
			9.4						
EBIT/Interest									
Net Profit + Depr., Dep., Amort./Cur. Mat. L /T/D									
Fixed/Worth			.1						
			.3						
			.8						
Debt/Worth			.4						
			1.0						
			1.8						
% Profit Before Taxes/Tangible Net Worth			30.4						
			15.5						
			5.6						
% Profit Before Taxes/Total Assets			17.1						
			7.8						
			2.0						
Sales/Net Fixed Assets			32.0						
			8.5						
			4.7						
Sales/Total Assets			2.1						
			1.8						
			1.5						
% Depr., Dep., Amort./Sales									
% Officers', Directors', Owners' Comp/Sales									
Net Sales ($)	1854M	15712M	91367M	192852M	158111M	650184M			
Total Assets ($)	762M	7613M	55603M	143684M	132455M	621341M			

© Robert Morris Associates 1995

M = $ thousand   MM = $ million

See Pages 1 through 15 for Explanation of Ratios and Data

Comparative Historical Data | Current Data Sorted By Sales

			# Postretirement Benefits					1	
		1	**Type of Statement**						
		12	Unqualified				4	4	4
		3	Reviewed			1	1	1	
		4	Compiled	2	1	1			
		1	Tax Returns			1			
		12	Other	1	2	1	1	1	6
4/1/92-3/31/93 ALL	4/1/93-3/31/94 ALL	4/1/94-3/31/95 ALL		0-1MM	16 (4/1-9/30/94) 1-3MM	3-5MM	5-10MM	16 (10/1/94-3/31/95) 10-25MM	25MM & OVER
		32	**NUMBER OF STATEMENTS**	3	3	4	6	6	10
%	%	%	**ASSETS**	%	%	%	%	%	%
D	D	16.5	Cash & Equivalents						20.4
A	A	27.2	Trade Receivables - (net)						24.1
T	T	26.9	Inventory						20.0
A	A	1.9	All Other Current						2.3
		72.6	Total Current						66.9
N	N	19.4	Fixed Assets (net)						23.4
O	O	2.1	Intangibles (net)						3.5
T	T	6.0	All Other Non-Current						6.3
		100.0	Total						100.0
A	A		**LIABILITIES**						
V	V	5.4	Notes Payable-Short Term						1.1
A	A	.9	Cur. Mat.-L /T/D						.7
I	I	10.0	Trade Payables						4.9
L	L	.6	Income Taxes Payable						.8
A	A	10.9	All Other Current						13.1
B	B	27.8	Total Current						20.7
L	L	7.0	Long Term Debt						3.5
E	E	.9	Deferred Taxes						1.2
		1.9	All Other-Non-Current						.7
		62.5	Net Worth						73.9
		100.0	Total Liabilities & Net Worth						100.0
			INCOME DATA						
		100.0	Net Sales						100.0
		49.4	Gross Profit						48.7
		40.9	Operating Expenses						37.5
		8.5	Operating Profit						11.2
		.5	All Other Expenses (net)						.4
		8.0	Profit Before Taxes						10.7
			RATIOS						
		4.5							4.5
		3.1	Current						3.9
		1.8							2.5
		2.7							3.2
		1.9	Quick						2.4
		1.0							1.5
	46	7.9						63	5.8
	62	5.9	Sales/Receivables					76	4.8
	79	4.6						85	4.3
	85	4.3						96	3.8
	114	3.2	Cost of Sales/Inventory					122	3.0
	152	2.4						152	2.4
	25	14.8						20	18.0
	33	10.9	Cost of Sales/Payables					27	13.7
	49	7.5						42	8.6
		2.2							1.9
		3.4	Sales/Working Capital						2.3
		6.6							3.6
		60.9							
	(23)	18.7	EBIT/Interest						
		1.8							
		10.7	Net Profit + Depr., Dep.,						
	(10)	3.9	Amort./Cur. Mat. L/T/D						
		1.7							
		.1							.3
		.3	Fixed/Worth						.3
		.4							.4
		.2							.2
		.4	Debt/Worth						.3
		1.6							.7
		27.6	% Profit Before Taxes/Tangible						25.1
		18.8	Net Worth						22.2
		11.8							12.7
		19.7	% Profit Before Taxes/Total						19.6
		10.3	Assets						14.8
		4.5							8.0
		25.3							8.7
		9.4	Sales/Net Fixed Assets						4.8
		4.5							3.5
		2.0							1.3
		1.4	Sales/Total Assets						1.2
		1.1							1.0
		1.4							
	(28)	2.3	% Depr., Dep., Amort./Sales						
		3.7							
			% Officers', Directors', Owners' Comp/Sales						
		1110080M	Net Sales ($)	2127M	5562M	13443M	46323M	100177M	942448M
		961458M	Total Assets ($)	2304M	2698M	5548M	31155M	68304M	851449M

© Robert Morris Associates 1995   M = $ thousand   MM = $ million
See Pages 1 through 15 for Explanation of Ratios and Data

Current Data Sorted By Assets | Comparative Historical Data

0-500M	500M-2MM	2-10MM	10-50MM	50-100MM	100-250MM		4/1/90-3/31/91 ALL	4/1/91-3/31/92 ALL
1					2	**# Postretirement Benefits**		
						Type of Statement		
	5		5		1	Unqualified	12	12
	5		2			Reviewed	8	5
4	2					Compiled	4	12
3	3	2	4		1	Tax Returns	1	2
						Other	14	13
	8 (4/1-9/30/94)		30 (10/1/94-3/31/95)					
7	10	8	11		2	**NUMBER OF STATEMENTS**	39	44
%	%	%	%	%	%	**ASSETS**	%	%
	11.5		4.9			Cash & Equivalents	8.3	7.8
	35.1		27.1			Trade Receivables - (net)	29.4	30.1
	28.8		33.0			Inventory	27.7	32.3
	.6		1.0			All Other Current	1.6	.9
	76.0		66.1			Total Current	67.0	71.0
	19.8		20.5			Fixed Assets (net)	24.0	20.7
	2.0		7.7			Intangibles (net)	2.0	2.2
	2.2		5.7			All Other Non-Current	7.1	6.0
	100.0		100.0			Total	100.0	100.0
						LIABILITIES		
	13.6		17.0			Notes Payable-Short Term	9.1	11.0
	4.0		2.1			Cur. Mat. -L/T/D	4.1	3.3
	16.6		12.7			Trade Payables	17.1	18.8
	.1		.4			Income Taxes Payable	.5	1.2
	10.7		9.1			All Other Current	9.4	8.1
	45.0		41.3			Total Current	40.3	42.4
	7.6		16.4			Long Term Debt	16.8	17.3
	.5		.1			Deferred Taxes	.9	.3
	5.5		8.9			All Other-Non-Current	3.8	5.1
	41.4		33.2			Net Worth	38.3	34.9
	100.0		100.0			Total Liabilities & Net Worth	100.0	100.0
						INCOME DATA		
	100.0		100.0			Net Sales	100.0	100.0
	34.1		36.0			Gross Profit	38.8	36.9
	28.3		28.8			Operating Expenses	32.6	32.8
	5.8		7.1			Operating Profit	6.2	4.1
	1.0		2.6			All Other Expenses (net)	.9	1.9
	4.8		4.5			Profit Before Taxes	5.3	2.2
						RATIOS		
	2.9		2.2			Current	2.8	2.7
	1.6		1.9				1.8	1.9
	1.4		1.2				1.2	1.3
	2.1		1.4			Quick	1.5	1.6
	1.1		1.2				.9	1.0
	.6		.5				.6	.6
	39 9.3		42 8.6			Sales/Receivables	36 10.2	32 11.3
	43 8.4		47 7.8				43 8.4	41 8.8
	53 6.9		64 5.7				55 6.6	51 7.2
	30 12.1		41 9.0			Cost of Sales/Inventory	34 10.8	39 9.4
	38 9.7		96 3.8				51 7.2	59 6.2
	74 4.9		166 2.2				146 2.5	146 2.5
	22 16.7		20 18.0			Cost of Sales/Payables	21 17.0	22 16.7
	26 13.9		29 12.5				40 9.1	35 10.3
	42 8.6		63 5.8				58 6.3	59 6.2
	5.9		5.3			Sales/Working Capital	5.7	4.7
	9.1		9.4				8.7	8.1
	28.8		15.6				28.2	24.4
			5.3			EBIT/Interest	(34) 12.0	(40) 5.0
			(10) 1.7				4.4	2.3
			.6				1.5	1.1
						Net Profit + Depr., Dep., Amort./Cur. Mat. L /T/D	(20) 7.9	(15) 4.4
							2.8	1.9
							1.6	1.5
	.2		.4			Fixed/Worth	.2	.2
	.6		.9				.7	.6
	1.0		3.8				3.2	1.7
	.5		1.2			Debt/Worth	.7	.7
	1.5		2.2				1.7	1.6
	49.2		12.4				6.2	4.3
						% Profit Before Taxes/Tangible Net Worth	(36) 61.4	(38) 32.5
							20.9	12.4
							7.4	1.7
	20.2		14.4			% Profit Before Taxes/Total Assets	17.7	11.9
	13.1		3.3				9.2	4.5
	.5		-.9				2.0	.4
	55.2		14.5			Sales/Net Fixed Assets	18.4	49.2
	20.1		11.8				13.1	14.3
	10.3		7.5				7.7	8.4
	3.4		3.1			Sales/Total Assets	3.2	3.5
	3.0		1.6				2.6	2.5
	2.5		1.4				1.8	1.6
	.5		1.3			% Depr., Dep., Amort./Sales	(34) 1.2	(38) .9
	1.3		(10) 1.9				1.9	1.5
	2.3		3.2				3.2	2.9
						% Officers', Directors', Owners' Comp/Sales	(12) 3.5	(16) 3.2
							5.1	5.6
							10.2	8.9
7603M	30856M	83378M	436116M		533816M	Net Sales ($)	903094M	767243M
2347M	11522M	41094M	253807M		348617M	Total Assets ($)	627678M	484152M

M = $ thousand   MM = $ million
See Pages 1 through 15 for Explanation of Ratios and Data

Comparative Historical Data				Current Data Sorted By Sales					
	2	3	# Postretirement Benefits	1					2
			Type of Statement						
9	18	11	Unqualified		1	1		3	6
11	9	8	Reviewed		4	1	1		2
17	5	6	Compiled	2	3	1			
2			Tax Returns						
7	7	13	Other	1	2	3	2		5
4/1/92-3/31/93	4/1/93-3/31/94	4/1/94-3/31/95			8 (4/1-9/30/94)		30 (10/1/94-3/31/95)		
ALL	ALL	ALL		0-1MM	1-3MM	3-5MM	5-10MM	10-25MM	25MM & OVER
46	39	38	**NUMBER OF STATEMENTS**	3	10	6	3	3	13
%	%	%	**ASSETS**	%	%	%	%	%	%
6.9	7.6	7.3	Cash & Equivalents		11.1				5.0
31.8	28.8	30.5	Trade Receivables - (net)		29.7				26.6
27.3	29.6	26.8	Inventory		22.4				31.7
1.3	1.3	2.8	All Other Current		.6				1.6
67.3	67.3	67.4	Total Current		63.8				64.9
22.0	22.9	23.4	Fixed Assets (net)		32.3				24.0
1.7	4.3	6.0	Intangibles (net)		3.3				7.0
8.9	5.6	3.2	All Other Non-Current		.6				4.0
100.0	100.0	100.0	Total		100.0				100.0
			LIABILITIES						
9.8	11.6	11.5	Notes Payable-Short Term		8.8				14.1
3.5	5.1	4.7	Cur. Mat.-L./T/D		6.1				2.4
17.8	18.1	14.1	Trade Payables		11.2				11.9
.4	1.2	.4	Income Taxes Payable		.1				.5
7.8	9.6	9.3	All Other Current		4.2				10.6
39.2	45.6	40.0	Total Current		30.3				39.6
16.7	12.6	14.8	Long Term Debt		15.4				15.7
.6	.6	.4	Deferred Taxes		.4				.7
1.9	5.6	5.7	All Other-Non-Current		7.6				8.4
41.6	35.5	39.1	Net Worth		46.3				35.6
100.0	100.0	100.0	Total Liabilities & Net Worth		100.0				100.0
			INCOME DATA						
100.0	100.0	100.0	Net Sales		100.0				100.0
35.6	35.5	35.7	Gross Profit		38.5				32.5
32.5	32.0	32.1	Operating Expenses		36.8				24.5
3.1	3.5	3.6	Operating Profit		1.7				8.0
.6	1.4	1.8	All Other Expenses (net)		1.4				2.5
2.5	2.1	1.8	Profit Before Taxes		.3				5.5
			RATIOS						
2.4	2.3	2.3	Current		2.9				2.1
1.9	1.7	1.7			1.9				1.8
1.2	1.2	1.4			1.6				1.3
1.6	1.3	1.4	Quick		2.1				1.3
1.1	.9	1.0			1.4				1.0
.7	.6	.6			.9				.5
35 10.3	36 10.1	39 9.4	Sales/Receivables		24 15.2				40 9.1
40 9.1	42 8.6	44 8.3			42 8.6				46 8.0
47 7.7	50 7.3	56 6.5			57 6.4				56 6.5
33 11.1	35 10.4	37 9.8	Cost of Sales/Inventory		26 14.3				43 8.4
51 7.2	63 5.8	64 5.7			37 10.0				94 3.9
89 4.1	126 2.9	126 2.9			70 5.2				126 2.9
20 18.7	22 16.7	22 16.5	Cost of Sales/Payables		23 16.0				20 18.3
33 10.9	35 10.4	28 12.9			28 13.2				28 13.0
49 7.5	63 5.8	53 6.9			38 9.7				31 11.7
6.3	5.3	6.1	Sales/Working Capital		6.6				5.8
10.0	11.4	9.3			7.6				9.4
21.8	32.4	14.2			12.4				14.4
12.3	6.5	5.8	EBIT/Interest						6.0
(43) 3.3	(36) 3.1	(33) 2.7						(12)	2.9
.7	.8	1.1							1.4
7.4	4.5	4.2	Net Profit + Depr., Dep.,						
(25) 2.6	(21) 2.2	(16) 2.7	Amort./Cur. Mat. L/T/D						
1.0	1.0	.4							
.2	.3	.4	Fixed/Worth		.3				.4
.6	.7	.9			1.0				.9
1.1	1.9	2.8			1.3				3.2
.7	.7	.7	Debt/Worth		.5				1.0
1.8	1.9	1.7			1.6				1.8
3.3	6.9	11.5			2.6				11.8
36.6	29.8	81.3	% Profit Before Taxes/Tangible		90.5				31.6
(34) 16.3	(34) 24.0	(34) 25.5	Net Worth		28.6			(11)	28.5
−4.1	8.1	12.9			13.7				13.0
15.8	11.6	15.7	% Profit Before Taxes/Total		24.2				14.5
7.5	6.3	6.3	Assets		13.1				5.4
−1.1	.9	.5			.5				2.4
26.5	19.7	19.8	Sales/Net Fixed Assets		21.1				13.7
14.9	12.6	11.9			10.7				11.2
7.7	7.0	7.1			6.5				5.6
3.8	3.1	3.3	Sales/Total Assets		3.8				3.1
2.7	2.3	2.5			3.2				1.6
2.1	1.5	1.5			1.6				1.4
.6	1.1	1.3	% Depr., Dep., Amort./Sales						1.3
(44) 1.6	(36) 2.0	(34) 2.1						(12)	2.2
2.6	3.1	2.9							3.5
2.2	.9		% Officers', Directors',						
(22) 4.4	(14) 3.0		Owners' Comp/Sales						
6.7	7.8								
859255M	1178552M	1091769M	Net Sales ($)	1307M	18307M	23182M	17845M	49172M	981956M
666291M	751003M	657387M	Total Assets ($)	736M	9986M	13559M	6315M	27341M	599450M

M = $ thousand   MM = $ million
See Pages 1 through 15 for Explanation of Ratios and Data

Current Data Sorted By Assets   Comparative Historical Data

	0-500M	500M-2MM	2-10MM	10-50MM	50-100MM	100-250MM		4/1/90-3/31/91 ALL	4/1/91-3/31/92 ALL
# Postretirement Benefits	1		3	2					
Type of Statement									
Unqualified	1		9	7	1	1		12	23
Reviewed	1	4	5					11	12
Compiled	3	4	1	1		1		6	7
Tax Returns									1
Other	2	6	6	4				3	4
	24 (4/1-9/30/94)			33 (10/1/94-3/31/95)					
NUMBER OF STATEMENTS	7	14	21	12	1	2		32	47
	%	%	%	%	%	%		%	%
ASSETS									
Cash & Equivalents		4.9	8.1	10.5				7.6	10.9
Trade Receivables - (net)		33.7	24.8	26.3				26.0	27.1
Inventory		30.8	29.9	22.0				30.1	31.5
All Other Current		2.9	6.3	4.6				4.7	1.6
Total Current		72.3	69.0	63.4				68.3	71.2
Fixed Assets (net)		18.3	23.9	28.7				24.3	23.0
Intangibles (net)		5.6	.5	4.3				1.5	1.5
All Other Non-Current		3.8	6.6	3.7				5.8	4.3
Total		100.0	100.0	100.0				100.0	100.0
LIABILITIES									
Notes Payable-Short Term		10.2	11.1	7.6				11.3	9.8
Cur. Mat. -L/T/D		1.9	4.8	8.6				2.8	4.0
Trade Payables		13.9	15.6	9.5				14.5	11.3
Income Taxes Payable		1.3	.2	.3				.6	.9
All Other Current		17.4	8.3	11.6				11.0	7.1
Total Current		44.6	39.9	37.6				40.2	33.2
Long Term Debt		11.5	14.1	8.7				12.7	13.3
Deferred Taxes		.3	.3	1.1				.5	.7
All Other-Non-Current		.6	3.8	2.4				2.7	2.6
Net Worth		43.0	41.8	50.1				43.9	50.1
Total Liabilities & Net Worth		100.0	100.0	100.0				100.0	100.0
INCOME DATA									
Net Sales		100.0	100.0	100.0				100.0	100.0
Gross Profit		39.1	35.4	32.1				38.2	39.9
Operating Expenses		32.3	31.1	34.8				35.8	34.5
Operating Profit		6.8	4.3	-2.7				2.4	5.4
All Other Expenses (net)		1.5	1.2	.7				1.3	1.5
Profit Before Taxes		5.4	3.1	-3.4				1.1	3.9
RATIOS									
Current		2.6	2.7	3.6				2.9	3.6
		1.5	1.4	2.2				2.0	2.3
		1.2	1.1	1.3				1.4	1.5
Quick		1.3	1.1	2.6				1.8	2.2
		.8	.8	1.4				1.0	1.1
		.4	.5	.7				.6	.8
Sales/Receivables	42	8.7	43 8.4	64 5.7				37 10.0	43 8.4
	51	7.1	56 6.5	73 5.0				48 7.6	55 6.6
	56	6.5	69 5.3	76 4.8				63 5.8	70 5.2
Cost of Sales/Inventory	40	9.1	53 6.9	73 5.0				44 8.3	65 5.6
	65	5.6	104 3.5	89 4.1				104 3.5	104 3.5
	111	3.3	166 2.2	111 3.3				166 2.2	166 2.2
Cost of Sales/Payables	15	25.1	17 22.1	20 18.0				17 20.9	20 18.6
	26	14.2	42 8.6	35 10.3				35 10.5	37 9.9
	35	10.4	91 4.0	60 6.1				54 6.7	52 7.0
Sales/Working Capital		7.2	2.9	2.9				4.0	2.5
		10.2	6.0	5.4				6.1	5.3
		13.9	31.9	13.2				11.6	8.5
EBIT/Interest		(12) 23.0	(17) 4.6	(11) 38.7				(30) 10.3	(41) 7.5
		3.0	2.2	16.8				2.8	2.9
		1.6	1.3	-5.2				.9	1.6
Net Profit + Depr., Dep., Amort./Cur. Mat. L./T/D			(11) 2.2					(19) 6.5	(23) 9.7
			1.3					1.7	2.7
			.3					.4	1.6
Fixed/Worth		.2	.3	.2				.3	.2
		.3	.8	.7				.5	.5
		1.1	1.2	2.3				1.0	1.1
Debt/Worth		.6	.7	.3				.5	.4
		1.7	1.9	.8				.9	1.0
		3.2	3.8	6.3				3.1	2.4
% Profit Before Taxes/Tangible Net Worth		(12) 52.9	26.9	(11) 45.8				(31) 29.7	(45) 29.1
		34.4	13.5	12.0				9.2	13.4
		9.9	3.3	-2.7				-.2	6.3
% Profit Before Taxes/Total Assets		23.4	7.4	16.3				10.9	12.9
		8.4	5.7	5.7				2.8	6.6
		3.9	1.1	-23.1				-.9	2.5
Sales/Net Fixed Assets		59.6	15.5	13.0				21.6	23.5
		29.7	6.3	3.9				9.2	10.1
		4.5	4.2	2.1				4.3	4.5
Sales/Total Assets		3.5	2.2	1.8				2.8	2.4
		2.8	1.6	1.0				2.0	1.7
		1.5	1.2	.8				1.2	1.3
% Depr., Dep., Amort./Sales		(12) .6	(18) 1.3	(11) 1.3				(30) 1.1	(45) 1.2
		1.9	3.1	6.5				2.1	2.2
		3.6	4.4	7.0				3.3	4.0
% Officers', Directors', Owners' Comp/Sales		(11) 2.5							(15) 2.8
		3.9							5.4
		6.6							8.6
Net Sales ($)	5000M	35903M	152119M	373648M	106340M	533816M		551547M	799770M
Total Assets ($)	2247M	15388M	94407M	302975M	79569M	348617M		484328M	677975M

M = $ thousand   MM = $ million
See Pages 1 through 15 for Explanation of Ratios and Data

Comparative Historical Data | Current Data Sorted By Sales

4/1/92-3/31/93 ALL	4/1/93-3/31/94 ALL	4/1/94-3/31/95 ALL		0-1MM	1-3MM	3-5MM	5-10MM	10-25MM	25MM & OVER
3	3	6	# Postretirement Benefits		1		3		2
			Type of Statement						
17	20	19	Unqualified		3		4	5	7
12	11	10	Reviewed	1	4	1	3	1	
7	9	10	Compiled	3	3	2	1		1
		1	Tax Returns						
9	8	18	Other	2	5	1	6	3	1
				24 (4/1-9/30/94)			33 (10/1/94-3/31/95)		
45	49	57	**NUMBER OF STATEMENTS**	6	15	4	13	10	9
%	%	%	**ASSETS**	%	%	%	%	%	%
10.2	12.5	7.9	Cash & Equivalents		10.5		1.7	10.4	
27.2	27.2	26.7	Trade Receivables - (net)		31.1		29.1	24.6	
29.2	28.2	28.7	Inventory		29.8		28.5	26.1	
2.7	2.6	4.2	All Other Current		2.5		9.0	5.3	
69.4	70.4	67.6	Total Current		74.0		68.2	66.4	
24.6	23.4	24.2	Fixed Assets (net)		16.7		24.3	26.6	
2.5	1.8	2.6	Intangibles (net)		4.9		.1	2.3	
3.5	4.3	5.6	All Other Non-Current		4.4		7.4	4.7	
100.0	100.0	100.0	Total		100.0		100.0	100.0	
			LIABILITIES						
7.6	6.3	10.3	Notes Payable-Short Term		7.7		16.2	6.8	
3.9	4.6	4.8	Cur. Mat.-L /T/D		2.7		4.5	9.3	
12.2	11.4	12.8	Trade Payables		10.9		22.2	8.0	
.6	1.6	.6	Income Taxes Payable		1.2		.1	.6	
8.6	9.0	14.4	All Other Current		16.6		8.0	9.7	
32.9	32.9	42.9	Total Current		39.1		51.0	34.4	
10.9	11.3	13.4	Long Term Debt		9.4		14.1	4.9	
.7	1.7	.6	Deferred Taxes		.3		.4	1.2	
3.0	1.9	2.1	All Other-Non-Current		1.5		5.0	.4	
52.5	52.2	40.9	Net Worth		49.6		29.4	59.2	
100.0	100.0	100.0	Total Liabilities & Net Worth		100.0		100.0	100.0	
			INCOME DATA						
100.0	100.0	100.0	Net Sales		100.0		100.0	100.0	
40.3	40.4	37.4	Gross Profit		40.7		30.5	36.5	
35.4	34.8	34.1	Operating Expenses		32.9		26.7	37.8	
4.9	5.7	3.3	Operating Profit		7.9		3.8	-1.4	
1.2	1.4	1.6	All Other Expenses (net)		1.3		1.8	.6	
3.7	4.2	1.7	Profit Before Taxes		6.6		1.9	-2.0	
			RATIOS						
4.1	4.4	2.7	Current		2.9		1.7	5.0	
2.4	2.1	1.6			1.6		1.3	3.2	
1.6	1.4	1.2			1.3		1.1	1.0	
2.2	2.5	1.6	Quick		2.0		.8	2.6	
1.2	1.2	.9			.9		.6	2.0	
.7	.6	.5			.4		.4	.4	
44 8.3	42 8.7	42 8.6	Sales/Receivables		47 7.8		40 9.1	59 6.2	
53 6.9	57 6.4	55 6.6			54 6.8		64 5.7	72 5.1	
65 5.6	74 4.9	70 5.2			61 6.0		72 5.1	74 4.9	
60 6.1	51 7.2	56 6.5	Cost of Sales/Inventory		47 7.8		44 8.3	59 6.2	
107 3.4	104 3.5	91 4.0			63 5.8		96 3.8	118 3.1	
146 2.5	166 2.2	159 2.3			192 1.9		107 3.4	183 2.0	
17 21.2	18 20.7	16 22.4	Cost of Sales/Payables		10 37.2		26 13.9	18 19.8	
38 9.6	34 10.7	28 13.0			19 19.7		83 4.4	29 12.4	
51 7.2	53 6.9	62 5.9			29 12.4		99 3.7	62 5.9	
3.1	2.9	4.0	Sales/Working Capital		4.0		5.7	2.2	
5.6	6.4	8.0			8.1		16.9	3.1	
8.8	13.7	18.8			13.5		31.9	NM	
7.1	13.2	12.8	EBIT/Interest		23.0		4.2		
(40) 2.6	(42) 3.7	(49) 3.0			(12) 3.0		(12) 2.5		
1.5	1.6	1.3			1.8		1.3		
6.4	3.7	9.8	Net Profit + Depr., Dep., Amort./Cur. Mat. L/T/D				2.2		
(27) 2.8	(18) 1.5	(27) 1.7					(10) 1.2		
1.6	-1.1	.3					.3		
.3	.1	.2	Fixed/Worth		.1		.4	.2	
.4	.4	.6			.2		.9	.4	
.8	.9	1.3			.9		1.6	1.4	
.4	.3	.5	Debt/Worth		.5		1.7	.3	
.8	1.0	1.5			1.4		2.2	.4	
2.6	2.1	5.3			2.0		6.1	2.8	
23.5	29.4	46.5	% Profit Before Taxes/Tangible Net Worth		52.1		46.2	26.1	
10.7	(47) 17.9	(52) 16.8			(13) 19.2		13.5	11.6	
3.1	8.1	3.9			8.3		3.2	-57.0	
10.3	14.8	16.0	% Profit Before Taxes/Total Assets		20.8		6.7	17.6	
4.6	6.6	6.1			7.3		4.9	8.6	
2.2	2.9	1.1			4.4		1.0	-5.0	
20.6	25.5	25.8	Sales/Net Fixed Assets		40.0		16.0	13.4	
8.3	8.2	6.7			32.6		9.3	5.5	
3.8	4.3	4.0			4.5		4.2	2.2	
2.4	2.4	2.5	Sales/Total Assets		3.5		2.5	1.7	
1.6	1.6	1.7			1.7		1.8	1.2	
1.3	1.1	1.2			1.2		1.3	.9	
1.8	.7	1.3	% Depr., Dep., Amort./Sales		.9		1.1		
(41) 2.7	(47) 2.5	(51) 3.1			(12) 1.9		(12) 2.9		
4.7	4.1	4.3			3.6		4.1		
2.4	1.6	2.5	% Officers', Directors', Owners' Comp/Sales						
(12) 8.0	(13) 5.8	(14) 5.0							
14.4	10.4	8.7							
920207M	1279050M	1206826M	Net Sales ($)	3873M	31728M	14513M	89252M	169848M	897612M
737912M	978142M	843203M	Total Assets ($)	1797M	18541M	10820M	50659M	149946M	611440M

Current Data Sorted By Assets   **Comparative Historical Data**

	0-500M	500M-2MM	2-10MM	10-50MM	50-100MM	100-250MM		4/1/90-3/31/91 ALL	4/1/91-3/31/92 ALL
			1	5	1	1	# Postretirement Benefits		
							Type of Statement		
	2	4	11	11	4	4	Unqualified	31	48
	1	8	11	1			Reviewed	15	16
	9	7	1			1	Compiled	15	14
	4	3					Tax Returns		1
	2	8	14	10	3	3	Other	19	14
		39 (4/1-9/30/94)			82 (10/1/94-3/31/95)				
	18	30	37	21	8	7	NUMBER OF STATEMENTS	80	93
	%	%	%	%	%	%	**ASSETS**	%	%
	12.4	6.2	7.0	8.4			Cash & Equivalents	6.6	10.5
	44.1	39.2	29.5	23.3			Trade Receivables - (net)	28.5	26.5
	14.7	24.2	29.3	27.7			Inventory	25.8	24.0
	1.5	2.2	1.8	3.8			All Other Current	1.1	2.3
	72.8	71.8	67.6	63.1			Total Current	62.1	63.2
	15.1	19.9	20.2	20.0			Fixed Assets (net)	25.6	22.5
	6.5	4.2	4.9	8.8			Intangibles (net)	6.1	6.8
	5.7	4.1	7.3	8.1			All Other Non-Current	6.3	7.5
	100.0	100.0	100.0	100.0			Total	100.0	100.0
							LIABILITIES		
	11.9	9.9	11.0	6.3			Notes Payable-Short Term	11.6	6.4
	3.6	3.1	2.8	3.5			Cur. Mat. -L/T/D	3.3	3.9
	11.9	17.4	16.4	10.6			Trade Payables	12.9	11.3
	.1	1.4	.5	1.5			Income Taxes Payable	.7	.7
	12.5	8.8	7.1	8.2			All Other Current	9.4	9.3
	40.1	40.5	37.8	30.0			Total Current	37.9	31.6
	10.0	16.4	13.2	13.4			Long Term Debt	21.8	15.3
	.4	.3	.5	.5			Deferred Taxes	.9	.7
	.1	2.8	3.3	3.7			All Other-Non-Current	4.3	1.7
	49.3	40.0	45.2	52.4			Net Worth	35.1	50.8
	100.0	100.0	100.0	100.0			Total Liabilities & Net Worth	100.0	100.0
							INCOME DATA		
	100.0	100.0	100.0	100.0			Net Sales	100.0	100.0
	56.3	44.6	39.0	42.2			Gross Profit	45.9	49.2
	47.7	40.1	31.7	37.0			Operating Expenses	39.8	41.2
	8.6	4.5	7.3	5.2			Operating Profit	6.1	8.0
	1.4	.3	1.5	.5			All Other Expenses (net)	2.9	1.9
	7.2	4.2	5.8	4.7			Profit Before Taxes	3.2	6.1
							RATIOS		
	4.9	2.3	3.3	3.6			Current	2.6	3.1
	1.9	2.0	1.9	2.1				1.8	2.3
	1.4	1.4	1.2	1.6				1.3	1.5
	3.1	1.6	1.7	1.9			Quick	1.6	1.9
	1.5	1.1	.9	1.0				.8	1.2
	.9	.9	.6	.6				.6	.8
	38 9.6	45 8.2	41 9.0	46 8.0			Sales/Receivables	43 8.5	41 8.9
	60 6.1	54 6.8	51 7.2	54 6.7				55 6.6	54 6.7
	76 4.8	69 5.3	72 5.1	68 5.4				68 5.4	69 5.3
	10 35.3	32 11.5	40 9.1	61 6.0			Cost of Sales/Inventory	62 5.9	59 6.2
	41 8.8	49 7.4	79 4.6	94 3.9				89 4.1	85 4.3
	87 4.2	94 3.9	146 2.5	183 2.5				130 2.8	146 2.5
	6 65.7	22 16.5	23 15.6	19 19.6			Cost of Sales/Payables	25 14.8	23 16.2
	17 20.9	37 9.8	43 8.4	37 9.8				39 9.3	38 9.7
	51 7.2	65 5.6	73 5.0	53 6.9				61 6.0	64 5.7
	5.4	5.7	4.3	3.5			Sales/Working Capital	4.2	3.5
	9.9	7.5	8.0	5.2				7.6	5.8
	19.0	14.5	22.8	7.1				17.2	10.6
	28.4	10.5	(33) 9.6	(20) 11.5			EBIT/Interest	(73) 6.6	(86) 12.3
	(14) 4.7	4.7	4.8	7.1				2.7	3.7
	.4	1.6	2.0	3.3				1.0	1.1
			(21) 11.3	(15) 7.0			Net Profit + Depr., Dep.,	(49) 6.1	(60) 10.5
			2.5	2.2			Amort./Cur. Mat. L /T/D	2.0	2.8
			1.4	1.1				.8	.6
	.1	.3	.2	.2			Fixed/Worth	.4	.3
	.3	.5	.5	.6				.8	.5
	1.1	.9	.9	1.0				2.1	.9
	.2	.9	.5	.4			Debt/Worth	.9	.5
	1.0	1.6	1.4	1.2				2.0	1.0
	2.7	2.6	3.6	2.7				6.9	2.5
	71.9	37.5	(35) 39.4	(19) 40.5			% Profit Before Taxes/Tangible	(68) 32.7	(86) 34.0
	(16) 31.0	(28) 21.9	18.5	20.1			Net Worth	20.3	19.0
	2.8	5.0	5.8	5.2				4.8	2.8
	38.5	18.0	16.4	12.7			% Profit Before Taxes/Total	12.4	15.8
	18.3	9.7	6.7	9.1			Assets	5.4	8.2
	-.0	2.1	2.5	3.5				-.2	.3
	59.8	36.1	23.6	15.0			Sales/Net Fixed Assets	13.7	18.1
	24.0	16.2	12.3	7.3				7.7	8.2
	12.8	6.6	6.3	4.7				4.9	5.1
	3.7	3.2	3.0	1.9			Sales/Total Assets	2.4	2.4
	3.0	2.7	2.1	1.5				1.8	1.7
	2.3	1.8	1.4	1.2				1.4	1.1
	1.0	.9	(34) .9	.9			% Depr., Dep., Amort./Sales	(72) 1.4	(86) 1.4
	(13) 1.7	(23) 1.9	1.9	(20) 3.1				2.1	2.2
	3.1	2.8	3.3	4.1				3.1	3.2
		(16) 1.6					% Officers', Directors',	(28) 3.8	(23) 4.2
		6.6					Owners' Comp/Sales	5.1	10.3
		9.0						12.4	13.7
	14977M	89622M	377940M	612933M	721764M	1159798M	Net Sales ($)	1991420M	2623414M
	4936M	34442M	183985M	417071M	544758M	1041058M	Total Assets ($)	1406759M	1975600M

M = $ thousand   MM = $ million
See Pages 1 through 15 for Explanation of Ratios and Data

Comparative Historical Data | Current Data Sorted By Sales

5	5	8	# Postretirement Benefits Type of Statement	1		1	3	2	2
44	42	36	Unqualified	1	4	1	7	8	15
16	21	20	Reviewed	1	4	6	5	4	
21	15	18	Compiled	9	5	2		1	1
1	3	7	Tax Returns	2	4	1			
26	32	40	Other	1	6	4	8	9	12

4/1/92-3/31/93 ALL	4/1/93-3/31/94 ALL	4/1/94-3/31/95 ALL		39 (4/1-9/30/94)			82 (10/1/94-3/31/95)		
				0-1MM	1-3MM	3-5MM	5-10MM	10-25MM	25MM & OVER
108	113	121	NUMBER OF STATEMENTS	14	23	14	20	22	28
%	%	%	ASSETS	%	%	%	%	%	%
11.1	10.1	8.4	Cash & Equivalents	15.0	5.0	9.3	10.8	5.8	7.8
28.9	29.2	32.1	Trade Receivables - (net)	39.0	41.1	32.6	32.2	28.4	23.7
24.0	23.7	24.7	Inventory	11.9	21.9	24.6	32.2	26.2	26.7
2.4	2.3	2.3	All Other Current	2.6	1.6	3.1	.8	2.1	3.7
66.3	65.4	67.5	Total Current	68.5	69.6	69.6	76.1	62.5	62.0
20.8	22.2	19.7	Fixed Assets (net)	20.0	18.8	20.0	15.4	20.7	22.2
5.1	5.1	5.9	Intangibles (net)	6.1	3.6	5.5	5.7	8.7	5.8
7.8	7.3	6.9	All Other Non-Current	5.4	8.0	4.9	2.8	8.0	10.0
100.0	100.0	100.0	Total	100.0	100.0	100.0	100.0	100.0	100.0
			LIABILITIES						
6.4	8.2	9.3	Notes Payable-Short Term	6.5	14.8	9.1	10.0	8.5	6.4
2.3	3.0	3.0	Cur. Mat.-L /T/D	3.9	3.1	3.6	2.2	2.5	3.2
10.7	14.1	13.7	Trade Payables	8.3	14.9	18.0	16.3	14.9	10.4
.7	2.4	.9	Income Taxes Payable	.1	.9	1.1	.9	1.0	.9
8.3	10.3	9.1	All Other Current	12.1	8.2	9.9	7.2	8.9	9.4
28.5	38.1	36.0	Total Current	30.9	42.0	41.6	36.6	35.8	30.4
15.2	11.7	13.5	Long Term Debt	12.0	17.2	10.8	12.7	13.2	13.4
.7	.6	.5	Deferred Taxes	.5	.2	.4	.7	.4	.9
2.5	3.9	2.5	All Other-Non-Current	.3	2.7	3.0	2.6	3.3	2.4
53.0	45.7	47.5	Net Worth	56.2	37.9	44.2	47.5	47.4	53.0
100.0	100.0	100.0	Total Liabilities & Net Worth	100.0	100.0	100.0	100.0	100.0	100.0
			INCOME DATA						
100.0	100.0	100.0	Net Sales	100.0	100.0	100.0	100.0	100.0	100.0
47.6	45.7	45.3	Gross Profit	59.1	49.1	40.2	38.9	41.2	45.5
39.9	38.9	38.2	Operating Expenses	49.4	43.0	35.1	35.2	33.2	36.4
7.6	6.9	7.0	Operating Profit	9.6	6.1	5.1	3.7	8.0	9.1
1.1	1.0	1.0	All Other Expenses (net)	1.0	1.9	-1.2	1.2	1.2	.9
6.5	5.9	6.1	Profit Before Taxes	8.6	4.2	6.3	2.5	6.8	8.2
			RATIOS						
4.0	3.0	3.4	Current	4.4	2.4	2.4	5.2	2.8	3.6
2.5	1.9	2.1		2.2	1.9	1.7	2.2	1.8	2.2
1.8	1.2	1.4		1.5	1.2	1.4	1.5	1.2	1.5
2.5	2.0	1.9	Quick	2.8	1.6	1.5	2.2	1.7	1.9
1.4	1.1	1.1		1.8	1.1	1.0	1.1	1.0	1.0
.9	.6	.7		1.2	.9	.7	.8	.7	.6
45 8.1	40 9.1	45 8.1	Sales/Receivables	42 8.7	51 7.1	40 9.2	39 9.3	45 8.2	47 7.7
54 6.8	52 7.0	56 6.5		60 6.1	68 5.4	49 7.5	54 6.8	51 7.2	56 6.5
68 5.4	63 5.8	72 5.1		96 3.8	73 5.0	55 6.6	79 4.6	68 5.4	69 5.3
47 7.8	45 8.2	40 9.1	Cost of Sales/Inventory	6 56.6	42 8.7	34 10.6	38 9.7	41 9.0	79 4.6
94 3.9	81 4.5	78 4.7		24 14.9	72 5.1	49 7.5	104 3.5	63 5.8	118 3.1
146 2.5	126 2.9	130 2.8		99 3.7	118 3.1	78 4.7	166 2.2	99 3.7	203 1.8
20 18.1	20 18.4	22 16.7	Cost of Sales/Payables	0 UND	17 21.6	21 17.6	24 15.0	20 18.7	29 12.6
34 10.6	40 9.1	37 10.0		22 16.3	42 8.6	47 7.7	37 9.8	39 9.3	36 10.1
53 6.9	64 5.7	58 6.3		47 7.8	79 4.6	69 5.3	62 5.9	58 6.3	47 7.7
2.8	3.8	4.0	Sales/Working Capital	4.5	5.3	5.7	2.1	4.0	3.3
5.2	7.6	6.5		7.7	6.6	9.1	6.1	8.0	4.1
8.9	25.3	13.6		10.7	18.9	15.5	11.9	31.4	8.3
17.6	11.8	12.6	EBIT/Interest	(10) 25.5	8.2	(17) 17.0	(20) 10.1	(26) 12.3	22.1
(100) 5.3	(96) 5.0	(110) 5.2		5.4	3.7	5.8	3.3	6.0	7.2
1.7	1.5	1.9		.3	1.2	1.3	1.2	2.1	4.1
10.6	7.8	19.0	Net Profit + Depr., Dep., Amort./Cur. Mat. L/T/D				(10) 7.2	(13) 13.8	(17) 24.9
(57) 4.1	(48) 2.7	(54) 3.8					2.3	2.5	6.3
1.5	1.1	1.5					-.6	2.0	1.5
.2	.3	.2	Fixed/Worth	.1	.3	.3	.1	.2	.2
.4	.5	.5		.3	.5	.4	.4	.6	.5
.9	1.1	.9		.8	1.1	.9	.6	1.8	.7
.4	.5	.5	Debt/Worth	.3	.7	.8	.5	.4	.4
1.0	1.2	1.3		.7	1.7	1.7	1.2	1.3	.8
2.1	3.0	2.6		1.5	2.8	2.7	3.1	5.7	2.1
31.1	42.7	40.5	% Profit Before Taxes/Tangible Net Worth	(13) 57.3	(21) 34.2	(13) 67.2	(19) 62.5	(19) 39.4	(27) 40.5
(103) 18.9	(106) 19.6	(112) 21.1		30.7	21.4	19.5	18.3	15.4	23.2
8.0	6.0	6.4		6.6	4.1	2.6	5.8	3.4	13.1
15.3	18.9	18.2	% Profit Before Taxes/Total Assets	38.5	17.0	24.0	14.9	22.0	13.6
8.4	7.9	8.9		14.8	9.9	10.6	6.2	6.4	10.5
3.1	2.1	2.7		-.0	.5	.8	.5	2.7	7.2
21.3	20.0	24.4	Sales/Net Fixed Assets	45.9	34.6	28.5	24.6	28.6	9.9
9.9	10.3	12.1		20.4	14.8	14.1	15.4	11.0	7.3
4.9	5.6	5.8		6.8	6.7	6.1	7.6	5.4	4.3
2.5	2.9	2.9	Sales/Total Assets	3.4	2.9	3.2	3.1	2.6	1.8
1.7	1.9	1.9		2.4	2.6	2.8	2.1	1.9	1.4
1.1	1.4	1.3		1.3	1.6	2.1	1.2	1.4	1.2
1.3	1.3	1.1	% Depr., Dep., Amort./Sales		(20) .8	(11) 1.3	(18) .9	(20) 1.1	(25) 1.9
(99) 2.2	(93) 2.3	(103) 2.5			1.7	2.7	1.7	2.6	3.1
3.8	3.2	3.8			2.9	3.6	3.3	3.9	4.0
1.7	4.9	2.2	% Officers', Directors', Owners' Comp/Sales		(11) 4.4				
(28) 7.1	(31) 7.2	(33) 6.8			6.6				
13.2	11.8	13.1			8.5				
2373027M	2526174M	2977034M	Net Sales ($)	8317M	42230M	58671M	138081M	351787M	2377948M
1903135M	1670639M	2226250M	Total Assets ($)	4175M	22374M	28381M	94735M	204853M	1871732M

M = $ thousand   MM = $ million
See Pages 1 through 15 for Explanation of Ratios and Data

Current Data Sorted By Assets							Comparative Historical Data	

0-500M	500M-2MM	2-10MM	10-50MM	50-100MM	100-250MM		4/1/90-3/31/91 ALL	4/1/91-3/31/92 ALL
	1	1			2	# Postretirement Benefits		
						Type of Statement		
	1	10	4	1	2	Unqualified	12	28
1	5	4	1			Reviewed	5	6
1	5	2				Compiled	11	11
						Tax Returns		1
1	3	5	2	2		Other	13	9
	18 (4/1-9/30/94)		32 (10/1/94-3/31/95)					
3	14	21	7	3	2	NUMBER OF STATEMENTS	41	55
%	%	%	%	%	%	ASSETS	%	%
	3.6	6.4				Cash & Equivalents	5.6	8.7
	27.1	28.6				Trade Receivables - (net)	28.0	24.8
	44.5	29.8				Inventory	29.6	27.8
	2.7	2.0				All Other Current	1.5	2.2
	78.0	66.8				Total Current	64.8	63.5
	17.7	26.8				Fixed Assets (net)	25.2	22.5
	1.9	1.3				Intangibles (net)	1.9	5.7
	2.5	5.1				All Other Non-Current	8.2	8.2
	100.0	100.0				Total	100.0	100.0
						LIABILITIES		
	12.3	11.5				Notes Payable-Short Term	14.2	11.2
	5.4	2.3				Cur. Mat. -L/T/D	5.6	4.8
	17.8	14.1				Trade Payables	13.3	11.0
	.3	.5				Income Taxes Payable	.8	.6
	11.9	11.6				All Other Current	9.3	11.1
	47.8	40.1				Total Current	43.1	38.7
	13.1	14.3				Long Term Debt	13.4	14.2
	.2	.2				Deferred Taxes	.7	.6
	1.1	1.6				All Other-Non-Current	2.3	2.3
	37.8	43.8				Net Worth	40.5	44.2
	100.0	100.0				Total Liabilities & Net Worth	100.0	100.0
						INCOME DATA		
	100.0	100.0				Net Sales	100.0	100.0
	31.3	36.4				Gross Profit	34.9	36.3
	26.3	33.6				Operating Expenses	32.3	33.1
	5.0	2.8				Operating Profit	2.6	3.2
	2.2	1.4				All Other Expenses (net)	2.0	1.9
	2.8	1.4				Profit Before Taxes	.6	1.3
						RATIOS		
	2.7	1.9				Current	3.1	2.7
	1.5	1.6					1.6	1.7
	1.1	1.3					1.1	1.3
	1.3	1.1				Quick	1.5	1.5
	.6	.9					.9	1.0
	.4	.4					.5	.6
	36 10.2	33 11.1				Sales/Receivables	35 10.5	38 9.5
	45 8.1	49 7.4					49 7.5	47 7.8
	53 6.9	65 5.6					66 5.5	59 6.2
	63 5.8	26 14.1				Cost of Sales/Inventory	41 8.9	36 10.2
	101 3.6	101 3.6					89 4.1	89 4.1
	174 2.1	140 2.6					130 2.8	152 2.4
	30 12.1	17 20.9				Cost of Sales/Payables	23 15.8	21 17.7
	42 8.7	37 9.9					31 11.7	30 12.3
	58 6.3	66 5.5					43 8.4	41 8.8
	3.3	5.3				Sales/Working Capital	4.0	3.8
	9.1	8.2					9.7	7.6
	59.0	19.5					91.2	17.1
	4.0	7.4				EBIT/Interest	7.2	4.5
	2.7	(17) 3.4					(37) 2.8	(47) 2.6
	1.1	1.3					-.3	1.1
						Net Profit + Depr., Dep.,	8.9	3.4
						Amort./Cur. Mat. L /T/D	(21) 2.3	(29) 1.5
							1.0	.3
	.1	.3				Fixed/Worth	.2	.2
	.7	.5					.6	.4
	NM	1.0					1.8	1.2
	.7	.7				Debt/Worth	.7	.6
	1.5	1.5					1.3	1.3
	NM	3.0					4.3	3.2
	30.4	42.1				% Profit Before Taxes/Tangible	33.4	24.1
	(11) 11.8	19.2				Net Worth	(37) 16.7	(49) 9.3
	.9	1.9					-2.4	2.2
	10.6	10.9				% Profit Before Taxes/Total	14.7	8.9
	4.1	5.5				Assets	6.7	3.5
	.4	.6					-3.5	.8
	46.2	29.4				Sales/Net Fixed Assets	23.4	17.4
	14.9	8.0					9.2	8.5
	7.3	3.4					4.8	5.6
	2.6	2.5				Sales/Total Assets	2.6	2.5
	2.1	2.0					1.9	1.8
	1.6	1.5					1.6	1.3
	.6	1.4				% Depr., Dep., Amort./Sales	1.6	1.9
	(13) 1.1	(18) 2.2					(34) 3.0	(47) 3.2
	3.1	5.3					5.0	4.7
						% Officers', Directors',		4.6
						Owners' Comp/Sales		(11) 6.3
								9.8
1920M	39343M	252970M	481806M	227317M	415453M	Net Sales ($)	1045669M	1589669M
1139M	17627M	111392M	159367M	198641M	286377M	Total Assets ($)	675469M	1066835M

M = $ thousand   MM = $ million
See Pages 1 through 15 for Explanation of Ratios and Data

Comparative Historical Data / Current Data Sorted By Sales

1	3	4	# Postretirement Benefits / Type of Statement	1	2			1	6
20	19	18	Unqualified			1	3	8	6
8	9	11	Reviewed	2	2	2	3	2	
7	3	8	Compiled	1	3	2	2		
			Tax Returns						
			Other	1	2	1	4	1	4

12	12	13		1	2	1	4	1	4
4/1/92-3/31/93	4/1/93-3/31/94	4/1/94-3/31/95			18 (4/1-9/30/94)			32 (10/1/94-3/31/95)	
ALL	ALL	ALL		0-1MM	1-3MM	3-5MM	5-10MM	10-25MM	25MM & OVER
47	43	50	NUMBER OF STATEMENTS	4	7	6	12	11	10
%	%	%	ASSETS	%	%	%	%	%	%
6.6	10.1	5.8	Cash & Equivalents				5.4	5.4	10.0
22.0	24.2	26.9	Trade Receivables - (net)				27.4	30.4	24.4
33.3	28.7	34.4	Inventory				34.0	25.8	27.5
1.4	1.9	2.2	All Other Current				2.7	.8	3.2
63.4	65.0	69.3	Total Current				69.6	62.4	65.1
26.2	25.8	22.3	Fixed Assets (net)				24.8	25.6	20.0
2.1	2.8	3.2	Intangibles (net)				1.6	3.5	7.5
8.3	6.4	5.1	All Other Non-Current				4.0	8.5	7.4
100.0	100.0	100.0	Total				100.0	100.0	100.0
			LIABILITIES						
8.5	8.8	11.3	Notes Payable-Short Term				13.9	6.3	6.7
6.5	4.5	3.8	Cur. Mat.-L /T/D				2.8	3.2	4.7
9.3	12.5	14.0	Trade Payables				15.3	11.5	12.6
.4	.9	.5	Income Taxes Payable				.2	.7	1.0
12.8	10.8	12.0	All Other Current				13.4	10.6	8.7
37.5	37.5	41.6	Total Current				45.7	32.3	33.7
14.9	13.1	13.9	Long Term Debt				8.7	21.3	14.7
.9	.9	.3	Deferred Taxes				.2	.6	.3
1.4	2.1	3.3	All Other-Non-Current				2.7	5.2	2.7
45.4	46.4	41.0	Net Worth				42.6	40.5	48.5
100.0	100.0	100.0	Total Liabilities & Net Worth				100.0	100.0	100.0
			INCOME DATA						
100.0	100.0	100.0	Net Sales				100.0	100.0	100.0
36.2	40.0	33.9	Gross Profit				35.1	37.0	28.8
33.2	35.5	31.0	Operating Expenses				33.1	31.5	23.4
3.1	4.5	2.9	Operating Profit				2.0	5.5	5.4
1.2	2.8	1.9	All Other Expenses (net)				2.4	1.0	2.9
1.8	1.7	1.0	Profit Before Taxes				-.4	4.5	2.5
			RATIOS						
3.0	2.3	2.4	Current				1.9	2.7	2.7
1.9	1.7	1.7					1.5	1.9	2.3
1.2	1.2	1.3					1.2	1.5	1.4
1.2	1.7	1.2	Quick				1.0	1.2	1.7
.8	.9	.8					.6	1.0	1.0
.5	.6	.5					.4	.9	.6
33 10.9	40 9.1	37 9.9	Sales/Receivables				24 15.0	45 8.2	29 12.4
43 8.5	45 8.1	47 7.7					41 8.8	49 7.4	50 7.3
60 6.1	61 6.0	62 5.9					76 4.8	66 5.5	79 4.6
76 4.8	39 9.3	48 7.6	Cost of Sales/Inventory				32 11.5	24 15.2	30 12.2
104 3.5	94 3.9	104 3.5					104 3.5	76 4.8	101 3.6
140 2.6	152 2.4	146 2.5					140 2.6	126 2.9	130 2.8
16 22.9	23 15.9	21 17.6	Cost of Sales/Payables				20 18.2	14 26.2	17 21.8
31 11.7	33 10.9	38 9.5					41 8.8	32 11.3	45 8.1
43 8.5	64 5.7	56 6.5					60 6.1	65 5.6	57 6.4
4.0	3.9	4.0	Sales/Working Capital				5.8	4.6	2.7
6.1	7.0	7.5					10.5	5.6	6.9
17.0	22.0	19.1					19.9	12.3	35.2
7.0	7.1	4.8	EBIT/Interest					17.9	
(45) 2.4	(40) 1.9	(45) 2.7						3.5	
-.2	-.3	.8						2.4	
3.0	5.2	4.4	Net Profit + Depr., Dep., Amort./Cur. Mat. L/T/D						
(27) 1.5	(23) 1.3	(17) 2.2							
.9	-.1	.3							
.2	.2	.3	Fixed/Worth				.3	.3	.2
.6	.6	.5					.5	.5	.4
1.3	1.2	1.1					.9	1.0	1.3
.7	.6	.7	Debt/Worth				.7	.7	.5
1.1	1.2	1.6					1.8	2.2	.8
3.7	2.4	3.1					2.9	4.3	5.1
22.1	21.8	32.2	% Profit Before Taxes/Tangible Net Worth				42.9	37.7	
(46) 8.9	(41) 7.9	(45) 16.1					11.9	29.9	
-4.7	-6.5	.3					-12.0	19.2	
7.8	9.3	11.2	% Profit Before Taxes/Total Assets				10.0	14.4	12.5
4.1	2.7	4.3					4.0	7.2	3.8
-2.3	-2.4	-.3					-3.1	3.9	-12.6
18.2	15.0	32.8	Sales/Net Fixed Assets				27.6	21.3	51.6
7.0	7.9	9.5					7.9	11.9	10.6
4.3	4.3	4.9					3.9	4.6	4.5
2.2	2.3	2.4	Sales/Total Assets				2.6	2.4	3.3
1.7	1.7	1.8					2.2	1.8	1.5
1.3	1.2	1.4					1.5	1.6	1.1
2.0	1.6	1.2	% Depr., Dep., Amort./Sales			(10) 1.4	1.4	1.3	
(44) 2.9	(38) 2.8	(41) 2.2					2.0	2.2	
3.9	4.7	4.1					5.7	4.1	
3.2		2.2	% Officers', Directors', Owners' Comp/Sales						
(10) 4.4		(14) 3.3							
8.7		8.8							
766341M	1345828M	1418809M	Net Sales ($)	2469M	13325M	21981M	83217M	166249M	1131568M
657202M	945717M	774543M	Total Assets ($)	1793M	8663M	9057M	46800M	118081M	590149M

M = $ thousand   MM = $ million
See Pages 1 through 15 for Explanation of Ratios and Data

| Current Data Sorted By Assets | | | | | | | Comparative Historical Data | |

Type of Statement / # Postretirement Benefits

0-500M	500M-2MM	2-10MM	10-50MM	50-100MM	100-250MM	# Postretirement Benefits / Type of Statement	4/1/90-3/31/91 ALL	4/1/91-3/31/92 ALL
	1	2	3	2	1			
	1	10	14	4	5	Unqualified	29	24
	3	4				Reviewed	15	5
1	1	3				Compiled	7	9
1	1					Tax Returns		1
	3	6	8	4	3	Other	8	10
	27 (4/1-9/30/94)			45 (10/1/94-3/31/95)				
							ALL	ALL
2	9	23	22	8	8	NUMBER OF STATEMENTS	59	49

Financial Data

0-500M %	500M-2MM %	2-10MM %	10-50MM %	50-100MM %	100-250MM %	Item	4/1/90-3/31/91 ALL %	4/1/91-3/31/92 ALL %
						ASSETS		
		9.3	7.9			Cash & Equivalents	9.3	9.6
		31.3	28.7			Trade Receivables - (net)	28.3	30.4
		26.9	29.8			Inventory	27.2	28.4
		9.0	4.4			All Other Current	3.2	3.3
		76.6	70.8			Total Current	68.0	71.7
		18.4	19.6			Fixed Assets (net)	22.7	21.4
		1.6	4.9			Intangibles (net)	3.4	2.6
		3.5	4.7			All Other Non-Current	5.9	4.3
		100.0	100.0			Total	100.0	100.0
						LIABILITIES		
		12.8	2.3			Notes Payable-Short Term	9.0	8.5
		2.5	4.5			Cur. Mat. -L/T/D	4.4	2.1
		13.6	11.4			Trade Payables	11.5	12.6
		1.2	.7			Income Taxes Payable	.7	.5
		11.2	10.7			All Other Current	11.9	13.8
		41.2	29.6			Total Current	37.4	37.5
		10.2	16.5			Long Term Debt	16.1	14.3
		1.1	.4			Deferred Taxes	.7	.8
		2.6	3.8			All Other-Non-Current	3.8	4.9
		45.0	49.7			Net Worth	42.0	42.5
		100.0	100.0			Total Liabilities & Net Worth	100.0	100.0
						INCOME DATA		
		100.0	100.0			Net Sales	100.0	100.0
		32.7	35.8			Gross Profit	36.0	35.2
		23.9	31.3			Operating Expenses	30.9	30.2
		8.8	4.5			Operating Profit	5.0	4.9
		.6	3.4			All Other Expenses (net)	2.3	1.8
		8.2	1.1			Profit Before Taxes	2.7	3.1
						RATIOS		
		3.5	3.9			Current	3.0	3.1
		2.0	2.5				1.9	2.2
		1.3	2.0				1.4	1.5
		2.0	1.9			Quick	1.6	1.9
		1.0	1.2				1.0	1.0
		.5	1.0				.7	.7
		35 10.3	55 6.6			Sales/Receivables	38 9.7	47 7.8
		57 6.4	68 5.4				50 7.3	57 6.4
		73 5.0	91 4.0				70 5.2	94 3.9
		14 26.5	72 5.1			Cost of Sales/Inventory	47 7.7	59 6.2
		76 4.8	118 3.1				99 3.7	94 3.9
		130 2.8	183 2.0				166 2.2	146 2.5
		21 17.7	29 12.5			Cost of Sales/Payables	19 19.0	23 16.0
		30 12.3	42 8.7				30 12.2	33 11.1
		54 6.7	58 6.3				51 7.2	59 6.2
		3.5	2.1			Sales/Working Capital	3.6	3.1
		5.5	3.3				5.5	4.5
		14.0	5.4				12.2	7.0
		15.0	8.3			EBIT/Interest	7.1	7.0
		(19) 4.0	(21) 3.4				(52) 2.9	(48) 3.3
		2.2	1.1				1.0	1.3
		13.8	10.5			Net Profit + Depr., Dep., Amort./Cur. Mat. L /T/D	11.7	6.2
		(11) 4.6	(14) 1.8				(35) 3.8	(30) 3.4
		1.6	.5				.6	1.4
		.2	.2			Fixed/Worth	.3	.3
		.4	.4				.6	.4
		.8	.8				1.4	1.4
		.5	.4			Debt/Worth	.6	.6
		1.4	1.0				1.6	1.0
		2.6	2.4				5.4	3.2
		65.1	31.0			% Profit Before Taxes/Tangible Net Worth	42.0	31.7
		31.0	(21) 7.7				(55) 19.0	(43) 14.4
		11.7	2.1				5.9	3.7
		27.0	13.8			% Profit Before Taxes/Total Assets	13.3	10.9
		10.5	3.9				6.8	6.4
		3.4	.5				.8	.9
		42.6	15.7			Sales/Net Fixed Assets	17.7	20.6
		10.8	9.6				6.6	8.3
		5.9	5.1				4.6	4.1
		2.5	1.7			Sales/Total Assets	2.2	2.3
		1.9	1.5				1.7	1.6
		1.5	1.0				1.3	1.1
		.9	2.4			% Depr., Dep., Amort./Sales	1.8	1.6
		(21) 2.1	(20) 3.2				(50) 2.7	(43) 2.8
		3.7	3.8				4.5	4.0
						% Officers', Directors', Owners' Comp/Sales	2.2	2.8
							(12) 4.5	(11) 4.0
							10.6	9.0
1606M	18200M	206466M	665219M	688016M	1394092M	Net Sales ($)	1048974M	2073986M
432M	10398M	102148M	468943M	516645M	1206665M	Total Assets ($)	792950M	1574687M

M = $ thousand   MM = $ million
See Pages 1 through 15 for Explanation of Ratios and Data

Comparative Historical Data / Current Data Sorted By Sales

	4/1/92-3/31/93 ALL	4/1/93-3/31/94 ALL	4/1/94-3/31/95 ALL	0-1MM	1-3MM	3-5MM	5-10MM	10-25MM	25MM & OVER
# Postretirement Benefits		5	9		1	1	1	2	4
Type of Statement									
Unqualified	31	22	34			1	4	11	17
Reviewed	8	6	7	1	1	1	4		
Compiled	7	3	5	1	1	1	2		
Tax Returns			2	2					
Other	10	14	24	1	1	4	1	9	9
					27 (4/1-9/30/94)			45 (10/1/94-3/31/95)	
NUMBER OF STATEMENTS	56	45	72	5	3	7	11	20	26
	%	%	%	%	%	%	%	%	%
ASSETS									
Cash & Equivalents	8.3	8.9	8.7				12.3	7.2	9.7
Trade Receivables - (net)	30.7	26.2	28.9				27.3	32.2	30.0
Inventory	25.4	27.8	26.6				31.9	23.0	22.4
All Other Current	5.0	5.5	6.4				7.2	7.9	5.1
Total Current	69.5	68.4	70.7				78.7	70.2	67.3
Fixed Assets (net)	20.8	24.3	19.6				18.1	20.9	18.4
Intangibles (net)	2.6	3.0	3.2				.2	4.3	4.5
All Other Non-Current	7.2	4.3	6.5				3.0	4.6	9.7
Total	100.0	100.0	100.0				100.0	100.0	100.0
LIABILITIES									
Notes Payable-Short Term	7.2	5.8	8.7				13.8	7.9	2.7
Cur. Mat.-L /T/D	3.7	3.4	3.0				3.6	3.7	1.9
Trade Payables	13.0	11.2	11.3				13.1	11.5	9.7
Income Taxes Payable	.7	1.3	.9				1.0	1.2	.8
All Other Current	11.6	10.9	11.1				5.2	13.1	12.4
Total Current	36.2	32.6	35.0				36.6	37.4	27.4
Long Term Debt	13.7	13.2	12.4				7.5	9.8	14.2
Deferred Taxes	.8	1.1	1.1				1.1	.9	.6
All Other-Non-Current	4.0	5.8	4.2				2.5	2.7	5.1
Net Worth	45.3	47.2	47.2				52.3	49.1	52.7
Total Liabilities & Net Worth	100.0	100.0	100.0				100.0	100.0	100.0
INCOME DATA									
Net Sales	100.0	100.0	100.0				100.0	100.0	100.0
Gross Profit	34.9	34.8	35.3				30.9	35.5	35.1
Operating Expenses	28.6	28.6	29.4				22.6	31.1	27.9
Operating Profit	6.3	6.2	5.9				8.3	4.5	7.2
All Other Expenses (net)	.5	1.4	2.3				.2	3.6	2.7
Profit Before Taxes	5.8	4.8	3.5				8.0	.9	4.5
RATIOS									
Current	3.7	3.0	3.4				5.5	3.4	3.4
	2.4	2.4	2.2				2.7	2.2	2.2
	1.4	1.5	1.5				1.2	1.3	1.9
Quick	2.3	2.0	2.0				2.9	1.8	2.0
	1.2	1.2	1.1				1.1	1.1	1.4
	.8	.5	.8				.4	.8	1.0
Sales/Receivables	51 7.2	39 9.3	50 7.3				24 15.2	55 6.6	58 6.3
	64 5.7	55 6.6	64 5.7				55 6.6	70 5.2	68 5.4
	99 3.7	79 4.6	81 4.5				73 5.0	85 4.3	99 3.7
Cost of Sales/Inventory	46 8.0	56 6.5	43 8.4				38 9.5	14 25.6	54 6.8
	89 4.1	101 3.6	96 3.8				111 3.3	91 4.0	91 4.0
	146 2.5	146 2.5	152 2.4				159 2.3	166 2.2	130 2.8
Cost of Sales/Payables	21 17.3	20 18.4	22 16.3				19 18.9	22 16.3	26 14.1
	30 12.1	31 11.9	35 10.5				21 17.3	38 9.6	37 9.8
	56 6.5	51 7.1	56 6.5				58 6.3	54 6.8	55 6.6
Sales/Working Capital	2.8	2.9	2.6				2.4	2.3	2.6
	4.2	4.6	4.2				4.0	5.1	3.8
	9.4	9.1	7.2				14.0	12.9	5.5
EBIT/Interest	8.5	9.1	10.8					8.8	26.3
	(52) 3.4	(40) 4.2	(64) 3.8					(19) 3.8	(24) 5.3
	1.8	2.1	1.3					1.3	1.4
Net Profit + Depr., Dep., Amort./Cur. Mat. L/T/D	10.7	9.9	11.2					13.0	10.9
	(30) 2.5	(28) 3.9	(38) 5.2					(12) 7.5	(16) 6.0
	.8	2.1	1.4					.7	1.7
Fixed/Worth	.3	.3	.2				.1	.3	.2
	.4	.5	.4				.3	.4	.4
	1.0	1.0	.7				.7	.8	.7
Debt/Worth	.4	.6	.5				.2	.5	.5
	1.5	1.3	1.1				1.0	1.1	1.0
	3.3	3.1	2.5				2.5	2.3	2.0
% Profit Before Taxes/Tangible Net Worth	36.1	26.8	32.4				50.6	42.2	26.1
	(52) 20.1	(43) 12.8	(69) 14.9				28.0	(19) 14.6	(25) 17.6
	8.4	3.7	5.2				.6	3.5	10.5
% Profit Before Taxes/Total Assets	13.0	13.3	13.1				32.2	18.3	13.1
	7.5	6.8	6.1				5.5	4.8	10.3
	4.0	1.7	.7				.5	.9	2.2
Sales/Net Fixed Assets	18.6	12.1	16.1				43.8	14.2	15.7
	8.8	6.8	9.5				10.8	9.3	9.6
	4.3	4.2	5.1				5.0	4.2	5.5
Sales/Total Assets	2.1	2.0	2.0				2.5	2.0	1.7
	1.6	1.7	1.6				2.0	1.4	1.6
	1.2	1.3	1.3				1.4	1.1	1.0
% Depr., Dep., Amort./Sales	1.4	2.1	1.4				.7	2.0	2.3
	(48) 2.6	(41) 3.0	(64) 3.0				(10) 2.0	(17) 3.2	(23) 3.0
	4.2	4.9	4.1				4.0	3.8	4.3
% Officers', Directors', Owners' Comp/Sales	1.7		4.8						
	(10) 3.6		(13) 5.7						
	13.3		9.4						
Net Sales ($)	2047212M	1639184M	2973599M	4357M	4827M	25540M	74982M	344706M	2519187M
Total Assets ($)	1690774M	1157174M	2305231M	3324M	2608M	14564M	40367M	259066M	1985302M

M = $ thousand   MM = $ million
See Pages 1 through 15 for Explanation of Ratios and Data

Current Data Sorted By Assets | **Comparative Historical Data**

		1		8		4		3	# Postretirement Benefits		
									Type of Statement		
2		1		43		31		14	6	Unqualified	64	82
2		14		24						Reviewed	33	29
5		15		8		1				Compiled	20	29
2				1						Tax Returns		2
6		9		14		17		1	2	Other	35	33

0-500M	500M-2MM	2-10MM	10-50MM	50-100MM	100-250MM		4/1/90-3/31/91 ALL	4/1/91-3/31/92 ALL
	80 (4/1-9/30/94)		138 (10/1/94-3/31/95)					
17	39	90	49	15	8	**NUMBER OF STATEMENTS**	152	175
%	%	%	%	%	%	**ASSETS**	%	%
18.3	5.6	9.7	12.1	10.7		Cash & Equivalents	8.5	9.8
26.6	30.2	28.9	21.6	20.1		Trade Receivables - (net)	29.3	27.9
32.2	30.5	29.3	23.9	19.0		Inventory	28.6	27.5
1.5	.8	2.1	2.5	1.9		All Other Current	2.1	1.6
78.6	67.2	70.0	60.1	51.7		Total Current	68.5	66.8
11.2	24.6	19.7	25.2	27.2		Fixed Assets (net)	21.6	22.8
5.5	3.0	3.8	6.3	16.7		Intangibles (net)	2.6	3.2
4.7	5.3	6.6	8.5	4.3		All Other Non-Current	7.4	7.2
100.0	100.0	100.0	100.0	100.0		Total	100.0	100.0
						LIABILITIES		
8.5	12.5	10.2	6.8	.9		Notes Payable-Short Term	10.3	8.3
5.7	5.7	2.5	2.9	2.2		Cur. Mat. -L/T/D	3.2	3.7
15.7	15.7	12.8	9.0	5.8		Trade Payables	13.4	11.8
1.3	.4	.9	.7	.5		Income Taxes Payable	.8	1.0
11.8	8.2	9.3	8.8	6.8		All Other Current	9.1	9.2
43.0	42.4	35.7	28.2	16.2		Total Current	36.8	33.9
10.3	13.3	12.4	10.3	13.8		Long Term Debt	13.7	12.3
.0	.1	.6	.9	1.8		Deferred Taxes	.8	.8
3.1	5.4	3.6	4.5	7.1		All Other-Non-Current	4.2	4.9
43.7	38.8	47.6	56.1	61.0		Net Worth	44.6	48.1
100.0	100.0	100.0	100.0	100.0		Total Liabilities & Net Worth	100.0	100.0
						INCOME DATA		
100.0	100.0	100.0	100.0	100.0		Net Sales	100.0	100.0
51.3	41.1	43.9	46.5	46.3		Gross Profit	44.8	45.4
45.8	31.3	41.4	36.7	36.4		Operating Expenses	37.2	37.6
5.5	9.8	2.5	9.8	9.9		Operating Profit	7.6	7.8
.1	1.6	.7	.4	1.8		All Other Expenses (net)	1.5	1.7
5.5	8.2	1.8	9.3	8.1		Profit Before Taxes	6.1	6.1
						RATIOS		
4.0	2.2	3.2	4.2	5.1		Current	2.9	3.2
1.6	1.6	1.9	2.0	3.4			2.0	2.1
1.2	1.1	1.4	1.5	2.3			1.4	1.5
1.5	1.2	1.9	3.0	3.6		Quick	1.7	2.0
1.0	.8	1.0	1.0	1.7			1.1	1.2
.6	.5	.8	.6	1.2			.7	.7
22 16.7	36 10.2	46 7.9	47 7.7	54 6.7		Sales/Receivables	45 8.2	45 8.1
35 10.5	47 7.7	55 6.6	58 6.3	68 5.4			58 6.3	55 6.6
51 7.2	60 6.1	72 5.1	70 5.2	79 4.6			72 5.1	68 5.4
31 11.7	54 6.8	73 5.0	79 4.6	99 3.7		Cost of Sales/Inventory	58 6.3	69 5.3
56 6.5	83 4.4	107 3.4	122 3.0	140 2.6			101 3.6	104 3.5
135 2.7	140 2.6	166 2.2	174 2.1	183 2.0			159 2.3	174 2.1
5 78.9	26 14.1	26 13.9	26 14.0	19 19.4		Cost of Sales/Payables	26 14.1	22 16.3
41 8.9	33 11.0	44 8.3	46 7.9	25 14.4			36 10.1	36 10.2
68 5.4	64 5.7	63 5.8	61 6.0	58 6.3			60 6.1	57 6.4
4.9	5.6	3.3	2.4	2.0		Sales/Working Capital	3.3	3.5
10.3	9.5	5.4	4.7	3.5			5.9	5.8
20.4	90.4	11.9	7.9	4.0			12.5	10.3
11.9	9.2	9.9	28.6	15.0		EBIT/Interest	8.7	11.0
(13) 5.0	(33) 3.5	(77) 3.9	(42) 6.3	(13) 9.8			(132) 3.7	(153) 4.7
2.5	2.0	1.1	3.3	2.2			1.5	1.6
	9.4	11.6	12.3	13.2		Net Profit + Depr., Dep.,	10.8	10.8
	(12) 2.2	(56) 2.9	(34) 3.0	(10) 8.7		Amort./Cur. Mat. L /T/D	(88) 2.8	(99) 3.4
	1.3	1.1	1.7	1.5			1.5	1.2
.1	.2	.2	.2	.4		Fixed/Worth	.2	.3
.2	.5	.4	.6	.5			.5	.5
.6	1.3	.8	.9	1.2			.9	.9
.4	.7	.5	.3	.2		Debt/Worth	.7	.5
1.3	1.5	1.3	.9	.6			1.3	1.2
4.1	3.1	2.9	2.4	2.6			2.9	2.4
71.3	72.9	36.6	40.5	33.7		% Profit Before Taxes/Tangible	41.2	44.2
(14) 19.5	(35) 25.2	(87) 15.8	(48) 21.4	(12) 14.4		Net Worth	(144) 24.4	(167) 22.7
6.8	14.2	2.0	8.4	7.9			5.8	7.5
19.0	25.7	14.9	15.1	17.2		% Profit Before Taxes/Total	18.3	18.3
6.4	9.4	6.6	8.6	8.5		Assets	10.0	10.1
2.2	5.0	.4	4.5	3.6			1.9	2.6
101.1	34.4	23.9	12.9	7.1		Sales/Net Fixed Assets	22.1	20.5
49.4	11.1	11.5	5.8	3.2			10.1	8.8
15.0	5.5	4.9	3.3	2.8			4.8	4.3
4.3	3.2	2.5	1.7	1.3		Sales/Total Assets	2.4	2.4
3.2	2.4	1.8	1.4	.9			1.8	1.7
1.8	1.7	1.1	1.0	.7			1.3	1.2
.6	.8	1.1	1.7	2.4		% Depr., Dep., Amort./Sales	1.2	1.4
(11) 1.4	(31) 1.5	(82) 2.0	(43) 3.4	(13) 3.7			(131) 2.3	(150) 2.3
1.7	3.9	4.1	5.0	7.7			3.4	3.6
	3.7	2.6				% Officers', Directors',	3.7	3.5
	(18) 5.2	(18) 4.5				Owners' Comp/Sales	(39) 6.3	(37) 7.1
	8.3	10.4					12.6	12.0
16265M	108863M	814839M	1444727M	1186153M	1545689M	Net Sales ($)	2656596M	4196887M
5170M	46927M	428564M	1054972M	1198150M	1349509M	Total Assets ($)	1877890M	3053759M

M = $thousand   MM = $million
See Pages 1 through 15 for Explanation of Ratios and Data

Comparative Historical Data				Current Data Sorted By Sales					
4	6	16		2	1	3	4	6	
			# Postretirement Benefits						
			Type of Statement						
102	81	97	Unqualified	2	7	9	15	23	41
36	39	40	Reviewed	1	11	8	11	7	2
33	34	29	Compiled	5	12	5	2	4	1
3	6	3	Tax Returns	1	1	1			
49	40	49	Other	7	5	8	8	11	10
4/1/92-3/31/93	4/1/93-3/31/94	4/1/94-3/31/95		**80 (4/1-9/30/94)**			**138 (10/1/94-3/31/95)**		
ALL	ALL	ALL		0-1MM	1-3MM	3-5MM	5-10MM	10-25MM	25MM & OVER
223	200	218	**NUMBER OF STATEMENTS**	16	36	31	36	45	54
%	%	%	**ASSETS**	%	%	%	%	%	%
12.7	9.9	10.1	Cash & Equivalents	15.4	10.4	10.5	8.9	10.1	8.8
27.6	28.5	26.4	Trade Receivables - (net)	24.6	26.9	23.8	30.9	27.5	24.1
27.3	25.6	27.5	Inventory	30.3	25.3	29.6	33.0	26.5	24.0
1.9	2.0	2.0	All Other Current	1.3	2.5	1.2	1.8	1.6	2.6
69.6	66.1	65.9	Total Current	71.6	65.0	65.0	74.5	65.8	59.6
21.8	22.2	22.3	Fixed Assets (net)	16.5	24.2	26.4	14.8	21.7	25.9
3.4	5.0	5.4	Intangibles (net)	6.9	4.3	1.7	4.8	4.9	8.6
5.2	6.7	6.4	All Other Non-Current	5.0	6.4	6.9	5.8	7.6	5.9
100.0	100.0	100.0	Total	100.0	100.0	100.0	100.0	100.0	100.0
			LIABILITIES						
7.2	7.7	8.8	Notes Payable-Short Term	8.9	10.4	6.9	10.8	9.3	7.0
3.7	3.0	3.4	Cur. Mat.-L /T/D	5.0	5.9	2.5	2.9	2.8	2.7
11.2	11.6	11.9	Trade Payables	13.7	13.1	11.8	17.2	10.9	7.8
.8	.7	.8	Income Taxes Payable	1.5	.7	.9	.5	.7	.7
9.7	10.0	9.1	All Other Current	8.0	9.6	7.7	6.7	11.8	9.2
32.5	33.0	33.9	Total Current	37.1	39.6	29.8	38.2	35.6	27.4
12.0	10.2	12.0	Long Term Debt	12.7	12.8	14.1	14.9	10.0	9.8
.6	.4	.7	Deferred Taxes	.0	.3	.3	.5	.9	1.3
2.8	4.1	4.3	All Other-Non-Current	3.3	6.3	2.6	6.2	3.2	3.7
52.0	52.3	49.1	Net Worth	46.9	40.9	53.2	40.2	50.3	57.8
100.0	100.0	100.0	Total Liabilities & Net Worth	100.0	100.0	100.0	100.0	100.0	100.0
			INCOME DATA						
100.0	100.0	100.0	Net Sales	100.0	100.0	100.0	100.0	100.0	100.0
45.5	46.4	45.0	Gross Profit	51.5	44.7	43.7	40.0	45.4	47.0
38.6	40.5	38.2	Operating Expenses	41.2	39.8	40.9	36.3	37.4	36.6
6.9	5.9	6.8	Operating Profit	10.2	4.9	2.8	3.6	8.0	10.4
1.3	.8	.9	All Other Expenses (net)	.2	1.3	-.1	1.2	1.0	.9
5.7	5.1	5.9	Profit Before Taxes	10.1	3.6	2.9	2.4	6.9	9.5
			RATIOS						
4.2	3.7	3.4		4.1	2.3	4.0	2.8	3.2	3.9
2.2	2.2	1.9	Current	2.0	1.5	2.5	1.9	1.8	2.1
1.5	1.5	1.4		.9	1.2	1.6	1.5	1.4	1.7
2.6	2.2	1.9		1.8	1.3	2.6	1.4	1.9	2.1
1.3	1.2	1.0	Quick	1.2	1.0	1.2	1.0	1.1	1.2
.8	.7	.7		.4	.6	.8	.8	.7	.7
43 8.5	42 8.6	45 8.2		29 12.5	36 10.2	41 8.8	43 8.4	46 7.9	50 7.3
54 6.8	54 6.8	55 6.6	Sales/Receivables	40 9.2	54 6.8	52 7.0	54 6.7	60 6.1	57 6.4
66 5.5	65 5.6	69 5.3		79 4.6	66 5.5	68 5.4	65 5.6	74 4.9	70 5.2
69 5.3	61 6.0	68 5.4		41 9.0	48 7.6	74 4.9	60 6.1	78 4.7	83 4.4
107 3.4	91 4.0	107 3.4	Cost of Sales/Inventory	114 3.2	79 4.6	122 3.0	101 3.6	107 3.4	122 3.0
159 2.3	146 2.5	159 2.3		159 2.3	146 2.5	166 2.2	146 2.5	159 2.3	166 2.2
23 15.8	21 17.4	25 14.4		4 88.4	27 13.4	26 14.0	28 13.1	25 14.7	17 21.7
35 10.4	35 10.5	41 9.0	Cost of Sales/Payables	37 9.8	41 9.0	46 7.9	45 8.1	41 8.9	30 12.3
52 7.0	57 6.4	61 6.0		114 3.2	54 6.7	64 5.7	62 5.9	58 6.3	58 6.3
2.8	3.3	3.4		4.1	4.6	2.1	4.2	3.7	3.0
5.1	5.8	5.6	Sales/Working Capital	7.0	9.2	4.6	6.1	5.6	4.2
10.2	10.6	10.9		NM	40.7	8.8	11.1	12.4	6.8
(194) 15.5	(174) 16.3	(186) 14.4		(10) 8.9	(32) 8.3	(22) 16.4	(34) 10.9	(40) 21.1	(48) 23.8
4.1	5.2	5.2	EBIT/Interest	4.8	3.8	5.5	2.8	5.4	9.3
1.3	2.0	1.8		.7	1.4	1.1	1.2	2.4	3.7
(119) 10.3	(94) 15.8	(121) 10.9			(13) 14.7	(18) 8.2	(21) 9.1	(29) 12.5	(37) 16.5
3.1	2.9	3.5	Net Profit + Depr., Dep., Amort./Cur. Mat. L/T/D		1.9	2.7	2.7	3.9	5.4
1.7	1.0	1.3			-.8	.4	1.3	1.5	1.7
.2	.2	.2		.1	.2	.2	.2	.2	.3
.4	.4	.4	Fixed/Worth	.2	.4	.5	.4	.5	.5
.9	.8	.9		13.4	1.6	.9	.7	1.0	.8
.3	.4	.5		.4	.8	.4	.7	.5	.3
.9	1.0	1.1	Debt/Worth	.7	1.7	.7	2.0	1.2	.7
2.4	2.3	2.8		25.4	3.2	1.7	4.4	2.6	2.2
(211) 38.5	(192) 33.4	(204) 43.7		(13) 80.2	(33) 66.4	(30) 42.7	(34) 39.9	(43) 44.7	(51) 39.6
19.9	17.9	20.9	% Profit Before Taxes/Tangible Net Worth	17.7	25.2	14.4	20.4	14.7	25.4
3.8	6.1	8.4		6.4	10.5	-8.8	9.0	5.5	12.6
20.1	17.1	18.4		16.4	20.9	19.5	15.3	13.8	21.4
8.9	7.4	8.5	% Profit Before Taxes/Total Assets	5.9	8.5	8.4	5.9	7.0	10.8
1.5	1.7	2.8		1.8	3.8	-.1	.8	2.2	5.2
18.5	22.4	21.0		96.9	37.8	11.6	32.4	20.5	12.5
8.6	9.4	9.5	Sales/Net Fixed Assets	26.4	12.5	6.9	16.3	9.0	4.7
4.8	4.6	3.9		5.2	4.1	3.6	9.7	4.0	3.2
2.5	2.6	2.5		3.2	3.3	2.4	2.8	2.3	1.9
1.7	1.9	1.7	Sales/Total Assets	1.9	2.0	1.6	2.1	1.7	1.3
1.1	1.3	1.1		1.5	1.1	.8	1.4	1.1	1.0
(199) 1.3	(180) 1.3	(187) 1.3			(31) .8	(28) 1.5	(31) .8	(41) 1.4	(47) 1.7
2.6	2.5	2.4	% Depr., Dep., Amort./Sales		2.2	2.4	1.8	2.5	3.1
4.0	4.1	4.7			8.0	4.5	2.9	4.4	4.8
(48) 3.6	(56) 4.2	(48) 3.3			(15) 4.3		(11) 3.1		
8.1	7.2	5.6	% Officers', Directors', Owners' Comp/Sales		5.3		7.5		
13.4	11.7	10.7			9.0		10.9		
5061684M	4591461M	5116536M	Net Sales ($)	10580M	74694M	123869M	270512M	707649M	3929232M
4052289M	3553876M	4083292M	Total Assets ($)	6750M	54595M	105552M	145904M	508445M	3262046M

Current Data Sorted By Assets | **Comparative Historical Data**

0-500M	500M-2MM	2-10MM	10-50MM	50-100MM	100-250MM		4/1/90-3/31/91 ALL	4/1/91-3/31/92 ALL
	1	5	5		3	# Postretirement Benefits		
						Type of Statement		
	5	9	8	5	8	Unqualified	36	31
	7	10	4			Reviewed	8	15
1	3	3	1			Compiled	12	11
						Tax Returns		1
	6	5	15	1	6	Other	27	21
	37 (4/1-9/30/94)		60 (10/1/94-3/31/95)					
1	21	27	28	6	14	**NUMBER OF STATEMENTS**	83	79
%	%	%	%	%	%	**ASSETS**	%	%
	6.3	7.8	3.6		3.8	Cash & Equivalents	6.3	7.0
	35.5	26.2	26.0		17.4	Trade Receivables - (net)	25.5	24.7
	18.0	27.6	28.9		25.1	Inventory	23.9	22.5
	4.1	1.5	1.7		1.4	All Other Current	1.7	1.9
	64.0	63.1	60.2		47.6	Total Current	57.4	56.1
	27.3	26.0	31.6		43.8	Fixed Assets (net)	32.8	35.0
	4.4	3.3	3.0		3.6	Intangibles (net)	2.4	2.0
	4.2	7.6	5.1		4.9	All Other Non-Current	7.4	6.9
	100.0	100.0	100.0		100.0	Total	100.0	100.0
						LIABILITIES		
	7.4	12.0	12.0		.7	Notes Payable-Short Term	10.7	9.3
	2.8	2.9	2.6		1.5	Cur. Mat. -L/T/D	4.3	4.7
	24.8	18.9	16.3		12.5	Trade Payables	16.2	13.9
	.3	.3	.4		.1	Income Taxes Payable	.5	.3
	9.3	7.5	10.6		6.8	All Other Current	7.7	9.7
	44.5	41.6	41.9		21.5	Total Current	39.3	37.9
	9.4	13.8	19.7		18.1	Long Term Debt	17.2	18.2
	.7	.9	.8		4.2	Deferred Taxes	1.7	1.1
	7.8	12.2	4.9		4.8	All Other-Non-Current	4.1	3.2
	37.7	31.5	32.6		51.4	Net Worth	37.7	39.6
	100.0	100.0	100.0		100.0	Total Liabilities & Net Worth	100.0	100.0
						INCOME DATA		
	100.0	100.0	100.0		100.0	Net Sales	100.0	100.0
	24.1	22.9	20.2		15.4	Gross Profit	20.8	21.4
	19.0	20.1	14.4		9.3	Operating Expenses	16.4	18.2
	5.1	2.8	5.8		6.2	Operating Profit	4.4	3.2
	.8	1.2	2.1		1.2	All Other Expenses (net)	1.7	1.4
	4.3	1.6	3.6		4.9	Profit Before Taxes	2.7	1.8
						RATIOS		
	2.2	2.1	2.2		2.8		2.4	2.5
	1.6	1.4	1.5		2.4	Current	1.5	1.6
	1.1	1.1	1.1		1.7		1.1	1.2
	1.3	1.1	1.3		1.3		1.4	1.4
	.9	.7	.8		1.0	Quick	.8	1.0
	.7	.6	.5		.8		.5	.5
	36 10.2	35 10.4	39 9.3		37 9.8		31 11.7	34 10.6
	43 8.4	42 8.6	54 6.8		45 8.2	Sales/Receivables	42 8.6	46 8.0
	51 7.1	55 6.6	60 6.1		56 6.5		57 6.4	55 6.6
	10 37.2	33 11.2	40 9.1		54 6.7		34 10.6	29 12.4
	37 9.8	73 5.0	61 6.0		73 5.0	Cost of Sales/Inventory	56 6.5	55 6.6
	62 5.9	89 4.1	114 3.2		99 3.7		76 4.8	85 4.3
	25 14.8	32 11.4	24 15.5		27 13.4		18 19.9	19 19.4
	40 9.1	41 8.8	35 10.5		35 10.4	Cost of Sales/Payables	34 10.8	28 12.9
	56 6.5	51 7.2	56 6.5		43 8.5		51 7.2	43 8.5
	6.9	5.6	3.9		4.1		5.8	4.6
	10.4	12.8	10.9		5.8	Sales/Working Capital	10.5	9.2
	49.2	59.9	112.1		9.9		48.6	35.9
	10.4	(25) 4.5	(27) 7.2		(13) 9.6		(74) 7.5	(74) 5.5
	(19) 6.5	2.6	3.6		7.2	EBIT/Interest	2.8	1.7
	3.2	1.6	2.0		2.6		1.5	.5
		(10) 7.6	(21) 4.3				(59) 5.9	(48) 2.5
		3.0	2.9			Net Profit + Depr., Dep., Amort./Cur. Mat. L /T/D	2.4	1.6
		1.1	1.5				.9	.7
	.4	.3	.6		.7		.3	.5
	.8	1.6	1.0		1.0	Fixed/Worth	1.0	1.0
	2.1	3.0	1.7		1.2		2.3	1.9
	1.0	1.5	1.2		.6		.9	.6
	2.0	3.4	2.3		.9	Debt/Worth	1.4	1.6
	4.1	5.9	5.3		1.8		5.7	4.7
	67.0	(25) 52.0	(25) 59.2		20.1		(72) 29.9	(71) 22.4
	(19) 33.9	23.5	20.4		15.1	% Profit Before Taxes/Tangible Net Worth	19.5	9.6
	10.3	9.6	13.5		6.5		7.8	-4.6
	19.1	14.9	15.6		10.3		10.3	10.2
	8.0	4.6	7.6		9.7	% Profit Before Taxes/Total Assets	7.0	2.7
	4.0	1.6	3.8		2.6		1.7	-2.6
	33.8	26.4	11.7		4.5		15.4	10.9
	10.6	11.0	4.7		3.2	Sales/Net Fixed Assets	6.7	4.9
	4.5	3.1	3.5		2.3		3.1	3.1
	4.0	2.9	2.6		1.6		2.6	2.3
	3.0	2.1	1.8		1.5	Sales/Total Assets	1.8	1.7
	1.6	1.2	1.3		1.1		1.4	1.3
	1.2	(25) .8	(25) 1.5		2.6		(77) 1.3	(72) 1.8
	(20) 2.5	1.8	2.8		(11) 3.1	% Depr., Dep., Amort./Sales	2.3	2.6
	4.0	3.1	3.6		4.0		3.9	4.0
		2.3					3.0	2.6
		(11) 4.7				% Officers', Directors', Owners' Comp/Sales	(18) 3.5	(18) 3.7
		8.9					6.0	6.7
2650M	65770M	234350M	1257619M	706832M	3257820M	Net Sales ($)	4168662M	4113719M
350M	24266M	109022M	641879M	415758M	2251417M	Total Assets ($)	2718535M	2885620M

M = $ thousand   MM = $ million
See Pages 1 through 15 for Explanation of Ratios and Data

Comparative Historical Data / Current Data Sorted By Sales

2	3	14	# Postretirement Benefits	1			4	3	6
			Type of Statement						
28	27	35	Unqualified	2	3	3	4	4	19
14	15	21	Reviewed	1	1	6	5	6	2
9	8	8	Compiled		2	2	2	1	1
1		2	Tax Returns						
23	23	33	Other		4	4	2	8	15
4/1/92-3/31/93 ALL	4/1/93-3/31/94 ALL	4/1/94-3/31/95 ALL		37 (4/1-9/30/94)			60 (10/1/94-3/31/95)		
				0-1MM	1-3MM	3-5MM	5-10MM	10-25MM	25MM & OVER
75	75	97	**NUMBER OF STATEMENTS**	3	10	15	13	19	37

4/1/92-3/31/93 ALL	4/1/93-3/31/94 ALL	4/1/94-3/31/95 ALL		0-1MM	1-3MM	3-5MM	5-10MM	10-25MM	25MM & OVER
%	%	%	**ASSETS**	%	%	%	%	%	%
4.8	3.7	5.7	Cash & Equivalents		8.3	7.7	5.5	7.0	3.7
27.3	33.0	26.6	Trade Receivables - (net)		34.1	25.6	29.8	28.2	22.4
21.4	22.1	25.0	Inventory		16.6	17.4	30.8	26.7	28.1
1.2	2.3	2.0	All Other Current		.4	4.8	1.1	2.1	1.5
54.6	61.1	59.4	Total Current		59.4	55.5	67.3	64.0	55.7
36.0	29.7	31.3	Fixed Assets (net)		29.0	30.5	26.5	28.7	35.6
1.5	3.7	3.4	Intangibles (net)		3.7	4.9	.8	3.5	2.6
7.8	5.5	6.0	All Other Non-Current		7.9	9.0	5.3	3.8	6.0
100.0	100.0	100.0	Total		100.0	100.0	100.0	100.0	100.0
			LIABILITIES						
11.7	13.5	8.5	Notes Payable-Short Term		7.2	4.2	14.2	13.4	5.7
4.2	3.0	2.6	Cur. Mat.-L /T/D		2.0	3.5	3.1	3.0	2.0
16.3	18.9	18.0	Trade Payables		18.7	18.1	22.4	19.5	14.7
.3	2.0	.3	Income Taxes Payable		.4	.3	.4	.2	.3
8.0	8.2	8.8	All Other Current		7.3	10.6	8.2	9.3	8.7
40.7	45.5	38.2	Total Current		35.6	36.8	48.3	45.5	31.5
17.7	15.4	14.9	Long Term Debt		10.7	12.5	13.7	16.8	16.6
.8	1.4	1.5	Deferred Taxes		.1	.8	1.0	.8	2.6
5.2	3.7	7.7	All Other-Non-Current		10.4	12.4	8.0	5.7	6.0
35.6	34.0	37.6	Net Worth		43.3	37.5	29.1	31.3	43.4
100.0	100.0	100.0	Total Liabilities & Net Worth		100.0	100.0	100.0	100.0	100.0
			INCOME DATA						
100.0	100.0	100.0	Net Sales		100.0	100.0	100.0	100.0	100.0
19.9	19.4	20.7	Gross Profit		25.4	27.7	23.0	20.5	16.1
16.3	15.5	16.1	Operating Expenses		20.3	23.7	21.2	15.8	10.8
3.5	3.9	4.6	Operating Profit		5.1	4.0	1.9	4.7	5.4
1.8	1.9	1.4	All Other Expenses (net)		1.0	1.2	1.0	1.5	1.5
1.7	2.0	3.3	Profit Before Taxes		4.1	2.8	.9	3.2	3.9
			RATIOS						
2.3 / 1.3 / 1.0	1.9 / 1.2 / 1.1	2.5 / 1.6 / 1.1	Current		2.4 / 2.0 / 1.2	2.5 / 1.6 / 1.1	1.8 / 1.2 / 1.0	2.2 / 1.4 / 1.0	2.6 / 2.1 / 1.3
1.1 / .8 / .5	1.1 / .8 / .6	1.2 / .9 / .6	Quick		2.2 / 1.2 / .8	1.5 / .7 / .6	.9 / .7 / .6	1.6 / .8 / .6	1.2 / .9 / .6
37 10.0 / 48 7.6 / 59 6.2	41 8.9 / 51 7.1 / 62 5.9	37 9.8 / 45 8.1 / 55 6.6	Sales/Receivables		35 10.4 / 44 8.3 / 64 5.7	35 10.4 / 40 9.1 / 47 7.7	34 10.6 / 41 8.8 / 51 7.1	41 8.8 / 54 6.8 / 70 5.2	39 9.4 / 45 8.1 / 55 6.6
23 15.8 / 61 6.0 / 85 4.3	23 16.2 / 52 7.0 / 74 4.9	34 10.8 / 58 6.3 / 87 4.2	Cost of Sales/Inventory		0 UND / 34 10.7 / 74 4.9	8 43.6 / 38 9.5 / 85 4.3	34 10.8 / 72 5.1 / 94 3.9	24 15.4 / 61 6.0 / 85 4.3	50 7.3 / 64 5.7 / 99 3.7
21 17.0 / 34 10.7 / 51 7.1	24 15.2 / 37 10.0 / 53 6.9	27 13.6 / 36 10.2 / 51 7.1	Cost of Sales/Payables		22 16.3 / 31 11.6 / 55 6.6	30 12.1 / 33 11.1 / 52 7.0	32 11.4 / 42 8.6 / 53 6.9	32 11.3 / 39 9.4 / 60 6.1	24 15.5 / 33 11.0 / 43 8.5
6.2 / 13.6 / UND	7.1 / 19.4 / 71.3	5.4 / 8.7 / 40.6	Sales/Working Capital		6.6 / 10.4 / 72.4	6.7 / 8.7 / 47.0	7.3 / 23.6 / NM	3.3 / 13.8 / -66.7	5.3 / 7.4 / 17.4
(71) 3.8 / 2.4 / .4	(70) 6.9 / 2.9 / 1.4	(90) 9.8 / 3.8 / 2.3	EBIT/Interest			(13) 5.3 / 3.1 / .6	6.7 / 3.8 / 2.4		(17) 9.9 / 3.3 / 1.6	(35) 10.5 / 4.5 / 2.5
(37) 3.2 / 2.0 / .5	(31) 7.7 / 1.5 / .1	(53) 9.4 / 3.4 / 1.8	Net Profit + Depr., Dep., Amort./Cur. Mat. L/T/D						(11) 7.5 / 2.5 / 1.1	(25) 10.8 / 3.7 / 2.5
.6 / 1.0 / 2.1	.5 / .9 / 1.7	.5 / 1.0 / 2.0	Fixed/Worth		.4 / .8 / 1.8	.4 / 1.5 / 3.8	.4 / 1.3 / 2.4	.4 / 1.0 / 3.6	.6 / 1.0 / 1.1
1.2 / 2.0 / 4.6	1.1 / 2.3 / 4.8	.9 / 2.1 / 4.8	Debt/Worth		.7 / 1.9 / 3.2	.8 / 2.0 / 6.4	1.6 / 3.9 / 6.8	1.5 / 3.3 / 7.6	.8 / 1.5 / 2.4
(71) 25.4 / 10.7 / -2.0	(69) 40.3 / 20.7 / 2.4	(90) 46.5 / 20.5 / 10.2	% Profit Before Taxes/Tangible Net Worth		64.2 / 28.3 / 12.4	(13) 61.6 / 11.3 / -6.4	86.4 / 33.5 / 20.5	(16) 62.9 / 26.6 / 16.2	(36) 24.6 / 16.5 / 9.4
8.1 / 3.3 / -1.5	11.7 / 4.7 / .6	14.5 / 8.0 / 3.0	% Profit Before Taxes/Total Assets		24.6 / 9.5 / 3.9	22.9 / 3.7 / .5	13.4 / 8.6 / 3.7	15.9 / 6.4 / 1.5	13.0 / 8.8 / 2.9
9.9 / 4.8 / 2.9	16.4 / 6.9 / 3.8	13.3 / 6.8 / 3.1	Sales/Net Fixed Assets		30.4 / 8.9 / 2.4	32.0 / 10.6 / 2.6	20.5 / 11.2 / 6.0	54.8 / 6.8 / 3.3	8.9 / 4.6 / 3.1
2.4 / 1.7 / 1.2	2.9 / 2.0 / 1.3	2.8 / 1.9 / 1.3	Sales/Total Assets		4.3 / 2.9 / 1.0	3.1 / 2.0 / 1.2	3.1 / 2.5 / 1.8	2.7 / 2.1 / 1.4	2.3 / 1.6 / 1.3
(66) 1.4 / 2.7 / 3.4	(61) 1.2 / 2.5 / 3.7	(88) 1.2 / 2.4 / 3.7	% Depr., Dep., Amort./Sales		1.0 / 2.0 / 3.5	(14) 1.5 / 3.7 / 5.1	(12) .8 / 1.5 / 2.3	(18) .9 / 2.3 / 3.9	(31) 1.3 / 2.8 / 3.6
(17) 3.0 / 4.4 / 6.2	(25) 2.2 / 3.6 / 5.2	(23) 2.5 / 4.9 / 8.9	% Officers', Directors', Owners' Comp/Sales						
3588337M / 2700863M	3895765M / 2832171M	5525041M / 3442692M	Net Sales ($) / Total Assets ($)	2292M / 1950M	23943M / 10345M	60331M / 34788M	96417M / 43205M	328596M / 203066M	5013462M / 3149338M

M = $ thousand   MM = $ million
See Pages 1 through 15 for Explanation of Ratios and Data

	Current Data Sorted By Assets						Comparative Historical Data	
2	1	2	2	1	3	# Postretirement Benefits		
						Type of Statement		
	2	3	7	4	8	Unqualified	20	25
1	5	3	3			Reviewed	4	6
3	1	2				Compiled	7	4
	1					Tax Returns		
1	2	5	5			Other	12	9
	16 (4/1-9/30/94)		40 (10/1/94-3/31/95)				4/1/90-3/31/91	4/1/91-3/31/92
0-500M	500M-2MM	2-10MM	10-50MM	50-100MM	100-250MM		ALL	ALL
5	11	13	15	4	8	NUMBER OF STATEMENTS	43	44
%	%	%	%	%	%	ASSETS	%	%
	4.0	5.4	3.1			Cash & Equivalents	4.1	4.6
	33.3	33.8	23.5			Trade Receivables - (net)	27.1	23.9
	32.2	29.3	29.4			Inventory	28.0	27.3
	.2	.9	4.2			All Other Current	1.2	1.2
	69.7	69.4	60.3			Total Current	60.3	57.0
	19.3	26.3	33.2			Fixed Assets (net)	32.2	34.9
	1.2	.4	.8			Intangibles (net)	1.1	1.1
	9.9	3.9	5.7			All Other Non-Current	6.3	7.0
	100.0	100.0	100.0			Total	100.0	100.0
						LIABILITIES		
	7.3	13.3	8.3			Notes Payable-Short Term	11.8	10.7
	2.5	3.5	3.4			Cur. Mat. -L/T/D	3.8	3.1
	29.3	20.6	20.1			Trade Payables	19.3	15.9
	.4	.3	.5			Income Taxes Payable	.3	1.2
	9.6	7.6	5.8			All Other Current	6.1	7.3
	49.1	45.4	38.2			Total Current	41.3	38.2
	7.9	12.5	17.1			Long Term Debt	15.0	13.2
	.7	.0	1.1			Deferred Taxes	2.5	2.1
	2.8	1.5	4.9			All Other-Non-Current	2.3	2.4
	39.5	40.6	38.7			Net Worth	38.8	44.2
	100.0	100.0	100.0			Total Liabilities & Net Worth	100.0	100.0
						INCOME DATA		
	100.0	100.0	100.0			Net Sales	100.0	100.0
	22.5	11.7	16.2			Gross Profit	19.9	16.6
	20.3	15.2	10.5			Operating Expenses	13.5	13.3
	2.3	-3.5	5.6			Operating Profit	6.4	3.2
	.5	1.3	1.3			All Other Expenses (net)	2.1	.9
	1.8	-4.8	4.3			Profit Before Taxes	4.3	2.3
						RATIOS		
	2.1	2.8	2.5				2.2	2.1
	1.7	1.7	1.6			Current	1.4	1.6
	.8	1.1	1.1				1.1	1.1
	1.4	1.6	1.1				1.1	1.1
	.8	.9	.7			Quick	.7	.8
	.4	.5	.5				.6	.5
	23 16.0	41 8.9	34 10.8				29 12.5	31 11.8
	41 9.0	47 7.7	38 9.6			Sales/Receivables	42 8.6	41 9.0
	54 6.8	63 5.8	45 8.1				54 6.7	54 6.8
	24 15.1	26 14.3	29 12.5				34 10.8	36 10.1
	56 6.5	46 8.0	55 6.6			Cost of Sales/Inventory	51 7.2	55 6.6
	64 5.7	70 5.2	76 4.8				81 4.5	79 4.6
	33 11.2	15 25.0	21 17.0				19 19.1	15 24.8
	39 9.4	27 13.3	38 9.7			Cost of Sales/Payables	34 10.7	31 11.7
	47 7.7	49 7.4	49 7.5				50 7.3	49 7.5
	6.2	6.4	6.0				5.6	5.9
	10.8	9.3	9.5			Sales/Working Capital	11.6	11.8
	-36.3	NM	89.1				67.4	41.3
		7.3	10.1				9.8	6.2
		(12) 2.0	(13) 3.7			EBIT/Interest	(39) 2.9	(37) 2.8
		-18.2	3.2				1.4	.9
							6.0	7.4
						Net Profit + Depr., Dep., Amort./Cur. Mat. L /T/D	(25) 2.6	(23) 2.5
							1.5	.8
	.1	.3	.5				.4	.5
	.7	.7	.9			Fixed/Worth	.9	.8
	1.7	1.3	1.3				1.6	1.4
	.6	.7	.8				.8	.7
	1.4	1.7	2.1			Debt/Worth	1.7	1.2
	3.4	3.3	2.8				4.2	2.9
	35.5	23.2	39.4				29.7	29.4
(10)	19.1	7.6	25.5			% Profit Before Taxes/Tangible Net Worth	(41) 20.5	(42) 12.9
	1.9	-131.1	15.1				3.2	-1.9
	13.4	12.9	12.8				13.8	10.9
	7.8	3.2	8.5			% Profit Before Taxes/Total Assets	7.3	6.1
	-4.1	-29.6	6.4				1.0	.0
	116.8	45.1	9.5				16.7	14.3
	19.8	9.9	6.9			Sales/Net Fixed Assets	6.4	5.5
	8.3	4.3	5.3				4.3	3.2
	4.8	3.3	2.7				3.2	3.1
	3.2	2.3	2.3			Sales/Total Assets	2.1	2.0
	2.4	1.5	2.0				1.6	1.4
		.7	1.1				1.1	1.0
		1.3	(13) 1.8			% Depr., Dep., Amort./Sales	(37) 2.0	(39) 1.9
		2.7	2.4				2.7	2.8
							1.2	1.3
						% Officers', Directors', Owners' Comp/Sales	(12) 3.2	(13) 3.1
							4.8	4.1
2647M	43695M	151687M	828443M	659201M	1802280M	Net Sales ($)	1731581M	1911511M
763M	12729M	61999M	381835M	307797M	1294169M	Total Assets ($)	1020048M	1254563M

M = $ thousand   MM = $ million
See Pages 1 through 15 for Explanation of Ratios and Data

Comparative Historical Data / Current Data Sorted By Sales

	4/1/92-3/31/93 ALL	4/1/93-3/31/94 ALL	4/1/94-3/31/95 ALL		0-1MM	1-3MM	3-5MM	5-10MM	10-25MM	25MM & OVER
# Postretirement Benefits	3	4	11		2	2		1		6
Type of Statement										
Unqualified	21	16	24			2	1	2		19
Reviewed	8	15	12		1	2	2	4	2	3
Compiled	4	7	6		2	1	1	1		1
Tax Returns	1		1			1				
Other	6	16	13		1	2	1	1	2	6
					16 (4/1-9/30/94)			40 (10/1/94-3/31/95)		
NUMBER OF STATEMENTS	40	54	56		4	6	5	8	4	29
ASSETS	%	%	%		%	%	%	%	%	%
Cash & Equivalents	6.4	3.9	4.5							4.0
Trade Receivables - (net)	24.8	27.3	28.9							25.8
Inventory	26.6	28.9	28.2							29.2
All Other Current	1.0	1.5	2.4							2.5
Total Current	58.8	61.6	64.1							61.5
Fixed Assets (net)	33.7	30.1	28.6							30.9
Intangibles (net)	1.5	1.5	1.0							1.4
All Other Non-Current	5.9	6.8	6.3							6.3
Total	100.0	100.0	100.0							100.0
LIABILITIES										
Notes Payable-Short Term	10.1	14.7	8.5							8.0
Cur. Mat.-L /T/D	2.2	2.8	3.2							2.3
Trade Payables	16.7	20.9	20.7							18.1
Income Taxes Payable	.5	.5	.4							.4
All Other Current	6.3	5.4	10.0							9.4
Total Current	35.8	44.3	42.9							38.2
Long Term Debt	16.2	14.8	14.5							17.6
Deferred Taxes	1.4	.6	.8							1.3
All Other-Non-Current	3.1	2.9	4.4							6.6
Net Worth	43.5	37.4	37.4							36.2
Total Liabilities & Net Worth	100.0	100.0	100.0							100.0
INCOME DATA										
Net Sales	100.0	100.0	100.0							100.0
Gross Profit	22.2	21.2	16.8							15.7
Operating Expenses	15.6	17.0	14.5							10.8
Operating Profit	6.6	4.2	2.3							4.9
All Other Expenses (net)	2.0	1.2	1.0							1.1
Profit Before Taxes	4.6	3.0	1.3							3.8
RATIOS										
Current	3.0	2.9	2.4							2.5
	1.7	1.5	1.7							1.7
	1.2	.9	1.0							1.2
Quick	1.6	1.3	1.2							1.2
	1.0	.7	.8							.8
	.5	.4	.5							.5
Sales/Receivables	31 11.8	36 10.2	34 10.8							35 10.4
	41 8.8	47 7.8	45 8.2							45 8.1
	54 6.7	55 6.6	54 6.8							54 6.8
Cost of Sales/Inventory	44 8.3	35 10.5	26 14.0							42 8.7
	60 6.1	60 6.1	55 6.6							69 5.3
	81 4.5	85 4.3	79 4.6							87 4.2
Cost of Sales/Payables	21 17.7	21 17.8	20 18.4							21 17.2
	33 11.1	38 9.7	35 10.4							37 9.8
	48 7.6	62 5.9	45 8.1							44 8.3
Sales/Working Capital	4.9	6.0	6.0							4.8
	10.4	10.7	9.8							9.3
	20.0	−69.5	UND							23.1
EBIT/Interest	(38) 11.1	(51) 7.4	(48) 10.6							(27) 11.8
	4.4	3.8	3.4							3.9
	2.1	1.3	1.3							2.8
Net Profit + Depr., Dep., Amort./Cur. Mat. L/T/D	(20) 7.3	(19) 5.2	(24) 18.5							(15) 29.0
	2.3	2.0	2.9							7.1
	1.6	.9	1.3							2.4
Fixed/Worth	.4	.4	.5							.5
	.8	.8	.8							.9
	1.4	1.9	1.3							1.2
Debt/Worth	.6	.6	.8							1.0
	1.2	2.2	1.8							2.3
	3.9	5.7	3.4							3.7
% Profit Before Taxes/Tangible Net Worth	(39) 38.4	(48) 40.6	(53) 33.4							(28) 35.6
	16.7	15.1	17.5							18.9
	7.5	4.1	3.9							11.5
% Profit Before Taxes/Total Assets	14.9	11.6	11.0							11.1
	6.4	6.1	6.9							8.2
	2.7	1.0	.9							4.7
Sales/Net Fixed Assets	17.1	24.5	22.8							11.1
	5.9	7.8	9.0							6.8
	3.5	3.8	4.4							3.8
Sales/Total Assets	2.9	2.7	3.2							2.8
	2.1	2.2	2.4							2.2
	1.4	1.5	1.7							1.4
% Depr., Dep., Amort./Sales	(36) 1.2	(51) .8	(49) 1.0							(26) 1.1
	1.9	1.4	1.8							1.8
	3.0	3.4	2.4							2.5
% Officers', Directors', Owners' Comp/Sales	(10) 1.1	(14) .9	(11) 2.7							
	3.3	2.3	3.2							
	8.8	4.3	6.1							
Net Sales ($)	1831121M	1712942M	3487953M		1516M	12343M	19020M	59357M	46555M	3349162M
Total Assets ($)	1102335M	1111439M	2059292M		435M	9838M	6038M	23905M	20131M	1998945M

M = $ thousand   MM = $ million
See Pages 1 through 15 for Explanation of Ratios and Data

MANUFACTURERS—IRON & STEEL FORGINGS. SIC# 3462

Current Data Sorted By Assets / Comparative Historical Data

0-500M	500M-2MM	2-10MM	10-50MM	50-100MM	100-250MM	# Postretirement Benefits / Type of Statement	4/1/90-3/31/91 ALL	4/1/91-3/31/92 ALL
1		3	1			# Postretirement Benefits		
	2	10	8	1	3	Unqualified	29	34
	9	6				Reviewed	15	19
3	6	2				Compiled	10	9
2						Tax Returns		
	4	9	8	2		Other	11	19
26 (4/1-9/30/94)			49 (10/1/94-3/31/95)					
5	21	27	16	3	3	NUMBER OF STATEMENTS	65	81
%	%	%	%	%	%	**ASSETS**	%	%
	11.7	4.5	4.1			Cash & Equivalents	6.7	5.5
	32.1	25.8	23.0			Trade Receivables - (net)	27.1	24.4
	18.6	24.9	28.7			Inventory	26.4	25.2
	4.3	1.2	2.8			All Other Current	2.5	2.5
	66.8	56.4	58.5			Total Current	62.7	57.7
	25.0	35.3	32.0			Fixed Assets (net)	30.2	33.7
	.4	.8	.9			Intangibles (net)	.7	.8
	7.8	7.5	8.6			All Other Non-Current	6.4	7.7
	100.0	100.0	100.0			Total	100.0	100.0
						LIABILITIES		
	9.8	8.1	12.7			Notes Payable-Short Term	12.6	12.8
	3.6	4.4	3.2			Cur. Mat. -L/T/D	4.6	4.4
	13.8	14.5	14.5			Trade Payables	15.2	15.0
	.6	.1	.9			Income Taxes Payable	.7	.6
	9.6	8.7	6.5			All Other Current	9.0	9.7
	37.5	35.9	37.8			Total Current	42.1	42.5
	11.5	20.2	21.6			Long Term Debt	14.7	15.9
	.4	1.1	3.3			Deferred Taxes	1.2	1.2
	4.3	.6	1.5			All Other-Non-Current	2.3	4.8
	46.4	42.3	35.8			Net Worth	39.7	35.6
	100.0	100.0	100.0			Total Liabilities & Net Worth	100.0	100.0
						INCOME DATA		
	100.0	100.0	100.0			Net Sales	100.0	100.0
	30.3	19.8	20.6			Gross Profit	22.9	20.3
	26.3	14.1	11.5			Operating Expenses	18.8	16.5
	3.9	5.7	9.0			Operating Profit	4.1	3.8
	.7	1.4	2.5			All Other Expenses (net)	1.0	1.5
	3.2	4.4	6.6			Profit Before Taxes	3.1	2.2
						RATIOS		
	3.9	2.3	2.5				2.7	2.5
	1.8	1.5	1.7			Current	1.4	1.5
	1.2	1.1	1.1				1.1	1.0
	2.6	1.3	1.3				1.2	1.5
	1.2	.8	.8			Quick	.8	.7
	.9	.5	.5				.6	.5
	27 13.4	45 8.2	41 9.0				39 9.4	38 9.7
	46 7.9	53 6.9	49 7.5			Sales/Receivables	49 7.5	47 7.7
	52 7.0	56 6.5	55 6.6				62 5.9	60 6.1
	10 36.6	37 9.8	51 7.2				40 9.1	35 10.3
	29 12.6	49 7.5	73 5.0			Cost of Sales/Inventory	57 6.4	53 6.9
	65 5.6	91 4.0	111 3.3				87 4.2	87 4.2
	11 34.2	25 14.6	28 12.9				17 21.9	21 17.5
	28 13.1	32 11.5	37 9.9			Cost of Sales/Payables	30 12.1	31 11.7
	46 8.0	41 8.9	44 8.3				47 7.8	45 8.2
	5.9	4.9	4.2				4.8	5.3
	7.8	11.8	7.4			Sales/Working Capital	9.9	10.9
	18.8	60.4	51.5				58.9	208.6
	8.5	10.6	10.0				7.5	3.8
	6.0	(26) 4.3	(15) 3.7			EBIT/Interest	(58) 2.4	(68) 1.6
	2.1	2.7	2.4				1.3	.5
	(13) 8.3	(14) 4.6					(40) 5.8	(41) 4.0
	3.7	2.9				Net Profit + Depr., Dep., Amort./Cur. Mat. L./T/D	2.3	1.6
	1.7	1.0					1.1	.7
	.2	.5	.7				.4	.5
	.4	.8	.9			Fixed/Worth	.7	.9
	1.0	1.5	2.2				1.6	1.9
	.6	.8	.9				.8	.8
	1.3	1.6	1.8			Debt/Worth	1.6	2.1
	2.5	2.2	4.6				4.2	6.2
	36.3	44.4	40.6				36.8	27.9
	22.2	(26) 17.1	(15) 28.3			% Profit Before Taxes/Tangible Net Worth	(62) 16.4	(72) 14.1
	6.0	8.0	14.1				3.0	1.7
	13.8	13.8	14.8				14.4	9.5
	9.1	9.2	9.1			% Profit Before Taxes/Total Assets	5.2	2.8
	2.7	3.7	4.8				1.0	-1.7
	18.8	10.0	5.7				12.2	10.5
	10.3	5.4	4.9			Sales/Net Fixed Assets	6.6	5.8
	7.0	3.5	4.0				4.1	3.4
	3.2	2.2	2.0				2.4	2.4
	2.5	1.9	1.6			Sales/Total Assets	2.0	1.8
	1.9	1.5	1.4				1.5	1.3
	1.3	1.8	1.9				1.4	1.5
	(19) 2.5	(26) 3.1	(13) 3.0			% Depr., Dep., Amort./Sales	(62) 2.6	(72) 3.0
	3.0	4.1	4.4				4.2	5.1
	5.1						2.3	2.4
	(12) 6.7					% Officers', Directors', Owners' Comp/Sales	(19) 5.0	(18) 6.4
	10.8						8.9	14.2
5750M	68070M	224212M	588443M	267266M	668504M	Net Sales ($)	2063256M	1888105M
1228M	25647M	121079M	370239M	208225M	431241M	Total Assets ($)	1254179M	1199950M

M = $ thousand   MM = $ million
See Pages 1 through 15 for Explanation of Ratios and Data

Comparative Historical Data | Current Data Sorted By Sales

	Hist 2	Hist 5		0-1MM	1-3MM	3-5MM	5-10MM	10-25MM	25MM & OVER
# Postretirement Benefits	2	5			1		3		1
Type of Statement									
Unqualified	17 / 21 / 24				2		4	8	10
Reviewed	9 / 14 / 15				4	4	6	1	
Compiled	7 / 5 / 11			2	4	3	2		
Tax Returns	— / — / 2			1	1				
Other	14 / 13 / 23				3	3	7	3	7
	4/1/92-3/31/93 ALL	4/1/93-3/31/94 ALL	4/1/94-3/31/95 ALL	*26 (4/1-9/30/94)*			*49 (10/1/94-3/31/95)*		
NUMBER OF STATEMENTS	47	53	75	3	14	10	19	12	17

ASSETS (%)

	Hist1	Hist2	Hist3	0-1MM	1-3MM	3-5MM	5-10MM	10-25MM	25MM & OVER
Cash & Equivalents	7.7	5.8	6.1		6.4	14.8	5.4	5.1	2.6
Trade Receivables - (net)	23.1	25.5	28.0		31.0	28.5	29.3	26.9	22.4
Inventory	24.1	24.6	22.9		19.2	18.8	20.7	31.4	24.7
All Other Current	1.9	1.0	2.6		3.0	5.5	1.0	.9	3.8
Total Current	56.9	57.0	59.6		59.6	67.7	56.5	64.3	53.6
Fixed Assets (net)	35.8	34.4	32.2		31.2	26.5	33.5	31.6	36.6
Intangibles (net)	.7	.9	.7		.7	.9	.7	.2	1.2
All Other Non-Current	6.6	7.7	7.4		8.5	4.9	9.3	3.9	8.6
Total	100.0	100.0	100.0		100.0	100.0	100.0	100.0	100.0

LIABILITIES

	Hist1	Hist2	Hist3	0-1MM	1-3MM	3-5MM	5-10MM	10-25MM	25MM & OVER
Notes Payable-Short Term	9.1	9.0	9.1		6.9	8.6	10.2	7.4	10.7
Cur. Mat.-L /T/D	4.5	3.7	4.0		4.7	3.9	4.5	3.0	3.0
Trade Payables	16.4	13.5	15.3		18.0	13.9	14.6	15.0	14.3
Income Taxes Payable	.7	1.8	.5		.1	.8	.3	.1	1.0
All Other Current	9.5	8.4	8.4		10.5	5.7	10.0	7.5	7.0
Total Current	40.3	36.4	37.3		40.1	32.8	39.6	33.0	36.1
Long Term Debt	17.6	17.6	17.8		12.5	14.9	21.0	21.0	16.2
Deferred Taxes	1.1	1.7	1.6		.7	.2	.7	1.8	4.2
All Other-Non-Current	4.5	5.3	3.9		7.3	2.3	1.4	.8	7.6
Net Worth	36.6	39.0	39.5		39.4	49.8	37.4	43.4	36.0
Total Liabilities & Net Worth	100.0	100.0	100.0		100.0	100.0	100.0	100.0	100.0

INCOME DATA

	Hist1	Hist2	Hist3	0-1MM	1-3MM	3-5MM	5-10MM	10-25MM	25MM & OVER
Net Sales	100.0	100.0	100.0		100.0	100.0	100.0	100.0	100.0
Gross Profit	22.4	21.2	22.8		30.5	27.9	20.6	21.7	17.3
Operating Expenses	18.0	16.8	17.6		28.4	20.6	16.5	12.6	9.9
Operating Profit	4.4	4.4	5.3		2.1	7.3	4.1	9.0	7.4
All Other Expenses (net)	1.3	1.6	1.4		1.0	.5	1.2	1.8	1.8
Profit Before Taxes	3.1	2.8	3.9		1.1	6.8	2.9	7.2	5.6

RATIOS

	Hist1	Hist2	Hist3	0-1MM	1-3MM	3-5MM	5-10MM	10-25MM	25MM & OVER
Current	2.2	2.8	2.3		3.8	3.7	1.8	2.8	2.3
	1.6	1.6	1.6		1.5	1.9	1.5	2.2	1.6
	.9	1.1	1.2		1.0	1.4	1.2	1.5	1.1
Quick	1.4	1.7	1.3		2.4	2.2	1.2	1.4	1.2
	.8	.9	.9		1.0	1.1	.8	1.1	.8
	.4	.5	.6		.5	.9	.5	.7	.5
Sales/Receivables	39 9.3	39 9.4	39 9.4		27 13.6	24 14.9	39 9.3	40 9.2	42 8.7
	46 7.9	46 7.9	49 7.5		41 8.8	50 7.3	50 7.3	54 6.7	49 7.5
	53 6.9	56 6.5	56 6.5		49 7.4	65 5.6	55 6.6	56 6.5	63 5.8
Cost of Sales/Inventory	33 11.0	36 10.1	29 12.6		5 73.4	11 32.9	28 13.1	41 8.8	44 8.3
	51 7.1	55 6.6	49 7.4		33 10.9	49 7.5	40 9.1	52 7.0	72 5.1
	94 3.9	78 4.7	78 4.7		81 4.5	61 6.0	78 4.7	140 2.6	83 4.4
Cost of Sales/Payables	26 14.3	16 23.5	24 14.9		22 16.3	19 19.3	25 14.6	23 16.1	26 14.2
	38 9.7	30 12.2	35 10.5		30 12.1	27 13.7	32 11.5	36 10.2	40 9.2
	55 6.6	43 8.4	45 8.1		43 8.4	45 8.1	46 7.9	43 8.5	50 7.3
Sales/Working Capital	4.5	5.3	5.4		5.1	5.4	6.6	4.4	5.4
	8.3	9.2	8.0		13.0	7.5	12.4	6.8	7.7
	−78.8	28.3	30.1		NM	13.8	35.7	10.9	45.8
EBIT/Interest	4.9	6.1	9.0		5.6	10.1	10.4	(11) 14.6	(16) 10.7
	(43) 3.2	3.2	(72) 4.5		1.9	8.1	4.1	4.3	5.2
	1.4	1.2	2.0		-2.5	5.3	2.1	3.6	1.8
Net Profit + Depr., Dep., Amort./Cur. Mat. L/T/D	3.6	3.3	5.3				(10) 6.0		(11) 7.7
	(26) 1.7	(27) 1.8	(42) 2.7				3.8		2.1
	1.2	.4	1.3				1.0		1.3
Fixed/Worth	.5	.4	.4		.3	.3	.5	.4	.7
	1.0	1.0	.9		.9	.5	.9	.8	.9
	2.0	2.0	1.5		1.6	1.1	1.6	1.5	2.0
Debt/Worth	.7	.8	.8		.6	.4	.9	.6	1.1
	2.3	1.8	1.6		2.1	1.0	1.9	1.5	1.6
	5.3	4.4	4.5		5.0	2.0	4.0	3.7	5.1
% Profit Before Taxes/Tangible Net Worth	27.9	34.9	40.5		36.2	37.1	38.3	50.3	40.3
	(43) 17.0	(50) 12.4	(69) 19.6	(13)	5.8	25.2	(18) 17.1	36.4	(15) 19.1
	5.7	2.2	9.1		-31.4	17.8	5.3	18.2	9.8
% Profit Before Taxes/Total Assets	12.0	8.5	13.3		10.8	13.9	13.8	17.0	10.6
	5.4	5.2	8.5		1.8	13.3	5.8	11.9	7.7
	1.1	.5	2.4		-9.2	9.0	1.4	8.8	3.6
Sales/Net Fixed Assets	9.0	12.4	10.7		17.3	21.5	11.6	9.8	5.4
	5.0	5.2	5.8		10.5	7.6	6.1	5.6	3.9
	2.8	3.2	3.9		6.0	5.3	3.5	4.4	3.0
Sales/Total Assets	2.3	2.5	2.6		3.0	2.9	2.6	2.6	1.9
	1.7	1.7	2.0		2.3	2.2	2.1	2.0	1.5
	1.4	1.4	1.5		1.6	1.8	1.6	1.5	1.2
% Depr., Dep., Amort./Sales	1.6	1.7	1.6		1.0		1.4	1.7	2.1
	(43) 3.5	(49) 3.1	(68) 2.8	(13)	2.6	(18)	2.8	2.7	(13) 3.8
	5.1	4.6	4.1		4.4		4.1	4.0	4.8
% Officers', Directors', Owners' Comp/Sales	5.1	3.8	2.3						
	(13) 8.0	(17) 6.5	(22) 5.8						
	13.4	10.0	10.0						
Net Sales ($)	1099925M	1449623M	1822245M	1716M	29890M	36000M	135814M	209627M	1409198M
Total Assets ($)	663399M	889658M	1157659M	683M	14527M	16031M	72235M	112347M	941836M

M = $ thousand   MM = $ million
See Pages 1 through 15 for Explanation of Ratios and Data

MANUFACTURERS—IRON & STEEL FOUNDRIES. SIC# 3321 (22,24,25)

Current Data Sorted By Assets							Comparative Historical Data	
	3	7	3		1	# Postretirement Benefits		
						Type of Statement		
	2	17	16	3	7	Unqualified	47	41
3	12	22	1			Reviewed	29	41
2	15	7	2			Compiled	22	24
						Tax Returns		
2	7	11	7	1	1	Other	32	27
	44 (4/1-9/30/94)		94 (10/1/94-3/31/95)				4/1/90-3/31/91	4/1/91-3/31/92
0-500M	500M-2MM	2-10MM	10-50MM	50-100MM	100-250MM		ALL	ALL
7	36	57	26	4	8	NUMBER OF STATEMENTS	130	133
%	%	%	%	%	%	ASSETS	%	%
	7.1	8.1	4.3			Cash & Equivalents	6.7	6.0
	29.1	28.1	25.9			Trade Receivables - (net)	28.3	26.8
	18.4	17.1	21.4			Inventory	18.7	19.3
	.7	1.8	.8			All Other Current	1.8	2.2
	55.3	55.1	52.4			Total Current	55.4	54.3
	36.4	37.1	39.2			Fixed Assets (net)	36.4	37.7
	.6	.8	1.2			Intangibles (net)	.8	.8
	7.6	7.1	7.3			All Other Non-Current	7.4	7.2
	100.0	100.0	100.0			Total	100.0	100.0
						LIABILITIES		
	4.4	6.4	10.9			Notes Payable-Short Term	8.7	8.5
	8.3	4.0	3.1			Cur. Mat. -L/T/D	3.8	4.7
	17.3	14.6	11.1			Trade Payables	14.5	14.6
	.3	.4	.2			Income Taxes Payable	.5	.4
	11.3	8.7	9.3			All Other Current	8.1	9.3
	41.6	34.1	34.7			Total Current	35.6	37.4
	22.8	15.9	15.2			Long Term Debt	19.2	19.7
	.7	1.3	1.6			Deferred Taxes	1.1	.7
	4.8	2.7	11.5			All Other-Non-Current	5.0	3.5
	30.1	46.0	37.0			Net Worth	39.1	38.7
	100.0	100.0	100.0			Total Liabilities & Net Worth	100.0	100.0
						INCOME DATA		
	100.0	100.0	100.0			Net Sales	100.0	100.0
	26.9	22.6	17.6			Gross Profit	22.4	21.5
	22.0	17.5	11.6			Operating Expenses	18.5	19.3
	4.9	5.1	6.1			Operating Profit	4.0	2.2
	1.5	1.4	1.3			All Other Expenses (net)	1.5	1.7
	3.4	3.7	4.8			Profit Before Taxes	2.4	.5
						RATIOS		
	2.3	2.5	2.1				2.5	2.2
	1.4	1.8	1.9			Current	1.7	1.5
	1.0	1.2	1.2				1.1	1.1
	1.7	2.0	1.4				1.7	1.3
	1.0	1.2	.9			Quick	1.0	.9
	.6	.7	.6				.7	.6
	34 10.6	44 8.3	41 9.0				40 9.1	39 9.4
	51 7.2	51 7.2	47 7.8			Sales/Receivables	48 7.6	48 7.6
	61 6.0	62 5.9	63 5.8				57 6.4	54 6.7
	20 18.5	25 14.7	22 16.3				21 17.5	26 14.3
	35 10.4	38 9.5	35 10.5			Cost of Sales/Inventory	34 10.8	38 9.6
	57 6.4	54 6.7	89 4.1				61 6.0	57 6.4
	18 20.6	22 16.4	17 21.0				19 18.9	22 16.5
	35 10.3	30 12.1	24 14.9			Cost of Sales/Payables	29 12.5	29 12.8
	52 7.0	41 8.9	33 11.2				41 9.0	39 9.4
	6.9	5.7	5.8				5.8	6.8
	10.7	9.7	9.4			Sales/Working Capital	9.9	11.5
	282.0	25.3	72.2				65.1	36.1
	5.5	10.4	15.3				7.8	6.0
	(34) 3.4	(52) 3.3	4.3			EBIT/Interest	(121) 2.4	(129) 2.2
	2.1	1.6	2.2				1.0	.9
	2.6	5.2	20.6				7.1	4.8
	(20) 1.6	(22) 3.0	(15) 5.0			Net Profit + Depr., Dep., Amort./Cur. Mat. L./T/D	(82) 2.8	(79) 1.9
	1.1	1.8	1.6				1.3	.7
	.6	.4	.7				.5	.5
	1.3	.8	1.1			Fixed/Worth	.9	.9
	2.4	2.0	1.8				2.1	2.3
	.9	.6	.9				.6	.7
	2.1	1.1	2.2			Debt/Worth	1.4	1.4
	4.0	2.6	3.9				4.0	3.9
	37.0	33.9	66.6				27.8	23.5
	(32) 20.2	(55) 18.0	(25) 33.9			% Profit Before Taxes/Tangible Net Worth	(119) 13.1	(122) 11.4
	9.7	5.9	12.8				2.0	1.8
	12.9	14.2	16.8				11.3	9.0
	7.8	5.9	8.1			% Profit Before Taxes/Total Assets	5.1	3.8
	4.3	1.4	4.0				.0	-.5
	11.1	8.5	7.9				10.4	8.9
	6.5	5.7	5.9			Sales/Net Fixed Assets	5.5	5.2
	3.9	4.0	2.8				3.9	3.6
	2.6	2.4	2.5				2.7	2.4
	2.3	2.1	1.8			Sales/Total Assets	2.0	2.0
	1.8	1.7	1.5				1.6	1.5
	1.0	1.9	1.7				1.5	1.9
	(35) 2.5	(54) 2.8	(25) 2.7			% Depr., Dep., Amort./Sales	(117) 2.9	(124) 2.9
	4.0	3.8	3.6				4.5	4.5
	1.2	1.6					1.3	2.2
	(18) 3.2	(21) 2.5				% Officers', Directors', Owners' Comp/Sales	(34) 3.6	(46) 3.9
	5.2	5.3					6.5	5.7
4626M	99900M	546598M	1027976M	513026M	1950397M	Net Sales ($)	2680093M	2895145M
1991M	44194M	284177M	515488M	262301M	1142901M	Total Assets ($)	1563609M	1680366M

M = $ thousand   MM = $ million
See Pages 1 through 15 for Explanation of Ratios and Data

Comparative Historical Data   Current Data Sorted By Sales

Postretirement Benefits — Type of Statement

Comp. Hist.			Type of Statement	0-1MM	1-3MM	3-5MM	5-10MM	10-25MM	25MM & OVER
3	16	14	(# Postretirement Benefits)		3	2	3	3	3
29	41	45	Unqualified	1	2		10	9	23
29	42	38	Reviewed	3	4	11	12	8	
16	15	26	Compiled	3	11	4	4	3	1
	1		Tax Returns						
30	31	29	Other	2	4	2	7	8	6

Dates / Periods:
- Historical: 4/1/92-3/31/93 (ALL), 4/1/93-3/31/94 (ALL), 4/1/94-3/31/95 (ALL)
- Current bands grouped: 44 (4/1-9/30/94) and 94 (10/1/94-3/31/95)

4/1/92-3/31/93 ALL	4/1/93-3/31/94 ALL	4/1/94-3/31/95 ALL	NUMBER OF STATEMENTS	0-1MM	1-3MM	3-5MM	5-10MM	10-25MM	25MM & OVER
104	130	138		9	21	17	33	28	30
%	%	%	**ASSETS**	%	%	%	%	%	%
7.2	6.4	6.9	Cash & Equivalents		7.7	4.8	11.4	5.6	3.2
26.1	28.6	28.0	Trade Receivables - (net)		29.9	28.4	27.7	27.2	26.6
18.5	18.6	18.1	Inventory		17.6	20.1	15.5	20.9	19.5
1.8	2.0	1.5	All Other Current		.7	1.2	2.0	1.2	1.3
53.6	55.6	54.5	Total Current		55.9	54.4	56.6	54.9	50.5
39.3	36.0	37.4	Fixed Assets (net)		36.1	39.9	34.3	37.9	40.8
1.4	1.5	.8	Intangibles (net)		.8	.3	1.2	.3	1.2
5.6	6.9	7.3	All Other Non-Current		7.2	5.3	7.9	6.9	7.5
100.0	100.0	100.0	Total		100.0	100.0	100.0	100.0	100.0
			LIABILITIES						
7.2	9.2	6.4	Notes Payable-Short Term		4.5	6.4	6.8	8.2	5.6
4.1	3.6	4.8	Cur. Mat.-L./T/D		6.6	7.7	5.0	3.3	2.7
13.0	14.9	14.5	Trade Payables		17.0	14.0	16.0	14.7	11.1
.5	.6	.3	Income Taxes Payable		.4	.1	.3	.5	.2
8.3	9.6	9.6	All Other Current		9.6	11.7	10.2	7.6	10.2
33.1	37.9	35.5	Total Current		38.1	39.8	38.4	34.2	29.9
20.5	15.7	17.0	Long Term Debt		23.8	17.1	12.8	19.5	14.2
1.0	1.0	1.3	Deferred Taxes		1.3	.8	.9	1.4	2.2
4.6	5.0	5.3	All Other-Non-Current		6.9	.5	4.4	4.4	9.5
40.7	40.4	40.9	Net Worth		29.9	41.8	43.5	40.6	44.2
100.0	100.0	100.0	Total Liabilities & Net Worth		100.0	100.0	100.0	100.0	100.0
			INCOME DATA						
100.0	100.0	100.0	Net Sales		100.0	100.0	100.0	100.0	100.0
20.9	21.6	22.8	Gross Profit		28.9	20.3	23.8	20.4	16.7
17.3	16.9	17.7	Operating Expenses		24.4	16.9	18.9	14.0	10.3
3.6	4.7	5.2	Operating Profit		4.5	3.4	4.9	6.4	6.4
1.3	1.1	1.3	All Other Expenses (net)		1.8	1.4	1.7	1.0	1.1
2.3	3.6	3.8	Profit Before Taxes		2.8	2.0	3.2	5.4	5.3

RATIOS

4/1/92-3/31/93	4/1/93-3/31/94	4/1/94-3/31/95	Ratio	0-1MM	1-3MM	3-5MM	5-10MM	10-25MM	25MM & OVER
2.6	2.3	2.3	Current		2.4	2.0	2.9	2.1	2.2
1.8	1.6	1.8			1.4	1.4	2.1	1.6	1.8
1.1	1.1	1.2			1.0	1.1	1.1	1.2	1.4
1.6	1.6	1.6	Quick		1.7	1.3	2.1	1.5	1.4
1.1	1.0	1.0			1.0	.8	1.2	.9	1.0
.6	.6	.7			.5	.5	.7	.7	.8
41 8.8	42 8.6	42 8.7	Sales/Receivables		41 8.8	41 8.8	41 8.8	41 9.0	42 8.7
48 7.6	51 7.1	50 7.3			54 6.8	47 7.8	51 7.2	50 7.3	47 7.7
57 6.4	59 6.2	61 6.0			69 5.3	54 6.7	64 5.7	63 5.8	60 6.1
26 14.0	23 15.7	23 16.2	Cost of Sales/Inventory		20 18.1	26 14.2	21 17.2	27 13.6	22 16.4
39 9.3	37 9.8	37 9.8			37 9.8	38 9.6	33 11.0	41 8.8	35 10.5
61 6.0	56 6.5	59 6.2			65 5.6	63 5.8	51 7.1	69 5.3	74 4.9
19 19.5	20 18.5	21 17.3	Cost of Sales/Payables		20 18.3	17 21.5	21 17.4	25 14.7	18 19.8
28 13.1	30 12.1	29 12.6			39 9.3	23 16.0	32 11.4	31 11.7	23 16.1
41 8.9	43 8.4	42 8.7			59 6.2	42 8.7	43 8.4	40 9.2	29 12.6
5.3	6.0	5.9	Sales/Working Capital		6.2	7.0	4.9	6.2	5.8
8.6	10.9	9.8			10.5	14.9	7.6	10.3	10.1
37.1	49.4	28.3			NM	73.8	32.4	25.3	17.0
(100) 5.7	(123) 9.0	(129) 8.2	EBIT/Interest		5.4	(15) 4.6	(28) 12.3	12.0	(28) 17.0
3.1	3.2	3.7			3.4	2.0	3.1	4.1	5.3
1.4	1.7	1.9			2.0	1.0	1.6	2.9	3.0
(50) 5.3	(63) 4.8	(66) 6.6	Net Profit + Depr., Dep., Amort./Cur. Mat. L/T/D		(11) 6.1			(17) 8.4	(17) 26.6
2.3	2.3	2.7			2.1			3.1	7.9
1.3	1.3	1.5			1.6			2.7	1.5
.6	.5	.5	Fixed/Worth		.6	.7	.4	.7	.7
.9	.9	.9			1.4	1.1	.6	.9	1.0
1.7	1.7	1.8			2.5	1.9	2.4	1.9	1.7
.6	.7	.7	Debt/Worth		1.1	.7	.4	.7	.6
1.2	1.5	1.5			1.9	1.7	1.1	1.6	1.6
3.1	3.3	3.3			3.9	2.7	5.1	2.8	3.3
(96) 25.1	(119) 31.8	(131) 35.8	% Profit Before Taxes/Tangible Net Worth		(19) 37.5	29.8	(29) 30.6	(27) 40.7	50.5
12.7	15.5	19.3			17.3	15.2	14.2	30.2	24.5
3.1	5.8	7.5			8.0	.6	2.1	15.5	11.8
9.9	13.8	14.6	% Profit Before Taxes/Total Assets		14.0	10.4	14.4	17.0	16.3
5.4	6.0	7.1			6.0	6.9	5.9	9.5	11.1
1.7	2.0	2.7			2.9	.2	.7	4.6	5.0
7.2	9.0	8.5	Sales/Net Fixed Assets		14.1	8.1	11.1	8.0	7.8
5.5	5.8	5.7			6.8	5.8	6.6	5.5	4.6
3.3	3.6	3.7			3.6	3.6	4.7	3.6	3.4
2.4	2.5	2.5	Sales/Total Assets		2.5	2.6	2.5	2.3	2.5
2.0	2.0	2.1			2.2	2.1	2.1	2.0	1.8
1.5	1.6	1.6			1.6	1.9	1.6	1.6	1.6
(94) 2.1	(124) 1.8	(128) 1.8	% Depr., Dep., Amort./Sales		(20) 1.6	1.0	(31) 1.7	(26) 2.0	(27) 1.8
3.3	2.9	2.7			3.4	2.2	2.7	2.9	2.8
4.7	4.0	3.8			6.0	3.8	3.8	3.4	3.7
(29) 1.5	(43) 2.1	(44) 1.7	% Officers', Directors', Owners' Comp/Sales		(10) 2.0		(17) 1.2		
3.2	4.0	2.8			3.2		2.5		
5.6	5.9	5.4			5.2		5.2		
2783085M	3899091M	4142523M	Net Sales ($)	6423M	43142M	66042M	230755M	445639M	3350522M
1800760M	2265062M	2251052M	Total Assets ($)	3408M	23921M	32109M	135334M	243233M	1813047M

M = $ thousand   MM = $ million
See Pages 1 through 15 for Explanation of Ratios and Data

Current Data Sorted By Assets						# Postretirement Benefits / Type of Statement	Comparative Historical Data	
	1		2	1			9	9
	1	6		4		Unqualified		
1	15	11				Reviewed	20	22
6	8	1	1			Compiled	8	16
						Tax Returns		
3	4	2	1			Other	8	10
	23 (4/1-9/30/94)			41 (10/1/94-3/31/95)			4/1/90-3/31/91	4/1/91-3/31/92
0-500M	500M-2MM	2-10MM	10-50MM	50-100MM	100-250MM		ALL	ALL
10	28	20	6			NUMBER OF STATEMENTS	45	57
%	%	%	%	%	%	ASSETS	%	%
13.9	11.7	11.0				Cash & Equivalents	8.1	8.4
42.0	32.0	24.8				Trade Receivables - (net)	29.1	27.7
6.3	3.1	9.3				Inventory	7.4	7.6
1.8	2.3	.7				All Other Current	2.1	1.0
63.9	49.1	45.8				Total Current	46.7	44.8
27.1	42.5	46.0				Fixed Assets (net)	44.3	44.6
.9	2.5	.4				Intangibles (net)	1.4	1.0
8.1	5.9	7.8				All Other Non-Current	7.7	9.6
100.0	100.0	100.0				Total	100.0	100.0
						LIABILITIES		
4.7	5.7	9.2				Notes Payable-Short Term	5.5	6.9
5.1	5.7	5.4				Cur. Mat. -L/T/D	4.9	7.1
21.7	12.5	13.4				Trade Payables	12.4	10.0
.6	.7	.5				Income Taxes Payable	.3	.4
8.5	8.0	4.8				All Other Current	6.0	6.0
40.6	32.5	33.3				Total Current	29.1	30.4
10.7	17.1	18.8				Long Term Debt	19.8	22.6
.1	1.4	.6				Deferred Taxes	1.4	1.0
3.6	2.8	2.8				All Other-Non-Current	2.7	3.1
45.1	46.1	44.5				Net Worth	47.1	42.9
100.0	100.0	100.0				Total Liabilities & Net Worth	100.0	100.0
						INCOME DATA		
100.0	100.0	100.0				Net Sales	100.0	100.0
40.2	32.1	29.6				Gross Profit	30.9	30.4
36.3	27.4	22.3				Operating Expenses	26.3	27.5
3.9	4.6	7.2				Operating Profit	4.5	3.0
.1	1.2	1.2				All Other Expenses (net)	1.6	1.6
3.8	3.4	6.0				Profit Before Taxes	3.0	1.3
						RATIOS		
4.1	2.3	2.4					2.5	2.2
1.8	1.6	1.2				Current	1.7	1.5
.8	1.0	.8					1.1	1.1
2.6	1.9	2.0					2.4	2.0
1.5	1.3	1.1				Quick	1.4	1.1
.8	1.0	.6					.8	.8
30 12.1	38 9.5	48 7.6					42 8.6	44 8.3
42 8.6	51 7.2	52 7.0				Sales/Receivables	49 7.5	51 7.1
49 7.4	69 5.3	60 6.1					63 5.8	56 6.5
0 UND	0 UND	0 UND					0 UND	0 UND
1 274.0	0 UND	0 UND				Cost of Sales/Inventory	2 190.6	2 223.6
7 55.1	12 31.2	32 11.5					23 15.6	32 11.4
10 35.9	17 20.9	18 20.3					14 25.7	13 27.8
22 16.8	29 12.7	34 10.7				Cost of Sales/Payables	27 13.6	21 17.5
60 6.1	46 8.0	58 6.3					47 7.8	34 10.6
5.1	6.1	4.1					6.1	7.2
10.2	12.6	27.3				Sales/Working Capital	10.4	14.0
-37.8	NM	NM					63.8	NM
	12.5	10.3					5.3	2.4
	(27) 4.1	(18) 3.0				EBIT/Interest	(42) 2.3	(52) 1.4
	1.8	1.5					1.2	.5
	6.1						3.7	3.0
	(11) 2.8					Net Profit + Depr., Dep., Amort./Cur. Mat. L /T/D	(30) 1.9	(30) 1.6
	1.3						1.3	.9
.2	.6	.6					.4	.6
.6	.8	1.1				Fixed/Worth	.8	1.0
NM	1.7	2.3					2.0	2.2
.5	.7	.6					.5	.6
.9	1.5	1.2				Debt/Worth	.9	1.4
NM	2.3	3.2					3.8	3.5
	31.3	43.5					30.7	18.9
	(27) 13.3	23.4				% Profit Before Taxes/Tangible Net Worth	(43) 10.3	(51) 3.2
	4.1	7.0					2.1	-1.1
16.1	12.5	17.5					11.2	7.3
8.4	5.9	6.4				% Profit Before Taxes/Total Assets	3.7	1.4
1.5	1.5	3.0					1.2	-1.3
40.0	7.6	7.7					9.0	7.1
15.0	4.1	3.3				Sales/Net Fixed Assets	4.1	4.5
8.5	2.4	1.8					2.6	2.3
5.2	2.4	2.3					2.6	2.5
3.9	2.0	1.6				Sales/Total Assets	2.0	1.8
3.0	1.4	1.0					1.4	1.3
	2.5	1.7					2.7	3.0
	(27) 4.4	4.2				% Depr., Dep., Amort./Sales	(40) 5.1	5.3
	6.7	6.2					6.5	7.0
	5.1						2.9	3.4
	(17) 9.3					% Officers', Directors', Owners' Comp/Sales	(19) 5.7	(30) 6.7
	12.3						8.6	9.8
10907M	72432M	124750M	249184M			Net Sales ($)	605010M	384219M
3044M	34312M	81811M	122368M			Total Assets ($)	310912M	302683M

M = $ thousand   MM = $ million
See Pages 1 through 15 for Explanation of Ratios and Data

Comparative Historical Data

Current Data Sorted By Sales

					# Postretirement Benefits						
	2		4		4		1		1	2	
					Type of Statement						
	14		10		11		Unqualified		1	4	1	2	3
	23		26		27		Reviewed	2	9	11	4	1	
	16		11		16		Compiled	5	8		2	1	
						Tax Returns						
	12		11		10		Other	2	5		1	1	1
	4/1/92-3/31/93		4/1/93-3/31/94		4/1/94-3/31/95			23 (4/1-9/30/94)		41 (10/1/94-3/31/95)		

	4/1/92-3/31/93 ALL	4/1/93-3/31/94 ALL	4/1/94-3/31/95 ALL	NUMBER OF STATEMENTS	0-1MM	1-3MM	3-5MM	5-10MM	10-25MM	25MM & OVER
	65	58	64		9	23	15	8	5	4
	%	%	%	ASSETS	%	%	%	%	%	%
	6.6	8.0	11.0	Cash & Equivalents		12.5	18.6			
	27.3	30.8	31.0	Trade Receivables - (net)		25.7	30.8			
	5.4	5.4	7.4	Inventory		3.0	4.8			
	1.2	1.0	1.7	All Other Current		1.1	1.5			
	40.6	45.2	51.0	Total Current		42.3	55.7			
	48.3	42.7	40.6	Fixed Assets (net)		50.0	34.3			
	1.2	1.2	1.6	Intangibles (net)		2.0	1.1			
	9.9	10.9	6.8	All Other Non-Current		5.7	8.9			
	100.0	100.0	100.0	Total		100.0	100.0			
				LIABILITIES						
	5.7	6.3	7.3	Notes Payable-Short Term		3.5	8.3			
	8.2	4.8	5.4	Cur. Mat.-L /T/D		6.2	4.7			
	10.2	10.7	13.6	Trade Payables		11.2	11.2			
	.2	.8	.5	Income Taxes Payable		.6	.1			
	6.3	7.7	7.6	All Other Current		4.5	10.8			
	30.5	30.2	34.4	Total Current		26.0	35.2			
	23.9	15.5	15.7	Long Term Debt		21.2	12.1			
	1.5	.3	.8	Deferred Taxes		1.0	1.0			
	3.1	2.2	3.0	All Other-Non-Current		1.2	4.2			
	41.0	51.7	46.0	Net Worth		50.7	47.5			
	100.0	100.0	100.0	Total Liabilities & Net Worth		100.0	100.0			
				INCOME DATA						
	100.0	100.0	100.0	Net Sales		100.0	100.0			
	37.1	31.7	31.3	Gross Profit		36.3	30.1			
	32.2	27.2	25.8	Operating Expenses		29.4	26.9			
	4.9	4.4	5.5	Operating Profit		6.9	3.2			
	1.1	.9	1.1	All Other Expenses (net)		1.3	.9			
	3.7	3.5	4.4	Profit Before Taxes		5.6	2.3			
				RATIOS						
	2.4	2.3	2.3			2.8	2.5			
	1.5	1.5	1.5	Current		1.9	1.5			
	.9	1.0	1.0			.9	1.0			
	1.8	2.0	2.0			2.8	2.5			
	1.2	1.3	1.2	Quick		1.8	1.2			
	.8	.9	.7			.7	.9			
47	7.7	44 8.3	41 9.0	Sales/Receivables	33 11.0	43 8.5				
57	6.4	52 7.0	50 7.3		47 7.8	52 7.0				
63	5.8	61 6.0	62 5.9		66 5.5	60 6.1				
0	UND	0 UND	0 UND	Cost of Sales/Inventory	0 UND	0 UND				
2	206.7	2 181.2	0 UND		0 UND	6 60.3				
29	12.8	15 25.0	15 24.5		3 129.9	14 25.8				
16	23.5	17 21.3	17 21.4	Cost of Sales/Payables	16 22.8	17 21.6				
29	12.6	22 16.4	26 14.3		29 12.7	26 14.2				
43	8.5	35 10.5	47 7.8		47 7.7	40 9.2				
	6.7	8.2	5.4	Sales/Working Capital		6.0	6.0			
	14.6	16.9	14.7			10.9	14.3			
	−66.0	−204.7	−999.8			−60.5	−999.8			
	5.3	12.0	13.0	EBIT/Interest		12.8	16.6			
(58)	2.6	(54) 4.0	(60) 4.0		(22) 6.3	(13) 2.5				
	1.6	1.9	1.6			1.9	1.5			
	4.2	5.7	7.6	Net Profit + Depr., Dep., Amort./Cur. Mat. L/T/D						
(33)	2.1	(24) 3.6	(26) 2.8							
	1.3	1.1	1.2							
	.7	.4	.5	Fixed/Worth		.7	.2			
	1.3	.8	.9			1.1	.7			
	2.7	1.3	1.5			1.8	1.4			
	.6	.4	.7	Debt/Worth		.6	.5			
	1.5	.9	1.1			.9	1.3			
	3.7	2.2	2.5			2.3	2.3			
	35.2	28.4	33.6	% Profit Before Taxes/Tangible Net Worth		31.7	34.1			
(60)	13.0	(56) 11.7	(61) 14.3		(22) 15.1	13.0				
	5.9	2.4	6.6			6.0	7.9			
	13.0	12.7	13.9	% Profit Before Taxes/Total Assets		14.1	13.2			
	4.5	6.8	6.2			8.9	5.7			
	2.1	1.4	1.6			2.2	2.9			
	6.1	7.3	11.0	Sales/Net Fixed Assets		9.8	8.4			
	3.9	5.1	4.9			3.4	7.4			
	2.1	3.1	2.5			2.2	4.5			
	2.2	2.6	2.7	Sales/Total Assets		2.4	2.7			
	1.7	1.9	2.0			1.9	2.0			
	1.3	1.5	1.2			1.2	1.2			
	3.7	2.6	1.7	% Depr., Dep., Amort./Sales		1.9	2.7			
(64)	5.4	(55) 4.2	(61) 3.8			5.3	(14) 3.8			
	7.9	5.9	6.1			7.3	6.1			
	5.3	5.6	4.8	% Officers', Directors', Owners' Comp/Sales		7.9	4.8			
(35)	8.0	(31) 8.2	(33) 8.6		(13) 10.2	(10) 7.2				
	13.5	13.4	12.2			12.3	13.9			
	625136M	359422M	457273M	Net Sales ($)	5513M	45017M	56596M	57787M	78923M	213437M
	403335M	211046M	241535M	Total Assets ($)	5077M	34110M	33575M	26232M	42806M	99735M

© Robert Morris Associates 1995   M = $ thousand   MM = $ million
See Pages 1 through 15 for Explanation of Ratios and Data

Current Data Sorted By Assets | Comparative Historical Data

0-500M	500M-2MM	2-10MM	10-50MM	50-100MM	100-250MM	# Postretirement Benefits / Type of Statement	4/1/90-3/31/91 ALL	4/1/91-3/31/92 ALL
		3	3	1	1	# Postretirement Benefits		
	4	18	20	4	2	Unqualified	36	40
2	14	21	7			Reviewed	37	40
7	16	8	3		1	Compiled	28	32
	1					Tax Returns		
1	8	21	8	1		Other	30	44
	60 (4/1-9/30/94)	107 (10/1/94-3/31/95)						
10	43	68	38	5	3	NUMBER OF STATEMENTS	131	156
%	%	%	%	%	%	**ASSETS**	%	%
12.7	7.7	8.1	6.2			Cash & Equivalents	6.5	6.1
31.1	32.9	28.9	27.0			Trade Receivables - (net)	28.3	28.0
11.1	18.2	20.1	17.2			Inventory	20.5	20.8
.8	1.5	1.0	2.2			All Other Current	1.5	1.5
55.7	60.3	58.0	52.6			Total Current	56.8	56.4
31.0	34.7	33.3	37.1			Fixed Assets (net)	34.6	36.6
1.2	.5	2.9	.7			Intangibles (net)	1.2	1.5
12.1	4.4	5.7	9.6			All Other Non-Current	7.3	5.5
100.0	100.0	100.0	100.0			Total	100.0	100.0
						LIABILITIES		
6.9	11.0	7.5	8.7			Notes Payable-Short Term	9.1	10.0
5.5	5.2	4.4	3.7			Cur. Mat. -L/T/D	3.8	5.7
18.5	19.9	18.3	17.1			Trade Payables	16.5	15.5
.6	.4	.3	.5			Income Taxes Payable	.3	.5
9.4	10.3	9.8	9.0			All Other Current	7.9	9.3
40.8	46.8	40.2	39.0			Total Current	37.8	41.0
18.0	17.6	15.1	18.6			Long Term Debt	22.1	18.4
.5	.2	.7	1.2			Deferred Taxes	.8	.8
3.2	4.9	3.7	1.1			All Other-Non-Current	3.5	4.1
37.4	30.4	40.3	40.2			Net Worth	35.9	35.7
100.0	100.0	100.0	100.0			Total Liabilities & Net Worth	100.0	100.0
						INCOME DATA		
100.0	100.0	100.0	100.0			Net Sales	100.0	100.0
31.0	27.0	21.1	21.4			Gross Profit	25.2	23.4
29.3	22.2	15.7	11.4			Operating Expenses	20.6	19.8
1.8	4.8	5.4	9.9			Operating Profit	4.6	3.6
.0	1.6	1.0	.7			All Other Expenses (net)	1.5	1.7
1.8	3.2	4.3	9.2			Profit Before Taxes	3.1	1.9
						RATIOS		
2.8	2.0	2.1	2.2			Current	2.2	2.2
1.5	1.2	1.4	1.3				1.5	1.5
.8	.9	1.0	1.1				1.2	1.0
2.1	1.5	1.4	1.5			Quick	1.3	1.4
1.0	.8	.8	.8				.9	.8
.7	.5	.6	.6				.6	.6
28 13.1	33 11.0	43 8.4	43 8.4			Sales/Receivables	39 9.4	38 9.6
43 8.4	51 7.2	52 7.0	51 7.1				48 7.6	48 7.6
64 5.7	66 5.5	61 6.0	58 6.3				59 6.2	57 6.4
5 75.0	15 24.7	24 15.5	29 12.4			Cost of Sales/Inventory	26 13.8	25 14.7
15 24.9	37 9.8	37 9.8	40 9.1				41 9.0	42 8.7
35 10.3	55 6.6	65 5.6	58 6.3				63 5.8	66 5.5
21 17.2	18 19.8	24 15.1	28 12.9			Cost of Sales/Payables	22 16.7	20 18.7
28 12.9	41 9.0	36 10.1	44 8.3				35 10.5	29 12.4
53 6.9	60 6.1	54 6.7	55 6.6				55 6.6	49 7.5
5.9	6.7	6.6	6.1			Sales/Working Capital	6.2	7.2
14.9	21.0	12.2	15.9				10.3	10.9
-43.6	-106.8	120.1	46.4				30.8	839.3
9.3	5.7	7.4	18.0			EBIT/Interest	5.5	4.6
5.8	(42) 3.2	(61) 3.3	(36) 6.8				(122) 2.2	(147) 1.9
.6	1.5	1.8	3.3				.9	.4
	3.3	3.3	14.1			Net Profit + Depr., Dep., Amort./Cur. Mat. L /T/D	7.8	3.7
	(20) 2.3	(32) 2.1	(18) 2.2				(77) 3.3	(80) 1.7
	1.4	1.1	1.6				1.0	.5
.4	.4	.5	.4			Fixed/Worth	.4	.6
1.1	1.2	1.0	1.1				1.1	1.0
-21.4	3.1	1.9	2.0				2.6	2.2
.4	.8	1.0	.8			Debt/Worth	.8	.8
2.5	2.2	1.8	1.6				1.9	2.0
-58.2	7.4	3.7	3.5				4.9	4.2
	41.5	46.8	65.5			% Profit Before Taxes/Tangible Net Worth	37.8	32.8
	(39) 22.4	(65) 20.0	(36) 42.2				(120) 14.9	(145) 9.6
	6.4	5.4	18.7				1.8	-4.8
11.6	13.7	17.2	27.6			% Profit Before Taxes/Total Assets	11.9	10.2
6.5	5.6	6.0	11.1				4.8	3.6
.8	1.3	1.8	5.0				.3	-3.0
17.7	22.0	9.6	8.6			Sales/Net Fixed Assets	10.7	10.0
10.7	7.2	6.2	5.5				5.6	5.7
4.9	3.8	4.7	3.7				3.7	3.8
3.7	3.3	2.4	2.3			Sales/Total Assets	2.5	2.6
2.5	2.4	2.2	2.0				2.1	2.1
2.1	1.7	1.8	1.4				1.6	1.6
1.2	1.1	1.9	1.9			% Depr., Dep., Amort./Sales	1.6	1.8
2.5	(41) 2.4	(64) 2.8	(34) 2.5				(121) 2.7	(144) 3.1
3.3	3.8	3.6	3.7				4.0	4.4
	4.2	1.0				% Officers', Directors', Owners' Comp/Sales	2.2	2.5
	(21) 5.1	(21) 3.0					(58) 4.8	(52) 4.2
	8.3	5.0					6.6	9.8
9071M	121344M	759015M	1383153M	428237M	543776M	Net Sales ($)	2243149M	2430330M
3134M	48465M	365085M	777844M	287929M	482429M	Total Assets ($)	1073645M	1333122M

M = $ thousand   MM = $ million
See Pages 1 through 15 for Explanation of Ratios and Data

Comparative Historical Data | **Current Data Sorted By Sales**

Comparative Historical Data				Current Data Sorted By Sales					
5	8	8	# Postretirement Benefits			1	2	1	4
			Type of Statement						
37	42	48	Unqualified	1	1	4	6	17	19
30	36	44	Reviewed	5	5	8	10	13	3
39	32	35	Compiled	7	11	7	6	1	3
	2	1	Tax Returns			1			
35	29	39	Other	2	4	5	6	14	8
4/1/92-3/31/93 ALL	4/1/93-3/31/94 ALL	4/1/94-3/31/95 ALL		60 (4/1-9/30/94) 0-1MM	1-3MM	3-5MM	107 (10/1/94-3/31/95) 5-10MM	10-25MM	25MM & OVER
141	141	167	**NUMBER OF STATEMENTS**	15	21	25	28	45	33
%	%	%	**ASSETS**	%	%	%	%	%	%
5.2	4.2	7.5	Cash & Equivalents	7.6	10.8	8.5	7.7	7.2	5.0
29.3	31.3	29.5	Trade Receivables - (net)	29.4	28.2	30.9	31.2	28.7	28.9
20.3	18.1	18.2	Inventory	13.6	16.4	22.5	18.6	18.4	17.5
.7	1.0	1.5	All Other Current	.8	.8	2.4	.7	1.3	2.3
55.5	54.5	56.7	Total Current	51.5	56.2	64.3	58.2	55.6	53.7
37.1	37.0	34.7	Fixed Assets (net)	42.2	35.4	29.9	32.9	33.4	37.9
1.5	2.1	1.9	Intangibles (net)	.2	.8	.6	3.8	2.1	2.3
6.0	6.4	6.7	All Other Non-Current	6.2	7.6	5.2	5.2	8.9	6.1
100.0	100.0	100.0	Total	100.0	100.0	100.0	100.0	100.0	100.0
			LIABILITIES						
9.7	9.5	8.5	Notes Payable-Short Term	7.0	12.6	10.2	7.1	7.5	7.7
5.1	5.5	4.4	Cur. Mat.-L /T/D	8.5	4.7	4.9	3.2	4.7	2.7
16.0	17.8	18.3	Trade Payables	16.9	19.2	17.3	20.5	18.3	17.1
.2	.6	.4	Income Taxes Payable	.5	.6	.0	.2	.4	.4
7.9	8.2	9.5	All Other Current	9.8	12.6	9.1	8.3	9.2	9.2
39.0	41.7	41.0	Total Current	42.8	49.8	41.6	39.3	40.1	37.0
19.3	18.5	17.3	Long Term Debt	22.3	18.3	14.1	11.0	18.9	20.0
.6	.7	.8	Deferred Taxes	.4	.4	.1	1.2	.8	1.3
3.6	3.7	3.5	All Other-Non-Current	2.9	6.0	2.4	3.1	4.0	2.6
37.5	35.4	37.4	Net Worth	31.7	25.5	41.9	45.4	36.2	39.0
100.0	100.0	100.0	Total Liabilities & Net Worth	100.0	100.0	100.0	100.0	100.0	100.0
			INCOME DATA						
100.0	100.0	100.0	Net Sales	100.0	100.0	100.0	100.0	100.0	100.0
24.8	23.1	23.1	Gross Profit	33.1	28.3	24.2	20.6	21.1	19.3
19.6	18.7	16.9	Operating Expenses	26.9	26.2	17.8	15.5	14.4	10.4
5.3	4.4	6.2	Operating Profit	6.2	2.1	6.4	5.0	6.7	8.8
1.3	1.2	1.1	All Other Expenses (net)	2.2	.9	1.3	.9	.9	.9
3.9	3.2	5.1	Profit Before Taxes	4.0	1.1	5.1	4.1	5.7	7.9
			RATIOS						
2.2	2.0	2.1		1.7	1.7	3.0	2.7	1.8	2.6
1.5	1.4	1.4	Current	1.1	1.1	1.4	1.4	1.3	1.5
1.0	1.0	1.0		.9	.8	1.0	1.0	1.1	1.1
1.5	1.2	1.5		1.4	1.2	2.3	1.5	1.2	1.8
.9	.9	.8	Quick	.8	.8	.9	.9	.8	.9
.6	.6	.6		.6	.5	.5	.6	.6	.6
41 9.0	38 9.6	38 9.5		54 6.7	22 16.8	38 9.7	45 8.1	42 8.7	45 8.1
50 7.3	48 7.6	52 7.0	Sales/Receivables	78 4.7	33 10.9	51 7.2	54 6.8	51 7.2	55 6.6
61 6.0	57 6.4	63 5.8		111 3.3	60 6.1	65 5.6	59 6.2	61 6.0	69 5.3
26 13.9	21 17.8	23 15.6		10 37.4	12 30.3	31 11.7	19 18.8	24 15.1	28 13.1
39 9.3	33 10.9	37 9.8	Cost of Sales/Inventory	57 6.4	29 12.7	49 7.5	35 10.3	34 10.6	37 9.9
64 5.7	51 7.1	61 6.0		114 3.2	53 6.9	70 5.2	51 7.2	60 6.1	56 6.5
20 18.4	21 17.6	24 15.3		24 15.3	18 19.8	21 17.7	20 18.5	26 14.1	30 12.2
31 11.9	31 11.7	38 9.5	Cost of Sales/Payables	64 5.7	36 10.1	39 9.4	38 9.7	36 10.1	44 8.3
49 7.5	49 7.5	55 6.6		94 3.9	51 7.2	50 7.3	61 6.0	57 6.4	51 7.2
6.5	8.5	6.2		5.2	6.4	5.5	6.5	9.6	5.4
12.5	18.6	13.6	Sales/Working Capital	14.8	85.8	14.5	10.3	13.4	11.1
165.2	−160.2	199.4		−26.7	−35.4	157.0	NM	43.6	78.3
7.0	7.0	8.6		8.9	6.2	5.5	10.4	13.2	17.6
(133) 2.9	(137) 3.0	(156) 4.1	EBIT/Interest	3.2	2.4	(22) 3.4	(25) 4.3	(43) 3.5	(30) 5.9
1.2	1.0	1.9		.9	−.7	1.7	2.1	2.0	2.5
3.0	4.0	4.2			5.8		2.7	3.4	28.1
(66) 1.8	(63) 1.5	(78) 2.2	Net Profit + Depr., Dep., Amort./Cur. Mat. L/T/D		(10) 3.4		(14) 1.7	(24) 2.0	(16) 3.1
1.0	.6	1.3			2.3		1.0	1.1	1.4
.6	.5	.5		.8	.5	.3	.4	.7	.5
1.0	1.2	1.1	Fixed/Worth	2.0	1.3	.9	.8	1.1	1.1
2.2	2.4	2.1		3.8	NM	1.4	1.6	2.0	2.4
.8	.7	.9		1.0	.8	.6	.5	1.2	.6
1.9	1.9	1.8	Debt/Worth	3.8	1.8	1.5	1.7	2.1	1.6
4.2	4.4	4.0		6.2	NM	3.4	3.6	3.9	3.6
39.1	43.0	48.2		55.3	34.6	35.0	40.4	67.8	62.0
(128) 21.0	(128) 20.6	(154) 26.0	% Profit Before Taxes/Tangible Net Worth	(13) 10.7	(16) 19.2	(24) 23.5	14.7	(43) 30.3	(30) 45.3
5.3	1.3	8.9		−2.1	8.9	5.0	5.6	10.3	18.4
15.0	12.6	16.2		12.7	10.3	17.1	15.1	20.6	25.9
6.7	5.9	7.1	% Profit Before Taxes/Total Assets	5.4	5.7	6.0	5.7	7.1	11.0
1.0	.1	2.3		−.3	−2.2	1.8	1.8	3.6	5.4
10.2	12.6	10.6		7.5	24.0	15.5	13.1	9.9	7.1
5.6	6.0	6.0	Sales/Net Fixed Assets	3.0	5.9	7.4	7.1	6.2	5.3
3.7	4.0	4.1		1.6	4.0	4.7	4.2	5.0	3.5
2.7	2.9	2.6		2.1	3.4	2.7	2.7	2.4	2.4
2.1	2.3	2.1	Sales/Total Assets	1.3	2.7	2.3	2.3	2.3	2.0
1.6	1.7	1.6		.7	2.0	1.9	1.7	1.8	1.5
1.9	1.7	1.6		2.6	1.2	1.0	1.5	1.7	2.1
(132) 3.1	(132) 2.8	(157) 2.6	% Depr., Dep., Amort./Sales	(14) 3.4	2.5	(23) 2.8	2.3	(40) 2.3	(31) 2.7
4.5	4.5	3.7		6.4	3.1	3.6	3.5	3.4	4.0
2.1	1.8	2.5			2.5	3.9	2.4		
(66) 4.6	(56) 4.2	(54) 4.4	% Officers', Directors', Owners' Comp/Sales		(12) 3.7	(11) 6.4	(12) 3.4		
7.4	7.1	6.7			8.9	10.4	4.9		
1964527M	2850865M	3244596M	Net Sales ($)	10789M	40486M	104090M	201979M	785791M	2101461M
1049691M	1616670M	1964886M	Total Assets ($)	9443M	17512M	61760M	105860M	412077M	1358234M

Current Data Sorted By Assets   Comparative Historical Data

0-500M	500M-2MM	2-10MM	10-50MM	50-100MM	100-250MM	# Postretirement Benefits / Type of Statement	6 / 4/1/90-3/31/91 ALL	7 / 4/1/91-3/31/92 ALL
		3	5	2		Unqualified	14	10
		6	1			Reviewed	4	4
1	2	2				Compiled	3	3
						Tax Returns		
	1	5	3			Other	6	7
	8 (4/1-9/30/94)			23 (10/1/94-3/31/95)				
1	3	16	9	2		NUMBER OF STATEMENTS	27	24
%	%	%	%	%	%	**ASSETS**	%	%
		3.2				Cash & Equivalents	5.0	5.4
		30.1				Trade Receivables - (net)	25.4	23.8
		24.8				Inventory	25.8	26.2
		2.7				All Other Current	2.2	1.8
		60.8				Total Current	58.5	57.2
		31.1				Fixed Assets (net)	36.2	33.7
		1.7				Intangibles (net)	.9	1.2
		6.4				All Other Non-Current	4.3	7.9
		100.0				Total	100.0	100.0
						LIABILITIES		
		10.5				Notes Payable-Short Term	12.0	12.2
		4.6				Cur. Mat. -L/T/D	3.6	3.6
		18.7				Trade Payables	11.8	8.1
		.1				Income Taxes Payable	.6	.3
		8.9				All Other Current	6.8	5.8
		42.8				Total Current	34.8	30.1
		10.7				Long Term Debt	12.9	13.2
		1.2				Deferred Taxes	1.6	1.2
		2.8				All Other-Non-Current	1.8	3.6
		42.6				Net Worth	49.0	52.0
		100.0				Total Liabilities & Net Worth	100.0	100.0
						INCOME DATA		
		100.0				Net Sales	100.0	100.0
		17.2				Gross Profit	22.8	22.9
		12.6				Operating Expenses	17.4	18.8
		4.6				Operating Profit	5.4	4.2
		1.0				All Other Expenses (net)	.5	1.4
		3.6				Profit Before Taxes	5.0	2.7
						RATIOS		
		2.3				Current	2.7	3.4
		1.6					1.9	2.0
		1.1					1.2	1.4
		1.3				Quick	1.7	1.6
		.8					.9	.9
		.6					.6	.8
		41 8.9				Sales/Receivables	47 7.8	37 9.9
		47 7.8					51 7.1	47 7.8
		60 6.1					69 5.3	60 6.1
		34 10.7				Cost of Sales/Inventory	47 7.7	35 10.5
		38 9.7					76 4.8	61 6.0
		73 5.0					126 2.9	122 3.0
		23 16.2				Cost of Sales/Payables	16 23.0	12 31.1
		34 10.8					26 14.3	21 17.0
		54 6.7					44 8.3	28 12.9
		6.4				Sales/Working Capital	3.5	4.2
		9.0					6.0	7.1
		NM					17.7	11.2
		12.0				EBIT/Interest	11.3	10.4
		(15) 4.8					(21) 5.1	(21) 1.9
		2.9					1.1	1.1
						Net Profit + Depr., Dep., Amort./Cur. Mat. L./T/D	7.6	19.3
							(17) 2.6	(13) 4.2
							1.2	1.2
		.5				Fixed/Worth	.5	.4
		.9					.7	.7
		1.4					1.1	1.0
		.6				Debt/Worth	.5	.5
		1.5					1.1	1.0
		3.7					1.9	1.8
		29.1				% Profit Before Taxes/Tangible Net Worth	33.4	23.4
		21.5					16.9	11.1
		7.1					1.3	.3
		12.7				% Profit Before Taxes/Total Assets	12.8	12.2
		8.9					7.2	4.0
		4.6					.6	-.1
		10.3				Sales/Net Fixed Assets	9.6	8.3
		7.3					4.9	6.0
		5.5					2.9	3.5
		2.7				Sales/Total Assets	2.3	2.3
		2.3					1.6	1.7
		1.8					1.1	1.2
		2.5				% Depr., Dep., Amort./Sales	1.6	2.4
	(11)	2.5					(24) 3.0	(21) 3.0
		3.1					4.4	4.5
						% Officers', Directors', Owners' Comp/Sales		
435M	11937M	194819M	518999M	211467M		Net Sales ($)	952504M	871397M
218M	3573M	88338M	259910M	120058M		Total Assets ($)	720165M	591342M

M = $ thousand   MM = $ million
See Pages 1 through 15 for Explanation of Ratios and Data

Comparative Historical Data / Current Data Sorted By Sales

2	1		# Postretirement Benefits — Type of Statement	0-1MM	1-3MM	3-5MM	5-10MM	10-25MM	25MM & OVER
11	9	10	Unqualified		1		4	4	5
6	3	7	Reviewed			1		1	1
3	4	5	Compiled	2	1		1	1	
			Tax Returns						
5	7	9	Other				1	5	3
4/1/92-3/31/93 ALL	4/1/93-3/31/94 ALL	4/1/94-3/31/95 ALL			8 (4/1-9/30/94)			23 (10/1/94-3/31/95)	
25	23	31	NUMBER OF STATEMENTS	2	2	1	6	11	9

Hist 2 %	Hist 1 %	Hist 3 %	ASSETS	0-1MM %	1-3MM %	3-5MM %	5-10MM %	10-25MM %	25MM %
4.5	3.7	7.1	Cash & Equivalents					3.5	
26.8	26.2	28.8	Trade Receivables - (net)					32.5	
26.4	25.4	25.0	Inventory					23.6	
2.5	2.8	2.3	All Other Current					1.8	
60.2	58.1	63.3	Total Current					61.4	
33.8	34.3	25.5	Fixed Assets (net)					30.2	
1.0	.9	3.8	Intangibles (net)					1.2	
5.0	6.7	7.4	All Other Non-Current					7.2	
100.0	100.0	100.0	Total					100.0	

Hist 2	Hist 1	Hist 3	LIABILITIES					10-25MM	
12.1	12.1	11.2	Notes Payable-Short Term					7.5	
2.2	2.9	3.4	Cur. Mat.-L/T/D					6.1	
12.6	11.5	18.1	Trade Payables					23.2	
.5	5.3	.1	Income Taxes Payable					.0	
7.4	8.2	7.2	All Other Current					7.9	
34.9	40.1	40.0	Total Current					44.7	
14.6	12.8	10.5	Long Term Debt					10.8	
.9	1.3	.8	Deferred Taxes					.9	
2.8	1.6	3.2	All Other-Non-Current					1.9	
46.8	44.2	45.5	Net Worth					41.8	
100.0	100.0	100.0	Total Liabilities & Net Worth					100.0	

Hist 2	Hist 1	Hist 3	INCOME DATA					10-25MM	
100.0	100.0	100.0	Net Sales					100.0	
20.8	21.9	21.7	Gross Profit					21.4	
18.1	17.7	16.1	Operating Expenses					16.1	
2.7	4.2	5.7	Operating Profit					5.3	
1.4	.9	1.3	All Other Expenses (net)					1.0	
1.2	3.3	4.4	Profit Before Taxes					4.3	

Hist 2	Hist 1	Hist 3	RATIOS					10-25MM	
3.9	2.4	2.6	Current					2.4	
1.6	1.4	1.6						1.6	
1.3	1.1	1.3						.9	
1.8	.9	1.3	Quick					1.5	
.9	.8	.9						.8	
.7	.6	.6						.6	
41 8.9	38 9.6	42 8.7	Sales/Receivables					43 8.4	
49 7.5	43 8.4	48 7.6						45 8.1	
65 5.6	51 7.2	55 6.6						61 6.0	
36 10.2	26 14.2	34 10.6	Cost of Sales/Inventory					30 12.0	
65 5.6	57 6.4	59 6.2						35 10.5	
101 3.6	78 4.7	89 4.1						65 5.6	
16 22.7	11 34.7	23 16.2	Cost of Sales/Payables					23 16.2	
26 14.3	23 15.6	34 10.6						35 10.5	
34 10.6	37 9.9	54 6.7						62 5.9	
3.9	8.2	4.2	Sales/Working Capital					7.1	
11.0	12.1	8.7						12.1	
16.0	48.9	18.2						-30.9	
(22) 6.6	(22) 11.8	(27) 24.8	EBIT/Interest				(10)	59.5	
2.3	2.9	4.1						6.4	
1.2	.9	3.1						3.1	
	(10) 3.9	(10) 6.7	Net Profit + Depr., Dep., Amort./Cur. Mat. L/T/D						
	1.9	2.9							
	.2	1.7							
.4	.5	.3	Fixed/Worth					.5	
.8	.7	.6						.7	
1.8	1.2	1.0						5.6	
.3	.8	.5	Debt/Worth					.5	
1.4	1.5	1.4						1.4	
4.5	1.9	3.2						11.6	
25.1	(22) 37.7	(30) 29.1	% Profit Before Taxes/Tangible Net Worth					28.7	
10.3	15.9	20.5						22.5	
1.4	.3	9.4						11.5	
8.5	12.7	12.8	% Profit Before Taxes/Total Assets					15.4	
2.2	6.3	8.5						8.1	
.7	-.0	4.7						4.7	
8.6	8.5	15.4	Sales/Net Fixed Assets					10.4	
5.3	5.6	8.1						7.4	
3.5	5.1	6.1						5.3	
2.3	2.6	2.6	Sales/Total Assets					2.7	
1.8	2.3	2.0						2.4	
1.3	1.8	1.6						1.8	
(22) 1.9	(22) 1.4	(25) 1.5	% Depr., Dep., Amort./Sales						
3.1	2.6	2.5							
5.6	3.2	3.1							
			% Officers', Directors', Owners' Comp/Sales						
682351M	935954M	937657M	Net Sales ($)	1244M	4416M	3529M	47564M	185843M	695061M
431330M	462385M	472097M	Total Assets ($)	782M	4755M	2165M	22939M	85132M	356324M

M = $ thousand   MM = $ million
See Pages 1 through 15 for Explanation of Ratios and Data

MANUFACTURERS—SECONDARY SMELTING & REFINING OF NONFERROUS METALS. SIC# 3341

	Current Data Sorted By Assets							Comparative Historical Data	
			2	2		1	**# Postretirement Benefits**		
							Type of Statement		
		1	7	5	1	2	Unqualified	15	16
		3	3	2			Reviewed	11	11
	1		2				Compiled	6	5
			1				Tax Returns	1	1
		3	4	6		1	Other	4	3
	16 (4/1-9/30/94)			26 (10/1/94-3/31/95)				4/1/90-3/31/91	4/1/91-3/31/92
	0-500M	500M-2MM	2-10MM	10-50MM	50-100MM	100-250MM		ALL	ALL
	1	7	17	13	2	2	**NUMBER OF STATEMENTS**	37	36
	%	%	%	%	%	%	**ASSETS**	%	%
			7.4	4.2			Cash & Equivalents	5.9	4.4
			27.3	30.5			Trade Receivables - (net)	26.2	27.7
			26.7	28.1			Inventory	29.1	27.6
			.7	3.9			All Other Current	2.2	2.6
			62.1	66.6			Total Current	63.5	62.3
			28.0	24.3			Fixed Assets (net)	30.1	26.9
			.4	.5			Intangibles (net)	1.2	1.2
			9.4	8.6			All Other Non-Current	5.3	9.6
			100.0	100.0			Total	100.0	100.0
							LIABILITIES		
			11.0	21.7			Notes Payable-Short Term	17.5	14.5
			1.8	1.6			Cur. Mat. -L/T/D	3.3	2.9
			24.8	14.3			Trade Payables	15.6	17.5
			.5	.1			Income Taxes Payable	.4	.4
			5.9	8.8			All Other Current	8.6	4.9
			44.1	46.5			Total Current	45.4	40.3
			9.1	7.7			Long Term Debt	14.1	10.2
			.6	.4			Deferred Taxes	.4	.7
			3.2	4.9			All Other-Non-Current	.7	2.4
			42.9	40.6			Net Worth	39.4	46.3
			100.0	100.0			Total Liabilities & Net Worth	100.0	100.0
							INCOME DATA		
			100.0	100.0			Net Sales	100.0	100.0
			21.8	11.6			Gross Profit	18.3	19.2
			15.9	8.7			Operating Expenses	16.0	17.3
			5.9	2.9			Operating Profit	2.3	1.9
			1.2	1.4			All Other Expenses (net)	.5	1.3
			4.7	1.6			Profit Before Taxes	1.8	.6
							RATIOS		
			1.9	2.3				2.2	2.4
			1.6	1.5			Current	1.5	1.5
			1.0	1.0				1.0	1.0
			1.2	1.1				1.2	1.2
			.8	.6			Quick	.8	.7
			.5	.4				.3	.6
			11 / 31.9	36 / 10.2				15 / 25.1	30 / 12.1
			46 / 7.9	59 / 6.2			Sales/Receivables	36 / 10.2	39 / 9.4
			57 / 6.4	69 / 5.3				51 / 7.2	54 / 6.8
			18 / 20.6	24 / 15.4				20 / 18.1	19 / 19.6
			31 / 11.8	48 / 7.6			Cost of Sales/Inventory	33 / 10.9	43 / 8.4
			59 / 6.2	60 / 6.1				68 / 5.4	73 / 5.0
			15 / 24.2	8 / 45.4				7 / 52.5	23 / 16.1
			49 / 7.5	21 / 17.8			Cost of Sales/Payables	22 / 16.5	29 / 12.4
			76 / 4.8	45 / 8.1				37 / 9.8	44 / 8.3
			7.8	6.0				7.4	6.9
			15.3	10.7			Sales/Working Capital	20.8	11.6
			NM	NM				130.3	358.1
			20.0	9.5				8.3	4.8
			(15) 6.4	(12) 3.3			EBIT/Interest	(32) 3.0	1.9
			2.8	1.1				.9	.9
							Net Profit + Depr., Dep.,	11.6	10.3
							Amort./Cur. Mat. L /T/D	(16) 3.7 / (19) 1.8	
								1.6	.8
			.3	.3				.3	.3
			.7	.5			Fixed/Worth	.6	.6
			1.2	1.5				1.5	1.1
			.8	.6				.8	.6
			1.6	1.4			Debt/Worth	1.6	1.2
			2.5	4.4				3.3	2.4
			58.5	25.9			% Profit Before Taxes/Tangible	34.6	10.2
			25.8	10.6			Net Worth	(35) 12.2 / (35) 4.6	
			6.6	2.7				.0	-1.0
			18.9	12.2			% Profit Before Taxes/Total	11.7	5.9
			11.1	5.5			Assets	6.2	1.9
			3.0	.5				-.4	-.4
			19.3	22.1				22.6	16.6
			8.8	9.1			Sales/Net Fixed Assets	9.7	9.7
			7.2	5.5				5.9	7.4
			3.6	2.9				3.7	3.6
			2.7	2.3			Sales/Total Assets	3.0	2.3
			2.2	1.6				1.8	1.7
			1.2	.9			% Depr., Dep., Amort./Sales	.7	1.1
			(16) 2.3	(12) 2.3				(31) 1.1 / (34) 2.0	
			2.6	3.4				3.1	2.7
							% Officers', Directors',	1.0	.8
							Owners' Comp/Sales	(17) 1.5 / (14) 1.4	
								2.7	3.6
	2643M	31146M	272066M	617923M	266974M	620763M	Net Sales ($)	1011893M	1455411M
	363M	8484M	86755M	262377M	162745M	292517M	Total Assets ($)	330512M	645268M

M = $ thousand   MM = $ million
See Pages 1 through 15 for Explanation of Ratios and Data

Comparative Historical Data | Current Data Sorted By Sales

 # Postretirement Benefits — (10-25MM) 2, (25MM & OVER) 3

Type of Statement

Hist 3	Hist 4	Hist 5	Type of Statement	0-1MM	1-3MM	3-5MM	5-10MM	10-25MM	25MM & OVER
22	19	16	Unqualified					6	9
8	8	8	Reviewed	1			1	4	2
8	8	3	Compiled		1		2		
1		1	Tax Returns			1			
7	5	14	Other		2	1		6	5
4/1/92-3/31/93 ALL	4/1/93-3/31/94 ALL	4/1/94-3/31/95 ALL		| 16 (4/1-9/30/94)			| 26 (10/1/94-3/31/95)		
46	40	42	**NUMBER OF STATEMENTS**	1	3	3	3	16	16

ASSETS

Hist 3 %	Hist 4 %	Hist 5 %	Item	0-1MM %	1-3MM %	3-5MM %	5-10MM %	10-25MM %	25MM & OVER %
6.1	6.3	5.2	Cash & Equivalents					7.4	3.1
24.6	27.6	31.8	Trade Receivables - (net)					31.5	26.7
24.0	21.1	25.4	Inventory					27.0	30.2
2.8	4.0	1.9	All Other Current					.3	3.5
57.4	58.9	64.3	Total Current					66.1	63.5
29.7	31.7	25.7	Fixed Assets (net)					23.9	24.3
1.2	1.1	1.4	Intangibles (net)					.2	2.9
11.7	8.3	8.5	All Other Non-Current					9.8	9.3
100.0	100.0	100.0	Total					100.0	100.0

LIABILITIES

Hist 3	Hist 4	Hist 5	Item	0-1MM	1-3MM	3-5MM	5-10MM	10-25MM	25MM & OVER
11.0	11.6	14.5	Notes Payable-Short Term					11.4	23.0
5.2	3.9	1.8	Cur. Mat.-L /T/D					2.0	1.5
16.0	15.8	19.3	Trade Payables					22.1	13.5
.1	.4	.4	Income Taxes Payable					.3	.1
7.2	6.2	6.5	All Other Current					5.4	8.5
39.5	38.0	42.5	Total Current					41.2	46.7
12.2	11.2	9.1	Long Term Debt					12.8	8.0
.7	1.0	.8	Deferred Taxes					.7	1.2
3.2	3.9	4.8	All Other-Non-Current					4.3	2.9
44.5	45.9	42.8	Net Worth					41.0	41.2
100.0	100.0	100.0	Total Liabilities & Net Worth					100.0	100.0

INCOME DATA

Hist 3	Hist 4	Hist 5	Item	0-1MM	1-3MM	3-5MM	5-10MM	10-25MM	25MM & OVER
100.0	100.0	100.0	Net Sales					100.0	100.0
22.7	25.1	17.9	Gross Profit					22.3	12.1
21.3	21.9	13.3	Operating Expenses					15.9	8.8
1.5	3.2	4.6	Operating Profit					6.4	3.3
.5	1.4	1.1	All Other Expenses (net)					1.3	1.6
.9	1.8	3.5	Profit Before Taxes					5.1	1.7

RATIOS

Hist 3	Hist 4	Hist 5	Item	0-1MM	1-3MM	3-5MM	5-10MM	10-25MM	25MM & OVER
2.4 / 1.6 / 1.1	2.5 / 1.4 / 1.2	2.3 / 1.5 / 1.0	Current					2.1 / 1.6 / 1.2	1.9 / 1.5 / 1.0
1.2 / .8 / .6	1.3 / .9 / .5	1.3 / .9 / .5	Quick					1.3 / 1.0 / .6	1.0 / .6 / .4
25 14.4 / 38 9.6 / 53 6.9	31 11.8 / 45 8.1 / 52 7.0	33 11.1 / 47 7.8 / 63 5.8	Sales/Receivables					28 13.0 / 47 7.8 / 65 5.6	32 11.4 / 48 7.6 / 63 5.8
19 19.4 / 39 9.4 / 79 4.6	18 20.4 / 32 11.5 / 51 7.1	17 21.2 / 33 11.1 / 59 6.2	Cost of Sales/Inventory					19 19.3 / 41 8.8 / 63 5.8	21 17.7 / 39 9.3 / 54 6.8
17 22.0 / 26 13.8 / 44 8.3	19 19.4 / 30 12.0 / 46 7.9	14 26.6 / 34 10.8 / 55 6.6	Cost of Sales/Payables					15 24.9 / 42 8.7 / 69 5.3	8 45.9 / 21 17.3 / 40 9.2
6.2 / 11.1 / 91.7	8.3 / 13.8 / 48.9	7.4 / 12.8 / 72.1	Sales/Working Capital					7.6 / 9.1 / 47.1	7.2 / 15.4 / 145.8
(45) 6.7 / 3.2 / .1	(36) 11.6 / 3.1 / -.9	(38) 17.4 / 4.9 / 1.3	EBIT/Interest				(15) 20.0 / 6.3 / 2.9		(14) 11.1 / 3.3 / 1.2
(18) 8.0 / .6 / -1.1	(17) 5.2 / 2.3 / 1.0	(13) 8.3 / 2.8 / 1.8	Net Profit + Depr., Dep., Amort./Cur. Mat. L/T/D						
.2 / .6 / 1.2	.3 / .6 / 1.2	.3 / .6 / 1.2	Fixed/Worth					.3 / .6 / 1.0	.2 / .6 / 1.2
.6 / 1.2 / 2.1	.6 / 1.3 / 2.5	.8 / 1.4 / 2.7	Debt/Worth					.9 / 1.5 / 2.4	.7 / 1.2 / 4.4
(44) 20.0 / 5.4 / -3.1	53.1 / 17.4 / -5.9	(41) 35.9 / 23.3 / 6.3	% Profit Before Taxes/Tangible Net Worth					65.6 / 26.6 / 11.4	(15) 27.3 / 12.0 / 4.7
7.8 / 2.8 / -1.9	16.6 / 5.4 / -2.2	14.4 / 8.1 / 2.3	% Profit Before Taxes/Total Assets					18.6 / 12.2 / 4.3	13.5 / 5.8 / 1.2
29.2 / 9.7 / 3.8	21.3 / 10.1 / 5.4	21.9 / 11.2 / 6.4	Sales/Net Fixed Assets					19.9 / 11.7 / 7.1	23.5 / 10.3 / 6.2
3.8 / 2.4 / 1.6	3.7 / 2.5 / 1.8	3.3 / 2.5 / 1.6	Sales/Total Assets					3.8 / 2.6 / 1.7	2.9 / 2.4 / 1.7
(44) .8 / 1.4 / 3.4	(37) .9 / 1.6 / 3.2	(38) .8 / 1.9 / 3.1	% Depr., Dep., Amort./Sales				(15) 1.1 / 2.3 / 3.2		(14) .7 / 1.7 / 3.1
(16) 1.1 / 1.6 / 6.1	(19) 1.9 / 3.9 / 5.4	(15) 1.8 / 3.3 / 4.0	% Officers', Directors', Owners' Comp/Sales						
1497671M / 994295M	1425815M / 623645M	1811515M / 813241M	Net Sales ($) / Total Assets ($)	705M / 826M	6345M / 2517M	11770M / 6404M	20860M / 6608M	254480M / 100133M	1517355M / 696753M

M = $ thousand   MM = $ million
See Pages 1 through 15 for Explanation of Ratios and Data

Current Data Sorted By Assets | | | | | | | **Comparative Historical Data**

Postretirement Benefits

Type of Statement	0-500M	500M-2MM	2-10MM	10-50MM	50-100MM	100-250MM		4/1/90-3/31/91 ALL	4/1/91-3/31/92 ALL
Unqualified		1	3	9	3	1			9
Reviewed		6	4						3
Compiled	1	2	5						1
Tax Returns									
Other		1	5	2	3	2			7
		20 (4/1-9/30/94)		28 (10/1/94-3/31/95)					
NUMBER OF STATEMENTS	1	10	17	11	6	3			20
ASSETS	%	%	%	%	%	%		%	%
Cash & Equivalents		6.2	4.7	4.4					8.3
Trade Receivables - (net)		32.4	34.2	23.3				D	21.4
Inventory		23.9	35.0	30.1				A	20.4
All Other Current		.6	1.3	1.3				T	1.2
Total Current		63.2	75.2	59.1				A	51.3
Fixed Assets (net)		27.5	19.3	31.2					36.6
Intangibles (net)		1.0	.8	1.1				N	2.8
All Other Non-Current		8.3	4.8	8.6				O	9.2
Total		100.0	100.0	100.0				T	100.0
LIABILITIES								A	
Notes Payable-Short Term		8.7	13.9	10.3				V	4.8
Cur. Mat. -L/T/D		2.7	2.0	2.8				A	2.9
Trade Payables		24.6	22.1	14.3				I	12.4
Income Taxes Payable		.9	.6	.9				L	.5
All Other Current		4.3	6.5	5.6				A	4.7
Total Current		41.2	45.0	33.9				B	25.3
Long Term Debt		11.8	10.6	19.5				L	22.4
Deferred Taxes		.2	.3	2.0				E	1.7
All Other-Non-Current		1.5	2.3	4.1					2.2
Net Worth		45.3	41.8	40.5					48.4
Total Liabilities & Net Worth		100.0	100.0	100.0					100.0
INCOME DATA									
Net Sales		100.0	100.0	100.0					100.0
Gross Profit		25.2	19.3	19.8					18.9
Operating Expenses		21.4	15.8	13.4					13.2
Operating Profit		3.8	3.4	6.4					5.7
All Other Expenses (net)		.1	.8	.6					2.5
Profit Before Taxes		3.7	2.7	5.8					3.2
RATIOS									
Current		2.1	1.9	2.4					3.0
		1.6	1.7	1.8					2.1
		1.4	1.4	1.3					1.3
Quick		1.4	1.1	1.5					2.2
		1.1	.9	.7					.8
		.7	.6	.6					.7
Sales/Receivables		35 10.5	41 8.9	36 10.1					39 9.3
		46 7.9	49 7.5	42 8.6					46 7.9
		55 6.6	61 6.0	49 7.5					56 6.5
Cost of Sales/Inventory		30 12.3	35 10.3	51 7.2					39 9.4
		39 9.4	60 6.1	81 4.5					51 7.2
		59 6.2	89 4.1	91 4.0					78 4.7
Cost of Sales/Payables		29 12.4	26 14.1	21 17.3					21 17.3
		38 9.5	37 9.9	26 13.8					35 10.5
		58 6.3	53 6.9	49 7.5					42 8.7
Sales/Working Capital		8.2	5.2	5.3					4.5
		10.4	8.4	8.6					5.7
		18.5	11.9	13.5					19.0
EBIT/Interest		11.0	18.1	15.0					11.6
		6.1	4.7	(10) 5.8					(19) 3.8
		3.3	1.4	2.5					1.2
Net Profit + Depr., Dep., Amort./Cur. Mat. L /T/D									17.6
									(12) 4.0
									.8
Fixed/Worth		.2	.2	.5					.5
		.5	.4	.8					.7
		1.1	1.0	1.7					2.1
Debt/Worth		.7	1.1	.9					.5
		1.1	1.4	2.1					1.1
		2.3	2.7	3.6					1.9
% Profit Before Taxes/Tangible Net Worth			41.2	47.3					25.5
			18.1	36.6					(19) 16.5
			4.0	21.6					8.6
% Profit Before Taxes/Total Assets		15.7	17.8	17.7					12.0
		7.0	8.1	9.7					7.1
		5.8	1.7	4.7					.2
Sales/Net Fixed Assets		34.4	29.2	10.0					8.6
		10.1	16.4	5.8					5.4
		4.9	8.4	4.9					3.3
Sales/Total Assets		3.0	3.2	2.3					2.0
		2.4	2.5	2.0					1.6
		2.2	2.2	1.6					1.1
% Depr., Dep., Amort./Sales			.8						1.7
		(15)	1.1						(17) 2.2
			1.9						3.8
% Officers', Directors', Owners' Comp/Sales									
Net Sales ($)	429M	39664M	195624M	519457M	664569M	859044M			1431813M
Total Assets ($)	156M	14191M	77415M	258616M	457560M	557329M			1205084M

M = $ thousand   MM = $ million
See Pages 1 through 15 for Explanation of Ratios and Data

Comparative Historical Data					Current Data Sorted By Sales					
		3	6	# Postretirement Benefits		1		2	3	
				Type of Statement						
	13	12	17	Unqualified				2	4	11
	6	8	10	Reviewed		3	2	4	1	
	5	6	8	Compiled	1	2		3	2	
		1		Tax Returns						
	7	13	13	Other	1	1		1	3	7
	4/1/92-3/31/93	4/1/93-3/31/94	4/1/94-3/31/95		20 (4/1-9/30/94)			28 (10/1/94-3/31/95)		
	ALL	ALL	ALL		0-1MM	1-3MM	3-5MM	5-10MM	10-25MM	25MM & OVER
NUMBER OF STATEMENTS	31	40	48		2	6	2	10	10	18

ASSETS

	H1 %	H2 %	H3 %		0-1MM %	1-3MM %	3-5MM %	5-10MM %	10-25MM %	25MM & OVER %
Cash & Equivalents	4.6	4.1	4.5					2.7	9.9	2.4
Trade Receivables - (net)	25.5	28.5	28.9					35.4	33.7	21.8
Inventory	29.1	28.6	29.0					39.7	26.5	27.7
All Other Current	2.0	1.1	1.1					.5	2.2	1.1
Total Current	61.3	62.3	63.5					78.3	72.3	52.9
Fixed Assets (net)	31.8	30.3	28.7					15.9	22.8	37.2
Intangibles (net)	1.6	1.0	1.5					.0	1.7	2.6
All Other Non-Current	5.3	6.4	6.2					5.7	3.1	7.3
Total	100.0	100.0	100.0					100.0	100.0	100.0

LIABILITIES

	H1	H2	H3		0-1MM	1-3MM	3-5MM	5-10MM	10-25MM	25MM & OVER
Notes Payable-Short Term	10.5	10.9	9.9					12.8	9.7	8.3
Cur. Mat.-L /T/D	3.1	3.6	2.6					1.3	2.3	3.0
Trade Payables	16.9	15.8	19.1					23.1	20.8	14.6
Income Taxes Payable	1.0	3.4	.7					1.1	1.2	.5
All Other Current	8.9	8.4	5.3					4.3	7.8	4.2
Total Current	40.4	42.1	37.7					42.6	41.8	30.7
Long Term Debt	17.3	17.4	15.8					10.9	7.4	22.9
Deferred Taxes	1.1	1.1	.9					.2	.9	1.7
All Other-Non-Current	3.1	3.8	2.8					1.4	2.5	4.5
Net Worth	38.1	35.6	42.8					44.9	47.3	40.2
Total Liabilities & Net Worth	100.0	100.0	100.0					100.0	100.0	100.0

INCOME DATA

	H1	H2	H3		0-1MM	1-3MM	3-5MM	5-10MM	10-25MM	25MM & OVER
Net Sales	100.0	100.0	100.0					100.0	100.0	100.0
Gross Profit	19.4	18.6	20.4					16.6	21.9	17.1
Operating Expenses	15.6	14.5	16.1					15.1	16.0	12.0
Operating Profit	3.8	4.1	4.2					1.5	5.9	5.0
All Other Expenses (net)	1.4	.9	.7					.8	.2	1.2
Profit Before Taxes	2.4	3.1	3.5					.7	5.7	3.8

RATIOS

	H1	H2	H3		0-1MM	1-3MM	3-5MM	5-10MM	10-25MM	25MM & OVER
Current	2.5 / 1.8 / 1.2	1.9 / 1.6 / 1.2	2.1 / 1.7 / 1.4					2.6 / 1.9 / 1.6	1.8 / 1.7 / 1.5	2.5 / 1.7 / 1.3
Quick	1.2 / .8 / .6	1.1 / .7 / .5	1.3 / .9 / .6					1.3 / 1.0 / .6	1.2 / 1.0 / .9	1.4 / .7 / .6
Sales/Receivables	36 10.2 / 48 7.6 / 61 6.0	37 9.9 / 44 8.3 / 57 6.4	40 9.1 / 45 8.2 / 56 6.5					39 9.4 / 45 8.2 / 60 6.1	41 8.8 / 50 7.3 / 60 6.1	38 9.7 / 42 8.7 / 49 7.5
Cost of Sales/Inventory	37 10.0 / 69 5.3 / 107 3.4	36 10.1 / 64 5.7 / 96 3.8	34 10.6 / 59 6.2 / 91 4.0					37 10.0 / 59 6.2 / 101 3.6	30 12.3 / 54 6.8 / 85 4.3	35 10.4 / 70 5.2 / 91 4.0
Cost of Sales/Payables	19 19.7 / 33 11.0 / 47 7.8	19 18.8 / 29 12.6 / 43 8.5	26 14.0 / 37 10.0 / 51 7.2					23 15.7 / 30 12.2 / 45 8.2	31 11.8 / 38 9.6 / 48 7.6	23 16.1 / 34 10.7 / 49 7.4
Sales/Working Capital	4.6 / 7.5 / 17.0	6.5 / 9.7 / 19.1	5.7 / 8.9 / 13.2					4.7 / 7.2 / 12.5	6.4 / 9.2 / 12.8	4.9 / 8.2 / 15.6
EBIT/Interest	(29) 9.1 / 3.0 / .5	(38) 6.8 / 2.9 / 1.4	(47) 10.8 / 5.3 / 2.1					11.6 / 4.3 / −.2		9.5 / 3.7 / 1.6
Net Profit + Depr., Dep., Amort./Cur. Mat. L/T/D	(14) 7.9 / 1.7 / .3	(17) 5.1 / 2.2 / 1.2	(26) 6.1 / 2.6 / 1.6						(12)	4.2 / 1.9 / 1.3
Fixed/Worth	.3 / .8 / 2.4	.2 / .9 / 2.0	.4 / .7 / 1.4					.2 / .3 / .8	.3 / .4 / .7	.7 / 1.1 / 1.8
Debt/Worth	.7 / 1.8 / 5.0	1.0 / 1.8 / 4.2	.9 / 1.4 / 2.5					.8 / 1.3 / 2.1	.9 / 1.2 / 1.7	.9 / 1.8 / 3.4
% Profit Before Taxes/Tangible Net Worth	(27) 31.5 / 15.0 / 4.5	(37) 33.0 / 14.6 / 6.6	(47) 42.2 / 23.7 / 9.5					30.1 / 12.5 / −53.8	48.8 / 33.9 / 14.0	48.4 / 30.4 / 4.9
% Profit Before Taxes/Total Assets	12.1 / 4.6 / −1.6	13.2 / 5.4 / 1.4	16.6 / 8.3 / 3.7					19.8 / 4.8 / −4.6	19.4 / 12.1 / 6.4	16.5 / 9.3 / 1.7
Sales/Net Fixed Assets	14.4 / 6.3 / 3.1	22.0 / 6.5 / 4.0	17.7 / 7.3 / 5.0					34.4 / 18.7 / 13.2	33.1 / 10.9 / 5.7	7.4 / 5.6 / 3.2
Sales/Total Assets	2.2 / 1.8 / 1.3	2.7 / 2.0 / 1.4	2.7 / 2.3 / 1.7					3.4 / 2.8 / 2.3	3.4 / 2.4 / 1.9	2.1 / 1.8 / 1.4
% Depr., Dep., Amort./Sales	(26) 1.5 / 2.2 / 3.6	(37) .9 / 2.1 / 3.1	(40) 1.1 / 1.8 / 2.7					.8 / 1.1 / 1.8	(14)	1.7 / 1.9 / 3.5
% Officers', Directors', Owners' Comp/Sales		(10) 2.0 / 3.7 / 6.1	(13) 1.3 / 3.1 / 7.8							
Net Sales ($)	1338153M	1911501M	2278787M		1426M	15695M	9349M	71919M	170542M	2009856M
Total Assets ($)	968240M	1295933M	1365267M		3189M	7234M	3436M	26833M	77415M	1247160M

M = $ thousand   MM = $ million
See Pages 1 through 15 for Explanation of Ratios and Data

Current Data Sorted By Assets | **Comparative Historical Data**

Type of Statement distribution (current data)

0-500M	500M-2MM	2-10MM	10-50MM	50-100MM	100-250MM	# Postretirement Benefits / Type of Statement	4/1/90-3/31/91 ALL	4/1/91-3/31/92 ALL
		3			1	Unqualified	11	18
	3	5	6	2		Reviewed	10	17
	2	5	1			Compiled	8	7
		2				Tax Returns		
1	2	1	2	1	1	Other	2	7
	10 (4/1-9/30/94)		24 (10/1/94-3/31/95)					
1	7	13	9	3	1	**NUMBER OF STATEMENTS**	31	49
%	%	%	%	%	%	**ASSETS**	%	%
		11.6				Cash & Equivalents	8.8	8.2
		26.7				Trade Receivables - (net)	25.2	25.2
		25.8				Inventory	32.6	28.5
		1.1				All Other Current	.6	.9
		65.2				Total Current	67.2	62.7
		29.8				Fixed Assets (net)	27.1	30.4
		.2				Intangibles (net)	.7	.8
		4.8				All Other Non-Current	5.0	6.0
		100.0				Total	100.0	100.0
						LIABILITIES		
		6.6				Notes Payable-Short Term	11.6	13.8
		2.4				Cur. Mat. -L/T/D	4.3	4.3
		11.3				Trade Payables	15.4	17.0
		1.5				Income Taxes Payable	.3	.5
		6.5				All Other Current	6.3	7.7
		28.3				Total Current	38.0	43.3
		14.2				Long Term Debt	15.3	14.2
		.2				Deferred Taxes	.9	.4
		1.3				All Other-Non-Current	1.7	.8
		56.0				Net Worth	44.1	41.3
		100.0				Total Liabilities & Net Worth	100.0	100.0
						INCOME DATA		
		100.0				Net Sales	100.0	100.0
		24.4				Gross Profit	25.0	26.2
		17.7				Operating Expenses	20.1	23.8
		6.7				Operating Profit	4.9	2.4
		.5				All Other Expenses (net)	1.0	1.2
		6.2				Profit Before Taxes	3.9	1.2
						RATIOS		
		3.9				Current	2.8	2.5
		3.2					1.8	1.5
		1.3					1.1	1.1
		2.5				Quick	1.4	1.6
		2.0					.8	.8
		.9					.5	.5
	30	12.3				Sales/Receivables	33 11.1	39 9.4
	41	9.0					47 7.8	46 7.9
	58	6.3					50 7.3	54 6.8
	31	11.8				Cost of Sales/Inventory	42 8.6	47 7.7
	58	6.3					72 5.1	69 5.3
	74	4.9					114 3.2	122 3.0
	15	24.7				Cost of Sales/Payables	23 15.7	19 19.5
	22	16.4					36 10.1	41 9.0
	30	12.1					49 7.5	54 6.7
		3.5				Sales/Working Capital	4.1	4.5
		5.8					7.8	10.4
		19.6					28.6	46.2
		55.7				EBIT/Interest	7.7	5.9
	(12)	14.6					(28) 2.6	(41) 1.5
		3.2					1.3	.1
						Net Profit + Depr., Dep., Amort./Cur. Mat. L /T/D	6.1	2.9
							(18) 2.1	(23) 1.8
							1.1	-.1
		.3				Fixed/Worth	.2	.4
		.5					.5	.7
		1.2					1.2	1.3
		.3				Debt/Worth	.7	.7
		.6					1.1	1.4
		2.2					2.7	2.8
		35.5				% Profit Before Taxes/Tangible Net Worth	31.5	18.0
		21.9					18.0 (45)	9.5
		8.2					4.9	.0
		24.8				% Profit Before Taxes/Total Assets	15.6	9.6
		6.5					7.0	2.9
		2.6					2.4	-2.0
		15.4				Sales/Net Fixed Assets	15.2	13.4
		8.9					7.9	7.4
		3.7					5.4	3.2
		3.2				Sales/Total Assets	2.6	2.3
		2.5					2.1	2.0
		1.4					1.6	1.4
		1.3				% Depr., Dep., Amort./Sales	1.1	1.3
		2.0					(28) 1.9	(44) 2.6
		4.7					2.9	4.3
						% Officers', Directors', Owners' Comp/Sales	4.0	4.6
							(10) 5.6	(16) 6.6
							9.3	9.3
59M	21256M	148463M	418392M	421790M	145389M	Net Sales ($)	812042M	1247887M
23M	8133M	71206M	201217M	239836M	102719M	Total Assets ($)	480724M	919939M

M = $ thousand   MM = $ million
See Pages 1 through 15 for Explanation of Ratios and Data

Comparative Historical Data | Current Data Sorted By Sales

Type of Statement

4/1/92-3/31/93	4/1/93-3/31/94	4/1/94-3/31/95	Item	0-1MM	1-3MM	3-5MM	5-10MM	10-25MM	25MM & OVER
1	1	4	# Postretirement Benefits				1	2	1
9	18	13	Unqualified			1	2	3	7
11	7	9	Reviewed		2		3	2	2
9	5	4	Compiled			2	2		
			Tax Returns						
4	3	8	Other	1	2			1	4

Date ranges: 4/1/92-3/31/93 (ALL); 4/1/93-3/31/94 (ALL); 4/1/94-3/31/95 (ALL)
Current data groups: 10 (4/1-9/30/94) covering 0-1MM, 1-3MM, 3-5MM; 24 (10/1/94-3/31/95) covering 5-10MM, 10-25MM, 25MM & OVER

4/1/92-3/31/93 ALL	4/1/93-3/31/94 ALL	4/1/94-3/31/95 ALL	Item	0-1MM	1-3MM	3-5MM	5-10MM	10-25MM	25MM & OVER
33	33	34	**NUMBER OF STATEMENTS**	1	4	3	7	6	13
%	%	%	**ASSETS**	%	%	%	%	%	%
4.4	5.7	6.3	Cash & Equivalents						2.1
30.0	27.8	27.0	Trade Receivables - (net)						27.8
28.9	25.9	25.7	Inventory						31.6
.7	.8	1.4	All Other Current						1.1
64.0	60.3	60.4	Total Current						62.6
28.6	32.1	32.7	Fixed Assets (net)						30.5
2.3	1.4	1.1	Intangibles (net)						2.0
5.1	6.3	5.8	All Other Non-Current						4.9
100.0	100.0	100.0	Total						100.0
			LIABILITIES						
10.8	7.6	5.9	Notes Payable-Short Term						8.4
2.7	3.5	5.7	Cur. Mat.-L/T/D						7.4
19.1	13.3	13.8	Trade Payables						12.2
.1	2.6	.6	Income Taxes Payable						.1
6.7	8.3	6.6	All Other Current						7.7
39.5	35.2	32.7	Total Current						35.8
22.9	15.7	20.8	Long Term Debt						24.7
.4	1.0	.4	Deferred Taxes						.6
1.8	2.8	3.2	All Other-Non-Current						7.1
35.4	45.3	42.9	Net Worth						31.8
100.0	100.0	100.0	Total Liabilities & Net Worth						100.0
			INCOME DATA						
100.0	100.0	100.0	Net Sales						100.0
23.6	26.2	23.0	Gross Profit						19.4
22.0	18.8	16.1	Operating Expenses						12.6
1.6	7.4	6.9	Operating Profit						6.9
1.4	1.0	1.6	All Other Expenses (net)						2.6
.2	6.4	5.3	Profit Before Taxes						4.3
			RATIOS						
2.9 1.6 1.2	3.7 1.8 1.3	3.3 2.1 1.2	Current						2.8 2.4 1.3
1.3 .9 .5	2.0 1.0 .6	2.0 1.2 .7	Quick						1.4 1.2 .7
41 9.0 51 7.1 59 6.2	40 9.1 46 7.9 54 6.7	35 10.4 44 8.3 61 6.0	Sales/Receivables						36 10.2 45 8.1 61 6.0
23 15.6 59 6.2 89 4.1	31 11.7 46 7.9 81 4.5	28 13.1 58 6.3 91 4.0	Cost of Sales/Inventory						38 9.6 65 5.6 104 3.5
22 16.5 33 11.1 49 7.4	14 25.6 28 13.0 41 9.0	17 21.4 26 14.1 44 8.3	Cost of Sales/Payables						17 21.4 29 12.7 32 11.4
4.4 11.6 22.5	5.4 8.2 22.7	4.6 6.9 23.9	Sales/Working Capital						4.6 6.7 17.2
(30) 3.8 1.5 -.0	(30) 20.9 4.8 1.3	(32) 17.2 4.2 2.3	EBIT/Interest						6.7 4.1 2.2
(14) 4.9 2.4 .6	(12) 4.8 1.7 .3	(19) 6.2 1.8 1.2	Net Profit + Depr., Dep., Amort./Cur. Mat. L/T/D						
.3 .7 1.7	.3 .7 2.1	.4 .7 1.9	Fixed/Worth						.5 1.1 2.4
.8 2.0 7.3	.3 1.3 3.2	.6 1.4 2.7	Debt/Worth						.7 2.2 5.3
(28) 25.2 6.8 -7.5	(29) 43.4 23.9 5.0	(33) 39.1 21.4 9.5	% Profit Before Taxes/Tangible Net Worth						(12) 51.5 27.4 16.3
7.9 2.0 -3.0	18.6 8.3 .6	15.8 7.0 3.1	% Profit Before Taxes/Total Assets						15.2 9.3 3.9
18.5 8.2 4.5	12.4 6.8 4.3	12.5 6.8 3.8	Sales/Net Fixed Assets						8.5 6.8 5.6
2.9 2.0 1.5	2.5 2.0 1.8	2.9 2.1 1.6	Sales/Total Assets						2.5 2.1 1.9
(31) 1.5 1.9 4.4	(29) 1.5 2.3 3.5	(31) 1.5 2.1 3.2	% Depr., Dep., Amort./Sales						(11) 1.8 2.1 2.2
(13) 1.9 5.8 8.2	(10) 4.5 7.0 11.2	(10) 2.3 4.5 7.0	% Officers', Directors', Owners' Comp/Sales						
555907M	1229184M	1155349M	Net Sales ($)	59M	7079M	12441M	55133M	85160M	995477M
329096M	605554M	623134M	Total Assets ($)	23M	4456M	7683M	28158M	56715M	526099M

M = $ thousand   MM = $ million
See Pages 1 through 15 for Explanation of Ratios and Data

MANUFACTURERS—ARCHITECTURAL & ORNAMENTAL METAL WORK. SIC# 3446

Current Data Sorted By Assets							# Postretirement Benefits Type of Statement	Comparative Historical Data	
		1							
1	2	6	3	2			Unqualified	10	14
1	10	8					Reviewed	29	23
2	5	1					Compiled	20	13
2	1						Tax Returns		
1	2	1	2				Other	10	5
0-500M	13 (4/1-9/30/94) 500M-2MM	2-10MM	36 (10/1/94-3/31/95) 10-50MM	50-100MM	100-250MM			4/1/90-3/31/91 ALL	4/1/91-3/31/92 ALL
6	20	16	5	2			**NUMBER OF STATEMENTS**	69	55
%	%	%	%	%	%		**ASSETS**	%	%
	5.9	6.8					Cash & Equivalents	6.6	8.8
	39.3	35.8					Trade Receivables - (net)	35.0	36.3
	14.4	29.1					Inventory	22.8	19.5
	11.2	4.9					All Other Current	4.0	4.5
	70.8	76.7					Total Current	68.3	69.1
	22.2	16.3					Fixed Assets (net)	22.8	22.0
	.1	1.6					Intangibles (net)	1.5	1.3
	6.9	5.5					All Other Non-Current	7.4	7.6
	100.0	100.0					Total	100.0	100.0
							LIABILITIES		
	9.2	10.8					Notes Payable-Short Term	7.7	8.7
	3.5	2.4					Cur. Mat. -L/T/D	3.3	3.0
	19.2	19.3					Trade Payables	17.0	17.7
	.2	.7					Income Taxes Payable	1.7	.5
	17.5	15.1					All Other Current	9.1	9.2
	49.6	48.2					Total Current	38.7	39.1
	15.7	10.6					Long Term Debt	13.9	13.2
	1.1	.6					Deferred Taxes	.4	.7
	.5	.4					All Other-Non-Current	3.9	.8
	33.1	40.1					Net Worth	43.1	46.1
	100.0	100.0					Total Liabilities & Net Worth	100.0	100.0
							INCOME DATA		
	100.0	100.0					Net Sales	100.0	100.0
	26.3	29.3					Gross Profit	29.0	27.2
	23.0	24.5					Operating Expenses	25.9	26.2
	3.3	4.8					Operating Profit	3.0	1.0
	.4	.9					All Other Expenses (net)	.6	.3
	2.9	3.9					Profit Before Taxes	2.4	.7
							RATIOS		
	2.1	2.6						2.7	2.5
	1.7	1.5					Current	1.7	1.8
	1.0	1.2						1.3	1.4
	1.4	1.3						1.5	1.5
	.9	.9					Quick	1.1	1.1
	.7	.6						.7	.9
	36 10.1	46 7.9						34 10.6	42 8.7
	65 5.6	57 6.4					Sales/Receivables	48 7.6	52 7.0
	85 4.3	94 3.9						73 5.0	76 4.8
	7 50.3	17 20.9						15 23.9	15 24.7
	19 19.1	78 4.7					Cost of Sales/Inventory	46 8.0	35 10.4
	45 8.2	111 3.3						83 4.4	64 5.7
	19 19.6	40 9.2						19 18.8	24 15.2
	40 9.2	49 7.5					Cost of Sales/Payables	31 11.6	31 11.7
	63 5.8	72 5.1						51 7.1	44 8.3
	5.9	5.0						5.5	5.4
	12.4	9.3					Sales/Working Capital	8.4	8.7
	NM	16.1						18.9	15.7
	11.7	8.8						8.9	6.1
	(17) 3.3	2.9					EBIT/Interest	(61) 3.0	(50) 2.2
	1.5	1.9						1.1	-.9
	3.2							6.2	3.9
	(10) 2.3						Net Profit + Depr., Dep., Amort./Cur. Mat. L./T/D	(34) 2.4	(26) 2.5
	1.0							.8	.4
	.2	.2						.2	.2
	.5	.4					Fixed/Worth	.5	.4
	2.2	.7						1.1	.9
	.9	1.1						.6	.6
	2.2	2.0					Debt/Worth	1.6	1.3
	4.1	3.1						2.5	2.1
	50.2	34.8						38.1	23.3
	(19) 26.0	22.5					% Profit Before Taxes/Tangible Net Worth	(65) 15.2	(52) 12.1
	9.1	5.8						1.1	-7.6
	17.3	14.4						15.9	9.5
	7.1	8.1					% Profit Before Taxes/Total Assets	4.8	4.8
	1.5	1.0						.0	-4.7
	35.0	34.4						31.5	23.6
	12.3	19.9					Sales/Net Fixed Assets	11.6	12.7
	6.0	8.2						6.1	6.1
	2.7	2.4						3.1	2.8
	2.4	1.9					Sales/Total Assets	2.3	2.4
	1.4	1.5						1.9	1.8
	.8	.8						.9	.7
	(19) 1.7	1.2					% Depr., Dep., Amort./Sales	(62) 1.3	(50) 1.7
	3.0	2.1						2.2	2.4
	2.8							4.1	2.3
	(10) 4.6						% Officers', Directors', Owners' Comp/Sales	(29) 5.0	(27) 4.0
	7.7							8.0	7.9
6958M	47177M	135266M	166170M	342061M			Net Sales ($)	632592M	369667M
2411M	20452M	68460M	107773M	129693M			Total Assets ($)	299108M	162433M

M = $ thousand   MM = $ million
See Pages 1 through 15 for Explanation of Ratios and Data

Comparative Historical Data

Current Data Sorted By Sales

				# Postretirement Benefits						
				Type of Statement		1				
	12	7	14	Unqualified	1	1	2		5	5
	19	15	20	Reviewed	3	5	4	8		
	13	7	8	Compiled	1	5	1	1		
	1	3	1	Tax Returns		1				
	8	11	6	Other	1	2		1	1	1
	4/1/92-3/31/93 ALL	4/1/93-3/31/94 ALL	4/1/94-3/31/95 ALL		0-1MM 13 (4/1-9/30/94)	1-3MM	3-5MM	5-10MM 36 (10/1/94-3/31/95)	10-25MM	25MM & OVER
	53	43	49	**NUMBER OF STATEMENTS**	6	14	7	10	6	6
	%	%	%	**ASSETS**	%	%	%	%	%	%
	8.3	8.0	6.1	Cash & Equivalents		6.5		5.9		
	36.4	35.6	35.6	Trade Receivables - (net)		39.7		36.0		
	19.0	20.8	21.6	Inventory		19.5		32.5		
	3.5	2.9	6.5	All Other Current		4.9		3.0		
	67.2	67.2	69.8	Total Current		70.6		77.4		
	24.7	25.8	21.4	Fixed Assets (net)		21.8		16.0		
	1.1	2.4	2.3	Intangibles (net)		.0		1.8		
	7.0	4.6	6.5	All Other Non-Current		7.6		4.7		
	100.0	100.0	100.0	Total		100.0		100.0		
				LIABILITIES						
	10.9	9.9	9.7	Notes Payable-Short Term		11.5		10.3		
	3.3	2.9	3.1	Cur. Mat.-L /T/D		5.5		2.7		
	15.4	14.6	17.9	Trade Payables		17.7		21.0		
	.4	2.5	.4	Income Taxes Payable		.2		1.0		
	8.2	10.2	13.9	All Other Current		18.0		16.2		
	38.1	40.1	45.0	Total Current		53.0		51.3		
	13.8	14.6	14.4	Long Term Debt		12.6		8.1		
	.3	.2	1.1	Deferred Taxes		.8		.8		
	2.9	5.6	3.0	All Other-Non-Current		5.9		.7		
	44.9	39.4	36.5	Net Worth		27.7		39.1		
	100.0	100.0	100.0	Total Liabilities & Net Worth		100.0		100.0		
				INCOME DATA						
	100.0	100.0	100.0	Net Sales		100.0		100.0		
	31.1	32.0	29.9	Gross Profit		32.4		33.2		
	27.9	29.0	25.8	Operating Expenses		30.1		26.5		
	3.2	3.0	4.1	Operating Profit		2.4		6.7		
	1.7	1.0	.8	All Other Expenses (net)		.7		.7		
	1.5	2.0	3.3	Profit Before Taxes		1.7		6.0		
				RATIOS						
	2.7	2.4	2.4			2.6		2.6		
	1.8	1.8	1.7	Current		1.5		1.3		
	1.3	1.3	1.1			.9		1.1		
	2.0	1.7	1.4			1.4		1.2		
	1.1	1.2	1.1	Quick		.9		.7		
	.8	.8	.7			.6		.5		
39	9.3	45 8.1	45 8.1		47 7.8			45 8.1		
54	6.7	56 6.5	57 6.4	Sales/Receivables	69 5.3			53 6.9		
68	5.4	72 5.1	78 4.7		89 4.1			78 4.7		
17	21.0	19 18.9	13 28.6		15 23.7			21 17.3		
39	9.3	48 7.6	42 8.6	Cost of Sales/Inventory	34 10.7			87 4.2		
74	4.9	81 4.5	91 4.0		79 4.6			126 2.9		
18	20.3	18 20.8	22 16.9		20 18.1			33 11.0		
32	11.4	30 12.0	45 8.2	Cost of Sales/Payables	38 9.5			51 7.1		
44	8.3	49 7.5	59 6.2		68 5.4			74 4.9		
	5.4	5.0	5.2			5.4		6.0		
	8.9	9.5	11.2	Sales/Working Capital		15.9		14.7		
	19.8	19.4	20.3			−22.7		23.3		
(48)	7.0 1.9 .7	(42) 6.5 3.3 1.3	(46) 9.5 3.2 1.7	EBIT/Interest	(13)	11.7 3.3 .9		14.7 7.8 2.8		
(24)	4.6 2.3 .9	(23) 4.8 1.7 1.0	(22) 7.9 2.7 2.0	Net Profit + Depr., Dep., Amort./Cur. Mat. L/T/D						
	.2	.3	.2			.4		.1		
	.4	.6	.5	Fixed/Worth		.6		.3		
	.8	1.7	1.6			3.9		.5		
	.7	.8	.9			.9		1.0		
	1.0	1.3	1.7	Debt/Worth		3.5		2.8		
	2.3	3.9	4.1			29.7		3.0		
(48)	27.7 5.6 −1.3	(40) 26.9 9.8 2.9	(46) 47.1 22.8 7.0	% Profit Before Taxes/Tangible Net Worth	(12)	67.9 26.9 3.3		51.5 31.6 20.2		
	10.7	10.3	15.8			17.7		20.0		
	2.7	4.5	7.5	% Profit Before Taxes/Total Assets		9.4		12.8		
	−.7	1.2	1.5			−.8		7.7		
	25.4	19.1	26.3			19.6		55.6		
	12.3	10.5	12.0	Sales/Net Fixed Assets		11.7		24.7		
	6.5	5.4	7.4			9.2		10.5		
	2.9	2.8	2.6			2.9		2.8		
	2.4	2.3	2.3	Sales/Total Assets		2.5		2.4		
	1.8	1.8	1.5			1.7		1.6		
(49)	.8 1.5 2.5	(41) 1.4 1.9 3.0	(47) .8 1.5 2.8	% Depr., Dep., Amort./Sales		1.1 2.0 2.8		.8 1.1 2.1		
(27)	2.3 5.1 10.8	(25) 2.8 4.0 8.1	(20) 2.7 3.9 6.8	% Officers', Directors', Owners' Comp/Sales						
	516048M 211983M	372221M 212672M	697632M 328789M	Net Sales ($) Total Assets ($)	4677M 3707M	23814M 10767M	28207M 12043M	66810M 32507M	86925M 46847M	487199M 222918M

M = $ thousand   MM = $ million
See Pages 1 through 15 for Explanation of Ratios and Data

Current Data Sorted By Assets						# Postretirement Benefits	Comparative Historical Data	
3	5	6	2			**Type of Statement**		
1	9	19	16	1	2	Unqualified	39	43
7	34	27	1			Reviewed	64	61
18	42	12				Compiled	66	67
4						Tax Returns		2
11	24	30	8	1	1	Other	42	44
0-500M	500M-2MM 82 (4/1-9/30/94)	2-10MM	10-50MM 187 (10/1/94-3/31/95)	50-100MM	100-250MM		4/1/90-3/31/91 ALL	4/1/91-3/31/92 ALL
41	109	88	26	2	3	**NUMBER OF STATEMENTS**	211	217
%	%	%	%	%	%	**ASSETS**	%	%
8.1	9.3	6.9	4.5			Cash & Equivalents	7.6	8.5
34.3	32.3	26.5	25.5			Trade Receivables - (net)	28.7	27.1
9.8	8.7	11.6	16.1			Inventory	10.4	10.2
3.8	1.0	2.2	.5			All Other Current	1.5	2.0
56.0	51.3	47.3	46.7			Total Current	48.2	47.7
36.9	40.1	43.3	43.6			Fixed Assets (net)	41.7	43.3
2.4	1.9	2.2	2.9			Intangibles (net)	1.7	2.0
4.7	6.7	7.1	6.9			All Other Non-Current	8.4	7.0
100.0	100.0	100.0	100.0			Total	100.0	100.0
						LIABILITIES		
9.2	6.9	6.8	5.8			Notes Payable-Short Term	9.6	9.1
5.9	5.1	4.4	3.4			Cur. Mat.-L/T/D	5.0	4.8
12.1	11.2	12.8	16.4			Trade Payables	12.2	10.7
1.2	.6	.3	.7			Income Taxes Payable	.4	.6
8.7	8.7	7.7	7.7			All Other Current	7.9	8.4
37.1	32.6	31.9	34.1			Total Current	35.1	33.7
15.8	19.2	20.2	18.8			Long Term Debt	18.8	20.1
.5	.5	.9	1.4			Deferred Taxes	.9	.8
8.3	3.7	3.8	3.2			All Other-Non-Current	3.3	4.3
38.3	43.9	43.3	42.5			Net Worth	42.0	41.0
100.0	100.0	100.0	100.0			Total Liabilities & Net Worth	100.0	100.0
						INCOME DATA		
100.0	100.0	100.0	100.0			Net Sales	100.0	100.0
49.1	35.8	32.3	26.8			Gross Profit	32.7	34.9
43.0	28.8	24.5	17.6			Operating Expenses	27.5	29.5
6.1	7.1	7.8	9.2			Operating Profit	5.1	5.3
1.5	1.3	1.3	2.6			All Other Expenses (net)	1.5	1.7
4.6	5.8	6.5	6.6			Profit Before Taxes	3.6	3.6
						RATIOS		
2.5	2.4	2.2	2.1			Current	2.5	2.4
1.8	1.6	1.5	1.4				1.4	1.5
1.1	1.1	1.0	1.0				.9	1.0
1.8	2.0	1.6	1.2			Quick	2.0	1.8
1.4	1.3	1.1	.8				1.1	1.0
.9	.8	.7	.7				.6	.7
36 10.1	39 9.4	40 9.1	43 8.4			Sales/Receivables	38 9.5	38 9.6
45 8.1	49 7.5	50 7.3	49 7.5				47 7.8	49 7.5
58 6.3	57 6.4	62 5.9	59 6.2				59 6.2	58 6.3
1 393.5	7 55.7	7 54.4	17 21.5			Cost of Sales/Inventory	8 45.2	8 47.5
20 18.3	13 27.3	21 17.7	32 11.3				18 20.7	18 20.0
38 9.7	26 14.0	51 7.2	69 5.3				33 10.9	42 8.7
13 29.2	14 27.0	18 20.3	30 12.3			Cost of Sales/Payables	15 24.1	14 26.0
26 13.9	22 16.3	30 12.3	36 10.1				26 13.9	26 14.1
55 6.6	37 9.8	47 7.8	46 7.9				39 9.4	42 8.7
6.4	7.4	7.3	6.0			Sales/Working Capital	7.2	6.9
11.4	14.0	14.5	13.3				15.4	14.3
150.8	77.5	134.1	−169.9				−81.7	−183.8
10.4	12.3	9.4	22.9			EBIT/Interest	7.1	6.1
(35) 5.0	(97) 4.1	(79) 3.8	(23) 5.7				(197) 2.3	(207) 2.4
1.1	2.1	1.9	2.4				1.2	.9
7.8	4.8	4.5	6.0			Net Profit + Depr., Dep.,	5.1	3.8
(13) 3.4	(52) 2.8	(33) 2.6	(17) 2.7			Amort./Cur. Mat. L /T/D	(112) 2.4	(110) 1.8
.9	1.4	1.5	1.8				1.0	.9
.5	.5	.5	.7			Fixed/Worth	.5	.5
1.0	1.0	1.0	1.1				1.0	1.1
3.7	1.8	2.4	2.0				2.0	2.4
.6	.6	.6	.6			Debt/Worth	.6	.7
1.6	1.3	1.6	1.8				1.3	1.6
7.2	3.7	3.8	3.4				3.3	3.3
59.6	52.5	44.4	49.7			% Profit Before Taxes/Tangible	36.4	31.7
(33) 35.9	(101) 24.4	(84) 22.4	(23) 18.8			Net Worth	(195) 14.2	(198) 16.4
8.1	7.7	9.7	12.1				3.7	−.2
23.9	18.6	16.3	16.1			% Profit Before Taxes/Total	14.3	13.0
10.5	7.9	8.9	9.8			Assets	5.0	5.7
.5	3.6	3.8	4.3				.9	−.4
14.4	9.7	7.3	6.4			Sales/Net Fixed Assets	11.4	9.4
8.5	6.6	4.6	3.6				5.4	4.4
4.3	3.6	2.6	3.0				2.9	2.8
3.2	3.0	2.4	2.2			Sales/Total Assets	2.9	2.6
2.7	2.4	1.8	1.6				2.1	2.0
2.0	1.7	1.4	1.2				1.5	1.5
1.8	2.0	2.2	2.2			% Depr., Dep., Amort./Sales	1.9	2.5
(39) 3.3	(104) 3.2	(81) 3.8	(25) 3.9				(200) 3.2	(206) 3.7
4.9	4.8	5.3	5.3				5.4	5.8
6.3	3.5	2.8				% Officers', Directors',	3.5	3.9
(22) 11.4	(61) 5.3	(39) 4.2				Owners' Comp/Sales	(100) 5.5	(111) 6.6
17.0	9.4	7.5					10.1	10.9
31642M	273216M	750895M	1145322M	315721M	734979M	Net Sales ($)	1327252M	1337751M
12380M	117782M	403042M	505286M	146149M	365007M	Total Assets ($)	754006M	763519M

M = $ thousand   MM = $ million
See Pages 1 through 15 for Explanation of Ratios and Data

Comparative Historical Data				Current Data Sorted By Sales					
6	8	16	# Postretirement Benefits	3	3	4	3	1	2
			Type of Statement						
41	37	48	Unqualified	1	7	5	8	14	13
79	62	69	Reviewed	8	19	21	9	11	1
69	73	73	Compiled	16	33	12	8	4	
2	5	4	Tax Returns	4					
49	47	75	Other	9	22	14	12	11	7
4/1/92-3/31/93	4/1/93-3/31/94	4/1/94-3/31/95		82 (4/1-9/30/94)			187 (10/1/94-3/31/95)		
ALL	ALL	ALL		0-1MM	1-3MM	3-5MM	5-10MM	10-25MM	25MM & OVER
240	224	269	**NUMBER OF STATEMENTS**	38	81	52	37	40	21
%	%	%	**ASSETS**	%	%	%	%	%	%
7.9	8.0	7.8	Cash & Equivalents	10.3	8.5	6.1	11.8	5.3	2.6
28.3	28.7	30.0	Trade Receivables - (net)	30.1	32.1	30.8	26.7	27.9	29.2
9.6	10.3	10.5	Inventory	7.7	8.6	10.6	8.0	16.8	15.2
1.3	1.5	1.8	All Other Current	2.5	2.0	1.8	1.7	1.5	.6
47.1	48.4	50.1	Total Current	50.6	51.2	49.3	48.1	51.5	47.7
43.3	41.8	41.2	Fixed Assets (net)	40.6	40.4	41.5	43.9	39.1	43.8
1.7	2.3	2.2	Intangibles (net)	2.8	2.1	1.6	1.0	3.5	2.5
7.9	7.5	6.5	All Other Non-Current	6.1	6.3	7.7	6.9	5.9	6.0
100.0	100.0	100.0	Total	100.0	100.0	100.0	100.0	100.0	100.0
			LIABILITIES						
8.7	7.9	7.0	Notes Payable-Short Term	9.2	7.3	7.1	4.8	7.0	5.5
4.7	4.8	4.9	Cur. Mat.-L/T/D	6.0	5.2	4.5	3.9	4.6	5.1
11.8	11.5	12.3	Trade Payables	9.5	11.7	11.4	11.2	15.3	18.4
.6	1.5	.6	Income Taxes Payable	.9	.5	.8	.2	.7	.2
8.9	8.3	8.3	All Other Current	10.8	7.5	7.4	10.3	6.3	9.6
34.6	34.0	33.2	Total Current	36.5	32.3	31.2	30.4	33.9	38.8
20.4	17.7	19.1	Long Term Debt	19.1	19.6	16.3	20.6	19.8	20.4
.8	.7	.7	Deferred Taxes	.6	.5	.9	.8	.9	1.0
4.7	5.4	4.3	All Other-Non-Current	6.6	4.9	1.8	3.1	6.4	2.3
39.6	42.2	42.6	Net Worth	37.2	42.6	49.8	45.1	39.0	37.5
100.0	100.0	100.0	Total Liabilities & Net Worth	100.0	100.0	100.0	100.0	100.0	100.0
			INCOME DATA						
100.0	100.0	100.0	Net Sales	100.0	100.0	100.0	100.0	100.0	100.0
36.3	35.2	35.8	Gross Profit	48.0	38.5	34.5	32.3	30.1	24.3
31.0	29.2	28.4	Operating Expenses	42.0	31.3	28.0	23.1	21.6	15.8
5.3	5.9	7.4	Operating Profit	6.0	7.2	6.5	9.2	8.5	8.4
1.3	1.3	1.5	All Other Expenses (net)	1.7	1.3	1.0	1.9	1.7	1.9
4.0	4.7	6.0	Profit Before Taxes	4.4	5.9	5.5	7.3	6.7	6.5
			RATIOS						
2.2	2.3	2.2	Current	2.7	2.4	2.1	2.7	2.1	1.9
1.4	1.5	1.5		1.6	1.6	1.5	1.5	1.5	1.3
1.0	1.0	1.0		1.0	1.1	1.0	1.2	1.1	.9
1.8	1.7	1.7	Quick	1.9	1.9	1.9	2.1	1.4	1.2
1.0	1.1	1.2		1.3	1.3	1.1	1.4	1.0	.8
.7	.7	.8		.7	.8	.8	.8	.7	.7
37 9.8	38 9.7	40 9.2	Sales/Receivables	37 9.9	39 9.4	40 9.2	39 9.4	41 8.8	42 8.6
47 7.8	47 7.8	48 7.6		45 8.2	51 7.2	52 7.0	46 8.0	46 8.0	48 7.6
56 6.5	57 6.4	60 6.1		57 6.4	66 5.5	62 5.9	58 6.3	55 6.6	60 6.1
7 51.5	7 49.1	7 52.9	Cost of Sales/Inventory	0 UND	5 70.5	9 39.4	6 57.0	13 27.5	16 22.4
18 20.1	19 19.2	17 20.9		18 20.7	14 26.1	19 19.6	13 28.4	35 10.4	25 14.6
39 9.3	36 10.2	40 9.2		37 9.8	29 12.6	35 10.4	34 10.7	61 6.0	56 6.5
14 26.5	14 25.7	16 23.0	Cost of Sales/Payables	10 37.9	15 24.9	15 24.4	15 24.8	19 18.9	25 14.5
26 14.1	24 15.2	27 13.7		26 14.1	25 14.4	25 14.4	23 15.8	33 11.1	33 10.9
46 8.0	40 9.2	42 8.7		54 6.8	43 8.4	38 9.7	39 9.3	54 6.8	42 8.7
7.8	7.5	7.2	Sales/Working Capital	6.5	6.5	7.4	7.6	7.6	7.5
17.1	15.1	13.3		11.8	13.5	14.8	12.1	12.4	22.9
-486.8	511.4	100.9		NM	58.4	243.5	40.4	36.4	-98.4
6.7	9.8	12.0	EBIT/Interest	11.5	12.3	8.0	22.1	17.1	15.7
(223) 2.9	(204) 3.7	(238) 4.6		(32) 4.6	(73) 4.7	(45) 3.1	(33) 3.7	(37) 5.9	(18) 4.7
.9	1.6	2.0		1.5	1.9	2.0	1.8	2.8	2.3
4.9	4.9	5.0	Net Profit + Depr., Dep.,	4.3	8.8	3.8	11.0	5.4	5.7
(101) 2.3	(100) 2.5	(119) 2.8	Amort./Cur. Mat. L/T/D	(14) 2.7	(43) 3.0	(19) 2.6	(12) 4.0	(18) 2.5	(13) 2.5
1.0	1.1	1.5		.9	1.8	1.4	1.5	1.2	1.8
.6	.6	.5	Fixed/Worth	.5	.5	.5	.5	.5	.8
1.2	1.0	1.0		1.1	1.0	1.0	.8	1.0	1.1
2.4	2.1	2.1		5.2	2.1	1.7	3.3	2.0	2.1
.7	.7	.6	Debt/Worth	.7	.6	.6	.4	.6	.7
1.7	1.5	1.5		2.1	1.4	1.2	1.5	1.7	1.8
3.3	3.4	3.8		7.4	3.9	2.2	4.5	5.3	3.5
41.6	48.2	49.5	% Profit Before Taxes/Tangible Net Worth	59.2	52.5	36.7	45.6	52.1	40.5
(217) 15.5	(208) 22.5	(245) 24.4		(31) 36.2	(73) 19.6	19.9	(36) 24.7	(35) 38.8	(18) 22.4
2.0	6.6	9.3		7.7	7.7	5.5	13.2	12.1	14.2
15.0	17.3	17.9	% Profit Before Taxes/Total Assets	21.3	19.8	15.1	24.0	17.0	21.5
6.3	7.3	8.7		7.8	7.9	7.6	9.4	10.2	11.7
.1	1.9	3.7		2.5	3.0	3.0	5.0	5.6	4.5
9.5	8.9	9.3	Sales/Net Fixed Assets	12.8	9.7	9.0	8.8	8.9	8.2
4.7	5.1	5.2		5.7	6.4	5.3	4.0	5.1	4.0
3.1	3.3	3.1		2.4	3.2	3.3	2.7	3.2	3.0
2.7	2.8	2.9	Sales/Total Assets	3.0	2.9	2.8	2.7	3.0	3.0
2.1	2.1	2.1		2.3	2.3	2.1	1.9	2.0	1.8
1.5	1.6	1.6		1.3	1.6	1.7	1.5	1.4	1.6
2.4	2.4	2.0	% Depr., Dep., Amort./Sales	1.9	2.2	2.0	2.4	1.9	1.7
(227) 3.8	(212) 3.7	(253) 3.4		(37) 3.6	(77) 3.6	(48) 3.3	(34) 3.4	(38) 3.2	(19) 2.7
5.4	5.2	5.0		5.2	5.4	5.0	5.1	5.0	4.2
3.7	3.8	3.2	% Officers', Directors', Owners' Comp/Sales	6.1	4.6	3.5	2.8		
(119) 6.4	(108) 6.5	(127) 5.4		(20) 11.1	(48) 6.2	(28) 4.3	(18) 4.3		
9.7	12.1	10.8		16.0	12.9	8.1	7.5		
1391769M	1553283M	3251775M	Net Sales ($)	25227M	153918M	197189M	276079M	564613M	2034749M
730639M	837748M	1549646M	Total Assets ($)	12926M	82982M	106245M	154721M	329655M	863117M

M = $ thousand   MM = $ million
See Pages 1 through 15 for Explanation of Ratios and Data

MANUFACTURERS—CUTLERY, HANDTOOLS & GENERAL HARDWARE. SIC# 3421 (23,25,29)

Current Data Sorted By Assets | Comparative Historical Data

						# Postretirement Benefits / Type of Statement		
1	4	3		1	1			
1	4	20	15	9	2	Unqualified	44	51
	13	21				Reviewed	31	40
7	16	3				Compiled	31	28
2		1				Tax Returns		
6	11	10	6	2		Other	33	32
	51 (4/1-9/30/94)		98 (10/1/94-3/31/95)				4/1/90-3/31/91	4/1/91-3/31/92
0-500M	500M-2MM	2-10MM	10-50MM	50-100MM	100-250MM		ALL	ALL
16	44	55	21	11	2	NUMBER OF STATEMENTS	139	151
%	%	%	%	%	%	**ASSETS**	%	%
6.7	6.7	4.2	7.0	2.8		Cash & Equivalents	6.3	5.7
37.1	31.2	28.8	22.9	23.8		Trade Receivables - (net)	23.8	24.9
22.6	31.8	32.8	28.0	27.7		Inventory	31.3	32.7
.4	.8	1.1	2.9	1.7		All Other Current	1.3	1.1
66.8	70.5	66.8	60.7	56.1		Total Current	62.7	64.5
24.7	24.8	24.3	27.2	27.0		Fixed Assets (net)	28.1	27.1
1.0	1.1	2.1	2.7	10.7		Intangibles (net)	1.7	1.6
7.6	3.6	6.7	9.4	6.2		All Other Non-Current	7.5	6.8
100.0	100.0	100.0	100.0	100.0		Total	100.0	100.0
						LIABILITIES		
15.8	10.9	13.4	7.5	2.6		Notes Payable-Short Term	7.4	9.5
5.0	3.8	4.1	1.3	2.3		Cur. Mat. -L/T/D	4.3	3.7
14.2	15.2	15.0	11.9	8.8		Trade Payables	12.5	13.5
.0	.5	1.5	.5	1.0		Income Taxes Payable	.7	.5
7.4	9.0	8.7	10.5	10.2		All Other Current	8.2	7.1
42.4	39.4	42.7	31.6	25.0		Total Current	33.2	34.2
19.8	18.5	12.4	10.4	26.0		Long Term Debt	16.4	16.7
.0	.1	.6	1.2	1.9		Deferred Taxes	.8	.8
3.6	5.8	1.8	7.3	12.2		All Other-Non-Current	4.1	3.8
34.1	36.3	42.5	49.5	34.9		Net Worth	45.5	44.5
100.0	100.0	100.0	100.0	100.0		Total Liabilities & Net Worth	100.0	100.0
						INCOME DATA		
100.0	100.0	100.0	100.0	100.0		Net Sales	100.0	100.0
40.0	33.6	31.8	34.6	35.9		Gross Profit	33.4	32.0
34.3	28.6	26.2	28.8	26.4		Operating Expenses	28.0	27.8
5.7	5.0	5.6	5.8	9.5		Operating Profit	5.4	4.2
.6	1.0	1.2	1.6	2.2		All Other Expenses (net)	1.3	1.5
5.1	4.1	4.4	4.3	7.3		Profit Before Taxes	4.1	2.7
						RATIOS		
3.0	3.1	2.0	3.2	3.3		Current	3.5	3.4
1.7	1.8	1.6	2.4	2.0			2.1	1.9
1.3	1.3	1.2	1.3	1.6			1.4	1.3
1.7	1.7	1.2	1.7	1.5		Quick	1.6	1.5
1.3	1.0	.8	1.0	1.3			1.1	.9
.8	.7	.6	.6	.7			.6	.6
31 11.8	37 9.8	42 8.6	45 8.2	51 7.1		Sales/Receivables	33 11.0	36 10.1
49 7.5	47 7.8	51 7.2	47 7.8	54 6.7			43 8.5	45 8.2
61 6.0	57 6.4	61 6.0	53 6.9	65 5.6			54 6.8	56 6.5
20 18.4	34 10.6	56 6.5	62 5.9	99 3.7		Cost of Sales/Inventory	51 7.2	55 6.6
52 7.0	81 4.5	81 4.5	91 4.0	126 2.9			85 4.3	91 4.0
81 4.5	126 2.9	130 2.8	101 3.6	159 2.3			122 3.0	140 2.6
15 24.4	16 23.4	21 17.7	18 20.5	21 17.4		Cost of Sales/Payables	16 23.5	18 20.3
23 15.6	30 12.0	34 10.6	29 12.5	27 13.5			27 13.5	30 12.0
46 7.9	43 8.4	54 6.8	54 6.7	58 6.3			43 8.5	48 7.6
4.7	4.9	5.9	3.5	3.2		Sales/Working Capital	4.1	3.7
11.9	7.5	7.8	7.3	5.0			6.4	6.1
27.9	17.5	14.9	18.5	9.2			14.4	14.1
(14) 11.4	(39) 6.4	(52) 8.9	(19) 11.2	6.3		EBIT/Interest	(126) 8.1	(138) 7.9
3.4	3.3	3.7	3.1	3.9			2.5	2.3
.5	1.5	1.8	1.9	2.2			1.2	1.1
	(23) 4.1	(26) 5.6	(13) 11.2			Net Profit + Depr., Dep., Amort./Cur. Mat. L /T/D	(83) 6.5	(82) 5.7
	2.0	2.4	4.6				2.5	2.4
	.9	1.3	3.0				.8	.7
.3	.2	.5	.3	.6		Fixed/Worth	.3	.3
.4	.6	.6	.5	.8			.5	.6
UND	1.4	.9	1.2	−14.8			1.2	1.2
1.1	.8	.7	.5	1.1		Debt/Worth	.6	.5
1.4	1.9	1.4	1.0	2.5			1.1	1.3
UND	4.0	2.8	2.8	−55.3			2.6	3.3
(13) 98.0	(40) 47.4	(52) 34.4	(20) 18.9			% Profit Before Taxes/Tangible Net Worth	(130) 28.7	(142) 25.7
23.7	18.7	19.2	15.7				15.0	13.1
7.7	7.4	5.7	9.1				4.7	2.1
19.5	17.6	13.2	10.6	15.0		% Profit Before Taxes/Total Assets	13.6	11.6
12.4	6.8	6.4	7.4	7.2			5.4	4.7
.9	1.5	2.0	3.6	5.0			.8	.4
35.4	26.6	14.1	11.2	7.4		Sales/Net Fixed Assets	15.9	17.0
25.0	13.2	9.4	6.2	5.4			7.2	7.4
3.8	5.5	5.2	4.4	3.8			4.8	4.3
3.9	2.9	2.5	2.3	1.8		Sales/Total Assets	2.6	2.4
3.0	2.1	2.0	1.8	1.5			2.0	1.8
1.8	1.8	1.6	1.4	1.1			1.5	1.5
(13) 1.0	(42) 1.1	(52) 1.2	(18) 1.8			% Depr., Dep., Amort./Sales	(126) 1.2	(131) 1.4
1.5	2.4	2.2	2.5				2.4	2.5
2.2	3.8	3.2	4.0				3.8	3.9
(10) 3.6	(26) 3.3	(18) 1.9				% Officers', Directors', Owners' Comp/Sales	(55) 3.4	(62) 2.1
8.1	4.9	4.5					5.1	4.0
14.8	7.0	6.1					7.8	8.4
12502M	123395M	540420M	761262M	1106083M	352448M	Net Sales ($)	2256521M	2652264M
4285M	52106M	267040M	436822M	760374M	317018M	Total Assets ($)	1458425M	1673948M

M = $ thousand   MM = $ million
See Pages 1 through 15 for Explanation of Ratios and Data

Comparative Historical Data				Current Data Sorted By Sales					
3	8	10	# Postretirement Benefits	1	3	2		2	2
			Type of Statement						
49	51	51	Unqualified	1	1	4	10	13	22
37	41	34	Reviewed		10	5	15	4	
27	27	26	Compiled	4	13	4	2	3	
1	4	3	Tax Returns	1	2				
24	32	35	Other	5	9	5	3	9	4
4/1/92-3/31/93	4/1/93-3/31/94	4/1/94-3/31/95		51 (4/1-9/30/94)			98 (10/1/94-3/31/95)		
ALL	ALL	ALL		0-1MM	1-3MM	3-5MM	5-10MM	10-25MM	25MM & OVER
138	155	149	**NUMBER OF STATEMENTS**	11	35	18	30	29	26
%	%	%	**ASSETS**	%	%	%	%	%	%
6.4	5.8	5.4	Cash & Equivalents	8.2	5.8	6.4	3.6	7.0	3.5
24.8	26.1	29.0	Trade Receivables - (net)	28.1	30.3	33.2	31.4	27.5	23.9
31.2	30.5	30.2	Inventory	24.2	30.9	32.4	32.2	29.7	28.4
1.6	2.1	1.2	All Other Current	.5	.8	.5	.6	1.6	3.0
64.0	64.5	65.9	Total Current	61.0	67.8	72.5	67.7	65.8	58.8
27.8	26.6	25.2	Fixed Assets (net)	27.0	27.8	20.4	23.4	25.0	26.5
1.8	2.8	2.7	Intangibles (net)	1.4	1.3	.9	2.7	2.0	7.3
6.4	6.1	6.2	All Other Non-Current	10.5	3.2	6.1	6.2	7.2	7.4
100.0	100.0	100.0	Total	100.0	100.0	100.0	100.0	100.0	100.0
			LIABILITIES						
9.7	10.1	11.1	Notes Payable-Short Term	19.4	9.7	11.7	14.0	11.8	4.9
3.4	3.9	3.5	Cur. Mat.-L /T/D	2.4	4.6	4.1	4.0	3.3	2.0
12.6	13.1	14.0	Trade Payables	13.1	12.8	18.9	16.9	11.9	11.6
.6	1.1	.9	Income Taxes Payable	.1	.3	3.1	.2	1.1	.8
8.4	9.0	9.0	All Other Current	5.4	10.5	5.5	9.3	9.9	9.5
34.7	37.3	38.5	Total Current	40.3	37.8	43.3	44.4	38.0	28.8
14.2	13.9	16.1	Long Term Debt	29.5	17.1	13.4	12.3	11.8	20.0
1.1	.9	.6	Deferred Taxes	.0	.0	.0	.8	.5	1.9
4.8	4.0	4.8	All Other-Non-Current	2.8	4.4	8.2	1.4	3.7	9.0
45.2	43.9	40.0	Net Worth	27.3	40.6	35.1	41.1	46.0	40.2
100.0	100.0	100.0	Total Liabilities & Net Worth	100.0	100.0	100.0	100.0	100.0	100.0
			INCOME DATA						
100.0	100.0	100.0	Net Sales	100.0	100.0	100.0	100.0	100.0	100.0
33.6	32.1	33.9	Gross Profit	36.7	36.0	33.0	32.4	32.4	34.0
27.9	27.5	28.1	Operating Expenses	29.4	30.8	28.7	26.7	26.9	26.3
5.6	4.5	5.8	Operating Profit	7.4	5.1	4.3	5.8	5.5	7.7
1.0	1.3	1.2	All Other Expenses (net)	2.3	.6	.7	1.5	1.1	1.7
4.7	3.3	4.6	Profit Before Taxes	5.1	4.5	3.7	4.2	4.4	6.0
			RATIOS						
3.2	2.9	2.9		4.1	3.1	2.5	2.0	3.1	3.0
1.9	1.8	1.7	Current	2.0	1.7	1.7	1.6	1.7	2.2
1.4	1.4	1.3		.9	1.3	1.3	1.2	1.3	1.6
1.6	1.5	1.4		2.1	1.7	1.5	1.1	1.3	1.4
.9	.8	.9	Quick	1.2	.9	1.0	.8	.9	1.1
.6	.5	.6		.4	.5	.8	.6	.6	.7
35 10.4	36 10.1	42 8.6		26 13.9	38 9.5	39 9.4	41 9.0	46 8.0	45 8.2
47 7.8	47 7.8	49 7.5	Sales/Receivables	49 7.5	47 7.7	47 7.7	53 6.9	50 7.3	52 7.0
55 6.6	57 6.4	59 6.2		74 4.9	53 6.9	54 6.8	64 5.7	57 6.4	62 5.9
51 7.1	43 8.4	50 7.3		22 16.5	38 9.7	35 10.4	59 6.2	49 7.4	73 5.0
87 4.2	79 4.6	81 4.5	Cost of Sales/Inventory	68 5.4	81 4.5	74 4.9	76 4.8	79 4.6	96 3.8
130 2.8	130 2.8	126 2.9		126 2.9	140 2.6	122 3.0	111 3.3	111 3.3	126 2.9
17 21.6	15 24.4	18 20.0		13 27.1	15 24.9	28 13.2	26 14.1	14 25.4	20 18.0
27 13.5	29 12.5	31 11.9	Cost of Sales/Payables	27 13.6	31 11.8	39 9.4	37 9.8	29 12.5	29 12.4
43 8.5	47 7.7	52 7.0		55 6.6	38 9.6	62 5.9	69 5.3	37 9.8	58 6.3
4.0	4.1	4.7		4.0	4.9	5.1	5.8	4.9	3.6
6.8	7.2	7.4	Sales/Working Capital	5.4	6.7	8.4	8.1	8.5	5.4
13.3	16.3	16.4		-42.6	20.2	17.9	23.6	14.7	9.4
(129) 7.8	(140) 7.1	(137) 9.0		(10) 5.4	(32) 9.8	(13) 5.0	9.3	(26) 10.8	10.9
3.9	3.8	3.6	EBIT/Interest	2.6	3.7	1.9	4.3	3.7	3.9
1.5	1.5	1.8		.5	1.9	.7	1.6	1.7	2.5
(81) 6.1	(72) 5.2	(73) 5.9	Net Profit + Depr., Dep.,		(15) 4.6		(15) 5.3	(13) 9.3	(20) 11.3
2.6	1.7	2.7	Amort./Cur. Mat. L/T/D		2.2		2.4	3.0	4.6
1.0	.8	1.5			.7		1.3	1.7	2.9
.3	.3	.4		.3	.3	.2	.4	.4	.4
.5	.6	.6	Fixed/Worth	1.3	.5	.7	.6	.6	.8
1.1	1.5	1.3		-9.0	1.3	1.3	.9	1.2	1.2
.5	.7	.7		1.2	.7	1.3	.7	.6	.9
1.2	1.3	1.5	Debt/Worth	2.4	1.2	2.2	1.3	1.3	1.8
2.6	3.2	3.7		-47.0	3.6	5.1	2.9	2.6	4.1
(130) 32.9	(144) 31.9	(134) 35.6	% Profit Before Taxes/Tangible		(31) 58.1	(17) 44.6	(28) 36.1	(28) 30.6	(22) 27.4
15.8	16.2	18.6	Net Worth		18.7	13.3	16.0	19.2	19.2
4.4	5.0	7.5			5.6	-3.3	5.3	9.6	12.5
13.9	13.0	14.1	% Profit Before Taxes/Total	16.5	19.1	21.2	15.2	12.9	12.2
7.2	6.4	7.4	Assets	9.5	7.4	2.4	4.4	7.4	8.6
1.7	1.4	2.5		.4	2.3	-1.6	1.5	4.0	4.4
15.0	16.7	18.8		28.1	29.8	25.2	19.2	14.1	9.8
7.1	7.8	8.4	Sales/Net Fixed Assets	20.7	7.5	13.5	9.7	7.7	6.2
4.2	4.7	5.0		3.3	4.3	8.8	5.1	5.6	3.9
2.5	2.6	2.6		3.2	2.9	3.3	2.5	2.6	2.2
1.9	2.0	2.0	Sales/Total Assets	2.3	2.0	2.5	2.0	2.0	1.6
1.5	1.5	1.5		1.4	1.7	1.8	1.6	1.6	1.2
(131) 1.3	(141) 1.4	(136) 1.2			(33) 1.6	.9	1.1	(24) 1.1	(23) 1.8
2.6	2.5	2.4	% Depr., Dep., Amort./Sales		2.5	1.7	2.1	2.2	3.1
3.4	3.7	3.8			4.5	3.8	3.2	3.4	4.0
(55) 3.0	(58) 2.8	(56) 2.9	% Officers', Directors',		(22) 3.8		(12) 2.5		
5.0	5.4	4.9	Owners' Comp/Sales		5.5		5.4		
8.2	8.0	7.0			8.4		7.2		
3142484M	2991108M	2896110M	Net Sales ($)	6176M	69071M	69682M	219272M	456557M	2075352M
1991701M	1976122M	1837645M	Total Assets ($)	2938M	38169M	30146M	112200M	259235M	1394957M

M = $ thousand   MM = $ million
See Pages 1 through 15 for Explanation of Ratios and Data

MANUFACTURERS—ENAMELED IRON, METAL SANITARY WARE & PLUMBING SUPPLIES. SIC# 3431 (32)

Current Data Sorted By Assets   Comparative Historical Data

Type of Statement distribution (top counts):

0-500M	500M-2MM	2-10MM	10-50MM	50-100MM	100-250MM	# Postretirement Benefits / Type of Statement	4/1/90-3/31/91	4/1/91-3/31/92
1		5	10	2	2	Unqualified	15	17
	3	5	2			Reviewed	7	12
4	4	1	2			Compiled	5	10
						Tax Returns	1	
		4	2	1		Other	10	4

0-500M	13 (4/1-9/30/94) 500M-2MM	2-10MM	35 (10/1/94-3/31/95) 10-50MM	50-100MM	100-250MM		4/1/90-3/31/91 ALL	4/1/91-3/31/92 ALL
5	7	15	16	3	2	NUMBER OF STATEMENTS	38	43
%	%	%	%	%	%	**ASSETS**	%	%
		5.7	2.9			Cash & Equivalents	7.3	7.9
		36.6	29.7			Trade Receivables - (net)	27.7	27.3
		26.9	35.0			Inventory	32.0	31.9
		4.0	.6			All Other Current	2.1	2.9
		73.2	68.1			Total Current	69.1	70.0
		20.0	27.3			Fixed Assets (net)	24.0	23.2
		.6	.4			Intangibles (net)	1.7	1.2
		6.3	4.1			All Other Non-Current	5.2	5.6
		100.0	100.0			Total	100.0	100.0
						LIABILITIES		
		16.1	11.6			Notes Payable-Short Term	10.4	12.6
		3.5	1.3			Cur. Mat. -L/T/D	4.0	3.2
		19.1	12.5			Trade Payables	16.9	14.0
		.4	.1			Income Taxes Payable	.5	.5
		7.6	7.5			All Other Current	6.0	8.4
		46.6	33.1			Total Current	37.7	38.7
		9.0	12.9			Long Term Debt	15.3	9.9
		.2	.7			Deferred Taxes	.8	.8
		6.5	.9			All Other-Non-Current	2.7	1.2
		37.7	52.3			Net Worth	43.4	49.4
		100.0	100.0			Total Liabilities & Net Worth	100.0	100.0
						INCOME DATA		
		100.0	100.0			Net Sales	100.0	100.0
		25.7	33.5			Gross Profit	30.8	31.5
		23.7	26.0			Operating Expenses	25.8	27.9
		2.0	7.5			Operating Profit	5.0	3.6
		.8	.9			All Other Expenses (net)	1.5	.8
		1.2	6.6			Profit Before Taxes	3.4	2.9
						RATIOS		
		1.8	4.8			Current	3.5	2.9
		1.4	1.9				1.9	1.9
		1.2	1.4				1.3	1.4
		1.2	2.0			Quick	1.6	1.5
		.8	1.0				.8	.9
		.6	.7				.6	.6
		47 7.7	54 6.8			Sales/Receivables	41 8.9	40 9.2
		55 6.6	60 6.1				50 7.3	49 7.5
		63 5.8	64 5.7				56 6.5	55 6.6
		24 15.3	74 4.9			Cost of Sales/Inventory	64 5.7	61 6.0
		63 5.8	107 3.4				87 4.2	87 4.2
		74 4.9	126 2.9				118 3.1	122 3.0
		25 14.7	20 18.1			Cost of Sales/Payables	21 17.6	16 23.4
		46 8.0	32 11.3				33 10.9	24 15.0
		60 6.1	48 7.6				53 6.9	42 8.7
		7.4	3.2			Sales/Working Capital	3.6	3.6
		11.1	7.2				6.5	7.4
		14.2	9.6				11.7	12.9
		6.8	13.7			EBIT/Interest	(34) 4.3	(39) 10.6
		3.0	(12) 4.7				1.8	3.2
		1.7	3.0				1.1	.6
						Net Profit + Depr., Dep., Amort./Cur. Mat. L./T/D	(21) 6.0	(23) 9.2
							2.7	3.0
							.6	-.1
		.1	.2			Fixed/Worth	.3	.3
		.5	.5				.5	.4
		1.0	.9				1.4	.8
		1.4	.3			Debt/Worth	.6	.4
		2.2	1.0				1.7	1.1
		3.0	2.4				3.6	2.2
		36.0	31.6			% Profit Before Taxes/Tangible Net Worth	(37) 22.0	(42) 25.2
		14.9	20.7				11.3	13.5
		4.8	11.6				2.9	-4.1
		12.1	16.1			% Profit Before Taxes/Total Assets	9.0	10.9
		5.0	8.8				4.3	6.3
		1.5	4.8				.4	-2.0
		34.8	18.4			Sales/Net Fixed Assets	16.8	20.9
		16.5	6.0				6.6	12.2
		6.5	4.2				5.2	5.1
		2.8	2.1			Sales/Total Assets	2.2	2.3
		2.5	1.9				1.9	2.0
		2.0	1.6				1.5	1.6
		.5	1.1			% Depr., Dep., Amort./Sales	(35) 1.2	(38) 1.2
		(14) 1.2	(13) 1.9				2.1	2.0
		2.1	3.1				3.3	3.1
						% Officers', Directors', Owners' Comp/Sales	(13) 2.5	(12) 2.4
							4.9	6.6
							9.2	9.9
4575M	25263M	194005M	604473M	348143M	683639M	Net Sales ($)	1795885M	1185012M
1309M	8878M	80659M	315160M	194248M	441395M	Total Assets ($)	1079906M	779714M

M = $ thousand   MM = $ million
See Pages 1 through 15 for Explanation of Ratios and Data

Comparative Historical Data / Current Data Sorted By Sales

4/1/92-3/31/93 ALL	4/1/93-3/31/94 ALL	4/1/94-3/31/95 ALL		0-1MM	1-3MM	3-5MM	5-10MM	10-25MM	25MM & OVER
2	1	1	# Postretirement Benefits					1	
			Type of Statement						
15	15	20	Unqualified		1		1	8	10
12	11	10	Reviewed		2	2	2	4	
10	3	11	Compiled	2	3	2	1	1	2
			Tax Returns						
			Other			1	1	2	3
7	9	7				13 (4/1-9/30/94)		35 (10/1/94-3/31/95)	
44	38	48	**NUMBER OF STATEMENTS**	2	6	5	5	15	15
%	%	%	**ASSETS**	%	%	%	%	%	%
4.2	7.7	6.4	Cash & Equivalents					4.4	3.3
30.6	27.5	32.4	Trade Receivables - (net)					33.7	29.3
32.9	33.5	31.4	Inventory					31.3	32.5
1.1	1.3	1.8	All Other Current					1.6	1.2
68.8	70.0	72.0	Total Current					71.1	66.3
23.8	22.9	22.1	Fixed Assets (net)					24.6	26.9
2.2	1.1	.9	Intangibles (net)					.5	1.0
5.2	5.9	5.0	All Other Non-Current					3.8	5.8
100.0	100.0	100.0	Total					100.0	100.0
			LIABILITIES						
12.0	8.2	11.5	Notes Payable-Short Term					8.1	12.5
3.0	2.9	3.2	Cur. Mat.-L /T/D					3.5	.7
14.6	13.8	16.4	Trade Payables					17.5	11.8
.6	1.6	.5	Income Taxes Payable					.3	.2
8.3	6.9	10.3	All Other Current					6.5	13.1
38.6	33.4	41.9	Total Current					35.9	38.4
12.8	11.3	11.8	Long Term Debt					12.8	8.5
1.0	.5	.7	Deferred Taxes					.1	1.3
5.0	2.9	4.2	All Other-Non-Current					4.6	1.4
42.7	51.9	41.4	Net Worth					46.5	50.4
100.0	100.0	100.0	Total Liabilities & Net Worth					100.0	100.0
			INCOME DATA						
100.0	100.0	100.0	Net Sales					100.0	100.0
29.3	32.1	30.3	Gross Profit					29.9	30.4
25.1	26.7	25.4	Operating Expenses					23.9	23.3
4.2	5.4	4.8	Operating Profit					6.0	7.1
.9	.6	1.2	All Other Expenses (net)					1.1	2.4
3.4	4.7	3.6	Profit Before Taxes					4.9	4.7
			RATIOS						
2.4	4.3	2.5						4.0	2.3
1.8	1.9	1.7	Current					1.8	2.0
1.4	1.4	1.4						1.4	1.4
1.3	2.4	1.4						2.0	1.3
.9	1.0	1.0	Quick					1.1	1.0
.7	.6	.7						.7	.6
41 8.9	36 10.1	43 8.5						50 7.3	45 8.1
50 7.3	51 7.1	54 6.8	Sales/Receivables					57 6.4	54 6.8
58 6.3	58 6.3	63 5.8						65 5.6	61 6.0
51 7.2	63 5.8	51 7.1						56 6.5	65 5.6
81 4.5	85 4.3	72 5.1	Cost of Sales/Inventory					74 4.9	85 4.3
114 3.2	140 2.6	107 3.4						118 3.1	114 3.2
21 17.7	16 22.2	20 18.0						22 16.7	18 20.2
29 12.8	26 14.1	35 10.5	Cost of Sales/Payables					39 9.4	32 11.3
41 8.8	48 7.6	52 7.0						57 6.4	45 8.1
4.7	3.6	5.3						3.5	5.0
7.2	6.2	7.7	Sales/Working Capital					7.6	6.9
13.7	9.9	13.7						11.1	10.0
(40) 7.7	(31) 11.5	(42) 14.1	EBIT/Interest				(14) 14.8		(12) 17.7
2.9	3.9	5.0						6.6	8.6
1.5	2.0	2.2						2.7	3.0
(23) 5.0	(17) 4.0	(16) 18.5	Net Profit + Depr., Dep.,						
3.1	2.3	2.6	Amort./Cur. Mat. L/T/D						
1.2	1.7	1.7							
.3	.3	.1						.3	.2
.5	.4	.6	Fixed/Worth					.6	.6
1.0	.7	1.0						.9	.9
.7	.3	.7						.7	.6
1.8	1.0	1.7	Debt/Worth					1.5	.8
3.5	2.2	2.9						2.5	2.5
(41) 28.0	(37) 29.1	(45) 36.1	% Profit Before Taxes/Tangible					42.9	(14) 32.1
18.7	18.1	20.6	Net Worth					29.3	21.1
7.9	9.0	10.2						9.3	16.5
15.1	13.6	16.1	% Profit Before Taxes/Total					23.6	16.4
6.1	7.0	7.8	Assets					11.9	11.4
2.4	3.8	2.7						4.2	5.9
19.4	20.8	39.0						29.4	21.7
10.8	8.9	8.5	Sales/Net Fixed Assets					6.9	6.1
6.1	5.4	5.2						5.8	4.3
2.6	2.5	2.7						2.6	2.1
2.2	2.0	2.1	Sales/Total Assets					2.2	2.0
1.7	1.6	1.8						1.8	1.7
(40) 1.2	(34) 1.1	(36) .9	% Depr., Dep., Amort./Sales				(12) .6		(10) .9
1.8	2.3	1.6						1.3	2.0
2.9	3.8	2.6						3.0	3.1
(15) 3.1	(10) 2.8	(17) 3.6	% Officers', Directors',						
4.8	5.2	5.4	Owners' Comp/Sales						
8.2	8.0	8.4							
1098025M	918115M	1860098M	Net Sales ($)	961M	9412M	19923M	36425M	271968M	1521409M
568158M	558263M	1041649M	Total Assets ($)	287M	5464M	8089M	13959M	139851M	873999M

© Robert Morris Associates 1995

M = $ thousand   MM = $ million
See Pages 1 through 15 for Explanation of Ratios and Data

Current Data Sorted By Assets						# Postretirement Benefits	Comparative Historical Data	
	5	2	1		1	**Type of Statement**		
	1	6	2	1	3	Unqualified	24	16
1	12	7				Reviewed	20	24
6	5	4				Compiled	18	10
1	1					Tax Returns		
	5	7				Other	19	13
	23 (4/1-9/30/94)		39 (10/1/94-3/31/95)				4/1/90-3/31/91	4/1/91-3/31/92
0-500M	500M-2MM	2-10MM	10-50MM	50-100MM	100-250MM		ALL	ALL
8	24	24	2	1	3	**NUMBER OF STATEMENTS**	81	63
%	%	%	%	%	%	**ASSETS**	%	%
	7.7	3.3				Cash & Equivalents	6.4	5.2
	35.0	33.2				Trade Receivables - (net)	31.5	31.7
	25.0	32.6				Inventory	27.2	27.4
	1.2	1.3				All Other Current	1.7	1.8
	68.9	70.4				Total Current	66.9	66.1
	23.7	23.3				Fixed Assets (net)	25.2	25.7
	2.2	.9				Intangibles (net)	.5	.7
	5.2	5.5				All Other Non-Current	7.4	7.6
	100.0	100.0				Total	100.0	100.0
						LIABILITIES		
	10.3	17.0				Notes Payable-Short Term	11.3	10.6
	3.7	3.2				Cur. Mat. -L/T/D	3.2	4.9
	18.7	16.7				Trade Payables	16.4	17.3
	.6	.2				Income Taxes Payable	.9	.3
	15.4	8.5				All Other Current	8.6	10.4
	48.7	45.6				Total Current	40.4	43.6
	12.6	11.2				Long Term Debt	15.8	15.1
	.8	.3				Deferred Taxes	.8	.7
	7.8	4.7				All Other-Non-Current	1.6	2.6
	30.1	38.1				Net Worth	41.5	37.9
	100.0	100.0				Total Liabilities & Net Worth	100.0	100.0
						INCOME DATA		
	100.0	100.0				Net Sales	100.0	100.0
	30.8	23.7				Gross Profit	24.5	25.2
	27.9	17.2				Operating Expenses	19.1	22.5
	2.9	6.5				Operating Profit	5.3	2.7
	.3	1.4				All Other Expenses (net)	1.6	.7
	2.7	5.1				Profit Before Taxes	3.7	2.0
						RATIOS		
	2.2	2.4				Current	2.2	2.3
	1.5	1.7					1.7	1.6
	1.0	1.3					1.3	1.2
	1.3	1.3				Quick	1.4	1.3
	.8	.8					.9	.9
	.6	.6					.6	.6
	40 9.1	41 9.0				Sales/Receivables	37 9.8	40 9.1
	51 7.1	49 7.5					47 7.8	51 7.2
	60 6.1	57 6.4					62 5.9	65 5.6
	21 17.8	46 8.0				Cost of Sales/Inventory	31 11.6	27 13.3
	49 7.4	62 5.9					54 6.7	55 6.6
	78 4.7	91 4.0					79 4.6	94 3.9
	21 17.1	24 15.1				Cost of Sales/Payables	18 20.4	18 20.4
	35 10.4	29 12.7					30 12.0	32 11.3
	63 5.8	43 8.4					44 8.3	49 7.5
	5.7	5.9				Sales/Working Capital	5.6	4.8
	12.0	8.6					8.2	8.6
	NM	15.7					17.9	30.5
	(22) 5.2	(23) 10.4				EBIT/Interest	(75) 6.3	(60) 5.4
	3.9	4.9					3.1	2.2
	1.8	2.8					1.2	1.0
	(14) 5.5					Net Profit + Depr., Dep., Amort./Cur. Mat. L./T/D	(45) 7.2	(37) 3.9
	2.6						3.0	2.0
	1.1						1.3	.6
	.4	.3				Fixed/Worth	.3	.3
	.7	.7					.5	.7
	1.7	1.2					1.0	1.3
	1.3	.9				Debt/Worth	.7	.8
	1.7	1.9					1.4	1.8
	7.3	3.1					3.2	3.8
	(22) 49.9	(23) 48.8				% Profit Before Taxes/Tangible Net Worth	(78) 30.1	(60) 27.9
	19.7	37.2					19.5	11.0
	5.1	13.7					2.4	.7
	11.0	19.2				% Profit Before Taxes/Total Assets	13.9	8.0
	6.7	13.2					6.1	4.9
	1.7	5.7					.7	.2
	24.7	14.1				Sales/Net Fixed Assets	17.0	15.2
	14.5	10.8					11.2	9.2
	8.6	7.4					6.1	5.4
	2.8	3.0				Sales/Total Assets	3.1	2.7
	2.4	2.3					2.4	2.2
	2.1	2.0					1.7	1.5
	(22) 1.0	1.1				% Depr., Dep., Amort./Sales	(75) 1.0	(56) 1.3
	2.2	1.6					1.9	2.0
	3.0	3.1					3.2	3.3
	(14) 5.1	(10) 1.1				% Officers', Directors', Owners' Comp/Sales	(35) 1.7	(28) 3.3
	7.4	2.8					3.5	4.9
	9.9	8.6					7.6	8.7
5370M	65178M	235260M	54899M	114519M	864526M	Net Sales ($)	1817362M	1466210M
2381M	25703M	98961M	30635M	62432M	418562M	Total Assets ($)	897726M	719733M

M = $ thousand   MM = $ million
See Pages 1 through 15 for Explanation of Ratios and Data

Comparative Historical Data / Current Data Sorted By Sales

Postretirement Benefits / Type of Statement

Comparative Historical Data			Type of Statement	0-1MM	1-3MM	3-5MM	5-10MM	10-25MM	25MM & OVER
4	2	9	# Postretirement Benefits		3	2	1	2	1
18	14	13	Unqualified		1		3	4	5
24	29	20	Reviewed	6	6	7	4	3	
17	25	15	Compiled	1	3	2	4		
2	2	2	Tax Returns		1				
19	19	12	Other		5		3	4	

Main Data

4/1/92- 3/31/93 ALL 80	4/1/93- 3/31/94 ALL 89	4/1/94- 3/31/95 ALL 62		0-1MM 7	1-3MM 16	3-5MM 9	5-10MM 14	10-25MM 11	25MM & OVER 5
			NUMBER OF STATEMENTS		23 (4/1-9/30/94)		39 (10/1/94-3/31/95)		
%	%	%	**ASSETS**	%	%	%	%	%	%
7.6	6.7	5.9	Cash & Equivalents		8.1		2.2	4.6	
31.2	31.0	33.7	Trade Receivables - (net)		35.4		30.0	36.3	
28.5	25.8	28.8	Inventory		20.5		35.9	27.8	
1.2	1.3	1.1	All Other Current		1.2		2.1	.1	
68.5	64.9	69.5	Total Current		65.2		70.2	68.8	
25.1	27.1	24.1	Fixed Assets (net)		27.1		24.8	23.6	
.9	1.8	1.2	Intangibles (net)		2.5		1.3	.1	
5.5	6.2	5.1	All Other Non-Current		5.3		3.7	7.4	
100.0	100.0	100.0	Total		100.0		100.0	100.0	
			LIABILITIES						
10.5	10.6	13.3	Notes Payable-Short Term		12.6		18.0	18.7	
3.5	3.0	3.3	Cur. Mat.-L /T/D		3.7		3.2	2.9	
16.1	15.4	17.6	Trade Payables		17.2		18.0	15.9	
.8	.9	.4	Income Taxes Payable		.4		.4	.0	
8.3	8.6	12.4	All Other Current		14.7		10.4	7.2	
39.2	38.5	46.9	Total Current		48.7		49.9	44.8	
14.3	13.3	11.5	Long Term Debt		12.9		11.3	10.1	
.6	.4	.5	Deferred Taxes		1.0		.4	.0	
3.3	4.7	7.2	All Other-Non-Current		10.2		4.9	4.1	
42.6	43.0	33.9	Net Worth		27.1		33.4	41.1	
100.0	100.0	100.0	Total Liabilities & Net Worth		100.0		100.0	100.0	
			INCOME DATA						
100.0	100.0	100.0	Net Sales		100.0		100.0	100.0	
26.5	28.6	27.2	Gross Profit		35.5		23.4	24.5	
22.9	25.1	22.7	Operating Expenses		32.4		16.1	19.1	
3.7	3.5	4.5	Operating Profit		3.1		7.3	5.4	
1.0	.8	.8	All Other Expenses (net)		.3		1.7	1.1	
2.6	2.8	3.7	Profit Before Taxes		2.8		5.6	4.3	
			RATIOS						
2.5	2.5	2.3	Current		2.2		2.2	2.4	
1.8	1.7	1.6			1.3		1.5	1.7	
1.3	1.3	1.0			.9		1.0	1.3	
1.6	1.5	1.3	Quick		1.7		1.0	1.6	
.9	.9	.8			.8		.7	1.1	
.7	.7	.6			.5		.5	.7	
35 10.3	36 10.2	40 9.1	Sales/Receivables		45 8.2		40 9.2	46 8.0	
45 8.1	47 7.7	49 7.4			52 7.0		49 7.4	48 7.6	
62 5.9	59 6.2	60 6.1			66 5.5		58 6.3	70 5.2	
35 10.4	31 11.7	33 11.1	Cost of Sales/Inventory		21 17.8		55 6.6	33 11.0	
57 6.4	51 7.1	58 6.3			47 7.7		78 4.7	52 7.0	
91 4.0	89 4.1	94 3.9			78 4.7		96 3.8	94 3.9	
17 21.7	19 19.4	25 14.8	Cost of Sales/Payables		27 13.3		27 13.7	23 15.7	
29 12.8	30 12.3	32 11.3			40 9.1		42 8.7	28 13.2	
50 7.3	45 8.2	53 6.9			63 5.8		51 7.1	41 9.0	
4.9	5.9	5.6	Sales/Working Capital		5.3		5.7	6.5	
7.7	8.0	9.9			17.6		8.5	9.6	
16.1	20.3	64.2			−87.6		292.9	15.7	
(72) 6.7	(82) 8.9	(58) 6.9	EBIT/Interest	(14) 5.3			7.8	(10) 26.4	
3.1	3.3	4.3			2.0		4.9	4.8	
1.4	2.0	1.9			.5		2.7	2.6	
(46) 4.1	(37) 4.1	(27) 4.9	Net Profit + Depr., Dep., Amort./Cur. Mat. L/T/D						
2.1	1.8	2.8							
1.1	.3	1.4							
.2	.3	.3	Fixed/Worth		.5		.5	.2	
.6	.6	.7			.9		.8	.3	
1.3	1.4	1.4			2.2		1.2	1.5	
.8	.7	1.1	Debt/Worth		1.5		.9	.6	
1.3	1.4	1.9			2.5		2.3	1.7	
3.0	3.2	5.5			7.9		3.2	3.4	
(75) 29.5	(86) 36.5	(57) 49.0	% Profit Before Taxes/Tangible Net Worth	(14) 55.1		(13)	51.0	60.9	
13.2	19.7	23.8			27.7		38.3	37.2	
3.3	6.0	9.8			−.9		17.8	8.7	
11.3	13.0	14.6	% Profit Before Taxes/Total Assets		13.5		16.6	19.3	
4.4	6.2	8.7			7.3		14.0	8.5	
.9	2.3	2.7			−1.4		5.0	2.9	
21.6	17.3	20.0	Sales/Net Fixed Assets		21.6		12.6	33.5	
9.2	9.7	11.4			12.7		9.4	11.8	
5.7	5.6	6.9			5.7		6.2	9.5	
2.8	2.8	2.9	Sales/Total Assets		2.5		2.9	3.0	
2.2	2.3	2.3			2.2		2.2	2.3	
1.7	1.9	2.0			1.8		2.0	2.1	
(75) 1.0	(80) 1.2	(60) 1.1	% Depr., Dep., Amort./Sales	(15) 1.9			1.1	1.1	
1.7	2.3	1.8			2.4		1.8	1.5	
3.3	3.3	3.1			3.5		3.4	2.8	
(31) 2.5	(39) 3.5	(29) 2.8	% Officers', Directors', Owners' Comp/Sales						
3.8	5.0	6.8							
7.2	9.6	9.7							
1624893M	887103M	1339752M	Net Sales ($)	4096M	31091M	35361M	101688M	149625M	1017891M
817071M	543234M	638674M	Total Assets ($)	1884M	15179M	11021M	45723M	66221M	498646M

M = $ thousand   MM = $ million
See Pages 1 through 15 for Explanation of Ratios and Data

Current Data Sorted By Assets   **Comparative Historical Data**

0-500M	500M-2MM	2-10MM	10-50MM	50-100MM	100-250MM	# Postretirement Benefits / Type of Statement	4/1/90-3/31/91 ALL	4/1/91-3/31/92 ALL
1	3	1	3		1	# Postretirement Benefits		
1	3	19	14	2	2	Unqualified	55	55
4	21	11		1		Reviewed	44	42
2	17	5				Compiled	29	36
1	1					Tax Returns	1	
2	14	11	8		1	Other	27	25
	51 (4/1-9/30/94)		89 (10/1/94-3/31/95)					
10	56	46	22	3	3	**NUMBER OF STATEMENTS**	156	158
%	%	%	%	%	%	**ASSETS**	%	%
9.3	7.0	6.2	5.2			Cash & Equivalents	8.5	7.7
35.0	35.8	29.0	28.7			Trade Receivables - (net)	30.4	31.2
20.1	22.1	21.7	23.2			Inventory	22.9	22.9
1.4	2.4	4.6	4.3			All Other Current	4.4	3.5
65.8	67.3	61.5	61.3			Total Current	66.2	65.3
27.0	26.7	28.9	27.8			Fixed Assets (net)	27.1	27.3
1.5	1.6	1.9	2.4			Intangibles (net)	1.2	1.2
5.7	4.4	7.7	8.5			All Other Non-Current	5.4	6.1
100.0	100.0	100.0	100.0			Total	100.0	100.0
						LIABILITIES		
8.2	9.4	10.9	7.5			Notes Payable-Short Term	10.1	9.2
3.2	4.9	3.8	5.2			Cur. Mat. -L/T/D	3.6	4.1
20.5	18.9	14.3	17.3			Trade Payables	17.4	15.0
.7	.6	.3	.2			Income Taxes Payable	.7	.6
9.2	9.4	9.8	13.2			All Other Current	11.4	10.2
41.9	43.2	39.1	43.4			Total Current	43.3	39.1
11.1	14.2	12.3	16.6			Long Term Debt	15.0	14.2
.8	.7	.9	1.8			Deferred Taxes	.7	.7
.4	3.1	2.4	2.5			All Other-Non-Current	2.4	2.5
45.9	38.8	45.4	35.7			Net Worth	38.7	43.5
100.0	100.0	100.0	100.0			Total Liabilities & Net Worth	100.0	100.0
						INCOME DATA		
100.0	100.0	100.0	100.0			Net Sales	100.0	100.0
37.7	29.2	22.5	19.5			Gross Profit	24.1	25.4
34.3	24.2	18.3	13.0			Operating Expenses	19.4	20.9
3.4	4.9	4.2	6.5			Operating Profit	4.7	4.5
.4	1.0	1.0	.4			All Other Expenses (net)	1.1	1.2
3.0	3.9	3.2	6.2			Profit Before Taxes	3.7	3.2
						RATIOS		
2.2	2.3	2.1	1.8			Current	2.2	2.6
1.6	1.5	1.5	1.3				1.5	1.7
1.1	1.1	1.2	1.2				1.2	1.2
1.7	1.8	1.1	1.1			Quick	1.3	1.6
.9	1.0	.8	.7				.9	1.0
.7	.7	.6	.5				.7	.7
29 12.6	36 10.1	38 9.6	40 9.2			Sales/Receivables	35 10.3	38 9.7
36 10.2	49 7.4	49 7.5	44 8.3				48 7.6	51 7.2
63 5.8	62 5.9	61 6.0	74 4.9				61 6.0	64 5.7
20 18.7	16 23.3	23 16.0	29 12.5			Cost of Sales/Inventory	25 14.8	24 15.3
38 9.6	38 9.6	43 8.4	68 5.4				47 7.7	47 7.7
65 5.6	76 4.8	68 5.4	87 4.2				74 4.9	76 4.8
29 12.6	23 15.9	18 19.8	30 12.1			Cost of Sales/Payables	22 16.7	18 20.3
41 8.8	34 10.7	30 12.3	38 9.6				32 11.3	30 12.3
48 7.6	50 7.3	41 8.9	66 5.5				46 7.9	38 9.5
5.0	5.2	6.5	6.3			Sales/Working Capital	5.6	5.2
15.5	10.0	9.9	10.9				10.4	8.8
43.0	48.4	24.7	25.2				23.7	20.2
	6.8	6.6	17.4			EBIT/Interest	8.4	11.7
	(50) 3.3	(42) 2.3	(20) 5.0				(139) 3.6	(145) 3.3
	1.8	1.0	3.0				1.6	1.2
	2.8	3.4	4.2			Net Profit + Depr., Dep., Amort./Cur. Mat. L./T/D	9.0	7.3
	(25) 1.6	(18) 1.4	(11) 1.7				(98) 3.2	(87) 2.4
	.9	.5	.8				1.3	.7
.4	.3	.4	.5			Fixed/Worth	.4	.3
.6	.7	.6	.6				.6	.6
.9	2.1	1.2	1.1				1.5	1.1
.6	.8	.8	.9			Debt/Worth	.8	.7
.9	1.8	1.3	2.2				1.7	1.2
3.6	4.3	2.4	3.6				3.5	2.6
	37.0	29.9	56.3			% Profit Before Taxes/Tangible Net Worth	45.6	34.1
	(53) 19.8	(45) 12.5	31.7				(148) 26.3	(152) 18.1
	5.9	1.9	12.7				8.8	3.1
18.2	15.0	13.6	14.8			% Profit Before Taxes/Total Assets	16.6	15.2
6.1	6.5	4.6	9.7				8.1	5.9
1.8	2.3	.7	4.5				2.2	.6
17.9	24.0	12.9	12.2			Sales/Net Fixed Assets	17.7	15.9
11.0	11.4	7.8	6.8				9.3	8.9
6.1	5.7	5.0	5.5				5.3	5.0
3.6	3.1	2.8	2.1			Sales/Total Assets	2.9	2.9
2.9	2.6	2.1	1.8				2.2	2.2
1.7	2.0	1.7	1.5				1.7	1.7
	.8	1.3	1.4			% Depr., Dep., Amort./Sales	1.2	1.3
	(52) 1.5	(44) 2.0	(19) 2.2				(141) 1.9	(147) 2.0
	2.9	3.3	2.9				3.1	3.2
	3.1	3.4				% Officers', Directors', Owners' Comp/Sales	2.4	2.9
	(34) 4.4	(15) 4.6					(47) 4.6	(58) 5.9
	8.2	7.0					6.8	9.1
7883M	159760M	458223M	809945M	237332M	981202M	Net Sales ($)	2515315M	2754336M
2762M	64668M	217266M	476812M	204855M	517848M	Total Assets ($)	1240279M	1477377M

M = $ thousand   MM = $ million

See Pages 1 through 15 for Explanation of Ratios and Data

Comparative Historical Data				Current Data Sorted By Sales					
5	6	9	# Postretirement Benefits		2	1	2		4
			Type of Statement						
46	45	41	Unqualified	1	3	3	6	12	16
33	41	37	Reviewed	3	12	12	6	3	1
37	31	24	Compiled	4	8	6	5	1	
2		2	Tax Returns	1	1				
25	28	36	Other	1	11	4	7	7	6
4/1/92-3/31/93 ALL	4/1/93-3/31/94 ALL	4/1/94-3/31/95 ALL		51 (4/1-9/30/94)			89 (10/1/94-3/31/95)		
				0-1MM	1-3MM	3-5MM	5-10MM	10-25MM	25MM & OVER
143	145	140	**NUMBER OF STATEMENTS**	10	35	25	24	23	23
%	%	%	**ASSETS**	%	%	%	%	%	%
6.5	8.1	7.1	Cash & Equivalents	7.5	8.5	4.5	9.1	6.0	6.5
33.8	33.3	32.3	Trade Receivables - (net)	27.2	34.8	37.5	26.6	30.9	32.3
19.9	19.6	21.7	Inventory	20.2	21.7	21.2	20.6	25.2	20.2
4.8	4.2	3.4	All Other Current	1.3	2.6	1.6	5.2	4.3	5.0
65.0	65.2	64.4	Total Current	56.2	67.6	64.7	61.5	66.4	63.9
28.4	27.6	27.4	Fixed Assets (net)	40.7	25.8	28.1	28.3	25.9	23.8
1.0	1.8	1.8	Intangibles (net)	1.6	1.6	1.5	1.9	1.8	2.6
5.7	5.5	6.3	All Other Non-Current	1.5	5.0	5.7	8.3	5.8	9.7
100.0	100.0	100.0	Total	100.0	100.0	100.0	100.0	100.0	100.0
			LIABILITIES						
6.4	9.3	9.2	Notes Payable-Short Term	11.4	5.4	12.9	8.3	13.0	6.9
5.5	3.8	4.4	Cur. Mat.-L/T/D	3.8	5.6	4.8	3.3	3.7	4.0
16.0	15.2	17.0	Trade Payables	12.3	17.4	19.4	17.0	14.9	17.7
.5	1.0	.5	Income Taxes Payable	.7	.8	.2	.4	.4	.5
10.6	9.8	10.3	All Other Current	10.7	9.0	7.9	12.2	10.6	12.4
39.1	39.1	41.3	Total Current	38.9	38.2	45.2	41.2	42.5	41.5
14.2	12.5	13.9	Long Term Debt	17.8	14.7	15.4	7.7	13.0	16.7
.9	1.1	1.0	Deferred Taxes	.8	1.0	.7	1.4	.4	1.6
3.1	2.5	2.9	All Other-Non-Current	1.8	2.5	3.8	3.1	.7	4.8
42.6	44.8	41.0	Net Worth	40.7	43.6	35.0	46.6	43.4	35.4
100.0	100.0	100.0	Total Liabilities & Net Worth	100.0	100.0	100.0	100.0	100.0	100.0
			INCOME DATA						
100.0	100.0	100.0	Net Sales	100.0	100.0	100.0	100.0	100.0	100.0
26.6	26.1	25.8	Gross Profit	39.8	31.6	25.9	23.7	20.6	18.1
22.4	22.4	21.0	Operating Expenses	33.6	26.4	22.2	18.3	16.5	13.1
4.3	3.7	4.8	Operating Profit	6.2	5.2	3.7	5.4	4.1	5.0
.6	.6	.8	All Other Expenses (net)	2.3	.4	1.3	.9	.8	.3
3.6	3.1	4.0	Profit Before Taxes	3.9	4.8	2.3	4.5	3.3	4.8
			RATIOS						
2.5	2.5	2.2	Current	2.8	2.8	2.0	1.9	2.0	1.8
1.9	1.8	1.5		1.8	1.8	1.5	1.5	1.6	1.6
1.2	1.2	1.2		1.1	1.2	1.1	1.1	1.2	1.2
1.5	1.5	1.3	Quick	1.9	1.9	1.1	1.2	1.1	1.2
1.1	1.1	.9		.9	1.3	.8	.7	.8	1.0
.7	.7	.6		.5	.7	.7	.5	.6	.6
37 10.0	38 9.6	38 9.7	Sales/Receivables	30 12.2	32 11.3	44 8.3	31 11.9	40 9.2	41 9.0
51 7.2	51 7.1	49 7.5		44 8.3	49 7.4	55 6.6	45 8.1	47 7.8	60 6.1
65 5.6	66 5.5	63 5.8		74 4.9	62 5.9	64 5.7	60 6.1	59 6.2	87 4.2
16 23.2	16 22.4	20 18.1	Cost of Sales/Inventory	24 15.3	16 22.9	13 28.0	19 18.8	24 15.3	27 13.7
44 8.3	44 8.3	43 8.4		61 6.0	41 9.0	34 10.8	42 8.6	62 5.9	60 6.1
64 5.7	70 5.2	72 5.1		104 3.5	78 4.7	69 5.3	66 5.5	73 5.0	76 4.8
19 18.8	18 20.0	23 16.2	Cost of Sales/Payables	20 18.3	24 15.3	20 18.2	19 19.4	18 19.9	28 12.9
27 13.3	29 12.4	34 10.7		38 9.5	33 11.1	40 9.5	31 11.6	30 12.2	39 9.4
45 8.2	45 8.2	48 7.6		54 6.7	46 7.9	53 6.9	47 7.8	39 9.4	65 5.6
5.2	5.2	5.6	Sales/Working Capital	4.4	4.4	8.5	6.9	5.6	5.8
8.5	7.7	9.9		12.9	7.2	11.9	11.9	9.9	10.6
25.9	22.4	26.3		NM	29.7	41.5	31.2	22.2	24.2
(131) 8.3	(131) 7.5	(124) 7.4	EBIT/Interest		(30) 11.8	(24) 4.5	(20) 7.7	(22) 7.4	(21) 15.8
3.4	3.9	3.4			4.4	2.3	3.3	3.5	4.6
1.5	1.9	1.8			2.0	1.5	1.5	.7	2.9
(73) 5.5	(72) 4.7	(62) 3.5	Net Profit + Depr., Dep., Amort./Cur. Mat. L/T/D		(17) 4.2	(13) 3.2			(13) 3.3
2.0	2.1	1.8			1.6	1.9			1.7
.8	1.1	.9			.9	.7			.7
.4	.3	.4	Fixed/Worth	.5	.3	.4	.3	.5	.5
.6	.6	.6		1.1	.5	.9	.6	.7	.6
1.1	1.3	1.3		7.8	1.8	1.5	1.3	1.0	1.0
.6	.7	.8	Debt/Worth	.6	.7	1.1	.7	.7	1.2
1.3	1.3	1.7		1.3	1.0	2.0	1.2	1.4	1.9
2.7	2.7	3.4		12.1	2.8	4.0	2.8	2.5	3.4
(135) 41.4	(140) 30.8	(135) 37.4	% Profit Before Taxes/Tangible Net Worth		(33) 34.3	(24) 26.2	40.2	(22) 36.7	48.2
14.4	15.2	19.1			16.5	19.5	17.1	21.7	23.5
5.5	4.3	3.9			6.9	2.8	3.3	-2.6	10.9
15.3	12.2	13.8	% Profit Before Taxes/Total Assets	21.1	14.9	10.0	16.1	15.7	12.7
6.2	6.2	6.3		2.5	6.4	4.3	4.9	10.2	7.2
1.7	1.8	1.7		-.3	2.5	1.3	1.5	-.5	2.3
14.9	16.6	18.4	Sales/Net Fixed Assets	9.6	22.8	20.3	17.9	12.7	17.1
8.7	8.3	8.8		6.1	12.6	9.9	9.9	8.6	7.6
5.5	5.4	5.4		3.2	5.7	5.1	4.3	6.2	5.0
3.0	2.7	2.8	Sales/Total Assets	2.6	3.0	3.1	3.4	2.8	2.1
2.2	2.2	2.1		1.7	2.5	2.6	2.3	2.1	1.8
1.7	1.7	1.7		.8	1.9	2.0	1.5	1.9	1.5
(137) 1.2	(137) 1.3	(128) 1.2	% Depr., Dep., Amort./Sales		(31) 1.3	.7	(22) 1.2	(22) 1.3	(19) 1.4
1.9	2.0	1.9			2.0	1.1	2.0	2.0	2.2
2.7	2.8	2.9			3.0	2.9	3.7	2.7	2.9
(57) 4.0	(55) 2.8	(55) 3.2	% Officers', Directors', Owners' Comp/Sales		(19) 3.2	(15) 3.4	(11) 3.6		
5.9	4.7	4.6			4.7	5.0	4.5		
9.3		7.7			8.8	8.0			
2318606M	2742925M	2654345M	Net Sales ($)	6190M	71301M	98471M	162821M	377968M	1937594M
1194741M	1471676M	1484211M	Total Assets ($)	5637M	47293M	41360M	84841M	171122M	1133958M

M = $ thousand   MM = $ million
See Pages 1 through 15 for Explanation of Ratios and Data

Current Data Sorted By Assets / Comparative Historical Data

Type of Statement

0-500M	500M-2MM	2-10MM	10-50MM	50-100MM	100-250MM	# Postretirement Benefits / Type of Statement	4/1/90-3/31/91 ALL	4/1/91-3/31/92 ALL
1	9	12	2		1			
	7	45	19	2	1	Unqualified	97	87
3	40	40	3			Reviewed	91	68
29	46	9	1			Compiled	75	73
2	5				1	Tax Returns	2	2
8	33	23	12	2	1	Other	54	49
42	131	117	35	4	3	NUMBER OF STATEMENTS	319	279

103 (4/1-9/30/94) covers 0-500M and 500M-2MM; 229 (10/1/94-3/31/95) covers remaining columns.

ASSETS

0-500M	500M-2MM	2-10MM	10-50MM	50-100MM	100-250MM	ASSETS	4/1/90-3/31/91 ALL	4/1/91-3/31/92 ALL
%	%	%	%	%	%		%	%
12.4	7.3	6.1	3.9			Cash & Equivalents	8.2	7.9
38.5	41.7	40.2	34.2			Trade Receivables - (net)	37.5	36.8
11.3	17.5	18.4	19.7			Inventory	18.3	17.1
.7	2.7	5.2	5.8			All Other Current	4.4	4.0
62.8	69.2	69.9	63.6			Total Current	68.5	65.8
31.3	24.1	23.3	25.7			Fixed Assets (net)	24.2	26.5
.7	.8	.6	1.1			Intangibles (net)	.9	.9
5.2	5.9	6.2	9.6			All Other Non-Current	6.4	6.7
100.0	100.0	100.0	100.0			Total	100.0	100.0

LIABILITIES

0-500M	500M-2MM	2-10MM	10-50MM	50-100MM	100-250MM	LIABILITIES	4/1/90-3/31/91 ALL	4/1/91-3/31/92 ALL
9.4	12.3	11.1	9.8			Notes Payable-Short Term	10.8	11.3
5.4	3.7	2.4	3.8			Cur. Mat. -L/T/D	3.3	4.0
21.5	20.5	19.8	15.1			Trade Payables	19.0	18.8
.3	.9	.3	.4			Income Taxes Payable	.8	.5
9.4	8.4	10.3	12.2			All Other Current	9.6	9.4
45.9	45.7	43.9	41.3			Total Current	43.4	43.9
15.5	12.0	9.9	13.0			Long Term Debt	13.7	13.0
.3	.3	.5	1.1			Deferred Taxes	.7	.6
2.2	3.8	3.6	1.3			All Other-Non-Current	1.8	2.5
36.1	38.2	42.0	43.3			Net Worth	40.4	40.0
100.0	100.0	100.0	100.0			Total Liabilities & Net Worth	100.0	100.0

INCOME DATA

0-500M	500M-2MM	2-10MM	10-50MM	50-100MM	100-250MM	INCOME DATA	4/1/90-3/31/91 ALL	4/1/91-3/31/92 ALL
100.0	100.0	100.0	100.0			Net Sales	100.0	100.0
35.6	26.5	19.6	21.4			Gross Profit	24.2	23.4
31.9	22.9	16.4	16.7			Operating Expenses	20.2	21.2
3.7	3.5	3.2	4.7			Operating Profit	4.1	2.2
.8	.8	.7	.7			All Other Expenses (net)	1.0	1.0
2.9	2.8	2.6	4.0			Profit Before Taxes	3.0	1.3

RATIOS

0-500M	500M-2MM	2-10MM	10-50MM	50-100MM	100-250MM	RATIOS	4/1/90-3/31/91 ALL	4/1/91-3/31/92 ALL
2.3	2.1	2.3	2.0			Current	2.3	2.3
1.4	1.6	1.5	1.6				1.6	1.5
.9	1.2	1.2	1.2				1.2	1.1
2.1	1.6	1.6	1.3			Quick	1.7	1.5
(41) 1.1	1.1	1.0	1.0				(318) 1.1	1.1
.8	.8	.7	.7				.7	.7
27 13.4	42 8.7	48 7.6	48 7.6			Sales/Receivables	38 9.7	38 9.5
42 8.6	52 7.0	59 6.2	63 5.8				50 7.3	54 6.8
70 5.2	70 5.2	79 4.6	79 4.6				68 5.4	69 5.3
1 465.2	12 31.1	17 21.9	21 17.7			Cost of Sales/Inventory	12 29.6	12 30.7
11 33.4	25 14.7	30 12.1	45 8.1				32 11.4	32 11.4
41 9.0	50 7.3	57 6.4	76 4.8				54 6.8	56 6.5
12 30.4	20 18.6	24 15.0	19 19.3			Cost of Sales/Payables	19 19.6	20 18.3
39 9.3	33 11.1	35 10.3	33 10.9				31 11.8	31 11.7
54 6.8	48 7.6	51 7.2	50 7.3				45 8.1	49 7.4
8.4	6.8	5.9	6.4			Sales/Working Capital	6.0	6.2
17.0	11.2	9.4	8.5				10.3	10.5
-36.6	26.6	21.3	20.8				23.6	36.8
9.1	9.5	6.3	7.0			EBIT/Interest	9.2	6.6
(37) 3.3	(116) 4.5	(103) 3.5	(31) 4.1				(296) 3.3	(255) 2.1
.1	1.9	1.7	1.3				1.4	.5
	5.7	4.1	6.1			Net Profit + Depr., Dep., Amort./Cur. Mat. L /T/D	6.6	4.2
	(45) 2.3	(59) 2.7	(16) 2.4				(183) 3.1	(149) 1.9
	1.2	1.3	1.2				1.2	.6
.3	.3	.3	.4			Fixed/Worth	.3	.3
.9	.5	.6	.6				.6	.6
5.5	1.2	1.0	1.0				1.1	1.3
.6	.8	.8	.8			Debt/Worth	.7	.7
1.5	1.6	1.5	1.3				1.6	1.5
9.5	3.4	3.0	2.3				3.1	3.2
59.7	39.1	27.4	30.6			% Profit Before Taxes/Tangible Net Worth	38.5	25.6
(35) 28.0	(123) 17.5	(115) 14.2	(34) 16.6				(304) 17.9	(265) 9.9
3.3	8.5	6.3	4.8				4.4	-2.1
20.5	12.0	9.9	12.3			% Profit Before Taxes/Total Assets	13.4	8.7
8.8	7.4	5.5	6.5				6.6	3.4
-1.4	2.9	1.9	1.2				1.2	-1.6
25.7	25.0	21.2	17.1			Sales/Net Fixed Assets	24.8	20.6
12.5	14.3	11.8	8.4				12.0	10.5
4.8	6.6	6.2	4.9				6.9	5.6
3.9	3.5	2.9	2.4			Sales/Total Assets	3.2	2.9
3.0	2.8	2.2	2.0				2.5	2.5
2.2	2.0	1.7	1.6				1.9	1.8
1.4	1.0	.8	1.1			% Depr., Dep., Amort./Sales	1.0	1.1
(36) 2.7	(121) 1.6	(111) 1.4	(30) 2.1				(292) 1.6	(251) 1.9
3.7	3.0	2.4	3.1				2.6	3.0
4.3	3.0	1.7				% Officers', Directors', Owners' Comp/Sales	2.2	2.4
(25) 7.6	(79) 4.7	(48) 2.8					(133) 4.6	(106) 4.4
15.3	6.6	4.7					8.4	7.9
41627M	412369M	1271953M	1317239M	461777M	1180579M	Net Sales ($)	4627673M	3591803M
12960M	148498M	548772M	684787M	256419M	539519M	Total Assets ($)	2257637M	1844712M

© Robert Morris Associates 1995

M = $ thousand   MM = $ million
See Pages 1 through 15 for Explanation of Ratios and Data

Comparative Historical Data				Current Data Sorted By Sales					
9	21	25	# Postretirement Benefits / Type of Statement	1	4	6	3	8	3
89	62	74	Unqualified		5	5	12	29	23
89	80	86	Reviewed	2	17	21	27	17	2
77	78	85	Compiled	18	38	17	10	1	1
2	7	8	Tax Returns	1	5	1		1	1
50	52	79	Other	9	18	19	6	16	11
4/1/92- 3/31/93	4/1/93- 3/31/94	4/1/94- 3/31/95		103 (4/1-9/30/94)			229 (10/1/94-3/31/95)		
ALL	ALL	ALL		0-1MM	1-3MM	3-5MM	5-10MM	10-25MM	25MM & OVER
307	279	332	NUMBER OF STATEMENTS	30	83	63	55	63	38
%	%	%	ASSETS	%	%	%	%	%	%
8.2	7.3	7.2	Cash & Equivalents	10.8	8.7	7.2	6.1	4.7	6.9
36.3	38.8	39.6	Trade Receivables - (net)	31.5	40.7	41.1	44.4	39.1	34.8
17.7	16.6	17.6	Inventory	14.0	15.8	16.7	17.2	21.2	20.4
3.9	3.9	3.6	All Other Current	.7	1.8	3.2	5.2	6.1	4.1
66.1	66.7	68.0	Total Current	57.2	66.9	68.2	72.9	71.1	66.2
26.6	25.2	24.9	Fixed Assets (net)	36.4	25.7	24.6	19.7	23.1	25.2
1.0	1.1	.8	Intangibles (net)	.7	1.0	.5	.4	1.0	1.2
6.3	7.0	6.3	All Other Non-Current	5.7	6.3	6.7	7.0	4.8	7.5
100.0	100.0	100.0	Total	100.0	100.0	100.0	100.0	100.0	100.0
			LIABILITIES						
10.6	11.2	11.2	Notes Payable-Short Term	11.3	11.6	11.1	11.5	12.5	7.6
4.3	4.2	3.5	Cur. Mat.-L /T/D	6.9	4.0	3.2	2.0	3.0	2.7
19.1	18.7	19.6	Trade Payables	16.9	20.5	22.2	18.6	19.7	17.3
.3	1.6	.5	Income Taxes Payable	.1	1.0	.4	.4	.4	.4
9.0	9.1	9.5	All Other Current	10.2	8.1	7.5	10.8	10.8	11.7
43.2	44.9	44.3	Total Current	45.4	45.2	44.3	43.2	46.4	39.8
13.3	13.0	11.9	Long Term Debt	20.1	12.0	12.2	8.5	10.0	12.9
.6	.5	.5	Deferred Taxes	.2	.1	.3	1.0	.5	1.0
2.5	3.4	3.2	All Other-Non-Current	2.8	3.2	4.3	3.3	3.2	1.6
40.3	38.2	40.1	Net Worth	31.4	39.5	38.8	44.0	39.8	44.7
100.0	100.0	100.0	Total Liabilities & Net Worth	100.0	100.0	100.0	100.0	100.0	100.0
			INCOME DATA						
100.0	100.0	100.0	Net Sales	100.0	100.0	100.0	100.0	100.0	100.0
24.4	24.0	24.5	Gross Profit	36.5	29.4	23.0	21.3	19.3	20.3
22.2	22.4	20.9	Operating Expenses	33.2	25.7	20.0	18.3	15.3	15.3
2.2	1.6	3.6	Operating Profit	3.3	3.7	3.0	3.0	4.1	5.0
.9	.7	.7	All Other Expenses (net)	1.4	.8	.5	.4	.9	.5
1.3	.9	2.9	Profit Before Taxes	1.9	2.9	2.5	2.6	3.2	4.5
			RATIOS						
2.2 / 1.5 / 1.2	2.2 / 1.5 / 1.2	2.2 / 1.6 / 1.2	Current	2.3 / 1.2 / .8	2.2 / 1.6 / 1.2	2.2 / 1.5 / 1.2	2.6 / 1.6 / 1.3	2.0 / 1.5 / 1.3	2.4 / 1.7 / 1.3
1.5 / 1.0 / .7	1.6 / 1.0 / .8	(331) 1.6 / 1.1 / .8	Quick	1.4 / .9 / .5	(82) 1.8 / 1.2 / .8	1.6 / 1.1 / .8	1.8 / 1.1 / .9	1.4 / .9 / .7	1.4 / 1.1 / .8
38 9.5 / 53 6.9 / 69 5.3	41 9.0 / 54 6.7 / 70 5.2	42 8.7 / 54 6.7 / 74 4.9	Sales/Receivables	28 13.1 / 47 7.7 / 79 4.6	41 9.0 / 54 6.8 / 72 5.1	41 8.9 / 54 6.8 / 73 5.0	48 7.6 / 56 6.5 / 76 4.8	43 8.4 / 56 6.5 / 78 4.7	43 8.4 / 55 6.6 / 73 5.0
14 26.8 / 29 12.5 / 56 6.5	11 32.8 / 28 13.2 / 53 6.9	12 29.7 / 29 12.8 / 54 6.8	Cost of Sales/Inventory	3 132.1 / 18 20.1 / 48 7.6	8 43.1 / 25 14.7 / 51 7.2	15 25.0 / 25 14.8 / 49 7.5	12 30.3 / 24 15.0 / 50 7.3	19 19.2 / 38 9.7 / 55 4.8	21 17.8 / 45 8.2 / 76 4.8
18 19.9 / 33 11.2 / 49 7.4	20 18.1 / 33 11.2 / 47 7.7	21 17.2 / 35 10.5 / 50 7.3	Cost of Sales/Payables	12 30.8 / 40 9.1 / 54 6.8	23 15.9 / 35 10.4 / 57 6.4	20 18.5 / 37 9.8 / 52 7.0	21 17.8 / 29 12.5 / 47 7.8	24 15.3 / 35 10.4 / 49 7.5	25 14.5 / 34 10.6 / 47 7.8
6.1 / 10.9 / 29.4	6.1 / 11.1 / 29.2	6.5 / 10.6 / 24.5	Sales/Working Capital	7.1 / 52.2 / -17.5	6.4 / 10.7 / 31.4	7.1 / 12.6 / 26.0	6.0 / 9.7 / 23.1	6.6 / 9.7 / 20.0	5.6 / 8.4 / 14.8
(278) 5.2 / 1.9 / .3	(253) 6.1 / 2.4 / .6	(293) 8.1 / 3.9 / 1.7	EBIT/Interest	(27) 6.5 / 1.7 / -1.6	(72) 9.9 / 4.4 / 1.8	(57) 7.7 / 3.9 / 2.1	(43) 10.2 / 2.7 / 1.4	(59) 6.5 / 3.8 / 2.6	(35) 7.9 / 4.9 / 1.7
(145) 3.3 / 1.6 / .5	(107) 2.9 / 1.4 / .1	(129) 4.4 / 2.5 / 1.2	Net Profit + Depr., Dep., Amort./Cur. Mat. L/T/D		(22) 2.8 / 1.3 / -.5	(30) 6.9 / 3.1 / 1.5	(22) 7.0 / 3.1 / 1.6	(32) 3.4 / 2.8 / 1.3	(17) 6.5 / 2.5 / 1.4
.3 / .6 / 1.1	.3 / .6 / 1.1	.3 / .6 / 1.1	Fixed/Worth	.4 / 1.1 / 9.5	.2 / .5 / 1.5	.3 / .6 / 1.3	.2 / .4 / .8	.3 / .6 / 1.0	.3 / .6 / 1.0
.8 / 1.6 / 3.3	.9 / 1.7 / 3.3	.8 / 1.5 / 3.0	Debt/Worth	1.0 / 2.5 / 13.3	.6 / 1.6 / 3.7	1.0 / 1.7 / 3.8	.7 / 1.3 / 2.2	.9 / 1.7 / 3.0	.7 / 1.2 / 2.4
(292) 21.8 / 8.3 / -1.6	(261) 24.3 / 9.6 / -.4	(314) 32.6 / 16.5 / 6.8	% Profit Before Taxes/Tangible Net Worth	(24) 31.1 / 12.6 / -3.3	(75) 48.2 / 21.0 / 7.8	(53) 27.8 / 16.9 / 9.2	(62) 27.8 / 12.1 / 3.7	(37) 32.9 / 16.3 / 7.7	31.3 / 16.7 / 9.0
8.6 / 3.3 / -1.3	8.5 / 3.3 / -1.4	11.8 / 6.6 / 1.8	% Profit Before Taxes/Total Assets	11.6 / 2.3 / -6.1	17.1 / 8.3 / 2.0	8.7 / 6.3 / 3.2	11.7 / 4.5 / 1.4	10.7 / 6.9 / 2.4	14.0 / 7.0 / 3.3
20.6 / 10.3 / 5.9	22.3 / 11.0 / 6.4	22.5 / 11.0 / 6.1	Sales/Net Fixed Assets	18.6 / 6.8 / 3.3	27.7 / 11.7 / 6.1	23.5 / 13.7 / 6.0	32.2 / 13.9 / 8.3	22.1 / 12.6 / 7.3	18.1 / 9.3 / 5.7
3.1 / 2.3 / 1.8	3.2 / 2.5 / 1.9	3.1 / 2.4 / 1.8	Sales/Total Assets	2.9 / 2.1 / 1.5	3.3 / 2.5 / 1.7	3.4 / 2.6 / 2.0	3.6 / 2.9 / 2.0	2.9 / 2.3 / 1.9	2.6 / 2.2 / 1.6
(290) 1.1 / 1.9 / 2.9	(261) 1.0 / 1.7 / 2.7	(303) 1.0 / 1.7 / 2.9	% Depr., Dep., Amort./Sales	(26) 1.5 / 2.8 / 3.9	(75) 1.3 / 1.9 / 3.9	(62) .8 / 1.5 / 2.3	(48) .8 / 1.4 / 2.4	(58) 1.0 / 1.4 / 2.3	(34) .8 / 1.8 / 2.6
(135) 2.7 / 5.1 / 7.5	(106) 2.4 / 4.7 / 9.9	(160) 2.1 / 3.9 / 6.8	% Officers', Directors', Owners' Comp/Sales	(18) 7.4 / 10.8 / 17.0	(57) 3.3 / 5.1 / 7.5	(35) 2.5 / 4.2 / 5.6	(19) 1.9 / 2.7 / 3.5	(25) 1.2 / 2.0 / 3.5	
3646582M / 1894098M	3128398M / 1687746M	4685544M / 2190955M	Net Sales ($) / Total Assets ($)	19004M / 10119M	159461M / 72562M	240939M / 101851M	387438M / 168641M	952598M / 427920M	2926104M / 1409862M

M = $ thousand   MM = $ million
See Pages 1 through 15 for Explanation of Ratios and Data

Current Data Sorted By Assets | **Comparative Historical Data**

0-500M	500M-2MM	2-10MM	10-50MM	50-100MM	100-250MM	# Postretirement Benefits / Type of Statement	4/1/90-3/31/91 ALL	4/1/91-3/31/92 ALL
		2 (10-50MM)				Unqualified	17	19
	1	9	10	2		Reviewed	14	15
	5	15	1			Compiled	13	10
7	4	3				Tax Returns		
1	1	1				Other	13	11
4	5	4	5			**NUMBER OF STATEMENTS**	57	55

Statement date ranges: 30 (4/1-9/30/94) covers 0-500M and 500M-2MM; 48 (10/1/94-3/31/95) covers 2-10MM through 50-100MM.

NUMBER OF STATEMENTS: 12 | 16 | 32 | 16 | 2 | | | 57 | 55

0-500M %	500M-2MM %	2-10MM %	10-50MM %	50-100MM %	100-250MM %	ASSETS	4/1/90-3/31/91 %	4/1/91-3/31/92 %
8.4	15.3	5.8	11.3			Cash & Equivalents	8.4	8.0
35.4	30.4	31.9	31.2			Trade Receivables - (net)	28.5	29.8
29.9	23.5	30.8	25.9			Inventory	34.1	32.8
.1	.6	1.8	2.1			All Other Current	2.5	2.2
73.8	69.7	70.2	70.5			Total Current	73.5	72.7
18.0	25.4	21.0	16.7			Fixed Assets (net)	17.1	20.2
2.7	1.5	4.0	5.6			Intangibles (net)	1.0	2.3
5.5	3.5	4.7	7.2			All Other Non-Current	8.4	4.8
100.0	100.0	100.0	100.0			Total	100.0	100.0
						LIABILITIES		
9.3	8.8	10.7	4.3			Notes Payable-Short Term	13.5	13.0
2.1	4.2	2.6	2.3			Cur. Mat. -L/T/D	2.8	2.6
26.1	15.0	13.9	13.6			Trade Payables	16.8	14.4
.2	1.0	.7	.8			Income Taxes Payable	.8	1.1
10.5	9.4	11.5	10.0			All Other Current	9.3	7.6
48.2	38.4	39.5	31.0			Total Current	43.0	38.7
19.2	17.9	10.9	12.1			Long Term Debt	11.5	14.0
.1	.3	.4	.1			Deferred Taxes	1.1	.2
5.5	4.8	6.9	1.2			All Other-Non-Current	2.9	2.2
27.0	38.6	42.4	55.6			Net Worth	41.5	44.9
100.0	100.0	100.0	100.0			Total Liabilities & Net Worth	100.0	100.0
						INCOME DATA		
100.0	100.0	100.0	100.0			Net Sales	100.0	100.0
35.7	32.7	29.0	30.3			Gross Profit	31.3	30.5
31.8	26.8	22.4	20.7			Operating Expenses	25.6	24.0
3.9	5.9	6.6	9.6			Operating Profit	5.8	6.4
.8	1.1	1.9	.9			All Other Expenses (net)	1.1	1.9
3.1	4.7	4.7	8.7			Profit Before Taxes	4.7	4.5

RATIOS

0-500M	500M-2MM	2-10MM	10-50MM	50-100MM	100-250MM	RATIO	4/1/90-3/31/91	4/1/91-3/31/92
2.9	3.2	2.5	4.7			Current	2.8	3.6
1.5	1.8	1.8	2.2				1.7	1.7
1.1	1.1	1.4	1.8				1.3	1.3
2.5	3.1	1.4	3.5			Quick	1.6	1.5
.9	.8	.9	1.3				.9	1.1
.6	.5	.7	1.0				.4	.6
11 31.9	22 16.6	39 9.3	45 8.2			Sales/Receivables	30 12.1	31 11.6
47 7.7	46 7.9	51 7.1	60 6.1				51 7.1	54 6.7
78 4.7	69 5.3	70 5.2	73 5.0				69 5.3	72 5.1
13 27.2	10 38.2	38 9.6	43 8.4			Cost of Sales/Inventory	41 8.9	45 8.1
54 6.8	59 6.2	81 4.5	72 5.1				81 4.5	76 4.8
96 3.8	96 3.8	111 3.3	99 3.7				111 3.3	130 2.8
19 19.6	16 22.6	21 17.4	22 16.8			Cost of Sales/Payables	24 15.4	21 17.3
39 9.3	27 13.5	28 13.2	30 12.1				35 10.3	29 12.8
74 4.9	38 9.6	40 9.1	54 6.8				57 6.4	51 7.2
5.6	4.9	5.2	3.3			Sales/Working Capital	4.4	4.2
14.2	7.7	7.6	5.1				6.2	6.0
100.6	199.8	12.4	8.7				16.5	14.9
(11) 9.5	(13) 7.5	(31) 15.5	(14) 21.5			EBIT/Interest	(55) 6.9	(49) 8.4
6.5	4.3	5.3	9.7				3.4	3.4
2.0	2.0	1.6	6.4				1.1	1.3
		(14) 6.5				Net Profit + Depr., Dep., Amort./Cur. Mat. L /T/D	(29) 11.1	(32) 5.6
		2.1					4.5	2.4
		1.1					1.3	1.0
.1	.1	.2	.2			Fixed/Worth	.2	.2
.6	.7	.4	.4				.4	.4
2.9	1.9	1.0	.5				.8	1.1
1.8	.9	.8	.5			Debt/Worth	.6	.5
2.5	2.3	1.5	1.1				1.4	1.6
8.8	3.9	3.4	1.9				4.0	3.6
(10) 81.4	(15) 52.6	(30) 53.8	59.0			% Profit Before Taxes/Tangible Net Worth	(53) 36.7	(52) 46.6
37.1	29.0	21.4	36.1				22.3	23.5
5.4	1.3	11.2	20.0				4.6	4.7
25.3	16.5	17.8	22.9			% Profit Before Taxes/Total Assets	12.8	17.7
7.7	11.1	8.5	14.4				7.6	7.9
2.1	.3	3.1	10.4				.4	1.1
68.3	29.9	23.8	18.6			Sales/Net Fixed Assets	43.6	33.9
30.0	8.9	12.5	11.5				16.2	11.4
14.7	7.0	6.6	9.3				7.1	6.7
5.0	3.1	2.7	2.4			Sales/Total Assets	2.8	2.7
3.1	2.1	2.2	1.8				2.2	2.0
1.8	1.4	1.6	1.5				1.6	1.5
(10) .6	(14) .8	.9	(14) 1.3			% Depr., Dep., Amort./Sales	(49) .8	(50) 1.0
.9	2.1	1.4	2.0				1.2	1.8
2.0	3.6	2.1	2.7				2.4	2.7
		(10) 1.5				% Officers', Directors', Owners' Comp/Sales	(20) 2.3	(18) 1.5
		2.9					4.2	3.3
		3.9					6.4	4.6
9276M	41614M	373378M	732121M	226179M		Net Sales ($)	2494102M	797471M
2966M	17752M	174971M	363171M	149178M		Total Assets ($)	557384M	426882M

M = $ thousand   MM = $ million
See Pages 1 through 15 for Explanation of Ratios and Data

Comparative Historical Data				Current Data Sorted By Sales					
2	2	2	# Postretirement Benefits / Type of Statement						2
17	18	22	Unqualified			1	5	6	10
8	16	21	Reviewed		4	2	7	8	
8	10	14	Compiled	6	3	2	2		1
		3	Tax Returns	1			1	1	
8	16	18	Other	3	6		1	5	3
4/1/92-3/31/93 ALL	4/1/93-3/31/94 ALL	4/1/94-3/31/95 ALL		30 (4/1-9/30/94)			48 (10/1/94-3/31/95)		
				0-1MM	1-3MM	3-5MM	5-10MM	10-25MM	25MM & OVER
41	60	78	**NUMBER OF STATEMENTS**	10	13	5	16	20	14
%	%	%	**ASSETS**	%	%	%	%	%	%
8.2	7.0	9.3	Cash & Equivalents	8.6	16.7		6.3	7.5	9.7
30.5	31.5	32.0	Trade Receivables - (net)	36.2	27.9		29.3	34.5	31.5
32.1	29.5	27.8	Inventory	29.6	24.4		25.5	31.6	27.4
1.7	2.4	1.3	All Other Current	.1	.4		2.3	1.7	2.0
72.6	70.3	70.4	Total Current	74.5	69.5		63.4	75.2	70.6
20.7	19.6	20.9	Fixed Assets (net)	16.6	24.9		24.3	15.8	19.8
1.5	3.5	3.7	Intangibles (net)	2.7	2.2		6.5	4.3	3.1
5.2	6.7	5.0	All Other Non-Current	6.2	3.5		5.9	4.7	6.5
100.0	100.0	100.0	Total	100.0	100.0		100.0	100.0	100.0
			LIABILITIES						
11.1	10.2	8.8	Notes Payable-Short Term	4.3	13.4		11.4	9.9	4.9
2.8	2.2	2.9	Cur. Mat.-L /T/D	1.9	4.5		3.8	1.0	3.7
13.2	14.9	15.9	Trade Payables	28.3	11.1		11.6	15.3	15.2
.7	1.0	.7	Income Taxes Payable	.2	.2		.6	.8	.5
10.1	10.3	10.7	All Other Current	11.0	7.5		12.8	11.2	8.4
38.0	38.6	38.9	Total Current	45.7	36.7		40.2	38.2	32.6
13.0	14.1	14.0	Long Term Debt	21.2	18.6		15.1	6.6	13.9
.4	.6	.3	Deferred Taxes	.1	.3		.4	.2	.3
3.8	2.5	5.0	All Other-Non-Current	4.2	5.5		5.4	7.0	2.4
44.9	44.2	41.8	Net Worth	28.7	38.9		39.0	48.1	50.8
100.0	100.0	100.0	Total Liabilities & Net Worth	100.0	100.0		100.0	100.0	100.0
			INCOME DATA						
100.0	100.0	100.0	Net Sales	100.0	100.0		100.0	100.0	100.0
31.2	29.1	30.8	Gross Profit	35.3	37.3		29.6	29.2	27.1
25.4	23.8	24.2	Operating Expenses	32.4	30.3		23.1	23.5	18.1
5.8	5.3	6.6	Operating Profit	3.0	7.0		6.5	5.7	8.9
.4	1.0	1.4	All Other Expenses (net)	.8	1.6		1.6	1.8	.8
5.4	4.3	5.2	Profit Before Taxes	2.2	5.3		4.9	3.9	8.2
			RATIOS						
2.8	2.5	2.6	Current	3.0	6.2		2.3	2.6	3.7
2.0	1.7	1.9		1.7	1.8		1.4	2.0	2.3
1.4	1.4	1.4		1.1	1.2		1.2	1.5	1.8
1.6	1.5	1.6	Quick	2.8	6.2		1.3	1.6	2.4
.9	1.0	1.0		.9	.9		.8	1.1	1.3
.6	.6	.7		.7	.6		.7	.8	1.0
31 11.9	35 10.4	37 10.0	Sales/Receivables	17 21.0	34 10.7		34 10.8	48 7.6	41 8.9
51 7.1	54 6.8	54 6.7		49 7.5	57 6.4		45 8.1	66 5.5	55 6.6
70 5.2	68 5.4	72 5.1		89 4.1	68 5.4		60 6.1	83 4.4	66 5.5
42 8.7	39 9.4	37 9.8	Cost of Sales/Inventory	10 35.3	10 36.0		27 13.7	51 7.1	45 8.1
72 5.1	64 5.7	68 5.4		59 6.2	73 5.0		53 6.9	87 4.2	61 6.0
118 3.1	101 3.6	101 3.6		104 3.5	111 3.3		111 3.3	104 3.5	94 3.9
20 18.7	19 19.7	21 17.6	Cost of Sales/Payables	27 13.6	10 35.9		19 19.7	22 16.5	22 16.6
26 13.8	29 12.8	29 12.7		50 7.3	19 19.1		23 15.8	30 12.0	30 12.1
43 8.4	42 8.7	48 7.6		83 4.4	37 10.0		31 11.6	49 7.5	56 6.5
4.6	4.4	4.5	Sales/Working Capital	3.8	3.2		5.2	4.0	4.0
6.5	7.3	7.2		11.2	7.1		11.8	6.5	5.5
13.4	14.7	17.0		47.4	142.1		26.5	9.6	9.4
(38) 10.6	(54) 8.6	(71) 12.2	EBIT/Interest		7.0		15.0	7.3	26.5
4.5	3.5	6.2		(10) 4.3			6.0	(17) 5.0	11.7
2.1	1.8	2.6		1.0			2.0	.8	7.8
(17) 10.5	(18) 6.4	(32) 7.0	Net Profit + Depr., Dep., Amort./Cur. Mat. L/T/D				14.3		
4.1	3.5	3.5		(11) 2.8					
1.8	2.0	1.2		1.3					
.1	.2	.2	Fixed/Worth	.1	.1		.3	.2	.3
.3	.4	.4		.4	.9		.5	.3	.4
.9	.9	1.1		NM	2.5		2.0	.8	.6
.6	.6	.8	Debt/Worth	1.5	.9		1.0	.5	.6
1.4	1.5	1.6		2.1	2.9		1.7	1.0	1.0
3.0	3.3	3.6		NM	5.5		4.1	2.4	1.9
(39) 37.2	(57) 42.5	(73) 53.5	% Profit Before Taxes/Tangible Net Worth		67.8		70.2	(19) 36.6	71.1
23.4	19.3	26.0		(12) 18.2		(15)	36.5	19.9	36.1
10.5	3.5	11.2		.4			12.5	11.0	18.4
14.6	15.3	18.0	% Profit Before Taxes/Total Assets	17.1	23.1		26.5	13.5	27.5
8.1	7.6	10.7		6.8	11.3		10.1	7.5	14.4
5.1	1.6	3.7		1.1	.1		4.7	2.2	11.0
40.4	42.7	26.8	Sales/Net Fixed Assets	92.9	27.5		20.7	26.9	17.9
14.4	14.3	12.8		34.0	9.7		8.3	13.6	11.0
6.2	7.2	7.2		12.2	5.8		6.3	10.2	5.6
2.9	3.0	2.9	Sales/Total Assets	4.7	2.8		3.0	2.4	2.6
2.2	2.1	2.1		2.8	2.0		2.3	2.0	1.8
1.4	1.5	1.6		1.6	1.3		1.5	1.6	1.6
(34) .9	(52) .9	(72) .8	% Depr., Dep., Amort./Sales		1.0		.4	.9	(12) 1.1
1.7	1.6	1.6		(11) 2.2			1.2	1.5	1.9
2.4	2.3	2.3		4.5			2.2	2.0	2.6
	(22) 2.1	(25) 1.4	% Officers', Directors', Owners' Comp/Sales						
	3.2	3.0							
	4.9	5.6							
730777M	1036569M	1382568M	Net Sales ($)	5996M	24133M	19480M	116512M	333781M	882666M
408837M	599420M	708038M	Total Assets ($)	2432M	12672M	9008M	58413M	172921M	452592M

© Robert Morris Associates 1995

M = $ thousand   MM = $ million

See Pages 1 through 15 for Explanation of Ratios and Data

Current Data Sorted By Assets / Comparative Historical Data

Type of Statement

0-500M	500M-2MM	2-10MM	10-50MM	50-100MM	100-250MM	# Postretirement Benefits / Type of Statement	4/1/90-3/31/91 ALL	4/1/91-3/31/92 ALL
	1	1	2	1		# Postretirement Benefits		
	5	14	9	2	3	Unqualified	36	32
1	19	21	5			Reviewed	42	32
5	10	7	1			Compiled	27	28
	1	2				Tax Returns		1
3	10	14	7	2		Other	26	14
	31 (4/1-9/30/94)		110 (10/1/94-3/31/95)					
9	45	58	22	4	3	NUMBER OF STATEMENTS	131	107

ASSETS (%)

0-500M	500M-2MM	2-10MM	10-50MM	50-100MM	100-250MM	ASSETS	4/1/90-3/31/91 ALL	4/1/91-3/31/92 ALL
%	%	%	%	%	%		%	%
	6.4	4.7	5.2			Cash & Equivalents	6.6	5.0
	31.0	31.0	24.2			Trade Receivables - (net)	29.0	30.8
	33.6	31.1	25.5			Inventory	30.5	30.9
	1.5	2.4	1.1			All Other Current	2.1	2.1
	72.4	69.3	55.9			Total Current	68.3	68.8
	20.5	24.4	36.8			Fixed Assets (net)	24.3	23.2
	2.1	.6	2.4			Intangibles (net)	1.9	2.3
	4.9	5.6	4.9			All Other Non-Current	5.5	5.6
	100.0	100.0	100.0			Total	100.0	100.0

LIABILITIES

0-500M	500M-2MM	2-10MM	10-50MM	50-100MM	100-250MM	LIABILITIES	4/1/90-3/31/91 ALL	4/1/91-3/31/92 ALL
	11.5	12.5	9.7			Notes Payable-Short Term	8.6	12.6
	3.9	4.3	4.0			Cur. Mat. -L/T/D	4.5	3.7
	19.1	17.1	13.9			Trade Payables	17.0	17.2
	1.7	.6	.1			Income Taxes Payable	.5	.6
	6.2	8.6	7.9			All Other Current	7.6	8.9
	42.4	43.0	35.7			Total Current	38.1	43.0
	12.4	14.2	16.7			Long Term Debt	17.1	17.2
	.4	.1	.4			Deferred Taxes	.8	.3
	4.8	3.4	3.0			All Other-Non-Current	4.0	2.9
	40.0	39.2	44.1			Net Worth	40.0	36.7
	100.0	100.0	100.0			Total Liabilities & Net Worth	100.0	100.0

INCOME DATA

0-500M	500M-2MM	2-10MM	10-50MM	50-100MM	100-250MM	INCOME DATA	4/1/90-3/31/91 ALL	4/1/91-3/31/92 ALL
	100.0	100.0	100.0			Net Sales	100.0	100.0
	27.3	26.7	29.9			Gross Profit	27.7	29.5
	22.6	22.2	21.9			Operating Expenses	22.8	26.4
	4.8	4.6	7.9			Operating Profit	4.9	3.1
	.8	.7	1.4			All Other Expenses (net)	1.1	1.6
	4.0	3.9	6.5			Profit Before Taxes	3.8	1.5

RATIOS

0-500M	500M-2MM	2-10MM	10-50MM	50-100MM	100-250MM	RATIOS	4/1/90-3/31/91 ALL	4/1/91-3/31/92 ALL
	2.4	2.1	2.4				2.7	2.3
	1.7	1.7	1.7			Current	1.9	1.6
	1.3	1.2	1.1				1.4	1.3
	1.3	1.2	1.2				1.5	1.3
	.9	.9	.9			Quick	.9	.9
	.6	.6	.6				.7	.6
(24) 14.9		(32) 11.5	(27) 13.4				(31) 11.9	(31) 11.6
(40) 9.1		(41) 8.9	(38) 9.7			Sales/Receivables	(42) 8.6	(46) 8.0
(62) 5.9		(63) 5.8	(43) 8.4				(59) 6.2	(63) 5.8
(41) 8.9		(45) 8.2	(49) 7.4				(38) 9.7	(36) 10.1
(56) 6.5		(56) 6.5	(63) 5.8			Cost of Sales/Inventory	(60) 6.1	(64) 5.7
(96) 3.8		(89) 4.1	(79) 4.6				(89) 4.1	(85) 4.3
(19) 19.2		(19) 19.6	(20) 18.5				(20) 18.2	(21) 17.8
(32) 11.5		(29) 12.4	(27) 13.5			Cost of Sales/Payables	(33) 11.2	(35) 10.4
(53) 6.9		(48) 7.6	(37) 10.0				(49) 7.5	(47) 7.7
	6.8	6.0	6.0				4.9	5.6
	9.4	9.4	10.1			Sales/Working Capital	7.4	9.2
	14.6	18.5	44.2				14.1	17.5
	10.5	9.0	25.1				5.2	4.2
(42)	3.5	(55) 3.0	(21) 5.6			EBIT/Interest	(121) 2.7	(99) 2.0
	1.2	1.5	2.2				1.3	1.1
	5.1	8.7	9.7			Net Profit + Depr., Dep.,		6.3	5.7
(17)	2.2	(17) 2.1	(11) 2.9			Amort./Cur. Mat. L /T/D	(78) 3.2	(48) 2.0
	.5	1.3	1.9				1.4	.4
	.2	.3	.6				.3	.3
	.4	.7	.8			Fixed/Worth	.5	.7
	.8	1.1	1.5				1.0	1.3
	.8	.9	.6				.9	.9
	1.3	1.6	1.4			Debt/Worth	1.4	1.8
	3.0	3.7	3.3				3.4	4.2
	43.5	46.8	47.4			% Profit Before Taxes/Tangible		34.3	23.5
(42)	22.4	(57) 14.5	(21) 26.6			Net Worth	(121) 19.2	(97) 11.0
	1.4	5.2	16.3				5.3	1.4
	22.6	19.3	26.4			% Profit Before Taxes/Total		13.7	10.6
	5.2	4.9	12.1			Assets	6.2	4.0
	.3	1.0	5.0				1.3	.2
	42.0	21.8	9.0				25.6	28.0
	20.0	10.8	7.0			Sales/Net Fixed Assets	11.1	12.7
	8.6	6.3	5.3				5.1	6.1
	3.3	3.3	2.9				2.9	3.3
	2.8	2.4	2.3			Sales/Total Assets	2.4	2.4
	2.1	2.0	1.9				1.7	1.9
	.7	.8	1.8				.9	1.1
(42)	1.3	(56) 1.4	(19) 2.1			% Depr., Dep., Amort./Sales	(117) 1.6	(96) 1.7
	1.7	2.1	3.3				3.0	2.5
	1.9	2.1				% Officers', Directors',		2.2	2.1
(23)	3.0	(24) 3.3				Owners' Comp/Sales	(49) 3.7	(46) 3.3
	4.8	4.3					7.1	7.0
12852M	151638M	615514M	1273609M	639634M	624567M	Net Sales ($)	3015071M	1641674M
3174M	56061M	238058M	561973M	282607M	423558M	Total Assets ($)	1522464M	728849M

M = $ thousand   MM = $ million
See Pages 1 through 15 for Explanation of Ratios and Data

Comparative Historical Data / Current Data Sorted By Sales

Hist 5	Hist 6	Hist 5	# Postretirement Benefits / Type of Statement		1	2	2
41	36	33	Unqualified		2 / 3	7	7	14
41	46	46	Reviewed		11 / 8	15	6	6
21	25	23	Compiled	2	10 / 5	4	1	1
1	2	3	Tax Returns		1 / 1	1		
22	31	36	Other	2	7 / 2	8	10	7

4/1/92-3/31/93 ALL	4/1/93-3/31/94 ALL	4/1/94-3/31/95 ALL		0-1MM	31 (4/1-9/30/94) 1-3MM	3-5MM	110 (10/1/94-3/31/95) 5-10MM	10-25MM	25MM & OVER
126	140	141	**NUMBER OF STATEMENTS**	4	31	19	35	24	28
%	%	%	**ASSETS**	%	%	%	%	%	%
5.4	8.1	5.6	Cash & Equivalents		7.0	6.3	5.8	3.5	5.0
30.8	27.0	29.7	Trade Receivables - (net)		30.4	34.2	29.7	26.4	28.1
31.5	31.0	30.3	Inventory		32.6	29.0	31.7	31.7	27.3
1.3	1.4	1.9	All Other Current		1.3	1.7	3.1	1.5	1.2
69.1	67.6	67.6	Total Current		71.2	71.0	70.3	63.2	61.5
22.0	23.8	25.0	Fixed Assets (net)		20.5	21.9	24.6	28.6	29.9
2.4	1.5	1.8	Intangibles (net)		4.9	.3	.2	1.1	2.2
6.4	7.2	5.6	All Other Non-Current		3.5	6.7	4.9	7.1	6.4
100.0	100.0	100.0	Total		100.0	100.0	100.0	100.0	100.0
			LIABILITIES						
10.1	8.2	11.0	Notes Payable-Short Term		8.7	10.1	16.4	9.9	8.7
4.3	4.0	4.3	Cur. Mat.-L /T/D		5.7	3.2	4.5	4.0	2.9
16.4	16.6	17.6	Trade Payables		22.9	17.5	15.6	16.5	15.9
.5	1.4	.9	Income Taxes Payable		1.9	.7	.6	.9	.1
8.7	7.7	7.8	All Other Current		6.0	7.0	9.0	7.1	8.9
39.9	37.9	41.6	Total Current		45.2	38.6	46.1	38.3	36.6
14.0	14.3	13.7	Long Term Debt		16.0	9.7	13.8	17.2	11.6
.4	.4	.3	Deferred Taxes		.5	.0	.3	.2	.4
4.5	2.2	3.6	All Other-Non-Current		5.1	5.4	3.0	2.7	2.6
41.3	45.1	40.8	Net Worth		33.2	46.3	36.9	41.6	48.8
100.0	100.0	100.0	Total Liabilities & Net Worth		100.0	100.0	100.0	100.0	100.0
			INCOME DATA						
100.0	100.0	100.0	Net Sales		100.0	100.0	100.0	100.0	100.0
28.6	30.2	28.3	Gross Profit		27.2	28.2	25.6	30.6	28.1
25.3	26.2	23.1	Operating Expenses		22.3	23.2	23.1	22.8	21.1
3.4	4.0	5.1	Operating Profit		5.0	4.9	2.5	7.7	7.0
.9	.7	.8	All Other Expenses (net)		.8	.7	1.2	1.1	.3
2.5	3.3	4.3	Profit Before Taxes		4.2	4.3	1.3	6.7	6.7
			RATIOS						
2.4	2.5	2.3	Current		2.4	2.5	2.0	2.3	2.7
1.7	1.8	1.7			1.7	1.9	1.7	1.6	1.9
1.4	1.3	1.3			1.3	1.4	1.2	1.2	1.3
1.4	1.4	1.2	Quick		1.4	1.4	1.1	1.1	1.4
.9	(139) 1.0	.9			.9	.9	.8	.7	.9
.6	.6	.6			.6	.8	.5	.5	.7
31 11.7	28 12.9	30 12.3	Sales/Receivables	24 15.4	32 11.4	28 13.0	20 18.4	35 10.4
44 8.3	40 9.2	40 9.1		41 9.0	47 7.8	38 9.6	38 9.6	38 9.5
59 6.2	56 6.5	56 6.5		65 5.6	68 5.4	54 6.7	41 8.8	47 7.8
45 8.1	40 9.1	41 8.8	Cost of Sales/Inventory	42 8.7	32 11.4	41 8.8	45 8.1	40 9.1
66 5.5	58 6.3	56 6.5		58 6.3	52 7.0	54 6.7	56 6.5	59 6.2
85 4.3	96 3.8	83 4.4		96 3.8	85 4.3	87 4.2	79 4.6	74 4.9
21 17.8	20 18.6	19 19.0	Cost of Sales/Payables	22 16.3	16 22.9	19 19.0	14 25.8	19 18.8
30 12.2	31 11.9	30 12.0		35 10.5	32 11.5	31 11.9	26 14.0	26 13.8
45 8.1	51 7.2	48 7.6		70 5.2	58 6.3	44 8.3	51 7.2	36 10.2
5.6	5.3	6.1	Sales/Working Capital		6.0	5.5	6.6	8.2	6.0
8.4	8.4	9.5			9.4	8.3	10.6	11.7	9.4
16.2	15.8	17.5			15.7	11.3	16.2	38.9	25.1
7.3	12.9	11.5	EBIT/Interest		12.1	8.5	5.4	27.8	27.8
(116) 3.4	(130) 3.6	(133) 4.3		(28) 3.8	(17) 2.7	(34) 2.6	(23) 6.4	(27) 11.4
1.3	1.4	1.5			1.3	1.0	.8	2.1	3.3
7.6	5.4	8.0	Net Profit + Depr., Dep., Amort./Cur. Mat. L/T/D		16.1		4.4		13.2
(50) 3.2	(60) 2.0	(50) 2.7		(10) 3.9		(13) 1.7		(15) 4.5
1.1	.6	1.3			.7		-.3		2.6
.3	.2	.3	Fixed/Worth		.2	.2	.4	.3	.4
.6	.6	.6			.4	.3	.7	.7	.6
1.0	1.0	1.1			4.8	.9	1.2	1.2	.8
.8	.6	.8	Debt/Worth		1.0	.8	1.0	.6	.6
1.6	1.2	1.4			2.2	1.2	1.7	1.4	1.0
3.2	2.8	3.3			11.1	2.2	4.3	3.3	2.4
34.2	35.6	45.5	% Profit Before Taxes/Tangible Net Worth		42.3	45.2	36.0	70.6	46.1
(117) 16.8	(134) 15.5	(133) 25.2		(25) 22.4	11.0	8.2	(22) 38.9	27.5
2.8	3.9	7.0			12.0	.6	-1.9	14.5	13.6
12.9	14.1	19.7	% Profit Before Taxes/Total Assets		14.6	26.8	13.5	35.9	25.7
6.1	6.4	7.7			8.5	4.8	4.2	12.3	13.7
.8	1.3	1.4			.5	.2	-.8	3.8	5.6
24.3	23.4	24.6	Sales/Net Fixed Assets		47.4	40.5	21.6	20.2	12.0
13.2	10.8	10.4			23.2	15.1	9.4	13.5	7.2
6.4	6.2	6.1			5.4	6.0	6.4	7.6	5.4
3.0	3.3	3.2	Sales/Total Assets		3.5	3.3	3.0	3.7	2.9
2.4	2.3	2.5			2.5	2.4	2.4	3.2	2.3
1.9	1.7	2.0			1.8	1.9	2.0	1.9	2.0
1.0	1.0	.8	% Depr., Dep., Amort./Sales		.7	.8	1.1	.8	1.3
(114) 1.5	(125) 1.7	(130) 1.5		(29) 1.2	(18) 1.3	(34) 1.5	(22) 1.7	(25) 2.0
2.4	2.7	2.3			1.6	2.1	2.2	2.4	2.7
2.1	1.9	2.0	% Officers', Directors', Owners' Comp/Sales		1.4	2.1	2.1		
(61) 3.8	(63) 3.5	(54) 3.3		(14) 3.4	(11) 3.3	(18) 3.3		
8.8	7.2	4.5			5.0	10.3	3.9		
3380499M	3357139M	3317814M	Net Sales ($)	3025M	65719M	76457M	254074M	366863M	2551676M
1722632M	1605799M	1565431M	Total Assets ($)	3255M	31292M	32385M	109295M	174652M	1214552M

M = $ thousand   MM = $ million
See Pages 1 through 15 for Explanation of Ratios and Data

MANUFACTURERS—METAL STAMPINGS. SIC# 3465 (66,69)

Current Data Sorted By Assets							Comparative Historical Data	
1	1	10	3			# Postretirement Benefits		
						Type of Statement		
	5	31	35		2	Unqualified	87	71
2	35	43	10			Reviewed	84	100
14	33	24	1			Compiled	65	60
2	4	4	1			Tax Returns		2
4	16	44	21	5	2	Other	45	56
	123 (4/1-9/30/94)		211 (10/1/94-3/31/95)				4/1/90-3/31/91	4/1/91-3/31/92
0-500M	500M-2MM	2-10MM	10-50MM	50-100MM	100-250MM		ALL	ALL
22	93	143	67	5	4	NUMBER OF STATEMENTS	281	289
%	%	%	%	%	%	**ASSETS**	%	%
6.8	7.5	5.9	5.6			Cash & Equivalents	7.0	7.2
32.2	29.8	29.2	26.1			Trade Receivables - (net)	26.3	27.6
15.0	20.0	21.9	20.9			Inventory	21.5	20.9
7.5	1.7	1.2	1.7			All Other Current	1.2	1.7
61.5	58.9	58.2	54.3			Total Current	56.0	57.4
36.1	34.0	34.5	39.3			Fixed Assets (net)	35.3	34.5
.8	1.3	1.2	1.7			Intangibles (net)	1.7	1.1
1.6	5.8	6.1	4.8			All Other Non-Current	7.0	7.0
100.0	100.0	100.0	100.0			Total	100.0	100.0
						LIABILITIES		
6.2	7.2	9.7	8.0			Notes Payable-Short Term	9.3	10.3
6.5	5.2	5.3	4.2			Cur. Mat. -L/T/D	5.1	4.9
19.8	16.9	18.2	17.9			Trade Payables	15.6	16.6
.9	.3	.3	.3			Income Taxes Payable	.7	.4
13.2	8.5	8.6	8.3			All Other Current	7.9	8.4
46.6	38.2	42.0	38.7			Total Current	38.6	40.6
21.4	14.6	14.5	18.3			Long Term Debt	19.0	16.8
.1	.4	.8	1.7			Deferred Taxes	1.0	.8
3.1	3.4	3.7	3.5			All Other-Non-Current	2.6	2.4
28.9	43.3	38.8	37.7			Net Worth	38.7	39.4
100.0	100.0	100.0	100.0			Total Liabilities & Net Worth	100.0	100.0
						INCOME DATA		
100.0	100.0	100.0	100.0			Net Sales	100.0	100.0
36.7	27.4	22.6	21.3			Gross Profit	24.3	23.8
29.5	22.8	17.2	13.4			Operating Expenses	19.8	20.3
7.2	4.7	5.5	7.8			Operating Profit	4.6	3.4
.9	1.0	1.1	1.2			All Other Expenses (net)	1.6	1.5
6.3	3.7	4.4	6.6			Profit Before Taxes	2.9	1.9
						RATIOS		
1.9	2.2	2.2	2.4			Current	2.1	2.2
1.5	1.6	1.3	1.4				1.5	1.4
.9	1.1	1.0	1.0				1.1	1.0
1.3	1.5	1.4	1.4			Quick	1.2	1.3
.9	.9	.8	.8				.8	.9
.5		.6	.5				.6	.6
15 23.9	34 10.6	38 9.7	42 8.7			Sales/Receivables	37 10.0	38 9.7
33 11.1	45 8.2	47 7.7	47 7.7				46 8.0	47 7.7
40 9.1	56 6.5	60 6.1	56 6.5				56 6.5	58 6.3
6 56.2	20 18.3	31 11.7	35 10.4			Cost of Sales/Inventory	29 12.4	29 12.6
16 22.8	37 10.0	45 8.1	47 7.8				46 7.9	43 8.5
28 13.1	58 6.3	61 6.0	64 5.7				66 5.5	63 5.8
9 38.9	21 17.6	22 16.6	23 15.6			Cost of Sales/Payables	21 17.5	20 18.6
35 10.5	33 11.2	37 9.8	39 9.4				32 11.5	30 12.2
44 8.3	47 7.7	51 7.2	57 6.4				45 8.1	49 7.4
11.7	7.6	6.6	6.3			Sales/Working Capital	6.7	6.8
17.8	11.0	16.5	12.3				12.0	12.6
-90.8	32.0	142.2	999.8				46.8	144.7
16.0	9.1	9.5	15.8			EBIT/Interest	4.8	5.3
(21) 6.3	(87) 3.9	(131) 3.5	(59) 4.8				(260) 2.2	(264) 2.1
1.2	1.3	1.7	2.5				.9	.8
	5.1	4.4	8.9			Net Profit + Depr., Dep.,		3.7	3.8
	(36) 1.6	(77) 2.4	(38) 3.5			Amort./Cur. Mat. L./T/D	(185) 2.0	(164) 1.9
	.7	1.4	1.7				1.0	.8
.5	.4	.5	.7			Fixed/Worth	.5	.5
1.1	.8	1.0	1.2				1.0	.9
3.2	1.4	1.8	2.8				1.9	1.8
.9	.7	.9	.8			Debt/Worth	.9	.9
1.7	1.2	1.8	1.8				1.7	1.7
8.4	3.1	4.0	5.0				3.8	3.4
92.3	33.5	40.4	59.0			% Profit Before Taxes/Tangible	31.2	26.0
(19) 55.4	(89) 15.9	(136) 19.3	(65) 30.9			Net Worth	(262) 15.0	(273) 11.3
2.5	4.2	6.8	15.3				.7	-1.3
39.0	16.6	13.8	17.6			% Profit Before Taxes/Total	12.1	10.7
22.0	6.0	5.9	9.9			Assets	4.7	3.6
1.1	1.3	1.8	5.6				-.1	-.9
22.4	13.6	9.9	6.7			Sales/Net Fixed Assets	10.1	9.8
12.6	6.9	6.9	4.7				5.6	6.2
7.1	4.1	3.9	3.7				3.8	4.3
5.0	3.0	2.7	2.3			Sales/Total Assets	2.5	2.5
3.4	2.4	2.2	1.9				2.1	2.1
2.3	1.9	1.7	1.5				1.7	1.7
1.6	1.9	2.1	1.9			% Depr., Dep., Amort./Sales	1.9	1.9
(20) 3.7	(84) 2.9	(133) 2.9	(60) 2.9				(266) 3.1	(268) 3.0
5.6	4.3	4.2	4.0				4.2	4.4
6.6	2.9	1.9	.9			% Officers', Directors',	2.1	2.1
(13) 7.9	(53) 4.4	(59) 3.1	(16) 1.4			Owners' Comp/Sales	(125) 4.4	(137) 4.4
17.6	8.3	6.0	2.6				8.2	7.0
19034M	269684M	1523301M	2648191M	620607M	824996M	Net Sales ($)	3983046M	4201121M
5610M	110876M	709306M	1410641M	343222M	620307M	Total Assets ($)	2484330M	2277720M

M = $ thousand   MM = $ million
See Pages 1 through 15 for Explanation of Ratios and Data

Comparative Historical Data				Current Data Sorted By Sales					
3	13	15	# Postretirement Benefits	1	1		4	6	3
			Type of Statement						
72	49	73	Unqualified		3	6	9	24	31
69	97	90	Reviewed	3	22	15	17	25	8
48	55	72	Compiled	12	24	11	15	9	1
2	1	7	Tax Returns	1	3	2	1		
62	78	92	Other	4	16	9	13	29	21
4/1/92-3/31/93	4/1/93-3/31/94	4/1/94-3/31/95		123 (4/1-9/30/94)			211 (10/1/94-3/31/95)		
ALL	ALL	ALL		0-1MM	1-3MM	3-5MM	5-10MM	10-25MM	25MM & OVER
253	280	334	NUMBER OF STATEMENTS	20	68	43	55	87	61
%	%	%	ASSETS	%	%	%	%	%	%
5.8	6.8	6.3	Cash & Equivalents	6.1	7.7	5.7	7.5	5.3	5.4
27.9	28.6	28.8	Trade Receivables - (net)	32.7	27.2	29.3	28.5	29.8	27.7
20.8	20.6	20.6	Inventory	13.9	18.0	23.8	20.4	22.4	21.0
1.1	1.9	1.9	All Other Current	8.0	2.0	.9	1.0	1.2	2.2
55.6	57.8	57.6	Total Current	60.7	54.9	59.7	57.4	58.8	56.4
36.0	34.9	35.4	Fixed Assets (net)	36.3	37.7	36.4	32.8	34.0	36.3
1.9	1.4	1.5	Intangibles (net)	.2	1.6	.8	2.0	1.5	2.1
6.5	5.8	5.5	All Other Non-Current	2.8	5.8	3.1	7.8	5.8	5.2
100.0	100.0	100.0	Total	100.0	100.0	100.0	100.0	100.0	100.0
			LIABILITIES						
10.4	9.0	8.3	Notes Payable-Short Term	5.0	7.5	8.9	8.1	9.1	8.7
5.5	4.5	5.1	Cur. Mat.-L /T/D	7.0	5.4	5.4	6.0	5.0	3.4
15.8	15.0	17.8	Trade Payables	19.3	15.5	17.6	16.7	18.7	19.5
.3	2.5	.4	Income Taxes Payable	.8	.3	.4	.2	.4	.3
7.9	8.2	8.8	All Other Current	12.3	10.5	7.2	7.1	9.1	7.9
39.9	39.2	40.3	Total Current	44.3	39.2	39.5	38.1	42.2	39.9
16.3	16.6	15.9	Long Term Debt	25.2	16.1	16.7	14.8	14.4	15.1
.8	1.0	.9	Deferred Taxes	.1	.5	.3	.6	1.0	1.9
3.3	3.9	3.6	All Other-Non-Current	5.2	3.3	2.1	3.8	3.9	4.0
39.7	39.3	39.4	Net Worth	25.2	40.9	41.3	42.7	38.4	39.2
100.0	100.0	100.0	Total Liabilities & Net Worth	100.0	100.0	100.0	100.0	100.0	100.0
			INCOME DATA						
100.0	100.0	100.0	Net Sales	100.0	100.0	100.0	100.0	100.0	100.0
24.9	24.8	24.6	Gross Profit	34.0	31.3	24.9	24.6	20.3	20.2
20.5	20.6	18.7	Operating Expenses	25.9	25.5	20.8	19.0	14.8	12.7
4.5	4.1	5.9	Operating Profit	8.0	5.7	4.1	5.5	5.5	7.5
1.1	.9	1.1	All Other Expenses (net)	.9	1.1	.9	1.1	1.2	1.0
3.4	3.3	4.8	Profit Before Taxes	7.1	4.6	3.2	4.4	4.3	6.6
			RATIOS						
2.0	2.3	2.2		2.0	2.1	2.1	2.6	1.9	2.4
1.4	1.5	1.4	Current	1.6	1.6	1.4	1.4	1.4	1.5
1.1	1.1	1.1		.9	1.1	1.1	1.1	1.0	1.0
1.3	1.4	1.4		1.4	1.5	1.3	1.5	1.3	1.5
.8	.9	.8	Quick	1.0	.8	.9	.9	.7	.9
.6	.6	.6		.7	.6	.6	.6	.6	.6
37 9.9	35 10.5	38 9.7		20 18.7	34 10.7	37 10.0	38 9.7	40 9.2	42 8.6
45 8.2	47 7.8	46 7.9	Sales/Receivables	37 9.9	44 8.3	45 8.2	46 8.0	47 7.8	48 7.6
54 6.7	55 6.6	58 6.3		81 4.5	60 6.1	56 6.5	59 6.2	57 6.4	55 6.6
29 12.7	29 12.8	28 13.0		12 30.4	16 23.4	31 11.6	23 15.8	31 11.6	32 11.4
42 8.7	41 8.9	42 8.6	Cost of Sales/Inventory	22 16.9	36 10.1	49 7.4	44 8.3	42 8.6	46 7.9
66 5.5	62 5.9	60 6.1		47 7.7	73 5.0	60 6.1	63 5.8	58 6.3	62 5.9
20 18.0	15 24.4	21 17.3		18 20.8	18 20.2	25 14.5	19 18.9	22 16.5	22 16.4
31 11.7	27 13.3	35 10.4	Cost of Sales/Payables	37 9.8	34 10.7	33 10.9	33 11.2	37 9.8	40 9.2
50 7.3	47 7.7	51 7.2		73 5.0	53 6.9	47 7.8	42 8.6	50 7.3	54 6.8
7.6	6.8	7.1		5.3	7.7	7.9	6.2	7.8	5.9
13.2	13.1	12.3	Sales/Working Capital	13.5	12.1	13.9	12.1	14.8	10.6
64.4	45.9	101.7		-69.6	49.2	63.8	73.0	139.6	NM
		6.6		14.6	10.1	7.4	9.5	11.1	15.8
(236) 2.9	(260) 3.2	(307) 4.0	EBIT/Interest	(19) 4.4	(64) 3.9	(39) 3.0	(52) 3.4	(78) 3.8	(55) 5.6
1.4	1.6	1.7		1.1	1.3	1.4	1.7	1.8	2.5
3.6	4.2	6.0			3.8	2.8	3.7	5.9	9.8
(140) 1.9	(131) 2.2	(159) 2.4	Net Profit + Depr., Dep., Amort./Cur. Mat. L/T/D		(27) 1.3	(17) 2.0	(29) 2.2	(45) 2.7	(35) 3.8
1.1	1.3	1.3			.8	.9	1.3	2.1	1.7
.5	.5	.5		.5	.5	.5	.4	.6	.6
1.0	.9	1.0	Fixed/Worth	1.2	.9	1.1	.8	1.0	1.0
1.7	1.9	2.0		3.4	1.9	1.7	1.8	1.8	2.6
.8	.8	.8		1.0	.6	.8	.8	1.0	.8
1.6	1.8	1.7	Debt/Worth	2.2	1.3	2.0	1.4	1.7	1.7
3.3	3.9	4.1		9.2	4.4	3.3	4.1	3.3	5.3
32.9	35.9	43.0	% Profit Before Taxes/Tangible Net Worth	87.4	40.2	35.6	35.0	46.5	49.3
(237) 15.7	(266) 16.8	(318) 21.1		(17) 19.1	(63) 18.1	(53) 15.6	(82) 18.6	(60) 19.6	31.2
5.1	4.6	7.9		2.9	4.2	4.0	7.0	7.6	20.5
12.6	12.9	16.7	% Profit Before Taxes/Total Assets	22.8	16.8	12.0	13.3	17.3	18.7
6.0	5.4	7.1		7.9	6.0	5.8	6.2	8.2	9.9
1.4	1.5	2.1		.8	.8	1.5	2.0	2.9	5.6
10.3	10.2	10.6		18.9	10.7	14.0	12.7	10.1	7.5
6.0	6.4	6.4	Sales/Net Fixed Assets	9.4	5.7	6.4	6.4	7.7	5.4
4.1	4.3	3.9		2.7	3.3	4.2	3.9	4.9	3.9
2.7	2.7	2.7		4.5	2.6	3.0	2.7	2.7	2.4
2.1	2.2	2.2	Sales/Total Assets	2.2	2.2	2.3	2.2	2.3	2.0
1.7	1.8	1.7		1.7	1.7	2.0	1.6	1.9	1.6
1.9	1.9	2.0		1.6	2.2	2.0	2.1	2.1	1.8
(232) 2.9	(262) 2.9	(302) 2.9	% Depr., Dep., Amort./Sales	(17) 4.4	(62) 3.0	(40) 3.4	(52) 3.1	(81) 2.7	(50) 2.6
4.1	4.3	4.3		5.5	5.1	4.1	5.2	3.9	3.4
2.6	2.6	2.0		4.0	3.4	2.2	2.1	1.2	.9
(114) 4.8	(136) 4.8	(141) 4.1	% Officers', Directors', Owners' Comp/Sales	(11) 7.9	(36) 5.4	(20) 4.4	(26) 3.9	(35) 2.7	(13) 2.0
7.8	8.3	6.8		17.8	11.1	5.5	7.9	4.1	2.9
3787694M	3363666M	5905813M	Net Sales ($)	12668M	138818M	171983M	392843M	1348512M	3840989M
2266006M	1841061M	3199962M	Total Assets ($)	10789M	90503M	76435M	207820M	645036M	2169379M

© Robert Morris Associates 1995

M = $ thousand   MM = $ million
See Pages 1 through 15 for Explanation of Ratios and Data

Current Data Sorted By Assets | **Comparative Historical Data**

Postretirement Benefits — Type of Statement

	0-500M	500M-2MM	2-10MM	10-50MM	50-100MM	100-250MM		4/1/90-3/31/91 ALL	4/1/91-3/31/92 ALL
	2	8	11	3		1			
Unqualified		15	44	22	4	4		75	73
Reviewed	7	42	62	6				95	97
Compiled	30	54	17	1		1		100	92
Tax Returns	10	3	1					3	3
Other	15	37	22	15	2	1		60	55
	114 (4/1-9/30/94)			300 (10/1/94-3/31/95)					
NUMBER OF STATEMENTS	62	151	146	43	6	6		333	320

ASSETS	%	%	%	%	%	%		%	%
Cash & Equivalents	10.3	4.9	6.1	5.0				6.8	6.3
Trade Receivables - (net)	31.8	30.6	30.9	24.6				28.3	28.9
Inventory	19.9	23.0	25.5	22.9				24.5	23.8
All Other Current	1.2	2.4	2.1	1.0				2.2	2.4
Total Current	63.1	60.9	64.7	53.5				61.8	61.5
Fixed Assets (net)	30.3	31.3	28.6	34.8				31.2	30.1
Intangibles (net)	1.0	2.3	1.5	2.5				1.4	2.2
All Other Non-Current	5.6	5.5	5.2	9.1				5.6	6.2
Total	100.0	100.0	100.0	100.0				100.0	100.0

LIABILITIES									
Notes Payable-Short Term	9.3	9.0	10.6	6.9				10.2	10.7
Cur. Mat. -L/T/D	5.8	4.3	4.5	4.4				5.1	4.6
Trade Payables	16.3	17.0	15.8	13.7				14.5	14.1
Income Taxes Payable	.7	.4	.4	.5				.7	.3
All Other Current	8.0	7.5	8.3	8.2				8.2	8.0
Total Current	40.0	38.2	39.6	33.7				38.6	37.7
Long Term Debt	16.8	18.3	14.7	18.0				18.1	17.0
Deferred Taxes	.1	.5	.6	1.7				.6	.7
All Other-Non-Current	4.3	3.5	2.4	5.8				3.4	3.4
Net Worth	38.8	39.5	42.7	40.8				39.3	41.2
Total Liabilities & Net Worth	100.0	100.0	100.0	100.0				100.0	100.0

INCOME DATA									
Net Sales	100.0	100.0	100.0	100.0				100.0	100.0
Gross Profit	45.8	31.8	25.3	23.5				29.5	29.0
Operating Expenses	39.0	26.2	19.0	16.5				23.8	25.3
Operating Profit	6.8	5.6	6.3	7.0				5.6	3.7
All Other Expenses (net)	1.5	1.0	1.0	1.3				1.9	1.4
Profit Before Taxes	5.4	4.6	5.3	5.7				3.7	2.3

RATIOS

Ratio	0-500M	500M-2MM	2-10MM	10-50MM	50-100MM	100-250MM		Hist 4/1/90-3/31/91	Hist 4/1/91-3/31/92
Current	2.8	2.4	2.5	2.4				2.5	2.7
	1.7	1.5	1.7	1.5				1.6	1.6
	1.2	1.2	1.3	1.2				1.2	1.2
Quick	1.8	1.5	1.4	1.4				1.4	1.6
	1.1	.9	.9	.9				.9	.9
	.6	.7	.7	.6				.6	.6
Sales/Receivables	27 / 13.3	35 / 10.3	39 / 9.4	38 / 9.7				34 / 10.8	35 / 10.3
	40 / 9.1	47 / 7.7	50 / 7.3	46 / 8.0				46 / 8.0	46 / 7.9
	56 / 6.5	60 / 6.1	62 / 5.9	54 / 6.8				57 / 6.4	56 / 6.5
Cost of Sales/Inventory	15 / 24.6	25 / 14.6	32 / 11.4	32 / 11.3				28 / 13.2	25 / 14.7
	37 / 9.9	47 / 7.7	52 / 7.0	49 / 7.5				55 / 6.6	49 / 7.5
	89 / 4.1	94 / 3.9	99 / 3.7	91 / 4.0				89 / 4.1	81 / 4.5
Cost of Sales/Payables	18 / 20.1	20 / 18.1	19 / 19.3	23 / 16.2				18 / 19.8	17 / 21.1
	33 / 11.0	33 / 11.2	32 / 11.5	32 / 11.4				29 / 12.7	28 / 12.9
	54 / 6.8	51 / 7.1	48 / 7.6	43 / 8.4				45 / 8.2	43 / 8.4
Sales/Working Capital	6.6	5.0	5.1	5.8				5.7	5.4
	11.6	10.5	7.9	8.4				10.7	10.1
	35.3	29.9	20.8	22.5				28.3	23.7
EBIT/Interest	(54) 7.3	(140) 9.9	(139) 10.3	(41) 29.0				(307) 5.6	(283) 5.4
	2.7	3.8	4.8	3.8				2.6	2.5
	1.3	1.8	2.2	2.7				1.2	1.1
Net Profit + Depr., Dep., Amort./Cur. Mat. L./T/D	(21) 5.1	(59) 3.6	(64) 6.7	(25) 16.9				(191) 5.0	(151) 4.1
	1.9	1.8	2.4	5.1				2.2	1.6
	.5	.8	1.2	1.5				1.0	.7
Fixed/Worth	.3	.4	.4	.4				.4	.4
	.7	.8	.6	.9				.8	.8
	1.8	1.7	1.3	1.8				1.7	1.5
Debt/Worth	.6	.7	.6	.7				.8	.7
	1.7	1.6	1.4	1.7				1.5	1.5
	4.7	3.6	3.4	3.4				3.4	3.4
% Profit Before Taxes/Tangible Net Worth	(55) 65.7	(138) 44.6	(141) 45.8	(41) 40.3				(312) 39.1	(298) 31.7
	29.7	21.0	24.8	25.7				20.0	13.1
	1.9	6.9	8.9	14.1				5.1	1.7
% Profit Before Taxes/Total Assets	23.2	15.5	17.6	17.8				14.6	12.0
	6.9	7.1	8.4	8.6				6.5	5.1
	.3	2.0	3.3	5.6				1.2	.1
Sales/Net Fixed Assets	20.7	16.6	16.1	8.5				16.2	17.2
	11.3	8.1	8.1	5.3				7.6	7.7
	6.2	4.4	4.5	4.3				4.4	4.3
Sales/Total Assets	3.6	3.1	2.6	2.6				2.8	2.8
	2.7	2.3	2.0	1.9				2.1	2.1
	2.0	1.6	1.6	1.4				1.7	1.6
% Depr., Dep., Amort./Sales	(57) 1.7	(141) 1.3	(133) 1.3	(41) 1.6				(307) 1.3	(288) 1.2
	2.7	2.3	2.0	2.6				2.5	2.4
	4.6	3.8	3.4	3.6				4.2	4.2
% Officers', Directors', Owners' Comp/Sales	(37) 4.9	(80) 2.7	(54) 1.7					(145) 2.8	(129) 3.0
	7.7	4.7	2.7					4.9	5.2
	15.9	7.9	5.0					8.7	8.3
Net Sales ($)	58637M	387051M	1403020M	1720674M	733912M	1300039M		3859394M	4691914M
Total Assets ($)	19908M	169582M	641044M	916114M	418027M	949541M		2247047M	2786994M

M = $ thousand   MM = $ million
See Pages 1 through 15 for Explanation of Ratios and Data

Comparative Historical Data				Current Data Sorted By Sales					
5	19	25	# Postretirement Benefits	2	4	4	5	8	2
			Type of Statement						
72	76	89	Unqualified		8	11	17	30	23
101	115	117	Reviewed	6	36	17	35	21	2
91	91	102	Compiled	31	35	21	9	4	2
5	7	14	Tax Returns	4	9		1		
58	80	92	Other	14	26	12	14	9	17
4/1/92-3/31/93 ALL	4/1/93-3/31/94 ALL	4/1/94-3/31/95 ALL		114 (4/1-9/30/94) 0-1MM	1-3MM	3-5MM	300 (10/1/94-3/31/95) 5-10MM	10-25MM	25MM & OVER
327	369	414	**NUMBER OF STATEMENTS**	55	114	61	76	64	44
%	%	%	**ASSETS**	%	%	%	%	%	%
7.0	7.1	6.1	Cash & Equivalents	7.5	6.1	6.6	6.6	5.2	4.5
27.2	29.5	30.1	Trade Receivables - (net)	26.8	31.5	29.5	30.3	32.8	26.9
25.4	23.1	23.6	Inventory	21.9	21.5	23.0	25.2	25.5	26.2
1.8	2.6	1.9	All Other Current	1.5	2.2	2.2	2.1	1.9	1.0
61.3	62.2	61.7	Total Current	57.7	61.4	61.3	64.2	65.4	58.6
29.6	29.4	30.6	Fixed Assets (net)	32.5	31.2	32.8	28.8	28.0	30.7
1.7	1.8	1.8	Intangibles (net)	2.2	2.1	1.2	1.7	1.6	2.1
7.4	6.5	5.8	All Other Non-Current	7.6	5.4	4.8	5.3	5.0	8.6
100.0	100.0	100.0	Total	100.0	100.0	100.0	100.0	100.0	100.0
			LIABILITIES						
10.1	9.0	9.4	Notes Payable-Short Term	11.9	9.1	7.8	7.2	13.0	7.5
4.4	3.6	4.6	Cur. Mat.-L /T/D	5.0	5.0	3.6	5.6	4.6	2.4
13.3	14.1	16.0	Trade Payables	12.3	17.4	15.5	16.7	16.9	14.8
.5	1.4	.5	Income Taxes Payable	.6	.5	.4	.3	.4	.6
8.2	8.6	8.0	All Other Current	7.5	7.3	8.3	8.0	8.9	8.5
36.5	36.6	38.3	Total Current	37.2	39.4	35.5	37.7	43.8	33.9
16.5	16.2	16.7	Long Term Debt	18.3	18.8	16.7	15.0	14.8	15.4
.5	.6	.6	Deferred Taxes	.2	.4	.7	.3	.8	1.6
2.9	3.4	3.6	All Other-Non-Current	4.9	4.0	1.2	3.5	2.2	5.7
43.5	43.2	40.8	Net Worth	39.3	37.4	45.9	43.5	38.3	43.4
100.0	100.0	100.0	Total Liabilities & Net Worth	100.0	100.0	100.0	100.0	100.0	100.0
			INCOME DATA						
100.0	100.0	100.0	Net Sales	100.0	100.0	100.0	100.0	100.0	100.0
30.9	30.9	30.4	Gross Profit	46.8	34.1	27.9	25.5	23.5	22.3
25.9	25.8	24.3	Operating Expenses	39.0	29.3	20.8	19.7	17.4	15.6
5.0	5.1	6.1	Operating Profit	7.8	4.8	7.0	5.9	6.1	6.7
1.1	1.0	1.1	All Other Expenses (net)	1.6	1.2	1.1	.8	.8	1.1
3.9	4.0	5.0	Profit Before Taxes	6.2	3.6	6.0	5.0	5.3	5.6
			RATIOS						
2.9	2.9	2.5		2.4	2.7	2.9	2.7	2.2	2.4
1.7	1.7	1.6	Current	1.7	1.5	1.7	1.7	1.6	1.9
1.2	1.2	1.2		1.2	1.1	1.4	1.2	1.2	1.3
1.6	1.7	1.5		1.5	1.6	1.8	1.5	1.3	1.4
1.0	1.0	.9	Quick	1.0	.9	1.0	1.0	.9	.9
.6	.7	.7		.6	.7	.7	.7	.6	.7
34 10.7	36 10.2	37 10.0		36 10.2	35 10.5	31 11.9	38 9.6	41 9.0	37 9.9
44 8.3	46 8.0	47 7.7	Sales/Receivables	47 7.8	47 7.8	45 8.1	52 7.0	46 7.9	46 7.9
56 6.5	59 6.2	60 6.1		66 5.5	59 6.2	61 6.0	60 6.1	61 6.0	56 6.5
33 11.1	27 13.7	26 14.1		39 9.3	23 16.2	26 13.9	29 12.8	30 12.0	34 10.8
60 6.1	53 6.9	49 7.4	Cost of Sales/Inventory	78 4.7	40 9.1	49 7.5	52 7.0	45 8.1	55 6.6
94 3.9	87 4.2	94 3.9		140 2.6	91 4.0	85 4.3	94 3.9	79 4.6	91 4.0
18 20.8	16 22.2	19 18.8		19 19.3	19 18.8	16 23.3	17 20.9	23 16.2	21 17.5
28 13.1	27 13.7	32 11.4	Cost of Sales/Payables	35 10.5	35 10.5	29 12.7	32 11.5	29 12.6	28 12.9
44 8.3	44 8.3	49 7.4		58 6.3	56 6.5	46 8.0	47 7.8	45 8.2	43 8.5
5.0	5.2	5.2		4.7	6.0	4.6	4.9	6.9	4.9
9.1	9.0	9.4	Sales/Working Capital	9.5	11.3	8.0	7.7	10.1	7.0
21.2	25.2	24.1		33.6	47.4	21.8	23.6	25.1	22.1
(292) 9.6	(338) 9.8	(385) 10.6		(46) 4.8	(105) 6.8	(60) 15.6	(71) 10.6	(61) 12.8	(42) 25.0
3.5	3.6	3.9	EBIT/Interest	2.4	3.5	4.7	4.5	5.0	6.3
1.4	1.6	1.8		1.3	1.3	2.4	2.2	2.0	3.1
(134) 5.5	(138) 5.1	(175) 5.5	Net Profit + Depr., Dep.,	(18) 3.7	(49) 4.0	(27) 5.4	(29) 9.1	(27) 10.9	(25) 20.2
2.5	2.1	2.3	Amort./Cur. Mat. L/T/D	1.8	1.8	2.6	2.2	2.7	6.4
1.3	1.2	1.0		.5	.6	1.0	.8	1.6	3.1
.3	.3	.4		.3	.4	.4	.3	.4	.4
.7	.7	.7	Fixed/Worth	.8	.8	.7	.6	.6	.8
1.4	1.5	1.6		3.4	1.9	1.4	1.5	1.3	1.5
.6	.7	.7		.6	.9	.6	.5	.7	.8
1.4	1.3	1.6	Debt/Worth	1.3	1.7	1.1	1.4	1.8	1.4
3.1	3.3	3.6		6.1	3.9	3.1	3.7	3.8	2.9
(306) 33.2	(347) 37.5	(387) 44.8	% Profit Before Taxes/Tangible	(49) 42.5	(102) 45.1	(58) 46.0	(73) 47.0	(61) 48.0	42.9
16.1	18.3	23.8	Net Worth	10.4	20.1	26.2	21.5	29.4	26.6
5.7	6.0	8.0		2.3	1.9	11.7	8.8	13.4	17.2
14.0	15.3	17.2	% Profit Before Taxes/Total	13.4	14.1	23.7	16.9	18.9	18.2
5.9	6.7	7.6	Assets	5.1	6.5	14.1	8.1	9.0	9.7
1.7	2.1	2.9		.5	.8	4.5	2.8	3.8	5.9
15.8	19.1	16.0		16.4	18.6	15.0	16.0	17.0	10.7
8.2	8.6	8.0	Sales/Net Fixed Assets	6.5	8.6	7.4	8.4	9.1	6.0
4.4	4.5	4.5		2.6	4.5	4.5	4.5	6.1	4.7
2.7	2.8	2.9		2.6	3.2	2.9	2.6	3.0	2.7
2.1	2.2	2.2	Sales/Total Assets	1.8	2.2	2.3	2.1	2.4	1.9
1.6	1.7	1.6		1.2	1.7	1.7	1.7	1.7	1.5
(301) 1.4	(331) 1.3	(378) 1.4	% Depr., Dep., Amort./Sales	(47) 1.7	(111) 1.4	(57) 1.4	(69) 1.2	(56) 1.1	(38) 1.3
2.4	2.2	2.3		2.9	2.6	2.2	1.8	2.1	2.5
4.0	4.0	3.7		6.1	3.8	3.9	3.7	3.3	3.1
(145) 2.6	(158) 2.9	(179) 2.5	% Officers', Directors',	(27) 5.6	(69) 3.2	(29) 2.9	(26) 2.0	(22) 1.4	
4.7	5.0	4.7	Owners' Comp/Sales	11.0	4.9	4.5	2.6	1.9	
8.5	8.7	7.9		16.7	7.2	8.5	5.7	4.5	
5136237M	4857232M	5603333M	Net Sales ($)	36763M	218092M	231589M	520280M	1018811M	3577796M
2890467M	2578817M	3114216M	Total Assets ($)	27508M	107424M	116420M	260914M	481428M	2120522M

M = $ thousand   MM = $ million
See Pages 1 through 15 for Explanation of Ratios and Data

Current Data Sorted By Assets | **Comparative Historical Data**

Postretirement Benefits
Type of Statement

	4	5	1			Type of Statement		
	4	10	9	3	2	Unqualified	48	39
4	14	23	2			Reviewed	32	30
5	13	6				Compiled	21	27
3	2	1				Tax Returns		1
4	3	13	4	2	1	Other	22	28

		36 (4/1-9/30/94)		92 (10/1/94-3/31/95)			4/1/90-3/31/91	4/1/91-3/31/92
0-500M	500M-2MM	2-10MM	10-50MM	50-100MM	100-250MM		ALL	ALL
16	36	53	15	5	3	NUMBER OF STATEMENTS	123	125
%	%	%	%	%	%	**ASSETS**	%	%
12.8	4.8	6.2	5.1			Cash & Equivalents	6.1	5.1
36.8	30.7	29.0	25.2			Trade Receivables - (net)	27.9	28.1
16.2	30.6	27.0	23.8			Inventory	28.1	28.1
2.3	1.1	1.0	.7			All Other Current	1.3	.8
68.1	67.1	63.1	54.8			Total Current	63.4	62.1
22.7	26.7	28.4	36.1			Fixed Assets (net)	27.1	30.2
2.1	1.3	2.3	2.0			Intangibles (net)	2.0	1.3
7.1	4.9	6.2	7.2			All Other Non-Current	7.5	6.3
100.0	100.0	100.0	100.0			Total	100.0	100.0
						LIABILITIES		
10.4	11.3	9.5	5.4			Notes Payable-Short Term	11.5	10.8
7.5	3.7	3.6	2.1			Cur. Mat. -L/T/D	5.0	3.6
15.0	15.8	15.2	11.1			Trade Payables	15.5	15.3
1.2	.3	.7	.1			Income Taxes Payable	.8	.3
8.8	8.5	7.1	7.4			All Other Current	7.9	9.4
42.9	39.6	36.1	26.1			Total Current	40.7	39.4
17.7	15.0	12.0	15.0			Long Term Debt	15.9	17.2
.3	.4	.4	2.1			Deferred Taxes	.7	.7
1.4	2.1	3.6	3.4			All Other-Non-Current	2.6	2.3
37.8	43.0	47.9	53.4			Net Worth	40.2	40.4
100.0	100.0	100.0	100.0			Total Liabilities & Net Worth	100.0	100.0
						INCOME DATA		
100.0	100.0	100.0	100.0			Net Sales	100.0	100.0
39.5	34.7	23.5	23.1			Gross Profit	25.0	26.1
32.0	28.7	19.3	16.8			Operating Expenses	19.9	21.9
7.5	6.0	4.2	6.3			Operating Profit	5.1	4.3
1.2	1.0	.8	.6			All Other Expenses (net)	1.6	1.5
6.3	5.1	3.3	5.7			Profit Before Taxes	3.5	2.8
						RATIOS		
2.1	2.4	2.9	3.3			Current	2.6	2.6
1.6	1.9	1.7	2.1				1.6	1.6
1.4	1.4	1.2	1.4				1.1	1.1
1.8	1.2	1.7	1.6			Quick	1.5	1.3
1.2	.9	1.1	1.2				.8	.8
.8	.6	.6	.9				.6	.6
28 13.1	33 11.1	38 9.6	41 8.8			Sales/Receivables	37 10.0	38 9.6
50 7.3	48 7.6	49 7.4	50 7.3				45 8.1	46 8.0
70 5.2	60 6.1	58 6.3	68 5.4				56 6.5	59 6.2
12 29.6	45 8.1	37 9.8	39 9.4			Cost of Sales/Inventory	39 9.3	41 9.0
30 12.0	72 5.1	59 6.2	73 5.0				59 6.2	59 6.2
59 6.2	99 3.7	91 4.0	89 4.1				85 4.3	91 4.0
9 41.3	21 17.4	19 19.6	20 18.3			Cost of Sales/Payables	20 18.7	21 17.3
23 15.7	33 11.2	27 13.3	26 13.8				29 12.4	32 11.3
54 6.7	53 6.9	40 9.1	42 8.6				43 8.5	49 7.4
7.2	5.8	4.8	3.2			Sales/Working Capital	5.3	5.2
10.0	8.1	9.1	6.2				9.4	9.8
20.8	13.3	19.3	15.2				34.1	27.1
15.8	7.1	12.7	10.6			EBIT/Interest	5.5	4.3
(13) 7.3	(31) 4.9	(46) 4.4	(12) 5.4				(116) 2.3	(114) 2.1
2.4	2.1	1.5	1.5				1.2	.8
	4.7	4.4				Net Profit + Depr., Dep.,	3.8	3.3
	(15) 2.3	(24) 2.1				Amort./Cur. Mat. L /T/D	(72) 2.5	(62) 1.5
	1.8	.8					1.1	.6
.3	.3	.3	.5			Fixed/Worth	.4	.4
.4	.6	.6	.6				.7	.7
1.7	1.3	1.4	1.1				1.5	1.9
.7	.8	.6	.6			Debt/Worth	.8	.7
1.2	1.4	1.1	.7				1.7	1.7
6.0	2.9	3.0	1.5				4.0	4.1
60.0	40.8	42.4	30.3			% Profit Before Taxes/Tangible	36.0	33.9
(13) 28.6	(35) 21.4	(51) 23.7	(12) 19.8			Net Worth	(117) 15.9	(119) 13.5
20.2	7.8	7.1	10.0				2.4	1.2
24.7	15.1	16.3	18.7			% Profit Before Taxes/Total	14.5	12.5
14.3	9.0	7.7	11.9			Assets	5.2	5.1
9.3	4.8	2.6	2.1				1.1	.4
34.4	23.1	16.7	6.6			Sales/Net Fixed Assets	16.9	14.3
21.8	10.8	6.6	4.7				8.7	6.9
6.4	5.5	4.6	3.0				5.2	4.4
4.4	2.9	2.6	2.2			Sales/Total Assets	2.7	2.8
3.1	2.4	2.3	1.6				2.3	2.2
2.3	1.8	1.6	1.4				1.7	1.5
1.2	1.1	1.2	2.1			% Depr., Dep., Amort./Sales	1.3	1.5
(15) 2.4	(34) 2.0	(51) 2.4	(12) 3.1				(112) 2.0	(112) 2.3
4.9	3.9	3.0	3.8				3.2	3.4
	4.4	2.5				% Officers', Directors',	2.2	1.9
	(19) 5.5	(18) 5.4				Owners' Comp/Sales	(43) 4.1	(48) 4.4
	8.6	9.4					7.2	7.9
15555M	98737M	567372M	495989M	770387M	764561M	Net Sales ($)	2667164M	2173430M
4681M	40306M	247770M	314371M	392211M	442611M	Total Assets ($)	1579123M	1236571M

M = $ thousand   MM = $ million
See Pages 1 through 15 for Explanation of Ratios and Data

Comparative Historical Data | Current Data Sorted By Sales

4	9	10	# Postretirement Benefits	0-1MM	1-3MM (2)	3-5MM (3)	5-10MM (3)	10-25MM (1)	25MM & OVER (1)
			Type of Statement						
40	32	28	Unqualified		1	3	1	12	11
37	38	43	Reviewed	2	9	11	14	6	1
25	30	24	Compiled	1	15	4	3	1	
5	1	6	Tax Returns	2	2	1	1		
25	24	27	Other	2	5	1	7	6	6
4/1/92-3/31/93	4/1/93-3/31/94	4/1/94-3/31/95		36 (4/1-9/30/94)			92 (10/1/94-3/31/95)		
ALL 132	ALL 125	ALL 128	**NUMBER OF STATEMENTS**	7	32	20	26	25	18
%	%	%	**ASSETS**	%	%	%	%	%	%
6.3	5.9	6.5	Cash & Equivalents		6.7	7.5	7.5	3.9	4.1
28.6	29.9	29.7	Trade Receivables - (net)		31.6	28.0	29.0	29.3	26.8
28.9	26.5	26.6	Inventory		28.7	27.1	27.8	25.3	29.5
2.1	1.2	1.1	All Other Current		1.5	.2	.9	1.2	.6
65.9	63.4	63.8	Total Current		68.6	62.7	65.3	59.7	60.9
27.8	30.0	28.2	Fixed Assets (net)		24.2	28.5	27.0	31.4	32.0
1.3	1.3	1.9	Intangibles (net)		1.8	4.6	1.0	2.0	1.0
5.0	5.3	6.0	All Other Non-Current		5.4	4.2	6.8	6.9	6.1
100.0	100.0	100.0	Total		100.0	100.0	100.0	100.0	100.0
			LIABILITIES						
10.5	9.0	9.5	Notes Payable-Short Term		9.8	12.2	7.3	9.5	8.9
3.8	3.0	3.9	Cur. Mat.-L/T/D		5.1	3.5	2.4	4.2	2.3
13.6	15.1	14.7	Trade Payables		15.0	15.7	13.8	15.9	14.6
.7	1.2	.5	Income Taxes Payable		.5	.7	.2	.9	.1
7.7	9.0	7.8	All Other Current		9.6	7.8	6.7	6.4	9.5
36.2	37.4	36.5	Total Current		39.8	39.9	30.3	36.9	35.4
15.4	14.1	14.0	Long Term Debt		16.4	13.1	10.8	13.0	13.8
.5	.6	.6	Deferred Taxes		.4	.2	.3	1.5	.9
4.7	5.2	2.8	All Other-Non-Current		2.0	4.9	3.1	2.8	2.0
43.3	42.8	46.1	Net Worth		41.4	41.8	55.5	45.8	47.9
100.0	100.0	100.0	Total Liabilities & Net Worth		100.0	100.0	100.0	100.0	100.0
			INCOME DATA						
100.0	100.0	100.0	Net Sales		100.0	100.0	100.0	100.0	100.0
27.1	27.7	28.6	Gross Profit		39.6	27.0	25.0	20.6	23.2
21.8	23.3	23.2	Operating Expenses		33.7	20.5	20.6	17.2	17.0
5.3	4.4	5.4	Operating Profit		5.9	6.4	4.4	3.4	6.3
1.1	1.0	.9	All Other Expenses (net)		.7	1.3	.7	.9	.7
4.1	3.4	4.5	Profit Before Taxes		5.2	5.2	3.6	2.5	5.6
			RATIOS						
3.3 / 1.9 / 1.3	2.8 / 1.7 / 1.2	2.5 / 1.9 / 1.3	Current		2.7 / 1.8 / 1.4	2.3 / 1.8 / 1.1	4.0 / 2.2 / 1.5	2.6 / 1.4 / 1.2	2.5 / 1.9 / 1.4
1.7 / 1.0 / .7	1.6 / 1.0 / .7	1.5 / 1.1 / .7	Quick		1.3 / 1.0 / .7	1.4 / 1.0 / .5	2.4 / 1.3 / .7	1.5 / .8 / .6	1.1 / 1.0 / .7
(38) 9.6 / (47) 7.8 / (60) 6.1	(37) 9.8 / (46) 7.9 / (55) 6.6	(37) 9.9 / (49) 7.4 / (59) 6.2	Sales/Receivables		(30) 12.2 / (45) 8.2 / (63) 5.8	(33) 11.1 / (49) 7.4 / (60) 6.1	(37) 9.8 / (49) 7.4 / (54) 6.8	(41) 8.8 / (51) 7.2 / (59) 6.2	(37) 10.0 / (44) 8.3 / (54) 6.8
(45) 8.2 / (61) 6.0 / (87) 4.2	(33) 11.2 / (57) 6.4 / (89) 4.1	(37) 10.0 / (62) 5.9 / (91) 4.0	Cost of Sales/Inventory		(40) 9.2 / (69) 5.3 / (101) 3.6	(46) 7.9 / (72) 5.1 / (94) 3.9	(34) 10.6 / (59) 6.2 / (76) 4.8	(35) 10.4 / (52) 7.0 / (89) 4.1	(41) 8.9 / (73) 5.0 / (94) 3.9
(16) 23.2 / (29) 12.8 / (43) 8.4	(20) 18.7 / (32) 11.5 / (46) 7.9	(20) 18.5 / (29) 12.8 / (45) 8.1	Cost of Sales/Payables		(20) 18.2 / (30) 12.1 / (58) 6.3	(21) 17.8 / (39) 9.3 / (51) 7.1	(15) 24.6 / (26) 14.0 / (33) 11.2	(22) 16.6 / (31) 11.8 / (45) 8.2	(19) 19.2 / (31) 11.9 / (42) 8.6
4.5 / 7.6 / 19.3	5.0 / 10.3 / 25.4	5.3 / 8.3 / 15.3	Sales/Working Capital		5.4 / 8.9 / 16.4	6.4 / 7.7 / NM	4.2 / 6.7 / 12.3	5.5 / 9.6 / 27.4	4.2 / 8.2 / 12.9
(119) 7.3 / 3.1 / 1.7	(114) 8.4 / 3.9 / 2.0	(110) 9.9 / 4.9 / 2.0	EBIT/Interest		(27) 10.1 / 4.9 / 2.5	(18) 11.7 / 3.8 / 1.2	(20) 12.7 / 4.9 / 2.3	(22) 6.5 / 4.0 / 1.7	10.4 / 6.6 / 3.2
(59) 4.7 / 2.5 / 1.3	(51) 5.0 / 3.3 / 1.7	(55) 4.7 / 2.3 / 1.2	Net Profit + Depr., Dep., Amort./Cur. Mat. L/T/D		(16) 7.1 / 2.3 / 1.3		(12) 3.0 / 2.1 / .8	(12) 4.4 / 2.1 / -3.3	
.3 / .7 / 1.3	.4 / .7 / 1.5	.4 / .6 / 1.3	Fixed/Worth		.3 / .5 / 1.5	.4 / .8 / 1.3	.2 / .4 / .9	.4 / .8 / 1.5	.5 / .6 / .9
.7 / 1.5 / 3.3	.6 / 1.5 / 3.2	.6 / 1.1 / 2.8	Debt/Worth		.8 / 1.2 / 2.9	.9 / 1.7 / 3.5	.3 / .8 / 1.8	.6 / 1.4 / 3.3	.6 / 1.1 / 1.6
(127) 37.7 / 15.2 / 5.2	(119) 32.5 / 16.8 / 4.4	(122) 41.1 / 23.2 / 8.0	% Profit Before Taxes/Tangible Net Worth		(29) 44.7 / 28.0 / 10.5	(19) 47.4 / 18.4 / 3.4	(25) 36.8 / 19.8 / 7.2	47.8 / 23.3 / 7.3	34.2 / 21.5 / 9.5
14.0 / 6.5 / 2.2	13.8 / 7.2 / 2.0	16.2 / 9.5 / 3.2	% Profit Before Taxes/Total Assets		18.1 / 9.7 / 6.7	12.9 / 5.8 / 1.1	20.6 / 8.8 / 3.2	15.6 / 8.6 / 2.5	16.3 / 10.3 / 3.2
17.8 / 8.2 / 4.7	16.6 / 7.1 / 4.7	17.9 / 7.5 / 4.7	Sales/Net Fixed Assets		27.5 / 13.0 / 6.4	21.3 / 7.4 / 3.5	26.0 / 9.2 / 4.2	11.7 / 5.6 / 4.9	9.1 / 5.2 / 4.7
2.8 / 2.1 / 1.7	2.9 / 2.2 / 1.7	2.7 / 2.3 / 1.6	Sales/Total Assets		3.0 / 2.5 / 2.1	2.6 / 2.0 / 1.4	2.6 / 2.4 / 1.8	2.7 / 2.3 / 1.4	2.3 / 2.1 / 1.7
(118) 1.3 / 2.1 / 3.3	(119) 1.4 / 2.5 / 3.4	(118) 1.3 / 2.4 / 3.5	% Depr., Dep., Amort./Sales		(30) 1.2 / 2.0 / 4.1	(18) .9 / 2.0 / 3.1	(25) 1.1 / 1.9 / 2.9	(23) 1.7 / 2.9 / 3.4	(15) 1.6 / 2.6 / 3.2
(52) 2.7 / 4.8 / 7.3	(53) 2.2 / 4.6 / 7.6	(46) 3.9 / 5.4 / 9.7	% Officers', Directors', Owners' Comp/Sales		(18) 4.6 / 6.5 / 10.2		(10) 2.5 / 5.4 / 10.8		
1769674M	2511871M	2712601M	Net Sales ($)	2856M	57465M	76267M	177661M	402439M	1995913M
1017178M	1346236M	1441950M	Total Assets ($)	1157M	24042M	46538M	84418M	233867M	1051928M

M = $ thousand   MM = $ million
See Pages 1 through 15 for Explanation of Ratios and Data

Current Data Sorted By Assets   **Comparative Historical Data**

0-500M	500M-2MM	2-10MM	10-50MM	50-100MM	100-250MM		4/1/90-3/31/91 ALL	4/1/91-3/31/92 ALL
	2	2				# Postretirement Benefits		
						Type of Statement		
	2	1	1			Unqualified		
	2	4				Reviewed		
2	6	3	1			Compiled		
						Tax Returns		
2	1	5	1	1		Other		
	9 (4/1-9/30/94)		23 (10/1/94-3/31/95)					
4	11	13	3	1		**NUMBER OF STATEMENTS**		
%	%	%	%	%	%	**ASSETS**	%	%
	4.5	6.2				Cash & Equivalents	D	D
	31.5	22.9				Trade Receivables - (net)	A	A
	23.4	24.8				Inventory	T	T
	.9	2.0				All Other Current	A	A
	60.3	55.9				Total Current		
	34.8	39.6				Fixed Assets (net)	N	N
	.3	1.4				Intangibles (net)	O	O
	4.6	3.0				All Other Non-Current	T	T
	100.0	100.0				Total		
						LIABILITIES	A	A
	10.4	7.7				Notes Payable-Short Term	V	V
	5.9	5.0				Cur. Mat. -L/T/D	A	A
	14.3	14.8				Trade Payables	I	I
	1.3	.3				Income Taxes Payable	L	L
	9.1	7.5				All Other Current	A	A
	41.1	35.3				Total Current	B	B
	10.3	20.9				Long Term Debt	L	L
	1.5	.3				Deferred Taxes	E	E
	2.8	.6				All Other-Non-Current		
	44.2	42.8				Net Worth		
	100.0	100.0				Total Liabilities & Net Worth		
						INCOME DATA		
	100.0	100.0				Net Sales		
	24.5	32.7				Gross Profit		
	19.3	25.6				Operating Expenses		
	5.1	7.1				Operating Profit		
	1.1	2.0				All Other Expenses (net)		
	4.0	5.1				Profit Before Taxes		
						RATIOS		
	3.1	3.0						
	1.7	2.0				Current		
	1.0	1.1						
	1.7	2.0						
	1.1	.8				Quick		
	.6	.4						
	42 8.7	30 12.3						
	47 7.7	43 8.4				Sales/Receivables		
	61 6.0	61 6.0						
	8 43.6	39 9.3						
	46 7.9	56 6.5				Cost of Sales/Inventory		
	94 3.9	146 2.5						
	20 18.6	19 19.4						
	23 16.0	29 12.5				Cost of Sales/Payables		
	29 12.5	101 3.6						
	5.8	4.9						
	11.1	6.2				Sales/Working Capital		
	−801.0	26.5						
	10.4	4.8						
	9.4 (11)	2.8				EBIT/Interest		
	1.9	1.1						
						Net Profit + Depr., Dep., Amort./Cur. Mat. L /T/D		
	.4	.3						
	.7	1.0				Fixed/Worth		
	1.4	2.9						
	1.0	.5						
	1.3	1.9				Debt/Worth		
	2.1	4.4						
	63.8	33.5				% Profit Before Taxes/Tangible		
	21.0	27.0				Net Worth		
	5.7	14.1						
	25.6	18.0				% Profit Before Taxes/Total		
	9.9	7.6				Assets		
	2.0	1.6						
	29.1	14.6						
	6.5	4.0				Sales/Net Fixed Assets		
	2.3	1.9						
	3.6	2.2						
	2.6	1.9				Sales/Total Assets		
	1.3	1.2						
		1.7						
	(12)	2.9				% Depr., Dep., Amort./Sales		
		4.8						
						% Officers', Directors', Owners' Comp/Sales		
3469M	30141M	97147M	117246M	116705M		Net Sales ($)		
1432M	12084M	51182M	72983M	69601M		Total Assets ($)		

M = $ thousand   MM = $ million
See Pages 1 through 15 for Explanation of Ratios and Data

Comparative Historical Data				Current Data Sorted By Sales					
		4	# Postretirement Benefits	1			3		
			Type of Statement						
		4	Unqualified			1	1	2	
		6	Reviewed	1	1	2	1	1	2
		12	Compiled	3	5	1	1	2	
			Tax Returns						
		10	Other		4	1	3		2
4/1/92-3/31/93 ALL	4/1/93-3/31/94 ALL	4/1/94-3/31/95 ALL		9 (4/1-9/30/94)			23 (10/1/94-3/31/95)		
				0-1MM	1-3MM	3-5MM	5-10MM	10-25MM	25MM & OVER
		32	NUMBER OF STATEMENTS	4	10	5	6	5	2
%	%	%	ASSETS	%	%	%	%	%	%
D A T A	D A T A	4.9	Cash & Equivalents		2.3				
		27.7	Trade Receivables - (net)		32.1				
		21.7	Inventory		22.0				
		1.3	All Other Current		.9				
		55.5	Total Current		57.2				
		39.3	Fixed Assets (net)		37.0				
N O T	N O T	1.1	Intangibles (net)		.2				
		4.1	All Other Non-Current		5.6				
		100.0	Total		100.0				
A V A I L A B L E	A V A I L A B L E		LIABILITIES						
		10.1	Notes Payable-Short Term		11.5				
		5.8	Cur. Mat.-L./T/D		4.9				
		15.5	Trade Payables		13.3				
		.6	Income Taxes Payable		.0				
		7.1	All Other Current		4.7				
		39.1	Total Current		34.5				
		18.6	Long Term Debt		21.1				
		.7	Deferred Taxes		1.7				
		3.3	All Other-Non-Current		3.1				
		38.3	Net Worth		39.6				
		100.0	Total Liabilities & Net Worth		100.0				
			INCOME DATA						
		100.0	Net Sales		100.0				
		27.6	Gross Profit		28.2				
		22.2	Operating Expenses		23.9				
		5.4	Operating Profit		4.3				
		2.1	All Other Expenses (net)		2.5				
		3.4	Profit Before Taxes		1.8				
			RATIOS						
		2.6			3.4				
		1.4	Current		1.6				
		1.0			1.3				
		1.6			1.8				
		.9	Quick		1.2				
		.5			.8				
	33	11.2		42	8.6				
	46	7.9	Sales/Receivables	56	6.5				
	62	5.9		63	5.8				
	18	20.6		13	29.0				
	47	7.8	Cost of Sales/Inventory	46	8.0				
	89	4.1		96	3.8				
	20	17.9		19	19.2				
	29	12.5	Cost of Sales/Payables	29	12.5				
	46	7.9		45	8.1				
		5.6			4.7				
		15.4	Sales/Working Capital		9.8				
		NM			18.4				
		9.4			5.7				
	(30)	2.5	EBIT/Interest		1.5				
		1.0			−1.1				
		3.2	Net Profit + Depr., Dep.,						
	(13)	1.6	Amort./Cur. Mat. L/T/D						
		.3							
		.4			.3				
		.9	Fixed/Worth		.8				
		2.7			1.5				
		.8			.9				
		1.7	Debt/Worth		1.3				
		4.4			2.0				
		39.3	% Profit Before Taxes/Tangible		43.4				
	(31)	21.0	Net Worth		9.8				
		.1			−13.4				
		18.5	% Profit Before Taxes/Total		13.2				
		5.9	Assets		1.6				
		.3			−5.9				
		14.7			23.9				
		4.9	Sales/Net Fixed Assets		6.0				
		2.4			1.9				
		2.7			2.7				
		2.0	Sales/Total Assets		2.2				
		1.4			1.2				
		1.5			1.3				
	(29)	2.8	% Depr., Dep., Amort./Sales		2.3				
		4.8			4.7				
		4.2	% Officers', Directors',						
	(14)	5.6	Owners' Comp/Sales						
		8.2							
		364708M	Net Sales ($)	2753M	18353M	21138M	44034M	84160M	194270M
		207282M	Total Assets ($)	2271M	11924M	11320M	20800M	49689M	111278M

M = $ thousand   MM = $ million
See Pages 1 through 15 for Explanation of Ratios and Data

Current Data Sorted By Assets   **Comparative Historical Data**

Postretirement Benefits
Type of Statement

Type of Statement	0-500M	500M-2MM	2-10MM	10-50MM	50-100MM	100-250MM		4/1/90-3/31/91 ALL	4/1/91-3/31/92 ALL
Unqualified			1	4				20	23
Reviewed			7	6		1		16	7
Compiled	1	3	1					12	11
Tax Returns	3	6	2						
Other		2	11	4	1			11	8

Periods: 11 (4/1-9/30/94) · 37 (10/1/94-3/31/95)

	0-500M	500M-2MM	2-10MM	10-50MM	50-100MM	100-250MM		4/1/90-3/31/91 ALL	4/1/91-3/31/92 ALL
NUMBER OF STATEMENTS	4	11	21	10	1	1		59	49
	%	%	%	%	%	%		%	%
ASSETS									
Cash & Equivalents		2.1	3.4	9.0				8.4	5.3
Trade Receivables - (net)		37.0	33.8	23.8				27.2	24.3
Inventory		26.7	30.0	17.2				22.3	23.1
All Other Current		3.8	.9	4.8				2.6	4.5
Total Current		69.6	68.1	54.9				60.5	57.1
Fixed Assets (net)		24.0	25.6	32.0				31.4	35.7
Intangibles (net)		.1	3.0	5.3				2.2	1.5
All Other Non-Current		6.3	3.2	7.8				5.8	5.6
Total		100.0	100.0	100.0				100.0	100.0
LIABILITIES									
Notes Payable-Short Term		11.2	11.3	4.7				12.7	11.1
Cur. Mat. -L/T/D		3.8	3.5	4.8				3.4	5.6
Trade Payables		24.3	19.1	14.9				16.7	14.1
Income Taxes Payable		.1	.4	.5				.8	.7
All Other Current		8.2	10.5	12.9				7.2	7.4
Total Current		47.6	44.8	37.8				40.6	38.8
Long Term Debt		18.5	17.2	11.8				20.3	23.4
Deferred Taxes		.5	.5	1.1				.6	.7
All Other-Non-Current		9.7	.7	2.4				2.0	3.4
Net Worth		23.8	36.7	47.0				36.4	33.7
Total Liabilities & Net Worth		100.0	100.0	100.0				100.0	100.0
INCOME DATA									
Net Sales		100.0	100.0	100.0				100.0	100.0
Gross Profit		26.8	25.5	22.8				28.3	27.4
Operating Expenses		22.7	20.8	14.9				23.7	23.3
Operating Profit		4.2	4.7	7.9				4.6	4.1
All Other Expenses (net)		.8	.7	1.5				1.7	1.7
Profit Before Taxes		3.4	4.1	6.4				2.9	2.3
RATIOS									
Current		1.9	1.7	2.1				2.2	2.4
		1.5	1.6	1.5				1.5	1.5
		1.2	1.3	1.0				1.1	1.0
Quick		1.1	1.1	1.3				1.2	1.2
		.9	.8	.8				.8	.6
		.7	.6	.5				.6	.4
Sales/Receivables	35	10.3	30 12.1	23 15.6				23 15.7	18 20.7
	51	7.2	42 8.7	35 10.4				37 9.8	41 8.9
	61	6.0	70 5.2	57 6.4				54 6.7	56 6.5
Cost of Sales/Inventory	34	10.6	30 12.2	21 17.7				24 14.9	25 14.5
	46	8.0	53 6.9	33 11.1				41 9.0	41 8.9
	78	4.7	85 4.3	49 7.5				68 5.4	72 5.1
Cost of Sales/Payables	30	12.0	23 15.6	18 20.7				18 20.5	17 21.2
	35	10.5	33 11.2	29 12.6				28 13.0	27 13.5
	59	6.2	52 7.0	38 9.5				46 7.9	33 11.1
Sales/Working Capital		7.1	7.6	6.7				7.6	6.1
		11.5	12.7	11.7				16.6	15.4
		28.7	20.8	NM				53.3	633.5
EBIT/Interest		4.1	11.1					4.8	3.6
		2.6	(20) 5.2					(54) 2.2	(45) 1.9
		2.0	2.4					1.2	.8
Net Profit + Depr., Dep., Amort./Cur. Mat. L /T/D								7.9	4.1
								(35) 2.1	(24) 2.0
								.7	1.0
Fixed/Worth		.5	.3	.4				.4	.6
		1.4	.5	.5				.8	.9
		1.5	1.9	2.3				1.6	3.3
Debt/Worth		1.9	1.2	.7				1.2	1.0
		4.1	1.7	1.0				2.0	2.6
		5.4	2.7	2.9				3.5	6.2
% Profit Before Taxes/Tangible Net Worth		53.6	53.3					36.3	28.2
		26.4	(20) 23.3					(55) 15.5	(46) 17.9
		19.3	9.3					3.1	-1.5
% Profit Before Taxes/Total Assets		11.0	20.0	19.2				12.1	13.5
		6.9	10.3	12.3				5.3	4.8
		3.4	3.3	6.9				1.0	-.6
Sales/Net Fixed Assets		35.0	25.1	16.0				20.0	13.7
		13.9	14.8	9.0				9.1	6.7
		7.4	5.5	3.9				4.4	3.9
Sales/Total Assets		3.5	3.0	2.9				3.6	3.0
		3.0	2.6	2.3				2.5	2.2
		2.4	1.8	1.1				1.7	1.7
% Depr., Dep., Amort./Sales		.8	.6	.4				1.0	1.3
		.9	(16) 1.1	.5				(50) 1.6	(43) 1.8
		1.6	2.3					2.9	2.5
% Officers', Directors', Owners' Comp/Sales								2.2	2.3
								(22) 4.3	(17) 5.0
								6.8	7.6
Net Sales ($)	2459M	31602M	274535M	348521M	167767M	170139M		1399885M	1121872M
Total Assets ($)	935M	10519M	107104M	187056M	63371M	102898M		980388M	634069M

M = $ thousand   MM = $ million
See Pages 1 through 15 for Explanation of Ratios and Data

Comparative Historical Data | | Current Data Sorted By Sales

			# Postretirement Benefits					1	4
4	5	5							
			Type of Statement						
22	13	14	Unqualified				2	4	8
8	6	5	Reviewed		4		1		
7	5	11	Compiled	3	4	2	2		
1			Tax Returns						
10	9	18	Other			3	5	6	4
4/1/92-3/31/93	4/1/93-3/31/94	4/1/94-3/31/95		0-1MM	1-3MM	3-5MM	5-10MM	10-25MM	25MM & OVER
ALL	ALL	ALL		11 (4/1-9/30/94)			37 (10/1/94-3/31/95)		
48	33	48	**NUMBER OF STATEMENTS**	3	8	5	10	10	12
%	%	%	**ASSETS**	%	%	%	%	%	%
8.6	4.1	4.7	Cash & Equivalents				2.2	3.4	9.1
25.8	28.3	32.4	Trade Receivables - (net)				38.1	28.5	27.7
25.0	26.0	24.1	Inventory				30.8	21.5	21.2
2.7	5.4	2.7	All Other Current				1.3	1.8	3.3
62.1	63.7	63.9	Total Current				72.3	55.3	61.4
29.3	31.1	28.8	Fixed Assets (net)				23.4	33.6	28.7
1.5	.5	2.6	Intangibles (net)				2.3	4.9	4.3
7.1	4.7	4.7	All Other Non-Current				2.0	6.1	5.6
100.0	100.0	100.0	Total				100.0	100.0	100.0
			LIABILITIES						
11.1	11.4	9.0	Notes Payable-Short Term				13.7	11.9	3.1
3.1	3.8	4.6	Cur. Mat.-L /T/D				2.3	5.3	4.5
16.5	19.1	20.1	Trade Payables				20.8	16.9	14.6
.5	1.9	.4	Income Taxes Payable				.7	.4	.6
8.8	7.5	10.8	All Other Current				7.9	7.4	14.4
39.9	43.6	44.8	Total Current				45.4	41.9	37.1
18.2	20.1	16.0	Long Term Debt				19.1	14.9	10.7
.6	.9	.8	Deferred Taxes				.3	1.6	.9
4.7	2.3	3.0	All Other-Non-Current				6.2	3.8	.0
36.6	33.0	35.4	Net Worth				29.0	37.9	51.3
100.0	100.0	100.0	Total Liabilities & Net Worth				100.0	100.0	100.0
			INCOME DATA						
100.0	100.0	100.0	Net Sales				100.0	100.0	100.0
26.0	25.6	27.6	Gross Profit				26.6	19.7	25.5
23.2	21.0	21.7	Operating Expenses				21.5	15.6	17.4
2.8	4.6	5.9	Operating Profit				5.1	4.2	8.2
1.3	.9	.9	All Other Expenses (net)				1.0	.2	1.0
1.6	3.6	5.0	Profit Before Taxes				4.1	4.0	7.2
			RATIOS						
2.4	1.9	1.8	Current				2.1	1.6	2.2
1.7	1.4	1.6					1.6	1.3	1.7
1.2	1.2	1.3					1.2	1.0	1.4
1.4	1.1	1.1	Quick				1.4	1.0	1.3
.9	.8	.9					.7	.8	1.1
.6	.5	.6					.6	.5	.7
24 15.2	24 15.2	31 11.7	Sales/Receivables				30 12.1	24 15.4	28 13.0
45 8.1	45 8.1	46 7.9					41 9.0	34 10.6	41 8.9
57 6.4	62 5.9	65 5.6					69 5.3	49 7.4	66 5.5
35 10.5	32 11.3	24 15.4	Cost of Sales/Inventory				26 14.1	23 16.2	28 13.1
49 7.5	45 8.1	40 9.1					51 7.1	34 10.6	38 9.6
74 4.9	79 4.6	74 4.9					79 4.6	54 6.7	63 5.8
22 16.9	25 14.8	24 15.4	Cost of Sales/Payables				28 12.9	18 19.8	22 16.9
30 12.3	32 11.3	34 10.8					38 9.7	28 13.1	26 13.8
49 7.5	61 6.0	49 7.5					51 7.2	38 9.7	35 10.3
5.9	7.4	7.3	Sales/Working Capital				6.9	12.7	6.2
10.3	12.1	12.1					10.6	17.8	8.6
21.6	25.2	23.1					25.1	NM	13.0
(40) 5.6	(31) 5.3	(45) 9.7	EBIT/Interest				8.0		(11) 21.9
2.1	2.7	4.4					4.3		19.2
1.2	1.6	2.5					2.7		6.8
(27) 6.4	(14) 4.0	(20) 5.8	Net Profit + Depr., Dep., Amort./Cur. Mat. L/T/D						
2.4	2.0	2.7							
1.7	.8	1.6							
.3	.4	.4	Fixed/Worth				.3	.5	.4
.8	.9	.6					1.3	.8	.4
2.5	2.3	1.7					UND	2.1	.8
.7	1.3	1.0	Debt/Worth				1.1	1.3	.6
2.1	2.8	1.8					2.0	1.8	.9
5.0	5.3	3.9					UND	3.0	2.0
(45) 25.4	36.8	(45) 47.0	% Profit Before Taxes/Tangible Net Worth					76.1	42.1
16.7	23.6	28.0						(11) 24.3	31.8
5.2	9.3	13.7						13.8	23.5
9.8	13.8	19.8	% Profit Before Taxes/Total Assets				22.2	13.4	20.7
5.3	5.6	10.3					10.3	7.1	17.0
1.3	2.6	4.5					1.0	5.8	10.3
21.8	16.8	20.5	Sales/Net Fixed Assets				39.8	16.2	16.3
8.6	8.1	10.2					15.0	7.7	9.0
4.2	4.7	4.6					8.1	4.3	7.9
2.9	2.9	3.1	Sales/Total Assets				3.6	3.1	2.8
2.3	2.3	2.6					2.9	2.8	2.5
1.7	1.9	1.8					2.0	2.1	1.8
(43) 1.0	(31) .9	(42) .8	% Depr., Dep., Amort./Sales				.5		(10) .9
1.8	1.3	1.3					1.3		1.3
3.2	2.0	2.6					2.4		2.4
(11) 4.2		(15) 2.5	% Officers', Directors', Owners' Comp/Sales						
5.2		5.2							
7.2		7.5							
1230695M	1667309M	995023M	Net Sales ($)	1300M	14393M	17026M	71168M	191813M	699323M
614086M	785927M	471883M	Total Assets ($)	566M	6111M	8713M	27909M	79630M	348954M

M = $ thousand   MM = $ million
See Pages 1 through 15 for Explanation of Ratios and Data

Current Data Sorted By Assets   **Comparative Historical Data**

1	2	3	3	1		# Postretirement Benefits		
						Type of Statement		
3	18	9	4	1		Unqualified	28	43
4	38	47	5			Reviewed	69	74
9	32	11	2			Compiled	69	63
2	3					Tax Returns		2
7	11	21	13	4	3	Other	32	31

0-500M	500M-2MM	2-10MM	10-50MM	50-100MM	100-250MM		4/1/90-3/31/91 ALL	4/1/91-3/31/92 ALL
\[89 (4/1-9/30/94)\]		\[158 (10/1/94-3/31/95)\]						
22	87	97	29	8	4	**NUMBER OF STATEMENTS**	198	213
%	%	%	%	%	%	**ASSETS**	%	%
6.8	7.4	4.7	5.1			Cash & Equivalents	6.6	6.0
28.3	31.8	24.8	22.9			Trade Receivables - (net)	28.1	24.9
22.3	25.2	28.5	26.9			Inventory	26.9	25.7
2.1	1.0	1.0	2.3			All Other Current	1.5	2.2
59.6	65.3	59.1	57.2			Total Current	63.1	58.8
30.5	29.1	33.6	36.3			Fixed Assets (net)	29.1	31.7
1.5	.9	1.6	1.5			Intangibles (net)	1.0	2.0
8.4	4.8	5.7	5.0			All Other Non-Current	6.8	7.5
100.0	100.0	100.0	100.0			Total	100.0	100.0
						LIABILITIES		
11.7	8.7	9.8	11.7			Notes Payable-Short Term	9.8	9.5
4.2	5.6	5.1	3.4			Cur. Mat. -L/T/D	5.3	5.2
17.2	17.5	14.7	12.4			Trade Payables	16.1	13.4
.6	.3	.5	.5			Income Taxes Payable	.3	.4
8.3	9.1	9.0	6.3			All Other Current	6.3	6.7
42.0	41.2	39.2	34.4			Total Current	37.8	35.2
18.7	17.4	16.2	16.8			Long Term Debt	16.0	18.1
.4	.3	1.0	.9			Deferred Taxes	.6	.8
5.6	5.5	3.3	4.4			All Other-Non-Current	3.6	2.4
33.2	35.5	40.3	43.5			Net Worth	42.0	43.5
100.0	100.0	100.0	100.0			Total Liabilities & Net Worth	100.0	100.0
						INCOME DATA		
100.0	100.0	100.0	100.0			Net Sales	100.0	100.0
36.2	26.7	24.7	24.6			Gross Profit	26.3	26.6
32.7	22.3	18.1	17.8			Operating Expenses	22.6	23.3
3.5	4.3	6.6	6.8			Operating Profit	3.7	3.3
.6	.8	1.7	2.3			All Other Expenses (net)	1.4	1.9
2.9	3.5	4.9	4.4			Profit Before Taxes	2.3	1.4
						RATIOS		
2.7	2.8	2.3	3.7				2.8	2.8
2.0	1.5	1.7	1.8			Current	1.7	1.8
1.0	1.1	1.1	1.4				1.2	1.2
2.4	1.7	1.2	2.0				1.5	1.4
1.3	1.0	.8	.9			Quick	.9	.9
.4	.6	.5	.6				.6	.6
31 11.9	36 10.2	37 10.0	42 8.7				35 10.4	34 10.7
40 9.1	46 8.0	44 8.3	49 7.5			Sales/Receivables	45 8.2	45 8.2
54 6.7	54 6.7	54 6.8	55 6.6				53 6.9	53 6.9
14 26.1	25 14.7	44 8.3	39 9.4				33 11.0	34 10.6
33 11.2	44 8.3	68 5.4	66 5.5			Cost of Sales/Inventory	55 6.6	57 6.4
74 4.9	61 6.0	91 4.0	111 3.3				85 4.3	87 4.2
8 45.1	19 19.7	20 18.0	19 19.3				16 22.3	16 23.1
26 14.0	30 12.0	33 11.1	29 12.6			Cost of Sales/Payables	28 13.0	26 14.0
44 8.3	43 8.5	48 7.6	45 8.2				47 7.8	44 8.3
6.5	6.1	5.6	2.9				5.6	5.3
10.5	11.1	8.5	8.1			Sales/Working Capital	9.1	8.6
NM	36.5	160.3	12.8				24.8	24.0
16.8	7.1	9.1	11.2				4.5	4.2
(20) 3.3	(82) 3.2	(92) 4.1	(26) 4.5			EBIT/Interest	(182) 2.1	(198) 1.9
-.4	1.8	2.0	1.6				1.0	.4
	5.3	5.2	4.3				3.3	3.7
	(46) 1.7	(60) 2.4	(15) 1.9			Net Profit + Depr., Dep., Amort./Cur. Mat. L /T/D	(123) 2.0	(115) 1.5
	1.2	1.3	1.4				1.0	.5
.5	.4	.5	.4				.3	.4
.9	.8	.8	.8			Fixed/Worth	.7	.8
3.5	1.9	1.8	1.6				1.6	1.6
.8	.9	.8	.4				.6	.6
1.8	1.7	1.4	1.3			Debt/Worth	1.5	1.5
7.3	4.1	3.4	3.8				4.4	3.2
42.7	37.9	47.0	33.4				24.6	22.9
(18) 24.2	(79) 23.6	(93) 22.3	(26) 23.9			% Profit Before Taxes/Tangible Net Worth	(184) 13.0	(199) 8.5
-2.4	11.1	8.8	9.9				2.0	-2.7
20.2	14.3	15.4	19.8				10.1	9.4
6.1	7.2	7.5	9.7			% Profit Before Taxes/Total Assets	4.6	3.2
-6.0	2.6	3.6	2.3				.3	-2.3
37.0	19.5	10.4	8.3				14.2	12.0
8.8	9.8	6.7	4.4			Sales/Net Fixed Assets	8.3	6.6
3.7	6.4	3.7	3.2				4.6	3.8
3.3	3.2	2.4	1.9				2.8	2.6
2.7	2.6	2.0	1.6			Sales/Total Assets	2.2	2.0
1.3	2.0	1.6	1.2				1.7	1.5
1.0	1.4	1.8	2.1				1.6	1.9
(20) 3.7	(81) 2.7	(91) 2.6	(26) 3.1			% Depr., Dep., Amort./Sales	(183) 2.8	(202) 3.1
7.4	4.0	3.9	4.5				4.4	4.6
6.8	3.4	2.4					3.1	3.3
(14) 10.5	(55) 6.8	(44) 4.6				% Officers', Directors', Owners' Comp/Sales	(97) 5.8	(97) 5.8
12.4	9.8	6.7					8.6	9.5
17417M	264813M	867258M	905437M	953086M	807417M	Net Sales ($)	1861439M	2026320M
6437M	101053M	443414M	558656M	590411M	476703M	Total Assets ($)	1096248M	1318377M

M = $ thousand   MM = $ million
See Pages 1 through 15 for Explanation of Ratios and Data

Comparative Historical Data   **Current Data Sorted By Sales**

6	7	10	# Postretirement Benefits / Type of Statement	0-1MM	1-3MM	3-5MM	5-10MM	10-25MM	25MM & OVER
					1	1		2	6
34	29	35	Unqualified		1	4	6	12	12
81	68	94	Reviewed	3	22	20	34	13	2
63	51	54	Compiled	7	23	9	11	3	1
1	2	5	Tax Returns	1	3		1		
32	41	59	Other	6	9	5	10	16	13
4/1/92-3/31/93 ALL	4/1/93-3/31/94 ALL	4/1/94-3/31/95 ALL	(89 = 4/1-9/30/94) (158 = 10/1/94-3/31/95)						
211	191	247	**NUMBER OF STATEMENTS**	17	58	38	62	44	28
%	%	%	**ASSETS**	%	%	%	%	%	%
5.7	6.7	5.8	Cash & Equivalents	5.4	8.6	6.0	5.5	4.5	2.9
25.0	26.2	27.3	Trade Receivables - (net)	24.1	30.3	29.3	27.2	24.9	24.1
27.5	25.8	26.3	Inventory	23.0	23.1	24.3	29.0	28.7	28.3
1.9	1.2	1.3	All Other Current	2.3	1.2	.5	1.0	1.5	2.4
60.0	59.9	60.8	Total Current	54.8	63.2	60.0	62.7	59.6	57.7
32.5	32.5	32.2	Fixed Assets (net)	38.3	29.8	33.1	30.5	34.4	32.9
1.5	1.6	1.4	Intangibles (net)	.5	1.7	1.2	.5	2.2	2.5
6.0	6.1	5.6	All Other Non-Current	6.5	5.3	5.7	6.3	3.8	6.9
100.0	100.0	100.0	Total	100.0	100.0	100.0	100.0	100.0	100.0
			LIABILITIES						
8.4	8.4	9.6	Notes Payable-Short Term	12.4	7.2	10.0	9.2	11.6	10.2
5.5	4.8	4.9	Cur. Mat.-L /T/D	5.0	4.8	6.7	5.1	4.3	2.9
13.6	12.2	15.6	Trade Payables	9.8	16.4	17.4	16.3	16.4	12.1
.6	1.9	.5	Income Taxes Payable	.8	.3	.2	.6	.6	.6
8.7	7.7	8.6	All Other Current	6.1	8.2	11.3	9.7	7.1	7.6
36.8	35.0	39.2	Total Current	34.0	36.9	45.6	41.0	40.0	33.5
15.9	15.2	16.9	Long Term Debt	23.6	18.2	14.7	17.9	14.3	14.7
.9	.7	.7	Deferred Taxes	.5	.4	.7	.7	1.0	1.3
2.8	3.4	4.7	All Other-Non-Current	7.2	3.3	10.2	2.9	3.3	4.5
43.6	45.7	38.5	Net Worth	34.7	41.3	28.9	37.6	41.3	46.0
100.0	100.0	100.0	Total Liabilities & Net Worth	100.0	100.0	100.0	100.0	100.0	100.0
			INCOME DATA						
100.0	100.0	100.0	Net Sales	100.0	100.0	100.0	100.0	100.0	100.0
28.2	27.0	26.2	Gross Profit	39.8	27.6	24.7	25.9	22.8	23.4
23.1	22.0	20.7	Operating Expenses	34.6	22.7	21.1	19.1	17.4	16.5
5.1	5.0	5.5	Operating Profit	5.1	4.8	3.6	6.8	5.4	7.0
1.3	1.2	1.3	All Other Expenses (net)	1.0	.8	1.4	1.6	1.9	1.0
3.8	3.9	4.2	Profit Before Taxes	4.1	4.0	2.2	5.2	3.5	5.9
			RATIOS						
2.5	2.5	2.5	Current	3.0	3.3	2.1	2.5	2.5	2.4
1.7	1.8	1.7		2.0	1.9	1.2	1.7	1.6	1.7
1.2	1.2	1.1		1.2	1.2	1.0	1.1	1.0	1.3
1.4	1.5	1.4	Quick	2.5	1.8	1.2	1.3	1.1	1.2
.9	1.0	.9		1.4	1.1	.8	.8	.8	.8
.7	.7	.6		.4	.7	.6	.5	.5	.7
35 10.4	38 9.5	37 9.8	Sales/Receivables	30 12.0	35 10.5	38 9.7	36 10.2	36 10.2	42 8.6
44 8.3	46 8.0	46 8.0		45 8.2	47 7.7	44 8.3	45 8.2	43 8.4	50 7.3
53 6.9	55 6.6	54 6.7		61 6.0	56 6.5	52 7.0	54 6.7	52 7.0	55 6.6
36 10.2	31 11.6	32 11.4	Cost of Sales/Inventory	8 47.6	19 19.3	33 11.0	40 9.2	42 8.7	43 8.5
64 5.7	55 6.6	54 6.7		55 6.6	40 9.2	48 7.6	64 5.7	68 5.4	62 5.9
89 4.1	89 4.1	81 4.5		126 2.9	65 5.6	69 5.3	89 4.1	94 3.9	107 3.4
19 19.3	14 25.5	19 19.1	Cost of Sales/Payables	7 55.0	16 22.2	22 16.3	21 17.8	23 15.9	16 22.7
29 12.6	27 13.7	31 11.9		26 13.9	27 13.6	35 10.4	31 11.8	37 9.9	27 13.4
43 8.4	41 9.0	46 8.0		41 8.8	47 7.7	42 8.7	48 7.6	50 7.3	43 8.5
5.1	5.4	5.6	Sales/Working Capital	4.8	5.4	7.2	5.7	5.3	4.8
8.9	8.1	8.9		10.0	8.1	20.3	8.6	8.2	8.5
24.0	19.7	37.6		57.4	25.4	-79.2	32.6	NM	14.2
(193) 7.0	(179) 9.0	(231) 8.2	EBIT/Interest	(15) 5.6	(56) 10.9	(36) 4.9	(57) 9.1	(41) 12.4	(26) 11.2
2.7	3.6	3.9		2.9	4.4	2.9	4.0	4.2	5.3
1.2	1.6	1.8		.5	1.7	1.8	2.0	2.9	2.1
(105) 3.6	(89) 4.4	(129) 5.3	Net Profit + Depr., Dep., Amort./Cur. Mat. L/T/D		(29) 3.9	(22) 4.3	(35) 6.0	(27) 5.3	(11) 5.4
1.9	2.1	2.2			1.7	1.5	2.6	2.2	2.0
1.0	1.2	1.3			1.1	1.1	1.5	1.4	1.8
.4	.4	.4	Fixed/Worth	.6	.4	.7	.4	.5	.4
.8	.8	.8		1.0	.7	1.2	.8	.8	.9
1.6	1.4	1.9		3.2	1.8	3.2	1.4	1.7	1.6
.7	.6	.8	Debt/Worth	.8	.6	1.1	1.0	.5	.7
1.4	1.2	1.6		1.8	1.6	2.0	1.6	1.4	1.5
3.3	3.1	3.7		6.9	2.8	9.9	3.7	3.6	2.9
(198) 31.3	(184) 33.0	(228) 39.9	% Profit Before Taxes/Tangible Net Worth	(15) 35.1	(53) 39.1	(31) 33.6	(60) 50.7	(42) 37.3	(27) 39.2
14.8	18.0	23.4		19.3	24.0	17.7	24.5	23.3	25.0
3.4	5.3	9.1		.0	10.4	10.8	9.4	10.2	8.9
12.8	13.1	16.3	% Profit Before Taxes/Total Assets	19.7	19.4	10.4	17.2	13.7	20.1
6.0	6.2	7.5		1.2	7.9	6.2	7.5	7.9	8.3
.9	1.7	2.6		-5.0	2.5	2.4	3.4	4.1	3.3
13.2	12.9	12.5	Sales/Net Fixed Assets	9.1	19.8	14.3	13.6	8.9	9.1
6.4	6.7	7.2		4.5	8.5	7.1	8.6	6.5	4.7
3.9	3.7	4.1		3.1	5.7	4.2	4.2	3.7	3.6
2.6	2.6	2.7	Sales/Total Assets	3.1	2.9	3.1	2.8	2.5	2.0
2.0	2.1	2.2		1.8	2.4	2.3	2.2	2.0	1.7
1.6	1.6	1.6		1.2	1.9	1.9	1.6	1.5	1.5
(200) 1.8	(176) 1.7	(225) 1.5	% Depr., Dep., Amort./Sales	(15) 3.5	(55) 1.2	(35) 1.4	(59) 1.4	(40) 2.1	(21) 1.4
2.9	2.8	2.8		5.1	2.8	2.7	2.3	2.8	3.0
4.6	4.4	4.0		9.1	4.0	4.2	3.7	4.0	3.4
(92) 2.8	(81) 3.2	(117) 2.6	% Officers', Directors', Owners' Comp/Sales	(11) 6.1	(33) 2.8	(25) 4.5	(30) 2.5	(17) 2.2	
4.8	5.6	5.6		10.2	5.6	7.1	5.2	2.8	
7.3	8.1	8.4		12.3	9.6	9.8	7.3	6.0	
2521943M	2546240M	3815428M	Net Sales ($)	9841M	120101M	151438M	426384M	679989M	2427675M
1504990M	1496509M	2176674M	Total Assets ($)	5031M	56369M	71339M	216402M	379022M	1448511M

Current Data Sorted By Assets							Comparative Historical Data	
3	10	6	1			# Postretirement Benefits		
						Type of Statement		
1	6	26	15	1		Unqualified	52	35
3	35	37	5			Reviewed	73	82
11	34	15	2			Compiled	79	58
	2	2				Tax Returns	1	1
9	20	15	2			Other	37	33
	86 (4/1-9/30/94)		155 (10/1/94-3/31/95)				4/1/90-3/31/91	4/1/91-3/31/92
0-500M	500M-2MM	2-10MM	10-50MM	50-100MM	100-250MM		ALL	ALL
24	97	95	24	1		**NUMBER OF STATEMENTS**	242	209
%	%	%	%	%	%	**ASSETS**	%	%
10.8	7.7	7.3	6.7			Cash & Equivalents	7.2	8.1
38.1	33.4	27.7	26.3			Trade Receivables - (net)	30.9	31.9
13.9	17.3	23.7	25.6			Inventory	21.1	20.8
2.9	2.0	1.7	2.5			All Other Current	2.7	2.3
65.8	60.5	60.4	61.0			Total Current	61.9	63.1
28.3	33.8	31.2	31.5			Fixed Assets (net)	30.5	29.4
.5	1.1	1.5	.9			Intangibles (net)	1.4	1.6
5.4	4.6	6.8	6.6			All Other Non-Current	6.3	5.8
100.0	100.0	100.0	100.0			Total	100.0	100.0
						LIABILITIES		
12.0	9.8	10.4	7.5			Notes Payable-Short Term	9.3	9.5
5.1	5.3	4.2	4.2			Cur. Mat. -L/T/D	4.6	4.9
16.3	16.2	16.0	17.0			Trade Payables	15.1	14.5
.9	.3	.6	.4			Income Taxes Payable	.7	.6
11.1	7.6	6.5	8.7			All Other Current	10.1	8.5
45.4	39.2	37.6	37.8			Total Current	39.8	38.0
17.7	18.7	15.0	16.5			Long Term Debt	16.7	15.8
.3	.6	.6	.9			Deferred Taxes	.6	.7
5.0	3.6	1.7	1.4			All Other-Non-Current	2.5	2.1
31.7	38.0	45.0	43.3			Net Worth	40.5	43.5
100.0	100.0	100.0	100.0			Total Liabilities & Net Worth	100.0	100.0
						INCOME DATA		
100.0	100.0	100.0	100.0			Net Sales	100.0	100.0
42.9	30.4	24.4	23.3			Gross Profit	28.0	27.9
35.0	25.9	20.0	15.6			Operating Expenses	23.6	24.1
7.9	4.5	4.5	7.7			Operating Profit	4.4	3.8
1.3	1.3	.7	.4			All Other Expenses (net)	1.3	1.2
6.6	3.2	3.8	7.3			Profit Before Taxes	3.1	2.5
						RATIOS		
2.5	2.7	2.7	2.8				2.6	2.8
1.6	1.7	1.5	1.6			Current	1.6	1.7
1.1	1.2	1.2	1.1				1.2	1.2
2.1	1.8	1.8	1.6				1.6	1.8
1.2	1.2	.9	.8			Quick	1.0	1.1
.6	.8	.6	.6				.6	.7
26 14.0	37 9.8	34 10.6	38 9.6				34 10.8	34 10.6
42 8.7	49 7.5	45 8.1	44 8.3			Sales/Receivables	47 7.8	48 7.6
56 6.5	63 5.8	57 6.4	60 6.1				59 6.2	61 6.0
2 161.3	14 26.1	31 11.8	34 10.7				23 16.2	19 19.4
31 11.6	31 11.9	49 7.5	64 5.7			Cost of Sales/Inventory	42 8.6	42 8.6
54 6.8	51 7.1	72 5.1	114 3.2				66 5.5	70 5.2
12 31.6	15 24.3	20 18.7	31 11.9				17 21.7	16 22.7
20 18.2	28 13.1	32 11.3	40 9.2			Cost of Sales/Payables	27 13.5	27 13.4
59 6.2	45 8.2	49 7.5	51 7.2				43 8.4	42 8.7
6.2	6.4	5.6	4.2				5.9	5.1
16.4	10.3	10.6	8.1			Sales/Working Capital	10.5	9.8
84.9	26.3	22.8	30.9				35.8	26.0
		7.9	18.3				6.4	6.0
(20) 7.4	(92) 6.4	(88) 3.7	(23) 7.4			EBIT/Interest	(217) 2.9	(190) 2.1
4.1 .7	3.3 1.6	1.3	2.7				1.3	1.1
	4.1	4.7	5.1				4.3	3.8
	(42) 2.1	(43) 2.3	(11) 1.8			Net Profit + Depr., Dep., Amort./Cur. Mat. L/T/D	(126) 2.1	(100) 1.6
	1.6	.8	1.3				.9	.8
.3	.4	.4	.4				.4	.3
.7	.8	.7	.9			Fixed/Worth	.7	.6
1.2	1.7	1.4	1.5				1.5	1.4
.9	.7	.6	.6				.6	.6
1.8	1.4	1.4	1.6			Debt/Worth	1.7	1.5
4.6	3.5	2.8	2.6				3.3	2.9
85.0	35.3	33.1	35.2				33.1	25.4
(21) 21.4	(88) 16.6	(92) 19.2	(23) 27.9			% Profit Before Taxes/Tangible Net Worth	(229) 16.7	(193) 13.1
2.0	3.8	4.5	9.5				5.3	1.7
21.6	13.9	13.6	21.7				13.1	12.1
5.0	6.8	8.0	9.2			% Profit Before Taxes/Total Assets	6.6	4.6
.0	1.8	1.4	3.4				1.6	.4
20.3	15.1	13.4	10.6				17.7	18.2
12.7	7.6	6.7	6.4			Sales/Net Fixed Assets	8.2	8.6
6.4	5.0	4.3	4.5				4.3	4.7
4.4	2.9	2.5	2.3				2.9	2.9
3.1	2.5	2.0	2.0			Sales/Total Assets	2.2	2.2
1.8	1.8	1.7	1.4				1.7	1.8
1.1	1.8	1.4	1.5				1.3	1.2
(18) 2.2	(92) 3.1	(83) 2.5	(21) 2.3			% Depr., Dep., Amort./Sales	(215) 2.4	(200) 2.2
3.2	4.4	3.8	3.3				4.0	3.8
3.6	3.4	2.2					3.3	2.7
(11) 9.3	(63) 6.0	(41) 3.8				% Officers', Directors', Owners' Comp/Sales	(116) 5.7	(116) 5.1
13.1	9.6	6.1					10.8	7.9
19164M	270066M	807609M	965598M	72111M		Net Sales ($)	2089300M	1826699M
6149M	109223M	381766M	498218M	61716M		Total Assets ($)	1055595M	918077M

M = $ thousand   MM = $ million
See Pages 1 through 15 for Explanation of Ratios and Data

Comparative Historical Data / Current Data Sorted By Sales

Hist 6/11/20				Current					
6	11	20	# Postretirement Benefits	2	4	6	3	4	1

Type of Statement

				0-1MM	1-3MM	3-5MM	5-10MM	10-25MM	25MM & OVER
44	48	49	Unqualified	1	6	5	13	10	14
72	85	80	Reviewed	3	18	25	19	12	3
61	61	62	Compiled	11	23	14	11	3	
5	6	4	Tax Returns			2	1		1
38	50	46	Other	10	13	7	6	8	2
4/1/92-3/31/93 ALL	4/1/93-3/31/94 ALL	4/1/94-3/31/95 ALL		86 (4/1-9/30/94)			155 (10/1/94-3/31/95)		
220	250	241	**NUMBER OF STATEMENTS**	25	62	52	49	34	19
%	%	%	**ASSETS**	%	%	%	%	%	%
9.3	8.4	7.8	Cash & Equivalents	9.4	9.8	7.3	7.0	6.4	4.9
30.0	30.5	30.9	Trade Receivables - (net)	28.7	33.0	30.5	30.4	31.1	28.5
19.3	22.1	20.2	Inventory	10.3	15.4	21.8	22.6	27.8	25.3
2.1	1.9	2.1	All Other Current	4.5	1.9	.8	2.1	2.0	2.5
60.6	62.9	60.9	Total Current	52.9	60.1	60.5	62.1	67.4	61.1
32.4	29.9	32.1	Fixed Assets (net)	40.4	33.2	32.1	31.1	25.8	31.1
1.4	1.3	1.2	Intangibles (net)	1.3	1.0	.7	1.8	1.2	1.1
5.6	5.9	5.8	All Other Non-Current	5.4	5.7	6.7	4.9	5.7	6.7
100.0	100.0	100.0	Total	100.0	100.0	100.0	100.0	100.0	100.0
			LIABILITIES						
8.3	8.9	10.0	Notes Payable-Short Term	15.6	7.0	10.3	11.3	8.6	10.0
4.6	4.0	4.7	Cur. Mat.-L/T/D	6.4	5.8	4.5	4.0	3.1	4.3
13.2	15.2	16.2	Trade Payables	11.3	15.1	15.7	17.1	19.8	18.4
.7	1.6	.5	Income Taxes Payable	.8	.4	.4	.4	.6	.5
8.8	9.4	7.6	All Other Current	10.0	7.7	5.7	7.0	9.0	8.6
35.7	39.0	38.9	Total Current	44.2	36.0	36.6	39.9	41.2	41.7
15.4	14.5	16.9	Long Term Debt	24.5	21.0	13.7	15.1	12.9	14.3
.4	.7	.6	Deferred Taxes	.3	.5	.9	.4	.6	1.2
1.6	2.4	2.8	All Other-Non-Current	3.0	4.0	3.1	2.0	2.0	.8
46.8	43.4	40.8	Net Worth	28.0	38.6	45.8	42.6	43.4	41.9
100.0	100.0	100.0	Total Liabilities & Net Worth	100.0	100.0	100.0	100.0	100.0	100.0
			INCOME DATA						
100.0	100.0	100.0	Net Sales	100.0	100.0	100.0	100.0	100.0	100.0
29.6	29.1	28.6	Gross Profit	41.3	34.0	25.9	25.6	19.8	25.1
25.6	25.1	23.5	Operating Expenses	31.4	29.5	22.0	21.2	15.5	17.2
4.1	4.0	5.1	Operating Profit	9.9	4.4	3.8	4.4	4.3	7.9
1.1	1.0	.9	All Other Expenses (net)	2.6	1.1	.8	.5	.4	.5
3.0	2.9	4.2	Profit Before Taxes	7.2	3.4	3.0	3.9	3.9	7.3
			RATIOS						
2.8	2.6	2.7	Current	2.4	2.8	2.7	2.1	2.8	2.7
1.9	1.7	1.6		1.4	1.9	1.6	1.5	1.6	1.4
1.2	1.2	1.2		.9	1.3	1.2	1.2	1.2	1.1
2.0	1.7	1.8	Quick	2.1	2.2	1.7	1.5	1.8	1.6
1.1	1.0	1.0		.8	1.4	1.1	.9	.8	.8
.7	.7	.7		.3	.9	.7	.6	.6	.6
33 11.0	34 10.6	36 10.2	Sales/Receivables	25 14.8	38 9.6	30 12.3	35 10.3	35 10.5	38 9.5
45 8.2	44 8.3	46 8.0		49 7.4	48 7.6	45 8.1	44 8.3	47 7.8	45 8.2
61 6.0	59 6.2	59 6.2		62 5.9	64 5.7	59 6.2	56 6.5	56 6.5	58 6.3
18 19.8	23 15.9	24 15.4	Cost of Sales/Inventory	3 114.1	13 28.6	26 14.3	27 13.6	29 12.6	30 12.3
38 9.7	47 7.7	42 8.6		32 11.5	27 13.3	45 8.2	42 8.7	54 6.7	51 7.1
63 5.8	73 5.0	68 5.4		57 6.4	65 6.1	60 6.1	73 5.0	74 4.9	79 4.6
13 28.5	16 22.3	18 19.8	Cost of Sales/Payables	6 64.8	15 24.7	19 19.3	19 19.2	22 16.9	31 11.6
23 16.1	27 13.5	31 11.6		18 20.2	25 14.4	32 11.5	30 12.3	37 10.0	38 9.5
39 9.3	44 8.3	46 8.0		54 6.8	49 7.4	43 8.5	45 8.1	53 6.9	47 7.7
5.5	5.4	5.8	Sales/Working Capital	5.7	5.4	5.9	6.2	5.8	5.2
9.4	10.2	10.5		15.9	8.2	11.0	11.8	10.6	11.4
24.6	30.2	29.0		-44.9	21.3	25.2	21.4	36.6	46.9
(196) 6.7	(217) 8.4	(224) 7.8	EBIT/Interest	(22) 7.8	(59) 4.9	(47) 6.5	(45) 10.4	(33) 10.7	(18) 19.5
2.7	3.6	3.6		3.3	3.2	3.4	3.1	6.0	9.4
1.2	1.2	1.6		.5	1.4	1.2	1.4	3.4	2.6
(110) 4.7	(101) 3.7	(103) 4.5	Net Profit + Depr., Dep., Amort./Cur. Mat. L/T/D		(30) 3.5	(21) 4.2	(18) 5.3	(18) 6.5	
2.0	1.8	2.1			2.0	1.9	2.9	2.3	
.7	.9	1.3			1.5	1.4	1.0	1.4	
.4	.3	.4	Fixed/Worth	.4	.4	.4	.4	.4	.4
.7	.7	.8		1.0	.8	.6	.8	.5	.8
1.3	1.3	1.6		5.5	1.8	1.3	1.7	1.0	1.3
.5	.6	.7	Debt/Worth	.8	.7	.7	.7	.5	.6
1.3	1.3	1.4		1.4	1.3	1.2	1.6	1.6	1.6
2.8	3.4	3.1		5.7	3.6	3.1	2.8	4.3	2.7
(214) 32.9	(238) 37.1	(225) 35.5	% Profit Before Taxes/Tangible Net Worth	(20) 84.2	(57) 34.8	(50) 28.8	(47) 31.4	(33) 43.9	(18) 43.1
13.4	16.4	20.0		24.0	16.0	12.8	21.7	24.9	30.5
2.4	5.1	4.2		4.6	2.5	2.9	7.6	12.7	14.7
12.9	13.9	14.9	% Profit Before Taxes/Total Assets	19.9	13.8	11.1	13.9	17.0	22.3
5.3	6.6	7.5		6.8	7.1	5.2	7.3	8.4	10.4
1.0	.9	1.8		-.7	1.2	.9	1.9	4.9	3.7
15.3	16.9	14.8	Sales/Net Fixed Assets	15.2	13.7	12.1	15.7	21.2	10.8
7.5	8.6	7.4		8.0	6.6	6.9	7.7	11.2	7.7
4.3	4.8	4.6		2.4	4.0	5.2	4.7	6.3	4.5
3.0	3.0	2.9	Sales/Total Assets	3.1	2.7	2.9	3.0	2.9	2.5
2.3	2.3	2.1		1.7	2.2	2.3	2.1	2.1	2.0
1.7	1.6	1.7		1.3	1.6	1.9	1.8	1.9	1.6
(207) 1.4	(234) 1.4	(215) 1.5	% Depr., Dep., Amort./Sales	(20) 2.0	(57) 1.9	(50) 1.8	(44) 1.6	(28) 1.2	(16) 1.4
2.4	2.4	2.7		3.2	3.0	3.2	2.7	1.6	2.0
4.0	3.7	3.9		5.5	4.5	3.9	3.6	3.1	3.3
(119) 3.1	(122) 2.9	(120) 3.0	% Officers', Directors', Owners' Comp/Sales		(38) 3.5	(37) 3.4	(24) 2.0		
5.5	5.0	5.1			6.0	5.2	4.6		
10.3	8.1	8.7			9.9	9.2	8.2		
1413323M	1903336M	2134548M	Net Sales ($)	14021M	122575M	209784M	335459M	494217M	958492M
758241M	927976M	1057072M	Total Assets ($)	9329M	62215M	99864M	161826M	232423M	491415M

M = $ thousand   MM = $ million
See Pages 1 through 15 for Explanation of Ratios and Data

274   MANUFACTURERS—VALVES & PIPE FITTINGS, EXCEPT PLUMBERS' BRASS GOODS.   SIC# 3494

Type of Statement

0-500M	500M-2MM	2-10MM	10-50MM	50-100MM	100-250MM	# Postretirement Benefits / Type of Statement	4/1/90-3/31/91 ALL	4/1/91-3/31/92 ALL
	7	3	6		1	# Postretirement Benefits		
	2	7	15	5	4	Unqualified	44	28
1	7	9	3			Reviewed	17	21
1	14	4				Compiled	14	11
1						Tax Returns		
2	5	9	9		2	Other	18	21
							4/1/90-3/31/91 ALL	4/1/91-3/31/92 ALL
5	28	29	27	5	6	**NUMBER OF STATEMENTS**	93	81

Current Data Sorted By Assets

Number of Statements current periods: 31 (4/1-9/30/94), 69 (10/1/94-3/31/95)

0-500M	500M-2MM	2-10MM	10-50MM	50-100MM	100-250MM		4/1/90-3/31/91 ALL	4/1/91-3/31/92 ALL
%	%	%	%	%	%	**ASSETS**	%	%
	7.1	7.1	6.2			Cash & Equivalents	7.0	6.3
	39.1	28.0	25.8			Trade Receivables - (net)	24.1	26.7
	33.9	33.7	30.6			Inventory	34.4	32.3
	.8	3.8	2.6			All Other Current	1.6	1.9
	80.8	72.6	65.2			Total Current	67.1	67.2
	13.3	22.5	22.5			Fixed Assets (net)	25.1	22.8
	1.5	.1	3.5			Intangibles (net)	1.4	2.8
	4.4	4.7	8.9			All Other Non-Current	6.5	7.3
	100.0	100.0	100.0			Total	100.0	100.0
						LIABILITIES		
	11.2	10.8	10.0			Notes Payable-Short Term	9.5	9.2
	3.4	3.8	2.6			Cur. Mat. -L/T/D	3.2	3.4
	19.7	12.3	12.1			Trade Payables	11.0	12.2
	.9	.5	.6			Income Taxes Payable	.7	.8
	9.0	6.2	10.1			All Other Current	9.0	10.4
	44.2	33.6	35.5			Total Current	33.3	36.0
	7.9	12.6	12.6			Long Term Debt	12.9	11.7
	.1	.5	.9			Deferred Taxes	.8	.8
	6.6	3.0	3.8			All Other-Non-Current	2.7	1.3
	41.1	50.3	47.2			Net Worth	50.3	50.2
	100.0	100.0	100.0			Total Liabilities & Net Worth	100.0	100.0
						INCOME DATA		
	100.0	100.0	100.0			Net Sales	100.0	100.0
	31.5	29.8	31.5			Gross Profit	31.7	30.1
	28.3	26.2	23.5			Operating Expenses	25.9	25.1
	3.3	3.6	8.1			Operating Profit	5.8	5.0
	.6	.8	1.5			All Other Expenses (net)	1.4	.8
	2.7	2.8	6.6			Profit Before Taxes	4.4	4.2
						RATIOS		
	2.6	3.9	2.9			Current	3.9	3.0
	2.0	2.1	1.7				2.1	1.9
	1.3	1.5	1.4				1.4	1.4
	1.5	2.0	1.3			Quick	1.7	1.5
	1.1	.9	.8				1.0	.9
	.8	.6	.5				.6	.6
	37 10.0	44 8.3	47 7.7			Sales/Receivables	39 9.3	40 9.2
	46 7.9	52 7.0	59 6.2				47 7.7	49 7.5
	68 5.4	61 6.0	69 5.3				58 6.3	62 5.9
	40 9.2	55 6.6	74 4.9			Cost of Sales/Inventory	70 5.2	62 5.9
	69 5.3	91 4.0	101 3.6				104 3.5	83 4.4
	114 3.2	118 3.1	152 2.4				140 2.6	135 2.7
	22 16.6	17 21.6	24 15.1			Cost of Sales/Payables	18 20.0	18 20.8
	35 10.4	31 11.9	37 9.9				27 13.7	28 13.1
	47 7.8	43 8.4	56 6.5				46 8.0	41 8.8
	4.6	3.1	3.7			Sales/Working Capital	3.2	4.0
	7.6	5.3	5.6				5.8	6.9
	13.3	9.1	9.5				10.4	11.1
	7.3	14.2	10.6			EBIT/Interest	12.4	12.1
	(25) 4.2	(26) 4.1	(24) 4.9				(86) 3.1	(78) 3.8
	-.4	1.3	2.3				1.5	1.2
		8.6	16.7			Net Profit + Depr., Dep., Amort./Cur. Mat. L./T/D	7.6	11.0
	(11)	1.6	(15) 4.2				(55) 3.0	(43) 3.2
		.2	1.0				1.1	1.3
	.1	.2	.4			Fixed/Worth	.2	.3
	.2	.4	.5				.5	.4
	.6	.7	.8				1.1	.9
	.7	.4	.7			Debt/Worth	.3	.4
	1.2	1.0	1.5				1.0	1.0
	5.9	1.9	2.0				2.6	2.3
	48.1	30.5	36.0			% Profit Before Taxes/Tangible Net Worth	26.6	24.7
	(25) 20.8	(28) 18.7	(26) 21.3				(91) 16.0	(77) 15.7
	-3.2	8.6	6.3				4.0	-.8
	15.7	15.4	15.9			% Profit Before Taxes/Total Assets	13.8	14.5
	5.3	8.4	7.4				7.2	8.6
	-6.4	1.7	3.3				1.7	1.2
	75.3	16.0	10.7			Sales/Net Fixed Assets	15.5	19.5
	31.9	9.6	7.1				6.9	8.5
	10.3	4.8	5.4				4.2	4.8
	3.6	2.3	1.8			Sales/Total Assets	2.1	2.6
	2.5	1.9	1.6				1.6	1.9
	2.1	1.4	1.4				1.3	1.4
	.6	.7	1.6			% Depr., Dep., Amort./Sales	1.5	1.2
	(24) 1.2	(26) 1.6	(24) 3.0				(80) 2.6	(68) 2.4
	2.7	3.1	3.7				3.7	3.8
	4.8					% Officers', Directors', Owners' Comp/Sales	4.1	3.0
	(15) 5.9						(29) 6.7	(23) 5.8
	13.1						9.9	11.1
5154M	90663M	281254M	885201M	422876M	912983M	Net Sales ($)	2416823M	2565068M
1582M	33996M	147880M	570228M	346488M	767550M	Total Assets ($)	1660068M	1782097M

© Robert Morris Associates 1995   M = $ thousand   MM = $ million   See Pages 1 through 15 for Explanation of Ratios and Data

Comparative Historical Data				Current Data Sorted By Sales					
4	9	17	# Postretirement Benefits		2	3	3	5	4
			Type of Statement						
30	31	33	Unqualified		2		6	6	19
22	27	20	Reviewed		4	6	3	5	2
18	12	19	Compiled	1	7	5	4	2	
		1	Tax Returns	1					
17	21	27	Other	1	4	3	5	7	7
4/1/92-3/31/93	4/1/93-3/31/94	4/1/94-3/31/95			31 (4/1-9/30/94)		69 (10/1/94-3/31/95)		
ALL	ALL	ALL		0-1MM	1-3MM	3-5MM	5-10MM	10-25MM	25MM & OVER
87	92	100	**NUMBER OF STATEMENTS**	3	17	14	18	20	28
%	%	%	**ASSETS**	%	%	%	%	%	%
6.7	7.2	6.4	Cash & Equivalents		7.4	6.1	3.9	8.6	6.4
26.2	28.4	30.0	Trade Receivables - (net)		39.5	34.5	27.4	29.3	24.0
33.5	34.0	32.9	Inventory		32.2	33.1	37.4	30.6	30.8
1.3	1.2	2.2	All Other Current		.3	3.1	3.2	3.9	1.4
67.7	70.8	71.5	Total Current		79.5	76.7	71.8	72.4	62.6
23.3	20.5	20.5	Fixed Assets (net)		14.2	19.3	22.1	17.3	27.3
3.5	2.5	1.5	Intangibles (net)		1.7	1.0	.8	2.6	1.4
5.5	6.1	6.6	All Other Non-Current		4.6	3.0	5.4	7.7	8.7
100.0	100.0	100.0	Total		100.0	100.0	100.0	100.0	100.0
			LIABILITIES						
9.3	9.6	10.9	Notes Payable-Short Term		12.7	13.0	11.5	11.4	7.7
3.4	2.4	2.9	Cur. Mat.-L./T/D		4.4	1.9	5.5	2.0	2.0
13.1	13.4	14.0	Trade Payables		15.2	17.6	16.6	11.9	10.8
.8	1.4	.7	Income Taxes Payable		.3	.6	1.1	.5	.8
8.4	8.9	8.6	All Other Current		12.7	5.5	5.3	8.5	10.4
35.0	35.5	37.2	Total Current		45.3	38.5	40.0	34.4	31.7
13.1	10.6	11.6	Long Term Debt		12.9	5.6	14.0	10.5	12.8
.7	.5	.5	Deferred Taxes		.0	.3	.6	.6	.8
2.0	3.2	3.8	All Other-Non-Current		7.8	3.1	3.9	3.2	2.6
49.2	50.2	46.9	Net Worth		33.9	52.5	41.6	51.3	52.0
100.0	100.0	100.0	Total Liabilities & Net Worth		100.0	100.0	100.0	100.0	100.0
			INCOME DATA						
100.0	100.0	100.0	Net Sales		100.0	100.0	100.0	100.0	100.0
32.1	31.0	29.6	Gross Profit		33.1	28.5	27.5	31.4	27.0
25.6	24.9	25.6	Operating Expenses		28.1	30.7	23.8	24.0	23.5
6.5	6.1	4.0	Operating Profit		5.0	-2.2	3.8	7.4	3.5
1.3	1.5	1.0	All Other Expenses (net)		.9	.5	1.2	.9	1.2
5.2	4.7	3.0	Profit Before Taxes		4.1	-2.7	2.6	6.5	2.3
			RATIOS						
3.5	3.6	3.1			2.6	5.8	2.8	3.3	3.6
2.2	1.9	1.9	Current		1.9	2.1	1.9	2.1	2.0
1.3	1.4	1.4			1.2	1.3	1.5	1.5	1.4
1.6	1.9	1.6			1.6	2.0	1.2	1.9	1.7
1.0	1.1	.9	Quick		.9	1.1	.9	1.0	1.0
.6	.7	.7			.7	.8	.5	.7	.5
40 9.2	41 8.8	41 8.9			35 10.3	37 9.9	43 8.5	47 7.8	47 7.7
46 7.9	51 7.1	54 6.8	Sales/Receivables		55 6.6	48 7.6	49 7.4	58 6.3	59 6.2
58 6.3	66 5.5	66 5.5			73 5.0	68 5.4	58 6.3	74 4.9	65 5.6
61 6.0	63 5.8	59 6.2			40 9.1	36 10.1	74 4.9	54 6.8	74 4.9
99 3.7	101 3.6	94 3.9	Cost of Sales/Inventory		70 5.2	73 5.0	94 3.9	91 4.0	104 3.5
135 2.7	140 2.6	140 2.6			152 2.4	99 3.7	126 2.9	140 2.6	140 2.6
21 17.5	18 20.3	21 17.6			14 25.6	11 31.9	24 15.5	21 17.6	21 17.8
30 12.0	30 12.0	36 10.2	Cost of Sales/Payables		35 10.5	23 15.6	37 9.9	37 9.8	34 10.7
44 8.3	50 7.3	50 7.3			45 8.2	48 7.6	58 6.9	53 6.9	47 7.7
3.8	3.2	3.5			4.4	3.7	3.6	3.1	3.1
5.6	5.6	5.6	Sales/Working Capital		8.5	5.6	5.6	5.3	5.0
10.8	9.7	10.5			21.1	23.4	11.5	8.6	9.6
(74) 13.2	(76) 12.9	(88) 9.9			(14) 7.9	9.1	(16) 9.2	(18) 11.7	(25) 14.9
3.6	3.9	4.1	EBIT/Interest		3.9	3.1	2.7	4.4	5.2
1.7	1.6	1.0			-.2	-17.1	.9	3.0	.8
(48) 5.4	(44) 11.4	(42) 8.8							(20) 15.7
2.2	3.2	2.7	Net Profit + Depr., Dep., Amort./Cur. Mat. L/T/D						4.5
.9	1.3	.7							2.3
.2	.2	.2			.2	.1	.2	.2	.4
.5	.4	.4	Fixed/Worth		.4	.2	.4	.4	.6
.7	.9	.7			1.4	1.2	.7	.6	.8
.5	.4	.6			.7	.4	.7	.6	.5
1.1	1.0	1.1	Debt/Worth		1.5	.9	1.2	1.0	1.0
2.4	2.5	2.4			9.1	2.0	2.8	1.8	1.9
(82) 29.0	(87) 29.2	(95) 35.4	% Profit Before Taxes/Tangible Net Worth		(14) 80.6	34.2	(17) 25.2	(19) 31.7	33.0
16.1	16.3	18.6			30.6	2.8	17.9	20.1	19.4
6.1	7.6	1.0			6.3	-56.7	2.6	10.5	-1.0
14.9	14.2	15.9	% Profit Before Taxes/Total Assets		19.5	16.7	11.5	20.3	16.0
7.4	6.8	7.3			6.5	1.9	7.4	6.7	12.2
2.7	2.8	.4			-.6	-16.5	.4	4.9	-.5
20.0	25.3	24.7			71.9	39.0	29.0	16.1	7.7
8.3	10.6	9.5	Sales/Net Fixed Assets		30.0	19.1	9.5	9.5	5.7
4.4	5.2	5.1			9.9	7.1	4.5	6.8	3.5
2.4	2.4	2.5			3.3	3.1	2.7	2.4	1.8
1.9	1.8	1.8	Sales/Total Assets		2.3	2.3	1.7	1.8	1.5
1.5	1.4	1.4			1.8	1.8	1.4	1.4	1.2
(77) .8	(85) .9	(88) .9	% Depr., Dep., Amort./Sales		(13) .8	.6	(16) .4	(17) 1.0	(25) 1.7
2.1	2.0	2.1			1.6	.9	1.6	2.2	3.0
3.8	3.1	3.6			3.6	5.8	3.0	3.4	4.2
(33) 2.6	(29) 2.3	(27) 1.8	% Officers', Directors', Owners' Comp/Sales						
6.1	4.8	5.2							
9.6	7.5	6.4							
2174085M	1915261M	2598131M	Net Sales ($)	1386M	35227M	57518M	131077M	326574M	2046349M
1529978M	1328537M	1867724M	Total Assets ($)	695M	15064M	25971M	78068M	213967M	1533959M

M = $ thousand   MM = $ million
See Pages 1 through 15 for Explanation of Ratios and Data

| Current Data Sorted By Assets | | | | | | | Comparative Historical Data | |

0-500M	500M-2MM	2-10MM	10-50MM	50-100MM	100-250MM		4/1/90-3/31/91 ALL	4/1/91-3/31/92 ALL
						# Postretirement Benefits		
						Type of Statement		
1	1	3		1		Unqualified	2	4
	6	6	1			Reviewed	8	16
4	3					Compiled	9	3
1						Tax Returns		
1	2	3	1			Other	3	3
	10 (4/1-9/30/94)		24 (10/1/94-3/31/95)				4/1/90-3/31/91	4/1/91-3/31/92
7	12	12	2	1		**NUMBER OF STATEMENTS**	22	26
%	%	%	%	%	%	**ASSETS**	%	%
	6.8	4.1				Cash & Equivalents	10.8	10.1
	27.8	25.5				Trade Receivables - (net)	25.4	26.6
	13.7	17.6				Inventory	20.9	19.8
	.9	.2				All Other Current	1.2	.9
	49.2	47.4				Total Current	58.2	57.4
	45.3	42.7				Fixed Assets (net)	32.9	34.8
	3.5	5.0				Intangibles (net)	2.6	1.9
	2.0	4.9				All Other Non-Current	6.2	5.9
	100.0	100.0				Total	100.0	100.0
						LIABILITIES		
	6.9	5.9				Notes Payable-Short Term	4.4	5.5
	6.9	5.7				Cur. Mat. -L/T/D	5.2	4.4
	14.6	12.2				Trade Payables	10.1	10.7
	.9	.3				Income Taxes Payable	.8	.8
	6.2	7.1				All Other Current	7.1	6.7
	35.5	31.2				Total Current	27.6	28.1
	34.7	22.2				Long Term Debt	15.9	16.2
	.5	1.0				Deferred Taxes	1.1	.8
	1.6	1.9				All Other-Non-Current	1.3	.5
	27.8	43.6				Net Worth	54.1	54.4
	100.0	100.0				Total Liabilities & Net Worth	100.0	100.0
						INCOME DATA		
	100.0	100.0				Net Sales	100.0	100.0
	33.8	27.4				Gross Profit	34.5	29.1
	28.7	19.6				Operating Expenses	28.2	25.3
	5.1	7.8				Operating Profit	6.2	3.8
	1.8	.6				All Other Expenses (net)	1.2	.5
	3.3	7.2				Profit Before Taxes	5.0	3.3
						RATIOS		
	1.7	2.1				Current	5.0	3.8
	1.4	1.5					2.0	2.0
	1.1	1.2					1.2	1.3
	1.2	1.2				Quick	3.0	2.7
	1.0	1.0					1.0	1.0
	.6	.7					.9	.8
47	47 7.8	41 8.8				Sales/Receivables	37 10.0	36 10.2
52	52 7.0	49 7.4					47 7.8	47 7.7
54	54 6.7	55 6.6					55 6.6	54 6.7
19	19 19.1	35 10.3				Cost of Sales/Inventory	35 10.3	29 12.7
40	40 9.1	41 8.8					46 7.9	48 7.6
54	54 6.7	58 6.3					58 6.3	64 5.7
28	28 13.0	18 20.3				Cost of Sales/Payables	13 29.0	14 25.4
34	34 10.6	26 14.3					25 14.6	21 17.3
46	46 8.0	44 8.3					33 11.2	33 11.0
	9.2	7.0				Sales/Working Capital	3.5	4.5
	16.5	12.2					8.8	8.5
	52.2	23.6					26.0	21.2
	6.3	11.7				EBIT/Interest	9.3	5.5
	2.3	(11) 5.1					(19) 3.0	(23) 1.8
	.7	2.7					2.3	1.0
	5.2					Net Profit + Depr., Dep., Amort./Cur. Mat. L./T/D	5.5	4.2
	(10) 1.9						(12) 2.6	(16) 2.0
	.7						2.0	1.2
	.8	.6				Fixed/Worth	.3	.3
	2.2	1.3					.6	.7
	12.7	2.6					1.5	1.2
	1.1	.5				Debt/Worth	.5	.4
	3.1	2.0					.9	.9
	19.0	3.9					1.8	2.0
	94.7	53.3				% Profit Before Taxes/Tangible Net Worth	34.6	29.0
	(11) 19.0	(11) 25.0					(21) 15.3	(25) 4.1
	7.2	13.0					10.4	.3
	14.6	13.5				% Profit Before Taxes/Total Assets	15.9	13.0
	3.8	9.7					9.2	2.4
	–2.0	6.7					5.7	.2
	6.9	6.4				Sales/Net Fixed Assets	12.5	15.1
	5.2	4.0					6.7	5.4
	2.6	3.3					5.0	3.5
	2.6	2.4				Sales/Total Assets	2.4	2.7
	2.2	1.8					2.1	2.0
	1.5	1.6					1.9	1.7
	2.2	3.0				% Depr., Dep., Amort./Sales	2.3	1.7
	6.1	3.3					(20) 3.5	(24) 3.2
	7.4	4.4					5.7	4.9
						% Officers', Directors', Owners' Comp/Sales	4.5	4.2
							(12) 7.5	(15) 7.7
							14.3	11.7
5511M	27799M	104012M	29784M	96865M		Net Sales ($)	709849M	215569M
1871M	13445M	52571M	24694M	53978M		Total Assets ($)	225115M	94450M

M = $ thousand MM = $ million
See Pages 1 through 15 for Explanation of Ratios and Data

Comparative Historical Data				Current Data Sorted By Sales					
	1	2	# Postretirement Benefits	1					1
			Type of Statement						
9	5	6	Unqualified	1	1	1	1	1	1
21	9	13	Reviewed		4	3	4	2	
3	3	7	Compiled	3	4				
		1	Tax Returns	1					
4	5	7	Other	2		2	1	2	
4/1/92-3/31/93 ALL	4/1/93-3/31/94 ALL	4/1/94-3/31/95 ALL		0-1MM	10 (4/1-9/30/94) 1-3MM	3-5MM	24 (10/1/94-3/31/95) 5-10MM	10-25MM	25MM & OVER
37	22	34	**NUMBER OF STATEMENTS**	7	9	6	6	5	1
%	%	%	**ASSETS**	%	%	%	%	%	%
6.8	3.3	5.5	Cash & Equivalents						
25.4	30.7	28.1	Trade Receivables - (net)						
18.0	21.4	17.5	Inventory						
.8	.3	.9	All Other Current						
51.0	55.7	51.9	Total Current						
37.8	34.0	39.9	Fixed Assets (net)						
3.3	2.1	3.4	Intangibles (net)						
7.8	8.2	4.8	All Other Non-Current						
100.0	100.0	100.0	Total						
			LIABILITIES						
5.0	9.3	5.9	Notes Payable-Short Term						
5.5	6.9	5.6	Cur. Mat.-L /T/D						
13.0	12.1	13.6	Trade Payables						
.9	2.1	.5	Income Taxes Payable						
7.9	9.6	7.1	All Other Current						
32.4	39.9	32.8	Total Current						
16.5	19.5	25.8	Long Term Debt						
1.3	1.4	.9	Deferred Taxes						
2.3	3.7	2.4	All Other-Non-Current						
47.5	35.5	38.2	Net Worth						
100.0	100.0	100.0	Total Liabilities & Net Worth						
			INCOME DATA						
100.0	100.0	100.0	Net Sales						
30.3	26.8	30.0	Gross Profit						
26.9	23.0	24.6	Operating Expenses						
3.4	3.8	5.4	Operating Profit						
1.6	1.5	1.2	All Other Expenses (net)						
1.8	2.3	4.2	Profit Before Taxes						
			RATIOS						
2.3	1.9	2.2							
1.5	1.5	1.5	Current						
1.2	1.0	1.2							
1.6	1.2	1.3							
1.0	.9	1.0	Quick						
.8	.6	.7							
37 9.8	43 8.4	43 8.5							
44 8.3	49 7.4	51 7.1	Sales/Receivables						
51 7.1	58 6.3	54 6.7							
26 14.0	33 10.9	29 12.4							
43 8.4	44 8.3	45 8.1	Cost of Sales/Inventory						
65 5.6	70 5.2	61 6.0							
12 30.0	13 28.9	21 17.1							
29 12.7	27 13.7	30 12.0	Cost of Sales/Payables						
41 8.8	47 7.8	43 8.4							
6.7	8.1	6.1							
14.3	11.6	12.9	Sales/Working Capital						
21.9	77.1	33.3							
6.2	5.7	7.9							
(32) 2.1	(21) 2.5	(30) 3.7	EBIT/Interest						
1.3	1.8	1.3							
3.2	3.9	3.0							
(23) 2.0	(10) 1.4	(18) 1.9	Net Profit + Depr., Dep., Amort./Cur. Mat. L/T/D						
.8	1.0	1.0							
.5	.6	.7							
1.0	1.0	1.2	Fixed/Worth						
1.6	7.1	2.9							
.7	1.0	.7							
1.1	1.6	2.2	Debt/Worth						
1.8	16.0	5.2							
30.7	39.2	52.8							
(34) 4.5	(20) 12.5	(31) 19.9	% Profit Before Taxes/Tangible Net Worth						
−1.1	3.3	9.0							
7.6	9.3	14.1							
2.5	5.8	7.8	% Profit Before Taxes/Total Assets						
.1	2.5	1.1							
11.8	13.2	7.3							
4.6	6.2	4.8	Sales/Net Fixed Assets						
3.6	3.6	3.4							
2.7	2.5	2.7							
2.1	2.2	2.1	Sales/Total Assets						
1.7	1.4	1.6							
2.5	1.5	2.9							
(31) 3.7	(20) 2.6	(31) 4.2	% Depr., Dep., Amort./Sales						
5.7	4.5	6.1							
4.5	2.2	3.3							
(16) 7.6	(10) 4.9	(18) 5.4	% Officers', Directors', Owners' Comp/Sales						
14.0	8.5	10.1							
372930M	169863M	263971M	Net Sales ($)	4723M	17400M	22595M	42373M	80015M	96865M
156460M	89904M	146559M	Total Assets ($)	2359M	8353M	13135M	24851M	43883M	53978M

M = $ thousand   MM = $ million
See Pages 1 through 15 for Explanation of Ratios and Data

Current Data Sorted By Assets — Comparative Historical Data

0-500M	500M-2MM	2-10MM	10-50MM	50-100MM	100-250MM		4/1/90-3/31/91 ALL	4/1/91-3/31/92 ALL
	1	4	2	2	2	# Postretirement Benefits		
						Type of Statement		
1	3	8	5	3	2	Unqualified	14	15
2	8	9	1			Reviewed	20	18
1	8	7	1			Compiled	17	13
	1	1				Tax Returns		1
	6	7	3	1	1	Other	6	8
	25 (4/1-9/30/94)		54 (10/1/94-3/31/95)					
4	26	32	10	4	3	NUMBER OF STATEMENTS	57	55
%	%	%	%	%	%		%	%
						ASSETS		
	7.9	2.5	6.3			Cash & Equivalents	8.6	6.8
	33.6	31.4	26.3			Trade Receivables - (net)	27.0	30.6
	22.2	22.2	19.8			Inventory	20.2	22.3
	.7	1.1	.9			All Other Current	1.6	1.7
	64.4	57.1	53.3			Total Current	57.3	61.4
	28.1	35.7	31.9			Fixed Assets (net)	33.3	30.5
	.9	1.1	2.4			Intangibles (net)	1.7	1.0
	6.6	6.1	12.4			All Other Non-Current	7.7	7.1
	100.0	100.0	100.0			Total	100.0	100.0
						LIABILITIES		
	7.1	11.8	3.8			Notes Payable-Short Term	8.2	6.8
	3.9	5.1	4.6			Cur. Mat. -L/T/D	5.4	4.2
	18.3	18.7	13.5			Trade Payables	16.5	15.7
	1.1	.8	.2			Income Taxes Payable	.4	.4
	9.9	5.6	6.5			All Other Current	7.8	8.3
	40.3	42.0	28.5			Total Current	38.2	35.3
	14.1	25.6	19.6			Long Term Debt	20.0	16.4
	.8	.3	1.0			Deferred Taxes	1.0	.6
	.8	3.7	1.2			All Other-Non-Current	4.2	4.0
	44.0	28.4	49.7			Net Worth	36.6	43.7
	100.0	100.0	100.0			Total Liabilities & Net Worth	100.0	100.0
						INCOME DATA		
	100.0	100.0	100.0			Net Sales	100.0	100.0
	29.4	28.5	27.0			Gross Profit	29.9	28.2
	26.5	22.1	20.6			Operating Expenses	25.3	23.7
	2.9	6.4	6.4			Operating Profit	4.7	4.5
	.9	1.8	1.1			All Other Expenses (net)	1.4	1.3
	2.0	4.6	5.3			Profit Before Taxes	3.3	3.2
						RATIOS		
	3.0	1.9	3.8			Current	2.4	2.5
	1.3	1.5	1.8				1.4	1.7
	1.0	1.0	1.4				1.1	1.3
	1.5	1.3	2.6			Quick	1.5	1.5
	1.0	.8	1.1				.9	1.0
	.6	.6	.7				.6	.8
	32 11.5	40 9.1	39 9.3			Sales/Receivables	37 10.0	35 10.3
	41 8.8	47 7.7	43 8.4				43 8.4	45 8.1
	54 6.8	59 6.2	52 7.0				50 7.3	51 7.2
	23 16.0	30 12.0	27 13.6			Cost of Sales/Inventory	31 11.8	33 11.2
	38 9.6	38 9.6	51 7.1				45 8.2	41 9.0
	64 5.7	72 5.1	72 5.1				63 5.8	62 5.9
	21 17.8	25 14.8	16 23.4			Cost of Sales/Payables	20 18.1	19 19.3
	28 12.9	38 9.7	37 9.9				39 9.4	26 14.3
	45 8.1	55 6.6	49 7.5				54 6.8	40 9.2
	5.5	9.6	6.2			Sales/Working Capital	6.2	5.6
	20.4	14.7	8.0				14.3	10.5
	587.3	390.5	11.0				46.3	20.1
	12.5	8.6				EBIT/Interest	5.6	9.3
	(24) 4.0	3.8					(53) 2.7	(54) 3.0
	-.2	1.5					1.3	1.2
	4.4	9.0				Net Profit + Depr., Dep.,	4.7	9.2
	(11) 1.8	(17) 3.0				Amort./Cur. Mat. L /T/D	(37) 2.5	(32) 2.6
	1.1	1.1					1.2	1.0
	.2	.5	.3			Fixed/Worth	.4	.4
	.7	1.4	.8				1.0	.7
	1.3	2.1	1.5				2.9	1.4
	.5	1.4	.2			Debt/Worth	.6	.5
	1.5	2.2	1.6				2.2	1.2
	3.2	4.4	2.5				5.0	2.7
	52.6	49.0	39.4			% Profit Before Taxes/Tangible	40.9	26.1
	(25) 21.0	(29) 32.7	22.3			Net Worth	(53) 15.5	(51) 12.6
	2.2	7.0	12.5				4.4	2.9
	15.0	15.4	16.5			% Profit Before Taxes/Total	14.7	10.5
	9.3	7.1	10.6			Assets	5.1	5.8
	-1.0	1.5	3.5				.8	.8
	22.6	14.9	8.2			Sales/Net Fixed Assets	15.5	17.4
	11.2	5.6	6.2				6.6	8.5
	6.1	3.6	4.8				4.3	4.6
	3.3	2.9	2.5			Sales/Total Assets	2.9	3.2
	2.9	2.3	1.9				2.2	2.2
	2.2	1.7	1.4				1.6	1.9
	.8	1.2				% Depr., Dep., Amort./Sales	1.7	1.3
	(25) 2.1	2.7					(55) 3.1	(51) 2.2
	3.1	3.7					4.0	3.6
	3.4	2.4				% Officers', Directors',	3.4	3.5
	(18) 7.0	(16) 4.1				Owners' Comp/Sales	(21) 6.8	(30) 4.9
	9.2	6.2					9.4	9.2
3593M	80077M	338577M	368293M	458593M	859043M	Net Sales ($)	1156916M	1554669M
1482M	30099M	155681M	203905M	351392M	470206M	Total Assets ($)	680026M	850678M

M = $ thousand   MM = $ million
See Pages 1 through 15 for Explanation of Ratios and Data

Comparative Historical Data   Current Data Sorted By Sales

 # Postretirement Benefits

	4/1/92-3/31/93	4/1/93-3/31/94	4/1/94-3/31/95		Current
Postretirement Benefits count	2	6	11		1, 2, 2, 6

Type of Statement

Type of Statement	4/1/92-3/31/93 ALL	4/1/93-3/31/94 ALL	4/1/94-3/31/95 ALL	0-1MM	1-3MM	3-5MM	5-10MM	10-25MM	25MM & OVER
Unqualified	20	18	22	1	2	2	3	4	10
Reviewed	19	17	20	1	4	5	4	5	1
Compiled	10	14	17		7	3	1	4	2
Tax Returns			2			1	1		
Other	6	16	18		5	1	5	2	5
					25 (4/1-9/30/94)			54 (10/1/94-3/31/95)	
NUMBER OF STATEMENTS	55	65	79	2	18	12	14	15	18

ASSETS (%)

	4/1/92-3/31/93	4/1/93-3/31/94	4/1/94-3/31/95	0-1MM	1-3MM	3-5MM	5-10MM	10-25MM	25MM & OVER
Cash & Equivalents	4.7	7.3	5.2		9.1	4.0	4.0	2.2	5.8
Trade Receivables - (net)	31.7	29.0	30.1		31.3	34.5	25.7	38.3	23.8
Inventory	22.0	19.9	21.4		23.9	19.9	17.6	25.8	20.0
All Other Current	1.0	1.7	1.2		.5	.8	1.7	.7	1.6
Total Current	59.4	57.8	57.8		64.8	59.2	48.9	67.0	51.2
Fixed Assets (net)	30.6	34.3	32.7		27.1	32.7	45.5	25.9	32.7
Intangibles (net)	1.4	1.9	2.1		.9	.7	1.3	1.2	5.2
All Other Non-Current	8.6	6.0	7.4		7.2	7.3	4.3	5.9	10.8
Total	100.0	100.0	100.0		100.0	100.0	100.0	100.0	100.0

LIABILITIES

	4/1/92-3/31/93	4/1/93-3/31/94	4/1/94-3/31/95	0-1MM	1-3MM	3-5MM	5-10MM	10-25MM	25MM & OVER
Notes Payable-Short Term	10.1	8.4	7.9		4.9	9.2	12.9	8.8	6.4
Cur. Mat.-L/T/D	3.9	4.6	4.7		4.9	4.3	5.7	4.0	4.8
Trade Payables	16.7	14.8	17.1		15.9	21.3	14.4	23.7	11.8
Income Taxes Payable	.4	1.0	.9		.6	1.6	.6	1.2	.5
All Other Current	7.5	7.1	7.3		9.7	8.4	3.3	7.8	7.0
Total Current	38.6	36.0	37.9		36.1	44.6	36.9	45.6	30.5
Long Term Debt	17.4	20.3	21.2		14.8	17.9	32.5	17.7	22.1
Deferred Taxes	1.0	.4	.6		.7	.3	.7	.4	1.0
All Other-Non-Current	1.7	2.6	2.7		.4	2.4	5.6	1.6	3.5
Net Worth	41.4	40.7	37.6		48.0	34.8	24.2	34.7	43.0
Total Liabilities & Net Worth	100.0	100.0	100.0		100.0	100.0	100.0	100.0	100.0

INCOME DATA

	4/1/92-3/31/93	4/1/93-3/31/94	4/1/94-3/31/95	0-1MM	1-3MM	3-5MM	5-10MM	10-25MM	25MM & OVER
Net Sales	100.0	100.0	100.0		100.0	100.0	100.0	100.0	100.0
Gross Profit	27.3	30.1	28.2		29.7	27.8	31.0	25.7	27.8
Operating Expenses	23.3	25.1	23.2		27.2	22.6	23.5	20.2	21.3
Operating Profit	4.0	5.0	5.0		2.4	5.2	7.6	5.5	6.6
All Other Expenses (net)	.9	1.8	1.5		.8	1.5	2.3	1.2	1.7
Profit Before Taxes	3.1	3.2	3.5		1.6	3.7	5.3	4.3	4.9

RATIOS

	4/1/92-3/31/93	4/1/93-3/31/94	4/1/94-3/31/95	0-1MM	1-3MM	3-5MM	5-10MM	10-25MM	25MM & OVER
Current	2.5	2.1	2.0		3.1	1.7	3.4	1.9	2.4
	1.5	1.6	1.5		1.7	1.3	1.2	1.6	1.7
	1.1	1.2	1.1		1.2	1.0	.7	1.2	1.4
Quick	1.5	1.5	1.4		1.5	1.3	1.8	1.0	1.7
	1.0	.8	.9		1.1	.9	.6	.9	.9
	.8	.7	.6		.8	.5	.3	.7	.5
Sales/Receivables	35 10.3	35 10.3	38 9.7		35 10.3	30 12.1	33 11.0	40 9.2	39 9.3
	44 8.3	43 8.5	46 8.0		43 8.4	42 8.6	47 7.8	48 7.6	46 8.0
	55 6.6	52 7.0	56 6.5		54 6.8	83 4.4	56 6.5	62 5.9	54 6.7
Cost of Sales/Inventory	29 12.7	28 13.0	30 12.2		26 13.8	11 33.3	22 16.4	31 11.8	37 9.9
	40 9.2	46 8.0	46 8.0		47 7.7	37 10.0	33 11.2	35 10.3	50 7.3
	63 5.8	65 5.6	69 5.3		83 4.4	64 5.7	69 5.3	68 5.4	87 4.2
Cost of Sales/Payables	17 21.2	19 19.0	24 15.3		21 17.6	22 16.6	15 23.6	29 12.5	23 15.8
	30 12.1	31 11.6	34 10.8		28 13.2	36 10.2	35 10.4	38 9.5	29 12.4
	44 8.3	44 8.3	51 7.2		43 8.4	73 5.0	54 6.8	55 6.6	46 7.9
Sales/Working Capital	6.7	6.0	6.9		5.0	8.3	7.6	9.8	5.4
	14.0	11.0	12.7		10.8	24.4	23.1	14.9	9.5
	40.8	34.4	31.8		28.1	-153.4	-8.5	24.5	16.1
EBIT/Interest	6.6	6.8	10.5		16.5	11.2	11.2	12.5	6.6
	(52) 2.6	(58) 3.0	(76) 3.6		(17) 3.9	4.9	(13) 2.8	4.1	(17) 3.1
	1.5	1.4	1.5		1.1	.3	1.2	3.0	2.0
Net Profit + Depr., Dep., Amort./Cur. Mat. L/T/D	3.7	3.1	7.9					5.5	15.3
	(30) 2.2	(33) 1.5	(40) 2.2					(10) 2.7	(10) 3.2
	1.5	.7	1.1					1.2	1.5
Fixed/Worth	.4	.4	.4		.2	.5	.9	.4	.5
	.7	.9	.9		.7	1.2	1.8	.6	.9
	1.6	1.6	1.7		1.1	1.6	NM	1.4	3.2
Debt/Worth	.6	.9	.9		.5	.8	.8	1.6	.9
	1.5	1.5	1.9		1.4	2.3	3.6	2.0	1.7
	3.7	2.6	3.6		2.2	7.5	NM	2.8	5.4
% Profit Before Taxes/Tangible Net Worth	25.6	32.2	48.2		45.8	55.9	55.1	47.4	29.6
	(53) 13.7	(59) 14.8	(74) 19.7		(11) 12.8	(11) 27.2	29.5	33.4	(17) 14.8
	4.4	6.4	6.8		3.0	7.2	6.4	12.6	7.7
% Profit Before Taxes/Total Assets	9.5	12.3	14.8		13.1	14.6	29.1	15.7	14.4
	5.3	5.3	7.4		9.3	8.2	6.9	10.0	5.9
	1.7	1.6	1.8		1.0	-2.8	1.2	4.0	2.4
Sales/Net Fixed Assets	18.2	13.7	14.5		27.2	11.6	12.6	41.7	7.7
	9.3	6.3	7.0		12.6	7.7	4.6	14.5	5.7
	4.8	3.9	4.5		6.9	5.6	2.3	4.5	4.1
Sales/Total Assets	3.3	2.9	3.1		3.3	3.2	3.0	3.5	2.4
	2.4	2.2	2.3		2.7	2.6	2.1	2.4	1.8
	1.9	1.7	1.7		2.0	2.0	1.2	1.9	1.3
% Depr., Dep., Amort./Sales	1.0	1.4	1.3		.7	1.2	2.0	.5	2.1
	2.1	(61) 2.8	(75) 2.6		(17) 2.4	2.2	3.7	2.1	(15) 3.2
	2.9	4.0	3.5		3.2	2.9	4.5	3.2	4.1
% Officers', Directors', Owners' Comp/Sales	3.1	3.4	2.3		6.1				
	(30) 5.2	(27) 7.2	(38) 4.8		(10) 8.2				
	8.0	13.4	7.4		11.0				
Net Sales ($)	703632M	2050231M	2108176M	815M	37305M	50693M	93368M	212942M	1713053M
Total Assets ($)	423252M	1166581M	1212765M	700M	16029M	23428M	55061M	82772M	1034775M

M = $ thousand   MM = $ million
See Pages 1 through 15 for Explanation of Ratios and Data

	Current Data Sorted By Assets							Comparative Historical Data	
	1		4		1		# Postretirement Benefits		
							Type of Statement		
		3	8	7	1		Unqualified	27	23
		5	15				Reviewed	14	18
	2	1	2	1			Compiled	7	8
	3	3	7	4			Tax Returns		
							Other	14	18
		18 (4/1-9/30/94)		44 (10/1/94-3/31/95)				4/1/90-3/31/91	4/1/91-3/31/92
	0-500M	500M-2MM	2-10MM	10-50MM	50-100MM	100-250MM		ALL	ALL
	5	12	32	12	1		NUMBER OF STATEMENTS	62	67
	%	%	%	%	%	%	ASSETS	%	%
		6.5	3.3	5.1			Cash & Equivalents	5.2	5.6
		33.7	27.6	26.1			Trade Receivables - (net)	30.5	25.2
		20.0	24.5	29.9			Inventory	27.4	28.8
		.8	.7	1.4			All Other Current	1.1	1.7
		60.9	56.0	62.6			Total Current	64.1	61.3
		37.0	36.5	30.9			Fixed Assets (net)	29.1	29.7
		.2	1.7	.3			Intangibles (net)	1.7	3.3
		1.9	5.8	6.2			All Other Non-Current	5.1	5.7
		100.0	100.0	100.0			Total	100.0	100.0
							LIABILITIES		
		15.6	13.2	6.1			Notes Payable-Short Term	14.4	11.6
		4.9	4.6	3.9			Cur. Mat. -L/T/D	3.8	3.9
		22.4	13.8	9.7			Trade Payables	14.5	12.6
		.1	.3	.4			Income Taxes Payable	.6	.3
		8.5	8.4	7.9			All Other Current	7.9	7.0
		51.5	40.4	28.0			Total Current	41.2	35.4
		16.2	18.6	16.5			Long Term Debt	15.3	19.5
		.1	1.0	1.0			Deferred Taxes	1.4	.7
		1.6	3.1	1.5			All Other-Non-Current	1.8	2.3
		30.6	37.0	53.0			Net Worth	40.3	42.2
		100.0	100.0	100.0			Total Liabilities & Net Worth	100.0	100.0
							INCOME DATA		
		100.0	100.0	100.0			Net Sales	100.0	100.0
		33.8	26.8	28.9			Gross Profit	26.8	27.6
		28.6	21.5	20.8			Operating Expenses	22.0	23.0
		5.2	5.3	8.2			Operating Profit	4.8	4.6
		1.5	1.1	1.0			All Other Expenses (net)	1.6	1.8
		3.7	4.3	7.2			Profit Before Taxes	3.2	2.7
							RATIOS		
		1.5	1.8	4.4				2.3	2.7
		1.3	1.4	2.2			Current	1.7	1.8
		1.0	1.1	1.5				1.3	1.2
		1.0	1.2	2.1				1.4	1.5
		.8	.8	1.1			Quick	.9	.9
		.6	.5	.7				.6	.5

										Sales/Receivables				
36	10.1	41	9.0	40	9.1				Sales/Receivables	34	10.7	37	9.9
43	8.4	46	8.0	48	7.6					45	8.1	43	8.5
51	7.1	54	6.7	56	6.5					54	6.7	49	7.5
24	15.0	33	10.9	51	7.2				Cost of Sales/Inventory	41	8.8	41	8.8
37	10.0	51	7.1	83	4.4					60	6.1	62	5.9
61	6.0	72	5.1	101	3.6					85	4.3	99	3.7
11	31.8	15	24.2	18	20.7				Cost of Sales/Payables	16	23.3	14	25.8
43	8.4	24	15.0	23	15.7					24	15.3	22	16.4
63	5.8	43	8.5	32	11.4					37	9.8	44	8.3

	10.3	8.4	3.8			Sales/Working Capital	6.2	4.9
	19.3	15.8	6.3				9.6	8.1
	NM	28.9	10.5				16.2	19.2

	7.7		6.2		30.7			8.2		5.2
(11)	5.6	(31)	2.7	(11)	4.7	EBIT/Interest	(58)	2.4	(63)	2.2
	.6		1.9		2.9			1.1		1.3

			3.7					5.4		5.2
		(16)	2.0			Net Profit + Depr., Dep., Amort./Cur. Mat. L./T/D	(32)	2.8	(31)	1.9
			1.4					1.3		.8

	.7	.5	.3				.4	.4
	.9	1.0	.7			Fixed/Worth	.8	.9
	2.4	2.3	1.0				1.3	1.4
	1.2	1.0	.4				.7	.7
	1.5	2.1	1.1			Debt/Worth	1.5	1.4
	4.0	3.6	1.5				3.6	3.6

	71.2		59.6		42.5			35.9		26.4
(10)	28.8	(31)	24.4		17.7	% Profit Before Taxes/Tangible Net Worth	(57)	19.4	(59)	13.6
	-1.1		13.1		14.8			5.6		5.4

	22.9	13.9	14.7			% Profit Before Taxes/Total Assets	15.1	10.6
	10.0	7.3	7.6				6.7	5.2
	-1.5	3.1	6.3				.5	1.2
	10.3	9.4	11.5			Sales/Net Fixed Assets	14.7	14.7
	7.2	5.9	7.7				7.0	6.2
	5.4	3.9	4.6				5.1	4.3
	3.2	2.5	2.4			Sales/Total Assets	2.8	2.7
	2.8	2.2	2.2				2.1	2.1
	2.1	1.7	1.8				1.7	1.5

	1.3		1.9					1.2		1.5
(10)	2.5	(28)	3.0			% Depr., Dep., Amort./Sales	(59)	2.0	(61)	2.3
	3.8		4.1					3.4		3.5

		2.7			% Officers', Directors', Owners' Comp/Sales	3.3	1.7
	(15)	3.0				(20) 4.5	(16) 2.9
		6.5				8.5	7.1

2681M	43669M	294435M	554738M	144899M		Net Sales ($)	1498447M	2290261M
1063M	15119M	133211M	286695M	71900M		Total Assets ($)	770494M	1328766M

© Robert Morris Associates 1995

M = $ thousand   MM = $ million
See Pages 1 through 15 for Explanation of Ratios and Data

Comparative Historical Data				Current Data Sorted By Sales					
2	2	6	**# Postretirement Benefits**				3	2	1
			Type of Statement	0-1MM	1-3MM	3-5MM	5-10MM	10-25MM	25MM & OVER
29	26	16	Unqualified			1	4	5	6
23	10	18	Reviewed		2	4	5	7	
8	9	10	Compiled	1	3	2	3		1
		1	Tax Returns			1			
10	18	17	Other	2	2	1	5	3	4
4/1/92-3/31/93 ALL	4/1/93-3/31/94 ALL	4/1/94-3/31/95 ALL		18 (4/1-9/30/94)			44 (10/1/94-3/31/95)		
70	63	62	**NUMBER OF STATEMENTS**	3	7	9	17	15	11
%	%	%	**ASSETS**	%	%	%	%	%	%
5.3	5.3	4.6	Cash & Equivalents				2.3	4.7	5.2
28.7	28.6	28.9	Trade Receivables - (net)				30.4	31.8	26.8
25.6	24.9	24.0	Inventory				24.5	26.1	26.7
1.4	1.0	1.0	All Other Current				.4	1.1	1.3
61.0	59.7	58.5	Total Current				57.5	63.7	60.0
32.3	33.1	35.1	Fixed Assets (net)				35.0	29.6	33.7
2.1	2.4	1.1	Intangibles (net)				3.1	.0	.4
4.6	4.8	5.4	All Other Non-Current				4.4	6.7	5.9
100.0	100.0	100.0	Total				100.0	100.0	100.0
			LIABILITIES						
12.0	9.4	11.4	Notes Payable-Short Term				16.7	14.3	5.2
4.9	4.0	4.4	Cur. Mat.-L/T/D				4.7	4.0	4.1
14.8	12.8	14.6	Trade Payables				13.9	16.2	10.2
.6	1.1	.3	Income Taxes Payable				.3	.6	.1
7.6	8.0	8.1	All Other Current				7.0	10.6	7.6
40.0	35.3	38.8	Total Current				42.5	45.7	27.3
17.4	14.8	18.3	Long Term Debt				19.6	11.0	19.1
.5	.7	.8	Deferred Taxes				.9	1.3	1.1
3.1	4.5	2.2	All Other-Non-Current				.9	4.4	1.2
39.0	44.6	39.9	Net Worth				36.1	37.6	51.4
100.0	100.0	100.0	Total Liabilities & Net Worth				100.0	100.0	100.0
			INCOME DATA						
100.0	100.0	100.0	Net Sales				100.0	100.0	100.0
30.1	28.8	29.7	Gross Profit				28.6	26.9	27.1
24.1	23.5	23.5	Operating Expenses				22.5	19.9	20.2
6.0	5.3	6.1	Operating Profit				6.1	7.0	7.0
1.5	1.2	1.0	All Other Expenses (net)				1.4	.7	1.0
4.5	4.1	5.2	Profit Before Taxes				4.7	6.3	6.0
			RATIOS						
2.3	2.9	2.1	Current				2.1	1.8	5.0
1.5	1.8	1.4					1.4	1.5	1.8
1.2	1.2	1.2					1.2	1.2	1.4
1.4	1.5	1.3	Quick				1.1	1.3	2.3
.9	1.0	.8					.7	.8	1.0
.6	.6	.6					.4	.4	.8
37 9.8	36 10.2	40 9.1	Sales/Receivables				38 9.6	41 8.8	42 8.6
47 7.8	45 8.1	46 7.9					45 8.1	46 7.9	49 7.5
61 6.0	53 6.9	54 6.7					54 6.8	56 6.5	58 6.3
33 11.0	31 11.7	33 11.1	Cost of Sales/Inventory				31 11.9	32 11.5	41 9.0
55 6.6	55 6.6	51 7.2					58 6.3	41 8.8	64 5.7
89 4.1	96 3.8	74 4.9					72 5.1	65 5.6	89 4.1
18 20.4	15 24.9	17 22.0	Cost of Sales/Payables				13 27.6	19 19.3	20 18.5
28 13.0	24 15.3	26 14.1					20 17.9	31 11.7	24 15.5
54 8.2	45 8.2	44 8.3					46 7.9	42 8.7	32 11.3
5.8	5.4	7.6	Sales/Working Capital				8.0	8.0	3.8
11.6	9.4	13.3					16.8	12.7	8.3
30.5	26.4	24.6					28.0	30.4	12.6
7.1	7.5	7.8	EBIT/Interest				7.6	10.5	12.8
(66) 3.8	(58) 4.0	(57) 3.6				(16)	3.7	3.6	(10) 4.4
1.3	1.4	2.2					2.3	2.6	3.0
9.8	3.2	5.5	Net Profit + Depr., Dep.,						
(36) 2.4	(30) 1.5	(26) 2.3	Amort./Cur. Mat. L/T/D						
1.0	1.0	1.4							
.6	.4	.5	Fixed/Worth				.6	.4	.7
1.0	.8	.9					.9	1.0	.8
1.9	1.4	1.7					2.2	1.3	1.0
.8	.5	.7	Debt/Worth				.8	1.1	.4
1.8	1.5	1.5					2.1	1.5	1.3
4.1	2.7	3.4					3.5	2.6	1.5
39.2	40.0	59.3	% Profit Before Taxes/Tangible				53.7	61.3	22.2
(64) 21.5	(61) 19.5	(58) 22.7	Net Worth			(15)	24.4	54.0	16.6
9.0	5.1	12.2					15.0	16.5	12.7
16.4	13.1	19.8	% Profit Before Taxes/Total				15.5	24.6	9.9
8.8	8.8	7.8	Assets				11.7	12.2	6.8
1.9	1.7	3.3					4.1	5.2	6.1
16.1	16.3	9.7	Sales/Net Fixed Assets				9.0	12.7	7.8
6.9	5.7	6.7					6.1	8.9	7.6
4.3	3.9	4.2					4.2	5.8	4.5
2.4	2.5	2.6	Sales/Total Assets				2.7	2.6	2.4
2.1	2.1	2.3					2.2	2.4	2.2
1.7	1.5	1.9					2.0	2.1	2.0
1.3	1.5	1.6	% Depr., Dep., Amort./Sales				2.1	1.3	
(66) 2.5	(57) 2.4	(50) 2.5				(13)	3.0	2.2	
4.0	4.3	3.8					4.9	3.0	
2.1	2.6	2.7	% Officers', Directors',						
(20) 2.8	(19) 3.6	(24) 3.1	Owners' Comp/Sales						
3.7	5.7	9.2							
1863409M	1486629M	1040422M	Net Sales ($)	350M	11636M	34855M	119370M	219885M	654326M
1093840M	855750M	507988M	Total Assets ($)	212M	6376M	18099M	54800M	93678M	334823M

M = $ thousand   MM = $ million
See Pages 1 through 15 for Explanation of Ratios and Data

Current Data Sorted By Assets   Comparative Historical Data

						# Postretirement Benefits		
	1					**Type of Statement**		
	3	2	3			Unqualified		
1	4	1				Reviewed		
	5	2				Compiled		
						Tax Returns		
	3	1	4		1	Other		
	7 (4/1-9/30/94)		23 (10/1/94-3/31/95)				4/1/90-3/31/91 ALL	4/1/91-3/31/92 ALL
0-500M	500M-2MM	2-10MM	10-50MM	50-100MM	100-250MM			
1	15	6	7		1	**NUMBER OF STATEMENTS**		
%	%	%	%	%	%	**ASSETS**	%	%
	8.5					Cash & Equivalents	D	D
	32.5					Trade Receivables - (net)	A	A
	28.0					Inventory	T	T
	1.3					All Other Current	A	A
	70.3					Total Current		
	20.0					Fixed Assets (net)	N	N
	1.1					Intangibles (net)	O	O
	8.6					All Other Non-Current	T	T
	100.0					Total		
						LIABILITIES	A	A
	12.7					Notes Payable-Short Term	V	V
	2.3					Cur. Mat. -L/T/D	A	A
	26.9					Trade Payables	I	I
	.9					Income Taxes Payable	L	L
	9.4					All Other Current	A	A
	52.2					Total Current	B	B
	6.8					Long Term Debt	L	L
	.0					Deferred Taxes	E	E
	1.3					All Other-Non-Current		
	39.8					Net Worth		
	100.0					Total Liabilities & Net Worth		
						INCOME DATA		
	100.0					Net Sales		
	28.0					Gross Profit		
	26.9					Operating Expenses		
	1.1					Operating Profit		
	.4					All Other Expenses (net)		
	.6					Profit Before Taxes		
						RATIOS		
	2.2							
	1.4					Current		
	1.1							
	1.2							
	.7					Quick		
	.5							
32	11.4							
40	9.1					Sales/Receivables		
45	8.1							
31	11.6							
47	7.7					Cost of Sales/Inventory		
72	5.1							
30	12.1							
37	10.0					Cost of Sales/Payables		
45	8.1							
	7.3							
	17.3					Sales/Working Capital		
	80.2							
	20.4							
(12)	3.6					EBIT/Interest		
	-8.3							
						Net Profit + Depr., Dep., Amort./Cur. Mat. L /T/D		
	.1							
	.2					Fixed/Worth		
	1.3							
	.8							
	1.4					Debt/Worth		
	2.7							
	37.6					% Profit Before Taxes/Tangible		
(14)	18.8					Net Worth		
	-9.7							
	17.7					% Profit Before Taxes/Total		
	3.5					Assets		
	-5.4							
	71.0							
	34.2					Sales/Net Fixed Assets		
	6.5							
	3.9							
	3.4					Sales/Total Assets		
	2.2							
	.7							
(13)	1.2					% Depr., Dep., Amort./Sales		
	3.8							
						% Officers', Directors', Owners' Comp/Sales		
818M	48811M	76464M	251599M		226016M	Net Sales ($)		
153M	15814M	31460M	135642M		122798M	Total Assets ($)		

© Robert Morris Associates 1995

M = $ thousand   MM = $ million
See Pages 1 through 15 for Explanation of Ratios and Data

Comparative Historical Data | Current Data Sorted By Sales

4/1/92-3/31/93 ALL	4/1/93-3/31/94 ALL	4/1/94-3/31/95 ALL	# Postretirement Benefits / Type of Statement	0-1MM	1-3MM	3-5MM	5-10MM	10-25MM	25MM & OVER
		1	(1)						
		8	Unqualified		3		1	1	3
		6	Reviewed	2		2	2		
		7	Compiled		3	1	2	1	
			Tax Returns						
		9	Other		2	1		3	3
		30	**NUMBER OF STATEMENTS**	2	8	4	5	5	6
%	%	%	**ASSETS**	%	%	%	%	%	%
D A T A N O T A V A I L A B L E	D A T A N O T A V A I L A B L E	7.9	Cash & Equivalents						
		30.4	Trade Receivables - (net)						
		25.7	Inventory						
		1.2	All Other Current						
		65.2	Total Current						
		27.6	Fixed Assets (net)						
		.6	Intangibles (net)						
		6.6	All Other Non-Current						
		100.0	Total						
			LIABILITIES						
		9.9	Notes Payable-Short Term						
		3.5	Cur. Mat.-L /T/D						
		20.4	Trade Payables						
		.9	Income Taxes Payable						
		9.6	All Other Current						
		44.3	Total Current						
		12.9	Long Term Debt						
		.3	Deferred Taxes						
		2.5	All Other-Non-Current						
		40.0	Net Worth						
		100.0	Total Liabilities & Net Worth						
			INCOME DATA						
		100.0	Net Sales						
		25.9	Gross Profit						
		21.5	Operating Expenses						
		4.4	Operating Profit						
		1.1	All Other Expenses (net)						
		3.4	Profit Before Taxes						
			RATIOS						
		2.3 / 1.4 / 1.1	Current						
		1.4 / .9 / .6	Quick						
		37 9.8 / 41 9.0 / 49 7.4	Sales/Receivables						
		32 11.4 / 49 7.5 / 68 5.4	Cost of Sales/Inventory						
		23 16.1 / 33 11.1 / 47 7.7	Cost of Sales/Payables						
		6.5 / 14.2 / 40.1	Sales/Working Capital						
		(27) 9.0 / 3.3 / 1.6	EBIT/Interest						
		(13) 4.3 / 1.3 / .6	Net Profit + Depr., Dep., Amort./Cur. Mat. L/T/D						
		.2 / .6 / 1.4	Fixed/Worth						
		.8 / 1.7 / 2.8	Debt/Worth						
		(29) 36.2 / 22.2 / 6.6	% Profit Before Taxes/Tangible Net Worth						
		15.2 / 8.1 / 2.2	% Profit Before Taxes/Total Assets						
		34.4 / 11.0 / 3.6	Sales/Net Fixed Assets						
		3.5 / 2.6 / 1.7	Sales/Total Assets						
		(28) .8 / 2.0 / 3.5	% Depr., Dep., Amort./Sales						
			% Officers', Directors', Owners' Comp/Sales						
		603708M	Net Sales ($)	1729M	17982M	15215M	35421M	94429M	438932M
		305867M	Total Assets ($)	1232M	7466M	5747M	10571M	54181M	226670M

7 (4/1-9/30/94) 23 (10/1/94-3/31/95)

M = $ thousand   MM = $ million
See Pages 1 through 15 for Explanation of Ratios and Data

	Current Data Sorted By Assets							Comparative Historical Data	
	1	5	9	6		2	# Postretirement Benefits / Type of Statement		
	1	8	31	27	7	7	Unqualified	64	68
	3	34	55	11			Reviewed	74	73
	12	29	15				Compiled	49	50
	1	1					Tax Returns	1	2
	5	21	41	16	2	1	Other	55	49
	0-500M	99 (4/1-9/30/94) 500M-2MM	2-10MM	231 (10/1/94-3/31/95) 10-50MM	50-100MM	100-250MM		4/1/90-3/31/91 ALL	4/1/91-3/31/92 ALL
	22	93	142	56	9	8	NUMBER OF STATEMENTS	243	242
	%	%	%	%	%	%	**ASSETS**	%	%
	11.8	5.4	5.8	5.1			Cash & Equivalents	6.4	5.5
	38.3	35.6	30.8	23.6			Trade Receivables - (net)	29.2	27.9
	18.8	21.4	19.5	19.5			Inventory	19.5	18.9
	1.4	1.2	1.2	1.6			All Other Current	1.7	1.3
	70.2	63.5	57.3	49.9			Total Current	56.8	53.7
	24.0	28.2	34.8	41.0			Fixed Assets (net)	34.6	37.1
	.2	.6	1.4	2.4			Intangibles (net)	2.7	2.0
	5.6	7.6	6.5	6.8			All Other Non-Current	5.9	7.2
	100.0	100.0	100.0	100.0			Total	100.0	100.0
							LIABILITIES		
	7.5	9.5	10.2	9.8			Notes Payable-Short Term	8.7	8.4
	4.9	4.4	4.4	4.9			Cur. Mat. -L/T/D	5.0	5.8
	25.7	26.0	19.5	14.3			Trade Payables	18.2	18.0
	2.1	.4	.4	.4			Income Taxes Payable	.5	.5
	10.4	7.7	7.9	7.2			All Other Current	6.0	6.7
	50.7	48.0	42.4	36.6			Total Current	38.4	39.4
	15.9	12.8	19.1	22.9			Long Term Debt	21.7	21.3
	.2	.6	.8	1.3			Deferred Taxes	1.0	.8
	5.4	4.5	2.8	2.3			All Other-Non-Current	2.7	2.5
	27.8	34.2	34.9	36.8			Net Worth	36.1	35.9
	100.0	100.0	100.0	100.0			Total Liabilities & Net Worth	100.0	100.0
							INCOME DATA		
	100.0	100.0	100.0	100.0			Net Sales	100.0	100.0
	35.3	26.8	23.9	23.6			Gross Profit	25.2	25.6
	29.9	23.1	19.4	17.3			Operating Expenses	20.8	21.2
	5.5	3.6	4.5	6.3			Operating Profit	4.4	4.4
	1.2	.9	1.1	1.6			All Other Expenses (net)	1.4	1.2
	4.3	2.7	3.4	4.7			Profit Before Taxes	2.9	3.1
							RATIOS		
	1.9	2.0	1.8	2.0			Current	2.2	2.1
	1.5	1.4	1.3	1.4				1.5	1.3
	1.1	1.1	1.1	1.0				1.1	1.0
	1.4	1.3	1.2	1.3			Quick	1.4	1.3
	1.0	.9	.8	.8				.9	.9
	.7	.7	.6	.5				.6	.6
	24 15.4	33 11.1	35 10.3	38 9.6			Sales/Receivables	32 11.4	30 12.0
	38 9.7	40 9.2	40 9.1	41 8.8				38 9.5	39 9.3
	46 8.0	47 7.8	51 7.2	57 6.4				46 7.9	47 7.8
	13 28.4	17 21.2	21 17.5	32 11.4			Cost of Sales/Inventory	20 18.6	21 17.7
	23 15.7	33 11.0	33 11.0	46 7.9				33 10.9	33 11.1
	34 10.6	53 6.9	56 6.5	69 5.3				57 6.4	49 7.4
	18 20.3	22 16.9	21 17.3	22 16.3			Cost of Sales/Payables	20 18.7	19 19.1
	43 8.5	41 9.0	35 10.4	37 9.8				30 12.1	30 12.1
	63 5.8	58 6.3	51 7.1	43 8.4				42 8.6	43 8.4
	9.2	9.5	9.0	6.4			Sales/Working Capital	7.8	9.1
	21.2	18.9	19.1	13.6				14.6	20.8
	93.3	70.1	71.9	NM				44.2	167.1
	(15) 26.5	(82) 8.9	(130) 8.7	(52) 8.2			EBIT/Interest	(223) 4.7	(221) 5.4
	5.3	3.8	3.3	3.6				2.4	2.5
	1.9	2.4	1.7	1.6				1.3	1.4
		(33) 9.2	(71) 3.1	(29) 4.7			Net Profit + Depr., Dep., Amort./Cur. Mat. L./T/D	(142) 4.2	(135) 3.8
		2.0	1.9	2.2				2.1	2.1
		1.3	1.0	1.4				1.1	1.2
	.3	.4	.5	.8			Fixed/Worth	.5	.5
	.7	.7	1.2	1.3				1.1	1.1
	2.7	2.4	2.4	2.2				2.3	2.2
	.9	.8	1.0	1.1			Debt/Worth	.9	.9
	2.3	2.1	2.1	2.2				2.0	2.0
	28.0	5.2	4.7	4.5				4.7	4.5
	(18) 103.8	(84) 55.0	(138) 46.4	41.3			% Profit Before Taxes/Tangible Net Worth	(223) 33.3	(224) 34.4
	73.3	26.8	23.7	24.3				16.7	19.4
	11.2	10.7	8.5	11.3				3.6	6.2
	32.8	16.0	13.9	14.0			% Profit Before Taxes/Total Assets	11.3	12.1
	17.9	7.2	6.6	6.9				5.8	5.8
	6.0	2.8	2.5	3.3				.8	1.3
	67.2	26.3	11.9	7.2			Sales/Net Fixed Assets	15.6	14.0
	19.8	13.5	7.4	4.3				7.0	7.1
	10.7	7.4	4.4	2.9				4.6	3.7
	4.8	3.9	3.2	2.3			Sales/Total Assets	3.3	3.4
	3.9	3.2	2.4	1.8				2.5	2.4
	3.3	2.5	1.9	1.4				1.9	1.8
	(17) .6	(82) .9	(136) 1.4	(53) 2.0			% Depr., Dep., Amort./Sales	(221) 1.5	(223) 1.6
	.9	2.0	2.3	3.4				2.5	2.6
	3.1	2.8	3.4	4.6				3.7	3.4
	(10) 4.5	(44) 2.7	(63) 1.6				% Officers', Directors', Owners' Comp/Sales	(85) 2.7	(76) 2.1
	6.6	4.7	2.7					4.5	3.6
	7.8	7.0	5.5					7.0	5.0
	30470M	359130M	1726704M	1996707M	955964M	1525122M	Net Sales ($)	4255159M	3672326M
	7312M	114976M	691304M	1128953M	591531M	1381178M	Total Assets ($)	2102837M	1826671M

M = $ thousand   MM = $ million
See Pages 1 through 15 for Explanation of Ratios and Data

Comparative Historical Data | | | Current Data Sorted By Sales

7	14	23	# Postretirement Benefits	0-1MM	1-3MM	3-5MM	5-10MM	10-25MM	25MM & OVER
					2	2	8	2	9
			Type of Statement						
75	80	81	Unqualified	1 / 5	7	4	26	38	
89	93	103	Reviewed	2 / 14	22	30	24	11	
64	57	58	Compiled	4 / 19	11	14	8	2	
1	4	2	Tax Returns	1 / 1					
59	67	86	Other	1 / 10	10	24	30	11	
4/1/92-3/31/93 ALL	4/1/93-3/31/94 ALL	4/1/94-3/31/95 ALL		99 (4/1-9/30/94)			231 (10/1/94-3/31/95)		
288	301	330	**NUMBER OF STATEMENTS**	9	49	50	72	88	62
%	%	%	**ASSETS**	%	%	%	%	%	%
5.6	5.7	5.9	Cash & Equivalents		8.3	7.8	3.7	5.5	5.1
28.8	28.1	30.7	Trade Receivables - (net)		29.9	33.0	33.4	30.4	26.2
19.4	19.9	19.8	Inventory		20.8	23.2	19.3	19.7	18.0
1.4	1.1	1.3	All Other Current		1.9	.7	1.4	1.1	1.4
55.2	54.8	57.7	Total Current		60.8	64.7	57.7	56.7	50.7
36.0	36.3	33.9	Fixed Assets (net)		30.3	26.8	33.5	36.6	39.0
1.9	1.5	1.4	Intangibles (net)		.6	1.4	1.0	1.5	2.4
6.9	7.5	7.0	All Other Non-Current		8.3	7.1	7.8	5.2	8.0
100.0	100.0	100.0	Total		100.0	100.0	100.0	100.0	100.0
			LIABILITIES						
8.1	8.4	9.3	Notes Payable-Short Term		9.3	11.0	9.9	9.3	7.8
5.5	5.3	4.4	Cur. Mat.-L /T/D		5.4	3.2	5.0	4.8	3.9
18.1	17.9	20.5	Trade Payables		22.3	22.9	22.6	19.0	16.4
.6	.5	.5	Income Taxes Payable		1.0	.3	.4	.6	.3
6.9	7.1	7.7	All Other Current		6.4	9.1	6.6	8.2	7.3
39.3	39.1	42.5	Total Current		44.3	46.5	44.4	41.9	35.6
21.6	21.7	18.3	Long Term Debt		16.6	11.4	20.1	18.1	22.6
.8	.8	.9	Deferred Taxes		.1	.7	.7	.9	1.9
3.2	3.1	3.3	All Other-Non-Current		2.5	5.5	3.7	2.9	1.5
35.2	35.2	35.0	Net Worth		36.4	36.0	31.1	36.2	38.4
100.0	100.0	100.0	Total Liabilities & Net Worth		100.0	100.0	100.0	100.0	100.0
			INCOME DATA						
100.0	100.0	100.0	Net Sales		100.0	100.0	100.0	100.0	100.0
26.1	24.6	25.3	Gross Profit		30.3	26.7	24.0	24.3	21.7
21.4	20.7	20.5	Operating Expenses		26.2	23.3	19.8	19.2	15.5
4.7	3.8	4.8	Operating Profit		4.1	3.3	4.2	5.1	6.1
1.1	1.2	1.1	All Other Expenses (net)		.9	.7	1.2	1.3	1.2
3.6	2.6	3.6	Profit Before Taxes		3.3	2.6	2.9	3.8	4.9
			RATIOS						
2.0	2.0	1.9			2.0	2.3	1.8	1.9	2.0
1.5	1.4	1.4	Current		1.4	1.4	1.3	1.3	1.7
1.1	1.0	1.1			1.1	1.1	1.0	1.1	1.2
1.4	1.3	1.2			1.3	1.3	1.1	1.2	1.3
.9	.9	.9	Quick		.9	1.0	.8	.9	.9
.6	.6	.6			.6	.6	.6		.7
31 — 11.9	32 — 11.5	35 — 10.4			29 — 12.7	35 — 10.3	36 — 10.1	33 — 10.9	37 — 9.9
39 — 9.4	38 — 9.5	41 — 9.0	Sales/Receivables		37 — 9.8	41 — 8.9	42 — 8.7	39 — 9.3	43 — 8.4
47 — 7.8	46 — 8.0	49 — 7.4			43 — 8.5	48 — 7.6	51 — 7.2	50 — 7.3	58 — 6.3
20 — 18.6	20 — 18.1	20 — 18.2			19 — 19.3	20 — 18.1	19 — 19.4	21 — 17.3	27 — 13.6
33 — 10.9	34 — 10.7	36 — 10.2	Cost of Sales/Inventory		32 — 11.5	41 — 8.8	32 — 11.5	38 — 9.5	40 — 9.1
54 — 6.7	60 — 6.1	57 — 6.4			62 — 5.9	66 — 5.5	51 — 7.1	53 — 6.9	60 — 6.1
17 — 21.2	18 — 20.2	22 — 16.8			20 — 18.5	17 — 21.1	23 — 16.1	21 — 17.5	23 — 15.6
30 — 12.1	33 — 11.2	37 — 9.9	Cost of Sales/Payables		40 — 9.1	41 — 8.8	41 — 8.9	31 — 11.6	38 — 9.7
45 — 8.1	45 — 8.1	52 — 7.0			58 — 6.3	60 — 6.3	54 — 6.8	43 — 8.5	48 — 7.6
9.0	8.2	7.8			7.1	6.4	12.3	7.9	7.3
15.7	15.5	17.7	Sales/Working Capital		19.3	16.9	23.8	18.5	12.0
48.1	136.1	70.0			61.3	121.3	182.8	58.2	35.6
(271) 7.6	(281) 6.3	(295) 8.7			(41) 14.4	(41) 10.0	(66) 7.5	(84) 11.5	(56) 8.3
3.2	2.9	3.5	EBIT/Interest		3.3	3.4	3.7	3.6	4.1
1.6	1.4	1.9			1.6	1.8	1.7	2.0	2.2
(141) 4.1	(141) 3.5	(149) 4.0			(21) 6.6	(19) 7.5	(37) 2.7	(40) 3.6	(29) 4.7
2.2	1.8	2.0	Net Profit + Depr., Dep., Amort./Cur. Mat. L/T/D		2.0	1.4	1.8	2.0	2.4
1.2	1.0	1.1			1.3	1.1	1.0	1.2	1.4
.6	.6	.5			.4	.3	.4	.6	.8
1.1	1.1	1.1	Fixed/Worth		.7	.6	1.1	1.2	1.1
2.1	2.3	2.3			2.5	1.9	2.8	2.4	1.7
1.1	1.1	1.0			.7	.8	1.5	1.1	1.1
2.0	1.9	2.1	Debt/Worth		2.1	1.9	2.3	1.8	2.0
4.6	4.3	4.6			4.8	5.2	4.7	4.7	3.2
(273) 40.6	(284) 38.6	(313) 50.2			(46) 68.4	(44) 54.1	(69) 45.4	(86) 48.2	40.1
23.4	20.3	25.2	% Profit Before Taxes/Tangible Net Worth		28.6	22.6	23.5	27.7	24.2
10.0	7.4	10.1			4.9	11.7	10.1	11.7	12.0
15.0	12.4	14.8			20.5	18.2	13.3	14.5	12.0
7.0	6.5	7.3	% Profit Before Taxes/Total Assets		6.3	8.9	7.2	7.5	7.3
2.1	1.9	3.0			2.2	2.4	3.2	3.4	4.7
13.8	14.6	14.8			19.1	22.3	17.7	11.9	8.3
7.3	7.3	7.8	Sales/Net Fixed Assets		11.8	12.6	8.3	6.7	4.9
4.2	4.1	4.1			6.3	5.3	4.9	4.1	3.1
3.4	3.2	3.4			3.8	3.6	3.6	3.4	2.5
2.5	2.5	2.5	Sales/Total Assets		3.1	2.9	3.1	2.4	2.0
1.9	1.8	1.8			2.0	2.1	1.9	1.8	1.5
(268) 1.6	(280) 1.6	(299) 1.4			(42) .8	(46) 1.1	(67) 1.3	(84) 1.5	(54) 1.8
2.4	2.5	2.4	% Depr., Dep., Amort./Sales		2.0	2.4	2.2	2.5	2.6
3.6	3.9	3.5			3.1	3.4	3.1	3.7	3.9
(108) 2.0	(120) 2.0	(126) 2.0			(21) 2.7	(28) 2.5	(36) 2.0	(31) 1.5	
3.7	3.5	3.2	% Officers', Directors', Owners' Comp/Sales		4.5	4.3	3.4	2.1	
6.6	5.7	6.7			6.5	8.2	6.7	4.0	
4703998M	5421011M	6594097M	Net Sales ($)	6729M	95063M	198357M	510245M	1443903M	4339780M
2421481M	2874640M	3915254M	Total Assets ($)	4498M	41479M	80339M	234622M	670317M	2883999M

Current Data Sorted By Assets

Comparative Historical Data

						# Postretirement Benefits		
						Type of Statement		
		5	1	2	1	Unqualified		
2	5	3				Reviewed		
	1	2	1			Compiled		
						Tax Returns		
		4	2	1		Other		
	9 (4/1-9/30/94)		21 (10/1/94-3/31/95)				4/1/90-3/31/91 ALL	4/1/91-3/31/92 ALL
0-500M	500M-2MM	2-10MM	10-50MM	50-100MM	100-250MM			
2	6	14	4	3	1	**NUMBER OF STATEMENTS**		
%	%	%	%	%	%	**ASSETS**	%	%
		3.8				Cash & Equivalents	D	D
		27.6				Trade Receivables - (net)	A	A
		21.6				Inventory	T	T
		.4				All Other Current	A	A
		53.5				Total Current		
		41.2				Fixed Assets (net)	N	N
		1.9				Intangibles (net)	O	O
		3.4				All Other Non-Current	T	T
		100.0				Total		
						LIABILITIES	A	A
		10.9				Notes Payable-Short Term	V	V
		5.7				Cur. Mat. -L/T/D	A	A
		13.6				Trade Payables	I	I
		.9				Income Taxes Payable	L	L
		7.3				All Other Current	A	A
		38.3				Total Current	B	B
		16.9				Long Term Debt	L	L
		.8				Deferred Taxes	E	E
		4.2				All Other-Non-Current		
		39.8				Net Worth		
		100.0				Total Liabilities & Net Worth		
						INCOME DATA		
		100.0				Net Sales		
		25.8				Gross Profit		
		20.0				Operating Expenses		
		5.8				Operating Profit		
		1.2				All Other Expenses (net)		
		4.7				Profit Before Taxes		
						RATIOS		
		2.3						
		1.5				Current		
		1.1						
		1.4						
		1.0				Quick		
		.6						
		34 10.6						
		49 7.4				Sales/Receivables		
		56 6.5						
		31 11.8						
		50 7.3				Cost of Sales/Inventory		
		61 6.0						
		16 22.4						
		26 14.0				Cost of Sales/Payables		
		49 7.4						
		7.7						
		13.6				Sales/Working Capital		
		NM						
		8.5						
	(13)	4.0				EBIT/Interest		
		2.6						
						Net Profit + Depr., Dep., Amort./Cur. Mat. L./T/D		
		.5						
		1.0				Fixed/Worth		
		3.4						
		.5						
		2.0				Debt/Worth		
		4.4						
		70.8						
	(13)	30.2				% Profit Before Taxes/Tangible Net Worth		
		8.8						
		18.1						
		7.7				% Profit Before Taxes/Total Assets		
		3.5						
		11.3						
		5.0				Sales/Net Fixed Assets		
		2.8						
		2.9						
		2.0				Sales/Total Assets		
		1.6						
		1.2						
		2.9				% Depr., Dep., Amort./Sales		
		6.1						
						% Officers', Directors', Owners' Comp/Sales		
2727M	27259M	126263M	140258M	349340M	226016M	Net Sales ($)		
878M	8714M	63317M	68190M	230952M	122797M	Total Assets ($)		

M = $ thousand   MM = $ million
See Pages 1 through 15 for Explanation of Ratios and Data

Comparative Historical Data | Current Data Sorted By Sales

	4/1/92-3/31/93 ALL	4/1/93-3/31/94 ALL	4/1/94-3/31/95 ALL	0-1MM	1-3MM	3-5MM	5-10MM	10-25MM	25MM & OVER
Type of Statement			1				1		
# Postretirement Benefits									
Unqualified			9			1	3	1	4
Reviewed			10		2	4	4		
Compiled			4				2	1	1
Tax Returns									
Other			7				3	3	1
NUMBER OF STATEMENTS			30		2	5	12	5	6
	%	%	%	%	%	%	%	%	%
ASSETS									
Cash & Equivalents	DATA NOT AVAILABLE	DATA NOT AVAILABLE	4.1				3.9		
Trade Receivables - (net)			30.7				33.2		
Inventory			23.0				23.2		
All Other Current			.8				.5		
Total Current			58.7				60.8		
Fixed Assets (net)			35.3				34.5		
Intangibles (net)			1.4				.4		
All Other Non-Current			4.7				4.3		
Total			100.0				100.0		
LIABILITIES									
Notes Payable-Short Term			10.5				13.8		
Cur. Mat.-L./T/D			5.0				5.9		
Trade Payables			18.1				16.6		
Income Taxes Payable			.6				.9		
All Other Current			6.4				7.1		
Total Current			40.5				44.4		
Long Term Debt			15.8				11.6		
Deferred Taxes			.9				.5		
All Other-Non-Current			4.1				7.5		
Net Worth			38.6				36.1		
Total Liabilities & Net Worth			100.0				100.0		
INCOME DATA									
Net Sales			100.0				100.0		
Gross Profit			26.2				28.0		
Operating Expenses			21.1				22.4		
Operating Profit			5.2				5.6		
All Other Expenses (net)			1.0				.9		
Profit Before Taxes			4.2				4.7		
RATIOS									
Current			2.0				1.8		
			1.4				1.5		
			1.1				1.1		
Quick			1.2				1.3		
			1.0				1.0		
			.6				.6		
Sales/Receivables			39 / 9.4				36 / 10.2		
			47 / 7.7				54 / 6.7		
			58 / 6.3				57 / 6.4		
Cost of Sales/Inventory			34 / 10.7				31 / 11.6		
			49 / 7.5				47 / 7.8		
			65 / 5.6				58 / 6.3		
Cost of Sales/Payables			23 / 15.8				17 / 21.9		
			38 / 9.6				32 / 11.4		
			51 / 7.2				52 / 7.0		
Sales/Working Capital			8.6				8.9		
			12.0				12.6		
			48.0				46.5		
EBIT/Interest			(29) 10.2				(11) 12.1		
			3.8				4.0		
			2.2				2.8		
Net Profit + Depr., Dep., Amort./Cur. Mat. L/T/D			(17) 2.4						
			1.8						
			1.3						
Fixed/Worth			.4				.5		
			.8				.7		
			2.3				2.7		
Debt/Worth			.8				1.1		
			2.0				2.2		
			4.4				4.1		
% Profit Before Taxes/Tangible Net Worth			(29) 50.7				(11) 66.2		
			26.2				34.2		
			8.8				8.5		
% Profit Before Taxes/Total Assets			14.2				23.3		
			7.7				11.5		
			3.1				2.7		
Sales/Net Fixed Assets			15.2				22.5		
			6.0				7.7		
			3.2				3.4		
Sales/Total Assets			2.9				3.1		
			2.2				2.6		
			1.7				1.8		
% Depr., Dep., Amort./Sales			1.7				1.2		
			3.2				2.3		
			4.9				4.3		
% Officers', Directors', Owners' Comp/Sales			(13) 2.1						
			4.0						
			5.4						
Net Sales ($)			871863M		2727M	18876M	85819M	91149M	673292M
Total Assets ($)			494848M		878M	8490M	42157M	46209M	397114M

M = $ thousand   MM = $ million
See Pages 1 through 15 for Explanation of Ratios and Data

Current Data Sorted By Assets   **Comparative Historical Data**

0-500M	500M-2MM	2-10MM	10-50MM	50-100MM	100-250MM		4/1/90-3/31/91 ALL	4/1/91-3/31/92 ALL
2	2	3	7	1		# Postretirement Benefits		
						Type of Statement		
2	4	20	18	10	12	Unqualified	61	46
	6	12				Reviewed	20	21
2	3	2				Compiled	16	11
1			1			Tax Returns		1
1	4	4	15	3	2	Other	22	23
	36 (4/1-9/30/94)		86 (10/1/94-3/31/95)					
6	17	38	34	13	14	NUMBER OF STATEMENTS	119	102
%	%	%	%	%	%	**ASSETS**	%	%
	6.2	4.7	7.9	2.9	5.9	Cash & Equivalents	7.3	7.5
	28.6	26.7	17.8	17.1	12.9	Trade Receivables - (net)	24.0	22.3
	18.9	23.2	16.9	19.0	12.7	Inventory	20.1	17.9
	1.1	.9	3.4	2.2	.7	All Other Current	2.1	2.0
	54.7	55.5	45.9	41.1	32.2	Total Current	53.5	49.7
	38.5	35.8	44.5	50.4	56.8	Fixed Assets (net)	36.9	39.8
	1.5	1.2	1.9	4.0	2.8	Intangibles (net)	1.5	2.7
	5.3	7.4	7.8	4.5	8.2	All Other Non-Current	8.1	7.7
	100.0	100.0	100.0	100.0	100.0	Total	100.0	100.0
						LIABILITIES		
	6.5	13.3	7.7	5.6	5.8	Notes Payable-Short Term	9.2	8.6
	3.8	4.1	3.1	2.2	1.8	Cur. Mat. -L/T/D	4.3	3.9
	18.8	16.8	15.0	12.5	6.6	Trade Payables	14.4	14.7
	.5	.4	.4	.4	.4	Income Taxes Payable	.6	.7
	5.6	7.8	7.4	9.3	5.0	All Other Current	6.3	6.3
	35.2	42.3	33.6	30.0	19.4	Total Current	34.8	34.2
	16.9	15.9	21.7	21.9	26.3	Long Term Debt	19.0	20.5
	2.0	1.5	2.1	2.9	3.9	Deferred Taxes	2.1	2.2
	4.6	6.0	4.5	6.6	8.5	All Other-Non-Current	3.2	3.5
	41.4	34.4	38.0	38.5	41.9	Net Worth	40.8	39.5
	100.0	100.0	100.0	100.0	100.0	Total Liabilities & Net Worth	100.0	100.0
						INCOME DATA		
	100.0	100.0	100.0	100.0	100.0	Net Sales	100.0	100.0
	28.6	21.4	23.3	18.6	20.2	Gross Profit	22.6	24.2
	25.0	16.8	16.1	13.8	10.2	Operating Expenses	16.2	18.1
	3.7	4.6	7.2	4.8	10.0	Operating Profit	6.4	6.2
	.7	1.3	1.1	1.2	2.0	All Other Expenses (net)	1.4	1.7
	2.9	3.3	6.1	3.6	8.0	Profit Before Taxes	5.1	4.5
						RATIOS		
	2.5	1.8	2.0	1.9	2.6	Current	2.5	2.2
	1.5	1.2	1.3	1.3	1.9		1.7	1.6
	1.2	1.0	1.0	1.1	1.6		1.0	1.1
	1.5	.9	1.3	1.0	1.7	Quick	1.5	1.4
	1.0	.7	.7	.7	1.3		.9	.8
	.7	.5	.6	.6	.7		.6	.6
	31 11.9	34 10.8	31 11.8	34 10.6	33 11.0	Sales/Receivables	29 12.5	31 11.7
	39 9.3	40 9.2	39 9.3	39 9.4	41 9.0		37 9.8	39 9.4
	46 7.9	47 7.8	47 7.7	46 8.0	51 7.1		49 7.5	47 7.8
	17 21.2	27 13.6	29 12.5	36 10.2	30 12.2	Cost of Sales/Inventory	27 13.4	22 16.7
	46 8.0	50 7.3	46 8.0	46 8.0	38 9.6		41 9.0	42 8.7
	63 5.8	64 5.7	63 5.8	69 5.3	54 6.7		59 6.2	62 5.9
	25 14.6	20 18.1	22 16.6	24 15.0	20 17.9	Cost of Sales/Payables	18 20.0	24 15.4
	37 9.9	29 12.7	36 10.1	33 10.9	27 13.6		30 12.3	32 11.5
	43 8.5	49 7.4	49 7.4	45 8.1	42 8.7		38 9.6	42 8.6
	6.4	9.3	7.2	7.5	6.0	Sales/Working Capital	6.5	7.1
	10.8	20.3	15.7	18.8	7.8		12.7	12.3
	51.1	NM	149.5	60.1	12.6		160.3	80.0
	11.4	5.5	8.1	8.7	7.4	EBIT/Interest	7.7	7.7
	(15) 3.7	(37) 3.0	(30) 4.1	2.7	(13) 4.4		(107) 2.7	(94) 3.2
	1.6	1.7	2.1	.3	1.8		1.6	1.4
		5.8	4.0			Net Profit + Depr., Dep.,	5.9	7.1
		(20) 2.2	(20) 2.8			Amort./Cur. Mat. L /T/D	(66) 3.3	(54) 3.3
		1.0	2.1				1.6	1.3
	.6	.7	.6	.9	1.2	Fixed/Worth	.4	.6
	1.3	1.3	1.2	1.6	1.4		1.0	1.1
	2.0	2.1	2.1	2.8	2.2		1.8	1.7
	.7	1.1	.8	.9	1.0	Debt/Worth	.7	.8
	1.5	2.2	1.9	2.5	1.7		1.4	1.7
	3.3	4.4	3.7	4.5	2.8		4.0	2.9
	47.0	37.9	30.5	24.7	50.4	% Profit Before Taxes/Tangible	38.0	35.2
	23.6	(37) 19.5	(32) 20.1	17.0	19.2	Net Worth	(112) 17.0	(94) 17.3
	10.2	7.9	10.3	–7.8	8.8		7.4	6.2
	18.0	12.4	13.0	11.3	13.5	% Profit Before Taxes/Total	13.4	15.3
	7.2	6.5	6.9	4.6	10.5	Assets	6.6	6.7
	1.8	1.8	2.4	–1.2	2.2		3.2	1.7
	13.9	17.8	6.1	4.0	2.9	Sales/Net Fixed Assets	18.1	12.4
	6.4	6.7	3.5	2.8	1.9		5.6	4.6
	2.8	3.7	1.9	2.2	.9		2.7	2.4
	3.3	2.8	1.9	1.9	1.5	Sales/Total Assets	2.8	2.6
	2.9	2.2	1.5	1.5	.9		2.2	1.8
	1.6	1.7	1.0	1.3	.7		1.4	1.2
	1.4	1.4	2.0	3.5		% Depr., Dep., Amort./Sales	1.3	1.5
	(15) 3.3	(37) 2.4	(28) 3.9	4.0			(96) 2.4	(85) 2.6
	5.7	4.0	5.3	4.4			4.0	4.7
		1.0				% Officers', Directors',	2.5	2.2
		(11) 2.2				Owners' Comp/Sales	(32) 3.5	(24) 4.7
		3.9					4.9	6.1
2261M	47473M	456456M	1332859M	1225105M	2588935M	Net Sales ($)	4424639M	4479884M
1313M	17749M	205379M	846947M	819941M	2330500M	Total Assets ($)	3089488M	3337465M

M = $ thousand   MM = $ million
See Pages 1 through 15 for Explanation of Ratios and Data

Comparative Historical Data — columns 5, 13, 15
Current Data Sorted By Sales — columns 2, 2, 3, 4, 4

5	13	15		0-1MM	1-3MM	3-5MM	5-10MM	10-25MM	25MM & OVER
5	13	15	# Postretirement Benefits		2	2	3	4	4
			Type of Statement						
44	43	66	Unqualified	3	4	1	7	16	35
22	10	18	Reviewed	1	3	4	2	7	1
7	19	7	Compiled	2	1		3	1	
1	2	2	Tax Returns	1					1
21	32	29	Other	1	4	1	1	5	17
4/1/92-3/31/93 ALL	4/1/93-3/31/94 ALL	4/1/94-3/31/95 ALL		36 (4/1-9/30/94)			86 (10/1/94-3/31/95)		
95	106	122	**NUMBER OF STATEMENTS**	8	11	7	13	29	54
%	%	%	**ASSETS**	%	%	%	%	%	%
7.2	7.1	5.8	Cash & Equivalents		6.6		7.0	4.0	6.0
23.3	22.4	22.0	Trade Receivables - (net)		21.7		29.7	24.1	17.9
21.0	18.2	18.5	Inventory		21.7		18.5	21.1	17.0
2.0	1.3	1.8	All Other Current		1.0		1.7	1.1	2.5
53.5	49.0	48.1	Total Current		51.1		57.0	50.3	43.5
37.1	41.5	42.8	Fixed Assets (net)		39.1		32.9	41.3	47.4
2.2	1.8	1.8	Intangibles (net)		1.8		3.1	.4	2.7
7.2	7.7	7.2	All Other Non-Current		8.0		7.0	8.0	6.4
100.0	100.0	100.0	Total		100.0		100.0	100.0	100.0
			LIABILITIES						
8.1	7.5	8.6	Notes Payable-Short Term		5.8		12.3	11.7	7.2
4.4	3.4	3.2	Cur. Mat.-L/T/D		2.6		3.8	4.4	2.5
16.0	15.1	15.0	Trade Payables		12.3		20.5	15.7	13.7
.4	1.1	.4	Income Taxes Payable		.2		.2	.5	.4
5.7	6.2	7.1	All Other Current		6.2		10.7	4.9	8.2
34.6	33.3	34.4	Total Current		27.1		47.6	37.3	32.0
18.5	18.6	19.5	Long Term Debt		15.6		12.6	21.7	21.8
1.7	1.7	2.1	Deferred Taxes		.8		2.6	1.6	2.6
5.1	3.4	5.5	All Other-Non-Current		5.3		7.0	4.9	6.1
40.0	43.0	38.6	Net Worth		51.3		30.1	34.6	37.5
100.0	100.0	100.0	Total Liabilities & Net Worth		100.0		100.0	100.0	100.0
			INCOME DATA						
100.0	100.0	100.0	Net Sales		100.0		100.0	100.0	100.0
23.6	25.2	23.0	Gross Profit		33.0		18.7	23.4	19.9
17.9	20.4	17.3	Operating Expenses		23.6		17.3	18.2	12.7
5.8	4.8	5.7	Operating Profit		9.4		1.5	5.2	7.2
1.3	1.1	1.2	All Other Expenses (net)		.7		.9	1.5	1.2
4.4	3.7	4.5	Profit Before Taxes		8.7		.6	3.7	6.0
			RATIOS						
2.6 1.7 1.1	2.2 1.6 1.1	2.0 1.3 1.1	Current		4.5 1.9 1.1		1.9 1.1 .9	1.8 1.4 1.1	2.0 1.7 1.1
1.5 .9 .6	1.3 .9 .6	1.2 .8 .6	Quick		2.6 1.0 .7		1.1 .6 .5	.9 .7 .6	1.3 .8 .6
29 12.7 36 10.2 46 8.0	31 11.7 38 9.6 47 7.8	33 11.1 40 9.2 47 7.7	Sales/Receivables		27 13.6 31 11.6 41 8.9		35 10.5 40 9.1 53 6.9	34 10.7 40 9.1 50 7.3	32 11.3 39 9.4 46 7.9
27 13.6 42 8.6 57 6.4	26 14.0 41 8.9 64 5.7	28 13.2 46 8.0 63 5.8	Cost of Sales/Inventory		32 11.4 51 7.1 74 4.9		21 17.1 47 7.8 58 6.3	25 14.8 42 8.6 66 5.5	31 11.7 45 8.1 60 6.1
21 17.2 28 12.9 42 8.6	19 18.9 31 11.8 45 8.1	22 16.8 32 11.3 47 7.8	Cost of Sales/Payables		19 19.1 26 14.2 39 9.3		18 20.7 41 8.9 52 7.0	27 13.6 38 9.7 47 7.7	22 16.9 29 12.8 46 8.0
5.4 11.9 50.1	7.2 13.4 49.9	7.4 14.2 115.2	Sales/Working Capital		5.5 10.1 79.5		8.7 88.6 -513.1	8.1 16.9 134.6	7.1 11.8 115.2
(85) 6.3 3.1 1.4	(101) 9.5 3.3 1.4	(111) 6.7 3.3 1.7	EBIT/Interest				(12) 5.1 2.3 1.1	(28) 5.2 2.7 1.9	(50) 7.9 3.2 1.7
(49) 4.2 2.5 .8	(52) 4.2 2.1 1.2	(62) 6.4 2.9 1.8	Net Profit + Depr., Dep., Amort./Cur. Mat. L/T/D					(17) 3.9 2.1 1.2	(26) 7.0 3.6 2.2
.5 1.0 1.9	.7 1.1 1.9	.8 1.3 2.2	Fixed/Worth		.5 .9 1.7		.6 1.3 1.9	1.0 1.5 2.5	.9 1.3 2.3
.7 1.7 4.0	.5 1.7 3.6	1.0 1.8 3.4	Debt/Worth		.5 1.1 1.8		1.3 1.6 5.0	1.3 2.2 5.0	1.1 2.2 3.4
(89) 27.7 17.0 5.1	(102) 29.6 15.3 4.4	(119) 35.6 18.2 6.1	% Profit Before Taxes/Tangible Net Worth		47.8 24.2 11.0		(12) 34.1 12.4 2.2	32.8 15.3 9.1	(52) 37.5 21.2 9.1
13.3 6.4 .9	11.4 7.5 1.5	12.5 6.6 1.4	% Profit Before Taxes/Total Assets		19.2 16.7 6.4		13.5 2.1 .4	9.9 6.0 2.4	13.5 7.8 1.5
17.7 4.7 2.6	11.6 4.6 2.5	8.5 4.1 2.5	Sales/Net Fixed Assets		12.1 5.8 2.1		21.7 14.6 1.7	8.7 4.3 3.3	5.3 2.9 1.9
2.8 1.8 1.3	2.8 1.8 1.3	2.6 1.8 1.2	Sales/Total Assets		3.0 2.1 1.2		3.5 2.8 1.1	2.5 2.1 1.4	2.0 1.5 1.1
(85) 1.3 2.5 4.0	(90) 1.4 2.8 4.8	(104) 1.8 3.2 4.5	% Depr., Dep., Amort./Sales				(12) 1.5 2.5 3.9	(28) 1.6 2.8 5.0	(44) 1.9 3.9 4.4
(31) 1.5 3.7 5.4	(35) 2.2 4.0 8.1	(29) 1.5 3.7 7.1	% Officers', Directors', Owners' Comp/Sales						
4336027M 2871931M	4398333M 3269242M	5653089M 4221829M	Net Sales ($) Total Assets ($)	3740M 2977M	20582M 12303M	29002M 13595M	88703M 49730M	456442M 303617M	5054620M 3839607M

M = $ thousand   MM = $ million
See Pages 1 through 15 for Explanation of Ratios and Data

Current Data Sorted By Assets — Comparative Historical Data

0-500M	500M-2MM	2-10MM	10-50MM	50-100MM	100-250MM		4/1/90-3/31/91 ALL	4/1/91-3/31/92 ALL
						# Postretirement Benefits		
	1					Type of Statement		
1	1	9	3		4	Unqualified	10	9
	1	5				Reviewed	6	12
1	4	1				Compiled	2	3
						Tax Returns		
		2	3			Other	4	5
	9 (4/1-9/30/94)		26 (10/1/94-3/31/95)					
2	6	17	6		4	NUMBER OF STATEMENTS	22	29
%	%	%	%	%	%	ASSETS	%	%
		10.6				Cash & Equivalents	7.8	11.3
		29.0				Trade Receivables - (net)	28.4	28.5
		26.6				Inventory	23.5	24.7
		1.8				All Other Current	2.4	3.0
		68.1				Total Current	62.2	67.5
		18.5				Fixed Assets (net)	27.8	23.2
		2.6				Intangibles (net)	2.2	.8
		10.8				All Other Non-Current	7.8	8.5
		100.0				Total	100.0	100.0
						LIABILITIES		
		13.2				Notes Payable-Short Term	13.1	11.3
		4.5				Cur. Mat. -L/T/D	2.7	3.7
		16.5				Trade Payables	18.0	15.8
		.4				Income Taxes Payable	.8	.5
		9.2				All Other Current	6.7	6.7
		43.7				Total Current	41.3	38.0
		15.8				Long Term Debt	10.3	8.8
		.5				Deferred Taxes	.7	.2
		2.3				All Other-Non-Current	6.3	3.4
		37.7				Net Worth	41.3	49.6
		100.0				Total Liabilities & Net Worth	100.0	100.0
						INCOME DATA		
		100.0				Net Sales	100.0	100.0
		25.0				Gross Profit	34.2	31.9
		19.8				Operating Expenses	30.4	28.4
		5.1				Operating Profit	3.8	3.5
		1.2				All Other Expenses (net)	.7	1.1
		3.9				Profit Before Taxes	3.1	2.4
						RATIOS		
		2.4				Current	2.1	2.9
		1.5					1.5	1.6
		1.1					1.1	1.2
		1.6				Quick	1.3	1.7
		.8					.8	.8
		.6					.6	.6
		37 9.9				Sales/Receivables	31 11.7	33 11.1
		45 8.2					38 9.5	46 8.0
		50 7.3					47 7.7	54 6.8
		27 13.3				Cost of Sales/Inventory	13 28.1	29 12.6
		54 6.8					33 10.9	51 7.1
		89 4.1					65 5.6	72 5.1
		21 17.5				Cost of Sales/Payables	22 16.7	19 19.4
		31 11.9					31 11.9	28 12.9
		43 8.4					46 8.0	54 6.8
		5.4				Sales/Working Capital	7.4	5.4
		12.7					16.0	8.8
		155.4					59.9	30.6
		11.6				EBIT/Interest	(19) 3.9	(26) 3.6
	(16)	3.3					2.8	1.6
		1.5					1.5	.7
						Net Profit + Depr., Dep., Amort./Cur. Mat. L./T/D		(16) 4.3
								1.3
								.2
		.3				Fixed/Worth	.4	.3
		.7					.7	.4
		1.0					2.2	.9
		.7				Debt/Worth	.6	.5
		1.9					1.6	.9
		4.1					4.5	1.9
		56.6				% Profit Before Taxes/Tangible Net Worth	(21) 32.9	(27) 14.7
	(16)	21.2					16.9	8.7
		7.2					5.7	1.5
		13.3				% Profit Before Taxes/Total Assets	10.6	8.1
		9.4					5.3	2.1
		1.8					2.6	-.1
		31.0				Sales/Net Fixed Assets	20.0	21.9
		14.0					11.8	12.3
		8.2					8.3	7.4
		3.4				Sales/Total Assets	3.6	3.0
		2.5					2.6	2.3
		1.5					2.1	1.9
		.8				% Depr., Dep., Amort./Sales	(19) .9	1.1
	(13)	1.2					1.7	1.5
		1.7					3.0	2.6
						% Officers', Directors', Owners' Comp/Sales		(11) 2.2
								4.0
								7.3
1035M	25289M	161005M	216844M		788120M	Net Sales ($)	290126M	513837M
510M	7646M	75179M	107877M		591647M	Total Assets ($)	130512M	289052M

M = $ thousand   MM = $ million
See Pages 1 through 15 for Explanation of Ratios and Data

Comparative Historical Data

Current Data Sorted By Sales

					# Postretirement Benefits						
				1	Type of Statement				1		
	13		9	18	Unqualified	1	1	1	7	2	6
	6		5	6	Reviewed		1		5		
	2		4	6	Compiled	1		3	1	1	
					Tax Returns						
					Other				1	2	2
	4		6	5			9 (4/1-9/30/94)			26 (10/1/94-3/31/95)	
	4/1/92-3/31/93		4/1/93-3/31/94	4/1/94-3/31/95							
	ALL		ALL	ALL		0-1MM	1-3MM	3-5MM	5-10MM	10-25MM	25MM & OVER
	25		24	35	NUMBER OF STATEMENTS	2	1	5	14	5	8
	%		%	%	ASSETS	%	%	%	%	%	%
	7.6		8.5	10.3	Cash & Equivalents				9.0		
	24.6		21.9	30.2	Trade Receivables - (net)				27.4		
	21.3		27.0	23.9	Inventory				25.5		
	2.1		1.7	1.4	All Other Current				2.0		
	55.7		59.2	65.8	Total Current				63.8		
	33.3		28.1	18.9	Fixed Assets (net)				15.9		
	1.7		1.7	3.2	Intangibles (net)				2.1		
	9.3		11.0	12.1	All Other Non-Current				18.1		
	100.0		100.0	100.0	Total				100.0		
					LIABILITIES						
	6.8		15.0	10.5	Notes Payable-Short Term				13.7		
	2.9		2.9	3.8	Cur. Mat.-L /T/D				4.6		
	13.4		13.3	17.1	Trade Payables				16.0		
	.2		.9	.9	Income Taxes Payable				.4		
	7.6		5.0	9.4	All Other Current				7.6		
	31.0		37.1	41.7	Total Current				42.4		
	16.1		18.5	12.8	Long Term Debt				15.9		
	.9		.7	.6	Deferred Taxes				.4		
	3.8		4.8	2.7	All Other-Non-Current				3.2		
	48.3		39.0	42.2	Net Worth				38.1		
	100.0		100.0	100.0	Total Liabilities & Net Worth				100.0		
					INCOME DATA						
	100.0		100.0	100.0	Net Sales				100.0		
	34.4		32.2	29.9	Gross Profit				26.0		
	29.9		29.6	24.6	Operating Expenses				19.5		
	4.4		2.6	5.3	Operating Profit				6.5		
	.5		1.1	.7	All Other Expenses (net)				1.6		
	3.9		1.5	4.6	Profit Before Taxes				4.9		
					RATIOS						
	2.6		2.4	2.2					2.4		
	1.8		1.7	1.5	Current				1.4		
	1.2		1.1	1.3					1.0		
	1.6		1.4	1.4					1.5		
	.9		.9	1.0	Quick				.8		
	.7		.5	.7					.6		
41	9.0	34	10.7	40 9.1					28 12.9		
46	8.0	43	8.5	47 7.8	Sales/Receivables				41 8.9		
59	6.2	54	6.8	57 6.4					48 7.6		
35	10.4	57	6.4	27 13.6					23 15.6		
53	6.9	70	5.2	54 6.8	Cost of Sales/Inventory				44 8.3		
87	4.2	101	3.6	68 5.4					70 5.2		
19	19.6	24	15.3	23 16.2					19 18.8		
33	11.2	31	11.8	38 9.6	Cost of Sales/Payables				25 14.4		
48	7.6	49	7.4	49 7.4					42 8.7		
	4.8		5.5	6.0					6.0		
	9.4		7.3	8.8	Sales/Working Capital				13.5		
	25.1		55.5	23.1					-541.1		
	4.7		6.7	12.8					12.5		
(23)	3.8	(22)	2.2	(31) 5.0	EBIT/Interest			(13)	4.0		
	1.9		.9	2.2					1.8		
	16.8		9.4	10.7	Net Profit + Depr., Dep.,						
(11)	2.6	(13)	3.8	(18) 4.2	Amort./Cur. Mat. L/T/D						
	1.8		1.6	1.9							
	.3		.5	.1					.1		
	.7		.8	.4	Fixed/Worth				.5		
	1.6		1.3	1.0					.8		
	.5		.6	.9					1.0		
	1.2		2.1	1.7	Debt/Worth				1.8		
	2.1		3.2	3.4					3.6		
	23.0		24.6	44.9	% Profit Before Taxes/Tangible				52.7		
(24)	15.2	(20)	8.9	(34) 21.4	Net Worth				21.4		
	6.1		3.6	9.0					6.5		
	10.9		8.8	13.6	% Profit Before Taxes/Total				16.0		
	6.1		4.6	8.5	Assets				9.1		
	2.7		.2	4.8					2.9		
	13.0		11.7	37.9					216.3		
	5.4		6.5	14.0	Sales/Net Fixed Assets				13.8		
	3.9		3.7	6.8					9.0		
	2.5		2.5	3.2					3.3		
	1.8		1.6	2.1	Sales/Total Assets				2.2		
	1.4		1.3	1.3					1.5		
	1.1		1.7	.8					.6		
	2.2	(22)	2.4	(30) 1.2	% Depr., Dep., Amort./Sales			(10)	1.3		
	3.7		3.5	1.9					1.9		
				1.2							
			(12)	3.0	% Officers', Directors',						
				4.7	Owners' Comp/Sales						
	989827M		723667M	1192293M	Net Sales ($)	1035M	2533M	19240M	121294M	70966M	977225M
	664952M		498587M	782859M	Total Assets ($)	510M	1342M	8338M	63821M	37593M	671255M

M = $ thousand   MM = $ million
See Pages 1 through 15 for Explanation of Ratios and Data

Current Data Sorted By Assets							Comparative Historical Data	
		2	4	2	3	# Postretirement Benefits		
						Type of Statement		
1	3	1	8	6	4	Unqualified	20	18
	3	5	1			Reviewed	5	1
1	3	1				Compiled	3	5
						Tax Returns		
		1	2	3	1	2 → Other	13	9
	18 (4/1-9/30/94)		28 (10/1/94-3/31/95)				4/1/90-3/31/91	4/1/91-3/31/92
0-500M	500M-2MM	2-10MM	10-50MM	50-100MM	100-250MM		ALL	ALL
2	10	9	12	7	6	NUMBER OF STATEMENTS	41	33
%	%	%	%	%	%	ASSETS	%	%
	5.7		5.4			Cash & Equivalents	8.6	8.2
	26.9		21.3			Trade Receivables - (net)	22.6	21.0
	14.0		18.2			Inventory	18.7	18.7
	1.9		1.8			All Other Current	2.7	1.7
	48.4		46.6			Total Current	52.7	49.6
	48.4		40.1			Fixed Assets (net)	35.0	38.5
	.0		.8			Intangibles (net)	1.9	4.5
	3.2		12.5			All Other Non-Current	10.5	7.4
	100.0		100.0			Total	100.0	100.0
						LIABILITIES		
	15.9		11.2			Notes Payable-Short Term	9.2	8.5
	2.9		2.8			Cur. Mat. -L/T/D	2.9	2.4
	26.5		19.8			Trade Payables	19.3	15.4
	1.0		.6			Income Taxes Payable	.7	.9
	3.2		7.7			All Other Current	7.2	15.1
	49.4		42.1			Total Current	39.2	42.2
	19.5		14.8			Long Term Debt	19.3	15.4
	.9		2.0			Deferred Taxes	2.2	2.1
	2.8		4.9			All Other-Non-Current	2.0	6.9
	27.4		36.1			Net Worth	37.3	33.3
	100.0		100.0			Total Liabilities & Net Worth	100.0	100.0
						INCOME DATA		
	100.0		100.0			Net Sales	100.0	100.0
	30.8		19.5			Gross Profit	25.9	15.5
	30.0		14.4			Operating Expenses	20.8	11.6
	.8		5.1			Operating Profit	5.0	3.9
	1.7		1.2			All Other Expenses (net)	1.3	2.1
	–.9		3.9			Profit Before Taxes	3.7	1.8
						RATIOS		
	1.5		1.5				1.8	1.7
	1.2		1.2			Current	1.4	1.3
	.9		1.0				1.1	.9
	1.0		.9				1.1	.9
	.7		.7			Quick	.7	.6
	.6		.4				.5	.4
22	16.9	19	19.0				26 13.9	19 19.4
42	8.7	30	12.0			Sales/Receivables	39 9.4	27 13.5
57	6.4	41	9.0				61 6.0	51 7.2
6	65.5	13	27.1				24 15.4	17 20.9
22	16.6	25	14.6			Cost of Sales/Inventory	44 8.3	24 15.1
38	9.6	51	7.2				76 4.8	39 9.3
29	12.4	22	16.4				24 15.2	14 26.5
40	9.1	32	11.3			Cost of Sales/Payables	39 9.3	21 17.1
63	5.8	61	6.0				78 4.7	39 9.4
	15.8		13.1				6.4	8.7
	24.9		35.1			Sales/Working Capital	16.7	30.2
	–38.3		NM				167.5	–47.9
	5.3		14.7				(39) 5.4	(32) 6.8
	3.2		5.1			EBIT/Interest	3.0	2.4
	–.2		3.2				1.3	.5
						Net Profit + Depr., Dep.,	(20) 8.8	(11) 5.8
						Amort./Cur. Mat. L./T/D	1.6	3.5
							.3	.7
	1.0		1.0				.5	.7
	1.5		1.3			Fixed/Worth	1.1	1.1
	4.2		1.5				1.9	3.4
	1.5		1.1				1.0	1.0
	2.5		1.6			Debt/Worth	1.5	1.6
	10.7		2.5				5.8	6.6
		(11)	39.9			% Profit Before Taxes/Tangible	(39) 39.5	(28) 33.3
			35.3			Net Worth	14.9	19.4
			17.2				1.3	–3.0
	10.8		16.6			% Profit Before Taxes/Total	12.6	10.2
	6.2		9.6			Assets	5.2	5.4
	–5.1		5.1				.8	–2.4
	10.6		16.5				17.6	11.8
	5.4		7.3			Sales/Net Fixed Assets	6.1	7.0
	3.0		2.5				3.3	4.5
	3.2		4.5				3.0	3.7
	2.5		2.1			Sales/Total Assets	1.9	2.8
	1.6		1.3				1.2	1.8
	1.5		1.0				(33) .9	(26) .7
	3.1		1.7			% Depr., Dep., Amort./Sales	2.2	1.1
	4.3		3.8				3.2	2.1
						% Officers', Directors',	(10) 1.0	
						Owners' Comp/Sales	2.5	
							4.4	
496M	32589M	146028M	790559M	849615M	3636716M	Net Sales ($)	4026860M	6286458M
276M	12581M	35189M	299730M	487091M	982590M	Total Assets ($)	1733969M	2169910M

M = $ thousand   MM = $ million
See Pages 1 through 15 for Explanation of Ratios and Data

Comparative Historical Data				Current Data Sorted By Sales					
2	2	11	**# Postretirement Benefits**				1		10
			Type of Statement						
13	14	23	Unqualified	1	2		1	2	17
4	6	9	Reviewed		1	1	2	3	2
3	2	5	Compiled	1	3			1	
			Tax Returns						
14	12	9	Other		1	1		1	6
4/1/92-3/31/93	4/1/93-3/31/94	4/1/94-3/31/95		18 (4/1-9/30/94)			28 (10/1/94-3/31/95)		
ALL	ALL	ALL		0-1MM	1-3MM	3-5MM	5-10MM	10-25MM	25MM & OVER
34	34	46	**NUMBER OF STATEMENTS**	2	7	2	3	7	25
%	%	%	**ASSETS**	%	%	%	%	%	%
4.5	7.2	7.7	Cash & Equivalents						5.3
19.1	27.3	23.7	Trade Receivables - (net)						21.6
15.1	21.5	17.2	Inventory						16.1
2.2	1.8	1.8	All Other Current						2.0
40.9	57.9	50.5	Total Current						45.0
50.1	31.8	41.3	Fixed Assets (net)						44.2
.3	.9	1.0	Intangibles (net)						1.5
8.6	9.4	7.3	All Other Non-Current						9.3
100.0	100.0	100.0	Total						100.0
			LIABILITIES						
4.6	6.0	10.8	Notes Payable-Short Term						8.3
4.2	3.3	2.8	Cur. Mat.-L/T/D						2.2
16.9	20.1	23.1	Trade Payables						20.1
1.2	1.2	.5	Income Taxes Payable						.4
7.0	8.1	5.5	All Other Current						7.2
33.9	38.7	42.7	Total Current						38.3
25.3	17.1	14.2	Long Term Debt						12.8
3.0	2.2	1.5	Deferred Taxes						1.9
3.6	1.5	2.8	All Other-Non-Current						3.7
34.3	40.5	38.7	Net Worth						43.3
100.0	100.0	100.0	Total Liabilities & Net Worth						100.0
			INCOME DATA						
100.0	100.0	100.0	Net Sales						100.0
23.0	22.3	23.2	Gross Profit						19.2
16.5	18.9	19.1	Operating Expenses						14.0
6.6	3.5	4.1	Operating Profit						5.2
2.9	1.0	1.0	All Other Expenses (net)						.9
3.7	2.4	3.1	Profit Before Taxes						4.3
			RATIOS						
1.6	2.6	1.6	Current						1.6
1.2	1.4	1.3							1.2
.9	1.1	1.0							1.0
.9	1.2	1.0	Quick						1.0
.6	.9	.8							.8
.4	.7	.6							.5
14 25.2	18 20.4	20 18.6	Sales/Receivables						19 19.0
29 12.7	32 11.4	37 10.0							26 14.0
40 9.2	51 7.2	45 8.2							41 8.9
16 23.1	19 19.1	15 23.7	Cost of Sales/Inventory						14 25.4
28 12.9	33 11.2	29 12.4							28 12.9
46 8.0	58 6.3	45 8.1							46 8.0
20 18.2	16 22.7	25 14.7	Cost of Sales/Payables						23 15.9
30 12.0	31 11.7	35 10.5							29 12.7
41 8.8	52 7.0	54 6.7							49 7.5
16.4	7.8	13.2	Sales/Working Capital						11.4
39.3	17.3	19.8							29.8
−44.0	62.6	NM							782.4
(29) 8.1	(31) 9.3	(42) 13.3	EBIT/Interest					(24) 18.1
3.4	4.5	3.8							6.9
1.1	1.1	2.4							2.8
(15) 7.7	(19) 4.3	(26) 26.5	Net Profit + Depr., Dep., Amort./Cur. Mat. L/T/D					(13) 107.5
2.8	1.4	3.6							9.1
1.6	.9	1.2							3.8
.9	.3	.6	Fixed/Worth						.8
1.3	.8	1.1							1.2
2.5	1.5	1.6							1.5
1.0	.9	.7	Debt/Worth						.7
1.5	1.8	1.6							1.3
3.7	2.8	3.3							2.3
(33) 35.8	(33) 35.4	(44) 37.4	% Profit Before Taxes/Tangible Net Worth						34.7
14.1	18.2	17.4							17.3
1.4	1.1	11.0							10.2
11.6	14.8	13.1	% Profit Before Taxes/Total Assets						15.3
4.2	6.5	6.9							8.0
.3	.4	3.1							3.1
7.7	26.1	16.0	Sales/Net Fixed Assets						11.7
4.5	8.4	6.1							4.4
2.0	3.9	2.6							2.4
3.2	3.3	3.9	Sales/Total Assets						4.2
2.1	2.5	2.5							2.1
1.2	1.5	1.4							1.3
(25) 1.0	(30) .8	(44) .9	% Depr., Dep., Amort./Sales					(24) .8
2.5	1.6	1.9							2.0
4.2	3.1	4.1							4.5
		(13) 1.3	% Officers', Directors', Owners' Comp/Sales						
		2.2							
		4.1							
4645670M	6108750M	5456003M	Net Sales ($)	496M	15002M	8999M	22071M	103962M	5305473M
2229805M	1730708M	1817457M	Total Assets ($)	276M	7558M	9107M	5673M	38049M	1756794M

© Robert Morris Associates 1995   M = $ thousand   MM = $ million
See Pages 1 through 15 for Explanation of Ratios and Data

Current Data Sorted By Assets | | | | | | | **Comparative Historical Data** |

0-500M	500M-2MM	2-10MM	10-50MM	50-100MM	100-250MM		4/1/90-3/31/91 ALL	4/1/91-3/31/92 ALL
1		1	1	2	1	# Postretirement Benefits		
						Type of Statement		
	2		8	2	1	Unqualified	10	10
		2	3		1	Reviewed	12	7
2			2	1		Compiled	11	11
1	1					Tax Returns		1
3	2		3	1	1	Other	3	7
	11 (4/1-9/30/94)		24 (10/1/94-3/31/95)				36	36
6	5	10	10	3	1	NUMBER OF STATEMENTS		
%	%	%	%	%	%	**ASSETS**	%	%
		3.9	3.7			Cash & Equivalents	7.6	6.9
		33.2	28.5			Trade Receivables - (net)	29.1	30.8
		19.6	14.4			Inventory	16.4	13.7
		3.0	.7			All Other Current	2.4	1.7
		59.7	47.3			Total Current	55.5	53.1
		34.3	38.7			Fixed Assets (net)	34.0	34.1
		2.2	2.9			Intangibles (net)	5.9	6.7
		3.8	11.0			All Other Non-Current	4.6	6.1
		100.0	100.0			Total	100.0	100.0
						LIABILITIES		
		7.2	8.0			Notes Payable-Short Term	6.7	8.8
		6.6	6.1			Cur. Mat. -L/T/D	5.3	8.0
		14.4	11.5			Trade Payables	12.2	12.8
		.4	.4			Income Taxes Payable	.4	.8
		15.8	8.5			All Other Current	8.2	8.6
		44.3	34.5			Total Current	32.8	38.9
		19.0	25.5			Long Term Debt	22.4	21.1
		.0	1.7			Deferred Taxes	1.3	.9
		2.5	3.1			All Other-Non-Current	3.6	3.6
		34.2	35.3			Net Worth	39.9	35.5
		100.0	100.0			Total Liabilities & Net Worth	100.0	100.0
						INCOME DATA		
		100.0	100.0			Net Sales	100.0	100.0
		30.6	25.7			Gross Profit	29.5	35.3
		23.5	20.2			Operating Expenses	24.2	31.3
		7.0	5.6			Operating Profit	5.3	4.1
		3.1	1.3			All Other Expenses (net)	2.1	1.9
		4.0	4.3			Profit Before Taxes	3.2	2.2
						RATIOS		
		2.9	1.9				2.9	2.4
		1.9	1.5			Current	1.8	1.5
		.9	1.1				1.2	1.1
		2.0	1.4				2.0	1.8
		1.0	1.0			Quick	1.1	1.1
		.6	.8				.7	.7
		47 7.8	49 7.4				42 8.7	34 10.7
		52 7.0	55 6.6			Sales/Receivables	56 6.5	55 6.6
		64 5.7	85 4.3				64 5.7	69 5.3
		20 17.9	25 14.7				22 16.5	17 21.2
		43 8.5	41 8.8			Cost of Sales/Inventory	29 12.8	26 13.9
		79 4.6	104 3.5				45 8.1	40 9.2
		21 17.3	25 14.7				20 18.1	22 16.4
		26 14.1	37 9.8			Cost of Sales/Payables	26 14.3	31 11.6
		32 11.3	65 5.6				40 9.2	42 8.7
		5.8	7.8				5.3	7.6
		8.5	13.8			Sales/Working Capital	9.7	11.9
		−57.4	NM				28.7	46.3
			9.1				4.5	5.9
			3.7			EBIT/Interest	(33) 2.3	2.5
			1.8				1.0	.8
							4.2	5.5
						Net Profit + Depr., Dep., Amort./Cur. Mat. L /T/D	(16) 1.9	(19) 2.3
							1.0	.9
		.4	.9				.6	.5
		1.0	1.3			Fixed/Worth	1.3	1.4
		−7.1	3.8				2.6	3.2
		.5	1.0				.7	.9
		1.7	2.5			Debt/Worth	2.0	2.2
		−10.5	6.2				6.3	6.0
							41.9	41.3
						% Profit Before Taxes/Tangible Net Worth	(31) 14.1	(31) 21.2
							4.7	−2.5
		17.1	9.4				13.7	14.7
		7.5	6.9			% Profit Before Taxes/Total Assets	5.7	8.1
		−2.3	1.7				.3	−1.9
		16.9	6.5				11.3	12.1
		7.5	4.2			Sales/Net Fixed Assets	6.8	7.2
		4.4	3.0				3.6	3.7
		3.1	2.0				2.5	2.9
		2.3	1.6			Sales/Total Assets	2.0	2.0
		1.9	1.2				1.6	1.6
							2.5	2.6
						% Depr., Dep., Amort./Sales	(34) 3.6	(33) 3.6
							5.8	5.3
							2.2	2.3
						% Officers', Directors', Owners' Comp/Sales	(13) 6.9	(13) 5.9
							10.9	12.2
3267M	13253M	82396M	426305M	368468M	294289M	Net Sales ($)	710650M	734845M
1404M	4869M	40333M	268626M	230949M	243940M	Total Assets ($)	396384M	448036M

M = $ thousand   MM = $ million
See Pages 1 through 15 for Explanation of Ratios and Data

Comparative Historical Data   Current Data Sorted By Sales

H1	H2	H3	Item	0-1MM	1-3MM	3-5MM	5-10MM	10-25MM	25MM & OVER
1	1	6	# Postretirement Benefits		1			1	4
			Type of Statement						
12	11	13	Unqualified				1	3	9
6	8	5	Reviewed		1		3	1	
5	2	5	Compiled	2			2	1	
1		2	Tax Returns	1	1				
4	7	10	Other	4	2		1	1	2
4/1/92-3/31/93 ALL	4/1/93-3/31/94 ALL	4/1/94-3/31/95 ALL		11 (4/1-9/30/94)			24 (10/1/94-3/31/95)		
28	28	35	**NUMBER OF STATEMENTS**	7	4		7	6	11
%	%	%	**ASSETS**	%	%	%	%	%	%
8.9	6.0	7.0	Cash & Equivalents						6.2
31.2	31.7	29.5	Trade Receivables - (net)						26.9
9.8	15.4	15.8	Inventory						14.2
1.3	2.2	2.6	All Other Current						3.0
51.2	55.4	54.9	Total Current						50.3
38.7	36.8	36.5	Fixed Assets (net)						37.0
4.2	.6	3.1	Intangibles (net)						4.1
5.9	7.1	5.4	All Other Non-Current						8.7
100.0	100.0	100.0	Total						100.0
			LIABILITIES						
5.2	8.3	6.5	Notes Payable-Short Term						6.4
6.6	4.0	6.8	Cur. Mat.-L /T/D						3.7
10.7	15.8	12.8	Trade Payables						11.5
.8	2.6	.5	Income Taxes Payable						.9
5.3	8.5	13.2	All Other Current						9.0
28.6	39.2	39.8	Total Current						31.5
26.8	19.1	21.6	Long Term Debt						21.5
1.2	1.3	.8	Deferred Taxes						2.0
3.5	2.4	3.2	All Other-Non-Current						4.5
39.8	38.1	34.6	Net Worth						40.4
100.0	100.0	100.0	Total Liabilities & Net Worth						100.0
			INCOME DATA						
100.0	100.0	100.0	Net Sales						100.0
36.1	24.6	34.5	Gross Profit						24.1
29.4	21.0	27.8	Operating Expenses						17.2
6.8	3.7	6.8	Operating Profit						6.8
1.4	1.2	1.8	All Other Expenses (net)						1.4
5.4	2.5	5.0	Profit Before Taxes						5.4
			RATIOS						
3.0 / 1.7 / 1.2	2.4 / 1.7 / 1.1	1.9 / 1.6 / 1.1	Current						2.3 / 1.6 / 1.1
2.3 / 1.4 / .9	1.6 / 1.2 / .6	1.4 / 1.0 / .7	Quick						1.4 / 1.0 / .8
43 8.5 / 61 6.0 / 69 5.3	47 7.8 / 62 5.9 / 70 5.2	45 8.1 / 52 7.0 / 64 5.7	Sales/Receivables						51 7.1 / 57 6.4 / 57 6.4
18 20.3 / 27 13.4 / 37 9.9	23 16.1 / 35 10.5 / 49 7.5	21 17.3 / 33 11.0 / 78 4.7	Cost of Sales/Inventory						27 13.4 / 32 11.4 / 47 7.7
15 23.6 / 24 15.5 / 38 9.7	24 14.9 / 33 11.2 / 45 8.2	24 15.4 / 30 12.3 / 46 8.0	Cost of Sales/Payables						22 16.7 / 35 10.5 / 46 8.0
5.4 / 8.7 / 25.1	6.1 / 9.2 / 78.7	5.3 / 9.6 / 46.0	Sales/Working Capital						4.9 / 9.6 / 27.0
6.9 / 3.8 / 1.8	7.8 / (26) 2.9 / .8	10.7 / (32) 3.8 / 1.1	EBIT/Interest						9.8 / 5.2 / .9
6.4 / (14) 2.8 / 1.5	5.8 / (13) 2.8 / .8	2.8 / (17) 1.1 / .8	Net Profit + Depr., Dep., Amort./Cur. Mat. L/T/D						
.5 / 1.1 / 2.2	.5 / .9 / 2.1	.4 / 1.2 / 6.8	Fixed/Worth						.5 / 1.2 / 2.1
.8 / 1.8 / 4.1	.7 / 1.7 / 4.1	1.0 / 2.3 / 8.7	Debt/Worth						1.1 / 2.3 / 3.9
57.8 / (24) 18.7 / 6.1	33.5 / (26) 13.4 / 4.5	41.5 / (28) 19.9 / 3.6	% Profit Before Taxes/Tangible Net Worth						44.2 / 20.6 / -1.4
14.3 / 7.7 / 2.1	9.4 / 5.3 / -1.1	12.2 / 5.1 / -.4	% Profit Before Taxes/Total Assets						9.1 / 7.0 / -.4
7.7 / 5.1 / 3.2	7.8 / 5.0 / 3.4	15.0 / 5.4 / 3.7	Sales/Net Fixed Assets						6.5 / 4.6 / 3.5
2.3 / 1.9 / 1.6	2.3 / 1.9 / 1.4	2.5 / 1.9 / 1.4	Sales/Total Assets						1.9 / 1.6 / 1.2
(26) 3.0 / 4.1 / 5.9	(22) 2.6 / 3.8 / 4.5	(29) 2.3 / 3.6 / 4.6	% Depr., Dep., Amort./Sales						3.2 / (10) 3.8 / 4.9
			% Officers', Directors', Owners' Comp/Sales						
742924M	816897M	1187978M	Net Sales ($)	3818M	9545M		46622M	96001M	1031992M
401409M	500092M	790121M	Total Assets ($)	2320M	8981M		21453M	65552M	691815M

M = $ thousand   MM = $ million
See Pages 1 through 15 for Explanation of Ratios and Data

Current Data Sorted By Assets							Comparative Historical Data	
						# Postretirement Benefits		
1	1	1				**Type of Statement**		
		4	1	1		Unqualified	8	11
	9	8				Reviewed	20	19
4	8	1				Compiled	17	17
1	1					Tax Returns		
1	3	4	3			Other	9	14
	17 (4/1-9/30/94)			32 (10/1/94-3/31/95)			9 4/1/90- 3/31/91 ALL	14 4/1/91- 3/31/92 ALL
0-500M	500M-2MM	2-10MM	10-50MM	50-100MM	100-250MM	**NUMBER OF STATEMENTS**	54	61
6	21	17	4	1				
%	%	%	%	%	%	**ASSETS**	%	%
	6.9	6.5				Cash & Equivalents	6.5	6.8
	29.9	33.0				Trade Receivables - (net)	31.0	28.5
	6.9	8.2				Inventory	10.1	9.2
	1.6	1.6				All Other Current	1.7	1.5
	45.2	49.3				Total Current	49.2	45.9
	41.1	42.7				Fixed Assets (net)	40.0	42.1
	2.2	.3				Intangibles (net)	2.6	2.5
	11.5	7.8				All Other Non-Current	8.2	9.5
	100.0	100.0				Total	100.0	100.0
						LIABILITIES		
	6.9	9.9				Notes Payable-Short Term	9.4	7.8
	8.8	5.5				Cur. Mat. -L/T/D	7.3	8.2
	9.8	10.7				Trade Payables	11.9	9.8
	.4	.6				Income Taxes Payable	.5	.2
	6.4	5.9				All Other Current	5.3	5.6
	32.3	32.5				Total Current	34.4	31.5
	20.8	24.2				Long Term Debt	26.7	24.7
	.5	.3				Deferred Taxes	.7	.7
	1.8	2.7				All Other-Non-Current	3.8	2.3
	44.5	40.3				Net Worth	34.4	40.8
	100.0	100.0				Total Liabilities & Net Worth	100.0	100.0
						INCOME DATA		
	100.0	100.0				Net Sales	100.0	100.0
	39.6	27.3				Gross Profit	35.0	33.4
	30.6	20.6				Operating Expenses	30.9	29.0
	9.0	6.7				Operating Profit	4.1	4.3
	3.1	1.4				All Other Expenses (net)	1.9	1.4
	5.9	5.3				Profit Before Taxes	2.2	2.9
						RATIOS		
	2.3	2.0					2.3	2.4
	1.4	1.4				Current	1.4	1.5
	.9	1.0					1.1	1.0
	1.9	1.7					1.6	2.0
	1.1	1.1				Quick	1.1	1.1
	.7	.8					.8	.8
	34 10.6	50 7.3					44 8.3	39 9.3
	48 7.6	65 5.6				Sales/Receivables	52 7.0	47 7.7
	59 6.2	73 5.0					66 5.5	58 6.3
	1 557.8	1 372.6					3 112.5	2 177.6
	13 28.7	9 38.6				Cost of Sales/Inventory	13 27.1	13 29.0
	32 11.4	40 9.1					37 9.8	27 13.7
	8 45.3	10 38.2					13 28.6	10 37.8
	23 15.9	28 12.9				Cost of Sales/Payables	29 12.4	19 19.6
	29 12.6	41 9.0					42 8.7	32 11.4
	9.1	5.9					7.6	8.6
	21.9	18.0				Sales/Working Capital	14.2	13.8
	-67.5	161.4					76.5	NM
	(19) 10.9	(16) 6.9					(52) 2.9	(57) 4.6
	3.9	4.2				EBIT/Interest	1.5	2.4
	2.3	2.2					.7	1.3
	(10) 5.3						(41) 2.6	(30) 2.1
	3.0					Net Profit + Depr., Dep., Amort./Cur. Mat. L./T/D	1.5	1.2
	1.7						.9	.8
	.6	.4					.5	.6
	.9	1.0				Fixed/Worth	1.2	1.1
	2.2	2.8					3.7	2.3
	.8	.8					1.1	.8
	1.0	1.4				Debt/Worth	2.2	1.4
	2.8	3.3					7.1	3.9
	54.2	44.2					(50) 29.9	(58) 30.7
	23.9	(16) 24.6				% Profit Before Taxes/Tangible Net Worth	12.2	12.9
	9.3	4.7					-.3	3.5
	16.0	12.2					9.5	10.3
	8.5	7.4				% Profit Before Taxes/Total Assets	3.1	4.0
	5.0	.7					-2.4	1.5
	8.0	10.7					9.5	11.1
	5.4	4.9				Sales/Net Fixed Assets	5.6	6.6
	3.4	2.2					2.8	3.1
	2.9	2.7					2.6	2.9
	2.0	1.9				Sales/Total Assets	2.0	2.3
	1.5	1.2					1.5	1.6
	(19) 3.1	(16) 2.1					(53) 2.4	(57) 1.9
	4.2	4.6				% Depr., Dep., Amort./Sales	3.9	4.0
	6.3	6.6					7.0	6.5
	(10) 3.7	(10) 1.8					(24) 2.9	(35) 3.2
	7.4	2.9				% Officers', Directors', Owners' Comp/Sales	5.1	6.6
	14.5	5.9					7.2	9.6
4195M	59693M	125006M	142681M	73540M		Net Sales ($)	307810M	251376M
1182M	26115M	67614M	120330M	59500M		Total Assets ($)	179059M	122638M

M = $ thousand   MM = $ million
See Pages 1 through 15 for Explanation of Ratios and Data

Comparative Historical Data | Current Data Sorted By Sales

	2	1	3		0-1MM	1-3MM	3-5MM	5-10MM	10-25MM	25MM & OVER
# Postretirement Benefits						1	2			
Type of Statement										
Unqualified	7	7	6				1		4	1
Reviewed	21	17	17			1	8	8		
Compiled	9	14	13		3	10				
Tax Returns	1	2	2		1		1			
Other	9	10	11		1	2	3	1	1	3
	4/1/92-3/31/93 ALL	4/1/93-3/31/94 ALL	4/1/94-3/31/95 ALL			17 (4/1-9/30/94)			32 (10/1/94-3/31/95)	
NUMBER OF STATEMENTS	47	50	49		5	13	13	9	5	4
	%	%	%		%	%	%	%	%	%
ASSETS										
Cash & Equivalents	7.7	8.9	7.9			8.8	5.8			
Trade Receivables - (net)	29.7	30.2	29.1			29.2	23.9			
Inventory	11.3	8.4	9.9			6.7	9.3			
All Other Current	2.1	1.0	1.8			1.5	2.9			
Total Current	50.8	48.5	48.7			46.3	41.9			
Fixed Assets (net)	39.7	42.7	41.3			40.2	46.7			
Intangibles (net)	1.7	2.4	1.1			2.4	1.4			
All Other Non-Current	7.8	6.3	8.8			11.1	10.0			
Total	100.0	100.0	100.0			100.0	100.0			
LIABILITIES										
Notes Payable-Short Term	11.7	10.7	9.1			7.4	8.1			
Cur. Mat.-L /T/D	5.4	5.6	6.5			7.1	8.0			
Trade Payables	11.2	11.5	10.1			8.3	7.9			
Income Taxes Payable	.4	.8	.4			.6	.6			
All Other Current	8.9	7.7	7.1			8.1	7.5			
Total Current	37.7	36.4	33.2			31.5	32.1			
Long Term Debt	23.5	23.4	20.9			23.6	21.8			
Deferred Taxes	.6	.9	.6			.7	.0			
All Other-Non-Current	2.2	3.2	2.5			3.5	1.3			
Net Worth	36.1	36.0	42.8			40.6	44.7			
Total Liabilities & Net Worth	100.0	100.0	100.0			100.0	100.0			
INCOME DATA										
Net Sales	100.0	100.0	100.0			100.0	100.0			
Gross Profit	37.2	33.6	36.9			34.3	42.8			
Operating Expenses	31.5	28.1	29.2			26.7	32.0			
Operating Profit	5.7	5.5	7.6			7.6	10.8			
All Other Expenses (net)	2.2	1.1	2.3			.9	4.1			
Profit Before Taxes	3.5	4.4	5.3			6.6	6.7			
RATIOS										
Current	2.0	1.9	2.2			3.9	1.6			
	1.5	1.5	1.4			1.4	1.3			
	1.1	.9	1.0			.9	1.0			
Quick	1.6	1.8	1.7			3.3	1.4			
	1.1	1.1	1.1			1.2	1.0			
	.8	.7	.8			.7	.8			
Sales/Receivables	37 9.8	36 10.1	38 9.6			36 10.1	28 13.0			
	47 7.7	47 7.7	52 7.0			57 6.4	42 8.7			
	56 6.5	63 5.8	70 5.2			62 5.9	58 6.3			
Cost of Sales/Inventory	3 111.1	0 UND	1 323.0			0 UND	2 227.2			
	17 21.9	10 37.5	17 21.3			5 72.5	28 13.2			
	43 8.5	28 13.2	44 8.3			25 14.8	61 6.0			
Cost of Sales/Payables	12 31.1	10 37.3	9 38.6			3 143.3	18 20.3			
	21 17.4	16 22.2	25 14.8			11 32.4	25 14.6			
	33 11.1	39 9.3	36 10.2			31 11.6	32 11.5			
Sales/Working Capital	8.7	7.1	7.8			5.1	8.4			
	15.5	20.3	21.9			20.4	22.1			
	90.3	−35.8	NM			−58.7	NM			
EBIT/Interest	(46) 6.4	(49) 5.7	(45) 6.7			(12) 17.9	7.3			
	2.1	2.9	3.5			3.5	4.0			
	1.1	1.4	2.1			1.7	2.4			
Net Profit + Depr., Dep., Amort./Cur. Mat. L/T/D	(27) 2.4	(19) 2.5	(19) 4.7							
	1.4	1.6	2.6							
	.9	.9	1.6							
Fixed/Worth	.5	.6	.5			.6	.7			
	1.0	1.2	1.0			.8	1.0			
	2.2	5.7	2.2			2.9	2.3			
Debt/Worth	1.0	.8	.7			.8	.7			
	1.8	1.5	1.4			1.4	1.0			
	3.9	12.4	3.0			3.6	2.9			
% Profit Before Taxes/Tangible Net Worth	(42) 28.1	(43) 48.3	(47) 47.5			(12) 58.0	42.8			
	12.6	17.4	22.2			19.5	20.3			
	6.9	8.5	9.3			6.8	15.3			
% Profit Before Taxes/Total Assets	11.3	11.7	12.9			19.8	12.2			
	3.6	5.8	8.5			7.9	10.0			
	1.4	1.6	4.5			3.6	6.4			
Sales/Net Fixed Assets	13.1	10.8	10.3			12.1	6.6			
	6.0	4.8	5.4			7.7	4.6			
	3.3	3.0	3.1			2.5	3.9			
Sales/Total Assets	2.9	2.7	2.9			3.1	2.5			
	2.2	2.1	1.9			1.8	1.9			
	1.6	1.6	1.4			1.2	1.5			
% Depr., Dep., Amort./Sales	(46) 2.3	(48) 1.9	(44) 2.6			(12) 2.8	3.3			
	3.3	4.2	4.0			3.8	5.1			
	6.3	7.4	5.7			4.6	7.2			
% Officers', Directors', Owners' Comp/Sales	(17) 4.1	(28) 3.0	(27) 2.7							
	6.5	5.5	6.1							
	7.8	8.1	9.1							
Net Sales ($)	176324M	266926M	405115M		2667M	23359M	45804M	57889M	80340M	195056M
Total Assets ($)	86367M	149164M	274741M		1068M	14314M	27689M	24371M	41748M	165551M

M = $ thousand   MM = $ million
See Pages 1 through 15 for Explanation of Ratios and Data

Current Data Sorted By Assets | Comparative Historical Data

0-500M	500M-2MM	2-10MM	10-50MM	50-100MM	100-250MM		4/1/90-3/31/91 ALL	4/1/91-3/31/92 ALL
2	1	3	1		1	# Postretirement Benefits Type of Statement		
	5	9	9	4	1	Unqualified	28	22
2	8	17	1			Reviewed	22	24
3	13	2				Compiled	16	20
2	3	1				Tax Returns	1	2
6	9	9	3		1	Other	11	10
	34 (4/1-9/30/94)		74 (10/1/94-3/31/95)					
13	38	38	13	4	2	NUMBER OF STATEMENTS	78	78
%	%	%	%	%	%	ASSETS	%	%
13.3	10.5	5.7	14.2			Cash & Equivalents	7.8	5.7
36.7	31.1	29.9	29.3			Trade Receivables - (net)	31.6	29.1
20.1	28.9	28.4	28.8			Inventory	25.9	31.4
4.4	3.8	3.5	1.5			All Other Current	2.5	2.2
74.4	74.3	67.4	73.7			Total Current	67.9	68.3
21.6	16.7	17.9	12.7			Fixed Assets (net)	20.1	18.7
2.9	3.6	5.5	4.8			Intangibles (net)	3.2	3.3
1.1	5.5	9.2	8.8			All Other Non-Current	8.8	9.6
100.0	100.0	100.0	100.0			Total	100.0	100.0
						LIABILITIES		
5.7	11.3	7.1	4.5			Notes Payable-Short Term	12.1	11.5
2.3	2.9	2.7	2.0			Cur. Mat.-L/T/D	4.7	3.5
12.4	17.5	14.3	13.7			Trade Payables	13.6	18.0
.7	.3	.5	.7			Income Taxes Payable	.4	.6
18.1	11.9	13.3	17.3			All Other Current	12.4	11.4
39.2	43.8	37.9	38.2			Total Current	43.3	44.9
20.8	13.4	11.6	11.3			Long Term Debt	16.5	14.1
.8	.2	.3	1.0			Deferred Taxes	.4	.4
1.3	7.5	9.6	2.5			All Other-Non-Current	4.1	3.6
37.9	35.1	40.6	47.0			Net Worth	35.5	36.9
100.0	100.0	100.0	100.0			Total Liabilities & Net Worth	100.0	100.0
						INCOME DATA		
100.0	100.0	100.0	100.0			Net Sales	100.0	100.0
55.1	46.6	50.8	47.4			Gross Profit	47.7	50.7
48.2	41.0	45.5	38.5			Operating Expenses	41.5	45.8
7.0	5.6	5.3	8.8			Operating Profit	6.2	4.9
-.3	2.0	.4	.9			All Other Expenses (net)	1.8	1.2
7.2	3.6	4.9	8.0			Profit Before Taxes	4.4	3.7
						RATIOS		
2.5	2.5	3.1	3.0				2.6	2.5
1.9	1.8	2.0	2.0			Current	1.5	1.6
1.5	1.4	1.3	1.3				1.2	1.1
2.0	1.5	1.7	1.6				1.4	1.2
1.3	1.0	1.1	1.1			Quick	.8	.8
1.0	.6	.6	.6				.5	.5
26 14.1	27 13.4	43 8.5	37 9.8			Sales/Receivables	41 9.0	30 12.0
46 7.9	46 7.9	57 6.4	65 5.6				55 6.6	49 7.4
79 4.6	76 4.8	87 4.2	104 3.5				79 4.6	73 5.0
12 30.0	21 17.0	70 5.2	47 7.8			Cost of Sales/Inventory	26 14.0	49 7.4
50 7.3	87 4.2	140 2.6	130 2.8				118 3.1	114 3.2
152 2.4	215 1.7	243 1.5	243 1.5				215 1.7	228 1.6
13 27.8	18 20.8	27 13.5	25 14.8			Cost of Sales/Payables	23 16.0	29 12.4
32 11.4	46 8.0	57 6.4	73 5.0				41 8.8	63 5.8
60 6.1	87 4.2	111 3.3	101 3.6				79 4.6	104 3.5
5.1	4.2	3.6	2.0			Sales/Working Capital	4.2	4.2
10.2	7.1	5.4	4.7				8.2	8.0
18.3	12.1	15.0	14.6				20.4	32.5
26.4	8.7	9.9	284.3			EBIT/Interest	7.3	7.3
(10) 13.1	(32) 3.6	(35) 4.2	(10) 4.3				(72) 3.1	(70) 2.6
2.1	1.4	1.8	2.9				1.3	1.3
	7.3	4.5				Net Profit + Depr., Dep., Amort./Cur. Mat. L /T/D	4.6	9.6
(11)	2.9	(15) 2.1					(40) 2.1	(29) 2.6
	1.1	1.9					.4	1.1
.0	.2	.2	.1			Fixed/Worth	.1	.1
.4	.4	.4	.2				.4	.5
1.7	1.0	1.3	.7				1.3	1.7
1.0	.8	.8	.6			Debt/Worth	.9	.8
1.5	1.8	1.5	1.7				2.0	1.9
2.6	5.5	4.6	2.8				3.5	4.4
98.5	34.5	43.3	51.8			% Profit Before Taxes/Tangible Net Worth	46.5	40.2
(11) 47.2	(35) 19.5	(35) 25.3	24.2				(72) 23.4	(70) 19.3
18.2	5.4	11.3	11.5				9.9	8.7
46.7	13.5	19.8	18.6			% Profit Before Taxes/Total Assets	18.8	13.8
12.7	6.9	7.9	8.4				7.8	5.9
5.2	1.6	2.5	4.2				1.8	1.4
UND	61.8	39.2	40.0			Sales/Net Fixed Assets	40.4	40.2
27.2	26.6	20.1	17.3				17.5	18.6
11.2	9.4	5.8	8.7				5.9	7.7
3.9	3.0	2.1	1.7			Sales/Total Assets	2.6	2.4
2.7	2.0	1.6	1.5				1.8	1.8
2.0	1.4	1.2	1.2				1.4	1.5
.7	.9	1.0	.6			% Depr., Dep., Amort./Sales	.9	.8
(10) 1.7	(33) 1.5	(32) 1.9	(12) 1.7				(62) 1.6	(66) 1.1
4.7	3.0	3.4	3.2				4.1	3.0
	3.7					% Officers', Directors', Owners' Comp/Sales	3.4	4.0
	(21) 7.1						(27) 6.5	(29) 7.8
	12.3						9.5	12.7
9996M	97916M	289933M	395448M	387950M	433989M	Net Sales ($)	1320811M	887399M
3057M	41746M	175410M	245258M	287424M	378833M	Total Assets ($)	933850M	538878M

M = $ thousand   MM = $ million
See Pages 1 through 15 for Explanation of Ratios and Data

Comparative Historical Data				Current Data Sorted By Sales					
	11	8	# Postretirement Benefits	2		2	1	2	1
			Type of Statement						
28	31	28	Unqualified		4	4	3	10	7
29	24	28	Reviewed	2	5	5	11	5	
19	24	18	Compiled	6	8	3	1		
3	4	6	Tax Returns	2	3		1		
17	24	28	Other	6	6	4	7	2	3
4/1/92-3/31/93 ALL	4/1/93-3/31/94 ALL	4/1/94-3/31/95 ALL		34 (4/1-9/30/94)			74 (10/1/94-3/31/95)		
96	107	108	**NUMBER OF STATEMENTS**	0-1MM 16	1-3MM 26	3-5MM 16	5-10MM 23	10-25MM 17	25MM & OVER 10
%	%	%	**ASSETS**	%	%	%	%	%	%
7.5	8.3	9.7	Cash & Equivalents	12.2	7.2	9.7	9.6	11.5	8.9
30.6	30.2	31.2	Trade Receivables - (net)	29.7	28.9	36.8	29.7	32.8	31.2
29.8	26.5	26.9	Inventory	24.2	34.8	24.8	25.4	24.2	22.0
1.5	3.8	3.7	All Other Current	5.7	2.3	4.2	2.7	4.3	4.4
69.4	68.8	71.4	Total Current	71.8	73.2	75.4	67.4	72.7	66.5
16.0	19.0	17.0	Fixed Assets (net)	22.0	18.0	14.2	17.4	12.3	18.5
4.0	5.5	4.7	Intangibles (net)	2.9	4.7	3.9	4.6	6.0	7.0
10.6	6.7	6.8	All Other Non-Current	3.3	4.1	6.5	10.6	8.9	8.0
100.0	100.0	100.0	Total	100.0	100.0	100.0	100.0	100.0	100.0
			LIABILITIES						
11.7	9.9	8.0	Notes Payable-Short Term	9.0	9.7	9.0	7.6	5.8	5.0
2.9	3.1	2.6	Cur. Mat.-L/T/D	2.8	2.1	3.3	2.6	2.6	2.0
16.8	15.0	15.1	Trade Payables	8.0	14.4	25.3	15.2	15.1	11.8
.7	.7	.6	Income Taxes Payable	.4	.5	.3	.7	.4	1.1
13.4	12.0	14.0	All Other Current	19.4	10.8	11.2	10.0	20.6	16.3
45.5	40.7	40.2	Total Current	39.6	37.6	49.0	35.9	44.5	36.2
10.8	15.0	13.1	Long Term Debt	17.3	13.0	12.9	12.2	10.0	14.1
.7	.9	.5	Deferred Taxes	.9	.1	.1	.1	.8	2.3
6.1	3.9	6.6	All Other-Non-Current	.7	6.5	11.0	11.3	4.8	1.4
36.9	39.5	39.6	Net Worth	41.5	42.8	27.0	40.4	39.9	46.0
100.0	100.0	100.0	Total Liabilities & Net Worth	100.0	100.0	100.0	100.0	100.0	100.0
			INCOME DATA						
100.0	100.0	100.0	Net Sales	100.0	100.0	100.0	100.0	100.0	100.0
47.3	48.7	50.3	Gross Profit	47.4	56.2	48.0	43.4	51.5	56.9
42.6	43.2	44.0	Operating Expenses	41.6	49.5	42.8	39.3	43.1	48.1
4.7	5.5	6.3	Operating Profit	5.8	6.8	5.2	4.1	8.4	8.9
.9	.6	.9	All Other Expenses (net)	.0	2.1	1.2	.3	.7	.7
3.8	4.8	5.3	Profit Before Taxes	5.9	4.7	4.0	3.7	7.6	8.1
			RATIOS						
2.3	2.7	2.5	Current	2.1	2.9	3.2	2.9	2.3	2.5
1.6	1.8	1.9		1.8	2.1	1.6	1.7	1.6	1.8
1.1	1.3	1.3		1.5	1.7	1.0	1.4	1.2	1.3
1.4	1.7	1.6	Quick	1.4	1.8	1.7	1.7	1.6	1.4
.8	1.0	1.1		1.1	1.1	1.0	1.2	1.0	1.1
.5	.6	.7		.9	.6	.7	.6	.6	.9
36 10.2	36 10.1	36 10.1	Sales/Receivables	31 11.8	26 14.1	29 12.5	36 10.2	41 8.9	51 7.2
55 6.6	57 6.4	55 6.6		49 7.5	56 6.5	51 7.1	53 6.9	65 5.6	57 6.4
76 4.8	73 5.0	81 4.5		91 4.0	87 4.2	76 4.8	72 5.1	96 3.8	140 2.6
43 8.5	35 10.3	38 9.6	Cost of Sales/Inventory	11 34.0	76 4.8	4 95.5	37 9.8	46 8.0	60 6.1
126 2.9	107 3.4	126 2.9		51 7.1	135 2.7	81 4.5	130 2.8	122 3.0	192 1.9
192 1.9	203 1.8	215 1.7		228 1.6	243 1.5	203 1.8	192 1.9	203 1.8	261 1.4
31 11.7	23 15.6	24 14.9	Cost of Sales/Payables	13 27.9	26 13.8	28 13.0	16 23.2	37 9.8	24 15.5
58 6.3	49 7.4	53 6.9		22 16.7	58 6.3	78 4.7	48 7.6	59 6.2	94 3.9
99 3.7	94 3.9	99 3.7		49 7.4	99 3.7	135 2.7	94 3.9	104 3.5	135 2.7
3.7	3.5	3.8	Sales/Working Capital	3.8	3.2	4.1	3.9	3.5	2.3
6.9	6.9	6.7		6.4	6.3	12.3	6.9	5.8	6.3
37.1	18.0	12.8		11.1	10.3	164.8	14.3	18.2	14.6
(82) 7.3	(94) 9.8	(91) 10.4	EBIT/Interest	(13) 13.6	(22) 7.7	(14) 9.9	(20) 10.3	(14) 18.1	
3.8	3.3	4.5		7.6	3.6	3.4	3.6	5.8	
1.6	1.4	2.0		2.0	1.2	.8	1.7	3.4	
(39) 7.2	(37) 6.3	(36) 5.9	Net Profit + Depr., Dep., Amort./Cur. Mat. L/T/D						
2.6	2.3	2.3							
.9	.8	1.6							
.1	.1	.1	Fixed/Worth	.0	.1	.2	.2	.1	.2
.4	.4	.4		.4	.3	.5	.4	.3	.4
1.1	1.4	1.1		1.4	.8	2.5	1.4	.9	1.2
.9	.7	.8	Debt/Worth	.8	.7	.8	.8	1.0	.7
2.0	2.0	1.6		1.1	1.6	3.1	1.6	2.1	1.7
5.3	5.0	3.8		2.3	2.6	12.8	4.6	3.6	3.3
(88) 37.8	(96) 40.1	(100) 46.5	% Profit Before Taxes/Tangible Net Worth	(14) 35.7	(25) 43.9	(13) 57.6	(22) 47.0	(16) 79.0	37.8
18.4	23.2	24.4		18.9	16.6	24.5	25.1	27.9	28.9
6.0	11.4	11.5		6.8	4.6	4.1	11.8	12.7	18.3
12.6	16.4	16.4	% Profit Before Taxes/Total Assets	16.5	20.2	15.2	16.0	19.9	13.4
7.4	7.5	8.2		9.1	6.1	7.9	7.5	10.0	9.8
1.4	2.0	2.9		4.9	1.0	.9	2.5	5.2	6.7
51.7	40.3	47.3	Sales/Net Fixed Assets	573.8	49.8	50.5	39.5	50.1	17.6
20.4	14.9	21.5		20.9	21.4	30.3	25.7	21.4	10.4
7.6	6.3	7.8		3.7	11.0	12.4	5.9	12.1	6.0
2.3	2.3	2.5	Sales/Total Assets	2.7	2.5	3.1	2.6	2.1	2.0
1.8	1.7	1.7		2.0	1.8	2.3	1.9	1.5	1.3
1.4	1.3	1.2		1.2	1.1	1.4	1.3	1.2	1.1
(80) .8	(87) .9	(92) .8	% Depr., Dep., Amort./Sales	(12) 1.1	(24) .7	(13) 1.0	(19) .5	(15) .6	
1.3	2.2	1.7		4.4	1.6	1.2	1.3	1.1	
3.0	3.4	3.3		5.0	2.9	2.6	3.4	4.1	
(39) 3.3	(45) 2.7	(40) 3.2	% Officers', Directors', Owners' Comp/Sales	(11) 4.9	(14) 2.9				
6.9	5.2	7.2		9.4	5.8				
11.8	12.6	14.2		13.7	11.5				
1730997M	1978470M	1615232M	Net Sales ($)	9464M	53673M	60135M	154809M	283325M	1053826M
1042818M	1476813M	1131728M	Total Assets ($)	6225M	32449M	32219M	89116M	182791M	788928M

M = $ thousand   MM = $ million
See Pages 1 through 15 for Explanation of Ratios and Data

Current Data Sorted By Assets						Comparative Historical Data		
1	11	10	4	1	2	# Postretirement Benefits		
						Type of Statement		
	12	25	22	3	2	Unqualified	49	38
10	45	35	4	1		Reviewed	56	71
42	55	16				Compiled	134	88
13	6					Tax Returns	1	4
25	28	26	17	2	1	Other	49	46
	141 (4/1-9/30/94)		249 (10/1/94-3/31/95)				4/1/90-3/31/91	4/1/91-3/31/92
0-500M	500M-2MM	2-10MM	10-50MM	50-100MM	100-250MM		ALL	ALL
90	146	102	43	6	3	**NUMBER OF STATEMENTS**	289	247
%	%	%	%	%	%	**ASSETS**	%	%
9.6	8.3	4.1	8.6			Cash & Equivalents	7.1	6.5
33.3	31.0	32.1	24.7			Trade Receivables - (net)	30.2	29.6
11.1	14.4	15.6	14.2			Inventory	12.3	13.2
1.2	1.1	.8	1.7			All Other Current	1.4	1.5
55.2	54.9	52.6	49.2			Total Current	51.0	50.8
36.2	37.9	39.3	41.9			Fixed Assets (net)	40.3	39.9
3.9	1.5	2.1	3.6			Intangibles (net)	2.8	2.0
4.7	5.7	6.0	5.3			All Other Non-Current	5.9	7.3
100.0	100.0	100.0	100.0			Total	100.0	100.0
						LIABILITIES		
8.5	7.8	11.1	4.3			Notes Payable-Short Term	8.4	8.6
6.2	7.2	5.7	4.1			Cur. Mat. -L/T/D	6.3	6.9
16.3	15.9	14.9	10.1			Trade Payables	13.0	16.0
.5	.4	.3	.3			Income Taxes Payable	.6	.5
7.6	6.8	7.7	9.0			All Other Current	7.9	7.2
39.0	38.1	39.7	27.8			Total Current	36.1	39.2
23.4	21.6	22.6	19.6			Long Term Debt	29.2	26.1
.2	.6	.9	1.6			Deferred Taxes	.7	.9
7.1	3.6	3.0	2.9			All Other-Non-Current	2.3	1.6
30.3	36.3	33.9	48.2			Net Worth	31.7	32.3
100.0	100.0	100.0	100.0			Total Liabilities & Net Worth	100.0	100.0
						INCOME DATA		
100.0	100.0	100.0	100.0			Net Sales	100.0	100.0
46.7	37.5	29.3	27.4			Gross Profit	38.6	35.8
42.0	33.3	23.3	20.5			Operating Expenses	32.6	31.2
4.7	4.3	6.0	6.9			Operating Profit	5.9	4.7
1.1	1.2	1.9	.9			All Other Expenses (net)	1.9	1.7
3.7	3.1	4.1	6.0			Profit Before Taxes	4.0	3.0
						RATIOS		
2.4	2.2	1.8	2.6			Current	2.2	1.9
1.4	1.4	1.3	1.7				1.5	1.3
1.0	1.1	1.0	1.3				1.1	1.0
1.9	1.6	1.4	2.0			Quick	1.5	1.5
1.2	1.0	.9	1.1		(288)		1.1	1.0
.8	.7	.7	.9				.7	.6
25 14.6	35 10.3	43 8.4	41 8.8			Sales/Receivables	36 10.2	34 10.7
36 10.2	45 8.1	53 6.9	54 6.8				46 7.9	46 7.9
51 7.2	54 6.7	64 5.7	61 6.0				59 6.2	58 6.3
7 49.2	10 35.6	17 21.4	20 17.9			Cost of Sales/Inventory	14 25.2	13 27.5
15 23.9	25 14.7	30 12.3	31 11.8				26 14.3	26 13.8
37 10.0	51 7.2	48 7.6	56 6.5				44 8.3	45 8.1
14 25.9	19 19.4	22 16.9	13 27.2			Cost of Sales/Payables	18 20.8	18 20.4
28 13.1	29 12.7	32 11.5	25 14.7				30 12.2	32 11.5
51 7.1	49 7.4	48 7.6	39 9.4				46 7.9	52 7.0
9.0	8.3	8.1	5.3			Sales/Working Capital	7.8	9.2
20.7	16.2	17.9	10.7				16.1	19.9
NM	90.1	-134.5	18.3				66.4	-125.2
9.3	5.9	6.3	11.7			EBIT/Interest	5.4	4.4
(85) 3.7	(143) 2.8	2.7	(41) 4.5			(272) 2.6	(232) 2.3
.8	1.4	1.5	2.3				1.2	1.2
3.4	3.3	3.0	8.0			Net Profit + Depr., Dep., Amort./Cur. Mat. L/T/D	3.5	2.7
(16) 1.7	(72) 1.4	(55) 1.7	(23) 2.8			(166) 2.0	(128) 1.7
.9	.9	1.1	1.3				1.0	1.0
.5	.6	.8	.6			Fixed/Worth	.7	.7
1.1	1.2	1.3	1.0				1.4	1.3
6.4	2.2	2.1	1.5				2.9	3.0
.7	.9	1.1	.6			Debt/Worth	1.1	1.1
2.4	1.8	2.2	1.2				2.2	2.2
13.8	4.5	4.4	2.1				5.2	5.2
100.0	43.7	37.8	35.4			% Profit Before Taxes/Tangible Net Worth	49.5	36.7
(71) 26.4	(134) 17.8	(98) 18.1	(42) 23.9			(253) 22.3	(218) 19.0
1.2	3.5	6.1	4.7				7.0	5.3
26.3	12.4	13.9	18.1			% Profit Before Taxes/Total Assets	15.2	12.0
9.2	6.2	5.2	9.8				7.0	5.9
-1.6	1.2	1.8	2.2				1.5	1.0
17.1	13.2	10.4	6.0			Sales/Net Fixed Assets	10.0	10.9
9.9	7.0	5.3	4.3				5.8	6.2
6.7	4.1	3.6	3.4				3.7	3.4
4.3	3.1	2.6	2.1			Sales/Total Assets	3.0	2.9
3.1	2.5	2.2	1.8				2.3	2.3
2.4	1.9	1.7	1.5				1.7	1.7
1.6	1.8	2.3	2.7			% Depr., Dep., Amort./Sales	2.1	2.2
(79) 3.3	(136) 3.1	(99) 3.4	(37) 4.2			(266) 3.8	(233) 3.7
5.2	4.7	4.5	5.3				5.0	5.0
5.9	4.0	2.1	1.9			% Officers', Directors', Owners' Comp/Sales	3.0	3.3
(50) 8.5	(76) 6.2	(43) 3.1	(10) 3.7			(130) 5.7	(114) 5.3
12.7	10.7	7.0	5.8				9.9	8.9
69805M	413208M	989543M	1531324M	727100M	799138M	Net Sales ($)	3112703M	2676318M
21986M	162675M	476455M	858211M	447041M	595246M	Total Assets ($)	1894705M	1351902M

M = $ thousand　　MM = $ million
See Pages 1 through 15 for Explanation of Ratios and Data

Comparative Historical Data | | | | **Current Data Sorted By Sales** | | | | | |

7	10	29	# Postretirement Benefits / Type of Statement	1	8	3	4	8	5
45	49	64	Unqualified		5	3	10	26	20
75	73	95	Reviewed	6	32	23	18	11	5
125	113	113	Compiled	35	43	16	17	2	
7	12	19	Tax Returns	11	7		1		
56	66	99	Other	22	24	11	13	12	17
4/1/92-3/31/93	4/1/93-3/31/94	4/1/94-3/31/95		141 (4/1-9/30/94)			249 (10/1/94-3/31/95)		
ALL	ALL	ALL		0-1MM	1-3MM	3-5MM	5-10MM	10-25MM	25MM & OVER
308	313	390	NUMBER OF STATEMENTS	74	111	53	59	51	42
%	%	%	**ASSETS**	%	%	%	%	%	%
7.5	7.2	7.6	Cash & Equivalents	11.1	7.6	6.4	5.0	4.9	10.2
30.9	29.8	31.0	Trade Receivables - (net)	29.8	31.0	34.5	33.9	30.8	24.7
12.3	13.5	13.9	Inventory	10.3	13.7	15.0	15.2	17.4	13.1
1.6	1.5	1.1	All Other Current	1.4	1.0	1.2	.9	.7	1.7
52.3	52.1	53.6	Total Current	52.6	53.3	57.1	55.0	53.8	49.6
39.4	40.0	38.2	Fixed Assets (net)	38.3	39.7	34.7	38.0	38.4	39.0
1.9	2.2	2.7	Intangibles (net)	4.2	1.8	1.6	1.8	1.9	6.0
6.4	5.8	5.5	All Other Non-Current	4.9	5.3	6.6	5.3	5.9	5.4
100.0	100.0	100.0	Total	100.0	100.0	100.0	100.0	100.0	100.0
			LIABILITIES						
7.8	8.7	8.4	Notes Payable-Short Term	7.8	7.3	10.4	10.3	11.3	3.8
7.1	6.2	6.2	Cur. Mat.-L/T/D	6.3	7.2	6.2	6.3	5.2	3.9
14.6	14.8	14.9	Trade Payables	15.5	15.0	15.7	17.7	13.4	10.3
.5	1.1	.4	Income Taxes Payable	.4	.4	.3	.4	.3	.3
8.0	8.0	7.5	All Other Current	8.4	6.5	5.8	7.3	9.1	8.5
37.9	38.8	37.3	Total Current	38.5	36.5	38.4	42.1	39.4	26.8
24.5	23.6	22.1	Long Term Debt	26.2	21.7	20.7	23.0	19.0	19.6
.9	.9	.7	Deferred Taxes	.3	.5	.8	.7	1.0	1.4
2.9	4.5	4.2	All Other-Non-Current	8.3	3.0	5.3	2.1	2.2	3.6
33.8	32.2	35.8	Net Worth	26.7	38.3	34.8	32.1	38.4	48.5
100.0	100.0	100.0	Total Liabilities & Net Worth	100.0	100.0	100.0	100.0	100.0	100.0
			INCOME DATA						
100.0	100.0	100.0	Net Sales	100.0	100.0	100.0	100.0	100.0	100.0
37.5	36.7	36.3	Gross Profit	49.5	38.2	36.2	28.5	28.5	28.6
32.3	32.1	31.1	Operating Expenses	44.6	34.4	30.7	23.1	22.4	21.0
5.1	4.7	5.2	Operating Profit	4.9	3.9	5.5	5.4	6.1	7.6
1.6	1.4	1.3	All Other Expenses (net)	1.4	1.0	1.6	1.5	1.9	.9
3.6	3.3	3.9	Profit Before Taxes	3.5	2.9	3.9	3.9	4.3	6.8
			RATIOS						
2.1	2.1	2.3	Current	2.4	2.3	2.4	1.9	1.8	3.1
1.4	1.4	1.4		1.4	1.5	1.4	1.3	1.6	1.6
1.0	1.0	1.1		1.0	1.0	1.1	1.0	1.1	1.3
1.5	1.5	1.7	Quick	1.8	1.9	1.9	1.3	1.4	2.2
1.1	(312) 1.0	1.1		1.2	1.1	.9	.9	.9	1.2
.7	.7	.7		.7	.7	.7	.7	.7	.8
34 10.7	35 10.3	35 10.3	Sales/Receivables	24 15.5	33 11.0	39 9.4	39 9.4	44 8.3	40 9.2
45 8.2	46 8.0	46 7.9		36 10.2	45 8.2	49 7.4	50 7.3	51 7.1	52 7.0
57 6.4	57 6.4	58 6.3		49 7.4	54 6.7	61 6.0	59 6.2	60 6.1	61 6.0
11 32.3	14 26.5	13 27.7	Cost of Sales/Inventory	7 50.8	10 34.8	11 32.0	17 21.7	18 19.9	21 17.7
22 16.9	24 15.0	27 13.7		15 23.8	23 15.9	32 11.3	27 13.6	31 11.8	30 12.2
38 9.7	46 8.0	48 7.6		53 6.9	46 8.0	65 5.6	39 9.4	55 6.6	54 6.7
18 20.1	19 19.5	19 19.6	Cost of Sales/Payables	15 24.6	17 21.3	19 19.5	23 16.2	18 20.5	18 20.3
30 12.1	31 11.9	30 12.2		31 11.7	30 12.2	29 12.8	32 11.4	27 13.6	27 13.7
49 7.5	47 7.8	46 7.9		58 6.3	47 7.8	49 7.4	48 7.6	41 8.8	39 9.3
8.7	8.9	7.9	Sales/Working Capital	8.8	8.2	7.5	9.3	8.1	4.1
17.9	18.3	15.8		20.9	15.8	12.6	19.3	14.0	10.9
242.4	-492.6	113.9		-120.5	546.5	82.5	298.9	48.6	19.2
5.7	6.0	7.0	EBIT/Interest	8.9	5.2	7.7	6.5	9.1	20.6
(289) 2.5	(296) 2.5	(380) 2.9		(69) 3.0	(110) 2.8	(51) 2.5	2.8	(40) 3.4	4.6
1.4	1.4	1.4		.8	1.1	1.5	1.5	1.7	2.3
2.8	4.2	3.6	Net Profit + Depr., Dep., Amort./Cur. Mat. L/T/D	2.6	3.0	3.5	2.8	4.4	8.7
(146) 1.9	(135) 1.8	(169) 1.7		(14) 1.2	(52) 1.4	(22) 1.6	(32) 1.7	(27) 1.8	(22) 3.5
1.2	1.1	1.0		.8	.9	1.1	1.0	1.2	1.2
.6	.7	.6	Fixed/Worth	.5	.6	.4	.8	.7	.5
1.3	1.3	1.2		1.2	1.3	1.1	1.4	1.1	1.0
2.7	2.9	2.4		13.5	2.4	2.0	2.0	1.6	1.7
1.0	1.1	.9	Debt/Worth	.8	.8	1.0	1.2	.9	.4
2.1	2.1	1.9		2.8	1.7	2.1	2.2	1.6	1.4
4.7	5.6	4.7		NM	4.0	4.5	3.8	4.1	2.7
45.4	39.3	45.0	% Profit Before Taxes/Tangible Net Worth	102.6	39.9	49.4	48.6	36.5	40.1
(278) 22.2	(276) 17.6	(352) 20.9		(56) 26.6	(103) 16.4	(49) 16.8	(55) 24.2	(50) 17.8	(39) 28.5
6.0	4.3	4.7		1.6	1.0	5.3	7.4	6.5	9.8
14.4	13.9	15.3	% Profit Before Taxes/Total Assets	25.4	12.4	13.0	14.4	14.7	19.6
6.6	5.6	6.5		8.1	6.0	6.1	6.1	6.1	10.6
1.8	.9	1.2		-1.3	.0	2.2	2.0	1.8	3.9
11.4	11.5	11.8	Sales/Net Fixed Assets	13.4	13.5	12.4	12.2	10.3	6.7
6.3	6.0	6.5		9.1	7.4	6.9	6.1	5.4	4.4
4.0	3.7	4.0		5.2	3.8	4.1	3.7	3.9	3.4
3.1	3.0	3.1	Sales/Total Assets	4.0	3.1	2.9	3.1	2.6	2.2
2.4	2.3	2.3		3.0	2.5	2.4	2.5	2.1	1.8
1.9	1.8	1.8		2.1	1.9	1.9	1.8	1.8	1.5
2.2	2.3	2.0	% Depr., Dep., Amort./Sales	1.8	1.9	1.6	1.9	2.2	2.9
(281) 3.5	(295) 3.6	(357) 3.5		(64) 3.9	(104) 3.4	(47) 2.6	(49) 3.3	(34) 3.5	4.0
5.3	5.4	4.9		5.8	4.9	4.7	4.1	4.3	5.3
3.5	3.5	3.3	% Officers', Directors', Owners' Comp/Sales	7.0	4.0	3.8	2.1	2.2	
(168) 5.6	(172) 5.1	(180) 5.9		(40) 9.8	(61) 6.2	(22)	(27) 4.2	(24) 3.0	
9.7	9.1	10.5		13.2	10.4	10.1	8.3	7.1	
2963557M	3209669M	4530118M	Net Sales ($)	44047M	215000M	205837M	419925M	768895M	2876414M
1491037M	1573943M	2561614M	Total Assets ($)	17973M	92444M	99329M	195247M	381246M	1775375M

M = $ thousand   MM = $ million
See Pages 1 through 15 for Explanation of Ratios and Data

Current Data Sorted By Assets							Comparative Historical Data	
5	10	36	5		1	# Postretirement Benefits		
						Type of Statement		
1	11	96	51	4	3	Unqualified	177	168
18	86	139	13			Reviewed	242	267
87	122	60	4			Compiled	282	267
11	8	5				Tax Returns	7	17
39	56	93	35	2	2	Other	188	175
	351 (4/1-9/30/94)			595 (10/1/94-3/31/95)			4/1/90-3/31/91	4/1/91-3/31/92
0-500M	500M-2MM	2-10MM	10-50MM	50-100MM	100-250MM		ALL	ALL
156	283	393	103	6	5	**NUMBER OF STATEMENTS**	896	894
%	%	%	%	%	%	**ASSETS**	%	%
9.4	7.5	6.2	4.3			Cash & Equivalents	7.3	7.6
35.4	32.7	29.9	29.1			Trade Receivables - (net)	31.5	30.2
8.6	10.4	11.1	12.8			Inventory	11.4	10.7
1.3	1.2	1.1	1.4			All Other Current	1.3	1.2
54.7	51.7	48.2	47.6			Total Current	51.5	49.7
36.0	41.6	44.5	43.2			Fixed Assets (net)	40.8	42.2
2.6	1.5	1.9	2.3			Intangibles (net)	1.5	1.7
6.7	5.2	5.5	6.9			All Other Non-Current	6.2	6.3
100.0	100.0	100.0	100.0			Total	100.0	100.0
						LIABILITIES		
5.6	6.0	7.8	7.2			Notes Payable-Short Term	7.2	8.0
8.0	8.1	7.2	6.6			Cur. Mat. -L/T/D	6.9	7.4
16.0	15.5	13.2	14.5			Trade Payables	14.6	13.4
.4	.4	.4	.4			Income Taxes Payable	.6	.4
9.1	7.3	7.6	8.2			All Other Current	7.4	7.4
39.2	37.2	36.2	36.9			Total Current	36.7	36.7
23.1	26.1	24.9	27.2			Long Term Debt	25.9	26.3
.2	.9	1.2	1.1			Deferred Taxes	.9	.8
5.6	2.6	2.5	2.7			All Other-Non-Current	2.6	2.8
31.9	33.1	35.2	32.2			Net Worth	33.9	33.3
100.0	100.0	100.0	100.0			Total Liabilities & Net Worth	100.0	100.0
						INCOME DATA		
100.0	100.0	100.0	100.0			Net Sales	100.0	100.0
45.2	35.8	29.2	24.2			Gross Profit	34.3	33.7
39.3	32.0	24.0	18.1			Operating Expenses	29.5	29.6
5.9	3.8	5.2	6.1			Operating Profit	4.8	4.1
1.1	1.3	1.7	1.6			All Other Expenses (net)	1.6	1.9
4.8	2.5	3.5	4.5			Profit Before Taxes	3.2	2.3
						RATIOS		
2.5	2.0	1.9	1.7				2.1	2.0
1.5	1.4	1.3	1.3			Current	1.4	1.4
1.0	1.0	1.0	1.0				1.1	1.0
1.9	1.7	1.5	1.3				1.6	1.6
1.3	1.1	1.0	.9			Quick	(895) 1.1	1.0
.8	.8	.8	.7				.8	.7
29 12.5	38 9.6	42 8.6	48 7.6				38 9.5	38 9.6
38 9.7	47 7.8	54 6.8	59 6.2			Sales/Receivables	49 7.4	49 7.5
49 7.4	59 6.2	66 5.5	69 5.3				62 5.9	60 6.1
4 89.3	11 34.3	17 21.6	21 17.8				13 27.3	14 26.6
13 28.7	20 18.6	25 14.4	30 12.0			Cost of Sales/Inventory	24 14.9	22 16.6
25 14.8	31 11.8	38 9.6	43 8.5				38 9.5	35 10.3
15 23.7	20 18.6	21 17.7	25 14.8				19 19.3	19 19.5
29 12.7	31 11.7	31 11.8	33 10.9			Cost of Sales/Payables	29 12.5	28 13.0
44 8.3	49 7.5	41 8.8	54 6.8				46 7.9	42 8.6
10.4	8.7	8.3	9.1				8.2	8.4
20.6	18.8	19.0	20.0			Sales/Working Capital	15.3	17.7
NM	158.9	115.0	165.7				82.2	UND
7.7	5.3	5.1	5.6				4.6	4.0
(146) 4.4	(276) 2.5	(383) 2.7	(98) 3.1			EBIT/Interest	(851) 2.2	(856) 1.9
1.5	1.2	1.3	1.7				1.2	.9
3.8	2.4	2.9	2.7			Net Profit + Depr., Dep.,	3.1	2.3
(39) 2.1	(162) 1.6	(220) 1.7	(59) 2.0			Amort./Cur. Mat. L /T/D	(563) 1.7	(498) 1.3
1.1	.9	1.1	1.5				1.0	.7
.6	.7	.8	.9				.7	.7
1.1	1.3	1.3	1.6			Fixed/Worth	1.3	1.4
3.4	2.7	2.7	2.7				2.6	2.8
.9	1.1	1.1	1.4				1.0	1.0
2.0	2.0	2.0	2.5			Debt/Worth	2.1	2.1
12.1	4.7	4.0	4.6				4.5	5.1
80.3	38.9	36.5	39.8			% Profit Before Taxes/Tangible	35.2	32.5
(135) 35.7	(256) 17.9	(372) 18.2	(99) 24.9			Net Worth	(820) 18.2	(810) 13.4
9.6	5.0	5.9	13.2				4.6	.5
25.5	11.9	11.1	12.0			% Profit Before Taxes/Total	11.9	10.4
10.3	6.0	5.8	6.9			Assets	5.7	3.7
2.6	1.0	1.4	3.4				.8	-.6
18.3	10.0	6.7	5.6				9.5	8.7
10.1	5.8	4.4	4.1			Sales/Net Fixed Assets	5.5	5.1
5.7	3.8	3.0	3.1				3.5	3.3
4.2	3.1	2.4	2.1				2.9	2.8
3.2	2.4	1.9	1.7			Sales/Total Assets	2.1	2.1
2.5	1.9	1.6	1.5				1.7	1.7
1.8	2.4	3.1	3.2				2.4	2.6
(140) 3.4	(272) 3.8	(377) 4.4	(88) 4.2			% Depr., Dep., Amort./Sales	(836) 3.8	(848) 4.0
5.6	6.0	5.8	5.0				5.3	5.6
4.4	3.6	2.5	1.2			% Officers', Directors',	3.0	2.7
(95) 7.9	(164) 5.9	(189) 4.1	(18) 2.3			Owners' Comp/Sales	(414) 5.3	(419) 5.3
11.8	8.4	6.7	3.8				8.9	8.8
139026M	793050M	3440878M	3748854M	778139M	1124546M	Net Sales ($)	8797038M	7565226M
42178M	325849M	1759804M	2114516M	455116M	818315M	Total Assets ($)	4805628M	4065597M

M = $ thousand   MM = $ million
See Pages 1 through 15 for Explanation of Ratios and Data

Comparative Historical Data				Current Data Sorted By Sales					
24	40	57	# Postretirement Benefits / Type of Statement	3	10	8	18	12	6
174	141	166	Unqualified	1	8	17	27	65	48
284	285	256	Reviewed	9	59	57	85	41	5
241	228	273	Compiled	57	118	48	37	10	3
20	23	24	Tax Returns	10	5	5	4		
181	207	227	Other	33	42	39	48	33	32
4/1/92-3/31/93 ALL	4/1/93-3/31/94 ALL	4/1/94-3/31/95 ALL		351 (4/1-9/30/94) 0-1MM	1-3MM	3-5MM	595 (10/1/94-3/31/95) 5-10MM	10-25MM	25MM & OVER
900	884	946	NUMBER OF STATEMENTS	110	232	166	201	149	88
%	%	%	ASSETS	%	%	%	%	%	%
7.6	6.6	6.9	Cash & Equivalents	8.9	8.3	6.8	6.8	4.6	4.7
30.5	31.3	31.5	Trade Receivables - (net)	31.7	32.4	31.5	29.5	32.9	31.2
11.2	10.8	10.6	Inventory	7.9	8.8	11.4	11.7	11.5	13.6
1.3	1.0	1.2	All Other Current	1.5	1.0	1.3	1.1	1.1	1.2
50.5	49.7	50.2	Total Current	50.0	50.5	50.9	49.1	50.1	50.7
41.9	42.7	42.0	Fixed Assets (net)	40.1	42.2	42.8	42.4	43.0	40.4
1.9	1.7	2.0	Intangibles (net)	3.3	1.4	2.1	1.7	1.7	2.5
5.6	5.9	5.8	All Other Non-Current	6.6	5.9	4.1	6.9	5.2	6.4
100.0	100.0	100.0	Total	100.0	100.0	100.0	100.0	100.0	100.0
			LIABILITIES						
7.1	7.0	6.8	Notes Payable-Short Term	5.1	5.6	6.8	7.2	9.0	7.5
7.1	7.0	7.5	Cur. Mat.-L/T/D	8.4	8.3	7.6	7.2	6.7	5.8
13.4	13.8	14.5	Trade Payables	14.1	14.6	15.0	13.3	15.2	15.0
.5	.9	.4	Income Taxes Payable	.5	.2	.4	.4	.5	.4
7.5	8.1	7.9	All Other Current	9.1	6.7	8.0	7.3	8.6	9.1
35.5	36.9	37.0	Total Current	37.2	35.6	37.8	35.4	40.0	37.8
26.4	25.7	25.2	Long Term Debt	27.7	27.0	24.7	23.2	24.3	24.3
.9	.9	.9	Deferred Taxes	.2	.7	1.2	1.2	1.0	1.3
2.9	3.3	3.1	All Other-Non-Current	5.3	3.5	2.2	2.7	2.3	3.2
34.4	33.1	33.7	Net Worth	29.6	33.1	34.0	37.5	32.4	33.3
100.0	100.0	100.0	Total Liabilities & Net Worth	100.0	100.0	100.0	100.0	100.0	100.0
			INCOME DATA						
100.0	100.0	100.0	Net Sales	100.0	100.0	100.0	100.0	100.0	100.0
34.6	34.5	33.2	Gross Profit	46.8	38.4	32.2	29.3	26.8	24.3
30.2	30.2	28.2	Operating Expenses	40.6	34.0	27.8	24.3	22.1	17.6
4.4	4.2	5.0	Operating Profit	6.2	4.4	4.4	5.0	4.7	6.7
1.5	1.5	1.4	All Other Expenses (net)	1.3	1.5	1.5	1.4	1.4	1.6
2.9	2.8	3.6	Profit Before Taxes	4.9	2.9	3.0	3.6	3.3	5.1
			RATIOS						
2.2 / 1.5 / 1.0	2.0 / 1.4 / 1.0	2.0 / 1.4 / 1.0	Current	2.5 / 1.4 / .9	2.1 / 1.5 / 1.1	2.0 / 1.4 / 1.0	2.0 / 1.4 / 1.1	1.8 / 1.2 / 1.0	1.7 / 1.3 / 1.0
1.6 / 1.1 / .7	1.6 / 1.0 / .7	1.6 / 1.0 / .7	Quick	2.0 / 1.1 / .7	1.7 / 1.2 / .8	1.6 / 1.1 / .8	1.5 / 1.0 / .8	1.4 / .9 / .7	1.3 / .9 / .7
38 9.7 / 48 7.6 / 61 6.0	39 9.3 / 50 7.3 / 63 5.8	38 9.5 / 49 7.4 / 63 5.8	Sales/Receivables	29 12.4 / 41 9.0 / 50 7.3	35 10.4 / 45 8.2 / 58 6.3	39 9.3 / 51 7.2 / 61 6.0	39 9.3 / 50 7.3 / 64 5.7	46 8.0 / 58 6.3 / 66 5.5	49 7.5 / 60 6.1 / 70 5.2
14 26.5 / 24 15.4 / 37 9.8	13 28.3 / 23 16.2 / 37 10.0	13 28.6 / 22 16.3 / 36 10.2	Cost of Sales/Inventory	5 69.8 / 14 25.8 / 29 12.4	8 46.6 / 18 20.6 / 29 12.8	14 25.4 / 23 16.1 / 36 10.1	17 21.7 / 23 14.0 / 39 9.4	17 22.0 / 23 15.8 / 36 10.2	23 16.0 / 30 12.0 / 43 8.4
19 19.4 / 27 13.5 / 43 8.4	20 18.6 / 30 12.3 / 46 8.0	21 17.6 / 31 11.7 / 46 8.0	Cost of Sales/Payables	18 19.9 / 32 11.5 / 45 8.1	18 20.0 / 30 12.3 / 49 7.4	20 18.3 / 32 11.4 / 45 8.2	20 18.2 / 29 12.4 / 39 9.3	23 15.8 / 31 11.7 / 46 8.0	26 14.2 / 34 10.6 / 53 6.9
7.9 / 16.1 / 130.3	8.3 / 17.6 / 774.8	8.8 / 19.2 / 147.7	Sales/Working Capital	10.0 / 21.9 / -124.9	8.8 / 18.8 / 126.7	8.0 / 18.1 / 136.8	8.5 / 16.6 / 82.5	10.5 / 24.7 / 188.4	8.6 / 16.3 / 129.6
(853) 5.0 / 2.3 / 1.1	(848) 5.1 / 2.4 / 1.1	(914) 5.7 / 2.8 / 1.4	EBIT/Interest	(102) 7.4 / 4.2 / 1.2	(224) 5.4 / 2.5 / 1.2	(162) 5.1 / 2.5 / 1.3	(197) 5.5 / 2.8 / 1.2	(145) 5.0 / 3.2 / 1.7	(84) 5.9 / 3.3 / 2.0
(460) 2.5 / 1.6 / 1.0	(421) 2.7 / 1.5 / .9	(485) 2.7 / 1.7 / 1.1	Net Profit + Depr., Dep., Amort./Cur. Mat. L/T/D	(27) 3.1 / 1.9 / .7	(108) 2.3 / 1.4 / .9	(109) 2.6 / 1.7 / 1.2	(110) 2.9 / 1.8 / 1.1	(85) 3.0 / 1.8 / 1.2	(46) 3.0 / 2.1 / 1.5
.7 / 1.3 / 2.8	.8 / 1.4 / 2.8	.8 / 1.3 / 2.7	Fixed/Worth	.7 / 1.7 / 7.0	.7 / 1.3 / 3.2	.8 / 1.3 / 2.4	.7 / 1.2 / 2.7	1.0 / 1.4 / 2.6	.8 / 1.4 / 2.3
1.0 / 2.0 / 4.8	1.1 / 2.2 / 4.4	1.1 / 2.1 / 4.5	Debt/Worth	1.0 / 2.6 / 19.2	1.0 / 1.9 / 5.7	1.2 / 2.0 / 4.1	1.0 / 1.9 / 3.9	1.2 / 2.3 / 4.1	1.4 / 2.3 / 4.1
(818) 38.4 / 17.0 / 3.7	(816) 37.4 / 16.7 / 3.6	(871) 40.9 / 20.8 / 6.6	% Profit Before Taxes/Tangible Net Worth	(92) 88.1 / 42.5 / 9.4	(209) 42.3 / 18.6 / 5.0	(153) 35.0 / 18.1 / 4.7	(189) 36.3 / 18.6 / 4.8	(144) 39.8 / 19.5 / 9.9	(84) 42.9 / 26.4 / 17.2
12.6 / 5.2 / .4	11.7 / 5.0 / .5	12.6 / 6.3 / 1.7	% Profit Before Taxes/Total Assets	26.7 / 10.3 / .8	12.2 / 6.0 / 1.1	10.8 / 6.0 / 1.1	11.9 / 5.9 / 1.0	11.4 / 5.9 / 2.3	13.0 / 8.8 / 4.4
8.9 / 5.2 / 3.3	8.9 / 5.3 / 3.2	9.1 / 5.3 / 3.3	Sales/Net Fixed Assets	14.0 / 7.2 / 4.0	10.8 / 5.9 / 3.5	8.6 / 5.1 / 3.2	7.6 / 5.0 / 3.2	7.6 / 4.8 / 3.3	5.9 / 4.5 / 3.2
2.8 / 2.2 / 1.7	2.8 / 2.2 / 1.7	2.8 / 2.2 / 1.7	Sales/Total Assets	3.7 / 2.7 / 1.9	3.2 / 2.5 / 1.8	2.9 / 2.2 / 1.6	2.5 / 2.1 / 1.6	2.5 / 2.1 / 1.7	2.2 / 1.8 / 1.6
(847) 2.6 / 3.9 / 5.5	(813) 2.7 / 4.0 / 5.7	(885) 2.7 / 4.1 / 5.8	% Depr., Dep., Amort./Sales	(95) 2.4 / 4.1 / 6.8	(222) 2.3 / 3.9 / 6.1	(163) 2.8 / 4.4 / 6.4	(191) 2.7 / 4.1 / 5.5	(143) 3.1 / 3.9 / 5.1	(71) 2.9 / 3.9 / 4.9
(432) 3.1 / 5.6 / 9.3	(416) 2.9 / 5.3 / 8.8	(469) 2.9 / 5.2 / 8.1	% Officers', Directors', Owners' Comp/Sales	(62) 5.3 / 8.1 / 11.8	(145) 4.1 / 6.2 / 8.9	(85) 2.8 / 4.3 / 7.2	(105) 2.6 / 3.9 / 7.0	(60) 2.0 / 3.2 / 5.8	(12) 1.3 / 2.2 / 3.8
9278773M	8404288M	10024493M	Net Sales ($)	65546M	448279M	668214M	1435911M	2225084M	5181459M
5121918M	4375563M	5515778M	Total Assets ($)	30572M	213420M	339372M	783150M	1111208M	3038056M

M = $ thousand   MM = $ million
See Pages 1 through 15 for Explanation of Ratios and Data

MANUFACTURERS—MANIFOLD BUSINESS FORMS. SIC# 2761

Current Data Sorted By Assets | Comparative Historical Data

# Postretirement Benefits / Type of Statement	0-500M	500M-2MM	2-10MM	10-50MM	50-100MM	100-250MM	4/1/90-3/31/91 ALL	4/1/91-3/31/92 ALL
# Postretirement Benefits		2	4	1				
Unqualified		1	15	7	1	1	30	31
Reviewed	2	6	14				19	22
Compiled	3	11	1				15	10
Tax Returns		1					1	1
Other	3	9	10	6		1	15	19
		29 (4/1-9/30/94)		63 (10/1/94-3/31/95)				
NUMBER OF STATEMENTS	8	28	40	13	1	2	80	83
ASSETS	%	%	%	%	%	%	%	%
Cash & Equivalents		5.1	5.5	7.4			8.4	5.1
Trade Receivables - (net)		38.5	27.7	27.3			28.9	31.8
Inventory		15.7	19.5	18.3			17.0	14.7
All Other Current		1.1	1.2	1.1			2.1	1.0
Total Current		60.4	54.0	54.1			56.4	52.7
Fixed Assets (net)		34.9	37.3	34.1			36.6	37.8
Intangibles (net)		.5	2.7	5.2			1.5	4.4
All Other Non-Current		4.2	6.0	6.6			5.5	5.2
Total		100.0	100.0	100.0			100.0	100.0
LIABILITIES								
Notes Payable-Short Term		10.8	11.9	6.6			8.3	7.5
Cur. Mat. -L/T/D		5.6	5.3	3.1			5.8	5.9
Trade Payables		21.3	15.2	10.7			13.5	16.4
Income Taxes Payable		.4	.3	.7			.7	.4
All Other Current		7.7	7.5	13.8			7.0	7.3
Total Current		45.7	40.2	34.9			35.4	37.5
Long Term Debt		16.6	18.4	18.3			21.3	21.8
Deferred Taxes		.6	1.2	2.0			1.3	1.4
All Other-Non-Current		4.9	3.1	3.4			4.4	3.6
Net Worth		32.2	37.1	41.4			37.6	35.8
Total Liabilities & Net Worth		100.0	100.0	100.0			100.0	100.0
INCOME DATA								
Net Sales		100.0	100.0	100.0			100.0	100.0
Gross Profit		27.2	24.1	20.9			28.5	29.7
Operating Expenses		24.1	21.4	15.1			24.9	27.1
Operating Profit		3.1	2.7	5.8			3.6	2.6
All Other Expenses (net)		.8	1.1	1.0			1.6	1.7
Profit Before Taxes		2.3	1.6	4.7			2.0	.8
RATIOS								
Current		1.9	1.7	2.5			2.5	2.3
		1.3	1.2	1.9			1.6	1.6
		1.1	1.1	1.0			1.2	1.1
Quick		1.3	1.1	1.7			1.6	1.6
		1.0	.8	1.2			1.0	1.0
		.7	.6	.8			.7	.7
Sales/Receivables		36 10.2	35 10.4	41 8.8			34 10.8	34 10.8
		40 9.2	41 8.8	47 7.7			41 8.9	42 8.7
		53 6.9	51 7.2	59 6.2			50 7.3	55 6.6
Cost of Sales/Inventory		17 21.4	24 14.9	23 15.7			29 12.7	18 20.0
		24 14.9	38 9.7	30 12.3			36 10.2	33 11.0
		41 8.9	54 6.8	50 7.3			51 7.2	56 6.5
Cost of Sales/Payables		25 14.7	20 18.5	13 28.3			17 21.7	17 21.5
		30 12.2	25 14.7	17 21.2			23 16.0	25 14.8
		41 9.0	39 9.4	37 10.0			38 9.7	52 7.0
Sales/Working Capital		12.2	9.6	7.1			5.8	7.2
		22.5	21.9	9.3			14.5	14.2
		197.2	88.2	294.1			33.1	115.1
EBIT/Interest		6.7	4.4	6.0			5.1	4.2
		(27) 3.9	(36) 2.2	(11) 2.6			(72) 1.9	(70) 2.0
		1.6	1.2	2.2			1.1	.2
Net Profit + Depr., Dep., Amort./Cur. Mat. L./T/D		3.0	3.8				3.7	2.7
		(14) 1.6	(16) 1.4				(47) 2.3	(38) 1.2
		.8	.4				1.1	.3
Fixed/Worth		.6	.6	.7			.5	.6
		1.2	1.2	1.1			.9	1.2
		2.3	1.7	1.9			1.9	2.3
Debt/Worth		1.0	1.1	.8			.7	.8
		2.3	1.9	1.3			1.8	1.9
		4.1	3.7	4.6			4.0	6.6
% Profit Before Taxes/Tangible Net Worth		36.3	27.8	50.3			26.6	23.6
		(27) 17.8	(38) 12.0	34.3			(72) 13.1	(72) 10.8
		13.0	.6	16.2			4.8	.6
% Profit Before Taxes/Total Assets		16.6	9.8	13.2			9.7	8.2
		5.6	5.1	7.6			3.6	2.6
		1.1	.3	3.8			.9	-3.1
Sales/Net Fixed Assets		18.8	9.5	9.7			10.9	10.3
		8.0	6.5	5.5			5.7	5.5
		5.6	4.0	3.2			4.1	3.5
Sales/Total Assets		4.2	2.6	2.5			2.9	3.0
		2.9	2.2	2.3			2.2	2.2
		2.5	1.9	1.4			1.8	1.6
% Depr., Dep., Amort./Sales		1.6	2.3	1.8			2.4	1.6
		(25) 2.9	(36) 3.1	(10) 2.7			(69) 3.3	(70) 3.2
		3.8	4.4	4.5			4.6	4.4
% Officers', Directors', Owners' Comp/Sales		2.7	2.8				2.8	1.6
		(18) 3.9	(13) 4.9				(22) 5.0	(26) 4.1
		5.6	7.9				7.6	7.6
Net Sales ($)	11196M	108824M	428808M	518350M	162235M	517044M	1970120M	2034827M
Total Assets ($)	2234M	34092M	190771M	262711M	77788M	277899M	1013583M	1166245M

M = $ thousand   MM = $ million
See Pages 1 through 15 for Explanation of Ratios and Data

Comparative Historical Data   **Current Data Sorted By Sales**

1	3	7							
			# Postretirement Benefits		2	2	2	1	
			Type of Statement						
25	19	25	Unqualified			2	9	8	6
18	14	22	Reviewed	1	2	4	10	5	
18	12	15	Compiled	1	6	4	4		
1	2	1	Tax Returns			1			
24	34	29	Other	3	6	2	4	7	7
4/1/92-3/31/93	4/1/93-3/31/94	4/1/94-3/31/95			**29 (4/1-9/30/94)**		**63 (10/1/94-3/31/95)**		
ALL	ALL	ALL		0-1MM	1-3MM	3-5MM	5-10MM	10-25MM	25MM & OVER
86	81	92	**NUMBER OF STATEMENTS**	5	14	13	27	20	13
%	%	%	**ASSETS**	%	%	%	%	%	%
6.5	7.4	6.5	Cash & Equivalents		10.6	4.3	7.6	5.7	4.9
32.4	30.8	32.9	Trade Receivables - (net)		38.1	34.4	32.8	26.9	29.1
17.4	14.9	17.1	Inventory		15.8	12.9	18.5	17.8	20.7
1.4	3.5	1.5	All Other Current		1.0	1.4	1.6	.6	3.5
57.6	56.7	57.9	Total Current		65.5	52.9	60.5	50.9	58.3
34.9	34.2	34.2	Fixed Assets (net)		29.6	40.6	34.4	37.0	30.0
1.7	2.8	2.3	Intangibles (net)		1.0	.5	1.3	3.6	6.4
5.8	6.4	5.6	All Other Non-Current		4.0	6.0	3.8	8.4	5.4
100.0	100.0	100.0	Total		100.0	100.0	100.0	100.0	100.0
			LIABILITIES						
7.9	8.4	10.2	Notes Payable-Short Term		9.0	10.0	11.0	11.3	6.6
5.9	5.9	5.0	Cur. Mat.-L /T/D		5.5	6.3	4.8	4.9	2.7
15.9	15.9	16.9	Trade Payables		16.6	18.2	20.0	14.5	11.0
.4	1.4	.4	Income Taxes Payable		.3	.5	.2	.8	.6
7.4	7.4	9.1	All Other Current		8.8	6.1	10.0	8.7	11.8
37.5	39.1	41.6	Total Current		40.2	41.1	45.9	40.2	32.8
19.0	16.6	17.5	Long Term Debt		16.6	21.1	13.5	19.0	18.4
1.0	1.0	1.0	Deferred Taxes		.0	.6	1.3	1.8	1.0
3.5	2.9	3.5	All Other-Non-Current		1.2	4.8	3.4	4.8	4.4
39.0	40.4	36.5	Net Worth		42.0	32.3	35.9	34.3	43.4
100.0	100.0	100.0	Total Liabilities & Net Worth		100.0	100.0	100.0	100.0	100.0
			INCOME DATA						
100.0	100.0	100.0	Net Sales		100.0	100.0	100.0	100.0	100.0
30.6	28.7	26.9	Gross Profit		31.1	22.1	23.9	27.5	25.3
26.8	25.7	23.5	Operating Expenses		28.7	20.9	21.1	22.5	20.0
3.7	3.0	3.4	Operating Profit		2.4	1.2	2.8	5.0	5.2
1.2	.8	1.0	All Other Expenses (net)		.1	1.5	1.0	1.0	1.3
2.5	2.2	2.5	Profit Before Taxes		2.3	-.3	1.8	4.0	3.9
			RATIOS						
2.5	2.4	2.0			2.5	1.5	2.0	1.7	2.9
1.6	1.5	1.3	Current		1.9	1.2	1.2	1.3	1.9
1.1	1.0	1.1			1.2	1.1	1.1	1.0	1.3
1.5	1.5	1.4			1.9	1.2	1.5	1.0	1.7
1.0	.9	.9	Quick		1.1	.8	.9	.8	1.2
.7	.6	.7			.8	.7	.7	.6	.8
35 10.4	33 11.1	36 10.2			37 10.0	37 9.9	34 10.8	34 10.7	41 9.0
43 8.5	42 8.6	43 8.5	Sales/Receivables		43 8.4	42 8.6	38 9.6	47 7.8	46 7.9
53 6.9	54 6.8	54 6.7			49 7.5	59 6.2	45 8.2	61 6.0	58 6.3
20 18.7	17 20.9	19 19.2			0 UND	16 22.7	18 19.9	24 15.4	27 13.3
32 11.4	28 12.9	28 13.0	Cost of Sales/Inventory		21 17.1	25 14.5	26 13.8	42 8.6	42 8.7
47 7.8	45 8.1	51 7.1			52 7.0	34 10.7	45 8.1	54 6.8	64 5.7
17 21.7	18 20.4	19 19.4			10 35.7	24 15.1	20 18.0	17 21.9	13 28.3
22 16.4	24 15.5	26 13.9	Cost of Sales/Payables		29 12.8	30 12.1	25 14.5	29 12.7	20 18.2
37 9.8	43 8.5	40 9.1			43 8.4	42 8.6	38 9.7	39 9.4	42 8.6
7.0	6.7	8.7			7.6	16.2	8.6	10.2	5.0
13.7	21.0	20.4	Sales/Working Capital		14.9	23.2	30.6	20.9	
63.3	135.5	88.2			100.7	165.8	62.3	130.0	269.5
(71) 5.0	(74) 7.8	(80) 5.7		(12) 6.7	(12) 4.7	(24) 6.7	(19) 5.7	(10) 4.8	
2.6	3.1	2.7	EBIT/Interest	4.0	2.5	2.5	3.7	2.3	
.1	.7	1.5		1.6	-3.0	1.0	1.5	.5	
(42) 2.9	(42) 3.8	(39) 2.8					(11) 6.7		
1.7	1.6	1.7	Net Profit + Depr., Dep., Amort./Cur. Mat. L/T/D				1.8		
1.0	.8	.8					1.3		
.4	.5	.6			.2	1.0	.6	.7	.5
.9	.8	1.1	Fixed/Worth		.5	1.4		1.5	.8
1.8	1.8	1.9			2.5	2.6	1.7	1.9	2.3
.7	.6	1.0			.4	1.3	1.0	1.2	.5
1.6	1.7	1.9	Debt/Worth		1.5	2.3	1.9	2.4	1.1
4.1	3.2	4.3			3.5	4.2	3.7	4.0	5.2
(77) 28.4	(74) 32.9	(87) 36.3		(13) 29.1	41.4	(25) 29.4	(19) 38.0	(12) 41.9	
12.0	12.9	17.4	% Profit Before Taxes/Tangible Net Worth	14.6	16.9	12.5	25.7	29.6	
-2.4	-.9	4.9		9.3	-12.0	2.0	9.2	4.7	
11.3	10.8	12.4			17.2	12.3	11.7	12.9	22.9
5.7	4.4	5.1	% Profit Before Taxes/Total Assets		3.9	6.5	3.8	6.9	6.3
-.9	-1.2	1.1			1.4	-6.5	.0	2.1	1.9
14.6	17.2	12.0			57.2	9.7	13.0	9.0	9.7
7.2	7.2	7.1	Sales/Net Fixed Assets		23.7	6.0	8.4	6.5	7.2
4.4	4.0	4.4			3.2	3.5	5.7	4.0	5.2
3.2	3.1	3.1			5.7	3.3	3.5	2.6	2.5
2.4	2.3	2.5	Sales/Total Assets		3.6	2.6	2.8	2.2	2.3
1.9	2.0	1.9			1.8	1.8	2.2	1.7	1.9
(73) 1.3	(72) 1.8	(80) 1.8		(12) 1.6	2.2	(22) 1.6	(19) 2.3		
3.4	2.9	3.0	% Depr., Dep., Amort./Sales	2.6	3.1	3.1	3.1		
4.4	4.2	4.2		4.2	3.8	4.1	5.3		
(33) 2.2	(31) 2.9	(36) 2.7			(10) 2.3	(11) 3.2			
4.5	4.0	4.2	% Officers', Directors', Owners' Comp/Sales		3.9	6.8			
7.4	8.1	7.6			6.4	9.4			
1924353M	1596895M	1746457M	Net Sales ($)	2901M	27515M	53272M	197282M	334964M	1130523M
937892M	792485M	845495M	Total Assets ($)	1548M	9642M	22685M	74726M	168074M	568820M

M = $ thousand   MM = $ million
See Pages 1 through 15 for Explanation of Ratios and Data

Current Data Sorted By Assets — **Comparative Historical Data**

0-500M	500M-2MM	2-10MM	10-50MM	50-100MM	100-250MM		4/1/90-3/31/91 ALL	4/1/91-3/31/92 ALL
						# Postretirement Benefits		
						Type of Statement		
		1	1		1			
		2	11	2	2	Unqualified		4
	5	8	5			Reviewed		5
5		8	5			Compiled		2
5		1				Tax Returns		
5	5	10	3		2	Other		3
							4/1/90-3/31/91 ALL	4/1/91-3/31/92 ALL
10	19	25	16	4	2	**NUMBER OF STATEMENTS**		14
19 (4/1-9/30/94)			57 (10/1/94-3/31/95)					

0-500M %	500M-2MM %	2-10MM %	10-50MM %	50-100MM %	100-250MM %	ASSETS	90-91 %	91-92 %
6.8	11.1	7.1	9.6			Cash & Equivalents		7.4
39.2	32.2	39.6	26.8			Trade Receivables - (net)		23.6
21.9	17.0	12.9	13.5			Inventory		16.8
2.1	3.8	1.0	1.7			All Other Current		1.0
70.0	64.1	60.6	51.7			Total Current		48.8
17.9	21.2	24.5	21.7			Fixed Assets (net)		40.6
4.5	4.6	7.4	10.5			Intangibles (net)		.7
7.5	10.1	7.6	16.1			All Other Non-Current		10.0
100.0	100.0	100.0	100.0			Total		100.0

(90-91 column: DATA NOT AVAILABLE)

						LIABILITIES		
11.1	11.4	14.1	4.9			Notes Payable-Short Term		6.0
3.4	3.9	1.8	3.6			Cur. Mat. -L/T/D		4.0
9.0	18.6	12.8	9.7			Trade Payables		11.2
.1	.8	.3	.3			Income Taxes Payable		.7
28.8	11.8	11.7	16.1			All Other Current		12.2
52.3	46.5	40.7	34.6			Total Current		34.0
12.6	11.0	16.4	18.9			Long Term Debt		21.9
.2	.1	.2	1.8			Deferred Taxes		1.5
.0	3.4	5.1	14.7			All Other-Non-Current		1.6
34.9	39.0	37.7	30.0			Net Worth		40.9
100.0	100.0	100.0	100.0			Total Liabilities & Net Worth		100.0

						INCOME DATA		
100.0	100.0	100.0	100.0			Net Sales		100.0
42.7	49.7	45.1	49.3			Gross Profit		44.0
37.3	44.0	40.0	45.5			Operating Expenses		37.7
5.4	5.7	5.0	3.7			Operating Profit		6.3
1.3	.9	1.6	2.3			All Other Expenses (net)		2.9
4.1	4.8	3.4	1.5			Profit Before Taxes		3.4

						RATIOS		
2.3	2.1	2.3	2.4			Current		2.5
1.4	1.3	1.3	1.4					1.6
.9	1.0	1.2	1.0					1.1
1.5	1.9	1.8	1.6			Quick		1.4
.9	1.1	1.2	1.0					1.0
.4	.5	.7	.7					.6
23 16.0	19 18.9	50 7.3	31 11.7			Sales/Receivables		32 11.3
34 10.7	50 7.3	58 6.3	69 5.3					43 8.4
54 6.7	63 5.8	87 4.2	85 4.3					54 6.8
0 UND	0 UND	6 62.1	32 11.3			Cost of Sales/Inventory		28 13.0
17 21.6	11 32.0	26 14.1	53 6.9					68 5.4
99 3.7	152 2.4	85 4.3	89 4.1					104 3.5
0 UND	18 20.5	14 26.5	29 12.7			Cost of Sales/Payables		7 51.7
24 15.5	26 13.8	37 9.9	49 7.5					22 16.7
34 10.7	81 4.5	66 5.5	70 5.2					40 9.2
7.8	5.6	5.2	4.8			Sales/Working Capital		5.1
12.9	10.4	10.8	13.4					10.7
-43.5	-104.9	22.2	NM					NM
	17.7	8.1	8.9			EBIT/Interest		5.4
	(18) 6.1	(22) 3.4	2.1					(13) 1.9
	3.0	1.0	.5					.7
						Net Profit + Depr., Dep., Amort./Cur. Mat. L/T/D		
.1	.3	.2	.4			Fixed/Worth		.8
.4	.6	.6	1.1					1.1
1.5	1.5	1.9	-1.5					2.0
1.1	.6	1.0	.6			Debt/Worth		.8
2.6	2.1	2.1	4.0					1.9
5.3	3.9	4.5	-8.6					2.7
	77.0	40.9	35.2			% Profit Before Taxes/Tangible Net Worth		28.1
	(16) 24.7	(23) 18.0	(10) 13.1					(13) 11.5
	14.0	.2	-3.0					2.6
13.6	17.0	13.2	9.2			% Profit Before Taxes/Total Assets		9.7
5.7	11.2	7.3	3.8					3.7
2.7	4.8	-.2	-1.5					-.1
42.1	31.5	20.7	13.1			Sales/Net Fixed Assets		7.5
21.6	14.5	8.2	8.0					4.1
15.1	9.9	5.0	5.7					2.4
4.8	3.4	2.2	1.9			Sales/Total Assets		2.3
2.3	2.4	1.8	1.5					1.5
1.0	1.2	1.5	1.2					1.4
	.6	1.1	1.9			% Depr., Dep., Amort./Sales		2.2
	(16) 2.0	(22) 3.8	(14) 2.7					(12) 3.7
	4.2	5.0	5.1					5.5
	3.8	3.5				% Officers', Directors', Owners' Comp/Sales		
	(11) 6.8	(14) 5.2						
	11.2	8.3						
7244M	46613M	204445M	463584M	573664M	346217M	Net Sales ($)		426545M
2450M	18802M	106572M	294649M	281903M	382766M	Total Assets ($)		294829M

M = $ thousand   MM = $ million

See Pages 1 through 15 for Explanation of Ratios and Data

Comparative Historical Data				Current Data Sorted By Sales					
1	2	3		1			1		1
			# Postretirement Benefits						
			Type of Statement						
12	13	17	Unqualified				2	7	8
13	15	15	Reviewed		5	2	6	1	1
8	12	18	Compiled	5	6	2	4	1	
	2	1	Tax Returns			1			
10	14	25	Other	5	5	1	4	5	5
4/1/92-	4/1/93-	4/1/94-			19 (4/1-9/30/94)			57 (10/1/94-3/31/95)	
3/31/93	3/31/94	3/31/95		0-1MM	1-3MM	3-5MM	5-10MM	10-25MM	25MM & OVER
ALL	ALL	ALL							
43	56	76	NUMBER OF STATEMENTS	10	16	6	16	14	14
%	%	%	ASSETS	%	%	%	%	%	%
8.4	11.8	8.7	Cash & Equivalents	3.7	9.7		10.7	9.4	9.0
31.2	32.6	32.9	Trade Receivables - (net)	26.3	41.0		30.8	34.7	21.8
16.2	17.5	15.0	Inventory	27.9	15.0		13.3	12.9	13.6
2.7	3.1	2.4	All Other Current	3.5	2.5		1.0	1.4	3.6
58.5	65.1	59.0	Total Current	61.5	68.1		55.8	58.4	48.0
25.4	22.7	23.7	Fixed Assets (net)	18.6	24.0		27.8	18.0	32.6
9.3	5.2	7.5	Intangibles (net)	4.6	3.8		7.3	12.3	9.9
6.8	7.0	9.7	All Other Non-Current	15.4	4.0		9.1	11.4	9.5
100.0	100.0	100.0	Total	100.0	100.0		100.0	100.0	100.0
			LIABILITIES						
8.2	8.6	10.0	Notes Payable-Short Term	13.0	11.6		11.0	11.6	2.2
5.6	3.2	3.2	Cur. Mat.-L./T/D	5.0	2.7		2.2	3.3	3.6
13.0	14.3	12.6	Trade Payables	9.4	10.2		15.1	11.3	10.0
.7	1.0	.4	Income Taxes Payable	.1	.8		.4	.1	.4
12.6	15.5	15.0	All Other Current	28.9	10.4		9.7	18.5	12.8
40.0	42.6	41.1	Total Current	56.4	35.8		38.4	44.8	29.0
17.8	13.7	15.6	Long Term Debt	9.4	13.2		19.0	20.5	15.6
1.5	.8	.7	Deferred Taxes	.2	.1		1.3	.2	2.1
3.6	5.2	6.2	All Other-Non-Current	.0	4.8		4.5	10.6	10.3
37.1	37.7	36.3	Net Worth	34.0	46.1		36.8	24.0	43.0
100.0	100.0	100.0	Total Liabilities & Net Worth	100.0	100.0		100.0	100.0	100.0
			INCOME DATA						
100.0	100.0	100.0	Net Sales	100.0	100.0		100.0	100.0	100.0
48.8	47.4	46.4	Gross Profit	41.5	52.0		41.0	52.9	42.2
43.8	44.4	40.6	Operating Expenses	36.6	44.1		38.7	48.0	33.1
5.0	3.0	5.8	Operating Profit	4.9	7.9		2.3	4.9	9.1
1.4	.9	1.6	All Other Expenses (net)	1.7	.8		1.6	1.9	2.1
3.5	2.1	4.2	Profit Before Taxes	3.2	7.1		.6	3.0	6.9
			RATIOS						
2.1	2.9	2.1		1.7	3.1		2.4	1.7	2.9
1.5	1.7	1.3	Current	1.1	1.9		1.3	1.3	1.7
1.0	1.0	1.0		.7	1.4		1.1	1.0	1.1
1.4	1.7	1.7		1.0	2.5		1.8	1.4	1.7
1.0	1.2	1.0	Quick	.5	1.7		1.1	.9	1.0
.7	.6	.6		.1	.6		.6	.7	.6
31 11.8	37 10.0	32 11.4		0 UND	27 13.6	38 9.6	41 8.9	21 17.4	
54 6.7	51 7.1	51 7.1	Sales/Receivables	43 8.5	48 7.6	57 6.4	73 5.0	39 9.4	
72 5.1	70 5.2	72 5.1		61 6.0	68 5.4	66 5.5	87 4.2	69 5.3	
16 22.7	11 33.1	4 100.9		0 UND	0 UND	12 30.5	0 UND	26 14.3	
31 11.8	36 10.1	31 11.9	Cost of Sales/Inventory	69 5.3	11 31.9	30 12.3	31 11.6	39 9.3	
85 4.3	130 2.8	94 3.9		730 .5	94 3.9	79 4.6	104 3.5	70 5.2	
19 19.7	10 36.5	19 19.7		19 35.0	10 35.0	24 15.5	19 19.3	20 18.0	
34 10.7	36 10.2	37 10.0	Cost of Sales/Payables	33 11.1	20 18.5	38 9.7	45 8.1	34 10.8	
65 5.6	62 5.9	64 5.7		70 5.2	44 8.3	56 6.5	68 5.4	62 5.9	
5.1	3.7	5.9		4.0	4.8		6.1	7.0	4.1
9.9	8.2	11.0	Sales/Working Capital	15.8	8.6		11.4	13.6	10.3
53.0	107.3	94.0		-32.9	14.2		42.3	-108.7	NM
7.2	13.5	11.1			13.1		8.0	9.1	58.8
(41) 3.3	(48) 3.2	(70) 3.9	EBIT/Interest	(15) 5.7		(15) 3.5	(13) 2.7	7.8	
1.5	1.3	1.5		2.3		.9	1.7	.7	
2.4	7.1	20.7							
(17) 1.9	(18) 2.5	(29) 6.3	Net Profit + Depr., Dep.,						
1.0	.6	1.1	Amort./Cur. Mat. L/T/D						
.4	.3	.3		.1	.2		.4	.3	.4
.9	.7	.7	Fixed/Worth	.4	.6		.7	1.1	.9
2.2	2.1	2.0		1.5	1.5		3.4	-2.6	1.8
.9	.8	.8		1.2	.6		1.0	2.0	.4
2.3	2.1	2.1	Debt/Worth	3.0	1.4		1.9	5.3	.9
6.9	6.5	5.8		5.3	2.6		8.4	-14.4	3.1
55.8	37.9	50.8			61.5		27.3		39.4
(36) 23.4	(49) 12.6	(63) 22.6	% Profit Before Taxes/Tangible	(14) 21.7		(14) 17.1	(12) 20.6		
6.3	2.2	7.0	Net Worth	5.6		-2.0	1.9		
15.0	10.3	13.2		10.3	24.1		10.2	14.5	27.7
7.6	4.7	7.4	% Profit Before Taxes/Total	5.7	11.3		4.0	5.8	8.0
1.2	.7	1.3	Assets	-4.3	4.0		-1.2	3.3	-.7
24.2	20.6	21.6		28.9	29.2		14.9	17.1	16.6
6.7	11.2	10.0	Sales/Net Fixed Assets	17.5	14.0		6.2	8.9	6.1
3.7	5.5	5.5		10.8	6.7		4.5	6.5	3.7
2.3	2.8	2.5		2.2	2.8		2.3	2.1	2.3
1.9	1.9	1.8	Sales/Total Assets	1.0	2.1		1.8	1.5	1.7
1.4	1.3	1.3		.8	1.2		1.6	1.3	1.2
1.3	1.7	1.2			1.1		2.8	1.3	2.0
(36) 2.8	(45) 2.6	(63) 3.0	% Depr., Dep., Amort./Sales	(14) 2.9		(15) 4.2	(12) 2.9	(11) 2.5	
5.6	4.9	4.9		4.8		5.4	4.9	5.1	
3.8	4.4	3.5							
(14) 6.0	(22) 8.7	(31) 6.0	% Officers', Directors',						
12.3	14.2	10.2	Owners' Comp/Sales						
926144M	699645M	1641767M	Net Sales ($)	4475M	30383M	24923M	116309M	224045M	1241632M
619646M	458910M	1087142M	Total Assets ($)	4096M	17130M	7907M	72982M	138897M	846130M

M = $ thousand   MM = $ million
See Pages 1 through 15 for Explanation of Ratios and Data

MANUFACTURERS—NEWSPAPERS: PUBLISHING, OR PUBLISHING & PRINTING. SIC# 2711

Statement Types

	0-500M	500M-2MM	2-10MM	10-50MM	50-100MM	100-250MM	4/1/90-3/31/91 ALL	4/1/91-3/31/92 ALL
# Postretirement Benefits		4	4	2	2	1		
Unqualified	1	4	9	7	2	3	20	24
Reviewed	1	6	3	4	1		18	18
Compiled	5	7	5	1			25	29
Tax Returns	1	1						1
Other	1	2	10	5	3	2	26	20

Current Data Sorted By Assets — 18 (4/1-9/30/94); 66 (10/1/94-3/31/95)
Comparative Historical Data

Financial Data

	0-500M	500M-2MM	2-10MM	10-50MM	50-100MM	100-250MM	4/1/90-3/31/91 ALL	4/1/91-3/31/92 ALL
NUMBER OF STATEMENTS	9	20	27	17	6	5	89	92
ASSETS %	%	%	%	%	%	%	%	%
Cash & Equivalents		7.7	11.7	11.0			9.8	10.6
Trade Receivables - (net)		37.7	18.7	16.3			26.1	26.7
Inventory		4.6	4.2	3.9			6.3	6.1
All Other Current		1.3	2.6	5.8			2.6	1.8
Total Current		51.3	37.2	37.0			44.7	45.1
Fixed Assets (net)		26.8	35.1	36.6			34.4	34.9
Intangibles (net)		9.8	14.5	15.5			10.1	10.0
All Other Non-Current		12.1	13.2	10.9			10.9	10.0
Total		100.0	100.0	100.0			100.0	100.0
LIABILITIES								
Notes Payable-Short Term		6.4	2.7	3.3			5.7	7.0
Cur. Mat. -L/T/D		4.8	3.6	4.0			5.1	5.0
Trade Payables		19.3	10.6	4.4			11.2	10.8
Income Taxes Payable		2.0	.4	.2			.8	.5
All Other Current		22.1	12.8	11.4			7.7	9.4
Total Current		54.6	30.0	23.4			30.5	32.8
Long Term Debt		18.9	24.0	24.9			29.5	30.0
Deferred Taxes		.1	.8	2.2			.7	.9
All Other-Non-Current		7.8	8.6	1.9			3.2	3.7
Net Worth		18.7	36.6	47.6			36.1	32.6
Total Liabilities & Net Worth		100.0	100.0	100.0			100.0	100.0
INCOME DATA								
Net Sales		100.0	100.0	100.0			100.0	100.0
Gross Profit		43.7	48.6	44.3			43.4	41.0
Operating Expenses		38.5	39.5	33.4			37.0	36.2
Operating Profit		5.1	9.1	10.9			6.4	4.8
All Other Expenses (net)		1.7	.6	2.5			2.8	2.8
Profit Before Taxes		3.5	8.5	8.4			3.5	2.0
RATIOS								
Current		1.7	1.9	2.5			2.3	2.5
		1.2	1.2	1.5			1.5	1.4
		.5	.9	1.0			.9	1.0
Quick		1.7	1.5	2.0			2.0	2.1
		1.1	1.0	1.1			1.1	1.1
		.4	.7	.8			.8	.7
Sales/Receivables	37 9.8	33 11.2	33 11.1				33 11.0	35 10.4
	47 7.8	38 9.5	38 9.5				40 9.2	41 8.8
	60 6.1	43 8.4	59 6.2				50 7.3	49 7.4
Cost of Sales/Inventory	0 UND	6 66.3	2 177.3				5 71.1	2 150.6
	5 81.0	11 32.0	12 30.7				13 27.3	11 33.4
	20 18.0	27 13.3	24 15.0				26 13.8	27 13.6
Cost of Sales/Payables	25 14.5	15 23.6	15 24.0				13 29.2	11 33.9
	42 8.7	35 10.4	23 15.7				23 15.9	24 14.9
	64 5.7	54 6.7	33 11.2				49 7.5	37 10.0
Sales/Working Capital		13.0	10.1	4.3			8.3	8.2
		54.0	43.9	18.4			15.9	18.6
		-10.7	-47.1	NM			-71.5	-302.4
EBIT/Interest		10.3	16.3	13.6			6.2	4.8
		(17) 3.0	(25) 6.9	(14) 4.8			(80) 2.4	(82) 2.1
		1.8	1.7	1.7			1.2	.3
Net Profit + Depr., Dep., Amort./Cur. Mat. L./T/D			22.1				6.7	4.4
		(12)	3.5				(46) 2.3	(45) 1.7
			1.1				1.0	.2
Fixed/Worth		.5	.5	.3			.6	.6
		2.0	1.4	1.3			1.3	1.6
		-1.0	7.0	NM			11.6	-8.4
Debt/Worth		1.0	.8	.5			.7	.9
		11.7	2.6	1.0			2.7	2.6
		-4.0	9.6	NM			21.9	-16.2
% Profit Before Taxes/Tangible Net Worth		59.6	87.4	50.8			53.1	37.6
	(12) 24.5	(21) 50.5	(13) 19.5				(72) 21.6	(66) 13.4
		8.2	11.7	10.0			6.7	-1.7
% Profit Before Taxes/Total Assets		11.2	21.1	22.5			14.0	12.6
		7.1	16.6	9.8			6.4	4.6
		3.1	5.4	4.4			1.2	-3.0
Sales/Net Fixed Assets		21.9	7.0	8.7			13.8	14.5
		13.5	5.6	3.3			6.0	6.3
		5.9	2.7	2.6			3.2	3.1
Sales/Total Assets		3.6	2.9	1.7			3.0	3.1
		2.6	1.7	1.3			2.1	1.9
		2.1	1.1	1.0			1.4	1.2
% Depr., Dep., Amort./Sales		.8	1.7	3.0			2.1	2.3
	(17) 2.2	(22) 4.3	(15) 4.1				(75) 3.2	(77) 3.3
		3.1	5.8	5.6			5.2	5.9
% Officers', Directors', Owners' Comp/Sales							3.1	4.0
							(31) 5.5	(22) 7.5
							9.7	15.4
Net Sales ($)	9096M	70515M	307009M	565733M	567000M	748336M	1654817M	2219965M
Total Assets ($)	2153M	25094M	151102M	441257M	444146M	673682M	1341882M	1850389M

M = $ thousand   MM = $ million
See Pages 1 through 15 for Explanation of Ratios and Data

Comparative Historical Data | | | | **Current Data Sorted By Sales** | | | | |

Type of Statement

5	8	13		0-1MM	1-3MM	3-5MM	5-10MM	10-25MM	25MM & OVER
5	8	13	# Postretirement Benefits		1	4	1	2	5
31	33	26	Unqualified	2	3	3	1	7	10
17	16	15	Reviewed	1	4	2	1	5	2
14	14	18	Compiled	4	4	3	4	3	
1	1	2	Tax Returns		1	1			
22	26	23	Other	1	2	2	5	2	11
4/1/92-3/31/93 ALL	4/1/93-3/31/94 ALL	4/1/94-3/31/95 ALL			18 (4/1-9/30/94)		66 (10/1/94-3/31/95)		
85	90	84	**NUMBER OF STATEMENTS**	8	14	11	11	17	23

ASSETS

5	8	13		0-1MM	1-3MM	3-5MM	5-10MM	10-25MM	25MM & OVER
%	%	%		%	%	%	%	%	%
10.3	9.7	10.9	Cash & Equivalents		9.7	8.9	15.9	9.1	12.5
24.6	23.6	24.3	Trade Receivables - (net)		27.7	35.7	29.8	21.0	15.6
5.1	5.2	4.4	Inventory		1.4	4.4	4.3	6.5	2.7
3.1	3.3	3.3	All Other Current		3.1	.9	1.3	5.9	4.6
43.0	41.8	42.9	Total Current		41.9	49.8	51.2	42.5	35.3
34.4	38.3	32.3	Fixed Assets (net)		23.9	22.8	29.2	39.2	37.4
12.1	8.7	11.8	Intangibles (net)		13.8	19.1	9.7	10.0	10.2
10.5	11.1	12.9	All Other Non-Current		20.5	8.2	9.9	8.3	17.1
100.0	100.0	100.0	Total		100.0	100.0	100.0	100.0	100.0

LIABILITIES

5	8	13		0-1MM	1-3MM	3-5MM	5-10MM	10-25MM	25MM & OVER
6.0	4.1	4.5	Notes Payable-Short Term		7.5	5.1	3.9	4.1	1.6
4.7	5.1	3.7	Cur. Mat.-L./T/D		4.5	2.8	3.1	3.9	3.2
11.5	11.2	11.9	Trade Payables		18.2	14.5	19.5	8.6	5.5
.8	.6	.9	Income Taxes Payable		2.9	.2	.0	.7	.4
10.4	9.9	14.6	All Other Current		24.4	12.3	10.8	10.3	12.9
33.4	30.9	35.5	Total Current		57.5	35.0	37.3	27.7	23.6
27.7	25.7	20.6	Long Term Debt		16.9	18.0	26.4	18.6	18.2
1.0	1.0	1.3	Deferred Taxes		.4	.5	.4	1.0	3.5
2.9	5.1	6.8	All Other-Non-Current		10.0	2.8	7.7	1.8	9.3
35.0	37.2	35.7	Net Worth		15.2	43.6	28.3	51.0	45.4
100.0	100.0	100.0	Total Liabilities & Net Worth		100.0	100.0	100.0	100.0	100.0

INCOME DATA

5	8	13		0-1MM	1-3MM	3-5MM	5-10MM	10-25MM	25MM & OVER
100.0	100.0	100.0	Net Sales		100.0	100.0	100.0	100.0	100.0
43.9	43.7	46.4	Gross Profit		42.6	45.4	50.8	48.9	45.4
36.9	37.2	37.6	Operating Expenses		39.1	40.7	43.9	38.0	31.1
7.0	6.5	8.7	Operating Profit		3.5	4.7	6.9	10.9	14.3
2.3	1.6	1.2	All Other Expenses (net)		.5	1.0	1.2	1.2	1.7
4.6	4.8	7.5	Profit Before Taxes		3.0	3.7	5.7	9.7	12.6

RATIOS

5	8	13		0-1MM	1-3MM	3-5MM	5-10MM	10-25MM	25MM & OVER
2.2 / 1.4 / 1.0	2.2 / 1.3 / 1.0	2.1 / 1.2 / .9	Current		1.2 / .9 / .7	2.6 / 1.7 / 1.0	1.9 / 1.3 / 1.1	2.3 / 1.3 / 1.0	2.2 / 1.3 / 1.0
1.7 / 1.1 / .7	1.8 / 1.1 / .7	1.7 / 1.1 / .7	Quick		1.2 / .7 / .5	2.1 / 1.6 / 1.0	1.6 / 1.2 / 1.1	1.6 / 1.1 / .8	1.9 / 1.1 / .8
31 11.7 / 37 9.9 / 48 7.6	31 11.7 / 38 9.6 / 49 7.5	33 11.2 / 40 9.2 / 52 7.0	Sales/Receivables		25 14.4 / 40 9.2 / 55 6.6	42 8.7 / 45 8.1 / 54 6.7	35 10.4 / 39 9.4 / 48 7.6	33 11.2 / 37 9.8 / 47 7.7	32 11.5 / 38 9.5 / 51 7.1
3 126.0 / 13 29.1 / 24 15.5	4 86.6 / 11 33.7 / 21 17.4	2 149.2 / 10 38.3 / 24 15.1	Cost of Sales/Inventory		0 UND / 4 85.5 / 12 31.3	0 UND / 2 163.8 / 17 22.1	5 77.4 / 12 30.6 / 33 10.9	8 46.9 / 22 16.5 / 27 13.3	5 73.7 / 12 30.7 / 24 15.2
13 27.7 / 25 14.5 / 49 7.5	16 23.5 / 27 13.3 / 46 8.0	16 22.4 / 29 12.7 / 53 6.9	Cost of Sales/Payables		21 17.4 / 36 10.1 / 70 5.2	15 23.6 / 29 12.6 / 36 10.1	32 11.3 / 50 7.3 / 73 5.0	15 24.0 / 23 16.0 / 46 7.9	12 30.9 / 24 15.4 / 48 7.6
8.3 / 21.8 / -132.0	8.7 / 26.3 / -238.1	8.7 / 35.2 / -72.0	Sales/Working Capital		58.9 / -44.5 / -13.8	8.9 / 16.0 / -281.9	12.9 / 20.6 / 77.7	6.9 / 25.4 / NM	4.8 / 49.2 / -85.2
(74) 7.9 / 2.7 / 1.5	(82) 7.4 / 2.8 / 1.6	(74) 10.8 / 4.9 / 1.6	EBIT/Interest		(13) 11.4 / 2.5 / .8		(10) 12.9 / 7.1 / 1.9	(16) 14.6 / 6.9 / 3.2	(19) 20.8 / 7.5 / 4.6
(39) 6.6 / 2.5 / 1.2	(43) 2.9 / 1.6 / 1.1	(37) 10.9 / 4.1 / 1.4	Net Profit + Depr., Dep., Amort./Cur. Mat. L/T/D					(10) 12.6 / 3.5 / 1.4	(10) 10.9 / 5.5 / 2.0
.8 / 1.6 / -12.5	.7 / 1.2 / 6.4	.5 / 1.2 / 26.1	Fixed/Worth		.7 / -2.8 / -.9	.5 / .7 / 4.1	.3 / 1.1 / 3.7	.5 / 1.0 / 1.8	.4 / 1.0 / 2.5
1.0 / 3.0 / -32.7	.7 / 1.8 / 25.2	.8 / 2.0 / 31.6	Debt/Worth		2.2 / -12.3 / -4.1	.4 / 1.6 / 14.2	1.3 / 2.1 / 7.9	.6 / .8 / 3.1	.5 / 1.1 / 3.1
(62) 40.3 / 20.8 / 8.9	(72) 67.9 / 24.4 / 7.8	(64) 63.8 / 29.9 / 12.9	% Profit Before Taxes/Tangible Net Worth					(15) 64.7 / 44.4 / 14.6	(19) 49.8 / 29.8 / 16.6
16.2 / 7.3 / 2.0	14.0 / 6.0 / 2.0	18.4 / 9.6 / 4.1	% Profit Before Taxes/Total Assets		8.9 / 6.2 / -1.0	13.8 / 8.4 / -3.3	18.8 / 7.4 / 4.1	23.2 / 16.6 / 5.5	26.8 / 15.1 / 8.2
15.0 / 5.8 / 3.3	10.5 / 5.0 / 2.9	14.6 / 5.8 / 2.7	Sales/Net Fixed Assets		30.8 / 13.5 / 2.7	51.9 / 9.0 / 5.4	22.3 / 11.7 / 2.9	9.5 / 5.3 / 2.8	6.8 / 3.9 / 2.4
3.1 / 1.9 / 1.2	2.8 / 1.9 / 1.1	2.9 / 1.8 / 1.1	Sales/Total Assets		3.9 / 2.1 / 1.0	3.1 / 2.5 / 1.3	4.0 / 3.4 / 1.5	2.7 / 1.7 / 1.2	2.0 / 1.4 / .9
(73) 1.9 / 3.3 / 5.0	(81) 2.2 / 3.7 / 5.9	(70) 1.9 / 3.3 / 5.5	% Depr., Dep., Amort./Sales		(11) 1.2 / 2.6 / 6.6		(10) 1.1 / 2.8 / 4.6	(16) 1.9 / 3.7 / 5.5	(18) 3.3 / 4.2 / 5.9
(28) 2.5 / 4.9 / 9.0	(26) 3.5 / 5.8 / 11.6	(18) 3.5 / 5.2 / 6.8	% Officers', Directors', Owners' Comp/Sales						
1964087M	2466279M	2267689M	Net Sales ($)	4849M	30664M	41364M	77387M	300989M	1812436M
1551909M	2147194M	1737434M	Total Assets ($)	3181M	20396M	20343M	41086M	193513M	1458915M

M = $ thousand   MM = $ million
See Pages 1 through 15 for Explanation of Ratios and Data

Current Data Sorted By Assets | **Comparative Historical Data**

0-500M	500M-2MM	2-10MM	10-50MM	50-100MM	100-250MM		4/1/90-3/31/91 ALL	4/1/91-3/31/92 ALL
	2	4	2	1	1	# Postretirement Benefits		
						Type of Statement		
	3	10	12	2	2	Unqualified	26	21
3	11	13				Reviewed	7	19
4	9	2				Compiled	15	20
1	1					Tax Returns	2	
3	9	7	2		1	Other	15	17
	38 (4/1-9/30/94)			57 (10/1/94-3/31/95)				
11	33	32	14	2	3	NUMBER OF STATEMENTS	65	77
%	%	%	%	%	%	ASSETS	%	%
14.2	12.8	12.6	8.5			Cash & Equivalents	9.8	11.3
28.4	41.9	38.2	22.2			Trade Receivables - (net)	28.2	29.2
5.3	5.3	7.6	12.3			Inventory	9.0	8.7
19.9	2.1	3.7	1.7			All Other Current	7.0	5.2
67.9	62.1	62.0	44.7			Total Current	54.0	54.4
21.1	19.4	22.2	32.1			Fixed Assets (net)	25.7	25.5
5.3	6.0	4.6	12.9			Intangibles (net)	7.4	8.9
5.8	12.6	11.2	10.3			All Other Non-Current	12.8	11.1
100.0	100.0	100.0	100.0			Total	100.0	100.0
						LIABILITIES		
9.2	3.3	7.4	5.5			Notes Payable-Short Term	8.1	5.3
5.5	5.2	3.8	3.9			Cur. Mat. -L/T/D	4.6	4.7
19.6	20.2	15.4	7.3			Trade Payables	14.1	14.2
.8	1.0	.3	.4			Income Taxes Payable	1.0	.7
33.0	24.0	23.1	13.2			All Other Current	16.6	18.5
68.1	53.7	50.0	30.2			Total Current	44.4	43.4
11.6	13.5	11.4	20.0			Long Term Debt	19.7	17.7
.0	.6	1.6	2.7			Deferred Taxes	.8	1.1
6.1	11.0	7.4	11.1			All Other-Non-Current	7.2	9.1
14.2	21.2	29.6	36.0			Net Worth	27.9	28.7
100.0	100.0	100.0	100.0			Total Liabilities & Net Worth	100.0	100.0
						INCOME DATA		
100.0	100.0	100.0	100.0			Net Sales	100.0	100.0
52.2	41.9	37.7	37.2			Gross Profit	36.8	41.4
52.8	36.8	33.5	31.2			Operating Expenses	33.1	36.7
-.6	5.1	4.2	6.0			Operating Profit	3.7	4.8
-.8	.1	.7	1.9			All Other Expenses (net)	1.8	.4
.3	5.0	3.5	4.1			Profit Before Taxes	1.9	4.4
						RATIOS		
1.9	1.5	1.7	2.4			Current	1.9	1.9
1.4	1.2	1.3	1.6				1.2	1.3
.6	.9	1.0	1.0				.9	.9
.9	1.3	1.3	1.5			Quick	1.4	1.4
.5	1.1	1.1	1.1				.9	1.0
.3	.7	.7	.8				.6	.6
0 UND	36 10.2	37 9.8	41 8.9			Sales/Receivables	28 13.2	32 11.4
21 17.0	46 7.9	47 7.7	53 6.9				43 8.5	44 8.3
45 8.1	59 6.2	63 5.8	79 4.6				64 5.7	58 6.3
0 UND	0 UND	0 UND	20 17.9			Cost of Sales/Inventory	0 UND	0 UND
0 UND	0 UND	4 92.4	29 12.5				10 37.6	14 25.7
5 71.4	16 22.7	21 17.7	114 3.2				36 10.1	34 10.8
10 35.9	20 18.5	18 20.6	23 15.9			Cost of Sales/Payables	14 26.9	17 22.0
56 6.5	34 10.8	31 11.8	31 11.7				31 11.8	26 14.0
65 5.6	65 5.6	58 6.3	43 8.4				52 7.0	54 6.8
12.6	13.1	10.1	3.8			Sales/Working Capital	8.3	8.6
14.7	30.9	18.8	8.8				17.4	19.7
-14.8	-43.4	763.9	NM				-35.8	-56.6
	23.8	17.0	14.4			EBIT/Interest	8.4	9.8
	(32) 11.1	(28) 5.5	(11) 2.1				(52) 2.1	(66) 3.3
	2.9	3.2	1.1				-.2	1.7
	6.1	4.2				Net Profit + Depr., Dep.,	3.3	5.5
	(12) 2.8	(14) 2.9				Amort./Cur. Mat. L./T/D	(30) 2.2	(34) 2.4
	1.7	1.2					.5	1.2
.5	.4	.3	.7			Fixed/Worth	.4	.6
2.3	1.0	.9	1.6				1.4	1.5
-1.3	3.5	3.0	-2.5				12.9	-4.1
1.8	1.8	1.4	.9			Debt/Worth	1.1	1.3
10.1	4.0	2.3	2.9				3.6	3.2
-5.9	17.7	7.2	-16.2				36.0	-13.5
	205.8	80.4	47.6			% Profit Before Taxes/Tangible	50.8	47.6
	(28) 61.5	(26) 41.7	(10) 17.4			Net Worth	(51) 20.0	(55) 17.5
	27.1	16.4	-3.0				-5.7	7.8
15.4	26.6	22.4	13.5			% Profit Before Taxes/Total	11.4	15.6
7.4	14.5	7.6	3.5			Assets	4.3	5.7
2.3	5.0	5.9	-.1				-2.5	2.3
53.7	44.2	36.2	11.4			Sales/Net Fixed Assets	28.1	33.9
24.6	26.5	15.4	4.3				10.2	11.6
9.9	11.7	8.4	2.4				3.7	4.9
7.0	4.3	3.8	1.8			Sales/Total Assets	2.9	3.4
4.0	3.1	3.0	1.3				1.9	2.3
2.5	2.1	2.2	.9				1.4	1.4
(10) .7	(30) 1.0	(26) 1.4	(13) 1.7			% Depr., Dep., Amort./Sales	(51) 1.4	(63) 1.0
1.4	1.5	1.8	3.7				2.3	2.2
3.0	2.4	2.3	7.4				4.1	3.9
	(18) 3.8	(10) 2.4				% Officers', Directors',	(17) 4.2	(23) 3.8
	5.5	4.2				Owners' Comp/Sales	5.9	7.4
	9.5	12.9					8.5	10.8
10694M	128064M	430429M	480881M	232887M	512449M	Net Sales ($)	1949015M	3391068M
2627M	38797M	150799M	351556M	161026M	370285M	Total Assets ($)	1235178M	1786238M

M = $ thousand   MM = $ million
See Pages 1 through 15 for Explanation of Ratios and Data

Comparative Historical Data				Current Data Sorted By Sales					
2	5	10	# Postretirement Benefits	1	2		3		4
			Type of Statement						
23	19	29	Unqualified		1	1	7	6	14
17	14	27	Reviewed	3	6	4	5	8	1
18	18	15	Compiled	2	8	1	3	1	
	1	2	Tax Returns	2					
16	18	22	Other	3	4	2	6	6	1
4/1/92- 3/31/93	4/1/93- 3/31/94	4/1/94- 3/31/95		38 (4/1-9/30/94)			57 (10/1/94-3/31/95)		
ALL	ALL	ALL		0-1MM	1-3MM	3-5MM	5-10MM	10-25MM	25MM & OVER
74	70	95	**NUMBER OF STATEMENTS**	10	19	8	21	21	16
%	%	%	**ASSETS**	%	%	%	%	%	%
11.9	13.6	11.9	Cash & Equivalents	18.7	11.1		13.1	12.6	9.0
28.3	34.8	35.4	Trade Receivables - (net)	26.4	38.5		43.3	31.2	27.8
7.8	7.4	7.5	Inventory	.8	7.6		5.9	9.8	11.3
6.4	3.6	4.9	All Other Current	17.2	3.3		5.1	1.1	3.6
54.4	59.4	59.7	Total Current	63.1	60.5		67.5	54.7	51.7
21.7	21.1	22.4	Fixed Assets (net)	27.6	19.2		20.2	28.1	22.1
10.7	8.8	7.1	Intangibles (net)	5.1	6.8		5.7	5.6	11.3
13.2	10.6	10.9	All Other Non-Current	4.2	13.5		6.7	11.7	14.9
100.0	100.0	100.0	Total	100.0	100.0		100.0	100.0	100.0
			LIABILITIES						
5.7	4.5	5.7	Notes Payable-Short Term	7.0	5.7		6.5	3.7	7.6
3.1	4.6	4.4	Cur. Mat.-L /T/D	5.9	5.9		2.8	4.3	2.9
13.7	14.8	16.5	Trade Payables	15.8	17.5		19.5	12.5	12.7
.5	.7	.6	Income Taxes Payable	.7	.5		.7	.7	.6
20.0	20.3	22.7	All Other Current	22.6	27.1		25.9	19.0	20.8
43.0	44.9	50.0	Total Current	52.0	56.7		55.4	40.1	44.5
15.1	13.6	13.6	Long Term Debt	14.8	16.1		8.2	15.6	13.9
.9	.6	1.2	Deferred Taxes	.0	.4		1.4	1.3	2.3
7.9	8.0	9.1	All Other-Non-Current	11.9	12.1		4.7	8.8	10.8
33.2	32.9	26.1	Net Worth	21.3	14.7		30.3	34.1	28.4
100.0	100.0	100.0	Total Liabilities & Net Worth	100.0	100.0		100.0	100.0	100.0
			INCOME DATA						
100.0	100.0	100.0	Net Sales	100.0	100.0		100.0	100.0	100.0
42.7	40.5	40.0	Gross Profit	54.5	45.5		40.4	38.0	30.9
37.9	35.7	35.8	Operating Expenses	53.5	42.1		35.9	31.6	27.3
4.8	4.9	4.2	Operating Profit	1.0	3.5		4.5	6.3	3.6
.6	.5	.5	All Other Expenses (net)	−.8	.8		1.0	.6	.9
4.2	4.4	3.6	Profit Before Taxes	1.8	2.7		3.5	5.7	2.7
			RATIOS						
2.2	2.0	1.7		2.6	1.6		1.7	1.8	1.7
1.2	1.3	1.2	Current	1.4	1.2		1.2	1.4	1.2
.8	.9	1.0		.5	.9		1.0	1.2	.9
1.7	1.5	1.3		1.3	1.3		1.3	1.4	1.4
1.0	1.0	1.1	Quick	.7	1.1		1.0	1.2	1.0
.5	.7	.7		.3	.7		.7	.8	.7
27 13.5	34 10.6	33 11.0		0 UND	33 11.0		38 9.7	33 11.0	37 9.8
39 9.4	47 7.8	47 7.7	Sales/Receivables	19 19.0	54 6.8		46 7.9	47 7.7	50 7.3
54 6.8	66 5.5	63 5.8		48 7.6	72 5.1		60 6.1	63 5.8	83 4.4
0 UND	0 UND	0 UND		0 UND	0 UND		0 UND	0 UND	0 UND
5 73.0	1 319.3	4 90.6	Cost of Sales/Inventory	0 UND	2 174.3		4 90.6	14 26.5	22 16.8
33 11.2	25 14.5	28 13.1		4 104.1	19 18.9		21 17.5	29 12.5	48 7.6
17 21.9	17 21.4	21 17.6		3 143.5	27 13.5		22 16.8	13 27.5	23 15.7
27 13.7	35 10.4	34 10.8	Cost of Sales/Payables	14 26.1	45 8.2		35 10.5	29 12.7	33 11.2
49 7.4	56 6.5	59 6.2		60 6.1	65 5.6		58 6.3	47 7.8	54 6.8
7.5	7.2	10.1		10.9	13.1		10.7	7.2	8.0
22.1	20.7	20.4	Sales/Working Capital	14.0	25.0		30.9	15.9	16.6
−56.3	−759.7	−113.0		−12.7	−26.9		−827.0	47.2	NM
12.9	14.1	16.7			9.8		(18) 25.5	(18) 50.6	(15) 6.6
(62) 3.8	(57) 4.8	(84) 5.8	EBIT/Interest		3.5		12.9	8.9	3.4
1.9	2.3	2.2			.5		2.5	3.8	.8
13.4	3.7	5.2					(11) 6.1		
(19) 4.5	(24) 1.8	(39) 3.0	Net Profit + Depr., Dep., Amort./Cur. Mat. L/T/D				4.0		
2.4	.8	1.2					1.2		
.3	.3	.4		.4	.5		.4	.4	.3
1.0	.8	1.2	Fixed/Worth	2.0	1.6		.7	1.1	1.5
2.8	NM	5.9		−1.0	−.5		4.0	1.7	NM
1.0	.8	1.7		1.6	1.5		1.7	1.0	2.0
3.1	3.1	3.3	Debt/Worth	2.2	4.0		2.5	1.9	3.1
17.9	NM	22.5		−5.2	−7.4		8.8	10.5	NM
65.0	66.0	87.2			(12) 58.0		(17) 91.2	(18) 90.4	(12) 56.6
(58) 26.7	(53) 31.2	(74) 40.3	% Profit Before Taxes/Tangible Net Worth		29.1		47.1	36.8	26.6
9.7	6.8	15.0			16.5		12.6	13.1	−8.7
16.6	19.2	19.9		27.4	16.0		27.3	23.7	14.4
8.7	8.1	8.9	% Profit Before Taxes/Total Assets	10.2	6.1		15.5	7.7	5.0
2.4	2.8	3.1		1.1	−.5		3.5	3.7	−6.6
41.2	46.6	35.8		35.1	38.1		42.8	26.8	34.8
16.5	17.7	18.8	Sales/Net Fixed Assets	21.7	26.5		21.6	8.7	12.3
6.2	6.3	7.3		5.1	8.7		9.4	4.7	4.4
3.4	3.5	3.7		5.7	3.3		4.6	3.5	2.0
2.3	2.5	2.5	Sales/Total Assets	3.0	2.3		3.7	2.5	1.6
1.6	1.6	1.6		1.7	1.6		2.3	1.6	1.3
.8	1.2	1.1			(18) 1.2		(19) 1.2	(17) 1.3	(12) 1.2
(61) 1.9	(58) 1.9	(82) 1.9	% Depr., Dep., Amort./Sales		2.1		1.4	2.1	2.6
3.6	3.7	2.8			2.8		2.2	4.2	3.8
3.4	2.1	2.8							
(18) 5.5	(25) 7.8	(35) 5.2	% Officers', Directors', Owners' Comp/Sales						
8.1	9.3	9.2							
2190852M	1483659M	1795424M	Net Sales ($)	6785M	42408M	30371M	159080M	327567M	1229213M
1386739M	845189M	1075090M	Total Assets ($)	2695M	19041M	10707M	82935M	164353M	795359M

M = $ thousand   MM = $ million
See Pages 1 through 15 for Explanation of Ratios and Data

	Current Data Sorted By Assets							Comparative Historical Data	
							# Postretirement Benefits		7
				2			**Type of Statement**		
		18	3 8				Unqualified		7
7		11	2				Reviewed		9
4		2	2				Compiled		7
		3	2				Tax Returns		
							Other	4/1/90-3/31/91	2 / 4/1/91-3/31/92
0-500M		19 (4/1-9/30/94) 500M-2MM	2-10MM	43 (10/1/94-3/31/95) 10-50MM	50-100MM	100-250MM		ALL	ALL
11		34	15	2			**NUMBER OF STATEMENTS**		25
%		%	%	%	%	%	**ASSETS**	%	%
11.3		8.8	4.7				Cash & Equivalents	D	8.2
36.1		31.8	28.0				Trade Receivables - (net)	A	30.8
8.1		7.2	10.9				Inventory	T	6.6
1.9		1.8	2.0				All Other Current	A	3.2
57.5		49.6	45.5				Total Current		48.7
36.5		41.4	46.7				Fixed Assets (net)	N	42.2
1.5		2.3	1.8				Intangibles (net)	O	1.6
4.6		6.7	6.0				All Other Non-Current	T	7.5
100.0		100.0	100.0				Total		100.0
							LIABILITIES	A	
7.2		6.0	7.3				Notes Payable-Short Term	V	9.0
3.1		10.2	7.7				Cur. Mat. -L/T/D	A	7.7
11.0		11.3	11.4				Trade Payables	I	9.7
.9		.1	.7				Income Taxes Payable	L	.6
11.5		7.9	9.6				All Other Current	A	10.1
33.6		35.5	36.8				Total Current	B	37.1
30.3		23.6	21.9				Long Term Debt	L	16.3
.0		.6	1.6				Deferred Taxes	E	.9
.2		5.8	2.2				All Other-Non-Current		2.9
35.8		34.5	37.5				Net Worth		42.8
100.0		100.0	100.0				Total Liabilities & Net Worth		100.0
							INCOME DATA		
100.0		100.0	100.0				Net Sales		100.0
61.6		40.7	39.0				Gross Profit		39.2
54.4		34.2	32.7				Operating Expenses		33.3
7.2		6.5	6.3				Operating Profit		5.8
1.9		2.5	1.7				All Other Expenses (net)		2.0
5.4		4.1	4.6				Profit Before Taxes		3.9
							RATIOS		
3.1		2.2	2.2						2.2
1.6		1.3	1.1				Current		1.3
1.0		1.0	.9						.9
2.4		1.7	1.1						1.6
1.6		1.0	.9				Quick		1.1
.7		.8	.7						.7
41　9.0		39　9.4	49　7.5					54　6.8	
48　7.6		48　7.6	57　6.4				Sales/Receivables	56　6.5	
59　6.2		60　6.1	66　5.5					66　5.5	
0　UND		8　45.1	16　22.6					10　36.2	
16　22.3		14　26.5	26　14.2				Cost of Sales/Inventory	17　21.2	
70　5.2		28　13.1	39　9.4					26　13.9	
12　30.5		12　30.8	18　20.0					18　20.1	
35　10.4		21　17.6	36　10.1				Cost of Sales/Payables	25　14.8	
152　2.4		41　8.9	54　6.8					42　8.6	
5.9		7.6	5.9						7.6
14.6		18.6	54.8				Sales/Working Capital		19.4
-206.5		-66.1	-31.1						NM
(10)　8.0		(32)　6.4	6.8					(23)　6.3	
5.3		3.3	2.7				EBIT/Interest	1.3	
.6		1.1	2.1					.8	
		(19)　2.9	(11)　1.9				Net Profit + Depr., Dep.,	(11)　2.4	
		1.3	1.3				Amort./Cur. Mat. L /T/D	1.1	
		.9	.7					-.4	
.2		.8	.6						.7
1.0		1.1	1.7				Fixed/Worth		1.0
2.1		2.6	3.2						1.8
.9		.9	1.3						.9
1.8		2.0	2.2				Debt/Worth		1.3
4.6		4.7	4.3						2.5
88.5		55.4	38.3				% Profit Before Taxes/Tangible		38.8
53.1		(31)　24.6	20.4				Net Worth	(23)　14.6	
-3.6		3.4	10.0						-3.0
31.2		16.1	13.4				% Profit Before Taxes/Total		15.6
16.0		7.1	6.5				Assets		6.3
-1.9		.7	3.9						-1.2
43.2		10.6	6.9						7.7
5.9		5.1	3.9				Sales/Net Fixed Assets		4.2
3.3		3.3	2.4						2.9
3.3		2.7	2.3						2.3
2.5		2.2	1.8				Sales/Total Assets		1.7
1.7		1.9	1.3						1.5
(10)　1.0		(33)　2.7	(14)　3.3				% Depr., Dep., Amort./Sales	(24)　3.1	
4.5		5.1	4.5					4.5	
10.6		8.1	6.4					5.7	
		(18)　2.4					% Officers', Directors',		
		6.7					Owners' Comp/Sales		
		11.1							
6476M		102521M	118639M	51108M			Net Sales ($)		124791M
3022M		44121M	66851M	32812M			Total Assets ($)		76856M

M = $ thousand　　MM = $ million
See Pages 1 through 15 for Explanation of Ratios and Data

Comparative Historical Data / Current Data Sorted By Sales

3	2	2	# Postretirement Benefits			1		1	
			Type of Statement	0-1MM	1-3MM	3-5MM	5-10MM	10-25MM	25MM & OVER
8	7	5	Unqualified				1	3	1
14	19	26	Reviewed		10	8	6	2	
13	8	20	Compiled	7	10	3	1		
1	1	6	Tax Returns	3	2		1		
3	8	5	Other			1	4		
4/1/92-3/31/93 ALL	4/1/93-3/31/94 ALL	4/1/94-3/31/95 ALL		19 (4/1-9/30/94)			43 (10/1/94-3/31/95)		
39	43	62	**NUMBER OF STATEMENTS**	10	22	12	12	5	1

Hist %	Hist %	Hist %	**ASSETS**	0-1MM %	1-3MM %	3-5MM %	5-10MM %	10-25MM %	25MM %
7.2	6.3	8.1	Cash & Equivalents	11.9	6.7	14.0	2.0		
32.6	28.8	31.9	Trade Receivables - (net)	32.5	28.9	30.2	38.6		
5.0	6.9	8.2	Inventory	8.0	5.9	6.7	15.0		
1.1	1.6	1.9	All Other Current	1.4	2.5	1.1	2.2		
45.9	43.6	50.1	Total Current	53.8	44.0	52.1	57.8		
45.8	48.0	41.5	Fixed Assets (net)	39.9	47.8	39.4	33.6		
1.4	1.8	1.9	Intangibles (net)	1.3	2.4	1.0	2.8		
6.9	6.7	6.5	All Other Non-Current	5.0	5.8	7.5	5.7		
100.0	100.0	100.0	Total	100.0	100.0	100.0	100.0		
			LIABILITIES						
8.1	5.7	6.8	Notes Payable-Short Term	5.5	6.3	3.7	9.8		
9.5	9.7	8.2	Cur. Mat.-L /T/D	3.4	10.1	11.5	7.2		
11.1	9.7	11.1	Trade Payables	10.6	6.4	13.3	19.9		
.9	.8	.4	Income Taxes Payable	1.0	.0	.3	.8		
8.4	6.4	9.0	All Other Current	12.1	5.9	8.1	12.5		
38.0	32.4	35.5	Total Current	32.5	28.6	36.9	50.3		
21.8	24.6	24.3	Long Term Debt	33.4	27.6	22.2	13.9		
1.8	.8	.8	Deferred Taxes	.0	.9	1.1	.6		
2.6	5.0	3.7	All Other-Non-Current	.2	5.2	3.1	5.8		
35.8	37.2	35.7	Net Worth	33.9	37.7	36.6	29.4		
100.0	100.0	100.0	Total Liabilities & Net Worth	100.0	100.0	100.0	100.0		
			INCOME DATA						
100.0	100.0	100.0	Net Sales	100.0	100.0	100.0	100.0		
40.0	37.0	43.9	Gross Profit	63.7	41.6	42.3	36.4		
34.4	33.5	37.3	Operating Expenses	56.1	35.3	36.5	29.6		
5.5	3.5	6.7	Operating Profit	7.6	6.3	5.8	6.8		
1.5	1.7	2.1	All Other Expenses (net)	2.0	2.5	1.1	3.2		
4.0	1.8	4.6	Profit Before Taxes	5.6	3.8	4.7	3.7		

RATIOS

Hist	Hist	Hist	Ratio	0-1MM	1-3MM	3-5MM	5-10MM	10-25MM	25MM
1.8	1.8	2.2	Current	3.2	2.4	1.9	2.0		
1.3	1.4	1.3		1.4	1.5	1.3	1.2		
.9	1.0	1.0		1.0	1.1	.9	.7		
1.5	1.6	1.7	Quick	2.6	1.9	1.7	1.1		
1.1	1.1	1.0		1.3	1.0	1.2	.9		
.8	.8	.8		.7	.8	.8	.6		
45 8.2	40 9.2	41 8.9	Sales/Receivables	40 9.2	35 10.3	43 8.5	41 8.8		
53 6.9	56 6.5	53 6.9		51 7.1	51 7.2	46 7.9	57 6.4		
64 5.7	64 5.7	64 5.7		60 6.1	70 5.2	60 6.1	63 5.8		
5 70.5	6 60.9	9 41.5	Cost of Sales/Inventory	0 UND	4 89.5	10 37.9	13 27.5		
13 28.4	15 24.1	17 21.2		21 17.0	14 26.1	14 26.2	27 13.4		
20 18.7	25 14.4	33 11.1		81 4.5	28 13.0	29 12.8	45 8.2		
18 20.2	13 28.6	13 28.1	Cost of Sales/Payables	0 UND	9 41.1	20 18.7	23 15.7		
25 14.6	24 15.0	24 15.2		38 9.6	15 24.3	34 10.8	40 9.2		
37 10.0	40 9.2	43 8.5		152 2.4	25 14.8	44 8.3	55 6.6		
7.8	9.7	7.6	Sales/Working Capital	5.5	7.0	8.1	9.9		
26.5	15.9	19.4		23.4	14.7	35.0	26.2		
-44.4	-999.8	-139.8		-177.2	110.4	-40.2	-27.4		
6.9	4.2	6.7	EBIT/Interest		4.9	6.4	10.3		
(37) 2.0	1.7	(59) 3.3			(20) 2.5	4.5	3.1		
1.0	.6	1.2			.4	1.8	2.2		
2.9	2.0	2.9	Net Profit + Depr., Dep., Amort./Cur. Mat. L/T/D		2.4	3.2			
(17) 1.6	(23) 1.1	(31) 1.3			(11) 1.0	(10) 1.4			
1.1	.6	.9			.7	.9			
.7	.9	.7	Fixed/Worth	.5	.8	.5	.9		
1.4	1.4	1.2		1.1	1.1	1.1	1.3		
2.4	2.5	2.2		3.8	3.0	1.8	2.0		
1.1	.8	1.1	Debt/Worth	1.0	.7	.8	1.5		
2.1	2.1	2.1		2.2	1.4	2.2	2.4		
4.1	3.7	4.3		7.3	4.0	4.4	9.7		
41.9	26.0	57.2	% Profit Before Taxes/Tangible Net Worth	115.3	33.6	37.6	79.3		
15.5	(42) 8.4	(59) 25.9		64.1	(20) 16.5	26.7	(11) 24.4		
.5	-2.9	3.8		-5.1	1.0	10.3	10.0		
15.5	9.5	16.5	% Profit Before Taxes/Total Assets	31.6	14.6	15.5	22.7		
5.8	2.7	8.4		16.1	3.8	9.5	7.9		
.1	-.9	1.1		-2.1	-1.6	4.3	4.2		
7.4	5.7	9.1	Sales/Net Fixed Assets	16.8	5.6	13.2	16.5		
4.4	4.2	4.9		5.6	3.8	5.3	8.8		
3.1	2.7	3.2		3.2	2.6	3.1	4.2		
2.5	2.1	2.7	Sales/Total Assets	2.9	2.3	2.7	3.2		
1.9	1.9	2.0		2.2	1.9	2.4	2.6		
1.6	1.7	1.6		1.6	1.3	1.8	2.1		
3.8	3.8	2.9	% Depr., Dep., Amort./Sales		4.0	2.5	2.3		
(35) 5.2	(41) 6.1	(59) 5.1			6.4	4.8	(11) 2.9		
7.9	8.5	7.5			9.1	7.0	4.0		
3.2	2.5	3.6	% Officers', Directors', Owners' Comp/Sales		4.0				
(17) 6.3	(21) 3.9	(34) 6.7			(11) 6.2				
10.8	12.7	13.2			8.2				
186935M	194386M	278744M	Net Sales ($)	5291M	44015M	46746M	73162M	76676M	32854M
103849M	106954M	146806M	Total Assets ($)	2822M	24315M	22336M	31395M	45381M	20557M

M = $ thousand   MM = $ million
See Pages 1 through 15 for Explanation of Ratios and Data

Current Data Sorted By Assets   Comparative Historical Data

0-500M	500M-2MM	2-10MM	10-50MM	50-100MM	100-250MM	# Postretirement Benefits / Type of Statement	4/1/90-3/31/91 ALL	4/1/91-3/31/92 ALL
2	1	1				Unqualified	11	9
1		4	2			Reviewed	22	16
2	7	1				Compiled	17	12
4	4	1				Tax Returns		1
1	5	3				Other	4	16
	7 (4/1-9/30/94)		28 (10/1/94-3/31/95)					
8	16	9	2			NUMBER OF STATEMENTS	54	54

0-500M %	500M-2MM %	2-10MM %	10-50MM %	50-100MM %	100-250MM %	Item	4/1/90-3/31/91 ALL %	4/1/91-3/31/92 ALL %
						ASSETS		
	2.9					Cash & Equivalents	6.3	6.6
	35.9					Trade Receivables - (net)	37.6	39.0
	6.8					Inventory	12.1	10.2
	.8					All Other Current	2.0	2.0
	46.3					Total Current	57.9	57.8
	46.9					Fixed Assets (net)	35.2	34.3
	1.1					Intangibles (net)	.5	.6
	5.7					All Other Non-Current	6.5	7.3
	100.0					Total	100.0	100.0
						LIABILITIES		
	12.4					Notes Payable-Short Term	10.7	11.6
	10.5					Cur. Mat. -L/T/D	7.1	6.7
	10.0					Trade Payables	10.5	9.6
	.2					Income Taxes Payable	1.2	.4
	4.9					All Other Current	11.1	10.5
	38.0					Total Current	40.6	38.9
	31.8					Long Term Debt	22.7	17.3
	1.9					Deferred Taxes	.2	.9
	2.6					All Other-Non-Current	2.3	1.0
	25.7					Net Worth	34.1	42.0
	100.0					Total Liabilities & Net Worth	100.0	100.0
						INCOME DATA		
	100.0					Net Sales	100.0	100.0
	42.0					Gross Profit	34.0	41.2
	39.3					Operating Expenses	30.4	37.0
	2.7					Operating Profit	3.6	4.1
	4.0					All Other Expenses (net)	1.9	2.8
	-1.3					Profit Before Taxes	1.7	1.3
						RATIOS		
	1.5					Current	2.4	2.7
	1.2						1.6	1.7
	.9						1.0	1.1
	1.3					Quick	1.9	1.9
	1.0						1.1	1.4
	.8						.8	.9
	52 7.0					Sales/Receivables	49 7.5	46 7.9
	64 5.7						62 5.9	57 6.4
	73 5.0						74 4.9	76 4.8
	3 134.4					Cost of Sales/Inventory	5 72.6	4 95.9
	16 23.5						19 19.6	14 26.3
	31 11.7						41 8.8	32 11.5
	13 27.3					Cost of Sales/Payables	13 28.7	9 39.2
	32 11.5						21 17.4	16 23.0
	47 7.8						37 9.9	43 8.4
	12.2					Sales/Working Capital	6.3	6.0
	41.3						12.6	10.9
	-82.9						-769.6	69.7
	2.4					EBIT/Interest	4.3	3.3
	(15) 1.3						(51) 1.5	(49) 1.7
	.5						.3	.0
						Net Profit + Depr., Dep., Amort./Cur. Mat. L /T/D	3.9	2.8
							(29) 1.5	(23) 1.3
							.8	.7
	1.1					Fixed/Worth	.6	.6
	1.9						1.0	.9
	5.3						2.1	1.5
	1.5					Debt/Worth	.9	.7
	3.1						2.2	1.4
	8.7						5.2	3.5
	21.9					% Profit Before Taxes/Tangible Net Worth	31.9	25.8
	(14) 5.0						(50) 11.8	(53) 5.1
	-65.9						-10.5	-15.2
	5.8					% Profit Before Taxes/Total Assets	12.5	8.3
	.6						2.3	2.3
	-7.5						-3.4	-6.4
	5.7					Sales/Net Fixed Assets	10.8	11.0
	4.6						6.2	7.7
	3.5						4.5	4.2
	2.7					Sales/Total Assets	2.7	2.8
	2.0						2.2	2.3
	1.6						1.8	1.8
	5.0					% Depr., Dep., Amort./Sales	2.6	3.0
	(15) 6.5						(53) 3.6	(46) 4.0
	9.9						5.6	6.2
	3.4					% Officers', Directors', Owners' Comp/Sales	4.2	4.0
	(11) 7.6						(16) 6.6	(24) 7.3
	11.5						11.3	13.4
4470M	42565M	58600M	62670M			Net Sales ($)	275043M	222235M
2037M	20037M	31171M	26341M			Total Assets ($)	126497M	104672M

M = $ thousand   MM = $ million
See Pages 1 through 15 for Explanation of Ratios and Data

Comparative Historical Data

Current Data Sorted By Sales

	92-93	93-94	94-95		0-1MM	1-3MM	3-5MM	5-10MM	10-25MM	25MM & OVER
	1	1	4	# Postretirement Benefits	1	2	1			
				Type of Statement						
	3	3	7	Unqualified	1		1	2	1	2
	13	12	10	Reviewed	1	4	4	1		
	12	10	9	Compiled	3	4	1	1		
			2	Tax Returns						
	6	7	9	Other	1	3	4	1		
	4/1/92- 3/31/93 ALL	4/1/93- 3/31/94 ALL	4/1/94- 3/31/95 ALL		7 (4/1-9/30/94)			28 (10/1/94-3/31/95)		
	34	34	35	NUMBER OF STATEMENTS	6	11	10	5	1	2
	%	%	%	ASSETS	%	%	%	%	%	%
	7.4	8.3	5.7	Cash & Equivalents		4.5	3.2			
	37.4	34.6	36.3	Trade Receivables - (net)		31.9	36.0			
	8.2	9.3	10.0	Inventory		10.5	10.9			
	1.0	1.4	1.3	All Other Current		1.5	.2			
	54.0	53.7	53.4	Total Current		48.3	50.2			
	40.5	37.9	39.4	Fixed Assets (net)		46.1	41.6			
	.5	1.1	1.3	Intangibles (net)		.4	2.5			
	5.0	7.3	6.0	All Other Non-Current		5.2	5.6			
	100.0	100.0	100.0	Total		100.0	100.0			
				LIABILITIES						
	10.4	10.9	9.1	Notes Payable-Short Term		12.0	7.3			
	8.0	6.1	8.6	Cur. Mat.-L./T/D		11.2	8.2			
	9.2	7.8	10.5	Trade Payables		9.4	9.8			
	.3	1.9	.7	Income Taxes Payable		.3	.0			
	9.2	11.6	8.5	All Other Current		4.3	12.8			
	37.0	38.2	37.4	Total Current		37.3	38.1			
	25.2	22.2	28.0	Long Term Debt		32.1	32.8			
	1.7	2.5	.9	Deferred Taxes		1.1	.0			
	4.4	4.0	2.0	All Other-Non-Current		2.6	1.2			
	31.7	33.0	31.7	Net Worth		26.9	27.9			
	100.0	100.0	100.0	Total Liabilities & Net Worth		100.0	100.0			
				INCOME DATA						
	100.0	100.0	100.0	Net Sales		100.0	100.0			
	37.6	38.7	41.1	Gross Profit		41.1	47.2			
	34.2	36.6	36.7	Operating Expenses		39.1	43.2			
	3.3	2.1	4.4	Operating Profit		2.0	4.0			
	1.1	1.3	2.4	All Other Expenses (net)		4.4	2.6			
	2.2	.9	2.0	Profit Before Taxes		-2.5	1.4			
				RATIOS						
	2.7	2.8	2.0	Current		1.9	1.6			
	1.9	1.6	1.4			1.2	1.3			
	.9	1.0	1.1			.9	1.1			
	2.4	2.3	1.5	Quick		1.3	1.2			
	1.5	1.5	1.1			.9	1.1			
	.9	.6	.8			.6	.8			
	49 7.5	49 7.4	52 7.0	Sales/Receivables		29 12.6	57 6.4			
	61 6.0	60 6.1	64 5.7			64 5.7	64 5.7			
	81 4.5	79 4.6	83 4.4			74 4.9	79 4.6			
	0 UND	9 41.7	8 44.0	Cost of Sales/Inventory		2 166.4	13 28.0			
	12 29.5	18 20.7	26 14.0			16 23.0	21 17.3			
	35 10.4	33 11.2	51 7.2			51 7.2	69 5.3			
	7 50.6	4 100.0	15 25.0	Cost of Sales/Payables		2 184.7	20 18.2			
	16 22.4	13 27.8	29 12.7			28 12.9	43 8.4			
	41 8.9	29 12.7	49 7.5			37 9.9	48 7.6			
	6.2	5.5	6.9	Sales/Working Capital		8.4	10.1			
	9.2	11.5	12.8			48.5	21.6			
	-48.7	NM	81.7			-26.0	56.7			
	6.4	4.2	4.6	EBIT/Interest		2.6	3.3			
(32)	2.0	(31) 2.5	(30) 2.3		(10)	1.4	1.6			
	.8	-.3	.8			.2	1.2			
	3.8	2.4	3.4	Net Profit + Depr., Dep., Amort./Cur. Mat. L/T/D						
(12)	1.5	(14) 1.4	(18) 1.9							
	.8	.6	1.2							
	.5	.5	.7	Fixed/Worth		.9	1.0			
	1.5	1.2	1.2			1.9	1.9			
	4.7	3.8	2.2			2.3	10.6			
	1.0	.7	1.4	Debt/Worth		1.7	1.3			
	2.0	2.1	2.3			2.9	2.7			
	8.4	6.4	7.4			8.3	25.0			
	24.3	45.9	36.9	% Profit Before Taxes/Tangible Net Worth		20.9				
(29)	18.4	(30) 13.6	(33) 16.4		(10)	2.2				
	-.7	1.5	-.1			-78.9				
	12.1	10.4	9.0	% Profit Before Taxes/Total Assets		6.5	3.4			
	4.2	5.8	4.4			-.7	1.9			
	-1.7	-2.7	-.9			-9.9	.9			
	8.9	9.3	9.2	Sales/Net Fixed Assets		8.2	5.4			
	6.1	4.6	5.2			4.9	4.4			
	3.9	4.2	4.0			2.6	4.1			
	2.5	2.3	2.5	Sales/Total Assets		2.9	2.2			
	2.1	2.1	2.0			2.0	1.9			
	1.9	1.6	1.5			1.5	1.5			
	2.9	3.5	3.6	% Depr., Dep., Amort./Sales		4.2	4.4			
(32)	4.1	(32) 4.7	(31) 5.3		(10)	7.8	5.2			
	6.0	7.5	8.0			11.9	6.9			
	3.0	4.5	5.1	% Officers', Directors', Owners' Comp/Sales						
(22)	6.0	(16) 7.1	(19) 7.6							
	9.3	12.3	11.9							
	107252M	124119M	168305M	Net Sales ($)	2389M	18121M	37218M	33241M	14666M	62670M
	53719M	63351M	79586M	Total Assets ($)	1272M	9229M	20079M	16119M	6546M	26341M

M = $ thousand   MM = $ million
See Pages 1 through 15 for Explanation of Ratios and Data

	Current Data Sorted By Assets						Comparative Historical Data	
1	3	2	2	1		# Postretirement Benefits		
						Type of Statement		
	2	7	5	2		Unqualified	8	14
	8	10	2			Reviewed	9	13
4	10	2	1	1		Compiled	15	10
1						Tax Returns		1
1	4	6	4	1	2	Other	7	9
							4/1/90-3/31/91	4/1/91-3/31/92
0-500M	23 (4/1-9/30/94) 500M-2MM	2-10MM	50 (10/1/94-3/31/95) 10-50MM	50-100MM	100-250MM		ALL	ALL
5	25	25	12	4	2	NUMBER OF STATEMENTS	39	47
%	%	%	%	%	%	ASSETS	%	%
	7.0	4.2	1.2			Cash & Equivalents	7.2	7.8
	36.3	29.0	25.7			Trade Receivables - (net)	28.9	27.1
	31.6	26.8	23.3			Inventory	30.7	26.5
	1.7	.6	.2			All Other Current	1.1	1.3
	76.6	60.7	50.4			Total Current	67.9	62.7
	17.8	31.6	31.1			Fixed Assets (net)	25.1	30.1
	.4	1.4	.8			Intangibles (net)	1.6	1.9
	5.2	6.3	17.6			All Other Non-Current	5.4	5.2
	100.0	100.0	100.0			Total	100.0	100.0
						LIABILITIES		
	8.2	11.4	8.7			Notes Payable-Short Term	10.0	13.1
	2.5	2.3	5.2			Cur. Mat. -L/T/D	3.6	4.0
	19.9	15.6	13.4			Trade Payables	17.6	14.3
	.6	.8	.0			Income Taxes Payable	.7	.2
	6.6	5.9	6.8			All Other Current	10.9	6.9
	37.7	36.0	34.2			Total Current	42.8	38.6
	9.9	14.0	23.1			Long Term Debt	11.1	11.3
	.1	.9	.7			Deferred Taxes	.6	1.0
	.6	3.4	5.9			All Other-Non-Current	2.9	2.9
	51.9	45.7	36.1			Net Worth	42.7	46.1
	100.0	100.0	100.0			Total Liabilities & Net Worth	100.0	100.0
						INCOME DATA		
	100.0	100.0	100.0			Net Sales	100.0	100.0
	28.7	28.1	31.9			Gross Profit	31.0	28.5
	25.1	23.7	29.4			Operating Expenses	27.8	24.7
	3.6	4.4	2.5			Operating Profit	3.1	3.8
	.9	1.1	−.6			All Other Expenses (net)	1.2	1.2
	2.7	3.2	3.1			Profit Before Taxes	1.9	2.6
						RATIOS		
	4.1	2.0	2.0				2.6	2.6
	1.8	1.7	1.4			Current	1.6	1.7
	1.6	1.3	.9				1.3	1.1
	2.3	1.5	1.0				1.2	1.4
	1.0	.9	.8			Quick	.8	.9
	.8	.7	.6				.6	.5
	37 9.9	36 10.2	42 8.6				33 11.1	35 10.3
	44 8.3	43 8.4	49 7.4			Sales/Receivables	41 8.8	44 8.3
	51 7.1	50 7.3	60 6.1				58 6.3	56 6.5
	32 11.3	37 9.9	35 10.5				50 7.3	37 9.9
	59 6.2	49 7.4	68 5.4			Cost of Sales/Inventory	66 5.5	57 6.4
	81 4.5	78 4.7	126 2.9				101 3.6	87 4.2
	17 21.2	21 17.4	20 18.6				17 21.3	19 19.0
	29 12.8	33 11.1	38 9.6			Cost of Sales/Payables	34 10.7	30 12.0
	50 7.3	45 8.2	76 4.8				55 6.6	52 7.0
	5.4	7.4	6.9				5.3	4.9
	7.0	10.1	15.6			Sales/Working Capital	10.7	9.3
	13.8	18.6	−289.6				24.6	43.6
	21.1	15.5	8.7				7.0	6.4
	(22) 8.1	(23) 4.8	(11) 5.0			EBIT/Interest	(38) 2.8	(45) 3.2
	3.7	2.9	1.8				1.2	1.6
		7.2					4.4	2.7
		(11) 2.4				Net Profit + Depr., Dep., Amort./Cur. Mat. L /T/D	(16) 2.2	(20) 1.8
		.4					1.1	.4
	.2	.3	.4				.3	.4
	.3	.7	.9			Fixed/Worth	.5	.7
	.6	1.6	2.0				1.2	1.3
	.4	.6	1.0				.6	.6
	1.1	1.3	2.2			Debt/Worth	1.3	1.2
	1.8	3.0	3.8				2.8	3.0
	47.9	50.0	70.7				(35) 25.0	(46) 36.7
	21.3	20.0	19.1			% Profit Before Taxes/Tangible Net Worth	12.2	13.7
	11.2	8.1	8.1				2.5	2.1
	15.1	15.3	26.0				10.5	12.9
	8.6	10.3	6.4			% Profit Before Taxes/Total Assets	5.6	5.2
	6.2	3.3	2.0				.9	.6
	43.6	13.8	9.2				23.0	16.6
	19.2	7.6	6.9			Sales/Net Fixed Assets	10.6	7.3
	9.3	4.7	4.0				5.5	3.8
	4.0	3.1	2.6				3.1	2.8
	3.1	2.2	2.0			Sales/Total Assets	2.5	2.2
	2.2	1.7	1.4				1.5	1.5
	.9	.7					1.0	1.1
	(23) 1.3	(23) 1.9				% Depr., Dep., Amort./Sales	(35) 2.2	(40) 2.7
	2.1	2.9					3.6	4.6
	3.9						3.2	3.3
	(12) 4.9					% Officers', Directors', Owners' Comp/Sales	(22) 5.3	(22) 4.6
	11.9						9.4	7.9
4311M	81641M	218241M	563429M	233119M	341788M	Net Sales ($)	262233M	482886M
1421M	27697M	94302M	292702M	259878M	255640M	Total Assets ($)	168926M	291495M

M = $ thousand   MM = $ million
See Pages 1 through 15 for Explanation of Ratios and Data

Type of Statement

	Comparative Historical Data 2	4	9	# Postretirement Benefits / Type of Statement		3	1	1	1	3
	8	12	16	Unqualified		1		6	4	5
	14	18	20	Reviewed	1	4	6	4	4	1
	15	20	18	Compiled	2	6	5	2	2	1
	3	2	1	Tax Returns				1		
	8	8	18	Other		5	2		4	7

Main Data

	4/1/92-3/31/93 ALL (2)	4/1/93-3/31/94 ALL (4)	4/1/94-3/31/95 ALL (9)	0-1MM	1-3MM 23 (4/1-9/30/94)	3-5MM	5-10MM 50 (10/1/94-3/31/95)	10-25MM	25MM & OVER
NUMBER OF STATEMENTS	48	60	73	3	16	13	13	14	14
ASSETS	%	%	%	%	%	%	%	%	%
Cash & Equivalents	4.6	5.5	4.6		4.8	5.1	3.0	5.0	1.9
Trade Receivables - (net)	30.8	33.5	30.6		32.8	30.5	34.0	31.1	24.1
Inventory	30.5	27.0	26.9		34.9	21.3	31.3	29.8	17.9
All Other Current	.7	1.1	1.1		2.9	.4	.4	.7	.6
Total Current	66.6	67.1	63.2		75.4	57.3	68.7	66.6	44.5
Fixed Assets (net)	25.3	25.5	26.5		21.4	35.3	15.1	30.1	34.0
Intangibles (net)	3.0	1.4	2.7		.2	.9	1.3	1.0	9.6
All Other Non-Current	5.2	6.0	7.6		3.1	6.6	15.0	2.3	11.9
Total	100.0	100.0	100.0		100.0	100.0	100.0	100.0	100.0
LIABILITIES									
Notes Payable-Short Term	6.1	10.1	8.7		7.1	6.2	17.4	7.7	7.4
Cur. Mat.-L /T/D	3.4	3.2	3.0		2.6	3.0	1.5	3.6	4.1
Trade Payables	16.7	18.1	16.6		21.4	12.6	20.8	13.8	11.7
Income Taxes Payable	.6	1.0	.5		.8	.4	.4	.9	.1
All Other Current	7.6	6.4	6.6		6.4	5.6	6.8	5.4	8.2
Total Current	34.4	38.8	35.3		38.2	27.7	46.9	31.5	31.5
Long Term Debt	12.5	12.2	16.1		12.5	20.9	8.5	17.8	23.6
Deferred Taxes	.6	.4	.5		.0	.8	.4	.6	.9
All Other-Non-Current	1.3	5.1	3.2		.4	5.2	1.7	.7	8.2
Net Worth	51.3	43.6	44.9		48.9	45.4	42.5	49.4	35.8
Total Liabilities & Net Worth	100.0	100.0	100.0		100.0	100.0	100.0	100.0	100.0
INCOME DATA									
Net Sales	100.0	100.0	100.0		100.0	100.0	100.0	100.0	100.0
Gross Profit	29.7	30.9	30.8		33.8	28.7	23.2	29.9	34.1
Operating Expenses	23.2	24.9	26.5		30.8	23.8	22.1	21.8	29.5
Operating Profit	6.5	6.0	4.3		3.0	5.0	1.1	8.0	4.6
All Other Expenses (net)	1.1	.9	.7		1.3	.7	.6	1.5	−.6
Profit Before Taxes	5.4	5.1	3.6		1.8	4.2	.4	6.6	5.2
RATIOS									
Current	3.7	2.2	2.4		2.7	3.0	2.0	3.6	1.9
	2.0	1.7	1.7		1.7	1.9	1.2	2.0	1.4
	1.3	1.3	1.4		1.6	1.6	1.1	1.7	1.2
Quick	2.1	1.5	1.4		1.5	1.9	.8	1.9	1.2
	1.0	1.0	.9		.9	1.2	.8	1.0	.9
	.7	.8	.7		.7	.8	.6	.9	.7
Sales/Receivables	37 9.9	39 9.4	39 9.3		34 10.7	41 8.8	38 9.7	35 10.5	47 7.8
	41 8.9	45 8.2	44 8.3		42 8.7	44 8.3	45 8.2	42 8.7	50 7.3
	48 7.6	52 7.0	52 7.0		50 7.3	49 7.5	53 6.9	51 7.1	62 5.9
Cost of Sales/Inventory	36 10.1	26 14.3	34 10.7		50 7.3	13 28.8	31 11.9	38 9.7	33 11.0
	58 6.3	47 7.7	55 6.6		62 5.9	54 6.8	59 6.2	51 7.2	54 6.8
	85 4.3	73 5.0	81 4.5		81 4.5	81 4.5	87 4.2	79 4.6	81 4.5
Cost of Sales/Payables	15 24.5	20 18.0	20 18.4		22 16.7	18 20.0	28 13.1	14 26.6	0 UND
	29 12.7	30 12.3	33 11.1		34 10.7	25 14.6	43 8.5	27 13.4	41 8.8
	49 7.4	45 8.1	52 7.0		64 5.7	43 8.4	57 6.4	37 9.8	68 5.4
Sales/Working Capital	5.1	6.1	6.3		5.5	6.4	6.7	6.0	7.8
	8.4	9.6	10.0		8.3	7.6	20.3	9.3	14.7
	20.1	19.5	16.4		12.7	12.3	151.1	11.5	NM
EBIT/Interest	(43) 13.7	(54) 10.4	(67) 16.2		(14) 14.3	(12) 15.2	14.2	(13) 18.3	(13) 41.0
	3.4	4.0	6.5		5.9	8.2	3.7	5.0	8.7
	1.9	2.2	2.9		3.0	2.9	2.1	4.1	2.0
Net Profit + Depr., Dep., Amort./Cur. Mat. L/T/D	(25) 3.4	(19) 3.4	(28) 6.9						
	1.8	2.4	3.0						
	1.1	1.8	1.2						
Fixed/Worth	.2	.3	.3		.2	.4	.2	.4	.6
	.5	.6	.6		.3	.7	.4	.5	1.1
	.9	1.1	1.2		.5	1.7	.7	1.3	2.3
Debt/Worth	.4	.6	.7		.7	.6	.5	.5	1.0
	1.0	1.2	1.3		1.2	1.1	2.0	1.1	2.2
	2.5	2.8	2.8		1.5	2.8	4.0	2.5	4.6
% Profit Before Taxes/Tangible Net Worth	35.4	(58) 43.8	(71) 48.2		49.2	54.7	48.4	58.6	64.9
	18.1	30.3	20.7		19.1	12.6	18.2	31.7	(12) 28.7
	8.8	11.3	9.4		6.8	10.2	2.6	19.2	8.1
% Profit Before Taxes/Total Assets	15.6	19.9	16.3		13.8	15.2	9.8	26.8	22.1
	6.5	8.9	9.1		9.4	8.4	6.1	15.3	10.9
	2.7	4.3	3.5		4.1	4.4	2.1	8.3	2.4
Sales/Net Fixed Assets	31.1	20.5	23.2		50.0	18.0	75.5	13.8	7.5
	12.6	11.0	9.1		20.6	6.0	23.9	9.6	4.5
	4.9	6.0	5.3		11.6	4.0	10.1	5.7	2.7
Sales/Total Assets	3.3	3.3	3.3		3.6	3.1	4.2	3.3	2.4
	2.4	2.6	2.3		2.9	1.9	2.7	2.7	1.6
	1.9	2.1	1.8		2.2	1.7	1.7	2.0	.8
% Depr., Dep., Amort./Sales	(42) .8	(56) 1.1	(61) 1.0		(13) .8	1.2	(12) .5	(12) 1.2	
	1.9	2.0	1.7		1.2	1.7	1.0	2.2	
	3.3	2.8	2.5		1.9	2.6	2.1	3.3	
% Officers', Directors', Owners' Comp/Sales	(24) 3.4	(31) 3.2	(27) 3.0						
	4.9	5.1	3.9						
	8.7	9.4	10.7						
Net Sales ($)	389126M	456899M	1442529M	1743M	31566M	48751M	93297M	204212M	1062960M
Total Assets ($)	183241M	198276M	931640M	1643M	13658M	23453M	56889M	88224M	747773M

M = $ thousand   MM = $ million
See Pages 1 through 15 for Explanation of Ratios and Data

MANUFACTURERS—MISCELLANEOUS PLASTIC PRODUCTS. SIC# 3089

	Current Data Sorted By Assets							Comparative Historical Data	
	2	14	14	11	6	3	**# Postretirement Benefits**		
							Type of Statement		
	2	14	86	75	28	9	Unqualified	172	202
	10	87	126	26			Reviewed	154	191
	28	65	47	5	1		Compiled	136	134
	2	8	5				Tax Returns	1	9
	11	52	66	68	17	4	Other	98	126
		277 (4/1-9/30/94)			565 (10/1/94-3/31/95)			4/1/90-3/31/91	4/1/91-3/31/92
	0-500M	500M-2MM	2-10MM	10-50MM	50-100MM	100-250MM	NUMBER OF STATEMENTS	ALL	ALL
	53	226	330	174	46	13		561	662
	%	%	%	%	%	%	**ASSETS**	%	%
	9.0	7.2	5.9	4.5	3.8	4.2	Cash & Equivalents	6.4	6.3
	31.2	29.1	26.8	25.4	23.2	23.3	Trade Receivables - (net)	26.8	26.3
	18.2	21.6	22.5	19.5	18.5	18.2	Inventory	21.7	20.8
	3.4	1.8	1.6	1.8	2.2	1.8	All Other Current	1.5	1.6
	61.8	59.8	56.7	51.2	47.7	47.4	Total Current	56.4	55.0
	32.2	32.6	36.9	38.6	40.8	41.9	Fixed Assets (net)	36.8	37.3
	1.3	2.1	1.9	3.3	5.1	5.4	Intangibles (net)	1.4	2.0
	4.6	5.5	4.5	6.9	6.4	5.3	All Other Non-Current	5.4	5.7
	100.0	100.0	100.0	100.0	100.0	100.0	Total	100.0	100.0
							LIABILITIES		
	8.4	8.9	9.8	9.0	6.0	1.6	Notes Payable-Short Term	9.6	9.0
	6.7	5.3	5.1	4.3	3.1	2.1	Cur. Mat. -L/T/D	5.2	5.6
	18.1	16.3	17.1	15.3	13.7	14.5	Trade Payables	15.9	15.5
	.8	.5	.5	.2	.3	.1	Income Taxes Payable	.6	.5
	11.0	8.9	6.7	7.7	7.9	9.0	All Other Current	7.8	7.8
	45.0	39.8	39.3	36.6	31.0	27.4	Total Current	39.1	38.4
	18.1	16.1	18.5	17.8	21.9	30.7	Long Term Debt	20.2	21.3
	.1	.3	.9	1.3	2.6	.7	Deferred Taxes	.9	.8
	3.7	3.5	3.9	3.6	3.1	5.9	All Other-Non-Current	3.1	3.6
	33.2	40.2	37.5	40.7	41.5	35.3	Net Worth	36.7	36.0
	100.0	100.0	100.0	100.0	100.0	100.0	Total Liabilities & Net Worth	100.0	100.0
							INCOME DATA		
	100.0	100.0	100.0	100.0	100.0	100.0	Net Sales	100.0	100.0
	36.9	30.8	24.8	23.4	24.8	27.6	Gross Profit	26.9	27.4
	33.4	24.5	19.5	16.7	17.0	17.9	Operating Expenses	21.2	22.1
	3.6	6.3	5.3	6.7	7.8	9.6	Operating Profit	5.8	5.3
	1.0	1.6	1.4	1.3	1.7	1.9	All Other Expenses (net)	1.9	1.9
	2.6	4.7	3.9	5.4	6.2	7.8	Profit Before Taxes	3.8	3.4
							RATIOS		
	2.4	2.2	2.1	2.0	2.1	2.3		2.2	2.2
	1.4	1.5	1.4	1.4	1.6	1.6	Current	1.4	1.5
	1.0	1.2	1.1	1.1	1.2	1.4		1.0	1.1
	1.6	1.4	1.3	1.1	1.2	1.3		1.3	1.3
	1.0	.9	.8	.8	.8	.9	Quick	.8	.8
	.5	.7	.6	.6	.7	.8		.6	.6
	25 14.7	34 10.8	39 9.4	41 8.8	42 8.7	43 8.5		34 10.7	35 10.5
	42 8.7	43 8.4	47 7.7	51 7.1	51 7.1	54 6.7	Sales/Receivables	43 8.5	45 8.1
	56 6.5	55 6.6	57 6.4	62 5.9	63 5.8	65 5.6		55 6.6	55 6.6
	16 22.3	29 12.8	36 10.2	35 10.4	40 9.2	36 10.1		32 11.4	31 11.6
	27 13.4	46 8.0	49 7.4	49 7.4	59 6.2	51 7.2	Cost of Sales/Inventory	47 7.7	46 8.0
	62 5.9	66 5.5	73 5.0	68 5.4	85 4.3	87 4.2		72 5.1	66 5.5
	15 24.6	17 21.0	24 15.3	28 12.9	32 11.3	34 10.6		21 17.3	22 16.3
	33 10.9	31 11.6	39 9.4	38 9.5	39 9.3	46 8.0	Cost of Sales/Payables	33 11.2	33 11.1
	57 6.4	48 7.6	53 6.9	51 7.2	54 6.7	56 6.5		49 7.5	48 7.6
	7.4	7.6	6.6	6.4	5.8	5.2		7.0	6.9
	15.5	13.0	12.0	13.6	9.7	8.6	Sales/Working Capital	13.8	13.1
	NM	31.5	59.4	100.3	21.0	14.5		78.7	85.4
	7.6	9.8	9.7	9.4	10.0	13.4		5.7	5.2
	(47) 2.9	(212) 4.0	(316) 3.9	(159) 4.2	(42) 4.6	5.3	EBIT/Interest	(535) 2.7	(615) 2.5
	.7	1.8	1.6	2.1	3.1	2.4		1.2	1.2
	3.6	3.5	3.9	4.5	8.0		Net Profit + Depr., Dep.,	4.4	4.2
	(19) 1.8	(103) 2.0	(161) 2.1	(95) 2.2	(37) 2.9		Amort./Cur. Mat. L /T/D	(328) 2.3	(361) 2.0
	.8	1.0	1.0	1.1	1.9			1.1	1.1
	.4	.5	.6	.7	.7	.9		.6	.6
	1.0	.9	1.1	1.1	1.3	1.3	Fixed/Worth	1.1	1.1
	3.7	1.7	1.9	2.0	2.1	4.3		2.2	2.4
	.8	.8	1.0	.8	1.0	1.4		.9	.9
	2.4	1.7	1.9	1.7	1.9	2.1	Debt/Worth	1.8	1.9
	9.7	3.7	3.8	3.3	3.3	7.7		4.3	4.2
	71.2	50.5	44.3	42.7	33.9	55.3	% Profit Before Taxes/Tangible	37.4	37.7
	(45) 23.9	(214) 24.5	(311) 22.5	(167) 23.4	(44) 26.8	(11) 35.7	Net Worth	(524) 19.3	(597) 18.8
	2.9	6.0	7.7	9.0	18.2	25.4		5.6	5.3
	24.7	18.7	15.4	15.3	14.2	18.7	% Profit Before Taxes/Total	13.8	12.6
	6.0	8.3	7.3	7.9	9.6	12.1	Assets	6.7	6.1
	-.3	2.1	1.9	3.6	5.5	4.6		1.1	1.0
	20.4	15.1	9.6	6.8	5.7	5.9		10.1	9.7
	11.6	7.6	5.5	4.4	3.9	3.7	Sales/Net Fixed Assets	5.9	5.7
	5.4	4.7	3.6	3.3	2.6	2.3		3.7	3.5
	4.0	3.0	2.4	2.2	1.8	1.9		2.6	2.6
	2.9	2.4	2.0	1.7	1.5	1.5	Sales/Total Assets	2.1	2.1
	2.1	1.8	1.6	1.3	1.2	1.1		1.6	1.6
	1.8	1.7	2.1	2.6	2.5			2.1	2.1
	(42) 2.5	(209) 2.8	(304) 3.1	(151) 3.6	(40) 4.0		% Depr., Dep., Amort./Sales	(517) 3.4	(618) 3.6
	5.8	4.5	4.8	5.2	5.0			4.9	5.2
	4.8	3.8	1.7	.9				2.7	2.7
	(33) 8.6	(127) 5.7	(122) 3.1	(31) 1.9			% Officers', Directors', Owners' Comp/Sales	(208) 4.5	(243) 4.5
	11.4	8.0	5.0	4.0				7.5	8.0
	48661M	626351M	3032686M	6173323M	5244850M	3144981M	Net Sales ($)	8733557M	10797557M
	16320M	259429M	1532202M	3567512M	3378790M	2016976M	Total Assets ($)	5126480M	6650824M

M = $ thousand   MM = $ million
See Pages 1 through 15 for Explanation of Ratios and Data

Comparative Historical Data				Current Data Sorted By Sales					
25	33	50		4	6	6	11	7	16
			# Postretirement Benefits						
			Type of Statement						
209	204	214	Unqualified	3	10	12	36	66	87
200	216	249	Reviewed	10	46	60	68	51	14
133	153	146	Compiled	21	53	29	24	13	6
10	11	15	Tax Returns	5	4	2	2	2	
156	178	218	Other	11	36	25	34	40	72
4/1/92-3/31/93 ALL	4/1/93-3/31/94 ALL	4/1/94-3/31/95 ALL		277 (4/1-9/30/94)		565 (10/1/94-3/31/95)			
				0-1MM	1-3MM	3-5MM	5-10MM	10-25MM	25MM & OVER
708	762	842	**NUMBER OF STATEMENTS**	50	149	128	164	172	179
%	%	%	**ASSETS**	%	%	%	%	%	%
6.0	5.7	6.0	Cash & Equivalents	6.6	7.5	6.8	6.4	5.6	4.0
26.7	27.1	27.1	Trade Receivables - (net)	28.4	26.7	28.2	29.1	26.1	25.6
21.0	21.0	21.1	Inventory	16.4	21.0	22.0	23.0	21.8	19.4
1.9	1.4	1.9	All Other Current	3.4	2.1	1.7	1.6	1.6	1.9
55.5	55.1	56.1	Total Current	54.7	57.3	58.7	60.0	55.1	50.9
36.6	37.1	36.1	Fixed Assets (net)	39.9	33.0	35.4	34.1	37.1	38.9
2.0	2.1	2.4	Intangibles (net)	.6	3.6	1.5	1.7	1.8	4.0
5.9	5.7	5.4	All Other Non-Current	4.8	6.1	4.4	4.2	6.0	6.2
100.0	100.0	100.0	Total	100.0	100.0	100.0	100.0	100.0	100.0
			LIABILITIES						
8.9	8.9	9.0	Notes Payable-Short Term	10.5	9.2	9.0	8.3	10.1	8.1
5.3	5.2	4.9	Cur. Mat.-L /T/D	7.2	4.8	5.8	5.4	4.1	4.1
15.8	14.8	16.4	Trade Payables	15.5	14.3	16.9	18.1	17.2	15.5
.6	1.2	.4	Income Taxes Payable	.6	.4	.5	.8	.3	.2
8.1	8.2	7.9	All Other Current	6.2	10.4	8.1	6.7	6.7	8.2
38.6	38.2	38.6	Total Current	39.9	39.1	40.4	39.2	38.4	36.1
19.3	19.8	18.0	Long Term Debt	21.4	16.6	17.0	17.6	17.9	19.5
.8	.9	.8	Deferred Taxes	.2	.3	.7	.9	.8	1.6
3.6	3.3	3.7	All Other-Non-Current	2.6	3.7	3.9	3.5	4.4	3.4
37.7	37.8	38.8	Net Worth	35.9	40.2	37.9	38.8	38.5	39.4
100.0	100.0	100.0	Total Liabilities & Net Worth	100.0	100.0	100.0	100.0	100.0	100.0
			INCOME DATA						
100.0	100.0	100.0	Net Sales	100.0	100.0	100.0	100.0	100.0	100.0
28.0	27.2	26.9	Gross Profit	39.6	32.3	26.7	25.4	23.4	23.9
22.2	21.6	21.0	Operating Expenses	32.4	26.9	21.3	20.1	17.5	16.7
5.7	5.7	6.0	Operating Profit	7.2	5.4	5.4	5.2	5.9	7.1
1.4	1.3	1.4	All Other Expenses (net)	2.0	1.8	1.2	1.2	1.3	1.5
4.3	4.4	4.5	Profit Before Taxes	5.2	3.7	4.1	4.1	4.6	5.6
			RATIOS						
2.2	2.1	2.1	Current	2.1	2.4	2.0	2.1	2.1	2.0
1.5	1.4	1.5		1.4	1.5	1.5	1.5	1.3	1.4
1.1	1.1	1.1		.9	1.1	1.2	1.1	1.1	1.1
1.3	1.3	1.3	Quick	1.5	1.4	1.2	1.3	1.4	1.1
.8	.9	.9		.9	1.0	.9	.9	.8	.8
.6	.6	.6		.5	.7	.7	.6	.6	.6
35 10.3	36 10.1	38 9.6	Sales/Receivables	31 11.6	33 11.2	38 9.7	38 9.7	41 9.0	41 8.9
45 8.1	45 8.1	47 7.8		55 6.6	45 8.2	43 8.5	47 7.8	47 7.7	51 7.2
55 6.6	56 6.5	58 6.3		81 4.5	56 6.5	55 6.6	57 6.4	56 6.5	61 6.0
30 12.2	30 12.0	32 11.3	Cost of Sales/Inventory	23 16.0	30 12.2	29 12.6	37 9.8	34 10.7	34 10.7
45 8.1	45 8.1	48 7.6		34 10.8	48 7.6	45 8.1	49 7.4	47 7.7	48 7.6
69 5.3	69 5.3	69 5.3		89 4.1	73 5.0	68 5.4	69 5.3	72 5.1	66 5.5
22 16.3	20 18.4	24 15.5	Cost of Sales/Payables	18 19.9	16 22.8	22 16.5	24 15.3	25 14.8	29 12.8
33 10.9	31 11.6	37 10.0		40 9.1	29 12.6	37 10.0	38 9.5	37 9.9	38 9.5
49 7.5	46 8.0	51 7.1		79 4.6	51 7.2	49 7.4	51 7.2	51 7.1	51 7.1
6.8	6.9	6.8	Sales/Working Capital	5.4	7.2	8.4	6.4	6.6	6.9
12.7	13.5	12.4		11.8	13.0	13.0	11.0	12.6	12.9
75.1	87.7	45.0		-30.3	46.0	29.5	31.9	60.5	63.7
(663) 6.9	(717) 7.7	(789) 9.8	EBIT/Interest	(45) 13.2	(138) 7.3	(122) 10.0	(156) 7.8	(163) 11.3	(165) 9.8
3.3	3.7	4.2		3.5	3.3	3.9	4.2	3.6	4.6
1.5	1.8	1.7		.2	1.2	1.9	1.9	1.5	2.5
(351) 4.2	(356) 3.9	(420) 4.0	Net Profit + Depr., Dep., Amort./Cur. Mat. L/T/D	(19) 1.9	(67) 4.0	(59) 3.8	(87) 3.7	(83) 4.9	(105) 4.6
2.2	2.2	2.1		1.5	2.3	1.6	2.3	1.8	2.8
1.1	1.4	1.1		.5	1.2	.8	1.3	1.0	1.5
.6	.5	.6	Fixed/Worth	.4	.4	.6	.5	.6	.8
1.1	1.1	1.1		1.2	1.0	1.1	.9	1.0	1.3
2.1	2.1	2.0		3.5	2.2	1.9	1.6	1.9	2.1
.9	.9	.9	Debt/Worth	.7	.7	.9	.9	.7	1.1
1.9	1.8	1.8		1.6	1.9	1.7	1.8	2.0	1.9
3.9	3.8	3.7		5.8	4.6	3.5	3.4	3.5	3.4
(659) 43.7	(711) 43.3	(792) 44.6	% Profit Before Taxes/Tangible Net Worth	(44) 62.1	(141) 49.6	(120) 44.2	(152) 46.0	(166) 41.1	(169) 44.6
21.3	22.3	23.9		21.4	22.6	22.7	25.2	21.4	26.7
7.2	8.9	8.4		2.5	3.9	6.6	8.7	7.1	15.9
14.8	14.8	15.7	% Profit Before Taxes/Total Assets	23.9	16.8	15.9	16.1	15.3	15.3
7.5	8.1	8.0		5.2	6.9	7.2	8.3	7.5	9.8
2.0	2.5	2.3		-1.8	1.7	2.2	2.4	1.9	4.7
10.6	10.5	10.1	Sales/Net Fixed Assets	12.4	15.7	11.0	10.8	9.0	6.5
5.8	5.6	5.7		4.6	7.1	6.2	6.4	5.6	4.5
3.7	3.6	3.6		1.7	4.3	3.9	4.1	3.5	3.3
2.7	2.7	2.6	Sales/Total Assets	2.9	2.9	2.7	2.6	2.4	2.2
2.1	2.1	2.1		1.5	2.3	2.2	2.1	2.0	1.8
1.6	1.6	1.5		.9	1.6	1.6	1.8	1.5	1.4
(659) 2.1	(687) 2.0	(753) 2.0	% Depr., Dep., Amort./Sales	(40) 2.4	(137) 1.6	(121) 2.2	(149) 1.9	(156) 2.3	(150) 2.5
3.2	3.2	3.2		4.2	2.8	3.0	3.0	3.1	3.5
5.0	5.1	4.8		6.2	5.0	4.9	4.7	4.7	4.7
(269) 2.6	(309) 2.3	(314) 2.3	% Officers', Directors', Owners' Comp/Sales	(30) 4.9	(76) 4.2	(73) 2.4	(58) 2.0	(60) 1.3	(17) .8
4.5	4.6	4.4		7.9	6.1	4.2	3.4	2.5	1.7
8.1	8.1	7.4		12.9	10.3	6.1	6.7	4.7	5.3
12146398M	13908962M	18270852M	Net Sales ($)	30946M	285038M	495818M	1176965M	2678922M	13603163M
7032292M	8570439M	10771229M	Total Assets ($)	26031M	164593M	267104M	595392M	1497499M	8220610M

M = $ thousand   MM = $ million
See Pages 1 through 15 for Explanation of Ratios and Data

Current Data Sorted By Assets   **Comparative Historical Data**

	0-500M	500M-2MM	2-10MM	10-50MM	50-100MM	100-250MM		4/1/90-3/31/91 ALL	4/1/91-3/31/92 ALL
		1		2			# Postretirement Benefits		
							Type of Statement		
		1	8	18			Unqualified		
	1	6	5	1			Reviewed		
	5	13	3				Compiled		
							Tax Returns		
		5	11	13	2	1	Other		
		36 (4/1-9/30/94)		57 (10/1/94-3/31/95)					
	6	25	27	32	2	1	**NUMBER OF STATEMENTS**		
%	%	%	%	%	%	%	**ASSETS**	%	%
		6.1	3.2	5.2			Cash & Equivalents	D	D
		36.4	30.4	25.8			Trade Receivables - (net)	A	A
		21.2	22.0	19.4			Inventory	T	T
		2.1	1.7	1.7			All Other Current	A	A
		65.8	57.3	52.2			Total Current		
		28.0	36.3	36.6			Fixed Assets (net)	N	N
		2.1	1.5	3.9			Intangibles (net)	O	O
		4.1	4.9	7.3			All Other Non-Current	T	T
		100.0	100.0	100.0			Total		
							LIABILITIES	A	A
		8.0	10.1	8.4			Notes Payable-Short Term	V	V
		4.1	4.3	3.3			Cur. Mat. -L/T/D	A	A
		23.7	20.9	16.0			Trade Payables	I	I
		.4	1.7	.5			Income Taxes Payable	L	L
		11.8	5.8	6.3			All Other Current	A	A
		48.0	42.8	34.5			Total Current	B	B
		14.9	16.6	16.8			Long Term Debt	L	L
		.8	.5	.6			Deferred Taxes	E	E
		4.1	2.8	5.0			All Other-Non-Current		
		32.2	37.3	43.1			Net Worth		
		100.0	100.0	100.0			Total Liabilities & Net Worth		
							INCOME DATA		
		100.0	100.0	100.0			Net Sales		
		31.0	30.0	25.8			Gross Profit		
		26.0	23.1	18.9			Operating Expenses		
		5.0	6.9	6.9			Operating Profit		
		.1	1.0	2.1			All Other Expenses (net)		
		5.0	5.9	4.8			Profit Before Taxes		
							RATIOS		
		2.0	2.0	2.1			Current		
		1.5	1.3	1.4					
		1.0	1.1	1.2					
		1.3	1.2	1.3			Quick		
		1.0	.7	1.0					
		.7	.6	.6					
		30 12.2	35 10.4	41 9.0			Sales/Receivables		
		40 9.2	42 8.7	47 7.8					
		53 6.9	50 7.3	59 6.2					
		19 19.6	33 10.9	35 10.4			Cost of Sales/Inventory		
		35 10.4	40 9.1	47 7.7					
		56 6.5	55 6.6	69 5.3					
		25 14.5	30 12.0	28 13.0			Cost of Sales/Payables		
		37 10.0	41 8.8	41 8.8					
		46 8.0	54 6.7	54 6.7					
		7.5	8.3	7.4			Sales/Working Capital		
		15.6	24.9	12.2					
		NM	91.8	31.5					
		(21) 10.9	(23) 12.4	(31) 16.7			EBIT/Interest		
		5.6	6.8	5.2					
		2.5	2.1	1.7					
			(11) 8.5	(14) 4.6			Net Profit + Depr., Dep., Amort./Cur. Mat. L /T/D		
			3.0	2.8					
			1.8	1.0					
		.4	.8	.6			Fixed/Worth		
		.8	.9	.7					
		1.8	1.4	2.0					
		1.2	.9	.6			Debt/Worth		
		2.6	2.1	1.3					
		4.4	2.9	3.8					
		(24) 81.1	(26) 46.5	(30) 44.4			% Profit Before Taxes/Tangible Net Worth		
		40.9	28.3	22.8					
		14.9	19.6	12.2					
		20.4	19.8	15.6			% Profit Before Taxes/Total Assets		
		12.4	12.6	10.0					
		5.2	4.5	3.4					
		25.2	13.1	7.8			Sales/Net Fixed Assets		
		17.9	8.2	5.3					
		6.6	3.8	3.3					
		4.1	3.3	2.5			Sales/Total Assets		
		3.4	2.5	1.9					
		2.2	1.6	1.4					
		(23) .9	(23) 1.9	(23) 1.7			% Depr., Dep., Amort./Sales		
		2.0	2.2	2.6					
		3.8	3.2	5.6					
		(13) 3.1					% Officers', Directors', Owners' Comp/Sales		
		5.5							
		8.3							
	5423M	92069M	268566M	1585201M	207835M	118844M	Net Sales ($)		
	1784M	29495M	111633M	789821M	155109M	138393M	Total Assets ($)		

© Robert Morris Associates 1995

M = $ thousand   MM = $ million
See Pages 1 through 15 for Explanation of Ratios and Data

Comparative Historical Data / Current Data Sorted By Sales

4/1/92-3/31/93 ALL	4/1/93-3/31/94 ALL	4/1/94-3/31/95 ALL		0-1MM	1-3MM	3-5MM	5-10MM	10-25MM	25MM & OVER
	4	3	# Postretirement Benefits		1				2
			Type of Statement						
10	10	27	Unqualified		1		4	11	11
5	18	13	Reviewed		3	4	3	2	1
6	13	21	Compiled	3	9	3	5	1	
	1		Tax Returns						
14	26	32	Other		5		6	4	16
				36 (4/1-9/30/94)			**57 (10/1/94-3/31/95)**		
35	68	93	**NUMBER OF STATEMENTS**	3	14	12	18	18	28
%	%	%	**ASSETS**	%	%	%	%	%	%
4.7	7.6	5.0	Cash & Equivalents		10.6	4.0	2.6	3.0	5.8
31.3	30.5	29.6	Trade Receivables - (net)		28.0	34.1	33.6	30.5	26.5
24.6	20.6	21.3	Inventory		23.8	23.2	22.3	18.5	20.7
1.1	1.6	1.7	All Other Current		2.6	.9	2.0	1.0	2.0
61.8	60.2	57.6	Total Current		65.0	62.3	60.5	53.0	55.0
31.2	29.8	34.0	Fixed Assets (net)		30.2	31.9	33.0	36.4	34.7
1.7	1.9	2.8	Intangibles (net)		.2	.5	1.6	5.0	3.6
5.3	8.1	5.6	All Other Non-Current		4.6	5.3	4.9	5.6	6.7
100.0	100.0	100.0	Total		100.0	100.0	100.0	100.0	100.0
			LIABILITIES						
9.8	10.1	9.7	Notes Payable-Short Term		14.6	12.0	5.1	10.7	8.4
3.7	3.3	3.9	Cur. Mat.-L /T/D		2.7	5.5	4.8	4.3	2.7
19.9	16.0	18.9	Trade Payables		10.9	26.1	26.1	19.4	15.8
1.0	4.2	.9	Income Taxes Payable		.1	.7	2.6	.1	.7
6.6	9.6	8.0	All Other Current		17.4	7.0	5.6	5.9	6.5
41.1	43.2	41.4	Total Current		45.7	51.2	44.3	40.5	34.1
17.8	16.8	16.0	Long Term Debt		14.0	14.9	18.7	18.0	14.5
.5	.6	.8	Deferred Taxes		.3	.4	.9	.7	.8
2.7	3.2	4.2	All Other-Non-Current		6.5	1.5	2.8	5.4	4.4
37.9	36.2	37.5	Net Worth		33.6	32.0	33.4	35.4	46.2
100.0	100.0	100.0	Total Liabilities & Net Worth		100.0	100.0	100.0	100.0	100.0
			INCOME DATA						
100.0	100.0	100.0	Net Sales		100.0	100.0	100.0	100.0	100.0
28.3	27.0	28.7	Gross Profit		32.2	31.8	30.6	26.0	26.1
22.5	21.2	22.5	Operating Expenses		25.4	27.7	23.7	19.6	18.7
5.8	5.8	6.1	Operating Profit		6.8	4.1	6.9	6.4	7.4
1.7	1.1	1.0	All Other Expenses (net)		.2	1.1	.9	1.9	1.7
4.1	4.7	5.1	Profit Before Taxes		6.5	3.0	6.0	4.5	5.7
			RATIOS						
2.2	2.2	2.0	Current		2.4	1.7	2.0	1.4	2.1
1.6	1.5	1.4			1.6	1.2	1.4	1.2	1.7
1.1	1.0	1.1			1.3	.8	1.2	1.0	1.2
1.4	1.4	1.2	Quick		1.5	1.0	1.2	.9	1.4
.8	.9	.9			1.0	.7	.8	.7	1.0
.6	.6	.6			.6	.6	.7	.6	.6
(33) 11.0	(34) 10.8	(35) 10.3	Sales/Receivables		(12) 30.4	(28) 13.1	(34) 10.7	(37) 9.9	(41) 8.9
(43) 8.4	(45) 8.2	(43) 8.5			(38) 9.7	(42) 8.6	(42) 8.6	(42) 8.7	(48) 7.6
(54) 6.7	(58) 6.3	(54) 6.8			(54) 6.8	(58) 6.3	(51) 7.2	(59) 6.2	(58) 6.3
(27) 13.5	(25) 14.6	(33) 11.1	Cost of Sales/Inventory		(19) 19.7	(30) 12.0	(34) 10.6	(28) 12.9	(35) 10.3
(54) 6.8	(39) 9.3	(43) 8.5			(36) 10.1	(46) 7.9	(41) 8.8	(40) 9.2	(52) 7.0
(72) 5.1	(62) 5.9	(63) 5.8			(68) 5.4	(57) 6.4	(56) 6.5	(66) 5.5	(69) 5.3
(26) 14.3	(12) 31.6	(28) 13.2	Cost of Sales/Payables		(3) 133.4	(34) 10.8	(37) 10.0	(26) 13.8	(28) 13.2
(37) 10.0	(27) 13.3	(39) 9.4			(25) 14.8	(42) 8.7	(44) 8.3	(43) 8.5	(34) 10.6
(52) 7.0	(42) 8.6	(51) 7.2			(35) 10.3	(55) 6.6	(55) 6.6	(56) 6.5	(49) 7.4
6.9	6.3	7.9	Sales/Working Capital		5.8	10.6	8.1	12.2	7.1
11.7	11.7	14.4			13.7	63.2	17.8	25.7	9.3
65.3	170.7	85.0			51.4	-19.4	36.6	NM	25.3
9.0	11.7	11.9	EBIT/Interest		7.0	9.9	11.1	12.2	18.5
(34) 3.9	(63) 4.1	(84) 5.8		(11)	(11) 5.5	(11) 2.5	(16) 6.5	(16) 4.0	(27) 7.8
1.4	2.0	2.0			2.0	1.8	3.3	1.8	2.0
8.5	6.3	5.2	Net Profit + Depr., Dep., Amort./Cur. Mat. L/T/D					8.5	6.5
(17) 2.1	(26) 2.8	(38) 2.9					(11) 3.0	(12) 3.8
1.5	1.5	1.6						1.3	1.8
.3	.5	.6	Fixed/Worth		.3	.5	.7	.7	.5
.9	.8	.9			.6	1.0	.9	1.4	.7
1.6	1.4	1.7			1.9	1.7	1.2	2.3	1.1
.9	1.1	1.0	Debt/Worth		1.1	1.2	1.6	1.3	.5
1.4	1.7	1.8			1.5	2.7	2.0	2.8	1.1
3.5	3.8	3.7			4.5	4.4	3.0	5.1	2.0
36.6	52.7	48.2	% Profit Before Taxes/Tangible Net Worth		128.3	46.8	44.4	57.0	42.6
(33) 21.1	(65) 21.8	(87) 27.9		(13)	54.1	19.7	(17) 35.5	(17) 27.9	(26) 21.3
2.8	8.3	14.2			13.0	10.2	21.9	17.0	12.7
15.4	16.9	19.1	% Profit Before Taxes/Total Assets		23.6	19.7	15.4	20.4	17.2
8.7	9.3	10.8			13.9	5.6	12.3	10.7	10.8
2.4	3.3	4.4			6.1	2.7	7.3	3.3	5.4
20.7	20.3	17.5	Sales/Net Fixed Assets		23.1	21.7	23.0	14.0	7.8
6.9	8.1	7.4			19.1	10.7	8.8	6.5	6.3
4.4	5.0	3.8			4.2	6.3	4.0	3.7	3.7
3.3	3.2	3.2	Sales/Total Assets		3.7	4.0	3.6	3.4	2.5
2.5	2.4	2.4			3.0	2.8	2.5	2.5	1.9
1.7	1.7	1.6			1.8	2.2	1.6	1.3	1.5
1.3	1.0	1.5	% Depr., Dep., Amort./Sales		1.3		1.0	1.9	1.7
(29) 2.7	(61) 2.2	(76) 2.3		(13)	2.5	(15) 2.1	(17) 3.1	(19) 1.8
3.4	3.3	3.8			4.3		2.7	6.2	3.1
2.4	2.5	1.7	% Officers', Directors', Owners' Comp/Sales						
(12) 4.3	(22) 4.3	(25) 4.4							
4.9	6.2	8.3							
909458M	1354959M	2277938M	Net Sales ($)	1961M	27235M	50385M	124587M	283863M	1789907M
472061M	720182M	1226235M	Total Assets ($)	1333M	10570M	21478M	55533M	151294M	986027M

M = $ thousand   MM = $ million
See Pages 1 through 15 for Explanation of Ratios and Data

Current Data Sorted By Assets   **Comparative Historical Data**

0-500M	500M-2MM	2-10MM	10-50MM	50-100MM	100-250MM	# Postretirement Benefits / Type of Statement	4/1/90-3/31/91 ALL	4/1/91-3/31/92 ALL
1	1	2	1	1	1	# Postretirement Benefits		
1	1	17	17	7	6	Unqualified	46	48
2	8	22	3			Reviewed	37	26
6	7	3				Compiled	29	25
1	1					Tax Returns		2
8	10	12	9	5		Other	35	36
	49 (4/1-9/30/94)			97 (10/1/94-3/31/95)				
18	27	54	29	12	6	**NUMBER OF STATEMENTS**	147	137
%	%	%	%	%	%	**ASSETS**	%	%
5.4	7.1	6.9	5.6	8.2		Cash & Equivalents	6.2	6.7
27.9	30.9	30.3	27.7	21.6		Trade Receivables - (net)	28.3	26.6
30.6	22.0	21.5	21.5	16.6		Inventory	24.4	23.9
3.2	1.2	1.3	2.0	2.4		All Other Current	.9	1.7
67.0	61.2	59.9	56.7	48.8		Total Current	59.9	58.9
25.8	32.5	31.1	30.3	35.0		Fixed Assets (net)	31.0	31.8
3.6	2.7	2.6	4.7	7.6		Intangibles (net)	2.6	2.6
3.6	3.6	6.5	8.3	8.6		All Other Non-Current	6.5	6.7
100.0	100.0	100.0	100.0	100.0		Total	100.0	100.0
						LIABILITIES		
5.6	6.3	9.4	7.8	2.7		Notes Payable-Short Term	10.3	9.2
4.1	4.5	4.2	3.2	3.7		Cur. Mat. -L/T/D	4.5	5.0
31.6	16.3	17.1	14.2	10.5		Trade Payables	14.4	15.9
.1	.4	.3	.5	.5		Income Taxes Payable	.4	.7
9.4	7.2	5.5	10.1	9.8		All Other Current	7.1	7.3
50.9	34.7	36.4	35.7	27.0		Total Current	36.8	38.1
11.7	17.1	18.5	15.6	21.1		Long Term Debt	18.7	17.8
.0	.3	.6	1.5	2.0		Deferred Taxes	.8	.8
5.3	8.7	2.3	5.0	12.6		All Other-Non-Current	3.6	3.5
32.2	39.3	42.1	42.2	37.3		Net Worth	40.2	39.9
100.0	100.0	100.0	100.0	100.0		Total Liabilities & Net Worth	100.0	100.0
						INCOME DATA		
100.0	100.0	100.0	100.0	100.0		Net Sales	100.0	100.0
37.5	33.7	27.5	23.6	28.3		Gross Profit	28.2	28.4
35.4	28.5	21.1	16.7	19.2		Operating Expenses	22.9	23.5
2.2	5.2	6.4	6.8	9.1		Operating Profit	5.2	4.8
1.5	.7	1.4	.9	2.3		All Other Expenses (net)	1.9	1.9
.7	4.5	4.9	6.0	6.8		Profit Before Taxes	3.4	2.9
						RATIOS		
2.3 / 1.3 / .9	3.2 / 2.0 / 1.4	2.2 / 1.7 / 1.3	2.3 / 1.7 / 1.1	3.3 / 1.7 / 1.3		Current	2.5 / 1.7 / 1.2	2.6 / 1.6 / 1.1
.9 / .7 / .5	2.1 / 1.4 / .8	1.5 / 1.0 / .7	1.5 / .9 / .6	1.9 / 1.0 / .7		Quick	1.5 / .9 / .6	1.5 / .9 / .5
25 14.7 / 33 10.9 / 51 7.2	35 10.3 / 42 8.6 / 54 6.8	45 8.2 / 51 7.1 / 60 6.1	44 8.3 / 49 7.4 / 59 6.2	43 8.5 / 53 6.9 / 58 6.3		Sales/Receivables	36 10.2 / 46 8.0 / 54 6.7	35 10.5 / 45 8.2 / 55 6.6
40 9.1 / 52 7.0 / 81 4.5	29 12.4 / 40 9.2 / 91 4.0	30 12.1 / 53 6.9 / 73 5.0	30 12.2 / 53 6.9 / 79 4.6	32 11.4 / 54 6.8 / 94 3.9		Cost of Sales/Inventory	31 11.6 / 48 7.6 / 83 4.4	33 10.9 / 49 7.5 / 83 4.4
30 12.2 / 46 7.9 / 89 4.1	17 21.3 / 29 12.7 / 41 9.0	24 15.1 / 33 11.0 / 49 7.5	23 16.0 / 30 12.1 / 46 7.9	29 12.5 / 34 10.6 / 40 9.2		Cost of Sales/Payables	19 19.2 / 28 13.0 / 42 8.6	20 17.9 / 30 12.0 / 49 7.4
7.2 / 19.3 / -29.1	5.8 / 9.2 / 15.7	8.3 / 17.5	5.4 / 8.9 / 38.7	3.6 / 10.5 / 20.7		Sales/Working Capital	6.1 / 9.4 / 22.6	6.0 / 10.0 / 77.3
6.4 / (16) 3.0 / -.1	13.4 / 4.0 / 2.1	10.0 / (52) 4.7 / 2.0	13.3 / (26) 5.5 / 2.0	13.6 / 4.4 / 1.5		EBIT/Interest	5.2 / (135) 2.1 / 1.3	4.6 / (127) 2.0 / .7
	(10) 3.0 / 1.9 / 1.6	(26) 5.9 / 2.4 / .9	(20) 4.8 / 3.8 / 2.0			Net Profit + Depr., Dep., Amort./Cur. Mat. L. /T/D	(86) 5.4 / 2.4 / 1.2	(74) 4.4 / 1.9 / .8
.3 / .8 / 3.9	.5 / .8 / 2.5	.4 / .8 / 1.6	.4 / 1.0 / 1.6	.5 / 1.4 / 6.0		Fixed/Worth	.3 / .8 / 1.9	.4 / .9 / 2.3
.9 / 3.5 / 11.1	.8 / 1.3 / 6.0	.8 / 1.3 / 3.3	.8 / 1.5 / 4.3	.8 / 2.5 / 9.2		Debt/Worth	.6 / 1.6 / 4.1	.6 / 1.7 / 4.9
58.1 / (17) 21.5 / -26.2	61.6 / (25) 29.7 / 5.1	44.3 / (52) 23.1 / 7.9	44.4 / (27) 26.3 / 8.4	46.5 / (10) 29.6 / 12.3		% Profit Before Taxes/Tangible Net Worth	38.6 / (134) 14.9 / 4.3	33.1 / (129) 14.1 / -3.3
10.8 / 5.3 / -10.2	19.8 / 5.0 / 1.3	15.6 / 10.1 / 2.7	14.5 / 9.4 / 3.7	16.7 / 8.2 / 3.4		% Profit Before Taxes/Total Assets	12.7 / 5.1 / 1.3	12.5 / 4.8 / -.7
52.8 / 12.0 / 6.1	12.9 / 7.5 / 4.4	12.2 / 7.3 / 4.5	14.0 / 5.9 / 4.4	6.7 / 4.5 / 2.6		Sales/Net Fixed Assets	17.2 / 8.1 / 4.2	13.5 / 6.6 / 3.9
3.7 / 2.9 / 1.9	3.1 / 2.4 / 1.9	2.5 / 2.1 / 1.6	2.3 / 1.9 / 1.4	2.1 / 1.3 / 1.1		Sales/Total Assets	2.8 / 2.1 / 1.7	2.7 / 2.0 / 1.6
1.0 / (16) 2.5 / 6.0	1.4 / (25) 2.4 / 3.5	1.4 / (45) 2.1 / 2.9	1.0 / (26) 3.0 / 4.1	2.3 / 3.8 / 5.3		% Depr., Dep., Amort./Sales	1.3 / (134) 2.4 / 4.0	1.3 / (124) 2.5 / 3.7
	(13) 3.4 / 4.8 / 7.9	(15) 1.7 / 3.2 / 6.5				% Officers', Directors', Owners' Comp/Sales	(41) 2.6 / 4.6 / 7.6	(34) 2.2 / 4.7 / 9.3
16850M	77258M	466758M	1235703M	1249265M	1679978M	Net Sales ($)	2730485M	3395677M
5995M	32135M	227295M	667271M	830238M	1010664M	Total Assets ($)	1592489M	1959340M

M = $ thousand   MM = $ million
See Pages 1 through 15 for Explanation of Ratios and Data

	Comparative Historical Data				Current Data Sorted By Sales					
# Postretirement Benefits	6	6	7		1	3		1	2	
Type of Statement										
Unqualified	51	53	49		1		2	9	10	27
Reviewed	27	32	35		2	4	7	16	3	3
Compiled	31	22	16		2	9	2	3		
Tax Returns	4	2	2		1	1				
Other	28	34	44		4	9	6	9	6	10
	4/1/92-3/31/93 ALL	4/1/93-3/31/94 ALL	4/1/94-3/31/95 ALL		49 (4/1-9/30/94)			97 (10/1/94-3/31/95)		
					0-1MM	1-3MM	3-5MM	5-10MM	10-25MM	25MM & OVER
NUMBER OF STATEMENTS	141	143	146		10	23	17	37	19	40
ASSETS	%	%	%		%	%	%	%	%	%
Cash & Equivalents	6.9	6.1	6.5		3.8	5.5	7.8	6.8	8.9	5.7
Trade Receivables - (net)	28.1	28.6	28.7		23.3	29.1	30.6	30.0	28.9	27.7
Inventory	24.1	23.0	22.3		20.2	30.1	23.5	20.1	21.4	20.3
All Other Current	1.7	1.3	1.7		1.7	2.0	2.1	1.0	1.4	2.2
Total Current	60.8	59.0	59.2		49.1	66.7	64.0	57.9	60.6	55.9
Fixed Assets (net)	29.6	33.4	30.9		40.5	25.6	29.9	33.3	26.1	31.9
Intangibles (net)	3.5	2.2	3.9		6.0	2.0	3.2	3.0	5.6	4.6
All Other Non-Current	6.1	5.4	6.1		4.3	5.7	2.9	5.8	7.6	7.6
Total	100.0	100.0	100.0		100.0	100.0	100.0	100.0	100.0	100.0
LIABILITIES										
Notes Payable-Short Term	10.3	9.9	7.2		3.8	7.0	7.3	9.8	6.9	6.0
Cur. Mat.-L /T/D	4.2	3.7	3.9		3.3	5.8	2.6	4.9	2.1	3.3
Trade Payables	16.0	15.1	17.6		28.5	20.4	16.6	17.3	15.0	15.0
Income Taxes Payable	.6	1.7	.4		.2	.0	.7	.3	.7	.3
All Other Current	8.3	8.2	7.5		12.5	5.6	7.9	5.3	6.5	9.8
Total Current	39.4	38.8	36.5		48.4	38.8	35.2	37.7	31.2	34.4
Long Term Debt	15.0	17.0	17.7		19.4	15.9	11.9	19.9	15.6	19.8
Deferred Taxes	.9	.7	.8		.0	.5	.5	.4	.5	1.8
All Other-Non-Current	2.9	3.7	5.4		11.4	5.4	6.1	2.6	5.9	6.0
Net Worth	41.8	39.8	39.5		20.8	39.3	46.3	39.4	46.8	38.1
Total Liabilities & Net Worth	100.0	100.0	100.0		100.0	100.0	100.0	100.0	100.0	100.0
INCOME DATA										
Net Sales	100.0	100.0	100.0		100.0	100.0	100.0	100.0	100.0	100.0
Gross Profit	28.6	27.9	28.8		44.1	31.2	34.8	27.2	28.0	22.9
Operating Expenses	23.1	22.7	22.9		41.7	27.0	28.3	21.9	20.4	15.7
Operating Profit	5.5	5.3	5.9		2.4	4.1	6.5	5.3	7.6	7.2
All Other Expenses (net)	1.3	1.5	1.3		4.2	.4	.0	1.6	1.1	1.3
Profit Before Taxes	4.2	3.8	4.6		–1.9	3.7	6.5	3.8	6.4	5.9
RATIOS										
Current	2.4	2.2	2.4		1.8	3.2	2.7	2.2	2.7	2.2
	1.6	1.6	1.7		1.0	2.2	1.9	1.6	1.8	1.7
	1.2	1.1	1.2		.8	1.3	1.6	1.2	1.4	1.1
Quick	1.4	1.4	1.5		.8	1.9	1.7	1.5	1.7	1.4
	.9	.9	1.0		.6	1.0	1.2	1.0	1.1	1.0
	.6	.6	.7		.5	.5	.8	.6	.8	.6
Sales/Receivables	37 9.9	39 9.3	42 8.7		15 24.2	28 12.9	39 9.3	43 8.5	46 7.9	43 8.4
	47 7.8	47 7.8	49 7.4		43 8.5	36 10.2	48 7.6	49 7.4	51 7.1	50 7.3
	56 6.5	57 6.4	58 6.3		58 6.3	52 7.0	58 6.3	57 6.4	68 5.4	58 6.3
Cost of Sales/Inventory	29 12.5	29 12.6	31 11.7		18 19.8	35 10.3	36 10.1	29 12.7	26 14.0	31 11.9
	49 7.4	54 6.7	52 7.0		45 8.2	68 5.4	51 7.2	45 8.2	58 6.3	53 6.9
	85 4.3	85 4.3	78 4.7		107 3.4	83 4.4	101 3.6	68 5.4	94 3.9	72 5.1
Cost of Sales/Payables	22 16.8	21 17.4	24 15.4		24 15.4	17 21.3	24 15.3	24 14.9	22 16.9	28 13.0
	33 11.0	32 11.3	34 10.8		44 8.3	34 10.8	33 11.2	33 11.0	39 9.3	32 11.5
	46 7.9	47 7.8	47 7.8		118 3.1	49 7.4	44 8.3	55 6.6	60 6.1	42 8.6
Sales/Working Capital	5.8	5.8	5.8		9.9	5.4	5.1	7.1	4.3	5.8
	9.7	10.3	8.9		–206.2	7.8	7.2	9.6	6.4	10.3
	27.0	43.5	26.5		–16.6	19.7	12.0	34.0	10.1	36.3
EBIT/Interest	(134) 9.2	(133) 6.9	(139) 9.7		2.8	(21) 7.5	20.9	(36) 10.0	(16) 9.7	(39) 8.6
	3.6	2.9	4.1		.7	3.4	9.6	4.1	5.3	4.9
	1.4	1.5	1.8		–1.4	1.3	2.4	1.3	2.6	1.9
Net Profit + Depr., Dep., Amort./Cur. Mat. L/T/D	(77) 4.9	(76) 4.0	(73) 5.2			(10) 9.8		(19) 5.3		(27) 5.2
	2.4	2.3	2.7			1.9		2.0		3.6
	1.0	1.3	1.7			1.5		.3		2.1
Fixed/Worth	.4	.5	.4		1.5	.3	.4	.5	.4	.4
	.7	.9	.8		3.0	.7	.7	.9	.7	1.1
	1.4	2.1	2.0		NM	1.6	1.1	1.9	1.5	2.2
Debt/Worth	.8	.8	.8		2.4	.8	.5	.9	.7	.9
	1.4	1.7	1.5		5.8	1.4	1.1	1.3	1.2	1.9
	3.2	4.0	5.0		NM	7.8	4.2	3.5	3.0	5.0
% Profit Before Taxes/Tangible Net Worth	(136) 41.4	(139) 37.0	(136) 47.5			(22) 66.6	52.4	(35) 48.1	(17) 40.0	(37) 59.8
	20.2	17.9	24.8			21.6	24.7	20.3	24.6	31.4
	4.7	6.5	8.0			3.6	13.7	5.2	13.6	11.4
% Profit Before Taxes/Total Assets	15.0	12.4	15.4		8.4	19.0	18.7	14.4	17.8	15.1
	7.2	5.6	8.6		–1.7	5.5	10.6	9.6	11.3	9.5
	1.5	1.7	2.6		–14.4	.9	3.1	1.3	4.7	3.8
Sales/Net Fixed Assets	16.7	13.3	13.2		9.7	52.7	13.6	12.2	16.1	11.8
	8.0	6.0	6.9		6.1	9.8	7.5	7.3	8.1	5.2
	4.8	4.1	4.5		2.5	4.3	5.0	4.7	4.5	4.1
Sales/Total Assets	2.9	2.6	2.6		2.9	3.4	2.7	2.6	2.5	2.4
	2.1	2.0	2.1		1.9	2.8	2.3	2.1	1.9	2.0
	1.7	1.6	1.6		1.3	1.9	1.8	1.6	1.3	1.3
% Depr., Dep., Amort./Sales	(131) 1.2	(135) 1.4	(128) 1.4		(20) 2.6	(14) 1.0	(32) 1.5	(16) 1.4	1.2	(36) 1.6
	2.3	2.3	2.4		5.9	2.5	2.2	2.2	2.0	2.5
	3.3	3.8	3.8		9.7	4.2	2.5	3.2	3.2	3.8
% Officers', Directors', Owners' Comp/Sales	(44) 1.7	(46) 2.0	(39) 1.9			(14) 4.6		(11) 1.5		
	4.4	3.5	5.0			6.8		2.4		
	9.1	7.0	8.5			8.6		5.0		
Net Sales ($)	3685844M	3542290M	4725812M		5796M	40867M	63327M	255133M	318874M	4041815M
Total Assets ($)	2039006M	2052778M	2773598M		3811M	18773M	31492M	138486M	208307M	2372729M

M = $ thousand   MM = $ million
See Pages 1 through 15 for Explanation of Ratios and Data

MANUFACTURERS—SIGNS & ADVERTISING SPECIALTIES. SIC# 3993

Current Data Sorted By Assets | | | | | | **Comparative Historical Data**

	0-500M	500M-2MM	2-10MM	10-50MM	50-100MM	100-250MM	4/1/90-3/31/91 ALL	4/1/91-3/31/92 ALL
# Postretirement Benefits	4	5	5	2				
Type of Statement								
Unqualified	2	5	20	13	1		30	34
Reviewed	4	22	18	2			49	58
Compiled	24	30	8				65	62
Tax Returns	6	3						3
Other	13	15	19	3			31	33
	69 (4/1-9/30/94)			139 (10/1/94-3/31/95)				
NUMBER OF STATEMENTS	49	75	65	18	1		175	190
ASSETS	%	%	%	%	%	%	%	%
Cash & Equivalents	13.3	7.7	5.0	5.8			6.5	7.4
Trade Receivables - (net)	33.2	37.2	36.3	33.4			35.9	33.3
Inventory	15.6	22.7	21.1	22.5			21.4	20.2
All Other Current	1.3	2.3	3.1	1.3			1.9	2.0
Total Current	63.4	69.9	65.4	63.0			65.7	62.9
Fixed Assets (net)	27.3	22.9	24.5	29.2			25.6	27.9
Intangibles (net)	2.3	1.3	2.4	1.1			1.3	2.0
All Other Non-Current	7.0	5.9	7.6	6.8			7.4	7.2
Total	100.0	100.0	100.0	100.0			100.0	100.0
LIABILITIES								
Notes Payable-Short Term	8.0	11.4	10.5	8.7			11.1	10.7
Cur. Mat. -L/T/D	4.4	5.3	2.9	3.1			6.0	5.3
Trade Payables	13.1	17.7	17.1	13.0			16.6	15.6
Income Taxes Payable	1.0	.4	.5	.2			.8	.8
All Other Current	10.1	15.2	12.6	9.9			11.5	10.7
Total Current	36.7	49.9	43.7	34.9			46.0	43.0
Long Term Debt	17.8	12.4	14.2	18.7			14.6	15.3
Deferred Taxes	.1	.4	.2	.4			.4	.4
All Other-Non-Current	10.4	2.8	2.2	3.0			2.7	3.7
Net Worth	35.0	34.5	39.7	43.0			36.3	37.6
Total Liabilities & Net Worth	100.0	100.0	100.0	100.0			100.0	100.0
INCOME DATA								
Net Sales	100.0	100.0	100.0	100.0			100.0	100.0
Gross Profit	48.1	37.9	30.3	34.6			38.5	40.6
Operating Expenses	42.3	34.1	25.6	27.0			34.1	36.4
Operating Profit	5.7	3.8	4.8	7.6			4.4	4.1
All Other Expenses (net)	.7	.6	.9	1.4			1.0	1.6
Profit Before Taxes	5.0	3.2	3.8	6.2			3.4	2.5
RATIOS								
Current	3.5	2.2	2.0	2.7			2.2	2.3
	1.8	1.6	1.5	1.7			1.5	1.6
	1.1	1.1	1.1	1.4			1.1	1.1
Quick	2.9	1.4	1.3	1.9			1.4	1.4
	1.1	1.0	1.0	1.0			.9	.9
	.7	.7	.7	.7			.6	.6
Sales/Receivables	24 14.9	39 9.3	45 8.2	46 8.0			38 9.7	33 11.2
	37 9.8	47 7.7	58 6.3	60 6.1			47 7.8	49 7.4
	56 6.5	62 5.9	76 4.8	79 4.6			62 5.9	61 6.0
Cost of Sales/Inventory	9 38.7	20 17.9	29 12.4	44 8.3			23 16.2	22 16.9
	28 13.0	42 8.6	52 7.0	70 5.2			42 8.7	46 8.0
	59 6.2	79 4.6	74 4.9	87 4.2			72 5.1	79 4.6
Cost of Sales/Payables	11 33.1	20 18.1	22 16.5	23 16.2			21 17.8	18 20.0
	26 13.9	34 10.8	36 10.2	36 10.1			33 10.9	33 11.2
	40 9.2	53 6.9	58 6.3	51 7.2			46 7.9	52 7.0
Sales/Working Capital	5.6	6.1	6.5	5.0			7.5	6.8
	9.7	10.0	9.4	6.7			12.7	13.0
	48.6	61.5	24.1	13.4			47.3	49.2
EBIT/Interest	(40) 9.6	(70) 7.6	(57) 11.1	(17) 8.2			(156) 5.0	(171) 6.9
	3.3	3.1	3.3	3.3			2.5	2.5
	1.3	1.4	1.8	1.4			1.1	.8
Net Profit + Depr., Dep., Amort./Cur. Mat. L /T/D		(36) 3.5	(26) 7.4	(11) 8.7			(97) 4.5	(82) 5.0
		2.0	3.3	4.0			2.0	1.9
		1.1	1.4	2.0			.8	.5
Fixed/Worth	.3	.3	.3	.4			.4	.4
	.7	.7	.7	.6			.7	.7
	3.1	1.7	1.3	1.2			1.4	1.7
Debt/Worth	.6	.9	.9	.5			.9	.8
	1.6	2.3	1.8	1.6			1.9	1.7
	7.6	4.6	3.6	3.0			3.4	4.1
% Profit Before Taxes/Tangible Net Worth	(42) 64.8	(68) 44.0	(64) 34.1	53.3			(160) 36.0	(171) 40.3
	27.1	22.1	22.1	23.6			17.8	15.6
	5.9	7.0	9.6	10.8			4.0	.0
% Profit Before Taxes/Total Assets	22.9	13.8	12.7	18.7			12.4	13.6
	10.4	6.1	6.9	9.9			6.2	5.2
	1.3	1.0	3.2	2.4			.7	–1.1
Sales/Net Fixed Assets	27.1	34.0	25.2	12.8			24.0	19.6
	13.9	14.7	10.4	7.5			13.3	11.4
	6.7	7.4	4.5	3.7			7.1	6.0
Sales/Total Assets	3.9	3.4	2.7	2.2			3.3	3.4
	3.1	2.5	2.1	1.7			2.7	2.6
	2.3	2.0	1.7	1.5			2.0	1.9
% Depr., Dep., Amort./Sales	(40) 1.5	(72) 1.1	(54) .9	(17) 1.5			(166) 1.2	(173) 1.1
	3.0	1.7	1.6	2.4			2.0	2.1
	4.0	2.9	2.9	4.1			3.3	3.4
% Officers', Directors', Owners' Comp/Sales	(28) 6.4	(38) 3.6	(19) 2.0				(78) 3.0	(84) 4.1
	9.2	6.6	3.0				5.9	6.5
	17.5	8.1	6.8				9.7	10.5
Net Sales ($)	39361M	217969M	603238M	665100M	110187M		1027453M	1041764M
Total Assets ($)	12665M	82349M	285403M	366663M	76039M		457469M	501924M

M = $ thousand   MM = $ million
See Pages 1 through 15 for Explanation of Ratios and Data

Comparative Historical Data				Current Data Sorted By Sales					
1	4	16	**# Postretirement Benefits**	1	7	2	1	3	2
			Type of Statement						
46	33	41	Unqualified	3	3	3	8	13	11
59	59	46	Reviewed	3	16	9	9	7	2
61	61	62	Compiled	17	25	9	8	3	
2	5	9	Tax Returns	5	3		1		
30	50	50	Other	10	13	4	12	9	2
4/1/92-3/31/93 ALL	**4/1/93-3/31/94 ALL**	**4/1/94-3/31/95 ALL**		**69 (4/1-9/30/94)**			**139 (10/1/94-3/31/95)**		
				0-1MM	**1-3MM**	**3-5MM**	**5-10MM**	**10-25MM**	**25MM & OVER**
198	208	208	**NUMBER OF STATEMENTS**	38	60	25	38	32	15
%	%	%	**ASSETS**	%	%	%	%	%	%
7.4	6.4	8.0	Cash & Equivalents	13.2	9.2	5.9	5.4	4.9	6.5
33.6	36.4	35.6	Trade Receivables - (net)	27.6	37.3	36.7	38.3	39.1	33.5
21.4	19.8	20.5	Inventory	14.7	20.5	23.7	21.1	23.4	22.6
2.4	2.3	2.2	All Other Current	2.1	1.6	3.0	3.4	2.0	1.5
64.9	65.0	66.3	Total Current	57.5	68.5	69.3	68.1	69.4	64.0
25.8	26.7	25.0	Fixed Assets (net)	31.9	24.1	23.7	21.2	22.3	29.2
2.2	2.0	1.9	Intangibles (net)	2.9	.8	1.7	3.3	1.4	1.1
7.1	6.3	6.8	All Other Non-Current	7.8	6.6	5.3	7.4	6.9	5.6
100.0	100.0	100.0	Total	100.0	100.0	100.0	100.0	100.0	100.0
			LIABILITIES						
10.2	11.2	10.0	Notes Payable-Short Term	11.5	7.8	11.0	12.0	10.3	7.8
4.6	4.2	4.2	Cur. Mat.-L/T/D	4.6	5.7	4.1	3.3	2.4	2.5
17.4	16.4	16.0	Trade Payables	8.5	18.5	13.9	20.2	17.8	13.1
.6	1.1	.5	Income Taxes Payable	.9	.4	.5	.4	.7	.2
10.8	11.9	12.7	All Other Current	9.0	13.9	15.6	14.6	11.5	9.9
43.7	44.8	43.4	Total Current	34.5	46.4	45.3	50.7	42.7	33.5
15.3	17.0	14.7	Long Term Debt	19.9	15.6	11.7	9.1	14.9	17.3
.4	.4	.3	Deferred Taxes	.1	.4	.1	.4	.3	.1
4.0	3.2	4.4	All Other-Non-Current	9.3	5.3	1.6	2.3	2.5	2.8
36.6	34.6	37.2	Net Worth	36.1	32.3	41.4	37.6	39.6	46.3
100.0	100.0	100.0	Total Liabilities & Net Worth	100.0	100.0	100.0	100.0	100.0	100.0
			INCOME DATA						
100.0	100.0	100.0	Net Sales	100.0	100.0	100.0	100.0	100.0	100.0
37.7	37.7	37.6	Gross Profit	50.3	38.9	36.0	31.5	30.2	34.2
33.2	33.6	32.7	Operating Expenses	44.1	34.4	32.7	28.0	24.3	26.7
4.5	4.0	4.9	Operating Profit	6.2	4.5	3.2	3.5	5.9	7.5
1.5	.9	.8	All Other Expenses (net)	.7	.9	.2	.7	1.2	1.2
2.9	3.1	4.1	Profit Before Taxes	5.5	3.6	3.1	2.8	4.7	6.3
			RATIOS						
2.3	2.1	2.6		3.8	2.6	2.0	1.7	2.1	2.7
1.6	1.6	1.6	Current	2.1	1.7	1.6	1.4	1.7	2.1
1.1	1.1	1.1		1.1	1.1	1.1	1.0	1.2	1.5
1.6	1.4	1.6		3.2	1.6	1.1	1.2	1.7	2.1
1.0	1.0	1.0	Quick	1.1	1.1	1.0	.8	1.1	1.0
.6	.7	.7		.6	.7	.7	.7	.6	.8
34 10.6	**35** 10.4	**37** 9.9		**24** 15.5	**35** 10.4	**40** 9.2	**39** 9.3	**46** 7.9	**46** 7.9
46 7.9	**48** 7.6	**49** 7.4	Sales/Receivables	**38** 9.5	**44** 8.3	**53** 6.9	**53** 6.9	**64** 5.7	**69** 5.3
61 6.0	**64** 5.7	**69** 5.3		**58** 6.3	**59** 6.2	**64** 5.7	**73** 5.0	**78** 4.7	**78** 4.7
20 18.4	**22** 16.6	**22** 16.5		**10** 36.8	**17** 21.9	**34** 10.8	**27** 13.4	**25** 14.4	**45** 8.1
45 8.2	**46** 8.0	**46** 7.9	Cost of Sales/Inventory	**33** 11.2	**34** 10.8	**58** 6.3	**44** 8.3	**57** 6.4	**69** 5.3
73 5.0	**69** 5.3	**76** 4.8		**62** 5.9	**78** 4.7	**79** 4.6	**65** 5.6	**79** 4.6	**81** 4.5
18 19.8	**19** 19.0	**20** 18.5		**7** 48.8	**22** 16.7	**15** 25.1	**23** 15.7	**20** 18.6	**21** 17.2
34 10.8	**32** 11.5	**33** 10.9	Cost of Sales/Payables	**23** 15.8	**37** 9.9	**31** 11.9	**37** 9.9	**38** 9.7	**35** 10.5
55 6.6	**47** 7.7	**51** 7.1		**37** 10.0	**51** 7.1	**43** 8.5	**63** 5.8	**54** 6.7	**50** 7.3
6.5	6.9	5.8		4.6	6.1	5.9	7.5	5.6	3.5
11.4	11.6	9.4	Sales/Working Capital	8.5	9.9	11.3	14.8	8.6	6.0
82.0	44.9	34.0		NM	39.4	29.5	687.1	16.1	12.7
7.7	6.9	8.4		11.1	7.7	5.2	9.3	11.1	8.2
(182) 2.7	(196) 3.1	(184) 3.3	EBIT/Interest	(33) 4.1	(54) 3.2	(22) 2.0	(33) 3.3	(29) 4.6	(13) 5.8
1.3	1.1	1.6		1.0	1.4	1.4	1.7	2.0	2.3
4.8	5.1	5.0		4.1	2.9	3.4	4.9	8.2	22.1
(92) 1.9	(94) 2.0	(83) 2.7	Net Profit + Depr., Dep., Amort./Cur. Mat. L/T/D	(12) 2.5	(18) 1.6	(12) 1.8	(16) 2.2	(15) 4.3	(10) 6.7
.7	.8	1.3		.8	.9	.9	.9	2.0	3.1
.3	.3	.3		.3	.3	.2	.3	.3	.4
.8	.8	.7	Fixed/Worth	.8	.8	.6	.7	.5	.5
1.8	1.7	1.4		3.9	2.1	1.3	1.2	1.2	1.2
.8	.8	.8		.6	.9	.8	1.2	.8	.5
1.8	2.0	1.8	Debt/Worth	1.5	2.3	1.8	2.0	2.0	1.5
4.6	4.8	3.9		6.5	4.9	2.6	4.5	3.4	3.0
42.4	40.5	43.3		52.5	54.0	28.7	37.6	37.6	51.7
(173) 16.0	(186) 19.2	(193) 22.2	% Profit Before Taxes/Tangible Net Worth	(31) 22.2	(55) 22.9	(23) 13.0	(37) 22.0	26.8	18.8
2.3	3.9	9.5		6.4	7.4	6.1	9.0	17.1	15.1
12.7	12.6	13.9		23.5	13.7	14.0	13.3	13.5	14.1
5.7	6.0	7.6	% Profit Before Taxes/Total Assets	7.5	8.4	4.3	5.1	10.1	10.2
.8	.4	2.3		.0	1.6	.9	1.9	4.1	4.7
24.3	23.7	26.8		16.6	37.2	36.1	28.6	32.3	13.0
13.6	12.6	11.2	Sales/Net Fixed Assets	7.8	12.7	12.9	13.0	12.3	7.6
6.7	5.6	5.8		4.4	6.8	4.9	7.0	4.9	3.8
3.3	3.4	3.3		3.6	3.5	3.3	3.4	2.9	2.3
2.5	2.6	2.4	Sales/Total Assets	2.4	2.7	2.3	2.5	2.1	1.7
1.9	1.9	1.8		1.5	2.0	1.9	2.0	1.8	1.5
1.2	1.0	1.1		2.1	1.1	1.1	.8	.9	1.4
(186) 1.9	(189) 1.9	(184) 2.1	% Depr., Dep., Amort./Sales	(32) 3.3	(54) 2.0	(24) 1.7	(32) 1.5	(27) 1.3	2.4
3.1	3.3	3.4		5.2	3.3	3.6	2.6	2.4	4.5
3.4	4.0	3.6		6.8	3.6	3.2	2.0		
(99) 6.2	(96) 7.1	(87) 6.8	% Officers', Directors', Owners' Comp/Sales	(23) 11.8	(30) 6.8	(14) 5.7	(11) 3.6		
9.7	11.4	10.4		19.2	9.1	7.7	7.2		
1198371M	**1392913M**	**1635875M**	Net Sales ($)	**22512M**	**117095M**	**94850M**	**261774M**	**449526M**	**690118M**
573256M	**621175M**	**823119M**	Total Assets ($)	**12115M**	**49625M**	**40831M**	**116834M**	**211678M**	**392036M**

© Robert Morris Associates 1995

M = $ thousand MM = $ million

See Pages 1 through 15 for Explanation of Ratios and Data

MANUFACTURERS—ABRASIVE PRODUCTS. SIC# 3291

	Current Data Sorted By Assets							Comparative Historical Data	
	1		3	1		1	# Postretirement Benefits		
							Type of Statement		
			5	4	1	1	Unqualified	11	13
	7		3				Reviewed	9	11
			1				Compiled	3	5
							Tax Returns	1	
3	3		4	2			Other	6	4
	8 (4/1-9/30/94)			26 (10/1/94-3/31/95)				4/1/90-3/31/91	4/1/91-3/31/92
0-500M	500M-2MM		2-10MM	10-50MM	50-100MM	100-250MM		ALL	ALL
3	10		13	6	1	1	NUMBER OF STATEMENTS	30	33
%	%		%	%	%	%	**ASSETS**	%	%
	5.9		5.9				Cash & Equivalents	5.7	5.4
	26.3		25.2				Trade Receivables - (net)	28.4	23.6
	36.7		28.1				Inventory	31.0	27.0
	.9		1.3				All Other Current	2.2	2.2
	69.9		60.5				Total Current	67.3	58.2
	21.1		33.5				Fixed Assets (net)	26.4	31.4
	.0		.4				Intangibles (net)	.9	1.7
	9.0		5.6				All Other Non-Current	5.4	8.7
	100.0		100.0				Total	100.0	100.0
							LIABILITIES		
	6.7		8.2				Notes Payable-Short Term	11.2	12.1
	4.2		8.8				Cur. Mat. -L/T/D	5.9	6.2
	12.9		13.6				Trade Payables	16.6	10.9
	.6		.5				Income Taxes Payable	.3	.3
	8.6		13.7				All Other Current	7.9	8.9
	33.0		44.8				Total Current	42.0	38.5
	7.1		12.2				Long Term Debt	15.0	15.3
	.2		.5				Deferred Taxes	.7	1.0
	4.1		2.0				All Other-Non-Current	1.5	2.6
	55.6		40.6				Net Worth	40.8	42.6
	100.0		100.0				Total Liabilities & Net Worth	100.0	100.0
							INCOME DATA		
	100.0		100.0				Net Sales	100.0	100.0
	33.1		30.1				Gross Profit	30.2	31.9
	28.6		24.6				Operating Expenses	24.3	27.8
	4.5		5.5				Operating Profit	5.9	4.2
	1.0		1.1				All Other Expenses (net)	1.1	1.7
	3.5		4.4				Profit Before Taxes	4.8	2.5
							RATIOS		
	3.5		2.5					3.1	2.8
	2.2		1.4				Current	1.5	1.7
	1.6		1.1					1.2	1.1
	1.5		1.3					1.4	1.5
	1.1		.7				Quick	.7	.6
	.6		.4					.5	.4
	30 12.1		38 9.7					40 9.2	35 10.3
	35 10.4		44 8.3				Sales/Receivables	47 7.7	44 8.3
	41 9.0		54 6.7					54 6.8	51 7.2
	29 12.4		44 8.3					51 7.1	45 8.1
	99 3.7		70 5.2				Cost of Sales/Inventory	66 5.5	78 4.7
	111 3.3		83 4.4					111 3.3	104 3.5
	18 20.1		17 21.8					25 14.5	12 29.5
	24 15.2		24 15.0				Cost of Sales/Payables	35 10.5	30 12.2
	32 11.5		55 6.6					47 7.7	42 8.7
	4.3		5.7					4.9	4.8
	6.7		12.2				Sales/Working Capital	9.7	7.6
	14.2		NM					28.3	56.4
		(10)	5.3					(25) 8.0	(31) 5.0
			2.8				EBIT/Interest	2.2	1.9
			1.8					1.1	.2
								(16) 6.1	(20) 3.2
							Net Profit + Depr., Dep., Amort./Cur. Mat. L./T/D	2.1	1.6
								.9	.1
	.1		.5					.3	.4
	.4		.7				Fixed/Worth	.8	.7
	.8		1.5					1.4	1.5
	.3		.7					.7	.7
	.9		1.7				Debt/Worth	1.7	1.5
	1.3		2.4					3.6	3.4
	23.2		30.0					(29) 36.8	(32) 26.2
	8.5	(12)	18.3				% Profit Before Taxes/Tangible Net Worth	16.9	12.4
	4.4		9.1					7.6	-3.4
	14.3		13.5					14.7	7.6
	5.2		5.8				% Profit Before Taxes/Total Assets	6.2	4.1
	2.3		3.3					1.0	-1.1
	39.8		11.6					15.0	14.0
	15.2		5.9				Sales/Net Fixed Assets	9.1	5.6
	8.1		3.6					5.0	3.9
	3.1		2.5					2.5	2.4
	2.7		1.9				Sales/Total Assets	2.0	1.8
	2.0		1.6					1.7	1.4
	.8		1.6					(25) 1.4	1.4
	2.2	(12)	2.3				% Depr., Dep., Amort./Sales	2.2	3.0
	3.2		4.1					3.1	3.9
							% Officers', Directors', Owners' Comp/Sales		
2001M	28549M		100972M	213295M	24908M	356638M	Net Sales ($)	546224M	549045M
799M	10931M		51256M	133253M	80758M	233541M	Total Assets ($)	334564M	400431M

M = $ thousand   MM = $ million
See Pages 1 through 15 for Explanation of Ratios and Data

Comparative Historical Data | | Current Data Sorted By Sales

	1		4		6	# Postretirement Benefits	1	1	1	2	1
						Type of Statement					
	9		11		11	Unqualified		1	3	3	4
	9		13		10	Reviewed	4	3	3		
	8		2		1	Compiled		1			
			1			Tax Returns					
	6		9		12	Other	2	4	1	2	2	1
	4/1/92- 3/31/93		4/1/93- 3/31/94		4/1/94- 3/31/95			8 (4/1-9/30/94)		26 (10/1/94-3/31/95)		
	ALL		ALL		ALL		0-1MM	1-3MM	3-5MM	5-10MM	10-25MM	25MM & OVER
	32		36		34	**NUMBER OF STATEMENTS**	2	8	6	8	5	5
	%		%		%	**ASSETS**	%	%	%	%	%	%
	6.0		6.4		4.9	Cash & Equivalents						
	27.6		24.9		25.1	Trade Receivables - (net)						
	26.4		29.3		30.4	Inventory						
	1.2		.6		1.7	All Other Current						
	61.2		61.3		62.1	Total Current						
	29.9		32.1		28.7	Fixed Assets (net)						
	1.9		1.5		2.7	Intangibles (net)						
	7.0		5.2		6.5	All Other Non-Current						
	100.0		100.0		100.0	Total						
						LIABILITIES						
	9.9		7.4		6.8	Notes Payable-Short Term						
	5.1		4.4		5.4	Cur. Mat.-L /T/D						
	15.5		13.0		13.9	Trade Payables						
	.6		2.4		.5	Income Taxes Payable						
	8.5		8.6		10.8	All Other Current						
	39.5		35.8		37.5	Total Current						
	13.0		11.8		14.2	Long Term Debt						
	.9		1.1		.8	Deferred Taxes						
	4.7		1.7		2.9	All Other-Non-Current						
	41.8		49.5		44.7	Net Worth						
	100.0		100.0		100.0	Total Liabilities & Net Worth						
						INCOME DATA						
	100.0		100.0		100.0	Net Sales						
	29.2		26.8		28.9	Gross Profit						
	24.7		23.2		23.3	Operating Expenses						
	4.5		3.6		5.6	Operating Profit						
	1.6		.5		1.2	All Other Expenses (net)						
	2.9		3.1		4.4	Profit Before Taxes						
						RATIOS						
	2.3		3.1		2.7							
	2.0		2.1		1.8	Current						
	1.2		1.2		1.3							
	1.3		1.9		1.3							
	.8		.8		.8	Quick						
	.6		.6		.5							
36	10.1	35	10.5	33	11.2							
42	8.6	42	8.7	41	9.0	Sales/Receivables						
51	7.2	53	6.9	54	6.8							
37	9.8	43	8.4	43	8.5							
68	5.4	70	5.2	78	4.7	Cost of Sales/Inventory						
99	3.7	104	3.5	111	3.3							
16	22.8	12	31.0	18	20.1							
28	12.9	27	13.5	27	13.5	Cost of Sales/Payables						
51	7.1	41	8.9	43	8.5							
	5.4		4.5		5.3							
	6.6		6.4		8.1	Sales/Working Capital						
	26.6		22.2		16.0							
(27)	4.9	(32)	8.0	(29)	7.3							
	2.5		3.1		3.2	EBIT/Interest						
	1.3		1.5		1.9							
(14)	7.8	(16)	5.5	(18)	8.3	Net Profit + Depr., Dep.,						
	2.4		1.5		1.7	Amort./Cur. Mat. L/T/D						
	1.1		.7		.9							
	.3		.4		.4							
	.7		.8		.7	Fixed/Worth						
	1.4		1.0		1.0							
	.7		.4		.7							
	1.4		1.0		1.4	Debt/Worth						
	2.9		2.5		2.4							
(30)	25.1	(34)	29.1	(32)	33.9	% Profit Before Taxes/Tangible						
	11.9		8.8		15.0	Net Worth						
	4.6		2.3		6.9							
	8.6		11.4		13.2	% Profit Before Taxes/Total						
	4.7		4.2		5.9	Assets						
	.7		1.1		2.9							
	14.9		16.2		13.4							
	7.4		5.7		7.5	Sales/Net Fixed Assets						
	4.3		3.8		4.4							
	2.5		2.6		2.6							
	2.0		1.9		2.1	Sales/Total Assets						
	1.6		1.4		1.5							
	1.7		1.6		1.4							
(28)	2.8	(35)	2.6	(30)	2.2	% Depr., Dep., Amort./Sales						
	4.1		3.8		3.6							
	5.3		3.5				% Officers', Directors',						
(14)	8.1	(16)	5.0			Owners' Comp/Sales						
	17.0		11.2										
	551140M		718802M		726363M	Net Sales ($)	829M	16627M	25322M	56308M	93863M	533414M
	342065M		494053M		510538M	Total Assets ($)	387M	7509M	15398M	22938M	131695M	332611M

M = $ thousand   MM = $ million
See Pages 1 through 15 for Explanation of Ratios and Data

Current Data Sorted By Assets   Comparative Historical Data

0-500M	500M-2MM	2-10MM	10-50MM	50-100MM	100-250MM		4/1/90-3/31/91 ALL	4/1/91-3/31/92 ALL
						# Postretirement Benefits		
						Type of Statement		
	1	1	2					
		1	8	2		Unqualified	11	14
1	1	3	1			Reviewed	2	6
	1		2			Compiled	7	2
						Tax Returns		
2	2	4	2		1	Other	9	6
8 (4/1-9/30/94)			23 (10/1/94-3/31/95)					
3	4	8	13	2	1	**NUMBER OF STATEMENTS**	29	28
%	%	%	%	%	%	**ASSETS**	%	%
			10.3			Cash & Equivalents	8.7	9.7
			14.3			Trade Receivables - (net)	17.6	17.3
			18.0			Inventory	24.3	26.6
			1.0			All Other Current	1.4	1.1
			43.6			Total Current	52.0	54.7
			40.8			Fixed Assets (net)	40.9	37.5
			1.1			Intangibles (net)	.6	1.9
			14.5			All Other Non-Current	6.4	5.9
			100.0			Total	100.0	100.0
						LIABILITIES		
			6.8			Notes Payable-Short Term	6.5	5.6
			6.9			Cur. Mat. -L/T/D	3.8	2.7
			6.5			Trade Payables	9.1	11.2
			.6			Income Taxes Payable	.5	.4
			4.7			All Other Current	6.5	6.6
			25.6			Total Current	26.6	26.4
			13.6			Long Term Debt	12.6	17.1
			1.0			Deferred Taxes	1.0	.8
			1.8			All Other-Non-Current	4.9	4.1
			58.0			Net Worth	54.9	51.7
			100.0			Total Liabilities & Net Worth	100.0	100.0
						INCOME DATA		
			100.0			Net Sales	100.0	100.0
			29.7			Gross Profit	30.5	25.6
			21.9			Operating Expenses	23.6	22.8
			7.8			Operating Profit	6.9	2.8
			.4			All Other Expenses (net)	1.1	1.6
			7.4			Profit Before Taxes	5.8	1.2
						RATIOS		
			5.7				3.0	4.9
			2.9			Current	1.8	2.8
			1.6				1.3	1.4
			2.9				1.4	2.0
			1.8			Quick	1.0	1.1
			.7				.5	.5
			37 10.0				33 11.1	36 10.1
			42 8.7			Sales/Receivables	40 9.1	42 8.6
			49 7.5				51 7.1	53 6.9
			45 8.1				72 5.1	70 5.2
			72 5.1			Cost of Sales/Inventory	89 4.1	111 3.3
			99 3.7				130 2.8	140 2.6
			14 25.4				19 19.4	21 17.8
			19 19.2			Cost of Sales/Payables	26 14.0	31 11.8
			33 11.1				39 9.3	60 6.1
			2.9				3.9	2.7
			4.8			Sales/Working Capital	5.7	3.9
			8.9				14.5	7.6
			21.0				8.0	6.0
		(10)	5.0			EBIT/Interest	(26) 2.4	(25) 2.4
			2.5				1.1	.0
							4.2	7.1
						Net Profit + Depr., Dep., Amort./Cur. Mat. L /T/D	(17) 1.7	(10) 1.7
							.5	.7
			.4				.5	.4
			.6			Fixed/Worth	.7	.5
			1.3				1.1	2.0
			.3				.4	.4
			.5			Debt/Worth	.9	1.1
			1.2				1.7	2.0
			23.2				19.8	20.2
		(12)	16.4			% Profit Before Taxes/Tangible Net Worth	10.4	5.9
			9.7				1.4	−8.1
			14.1				14.6	10.1
			8.8			% Profit Before Taxes/Total Assets	5.0	3.0
			4.2				.5	−4.1
			5.2				6.1	6.1
			3.5			Sales/Net Fixed Assets	4.2	3.3
			1.9				1.7	1.5
			1.6				1.9	1.7
			1.3			Sales/Total Assets	1.4	1.3
			.7				1.0	.8
			2.1				2.7	1.9
		(11)	3.6			% Depr., Dep., Amort./Sales	(26) 5.0	(27) 5.0
			7.2				6.7	6.8
								1.0
						% Officers', Directors', Owners' Comp/Sales		(11) 3.2
								4.3
3432M	18555M	42021M	308549M	92929M	113014M	Net Sales ($)	719368M	400895M
1156M	6337M	32152M	245823M	133616M	152823M	Total Assets ($)	561940M	389547M

M = $ thousand   MM = $ million

See Pages 1 through 15 for Explanation of Ratios and Data

Comparative Historical Data | **Current Data Sorted By Sales**

Comparative Historical Data				Current Data Sorted By Sales					
		4	# Postretirement Benefits		1		1		2
			Type of Statement						
24	15	11	Unqualified					7	4
3	6	6	Reviewed		4	1		1	
6	4	3	Compiled	1			1	1	
			Tax Returns						
6	12	11	Other	1	1	3	1	2	3
6	12	11			8 (4/1-9/30/94)			23 (10/1/94-3/31/95)	
4/1/92- 3/31/93 ALL	4/1/93- 3/31/94 ALL	4/1/94- 3/31/95 ALL		0-1MM	1-3MM	3-5MM	5-10MM	10-25MM	25MM & OVER
39	37	31	**NUMBER OF STATEMENTS**	2	5	4	2	11	7
%	%	%	**ASSETS**	%	%	%	%	%	%
10.7	9.5	10.5	Cash & Equivalents					13.8	
19.4	17.9	18.0	Trade Receivables - (net)					18.7	
19.7	22.4	21.4	Inventory					19.9	
.7	2.0	.8	All Other Current					.3	
50.5	51.9	50.7	Total Current					52.7	
38.4	38.0	35.8	Fixed Assets (net)					34.0	
1.6	2.1	3.1	Intangibles (net)					1.1	
9.4	8.0	10.4	All Other Non-Current					12.2	
100.0	100.0	100.0	Total					100.0	
			LIABILITIES						
7.4	6.0	9.5	Notes Payable-Short Term					6.5	
2.7	2.7	4.4	Cur. Mat.-L/T/D					8.0	
9.9	7.3	9.9	Trade Payables					9.5	
.2	1.8	.5	Income Taxes Payable					1.2	
6.5	6.0	7.8	All Other Current					7.6	
26.6	23.8	32.0	Total Current					32.8	
16.9	16.2	14.3	Long Term Debt					10.4	
.5	.9	.6	Deferred Taxes					1.1	
3.4	3.9	2.5	All Other-Non-Current					.6	
52.5	55.2	50.7	Net Worth					55.1	
100.0	100.0	100.0	Total Liabilities & Net Worth					100.0	
			INCOME DATA						
100.0	100.0	100.0	Net Sales					100.0	
29.3	25.6	30.5	Gross Profit					31.1	
23.7	21.5	24.6	Operating Expenses					23.7	
5.6	4.2	5.9	Operating Profit					7.5	
1.3	.3	.8	All Other Expenses (net)					.1	
4.3	3.9	5.1	Profit Before Taxes					7.4	
			RATIOS						
3.8 / 2.3 / 1.4	4.6 / 2.6 / 1.5	3.4 / 2.4 / 1.2	Current					3.4 / 2.9 / 1.5	
1.9 / 1.3 / .6	2.4 / 1.3 / .6	2.0 / 1.0 / .6	Quick					2.1 / 1.8 / .8	
38 9.5 / 45 8.2 / 60 6.1	37 10.0 / 49 7.4 / 60 6.1	33 11.1 / 42 8.7 / 55 6.6	Sales/Receivables					41 9.0 / 42 8.7 / 49 7.5	
45 8.1 / 79 4.6 / 122 3.0	49 7.5 / 76 4.8 / 140 2.6	41 9.0 / 72 5.1 / 107 3.4	Cost of Sales/Inventory					51 7.2 / 72 5.1 / 114 3.2	
17 22.0 / 27 13.3 / 50 7.3	16 23.3 / 23 15.8 / 37 9.8	18 20.3 / 28 13.1 / 37 10.0	Cost of Sales/Payables					18 20.3 / 28 13.1 / 32 11.3	
3.7 / 5.0 / 11.9	2.8 / 4.1 / 8.0	3.2 / 5.4 / 29.7	Sales/Working Capital					3.2 / 4.8 / 6.4	
(33) 5.5 / 2.2 / .5	(32) 14.6 / 2.3 / .3	(25) 8.1 / 2.9 / 1.3	EBIT/Interest						
(13) 3.1 / 1.7 / 1.3	(15) 3.0 / 2.3 / .7	(11) 29.1 / 2.9 / .9	Net Profit + Depr., Dep., Amort./Cur. Mat. L/T/D						
.4 / .6 / 1.3	.4 / .7 / 1.6	.3 / .6 / 1.6	Fixed/Worth					.4 / .6 / .9	
.3 / .9 / 2.4	.4 / .7 / 2.0	.3 / 1.1 / 2.6	Debt/Worth					.3 / .4 / 1.4	
(37) 18.6 / 9.4 / -2.4	(36) 15.1 / 8.4 / 1.3	(29) 20.0 / 12.3 / 5.3	% Profit Before Taxes/Tangible Net Worth				(10)	25.6 / 15.4 / 11.6	
10.0 / 4.0 / -1.9	10.1 / 4.0 / -1.1	11.9 / 6.0 / 1.8	% Profit Before Taxes/Total Assets					18.1 / 9.2 / 2.1	
6.3 / 4.0 / 1.6	6.8 / 3.7 / 1.8	8.7 / 4.1 / 1.8	Sales/Net Fixed Assets					8.7 / 4.1 / 2.3	
1.7 / 1.3 / .8	1.6 / 1.2 / .9	1.8 / 1.3 / .8	Sales/Total Assets					1.8 / 1.3 / .7	
(36) 2.7 / 4.2 / 5.9	(33) 2.8 / 4.4 / 6.9	(28) 2.1 / 3.6 / 6.7	% Depr., Dep., Amort./Sales				(10)	1.0 / 2.7 / 5.5	
(18) 1.9 / 3.4 / 5.2	(10) 1.2 / 2.5 / 5.8		% Officers', Directors', Owners' Comp/Sales						
673790M	612103M	578500M	Net Sales ($)	1518M	11199M	14934M	14602M	159310M	376937M
749056M	578243M	571907M	Total Assets ($)	1663M	8321M	12441M	15513M	143972M	389997M

M = $ thousand   MM = $ million
See Pages 1 through 15 for Explanation of Ratios and Data

MANUFACTURERS—CONCRETE BRICK, BLOCK & OTHER PRODUCTS. SIC# 3271 (72)

Current Data Sorted By Assets   **Comparative Historical Data**

0-500M	500M-2MM	2-10MM	10-50MM	50-100MM	100-250MM	# Postretirement Benefits / Type of Statement	4/1/90-3/31/91 ALL	4/1/91-3/31/92 ALL
2	5	10	5		1			
	6	47	21	3	1	Unqualified	70	51
1	25	32	8	1		Reviewed	70	72
11	33	21	1			Compiled	69	53
3	4	1	1			Tax Returns	1	3
4	15	19	10	4		Other	41	46
	86 (4/1-9/30/94)		185 (10/1/94-3/31/95)					
19	83	120	41	7	1	**NUMBER OF STATEMENTS**	251	225
%	%	%	%	%	%	**ASSETS**	%	%
11.2	8.0	5.6	3.4			Cash & Equivalents	6.7	6.4
30.5	27.9	30.4	30.3			Trade Receivables - (net)	26.6	26.3
16.2	18.0	16.5	13.6			Inventory	18.6	18.4
4.4	1.3	1.6	4.3			All Other Current	2.0	1.7
62.3	55.2	54.1	51.5			Total Current	53.9	52.9
30.2	35.1	36.9	36.5			Fixed Assets (net)	37.3	38.1
1.4	1.3	1.1	1.6			Intangibles (net)	1.3	1.7
6.1	8.3	8.0	10.3			All Other Non-Current	7.5	7.3
100.0	100.0	100.0	100.0			Total	100.0	100.0
						LIABILITIES		
14.1	6.9	7.5	6.9			Notes Payable-Short Term	8.8	9.0
3.8	5.1	4.5	4.8			Cur. Mat. -L/T/D	4.7	5.2
13.0	14.2	15.0	14.0			Trade Payables	13.4	12.1
.2	.5	.4	.3			Income Taxes Payable	.6	.3
8.0	7.2	6.9	8.5			All Other Current	7.7	6.9
39.0	34.0	34.3	34.5			Total Current	35.2	33.5
17.7	19.4	18.2	15.0			Long Term Debt	20.9	18.4
.2	.6	.8	2.2			Deferred Taxes	.9	.8
8.9	2.8	3.7	3.7			All Other-Non-Current	3.4	2.8
34.2	43.2	43.0	44.5			Net Worth	39.6	44.4
100.0	100.0	100.0	100.0			Total Liabilities & Net Worth	100.0	100.0
						INCOME DATA		
100.0	100.0	100.0	100.0			Net Sales	100.0	100.0
41.0	31.5	27.8	22.8			Gross Profit	30.8	29.2
34.7	26.9	23.1	17.4			Operating Expenses	26.3	26.5
6.3	4.6	4.7	5.3			Operating Profit	4.5	2.6
1.4	.3	.9	.9			All Other Expenses (net)	1.4	1.3
4.9	4.3	3.8	4.4			Profit Before Taxes	3.1	1.3
						RATIOS		
3.8	2.8	2.5	2.2			Current	2.4	2.6
1.5	1.6	1.6	1.5				1.6	1.7
.8	1.1	1.1	1.1				1.2	1.2
2.2	1.6	1.5	1.4			Quick	1.5	1.7
.9	1.0	1.0	1.0				1.0	1.1
.6	.6	.7	.7				.6	.6
17 21.4	31 11.9	40 9.1	46 7.9			Sales/Receivables	34 10.6	38 9.6
37 9.9	45 8.2	51 7.2	57 6.4				46 7.9	50 7.3
48 7.6	60 6.1	69 5.3	79 4.6				62 5.9	65 5.6
16 23.4	19 19.6	17 21.0	18 20.5			Cost of Sales/Inventory	26 14.1	27 13.3
40 9.2	39 9.3	44 8.3	42 8.7				48 7.6	52 7.0
70 5.2	74 4.9	72 5.1	68 5.4				79 4.6	89 4.1
9 41.4	17 21.3	24 14.9	25 14.8			Cost of Sales/Payables	18 20.4	18 20.0
23 16.2	27 13.3	34 10.8	34 10.8				29 12.8	28 13.0
30 12.2	49 7.4	46 7.9	47 7.8				46 8.0	43 8.4
5.5	5.2	5.6	5.3			Sales/Working Capital	6.2	5.7
16.9	11.8	9.9	12.9				10.0	8.7
-38.4	40.0	35.6	28.6				29.5	27.4
(15) 22.3	(77) 6.6	(110) 6.4	10.8			EBIT/Interest	(227) 5.4	(212) 3.9
4.3	3.3	3.4	3.7				2.2	1.6
1.9	1.7	1.6	1.4				.8	.2
	(39) 3.1	(51) 4.1	(24) 8.0			Net Profit + Depr., Dep., Amort./Cur. Mat. L /T/D	(144) 4.2	(122) 3.8
	2.0	2.2	2.7				1.7	1.8
	1.5	1.1	.7				.9	.7
.1	.5	.5	.5			Fixed/Worth	.5	.5
.6	.8	.9	.8				1.0	.8
5.1	1.7	1.6	1.7				2.0	1.5
.3	.7	.7	.7			Debt/Worth	.7	.6
1.7	1.4	1.5	1.1				1.6	1.3
9.8	2.7	2.8	3.1				3.7	2.7
(16) 73.3	(77) 32.8	(116) 30.7	(39) 35.1			% Profit Before Taxes/Tangible Net Worth	(229) 27.3	(212) 17.8
42.1	14.6	17.5	13.5				14.0	6.7
21.9	7.3	5.4	3.9				-.0	-5.7
22.8	12.3	12.6	15.1			% Profit Before Taxes/Total Assets	11.4	7.9
14.4	6.5	6.2	6.2				4.6	2.3
3.7	2.1	2.0	1.2				-1.0	-3.0
53.7	10.0	7.7	8.3			Sales/Net Fixed Assets	9.8	8.6
16.7	6.0	5.5	5.1				5.5	5.0
6.5	3.5	3.5	3.1				3.2	3.0
4.0	2.9	2.3	2.2			Sales/Total Assets	2.5	2.3
2.9	2.2	1.9	1.8				1.9	1.8
2.1	1.6	1.6	1.2				1.4	1.3
(15) .6	(79) 2.1	(109) 2.2	(38) 2.4			% Depr., Dep., Amort./Sales	(232) 2.3	(215) 2.4
3.5	3.5	3.5	3.4				3.6	3.9
7.1	4.9	4.4	5.1				5.6	6.1
(10) 6.0	(38) 2.6	(44) 1.8				% Officers', Directors', Owners' Comp/Sales	(92) 2.0	(94) 2.1
7.5	4.4	3.5					4.0	3.9
14.6	6.3	5.3					7.1	6.8
15521M	213330M	1133037M	1386153M	683386M	207085M	Net Sales ($)	3049043M	2415050M
5214M	97346M	586816M	794863M	422245M	120981M	Total Assets ($)	1909439M	1629647M

M = $ thousand   MM = $ million
See Pages 1 through 15 for Explanation of Ratios and Data

Comparative Historical Data | **Current Data Sorted By Sales**

4	18	23	# Postretirement Benefits	1	4	3	6	6	3
			Type of Statement						
56	68	78	Unqualified		4	8	20	28	18
63	65	66	Reviewed	1	20	10	18	15	2
63	56	66	Compiled	9	30	10	14	2	1
4	6	9	Tax Returns	2	3	2	1	1	
51	47	52	Other	5	10	7	11	9	10
4/1/92-3/31/93	4/1/93-3/31/94	4/1/94-3/31/95		86 (4/1-9/30/94)			185 (10/1/94-3/31/95)		
ALL	ALL	ALL		0-1MM	1-3MM	3-5MM	5-10MM	10-25MM	25MM & OVER
237	242	271	**NUMBER OF STATEMENTS**	17	67	37	64	55	31
%	%	%	**ASSETS**	%	%	%	%	%	%
6.4	6.4	6.5	Cash & Equivalents	12.9	8.6	5.6	6.2	4.2	4.2
26.6	28.7	29.3	Trade Receivables - (net)	20.5	28.6	26.5	29.7	33.5	30.8
19.5	18.8	16.5	Inventory	14.1	16.6	18.2	16.9	16.4	14.8
1.7	1.9	2.1	All Other Current	3.9	1.8	.7	1.3	2.4	4.7
54.1	55.8	54.4	Total Current	51.4	55.5	51.1	54.1	56.4	54.5
37.1	35.4	36.0	Fixed Assets (net)	34.0	35.8	39.3	37.2	33.3	36.3
1.3	1.4	1.3	Intangibles (net)	3.3	1.4	1.0	.8	.8	2.1
7.5	7.4	8.3	All Other Non-Current	11.2	7.3	8.7	7.9	9.4	7.1
100.0	100.0	100.0	Total	100.0	100.0	100.0	100.0	100.0	100.0
			LIABILITIES						
9.0	8.7	7.8	Notes Payable-Short Term	10.7	6.6	9.0	7.9	7.1	8.1
5.2	5.0	4.7	Cur. Mat.-L./T/D	5.3	5.1	3.7	5.0	4.2	4.6
13.7	14.9	14.3	Trade Payables	9.8	12.6	13.2	15.6	17.8	13.0
.4	.7	.4	Income Taxes Payable	.2	.4	.7	.3	.4	.4
6.6	8.0	7.3	All Other Current	6.9	7.3	7.3	5.2	7.9	10.9
34.9	37.2	34.5	Total Current	32.9	32.0	33.9	34.0	37.4	36.9
18.6	16.0	17.9	Long Term Debt	23.8	20.3	19.1	19.3	13.5	13.2
.8	1.0	.9	Deferred Taxes	.2	.6	.6	.8	1.4	1.9
3.0	3.4	3.7	All Other-Non-Current	9.9	3.3	3.2	2.7	4.7	2.2
42.7	42.3	42.9	Net Worth	33.2	43.7	43.2	43.1	42.9	45.8
100.0	100.0	100.0	Total Liabilities & Net Worth	100.0	100.0	100.0	100.0	100.0	100.0
			INCOME DATA						
100.0	100.0	100.0	Net Sales	100.0	100.0	100.0	100.0	100.0	100.0
31.8	30.0	29.1	Gross Profit	44.0	32.0	29.7	29.5	23.7	22.6
28.5	26.6	24.1	Operating Expenses	36.8	27.2	24.8	24.4	20.0	16.2
3.3	3.4	5.0	Operating Profit	7.2	4.8	4.9	5.1	3.7	6.4
1.0	.7	.8	All Other Expenses (net)	.3	.6	.9	1.0	.5	1.2
2.3	2.7	4.2	Profit Before Taxes	6.9	4.2	4.0	4.1	3.2	5.1
			RATIOS						
2.5	2.5	2.5		4.8	2.9	2.3	2.4	2.6	2.1
1.6	1.6	1.6	Current	1.2	1.7	1.4	1.6	1.5	1.5
1.2	1.1	1.1		.6	1.3	1.1	1.1	1.2	1.1
1.5	1.5	1.5		3.3	1.9	1.4	1.6	1.5	1.3
1.0	1.0	1.0	Quick	.9	1.3	.9	.9	1.1	1.0
.6	.6	.7		.4	.7	.7	.7	.7	.5
35 · 10.4	37 · 10.0	37 · 9.8		6 · 61.4	37 · 10.0	34 · 10.7	40 · 9.2	42 · 8.7	45 · 8.1
46 · 8.0	48 · 7.6	49 · 7.5	Sales/Receivables	36 · 10.2	50 · 7.3	40 · 9.2	49 · 7.5	57 · 6.4	48 · 7.6
61 · 6.0	65 · 5.6	63 · 5.8		52 · 7.0	65 · 5.6	57 · 6.4	61 · 6.0	78 · 4.7	64 · 5.7
25 · 14.8	26 · 14.3	18 · 19.8		15 · 24.5	14 · 25.9	23 · 15.8	19 · 18.9	18 · 20.5	16 · 23.4
52 · 7.0	50 · 7.3	41 · 8.9	Cost of Sales/Inventory	40 · 9.2	40 · 9.1	44 · 8.3	41 · 9.0	43 · 8.5	39 · 9.3
81 · 4.5	79 · 4.6	70 · 5.2		74 · 4.9	74 · 4.9	76 · 4.8	69 · 5.3	63 · 5.8	66 · 5.5
20 · 18.5	19 · 19.1	21 · 17.7		8 · 44.1	17 · 21.3	19 · 19.1	27 · 13.3	27 · 13.7	21 · 17.7
32 · 11.3	31 · 11.7	31 · 11.7	Cost of Sales/Payables	29 · 12.7	26 · 14.1	29 · 12.7	37 · 9.9	37 · 9.9	27 · 13.7
46 · 8.0	55 · 6.6	46 · 7.9		36 · 10.1	46 · 8.0	45 · 8.1	49 · 7.5	52 · 7.0	41 · 9.0
5.3	5.3	5.5		3.6	4.7	6.5	6.0	5.2	7.2
9.8	10.3	11.0	Sales/Working Capital	38.8	7.7	15.4	12.4	11.0	14.1
32.0	34.9	38.8		−16.4	17.1	66.6	34.3	35.8	31.5
5.0	7.6	7.5		9.3	7.1	6.1	7.0	7.5	21.4
(218) 2.3	(231) 2.8	(251) 3.4	EBIT/Interest	(13) 3.2	(60) 3.3	3.2	(56) 3.2	(54) 3.8	4.7
1.0	1.4	1.6		.9	1.7	1.3	1.8	1.1	2.0
4.3	4.6	4.2			3.2	5.9	3.6	6.1	14.1
(123) 1.9	(117) 2.3	(122) 2.1	Net Profit + Depr., Dep., Amort./Cur. Mat. L/T/D		(30) 1.9	(17) 2.2	(27) 2.4	(29) 1.2	(19) 3.7
.9	1.0	1.2			1.4	1.5	1.1	.5	1.4
.6	.5	.5		.1	.5	.5	.5	.5	.5
.8	.8	.9	Fixed/Worth	2.0	.8	.9	.8	.9	.9
1.5	1.8	1.7		NM	1.9	1.7	1.6	1.3	1.4
.7	.6	.7		.3	.6	.8	.7	.7	.7
1.4	1.5	1.4	Debt/Worth	2.6	1.5	1.3	1.6	1.3	1.3
2.7	3.2	3.0		NM	3.3	2.6	2.9	2.7	2.4
25.9	26.3	32.2		68.3	34.5	23.8	29.2	32.5	37.6
(226) 13.8	(227) 12.1	(256) 17.4	% Profit Before Taxes/Tangible Net Worth	(13) 30.7	(63) 17.5	(35) 13.6	(61) 17.6	(53) 14.2	26.6
.8	3.2	7.0		10.8	7.0	3.1	10.8	1.7	7.8
9.9	10.5	13.5		21.8	13.3	10.4	13.9	11.1	20.3
5.0	4.7	6.6	% Profit Before Taxes/Total Assets	14.0	6.9	6.2	6.9	6.0	9.6
.1	.9	2.1		−.7	2.1	1.2	3.3	.3	2.6
8.8	9.1	9.3		35.8	10.0	8.3	8.6	9.2	10.5
6.0	5.9	5.6	Sales/Net Fixed Assets	6.5	5.5	5.8	5.5	5.7	5.1
3.6	3.7	3.4		3.2	3.2	3.4	3.6	4.2	3.3
2.6	2.5	2.5		2.9	2.8	2.5	2.6	2.4	2.4
2.0	1.9	2.0	Sales/Total Assets	2.1	1.9	2.1	1.9	2.0	1.9
1.5	1.5	1.5		1.2	1.3	1.6	1.6	1.6	1.5
2.4	2.1	2.3		.4	2.4	2.4	2.2	1.7	2.5
(225) 3.7	(230) 3.6	(249) 3.5	% Depr., Dep., Amort./Sales	(13) 3.5	(62) 3.8	(35) 3.7	(61) 3.5	(51) 2.8	(27) 3.7
5.7	5.2	4.6		6.2	5.3	4.9	4.3	4.4	4.6
2.3	2.2	2.0			3.6	1.8	1.3	1.9	
(92) 4.4	(89) 4.8	(97) 4.2	% Officers', Directors', Owners' Comp/Sales		(31) 5.2	(17) 2.8	(28) 2.9	(14) 2.9	
7.9	7.3	6.9			7.6	5.1	5.9	6.1	
2637305M	3041439M	3638512M	Net Sales ($)	9352M	130154M	148166M	467099M	914874M	1968867M
1745686M	1837167M	2027465M	Total Assets ($)	5706M	74878M	85711M	265643M	521979M	1073548M

See Pages 1 through 15 for Explanation of Ratios and Data

Current Data Sorted By Assets							Comparative Historical Data	
						# Postretirement Benefits **Type of Statement**		
	2	7		1		Unqualified	5	12
1	9	2	1			Reviewed	14	13
6	6	1				Compiled	22	20
	1	1				Tax Returns	1	1
1	3	3		1		Other	8	6
0-500M	16 (4/1-9/30/94) 500M-2MM	2-10MM	30 (10/1/94-3/31/95) 10-50MM	50-100MM	100-250MM		4/1/90-3/31/91 ALL	4/1/91-3/31/92 ALL
8	21	14	2	1		**NUMBER OF STATEMENTS**	50	52
%	%	%	%	%	%	**ASSETS**	%	%
	6.6	5.7				Cash & Equivalents	5.4	7.2
	26.9	31.7				Trade Receivables - (net)	27.7	23.2
	22.0	23.3				Inventory	19.7	17.8
	1.0	.6				All Other Current	1.7	1.9
	56.6	61.3				Total Current	54.5	50.1
	37.5	28.8				Fixed Assets (net)	37.1	40.9
	.5	2.4				Intangibles (net)	1.3	1.1
	5.4	7.5				All Other Non-Current	7.1	7.9
	100.0	100.0				Total	100.0	100.0
						LIABILITIES		
	10.0	7.7				Notes Payable-Short Term	9.3	7.1
	5.3	4.5				Cur. Mat. -L/T/D	6.3	5.8
	15.2	21.6				Trade Payables	16.2	12.2
	.6	.2				Income Taxes Payable	.5	.4
	5.8	7.6				All Other Current	7.4	6.9
	36.9	41.6				Total Current	39.6	32.4
	16.1	14.1				Long Term Debt	25.6	27.7
	.4	.3				Deferred Taxes	.4	.5
	8.7	5.3				All Other-Non-Current	3.7	4.3
	38.0	38.6				Net Worth	30.6	35.0
	100.0	100.0				Total Liabilities & Net Worth	100.0	100.0
						INCOME DATA		
	100.0	100.0				Net Sales	100.0	100.0
	37.3	22.3				Gross Profit	34.5	30.5
	31.5	16.0				Operating Expenses	28.9	26.4
	5.8	6.2				Operating Profit	5.6	4.1
	1.3	1.3				All Other Expenses (net)	2.2	1.5
	4.5	4.9				Profit Before Taxes	3.4	2.6
						RATIOS		
	2.7	2.5				Current	2.1	2.8
	1.5	1.5					1.4	1.6
	1.2	1.1					1.1	1.0
	1.8	1.2				Quick	1.4	1.7
	.9	.8					.9	1.0
	.6	.6					.5	.5
	25 14.7	30 12.3				Sales/Receivables	30 12.0	31 11.9
	45 8.2	39 9.3					43 8.5	42 8.6
	61 6.0	59 6.2					53 6.9	61 6.0
	26 13.8	9 41.5				Cost of Sales/Inventory	18 19.8	22 16.6
	51 7.1	36 10.2					43 8.4	39 9.3
	79 4.6	99 3.7					79 4.6	70 5.2
	24 15.3	26 14.3				Cost of Sales/Payables	18 20.2	16 23.1
	33 11.2	37 9.9					30 12.0	27 13.7
	43 8.5	47 7.7					51 7.2	46 7.9
	6.3	4.7				Sales/Working Capital	6.6	5.4
	11.4	10.2					16.1	9.8
	NM	NM					60.4	580.3
	6.2	6.0				EBIT/Interest	3.8	4.4
	(19) 2.1	(12) 3.3					1.9	(49) 1.8
	1.0	1.8					1.0	.5
						Net Profit + Depr., Dep., Amort./Cur. Mat. L./T/D	(31) 3.6	2.1
							2.0	(22) 1.1
							.9	.4
	.4	.2				Fixed/Worth	.7	.5
	1.0	.6					1.1	1.0
	2.1	1.9					3.3	4.6
	.8	1.2				Debt/Worth	1.0	.6
	2.0	2.5					2.1	1.7
	4.1	3.0					7.4	5.5
	50.4	36.4				% Profit Before Taxes/Tangible Net Worth	36.2	30.9
	21.0	29.0					(47) 14.8	(46) 8.7
	.9	5.9					.3	-3.5
	14.9	13.5				% Profit Before Taxes/Total Assets	10.9	10.3
	4.7	5.5					4.5	3.3
	.2	2.4					-.3	-2.1
	21.4	30.8				Sales/Net Fixed Assets	12.7	12.6
	8.6	13.6					7.2	4.3
	2.7	3.1					2.6	2.9
	2.9	3.1				Sales/Total Assets	3.1	2.6
	2.1	1.9					2.1	1.8
	1.7	1.2					1.6	1.3
	1.5	1.2				% Depr., Dep., Amort./Sales	1.3	1.8
	(19) 3.5	1.8					(49) 2.5	(47) 3.1
	4.7	7.1					4.1	4.9
	4.2					% Officers', Directors', Owners' Comp/Sales	2.6	2.5
	(13) 7.5						(29) 6.2	(28) 4.4
	9.2						8.5	8.8
7240M	45259M	198045M	31522M	64848M		Net Sales ($)	246308M	289714M
2176M	22427M	64977M	62130M	98589M		Total Assets ($)	228782M	338347M

M = $ thousand   MM = $ million
See Pages 1 through 15 for Explanation of Ratios and Data

Comparative Historical Data				Current Data Sorted By Sales					
3	5		# Postretirement Benefits						
			Type of Statement						
10	7	10	Unqualified		3	2	2	1	2
19	13	13	Reviewed	1	7	3		1	1
13	13	13	Compiled	2	9	1	1		
6	5	2	Tax Returns	1			1		
7	7	8	Other	1	2	2	1	2	
4/1/92-3/31/93	4/1/93-3/31/94	4/1/94-3/31/95			16 (4/1-9/30/94)		30 (10/1/94-3/31/95)		
ALL	ALL	ALL		0-1MM	1-3MM	3-5MM	5-10MM	10-25MM	25MM & OVER
55	45	46	**NUMBER OF STATEMENTS**	5	21	8	5	4	3
%	%	%	**ASSETS**	%	%	%	%	%	%
7.2	7.0	7.6	Cash & Equivalents		7.2				
30.0	30.0	24.6	Trade Receivables - (net)		22.7				
20.1	20.0	24.7	Inventory		25.1				
.7	2.1	.8	All Other Current		1.2				
58.1	59.1	57.7	Total Current		56.3				
33.2	30.9	32.9	Fixed Assets (net)		35.3				
.6	1.8	1.9	Intangibles (net)		2.0				
8.0	8.2	7.5	All Other Non-Current		6.4				
100.0	100.0	100.0	Total		100.0				
			LIABILITIES						
9.5	6.0	8.5	Notes Payable-Short Term		10.0				
5.2	3.8	5.4	Cur. Mat.-L./T/D		5.8				
15.7	15.8	16.3	Trade Payables		15.4				
.8	1.3	.5	Income Taxes Payable		.5				
9.3	7.0	6.1	All Other Current		5.9				
40.5	34.0	36.8	Total Current		37.5				
18.8	20.1	16.8	Long Term Debt		19.9				
.6	.6	.3	Deferred Taxes		.4				
1.9	5.7	7.7	All Other-Non-Current		8.4				
38.1	39.5	38.5	Net Worth		33.8				
100.0	100.0	100.0	Total Liabilities & Net Worth		100.0				
			INCOME DATA						
100.0	100.0	100.0	Net Sales		100.0				
33.0	31.2	30.8	Gross Profit		33.9				
29.3	26.9	24.9	Operating Expenses		28.0				
3.7	4.3	5.9	Operating Profit		5.9				
1.0	.7	1.0	All Other Expenses (net)		1.8				
2.7	3.6	4.8	Profit Before Taxes		4.2				
			RATIOS						
2.5	3.1	2.7			2.7				
1.6	1.9	1.6	Current		1.5				
1.1	1.3	1.3			1.2				
1.5	1.9	1.5			1.5				
1.1	1.0	.9	Quick		.9				
.6	.7	.6			.5				
37 10.0	30 12.2	24 14.9			23 15.8				
46 8.0	40 9.2	39 9.3	Sales/Receivables		41 9.0				
60 6.1	58 6.3	55 6.6			61 6.0				
22 16.9	26 13.9	20 18.1			23 15.8				
37 9.8	42 8.7	49 7.4	Cost of Sales/Inventory		51 7.1				
83 4.4	78 4.7	83 4.4			81 4.5				
12 29.3	16 23.0	24 15.3			25 14.8				
28 13.1	31 11.9	31 11.7	Cost of Sales/Payables		33 11.1				
53 6.9	41 8.9	43 8.4			43 8.4				
5.9	6.2	4.7			6.4				
10.6	9.8	10.4	Sales/Working Capital		12.1				
64.8	17.1	40.8			NM				
5.6	6.3	7.5			3.6				
(51) 2.5	(42) 2.5	(42) 2.7	EBIT/Interest	(19) 1.7					
.8	.9	.9			.2				
3.2	4.6	4.0	Net Profit + Depr., Dep.,						
(29) 1.7	(23) 2.1	(14) 2.6	Amort./Cur. Mat. L/T/D						
.9	1.1	.9							
.4	.3	.3			.3				
.8	.8	.9	Fixed/Worth		1.0				
1.4	3.1	2.1			4.9				
.7	.6	.7			.9				
1.6	1.7	2.3	Debt/Worth		2.6				
6.3	6.0	3.8			8.6				
40.5	42.1	40.2	% Profit Before Taxes/Tangible		40.5				
(51) 13.7	(43) 15.2	(45) 18.6	Net Worth	(20) 14.3					
2.6	1.3	.9			-.9				
13.7	12.4	14.6	% Profit Before Taxes/Total		13.9				
4.0	4.5	5.0	Assets		3.0				
-.1	.1	-.3			-2.6				
18.5	20.8	21.9			23.5				
8.1	10.0	8.7	Sales/Net Fixed Assets		9.5				
3.9	4.0	2.9			2.4				
3.3	3.3	3.1			3.2				
2.2	2.2	2.1	Sales/Total Assets		2.1				
1.5	1.6	1.3			1.5				
1.6	1.1	1.5			1.3				
(51) 2.6	(42) 2.1	(41) 2.2	% Depr., Dep., Amort./Sales	(18) 4.0					
5.1	4.0	5.5			5.6				
2.9	2.5	2.9			4.0				
(31) 4.9	(31) 4.9	(23) 4.6	% Officers', Directors',	(13) 5.2					
9.6	9.9	7.8	Owners' Comp/Sales		7.9				
291613M	390140M	346914M	Net Sales ($)	3042M	36070M	30435M	37079M	64002M	176286M
191042M	264732M	250299M	Total Assets ($)	1368M	23825M	16858M	15280M	78815M	114153M

M = $ thousand   MM = $ million
See Pages 1 through 15 for Explanation of Ratios and Data

MANUFACTURERS—GLASS PRODUCTS MADE OF PURCHASED GLASS. SIC# 3231

	Current Data Sorted By Assets							Comparative Historical Data	
							# Postretirement Benefits		
							Type of Statement		
2	2								
1	4	7	3		4	Unqualified	27	19
2	11	5	2			Reviewed	16	23
8	6	3				Compiled	15	15
	1					Tax Returns	1	
4	2	8	4		1	Other	11	13
	22 (4/1-9/30/94)		54 (10/1/94-3/31/95)				4/1/90-3/31/91	4/1/91-3/31/92
0-500M	500M-2MM	2-10MM	10-50MM	50-100MM	100-250MM		ALL	ALL
15	24	23	9		5	NUMBER OF STATEMENTS	70	70
%	%	%	%	%	%	ASSETS	%	%
10.9	9.1	7.5				Cash & Equivalents	8.2	9.4
25.9	27.7	31.8				Trade Receivables - (net)	28.0	26.7
31.0	31.4	20.6				Inventory	24.6	24.0
1.1	1.6	1.7				All Other Current	1.9	2.7
68.9	69.8	61.6				Total Current	62.6	62.8
23.9	24.2	32.3				Fixed Assets (net)	30.4	28.3
4.2	.8	1.0				Intangibles (net)	1.3	1.5
3.0	5.2	5.1				All Other Non-Current	5.8	7.3
100.0	100.0	100.0				Total	100.0	100.0
						LIABILITIES		
15.4	8.4	6.4				Notes Payable-Short Term	12.6	11.1
6.7	4.4	4.9				Cur. Mat.-L/T/D	4.2	4.9
22.1	19.5	16.3				Trade Payables	15.7	16.3
.2	.2	.4				Income Taxes Payable	1.4	.4
7.3	6.8	9.2				All Other Current	9.3	7.6
51.7	39.3	37.2				Total Current	43.2	40.3
21.5	15.9	13.9				Long Term Debt	17.3	16.4
.0	.6	.8				Deferred Taxes	.7	.7
2.5	6.5	3.5				All Other-Non-Current	2.9	5.4
24.2	37.6	44.5				Net Worth	35.9	37.2
100.0	100.0	100.0				Total Liabilities & Net Worth	100.0	100.0
						INCOME DATA		
100.0	100.0	100.0				Net Sales	100.0	100.0
37.5	32.8	27.9				Gross Profit	32.5	30.7
32.5	28.8	22.1				Operating Expenses	26.4	27.3
5.0	4.0	5.8				Operating Profit	6.1	3.4
1.0	1.1	.3				All Other Expenses (net)	2.0	1.6
4.0	2.9	5.5				Profit Before Taxes	4.1	1.9
						RATIOS		
2.5	2.5	3.1					2.4	2.8
1.3	1.7	1.9				Current	1.6	1.6
1.1	1.4	1.2					1.2	1.1
1.4	1.3	2.3					1.3	1.6
.7	.8	1.0				Quick	.9	.9
.3	.6	.6					.5	.6
11	33.0	24	15.1	32	11.5	Sales/Receivables	33	11.2	31	11.8
33	11.0	37	9.8	41	8.8		42	8.7	40	9.1
42	8.7	56	6.5	53	6.9		54	6.7	52	7.0
32	11.3	44	8.3	15	23.9	Cost of Sales/Inventory	37	10.0	32	11.5
48	7.6	62	5.9	35	10.4		53	6.9	56	6.5
76	4.8	96	3.8	61	6.0		81	4.5	94	3.9
8	45.1	27	13.7	14	26.1	Cost of Sales/Payables	15	23.9	21	17.8
33	11.1	36	10.1	20	18.3		29	12.6	34	10.7
50	7.3	59	6.2	42	8.6		57	6.4	55	6.6
8.3	5.3	5.8				Sales/Working Capital	5.4	4.9
17.4	7.7	9.1					10.6	9.8
59.4	13.9	45.5					39.7	45.5
	9.0		5.7		13.2	EBIT/Interest		6.6		5.2
(14)	2.2	(23)	2.8	(20)	5.3		(66)	2.7	(65)	1.9
	.5		1.3		3.0			1.5		.9
						Net Profit + Depr., Dep., Amort./Cur. Mat. L /T/D		5.4		5.5
							(40)	2.0	(35)	2.3
								1.4		.7
.3	.2	.3				Fixed/Worth	.5	.4
.8	.5	.7					.9	.9
-4.1	1.4	1.2					1.5	1.5
.9	.9	.5				Debt/Worth	.7	.8
2.4	2.1	1.3					2.0	1.7
-6.4	3.8	3.5					5.1	5.1
	44.8		29.5		50.9	% Profit Before Taxes/Tangible Net Worth		56.5		30.6
(11)	16.3		16.1	(21)	30.8		(63)	21.8	(64)	12.3
	-2.9		1.4		15.2			7.4		.3
18.9	9.5	22.9				% Profit Before Taxes/Total Assets	19.7	11.0
5.6	5.4	9.6					7.8	2.9
-.8	.8	6.2					1.9	-.7
39.1	28.1	20.1				Sales/Net Fixed Assets	16.6	20.7
22.6	13.0	6.5					9.5	9.9
8.6	6.5	5.3					4.0	4.6
5.0	3.1	3.2				Sales/Total Assets	3.1	3.0
3.5	2.5	2.9					2.5	2.4
2.3	1.7	2.0					1.6	1.6
	.6		.8		.9	% Depr., Dep., Amort./Sales		1.3		1.3
(14)	1.2	(22)	1.7	(18)	2.4		(65)	2.0	(64)	2.0
	4.3		3.8		3.4			3.7		3.5
			2.6			% Officers', Directors', Owners' Comp/Sales		2.6		2.6
		(16)	4.2				(25)	4.2	(39)	4.2
			7.2					6.6		11.6
14572M	67118M	289966M	386447M		1430369M	Net Sales ($)	1017037M	1854907M
3840M	28595M	114470M	207755M		966471M	Total Assets ($)	660866M	924539M

© Robert Morris Associates 1995

M = $ thousand   MM = $ million
See Pages 1 through 15 for Explanation of Ratios and Data

Comparative Historical Data / Current Data Sorted By Sales

			# Postretirement Benefits		3	1			
4	3	4	Type of Statement						
21	26	19	Unqualified	1	2	2	1	6	7
26	17	20	Reviewed	1	7	4	4	3	1
9	17	17	Compiled	5	8	2		2	
1	1	1	Tax Returns		1				
17	27	19	Other	3	2	1	1	8	4
4/1/92-3/31/93 ALL	4/1/93-3/31/94 ALL	4/1/94-3/31/95 ALL		0-1MM	1-3MM	3-5MM	5-10MM	10-25MM	25MM & OVER
				22 (4/1-9/30/94)		54 (10/1/94-3/31/95)			
74	88	76	NUMBER OF STATEMENTS	10	20	9	6	19	12
%	%	%	ASSETS	%	%	%	%	%	%
7.7	6.6	7.7	Cash & Equivalents	10.7	10.9			6.7	2.7
28.6	28.6	27.9	Trade Receivables - (net)	22.8	24.9			32.2	24.4
24.0	23.2	26.2	Inventory	33.0	28.7			21.7	20.8
2.7	1.7	1.7	All Other Current	1.0	2.0			.7	2.5
63.0	60.1	63.6	Total Current	67.5	66.5			61.3	50.3
27.5	31.3	29.6	Fixed Assets (net)	23.7	26.7			32.5	42.0
1.4	1.8	2.1	Intangibles (net)	4.2	1.4			2.4	2.0
8.1	6.7	4.8	All Other Non-Current	4.6	5.4			3.8	5.6
100.0	100.0	100.0	Total	100.0	100.0			100.0	100.0
			LIABILITIES						
10.3	8.7	8.7	Notes Payable-Short Term	21.5	6.5			8.5	4.4
4.9	4.0	4.8	Cur. Mat.-L /T/D	4.8	5.3			5.2	3.4
17.2	13.2	17.6	Trade Payables	16.5	23.0			15.9	11.4
.3	.5	.3	Income Taxes Payable	.2	.1			.4	.3
8.7	10.3	9.6	All Other Current	3.7	8.2			8.3	19.1
41.4	36.7	41.0	Total Current	46.7	43.2			38.4	38.6
15.0	16.9	17.2	Long Term Debt	20.3	19.2			14.0	20.3
.7	.7	.5	Deferred Taxes	.1	.0			.8	.3
3.3	6.2	4.4	All Other-Non-Current	.0	6.6			4.0	2.0
39.7	39.5	36.9	Net Worth	32.9	31.0			42.8	38.9
100.0	100.0	100.0	Total Liabilities & Net Worth	100.0	100.0			100.0	100.0
			INCOME DATA						
100.0	100.0	100.0	Net Sales	100.0	100.0			100.0	100.0
30.2	28.5	30.5	Gross Profit	33.6	39.1			27.5	22.1
27.3	25.1	25.0	Operating Expenses	30.4	34.1			20.6	14.1
2.9	3.4	5.5	Operating Profit	3.2	4.9			6.9	7.9
.9	1.6	1.0	All Other Expenses (net)	1.3	.3			1.0	1.9
2.0	1.8	4.5	Profit Before Taxes	1.9	4.6			5.9	6.0
			RATIOS						
2.2	2.5	2.7	Current	2.0	2.8			2.8	2.9
1.6	1.7	1.7		1.3	1.7			1.9	1.7
1.2	1.3	1.2		1.2	1.0			1.2	.9
1.4	1.7	1.6	Quick	1.0	1.6			2.3	1.7
.8	1.0	.8		.7	.8			1.0	.8
.6	.6	.5		.3	.3			.6	.4
29 12.8	32 11.4	28 12.9	Sales/Receivables	0 UND	15 23.7			32 11.5	29 12.8
43 8.5	45 8.2	38 9.5		34 10.7	29 12.7			40 9.1	50 7.3
52 7.0	58 6.3	55 6.6		48 7.6	43 8.5			53 6.9	59 6.2
29 12.4	25 14.6	31 11.7	Cost of Sales/Inventory	46 8.0	32 11.3			15 24.0	31 11.7
53 6.9	49 7.5	51 7.1		70 5.2	49 7.4			42 8.7	57 6.4
79 4.6	81 4.5	85 4.3		96 3.8	89 4.1			61 6.0	83 4.4
22 16.5	17 22.0	14 25.2	Cost of Sales/Payables	0 UND	12 31.0			15 24.9	14 26.2
31 11.6	25 14.6	29 12.7		35 10.3	40 9.1			22 16.4	23 15.7
51 7.1	44 8.3	51 7.1		63 5.8	76 4.8			38 9.5	41 8.9
6.1	5.8	5.9	Sales/Working Capital	6.9	6.3			5.8	4.2
11.4	9.7	9.2		15.9	9.8			10.8	11.3
28.8	16.3	33.2		27.0	NM			45.5	NM
(71) 5.3	(78) 8.7	(71) 7.9	EBIT/Interest		6.2		(18)	14.7	8.8
2.4	3.2	3.2			3.0			4.8	3.1
.4	.7	1.5			1.4			2.9	1.8
(34) 7.0	(39) 6.4	(30) 3.9	Net Profit + Depr., Dep., Amort./Cur. Mat. L/T/D						
1.7	2.9	1.5							
1.0	.4	.6							
.4	.4	.3	Fixed/Worth	.1	.3			.5	.5
.7	.8	.8		.8	.8			.7	1.3
1.2	1.9	2.2		NM	2.4			1.2	4.1
.9	.6	.8	Debt/Worth	1.0	.7			.7	.6
1.6	1.4	2.2		2.1	2.5			1.3	3.0
3.5	5.2	4.6		NM	4.6			3.5	5.3
(72) 28.2	(80) 38.1	(70) 46.8	% Profit Before Taxes/Tangible Net Worth		(18) 50.8		(17)	77.5	63.8
11.4	18.0	22.6			12.9			34.2	40.1
-.5	-1.0	9.3			1.6			19.4	12.6
9.2	16.7	17.4	% Profit Before Taxes/Total Assets	21.7	17.7			26.2	17.7
4.5	5.3	6.6		2.6	5.6			13.0	6.8
-2.5	-1.0	2.2		-1.8	1.1			6.6	3.5
20.6	17.4	24.6	Sales/Net Fixed Assets	49.0	38.5			20.1	7.5
9.9	7.3	9.5		17.8	13.0			6.5	4.8
5.0	4.3	5.4		8.2	5.9			5.4	2.7
3.0	3.0	3.2	Sales/Total Assets	3.5	3.9			3.4	2.1
2.3	2.1	2.5		2.5	3.0			2.9	1.8
1.9	1.6	1.8		2.0	1.8			2.1	1.2
(68) 1.4	(77) 1.4	(63) .9	% Depr., Dep., Amort./Sales		(18) .6		(13)	1.3	
2.0	2.5	2.1			1.2			2.7	
3.2	4.0	3.6			3.2			3.6	
(29) 3.0	(33) 2.1	(32) 2.3	% Officers', Directors', Owners' Comp/Sales		(13) 2.5				
4.4	4.0	4.6			4.6				
8.1	5.7	8.0			7.6				
1370183M	2077002M	2188472M	Net Sales ($)	6582M	39090M	32464M	46762M	290355M	1773219M
617357M	1447253M	1321131M	Total Assets ($)	2661M	16446M	13902M	25576M	114734M	1147812M

M = $ thousand   MM = $ million
See Pages 1 through 15 for Explanation of Ratios and Data

Current Data Sorted By Assets | Comparative Historical Data

0-500M	500M-2MM	2-10MM	10-50MM	50-100MM	100-250MM	# Postretirement Benefits / Type of Statement	4/1/90-3/31/91 ALL	4/1/91-3/31/92 ALL
	1	3				# Postretirement Benefits		
						Type of Statement		
	1	4		1		Unqualified	3	5
1	1	4				Reviewed	4	5
2	2	3				Compiled	7	6
		1				Tax Returns		
	5	6		2		Other	4	3
	10 (4/1-9/30/94)		23 (10/1/94-3/31/95)					
3	9	18		3		**NUMBER OF STATEMENTS**	18	19
%	%	%	%	%	%	**ASSETS**	%	%
		4.6				Cash & Equivalents	8.1	5.2
		29.4				Trade Receivables - (net)	31.6	26.3
		30.8				Inventory	20.5	30.3
		3.4				All Other Current	1.4	1.3
		68.3				Total Current	61.7	63.2
		22.8				Fixed Assets (net)	29.0	30.7
		2.2				Intangibles (net)	2.3	2.4
		6.6				All Other Non-Current	7.0	3.8
		100.0				Total	100.0	100.0
						LIABILITIES		
		6.2				Notes Payable-Short Term	11.5	10.0
		1.4				Cur. Mat. -L/T/D	1.7	3.8
		17.8				Trade Payables	18.1	13.3
		1.9				Income Taxes Payable	1.0	.4
		8.8				All Other Current	5.2	13.1
		36.1				Total Current	37.4	40.6
		14.8				Long Term Debt	11.2	16.1
		.5				Deferred Taxes	.5	1.4
		6.4				All Other-Non-Current	5.9	3.7
		42.1				Net Worth	45.0	38.3
		100.0				Total Liabilities & Net Worth	100.0	100.0
						INCOME DATA		
		100.0				Net Sales	100.0	100.0
		32.5				Gross Profit	36.2	39.2
		26.2				Operating Expenses	31.6	33.4
		6.3				Operating Profit	4.6	5.8
		.6				All Other Expenses (net)	1.3	1.5
		5.8				Profit Before Taxes	3.3	4.3
						RATIOS		
		2.8					2.7	2.3
		2.0				Current	2.1	1.8
		1.3					1.1	1.1
		1.3					1.7	1.2
		1.0				Quick	.8	.9
		.8					.7	.5
		36 10.2					27 13.3	24 15.4
		39 9.4				Sales/Receivables	43 8.5	43 8.4
		54 6.8					54 6.7	52 7.0
		33 10.9					18 20.1	45 8.1
		73 5.0				Cost of Sales/Inventory	39 9.3	64 5.7
		107 3.4					118 3.1	126 2.9
		19 19.3					25 14.5	22 16.3
		35 10.5				Cost of Sales/Payables	36 10.1	30 12.3
		47 7.7					49 7.4	46 7.9
		4.3					5.7	4.6
		8.6				Sales/Working Capital	8.2	12.7
		16.7					NM	37.4
		24.1					9.6	7.5
	(16)	6.2				EBIT/Interest	(17) 3.5	(18) 3.2
		3.0					.2	2.0
						Net Profit + Depr., Dep., Amort./Cur. Mat. L./T/D		
		.2					.2	.5
		.5				Fixed/Worth	.8	.9
		1.1					1.4	2.0
		.5					.6	.8
		1.2				Debt/Worth	1.2	1.7
		5.2					2.0	6.0
		44.7					28.8	32.3
	(15)	27.6				% Profit Before Taxes/Tangible Net Worth	(17) 17.0	(18) 25.1
		8.7					-.7	11.0
		20.4					12.3	15.2
		9.8				% Profit Before Taxes/Total Assets	5.1	5.6
		4.1					-.7	3.7
		34.1					36.1	20.4
		11.6				Sales/Net Fixed Assets	8.0	9.0
		4.5					4.7	4.7
		2.9					3.2	3.3
		2.4				Sales/Total Assets	2.2	2.2
		1.7					1.7	1.4
		.4					1.2	1.2
	(14)	2.7				% Depr., Dep., Amort./Sales	(14) 2.4	(17) 1.7
		4.6					4.1	3.6
								7.1
						% Officers', Directors', Owners' Comp/Sales		(10) 8.2
								9.5
1974M	30903M	193798M		282964M		Net Sales ($)	297473M	346957M
595M	11091M	76798M		248337M		Total Assets ($)	172138M	219001M

M = $ thousand   MM = $ million
See Pages 1 through 15 for Explanation of Ratios and Data

Comparative Historical Data | | Current Data Sorted By Sales

	1			4	# Postretirement Benefits			2		2	
					Type of Statement						
	3		8	6	Unqualified			2	1	2	1
	4		8	6	Reviewed	1	1	2	1	1	
	2		7	7	Compiled	1	2	2	1	1	
	1			1	Tax Returns					1	
	5		8	13	Other		1		3		3
	4/1/92- 3/31/93		4/1/93- 3/31/94	4/1/94- 3/31/95			10 (4/1-9/30/94)			23 (10/1/94-3/31/95)	
	ALL		ALL	ALL		0-1MM	1-3MM	3-5MM	5-10MM	10-25MM	25MM & OVER
	15		31	33	**NUMBER OF STATEMENTS**	2	4	9	7	7	4
	%		%	%	**ASSETS**	%	%	%	%	%	%
	4.6		6.2	8.1	Cash & Equivalents						
	19.7		29.2	29.7	Trade Receivables - (net)						
	20.3		23.8	27.0	Inventory						
	2.1		2.0	2.2	All Other Current						
	46.7		61.1	67.1	Total Current						
	38.8		27.3	22.9	Fixed Assets (net)						
	5.2		2.2	2.0	Intangibles (net)						
	9.3		9.4	8.0	All Other Non-Current						
	100.0		100.0	100.0	Total						
					LIABILITIES						
	3.6		11.0	9.0	Notes Payable-Short Term						
	3.7		3.1	1.8	Cur. Mat.-L /T/D						
	13.4		15.4	18.1	Trade Payables						
	.2		.7	1.1	Income Taxes Payable						
	19.1		7.9	8.6	All Other Current						
	40.0		38.1	38.6	Total Current						
	12.3		19.8	11.5	Long Term Debt						
	1.2		1.0	.8	Deferred Taxes						
	3.0		4.2	5.0	All Other-Non-Current						
	43.4		36.9	44.1	Net Worth						
	100.0		100.0	100.0	Total Liabilities & Net Worth						
					INCOME DATA						
	100.0		100.0	100.0	Net Sales						
	26.4		32.9	31.6	Gross Profit						
	26.0		26.5	25.1	Operating Expenses						
	.5		6.4	6.4	Operating Profit						
	2.2		2.0	1.2	All Other Expenses (net)						
	-1.7		4.4	5.3	Profit Before Taxes						
					RATIOS						
	1.6		2.5	2.7							
	1.0		1.7	1.8	Current						
	.6		1.2	1.3							
	.9		1.3	1.4							
	.5		.8	1.0	Quick						
	.2		.7	.8							
21	17.6	33	11.2	36 10.2							
33	11.0	43	8.4	41 8.8	Sales/Receivables						
49	7.5	51	7.2	54 6.8							
28	13.1	43	8.4	33 10.9							
40	9.2	69	5.3	55 6.6	Cost of Sales/Inventory						
79	4.6	99	3.7	83 4.4							
15	24.9	23	15.8	17 21.9							
31	11.9	33	10.9	42 8.6	Cost of Sales/Payables						
48	7.6	46	8.0	52 7.0							
	9.6		5.5	5.0							
	675.0		10.5	7.8	Sales/Working Capital						
	-6.6		19.1	21.1							
	8.8		7.9	23.3							
(13)	2.2	(29)	3.0	(27) 7.5	EBIT/Interest						
	.8		1.6	1.9							
					Net Profit + Depr., Dep., Amort./Cur. Mat. L/T/D						
	.5		.3	.2							
	.9		.6	.5	Fixed/Worth						
	1.9		1.5	1.0							
	.6		1.0	.5							
	1.6		1.4	1.1	Debt/Worth						
	2.6		3.2	3.2							
	29.0		44.2	43.3							
(14)	5.9	(28)	18.7	(29) 27.6	% Profit Before Taxes/Tangible Net Worth						
	-9.5		1.4	8.6							
	12.3		16.1	17.9							
	1.7		9.9	10.5	% Profit Before Taxes/Total Assets						
	-1.1		1.0	3.2							
	11.6		19.3	32.7							
	7.0		8.7	11.2	Sales/Net Fixed Assets						
	2.3		4.5	5.6							
	2.6		3.2	3.1							
	2.1		2.6	2.7	Sales/Total Assets						
	1.4		1.6	1.6							
	2.4		1.3	1.0							
(14)	3.4	(23)	1.8	(27) 2.9	% Depr., Dep., Amort./Sales						
	8.4		2.6	4.5							
			2.3	2.3							
		(11)	3.3	(16) 5.0	% Officers', Directors', Owners' Comp/Sales						
			6.0	10.1							
	294524M		978893M	509639M	Net Sales ($)	612M	6991M	34455M	49683M	108468M	309430M
	163314M		723575M	336821M	Total Assets ($)	216M	3381M	19074M	18718M	40229M	255203M

M = $ thousand   MM = $ million
See Pages 1 through 15 for Explanation of Ratios and Data

Current Data Sorted By Assets   Comparative Historical Data

0-500M	500M-2MM	2-10MM	10-50MM	50-100MM	100-250MM	# Postretirement Benefits / Type of Statement	4/1/90-3/31/91 ALL	4/1/91-3/31/92 ALL
	1	7	4		1	# Postretirement Benefits		
	6	15	18		3	Unqualified	48	45
2	10	32	3		1	Reviewed	30	41
5	25	23	1			Compiled	48	42
3	2					Tax Returns		4
6	20	13	9		1	Other	35	28
	61 (4/1-9/30/94)		137 (10/1/94-3/31/95)					
16	63	83	31		5	**NUMBER OF STATEMENTS**	161	160
%	%	%	%	%	%	**ASSETS**	%	%
5.2	10.6	9.0	7.0			Cash & Equivalents	8.2	6.5
31.7	28.7	29.5	23.5			Trade Receivables - (net)	23.7	25.9
5.9	6.7	6.6	8.6			Inventory	8.2	8.4
5.2	2.8	1.9	1.0			All Other Current	2.0	3.1
48.0	48.8	47.0	40.1			Total Current	42.1	43.9
45.7	39.7	43.8	48.3			Fixed Assets (net)	48.8	45.7
2.2	2.3	1.4	2.4			Intangibles (net)	1.5	2.1
4.1	9.2	7.9	9.2			All Other Non-Current	7.6	8.3
100.0	100.0	100.0	100.0			Total	100.0	100.0
						LIABILITIES		
3.2	5.6	4.2	8.0			Notes Payable-Short Term	5.9	7.2
7.9	7.4	6.2	5.5			Cur. Mat. -L/T/D	6.2	6.8
22.8	15.1	16.3	12.8			Trade Payables	13.0	14.8
.5	.3	.5	.2			Income Taxes Payable	.5	.4
4.4	6.4	5.6	4.9			All Other Current	5.8	5.9
38.9	34.9	32.7	31.4			Total Current	31.4	35.2
31.8	17.6	16.3	19.7			Long Term Debt	20.9	19.7
.0	.6	1.0	3.1			Deferred Taxes	1.3	1.0
1.4	3.5	1.8	2.1			All Other-Non-Current	2.9	2.9
27.9	43.5	48.2	43.7			Net Worth	43.5	41.2
100.0	100.0	100.0	100.0			Total Liabilities & Net Worth	100.0	100.0
						INCOME DATA		
100.0	100.0	100.0	100.0			Net Sales	100.0	100.0
31.7	37.4	29.4	22.7			Gross Profit	29.1	29.3
30.6	33.0	24.8	15.7			Operating Expenses	26.5	26.2
1.1	4.4	4.6	7.0			Operating Profit	2.7	3.0
.9	.1	.1	1.3			All Other Expenses (net)	1.0	1.4
.2	4.3	4.5	5.7			Profit Before Taxes	1.7	1.7
						RATIOS		
2.0	2.1	2.1	1.9			Current	2.4	2.1
1.1	1.5	1.5	1.2				1.5	1.4
.8	1.1	1.1	.9				.9	.8
1.7	1.8	1.7	1.4			Quick	1.8	1.5
.8	1.3	1.2	.9				1.0	1.0
.6	.7	.9	.7				.7	.6
26 14.1	31 11.8	37 10.0	42 8.7			Sales/Receivables	33 11.2	33 10.9
41 8.8	41 8.8	44 8.3	49 7.4				42 8.6	43 8.4
54 6.8	51 7.2	57 6.4	59 6.2				55 6.6	56 6.5
0 UND	6 63.9	6 65.9	10 35.9			Cost of Sales/Inventory	9 39.0	7 54.9
6 60.7	11 32.5	11 34.2	21 17.7				19 19.0	15 24.6
42 8.7	20 18.1	22 16.3	33 11.1				39 9.3	31 11.6
10 36.2	20 17.9	24 15.0	22 16.3			Cost of Sales/Payables	16 23.3	20 18.6
52 7.0	33 11.2	32 11.3	28 13.0				31 11.7	31 11.9
65 5.6	51 7.2	47 7.8	47 7.8				48 7.6	51 7.2
14.7	9.8	9.0	9.5			Sales/Working Capital	7.4	8.1
58.0	16.2	15.5	28.7				16.8	20.7
-73.5	116.2	44.6	-74.5				-48.3	-26.3
5.6	11.4	9.6	8.6			EBIT/Interest	4.8	5.0
1.9	(58) 4.2	(70) 5.8	(30) 3.6				(152) 2.0	(153) 2.3
-2.0	2.2	2.7	1.9				.4	1.0
	4.8	4.9	4.7			Net Profit + Depr., Dep., Amort./Cur. Mat. L /T/D	4.1	3.7
	(23) 1.9	(41) 2.1	(18) 2.0				(97) 1.8	(97) 1.7
	1.3	1.3	1.2				1.1	.7
.6	.5	.6	.9			Fixed/Worth	.7	.6
2.8	1.0	.9	1.2				1.2	1.1
10.1	1.9	1.5	2.0				2.3	2.5
.7	.7	.5	.8			Debt/Worth	.7	.6
3.9	1.1	1.2	1.6				1.4	1.7
43.0	3.4	2.0	3.0				3.2	3.6
(13) 59.1	(62) 57.2	(81) 31.8	(30) 30.8			% Profit Before Taxes/Tangible Net Worth	(151) 21.5	(153) 24.5
15.4	29.9	20.8	18.0				9.8	9.0
7.4	11.8	8.9	6.2				-1.4	1.4
13.6	23.1	14.5	15.2			% Profit Before Taxes/Total Assets	8.9	8.7
3.6	10.3	9.4	6.2				4.2	4.1
-10.0	3.0	3.9	2.7				-2.1	.1
20.9	10.1	8.6	4.7			Sales/Net Fixed Assets	5.8	6.8
5.4	6.8	5.3	3.7				4.0	4.4
3.5	5.2	3.4	2.8				2.9	2.9
4.1	3.1	2.6	2.1			Sales/Total Assets	2.5	2.8
2.8	2.6	2.3	1.7				1.9	2.0
2.1	2.0	1.8	1.4				1.4	1.5
2.0	2.4	2.8	3.6			% Depr., Dep., Amort./Sales	3.7	2.9
3.5	(60) 3.8	(80) 4.3	(30) 4.3				(150) 5.3	(155) 4.7
6.1	5.8	5.4	5.8				7.3	6.5
	2.6	1.7				% Officers', Directors', Owners' Comp/Sales	1.8	2.1
	(30) 4.3	(33) 3.2					(58) 3.2	(74) 3.2
	6.3	5.1					6.2	5.3
18915M	184008M	807663M	1060320M		696784M	Net Sales ($)	2999302M	2404190M
5676M	69706M	348491M	631905M		709071M	Total Assets ($)	2217186M	1833765M

M = $ thousand   MM = $ million
See Pages 1 through 15 for Explanation of Ratios and Data

MANUFACTURERS—READY-MIXED CONCRETE

Comparative Historical Data / Current Data

Type of Statement

4	8	13	Type of Statement	# Postretirement Benefits
40	53	42	Unqualified	
38	41	48	Reviewed	2
39	45	54	Compiled	4
2	7	5	Tax Returns	
31	40	49	Other	6

Main Data

4/1/92-3/31/93 ALL	4/1/93-3/31/94 ALL	4/1/94-3/31/95 ALL		0-1MM					
150	186	198	NUMBER OF STATEMENTS	12					
%	**%**	**%**	**ASSETS**	**%**					
8.6	7.5	8.8	Cash & Equivalents	7.6					
25.9	26.3	28.1	Trade Receivables - (net)	21.5					
7.9	7.8	6.9	Inventory	7.1					
2.0	1.8	2.3	All Other Current	7.4					
44.4	43.5	46.2	Total Current	43.6					
45.0	46.2	43.6	Fixed Assets (net)	45.					
1.7	2.1	2.0	Intangibles (net)	1					
8.9	8.2	8.2	All Other Non-Current						
100.0	100.0	100.0	Total	100.0					
			LIABILITIES						
5.9	5.7	5.1	Notes Payable-Short Term		4.2				
7.0	6.0	6.6	Cur. Mat.-L /T/D		7.9				
14.1	14.0	15.6	Trade Payables		16.2				
.3	.9	.4	Income Taxes Payable						
5.3	5.0	5.6	All Other Current	3.8	5.5		4.9		
32.6	31.5	33.3	Total Current	30.4	34.1		33.0		
18.3	20.2	18.6	Long Term Debt	30.1	21.9		18.9	17.2	
1.3	1.2	1.2	Deferred Taxes	.0	.6	.4		1.0	
2.5	2.5	2.6	All Other-Non-Current	1.9	3.7	3.1	.9		45.7
45.3	44.6	44.3	Net Worth	37.6	39.7	44.3	46.0		
100.0	100.0	100.0	Total Liabilities & Net Worth	100.0	100.0	100.0	100.0	100.0	100.0
			INCOME DATA						
100.0	100.0	100.0	Net Sales	100.0	100.0	100.0	100.0	100.0	100.0
31.4	30.3	31.0	Gross Profit	36.8	37.1	34.1	30.9	26.9	21.0
28.4	25.7	26.2	Operating Expenses	40.3	32.8	29.5	25.4	20.9	13.9
3.0	4.6	4.9	Operating Profit	-3.5	4.3	4.6	5.4	6.0	7.1
.5	.6	.4	All Other Expenses (net)	1.0	.1	-.1	.4	.6	1.1
2.5	4.0	4.5	Profit Before Taxes	-4.5	4.3	4.7	5.1	5.4	6.1
			RATIOS						
2.3	2.3	2.1	Current	3.7	2.1	2.0	2.1	2.3	2.4
1.5	1.4	1.4		1.5	1.4	1.4	1.5	1.5	1.2
1.0	1.0	1.1		.7	1.0	.9	1.1	1.2	1.1
1.7	1.6	1.7	Quick	2.2	1.7	1.5	1.8	1.8	1.8
1.1	1.1	1.1		.7	1.1	1.2	1.2	1.2	.9
.7	.8	.8		.5	.7	.7	.9	.9	.6
36 10.2	35 10.5	36 10.2	Sales/Receivables	26 14.1	33 11.0	31 11.9	37 10.0	38 9.7	43 8.5
41 8.8	44 8.3	44 8.3		46 7.9	43 8.5	39 9.4	42 8.7	45 8.1	50 7.3
53 6.9	54 6.7	54 6.8		60 6.1	50 7.3	51 7.2	54 6.8	54 6.8	63 5.8
7 49.0	6 56.9	6 65.0	Cost of Sales/Inventory	0 UND	5 71.5	5 77.7	6 64.8	6 65.0	10 37.6
17 22.0	13 28.3	12 29.5		19 19.4	12 30.3	8 44.9	12 31.6	16 22.2	18 20.3
30 12.0	31 11.7	26 13.8		65 5.6	26 14.1	16 22.3	20 18.3	31 11.9	31 11.7
20 18.7	21 17.5	22 16.4	Cost of Sales/Payables	0 UND	21 17.1	21 17.8	23 15.8	22 16.7	23 15.6
30 12.1	29 12.5	32 11.3		56 6.5	38 9.7	35 10.4	29 12.6	31 11.6	28 13.1
47 7.8	45 8.2	49 7.5		70 5.2	51 7.1	56 6.5	43 8.4	38 9.5	36 10.1
7.5	8.5	9.3	Sales/Working Capital	4.2	10.0	12.5	9.2	8.5	6.2
17.3	17.3	18.4		22.8	16.2	23.8	15.6	14.4	23.7
-191.3	-842.9	92.5		-14.5	NM	-30.5	55.2	32.3	88.5
6.0	8.9	9.2	EBIT/Interest	3.4	10.9	6.9	9.5	9.7	10.3
(141) 2.7	(169) 3.4	(179) 4.1		(11) 1.0	(39) 3.5	(33) 5.0	(41) 4.9	(32) 6.3	(23) 3.0
1.2	1.7	2.3		-2.0	1.6	2.4	2.9	2.7	2.3
3.7	3.8	4.5	Net Profit + Depr., Dep., Amort./Cur. Mat. L/T/D		5.2	3.3	6.0	3.0	5.1
(73) 1.8	(89) 2.1	(89) 2.0			(15) 2.4	(15) 1.7	(22) 2.7	(17) 2.0	(16) 2.0
1.0	1.1	1.3			1.4	1.3	1.5	1.3	1.1
.7	.7	.6	Fixed/Worth	.3	.6	.6	.7	.5	.7
1.0	1.1	1.0		2.0	1.2	1.0	1.1	.9	1.2
1.8	2.0	1.9		8.9	2.8	1.6	1.5	1.8	2.0
.6	.6	.7	Debt/Worth	.5	.8	.8	.6	.6	.6
1.1	1.3	1.3		2.0	1.5	1.1	1.3	1.1	1.3
3.1	2.9	2.8		13.0	6.1	2.1	2.2	2.1	3.0
21.1	34.4	42.2	% Profit Before Taxes/Tangible Net Worth	28.3	56.2	47.0	50.1	38.5	28.6
(144) 8.4	(179) 16.7	(191) 21.8		(10) 6.6	(40) 23.4	(35) 26.9	(43) 24.9	(37) 20.0	(26) 16.0
1.6	4.4	8.5		-10.8	6.8	8.8	14.0	9.3	7.1
9.4	13.5	16.0	% Profit Before Taxes/Total Assets	9.6	17.0	20.1	15.2	15.3	15.9
4.0	5.9	8.7		-1.5	7.8	10.7	9.8	10.5	6.7
.6	2.0	3.4		-11.7	2.4	3.8	5.6	4.1	3.1
7.1	7.3	8.4	Sales/Net Fixed Assets	15.8	9.1	9.2	7.6	9.6	5.6
4.3	4.4	5.3		4.0	6.5	5.5	5.5	4.9	4.2
3.0	2.9	3.5		2.2	4.3	4.2	3.6	3.1	3.4
2.6	2.6	2.8	Sales/Total Assets	2.7	2.9	3.1	2.7	2.6	2.3
2.0	2.1	2.3		1.7	2.4	2.7	2.4	2.2	1.8
1.6	1.5	1.7		1.1	2.0	1.7	1.9	1.7	1.5
3.3	3.2	2.8	% Depr., Dep., Amort./Sales	3.4	2.4	2.8	2.9	1.9	3.6
(144) 4.9	(174) 4.5	(188) 4.2		(11) 4.7	(40) 3.9	(35) 4.0	(35) 4.5	(23) 3.9	4.3
6.6	6.5	5.6		6.6	6.0	5.2	5.5	5.3	5.5
2.2	1.8	2.1	% Officers', Directors', Owners' Comp/Sales		2.7	2.4	1.6	1.3	
(59) 3.5	(71) 3.1	(76) 3.3		(18) 4.2	(22) 3.5	(19) 3.8	(10) 2.0		
5.7	4.9	5.2		5.7	6.4	5.3	2.6		
1747389M	2510420M	2767690M	Net Sales ($)	7016M	82105M	140845M	320765M	613778M	1603181M
1326178M	2101720M	1764849M	Total Assets ($)	4815M	39879M	60512M	147712M	308865M	1203066M

...By Assets — **Comparative Historical Data**

Postretirement Benefits

Type of Statement	2-10MM	10-50MM	50-100MM	100-250MM	4/1/90-3/31/91 ALL	4/1/91-3/31/92 ALL
Unqualified		14	6	5	64	49
Reviewed		2	1		22	11
Compiled					14	11
Tax Returns						1
Other		8	3	4	20	22

63 (10/1/94-3/31/95)

(—)	(—)	2-10MM	10-50MM	50-100MM	100-250MM		4/1/90-3/31/91 ALL	4/1/91-3/31/92 ALL
		30	24	10	9	**NUMBER OF STATEMENTS**	120	94
		%	%	%	%	**ASSETS**	%	%
		4.7	2.8	3.1		Cash & Equivalents	5.9	4.5
		23.9	21.6	29.3		Trade Receivables - (net)	24.3	24.2
		29.7	32.0	31.6		Inventory	28.1	30.3
		1.8	1.8	.8		All Other Current	2.6	2.0
		63.6	60.1	58.3	64.7	Total Current	60.8	61.0
		26.4	34.1	33.6	31.9	Fixed Assets (net)	30.9	30.6
		3.3	.3	1.8	.6	Intangibles (net)	2.0	1.8
		6.6	5.5	6.4	2.7	All Other Non-Current	6.3	6.6
		100.0	100.0	100.0	100.0	Total	100.0	100.0
						LIABILITIES		
		8.7	11.1	7.6	8.7	Notes Payable-Short Term	8.6	10.9
		3.1	4.8	3.2	3.4	Cur. Mat. -L/T/D	3.7	4.5
		16.6	16.9	14.2	13.8	Trade Payables	13.5	15.1
		.3	.3	.6	.3	Income Taxes Payable	.6	.3
		11.2	5.8	7.2	7.3	All Other Current	6.0	5.8
		39.9	38.9	32.8	33.5	Total Current	32.5	36.6
		19.1	16.8	22.2	20.4	Long Term Debt	19.4	16.3
		.7	.6	1.3	1.2	Deferred Taxes	1.9	1.4
		4.9	2.5	5.0	1.0	All Other-Non-Current	3.5	4.6
		35.4	41.2	38.7	43.9	Net Worth	42.8	41.2
		100.0	100.0	100.0	100.0	Total Liabilities & Net Worth	100.0	100.0
						INCOME DATA		
		100.0	100.0	100.0	100.0	Net Sales	100.0	100.0
		24.0	17.7	17.4	15.5	Gross Profit	20.6	20.2
		19.6	17.9	13.4	9.8	Operating Expenses	14.3	16.1
		4.4	-.1	4.0	5.7	Operating Profit	6.2	4.1
		1.6	1.5	2.2	1.1	All Other Expenses (net)	2.2	1.9
		2.8	-1.6	1.8	4.6	Profit Before Taxes	4.0	2.2
						RATIOS		
	2.5	2.6	2.3	3.0		Current	2.9	2.6
	1.7	1.6	1.8	2.3			2.0	1.7
	1.2	1.1	1.3	1.3			1.5	1.3
	1.3	1.1	1.2	1.3		Quick	1.6	1.1
	1.0	.8	.9	1.1			1.0	.8
	.7	.5	.5	.6			.6	.5
	35 10.4	29 12.8	24 15.3	47 7.7		Sales/Receivables	31 11.7	32 11.3
	51 7.1	39 9.4	38 9.5	56 6.5			46 8.0	51 7.2
	76 4.8	52 7.0	62 5.9	64 5.7			60 6.1	64 5.7
	24 15.0	35 10.4	38 9.6	51 7.1		Cost of Sales/Inventory	36 10.2	49 7.4
	50 7.3	63 5.8	62 5.9	81 4.5			58 6.3	69 5.3
	81 4.5	85 4.3	87 4.2	94 3.9			96 3.8	96 3.8
	21 17.3	21 17.4	17 22.1	20 18.5		Cost of Sales/Payables	15 23.9	18 19.9
	34 10.6	33 11.2	24 15.5	24 15.4			24 15.2	27 13.3
	55 6.6	48 7.6	43 8.5	39 9.4			42 8.7	46 8.0
	5.4	6.7	5.6	4.2		Sales/Working Capital	4.8	5.3
	10.2	10.5	8.3	5.0			7.0	9.0
	29.4	57.6	13.6	11.8			13.2	15.5
	(16) 9.4	(28) 4.9	(23) 6.3		EBIT/Interest	(112) 7.3	(87) 4.9
	2.9	2.1	2.8			2.5	1.9
	2.0	.4	.2			1.1	1.1
		(15) 2.7	(13) 8.9		Net Profit + Depr., Dep., Amort./Cur. Mat. L /T/D	(71) 4.7	(47) 2.9
		1.5	2.9			2.6	1.7
		-2.7	1.3			1.0	.6
	.2	.5	.4	.2	Fixed/Worth	.3	.4
	.6	.8	.7	.6		.7	.8
	2.8	1.3	1.2	1.4		1.5	1.5
	1.0	.8	.6	.6	Debt/Worth	.7	.7
	2.4	1.5	1.2	1.2		1.5	1.5
	8.6	2.9	3.3	3.2		3.2	2.9
	(16) 57.8	(29) 24.6	(21) 30.3	26.5	% Profit Before Taxes/Tangible Net Worth	(116) 32.1	(87) 20.7
	19.3	7.2	14.6	15.2		15.4	11.4
	7.9	-3.1	-11.4	9.9		1.6	3.1
	10.2	9.5	16.6	11.5	% Profit Before Taxes/Total Assets	13.9	9.8
	5.9	2.9	6.1	7.8		6.6	4.5
	2.5	-.7	-1.9	2.5		.3	.4
	44.6	14.2	12.8	44.1	Sales/Net Fixed Assets	12.7	14.3
	8.9	6.0	7.2	6.0		6.2	5.9
	3.2	3.6	3.6	3.0		3.8	3.2
	3.1	2.7	2.5	2.3	Sales/Total Assets	2.6	2.5
	1.9	2.1	2.2	1.8		1.9	1.8
	1.5	1.7	1.7	1.4		1.5	1.3
	(12) .9	(28) 1.0	(22) 1.6	.8	% Depr., Dep., Amort./Sales	(99) 1.6	(82) 1.3
	1.6	2.3	2.8	3.1		2.5	2.9
	4.7	3.8	4.3	4.5		4.3	4.5
			(20) 1.9		% Officers', Directors', Owners' Comp/Sales	(26) 1.2	(25) 1.3
			3.0			2.2	2.5
			4.1			4.9	5.4
3128M	58866M	297948M	1164726M	1327050M	2516757M	Net Sales ($)	7781534M	4568266M
913M	22685M	128438M	522761M	689503M	1497790M	Total Assets ($)	4532894M	2802502M

M = $ thousand   MM = $ million
See Pages 1 through 15 for Explanation of Ratios and Data

	Comparative Historical Data			Current Data Sorted By Sales					
# Postretirement Benefits	4	8	7		1	1	1	1	4
Type of Statement									
Unqualified	74	47	40	1	1	2	8	4	24
Reviewed	23	25	21		4	5	4	4	4
Compiled	10	16	6	1	1	2	1	1	
Tax Returns		2	2		1		1		
Other	14	31	23		3	2	1	3	14
	4/1/92-3/31/93 ALL	4/1/93-3/31/94 ALL	4/1/94-3/31/95 ALL	29 (4/1-9/30/94)			63 (10/1/94-3/31/95)		
				0-1MM	1-3MM	3-5MM	5-10MM	10-25MM	25MM & OVER
NUMBER OF STATEMENTS	121	121	92	2	10	11	15	12	42
ASSETS	%	%	%	%	%	%	%	%	%
Cash & Equivalents	4.8	4.4	3.6		1.4	3.4	5.6	6.1	2.9
Trade Receivables - (net)	23.9	26.8	25.6		30.7	31.1	25.2	22.7	24.1
Inventory	31.1	28.5	27.6		21.4	24.0	30.4	29.7	29.0
All Other Current	4.5	2.2	2.4		1.8	2.5	4.6	2.4	1.5
Total Current	64.3	61.9	59.3		55.3	60.9	65.8	61.0	57.5
Fixed Assets (net)	29.5	29.0	33.1		36.5	32.5	28.7	35.3	33.9
Intangibles (net)	1.0	2.7	2.1		.1	.4	.3	.1	3.1
All Other Non-Current	5.2	6.4	5.5		8.1	6.2	5.2	3.7	5.6
Total	100.0	100.0	100.0		100.0	100.0	100.0	100.0	100.0
LIABILITIES									
Notes Payable-Short Term	9.4	9.0	8.5		2.5	14.4	16.7	5.6	6.7
Cur. Mat.-L/T/D	3.7	3.4	3.7		5.6	3.9	4.4	3.0	3.2
Trade Payables	15.5	14.0	15.0		17.8	14.4	18.1	15.2	13.8
Income Taxes Payable	.7	1.1	.4		.3	.1	.5	.2	.5
All Other Current	6.9	8.1	7.5		8.0	12.0	5.4	7.6	6.7
Total Current	36.3	35.6	35.1		34.2	44.6	45.1	31.6	30.9
Long Term Debt	14.3	18.8	20.6		29.0	15.4	11.0	23.8	22.0
Deferred Taxes	.9	1.0	1.1		.8	.3	.7	.5	1.7
All Other-Non-Current	3.0	4.0	3.5		6.6	2.8	4.1	1.2	3.6
Net Worth	45.5	40.6	39.7		29.4	36.8	39.1	42.9	41.7
Total Liabilities & Net Worth	100.0	100.0	100.0		100.0	100.0	100.0	100.0	100.0
INCOME DATA									
Net Sales	100.0	100.0	100.0		100.0	100.0	100.0	100.0	100.0
Gross Profit	21.3	21.4	19.5		26.9	18.1	17.1	20.9	18.2
Operating Expenses	15.8	17.9	16.3		24.9	18.2	17.5	17.7	12.8
Operating Profit	5.5	3.6	3.1		1.9	-.1	-.4	3.2	5.4
All Other Expenses (net)	1.6	1.3	1.6		1.7	1.1	2.2	1.1	1.7
Profit Before Taxes	3.9	2.3	1.5		.2	-1.2	-2.5	2.0	3.7
RATIOS									
Current	2.7	2.7	2.6		2.2	1.8	2.4	3.2	2.6
	1.9	2.0	1.8		1.6	1.4	1.3	1.9	2.1
	1.4	1.3	1.3		1.2	1.1	1.0	1.6	1.3
Quick	1.5	1.4	1.3		1.2	.9	1.3	1.2	1.4
	.9	1.0	.9		1.0	.8	.6	.9	1.0
	.5	.6	.6		.7	.6	.5	.7	.6
Sales/Receivables	27 13.5	32 11.5	31 11.9		37 9.8	34 10.8	31 11.7	16 22.9	26 13.9
	47 7.8	49 7.5	43 8.4		50 7.3	51 7.2	40 9.1	38 9.6	46 7.9
	57 6.4	64 5.7	60 6.1		66 5.5	72 5.1	57 6.4	48 7.6	63 5.8
Cost of Sales/Inventory	38 9.5	38 9.5	38 9.6		45 8.2	35 10.4	33 10.9	32 11.3	41 9.0
	62 5.9	59 6.2	61 6.0		69 5.3	50 7.3	61 6.0	79 4.6	59 6.2
	89 4.1	89 4.1	85 4.3		89 4.1	76 4.8	72 5.1	101 3.6	85 4.3
Cost of Sales/Payables	18 20.6	15 24.6	20 18.4		28 13.0	20 18.6	12 30.8	17 21.4	19 19.1
	26 14.0	26 13.8	29 12.4		38 9.7	32 11.4	38 9.7	27 13.7	24 15.5
	43 8.5	39 9.4	44 8.3		56 6.5	48 7.6	54 6.8	35 10.5	39 9.3
Sales/Working Capital	5.4	4.9	5.6		4.2	7.2	7.4	6.3	4.5
	8.6	7.2	8.7		9.9	11.1	14.0	7.6	8.1
	15.3	13.9	18.8		29.3	61.7	94.7	17.3	12.8
EBIT/Interest	(113) 7.6	(110) 6.2	(86) 5.9		5.4	2.5	3.1	10.8	(39) 6.5
	3.8	4.0	2.8		2.9	(10) 1.9	(11) 2.3	3.1	3.7
	1.7	1.7	1.3		1.8	.3	-1.1	1.2	1.3
Net Profit + Depr., Dep., Amort./Cur. Mat. L/T/D	(55) 4.1	(53) 3.9	(42) 5.3						(18) 5.9
	2.5	2.4	1.8						2.6
	1.1	1.4	.8						1.1
Fixed/Worth	.3	.4	.4			.6	.4	.3	.4
	.6	.7	.8			1.0	.7	.6	.8
	1.1	1.4	1.5			2.6	1.6	1.3	1.4
Debt/Worth	.7	.7	.8			1.1	1.0	.5	1.0
	1.1	1.5	1.5			2.7	2.0	1.9	1.2
	2.3	3.6	3.3			6.6	3.3	4.6	1.9
% Profit Before Taxes/Tangible Net Worth	(115) 31.3	(109) 31.2	(87) 29.4			22.7	19.9	32.3	(39) 30.7
	17.8	18.8	15.4			6.1	(14) 8.3	15.5	25.1
	6.5	5.5	.3			-2.6	-57.7	3.9	9.5
% Profit Before Taxes/Total Assets	14.5	12.7	12.4			9.3	5.3	7.9	14.8
	7.3	6.4	6.0			6.7	1.7	3.2	6.9
	2.4	2.5	1.2			1.8	-1.2	-13.5	1.6
Sales/Net Fixed Assets	25.7	19.3	13.8		13.6	32.0	17.6	21.4	12.9
	7.2	6.7	6.3		4.2	6.5	8.9	6.2	6.3
	4.1	4.2	3.4		2.7	3.4	4.8	3.8	3.0
Sales/Total Assets	2.9	2.7	2.6		2.4	2.8	2.7	3.1	2.5
	2.2	2.0	2.0		1.7	2.0	2.1	2.4	2.0
	1.6	1.5	1.6		1.3	1.6	1.8	1.8	1.5
% Depr., Dep., Amort./Sales	(102) .9	(109) 1.0	(77) 1.0				(14) .6	(11) 1.4	(34) 1.0
	2.1	2.5	2.8				1.4	3.8	2.8
	3.8	3.8	3.8				2.8	5.1	3.8
% Officers', Directors', Owners' Comp/Sales	(34) 1.1	(41) 1.7	(29) 1.5						
	1.9	3.6	3.0						
	3.7	9.2	4.2						
Net Sales ($)	6357836M	6714814M	5368475M	744M	20246M	44769M	106006M	188243M	5008467M
Total Assets ($)	3390565M	3983613M	2862090M	1591M	13421M	25332M	49205M	99667M	2672874M

M = $ thousand   MM = $ million

See Pages 1 through 15 for Explanation of Ratios and Data

MANUFACTURERS—CARPETS & RUGS. SIC# 2273

Current Data Sorted By Assets							Comparative Historical Data	
	2		1			2	# Postretirement Benefits	
							Type of Statement	
2	1	3	7	1	3		Unqualified	39 / 34
	1	4					Reviewed	9 / 9
8	3	1					Compiled	7 / 6
1							Tax Returns	/ 1
4	5	5	1	2	1		Other	5 / 9
0-500M	**20 (4/1-9/30/94)** **500M-2MM**	**2-10MM**	**10-50MM**	**33 (10/1/94-3/31/95)** **50-100MM**	**100-250MM**		**4/1/90-3/31/91 ALL**	**4/1/91-3/31/92 ALL**
15	10	13	8	3	4	**NUMBER OF STATEMENTS**	60	59
%	%	%	%	%	%	**ASSETS**	%	%
9.6	4.6	2.8				Cash & Equivalents	5.3	5.6
23.2	34.7	28.0				Trade Receivables - (net)	21.6	24.1
29.1	34.9	40.0				Inventory	37.1	32.8
3.5	1.8	.4				All Other Current	3.3	1.2
65.3	75.9	71.1				Total Current	67.3	63.7
29.1	17.9	19.4				Fixed Assets (net)	25.8	28.9
2.1	3.3	5.8				Intangibles (net)	1.2	.9
3.5	2.9	3.8				All Other Non-Current	5.8	6.5
100.0	100.0	100.0				Total	100.0	100.0
						LIABILITIES		
14.4	13.1	8.2				Notes Payable-Short Term	7.3	4.5
6.1	3.0	6.7				Cur. Mat. -L/T/D	3.9	5.9
24.8	15.6	29.3				Trade Payables	23.0	22.2
.5	.0	.3				Income Taxes Payable	.4	.4
5.9	9.3	7.2				All Other Current	7.7	5.9
51.6	41.1	51.7				Total Current	42.3	38.9
13.3	11.1	16.7				Long Term Debt	16.7	16.2
.0	.0	.3				Deferred Taxes	.5	.9
3.8	2.9	4.2				All Other-Non-Current	1.9	6.0
31.3	44.9	27.1				Net Worth	38.5	38.0
100.0	100.0	100.0				Total Liabilities & Net Worth	100.0	100.0
						INCOME DATA		
100.0	100.0	100.0				Net Sales	100.0	100.0
36.4	24.2	23.5				Gross Profit	22.4	24.8
31.9	20.8	20.7				Operating Expenses	17.8	20.4
4.5	3.4	2.7				Operating Profit	4.5	4.4
1.7	.9	1.8				All Other Expenses (net)	1.7	1.4
2.8	2.4	.9				Profit Before Taxes	2.8	3.0
						RATIOS		
2.0 / 1.5 / 1.0	2.7 / 2.1 / 1.4	1.6 / 1.5 / 1.1				Current	2.3 / 1.6 / 1.2	2.6 / 1.7 / 1.2
1.0 / .7 / .4	1.4 / 1.0 / .7	.9 / .6 / .4				Quick	1.1 / .7 / .3	1.3 / .8 / .5
14 25.4 / 21 17.5 / 35 10.5	28 13.0 / 37 9.8 / 52 7.0	20 18.1 / 38 9.6 / 41 9.0				Sales/Receivables	16 22.4 / 31 11.6 / 48 7.6	21 17.5 / 41 9.0 / 52 7.0
12 31.0 / 29 12.5 / 91 4.0	35 10.3 / 53 6.9 / 78 4.7	58 6.3 / 61 6.0 / 89 4.1				Cost of Sales/Inventory	45 8.1 / 63 5.8 / 94 3.9	46 8.0 / 72 5.1 / 91 4.0
11 34.0 / 41 8.9 / 49 7.4	14 25.8 / 18 20.0 / 27 13.7	36 10.1 / 47 7.7 / 52 7.0				Cost of Sales/Payables	23 15.6 / 34 10.6 / 50 7.3	25 14.5 / 36 10.1 / 51 7.2
9.5 / 43.6 / -194.1	6.2 / 8.0 / 14.0	10.6 / 14.0 / 507.8				Sales/Working Capital	6.7 / 12.3 / 23.1	5.6 / 8.4 / 21.4
(13) 6.9 / 2.9 / 1.1	8.6 / 3.8 / 1.8	(12) 5.6 / 1.8 / 1.1				EBIT/Interest	(56) 7.6 / 2.2 / 1.2	(55) 4.5 / 2.3 / 1.2
						Net Profit + Depr., Dep., Amort./Cur. Mat. L./T/D	(31) 4.7 / 2.4 / .7	(34) 4.2 / 2.6 / 1.0
.2 / .4 / 3.6	.2 / .5 / .8	.3 / .9 / 2.4				Fixed/Worth	.3 / .7 / 1.2	.3 / .8 / 1.9
.8 / 2.9 / 105.7	.6 / 1.3 / 4.2	1.4 / 2.5 / 9.9				Debt/Worth	1.1 / 1.9 / 3.1	.8 / 1.8 / 3.0
(12) 59.3 / 8.0 / 1.4	33.5 / 17.2 / 5.8	(11) 45.5 / 31.9 / 3.0				% Profit Before Taxes/Tangible Net Worth	(58) 29.1 / 15.1 / 6.1	(55) 26.7 / 13.7 / 4.2
15.6 / 4.0 / .0	12.3 / 7.5 / 2.8	10.1 / 1.8 / .6				% Profit Before Taxes/Total Assets	12.3 / 5.3 / 1.9	11.7 / 5.6 / 1.1
73.4 / 26.1 / 5.8	34.5 / 22.9 / 13.0	44.9 / 15.9 / 8.6				Sales/Net Fixed Assets	29.6 / 9.3 / 6.3	24.7 / 7.4 / 5.4
5.9 / 4.0 / 2.2	3.9 / 3.0 / 2.5	3.6 / 2.9 / 2.3				Sales/Total Assets	3.2 / 2.4 / 2.0	3.1 / 2.3 / 1.7
(12) .5 / 1.6 / 3.6	.5 / .7 / 1.4	(11) .9 / 2.0 / 2.2				% Depr., Dep., Amort./Sales	(43) .7 / 1.4 / 2.4	(52) 1.1 / 2.0 / 3.2
						% Officers', Directors', Owners' Comp/Sales	(14) .7 / 1.9 / 4.5	(16) 1.0 / 2.0 / 3.3
16635M	42157M	191605M	354470M	331210M	1280691M	Net Sales ($)	3360768M	3380232M
4044M	13596M	55259M	158131M	212169M	679852M	Total Assets ($)	1641522M	1797828M

M = $ thousand   MM = $ million
See Pages 1 through 15 for Explanation of Ratios and Data

Comparative Historical Data / Current Data Sorted By Sales

4/1/92-3/31/93 ALL (48)	4/1/93-3/31/94 ALL (52)	4/1/94-3/31/95 ALL (53)		0-1MM (8)	1-3MM (8)	3-5MM (6)	5-10MM (9)	10-25MM (6)	25MM & OVER (16)
2	1	5	# Postretirement Benefits	1		1			3
			Type of Statement						
33	22	17	Unqualified	2			2	3	10
3	8	5	Reviewed				2	2	1
6	7	12	Compiled	3	6	2	1		
		1	Tax Returns	1					
6	15	18	Other	2	2	4	4	1	5
48	52	53	**NUMBER OF STATEMENTS**	8	8	6	9	6	16
%	%	%	**ASSETS**	%	%	%	%	%	%
3.9	6.3	4.7	Cash & Equivalents						1.7
23.3	22.4	26.2	Trade Receivables - (net)						26.0
34.6	36.2	33.8	Inventory						32.1
2.5	2.2	2.2	All Other Current						2.5
64.2	67.1	66.8	Total Current						62.3
26.3	27.4	25.5	Fixed Assets (net)						28.7
3.5	.6	2.9	Intangibles (net)						1.0
6.0	4.9	4.7	All Other Non-Current						8.0
100.0	100.0	100.0	Total						100.0
			LIABILITIES						
5.4	7.4	10.5	Notes Payable-Short Term						7.0
5.2	4.1	4.9	Cur. Mat.-L /T/D						2.9
20.0	18.6	21.6	Trade Payables						19.2
.4	3.0	.3	Income Taxes Payable						.3
7.8	8.6	7.1	All Other Current						7.0
38.8	41.7	44.5	Total Current						36.4
18.2	17.0	15.8	Long Term Debt						18.1
.3	.9	.5	Deferred Taxes						1.2
2.8	3.3	3.6	All Other-Non-Current						3.0
39.9	37.1	35.7	Net Worth						41.4
100.0	100.0	100.0	Total Liabilities & Net Worth						100.0
			INCOME DATA						
100.0	100.0	100.0	Net Sales						100.0
27.3	22.7	26.5	Gross Profit						19.7
22.1	19.0	23.1	Operating Expenses						17.7
5.2	3.7	3.3	Operating Profit						2.0
1.6	1.1	1.4	All Other Expenses (net)						.6
3.6	2.6	2.0	Profit Before Taxes						1.4
			RATIOS						
2.4	2.3	2.2							2.2
1.8	1.5	1.6	Current						1.9
1.3	1.3	1.2							1.3
1.2	1.0	1.0							1.0
.7	.7	.7	Quick						.8
.4	.5	.5							.6
21 17.0	20 18.0	21 17.4							30 12.0
34 10.7	33 11.2	36 10.1	Sales/Receivables						45 8.1
50 7.3	45 8.2	46 7.9							47 7.8
42 8.7	38 9.5	39 9.4							50 7.3
73 5.0	70 5.2	61 6.0	Cost of Sales/Inventory						74 4.9
96 3.8	96 3.8	89 4.1							94 3.9
23 15.7	14 25.3	18 20.0							23 15.9
38 9.5	33 11.2	37 10.0	Cost of Sales/Payables						35 10.3
51 7.2	46 8.0	46 7.9							40 9.2
5.1	7.1	7.1							5.2
8.9	12.6	12.2	Sales/Working Capital						7.4
24.4	32.0	41.2							17.7
6.0	(50) 7.4	(50) 5.6							5.4
(47) 3.0	2.6	3.1	EBIT/Interest						3.1
1.5	1.5	1.1							1.1
3.9	6.2	6.9							
(28) 2.3	(18) 2.5	(18) 2.9	Net Profit + Depr., Dep., Amort./Cur. Mat. L/T/D						
1.4	.3	1.7							
.3	.3	.3							.4
.6	.8	.6	Fixed/Worth						.7
1.5	1.5	1.7							1.6
.7	.9	.9							.8
1.6	1.7	1.8	Debt/Worth						1.4
3.6	4.1	4.1							3.0
37.6	39.1	40.0							31.7
(45) 21.1	(49) 16.0	(48) 13.3	% Profit Before Taxes/Tangible Net Worth						8.0
5.6	6.6	1.7							.3
12.2	14.1	10.2							9.6
5.4	5.4	4.8	% Profit Before Taxes/Total Assets						4.3
1.8	1.6	.4							.1
26.5	39.1	43.4							44.9
10.9	10.4	15.3	Sales/Net Fixed Assets						6.6
4.8	5.3	5.8							4.3
3.3	3.5	3.8							2.8
2.4	2.6	2.7	Sales/Total Assets						2.0
1.8	1.9	2.0							1.6
.8	.5	.6							.6
(43) 1.8	(45) 1.4	(43) 1.2	% Depr., Dep., Amort./Sales					(11)	.9
2.8	2.7	2.7							3.4
.9		1.5							
(12) 3.5		(18) 3.2	% Officers', Directors', Owners' Comp/Sales						
7.1		4.4							
2446837M	3354851M	2216768M	Net Sales ($)	3435M	14999M	24648M	63109M	80869M	2029708M
1269496M	1696414M	1123051M	Total Assets ($)	1330M	5158M	6113M	23549M	34543M	1052358M

M = $ thousand   MM = $ million
See Pages 1 through 15 for Explanation of Ratios and Data

Current Data Sorted By Assets | Comparative Historical Data

						# Postretirement Benefits Type of Statement		
	1	2	1	2				
		6	8	4	1	Unqualified	27	27
	8	10	3	1		Reviewed	8	12
2	3	2				Compiled	10	13
1						Tax Returns		
3	4	5	1	1		Other	10	10

0-500M	16 (4/1-9/30/94) 500M-2MM	2-10MM	47 (10/1/94-3/31/95) 10-50MM	50-100MM	100-250MM		4/1/90-3/31/91 ALL	4/1/91-3/31/92 ALL
6	15	23	12	6	1	NUMBER OF STATEMENTS	55	62
%	%	%	%	%	%	**ASSETS**	%	%
	4.0	4.5	4.6			Cash & Equivalents	6.8	7.4
	35.0	24.9	28.1			Trade Receivables - (net)	26.6	28.0
	22.9	18.6	25.4			Inventory	23.0	21.4
	.3	1.2	2.6			All Other Current	1.7	1.3
	62.3	49.2	60.7			Total Current	58.1	58.1
	32.8	43.6	33.0			Fixed Assets (net)	35.0	34.5
	.7	3.1	.2			Intangibles (net)	1.9	1.1
	4.2	4.1	6.1			All Other Non-Current	5.1	6.3
	100.0	100.0	100.0			Total	100.0	100.0
						LIABILITIES		
	13.0	6.0	12.8			Notes Payable-Short Term	13.2	8.5
	3.9	4.9	4.0			Cur. Mat. -L/T/D	4.5	5.5
	21.5	18.4	16.2			Trade Payables	15.8	16.7
	.7	.3	.0			Income Taxes Payable	.5	.6
	4.6	5.4	4.2			All Other Current	6.7	7.4
	43.6	35.0	37.2			Total Current	40.7	38.6
	14.4	20.1	18.5			Long Term Debt	18.2	17.7
	.0	.4	1.0			Deferred Taxes	.9	.8
	6.4	4.7	3.7			All Other-Non-Current	4.1	4.0
	35.6	39.8	39.6			Net Worth	36.0	38.8
	100.0	100.0	100.0			Total Liabilities & Net Worth	100.0	100.0
						INCOME DATA		
	100.0	100.0	100.0			Net Sales	100.0	100.0
	31.8	23.2	17.6			Gross Profit	26.7	28.1
	27.8	17.5	13.9			Operating Expenses	22.1	23.0
	4.0	5.7	3.7			Operating Profit	4.5	5.1
	1.5	1.4	1.1			All Other Expenses (net)	1.7	1.4
	2.4	4.3	2.6			Profit Before Taxes	2.8	3.7
						RATIOS		
	2.2	2.3	2.0				2.4	2.6
	1.4	1.3	1.5			Current	1.4	1.4
	1.1	.9	1.2				1.1	1.2
	1.6	1.5	1.2				1.6	1.6
	1.0	.9	1.0			Quick	.8	1.0
	.5	.4	.5				.5	.6
	34 10.8	29 12.5	37 10.0				26 14.0	31 11.8
	43 8.4	40 9.2	48 7.6			Sales/Receivables	38 9.7	41 8.8
	55 6.6	49 7.5	57 6.4				53 6.9	54 6.8
	17 21.8	7 50.1	17 22.0				22 16.8	16 23.4
	29 12.6	29 12.8	62 5.9			Cost of Sales/Inventory	45 8.2	35 10.3
	79 4.6	54 6.7	79 4.6				85 4.3	69 5.3
	24 15.2	20 18.6	23 16.2				16 23.5	17 20.9
	32 11.4	37 10.0	39 9.4			Cost of Sales/Payables	32 11.3	26 14.1
	61 6.0	51 7.1	47 7.8				45 8.1	44 8.3
	7.5	7.7	4.8				6.3	7.5
	10.1	22.4	10.1			Sales/Working Capital	12.3	16.4
	29.3	-63.9	20.9				74.9	33.8
	9.3	9.9	5.3				4.1	5.8
(14)	1.8	(21) 3.9	(10) 4.9			EBIT/Interest	(53) 2.7	(57) 2.8
	.6	1.7	2.6				1.5	1.5
							5.6	4.2
						Net Profit + Depr., Dep., Amort./Cur. Mat. L /T/D	(31) 2.6	(29) 1.9
							1.3	1.1
	.5	.7	.3				.6	.5
	.7	1.4	1.0			Fixed/Worth	.9	.9
	2.4	2.3	1.6				1.9	1.6
	1.1	.6	1.3				.8	.8
	2.0	2.3	1.7			Debt/Worth	2.3	1.9
	4.4	3.5	2.8				5.5	3.2
	36.9	59.8	30.9				53.7	49.1
	18.0	25.7	20.6			% Profit Before Taxes/Tangible Net Worth	(50) 24.4	(57) 19.2
	-9.4	8.2	-.7				6.5	9.4
	17.2	14.1	10.6				14.8	16.7
	6.4	6.5	7.1			% Profit Before Taxes/Total Assets	6.3	7.9
	-1.1	3.6	.2				1.6	2.7
	15.6	10.4	12.4				14.0	13.0
	9.5	5.5	7.1			Sales/Net Fixed Assets	7.3	7.5
	5.6	3.1	2.7				4.6	4.7
	3.4	2.6	2.6				3.2	3.2
	2.6	2.3	2.2			Sales/Total Assets	2.5	2.3
	1.4	1.8	1.2				1.7	1.8
	1.2	2.2	2.1				1.0	1.4
(14)	1.6	(22) 3.7	2.6			% Depr., Dep., Amort./Sales	(49) 1.9	(55) 2.3
	2.9	6.2	4.5				3.3	4.2
		1.8					1.1	2.3
	(12)	4.1				% Officers', Directors', Owners' Comp/Sales	(20) 3.8	(22) 4.9
		5.8					8.2	8.0
6164M	45806M	256031M	480095M	834802M	253471M	Net Sales ($)	1159108M	1754539M
1505M	17668M	119876M	248561M	438835M	167337M	Total Assets ($)	625195M	830926M

M = $ thousand   MM = $ million
See Pages 1 through 15 for Explanation of Ratios and Data

Comparative Historical Data / Current Data Sorted By Sales

Hist 1	Hist 6	Hist 6		0-1MM	1-3MM	3-5MM	5-10MM	10-25MM	25MM & OVER
1	6	6	# Postretirement Benefits	1			1	1	3
			Type of Statement						
32	23	19	Unqualified			1	2	4	12
14	16	22	Reviewed	1	4	4	4	6	3
16	13	7	Compiled	2	2	2	1		
		1	Tax Returns		1				
16	12	14	Other	1	4	2		6	1
16	12	14		16 (4/1-9/30/94)			47 (10/1/94-3/31/95)		
4/1/92-3/31/93 ALL	4/1/93-3/31/94 ALL	4/1/94-3/31/95 ALL		0-1MM	1-3MM	3-5MM	5-10MM	10-25MM	25MM & OVER
78	64	63	**NUMBER OF STATEMENTS**	4	11	7	8	17	16
%	%	%	**ASSETS**	%	%	%	%	%	%
6.6	6.3	5.3	Cash & Equivalents		3.2			5.7	4.0
27.0	28.2	29.7	Trade Receivables - (net)		40.2			24.3	31.9
21.2	22.9	21.6	Inventory		22.3			13.4	28.7
3.2	3.5	1.4	All Other Current		.4			1.9	2.4
58.1	60.9	58.0	Total Current		66.1			45.2	67.1
33.9	32.6	35.5	Fixed Assets (net)		30.5			47.7	28.3
1.9	1.6	1.4	Intangibles (net)		.4			1.9	.3
6.1	4.8	5.1	All Other Non-Current		3.1			5.1	4.3
100.0	100.0	100.0	Total		100.0			100.0	100.0
			LIABILITIES						
10.9	10.2	9.0	Notes Payable-Short Term		13.8			3.4	10.2
4.1	4.0	4.2	Cur. Mat.-L /T/D		3.9			5.1	3.2
15.8	16.0	17.9	Trade Payables		24.2			16.3	15.8
.5	3.2	.3	Income Taxes Payable		.0			.4	.1
5.8	9.2	4.7	All Other Current		4.7			4.9	4.7
37.1	42.6	36.2	Total Current		46.6			30.1	34.0
14.5	15.7	18.3	Long Term Debt		19.6			20.8	17.9
1.2	.8	.4	Deferred Taxes		.0			.9	.7
3.8	4.2	4.3	All Other-Non-Current		3.8			5.9	1.9
43.4	36.7	40.9	Net Worth		29.9			42.2	45.5
100.0	100.0	100.0	Total Liabilities & Net Worth		100.0			100.0	100.0
			INCOME DATA						
100.0	100.0	100.0	Net Sales		100.0			100.0	100.0
26.6	23.2	25.5	Gross Profit		32.8			19.2	19.7
21.5	19.2	20.3	Operating Expenses		32.2			14.3	13.0
5.2	4.0	5.2	Operating Profit		.6			4.9	6.6
1.1	1.3	1.2	All Other Expenses (net)		1.2			1.4	.9
4.1	2.7	4.0	Profit Before Taxes		-.6			3.5	5.7
			RATIOS						
2.5 / 1.6 / 1.1	2.1 / 1.5 / 1.1	2.3 / 1.6 / 1.1	Current		2.0 / 1.4 / 1.0			2.2 / 1.6 / 1.0	3.5 / 2.1 / 1.4
1.8 / 1.0 / .5	1.5 / .8 / .5	1.6 / 1.0 / .5	Quick		1.6 / 1.0 / .5			1.6 / 1.0 / .5	1.9 / 1.1 / .7
31/11.6 · 45/8.2 · 54/6.8	24/15.1 · 43/8.4 · 54/6.8	34/10.8 · 43/8.4 · 54/6.7	Sales/Receivables		37/9.8 · 45/8.1 · 61/6.0			31/11.7 · 43/8.5 · 53/6.9	41/9.0 · 52/7.0 · 64/5.7
14/25.6 · 37/9.9 · 76/4.8	17/21.5 · 36/10.2 · 63/5.8	16/22.2 · 40/9.2 · 76/4.8	Cost of Sales/Inventory		17/21.8 · 29/12.5 · 76/4.8			10/38.2 · 29/12.8 · 41/8.8	46/7.9 · 68/5.4 · 79/4.6
20/18.2 · 26/14.1 · 39/9.3	15/24.0 · 29/12.8 · 44/8.3	22/16.9 · 33/11.0 · 51/7.1	Cost of Sales/Payables		28/12.9 · 50/7.3 · 65/5.6			21/17.5 · 33/11.0 · 49/7.4	22/16.8 · 31/11.6 · 47/7.8
6.6 / 10.8 / 38.4	7.2 / 13.4 / 84.6	6.1 / 11.4 / 55.6	Sales/Working Capital		7.8 / 11.4 / 211.0			7.7 / 14.9 / NM	3.3 / 5.7 / 14.9
(73) 8.0 / 3.6 / 1.4	(54) 9.7 / 3.0 / 1.3	(54) 7.1 / 3.9 / 1.7	EBIT/Interest	(10) 5.1 / 2.2 / .0			(15) 26.3 / 4.8 / -.2		(13) 8.6 / 5.2 / 3.5
(35) 6.6 / 3.1 / 1.5	(23) 4.3 / 2.4 / 1.3	(23) 4.0 / 2.3 / 1.3	Net Profit + Depr., Dep., Amort./Cur. Mat. L/T/D						
.4 / .8 / 1.3	.3 / .7 / 2.0	.4 / .8 / 2.0	Fixed/Worth		.5 / .8 / 2.9			.6 / 1.4 / 2.2	.3 / .6 / 1.1
.7 / 1.4 / 2.7	.9 / 1.8 / 3.5	.8 / 1.7 / 3.1	Debt/Worth		1.1 / 2.1 / 7.8			.7 / 1.7 / 3.0	1.0 / 1.4 / 2.4
(74) 41.8 / 20.5 / 3.7	(60) 52.4 / 26.8 / 6.8	48.2 / 24.1 / 7.8	% Profit Before Taxes/Tangible Net Worth		36.9 / 18.0 / -12.8			50.2 / 20.8 / -6.7	33.7 / 23.1 / 16.8
16.3 / 8.7 / 1.4	14.2 / 7.7 / 1.8	15.0 / 7.2 / 2.4	% Profit Before Taxes/Total Assets		10.6 / 5.0 / -4.0			22.8 / 7.0 / -3.6	15.6 / 10.4 / 5.4
20.1 / 6.9 / 4.4	18.3 / 8.5 / 4.9	13.1 / 6.4 / 4.3	Sales/Net Fixed Assets		15.6 / 9.1 / 6.0			7.9 / 3.6 / 2.5	10.8 / 8.1 / 5.7
3.1 / 2.3 / 1.7	3.4 / 2.4 / 1.8	3.0 / 2.3 / 1.7	Sales/Total Assets		4.3 / 3.0 / 1.4			2.6 / 1.9 / 1.6	2.3 / 2.2 / 1.7
(67) 1.2 / 2.3 / 3.8	(53) 1.4 / 1.8 / 3.7	(60) 1.6 / 2.7 / 4.4	% Depr., Dep., Amort./Sales		1.0 / 1.6 / 3.6			(16) 2.5 / 4.1 / 6.3	(15) 1.8 / 2.4 / 3.3
(23) 3.3 / 5.3 / 8.9	(21) 2.0 / 3.5 / 5.0	(26) 2.0 / 3.9 / 5.9	% Officers', Directors', Owners' Comp/Sales						
2426541M	2044127M	1876369M	Net Sales ($)	2261M	21667M	29273M	53896M	246609M	1522663M
1270225M	954484M	993782M	Total Assets ($)	1043M	9004M	11797M	22605M	134364M	814969M

Current Data Sorted By Assets | **Comparative Historical Data**

0-500M	500M-2MM	2-10MM	10-50MM	50-100MM	100-250MM	# Postretirement Benefits / Type of Statement	4/1/90-3/31/91 ALL	4/1/91-3/31/92 ALL
2	2	3		1		Unqualified	22	12
	1	3	6	1		Reviewed	7	5
1	2	4	1			Compiled	11	11
	2	2				Tax Returns		
3	4	7	2			Other	2	5
	16 (4/1-9/30/94)			21 (10/1/94-3/31/95)				
4	7	16	9	1		NUMBER OF STATEMENTS	42	33
%	%	%	%	%	%		%	%

0-500M	500M-2MM	2-10MM	10-50MM	50-100MM	100-250MM		4/1/90-3/31/91 ALL 42	4/1/91-3/31/92 ALL 33
						ASSETS		
		10.9				Cash & Equivalents	5.6	5.3
		24.6				Trade Receivables - (net)	24.5	25.9
		26.4				Inventory	32.1	32.9
		1.1				All Other Current	1.1	.7
		63.0				Total Current	63.3	64.8
		30.8				Fixed Assets (net)	31.7	28.8
		.4				Intangibles (net)	.8	.5
		5.7				All Other Non-Current	4.2	6.0
		100.0				Total	100.0	100.0
						LIABILITIES		
		9.7				Notes Payable-Short Term	13.1	8.9
		4.8				Cur. Mat. -L/T/D	4.3	4.1
		12.4				Trade Payables	15.0	16.4
		.3				Income Taxes Payable	.7	.8
		6.9				All Other Current	4.4	7.2
		34.2				Total Current	37.5	37.4
		14.4				Long Term Debt	19.6	17.9
		.4				Deferred Taxes	.9	.7
		2.8				All Other-Non-Current	2.0	1.3
		48.3				Net Worth	39.9	42.7
		100.0				Total Liabilities & Net Worth	100.0	100.0
						INCOME DATA		
		100.0				Net Sales	100.0	100.0
		15.0				Gross Profit	19.1	19.6
		13.2				Operating Expenses	15.0	14.2
		1.8				Operating Profit	4.1	5.4
		-.1				All Other Expenses (net)	1.4	1.2
		1.9				Profit Before Taxes	2.7	4.2
						RATIOS		
		3.2					3.2	2.7
		1.7				Current	1.7	1.5
		1.3					1.2	1.2
		1.6					1.5	1.3
		.9				Quick	.8	.8
		.5					.5	.4
		31 11.7					26 13.9	25 14.8
		41 8.9				Sales/Receivables	42 8.6	43 8.4
		46 7.9					57 6.4	54 6.8
		20 18.2					42 8.6	39 9.3
		47 7.8				Cost of Sales/Inventory	60 6.1	54 6.8
		83 4.4					99 3.7	87 4.2
		12 30.0					18 20.7	16 22.9
		18 20.7				Cost of Sales/Payables	24 15.5	26 13.8
		26 14.0					41 8.9	47 7.8
		5.1					4.8	5.5
		12.2				Sales/Working Capital	8.7	9.6
		16.7					25.9	24.1
		11.5					3.5	5.5
	(14)	2.2				EBIT/Interest	(37) 2.2	(29) 2.7
		1.0					1.1	2.1
							3.8	4.1
						Net Profit + Depr., Dep., Amort./Cur. Mat. L /T/D	(30) 2.0	(19) 3.2
							1.1	1.4
		.3					.5	.3
		.6				Fixed/Worth	.8	.7
		1.1					1.6	1.3
		.4					.6	.9
		1.1				Debt/Worth	1.8	1.4
		1.9					3.3	2.4
		15.1					30.3	32.8
	(15)	5.6				% Profit Before Taxes/Tangible Net Worth	(39) 15.0	(32) 20.4
		3.6					3.1	10.1
		8.6					10.8	16.2
		3.1				% Profit Before Taxes/Total Assets	5.6	7.3
		.5					.3	3.4
		12.7					11.6	18.9
		8.0				Sales/Net Fixed Assets	7.2	9.5
		5.8					4.9	5.9
		2.8					2.8	3.1
		2.4				Sales/Total Assets	2.2	2.1
		2.1					1.6	1.7
		1.5					1.4	1.5
	(14)	3.1				% Depr., Dep., Amort./Sales	(39) 2.5	(31) 2.2
		4.7					3.3	3.2
		1.2					1.3	1.3
	(10)	2.8				% Officers', Directors', Owners' Comp/Sales	(18) 1.6	(17) 1.9
		3.9					3.7	3.5
2960M	26361M	191367M	349831M	125560M		Net Sales ($)	752706M	453831M
664M	9183M	78832M	170765M	67084M		Total Assets ($)	429333M	218443M

M = $ thousand   MM = $ million
See Pages 1 through 15 for Explanation of Ratios and Data

	Comparative Historical Data				Current Data Sorted By Sales					
	1	1	8	# Postretirement Benefits	2	1	2	1	1	1
				Type of Statement						
	17	11	11	Unqualified		1		1	3	6
	5	8	6	Reviewed		1		3	1	1
	8	6	4	Compiled		1	1	1		1
			2	Tax Returns						
	5	16	16	Other	3	3	1	3	6	
	4/1/92-3/31/93	4/1/93-3/31/94	4/1/94-3/31/95		16 (4/1-9/30/94)			21 (10/1/94-3/31/95)		
	ALL	ALL	ALL		0-1MM	1-3MM	3-5MM	5-10MM	10-25MM	25MM & OVER
	35	43	37	**NUMBER OF STATEMENTS**	3	6	2	8	10	8
	%	%	%	**ASSETS**	%	%	%	%	%	%
	4.4	7.2	8.3	Cash & Equivalents					3.1	
	23.8	22.4	26.2	Trade Receivables - (net)					27.4	
	31.1	28.9	28.3	Inventory					30.2	
	1.5	2.5	.9	All Other Current					1.5	
	60.8	61.1	63.6	Total Current					62.1	
	33.7	33.3	29.5	Fixed Assets (net)					31.8	
	.0	.2	.3	Intangibles (net)					.6	
	5.4	5.4	6.6	All Other Non-Current					5.4	
	100.0	100.0	100.0	Total					100.0	
				LIABILITIES						
	9.5	9.5	9.3	Notes Payable-Short Term					15.0	
	4.2	4.5	4.3	Cur. Mat.-L./T/D					5.0	
	16.6	15.9	12.6	Trade Payables					14.3	
	.9	2.6	.4	Income Taxes Payable					.3	
	4.5	6.8	7.5	All Other Current					4.6	
	35.8	39.4	34.2	Total Current					39.3	
	15.7	19.2	16.7	Long Term Debt					15.1	
	1.1	.4	.6	Deferred Taxes					.8	
	.8	1.5	1.9	All Other-Non-Current					4.5	
	46.7	39.5	46.7	Net Worth					40.3	
	100.0	100.0	100.0	Total Liabilities & Net Worth					100.0	
				INCOME DATA						
	100.0	100.0	100.0	Net Sales					100.0	
	15.9	19.7	17.3	Gross Profit					14.5	
	12.5	16.5	13.9	Operating Expenses					11.7	
	3.4	3.2	3.4	Operating Profit					2.8	
	.4	1.0	.5	All Other Expenses (net)					.8	
	2.9	2.2	2.8	Profit Before Taxes					2.1	
				RATIOS						
	2.2	2.8	2.8						2.1	
	1.6	1.6	1.9	Current					1.9	
	1.4	1.0	1.4						1.2	
	1.4	1.2	1.5						1.2	
	.7	.8	.9	Quick					.8	
	.4	.4	.6						.5	
24	15.0	26 14.3	31 11.6						33 10.9	
36	10.1	41 8.9	37 9.8	Sales/Receivables					46 7.9	
49	7.5	51 7.1	54 6.7						56 6.5	
31	11.7	24 15.3	21 17.0						29 12.7	
49	7.4	70 5.2	63 5.8	Cost of Sales/Inventory					58 6.3	
78	4.7	101 3.6	87 4.2						85 4.3	
16	22.5	15 25.0	13 29.1						18 19.8	
24	15.4	26 14.1	18 19.8	Cost of Sales/Payables					23 15.7	
37	9.9	43 8.5	29 12.4						29 12.6	
	6.7	4.9	5.1						5.3	
	11.3	10.1	9.4	Sales/Working Capital					10.0	
	17.9	−153.7	16.6						24.8	
(29)	7.1	(37) 5.4	(31) 9.0							
	3.9	3.8	2.8	EBIT/Interest						
	1.4	.9	1.6							
(20)	3.2	(18) 4.9	(18) 4.8	Net Profit + Depr., Dep.,						
	2.2	2.4	1.9	Amort./Cur. Mat. L/T/D						
	1.2	1.1	1.1							
	.3	.4	.3						.3	
	.8	.7	.6	Fixed/Worth					.6	
	1.2	1.8	1.2						2.2	
	.5	.5	.5						.5	
	1.3	1.6	1.4	Debt/Worth					1.3	
	2.2	3.1	2.1						3.4	
(34)	32.4	(39) 25.4	(36) 29.4	% Profit Before Taxes/Tangible						
	17.3	11.7	13.9	Net Worth						
	8.2	3.8	4.5							
	15.1	10.0	11.4	% Profit Before Taxes/Total					8.7	
	9.0	6.7	6.6	Assets					6.6	
	2.7	.2	2.0						1.2	
	12.8	11.9	15.1						9.5	
	8.6	8.4	9.1	Sales/Net Fixed Assets					8.7	
	4.7	4.9	5.6						6.2	
	3.2	2.5	2.9						2.6	
	2.2	2.1	2.3	Sales/Total Assets					2.3	
	1.8	1.6	1.8						2.0	
(33)	1.2	(40) 1.5	(32) 1.3	% Depr., Dep., Amort./Sales						
	2.1	2.6	2.2							
	3.6	4.7	4.0							
(17)	1.3	(16) 1.3	(19) 1.5	% Officers', Directors',						
	2.8	2.9	3.0	Owners' Comp/Sales						
	4.3	5.7	4.0							
	708929M	732560M	696079M	Net Sales ($)	1438M	9848M	9115M	57300M	187523M	430855M
	323526M	359436M	326528M	Total Assets ($)	828M	8374M	4082M	23867M	83492M	205885M

© Robert Morris Associates 1995   M = $ thousand   MM = $ million
See Pages 1 through 15 for Explanation of Ratios and Data

Current Data Sorted By Assets / Comparative Historical Data

Postretirement Benefits — Type of Statement

	0-500M	500M-2MM	2-10MM	10-50MM	50-100MM	100-250MM		4/1/90-3/31/91 ALL	4/1/91-3/31/92 ALL
		1		2					
Unqualified	1		1	4		1		17	15
Reviewed		1	2						5
Compiled	1	7	1					6	5
Tax Returns									
Other	1		5	10				9	5
	13 (4/1-9/30/94)			22 (10/1/94-3/31/95)					
NUMBER OF STATEMENTS	3	8	9	14	1			32	30

ASSETS (%)

	0-500M %	500M-2MM %	2-10MM %	10-50MM %	50-100MM %	100-250MM %		4/1/90-3/31/91 ALL %	4/1/91-3/31/92 ALL %
Cash & Equivalents				3.8				5.8	4.0
Trade Receivables - (net)				24.5				21.1	26.1
Inventory				34.6				34.0	31.5
All Other Current				1.2				1.5	1.0
Total Current				64.1				62.3	62.6
Fixed Assets (net)				24.1				30.0	29.3
Intangibles (net)				1.9				2.1	1.1
All Other Non-Current				9.9				5.6	7.0
Total				100.0				100.0	100.0

LIABILITIES

	10-50MM		4/1/90-3/31/91	4/1/91-3/31/92
Notes Payable-Short Term	15.0		13.9	10.9
Cur. Mat. -L/T/D	3.4		3.9	5.4
Trade Payables	9.1		19.3	15.8
Income Taxes Payable	.3		1.1	1.4
All Other Current	7.9		9.5	8.3
Total Current	35.7		47.7	41.7
Long Term Debt	15.1		17.1	16.3
Deferred Taxes	1.0		.9	1.4
All Other-Non-Current	6.4		2.4	4.0
Net Worth	41.9		31.8	36.7
Total Liabilities & Net Worth	100.0		100.0	100.0

INCOME DATA

	10-50MM		4/1/90-3/31/91	4/1/91-3/31/92
Net Sales	100.0		100.0	100.0
Gross Profit	25.2		20.4	19.3
Operating Expenses	17.5		16.2	14.2
Operating Profit	7.7		4.2	5.1
All Other Expenses (net)	1.3		2.2	1.0
Profit Before Taxes	6.4		2.0	4.0

RATIOS

	2-10MM	10-50MM		4/1/90-3/31/91	4/1/91-3/31/92
Current		3.3		2.1	2.2
		1.6		1.4	1.6
		1.2		1.1	1.2
Quick		1.7		1.1	1.4
		.6		.6	.8
		.5		.3	.5
Sales/Receivables		32 11.3		12 29.5	27 13.3
		56 6.5		43 8.5	45 8.2
		62 5.9		54 6.7	52 7.0
Cost of Sales/Inventory		64 5.7		48 7.6	38 9.6
		87 4.2		65 5.6	63 5.8
		107 3.4		83 4.4	85 4.3
Cost of Sales/Payables		17 21.5		16 22.3	15 24.4
		22 16.4		25 14.5	24 15.4
		33 11.0		47 7.7	41 8.9
Sales/Working Capital		3.8		6.1	5.9
		10.5		10.7	10.6
		16.9		55.3	46.7
EBIT/Interest	(11)	7.4		(29) 2.8	(27) 5.0
		2.5		1.8	2.8
		1.2		1.0	1.3
Net Profit + Depr., Dep., Amort./Cur. Mat. L /T/D				(22) 2.8	(22) 4.6
				1.7	2.4
				.8	1.1
Fixed/Worth		.3		.6	.5
		.8		.9	.7
		1.3		2.6	1.6
Debt/Worth		.6		.9	1.0
		1.5		2.2	1.7
		4.7		7.2	4.6
% Profit Before Taxes/Tangible Net Worth		37.8		(27) 25.4	(29) 43.0
		22.4		14.3	22.1
		8.7		7.1	4.3
% Profit Before Taxes/Total Assets		12.4		5.9	12.2
		8.0		4.2	6.3
		4.4		.8	.7
Sales/Net Fixed Assets		11.3		11.9	13.1
		8.4		7.6	8.7
		6.7		5.6	6.7
Sales/Total Assets		2.4		3.2	3.0
		1.9		2.2	2.4
		1.5		1.9	1.9
% Depr., Dep., Amort./Sales	(13)	2.2		(30) 1.7	(29) 1.3
		2.3		2.4	2.1
		3.0		3.0	3.1
% Officers', Directors', Owners' Comp/Sales				(11) 1.3	(12) 1.3
				3.0	3.4
				3.8	4.2

	0-500M	500M-2MM	2-10MM	10-50MM	50-100MM		4/1/90-3/31/91	4/1/91-3/31/92
Net Sales ($)	1245M	27548M	82743M	582772M	125000M		607707M	707219M
Total Assets ($)	315M	9986M	32608M	298520M	74740M		313591M	356956M

M = $ thousand   MM = $ million
See Pages 1 through 15 for Explanation of Ratios and Data

Comparative Historical Data				Current Data Sorted By Sales					
2	2	3	# Postretirement Benefits			1		1	1
			Type of Statement						
17	13	7	Unqualified	1		1		1	4
2	1	3	Reviewed			1	2		
6	4	9	Compiled	1	3	4	1		
	1		Tax Returns						
6	13	16	Other	1		1	2	6	6
4/1/92- 3/31/93 ALL	4/1/93- 3/31/94 ALL	4/1/94- 3/31/95 ALL		13 (4/1-9/30/94)			22 (10/1/94-3/31/95)		
				0-1MM	1-3MM	3-5MM	5-10MM	10-25MM	25MM & OVER
31	32	35	NUMBER OF STATEMENTS	3	3	7	5	7	10
%	%	%	ASSETS	%	%	%	%	%	%
4.7	3.9	3.8	Cash & Equivalents						1.6
26.9	28.1	30.1	Trade Receivables - (net)						25.3
33.8	33.2	29.9	Inventory						34.5
1.0	3.3	1.9	All Other Current						5.5
66.5	68.5	65.7	Total Current						66.9
28.2	23.2	24.5	Fixed Assets (net)						27.3
.3	1.5	3.3	Intangibles (net)						2.6
5.0	6.8	6.5	All Other Non-Current						3.3
100.0	100.0	100.0	Total						100.0
			LIABILITIES						
7.8	11.0	12.4	Notes Payable-Short Term						13.0
3.8	2.9	4.5	Cur. Mat.-L /T/D						3.6
13.4	14.6	17.0	Trade Payables						10.3
.7	4.2	.2	Income Taxes Payable						.5
10.4	9.5	6.4	All Other Current						8.8
36.0	42.2	40.4	Total Current						36.1
15.1	17.7	16.9	Long Term Debt						14.0
1.4	1.2	.6	Deferred Taxes						.3
4.0	2.5	7.1	All Other-Non-Current						8.4
43.5	36.4	35.0	Net Worth						41.2
100.0	100.0	100.0	Total Liabilities & Net Worth						100.0
			INCOME DATA						
100.0	100.0	100.0	Net Sales						100.0
19.1	21.9	22.8	Gross Profit						24.4
14.4	17.0	17.7	Operating Expenses						17.4
4.7	4.9	5.1	Operating Profit						7.0
1.0	.9	1.5	All Other Expenses (net)						1.6
3.7	3.9	3.6	Profit Before Taxes						5.4
			RATIOS						
2.8	2.5	2.7	Current						3.7
2.0	1.6	1.5							1.6
1.4	1.2	1.1							1.4
1.4	1.2	1.5	Quick						1.3
1.0	.8	.8							.6
.5	.5	.5							.5
35 10.5	37 9.9	31 11.8	Sales/Receivables						30 12.1
46 7.9	50 7.3	45 8.1							49 7.5
60 6.1	62 5.9	68 5.4							63 5.8
60 6.1	33 11.2	33 11.0	Cost of Sales/Inventory						58 6.3
72 5.1	57 6.4	64 5.7							78 4.7
85 4.3	94 3.9	99 3.7							101 3.6
16 22.7	13 29.0	16 22.6	Cost of Sales/Payables						15 24.3
22 16.6	26 14.0	28 13.2							19 19.3
36 10.2	38 9.5	46 7.9							32 11.3
4.8	5.7	4.4	Sales/Working Capital						3.8
7.8	7.0	12.3							10.5
12.3	20.2	26.6							14.2
(27) 7.0	(29) 9.1	(32) 4.5	EBIT/Interest						
3.6	3.1	2.5							
2.0	1.6	1.0							
(23) 5.0	(14) 2.7	(15) 5.7	Net Profit + Depr., Dep., Amort./Cur. Mat. L/T/D						
2.3	1.9	2.3							
1.3	−.4	1.5							
.3	.3	.3	Fixed/Worth						.4
.6	.7	.7							.8
1.2	1.3	1.5							1.5
.7	1.0	.9	Debt/Worth						.8
1.4	1.6	3.0							1.5
2.3	6.6	5.6							3.7
(30) 33.8	(29) 45.1	(31) 38.9	% Profit Before Taxes/Tangible Net Worth						46.2
17.3	20.0	11.9							28.0
10.5	5.7	3.0							14.0
11.0	14.0	11.2	% Profit Before Taxes/Total Assets						12.4
8.1	6.2	7.1							10.5
3.2	1.6	.0							6.8
11.1	20.8	17.0	Sales/Net Fixed Assets						10.5
9.0	10.4	10.0							7.6
6.1	6.6	6.5							6.0
2.6	2.9	2.9	Sales/Total Assets						2.6
2.2	2.4	2.1							2.0
1.8	1.9	1.7							1.6
(30) 1.4	(31) 1.3	(30) 1.4	% Depr., Dep., Amort./Sales						1.7
2.6	2.1	2.7							2.3
3.4	3.2	3.4							3.0
		(12) 1.4	% Officers', Directors', Owners' Comp/Sales						
		2.2							
		5.0							
908586M	804323M	819308M	Net Sales ($)	1245M	4406M	28356M	36968M	131730M	616603M
448667M	396112M	416169M	Total Assets ($)	315M	2227M	21483M	13083M	67135M	311926M

© Robert Morris Associates 1995

M = $ thousand   MM = $ million

See Pages 1 through 15 for Explanation of Ratios and Data

Current Data Sorted By Assets   **Comparative Historical Data**

0-500M	500M-2MM	2-10MM	10-50MM	50-100MM	100-250MM	# Postretirement Benefits / Type of Statement	4/1/90-3/31/91 ALL	4/1/91-3/31/92 ALL
	3	9	14	1	4	Unqualified	37	35
2	9	8	4			Reviewed	21	21
1	3	2				Compiled	15	14
1						Tax Returns	1	1
1	4	13	8		1	Other	11	13
	23 (4/1-9/30/94)		65 (10/1/94-3/31/95)					
5	19	32	26	1	5	NUMBER OF STATEMENTS	85	84
%	%	%	%	%	%	**ASSETS**	%	%
	8.7	11.2	7.5			Cash & Equivalents	6.7	8.8
	29.8	24.5	24.1			Trade Receivables - (net)	25.4	27.2
	32.8	24.0	30.2			Inventory	25.9	26.2
	.5	1.4	2.3			All Other Current	2.0	2.2
	71.7	61.1	64.1			Total Current	60.0	64.4
	23.3	32.7	27.9			Fixed Assets (net)	31.5	30.2
	.4	1.8	2.4			Intangibles (net)	1.4	1.0
	4.5	4.4	5.6			All Other Non-Current	7.1	4.4
	100.0	100.0	100.0			Total	100.0	100.0
						LIABILITIES		
	14.2	8.0	8.3			Notes Payable-Short Term	9.5	9.7
	3.3	5.9	4.0			Cur. Mat. -L/T/D	5.3	5.3
	8.2	15.4	11.3			Trade Payables	13.9	15.4
	.4	.3	.2			Income Taxes Payable	.7	.8
	10.0	5.4	5.7			All Other Current	8.7	9.0
	36.1	35.1	29.6			Total Current	38.1	40.2
	8.9	12.2	15.3			Long Term Debt	14.9	13.2
	.6	.8	1.9			Deferred Taxes	.9	.7
	7.6	.5	2.8			All Other-Non-Current	1.9	1.3
	46.8	51.3	50.4			Net Worth	44.1	44.5
	100.0	100.0	100.0			Total Liabilities & Net Worth	100.0	100.0
						INCOME DATA		
	100.0	100.0	100.0			Net Sales	100.0	100.0
	23.7	22.2	21.1			Gross Profit	22.7	24.3
	18.1	16.1	15.1			Operating Expenses	16.7	18.6
	5.6	6.2	6.0			Operating Profit	6.0	5.7
	.7	1.7	1.0			All Other Expenses (net)	2.1	1.1
	4.9	4.5	5.1			Profit Before Taxes	3.9	4.5
						RATIOS		
	4.3 / 2.5 / 1.5	3.8 / 1.8 / 1.2	3.7 / 2.3 / 1.4			Current	2.7 / 1.6 / 1.2	2.6 / 1.7 / 1.1
	2.4 / 1.2 / .8	2.5 / 1.1 / .5	2.2 / 1.0 / .6			Quick	1.7 / .9 / .5	1.5 / .9 / .6
36 / 47 / 57	10.2 / 7.8 / 6.4	29 / 41 / 56 → 12.8 / 8.9 / 6.5	38 / 54 / 69 → 9.7 / 6.7 / 5.3			Sales/Receivables	26 / 38 / 58 → 14.2 / 9.6 / 6.3	24 / 46 / 69 → 15.4 / 8.0 / 5.3
25 / 70 / 135	14.5 / 5.2 / 2.7	20 / 41 / 89 → 18.2 / 8.9 / 4.1	51 / 72 / 111 → 7.1 / 5.1 / 3.3			Cost of Sales/Inventory	24 / 51 / 81 → 14.9 / 7.2 / 4.5	20 / 53 / 91 → 18.4 / 6.9 / 4.0
6 / 15 / 26	57.4 / 24.2 / 14.3	18 / 26 / 45 → 20.4 / 14.3 / 8.1	17 / 25 / 37 → 21.0 / 14.4 / 10.0			Cost of Sales/Payables	13 / 22 / 37 → 28.0 / 16.4 / 9.8	17 / 25 / 39 → 21.7 / 14.6 / 9.4
	3.6 / 5.4 / 11.4	4.2 / 11.0 / 31.8	3.3 / 5.3 / 11.7			Sales/Working Capital	5.5 / 9.8 / 23.3	4.8 / 7.5 / 41.2
	(17) 6.5 / 3.7 / 1.9	(31) 14.0 / 3.8 / 1.4	10.3 / 3.2 / 2.1			EBIT/Interest	(76) 6.2 / 2.8 / .7	(76) 9.2 / 2.7 / 1.8
			(15) 5.6 / 2.9 / 1.7			Net Profit + Depr., Dep., Amort./Cur. Mat. L /T/D	(46) 5.5 / 2.3 / .6	(45) 6.5 / 3.1 / 1.9
	.2 / .3 / .7	.4 / .7 / 1.2	.3 / .5 / .7			Fixed/Worth	.3 / .6 / 1.4	.2 / .7 / 1.4
	.6 / 1.1 / 1.8	.3 / 1.3 / 2.4	.5 / 1.0 / 1.7			Debt/Worth	.7 / 1.3 / 2.3	.6 / 1.2 / 2.6
	(18) 42.3 / 13.1 / 2.5	41.4 / 17.8 / 8.1	28.7 / 17.1 / 7.5			% Profit Before Taxes/Tangible Net Worth	(81) 38.9 / 16.0 / .3	(80) 36.3 / 18.0 / 8.3
	16.5 / 8.5 / 2.0	20.8 / 7.2 / 2.5	13.9 / 5.9 / 2.9			% Profit Before Taxes/Total Assets	14.7 / 7.7 / -.6	15.7 / 7.1 / 3.4
	29.5 / 14.9 / 4.0	15.6 / 9.9 / 4.2	12.3 / 6.8 / 4.1			Sales/Net Fixed Assets	17.8 / 8.1 / 4.0	26.5 / 9.6 / 3.7
	3.3 / 2.0 / 1.5	2.8 / 2.1 / 1.5	2.2 / 1.8 / 1.2			Sales/Total Assets	3.1 / 2.3 / 1.5	2.9 / 2.2 / 1.5
	(16) 1.0 / 2.5 / 5.7	(29) 1.4 / 2.5 / 6.3	(24) 1.5 / 2.8 / 5.0			% Depr., Dep., Amort./Sales	(81) 1.2 / 2.1 / 4.9	(83) .9 / 1.8 / 4.5
	(10) 1.2 / 1.6 / 5.5	(11) 1.5 / 2.0 / 4.5				% Officers', Directors', Owners' Comp/Sales	(28) 2.3 / 3.5 / 9.5	(38) 2.5 / 4.0 / 5.8
6087M	51929M	371906M	1023917M	127953M	1327860M	Net Sales ($)	2582334M	1953726M
1702M	22622M	163868M	577947M	62634M	918942M	Total Assets ($)	1404230M	1007907M

M = $ thousand   MM = $ million
See Pages 1 through 15 for Explanation of Ratios and Data

Comparative Historical Data / Current Data Sorted By Sales

		1	7	# Postretirement Benefits	1		1	3	2
				Type of Statement					
	32	35	31	Unqualified	3	2	1	7	18
	23	24	23	Reviewed	7	2	6	8	
	18	12	6	Compiled	4	1		1	
		2	1	Tax Returns	1				
	9	22	27	Other	1	2	3	4	10	7
	4/1/92-3/31/93	4/1/93-3/31/94	4/1/94-3/31/95			23 (4/1-9/30/94)		65 (10/1/94-3/31/95)		
	ALL	ALL	ALL		0-1MM	1-3MM	3-5MM	5-10MM	10-25MM	25MM & OVER
	82	95	88	**NUMBER OF STATEMENTS**	2	16	8	11	26	25
	%	%	%	**ASSETS**	%	%	%	%	%	%
	7.9	7.3	9.6	Cash & Equivalents		10.1		17.9	6.4	7.3
	25.0	26.3	25.7	Trade Receivables - (net)		26.1		28.1	25.0	26.6
	26.1	26.1	28.3	Inventory		29.9		19.5	29.6	28.9
	3.0	1.1	1.6	All Other Current		1.0		.1	2.0	2.4
	62.0	60.8	65.2	Total Current		67.0		65.7	63.0	65.3
	30.5	32.1	27.9	Fixed Assets (net)		27.5		30.7	28.3	25.9
	.9	1.1	1.5	Intangibles (net)		.6		.2	2.1	2.4
	6.5	6.0	5.4	All Other Non-Current		4.9		3.5	6.7	6.4
	100.0	100.0	100.0	Total		100.0		100.0	100.0	100.0
				LIABILITIES						
	9.3	10.0	9.6	Notes Payable-Short Term		12.5		13.1	10.0	5.0
	5.4	3.6	4.9	Cur. Mat.-L/T/D		8.0		6.4	4.1	3.2
	12.9	13.0	12.0	Trade Payables		7.3		11.5	16.3	12.3
	.6	1.3	.5	Income Taxes Payable		.6		.4	.4	.4
	5.7	6.3	6.8	All Other Current		6.9		7.2	4.7	7.7
	34.0	34.2	33.8	Total Current		35.2		38.7	35.6	28.5
	16.1	13.9	13.2	Long Term Debt		17.3		4.0	15.9	12.8
	.7	.9	1.2	Deferred Taxes		.7		.9	1.4	1.7
	3.6	4.5	3.5	All Other-Non-Current		5.6		3.5	.8	2.7
	45.6	46.5	48.3	Net Worth		41.2		52.9	46.3	54.4
	100.0	100.0	100.0	Total Liabilities & Net Worth		100.0		100.0	100.0	100.0
				INCOME DATA						
	100.0	100.0	100.0	Net Sales		100.0		100.0	100.0	100.0
	24.3	23.4	23.2	Gross Profit		25.9		25.6	21.0	22.0
	17.9	18.2	17.1	Operating Expenses		19.9		16.1	14.8	16.1
	6.4	5.2	6.1	Operating Profit		6.0		9.5	6.3	5.9
	1.0	1.2	1.3	All Other Expenses (net)		1.4		.5	1.4	1.1
	5.5	4.0	4.8	Profit Before Taxes		4.6		8.9	4.9	4.7
				RATIOS						
	2.9	2.9	3.6			4.0		2.7	3.8	3.6
	1.8	1.8	2.3	Current		2.6		1.8	1.5	2.5
	1.3	1.3	1.4			1.5		1.5	1.2	1.8
	1.5	1.8	2.3			2.3		2.7	2.1	2.3
	1.0	1.1	1.2	Quick		1.2		1.3	.8	1.4
	.6	.6	.6			.6		.8	.5	.7
	27 13.5	32 11.4	30 12.3		32 11.3		25 14.5	29 12.7	38 9.7
	43 8.4	51 7.2	47 7.8	Sales/Receivables	46 7.9		48 7.6	43 8.4	57 6.4
	60 6.1	65 5.6	62 5.9		58 6.3		54 6.7	61 6.0	66 5.5
	23 16.2	26 14.3	35 10.5		16 22.2		13 29.0	40 9.1	46 7.9
	48 7.6	58 6.3	63 5.8	Cost of Sales/Inventory	70 5.2		33 11.0	61 6.0	70 5.2
	89 4.1	94 3.9	99 3.7		140 2.6		72 5.1	107 3.4	101 3.6
	14 26.4	14 27.0	14 25.4		6 59.4		16 22.6	21 17.6	17 21.2
	21 17.2	21 17.0	24 15.3	Cost of Sales/Payables	15 25.0		19 19.0	26 14.2	27 13.5
	34 10.7	44 8.3	35 10.3		28 13.2		34 10.6	45 8.2	34 10.8
	4.8	4.5	3.7			3.6		4.2	3.3	3.7
	6.8	7.8	6.1	Sales/Working Capital		4.8		7.0	11.1	5.2
	18.1	20.0	14.7			11.1		17.9	23.3	7.4
	6.7	7.8	10.2		(15) 7.5		56.3	13.0	10.4
(78)	3.8	(90) 3.4	(84) 3.7	EBIT/Interest	2.8		(10) 7.9	3.4	(24) 3.7
	1.6	1.2	1.7		1.5		1.2	1.4	2.2
	4.2	4.8	6.4	Net Profit + Depr., Dep.,				(11) 7.1	(12) 5.1
(37)	2.7	(29) 1.6	(33) 2.9	Amort./Cur. Mat. L/T/D				2.7	3.2
	1.8	.7	1.5					1.1	2.1
	.3	.3	.3			.3		.1	.4	.3
	.5	.6	.6	Fixed/Worth		.7		.5	.6	.5
	1.4	1.3	1.0			1.1		.9	1.2	.7
	.5	.6	.5			.6		.2	.5	.4
	1.4	1.2	1.2	Debt/Worth		1.2		1.2	1.8	.9
	2.2	2.3	2.2			5.3		1.9	2.5	1.4
	36.4	28.7	31.9	% Profit Before Taxes/Tangible	49.7		43.9	31.6	28.9
(78)	17.9	(92) 17.3	(85) 17.3	Net Worth	(14) 9.6		25.6	20.5	17.3
	7.5	3.1	5.3		1.3		8.1	2.9	9.0
	16.0	14.3	17.2	% Profit Before Taxes/Total		15.4		27.7	17.6	14.0
	8.9	5.6	7.2	Assets		5.0		16.8	6.7	7.4
	2.7	.8	2.0			1.2		2.0	1.1	3.8
	19.4	14.3	20.6			27.4		28.1	14.5	14.0
	8.4	7.8	7.9	Sales/Net Fixed Assets		11.0		10.0	9.4	6.9
	3.9	4.1	4.5			3.7		3.2	4.8	5.2
	3.0	2.6	2.6			2.5		3.4	2.7	2.3
	2.2	1.9	2.0	Sales/Total Assets		2.0		2.2	2.1	2.0
	1.5	1.4	1.5			1.5		1.7	1.3	1.6
	1.1	1.5	1.4	% Depr., Dep., Amort./Sales	(15) 1.0		.7	(23) 1.4	(24) 1.8
(79)	2.2	(90) 2.4	(79) 2.6		2.4		2.3	2.5	2.7
	4.2	4.5	4.5		6.1		7.1	4.8	2.9
	2.4	1.6	1.3	% Officers', Directors',					
(28)	3.4	(36) 4.0	(27) 2.0	Owners' Comp/Sales					
	8.8	6.6	4.5						
	2001469M	2547164M	2909652M	Net Sales ($)	1550M	28029M	34070M	74433M	388194M	2383376M
	1106500M	1692283M	1747715M	Total Assets ($)	310M	15222M	23016M	37341M	223412M	1448414M

M = $ thousand   MM = $ million
See Pages 1 through 15 for Explanation of Ratios and Data

352 MANUFACTURERS—NARROW FABRIC & OTHER SMALLWARES. SIC# 2241

Current Data Sorted By Assets / Comparative Historical Data

0-500M	500M-2MM	2-10MM	10-50MM	50-100MM	100-250MM	# Postretirement Benefits / Type of Statement	4/1/90-3/31/91 ALL	4/1/91-3/31/92 ALL
		1	1	1				
		9	5	2		Unqualified	8	10
	4	5		1		Reviewed	11	6
1	4		1			Compiled	10	9
						Tax Returns		1
1		1	3			Other	10	7
12 (4/1-9/30/94)		25 (10/1/94-3/31/95)						
2	8	15	9	3		NUMBER OF STATEMENTS	39	33
%	%	%	%	%	%	ASSETS	%	%
		6.2				Cash & Equivalents	4.2	3.8
		28.8				Trade Receivables - (net)	27.2	27.1
		31.5				Inventory	32.6	31.2
		.6				All Other Current	1.2	.7
		67.1				Total Current	65.3	62.8
		21.7				Fixed Assets (net)	25.6	27.2
		2.4				Intangibles (net)	1.0	3.6
		8.8				All Other Non-Current	8.1	6.4
		100.0				Total	100.0	100.0
						LIABILITIES		
		12.8				Notes Payable-Short Term	6.1	6.3
		3.5				Cur. Mat. -L/T/D	3.2	4.1
		15.2				Trade Payables	13.9	14.2
		.5				Income Taxes Payable	.6	.1
		7.4				All Other Current	6.6	4.7
		39.4				Total Current	30.4	29.4
		19.7				Long Term Debt	16.4	20.7
		.3				Deferred Taxes	1.1	.8
		1.0				All Other-Non-Current	1.0	1.7
		39.5				Net Worth	51.1	47.3
		100.0				Total Liabilities & Net Worth	100.0	100.0
						INCOME DATA		
		100.0				Net Sales	100.0	100.0
		21.7				Gross Profit	25.9	28.8
		17.9				Operating Expenses	21.3	25.1
		3.8				Operating Profit	4.6	3.7
		2.3				All Other Expenses (net)	1.0	1.0
		1.6				Profit Before Taxes	3.6	2.7
						RATIOS		
		3.4				Current	2.9	3.1
		1.8					2.2	2.1
		1.0					1.8	1.6
		1.8				Quick	1.6	1.5
		.8					1.1	1.1
		.4					.7	.6
		34 10.8				Sales/Receivables	31 11.7	36 10.2
		51 7.1					45 8.1	47 7.8
		62 5.9					54 6.8	56 6.5
		44 8.3				Cost of Sales/Inventory	47 7.8	51 7.2
		76 4.8					65 5.6	81 4.5
		118 3.1					107 3.4	104 3.5
		17 22.0				Cost of Sales/Payables	16 23.4	21 17.6
		26 14.2					25 14.6	29 12.6
		39 9.3					40 9.1	42 8.6
		4.9				Sales/Working Capital	4.7	4.5
		6.3					6.8	6.6
		-67.5					10.7	9.9
	(13)	17.8				EBIT/Interest	(36) 5.4	(31) 6.0
		4.5					3.3	2.2
		.0					1.4	1.0
						Net Profit + Depr., Dep., Amort./Cur. Mat. L./T/D	(21) 8.3	(19) 5.1
							2.9	2.2
							1.1	.2
		.2				Fixed/Worth	.2	.2
		.3					.4	.6
		3.9					1.0	1.3
		.5				Debt/Worth	.5	.6
		1.2					1.2	1.3
		9.5					2.1	2.0
	(12)	46.9				% Profit Before Taxes/Tangible Net Worth	31.4	27.6
		21.2					10.6	(31) 13.2
		-30.3					3.6	.0
		25.5				% Profit Before Taxes/Total Assets	10.8	12.5
		8.2					5.5	4.5
		-1.2					2.0	-.9
		26.7				Sales/Net Fixed Assets	20.3	26.4
		12.0					10.6	8.0
		5.0					7.1	3.8
		2.9				Sales/Total Assets	2.9	2.6
		2.0					2.4	2.0
		1.8					1.6	1.6
	(13)	1.1				% Depr., Dep., Amort./Sales	(36) 1.1	(32) .7
		1.8					1.8	1.8
		2.3					3.0	4.5
						% Officers', Directors', Owners' Comp/Sales	(18) 2.2	(16) 1.9
							4.3	3.5
							11.3	9.9
2884M	30194M	158059M	264149M	316160M		Net Sales ($)	621804M	284020M
534M	9604M	71733M	149445M	175353M		Total Assets ($)	311363M	162405M

© Robert Morris Associates 1995

M = $ thousand   MM = $ million
See Pages 1 through 15 for Explanation of Ratios and Data

Comparative Historical Data				Current Data Sorted By Sales					
2	1	3	# Postretirement Benefits				1		2
			Type of Statement						
16	13	16	Unqualified		1	7	2		6
11	10	10	Reviewed	2	2	1	4		1
10	8	6	Compiled	2	2	1	1		
1	1		Tax Returns						
8	4	5	Other	1			3		1
4/1/92-3/31/93 ALL	4/1/93-3/31/94 ALL	4/1/94-3/31/95 ALL		0-1MM	12 (4/1-9/30/94) 1-3MM	3-5MM	5-10MM	25 (10/1/94-3/31/95) 10-25MM	25MM & OVER
46	36	37	NUMBER OF STATEMENTS		5	5	9	10	8
%	%	%	ASSETS	%	%	%	%	%	%
3.0	4.3	5.5	Cash & Equivalents					5.7	
28.6	26.3	29.0	Trade Receivables - (net)					26.5	
34.1	32.6	30.4	Inventory					29.8	
1.4	1.5	1.4	All Other Current					.6	
67.2	64.8	66.3	Total Current					62.6	
25.8	23.9	24.6	Fixed Assets (net)					25.3	
1.4	2.5	1.2	Intangibles (net)					.4	
5.6	8.8	7.9	All Other Non-Current					11.7	
100.0	100.0	100.0	Total					100.0	
			LIABILITIES						
8.3	9.9	10.6	Notes Payable-Short Term					6.1	
3.5	2.8	3.2	Cur. Mat.-L /T/D					3.0	
17.1	15.5	17.9	Trade Payables					12.9	
.3	.8	.3	Income Taxes Payable					.1	
7.2	8.4	8.2	All Other Current					10.3	
36.4	37.4	40.3	Total Current					32.4	
18.1	19.9	15.8	Long Term Debt					19.6	
.9	.7	.3	Deferred Taxes					.2	
2.0	1.7	4.6	All Other-Non-Current					3.7	
42.6	40.3	39.0	Net Worth					44.1	
100.0	100.0	100.0	Total Liabilities & Net Worth					100.0	
			INCOME DATA						
100.0	100.0	100.0	Net Sales					100.0	
24.6	24.2	23.8	Gross Profit					18.5	
19.7	21.1	19.2	Operating Expenses					16.9	
5.0	3.1	4.6	Operating Profit					1.7	
1.4	1.2	1.4	All Other Expenses (net)					1.5	
3.6	1.8	3.2	Profit Before Taxes					.2	
			RATIOS						
3.0	3.6	2.5						2.9	
1.8	1.8	1.6	Current					2.2	
1.4	1.3	1.2						1.6	
1.5	1.6	1.5						1.4	
.9	1.2	.8	Quick					.9	
.6	.5	.5						.8	
35 10.5	32 11.5	33 11.2						37 9.8	
47 7.7	47 7.7	47 7.7	Sales/Receivables					46 7.9	
55 6.6	62 5.9	57 6.4						54 6.8	
52 7.0	40 9.1	39 9.3						46 7.9	
74 4.9	72 5.1	64 5.7	Cost of Sales/Inventory					57 6.4	
94 3.9	122 3.0	96 3.8						107 3.4	
19 19.5	17 21.1	17 21.4						16 23.4	
31 11.7	31 11.6	29 12.8	Cost of Sales/Payables					22 16.6	
41 8.8	40 9.2	47 7.8						26 13.9	
5.2	3.7	5.0						4.6	
7.2	6.0	7.7	Sales/Working Capital					6.2	
12.6	12.8	27.8						11.9	
5.5	6.9	8.1							
(43) 3.4	(35) 2.8	(31) 4.5	EBIT/Interest						
1.6	1.4	1.5							
5.7	4.4	4.0	Net Profit + Depr., Dep.,						
(27) 2.7	(15) 2.1	(16) 1.5	Amort./Cur. Mat. L/T/D						
1.2	1.3	.2							
.2	.2	.2						.1	
.6	.5	.6	Fixed/Worth					.5	
1.1	1.8	1.7						4.0	
.8	.7	.7						.5	
1.5	1.5	1.4	Debt/Worth					.9	
2.6	3.9	3.8						6.2	
36.7	29.3	41.2	% Profit Before Taxes/Tangible						
(45) 13.6	(31) 11.8	(33) 18.0	Net Worth						
4.7	3.7	3.8							
11.3	10.0	17.2						16.9	
7.1	5.1	4.8	% Profit Before Taxes/Total Assets					5.8	
1.3	1.7	2.1						2.6	
25.9	24.7	24.3						28.2	
9.8	13.2	11.0	Sales/Net Fixed Assets					9.4	
5.5	5.2	5.7						5.1	
3.0	2.8	3.0						2.9	
2.2	2.1	2.0	Sales/Total Assets					2.0	
1.8	1.5	1.8						1.7	
.7	.9	1.1							
(43) 1.8	(31) 1.8	(33) 1.9	% Depr., Dep., Amort./Sales						
3.1	3.3	2.7							
1.5	2.6	2.1							
(22) 2.9	(16) 4.3	(15) 4.1	% Officers', Directors', Owners' Comp/Sales						
4.7	5.7	8.9							
752866M	677089M	771446M	Net Sales ($)	8375M	21174M	71949M	161994M		507954M
354392M	583136M	406669M	Total Assets ($)	2429M	9151M	37196M	78282M		279611M

© Robert Morris Associates 1995   M = $ thousand   MM = $ million

See Pages 1 through 15 for Explanation of Ratios and Data

Current Data Sorted By Assets   Comparative Historical Data

0-500M	500M-2MM	2-10MM	10-50MM	50-100MM	100-250MM		4/1/90-3/31/91 ALL	4/1/91-3/31/92 ALL
				1	2	# Postretirement Benefits		
						Type of Statement		
1	1	5	2	1		Unqualified	28	23
		3			1	Reviewed	7	7
1		1	1			Compiled	1	4
						Tax Returns		1
1	2	2	6		3	Other	11	8
	9 (4/1-9/30/94)		22 (10/1/94-3/31/95)					
3	3	11	9	1	4	**NUMBER OF STATEMENTS**	47	43
%	%	%	%	%	%	**ASSETS**	%	%
		2.7				Cash & Equivalents	4.9	4.0
		24.3				Trade Receivables - (net)	22.1	24.7
		20.9				Inventory	18.2	18.3
		3.5				All Other Current	.5	1.0
		51.4				Total Current	45.7	48.1
		42.7				Fixed Assets (net)	49.3	46.8
		1.1				Intangibles (net)	.7	.1
		4.8				All Other Non-Current	4.3	5.0
		100.0				Total	100.0	100.0
						LIABILITIES		
		10.3				Notes Payable-Short Term	8.6	7.2
		5.4				Cur. Mat. -L/T/D	3.7	8.5
		15.3				Trade Payables	12.1	14.2
		.4				Income Taxes Payable	.2	.2
		6.9				All Other Current	5.9	8.2
		38.3				Total Current	30.5	38.3
		22.9				Long Term Debt	21.7	16.6
		.9				Deferred Taxes	2.0	1.4
		1.0				All Other-Non-Current	2.9	2.4
		36.7				Net Worth	42.9	41.4
		100.0				Total Liabilities & Net Worth	100.0	100.0
						INCOME DATA		
		100.0				Net Sales	100.0	100.0
		21.6				Gross Profit	13.3	10.2
		16.6				Operating Expenses	9.8	8.9
		4.9				Operating Profit	3.5	1.3
		1.3				All Other Expenses (net)	1.3	1.1
		3.7				Profit Before Taxes	2.1	.2
						RATIOS		
		1.4					2.8	2.7
		1.4				Current	1.9	1.6
		1.1					1.0	.9
		1.0					1.8	1.6
		.8				Quick	1.1	1.0
		.2					.4	.6
	21	17.6					28 12.9	32 11.5
	39	9.4				Sales/Receivables	41 8.8	43 8.4
	46	8.0					53 6.9	58 6.3
	18	19.9					21 17.2	17 21.5
	32	11.5				Cost of Sales/Inventory	33 11.0	30 12.3
	72	5.1					51 7.1	46 8.0
	17	21.4					11 31.9	13 28.1
	28	13.2				Cost of Sales/Payables	22 16.6	21 17.3
	39	9.4					34 10.8	31 11.6
		13.0					6.2	6.9
		22.7				Sales/Working Capital	10.8	13.1
		49.6					-999.8	-61.0
		13.2					4.6	3.2
		3.2				EBIT/Interest	(43) 1.8	(39) 1.1
		2.2					-.4	-.9
						Net Profit + Depr., Dep.,	2.6	5.3
						Amort./Cur. Mat. L/T/D	(21) 1.4	(22) 1.1
							.8	.3
		.6					.7	.6
		1.2				Fixed/Worth	1.2	1.1
		1.6					1.6	2.1
		.9					.7	.7
		1.8				Debt/Worth	1.3	1.4
		2.1					3.6	3.0
		39.3				% Profit Before Taxes/Tangible	26.9	12.9
	(10)	18.4				Net Worth	7.4	(42) .5
		13.8					-11.4	-9.4
		19.8				% Profit Before Taxes/Total	11.0	5.5
		6.3				Assets	2.5	.2
		3.5					-4.7	-5.5
		12.6					6.7	8.6
		5.4				Sales/Net Fixed Assets	3.4	4.6
		3.1					2.4	2.5
		3.5					2.3	2.7
		2.5				Sales/Total Assets	1.9	2.0
		1.4					1.4	1.6
		1.8					3.5	2.5
		3.0				% Depr., Dep., Amort./Sales	(32) 4.2	(37) 4.1
		3.8					5.9	6.3
						% Officers', Directors',		1.4
						Owners' Comp/Sales		(12) 2.1
								3.5
1403M	7085M	136468M	489973M	112475M	988406M	Net Sales ($)	2889380M	2699406M
545M	3815M	60219M	244076M	94798M	652364M	Total Assets ($)	1651518M	1629863M

M = $ thousand   MM = $ million
See Pages 1 through 15 for Explanation of Ratios and Data

Comparative Historical Data / Current Data Sorted By Sales

	2	2	3							3
Type of Statement				**# Postretirement Benefits**						
Unqualified	25	19	10		1	1		2	4	2
Reviewed	9	7	4						3	1
Compiled	4	2	3		1			1		1
Tax Returns										
Other	8	9	14		1	1	1	2		9

	4/1/92-3/31/93 ALL	4/1/93-3/31/94 ALL	4/1/94-3/31/95 ALL		0-1MM	1-3MM	3-5MM	5-10MM	10-25MM	25MM & OVER
					9 (4/1-9/30/94)			22 (10/1/94-3/31/95)		
NUMBER OF STATEMENTS	46	37	31		3	2	1	5	7	13
ASSETS	%	%	%		%	%	%	%	%	%
Cash & Equivalents	6.5	4.2	5.1							4.8
Trade Receivables - (net)	22.2	22.8	22.9							19.2
Inventory	21.8	22.0	17.9							19.4
All Other Current	1.2	.8	2.0							1.3
Total Current	51.6	49.8	47.9							44.6
Fixed Assets (net)	43.2	43.2	47.4							50.5
Intangibles (net)	1.3	.2	.7							.7
All Other Non-Current	3.9	6.8	3.9							4.1
Total	100.0	100.0	100.0							100.0
LIABILITIES										
Notes Payable-Short Term	4.7	7.2	6.5							2.2
Cur. Mat.-L /T/D	3.8	1.9	4.6							5.3
Trade Payables	14.0	14.9	13.5							12.0
Income Taxes Payable	.8	2.3	.2							.2
All Other Current	6.7	6.4	6.4							3.1
Total Current	30.0	32.7	31.2							22.8
Long Term Debt	19.7	19.3	26.6							34.8
Deferred Taxes	1.2	1.0	1.3							1.6
All Other-Non-Current	3.9	2.3	1.6							2.4
Net Worth	45.2	44.7	39.3							38.3
Total Liabilities & Net Worth	100.0	100.0	100.0							100.0
INCOME DATA										
Net Sales	100.0	100.0	100.0							100.0
Gross Profit	20.6	14.1	19.0							13.9
Operating Expenses	12.2	10.6	13.8							8.9
Operating Profit	8.4	3.5	5.2							4.9
All Other Expenses (net)	1.2	.8	1.4							1.7
Profit Before Taxes	7.2	2.7	3.7							3.2
RATIOS										
Current	2.6	2.6	2.5							2.5
	1.7	1.8	1.4							1.8
	1.3	1.3	1.2							1.5
Quick	1.7	1.5	1.1							1.2
	.9	1.1	.9							1.0
	.6	.5	.7							.8
Sales/Receivables	23 16.2	27 13.5	32 11.3							28 13.0
	37 9.9	37 10.0	41 8.8							41 8.8
	46 8.0	47 7.8	48 7.6							47 7.8
Cost of Sales/Inventory	19 19.5	28 12.9	20 18.7							32 11.4
	37 9.9	44 8.3	33 11.1							51 7.1
	57 6.4	69 5.3	68 5.4							78 4.7
Cost of Sales/Payables	15 24.9	15 24.4	17 21.4							19 19.6
	23 16.1	28 13.2	24 15.3							22 16.6
	35 10.3	41 9.0	37 9.9							39 9.4
Sales/Working Capital	6.3	5.8	7.2							5.0
	10.1	10.0	14.3							8.3
	20.8	23.5	40.4							13.0
EBIT/Interest	9.0	8.9	8.1							6.9
	(42) 5.4	(35) 3.5	(29) 2.8						(12)	2.4
	2.2	1.4	1.6							.7
Net Profit + Depr., Dep., Amort./Cur. Mat. L/T/D	8.6	14.0	4.5							
	(24) 3.2	(12) 1.8	(16) 2.2							
	2.0	1.7	1.3							
Fixed/Worth	.5	.7	.7							.9
	.9	.8	1.2							1.2
	1.6	1.5	2.0							3.5
Debt/Worth	.8	.7	.9							1.0
	1.3	1.3	1.6							1.6
	2.6	2.4	3.2							4.0
% Profit Before Taxes/Tangible Net Worth	62.6	28.3	50.0							56.3
	31.7	(35) 12.8	(29) 18.3							17.7
	14.7	3.1	10.5							.6
% Profit Before Taxes/Total Assets	23.2	12.6	13.8							11.8
	11.6	5.0	5.6							5.6
	4.9	.8	3.2							.7
Sales/Net Fixed Assets	12.5	8.0	7.1							6.5
	4.6	5.0	4.8							4.5
	3.4	3.1	2.3							1.8
Sales/Total Assets	2.7	2.7	2.9							2.2
	2.1	2.1	2.1							1.8
	1.7	1.4	1.3							1.2
% Depr., Dep., Amort./Sales	1.7	2.0	1.8							
	(41) 3.5	(31) 3.4	(26) 3.5							
	5.0	6.6	6.3							
% Officers', Directors', Owners' Comp/Sales	2.1	2.1								
	(12) 2.6	(12) 3.1								
	5.1	4.6								
Net Sales ($)	2537783M	1744611M	1735810M		1403M	3495M	3590M	40514M	114004M	1572804M
Total Assets ($)	1351963M	1092279M	1055817M		545M	2479M	1336M	26369M	45281M	979607M

© Robert Morris Associates 1995
M = $ thousand   MM = $ million
See Pages 1 through 15 for Explanation of Ratios and Data

Current Data Sorted By Assets   Comparative Historical Data

Type of Statement

0-500M	500M-2MM	2-10MM	10-50MM	50-100MM	100-250MM		4/1/90-3/31/91 ALL	4/1/91-3/31/92 ALL
	1	2	1	2		# Postretirement Benefits / Type of Statement		
		7	12	2	1	Unqualified	17	19
1	6	11	2		1	Reviewed	11	21
2	2	2				Compiled	2	7
1	1					Tax Returns		1
3	4	7	3	5		Other	17	20
							4/1/90-3/31/91 ALL	4/1/91-3/31/92 ALL
7	13	27	17	7	2	NUMBER OF STATEMENTS	47	68

ASSETS

0-500M	500M-2MM	2-10MM	10-50MM	50-100MM	100-250MM		90-91	91-92
%	%	%	%	%	%		%	%
	1.9	8.6	7.8			Cash & Equivalents	7.1	8.9
	33.1	33.4	37.3			Trade Receivables - (net)	27.0	30.9
	36.0	33.2	29.9			Inventory	31.9	30.4
	1.2	2.2	1.2			All Other Current	2.1	1.9
	72.1	77.4	76.3			Total Current	68.1	72.1
	20.7	12.1	17.1			Fixed Assets (net)	19.2	17.5
	3.1	2.3	2.2			Intangibles (net)	4.2	3.7
	4.1	8.1	4.4			All Other Non-Current	8.5	6.7
	100.0	100.0	100.0			Total	100.0	100.0

LIABILITIES

0-500M	500M-2MM	2-10MM	10-50MM	50-100MM	100-250MM		90-91	91-92
	16.1	18.9	19.0			Notes Payable-Short Term	16.4	12.6
	6.1	2.9	3.4			Cur. Mat. -L/T/D	3.4	2.3
	20.1	14.0	11.3			Trade Payables	11.7	13.1
	.1	.8	.3			Income Taxes Payable	.7	.9
	5.8	7.2	6.5			All Other Current	8.1	9.0
	48.1	43.8	40.5			Total Current	40.3	38.0
	15.9	7.0	8.9			Long Term Debt	13.2	13.4
	.1	.2	1.4			Deferred Taxes	1.2	.5
	7.4	5.7	1.7			All Other-Non-Current	2.8	5.3
	28.4	43.2	47.5			Net Worth	42.4	42.9
	100.0	100.0	100.0			Total Liabilities & Net Worth	100.0	100.0

INCOME DATA

0-500M	500M-2MM	2-10MM	10-50MM	50-100MM	100-250MM		90-91	91-92
	100.0	100.0	100.0			Net Sales	100.0	100.0
	34.5	37.2	33.1			Gross Profit	35.5	37.2
	30.1	32.7	27.4			Operating Expenses	28.5	29.3
	4.4	4.4	5.7			Operating Profit	6.9	7.9
	1.6	1.2	1.6			All Other Expenses (net)	3.3	1.8
	2.8	3.2	4.1			Profit Before Taxes	3.7	6.1

RATIOS

0-500M	500M-2MM	2-10MM	10-50MM	50-100MM	100-250MM		90-91	91-92
	2.0	2.9	2.7			Current	2.5	2.8
	1.5	1.7	1.7				1.7	1.9
	1.1	1.4	1.4				1.2	1.3
	.9	1.2	1.7			Quick	1.4	1.7
	.7	.9	1.0				.8	1.1
	.5	.7	.7				.6	.7
	30 12.1	37 9.9	62 5.9			Sales/Receivables	34 10.6	31 11.6
	43 8.5	63 5.8	85 4.3				55 6.6	49 7.4
	79 4.6	81 4.5	107 3.4				85 4.3	85 4.3
	37 9.8	62 5.9	81 4.5			Cost of Sales/Inventory	62 5.9	55 6.6
	85 4.3	111 3.3	101 3.6				104 3.5	85 4.3
	146 2.5	166 2.2	130 2.8				146 2.5	152 2.4
	15 24.6	19 19.5	22 16.6			Cost of Sales/Payables	21 17.0	21 17.7
	42 8.6	28 13.2	33 11.0				29 12.4	27 13.3
	87 4.2	68 5.4	60 6.1				50 7.3	47 7.8
	5.2	3.8	3.2			Sales/Working Capital	3.9	3.4
	10.5	6.8	4.7				7.6	6.2
	35.1	18.2	6.6				17.5	10.8
	4.1	(25) 6.3	(15) 6.8			EBIT/Interest	(44) 7.1	(66) 10.1
	2.2	1.4	2.9				2.4	3.4
	1.2	.2	1.7				1.0	1.5
		(11) 23.8				Net Profit + Depr., Dep., Amort./Cur. Mat. L./T/D	(23) 8.9	(34) 13.3
		8.0					2.8	3.3
		1.1					.5	1.8
	.2	.2	.2			Fixed/Worth	.2	.2
	.6	.2	.4				.6	.4
	32.9	.8	.7				.8	.8
	1.0	.5	.5			Debt/Worth	.9	.8
	2.3	1.6	1.7				2.0	1.6
	44.0	3.2	2.1				3.0	3.3
	(11) 50.0	(24) 34.5	22.9			% Profit Before Taxes/Tangible Net Worth	(45) 34.5	(65) 52.8
	18.4	12.4	11.9				16.2	26.1
	9.3	−.2	5.6				−1.1	7.0
	11.5	15.1	8.8			% Profit Before Taxes/Total Assets	11.7	20.5
	4.8	2.6	6.2				5.5	10.8
	.9	−1.5	2.4				−.4	1.9
	39.5	33.3	23.2			Sales/Net Fixed Assets	20.1	44.3
	15.3	25.2	9.2				9.8	15.6
	9.7	8.9	6.1				6.5	7.3
	2.9	2.7	1.8			Sales/Total Assets	2.1	2.5
	2.3	1.9	1.4				1.6	2.0
	1.7	1.6	1.2				1.3	1.5
	(12) .6	(25) .7	(16) 1.1			% Depr., Dep., Amort./Sales	(36) 1.1	(61) .8
	2.0	1.3	1.8				2.1	1.7
	4.0	2.5	3.3				2.9	
		(11) 2.3				% Officers', Directors', Owners' Comp/Sales	(12) 1.8	(23) 2.4
		2.8					4.3	4.1
		3.8					6.7	9.5

0-500M	500M-2MM	2-10MM	10-50MM	50-100MM	100-250MM		90-91	91-92
4012M	38711M	281000M	667117M	822378M	512148M	Net Sales ($)	1537661M	1883457M
1579M	15651M	135671M	426806M	532939M	313909M	Total Assets ($)	1092333M	1169085M

© Robert Morris Associates 1995

M = $ thousand   MM = $ million
See Pages 1 through 15 for Explanation of Ratios and Data

Comparative Historical Data / Current Data Sorted By Sales

Type of Statement (# Postretirement Benefits)

	1	4	6	Type of Statement	0-1MM	1-3MM	3-5MM	5-10MM	10-25MM	25MM & OVER
	19	25	22	Unqualified			2	2	11	7
	24	18	19	Reviewed	2	1	4	6	5	1
	14	4	8	Compiled	2	2	1		1	2
		1	2	Tax Returns	2					
	18	20	22	Other	1	5	2	5	1	8

Historical periods: 1 = 4/1/92-3/31/93 ALL; 4 = 4/1/93-3/31/94 ALL; 6 = 4/1/94-3/31/95 ALL
Current periods: 15 (4/1-9/30/94) covers 0-1MM, 1-3MM, 3-5MM; 58 (10/1/94-3/31/95) covers 5-10MM, 10-25MM, 25MM & OVER

	1 (75)	4 (68)	6 (73)	NUMBER OF STATEMENTS	0-1MM (7)	1-3MM (8)	3-5MM (9)	5-10MM (13)	10-25MM (18)	25MM & OVER (18)
	%	%	%	**ASSETS**	%	%	%	%	%	%
	7.2	9.0	7.0	Cash & Equivalents				7.9	9.1	3.0
	31.8	31.8	33.9	Trade Receivables - (net)				27.8	35.1	43.8
	35.3	31.5	32.0	Inventory				34.9	33.5	26.6
	1.7	1.9	1.7	All Other Current				4.4	1.0	1.8
	76.1	74.2	74.5	Total Current				75.1	78.8	75.3
	16.7	18.7	16.2	Fixed Assets (net)				10.8	14.4	15.5
	3.1	3.1	3.4	Intangibles (net)				2.9	.7	5.5
	4.1	4.0	5.9	All Other Non-Current				11.2	6.1	3.8
	100.0	100.0	100.0	Total				100.0	100.0	100.0
				LIABILITIES						
	14.0	14.7	18.1	Notes Payable-Short Term				20.7	18.2	20.2
	3.0	2.0	3.8	Cur. Mat.-L /T/D				2.6	1.9	4.2
	14.6	15.8	15.3	Trade Payables				13.9	14.1	12.6
	.6	1.4	.6	Income Taxes Payable				.0	1.0	.8
	11.1	8.9	6.6	All Other Current				5.8	5.8	6.8
	43.2	42.7	44.3	Total Current				43.0	41.1	44.7
	12.2	11.1	9.8	Long Term Debt				3.1	9.5	8.7
	.4	.2	.5	Deferred Taxes				.1	1.3	.6
	3.5	5.9	6.5	All Other-Non-Current				7.6	1.8	4.6
	40.6	40.1	38.8	Net Worth				46.2	46.3	41.5
	100.0	100.0	100.0	Total Liabilities & Net Worth				100.0	100.0	100.0
				INCOME DATA						
	100.0	100.0	100.0	Net Sales				100.0	100.0	100.0
	36.0	35.0	33.8	Gross Profit				37.7	32.8	32.9
	30.2	29.6	29.2	Operating Expenses				33.8	26.9	25.6
	5.8	5.4	4.7	Operating Profit				3.9	5.8	7.3
	1.2	1.7	1.4	All Other Expenses (net)				1.2	1.2	1.5
	4.6	3.7	3.2	Profit Before Taxes				2.7	4.6	5.8
				RATIOS						
	2.9 / 1.8 / 1.3	3.1 / 1.8 / 1.2	2.5 / 1.7 / 1.3	Current				3.3 / 1.7 / 1.2	2.9 / 1.8 / 1.5	2.6 / 1.8 / 1.3
	1.4 / .8 / .6	1.8 / .9 / .6	1.4 / .9 / .6	Quick				1.0 / .7 / .4	1.5 / .9 / .7	1.6 / 1.1 / .8
	34 10.8 / 56 6.5 / 85 4.3	40 9.1 / 61 6.0 / 89 4.1	39 9.3 / 63 5.8 / 94 3.9	Sales/Receivables				22 16.5 / 49 7.4 / 78 4.7	47 7.8 / 68 5.4 / 83 4.4	63 5.8 / 101 3.6 / 130 2.8
	63 5.8 / 94 3.9 / 146 2.5	55 6.6 / 89 4.1 / 135 2.7	56 6.5 / 101 3.6 / 135 2.7	Cost of Sales/Inventory				39 9.4 / 122 3.0 / 183 2.0	65 5.6 / 104 3.5 / 135 2.7	57 6.4 / 101 3.6 / 118 3.1
	18 20.1 / 30 12.3 / 61 6.0	22 16.4 / 37 9.8 / 65 5.6	19 19.5 / 33 11.0 / 69 5.3	Cost of Sales/Payables				20 18.3 / 28 13.2 / 73 5.0	21 17.2 / 28 13.1 / 46 7.9	21 17.2 / 45 8.1 / 70 5.2
	3.3 / 6.3 / 13.8	3.8 / 5.6 / 21.1	4.2 / 6.8 / 13.8	Sales/Working Capital				3.8 / 7.2 / 58.1	4.0 / 5.0 / 7.6	3.7 / 4.9 / 11.0
	(69) 9.0 / 3.6 / 1.5	(64) 13.3 / 2.1 / 1.0	(67) 5.5 / 2.3 / 1.2	EBIT/Interest				5.3 / 1.7 / 1.0	(16) 10.8 / 2.5 / .7	(16) 9.4 / 3.5 / 1.6
	(24) 13.1 / 2.8 / 1.2	(22) 11.6 / 3.4 / 1.0	(33) 13.0 / 3.8 / .8	Net Profit + Depr., Dep., Amort./Cur. Mat. L/T/D						(11) 24.9 / 10.1 / 2.9
	.1 / .5 / 1.0	.2 / .5 / 1.0	.2 / .4 / .9	Fixed/Worth				.1 / .2 / 1.5	.2 / .3 / .6	.2 / .4 / .9
	1.0 / 1.8 / 3.3	.8 / 1.7 / 7.7	.8 / 1.7 / 3.9	Debt/Worth				.3 / 1.3 / 17.3	.8 / 1.4 / 2.0	.8 / 1.9 / 4.7
	(70) 39.9 / 22.8 / 4.6	(62) 52.7 / 15.7 / 3.2	(65) 38.7 / 16.9 / 4.4	% Profit Before Taxes/Tangible Net Worth			(11)	42.0 / 29.6 / .8	(17) 26.9 / 10.5 / 1.5	43.5 / 27.2 / 8.5
	17.0 / 7.6 / 1.5	18.0 / 4.6 / .1	11.9 / 5.4 / .8	% Profit Before Taxes/Total Assets				17.7 / 5.0 / .2	10.2 / 6.0 / .5	14.1 / 6.7 / 2.0
	35.8 / 17.1 / 7.5	28.7 / 13.1 / 6.9	34.4 / 15.3 / 7.7	Sales/Net Fixed Assets				44.9 / 29.4 / 10.5	36.0 / 22.1 / 7.6	22.4 / 10.6 / 5.9
	2.6 / 2.0 / 1.6	2.3 / 1.9 / 1.4	2.4 / 1.9 / 1.4	Sales/Total Assets				3.1 / 2.0 / 1.5	2.5 / 1.8 / 1.5	2.1 / 1.7 / 1.2
	(61) .7 / 1.6 / 2.8	(58) .6 / 1.9 / 3.3	(65) .8 / 1.7 / 3.3	% Depr., Dep., Amort./Sales			(12)	.5 / 1.3 / 2.7	(17) .5 / 1.1 / 1.9	(17) 1.1 / 2.0 / 2.9
	(30) 2.7 / 4.5 / 7.8	(24) 2.3 / 3.6 / 8.2	(23) 1.9 / 2.9 / 7.6	% Officers', Directors', Owners' Comp/Sales						
	1840680M	1875845M	2325366M	Net Sales ($)	3365M	14996M	36189M	98027M	323361M	1849428M
	1136958M	1328476M	1426555M	Total Assets ($)	1834M	8276M	19876M	55321M	178614M	1162634M

M = $ thousand   MM = $ million
See Pages 1 through 15 for Explanation of Ratios and Data

MANUFACTURERS—SPORTING & ATHLETIC GOODS. SIC# 3949

Current Data Sorted By Assets | **Comparative Historical Data**

		1	4	5	2		# Postretirement Benefits Type of Statement		
	2	8	24	23	7	8	Unqualified	54	42
	2	9	14				Reviewed	32	30
	8	20	8	1	1		Compiled	29	22
	1		1	1			Tax Returns		3
	8	15	21	10	2	3	Other	27	33
		68 (4/1-9/30/94)		129 (10/1/94-3/31/95)				4/1/90-3/31/91	4/1/91-3/31/92
	0-500M	500M-2MM	2-10MM	10-50MM	50-100MM	100-250MM		ALL	ALL
NUMBER OF STATEMENTS	21	52	68	35	10	11		142	130

	0-500M %	500M-2MM %	2-10MM %	10-50MM %	50-100MM %	100-250MM %		4/1/90-3/31/91 ALL %	4/1/91-3/31/92 ALL %
ASSETS									
Cash & Equivalents	16.3	8.1	4.6	4.9	2.6	8.0		5.8	6.1
Trade Receivables - (net)	19.7	24.0	28.2	33.4	29.4	26.5		25.1	26.4
Inventory	38.8	42.7	38.5	25.8	28.2	28.7		38.2	39.4
All Other Current	.8	1.1	1.2	.9	1.7	5.6		1.4	1.4
Total Current	75.6	75.9	72.6	65.0	61.8	68.7		70.6	73.4
Fixed Assets (net)	13.8	16.4	18.4	24.2	17.8	14.3		18.9	17.2
Intangibles (net)	2.9	2.4	3.0	4.5	9.0	10.2		2.8	3.6
All Other Non-Current	7.7	5.3	6.1	6.3	11.3	6.8		7.8	5.8
Total	100.0	100.0	100.0	100.0	100.0	100.0		100.0	100.0
LIABILITIES									
Notes Payable-Short Term	4.9	16.9	18.5	14.0	12.2	12.8		14.7	15.5
Cur. Mat. -L/T/D	4.4	2.5	2.6	2.5	1.7	5.7		3.5	2.7
Trade Payables	18.4	14.7	14.8	11.9	7.6	9.4		12.0	11.8
Income Taxes Payable	.4	.6	.4	.5	.2	1.2		.9	.7
All Other Current	7.7	7.1	8.5	10.1	9.1	8.8		9.7	8.6
Total Current	35.8	41.9	44.9	39.0	30.8	37.8		40.9	39.4
Long Term Debt	16.9	10.0	12.6	14.4	18.6	15.0		12.4	13.5
Deferred Taxes	.1	.1	.3	.8	.3	.2		.3	.4
All Other-Non-Current	4.5	6.5	3.7	1.7	4.0	6.2		4.2	3.3
Net Worth	42.7	41.6	38.5	44.1	46.3	40.9		42.2	43.4
Total Liabilities & Net Worth	100.0	100.0	100.0	100.0	100.0	100.0		100.0	100.0
INCOME DATA									
Net Sales	100.0	100.0	100.0	100.0	100.0	100.0		100.0	100.0
Gross Profit	43.1	34.7	34.0	32.9	37.1	37.4		35.2	35.3
Operating Expenses	37.9	30.8	28.8	26.6	27.8	28.5		29.8	28.9
Operating Profit	5.2	3.9	5.2	6.3	9.4	8.9		5.4	6.4
All Other Expenses (net)	.3	1.0	1.7	1.8	1.6	1.8		2.1	1.8
Profit Before Taxes	4.9	2.9	3.6	4.5	7.8	7.1		3.3	4.6
RATIOS									
Current	5.0	3.1	2.5	2.6	4.0	3.3		2.7	3.0
	2.3	1.8	1.7	1.6	2.9	2.5		1.7	1.8
	1.8	1.3	1.2	1.2	1.2	1.5		1.3	1.3
Quick	1.9	1.2	1.1	1.5	1.9	1.6		1.4	1.4
	1.2	.7	.7	1.0	1.4	1.3		.7	.8
	.5	.4	.5	.7	.7	.6		.5	.5
Sales/Receivables	8 — 45.1	19 — 19.4	36 — 10.1	56 — 6.5	47 — 7.8	55 — 6.6		29 — 12.7	33 — 11.0
	20 — 18.5	37 — 9.9	55 — 6.6	76 — 4.8	68 — 5.4	79 — 4.6		45 — 8.2	52 — 7.0
	38 — 9.6	54 — 6.7	66 — 5.5	99 — 3.7	89 — 4.1	94 — 3.9		72 — 5.1	66 — 5.5
Cost of Sales/Inventory	46 — 8.0	63 — 5.8	83 — 4.4	58 — 6.3	79 — 4.6	89 — 4.1		74 — 4.9	78 — 4.7
	74 — 4.9	89 — 4.1	122 — 3.0	91 — 4.0	111 — 3.3	130 — 2.8		111 — 3.3	104 — 3.5
	118 — 3.1	146 — 2.5	166 — 2.2	126 — 2.9	130 — 2.8	183 — 2.0		174 — 2.1	166 — 2.2
Cost of Sales/Payables	6 — 58.4	13 — 27.6	20 — 18.1	21 — 17.7	15 — 24.9	28 — 13.0		16 — 22.9	14 — 25.7
	31 — 11.6	30 — 12.1	33 — 10.9	37 — 9.8	20 — 18.5	41 — 8.9		28 — 13.0	25 — 14.6
	69 — 5.3	51 — 7.1	55 — 6.6	52 — 7.0	41 — 9.0	58 — 6.3		51 — 7.2	48 — 7.6
Sales/Working Capital	3.9	4.6	3.8	3.6	2.8	2.2		3.5	3.6
	6.8	7.1	7.1	7.5	4.1	4.3		6.2	5.8
	16.8	14.9	14.7	13.1	NM	7.2		14.4	12.7
EBIT/Interest	(13) 5.8	(50) 9.5	(65) 5.1	(34) 11.3	15.2	6.7		(131) 5.2	(118) 5.4
	2.0	2.9	2.2	2.4	8.3	3.6		2.3	2.6
	.4	1.1	1.1	1.6	2.0	.1		1.2	1.4
Net Profit + Depr., Dep., Amort./Cur. Mat. L /T/D		(18) 10.9	(34) 6.2	(17) 39.4				(87) 9.3	(62) 8.2
		3.5	2.2	3.8				2.9	3.4
		.8	1.2	1.0				1.6	1.7
Fixed/Worth	.1	.1	.2	.3	.3	.3		.2	.2
	.4	.3	.5	.6	.5	.4		.5	.5
	.6	1.0	.9	1.5	.8	1.2		.8	.9
Debt/Worth	.4	.6	.9	.7	.9	1.1		.7	.7
	1.2	1.2	1.9	1.5	1.3	1.9		1.5	1.7
	NM	4.9	3.2	3.7	2.5	4.0		3.2	3.5
% Profit Before Taxes/Tangible Net Worth	(16) 64.1	(48) 36.6	(63) 40.5	(34) 38.4		(10) 75.8		(133) 39.9	(123) 37.0
	34.0	14.5	13.9	18.0		26.7		17.3	18.9
	3.4	2.9	1.4	4.7		12.5		4.2	6.1
% Profit Before Taxes/Total Assets	27.4	15.3	14.8	17.0	20.2	13.5		14.1	15.5
	10.1	5.3	4.2	4.1	10.5	8.8		6.3	7.5
	-.1	.3	.4	1.8	1.9	-1.3		1.1	2.1
Sales/Net Fixed Assets	65.4	41.1	19.1	19.8	21.9	13.9		24.5	31.1
	25.1	21.3	10.3	8.0	9.1	8.9		12.0	12.1
	19.0	9.4	7.3	3.8	6.9	6.2		6.6	6.9
Sales/Total Assets	4.5	3.3	2.2	1.9	1.8	1.8		2.5	2.3
	2.8	2.4	1.8	1.5	1.6	1.3		1.8	1.9
	2.0	1.5	1.4	1.2	1.3	.8		1.3	1.5
% Depr., Dep., Amort./Sales	(16) .6	(46) .8	(60) 1.0	(30) 1.5				(127) 1.0	(107) .9
	1.3	1.2	1.9	2.2				1.6	1.6
	2.5	2.1	2.7	2.8				3.0	2.7
% Officers', Directors', Owners' Comp/Sales	(11) 3.2	(19) 2.6	(20) 1.3					(43) 2.3	(41) 2.0
	6.2	4.3	2.9					4.4	4.4
	9.6	8.3	6.0					8.0	6.9
Net Sales ($)	15436M	145466M	631242M	1135027M	1125658M	2396964M		3188297M	3151359M
Total Assets ($)	5271M	58370M	348468M	691826M	705176M	1891278M		2231343M	1961035M

M = $ thousand   MM = $ million
See Pages 1 through 15 for Explanation of Ratios and Data

Comparative Historical Data / **Current Data Sorted By Sales**

	3	4	12	# Postretirement Benefits / Type of Statement	1	2	4	5		
	42	48	72	Unqualified	3	6	9	7	17	30
	34	33	25	Reviewed	3	2	8	7	5	
	29	37	38	Compiled	6	15	6	4	6	1
	1	2	3	Tax Returns		1			2	
	36	38	59	Other	8	11	7	10	15	8
	4/1/92-3/31/93	4/1/93-3/31/94	4/1/94-3/31/95		68 (4/1-9/30/94)			129 (10/1/94-3/31/95)		
	ALL	ALL	ALL		0-1MM	1-3MM	3-5MM	5-10MM	10-25MM	25MM & OVER
	142	158	197	NUMBER OF STATEMENTS	20	35	30	28	45	39
	%	%	%	ASSETS	%	%	%	%	%	%
	5.5	6.3	6.9	Cash & Equivalents	12.0	9.6	5.5	6.4	6.0	4.5
	28.8	28.5	27.1	Trade Receivables - (net)	18.9	24.6	25.1	27.6	28.4	33.1
	37.9	36.1	36.3	Inventory	44.3	35.9	42.3	40.2	33.9	28.1
	1.7	1.6	1.3	All Other Current	2.0	.5	.4	1.5	1.4	2.3
	73.8	72.5	71.7	Total Current	77.2	70.6	73.3	75.6	69.6	68.0
	17.3	17.8	18.1	Fixed Assets (net)	13.5	21.6	15.8	15.1	22.0	16.9
	2.6	3.6	3.8	Intangibles (net)	4.5	1.0	4.1	2.6	3.7	6.6
	6.2	6.1	6.4	All Other Non-Current	4.7	6.8	6.7	6.6	4.7	8.5
	100.0	100.0	100.0	Total	100.0	100.0	100.0	100.0	100.0	100.0
				LIABILITIES						
	14.3	15.4	15.2	Notes Payable-Short Term	11.0	14.2	14.4	20.5	17.1	12.7
	2.8	3.2	2.9	Cur. Mat.-L /T/D	3.2	3.1	4.2	2.1	2.3	2.9
	11.6	13.5	14.0	Trade Payables	17.8	13.3	15.3	16.5	14.4	9.4
	.7	.4	.5	Income Taxes Payable	.4	.2	.7	.5	.4	.8
	7.9	10.7	8.4	All Other Current	10.5	6.4	5.2	9.5	7.9	11.3
	37.3	43.3	41.0	Total Current	43.0	37.2	39.8	49.1	42.1	37.1
	14.0	13.0	13.1	Long Term Debt	15.2	14.6	13.4	10.2	10.9	15.2
	.4	.3	.3	Deferred Taxes	.1	.1	.2	.2	.6	.4
	4.1	2.8	4.3	All Other-Non-Current	3.8	5.9	5.7	6.5	2.1	3.1
	44.1	40.6	41.3	Net Worth	38.0	42.2	40.9	34.0	44.4	44.3
	100.0	100.0	100.0	Total Liabilities & Net Worth	100.0	100.0	100.0	100.0	100.0	100.0
				INCOME DATA						
	100.0	100.0	100.0	Net Sales	100.0	100.0	100.0	100.0	100.0	100.0
	36.8	34.1	35.3	Gross Profit	41.1	39.4	34.5	32.4	31.2	36.1
	30.1	29.6	29.8	Operating Expenses	35.9	34.5	30.2	28.2	26.3	27.5
	6.7	4.5	5.5	Operating Profit	5.3	4.9	4.3	4.2	5.0	8.6
	1.9	1.6	1.4	All Other Expenses (net)	1.1	.8	1.5	2.2	1.3	1.5
	4.9	2.9	4.1	Profit Before Taxes	4.2	4.1	2.8	2.0	3.7	7.1
				RATIOS						
	2.9	2.9	2.9	Current	3.9	3.7	2.7	2.3	2.2	3.3
	2.1	1.8	1.9		2.4	2.0	1.8	1.5	1.5	2.4
	1.4	1.3	1.3		1.3	1.3	1.3	1.2	1.2	1.4
	1.6	1.4	1.4	Quick	1.6	1.4	1.2	.8	1.1	1.7
	.9	.8	.8		.9	.9	.8	.6	.7	1.3
	.6	.6	.6		.2	.6	.4	.5	.6	.8
	33 10.9	33 11.1	32 11.4	Sales/Receivables	8 47.7	30 12.0	29 12.6	22 16.3	37 9.8	57 6.4
	54 6.8	51 7.2	51 7.1		24 15.0	39 9.3	39 9.3	47 7.7	56 6.5	74 4.9
	70 5.2	76 4.8	74 4.9		51 7.2	55 6.6	62 5.9	74 4.9	78 4.7	91 4.0
	69 5.3	66 5.5	69 5.3	Cost of Sales/Inventory	59 6.2	63 5.8	72 5.1	68 5.4	72 5.1	69 5.3
	111 3.3	104 3.5	101 3.6		99 3.7	94 3.9	104 3.5	99 3.7	101 3.6	104 3.5
	166 2.2	159 2.3	146 2.5		332 1.1	146 2.5	174 2.1	140 2.6	140 2.6	140 2.6
	18 19.8	18 20.7	17 20.9	Cost of Sales/Payables	9 42.5	17 22.0	14 25.4	13 28.2	21 17.8	18 20.4
	30 12.3	30 12.0	33 11.1		35 10.4	31 11.6	34 10.8	29 12.6	40 9.2	31 11.6
	49 7.4	49 7.4	52 7.0		78 4.7	76 4.8	51 7.1	56 6.5	55 6.6	45 8.1
	3.6	3.6	3.6	Sales/Working Capital	2.5	3.4	5.0	5.2	5.0	3.4
	5.3	5.9	6.8		6.1	6.1	6.7	8.1	7.2	4.8
	10.2	15.6	14.7		24.1	14.9	12.5	16.3	16.5	10.0
	9.4	7.5	7.4	EBIT/Interest	4.4	11.6	5.4	4.9	6.5	12.2
	(131) 3.6	(141) 3.1	(183) 2.6		(13) 2.0	(33) 3.6	(29) 2.0	(41) 2.0	2.4	5.0
	2.0	1.1	1.2		-.5	1.1	1.1	.5	1.4	2.1
	9.2	4.5	12.3	Net Profit + Depr., Dep., Amort./Cur. Mat. L/T/D			18.9	5.2	4.9	65.3
	(73) 3.5	(65) 2.4	(82) 3.3			(14) 5.1	(14) 2.7	(23) 2.1	(20) 12.5	
	1.5	1.0	1.2			1.4	1.7	.9	3.0	
	.2	.2	.2	Fixed/Worth	.1	.2	.2	.1	.3	.2
	.4	.5	.4		.4	.6	.4	.4	.6	.4
	.8	1.2	1.0		-10.0	1.3	.8	1.1	1.5	.9
	.7	.7	.7	Debt/Worth	.5	.6	.7	1.1	.6	.9
	1.4	1.6	1.7		.9	1.7	1.8	2.1	1.7	1.3
	2.5	4.4	3.5		-8.4	4.2	2.9	4.3	3.4	2.4
	45.4	42.4	42.2	% Profit Before Taxes/Tangible Net Worth	57.4	45.7	29.3	43.5	30.7	69.1
	(134) 21.4	(144) 16.8	(180) 17.3		(13) 41.3	(34) 13.4	(28) 12.3	(26) 15.5	(43) 16.2	(36) 30.2
	11.0	2.6	2.9		3.7	2.5	.5	-.6	3.6	10.0
	16.2	15.3	16.9	% Profit Before Taxes/Total Assets	24.8	15.6	13.5	14.3	15.1	22.4
	8.3	6.4	5.6		6.9	5.6	3.1	3.4	5.1	10.8
	3.8	.1	.5		-2.5	.7	.4	-.9	1.4	2.5
	27.2	26.8	26.9	Sales/Net Fixed Assets	50.5	33.7	28.7	42.4	14.8	23.2
	11.5	12.8	11.6		22.6	11.6	18.7	15.1	8.6	9.3
	7.5	6.7	7.0		10.9	5.7	8.5	8.8	6.0	6.2
	2.4	2.5	2.6	Sales/Total Assets	4.2	2.8	3.4	2.7	2.1	1.9
	2.0	1.8	1.8		2.0	2.3	2.1	2.0	1.7	1.6
	1.4	1.4	1.4		1.2	1.4	1.6	1.6	1.4	1.3
	1.0	.8	1.0	% Depr., Dep., Amort./Sales	.8	.8	1.0	1.0	1.1	1.2
	(121) 1.8	(138) 1.6	(169) 1.7		(15) 1.5	(33) 1.3	(26) 1.4	(23) 1.6	(42) 2.1	(30) 2.1
	2.7	2.6	2.7		3.1	3.0	2.8	2.4	2.7	3.0
	2.7	2.3	2.2	% Officers', Directors', Owners' Comp/Sales	3.1	2.2	2.8			
	(49) 4.1	(54) 3.8	(54) 4.2		(10) 6.8	(13) 4.8	(13) 4.3			
	7.0	6.7	8.1		11.0	8.7	8.5			
	3876554M	3816783M	5449793M	Net Sales ($)	10859M	68127M	116176M	199518M	705812M	4349301M
	2452997M	2441625M	3700389M	Total Assets ($)	6643M	56599M	59532M	106079M	441246M	3030290M

M = $ thousand   MM = $ million
See Pages 1 through 15 for Explanation of Ratios and Data

Current Data Sorted By Assets   Comparative Historical Data

			3	2		1	# Postretirement Benefits / Type of Statement		
	1		4	8	1	1	Unqualified	16	16
	1		8				Reviewed	12	9
1		4	4				Compiled	7	4
							Tax Returns		
		2	6	5		1	Other	11	9

	0-500M	500M-2MM	2-10MM	10-50MM	50-100MM	100-250MM		4/1/90-3/31/91 ALL	4/1/91-3/31/92 ALL
		14 (4/1-9/30/94)		33 (10/1/94-3/31/95)					
NUMBER OF STATEMENTS	1	8	22	13	1	2		46	38
	%	%	%	%	%	%	**ASSETS**	%	%
			8.1	7.8			Cash & Equivalents	3.9	6.8
			23.4	20.9			Trade Receivables - (net)	22.7	21.3
			28.0	28.3			Inventory	35.3	37.0
			2.5	2.3			All Other Current	2.3	1.3
			61.9	59.3			Total Current	64.2	66.4
			32.8	24.8			Fixed Assets (net)	26.7	26.7
			.3	6.0			Intangibles (net)	1.4	.5
			5.0	9.9			All Other Non-Current	7.6	6.4
			100.0	100.0			Total	100.0	100.0
							LIABILITIES		
			10.0	5.0			Notes Payable-Short Term	10.6	9.4
			5.0	3.9			Cur. Mat.-L/T/D	3.9	4.4
			10.9	9.0			Trade Payables	13.8	9.6
			.3	.7			Income Taxes Payable	.4	.6
			8.6	12.1			All Other Current	7.3	8.7
			34.9	30.6			Total Current	36.0	32.8
			17.7	18.8			Long Term Debt	23.1	18.2
			.9	1.7			Deferred Taxes	1.7	1.1
			3.2	9.6			All Other-Non-Current	2.3	1.2
			43.3	39.3			Net Worth	36.9	46.7
			100.0	100.0			Total Liabilities & Net Worth	100.0	100.0
							INCOME DATA		
			100.0	100.0			Net Sales	100.0	100.0
			27.2	25.1			Gross Profit	23.6	24.6
			23.1	18.7			Operating Expenses	19.1	19.2
			4.1	6.4			Operating Profit	4.5	5.4
			1.1	2.4			All Other Expenses (net)	2.2	1.6
			3.0	4.0			Profit Before Taxes	2.3	3.8
							RATIOS		
			3.0	3.0				2.5	3.5
			1.7	1.8			Current	1.8	2.1
			1.2	1.3				1.2	1.3
			2.2	1.8				1.2	1.6
			.8	.6			Quick	.7	1.0
			.5	.6				.5	.5
			45 8.1	47 7.7				37 10.0	37 10.0
			56 6.5	64 5.7			Sales/Receivables	52 7.0	47 7.7
			69 5.3	74 4.9				61 6.0	58 6.3
			44 8.3	73 5.0				69 5.3	79 4.6
			91 4.0	96 3.8			Cost of Sales/Inventory	107 3.4	126 2.9
			159 2.3	166 2.2				152 2.4	183 2.0
			13 27.8	21 17.5				22 16.8	15 25.0
			37 10.0	41 8.9			Cost of Sales/Payables	33 11.0	25 14.5
			49 7.4	54 6.8				46 7.9	43 8.4
			3.0	2.8				3.8	2.8
			5.4	3.7			Sales/Working Capital	6.4	4.7
			23.2	10.5				15.9	12.5
			5.5	9.9				(41) 2.8	(36) 15.3
			(19) 2.1	3.3			EBIT/Interest	1.8	2.3
			.6	1.5				.9	1.4
			9.8					(29) 5.8	(20) 4.0
			(10) 1.6				Net Profit + Depr., Dep., Amort./Cur. Mat. L./T/D	1.8	2.1
			.7					1.2	1.2
			.3	.3				.3	.3
			.8	.9			Fixed/Worth	.7	.5
			1.6	2.9				1.9	1.2
			.6	.7				.9	.4
			1.3	2.2			Debt/Worth	2.1	1.2
			3.1	6.7				4.6	3.1
			28.0	59.5				(44) 37.9	28.8
			(20) 4.8	(12) 17.9			% Profit Before Taxes/Tangible Net Worth	10.5	13.4
			-8.0	6.3				1.8	6.2
			11.3	7.8				7.4	10.2
			2.0	5.7			% Profit Before Taxes/Total Assets	4.5	6.6
			-2.1	1.5				-.1	2.0
			8.5	7.8				15.9	9.2
			5.7	4.3			Sales/Net Fixed Assets	7.2	5.9
			2.8	3.0				3.6	4.0
			1.7	1.4				2.0	2.0
			1.4	1.1			Sales/Total Assets	1.5	1.4
			1.2	.7				1.3	1.2
			2.5	3.5				(44) 2.3	(37) 1.4
			4.0	4.3			% Depr., Dep., Amort./Sales	3.9	3.4
			5.2	5.2				6.1	4.5
			2.8					(16) 3.0	(12) 2.2
			(12) 5.6				% Officers', Directors', Owners' Comp/Sales	5.2	4.6
			10.4					9.5	8.2
	408M	20715M	166593M	275599M	61429M	260698M	Net Sales ($)	457511M	717972M
	138M	10491M	111185M	243416M	55784M	428087M	Total Assets ($)	283372M	587488M

M = $ thousand   MM = $ million
See Pages 1 through 15 for Explanation of Ratios and Data

	Comparative Historical Data				Current Data Sorted By Sales					
	1	2	6	# Postretirement Benefits	1	1	1	1	1	2
				Type of Statement						
	22	13	15	Unqualified		1	2	2	6	4
	8	6	9	Reviewed		1	2	3	3	
	5	4	9	Compiled	1	2	4	2		
	1			Tax Returns						
	5	8	14	Other	1	2	1	2	5	3
	4/1/92- 3/31/93 ALL	4/1/93- 3/31/94 ALL	4/1/94- 3/31/95 ALL		2	14 (4/1-9/30/94) 6	9	33 (10/1/94-3/31/95) 9	14	7
					0-1MM	1-3MM	3-5MM	5-10MM	10-25MM	25MM & OVER
	41	31	47	**NUMBER OF STATEMENTS**	2	6	9	9	14	7
	%	%	%	**ASSETS**	%	%	%	%	%	%
	10.4	10.7	7.8	Cash & Equivalents					4.8	
	21.3	21.0	23.9	Trade Receivables - (net)					23.1	
	32.0	31.5	26.8	Inventory					27.8	
	2.4	2.6	2.1	All Other Current					3.4	
	66.0	65.7	60.7	Total Current					59.2	
	24.0	23.9	29.5	Fixed Assets (net)					25.8	
	1.7	2.7	2.6	Intangibles (net)					4.8	
	8.3	7.7	7.3	All Other Non-Current					10.2	
	100.0	100.0	100.0	Total					100.0	
				LIABILITIES						
	5.5	8.6	8.2	Notes Payable-Short Term					12.7	
	5.7	5.2	4.9	Cur. Mat.-L /T/D					1.9	
	9.4	9.6	12.7	Trade Payables					10.0	
	.5	.3	.6	Income Taxes Payable					.4	
	9.1	11.8	9.6	All Other Current					11.5	
	30.2	35.6	36.0	Total Current					36.4	
	17.8	12.8	17.6	Long Term Debt					12.7	
	1.1	.9	1.0	Deferred Taxes					1.8	
	3.4	5.3	5.8	All Other-Non-Current					9.0	
	47.6	45.4	39.7	Net Worth					40.1	
	100.0	100.0	100.0	Total Liabilities & Net Worth					100.0	
				INCOME DATA						
	100.0	100.0	100.0	Net Sales					100.0	
	27.8	24.3	27.4	Gross Profit					24.0	
	23.4	21.5	22.6	Operating Expenses					19.3	
	4.4	2.8	4.8	Operating Profit					4.8	
	1.1	2.0	1.3	All Other Expenses (net)					1.3	
	3.4	.8	3.5	Profit Before Taxes					3.5	
				RATIOS						
	3.7	4.3	2.7						2.1	
	2.6	2.2	1.7	Current					1.3	
	1.7	1.2	1.2						1.2	
	1.8	2.5	1.7						.9	
	1.3	1.0	.8	Quick					.6	
	.6	.4	.6						.5	
	33 11.0	40 9.1	45 8.2						54 6.8	
	48 7.6	47 7.7	56 6.5	Sales/Receivables					61 6.0	
	69 5.3	58 6.3	70 5.2						72 5.1	
	66 5.5	74 4.9	62 5.9						57 6.4	
	118 3.1	107 3.4	91 4.0	Cost of Sales/Inventory					118 3.1	
	159 2.3	140 2.6	140 2.6						174 2.1	
	13 28.8	11 31.9	18 19.8						15 24.4	
	25 14.5	23 16.2	37 9.8	Cost of Sales/Payables					39 9.4	
	38 9.6	45 8.2	49 7.4						46 7.9	
	2.3	2.5	3.1						3.3	
	3.6	6.0	6.5	Sales/Working Capital					9.3	
	7.2	17.5	15.6						13.7	
	7.2	4.3	5.9						6.6	
(38)	3.0	(28) 3.2	(43) 2.1	EBIT/Interest					3.5	
	1.0	1.3	1.0						1.0	
	4.4	2.4	8.5						11.8	
(21)	2.4	(14) 1.6	(24) 2.2	Net Profit + Depr., Dep., Amort./Cur. Mat. L/T/D				(10)	8.1	
	.3	.6	1.5						1.7	
	.3	.3	.3						.3	
	.5	.5	.8	Fixed/Worth					.9	
	1.1	1.8	2.0						1.9	
	.5	.4	.7						.7	
	.8	1.0	1.8	Debt/Worth					2.3	
	3.4	11.0	5.3						6.3	
	28.0	17.3	31.1						53.5	
(38)	11.8	(27) 5.1	(44) 10.9	% Profit Before Taxes/Tangible Net Worth				(13)	24.8	
	2.1	1.3	.9						.9	
	10.2	7.1	9.4						10.0	
	3.4	2.0	3.2	% Profit Before Taxes/Total Assets					4.9	
	-.4	.6	.2						-.1	
	9.5	12.0	8.3						8.5	
	6.7	6.9	4.7	Sales/Net Fixed Assets					5.7	
	3.9	3.7	2.9						3.0	
	1.9	1.8	1.8						1.6	
	1.4	1.4	1.4	Sales/Total Assets					1.3	
	1.0	1.0	1.0						.9	
	1.7	2.0	2.6						2.9	
(37)	2.7	(24) 2.8	(45) 4.3	% Depr., Dep., Amort./Sales					4.1	
	5.7	4.5	5.2						4.7	
	2.4	3.5	3.6							
(10)	4.7	(11) 4.5	(17) 5.9	% Officers', Directors', Owners' Comp/Sales						
	14.0	13.6	10.6							
	823580M	644451M	785442M	Net Sales ($)	1181M	14070M	35525M	60195M	208409M	466062M
	959902M	729269M	849101M	Total Assets ($)	3622M	7833M	28986M	55561M	175781M	577318M

M = $ thousand   MM = $ million
See Pages 1 through 15 for Explanation of Ratios and Data

Current Data Sorted By Assets   **Comparative Historical Data**

Type of Statement (# Postretirement Benefits)

0-500M	500M-2MM	2-10MM	10-50MM	50-100MM	100-250MM	Type of Statement	4/1/90-3/31/91 ALL	4/1/91-3/31/92 ALL
	1	2	4	2	3			
		13	13	1	4	Unqualified	33	32
1	12	18	3			Reviewed	38	36
4	10	4	1		1	Compiled	16	15
	1					Tax Returns		
4	5	12	9	2	3	Other	27	23

Current Data dates: 46 (4/1-9/30/94) covers 0-500M & 500M-2MM; 75 (10/1/94-3/31/95) covers 10-50MM & 50-100MM.

0-500M	500M-2MM	2-10MM	10-50MM	50-100MM	100-250MM		4/1/90-3/31/91 ALL	4/1/91-3/31/92 ALL
9	28	47	26	3	8	**NUMBER OF STATEMENTS**	114	106
%	%	%	%	%	%	**ASSETS**	%	%
	5.0	7.7	6.4			Cash & Equivalents	8.3	7.7
	24.4	22.4	18.6			Trade Receivables - (net)	22.3	22.1
	30.2	37.4	31.3			Inventory	30.1	30.0
	1.2	1.6	4.0			All Other Current	3.3	1.7
	60.8	69.1	60.3			Total Current	63.9	61.5
	32.7	22.4	26.2			Fixed Assets (net)	26.9	27.9
	1.1	1.5	5.5			Intangibles (net)	2.2	2.7
	5.4	7.0	8.1			All Other Non-Current	6.9	7.9
	100.0	100.0	100.0			Total	100.0	100.0
						LIABILITIES		
	7.4	9.2	8.4			Notes Payable-Short Term	9.1	11.1
	4.5	5.0	4.1			Cur. Mat. -L/T/D	5.0	5.6
	13.4	11.5	9.0			Trade Payables	10.5	11.4
	.5	.3	.2			Income Taxes Payable	.7	.5
	8.5	8.7	11.9			All Other Current	9.1	8.1
	34.4	34.7	33.6			Total Current	34.5	36.6
	17.9	10.3	18.1			Long Term Debt	16.5	17.9
	.3	1.0	1.0			Deferred Taxes	1.4	.9
	2.7	4.2	2.1			All Other-Non-Current	2.8	4.1
	44.7	49.8	45.2			Net Worth	44.8	40.5
	100.0	100.0	100.0			Total Liabilities & Net Worth	100.0	100.0
						INCOME DATA		
	100.0	100.0	100.0			Net Sales	100.0	100.0
	35.2	28.3	23.1			Gross Profit	28.9	28.7
	31.5	22.0	17.5			Operating Expenses	20.3	22.3
	3.7	6.3	5.6			Operating Profit	8.6	6.4
	1.5	1.3	2.6			All Other Expenses (net)	2.0	2.0
	2.2	5.0	3.0			Profit Before Taxes	6.7	4.4
						RATIOS		
	2.8	3.5	2.7				2.9	2.6
	1.9	2.0	2.1			Current	2.0	1.7
	1.3	1.5	1.2				1.4	1.2
	1.6	1.9	1.2				1.6	1.3
	.8	1.0	.8			Quick	.9	.8
	.5	.5	.4				.6	.5
	34 10.8	40 9.2	38 9.7				30 12.0	35 10.3
	45 8.2	51 7.1	48 7.6			Sales/Receivables	45 8.1	43 8.4
	57 6.4	69 5.3	61 6.0				64 5.7	59 6.2
	46 7.9	73 5.0	61 6.0				51 7.1	46 7.9
	83 4.4	118 3.1	94 3.9			Cost of Sales/Inventory	94 3.9	94 3.9
	159 2.3	192 1.9	152 2.4				146 2.5	140 2.6
	25 14.4	15 24.5	14 26.9				17 21.2	17 21.4
	34 10.8	37 9.9	33 11.1			Cost of Sales/Payables	27 13.7	28 12.9
	57 6.4	54 6.8	43 8.5				40 9.1	42 8.7
	3.7	3.1	3.6				3.9	4.2
	6.9	5.2	5.4			Sales/Working Capital	5.4	7.1
	23.1	8.9	11.6				12.2	18.9
	(24) 5.4	(44) 13.7	(22) 4.9				(104) 7.8	(101) 5.6
	3.0	3.0	1.6			EBIT/Interest	3.0	2.5
	.9	1.2	.3				1.3	1.3
	(14) 5.2	(19) 9.7	(13) 3.9				(65) 7.8	(61) 3.7
	2.2	3.2	.7			Net Profit + Depr., Dep., Amort./Cur. Mat. L /T/D	2.4	1.6
	.5	.7	.6				1.1	.9
	.3	.2	.2				.4	.4
	.6	.3	.7			Fixed/Worth	.7	.7
	1.7	1.1	1.0				1.2	1.3
	.6	.5	.6				.7	.8
	1.4	.9	1.0			Debt/Worth	1.2	1.6
	2.3	2.4	5.0				3.3	3.4
	31.9	27.2	34.6				39.4	32.0
	(46) 9.0	(24) 12.5	4.0			% Profit Before Taxes/Tangible Net Worth	(112) 18.9	(98) 15.2
	-1.0	2.1	-9.2				5.8	4.2
	14.0	13.8	11.4				16.6	12.2
	4.1	4.3	2.3			% Profit Before Taxes/Total Assets	6.6	5.0
	-.3	.3	-2.8				2.0	1.9
	18.8	18.0	13.0				13.1	12.7
	7.1	6.7	4.4			Sales/Net Fixed Assets	6.4	6.4
	2.9	4.7	2.7				4.1	3.9
	2.3	2.0	1.7				2.3	2.3
	1.9	1.5	1.3			Sales/Total Assets	1.6	1.7
	1.3	1.1	1.0				1.2	1.3
	1.6	1.4	2.1				1.8	1.8
	(26) 2.8	(42) 2.3	(20) 4.8			% Depr., Dep., Amort./Sales	(96) 2.9	(96) 3.2
	4.3	3.8	7.2				4.5	4.8
	5.5	2.7					2.8	2.1
	(10) 8.6	(10) 4.6				% Officers', Directors', Owners' Comp/Sales	(43) 5.5	(40) 5.1
	12.9	8.5					7.8	7.0
7551M	67551M	364220M	702307M	194362M	1340302M	Net Sales ($)	1730179M	3154018M
2802M	35255M	242367M	528677M	231706M	1258110M	Total Assets ($)	1413658M	1335371M

M = $ thousand   MM = $ million

See Pages 1 through 15 for Explanation of Ratios and Data

Comparative Historical Data   **Current Data Sorted By Sales**

Hist	Hist	Hist		0-1MM	1-3MM	3-5MM	5-10MM	10-25MM	25MM & OVER
4	7	12	# Postretirement Benefits			1	1	3	7
			Type of Statement						
24	25	31	Unqualified		1	3	6	12	9
38	38	34	Reviewed	1	7	13	7	5	1
17	18	20	Compiled	4	9	2	3	1	1
1	4	1	Tax Returns		1				
29	27	35	Other	6	2	3	6	7	11
4/1/92-3/31/93 ALL	4/1/93-3/31/94 ALL	4/1/94-3/31/95 ALL		46 (4/1-9/30/94)			75 (10/1/94-3/31/95)		
109	112	121	**NUMBER OF STATEMENTS**	11	20	21	22	25	22
%	%	%	**ASSETS**	%	%	%	%	%	%
6.5	8.4	6.3	Cash & Equivalents	5.6	4.6	9.5	6.9	4.9	6.1
21.2	23.5	22.3	Trade Receivables - (net)	24.2	25.0	22.3	21.5	22.1	20.1
31.0	28.4	32.5	Inventory	26.5	30.2	35.5	41.0	35.9	22.4
2.2	2.3	2.5	All Other Current	.3	2.6	1.0	1.0	2.1	6.8
60.9	62.6	63.6	Total Current	56.5	62.4	68.3	70.4	65.0	55.3
30.5	28.4	26.4	Fixed Assets (net)	35.1	30.8	26.7	19.7	25.7	25.1
2.6	2.4	3.3	Intangibles (net)	2.7	1.5	1.2	1.2	3.1	9.3
6.0	6.7	6.8	All Other Non-Current	5.7	5.4	3.7	8.7	6.2	10.2
100.0	100.0	100.0	Total	100.0	100.0	100.0	100.0	100.0	100.0
			LIABILITIES						
9.8	8.9	7.8	Notes Payable-Short Term	8.0	6.9	6.7	11.4	7.7	6.3
4.5	4.0	4.7	Cur. Mat.-L /T/D	2.3	5.4	7.3	3.6	3.4	5.4
10.6	10.2	11.2	Trade Payables	7.7	14.0	9.1	11.8	12.9	9.7
.4	.7	.3	Income Taxes Payable	.1	.2	.6	.3	.2	.3
7.6	8.5	9.0	All Other Current	5.1	6.2	7.5	11.7	10.8	10.3
32.9	32.3	33.0	Total Current	23.2	32.6	31.2	38.7	35.0	31.9
18.4	16.6	18.1	Long Term Debt	31.9	20.5	16.0	9.0	13.3	25.6
1.1	.7	.9	Deferred Taxes	.2	.7	.5	.5	1.3	1.6
3.0	4.1	3.6	All Other-Non-Current	5.3	2.0	4.6	2.7	3.9	3.7
44.5	46.4	44.4	Net Worth	39.3	44.2	47.7	49.2	46.4	37.1
100.0	100.0	100.0	Total Liabilities & Net Worth	100.0	100.0	100.0	100.0	100.0	100.0
			INCOME DATA						
100.0	100.0	100.0	Net Sales	100.0	100.0	100.0	100.0	100.0	100.0
28.8	31.3	30.0	Gross Profit	34.5	33.4	33.7	27.0	25.7	28.8
23.5	26.6	24.1	Operating Expenses	28.8	29.8	26.8	20.7	19.6	22.5
5.3	4.7	5.9	Operating Profit	5.7	3.6	6.9	6.3	6.1	6.3
2.0	1.5	2.0	All Other Expenses (net)	1.7	1.5	1.8	1.3	1.9	3.6
3.3	3.2	3.9	Profit Before Taxes	4.0	2.1	5.1	5.1	4.2	2.7
			RATIOS						
2.8 / 2.0 / 1.4	3.0 / 2.1 / 1.5	2.9 / 2.0 / 1.4	Current	3.8 / 2.1 / 1.7	3.3 / 2.3 / 1.5	3.7 / 2.1 / 1.5	2.3 / 1.9 / 1.4	2.9 / 2.1 / 1.3	2.6 / 2.0 / 1.2
1.5 / .8 / .5	1.5 / 1.0 / .6	1.6 / .9 / .5	Quick	2.8 / 1.0 / .5	1.9 / .9 / .7	2.1 / 1.0 / .6	1.1 / .9 / .4	1.6 / .7 / .5	1.2 / .9 / .5
29 12.7 / 46 8.0 / 58 6.3	34 10.7 / 45 8.1 / 65 5.6	37 9.9 / 49 7.4 / 64 5.7	Sales/Receivables	18 20.6 / 34 10.7 / 68 5.4	34 10.6 / 45 8.2 / 58 6.3	37 10.0 / 49 7.4 / 69 5.3	40 9.2 / 47 7.7 / 83 4.4	37 10.0 / 49 7.4 / 58 6.3	41 8.8 / 59 6.2 / 69 5.3
49 7.5 / 94 3.9 / 146 2.5	46 7.9 / 91 4.0 / 146 2.5	61 6.0 / 99 3.7 / 166 2.2	Cost of Sales/Inventory	24 14.9 / 79 4.6 / 174 2.1	46 8.0 / 65 5.6 / 159 2.3	96 3.8 / 111 3.3 / 192 1.9	72 5.1 / 135 2.7 / 192 1.9	64 5.7 / 94 3.9 / 174 2.1	40 9.1 / 94 3.9 / 130 2.8
14 26.1 / 26 14.3 / 42 8.6	16 23.4 / 27 13.5 / 44 8.3	16 23.0 / 34 10.8 / 52 7.0	Cost of Sales/Payables	8 43.2 / 12 29.8 / 46 8.0	24 15.4 / 31 11.7 / 47 7.7	16 22.9 / 30 12.2 / 47 7.7	14 27.0 / 38 9.5 / 62 5.9	17 21.0 / 36 10.1 / 53 6.9	26 13.9 / 39 9.4 / 52 7.0
3.6 / 5.9 / 11.5	3.6 / 5.4 / 10.8	3.4 / 5.5 / 9.5	Sales/Working Capital	2.3 / 7.5 / 26.3	3.5 / 6.3 / 11.3	3.1 / 5.0 / 8.5	3.1 / 5.5 / 9.0	3.6 / 5.1 / 10.0	2.8 / 4.8 / 21.5
(104) 7.0 / 2.2 / .9	(100) 6.2 / 2.3 / 1.1	(108) 7.3 / 3.0 / 1.1	EBIT/Interest		(17) 6.5 / 3.1 / 1.0	(19) 9.3 / 2.9 / .8	14.7 / 2.2 / 1.4	(23) 10.8 / 3.1 / 1.2	(19) 5.8 / 2.3 / .2
(56) 3.6 / 1.7 / .7	(56) 5.4 / 2.0 / 1.0	(54) 4.1 / 1.8 / .6	Net Profit + Depr., Dep., Amort./Cur. Mat. L/T/D		(10) 1.6 / 1.1 / -1.8	(10) 7.8 / 3.5 / 1.0	(10) 5.1 / 1.7 / .4	(11) 29.0 / 3.8 / 2.5	(11) 1.4 / .7 / .4
.3 / .6 / 1.3	.3 / .7 / 1.2	.3 / .6 / 1.5	Fixed/Worth	.6 / 1.8 / 3.6	.3 / .6 / 1.9	.3 / .4 / 1.5	.2 / .4 / .6	.2 / .7 / 1.0	.2 / 1.0 / 5.4
.6 / 1.3 / 3.4	.6 / 1.3 / 3.0	.6 / 1.2 / 3.8	Debt/Worth	.6 / 1.5 / 8.6	.5 / 1.3 / 2.9	.6 / 1.1 / 2.2	.7 / 1.1 / 2.1	.5 / .7 / 4.8	1.2 / 2.2 / 13.5
(104) 32.2 / 15.8 / 1.6	(107) 27.2 / 9.6 / 1.9	(117) 36.4 / 12.4 / .4	% Profit Before Taxes/Tangible Net Worth	108.3 / 9.2 / .6	(19) 30.7 / 9.0 / -16.6	43.7 / 18.5 / -.9	(23) 20.5 / 10.6 / 2.2	26.2 / 16.3 / 1.8	(21) 47.4 / 20.9 / -8.8
13.7 / 5.2 / -.1	9.5 / 4.0 / .3	13.7 / 4.5 / .1	% Profit Before Taxes/Total Assets	17.0 / 4.7 / .3	14.0 / 6.7 / -.2	17.0 / 6.2 / -.4	14.7 / 3.5 / 1.2	16.3 / 7.5 / .4	9.2 / 3.7 / -3.1
10.7 / 5.6 / 3.5	13.8 / 6.0 / 3.0	16.9 / 6.5 / 3.2	Sales/Net Fixed Assets	23.4 / 6.3 / 1.8	19.1 / 5.3 / 2.7	12.2 / 6.7 / 4.3	20.1 / 8.8 / 5.0	26.9 / 6.4 / 3.4	12.4 / 4.4 / 3.1
2.2 / 1.6 / 1.1	2.3 / 1.6 / 1.1	2.0 / 1.5 / 1.1	Sales/Total Assets	2.1 / 1.6 / 1.0	2.8 / 1.6 / 1.2	2.1 / 1.5 / 1.0	2.0 / 1.6 / 1.0	2.0 / 1.6 / 1.3	1.6 / 1.2 / .8
(97) 1.8 / 3.2 / 5.2	(98) 1.8 / 3.3 / 5.5	(102) 1.8 / 2.9 / 4.7	% Depr., Dep., Amort./Sales		(19) 1.1 / 3.2 / 4.5	(20) 1.5 / 2.7 / 5.1	(19) 1.4 / 2.1 / 3.1	(21) 1.6 / 2.4 / 5.2	(14) 2.8 / 4.4 / 5.5
(38) 3.2 / 5.1 / 10.2	(36) 3.5 / 5.5 / 8.9	(25) 3.4 / 6.3 / 9.7	% Officers', Directors', Owners' Comp/Sales						
1847337M	1707088M	2676293M	Net Sales ($)	7416M	40281M	81268M	160798M	386130M	2000400M
1482478M	1470508M	2298917M	Total Assets ($)	5000M	28017M	61442M	130344M	261616M	1812498M

M = $ thousand   MM = $ million
See Pages 1 through 15 for Explanation of Ratios and Data

Current Data Sorted By Assets | Comparative Historical Data

0-500M	500M-2MM	2-10MM	10-50MM	50-100MM	100-250MM	# Postretirement Benefits / Type of Statement	4/1/90-3/31/91 ALL	4/1/91-3/31/92 ALL
1		4	14	6	4	Unqualified	27	16
	3	2			1	Reviewed	13	7
1	5	3				Compiled	5	8
	1					Tax Returns	1	
2	5	1	4	1	1	Other	13	8
	19 (4/1-9/30/94)		40 (10/1/94-3/31/95)					
4	14	10	18	7	6	**NUMBER OF STATEMENTS**	59	39
%	%	%	%	%	%	**ASSETS**	%	%
	6.0	8.3	10.3			Cash & Equivalents	12.6	12.2
	28.2	16.8	19.7			Trade Receivables - (net)	23.0	19.4
	47.0	33.9	29.8			Inventory	28.4	32.8
	1.8	2.1	2.6			All Other Current	2.2	2.8
	83.0	61.0	62.3			Total Current	66.3	67.2
	11.8	33.2	19.0			Fixed Assets (net)	25.3	21.5
	2.7	.5	7.0			Intangibles (net)	1.0	1.7
	2.4	5.3	11.6			All Other Non-Current	7.5	9.6
	100.0	100.0	100.0			Total	100.0	100.0
						LIABILITIES		
	13.3	13.1	6.2			Notes Payable-Short Term	9.6	12.9
	1.8	1.9	2.7			Cur. Mat. -L/T/D	2.2	2.8
	20.0	11.7	16.2			Trade Payables	15.1	13.7
	.3	.0	1.2			Income Taxes Payable	.6	.6
	12.8	13.2	18.9			All Other Current	15.2	12.1
	48.1	40.0	45.1			Total Current	42.6	42.2
	9.1	15.0	9.4			Long Term Debt	12.5	11.5
	.0	.4	1.0			Deferred Taxes	.6	.4
	1.9	.0	6.4			All Other-Non-Current	1.6	2.0
	40.9	44.7	38.1			Net Worth	42.7	44.0
	100.0	100.0	100.0			Total Liabilities & Net Worth	100.0	100.0
						INCOME DATA		
	100.0	100.0	100.0			Net Sales	100.0	100.0
	22.9	16.5	18.5			Gross Profit	15.9	18.7
	21.0	15.8	12.6			Operating Expenses	14.0	17.7
	1.9	.7	5.9			Operating Profit	1.9	1.0
	.5	-.1	-.6			All Other Expenses (net)	.4	.1
	1.4	.8	6.5			Profit Before Taxes	1.5	.9
						RATIOS		
	2.5	1.9	2.3			Current	2.0	2.4
	1.8	1.4	1.4				1.6	1.6
	1.4	1.2	1.0				1.2	1.2
	1.1	.9	1.2			Quick	1.2	1.1
	.6	.6	.7				.8	.8
	.4	.4	.6				.5	.4
	14 26.1	11 33.0	17 21.7			Sales/Receivables	15 24.6	8 47.0
	19 19.4	19 19.6	20 18.4				25 14.7	20 18.5
	54 6.7	29 12.6	26 14.0				47 7.8	38 9.7
	33 11.0	18 20.7	17 22.0			Cost of Sales/Inventory	24 15.2	18 20.3
	74 4.9	40 9.2	37 9.8				32 11.5	28 13.0
	183 2.0	87 4.2	63 5.8				58 6.3	89 4.1
	8 47.0	9 40.6	15 24.4			Cost of Sales/Payables	10 35.3	11 32.5
	22 16.4	14 25.7	22 16.9				17 21.4	18 20.1
	43 8.4	21 17.0	28 13.2				29 12.4	27 13.7
	5.6	8.8	8.0			Sales/Working Capital	7.6	6.4
	10.3	23.8	17.2				16.8	12.8
	23.3	34.6	-792.6				45.6	42.6
	22.3		58.6			EBIT/Interest	6.1	8.4
	(12) 3.1		(17) 20.5				(51) 3.1	(34) 2.5
	1.6		8.1				1.2	.4
						Net Profit + Depr., Dep., Amort./Cur. Mat. L /T/D	7.1	5.0
							(32) 3.3	(15) 2.3
							.5	1.4
	.1	.4	.3			Fixed/Worth	.2	.1
	.2	.7	.5				.5	.5
	.7	1.3	1.0				1.2	1.0
	.8	.7	.7			Debt/Worth	.8	.6
	1.8	1.3	1.7				1.3	1.3
	3.0	2.8	5.4				2.3	2.4
	53.6	42.8	66.2			% Profit Before Taxes/Tangible Net Worth	33.7	38.0
	(12) 13.9	25.4	(15) 38.8				(56) 13.4	(37) 11.4
	7.0	-4.2	14.8				3.1	-.3
	17.4	19.8	24.9			% Profit Before Taxes/Total Assets	13.6	15.2
	5.2	7.2	18.8				5.3	2.6
	2.0	-2.9	7.3				1.2	-1.3
	65.5	20.4	26.2			Sales/Net Fixed Assets	33.0	46.7
	30.5	11.8	15.4				15.7	16.9
	12.2	5.9	11.7				7.8	7.7
	4.8	4.7	4.5			Sales/Total Assets	4.5	4.1
	3.8	4.2	3.6				3.2	3.2
	1.4	1.3	2.1				2.2	2.0
	.3		.4			% Depr., Dep., Amort./Sales	.6	.6
	(12) .7		(16) .6				(53) .9	(34) .9
	1.3		1.3				1.2	1.6
						% Officers', Directors', Owners' Comp/Sales	1.1	.8
							(19) 1.7	(10) 2.6
							3.2	4.5
3530M	59854M	159007M	1332758M	1609566M	2460773M	Net Sales ($)	2968111M	1126558M
521M	16906M	40776M	434014M	495297M	941018M	Total Assets ($)	1284240M	409599M

M = $ thousand   MM = $ million
See Pages 1 through 15 for Explanation of Ratios and Data

Comparative Historical Data				Current Data Sorted By Sales					
		2	# Postretirement Benefits					1	1
			Type of Statement						
21	26	29	Unqualified	1	1		1	1	25
10	6	6	Reviewed				3	2	1
9	9	9	Compiled		4		3	2	
		1	Tax Returns			1			
15	11	14	Other	3	3	1	1	2	4
4/1/92-	4/1/93-	4/1/94-		19 (4/1-9/30/94)			40 (10/1/94-3/31/95)		
3/31/93	3/31/94	3/31/95							
ALL	ALL	ALL		0-1MM	1-3MM	3-5MM	5-10MM	10-25MM	25MM & OVER
55	53	59	NUMBER OF STATEMENTS	4	8	2	8	7	30
%	%	%	ASSETS	%	%	%	%	%	%
13.1	15.1	8.8	Cash & Equivalents						10.9
20.2	20.0	20.3	Trade Receivables - (net)						19.4
31.3	31.5	34.9	Inventory						26.2
1.7	2.4	2.6	All Other Current						2.8
66.3	68.9	66.6	Total Current						59.4
25.6	21.5	21.7	Fixed Assets (net)						26.4
1.2	2.3	3.8	Intangibles (net)						5.9
6.9	7.3	7.9	All Other Non-Current						8.3
100.0	100.0	100.0	Total						100.0
			LIABILITIES						
9.0	6.8	8.7	Notes Payable-Short Term						4.5
3.2	1.8	1.9	Cur. Mat.-L /T/D						2.0
19.8	15.6	16.9	Trade Payables						17.0
.6	1.5	.6	Income Taxes Payable						.9
13.6	14.3	15.9	All Other Current						19.2
46.2	40.0	43.9	Total Current						43.5
11.4	8.6	11.0	Long Term Debt						7.8
.4	.6	1.0	Deferred Taxes						1.6
1.4	1.4	3.0	All Other-Non-Current						4.8
40.6	49.3	41.1	Net Worth						42.4
100.0	100.0	100.0	Total Liabilities & Net Worth						100.0
			INCOME DATA						
100.0	100.0	100.0	Net Sales						100.0
16.5	18.4	18.4	Gross Profit						16.7
14.8	14.1	15.1	Operating Expenses						11.7
1.7	4.3	3.3	Operating Profit						4.9
1.0	.2	.0	All Other Expenses (net)						.0
.7	4.1	3.2	Profit Before Taxes						4.9
			RATIOS						
2.2	2.4	2.2							2.2
1.5	1.7	1.5	Current						1.4
1.2	1.2	1.1							1.0
1.0	1.6	1.0							1.2
.7	.8	.7	Quick						.7
.5	.6	.5							.5
11 33.3	12 31.7	14 26.2							15 24.4
18 20.7	19 19.6	19 18.9	Sales/Receivables						19 18.9
27 13.7	25 14.7	26 13.0							26 13.9
21 17.1	18 20.5	22 16.7							17 22.0
31 11.8	31 11.8	41 8.9	Cost of Sales/Inventory						27 13.4
49 7.5	64 5.7	76 4.8							49 7.5
10 34.9	8 43.7	13 28.6							14 26.3
22 16.4	17 21.1	21 17.8	Cost of Sales/Payables						20 18.0
32 11.3	25 14.4	32 11.5							27 13.6
8.9	8.8	8.5							10.9
18.4	11.2	16.5	Sales/Working Capital						26.6
63.1	29.3	34.6							373.0
	44.0	29.3							43.3
(47) 12.3 3.9	(44) 10.8	(53) 10.0	EBIT/Interest					(28) 22.3	
1.8	3.8	2.4							15.1
7.3	6.8	8.9							9.0
(19) 2.3	(15) 2.9	(23) 4.3	Net Profit + Depr., Dep., Amort./Cur. Mat. L/T/D					(15) 5.5	
.5	1.5	2.4							2.5
.3	.2	.2							.4
.6	.4	.5	Fixed/Worth						.7
1.2	.9	1.0							1.1
.6	.5	.8							.8
1.5	1.3	1.4	Debt/Worth						1.4
2.4	2.1	2.9							2.9
52.6	40.8	52.2							55.3
(50) 20.3	(51) 27.4	(53) 30.2	% Profit Before Taxes/Tangible Net Worth					(27) 39.4	
8.5	13.8	7.7							25.2
16.7	18.8	19.3							20.1
7.4	12.5	12.0	% Profit Before Taxes/Total Assets						17.8
2.8	6.5	3.8							11.4
29.0	43.9	30.8							20.6
17.5	21.4	15.6	Sales/Net Fixed Assets						15.3
8.3	12.4	10.4							11.7
5.5	5.3	4.5							4.5
3.4	3.7	3.6	Sales/Total Assets						3.6
2.2	2.8	2.0							2.2
.5	.5	.5							.6
(47) .7	(46) .6	(53) .8	% Depr., Dep., Amort./Sales					(29) .8	
1.5	1.2	1.3							1.1
1.6	1.1	2.0							
(11) 2.3	(15) 3.2	(12) 4.5	% Officers', Directors', Owners' Comp/Sales						
4.5	6.7	6.0							
2051657M	4204505M	5625488M	Net Sales ($)	2480M	15675M	7733M	53270M	119312M	5427018M
647001M	1331379M	1928532M	Total Assets ($)	2049M	8918M	1742M	55751M	32838M	1827234M

M = $ thousand   MM = $ million
See Pages 1 through 15 for Explanation of Ratios and Data

Current Data Sorted By Assets							Comparative Historical Data	
4	6	6	5	3	5	# Postretirement Benefits		
						Type of Statement		
2	6	24	34	14	11	Unqualified	72	94
1	16	35	5	1	1	Reviewed	47	56
8	30	15	4			Compiled	46	47
5	1					Tax Returns		3
4	25	25	24	10	10	Other	47	56
	103 (4/1-9/30/94)			208 (10/1/94-3/31/95)			4/1/90-3/31/91 ALL	4/1/91-3/31/92 ALL
0-500M	500M-2MM	2-10MM	10-50MM	50-100MM	100-250MM			
20	78	99	67	25	22	**NUMBER OF STATEMENTS**	212	256
%	%	%	%	%	%	**ASSETS**	%	%
10.2	6.4	5.4	5.6	5.5	4.2	Cash & Equivalents	5.1	5.5
14.3	25.3	28.1	27.3	23.1	26.0	Trade Receivables - (net)	25.9	24.2
37.3	33.6	32.5	26.7	20.2	20.9	Inventory	30.7	29.6
2.2	1.7	1.8	2.4	2.9	2.9	All Other Current	1.5	1.8
64.0	67.1	67.9	62.0	51.8	53.9	Total Current	63.3	61.2
27.2	22.9	26.3	30.6	36.3	33.3	Fixed Assets (net)	28.1	29.1
1.3	3.7	1.1	3.1	4.3	6.4	Intangibles (net)	2.2	3.2
7.4	6.3	4.7	4.3	7.6	6.3	All Other Non-Current	6.3	6.5
100.0	100.0	100.0	100.0	100.0	100.0	Total	100.0	100.0
						LIABILITIES		
11.4	10.4	12.8	9.2	6.0	3.2	Notes Payable-Short Term	12.4	10.6
3.2	3.0	3.7	3.8	1.9	2.0	Cur. Mat. -L/T/D	3.8	4.4
16.4	19.0	18.1	14.9	12.4	12.3	Trade Payables	15.9	15.1
2.9	.5	.8	.8	.5	.9	Income Taxes Payable	.5	.4
10.9	7.5	10.2	6.8	12.9	9.0	All Other Current	7.9	7.7
44.8	40.4	45.6	35.4	33.7	27.4	Total Current	40.5	38.2
19.3	13.0	14.1	15.6	16.7	17.8	Long Term Debt	15.9	17.2
.2	.3	.7	1.0	1.3	1.3	Deferred Taxes	.7	.6
2.9	7.3	3.1	6.8	5.4	6.6	All Other-Non-Current	3.4	3.9
32.7	39.0	36.4	41.3	42.8	47.0	Net Worth	39.5	40.1
100.0	100.0	100.0	100.0	100.0	100.0	Total Liabilities & Net Worth	100.0	100.0
						INCOME DATA		
100.0	100.0	100.0	100.0	100.0	100.0	Net Sales	100.0	100.0
43.6	32.6	26.1	25.1	23.5	23.5	Gross Profit	27.9	27.1
38.9	28.0	20.7	16.8	15.4	15.5	Operating Expenses	22.7	23.2
4.7	4.5	5.4	8.3	8.0	8.0	Operating Profit	5.2	4.0
1.0	.9	1.0	1.2	1.0	1.2	All Other Expenses (net)	1.6	2.0
3.7	3.6	4.4	7.1	7.0	6.8	Profit Before Taxes	3.6	2.0
						RATIOS		
2.6	2.5	2.0	2.5	2.2	2.8		2.6	2.4
1.6	1.8	1.5	1.9	1.6	2.0	Current	1.5	1.7
1.0	1.2	1.2	1.3	1.2	1.6		1.1	1.2
(19) 1.2	1.1	1.0	1.3	1.3	1.6		1.3	1.3
.8	.8	.7	.9	.9	1.1	Quick	(211) .7	.8
.2	.5	.5	.7	.6	.9		.5	.5
5 80.9	26 13.9	30 12.1	45 8.2	38 9.6	49 7.4		32 11.3	34 10.6
13 29.2	38 9.6	43 8.5	56 6.5	52 7.0	59 6.2	Sales/Receivables	43 8.4	46 7.9
32 11.5	51 7.2	56 6.5	68 5.4	62 5.9	63 5.8		54 6.8	55 6.6
23 16.1	41 9.0	34 10.6	50 7.3	29 12.6	42 8.7		41 8.8	45 8.1
76 4.8	64 5.7	65 5.6	74 4.9	51 7.2	59 6.2	Cost of Sales/Inventory	69 5.3	74 4.9
183 2.0	126 2.9	104 3.5	101 3.6	78 4.7	79 4.6		107 3.4	107 3.4
14 25.3	24 14.9	22 16.6	23 16.1	19 19.6	24 15.1		21 17.8	22 16.4
30 12.1	38 9.6	35 10.5	35 10.5	33 11.1	29 12.5	Cost of Sales/Payables	34 10.8	33 11.1
57 6.4	60 6.1	50 7.3	51 7.2	54 6.8	38 9.7		46 7.9	51 7.1
5.2	5.3	6.0	4.5	5.9	4.4		5.2	5.0
18.1	9.2	11.8	6.7	9.4	5.9	Sales/Working Capital	10.1	9.4
NM	37.7	26.1	12.9	34.6	12.3		35.5	26.3
(17) 8.8	(73) 10.5	(92) 16.6	(58) 11.7	(24) 7.7	(20) 12.5		(192) 4.8	(240) 5.2
3.3	3.8	5.1	7.1	4.8	6.9	EBIT/Interest	2.2	2.1
1.5	1.4	2.4	2.3	3.7	2.1		1.1	1.0
	(26) 10.8	(52) 7.7	(36) 10.4	(15) 28.8	(11) 8.7		(126) 5.3	(137) 3.5
	2.9	3.5	4.1	5.7	3.7	Net Profit + Depr., Dep., Amort./Cur. Mat. L /T/D	2.4	1.7
	1.1	1.9	1.7	3.5	.4		1.0	.7
.2	.3	.4	.4	.6	.5		.4	.3
.5	.5	.7	.7	1.1	.8	Fixed/Worth	.7	.8
2.5	1.3	1.4	1.5	2.1	2.2		1.6	1.6
.8	.8	1.0	.7	.6	.4		.8	.8
1.7	1.5	1.9	1.5	1.4	1.4	Debt/Worth	1.8	1.6
15.2	4.7	3.3	3.3	3.9	4.6		3.6	3.6
(16) 58.9	(72) 45.9	(91) 51.9	(63) 50.4	(24) 52.4	(21) 45.6	% Profit Before Taxes/Tangible Net Worth	(199) 35.2	(235) 29.1
31.7	22.8	29.4	29.6	26.1	24.5		14.7	12.1
5.3	6.4	15.8	12.8	10.2	21.1		4.0	1.5
22.8	15.5	21.7	19.2	15.9	17.7	% Profit Before Taxes/Total Assets	12.1	10.2
12.8	6.3	11.3	10.6	9.3	10.8		5.3	4.3
.1	2.2	4.2	4.2	4.9	3.8		.6	-.2
36.8	30.5	18.1	11.2	7.1	6.9		18.4	16.5
22.1	15.9	10.5	6.0	4.8	5.5	Sales/Net Fixed Assets	7.9	7.4
11.7	5.6	6.1	3.8	3.3	4.7		4.4	3.7
6.0	3.1	2.9	2.1	1.9	2.0		2.8	2.6
2.7	2.4	2.4	1.8	1.6	1.7	Sales/Total Assets	2.1	1.9
2.1	1.7	1.9	1.4	1.3	1.6		1.6	1.4
(17) .9	(71) .9	(93) 1.1	(60) 1.2	(21) 2.6	(13) 2.0	% Depr., Dep., Amort./Sales	(188) 1.2	(234) 1.2
1.8	1.9	1.8	2.4	3.2	2.7		2.0	2.3
3.0	3.5	3.0	3.6	4.3	3.4		3.9	4.1
(11) 4.9	(34) 2.8	(41) 1.6	(11) 1.3			% Officers', Directors', Owners' Comp/Sales	(78) 2.3	(85) 2.4
7.9	5.1	3.7	2.1				4.4	4.6
12.5	7.9	5.1	6.9				8.9	6.8
16146M	214937M	1240073M	2806986M	9436463M	6305898M	Net Sales ($)	5445838M	7084826M
5017M	86115M	500613M	1635768M	1718904M	3594107M	Total Assets ($)	3386027M	4565330M

© Robert Morris Associates 1995

M = $ thousand   MM = $ million

See Pages 1 through 15 for Explanation of Ratios and Data

Comparative Historical Data				Current Data Sorted By Sales					
11	25	29	# Postretirement Benefits	3	6	1	2	5	12
			Type of Statement						
93	93	91	Unqualified	2	3	4	7	23	52
52	66	59	Reviewed	1	6	11	18	15	8
43	56	57	Compiled	10	22	3	12	7	3
3	1	6	Tax Returns	4	2				
59	89	98	Other	8	13	11	8	20	38
4/1/92-3/31/93	4/1/93-3/31/94	4/1/94-3/31/95		103 (4/1-9/30/94)			208 (10/1/94-3/31/95)		
ALL	ALL	ALL		0-1MM	1-3MM	3-5MM	5-10MM	10-25MM	25MM & OVER
250	305	311	**NUMBER OF STATEMENTS**	25	46	29	45	65	101
%	%	%	**ASSETS**	%	%	%	%	%	%
5.9	6.1	5.9	Cash & Equivalents	7.3	6.9	8.4	6.4	4.6	5.2
24.9	25.6	25.8	Trade Receivables - (net)	17.1	23.6	25.2	28.1	27.6	26.9
28.8	28.3	30.0	Inventory	30.5	35.3	34.0	31.3	30.4	25.5
2.5	1.9	2.1	All Other Current	3.6	1.6	3.0	1.3	1.3	2.6
62.0	61.9	63.9	Total Current	58.6	67.3	70.6	67.1	64.0	60.2
29.1	29.5	27.8	Fixed Assets (net)	33.3	21.5	22.5	26.4	29.4	30.3
2.9	2.8	2.8	Intangibles (net)	3.3	4.9	1.0	.5	1.8	4.0
5.9	5.8	5.5	All Other Non-Current	4.8	6.3	5.9	6.0	4.8	5.6
100.0	100.0	100.0	Total	100.0	100.0	100.0	100.0	100.0	100.0
			LIABILITIES						
10.2	9.8	10.1	Notes Payable-Short Term	15.0	7.7	9.9	12.2	11.9	7.9
5.0	3.4	3.2	Cur. Mat.-L /T/D	3.7	2.5	3.5	3.7	3.9	2.8
16.1	15.5	16.7	Trade Payables	11.9	18.4	18.8	20.4	17.4	14.3
.5	1.2	.9	Income Taxes Payable	2.3	.5	.3	.8	1.0	.8
8.1	8.8	9.0	All Other Current	9.4	8.4	9.5	9.5	8.8	9.1
39.9	38.6	39.8	Total Current	42.3	37.5	42.1	46.1	42.9	34.8
17.5	14.7	14.9	Long Term Debt	23.6	12.3	12.4	15.4	14.1	15.1
.8	.8	.7	Deferred Taxes	.2	.4	.8	.3	.7	1.1
3.4	4.1	5.4	All Other-Non-Current	8.5	6.2	5.1	3.9	4.9	5.2
38.3	41.7	39.1	Net Worth	25.3	43.5	39.6	34.3	37.4	43.8
100.0	100.0	100.0	Total Liabilities & Net Worth	100.0	100.0	100.0	100.0	100.0	100.0
			INCOME DATA						
100.0	100.0	100.0	Net Sales	100.0	100.0	100.0	100.0	100.0	100.0
27.4	28.3	28.2	Gross Profit	40.7	36.7	26.7	26.0	26.1	24.0
22.5	22.4	22.1	Operating Expenses	36.1	31.8	25.3	20.0	19.6	15.7
4.9	5.8	6.2	Operating Profit	4.6	4.8	1.4	6.1	6.5	8.3
1.5	1.3	1.0	All Other Expenses (net)	1.3	.8	.6	1.0	1.3	1.0
3.4	4.5	5.1	Profit Before Taxes	3.3	4.0	.8	5.1	5.3	7.2
			RATIOS						
2.5	2.5	2.4		2.5	2.7	2.6	2.2	2.0	2.5
1.6	1.6	1.7	Current	1.6	1.9	1.6	1.6	1.5	1.8
1.2	1.1	1.2		.9	1.3	1.2	1.2	1.2	1.3
1.3	1.3	1.2		1.2	1.1	1.3	1.3	1.1	1.3
.8 (304)	.8 (310)	.8	Quick (24)	.8	.8	.7	.8	.7	1.0
.5	.6	.6		.3	.5	.5	.5	.5	.7
35 10.3	33 11.1	31 11.6		11 33.3	24 15.3	26 14.2	28 12.9	34 10.6	43 8.4
47 7.8	47 7.7	46 7.9	Sales/Receivables	31 11.6	36 10.1	41 9.0	42 8.6	46 8.0	54 6.7
61 6.0	57 6.4	60 6.1		76 4.8	50 7.3	56 6.5	55 6.6	59 6.2	63 5.8
44 8.3	40 9.2	39 9.4		36 10.1	44 8.3	46 7.9	23 15.7	38 9.7	39 9.3
65 5.6	62 5.9	66 5.5	Cost of Sales/Inventory	79 4.6	91 4.0	74 4.9	54 6.7	69 5.3	59 6.2
101 3.6	101 3.6	104 3.5		192 1.9	130 2.8	126 2.9	96 3.8	101 3.6	87 4.2
23 16.0	20 18.3	23 15.8		13 29.2	24 15.1	31 11.6	19 19.1	23 15.8	20 18.2
35 10.4	31 11.7	35 10.5	Cost of Sales/Payables	37 9.8	38 9.7	42 8.7	33 11.2	37 9.9	31 11.7
51 7.2	47 7.8	53 6.9		85 4.3	59 6.2	60 6.1	54 6.7	49 7.4	45 8.2
5.1	5.4	5.3		3.6	4.6	5.3	5.8	5.9	4.6
9.2	9.6	9.1	Sales/Working Capital	13.3	8.9	6.6	10.2	11.8	7.3
24.2	27.1	23.6		−38.0	22.3	31.6	27.5	25.0	15.5
7.0	10.9	11.4		7.1	10.1	8.0	16.0	15.7	12.6
(232) 2.9	(279) 4.3	(284) 5.0	EBIT/Interest	(23) 3.0	(42) 3.7	(24) 3.2	(42) 4.5	(61) 5.3	(92) 7.4
1.5	1.9	2.3		1.4	1.8	1.1	2.1	2.3	3.4
3.7	7.8	8.7		10.1	15.1	6.6	7.4	6.0	19.0
(136) 2.0	(137) 3.3	(145) 3.8	Net Profit + Depr., Dep., Amort./Cur. Mat. L/T/D	(10) 2.8	(15) 2.4	(10) 2.6	(22) 3.2	(35) 3.3	(53) 4.4
1.2	1.4	1.8		1.1	1.0	1.4	1.1	1.8	2.8
.4	.4	.4		.2	.2	.2	.4	.4	.4
.8	.7	.7	Fixed/Worth	.9	.5	.4	.6	.8	.8
1.8	1.4	1.5		21.5	1.1	1.1	1.5	1.6	1.5
1.0	.8	.8		1.0	.8	.8	1.0	.9	.7
1.8	1.5	1.6	Debt/Worth	5.2	1.2	1.6	1.9	1.9	1.4
4.0	3.0	3.4		33.7	2.9	3.1	3.9	3.4	3.2
36.8	43.1	50.6		62.7	45.8	37.4	56.5	51.7	51.7
(229) 18.9	(289) 23.1	(287) 27.2	% Profit Before Taxes/Tangible Net Worth	(20) 25.6	(44) 20.3	(26) 21.9	(40) 27.7	(61) 31.6	(96) 29.5
6.0	10.5	12.0		4.6	5.1	3.3	10.2	15.9	15.9
12.3	16.4	18.7		17.8	14.8	14.0	22.3	21.4	20.1
6.2	8.7	9.8	% Profit Before Taxes/Total Assets	8.5	5.8	7.5	7.8	11.9	11.1
1.6	3.1	3.8		.3	2.5	.3	3.5	4.3	5.0
16.2	16.4	19.4		34.8	32.2	29.7	30.1	13.1	9.6
7.3	7.9	8.6	Sales/Net Fixed Assets	11.6	15.4	13.3	16.6	8.5	6.1
4.0	4.2	4.8		2.9	7.2	7.3	5.1	5.3	4.7
2.6	2.6	2.7		2.7	2.9	2.6	3.4	2.7	2.1
1.9	2.0	2.1	Sales/Total Assets	1.8	2.3	2.2	2.5	2.2	1.8
1.4	1.6	1.6		1.1	1.7	1.8	1.9	1.6	1.5
1.4	1.4	1.1		1.1	1.0	1.3	.8	1.3	1.3
(221) 2.4	(273) 2.3	(275) 2.1	% Depr., Dep., Amort./Sales	(22) 2.9	(41) 1.9	(25) 2.0	(43) 1.2	(63) 1.9	(81) 2.7
4.1	4.0	3.4		4.5	2.9	2.8	3.2	3.4	3.6
2.0	1.7	1.8		4.9	2.8	4.8	2.9	1.1	
(80) 4.2	(106) 4.0	(98) 4.3	% Officers', Directors', Owners' Comp/Sales	(10) 7.4	(24) 6.5	(11) 5.0	(19) 4.1	(25) 1.7	
7.2	7.1	7.5		11.5	11.3	7.5	7.3	4.0	
7831450M	11810560M	20020503M	Net Sales ($)	15820M	88460M	120499M	313431M	1090633M	18391660M
4785236M	6890166M	7540524M	Total Assets ($)	10480M	40572M	65053M	158714M	585467M	6680238M

M = $ thousand   MM = $ million
See Pages 1 through 15 for Explanation of Ratios and Data

Current Data Sorted By Assets							Comparative Historical Data	
		1	2		1	**# Postretirement Benefits**		
						Type of Statement		
		4	6	2		Unqualified	15	16
	2	4	1			Reviewed	6	6
	4					Compiled	5	6
		1				Tax Returns		
1	3	3	4	5	3	Other	5	7
	14 (4/1-9/30/94)		29 (10/1/94-3/31/95)				**4/1/90-3/31/91**	**4/1/91-3/31/92**
0-500M	**500M-2MM**	**2-10MM**	**10-50MM**	**50-100MM**	**100-250MM**		**ALL**	**ALL**
1	9	12	11	7	3	**NUMBER OF STATEMENTS**	31	35
%	%	%	%	%	%	**ASSETS**	%	%
		3.8	4.9			Cash & Equivalents	5.4	6.6
		27.4	29.2			Trade Receivables - (net)	20.7	20.5
		31.3	31.3			Inventory	36.0	40.4
		3.8	1.1			All Other Current	3.0	1.7
		66.3	66.5			Total Current	65.1	69.2
		21.0	23.6			Fixed Assets (net)	21.9	19.1
		1.3	4.1			Intangibles (net)	1.5	1.0
		11.4	5.8			All Other Non-Current	11.5	10.7
		100.0	100.0			Total	100.0	100.0
						LIABILITIES		
		22.0	14.8			Notes Payable-Short Term	21.1	20.1
		2.5	3.3			Cur. Mat. -L/T/D	3.4	2.7
		17.5	19.2			Trade Payables	14.5	15.9
		.2	.1			Income Taxes Payable	.6	.6
		13.9	8.4			All Other Current	13.7	13.9
		56.0	45.9			Total Current	53.2	53.2
		17.9	15.6			Long Term Debt	12.2	12.3
		1.0	.4			Deferred Taxes	.6	.6
		6.4	5.3			All Other-Non-Current	2.6	6.5
		18.7	32.8			Net Worth	31.4	27.5
		100.0	100.0			Total Liabilities & Net Worth	100.0	100.0
						INCOME DATA		
		100.0	100.0			Net Sales	100.0	100.0
		19.3	21.7			Gross Profit	20.0	15.6
		16.1	14.0			Operating Expenses	15.1	12.1
		3.2	7.7			Operating Profit	4.9	3.6
		1.0	1.3			All Other Expenses (net)	2.1	1.3
		2.2	6.4			Profit Before Taxes	2.8	2.2
						RATIOS		
		1.5	2.7				1.5	1.9
		1.2	1.3			Current	1.3	1.2
		1.0	.8				1.0	1.0
		.9	1.3				.8	.9
		.4	.8			Quick	.5	.6
		.3	.5				.3	.3
		11 33.9	**47** 7.8				**11** 34.1	**13** 28.0
		26 14.1	**49** 7.4			Sales/Receivables	**31** 11.9	**30** 12.0
		94 3.9	**68** 5.4				**57** 6.4	**52** 7.0
		27 13.7	**32** 11.3				**38** 9.5	**38** 9.7
		48 7.6	**54** 6.8			Cost of Sales/Inventory	**54** 6.7	**66** 5.5
		68 5.4	**130** 2.8				**94** 3.9	**114** 3.2
		10 37.7	**29** 12.7				**16** 23.1	**12** 30.9
		24 15.1	**41** 8.9			Cost of Sales/Payables	**25** 14.4	**30** 12.1
		60 6.1	**66** 5.5				**52** 7.0	**41** 9.0
		9.3	4.2				9.1	6.3
		24.4	16.6			Sales/Working Capital	18.6	26.1
		UND	-24.2				95.8	-355.7
		3.1	17.4				4.8	4.4
		(11) 2.2	7.0			EBIT/Interest	(28) 2.0	(29) 2.6
		1.4	3.2				1.0	1.0
							5.2	3.6
						Net Profit + Depr., Dep., Amort./Cur. Mat. L /T/D	(18) 2.6	(15) 1.3
							.6	.7
		.5	.3				.5	.2
		1.5	.5			Fixed/Worth	.8	.9
		2.2	3.0				1.4	2.0
		3.3	1.1				1.1	1.2
		3.9	2.7			Debt/Worth	2.5	3.7
		9.5	5.4				6.7	8.2
		46.7					28.6	44.3
		(11) 31.1				% Profit Before Taxes/Tangible Net Worth	13.8	(31) 11.6
		8.5					1.3	1.1
		6.0	20.9				9.5	10.4
		3.5	14.4			% Profit Before Taxes/Total Assets	3.5	5.2
		2.7	4.9				.4	-.7
		30.9	34.7				30.2	35.5
		12.5	9.5			Sales/Net Fixed Assets	11.4	16.4
		8.7	4.8				5.4	6.6
		4.0	2.4				3.2	3.3
		2.7	1.7			Sales/Total Assets	2.2	2.4
		1.7	1.3				1.2	1.3
		.6	.6				.8	.4
		(11) 1.2	1.3			% Depr., Dep., Amort./Sales	(24) 1.7	(31) .8
		1.4	3.5				4.4	1.8
								.9
						% Officers', Directors', Owners' Comp/Sales		(11) 1.5
								6.3
1800M	**39098M**	**191528M**	**659319M**	**1613501M**	**1107863M**	Net Sales ($)	**1079886M**	**1912620M**
410M	**10638M**	**68932M**	**348008M**	**468156M**	**563538M**	Total Assets ($)	**620355M**	**1092892M**

M = $ thousand MM = $ million

See Pages 1 through 15 for Explanation of Ratios and Data

Comparative Historical Data / Current Data Sorted By Sales

	2	1	4					1		3
# Postretirement Benefits										
Type of Statement										
Unqualified	20	12	12					2	2	8
Reviewed	7	5	7					4	2	1
Compiled	7	6	4			2	2			
Tax Returns	1	1	1						1	
Other	9	9	19		1	1	3			14
	4/1/92-3/31/93 ALL	4/1/93-3/31/94 ALL	4/1/94-3/31/95 ALL		14 (4/1-9/30/94)			29 (10/1/94-3/31/95)		
				0-1MM	1-3MM	3-5MM	5-10MM	10-25MM		25MM & OVER
NUMBER OF STATEMENTS	44	33	43	1	3	5	6	5		23
ASSETS	%	%	%	%	%	%	%	%		%
Cash & Equivalents	7.2	4.3	5.3							4.9
Trade Receivables - (net)	17.4	20.1	26.6							25.8
Inventory	31.9	37.2	34.8							34.3
All Other Current	3.6	2.8	2.0							2.0
Total Current	60.1	64.4	68.7							67.1
Fixed Assets (net)	25.1	22.2	21.3							22.4
Intangibles (net)	2.9	4.7	2.7							4.2
All Other Non-Current	11.9	8.7	7.3							6.2
Total	100.0	100.0	100.0							100.0
LIABILITIES										
Notes Payable-Short Term	16.0	16.2	16.9							18.4
Cur. Mat.-L/T/D	2.9	3.0	2.3							2.3
Trade Payables	15.0	16.7	20.4							21.1
Income Taxes Payable	.6	1.2	.3							.1
All Other Current	12.7	12.1	12.9							10.8
Total Current	47.2	49.1	52.8							52.8
Long Term Debt	17.9	16.2	15.2							13.4
Deferred Taxes	.7	.5	.6							.5
All Other-Non-Current	6.7	6.7	6.7							7.5
Net Worth	27.4	27.5	24.7							25.9
Total Liabilities & Net Worth	100.0	100.0	100.0							100.0
INCOME DATA										
Net Sales	100.0	100.0	100.0							100.0
Gross Profit	18.7	20.5	18.8							16.4
Operating Expenses	15.2	16.7	15.2							11.5
Operating Profit	3.4	3.8	3.5							4.9
All Other Expenses (net)	2.0	1.3	1.4							1.1
Profit Before Taxes	1.4	2.4	2.1							3.8
RATIOS										
Current	1.7 / 1.2 / .9	1.8 / 1.3 / 1.0	1.7 / 1.3 / 1.0							1.9 / 1.2 / .9
Quick	.8 / .5 / .3	.8 / .5 / .3	1.0 / .7 / .3							1.2 / .5 / .3
Sales/Receivables	10 35.5 / 30 12.0 / 46 7.9	13 28.3 / 25 14.7 / 45 8.2	17 21.4 / 33 10.9 / 53 6.9							19 18.8 / 46 7.9 / 58 6.3
Cost of Sales/Inventory	32 11.3 / 54 6.7 / 87 4.2	37 10.0 / 62 5.9 / 99 3.7	32 11.3 / 50 7.3 / 73 5.0							34 10.8 / 45 8.2 / 74 4.9
Cost of Sales/Payables	17 20.9 / 29 12.7 / 39 9.3	17 21.2 / 31 11.7 / 37 9.8	17 21.4 / 30 12.1 / 51 7.1							17 21.4 / 40 9.1 / 66 5.5
Sales/Working Capital	7.0 / 27.9 / -60.2	8.2 / 17.2 / -253.1	8.6 / 19.5 / UND							5.6 / 19.5 / -47.1
EBIT/Interest	3.7 / 2.0 / .7	(32) 4.9 / 2.5 / 1.1	(41) 7.4 / 3.1 / 1.3						(22)	14.4 / 4.1 / .9
Net Profit + Depr., Dep., Amort./Cur. Mat. L/T/D	(21) 3.8 / 1.9 / .6	(14) 6.8 / 1.6 / .8	(16) 6.4 / 1.7 / .8						(11)	13.6 / 2.1 / .9
Fixed/Worth	.6 / 1.3 / 4.2	.5 / 1.2 / 4.3	.3 / 1.3 / 2.3							.3 / 1.5 / 3.0
Debt/Worth	1.4 / 4.1 / 21.7	1.4 / 4.8 / 12.3	1.7 / 3.6 / 8.8							1.3 / 4.6 / 11.0
% Profit Before Taxes/Tangible Net Worth	(35) 44.7 / 14.9 / 3.9	(29) 62.5 / 23.2 / 5.8	(37) 60.4 / 30.2 / 9.9						(18)	70.0 / 32.9 / 15.6
% Profit Before Taxes/Total Assets	4.9 / 3.3 / -.8	12.0 / 4.7 / .5	14.5 / 4.9 / 1.8							17.3 / 10.1 / -.8
Sales/Net Fixed Assets	17.5 / 8.9 / 4.6	20.4 / 10.7 / 6.4	34.7 / 13.1 / 6.9							23.4 / 10.9 / 6.0
Sales/Total Assets	2.9 / 2.3 / 1.1	3.6 / 2.5 / 1.6	3.8 / 2.4 / 1.7							3.4 / 2.3 / 1.7
% Depr., Dep., Amort./Sales	(39) .8 / 2.1 / 4.3	(31) .9 / 1.6 / 2.3	(38) .6 / 1.2 / 2.2						(21)	.6 / 1.3 / 3.0
% Officers', Directors', Owners' Comp/Sales	(10) 1.3 / 2.2 / 5.3									
Net Sales ($)	2495640M	1301453M	3613109M	845M	7029M	20330M	47499M	90591M		3446815M
Total Assets ($)	1910460M	884626M	1459682M	895M	2698M	6030M	24112M	32633M		1393314M

M = $ thousand   MM = $ million
See Pages 1 through 15 for Explanation of Ratios and Data

Current Data Sorted By Assets

						# Postretirement Benefits		
	2	1			1	Type of Statement		
1		3	4	2	2	Unqualified		
	1	1				Reviewed		
	4	3		1		Compiled		
						Tax Returns		
	3		2	2	2	Other		

Comparative Historical Data

0-500M	4 (4/1-9/30/94) 500M-2MM	2-10MM	27 (10/1/94-3/31/95) 10-50MM	50-100MM	100-250MM		4/1/90- 3/31/91 ALL	4/1/91- 3/31/92 ALL
1	8	7	6	5	4	**NUMBER OF STATEMENTS**		
%	%	%	%	%	%	**ASSETS**	%	%
						Cash & Equivalents	D	D
						Trade Receivables - (net)	A	A
						Inventory	T	T
						All Other Current	A	A
						Total Current		
						Fixed Assets (net)	N	N
						Intangibles (net)	O	O
						All Other Non-Current	T	T
						Total		
						LIABILITIES	A	A
						Notes Payable-Short Term	V	V
						Cur. Mat. -L/T/D	A	A
						Trade Payables	I	I
						Income Taxes Payable	L	L
						All Other Current	A	A
						Total Current	B	B
						Long Term Debt	L	L
						Deferred Taxes	E	E
						All Other-Non-Current		
						Net Worth		
						Total Liabilities & Net Worth		
						INCOME DATA		
						Net Sales		
						Gross Profit		
						Operating Expenses		
						Operating Profit		
						All Other Expenses (net)		
						Profit Before Taxes		
						RATIOS		
						Current		
						Quick		
						Sales/Receivables		
						Cost of Sales/Inventory		
						Cost of Sales/Payables		
						Sales/Working Capital		
						EBIT/Interest		
						Net Profit + Depr., Dep., Amort./Cur. Mat. L /T/D		
						Fixed/Worth		
						Debt/Worth		
						% Profit Before Taxes/Tangible Net Worth		
						% Profit Before Taxes/Total Assets		
						Sales/Net Fixed Assets		
						Sales/Total Assets		
						% Depr., Dep., Amort./Sales		
						% Officers', Directors', Owners' Comp/Sales		
734M	24513M	57896M	137066M	576544M	1172727M	Net Sales ($)		
425M	10507M	30432M	99614M	379966M	589835M	Total Assets ($)		

M = $ thousand   MM = $ million
See Pages 1 through 15 for Explanation of Ratios and Data

Comparative Historical Data   Current Data Sorted By Sales

4/1/92-3/31/93 ALL	4/1/93-3/31/94 ALL	4/1/94-3/31/95 ALL		0-1MM	1-3MM	3-5MM	5-10MM	10-25MM	25MM & OVER
		4	# Postretirement Benefits			1	1	1	1
			Type of Statement						
		12	Unqualified	1		3	1	2	5
		2	Reviewed		1		1		
		8	Compiled	1	1	2	2	2	
			Tax Returns						
		9	Other			2	1	1	5
				4 (4/1-9/30/94)			27 (10/1/94-3/31/95)		
		31	**NUMBER OF STATEMENTS**	2	2	7	5	5	10
%	%	%	**ASSETS**	%	%	%	%	%	%
		7.2	Cash & Equivalents						3.0
		23.7	Trade Receivables - (net)						21.8
D	D	28.5	Inventory						28.5
A	A	3.2	All Other Current						5.8
T	T	62.6	Total Current						59.2
A	A	24.9	Fixed Assets (net)						28.9
		4.6	Intangibles (net)						5.8
N	N	7.9	All Other Non-Current						6.1
O	O	100.0	Total						100.0
T	T		**LIABILITIES**						
		9.8	Notes Payable-Short Term						4.3
A	A	4.2	Cur. Mat.-L /T/D						1.9
V	V	16.5	Trade Payables						14.4
A	A	.4	Income Taxes Payable						.6
I	I	9.8	All Other Current						12.8
L	L	40.5	Total Current						34.0
A	A	18.6	Long Term Debt						19.8
B	B	1.9	Deferred Taxes						3.0
L	L	4.1	All Other-Non-Current						7.3
E	E	34.9	Net Worth						36.0
		100.0	Total Liabilities & Net Worth						100.0
			INCOME DATA						
		100.0	Net Sales						100.0
		31.0	Gross Profit						22.7
		24.8	Operating Expenses						15.5
		6.2	Operating Profit						7.2
		1.8	All Other Expenses (net)						1.8
		4.4	Profit Before Taxes						5.4
			RATIOS						
		2.4							2.5
		1.7	Current						1.8
		1.1							1.3
		1.3							1.2
		.8	Quick						.6
		.5							.6
		31 11.6							31 11.8
		49 7.4	Sales/Receivables						49 7.4
		61 6.0							54 6.7
		52 7.0							52 7.0
		70 5.2	Cost of Sales/Inventory						68 5.4
		135 2.7							111 3.3
		25 14.5							31 11.6
		41 9.0	Cost of Sales/Payables						37 10.0
		58 6.3							39 9.3
		3.8							4.1
		7.0	Sales/Working Capital						6.9
		21.0							29.6
		9.8							8.0
	(28)	4.7	EBIT/Interest						4.9
		1.5							2.8
		19.5	Net Profit + Depr., Dep.,						
	(15)	4.8	Amort./Cur. Mat. L/T/D						
		.4							
		.3							.6
		.8	Fixed/Worth						.9
		1.3							1.6
		.8							1.1
		2.3	Debt/Worth						2.2
		4.7							4.7
		41.9	% Profit Before Taxes/Tangible						
	(27)	21.4	Net Worth						
		13.6							
		13.6	% Profit Before Taxes/Total						11.7
		6.6	Assets						8.0
		1.5							5.3
		14.0							13.1
		8.0	Sales/Net Fixed Assets						7.0
		3.8							4.4
		2.4							2.6
		1.8	Sales/Total Assets						1.6
		1.2							1.3
		1.2							
	(26)	2.6	% Depr., Dep., Amort./Sales						
		3.6							
		1.8	% Officers', Directors',						
	(10)	3.6	Owners' Comp/Sales						
		6.6							
		1969480M	Net Sales ($)	1667M	3194M	26114M	28762M	95755M	1813988M
		1110779M	Total Assets ($)	1491M	1664M	32779M	19037M	103220M	952588M

M = $ thousand   MM = $ million
See Pages 1 through 15 for Explanation of Ratios and Data

	Current Data Sorted By Assets						# Postretirement Benefits	Comparative Historical Data	
							Type of Statement		
1	1	3		1			Unqualified	28	28
	4	19	10	4	2		Reviewed	27	33
1	5	11	3				Compiled	23	17
5	11	3	1				Tax Returns		2
3	1						Other	26	24
1	13	7	7	4				4/1/90-	4/1/91-
	44 (4/1-9/30/94)		71 (10/1/94-3/31/95)					3/31/91	3/31/92
0-500M	500M-2MM	2-10MM	10-50MM	50-100MM	100-250MM			ALL	ALL
10	34	40	21	8	2		NUMBER OF STATEMENTS	104	104
%	%	%	%	%	%		ASSETS	%	%
8.3	8.6	7.6	6.0				Cash & Equivalents	8.5	7.4
19.5	19.4	25.9	18.2				Trade Receivables - (net)	18.5	19.5
26.5	33.8	22.6	16.2				Inventory	27.3	25.6
.2	3.2	6.9	10.0				All Other Current	4.5	5.2
54.4	65.0	63.0	50.4				Total Current	58.7	57.7
34.7	27.3	27.4	36.0				Fixed Assets (net)	32.4	33.2
1.7	1.0	.9	.6				Intangibles (net)	.5	1.0
9.1	6.7	8.6	13.0				All Other Non-Current	8.4	8.1
100.0	100.0	100.0	100.0				Total	100.0	100.0
							LIABILITIES		
9.0	14.7	9.5	9.8				Notes Payable-Short Term	10.5	9.5
4.2	1.9	2.0	4.3				Cur. Mat. -L/T/D	3.6	3.6
8.4	14.8	14.8	9.2				Trade Payables	15.4	15.7
.0	.2	.1	.2				Income Taxes Payable	.6	.9
20.4	13.4	17.3	17.1				All Other Current	11.9	10.6
41.9	45.0	43.8	40.7				Total Current	42.0	42.3
16.0	15.3	11.5	16.5				Long Term Debt	16.0	17.3
.0	.5	1.0	1.2				Deferred Taxes	.8	.5
1.8	5.6	2.9	4.7				All Other-Non-Current	2.4	3.3
40.2	33.6	40.9	36.9				Net Worth	38.8	36.6
100.0	100.0	100.0	100.0				Total Liabilities & Net Worth	100.0	100.0
							INCOME DATA		
100.0	100.0	100.0	100.0				Net Sales	100.0	100.0
33.1	24.5	22.7	22.0				Gross Profit	27.6	24.0
28.7	22.5	18.6	16.3				Operating Expenses	25.4	21.2
4.3	2.0	4.1	5.7				Operating Profit	2.2	2.9
.8	.6	1.2	2.1				All Other Expenses (net)	1.6	1.7
3.5	1.4	2.9	3.6				Profit Before Taxes	.5	1.2
							RATIOS		
4.0	2.9	1.8	2.4					2.4	2.0
1.2	1.7	1.5	1.1				Current	1.3	1.3
.7	1.0	1.1	.9					1.0	1.0
1.2	1.4	1.3	1.4					1.0	1.1
.5	(33) .8	.7	.5				Quick	.5	.7
.2	.3	.4	.3					.3	.3
2 198.1	11 34.5	18 20.6	23 15.8					13 29.2	14 26.8
14 26.3	25 14.7	30 12.0	34 10.8				Sales/Receivables	23 16.1	30 12.1
46 8.0	47 7.7	54 6.7	44 8.3					40 9.1	51 7.2
6 64.5	14 26.3	0 786.3	8 44.4					17 21.1	14 26.7
52 7.0	64 5.7	42 8.7	38 9.5				Cost of Sales/Inventory	49 7.5	45 8.2
126 2.9	118 3.1	89 4.1	66 5.5					87 4.2	85 4.3
6 63.7	10 36.5	16 23.0	12 31.6					15 23.7	19 18.9
13 29.2	19 18.9	26 14.1	22 16.4				Cost of Sales/Payables	28 13.2	29 12.6
30 12.0	37 10.0	37 9.9	33 11.2					41 9.0	43 8.4
8.8	5.3	7.1	6.9					7.0	7.5
46.5	8.9	12.7	63.7				Sales/Working Capital	19.4	18.9
-21.4	-117.6	49.0	-31.0					NM	212.9
	5.5	9.0	6.5					4.5	7.2
	(27) 2.2	(36) 2.8	(19) 2.8				EBIT/Interest	(94) 1.9	(98) 2.0
	1.2	1.4	.8					.2	.0
		3.5						4.4	6.7
		(14) 1.7					Net Profit + Depr., Dep.,	(56) 2.4	(56) 2.2
		.6					Amort./Cur. Mat. L /T/D	.1	.4
.4	.3	.4	.5					.4	.5
.8	.9	.8	1.2				Fixed/Worth	.9	.8
1.4	NM	1.2	2.9					1.5	1.9
.9	.6	.7	.6					.8	.8
1.4	1.5	1.7	2.2				Debt/Worth	1.9	1.6
4.2	NM	3.3	8.6					3.3	4.2
	49.3	40.9	23.1					30.3	34.0
	(26) 11.3	19.3	6.9				% Profit Before Taxes/Tangible	(100) 8.7	(95) 13.9
	.6	3.6	-8.4				Net Worth	-12.8	-5.3
20.4	9.7	15.5	10.3					10.0	12.1
7.5	3.2	5.9	4.6				% Profit Before Taxes/Total	3.1	4.7
2.2	.4	1.1	-.5				Assets	-5.3	-4.9
23.2	27.1	23.1	14.3					15.1	13.8
10.5	13.7	8.9	4.4				Sales/Net Fixed Assets	9.2	8.0
3.3	5.1	5.0	2.8					5.1	4.2
4.9	3.7	3.2	2.8					3.4	2.9
2.7	2.2	2.6	1.7				Sales/Total Assets	2.7	2.2
1.8	1.6	1.8	1.3					1.7	1.6
	.9	.7	1.7					.9	1.2
	(27) 1.8	(36) 1.6	(19) 2.4				% Depr., Dep., Amort./Sales	(95) 1.7	(97) 2.4
	4.1	2.8	3.9					2.8	3.6
	1.3	1.7						1.7	2.2
	(14) 3.7	(15) 2.9					% Officers', Directors',	(33) 3.2	(44) 3.6
	6.5	4.3					Owners' Comp/Sales	5.5	5.4
9048M	83221M	472351M	725906M	622682M	288375M		Net Sales ($)	1582805M	1955663M
2843M	34115M	182577M	403970M	527162M	254183M		Total Assets ($)	767126M	1245207M

M = $ thousand   MM = $ million
See Pages 1 through 15 for Explanation of Ratios and Data

Comparative Historical Data				Current Data Sorted By Sales					
5	8	6	# Postretirement Benefits		3			2	1
			Type of Statement						
34	36	39	Unqualified		3	4	4	13	15
26	27	20	Reviewed	2	1	3	10	3	1
20	22	20	Compiled	3	12	3	1		1
		1	Tax Returns	3	1				
28	22	32	Other	3	7	3	4	8	7
4/1/92-3/31/93	4/1/93-3/31/94	4/1/94-3/31/95		44 (4/1-9/30/94)			71 (10/1/94-3/31/95)		
ALL	ALL	ALL		0-1MM	1-3MM	3-5MM	5-10MM	10-25MM	25MM & OVER
108	108	115	**NUMBER OF STATEMENTS**	11	24	13	19	24	24
%	%	%	**ASSETS**	%	%	%	%	%	%
7.4	9.9	7.6	Cash & Equivalents	7.9	6.5	13.1	5.3	6.5	8.8
23.3	20.8	22.1	Trade Receivables - (net)	8.6	18.4	27.6	28.3	23.0	23.0
19.9	22.3	23.5	Inventory	18.7	42.8	18.9	24.5	15.2	16.3
7.1	5.4	5.7	All Other Current	4.8	1.4	4.8	5.0	8.6	8.5
57.7	58.3	58.8	Total Current	40.1	69.0	64.4	63.0	53.2	56.5
32.2	30.9	31.0	Fixed Assets (net)	47.4	24.1	25.1	29.8	34.1	31.5
1.5	1.0	1.0	Intangibles (net)	.6	2.5	.2	.5	.8	.6
8.6	9.8	9.2	All Other Non-Current	11.9	4.5	10.2	6.7	11.9	11.5
100.0	100.0	100.0	Total	100.0	100.0	100.0	100.0	100.0	100.0
			LIABILITIES						
11.7	13.0	10.6	Notes Payable-Short Term	14.8	15.2	9.3	9.3	10.2	6.0
4.6	2.9	2.7	Cur. Mat.-L /T/D	3.0	1.6	1.8	4.0	3.7	2.4
16.1	12.7	13.3	Trade Payables	6.1	14.3	12.6	18.7	11.8	13.3
.5	1.2	.3	Income Taxes Payable	.0	.2	.1	.2	.0	.8
10.2	10.8	15.4	All Other Current	17.3	10.8	21.6	13.2	15.0	17.8
43.1	40.6	42.2	Total Current	41.1	42.1	45.5	45.4	40.7	40.2
18.5	14.1	14.6	Long Term Debt	18.0	15.6	7.6	19.1	12.9	13.8
.9	.6	.8	Deferred Taxes	1.1	.3	1.4	.7	1.2	.5
4.2	3.4	4.0	All Other-Non-Current	7.0	5.0	2.9	1.1	6.0	2.4
33.3	41.3	38.4	Net Worth	32.9	37.1	42.6	33.7	39.2	43.1
100.0	100.0	100.0	Total Liabilities & Net Worth	100.0	100.0	100.0	100.0	100.0	100.0
			INCOME DATA						
100.0	100.0	100.0	Net Sales	100.0	100.0	100.0	100.0	100.0	100.0
22.7	26.2	24.8	Gross Profit	34.9	26.4	18.9	25.3	22.5	23.7
20.0	25.6	20.3	Operating Expenses	32.9	23.8	18.3	19.5	16.3	16.8
2.8	.5	4.5	Operating Profit	1.9	2.6	.7	5.8	6.2	6.8
.8	.5	1.1	All Other Expenses (net)	2.0	.6	.3	1.0	1.8	1.1
2.0	.0	3.4	Profit Before Taxes	.0	2.0	.3	4.8	4.4	5.7
			RATIOS						
2.1	2.1	2.3	Current	1.7	3.6	2.4	1.7	2.1	2.4
1.4	1.5	1.5		.9	1.9	1.5	1.4	1.2	1.5
1.0	1.0	1.0		.7	1.4	1.0	1.2	.9	.9
1.3	1.3	1.4	Quick	.9	1.2	2.0	1.3	1.5	1.7
.7 (107)	.8 (114)	.8		.3 (23)	.8	.8	.7	.6	.9
.4	.4	.3		.1	.4	.5	.4	.3	.3
18 20.3	12 31.2	17 21.3	Sales/Receivables	2 148.0	6 59.7	13 27.9	19 19.2	17 22.0	18 20.5
35 10.4	27 13.4	31 11.7		18 20.7	27 13.6	25 14.7	34 10.7	35 10.5	34 10.7
55 6.6	50 7.3	49 7.5		49 7.5	42 8.7	62 5.9	76 4.8	50 7.3	49 7.5
3 134.2	6 65.8	5 75.7	Cost of Sales/Inventory	0 UND	64 5.7	2 179.9	3 123.4	0 UND	6 62.9
33 11.1	38 9.5	41 9.0		33 11.0	83 4.4	29 12.8	30 12.1	8 45.7	28 13.0
70 5.2	81 4.5	85 4.3		89 4.1	122 3.0	74 4.9	89 4.1	68 5.4	51 7.2
17 21.0	14 27.0	13 28.5	Cost of Sales/Payables	2 152.0	8 43.8	15 25.1	21 17.6	11 34.6	14 26.6
29 12.5	26 14.1	22 16.4		15 23.8	16 22.4	20 18.2	29 12.4	20 18.1	24 15.5
45 8.2	36 10.1	39 9.4		54 6.7	42 8.7	31 11.7	44 8.3	33 11.2	43 8.5
7.5	5.6	6.2	Sales/Working Capital	9.3	5.1	5.4	7.1	9.2	5.6
18.3	12.5	11.9		-43.0	7.0	6.7	12.8	42.7	13.0
-74.9	220.5	-138.9		-3.9	17.0	NM	30.8	-50.6	-86.1
7.4	6.6	7.8	EBIT/Interest		6.1	15.6	12.3	4.9	11.6
2.3 (104)	1.8 (100)	2.7 (98)		(22)	2.3	1.8 (10)	3.5	2.2 (21)	5.2 (18)
.6	-1.2	1.2			1.2	-.0	2.1	.6	1.1
4.6	3.1	4.0	Net Profit + Depr., Dep., Amort./Cur. Mat. L/T/D						
1.8 (51)	1.0 (41)	1.9 (32)							
.4	-1.2	.6							
.4	.3	.4	Fixed/Worth	.6	.4	.4	.4	.4	.3
1.0	.8	.8		1.1	.9	.6	.8	.9	.8
2.0	1.6	1.7		UND	1.2	2.7	1.7	2.1	1.7
.8	.7	.6	Debt/Worth	.8	.8	.4	1.2	.6	.6
1.7	1.4	1.6		1.5	1.4	1.4	2.1	1.7	1.7
5.2	3.7	4.0		UND	4.5	7.8	3.9	6.8	3.0
44.5	30.4	37.5	% Profit Before Taxes/Tangible Net Worth		47.3	49.0	54.3	29.9	52.1
14.5 (94)	6.5 (102)	15.4 (106)		(20)	7.1	8.1 (11)	25.9 (18)	9.8	15.3
1.2	-14.5	1.5			1.1	-5.8	11.9	-15.9	-1.4
13.1	11.7	11.5	% Profit Before Taxes/Total Assets	9.8	10.6	12.8	15.5	11.2	16.9
4.7	2.6	5.0		4.2	3.5	2.7	9.2	3.0	5.5
-1.8	-5.9	.6		-1.4	.7	-3.5	5.0	-3.0	-.8
17.2	17.0	21.8	Sales/Net Fixed Assets	13.2	63.1	27.9	23.3	22.3	18.7
6.7	7.9	7.4		3.5	13.6	12.8	7.3	9.8	6.7
4.4	4.3	4.0		.6	4.8	5.1	5.9	2.8	4.1
3.2	3.0	3.0	Sales/Total Assets	2.3	3.4	4.4	2.8	3.3	3.0
2.2	2.3	2.2		1.4	2.2	2.2	2.6	2.4	1.8
1.6	1.5	1.5		.3	1.6	1.8	1.8	1.6	1.3
1.1	.8	1.0	% Depr., Dep., Amort./Sales	1.3	1.1		.7	1.5	.6
2.0 (99)	1.8 (100)	2.0 (99)		3.5 (20)	2.0		1.5 (19)	2.0 (21)	2.3
3.4	3.5	3.6		13.4	4.4		2.9	3.0	3.8
2.5	2.2	1.7	% Officers', Directors', Owners' Comp/Sales		2.2				
3.9 (46)	3.7 (36)	3.2 (43)		(15)	3.7				
5.7	6.8	6.5			6.4				
2231857M	2415750M	2201583M	Net Sales ($)	5667M	48025M	48013M	142649M	405066M	1552163M
1273315M	1417321M	1404850M	Total Assets ($)	6104M	22059M	24655M	69927M	291271M	990834M

M = $ thousand   MM = $ million
See Pages 1 through 15 for Explanation of Ratios and Data

Current Data Sorted By Assets / Comparative Historical Data

						# Postretirement Benefits / Type of Statement		
	1	1	2					
	4	8	8	3		Unqualified	22	22
2	10	5	2			Reviewed	11	18
1	5	4	1			Compiled	12	8
1						Tax Returns		
1	5	11	3		1	Other	14	14
	32 (4/1-9/30/94)		42 (10/1/94-3/31/95)				4/1/90-3/31/91	4/1/91-3/31/92
0-500M	500M-2MM	2-10MM	10-50MM	50-100MM	100-250MM		ALL	ALL
4	24	28	14	3	1	NUMBER OF STATEMENTS	59	62
%	%	%	%	%	%	**ASSETS**	%	%
	7.8	5.7	7.2			Cash & Equivalents	7.1	8.1
	24.7	23.5	26.7			Trade Receivables - (net)	23.7	21.5
	41.4	36.0	35.3			Inventory	38.1	39.2
	1.8	2.0	1.8			All Other Current	2.0	1.6
	75.7	67.1	70.9			Total Current	70.9	70.5
	18.9	27.7	20.0			Fixed Assets (net)	22.7	22.1
	.4	.9	1.3			Intangibles (net)	1.2	1.6
	5.0	4.4	7.8			All Other Non-Current	5.3	5.9
	100.0	100.0	100.0			Total	100.0	100.0
						LIABILITIES		
	11.0	12.5	17.0			Notes Payable-Short Term	15.1	11.0
	6.9	4.0	1.8			Cur. Mat. -L/T/D	3.2	2.7
	20.1	17.2	18.7			Trade Payables	17.8	17.3
	.4	.4	.5			Income Taxes Payable	.8	.2
	11.4	10.2	8.6			All Other Current	10.4	9.4
	49.8	44.2	46.6			Total Current	47.4	40.6
	7.6	16.4	17.0			Long Term Debt	16.9	15.2
	.6	.3	.7			Deferred Taxes	.7	.4
	5.3	2.6	3.7			All Other-Non-Current	2.3	3.5
	36.7	36.6	32.0			Net Worth	32.7	40.4
	100.0	100.0	100.0			Total Liabilities & Net Worth	100.0	100.0
						INCOME DATA		
	100.0	100.0	100.0			Net Sales	100.0	100.0
	23.6	21.2	19.1			Gross Profit	20.0	20.3
	21.1	17.6	15.0			Operating Expenses	16.5	19.3
	2.4	3.5	4.1			Operating Profit	3.4	1.0
	-.1	1.0	.0			All Other Expenses (net)	1.5	.9
	2.5	2.5	4.1			Profit Before Taxes	2.0	.1
						RATIOS		
	2.2	2.2	3.5				2.2	3.7
	1.5	1.4	1.5			Current	1.5	1.7
	1.1	1.1	1.1				1.2	1.2
	1.0	1.1	1.8				1.0	1.5
	.6	.6	.7			Quick	.7	.6
	.4	.5	.5				.5	.4
	19 19.4	28 13.2	36 10.2				21 17.7	23 16.0
	30 12.3	39 9.4	44 8.3			Sales/Receivables	26 13.8	30 12.0
	46 7.9	49 7.4	54 6.8				41 8.9	45 8.1
	44 8.3	54 6.7	60 6.1				32 11.3	46 7.9
	65 5.6	78 4.7	74 4.9			Cost of Sales/Inventory	57 6.4	63 5.8
	94 3.9	96 3.8	89 4.1				83 4.4	111 3.3
	16 22.2	19 19.0	25 14.6				12 29.8	16 22.4
	29 12.7	29 12.8	38 9.7			Cost of Sales/Payables	24 14.9	25 14.4
	52 7.0	41 8.8	47 7.7				33 11.1	44 8.3
	6.1	5.5	4.9				7.1	4.2
	12.6	11.3	10.4			Sales/Working Capital	15.4	10.0
	27.3	57.3	30.9				30.7	22.4
	11.8	8.7	24.4				4.4	4.5
	(23) 4.4	(26) 2.7	(13) 7.6			EBIT/Interest	(55) 2.0	(56) 1.1
	1.3	.8	1.6				.5	-.7
		4.6	23.7				7.8	5.6
		(13) 3.9	(10) 2.9			Net Profit + Depr., Dep., Amort./Cur. Mat. L /T/D	(37) 2.1	(33) 1.4
		.8	1.7				.9	-.6
	.2	.3	.3				.3	.2
	.4	.7	.6			Fixed/Worth	.6	.5
	1.3	1.5	1.1				1.3	1.4
	.7	1.1	1.3				1.0	.5
	1.6	2.2	1.9			Debt/Worth	2.0	1.4
	3.8	4.5	4.1				4.8	4.8
	39.6	40.0	52.6				31.4	18.1
	(22) 17.0	16.3	(12) 25.7			% Profit Before Taxes/Tangible Net Worth	(54) 19.3	(57) 4.6
	2.4	-6.8	8.7				1.8	-16.7
	22.8	13.5	18.8				15.4	7.4
	6.0	3.9	9.4			% Profit Before Taxes/Total Assets	5.7	.7
	.9	-1.9	2.5				-1.3	-8.7
	44.3	24.0	14.2				32.8	28.3
	23.7	7.6	10.8			Sales/Net Fixed Assets	17.3	15.5
	8.1	4.9	9.1				7.8	6.7
	3.7	2.9	2.5				3.6	3.1
	2.8	2.0	2.1			Sales/Total Assets	2.8	2.3
	2.1	1.6	1.8				2.2	1.7
	.6	.8	.7				.9	1.0
	(21) 1.1	(24) 1.3	(13) 1.1			% Depr., Dep., Amort./Sales	(53) 1.2	(55) 1.5
	1.9	2.7	2.6				1.9	2.8
	1.3						1.4	1.6
	(12) 3.2					% Officers', Directors', Owners' Comp/Sales	(17) 2.4	(23) 4.7
	7.1						8.2	8.6
5371M	94873M	285947M	666844M	329489M	190073M	Net Sales ($)	1843295M	1578116M
1174M	30912M	124550M	321309M	171416M	100826M	Total Assets ($)	771413M	700151M

M = $ thousand   MM = $ million
See Pages 1 through 15 for Explanation of Ratios and Data

Comparative Historical Data

Current Data Sorted By Sales

Hist 1	Hist 2	Hist 3		0-1MM	1-3MM	3-5MM	5-10MM	10-25MM	25MM & OVER
3	5	4	# Postretirement Benefits	1			1		2
			Type of Statement						
21	24	23	Unqualified		2	3	3	5	10
18	10	19	Reviewed	1	5	3	7	1	2
15	16	10	Compiled		2	3	1	3	1
1	2	1	Tax Returns		1				
19	18	21	Other		4	5	3	5	4
4/1/92-3/31/93 ALL	4/1/93-3/31/94 ALL	4/1/94-3/31/95 ALL		32 (4/1-9/30/94)			42 (10/1/94-3/31/95)		
74	70	74	**NUMBER OF STATEMENTS**	1	14	14	14	14	17
%	%	%	**ASSETS**	%	%	%	%	%	%
7.4	7.8	7.1	Cash & Equivalents		11.0	7.9	4.5	6.2	5.6
24.3	23.3	25.0	Trade Receivables - (net)		22.2	21.9	30.7	25.3	26.2
37.9	36.9	37.7	Inventory		35.2	35.9	41.3	39.9	35.5
1.3	3.0	2.0	All Other Current		1.3	3.0	1.3	1.6	2.8
71.0	71.0	71.8	Total Current		69.7	68.6	77.8	73.0	70.1
21.3	20.7	22.2	Fixed Assets (net)		26.2	24.0	16.4	23.7	21.2
1.6	.8	.8	Intangibles (net)		.4	1.6	.3	.2	1.3
6.1	7.5	5.2	All Other Non-Current		3.7	5.8	5.6	3.1	7.3
100.0	100.0	100.0	Total		100.0	100.0	100.0	100.0	100.0
			LIABILITIES						
14.1	13.0	12.1	Notes Payable-Short Term		11.6	6.5	14.7	10.8	14.8
3.4	3.2	4.5	Cur. Mat.-L /T/D		4.8	8.5	4.3	2.3	3.1
18.2	20.9	19.0	Trade Payables		19.3	14.3	24.4	17.0	20.3
.3	1.1	.4	Income Taxes Payable		.2	1.1	.1	.3	.4
10.9	11.4	10.7	All Other Current		12.8	9.8	10.7	10.9	10.2
46.9	49.6	46.7	Total Current		48.7	40.1	54.1	41.3	48.7
11.2	14.2	13.4	Long Term Debt		11.3	21.5	7.6	6.0	19.9
.4	.3	.5	Deferred Taxes		.8	.5	.1	.2	.8
3.6	2.9	4.1	All Other-Non-Current		5.1	3.6	5.3	1.8	4.7
37.9	32.9	35.4	Net Worth		34.1	34.3	33.0	50.7	25.9
100.0	100.0	100.0	Total Liabilities & Net Worth		100.0	100.0	100.0	100.0	100.0
			INCOME DATA						
100.0	100.0	100.0	Net Sales		100.0	100.0	100.0	100.0	100.0
21.6	22.1	21.2	Gross Profit		24.3	27.6	20.2	18.1	17.6
19.6	18.4	17.8	Operating Expenses		21.1	22.4	17.6	15.6	13.7
2.0	3.7	3.4	Operating Profit		3.2	5.2	2.7	2.5	3.9
.6	.7	.5	All Other Expenses (net)		.6	.4	.4	.5	.3
1.4	2.9	2.9	Profit Before Taxes		2.5	4.8	2.2	2.0	3.6
			RATIOS						
2.1	2.0	2.5	Current		2.3	3.5	1.9	3.1	3.0
1.5	1.4	1.5			1.3	1.9	1.3	1.9	1.6
1.1	1.1	1.1			1.0	1.2	1.2	1.3	1.1
.9	.9	1.1	Quick		1.3	1.4	.9	1.3	1.4
.7	.6	.6			.6	.7	.6	.9	.8
.4	.4	.4			.4	.4	.5	.5	.5
25 14.5	22 16.4	27 13.7	Sales/Receivables	12 29.8	22 16.7	28 13.0	25 14.4	35 10.3	
33 11.1	38 9.6	38 9.5		31 11.6	35 10.3	35 10.3	35 10.4	43 8.5	
45 8.1	47 7.7	49 7.4		50 7.3	50 7.3	45 8.1	49 7.4	58 6.3	
48 7.6	51 7.2	53 6.9	Cost of Sales/Inventory	40 9.2	64 5.7	37 9.9	50 7.3	62 5.9	
68 5.4	64 5.7	72 5.1		81 4.5	78 4.7	54 6.8	61 6.0	69 5.3	
85 4.3	111 3.3	94 3.9		96 3.8	118 3.1	83 4.4	85 4.3	91 4.0	
17 21.6	21 17.3	20 18.0	Cost of Sales/Payables	6 61.5	13 27.5	21 17.6	18 20.3	28 13.1	
28 13.0	37 10.0	31 11.8		45 8.1	31 11.8	31 11.9	24 15.2	38 9.6	
43 8.4	54 6.8	49 7.5		69 5.3	48 7.6	45 8.2	30 12.2	58 6.3	
6.5	5.7	5.6	Sales/Working Capital		8.6	4.6	9.5	4.0	4.8
10.3	12.6	11.2			15.4	7.2	20.6	9.5	9.8
35.1	34.8	28.2			NM	23.5	26.4	40.1	31.4
5.4	7.9	10.6	EBIT/Interest		10.2	11.0	7.4	30.6	12.5
(71) 1.9	(67) 3.5	(70) 4.2			3.5	3.0 (12)	3.6 (13)	8.0 (16)	6.6
.6	1.3	1.3			1.5	1.4	.5	1.3	1.2
4.4	4.6	4.8	Net Profit + Depr., Dep., Amort./Cur. Mat. L/T/D						10.0
(30) 2.2	(30) 2.6	(34) 2.8						(13)	2.9
.6	.3	.6							1.5
.2	.3	.3	Fixed/Worth		.2	.3	.2	.2	.5
.4	.5	.6			.5	.8	.5	.5	.7
1.2	1.0	1.4			2.9	1.7	1.1	.9	1.2
.7	1.1	1.0	Debt/Worth		1.0	1.1	1.1	.3	1.4
2.1	2.1	1.9			1.9	1.9	2.6	1.1	1.9
4.2	4.6	3.8			5.7	6.7	3.7	2.9	4.4
23.7	42.6	40.8	% Profit Before Taxes/Tangible Net Worth		40.0	64.4	33.8	36.7	50.2
(67) 9.5	(66) 18.6	(69) 19.0		(13) 18.4	9.1	16.8 (13)	21.0	26.2 (14)	
1.7	6.7	4.2			9.3	-.3	-2.4	-1.7	10.8
10.5	12.7	16.1	% Profit Before Taxes/Total Assets		12.8	18.9	15.0	17.2	17.5
3.2	5.6	5.5			5.4	3.0	6.8	8.0	8.0
-.8	1.3	.9			2.5	.8	.1	-1.9	1.6
35.0	33.6	33.4	Sales/Net Fixed Assets		43.5	28.8	46.1	34.8	12.1
18.5	13.7	12.0			19.8	8.1	32.3	12.0	10.2
6.4	7.2	7.0			2.6	5.6	10.7	6.9	8.2
3.4	3.1	3.3	Sales/Total Assets		3.7	2.9	4.1	4.3	2.4
2.5	2.4	2.3			2.6	2.2	3.1	2.4	2.1
1.9	1.8	1.7			1.4	1.8	2.2	1.9	1.8
.7	.8	.8	% Depr., Dep., Amort./Sales		.6	.5	.8	.8	.8
(66) 1.4	(61) 1.3	(66) 1.1		(12) 1.0	1.3 (11)	1.1 (12)	1.0	1.1 (16)	
2.3	2.5	2.3			3.2	1.7	2.7	2.5	2.3
1.4	1.2	1.2	% Officers', Directors', Owners' Comp/Sales						
(24) 3.2	(25) 2.1	(24) 2.5							
5.7	3.8	6.0							
1530261M	1240127M	1572597M	Net Sales ($)	872M	29087M	57625M	94486M	229014M	1161513M
614152M	597813M	750187M	Total Assets ($)	564M	15206M	29983M	35837M	87959M	580638M

M = $ thousand   MM = $ million
See Pages 1 through 15 for Explanation of Ratios and Data

Current Data Sorted By Assets   **Comparative Historical Data**

Asset-size period groupings: 17 (4/1-9/30/94)   34 (10/1/94-3/31/95)

Historical columns: **6** = 4/1/90-3/31/91 ALL   **7** = 4/1/91-3/31/92 ALL

Type of Statement / Number of Statements

	0-500M	500M-2MM	2-10MM	10-50MM	50-100MM	100-250MM		4/1/90-3/31/91 ALL	4/1/91-3/31/92 ALL
# Postretirement Benefits			1	2		1			
Unqualified		1	6	7		4		14	16
Reviewed		1	8	3				8	5
Compiled	2	7	1	1				7	13
Tax Returns		1							
Other	3	2	4					6	7
NUMBER OF STATEMENTS	5	12	19	11		4		35	41

Common-Size Data (%)

	0-500M	500M-2MM	2-10MM	10-50MM	50-100MM	100-250MM		4/1/90-3/31/91	4/1/91-3/31/92
	%	%	%	%	%	%		%	%
ASSETS									
Cash & Equivalents		8.0	8.3	6.0				4.8	3.9
Trade Receivables - (net)		20.3	21.1	17.7				20.9	20.3
Inventory		46.9	38.3	43.5				43.3	42.4
All Other Current		6.3	1.6	4.5				1.5	1.2
Total Current		81.5	69.3	71.8				70.5	67.7
Fixed Assets (net)		12.6	25.3	20.1				22.0	22.8
Intangibles (net)		3.1	.6	.8				1.0	2.2
All Other Non-Current		2.8	4.8	7.3				6.5	7.4
Total		100.0	100.0	100.0				100.0	100.0
LIABILITIES									
Notes Payable-Short Term		11.6	11.8	10.7				14.9	11.8
Cur. Mat. -L/T/D		3.8	2.2	3.9				3.1	3.8
Trade Payables		18.0	18.3	18.2				18.4	17.5
Income Taxes Payable		.3	.7	.6				.5	.6
All Other Current		12.5	8.4	10.0				7.8	8.8
Total Current		46.1	41.4	43.4				44.6	42.4
Long Term Debt		9.6	12.7	16.4				17.2	16.9
Deferred Taxes		.5	.2	.3				.2	.9
All Other-Non-Current		3.4	3.9	1.6				1.2	1.9
Net Worth		40.5	41.8	38.3				36.8	37.8
Total Liabilities & Net Worth		100.0	100.0	100.0				100.0	100.0
INCOME DATA									
Net Sales		100.0	100.0	100.0				100.0	100.0
Gross Profit		18.5	20.9	17.8				16.3	14.8
Operating Expenses		16.8	16.3	11.0				13.4	15.8
Operating Profit		1.7	4.5	6.9				2.9	-1.0
All Other Expenses (net)		.2	1.1	.6				.6	.9
Profit Before Taxes		1.6	3.4	6.3				2.3	-1.9

RATIOS

Ratio	0-500M	500M-2MM	2-10MM	10-50MM	50-100MM	100-250MM		4/1/90-3/31/91	4/1/91-3/31/92
Current		3.6	2.8	2.0				2.3	2.1
		1.7	1.6	1.8				1.7	1.7
		1.4	1.3	1.4				1.1	1.3
Quick		1.2	1.2	.7				.8	.9
		.6	.7	.6				.5	.5
		.4	.5	.4				.4	.4
Sales/Receivables		10 35.4	13 28.1	17 20.9				20 18.0	15 24.0
		13 27.2	26 14.1	25 14.7				27 13.3	30 12.2
		25 14.4	41 8.9	35 10.5				38 9.6	47 7.8
Cost of Sales/Inventory		29 12.6	38 9.6	53 6.9				43 8.4	50 7.3
		62 5.9	51 7.1	83 4.4				72 5.1	66 5.5
		91 4.0	83 4.4	94 3.9				85 4.3	87 4.2
Cost of Sales/Payables		7 49.4	20 18.6	21 17.7				17 21.3	15 24.2
		15 24.5	27 13.3	23 16.2				24 15.1	24 15.3
		21 17.4	40 9.1	34 10.6				34 10.6	40 9.2
Sales/Working Capital		5.9	5.1	5.2				6.6	6.5
		11.4	10.5	9.1				11.2	9.3
		29.2	20.4	10.9				32.6	19.6
EBIT/Interest		6.7	31.3	14.5				4.7	3.1
		3.5	(18) 8.6	5.7				2.6	(39) 1.6
		1.8	1.7	4.2				1.7	-1.0
Net Profit + Depr., Dep., Amort./Cur. Mat. L /T/D			(18)					(18) 4.8	(19) 5.8
								3.0	1.1
								1.8	-.4
Fixed/Worth		.1	.2	.3				.3	.2
		.4	.6	.5				.6	.6
		.7	1.1	1.0				.9	1.1
Debt/Worth		.7	.8	1.0				1.0	.8
		1.8	1.7	1.7				1.4	1.4
		5.2	2.9	3.0				3.7	3.8
% Profit Before Taxes/Tangible Net Worth		55.5	40.6	55.7				(34) 42.2	(38) 21.3
		28.3	25.2	25.7				17.8	4.7
		3.7	6.9	23.4				6.0	-9.6
% Profit Before Taxes/Total Assets		10.5	18.0	17.9				14.6	7.1
		6.8	6.9	12.2				5.5	.9
		1.4	2.6	8.9				2.5	-9.3
Sales/Net Fixed Assets		104.5	43.4	30.3				28.0	27.7
		40.7	15.4	13.3				14.4	11.4
		25.7	4.8	6.8				8.0	7.0
Sales/Total Assets		7.4	3.5	2.9				3.3	3.4
		3.8	2.9	2.3				2.6	2.5
		2.6	1.7	1.9				2.2	1.9
% Depr., Dep., Amort./Sales		(10) .2	.3					(30) .7	(37) .8
		.5	.9					1.1	1.1
		1.9	1.9					1.4	1.8
% Officers', Directors', Owners' Comp/Sales									1.2
									(15) 2.2
									3.6
Net Sales ($)	7755M	70767M	228331M	677053M		1603153M		1097208M	1218831M
Total Assets ($)	1815M	14590M	85444M	261692M		736733M		457364M	640485M

M = $ thousand   MM = $ million

See Pages 1 through 15 for Explanation of Ratios and Data

Comparative Historical Data | | | # Postretirement Benefits | Current Data Sorted By Sales

Comparative Historical Data				Current Data Sorted By Sales					
2	1	4	# Postretirement Benefits					1	3
			Type of Statement						
12	13	18	Unqualified		2		2	5	11
9	11	12	Reviewed		2	1	2	4	3
9	5	11	Compiled		5	2	2	1	1
6	2	1	Tax Returns		1				
4	4	9	Other	1			4	2	
4/1/92-3/31/93 ALL	4/1/93-3/31/94 ALL	4/1/94-3/31/95 ALL		0-1MM	17 (4/1-9/30/94) 1-3MM	3-5MM	34 (10/1/94-3/31/95) 5-10MM	10-25MM	25MM & OVER
36	35	51	**NUMBER OF STATEMENTS**	1	10	3	10	12	15
%	%	%	**ASSETS**	%	%	%	%	%	%
6.1	6.3	9.5	Cash & Equivalents		11.3		7.5	10.9	9.3
20.4	20.8	19.4	Trade Receivables - (net)		16.9		21.3	24.3	18.9
40.5	39.8	39.8	Inventory		45.5		43.2	31.0	38.0
2.3	1.4	3.4	All Other Current		1.6		.8	7.7	3.7
69.3	68.4	72.0	Total Current		75.4		72.8	74.0	69.8
21.4	21.2	21.3	Fixed Assets (net)		20.0		20.5	21.0	19.8
1.4	3.0	1.3	Intangibles (net)		3.4		.5	.8	.8
7.9	7.4	5.4	All Other Non-Current		1.2		6.2	4.2	9.6
100.0	100.0	100.0	Total		100.0		100.0	100.0	100.0
			LIABILITIES						
8.1	11.4	11.1	Notes Payable-Short Term		10.1		14.2	9.1	8.0
4.2	4.9	3.9	Cur. Mat.-L /T/D		5.5		4.2	3.6	3.7
17.8	15.3	17.3	Trade Payables		14.2		21.0	21.0	17.3
.6	2.0	.5	Income Taxes Payable		.0		.0	1.1	.5
7.5	8.8	10.6	All Other Current		12.9		6.9	13.1	11.0
38.2	42.5	43.4	Total Current		42.8		46.3	47.9	40.4
14.7	14.3	13.4	Long Term Debt		10.4		10.3	9.7	16.9
.4	.8	.5	Deferred Taxes		.0		.6	.3	1.0
1.7	6.2	3.2	All Other-Non-Current		2.2		7.2	.9	2.1
44.9	36.2	39.5	Net Worth		44.6		35.5	41.3	39.6
100.0	100.0	100.0	Total Liabilities & Net Worth		100.0		100.0	100.0	100.0
			INCOME DATA						
100.0	100.0	100.0	Net Sales		100.0		100.0	100.0	100.0
19.6	17.1	19.4	Gross Profit		25.3		20.6	17.5	16.5
16.1	14.3	14.9	Operating Expenses		21.7		18.5	12.5	9.7
3.6	2.8	4.4	Operating Profit		3.6		2.1	4.9	6.8
.5	.3	.5	All Other Expenses (net)		.9		.0	1.3	.4
3.1	2.5	3.9	Profit Before Taxes		2.8		2.0	3.7	6.4
			RATIOS						
2.9 / 1.8 / 1.5	2.3 / 1.6 / 1.3	2.3 / 1.7 / 1.3	Current		3.5 / 1.5 / 1.2		2.7 / 1.7 / 1.2	2.3 / 1.4 / 1.2	2.1 / 1.8 / 1.5
1.1 / .8 / .5	.9 / .7 / .5	1.1 / .7 / .4	Quick		1.2 / .7 / .3		1.3 / .7 / .5	1.2 / .8 / .5	.9 / .7 / .5
(13) 28.5 / (24) 15.0 / (46) 8.0	(19) 18.8 / (27) 13.6 / (40) 9.1	(13) 28.7 / (22) 16.7 / (35) 10.4	Sales/Receivables		(1) 275.8 / (21) 17.7 / (32) 11.3		(9) 39.0 / (26) 13.9 / (41) 8.9	(12) 31.3 / (22) 16.9 / (37) 9.8	(17) 20.9 / (33) 10.9 / (35) 10.4
(43) 8.4 / (53) 6.9 / (78) 4.7	(49) 7.5 / (57) 6.4 / (85) 4.3	(34) 10.6 / (59) 6.2 / (85) 4.3	Cost of Sales/Inventory		(19) 19.7 / (69) 5.3 / (192) 1.9		(29) 12.5 / (50) 7.3 / (87) 4.2	(19) 19.0 / (45) 8.2 / (53) 6.9	(38) 9.6 / (76) 4.8 / (89) 4.1
(16) 22.4 / (27) 13.4 / (37) 9.9	(16) 23.3 / (22) 16.8 / (37) 9.9	(14) 25.6 / (22) 16.6 / (34) 10.6	Cost of Sales/Payables		(1) 275.4 / (23) 16.1 / (31) 11.7		(15) 25.1 / (20) 18.7 / (57) 6.4	(13) 27.7 / (28) 13.2 / (39) 9.3	(21) 17.7 / (23) 15.9 / (35) 10.4
6.0 / 9.1 / 14.6	6.7 / 11.2 / 15.2	5.9 / 10.2 / 21.6	Sales/Working Capital		2.7 / 11.0 / 114.7		5.0 / 16.1 / NM	7.7 / 13.2 / 31.4	5.2 / 9.1 / 10.4
(33) 9.5 / 3.1 / 1.7	(34) 13.9 / 3.4 / 1.4	(49) 22.1 / 5.5 / 2.6	EBIT/Interest					34.6 / 14.6 / 4.1	14.5 / 5.8 / 4.2
(16) 4.5 / 1.6 / .7	(15) 3.6 / 1.1 / .0	(20) 7.2 / 2.2 / 1.0	Net Profit + Depr., Dep., Amort./Cur. Mat. L/TD						
.2 / .4 / .9	.3 / .6 / 1.3	.3 / .6 / .9	Fixed/Worth		.1 / .6 / 1.2		.1 / .7 / 1.1	.2 / .4 / .6	.3 / .5 / .8
.8 / 1.3 / 2.2	1.0 / 1.8 / 3.3	.8 / 1.7 / 3.3	Debt/Worth		.7 / 1.5 / 4.0		1.0 / 2.5 / 4.0	.7 / 1.9 / 3.2	1.0 / 1.7 / 3.0
(35) 39.7 / 15.8 / 5.7	(33) 35.7 / 21.7 / 4.8	(50) 48.1 / 27.7 / 9.1	% Profit Before Taxes/Tangible Net Worth		81.8 / 6.7 / 2.1		46.1 / 19.7 / 6.2	49.8 / 33.0 / 25.9	47.0 / 27.6 / 23.4
20.8 / 5.2 / 1.3	15.6 / 7.2 / 1.7	15.1 / 9.3 / 3.8	% Profit Before Taxes/Total Assets		14.5 / 3.2 / .8		12.4 / 7.5 / 1.4	19.5 / 11.0 / 5.0	16.9 / 12.2 / 8.9
31.0 / 13.9 / 9.7	29.4 / 12.5 / 7.7	32.0 / 19.5 / 7.3	Sales/Net Fixed Assets		37.0 / 21.1 / 12.7		87.6 / 26.7 / 6.1	95.3 / 23.7 / 6.8	25.2 / 13.3 / 7.3
3.6 / 3.0 / 2.1	3.3 / 2.6 / 1.8	4.1 / 2.9 / 1.9	Sales/Total Assets		5.5 / 2.9 / 1.5		6.9 / 3.2 / 1.9	4.3 / 3.4 / 2.9	2.9 / 2.3 / 1.8
(30) .7 / 1.0 / 1.2	(33) .8 / 1.0 / 2.1	(45) .4 / .9 / 1.9	% Depr., Dep., Amort./Sales					.2 / .4 / 1.0	(12) .7 / 1.1 / 1.6
(12) 2.2 / 2.8 / 4.1	(11) .6 / 2.2 / 3.3	(14) 1.7 / 4.6 / 6.8	% Officers', Directors', Owners' Comp/Sales						
1547836M / 878504M	1909858M / 939766M	2587059M / 1100274M	Net Sales ($) / Total Assets ($)	741M / 378M	19620M / 9922M	13329M / 5942M	71367M / 23301M	201796M / 62306M	2280206M / 998425M

© Robert Morris Associates 1995   M = $ thousand   MM = $ million
See Pages 1 through 15 for Explanation of Ratios and Data

PART II

WHOLESALING INDUSTRIES

Current Data Sorted By Assets / Comparative Historical Data

	0-500M	500M-2MM	2-10MM	10-50MM	50-100MM	100-250MM		4/1/90-3/31/91 ALL 188	4/1/91-3/31/92 ALL 181
		60 (4/1-9/30/94)	144 (10/1/94-3/31/95)				# Postretirement Benefits		
# Postretirement Benefits	1	4	8	4					
							Type of Statement		
	1	4	17	17		7	Unqualified	26	36
	1	15	31	4		1	Reviewed	68	50
	7	32	10	1			Compiled	56	51
	1	3					Tax Returns		7
	4	19	19	9		1	Other	38	37
NUMBER OF STATEMENTS	14	73	77	31		9		188	181
	%	%	%	%	%	%	**ASSETS**	%	%
	8.8	8.0	6.4	2.8			Cash & Equivalents	7.9	6.3
	15.6	20.8	20.9	21.2			Trade Receivables - (net)	20.4	23.4
	50.0	41.0	50.6	47.5			Inventory	45.7	46.0
	.7	4.5	2.0	2.2			All Other Current	2.6	2.4
	75.0	74.3	79.8	73.7			Total Current	76.5	78.1
	19.3	16.8	14.1	18.9			Fixed Assets (net)	16.9	15.4
	.1	1.5	1.3	1.3			Intangibles (net)	.3	.7
	5.5	7.4	4.9	6.1			All Other Non-Current	6.3	5.8
	100.0	100.0	100.0	100.0			Total	100.0	100.0
							LIABILITIES		
	19.8	19.5	35.8	32.1			Notes Payable-Short Term	27.6	28.3
	1.8	2.7	2.9	3.7			Cur. Mat. -L/T/D	4.1	3.7
	11.9	15.6	12.6	9.8			Trade Payables	13.9	12.7
	.1	.2	.5	.1			Income Taxes Payable	.4	.5
	4.5	7.1	7.9	12.7			All Other Current	7.4	7.0
	38.1	45.1	59.7	58.4			Total Current	53.4	52.3
	13.8	11.3	9.3	16.1			Long Term Debt	13.6	10.3
	.0	.3	.6	.6			Deferred Taxes	.2	.2
	1.2	3.8	1.4	2.5			All Other-Non-Current	2.2	2.8
	46.8	39.5	29.0	22.4			Net Worth	30.6	34.4
	100.0	100.0	100.0	100.0			Total Liabilities & Net Worth	100.0	100.0
							INCOME DATA		
	100.0	100.0	100.0	100.0			Net Sales	100.0	100.0
	14.3	17.0	15.8	16.5			Gross Profit	19.9	20.2
	11.3	14.6	13.5	12.7			Operating Expenses	17.7	18.5
	2.9	2.4	2.3	3.9			Operating Profit	2.3	1.6
	.4	.7	.1	.9			All Other Expenses (net)	.9	.6
	2.5	1.7	2.2	3.0			Profit Before Taxes	1.3	1.1
							RATIOS		
	9.2 / 2.1 / 1.4	2.6 / 1.6 / 1.2	1.7 / 1.3 / 1.1	1.6 / 1.2 / 1.0			Current	2.0 / 1.4 / 1.1	2.1 / 1.4 / 1.2
	2.4 / .9 / .1	1.1 / .6 / .3	.8 / .5 / .2	.5 / .4 / .3			Quick	(187) .9 / .5 / .3	.9 / .5 / .3
	0 UND / 1 528.8 / 24 15.2	4 86.6 / 13 28.8 / 28 13.1	10 35.6 / 15 24.0 / 26 13.8	6 57.8 / 19 19.6 / 47 7.7			Sales/Receivables	8 45.1 / 17 21.2 / 33 11.1	9 41.9 / 19 19.1 / 32 11.3
	10 36.9 / 21 17.3 / 36 10.2	15 25.1 / 29 12.4 / 63 5.8	33 10.9 / 49 7.5 / 81 4.5	34 10.7 / 50 7.3 / 87 4.2			Cost of Sales/Inventory	27 13.7 / 57 6.4 / 83 4.4	25 14.8 / 54 6.7 / 81 4.5
	0 UND / 1 615.3 / 26 13.8	2 156.5 / 10 37.5 / 27 13.3	4 93.7 / 10 37.9 / 16 23.2	4 90.5 / 8 47.8 / 13 28.1			Cost of Sales/Payables	4 93.7 / 10 34.8 / 26 13.8	4 97.6 / 11 33.9 / 24 14.9
	11.8 / 28.2 / 106.7	10.8 / 22.9 / 74.6	13.4 / 22.7 / 53.8	11.1 / 33.1 / 135.9			Sales/Working Capital	8.3 / 20.2 / 75.4	8.8 / 17.7 / 50.3
	(11) 11.3 / 3.8 / 2.8	(71) 9.0 / 3.7 / 1.8	(68) 6.8 / 2.5 / 1.7	(28) 4.8 / 2.7 / 1.5			EBIT/Interest	(169) 3.9 / 1.8 / 1.0	(166) 3.2 / 1.8 / 1.1
		(17) 2.6 / 1.6 / 1.3	(32) 4.8 / 1.9 / 1.0	(22) 7.8 / 1.9 / 1.2			Net Profit + Depr., Dep., Amort./Cur. Mat. L /T/D	(71) 3.0 / 1.2 / .2	(72) 6.4 / 1.5 / .6
	.2 / .4 / .8	.1 / .4 / 1.1	.2 / .4 / 1.0	.5 / .8 / 1.4			Fixed/Worth	.1 / .4 / 1.3	.1 / .3 / .9
	.4 / 1.4 / 3.0	.7 / 1.7 / 5.0	1.4 / 3.2 / 7.3	2.1 / 5.0 / 12.7			Debt/Worth	1.3 / 2.7 / 7.1	1.0 / 2.5 / 4.9
	(13) 102.4 / 41.4 / 19.5	(70) 46.5 / 23.8 / 11.3	(75) 45.2 / 27.5 / 14.8	(30) 55.2 / 39.6 / 18.1			% Profit Before Taxes/Tangible Net Worth	(179) 31.3 / 11.7 / 1.6	(170) 26.8 / 11.3 / 2.0
	29.5 / 18.7 / 6.9	13.5 / 8.4 / 3.6	11.8 / 5.5 / 2.3	9.4 / 5.8 / 2.4			% Profit Before Taxes/Total Assets	8.6 / 3.2 / -.1	7.6 / 3.8 / .3
	198.1 / 115.4 / 35.6	160.5 / 67.6 / 18.1	102.1 / 47.2 / 18.2	46.6 / 21.1 / 12.7			Sales/Net Fixed Assets	115.2 / 40.0 / 11.6	115.1 / 40.7 / 18.2
	17.1 / 7.7 / 3.2	10.0 / 4.1 / 2.9	5.2 / 3.9 / 2.9	5.2 / 3.2 / 2.2			Sales/Total Assets	5.1 / 3.4 / 2.3	5.7 / 3.8 / 2.6
	(10) .1 / .4 / .7	(58) .2 / .6 / 1.0	(72) .2 / .4 / .9	(29) .2 / .6 / 1.2			% Depr., Dep., Amort./Sales	(163) .3 / .6 / 1.5	(157) .2 / .5 / 1.3
		(45) .8 / 1.4 / 3.2	(31) .5 / 1.6 / 2.9				% Officers', Directors', Owners' Comp/Sales	(98) 1.0 / 2.0 / 4.3	(86) .9 / 1.9 / 3.4
	53917M	550559M	1620548M	2164751M		4821190M	Net Sales ($)	3066598M	5012065M
	4215M	86339M	369281M	615530M		1476308M	Total Assets ($)	1109453M	1252909M

© Robert Morris Associates 1995

M = $ thousand   MM = $ million
See Pages 1 through 15 for Explanation of Ratios and Data

Comparative Historical Data				Current Data Sorted By Sales					
2	9	17		1	2	3		5	6
			# Postretirement Benefits						
			Type of Statement						
45	39	46	Unqualified	3	2	3		12	26
45	49	52	Reviewed		5	8		25	14
63	50	50	Compiled	5 / 7	11	13		11	3
1	9	4	Tax Returns	2		1		1	
42	61	52	Other	1 / 3	6	13		13	16
4/1/92-3/31/93 ALL	4/1/93-3/31/94 ALL	4/1/94-3/31/95 ALL		**60 (4/1-9/30/94)**			**144 (10/1/94-3/31/95)**		
196	208	204	**NUMBER OF STATEMENTS**	0-1MM: 6 / 1-3MM: 15	3-5MM: 24	5-10MM: 38		10-25MM: 62	25MM & OVER: 59

Columns for current data below: 0-1MM, 1-3MM, 3-5MM, 5-10MM, 10-25MM, 25MM & OVER.

2	9	17		0-1MM	1-3MM	3-5MM	5-10MM	10-25MM	25MM & OVER
%	%	%	**ASSETS**	%	%	%	%	%	%
6.6	8.2	6.6	Cash & Equivalents		5.7	8.6	6.8	7.5	5.1
21.9	20.0	20.8	Trade Receivables - (net)		25.8	16.3	18.0	22.0	21.6
46.5	46.2	45.3	Inventory		37.6	37.2	53.8	44.2	47.8
1.6	2.6	2.9	All Other Current		2.7	2.0	2.8	3.8	2.6
76.7	77.0	75.6	Total Current		71.8	64.1	81.4	77.5	77.1
15.9	16.0	16.8	Fixed Assets (net)		14.0	24.1	12.2	16.3	16.5
1.0	.4	1.6	Intangibles (net)		3.7	4.3	.3	.9	1.7
6.4	6.7	6.0	All Other Non-Current		10.5	7.6	6.0	5.2	4.8
100.0	100.0	100.0	Total		100.0	100.0	100.0	100.0	100.0
			LIABILITIES						
27.7	29.8	27.4	Notes Payable-Short Term		15.1	20.5	21.7	32.8	33.9
3.0	2.4	3.0	Cur. Mat.-L/T/D		4.2	2.1	2.9	2.7	3.6
15.0	12.3	13.2	Trade Payables		18.7	16.9	13.4	12.7	10.9
.3	.9	.3	Income Taxes Payable		.1	.1	.4	.3	.5
9.4	9.5	8.3	All Other Current		3.0	5.8	7.4	8.0	11.7
55.4	54.9	52.1	Total Current		41.0	45.4	45.8	56.4	60.6
10.5	11.3	11.8	Long Term Debt		14.6	12.8	11.4	9.0	12.9
.2	.2	.5	Deferred Taxes		.1	.9	.0	.3	1.0
3.0	1.4	2.4	All Other-Non-Current		3.1	3.6	2.3	1.8	2.8
30.9	32.3	33.1	Net Worth		41.3	37.3	40.5	32.5	22.7
100.0	100.0	100.0	Total Liabilities & Net Worth		100.0	100.0	100.0	100.0	100.0
			INCOME DATA						
100.0	100.0	100.0	Net Sales		100.0	100.0	100.0	100.0	100.0
19.8	19.0	16.7	Gross Profit		25.3	22.2	16.5	13.8	14.4
17.7	16.3	13.8	Operating Expenses		24.3	17.9	13.9	11.4	11.2
2.1	2.7	2.9	Operating Profit		.9	4.3	2.6	2.5	3.1
.5	.4	.6	All Other Expenses (net)		1.6	.4	.0	.3	.9
1.6	2.4	2.4	Profit Before Taxes		-.7	3.9	2.6	2.2	2.2
			RATIOS						
1.8 / 1.3 / 1.1	1.8 / 1.3 / 1.1	2.0 / 1.4 / 1.1	Current		3.3 / 1.6 / 1.2	2.1 / 1.3 / 1.0	2.4 / 1.8 / 1.4	1.7 / 1.4 / 1.1	1.4 / 1.2 / 1.0
(195) .9 / .5 / .2	(207) .9 / .5 / .3	1.0 / .5 / .2	Quick		1.8 / .9 / .4	1.1 / .6 / .2	1.0 / .5 / .2	.9 / .5 / .2	.7 / .4 / .2
7/49.2 / 17/21.0 / 34/10.6	5/66.5 / 16/23.1 / 28/13.0	6/60.4 / 15/24.7 / 29/12.5	Sales/Receivables		13/27.6 / 33/11.2 / 46/7.9	7/53.0 / 14/25.2 / 26/14.3	2/172.5 / 13/28.4 / 24/15.2	6/58.7 / 15/25.0 / 27/13.7	6/66.2 / 13/29.1 / 29/12.5
26/14.0 / 52/7.0 / 89/4.1	25/14.4 / 46/8.0 / 76/4.8	21/17.3 / 41/8.9 / 76/4.8	Cost of Sales/Inventory		22/16.4 / 46/7.9 / 126/2.9	17/21.1 / 35/10.4 / 99/3.7	24/15.1 / 45/8.1 / 79/4.6	17/22.0 / 35/10.3 / 74/4.9	25/14.8 / 41/8.8 / 74/4.9
5/81.0 / 12/29.4 / 27/13.5	3/116.6 / 9/39.8 / 21/17.4	3/104.7 / 9/40.1 / 21/17.4	Cost of Sales/Payables		10/35.6 / 35/10.5 / 54/6.8	2/211.8 / 12/31.3 / 37/10.0	2/188.2 / 10/37.3 / 20/17.9	4/101.0 / 9/41.0 / 13/27.7	4/103.8 / 7/52.1 / 15/24.1
11.7 / 22.5 / 90.4	11.0 / 25.9 / 73.9	11.5 / 23.5 / 76.8	Sales/Working Capital		4.5 / 12.7 / 27.3	13.5 / 26.2 / 682.2	8.2 / 14.8 / 29.3	15.5 / 25.5 / 66.5	19.5 / 36.0 / 308.6
(182) 4.4 / 2.0 / 1.3	(199) 7.1 / 3.1 / 1.6	(186) 7.0 / 3.0 / 1.8	EBIT/Interest		(14) 5.5 / 3.2 / 1.8	8.6 / 3.7 / 1.7	(34) 9.4 / 4.3 / 2.4	(57) 7.1 / 2.8 / 1.7	(53) 5.3 / 3.1 / 1.7
(69) 3.8 / 1.4 / .8	(56) 5.7 / 1.7 / .8	(80) 4.7 / 1.9 / 1.1	Net Profit + Depr., Dep., Amort./Cur. Mat. L/T/D					(26) 2.8 / 1.9 / 1.1	(32) 5.9 / 1.9 / 1.1
.1 / .4 / 1.0	.1 / .3 / 1.0	.2 / .5 / 1.1	Fixed/Worth		.1 / .3 / 1.2	.4 / .7 / 1.4	.1 / .2 / .6	.2 / .4 / 1.0	.3 / .8 / 1.4
1.2 / 2.7 / 5.9	1.3 / 2.5 / 5.4	1.1 / 2.5 / 6.7	Debt/Worth		.6 / 1.9 / 5.4	.9 / 1.7 / 4.0	.8 / 1.6 / 2.4	1.1 / 3.5 / 6.6	2.1 / 4.0 / 9.2
(186) 33.4 / 14.3 / 4.2	(201) 41.3 / 21.6 / 6.3	(197) 49.2 / 29.9 / 13.8	% Profit Before Taxes/Tangible Net Worth		(13) 41.7 / 17.5 / 4.6	(23) 108.8 / 27.0 / 9.2	(37) 41.0 / 27.9 / 13.0	(61) 52.0 / 25.7 / 12.7	(58) 54.1 / 38.1 / 23.4
8.7 / 3.7 / .8	11.3 / 5.0 / 2.1	13.0 / 6.6 / 2.9	% Profit Before Taxes/Total Assets		14.8 / 5.1 / 1.4	21.8 / 10.6 / 2.3	16.1 / 10.3 / 4.1	10.1 / 6.0 / 2.8	9.9 / 5.7 / 3.0
137.7 / 34.7 / 15.2	144.8 / 53.7 / 15.9	108.1 / 44.7 / 15.9	Sales/Net Fixed Assets		86.7 / 26.4 / 7.7	45.7 / 20.8 / 8.0	172.1 / 71.1 / 27.4	143.4 / 62.4 / 17.1	102.6 / 40.7 / 18.9
5.8 / 3.7 / 2.6	6.3 / 3.9 / 2.7	6.2 / 3.9 / 2.7	Sales/Total Assets		3.3 / 2.2 / 1.4	4.3 / 3.7 / 2.4	6.6 / 4.3 / 3.6	8.2 / 3.9 / 2.9	6.4 / 4.6 / 2.7
(167) .3 / .5 / 1.4	(179) .2 / .5 / 1.4	(177) .2 / .5 / 1.0	% Depr., Dep., Amort./Sales		(11) .7 / .9 / 1.8	(22) .6 / .8 / 1.6	(29) .2 / .5 / .7	(55) .2 / .4 / 1.0	(55) .1 / .3 / .8
(94) 1.0 / 2.0 / 3.5	(101) .7 / 1.4 / 2.6	(86) .6 / 1.4 / 3.0	% Officers', Directors', Owners' Comp/Sales				(22) .8 / 1.5 / 2.5	(29) .8 / 1.2	(17) .2 / .5 / 1.5
4359094M	6048082M	9210965M	Net Sales ($)	3354M	31623M	91381M	284571M	1019635M	7780401M
1344335M	1730580M	2551673M	Total Assets ($)	2239M	15989M	31131M	64355M	280862M	2157097M

M = $ thousand   MM = $ million
See Pages 1 through 15 for Explanation of Ratios and Data

WHOLESALERS—MOTOR VEHICLE SUPPLIES & NEW PARTS. SIC# 5013

Current Data Sorted By Assets							Comparative Historical Data	
5	15	14	3		1	# Postretirement Benefits	85	90
						Type of Statement		
3	11	44	18	5	5	Unqualified	85	90
7	68	79	7			Reviewed	181	196
53	123	52	7	2	1	Compiled	229	205
10	13	3				Tax Returns	6	11
23	54	56	14	1	2	Other	129	128
	223 (4/1-9/30/94)		438 (10/1/94-3/31/95)				4/1/90-3/31/91	4/1/91-3/31/92
0-500M	500M-2MM	2-10MM	10-50MM	50-100MM	100-250MM		ALL	ALL
96	269	234	46	8	8	**NUMBER OF STATEMENTS**	630	630
%	%	%	%	%	%	**ASSETS**	%	%
7.6	5.0	4.5	2.3			Cash & Equivalents	5.0	4.6
25.3	25.8	24.7	27.7			Trade Receivables - (net)	24.4	24.1
46.0	48.2	51.4	44.7			Inventory	49.7	49.6
.5	1.1	1.3	1.9			All Other Current	1.3	1.4
79.3	80.1	81.9	76.6			Total Current	80.4	79.7
16.2	13.0	11.5	15.5			Fixed Assets (net)	12.5	12.2
.8	1.4	1.6	2.5			Intangibles (net)	1.3	1.5
3.7	5.5	5.0	5.3			All Other Non-Current	5.8	6.6
100.0	100.0	100.0	100.0			Total	100.0	100.0
						LIABILITIES		
7.4	11.6	15.8	16.3			Notes Payable-Short Term	12.6	13.0
4.4	3.2	2.1	2.1			Cur. Mat. -L/T/D	3.4	3.5
19.5	23.2	25.4	21.9			Trade Payables	23.4	23.3
.3	.5	.4	.2			Income Taxes Payable	.5	.3
9.4	5.9	6.4	6.1			All Other Current	6.2	6.4
41.0	44.4	50.1	46.7			Total Current	46.1	46.5
16.8	12.7	8.5	9.1			Long Term Debt	13.6	12.1
.1	.1	.1	.2			Deferred Taxes	.1	.2
5.8	3.4	3.2	6.5			All Other-Non-Current	2.2	3.0
36.3	39.5	38.1	37.5			Net Worth	38.0	38.1
100.0	100.0	100.0	100.0			Total Liabilities & Net Worth	100.0	100.0
						INCOME DATA		
100.0	100.0	100.0	100.0			Net Sales	100.0	100.0
35.2	31.8	28.8	27.4			Gross Profit	32.0	31.8
31.1	28.6	25.5	23.5			Operating Expenses	28.5	29.1
4.1	3.3	3.3	3.9			Operating Profit	3.6	2.7
.8	.4	.8	1.7			All Other Expenses (net)	.9	.9
3.3	2.9	2.6	2.2			Profit Before Taxes	2.7	1.7
						RATIOS		
3.2	2.5	2.3	2.2				2.6	2.6
2.1	1.8	1.6	1.7			Current	1.8	1.8
1.4	1.4	1.3	1.3				1.3	1.3
1.2	1.0	.9	1.0				1.0	.9
.8	.7	(233) .6	.6			Quick	.6	.6
.5	.5	.4	.4				.4	.4
19 19.6	24 15.1	26 14.3	38 9.7				23 15.7	23 15.6
28 13.0	32 11.4	35 10.5	45 8.1			Sales/Receivables	31 11.7	33 10.9
38 9.6	41 8.8	47 7.8	60 6.1				41 8.8	45 8.2
56 6.5	59 6.2	72 5.1	81 4.5				72 5.1	74 4.9
91 4.0	94 3.9	107 3.4	101 3.6			Cost of Sales/Inventory	104 3.5	107 3.4
152 2.4	140 2.6	146 2.5	140 2.6				140 2.6	152 2.4
22 16.9	28 13.0	32 11.4	31 11.6				28 13.2	28 12.9
34 10.8	40 9.2	46 7.9	54 6.7			Cost of Sales/Payables	41 8.8	44 8.3
46 7.9	62 5.9	69 5.3	65 5.6				65 5.6	65 5.6
4.4	5.0	5.2	4.3				5.0	4.9
7.4	7.6	8.6	6.6			Sales/Working Capital	7.8	7.5
15.5	13.5	16.0	10.0				16.4	15.7
10.0	9.1	9.3	6.8				6.4	5.5
(80) 2.7	(253) 3.5	(215) 3.6	(45) 3.5			EBIT/Interest	(584) 2.5	(588) 2.2
1.1	1.6	1.8	2.1				1.3	1.2
3.9	5.7	7.0	4.9				5.0	3.8
(15) 1.3	(97) 2.1	(107) 2.4	(15) 1.6			Net Profit + Depr., Dep., Amort./Cur. Mat. L /T/D	(334) 2.0	(296) 1.6
.4	1.0	1.4	1.0				.9	.6
.1	.1	.1	.2				.1	.1
.3	.3	.3	.3			Fixed/Worth	.3	.3
1.3	.6	.5	.7				.7	.6
.7	.8	1.0	1.0				.9	.9
1.3	1.8	2.0	1.8			Debt/Worth	1.8	1.8
7.3	3.2	3.4	3.8				4.0	3.7
66.1	31.8	34.0	37.0				30.3	26.5
(84) 24.9	(256) 15.1	(225) 16.3	18.8			% Profit Before Taxes/Tangible Net Worth	(588) 14.1	(600) 12.4
2.7	6.6	8.0	9.5				4.2	2.4
21.0	11.3	10.9	10.9				10.8	8.8
7.8	5.4	5.5	5.6			% Profit Before Taxes/Total Assets	5.3	3.7
.5	2.3	2.3	2.7				1.2	.7
105.8	60.5	52.5	36.0				58.3	59.3
38.2	30.5	30.4	22.2			Sales/Net Fixed Assets	30.5	28.7
13.9	16.9	17.0	9.3				15.3	15.0
4.4	3.5	3.1	2.5				3.3	3.2
2.9	2.8	2.5	2.2			Sales/Total Assets	2.6	2.5
1.9	2.1	2.0	1.7				2.0	1.9
.5	.6	.5	.7				.6	.6
(75) 1.2	(240) 1.1	(218) .9	(39) .9			% Depr., Dep., Amort./Sales	(568) 1.1	(572) 1.0
2.4	1.7	1.3	1.7				1.6	1.6
3.9	2.4	1.5	.7				2.0	2.0
(45) 5.5	(159) 4.0	(98) 2.5	(11) 1.9			% Officers', Directors', Owners' Comp/Sales	(288) 3.6	(306) 3.8
9.9	6.2	4.1					5.8	6.5
84692M	883061M	2629264M	1961352M	978842M	2989397M	Net Sales ($)	6155150M	6988927M
28175M	307948M	1043948M	960551M	539103M	1289036M	Total Assets ($)	2882545M	3407281M

M = $ thousand   MM = $ million
See Pages 1 through 15 for Explanation of Ratios and Data

Comparative Historical Data				Current Data Sorted By Sales					
10	32	38	# Postretirement Benefits	3	12	3	7	10	3
			Type of Statement						
80	81	86	Unqualified	2	7	7	15	28	27
183	172	161	Reviewed	4	32	30	54	33	8
238	206	238	Compiled	44	85	41	34	27	7
21	27	26	Tax Returns	9	8	4	3	2	
149	135	150	Other	17	33	30	21	33	16
4/1/92-3/31/93 ALL	4/1/93-3/31/94 ALL	4/1/94-3/31/95 ALL		223 (4/1-9/30/94) 0-1MM	1-3MM	3-5MM	438 (10/1/94-3/31/95) 5-10MM	10-25MM	25MM & OVER
671	621	661	**NUMBER OF STATEMENTS**	76	165	112	127	123	58
%	%	%	**ASSETS**	%	%	%	%	%	%
4.9	5.0	5.0	Cash & Equivalents	7.1	5.0	5.1	5.6	3.9	2.8
23.8	23.8	25.3	Trade Receivables - (net)	22.3	24.5	26.9	27.1	24.5	26.0
50.2	48.4	48.6	Inventory	46.8	48.6	48.1	48.6	52.3	44.5
1.2	1.5	1.1	All Other Current	.6	1.3	.7	1.0	1.6	1.4
80.1	78.8	80.0	Total Current	76.8	79.3	80.7	82.3	82.4	74.8
12.7	13.6	13.3	Fixed Assets (net)	18.5	13.1	12.6	11.6	10.7	17.4
1.6	1.6	1.5	Intangibles (net)	.7	2.1	.9	1.8	1.4	1.7
5.5	6.1	5.2	All Other Non-Current	4.0	5.4	5.8	4.3	5.6	6.1
100.0	100.0	100.0	Total	100.0	100.0	100.0	100.0	100.0	100.0
			LIABILITIES						
11.6	10.7	12.6	Notes Payable-Short Term	9.4	10.1	11.5	15.2	17.1	11.2
3.7	3.5	2.8	Cur. Mat.-L /T/D	4.8	3.5	2.8	2.2	1.9	2.0
22.1	21.3	23.2	Trade Payables	17.4	21.9	23.8	26.1	24.9	23.4
.3	1.8	.4	Income Taxes Payable	.3	.4	.5	.4	.4	.3
7.9	7.2	6.6	All Other Current	7.1	5.9	7.9	6.1	6.8	6.4
45.7	44.5	45.7	Total Current	39.0	41.8	46.4	50.0	51.1	43.3
12.8	12.6	11.7	Long Term Debt	19.3	15.0	10.0	9.0	6.7	12.3
.3	.2	.1	Deferred Taxes	.1	.1	.1	.1	.1	.5
3.8	3.5	3.9	All Other-Non-Current	6.5	4.0	2.3	2.8	4.3	4.8
37.4	39.3	38.6	Net Worth	35.1	39.0	41.2	38.2	37.8	39.0
100.0	100.0	100.0	Total Liabilities & Net Worth	100.0	100.0	100.0	100.0	100.0	100.0
			INCOME DATA						
100.0	100.0	100.0	Net Sales	100.0	100.0	100.0	100.0	100.0	100.0
32.0	31.6	30.9	Gross Profit	36.8	33.9	29.8	28.7	28.5	26.6
29.4	28.7	27.3	Operating Expenses	31.7	30.7	27.1	25.2	25.1	22.1
2.7	2.9	3.6	Operating Profit	5.1	3.2	2.7	3.5	3.5	4.5
.6	.6	.7	All Other Expenses (net)	1.4	.5	.1	.8	1.0	.4
2.0	2.3	2.9	Profit Before Taxes	3.7	2.7	2.7	2.7	2.4	4.1
			RATIOS						
2.7	2.6	2.6	Current	3.5	3.0	2.5	2.2	2.2	2.6
1.9	1.9	1.8		2.1	2.1	1.7	1.6	1.6	1.7
1.3	1.4	1.3		1.4	1.5	1.4	1.3	1.2	1.3
1.0	1.0	1.0	Quick	1.3	1.0	.9	1.0	.8	1.1
(670) .6	(620) .6	(660) .7		.8	.7	.7 (126)	.6	.5	.8
.4	.4	.4		.5	.5	.5	.4	.4	.4
22 16.3	23 15.9	24 15.1	Sales/Receivables	19 15.9	24 15.1	24 15.0	24 14.9	24 15.0	30 12.3
32 11.5	32 11.3	33 10.9		30 12.3	31 11.6	33 11.1	35 10.4	34 10.6	43 8.5
43 8.5	42 8.7	45 8.2		43 8.5	42 8.6	42 8.6	46 7.9	42 8.7	58 6.3
73 5.0	68 5.4	65 5.6	Cost of Sales/Inventory	64 5.7	69 5.3	57 6.4	62 5.9	68 5.4	74 4.9
107 3.4	104 3.5	101 3.6		114 3.2	107 3.4	91 4.0	91 4.0	104 3.5	99 3.7
146 2.5	140 2.6	146 2.5		192 1.9	152 2.4	130 2.8	135 2.7	135 2.7	135 2.7
26 13.8	24 15.4	29 12.7	Cost of Sales/Payables	23 15.9	29 12.7	30 12.0	30 12.0	30 12.3	31 11.9
41 9.0	38 9.7	42 8.7		37 10.0	41 8.8	41 8.8	42 8.7	42 8.6	51 7.1
60 6.1	61 6.0	63 5.8		56 6.5	68 5.4	60 6.1	63 5.8	61 6.0	63 5.8
4.7	4.9	4.9	Sales/Working Capital	3.7	4.4	5.0	6.2	5.8	4.2
7.1	7.5	7.6		5.6	6.5	8.3	9.5	9.3	7.5
15.3	14.2	14.1		13.4	10.7	14.6	15.6	17.7	11.6
6.1	7.1	9.2	EBIT/Interest	8.1	8.3	8.6	9.8	10.2	13.8
(611) 2.5	(573) 3.1	(608) 3.5		(66) 2.4	(151) 2.9	(104) 3.7	(118) 3.6	(113) 3.8	(56) 4.7
1.3	1.4	1.7		1.1	1.5	2.0	1.6	2.1	2.5
3.5	4.4	5.9	Net Profit + Depr., Dep., Amort./Cur. Mat. L/T/D	3.7	3.0	6.2	7.2	9.3	5.9
(283) 1.7	(248) 1.6	(242) 2.1		(12) 1.0	(56) 1.3	(44) 2.9	(58) 2.6	(53) 2.5	(19) 3.7
.6	.7	1.1		.4	.7	1.3	1.2	1.4	1.5
.1	.1	.1	Fixed/Worth	.1	.1	.1	.1	.1	.2
.3	.3	.3		.4	.3	.3	.3	.3	.4
.7	.7	.7		2.5	.7	.5	.6	.5	.8
.9	.8	.9	Debt/Worth	.8	.7	.9	1.0	1.0	.9
1.8	1.6	1.8		1.7	1.8	1.5	2.0	2.0	1.7
4.0	3.4	3.4		9.4	3.7	3.0	3.2	3.6	3.1
28.4	29.3	36.6	% Profit Before Taxes/Tangible Net Worth	61.4	27.9	32.4	36.9	38.1	42.4
(628) 13.3	(587) 13.7	(627) 16.8		(66) 19.3	(152) 13.7	(110) 14.9	(118) 15.3	19.8	23.2
3.7	4.1	7.3		.9	3.9	7.8	7.8	8.8	11.6
9.4	10.2	11.9	% Profit Before Taxes/Total Assets	19.2	11.8	11.1	11.4	11.5	15.3
4.0	4.3	5.9		6.8	5.4	6.3	5.0	6.9	7.9
.9	1.4	2.2		.5	1.3	2.7	2.2	2.9	4.1
59.7	59.9	58.0	Sales/Net Fixed Assets	94.9	62.3	60.7	52.5	54.3	42.0
30.3	28.1	29.7		25.8	28.4	33.7	32.3	30.7	16.8
15.0	13.7	15.0		9.3	14.3	19.5	18.3	19.2	6.3
3.3	3.2	3.3	Sales/Total Assets	3.3	3.2	3.5	3.5	3.3	2.8
2.5	2.6	2.6		2.3	2.5	2.8	2.8	2.7	2.2
2.0	2.0	2.0		1.7	1.9	2.2	2.1	2.2	1.7
.5	.6	.6	% Depr., Dep., Amort./Sales	.8	.6	.5	.5	.5	.7
(602) 1.0	(568) 1.0	(584) 1.0		(61) 1.5	(139) 1.2	(104) 1.0	(119) .9	(115) .9	(46) 1.0
1.6	1.6	1.6		2.7	1.8	1.5	1.4	1.3	2.0
2.3	1.9	1.9	% Officers', Directors', Owners' Comp/Sales	4.5	2.7	2.0	1.4	1.4	.7
(328) 4.1	(299) 3.9	(315) 3.6		(34) 7.1	(97) 4.4	(61) 3.2	(69) 2.6	(43) 2.4	(11) 1.9
7.1	6.5	6.1		11.0	6.3	6.2	5.0	3.7	7.6
7068675M	6697249M	9526608M	Net Sales ($)	48705M	316635M	439593M	931548M	1869415M	5920712M
3342010M	2825712M	4168761M	Total Assets ($)	25860M	146423M	169335M	369749M	767119M	2690275M

M = $ thousand   MM = $ million
See Pages 1 through 15 for Explanation of Ratios and Data

WHOLESALERS—TIRES & TUBES. SIC# 5014

Current Data Sorted By Assets							Comparative Historical Data	
4	3	6	1			**# Postretirement Benefits**		
						Type of Statement		
3	4	10	8	2	1	Unqualified	28	26
7	10	25	7		1	Reviewed	32	50
7	31	15	1			Compiled	62	66
3	1	2				Tax Returns	1	4
4	9	19	14	1	1	Other	26	32
	44 (4/1-9/30/94)		141 (10/1/94-3/31/95)				4/1/90-3/31/91	4/1/91-3/31/92
0-500M	500M-2MM	2-10MM	10-50MM	50-100MM	100-250MM		ALL	ALL
24	55	71	30	3	2	**NUMBER OF STATEMENTS**	149	178
%	%	%	%	%	%	**ASSETS**	%	%
5.2	6.0	5.0	5.7			Cash & Equivalents	5.5	6.3
26.4	32.3	31.3	31.7			Trade Receivables - (net)	33.4	29.7
36.4	36.6	39.1	40.7			Inventory	37.7	39.2
1.8	.8	2.8	1.3			All Other Current	1.7	1.7
69.8	75.6	78.2	79.4			Total Current	78.4	76.8
19.5	16.7	15.6	15.3			Fixed Assets (net)	14.8	16.8
3.5	1.4	.5	.2			Intangibles (net)	.6	.7
7.3	6.2	5.7	5.1			All Other Non-Current	6.3	5.7
100.0	100.0	100.0	100.0			Total	100.0	100.0
						LIABILITIES		
8.6	6.7	11.1	10.5			Notes Payable-Short Term	12.0	11.2
4.0	3.3	2.1	4.3			Cur. Mat. -L/T/D	2.7	3.5
39.6	36.7	34.1	35.5			Trade Payables	36.0	33.7
.0	.3	.1	.1			Income Taxes Payable	.4	.5
9.1	4.9	6.2	5.3			All Other Current	8.2	6.2
61.4	51.9	53.6	55.8			Total Current	59.4	55.2
14.9	13.2	6.4	10.3			Long Term Debt	11.5	10.9
.0	.3	.2	.2			Deferred Taxes	.3	.1
1.2	2.0	2.6	1.4			All Other-Non-Current	2.1	1.7
22.5	32.6	37.2	32.3			Net Worth	26.8	32.1
100.0	100.0	100.0	100.0			Total Liabilities & Net Worth	100.0	100.0
						INCOME DATA		
100.0	100.0	100.0	100.0			Net Sales	100.0	100.0
30.6	27.7	24.7	21.4			Gross Profit	25.4	27.6
27.8	25.5	22.4	18.8			Operating Expenses	23.4	25.4
2.8	2.3	2.3	2.6			Operating Profit	2.0	2.1
.3	.0	-.1	.0			All Other Expenses (net)	.1	.5
2.6	2.3	2.4	2.6			Profit Before Taxes	1.9	1.6
						RATIOS		
1.7	1.9	1.9	1.8				1.7	1.8
1.3	1.5	1.3	1.3			Current	1.3	1.4
.9	1.2	1.2	1.2				1.1	1.1
.8	.9	.8	1.0				.9	.9
.5	.7	.6	.6			Quick	.6	.6
.4	.6	.5	.5				.5	.4
13 28.2	30 12.3	30 12.1	27 13.3				27 13.3	25 14.4
21 17.8	36 10.2	38 9.5	42 8.7			Sales/Receivables	40 9.1	38 9.6
37 10.0	47 7.8	54 6.7	64 5.7				55 6.6	47 7.7
29 12.5	38 9.7	45 8.2	47 7.8				45 8.2	51 7.2
46 7.9	63 5.8	66 5.5	72 5.1			Cost of Sales/Inventory	61 6.0	72 5.1
78 4.7	87 4.2	87 4.2	94 3.9				91 4.0	96 3.8
28 12.9	40 9.2	37 9.8	32 11.5				44 8.3	40 9.1
45 8.1	62 5.9	59 6.2	65 5.6			Cost of Sales/Payables	62 5.9	59 6.2
58 6.3	76 4.8	79 4.6	87 4.2				85 4.3	79 4.6
7.2	8.0	7.1	6.5				8.3	8.0
29.8	15.2	15.3	13.5			Sales/Working Capital	15.8	14.0
-73.5	30.7	27.2	33.2				42.6	44.7
(22) 6.0	(51) 7.9	(63) 8.1	(24) 9.6				(130) 4.5	(163) 5.3
2.6	3.8	3.5	5.1			EBIT/Interest	2.5	2.3
.6	2.2	1.7	1.6				1.1	1.1
	(23) 7.1	(22) 4.4	(13) 3.4				(68) 4.9	(81) 4.6
	2.9	2.1	2.7			Net Profit + Depr., Dep., Amort./Cur. Mat. L /T/D	2.0	2.0
	2.1	1.3	.4				1.0	.7
.3	.2	.2	.2				.2	.2
.8	.4	.3	.4			Fixed/Worth	.4	.5
5.9	1.1	.9	1.4				1.0	1.0
1.2	1.3	.9	1.1				1.6	1.3
4.4	2.3	2.3	2.6			Debt/Worth	2.9	2.5
96.6	4.7	3.8	6.2				5.7	4.7
(19) 50.0	(53) 41.7	(70) 27.6	39.9				(139) 34.1	(171) 31.3
29.3	22.5	16.0	16.6			% Profit Before Taxes/Tangible Net Worth	15.6	11.6
-3.1	10.7	8.3	7.0				6.4	2.6
12.4	10.6	9.8	10.3				7.8	7.8
4.1	6.3	5.0	4.3			% Profit Before Taxes/Total Assets	3.7	3.0
-1.9	3.5	1.5	1.9				.7	.5
60.9	56.2	46.1	51.4				66.5	57.2
28.7	22.8	22.4	26.0			Sales/Net Fixed Assets	25.3	23.6
14.0	11.9	12.2	11.5				13.9	11.8
5.6	4.1	3.5	3.4				3.6	3.7
4.0	3.1	2.8	2.8			Sales/Total Assets	2.9	2.8
3.1	2.1	2.2	2.3				2.3	2.2
(20) .5	(51) .6	(68) .5	(28) .5				(137) .5	(167) .6
1.0	1.0	.9	.7			% Depr., Dep., Amort./Sales	1.1	1.1
1.8	1.8	1.6	1.1				1.7	1.7
(12) 3.9	(27) 1.5	(38) .9	(10) .5				(59) 1.4	(79) 1.4
5.1	3.3	1.4	1.7			% Officers', Directors', Owners' Comp/Sales	2.0	2.7
6.4	6.2	2.1	10.3				4.0	4.6
28593M	210121M	947716M	1729644M	595020M	825974M	Net Sales ($)	4108763M	3066633M
6423M	66506M	324526M	632085M	227855M	341709M	Total Assets ($)	1355981M	1092380M

M = $ thousand   MM = $ million
See Pages 1 through 15 for Explanation of Ratios and Data

Comparative Historical Data				Current Data Sorted By Sales					
4	10	14	# Postretirement Benefits Type of Statement	1	4	1	3	3	2
27	33	28	Unqualified	1	4	2	4	8	9
52	56	49	Reviewed	2	6	7	12	13	9
68	58	54	Compiled	1	25	10	14	3	1
3	3	6	Tax Returns	3	1		1	1	
34	28	48	Other	4	2	4	9	12	17
4/1/92-3/31/93 ALL	4/1/93-3/31/94 ALL	4/1/94-3/31/95 ALL		44 (4/1-9/30/94) 0-1MM	1-3MM	141 (10/1/94-3/31/95) 3-5MM	5-10MM	10-25MM	25MM & OVER
184	178	185	**NUMBER OF STATEMENTS**	11	38	23	40	37	36
%	%	%	**ASSETS**	%	%	%	%	%	%
4.8	5.8	5.3	Cash & Equivalents	4.4	6.7	6.3	4.1	4.7	5.6
32.2	30.4	31.0	Trade Receivables - (net)	30.5	27.6	30.4	33.1	33.5	30.4
36.7	37.7	38.0	Inventory	35.6	37.6	36.6	38.6	39.1	38.2
1.5	1.3	1.8	All Other Current	2.8	.7	3.2	2.1	1.7	1.5
75.1	75.2	76.1	Total Current	73.2	72.6	76.5	77.8	78.9	75.7
18.4	17.8	16.6	Fixed Assets (net)	16.0	20.7	13.1	13.9	15.5	18.7
.7	1.2	1.2	Intangibles (net)	.6	1.1	4.3	1.0	.3	.9
5.8	5.8	6.1	All Other Non-Current	10.3	5.6	6.2	7.3	5.2	4.8
100.0	100.0	100.0	Total	100.0	100.0	100.0	100.0	100.0	100.0
			LIABILITIES						
10.4	10.8	9.3	Notes Payable-Short Term	10.8	6.7	5.1	9.6	12.4	10.7
4.1	3.4	3.1	Cur. Mat.-L /T/D	3.5	3.8	3.6	2.1	2.6	3.5
35.3	31.3	35.4	Trade Payables	40.0	31.9	40.7	37.3	33.6	34.2
.3	1.7	.2	Income Taxes Payable	.0	.4	.1	.1	.2	.2
7.0	6.5	6.1	All Other Current	13.4	5.1	6.6	5.1	5.6	6.2
57.1	53.7	54.0	Total Current	67.7	47.8	56.1	54.1	54.4	54.7
10.5	12.0	10.2	Long Term Debt	16.1	15.2	11.6	6.4	6.5	10.4
.2	.1	.2	Deferred Taxes	.0	.1	.3	.2	.2	.2
2.1	2.6	2.0	All Other-Non-Current	.3	2.2	1.4	3.0	1.5	2.1
30.1	31.6	33.5	Net Worth	15.9	34.6	30.6	36.2	37.5	32.5
100.0	100.0	100.0	Total Liabilities & Net Worth	100.0	100.0	100.0	100.0	100.0	100.0
			INCOME DATA						
100.0	100.0	100.0	Net Sales	100.0	100.0	100.0	100.0	100.0	100.0
26.6	28.0	25.8	Gross Profit	32.4	32.0	24.7	22.5	23.9	23.6
24.7	26.0	23.3	Operating Expenses	30.3	28.7	23.3	20.0	21.6	21.1
1.9	2.0	2.5	Operating Profit	2.1	3.3	1.4	2.5	2.4	2.5
.1	.3	.0	All Other Expenses (net)	.2	.1	−.2	−.2	.1	.0
1.8	1.7	2.5	Profit Before Taxes	1.9	3.2	1.6	2.7	2.2	2.5
			RATIOS						
1.7 1.3 1.1	1.9 1.4 1.2	1.9 1.4 1.2	Current	1.8 1.4 .8	2.1 1.5 1.3	1.8 1.3 1.1	1.7 1.4 1.2	2.1 1.3 1.2	1.9 1.3 1.1
.9 .6 .5	.9 .6 .5	.9 .6 .5	Quick	1.1 .5 .4	1.1 .7 .5	.7 .6 .4	.9 .7 .6	1.0 .6 .5	1.0 .6 .4
26 14.2 38 9.6 52 7.0	28 13.2 38 9.7 49 7.4	26 14.0 37 9.8 49 7.4	Sales/Receivables	12 29.9 27 13.3 58 6.3	19 19.7 35 10.5 43 8.4	31 11.8 38 9.7 47 7.8	30 12.2 38 9.5 54 6.8	30 12.1 42 8.6 61 6.0	19 19.6 38 9.6 49 7.4
42 8.6 64 5.7 83 4.4	47 7.8 65 5.6 94 3.9	42 8.6 64 5.7 87 4.2	Cost of Sales/Inventory	29 12.5 65 5.6 78 4.7	38 9.7 64 5.7 99 3.7	40 9.1 65 5.6 104 3.5	43 8.5 63 5.8 83 4.4	47 7.8 64 5.7 87 4.2	46 8.0 61 6.0 78 4.7
41 8.8 57 6.4 78 4.7	31 11.7 55 6.6 78 4.7	37 9.9 59 6.2 76 4.8	Cost of Sales/Payables	30 12.0 45 8.1 64 5.7	37 9.9 51 7.1 74 4.9	47 7.7 63 5.8 89 4.1	33 11.0 59 6.2 78 4.7	37 9.9 59 6.2 73 5.0	25 14.6 60 6.1 85 4.3
9.1 15.4 53.2	7.1 13.1 31.6	7.2 15.7 32.0	Sales/Working Capital	5.7 23.0 −24.5	6.7 12.8 32.6	7.2 17.0 40.6	8.3 15.8 29.9	5.7 15.7 25.5	7.4 16.5 53.4
(173) 6.5 2.6 1.2	(172) 5.5 2.3 1.3	(165) 8.1 3.7 1.7	EBIT/Interest		(37) 7.7 3.5 1.7	(21) 7.4 3.4 1.3	(34) 12.1 3.9 2.4	(32) 7.5 3.3 1.6	(32) 9.6 5.1 1.6
(85) 3.4 1.6 .9	(62) 4.1 1.6 .8	(67) 4.4 2.7 1.5	Net Profit + Depr., Dep., Amort./Cur. Mat. L/T/D		(14) 7.7 3.4 2.1		(13) 7.8 2.9 .7	(14) 3.0 2.2 1.4	(16) 7.6 2.4 1.0
.2 .5 1.1	.2 .6 1.1	.2 .5 1.1	Fixed/Worth	.2 .5 3.2	.3 .5 1.4	.2 .5 1.3	.2 .3 .7	.2 .5 1.0	.3 .5 1.4
1.3 2.6 5.4	1.2 2.5 4.5	1.1 2.5 5.3	Debt/Worth	1.5 3.8 −9.1	1.0 2.1 5.1	1.3 2.6 6.5	1.2 2.4 3.6	.8 2.2 3.8	1.1 2.7 6.2
(174) 31.3 12.9 3.0	(169) 24.4 13.1 4.1	(177) 35.3 18.6 8.9	% Profit Before Taxes/Tangible Net Worth		(36) 43.0 23.1 6.0	(21) 47.0 16.1 6.4	34.8 19.3 10.1	(36) 26.5 13.7 8.8	39.1 18.6 7.7
8.9 3.1 .8	8.2 3.5 1.0	10.4 5.3 1.7	% Profit Before Taxes/Total Assets	12.5 4.2 −2.6	13.1 6.8 2.3	7.4 5.0 .5	11.3 5.2 2.9	9.0 5.2 1.3	11.5 4.3 2.2
37.7 19.5 11.6	33.7 19.8 11.6	52.0 22.6 12.0	Sales/Net Fixed Assets	61.0 33.4 15.0	45.3 17.8 7.8	56.2 22.5 14.0	56.3 24.5 14.7	52.5 22.4 13.2	47.6 21.7 11.0
3.6 2.9 2.3	3.4 2.7 2.3	3.8 3.0 2.2	Sales/Total Assets	5.0 3.3 2.0	4.3 3.0 2.0	3.9 2.7 2.1	3.7 3.0 2.3	3.5 2.8 2.1	3.7 3.0 2.4
(173) .6 1.1 1.9	(166) .7 1.1 1.8	(172) .5 .9 1.6	% Depr., Dep., Amort./Sales		(35) .8 1.4 2.2	(21) .5 1.0 1.5	(39) .5 .7 1.2	(35) .5 .8 1.5	(34) .6 .8 1.5
(87) 1.4 2.4 4.6	(87) 1.4 2.5 4.3	(87) 1.1 2.0 5.0	% Officers', Directors', Owners' Comp/Sales		(19) 2.0 4.1 6.2	(12) 1.4 3.2 4.4	(20) 1.1 1.8 2.5	(20) .9 1.2 3.7	(10) .7 1.4 5.5
3372223M 1286216M	2894625M 1106944M	4337068M 1599104M	Net Sales ($) Total Assets ($)	5353M 1684M	79619M 28756M	96598M 36204M	308818M 109983M	626671M 242428M	3220009M 1180049M

M = $ thousand   MM = $ million
See Pages 1 through 15 for Explanation of Ratios and Data

Current Data Sorted By Assets   Comparative Historical Data

0-500M	500M-2MM	2-10MM	10-50MM	50-100MM	100-250MM	# Postretirement Benefits / Type of Statement	4/1/90-3/31/91 ALL	4/1/91-3/31/92 ALL
	1	3				# Postretirement Benefits		
						Type of Statement		
1	2	4	4			Unqualified	4	5
	5	7	3			Reviewed	15	16
3	9	3				Compiled	16	15
1		1				Tax Returns	2	
3	5	1				Other	7	8
	17 (4/1-9/30/94)		35 (10/1/94-3/31/95)					
8	21	16	7			NUMBER OF STATEMENTS	44	44

0-500M %	500M-2MM %	2-10MM %	10-50MM %	50-100MM %	100-250MM %		%	%
						ASSETS		
	8.5	.1				Cash & Equivalents	3.9	3.3
	29.4	21.8				Trade Receivables - (net)	27.3	26.7
	40.0	52.5				Inventory	44.2	49.7
	.8	.9				All Other Current	1.6	1.7
	78.7	75.3				Total Current	77.0	81.4
	9.3	17.4				Fixed Assets (net)	15.2	11.2
	6.1	1.7				Intangibles (net)	2.6	1.9
	5.9	5.7				All Other Non-Current	5.2	5.4
	100.0	100.0				Total	100.0	100.0
						LIABILITIES		
	13.2	17.5				Notes Payable-Short Term	15.3	15.4
	2.5	2.3				Cur. Mat. -L/T/D	2.8	3.2
	18.3	18.7				Trade Payables	20.8	24.2
	.4	.3				Income Taxes Payable	.3	.6
	4.9	10.8				All Other Current	10.0	5.4
	39.3	49.4				Total Current	49.3	48.9
	10.1	12.7				Long Term Debt	11.8	13.7
	.0	.1				Deferred Taxes	.1	.0
	5.0	2.9				All Other-Non-Current	3.6	3.9
	45.6	34.9				Net Worth	35.3	33.5
	100.0	100.0				Total Liabilities & Net Worth	100.0	100.0
						INCOME DATA		
	100.0	100.0				Net Sales	100.0	100.0
	32.7	39.5				Gross Profit	38.7	38.7
	30.6	37.1				Operating Expenses	36.1	35.9
	2.1	2.4				Operating Profit	2.6	2.9
	.6	.3				All Other Expenses (net)	.9	.8
	1.6	2.1				Profit Before Taxes	1.7	2.1
						RATIOS		
	2.7	2.0					2.5	2.2
	2.0	1.5				Current	1.5	1.6
	1.5	1.2					1.1	1.3
	1.6	.7					1.0	.9
	.8	.5				Quick	.6	.6
	.6	.2					.4	.4
18	20.3	17 21.6					20 18.0	17 21.0
24	15.2	20 18.1				Sales/Receivables	30 12.2	30 12.3
41	8.8	29 12.5					54 6.8	37 10.0
41	8.8	74 4.9					51 7.1	61 6.0
66	5.5	94 3.9				Cost of Sales/Inventory	74 4.9	104 3.5
94	3.9	126 2.9					130 2.8	126 2.9
11	33.8	20 18.7					23 16.0	31 11.9
23	15.9	31 11.6				Cost of Sales/Payables	41 9.0	45 8.2
42	8.6	40 9.2					54 6.7	59 6.2
	7.2	8.3					5.8	6.0
	10.2	14.7				Sales/Working Capital	12.3	9.9
	16.3	31.3					40.9	17.2
	3.5	6.7					5.3	5.9
	(17) 2.6	2.5				EBIT/Interest	(40) 2.1	(40) 2.6
	.1	1.1					1.1	1.2
	3.1	7.9					4.5	3.4
	(11) 2.0	(11) 2.3				Net Profit + Depr., Dep., Amort./Cur. Mat. L /T/D	(29) 1.7	(24) 1.8
	.7	1.3					.6	.7
	.1	.3					.2	.2
	.2	.5				Fixed/Worth	.4	.3
	.4	.6					.8	.9
	.6	1.6					1.0	1.6
	1.7	2.5				Debt/Worth	2.3	2.0
	3.7	3.1					8.0	3.8
	27.9	31.7					26.6	41.2
	(18) 9.9	18.3				% Profit Before Taxes/Tangible Net Worth	(40) 13.5	(42) 14.7
	−1.6	1.4					1.1	5.5
	7.6	12.4					10.7	12.3
	5.5	4.9				% Profit Before Taxes/Total Assets	4.5	4.1
	.6	.4					.4	1.0
	157.4	36.6					64.4	69.0
	44.6	22.3				Sales/Net Fixed Assets	27.1	27.5
	30.4	15.4					15.2	19.9
	4.9	4.1					3.9	4.4
	4.0	3.3				Sales/Total Assets	2.8	3.2
	2.4	2.9					2.1	2.5
	.4	.7					.6	.5
	(17) .8	1.0				% Depr., Dep., Amort./Sales	(39) .9	(39) .9
	1.1	1.2					1.2	1.3
	3.4						2.2	1.6
	(13) 7.1					% Officers', Directors', Owners' Comp/Sales	(23) 4.0	(23) 4.0
	12.2						6.7	5.5
8708M	82027M	206769M	353692M			Net Sales ($)	408457M	405477M
2059M	21297M	60853M	117412M			Total Assets ($)	156328M	124035M

M = $ thousand   MM = $ million
See Pages 1 through 15 for Explanation of Ratios and Data

Comparative Historical Data | Current Data Sorted By Sales

3	4	4	# Postretirement Benefits	1	2	1			
			Type of Statement						
7	11	11	Unqualified		2	1		4	4
16	15	15	Reviewed	1		2	3	6	3
16	14	15	Compiled	1	5	5	3	1	
2	2	2	Tax Returns	1				1	
14	11	9	Other	3	3		2		
4/1/92-3/31/93 ALL	4/1/93-3/31/94 ALL	4/1/94-3/31/95 ALL		17 (4/1-9/30/94)			35 (10/1/94-3/31/95)		
				0-1MM	1-3MM	3-5MM	5-10MM	10-25MM	25MM & OVER
55	53	52	**NUMBER OF STATEMENTS**	6	10	9	8	12	7

ASSETS

Hist 1 %	Hist 2 %	Hist 3 %		0-1MM %	1-3MM %	3-5MM %	5-10MM %	10-25MM %	25MM & OVER %
6.3	7.8	6.5	Cash & Equivalents		11.7			.2	
22.4	28.3	24.4	Trade Receivables - (net)		23.7			23.2	
50.7	39.3	44.3	Inventory		39.3			50.7	
1.9	1.9	1.0	All Other Current		.2			1.0	
81.3	77.3	76.2	Total Current		74.8			75.1	
11.6	14.4	12.6	Fixed Assets (net)		13.1			17.3	
3.0	1.7	3.7	Intangibles (net)		2.7			1.8	
4.1	6.6	7.5	All Other Non-Current		9.4			5.7	
100.0	100.0	100.0	Total		100.0			100.0	

LIABILITIES

Hist 1	Hist 2	Hist 3		0-1MM	1-3MM	3-5MM	5-10MM	10-25MM	25MM & OVER
12.9	12.9	14.4	Notes Payable-Short Term		3.9			18.1	
4.0	3.1	2.6	Cur. Mat.-L /T/D		2.7			2.4	
21.3	21.7	18.0	Trade Payables		21.5			19.0	
.6	.9	.3	Income Taxes Payable		.3			.4	
7.1	7.8	8.0	All Other Current		10.4			9.2	
45.9	46.4	43.3	Total Current		38.8			49.1	
13.1	8.9	11.7	Long Term Debt		13.8			14.0	
.1	.2	.0	Deferred Taxes		.0			.1	
4.1	5.5	3.7	All Other-Non-Current		2.5			1.6	
36.8	39.0	41.2	Net Worth		44.9			35.3	
100.0	100.0	100.0	Total Liabilities & Net Worth		100.0			100.0	

INCOME DATA

Hist 1	Hist 2	Hist 3		0-1MM	1-3MM	3-5MM	5-10MM	10-25MM	25MM & OVER
100.0	100.0	100.0	Net Sales		100.0			100.0	
36.5	35.1	35.6	Gross Profit		33.2			40.9	
33.3	34.2	32.8	Operating Expenses		29.5			38.4	
3.2	.9	2.8	Operating Profit		3.7			2.5	
.5	–.2	.8	All Other Expenses (net)		.3			.6	
2.8	1.1	2.0	Profit Before Taxes		3.3			2.0	

RATIOS

Hist 1	Hist 2	Hist 3		0-1MM	1-3MM	3-5MM	5-10MM	10-25MM	25MM & OVER
2.8	2.4	2.7	Current		3.5			2.2	
1.9	1.7	1.6			1.9			1.4	
1.3	1.3	1.3			1.3			1.2	
1.1	1.1	1.1	Quick		2.4			.7	
.7	.7	.7			.9			.6	
.3	.5	.5			.5			.3	
18 20.7	19 18.9	16 22.9	Sales/Receivables		16 22.5			17 21.6	
31 11.9	29 12.4	21 17.5			33 11.2			20 18.1	
38 9.5	41 8.9	36 10.2			39 9.3			29 12.5	
78 4.7	42 8.6	46 8.0	Cost of Sales/Inventory		35 10.5			51 7.2	
101 3.6	69 5.3	76 4.8			58 6.3			87 4.2	
126 2.9	96 3.8	101 3.6			89 4.1			114 3.2	
17 20.9	20 18.6	13 27.9	Cost of Sales/Payables		11 33.6			20 18.7	
39 9.4	30 12.1	27 13.3			33 11.2			30 12.2	
57 6.4	51 7.2	40 9.1			52 7.0			40 9.2	
4.9	5.7	6.9	Sales/Working Capital		5.7			7.9	
8.1	11.2	10.4			8.6			18.7	
16.7	36.3	19.5			17.3			31.3	
7.4	9.0	7.5	EBIT/Interest					6.7	
(50) 2.1	(49) 2.7	(46) 3.0						2.6	
.9	1.4	1.4						1.1	
6.6	9.2	6.3	Net Profit + Depr., Dep.,						
(25) 1.9	(34) 3.7	(29) 2.2	Amort./Cur. Mat. L/T/D						
.4	1.3	1.3							
.1	.1	.2	Fixed/Worth		.0			.3	
.3	.3	.3			.3			.4	
.8	.6	.6			.8			.8	
.6	1.0	.8	Debt/Worth		.6			1.5	
2.3	1.8	1.9			1.5			2.1	
5.2	3.1	2.9			2.3			2.7	
32.6	27.2	32.3	% Profit Before Taxes/Tangible					30.4	
(51) 11.5	(51) 12.3	(49) 18.2	Net Worth					12.9	
1.7	2.7	4.8						1.4	
12.5	11.2	12.4	% Profit Before Taxes/Total		16.2			12.4	
4.0	4.8	5.7	Assets		10.1			4.0	
.0	1.1	1.3			6.2			.4	
85.1	67.1	63.0	Sales/Net Fixed Assets		303.5			49.0	
34.9	30.5	34.7			47.8			27.6	
18.9	17.6	17.6			17.5			13.8	
3.6	4.3	4.5	Sales/Total Assets		4.5			4.5	
2.8	3.3	3.4			3.2			3.6	
2.3	2.4	2.6			2.4			3.1	
.4	.5	.6	% Depr., Dep., Amort./Sales					.6	
(46) .8	(50) .9	(45) .8						.8	
1.2	1.2	1.2						1.2	
2.0	2.4	1.3	% Officers', Directors',						
(27) 4.8	(30) 3.8	(26) 4.6	Owners' Comp/Sales						
7.7	6.7	8.1							
584000M	441967M	651196M	Net Sales ($)	3749M	20974M	35428M	59607M	177746M	353692M
223548M	143699M	201621M	Total Assets ($)	2034M	6616M	9464M	16362M	49733M	117412M

M = $ thousand   MM = $ million
See Pages 1 through 15 for Explanation of Ratios and Data

Current Data Sorted By Assets							Comparative Historical Data	
	1	6	2			# Postretirement Benefits		
						Type of Statement		
	3	5	8		2	Unqualified		8
	5	6	1	1		Reviewed		4
	8	8	1			Compiled		8
3	1	2				Tax Returns		
	6	8	4			Other		7
	26 (4/1-9/30/94)		46 (10/1/94-3/31/95)				4/1/90-3/31/91	4/1/91-3/31/92
0-500M	500M-2MM	2-10MM	10-50MM	50-100MM	100-250MM		ALL	ALL
3	23	29	14	1	2	NUMBER OF STATEMENTS		27
%	%	%	%	%	%	**ASSETS**	%	%
	7.1	11.0	17.4			Cash & Equivalents	DATA NOT AVAILABLE	6.6
	42.3	33.4	27.4			Trade Receivables - (net)		27.9
	21.7	26.1	28.2			Inventory		25.8
	3.3	1.4	3.1			All Other Current		2.2
	74.5	71.9	76.1			Total Current		62.5
	14.9	13.7	16.9			Fixed Assets (net)		21.0
	3.7	4.2	1.6			Intangibles (net)		5.4
	6.9	10.2	5.5			All Other Non-Current		11.0
	100.0	100.0	100.0			Total		100.0
						LIABILITIES		
	8.2	5.0	4.0			Notes Payable-Short Term		8.8
	2.4	3.8	1.0			Cur. Mat. -L/T/D		3.6
	29.7	37.2	42.3			Trade Payables		33.5
	.1	.4	.1			Income Taxes Payable		.2
	8.6	10.4	13.8			All Other Current		8.3
	48.9	56.8	61.1			Total Current		54.3
	10.7	9.4	6.5			Long Term Debt		14.4
	3.7	.1	1.0			Deferred Taxes		.1
	4.9	5.1	.7			All Other-Non-Current		4.2
	31.8	28.7	30.7			Net Worth		26.9
	100.0	100.0	100.0			Total Liabilities & Net Worth		100.0
						INCOME DATA		
	100.0	100.0	100.0			Net Sales		100.0
	32.1	31.5	25.8			Gross Profit		27.2
	30.0	27.6	21.4			Operating Expenses		24.5
	2.1	3.9	4.3			Operating Profit		2.6
	.1	.2	-.4			All Other Expenses (net)		.4
	2.0	3.7	4.7			Profit Before Taxes		2.3
						RATIOS		
	2.6	1.8	1.6					1.6
	1.4	1.2	1.3			Current		1.1
	1.2	1.0	.9					.9
	1.4	1.2	1.1					1.0
	1.0	.8	.7			Quick		.6
	.7	.5	.6					.4
	30 12.1	**26** 13.9	**20** 18.1					**16** 22.8
	46 7.9	**41** 9.0	**33** 11.1			Sales/Receivables		**35** 10.5
	74 4.9	**63** 5.8	**47** 7.7					**51** 7.2
	2 215.3	**20** 18.5	**30** 12.0					**27** 13.7
	15 23.9	**40** 9.1	**45** 8.1			Cost of Sales/Inventory		**42** 8.6
	99 3.7	**99** 3.7	**78** 4.7					**76** 4.8
	24 15.1	**47** 7.8	**52** 7.0					**28** 13.0
	48 7.6	**74** 4.9	**72** 5.1			Cost of Sales/Payables		**68** 5.4
	81 4.5	**94** 3.9	**91** 4.0					**89** 4.1
	8.1	7.0	10.8					15.2
	13.7	22.8	18.2			Sales/Working Capital		44.4
	46.7	-646.9	-56.6					-39.3
	26.5	22.3	50.8					5.9
	(22) 5.1	(27) 6.0	(11) 10.2			EBIT/Interest		(22) 3.3
	1.9	2.5	6.6					.9
		5.1						9.7
		(11) 3.0				Net Profit + Depr., Dep., Amort./Cur. Mat. L /T/D		(10) 1.5
		1.5						.8
	.2	.3	.3					.3
	.6	.6	.5			Fixed/Worth		.7
	1.7	3.8	2.4					2.2
	.9	1.5	.9					2.5
	2.6	3.6	3.3			Debt/Worth		3.4
	12.2	12.5	11.3					9.0
	40.3	61.3	85.4					55.4
	(20) 25.9	(23) 30.6	(13) 39.6			% Profit Before Taxes/Tangible Net Worth		(25) 28.5
	14.9	12.5	15.4					.7
	11.2	15.3	18.9					9.3
	5.0	8.4	8.0			% Profit Before Taxes/Total Assets		4.2
	1.9	1.2	5.4					-.3
	49.1	33.2	39.8					44.8
	26.4	24.3	27.8			Sales/Net Fixed Assets		24.5
	17.8	14.3	18.6					14.7
	3.7	3.6	3.0					3.5
	3.0	2.8	2.8			Sales/Total Assets		2.9
	1.7	1.9	2.5					2.2
	.6	.8	.5					.6
	(21) 1.1	(28) 1.1	.6			% Depr., Dep., Amort./Sales		(24) 1.2
	1.6	1.5	1.0					1.6
	2.4	.9						2.4
	(14) 5.3	(11) 1.3				% Officers', Directors', Owners' Comp/Sales		(11) 4.7
	8.5	4.2						12.1
2896M	110041M	416384M	744349M	125476M	1496851M	Net Sales ($)		1281670M
891M	29835M	145716M	248344M	61184M	436065M	Total Assets ($)		435803M

M = $ thousand MM = $ million

See Pages 1 through 15 for Explanation of Ratios and Data

Comparative Historical Data / Current Data Sorted By Sales

1	2	9	# Postretirement Benefits / Type of Statement	0-1MM	1-3MM	3-5MM	5-10MM	10-25MM	25MM & OVER
					2			5	2
12	10	18	Unqualified		1	2		4	11
10	8	13	Reviewed		2	1	2	5	3
10	8	17	Compiled		5	3	3	4	2
2	2	6	Tax Returns	3	1			2	
4	12	18	Other	1	2		2	5	4
4/1/92-3/31/93 ALL	4/1/93-3/31/94 ALL	4/1/94-3/31/95 ALL			26 (4/1-9/30/94)			46 (10/1/94-3/31/95)	
38	40	72	NUMBER OF STATEMENTS	4	11	8	9	20	20
%	%	%	ASSETS	%	%	%	%	%	%
11.7	10.0	11.0	Cash & Equivalents		7.1			8.8	15.4
27.6	34.1	35.5	Trade Receivables - (net)		44.2			33.9	31.0
30.4	32.8	25.3	Inventory		12.9			26.8	26.8
3.5	1.7	2.2	All Other Current		1.3			1.8	2.7
73.2	78.6	74.1	Total Current		65.5			71.2	75.9
13.8	11.4	14.3	Fixed Assets (net)		18.4			13.7	14.3
3.8	3.1	3.4	Intangibles (net)		4.9			2.6	3.5
9.2	6.9	8.2	All Other Non-Current		11.1			12.4	6.3
100.0	100.0	100.0	Total		100.0			100.0	100.0
			LIABILITIES						
8.4	9.5	5.7	Notes Payable-Short Term		6.9			5.6	4.7
2.8	2.2	2.5	Cur. Mat.-L./T/D		2.5			3.5	1.1
31.6	29.1	37.0	Trade Payables		28.0			42.7	41.9
.7	2.6	.3	Income Taxes Payable		.1			.4	.1
9.0	10.1	10.4	All Other Current		8.9			6.4	15.4
52.6	53.4	56.1	Total Current		46.5			58.7	63.2
7.1	6.2	9.2	Long Term Debt		15.6			9.7	6.4
1.4	.7	1.4	Deferred Taxes		7.5			.0	.8
2.3	2.4	3.8	All Other-Non-Current		3.5			7.6	1.8
36.7	37.3	29.6	Net Worth		26.9			23.9	27.8
100.0	100.0	100.0	Total Liabilities & Net Worth		100.0			100.0	100.0
			INCOME DATA						
100.0	100.0	100.0	Net Sales		100.0			100.0	100.0
27.4	33.0	30.3	Gross Profit		35.4			30.2	22.7
24.7	30.2	27.2	Operating Expenses		33.8			26.5	19.4
2.7	2.8	3.1	Operating Profit		1.6			3.7	3.3
-.1	.4	.1	All Other Expenses (net)		-.1			.4	-.2
2.8	2.4	3.1	Profit Before Taxes		1.7			3.3	3.5
			RATIOS						
1.9	2.3	1.9	Current		2.0			1.4	1.5
1.5	1.5	1.3			1.6			1.2	1.2
1.1	1.1	1.0			1.0			1.0	.9
1.3	1.2	1.2	Quick		1.7			1.0	1.2
.8	.8	.8			1.1			.8	.7
.5	.6	.6			.7			.5	.5
20 17.9	28 13.0	26 13.9	Sales/Receivables	46 7.9				25 14.7	21 17.5
34 10.8	41 8.9	39 9.3		62 5.9				34 10.8	33 11.1
62 5.9	62 5.9	62 5.9		159 2.3				46 8.0	43 8.4
25 14.7	35 10.5	10 37.0	Cost of Sales/Inventory	0 UND				16 22.9	10 36.1
51 7.1	62 5.9	38 9.6		5 80.9				35 10.5	37 9.8
111 3.3	107 3.4	94 3.9		99 3.7				79 4.6	70 5.2
25 14.8	18 20.6	43 8.5	Cost of Sales/Payables	24 15.1				45 8.2	44 8.3
59 6.2	51 7.1	72 5.1		46 8.0				78 4.7	66 5.5
85 4.3	96 3.8	94 3.9		203 1.8				94 3.9	94 3.9
5.6	5.3	9.2	Sales/Working Capital		4.7			12.7	16.9
11.9	12.2	19.9			10.8			23.6	21.6
39.3	44.1	219.3			999.8			132.4	-51.8
(32) 6.3	(36) 12.1	(66) 22.1	EBIT/Interest		22.0			(19) 9.8	(17) 35.9
4.7	4.2	6.6			5.5			6.0	10.2
1.3	1.2	2.4			2.3			2.5	5.5
(16) 24.7	(16) 8.3	(29) 9.4	Net Profit + Depr., Dep., Amort./Cur. Mat. L/T/D						(13) 36.8
3.4	2.4	3.4							9.2
.7	1.7	1.6							4.1
.2	.2	.3	Fixed/Worth		.3			.3	.3
.4	.3	.6			.7			.6	.6
1.0	.6	2.0			2.7			1.9	3.1
.9	1.0	1.1	Debt/Worth		.9			1.8	1.5
2.6	1.9	3.6			4.7			3.7	3.5
8.3	5.1	11.7			17.6			6.8	16.0
(33) 36.0	(37) 40.6	(62) 59.7	% Profit Before Taxes/Tangible Net Worth					(16) 64.0	(19) 89.4
18.4	21.0	29.2						31.8	49.0
6.1	3.8	14.8						10.4	22.3
10.3	14.9	12.1	% Profit Before Taxes/Total Assets		7.8			16.5	14.8
4.9	4.1	7.1			3.5			8.2	6.9
-.0	.4	2.4			2.7			.8	4.5
46.2	50.5	39.4	Sales/Net Fixed Assets		30.9			41.7	40.5
30.8	30.3	26.1			19.6			26.2	27.3
17.8	17.3	16.4			6.2			15.7	18.7
3.8	3.5	3.5	Sales/Total Assets		3.7			3.7	3.7
2.7	2.7	2.9			1.7			3.0	3.0
1.9	2.2	2.0			1.4			2.5	2.7
(36) .6	(34) .5	(68) .6	% Depr., Dep., Amort./Sales					(19) .8	.5
.8	1.0	1.0						1.0	.6
1.3	1.5	1.5						1.5	1.0
(15) 1.9	(12) 1.2	(33) 1.3	% Officers', Directors', Owners' Comp/Sales					(10) .9	
4.4	2.5	3.0						1.3	
9.6	5.1	7.8						3.6	
2519975M	2111007M	2895997M	Net Sales ($)	2533M	21985M	30316M	54778M	297680M	2488705M
867870M	784081M	922035M	Total Assets ($)	3378M	12302M	12011M	27338M	110037M	756969M

M = $ thousand   MM = $ million
See Pages 1 through 15 for Explanation of Ratios and Data

Current Data Sorted By Assets							Comparative Historical Data	
2	4	5	7	1	1	**# Postretirement Benefits**		
						Type of Statement		
2	14	17	20	3	2	Unqualified	40	39
8	20	46	5			Reviewed	67	82
21	23	8	2			Compiled	49	62
2	2	1				Tax Returns	4	1
6	24	16	11		1	Other	35	35
	90 (4/1-9/30/94)		164 (10/1/94-3/31/95)				4/1/90-3/31/91 ALL	4/1/91-3/31/92 ALL
0-500M	500M-2MM	2-10MM	10-50MM	50-100MM	100-250MM	**NUMBER OF STATEMENTS**		
39	83	88	38	3	3		195	219
%	%	%	%	%	%	**ASSETS**	%	%
13.9	7.5	6.6	3.3			Cash & Equivalents	6.5	7.7
40.0	42.9	41.5	32.0			Trade Receivables - (net)	38.4	40.6
16.0	26.0	24.4	21.4			Inventory	25.5	25.1
2.0	.7	.9	2.1			All Other Current	1.8	1.0
72.0	77.1	73.4	58.8			Total Current	72.2	74.4
18.5	15.1	18.6	33.2			Fixed Assets (net)	19.4	16.8
.4	2.6	1.9	.8			Intangibles (net)	1.6	1.5
9.2	5.2	6.0	7.1			All Other Non-Current	6.8	7.3
100.0	100.0	100.0	100.0			Total	100.0	100.0
						LIABILITIES		
11.5	13.0	11.8	10.9			Notes Payable-Short Term	11.9	11.0
3.9	4.4	2.3	3.2			Cur. Mat. -L/T/D	3.7	3.1
27.7	30.0	31.7	21.5			Trade Payables	26.9	29.4
1.3	.5	.3	.2			Income Taxes Payable	.6	.6
9.2	7.5	7.4	6.3			All Other Current	6.6	7.8
53.5	55.5	53.5	42.1			Total Current	49.7	51.9
10.1	10.3	8.6	16.4			Long Term Debt	11.2	9.5
.1	.2	.4	1.0			Deferred Taxes	.5	.3
.4	2.4	3.2	.5			All Other-Non-Current	2.2	2.3
35.8	31.7	34.2	40.0			Net Worth	36.3	36.0
100.0	100.0	100.0	100.0			Total Liabilities & Net Worth	100.0	100.0
						INCOME DATA		
100.0	100.0	100.0	100.0			Net Sales	100.0	100.0
34.7	30.4	25.5	27.7			Gross Profit	29.2	28.5
31.4	27.6	22.6	23.4			Operating Expenses	26.1	25.7
3.4	2.7	2.9	4.3			Operating Profit	3.0	2.8
.3	.3	.3	.7			All Other Expenses (net)	.7	.6
3.1	2.5	2.6	3.6			Profit Before Taxes	2.4	2.1
						RATIOS		
2.1	2.0	1.7	1.9			Current	2.0	2.0
1.2	1.4	1.3	1.3				1.5	1.4
.9	1.1	1.2	1.1				1.2	1.1
1.7	1.3	1.1	1.0			Quick	1.2	1.3
.9	1.0	.9	.8				.9	.9
.6	.7	.7	.7				.7	.7
28 13.2	36 10.1	39 9.3	38 9.7			Sales/Receivables	34 10.6	35 10.5
38 9.5	45 8.1	47 7.8	45 8.2				42 8.6	42 8.6
54 6.8	54 6.7	60 6.1	51 7.2				52 7.0	52 7.0
9 41.5	20 17.9	24 15.5	29 12.4			Cost of Sales/Inventory	23 15.6	20 18.2
24 15.1	38 9.7	37 10.0	46 7.9				43 8.5	37 9.9
40 9.2	63 5.8	59 6.2	61 6.0				64 5.7	59 6.2
22 16.5	27 13.4	34 10.7	31 11.9			Cost of Sales/Payables	27 13.6	27 13.6
39 9.4	45 8.2	47 7.8	42 8.6				39 9.4	41 8.9
61 6.0	57 6.4	60 6.1	53 6.9				54 6.7	57 6.4
10.8	7.7	9.6	8.5			Sales/Working Capital	8.3	8.0
34.3	15.6	19.5	18.9				15.5	17.3
−71.3	52.2	28.7	29.6				34.6	44.8
(26) 6.5	(75) 5.8	(83) 10.4	(36) 7.8			EBIT/Interest	(171) 7.1	(201) 7.8
3.6	3.5	4.9	4.3				2.9	3.4
1.3	1.9	2.0	2.6				1.4	1.4
	(29) 6.3	(37) 6.7	(20) 5.3			Net Profit + Depr., Dep., Amort./Cur. Mat. L /T/D	(93) 5.8	(101) 6.7
	2.4	2.7	3.0				2.5	2.5
	1.1	1.6	1.5				1.0	1.2
.1	.1	.1	.5			Fixed/Worth	.2	.1
.5	.5	.4	.7				.5	.4
1.8	1.1	.9	1.3				1.0	.9
.7	1.0	1.2	1.1			Debt/Worth	1.0	.9
2.2	2.4	2.4	1.6				1.7	2.0
5.7	6.1	4.5	2.5				3.8	4.1
(35) 49.2	(74) 34.7	39.2	27.6			% Profit Before Taxes/Tangible Net Worth	(182) 32.1	(208) 30.0
20.5	18.8	19.9	16.9				18.4	15.8
5.6	7.3	7.4	11.6				6.7	6.2
13.6	12.3	13.1	12.4			% Profit Before Taxes/Total Assets	11.7	10.8
6.7	4.7	7.3	6.5				5.8	4.7
.3	2.4	2.3	4.2				1.5	1.3
112.1	113.9	102.5	19.9			Sales/Net Fixed Assets	53.1	93.3
30.4	38.9	28.4	7.4				21.5	30.8
8.3	11.3	8.3	3.6				10.0	10.7
5.4	4.4	3.8	3.1			Sales/Total Assets	4.0	4.4
4.3	3.4	3.1	2.3				3.1	3.5
2.5	2.5	2.1	1.6				2.3	2.5
(30) .4	(72) .4	(83) .3	(34) 1.1			% Depr., Dep., Amort./Sales	(173) .6	(193) .4
.6	.9	.7	2.0				1.2	.9
3.1	1.9	1.6	3.9				2.3	1.7
(21) 3.7	(43) 3.1	(43) 1.2				% Officers', Directors', Owners' Comp/Sales	(88) 2.1	(113) 1.8
5.5	4.0	2.3					4.3	3.6
13.3	8.4	4.6					8.4	7.8
49337M	351323M	1189789M	1970228M	376926M	729342M	Net Sales ($)	3571375M	3368501M
12108M	92062M	409762M	780451M	178888M	510916M	Total Assets ($)	1402259M	1264244M

M = $ thousand   MM = $ million
See Pages 1 through 15 for Explanation of Ratios and Data

Comparative Historical Data				Current Data Sorted By Sales					
4	11	20	**# Postretirement Benefits**		4	1	3	3	9
			Type of Statement						
47	42	58	Unqualified	1	6	5	11	10	25
81	68	79	Reviewed	4	13	8	14	31	9
60	54	54	Compiled	7	26	3	12	5	1
3	11	5	Tax Returns		2	1	1	1	
42	65	58	Other	3	12	10	9	14	10
				90 (4/1-9/30/94)		164 (10/1/94-3/31/95)			
4/1/92-3/31/93 ALL	**4/1/93-3/31/94 ALL**	**4/1/94-3/31/95 ALL**		**0-1MM**	**1-3MM**	**3-5MM**	**5-10MM**	**10-25MM**	**25MM & OVER**
233	240	254	**NUMBER OF STATEMENTS**	15	59	27	47	61	45
%	%	%	**ASSETS**	%	%	%	%	%	%
7.6	7.2	7.5	Cash & Equivalents	9.1	11.3	5.2	8.8	5.5	4.6
38.8	38.6	39.9	Trade Receivables - (net)	38.2	36.8	42.2	44.0	43.8	33.3
25.3	24.9	23.3	Inventory	17.2	21.9	26.3	22.3	23.6	26.0
1.3	1.4	1.2	All Other Current	2.4	1.0	.8	.9	.9	2.1
73.0	72.1	71.8	Total Current	66.9	71.1	74.5	76.0	73.7	66.0
18.6	19.3	19.9	Fixed Assets (net)	22.8	19.1	19.6	15.5	18.7	26.4
1.3	1.8	1.8	Intangibles (net)	1.0	2.9	2.2	1.3	1.8	1.2
7.1	6.8	6.5	All Other Non-Current	9.3	7.0	3.7	7.2	5.8	6.5
100.0	100.0	100.0	Total	100.0	100.0	100.0	100.0	100.0	100.0
			LIABILITIES						
12.2	11.2	11.9	Notes Payable-Short Term	14.5	15.1	10.5	7.3	13.4	10.2
3.0	3.0	3.4	Cur. Mat.-L/T/D	5.9	4.3	5.4	2.5	2.6	1.9
27.1	26.7	28.7	Trade Payables	21.0	25.6	26.4	34.2	32.6	25.6
.4	2.0	.5	Income Taxes Payable	2.6	.3	.8	.3	.3	.5
7.9	8.4	7.6	All Other Current	4.3	8.8	8.7	7.4	7.7	6.7
50.7	51.3	52.1	Total Current	48.3	54.1	51.8	51.8	56.6	45.0
9.7	8.8	10.7	Long Term Debt	10.6	12.1	10.9	9.4	8.4	13.0
.5	.5	.4	Deferred Taxes	.0	.4	.2	.2	.5	.8
2.8	2.8	2.2	All Other-Non-Current	2.8	.8	2.6	2.7	3.3	1.4
36.3	36.5	34.7	Net Worth	38.3	32.6	34.5	36.0	31.2	39.9
100.0	100.0	100.0	Total Liabilities & Net Worth	100.0	100.0	100.0	100.0	100.0	100.0
			INCOME DATA						
100.0	100.0	100.0	Net Sales	100.0	100.0	100.0	100.0	100.0	100.0
29.8	28.9	28.8	Gross Profit	51.1	31.8	33.7	27.2	24.1	22.7
27.2	26.1	25.7	Operating Expenses	43.7	29.3	29.6	24.4	22.1	19.0
2.6	2.8	3.1	Operating Profit	7.3	2.6	4.0	2.8	2.0	3.7
.4	.4	.3	All Other Expenses (net)	.9	.5	.7	-.1	.2	.4
2.2	2.4	2.8	Profit Before Taxes	6.4	2.1	3.4	2.9	1.8	3.3
			RATIOS						
2.1	1.9	1.8		2.4	1.9	2.0	2.0	1.6	1.9
1.4	1.4	1.3	Current	1.2	1.3	1.5	1.4	1.3	1.4
1.2	1.1	1.1		.8	1.0	1.0	1.2	1.1	1.2
1.3	1.3	1.2		1.5	1.4	1.3	1.3	1.0	1.0
.9	.9	.9	Quick	.8	.9	.9	1.0	.8	.8
.6	.6	.7		.6	.5	.7	.8	.7	.7
35 10.4	**33** 10.9	**37** 9.9		**41** 8.8	**31** 11.7	**35** 10.3	**34** 10.6	**43** 8.5	**36** 10.2
42 8.6	**43** 8.5	**46** 8.0	Sales/Receivables	**58** 6.3	**43** 8.5	**46** 7.9	**45** 8.2	**48** 7.6	**43** 8.4
51 7.1	**51** 7.2	**56** 6.5		**114** 3.2	**50** 7.3	**58** 6.3	**57** 6.4	**61** 6.0	**49** 7.5
22 16.9	**23** 16.2	**21** 17.4		**16** 23.0	**12** 31.2	**29** 12.8	**14** 25.2	**21** 17.4	**31** 11.6
42 8.7	**41** 9.0	**36** 10.1	Cost of Sales/Inventory	**36** 10.2	**36** 10.2	**42** 8.7	**33** 11.1	**29** 12.4	**45** 8.1
72 5.1	**63** 5.8	**59** 6.2		**243** 1.5	**56** 6.5	**61** 6.0	**51** 7.2	**58** 6.3	**55** 6.6
24 15.5	**23** 15.9	**30** 12.1		**36** 10.1	**20** 18.1	**31** 11.7	**30** 12.2	**35** 10.5	**30** 12.1
39 9.3	**37** 10.0	**43** 8.5	Cost of Sales/Payables	**83** 4.4	**39** 9.4	**35** 10.3	**46** 7.9	**47** 7.8	**40** 9.1
59 6.2	**58** 6.3	**58** 6.3		**152** 2.4	**59** 6.2	**57** 6.4	**55** 6.6	**59** 6.2	**54** 6.7
7.4	8.3	8.5		4.2	8.2	7.2	8.4	12.5	7.3
14.8	16.7	17.7	Sales/Working Capital	33.0	17.7	15.8	16.3	21.5	17.4
43.9	42.2	45.0		-19.8	-999.8	158.2	38.9	32.3	27.1
7.8	8.0	8.6			5.4	8.7	17.2	10.4	11.6
(209) 3.4	(210) 3.2	(226) 3.9	EBIT/Interest		(50) 3.1	(25) 3.5	(41) 3.9	(59) 4.6	(42) 4.3
1.6	1.4	2.0			1.4	2.1	2.3	2.0	2.8
6.7	3.8	5.4			5.1	3.6	7.5	6.0	7.9
(96) 2.4	(85) 2.2	(98) 2.7	Net Profit + Depr., Dep., Amort./Cur. Mat. L/T/D		(17) 2.0	(12) 2.2	(17) 3.7	(22) 2.7	(26) 3.6
1.2	1.3	1.5			.6	1.9	1.6	1.3	2.5
.2	.2	.2		.1	.1	.1	.1	.2	.4
.4	.5	.5	Fixed/Worth	.5	.6	.6	.3	.4	.6
.9	1.0	1.2		1.5	3.8	1.2	1.2	.9	1.0
1.0	.9	1.1		.7	1.0	.9	.8	1.7	1.0
1.9	2.0	2.2	Debt/Worth	1.4	2.3	2.4	2.0	2.5	1.7
4.4	4.2	4.2		10.9	6.9	5.6	3.7	4.4	2.9
34.6	34.7	37.2		87.5	33.7	37.7	37.2	49.7	29.1
(219) 16.7	(228) 15.2	(241) 18.9	% Profit Before Taxes/Tangible Net Worth	(14) 18.0	(51) 13.8	(26) 24.4	(44) 22.2	19.0	18.9
5.3	6.4	7.7		6.6	4.6	4.1	8.7	7.9	10.9
11.0	10.2	12.3		21.0	10.6	11.0	15.2	12.8	12.5
5.3	4.9	6.2	% Profit Before Taxes/Total Assets	6.7	4.7	5.2	6.2	6.8	7.1
1.4	1.5	2.3		.7	1.4	.6	2.6	2.4	2.9
71.1	75.7	97.9		111.0	99.9	123.7	97.1	138.1	42.8
25.1	23.0	23.0	Sales/Net Fixed Assets	6.2	23.2	34.1	46.1	32.0	9.6
10.3	10.0	7.1		4.1	9.3	7.1	11.0	8.3	5.7
4.2	4.4	4.1		3.1	4.4	4.4	4.7	4.0	3.5
3.2	3.1	3.1	Sales/Total Assets	2.1	3.2	3.3	3.6	3.2	2.8
2.3	2.3	2.2		1.0	2.4	2.4	2.7	2.2	1.9
.5	.4	.4		.5	.5	.3	.4	.2	.5
(205) 1.1	(209) 1.0	(224) .9	% Depr., Dep., Amort./Sales	(10) 4.1	(50) 1.0	(25) 1.1	(43) .7	(55) .6	(41) 1.4
2.0	2.4	2.3		5.1	2.3	2.9	1.9	1.5	2.9
1.8	1.7	1.9			3.1	2.2	2.0	1.2	1.4
(99) 4.4	(114) 3.8	(114) 3.6	% Officers', Directors', Owners' Comp/Sales		(29) 5.2	(14) 3.9	(26) 3.4	(29) 2.5	(12) 1.9
8.8	6.6	7.5			8.5	11.1	5.3	4.8	4.5
4195395M	**4557404M**	**4666945M**	Net Sales ($)	**7190M**	**110225M**	**105318M**	**334878M**	**936609M**	**3172725M**
1579633M	**1883956M**	**1984187M**	Total Assets ($)	**4257M**	**38951M**	**41888M**	**109449M**	**351158M**	**1438484M**

© Robert Morris Associates 1995

M = $ thousand MM = $ million

See Pages 1 through 15 for Explanation of Ratios and Data

	Current Data Sorted By Assets							Comparative Historical Data	

 # Postretirement Benefits: 1 | 2 | 3 | 1

Type of Statement

	0-500M	500M-2MM	2-10MM	10-50MM	50-100MM	100-250MM		4/1/90-3/31/91 ALL	4/1/91-3/31/92 ALL
Unqualified		2	5	4	1			5	
Reviewed	1	12	5					12	18
Compiled	6	9	3					10	6
Tax Returns	1	1	1					1	
Other	3	7	8	1	1			2	9

Size groups: 23 (4/1-9/30/94) spans 500M-2MM; 48 (10/1/94-3/31/95) spans 2-10MM through 100-250MM.

0-500M	500M-2MM	2-10MM	10-50MM	50-100MM	100-250MM		4/1/90-3/31/91 ALL	4/1/91-3/31/92 ALL
11	31	22	5	2		**NUMBER OF STATEMENTS**	30	33
%	%	%	%	%	%	**ASSETS**	%	%
13.1	7.6	4.5				Cash & Equivalents	9.3	8.0
38.1	44.3	42.9				Trade Receivables - (net)	40.9	38.7
36.0	28.9	28.5				Inventory	30.3	29.9
1.5	1.3	.5				All Other Current	2.3	1.3
88.6	82.0	76.4				Total Current	82.8	78.0
7.9	12.9	17.2				Fixed Assets (net)	9.6	13.6
.8	1.7	1.0				Intangibles (net)	2.5	2.5
2.6	3.4	5.3				All Other Non-Current	5.0	5.9
100.0	100.0	100.0				Total	100.0	100.0
						LIABILITIES		
9.5	12.6	13.5				Notes Payable-Short Term	14.1	15.6
1.5	2.1	2.9				Cur. Mat. -L/T/D	2.6	3.1
25.7	31.6	30.9				Trade Payables	27.6	30.6
.0	.9	.1				Income Taxes Payable	2.0	.2
10.6	2.9	7.4				All Other Current	5.9	7.2
47.4	50.1	54.8				Total Current	52.3	56.7
9.3	7.5	7.2				Long Term Debt	10.7	14.6
.1	.0	.3				Deferred Taxes	.3	.1
5.6	4.0	3.5				All Other-Non-Current	3.0	3.7
37.7	38.4	34.1				Net Worth	33.7	24.9
100.0	100.0	100.0				Total Liabilities & Net Worth	100.0	100.0
						INCOME DATA		
100.0	100.0	100.0				Net Sales	100.0	100.0
39.6	25.1	28.8				Gross Profit	26.7	26.0
34.6	21.5	24.1				Operating Expenses	21.8	25.0
5.0	3.6	4.8				Operating Profit	4.9	1.0
1.2	.3	-.2				All Other Expenses (net)	.8	1.1
3.8	3.4	5.0				Profit Before Taxes	4.1	.0
						RATIOS		
5.4	2.7	2.0				Current	2.2	2.2
1.9	1.9	1.3					1.5	1.4
1.2	1.2	1.0					1.3	1.1
1.8	1.9	1.0				Quick	1.3	1.2
1.0	1.0	.7					.9	.9
.9	.7	.6					.7	.6
29 12.4	36 10.1	42 8.6				Sales/Receivables	35 10.3	31 11.8
44 8.3	45 8.2	50 7.3					41 9.0	50 7.3
53 6.9	73 5.0	64 5.7					58 6.3	58 6.3
25 14.5	29 12.6	19 18.8				Cost of Sales/Inventory	31 11.8	24 15.0
49 7.4	49 7.5	45 8.2					43 8.4	39 9.3
215 1.7	68 5.4	78 4.7					65 5.6	76 4.8
19 19.4	28 13.2	35 10.5				Cost of Sales/Payables	26 14.3	33 11.1
49 7.4	36 10.2	54 6.7					37 9.8	49 7.4
60 6.1	57 6.4	70 5.2					55 6.6	70 5.2
3.6	4.7	7.9				Sales/Working Capital	7.9	7.2
9.7	10.2	18.2					9.8	14.0
41.9	17.7	-277.6					17.1	47.7
	17.1	8.6				EBIT/Interest	10.2	2.9
	(25) 6.4	(20) 4.3					(29) 3.9	(31) 1.8
	2.5	1.3					1.3	-.2
						Net Profit + Depr., Dep., Amort./Cur. Mat. L./T/D		5.5
								(14) 2.3
								.5
.1	.2	.1				Fixed/Worth	.1	.2
.1	.3	.3					.3	.5
12.0	.7	1.4					1.2	-24.8
.5	1.0	.9				Debt/Worth	.9	1.3
1.3	1.8	3.0					2.0	2.9
59.3	7.1	5.2					5.7	-96.6
	30.9	50.1				% Profit Before Taxes/Tangible Net Worth	42.3	33.1
	(29) 13.7	22.8					(26) 22.5	(24) 11.5
	6.3	4.7					6.8	-8.3
26.9	14.1	13.7				% Profit Before Taxes/Total Assets	20.8	8.5
9.1	6.6	7.3					7.0	3.2
1.1	1.3	1.2					1.6	-4.6
142.0	74.3	94.3				Sales/Net Fixed Assets	243.3	69.3
75.5	39.9	23.7					52.0	31.2
28.8	19.3	8.5					23.2	14.7
5.0	4.2	3.7				Sales/Total Assets	4.1	3.7
3.0	3.2	3.0					3.2	3.0
2.4	2.2	2.1					2.2	2.6
	.5	.3				% Depr., Dep., Amort./Sales	.2	.5
	(27) .6	(18) .6					(21) .7	(28) .7
	1.3	2.1					1.3	2.0
	1.5	1.1				% Officers', Directors', Owners' Comp/Sales	2.2	.9
	(19) 3.6	(14) 2.4					(14) 3.5	(21) 2.6
	6.6	4.5					6.0	11.2
12905M	130046M	238300M	407980M	314186M		Net Sales ($)	240410M	677168M
3149M	39311M	87067M	102666M	136710M		Total Assets ($)	67724M	228041M

M = $ thousand   MM = $ million
See Pages 1 through 15 for Explanation of Ratios and Data

	Comparative Historical Data			Current Data Sorted By Sales					
# Postretirement Benefits		1	7		2	2	2		1
Type of Statement									
Unqualified	9	4	12			1	3	3	5
Reviewed	18	14	18		4	6	6	2	
Compiled	16	16	18	4	7	2	3	2	
Tax Returns	1	3	3		1		2		
Other	19	15	20	3	3	3	3	6	2
	4/1/92-3/31/93 ALL	4/1/93-3/31/94 ALL	4/1/94-3/31/95 ALL		23 (4/1-9/30/94)			48 (10/1/94-3/31/95)	
				0-1MM	1-3MM	3-5MM	5-10MM	10-25MM	25MM & OVER
NUMBER OF STATEMENTS	63	52	71	7	15	12	17	13	7
	%	%	%	%	%	%	%	%	%
ASSETS									
Cash & Equivalents	4.6	6.8	7.0		14.8	4.4	5.2	2.6	
Trade Receivables - (net)	38.3	35.1	42.9		43.5	43.4	43.1	44.3	
Inventory	31.0	31.3	30.2		21.7	30.5	37.9	23.7	
All Other Current	2.4	1.0	1.0		.2	1.4	.6	1.3	
Total Current	76.2	74.3	81.0		80.1	79.7	86.9	71.9	
Fixed Assets (net)	15.6	19.5	13.1		16.1	13.4	9.9	19.3	
Intangibles (net)	2.2	.6	1.5		.2	3.4	.1	2.4	
All Other Non-Current	6.0	5.6	4.4		3.6	3.5	3.1	6.4	
Total	100.0	100.0	100.0		100.0	100.0	100.0	100.0	
LIABILITIES									
Notes Payable-Short Term	13.6	15.4	12.5		6.8	15.5	14.3	15.2	
Cur. Mat.-L /T/D	3.1	3.1	2.1		1.9	1.5	2.1	4.5	
Trade Payables	27.6	28.4	30.2		26.1	25.4	35.2	35.7	
Income Taxes Payable	.1	1.2	.5		.0	1.2	.2	.9	
All Other Current	5.7	5.3	6.4		7.5	2.1	7.1	6.0	
Total Current	50.1	53.5	51.7		42.4	45.8	58.9	62.3	
Long Term Debt	11.3	10.6	7.7		11.1	5.6	6.8	9.8	
Deferred Taxes	.3	.1	.2		.1	.0	.0	.5	
All Other-Non-Current	2.6	2.2	3.7		4.1	9.9	.3	3.3	
Net Worth	35.8	33.7	36.6		42.3	38.7	34.1	24.0	
Total Liabilities & Net Worth	100.0	100.0	100.0		100.0	100.0	100.0	100.0	
INCOME DATA									
Net Sales	100.0	100.0	100.0		100.0	100.0	100.0	100.0	
Gross Profit	24.7	24.3	27.4		32.8	27.0	24.7	20.8	
Operating Expenses	21.7	21.0	23.2		27.2	25.8	20.2	19.2	
Operating Profit	3.0	3.3	4.3		5.6	1.2	4.6	1.6	
All Other Expenses (net)	1.0	.9	.3		.8	−.8	.4	.4	
Profit Before Taxes	2.0	2.4	4.0		4.8	2.0	4.2	1.2	
RATIOS									
Current	2.4	1.8	2.3		4.0	2.1	2.0	1.6	
	1.5	1.4	1.5		2.4	2.0	1.4	1.1	
	1.1	1.0	1.2		1.2	1.2	1.1	.9	
Quick	1.3	1.1	1.5		2.6	1.4	1.0	1.0	
	.8	.7	1.0		1.9	1.0	.7	.6	
	.6	.5	.6		.9	.8	.6	.5	
Sales/Receivables	33 11.1	32 11.3	37 9.8		41 9.0	36 10.2	37 9.8	39 9.4	
	42 8.7	43 8.5	47 7.7		53 6.9	46 7.9	44 8.3	46 7.9	
	51 7.2	51 7.2	64 5.7		104 3.5	69 5.3	56 6.5	60 6.1	
Cost of Sales/Inventory	31 11.7	21 17.2	29 12.6		11 32.7	29 12.5	27 13.3	14 25.3	
	45 8.2	51 7.2	49 7.4		49 7.4	35 10.3	51 7.1	41 8.8	
	72 5.1	72 5.1	78 4.7		104 3.5	55 6.6	79 4.6	56 6.5	
Cost of Sales/Payables	22 16.9	22 16.9	30 12.0		28 13.0	19 19.0	34 10.7	29 12.4	
	43 8.5	41 8.8	41 8.8		36 10.2	36 10.2	46 8.0	39 9.3	
	54 6.8	57 6.4	66 5.5		57 6.4	59 6.2	65 5.6	68 5.4	
Sales/Working Capital	7.8	9.3	5.3		3.2	5.9	6.4	15.9	
	13.1	15.6	11.1		6.1	9.4	12.4	40.2	
	43.3	693.5	41.9		41.9	25.5	51.6	−55.9	
EBIT/Interest	(59) 6.8	12.2	11.5		(12) 40.6	(11) 22.5	(16) 11.0	(11) 5.0	
	3.1	(47) 3.5	(60) 5.0		2.8	5.0	6.0	2.1	
	1.2	1.7	1.6		2.0	1.5	2.7	1.2	
Net Profit + Depr., Dep., Amort./Cur. Mat. L/T/D	(24) 4.1	(16) 4.5	(20) 3.6						
	2.0	2.6	2.1						
	.4	.8	1.0						
Fixed/Worth	.1	.1	.1		.1	.1	.1	.2	
	.6	.4	.3		.4	.3	.3	.7	
	1.2	1.2	1.1		12.0	.7	.6	2.3	
Debt/Worth	1.0	1.3	.9		.3	1.1	.9	2.1	
	2.1	2.2	2.1		1.3	1.6	2.1	3.4	
	6.1	3.8	5.9		59.3	6.1	5.3	7.7	
% Profit Before Taxes/Tangible Net Worth	(59) 40.0	43.4	46.9		(13) 23.2	47.1	(16) 48.8	(12) 46.1	
	14.3	(50) 19.3	(67) 22.2		13.7	14.6	27.1	12.7	
	3.9	5.0	8.9		9.3	3.7	10.8	.6	
% Profit Before Taxes/Total Assets	11.1	13.4	15.1		13.7	21.0	19.4	10.3	
	4.2	6.7	6.8		6.6	4.3	9.2	3.8	
	1.1	1.2	1.5		1.1	.5	2.4	.2	
Sales/Net Fixed Assets	72.9	89.8	92.7		83.1	72.0	111.7	99.1	
	31.3	30.2	35.8		26.5	40.7	55.3	23.3	
	17.7	10.8	16.9		6.6	20.1	25.0	7.4	
Sales/Total Assets	4.0	3.9	3.8		3.2	4.6	3.8	4.1	
	3.4	3.1	2.9		2.5	3.4	3.4	3.7	
	2.7	2.3	2.2		2.1	2.3	3.0	2.4	
% Depr., Dep., Amort./Sales	(53) .5	(47) .4	(57) .4		(12) .5		(10) .4	.5	
	1.0	.7	.6		1.0		.5	1.8	
	1.9	1.9	1.4		2.9		.6	3.2	
% Officers', Directors', Owners' Comp/Sales	(38) 2.1	(33) 2.2	(42) 1.6		(13) 2.4	(10) 1.9	(10) 1.9		
	3.8	3.5	3.5		6.0	4.3	2.4		
	7.9	6.1	7.1		9.8	7.2	4.5		
Net Sales ($)	1248494M	807614M	1103417M	3851M	22941M	46425M	120039M	187995M	722166M
Total Assets ($)	420358M	268976M	368903M	3437M	11662M	15343M	36757M	62328M	239376M

© Robert Morris Associates 1995

M = $ thousand   MM = $ million

See Pages 1 through 15 for Explanation of Ratios and Data

| Current Data Sorted By Assets | | | | | | | Comparative Historical Data | |

Type of Statement (# Postretirement Benefits)

0-500M	500M-2MM	2-10MM	10-50MM	50-100MM	100-250MM		4/1/90-3/31/91 ALL	4/1/91-3/31/92 ALL
		1		1	1	# Postretirement Benefits — Type of Statement		
9	9	27	19	7	4	Unqualified	55	57
1	9	11	5	1		Reviewed	34	33
10	12	4	1			Compiled	34	34
3	1		1			Tax Returns		2
6	11	9		1		Other	28	33
67 (4/1-9/30/94)		94 (10/1/94-3/31/95)					151	159
20	42	51	35	9	4	NUMBER OF STATEMENTS	151	159

ASSETS

0-500M %	500M-2MM %	2-10MM %	10-50MM %	50-100MM %	100-250MM %	ASSETS	%	%
9.2	6.5	7.4	4.8			Cash & Equivalents	5.4	6.0
38.4	38.6	37.2	33.8			Trade Receivables - (net)	34.8	34.0
36.1	32.3	33.9	37.2			Inventory	38.5	40.2
1.0	4.0	2.2	1.5			All Other Current	1.8	2.8
84.6	81.3	80.8	77.3			Total Current	80.5	83.0
10.7	10.7	11.2	13.3			Fixed Assets (net)	11.4	9.8
.7	3.6	2.1	3.5			Intangibles (net)	2.6	2.4
3.9	4.5	5.9	5.9			All Other Non-Current	5.6	4.8
100.0	100.0	100.0	100.0			Total	100.0	100.0

LIABILITIES

0-500M	500M-2MM	2-10MM	10-50MM	50-100MM	100-250MM	LIABILITIES	Hist	Hist
13.0	8.3	12.6	16.8			Notes Payable-Short Term	15.6	13.9
3.1	3.2	2.5	1.3			Cur. Mat. -L/T/D	4.0	3.4
29.2	27.7	33.9	27.0			Trade Payables	27.3	28.9
.7	.4	.5	.7			Income Taxes Payable	.7	.7
9.4	7.1	5.9	10.5			All Other Current	6.1	6.6
55.6	46.7	55.4	56.3			Total Current	53.7	53.5
15.6	8.4	9.2	8.6			Long Term Debt	11.0	11.2
.0	.1	.4	.4			Deferred Taxes	.2	.2
1.3	6.0	3.3	2.5			All Other-Non-Current	3.3	2.0
27.5	38.7	31.7	32.2			Net Worth	31.7	33.0
100.0	100.0	100.0	100.0			Total Liabilities & Net Worth	100.0	100.0

INCOME DATA

0-500M	500M-2MM	2-10MM	10-50MM	50-100MM	100-250MM	INCOME DATA	Hist	Hist
100.0	100.0	100.0	100.0			Net Sales	100.0	100.0
35.5	32.0	27.5	27.5			Gross Profit	27.9	24.7
32.5	27.8	23.7	21.9			Operating Expenses	24.4	20.9
3.0	4.1	3.8	5.6			Operating Profit	3.5	3.8
.5	.4	.7	.4			All Other Expenses (net)	1.1	1.2
2.5	3.8	3.1	5.2			Profit Before Taxes	2.4	2.6

RATIOS

0-500M	500M-2MM	2-10MM	10-50MM	50-100MM	100-250MM	RATIOS	Hist	Hist
2.8	2.7	1.8	1.8			Current	1.9	2.1
1.6	1.8	1.5	1.4				1.5	1.5
1.1	1.3	1.2	1.2				1.2	1.2
1.3	1.6	1.0	1.0			Quick	1.0	1.1
.9	.9	.7	.8				.7	.7
.6	.7	.6	.4				.5	.5
24 14.9	24 15.1	31 11.7	22 16.6			Sales/Receivables	24 14.9	24 15.0
35 10.5	43 8.5	42 8.7	32 11.4				36 10.1	35 10.4
41 8.8	68 5.4	54 6.7	56 6.5				54 6.8	47 7.7
19 19.5	29 12.4	33 11.1	39 9.3			Cost of Sales/Inventory	35 10.5	33 10.9
51 7.1	48 7.6	54 6.8	55 6.6				57 6.4	52 7.0
94 3.9	85 4.3	74 4.9	83 4.4				96 3.8	91 4.0
16 23.2	19 18.9	32 11.4	28 12.9			Cost of Sales/Payables	25 14.4	27 13.3
42 8.7	39 9.4	49 7.5	37 10.0				37 9.9	36 10.2
64 5.7	81 4.5	69 5.3	56 6.5				56 6.5	54 6.8
7.5	6.2	8.1	8.7			Sales/Working Capital	7.4	6.9
13.9	8.9	13.2	18.1				14.1	12.7
97.6	23.1	21.5	27.7				33.8	27.0
24.0	9.6	8.2	31.7			EBIT/Interest	5.8	6.8
(15) 3.5	(38) 5.4	(47) 4.8	(32) 4.4				(132) 2.4	(147) 3.0
-.8	1.2	1.5	2.5				1.2	1.4
		5.3	6.7			Net Profit + Depr., Dep., Amort./Cur. Mat. L /T/D	6.0	6.8
		(22) 2.9	(17) 2.5				(64) 2.1	(77) 2.1
		1.2	1.3				.5	.5
.1	.1	.1	.1			Fixed/Worth	.1	.1
.3	.2	.3	.4				.3	.3
1.1	.8	.7	.9				.8	.7
.7	.7	1.4	1.5			Debt/Worth	1.1	1.3
2.2	2.5	3.0	2.4				2.5	2.4
14.3	4.3	3.8	7.2				6.3	4.5
74.9	49.9	57.8	86.3			% Profit Before Taxes/Tangible Net Worth	36.4	41.8
(16) 26.2	(38) 23.2	(50) 25.3	(32) 30.2				(137) 17.0	(147) 23.4
1.4	2.8	6.1	12.5				4.8	6.8
18.9	17.3	14.9	25.2			% Profit Before Taxes/Total Assets	11.4	14.0
8.1	6.6	6.1	6.4				5.2	5.9
-2.7	.8	1.5	2.5				.8	1.5
91.5	149.0	84.3	171.7			Sales/Net Fixed Assets	109.0	131.0
40.8	42.4	42.2	49.5				44.8	52.2
20.9	19.9	21.8	17.4				17.6	25.1
4.9	3.9	4.1	4.6			Sales/Total Assets	4.5	4.8
4.4	3.1	3.2	3.5				3.3	3.5
2.9	2.4	2.2	2.5				2.4	2.4
.4	.3	.3	.2			% Depr., Dep., Amort./Sales	.3	.2
(15) .7	(32) .9	(50) .6	(29) .5				(132) .6	(140) .5
1.2	1.7	1.1	1.8				1.1	1.1
	2.6	.8				% Officers', Directors', Owners' Comp/Sales	.9	1.1
	(20) 4.3	(14) 1.6					(54) 2.8	(60) 2.6
	8.7	4.4					5.2	5.5
19361M	166415M	870836M	2849021M	1368465M	1725777M	Net Sales ($)	7393924M	10735359M
4786M	51123M	253335M	812799M	568501M	559655M	Total Assets ($)	2298354M	2843482M

© Robert Morris Associates 1995

M = $ thousand   MM = $ million
See Pages 1 through 15 for Explanation of Ratios and Data

Comparative Historical Data				Current Data Sorted By Sales					
3	7	3	# Postretirement Benefits						3
			Type of Statement						
49	58	66	Unqualified	1	1	6	7	15	36
26	29	27	Reviewed	1	4	3	9	2	8
28	28	27	Compiled	4	10	4	4	3	2
5	3	5	Tax Returns	2	2				1
20	25	36	Other	3	10	3	6	2	12
4/1/92-3/31/93 ALL	4/1/93-3/31/94 ALL	4/1/94-3/31/95 ALL		67 (4/1-9/30/94)			94 (10/1/94-3/31/95)		
				0-1MM	1-3MM	3-5MM	5-10MM	10-25MM	25MM & OVER
128	143	161	NUMBER OF STATEMENTS	11	27	16	26	22	59
%	%	%	**ASSETS**	%	%	%	%	%	%
7.6	7.3	6.8	Cash & Equivalents	8.4	8.9	6.5	7.9	6.7	5.1
34.4	34.8	36.6	Trade Receivables - (net)	40.4	32.1	39.9	42.3	34.9	35.3
38.9	35.1	34.4	Inventory	29.2	35.4	32.3	29.8	38.0	36.0
1.5	1.5	2.3	All Other Current	1.1	5.6	1.6	1.6	1.5	1.9
82.3	78.7	80.1	Total Current	79.1	82.0	80.3	81.6	81.1	78.4
10.9	9.9	11.1	Fixed Assets (net)	9.6	13.4	9.0	12.2	9.6	11.0
1.8	4.3	3.1	Intangibles (net)	7.9	.4	4.6	1.6	2.5	4.0
5.0	7.1	5.6	All Other Non-Current	3.4	4.2	6.1	4.6	6.8	6.6
100.0	100.0	100.0	Total	100.0	100.0	100.0	100.0	100.0	100.0
			LIABILITIES						
14.0	11.4	12.3	Notes Payable-Short Term	16.0	7.8	5.8	13.8	14.4	14.1
1.9	3.1	2.6	Cur. Mat.-L/T/D	3.1	3.3	4.4	2.7	2.4	1.6
29.3	26.0	29.4	Trade Payables	24.0	26.7	31.4	29.4	31.7	30.3
.8	1.8	.5	Income Taxes Payable	1.1	.4	.7	.6	.4	.5
8.1	7.2	7.4	All Other Current	12.2	10.4	2.5	5.3	6.4	7.8
54.0	49.4	52.3	Total Current	56.4	48.6	44.8	51.9	55.4	54.3
9.1	9.7	9.7	Long Term Debt	19.8	9.4	11.3	8.3	8.3	8.7
.5	.4	.3	Deferred Taxes	.0	.0	.3	.5	.2	.4
1.9	2.2	3.4	All Other-Non-Current	3.2	3.8	5.1	3.9	3.1	2.6
34.4	38.3	34.3	Net Worth	20.5	38.2	38.5	35.4	33.1	33.9
100.0	100.0	100.0	Total Liabilities & Net Worth	100.0	100.0	100.0	100.0	100.0	100.0
			INCOME DATA						
100.0	100.0	100.0	Net Sales	100.0	100.0	100.0	100.0	100.0	100.0
24.6	29.9	29.3	Gross Profit	35.6	38.7	33.2	27.9	29.8	23.3
21.6	25.8	25.0	Operating Expenses	30.0	36.0	29.7	24.5	24.7	18.1
3.1	4.1	4.4	Operating Profit	5.6	2.7	3.5	3.5	5.1	5.3
.7	.3	.5	All Other Expenses (net)	.7	.2	.5	.5	1.4	.3
2.4	3.8	3.8	Profit Before Taxes	4.9	2.5	3.0	3.0	3.7	4.9
			RATIOS						
2.0	2.2	2.2	Current	2.8	2.9	2.4	2.2	1.8	1.9
1.5	1.5	1.6		1.6	1.8	1.8	1.5	1.4	1.5
1.2	1.2	1.2		1.1	1.1	1.4	1.2	1.2	1.2
1.1	1.2	1.1	Quick	1.4	1.3	1.6	1.4	.8	1.0
.8	.8	.8		.9	.9	1.0	.8	.6	.8
.6	.6	.6		.6	.7	.6	.7	.5	.5
24 14.9	27 13.5	25 14.4	Sales/Receivables	35 10.5	22 16.5	35 10.4	38 9.7	30 12.3	23 15.7
33 11.2	40 9.1	41 8.9		41 8.8	36 10.1	41 9.0	48 7.6	42 8.7	33 10.9
45 8.1	54 6.8	58 6.3		54 6.7	58 6.3	81 4.5	59 6.2	56 6.5	56 6.5
28 12.9	32 11.3	31 11.6	Cost of Sales/Inventory	18 20.5	32 11.4	24 15.3	31 11.7	42 8.7	30 12.1
50 7.3	54 6.7	54 6.8		51 7.1	70 5.2	57 6.4	51 7.2	63 5.8	49 7.4
85 4.3	91 4.0	81 4.5		96 3.8	104 3.5	94 3.9	68 5.4	79 4.6	70 5.2
24 14.9	26 14.3	26 14.3	Cost of Sales/Payables	10 38.4	26 14.2	20 18.0	24 15.2	31 11.7	28 12.9
34 10.6	37 9.9	40 9.1		31 11.7	51 7.1	50 7.3	39 9.3	49 7.4	39 9.4
51 7.2	52 7.0	63 5.8		54 6.7	79 4.6	104 3.5	61 6.0	66 5.5	54 6.7
8.0	6.2	7.2	Sales/Working Capital	5.0	6.4	5.9	7.1	8.0	8.3
15.4	11.3	12.3		9.8	10.4	8.6	11.1	14.8	17.9
28.1	26.7	25.0		137.0	23.4	13.2	25.1	22.7	27.3
(115) 10.4	(130) 11.3	(144) 12.5	EBIT/Interest		(22) 9.6	(15) 15.1	(24) 8.0	12.1	(53) 22.0
4.3	5.1	4.5			4.7	5.8	5.0	4.2	4.2
1.9	1.8	1.6			.6	.4	1.3	2.0	2.1
(57) 8.3	(63) 10.0	(61) 6.2	Net Profit + Depr., Dep., Amort./Cur. Mat. L/T/D				(12) 12.8		(25) 6.4
3.6	2.6	2.5					3.2		2.5
1.5	1.0	1.1					1.3		1.3
.1	.1	.1	Fixed/Worth	.1	.1	.1	.1	.1	.1
.3	.2	.3		.4	.3	.2	.2	.3	.2
.7	.6	.7		3.5	.8	.5	.7	.6	.8
1.0	1.0	1.0	Debt/Worth	1.5	.6	.7	1.0	1.3	1.1
2.0	1.9	2.6		3.4	1.7	2.2	2.7	3.1	2.3
4.7	4.2	4.3		-3.8	4.0	3.9	4.3	4.1	5.4
(124) 45.6	(136) 43.9	(149) 58.8	% Profit Before Taxes/Tangible Net Worth		(23) 57.5	(15) 48.9	34.5	57.2	(55) 66.8
22.0	19.5	25.4			21.1	26.2	19.7	34.2	28.4
7.4	7.9	6.3			.5	-3.1	4.9	12.9	8.2
12.3	14.0	16.2	% Profit Before Taxes/Total Assets	30.1	17.6	22.7	14.2	15.1	21.8
6.3	6.5	6.4		7.9	8.3	5.6	6.3	7.7	5.5
1.7	1.8	1.7		-3.1	.3	-1.7	1.3	2.9	1.7
157.2	109.3	105.5	Sales/Net Fixed Assets	91.5	84.3	116.3	274.3	66.1	161.7
66.3	44.4	42.3		32.8	40.9	41.0	50.5	37.1	51.4
21.5	23.6	19.6		13.7	18.6	20.4	22.5	21.0	18.5
5.1	4.3	4.4	Sales/Total Assets	4.9	4.5	3.7	4.2	4.0	4.8
3.8	3.2	3.2		2.9	3.1	2.9	3.2	3.1	3.7
2.4	2.2	2.4		2.6	2.3	2.1	2.3	2.4	2.5
(114) .2	(130) .3	(137) .3	% Depr., Dep., Amort./Sales		(21) .3	(14) .5	(22) .3	(21) .3	(52) .2
.5	.5	.6			.7	.9	1.0	.8	.3
1.0	1.5	1.3			1.8	2.0	1.4	1.1	1.1
(51) .8	(61) 1.7	(50) 1.3	% Officers', Directors', Owners' Comp/Sales		(15) 4.6				(10) .5
5.0	4.4	4.1			6.5				.9
8.9	7.1	6.7			8.9				2.2
8348839M	8206237M	6999875M	Net Sales ($)	5141M	53638M	65790M	190174M	355041M	6330091M
2053177M	2388825M	2250199M	Total Assets ($)	2116M	20109M	25656M	70422M	123861M	2008035M

© Robert Morris Associates 1995

M = $ thousand   MM = $ million

See Pages 1 through 15 for Explanation of Ratios and Data

WHOLESALERS—ELECTRICAL SUPPLIES & APPARATUS. SIC# 5063

Current Data Sorted By Assets						# Postretirement Benefits	Comparative Historical Data	
3	13	14	8	2		Type of Statement		
3	9	54	30	2	3	Unqualified	120	89
5	65	79	13	2		Reviewed	194	193
31	69	32				Compiled	173	168
9	7					Tax Returns	2	8
13	36	48	21	2	2	Other	90	103
	173 (4/1-9/30/94)		362 (10/1/94-3/31/95)				4/1/90-3/31/91	4/1/91-3/31/92
0-500M	500M-2MM	2-10MM	10-50MM	50-100MM	100-250MM		ALL	ALL
61	186	213	64	6	5	NUMBER OF STATEMENTS	579	561
%	%	%	%	%	%	ASSETS	%	%
8.4	6.4	4.9	3.2			Cash & Equivalents	5.3	6.1
37.4	39.4	42.2	41.0			Trade Receivables - (net)	37.9	38.0
32.5	37.6	36.3	35.9			Inventory	37.7	37.3
1.9	.8	.9	1.4			All Other Current	1.6	1.0
80.2	84.2	84.2	81.5			Total Current	82.5	82.3
13.7	10.9	10.4	12.0			Fixed Assets (net)	12.3	12.6
.9	.5	.9	1.1			Intangibles (net)	.9	.9
5.2	4.4	4.4	5.4			All Other Non-Current	4.3	4.2
100.0	100.0	100.0	100.0			Total	100.0	100.0
						LIABILITIES		
10.3	11.3	16.0	18.9			Notes Payable-Short Term	15.7	14.8
3.2	2.6	2.1	1.4			Cur. Mat. -L/T/D	2.8	2.8
29.3	28.5	26.5	24.3			Trade Payables	25.5	25.1
.1	.4	.5	.5			Income Taxes Payable	.5	.3
10.8	7.0	7.0	8.3			All Other Current	6.9	6.6
53.7	49.9	52.0	53.4			Total Current	51.5	49.7
10.8	10.1	8.6	7.1			Long Term Debt	9.9	9.7
.1	.3	.1	.2			Deferred Taxes	.2	.2
2.4	2.5	2.2	3.3			All Other-Non-Current	2.3	2.9
33.1	37.3	37.1	36.0			Net Worth	36.1	37.6
100.0	100.0	100.0	100.0			Total Liabilities & Net Worth	100.0	100.0
						INCOME DATA		
100.0	100.0	100.0	100.0			Net Sales	100.0	100.0
29.3	27.2	23.0	22.7			Gross Profit	26.4	27.6
28.7	25.3	20.7	20.0			Operating Expenses	23.7	25.3
.6	1.9	2.3	2.7			Operating Profit	2.7	2.3
.5	.4	.4	.6			All Other Expenses (net)	.9	.6
.1	1.5	1.9	2.2			Profit Before Taxes	1.8	1.7
						RATIOS		
2.0	2.4	2.2	2.0				2.2	2.4
1.4	1.7	1.6	1.4			Current	1.6	1.6
1.2	1.3	1.3	1.3				1.3	1.3
1.2	1.3	1.2	1.1				1.2	1.3
.8	.9	.9	.8			Quick	(578) .8	.9
.6	.7	.7	.7				.6	.7

28	13.2	36	10.1	41	8.9	47	7.8			Sales/Receivables	37	9.8	36	10.2

Sales/Receivables
28 13.2	36 10.1	41 8.9	47 7.8			Sales/Receivables	37 9.8	36 10.2
36 10.1	45 8.1	49 7.4	52 7.0				45 8.1	45 8.2
51 7.1	56 6.5	58 6.3	58 6.3				55 6.6	56 6.5

24 15.1	38 9.7	43 8.5	43 8.5			Cost of Sales/Inventory	41 8.8	38 9.5
49 7.5	59 6.2	57 6.4	54 6.7				60 6.1	60 6.1
79 4.6	91 4.0	76 4.8	87 4.2				89 4.1	94 3.9

20 18.5	31 11.7	31 11.9	28 13.1			Cost of Sales/Payables	28 13.1	27 13.6
39 9.3	43 8.5	41 9.0	39 9.4				38 9.7	38 9.6
69 5.3	57 6.4	53 6.9	47 7.7				53 6.9	53 6.9

7.6	5.7	6.1	7.1			Sales/Working Capital	6.2	5.8
14.2	8.8	10.0	10.8				10.0	9.6
37.2	18.2	18.4	17.2				19.2	17.7

(52) 8.8	(172) 8.1	(191) 8.3	(61) 8.6			EBIT/Interest	(529) 4.8	(517) 5.6
3.0	3.3	3.2	3.6				2.1	2.1
.6	1.5	1.7	1.6				1.1	1.1

(10) 11.7	(62) 5.8	(98) 5.7	(36) 11.2			Net Profit + Depr., Dep., Amort./Cur. Mat. L /T/D	(308) 4.7	(243) 5.1
1.1	2.7	2.8	3.1				1.8	1.5
.3	1.2	1.3	1.4				.7	.5

.1	.1	.1	.2			Fixed/Worth	.1	.1
.3	.2	.2	.3				.3	.3
.9	.5	.5	.6				.6	.6

1.0	1.0	1.0	1.1			Debt/Worth	.9	.9
2.2	1.9	2.1	2.2				2.0	1.8
5.9	3.6	3.5	3.6				3.9	3.7

(57) 47.8	(184) 30.4	(208) 31.7	(63) 39.0			% Profit Before Taxes/Tangible Net Worth	(556) 26.3	(530) 25.6
15.9	15.5	16.6	22.5				12.6	11.9
-2.3	4.4	7.9	7.7				3.8	2.0

14.3	10.9	9.9	11.9			% Profit Before Taxes/Total Assets	9.5	8.2
4.1	4.7	5.3	5.9				4.0	3.6
-1.7	1.1	1.9	2.3				.8	.5

138.6	91.5	84.2	47.3			Sales/Net Fixed Assets	73.4	69.8
36.1	42.0	45.0	34.4				37.3	37.9
17.4	24.2	24.1	16.5				17.9	18.0

4.4	3.8	3.5	3.5			Sales/Total Assets	3.7	3.8
3.5	3.1	3.0	2.8				3.0	3.0
2.4	2.5	2.5	2.2				2.3	2.4

(48) .5	(170) .4	(198) .3	(60) .5			% Depr., Dep., Amort./Sales	(525) .4	(507) .4
1.0	.6	.5	.7				.7	.8
1.6	1.1	.9	1.0				1.2	1.2

(33) 4.5	(91) 2.2	(94) 1.2	(18) .7			% Officers', Directors', Owners' Comp/Sales	(249) 1.9	(256) 2.0
6.2	3.8	2.2	1.5				3.2	3.7
10.2	8.3	3.6	3.3				6.3	6.6

| 71355M | 720353M | 3120835M | 3259056M | 1033381M | 1608722M | Net Sales ($) | 9022384M | 7881045M |
| 19415M | 226760M | 1002615M | 1143169M | 371531M | 645498M | Total Assets ($) | 3430618M | 3097947M |

M = $ thousand   MM = $ million

See Pages 1 through 15 for Explanation of Ratios and Data

Comparative Historical Data				Current Data Sorted By Sales					
13	25	40	# Postretirement Benefits	3	5	8	4	11	9
			Type of Statement						
92	102	101	Unqualified	2	5	6	11	31	46
182	185	164	Reviewed	4	32	23	38	42	25
145	126	132	Compiled	15	41	34	28	14	
9	17	16	Tax Returns	5	8	3			
99	98	122	Other	7	19	12	28	30	26
4/1/92-3/31/93	4/1/93-3/31/94	4/1/94-3/31/95		173 (4/1-9/30/94)			362 (10/1/94-3/31/95)		
ALL	ALL	* ALL		0-1MM	1-3MM	3-5MM	5-10MM	10-25MM	25MM & OVER
527	528	535	**NUMBER OF STATEMENTS**	33	105	78	105	117	97
%	%	%	**ASSETS**	%	%	%	%	%	%
5.2	5.1	5.6	Cash & Equivalents	4.6	8.4	8.2	5.2	4.0	3.0
38.8	39.4	40.5	Trade Receivables - (net)	31.0	37.6	36.3	42.6	45.4	42.2
37.6	37.0	36.2	Inventory	34.5	34.0	39.8	37.9	35.3	35.6
1.2	1.5	1.1	All Other Current	3.5	.5	1.2	.7	1.0	1.2
82.8	82.9	83.3	Total Current	73.6	80.5	85.4	86.3	85.7	82.1
11.3	11.1	11.2	Fixed Assets (net)	19.3	13.3	10.8	8.8	9.1	11.4
1.3	1.0	.8	Intangibles (net)	1.2	.8	.4	.7	.8	1.3
4.5	5.0	4.7	All Other Non-Current	5.9	5.4	3.4	4.2	4.4	5.2
100.0	100.0	100.0	Total	100.0	100.0	100.0	100.0	100.0	100.0
			LIABILITIES						
15.0	14.3	14.1	Notes Payable-Short Term	8.1	11.0	10.8	14.5	17.1	18.1
2.5	2.4	2.3	Cur. Mat.-L /T/D	4.3	2.7	3.0	1.8	2.0	1.6
26.8	25.5	27.2	Trade Payables	26.1	27.1	27.5	29.2	26.6	26.3
.4	1.7	.4	Income Taxes Payable	.1	.4	.4	.4	.6	.3
6.9	7.1	7.6	All Other Current	10.6	7.3	7.8	7.1	6.9	8.2
51.6	51.0	51.7	Total Current	49.2	48.5	49.5	52.9	53.2	54.4
8.3	7.6	9.1	Long Term Debt	13.8	12.6	9.3	7.2	7.9	7.2
.2	.2	.2	Deferred Taxes	.9	.1	.1	.1	.1	.1
2.9	3.4	2.5	All Other-Non-Current	2.7	3.1	1.5	2.4	2.8	2.5
37.1	37.8	36.5	Net Worth	33.4	35.7	39.5	37.3	35.9	35.7
100.0	100.0	100.0	Total Liabilities & Net Worth	100.0	100.0	100.0	100.0	100.0	100.0
			INCOME DATA						
100.0	100.0	100.0	Net Sales	100.0	100.0	100.0	100.0	100.0	100.0
26.5	26.0	25.0	Gross Profit	35.4	30.1	27.1	23.0	22.0	20.2
24.4	24.1	23.1	Operating Expenses	35.2	27.7	25.8	21.4	19.4	18.1
2.1	1.9	1.9	Operating Profit	.2	2.4	1.3	1.6	2.6	2.1
.4	.4	.4	All Other Expenses (net)	.9	.5	.4	.4	.3	.4
1.8	1.5	1.5	Profit Before Taxes	-.7	1.8	.9	1.2	2.2	1.7
			RATIOS						
2.3	2.2	2.2	Current	2.2	2.5	2.4	2.3	2.2	1.9
1.6	1.6	1.6		1.5	1.5	1.7	1.6	1.6	1.4
1.3	1.3	1.3		1.1	1.3	1.4	1.3	1.2	1.3
1.2	1.2	1.2	Quick	1.2	1.3	1.3	1.2	1.2	1.1
.9	.9 (534)	.9		.8	.9 (77)	.9	.9	.9	.9
.6	.6	.7		.5	.7	.6	.7	.7	.7
38 9.7	39 9.4	38 9.5	Sales/Receivables	28 12.9	34 10.8	38 9.6	39 9.3	44 8.3	42 8.7
46 8.0	47 7.8	48 7.6		36 10.1	43 8.4	47 7.8	47 7.7	51 7.2	51 7.1
56 6.5	58 6.3	56 6.5		53 6.9	57 6.4	56 6.5	57 6.4	59 6.2	56 6.5
41 9.0	40 9.2	40 9.1	Cost of Sales/Inventory	40 9.1	29 12.4	44 8.3	45 8.2	39 9.3	41 8.9
59 6.2	60 6.1	56 6.5		76 4.8	58 6.3	66 5.5	59 6.2	54 6.7	49 7.4
91 4.0	91 4.0	81 4.5		122 3.0	96 3.8	101 3.6	78 4.7	72 5.1	72 5.1
29 12.4	27 13.6	30 12.2	Cost of Sales/Payables	25 14.8	27 13.5	33 11.2	33 11.0	30 12.3	28 13.2
39 9.3	40 9.2	41 9.0		51 7.1	43 8.5	46 8.0	45 8.2	38 9.7	37 10.0
57 6.4	55 6.6	55 6.6		78 4.7	57 6.4	63 5.8	58 6.3	49 7.4	43 8.4
5.9	6.1	6.3	Sales/Working Capital	6.6	5.4	5.1	6.7	6.2	8.0
10.0	9.6	10.2		13.5	9.9	8.2	9.5	10.4	11.0
18.8	17.8	18.7		32.8	23.2	13.5	18.4	18.6	18.7
(476) 5.8	(483) 7.0	(486) 8.3	EBIT/Interest	(28) 5.0	(95) 7.2	(72) 9.4	(94) 7.7	(103) 8.8	(94) 10.1
2.6	3.1	3.3		2.0	4.1	2.6	3.0	3.4	4.2
1.4	1.5	1.6		-.3	1.5	1.0	1.6	2.0	1.7
(217) 5.2	(206) 5.7	(214) 7.4	Net Profit + Depr., Dep., Amort./Cur. Mat. L/T/D		(30) 6.1	(27) 5.0	(45) 7.9	(53) 5.1	(52) 11.4
2.0	2.0	2.8			2.3	2.8	2.9	2.6	3.1
.8	.6	1.2			.8	1.2	1.3	1.3	1.6
.1	.1	.1	Fixed/Worth	.2	.1	.1	.1	.1	.2
.2	.2	.2		.4	.3	.2	.2	.2	.3
.6	.5	.5		1.1	.8	.4	.5	.5	.5
.9	1.0	1.0	Debt/Worth	.9	1.0	.9	.9	1.1	1.2
1.9	1.9	2.0		2.0	2.2	1.6	1.9	2.2	2.1
3.8	3.3	3.6		7.4	4.5	2.9	3.5	3.7	3.5
(503) 26.6	(512) 28.6	(523) 32.6	% Profit Before Taxes/Tangible Net Worth	(30) 24.0	(103) 42.2	(77) 24.9	(101) 28.5	(116) 34.3	(96) 43.1
11.9	13.6	17.2		12.7	20.1	9.7	13.7	19.8	22.1
3.2	4.4	5.5		-10.2	4.9	-.9	4.2	9.7	9.4
8.7	9.8	10.7	% Profit Before Taxes/Total Assets	9.0	12.7	8.8	8.3	9.7	13.1
3.9	4.5	5.2		1.7	6.7	3.4	3.9	5.9	7.3
.9	1.2	1.6		-4.7	1.6	-.1	1.1	2.7	2.1
80.6	78.3	79.7	Sales/Net Fixed Assets	57.8	85.4	97.2	94.3	82.6	52.7
42.3	43.2	42.0		21.9	36.1	41.7	49.1	49.2	37.5
20.0	19.0	21.6		8.6	20.1	24.1	28.4	25.4	19.8
3.6	3.6	3.7	Sales/Total Assets	3.5	3.9	3.5	3.8	3.7	3.7
3.0	2.9	3.0		2.4	3.0	2.8	3.1	3.1	3.1
2.4	2.4	2.4		2.0	2.2	2.2	2.6	2.6	2.6
(467) .4	(464) .4	(485) .4	% Depr., Dep., Amort./Sales	(26) .5	(92) .5	(70) .4	(97) .3	(111) .3	(89) .4
.6	.7	.6		1.5	.8	.6	.6	.5	.6
1.1	1.2	1.0		2.1	1.3	1.1	.9	.8	.8
(231) 1.8	(229) 1.7	(238) 1.7	% Officers', Directors', Owners' Comp/Sales	(17) 4.9	(48) 3.3	(43) 1.7	(55) 2.0	(50) 1.1	(25) .7
3.7	3.1	2.8		6.4	5.6	2.7	2.8	2.1	1.1
6.7	6.1	6.4		13.2	9.8	7.1	4.6	3.0	2.9
8136723M	8815996M	9813702M	Net Sales ($)	23173M	211378M	304621M	732491M	1887215M	6654824M
2980870M	3358260M	3408988M	Total Assets ($)	10658M	77598M	122657M	244917M	648583M	2304575M

M = $ thousand   MM = $ million
See Pages 1 through 15 for Explanation of Ratios and Data

Current Data Sorted By Assets   Comparative Historical Data

Postretirement Benefits / Type of Statement

Type of Statement	0-500M	500M-2MM	2-10MM	10-50MM	50-100MM	100-250MM		4/1/90-3/31/91 ALL	4/1/91-3/31/92 ALL
# Postretirement Benefits		1	1	1					
Unqualified	1	3	12	10	1			33	38
Reviewed	5	9	27	8	2			39	46
Compiled	3	19	7					31	35
Tax Returns	3		1					1	3
Other		16	13	10				32	24
	58 (4/1-9/30/94)			92 (10/1/94-3/31/95)					
NUMBER OF STATEMENTS	12	47	60	28	3			136	146

Financial Data

	0-500M	500M-2MM	2-10MM	10-50MM	50-100MM	100-250MM		4/1/90-3/31/91 ALL	4/1/91-3/31/92 ALL
	%	%	%	%	%	%		%	%
ASSETS									
Cash & Equivalents	3.4	4.9	6.4	5.9				5.6	6.1
Trade Receivables - (net)	39.1	29.5	32.5	41.1				34.8	32.5
Inventory	32.0	46.8	43.5	36.0				44.0	43.5
All Other Current	.1	1.3	1.1	4.2				1.4	1.5
Total Current	74.7	82.5	83.5	87.3				85.8	83.7
Fixed Assets (net)	16.8	10.6	9.5	5.7				8.1	9.3
Intangibles (net)	.3	.4	.3	.6				.6	1.2
All Other Non-Current	8.2	6.6	6.7	6.4				5.6	5.8
Total	100.0	100.0	100.0	100.0				100.0	100.0
LIABILITIES									
Notes Payable-Short Term	6.1	14.2	13.9	16.7				17.2	16.7
Cur. Mat. -L/T/D	2.3	1.5	1.1	.5				1.1	1.7
Trade Payables	29.4	33.0	27.5	29.4				29.9	29.4
Income Taxes Payable	.5	.1	.2	.3				.3	.2
All Other Current	9.6	5.0	6.7	10.3				7.7	6.3
Total Current	47.9	53.8	49.4	57.1				56.2	54.5
Long Term Debt	13.1	6.7	4.9	2.8				6.4	7.5
Deferred Taxes	1.3	.1	.2	.1				.2	.0
All Other-Non-Current	3.2	4.2	3.2	1.5				2.4	2.9
Net Worth	34.5	35.2	42.4	38.5				34.8	35.1
Total Liabilities & Net Worth	100.0	100.0	100.0	100.0				100.0	100.0
INCOME DATA									
Net Sales	100.0	100.0	100.0	100.0				100.0	100.0
Gross Profit	31.3	23.6	19.8	21.3				22.1	21.1
Operating Expenses	30.0	21.8	17.3	18.2				19.6	19.2
Operating Profit	1.3	1.7	2.4	3.1				2.5	1.9
All Other Expenses (net)	.0	.1	.2	.4				.7	.5
Profit Before Taxes	1.3	1.7	2.3	2.7				1.8	1.4
RATIOS									
Current	2.4	2.6	2.3	2.2				2.2	2.0
	1.7	1.8	1.7	1.5				1.4	1.5
	1.2	1.1	1.4	1.2				1.2	1.2
Quick	1.3	1.1	1.2	1.2				1.0	1.1
	1.0	.6	.8	.8				.6	.7
	.6	.4	.6	.7				.5	.5
Sales/Receivables	7 55.4	22 16.9	28 12.9	38 9.5				25 14.4	22 16.4
	37 10.0	32 11.4	34 10.6	51 7.1				35 10.5	33 11.0
	51 7.2	45 8.1	52 7.0	65 5.6				53 6.9	47 7.7
Cost of Sales/Inventory	18 19.9	45 8.2	49 7.5	45 8.1				46 8.0	38 9.6
	38 9.7	73 5.0	61 6.0	64 5.7				66 5.5	55 6.6
	63 5.8	101 3.6	81 4.5	89 4.1				91 4.0	89 4.1
Cost of Sales/Payables	21 17.4	32 11.5	23 15.8	26 13.9				28 13.0	22 16.3
	37 9.8	44 8.3	38 9.5	37 9.9				39 9.4	36 10.1
	51 7.2	72 5.1	49 7.4	58 6.3				58 6.3	51 7.1
Sales/Working Capital	8.9	5.3	6.0	5.4				6.9	7.2
	14.7	11.4	10.8	10.5				14.2	13.6
	37.4	65.8	15.4	18.9				22.4	25.2
EBIT/Interest	5.5	8.6	10.5	11.3				4.9	4.5
	(11) 3.8	(42) 2.4	(55) 3.9	(24) 5.1				(126) 2.1	(137) 1.9
	1.0	.9	1.9	2.2				1.2	1.0
Net Profit + Depr., Dep., Amort./Cur. Mat. L./T/D			6.8					10.7	5.2
			(23) 2.6					(50) 3.7	(56) 2.2
			1.0					1.0	.7
Fixed/Worth	.0	.1	.1	.1				.1	.1
	.5	.2	.2	.1				.2	.2
	.7	1.6	.4	.2				.3	.4
Debt/Worth	1.1	.9	.7	.8				1.0	1.1
	1.7	2.2	1.6	1.9				2.4	2.1
	7.0	6.6	3.6	4.3				4.1	3.8
% Profit Before Taxes/Tangible Net Worth	23.8	25.1	31.5	33.7				27.7	23.8
	13.6	(46) 9.3	16.9	16.9				(133) 11.2	(143) 8.4
	.0	1.4	5.7	6.3				1.7	-.3
% Profit Before Taxes/Total Assets	15.6	7.6	11.8	8.7				7.9	7.0
	3.4	3.3	6.2	5.6				3.7	2.8
	.0	.2	1.8	2.0				.6	-.1
Sales/Net Fixed Assets	UND	125.5	138.5	140.5				178.1	169.9
	25.6	66.7	68.5	73.0				73.7	78.0
	13.9	26.4	25.2	27.7				28.8	25.4
Sales/Total Assets	5.3	3.4	3.9	3.2				4.1	4.4
	4.4	3.0	3.2	2.6				3.2	3.4
	3.0	2.5	2.3	2.2				2.5	2.5
% Depr., Dep., Amort./Sales		.3	.3	.2				.2	.2
		(41) .4	(54) .4	(25) .4				(116) .4	(127) .4
		1.3	.8	.7				.8	.9
% Officers', Directors', Owners' Comp/Sales		2.3	.9					1.4	1.6
		(27) 3.4	(30) 1.7					(54) 3.4	(66) 2.7
		6.5	4.9					5.7	5.5
Net Sales ($)	11683M	181116M	845891M	1511435M	614388M			3074426M	3038934M
Total Assets ($)	2922M	58647M	266530M	505455M	202680M			1038970M	913036M

M = $ thousand   MM = $ million
See Pages 1 through 15 for Explanation of Ratios and Data

	Comparative Historical Data				Current Data Sorted By Sales					
# Postretirement Benefits	5	5	3				2			1
Type of Statement										
Unqualified	34	40	26			1	4	10	11	
Reviewed	43	37	47	1	3	5	12	15	11	
Compiled	37	31	31	4	7	9	6	4	1	
Tax Returns	4	4	4	1	2			1		
Other	27	33	42	1		9	8	5	12	
	4/1/92-3/31/93 ALL	4/1/93-3/31/94 ALL	4/1/94-3/31/95 ALL	58 (4/1-9/30/94) 0-1MM	1-3MM	3-5MM	92 (10/1/94-3/31/95) 5-10MM	10-25MM	25MM & OVER	
NUMBER OF STATEMENTS	145	145	150	7	19	24	30	35	35	
ASSETS	%	%	%	%	%	%	%	%	%	
Cash & Equivalents	6.8	7.8	5.6		3.2	5.9	4.9	8.2	5.1	
Trade Receivables - (net)	33.4	33.2	33.9		24.9	33.5	28.9	36.4	40.2	
Inventory	42.4	39.9	42.2		52.6	40.0	46.1	39.8	40.4	
All Other Current	1.2	2.6	1.6		.6	1.1	1.1	1.4	3.5	
Total Current	83.8	83.5	83.3		81.3	80.6	81.1	85.8	89.4	
Fixed Assets (net)	9.1	9.1	9.6		13.0	12.9	9.4	7.7	4.9	
Intangibles (net)	.8	.7	.4		.2	.5	.4	.3	.7	
All Other Non-Current	6.3	6.7	6.7		5.5	6.0	9.1	6.2	5.1	
Total	100.0	100.0	100.0		100.0	100.0	100.0	100.0	100.0	
LIABILITIES										
Notes Payable-Short Term	15.3	13.6	13.6		8.8	15.4	11.3	16.7	15.1	
Cur. Mat.-L /T/D	1.9	1.6	1.3		2.1	1.9	.7	.9	.8	
Trade Payables	28.4	25.7	30.1		30.3	32.3	29.2	28.2	32.6	
Income Taxes Payable	.2	2.1	.2		.2	.2	.2	.2	.2	
All Other Current	7.0	7.4	7.1		8.8	4.7	7.5	4.5	10.2	
Total Current	52.8	50.4	52.2		50.2	54.5	48.9	50.6	58.9	
Long Term Debt	5.8	4.9	5.8		12.7	7.7	4.3	3.8	2.8	
Deferred Taxes	.1	.2	.2		.9	.1	.2	.1	.0	
All Other-Non-Current	3.5	3.5	3.1		2.2	6.3	2.7	2.7	1.9	
Net Worth	37.9	41.1	38.7		34.1	31.4	43.8	42.8	36.3	
Total Liabilities & Net Worth	100.0	100.0	100.0		100.0	100.0	100.0	100.0	100.0	
INCOME DATA										
Net Sales	100.0	100.0	100.0		100.0	100.0	100.0	100.0	100.0	
Gross Profit	21.3	22.4	22.0		31.2	21.5	20.3	19.5	19.1	
Operating Expenses	19.1	20.4	19.8		29.8	19.0	17.9	17.7	16.1	
Operating Profit	2.2	2.0	2.2		1.4	2.5	2.4	1.8	2.9	
All Other Expenses (net)	.3	.3	.2		-.3	.6	-.3	.2	.5	
Profit Before Taxes	1.9	1.7	2.1		1.7	1.9	2.7	1.7	2.4	
RATIOS										
Current	2.2	2.4	2.3		2.8	2.2	2.5	2.2	2.2	
	1.6	1.6	1.6		2.0	1.7	1.8	1.6	1.5	
	1.2	1.2	1.2		1.0	1.1	1.3	1.4	1.2	
Quick	1.1	1.3	1.1		1.1	1.1	1.2	1.3	1.1	
	.7	.8	.8		.6	.8	.8	.8	.8	
	.5	.5	.6		.2	.6	.5	.7	.6	
Sales/Receivables	23 15.6	27 13.6	27 13.5	17 22.1	29 12.8	27 13.3	30 12.1	32 11.5		
	35 10.3	34 10.7	38 9.7	24 15.1	39 9.3	34 10.7	40 9.2	47 7.7		
	46 7.9	46 7.9	54 6.8	39 9.3	53 6.9	54 6.8	54 6.7	62 5.9		
Cost of Sales/Inventory	40 9.2	38 9.7	44 8.3	51 7.2	40 9.2	53 6.9	41 8.9	43 8.4		
	55 6.6	57 6.4	62 5.9	101 3.6	65 5.6	69 5.3	59 6.2	60 6.1		
	81 4.5	79 4.6	91 4.0	146 2.5	89 4.1	87 4.2	72 5.1	73 5.0		
Cost of Sales/Payables	22 16.7	16 23.3	27 13.6	29 12.7	20 18.2	26 14.3	31 11.7	24 14.9		
	36 10.1	33 11.0	39 9.3	49 7.5	45 8.1	37 9.8	40 9.2	37 9.9		
	49 7.4	50 7.3	57 6.4	79 4.6	73 5.0	58 6.3	45 8.2	57 6.4		
Sales/Working Capital	7.1	6.5	5.8		4.7	5.6	5.4	7.7	6.3	
	12.4	11.0	11.2		8.6	12.2	8.5	11.5	14.4	
	25.7	26.1	22.7		-422.5	61.0	21.3	14.1	25.0	
EBIT/Interest	(133) 4.8	(131) 10.3	(134) 9.0	(17) 4.7	(22) 8.6	(25) 14.7	(34) 10.8	(30) 11.9		
	2.3	3.3	3.3	1.4	2.6	4.0	3.2	5.1		
	1.2	1.6	1.4	.7	.7	1.8	1.4	2.3		
Net Profit + Depr., Dep., Amort./Cur. Mat. L/T/D	(44) 9.6	(35) 9.1	(41) 7.6				(15) 6.8			
	2.4	3.6	2.7				2.8			
	.6	1.5	1.1				.9			
Fixed/Worth	.1	.1	.1		.1	.1	.1	.1	.1	
	.1	.1	.2		.2	.5	.1	.2	.1	
	.4	.4	.5		1.2	2.3	.4	.3	.2	
Debt/Worth	.9	.8	.8		1.0	.9	.7	.7	.8	
	1.9	1.8	1.9		2.6	4.0	1.3	1.5	2.4	
	3.7	3.7	3.8		4.0	16.0	3.3	2.8	4.5	
% Profit Before Taxes/Tangible Net Worth	(142) 28.4	(143) 24.6	(149) 27.1		16.4	(23) 50.8	22.7	33.8	33.7	
	11.1	10.3	14.9		6.4	11.1	11.6	18.3	16.9	
	2.1	4.0	3.1		.7	-.4	5.4	2.7	6.3	
% Profit Before Taxes/Total Assets	8.9	9.2	9.7		5.7	10.0	8.7	15.2	9.9	
	3.7	4.2	5.1		1.8	3.0	5.1	5.9	6.3	
	.5	.9	1.0		.2	-1.2	1.7	.9	2.2	
Sales/Net Fixed Assets	178.6	173.3	134.6		145.3	116.5	127.5	114.2	163.5	
	80.1	72.6	67.3		31.9	57.6	66.1	67.2	111.1	
	26.0	24.3	26.4		18.5	19.3	21.7	27.4	51.8	
Sales/Total Assets	4.4	4.1	3.9		3.9	3.3	3.5	3.7	4.3	
	3.3	3.3	3.1		2.6	2.9	3.0	3.2	3.0	
	2.5	2.4	2.4		2.2	2.5	2.1	2.4	2.4	
% Depr., Dep., Amort./Sales	(129) .2	(129) .2	(130) .3		(17) .4	(19) .3	(25) .3	.2	(30) .2	
	.4	.4	.4		1.1	.4	.4	.4	.3	
	.7	.9	.8		1.8	.9	.8	.8	.6	
% Officers', Directors', Owners' Comp/Sales	(65) 1.3	(71) 1.3	(70) 1.2		(13) 2.9	(10) 1.1	(17) 1.5	(20) .9		
	2.9	2.4	2.8		6.5	2.6	2.9	1.8		
	5.5	5.7	6.5		7.3	4.5	5.2	5.3		
Net Sales ($)	2782043M	2823729M	3164513M	4021M	38241M	94466M	210477M	541471M	2275837M	
Total Assets ($)	921188M	993571M	1036234M	993M	14789M	33209M	80289M	185598M	721356M	

M = $ thousand   MM = $ million
See Pages 1 through 15 for Explanation of Ratios and Data

WHOLESALERS—ELECTRONIC PARTS & EQUIPMENT. SIC# 5065

Current Data Sorted By Assets							Comparative Historical Data	
2	3	9	2	1	1	# Postretirement Benefits		
						Type of Statement		
4	5	33	23	6	1	Unqualified	66	72
	46	45	5	1		Reviewed	94	102
25	62	12	2			Compiled	84	82
3	5	1				Tax Returns	2	4
14	31	34	9	1	4	Other	73	76
	130 (4/1-9/30/94)		242 (10/1/94-3/31/95)				4/1/90-3/31/91	4/1/91-3/31/92
0-500M	500M-2MM	2-10MM	10-50MM	50-100MM	100-250MM		ALL	ALL
46	149	125	39	8	5	**NUMBER OF STATEMENTS**	319	336
%	%	%	%	%	%	**ASSETS**	%	%
12.3	7.5	6.9	9.5			Cash & Equivalents	6.9	7.5
38.6	39.6	40.5	36.7			Trade Receivables - (net)	34.8	34.4
25.7	34.8	34.2	34.4			Inventory	37.6	35.1
.9	1.5	1.5	1.3			All Other Current	1.6	1.6
77.4	83.4	83.1	82.0			Total Current	80.9	78.7
13.9	11.6	10.4	12.0			Fixed Assets (net)	11.6	12.5
1.5	1.5	1.6	1.7			Intangibles (net)	1.4	1.8
7.3	3.4	4.9	4.3			All Other Non-Current	6.1	7.0
100.0	100.0	100.0	100.0			Total	100.0	100.0
						LIABILITIES		
9.1	12.7	14.1	11.9			Notes Payable-Short Term	16.8	14.2
3.1	2.8	2.7	2.0			Cur. Mat. -L/T/D	3.4	3.1
27.6	24.7	25.9	26.0			Trade Payables	22.9	23.3
.5	.8	.4	.3			Income Taxes Payable	.8	.5
5.9	9.9	9.1	8.2			All Other Current	8.6	8.6
46.2	50.8	52.3	48.5			Total Current	52.5	49.7
11.8	8.6	6.1	6.0			Long Term Debt	8.5	11.0
.0	.2	.2	.4			Deferred Taxes	.4	.4
4.5	3.3	3.4	2.0			All Other-Non-Current	3.7	3.0
37.5	37.1	38.0	43.2			Net Worth	35.1	35.9
100.0	100.0	100.0	100.0			Total Liabilities & Net Worth	100.0	100.0
						INCOME DATA		
100.0	100.0	100.0	100.0			Net Sales	100.0	100.0
34.7	33.1	25.8	23.8			Gross Profit	31.8	30.8
34.5	30.2	22.3	19.6			Operating Expenses	28.1	28.0
.3	3.0	3.6	4.3			Operating Profit	3.7	2.9
.6	.4	.6	.5			All Other Expenses (net)	1.0	1.0
-.4	2.5	3.0	3.8			Profit Before Taxes	2.7	1.9
						RATIOS		
2.6	2.2	2.2	2.3			Current	2.2	2.3
1.9	1.7	1.6	1.7				1.6	1.6
1.1	1.2	1.2	1.2				1.2	1.2
1.8	1.3	1.3	1.3			Quick	1.2	1.2
1.1	.9	.9	1.0				.8	.8
.8	.7	.6	.6				.5	.6
24 15.2	31 11.7	38 9.7	42 8.6			Sales/Receivables	33 11.2	30 12.1
36 10.2	43 8.4	46 7.9	56 6.5				43 8.5	41 8.9
54 6.7	56 6.5	61 6.0	68 5.4				55 6.6	55 6.6
16 22.6	31 11.6	35 10.5	47 7.7			Cost of Sales/Inventory	41 9.0	33 11.0
42 8.7	58 6.3	50 7.3	69 5.3				66 5.5	61 6.0
72 5.1	89 4.1	79 4.6	107 3.4				101 3.6	99 3.7
23 16.1	24 15.0	26 13.8	27 13.7			Cost of Sales/Payables	22 16.3	21 17.4
36 10.1	40 9.2	37 9.9	38 9.5				38 9.5	35 10.4
65 5.6	59 6.2	53 6.9	62 5.9				56 6.5	53 6.9
5.2	6.0	6.7	4.3			Sales/Working Capital	6.1	6.1
14.2	9.9	11.2	8.1				10.5	10.8
36.3	19.0	23.1	18.2				23.7	26.0
4.5	11.6	11.5	49.5			EBIT/Interest	6.0	6.3
(38) 1.5	(136) 4.3	(110) 3.9	(32) 9.8				(279) 2.7	(296) 2.3
.0	1.9	1.9	3.1				1.3	1.2
1.8	6.6	6.5	32.9			Net Profit + Depr., Dep., Amort./Cur. Mat. L /T/D	4.4	5.7
(13) 1.1	(44) 2.6	(49) 2.1	(17) 9.8				(153) 2.1	(126) 2.1
.0	.7	.9	4.0				.9	.3
.1	.1	.1	.1			Fixed/Worth	.1	.1
.3	.2	.2	.2				.2	.3
.7	.7	.5	.4				.6	.7
.7	1.0	1.0	.8			Debt/Worth	1.0	1.0
1.7	1.7	1.7	1.5				2.0	1.9
4.9	3.8	3.8	3.4				4.7	5.0
30.0	51.7	40.6	40.5			% Profit Before Taxes/Tangible Net Worth	41.3	39.0
(41) 6.3	(142) 28.6	(121) 22.4	(38) 30.2				(298) 19.3	(309) 12.8
-3.7	5.6	9.6	11.5				7.4	2.8
9.8	16.0	13.7	15.6			% Profit Before Taxes/Total Assets	12.3	11.9
1.4	7.1	6.9	9.4				5.9	4.2
-1.8	2.0	2.1	4.2				1.5	.6
101.2	111.1	101.0	87.9			Sales/Net Fixed Assets	94.5	92.1
42.0	51.9	46.7	40.4				40.9	38.1
16.0	22.1	20.1	14.4				18.4	19.1
5.0	4.0	3.8	3.3			Sales/Total Assets	3.7	3.8
3.4	3.2	3.2	2.5				2.8	2.9
2.5	2.5	2.3	1.5				2.2	2.2
.4	.4	.3	.4			% Depr., Dep., Amort./Sales	.4	.4
(36) 1.0	(129) .7	(112) .6	(37) .6				(273) .9	(288) .7
1.8	1.2	1.1	1.2				1.8	1.4
4.6	3.1	1.4				% Officers', Directors', Owners' Comp/Sales	2.9	2.7
(26) 9.3	(73) 4.2	(53) 2.5					(126) 4.9	(147) 4.2
13.3	8.3	4.7					8.6	7.9
51174M	543867M	1764481M	2490191M	1371435M	1878870M	Net Sales ($)	4688476M	6094364M
13325M	164898M	556138M	992757M	584801M	912199M	Total Assets ($)	1892920M	2649972M

© Robert Morris Associates 1995

M = $ thousand   MM = $ million
See Pages 1 through 15 for Explanation of Ratios and Data

Comparative Historical Data / Current Data Sorted By Sales

9	8	18	# Postretirement Benefits / Type of Statement	3	1	4	5	5
73	78	72	Unqualified	3	1	3	10	23	32
120	116	97	Reviewed	2	16	12	41	21	5
89	77	101	Compiled	16	40	25	11	6	3
	13	9	Tax Returns	2	5	1		1	
77	75	93	Other	9	19	12	23	10	20
4/1/92-3/31/93	4/1/93-3/31/94	4/1/94-3/31/95		130 (4/1-9/30/94)			242 (10/1/94-3/31/95)		
ALL	ALL	ALL		0-1MM	1-3MM	3-5MM	5-10MM	10-25MM	25MM & OVER
359	359	372	**NUMBER OF STATEMENTS**	32	81	53	85	61	60

ASSETS
9	8	18		0-1MM	1-3MM	3-5MM	5-10MM	10-25MM	25MM & OVER
%	%	%		%	%	%	%	%	%
8.0	6.4	8.1	Cash & Equivalents	11.8	9.2	5.6	8.2	8.5	6.2
37.3	38.8	39.2	Trade Receivables - (net)	31.4	36.1	46.4	41.0	39.1	38.8
34.0	35.1	33.6	Inventory	26.6	34.1	34.1	34.1	30.7	38.6
1.6	1.5	1.4	All Other Current	.6	1.3	1.6	1.8	1.5	1.4
80.9	81.8	82.4	Total Current	70.4	80.8	87.8	85.1	79.8	85.1
11.8	11.6	11.5	Fixed Assets (net)	17.4	13.5	8.3	8.8	14.0	9.4
1.6	1.5	1.6	Intangibles (net)	1.2	2.3	1.3	1.7	1.4	1.1
5.7	5.1	4.6	All Other Non-Current	11.1	3.4	2.6	4.4	4.8	4.4
100.0	100.0	100.0	Total	100.0	100.0	100.0	100.0	100.0	100.0

LIABILITIES
9	8	18		0-1MM	1-3MM	3-5MM	5-10MM	10-25MM	25MM & OVER
14.3	14.4	12.3	Notes Payable-Short Term	8.9	9.9	15.5	12.5	15.1	11.4
2.7	2.6	2.7	Cur. Mat.-L/T/D	3.5	3.7	1.7	2.5	2.1	2.6
24.0	25.7	25.5	Trade Payables	25.2	23.3	26.2	26.6	25.5	26.2
.6	1.7	.6	Income Taxes Payable	.7	.5	.4	1.0	.3	.5
9.1	9.0	8.8	All Other Current	6.2	10.2	7.6	9.8	9.5	7.3
50.7	53.4	49.8	Total Current	44.4	47.5	51.4	52.3	52.5	48.0
9.4	8.0	8.2	Long Term Debt	15.5	10.6	6.5	5.3	6.6	8.2
.4	.2	.2	Deferred Taxes	.0	.3	.0	.2	.4	.2
2.3	3.1	3.3	All Other-Non-Current	6.1	3.1	3.3	4.4	2.4	1.7
37.2	35.3	38.5	Net Worth	33.9	38.4	38.7	37.8	38.1	42.0
100.0	100.0	100.0	Total Liabilities & Net Worth	100.0	100.0	100.0	100.0	100.0	100.0

INCOME DATA
9	8	18		0-1MM	1-3MM	3-5MM	5-10MM	10-25MM	25MM & OVER
100.0	100.0	100.0	Net Sales	100.0	100.0	100.0	100.0	100.0	100.0
30.6	28.1	29.7	Gross Profit	38.7	35.2	30.3	29.1	26.0	21.3
27.2	25.9	26.5	Operating Expenses	39.6	32.5	26.3	25.8	22.7	16.7
3.4	2.2	3.2	Operating Profit	-.8	2.7	4.0	3.3	3.3	4.7
.6	.7	.5	All Other Expenses (net)	1.9	.3	.1	.5	.5	.7
2.8	1.5	2.6	Profit Before Taxes	-2.7	2.4	4.0	2.8	2.8	4.0

RATIOS
9	8	18		0-1MM	1-3MM	3-5MM	5-10MM	10-25MM	25MM & OVER
2.4	2.1	2.3	Current	2.7	2.5	2.2	2.3	2.0	2.6
1.5	1.5	1.7		1.7	1.7	1.8	1.6	1.5	1.8
1.2	1.3	1.2		1.1	1.2	1.3	1.2	1.2	1.4
1.3	1.2	1.4	Quick	1.7	1.5	1.3	1.4	1.2	1.4
.8	.8	.9		.9	.9	1.0	.9	.9	1.0
.7	.6	.7		.7	.6	.8	.7	.6	.8
35 10.5	32 11.3	33 10.9	Sales/Receivables	23 15.7	28 13.1	40 9.1	38 9.7	36 10.2	41 9.0
46 8.0	46 8.0	46 8.0		42 8.7	47 9.1	47 7.8	43 8.4	49 7.5	50 7.3
58 6.3	58 6.3	60 6.1		65 5.6	59 6.2	60 6.1	59 6.2	61 6.0	61 6.0
36 10.2	34 10.8	34 10.6	Cost of Sales/Inventory	35 10.4	24 15.3	33 11.0	32 11.4	35 10.5	37 10.0
61 6.0	52 7.0	54 6.7		60 6.1	63 5.8	52 7.0	55 6.6	50 7.3	63 5.8
94 3.9	87 4.2	89 4.1		107 3.4	111 3.3	70 5.2	89 4.1	70 5.2	89 4.1
23 15.8	23 15.6	25 14.5	Cost of Sales/Payables	28 12.9	24 15.2	25 14.5	25 14.7	29 12.6	25 14.7
40 9.2	40 9.2	37 9.8		49 7.4	36 10.1	39 9.3	39 9.4	37 9.8	34 10.6
57 6.4	55 6.6	58 6.3		89 4.1	63 5.8	54 6.8	55 6.6	51 7.1	50 7.3
5.9	6.5	5.7	Sales/Working Capital	4.8	5.6	6.4	6.3	7.0	4.9
9.7	10.8	10.1		8.7	9.9	9.0	10.2	12.6	8.2
21.6	24.3	21.9		65.5	21.6	17.6	21.8	29.7	19.3
(321) 8.0	(331) 9.0	(329) 11.2	EBIT/Interest	(26) 2.8	(72) 9.3	(49) 15.3	(78) 14.0	(49) 10.8	(55) 37.6
3.0	3.9	4.3		1.1	3.4	6.1	3.8	3.6	9.4
1.5	1.5	1.8		-3.7	1.4	2.6	1.7	1.9	4.5
(142) 6.8	(124) 7.1	(134) 9.2	Net Profit + Depr., Dep., Amort./Cur. Mat. L/T/D		(30) 2.7	(17) 24.9	(27) 7.0	(23) 6.0	(31) 41.4
2.4	2.7	2.7			1.5	3.3	1.5	3.1	8.0
1.4	1.0	.9			.7	1.4	.6	1.5	3.5
.1	.1	.1	Fixed/Worth	.1	.1	.1	.1	.1	.1
.2	.3	.2		.5	.4	.2	.2	.2	.2
.6	.6	.6		1.5	.8	.4	.4	.8	.4
1.0	1.0	.9	Debt/Worth	.8	.9	.9	.9	1.0	.9
1.9	2.0	1.6		1.7	1.7	1.5	1.7	1.7	1.5
4.5	4.3	3.7		25.2	3.5	3.3	4.9	4.1	2.5
(346) 43.0	(338) 37.4	(355) 44.2	% Profit Before Taxes/Tangible Net Worth	(25) 28.0	(76) 49.4	54.5	(82) 41.4	(59) 35.4	43.9
17.4	18.8	24.9		5.2	21.8	38.5	22.8	17.7	30.8
5.4	5.4	6.3		-23.2	3.1	11.6	7.5	8.5	17.4
13.2	12.4	14.5	% Profit Before Taxes/Total Assets	8.6	14.3	17.9	13.5	14.4	16.5
5.0	6.1	7.1		1.1	7.6	9.9	6.2	4.3	12.0
1.6	1.3	1.7		-6.9	1.0	3.1	1.9	1.7	6.0
84.0	106.0	100.8	Sales/Net Fixed Assets	76.0	80.0	140.2	121.8	100.1	89.3
41.0	44.9	46.9		21.0	42.5	63.3	57.5	41.9	47.9
17.5	19.7	19.9		6.8	19.1	25.9	26.4	14.5	20.5
3.8	4.0	3.9	Sales/Total Assets	3.5	3.8	4.0	3.8	3.9	4.0
2.9	3.1	3.1		2.5	3.0	3.3	3.2	3.2	3.1
2.2	2.3	2.4		1.7	2.2	2.7	2.6	2.1	2.2
(314) .4	(308) .3	(327) .4	% Depr., Dep., Amort./Sales	(26) .5	(69) .5	(45) .3	(75) .2	(54) .4	(58) .3
.7	.6	.7		1.6	.8	.6	.5	.6	.6
1.5	1.3	1.2		3.7	1.6	1.1	1.1	1.3	.9
(168) 2.4	(170) 2.4	(161) 2.3	% Officers', Directors', Owners' Comp/Sales	(15) 4.7	(48) 3.3	(23) 3.8	(39) 2.0	(22) 1.3	(14) .9
5.0	4.5	4.0		11.2	5.1	4.2	3.2	2.6	1.2
8.0	7.3	8.4		15.4	9.7	8.1	5.9	3.9	2.0
6193827M	7265162M	8100018M	Net Sales ($)	20036M	166220M	203919M	615452M	943379M	6151012M
2827976M	2913875M	3224118M	Total Assets ($)	11620M	62428M	63678M	222073M	412091M	2452228M

M = $ thousand   MM = $ million
See Pages 1 through 15 for Explanation of Ratios and Data

Current Data Sorted By Assets   **Comparative Historical Data**

	2	13	10	9	3	2	# Postretirement Benefits / Type of Statement		
	1	16	44	29	5	5	Unqualified	85	92
	5	36	42	3			Reviewed	79	85
	16	58	14	2			Compiled	73	89
	4	4					Tax Returns	3	1
	14	34	24	10		1	Other	57	65

	0-500M	184 (4/1-9/30/94) 500M-2MM	2-10MM	183 (10/1/94-3/31/95) 10-50MM	50-100MM	100-250MM		4/1/90-3/31/91 ALL	4/1/91-3/31/92 ALL
NUMBER OF STATEMENTS	40	148	124	44	5	6		297	332
	%	%	%	%	%	%	**ASSETS**	%	%
	10.7	7.4	6.9	5.5			Cash & Equivalents	6.4	6.7
	29.7	28.6	27.7	31.9			Trade Receivables - (net)	29.3	28.9
	32.1	25.4	28.8	32.4			Inventory	30.2	29.5
	2.1	1.9	3.1	3.2			All Other Current	2.6	2.5
	74.6	63.3	66.4	73.0			Total Current	68.4	67.6
	18.2	28.0	24.3	18.2			Fixed Assets (net)	22.8	24.5
	1.7	1.0	.8	1.6			Intangibles (net)	1.1	1.2
	5.5	7.7	8.4	7.3			All Other Non-Current	7.7	6.7
	100.0	100.0	100.0	100.0			Total	100.0	100.0
							LIABILITIES		
	12.9	11.3	14.4	23.1			Notes Payable-Short Term	16.4	16.9
	2.4	3.6	2.0	1.8			Cur. Mat. -L/T/D	2.9	3.4
	21.4	17.4	19.3	22.2			Trade Payables	17.8	17.9
	.2	.4	.5	.3			Income Taxes Payable	.5	.4
	9.0	8.1	7.7	11.1			All Other Current	8.5	8.7
	45.9	40.8	43.8	58.5			Total Current	46.2	47.3
	15.1	11.3	10.3	8.0			Long Term Debt	12.7	12.4
	.0	.2	.4	.7			Deferred Taxes	.5	.5
	3.0	3.0	1.9	1.8			All Other-Non-Current	2.5	2.5
	36.0	44.6	43.6	31.0			Net Worth	38.2	37.3
	100.0	100.0	100.0	100.0			Total Liabilities & Net Worth	100.0	100.0
							INCOME DATA		
	100.0	100.0	100.0	100.0			Net Sales	100.0	100.0
	21.4	22.7	22.2	16.6			Gross Profit	21.6	21.6
	19.6	20.1	19.8	14.4			Operating Expenses	19.3	19.3
	1.9	2.6	2.4	2.2			Operating Profit	2.3	2.3
	.6	.0	−.2	.2			All Other Expenses (net)	.5	.8
	1.2	2.6	2.5	2.1			Profit Before Taxes	1.8	1.4
							RATIOS		
	2.7	2.3	2.2	1.4				2.1	2.1
	1.6	1.5	1.5	1.2			Current	1.5	1.4
	1.3	1.1	1.2	1.1				1.1	1.1
	1.5	1.5	1.1	.9				1.1	1.2
	.9	.9	.8	.6			Quick	.8	.7
	.6	.5	.5	.4				.5	.4
	8 45.3	20 18.6	21 17.4	21 17.6				20 18.2	19 19.3
	31 11.6	30 12.3	34 10.6	39 9.4			Sales/Receivables	32 11.5	30 12.0
	42 8.7	45 8.2	51 7.1	69 5.3				51 7.1	48 7.6
	12 29.7	16 23.5	26 13.8	31 11.8				23 15.9	22 16.4
	40 9.2	32 11.5	43 8.4	45 8.1			Cost of Sales/Inventory	44 8.3	42 8.7
	62 5.9	62 5.9	94 3.9	78 4.7				74 4.9	76 4.8
	9 39.6	8 44.7	12 31.1	17 21.7				11 32.8	11 33.9
	23 15.8	23 15.9	24 15.2	27 13.6			Cost of Sales/Payables	23 16.0	22 16.3
	39 9.4	41 9.0	46 7.9	51 7.1				39 9.4	38 9.5
	8.4	7.8	6.7	12.5				7.6	7.9
	12.8	16.8	14.1	24.6			Sales/Working Capital	15.2	15.6
	19.6	48.2	27.8	48.9				47.5	45.6
	4.2	(136) 7.9	(114) 5.8	(43) 4.7				(281) 4.0	(309) 3.5
	(37) 2.2	3.0	3.0	3.1			EBIT/Interest	2.0	1.9
	.3	1.8	1.5	1.8				1.3	1.1
		(58) 4.9	(58) 6.6	(24) 6.2			Net Profit + Depr., Dep., Amort./Cur. Mat. L./T/D	(141) 5.9	(148) 6.3
		2.2	3.4	3.4				2.2	2.3
		1.0	1.7	2.1				1.1	1.0
	.1	.3	.3	.4				.3	.3
	.5	.6	.5	.5			Fixed/Worth	.6	.6
	1.0	1.1	.9	1.0				1.2	1.3
	1.0	.6	.7	1.5				1.0	.9
	1.7	1.2	1.2	2.5			Debt/Worth	1.8	2.0
	4.3	3.5	2.9	4.9				3.3	4.1
	36.1	29.4	24.4	24.9				23.2	23.5
	(36) 9.4	(144) 14.7	(123) 12.7	(41) 17.5			% Profit Before Taxes/Tangible Net Worth	(283) 13.2	(317) 10.2
	−2.2	4.6	4.5	9.2				4.8	2.5
	11.9	10.5	8.9	7.6				8.4	7.5
	3.0	5.7	4.8	4.9			% Profit Before Taxes/Total Assets	4.3	3.2
	−.9	2.6	1.8	2.1				1.4	.6
	140.9	25.7	25.3	31.3				34.3	34.9
	29.1	11.8	11.6	14.7			Sales/Net Fixed Assets	16.3	14.3
	9.3	6.7	6.9	10.2				8.6	7.6
	5.2	3.9	3.7	3.4				3.9	3.9
	3.6	2.9	2.6	2.8			Sales/Total Assets	3.0	2.9
	2.5	2.2	1.8	2.0				2.1	2.2
	.5	1.0	.8	.6				.7	.7
	(31) 1.2	(136) 1.8	(118) 1.4	(39) 1.1			% Depr., Dep., Amort./Sales	(281) 1.3	(313) 1.4
	2.5	2.9	2.3	1.7				2.3	2.4
	2.4	1.4	1.0					1.3	1.4
	(15) 3.3	(67) 3.5	(52) 1.5				% Officers', Directors', Owners' Comp/Sales	(114) 2.4	(125) 2.7
	4.9	5.7	2.4					5.2	5.5
	50124M	538350M	1786338M	2429430M	1253151M	1784008M	Net Sales ($)	9017673M	10447813M
	11129M	170534M	593656M	905963M	354791M	822598M	Total Assets ($)	3007078M	3425196M

© Robert Morris Associates 1995

M = $ thousand   MM = $ million
See Pages 1 through 15 for Explanation of Ratios and Data

Comparative Historical Data | | | | Current Data Sorted By Sales

5	17	39	# Postretirement Benefits	1	5	5	6	9	13
			Type of Statement						
77	82	100	Unqualified	1	4	9	23	20	43
88	96	86	Reviewed	5	15	22	14	23	7
80	82	90	Compiled	6	42	17	18	6	1
5	12	8	Tax Returns	1	5	2			
48	76	83	Other	8	22	12	15	11	15
4/1/92-3/31/93 ALL	4/1/93-3/31/94 ALL	4/1/94-3/31/95 ALL		184 (4/1-9/30/94) 0-1MM	1-3MM	3-5MM	183 (10/1/94-3/31/95) 5-10MM	10-25MM	25MM & OVER
298	348	367	**NUMBER OF STATEMENTS**	21	88	62	70	60	66
%	%	%	**ASSETS**	%	%	%	%	%	%
6.4	7.1	7.3	Cash & Equivalents	8.2	9.0	6.7	5.2	8.4	6.4
29.0	28.7	28.7	Trade Receivables - (net)	23.6	26.8	28.6	28.9	31.7	30.2
30.0	30.2	28.3	Inventory	38.8	24.0	27.9	30.4	24.8	31.9
2.6	2.4	2.4	All Other Current	.9	2.2	1.9	1.4	4.6	2.9
68.0	68.4	66.7	Total Current	71.6	62.0	65.0	65.9	69.5	71.5
22.7	23.7	24.5	Fixed Assets (net)	23.7	28.1	25.2	26.4	22.2	19.2
1.2	1.1	1.1	Intangibles (net)	.7	1.7	.8	.5	.9	1.5
8.1	6.8	7.7	All Other Non-Current	4.1	8.1	9.0	7.1	7.5	7.8
100.0	100.0	100.0	Total	100.0	100.0	100.0	100.0	100.0	100.0
			LIABILITIES						
16.7	16.8	14.0	Notes Payable-Short Term	16.3	10.3	14.2	12.9	13.5	19.9
2.6	2.4	2.7	Cur. Mat.-L/T/D	3.8	3.2	4.0	2.1	1.9	1.7
18.5	18.8	19.1	Trade Payables	19.7	15.6	17.6	18.7	23.7	20.9
.3	1.4	.4	Income Taxes Payable	.1	.2	.6	.4	.5	.4
9.0	10.0	8.4	All Other Current	3.7	7.3	9.7	7.2	7.9	11.9
47.2	49.5	44.6	Total Current	43.7	36.6	46.1	41.2	47.5	54.8
10.2	11.0	11.2	Long Term Debt	20.0	11.6	12.0	11.6	8.1	9.6
.4	.5	.4	Deferred Taxes	.0	.2	.4	.3	.4	.8
3.1	2.1	2.5	All Other-Non-Current	4.5	3.9	1.7	1.9	1.5	2.1
39.1	37.0	41.4	Net Worth	31.9	47.7	39.8	44.9	42.5	32.8
100.0	100.0	100.0	Total Liabilities & Net Worth	100.0	100.0	100.0	100.0	100.0	100.0
			INCOME DATA						
100.0	100.0	100.0	Net Sales	100.0	100.0	100.0	100.0	100.0	100.0
21.8	21.2	21.5	Gross Profit	26.9	24.7	21.8	22.9	19.9	15.1
19.3	19.4	19.1	Operating Expenses	27.3	21.7	19.4	20.2	17.6	12.9
2.5	1.8	2.4	Operating Profit	-.4	3.0	2.4	2.7	2.3	2.2
.3	.0	.0	All Other Expenses (net)	.4	-.1	.2	.1	-.4	.3
2.2	1.8	2.4	Profit Before Taxes	-.8	3.2	2.2	2.6	2.7	1.9
			RATIOS						
1.9	1.8	2.1		2.2	2.8	1.9	2.2	2.1	1.6
1.4	1.4	1.4	Current	1.5	1.7	1.4	1.6	1.4	1.3
1.2	1.1	1.2		1.3	1.2	1.1	1.3	1.2	1.1
1.1	1.1	1.2		1.2	2.1	1.3	1.1	1.2	1.0
.7	.7	.8	Quick	.6	1.0	.8	.8	.8	.6
.5	.5	.5		.3	.3	.6	.6	.5	.4
19 19.6 / 31 11.6 / 49 7.4	20 17.9 / 31 11.6 / 50 7.3	20 18.3 / 33 11.2 / 50 7.3	Sales/Receivables	5 75.7 / 33 11.2 / 44 8.3	18 20.1 / 32 11.4 / 51 7.1	21 17.1 / 31 11.7 / 41 8.9	22 16.8 / 34 10.8 / 51 7.1	21 17.0 / 34 10.6 / 45 8.2	18 20.2 / 29 12.8 / 57 6.4
22 16.3 / 42 8.7 / 78 4.7	23 16.1 / 42 8.7 / 73 5.0	20 18.4 / 39 9.3 / 72 5.1	Cost of Sales/Inventory	27 13.5 / 63 5.8 / 140 2.6	13 27.1 / 33 10.9 / 70 5.2	21 17.3 / 36 10.1 / 64 5.7	18 19.9 / 46 7.9 / 111 3.3	17 21.2 / 35 10.5 / 60 6.1	24 15.2 / 43 8.5 / 64 5.7
10 37.1 / 23 15.6 / 40 9.2	11 32.6 / 22 16.9 / 42 8.7	11 32.6 / 24 15.2 / 43 8.5	Cost of Sales/Payables	10 37.8 / 35 10.4 / 66 5.5	9 40.1 / 21 17.2 / 43 8.5	9 42.2 / 25 14.7 / 38 9.5	8 47.1 / 24 14.9 / 42 7.5	15 23.9 / 26 14.1 / 49 7.5	15 24.7 / 23 15.9 / 44 8.3
9.1 / 16.4 / 38.5	8.9 / 18.6 / 48.7	7.8 / 15.2 / 38.4	Sales/Working Capital	7.1 / 10.7 / 17.5	6.3 / 11.8 / 46.2	10.1 / 21.2 / 68.5	6.7 / 14.8 / 23.6	9.0 / 14.2 / 29.7	12.1 / 25.5 / 49.3
(283) 4.5 / 2.3 / 1.5	(333) 5.0 / 2.5 / 1.5	(341) 5.8 / 3.0 / 1.6	EBIT/Interest	(19) 3.0 / 1.5 / -.4	(80) 8.5 / 2.9 / 1.7	(58) 5.3 / 2.7 / 1.7	(66) 6.5 / 3.3 / 1.6	(54) 6.9 / 3.1 / 1.7	(64) 5.2 / 3.1 / 1.7
(123) 5.3 / 2.5 / 1.2	(130) 5.2 / 2.4 / 1.4	(157) 5.6 / 2.8 / 1.5	Net Profit + Depr., Dep., Amort./Cur. Mat. L/T/D		(26) 4.9 / 2.5 / 1.2	(28) 4.5 / 1.8 / .8	(31) 4.7 / 3.0 / 1.9	(30) 8.5 / 3.5 / 1.4	(38) 6.7 / 3.5 / 2.0
.2 / .6 / 1.0	.3 / .6 / 1.1	.3 / .5 / 1.0	Fixed/Worth	.1 / .6 / 2.4	.3 / .5 / 1.0	.3 / .7 / 1.1	.4 / .6 / .9	.3 / .5 / .9	.4 / .5 / 1.1
.9 / 1.7 / 3.4	1.0 / 1.9 / 4.0	.8 / 1.4 / 3.6	Debt/Worth	1.1 / 2.2 / 6.7	.5 / 1.1 / 2.4	.7 / 1.4 / 4.4	.8 / 1.2 / 2.6	.7 / 1.5 / 3.4	1.2 / 2.4 / 4.8
(292) 29.2 / 13.4 / 4.5	(334) 26.2 / 12.8 / 4.8	(355) 25.3 / 14.1 / 5.1	% Profit Before Taxes/Tangible Net Worth	(19) 20.0 / 1.9 / -25.7	(86) 25.5 / 13.0 / 4.0	(58) 32.2 / 12.7 / 3.0	28.0 / 13.0 / 6.1	(59) 25.2 / 15.4 / 7.7	(63) 24.2 / 16.7 / 9.7
8.9 / 4.0 / 1.6	8.5 / 4.1 / 1.6	9.1 / 5.1 / 1.9	% Profit Before Taxes/Total Assets	6.5 / .7 / -6.6	9.8 / 5.0 / 2.0	10.1 / 5.2 / 1.8	9.8 / 5.7 / 2.2	10.1 / 4.9 / 1.8	7.9 / 5.6 / 2.1
35.6 / 15.0 / 7.9	32.2 / 14.0 / 7.6	29.1 / 13.4 / 7.6	Sales/Net Fixed Assets	61.0 / 14.3 / 6.5	28.2 / 10.0 / 5.6	26.2 / 13.7 / 7.3	18.9 / 9.9 / 6.8	33.2 / 15.4 / 8.5	32.3 / 18.8 / 10.3
4.0 / 3.0 / 2.2	3.9 / 2.9 / 2.1	3.8 / 2.8 / 2.0	Sales/Total Assets	3.6 / 2.5 / 1.8	3.5 / 2.5 / 1.7	4.9 / 3.1 / 2.3	3.7 / 2.7 / 1.8	4.4 / 2.8 / 2.3	4.2 / 3.0 / 2.3
(282) .7 / 1.4 / 2.2	(329) .7 / 1.4 / 2.4	(334) .7 / 1.5 / 2.4	% Depr., Dep., Amort./Sales	(16) 1.0 / 1.6 / 4.9	(78) .8 / 2.3 / 3.5	(57) 1.0 / 1.6 / 2.4	(66) 1.0 / 1.6 / 2.2	(56) .7 / 1.3 / 1.9	(61) .5 / .9 / 1.5
(125) 1.3 / 2.3 / 3.8	(134) 1.5 / 2.4 / 4.7	(140) 1.2 / 2.4 / 4.8	% Officers', Directors', Owners' Comp/Sales		(36) 1.5 / 3.7 / 5.7	(29) 1.3 / 3.3 / 6.6	(31) 1.1 / 2.0 / 4.5	(28) 1.1 / 1.6 / 2.4	(10) .6 / .9 / 1.3
6757888M	7406658M	7841401M	Net Sales ($)	11849M	178326M	238169M	501587M	936754M	5974716M
2554536M	2854730M	2858671M	Total Assets ($)	6389M	78677M	82202M	221097M	331894M	2138412M

M = $ thousand   MM = $ million
See Pages 1 through 15 for Explanation of Ratios and Data

Current Data Sorted By Assets   **Comparative Historical Data**

Type of Statement (# Postretirement Benefits)

0-500M	500M-2MM	2-10MM	10-50MM	50-100MM	100-250MM	Type of Statement	4/1/90-3/31/91 ALL	4/1/91-3/31/92 ALL
2	1	3			1			
	3	14	4		1	Unqualified	14	16
1	18	17	5			Reviewed	51	41
17	21	10				Compiled	44	49
7	3	1				Tax Returns	3	
4	10	20	5			Other	17	24

0-500M	500M-2MM	2-10MM	10-50MM	50-100MM	100-250MM		4/1/90-3/31/91	4/1/91-3/31/92
70 (4/1-9/30/94)		91 (10/1/94-3/31/95)					ALL	ALL
29	55	62	14		1	**NUMBER OF STATEMENTS**	129	130

0-500M	500M-2MM	2-10MM	10-50MM	50-100MM	100-250MM		4/1/90-3/31/91 ALL	4/1/91-3/31/92 ALL
%	%	%	%	%	%	**ASSETS**	%	%
6.6	8.2	5.2	7.0			Cash & Equivalents	5.3	5.5
25.3	25.1	25.6	21.2			Trade Receivables - (net)	26.5	26.2
23.0	29.2	29.0	38.7			Inventory	31.5	29.9
.4	2.5	.8	.5			All Other Current	1.5	1.9
55.3	65.0	60.7	67.4			Total Current	64.8	63.5
34.6	27.7	27.5	26.5			Fixed Assets (net)	27.1	27.3
.5	.6	3.2	1.4			Intangibles (net)	1.3	1.1
9.6	6.7	8.5	4.7			All Other Non-Current	6.7	8.1
100.0	100.0	100.0	100.0			Total	100.0	100.0
						LIABILITIES		
14.9	11.7	17.6	7.4			Notes Payable-Short Term	14.5	14.3
3.2	4.1	2.3	4.7			Cur. Mat. -L/T/D	3.0	4.1
15.5	16.1	16.4	12.4			Trade Payables	17.7	18.5
.3	.3	1.2	.5			Income Taxes Payable	.5	.7
6.3	7.1	5.0	3.8			All Other Current	6.6	6.9
40.0	39.3	42.5	28.8			Total Current	42.3	44.5
17.7	17.7	15.3	13.0			Long Term Debt	17.2	16.4
.1	.2	.8	2.1			Deferred Taxes	1.0	1.1
2.2	2.6	4.1	6.8			All Other-Non-Current	2.6	3.1
40.0	40.2	37.2	49.4			Net Worth	36.9	34.9
100.0	100.0	100.0	100.0			Total Liabilities & Net Worth	100.0	100.0
						INCOME DATA		
100.0	100.0	100.0	100.0			Net Sales	100.0	100.0
40.9	36.3	28.1	34.1			Gross Profit	33.9	35.2
36.6	34.1	25.9	23.4			Operating Expenses	30.5	32.5
4.3	2.3	2.2	10.7			Operating Profit	3.4	2.7
.7	.2	1.2	2.9			All Other Expenses (net)	1.7	1.0
3.6	2.1	1.0	7.8			Profit Before Taxes	1.7	1.7
						RATIOS		
3.1	2.6	1.7	4.0			Current	2.4	2.2
1.7	1.9	1.4	2.6				1.5	1.4
.9	1.2	1.2	1.3				1.1	1.1
1.7	1.7	1.2	1.8			Quick	1.3	1.1
.9	1.0	.7	.8				.7	.7
.3		.4	.5				.4	.5
6 64.6	17 21.4	25 14.7	23 16.0			Sales/Receivables	22 16.9	22 16.3
22 16.8	32 11.4	35 10.4	43 8.4				33 11.1	32 11.3
40 9.2	50 7.3	52 7.0	76 4.8				46 8.0	46 7.9
5 68.6	21 17.6	24 15.4	46 8.0			Cost of Sales/Inventory	27 13.5	25 14.6
20 18.4	36 10.1	49 7.4	140 2.6				59 6.2	63 5.8
78 4.7	107 3.4	130 2.8	332 1.1				118 3.1	111 3.3
0 UND	13 28.2	17 21.7	20 18.4			Cost of Sales/Payables	16 23.0	18 20.3
19 19.2	27 13.7	26 13.8	26 14.0				28 12.9	31 11.7
49 7.4	51 7.2	45 8.2	85 4.3				51 7.2	52 7.0
8.1	4.5	6.8	1.8			Sales/Working Capital	6.1	7.5
16.0	9.4	14.8	3.2				15.4	17.3
-57.1	40.4	38.9	11.3				57.7	62.4
(24) 12.4	(52) 5.7	(57) 4.6	9.5			EBIT/Interest	(123) 3.8	(122) 3.2
5.1	2.3	2.7	4.4				1.9	1.8
1.9	.2	1.4	3.0				1.1	1.1
	(18) 9.6	(28) 5.3				Net Profit + Depr., Dep., Amort./Cur. Mat. L./T/D	(67) 5.7	(66) 3.1
	1.0	3.6					2.0	1.7
	.3	2.0					1.0	.5
.3	.2	.3	.2			Fixed/Worth	.3	.3
1.1	.5	.7	.4				.6	.8
1.6	1.4	1.4	1.2				1.8	1.6
.6	.5	1.1	.5			Debt/Worth	.9	1.0
1.6	1.3	2.1	.8				1.9	2.0
4.9	3.8	3.7	3.3				4.1	4.6
(27) 61.2	(50) 21.3	(58) 24.8	33.1			% Profit Before Taxes/Tangible Net Worth	(118) 22.9	(121) 22.9
36.9	10.0	15.3	17.6				12.5	13.3
14.9	-1.9	4.6	5.8				1.7	2.4
22.4	8.3	8.4	13.5			% Profit Before Taxes/Total Assets	7.8	7.2
13.6	3.7	4.1	11.4				4.1	3.5
4.9	-3.5	1.3	3.2				.3	.3
26.7	38.0	28.5	11.8			Sales/Net Fixed Assets	32.5	29.0
11.9	15.6	13.3	5.5				13.2	14.2
6.4	4.7	3.9	3.0				5.8	5.5
5.0	3.4	3.2	2.3			Sales/Total Assets	3.5	3.7
3.4	2.5	2.3	1.2				2.6	2.5
2.4	1.6	1.7	.8				1.8	1.8
(26) 1.1	(53) .9	(58) .7	1.1			% Depr., Dep., Amort./Sales	(120) .6	(120) .8
2.1	1.8	1.3	2.2				1.6	1.4
3.1	3.8	3.2	4.7				2.7	2.7
(17) 2.8	(34) 3.1	(26) 2.2				% Officers', Directors', Owners' Comp/Sales	(61) 2.5	(63) 2.2
4.6	4.1	4.0					3.5	3.9
9.4	5.9	5.6					6.7	6.4
29734M	154342M	767599M	444960M		167329M	Net Sales ($)	1121549M	1016880M
8054M	62125M	289835M	271969M		135505M	Total Assets ($)	432495M	376871M

M = $ thousand   MM = $ million
See Pages 1 through 15 for Explanation of Ratios and Data

Comparative Historical Data / Current Data Sorted By Sales

6	4	6	# Postretirement Benefits	2		3		1	
			Type of Statement						
17	27	22	Unqualified	1	1	3	2	8	7
40	55	41	Reviewed	3	6	6	14	8	4
65	56	48	Compiled	9	25	6	6	2	
4	9	11	Tax Returns	6	3	1	1		
34	41	39	Other	4	9	5	9	9	3
4/1/92-3/31/93 ALL	4/1/93-3/31/94 ALL	4/1/94-3/31/95 ALL		70 (4/1-9/30/94)			91 (10/1/94-3/31/95)		
				0-1MM	1-3MM	3-5MM	5-10MM	10-25MM	25MM & OVER
160	188	161	NUMBER OF STATEMENTS	23	44	21	31	28	14
%	%	%	ASSETS	%	%	%	%	%	%
7.3	7.5	6.8	Cash & Equivalents	5.0	7.9	9.4	5.3	5.5	8.9
24.6	22.6	24.9	Trade Receivables - (net)	13.1	26.8	19.4	29.2	30.1	27.2
29.3	28.6	28.7	Inventory	28.2	23.2	32.8	34.4	27.8	29.9
1.0	2.2	1.3	All Other Current	.1	2.9	.4	1.4	.3	1.5
62.2	60.9	61.8	Total Current	46.4	60.7	62.0	70.3	63.6	67.6
29.4	29.5	28.8	Fixed Assets (net)	39.5	30.9	31.3	24.1	22.7	23.7
.8	1.4	1.7	Intangibles (net)	.3	.6	2.0	.7	5.2	1.5
7.7	8.3	7.7	All Other Non-Current	13.7	7.8	4.7	4.9	8.4	7.2
100.0	100.0	100.0	Total	100.0	100.0	100.0	100.0	100.0	100.0
			LIABILITIES						
12.6	11.6	14.1	Notes Payable-Short Term	13.6	13.4	11.6	18.4	15.6	7.9
3.9	3.3	3.3	Cur. Mat.-L /T/D	3.7	4.1	2.1	3.5	2.5	3.0
16.9	15.8	15.8	Trade Payables	8.0	15.2	19.2	16.6	17.0	21.7
.8	.5	.7	Income Taxes Payable	.3	.3	.2	1.1	1.6	.2
7.1	6.6	5.9	All Other Current	4.5	6.5	3.9	7.3	4.9	8.5
41.3	37.8	39.8	Total Current	30.2	39.4	37.1	46.9	41.7	41.3
13.8	13.3	16.4	Long Term Debt	18.9	20.8	20.1	11.6	13.3	10.0
.9	1.3	.6	Deferred Taxes	.1	.2	.2	1.6	.8	.4
3.6	3.6	3.5	All Other-Non-Current	1.2	2.1	7.9	2.9	4.7	3.4
40.4	44.0	39.7	Net Worth	49.7	37.4	34.7	37.0	39.5	44.9
100.0	100.0	100.0	Total Liabilities & Net Worth	100.0	100.0	100.0	100.0	100.0	100.0
			INCOME DATA						
100.0	100.0	100.0	Net Sales	100.0	100.0	100.0	100.0	100.0	100.0
36.2	37.3	33.7	Gross Profit	47.2	34.4	29.6	32.4	29.2	27.2
32.8	33.9	30.3	Operating Expenses	39.4	35.1	25.5	29.8	24.6	20.6
3.4	3.4	3.4	Operating Profit	7.8	-.7	4.1	2.7	4.6	6.6
.5	.6	.9	All Other Expenses (net)	1.5	.0	1.7	.6	.8	2.6
2.8	2.8	2.4	Profit Before Taxes	6.4	-.7	2.4	2.1	3.7	4.1
			RATIOS						
2.4	2.6	2.6	Current	3.5	2.6	3.0	2.2	1.9	2.5
1.5	1.5	1.6		1.9	1.7	1.7	1.4	1.4	1.5
1.1	1.2	1.2		.8	1.0	1.2	1.2	1.2	1.3
1.2	1.4	1.5	Quick	1.8	1.7	1.3	1.2	1.4	1.2
.8	.8	.8		.6	1.0	.8	.7	.8	.9
.5	.4	.4		.2	.5	.5	.4	.4	.5
24 15.4 / 19 19.2 / 19 19.6			Sales/Receivables	6 66.2 / 15 24.8 / 15 24.2			29 12.7 / 26 14.2 / 23 16.0		
33 11.2 / 31 11.6 / 33 11.0				14 25.3 / 31 11.8 / 32 11.4			39 9.4 / 35 10.4 / 29 12.5		
46 8.0 / 42 8.6 / 50 7.3				43 8.5 / 47 7.8 / 57 6.4			56 6.5 / 52 7.0 / 41 9.0		
21 17.1 / 22 16.8 / 19 19.7			Cost of Sales/Inventory	0 UND / 8 45.9 / 21 17.0			34 10.6 / 15 23.6 / 21 17.3		
58 6.3 / 54 6.7 / 47 7.8				63 5.8 / 26 13.8 / 61 6.0			76 4.8 / 49 7.4 / 31 11.6		
130 2.8 / 126 2.9 / 118 3.1				111 3.3 / 83 4.4 / 146 2.5			146 2.5 / 114 3.2 / 94 3.9		
15 24.5 / 14 25.6 / 14 25.9			Cost of Sales/Payables	0 UND / 11 32.8 / 7 51.5			18 20.4 / 21 17.3 / 18 19.8		
29 12.7 / 28 13.1 / 26 13.8				18 20.5 / 26 13.8 / 35 10.4			35 10.5 / 27 13.5 / 23 15.7		
51 7.1 / 54 6.8 / 49 7.5				49 7.4 / 54 6.8 / 46 7.9			63 5.8 / 38 9.6 / 46 7.9		
5.3	5.8	6.1	Sales/Working Capital	4.2	5.8	4.6	5.7	7.5	7.2
12.9	11.2	11.7		10.4	11.6	9.2	11.2	14.8	13.2
113.7	34.3	42.8		-20.0	NM	39.0	21.6	36.3	31.2
(148) 4.9	(173) 6.9	(148) 6.5	EBIT/Interest	(19) 13.0	(42) 7.6	(20) 5.5	(30) 3.6	(25) 7.9	(12) 8.3
2.6	2.6	3.0		4.0	2.3	2.3	2.3	3.9	4.6
1.3	1.2	1.2		1.8	.2	.9	1.1	2.6	2.7
(72) 4.9	(85) 5.0	(57) 4.8	Net Profit + Depr., Dep., Amort./Cur. Mat. L/T/D		(11) 2.7		(15) 6.6	(14) 5.0	
2.0	2.2	2.5			1.0		3.1	3.6	
1.1	1.0	1.3			-1.1		1.7	2.0	
.3	.2	.3	Fixed/Worth	.3	.2	.3	.2	.3	.2
.6	.6	.6		1.1	.6	.8	.5	.6	.5
1.5	1.3	1.4		1.5	1.6	2.5	1.6	1.1	1.0
.7	.5	.6	Debt/Worth	.3	.7	.6	.7	1.0	.5
1.7	1.3	1.7		1.0	1.4	3.0	1.9	1.9	1.4
3.1	2.9	3.6		2.7	3.6	5.0	3.6	4.4	3.1
(151) 26.9	(178) 25.5	(150) 29.5	% Profit Before Taxes/Tangible Net Worth	(22) 40.2	(39) 36.9	(19) 26.7	(30) 21.8	(26) 33.0	29.9
13.5	12.4	15.5		23.3	10.7	16.2	12.5	19.6	15.4
3.5	1.7	3.1		6.7	-1.8	2.1	1.1	7.0	5.8
9.3	11.3	11.7	% Profit Before Taxes/Total Assets	16.7	13.3	8.5	6.7	12.5	12.3
4.6	4.5	5.0		6.5	4.6	3.5	3.9	6.4	8.8
1.1	.6	.9		2.8	-4.8	-.7	.5	2.5	3.2
27.0	27.3	28.5	Sales/Net Fixed Assets	12.2	29.7	23.0	40.4	22.2	41.4
11.5	11.7	13.0		6.8	12.9	13.0	14.2	14.3	19.6
4.2	4.1	4.1		2.5	4.9	3.1	4.4	5.0	9.2
3.7	3.5	3.5	Sales/Total Assets	3.0	4.3	3.1	3.1	3.5	5.0
2.4	2.3	2.5		2.4	2.7	2.1	2.4	2.5	3.2
1.7	1.5	1.7		.8	1.7	1.4	1.8	1.7	1.9
(150) .9	(178) .8	(151) .8	% Depr., Dep., Amort./Sales	(20) 1.8	(43) 1.0	(30) 1.6	(25) .7	(12) .7	.6
1.9	1.7	1.7		3.3	2.0	1.9	1.4	1.3	.9
3.2	3.7	3.6		5.4	3.4	4.7	3.2	2.1	1.3
(82) 2.5	(98) 2.6	(83) 2.6	% Officers', Directors', Owners' Comp/Sales	(12) 4.2	(27) 3.0	(14) 3.2	(13) 2.1	(11) 2.1	
4.4	4.3	4.1		5.6	4.7	4.0	3.5	2.8	
8.6	8.0	5.8		9.6	6.9	5.5	5.4	3.8	
1235812M	1630165M	1563964M	Net Sales ($)	15032M	82764M	85003M	215921M	424548M	740696M
537002M	804648M	767488M	Total Assets ($)	12451M	37432M	48078M	120207M	195927M	353393M

© Robert Morris Associates 1995

M = $ thousand   MM = $ million
See Pages 1 through 15 for Explanation of Ratios and Data

WHOLESALERS—COFFEE, TEA & SPICES. SIC# 5149

| Current Data Sorted By Assets | | | | | | | Comparative Historical Data | |

	0-500M	500M-2MM	2-10MM	10-50MM	50-100MM	100-250MM		4/1/90-3/31/91 ALL	4/1/91-3/31/92 ALL
	1	2	6			1	# Postretirement Benefits		
							Type of Statement		
		2	19	14	2	3	Unqualified	37	36
	2	12	19	2			Reviewed	40	34
	17	22	10	1			Compiled	29	38
	5						Tax Returns		1
	5	6	13	5	1		Other	20	30
		52 (4/1-9/30/94)		108 (10/1/94-3/31/95)					
	29	42	61	22	3	3	**NUMBER OF STATEMENTS**	126	139
	%	%	%	%	%	%	**ASSETS**	%	%
	11.1	6.2	6.2	3.1			Cash & Equivalents	5.6	6.5
	29.6	30.2	29.9	26.5			Trade Receivables - (net)	30.4	28.4
	24.0	28.0	30.2	36.1			Inventory	30.2	28.1
	2.5	2.7	1.5	3.2			All Other Current	1.1	2.0
	67.3	67.2	67.8	68.9			Total Current	67.2	64.9
	26.0	25.1	23.9	24.1			Fixed Assets (net)	24.0	26.3
	2.4	1.8	2.3	1.6			Intangibles (net)	2.4	2.3
	4.3	5.8	5.9	5.4			All Other Non-Current	6.4	6.5
	100.0	100.0	100.0	100.0			Total	100.0	100.0
							LIABILITIES		
	11.6	10.3	14.4	27.9			Notes Payable-Short Term	15.4	15.7
	6.3	6.1	2.9	2.0			Cur. Mat.-L/T/D	4.9	3.4
	19.2	19.9	21.0	16.1			Trade Payables	19.4	19.3
	.2	.2	.7	.3			Income Taxes Payable	.4	.4
	14.8	7.0	7.2	7.3			All Other Current	6.0	6.7
	52.2	43.5	46.3	53.6			Total Current	46.1	45.4
	15.0	14.9	10.3	15.4			Long Term Debt	13.1	13.4
	.3	.1	.6	.4			Deferred Taxes	.3	.4
	3.0	3.5	6.0	2.0			All Other-Non-Current	2.0	2.6
	29.4	38.0	36.8	28.5			Net Worth	38.5	38.2
	100.0	100.0	100.0	100.0			Total Liabilities & Net Worth	100.0	100.0
							INCOME DATA		
	100.0	100.0	100.0	100.0			Net Sales	100.0	100.0
	32.6	30.8	27.6	23.0			Gross Profit	26.9	28.4
	29.0	26.5	24.1	21.2			Operating Expenses	23.8	24.8
	3.6	4.3	3.5	1.8			Operating Profit	3.2	3.7
	1.2	1.5	.8	.7			All Other Expenses (net)	.8	.9
	2.4	2.9	2.6	1.0			Profit Before Taxes	2.4	2.8
							RATIOS		
	2.3	2.2	2.2	1.8				1.9	2.2
	1.5	1.4	1.6	1.2			Current	1.5	1.4
	.8	1.1	1.1	1.0				1.1	1.1
	1.3	1.2	1.2	1.1				1.1	1.2
	.8	.8	.8	.5			Quick	.7 (138)	.7
	.5	.6	.6	.4				.5	.5
18	20.6	24 15.1	25 14.4	28 12.9				22 16.9	22 16.9
29	12.5	35 10.5	35 10.5	34 10.7			Sales/Receivables	29 12.7	29 12.8
41	8.9	40 9.1	43 8.5	41 9.0				38 9.5	38 9.7
18	19.9	30 12.2	24 15.5	34 10.8				24 15.3	23 15.8
34	10.8	44 8.3	45 8.2	64 5.7			Cost of Sales/Inventory	38 9.5	38 9.5
81	4.5	65 5.6	78 4.7	111 3.3				63 5.8	74 4.9
11	34.3	12 30.9	14 26.0	10 35.9				12 31.6	14 26.4
21	17.6	25 14.4	28 13.1	23 16.0			Cost of Sales/Payables	24 15.5	23 16.2
36	10.1	50 7.3	57 6.4	39 9.4				40 9.1	40 9.1
	7.3	7.9	7.6	10.5				11.3	8.6
	25.7	20.0	13.5	22.3			Sales/Working Capital	19.9	23.5
	-24.7	89.4	55.3	NM				44.7	83.3
	7.9	6.0	10.2	4.6				5.6	6.1
(25)	3.3	(37) 3.3	(53) 3.3	(19) 1.8			EBIT/Interest	(115) 2.6	(120) 2.7
	1.1	2.1	1.4	1.4				1.5	1.4
		(16) 5.6	(18) 7.5	(10) 8.9			Net Profit + Depr., Dep.,	(61) 6.3	(53) 5.2
		2.0	3.8	3.6			Amort./Cur. Mat. L./T/D	2.1	2.4
		.7	.4	3.0				.9	1.3
	.2	.2	.3	.3				.2	.3
	1.1	.5	.6	.8			Fixed/Worth	.6	.5
	5.2	1.6	1.2	1.8				1.3	1.3
	.7	1.0	.9	1.7				1.0	.9
	2.4	2.0	1.6	3.2			Debt/Worth	1.7	1.9
	19.7	4.6	4.3	8.7				3.9	4.3
	49.6	35.7	38.0	42.4			% Profit Before Taxes/Tangible	33.2	39.6
(23)	25.0	(41) 21.1	(55) 21.1	(21) 21.2			Net Worth	(118) 18.3	(131) 16.0
	4.1	9.7	7.0	11.0				7.4	5.5
	16.5	11.5	16.8	11.3			% Profit Before Taxes/Total	12.6	10.3
	4.8	6.7	5.7	3.7			Assets	6.7	4.9
	-.9	4.6	1.0	1.3				2.0	1.5
	61.6	65.7	43.9	51.2				56.0	55.4
	14.9	14.4	17.9	12.1			Sales/Net Fixed Assets	17.8	18.6
	9.3	6.4	6.3	5.3				7.9	5.7
	4.9	4.2	4.6	3.8				5.1	5.3
	3.3	3.2	2.8	2.4			Sales/Total Assets	3.4	3.0
	2.2	2.3	2.2	1.8				2.4	2.1
	.6	.6	.6	.5				.5	.4
(23)	1.7	(37) 1.8	(56) 1.1	(19) 1.4			% Depr., Dep., Amort./Sales	(106) 1.3	(121) 1.1
	4.0	4.3	3.5	5.1				2.6	3.1
	1.5	2.1	1.0					1.3	1.5
(15)	3.7	(20) 4.0	(25) 2.1				% Officers', Directors',	(44) 2.2	(62) 3.2
	7.7	7.5	4.9				Owners' Comp/Sales	4.7	6.3
	42102M	160788M	980288M	1207509M	537685M	2116265M	Net Sales ($)	3322217M	4587719M
	8759M	48694M	293577M	426932M	189150M	545452M	Total Assets ($)	889315M	1632749M

© Robert Morris Associates 1995

M = $ thousand   MM = $ million

See Pages 1 through 15 for Explanation of Ratios and Data

Comparative Historical Data				Current Data Sorted By Sales					
1	5	10	# Postretirement Benefits	1	1	3	3	2	
			Type of Statement						
26	19	40	Unqualified	1	1	4	13	21	
40	25	35	Reviewed	1 3	6	9	14	2	
46	34	50	Compiled	7 14	14	11	2	2	
2	1	5	Tax Returns	4 1					
29	16	30	Other	3 9		4	8	6	
4/1/92-3/31/93 ALL	4/1/93-3/31/94 ALL	4/1/94-3/31/95 ALL		52 (4/1-9/30/94)		108 (10/1/94-3/31/95)			
				0-1MM	1-3MM	3-5MM	5-10MM	10-25MM	25MM & OVER
143	95	160	NUMBER OF STATEMENTS	15	28	21	28	37	31
%	%	%	ASSETS	%	%	%	%	%	%
7.2	5.6	6.6	Cash & Equivalents	8.1	7.0	5.2	9.7	6.7	3.4
28.1	29.2	28.9	Trade Receivables - (net)	30.9	24.9	32.3	29.4	29.5	28.1
27.6	26.9	28.9	Inventory	19.6	24.8	33.2	24.3	33.3	32.9
2.0	1.5	2.3	All Other Current	.7	3.0	4.1	.8	1.4	3.6
64.9	63.2	66.7	Total Current	59.4	59.8	74.8	64.2	71.0	67.9
25.3	27.0	25.0	Fixed Assets (net)	29.7	33.6	17.8	28.3	20.6	22.3
2.8	3.3	2.8	Intangibles (net)	3.0	2.5	1.3	2.1	3.1	4.3
7.0	6.4	5.5	All Other Non-Current	7.9	4.0	6.1	5.5	5.3	5.5
100.0	100.0	100.0	Total	100.0	100.0	100.0	100.0	100.0	100.0
			LIABILITIES						
12.7	13.1	14.3	Notes Payable-Short Term	12.7	9.3	10.2	11.7	16.9	21.4
3.8	5.6	4.2	Cur. Mat.-L./T/D	8.3	7.5	4.6	3.3	2.6	1.7
21.9	19.9	19.6	Trade Payables	15.7	18.6	20.2	19.9	21.7	19.2
.2	2.6	.4	Income Taxes Payable	.2	.2	.2	1.2	.2	.2
7.3	7.5	8.6	All Other Current	17.5	6.9	7.8	9.3	7.4	7.3
45.9	48.7	47.1	Total Current	54.4	42.5	43.1	45.5	48.8	49.8
13.9	11.9	14.1	Long Term Debt	17.3	21.2	7.5	12.2	11.5	15.5
.3	.2	.4	Deferred Taxes	.3	.2	.3	.3	.3	.7
3.2	4.6	4.3	All Other-Non-Current	3.6	3.5	3.3	6.9	4.2	3.7
36.6	34.6	34.2	Net Worth	24.4	32.6	45.8	35.0	35.2	30.4
100.0	100.0	100.0	Total Liabilities & Net Worth	100.0	100.0	100.0	100.0	100.0	100.0
			INCOME DATA						
100.0	100.0	100.0	Net Sales	100.0	100.0	100.0	100.0	100.0	100.0
28.9	31.5	29.0	Gross Profit	41.5	34.7	27.9	28.2	27.6	20.8
26.4	28.8	25.4	Operating Expenses	36.7	30.6	22.8	24.5	24.7	18.5
2.5	2.6	3.6	Operating Profit	4.8	4.1	5.1	3.7	2.9	2.3
.7	.6	1.1	All Other Expenses (net)	1.3	1.4	1.8	.8	.6	1.3
1.9	2.1	2.5	Profit Before Taxes	3.5	2.7	3.2	2.9	2.3	1.0
			RATIOS						
2.3	2.0	2.0		1.5	2.5	2.6	1.7	2.1	2.0
1.3	1.4	1.5	Current	.9	1.3	1.7	1.4	1.6	1.3
1.1	1.0	1.1		.7	.9	1.3	1.1	1.1	1.1
1.2	1.2	1.1		1.0	1.2	1.3	1.5	1.1	1.0
.7	.7	.8	Quick	.6	.7	.9	.9	.8	.6
.5	.5	.5		.5	.5	.7	.5	.5	.4
21 17.0	25 14.7	23 15.6		28 13.1	22 16.5	28 12.9	21 17.8	24 15.0	22 16.5
29 12.6	31 11.9	33 11.1	Sales/Receivables	41 8.8	32 11.3	34 10.7	35 10.5	33 10.9	30 12.2
37 10.0	39 9.3	41 8.8		70 5.2	38 9.7	43 8.5	48 7.6	42 8.7	37 10.0
19 18.8	23 15.9	24 14.9		22 16.5	21 17.7	31 11.6	17 21.7	30 12.3	24 15.0
35 10.5	41 9.0	43 8.4	Cost of Sales/Inventory	41 8.8	45 8.1	50 7.3	38 9.5	46 7.9	34 10.7
61 6.0	63 5.8	76 4.8		99 3.7	79 4.6	68 5.4	81 4.5	81 4.5	66 5.5
16 23.0	14 25.7	13 29.1		13 28.7	11 34.4	12 29.9	13 28.3	17 21.1	14 27.0
29 12.7	26 13.8	25 14.4	Cost of Sales/Payables	25 14.5	26 14.0	21 17.3	31 11.8	27 13.7	21 17.3
49 7.5	48 7.6	49 7.4		64 5.7	49 7.5	36 10.2	63 5.8	56 6.5	33 10.9
8.9	8.7	8.2		6.4	7.2	6.5	9.4	7.9	11.3
19.5	22.7	17.8	Sales/Working Capital	-36.7	24.4	11.8	19.0	13.2	23.2
97.4	999.8	102.8		-14.5	-53.0	25.8	205.1	64.9	65.2
	6.3	6.8		9.2	4.8	13.0	7.1	6.8	6.1
(125) 5.7 2.2	(85) 3.2	(138) 3.3	EBIT/Interest	(14) 2.5	(24) 3.3	(18) 4.4	(25) 3.5	(31) 3.2	(26) 2.7
1.1	1.4	1.6		.8	1.5	2.8	1.8	1.6	1.4
	4.1	6.4						11.8	8.2
(50) 4.5 2.1	(31) 2.0	(52) 3.4	Net Profit + Depr., Dep., Amort./Cur. Mat. L/T/D				(12) 5.2	(12) 3.6	
.9	.9	1.0						2.5	2.5
.3	.3	.3		.3	.5	.1	.2	.2	.3
.6	.8	.7	Fixed/Worth	2.2	1.3	.3	.6	.7	.6
1.7	1.8	1.9		5.4	5.1	.6	1.2	1.4	2.1
.9	1.0	1.0		.8	.8	.6	1.1	1.0	1.1
2.1	2.2	2.2	Debt/Worth	6.1	2.6	1.1	1.9	1.7	3.4
4.5	5.1	6.1		22.3	10.5	2.9	4.2	4.3	7.2
29.0	31.2	40.7		47.4	50.4	32.9	51.7	36.4	41.9
(130) 14.2	(84) 12.7	(144) 21.8	% Profit Before Taxes/Tangible Net Worth	(12) 19.2	(24) 19.4	24.4	(26) 26.4	(32) 16.3	(29) 25.6
2.5	2.7	8.1		4.4	4.3	10.6	11.2	7.8	14.4
11.5	11.4	13.1		11.3	12.9	11.8	16.9	13.2	12.7
4.8	4.2	6.6	% Profit Before Taxes/Total Assets	3.0	5.7	7.8	8.2	4.0	7.7
.6	.7	1.7		-1.3	.5	4.8	2.3	1.3	1.6
48.3	45.5	49.6		40.8	21.4	83.1	59.5	66.3	39.1
15.8	14.6	14.9	Sales/Net Fixed Assets	10.8	9.9	19.7	13.2	18.8	21.6
7.1	6.2	6.2		4.8	5.2	11.7	4.8	8.3	7.6
4.6	4.7	4.4		3.5	4.5	4.4	3.5	4.8	5.8
3.1	3.2	2.9	Sales/Total Assets	2.5	3.0	3.3	2.6	3.0	3.8
2.2	2.5	2.2		1.7	1.8	2.4	2.1	2.3	2.3
.6	.6	.6		.6	.8	.5	.8	.3	.3
(127) 1.6	(86) 1.7	(138) 1.4	% Depr., Dep., Amort./Sales	(11) 3.8	(26) 2.5	(20) 1.4	(23) 1.8	(33) 1.0	(25) .8
3.7	3.9	4.0		5.2	5.1	2.6	3.9	4.1	1.7
1.5	3.0	1.4			1.4	2.0	1.9	1.0	
(59) 2.8	(42) 4.7	(66) 2.6	% Officers', Directors', Owners' Comp/Sales	(15) 3.7	(11) 2.4	(10) 4.2	(18) 1.8		
7.1	8.7	6.7		7.8	5.9	7.8	4.2		
5413445M	1896602M	5044637M	Net Sales ($)	9173M	49458M	80481M	213021M	630669M	4061835M
1360449M	636656M	1512564M	Total Assets ($)	5665M	20247M	26153M	81994M	232660M	1145845M

© Robert Morris Associates 1995

M = $ thousand   MM = $ million

See Pages 1 through 15 for Explanation of Ratios and Data

WHOLESALERS—CONFECTIONERY. SIC# 5145

Current Data Sorted By Assets | **Comparative Historical Data**

Type of Statement

Type of Statement	0-500M	500M-2MM	2-10MM	10-50MM	50-100MM	100-250MM	4/1/90-3/31/91 ALL	4/1/91-3/31/92 ALL
			3	2	1			
Unqualified			7	2	1		13	8
Reviewed	1	7	12	1			20	28
Compiled	4	12	4	1			36	32
Tax Returns	1						2	2
Other	4	4	3	3			24	21

Periods: 22 (4/1-9/30/94); 45 (10/1/94-3/31/95)

	0-500M	500M-2MM	2-10MM	10-50MM	50-100MM	100-250MM		4/1/90-3/31/91 ALL	4/1/91-3/31/92 ALL
NUMBER OF STATEMENTS	10	23	26	7	1			95	91
ASSETS	%	%	%	%	%	%		%	%
Cash & Equivalents	4.3	7.2	6.2					4.8	5.8
Trade Receivables - (net)	25.3	31.5	27.0					25.6	27.6
Inventory	34.2	33.9	38.1					36.5	34.3
All Other Current	.1	.8	1.5					1.1	1.3
Total Current	63.8	73.5	72.8					67.9	69.0
Fixed Assets (net)	27.8	19.0	18.3					22.0	21.4
Intangibles (net)	.7	2.1	1.4					3.9	3.0
All Other Non-Current	7.6	5.4	7.4					6.2	6.5
Total	100.0	100.0	100.0					100.0	100.0
LIABILITIES									
Notes Payable-Short Term	13.9	12.0	14.4					12.1	16.2
Cur. Mat. -L/T/D	2.1	4.8	2.7					4.0	3.2
Trade Payables	26.6	23.4	22.9					21.9	22.2
Income Taxes Payable	.4	.0	.2					.6	.4
All Other Current	6.1	6.4	11.4					6.9	5.9
Total Current	49.0	46.6	51.7					45.6	47.9
Long Term Debt	17.8	14.1	9.5					13.3	13.7
Deferred Taxes	.0	1.3	.4					.2	.3
All Other-Non-Current	9.7	7.7	4.9					5.8	3.1
Net Worth	23.5	30.4	33.5					35.1	34.9
Total Liabilities & Net Worth	100.0	100.0	100.0					100.0	100.0
INCOME DATA									
Net Sales	100.0	100.0	100.0					100.0	100.0
Gross Profit	39.7	23.7	21.3					23.7	21.5
Operating Expenses	31.0	21.9	19.8					21.5	18.1
Operating Profit	8.7	1.8	1.6					2.2	3.4
All Other Expenses (net)	.8	.3	.4					1.0	1.0
Profit Before Taxes	7.9	1.5	1.2					1.1	2.5
RATIOS									
Current	2.2 / 1.4 / .9	2.3 / 1.7 / 1.1	2.2 / 1.3 / 1.0					2.2 / 1.5 / 1.1	2.5 / 1.5 / 1.0
Quick	1.6 / .6 / .4	1.1 / .7 / .5	1.2 / .5 / .4				(94)	1.2 / .6 / .4	1.1 / .6 / .4
Sales/Receivables	8 45.6	15 24.4	19 19.3					12 31.7	14 26.8
	30 12.0	23 15.8	36 10.2					20 18.1	24 15.4
	42 8.7	37 9.9	46 7.9					30 12.2	34 10.6
Cost of Sales/Inventory	21 17.0	18 19.8	34 10.8					24 15.5	23 16.1
	59 6.2	27 13.3	66 5.5					38 9.7	34 10.7
	159 2.3	85 4.3	85 4.3					58 6.3	51 7.2
Cost of Sales/Payables	0 UND	9 39.4	15 23.8					11 32.3	10 38.0
	27 13.7	24 15.5	35 10.5					22 16.7	21 17.6
	58 6.3	49 7.5	63 5.8					46 7.9	38 9.5
Sales/Working Capital	6.8	9.8	6.9					10.1	11.8
	62.0	19.3	25.2					23.6	21.2
	-79.8	91.7	-445.8					93.3	152.8
EBIT/Interest		(22) 5.4 / 2.6 / .8	(21) 5.3 / 2.8 / 1.6				(84)	6.0 / 2.1 / .8	(85) 5.6 / 2.5 / 1.1
Net Profit + Depr., Dep., Amort./Cur. Mat. L /T/D			(12) 11.4 / 2.7 / .9				(40)	4.9 / 2.4 / .9	(32) 3.6 / 2.4 / 1.3
Fixed/Worth	.5 / 1.0 / NM	.2 / .6 / UND	.1 / .3 / 2.0					.2 / .7 / 1.5	.2 / .8 / 1.5
Debt/Worth	.7 / 2.7 / NM	.9 / 1.3 / UND	.9 / 1.9 / 4.8					.9 / 2.3 / 6.5	1.0 / 2.2 / 4.7
% Profit Before Taxes/Tangible Net Worth		(18) 59.8 / 31.9 / 8.8	(24) 26.8 / 13.5 / 2.8				(84)	29.9 / 17.7 / 2.0	(83) 36.9 / 16.0 / 3.8
% Profit Before Taxes/Total Assets	14.5 / 8.4 / 1.6	15.4 / 4.2 / .2	9.0 / 3.2 / .2					10.8 / 5.9 / .0	11.2 / 6.1 / .6
Sales/Net Fixed Assets	35.7 / 11.6 / 6.4	73.5 / 32.7 / 12.5	97.9 / 30.8 / 6.9					99.3 / 33.5 / 9.0	68.4 / 26.8 / 8.8
Sales/Total Assets	5.7 / 4.3 / 1.4	6.2 / 4.5 / 3.1	4.0 / 2.6 / 1.7					6.4 / 4.3 / 2.7	6.8 / 4.3 / 2.6
% Depr., Dep., Amort./Sales	.9 / 1.3 / 4.3	(22) .4 / .7 / 1.3	(23) .5 / .8 / 1.4				(83)	.4 / 1.0 / 1.8	(86) .4 / .8 / 1.6
% Officers', Directors', Owners' Comp/Sales		(12) 2.0 / 2.8 / 4.6					(41)	1.5 / 2.6 / 4.6	(36) .8 / 1.7 / 5.1
Net Sales ($)	8918M	108403M	442873M	422258M	58110M			2243698M	1549416M
Total Assets ($)	2284M	24034M	127187M	166480M	69489M			1006019M	648391M

Postretirement Benefits

M = $ thousand   MM = $ million
See Pages 1 through 15 for Explanation of Ratios and Data

Comparative Historical Data | **Current Data Sorted By Sales**

4/1/92-3/31/93 ALL	4/1/93-3/31/94 ALL	4/1/94-3/31/95 ALL		0-1MM	1-3MM	3-5MM	5-10MM	10-25MM	25MM & OVER
			# Postretirement Benefits				2	1	3
			Type of Statement						
11	8	10	Unqualified				1	5	4
25	26	21	Reviewed	1	1	4	4	8	3
33	28	21	Compiled	2	7	2	5	4	1
3	1	1	Tax Returns	1					
7	11	14	Other	3	2	3	3		3
				22 (4/1-9/30/94)			**45 (10/1/94-3/31/95)**		
79	**74**	**67**	**NUMBER OF STATEMENTS**	7	10	9	13	17	11
%	%	%	**ASSETS**	%	%	%	%	%	%
6.0	7.4	6.0	Cash & Equivalents		10.7		8.1	4.6	4.8
28.2	27.9	27.1	Trade Receivables - (net)		27.4		31.0	22.7	25.6
36.8	32.7	35.4	Inventory		27.0		34.6	43.9	34.7
1.5	.8	2.2	All Other Current		.0		2.5	1.1	7.9
72.5	68.9	70.7	Total Current		65.2		76.3	72.3	73.0
18.4	22.8	21.2	Fixed Assets (net)		28.4		17.0	20.9	19.9
3.3	2.0	1.4	Intangibles (net)		4.2		.8	.2	.1
5.8	6.4	6.7	All Other Non-Current		2.2		5.9	6.6	6.9
100.0	100.0	100.0	Total		100.0		100.0	100.0	100.0
			LIABILITIES						
15.3	16.1	13.6	Notes Payable-Short Term		8.3		15.5	14.6	17.3
3.6	2.8	3.2	Cur. Mat.-L /T/D		7.5		2.9	2.6	1.6
21.6	21.3	23.4	Trade Payables		27.6		21.5	22.1	23.5
.6	1.0	.2	Income Taxes Payable		.0		.1	.2	.1
5.9	6.6	9.5	All Other Current		8.0		13.0	10.8	10.9
47.0	47.7	50.0	Total Current		51.4		53.0	50.4	53.5
10.8	11.2	11.7	Long Term Debt		19.0		10.6	11.4	2.6
.3	.7	.6	Deferred Taxes		.0		.1	.5	.0
2.0	3.9	6.3	All Other-Non-Current		6.5		9.8	4.0	1.6
39.8	36.5	31.4	Net Worth		23.1		26.5	33.7	42.3
100.0	100.0	100.0	Total Liabilities & Net Worth		100.0		100.0	100.0	100.0
			INCOME DATA						
100.0	100.0	100.0	Net Sales		100.0		100.0	100.0	100.0
21.9	21.0	24.8	Gross Profit		31.7		20.1	20.3	16.9
18.2	18.9	22.1	Operating Expenses		29.3		19.9	17.7	15.7
3.7	2.2	2.7	Operating Profit		2.4		.2	2.7	1.2
.7	.3	.4	All Other Expenses (net)		.1		.2	.9	.0
3.1	1.8	2.3	Profit Before Taxes		2.3		-.1	1.7	1.2
			RATIOS						
2.6 / 1.6 / 1.1	2.4 / 1.4 / 1.1	2.2 / 1.3 / 1.0	Current		2.4 / 1.3 / .9		2.8 / 1.2 / .9	2.0 / 1.5 / 1.1	2.2 / 1.2 / 1.1
1.1 / .7 / .5	1.2 / .7 / .4	1.1 / .6 / .4	Quick		1.5 / .7 / .4		1.9 / .6 / .4	.9 / .5 / .3	1.3 / .5 / .4
17 22.1 / 24 15.1 / 37 9.8	14 26.6 / 22 16.7 / 35 10.3	16 23.4 / 31 11.9 / 42 8.6	Sales/Receivables		12 30.1 / 24 15.2 / 33 11.2		18 19.9 / 42 8.6 / 52 7.0	17 21.8 / 32 11.4 / 43 8.5	14 26.9 / 21 17.6 / 40 9.1
23 15.9 / 38 9.5 / 62 5.9	15 24.4 / 33 11.1 / 54 6.8	23 16.0 / 55 6.6 / 94 3.9	Cost of Sales/Inventory		12 31.2 / 24 15.2 / 87 4.2		25 14.4 / 30 12.1 / 83 4.4	35 10.4 / 72 5.1 / 107 3.4	18 20.3 / 29 12.8 / 74 4.9
13 29.0 / 21 17.3 / 37 9.9	10 35.9 / 20 18.0 / 38 9.6	11 33.0 / 27 13.4 / 55 6.6	Cost of Sales/Payables		10 35.4 / 37 10.0 / 54 6.8		13 28.2 / 27 13.7 / 61 6.0	11 34.0 / 26 13.8 / 56 6.5	12 31.3 / 16 21.8 / 33 10.9
7.6 / 15.7 / 116.7	12.9 / 20.8 / 148.0	8.2 / 21.4 / -580.9	Sales/Working Capital		7.9 / 52.4 / -48.7		7.6 / 23.0 / -38.5	7.7 / 19.2 / 92.7	17.5 / 27.1 / 58.1
(76) 7.1 / 3.1 / 1.4	(67) 5.1 / 2.8 / 1.4	(59) 6.6 / 2.9 / 1.2	EBIT/Interest		14.0 / 4.1 / 1.2		(10) 5.5 / 2.8 / -2.3	(15) 5.9 / 2.2 / .8	
(31) 5.3 / 2.4 / 1.3	(30) 3.8 / 1.6 / .6	(22) 5.1 / 2.2 / .8	Net Profit + Depr., Dep., Amort./Cur. Mat. L/T/D						
.1 / .5 / 1.3	.2 / .6 / 1.4	.2 / .6 / 1.8	Fixed/Worth		.6 / 1.4 / -2.9		.0 / 1.2 / NM	.2 / .5 / 1.8	.1 / .4 / .6
.8 / 1.7 / 3.8	1.1 / 2.1 / 3.9	.9 / 1.9 / 6.0	Debt/Worth		.8 / 3.6 / -13.0		.5 / 2.5 / NM	1.2 / 1.9 / 4.8	.7 / 1.5 / 2.2
(71) 33.6 / 19.3 / 7.1	(70) 32.3 / 17.3 / 2.8	(58) 32.6 / 12.4 / 4.7	% Profit Before Taxes/Tangible Net Worth		(10)		31.9 / 13.6 / 7.0	30.9 / 5.8 / -.5	15.1 / 11.7 / 5.8
13.1 / 5.5 / 1.5	9.7 / 4.4 / .6	9.9 / 3.6 / .5	% Profit Before Taxes/Total Assets		15.3 / 8.2 / 1.5		9.4 / 5.3 / -21.4	11.0 / 2.6 / -.2	6.1 / 4.0 / 2.1
67.8 / 34.5 / 10.4	63.5 / 25.9 / 8.7	59.5 / 25.2 / 8.7	Sales/Net Fixed Assets		22.9 / 12.9 / 8.8		137.0 / 32.7 / 11.3	57.9 / 29.4 / 6.6	163.4 / 32.0 / 7.6
5.3 / 3.9 / 2.3	6.4 / 4.1 / 2.5	5.3 / 3.3 / 2.1	Sales/Total Assets		5.1 / 3.9 / 3.4		4.7 / 3.1 / 2.0	5.3 / 2.7 / 2.0	6.6 / 4.1 / 2.1
(74) .4 / .9 / 1.8	(73) .5 / .8 / 2.0	(62) .5 / 1.0 / 2.0	% Depr., Dep., Amort./Sales		1.0 / 1.3 / 2.0		(10) .4 / .7 / 1.4	.5 / 1.0 / 1.9	(10) .3 / .5 / 2.7
(38) 1.3 / 1.9 / 5.0	(36) .9 / 2.0 / 5.2	(25) 1.8 / 3.2 / 5.7	% Officers', Directors', Owners' Comp/Sales						
1677683M	1339640M	1040562M	Net Sales ($)	2481M	21301M	32780M	85331M	224451M	674218M
708547M	499772M	389474M	Total Assets ($)	1671M	6104M	12261M	30236M	97613M	241589M

Current Data Sorted By Assets   **Comparative Historical Data**

0-500M	500M-2MM	2-10MM	10-50MM	50-100MM	100-250MM		4/1/90-3/31/91 ALL	4/1/91-3/31/92 ALL
						# Postretirement Benefits		
1	3	1	3	1		**Type of Statement**		
	2	7	5	4	3	Unqualified	34	26
1	9	6	4			Reviewed	19	28
5	14	8	1			Compiled	24	22
2	1					Tax Returns	3	2
2	3	5	6			Other	15	17
33 (4/1-9/30/94)			55 (10/1/94-3/31/95)					
10	29	26	16	4	3	**NUMBER OF STATEMENTS**	95	95
%	%	%	%	%	%	**ASSETS**	%	%
11.1	3.4	6.5	6.0			Cash & Equivalents	8.0	7.8
35.9	35.2	39.6	41.6			Trade Receivables - (net)	32.0	31.6
23.6	21.7	23.4	15.7			Inventory	19.7	21.2
1.3	.9	2.1	1.4			All Other Current	.9	1.4
71.9	61.1	71.6	64.8			Total Current	60.5	62.0
13.6	26.4	21.8	27.2			Fixed Assets (net)	31.7	27.6
10.5	2.4	1.7	1.4			Intangibles (net)	1.7	3.3
4.1	10.1	4.8	6.6			All Other Non-Current	6.1	7.2
100.0	100.0	100.0	100.0			Total	100.0	100.0
						LIABILITIES		
7.0	14.4	13.9	9.7			Notes Payable-Short Term	12.5	13.6
7.0	4.6	2.7	2.9			Cur. Mat. -L/T/D	3.5	4.3
37.6	33.3	36.4	35.9			Trade Payables	25.5	28.1
1.6	.6	.2	.3			Income Taxes Payable	.5	.2
22.0	6.9	6.2	7.7			All Other Current	9.1	6.5
75.2	59.8	59.3	56.5			Total Current	51.2	52.6
10.5	16.1	13.3	12.7			Long Term Debt	16.0	15.3
.0	.1	.2	.9			Deferred Taxes	.4	.2
3.1	2.5	.9	1.7			All Other-Non-Current	2.6	3.4
11.2	21.4	26.3	28.3			Net Worth	29.8	28.4
100.0	100.0	100.0	100.0			Total Liabilities & Net Worth	100.0	100.0
						INCOME DATA		
100.0	100.0	100.0	100.0			Net Sales	100.0	100.0
21.2	22.7	13.7	14.8			Gross Profit	21.3	18.7
18.6	21.3	12.9	12.7			Operating Expenses	18.4	16.6
2.6	1.4	.8	2.0			Operating Profit	2.8	2.1
1.2	1.5	.5	.4			All Other Expenses (net)	1.1	.7
1.4	.0	.3	1.6			Profit Before Taxes	1.7	1.4
						RATIOS		
1.4	1.4	1.5	1.4				1.6	1.4
.9	1.0	1.1	1.2			Current	1.2	1.2
.6	.8	.9	.9				.9	.9
1.0	.8	1.1	1.3				1.1	1.0
.7	.6	.7	.9			Quick	.8	.7
.2	.5	.5	.5				.5	.5
6 64.3	18 20.7	20 17.9	20 18.1				16 23.5	17 20.9
24 15.4	25 14.7	28 13.1	26 14.3			Sales/Receivables	23 15.8	24 14.9
32 11.4	35 10.5	35 10.4	29 12.4				31 11.6	31 11.9
4 87.1	11 31.9	9 41.8	1 284.0				8 43.9	8 48.4
12 31.1	21 17.6	14 25.6	16 22.6			Cost of Sales/Inventory	18 20.3	16 22.4
40 9.2	35 10.3	33 10.9	23 15.9				38 9.7	32 11.4
12 31.4	17 21.7	21 17.6	20 17.9				15 25.1	17 21.4
33 11.1	25 14.5	26 14.1	23 16.1			Cost of Sales/Payables	24 15.1	24 15.4
50 7.3	41 8.8	39 9.3	30 12.1				32 11.5	31 11.6
22.3	29.2	13.8	17.6				18.2	24.1
-531.9	552.3	93.7	64.6			Sales/Working Capital	66.3	62.6
-6.7	-25.1	-177.1	-103.3				-96.5	-159.3
	4.8	5.1	33.1				7.9	4.7
	(28) 1.9	(25) 2.1	(15) 4.2			EBIT/Interest	(86) 2.4	(88) 2.5
	.9	-.4	1.8				1.3	1.1
	9.6	7.5				Net Profit + Depr., Dep.,	5.7	4.1
	(11) 2.2	(14) 1.7				Amort./Cur. Mat. L /T/D	(46) 3.1	(43) 2.1
	1.6	.7					1.1	.5
.2	.3	.3	.5				.4	.4
.6	1.7	.8	1.1			Fixed/Worth	1.1	1.0
-22.7	5.1	1.6	2.2				2.2	1.9
2.1	2.1	1.8	1.2				1.2	1.5
29.5	4.6	2.7	2.9			Debt/Worth	2.8	2.6
-3.0	17.3	9.3	6.0				5.7	6.3
	40.9	33.4	37.9			% Profit Before Taxes/Tangible	39.4	34.5
	(24) 20.0	(22) 8.3	(14) 30.5			Net Worth	(85) 17.1	(84) 16.8
	-.9	-9.6	16.0				6.5	4.5
24.0	8.3	6.4	14.4			% Profit Before Taxes/Total	10.7	9.8
6.0	3.2	2.5	7.7			Assets	5.3	4.0
1.4	-.3	-3.5	1.7				.6	.8
117.2	52.1	95.4	307.5				44.7	74.6
67.0	15.9	37.9	15.7			Sales/Net Fixed Assets	17.1	18.0
33.2	9.9	12.5	7.5				6.9	8.5
10.1	6.8	6.5	8.4				6.9	6.5
6.3	4.8	4.7	4.8			Sales/Total Assets	4.4	4.6
3.7	3.5	3.5	3.3				3.0	3.3
	.6	.5	.2				.6	.4
	(26) 1.4	(23) .6	(15) 1.4			% Depr., Dep., Amort./Sales	(80) 1.3	(86) 1.1
	2.7	1.2	2.2				2.3	2.2
	1.4	.7					1.1	.9
	(15) 2.2	(13) 1.8				% Officers', Directors',	(36) 2.2	(37) 1.8
	5.2	4.0				Owners' Comp/Sales	4.2	4.0
27585M	163525M	613071M	1527154M	1488187M	1781488M	Net Sales ($)	6854118M	5957208M
3446M	32064M	114372M	258603M	351564M	420638M	Total Assets ($)	1534940M	1463082M

M = $ thousand   MM = $ million
See Pages 1 through 15 for Explanation of Ratios and Data

WHOLESALERS—DAIRY PRODUCTS. SIC# 5143   411

Comparative Historical Data				Current Data Sorted By Sales					
4	10	9	# Postretirement Benefits			2	1	2	4
			Type of Statement						
25	22	21	Unqualified				1	4	16
25	26	20	Reviewed	1	2	3	4	2	8
23	27	28	Compiled	2	2	8	8	6	2
3	4	3	Tax Returns	1	1	1			
9	10	16	Other		2	3	1	3	7
4/1/92-3/31/93	4/1/93-3/31/94	4/1/94-3/31/95		33 (4/1-9/30/94)			55 (10/1/94-3/31/95)		
ALL	ALL	ALL		0-1MM	1-3MM	3-5MM	5-10MM	10-25MM	25MM & OVER
85	89	88	NUMBER OF STATEMENTS	4	7	15	14	15	33
%	%	%	ASSETS	%	%	%	%	%	%
5.4	5.0	5.7	Cash & Equivalents			12.8	3.2	5.0	4.7
34.1	35.1	37.8	Trade Receivables - (net)			27.5	37.4	43.3	42.6
21.9	21.6	21.3	Inventory			18.0	24.7	25.4	17.6
.9	.8	1.4	All Other Current			.9	2.6	.7	1.5
62.2	62.4	66.2	Total Current			59.1	67.9	74.3	66.4
27.5	28.1	23.8	Fixed Assets (net)			26.4	25.3	16.8	25.7
2.7	1.9	2.8	Intangibles (net)			1.2	2.4	1.9	1.2
7.6	7.6	7.1	All Other Non-Current			13.3	4.4	6.9	6.7
100.0	100.0	100.0	Total			100.0	100.0	100.0	100.0
			LIABILITIES						
10.8	12.0	11.9	Notes Payable-Short Term			10.0	7.7	16.1	9.9
4.0	4.6	3.8	Cur. Mat.-L /T/D			7.1	2.9	2.0	2.6
31.0	31.7	34.6	Trade Payables			30.9	36.6	32.3	39.2
.2	1.6	.9	Income Taxes Payable			1.3	.7	.1	1.2
6.5	5.5	8.7	All Other Current			4.4	7.6	8.9	6.9
52.6	55.4	59.9	Total Current			53.8	55.5	59.3	59.8
13.7	13.5	13.5	Long Term Debt			17.5	14.8	7.5	10.5
1.3	.2	.3	Deferred Taxes			.0	.2	.1	.7
2.7	2.8	1.9	All Other-Non-Current			4.8	.7	1.7	1.4
29.6	28.1	24.4	Net Worth			23.9	28.9	31.4	27.7
100.0	100.0	100.0	Total Liabilities & Net Worth			100.0	100.0	100.0	100.0
			INCOME DATA						
100.0	100.0	100.0	Net Sales			100.0	100.0	100.0	100.0
19.7	18.9	17.5	Gross Profit			22.1	18.2	14.4	12.9
18.0	17.6	16.0	Operating Expenses			21.3	16.6	13.8	11.4
1.7	1.3	1.5	Operating Profit			.9	1.7	.6	1.5
.1	.5	.9	All Other Expenses (net)			.2	.6	.2	.2
1.6	.8	.7	Profit Before Taxes			.6	1.0	.4	1.3
			RATIOS						
1.5	1.5	1.4				1.3	1.8	1.7	1.4
1.1	1.2	1.1	Current			1.1	1.4	1.3	1.0
1.0	.9	.9				.6	.9	1.0	.9
.9	1.0	1.0				.8	1.2	1.3	1.1
.7	.8	.7	Quick			.6	.7	.8	.8
.5	.5	.5				.3	.4	.6	.6
17 22.1	18 20.0	20 18.0				17 21.0	23 15.7	23 16.1	20 18.1
24 15.5	25 14.4	26 14.1	Sales/Receivables			22 16.8	29 12.5	29 12.8	25 14.4
31 11.9	34 10.8	34 10.8				27 13.4	38 9.7	35 10.5	31 11.9
9 40.5	8 47.5	8 44.4				4 96.1	11 34.6	10 36.0	6 65.8
16 23.2	17 21.7	17 21.4	Cost of Sales/Inventory			18 20.8	22 16.7	15 25.1	14 25.3
27 13.5	32 11.5	33 11.2				34 10.6	31 11.8	34 10.8	22 16.3
18 19.9	18 19.9	17 21.0				8 46.8	15 24.5	15 23.6	21 17.3
25 14.6	25 14.8	25 14.6	Cost of Sales/Payables			25 14.5	25 14.5	24 15.1	25 14.7
34 10.6	33 11.1	38 9.6				47 7.8	46 7.9	34 10.7	30 12.1
23.1	22.8	21.9				20.8	12.9	13.8	31.1
73.2	46.6	129.1	Sales/Working Capital			132.1	30.3	41.0	158.0
NM	-90.4	-75.8				-16.0	-107.9	-557.2	-167.7
	4.7	6.1	6.3			4.7	6.5	4.3	11.0
(79) 1.8	(82) 2.8	(84) 3.2	EBIT/Interest	(13) 2.5		2.5	2.6	(14) 2.2	(32) 4.4
1.0	1.1	1.3				.6	-1.3	-.2	2.0
4.9	9.0	9.9							10.4
(42) 2.2	(37) 2.5	(41) 2.2	Net Profit + Depr., Dep., Amort./Cur. Mat. L/T/D					(20) 2.9	
1.0	.9	.9							1.2
.4	.4	.4				.3	.3	.3	.5
1.0	.9	1.1	Fixed/Worth			1.2	.8	.5	1.1
1.9	1.7	2.7				2.7	6.3	1.2	1.5
1.5	1.4	1.6				2.0	.9	1.5	1.3
2.7	2.3	3.2	Debt/Worth			2.7	5.7	2.7	2.7
6.0	4.2	11.5				11.0	18.6	4.1	6.0
27.1	34.3	37.4	% Profit Before Taxes/Tangible Net Worth			45.7	40.9	38.3	33.5
(76) 13.7	(80) 16.6	(73) 22.2		(12) 16.2	(12) 21.4			(14) 5.1	(29) 22.8
2.0	3.9	2.8				-.9	-9.2	-10.9	11.0
6.6	9.1	9.3				8.3	17.3	4.8	9.2
3.1	4.6	3.9	% Profit Before Taxes/Total Assets			3.9	2.3	2.3	5.6
.2	.3	.5				-.4	-1.6	-3.2	1.5
53.2	52.5	69.5				97.9	56.9	130.9	75.8
21.3	20.0	23.6	Sales/Net Fixed Assets			17.3	29.3	44.5	15.9
10.3	9.3	11.0				10.3	9.3	25.7	11.9
7.4	7.1	7.4				6.5	5.7	7.8	8.3
4.8	4.7	4.8	Sales/Total Assets			4.8	4.4	5.6	5.1
3.5	3.5	3.6				2.5	3.5	3.7	3.9
.4	.5	.4				.4	.6	.4	.4
(79) 1.0	(81) 1.2	(80) 1.0	% Depr., Dep., Amort./Sales	(13) 1.1	(13) .9	1.1	.9	(14) .6	(30) .9
1.9	2.0	1.8				2.7	1.2	1.0	1.5
.8	1.2	.8						.7	
(39) 1.9	(41) 2.5	(38) 1.9	% Officers', Directors', Owners' Comp/Sales					(10) 1.3	
3.8	5.9	4.3						2.1	
5722153M	6286381M	5601010M	Net Sales ($)	2232M	12902M	60142M	92661M	236724M	5196349M
1197094M	1520174M	1180687M	Total Assets ($)	1782M	3427M	16453M	21743M	48187M	1089095M

M = $ thousand   MM = $ million
See Pages 1 through 15 for Explanation of Ratios and Data

Current Data Sorted By Assets / Comparative Historical Data

 # Postretirement Benefits — Type of Statement

Type of Statement	0-500M	500M-2MM	2-10MM	10-50MM	50-100MM	100-250MM	4/1/90-3/31/91 ALL	4/1/91-3/31/92 ALL
# Postretirement Benefits		3	1					
Unqualified		7	17	16	1		37	42
Reviewed	6	23	29	5			54	50
Compiled	9	22	6				50	50
Tax Returns	5	4	1				2	4
Other	1	18	11	7		1	33	28

Current data periods: 64 (4/1-9/30/94) ; 125 (10/1/94-3/31/95)

	0-500M	500M-2MM	2-10MM	10-50MM	50-100MM	100-250MM		4/1/90-3/31/91 ALL	4/1/91-3/31/92 ALL
NUMBER OF STATEMENTS	21	74	64	28	1	1		176	174
	%	%	%	%	%	%	**ASSETS**	%	%
	14.5	9.7	5.2	4.1			Cash & Equivalents	8.5	7.0
	33.2	40.5	39.1	29.4			Trade Receivables - (net)	36.6	38.4
	18.2	21.8	30.3	38.3			Inventory	25.8	26.9
	2.7	1.6	3.0	1.6			All Other Current	1.6	1.8
	68.5	73.7	77.6	73.5			Total Current	72.5	74.1
	22.1	18.2	16.2	17.3			Fixed Assets (net)	20.5	19.5
	2.2	.5	.6	.5			Intangibles (net)	1.1	1.2
	7.2	7.7	5.5	8.7			All Other Non-Current	5.9	5.1
	100.0	100.0	100.0	100.0			Total	100.0	100.0
							LIABILITIES		
	8.2	14.7	18.6	27.7			Notes Payable-Short Term	18.0	18.3
	6.2	3.9	2.4	1.8			Cur. Mat. -L/T/D	3.4	2.9
	21.6	23.5	26.3	16.5			Trade Payables	26.4	26.0
	.0	.6	.2	.0			Income Taxes Payable	.4	.3
	6.4	8.8	11.2	9.1			All Other Current	5.3	8.1
	42.4	51.5	58.8	55.1			Total Current	53.5	55.6
	14.7	9.0	8.0	11.6			Long Term Debt	10.7	9.6
	.7	.3	.2	1.3			Deferred Taxes	.3	.3
	5.5	2.9	2.3	2.8			All Other-Non-Current	3.8	3.2
	36.6	36.3	30.9	29.2			Net Worth	31.6	31.3
	100.0	100.0	100.0	100.0			Total Liabilities & Net Worth	100.0	100.0
							INCOME DATA		
	100.0	100.0	100.0	100.0			Net Sales	100.0	100.0
	24.7	15.8	13.7	9.9			Gross Profit	16.0	15.8
	20.5	13.6	11.4	9.0			Operating Expenses	14.2	14.0
	4.2	2.2	2.2	.9			Operating Profit	1.8	1.8
	.4	.2	.6	.6			All Other Expenses (net)	.7	.4
	3.7	2.0	1.6	.4			Profit Before Taxes	1.1	1.4
							RATIOS		
	2.9 / 1.6 / 1.1	2.2 / 1.3 / 1.1	1.7 / 1.3 / 1.1	1.8 / 1.3 / 1.0			Current	1.9 / 1.4 / 1.1	1.7 / 1.3 / 1.1
	2.1 / 1.0 / .6	1.4 / .9 / .7	.9 / .7 / .6	.8 / .6 / .4			Quick	1.3 / .8 / .5	1.2 / .8 / .5
	0 UND / 23 16.2 / 35 10.3	18 20.3 / 26 13.9 / 39 9.4	23 16.2 / 31 11.8 / 37 10.0	29 12.7 / 33 11.0 / 39 9.4			Sales/Receivables	17 21.9 / 26 13.9 / 34 10.6	19 19.7 / 27 13.3 / 37 9.8
	0 UND / 9 40.4 / 27 13.4	7 53.9 / 10 36.1 / 36 10.1	12 29.4 / 25 14.6 / 43 8.5	27 13.7 / 43 8.4 / 83 4.4			Cost of Sales/Inventory	8 45.6 / 21 17.7 / 41 8.8	7 49.1 / 23 16.0 / 43 8.4
	0 UND / 19 19.7 / 28 13.2	5 80.8 / 14 26.7 / 29 12.5	11 33.5 / 22 16.9 / 33 11.2	12 31.3 / 20 18.5 / 33 11.1			Cost of Sales/Payables	10 37.9 / 20 18.1 / 31 11.9	10 35.8 / 20 18.5 / 31 11.7
	12.2 / 24.0 / 103.1	10.7 / 31.4 / 156.5	15.7 / 26.6 / 94.3	11.2 / 21.7 / 140.1			Sales/Working Capital	15.1 / 31.2 / 100.1	13.5 / 31.6 / 125.3
	(18) 11.1 / 4.7 / 1.8	(60) 9.1 / 3.1 / 1.5	(59) 5.0 / 2.2 / 1.3	(27) 11.4 / 2.1 / 1.1			EBIT/Interest	(162) 5.5 / 2.0 / .9	(150) 5.0 / 1.9 / 1.0
		(17) 6.5 / 1.7 / 1.1	(23) 8.2 / 1.8 / 1.1	(11) 2.6 / 1.5 / .1			Net Profit + Depr., Dep., Amort./Cur. Mat. L /T/D	(71) 9.3 / 2.5 / .9	(62) 11.7 / 2.4 / .5
	.1 / .2 / 1.7	.1 / .5 / 1.2	.1 / .4 / 1.0	.1 / .2 / 1.0			Fixed/Worth	.2 / .6 / 1.2	.2 / .5 / 1.0
	.7 / 1.8 / 3.8	.9 / 2.0 / 4.5	1.4 / 2.5 / 5.4	1.3 / 3.0 / 8.4			Debt/Worth	1.1 / 2.6 / 5.7	1.0 / 2.6 / 7.9
	(19) 55.7 / 14.7 / 5.1	(71) 47.5 / 18.8 / 5.2	(62) 29.9 / 18.4 / 3.3	(27) 34.0 / 28.4 / 1.9			% Profit Before Taxes/Tangible Net Worth	(163) 36.1 / 15.1 / 2.4	(163) 35.5 / 12.3 / 2.5
	22.7 / 7.5 / 2.2	12.4 / 5.9 / 1.9	8.2 / 3.2 / .6	9.8 / 4.0 / .4			% Profit Before Taxes/Total Assets	11.5 / 3.4 / -.4	8.7 / 3.3 / .1
	413.9 / 63.6 / 36.2	174.0 / 36.4 / 17.7	138.3 / 46.2 / 15.5	940.1 / 76.9 / 7.3			Sales/Net Fixed Assets	129.0 / 39.0 / 14.7	111.1 / 38.5 / 16.1
	7.9 / 6.2 / 2.9	8.2 / 5.1 / 3.5	6.4 / 4.8 / 3.4	4.2 / 3.3 / 2.4			Sales/Total Assets	6.9 / 5.1 / 3.3	6.6 / 5.1 / 3.1
	(16) .2 / .5 / 1.8	(57) .3 / .6 / 1.1	(58) .2 / .5 / 1.0	(22) .0 / .3 / 1.6			% Depr., Dep., Amort./Sales	(156) .2 / .7 / 1.4	(157) .3 / .6 / 1.4
	(13) 1.5 / 2.8 / 5.9	(42) 1.3 / 1.8 / 3.1	(31) .7 / 1.4 / 2.6				% Officers', Directors', Owners' Comp/Sales	(79) 1.0 / 1.9 / 3.3	(87) 1.0 / 1.8 / 3.5
	39552M	509179M	1553681M	1997943M	174823M	511952M	Net Sales ($)	3658754M	4265587M
	6164M	83043M	273256M	600318M	78651M	168962M	Total Assets ($)	913209M	1221372M

M = $ thousand   MM = $ million
See Pages 1 through 15 for Explanation of Ratios and Data

Comparative Historical Data / Current Data Sorted By Sales

	6	6	4	# Postretirement Benefits		1	1	2
				Type of Statement				
Unqualified	36	37	41		3	5	8	25
Reviewed	70	66	63	10 / 8	11	23	11	
Compiled	56	46	37	2 / 13 / 6	9	6	1	
Tax Returns	4	11	10	2 / 4 / 1	2	1		
Other	26	29	38	1 / 3 / 5	10	10	9	

Comparative periods (ALL): 4/1/92-3/31/93 | 4/1/93-3/31/94 | 4/1/94-3/31/95
Current periods: 64 (4/1-9/30/94) covers 0-1MM, 1-3MM, 3-5MM | 125 (10/1/94-3/31/95) covers 5-10MM, 10-25MM, 25MM & OVER

	4/1/92-3/31/93 ALL	4/1/93-3/31/94 ALL	4/1/94-3/31/95 ALL	0-1MM	1-3MM	3-5MM	5-10MM	10-25MM	25MM & OVER
NUMBER OF STATEMENTS	192	189	189	5	30	23	37	48	46
ASSETS	%	%	%	%	%	%	%	%	%
Cash & Equivalents	7.1	7.0	7.9		14.4	7.2	10.0	5.4	4.2
Trade Receivables - (net)	36.6	39.6	37.4		32.5	38.1	40.1	39.6	38.1
Inventory	27.7	26.2	26.9		19.1	26.9	22.4	28.3	36.2
All Other Current	1.4	2.0	2.2		4.0	2.1	2.4	1.4	1.9
Total Current	72.8	74.8	74.3		70.0	74.2	74.8	74.7	80.4
Fixed Assets (net)	19.6	17.9	17.8		19.7	16.2	17.6	20.2	11.5
Intangibles (net)	1.1	.9	.7		1.1	.7	.6	.2	.9
All Other Non-Current	6.4	6.4	7.1		9.2	8.8	7.0	4.8	7.2
Total	100.0	100.0	100.0		100.0	100.0	100.0	100.0	100.0
LIABILITIES									
Notes Payable-Short Term	20.5	20.4	17.3		12.2	13.8	12.2	20.2	24.9
Cur. Mat.-L/T/D	3.4	2.7	3.4		5.5	5.2	1.8	2.3	2.6
Trade Payables	23.7	22.7	23.1		18.5	21.6	23.4	26.0	25.4
Income Taxes Payable	.3	1.8	.3		.1	.3	.8	.2	.1
All Other Current	6.6	6.7	9.5		6.8	7.1	13.6	10.5	8.8
Total Current	54.4	54.3	53.6		43.1	48.1	51.7	59.3	61.9
Long Term Debt	11.7	10.0	9.7		12.4	13.9	10.2	6.7	7.2
Deferred Taxes	.4	.3	.5		.5	.0	.5	.4	.7
All Other-Non-Current	3.2	3.0	3.0		3.0	1.9	1.7	3.0	2.7
Net Worth	30.4	32.4	33.3		41.0	36.0	35.9	30.6	27.6
Total Liabilities & Net Worth	100.0	100.0	100.0		100.0	100.0	100.0	100.0	100.0
INCOME DATA									
Net Sales	100.0	100.0	100.0		100.0	100.0	100.0	100.0	100.0
Gross Profit	15.3	15.2	15.2		21.4	16.7	13.6	13.4	9.6
Operating Expenses	13.7	13.4	12.9		18.3	13.2	12.0	11.7	8.6
Operating Profit	1.6	1.8	2.3		3.2	3.5	1.6	1.7	1.0
All Other Expenses (net)	.8	.5	.4		.3	.1	.3	.8	.4
Profit Before Taxes	.8	1.3	1.8		2.9	3.4	1.3	.9	.6
RATIOS									
Current	1.9	1.7	1.8		3.4	2.9	2.5	1.6	1.6
	1.3	1.3	1.3		1.7	1.4	1.3	1.3	1.2
	1.0	1.1	1.1		1.1	1.2	1.0	1.1	1.1
Quick	1.1	1.3	1.2		2.1	1.2	1.3	1.0	.9
	(191) .8	.8	.8		1.2	.8	.9	.7	.7
	.6	.6	.6		.7	.5	.7	.6	.5
Sales/Receivables	19 19.6	21 17.5	20 18.1		17 20.9	21 17.2	20 17.9	20 18.4	23 15.7
	27 13.6	29 12.4	29 12.6		26 14.3	28 13.1	31 11.8	28 12.9	33 11.2
	35 10.4	41 8.8	37 9.9		48 7.6	38 9.6	37 10.0	33 10.9	37 9.9
Cost of Sales/Inventory	9 40.9	6 63.1	8 44.3		6 60.9	7 54.3	7 52.7	10 38.1	18 20.2
	22 16.4	24 15.4	22 16.5		20 17.9	25 14.5	12 29.8	18 19.8	31 11.9
	47 7.7	42 8.7	44 8.3		46 7.9	44 8.3	38 9.5	37 9.9	63 5.8
Cost of Sales/Payables	9 40.5	7 54.7	8 46.1		5 74.0	4 82.8	8 44.5	8 44.3	12 30.5
	17 20.9	19 19.6	19 19.6		16 22.8	17 21.6	20 18.3	18 20.3	21 17.6
	29 12.5	31 11.8	30 12.1		29 12.8	31 11.6	32 11.5	27 13.4	34 10.7
Sales/Working Capital	14.9	12.3	13.2		5.5	10.7	11.0	20.5	16.8
	28.8	25.8	27.9		18.4	27.1	30.5	34.1	33.0
	228.7	74.3	114.3		60.4	44.7	UND	98.4	167.3
EBIT/Interest	(187) 4.8	(176) 4.8	(166) 6.0		(23) 8.0	(20) 11.2	(28) 9.7	(46) 3.9	(44) 5.5
	2.0	2.6	2.6		3.4	4.4	3.0	1.7	2.4
	1.1	1.4	1.4		1.3	1.8	1.4	1.1	1.6
Net Profit + Depr., Dep., Amort./Cur. Mat. L/T/D	(75) 6.2	(56) 4.4	(54) 4.7					(21) 4.9	(17) 5.6
	2.0	2.2	1.5					1.4	1.5
	.5	.6	1.1					1.1	.6
Fixed/Worth	.2	.1	.1		.1	.1	.2	.2	.1
	.5	.4	.4		.4	.3	.5	.6	.2
	1.2	1.1	1.0		.8	.8	1.4	1.1	.9
Debt/Worth	1.1	1.2	1.1		.7	1.1	.9	1.2	2.1
	2.8	2.3	2.3		1.5	2.0	1.9	2.4	3.4
	7.3	5.8	5.3		2.6	4.5	5.6	5.9	7.0
% Profit Before Taxes/Tangible Net Worth	(178) 34.5	(176) 30.5	(181) 37.3		(28) 26.1	(22) 52.0	(34) 45.4	(46) 27.6	38.6
	13.5	16.8	18.9		16.1	19.4	20.5	15.1	27.0
	2.1	4.7	4.6		2.6	4.5	4.5	1.2	10.8
% Profit Before Taxes/Total Assets	9.1	9.3	10.5		11.7	17.4	11.8	10.2	8.3
	3.0	4.3	4.8		6.9	5.2	6.7	2.7	4.4
	.2	1.1	1.4		1.3	3.1	1.7	.5	2.5
Sales/Net Fixed Assets	160.2	227.1	207.0		259.1	126.0	123.7	199.7	766.7
	43.5	56.6	48.6		38.1	33.3	40.1	46.2	93.0
	17.6	17.8	17.1		7.8	14.9	20.3	14.9	28.0
Sales/Total Assets	7.0	6.5	6.7		7.1	6.0	7.4	7.3	6.0
	4.9	4.6	4.5		3.6	4.0	4.7	5.5	4.2
	3.4	3.2	3.1		2.1	3.4	3.3	4.3	3.0
% Depr., Dep., Amort./Sales	(170) .2	(165) .2	(154) .2		(22) .4	(14) .3	(33) .3	(44) .2	(37) .1
	.6	.5	.5		.8	.6	.6	.5	.2
	1.1	1.3	1.1		2.0	1.3	1.0	1.1	.9
% Officers', Directors', Owners' Comp/Sales	(103) 1.3	(99) 1.2	(95) .8		(20) 1.5	(15) 1.2	(21) .5	(20) .9	(18) .6
	2.4	2.0	1.8		2.8	1.4	1.7	1.5	1.2
	3.8	3.4	3.0		4.2	2.8	3.2	2.3	2.6
Net Sales ($)	4295769M	3878599M	4787130M	2124M	61088M	96963M	260806M	799450M	3566699M
Total Assets ($)	1127660M	1067625M	1210394M	898M	21686M	30683M	67413M	178277M	911437M

M = $ thousand   MM = $ million
See Pages 1 through 15 for Explanation of Ratios and Data

Current Data Sorted By Assets

Comparative Historical Data

	4	8	5		4	# Postretirement Benefits — Type of Statement		
	3	3	14	9		4	Unqualified	25	24
	1	26	32	13	1		Reviewed	43	63
	12	49	31	1			Compiled	70	82
		1	1				Tax Returns	3	2
	7	13	25	7	1		Other	43	38

	0-500M	110 (4/1-9/30/94) 500M-2MM	2-10MM	143 (10/1/94-3/31/95) 10-50MM	50-100MM	100-250MM		ALL 4/1/90-3/31/91	ALL 4/1/91-3/31/92
NUMBER OF STATEMENTS	23	92	103	30	1	4		184	209
	%	%	%	%	%	%	**ASSETS**	%	%
	13.0	10.2	7.0	4.8			Cash & Equivalents	9.3	8.5
	38.0	43.5	41.6	32.3			Trade Receivables - (net)	37.5	39.3
	13.6	10.2	11.6	14.2			Inventory	13.5	11.7
	.9	2.4	2.1	3.5			All Other Current	2.3	2.6
	65.3	66.2	62.4	54.8			Total Current	62.5	62.1
	28.6	24.1	26.5	26.9			Fixed Assets (net)	26.6	26.6
	1.1	.8	1.6	6.5			Intangibles (net)	1.2	1.2
	5.0	8.8	9.5	11.8			All Other Non-Current	9.7	10.2
	100.0	100.0	100.0	100.0			Total	100.0	100.0
							LIABILITIES		
	6.8	10.0	8.0	13.3			Notes Payable-Short Term	11.4	11.9
	2.8	3.4	3.1	3.6			Cur. Mat. -L/T/D	3.2	4.1
	30.5	33.6	32.8	20.0			Trade Payables	27.7	28.6
	.5	.6	.2	.2			Income Taxes Payable	.6	.5
	8.6	7.6	7.3	8.4			All Other Current	8.4	7.1
	49.3	55.2	51.4	45.4			Total Current	51.3	52.3
	12.5	11.1	10.2	14.8			Long Term Debt	13.2	12.4
	.1	.2	.5	.5			Deferred Taxes	.3	.4
	2.1	4.4	3.3	4.1			All Other-Non-Current	1.5	2.5
	36.0	29.1	34.5	35.3			Net Worth	33.7	32.4
	100.0	100.0	100.0	100.0			Total Liabilities & Net Worth	100.0	100.0
							INCOME DATA		
	100.0	100.0	100.0	100.0			Net Sales	100.0	100.0
	19.3	19.7	18.4	16.5			Gross Profit	22.0	20.4
	20.3	17.9	16.7	12.5			Operating Expenses	19.4	17.7
	−1.0	1.8	1.7	4.0			Operating Profit	2.5	2.6
	−.4	.4	.5	1.0			All Other Expenses (net)	1.0	.8
	−.6	1.4	1.2	3.0			Profit Before Taxes	1.6	1.9
							RATIOS		
	3.2	1.9	1.6	1.4			Current	1.7	1.7
	1.5	1.2	1.2	1.3				1.2	1.2
	.8	1.0	.9	1.0				1.0	1.0
	1.7	1.4	1.2	1.2			Quick	1.4	1.3
	1.0	1.0	.9	.9			(183)	1.0	.9
	.5	.7	.7	.5				.6	.6
	11 32.3	19 19.7	21 17.0	20 17.9			Sales/Receivables	16 23.0	16 22.5
	29 12.8	27 13.3	28 13.1	26 13.8				24 15.3	25 14.4
	39 9.3	39 9.3	37 10.0	39 9.3				35 10.4	35 10.5
	4 98.3	1 426.5	4 84.9	4 92.0			Cost of Sales/Inventory	3 125.7	1 264.5
	7 50.9	5 72.7	7 50.1	9 39.9				7 52.6	5 70.3
	22 16.4	12 31.2	16 23.5	35 10.5				19 19.5	12 30.0
	8 43.7	13 29.0	19 19.6	13 28.5			Cost of Sales/Payables	11 32.9	14 25.8
	22 16.5	23 16.0	26 14.2	22 16.6				20 18.0	21 17.7
	46 8.0	34 10.6	38 9.6	30 12.1				33 11.0	31 11.6
	13.9	20.2	19.2	22.4			Sales/Working Capital	18.5	22.7
	36.4	51.5	48.5	40.6				59.9	68.5
	−26.4	−343.5	−92.2	NM				−163.2	−301.4
	(19) 4.6	(86) 7.6	(94) 11.6	(27) 5.1			EBIT/Interest	(163) 7.1	(187) 8.6
	1.2	3.8	3.4	3.1				2.3	2.8
	−4.8	1.5	.8	1.5				1.1	1.2
		(28) 4.1	(41) 4.5	(13) 10.1			Net Profit + Depr., Dep., Amort./Cur. Mat. L /T/D	(75) 4.3	(72) 4.6
		2.0	2.4	3.1				2.0	2.9
		.9	.6	1.1				.8	.6
	.1	.3	.4	.4			Fixed/Worth	.3	.3
	.5	.8	.8	1.0				.8	.8
	4.2	1.7	1.6	1.6				1.7	1.7
	.7	1.2	1.1	1.2			Debt/Worth	.9	1.1
	1.9	2.8	2.2	2.5				2.1	2.4
	15.7	6.7	4.7	4.5				6.8	5.8
	(19) 24.7	(86) 60.0	(99) 33.0	(28) 31.9			% Profit Before Taxes/Tangible Net Worth	(171) 31.8	(196) 44.2
	6.8	26.9	15.1	19.8				11.3	19.6
	−12.8	6.2	.9	5.2				1.3	2.5
	17.2	15.3	11.8	9.0			% Profit Before Taxes/Total Assets	11.0	11.9
	5.5	6.1	4.0	6.3				3.4	5.3
	−5.6	1.7	.1	1.6				.2	.6
	246.6	95.3	45.9	64.3			Sales/Net Fixed Assets	67.9	80.5
	18.9	35.1	25.8	14.7				28.5	26.6
	6.7	12.7	9.8	7.1				9.2	10.6
	8.8	7.8	6.9	5.8			Sales/Total Assets	7.8	7.7
	5.5	5.8	5.6	3.8				5.3	5.4
	3.3	3.9	3.3	2.5				3.1	3.3
	(18) .3	(83) .3	(98) .4	.4			% Depr., Dep., Amort./Sales	(163) .5	(196) .3
	1.4	.6	.9	.8				1.0	.8
	2.2	1.4	1.7	2.3				2.1	1.5
		(48) 1.0	(54) .7				% Officers', Directors', Owners' Comp/Sales	(85) 1.2	(103) 1.2
		1.9	1.7					1.9	2.1
		3.4	3.3					4.1	3.7
	44078M	663522M	2300899M	2097137M	501100M	2539503M	Net Sales ($)	4082980M	4116402M
	7034M	106006M	436561M	520863M	66200M	674349M	Total Assets ($)	1296617M	1145686M

M = $ thousand   MM = $ million
See Pages 1 through 15 for Explanation of Ratios and Data

Comparative Historical Data | Current Data Sorted By Sales

4	7	17	# Postretirement Benefits	2	1	2	6	6

Type of Statement

Hist 1	Hist 2	Hist 3	Type of Statement	0-1MM	1-3MM	3-5MM	5-10MM	10-25MM	25MM & OVER
33	30	33	Unqualified	2	4	1	2	7	17
71	60	72	Reviewed		6	5	14	23	24
90	85	93	Compiled	6	12	16	22	33	4
8	11	2	Tax Returns				1	1	
39	67	53	Other	2	8	5	4	19	15

Historical periods: 4/1/92-3/31/93 ALL (241) · 4/1/93-3/31/94 ALL (253) · 4/1/94-3/31/95 ALL (253)

Current periods: 110 (4/1-9/30/94) · 143 (10/1/94-3/31/95)

NUMBER OF STATEMENTS — 0-1MM: 10 · 1-3MM: 30 · 3-5MM: 27 · 5-10MM: 43 · 10-25MM: 83 · 25MM & OVER: 60

Hist (4)	Hist (7)	Hist (17)		0-1MM	1-3MM	3-5MM	5-10MM	10-25MM	25MM & OVER
%	%	%	**ASSETS**	%	%	%	%	%	%
8.6	7.5	8.3	Cash & Equivalents	6.2	9.9	9.0	12.3	6.6	7.1
39.9	40.2	40.6	Trade Receivables - (net)	19.8	33.6	39.9	44.2	43.1	42.0
11.6	11.9	12.0	Inventory	14.7	15.0	8.3	9.3	11.7	14.0
2.1	2.7	2.3	All Other Current	.8	.7	4.1	1.7	2.9	2.2
62.2	62.4	63.3	Total Current	41.6	59.1	61.2	67.4	64.4	65.3
25.0	25.3	25.7	Fixed Assets (net)	50.6	32.3	30.1	20.8	25.1	20.5
1.2	1.6	1.9	Intangibles (net)	.1	.6	1.0	2.3	.7	4.5
11.7	10.7	9.2	All Other Non-Current	7.7	8.0	7.7	9.4	9.7	9.7
100.0	100.0	100.0	Total	100.0	100.0	100.0	100.0	100.0	100.0
			LIABILITIES						
9.5	8.9	9.6	Notes Payable-Short Term	12.4	9.3	7.6	9.0	10.0	9.9
2.8	3.3	3.3	Cur. Mat.-L /T/D	2.2	4.3	6.5	2.8	2.6	2.8
30.0	31.9	30.9	Trade Payables	18.9	23.0	29.8	34.2	34.1	30.3
.4	1.3	.4	Income Taxes Payable	.2	.7	.1	.8	.3	.2
7.6	8.2	7.8	All Other Current	9.8	6.1	9.1	7.6	6.3	9.8
50.3	53.6	51.8	Total Current	43.5	43.4	53.2	54.4	53.3	53.0
11.5	11.9	11.2	Long Term Debt	19.1	17.0	15.1	9.3	9.6	8.6
.5	.3	.4	Deferred Taxes	.2	.4	.5	.2	.5	.3
3.2	2.4	3.6	All Other-Non-Current	.1	2.7	3.1	6.8	2.6	4.2
34.6	31.8	33.0	Net Worth	37.1	36.5	28.2	29.3	34.1	33.9
100.0	100.0	100.0	Total Liabilities & Net Worth	100.0	100.0	100.0	100.0	100.0	100.0
			INCOME DATA						
100.0	100.0	100.0	Net Sales	100.0	100.0	100.0	100.0	100.0	100.0
21.7	19.4	19.2	Gross Profit	31.2	25.2	21.4	17.3	17.3	17.1
18.8	17.5	16.9	Operating Expenses	35.1	22.5	18.8	15.3	15.4	13.2
2.9	1.9	2.3	Operating Profit	-3.8	2.7	2.6	2.0	1.8	3.9
.3	.5	1.0	All Other Expenses (net)	.6	.9	1.0	.0	.4	2.8
2.6	1.5	1.3	Profit Before Taxes	-4.4	1.8	1.7	2.0	1.4	1.1
			RATIOS						
1.7	1.6	1.7	Current	1.7	3.3	1.9	1.6	1.7	1.5
1.2	1.2	1.2		.8	1.3	1.3	1.2	1.2	1.3
1.0	.9	.9		.6	.9	.8	1.0	.9	1.1
1.3	1.2	1.3	Quick	1.1	2.2	1.4	1.4	1.3	1.2
1.0 (252)	.9	.9		.5	.9	.8	1.0	.9	1.0
.7	.6	.7		.2	.5	.6	.8	.7	.7
19 19.2	19 19.7	20 18.6	Sales/Receivables	15 24.8	17 21.5	18 20.4	22 16.8	20 18.5	20 18.6
28 13.2	26 13.9	28 13.1		41 8.9	35 10.5	30 12.3	29 12.6	27 13.5	27 13.5
35 10.3	36 10.2	38 9.7		53 6.9	68 5.4	51 7.1	39 9.4	35 10.5	33 10.9
3 141.9	3 109.0	3 118.7	Cost of Sales/Inventory	8 44.6	0 UND	2 193.4	2 171.3	3 106.4	3 124.8
6 58.1	7 53.9	7 53.7		24 15.2	8 44.8	5 72.1	6 63.8	7 55.6	7 55.9
17 22.1	15 24.5	16 23.5		83 4.4	45 8.2	16 23.4	12 30.5	12 29.7	17 21.2
15 25.1	16 23.1	15 23.7	Cost of Sales/Payables	22 16.3	6 60.0	20 18.3	14 25.3	18 20.0	14 26.0
23 15.8	24 14.9	24 15.3		40 9.2	18 20.3	29 12.4	23 15.7	25 14.7	22 16.6
34 10.6	37 10.0	36 10.1		51 7.2	62 5.9	43 8.4	35 10.5	39 9.4	28 12.9
20.7	23.9	18.9	Sales/Working Capital	10.9	9.0	15.0	19.6	19.2	26.0
52.9	69.6	47.8		-31.9	21.2	46.6	60.2	53.1	44.0
-257.6	-143.4	-114.9		-3.8	-52.4	-20.3	-300.4	-133.2	196.0
9.9	10.2	7.8	EBIT/Interest		6.2	6.5	9.2	12.8	5.2
(217) 3.4	(224) 4.7	(231) 3.2			(27) 1.6	(26) 4.2	(38) 4.8	(81) 3.9	(51) 3.0
1.4	1.6	1.1			.5	-1.6	1.9	1.3	1.2
5.7	5.1	4.6	Net Profit + Depr., Dep., Amort./Cur. Mat. L/T/D			2.4	6.6	3.5	6.2
(79) 2.1	(87) 2.5	(86) 2.4			(11) .7	(15) 3.1	(27) 1.8	(26) 3.3	
1.0	.8	.8				-.2	1.2	.5	1.6
.3	.3	.4	Fixed/Worth	.9	.4	.3	.3	.3	.3
.7	.9	.8		1.7	1.0	1.2	.6	.8	.7
1.5	1.9	1.7		5.8	2.8	2.8	1.5	1.6	1.1
1.1	1.0	1.1	Debt/Worth	.6	.7	.9	1.5	1.1	1.3
2.1	2.4	2.4		2.3	1.4	2.7	3.1	2.2	2.5
5.0	6.9	5.1		7.7	17.3	7.8	6.9	4.6	4.4
45.5	42.3	39.3	% Profit Before Taxes/Tangible Net Worth	25.1	49.6	44.7	65.2	39.1	32.8
(231) 20.8	(230) 18.5	(237) 19.1		2.5	(24) 9.2	(23) 20.3	(41) 30.8	(82) 17.8	(57) 17.6
4.2	6.0	3.4		-17.2	-2.0	-7.3	14.1	2.6	3.7
12.2	13.4	12.6	% Profit Before Taxes/Total Assets	6.6	18.7	13.1	15.6	14.3	9.6
5.1	5.4	5.0		1.6	5.0	7.1	5.8	4.3	3.9
1.0	1.7	.5		-4.7	-1.2	-8.4	3.3	.6	.8
62.2	65.6	73.6	Sales/Net Fixed Assets	7.6	38.4	97.8	111.7	57.9	80.8
27.0	27.5	28.1		2.3	15.9	17.3	35.1	28.5	35.5
10.1	12.0	9.6		.9	4.4	6.1	12.1	13.9	18.1
7.8	7.6	7.0	Sales/Total Assets	2.8	5.2	6.7	7.0	8.3	7.6
5.3	5.5	5.5		1.4	3.9	5.2	5.4	6.1	6.1
2.6	3.4	3.3		.5	2.1	1.8	3.6	3.9	4.1
.4	.4	.4	% Depr., Dep., Amort./Sales		.4	.6	.3	.4	.3
(218) .8	(228) .7	(233) .8			(27) 1.4	(24) 1.5	(41) .8	(76) .7	(57) .6
1.6	1.5	1.7			2.7	2.9	1.3	1.4	.9
1.1	1.1	.8	% Officers', Directors', Owners' Comp/Sales		2.6	1.6	.9	.7	.6
(114) 2.6	(122) 2.3	(118) 2.4			(12) 4.4	(13) 3.1	(21) 1.9	(45) 1.5	(24) 1.0
4.0	5.2	3.3			9.2	3.5	3.4	2.8	2.5
6702219M	6882231M	8146239M	Net Sales ($)	4942M	58966M	108539M	305452M	1366851M	6301489M
2011564M	1865267M	1811013M	Total Assets ($)	5869M	28931M	52258M	67277M	300063M	1356615M

M = $ thousand   MM = $ million
See Pages 1 through 15 for Explanation of Ratios and Data

Current Data Sorted By Assets   Comparative Historical Data

# Postretirement Benefits	2	7	19	4	2	3			
Type of Statement									
Unqualified	4	12	36	55	17	8		120	115
Reviewed	1	20	54	8	1			77	91
Compiled	15	38	31	2		1		95	85
Tax Returns	7	3			1			3	3
Other	5	26	35	17	5	5		64	63

	0-500M	500M-2MM	2-10MM	10-50MM	50-100MM	100-250MM		4/1/90-3/31/91 ALL	4/1/91-3/31/92 ALL
	180 (4/1-9/30/94)			227 (10/1/94-3/31/95)					
NUMBER OF STATEMENTS	32	99	156	82	24	14		359	357
ASSETS	%	%	%	%	%	%		%	%
Cash & Equivalents	8.7	6.3	4.8	4.0	8.5	4.9		5.0	5.1
Trade Receivables - (net)	24.5	29.7	33.0	31.8	25.5	23.8		32.2	30.9
Inventory	36.2	33.7	33.4	31.3	28.0	34.5		33.9	34.0
All Other Current	.8	1.7	1.7	1.2	3.1	1.7		1.8	1.4
Total Current	70.2	71.5	72.9	68.3	65.0	64.8		72.8	71.4
Fixed Assets (net)	20.6	19.4	19.1	21.8	22.3	24.0		20.3	20.8
Intangibles (net)	2.4	2.2	1.7	2.4	3.2	1.4		1.2	1.4
All Other Non-Current	6.8	6.9	6.3	7.5	9.5	9.8		5.7	6.4
Total	100.0	100.0	100.0	100.0	100.0	100.0		100.0	100.0
LIABILITIES									
Notes Payable-Short Term	13.0	9.9	17.6	13.7	10.1	8.4		16.1	13.8
Cur. Mat. -L/T/D	2.7	4.2	2.7	2.8	2.5	4.1		3.1	3.5
Trade Payables	24.6	25.1	24.5	22.1	24.6	28.5		24.4	23.8
Income Taxes Payable	.9	.1	.3	.2	.3	.1		.4	.4
All Other Current	12.5	6.0	7.6	8.5	9.0	12.5		7.5	7.9
Total Current	53.8	45.4	52.7	47.4	46.5	53.6		51.6	49.5
Long Term Debt	19.2	17.0	12.3	13.1	17.1	17.7		15.4	14.8
Deferred Taxes	.0	.3	.2	.7	.8	.4		.4	.4
All Other-Non-Current	5.9	3.1	2.7	3.4	3.4	5.6		2.2	2.6
Net Worth	21.1	34.3	32.1	35.5	32.2	22.7		30.4	32.7
Total Liabilities & Net Worth	100.0	100.0	100.0	100.0	100.0	100.0		100.0	100.0
INCOME DATA									
Net Sales	100.0	100.0	100.0	100.0	100.0	100.0		100.0	100.0
Gross Profit	30.8	18.7	17.4	16.8	13.0	12.9		17.1	17.8
Operating Expenses	27.9	16.7	16.0	14.8	10.6	10.1		15.4	16.2
Operating Profit	2.9	2.1	1.4	2.0	2.4	2.8		1.6	1.7
All Other Expenses (net)	1.1	.4	.4	.1	.4	.7		.6	.4
Profit Before Taxes	1.8	1.7	1.0	1.9	2.0	2.1		1.1	1.3

RATIOS

	0-500M	500M-2MM	2-10MM	10-50MM	50-100MM	100-250MM		4/1/90-3/31/91 ALL	4/1/91-3/31/92 ALL
Current	2.3 / 1.6 / 1.0	2.3 / 1.6 / 1.1	1.8 / 1.4 / 1.1	1.8 / 1.4 / 1.2	1.6 / 1.4 / 1.2	1.5 / 1.2 / 1.1		1.9 / 1.4 / 1.1	2.0 / 1.4 / 1.1
Quick	1.1 / .7 / .4	(98) 1.2 / .7 / .5	1.0 / .7 / .5	1.0 / .8 / .5	.8 / .6 / .4	.7 / .6 / .4		1.0 / .7 / .5	1.0 / .7 / .5
Sales/Receivables	8 48.0 / 18 19.8 / 29 12.5	12 31.4 / 21 17.8 / 28 13.0	16 22.7 / 24 15.0 / 35 10.4	13 28.5 / 25 14.4 / 33 11.2	9 41.5 / 18 19.9 / 24 14.9	10 36.6 / 13 28.6 / 22 16.7		14 26.9 / 20 17.9 / 32 11.5	13 27.6 / 23 16.1 / 32 11.5
Cost of Sales/Inventory	20 18.5 / 26 13.9 / 47 7.7	18 20.8 / 29 12.4 / 46 8.0	20 18.3 / 28 13.1 / 41 9.0	19 18.9 / 27 13.7 / 37 9.8	17 21.1 / 21 17.2 / 24 15.1	20 18.1 / 24 15.2 / 32 11.4		19 19.0 / 27 13.5 / 39 9.4	19 19.5 / 28 13.2 / 40 9.2
Cost of Sales/Payables	13 28.3 / 26 14.1 / 41 8.9	11 32.3 / 19 19.4 / 33 10.9	12 31.7 / 19 19.7 / 30 12.0	13 28.6 / 17 21.3 / 24 15.5	13 28.7 / 18 20.6 / 26 14.0	14 26.9 / 21 17.3 / 28 13.2		12 31.6 / 18 19.8 / 29 12.4	12 30.4 / 18 20.2 / 27 13.3
Sales/Working Capital	12.0 / 22.6 / 848.2	11.0 / 23.0 / 74.7	14.1 / 23.4 / 68.6	16.2 / 25.8 / 58.1	25.3 / 31.2 / 75.9	21.9 / 32.3 / 292.4		13.7 / 25.8 / 75.6	12.9 / 24.5 / 64.7
EBIT/Interest	(24) 3.4 / 2.2 / .9	(88) 5.5 / 2.6 / 1.7	(145) 5.1 / 2.3 / 1.4	(73) 6.2 / 3.5 / 1.5	(23) 10.9 / 3.9 / 2.0	11.8 / 3.8 / 1.4		(332) 3.7 / 2.2 / 1.3	(325) 4.4 / 2.3 / 1.3
Net Profit + Depr., Dep., Amort./Cur. Mat. L /T/D		(34) 3.9 / 1.6 / 1.2	(74) 4.2 / 2.2 / 1.1	(49) 5.1 / 2.2 / 1.0	(17) 10.1 / 5.5 / 2.1			(208) 6.0 / 2.4 / 1.2	(189) 5.5 / 2.5 / 1.0
Fixed/Worth	.3 / .8 / NM	.2 / .5 / 1.8	.2 / .6 / 1.3	.4 / .7 / 1.2	.3 / .8 / 1.5	.7 / 1.2 / 2.9		.3 / .7 / 1.3	.3 / .6 / 1.4
Debt/Worth	1.1 / 3.3 / NM	1.0 / 2.5 / 7.6	1.1 / 2.4 / 5.0	1.3 / 2.2 / 3.7	1.3 / 2.1 / 3.9	2.6 / 3.8 / 12.8		1.3 / 2.6 / 5.9	1.2 / 2.4 / 5.1
% Profit Before Taxes/Tangible Net Worth	(24) 63.6 / 13.5 / 1.2	(87) 36.2 / 15.6 / 5.6	(144) 29.0 / 13.7 / 5.2	(79) 31.2 / 18.3 / 4.5	(21) 33.3 / 21.6 / 11.8	60.8 / 22.3 / 8.4		(333) 29.7 / 14.4 / 5.4	(336) 26.7 / 13.5 / 4.7
% Profit Before Taxes/Total Assets	14.3 / 5.1 / .7	9.2 / 4.8 / 2.4	7.9 / 3.7 / 1.4	10.3 / 5.9 / 2.1	14.1 / 7.7 / 3.4	12.4 / 7.6 / 1.4		8.5 / 4.0 / 1.1	9.3 / 3.7 / 1.1
Sales/Net Fixed Assets	59.1 / 35.3 / 22.5	124.1 / 46.3 / 15.7	79.3 / 36.4 / 16.7	51.7 / 27.7 / 14.0	92.8 / 19.7 / 15.9	57.1 / 27.0 / 17.3		74.8 / 31.0 / 15.4	66.3 / 30.3 / 14.8
Sales/Total Assets	6.5 / 5.4 / 3.5	7.2 / 5.2 / 3.8	6.4 / 5.2 / 3.8	6.4 / 5.0 / 3.7	6.6 / 5.6 / 4.8	7.4 / 5.6 / 4.7		6.9 / 5.1 / 3.6	6.6 / 5.0 / 3.5
% Depr., Dep., Amort./Sales	(24) .6 / .8 / 1.4	(87) .3 / .6 / 1.1	(147) .3 / .6 / .9	(77) .4 / .7 / 1.1	(19) .5 / .7 / 1.1	(12) .3 / .5 / .9		(328) .4 / .7 / 1.1	(329) .4 / .6 / 1.1
% Officers', Directors', Owners' Comp/Sales	(15) 3.3 / 5.3 / 11.3	(44) 1.2 / 1.6 / 3.1	(59) .6 / 1.3 / 2.4	(15) .8 / 1.6 / 3.7				(122) .7 / 1.5 / 2.8	(124) 1.0 / 1.7 / 3.8
Net Sales ($)	43474M	672064M	3669739M	10871460M	10506172M	14874200M		29065602M	33171597M
Total Assets ($)	8326M	121401M	712694M	1870926M	1743637M	2561837M		5470558M	5880003M

M = $ thousand   MM = $ million
See Pages 1 through 15 for Explanation of Ratios and Data

Comparative Historical Data				Current Data Sorted By Sales					
9	22	37	# Postretirement Benefits	2	2	1	7	7	18
			Type of Statement						
116	135	132	Unqualified	1	5	3	7	14	102
87	101	84	Reviewed	1	1	7	18	28	29
90	88	87	Compiled	7	15	9	19	29	8
8	17	11	Tax Returns	3	5	1		1	1
81	78	93	Other	3	3	14	16	21	36
4/1/92-3/31/93 ALL	4/1/93-3/31/94 ALL	4/1/94-3/31/95 ALL		180 (4/1-9/30/94)			227 (10/1/94-3/31/95)		
				0-1MM	1-3MM	3-5MM	5-10MM	10-25MM	25MM & OVER
382	419	407	**NUMBER OF STATEMENTS**	15	29	34	60	93	176
%	%	%	**ASSETS**	%	%	%	%	%	%
4.9	6.0	5.5	Cash & Equivalents	9.1	11.5	5.4	4.7	5.4	4.6
32.7	32.8	30.6	Trade Receivables - (net)	23.7	22.0	27.6	31.1	32.9	31.7
33.6	32.5	33.0	Inventory	27.0	33.1	36.1	32.1	34.6	32.3
1.2	1.2	1.6	All Other Current	1.0	.7	1.2	1.0	1.7	2.0
72.4	72.4	70.7	Total Current	60.8	67.2	70.2	69.0	74.6	70.7
19.3	18.4	20.2	Fixed Assets (net)	30.3	22.9	18.5	22.7	16.7	20.3
2.1	2.0	2.1	Intangibles (net)	.7	3.0	4.1	2.5	2.3	1.4
6.2	7.2	7.0	All Other Non-Current	8.2	6.9	7.3	5.8	6.4	7.7
100.0	100.0	100.0	Total	100.0	100.0	100.0	100.0	100.0	100.0
			LIABILITIES						
15.2	14.6	13.8	Notes Payable-Short Term	8.3	12.5	9.5	13.5	14.2	15.3
3.0	3.6	3.1	Cur. Mat.-L/T/D	3.1	3.1	4.5	4.0	2.7	2.8
24.1	22.7	24.3	Trade Payables	15.5	23.3	26.5	23.1	27.7	23.5
.3	1.2	.3	Income Taxes Payable	1.6	.2	.2	.1	.2	.3
7.5	7.5	8.0	All Other Current	6.9	10.6	8.2	7.2	7.0	8.5
50.1	49.6	49.6	Total Current	35.3	49.7	48.8	48.0	51.8	50.3
13.6	12.6	14.6	Long Term Debt	21.2	23.2	17.1	17.3	11.0	13.2
.4	.4	.3	Deferred Taxes	.3	.0	.3	.4	.2	.5
3.8	3.4	3.3	All Other-Non-Current	5.7	6.6	3.5	2.3	1.8	3.7
32.2	33.9	32.1	Net Worth	37.6	20.5	30.3	32.1	35.2	32.3
100.0	100.0	100.0	Total Liabilities & Net Worth	100.0	100.0	100.0	100.0	100.0	100.0
			INCOME DATA						
100.0	100.0	100.0	Net Sales	100.0	100.0	100.0	100.0	100.0	100.0
18.7	18.8	18.2	Gross Profit	39.3	25.2	20.1	19.6	17.4	14.9
17.2	17.1	16.4	Operating Expenses	34.3	21.5	18.2	18.3	15.8	13.2
1.5	1.7	1.9	Operating Profit	5.0	3.7	1.8	1.3	1.5	1.7
.4	.3	.4	All Other Expenses (net)	.8	1.1	.6	.5	.3	.2
1.1	1.4	1.5	Profit Before Taxes	4.2	2.6	1.2	.8	1.3	1.5
			RATIOS						
1.9	2.0	1.9	Current	2.7	3.0	2.2	2.0	2.0	1.7
1.4	1.4	1.4		1.7	1.6	1.4	1.5	1.4	1.4
1.1	1.1	1.1		1.5	.8	.9	1.1	1.1	1.1
1.1	1.1	1.0	Quick	2.0	1.2	1.1	1.1	1.0	.9
(381) .7	.8	(406) .7		.9	.7	.6	.7	(92) .7	.7
.5	.5	.5		.4	.4	.4	.5	.5	.5
14 25.9	15 24.1	13 28.5	Sales/Receivables	0 UND	12 30.6	16 23.4	15 24.4	16 22.7	11 32.1
23 16.1	24 14.9	23 16.1		30 12.1	19 19.3	23 16.2	27 13.7	24 15.3	20 17.9
32 11.5	35 10.5	31 11.8		50 7.3	26 14.1	32 11.4	40 9.1	31 11.9	29 12.6
18 20.6	18 19.9	19 19.5	Cost of Sales/Inventory	9 38.7	20 18.3	23 15.9	22 16.9	20 18.5	18 20.3
27 13.6	28 13.2	27 13.5		27 13.5	30 12.3	40 9.2	33 10.9	28 13.1	24 15.3
43 8.5	44 8.3	41 9.0		73 5.0	45 8.1	58 6.3	47 7.8	39 9.4	31 11.6
12 31.0	11 32.7	12 30.0	Cost of Sales/Payables	0 UND	13 28.9	12 29.8	14 25.5	13 28.8	11 32.4
18 19.8	18 20.2	19 19.7		40 9.2	21 17.4	24 15.1	21 17.0	19 19.0	17 22.1
29 12.8	29 12.4	30 12.3		72 5.1	38 9.6	40 9.1	32 11.3	32 11.4	23 15.6
13.6	12.1	14.0	Sales/Working Capital	6.5	9.1	9.9	12.0	12.7	20.9
26.3	25.2	25.7		13.9	19.9	19.3	21.6	21.5	29.0
82.3	71.0	72.9		48.0	-30.7	-74.5	68.8	79.0	68.2
5.2	6.9	5.7	EBIT/Interest	6.3	3.5	6.4	3.8	6.1	6.5
(349) 2.5	(384) 2.7	(367) 2.6		(10) 2.4	(23) 2.0	(30) 2.7	(56) 2.0	(84) 3.1	(164) 3.2
1.4	1.2	1.5		1.4	.9	1.8	1.3	1.7	1.5
4.9	5.2	4.4	Net Profit + Depr., Dep., Amort./Cur. Mat. L/T/D				3.9	5.7	5.9
(172) 2.1	(186) 2.1	(187) 2.2					(28) 1.8	(42) 2.1	(101) 2.7
1.2	.8	1.1					1.4	1.1	1.2
.2	.2	.2	Fixed/Worth	.2	.3	.3	.2	.2	.3
.6	.5	.6		.8	.8	.7	.6	.5	.8
1.3	1.2	1.5		3.3	-4.9	2.4	1.6	1.0	1.2
1.3	1.1	1.2	Debt/Worth	.4	.9	1.4	1.2	1.0	1.3
2.4	2.3	2.5		1.9	3.8	2.6	2.6	2.1	2.4
5.1	4.7	5.0		6.2	-9.7	12.5	6.9	5.0	3.9
30.0	29.7	31.3	% Profit Before Taxes/Tangible Net Worth	76.2	74.8	36.8	28.4	29.2	31.3
(358) 15.1	(394) 16.1	(369) 15.8		(14) 37.9	(20) 11.5	(28) 17.2	(53) 11.2	(86) 15.8	(168) 17.0
4.7	4.2	5.6		3.4	2.9	5.4	3.8	5.6	7.4
8.1	9.5	9.6	% Profit Before Taxes/Total Assets	12.6	15.4	8.2	7.7	9.5	10.0
4.0	4.4	4.8		6.7	4.1	5.2	2.9	4.8	5.4
1.2	.8	1.9		1.9	.7	2.4	1.2	1.8	2.0
75.1	79.4	75.4	Sales/Net Fixed Assets	60.3	71.6	96.2	105.6	86.2	66.6
35.3	34.7	34.6		30.0	33.3	39.6	29.3	42.6	32.7
16.2	15.8	16.1		7.2	11.6	12.4	12.0	21.1	16.5
6.8	6.9	6.6	Sales/Total Assets	5.0	6.2	5.6	5.8	6.8	7.0
5.2	4.8	5.3		3.1	5.2	4.0	4.3	5.5	5.7
3.6	3.4	3.8		1.3	2.9	2.9	3.0	4.1	4.4
(346) .4	(378) .4	(366) .3	% Depr., Dep., Amort./Sales		(25) .4	(30) .4	(55) .4	(87) .4	(162) .3
.6	.6	.6			.6	.9	.6	.6	.6
1.1	1.1	1.1			1.3	1.6	1.1	1.0	.9
(142) .9	(146) .9	(136) .9	% Officers', Directors', Owners' Comp/Sales		(11) 1.5	(13) 1.2	(30) 1.2	(36) .8	(37) .5
2.0	1.7	1.7			3.4	1.6	2.0	1.5	1.2
3.9	3.4	3.4			7.1	5.1	3.2	2.4	2.4
33550925M	34777594M	40637109M	Net Sales ($)	10378M	52281M	138460M	435353M	1503395M	38497242M
6387529M	6075366M	7018821M	Total Assets ($)	5721M	15677M	38358M	124844M	335784M	6498437M

M = $ thousand   MM = $ million
See Pages 1 through 15 for Explanation of Ratios and Data

Current Data Sorted By Assets							Comparative Historical Data	
2	1	6	6		4	# Postretirement Benefits / Type of Statement		
1	22	47	25	1	3	Unqualified	90	87
9	36	27				Reviewed	67	63
5	16	14				Compiled	29	28
1	2		1			Tax Returns	1	3
3	10	16	12	1	1	Other	35	30
151 (4/1-9/30/94)			102 (10/1/94-3/31/95)				4/1/90-3/31/91	4/1/91-3/31/92
0-500M	500M-2MM	2-10MM	10-50MM	50-100MM	100-250MM		ALL	ALL
19	86	104	38	2	4	NUMBER OF STATEMENTS	222	211
%	%	%	%	%	%	ASSETS	%	%
10.8	12.3	7.0	6.0			Cash & Equivalents	10.0	10.0
22.1	21.8	18.9	17.1			Trade Receivables - (net)	21.6	20.7
23.8	27.6	31.5	30.3			Inventory	26.1	29.4
.5	3.7	6.3	5.6			All Other Current	3.7	2.6
57.2	65.4	63.7	59.0			Total Current	61.3	62.7
31.5	27.6	28.3	32.7			Fixed Assets (net)	30.3	30.5
1.2	.8	.7	1.4			Intangibles (net)	.7	.2
10.1	6.2	7.3	7.0			All Other Non-Current	7.7	6.5
100.0	100.0	100.0	100.0			Total	100.0	100.0
						LIABILITIES		
9.8	14.0	16.5	14.5			Notes Payable-Short Term	16.4	14.6
3.2	1.9	1.9	5.0			Cur. Mat. -L/T/D	2.7	2.1
14.6	16.2	15.9	11.4			Trade Payables	17.1	16.9
.1	.3	.3	.2			Income Taxes Payable	.3	.3
8.4	7.4	11.1	12.9			All Other Current	8.0	8.1
36.1	39.7	45.7	44.1			Total Current	44.5	41.9
15.6	8.0	9.3	14.2			Long Term Debt	10.9	10.6
.4	1.1	.7	1.9			Deferred Taxes	.9	1.0
6.0	.9	1.2	1.0			All Other-Non-Current	1.5	1.6
41.9	50.3	43.0	38.8			Net Worth	42.1	44.8
100.0	100.0	100.0	100.0			Total Liabilities & Net Worth	100.0	100.0
						INCOME DATA		
100.0	100.0	100.0	100.0			Net Sales	100.0	100.0
17.1	12.9	11.7	12.0			Gross Profit	10.5	12.1
16.4	11.7	9.9	9.9			Operating Expenses	9.4	10.6
.7	1.2	1.8	2.1			Operating Profit	1.1	1.5
−.3	.0	.3	.4			All Other Expenses (net)	.3	.4
1.0	1.2	1.6	1.7			Profit Before Taxes	.7	1.1
						RATIOS		
2.4	2.5	1.7	1.6			Current	2.1	2.2
1.6	1.6	1.3	1.3				1.3	1.4
1.3	1.2	1.1	1.1				1.1	1.1
1.3	1.5	1.0	.8			Quick	1.1	1.2
1.0	.8	.5	.4				.8 (210)	.7
.5	.5	.2	.2				.4	.4
4 100.7	5 70.4	6 59.9	6 57.4			Sales/Receivables	7 55.1	7 53.9
10 36.0	15 25.0	14 25.5	13 27.7				14 26.7	13 27.8
26 13.8	31 11.9	30 12.1	38 9.5				25 14.7	28 13.2
4 83.0	7 49.9	15 23.8	23 15.6			Cost of Sales/Inventory	8 45.5	11 33.0
16 22.9	23 16.0	35 10.3	33 11.0				20 18.2	27 13.7
46 7.9	50 7.3	69 5.3	70 5.2				49 7.5	56 6.5
2 236.5	3 116.2	4 86.0	5 74.9			Cost of Sales/Payables	4 98.0	5 77.6
6 59.1	10 38.1	12 31.6	14 26.8				11 33.3	12 29.9
21 17.7	27 13.4	34 10.7	21 17.6				25 14.5	24 15.1
13.6	8.7	13.0	12.5			Sales/Working Capital	14.9	10.6
20.7	21.3	24.8	28.6				31.8	26.2
95.5	73.0	51.9	95.4				144.7	71.7
(17) 5.0	(83) 5.0	(99) 8.5	4.3			EBIT/Interest	(207) 3.8	(196) 3.6
1.9	2.4	2.7	2.6				1.8	1.9
−1.9	1.4	1.1	1.3				.9	1.1
	(28) 6.1	(49) 5.9	(24) 12.3			Net Profit + Depr., Dep., Amort./Cur. Mat. L /T/D	(114) 5.0	(106) 6.7
	2.7	3.0	2.8				2.2	2.9
	1.6	1.1	1.5				.9	1.4
.3	.3	.3	.7			Fixed/Worth	.4	.4
.8	.6	.7	.9				.7	.7
1.7	.9	1.2	1.3				1.4	1.2
.6	.6	.9	1.0			Debt/Worth	.7	.7
1.5	1.0	1.4	1.7				1.7	1.3
3.9	1.9	2.5	3.3				3.6	2.7
43.6	16.9	18.5	20.4			% Profit Before Taxes/Tangible Net Worth	(218) 15.6	(207) 14.2
9.8	9.1	9.8	12.1				8.4	6.3
−18.2	2.9	1.4	4.7				−.8	1.1
12.9	6.8	8.3	7.9			% Profit Before Taxes/Total Assets	6.4	7.4
6.5	4.0	3.9	3.9				3.0	3.1
−8.1	1.6	.4	1.3				−.5	.4
64.3	31.3	26.2	13.7			Sales/Net Fixed Assets	30.2	27.9
23.9	17.9	13.9	10.3				14.9	12.6
6.9	10.9	8.0	7.5				8.5	8.8
9.6	5.7	5.2	4.3			Sales/Total Assets	6.2	5.6
5.0	4.4	3.3	2.9				4.1	3.9
3.2	2.7	2.3	2.4				2.9	2.6
(17) .3	(79) .6	(102) .7	(35) .9			% Depr., Dep., Amort./Sales	(208) .6	(199) .7
1.9	1.1	1.1	1.2				1.1	1.2
2.2	1.6	1.5	1.9				1.7	1.7
(10) 1.3	(28) .4	(24) .4				% Officers', Directors', Owners' Comp/Sales	(58) .7	(71) .6
2.7	1.2	.8					1.5	1.4
3.3	2.6	1.6					2.8	2.9
45572M	484018M	1708996M	3077021M	1155219M	2314588M	Net Sales ($)	11748047M	7651047M
6686M	100583M	454497M	807652M	122784M	659046M	Total Assets ($)	2346651M	1925678M

M = $ thousand   MM = $ million
See Pages 1 through 15 for Explanation of Ratios and Data

Comparative Historical Data				Current Data Sorted By Sales					
6	19	19	# Postretirement Benefits	1	2		6		10
			Type of Statement						
95	98	99	Unqualified		5	6	23	28	37
69	74	72	Reviewed	3	17	10	21	18	3
28	38	35	Compiled		13	5	9	7	1
	2	4	Tax Returns	1		1	1	1	
21	29	43	Other	1	2	5	9	12	14
4/1/92-3/31/93 ALL	4/1/93-3/31/94 ALL	4/1/94-3/31/95 ALL		0-1MM	151 (4/1-9/30/94) 1-3MM	3-5MM	102 (10/1/94-3/31/95) 5-10MM	10-25MM	25MM & OVER
213	241	253	**NUMBER OF STATEMENTS**	5	37	27	63	66	55
%	%	%	**ASSETS**	%	%	%	%	%	%
10.6	9.0	8.9	Cash & Equivalents		10.5	15.3	8.6	6.3	8.4
20.6	20.4	20.3	Trade Receivables - (net)		21.7	19.5	17.3	20.9	22.2
28.2	33.8	29.2	Inventory		30.6	27.8	27.8	31.5	27.7
2.8	2.8	4.9	All Other Current		3.2	4.4	4.5	6.3	5.0
62.3	65.9	63.2	Total Current		65.9	67.0	58.2	64.9	63.3
30.3	27.0	28.6	Fixed Assets (net)		24.9	22.6	34.5	27.8	28.0
.6	1.0	.9	Intangibles (net)		.8	2.5	.7	.5	.9
6.8	6.1	7.3	All Other Non-Current		8.4	8.0	6.6	6.7	7.8
100.0	100.0	100.0	Total		100.0	100.0	100.0	100.0	100.0
			LIABILITIES						
14.3	19.2	14.8	Notes Payable-Short Term		20.5	9.1	11.6	18.3	13.6
2.3	2.0	2.5	Cur. Mat.-L /T/D		1.7	1.8	2.1	2.7	3.2
17.5	15.3	15.4	Trade Payables		10.3	22.7	16.4	13.8	17.0
.3	1.3	.3	Income Taxes Payable		.2	.3	.2	.4	.3
8.7	8.2	10.0	All Other Current		5.2	8.1	11.2	10.4	12.2
43.2	46.0	42.9	Total Current		37.9	41.9	41.4	45.5	46.2
9.5	9.1	10.1	Long Term Debt		11.7	10.1	8.1	10.5	10.8
.9	.9	1.0	Deferred Taxes		.2	.6	1.2	1.1	1.5
1.6	1.4	1.5	All Other-Non-Current		1.6	.2	1.7	.8	1.6
44.8	42.6	44.5	Net Worth		48.6	47.1	47.7	42.1	39.9
100.0	100.0	100.0	Total Liabilities & Net Worth		100.0	100.0	100.0	100.0	100.0
			INCOME DATA						
100.0	100.0	100.0	Net Sales		100.0	100.0	100.0	100.0	100.0
12.3	13.2	12.8	Gross Profit		18.1	12.5	12.6	11.0	9.4
11.7	11.5	11.2	Operating Expenses		16.0	10.0	11.8	9.7	8.1
.6	1.8	1.6	Operating Profit		2.0	2.5	.9	1.3	1.3
.1	.3	.1	All Other Expenses (net)		.3	.0	-.2	.4	.2
.5	1.5	1.4	Profit Before Taxes		1.7	2.4	1.1	1.0	1.1
			RATIOS						
2.0	2.0	1.9			3.0	3.8	1.9	1.8	1.6
1.4	1.3	1.4	Current		1.6	1.4	1.4	1.3	1.4
1.1	1.1	1.1			1.2	1.1	1.1	1.1	1.2
1.1	1.0	1.2			1.3	2.5	1.2	1.0	1.1
.7	.6	.6	Quick		.8	.8	.6	.5	.7
.4	.4	.3			.4	.4	.2	.2	.3
7 53.0	7 50.0	6 60.0		8 44.6	3 141.4	5 76.2	7 52.5		6 58.1
14 26.0	15 23.6	14 25.4	Sales/Receivables	26 14.2	19 18.9	10 35.4	16 23.5		14 27.0
28 12.9	28 13.1	31 11.7		54 6.7	32 11.3	20 18.7	32 11.4		28 13.1
11 32.0	14 26.8	12 29.7		16 23.3	8 46.3	10 35.3	18 20.3		8 47.3
27 13.3	34 10.7	29 12.4	Cost of Sales/Inventory	29 12.4	28 13.0	26 14.2	35 10.4		27 13.4
51 7.2	66 5.5	60 6.1		140 2.6	54 6.7	63 5.8	60 6.1		47 7.7
4 92.8	3 108.3	4 102.6		3 113.1	4 86.1	2 181.3	4 90.0		5 78.8
12 30.1	12 31.6	11 32.3	Cost of Sales/Payables	16 23.0	13 29.2	11 32.5	8 47.5		11 32.2
31 11.6	26 14.2	27 13.4		35 10.3	45 8.1	32 11.3	21 17.4		20 17.9
11.5	11.5	11.1			4.0	10.7	16.3	11.2	16.7
25.1	24.9	23.1	Sales/Working Capital		10.1	16.5	24.1	28.5	31.3
80.0	67.8	64.2			30.3	95.3	77.1	65.1	59.9
3.9	5.5	5.2		4.9	6.0	6.6	4.4		4.6
(196) 1.9	(227) 2.2	(243) 2.4	EBIT/Interest	(33) 1.8	(26) 3.1	(61) 2.6	1.7	(52) 2.7
1.1	1.3	1.2		-.7	2.0	1.6	.7		1.6
5.9	6.7	6.1				7.9	4.3		14.7
(88) 2.8	(92) 3.4	(110) 2.8	Net Profit + Depr., Dep., Amort./Cur. Mat. L/T/D			(30) 3.3	(34) 2.1	(33) 3.7
1.0	1.3	1.4				1.7	.9		1.5
.4	.4	.4			.2	.2	.4	.3	.4
.7	.7	.7	Fixed/Worth		.4	.5	.7	.7	.8
1.2	1.1	1.1			1.1	.9	1.2	1.1	1.1
.8	.8	.7			.6	.5	.7	.8	1.0
1.2	1.6	1.3	Debt/Worth		1.2	1.5	1.1	1.5	1.8
2.7	3.0	2.5			2.4	2.7	1.8	3.0	3.0
16.0	20.0	18.8			18.7	33.2	17.4	14.3	20.1
(212) 7.9	(238) 10.1	9.6	% Profit Before Taxes/Tangible Net Worth		9.1	16.6	9.0	6.0	11.2
1.0	3.5	2.1			-6.3	7.9	3.4	-1.6	6.6
5.8	7.7	7.4			7.4	10.0	6.9	6.9	6.9
2.9	3.6	3.9	% Profit Before Taxes/Total Assets		4.0	5.8	4.3	1.9	4.0
.5	1.0	.7			-3.3	2.7	1.7	-.4	1.9
27.1	35.0	28.4			26.5	64.3	24.5	27.4	29.1
14.4	14.6	13.7	Sales/Net Fixed Assets		12.5	23.1	14.3	14.0	12.6
7.5	8.8	8.5			6.6	12.5	7.8	8.2	10.0
5.3	5.3	5.4			3.8	5.3	6.0	5.3	7.2
3.8	3.6	3.7	Sales/Total Assets		2.5	4.2	4.1	3.6	4.3
2.8	2.4	2.5			1.3	2.5	2.7	2.4	2.7
.6	.6	.7		.6	.7	.9	.8		.5
(208) 1.2	(230) 1.2	(239) 1.1	% Depr., Dep., Amort./Sales	(33) 1.4	(25) 1.0	(60) 1.2	(65) 1.1	(51) .9
1.8	1.7	1.6		2.4	1.4	1.8	1.5		1.3
.5	.7	.5		1.2	.5	.5	.3		.1
(63) 1.1	(81) 1.6	(68) 1.2	% Officers', Directors', Owners' Comp/Sales	(12) 2.1	(13) 1.5	(17) .8	(14) .7	(10) .8
2.4	2.8	2.5		3.3	2.8	2.0	1.5		1.9
5814189M	6363053M	8785414M	Net Sales ($)	3074M	72165M	106920M	443769M	1082449M	7077037M
1620726M	1388925M	2151248M	Total Assets ($)	1495M	48314M	34408M	128461M	352120M	1586450M

M = $ thousand   MM = $ million
See Pages 1 through 15 for Explanation of Ratios and Data

Current Data Sorted By Assets   Comparative Historical Data

# Postretirement Benefits / Type of Statement	0-500M	500M-2MM	2-10MM	10-50MM	50-100MM	100-250MM	4/1/90-3/31/91 ALL	4/1/91-3/31/92 ALL
# Postretirement Benefits		4	1	2		1		
Unqualified		4	17	20	3	1	56	54
Reviewed		25	29	2			66	74
Compiled	14	44	14			1	65	67
Tax Returns	1	2						3
Other	3	8	20		9		44	34

77 (4/1-9/30/94)   140 (10/1/94-3/31/95)

	0-500M	500M-2MM	2-10MM	10-50MM	50-100MM	100-250MM	ITEM	4/1/90-3/31/91 ALL	4/1/91-3/31/92 ALL
NUMBER OF STATEMENTS	18	83	80	32	3	1	NUMBER OF STATEMENTS	231	232
	%	%	%	%	%	%	**ASSETS**	%	%
	13.7	7.3	5.5	5.4			Cash & Equivalents	5.0	6.2
	32.6	40.4	40.8	35.9			Trade Receivables - (net)	40.7	40.6
	17.0	24.1	26.7	30.3			Inventory	24.8	25.7
	1.2	1.5	1.1	2.6			All Other Current	1.5	1.0
	64.5	73.4	74.0	74.1			Total Current	72.1	73.5
	30.9	20.0	20.4	16.9			Fixed Assets (net)	20.2	18.7
	1.7	.9	.9	1.1			Intangibles (net)	.5	1.1
	2.9	5.7	4.7	7.9			All Other Non-Current	7.3	6.6
	100.0	100.0	100.0	100.0			Total	100.0	100.0
							LIABILITIES		
	9.2	16.2	19.6	26.6			Notes Payable-Short Term	17.2	16.8
	6.1	3.1	2.0	.9			Cur. Mat. -L/T/D	3.4	2.1
	17.9	23.3	21.0	19.9			Trade Payables	23.7	23.4
	.1	.3	.3	.2			Income Taxes Payable	.4	.3
	4.7	4.4	6.5	6.1			All Other Current	7.3	5.3
	38.0	47.2	49.5	53.7			Total Current	51.9	48.0
	16.8	9.8	10.7	8.8			Long Term Debt	11.7	11.8
	.1	.2	.2	.3			Deferred Taxes	.5	.4
	3.2	3.1	3.5	2.0			All Other-Non-Current	2.8	2.7
	41.9	39.7	36.2	35.1			Net Worth	33.1	37.1
	100.0	100.0	100.0	100.0			Total Liabilities & Net Worth	100.0	100.0
							INCOME DATA		
	100.0	100.0	100.0	100.0			Net Sales	100.0	100.0
	23.8	14.7	12.0	10.1			Gross Profit	13.1	12.9
	21.8	13.9	10.4	9.1			Operating Expenses	11.8	11.4
	2.0	.8	1.6	1.0			Operating Profit	1.3	1.4
	.5	.4	.5	.0			All Other Expenses (net)	.4	.5
	1.6	.5	1.1	.9			Profit Before Taxes	.8	1.0
							RATIOS		
	3.1	2.0	2.2	1.8			Current	2.0	2.2
	1.7	1.6	1.4	1.4				1.4	1.5
	1.1	1.2	1.1	1.1				1.1	1.2
	2.6	1.4	1.3	1.0			Quick	1.3	1.5
	1.0	1.0	.9	.7	(230)			.9	.9
	.5	.7	.7	.6				.6	.7
	7 50.1	15 24.4	16 23.0	18 20.8			Sales/Receivables	15 25.1	14 27.0
	11 31.8	19 19.3	21 17.4	20 18.5				21 17.7	19 19.3
	18 20.1	24 14.9	31 11.8	24 15.5				28 13.2	26 14.1
	0 UND	8 45.9	9 39.1	12 30.7			Cost of Sales/Inventory	8 45.1	8 45.2
	6 61.6	14 25.9	17 22.1	18 19.9				14 25.3	14 26.0
	21 17.4	23 15.8	23 15.7	27 13.7				23 16.0	24 15.5
	0 UND	6 60.0	8 48.4	9 42.1			Cost of Sales/Payables	7 49.7	7 49.0
	11 34.1	12 31.6	13 28.4	13 28.5				13 28.5	12 30.0
	13 27.1	21 17.5	20 18.3	17 21.9				20 18.6	18 20.3
	10.3	16.9	13.0	15.1			Sales/Working Capital	18.3	16.3
	36.0	32.5	35.6	35.8				39.1	31.1
	NM	68.7	99.6	97.4				104.1	70.9
	7.3	5.0	4.8	11.7			EBIT/Interest	4.5	5.7
(15) 2.4		(81) 2.5	(72) 2.0	(31) 3.2				(212) 2.2	(215) 2.1
	-1.1	1.1	1.1	1.7				1.1	1.3
		3.9	4.2				Net Profit + Depr., Dep., Amort./Cur. Mat. L /T/D	4.6	6.2
	(31) 1.6		(28) 2.2					(113) 2.3	(99) 2.1
		.5	1.5					.9	.9
	.3	.2	.1	.2			Fixed/Worth	.2	.2
	.5	.5	.5	.5				.6	.4
	2.4	1.1	1.2	1.1				1.1	1.0
	.4	.8	1.0	1.0			Debt/Worth	1.2	.9
	1.3	1.7	2.7	2.1				2.2	1.9
	6.2	4.5	5.1	4.1				4.5	4.2
	55.3	24.1	31.4	33.3			% Profit Before Taxes/Tangible Net Worth	32.6	27.8
(15) 15.9		(80) 7.8	(79) 15.2	(31) 17.5				(219) 16.3	(224) 12.6
	-3.6	1.4	2.7	6.9				3.2	2.6
	18.4	6.9	12.2	12.4			% Profit Before Taxes/Total Assets	11.2	8.7
	9.9	3.1	3.6	5.7				4.5	3.9
	-6.8	.6	.8	1.0				1.8	2.6
	137.2	152.7	132.4	255.6			Sales/Net Fixed Assets	127.4	150.8
	22.7	46.7	46.1	42.9				44.6	52.4
	7.5	20.0	19.7	18.5				21.1	22.3
	9.2	9.5	9.0	9.0			Sales/Total Assets	9.6	9.9
	6.7	7.0	6.4	6.1				6.7	6.8
	3.3	4.9	4.6	4.1				4.8	5.0
	.5	.2	.2	.1			% Depr., Dep., Amort./Sales	.3	.2
(14) 1.0		(75) .5	(73) .5	(29) .4				(209) .5	(212) .5
	2.4	1.2	.8	.9				.9	.9
	1.0	.9	.5				% Officers', Directors', Owners' Comp/Sales	.7	.7
(12) 2.4		(52) 1.5	(36) 1.3					(107) 1.5	(111) 1.5
	4.5	3.1	1.8					2.7	2.7
Net Sales ($)	48121M	753262M	2292911M	4485714M	1406829M	1523513M	Net Sales ($)	7976251M	10813926M
Total Assets ($)	4801M	93663M	344259M	675137M	207396M	247948M	Total Assets ($)	1187175M	1649410M

M = $ thousand   MM = $ million
See Pages 1 through 15 for Explanation of Ratios and Data

Comparative Historical Data | **Current Data Sorted By Sales**

Current data periods: **77 (4/1-9/30/94)** covers 0-1MM & 1-3MM; **140 (10/1/94-3/31/95)** covers 3-5MM through 25MM & Over.

	4/1/92-3/31/93 ALL	4/1/93-3/31/94 ALL	4/1/94-3/31/95 ALL	0-1MM	1-3MM	3-5MM	5-10MM	10-25MM	25MM & OVER
# Postretirement Benefits	7	4	8			1	3	1	3
Type of Statement									
Unqualified	42	52	45			1	2	3	39
Reviewed	68	66	56		1	6	9	24	16
Compiled	61	52	73	7	7	17	17	19	6
Tax Returns	6	6	3		1		2		
Other	35	31	40	1	1	4	4	13	17
NUMBER OF STATEMENTS	212	207	217	8	10	28	34	59	78
ASSETS	%	%	%	%	%	%	%	%	%
Cash & Equivalents	5.4	5.3	6.9		6.2	6.9	7.1	7.1	5.0
Trade Receivables - (net)	40.6	40.3	38.9		27.0	30.5	39.4	44.6	41.1
Inventory	25.5	26.2	25.4		27.6	23.5	21.4	26.5	28.3
All Other Current	1.3	1.2	1.4		.4	2.8	1.5	.8	1.6
Total Current	72.8	73.0	72.7		61.2	63.8	69.3	79.0	76.0
Fixed Assets (net)	19.4	18.5	20.8		32.4	27.5	23.2	15.9	17.1
Intangibles (net)	1.6	1.9	1.0		2.6	1.2	1.1	.7	1.1
All Other Non-Current	6.2	6.6	5.5		3.8	7.5	6.4	4.4	5.7
Total	100.0	100.0	100.0		100.0	100.0	100.0	100.0	100.0
LIABILITIES									
Notes Payable-Short Term	18.2	18.4	18.1		12.9	14.0	20.2	14.7	23.3
Cur. Mat.-L./T/D	2.7	2.3	2.6		2.2	2.4	3.7	2.5	1.4
Trade Payables	22.0	21.6	21.8		17.9	15.4	21.9	26.0	23.2
Income Taxes Payable	.4	1.2	.3		.0	.1	.2	.2	.4
All Other Current	5.3	5.6	5.5		4.1	4.8	3.1	5.4	7.2
Total Current	48.7	49.1	48.3		37.2	36.7	49.1	48.8	55.6
Long Term Debt	10.5	10.4	10.6		19.3	15.1	13.1	7.4	8.3
Deferred Taxes	.4	.2	.2		.2	.2	.2	.1	.3
All Other-Non-Current	2.6	4.8	3.1		1.8	3.5	5.1	3.3	2.3
Net Worth	37.9	35.5	37.8		41.6	44.6	32.5	40.4	33.4
Total Liabilities & Net Worth	100.0	100.0	100.0		100.0	100.0	100.0	100.0	100.0
INCOME DATA									
Net Sales	100.0	100.0	100.0		100.0	100.0	100.0	100.0	100.0
Gross Profit	13.5	13.2	13.6		21.1	20.4	14.5	12.2	8.8
Operating Expenses	12.0	12.3	12.4		19.1	18.9	13.9	11.1	7.8
Operating Profit	1.5	.9	1.2		2.0	1.5	.7	1.2	.9
All Other Expenses (net)	.5	.4	.4		.6	.5	.5	.3	.3
Profit Before Taxes	1.0	.5	.8		1.4	1.0	.2	.8	.7
RATIOS									
Current	2.0 / 1.4 / 1.2	2.0 / 1.5 / 1.2	2.0 / 1.5 / 1.2		2.4 / 1.5 / 1.4	2.7 / 1.8 / 1.1	2.0 / 1.6 / 1.2	2.2 / 1.6 / 1.2	1.7 / 1.3 / 1.1
Quick	1.3 / .9 / .7	1.4 / (206) .9 / .7	1.3 / .9 / .7		1.6 / .9 / .7	1.5 / .9 / .7	1.3 / .9 / .6	1.4 / 1.0 / .7	1.1 / .8 / .6
Sales/Receivables	15 23.7 / 20 18.2 / 27 13.7	14 25.6 / 20 18.1 / 27 13.7	15 24.4 / 19 19.1 / 27 13.7		9 42.2 / 17 21.7 / 29 12.7	16 22.5 / 20 18.2 / 29 12.6	16 22.2 / 19 18.9 / 27 13.5	15 24.5 / 20 18.0 / 31 11.6	15 24.1 / 20 19.4 / 24 15.3
Cost of Sales/Inventory	7 48.7 / 15 24.4 / 25 14.5	8 43.6 / 16 23.3 / 26 14.1	9 41.0 / 16 22.6 / 24 15.4		19 19.6 / 27 13.4 / 39 9.3	12 31.1 / 19 19.7 / 28 13.0	6 62.5 / 14 25.5 / 24 15.3	8 45.9 / 15 24.9 / 22 16.4	9 41.1 / 15 23.6 / 22 16.3
Cost of Sales/Payables	7 54.7 / 12 29.9 / 18 20.6	7 55.7 / 13 28.9 / 19 19.6	7 50.7 / 12 30.0 / 19 19.0		5 76.9 / 15 24.4 / 31 11.7	5 74.9 / 12 30.2 / 21 17.2	8 48.5 / 11 31.9 / 21 17.5	8 47.7 / 13 28.6 / 21 17.7	7 49.4 / 12 30.1 / 17 22.0
Sales/Working Capital	17.6 / 31.8 / 72.0	16.9 / 30.0 / 67.2	14.9 / 34.9 / 83.9		14.2 / 20.4 / 38.9	9.9 / 22.7 / 76.2	14.5 / 29.7 / 73.4	14.9 / 31.1 / 76.0	24.5 / 45.0 / 100.0
EBIT/Interest	5.8 / (193) 2.4 / 1.4	6.0 / (196) 2.8 / 1.3	5.6 / (203) 2.5 / 1.1			3.9 / (27) 2.2 / 1.0	4.6 / 1.9 / -.0	6.3 / (53) 2.3 / 1.4	6.6 / (74) 3.0 / 1.1
Net Profit + Depr., Dep., Amort./Cur. Mat. L/T/D	6.9 / (80) 2.4 / 1.2	7.8 / (70) 2.7 / .8	4.2 / (72) 1.9 / .8			3.3 / (11) 1.7 / .7	4.2 / (12) 1.1 / .2	4.5 / (21) 1.9 / 1.3	13.8 / (25) 3.1 / 1.2
Fixed/Worth	.2 / .4 / 1.1	.1 / .4 / 1.2	.2 / .5 / 1.2		.2 / .8 / 1.8	.2 / .6 / 2.1	.2 / .6 / 1.9	.1 / .4 / .8	.1 / .4 / 1.1
Debt/Worth	.8 / 1.9 / 3.9	.9 / 2.1 / 4.5	.8 / 1.8 / 4.8		.9 / 1.6 / 4.8	.5 / 1.0 / 5.6	1.0 / 1.7 / 7.5	.7 / 1.8 / 5.3	1.2 / 2.7 / 4.4
% Profit Before Taxes/Tangible Net Worth	30.9 / (203) 14.3 / 4.0	29.0 / (194) 14.3 / 3.6	31.2 / (209) 13.5 / 2.0		80.2 / 20.6 / -1.8	15.3 / (30) 7.6 / -.6	27.4 / (58) 7.1 / 3.3	29.2 / (77) 15.2 / 2.3	35.1 / 17.7 / 4.7
% Profit Before Taxes/Total Assets	9.7 / 4.4 / 1.5	9.7 / 4.3 / .8	10.9 / 4.0 / .7		15.6 / 4.8 / -.7	8.5 / 3.3 / -.1	5.6 / 2.8 / -1.6	11.2 / 3.7 / 1.0	12.0 / 5.8 / .7
Sales/Net Fixed Assets	149.3 / 43.4 / 18.5	170.5 / 56.6 / 20.4	153.3 / 43.9 / 17.2		UND / 30.6 / 6.8	55.3 / 22.8 / 12.4	153.0 / 37.8 / 11.2	163.4 / 57.6 / 24.8	295.1 / 61.2 / 22.9
Sales/Total Assets	10.1 / 6.6 / 5.0	9.7 / 6.6 / 4.6	9.0 / 6.5 / 4.5		7.8 / 4.9 / 2.6	6.4 / 5.3 / 3.9	8.0 / 6.7 / 4.2	9.9 / 7.2 / 5.0	10.1 / 7.7 / 5.3
% Depr., Dep., Amort./Sales	.2 / (194) .5 / .9	.2 / (184) .5 / 1.0	.2 / (194) .5 / 1.1			.5 / (27) .6 / 1.8	.2 / (31) .7 / 1.5	.2 / (52) .5 / .8	.1 / (71) .3 / .7
% Officers', Directors', Owners' Comp/Sales	.6 / (106) 1.5 / 3.1	.9 / (98) 1.6 / 2.7	.7 / (108) 1.4 / 2.4			1.0 / (20) 2.8 / 3.8	1.1 / (18) 1.5 / 2.2	.7 / (34) 1.2 / 1.7	.3 / (24) .6 / 1.5
Net Sales ($)	10758539M	11837707M	10510350M	4169M	22231M	109925M	259029M	995485M	9119511M
Total Assets ($)	1919846M	1824658M	1573204M	1207M	7630M	23619M	56707M	153382M	1330659M

M = $ thousand   MM = $ million
See Pages 1 through 15 for Explanation of Ratios and Data

Current Data Sorted By Assets / Comparative Historical Data

Type of Statement

# Postretirement Benefits	0-500M	500M-2MM	2-10MM	10-50MM	50-100MM	100-250MM		4/1/90-3/31/91 ALL	4/1/91-3/31/92 ALL
(# Postretirement Benefits)		4	3	3					
Unqualified		2	13	9	1	5		21	21
Reviewed		8	17	4				25	24
Compiled	6	6	6					22	17
Tax Returns	1							1	2
Other	2	5	9	3	1			18	14
Period label		43 (4/1-9/30/94)		55 (10/1/94-3/31/95)					
NUMBER OF STATEMENTS	9	21	45	16	2	5		87	78

ASSETS (%)

	500M-2MM	2-10MM	10-50MM		4/1/90-3/31/91 ALL	4/1/91-3/31/92 ALL
Cash & Equivalents	4.1	4.2	5.1		6.2	6.9
Trade Receivables - (net)	38.8	37.3	30.4		31.3	31.5
Inventory	31.4	31.4	28.5		31.3	29.9
All Other Current	.6	1.1	.6		2.1	1.6
Total Current	74.8	74.1	64.6		70.9	69.9
Fixed Assets (net)	18.6	18.6	27.0		21.6	22.5
Intangibles (net)	1.5	2.8	4.1		1.8	1.8
All Other Non-Current	5.1	4.6	4.3		5.8	5.8
Total	100.0	100.0	100.0		100.0	100.0

LIABILITIES (%)

	500M-2MM	2-10MM	10-50MM		4/1/90-3/31/91 ALL	4/1/91-3/31/92 ALL
Notes Payable-Short Term	11.0	17.2	12.1		15.3	14.0
Cur. Mat. -L/T/D	2.0	1.8	3.3		4.7	3.8
Trade Payables	27.3	24.9	22.9		21.6	20.0
Income Taxes Payable	.4	.3	.1		.4	.2
All Other Current	11.7	5.4	6.2		5.6	5.9
Total Current	52.4	49.4	44.6		47.8	43.9
Long Term Debt	5.6	11.8	22.5		15.1	17.1
Deferred Taxes	.1	.4	1.7		.4	.4
All Other-Non-Current	7.3	4.4	3.0		2.9	1.4
Net Worth	34.7	34.0	28.3		33.8	37.1
Total Liabilities & Net Worth	100.0	100.0	100.0		100.0	100.0

INCOME DATA (%)

	500M-2MM	2-10MM	10-50MM		4/1/90-3/31/91 ALL	4/1/91-3/31/92 ALL
Net Sales	100.0	100.0	100.0		100.0	100.0
Gross Profit	19.3	17.6	17.7		18.6	17.3
Operating Expenses	17.7	15.3	15.9		15.7	14.9
Operating Profit	1.6	2.2	1.8		2.8	2.4
All Other Expenses (net)	.6	.6	.6		.5	1.0
Profit Before Taxes	1.0	1.6	1.2		2.4	1.4

RATIOS

	500M-2MM	2-10MM	10-50MM		4/1/90-3/31/91 ALL	4/1/91-3/31/92 ALL
Current	2.1	2.2	2.0		2.2	2.7
	1.3	1.6	1.5		1.4	1.6
	1.1	1.2	1.1		1.1	1.2
Quick	1.0	1.2	1.0		1.2	1.3
	.9	.9	.9		.8	.9
	.5	.6	.6		.6	.7
Sales/Receivables	12 31.0	20 18.2	19 18.8		17 21.1	17 20.9
	21 17.2	27 13.4	24 15.4		23 15.8	21 17.2
	31 11.7	36 10.1	28 13.0		31 11.7	30 12.2
Cost of Sales/Inventory	13 27.3	18 20.4	19 19.4		18 20.5	16 23.4
	26 14.0	27 13.4	22 16.9		30 12.3	29 12.6
	35 10.3	42 8.7	50 7.3		47 7.8	43 8.5
Cost of Sales/Payables	9 40.0	12 29.3	18 20.7		11 32.6	9 40.7
	13 27.8	21 17.6	20 18.2		18 20.0	17 21.4
	22 16.5	31 11.8	22 16.7		28 13.0	26 14.0
Sales/Working Capital	15.2	11.2	10.4		10.8	11.2
	37.6	18.8	28.7		24.4	22.1
	121.2	56.1	114.6		65.3	51.0
EBIT/Interest	7.3	5.4	3.3		4.0	3.6
	2.5	(42) 2.8	(15) 2.0		(81) 2.5	(75) 2.1
	1.2	1.3	1.4		1.3	1.3
Net Profit + Depr., Dep., Amort./Cur. Mat. L./T/D		7.1			8.0	4.5
		(18) 3.9			(54) 2.6	(35) 2.1
		2.6			.8	.5
Fixed/Worth	.2	.2	.6		.2	.2
	.4	.6	1.0		.6	.7
	1.4	1.2	1.4		1.8	1.5
Debt/Worth	1.1	1.1	1.5		1.2	1.0
	2.7	2.9	2.8		2.2	2.1
	5.7	4.9	4.9		5.4	4.4
% Profit Before Taxes/Tangible Net Worth	46.0	35.6	30.5		33.3	26.5
	9.4	(43) 15.3	(14) 14.9		(79) 17.4	(75) 9.4
	.8	6.0	4.7		6.7	4.1
% Profit Before Taxes/Total Assets	11.7	10.3	7.8		9.6	6.5
	2.0	4.0	3.8		4.4	3.4
	.5	1.3	1.4		1.2	1.3
Sales/Net Fixed Assets	152.2	105.2	36.8		102.1	96.1
	51.1	38.2	18.5		24.0	25.8
	17.8	14.6	9.1		11.5	11.1
Sales/Total Assets	7.6	6.3	6.6		6.1	6.7
	5.9	4.7	4.4		4.7	5.0
	3.9	3.5	3.0		3.5	3.4
% Depr., Dep., Amort./Sales	.2	.4	.5		.4	.4
	(20) .5	(41) .6	(12) .7		(85) .9	(73) .8
	.8	1.0	1.2		1.8	1.4
% Officers', Directors', Owners' Comp/Sales	1.3	.9			.8	.8
	(15) 3.2	(23) 1.4			(31) 1.5	(38) 1.0
	4.7	2.1			2.2	2.1

Dollar Totals

	0-500M	500M-2MM	2-10MM	10-50MM	50-100MM	100-250MM		4/1/90-3/31/91	4/1/91-3/31/92
Net Sales ($)	15153M	170797M	1054802M	1787866M	524702M	2899965M		4693652M	2914093M
Total Assets ($)	2733M	23890M	210507M	348546M	114231M	701723M		958652M	600518M

M = $ thousand   MM = $ million
See Pages 1 through 15 for Explanation of Ratios and Data

Comparative Historical Data   **Current Data Sorted By Sales**

3	6	10		0-1MM	1-3MM	3-5MM	5-10MM	10-25MM	25MM & OVER
			# Postretirement Benefits		1	1	1	3	4
			Type of Statement						
31	26	30	Unqualified			2	2	10	16
22	25	29	Reviewed			2	4	10	13
16	11	18	Compiled	1	5	6	2	3	1
	1	1	Tax Returns		1				
20	17	20	Other	2	2	2	2	6	6
4/1/92-3/31/93 ALL	4/1/93-3/31/94 ALL	4/1/94-3/31/95 ALL		43 (4/1-9/30/94)		55 (10/1/94-3/31/95)			
89	80	98	**NUMBER OF STATEMENTS**	3	8	12	10	29	36
%	%	%	**ASSETS**	%	%	%	%	%	%
4.9	4.6	4.3	Cash & Equivalents			2.9	2.2	5.0	3.7
37.7	31.2	35.9	Trade Receivables - (net)			40.4	35.4	36.8	33.7
28.8	29.4	30.0	Inventory			35.7	27.5	33.4	30.5
1.5	1.3	1.2	All Other Current			.9	.3	1.3	.9
72.9	66.4	71.4	Total Current			79.9	65.2	76.6	68.8
19.6	26.2	20.6	Fixed Assets (net)			14.0	28.4	16.2	23.2
2.1	1.9	2.5	Intangibles (net)			1.6	3.4	3.1	2.5
5.4	5.5	5.5	All Other Non-Current			4.5	2.9	4.2	5.5
100.0	100.0	100.0	Total			100.0	100.0	100.0	100.0
			LIABILITIES						
16.4	15.0	13.7	Notes Payable-Short Term			12.1	15.2	11.7	15.6
3.0	3.0	2.6	Cur. Mat.-L /T/D			2.7	2.6	1.0	3.5
23.0	21.2	25.0	Trade Payables			23.9	20.2	29.7	23.6
.3	1.8	.2	Income Taxes Payable			.4	.4	.2	.2
7.5	8.0	7.7	All Other Current			12.3	3.3	5.8	6.3
50.3	48.9	49.2	Total Current			51.5	41.7	48.4	49.1
11.2	15.5	12.8	Long Term Debt			4.5	14.6	9.2	17.7
.4	.5	.5	Deferred Taxes			.1	.1	.4	1.0
5.3	3.7	4.2	All Other-Non-Current			2.2	7.6	7.1	2.7
32.9	31.5	33.3	Net Worth			41.6	36.0	34.9	29.6
100.0	100.0	100.0	Total Liabilities & Net Worth			100.0	100.0	100.0	100.0
			INCOME DATA						
100.0	100.0	100.0	Net Sales			100.0	100.0	100.0	100.0
17.9	21.3	19.4	Gross Profit			21.9	19.6	16.3	16.8
15.3	18.8	16.9	Operating Expenses			20.8	17.4	14.0	15.0
2.7	2.5	2.5	Operating Profit			1.1	2.2	2.3	1.8
.6	.7	.7	All Other Expenses (net)			1.1	1.0	.3	.4
2.1	1.8	1.7	Profit Before Taxes			.0	1.2	2.0	1.4
			RATIOS						
2.2	1.9	2.0				2.3	3.6	2.3	1.8
1.5	1.4	1.5	Current			1.8	1.6	1.7	1.4
1.1	1.1	1.1				1.1	1.1	1.2	1.2
1.2	1.0	1.1				1.0	1.9	1.3	1.0
.8	.8	.9	Quick			.9	.9	1.0	.8
.6	.5	.6				.7	.6	.6	.6
19 18.8	18 20.8	19 19.4				19 19.6	27 13.6	18 19.8	19 18.8
25 14.4	24 15.3	25 14.6	Sales/Receivables			23 15.8	32 11.5	24 15.5	24 14.9
33 11.2	31 11.7	33 10.9				46 8.0	41 9.0	33 11.2	28 13.0
15 23.6	17 22.0	17 21.6				21 17.5	17 21.7	17 21.1	17 21.9
29 12.5	27 13.5	26 14.1	Cost of Sales/Inventory			31 11.6	31 11.8	29 12.8	22 16.9
38 9.6	37 9.9	42 8.7				63 5.8	46 7.9	40 9.2	44 8.3
13 28.6	11 32.7	12 29.3				9 41.1	6 57.8	13 27.2	15 23.9
20 18.6	19 18.9	20 18.0	Cost of Sales/Payables			14 25.5	15 23.9	25 14.5	20 18.5
26 13.9	25 14.4	29 12.6				41 8.8	32 11.4	33 11.1	23 15.7
12.0	13.3	12.4				11.2	8.7	11.2	13.4
20.1	26.7	23.2	Sales/Working Capital			18.5	18.0	20.7	29.2
116.3	115.8	75.5				94.5	NM	57.8	59.0
4.6	5.2	5.4				3.3	6.3	11.0	3.6
(82) 2.4	(76) 2.3	(93) 2.6	EBIT/Interest			1.5	2.5	(27) 3.4	(34) 2.4
1.5	1.3	1.3				.6	.9	1.5	1.4
6.5	4.8	5.7							5.9
(38) 2.8	(33) 3.0	(35) 2.7	Net Profit + Depr., Dep., Amort./Cur. Mat. L/T/D						(21) 2.5
1.6	1.4	1.7							1.7
.2	.3	.2				.2	.5	.1	.4
.5	.9	.6	Fixed/Worth			.3	.8	.4	1.0
1.3	1.6	1.3				.5	2.0	1.2	1.4
1.1	1.3	1.1				.6	1.0	1.1	1.2
2.4	2.6	2.6	Debt/Worth			1.3	2.6	2.9	2.8
4.9	5.5	4.9				5.3	4.9	4.9	4.9
29.8	33.3	36.7				11.6	36.1	56.2	29.4
(83) 16.5	(75) 11.7	(93) 15.3	% Profit Before Taxes/Tangible Net Worth			5.0	8.4	(28) 16.6	(33) 15.8
5.0	1.6	4.9				−1.0	−1.6	5.7	6.2
9.9	9.4	9.6				2.5	14.2	12.1	8.0
4.6	4.0	4.2	% Profit Before Taxes/Total Assets			1.3	3.5	6.2	4.4
1.9	.6	1.3				−.6	.2	2.4	1.4
121.5	65.4	86.8				77.3	35.1	183.3	52.4
44.4	25.2	36.8	Sales/Net Fixed Assets			51.5	15.0	56.0	26.9
14.1	10.6	12.5				30.9	8.4	18.5	11.8
6.7	6.2	6.5				6.8	5.2	7.2	6.8
4.9	4.9	4.8	Sales/Total Assets			5.4	4.0	4.8	5.3
3.6	3.2	3.5				3.4	3.0	4.0	3.4
.2	.5	.3				(11) .2	.5	(26) .2	(31) .4
(79) .7	(70) .9	(86) .6	% Depr., Dep., Amort./Sales			.5	.9	.5	.6
1.3	1.6	1.1				1.2	2.3	1.0	1.1
.7	1.1	1.0						(15) .9	(11) .9
(40) 1.9	(31) 1.5	(44) 1.9	% Officers', Directors', Owners' Comp/Sales					1.8	1.4
3.9	5.6	3.5						2.4	2.1
4262855M	3767919M	6453285M	Net Sales ($)	2041M	17350M	52270M	81435M	518131M	5782058M
1101730M	853387M	1401630M	Total Assets ($)	583M	5748M	12481M	21481M	111057M	1250280M

M = $ thousand   MM = $ million
See Pages 1 through 15 for Explanation of Ratios and Data

WHOLESALERS—POULTRY & POULTRY PRODUCTS. SIC# 5144

Current Data Sorted By Assets							Comparative Historical Data	
1			3	1		# Postretirement Benefits		
						Type of Statement		
	1		8	4		1	Unqualified	15	10
2	4		10	3			Reviewed	23	21
5	4		10	1			Compiled	18	23
	2		1				Tax Returns		2
3	7		7	4	1	1	Other	13	12
	26 (4/1-9/30/94)			53 (10/1/94-3/31/95)				4/1/90-3/31/91	4/1/91-3/31/92
0-500M	500M-2MM	2-10MM	10-50MM	50-100MM	100-250MM		ALL	ALL
10	18	36	12	1	2	**NUMBER OF STATEMENTS**	69	68
%	%	%	%	%	%	**ASSETS**	%	%
9.5	5.2	6.3	8.6			Cash & Equivalents	6.5	8.4
48.5	50.2	39.3	30.3			Trade Receivables - (net)	39.4	35.8
8.6	10.3	18.0	20.4			Inventory	20.6	19.9
3.6	1.9	6.9	2.0			All Other Current	2.1	2.9
70.3	67.6	70.5	61.3			Total Current	68.6	67.0
13.9	23.4	23.7	26.8			Fixed Assets (net)	22.7	24.7
2.4	1.5	.3	.7			Intangibles (net)	1.1	1.0
13.3	7.4	5.5	11.2			All Other Non-Current	7.6	7.2
100.0	100.0	100.0	100.0			Total	100.0	100.0
						LIABILITIES		
11.6	10.1	14.0	21.4			Notes Payable-Short Term	12.9	13.7
3.2	4.0	1.5	3.1			Cur. Mat. -L/T/D	3.7	2.1
28.4	28.6	29.3	15.4			Trade Payables	28.5	24.6
.3	.0	.2	.1			Income Taxes Payable	.5	.5
9.5	6.0	5.5	6.7			All Other Current	5.5	6.3
52.9	48.8	50.5	46.7			Total Current	51.1	47.1
6.9	11.9	12.0	9.8			Long Term Debt	14.7	12.6
.0	.0	.7	1.7			Deferred Taxes	.8	.6
2.9	1.5	1.1	1.4			All Other-Non-Current	1.6	.3
37.3	37.8	35.7	40.3			Net Worth	31.7	39.4
100.0	100.0	100.0	100.0			Total Liabilities & Net Worth	100.0	100.0
						INCOME DATA		
100.0	100.0	100.0	100.0			Net Sales	100.0	100.0
14.7	16.5	12.2	14.5			Gross Profit	16.2	12.9
13.0	14.4	11.3	11.2			Operating Expenses	13.5	11.3
1.7	2.1	.9	3.4			Operating Profit	2.8	1.6
.2	1.1	.5	2.2			All Other Expenses (net)	.5	.0
1.5	1.0	.4	1.2			Profit Before Taxes	2.3	1.6
						RATIOS		
2.8	1.7	1.9	2.1				2.1	2.2
1.3	1.3	1.4	1.3			Current	1.3	1.4
1.0	1.1	1.1	.9				1.0	1.1
1.7	1.5	1.1	1.6				1.2	1.5
1.1	1.2	.9	.9			Quick	.9	.9
.8	.8	.6	.4				.6	.6
12 30.0	15 24.9	19 19.1	15 23.8				15 24.0	17 22.0
21 17.5	18 20.7	21 17.2	23 15.7			Sales/Receivables	19 19.6	20 18.6
28 13.0	23 16.2	26 14.2	30 12.0				26 13.9	26 14.8
0 UND	1 629.5	4 101.8	8 46.4				5 68.8	5 73.1
3 110.8	3 104.6	12 31.3	20 17.9			Cost of Sales/Inventory	10 35.1	10 35.4
11 33.8	10 37.4	24 15.5	43 8.5				26 13.8	22 16.4
7 51.9	4 85.7	13 27.4	6 60.2				11 34.6	10 38.3
12 30.7	13 28.8	17 21.6	13 29.2			Cost of Sales/Payables	17 21.1	16 23.1
19 18.9	16 22.2	21 17.1	18 20.2				22 16.4	19 19.0
20.1	26.6	15.7	12.7				14.7	15.1
70.9	42.9	37.2	41.3			Sales/Working Capital	41.3	42.3
NM	164.4	127.2	NM				314.1	251.2
	10.3	6.1	13.7				6.8	8.0
	(15) 3.0	(30) 1.7	(10) 3.0			EBIT/Interest	(61) 2.9	(55) 3.2
	1.0	-.6	.5				1.3	1.1
		4.5					7.8	8.0
		(15) 1.4				Net Profit + Depr., Dep., Amort./Cur. Mat. L./T/D	(28) 4.0	(25) 2.8
		-.6					2.4	1.5
.0	.1	.2	.4				.3	.3
.6	.5	.5	.7			Fixed/Worth	.6	.6
.9	1.3	1.3	1.1				1.2	1.3
.6	1.1	1.0	.7				1.1	.9
2.6	1.9	1.9	1.6			Debt/Worth	2.0	1.7
9.0	2.9	4.5	4.3				5.1	3.8
112.1	27.4	17.2	25.3				49.4	29.1
24.3	(17) 16.5	(35) 9.6	12.9			% Profit Before Taxes/Tangible Net Worth	(61) 22.9	(65) 14.4
-13.9	.4	-8.6	6.3				9.0	3.0
28.7	8.8	8.1	6.9				13.8	11.5
11.5	4.1	2.2	6.2			% Profit Before Taxes/Total Assets	6.6	5.3
-2.0	.1	-2.7	1.0				1.7	.7
UND	345.5	79.0	66.0				96.0	99.3
79.1	64.4	30.5	20.6			Sales/Net Fixed Assets	42.3	31.8
30.2	26.4	15.1	4.8				10.7	11.4
14.4	13.9	10.2	6.7				10.4	9.1
9.4	9.5	6.2	5.3			Sales/Total Assets	6.3	6.2
5.0	7.0	3.9	2.0				3.8	3.7
	.1	.2	.2				.3	.3
	(16) .5	(33) .4	(10) .6			% Depr., Dep., Amort./Sales	(59) .8	(54) .7
	1.0	1.1	3.5				1.5	1.5
		.8					.9	.7
		(11) 1.7				% Officers', Directors', Owners' Comp/Sales	(19) 1.4	(25) 1.4
		2.8					3.3	3.2
34444M	224932M	1351636M	1123668M	95707M	818641M	Net Sales ($)	2145444M	3562418M
3610M	22803M	192767M	249213M	56598M	336209M	Total Assets ($)	438565M	714594M

M = $ thousand   MM = $ million
See Pages 1 through 15 for Explanation of Ratios and Data

Comparative Historical Data				Current Data Sorted By Sales					
1	1	6	# Postretirement Benefits		1	1	1	1	2
			Type of Statement						
6	14	14	Unqualified					5	9
23	23	19	Reviewed		1	2	2	3	11
19	16	20	Compiled		2	1	8	2	7
	2	3	Tax Returns				2	1	
10	15	23	Other	2	2	1	1	6	11
4/1/92-3/31/93 ALL	4/1/93-3/31/94 ALL	4/1/94-3/31/95 ALL		26 (4/1-9/30/94)			53 (10/1/94-3/31/95)		
				0-1MM	1-3MM	3-5MM	5-10MM	10-25MM	25MM & OVER
58	70	79	NUMBER OF STATEMENTS	2	5	4	13	17	38
%	%	%	**ASSETS**	%	%	%	%	%	%
6.1	4.1	6.6	Cash & Equivalents				9.2	2.4	7.0
39.0	41.4	40.5	Trade Receivables - (net)				36.1	42.9	41.9
18.8	18.7	15.5	Inventory				14.0	18.9	16.4
2.3	2.6	4.4	All Other Current				2.8	5.0	4.9
66.2	66.8	67.0	Total Current				62.1	69.2	70.1
25.3	24.5	24.2	Fixed Assets (net)				28.3	20.6	22.4
.5	.5	1.1	Intangibles (net)				2.2	1.4	.9
8.0	8.3	7.7	All Other Non-Current				7.4	8.8	6.5
100.0	100.0	100.0	Total				100.0	100.0	100.0
			LIABILITIES						
14.8	14.9	13.5	Notes Payable-Short Term				9.0	18.3	14.2
3.1	4.0	2.6	Cur. Mat.-L /T/D				4.3	3.3	1.8
25.7	29.3	26.2	Trade Payables				18.6	26.3	30.6
.2	.5	.2	Income Taxes Payable				.0	.4	.1
6.4	4.8	6.3	All Other Current				5.8	6.1	5.8
50.2	53.4	48.8	Total Current				37.6	54.3	52.5
12.1	12.1	11.4	Long Term Debt				15.9	12.4	9.3
1.7	.7	.8	Deferred Taxes				.0	.2	1.4
1.1	2.5	1.8	All Other-Non-Current				1.1	1.4	1.7
35.0	31.3	37.3	Net Worth				45.4	31.8	35.1
100.0	100.0	100.0	Total Liabilities & Net Worth				100.0	100.0	100.0
			INCOME DATA						
100.0	100.0	100.0	Net Sales				100.0	100.0	100.0
12.5	12.1	13.8	Gross Profit				11.9	15.3	9.9
13.0	10.7	12.1	Operating Expenses				10.9	13.5	8.5
–.4	1.5	1.7	Operating Profit				1.1	1.8	1.4
.1	.5	.9	All Other Expenses (net)				.3	1.3	.6
–.5	1.0	.8	Profit Before Taxes				.8	.5	.8
			RATIOS						
1.8	1.9	2.0					2.7	1.6	2.0
1.3	1.2	1.3	Current				1.7	1.3	1.3
1.0	1.0	1.1					1.3	1.0	1.1
1.2	1.1	1.3					1.7	1.2	1.2
.9	.9	1.0	Quick				1.1	.8	.9
.6	.6	.7					.8	.5	.6
15 23.6	17 20.9	16 22.6					14 27.0	18 20.7	16 23.2
21 17.1	22 16.5	21 17.3	Sales/Receivables				19 19.2	21 17.2	21 17.4
28 13.0	28 13.2	26 14.1					25 14.6	30 12.0	24 15.4
5 75.4	5 67.3	3 121.9					3 122.0	2 167.0	3 107.7
14 25.6	12 31.6	9 38.5	Cost of Sales/Inventory				9 41.2	15 24.2	10 38.2
26 14.0	22 16.7	22 16.8					21 17.1	63 5.8	17 21.2
11 33.3	12 31.5	8 43.0					5 76.8	4 93.1	13 29.2
15 24.6	17 21.6	16 23.5	Cost of Sales/Payables				12 29.6	16 22.5	16 22.7
24 15.5	21 17.1	20 18.6					17 21.7	25 14.5	18 19.8
19.2	22.7	18.0					12.9	19.4	19.3
42.7	55.7	41.4	Sales/Working Capital				23.8	46.0	53.0
302.8	578.5	128.0					50.5	NM	173.3
(54) 5.1	(68) 5.6	(65) 8.0					9.3	(15) 8.0	(29) 7.9
1.7	2.8	2.3	EBIT/Interest				2.3	1.8	2.7
–.7	1.2	–.3					.0	–.9	.4
(22) 6.4	(30) 4.0	(30) 5.7							(15) 6.4
2.8	2.0	1.4	Net Profit + Depr., Dep., Amort./Cur. Mat. L/T/D						3.0
.8	.4	.1							.8
.3	.3	.2					.4	.1	.2
.7	.8	.5	Fixed/Worth				.6	.5	.5
1.1	1.6	1.2					1.1	1.4	1.1
1.0	1.0	.8					.6	1.4	.8
2.0	2.3	1.9	Debt/Worth				1.5	2.0	2.1
4.1	4.2	3.9					2.7	5.2	4.5
(56) 20.2	(64) 21.8	(76) 27.1					35.7	(16) 34.5	(36) 21.1
4.4	10.8	12.8	% Profit Before Taxes/Tangible Net Worth				16.5	8.3	12.8
–16.8	2.3	.1					–4.5	–21.3	5.3
7.4	6.6	8.9					13.9	8.5	7.2
1.3	3.2	3.9	% Profit Before Taxes/Total Assets				3.9	2.0	4.7
–5.5	.5	–1.2					–2.3	–5.5	1.4
91.1	75.7	204.7					80.7	284.0	290.0
27.5	31.3	31.7	Sales/Net Fixed Assets				33.9	30.1	37.5
9.6	11.3	11.9					8.2	8.9	17.8
9.8	9.9	10.5					10.3	11.6	11.0
6.1	6.5	6.7	Sales/Total Assets				7.3	6.1	6.8
3.5	4.0	3.9					3.7	2.5	5.5
(50) .2	(68) .3	(67) .2					(12) .5	(15) .1	(32) .2
.7	.6	.5	% Depr., Dep., Amort./Sales				.8	.3	.3
1.7	1.4	1.0					1.2	1.1	.8
(20) .6	(26) .8	(25) .8							
1.1	1.2	1.5	% Officers', Directors', Owners' Comp/Sales						
1.8	2.4	2.4							
2167518M	2750223M	3649028M	Net Sales ($)	541M	10844M	15737M	103032M	289024M	3229850M
517558M	605239M	861200M	Total Assets ($)	1539M	1611M	7014M	19984M	88582M	742470M

M = $ thousand   MM = $ million

See Pages 1 through 15 for Explanation of Ratios and Data

WHOLESALERS—TOBACCO & TOBACCO PRODUCTS, EXCEPT LEAF. SIC# 5194

	Current Data Sorted By Assets							Comparative Historical Data		
	2		5		1			# Postretirement Benefits		
			3		10	1	1	Type of Statement		
1	15		21		1	1		Unqualified	20	27
2	17		15		1			Reviewed	37	39
1								Compiled	41	51
1	6		7		3		1	Tax Returns	1	
								Other	15	9
	37 (4/1-9/30/94)				71 (10/1/94-3/31/95)				4/1/90-3/31/91	4/1/91-3/31/92
0-500M	500M-2MM		2-10MM		10-50MM	50-100MM	100-250MM		ALL	ALL
5	38		46		15	2	2	NUMBER OF STATEMENTS	114	126
%	%		%		%	%	%	ASSETS	%	%
	9.1		5.5		4.4			Cash & Equivalents	4.8	5.2
	30.4		35.8		31.5			Trade Receivables - (net)	30.7	27.3
	42.2		39.0		32.7			Inventory	44.7	47.6
	1.5		1.8		2.0			All Other Current	1.8	1.7
	83.3		82.1		70.6			Total Current	82.0	81.7
	10.8		13.2		18.8			Fixed Assets (net)	12.3	12.7
	.5		.4		6.5			Intangibles (net)	1.3	1.0
	5.4		4.3		4.0			All Other Non-Current	4.4	4.6
	100.0		100.0		100.0			Total	100.0	100.0
								LIABILITIES		
	12.9		20.7		26.9			Notes Payable-Short Term	21.8	18.9
	2.6		3.6		3.2			Cur. Mat. -L/T/D	2.5	2.9
	21.5		17.5		18.1			Trade Payables	23.9	26.7
	.2		1.0		.4			Income Taxes Payable	.6	.6
	6.0		5.6		4.6			All Other Current	6.5	7.1
	43.2		48.4		53.1			Total Current	55.3	56.1
	6.8		7.5		17.2			Long Term Debt	10.3	10.7
	.0		.1		1.4			Deferred Taxes	.4	.2
	1.5		1.3		2.7			All Other-Non-Current	2.5	1.8
	48.5		42.7		25.5			Net Worth	31.5	31.2
	100.0		100.0		100.0			Total Liabilities & Net Worth	100.0	100.0
								INCOME DATA		
	100.0		100.0		100.0			Net Sales	100.0	100.0
	8.1		8.8		15.2			Gross Profit	11.7	9.2
	8.1		7.9		13.2			Operating Expenses	10.0	8.7
	.0		.8		2.0			Operating Profit	1.7	.5
	–.3		.2		1.2			All Other Expenses (net)	.4	.2
	.3		.7		.7			Profit Before Taxes	1.4	.4
								RATIOS		
	2.9		2.9		1.5				1.9	2.0
	1.9		1.6		1.2			Current	1.5	1.4
	1.4		1.2		1.1				1.2	1.1
	1.3		1.6		.8				.9	.8
	.9		.8		.6			Quick	.6	.6
	.6		.5		.5				.5	.4
9	42.0	13	27.6	14	25.5				12 29.9	11 32.2
14	25.9	16	22.2	18	20.7			Sales/Receivables	17 21.8	15 24.7
19	19.5	21	17.2	21	17.8				21 17.0	19 19.4
16	23.4	16	22.9	16	22.5				20 18.4	19 19.3
19	18.9	21	17.5	23	16.1			Cost of Sales/Inventory	26 14.3	27 13.6
26	14.2	27	13.6	26	14.3				37 9.8	38 9.5
5	75.6	4	88.7	8	43.4				8 43.2	9 39.4
9	40.0	9	41.7	9	38.5			Cost of Sales/Payables	14 26.7	14 25.7
14	25.6	13	27.7	21	17.4				21 17.7	19 19.0
	14.8		12.9		29.2				13.8	16.2
	20.0		25.9		82.9			Sales/Working Capital	24.4	26.3
	37.6		64.7		126.5				54.6	73.7
	8.6		4.5		2.3				4.6	4.4
(35)	2.5	(43)	2.8		1.8			EBIT/Interest	(106) 2.4	(116) 2.1
	1.4		1.2		1.4				1.3	1.3
	2.9		3.1		4.2				8.5	3.9
(14)	1.2	(22)	1.5	(10)	1.9			Net Profit + Depr., Dep., Amort./Cur. Mat. L./T/D	(62) 2.7	(65) 2.3
	–.5		.4		1.0				1.4	.7
	.1		.1		.4				.2	.2
	.2		.3		.8			Fixed/Worth	.4	.4
	.5		.5		1.6				.9	1.0
	.7		.6		2.7				1.4	1.2
	1.2		1.9		5.1			Debt/Worth	2.4	2.8
	2.2		3.7		6.1				5.3	5.9
	22.7		15.7		33.4				29.9	29.1
	12.9		9.1	(14)	20.3			% Profit Before Taxes/Tangible Net Worth	(108) 15.8	(120) 15.6
	.6		1.8		6.6				5.4	6.2
	9.7		6.9		7.3				9.4	7.9
	5.3		3.5		3.9			% Profit Before Taxes/Total Assets	4.6	3.8
	.3		.6		1.4				1.4	1.1
	192.5		136.8		82.9				158.6	141.9
	106.1		69.7		52.0			Sales/Net Fixed Assets	70.7	66.7
	53.3		33.2		16.8				34.1	34.2
	11.2		9.4		9.0				8.5	8.5
	7.8		7.4		7.3			Sales/Total Assets	6.5	6.8
	6.4		6.1		5.0				5.4	5.3
	.2		.2		.3				.2	.2
(37)	.2	(45)	.3	(14)	.5			% Depr., Dep., Amort./Sales	(106) .3	(121) .3
	.5		.5		.8				.6	.5
	.6		.5							.5	.5
(21)	1.2	(23)	1.1					% Officers', Directors', Owners' Comp/Sales	(50) .9	(66) .8
	1.5		1.7							1.5	1.5
13388M	412350M		1468129M		1683566M	1215891M	1486692M	Net Sales ($)	4907926M	6271863M
1771M	46402M		197867M		308508M	168493M	245665M	Total Assets ($)	1164902M	1146916M

M = $ thousand   MM = $ million
See Pages 1 through 15 for Explanation of Ratios and Data

Comparative Historical Data | Current Data Sorted By Sales

3	7	8	# Postretirement Benefits / Type of Statement	0-1MM	1-3MM	3-5MM	5-10MM	10-25MM	25MM & OVER
17	22	15	Unqualified					2	13
40	35	39	Reviewed		1		6	15	17
28	30	35	Compiled		1	3	11	14	6
3		1	Tax Returns			1			
14	21	18	Other	1		2	1	6	8
4/1/92-3/31/93 ALL	4/1/93-3/31/94 ALL	4/1/94-3/31/95 ALL		37 (4/1-9/30/94)			71 (10/1/94-3/31/95)		
102	108	108	NUMBER OF STATEMENTS	1	2	6	18	37	44
%	%	%	**ASSETS**	%	%	%	%	%	%
4.8	5.9	6.8	Cash & Equivalents				5.7	7.6	6.1
30.8	32.0	32.5	Trade Receivables - (net)				26.6	32.3	36.0
45.3	42.5	39.9	Inventory				41.0	40.7	37.5
1.6	1.5	1.6	All Other Current				3.1	1.2	1.7
82.4	81.7	80.8	Total Current				76.4	81.7	81.2
11.8	12.2	13.0	Fixed Assets (net)				14.4	12.9	12.9
1.0	2.2	1.3	Intangibles (net)				.6	2.5	.7
4.8	3.9	4.9	All Other Non-Current				8.6	2.9	5.2
100.0	100.0	100.0	Total				100.0	100.0	100.0
			LIABILITIES						
20.1	16.7	19.5	Notes Payable-Short Term				11.4	13.7	27.0
2.7	2.9	2.9	Cur. Mat.-L /T/D				2.4	3.9	2.6
23.5	18.4	18.8	Trade Payables				18.3	18.7	19.9
.4	1.2	.6	Income Taxes Payable				.1	.3	1.1
6.8	5.9	6.3	All Other Current				5.0	7.2	6.1
53.5	45.2	48.2	Total Current				37.3	43.6	56.7
9.3	8.0	9.0	Long Term Debt				7.8	9.7	9.6
.1	.2	.3	Deferred Taxes				.3	.5	.2
1.9	2.4	1.7	All Other-Non-Current				.3	2.7	1.2
35.2	44.2	40.9	Net Worth				54.3	43.5	32.3
100.0	100.0	100.0	Total Liabilities & Net Worth				100.0	100.0	100.0
			INCOME DATA						
100.0	100.0	100.0	Net Sales				100.0	100.0	100.0
10.0	9.8	9.4	Gross Profit				10.7	11.1	7.2
8.8	8.4	8.7	Operating Expenses				10.3	10.2	6.5
1.2	1.4	.7	Operating Profit				.3	.9	.7
.2	.3	.2	All Other Expenses (net)				−.7	.5	.3
1.1	1.1	.5	Profit Before Taxes				1.0	.4	.4
			RATIOS						
2.2	3.0	2.5	Current				3.0	3.1	1.7
1.5	1.9	1.6					2.2	1.8	1.3
1.2	1.3	1.2					1.7	1.3	1.1
1.0	1.4	1.2	Quick				1.3	1.5	1.0
.7	.8	.8					.9	.9	.7
.5	.6	.6					.5	.6	.5
13 28.9	12 31.7	12 30.0	Sales/Receivables				10 37.3	11 32.4	13 28.2
17 22.0	15 24.3	16 23.2					15 23.9	16 22.4	16 22.8
21 17.2	19 19.5	20 18.3					20 18.3	21 17.3	20 18.4
18 19.8	16 22.5	16 22.6	Cost of Sales/Inventory				18 19.8	16 22.7	13 27.2
27 13.7	20 17.9	21 17.4					22 16.7	21 17.6	20 18.0
37 10.0	28 13.2	26 13.9					33 11.2	29 12.6	25 14.7
8 47.2	5 73.9	5 71.6	Cost of Sales/Payables				5 75.6	5 69.3	5 71.2
12 30.4	9 42.5	9 39.5					9 39.3	9 39.1	9 39.3
19 18.9	12 31.1	13 27.2					16 23.2	15 24.4	13 29.2
13.5	13.8	14.9	Sales/Working Capital				11.0	13.7	21.8
25.0	21.7	29.0					17.4	25.6	44.2
59.7	57.7	65.3					27.6	40.8	93.5
(97) 7.1	8.7	(102) 5.7	EBIT/Interest				(16) 7.9	(34) 6.2	(43) 3.6
3.4	3.6	2.4					2.8	2.5	2.3
1.9	2.0	1.4					1.4	1.2	1.6
(44) 9.9	(46) 5.1	(47) 3.2	Net Profit + Depr., Dep., Amort./Cur. Mat. L/T/D					(17) 1.5	(19) 3.6
2.8	2.1	1.6						.9	2.3
1.2	1.0	.7						−.5	1.0
.1	.1	.1	Fixed/Worth				.1	.1	.2
.3	.3	.3					.2	.3	.4
.7	.6	.6					.5	.6	.8
1.0	.6	.8	Debt/Worth				.5	.7	2.0
2.1	1.4	2.0					.9	1.5	3.2
5.0	3.7	4.0					1.3	4.0	4.9
(98) 30.4	(103) 27.0	(107) 22.6	% Profit Before Taxes/Tangible Net Worth				18.4	20.1	28.5
17.5	16.2	11.5					8.8	(36) 8.8	12.6
8.1	7.3	1.8					.2	.8	5.6
8.8	10.7	7.8	% Profit Before Taxes/Total Assets				8.3	6.8	8.5
5.7	6.6	4.1					5.7	3.9	4.0
2.8	3.2	.7					.0	.7	1.3
177.3	167.2	137.3	Sales/Net Fixed Assets				192.5	151.4	133.8
82.9	86.2	74.5					81.3	79.1	66.5
33.4	39.2	38.9					35.4	35.7	49.8
8.6	9.7	9.4	Sales/Total Assets				8.1	10.0	9.5
6.8	7.9	7.7					6.8	7.9	8.0
5.1	6.4	6.1					5.8	6.2	6.4
(96) .2	(98) .2	(103) .2	% Depr., Dep., Amort./Sales				.2	.2	(40) .2
.3	.3	.3					.4	.3	.3
.5	.6	.5					.5	.5	.5
(47) .5	(40) .6	(49) .6	% Officers', Directors', Owners' Comp/Sales				(10) 1.2	(16) .5	(19) .4
.8	1.0	1.1					1.3	.9	1.2
1.3	1.7	1.6					2.5	1.5	
5941169M	6851465M	6280016M	Net Sales ($)	620M	3829M	26080M	145007M	621896M	5482584M
984388M	1095180M	968706M	Total Assets ($)	433M	405M	3757M	27528M	148231M	788352M

M = $ thousand   MM = $ million
See Pages 1 through 15 for Explanation of Ratios and Data

WHOLESALERS—WINE, LIQUOR & BEER. SIC# 5181 (82)

Current Data Sorted By Assets							Comparative Historical Data	
3	8	28	15		1	**# Postretirement Benefits**		
						Type of Statement		
1	15	64	49	4	1	Unqualified	117	142
6	46	83	14			Reviewed	157	126
19	79	29	7			Compiled	147	119
4	3	2				Tax Returns	2	4
5	34	65	29	4	1	Other	84	80
	138 (4/1-9/30/94)		426 (10/1/94-3/31/95)				4/1/90-3/31/91	4/1/91-3/31/92
0-500M	500M-2MM	2-10MM	10-50MM	50-100MM	100-250MM		ALL	ALL
35	177	243	99	8	2	**NUMBER OF STATEMENTS**	507	471
%	%	%	%	%	%	**ASSETS**	%	%
9.9	10.8	10.4	8.4			Cash & Equivalents	10.6	9.4
12.7	10.9	13.1	18.1			Trade Receivables - (net)	13.1	12.7
49.0	35.9	27.7	23.2			Inventory	30.1	33.1
1.5	1.1	1.7	2.0			All Other Current	2.1	1.6
73.0	58.7	52.9	51.8			Total Current	55.9	56.7
15.3	22.9	25.6	24.5			Fixed Assets (net)	24.7	24.9
4.7	10.3	11.3	12.7			Intangibles (net)	8.7	8.9
7.1	8.1	10.2	11.0			All Other Non-Current	10.6	9.6
100.0	100.0	100.0	100.0			Total	100.0	100.0
						LIABILITIES		
8.9	11.8	10.0	7.1			Notes Payable-Short Term	11.3	10.4
4.7	5.3	5.0	3.6			Cur. Mat. -L/T/D	4.0	4.4
19.8	12.3	13.6	13.2			Trade Payables	14.9	14.3
.8	.3	.3	.3			Income Taxes Payable	.5	.5
9.6	7.6	7.3	8.5			All Other Current	7.6	7.7
43.7	37.3	36.2	32.7			Total Current	38.2	37.2
14.8	14.9	17.2	19.3			Long Term Debt	18.5	17.3
.0	.3	.3	.5			Deferred Taxes	.4	.3
7.2	4.7	3.8	4.2			All Other-Non-Current	2.9	2.8
34.3	42.8	42.5	43.2			Net Worth	39.9	42.5
100.0	100.0	100.0	100.0			Total Liabilities & Net Worth	100.0	100.0
						INCOME DATA		
100.0	100.0	100.0	100.0			Net Sales	100.0	100.0
23.2	24.8	23.5	22.9			Gross Profit	24.0	23.4
22.4	22.4	20.5	18.8			Operating Expenses	21.1	20.4
.8	2.5	3.0	4.1			Operating Profit	2.9	2.9
.5	.4	.5	.4			All Other Expenses (net)	.6	.6
.4	2.1	2.5	3.7			Profit Before Taxes	2.3	2.3
						RATIOS		
2.9	2.7	2.2	2.3			Current	2.3	2.3
1.6	1.7	1.5	1.6				1.5	1.6
1.3	1.1	1.1	1.1				1.1	1.1
1.0	1.0	1.1	1.3			Quick	1.1	1.0
.5	.6	.6	(98) .7				(505) .6	.6
.3	.3	.3	.5				.3	.3
0 UND	1 353.3	2 210.0	4 90.2			Sales/Receivables	2 238.7	2 230.0
5 73.5	3 112.9	5 69.1	18 19.8				6 61.2	6 60.2
23 15.9	12 29.6	22 16.9	31 11.7				22 16.4	21 17.2
28 13.2	22 16.8	20 18.5	19 19.3			Cost of Sales/Inventory	18 20.0	22 16.5
42 8.7	32 11.5	26 14.1	26 14.3				30 12.2	30 12.1
89 4.1	45 8.1	38 9.6	47 7.7				45 8.1	46 7.9
2 191.6	3 116.2	7 53.0	9 38.7			Cost of Sales/Payables	6 60.4	6 57.0
22 16.4	9 39.7	12 30.7	16 22.2				14 25.8	13 28.6
43 8.5	17 21.2	19 19.6	25 14.4				26 14.2	23 15.7
9.9	11.9	13.0	9.7			Sales/Working Capital	12.5	12.0
16.1	25.0	27.4	19.9				24.4	24.2
29.8	98.4	126.6	84.9				133.2	143.6
6.0	7.8	8.7	12.5			EBIT/Interest	6.3	7.9
(30) 1.6	(162) 3.3	(216) 3.4	(90) 4.8				(464) 2.8	(432) 3.2
.2	1.4	1.8	2.3				1.3	1.6
3.2	3.7	4.1	10.2			Net Profit + Depr., Dep.,	7.3	5.5
(11) .9	(61) 2.6	(79) 2.0	(35) 3.5			Amort./Cur. Mat. L /T/D	(248) 2.2	(204) 2.5
.3	.9	1.0	1.4				1.1	1.2
.1	.3	.3	.2			Fixed/Worth	.3	.3
.4	.7	.7	.7				.7	.7
1.7	1.7	3.2	1.8				2.6	2.1
.9	.7	.6	.6			Debt/Worth	.8	.7
2.4	1.9	1.8	1.5				1.8	1.7
6.9	4.8	9.1	5.2				7.4	6.3
32.8	48.2	42.8	38.3			% Profit Before Taxes/Tangible	40.8	46.6
(28) 13.8	(150) 21.7	(199) 23.9	(83) 26.1			Net Worth	(424) 19.5	(404) 22.3
-2.1	6.2	8.4	14.5				7.7	9.2
12.1	15.1	16.8	17.7			% Profit Before Taxes/Total	13.4	15.2
3.2	6.2	8.0	10.4			Assets	6.7	7.3
-2.5	2.0	3.1	5.2				1.6	2.6
82.8	48.1	42.4	30.4			Sales/Net Fixed Assets	41.7	41.8
40.5	28.9	21.2	14.7				20.9	21.3
23.6	13.5	9.4	8.2				10.7	10.8
7.3	6.2	5.2	4.0			Sales/Total Assets	5.4	5.5
4.2	4.9	4.1	3.4				4.0	4.1
2.7	3.8	3.1	2.5				3.0	3.2
.6	.7	.6	.7			% Depr., Dep., Amort./Sales	.7	.7
(30) .9	(158) 1.1	(224) 1.1	(87) 1.1				(465) 1.2	(435) 1.2
1.8	1.8	1.7	1.8				1.8	1.7
1.5	1.6	1.3	.9			% Officers', Directors',	1.4	1.4
(17) 3.5	(98) 2.7	(87) 2.5	(23) 1.4			Owners' Comp/Sales	(209) 2.5	(212) 2.3
4.5	4.1	3.4	2.5				4.0	3.8
57474M	1141308M	4933443M	7153624M	1535387M	1156176M	Net Sales ($)	12647830M	12996843M
11584M	217040M	1145083M	2158933M	518724M	346265M	Total Assets ($)	3698329M	3509598M

M = $ thousand   MM = $ million
See Pages 1 through 15 for Explanation of Ratios and Data

Comparative Historical Data / **Current Data Sorted By Sales**

Hist 20	Hist 29	Hist 55	# Postretirement Benefits / Type of Statement	C 5	C 2	C 6	C 22	C 20	
157	132	134	Unqualified		1	1	15	41	76
146	128	149	Reviewed	2	9	9	37	63	29
126	108	134	Compiled	7	19	28	47	24	9
4	5	9	Tax Returns	3	2	1	1	2	
92	124	138	Other	2	10	11	28	35	52

Historical periods: 4/1/92-3/31/93 ALL | 4/1/93-3/31/94 ALL | 4/1/94-3/31/95 ALL
Current split: 138 (4/1-9/30/94) | 426 (10/1/94-3/31/95)

4/1/92-3/31/93 ALL	4/1/93-3/31/94 ALL	4/1/94-3/31/95 ALL	Item	0-1MM	1-3MM	3-5MM	5-10MM	10-25MM	25MM & OVER
525	497	564	**NUMBER OF STATEMENTS**	14	41	50	128	165	166
%	%	%	**ASSETS**	%	%	%	%	%	%
10.3	10.0	10.0	Cash & Equivalents	11.9	7.9	10.2	9.8	11.9	8.5
12.7	14.3	13.5	Trade Receivables - (net)	16.9	15.1	11.7	9.8	12.0	17.7
31.1	31.7	31.0	Inventory	46.4	37.4	38.1	33.3	28.3	27.1
1.7	1.6	1.5	All Other Current	1.0	2.0	.5	1.5	1.6	1.8
55.9	57.6	56.1	Total Current	76.2	62.4	60.5	54.4	53.8	55.1
25.0	23.7	23.8	Fixed Assets (net)	9.8	19.7	19.2	26.0	25.4	24.1
8.7	9.6	10.7	Intangibles (net)	2.8	9.7	12.7	11.7	10.6	10.5
10.4	9.1	9.4	All Other Non-Current	11.3	8.1	7.7	8.0	10.3	10.3
100.0	100.0	100.0	Total	100.0	100.0	100.0	100.0	100.0	100.0
			LIABILITIES						
10.4	11.5	10.2	Notes Payable-Short Term	6.6	8.7	15.4	10.8	10.1	9.0
4.3	4.3	4.7	Cur. Mat.-L /T/D	2.4	5.9	5.0	5.5	5.4	3.3
13.9	14.8	13.7	Trade Payables	22.6	16.5	12.8	12.8	11.9	15.1
.4	.8	.3	Income Taxes Payable	.3	.5	.3	.3	.4	.2
8.2	8.0	7.8	All Other Current	15.5	5.3	7.2	6.7	7.9	8.5
37.2	39.5	36.8	Total Current	47.4	36.9	40.8	36.1	35.7	36.2
16.6	16.2	16.6	Long Term Debt	9.8	21.1	14.0	16.1	17.3	16.5
.2	.2	.3	Deferred Taxes	.0	.2	.1	.4	.1	.5
2.3	3.1	4.3	All Other-Non-Current	12.5	8.0	5.1	4.1	3.7	3.3
43.6	41.0	42.0	Net Worth	30.3	33.8	40.0	43.3	43.1	43.4
100.0	100.0	100.0	Total Liabilities & Net Worth	100.0	100.0	100.0	100.0	100.0	100.0
			INCOME DATA						
100.0	100.0	100.0	Net Sales	100.0	100.0	100.0	100.0	100.0	100.0
23.5	23.0	23.7	Gross Profit	26.0	27.5	24.2	24.8	23.2	22.1
20.6	20.7	20.9	Operating Expenses	25.8	24.0	21.8	22.3	20.6	18.6
2.9	2.3	2.8	Operating Profit	.1	3.5	2.4	2.5	2.6	3.5
.5	.4	.4	All Other Expenses (net)	.5	.8	.3	.4	.4	.5
2.4	2.0	2.4	Profit Before Taxes	-.4	2.7	2.1	2.1	2.2	3.0
			RATIOS						
2.3	2.1	2.4	Current	3.8	2.8	2.4	2.4	2.4	2.1
1.5	1.5	1.6		1.7	1.8	1.5	1.5	1.6	1.5
1.1	1.1	1.1		1.1	1.3	1.1	1.1	1.1	1.2
1.1	1.0	1.1	Quick	.8	1.1	1.0	.9	1.3	1.1
(524) .6	(496) .6	(563) .6		.6	.8	.6	.5	(165) .7	.7
.3	.3	.3		.3	.3	.3	.2	.3	.4
2 195.7	2 192.8	2 215.6	Sales/Receivables	0 UND	0 UND	1 349.4	1 375.9	2 218.8	3 117.5
6 65.0	6 59.5	5 69.4		22 16.4	7 49.3	5 75.5	3 106.1	4 97.1	14 25.8
21 17.7	22 16.4	22 16.3		48 7.6	29 12.5	19 19.1	14 26.8	19 19.1	28 13.1
20 18.0	21 17.6	20 17.9	Cost of Sales/Inventory	55 6.6	31 11.9	26 14.1	22 16.8	20 18.6	19 19.6
28 13.2	28 13.1	28 13.2		76 4.8	44 8.3	38 9.7	28 13.0	26 14.3	25 14.6
41 8.8	42 8.6	44 8.3		183 2.0	73 5.0	47 7.8	43 8.4	34 10.8	42 8.7
6 57.0	7 50.6	6 60.8	Cost of Sales/Payables	8 46.2	4 97.5	6 62.2	4 97.7	6 59.4	8 43.1
12 30.4	13 28.2	12 30.7		43 8.5	23 15.8	10 35.0	10 36.9	11 33.5	15 23.8
20 18.4	21 17.1	22 16.9		61 6.0	47 7.8	17 21.3	18 20.1	17 21.4	25 14.4
12.4	12.9	11.5	Sales/Working Capital	5.0	9.6	11.2	13.3	11.8	12.7
23.4	25.0	24.1		10.0	15.2	25.6	27.2	27.0	25.0
135.9	120.8	94.9		NM	27.2	111.5	92.8	186.6	78.2
8.2	7.1	8.8	EBIT/Interest	8.5	6.9	5.9	7.9	7.6	12.4
(469) 3.6	(446) 3.2	(507) 3.4		(11) 1.3	(37) 2.4	(45) 3.4	(118) 3.4	(147) 3.0	(149) 4.9
1.7	1.4	1.7		-1.6	1.6	1.1	1.6	1.6	2.2
4.5	5.4	4.9	Net Profit + Depr., Dep., Amort./Cur. Mat. L/T/D		3.3	11.4	3.5	3.2	9.2
(190) 2.0	(156) 2.2	(192) 2.2			(18) 2.3	(16) 3.3	(50) 2.0	(50) 1.7	(54) 3.5
1.1	1.0	1.0			.9	1.5	.8	.9	1.4
.3	.3	.3	Fixed/Worth	.0	.3	.3	.3	.3	.3
.6	.7	.7		.1	.6	.7	.7	.7	.7
1.7	2.5	2.1		NM	2.8	3.2	2.1	3.6	1.7
.6	.7	.7	Debt/Worth	.5	1.2	.8	.6	.6	.7
1.6	1.8	1.9		3.0	3.0	2.3	1.9	1.6	1.6
5.3	7.5	6.3		-10.0	6.5	10.8	5.9	10.3	4.9
49.0	45.2	42.6	% Profit Before Taxes/Tangible Net Worth	18.9	67.5	38.5	45.3	34.2	43.2
(457) 22.6	(418) 18.8	(470) 22.3		(10) 7.3	(34) 24.3	(41) 20.5	(106) 22.3	(132) 17.7	(147) 27.1
9.1	6.2	8.0		-18.2	12.1	4.7	7.3	6.1	15.3
15.8	13.5	15.8	% Profit Before Taxes/Total Assets	8.2	14.6	11.1	14.8	16.6	18.6
7.6	6.2	7.9		2.7	4.9	7.5	6.2	7.4	9.8
2.7	1.4	2.4		-4.9	2.4	.8	2.2	1.9	5.1
43.4	49.8	44.3	Sales/Net Fixed Assets	190.6	46.6	48.1	42.0	42.7	41.8
21.7	23.1	22.6		47.0	25.8	30.3	21.3	22.1	20.6
11.2	11.1	10.9		20.6	11.3	14.5	11.4	9.6	9.9
5.6	5.5	5.5	Sales/Total Assets	3.5	4.5	5.5	5.7	6.0	5.3
4.3	4.3	4.2		2.4	3.6	4.4	4.5	4.3	3.7
3.3	3.1	3.1		1.8	2.4	3.5	3.5	3.1	3.0
.7	.7	.7	% Depr., Dep., Amort./Sales	.6	.7	.5	.8	.7	.6
(477) 1.2	(454) 1.2	(509) 1.1		(11) 1.2	(37) 1.4	(44) 1.1	(116) 1.2	(154) 1.2	(147) 1.0
1.8	1.8	1.8		2.4	2.3	1.9	1.8	1.8	1.5
1.5	1.5	1.4	% Officers', Directors', Owners' Comp/Sales		2.7	1.1	1.6	1.3	.9
(220) 2.6	(202) 2.4	(228) 2.4			(23) 3.6	(30) 2.0	(67) 2.3	(61) 2.5	(42) 1.6
4.6	4.3	3.8			4.4	3.4	3.9	3.6	3.2
13212161M	13104931M	15977412M	Net Sales ($)	8883M	84900M	203113M	943036M	2632192M	12105288M
3522530M	3403717M	4397629M	Total Assets ($)	3744M	30724M	51395M	224325M	727107M	3360334M

M = $ thousand   MM = $ million
See Pages 1 through 15 for Explanation of Ratios and Data

WHOLESALERS—FLOOR COVERINGS. SIC# 5023

Current Data Sorted By Assets							Comparative Historical Data		
1	3	4	1			# Postretirement Benefits			
						Type of Statement			
	4	15	11	2	2	Unqualified		39	38
1	22	36	4			Reviewed		72	60
10	34	8	2			Compiled		58	59
3	1					Tax Returns		1	1
6	10	11	10		1	Other		40	38
	61 (4/1-9/30/94)		132 (10/1/94-3/31/95)					4/1/90-3/31/91	4/1/91-3/31/92
0-500M	500M-2MM	2-10MM	10-50MM	50-100MM	100-250MM			ALL	ALL
20	71	70	27	2	3	NUMBER OF STATEMENTS		210	196
%	%	%	%	%	%	**ASSETS**		%	%
7.6	5.2	3.2	4.3			Cash & Equivalents		5.7	6.1
42.8	33.3	38.6	34.0			Trade Receivables - (net)		35.4	35.6
33.4	41.7	41.5	38.5			Inventory		39.0	38.6
.6	2.3	1.6	2.3			All Other Current		2.3	1.2
84.4	82.4	84.9	79.1			Total Current		82.4	81.4
10.4	12.1	9.3	14.2			Fixed Assets (net)		12.1	12.2
.1	1.0	.5	1.3			Intangibles (net)		.5	.7
5.0	4.5	5.2	5.4			All Other Non-Current		5.0	5.8
100.0	100.0	100.0	100.0			Total		100.0	100.0
						LIABILITIES			
12.0	13.9	20.9	19.2			Notes Payable-Short Term		17.5	17.7
1.5	2.7	2.2	1.5			Cur. Mat. -L/T/D		3.5	3.0
28.0	21.9	19.6	16.1			Trade Payables		21.9	19.8
.8	.3	.3	.5			Income Taxes Payable		.4	.5
9.7	8.2	10.8	11.6			All Other Current		8.9	7.4
52.0	46.9	53.8	48.8			Total Current		52.3	48.4
8.5	9.3	5.9	13.8			Long Term Debt		9.6	8.6
.0	.2	.0	.1			Deferred Taxes		.3	.2
4.1	5.9	3.7	3.9			All Other-Non-Current		3.1	2.1
35.4	37.7	36.6	33.3			Net Worth		34.7	40.6
100.0	100.0	100.0	100.0			Total Liabilities & Net Worth		100.0	100.0
						INCOME DATA			
100.0	100.0	100.0	100.0			Net Sales		100.0	100.0
29.1	27.3	24.2	25.4			Gross Profit		27.0	26.9
26.1	25.1	21.3	21.1			Operating Expenses		25.2	25.2
3.0	2.2	2.9	4.3			Operating Profit		1.7	1.6
.1	.4	.6	1.0			All Other Expenses (net)		.6	.5
2.9	1.8	2.3	3.4			Profit Before Taxes		1.1	1.2
						RATIOS			
2.5	2.4	2.1	2.4					2.1	2.4
1.7	1.8	1.5	1.8			Current		1.6	1.7
1.4	1.4	1.3	1.2					1.2	1.3
1.4	1.2	1.1	1.0					1.1	1.4
1.0	.8	.8	.8			Quick		.7	.8
.7	.6	.5	.6					.5	.6
17 21.1	25 14.4	33 11.1	40 9.2					32 11.4	31 11.7
45 8.1	38 9.6	41 8.8	47 7.7			Sales/Receivables		41 9.0	40 9.1
60 6.1	51 7.1	54 6.8	62 5.9					49 7.5	51 7.2
22 16.5	35 10.4	42 8.6	47 7.7					37 10.0	36 10.1
46 7.9	72 5.1	61 6.0	79 4.6			Cost of Sales/Inventory		65 5.6	63 5.8
87 4.2	94 3.9	89 4.1	118 3.1					96 3.8	96 3.8
20 18.1	20 18.5	14 25.4	19 19.7					18 20.7	17 20.9
35 10.5	31 11.6	24 15.1	23 16.1			Cost of Sales/Payables		31 11.9	29 12.6
55 6.6	44 8.3	43 8.5	51 7.1					49 7.4	45 8.1
5.6	5.5	7.3	4.4					6.4	6.0
13.2	8.7	9.7	9.7			Sales/Working Capital		10.8	10.2
29.9	17.6	17.5	20.6					23.3	19.9
10.8	5.8	6.9	7.2					4.0	4.1
(18) 4.2	(68) 2.9	(69) 3.7	(24) 3.1			EBIT/Interest		(186) 1.9	(175) 1.9
1.4	1.9	1.8	1.5					1.0	1.0
	3.2	7.4	9.2					5.0	3.8
	(24) 1.3	(19) 3.4	(11) 7.2			Net Profit + Depr., Dep., Amort./Cur. Mat. L /T/D		(109) 1.6	(95) 1.3
	.7	1.3	3.0					.4	.2
.1	.1	.1	.2					.1	.1
.2	.2	.2	.4			Fixed/Worth		.3	.3
.4	.7	.4	.8					.6	.5
1.0	.8	1.0	1.3					1.0	.7
1.8	1.8	1.8	2.7			Debt/Worth		2.1	1.6
3.5	3.8	4.0	5.3					4.1	3.3
43.0	26.7	31.0	34.8					23.3	20.2
(18) 22.5	(66) 15.9	(69) 17.3	(25) 18.6			% Profit Before Taxes/Tangible Net Worth		(195) 10.9	(190) 7.1
2.5	6.8	8.9	6.2					2.0	1.5
13.1	11.4	10.2	10.6					8.2	7.9
8.0	5.6	6.1	6.9			% Profit Before Taxes/Total Assets		2.9	2.6
.8	2.8	2.6	2.1					−.1	.3
119.6	100.0	106.3	42.3					71.5	73.8
54.9	50.6	49.4	19.3			Sales/Net Fixed Assets		39.6	40.4
28.8	20.7	26.1	11.1					18.2	19.3
5.1	3.8	4.0	3.2					3.9	3.9
3.6	3.0	3.2	2.3			Sales/Total Assets		3.1	3.1
2.9	2.5	2.3	1.6					2.4	2.3
.2	.4	.3	.5					.4	.4
(17) .6	(59) .6	(66) .5	(24) .8			% Depr., Dep., Amort./Sales		(185) .7	(167) .7
.8	1.0	.8	1.4					1.1	1.1
2.9	2.4	1.1						2.0	2.2
(13) 6.6	(42) 3.7	(38) 2.1				% Officers', Directors', Owners' Comp/Sales		(98) 3.3	(93) 3.9
8.6	6.4	3.6						6.3	6.3
26793M	270706M	1002547M	1329085M	297900M	2180474M	Net Sales ($)		2397628M	2077604M
6147M	82629M	312089M	581081M	126996M	663670M	Total Assets ($)		930059M	761686M

M = $ thousand   MM = $ million
See Pages 1 through 15 for Explanation of Ratios and Data

WHOLESALERS—FLOOR COVERINGS. SIC# 5023

Comparative Historical Data				# Postretirement Benefits	Current Data Sorted By Sales					
1	10	9		Type of Statement	1	2	2	3	1
36	40	34		Unqualified	1	1	8	7	17
61	64	63		Reviewed	9	15	12	18	9
54	52	54		Compiled	6	21	10	12	4	1
2	1	4		Tax Returns	3	1			
42	28	38		Other	3	8	5	3	9	10
4/1/92-3/31/93 ALL	4/1/93-3/31/94 ALL	4/1/94-3/31/95 ALL			61 (4/1-9/30/94)			132 (10/1/94-3/31/95)		
					0-1MM	1-3MM	3-5MM	5-10MM	10-25MM	25MM & OVER
195	185	193		NUMBER OF STATEMENTS	9	42	32	35	38	37
%	%	%		ASSETS	%	%	%	%	%	%
4.1	4.6	4.6		Cash & Equivalents		5.6	5.0	2.9	5.3	2.9
37.4	38.5	36.4		Trade Receivables - (net)		35.6	30.5	36.1	41.5	35.9
40.1	37.7	40.0		Inventory		39.0	40.4	45.1	38.8	39.4
1.5	1.8	1.8		All Other Current		2.4	2.4	1.3	1.2	1.9
83.1	82.6	82.7		Total Current		82.7	78.3	85.4	86.8	80.0
10.3	11.0	11.6		Fixed Assets (net)		10.4	16.7	8.5	8.4	14.1
1.3	1.0	.7		Intangibles (net)		.3	.3	1.7	.8	.9
5.3	5.5	5.0		All Other Non-Current		6.6	4.7	4.3	4.1	5.0
100.0	100.0	100.0		Total		100.0	100.0	100.0	100.0	100.0
				LIABILITIES						
17.2	15.2	16.8		Notes Payable-Short Term		13.4	12.4	17.2	22.2	19.3
3.7	2.3	2.2		Cur. Mat.-L /T/D		3.2	2.3	2.6	1.6	1.7
21.3	20.0	20.6		Trade Payables		25.2	19.7	22.5	17.8	16.5
.5	1.8	.4		Income Taxes Payable		.4	.1	.5	.2	.5
8.5	8.9	9.7		All Other Current		8.1	8.6	12.9	12.1	7.6
51.1	48.2	49.7		Total Current		50.4	43.1	55.6	53.9	45.6
8.2	10.1	8.7		Long Term Debt		9.6	12.2	5.1	4.7	11.6
.1	.1	.1		Deferred Taxes		.2	.1	.0	.0	.2
2.5	2.7	4.5		All Other-Non-Current		5.0	5.9	4.6	4.6	3.7
38.1	38.9	37.0		Net Worth		34.9	38.6	34.6	36.7	39.0
100.0	100.0	100.0		Total Liabilities & Net Worth		100.0	100.0	100.0	100.0	100.0
				INCOME DATA						
100.0	100.0	100.0		Net Sales		100.0	100.0	100.0	100.0	100.0
27.5	25.4	25.9		Gross Profit		28.1	27.4	26.2	24.1	23.6
24.6	23.6	23.1		Operating Expenses		26.1	24.6	23.8	21.0	19.8
3.0	1.8	2.8		Operating Profit		2.0	2.8	2.4	3.1	3.8
.9	.4	.5		All Other Expenses (net)		.7	.0	.5	.5	.6
2.1	1.4	2.4		Profit Before Taxes		1.3	2.8	1.9	2.5	3.2
				RATIOS						
2.3	2.6	2.3				2.4	2.8	2.1	2.2	2.3
1.6	1.8	1.7		Current		1.6	1.7	1.6	1.5	1.9
1.3	1.3	1.3				1.3	1.3	1.3	1.3	1.3
1.2	1.5	1.1				1.2	1.2	1.0	1.3	1.0
.8	.9	.8		Quick		.7	.8	.7	.8	.8
.6	.6	.6				.5	.6	.5	.5	.7

34	10.8	33	11.0	30	12.0	Sales/Receivables	26	14.1	26	13.8	26	14.1	33	11.1	34	10.8
42	8.6	42	8.6	41	8.9		42	8.6	38	9.5	39	9.3	43	8.4	42	8.6
54	6.7	53	6.9	54	6.8		57	6.4	47	7.7	56	6.5	58	6.3	50	7.3
41	8.8	32	11.5	38	9.5	Cost of Sales/Inventory	28	12.9	38	9.6	42	8.7	40	9.1	44	8.3
62	5.9	57	6.4	65	5.6		64	5.7	78	4.7	78	4.7	55	6.6	59	6.2
96	3.8	81	4.5	94	3.9		111	3.3	101	3.6	89	4.1	83	4.4	99	3.7
19	19.4	15	24.0	19	19.7	Cost of Sales/Payables	26	14.2	12	31.3	20	18.4	14	26.6	16	23.2
30	12.2	24	15.1	27	13.3		37	10.0	32	11.3	30	12.2	24	15.3	22	16.3
47	7.7	42	8.6	47	7.8		59	6.2	61	6.0	45	8.1	34	10.8	39	9.3

6.3		5.7		5.8	Sales/Working Capital		5.2	4.8	6.9	7.4	5.1
10.2		9.3		9.5			8.8	8.6	9.7	9.7	10.0
19.0		16.5		17.6			21.4	18.4	16.4	18.0	18.9

	5.9		7.2		7.1	EBIT/Interest		6.1		5.9		5.9		9.2		7.9
(186)	2.6	(169)	3.1	(184)	3.3		(41)	2.8	(31)	3.2	(34)	4.0		3.4	(33)	3.1
	1.3		1.6		1.9			1.6		1.8		2.2		1.8		1.8
	4.6		9.1		6.8	Net Profit + Depr., Dep., Amort./Cur. Mat. L/T/D				4.3		6.8		7.9		9.3
(73)	1.9	(77)	2.4	(59)	3.0			(10)	1.3	(11)	1.9	(10)	3.3	(18)	7.0
	.7		.9		1.1				.8		1.0		1.0		3.3
	.1		.1		.1	Fixed/Worth		.1	.1	.1	.1	.2
	.2		.2		.2			.2	.3	.2	.2	.4
	.5		.5		.5			.9	.8	.3	.4	.7
	1.0		.9		1.0	Debt/Worth		.8	.9	1.2	1.0	1.0
	1.8		1.7		1.8			2.0	1.7	2.1	2.2	1.4
	3.4		3.3		3.8			4.7	3.9	2.9	4.7	3.5

	29.2		27.2		29.7	% Profit Before Taxes/Tangible Net Worth		43.1		23.9	25.2	40.3	35.4
(186)	12.2	(176)	13.5	(183)	17.3		(37)	20.7	(31)	14.7	(33) 18.3	17.8	(35) 17.0
	3.4		3.8		7.8			5.5		5.3	9.0	7.9	8.4
	10.1		10.4		11.2	% Profit Before Taxes/Total Assets		12.6	8.6	10.5	9.8	13.1
	4.4		4.5		6.0			5.8	5.3	5.7	7.4	6.9
	.8		1.4		2.6			1.5	3.0	3.1	2.5	3.8
	85.2		85.6		94.8	Sales/Net Fixed Assets		143.4	91.3	68.1	114.7	62.3
	45.8		45.7		46.1			54.9	30.6	46.9	60.1	23.6
	20.9		22.1		20.3			21.1	10.8	30.0	27.6	11.1
	3.9		4.1		3.9	Sales/Total Assets		3.6	3.6	3.6	4.3	4.1
	3.2		3.1		3.0			3.0	2.9	3.2	3.4	3.1
	2.4		2.5		2.3			2.3	2.1	2.6	2.8	2.2

	.4		.4		.3	% Depr., Dep., Amort./Sales		.3		.3		.5		.3	.4
(171)	.7	(169)	.6	(168)	.6		(34)	.5	(28)	.7	(33)	.6	(34) .5	(31) .8
	1.0		1.0		.9			.8		1.1		.9		.7	1.0
	1.5		1.7		1.6	% Officers', Directors', Owners' Comp/Sales		2.2		2.6		1.8	1.0
(95)	3.1	(96)	3.0	(100)	3.0		(29)	3.1	(21)	3.9	(17) 3.1	(23) 1.6
	6.0		5.7		6.0			7.1		7.6		5.1	3.3

2264719M	2849106M	5107505M		Net Sales ($)	5251M	82824M	122342M	258772M	616624M	4021692M
823834M	1070612M	1772612M		Total Assets ($)	2761M	31904M	47867M	92971M	254109M	1343000M

M = $ thousand   MM = $ million
See Pages 1 through 15 for Explanation of Ratios and Data

WHOLESALERS—FURNITURE. SIC# 5021

Current Data Sorted By Assets						# Postretirement Benefits / Type of Statement	Comparative Historical Data	
1	4	6	3			# Postretirement Benefits		
	8	15	8	2		Unqualified	34	50
4	32	33	3	1		Reviewed	79	74
16	25	6	2			Compiled	69	62
2	4	1				Tax Returns		1
7	24	24	6			Other	38	39
0-500M	80 (4/1-9/30/94) 500M-2MM	2-10MM	143 (10/1/94-3/31/95) 10-50MM	50-100MM	100-250MM		4/1/90-3/31/91 ALL	4/1/91-3/31/92 ALL
29	93	79	19	3		NUMBER OF STATEMENTS	220	226
%	%	%	%	%	%	ASSETS	%	%
10.4	8.1	5.8	5.3			Cash & Equivalents	7.5	7.6
36.7	38.0	41.9	42.6			Trade Receivables - (net)	38.9	37.6
33.2	29.0	30.9	24.8			Inventory	30.8	31.8
4.6	2.5	1.6	1.5			All Other Current	2.6	2.0
84.8	77.6	80.3	74.1			Total Current	79.6	79.0
9.3	14.0	12.2	14.7			Fixed Assets (net)	12.7	13.3
1.1	1.5	1.0	1.6			Intangibles (net)	1.4	1.4
4.8	6.8	6.5	9.6			All Other Non-Current	6.3	6.4
100.0	100.0	100.0	100.0			Total	100.0	100.0
						LIABILITIES		
16.2	14.1	19.2	14.7			Notes Payable-Short Term	14.9	17.5
1.4	2.1	3.5	2.4			Cur. Mat. -L/T/D	2.5	1.9
19.9	25.4	22.0	20.7			Trade Payables	22.5	21.7
.4	1.2	.5	.4			Income Taxes Payable	.6	.4
10.0	11.2	11.1	10.6			All Other Current	10.4	10.4
47.9	54.0	56.3	48.7			Total Current	51.0	51.9
4.9	10.0	6.7	9.8			Long Term Debt	9.8	10.5
.1	.4	.2	1.3			Deferred Taxes	.5	.2
4.1	2.9	5.0	1.6			All Other-Non-Current	2.7	3.3
43.0	32.7	31.7	38.6			Net Worth	36.1	34.1
100.0	100.0	100.0	100.0			Total Liabilities & Net Worth	100.0	100.0
						INCOME DATA		
100.0	100.0	100.0	100.0			Net Sales	100.0	100.0
30.3	28.3	27.1	23.0			Gross Profit	29.9	29.8
29.1	26.8	25.4	19.9			Operating Expenses	27.3	27.8
1.1	1.5	1.6	3.1			Operating Profit	2.5	1.9
-.6	.5	.3	.2			All Other Expenses (net)	.5	.7
1.7	1.0	1.3	2.9			Profit Before Taxes	2.0	1.2
						RATIOS		
3.0	1.9	1.9	2.0			Current	2.4	2.3
1.9	1.4	1.5	1.3				1.5	1.5
1.2	1.1	1.1	1.2				1.2	1.2
2.1	1.3	1.1	1.3			Quick	1.5	1.3
1.0	.9	.8	1.0				.9	.9
.6	.6	.6	.6				.6	.6
22 16.7	22 16.6	33 11.0	37 9.9			Sales/Receivables	27 13.4	31 11.7
31 11.8	34 10.8	46 8.0	55 6.6				41 8.9	41 8.8
40 9.2	61 6.0	66 5.5	69 5.3				56 6.5	56 6.5
1 567.4	16 22.4	20 18.5	20 18.7			Cost of Sales/Inventory	17 21.4	20 18.1
43 8.5	35 10.4	46 7.9	38 9.7				45 8.1	49 7.5
87 4.2	79 4.6	101 3.6	63 5.8				81 4.5	87 4.2
5 69.0	19 19.6	21 17.5	19 19.6			Cost of Sales/Payables	16 22.9	18 20.1
23 15.8	32 11.4	34 10.8	30 12.3				32 11.5	31 11.7
49 7.5	50 7.3	48 7.6	48 7.6				52 7.0	48 7.6
5.4	7.1	7.0	6.9			Sales/Working Capital	6.2	6.5
13.3	15.5	13.3	12.9				13.4	11.3
54.7	46.8	41.2	23.6				31.6	29.2
6.5	7.1	5.3	8.5			EBIT/Interest	6.8	5.1
(21) 2.9	(82) 2.6	(71) 2.6	(17) 3.5				(204) 2.6	(211) 2.1
-1.3	.8	1.6	2.4				1.3	1.0
	7.8	5.3				Net Profit + Depr., Dep., Amort./Cur. Mat. L./T/D	10.4	4.8
	(36) 2.1	(33) 2.0					(103) 2.9	(85) 2.2
	-.2	.7					1.3	.8
.0	.1	.2	.1			Fixed/Worth	.1	.1
.2	.3	.3	.4				.3	.3
.5	.9	.5	.7				.8	.8
.6	1.2	1.0	1.0			Debt/Worth	.9	.9
1.3	2.1	2.9	1.8				2.2	2.1
2.7	4.3	6.1	4.3				4.9	5.0
61.9	29.2	39.8	31.3			% Profit Before Taxes/Tangible Net Worth	31.2	28.8
(26) 16.9	(86) 10.6	(76) 19.7	(18) 22.0				(207) 16.6	(210) 13.5
-3.2	.1	8.1	13.3				3.4	.7
18.7	8.0	9.7	11.0			% Profit Before Taxes/Total Assets	10.5	8.9
5.4	3.3	4.5	8.2				5.1	4.0
-7.5	-.2	1.8	3.1				1.1	.0
281.8	96.9	90.8	75.6			Sales/Net Fixed Assets	77.4	77.6
63.7	42.7	52.0	35.9				38.6	35.3
31.0	20.1	19.2	10.0				18.6	15.8
6.5	4.8	3.6	3.5			Sales/Total Assets	4.4	4.1
4.7	3.4	3.1	2.8				3.3	3.1
2.7	2.4	2.3	2.2				2.4	2.2
.3	.4	.3	.5			% Depr., Dep., Amort./Sales	.4	.4
(18) .6	(84) .6	(73) .5	(16) .8				(192) .7	(203) .8
1.0	1.2	1.1	1.1				1.2	1.3
2.7	1.9	1.4				% Officers', Directors', Owners' Comp/Sales	2.6	2.2
(18) 3.9	(46) 3.4	(40) 2.7					(92) 4.1	(104) 3.9
6.4	5.9	4.5					6.4	6.8
44799M	406472M	1092504M	1004037M	359995M		Net Sales ($)	2081344M	2619351M
9409M	105706M	352983M	371833M	196794M		Total Assets ($)	647123M	857842M

M = $ thousand   MM = $ million
See Pages 1 through 15 for Explanation of Ratios and Data

Comparative Historical Data			# Postretirement Benefits	Current Data Sorted By Sales					
6	10	14		3			5	3	3
			Type of Statement						
40	40	33	Unqualified		4		7	8	14
79	84	73	Reviewed	1	12	14	25	16	5
77	54	49	Compiled	4	24	10	7	3	1
1	1	7	Tax Returns	1	3	2		1	
37	51	61	Other	5	11	6	18	10	11
4/1/92-3/31/93 ALL	4/1/93-3/31/94 ALL	4/1/94-3/31/95 ALL		80 (4/1-9/30/94)			143 (10/1/94-3/31/95)		
				0-1MM	1-3MM	3-5MM	5-10MM	10-25MM	25MM & OVER
234	230	223	**NUMBER OF STATEMENTS**	11	54	32	57	38	31
%	%	%	**ASSETS**	%	%	%	%	%	%
6.8	8.0	7.3	Cash & Equivalents	9.4	8.6	9.2	7.8	4.6	4.4
39.6	36.9	39.4	Trade Receivables - (net)	34.6	32.3	37.0	40.2	46.3	45.8
31.4	31.7	29.9	Inventory	31.9	33.2	24.6	35.4	24.6	25.0
1.9	2.3	2.3	All Other Current	.7	4.6	1.6	1.5	1.9	1.7
79.8	78.9	78.8	Total Current	76.6	78.7	72.4	84.9	77.4	77.0
12.1	12.8	13.0	Fixed Assets (net)	9.0	14.4	17.2	10.3	11.3	14.4
1.5	1.6	1.3	Intangibles (net)	6.2	.7	2.2	.7	.7	1.2
6.7	6.6	6.9	All Other Non-Current	8.2	6.1	8.1	4.1	10.6	7.4
100.0	100.0	100.0	Total	100.0	100.0	100.0	100.0	100.0	100.0
			LIABILITIES						
14.5	13.4	16.1	Notes Payable-Short Term	4.2	16.7	12.0	15.9	21.7	17.2
3.0	1.6	2.5	Cur. Mat.-L./T/D	4.0	2.0	1.8	4.0	1.6	2.2
21.9	19.2	23.0	Trade Payables	21.2	21.8	19.2	25.0	25.9	22.4
.5	1.9	.8	Income Taxes Payable	.2	1.3	1.1	.4	.4	.9
10.6	11.8	11.0	All Other Current	4.2	9.0	12.3	13.1	10.2	12.5
50.5	47.8	53.4	Total Current	33.8	50.8	46.4	58.4	59.7	55.3
9.0	8.4	8.2	Long Term Debt	16.6	9.6	10.6	5.9	5.8	7.5
.3	.4	.4	Deferred Taxes	.0	.4	.8	.0	.6	.8
3.1	4.0	3.7	All Other-Non-Current	10.3	3.0	5.7	3.9	2.5	1.6
37.1	39.4	34.3	Net Worth	39.3	36.2	36.5	31.8	31.3	34.8
100.0	100.0	100.0	Total Liabilities & Net Worth	100.0	100.0	100.0	100.0	100.0	100.0
			INCOME DATA						
100.0	100.0	100.0	Net Sales	100.0	100.0	100.0	100.0	100.0	100.0
28.9	27.9	27.6	Gross Profit	36.3	31.2	30.4	26.8	22.1	23.7
26.6	26.2	26.0	Operating Expenses	34.8	29.2	29.8	25.4	20.8	20.9
2.3	1.7	1.6	Operating Profit	1.5	2.0	.6	1.4	1.3	2.8
.2	.2	.3	All Other Expenses (net)	.4	.4	-.1	.4	.1	.7
2.1	1.5	1.3	Profit Before Taxes	1.1	1.6	.7	1.0	1.1	2.1
			RATIOS						
2.3 / 1.5 / 1.2	2.3 / 1.7 / 1.2	2.0 / 1.5 / 1.2	Current	3.7 / 2.1 / 1.6	2.3 / 1.6 / 1.1	2.5 / 1.7 / 1.1	1.8 / 1.5 / 1.2	1.5 / 1.2 / 1.1	1.8 / 1.3 / 1.2
1.3 / 1.0 / .6	1.4 / .9 / .6	1.2 / .9 / .6	Quick	2.8 / 1.1 / .7	1.4 / .8 / .5	1.6 / 1.0 / .7	1.1 / .8 / .5	1.1 / .8 / .7	1.1 / 1.0 / .7
12.3 (30) / 9.1 (40) / 6.7 (54)	13.1 (28) / 9.3 (39) / 6.7 (54)	14.6 (25) / 9.1 (40) / 5.9 (62)	Sales/Receivables	13.7 (27) / 6.4 (57) / 2.6 (140)	17.5 (21) / 11.2 (33) / 6.1 (60)	17.5 (21) / 11.4 (32) / 7.8 (47)	16.3 (22) / 9.1 (40) / 5.7 (64)	11.1 (33) / 8.2 (45) / 6.3 (58)	10.2 (36) / 6.7 (54) / 5.3 (69)
20.0 (18) / 7.8 (47) / 4.1 (89)	21.7 (17) / 7.6 (48) / 4.0 (91)	21.2 (17) / 8.9 (41) / 4.5 (81)	Cost of Sales/Inventory	10.1 (36) / 3.3 (111) / 1.9 (192)	23.3 (16) / 6.8 (54) / 3.6 (101)	25.0 (15) / 12.0 (30) / 5.6 (65)	18.0 (20) / 7.7 (47) / 3.6 (101)	26.1 (14) / 12.4 (29) / 6.5 (56)	21.2 (17) / 9.1 (40) / 6.9 (53)
21.8 (17) / 12.4 (29) / 7.9 (46)	25.7 (14) / 14.4 (25) / 8.6 (42)	19.4 (19) / 11.6 (31) / 7.5 (49)	Cost of Sales/Payables	17.3 (21) / 7.3 (50) / 5.3 (69)	21.3 (17) / 9.7 (38) / 5.6 (65)	23.3 (16) / 15.8 (23) / 7.8 (47)	17.0 (21) / 9.8 (37) / 7.9 (46)	20.0 (18) / 12.8 (29) / 8.5 (43)	18.6 (20) / 12.3 (30) / 7.7 (47)
6.5 / 11.9 / 27.8	6.6 / 11.0 / 29.9	7.0 / 13.7 / 39.6	Sales/Working Capital	2.1 / 5.4 / 6.1	5.3 / 12.3 / 32.8	6.6 / 15.3 / 70.4	7.5 / 13.7 / 35.3	11.7 / 25.4 / 97.1	8.2 / 15.3 / 29.9
(218) 6.7 / 2.9 / 1.3	(213) 7.4 / 3.0 / 1.3	(193) 6.0 / 2.9 / 1.2	EBIT/Interest		(46) 6.2 / 2.3 / .8	(29) 7.3 / 1.6 / .1	(48) 5.4 / 2.6 / 1.1	(33) 6.0 / 3.0 / 1.6	(28) 8.4 / 3.5 / 1.9
(83) 6.1 / 2.1 / 1.0	(72) 8.7 / 2.4 / .6	(78) 7.0 / 2.0 / .1	Net Profit + Depr., Dep., Amort./Cur. Mat. L/T/D		(16) 3.0 / 1.2 / -1.8	(12) 7.2 / 1.6 / -1.0	(20) 24.5 / 2.5 / .1	(18) 6.0 / 2.2 / 1.0	(10) 9.1 / 6.2 / -2.7
.1 / .3 / .6	.1 / .2 / .7	.1 / .3 / .6	Fixed/Worth	.0 / .1 / 3.0	.1 / .3 / 1.3	.2 / .4 / 1.0	.1 / .2 / .5	.1 / .4 / .6	.2 / .5 / .7
.8 / 1.9 / 4.1	.8 / 1.7 / 3.6	1.1 / 2.2 / 4.6	Debt/Worth	.6 / 1.7 / 14.6	.9 / 1.7 / 3.5	.9 / 1.8 / 4.7	1.2 / 2.7 / 4.9	1.3 / 2.9 / 5.1	1.0 / 2.0 / 4.4
(221) 36.5 / 15.6 / 4.2	(220) 28.5 / 12.6 / 2.5	(209) 36.4 / 16.1 / 2.4	% Profit Before Taxes/Tangible Net Worth		(48) 26.0 / 10.6 / 2.3	(30) 24.6 / 6.7 / -6.4	(56) 44.3 / 23.0 / 3.7	(37) 37.5 / 17.8 / 7.5	(29) 32.1 / 21.5 / 8.8
11.0 / 4.3 / .7	11.7 / 4.3 / .8	9.8 / 4.5 / .7	% Profit Before Taxes/Total Assets	6.5 / 3.6 / -4.5	8.8 / 3.3 / .3	11.8 / 1.7 / -2.4	8.5 / 5.0 / 1.5	10.0 / 4.3 / 1.6	10.9 / 6.6 / 2.0
90.0 / 47.4 / 19.8	90.6 / 41.5 / 20.6	94.8 / 45.8 / 19.6	Sales/Net Fixed Assets	UND / 26.9 / 15.1	116.1 / 40.3 / 19.2	90.2 / 37.4 / 15.1	101.4 / 67.6 / 25.9	138.3 / 59.1 / 18.2	57.6 / 30.0 / 15.1
4.2 / 3.2 / 2.5	4.6 / 3.3 / 2.4	4.5 / 3.2 / 2.4	Sales/Total Assets	3.9 / 1.9 / 1.1	4.7 / 2.6 / 2.1	5.6 / 3.6 / 2.3	4.4 / 3.3 / 2.5	5.0 / 3.4 / 2.7	3.8 / 3.2 / 2.5
(203) .4 / .7 / 1.2	(199) .4 / .6 / 1.1	(194) .4 / .6 / 1.2	% Depr., Dep., Amort./Sales		(47) .4 / .7 / 1.4	(29) .3 / .8 / 1.4	(51) .3 / .5 / .9	(34) .4 / .5 / 1.1	(28) .5 / .8 / 1.4
(97) 1.9 / 3.5 / 6.9	(104) 1.7 / 3.4 / 6.5	(109) 1.8 / 3.1 / 5.2	% Officers', Directors', Owners' Comp/Sales		(35) 2.7 / 4.5 / 7.1	(17) 1.9 / 3.2 / 5.9	(27) 1.4 / 2.3 / 5.0	(19) .9 / 2.6 / 3.3	
2415770M / 800145M	3061009M / 1052749M	2907807M / 1036725M	Net Sales ($) / Total Assets ($)	6334M / 4216M	102941M / 41949M	129800M / 43689M	399953M / 130652M	593850M / 234486M	1674929M / 581733M

M = $ thousand   MM = $ million

See Pages 1 through 15 for Explanation of Ratios and Data

Current Data Sorted By Assets / Comparative Historical Data

	0-500M	500M-2MM	2-10MM	10-50MM	50-100MM	100-250MM		4/1/90-3/31/91 ALL	4/1/91-3/31/92 ALL
	2	9	6	3		2	# Postretirement Benefits		
							Type of Statement		
	1	16	28	22	4	2	Unqualified	65	53
	10	50	60	10			Reviewed	123	119
	40	61	18	1			Compiled	125	130
	7	2	1				Tax Returns	7	7
	29	30	37	7			Other	76	87
		149 (4/1-9/30/94)		287 (10/1/94-3/31/95)					
	87	159	144	40	4	2	**NUMBER OF STATEMENTS**	396	396
	%	%	%	%	%	%	**ASSETS**	%	%
	9.5	8.1	5.5	5.8			Cash & Equivalents	7.7	7.6
	28.2	32.9	31.6	25.5			Trade Receivables - (net)	28.7	31.8
	34.6	40.7	37.1	39.7			Inventory	37.9	35.8
	2.9	1.6	2.2	2.8			All Other Current	2.5	1.9
	75.3	83.3	76.4	73.8			Total Current	76.7	77.1
	16.5	10.5	15.0	16.9			Fixed Assets (net)	15.7	14.0
	2.0	1.3	1.5	2.7			Intangibles (net)	1.5	1.4
	6.3	4.9	7.1	6.6			All Other Non-Current	6.1	7.5
	100.0	100.0	100.0	100.0			Total	100.0	100.0
							LIABILITIES		
	15.8	13.5	16.6	21.5			Notes Payable-Short Term	18.4	16.3
	4.7	3.0	2.1	2.8			Cur. Mat. -L/T/D	3.2	3.7
	17.1	23.2	18.9	14.6			Trade Payables	19.9	21.1
	.3	.4	.4	.4			Income Taxes Payable	.8	.7
	8.8	8.7	8.0	7.2			All Other Current	8.1	8.8
	46.7	48.8	46.2	46.6			Total Current	50.4	50.6
	12.6	8.9	8.7	9.7			Long Term Debt	8.9	9.0
	.1	.2	.3	.4			Deferred Taxes	.3	.3
	2.7	6.2	5.0	4.4			All Other-Non-Current	4.0	4.6
	37.9	35.9	39.9	38.9			Net Worth	36.5	35.5
	100.0	100.0	100.0	100.0			Total Liabilities & Net Worth	100.0	100.0
							INCOME DATA		
	100.0	100.0	100.0	100.0			Net Sales	100.0	100.0
	38.6	30.1	29.2	29.5			Gross Profit	32.9	31.8
	35.7	28.3	25.7	24.0			Operating Expenses	29.0	27.6
	2.8	1.7	3.5	5.6			Operating Profit	3.9	4.2
	.5	.7	.7	1.4			All Other Expenses (net)	1.3	1.0
	2.3	1.0	2.8	4.2			Profit Before Taxes	2.6	3.2
							RATIOS		
	3.3	2.7	2.3	2.3			Current	2.2	2.2
	1.7	1.7	1.6	1.5				1.5	1.5
	1.1	1.3	1.3	1.3				1.2	1.1
	1.4	1.3	1.2	.9			Quick	1.1	1.2
	.8	.8	.8	.6				.7	.7
	.5	.5	.5	.4				.4	.5
	14 26.8	24 15.4	26 13.8	26 14.1			Sales/Receivables	21 17.6	24 15.0
	30 12.2	37 10.0	40 9.1	45 8.2				35 10.5	38 9.6
	41 8.8	57 6.4	53 6.9	49 7.5				51 7.2	53 6.9
	22 16.7	31 11.7	36 10.1	49 7.5			Cost of Sales/Inventory	35 10.5	28 13.1
	54 6.8	78 4.7	64 5.7	96 3.8				70 5.2	63 5.8
	118 3.1	126 2.9	118 3.1	118 3.1				126 2.9	118 3.1
	7 52.3	15 24.4	16 23.1	21 17.3			Cost of Sales/Payables	14 26.2	14 25.8
	20 18.0	37 9.8	30 12.1	27 13.6				29 12.5	31 11.6
	42 8.7	61 6.0	44 8.3	41 9.0				55 6.6	55 6.6
	6.7	5.0	5.9	5.8			Sales/Working Capital	5.7	6.1
	10.4	9.7	9.3	9.5				11.8	11.5
	117.4	18.7	16.4	15.2				36.5	35.0
	6.1	5.2	8.2	6.7			EBIT/Interest	5.7	6.1
	(73) 3.2	(149) 2.6	(140) 2.9	(38) 3.3				(362) 2.7	(362) 2.7
	1.3	1.3	1.6	1.8				1.1	1.2
	3.6	5.3	9.6	6.3			Net Profit + Depr., Dep., Amort./Cur. Mat. L./T/D	5.7	5.2
	(18) 1.6	(52) 1.9	(42) 2.7	(21) 2.8				(164) 2.3	(151) 1.9
	.1	.8	1.2	1.7				.7	.5
	.1	.1	.1	.2			Fixed/Worth	.1	.1
	.4	.2	.3	.4				.3	.3
	1.2	.6	.7	.8				.9	.9
	.7	1.0	.9	1.0			Debt/Worth	.8	.9
	1.5	2.0	1.8	1.8				1.8	2.2
	5.3	4.7	3.5	3.6				4.5	4.7
	35.7	32.7	33.4	39.4			% Profit Before Taxes/Tangible Net Worth	33.8	37.8
	(78) 17.6	(150) 13.4	(137) 18.2	(39) 23.6				(361) 15.4	(373) 16.5
	2.7	3.2	7.4	13.9				4.0	4.6
	12.4	9.0	12.9	14.4			% Profit Before Taxes/Total Assets	12.9	13.4
	4.7	4.1	5.6	7.6				5.4	4.9
	.0	.6	2.3	3.7				.5	.9
	67.8	131.4	84.3	56.0			Sales/Net Fixed Assets	71.0	84.9
	30.7	52.9	33.6	16.7				31.6	34.8
	19.9	24.0	12.8	8.9				14.6	16.5
	4.8	4.0	3.5	2.9			Sales/Total Assets	3.9	4.0
	3.6	2.9	2.7	2.4				2.8	2.8
	2.4	2.1	2.0	1.8				1.9	1.9
	.7	.3	.4	.6			% Depr., Dep., Amort./Sales	.5	.4
	(68) 1.2	(134) .6	(126) .7	(36) 1.0				(343) .9	(344) .8
	1.8	1.1	1.3	1.6				1.6	1.5
	3.2	2.0	1.4	.8			% Officers', Directors', Owners' Comp/Sales	2.3	2.2
	(39) 6.0	(87) 4.5	(76) 2.3	(14) 1.0				(197) 4.4	(185) 3.9
	12.5	6.5	4.2	3.4				7.4	7.1
	86569M	656234M	1760747M	2012994M	763937M	687488M	Net Sales ($)	4094937M	4799924M
	24333M	192746M	607445M	783826M	289010M	380347M	Total Assets ($)	1735074M	1977814M

M = $ thousand   MM = $ million
See Pages 1 through 15 for Explanation of Ratios and Data

Comparative Historical Data				Current Data Sorted By Sales					
9	11	22	# Postretirement Benefits	1	2	3	7	3	6
			Type of Statement						
54	54	73	Unqualified	2	5	6	9	21	30
116	109	130	Reviewed	5	24	21	42	25	13
106	119	120	Compiled	25	44	22	19	9	1
10	16	10	Tax Returns	6	3		1		
62	87	103	Other	18	26	10	25	15	9
4/1/92-3/31/93	4/1/93-3/31/94	4/1/94-3/31/95		149 (4/1-9/30/94)			287 (10/1/94-3/31/95)		
ALL	ALL	ALL		0-1MM	1-3MM	3-5MM	5-10MM	10-25MM	25MM & OVER
348	385	436	**NUMBER OF STATEMENTS**	56	102	59	96	70	53
%	%	%	**ASSETS**	%	%	%	%	%	%
7.7	7.6	7.3	Cash & Equivalents	10.3	8.6	6.3	6.2	5.8	6.3
29.6	33.1	30.9	Trade Receivables - (net)	25.1	29.1	35.0	31.3	34.6	30.5
37.1	35.9	38.2	Inventory	33.9	39.5	40.3	37.7	40.2	36.1
1.6	1.8	2.2	All Other Current	2.5	2.2	1.7	2.4	1.3	3.0
76.1	78.3	78.5	Total Current	71.9	79.4	83.3	77.6	81.9	75.9
15.3	13.8	13.7	Fixed Assets (net)	17.4	13.9	10.6	14.1	12.0	14.7
1.6	1.4	1.6	Intangibles (net)	2.3	1.1	1.7	1.2	1.4	2.7
7.0	6.4	6.1	All Other Non-Current	8.5	5.6	4.3	7.0	4.6	6.7
100.0	100.0	100.0	Total	100.0	100.0	100.0	100.0	100.0	100.0
			LIABILITIES						
16.9	17.0	15.7	Notes Payable-Short Term	18.4	11.8	15.7	17.1	14.7	19.3
3.0	2.5	3.0	Cur. Mat.-L /T/D	5.2	3.8	2.0	2.3	2.4	2.4
19.7	18.4	19.8	Trade Payables	14.8	19.4	23.2	17.3	24.5	20.3
.6	2.5	.4	Income Taxes Payable	.1	.4	.3	.5	.3	.4
8.9	9.4	8.4	All Other Current	7.9	9.1	11.1	7.4	7.0	8.0
49.1	49.9	47.3	Total Current	46.5	44.5	52.4	44.6	49.1	50.5
9.3	8.1	9.7	Long Term Debt	13.9	11.5	7.9	8.4	7.6	8.5
.4	.2	.2	Deferred Taxes	.0	.1	.4	.2	.2	.4
3.8	4.9	5.1	All Other-Non-Current	2.4	6.4	4.7	6.1	3.8	5.4
37.4	36.9	37.8	Net Worth	37.3	37.5	34.5	40.6	39.3	35.2
100.0	100.0	100.0	Total Liabilities & Net Worth	100.0	100.0	100.0	100.0	100.0	100.0
			INCOME DATA						
100.0	100.0	100.0	Net Sales	100.0	100.0	100.0	100.0	100.0	100.0
33.1	30.4	31.3	Gross Profit	41.0	35.3	31.1	29.7	24.6	25.3
29.5	27.0	28.4	Operating Expenses	38.5	33.5	28.2	26.3	20.8	21.7
3.5	3.4	2.9	Operating Profit	2.5	1.8	2.9	3.4	3.8	3.7
.8	.8	.7	All Other Expenses (net)	.4	.6	.9	.8	.8	.8
2.8	2.6	2.2	Profit Before Taxes	2.0	1.1	2.0	2.6	3.0	2.8
			RATIOS						
2.3 / 1.6 / 1.2	2.3 / 1.5 / 1.2	2.6 / 1.6 / 1.3	Current	3.5 / 1.7 / 1.0	2.8 / 2.1 / 1.2	2.1 / 1.6 / 1.3	2.8 / 1.6 / 1.3	2.3 / 1.6 / 1.3	1.9 / 1.5 / 1.3
1.3 / .8 / .5	1.2 / .8 / .5	1.2 / .8 / .5	Quick	1.1 / .8 / .4	1.6 / .8 / .5	1.3 / .7 / .5	1.2 / .8 / .5	1.2 / .8 / .6	.9 / .6 / .4
22 16.3 / 37 9.9 / 52 7.0	24 15.0 / 39 9.3 / 53 6.9	24 15.5 / 37 9.9 / 51 7.1	Sales/Receivables	10 36.2 / 32 11.5 / 45 8.2	20 18.2 / 35 10.5 / 54 6.8	27 13.4 / 46 7.9 / 63 5.8	26 13.8 / 37 10.0 / 53 6.9	20 18.4 / 38 9.7 / 50 7.3	26 14.3 / 45 8.1 / 50 7.3
33 11.2 / 73 5.0 / 122 3.0	28 13.2 / 63 5.8 / 118 3.1	33 11.1 / 70 5.2 / 122 3.0	Cost of Sales/Inventory	23 15.8 / 68 5.4 / 135 2.7	35 10.3 / 83 4.4 / 152 2.4	32 11.5 / 81 4.5 / 126 2.9	35 10.4 / 61 6.0 / 111 3.3	32 11.5 / 58 6.3 / 96 3.8	41 8.9 / 68 5.4 / 107 3.4
15 23.9 / 31 11.8 / 52 7.0	10 35.4 / 24 15.4 / 47 7.8	14 25.7 / 29 12.5 / 51 7.2	Cost of Sales/Payables	6 58.2 / 20 18.4 / 54 6.8	14 25.4 / 31 11.9 / 63 5.8	18 20.3 / 38 9.6 / 60 6.1	13 27.4 / 27 13.7 / 43 8.4	14 25.5 / 30 12.0 / 46 8.0	21 17.5 / 32 11.5 / 43 8.5
5.7 / 10.1 / 32.5	5.7 / 11.1 / 25.0	5.7 / 9.5 / 19.8	Sales/Working Capital	5.0 / 9.2 / -193.5	4.4 / 8.4 / 18.6	5.7 / 10.1 / 18.2	6.0 / 8.8 / 16.7	6.8 / 11.2 / 21.0	6.5 / 11.4 / 19.6
(319) 8.0 / 3.4 / 1.4	(345) 8.3 / 3.5 / 1.6	(406) 6.5 / 2.9 / 1.5	EBIT/Interest	(42) 5.4 / 2.3 / 1.2	(98) 5.1 / 2.4 / 1.0	(56) 6.0 / 2.7 / 1.3	(92) 8.1 / 2.8 / 1.7	(67) 8.3 / 4.1 / 2.1	(51) 6.1 / 3.2 / 1.7
(121) 5.2 / 2.1 / .9	(110) 9.2 / 3.3 / 1.3	(137) 5.6 / 2.2 / 1.0	Net Profit + Depr., Dep., Amort./Cur. Mat. L/T/D		(35) 4.3 / 1.6 / .5	(12) 3.2 / 1.9 / 1.2	(41) 10.0 / 4.6 / 1.3	(15) 9.5 / 1.9 / .6	(28) 6.5 / 2.9 / 1.7
.1 / .3 / .8	.1 / .3 / .7	.1 / .3 / .7	Fixed/Worth	.1 / .4 / 1.6	.1 / .3 / .8	.1 / .2 / .6	.1 / .3 / .6	.1 / .2 / .5	.2 / .4 / .8
.8 / 1.8 / 3.6	.9 / 2.0 / 3.7	.9 / 1.8 / 3.9	Debt/Worth	.6 / 1.5 / 8.6	.8 / 1.6 / 4.0	1.2 / 1.8 / 5.4	.7 / 1.8 / 3.5	.8 / 1.7 / 3.5	1.1 / 2.0 / 4.2
(327) 39.9 / 18.2 / 6.6	(361) 39.8 / 17.0 / 5.0	(410) 33.4 / 15.8 / 5.7	% Profit Before Taxes/Tangible Net Worth	(49) 38.1 / 11.1 / 1.5	(95) 25.3 / 11.4 / 1.1	(54) 33.4 / 14.2 / 3.7	(94) 32.6 / 17.4 / 7.9	(66) 44.2 / 19.3 / 8.7	(52) 40.0 / 21.4 / 10.0
13.4 / 5.6 / 1.6	12.9 / 5.3 / 1.3	11.3 / 5.0 / 1.4	% Profit Before Taxes/Total Assets	10.7 / 4.3 / -1.9	9.4 / 3.5 / .1	11.2 / 5.8 / 1.3	10.8 / 5.0 / 2.4	13.9 / 8.5 / 3.0	12.9 / 7.3 / 2.2
82.3 / 34.5 / 13.6	99.0 / 40.8 / 16.8	88.8 / 37.5 / 16.5	Sales/Net Fixed Assets	70.7 / 29.1 / 12.8	69.6 / 35.1 / 18.6	143.6 / 42.4 / 26.7	96.2 / 48.1 / 13.6	123.6 / 51.7 / 19.8	69.3 / 28.5 / 12.0
3.8 / 2.8 / 2.0	4.1 / 2.8 / 2.2	3.8 / 2.9 / 2.1	Sales/Total Assets	3.7 / 2.4 / 1.6	3.9 / 2.7 / 1.8	3.5 / 2.8 / 2.2	3.6 / 2.9 / 2.0	4.7 / 3.4 / 2.5	3.4 / 2.7 / 2.2
(310) .3 / .8 / 1.5	(335) .3 / .7 / 1.3	(369) .4 / .7 / 1.4	% Depr., Dep., Amort./Sales	(44) .6 / 1.2 / 2.1	(85) .4 / .9 / 1.6	(49) .3 / .5 / 1.2	(86) .4 / .6 / 1.3	(57) .3 / .7 / 1.1	(48) .4 / .8 / 1.5
(173) 2.2 / 4.0 / 7.8	(206) 1.8 / 3.7 / 7.3	(216) 1.6 / 3.4 / 6.0	% Officers', Directors', Owners' Comp/Sales	(24) 2.9 / 4.0 / 14.0	(48) 3.9 / 5.3 / 6.7	(37) 1.6 / 4.0 / 4.6	(53) 1.3 / 2.6 / 4.5	(35) 1.4 / 2.2 /	(19) .8 / 1.2 / 2.5
5483399M / 1741785M	6584116M / 2166003M	5967969M / 2277707M	Net Sales ($) / Total Assets ($)	32244M / 15827M	187079M / 78937M	228008M / 85647M	671804M / 266623M	1101183M / 363376M	3747651M / 1467297M

© Robert Morris Associates 1995   M = $ thousand   MM = $ million
See Pages 1 through 15 for Explanation of Ratios and Data

Current Data Sorted By Assets   **Comparative Historical Data**

	0-500M	500M-2MM	2-10MM	10-50MM	50-100MM	100-250MM	# Postretirement Benefits / Type of Statement	4/1/90-3/31/91 ALL	4/1/91-3/31/92 ALL
	3	8	3	6					
	6	11	28	24	2	2	Unqualified	60	56
	12	48	49	3			Reviewed	102	102
	20	53	15	1			Compiled	93	77
	4	1	1	1		1	Tax Returns	3	2
	12	25	21	5	1	2	Other	57	57
		89 (4/1-9/30/94)			257 (10/1/94-3/31/95)				
NUMBER OF STATEMENTS	54	138	114	32	3	5		315	294

ASSETS (%)

Item	0-500M	500M-2MM	2-10MM	10-50MM	50-100MM	100-250MM	4/1/90-3/31/91 ALL	4/1/91-3/31/92 ALL
Cash & Equivalents	9.4	6.7	3.6	3.9			5.7	5.9
Trade Receivables - (net)	40.2	39.4	36.6	32.9			35.3	37.4
Inventory	32.8	33.8	43.5	42.0			39.4	37.2
All Other Current	1.4	1.6	1.0	1.5			2.0	2.1
Total Current	83.7	81.5	84.7	80.3			82.4	82.5
Fixed Assets (net)	11.6	11.7	9.7	13.2			11.4	11.4
Intangibles (net)	.7	1.2	.6	1.6			1.2	1.3
All Other Non-Current	4.1	5.6	5.0	4.9			5.0	4.8
Total	100.0	100.0	100.0	100.0			100.0	100.0

LIABILITIES

Item	0-500M	500M-2MM	2-10MM	10-50MM	50-100MM	100-250MM	4/1/90-3/31/91 ALL	4/1/91-3/31/92 ALL
Notes Payable-Short Term	9.1	11.6	17.4	19.5			17.0	16.3
Cur. Mat. -L/T/D	3.2	2.9	2.3	1.4			2.7	3.3
Trade Payables	28.3	26.6	25.4	16.6			22.9	22.4
Income Taxes Payable	.6	.9	.4	.3			.6	.3
All Other Current	7.9	9.5	8.7	9.3			7.9	8.1
Total Current	49.1	51.4	54.2	47.1			51.1	50.4
Long Term Debt	9.3	8.8	5.1	8.2			8.7	8.6
Deferred Taxes	.0	.2	.2	.8			.4	.4
All Other-Non-Current	2.7	2.5	3.2	2.4			1.5	2.3
Net Worth	38.8	37.2	37.3	41.5			38.3	38.2
Total Liabilities & Net Worth	100.0	100.0	100.0	100.0			100.0	100.0

INCOME DATA

Item	0-500M	500M-2MM	2-10MM	10-50MM	50-100MM	100-250MM	4/1/90-3/31/91 ALL	4/1/91-3/31/92 ALL
Net Sales	100.0	100.0	100.0	100.0			100.0	100.0
Gross Profit	28.6	26.9	24.5	21.6			26.9	27.5
Operating Expenses	25.9	24.6	21.4	18.1			24.4	25.5
Operating Profit	2.7	2.4	3.1	3.5			2.5	2.0
All Other Expenses (net)	.1	.1	.4	.6			.5	.5
Profit Before Taxes	2.6	2.3	2.7	2.9			2.0	1.5

RATIOS

Item	0-500M	500M-2MM	2-10MM	10-50MM	50-100MM	100-250MM	4/1/90-3/31/91 ALL	4/1/91-3/31/92 ALL
Current	2.8	2.0	1.9	2.4			2.3	2.3
	1.8	1.6	1.5	1.6			1.6	1.6
	1.4	1.3	1.3	1.4			1.3	1.3
Quick	1.4	1.3	1.0	1.1			1.2	1.3
	1.1	.9	.8	.7			.8	.9
	.7	.7	.5	.6			.5	.6
Sales/Receivables	23 16.1	32 11.5	35 10.4	36 10.1			32 11.3	36 10.1
	33 10.9	42 8.7	43 8.4	41 8.8			42 8.6	46 7.9
	48 7.6	59 6.2	57 6.4	54 6.8			55 6.6	57 6.4
Cost of Sales/Inventory	13 28.9	29 12.5	47 7.8	60 6.1			38 9.7	36 10.1
	39 9.4	49 7.5	74 4.9	79 4.6			76 4.8	73 5.0
	70 5.2	79 4.6	118 3.1	99 3.7			107 3.4	107 3.4
Cost of Sales/Payables	18 20.5	24 14.9	24 15.2	15 24.1			22 16.7	22 16.5
	31 11.8	40 9.2	38 9.5	24 15.1			34 10.6	36 10.2
	51 7.2	54 6.7	60 6.1	39 9.4			53 6.9	57 6.4
Sales/Working Capital	7.2	6.5	6.2	5.7			6.1	5.8
	12.1	11.2	9.3	9.1			9.4	8.8
	27.0	22.8	16.1	14.0			18.5	16.3
EBIT/Interest	11.8	7.8	5.6	10.9			5.2	4.0
	(49) 4.0	(129) 3.1	(106) 3.1	(29) 3.6			(290) 2.6	(274) 2.0
	1.6	1.9	2.1	2.1			1.4	1.1
Net Profit + Depr., Dep., Amort./Cur. Mat. L /T/D	3.1	3.8	8.9	13.4			7.2	4.9
	(18) 2.4	(60) 2.1	(47) 3.4	(20) 4.3			(182) 2.6	(157) 2.1
	1.5	1.3	1.6	2.3			1.2	.6
Fixed/Worth	.1	.1	.1	.1			.1	.1
	.3	.3	.2	.2			.2	.2
	.5	.6	.4	.6			.6	.5
Debt/Worth	.7	1.1	1.2	.9			.9	.9
	1.4	1.8	2.1	1.9			1.9	1.8
	3.3	3.8	3.4	3.2			3.2	3.5
% Profit Before Taxes/Tangible Net Worth	47.6	30.8	29.1	34.4			28.7	21.1
	(50) 19.3	(128) 15.4	(113) 16.8	(31) 23.2			(306) 15.1	(279) 9.4
	4.2	7.2	7.4	12.1			4.9	1.5
% Profit Before Taxes/Total Assets	15.3	11.1	10.0	12.5			9.3	7.6
	5.1	5.7	4.8	8.2			5.1	3.1
	1.6	2.3	2.2	4.9			1.8	.3
Sales/Net Fixed Assets	120.1	79.6	84.9	58.0			70.4	77.6
	44.9	36.1	36.0	41.1			37.4	36.5
	25.2	20.8	18.2	15.5			18.6	19.3
Sales/Total Assets	4.9	4.0	3.4	3.3			3.5	3.5
	3.9	3.2	2.8	2.7			2.8	2.7
	2.8	2.4	2.2	2.2			2.3	2.3
% Depr., Dep., Amort./Sales	.4	.4	.4	.3			.4	.5
	(43) .7	(118) .7	(107) .6	(30) .6			(284) .7	(266) .7
	1.3	1.1	.9	.8			1.2	1.2
% Officers', Directors', Owners' Comp/Sales	2.8	3.0	1.6	1.3			2.1	2.3
	(27) 5.4	(80) 4.7	(53) 2.7	(12) 2.7			(150) 4.0	(125) 4.1
	9.7	8.9	4.8	5.1			6.6	8.2
Net Sales ($)	72772M	498491M	1411714M	1949229M	476542M	2387873M	4154459M	3845927M
Total Assets ($)	16927M	155001M	510060M	727915M	203077M	1021140M	1680258M	1550910M

M = $ thousand   MM = $ million
See Pages 1 through 15 for Explanation of Ratios and Data

Comparative Historical Data						# Postretirement Benefits	Current Data Sorted By Sales											
7		5		20			2		3		3		4		3		5	
						Type of Statement												
65		60		73		Unqualified	2		8		6		9		16		32	
94		90		112		Reviewed	5		23		19		34		28		3	
74		95		88		Compiled	7		42		18		15		6			
5		8		7		Tax Returns	1		4				1				1	
51		61		66		Other	4		16		16		12		11		7	
	4/1/92-3/31/93 ALL		4/1/93-3/31/94 ALL		4/1/94-3/31/95 ALL		89 (4/1-9/30/94) 0-1MM		1-3MM		3-5MM		257 (10/1/94-3/31/95) 5-10MM		10-25MM		25MM & OVER	
	289		314		346	**NUMBER OF STATEMENTS**	19		93		59		71		61		43	
	%		%		%	**ASSETS**	%		%		%		%		%		%	
	5.5		6.8		5.7	Cash & Equivalents	8.9		7.2		5.6		6.7		3.2		3.2	
	37.0		36.1		37.9	Trade Receivables - (net)	37.7		35.5		43.9		39.1		36.1		35.2	
	38.4		38.0		37.9	Inventory	39.9		35.3		32.0		38.1		42.8		43.3	
	2.2		1.8		1.4	All Other Current	.9		1.7		1.4		1.1		1.2		1.4	
	83.1		82.7		82.8	Total Current	87.4		79.8		82.9		85.0		83.2		83.2	
	10.9		10.9		11.1	Fixed Assets (net)	11.0		12.6		10.7		9.5		11.4		10.9	
	1.0		1.0		1.0	Intangibles (net)	.1		1.3		1.2		.3		.9		1.3	
	5.0		5.4		5.1	All Other Non-Current	1.5		6.2		5.2		5.2		4.5		4.6	
	100.0		100.0		100.0	Total	100.0		100.0		100.0		100.0		100.0		100.0	
						LIABILITIES												
	15.5		13.4		14.1	Notes Payable-Short Term	15.5		10.2		11.9		11.3		18.4		23.6	
	2.7		2.1		2.6	Cur. Mat.-L /T/D	2.6		3.2		3.0		1.7		3.2		1.2	
	24.1		22.0		25.4	Trade Payables	24.7		25.0		27.2		28.2		26.8		17.2	
	.4		2.0		.6	Income Taxes Payable	.2		1.0		.9		.5		.3		.3	
	8.3		8.5		8.9	All Other Current	8.3		7.8		9.8		10.4		8.1		9.3	
	51.1		48.0		51.6	Total Current	51.3		47.1		52.8		52.2		56.9		51.7	
	8.8		7.7		7.6	Long Term Debt	16.5		9.8		6.5		4.7		7.0		6.4	
	.2		.3		.2	Deferred Taxes	.0		.2		.3		.1		.1		.7	
	2.3		3.0		2.7	All Other-Non-Current	2.6		1.9		5.4		2.7		1.7		2.0	
	37.7		41.0		37.8	Net Worth	29.6		41.0		35.0		40.3		34.2		39.2	
	100.0		100.0		100.0	Total Liabilities & Net Worth	100.0		100.0		100.0		100.0		100.0		100.0	
						INCOME DATA												
	100.0		100.0		100.0	Net Sales	100.0		100.0		100.0		100.0		100.0		100.0	
	26.0		27.5		25.8	Gross Profit	32.6		27.3		27.9		25.7		22.3		21.5	
	23.8		25.1		23.0	Operating Expenses	29.7		24.8		24.7		23.4		19.5		18.2	
	2.2		2.5		2.8	Operating Profit	2.9		2.6		3.2		2.4		2.9		3.3	
	.4		.2		.2	All Other Expenses (net)	.1		.2		.3		-.2		.6		.5	
	1.8		2.3		2.6	Profit Before Taxes	2.8		2.4		2.9		2.6		2.3		2.9	
						RATIOS												
	2.2		2.5		2.1	Current	3.1		2.1		1.9		2.6		1.7		2.2	
	1.6		1.7		1.6		2.0		1.7		1.6		1.5		1.4		1.6	
	1.3		1.3		1.3		1.1		1.4		1.3		1.3		1.2		1.3	
	1.2		1.3		1.2	Quick	1.4		1.3		1.3		1.3		1.0		1.0	
	.8		.9		.8		.9		1.0		.9		.9		.7		.7	
	.6		.6		.6		.7		.7		.7		.6		.5		.6	
36	10.2	33	11.0	33	11.1	Sales/Receivables	25	14.5	29	12.6	32	11.5	33	11.0	35	10.4	37	9.8
46	8.0	43	8.5	41	8.8		37	10.0	38	9.7	47	7.7	42	8.7	43	8.5	42	8.7
59	6.2	56	6.5	56	6.5		62	5.9	51	7.1	69	5.3	54	6.8	55	6.6	55	6.6
35	10.5	35	10.4	33	11.0	Cost of Sales/Inventory	36	10.2	30	12.2	28	13.0	31	11.9	44	8.3	58	6.3
73	5.0	73	5.0	63	5.8		61	6.0	56	6.5	49	7.5	51	7.2	65	5.6	74	4.9
111	3.3	111	3.3	99	3.7		140	2.6	89	4.1	89	4.1	101	3.6	101	3.6	99	3.7
24	14.9	20	18.4	23	16.2	Cost of Sales/Payables	15	24.5	24	15.4	27	13.6	21	17.4	27	13.3	15	24.1
38	9.7	33	10.9	37	9.8		34	10.7	37	9.8	46	8.0	36	10.1	38	9.5	26	13.8
58	6.3	54	6.7	54	6.5		68	5.4	52	7.0	56	6.5	59	6.2	57	6.4	39	9.4
	5.2		5.4		6.5	Sales/Working Capital		4.3		6.1		6.1		6.5		7.5		6.6
	9.1		8.5		10.7			7.4		10.0		11.1		11.2		12.0		9.7
	15.9		15.8		18.6			29.9		20.5		22.2		18.5		21.7		14.1
	6.2		7.7		7.0	EBIT/Interest		6.6		8.9		5.5		9.7		5.1		10.9
(274)	2.5	(284)	3.2	(321)	3.4		(16)	2.6	(87)	3.4	(55)	3.1	(64)	4.5	(58)	2.9	(41)	3.9
	1.4		1.6		2.0			1.4		1.5		2.1		2.3		2.0		2.2
	4.4		6.8		5.5	Net Profit + Depr., Dep., Amort./Cur. Mat. L/T/D				3.0		3.8		6.6		5.3		10.2
(127)	1.9	(123)	2.4	(150)	2.6				(37)	2.3	(27)	2.1	(29)	3.1	(28)	3.0	(26)	4.5
	.8		1.1		1.5					1.3		1.1		1.9		1.4		2.8
	.1		.1		.1	Fixed/Worth		.2		.1		.1		.1		.1		.1
	.2		.2		.3			.3		.2		.3		.2		.3		.2
	.5		.5		.5			.7		.6		.6		.4		.5		.5
	.9		.8		.9	Debt/Worth		.7		.8		1.3		.8		1.3		.9
	1.7		1.7		1.9			2.9		1.5		1.9		1.7		2.3		2.1
	3.4		3.2		3.4			6.0		3.0		4.1		2.9		4.3		3.3
	24.2		28.9		33.1	% Profit Before Taxes/Tangible Net Worth		45.0		30.9		37.2		35.6		28.9		41.5
(273)	10.7	(305)	14.0	(330)	17.4		(16)	10.4	(87)	15.7	(56)	15.8	(68)	14.5	(60)	18.9		23.2
	3.3		4.8		7.3			4.3		4.8		6.1		7.4		8.1		12.1
	9.1		10.2		11.4	% Profit Before Taxes/Total Assets		11.5		12.6		11.8		11.0		9.6		12.3
	4.1		5.1		5.8			3.5		5.7		5.7		5.4		5.1		8.5
	.9		1.7		2.3			1.6		1.8		2.3		2.5		2.4		4.4
	76.9		74.4		76.2	Sales/Net Fixed Assets		51.5		80.4		72.6		84.3		89.6		60.2
	39.8		40.9		37.9			26.7		37.8		35.1		41.4		35.1		45.0
	19.9		19.3		18.8			19.5		18.2		18.6		26.2		17.0		16.7
	3.5		3.5		3.7	Sales/Total Assets		3.7		4.3		3.8		4.0		3.5		3.5
	2.7		2.8		3.0			2.8		3.1		3.1		3.2		3.0		2.8
	2.3		2.3		2.3			2.0		2.4		2.4		2.4		2.3		2.2
	.5		.4		.4	% Depr., Dep., Amort./Sales		.6		.4		.4		.4		.4		.2
(271)	.7	(285)	.7	(306)	.6		(14)	1.1	(80)	.7	(50)	.8	(63)	.7	(57)	.5	(42)	.5
	1.2		1.1		1.0			1.6		1.1		1.2		1.0		.8		.8
	2.4		2.4		2.3	% Officers', Directors', Owners' Comp/Sales		2.6		2.8		3.1		1.8		1.4		1.2
(135)	4.4	(158)	4.8	(173)	4.0		(10)	4.8	(55)	4.9	(31)	4.3	(34)	4.1	(26)	2.9	(17)	2.5
	7.5		7.1		7.1			10.5		8.8		9.5		5.6		4.3		5.1
	3804110M		4223828M		6796621M	Net Sales ($)	11869M		176291M		236217M		500653M		931215M		4940376M	
	1548285M		1639847M		2634120M	Total Assets ($)	4482M		62450M		91637M		167316M		336135M		1972100M	

© Robert Morris Associates 1995

M = $ thousand   MM = $ million
See Pages 1 through 15 for Explanation of Ratios and Data

Current Data Sorted By Assets							Comparative Historical Data	
		4	4	1	1	# Postretirement Benefits Type of Statement Unqualified	8	3
	3	6				Reviewed	4	3
2	2					Compiled	4	1
1	1	1				Tax Returns		
1	2	9	1			Other	4	4
	7 (4/1-9/30/94)		32 (10/1/94-3/31/95)				4 4/1/90- 3/31/91 ALL	4 4/1/91- 3/31/92 ALL
0-500M	500M-2MM	2-10MM	10-50MM	50-100MM	100-250MM			
4	8	20	5	1	1	NUMBER OF STATEMENTS	20	11
%	%	%	%	%	%	**ASSETS**	%	%
		6.0				Cash & Equivalents	7.5	3.8
		43.7				Trade Receivables - (net)	42.1	40.2
		12.0				Inventory	26.1	15.9
		2.5				All Other Current	.8	3.0
		64.2				Total Current	76.5	63.0
		20.6				Fixed Assets (net)	18.5	29.6
		.7				Intangibles (net)	.6	.4
		14.5				All Other Non-Current	4.4	7.0
		100.0				Total	100.0	100.0
						LIABILITIES		
		12.9				Notes Payable-Short Term	28.2	22.1
		4.8				Cur. Mat. -L/T/D	2.5	1.9
		31.3				Trade Payables	28.0	22.2
		.3				Income Taxes Payable	.1	.0
		4.2				All Other Current	7.7	4.2
		53.5				Total Current	66.6	50.4
		10.5				Long Term Debt	9.5	13.1
		.1				Deferred Taxes	.0	3.9
		4.9				All Other-Non-Current	1.9	6.9
		31.0				Net Worth	22.1	25.8
		100.0				Total Liabilities & Net Worth	100.0	100.0
						INCOME DATA		
		100.0				Net Sales	100.0	100.0
		12.3				Gross Profit	11.6	11.8
		8.9				Operating Expenses	9.2	7.6
		3.3				Operating Profit	2.4	4.2
		.4				All Other Expenses (net)	1.4	.7
		2.9				Profit Before Taxes	1.0	3.5
						RATIOS		
		1.7				Current	1.4	2.3
		1.2					1.2	1.4
		1.0					1.0	1.0
		1.3				Quick	1.1	2.2
		1.0					.7	.7
		.6					.5	.6
	23	15.7				Sales/Receivables	24 15.5	28 13.2
	38	9.5					38 9.5	36 10.2
	59	6.2					55 6.6	38 9.5
	0	UND				Cost of Sales/Inventory	0 UND	0 UND
	7	53.3					29 12.4	16 22.4
	26	13.8					69 5.3	47 7.8
	16	22.4				Cost of Sales/Payables	12 29.5	17 21.3
	38	9.6					18 20.0	26 14.1
	50	7.3					31 11.6	35 10.5
		16.1				Sales/Working Capital	13.4	9.0
		37.2					29.9	13.9
		-146.2					349.6	-743.6
	(19)	7.6				EBIT/Interest	(18) 2.7	(10) 5.1
		3.1					1.4	3.9
		1.3					.2	1.2
						Net Profit + Depr., Dep., Amort./Cur. Mat. L /T/D	(10) 13.1	
							.4	
							-2.2	
		.2				Fixed/Worth	.1	.4
		.7					.5	1.3
		1.7					2.8	1.7
		1.2				Debt/Worth	2.1	.9
		2.1					4.9	2.0
		8.3					22.2	53.3
		44.0				% Profit Before Taxes/Tangible Net Worth	(18) 46.0	(10) 132.2
	(18)	19.7					14.7	24.9
		5.6					2.3	4.2
		13.7				% Profit Before Taxes/Total Assets	6.7	13.1
		5.8					2.3	8.5
		.1					-2.8	2.0
		250.4				Sales/Net Fixed Assets	317.8	203.4
		31.8					44.3	18.5
		8.6					9.1	2.7
		5.6				Sales/Total Assets	5.5	6.0
		3.3					3.5	3.1
		2.5					2.0	1.5
		.2				% Depr., Dep., Amort./Sales	(18) .2	
	(17)	1.2					.7	
		2.0					1.3	
						% Officers', Directors', Owners' Comp/Sales		
15616M	54462M	377742M	165074M	144230M	99224M	Net Sales ($)	354583M	969637M
1029M	9532M	101704M	91382M	96745M	112445M	Total Assets ($)	121275M	637316M

M = $ thousand   MM = $ million
See Pages 1 through 15 for Explanation of Ratios and Data

Comparative Historical Data   /   Current Data Sorted By Sales

 # Postretirement Benefits — Type of Statement

Type of Statement	4/1/92-3/31/93	4/1/93-3/31/94	4/1/94-3/31/95	0-1MM	1-3MM	3-5MM	5-10MM	10-25MM	25MM & OVER
Unqualified	8	14	10			1		3	6
Reviewed	7	3	9			2	1	6	
Compiled	5	4	4		1	2		1	
Tax Returns			3		1	1	1		
Other	2	5	13			2	3	6	2
	22	26	39						
Date range				\<—— 7 (4/1-9/30/94) ——\>			\<—— 32 (10/1/94-3/31/95) ——\>		
NUMBER OF STATEMENTS	22	26	39		2	8	5	16	8

Main Data

(Quartile rows are listed upper / median / lower. Only the 10-25MM column of the current-data section contains percentage data.)

Item	4/1/92-3/31/93	4/1/93-3/31/94	4/1/94-3/31/95	10-25MM
ASSETS (%)	%	%	%	%
Cash & Equivalents	4.4	8.5	8.6	6.9
Trade Receivables - (net)	42.8	40.3	44.0	45.6
Inventory	15.6	16.7	13.8	8.8
All Other Current	2.6	2.8	1.8	2.4
Total Current	65.5	68.4	68.2	63.7
Fixed Assets (net)	21.3	25.6	19.9	21.9
Intangibles (net)	2.2	.3	2.5	2.5
All Other Non-Current	11.1	5.7	9.4	11.8
Total	100.0	100.0	100.0	100.0
LIABILITIES				
Notes Payable-Short Term	14.5	12.1	17.5	9.3
Cur. Mat.-L /T/D	3.5	2.2	3.4	3.7
Trade Payables	30.5	27.0	28.3	31.0
Income Taxes Payable	.7	1.8	.2	.4
All Other Current	3.9	8.9	5.6	4.3
Total Current	53.1	52.0	55.0	48.7
Long Term Debt	6.8	15.6	8.6	9.7
Deferred Taxes	1.5	1.0	.1	.1
All Other-Non-Current	3.1	2.7	4.7	4.3
Net Worth	35.5	28.6	31.5	37.3
Total Liabilities & Net Worth	100.0	100.0	100.0	100.0
INCOME DATA				
Net Sales	100.0	100.0	100.0	100.0
Gross Profit	12.5	16.0	12.9	12.9
Operating Expenses	11.0	12.6	9.3	10.0
Operating Profit	1.5	3.3	3.6	2.9
All Other Expenses (net)	.6	.5	.6	.4
Profit Before Taxes	.9	2.8	3.0	2.5
RATIOS				
Current	1.8	1.9	1.8	1.9
	1.1	1.2	1.2	1.4
	.9	1.0	1.0	1.0
Quick	1.2	1.3	1.3	1.4
	.8	1.1	.9	1.1
	.7	.6	.6	.7
Sales/Receivables	29 12.5	30 12.2	28 13.1	21 17.2
	48 7.6	52 7.0	35 10.4	33 11.0
	57 6.4	65 5.6	61 6.0	54 6.7
Cost of Sales/Inventory	0 UND	0 UND	0 UND	0 UND
	10 36.2	28 13.1	9 42.7	7 52.2
	65 5.6	53 6.9	57 6.4	21 17.1
Cost of Sales/Payables	23 16.1	24 15.4	11 32.2	12 30.4
	33 11.1	34 10.8	37 9.8	33 11.2
	58 6.3	56 6.5	48 7.6	41 8.9
Sales/Working Capital	8.6	9.3	14.3	14.9
	31.0	24.2	68.3	37.2
	-77.6	-463.5	-212.1	-216.3
EBIT/Interest	(20) 4.5	(23) 7.4	(36) 9.4	(15) 8.4
	2.6	3.7	2.9	3.8
	-.0	2.4	1.5	1.3
Net Profit + Depr., Dep., Amort./Cur. Mat. L/T/D	(11) 20.2			
	4.4			
	1.1			
Fixed/Worth	.1	.2	.1	.2
	.5	.9	.5	.7
	1.2	1.5	1.5	1.4
Debt/Worth	1.2	1.2	1.1	.9
	2.1	2.7	2.1	1.4
	5.4	10.8	8.5	6.2
% Profit Before Taxes/Tangible Net Worth	(21) 30.0	(25) 38.0	(36) 62.4	(14) 44.8
	8.7	24.0	26.9	19.7
	-7.7	6.8	9.9	4.6
% Profit Before Taxes/Total Assets	8.0	9.1	12.8	15.1
	3.7	3.7	5.1	6.1
	-.8	2.0	1.1	-.2
Sales/Net Fixed Assets	178.6	110.5	601.7	250.4
	20.4	21.6	28.6	22.4
	9.3	2.4	7.9	7.5
Sales/Total Assets	5.9	3.5	5.8	5.8
	2.5	2.3	3.4	3.3
	1.6	1.6	2.2	2.5
% Depr., Dep., Amort./Sales	(20) .1	(21) .4	(31) .2	(15) .2
	1.0	1.0	1.2	1.3
	2.2	5.3	2.3	3.9
% Officers', Directors', Owners' Comp/Sales			(10) .9	
			1.4	
			4.1	
Net Sales ($)	1240638M	1485422M	856348M	253929M
Total Assets ($)	785801M	876918M	412837M	87956M

Current-data dollar figures (sorted by sales):

	0-1MM	1-3MM	3-5MM	5-10MM	10-25MM	25MM & OVER
Net Sales ($)		4076M	32518M	34602M	253929M	531223M
Total Assets ($)		752M	28923M	15251M	87956M	279955M

© Robert Morris Associates 1995

M = $ thousand   MM = $ million
See Pages 1 through 15 for Explanation of Ratios and Data

WHOLESALERS—HARDWARE & PAINTS. SIC# 5072, 5198

	Current Data Sorted By Assets							Comparative Historical Data	
	2	7	10	3	2		# Postretirement Benefits		
							Type of Statement		
	1	10	29	19	6	2	Unqualified	69	64
	6	42	57	7			Reviewed	107	109
	21	58	19	1	1		Compiled	117	109
	2	3	2	1			Tax Returns	4	1
	10	25	23	4	2	1	Other	60	55
		98 (4/1-9/30/94)			254 (10/1/94-3/31/95)			4/1/90-3/31/91 ALL	4/1/91-3/31/92 ALL
	0-500M	500M-2MM	2-10MM	10-50MM	50-100MM	100-250MM	**NUMBER OF STATEMENTS**		
	40	138	130	32	9	3		357	338
	%	%	%	%	%	%	**ASSETS**	%	%
	8.3	5.4	4.1	2.8			Cash & Equivalents	5.7	5.2
	31.5	34.5	31.0	30.7			Trade Receivables - (net)	31.7	32.0
	40.0	43.4	46.9	46.6			Inventory	43.2	43.1
	2.4	.8	1.1	1.5			All Other Current	1.3	1.1
	82.1	84.2	83.1	81.7			Total Current	81.9	81.4
	13.4	10.4	11.1	12.0			Fixed Assets (net)	12.3	12.2
	.9	1.1	1.0	1.6			Intangibles (net)	1.0	1.0
	3.5	4.3	4.7	4.7			All Other Non-Current	4.7	5.4
	100.0	100.0	100.0	100.0			Total	100.0	100.0
							LIABILITIES		
	12.0	12.4	19.6	15.7			Notes Payable-Short Term	13.5	13.7
	3.9	1.9	2.1	2.0			Cur. Mat. -L/T/D	3.0	3.2
	20.1	22.3	21.4	22.6			Trade Payables	21.9	21.3
	.1	.4	.4	.1			Income Taxes Payable	.5	.4
	13.9	7.3	7.2	4.2			All Other Current	7.0	7.5
	50.1	44.3	50.7	44.8			Total Current	45.9	46.0
	12.6	9.1	6.8	7.5			Long Term Debt	10.0	10.2
	.0	.1	.2	.3			Deferred Taxes	.2	.3
	3.8	3.6	4.6	1.7			All Other-Non-Current	2.6	2.7
	33.6	42.9	37.7	45.8			Net Worth	41.3	40.8
	100.0	100.0	100.0	100.0			Total Liabilities & Net Worth	100.0	100.0
							INCOME DATA		
	100.0	100.0	100.0	100.0			Net Sales	100.0	100.0
	31.0	31.9	28.3	27.2			Gross Profit	31.4	30.8
	28.1	29.6	25.2	22.2			Operating Expenses	28.3	28.3
	2.9	2.3	3.1	5.1			Operating Profit	3.1	2.5
	.4	.3	.9	.6			All Other Expenses (net)	.8	.9
	2.5	1.9	2.2	4.5			Profit Before Taxes	2.3	1.7
							RATIOS		
	3.0	2.8	2.3	2.8			Current	2.6	2.7
	1.6	1.9	1.6	1.8				1.8	1.8
	1.2	1.5	1.3	1.4				1.4	1.3
	1.3	1.4	1.1	1.2			Quick	1.3	1.2
	.8	1.0	.6	.7				.8	.8
	.4	.6	.5	.6				.5	.5
	28 13.1	31 11.6	33 11.1	41 8.9			Sales/Receivables	32 11.5	32 11.5
	36 10.2	41 9.0	42 8.7	46 8.0				40 9.1	41 8.9
	47 7.8	53 6.9	53 6.9	60 6.1				51 7.2	51 7.1
	29 12.7	59 6.2	64 5.7	69 5.3			Cost of Sales/Inventory	53 6.9	54 6.8
	74 4.9	76 4.8	91 4.0	89 4.1				85 4.3	83 4.4
	111 3.3	114 3.2	140 2.6	140 2.6				126 2.9	122 3.0
	13 29.1	22 16.3	26 14.2	29 12.8			Cost of Sales/Payables	25 14.4	21 17.0
	35 10.5	37 9.8	39 9.3	46 7.9				39 9.3	37 10.0
	52 7.0	57 6.4	55 6.6	63 5.8				58 6.3	56 6.5
	5.2	5.2	5.2	3.6			Sales/Working Capital	5.2	4.9
	9.4	7.3	8.9	6.6				7.6	8.0
	43.2	11.4	14.5	11.8				13.9	15.8
(31)	8.0	(125) 9.4	(121) 8.1	(31) 13.5			EBIT/Interest	(324) 6.1	(321) 5.1
	2.7	3.1	2.7	6.7				2.8	2.2
	1.0	1.4	1.5	1.8				1.3	.9
		(49) 6.0	(57) 8.3	(13) 7.2			Net Profit + Depr., Dep., Amort./Cur. Mat. L /T/D	(187) 5.8	(146) 4.6
		1.9	2.8	2.5				2.2	1.7
		1.1	1.2	1.0				.7	.4
	.1	.1	.1	.1			Fixed/Worth	.1	.1
	.3	.2	.2	.3				.3	.2
	1.0	.4	.5	.6				.6	.6
	.7	.7	1.0	.7			Debt/Worth	.8	.7
	1.9	1.3	1.8	1.2				1.5	1.5
	9.1	3.2	3.6	2.9				3.2	3.4
(35)	59.7	(135) 29.2	(124) 32.0	(31) 31.8			% Profit Before Taxes/Tangible Net Worth	(345) 26.8	(319) 22.8
	16.5	12.1	15.6	15.7				11.8	10.1
	5.2	3.3	5.0	7.8				4.2	1.8
	15.1	10.4	12.1	17.1			% Profit Before Taxes/Total Assets	10.3	8.8
	5.7	4.5	4.5	7.7				4.6	3.8
	.5	1.0	1.4	2.6				1.0	.0
	121.2	69.2	70.6	41.7			Sales/Net Fixed Assets	56.9	59.4
	44.7	36.9	32.8	21.9				32.9	32.3
	18.1	23.3	15.4	14.0				16.6	16.5
	4.1	3.5	3.3	2.8			Sales/Total Assets	3.4	3.2
	3.3	2.9	2.7	2.4				2.6	2.7
	2.4	2.4	1.9	1.9				2.0	2.2
(29)	.5	(127) .4	(121) .4	(30) .6			% Depr., Dep., Amort./Sales	(324) .5	(308) .5
	.9	.7	.7	.8				.9	.9
	1.7	1.4	1.1	1.1				1.4	1.4
(24)	3.6	(73) 2.8	(59) 2.1	(10) 1.6			% Officers', Directors', Owners' Comp/Sales	(153) 2.5	(153) 2.4
	4.8	4.8	3.6	2.0				4.8	4.4
	10.0	7.3	5.1	6.9				7.4	6.9
	39184M	489844M	1480503M	1611338M	1270046M	622248M	Net Sales ($)	3767606M	3728111M
	11175M	162408M	558025M	651051M	567472M	356957M	Total Assets ($)	1457500M	1607626M

M = $ thousand   MM = $ million
See Pages 1 through 15 for Explanation of Ratios and Data

Comparative Historical Data				Current Data Sorted By Sales					
8	9	24	# Postretirement Benefits	2	3	3	5	6	5
			Type of Statement						
72	63	67	Unqualified		6	6	14	12	29
110	107	112	Reviewed	5	16	17	42	27	5
118	94	100	Compiled	12	37	22	16	11	2
9	3	8	Tax Returns		5		1	1	1
57	68	65	Other	7	16	8	15	11	8
4/1/92-3/31/93 ALL	4/1/93-3/31/94 ALL	4/1/94-3/31/95 ALL		98 (4/1-9/30/94) 0-1MM	1-3MM	3-5MM	254 (10/1/94-3/31/95) 5-10MM	10-25MM	25MM & OVER
366	335	352	**NUMBER OF STATEMENTS**	24	80	53	88	62	45
%	%	%	**ASSETS**	%	%	%	%	%	%
4.7	5.0	5.0	Cash & Equivalents	7.0	7.5	4.2	4.7	3.6	2.5
31.4	32.2	32.3	Trade Receivables - (net)	29.5	32.6	33.3	31.9	34.2	30.3
44.6	43.0	44.3	Inventory	41.5	42.5	44.0	47.8	43.1	44.6
1.3	1.5	1.2	All Other Current	2.3	.9	.2	1.3	1.7	1.4
82.0	81.6	82.8	Total Current	80.3	83.5	81.8	85.6	82.6	78.7
11.8	12.0	11.5	Fixed Assets (net)	15.3	10.6	12.6	9.2	11.6	13.8
1.2	1.3	1.2	Intangibles (net)	.9	1.4	.8	1.1	1.2	1.8
5.0	5.1	4.5	All Other Non-Current	3.6	4.5	4.8	4.1	4.7	5.6
100.0	100.0	100.0	Total	100.0	100.0	100.0	100.0	100.0	100.0
			LIABILITIES						
15.0	14.7	15.0	Notes Payable-Short Term	16.1	9.2	15.8	18.8	17.1	13.3
2.7	1.9	2.2	Cur. Mat.-L./T/D	3.4	2.0	3.0	1.8	2.4	1.6
21.9	21.2	21.7	Trade Payables	17.0	21.9	21.5	20.9	22.6	24.4
.4	1.6	.4	Income Taxes Payable	.1	.4	.3	.5	.3	.3
6.8	6.3	7.8	All Other Current	14.1	10.1	5.7	7.2	6.1	6.2
46.8	45.6	47.1	Total Current	50.7	43.6	46.4	49.2	48.5	45.8
8.6	8.7	8.8	Long Term Debt	13.3	11.6	9.1	5.5	7.0	10.1
.1	.2	.2	Deferred Taxes	.0	.0	.1	.2	.1	.4
3.1	2.4	3.7	All Other-Non-Current	4.3	3.5	2.6	5.7	2.7	2.6
41.3	43.1	40.2	Net Worth	31.6	41.2	41.7	39.3	41.6	41.1
100.0	100.0	100.0	Total Liabilities & Net Worth	100.0	100.0	100.0	100.0	100.0	100.0
			INCOME DATA						
100.0	100.0	100.0	Net Sales	100.0	100.0	100.0	100.0	100.0	100.0
30.6	29.4	29.9	Gross Profit	35.7	31.9	30.6	30.2	27.9	24.2
27.8	27.3	26.8	Operating Expenses	32.5	28.9	28.8	28.1	23.6	19.6
2.8	2.1	3.1	Operating Profit	3.2	3.0	1.8	2.2	4.4	4.6
.8	.5	.6	All Other Expenses (net)	.6	.4	.7	.6	.8	.7
2.0	1.6	2.4	Profit Before Taxes	2.6	2.6	1.1	1.6	3.6	3.9
			RATIOS						
2.5	2.7	2.6	Current	3.0	3.1	2.1	2.4	2.3	2.9
1.7	1.8	1.8		1.5	1.9	1.8	1.7	1.8	1.7
1.3	1.4	1.4		1.0	1.4	1.4	1.4	1.4	1.4
1.2	1.2	1.2	Quick	1.6	1.5	1.2	1.1	1.2	1.2
.7	.8	.8		.6	1.0	.8	.7	.8	.7
.5	.5	.5		.3	.6	.5	.5	.5	.5
32 11.3	32 11.3	33 11.1	Sales/Receivables	28 13.0	31 11.6	33 11.2	32 11.5	34 10.7	37 9.8
41 8.9	42 8.7	42 8.7		36 10.1	39 9.3	43 8.5	41 8.8	41 8.9	45 8.2
52 7.0	52 7.0	54 6.8		66 5.5	60 6.1	54 6.8	54 6.7	49 7.5	53 6.9
57 6.4	53 6.9	61 6.0	Cost of Sales/Inventory	69 5.3	54 6.8	61 6.0	68 5.4	53 6.9	64 5.7
87 4.2	79 4.6	85 4.3		111 3.3	83 4.4	76 4.8	89 4.1	79 4.6	83 4.4
122 3.0	114 3.2	130 2.8		146 2.5	130 2.8	118 3.1	140 2.6	101 3.6	122 3.0
24 15.4	20 18.0	24 15.0	Cost of Sales/Payables	6 60.8	25 14.7	23 15.6	22 16.7	25 14.8	26 14.0
38 9.5	36 10.2	39 9.4		42 8.7	36 10.1	42 8.7	39 9.3	39 9.5	39 9.3
56 6.5	55 6.6	57 6.4		66 5.5	62 5.9	55 6.6	57 6.4	49 7.4	59 6.2
4.7	4.9	5.1	Sales/Working Capital	4.0	3.9	5.7	5.2	5.7	4.9
7.9	7.8	7.9		8.6	6.6	7.7	8.0	9.3	9.4
16.2	13.8	13.3		313.5	10.2	11.8	12.7	15.4	14.1
(336) 6.0	(307) 7.3	(318) 8.9	EBIT/Interest	(19) 4.8	(68) 8.9	(50) 6.0	(82) 8.5	(57) 12.1	(42) 10.6
2.8	3.1	3.1		2.1	2.7	2.6	2.8	4.2	4.8
1.3	1.5	1.5		1.2	1.1	1.3	1.6	1.9	1.9
(150) 5.4	(115) 6.2	(131) 6.5	Net Profit + Depr., Dep., Amort./Cur. Mat. L/T/D		(18) 5.7	(25) 6.0	(34) 8.8	(27) 9.3	(21) 4.8
2.0	2.3	2.5			1.8	1.3	3.7	2.9	2.9
.7	1.0	1.2			1.0	.7	1.5	1.2	1.2
.1	.1	.1	Fixed/Worth	.0	.1	.1	.1	.1	.1
.3	.2	.2		.2	.2	.2	.2	.2	.5
.6	.5	.5		1.2	.4	.5	.4	.5	.7
.8	.7	.8	Debt/Worth	.6	.7	1.0	.8	.8	.9
1.6	1.4	1.5		3.0	1.4	1.5	1.5	1.5	1.9
3.3	2.8	3.4		10.1	3.9	2.6	3.5	3.2	3.4
(354) 25.3	(326) 26.0	(337) 30.8	% Profit Before Taxes/Tangible Net Worth	(20) 47.0	(76) 29.5	(86) 27.5	(59) 31.2	(43) 37.0	28.5
11.0	11.4	14.8		13.1	10.4	9.4	15.0	21.8	18.6
2.3	3.4	4.5		1.9	3.4	2.4	6.1	6.1	11.6
8.1	9.2	11.7	% Profit Before Taxes/Total Assets	9.6	11.6	9.0	10.2	14.0	13.5
4.3	4.8	4.7		3.4	4.5	4.1	4.9	7.7	6.1
.7	1.1	1.3		.5	.5	1.0	1.3	2.3	2.8
68.4	65.6	65.4	Sales/Net Fixed Assets	180.8	60.6	60.1	82.0	69.9	39.1
34.4	32.6	32.7		34.2	39.2	32.4	36.7	32.6	19.8
15.3	16.1	17.8		14.4	17.7	17.6	22.5	18.4	14.7
3.3	3.3	3.4	Sales/Total Assets	3.3	3.4	3.4	3.5	3.6	3.2
2.7	2.7	2.8		2.4	2.7	2.7	2.9	2.9	2.6
2.2	2.2	2.1		1.5	1.9	2.3	1.9	2.3	2.0
(335) .5	(299) .5	(318) .4	% Depr., Dep., Amort./Sales	(19) .8	(68) .5	(47) .5	(81) .4	(61) .4	(42) .5
.8	.8	.7		1.4	.8	.7	.6	.6	.8
1.3	1.3	1.3		2.5	1.5	1.4	1.1	1.1	1.2
(173) 3.0	(169) 2.6	(166) 2.4	% Officers', Directors', Owners' Comp/Sales	(15) 3.5	(36) 2.6	(28) 2.8	(53) 2.4	(28) 1.7	
4.9	4.5	4.2		4.7	4.8	4.4	4.2	3.5	
7.7	7.6	6.2		11.2	6.6	7.6	5.5	6.0	
4202991M	3841216M	5513163M	Net Sales ($)	13221M	146321M	201853M	605560M	874324M	3671884M
1849105M	1538675M	2307088M	Total Assets ($)	6114M	64695M	80683M	255968M	332440M	1567188M

M = $ thousand   MM = $ million
See Pages 1 through 15 for Explanation of Ratios and Data

Current Data Sorted By Assets   Comparative Historical Data

# Postretirement Benefits	4	11	10	3			
Type of Statement							
Unqualified	2	6	45	57	6	6	120 / 124
Reviewed	2	37	82	15	1		133 / 122
Compiled	25	54	34	5			109 / 112
Tax Returns	2	5					1 / 4
Other	9	29	32	30	6	6	73 / 88

170 (4/1-9/30/94)   326 (10/1/94-3/31/95)   4/1/90-3/31/91 ALL   4/1/91-3/31/92 ALL

	0-500M	500M-2MM	2-10MM	10-50MM	50-100MM	100-250MM	4/1/90-3/31/91 ALL	4/1/91-3/31/92 ALL
NUMBER OF STATEMENTS	40	131	193	107	13	12	436	450
ASSETS	%	%	%	%	%	%	%	%
Cash & Equivalents	7.7	5.1	4.8	4.2	2.3	3.4	5.6	4.9
Trade Receivables - (net)	46.4	37.4	37.8	32.9	28.8	28.3	34.8	34.7
Inventory	22.7	36.9	39.5	38.5	39.3	41.9	36.6	37.8
All Other Current	1.6	1.2	1.1	1.7	2.6	1.2	1.6	1.6
Total Current	78.4	80.6	83.1	77.2	73.0	74.8	78.5	79.0
Fixed Assets (net)	15.5	13.2	12.3	16.7	21.5	16.9	15.2	15.1
Intangibles (net)	1.0	.6	.7	1.3	.3	4.5	.8	.7
All Other Non-Current	5.2	5.5	3.8	4.7	5.1	3.8	5.4	5.2
Total	100.0	100.0	100.0	100.0	100.0	100.0	100.0	100.0
LIABILITIES								
Notes Payable-Short Term	14.2	16.5	21.5	19.9	14.8	10.6	19.4	20.5
Cur. Mat. -L/T/D	3.3	2.2	2.1	1.8	1.5	2.5	2.6	2.7
Trade Payables	28.8	25.8	26.2	22.5	19.3	21.3	24.4	23.3
Income Taxes Payable	.2	.4	.3	.4	.7	.6	.4	.4
All Other Current	9.0	5.5	6.7	6.0	8.1	3.7	7.0	6.3
Total Current	55.5	50.4	56.8	50.6	44.4	38.8	53.7	53.1
Long Term Debt	7.0	8.4	7.4	10.6	18.4	13.3	10.1	9.5
Deferred Taxes	.1	.3	.2	.7	.5	.8	.4	.3
All Other-Non-Current	3.4	2.7	2.8	2.9	2.1	5.6	2.6	2.7
Net Worth	33.9	38.2	32.8	35.2	34.6	41.6	33.2	34.4
Total Liabilities & Net Worth	100.0	100.0	100.0	100.0	100.0	100.0	100.0	100.0
INCOME DATA								
Net Sales	100.0	100.0	100.0	100.0	100.0	100.0	100.0	100.0
Gross Profit	25.4	24.2	20.0	16.1	13.6	20.7	21.4	21.9
Operating Expenses	20.5	22.0	17.6	13.1	9.5	16.4	18.6	19.8
Operating Profit	4.8	2.2	2.4	3.0	4.1	4.3	2.8	2.0
All Other Expenses (net)	.8	.5	.7	.6	1.0	.6	1.0	1.3
Profit Before Taxes	4.0	1.7	1.8	2.4	3.1	3.7	1.8	.8
RATIOS								
Current	2.1	2.3	1.9	2.3	2.3	2.8	2.0	2.2
	1.5	1.6	1.3	1.5	1.7	2.1	1.4	1.5
	1.0	1.3	1.2	1.2	1.2	1.5	1.2	1.1
Quick	1.5	1.2	1.0	1.1	1.0	1.2	1.1	1.1
	1.0	.8	.7	.8	.7	.8	.7	.7
	.5	.6	.5	.5	.5	.6	.5	.5
Sales/Receivables	25 / 14.7	35 / 10.4	38 / 9.5	41 / 8.9	36 / 10.1	37 / 9.9	33 / 11.0	35 / 10.4
	36 / 10.2	45 / 8.2	47 / 7.7	47 / 7.8	42 / 8.6	42 / 8.6	42 / 8.7	43 / 8.4
	52 / 7.0	54 / 6.7	57 / 6.4	53 / 6.9	52 / 7.0	47 / 7.7	51 / 7.1	53 / 6.9
Cost of Sales/Inventory	3 / 117.9	31 / 11.7	42 / 8.7	54 / 6.7	49 / 7.5	63 / 5.8	36 / 10.1	42 / 8.6
	16 / 22.6	62 / 5.9	62 / 5.9	76 / 4.8	64 / 5.7	89 / 4.1	59 / 6.2	65 / 5.6
	57 / 6.4	99 / 3.7	96 / 3.8	91 / 4.0	107 / 3.4	104 / 3.5	91 / 4.0	99 / 3.7
Cost of Sales/Payables	3 / 104.4	26 / 13.8	22 / 16.6	27 / 13.5	15 / 23.9	30 / 12.3	23 / 15.7	22 / 16.8
	25 / 14.7	38 / 9.5	38 / 9.6	36 / 10.2	33 / 11.0	37 / 10.0	36 / 10.1	34 / 10.6
	45 / 8.1	58 / 6.3	55 / 6.6	48 / 7.6	46 / 7.9	54 / 6.8	49 / 7.4	49 / 7.4
Sales/Working Capital	9.2	6.0	7.1	5.6	6.6	4.8	6.8	6.3
	17.8	10.3	14.3	10.2	7.7	6.3	13.1	11.6
	831.0	23.0	29.6	20.6	17.9	7.1	31.0	36.8
EBIT/Interest	(30) 11.0	(119) 8.7	(183) 6.3	(98) 8.0	7.8	(11) 7.4	(405) 4.3	(409) 3.9
	4.6	3.8	3.2	3.6	3.5	4.9	2.1	1.6
	2.6	1.3	1.7	2.1	2.3	3.9	1.1	1.0
Net Profit + Depr., Dep., Amort./Cur. Mat. L/T/D		(38) 6.5	(72) 7.3	(46) 8.1			(217) 6.7	(187) 4.7
		2.6	3.3	3.0			2.4	2.0
		.9	1.9	1.5			.9	.7
Fixed/Worth	.1	.1	.1	.1	.4	.3	.2	.2
	.4	.3	.3	.5	.6	.5	.4	.4
	1.1	.7	.8	.8	.8	.6	.9	.9
Debt/Worth	1.0	.8	1.2	1.1	1.5	1.3	1.2	1.0
	2.0	1.9	2.5	2.1	2.7	1.8	2.4	2.1
	6.6	3.7	5.3	5.1	3.4	2.6	5.3	4.8
% Profit Before Taxes/Tangible Net Worth	(36) 92.9	(126) 32.4	(186) 38.2	(104) 34.2	32.8	30.0	(417) 30.8	(428) 20.5
	50.7	15.4	19.4	21.1	16.8	19.8	14.4	9.4
	15.1	5.9	8.7	9.2	13.4	14.7	2.9	.6
% Profit Before Taxes/Total Assets	27.3	11.3	10.1	12.9	9.8	11.3	8.9	7.7
	15.4	5.5	5.1	6.0	7.1	7.2	4.4	2.3
	4.3	1.1	2.2	2.5	3.6	5.7	.5	.0
Sales/Net Fixed Assets	285.5	86.3	76.6	59.8	18.4	17.4	63.9	64.5
	51.2	28.1	31.7	17.5	12.9	12.6	27.4	26.3
	21.2	13.7	16.2	8.9	6.0	9.9	12.2	11.3
Sales/Total Assets	6.2	3.6	3.4	3.0	2.8	2.6	3.7	3.5
	4.3	3.0	2.8	2.4	2.3	2.4	2.8	2.7
	3.1	2.3	2.2	2.0	1.9	2.0	2.2	2.1
% Depr., Dep., Amort./Sales	(27) .3	(113) .4	(178) .4	(100) .3		(11) .5	(390) .5	(403) .5
	.7	.9	.7	.8		.8	.9	.9
	1.6	1.4	1.1	1.4		1.0	1.5	1.4
% Officers', Directors', Owners' Comp/Sales	(18) 2.7	(67) 2.6	(94) 1.3	(17) .9			(174) 1.7	(188) 1.9
	4.2	4.5	2.2	1.6			3.1	3.3
	9.0	6.8	4.9	2.4			6.3	5.9
Net Sales ($)	67035M	502699M	2461477M	6349424M	2197900M	4631787M	12495911M	12696873M
Total Assets ($)	12643M	162198M	863387M	2443778M	941885M	2001087M	4593375M	4859268M

M = $ thousand   MM = $ million
See Pages 1 through 15 for Explanation of Ratios and Data

Comparative Historical Data				Current Data Sorted By Sales					
8	11	28	# Postretirement Benefits Type of Statement		2	7	5	14	
102	112	122	Unqualified	3	3	7	13	25	71
128	144	137	Reviewed	2	13	15	47	41	19
107	96	118	Compiled	11	37	20	27	19	4
4	7	7	Tax Returns			4		2	1
94	95	112	Other	2	17	12	20	19	42
4/1/92-3/31/93	4/1/93-3/31/94	4/1/94-3/31/95		170 (4/1-9/30/94)			326 (10/1/94-3/31/95)		
ALL	ALL	ALL		0-1MM	1-3MM	3-5MM	5-10MM	10-25MM	25MM & OVER
435	454	496	NUMBER OF STATEMENTS	18	74	54	109	105	136
%	%	%	ASSETS	%	%	%	%	%	%
5.4	5.4	4.9	Cash & Equivalents	7.2	5.8	5.1	5.6	4.8	3.3
34.9	36.3	36.9	Trade Receivables - (net)	30.2	37.9	35.4	39.5	38.2	34.6
38.1	37.2	37.3	Inventory	36.3	34.1	37.3	36.9	37.8	39.0
1.5	1.1	1.3	All Other Current	2.3	1.3	1.5	.7	1.6	1.5
80.0	80.0	80.3	Total Current	76.0	79.1	79.5	82.8	82.4	78.4
14.0	14.2	14.1	Fixed Assets (net)	14.8	15.4	14.5	12.2	12.0	16.3
.9	.9	.9	Intangibles (net)	2.2	.8	.9	.5	1.0	1.1
5.1	4.9	4.6	All Other Non-Current	7.0	4.8	5.1	4.5	4.6	4.2
100.0	100.0	100.0	Total	100.0	100.0	100.0	100.0	100.0	100.0
			LIABILITIES						
19.0	18.0	18.8	Notes Payable-Short Term	12.8	14.4	20.3	16.6	23.8	19.3
2.5	2.3	2.1	Cur. Mat.-L/T/D	3.9	2.8	1.6	2.7	1.6	1.8
22.9	22.3	25.2	Trade Payables	18.6	25.7	23.4	28.3	26.8	22.9
.3	2.2	.4	Income Taxes Payable	.2	.3	.5	.3	.4	.4
6.7	7.4	6.3	All Other Current	11.0	6.9	4.5	5.5	6.8	6.5
51.3	52.3	52.9	Total Current	46.5	50.1	50.3	53.4	59.4	50.8
8.8	9.2	8.7	Long Term Debt	8.6	10.9	5.1	8.0	6.5	11.4
.2	.4	.4	Deferred Taxes	.3	.2	.5	.2	.2	.7
3.3	3.2	2.9	All Other-Non-Current	.0	4.5	2.8	2.3	2.9	2.9
36.4	35.0	35.1	Net Worth	44.7	34.3	41.3	36.1	30.9	34.2
100.0	100.0	100.0	Total Liabilities & Net Worth	100.0	100.0	100.0	100.0	100.0	100.0
			INCOME DATA						
100.0	100.0	100.0	Net Sales	100.0	100.0	100.0	100.0	100.0	100.0
21.4	20.6	20.6	Gross Profit	30.0	26.0	23.4	22.9	17.3	15.9
18.8	18.4	17.8	Operating Expenses	27.1	22.7	21.5	20.3	14.6	12.8
2.6	2.2	2.8	Operating Profit	2.9	3.3	1.9	2.6	2.7	3.1
.8	.6	.6	All Other Expenses (net)	1.0	.8	.2	.7	.4	.8
1.7	1.6	2.1	Profit Before Taxes	1.8	2.5	1.6	1.9	2.2	2.3
			RATIOS						
2.4	2.1	2.2	Current	2.5	2.4	2.3	2.1	1.8	2.3
1.5	1.4	1.5		1.9	1.7	1.5	1.5	1.3	1.5
1.2	1.2	1.2		1.1	1.2	1.3	1.2	1.1	1.2
1.2	1.1	1.1	Quick	1.4	1.3	1.1	1.2	1.0	1.1
.8	.8	.8		.9	.8	.8	.8	.7	.8
.5	.6	.5		.6	.5	.7	.6	.5	.5
36 10.1	37 9.9	37 10.0	Sales/Receivables	33 11.1	33 11.0	35 10.4	38 9.6	37 10.0	39 9.3
46 8.0	46 7.9	46 8.0		49 7.4	44 8.3	46 7.9	46 8.0	46 8.0	46 7.9
56 6.5	56 6.5	54 6.7		96 3.8	54 6.7	54 6.7	56 6.5	57 6.4	52 7.0
40 9.2	38 9.6	39 9.4	Cost of Sales/Inventory	33 10.9	22 16.3	31 11.8	35 10.4	37 9.8	52 7.0
66 5.5	64 5.7	64 5.7		79 4.6	59 6.2	65 5.6	58 6.3	58 6.3	72 5.1
99 3.7	94 3.9	94 3.9		228 1.6	111 3.3	99 3.7	96 3.8	81 4.5	91 4.0
22 16.6	19 19.1	24 15.4	Cost of Sales/Payables	19 19.3	23 16.2	22 16.8	21 17.5	25 14.6	26 14.3
35 10.3	34 10.8	37 10.0		31 11.8	38 9.6	35 10.5	45 8.2	39 9.4	35 10.5
51 7.1	50 7.3	54 6.8		78 4.7	65 5.6	54 6.7	60 6.1	51 7.2	46 7.9
5.5	6.1	6.2	Sales/Working Capital	2.7	5.4	6.0	6.2	8.0	5.9
11.0	11.3	11.3		9.0	10.4	9.9	12.1	16.6	9.9
26.0	25.6	24.8		70.7	23.9	22.4	30.9	34.6	20.6
(391) 4.1	(401) 5.9	(454) 7.8	EBIT/Interest	(14) 9.0	(64) 9.5	(52) 7.6	(99) 8.1	(96) 6.1	(129) 7.5
2.2	2.9	3.5		3.9	3.6	4.3	3.5	3.1	3.8
1.3	1.5	1.8		1.5	1.3	1.5	1.5	1.7	2.2
(159) 5.9	(176) 6.5	(174) 7.4	Net Profit + Depr., Dep., Amort./Cur. Mat. L/T/D		(18) 4.5	(16) 10.6	(31) 6.3	(44) 6.6	(62) 8.3
2.3	2.4	3.2			2.3	3.9	2.4	3.3	3.3
1.2	.9	1.7			.5	1.4	.7	2.3	1.6
.1	.1	.1	Fixed/Worth	.1	.1	.1	.1	.1	.2
.3	.3	.4		.3	.3	.3	.3	.3	.5
.8	.8	.8		.9	1.0	.5	.7	.8	.8
1.0	1.1	1.0	Debt/Worth	.7	.9	.7	.8	1.4	1.2
2.1	2.3	2.2		1.1	2.1	1.5	2.5	2.8	2.3
4.7	4.8	4.8		6.3	6.0	2.8	5.3	5.5	4.0
(418) 24.4	(444) 32.4	(477) 37.5	% Profit Before Taxes/Tangible Net Worth	(17) 47.5	(69) 61.0	(52) 32.5	(105) 36.8	(101) 40.5	(133) 34.8
12.2	14.7	19.5		17.8	20.6	19.0	16.6	21.2	21.3
2.9	5.3	8.2		6.9	7.5	6.4	6.2	9.8	11.3
7.7	9.6	11.9	% Profit Before Taxes/Total Assets	22.9	16.5	13.5	11.2	10.0	11.6
3.5	4.6	6.1		6.8	6.8	5.9	4.8	5.0	6.8
.9	1.3	2.3		.4	1.4	2.1	1.4	2.2	3.0
69.6	69.4	75.7	Sales/Net Fixed Assets	34.9	111.7	102.5	93.4	94.1	46.1
26.5	27.3	27.8		19.5	30.7	30.0	33.9	32.4	17.5
12.3	12.1	12.8		9.2	10.7	16.8	18.6	16.2	9.7
3.4	3.6	3.5	Sales/Total Assets	3.1	4.3	3.4	3.6	3.8	3.1
2.6	2.7	2.8		2.0	2.9	2.7	3.0	2.8	2.6
2.0	2.1	2.2		1.0	2.0	2.3	2.5	2.2	2.1
(378) .4	(394) .5	(438) .4	% Depr., Dep., Amort./Sales	(12) .7	(61) .5	(47) .5	(95) .4	(99) .3	(124) .4
.9	.9	.8		1.1	1.0	.9	.7	.7	.8
1.4	1.4	1.3		2.6	1.9	1.3	1.2	1.1	1.2
(193) 1.7	(180) 1.9	(197) 1.6	% Officers', Directors', Owners' Comp/Sales	(12) 2.7	(38) 3.1	(25) 2.0	(54) 1.9	(45) 1.1	(23) .9
3.6	3.3	2.8		6.7	4.4	5.2	3.5	1.8	1.5
6.2	5.9	5.8		10.7	6.1	7.3	5.4	2.8	2.2
11933855M	15610773M	16210322M	Net Sales ($)	12440M	150428M	205632M	797998M	1628075M	13415749M
4784357M	5684911M	6424978M	Total Assets ($)	11481M	61872M	78605M	325125M	631426M	5316469M

© Robert Morris Associates 1995   M = $ thousand   MM = $ million
See Pages 1 through 15 for Explanation of Ratios and Data

WHOLESALERS—SCRAP & WASTE MATERIALS. SIC# 5093

Current Data Sorted By Assets							Comparative Historical Data	
2	2	1	1			# Postretirement Benefits		
						Type of Statement		
	1	11	10	1	1	Unqualified	30	17
2	21	32	4			Reviewed	57	38
8	16	19	2			Compiled	60	61
3	4					Tax Returns		1
1	9	20	5	1		Other	27	24
	66 (4/1-9/30/94)		105 (10/1/94-3/31/95)				4/1/90-3/31/91	4/1/91-3/31/92
0-500M	500M-2MM	2-10MM	10-50MM	50-100MM	100-250MM		ALL	ALL
14	51	82	21	2	1	NUMBER OF STATEMENTS	174	141
%	%	%	%	%	%	ASSETS	%	%
8.0	9.4	6.6	3.1			Cash & Equivalents	8.5	8.8
26.3	29.7	32.3	36.6			Trade Receivables - (net)	25.5	22.4
26.5	23.7	21.1	21.8			Inventory	19.5	21.1
3.1	1.4	1.0	1.3			All Other Current	3.2	4.2
63.8	64.2	61.0	62.8			Total Current	56.7	56.5
29.8	29.5	30.9	26.6			Fixed Assets (net)	33.8	34.0
2.1	.7	1.3	.8			Intangibles (net)	.5	1.1
4.3	5.6	6.7	9.8			All Other Non-Current	9.0	8.3
100.0	100.0	100.0	100.0			Total	100.0	100.0
						LIABILITIES		
8.3	12.6	11.5	12.2			Notes Payable-Short Term	12.2	12.6
6.1	3.8	4.1	2.4			Cur. Mat. -L/T/D	3.9	4.3
13.8	16.8	17.2	17.6			Trade Payables	16.0	12.2
.1	.8	.9	.6			Income Taxes Payable	.3	.3
5.1	5.1	5.6	8.7			All Other Current	7.3	5.7
33.3	39.1	39.3	41.4			Total Current	39.7	35.1
19.8	11.2	11.2	11.1			Long Term Debt	13.0	14.3
.0	.2	.5	.9			Deferred Taxes	.3	.3
4.3	2.6	3.4	1.8			All Other-Non-Current	3.0	4.0
42.6	46.9	45.6	44.7			Net Worth	44.1	46.3
100.0	100.0	100.0	100.0			Total Liabilities & Net Worth	100.0	100.0
						INCOME DATA		
100.0	100.0	100.0	100.0			Net Sales	100.0	100.0
30.8	29.4	23.9	16.2			Gross Profit	24.1	25.4
25.7	23.1	18.9	13.8			Operating Expenses	21.1	25.1
5.0	6.3	5.0	2.3			Operating Profit	3.0	.3
1.0	.4	.5	.0			All Other Expenses (net)	.6	.5
4.1	5.9	4.4	2.4			Profit Before Taxes	2.4	−.2
						RATIOS		
4.3	2.2	2.3	2.2				2.2	2.7
1.6	1.5	1.6	1.5			Current	1.5	1.6
1.1	1.2	1.1	1.2				1.0	1.1
1.8	1.4	1.4	1.5				1.4	1.5
1.2	1.0	1.1	1.0			Quick	.8	.9
.6	.6	.7	.7				.5	.5
4	97.7	20	18.0	25	14.7	41	9.0				17	21.3	16	22.2
25	14.8	30	12.0	40	9.1	48	7.6			Sales/Receivables	27	13.6	24	15.3
36	10.2	40	9.1	54	6.7	59	6.2				40	9.1	36	10.1
8	43.5	11	33.6	16	22.7	13	28.6				11	32.3	10	36.5
20	18.5	32	11.4	29	12.8	34	10.7			Cost of Sales/Inventory	26	14.2	30	12.2
61	6.0	69	5.3	52	7.0	54	6.8				48	7.6	59	6.2
0	UND	11	34.1	12	30.1	15	24.1				8	44.4	6	66.0
10	34.9	19	19.1	24	15.2	26	14.0			Cost of Sales/Payables	20	18.1	15	23.9
31	11.6	43	8.5	41	8.9	54	6.8				37	9.9	30	12.3
8.1	7.2	8.2	8.5				9.1	7.1
19.1	17.4	14.8	11.9			Sales/Working Capital	18.3	15.3
NM	68.3	48.2	25.6				999.8	76.2
11.9	11.8	13.0	10.8				5.8	3.8
6.1	(42) 4.6	(76) 4.8	(19) 3.1			EBIT/Interest	(164) 2.7	(125) 1.5
2.8	1.6	2.7	1.5				1.1	.2
	4.0	8.2					5.7	3.6
	(13) 2.9	(32) 3.4				Net Profit + Depr., Dep., Amort./Cur. Mat. L /T/D	(88) 2.6	(58) 1.0
	1.9	1.4					1.0	.2
.3	.1	.4	.3				.3	.3
.7	.5	.6	.6			Fixed/Worth	.8	.7
7.4	1.4	1.2	1.3				1.5	1.5
.5	.6	.7	.6				.6	.4
1.4	1.3	1.2	1.4			Debt/Worth	1.4	1.4
11.0	2.4	2.2	2.4				2.9	2.5
267.6	47.8	48.7	32.6				24.8	12.6
45.9	27.6	(81) 26.6	14.0			% Profit Before Taxes/Tangible Net Worth	(169) 12.8	(135) 4.8
16.6	8.9	10.6	6.0				2.7	−8.3
22.1	19.5	21.3	13.9				10.4	7.0
11.9	11.1	10.5	6.3			% Profit Before Taxes/Total Assets	4.9	1.7
7.5	3.1	4.5	2.5				.5	−4.2
93.5	31.8	19.2	15.7				23.2	21.4
19.6	13.5	10.1	11.6			Sales/Net Fixed Assets	11.4	9.6
6.1	6.0	4.6	5.9				5.7	5.2
7.7	4.2	3.8	3.5				4.4	4.0
5.1	3.3	2.8	2.5			Sales/Total Assets	3.1	2.8
2.3	1.9	2.1	2.1				2.2	2.0
1.5	1.3	.9	1.0				.9	1.1
(10) 3.0	(43) 2.0	(78) 2.2	(19) 1.6			% Depr., Dep., Amort./Sales	(163) 1.9	(132) 2.2
5.0	3.5	3.4	2.2				3.4	3.5
	1.6	1.4					2.1	2.0
	(22) 2.9	(46) 2.7				% Officers', Directors', Owners' Comp/Sales	(94) 3.5	(66) 3.7
	4.8	4.7					6.7	6.0
23681M	206213M	1107636M	1106353M	401887M	423514M	Net Sales ($)	3688089M	2998910M
4530M	59683M	371665M	436038M	150412M	168378M	Total Assets ($)	1274596M	1046570M

M = $ thousand   MM = $ million
See Pages 1 through 15 for Explanation of Ratios and Data

Comparative Historical Data				Current Data Sorted By Sales					
1	6	6	# Postretirement Benefits		1	1	1	2	1
			Type of Statement	0-1MM	1-3MM	3-5MM	5-10MM	10-25MM	25MM & OVER
22	20	24	Unqualified			1	3	7	13
57	54	59	Reviewed	2	6	9	18	17	7
49	59	45	Compiled	3	15	6	10	8	3
3	6	7	Tax Returns	1	5		1		
24	29	36	Other	3	6	3	8	7	9
4/1/92- 3/31/93 ALL	4/1/93- 3/31/94 ALL	4/1/94- 3/31/95 ALL			66 (4/1-9/30/94)		105 (10/1/94-3/31/95)		
155	168	171	**NUMBER OF STATEMENTS**	9	32	19	40	39	32
%	%	%	**ASSETS**	%	%	%	%	%	%
5.9	8.1	7.1	Cash & Equivalents		8.4	11.6	7.1	6.6	3.4
26.3	23.9	31.6	Trade Receivables - (net)		25.0	22.3	33.5	37.1	39.4
21.9	23.6	22.4	Inventory		24.7	22.7	22.3	21.7	20.4
3.0	2.0	1.4	All Other Current		1.4	2.1	.8	1.5	1.2
57.2	57.6	62.5	Total Current		59.5	58.7	63.7	66.9	64.4
34.9	33.5	29.8	Fixed Assets (net)		34.0	34.0	30.2	24.9	24.6
1.1	1.0	1.1	Intangibles (net)		1.4	.5	.4	2.3	1.0
6.9	8.0	6.6	All Other Non-Current		5.2	6.7	5.7	6.0	10.0
100.0	100.0	100.0	Total		100.0	100.0	100.0	100.0	100.0
			LIABILITIES						
14.1	11.4	11.6	Notes Payable-Short Term		11.7	10.2	13.3	10.1	11.9
4.7	3.8	3.9	Cur. Mat.-L /T/D		5.9	3.6	4.4	2.0	3.7
14.2	15.1	17.0	Trade Payables		10.4	14.7	22.8	18.0	19.3
.3	.4	.8	Income Taxes Payable		.2	1.6	1.0	1.0	.5
7.7	6.6	5.8	All Other Current		4.1	5.9	4.6	6.7	8.2
41.0	37.3	39.1	Total Current		32.4	36.0	46.1	37.8	43.5
14.0	15.0	12.0	Long Term Debt		17.7	12.0	11.6	8.2	10.9
.4	.5	.4	Deferred Taxes		.1	.3	.8	.4	.5
4.3	2.8	3.0	All Other-Non-Current		2.7	6.2	2.1	2.2	2.9
40.3	44.3	45.5	Net Worth		47.0	45.5	39.4	51.4	42.1
100.0	100.0	100.0	Total Liabilities & Net Worth		100.0	100.0	100.0	100.0	100.0
			INCOME DATA						
100.0	100.0	100.0	Net Sales		100.0	100.0	100.0	100.0	100.0
24.2	27.3	24.9	Gross Profit		29.8	36.7	21.8	20.4	14.3
23.2	25.7	19.9	Operating Expenses		24.2	29.5	18.6	15.9	11.5
.9	1.5	5.0	Operating Profit		5.7	7.2	3.3	4.5	2.7
.6	.2	.5	All Other Expenses (net)		.1	1.1	.5	.3	.1
.3	1.3	4.5	Profit Before Taxes		5.5	6.1	2.8	4.2	2.7
			RATIOS						
2.2 / 1.4 / .9	3.0 / 1.6 / 1.0	2.3 / 1.5 / 1.2	Current		4.0 / 1.4 / 1.0	2.1 / 1.6 / 1.2	2.0 / 1.4 / 1.1	2.4 / 1.8 / 1.3	2.3 / 1.5 / 1.2
1.3 / .8 / .5	1.5 / .9 / .6	1.4 / 1.0 / .7	Quick		1.8 / 1.0 / .6	1.4 / 1.2 / .7	1.3 / .9 / .7	1.5 / 1.1 / .9	1.6 / 1.0 / .7
16 23.0 / 29 12.6 / 41 9.0	18 20.3 / 30 12.2 / 42 8.7	24 14.9 / 37 10.0 / 49 7.5	Sales/Receivables		14 25.6 / 28 12.9 / 38 9.5	17 22.0 / 41 8.9 / 51 7.1	20 18.7 / 34 10.8 / 49 7.5	27 13.6 / 41 8.9 / 53 6.9	36 10.2 / 42 8.6 / 53 6.9
13 28.1 / 30 12.1 / 55 6.6	16 22.2 / 36 10.1 / 70 5.2	14 26.9 / 29 12.5 / 57 6.4	Cost of Sales/Inventory		11 31.9 / 57 6.4 / 94 3.9	18 20.3 / 35 10.3 / 94 3.9	14 25.8 / 25 14.7 / 48 7.6	13 28.6 / 28 13.1 / 49 7.5	15 24.0 / 27 13.4 / 52 7.0
7 49.6 / 18 20.3 / 32 11.5	7 55.4 / 18 20.0 / 37 10.0	12 31.7 / 23 15.9 / 40 9.1	Cost of Sales/Payables		5 77.0 / 14 25.6 / 32 11.3	21 17.5 / 31 11.7 / 61 6.0	13 28.4 / 24 15.4 / 48 7.6	11 33.3 / 21 17.6 / 35 10.3	12 30.4 / 24 15.4 / 35 10.3
8.7 / 21.8 / -66.8	6.5 / 14.8 / 286.9	8.2 / 15.7 / 48.7	Sales/Working Capital		7.3 / 14.4 / UND	7.2 / 14.0 / 58.1	9.4 / 20.6 / 91.6	7.9 / 13.1 / 23.9	10.1 / 16.0 / 33.8
(139) 3.3 / 1.4 / .1	(151) 5.6 / 2.4 / .6	(154) 11.5 / 4.8 / 2.3	EBIT/Interest		(27) 7.0 / 3.7 / 2.1	(16) 19.6 / 5.7 / 3.0	(39) 7.6 / 4.6 / 1.9	(35) 32.3 / 6.3 / 2.5	(29) 12.3 / 5.0 / 2.3
(55) 4.8 / 1.9 / .8	(63) 4.9 / 1.9 / 1.0	(57) 8.1 / 3.5 / 1.8	Net Profit + Depr., Dep., Amort./Cur. Mat. L/T/D				(19) 7.2 / 3.5 / 1.7	(12) 18.3 / 5.2 / 1.3	(11) 9.4 / 6.9 / 2.1
.3 / .8 / 1.8	.3 / .6 / 1.5	.3 / .6 / 1.2	Fixed/Worth		.2 / .8 / 1.7	.3 / .6 / 2.1	.4 / .8 / 1.3	.2 / .4 / .9	.3 / .6 / 1.1
.8 / 1.6 / 3.4	.5 / 1.2 / 2.8	.7 / 1.3 / 2.4	Debt/Worth		.6 / 1.4 / 2.2	.6 / 1.0 / 2.7	.9 / 1.6 / 2.5	.5 / 1.0 / 1.7	.7 / 1.7 / 2.5
(145) 15.7 / 4.6 / -5.0	(157) 22.5 / 7.7 / -.2	(170) 47.8 / 23.5 / 9.4	% Profit Before Taxes/Tangible Net Worth		77.3 / 24.9 / 5.2	(18) 45.8 / 23.6 / 17.2	45.2 / 19.2 / 9.1	48.8 / 26.6 / 9.3	40.1 / 24.8 / 9.0
5.3 / 1.6 / -2.9	8.9 / 2.8 / -1.0	19.3 / 9.7 / 4.2	% Profit Before Taxes/Total Assets		21.8 / 11.0 / 2.9	19.3 / 11.1 / 5.1	15.3 / 8.0 / 3.5	26.6 / 11.7 / 4.7	15.1 / 8.3 / 4.1
20.6 / 9.3 / 4.6	17.2 / 9.2 / 5.6	23.6 / 11.0 / 5.9	Sales/Net Fixed Assets		26.3 / 8.3 / 4.1	13.5 / 8.3 / 3.6	22.9 / 10.1 / 4.8	26.9 / 14.0 / 8.9	22.1 / 12.9 / 8.1
4.4 / 3.0 / 2.0	3.7 / 2.7 / 1.8	4.0 / 2.9 / 2.0	Sales/Total Assets		4.1 / 2.8 / 1.7	2.9 / 2.0 / 1.7	4.3 / 3.2 / 2.3	5.0 / 3.2 / 2.6	4.0 / 3.0 / 2.3
(149) 1.1 / 2.2 / 3.9	(163) 1.3 / 2.4 / 3.9	(153) 1.0 / 2.1 / 3.4	% Depr., Dep., Amort./Sales		(28) 1.7 / 2.9 / 5.5	(18) 1.3 / 3.1 / 4.0	(36) 1.3 / 2.2 / 3.4	(35) .7 / 1.6 / 2.5	(30) .6 / 1.5 / 2.2
(81) 2.9 / 5.2	(92) 2.0 / 3.9 / 5.6	(83) 1.5 / 2.7 / 4.7	% Officers', Directors', Owners' Comp/Sales		(16) 1.4 / 2.8 / 4.4		(22) 1.6 / 2.7 / 3.9	(22) 1.1 / 2.2 / 3.5	(11) .8 / 1.4 / 2.3
2615943M / 1032487M	2843518M / 1112328M	3269284M / 1190706M	Net Sales ($) / Total Assets ($)	6012M / 3503M	68804M / 30161M	77609M / 42176M	292705M / 127745M	595488M / 198051M	2228666M / 789070M

M = $ thousand   MM = $ million
See Pages 1 through 15 for Explanation of Ratios and Data

Current Data Sorted By Assets | | Comparative Historical Data

						# Postretirement Benefits		
	1	3				**Type of Statement**		
	1	3	2			Unqualified	5	9
1	21	5	1			Reviewed	30	17
10	21	3				Compiled	44	44
2	2					Tax Returns		
7	12	5	1			Other	15	12
	36 (4/1-9/30/94)		61 (10/1/94-3/31/95)				4/1/90-3/31/91	4/1/91-3/31/92
0-500M	500M-2MM	2-10MM	10-50MM	50-100MM	100-250MM		ALL	ALL
20	57	16	4			**NUMBER OF STATEMENTS**	94	82
%	%	%	%	%	%	**ASSETS**	%	%
5.8	3.8	4.1				Cash & Equivalents	5.9	5.7
36.7	38.2	36.6				Trade Receivables - (net)	35.4	33.3
38.2	38.5	37.8				Inventory	36.7	34.8
1.3	1.8	1.2				All Other Current	1.7	1.5
82.1	82.4	79.7				Total Current	79.7	75.3
10.9	10.8	12.8				Fixed Assets (net)	13.2	14.6
3.5	1.7	2.6				Intangibles (net)	1.5	4.0
3.5	5.1	4.9				All Other Non-Current	5.6	6.1
100.0	100.0	100.0				Total	100.0	100.0
						LIABILITIES		
7.8	13.8	13.2				Notes Payable-Short Term	13.0	11.6
6.6	3.8	2.4				Cur. Mat. -L/T/D	4.0	4.4
26.1	23.7	21.6				Trade Payables	22.5	21.0
.1	.2	.2				Income Taxes Payable	.8	.5
11.4	5.9	7.4				All Other Current	8.6	8.6
52.0	47.4	44.8				Total Current	48.8	46.1
15.4	11.7	11.9				Long Term Debt	14.5	17.3
.0	.2	.0				Deferred Taxes	.1	.1
4.3	3.7	6.6				All Other-Non-Current	2.1	3.4
28.3	37.0	36.7				Net Worth	34.6	33.1
100.0	100.0	100.0				Total Liabilities & Net Worth	100.0	100.0
						INCOME DATA		
100.0	100.0	100.0				Net Sales	100.0	100.0
36.6	31.7	31.1				Gross Profit	33.7	33.9
33.9	31.0	30.2				Operating Expenses	30.5	31.8
2.6	.7	.9				Operating Profit	3.1	2.0
1.0	.3	.1				All Other Expenses (net)	.9	.4
1.6	.4	.8				Profit Before Taxes	2.3	1.6
						RATIOS		
2.4 2.0 1.3	2.7 1.8 1.3	2.9 1.7 1.5				Current	2.3 1.6 1.3	2.3 1.7 1.3
1.3 1.0 .6	1.3 .9 .7	1.6 .8 .7				Quick	1.1 .8 .6	1.2 .9 .7
29 12.4 36 10.2 42 8.7	35 10.5 41 9.0 49 7.5	34 10.8 38 9.7 44 8.3				Sales/Receivables	34 10.8 40 9.2 48 7.6	31 11.8 38 9.7 46 8.0
45 8.1 56 6.5 78 4.7	49 7.5 63 5.8 94 3.9	49 7.4 59 6.2 72 5.1				Cost of Sales/Inventory	43 8.5 64 5.7 89 4.1	42 8.7 60 6.1 78 4.7
22 16.7 36 10.1 59 6.2	22 16.3 34 10.7 51 7.2	25 14.8 33 11.0 38 9.6				Cost of Sales/Payables	21 17.1 34 10.6 53 6.9	22 16.9 32 11.5 51 7.2
7.6 9.8 17.8	5.8 9.8 19.1	7.3 9.4 14.4				Sales/Working Capital	7.0 11.2 18.6	7.0 11.7 18.0
12.5 (19) 2.4 1.5	6.3 (54) 2.3 1.4	14.1 3.4 1.2				EBIT/Interest	5.3 (86) 2.5 1.4	4.6 (78) 1.9 1.9
	3.3 (30) 1.6 .4					Net Profit + Depr., Dep., Amort./Cur. Mat. L./T/D	3.5 (49) 1.6 .9	3.8 (42) 1.2 .5
.1 .5 15.5	.2 .3 .6	.1 .3 .9				Fixed/Worth	.1 .3 .7	.2 .4 1.2
.9 3.7 73.0	.9 2.2 3.7	.8 2.2 5.3				Debt/Worth	1.1 2.0 4.4	1.0 2.2 6.5
62.7 (16) 29.4 16.2	21.9 (53) 8.9 4.1	34.7 (15) 13.4 6.0				% Profit Before Taxes/Tangible Net Worth	26.2 (86) 15.4 6.7	34.5 (72) 15.2 2.5
12.4 6.5 1.4	6.8 3.8 1.1	11.3 5.7 .3				% Profit Before Taxes/Total Assets	11.0 4.2 2.1	10.4 3.9 .1
67.4 41.1 25.1	62.6 33.5 21.6	67.4 31.0 17.9				Sales/Net Fixed Assets	58.9 38.5 19.6	50.2 28.3 16.5
4.3 3.8 3.1	3.7 3.3 2.6	3.9 3.4 2.7				Sales/Total Assets	4.0 3.2 2.7	4.2 3.2 2.6
.5 (17) 1.0 1.8	.6 (55) .9 1.3	.8 (14) 1.0 1.4				% Depr., Dep., Amort./Sales	.6 (82) .9 1.4	.8 (72) 1.1 1.8
	1.9 (30) 3.3 7.3					% Officers', Directors', Owners' Comp/Sales	2.7 (51) 4.8 6.4	3.5 (44) 4.6 6.4
22291M 6126M	212890M 66179M	209719M 62743M	180770M 52684M			Net Sales ($) Total Assets ($)	442704M 143982M	319056M 102572M

M = $ thousand   MM = $ million
See Pages 1 through 15 for Explanation of Ratios and Data

	Comparative Historical Data			Current Data Sorted By Sales					
	1	2	4	1	1	2			
# Postretirement Benefits									
Type of Statement									
Unqualified	5	4	6		1		2	1	2
Reviewed	22	20	28	1	4	12	7	2	2
Compiled	31	26	34	4	17	4	7	2	
Tax Returns	2	4	4	1	2	1			
Other	10	13	25	3	7	8	3	2	2
	4/1/92-3/31/93 ALL	4/1/93-3/31/94 ALL	4/1/94-3/31/95 ALL	36 (4/1-9/30/94) 0-1MM	1-3MM	3-5MM	61 (10/1/94-3/31/95) 5-10MM	10-25MM	25MM & OVER
NUMBER OF STATEMENTS	70	67	97	9	31	25	19	7	6
ASSETS	%	%	%	%	%	%	%	%	%
Cash & Equivalents	5.1	4.3	4.1		5.0	3.0	4.4		
Trade Receivables - (net)	34.4	34.1	37.7		32.1	39.4	42.0		
Inventory	35.6	35.1	38.5		41.7	36.8	34.4		
All Other Current	1.0	1.4	1.7		1.9	1.4	1.1		
Total Current	76.1	74.9	82.0		80.6	80.6	81.9		
Fixed Assets (net)	16.0	15.9	11.1		10.6	12.1	11.3		
Intangibles (net)	2.6	2.5	2.2		4.6	.7	1.9		
All Other Non-Current	5.3	6.8	4.7		4.2	6.7	4.8		
Total	100.0	100.0	100.0		100.0	100.0	100.0		
LIABILITIES									
Notes Payable-Short Term	11.8	14.3	13.2		6.9	18.6	15.8		
Cur. Mat.-L/T/D	4.4	3.6	4.0		5.0	4.5	2.4		
Trade Payables	20.8	19.9	23.6		24.7	23.5	25.4		
Income Taxes Payable	.3	.7	.2		.2	.3	.1		
All Other Current	6.6	8.2	7.3		5.5	6.9	6.1		
Total Current	43.9	46.7	48.4		42.4	53.8	49.7		
Long Term Debt	14.7	11.4	12.3		16.9	8.4	12.8		
Deferred Taxes	.0	.1	.1		.2	.1	.2		
All Other-Non-Current	6.6	1.7	4.2		2.7	2.6	7.2		
Net Worth	34.7	40.1	35.0		37.9	35.1	30.0		
Total Liabilities & Net Worth	100.0	100.0	100.0		100.0	100.0	100.0		
INCOME DATA									
Net Sales	100.0	100.0	100.0		100.0	100.0	100.0		
Gross Profit	36.5	34.4	32.4		34.6	31.1	31.5		
Operating Expenses	34.2	32.9	31.2		33.0	30.6	31.3		
Operating Profit	2.3	1.5	1.2		1.7	.5	.2		
All Other Expenses (net)	.5	-.2	.4		.6	.3	.3		
Profit Before Taxes	1.8	1.7	.8		1.0	.2	-.1		
RATIOS									
Current	2.3	2.2	2.6		3.1	2.4	2.1		
	1.7	1.7	1.8		2.2	1.5	1.7		
	1.3	1.3	1.3		1.4	1.1	1.4		
Quick	1.3	1.1	1.3		1.3	1.1	1.2		
	.8	.8	.9		1.0	.7	.9		
	.6	.6	.7		.6	.7	.7		
Sales/Receivables	31 11.7	30 12.1	34 10.7		31 11.7	36 10.1	37 10.0		
	37 10.0	36 10.2	40 9.2		39 9.3	41 9.0	43 8.5		
	44 8.3	44 8.3	47 7.8		46 7.9	51 7.1	48 7.6		
Cost of Sales/Inventory	44 8.3	40 9.1	48 7.6		51 7.1	47 7.8	41 8.8		
	58 6.3	61 6.0	62 5.9		79 4.6	62 5.9	54 6.8		
	81 4.5	78 4.7	85 4.3		96 3.8	81 4.5	68 5.4		
Cost of Sales/Payables	20 18.6	21 17.0	22 16.6		22 16.8	22 16.3	24 15.3		
	31 11.9	34 10.7	33 11.0		43 8.4	33 11.2	34 10.7		
	59 6.2	46 7.9	51 7.2		64 5.7	50 7.3	52 7.0		
Sales/Working Capital	6.6	7.7	6.9		5.1	7.9	7.9		
	10.4	12.3	9.8		6.9	12.6	10.9		
	20.7	21.5	18.2		11.9	34.4	15.3		
EBIT/Interest	(65) 5.9	(63) 5.0	(93) 6.5		(29) 6.4	5.1	(18) 5.0		
	2.1	2.1	2.4		1.9	2.4	2.1		
	1.1	1.0	1.4		1.2	1.3	1.2		
Net Profit + Depr., Dep., Amort./Cur. Mat. L/T/D	(32) 3.1	(26) 3.6	(44) 3.8		(17) 3.4	(11) 1.8			
	2.0	1.2	1.6		1.4	1.1			
	.7	.6	.5		.3	.1			
Fixed/Worth	.2	.1	.1		.1	.2	.2		
	.4	.4	.3		.3	.3	.5		
	1.6	.8	.8		1.6	.7	.9		
Debt/Worth	.8	.8	.9		.6	1.0	1.7		
	2.1	1.8	2.2		2.3	2.2	2.4		
	13.3	3.2	5.4		8.2	3.6	5.4		
% Profit Before Taxes/Tangible Net Worth	(60) 29.9	(64) 28.1	(88) 30.8		(26) 24.9	(24) 29.3	(17) 21.0		
	13.3	10.7	12.6		11.6	8.0	15.8		
	3.1	1.3	5.1		3.9	3.9	4.6		
% Profit Before Taxes/Total Assets	9.9	9.3	8.8		7.2	6.9	6.9		
	3.6	4.1	4.0		3.2	3.8	3.8		
	.3	.5	1.2		.4	1.1	.7		
Sales/Net Fixed Assets	52.0	71.4	65.5		50.1	80.6	92.1		
	32.5	30.7	33.2		31.9	33.5	32.1		
	13.2	16.2	22.8		25.0	18.7	21.2		
Sales/Total Assets	4.0	4.3	4.0		3.8	3.8	4.5		
	3.3	3.6	3.4		3.0	3.4	3.5		
	2.6	2.6	2.7		2.5	2.6	2.9		
% Depr., Dep., Amort./Sales	(66) .7	(59) .6	(90) .6		(29) .6	(24) .4	.6		
	1.0	1.1	.9		1.0	.9	1.0		
	1.6	1.8	1.6		1.6	1.3	1.3		
% Officers', Directors', Owners' Comp/Sales	(35) 3.0	(34) 2.3	(44) 2.1		(16) 3.0	(13) 1.8			
	4.9	4.5	3.6		4.6	2.5			
	7.3	6.7			7.0	4.3			
Net Sales ($)	246161M	268065M	625670M	6846M	55185M	100847M	127266M	103225M	232301M
Total Assets ($)	76372M	82100M	187732M	1984M	19403M	32362M	37304M	26923M	69756M

M = $ thousand   MM = $ million
See Pages 1 through 15 for Explanation of Ratios and Data

WHOLESALERS—JEWELRY. SIC# 5094

	Current Data Sorted By Assets							Comparative Historical Data	
	2	4	1	1	1		**# Postretirement Benefits**		
							Type of Statement		
		2	14	7	4		Unqualified	18	15
	4	18	30	5	1		Reviewed	53	64
	4	28	8				Compiled	51	43
	5	4					Tax Returns		2
	6	6	9	1	2	1	Other	20	34
		57 (4/1-9/30/94)			102 (10/1/94-3/31/95)			4/1/90-3/31/91	4/1/91-3/31/92
	0-500M	500M-2MM	2-10MM	10-50MM	50-100MM	100-250MM		ALL	ALL
	19	58	61	13	7	1	**NUMBER OF STATEMENTS**	142	158
	%	%	%	%	%	%	**ASSETS**	%	%
	7.7	4.7	4.1	3.8			Cash & Equivalents	6.4	6.5
	19.3	26.9	33.8	40.4			Trade Receivables - (net)	29.0	29.9
	51.8	52.9	48.7	43.7			Inventory	50.5	48.9
	2.2	1.1	1.7	.2			All Other Current	1.0	1.0
	81.0	85.6	88.3	88.0			Total Current	86.9	86.3
	12.7	8.3	5.4	4.3			Fixed Assets (net)	8.0	7.6
	.7	1.6	1.5	2.7			Intangibles (net)	.5	.9
	5.5	4.6	4.8	5.0			All Other Non-Current	4.6	5.3
	100.0	100.0	100.0	100.0			Total	100.0	100.0
							LIABILITIES		
	23.5	15.8	26.7	23.3			Notes Payable-Short Term	19.2	16.5
	1.9	2.5	1.0	.5			Cur. Mat. -L/T/D	2.6	1.6
	26.1	19.2	21.0	20.1			Trade Payables	20.5	19.1
	.1	.1	.5	.2			Income Taxes Payable	.4	.3
	5.7	7.8	4.8	13.0			All Other Current	6.3	7.8
	57.3	45.5	54.1	57.0			Total Current	49.0	45.3
	11.6	8.2	3.1	4.7			Long Term Debt	5.6	6.8
	.1	.0	.1	.0			Deferred Taxes	.2	.2
	3.8	4.9	6.6	2.7			All Other-Non-Current	3.0	4.7
	27.2	41.5	36.1	35.6			Net Worth	42.2	43.0
	100.0	100.0	100.0	100.0			Total Liabilities & Net Worth	100.0	100.0
							INCOME DATA		
	100.0	100.0	100.0	100.0			Net Sales	100.0	100.0
	36.8	30.1	24.0	28.6			Gross Profit	29.1	29.9
	33.5	27.4	20.1	23.0			Operating Expenses	25.8	26.4
	3.3	2.7	3.9	5.6			Operating Profit	3.3	3.5
	1.0	1.0	.8	1.0			All Other Expenses (net)	1.1	1.3
	2.3	1.7	3.1	4.5			Profit Before Taxes	2.1	2.2
							RATIOS		
	3.0	2.9	2.0	2.4			Current	2.5	3.1
	1.6	1.9	1.6	1.3				1.8	1.9
	1.0	1.4	1.3	1.3				1.4	1.4
	1.3	1.0	1.1	1.0			Quick	1.2	1.4
	.6	.6	.7	.8			(141)	.7	.8
	.1	.4	.5	.6				.4	.4
1	342.5	11 32.1	38 9.6	50 7.3			Sales/Receivables	23 16.1	25 14.6
20	18.6	37 9.8	52 7.0	70 5.2				40 9.2	43 8.4
36	10.1	61 6.0	78 4.7	101 3.6				62 5.9	68 5.4
49	7.5	53 6.9	68 5.4	96 3.8			Cost of Sales/Inventory	68 5.4	55 6.6
101	3.6	130 2.8	126 2.9	114 3.2				111 3.3	122 3.0
159	2.3	174 2.1	166 2.2	152 2.4				174 2.1	203 1.8
5	80.2	7 52.9	16 22.6	20 18.6			Cost of Sales/Payables	16 23.2	12 29.5
29	12.8	35 10.4	43 8.5	56 6.5				37 9.9	31 11.7
87	4.2	89 4.1	60 6.1	74 4.9				72 5.1	64 5.7
	4.1	4.1	4.1	4.6			Sales/Working Capital	4.4	3.0
	11.3	6.9	6.9	6.3				6.8	5.8
	−107.6	14.9	11.6	11.1				10.5	12.4
	4.8	6.5	5.2	11.1			EBIT/Interest	4.1	4.6
(14)	1.2	(54) 3.2	(57) 2.2	(12) 3.5			(129)	2.0	(145) 2.1
	−1.1	1.3	1.3	2.1				1.1	1.2
		3.0	16.3				Net Profit + Depr., Dep.,	6.6	11.9
		(11) 1.0	(15) 7.5				Amort./Cur. Mat. L /T/D (47)	1.3	(38) 3.0
		.3	.9					.4	.9
	.0	.0	.0	.0			Fixed/Worth	.0	.0
	.3	.1	.1	.1				.1	.1
	1.8	.4	.3	.2				.3	.3
	.8	.6	1.0	1.2			Debt/Worth	.8	.6
	3.0	2.0	2.2	2.5				1.4	1.5
	−79.0	3.8	4.0	4.7				3.2	3.3
	37.2	31.2	22.3	43.8			% Profit Before Taxes/Tangible	25.3	23.3
(14)	15.9	(57) 12.0	(58) 10.1	29.1			Net Worth (140)	9.5	(153) 10.0
	−1.0	2.9	2.8	6.9				1.1	2.6
	7.4	7.7	8.5	16.7			% Profit Before Taxes/Total	9.9	8.0
	2.2	4.2	2.7	6.0			Assets	3.5	3.3
	−3.0	.9	.9	2.3				.3	.6
	576.3	171.8	479.6	273.1			Sales/Net Fixed Assets	214.8	213.2
	48.8	61.8	105.5	68.7				64.2	63.9
	20.2	20.5	37.5	36.3				29.4	26.0
	3.8	3.2	3.0	2.5			Sales/Total Assets	3.3	3.2
	2.7	2.3	2.1	1.9				2.4	2.2
	1.9	1.5	1.4	1.5				1.6	1.5
	.3	.2	.1	.1			% Depr., Dep., Amort./Sales	.2	.2
(12)	.6	(48) .5	(53) .3	(10) .4			(123)	.5	(131) .5
	1.1	.9	.6	.5				1.0	.9
	1.9	2.8	1.2				% Officers', Directors',	2.0	1.5
(11)	3.1	(36) 4.4	(41) 1.9				Owners' Comp/Sales (73)	3.9	(83) 3.6
	10.9	6.6	5.5					7.7	7.0
	24757M	212109M	825876M	468294M	747475M	326850M	Net Sales ($)	1838217M	1680964M
	5621M	67475M	280606M	242353M	488669M	168718M	Total Assets ($)	943159M	889429M

© Robert Morris Associates 1995

M = $ thousand   MM = $ million
See Pages 1 through 15 for Explanation of Ratios and Data

‖‖‖

S REPLY MAIL

NO. 26639 PHILA., PA

By

S ASSOCIATES
ACE
REET, 23RD FLOOR
A 19103-9734

‖‖‖

S REPLY MAIL

IT NO. 26639 PHILA., PA

d By

IS ASSOCIATES
LACE
STREET, 23RD FLOOR
PA 19103-9734

Comparative Historical Data				Current Data Sorted By Sales					
4	5	9	# Postretirement Benefits / Type of Statement	1	2	1	1	2	2
20	19	27	Unqualified		2	3	6	5	11
60	53	58	Reviewed	4	9	12	11	16	6
44	44	40	Compiled	6	19	4	7	3	1
6	6	9	Tax Returns	3	3	2			1
20	28	25	Other	4	2	2	5	5	4
4/1/92-3/31/93 ALL	4/1/93-3/31/94 ALL	4/1/94-3/31/95 ALL		57 (4/1-9/30/94)			102 (10/1/94-3/31/95)		
				0-1MM	1-3MM	3-5MM	5-10MM	10-25MM	25MM & OVER
150	150	159	**NUMBER OF STATEMENTS**	17	38	23	29	29	23
%	%	%	**ASSETS**	%	%	%	%	%	%
6.3	4.9	4.7	Cash & Equivalents	6.9	4.5	3.6	4.5	4.6	4.2
30.4	30.5	30.0	Trade Receivables - (net)	12.9	22.9	32.6	32.6	39.5	36.7
46.8	51.7	50.0	Inventory	61.6	53.1	49.9	48.3	44.8	45.2
1.3	1.4	1.5	All Other Current	2.4	1.5	1.5	2.2	.3	1.7
84.7	88.5	86.3	Total Current	83.8	82.5	87.6	87.6	89.3	87.8
8.4	6.3	7.3	Fixed Assets (net)	11.9	9.0	5.8	6.1	6.3	5.6
.3	1.0	1.5	Intangibles (net)	.9	3.5	.0	1.0	.8	1.9
6.7	4.2	4.9	All Other Non-Current	3.4	5.1	6.6	5.4	3.7	4.7
100.0	100.0	100.0	Total	100.0	100.0	100.0	100.0	100.0	100.0
			LIABILITIES						
17.2	19.5	22.1	Notes Payable-Short Term	14.8	18.1	32.9	20.5	24.7	21.9
1.8	1.6	1.6	Cur. Mat.-L /T/D	1.9	3.8	.4	.7	1.4	.5
18.3	19.2	20.3	Trade Payables	23.0	20.8	18.4	19.1	21.5	19.4
.2	2.1	.3	Income Taxes Payable	.0	.1	.1	.1	1.0	.2
8.0	6.9	7.2	All Other Current	7.4	6.0	7.1	4.9	6.2	13.4
45.5	49.4	51.5	Total Current	47.2	48.9	58.9	45.3	54.8	55.3
7.8	5.6	6.2	Long Term Debt	12.8	11.3	3.3	2.6	3.3	4.1
.0	.1	.1	Deferred Taxes	.1	.0	.0	.2	.0	.0
2.9	4.2	5.1	All Other-Non-Current	1.9	4.3	6.8	6.9	7.7	1.3
43.7	40.7	37.1	Net Worth	38.1	35.4	31.0	45.0	34.2	39.3
100.0	100.0	100.0	Total Liabilities & Net Worth	100.0	100.0	100.0	100.0	100.0	100.0
			INCOME DATA						
100.0	100.0	100.0	Net Sales	100.0	100.0	100.0	100.0	100.0	100.0
30.1	28.7	28.2	Gross Profit	44.5	34.8	22.6	24.4	23.8	21.2
26.1	25.3	24.6	Operating Expenses	42.0	30.4	20.4	20.6	20.0	17.2
4.0	3.5	3.6	Operating Profit	2.5	4.4	2.2	3.8	3.8	4.0
.8	.9	.9	All Other Expenses (net)	1.4	1.1	1.2	.4	.9	.8
3.2	2.6	2.7	Profit Before Taxes	1.1	3.3	1.0	3.4	2.9	3.3
			RATIOS						
2.7	2.6	2.4	Current	3.7	2.5	2.0	2.6	2.7	2.3
1.8	1.8	1.6		2.0	1.8	1.5	1.8	1.5	1.4
1.4	1.4	1.3		1.2	1.3	1.3	1.5	1.3	1.2
1.2	1.1	1.0	Quick	1.3	.8	1.0	1.2	1.2	1.1
.8	.7	.7		.5	.5	.6	.7	.7	.8
.5	.5	.4		.1	.4	.4	.5	.5	.6
21 17.3	24 15.4	21 17.4	Sales/Receivables	0 UND	9 38.9	27 13.3	28 13.2	40 9.1	39 9.4
46 7.9	46 7.9	46 7.9		21 17.4	39 9.3	49 7.4	49 7.5	55 6.6	59 6.2
74 4.9	76 4.8	70 5.2		46 8.0	69 5.3	87 4.2	85 4.3	68 5.4	89 4.1
63 5.8	68 5.4	66 5.5	Cost of Sales/Inventory	104 3.5	99 3.7	60 6.1	53 6.9	53 6.9	37 10.0
104 3.5	107 3.4	126 2.9		261 1.4	146 2.5	126 2.9	99 3.7	99 3.7	104 3.5
166 2.2	215 1.7	166 2.2		521 .7	215 1.7	159 2.3	183 2.0	130 2.8	152 2.4
14 25.9	12 29.5	13 27.6	Cost of Sales/Payables	2 163.5	17 21.9	4 97.8	10 36.0	19 19.1	8 46.6
34 10.7	35 10.5	37 9.8		44 8.3	39 9.3	28 13.0	41 8.8	37 10.0	24 15.5
60 6.1	66 5.5	73 5.0		135 2.7	107 3.4	58 6.3	64 5.7	60 6.1	56 6.5
3.4	3.7	4.1	Sales/Working Capital	2.3	3.7	6.0	3.3	6.3	4.2
6.6	6.6	7.1		4.1	5.4	8.0	6.6	10.4	10.7
11.2	11.4	12.5		18.7	11.2	12.1	9.5	13.8	28.0
(139) 7.2	(144) 7.6	(145) 5.8	EBIT/Interest	(11) 5.4	(36) 7.3	3.3	(25) 5.2	(28) 6.8	(22) 9.3
2.9	3.0	2.5		1.2	3.2	1.6	2.2	2.4	3.5
1.3	1.5	1.3		.7	1.3	1.0	1.4	1.6	1.6
(38) 12.9	(31) 7.1	(35) 15.1	Net Profit + Depr., Dep., Amort./Cur. Mat. L/T/D		(11) 1.7				
2.4	2.6	2.7			.7				
.9	.4	.3			.0				
.0	.0	.0	Fixed/Worth	.0	.0	.0	.0	.0	.0
.1	.1	.1		.2	.2	.1	.1	.1	.2
.2	.2	.3		1.0	.6	.3	.2	.3	.3
.8	.7	.8	Debt/Worth	.6	.7	1.5	.8	.8	.8
1.4	1.8	2.2		1.9	2.2	3.4	1.4	3.0	2.3
2.2	3.3	4.0		13.9	5.1	4.2	2.6	4.7	4.4
(149) 25.9	(145) 27.9	(150) 29.6	% Profit Before Taxes/Tangible Net Worth	(14) 37.2	(34) 33.4	16.9	35.7	(27) 23.6	36.7
13.9	12.0	12.2		6.4	15.6	10.2	12.0	13.4	10.1
3.2	3.3	3.3		-1.3	3.6	-.3	2.8	5.7	5.1
11.8	9.2	8.5	% Profit Before Taxes/Total Assets	7.3	8.6	4.9	11.9	8.9	13.8
4.9	4.6	3.5		1.1	4.7	2.3	4.1	3.7	3.6
1.1	1.4	.9		-2.1	.9	-.1	1.1	1.8	1.6
214.1	222.6	269.9	Sales/Net Fixed Assets	114.2	263.3	479.6	226.2	294.8	512.9
60.9	88.4	72.3		33.9	38.1	159.5	77.5	82.8	75.5
26.7	33.8	26.5		8.5	21.0	32.7	26.3	39.3	33.8
2.9	3.2	3.1	Sales/Total Assets	2.5	2.6	3.2	3.6	3.9	3.1
2.2	2.3	2.2		1.6	2.0	2.3	2.1	2.6	2.2
1.7	1.5	1.5		1.0	1.4	1.6	1.4	2.0	1.5
(126) .2	(116) .2	(130) .2	% Depr., Dep., Amort./Sales	(11) .3	(28) .3	(21) .1	(27) .2	(24) .1	(19) .1
.4	.4	.4		1.0	.6	.2	.4	.3	.4
1.0	.7	.8		1.8	.9	.5	.8	.6	.9
(83) 2.3	(90) 1.6	(98) 1.5	% Officers', Directors', Owners' Comp/Sales		(24) 3.9	(18) 2.3	(21) 1.3	(17) 1.1	(11) .4
4.6	3.0	3.5			5.2	3.6	1.9	1.7	.5
8.0	6.3	5.9			7.2	6.2	4.5	4.7	3.0
1895016M	2001859M	2605361M	Net Sales ($)	9513M	74584M	87920M	202845M	446946M	1783553M
950391M	994836M	1253442M	Total Assets ($)	7205M	42525M	45947M	100812M	180412M	876541M

M = $ thousand   MM = $ million
See Pages 1 through 15 for Explanation of Ratios and Data

WHOLESALERS—BUILDING MATERIALS. SIC# 5032

| Current Data Sorted By Assets | | | | | | | Comparative Historical Data | |

0-500M	500M-2MM	2-10MM	10-50MM	50-100MM	100-250MM	# Postretirement Benefits / Type of Statement	4/1/90-3/31/91 ALL	4/1/91-3/31/92 ALL
1	2	5	5	1		# Postretirement Benefits		
1	4	36	12	4	1	Unqualified	59	41
3	42	54	3	2		Reviewed	89	69
21	51	19	2			Compiled	104	81
4	5	1				Tax Returns	6	2
14	16	24	4			Other	40	40
	80 (4/1-9/30/94)		241 (10/1/94-3/31/95)					
43	118	134	21	4	1	**NUMBER OF STATEMENTS**	298	233
%	%	%	%	%	%	**ASSETS**	%	%
11.1	5.7	5.5	4.6			Cash & Equivalents	7.4	6.3
33.5	36.4	36.7	28.3			Trade Receivables - (net)	33.8	31.4
26.3	32.5	30.1	26.4			Inventory	29.8	30.5
1.6	1.5	1.7	.9			All Other Current	2.1	1.3
72.6	76.1	74.0	60.2			Total Current	73.1	69.5
20.4	17.9	18.1	27.0			Fixed Assets (net)	19.8	22.5
1.6	.8	1.2	2.8			Intangibles (net)	.8	1.0
5.5	5.2	6.6	10.1			All Other Non-Current	6.3	6.9
100.0	100.0	100.0	100.0			Total	100.0	100.0
						LIABILITIES		
11.3	9.9	14.0	11.0			Notes Payable-Short Term	13.3	12.5
2.5	3.4	2.9	2.1			Cur. Mat. -L/T/D	3.4	4.2
23.3	24.9	20.4	15.2			Trade Payables	22.1	19.1
.0	.3	.4	.7			Income Taxes Payable	.5	.3
6.0	7.4	7.3	5.6			All Other Current	6.7	7.2
43.1	45.9	45.1	34.6			Total Current	46.0	43.2
12.8	11.0	9.7	19.0			Long Term Debt	11.6	14.6
.0	.3	.4	.5			Deferred Taxes	.3	.2
3.2	4.1	3.4	.8			All Other-Non-Current	2.4	3.4
40.9	38.9	41.4	45.1			Net Worth	39.7	38.7
100.0	100.0	100.0	100.0			Total Liabilities & Net Worth	100.0	100.0
						INCOME DATA		
100.9	100.0	100.0	100.0			Net Sales	100.0	100.0
33.6	25.8	22.8	22.9			Gross Profit	26.3	27.4
31.3	22.7	20.4	18.1			Operating Expenses	23.7	24.6
2.3	3.1	2.3	4.9			Operating Profit	2.5	2.8
.1	.7	.3	.8			All Other Expenses (net)	.6	1.2
2.2	2.4	2.0	4.0			Profit Before Taxes	2.0	1.6
						RATIOS		
3.1	2.6	2.3	2.8				2.4	2.5
1.7	1.6	1.7	1.7			Current	1.6	1.7
1.2	1.3	1.3	1.3				1.2	1.2
1.5	1.4	1.3	1.2				1.4	1.4
1.1	.9	.9	.9			Quick	.9	.9
.6	.7	.7	.7				.6	.6
20 18.1	32 11.5	35 10.3	34 10.7				30 12.1	31 11.9
33 11.1	43 8.5	45 8.1	49 7.5			Sales/Receivables	39 9.3	41 8.8
45 8.1	54 6.7	57 6.4	61 6.0				53 6.9	56 6.5
10 34.8	24 15.2	27 13.3	37 9.8				25 14.7	29 12.5
38 9.5	47 7.7	44 8.3	53 6.9			Cost of Sales/Inventory	47 7.7	55 6.6
79 4.6	89 4.1	66 5.5	83 4.4				74 4.9	94 3.9
19 19.4	21 17.8	20 18.3	18 20.8				19 18.8	19 19.6
42 8.7	34 10.7	32 11.5	33 11.2			Cost of Sales/Payables	30 12.1	30 12.1
60 6.1	54 6.7	45 8.1	55 6.6				54 6.8	49 7.5
6.6	6.2	6.1	4.5				6.3	5.4
10.1	10.4	9.9	10.0			Sales/Working Capital	10.9	10.6
34.8	24.1	22.9	19.5				30.2	28.0
(38) 10.0	(103) 7.5	(120) 7.4	(20) 12.6				(261) 5.7	(212) 3.8
3.5	3.4	3.3	3.0			EBIT/Interest	2.5	1.9
1.7	2.0	1.7	1.9				1.0	1.0
	(48) 3.9	(50) 5.2	(13) 13.8				(158) 5.9	(112) 3.0
	1.8	2.1	4.4			Net Profit + Depr., Dep., Amort./Cur. Mat. L./T/D	2.0	1.6
	1.2	1.5	2.0				.9	.5
.2	.2	.2	.2				.2	.2
.4	.4	.4	.7			Fixed/Worth	.4	.5
1.3	1.0	.7	1.3				.9	1.1
.7	.8	.9	.6				.8	.8
1.2	1.7	1.6	1.7			Debt/Worth	1.7	1.7
4.7	3.4	3.1	3.0				3.3	3.8
(41) 54.9	(113) 42.8	(132) 27.2	36.8				(281) 33.5	(217) 27.2
24.4	19.7	17.2	18.6			% Profit Before Taxes/Tangible Net Worth	14.5	9.3
2.8	8.3	7.6	6.1				1.7	2.5
20.7	14.8	12.2	10.1				12.5	7.1
6.6	6.1	6.3	5.3			% Profit Before Taxes/Total Assets	4.4	3.1
1.0	2.7	2.2	2.7				.3	.4
39.1	56.5	40.2	22.1				47.5	36.2
20.4	26.5	22.2	14.8			Sales/Net Fixed Assets	21.8	17.1
13.3	10.4	10.7	2.6				9.7	7.4
4.1	3.8	3.8	2.5				3.8	3.5
3.5	2.9	2.8	2.1			Sales/Total Assets	3.0	2.5
2.3	2.3	2.1	1.3				2.1	1.8
(37) .8	(108) .5	(127) .5	(20) .6				(271) .6	(222) .7
1.4	1.0	.9	.9			% Depr., Dep., Amort./Sales	1.1	1.2
2.0	2.0	1.4	5.7				1.9	1.8
(22) 5.5	(61) 2.0	(62) 1.1					(120) 1.8	(106) 2.0
9.2	3.5	1.9				% Officers', Directors', Owners' Comp/Sales	3.5	3.6
12.2	4.8	3.1					6.6	5.2
44029M	435527M	1653041M	831402M	350749M	365237M	Net Sales ($)	3107907M	1858615M
12925M	141039M	564400M	405627M	307300M	110294M	Total Assets ($)	1279473M	793500M

M = $ thousand   MM = $ million
See Pages 1 through 15 for Explanation of Ratios and Data

Comparative Historical Data				Current Data Sorted By Sales					
2	17	14	# Postretirement Benefits	1	1	1	4	3	4
			Type of Statement						
57	58	58	Unqualified	1	4	4	13	22	14
78	96	102	Reviewed	2	17	20	30	26	7
71	109	93	Compiled	13	37	16	16	8	3
2	9	10	Tax Returns	2	3	3	2		
49	65	58	Other	3	15	8	14	16	2
4/1/92-3/31/93 ALL	4/1/93-3/31/94 ALL	4/1/94-3/31/95 ALL		80 (4/1-9/30/94)			241 (10/1/94-3/31/95)		
				0-1MM	1-3MM	3-5MM	5-10MM	10-25MM	25MM & OVER
257	337	321	NUMBER OF STATEMENTS	21	76	51	75	72	26
%	%	%	**ASSETS**	%	%	%	%	%	%
7.5	6.7	6.3	Cash & Equivalents	12.7	6.5	5.3	6.6	4.8	5.3
33.0	34.4	35.4	Trade Receivables - (net)	28.2	33.6	33.3	37.8	38.0	36.2
30.1	31.1	30.0	Inventory	18.3	33.0	31.7	31.1	29.5	25.4
1.5	1.9	1.6	All Other Current	2.4	1.7	1.1	1.5	1.7	1.5
72.1	74.1	73.2	Total Current	61.6	74.8	71.4	76.9	74.0	68.4
19.7	18.0	19.4	Fixed Assets (net)	27.0	18.3	22.2	16.1	18.0	24.9
1.2	1.3	1.3	Intangibles (net)	1.9	1.3	.4	1.2	1.7	1.0
7.0	6.5	6.1	All Other Non-Current	9.6	5.5	6.0	5.8	6.3	5.7
100.0	100.0	100.0	Total	100.0	100.0	100.0	100.0	100.0	100.0
			LIABILITIES						
13.1	12.8	11.8	Notes Payable-Short Term	12.1	9.3	9.6	13.5	15.2	9.1
3.6	3.5	3.0	Cur. Mat.-L /T/D	3.1	3.1	3.4	3.1	2.6	2.2
19.8	20.7	22.0	Trade Payables	20.6	24.8	21.3	21.6	21.0	19.9
.3	.6	.3	Income Taxes Payable	.0	.2	.2	.2	.7	.6
7.1	7.2	7.0	All Other Current	7.6	5.9	7.2	7.9	7.4	5.9
44.0	44.8	44.1	Total Current	43.5	43.3	41.7	46.4	46.9	37.7
11.1	9.9	11.3	Long Term Debt	13.5	13.1	12.0	7.3	10.9	15.7
.2	.2	.3	Deferred Taxes	.1	.4	.1	.1	.6	.7
3.1	3.1	3.4	All Other-Non-Current	2.8	4.4	4.1	2.6	3.7	1.1
41.6	42.0	40.8	Net Worth	40.1	38.9	42.1	43.6	37.9	44.9
100.0	100.0	100.0	Total Liabilities & Net Worth	100.0	100.0	100.0	100.0	100.0	100.0
			INCOME DATA						
100.0	100.0	100.0	Net Sales	100.0	100.0	100.0	100.0	100.0	100.0
26.3	26.1	25.3	Gross Profit	37.8	30.1	26.5	21.8	21.0	20.4
24.4	23.9	22.5	Operating Expenses	36.5	26.0	22.5	19.8	19.4	17.2
1.9	2.2	2.8	Operating Profit	1.2	4.1	4.0	2.0	1.5	3.2
.5	.2	.4	All Other Expenses (net)	.3	.7	.4	.1	.7	.3
1.4	2.0	2.3	Profit Before Taxes	.9	3.3	3.7	1.9	.9	2.9
			RATIOS						
2.4	2.5	2.5	Current	2.3	3.0	2.3	2.3	2.2	2.7
1.7	1.7	1.6		1.3	1.8	1.7	1.6	1.5	1.7
1.2	1.3	1.3		1.1	1.2	1.4	1.3	1.3	1.4
1.5	1.4	1.4	Quick	1.3	1.6	1.4	1.4	1.2	1.4
.9	.9	.9		.9	1.0	.9	.9	.9	1.0
.6	.6	.7		.6	.6	.6	.7	.7	.9
32　11.5	33　11.2	32　11.3	Sales/Receivables	19　19.2	31　11.9	28　13.1	35　10.4	33　11.2	37　10.0
41　8.8	44　8.3	43　8.4		34　10.6	43　8.4	40　9.1	43　8.5	46　8.0	46　7.9
55　6.6	55　6.6	55　6.6		51　7.1	56　6.5	54　6.7	58　6.3	51　7.1	60　6.1
29　12.7	30　12.3	25　14.5	Cost of Sales/Inventory	0　UND	24　15.0	27　13.5	23　15.7	29　12.7	26　14.3
46　8.0	51　7.1	45　8.1		33　10.9	59　6.2	54　6.8	44　8.3	43　8.4	34　10.6
78　4.7	78　4.7	79　4.6		87　4.2	94　3.9	91　4.0	68　5.4	58　6.3	54　6.7
19　18.8	20　18.4	20　18.3	Cost of Sales/Payables	21　17.1	23　15.6	17　21.1	21　17.4	18　20.2	19　19.2
32　11.4	33　11.1	33　11.1		51　7.1	43　8.5	35　10.4	28　13.0	29　12.4	34　10.7
47　7.7	50　7.3	51　7.1		73　5.0	63　5.8	54　6.7	45　8.1	41　8.9	42　8.7
6.0	6.1	6.1	Sales/Working Capital	5.9	5.4	6.7	6.0	7.6	6.6
10.6	9.7	10.0		19.2	8.3	9.9	9.9	14.3	9.4
30.8	19.0	23.3		252.2	29.4	16.4	23.3	26.2	17.2
(240)　6.2	(305)　6.5	(286)　7.8	EBIT/Interest	(19)　9.0	(65)　6.2	(45)　9.1	(69)　9.3	(63)　7.2	(25)　11.6
2.6	2.9	3.3		2.2	3.1	4.2	3.5	2.9	3.4
1.1	1.6	1.9		−1.7	1.5	2.1	2.0	1.6	2.6
(111)　8.1	(118)　5.2	(122)　5.0	Net Profit + Depr., Dep., Amort./Cur. Mat. L/T/D		(25)　5.5	(18)　4.5	(29)　3.4	(33)　5.2	(14)　8.8
2.4	2.0	2.0			1.9	2.6	1.8	2.1	4.8
1.0	1.2	1.5			1.5	1.2	1.3	1.6	1.9
.2	.2	.2	Fixed/Worth	.2	.2	.2	.2	.3	.2
.4	.4	.4		.9	.4	.5	.4	.5	.5
1.0	.8	.9		1.3	1.4	1.0	.6	.9	.9
.7	.7	.8	Debt/Worth	.6	.7	.7	.8	1.0	.6
1.5	1.6	1.7		1.2	1.7	1.7	1.6	1.8	1.6
3.6	3.1	3.1		4.2	4.8	2.7	2.9	3.4	2.8
(247)　30.4	(322)　31.5	(312)　36.4	% Profit Before Taxes/Tangible Net Worth	(19)　48.1	(71)　40.6	37.7	(70)　33.8	30.3	30.9
10.9	14.2	18.6		13.6	17.2	20.6	17.0	19.1	20.7
.9	4.2	7.6		−7.5	3.9	9.6	8.0	6.4	8.9
10.3	11.4	12.6	% Profit Before Taxes/Total Assets	13.3	14.7	12.8	12.5	12.3	12.1
4.2	4.9	6.1		6.1	6.0	6.6	5.9	5.9	6.5
.3	1.6	2.3		−8.3	1.4	3.5	2.6	1.7	4.6
43.1	46.4	44.4	Sales/Net Fixed Assets	38.1	52.1	75.2	49.2	35.9	49.3
19.6	23.5	22.0		14.8	21.0	15.1	26.9	23.7	15.3
10.0	10.4	10.5		8.6	10.7	5.1	15.0	14.3	8.7
3.9	3.6	3.8	Sales/Total Assets	3.9	3.4	3.6	4.1	4.1	3.6
2.8	2.9	2.8		2.3	2.7	2.8	3.1	3.2	2.9
2.0	2.1	2.2		1.8	2.1	1.9	2.2	2.5	1.5
(240)　.7	(316)　.6	(297)　.6	% Depr., Dep., Amort./Sales	(18)　.9	(66)　.8	(48)　.4	(73)　.5	(67)　.6	(25)　.5
1.1	1.0	1.0		1.4	1.4	1.0	.9	.9	.7
2.0	1.8	1.7		2.5	2.5	2.1	1.4	1.2	1.3
(113)　1.9	(156)　1.9	(149)　1.6	% Officers', Directors', Owners' Comp/Sales		(38)　2.6	(29)　1.8	(38)　.9	(31)　1.2	
3.5	3.2	2.9			4.0	3.1	2.2	1.7	
7.2	6.9	5.5			9.3	4.3	4.1	2.8	
2484304M	5029490M	3679985M	Net Sales ($)	12262M	147029M	197258M	538048M	1127058M	1658330M
1119655M	2185381M	1541585M	Total Assets ($)	4959M	64272M	90766M	196936M	393968M	790684M

M = $ thousand　　MM = $ million
See Pages 1 through 15 for Explanation of Ratios and Data

WHOLESALERS—LUMBER & MILLWORK. SIC# 5031

Current Data Sorted By Assets | Comparative Historical Data

2	16	18	12	2	4	# Postretirement Benefits		
						Type of Statement		
1	13	87	71	4	9	Unqualified	152	162
7	86	147	20	1		Reviewed	229	238
33	135	69	3			Compiled	176	178
8	15	5				Tax Returns	4	12
16	57	76	22	3	2	Other	135	137
	214 (4/1-9/30/94)		676 (10/1/94-3/31/95)				4/1/90-3/31/91	4/1/91-3/31/92
0-500M	500M-2MM	2-10MM	10-50MM	50-100MM	100-250MM		ALL	ALL
65	306	384	116	8	11	**NUMBER OF STATEMENTS**	696	727
%	%	%	%	%	%	**ASSETS**	%	%
8.3	6.7	4.2	3.5		.9	Cash & Equivalents	6.1	5.6
42.7	39.6	35.8	33.1		37.7	Trade Receivables - (net)	35.3	34.9
25.7	31.8	36.6	34.1		34.1	Inventory	33.2	33.8
1.4	1.4	1.4	2.2		2.7	All Other Current	2.0	1.7
78.1	79.4	78.0	72.8		75.4	Total Current	76.6	76.1
13.4	13.8	15.5	19.8		15.6	Fixed Assets (net)	16.1	17.1
1.4	.6	.9	1.8		.4	Intangibles (net)	.6	.8
7.1	6.2	5.5	5.6		8.6	All Other Non-Current	6.8	6.0
100.0	100.0	100.0	100.0		100.0	Total	100.0	100.0
						LIABILITIES		
21.2	17.4	21.9	21.7		11.6	Notes Payable-Short Term	20.1	20.4
5.1	2.7	2.6	2.9		2.2	Cur. Mat. -L/T/D	3.3	3.4
18.2	18.3	15.1	13.9		22.9	Trade Payables	15.7	15.5
.3	.5	.3	.6		.9	Income Taxes Payable	.4	.3
6.1	7.9	7.2	6.3		8.0	All Other Current	7.2	6.8
51.0	46.9	47.1	45.4		45.7	Total Current	46.8	46.4
12.9	9.3	8.1	13.4		26.4	Long Term Debt	11.1	11.0
.0	.3	.2	.4		.3	Deferred Taxes	.3	.3
3.8	3.0	2.7	1.7		.9	All Other-Non-Current	2.2	2.6
32.3	40.5	42.0	39.1		26.8	Net Worth	39.5	39.7
100.0	100.0	100.0	100.0		100.0	Total Liabilities & Net Worth	100.0	100.0
						INCOME DATA		
100.0	100.0	100.0	100.0		100.0	Net Sales	100.0	100.0
22.8	19.7	19.2	18.6		11.8	Gross Profit	19.5	20.2
19.9	16.7	16.3	14.4		8.8	Operating Expenses	17.6	18.4
2.9	2.9	2.8	4.2		3.0	Operating Profit	1.9	1.7
.6	.4	.5	.8		.8	All Other Expenses (net)	.7	.8
2.3	2.5	2.4	3.3		2.2	Profit Before Taxes	1.2	.9
						RATIOS		
2.6	2.8	2.3	2.6		3.1	Current	2.5	2.5
1.6	1.7	1.6	1.5		1.6		1.6	1.6
1.1	1.3	1.3	1.2		1.3		1.3	1.2
1.5	1.6	1.3	1.2		1.0	Quick	1.4	1.3
1.0	1.0	.8	.7		.8		.9	.8
.7	.7	.6	.6		.6		.6	.6
16 23.0	23 15.7	27 13.4	28 13.0		19 19.1	Sales/Receivables	24 15.5	26 13.9
30 12.3	33 11.2	35 10.4	36 10.2		30 12.3		33 11.1	35 10.4
43 8.4	47 7.8	47 7.8	42 8.7		39 9.4		43 8.5	46 7.9
3 141.8	17 21.4	32 11.3	33 11.0		19 19.1	Cost of Sales/Inventory	23 15.6	27 13.5
30 12.0	38 9.7	51 7.2	52 7.0		53 6.9		45 8.1	50 7.3
47 7.7	64 5.7	74 4.9	78 4.7		66 5.5		73 5.0	74 4.9
2 187.7	8 43.0	10 36.7	10 35.1		8 43.7	Cost of Sales/Payables	8 43.4	8 43.4
11 34.4	15 24.5	17 22.0	17 21.9		16 22.4		15 23.9	17 22.0
32 11.5	33 11.2	28 13.1	23 16.2		20 18.3		29 12.7	29 12.8
8.7	6.3	6.8	6.3		5.2	Sales/Working Capital	7.4	6.9
23.0	12.6	12.2	13.4		14.7		13.0	12.7
83.8	30.6	24.5	29.5		20.2		31.2	27.7
8.7	7.9	7.6	7.9		4.5	EBIT/Interest	3.7	4.0
(57) 3.6	(279) 3.3	(366) 3.2	(109) 3.4		4.1		(646) 2.0	(680) 1.9
1.0	1.7	1.7	2.1		2.3		1.1	1.0
	6.2	6.1	10.0			Net Profit + Depr., Dep.,	5.8	5.4
	(100) 2.5	(119) 2.6	(61) 3.5			Amort./Cur. Mat. L /T/D	(360) 2.2	(316) 1.6
	1.0	1.3	1.9				.8	.3
.1	.1	.1	.3		.3	Fixed/Worth	.1	.1
.3	.2	.3	.5		.5		.3	.4
1.4	.6	.6	.8		.7		.8	.8
.9	.7	.8	1.0		1.4	Debt/Worth	.8	.8
2.4	1.5	1.6	1.9		2.6		1.8	1.7
7.0	3.6	3.0	3.3		6.5		3.6	3.6
84.6	39.2	32.6	39.3		40.4	% Profit Before Taxes/Tangible	25.5	22.1
(57) 40.0	(292) 19.1	(377) 17.5	(113) 22.2		25.5	Net Worth	(676) 13.3	(690) 10.0
9.1	6.8	7.3	12.3		20.3		1.9	.9
20.5	15.0	13.4	14.0		10.8	% Profit Before Taxes/Total	9.5	8.4
11.3	6.3	6.3	8.4		7.6	Assets	4.4	3.3
.3	2.5	2.4	3.6		6.3		.5	.0
422.0	123.9	70.2	51.7		257.0	Sales/Net Fixed Assets	72.6	71.0
58.3	45.9	28.4	19.2		15.8		30.0	25.4
20.8	19.2	13.9	10.4		11.1		13.6	11.3
6.8	5.4	4.3	4.4		6.1	Sales/Total Assets	5.0	4.5
4.3	3.6	3.3	3.1		3.1		3.4	3.2
3.1	2.7	2.5	2.2		2.6		2.5	2.3
.2	.3	.3	.4		.1	% Depr., Dep., Amort./Sales	.4	.4
(44) .8	(278) .6	(361) .6	(107) .8	(10)	.6		(638) .8	(676) .8
1.4	1.1	1.1	1.1		.8		1.4	1.5
3.0	1.4	1.1	.7			% Officers', Directors',	1.5	1.4
(32) 4.9	(165) 2.6	(179) 2.3	(32) 1.6			Owners' Comp/Sales	(290) 2.4	(330) 2.6
6.7	4.4	4.0	2.3				4.3	4.8
118984M	1680645M	6191952M	7898495M	1175475M	8098503M	Net Sales ($)	14145261M	14857342M
19276M	357826M	1704066M	2336048M	585464M	1637359M	Total Assets ($)	4266917M	4467029M

M = $ thousand   MM = $ million
See Pages 1 through 15 for Explanation of Ratios and Data

Comparative Historical Data				Current Data Sorted By Sales					
12	26	54	# Postretirement Benefits	2	5	4	9	11	23
			Type of Statement						
170	160	185	Unqualified	1	2	7	21	58	96
220	245	261	Reviewed	5	20	27	77	90	42
196	222	240	Compiled	14	67	49	52	51	7
10	20	28	Tax Returns	4	6	6	8	4	
148	158	176	Other	9	28	19	41	42	37
4/1/92-3/31/93 ALL	4/1/93-3/31/94 ALL	4/1/94-3/31/95 ALL		214 (4/1-9/30/94)			676 (10/1/94-3/31/95)		
				0-1MM	1-3MM	3-5MM	5-10MM	10-25MM	25MM & OVER
744	805	890	**NUMBER OF STATEMENTS**	33	123	108	199	245	182
%	%	%	**ASSETS**	%	%	%	%	%	%
5.5	4.9	5.2	Cash & Equivalents	6.4	7.7	7.2	5.1	4.6	3.1
36.8	38.7	37.1	Trade Receivables - (net)	31.7	33.0	36.4	37.6	38.9	38.5
34.4	33.3	33.7	Inventory	28.8	35.2	31.3	34.3	33.9	34.2
1.2	1.5	1.6	All Other Current	2.9	1.0	1.4	1.2	1.4	2.5
78.0	78.5	77.7	Total Current	69.8	76.8	76.4	78.2	78.7	78.3
14.6	15.1	15.4	Fixed Assets (net)	19.2	16.3	14.9	15.6	14.5	15.4
.9	.7	1.0	Intangibles (net)	2.1	.6	.9	.6	1.3	.9
6.5	5.8	6.0	All Other Non-Current	9.0	6.2	7.9	5.5	5.5	5.4
100.0	100.0	100.0	Total	100.0	100.0	100.0	100.0	100.0	100.0
			LIABILITIES						
20.8	20.5	20.0	Notes Payable-Short Term	17.1	15.3	20.0	19.8	20.7	23.3
3.1	2.7	2.9	Cur. Mat.-L./T/D	4.3	4.0	3.8	2.7	2.4	2.1
17.0	17.1	16.3	Trade Payables	19.6	17.2	15.5	15.6	16.7	15.9
.3	1.6	.4	Income Taxes Payable	.2	.3	.7	.3	.4	.5
7.0	7.2	7.2	All Other Current	7.8	7.2	4.5	7.4	7.8	7.8
48.2	49.1	46.9	Total Current	49.0	44.0	44.5	45.8	48.0	49.6
10.1	9.8	9.8	Long Term Debt	16.0	11.2	11.2	9.2	7.8	10.5
.2	.2	.2	Deferred Taxes	.0	.1	.4	.2	.2	.3
3.3	3.2	2.8	All Other-Non-Current	7.0	3.5	2.9	3.2	2.0	1.9
38.1	37.6	40.3	Net Worth	28.0	41.1	40.9	41.7	42.0	37.6
100.0	100.0	100.0	Total Liabilities & Net Worth	100.0	100.0	100.0	100.0	100.0	100.0
			INCOME DATA						
100.0	100.0	100.0	Net Sales	100.0	100.0	100.0	100.0	100.0	100.0
19.6	19.2	19.4	Gross Profit	30.8	24.8	20.4	19.6	17.4	15.7
17.2	16.7	16.4	Operating Expenses	25.9	20.9	17.5	16.8	14.9	12.3
2.4	2.5	3.1	Operating Profit	4.9	3.9	2.9	2.8	2.5	3.4
.5	.4	.5	All Other Expenses (net)	2.4	.2	.4	.5	.5	.5
1.9	2.1	2.6	Profit Before Taxes	2.5	3.6	2.4	2.3	2.0	2.9
			RATIOS						
2.5 / 1.6 / 1.2	2.4 / 1.6 / 1.2	2.6 / 1.6 / 1.3	Current	2.6 / 1.5 / 1.2	3.0 / 1.8 / 1.2	2.9 / 1.8 / 1.3	2.4 / 1.7 / 1.3	2.3 / 1.6 / 1.2	2.3 / 1.5 / 1.2
1.3 / .9 / .6	1.3 / .9 / .6	1.4 / .9 / .6	Quick	1.5 / .7 / .4	1.5 / .9 / .6	1.6 / 1.1 / .6	1.4 / .9 / .6	1.4 / .9 / .6	1.2 / .8 / .6
24 14.9 / 33 10.9 / 45 8.1	26 14.0 / 35 10.5 / 46 7.9	25 14.5 / 34 10.7 / 46 7.9	Sales/Receivables	22 16.5 / 36 10.1 / 56 6.5	26 14.3 / 35 10.4 / 54 6.7	24 15.0 / 34 10.8 / 50 7.3	27 13.7 / 35 10.5 / 47 7.7	25 14.8 / 33 11.0 / 45 8.1	25 14.7 / 34 10.8 / 40 9.1
26 14.3 / 48 7.6 / 70 5.2	22 16.5 / 45 8.1 / 69 5.3	24 15.2 / 45 8.1 / 70 5.2	Cost of Sales/Inventory	17 21.5 / 41 8.8 / 111 3.3	30 12.0 / 55 6.6 / 107 3.4	19 19.6 / 42 8.6 / 72 5.1	24 15.3 / 46 7.9 / 70 5.2	27 13.6 / 44 8.3 / 64 5.7	23 16.1 / 39 9.4 / 60 6.1
8 44.1 / 17 21.2 / 29 12.7	8 44.1 / 17 21.8 / 29 12.6	9 40.2 / 16 22.4 / 28 13.0	Cost of Sales/Payables	4 94.1 / 37 9.9 / 94 3.9	11 34.4 / 23 15.7 / 41 8.9	8 48.1 / 16 23.0 / 34 10.8	9 42.7 / 17 22.0 / 31 11.9	9 39.1 / 15 23.8 / 25 14.4	10 37.5 / 15 24.8 / 21 17.7
7.1 / 13.2 / 32.3	7.4 / 13.8 / 34.1	6.7 / 12.5 / 28.9	Sales/Working Capital	5.2 / 12.5 / 28.2	4.5 / 8.5 / 25.4	6.0 / 11.2 / 39.7	6.8 / 11.6 / 21.4	8.1 / 13.8 / 29.2	8.9 / 16.1 / 37.5
(689) 5.5 / 2.7 / 1.5	(754) 7.1 / 3.1 / 1.7	(830) 7.8 / 3.3 / 1.8	EBIT/Interest	(26) 6.3 / 2.1 / -2.0	(113) 8.9 / 3.6 / 1.5	(98) 6.7 / 3.0 / 1.6	(182) 6.8 / 3.0 / 1.5	(234) 9.9 / 3.5 / 1.9	(177) 8.4 / 3.7 / 2.2
(290) 5.7 / 2.4 / 1.1	(278) 7.4 / 3.0 / 1.1	(299) 6.6 / 2.7 / 1.3	Net Profit + Depr., Dep., Amort./Cur. Mat. L/T/D		(38) 5.1 / 2.0 / .8	(35) 5.9 / 2.1 / 1.2	(59) 4.8 / 2.2 / .8	(82) 6.2 / 2.7 / 1.4	(79) 10.2 / 4.4 / 2.0
.1 / .3 / .7	.1 / .3 / .7	.1 / .3 / .7	Fixed/Worth	.1 / .4 / 23.9	.1 / .3 / .9	.1 / .3 / .7	.1 / .3 / .7	.1 / .3 / .6	.2 / .4 / .7
.9 / 1.8 / 3.6	.9 / 1.9 / 3.6	.8 / 1.7 / 3.3	Debt/Worth	.9 / 2.4 / 52.2	.6 / 1.5 / 5.2	.7 / 1.5 / 3.8	.7 / 1.6 / 2.9	.8 / 1.7 / 2.8	1.0 / 2.0 / 3.4
(712) 31.9 / 15.9 / 5.7	(769) 35.7 / 18.6 / 7.6	(858) 38.3 / 19.4 / 7.7	% Profit Before Taxes/Tangible Net Worth	(27) 55.6 / 16.6 / -5.5	(114) 45.2 / 17.9 / 5.3	(102) 43.5 / 18.7 / 5.5	(192) 34.4 / 15.5 / 5.9	(242) 32.3 / 19.0 / 8.3	(181) 41.8 / 24.8 / 14.4
10.8 / 5.1 / 1.8	12.4 / 6.3 / 2.2	14.1 / 6.7 / 2.6	% Profit Before Taxes/Total Assets	13.4 / 4.8 / -3.8	14.7 / 6.7 / 1.3	14.9 / 7.5 / 2.5	14.5 / 5.6 / 2.0	14.0 / 6.5 / 2.4	14.2 / 8.6 / 4.1
101.0 / 33.7 / 14.5	97.0 / 33.3 / 14.3	84.2 / 32.5 / 14.4	Sales/Net Fixed Assets	263.8 / 22.7 / 8.3	66.4 / 28.8 / 10.2	102.2 / 42.0 / 14.9	76.9 / 33.5 / 14.0	99.3 / 37.5 / 16.8	78.9 / 25.8 / 14.4
5.0 / 3.5 / 2.5	4.9 / 3.5 / 2.6	4.7 / 3.4 / 2.5	Sales/Total Assets	3.9 / 2.5 / 1.4	3.7 / 3.0 / 2.0	4.9 / 3.4 / 2.7	4.7 / 3.3 / 2.6	4.9 / 3.6 / 2.8	5.5 / 3.7 / 2.8
(668) .3 / .7 / 1.2	(752) .3 / .7 / 1.1	(807) .3 / .6 / 1.1	% Depr., Dep., Amort./Sales	(23) .6 / 1.3 / 3.6	(106) .6 / 1.1 / 1.6	(98) .4 / .7 / 1.3	(190) .3 / .6 / 1.1	(224) .3 / .5 / 1.0	(166) .2 / .6 / 1.0
(329) 1.3 / 2.3 / 4.5	(386) 1.4 / 2.6 / 4.7	(408) 1.3 / 2.5 / 4.4	% Officers', Directors', Owners' Comp/Sales	(15) 3.4 / 5.6 / 6.8	(65) 2.5 / 4.4 / 6.0	(60) 1.5 / 2.7 / 4.6	(101) 1.3 / 2.5 / 3.7	(111) 1.0 / 2.0 / 3.6	(56) .5 / 1.4 / 2.6
17128226M	21924313M	25164054M	Net Sales ($)	20192M	252400M	421792M	1433653M	3912414M	19123603M
4911314M	5446242M	6640039M	Total Assets ($)	11695M	117602M	132355M	501342M	1123323M	4753722M

M = $ thousand   MM = $ million
See Pages 1 through 15 for Explanation of Ratios and Data

Current Data Sorted By Assets

Comparative Historical Data

						# Postretirement Benefits Type of Statement		
	5	4	1					
	2	9	4		1	Unqualified	20	26
	13	19	2			Reviewed	36	49
4	20	8				Compiled	30	24
2	2					Tax Returns		
6	13	17	4			Other	21	22

0-500M	500M-2MM	2-10MM	10-50MM	50-100MM	100-250MM		4/1/90-3/31/91 ALL	4/1/91-3/31/92 ALL
	21 (4/1-9/30/94)		105 (10/1/94-3/31/95)					
12	50	53	10		1	NUMBER OF STATEMENTS	107	121
%	%	%	%	%	%	**ASSETS**	%	%
5.7	4.8	5.7	4.7			Cash & Equivalents	6.1	6.7
38.4	41.8	44.9	39.2			Trade Receivables - (net)	41.2	42.8
41.8	33.7	30.1	27.3			Inventory	28.4	28.6
3.6	.9	.7	4.0			All Other Current	1.6	1.5
89.5	81.2	81.4	75.3			Total Current	77.2	79.7
7.0	12.7	12.3	17.0			Fixed Assets (net)	15.8	13.1
.2	.5	1.1	.9			Intangibles (net)	1.5	.9
3.3	5.6	5.2	6.9			All Other Non-Current	5.5	6.4
100.0	100.0	100.0	100.0			Total	100.0	100.0
						LIABILITIES		
29.1	11.2	14.0	11.4			Notes Payable-Short Term	13.7	15.2
1.4	1.9	2.1	2.4			Cur. Mat. -L/T/D	3.0	2.5
29.5	31.9	34.5	28.8			Trade Payables	29.7	27.8
.4	.3	.7	.1			Income Taxes Payable	.6	.5
12.7	6.3	6.7	6.8			All Other Current	6.7	7.2
73.0	51.7	58.1	49.4			Total Current	53.7	53.1
3.6	10.1	5.4	5.9			Long Term Debt	12.4	7.6
.0	.1	.7	.2			Deferred Taxes	.4	.2
.0	2.7	3.1	3.4			All Other-Non-Current	1.5	2.6
23.4	35.5	32.7	41.2			Net Worth	32.0	36.5
100.0	100.0	100.0	100.0			Total Liabilities & Net Worth	100.0	100.0
						INCOME DATA		
100.0	100.0	100.0	100.0			Net Sales	100.0	100.0
30.1	22.5	21.4	22.5			Gross Profit	22.2	20.8
28.2	19.3	18.9	20.1			Operating Expenses	19.6	18.8
1.9	3.2	2.5	2.4			Operating Profit	2.6	1.9
.0	.3	.0	−.9			All Other Expenses (net)	.8	.4
1.9	3.0	2.5	3.4			Profit Before Taxes	1.8	1.6
						RATIOS		
2.0	2.2	1.7	2.0				1.9	2.0
1.2	1.6	1.3	1.6			Current	1.4	1.4
.9	1.2	1.2	1.2				1.1	1.2
1.2	1.1	1.1	1.1				1.1	1.2
.7	.9	.8	1.0			Quick	.9	.9
.4	.7	.6	.7				.6	.7
30 12.0	28 13.0	37 9.9	32 11.5				33 11.1	35 10.5
44 8.3	41 8.9	52 7.0	47 7.8			Sales/Receivables	42 8.6	46 8.0
48 7.6	55 6.6	68 5.4	56 6.5				61 6.0	57 6.4
45 8.1	27 13.4	32 11.3	27 13.4				22 16.4	22 16.7
56 6.5	41 8.9	47 7.7	40 9.2			Cost of Sales/Inventory	39 9.3	37 9.9
69 5.3	65 5.6	61 6.0	54 6.8				63 5.8	62 5.9
27 13.5	25 14.8	37 9.8	33 11.0				30 12.3	25 14.6
40 9.2	41 8.9	49 7.5	41 9.0			Cost of Sales/Payables	38 9.6	34 10.7
50 7.3	58 6.3	64 5.7	47 7.7				52 7.0	49 7.5
7.9	8.0	8.4	9.5				8.4	7.9
26.2	11.4	15.1	10.3			Sales/Working Capital	14.6	13.7
−67.3	26.4	25.2	20.8				38.1	26.2
4.8	11.0	11.4					5.4	6.6
(11) 3.8	(46) 4.5	(50) 4.6				EBIT/Interest	(101) 2.5	(111) 3.0
2.0	2.5	2.3					1.2	1.2
	5.6	15.9					4.5	5.5
	(22) 2.6	(23) 3.1				Net Profit + Depr., Dep., Amort./Cur. Mat. L /T/D	(59) 2.0	(54) 2.3
	1.5	1.5					1.0	.6
.0	.2	.2	.2				.2	.1
.3	.3	.3	.3			Fixed/Worth	.4	.3
3.4	.8	.7	.9				.8	.6
1.3	1.0	1.3	.8				1.2	1.1
4.4	2.0	2.5	1.4			Debt/Worth	2.1	1.8
37.3	4.4	4.1	2.5				4.4	3.9
256.0	44.2	33.5	28.2				37.3	33.9
(11) 29.8	(47) 25.4	(52) 20.2	20.3			% Profit Before Taxes/Tangible Net Worth	(102) 18.8	(117) 15.7
2.4	8.4	10.6	6.1				4.9	3.1
18.4	15.8	10.6	16.0				11.9	11.9
8.0	9.0	6.4	8.2			% Profit Before Taxes/Total Assets	5.3	5.4
1.4	3.1	2.5	2.3				1.1	1.0
858.9	87.0	69.1	46.9				55.0	68.1
54.0	43.5	39.4	22.3			Sales/Net Fixed Assets	32.6	34.9
24.4	20.6	16.1	10.8				16.5	20.4
4.2	4.3	3.5	3.9				4.4	4.3
3.5	3.3	3.1	3.4			Sales/Total Assets	3.2	3.4
2.5	2.7	2.8	2.6				2.6	2.6
	.6	.4					.6	.5
	(44) .8	(49) .7				% Depr., Dep., Amort./Sales	(94) .8	(107) .8
	1.3	1.0					1.2	1.2
	2.1	1.0					1.6	1.2
	(20) 2.9	(19) 2.4				% Officers', Directors', Owners' Comp/Sales	(50) 2.7	(56) 2.7
	4.0	4.0					3.9	4.8
12894M	227871M	717480M	523845M		329490M	Net Sales ($)	1835028M	1876165M
3482M	64873M	226853M	168378M		129971M	Total Assets ($)	671274M	639460M

M = $ thousand   MM = $ million
See Pages 1 through 15 for Explanation of Ratios and Data

Comparative Historical Data / Current Data Sorted By Sales

	2	10	# Postretirement Benefits / Type of Statement		2	1	3	3	1
25	18	16	Unqualified		1		3	8	4
44	44	34	Reviewed		2	5	10	12	5
27	26	32	Compiled	3	10	7	7	5	
2	1	4	Tax Returns	2	1		1		
27	36	40	Other	1	7	9	11	8	4

4/1/92-3/31/93 ALL	4/1/93-3/31/94 ALL	4/1/94-3/31/95 ALL		21 (4/1-9/30/94)		105 (10/1/94-3/31/95)			
				0-1MM	1-3MM	3-5MM	5-10MM	10-25MM	25MM & OVER
125	125	126	**NUMBER OF STATEMENTS**	6	21	21	32	33	13

%	%	%	**ASSETS**	%	%	%	%	%	%
5.5	4.6	5.2	Cash & Equivalents		2.4	6.1	4.7	6.1	5.3
42.0	41.2	42.6	Trade Receivables - (net)		35.6	45.7	43.7	46.6	41.1
31.4	32.7	32.3	Inventory		37.7	31.6	32.9	28.8	29.4
1.6	1.6	1.3	All Other Current		1.9	.6	.6	1.7	.7
80.5	80.1	81.5	Total Current		77.7	83.9	82.0	83.2	76.5
13.4	14.0	12.4	Fixed Assets (net)		14.8	12.3	11.0	10.7	18.3
1.1	1.4	.8	Intangibles (net)		.3	.4	1.5	.8	.7
4.9	4.6	5.3	All Other Non-Current		7.2	3.3	5.5	5.3	4.5
100.0	100.0	100.0	Total		100.0	100.0	100.0	100.0	100.0

			LIABILITIES						
12.0	15.6	14.0	Notes Payable-Short Term		13.7	13.6	11.2	15.1	8.7
2.4	1.9	2.0	Cur. Mat.-L/T/D		2.0	2.3	1.4	2.3	2.4
30.5	29.0	32.5	Trade Payables		26.5	34.5	34.0	35.9	30.4
.5	.9	.5	Income Taxes Payable		.4	.5	.6	.7	.1
7.9	7.0	7.1	All Other Current		7.8	5.5	7.7	6.9	4.9
53.3	54.3	56.1	Total Current		50.4	56.5	54.9	60.9	46.5
8.2	7.9	7.5	Long Term Debt		12.9	8.7	4.4	6.5	7.9
.2	.2	.4	Deferred Taxes		.1	.2	1.1	.1	.2
2.2	1.9	2.6	All Other-Non-Current		.2	7.9	1.8	2.2	2.6
36.1	35.8	33.4	Net Worth		36.4	26.8	37.9	30.3	42.9
100.0	100.0	100.0	Total Liabilities & Net Worth		100.0	100.0	100.0	100.0	100.0

			INCOME DATA						
100.0	100.0	100.0	Net Sales		100.0	100.0	100.0	100.0	100.0
23.3	22.0	22.7	Gross Profit		24.2	23.7	20.8	20.1	23.0
20.8	20.2	20.0	Operating Expenses		21.0	19.4	18.7	17.9	20.3
2.5	1.8	2.7	Operating Profit		3.3	4.3	2.1	2.2	2.7
.4	.1	.0	All Other Expenses (net)		-.1	.4	.0	-.1	-.2
2.1	1.8	2.7	Profit Before Taxes		3.3	3.9	2.2	2.3	2.9

			RATIOS						
2.2	1.9	2.1	Current		2.2	2.0	2.2	1.5	2.1
1.5	1.4	1.4			1.7	1.4	1.5	1.3	1.8
1.2	1.2	1.2			1.2	1.1	1.1	1.2	1.4
1.2	1.2	1.1	Quick		1.1	1.0	1.2	1.1	1.3
.9	.8	.8			.8	.8	.8	.9	1.1
.7	.6	.6			.6	.8	.6	.6	.8
34 10.7	30 12.2	35 10.5	Sales/Receivables		25 14.5	36 10.1	34 10.6	37 9.9	31 11.8
45 8.2	42 8.6	45 8.2			42 8.7	52 7.0	40 9.1	48 7.6	50 7.3
57 6.4	56 6.5	61 6.0			50 7.3	73 5.0	64 5.7	62 5.9	55 6.6
30 12.2	34 10.6	29 12.6	Cost of Sales/Inventory		31 11.8	29 12.6	27 13.3	18 20.3	36 10.1
43 8.5	44 8.3	46 8.0			59 6.2	42 8.7	43 8.4	44 8.3	41 8.9
62 5.9	56 6.5	62 5.9			89 4.1	58 6.3	62 5.9	53 6.9	51 7.1
27 13.5	27 13.7	33 11.2	Cost of Sales/Payables		23 15.7	37 10.0	27 13.3	35 10.4	36 10.2
40 9.1	37 9.8	44 8.3			40 9.2	49 7.5	46 7.9	47 7.8	40 9.1
59 6.2	49 7.4	58 6.3			54 6.7	85 4.3	62 5.9	61 6.0	47 7.7
7.5	7.8	8.2	Sales/Working Capital		6.9	7.9	8.1	11.4	8.1
13.5	14.6	13.4			10.4	11.6	13.0	17.0	9.9
26.8	34.9	25.6			29.9	25.4	37.3	25.5	16.6
7.9	9.2	10.7	EBIT/Interest		(19) 11.0	(20) 11.0	(29) 12.0	(32) 13.3	(10) 10.6
(112) 2.8	(116) 3.4	(116) 4.2			3.8	5.0	4.6	4.1	3.1
1.6	1.7	2.2			1.3	3.5	1.9	2.4	2.0
6.8	7.7	7.6	Net Profit + Depr., Dep., Amort./Cur. Mat. L/T/D				(15) 5.4	(15) 22.4	
(52) 2.5	(48) 2.5	(48) 3.0					2.3	5.4	
1.1	1.6	1.6					1.2	1.9	
.2	.2	.2	Fixed/Worth		.1	.2	.1	.2	.3
.3	.4	.3			.3	.5	.3	.3	.3
.8	.9	.8			.8	1.7	.6	.5	.9
1.1	1.1	1.1	Debt/Worth		.9	1.5	.8	1.7	.7
2.1	2.1	2.3			1.8	3.3	2.0	2.6	1.2
4.4	4.3	4.2			3.9	5.4	3.9	4.1	2.8
32.8	35.5	37.8	% Profit Before Taxes/Tangible Net Worth		(20) 43.3	(17) 63.4	30.9	35.1	28.7
(122) 16.9	(119) 19.0	(121) 24.0			22.7	40.1	18.8	22.7	20.2
6.4	8.2	8.3			3.9	18.1	7.4	11.0	4.7
11.4	11.0	13.4	% Profit Before Taxes/Total Assets		19.1	16.0	10.8	10.9	11.6
4.4	5.6	7.4			7.7	13.1	6.1	6.1	7.7
2.0	2.4	2.6			1.1	7.0	2.0	2.6	1.8
72.1	66.3	77.6	Sales/Net Fixed Assets		80.4	78.3	83.2	82.9	32.4
34.5	33.0	39.0			43.5	33.2	54.3	46.5	22.1
17.9	16.6	17.1			13.1	15.4	22.3	17.7	10.9
4.1	4.1	3.9	Sales/Total Assets		3.7	3.8	4.2	3.9	3.7
3.5	3.5	3.2			3.0	3.0	3.4	3.2	3.5
2.6	2.7	2.7			2.5	2.3	2.5	3.0	2.9
.5	.5	.5	% Depr., Dep., Amort./Sales		(18) .6	(16) .7	(30) .5	(30) .4	(10) .8
(111) .8	(113) .9	(107) .8			1.0	1.0	.7	.6	.9
1.2	1.2	1.3			1.5	1.3	1.0	.9	1.6
1.6	1.2	1.6	% Officers', Directors', Owners' Comp/Sales			(10) 1.8	(11) 2.3	(12) .9	
(58) 2.6	(47) 2.9	(51) 2.8				2.9	3.0	1.9	
4.5	4.9	4.2				4.3	6.8	3.8	
2467846M	3309759M	1811580M	Net Sales ($)	3079M	43487M	85644M	235389M	522423M	921558M
858179M	1001271M	593557M	Total Assets ($)	1135M	16177M	29338M	72871M	164183M	309853M

M = $ thousand   MM = $ million
See Pages 1 through 15 for Explanation of Ratios and Data

Current Data Sorted By Assets   **Comparative Historical Data**

	0-500M	500M-2MM	2-10MM	10-50MM	50-100MM	100-250MM	Item	4/1/90-3/31/91 ALL	4/1/91-3/31/92 ALL
	4	9	8	1	1		# Postretirement Benefits		
							Type of Statement		
	1	12	29	14	6	6	Unqualified	34	49
	2	24	29	5	1		Reviewed	48	53
	21	29	14				Compiled	44	53
	2	3	2				Tax Returns	2	3
	22	34	22	11	7	2	Other	55	53
		83 (4/1-9/30/94)			215 (10/1/94-3/31/95)				
	48	102	96	30	14	8	NUMBER OF STATEMENTS	183	211
	%	%	%	%	%	%	ASSETS	%	%
	10.5	6.7	9.1	9.8	8.3		Cash & Equivalents	8.6	8.1
	50.2	50.9	45.3	42.9	39.9		Trade Receivables - (net)	39.0	41.5
	19.9	24.4	26.6	26.4	32.3		Inventory	28.8	28.4
	1.2	1.0	3.6	2.4	2.1		All Other Current	1.4	1.8
	81.8	83.0	84.6	81.6	82.6		Total Current	77.8	79.8
	12.3	10.2	8.1	9.4	10.0		Fixed Assets (net)	14.5	12.0
	1.9	.9	2.7	2.1	3.6		Intangibles (net)	1.5	2.1
	4.0	6.0	4.6	6.8	3.8		All Other Non-Current	6.1	6.1
	100.0	100.0	100.0	100.0	100.0		Total	100.0	100.0
							LIABILITIES		
	14.7	18.3	14.7	15.5	17.1		Notes Payable-Short Term	13.5	15.8
	4.3	2.2	1.5	1.4	.5		Cur. Mat. -L/T/D	3.1	2.4
	22.7	27.6	31.7	30.3	26.0		Trade Payables	27.7	29.5
	.5	.4	.7	.9	.5		Income Taxes Payable	.6	.7
	15.8	11.0	11.1	10.5	6.2		All Other Current	11.1	9.6
	57.9	59.4	59.7	58.5	50.3		Total Current	55.9	57.9
	8.2	6.0	5.9	3.6	8.1		Long Term Debt	8.3	8.1
	.5	.6	.3	.2	.5		Deferred Taxes	.4	.3
	2.4	4.2	4.7	3.4	1.1		All Other-Non-Current	2.5	3.1
	31.0	29.7	29.4	34.4	40.0		Net Worth	32.8	30.6
	100.0	100.0	100.0	100.0	100.0		Total Liabilities & Net Worth	100.0	100.0
							INCOME DATA		
	100.0	100.0	100.0	100.0	100.0		Net Sales	100.0	100.0
	37.7	30.2	24.5	22.1	24.3		Gross Profit	32.9	30.0
	33.8	28.0	22.5	19.6	18.9		Operating Expenses	29.1	27.9
	3.9	2.2	2.1	2.5	5.4		Operating Profit	3.8	2.2
	.4	.2	.4	.4	.7		All Other Expenses (net)	.6	.7
	3.6	2.0	1.7	2.1	4.7		Profit Before Taxes	3.2	1.5
							RATIOS		
	2.3	1.9	1.8	1.8	2.8			2.0	2.0
	1.4	1.3	1.3	1.3	1.6		Current	1.3	1.4
	1.1	1.1	1.2	1.2	1.2			1.1	1.1
	1.7	1.4	1.2	1.2	1.5			1.2	1.2
	1.1	1.0	.9	.9	1.0		Quick	.8	.9
	.8	.7	.7	.6	.6			.6	.6
	27 13.5	32 11.5	35 10.5	38 9.7	39 9.3			26 13.8	31 11.8
	40 9.2	45 8.2	48 7.6	54 6.8	53 6.9		Sales/Receivables	41 9.0	43 8.4
	58 6.3	62 5.9	60 6.1	78 4.7	72 5.1			57 6.4	58 6.3
	2 200.9	10 36.7	13 28.3	17 21.5	27 13.3			21 17.0	21 17.1
	20 18.4	30 12.0	33 10.9	32 11.3	61 6.0		Cost of Sales/Inventory	41 9.0	40 9.2
	41 8.8	50 7.3	47 7.8	49 7.4	87 4.2			74 4.9	65 5.6
	7 50.3	16 22.4	27 13.5	26 14.2	33 10.9			21 17.2	26 13.9
	20 18.5	34 10.8	40 9.2	39 9.3	43 8.5		Cost of Sales/Payables	41 9.0	41 8.8
	49 7.4	53 6.9	59 6.2	64 5.7	52 7.0			70 5.2	61 6.0
	8.4	9.7	10.6	8.2	4.9			9.6	8.9
	21.4	22.0	18.4	14.2	12.8		Sales/Working Capital	16.6	18.6
	133.0	59.2	30.5	46.0	20.5			43.9	50.0
	9.0	9.7	10.6	14.4	36.9			11.9	7.7
	(34) 4.0	(92) 3.0	(89) 4.0	(26) 4.5	9.8		EBIT/Interest	(152) 3.3	(187) 3.0
	1.5	1.1	1.7	2.3	2.2			1.6	1.3
		4.0	8.3	11.9			Net Profit + Depr., Dep.,	9.5	11.9
		(25) 1.5	(32) 4.5	(10) 8.0			Amort./Cur. Mat. L /T/D	(72) 2.5	(64) 2.3
		.3	1.6	1.9				.8	.5
	.1	.1	.1	.1	.1			.1	.1
	.3	.2	.3	.2	.2		Fixed/Worth	.3	.3
	.8	.6	.5	.5	.6			.8	.8
	1.1	1.2	1.8	1.4	.9			1.0	1.3
	2.0	2.9	3.0	2.6	2.0		Debt/Worth	2.8	2.7
	4.7	5.6	6.1	4.3	4.8			5.5	5.7
	91.2	56.3	57.4	39.6	46.5		% Profit Before Taxes/Tangible	57.9	47.6
	(41) 43.8	(94) 14.9	(92) 21.8	20.8	32.4		Net Worth	(171) 33.1	(199) 22.2
	15.4	3.0	8.0	9.6	10.4			11.1	4.9
	33.5	14.1	12.1	12.0	19.3		% Profit Before Taxes/Total	16.3	11.9
	12.7	5.0	5.2	4.6	8.9		Assets	7.1	4.9
	3.6	.5	1.6	3.0	2.8			2.0	1.0
	194.8	179.4	134.9	147.2	187.7			108.6	113.8
	45.9	68.3	61.4	72.7	26.1		Sales/Net Fixed Assets	42.9	48.7
	24.9	26.2	31.3	21.6	19.1			16.0	19.5
	6.4	5.1	4.5	4.4	4.4			4.4	4.6
	4.9	4.0	3.5	3.1	3.1		Sales/Total Assets	3.4	3.5
	3.2	2.8	2.5	2.1	1.6			2.3	2.5
	.5	.2	.2	.2	.2			.3	.3
	(33) .9	(78) .6	(84) .5	(27) .3	(13) .8		% Depr., Dep., Amort./Sales	(148) .8	(174) .6
	1.7	1.2	1.0	1.1	1.4			1.9	1.4
	5.2	1.9	1.4					2.3	2.2
	(17) 9.0	(43) 4.1	(28) 2.1				% Officers', Directors',	(63) 4.3	(83) 4.2
	13.3	6.9	3.7				Owners' Comp/Sales	7.0	7.1
	62667M	467112M	1607497M	2169107M	2899862M	1905782M	Net Sales ($)	6180651M	7882789M
	12151M	108514M	412793M	611167M	953775M	1327478M	Total Assets ($)	1820135M	2795640M

M = $ thousand   MM = $ million
See Pages 1 through 15 for Explanation of Ratios and Data

Comparative Historical Data				Current Data Sorted By Sales					
4	10	23	# Postretirement Benefits	5	3	5	2	5	3
			Type of Statement						
68	64	68	Unqualified	2	6	2	11	14	33
63	49	61	Reviewed	1	9	8	17	16	10
63	59	64	Compiled	8	19	16	7	11	3
8	6	7	Tax Returns	1	3		1	1	1
83	86	98	Other	11	29	10	13	14	21
4/1/92-3/31/93	4/1/93-3/31/94	4/1/94-3/31/95		83 (4/1-9/30/94)		215 (10/1/94-3/31/95)			
ALL	ALL	ALL		0-1MM	1-3MM	3-5MM	5-10MM	10-25MM	25MM & OVER
285	264	298	**NUMBER OF STATEMENTS**	23	66	36	49	56	68
%	%	%	**ASSETS**	%	%	%	%	%	%
10.0	9.4	8.5	Cash & Equivalents	11.3	8.5	7.0	9.3	8.4	7.8
40.8	43.8	46.9	Trade Receivables - (net)	45.7	46.5	54.7	44.5	52.5	40.6
27.1	27.8	24.7	Inventory	22.3	23.5	20.7	25.2	25.3	27.9
1.5	1.8	2.2	All Other Current	1.2	1.2	2.0	2.6	1.6	3.7
79.3	82.9	82.2	Total Current	80.5	79.8	84.4	81.7	87.7	79.9
12.0	10.0	9.9	Fixed Assets (net)	13.9	12.3	8.6	9.0	6.6	10.1
3.0	1.8	2.0	Intangibles (net)	.5	1.9	1.6	3.5	1.1	2.5
5.8	5.3	5.9	All Other Non-Current	5.2	6.1	5.3	5.9	4.6	7.5
100.0	100.0	100.0	Total	100.0	100.0	100.0	100.0	100.0	100.0
			LIABILITIES						
13.8	13.1	16.0	Notes Payable-Short Term	19.0	13.6	20.4	13.3	15.2	17.7
3.2	1.9	2.1	Cur. Mat.-L /T/D	5.2	2.6	2.2	2.7	1.2	.9
27.3	28.2	28.0	Trade Payables	20.8	25.0	23.0	31.3	34.3	28.2
.7	1.7	.5	Income Taxes Payable	.9	.5	.5	.6	.6	.5
10.2	11.6	11.4	All Other Current	15.5	12.2	13.6	11.9	11.0	8.0
55.3	56.5	58.0	Total Current	61.3	53.8	59.7	59.8	62.5	55.2
8.6	6.7	6.5	Long Term Debt	13.7	5.2	6.5	8.9	2.8	6.6
.4	.3	.5	Deferred Taxes	.0	.5	1.0	.7	.2	.3
3.3	4.3	4.0	All Other-Non-Current	3.0	4.3	3.4	4.4	4.5	3.6
32.4	32.3	31.0	Net Worth	22.0	36.2	29.4	26.2	30.0	34.2
100.0	100.0	100.0	Total Liabilities & Net Worth	100.0	100.0	100.0	100.0	100.0	100.0
			INCOME DATA						
100.0	100.0	100.0	Net Sales	100.0	100.0	100.0	100.0	100.0	100.0
30.9	29.8	28.4	Gross Profit	39.1	37.3	30.6	31.7	19.5	19.9
27.2	26.4	25.7	Operating Expenses	34.1	35.2	26.9	28.7	18.8	16.5
3.7	3.4	2.7	Operating Profit	5.0	2.1	3.6	3.0	.7	3.5
.7	.5	.4	All Other Expenses (net)	.1	.1	.5	.7	.1	.8
3.0	2.9	2.3	Profit Before Taxes	4.9	2.0	3.1	2.3	.6	2.7
			RATIOS						
1.9	2.0	1.9		2.1	2.7	2.0	1.8	1.6	2.0
1.4	1.4	1.4	Current	1.2	1.4	1.4	1.4	1.3	1.4
1.2	1.2	1.2		1.0	1.1	1.2	1.1	1.2	1.2
1.2	1.3	1.3		1.6	1.5	1.5	1.2	1.2	1.2
.9	.9	.9	Quick	.8	1.0	1.1	.9	1.0	.8
.7	.7	.7		.6	.7	.7	.7	.8	.6
27 13.6	28 12.9	31 11.7		29 12.8	31 11.6	36 10.2	30 12.3	29 12.7	30 12.2
42 8.7	45 8.2	45 8.1	Sales/Receivables	48 7.6	42 8.7	46 8.0	43 8.5	50 7.3	48 7.6
57 6.4	64 5.7	61 6.0		85 4.3	62 5.9	65 5.6	54 6.7	62 5.9	58 6.3
17 21.2	18 20.1	12 31.5		0 UND	10 38.1	6 63.0	10 37.3	13 29.0	20 18.7
34 10.8	36 10.1	31 11.8	Cost of Sales/Inventory	37 9.8	30 12.3	26 13.9	35 10.5	26 14.2	37 9.8
55 6.6	60 6.1	50 7.3		78 4.7	58 6.3	46 7.9	61 6.0	38 9.7	51 7.2
20 18.0	20 18.2	18 20.3		12 29.4	18 19.8	14 27.0	22 16.8	18 20.8	25 14.8
34 10.7	37 9.8	37 9.9	Cost of Sales/Payables	24 15.0	38 9.6	28 13.0	40 9.1	34 10.6	39 9.4
54 6.7	59 6.2	56 6.5		69 5.3	60 6.1	46 7.9	65 5.6	53 6.9	48 7.6
8.8	8.3	8.7		4.3	6.9	9.4	10.3	13.1	8.2
17.7	16.8	17.8	Sales/Working Capital	17.1	19.3	18.3	17.5	19.9	15.6
41.2	42.0	49.9		-185.3	103.8	52.1	42.9	38.1	38.7
10.9	11.9	11.0		8.3	8.2	15.6	14.0	11.3	15.1
(254) 3.8	(231) 4.6	(263) 4.0	EBIT/Interest	(17) 3.2	(53) 3.0	(31) 4.3	(44) 3.8	(54) 3.9	(64) 4.8
1.6	1.9	1.5		1.5	1.0	.5	1.7	1.5	2.1
12.8	13.2	10.0			3.4		8.1	10.1	20.2
(84) 3.8	(68) 4.9	(80) 3.1	Net Profit + Depr., Dep., Amort./Cur. Mat. L/T/D		(12) 1.9		(17) 2.3	(21) 4.6	(20) 9.6
1.0	1.4	1.3			.8		1.1	1.6	3.1
.1	.1	.1		.1	.1	.1	.2	.1	.1
.3	.3	.3	Fixed/Worth	.4	.2	.2	.3	.2	.2
.8	.7	.6		.9	.7	.4	.6	.4	.7
1.3	1.3	1.3		1.3	.8	1.3	2.2	1.8	1.2
2.4	2.6	2.7	Debt/Worth	3.0	1.8	3.1	3.3	2.8	2.6
5.3	4.8	5.5		48.3	5.0	5.4	5.7	5.7	5.5
51.4	55.4	55.5		100.0	46.9	76.5	62.4	41.6	45.0
(260) 25.7	(249) 26.3	(279) 22.7	% Profit Before Taxes/Tangible Net Worth	(19) 36.1	(57) 15.5	(35) 31.9	(45) 34.5	(55) 17.5	23.2
10.4	9.3	6.9		7.5	2.3	3.0	9.3	6.9	8.4
14.6	13.7	15.2		45.1	15.3	22.7	15.9	10.0	13.0
6.8	7.1	5.4	% Profit Before Taxes/Total Assets	8.0	5.1	7.9	5.8	4.6	6.1
1.7	2.6	1.6		3.7	.8	.5	2.1	1.3	2.7
126.7	132.4	160.9		70.9	109.9	212.1	95.3	263.0	167.9
50.5	54.7	58.2	Sales/Net Fixed Assets	24.0	41.5	74.9	56.3	109.7	63.0
18.8	22.2	25.4		11.8	20.4	34.9	29.1	49.1	22.1
5.0	5.1	5.1		5.0	4.9	5.7	4.3	6.3	4.6
3.7	3.5	3.8	Sales/Total Assets	3.1	3.8	4.2	3.5	4.1	3.6
2.7	2.5	2.7		1.9	2.6	2.8	3.0	3.3	2.3
.2	.2	.2		.9	.7	.2	.2	.2	.2
(221) .6	(211) .5	(241) .5	% Depr., Dep., Amort./Sales	(13) 1.7	(48) 1.0	(28) .4	(42) .5	(50) .4	(60) .4
1.5	1.5	1.3		3.0	1.7	1.0	1.1	.7	1.1
1.6	1.4	1.8			3.9	2.0	1.9	1.6	.6
(113) 3.3	(95) 2.7	(93) 3.5	% Officers', Directors', Owners' Comp/Sales		(28) 5.8	(16) 4.7	(16) 3.0	(16) 2.0	(12) 1.0
7.7	7.6	7.3			9.4	7.1	4.8	3.3	1.4
9089939M	7128953M	9112027M	Net Sales ($)	12654M	132712M	143197M	345551M	907457M	7570456M
3041573M	2654820M	3425878M	Total Assets ($)	6711M	54368M	43616M	105043M	247170M	2968970M

M = $ thousand   MM = $ million
See Pages 1 through 15 for Explanation of Ratios and Data

Current Data Sorted By Assets							Comparative Historical Data	
	2		1	1	1	# Postretirement Benefits		
						Type of Statement		
		6	5	3	5	Unqualified		
		6	3			Reviewed		
1	5	3				Compiled		
	1					Tax Returns		
1	2	7	3			Other		
	10 (4/1-9/30/94)		41 (10/1/94-3/31/95)				4/1/90-3/31/91 ALL	4/1/91-3/31/92 ALL
0-500M	500M-2MM	2-10MM	10-50MM	50-100MM	100-250MM			
2	8	22	11	3	5	NUMBER OF STATEMENTS		
%	%	%	%	%	%	ASSETS	%	%
		3.2	2.8			Cash & Equivalents	D	D
		21.2	17.0			Trade Receivables - (net)	A	A
		34.8	51.2			Inventory	T	T
		3.3	2.0			All Other Current	A	A
		62.5	72.9			Total Current		
		30.7	22.5			Fixed Assets (net)	N	N
		.5	.4			Intangibles (net)	O	O
		6.3	4.2			All Other Non-Current	T	T
		100.0	100.0			Total		
						LIABILITIES	A	A
		18.4	38.2			Notes Payable-Short Term	V	V
		5.9	10.0			Cur. Mat. -L/T/D	A	A
		11.8	7.5			Trade Payables	I	I
		.5	.7			Income Taxes Payable	L	L
		9.4	3.9			All Other Current	A	A
		45.9	60.2			Total Current	B	B
		16.0	10.4			Long Term Debt	L	L
		.7	1.2			Deferred Taxes	E	E
		3.7	.4			All Other-Non-Current		
		33.6	27.8			Net Worth		
		100.0	100.0			Total Liabilities & Net Worth		
						INCOME DATA		
		100.0	100.0			Net Sales		
		30.9	29.5			Gross Profit		
		25.1	22.9			Operating Expenses		
		5.8	6.6			Operating Profit		
		1.1	1.5			All Other Expenses (net)		
		4.7	5.1			Profit Before Taxes		
						RATIOS		
		1.7	1.3					
		1.3	1.3			Current		
		1.1	.9					
		.9	.6					
		.6	.3			Quick		
		.3	.2					
		25 14.7	31 11.6					
		35 10.5	41 9.0			Sales/Receivables		
		68 5.4	58 6.3					
		51 7.1	114 3.2					
		73 5.0	174 2.1			Cost of Sales/Inventory		
		126 2.9	192 1.9					
		12 29.6	10 35.5					
		27 13.5	23 15.9			Cost of Sales/Payables		
		47 7.8	31 11.9					
		6.3	7.9					
		13.1	12.1			Sales/Working Capital		
		29.4	–33.8					
		8.7	4.7					
		2.8	(10) 3.1			EBIT/Interest		
		1.9	2.3					
						Net Profit + Depr., Dep., Amort./Cur. Mat. L /T/D		
		.3	.2					
		.7	.5			Fixed/Worth		
		1.5	1.8					
		1.1	2.0					
		2.2	2.9			Debt/Worth		
		3.7	3.6					
		38.2	34.2			% Profit Before Taxes/Tangible Net Worth		
		24.1	23.8					
		10.4	11.1					
		12.8	11.0			% Profit Before Taxes/Total Assets		
		5.8	5.7					
		2.6	2.8					
		19.3	35.7			Sales/Net Fixed Assets		
		10.6	19.4					
		3.2	2.8					
		2.4	2.0			Sales/Total Assets		
		1.9	1.8					
		1.3	1.5					
		1.1						
	(17)	2.9				% Depr., Dep., Amort./Sales		
		5.8						
						% Officers', Directors', Owners' Comp/Sales		
2553M	17646M	192500M	449013M	339776M	1052254M	Net Sales ($)		
731M	7569M	103713M	288043M	223743M	756313M	Total Assets ($)		

M = $ thousand   MM = $ million
See Pages 1 through 15 for Explanation of Ratios and Data

Comparative Historical Data — **Current Data Sorted By Sales**

4/1/92-3/31/93 ALL	4/1/93-3/31/94 ALL	4/1/94-3/31/95 ALL		0-1MM	1-3MM	3-5MM	5-10MM	10-25MM	25MM & OVER
		5	# Postretirement Benefits	1			1		3
			Type of Statement						
		19	Unqualified		1		5	3	10
		9	Reviewed		3		3		3
		9	Compiled	2	3	1	2	1	
		1	Tax Returns			1			
		13	Other		3		2	6	2
					10 (4/1-9/30/94)			41 (10/1/94-3/31/95)	
		51	**NUMBER OF STATEMENTS**	2	6	6	12	10	15
%	%	%	**ASSETS**	%	%	%	%	%	%
		4.3	Cash & Equivalents				3.3	2.3	3.3
D	D	21.3	Trade Receivables - (net)				18.7	17.2	18.8
A	A	39.6	Inventory				41.1	44.8	50.6
T	T	2.3	All Other Current				.4	7.1	2.1
A	A	67.5	Total Current				63.4	71.3	74.9
		23.8	Fixed Assets (net)				30.6	22.0	16.3
N	N	1.7	Intangibles (net)				.1	1.1	1.5
O	O	7.1	All Other Non-Current				6.0	5.6	7.3
T	T	100.0	Total				100.0	100.0	100.0
			LIABILITIES						
A	A	19.3	Notes Payable-Short Term				15.9	35.5	25.0
V	V	5.6	Cur. Mat.-L./T/D				6.1	3.1	6.7
A	A	14.8	Trade Payables				15.2	6.9	17.3
I	I	.4	Income Taxes Payable				.4	.8	.6
L	L	6.5	All Other Current				10.7	4.4	5.4
A	A	46.8	Total Current				48.2	50.8	55.0
B	B	15.5	Long Term Debt				14.7	15.2	14.3
L	L	.8	Deferred Taxes				.3	2.5	.7
E	E	2.8	All Other-Non-Current				3.9	1.3	.6
		34.1	Net Worth				32.8	30.2	29.5
		100.0	Total Liabilities & Net Worth				100.0	100.0	100.0
			INCOME DATA						
		100.0	Net Sales				100.0	100.0	100.0
		30.3	Gross Profit				28.0	32.3	23.5
		24.5	Operating Expenses				22.6	26.1	18.4
		5.8	Operating Profit				5.4	6.3	5.0
		.8	All Other Expenses (net)				1.1	1.2	.5
		5.0	Profit Before Taxes				4.3	5.0	4.5
			RATIOS						
		1.9					1.8	2.1	1.6
		1.3	Current				1.3	1.3	1.4
		1.2					1.1	1.1	1.1
		.9					.8	.8	.6
		.6	Quick				.5	.3	.4
		.3					.3	.3	.3
	29	12.8					26 14.0	18 20.0	34 10.8
	42	8.6	Sales/Receivables				32 11.5	39 9.3	42 8.6
	58	6.3					43 8.5	53 6.9	55 6.6
	54	6.8					62 5.9	59 6.2	114 3.2
	107	3.4	Cost of Sales/Inventory				91 4.0	130 2.8	174 2.1
	174	2.1					146 2.5	192 1.9	203 1.8
	16	22.8					18 20.7	5 78.3	23 15.9
	31	11.9	Cost of Sales/Payables				30 12.1	14 26.5	47 7.8
	70	5.2					53 6.9	43 8.5	99 3.7
		4.5					7.3	5.1	4.4
		11.2	Sales/Working Capital				18.1	10.5	8.3
		28.3					31.5	NM	26.6
		7.3					7.7		5.5
	(48)	3.7	EBIT/Interest				2.4		4.2
		2.1					1.6		2.5
		5.3	Net Profit + Depr., Dep.,						
	(17)	1.9	Amort./Cur. Mat. L/T/D						
		1.3							
		.2					.3	.3	.2
		.4	Fixed/Worth				.7	.5	.4
		1.2					2.0	1.5	.5
		1.3					1.0	1.4	2.3
		2.5	Debt/Worth				2.5	2.5	2.9
		3.4					3.6	4.8	3.2
		35.5	% Profit Before Taxes/Tangible				38.8	35.0	31.2
	(50)	24.2	Net Worth				18.3	28.2	24.1
		11.0					10.0	7.7	19.2
		12.5	% Profit Before Taxes/Total				13.3	11.1	9.9
		5.9	Assets				4.7	6.3	5.9
		3.3					2.0	2.5	4.8
		35.7					20.2	42.2	29.0
		13.7	Sales/Net Fixed Assets				9.5	13.4	19.4
		4.0					3.6	9.7	9.2
		2.2					2.4	2.5	1.8
		1.7	Sales/Total Assets				2.0	1.9	1.5
		1.5					1.4	1.5	1.4
		.7					1.1		.7
	(42)	1.6	% Depr., Dep., Amort./Sales				(11) 2.2		(14) .9
		5.5					4.1		2.3
		2.3	% Officers', Directors',						
	(13)	5.7	Owners' Comp/Sales						
		7.9							
		2053742M	Net Sales ($)	1724M	12067M	23098M	93988M	160851M	1762014M
		1380112M	Total Assets ($)	1039M	4784M	14419M	54313M	103244M	1202313M

M = $ thousand   MM = $ million
See Pages 1 through 15 for Explanation of Ratios and Data

Current Data Sorted By Assets | Comparative Historical Data

	5	40	35	12	2	1	# Postretirement Benefits Type of Statement		
	3	25	105	82	9	8	Unqualified	240	238
	18	171	176	16			Reviewed	389	424
	72	168	61	2			Compiled	368	364
	19	15	5	1			Tax Returns	7	14
	45	126	100	49	1	1	Other	234	229
		444 (4/1-9/30/94)			834 (10/1/94-3/31/95)			4/1/90- 3/31/91	4/1/91- 3/31/92
	0-500M	500M-2MM	2-10MM	10-50MM	50-100MM	100-250MM		ALL	ALL
	157	505	447	150	10	9	NUMBER OF STATEMENTS	1238	1269
	%	%	%	%	%	%	ASSETS	%	%
	12.1	7.1	5.6	4.8	2.0		Cash & Equivalents	6.1	6.7
	35.3	36.8	34.2	27.5	24.8		Trade Receivables - (net)	33.1	32.8
	30.2	35.1	34.9	36.9	44.7		Inventory	36.4	36.1
	1.8	1.6	1.7	2.1	2.6		All Other Current	1.9	1.8
	79.4	80.6	76.4	71.4	74.1		Total Current	77.5	77.5
	13.4	13.0	15.6	19.9	18.7		Fixed Assets (net)	15.6	15.7
	1.2	1.0	.9	2.5	3.3		Intangibles (net)	.9	.8
	6.0	5.3	7.2	6.2	4.0		All Other Non-Current	6.1	6.0
	100.0	100.0	100.0	100.0	100.0		Total	100.0	100.0
							LIABILITIES		
	11.8	12.5	15.6	15.0	17.1		Notes Payable-Short Term	15.8	14.6
	4.5	3.1	3.4	3.8	4.8		Cur. Mat.-L/T/D	4.0	3.7
	25.8	25.3	22.8	16.5	28.0		Trade Payables	22.3	22.3
	.3	.4	.4	.6	.5		Income Taxes Payable	.6	.5
	10.6	8.5	9.0	11.3	5.4		All Other Current	8.6	8.3
	53.0	49.8	51.2	47.1	55.8		Total Current	51.4	49.4
	9.1	8.4	9.1	14.2	12.5		Long Term Debt	11.6	10.7
	.2	.4	.4	.5	.5		Deferred Taxes	.3	.3
	2.5	3.2	2.1	3.1	.9		All Other-Non-Current	2.1	2.5
	35.2	38.3	37.2	35.0	30.2		Net Worth	34.7	37.0
	100.0	100.0	100.0	100.0	100.0		Total Liabilities & Net Worth	100.0	100.0
							INCOME DATA		
	100.0	100.0	100.0	100.0	100.0		Net Sales	100.0	100.0
	33.7	29.1	27.5	27.5	24.5		Gross Profit	28.8	29.8
	30.8	25.9	24.2	22.2	20.1		Operating Expenses	25.9	27.2
	2.9	3.2	3.3	5.3	4.3		Operating Profit	2.9	2.6
	.4	.5	.3	.8	.4		All Other Expenses (net)	.8	.8
	2.5	2.7	3.0	4.5	3.9		Profit Before Taxes	2.1	1.8
							RATIOS		
	2.3	2.2	1.9	2.0	1.5			2.1	2.3
	1.5	1.6	1.4	1.4	1.2		Current	1.5	1.5
	1.1	1.3	1.2	1.2	1.1			1.2	1.2
	1.4	1.2	1.1	1.1	.7			1.2	1.2
(156)	.9	(504) .9	.8	.7	.5		Quick	.8	.8
	.6	.6	.5	.4	.3			.5	.5
19	19.1	32 11.5	37 10.0	37 9.8	36 10.1			33 11.2	33 11.1
34	10.6	45 8.2	46 7.9	45 8.2	47 7.7		Sales/Receivables	42 8.6	42 8.7
46	7.9	55 6.6	57 6.4	55 6.6	55 6.6			54 6.7	53 6.9
9	40.9	33 11.1	43 8.5	50 7.3	50 7.3			39 9.4	40 9.1
39	9.4	56 6.5	64 5.7	74 4.9	122 3.0		Cost of Sales/Inventory	65 5.6	65 5.6
73	5.0	89 4.1	99 3.7	126 2.9	203 1.8			104 3.5	104 3.5
13	27.5	23 16.2	24 15.4	22 16.9	43 8.4			21 17.7	21 17.1
31	11.6	37 9.8	38 9.5	31 11.7	69 5.3		Cost of Sales/Payables	37 10.0	37 10.0
56	6.5	56 6.5	59 6.2	50 7.3	111 3.3			56 6.5	57 6.4
	9.0	6.1	6.0	6.0	6.1			6.3	6.0
	17.6	10.8	11.4	9.7	17.8		Sales/Working Capital	11.1	10.6
	45.1	21.3	22.3	20.9	23.2			25.1	23.3
	8.5	7.6	8.4	8.1				4.9	4.8
(133)	3.4	(462) 3.3	(419) 3.5	(142) 3.4			EBIT/Interest	(1144) 2.3	(1172) 2.2
	1.4	1.7	1.8	2.0				1.3	1.1
	5.6	4.9	5.0	6.8				4.8	4.2
(33)	1.6	(214) 2.2	(210) 2.4	(72) 2.6			Net Profit + Depr., Dep., Amort./Cur. Mat. L /T/D	(662) 2.0	(591) 1.7
	.8	1.2	1.0	1.1				.7	.6
	.1	.1	.1	.2	.1			.2	.1
	.3	.3	.3	.5	.8		Fixed/Worth	.3	.3
	1.0	.6	.8	1.2	1.4			.9	.8
	.8	1.0	1.0	1.0	1.9			1.0	.9
	1.9	1.7	2.1	2.4	3.2		Debt/Worth	2.1	1.8
	5.9	3.2	3.4	4.4	4.8			4.4	4.0
	51.2	35.3	32.3	35.8	28.8		% Profit Before Taxes/Tangible	30.0	25.4
(142)	23.8	(486) 17.0	(433) 17.7	(146) 22.0	20.0		Net Worth	(1168) 14.3	(1209) 11.1
	4.4	6.0	7.3	12.7	13.3			4.7	2.2
	16.8	11.7	10.6	11.8	9.4		% Profit Before Taxes/Total	9.6	8.7
	7.0	5.6	5.7	6.6	5.8		Assets	4.4	3.5
	1.1	2.1	2.0	3.4	2.6			1.2	.4
	139.2	72.4	59.8	37.1	53.7			63.3	59.6
	43.3	38.4	25.5	15.1	14.2		Sales/Net Fixed Assets	28.5	26.8
	23.4	17.4	10.1	6.1	4.8			10.7	11.1
	5.1	3.8	3.2	2.8	1.9			3.5	3.5
	4.0	3.1	2.6	2.0	1.6		Sales/Total Assets	2.8	2.7
	3.0	2.3	2.0	1.5	1.6			2.0	2.0
	.4	.5	.5	.6				.6	.6
(119)	.8	(447) .8	(413) .9	(134) 1.2			% Depr., Dep., Amort./Sales	(1079) 1.0	(1159) 1.0
	1.7	1.6	1.8	3.2				1.8	2.0
	4.5	2.5	1.8	1.1				2.2	2.5
(94)	6.7	(290) 4.4	(156) 3.0	(28) 1.8			% Officers', Directors', Owners' Comp/Sales	(505) 4.1	(554) 4.1
	9.5	6.9	5.9	2.7				7.2	6.8
	214869M	1864025M	4932866M	6656010M	1245600M	1813640M	Net Sales ($)	13953673M	12817981M
	48510M	604710M	1931054M	3145453M	704330M	1299323M	Total Assets ($)	7234167M	6215508M

M = $ thousand   MM = $ million
See Pages 1 through 15 for Explanation of Ratios and Data

Comparative Historical Data				Current Data Sorted By Sales					
19	66	95	# Postretirement Benefits	4	19	16	26	18	12
			Type of Statement						
234	226	232	Unqualified	2	9	12	53	69	87
391	403	381	Reviewed	5	74	86	114	82	20
344	336	303	Compiled	26	127	64	64	19	3
25	29	40	Tax Returns	9	18	5	7	1	
227	260	322	Other	28	77	56	63	55	43
4/1/92-3/31/93 ALL	4/1/93-3/31/94 ALL	4/1/94-3/31/95 ALL		444 (4/1-9/30/94)			834 (10/1/94-3/31/95)		
				0-1MM	1-3MM	3-5MM	5-10MM	10-25MM	25MM & OVER
1221	1254	1278	**NUMBER OF STATEMENTS**	70	305	223	301	226	153
%	%	%	**ASSETS**	%	%	%	%	%	%
6.1	6.2	6.8	Cash & Equivalents	11.2	8.4	7.7	6.1	5.3	4.0
33.9	34.8	34.4	Trade Receivables - (net)	28.9	34.5	35.4	35.2	35.9	31.5
36.4	35.2	34.8	Inventory	33.0	33.1	35.4	35.5	34.6	37.3
1.6	1.6	1.8	All Other Current	2.7	2.0	1.6	1.5	1.6	2.2
78.0	77.9	77.9	Total Current	75.7	78.0	80.1	78.3	77.4	75.0
15.6	15.3	14.8	Fixed Assets (net)	14.6	14.5	13.6	13.9	16.2	16.9
.9	1.1	1.2	Intangibles (net)	1.8	1.3	.9	.8	.8	2.5
5.5	5.7	6.2	All Other Non-Current	7.8	6.2	5.4	6.9	5.6	5.7
100.0	100.0	100.0	Total	100.0	100.0	100.0	100.0	100.0	100.0
			LIABILITIES						
14.7	13.5	13.9	Notes Payable-Short Term	12.6	11.0	13.1	15.6	15.7	15.3
3.5	3.4	3.5	Cur. Mat.-L /T/D	4.4	3.7	3.0	3.5	3.6	3.0
23.2	21.8	23.4	Trade Payables	21.7	25.1	23.5	23.8	23.1	20.6
.5	1.6	.4	Income Taxes Payable	.2	.3	.5	.4	.6	.4
8.5	9.2	9.2	All Other Current	11.5	7.9	8.6	9.0	9.8	11.1
50.3	49.4	50.4	Total Current	50.4	48.1	48.8	52.2	52.7	50.3
10.0	10.2	9.4	Long Term Debt	9.4	10.3	7.7	8.4	9.2	12.3
.3	.3	.4	Deferred Taxes	.3	.4	.4	.2	.4	.5
2.8	2.7	2.8	All Other-Non-Current	3.1	3.4	2.3	2.8	2.1	3.1
36.7	37.4	37.1	Net Worth	36.8	37.8	40.8	36.4	35.6	33.8
100.0	100.0	100.0	Total Liabilities & Net Worth	100.0	100.0	100.0	100.0	100.0	100.0
			INCOME DATA						
100.0	100.0	100.0	Net Sales	100.0	100.0	100.0	100.0	100.0	100.0
29.2	29.4	28.8	Gross Profit	40.6	32.1	29.0	26.3	26.5	25.1
26.6	26.5	25.4	Operating Expenses	35.3	28.7	26.0	23.4	22.9	20.5
2.7	2.9	3.5	Operating Profit	5.2	3.4	3.0	2.9	3.6	4.6
.5	.4	.4	All Other Expenses (net)	.9	.4	.3	.4	.3	.6
2.1	2.5	3.1	Profit Before Taxes	4.3	3.0	2.6	2.5	3.2	4.0
			RATIOS						
2.2	2.2	2.1	Current	3.5	2.3	2.2	2.0	1.9	2.0
1.5	1.5	1.5		1.6	1.6	1.6	1.4	1.4	1.5
1.2	1.2	1.2		1.1	1.3	1.2	1.2	1.2	1.2
1.1	1.2	1.2	Quick	1.5	1.3	1.3	1.1	1.1	1.1
.8	.8 (1276)	.8		(69).9	(304).9	.8	.8	.8	.7
.5	.6	.6		.4	.6	.6	.6	.6	.5
34 10.8	35 10.5	33 11.1	Sales/Receivables	16 22.2	29 12.5	33 11.1	33 10.9	37 9.9	37 9.9
43 8.5	45 8.2	45 8.2		35 10.4	45 8.2	45 8.2	44 8.3	45 8.1	46 7.9
54 6.8	54 6.7	55 6.6		50 7.3	57 6.4	55 6.6	53 6.9	55 6.6	55 6.6
39 9.3	37 9.9	37 10.0	Cost of Sales/Inventory	9 40.6	28 13.2	38 9.6	37 9.8	41 8.8	43 8.5
64 5.7	61 6.0	60 6.1		74 4.9	56 6.5	64 5.7	57 6.4	61 6.0	72 5.1
104 3.5	99 3.7	96 3.8		215 1.7	107 3.4	96 3.8	85 4.3	85 4.3	114 3.2
23 15.9	19 19.3	22 16.7	Cost of Sales/Payables	14 25.2	22 16.8	23 16.2	21 17.1	21 17.4	23 15.8
37 9.8	36 10.2	37 9.9		38 9.7	40 9.2	37 10.0	36 10.2	36 10.1	37 9.9
58 6.3	54 6.7	57 6.4		66 5.5	65 5.6	54 6.7	54 6.8	55 6.6	53 6.9
6.0	6.1	6.4	Sales/Working Capital	4.1	5.4	6.0	7.0	7.7	6.5
10.6	10.3	11.4		11.7	10.3	10.0	12.1	14.2	10.1
23.7	21.2	22.8		85.0	24.2	22.2	21.8	26.6	21.2
5.7	7.2	8.1	EBIT/Interest	9.0	7.5	7.5	7.4	8.8	9.7
(1117)2.6	(1142)3.1	(1174)3.5		(55)3.8	(275)3.1	(202)4.0	(284)3.1	(212)3.7	(146)4.2
1.4	1.5	1.8		1.2	1.6	1.5	1.7	2.0	2.4
4.2	4.7	5.2	Net Profit + Depr., Dep., Amort./Cur. Mat. L/T/D	3.8	4.7	5.2	4.3	5.6	9.3
(521)1.7	(515)2.1	(537)2.4		(11)2.5	(108)1.7	(90)2.6	(147)2.0	(109)2.7	(72)2.8
.7	.9	1.1		.7	.8	1.4	1.0	1.0	1.3
.1	.1	.1	Fixed/Worth	.1	.1	.1	.1	.2	.2
.4	.3	.3		.3	.3	.2	.3	.4	.4
.8	.7	.8		1.0	.8	.7	.7	.8	.9
.9	.9	1.0	Debt/Worth	.6	.9	.9	1.0	1.1	1.2
1.9	1.9	1.9		1.7	1.6	1.7	2.1	2.0	2.5
3.9	3.7	3.6		8.8	4.2	2.8	3.4	3.7	4.2
26.4	30.2	35.2	% Profit Before Taxes/Tangible Net Worth	74.1	38.6	33.4	30.1	35.9	40.5
(1168)11.8	(1201)15.4	(1226)18.8		(63)22.5	(286)19.5	(216)15.5	(290)17.0	(222)19.8	(149)24.5
3.4	5.3	7.3		3.5	6.3	4.5	5.9	9.8	14.6
8.9	10.4	11.7	% Profit Before Taxes/Total Assets	18.7	13.3	11.7	10.0	11.0	11.9
3.9	4.9	5.9		7.2	6.0	5.6	5.1	6.1	6.9
1.1	1.6	2.2		.8	1.7	1.9	1.9	3.0	3.9
59.6	63.1	67.1	Sales/Net Fixed Assets	94.0	73.5	75.0	65.0	61.2	57.3
26.9	29.7	29.9		29.8	35.9	33.0	32.2	24.2	22.8
11.0	11.8	12.7		16.1	14.9	15.2	14.9	10.6	8.7
3.6	3.6	3.6	Sales/Total Assets	4.1	3.8	3.8	3.8	3.5	3.1
2.7	2.8	2.8		2.7	2.9	2.9	3.1	2.7	2.4
2.0	2.0	2.0		1.6	2.0	2.2	2.3	2.0	1.7
.5	.5	.5	% Depr., Dep., Amort./Sales	.6	.5	.4	.5	.5	.4
(1091).9	(1115).9	(1127).9		(50)1.2	(255)1.0	(201).9	(276).8	(211).8	(134).8
1.8	1.8	1.7		2.2	1.7	1.6	1.5	1.8	2.0
2.5	2.6	2.3	% Officers', Directors', Owners' Comp/Sales	4.1	3.4	2.5	2.3	1.4	1.1
(525)4.4	(546)4.4	(568)4.2		(37)8.0	(186)5.5	(113)4.2	(141)3.4	(65)2.3	(26)1.7
7.6	7.6	7.2		10.5	8.3	7.0	5.9	3.7	2.5
13737107M	13839972M	16727010M	Net Sales ($)	44887M	590457M	872110M	2152144M	3442117M	9625295M
6767726M	6570011M	7733380M	Total Assets ($)	22934M	253554M	347196M	839328M	1469487M	4800881M

WHOLESALERS—INDUSTRIAL SUPPLIES. SIC# 5085

Current Data Sorted By Assets							Comparative Historical Data	
3	18	19	9	1	1	**# Postretirement Benefits**		
						Type of Statement		
2	22	58	29	1	2	Unqualified	100	86
11	92	110	12			Reviewed	186	195
35	87	49	4			Compiled	183	189
3	5	1				Tax Returns	8	3
20	51	61	14		3	Other	105	115
	215 (4/1-9/30/94)			457 (10/1/94-3/31/95)			4/1/90-3/31/91	4/1/91-3/31/92
0-500M	500M-2MM	2-10MM	10-50MM	50-100MM	100-250MM		ALL	ALL
71	257	279	59	1	5	**NUMBER OF STATEMENTS**	582	588
%	%	%	%	%	%	**ASSETS**	%	%
9.6	5.4	5.1	5.2			Cash & Equivalents	4.7	5.2
37.2	38.3	36.3	30.9			Trade Receivables - (net)	34.5	34.6
31.8	38.1	37.9	38.6			Inventory	40.1	39.6
.8	1.0	1.1	1.8			All Other Current	1.4	1.1
79.4	82.8	80.4	76.5			Total Current	80.7	80.5
14.1	11.3	12.5	15.3			Fixed Assets (net)	13.3	12.9
.9	1.2	1.1	3.2			Intangibles (net)	.8	1.2
5.6	4.6	6.0	5.0			All Other Non-Current	5.2	5.4
100.0	100.0	100.0	100.0			Total	100.0	100.0
						LIABILITIES		
9.4	13.8	16.8	18.4			Notes Payable-Short Term	15.5	14.1
4.9	3.0	2.4	2.1			Cur. Mat. -L/T/D	3.4	3.5
23.6	26.3	23.6	19.2			Trade Payables	23.3	24.4
.5	.5	.5	.3			Income Taxes Payable	.5	.4
10.9	7.2	6.5	6.7			All Other Current	6.6	5.8
49.3	50.8	49.8	46.6			Total Current	49.3	48.2
13.9	9.3	8.1	8.8			Long Term Debt	11.0	11.3
.0	.1	.2	.6			Deferred Taxes	.3	.2
2.7	2.5	2.8	4.1			All Other-Non-Current	2.4	2.0
34.1	37.3	39.1	39.8			Net Worth	37.1	38.4
100.0	100.0	100.0	100.0			Total Liabilities & Net Worth	100.0	100.0
						INCOME DATA		
100.0	100.0	100.0	100.0			Net Sales	100.0	100.0
32.4	29.5	26.0	26.7			Gross Profit	29.6	29.9
29.1	27.0	23.3	21.5			Operating Expenses	26.6	27.4
3.2	2.5	2.7	5.2			Operating Profit	3.0	2.5
.7	.8	.4	.9			All Other Expenses (net)	1.0	.8
2.5	1.8	2.3	4.3			Profit Before Taxes	2.1	1.7
						RATIOS		
2.8	2.3	2.2	2.6				2.5	2.6
1.6	1.6	1.6	1.6			Current	1.7	1.7
1.2	1.3	1.3	1.3				1.2	1.3
1.6	1.2	1.2	1.2				1.2	1.3
1.0	.9	.8	.8			Quick	.8	.8
.6	.6	.6	.5				.6	.6
29 12.5	37 10.0	38 9.5	40 9.1				34 10.7	34 10.8
39 9.3	43 8.4	45 8.2	46 8.0			Sales/Receivables	40 9.1	41 9.0
50 7.3	51 7.1	54 6.8	57 6.4				50 7.3	48 7.6
21 17.0	41 8.9	41 8.8	51 7.1				45 8.1	43 8.4
46 8.0	60 6.1	60 6.1	70 5.2			Cost of Sales/Inventory	69 5.3	69 5.3
83 4.4	96 3.8	94 3.9	104 3.5				104 3.5	99 3.7
14 25.6	27 13.3	26 13.8	23 16.2				24 15.5	24 15.2
31 11.6	41 8.9	37 10.0	35 10.5			Cost of Sales/Payables	37 10.0	38 9.6
57 6.4	58 6.3	52 7.0	50 7.3				53 6.9	54 6.7
6.0	6.0	5.8	5.2				5.7	5.7
11.5	10.1	9.3	8.2			Sales/Working Capital	9.7	9.5
27.8	19.7	18.0	16.4				20.6	18.6
8.4	7.8	7.2	6.7				5.2	4.6
(59) 4.4	(239) 3.2	(254) 3.5	(53) 3.8			EBIT/Interest	(540) 2.4	(545) 2.1
1.4	1.7	1.7	1.9				1.3	1.1
9.3	4.3	6.6	8.8				5.6	4.4
(16) 4.9	(114) 1.9	(133) 2.7	(32) 3.1			Net Profit + Depr., Dep., Amort./Cur. Mat. L /T/D	(340) 2.2	(300) 1.7
1.2	.8	1.3	1.5				.9	.6
.1	.1	.1	.2				.1	.1
.3	.3	.3	.4			Fixed/Worth	.3	.3
1.2	.6	.5	.7				.6	.7
1.0	.9	.9	.9				.9	.8
2.1	1.8	1.8	1.9			Debt/Worth	1.8	1.8
6.6	3.4	3.2	4.0				3.8	3.7
80.6	32.2	31.9	36.5				30.2	26.4
(65) 27.7	(240) 16.4	(270) 16.8	(56) 18.4			% Profit Before Taxes/Tangible Net Worth	(552) 15.0	(563) 11.3
7.8	6.1	5.4	9.3				3.9	1.5
16.8	10.8	11.4	13.5				10.9	9.4
9.5	6.0	5.9	6.2			% Profit Before Taxes/Total Assets	5.0	3.6
1.4	1.8	1.8	3.1				1.0	.2
141.7	71.7	64.1	40.6				63.9	65.2
47.2	35.6	31.8	22.6			Sales/Net Fixed Assets	31.6	34.4
13.7	20.1	16.8	13.2				14.8	14.8
4.4	3.8	3.5	3.1				3.7	3.7
3.5	3.2	2.9	2.4			Sales/Total Assets	3.0	3.0
2.4	2.4	2.3	1.9				2.3	2.3
.4	.4	.4	.5				.5	.5
(55) .9	(230) .8	(255) .7	(53) .9			% Depr., Dep., Amort./Sales	(539) .8	(540) .8
1.8	1.4	1.1	1.3				1.4	1.4
4.1	3.1	1.7	1.0				2.3	2.3
(28) 5.5	(139) 4.7	(114) 3.4	(13) 2.6			% Officers', Directors', Owners' Comp/Sales	(257) 4.1	(269) 4.3
8.2	6.3	5.9	3.2				7.1	7.1
81621M	933349M	3272172M	2744595M	174682M	1376269M	Net Sales ($)	5312512M	6028268M
22697M	301142M	1122345M	1128728M	91107M	697977M	Total Assets ($)	2140279M	2287360M

M = $ thousand   MM = $ million
See Pages 1 through 15 for Explanation of Ratios and Data

Comparative Historical Data				Current Data Sorted By Sales					
13	38	51	# Postretirement Benefits	1	9	7	14	11	9
			Type of Statement						
97	99	114	Unqualified	2	9	9	29	35	30
176	197	225	Reviewed	8	41	38	71	51	16
200	189	175	Compiled	21	59	36	42	14	3
10	14	9	Tax Returns	3	2	3	1		
107	136	149	Other	6	35	22	41	27	18
4/1/92-3/31/93 ALL	4/1/93-3/31/94 ALL	4/1/94-3/31/95 ALL		215 (4/1-9/30/94) 0-1MM	1-3MM	3-5MM	457 (10/1/94-3/31/95) 5-10MM	10-25MM	25MM & OVER
590	635	672	**NUMBER OF STATEMENTS**	40	146	108	184	127	67
%	%	%	**ASSETS**	%	%	%	%	%	%
5.2	5.0	5.7	Cash & Equivalents	9.2	6.8	6.5	5.2	4.5	3.4
35.0	37.0	36.6	Trade Receivables - (net)	28.3	37.3	37.0	37.3	37.7	35.4
38.3	37.2	37.4	Inventory	38.3	37.5	35.6	37.9	37.0	38.9
1.0	1.1	1.1	All Other Current	.7	.7	1.5	1.2	.9	1.7
79.4	80.3	80.8	Total Current	76.4	82.2	80.7	81.6	80.1	79.3
13.6	13.5	12.5	Fixed Assets (net)	13.8	12.2	13.8	11.5	12.2	13.2
1.7	1.1	1.3	Intangibles (net)	1.8	1.4	.8	.8	1.6	2.4
5.4	5.1	5.5	All Other Non-Current	8.0	4.1	4.8	6.2	6.0	5.1
100.0	100.0	100.0	Total	100.0	100.0	100.0	100.0	100.0	100.0
			LIABILITIES						
15.1	14.2	14.9	Notes Payable-Short Term	10.1	11.4	11.7	17.3	18.9	16.4
3.5	3.0	2.9	Cur. Mat.-L./T/D	5.1	3.5	3.8	1.9	2.4	2.1
23.7	23.9	24.1	Trade Payables	18.8	23.7	24.1	26.5	24.5	21.2
.4	1.8	.5	Income Taxes Payable	.2	.5	.5	.5	.5	.2
6.4	6.6	7.3	All Other Current	13.0	7.8	6.7	5.9	7.3	7.3
49.1	49.6	49.6	Total Current	47.2	46.8	46.8	52.2	53.7	47.2
10.6	8.8	9.3	Long Term Debt	15.8	11.4	9.6	7.9	6.7	9.1
.3	.3	.2	Deferred Taxes	.0	.1	.1	.2	.2	.6
2.1	3.0	2.8	All Other-Non-Current	3.3	3.6	2.0	2.2	2.5	4.4
38.0	38.4	38.1	Net Worth	33.6	38.0	41.5	37.6	37.0	38.7
100.0	100.0	100.0	Total Liabilities & Net Worth	100.0	100.0	100.0	100.0	100.0	100.0
			INCOME DATA						
100.0	100.0	100.0	Net Sales	100.0	100.0	100.0	100.0	100.0	100.0
30.3	29.2	28.2	Gross Profit	35.3	32.1	29.5	26.5	25.1	23.7
27.5	26.7	25.2	Operating Expenses	32.5	28.6	26.8	23.9	22.2	19.8
2.9	2.5	3.0	Operating Profit	2.8	3.5	2.8	2.6	2.8	4.0
.7	.5	.6	All Other Expenses (net)	2.1	.7	.7	.2	.5	.7
2.2	1.9	2.4	Profit Before Taxes	.7	2.8	2.1	2.4	2.3	3.2
			RATIOS						
2.3	2.4	2.3	Current	2.8	2.7	2.4	2.2	2.0	2.6
1.6	1.7	1.6		1.7	1.8	1.8	1.5	1.5	1.6
1.3	1.2	1.3		1.2	1.3	1.3	1.3	1.2	1.3
1.2	1.2	1.3	Quick	1.5	1.5	1.3	1.2	1.1	1.2
.8	.9	.9		.9	1.0	1.0	.8	.8	.8
.6	.6	.6		.4	.7	.7	.6	.6	.6
34 10.6	36 10.2	37 9.8	Sales/Receivables	30 12.2	37 9.9	36 10.1	37 9.8	39 9.4	38 9.6
41 9.0	42 8.7	44 8.3		37 9.8	45 8.1	43 8.4	43 8.5	45 8.2	45 8.2
49 7.4	49 7.4	52 7.0		50 7.3	55 6.6	53 6.9	52 7.0	54 6.7	50 7.3
41 9.0	38 9.6	41 9.0	Cost of Sales/Inventory	38 9.6	42 8.7	40 9.1	40 9.2	38 9.6	45 8.2
66 5.5	61 6.0	61 6.0		87 4.2	70 5.2	60 6.1	58 6.3	57 6.4	61 6.0
99 3.7	94 3.9	94 3.9		166 2.2	114 3.2	99 3.7	89 4.1	89 4.1	85 4.3
24 14.9	24 15.2	26 14.3	Cost of Sales/Payables	24 15.1	24 15.5	26 14.3	27 13.3	26 14.2	24 15.2
37 9.9	37 10.0	37 9.8		38 9.7	40 9.1	38 9.6	39 9.4	37 9.8	31 11.7
54 6.7	55 6.6	54 6.7		63 5.8	63 5.8	55 6.6	54 6.7	51 7.2	46 8.0
6.1	6.3	5.8	Sales/Working Capital	4.3	5.0	5.8	6.4	6.9	5.7
9.8	10.8	9.7		8.4	8.4	9.0	10.9	12.2	9.7
20.4	21.1	18.8		30.8	16.7	16.1	19.9	21.5	18.9
5.8	5.9	7.7	EBIT/Interest	(34) 8.3	(130) 7.6	(96) 8.2	(174) 8.5	(114) 6.6	(62) 6.7
(551) 2.7	(575) 3.0	(610) 3.5		2.0	3.8	4.8	3.2	3.5	3.5
1.3	1.5	1.7		.5	1.4	1.9	2.0	1.8	1.9
4.5	6.0	6.0	Net Profit + Depr., Dep., Amort./Cur. Mat. L/T/D		(61) 4.3	(49) 4.6	(77) 6.2	(64) 6.5	(40) 10.3
(274) 1.9	(286) 2.1	(300) 2.5			1.9	1.9	2.5	2.7	3.5
.8	1.0	1.1			.9	.5	1.4	1.4	1.6
.1	.1	.1	Fixed/Worth	.1	.1	.1	.1	.1	.2
.3	.3	.3		.4	.3	.3	.3	.3	.3
.7	.7	.6		1.9	.6	.6	.5	.6	.6
.9	.9	.9	Debt/Worth	.7	.9	.8	1.0	1.0	.9
1.8	1.8	1.8		2.3	1.7	1.7	2.0	1.9	2.0
3.8	3.8	3.5		7.1	3.6	3.0	3.5	3.5	4.0
29.0	26.5	33.5	% Profit Before Taxes/Tangible Net Worth	(35) 36.3	(133) 42.4	(106) 33.2	(176) 31.9	(123) 31.3	(64) 37.9
(558) 12.8	(607) 15.0	(637) 17.4		13.9	18.4	15.8	18.9	16.9	17.3
3.6	4.9	6.1		.0	6.1	4.9	6.5	7.6	7.9
9.8	9.7	12.1	% Profit Before Taxes/Total Assets	12.7	13.6	11.5	11.5	11.2	13.5
4.3	4.5	6.1		3.0	6.9	6.2	6.2	5.7	6.2
.9	1.4	1.8		-1.9	1.6	1.7	2.3	2.2	2.0
61.1	62.1	67.3	Sales/Net Fixed Assets	113.3	79.9	59.3	73.5	66.8	53.4
30.3	31.7	32.5		26.9	34.0	32.2	35.7	32.5	29.4
14.9	16.1	16.5		9.0	15.5	16.0	20.4	16.6	16.8
3.8	3.8	3.6	Sales/Total Assets	3.3	3.7	3.7	3.6	3.6	3.5
3.0	3.1	3.0		2.3	3.0	2.9	3.1	3.1	2.9
2.2	2.4	2.3		1.6	2.3	2.3	2.6	2.5	2.3
.5	.4	.4	% Depr., Dep., Amort./Sales	(28) .9	(124) .5	(100) .4	(172) .4	(111) .4	(64) .4
(540) .9	(581) .8	(599) .8		1.4	.9	.8	.7	.7	.8
1.4	1.3	1.2		2.7	1.7	1.3	1.1	1.0	1.1
2.5	2.4	2.5	% Officers', Directors', Owners' Comp/Sales	(10) 4.6	(80) 3.6	(56) 3.2	(87) 2.5	(49) 1.3	(12) 1.0
(275) 4.3	(283) 4.2	(294) 4.2		6.0	5.4	4.5	4.0	2.0	2.3
7.3	6.6	6.4		9.6	7.5	7.1	5.8	3.9	3.3
5709819M	7020730M	8582688M	Net Sales ($)	27706M	290408M	428349M	1343975M	1962450M	4529800M
2268851M	2602972M	3363996M	Total Assets ($)	17101M	113569M	163390M	595377M	738151M	1736408M

M = $ thousand   MM = $ million
See Pages 1 through 15 for Explanation of Ratios and Data

WHOLESALERS—LAUNDRY & DRY CLEANING EQUIPMENT & SUPPLIES. SIC# 5087

	Current Data Sorted By Assets						Comparative Historical Data	
	3	3				# Postretirement Benefits		
						Type of Statement		
1	1	4				Unqualified	12	11
1	7	8	2			Reviewed	31	28
5	9	5				Compiled	22	22
1	1					Tax Returns		1
1	9	5				Other	21	13
0-500M	21 (4/1-9/30/94) 500M-2MM	2-10MM	39 (10/1/94-3/31/95) 10-50MM	50-100MM	100-250MM		4/1/90- 3/31/91 ALL	4/1/91- 3/31/92 ALL
9	27	22	2			NUMBER OF STATEMENTS	86	75
%	%	%	%	%	%	**ASSETS**	%	%
	7.2	5.5				Cash & Equivalents	6.8	7.4
	32.2	31.6				Trade Receivables - (net)	34.3	37.3
	31.6	36.7				Inventory	35.5	32.3
	.7	1.6				All Other Current	1.9	1.2
	71.7	75.3				Total Current	78.4	78.2
	23.4	13.8				Fixed Assets (net)	14.2	12.5
	.8	2.0				Intangibles (net)	1.1	2.7
	4.2	8.9				All Other Non-Current	6.2	6.7
	100.0	100.0				Total	100.0	100.0
						LIABILITIES		
	7.9	10.1				Notes Payable-Short Term	13.7	12.7
	6.4	2.6				Cur. Mat.-L/T/D	4.8	3.9
	19.6	20.6				Trade Payables	23.4	21.4
	.3	.5				Income Taxes Payable	.6	.4
	6.5	7.1				All Other Current	7.7	9.6
	40.7	40.9				Total Current	50.2	48.0
	12.6	14.6				Long Term Debt	12.1	11.8
	.1	.1				Deferred Taxes	.1	.7
	3.9	4.6				All Other-Non-Current	3.6	3.1
	42.8	39.7				Net Worth	34.0	36.4
	100.0	100.0				Total Liabilities & Net Worth	100.0	100.0
						INCOME DATA		
	100.0	100.0				Net Sales	100.0	100.0
	29.3	29.7				Gross Profit	32.1	31.3
	28.6	28.7				Operating Expenses	30.7	29.7
	.7	1.0				Operating Profit	1.4	1.6
	.0	−.2				All Other Expenses (net)	.4	.5
	.7	1.1				Profit Before Taxes	1.0	1.1
						RATIOS		
	3.1	2.5					2.6	2.7
	1.5	2.0				Current	1.5	1.5
	1.2	1.5					1.2	1.3
	1.6	1.7					1.4	1.6
	.9	1.0				Quick	.9	.9
	.6	.5					.6	.6
	28 12.9	33 10.9					29 12.5	33 11.1
	41 8.9	46 7.9				Sales/Receivables	39 9.3	42 8.6
	54 6.7	63 5.8					48 7.6	53 6.9
	33 11.0	35 10.5					37 10.0	37 10.0
	47 7.8	54 6.8				Cost of Sales/Inventory	52 7.0	57 6.4
	87 4.2	111 3.3					91 4.0	94 3.9
	12 29.5	18 20.5					21 17.2	17 21.0
	36 10.2	38 9.7				Cost of Sales/Payables	36 10.1	32 11.3
	56 6.5	69 5.3					52 7.0	50 7.3
	4.9	5.5					6.6	5.5
	12.3	6.6				Sales/Working Capital	12.6	11.2
	22.7	13.4					27.6	22.0
	3.7	9.8					4.4	3.6
	(25) 1.9	(20) 2.6				EBIT/Interest	(81) 2.3	(66) 1.9
	1.1	.8					.8	.9
	6.8	8.0					4.6	3.4
	(13) 2.4	(10) 2.1				Net Profit + Depr., Dep., Amort./Cur. Mat. L /T/D	(49) 1.8	(43) 1.5
	.3	.8					.7	.7
	.2	.2					.1	.1
	.4	.3				Fixed/Worth	.4	.3
	1.3	.6					1.0	.8
	.5	.9					.8	.9
	1.7	1.6				Debt/Worth	1.9	2.0
	2.8	4.8					4.8	4.2
	17.9	25.9					(77) 27.2	(70) 26.1
	6.7	11.2				% Profit Before Taxes/Tangible Net Worth	15.5	9.4
	.9	−.6					5.1	.1
	6.8	10.1					9.5	7.4
	2.4	4.3				% Profit Before Taxes/Total Assets	4.6	3.3
	.3	−.1					−.3	−.2
	57.0	66.0					77.4	64.2
	19.0	27.0				Sales/Net Fixed Assets	36.7	34.8
	6.6	14.5					16.8	20.0
	3.6	3.4					4.0	3.9
	2.8	3.1				Sales/Total Assets	3.2	3.0
	2.2	2.0					2.6	2.2
	.6	.5					(80) .6	(69) .6
	(25) 1.1	(21) .9				% Depr., Dep., Amort./Sales	.9	.9
	2.0	1.2					1.7	1.8
	1.9	1.6					2.4	1.9
	(15) 3.6	(13) 2.0				% Officers', Directors', Owners' Comp/Sales	(43) 4.2	(30) 3.7
	5.4	4.0					6.0	6.0
11208M	90671M	236063M	19062M			Net Sales ($)	507424M	610887M
3133M	31317M	90181M	23183M			Total Assets ($)	184937M	231982M

M = $ thousand   MM = $ million
See Pages 1 through 15 for Explanation of Ratios and Data

Comparative Historical Data | | | | **Current Data Sorted By Sales**

				# Postretirement Benefits	1		1	3	1
	1		6	**Type of Statement**					
8	3		6	Unqualified		1		2	2
24	18		18	Reviewed		3	4	6	5
22	20		19	Compiled	2	10		6	1
2	3		2	Tax Returns		2			
13	14		15	Other	2	4	4	3	1	1

Comparative Historical Data			Current Data Sorted By Sales						
4/1/92-3/31/93 ALL	4/1/93-3/31/94 ALL	4/1/94-3/31/95 ALL		21 (4/1-9/30/94)		39 (10/1/94-3/31/95)			
				0-1MM	1-3MM	3-5MM	5-10MM	10-25MM	25MM & OVER
69	58	60	**NUMBER OF STATEMENTS**	4	20	9	17	9	1

%	%	%	**ASSETS**	%	%	%	%	%	%
7.1	5.0	6.6	Cash & Equivalents		9.0		6.3		
34.2	33.1	33.2	Trade Receivables - (net)		32.1		31.0		
34.6	37.1	33.5	Inventory		33.6		34.6		
1.1	.5	1.0	All Other Current		.3		1.4		
77.0	75.7	74.4	Total Current		75.1		73.3		
15.3	14.5	18.4	Fixed Assets (net)		19.0		14.6		
1.3	2.8	1.5	Intangibles (net)		1.9		1.1		
6.3	7.1	5.7	All Other Non-Current		4.0		11.0		
100.0	100.0	100.0	Total		100.0		100.0		

			LIABILITIES						
11.0	14.1	9.9	Notes Payable-Short Term		6.8		12.7		
7.1	3.3	5.2	Cur. Mat.-L/T/D		6.9		2.3		
23.4	20.2	21.2	Trade Payables		19.0		26.3		
.5	2.6	.4	Income Taxes Payable		.2		.4		
7.2	7.8	7.2	All Other Current		9.2		6.6		
49.3	48.0	43.8	Total Current		42.0		48.4		
12.1	12.8	14.6	Long Term Debt		13.5		8.8		
.9	.5	.5	Deferred Taxes		.1		.2		
4.1	6.1	4.2	All Other-Non-Current		6.9		4.3		
33.6	32.6	37.0	Net Worth		37.5		38.2		
100.0	100.0	100.0	Total Liabilities & Net Worth		100.0		100.0		

			INCOME DATA						
100.0	100.0	100.0	Net Sales		100.0		100.0		
32.5	31.9	30.8	Gross Profit		33.2		30.0		
30.8	31.3	29.7	Operating Expenses		31.6		28.2		
1.7	.5	1.1	Operating Profit		1.6		1.8		
.2	.5	.2	All Other Expenses (net)		-.1		-.4		
1.5	.1	.9	Profit Before Taxes		1.8		2.2		

			RATIOS						
2.1	2.1	2.4	Current		2.9		2.1		
1.6	1.6	1.7			1.8		1.5		
1.3	1.2	1.2			1.3		1.2		
1.3	1.2	1.4	Quick		1.6		1.1		
.9	.8	.9			.9		.7		
.6	.5	.6			.6		.5		
31 11.6	25 14.5	30 12.3	Sales/Receivables	24 15.0		28 13.2			
42 8.7	39 9.4	43 8.5		35 10.5		44 8.3			
51 7.2	49 7.4	57 6.4		57 6.4		60 6.1			
38 9.6	35 10.3	35 10.3	Cost of Sales/Inventory	39 9.4		30 12.0			
56 6.5	61 6.0	47 7.7		47 7.7		54 6.7			
96 3.8	91 4.0	99 3.7		85 4.3		99 3.7			
20 18.2	17 22.1	21 17.3	Cost of Sales/Payables	14 26.3		35 10.4			
33 11.2	32 11.5	37 9.9		33 11.2		48 7.6			
64 5.7	58 6.3	62 5.9		49 7.4		72 5.1			
6.4	6.7	5.3	Sales/Working Capital	5.1		6.1			
10.9	11.6	9.5		10.4		10.9			
19.9	26.6	24.1		26.2		28.9			
4.7	6.2	6.8	EBIT/Interest	(19) 4.6		(15) 8.1			
(64) 2.5	(54) 2.3	(55) 2.5		1.6		3.5			
1.2	.4	1.1		-.5		1.7			
3.3	2.1	6.8	Net Profit + Depr., Dep., Amort./Cur. Mat. L/T/D			(10) 6.4			
(34) 1.3	(17) 1.2	(25) 2.0				2.6			
.6	-1.4	.4				1.8			
.2	.1	.2	Fixed/Worth	.2		.2			
.4	.4	.4		.4		.4			
.7	1.0	1.0		2.1		.7			
1.0	1.0	.9	Debt/Worth	.6		1.1			
1.8	2.2	1.9		2.2		1.9			
3.8	7.4	4.7		5.3		4.3			
25.7	42.8	22.6	% Profit Before Taxes/Tangible Net Worth	(18) 33.9		23.2			
(62) 13.1	(52) 13.2	(57) 11.2		6.3		11.2			
2.9	.8	1.5		.1		6.2			
8.1	10.3	10.0	% Profit Before Taxes/Total Assets	16.2		8.0			
4.8	3.4	3.9		2.6		3.8			
.2	-1.9	.3		-.8		.9			
60.4	62.4	59.9	Sales/Net Fixed Assets	74.3		62.1			
25.8	31.4	25.9		35.3		31.9			
12.3	15.5	9.1		9.1		8.3			
3.7	3.9	3.6	Sales/Total Assets	3.8		3.5			
3.1	3.2	3.0		3.0		3.0			
2.6	2.3	2.2		2.5		2.3			
.5	.5	.6	% Depr., Dep., Amort./Sales	(19) .6		(16) .5			
(63) 1.0	(52) .8	(57) .9		.9		.8			
2.3	1.6	1.5		1.4		1.3			
2.8	3.2	1.8	% Officers', Directors', Owners' Comp/Sales	(10) 2.8		(11) 1.6			
(35) 4.6	(24) 4.2	(34) 3.3		4.7		2.0			
7.2	6.9	5.3		11.5		3.6			
530278M	265146M	357004M	Net Sales ($)	3105M	36412M	37723M	120243M	133646M	25875M
209240M	103843M	147814M	Total Assets ($)	2260M	12494M	27429M	50886M	46507M	8238M

© Robert Morris Associates 1995

M = $ thousand   MM = $ million
See Pages 1 through 15 for Explanation of Ratios and Data

WHOLESALERS—MEDICAL, DENTAL & HOSPITAL EQUIPMENT & SUPPLIES. SIC# 5047

Current Data Sorted By Assets						# Postretirement Benefits / Type of Statement	Comparative Historical Data	
4	6	9	1					
3	8	41	20	2	2	Unqualified	52	57
9	28	41	6			Reviewed	71	77
27	53	9	3			Compiled	92	87
6	3					Tax Returns	2	5
19	29	20	12	3		Other	53	71
	129 (4/1-9/30/94)		215 (10/1/94-3/31/95)				4/1/90-3/31/91	4/1/91-3/31/92
0-500M	500M-2MM	2-10MM	10-50MM	50-100MM	100-250MM		ALL	ALL
64	121	111	41	5	2	NUMBER OF STATEMENTS	270	297
%	%	%	%	%	%	ASSETS	%	%
8.1	4.5	4.8	4.8			Cash & Equivalents	5.2	6.2
39.3	39.0	40.5	34.9			Trade Receivables - (net)	40.3	39.6
29.1	35.7	33.6	30.1			Inventory	32.9	32.6
1.4	1.9	1.4	3.1			All Other Current	1.3	1.4
77.9	81.2	80.3	72.8			Total Current	79.7	79.9
16.7	11.5	11.2	13.7			Fixed Assets (net)	14.2	13.7
1.6	2.1	1.4	6.6			Intangibles (net)	1.3	2.4
3.9	5.2	7.1	6.9			All Other Non-Current	4.8	4.1
100.0	100.0	100.0	100.0			Total	100.0	100.0
						LIABILITIES		
13.9	17.0	16.5	16.9			Notes Payable-Short Term	15.7	14.8
4.9	3.6	2.9	3.6			Cur. Mat. -L/T/D	3.7	3.7
24.2	27.0	26.8	17.6			Trade Payables	25.8	23.9
.4	.5	.5	.7			Income Taxes Payable	.5	.5
10.4	9.0	7.5	8.6			All Other Current	7.2	8.3
53.7	57.1	54.2	47.4			Total Current	53.0	51.2
11.8	6.4	7.6	12.6			Long Term Debt	11.8	11.3
.0	.2	.2	.3			Deferred Taxes	.4	.2
3.4	2.2	3.1	2.6			All Other-Non-Current	1.5	2.7
31.0	34.1	34.9	37.1			Net Worth	33.4	34.7
100.0	100.0	100.0	100.0			Total Liabilities & Net Worth	100.0	100.0
						INCOME DATA		
100.0	100.0	100.0	100.0			Net Sales	100.0	100.0
40.8	35.2	30.1	31.8			Gross Profit	37.1	36.6
38.7	32.7	27.4	28.1			Operating Expenses	33.4	32.2
2.2	2.5	2.6	3.7			Operating Profit	3.6	4.4
.6	.4	.8	.9			All Other Expenses (net)	1.0	1.1
1.6	2.1	1.9	2.8			Profit Before Taxes	2.7	3.3
						RATIOS		
2.0	1.8	2.0	2.4				2.1	2.1
1.5	1.4	1.4	1.5			Current	1.5	1.6
1.2	1.1	1.2	1.2				1.2	1.2
1.3	1.1	1.2	1.1				1.2	1.2
.9	.8	.8	.8			Quick	.8	.9
.5	.5	.6	.6				.6	.7
29 12.4	33 11.1	39 9.3	47 7.8				39 9.3	37 9.8
46 8.0	45 8.1	48 7.6	51 7.1			Sales/Receivables	49 7.4	49 7.5
57 6.4	63 5.8	64 5.7	63 5.8				62 5.9	64 5.7
20 17.9	45 8.2	40 9.2	54 6.7				41 8.8	38 9.7
43 8.4	60 6.1	58 6.3	70 5.2			Cost of Sales/Inventory	65 5.6	58 6.3
99 3.7	99 3.7	87 4.2	107 3.4				96 3.8	94 3.9
19 19.6	29 12.5	31 11.9	26 14.0				30 12.0	27 13.6
36 10.1	46 7.9	46 8.0	38 9.5			Cost of Sales/Payables	46 8.0	41 9.0
57 6.4	69 5.3	65 5.6	47 7.8				72 5.1	61 6.0
7.9	8.2	6.4	4.6				6.5	6.3
14.8	13.1	11.9	9.2			Sales/Working Capital	11.8	11.0
55.9	27.4	29.6	20.0				25.6	23.7
(52) 7.6	(111) 6.8	(106) 8.6	(40) 8.6				(255) 5.7	(283) 6.9
2.9	2.9	3.2	3.4			EBIT/Interest	2.5	2.6
.1	1.4	1.4	1.5				1.2	1.6
(12) 3.8	(37) 3.7	(54) 6.3	(19) 12.7			Net Profit + Depr., Dep.,	(145) 4.8	(138) 5.8
1.3	1.8	2.3	2.6			Amort./Cur. Mat. L/T/D	2.1	2.2
-2.5	.7	1.3	1.4				.6	.8
.2	.1	.1	.2				.2	.2
.4	.3	.3	.5			Fixed/Worth	.4	.3
1.2	.7	.7	.9				.9	.7
.9	1.1	.9	1.1				1.1	1.0
2.3	2.2	2.4	2.2			Debt/Worth	2.3	2.1
6.1	4.8	4.2	6.5				4.5	5.2
(53) 49.0	(113) 43.1	(106) 33.8	(37) 36.6			% Profit Before Taxes/Tangible	(254) 42.8	(282) 40.3
28.3	17.5	14.5	21.6			Net Worth	16.2	20.1
-6.3	4.8	5.6	7.7				4.4	7.8
13.8	11.7	11.2	11.5			% Profit Before Taxes/Total	12.5	12.4
8.0	5.0	4.7	7.8			Assets	4.7	5.9
-1.6	1.2	1.1	1.7				.8	1.8
84.3	99.5	73.5	53.0				69.0	68.5
35.5	49.1	37.9	23.2			Sales/Net Fixed Assets	32.0	32.6
11.6	17.6	15.7	9.5				13.5	14.9
4.7	4.0	3.6	3.1				3.7	4.0
3.6	3.1	2.8	2.5			Sales/Total Assets	2.9	2.9
2.4	2.1	2.1	1.2				2.2	2.1
(49) .4	(104) .4	(100) .4	(38) .5			% Depr., Dep., Amort./Sales	(236) .6	(266) .5
1.1	.8	.7	1.0				1.1	.9
2.6	1.6	1.6	2.5				2.2	1.8
(36) 4.2	(63) 3.6	(41) 1.5	(10) 1.6			% Officers', Directors',	(116) 2.1	(130) 2.2
7.2	5.1	2.7	3.1			Owners' Comp/Sales	4.1	4.5
9.9	9.7	4.6	7.1				6.9	7.9
63495M	420278M	1450649M	2068915M	789436M	1002061M	Net Sales ($)	3122765M	4843369M
17518M	134078M	501893M	904061M	384413M	309571M	Total Assets ($)	1290818M	1929696M

© Robert Morris Associates 1995

M = $ thousand   MM = $ million
See Pages 1 through 15 for Explanation of Ratios and Data

Comparative Historical Data				Current Data Sorted By Sales					
4	13	20	# Postretirement Benefits	2	6	2	5	3	2
			Type of Statement						
70	73	76	Unqualified	2	3	9	15	23	24
90	91	84	Reviewed	2	19	11	26	19	7
78	88	92	Compiled	18	43	14	8	7	2
7	9	9	Tax Returns	6	1	2			
63	73	83	Other	13	18	11	10	16	15
4/1/92-3/31/93	4/1/93-3/31/94	4/1/94-3/31/95		129 (4/1-9/30/94)			215 (10/1/94-3/31/95)		
ALL	ALL	ALL		0-1MM	1-3MM	3-5MM	5-10MM	10-25MM	25MM & OVER
308	334	344	**NUMBER OF STATEMENTS**	41	84	47	59	65	48
%	%	%	**ASSETS**	%	%	%	%	%	%
6.3	4.8	5.3	Cash & Equivalents	7.5	5.7	5.0	4.0	5.5	4.4
38.9	38.5	39.0	Trade Receivables - (net)	34.3	40.9	38.5	39.1	39.7	39.3
32.5	33.6	33.0	Inventory	30.9	31.4	35.0	36.1	31.8	33.3
1.2	1.6	1.8	All Other Current	1.3	1.8	2.5	.9	2.2	2.1
79.0	78.5	79.1	Total Current	73.9	79.8	81.0	80.2	79.2	79.0
13.4	13.7	12.8	Fixed Assets (net)	20.0	12.5	9.2	12.4	12.6	11.6
2.0	2.2	2.3	Intangibles (net)	1.5	2.1	3.5	.7	3.3	2.9
5.6	5.6	5.7	All Other Non-Current	4.6	5.5	6.3	6.7	4.9	6.4
100.0	100.0	100.0	Total	100.0	100.0	100.0	100.0	100.0	100.0
			LIABILITIES						
15.1	15.1	15.9	Notes Payable-Short Term	15.5	15.9	14.2	16.9	16.1	16.5
3.0	2.8	3.6	Cur. Mat.-L /T/D	5.6	4.6	2.3	3.8	3.0	1.7
25.0	22.7	25.1	Trade Payables	20.2	25.8	29.5	25.3	26.0	22.3
.6	1.4	.5	Income Taxes Payable	.4	.2	.7	.7	.6	.6
8.2	7.5	8.7	All Other Current	10.8	9.5	8.8	6.7	8.3	8.2
51.8	49.5	53.7	Total Current	52.4	55.8	55.5	53.4	54.1	49.4
10.1	9.9	8.9	Long Term Debt	12.6	8.9	4.6	8.9	8.7	10.2
.2	.4	.2	Deferred Taxes	.0	.1	.1	.3	.2	.7
2.7	2.8	2.8	All Other-Non-Current	4.2	3.2	3.5	2.0	1.9	2.2
35.2	37.4	34.4	Net Worth	30.8	32.0	36.3	35.2	35.2	37.5
100.0	100.0	100.0	Total Liabilities & Net Worth	100.0	100.0	100.0	100.0	100.0	100.0
			INCOME DATA						
100.0	100.0	100.0	Net Sales	100.0	100.0	100.0	100.0	100.0	100.0
35.1	34.2	34.1	Gross Profit	45.0	37.1	34.8	30.7	31.1	27.2
30.6	31.0	31.4	Operating Expenses	43.0	34.6	32.5	28.6	28.1	22.9
4.5	3.2	2.7	Operating Profit	2.0	2.5	2.3	2.1	3.0	4.3
.7	.4	.6	All Other Expenses (net)	.9	.6	.6	.3	.8	.4
3.8	2.8	2.1	Profit Before Taxes	1.2	1.9	1.7	1.8	2.2	3.9
			RATIOS						
2.2	2.4	2.0	Current	2.3	1.8	2.0	2.3	2.0	2.6
1.6	1.6	1.5		1.5	1.4	1.4	1.5	1.4	1.5
1.2	1.2	1.2		.9	1.2	1.2	1.1	1.2	1.2
1.3	1.3	1.2	Quick	1.7	1.1	1.2	1.2	1.2	1.4
.9	.9	.8		.8	.9	.8	.8	.8	.9
.7	.6	.6		.5	.6	.5	.6	.6	.7
34 10.6	36 10.1	37 9.8	Sales/Receivables	30 12.0	38 9.7	34 10.7	38 9.5	37 9.8	45 8.1
46 8.0	46 8.0	48 7.6		47 7.7	48 7.6	41 8.8	49 7.4	46 7.9	50 7.3
61 6.0	61 6.0	62 5.9		61 6.0	72 5.1	59 6.2	66 5.5	58 6.3	61 6.0
33 10.9	37 9.8	38 9.5	Cost of Sales/Inventory	23 15.9	31 11.9	41 9.0	49 7.5	37 9.8	43 8.4
56 6.5	59 6.2	59 6.2		61 6.0	58 6.3	58 6.3	65 5.6	55 6.6	59 6.2
87 4.2	89 4.1	91 4.0		126 2.9	107 3.4	99 3.7	89 4.1	79 4.6	81 4.5
26 13.8	26 13.9	29 12.8	Cost of Sales/Payables	12 29.8	31 11.7	29 12.4	27 13.3	30 12.3	28 13.2
41 8.8	39 9.4	43 8.5		43 8.5	46 7.9	51 7.1	45 8.2	41 8.9	37 9.8
64 5.7	60 6.1	64 5.7		78 4.7	68 5.4	72 5.1	69 5.3	60 6.1	47 7.8
6.8	6.2	6.8	Sales/Working Capital	5.9	7.8	8.0	7.4	6.2	4.9
11.2	11.0	12.6		13.9	13.0	14.0	12.5	12.6	10.0
22.5	23.6	27.8		-72.9	26.7	27.4	29.6	27.7	21.8
9.7	7.2	8.4	EBIT/Interest	7.2	5.9	12.2	6.9	8.4	15.6
(283) 3.8	(302) 3.0	(315) 3.1		(32) 2.0	(77) 2.8	(41) 3.9	(58) 2.5	(61) 3.2	(46) 4.0
1.6	1.3	1.4		-1.8	.9	1.8	1.4	1.1	2.1
7.5	6.2	6.0	Net Profit + Depr., Dep., Amort./Cur. Mat. L/T/D		4.5	7.4	2.8	8.8	13.0
(128) 2.5	(142) 2.4	(126) 2.2		(28) 1.7	(10) 1.7	(29) 2.2	(32) 2.3	(21) 5.7	
1.0	.8	.9			.9	.5	.8	1.4	1.9
.1	.1	.1	Fixed/Worth	.2	.1	.1	.1	.1	.2
.3	.3	.3		.5	.3	.2	.4	.3	.3
.8	.7	.8		-21.6	.8	.7	.7	.8	.6
1.0	.9	1.0	Debt/Worth	.8	1.3	.8	.9	1.0	1.0
2.0	2.0	2.2		1.7	2.6	2.2	2.0	2.6	2.1
4.6	4.4	4.8		-230.5	5.1	5.4	4.8	4.1	4.3
45.2	39.6	41.1	% Profit Before Taxes/Tangible Net Worth	42.9	48.7	36.2	29.6	41.9	39.6
(289) 20.1	(317) 17.5	(316) 18.0		(30) 14.0	(79) 17.5	(42) 21.2	(58) 12.8	(60) 19.0	(47) 21.8
6.6	5.3	5.1		-12.7	.8	7.6	5.8	2.1	8.8
14.6	12.7	12.2	% Profit Before Taxes/Total Assets	13.9	12.2	11.7	8.7	13.4	15.0
5.9	5.1	5.4		5.0	5.5	5.2	3.9	5.1	7.8
1.9	1.2	1.1		-5.1	-.2	2.8	1.5	.5	2.9
74.4	75.1	80.2	Sales/Net Fixed Assets	70.6	88.0	169.5	59.3	74.9	56.6
34.4	35.6	37.8		23.7	42.2	60.7	36.9	37.9	33.4
14.6	14.4	13.9		11.0	11.0	17.3	13.9	13.7	14.2
4.0	3.8	3.8	Sales/Total Assets	4.6	4.1	4.1	3.5	3.8	3.4
3.1	3.0	3.0		2.9	3.0	3.2	2.8	3.0	2.8
2.2	2.2	2.1		1.9	1.9	2.5	2.2	2.0	2.2
.4	.4	.4	% Depr., Dep., Amort./Sales	.5	.5	.3	.4	.4	.4
(270) .8	(288) .9	(296) .8		(31) 1.4	(73) 1.1	(37) .8	(55) .7	(60) .7	(40) .7
1.7	2.0	1.8		3.4	1.8	1.4	1.6	2.0	1.7
2.5	2.6	2.6	% Officers', Directors', Owners' Comp/Sales	6.8	3.8	2.6	1.6	1.5	1.5
(139) 4.8	(148) 4.6	(150) 4.6		(22) 8.7	(50) 4.8	(22) 4.4	(24) 2.7	(22) 3.0	(10) 2.3
8.2	8.5	8.4		18.0	8.1	8.1	5.5	5.8	7.0
6055306M	6507349M	5794834M	Net Sales ($)	23693M	165448M	180628M	418489M	1007668M	3998908M
2102788M	2159715M	2251534M	Total Assets ($)	9034M	65725M	66761M	161651M	435464M	1512899M

M = $ thousand   MM = $ million
See Pages 1 through 15 for Explanation of Ratios and Data

WHOLESALERS—OFFICE EQUIPMENT. SIC# 5044

Current Data Sorted By Assets							Comparative Historical Data	
3	6	8				# Postretirement Benefits		
						Type of Statement		
1	7	21				Unqualified	29	21
7	32	32	6	3		Reviewed	67	79
27	51	5	2	1		Compiled	101	95
4	4					Tax Returns	1	1
13	17	19	1			Other	49	52
107 (4/1-9/30/94)			**146 (10/1/94-3/31/95)**				4/1/90-3/31/91	4/1/91-3/31/92
0-500M	500M-2MM	2-10MM	10-50MM	50-100MM	100-250MM		ALL	ALL
52	111	77	9	4		**NUMBER OF STATEMENTS**	247	248
%	%	%	%	%	%	**ASSETS**	%	%
7.7	5.6	4.7				Cash & Equivalents	6.4	6.8
34.0	34.5	31.1				Trade Receivables - (net)	29.1	30.1
37.8	38.8	33.3				Inventory	39.3	38.4
.5	1.3	2.4				All Other Current	2.1	1.6
80.0	80.2	71.5				Total Current	76.9	76.9
12.8	11.6	18.0				Fixed Assets (net)	15.1	15.6
2.9	2.0	2.2				Intangibles (net)	1.5	1.4
4.3	6.3	8.4				All Other Non-Current	6.5	6.1
100.0	100.0	100.0				Total	100.0	100.0
						LIABILITIES		
11.3	11.3	12.7				Notes Payable-Short Term	12.5	11.5
4.8	5.0	4.5				Cur. Mat. -L/T/D	4.5	4.7
23.7	21.6	16.9				Trade Payables	18.4	17.7
.6	.3	.2				Income Taxes Payable	.6	.4
12.4	14.2	15.4				All Other Current	13.8	14.2
52.9	52.4	49.7				Total Current	49.8	48.5
13.8	8.8	12.0				Long Term Debt	11.0	11.5
.0	.4	.2				Deferred Taxes	.7	.4
4.0	4.9	6.7				All Other-Non-Current	4.0	4.4
29.2	33.6	31.4				Net Worth	34.5	35.2
100.0	100.0	100.0				Total Liabilities & Net Worth	100.0	100.0
						INCOME DATA		
100.0	100.0	100.0				Net Sales	100.0	100.0
41.9	38.1	35.5				Gross Profit	40.9	41.0
38.6	35.6	31.8				Operating Expenses	38.1	38.5
3.3	2.4	3.7				Operating Profit	2.7	2.5
.4	.3	.9				All Other Expenses (net)	.5	.6
2.9	2.1	2.8				Profit Before Taxes	2.2	1.9
						RATIOS		
2.4	2.1	1.9					2.1	2.2
1.6	1.5	1.3				Current	1.5	1.6
1.3	1.3	1.1					1.2	1.2
1.2	1.1	.9					1.1	1.1
.8	.7	.7				Quick	.7	.7
.6	.5	.5					.5	.5
24 15.1	31 11.9	31 11.6					29 12.6	29 12.4
31 11.7	39 9.3	41 8.8				Sales/Receivables	37 9.9	38 9.7
40 9.2	48 7.6	53 6.9					45 8.1	47 7.8
42 8.7	45 8.2	49 7.4					58 6.3	58 6.3
74 4.9	79 4.6	74 4.9				Cost of Sales/Inventory	96 3.8	89 4.1
114 3.2	122 3.0	99 3.7					135 2.7	130 2.8
13 27.6	20 17.9	16 22.7					19 19.7	19 19.6
34 10.6	37 10.0	33 11.2				Cost of Sales/Payables	35 10.5	31 11.7
56 6.5	58 6.3	51 7.1					59 6.2	54 6.8
6.7	6.6	7.9					6.9	6.2
12.6	12.1	14.0				Sales/Working Capital	10.7	10.9
22.1	18.9	37.7					25.9	21.0
(49) 9.5	(104) 6.8	(69) 4.3					(222) 4.2	(222) 4.6
3.1	2.9	2.4				EBIT/Interest	2.1	2.2
1.4	1.8	1.6					1.2	1.1
(11) 2.7	(54) 3.5	(43) 3.5				Net Profit + Depr., Dep.,	(122) 3.5	(110) 2.9
1.2	1.4	1.8				Amort./Cur. Mat. L /T/D	1.5	1.2
.5	.4	1.1					.6	.6
.2	.2	.2					.2	.2
.3	.3	.5				Fixed/Worth	.4	.4
1.3	.6	1.2					1.0	.9
1.0	1.1	1.4					1.2	1.1
2.4	2.3	2.9				Debt/Worth	2.2	2.0
13.6	4.4	4.0					4.7	4.4
(45) 79.0	(106) 33.5	(74) 29.5				% Profit Before Taxes/Tangible	(232) 31.0	(239) 32.0
21.7	17.7	13.5				Net Worth	14.4	13.8
6.2	7.0	7.1					3.0	1.8
20.8	9.4	10.9					9.2	9.3
7.8	5.1	3.6				% Profit Before Taxes/Total	4.1	3.8
1.8	2.2	1.7				Assets	1.1	.5
79.1	56.2	49.8					45.2	45.8
35.5	34.2	20.6				Sales/Net Fixed Assets	24.0	26.7
24.1	17.7	8.7					12.7	11.6
4.9	3.8	3.2					3.5	3.4
3.5	3.0	2.5				Sales/Total Assets	2.8	2.8
2.8	2.3	2.1					2.0	2.2
(41) .6	(99) .8	(68) .6					(216) .8	(212) .8
1.0	1.1	1.4				% Depr., Dep., Amort./Sales	1.5	1.3
1.6	1.7	2.5					2.6	2.1
(25) 3.9	(62) 2.8	(27) 1.5					(115) 3.2	(119) 2.6
7.6	3.9	3.8				% Officers', Directors',	5.3	4.9
14.5	6.7	4.8				Owners' Comp/Sales	8.0	8.4
56309M	389162M	854857M	303314M	467729M		Net Sales ($)	1826461M	1999297M
13981M	125580M	328894M	150226M	284036M		Total Assets ($)	828305M	823735M

M = $ thousand   MM = $ million
See Pages 1 through 15 for Explanation of Ratios and Data

Comparative Historical Data				Current Data Sorted By Sales					
4	9	17	# Postretirement Benefits	2	4	3	5	3	
			Type of Statement		1	7	7	17	6
31	27	38	Unqualified		17	13	30	9	2
77	80	73	Reviewed	2	34	19	8	4	
92	88	84	Compiled	19	4	1			
4	9	8	Tax Returns	3					
49	61	50	Other	9	12	8	11	8	2
4/1/92-	4/1/93-	4/1/94-			107 (4/1-9/30/94)		146 (10/1/94-3/31/95)		
3/31/93	3/31/94	3/31/95		0-1MM	1-3MM	3-5MM	5-10MM	10-25MM	25MM & OVER
ALL	ALL	ALL							
253	265	253	NUMBER OF STATEMENTS	33	68	48	56	38	10
%	%	%	ASSETS	%	%	%	%	%	%
6.3	5.9	5.8	Cash & Equivalents	8.2	4.6	7.3	6.1	3.4	6.7
30.6	32.7	33.1	Trade Receivables - (net)	29.7	32.3	35.2	35.2	31.6	33.0
37.2	37.3	36.1	Inventory	36.9	41.5	34.8	34.4	33.3	22.1
1.4	1.6	1.6	All Other Current	.4	1.1	1.5	2.2	1.8	5.5
75.4	77.5	76.5	Total Current	75.1	79.5	78.8	77.9	70.1	67.3
15.7	14.3	14.2	Fixed Assets (net)	15.4	12.2	11.2	15.7	18.1	14.6
2.0	1.6	2.2	Intangibles (net)	3.1	1.9	2.6	1.7	2.3	1.0
6.8	6.6	7.1	All Other Non-Current	6.4	6.4	7.4	4.7	9.5	17.1
100.0	100.0	100.0	Total	100.0	100.0	100.0	100.0	100.0	100.0
			LIABILITIES						
11.1	13.3	11.7	Notes Payable-Short Term	9.8	11.6	12.2	10.4	15.7	8.1
4.9	3.9	4.8	Cur. Mat.-L /T/D	5.2	5.9	3.1	5.6	3.3	5.4
17.0	17.9	20.1	Trade Payables	19.0	21.5	20.6	23.2	15.6	11.6
.4	1.3	.4	Income Taxes Payable	.6	.4	.3	.3	.4	.2
13.3	15.2	14.3	All Other Current	14.3	12.7	15.8	14.5	13.8	18.3
46.7	51.6	51.3	Total Current	48.9	52.1	52.0	54.1	48.8	43.5
10.2	10.5	11.0	Long Term Debt	19.9	11.8	5.4	7.7	13.8	12.4
.7	.5	.3	Deferred Taxes	.0	.4	.1	.1	.3	2.2
4.8	5.1	5.2	All Other-Non-Current	3.0	5.4	5.2	5.9	5.9	3.1
37.5	32.3	32.2	Net Worth	28.1	30.3	37.3	32.1	31.1	38.8
100.0	100.0	100.0	Total Liabilities & Net Worth	100.0	100.0	100.0	100.0	100.0	100.0
			INCOME DATA						
100.0	100.0	100.0	Net Sales	100.0	100.0	100.0	100.0	100.0	100.0
40.7	38.9	38.3	Gross Profit	49.2	39.8	34.4	36.8	32.9	39.4
37.7	36.1	35.1	Operating Expenses	42.4	37.6	32.0	34.2	29.9	33.4
2.9	2.8	3.2	Operating Profit	6.9	2.2	2.5	2.6	3.0	6.0
.3	.4	.5	All Other Expenses (net)	2.1	.3	.1	.6	.1	.6
2.7	2.4	2.7	Profit Before Taxes	4.7	1.9	2.4	2.0	2.8	5.4
			RATIOS						
2.3	2.1	2.1		3.0	2.0	2.1	1.9	2.1	2.4
1.7	1.5	1.5	Current	1.7	1.5	1.4	1.3	1.4	1.6
1.2	1.2	1.2		1.2	1.3	1.3	1.2	1.1	1.2
1.2	1.0	1.0		1.1	.9	1.3	1.1	1.0	1.4
(252) .8	.7	.7	Quick	.8	.7	.7	.7	.8	.8
.5	.5	.5		.6	.5	.5	.5	.5	.5
30 12.3	31 11.9	30 12.3		22 16.8	30 12.3	29 12.6	32 11.5	32 11.3	40 9.1
38 9.7	38 9.5	39 9.3	Sales/Receivables	31 11.8	38 9.6	39 9.3	39 9.3	42 8.6	49 7.4
47 7.7	48 7.6	49 7.4		43 8.4	46 7.9	49 7.4	49 7.4	54 6.7	66 5.5
57 6.4	51 7.1	45 8.2		43 8.4	54 6.7	32 11.4	40 9.1	48 7.6	41 9.0
87 4.2	83 4.4	78 4.7	Cost of Sales/Inventory	91 4.0	101 3.6	63 5.8	76 4.8	64 5.7	61 6.0
122 3.0	114 3.2	111 3.3		140 2.6	130 2.8	94 3.9	111 3.3	85 4.3	91 4.0
19 19.4	17 21.1	17 20.9		12 30.9	24 15.5	14 26.1	26 14.1	14 25.6	12 31.2
33 10.9	31 11.8	35 10.4	Cost of Sales/Payables	34 10.7	39 9.4	26 14.2	42 8.6	27 13.7	25 14.4
51 7.2	51 7.2	55 6.6		64 5.7	64 5.7	43 8.5	64 5.7	43 8.4	40 9.2
5.9	6.8	6.8		5.4	5.8	8.5	9.2	7.7	4.7
9.7	11.3	12.5	Sales/Working Capital	11.6	10.8	14.4	16.4	13.4	8.4
21.9	30.2	21.8		23.7	20.0	20.6	24.1	61.7	NM
7.7	5.7	6.3		10.0	5.0	10.6	5.0	5.9	
(232) 2.6	(244) 2.7	(234) 2.9	EBIT/Interest	(31) 3.3	(65) 2.5	(44) 4.6	(50) 2.3	(35) 3.1	
1.4	1.3	1.8		1.4	1.3	2.6	1.6	1.8	
3.5	3.9	3.5	Net Profit + Depr., Dep.,		2.2	3.7	4.4	4.5	
(120) 1.3	(108) 1.4	(116) 1.5	Amort./Cur. Mat. L/T/D	(31) 1.1	(20) 1.5	(35) 1.9	(18) 1.6		
.7	.7	.7		.3	.2	1.1	1.1		
.2	.2	.2		.1	.2	.2	.2	.2	.3
.4	.4	.4	Fixed/Worth	.3	.4	.3	.4	.5	.5
.9	.9	.9		2.2	.8	.6	.8	1.5	.6
.9	1.2	1.1		.8	1.5	.8	1.7	1.2	.6
2.1	2.3	2.5	Debt/Worth	3.2	2.4	1.9	2.5	3.3	2.3
4.1	4.9	4.4		17.3	4.3	5.2	3.7	4.2	3.5
30.3	34.6	35.7	% Profit Before Taxes/Tangible	94.4	28.6	41.2	27.8	33.9	
(234) 14.0	(250) 14.4	(237) 17.7	Net Worth	(29) 33.3	(63) 14.0	(45) 24.1	(55) 13.4	(36) 22.0	
3.9	5.0	7.4		8.5	4.4	7.9	7.5	8.7	
10.2	11.3	11.3	% Profit Before Taxes/Total	18.4	8.6	15.8	9.1	11.7	19.6
4.3	4.4	5.1	Assets	5.7	4.0	6.2	3.6	6.0	8.8
1.2	1.2	2.0		2.3	1.3	3.0	1.7	2.5	3.8
44.8	56.2	56.0		111.7	54.8	65.5	49.4	51.5	26.3
24.5	29.3	31.9	Sales/Net Fixed Assets	35.4	31.8	38.3	27.6	17.6	14.3
11.9	14.5	14.2		15.3	14.4	20.0	14.8	7.4	10.0
3.5	3.6	3.7		4.6	3.5	4.0	3.5	3.5	3.0
2.7	2.9	2.9	Sales/Total Assets	3.0	2.7	3.3	2.9	2.6	2.0
2.2	2.2	2.1		2.1	2.1	2.5	2.2	2.0	1.3
.7	.7	.7		.7	.8	.7	.6	.5	
(228) 1.3	(236) 1.2	(218) 1.2	% Depr., Dep., Amort./Sales	(25) 1.3	(60) 1.2	(42) 1.1	(50) 1.2	(33) 1.1	
2.5	2.0	1.9		3.1	1.9	1.5	1.8	2.7	
3.2	3.2	2.7	% Officers', Directors',	3.7	3.9	1.9	2.2	1.2	
(130) 5.1	(134) 5.2	(117) 4.3	Owners' Comp/Sales	(14) 9.0	(45) 5.3	(21) 3.4	(23) 3.3	(13) 2.2	
8.6	7.9	7.4		18.4	8.4	5.4	5.3	4.4	
3180735M	2467614M	2071371M	Net Sales ($)	21581M	132301M	184225M	397591M	598933M	736740M
1336509M	1000700M	902717M	Total Assets ($)	13556M	53076M	60867M	144930M	234735M	395553M

© Robert Morris Associates 1995

M = $ thousand   MM = $ million
See Pages 1 through 15 for Explanation of Ratios and Data

Current Data Sorted By Assets   Comparative Historical Data

	0-500M	500M-2MM	2-10MM	10-50MM	50-100MM	100-250MM		4/1/90-3/31/91 ALL	4/1/91-3/31/92 ALL
# Postretirement Benefits		5	3	1			Type of Statement		
Unqualified		3	8	2	1			16	17
Reviewed		27	16					51	47
Compiled	12	26	8	1				50	40
Tax Returns	4	2	1					2	2
Other	6	8	10	2				24	24
		49 (4/1-9/30/94)		88 (10/1/94-3/31/95)					
NUMBER OF STATEMENTS	22	66	43	5	1			143	130

ASSETS
	0-500M %	500M-2MM %	2-10MM %	10-50MM %	50-100MM %	100-250MM %		ALL %	ALL %
Cash & Equivalents	10.8	7.3	4.6					5.7	7.0
Trade Receivables - (net)	30.1	35.5	30.6					35.0	33.6
Inventory	38.2	35.8	38.5					37.0	37.0
All Other Current	.1	3.2	1.1					1.9	1.7
Total Current	79.3	81.8	74.8					79.7	79.3
Fixed Assets (net)	13.7	11.5	16.8					13.3	14.6
Intangibles (net)	2.4	1.0	1.8					1.4	1.5
All Other Non-Current	4.7	5.6	6.6					5.6	4.6
Total	100.0	100.0	100.0					100.0	100.0

LIABILITIES
	0-500M	500M-2MM	2-10MM					ALL	ALL
Notes Payable-Short Term	9.7	9.1	14.1					13.4	12.6
Cur. Mat. -L/T/D	4.6	3.2	2.6					4.1	3.1
Trade Payables	31.7	25.7	19.4					22.7	20.9
Income Taxes Payable	.4	.6	.2					.7	.4
All Other Current	14.2	8.0	9.5					7.7	7.2
Total Current	60.6	46.6	45.7					48.7	44.1
Long Term Debt	12.2	10.8	10.7					11.0	11.4
Deferred Taxes	.0	.2	.5					.2	.1
All Other-Non-Current	2.6	4.6	3.0					3.3	3.6
Net Worth	24.5	37.8	40.1					36.8	40.8
Total Liabilities & Net Worth	100.0	100.0	100.0					100.0	100.0

INCOME DATA
	0-500M	500M-2MM	2-10MM					ALL	ALL
Net Sales	100.0	100.0	100.0					100.0	100.0
Gross Profit	36.6	28.1	27.0					30.6	30.6
Operating Expenses	33.7	25.3	24.2					28.0	28.7
Operating Profit	2.9	2.8	2.9					2.6	1.9
All Other Expenses (net)	.7	.8	.2					.4	.4
Profit Before Taxes	2.1	2.0	2.6					2.2	1.4

RATIOS
	0-500M	500M-2MM	2-10MM					ALL	ALL
Current	2.3	2.5	2.3					2.4	2.6
	1.5	1.8	1.6					1.7	1.9
	1.0	1.4	1.2					1.2	1.3
Quick	1.1	1.3	1.0					1.3	1.4
	.8	.9	.7					.8	.9
	.4	.7	.5					.6	.5
Sales/Receivables	18 19.8	27 13.7	29 12.8					29 12.5	29 12.5
	24 15.2	39 9.4	39 9.4					41 9.0	40 9.2
	38 9.6	51 7.2	52 7.0					54 6.8	49 7.4
Cost of Sales/Inventory	25 14.6	32 11.4	40 9.2					38 9.5	37 9.8
	48 7.6	58 6.3	63 5.8					59 6.2	64 5.7
	114 3.2	94 3.9	96 3.8					96 3.8	96 3.8
Cost of Sales/Payables	23 15.8	21 17.0	20 18.3					21 17.6	20 18.0
	42 8.7	35 10.5	30 12.2					36 10.1	32 11.4
	87 4.2	51 7.1	43 8.4					59 6.2	50 7.3
Sales/Working Capital	6.8	6.3	6.0					6.3	5.3
	12.7	8.4	11.4					10.3	8.6
	NM	15.8	27.3					21.2	17.8
EBIT/Interest	(20) 7.7	(61) 8.3	(42) 7.4					(130) 5.5	(117) 4.9
	2.1	3.5	3.2					2.3	2.1
	1.3	1.9	1.4					1.3	.8
Net Profit + Depr., Dep., Amort./Cur. Mat. L /T/D		(27) 5.5	(22) 4.4					(87) 5.3	(52) 5.1
		2.8	2.2					2.0	1.8
		.9	.9					.6	.8
Fixed/Worth	.1	.1	.1					.1	.1
	.7	.2	.3					.3	.3
	-1.1	.8	.8					.6	.7
Debt/Worth	1.0	.8	.7					.9	.7
	3.5	1.4	1.9					1.7	1.5
	-11.6	3.6	3.3					3.9	4.1
% Profit Before Taxes/Tangible Net Worth	(16) 64.5	(62) 34.4	39.8					(134) 31.9	(122) 21.6
	27.6	17.5	10.3					14.0	9.4
	4.3	5.6	2.6					3.9	.3
% Profit Before Taxes/Total Assets	14.4	9.9	12.4					10.2	9.1
	4.4	5.2	4.5					3.9	3.2
	1.7	1.9	.6					1.0	-.0
Sales/Net Fixed Assets	123.7	172.0	72.0					74.6	70.7
	37.0	49.5	34.8					39.0	33.6
	15.0	17.1	13.2					16.7	14.4
Sales/Total Assets	4.9	4.2	4.1					3.9	3.9
	3.7	3.1	3.1					3.1	3.0
	2.1	2.2	2.1					2.4	2.3
% Depr., Dep., Amort./Sales	(16) .4	(55) .3	(41) .4					(132) .5	(117) .4
	.8	.7	.6					.8	.8
	1.7	1.3	1.3					1.4	1.7
% Officers', Directors', Owners' Comp/Sales	(16) 2.7	(37) 2.3	(30) 1.5					(67) 2.0	(68) 2.4
	4.7	4.1	2.4					4.4	4.0
	8.3	5.6	3.9					7.4	7.5
Net Sales ($)	25053M	267996M	525997M	291079M	163389M			1293505M	906766M
Total Assets ($)	7092M	75289M	172256M	108697M	53390M			500846M	345211M

© Robert Morris Associates 1995

M = $ thousand   MM = $ million
See Pages 1 through 15 for Explanation of Ratios and Data

WHOLESALERS—RESTAURANT & HOTEL SUPPLIES, FIXTURES & EQUIPMENT. SIC# 5046

Comparative Historical Data 1	5	9	# Postretirement Benefits	Current Data Sorted By Sales 1	3	2	2	1	
			Type of Statement						
13	13	14	Unqualified		1	1	3	4	5
60	53	43	Reviewed		8	14	11	9	1
54	40	47	Compiled	7	21	7	9	2	1
3	6	7	Tax Returns	1	4	1	1		
34	29	26	Other	4	3	7	7	3	2
4/1/92-3/31/93	4/1/93-3/31/94	4/1/94-3/31/95		49 (4/1-9/30/94)			88 (10/1/94-3/31/95)		
ALL	ALL	ALL		0-1MM	1-3MM	3-5MM	5-10MM	10-25MM	25MM & OVER
164	141	137	**NUMBER OF STATEMENTS**	12	37	30	31	18	9
%	%	%	**ASSETS**	%	%	%	%	%	%
5.6	6.3	7.0	Cash & Equivalents	9.6	8.3	4.6	6.6	7.4	
34.1	34.7	32.7	Trade Receivables - (net)	23.9	30.1	40.8	32.2	33.9	
38.6	37.4	36.8	Inventory	39.3	37.2	35.4	37.9	38.3	
1.8	1.7	2.0	All Other Current	.9	2.0	4.0	.9	1.0	
80.2	80.0	78.4	Total Current	73.7	77.7	84.9	77.6	80.6	
12.6	13.3	14.4	Fixed Assets (net)	14.7	14.8	10.0	16.4	10.1	
1.5	1.3	1.6	Intangibles (net)	2.4	2.0	.9	.7	.8	
5.7	5.4	5.6	All Other Non-Current	9.2	5.5	4.2	5.3	8.4	
100.0	100.0	100.0	Total	100.0	100.0	100.0	100.0	100.0	
			LIABILITIES						
12.8	12.9	10.8	Notes Payable-Short Term	11.8	7.8	9.0	11.0	18.9	
3.0	3.6	3.2	Cur. Mat.-L/T/D	1.9	5.1	2.8	2.8	2.2	
23.9	20.0	24.4	Trade Payables	25.0	25.3	25.4	22.4	25.3	
.3	.6	.4	Income Taxes Payable	.7	.6	.4	.4	.3	
7.9	8.0	9.8	All Other Current	10.0	11.7	7.9	7.3	11.1	
47.9	45.2	48.7	Total Current	49.5	50.6	45.5	43.9	57.8	
12.7	11.6	11.1	Long Term Debt	18.4	11.1	11.5	8.5	7.9	
.2	.1	.3	Deferred Taxes	.0	.0	.2	.7	.0	
2.8	3.5	3.6	All Other-Non-Current	2.4	4.2	4.4	3.9	2.2	
36.4	39.7	36.3	Net Worth	29.8	34.1	38.4	43.0	32.1	
100.0	100.0	100.0	Total Liabilities & Net Worth	100.0	100.0	100.0	100.0	100.0	
			INCOME DATA						
100.0	100.0	100.0	Net Sales	100.0	100.0	100.0	100.0	100.0	
29.3	28.6	28.9	Gross Profit	42.5	33.1	25.6	26.3	24.9	
27.0	26.5	26.0	Operating Expenses	35.1	30.7	23.1	23.9	22.7	
2.3	2.1	2.9	Operating Profit	7.4	2.4	2.5	2.4	2.2	
.3	.3	.6	All Other Expenses (net)	3.1	.7	.1	.0	.5	
1.9	1.8	2.3	Profit Before Taxes	4.3	1.6	2.4	2.4	1.7	
			RATIOS						
2.7	2.8	2.4	Current	3.3	2.5	3.2	2.3	2.1	
1.7	1.8	1.6		1.7	1.6	1.8	1.8	1.3	
1.2	1.4	1.2		.9	1.1	1.5	1.4	1.0	
1.5	1.3	1.2	Quick	1.3	1.3	1.6	1.1	1.0	
.9	.9	.9		.6	.9	1.0	.9	.7	
.5	.6	.5		.3	.5	.7	.7	.5	
30 12.1	25 14.5	23 15.6	Sales/Receivables	19 19.7	22 16.5	34 10.8	28 13.0	21 17.3	
41 9.0	39 9.3	37 9.8		26 14.3	34 10.6	47 7.7	38 9.6	31 11.7	
54 6.7	51 7.2	50 7.3		76 4.8	41 8.8	60 6.1	46 7.9	45 8.1	
38 9.6	39 9.4	33 10.9	Cost of Sales/Inventory	24 14.9	41 8.8	32 11.3	34 10.6	30 12.0	
60 6.1	58 6.3	58 6.3		174 2.1	57 6.4	68 5.4	53 6.9	42 8.7	
107 3.4	85 4.3	91 4.0		243 1.5	114 3.2	83 4.4	83 4.4	68 5.4	
23 15.7	17 21.6	22 16.9	Cost of Sales/Payables	20 18.2	20 18.1	23 15.6	19 19.3	20 17.9	
39 9.3	26 13.8	33 11.0		78 4.7	35 10.3	39 9.4	30 12.5	29 12.5	
54 6.7	40 9.1	50 7.3		126 2.9	70 5.2	52 7.0	43 8.5	35 10.3	
5.4	5.9	6.4	Sales/Working Capital	2.4	6.0	6.6	7.7	7.2	
8.8	8.9	10.9		7.4	9.0	8.3	9.6	20.3	
21.4	16.9	27.8		NM	37.7	12.9	17.2	462.5	
(145) 5.0	(131) 7.5	(129) 8.0	EBIT/Interest	(10) 4.9	(36) 9.4	(29) 7.8	(28) 8.4	(17) 7.6	
2.5	3.1	3.3		2.3	2.5	3.5	3.8	1.7	
1.0	1.6	1.6		1.3	1.3	1.6	1.8	1.2	
(71) 3.1	(55) 3.3	(57) 6.5	Net Profit + Depr., Dep., Amort./Cur. Mat. L/T/D		(12) 9.3		(21) 4.8		
1.3	1.5	2.6			1.4		2.2		
.4	.7	1.0			.7		1.0		
.1	.1	.1	Fixed/Worth	.1	.1	.1	.1	.1	
.4	.3	.3		.7	.4	.2	.2	.2	
.9	.8	.9		NM	1.4	.7	.6	.8	
.8	.7	.8	Debt/Worth	.7	.7	.7	.7	1.1	
2.0	1.6	1.9		2.1	1.4	1.7	1.2	2.7	
5.6	3.6	3.9		NM	4.0	3.3	2.8	6.4	
(148) 30.1	(132) 34.4	(127) 37.5	% Profit Before Taxes/Tangible Net Worth		(31) 37.5	(29) 42.5	34.7	41.5	
13.2	13.1	17.6			16.2	17.4	17.6	15.5	
2.4	4.6	5.4			2.5	3.0	6.1	2.6	
9.1	10.7	10.5	% Profit Before Taxes/Total Assets	12.6	11.8	8.5	11.6	11.9	
3.7	4.6	4.9		2.1	5.4	4.4	5.3	3.5	
.3	1.6	1.5		1.8	.7	1.1	3.2	.6	
69.5	70.6	113.5	Sales/Net Fixed Assets	232.8	78.3	142.9	78.7	179.7	
37.7	32.9	36.5		17.1	28.5	62.2	35.4	57.0	
17.1	16.1	15.0		4.9	16.0	14.3	13.2	22.3	
3.8	4.0	4.2	Sales/Total Assets	3.2	4.3	4.0	4.3	4.5	
3.0	3.1	3.1		1.9	2.9	3.1	3.3	4.1	
2.2	2.4	2.2		.8	2.1	2.4	2.8	3.1	
(144) .4	(124) .5	(118) .4	% Depr., Dep., Amort./Sales		(29) .4	(25) .5	(30) .3	(17) .3	
.7	.7	.7			1.0	.7	.5	.7	
1.3	1.4	1.3			1.9	1.3	1.2	.8	
(83) 3.0	(74) 2.3	(85) 2.1	% Officers', Directors', Owners' Comp/Sales		(24) 2.5	(20) 2.1	(18) 1.8	(13) 1.7	
4.5	4.1	3.5			4.1	3.0	2.8	2.5	
6.7	7.0	5.6			6.1	5.7	6.4	3.9	
1423633M	1684694M	1273514M	Net Sales ($)	7271M	71506M	119286M	223716M	313609M	538126M
512180M	551454M	416724M	Total Assets ($)	4700M	27111M	43671M	76837M	86104M	178301M

M = $ thousand   MM = $ million
See Pages 1 through 15 for Explanation of Ratios and Data

WHOLESALERS—TRANSPORTATION EQUIPMENT & SUPPLIES, EXCEPT MOTOR VEHICLES. SIC# 5088

Current Data Sorted By Assets | **Comparative Historical Data**

						# Postretirement Benefits / Type of Statement		
1	5	1	2					
1	4	10	6		1	Unqualified	30	26
7	14	17	4			Reviewed	44	52
3	19	6	1			Compiled	40	35
6	1	1				Tax Returns	3	
	9	11	5		1	Other	22	23
	46 (4/1-9/30/94)		81 (10/1/94-3/31/95)				4/1/90-3/31/91	4/1/91-3/31/92
0-500M	500M-2MM	2-10MM	10-50MM	50-100MM	100-250MM		ALL	ALL
17	47	45	16		2	NUMBER OF STATEMENTS	139	136

%	%	%	%	%	%	ASSETS	%	%
13.5	7.3	5.3	6.7			Cash & Equivalents	6.6	7.7
33.9	28.0	28.4	25.6			Trade Receivables - (net)	29.4	27.6
25.2	37.9	44.1	46.6			Inventory	39.5	41.6
1.6	2.2	1.8	1.4			All Other Current	2.9	1.6
74.3	75.3	79.7	80.2			Total Current	78.4	78.5
7.8	18.2	13.9	14.2			Fixed Assets (net)	14.4	14.4
2.3	.1	.3	1.1			Intangibles (net)	1.1	.8
15.7	6.4	6.1	4.4			All Other Non-Current	6.2	6.3
100.0	100.0	100.0	100.0			Total	100.0	100.0

						LIABILITIES		
15.6	11.8	17.9	19.6			Notes Payable-Short Term	16.6	18.3
4.8	3.3	2.5	1.9			Cur. Mat. -L/T/D	3.4	4.6
20.3	23.5	21.6	19.8			Trade Payables	22.8	21.0
1.1	.4	.7	.4			Income Taxes Payable	.6	.4
9.0	5.6	8.4	6.3			All Other Current	7.1	8.3
50.8	44.7	51.1	48.0			Total Current	50.5	52.6
7.3	13.4	9.0	10.5			Long Term Debt	13.6	10.0
.6	.5	.1	.4			Deferred Taxes	.2	.3
.0	.8	2.4	.4			All Other-Non-Current	3.6	2.1
41.3	40.6	37.3	40.7			Net Worth	32.1	35.1
100.0	100.0	100.0	100.0			Total Liabilities & Net Worth	100.0	100.0

						INCOME DATA		
100.0	100.0	100.0	100.0			Net Sales	100.0	100.0
35.4	25.4	28.2	27.4			Gross Profit	27.8	28.8
32.9	22.6	23.4	21.8			Operating Expenses	24.5	25.6
2.5	2.9	4.8	5.6			Operating Profit	3.2	3.2
.4	1.0	1.2	.4			All Other Expenses (net)	1.0	1.4
2.1	1.9	3.6	5.2			Profit Before Taxes	2.2	1.7

						RATIOS		
3.1	2.5	2.0	2.1				2.3	2.3
1.4	1.7	1.5	1.5			Current	1.5	1.5
1.0	1.2	1.2	1.2				1.2	1.2
2.6	1.1	1.0	.8				1.2	1.1
1.2	.8	.6	.6			Quick	.7	.7
.4	.6	.4	.4				.4	.4
0 UND	18 20.5	27 13.6	37 9.9				26 13.9	26 13.8
25 14.4	37 9.8	45 8.1	48 7.6			Sales/Receivables	37 9.8	42 8.6
62 5.9	50 7.3	63 5.8	59 6.2				54 6.8	54 6.7
0 UND	33 11.0	41 8.8	72 5.1				41 8.9	49 7.4
20 18.7	57 6.4	94 3.9	94 3.9			Cost of Sales/Inventory	73 5.0	87 4.2
64 5.7	101 3.6	159 2.3	159 2.3				114 3.2	140 2.6
14 27.0	17 21.1	30 12.3	25 14.8				23 15.9	20 18.4
32 11.4	32 11.5	42 8.7	35 10.4			Cost of Sales/Payables	37 10.0	38 9.5
59 6.2	59 6.2	62 5.9	51 7.2				60 6.1	60 6.1
6.9	5.9	4.2	3.3				5.4	5.3
19.7	9.1	8.9	9.2			Sales/Working Capital	10.1	9.0
-113.6	39.0	19.5	27.8				25.8	30.5
(13) 13.9	(45) 6.0	(41) 8.4	(12) 14.0				(132) 5.4	(128) 4.7
4.7	2.6	2.8	3.9			EBIT/Interest	1.9	1.7
1.2	1.5	1.3	2.7				1.1	.9
	(19) 5.3	(19) 6.3				Net Profit + Depr., Dep.,	(79) 5.8	(54) 3.0
	1.4	2.2				Amort./Cur. Mat. L /T/D	1.8	1.2
	.9	.6					.4	.3
.1	.1	.1	.1				.1	.1
.2	.3	.2	.5			Fixed/Worth	.4	.3
.4	.8	.6	.8				1.0	.9
.5	.7	1.0	.7				1.0	.9
1.7	1.8	1.8	2.5			Debt/Worth	2.1	1.9
6.4	3.0	3.7	3.8				5.6	5.4
(16) 40.2	32.6	44.8	45.1			% Profit Before Taxes/Tangible	(130) 33.5	(128) 32.5
23.1	14.8	15.0	25.8			Net Worth	16.5	12.7
1.8	4.8	5.8	10.0				3.0	1.6
17.4	11.9	11.5	11.3			% Profit Before Taxes/Total	11.2	9.0
7.8	5.9	5.3	8.3			Assets	4.2	3.2
.4	1.8	1.6	4.2				.7	-.3
192.8	59.2	79.5	34.4				57.1	65.7
82.2	24.4	43.9	19.7			Sales/Net Fixed Assets	29.3	26.9
35.9	11.7	13.8	9.5				12.5	9.9
5.2	3.8	3.1	3.1				3.6	3.3
3.2	3.0	2.4	2.3			Sales/Total Assets	2.5	2.4
1.7	2.1	1.6	1.3				1.8	1.8
(13) .2	(44) .4	(41) .4	(14) .7				(126) .5	(124) .5
.6	.8	.7	1.0			% Depr., Dep., Amort./Sales	.9	.9
.7	1.3	1.2	1.7				1.5	1.8
(10) 1.9	(23) 2.1	(23) 1.6				% Officers', Directors',	(69) 2.3	(58) 2.6
4.6	3.7	3.4				Owners' Comp/Sales	4.2	4.2
14.4	5.8	6.3					6.2	7.1
26642M	166308M	470750M	618884M		431673M	Net Sales ($)	1680454M	1309436M
5638M	57617M	195928M	282962M		295733M	Total Assets ($)	867760M	702483M

M = $ thousand   MM = $ million
See Pages 1 through 15 for Explanation of Ratios and Data

Comparative Historical Data | **Current Data Sorted By Sales**

	8	9	# Postretirement Benefits / Type of Statement	2	1	1	2	2	1
12	18	21	Unqualified	1		4	2	8	6
37	36	36	Reviewed	1	7	8	9	8	3
28	35	33	Compiled	2	12	11	3	4	1
	6	5	Tax Returns		3		2		
33	30	32	Other	3	6	4	10	4	5
4/1/92-3/31/93 ALL	4/1/93-3/31/94 ALL	4/1/94-3/31/95 ALL		46 (4/1-9/30/94)			81 (10/1/94-3/31/95)		
				0-1MM	1-3MM	3-5MM	5-10MM	10-25MM	25MM & OVER
110	125	127	NUMBER OF STATEMENTS	7	28	27	26	24	15
%	%	%	**ASSETS**	%	%	%	%	%	%
6.5	5.8	7.5	Cash & Equivalents		7.2	7.0	7.8	8.1	4.3
30.6	26.2	28.4	Trade Receivables - (net)		38.2	26.0	26.6	31.3	24.5
40.5	43.0	39.3	Inventory		28.8	40.2	46.7	43.1	44.5
1.6	1.6	2.1	All Other Current		2.7	2.0	1.8	.9	3.5
79.2	76.7	77.3	Total Current		76.9	75.2	82.8	83.4	76.9
14.2	17.3	14.8	Fixed Assets (net)		16.0	19.0	9.8	11.0	16.8
.3	.5	.7	Intangibles (net)		.8	.4	.1	.3	2.2
6.3	5.5	7.2	All Other Non-Current		6.2	5.4	7.3	5.3	4.1
100.0	100.0	100.0	Total		100.0	100.0	100.0	100.0	100.0
			LIABILITIES						
18.6	16.4	15.4	Notes Payable-Short Term		12.5	10.9	15.4	17.8	23.8
3.2	3.1	3.0	Cur. Mat.-L/T/D		4.1	3.2	1.7	2.5	2.4
19.7	18.9	21.7	Trade Payables		23.0	21.3	21.8	23.1	20.9
.6	.8	.6	Income Taxes Payable		.7	.8	.7	.4	.4
7.2	8.0	7.7	All Other Current		6.9	6.1	8.6	6.8	11.4
49.3	47.2	48.3	Total Current		47.3	42.4	48.2	50.6	58.9
8.6	12.4	10.8	Long Term Debt		11.0	14.2	6.4	8.8	11.0
.2	.5	.4	Deferred Taxes		.8	.4	.1	.1	.5
1.8	3.0	1.2	All Other-Non-Current		.4	.8	1.6	3.1	.4
40.0	37.0	39.2	Net Worth		40.5	42.2	43.6	37.4	29.1
100.0	100.0	100.0	Total Liabilities & Net Worth		100.0	100.0	100.0	100.0	100.0
			INCOME DATA						
100.0	100.0	100.0	Net Sales		100.0	100.0	100.0	100.0	100.0
29.4	29.2	27.8	Gross Profit		31.4	26.3	25.9	25.6	22.0
26.2	27.0	24.0	Operating Expenses		28.6	23.4	21.4	20.4	18.7
3.2	2.2	3.8	Operating Profit		2.8	2.9	4.5	5.1	3.4
.9	.6	.9	All Other Expenses (net)		.1	.9	1.4	.5	.8
2.3	1.6	2.9	Profit Before Taxes		2.6	2.0	3.2	4.6	2.5
			RATIOS						
2.3	2.5	2.4	Current		2.3	2.9	2.6	2.3	1.5
1.7	1.7	1.5			1.7	1.7	1.7	1.5	1.3
1.2	1.2	1.2			1.3	1.3	1.3	1.2	1.2
1.2	1.0	1.1	Quick		1.3	1.1	1.1	1.1	.7
.8	.7	.7			.9	.8	.7	.8	.5
.4	.4	.4			.7	.4	.4	.5	.3
28 13.0	22 16.3	21 17.8	Sales/Receivables		31 11.6	14 26.0	24 15.4	27 13.5	20 18.2
41 8.9	37 10.0	40 9.1			39 9.4	39 9.3	43 8.5	50 7.3	40 9.1
56 6.5	51 7.2	55 6.6			65 5.6	49 7.5	51 7.1	63 5.8	50 7.3
34 10.8	38 9.6	33 11.1	Cost of Sales/Inventory		13 28.7	33 11.0	50 7.3	35 10.5	45 8.2
78 4.7	87 4.2	72 5.1			58 6.3	54 6.8	81 4.5	91 4.0	78 4.7
130 2.8	140 2.6	122 3.0			101 3.6	111 3.3	166 2.2	122 3.0	111 3.3
23 16.0	17 20.9	22 16.6	Cost of Sales/Payables		20 18.1	16 22.9	24 15.0	24 14.9	19 19.5
35 10.3	34 10.7	36 10.2			39 9.3	31 11.8	40 9.2	38 9.6	31 11.7
54 6.7	51 7.2	59 6.2			61 6.0	50 7.3	62 5.9	57 6.4	47 7.8
4.5	5.2	5.6	Sales/Working Capital		5.8	4.9	3.9	5.2	8.5
8.7	8.7	10.1			12.7	8.5	8.9	10.8	13.0
24.2	26.0	23.7			26.2	18.3	13.7	20.5	35.6
(102) 6.9	(119) 4.6	(113) 7.5	EBIT/Interest		(25) 5.5	(24) 4.2	(24) 9.9	(22) 20.1	(13) 7.8
2.6	2.1	2.8			2.0	2.7	4.6	2.9	3.7
1.2	1.0	1.4			1.2	1.6	2.0	1.3	2.4
(47) 3.4	(54) 8.5	(48) 5.3	Net Profit + Depr., Dep., Amort./Cur. Mat. L/T/D			(14) 5.4		(10) 13.7	
1.5	1.5	1.9				1.5		1.9	
.7	.5	.7				.9		.6	
.1	.1	.1	Fixed/Worth		.1	.1	.1	.1	.4
.3	.4	.3			.3	.3	.2	.2	.6
.7	.8	.7			.7	1.2	.5	.5	.9
.7	.9	.9	Debt/Worth		.7	.6	.7	1.0	2.3
1.7	1.9	1.9			2.1	1.7	1.4	2.2	3.0
3.4	4.1	3.5			2.8	3.1	2.3	4.4	4.8
(108) 29.5	(120) 25.3	(126) 40.0	% Profit Before Taxes/Tangible Net Worth		34.6	31.9	39.3	56.2	46.9
12.2	9.1	17.4			8.7	18.7	12.4	28.9	31.3
2.5	.7	4.8			2.6	6.7	5.6	9.5	4.0
11.3	7.3	11.7	% Profit Before Taxes/Total Assets		10.8	11.6	12.5	21.9	9.8
4.8	2.9	5.5			3.4	6.1	5.5	5.7	8.2
1.0	.1	1.6			.9	3.1	2.6	1.4	2.6
66.4	59.7	73.5	Sales/Net Fixed Assets		151.4	60.8	70.3	92.4	34.9
30.3	26.5	32.7			33.9	31.1	45.9	36.0	19.4
10.7	11.1	13.2			13.7	7.5	16.4	18.3	6.1
3.6	3.5	3.6	Sales/Total Assets		4.2	3.6	3.3	3.5	3.8
2.6	2.6	2.6			3.1	2.7	2.7	2.7	2.4
1.7	1.7	1.8			1.8	2.0	1.8	1.7	2.0
(96) .5	(118) .5	(112) .4	% Depr., Dep., Amort./Sales		(24) .3	(26) .4	(24) .3	(21) .3	(12) .6
.8	1.0	.7			.7	.6	.6	.8	1.2
1.8	1.7	1.3			1.1	1.3	.9	1.2	1.5
(55) 2.0	(66) 2.2	(61) 1.9	% Officers', Directors', Owners' Comp/Sales		(17) 1.9	(10) 2.1	(17) 1.9	(11) 1.6	
4.1	4.1	3.4			3.4	4.6	3.2	3.3	
6.4	6.4	6.0			6.8	6.0	7.7	4.7	
923062M	906726M	1714257M	Net Sales ($)	2890M	55334M	104309M	173083M	349701M	1028940M
524976M	437648M	837878M	Total Assets ($)	1964M	22641M	46794M	76526M	155262M	534691M

© Robert Morris Associates 1995

M = $ thousand   MM = $ million
See Pages 1 through 15 for Explanation of Ratios and Data

Current Data Sorted By Assets   **Comparative Historical Data**

0-500M	500M-2MM	2-10MM	10-50MM	50-100MM	100-250MM	# Postretirement Benefits / Type of Statement	4/1/90-3/31/91 ALL	4/1/91-3/31/92 ALL
1	4	12	10	2		Unqualified	28	28
4	28	32	1			Reviewed	72	63
15	29	16	1			Compiled	67	63
1	4	1				Tax Returns	1	2
10	16	12	3	1		Other	25	45
	73 (4/1-9/30/94)		129 (10/1/94-3/31/95)					
31	81	73	14	3		**NUMBER OF STATEMENTS**	193	201
%	%	%	%	%	%	**ASSETS**	%	%
5.4	4.3	4.4	1.6			Cash & Equivalents	5.2	5.9
42.5	43.2	45.2	47.5			Trade Receivables - (net)	39.1	39.0
26.3	31.2	28.5	27.6			Inventory	32.2	29.4
.4	1.3	1.0	1.1			All Other Current	.9	1.1
74.6	80.0	79.1	77.7			Total Current	77.4	75.5
16.2	13.5	13.6	14.5			Fixed Assets (net)	14.9	16.2
2.5	.8	1.4	.5			Intangibles (net)	1.6	2.0
6.7	5.7	5.9	7.3			All Other Non-Current	6.1	6.3
100.0	100.0	100.0	100.0			Total	100.0	100.0
						LIABILITIES		
10.0	12.9	16.2	19.9			Notes Payable-Short Term	12.9	12.7
6.5	2.8	1.7	1.1			Cur. Mat. -L/T/D	3.7	3.1
27.5	30.4	30.4	31.5			Trade Payables	25.4	28.6
.4	.1	.2	.2			Income Taxes Payable	.5	.5
10.3	6.3	6.6	8.1			All Other Current	6.3	6.6
54.6	52.6	55.0	60.8			Total Current	48.7	51.5
10.6	10.7	12.4	5.3			Long Term Debt	11.6	11.8
.1	.3	.2	.0			Deferred Taxes	.3	.3
1.7	2.9	2.8	4.2			All Other-Non-Current	3.4	2.2
32.9	33.5	29.5	29.7			Net Worth	36.0	34.2
100.0	100.0	100.0	100.0			Total Liabilities & Net Worth	100.0	100.0
						INCOME DATA		
100.0	100.0	100.0	100.0			Net Sales	100.0	100.0
27.6	26.7	20.7	17.1			Gross Profit	26.1	25.6
24.4	25.0	19.1	14.8			Operating Expenses	23.9	23.8
3.2	1.7	1.6	2.4			Operating Profit	2.2	1.8
.4	.4	.4	.6			All Other Expenses (net)	.5	.6
2.8	1.3	1.3	1.7			Profit Before Taxes	1.7	1.3
						RATIOS		
2.6	2.0	1.9	1.7			Current	2.3	2.1
1.3	1.5	1.5	1.3				1.6	1.5
.9	1.2	1.2	1.1				1.3	1.1
1.3	1.3	1.1	1.0			Quick	1.4	1.4
.9	.9	.9	.8				.9	.9
.6	.7	.7	.6				.6	.6
30 12.0	33 11.1	32 11.3	33 11.0			Sales/Receivables	30 12.3	30 12.2
36 10.2	41 9.0	41 8.9	43 8.5				37 9.9	37 9.8
43 8.4	50 7.3	51 7.2	50 7.3				46 8.0	46 7.9
11 33.2	29 12.4	26 14.3	13 28.6			Cost of Sales/Inventory	24 15.2	23 16.2
34 10.6	44 8.3	39 9.4	31 11.7				39 9.3	37 9.8
50 7.3	64 5.7	51 7.2	62 5.9				60 6.1	59 6.2
18 20.6	23 16.2	22 16.4	21 17.0			Cost of Sales/Payables	16 22.2	20 18.5
29 12.5	39 9.4	33 11.0	27 13.4				27 13.4	32 11.3
55 6.6	54 6.8	47 7.7	51 7.1				46 7.9	51 7.2
9.5	8.3	9.6	10.0			Sales/Working Capital	8.3	9.0
19.7	14.8	15.0	19.0				13.2	15.4
-54.6	28.4	30.2	NM				29.5	40.0
8.1	7.2	6.0	10.0			EBIT/Interest	7.0	5.5
(27) 3.8	(77) 2.0	(69) 2.5	2.6				(179) 2.6	(182) 2.4
1.1	.9	1.5	1.5				1.2	1.2
	4.4	7.0				Net Profit + Depr., Dep., Amort./Cur. Mat. L /T/D	5.7	7.4
	(33) 1.2	(32) 3.0					(101) 2.4	(85) 2.2
	.1	1.6					1.2	.9
.1	.1	.1	.2			Fixed/Worth	.2	.2
.2	.3	.2	.6				.3	.4
1.1	1.0	.8	1.2				1.0	1.1
1.2	1.1	1.3	1.1			Debt/Worth	.8	1.0
2.5	1.9	2.4	3.1				2.1	2.1
4.3	4.1	4.9	11.9				4.5	4.6
49.8	24.5	33.1	32.7			% Profit Before Taxes/Tangible Net Worth	31.3	28.5
(28) 17.1	(74) 7.8	(67) 14.1	(13) 13.4				(180) 15.0	(184) 14.7
1.2	.1	5.5	5.8				4.3	3.0
16.8	8.8	10.0	10.7			% Profit Before Taxes/Total Assets	10.7	9.8
5.4	3.0	4.4	3.1				4.6	4.3
.3	-.1	2.0	1.8				.8	.5
129.3	82.1	121.9	73.8			Sales/Net Fixed Assets	76.6	74.5
41.8	40.0	49.5	28.4				38.2	36.7
20.6	21.4	13.7	21.2				17.6	16.6
5.2	4.3	4.6	4.2			Sales/Total Assets	4.7	4.7
4.3	3.7	3.8	3.5				3.8	3.7
3.1	3.1	2.8	2.9				2.9	2.9
.5	.3	.3	.2			% Depr., Dep., Amort./Sales	.4	.4
(24) .9	(74) .7	(67) .5	(10) .6				(168) .8	(182) .7
1.3	.9	.9	1.0				1.3	1.1
3.6	1.8	1.2				% Officers', Directors', Owners' Comp/Sales	1.9	2.0
(18) 4.7	(47) 3.2	(32) 2.8					(95) 3.3	(89) 3.3
7.6	4.4	4.3					4.9	5.7
38806M	358665M	1241840M	1098217M	486991M		Net Sales ($)	2752623M	2680414M
9313M	93060M	325731M	305531M	240386M		Total Assets ($)	691770M	694510M

© Robert Morris Associates 1995

M = $ thousand   MM = $ million
See Pages 1 through 15 for Explanation of Ratios and Data

Comparative Historical Data — columns 1, 5, 17
Current Data Sorted By Sales — columns 1, 4, 2, 2, 7, 1

# Postretirement Benefits / Type of Statement	1	5	17	1	4	2	2	7	1
Unqualified	35	34	29	1		4	1	6	17
Reviewed	75	74	64	1	7	10	20	22	4
Compiled	57	56	61	6	18	11	14	7	5
Tax Returns	4	1	6		3	2	1		
Other	38	36	42	6	13	6	5	7	5

	4/1/92-3/31/93 ALL	4/1/93-3/31/94 ALL	4/1/94-3/31/95 ALL		73 (4/1-9/30/94)			129 (10/1/94-3/31/95)		
				0-1MM	1-3MM	3-5MM	5-10MM	10-25MM	25MM & OVER
NUMBER OF STATEMENTS	209	201	202	14	41	33	41	42	31

ASSETS (%)

Line item	Hist 92-93	Hist 93-94	Hist 94-95	0-1MM	1-3MM	3-5MM	5-10MM	10-25MM	25MM & OVER
Cash & Equivalents	5.5	5.7	4.3	3.7	5.6	4.6	5.4	3.0	2.7
Trade Receivables - (net)	41.0	42.1	43.8	40.9	41.3	41.9	44.2	45.0	48.1
Inventory	30.3	28.4	29.2	23.6	29.3	30.6	31.0	30.2	26.2
All Other Current	1.0	1.4	1.1	.6	1.4	.5	1.1	1.0	1.3
Total Current	77.8	77.6	78.3	68.9	77.5	77.7	81.7	79.2	78.4
Fixed Assets (net)	14.6	14.5	14.3	20.1	15.9	15.7	10.4	14.7	12.8
Intangibles (net)	1.3	1.3	1.2	2.0	1.7	.8	1.9	.6	.8
All Other Non-Current	6.3	6.7	6.1	9.1	4.8	5.8	6.0	5.4	8.0
Total	100.0	100.0	100.0	100.0	100.0	100.0	100.0	100.0	100.0

LIABILITIES

Line item	Hist 92-93	Hist 93-94	Hist 94-95	0-1MM	1-3MM	3-5MM	5-10MM	10-25MM	25MM & OVER
Notes Payable-Short Term	14.3	14.0	14.0	11.7	9.1	10.2	15.2	17.3	19.2
Cur. Mat.-L/T/D	2.2	3.0	2.9	9.0	4.0	3.3	1.6	1.9	1.2
Trade Payables	27.1	26.9	29.8	24.2	29.2	28.7	32.6	28.1	32.9
Income Taxes Payable	.5	1.3	.2	.6	.1	.2	.1	.1	.3
All Other Current	6.6	7.0	7.1	12.7	7.8	5.4	7.0	6.0	7.3
Total Current	50.7	52.1	53.9	58.1	50.3	47.8	56.5	53.4	60.8
Long Term Debt	10.4	10.2	11.3	9.9	14.9	12.1	9.2	12.1	8.0
Deferred Taxes	.1	.2	.2	.0	.2	.6	.0	.3	.3
All Other-Non-Current	3.2	3.0	2.8	1.7	3.3	2.3	3.4	2.4	2.8
Net Worth	35.6	34.5	31.7	30.3	31.3	37.3	30.9	31.8	28.2
Total Liabilities & Net Worth	100.0	100.0	100.0	100.0	100.0	100.0	100.0	100.0	100.0

INCOME DATA

Line item	Hist 92-93	Hist 93-94	Hist 94-95	0-1MM	1-3MM	3-5MM	5-10MM	10-25MM	25MM & OVER
Net Sales	100.0	100.0	100.0	100.0	100.0	100.0	100.0	100.0	100.0
Gross Profit	25.0	23.5	23.9	28.6	28.3	25.8	24.3	20.3	18.1
Operating Expenses	22.6	22.2	21.9	25.3	25.2	24.2	23.6	18.5	15.7
Operating Profit	2.4	1.3	2.0	3.3	3.1	1.5	.7	1.8	2.4
All Other Expenses (net)	.5	.4	.4	.3	.5	.3	.5	.5	.3
Profit Before Taxes	1.9	.9	1.6	3.0	2.6	1.2	.2	1.4	2.1

RATIOS

Ratio	Hist 92-93	Hist 93-94	Hist 94-95	0-1MM	1-3MM	3-5MM	5-10MM	10-25MM	25MM & OVER
Current	2.1	2.1	2.0	2.7	2.3	2.4	1.8	1.8	1.8
	1.5	1.5	1.5	1.1	1.5	1.7	1.5	1.5	1.3
	1.2	1.2	1.2	.8	1.2	1.2	1.2	1.2	1.1
Quick	1.3	1.2	1.2	1.7	1.2	1.4	1.1	1.1	1.1
	.9	.9	.9	.7	.9	1.0	.9	.9	.8
	.6	.7	.7	.4	.7	.8	.7	.7	.7
Sales/Receivables	29 12.5	33 11.0	32 11.3	30 12.1	32 11.3	33 11.1	32 11.4	32 11.5	33 11.1
	38 9.7	38 9.5	40 9.1	37 9.9	40 9.1	43 8.5	40 9.1	39 9.4	41 9.0
	47 7.8	46 7.9	49 7.5	46 7.9	51 7.1	54 6.8	47 7.7	46 7.9	47 7.8
Cost of Sales/Inventory	22 16.7	24 14.9	25 14.4	6 64.5	25 14.8	26 13.9	29 12.7	25 14.7	13 27.4
	37 9.8	36 10.2	39 9.3	35 10.3	47 7.8	38 9.5	44 8.3	37 9.8	37 9.8
	56 6.5	54 6.8	56 6.5	70 5.2	63 5.8	69 5.3	55 6.6	49 7.5	55 6.6
Cost of Sales/Payables	18 20.2	19 19.0	22 16.8	9 39.7	20 18.2	24 14.9	26 13.8	20 18.2	21 17.2
	30 12.1	30 12.0	35 10.5	34 10.8	36 10.2	42 8.7	39 9.4	29 12.5	29 12.4
	43 8.4	43 8.5	51 7.1	76 4.8	63 5.8	51 7.1	54 6.8	42 8.6	50 7.3
Sales/Working Capital	9.4	8.7	9.1	8.4	6.9	7.2	9.8	11.1	9.3
	14.8	14.7	15.3	48.7	13.9	13.2	16.3	15.6	17.3
	32.1	35.5	36.5	-20.5	41.1	22.9	27.7	29.8	53.8
EBIT/Interest	(195) 7.0	(190) 7.2	(190) 6.9	(10) 7.0	(40) 7.5	(31) 7.5	(39) 7.4	(41) 4.8	(29) 11.7
	2.6	2.6	2.5	.8	3.7	2.4	2.0	2.6	3.4
	1.3	1.2	1.4	-1.0	1.2	1.1	.6	1.5	1.8
Net Profit + Depr., Dep., Amort./Cur. Mat. L/T/D	(78) 4.8	(68) 5.0	(78) 5.0		(12) 2.6	(16) 10.9	(12) 3.9	(24) 7.0	(11) 10.0
	3.0	1.7	2.3		1.0	2.1	2.4	2.3	2.4
	1.0	.4	1.0		-.3	.7	-1.0	1.5	
Fixed/Worth	.1	.1	.1	.0	.1	.1	.1	.1	.1
	.3	.3	.3	.3	.4	.3	.2	.2	.3
	.9	.9	1.0	6.3	1.5	.9	.8	.8	.9
Debt/Worth	1.0	.9	1.2	.6	1.2	.9	1.2	1.4	1.1
	1.9	2.2	2.3	3.0	2.3	1.6	2.2	2.3	2.5
	4.0	5.6	4.3	17.1	4.0	4.0	5.1	4.0	5.7
% Profit Before Taxes/Tangible Net Worth	(199) 33.2	(190) 30.1	(185) 30.2	(12) 49.8	(36) 41.6	(31) 28.0	(37) 19.4	(41) 32.7	(28) 41.7
	16.0	14.2	12.6	.6	18.0	20.4	9.1	11.0	18.2
	3.4	2.3	3.5	-3.9	3.6	2.4	.7	5.1	7.8
% Profit Before Taxes/Total Assets	10.7	8.6	10.3	39.0	12.6	11.3	6.2	8.6	11.3
	4.9	3.4	3.9	.6	5.5	3.5	2.6	4.1	5.1
	1.0	.3	.9	-1.1	.3	.5	-.5	1.5	2.2
Sales/Net Fixed Assets	104.8	96.6	91.6	268.2	71.2	94.4	91.4	122.7	119.3
	40.2	40.4	41.7	37.0	36.9	34.1	61.1	51.7	46.1
	18.5	17.5	15.7	9.2	14.2	13.6	35.7	13.8	25.5
Sales/Total Assets	5.0	4.7	4.6	4.8	4.6	3.9	3.9	5.0	4.5
	3.9	3.7	3.8	3.6	3.6	3.5	3.9	3.9	3.7
	3.0	3.0	3.0	2.0	2.7	3.1	3.1	3.3	3.0
% Depr., Dep., Amort./Sales	(182) .4	(175) .4	(177) .3		(37) .3	(31) .3	(36) .4	(40) .2	(24) .2
	.7	.6	.6		.7	.7	.8	.5	.4
	1.0	1.1	1.0		1.3	1.1	.9	.9	.9
% Officers', Directors', Owners' Comp/Sales	(97) 1.9	(103) 1.8	(101) 1.7		(26) 2.4	(16) 2.4	(25) 1.7	(21) .9	
	2.8	3.2	3.2		4.0	3.8	3.1	1.6	
	4.9	4.9	4.7		7.0	5.7	4.1	2.9	
Net Sales ($)	3427961M	3505849M	3224519M	8318M	78047M	133452M	286635M	652551M	2065516M
Total Assets ($)	850819M	1048770M	974021M	3262M	25413M	39457M	81601M	175584M	648704M

M = $ thousand   MM = $ million
See Pages 1 through 15 for Explanation of Ratios and Data

WHOLESALERS—PRINTING & WRITING PAPER. SIC# 5111

Current Data Sorted By Assets   **Comparative Historical Data**

Type of Statement / # Postretirement Benefits

Type of Statement	0-500M	500M-2MM	2-10MM	10-50MM	50-100MM	100-250MM	4/1/90-3/31/91 ALL	4/1/91-3/31/92 ALL
Unqualified		1	14	8		2	20	27
Reviewed	3	8	9	1			22	23
Compiled	5	10	3	1			26	18
Tax Returns							1	1
Other	3	1	10	7			18	21

Date ranges: 30 (4/1-9/30/94) · 56 (10/1/94-3/31/95)

Main Table

	0-500M	500M-2MM	2-10MM	10-50MM	50-100MM	100-250MM	4/1/90-3/31/91 ALL	4/1/91-3/31/92 ALL
NUMBER OF STATEMENTS	11	20	36	17		2	87	90
ASSETS	%	%	%	%	%	%	%	%
Cash & Equivalents	7.2	6.0	4.1	1.8			4.4	5.1
Trade Receivables - (net)	38.6	45.9	48.5	54.1			43.9	42.4
Inventory	17.0	30.2	28.9	26.3			28.1	30.4
All Other Current	2.1	.4	.8	1.1			1.8	2.3
Total Current	64.9	82.4	82.3	83.2			78.2	80.2
Fixed Assets (net)	23.6	13.2	11.2	10.2			15.1	11.0
Intangibles (net)	3.8	.8	1.2	.7			.8	1.0
All Other Non-Current	7.7	3.5	5.3	5.8			6.0	7.7
Total	100.0	100.0	100.0	100.0			100.0	100.0
LIABILITIES								
Notes Payable-Short Term	18.9	17.1	22.6	19.7			16.5	18.1
Cur. Mat. -L/T/D	2.3	3.9	1.3	.9			2.4	1.7
Trade Payables	21.1	31.6	25.6	28.8			24.9	24.0
Income Taxes Payable	1.1	.4	.3	.2			.5	.5
All Other Current	6.9	6.0	7.7	4.1			5.4	7.5
Total Current	50.3	59.0	57.5	53.7			49.7	51.8
Long Term Debt	19.5	9.2	4.7	6.4			12.1	11.0
Deferred Taxes	.0	.4	.4	.1			.3	.2
All Other-Non-Current	5.2	6.0	4.2	3.7			3.9	2.2
Net Worth	25.0	25.4	33.1	36.1			34.0	34.8
Total Liabilities & Net Worth	100.0	100.0	100.0	100.0			100.0	100.0
INCOME DATA								
Net Sales	100.0	100.0	100.0	100.0			100.0	100.0
Gross Profit	39.8	28.6	19.1	14.8			21.0	21.1
Operating Expenses	33.5	27.1	16.2	13.7			18.8	19.7
Operating Profit	6.3	1.5	2.9	1.1			2.1	1.4
All Other Expenses (net)	3.0	.9	.5	.2			.9	.5
Profit Before Taxes	3.4	.6	2.4	.9			1.2	.9
RATIOS								
Current	1.8	1.8	1.7	1.9			2.4	2.1
	1.4	1.3	1.4	1.7			1.6	1.6
	.9	1.1	1.2	1.2			1.2	1.2
Quick	1.2	1.1	1.3	1.2			1.4	1.5
	1.0	.8	.9	1.0			1.0	.9
	.8	.6	.7	.9			.7	.6
Sales/Receivables	13 27.5	30 12.1	42 8.7	41 9.0			34 10.6	32 11.3
	35 10.4	41 8.8	47 7.8	46 8.0			41 8.8	39 9.3
	59 6.2	50 7.3	60 6.1	50 7.3			54 6.7	48 7.6
Cost of Sales/Inventory	4 87.3	27 13.7	21 17.4	23 16.1			20 18.7	18 20.1
	23 15.9	43 8.4	34 10.6	28 13.2			33 11.2	34 10.6
	33 11.0	55 6.6	59 6.2	40 9.2			58 6.3	64 5.7
Cost of Sales/Payables	9 41.6	19 19.1	19 19.4	20 18.0			18 20.3	17 21.3
	33 10.9	41 8.9	26 13.9	28 13.2			30 12.3	24 14.9
	51 7.1	59 6.2	38 9.7	31 11.8			43 8.4	39 9.4
Sales/Working Capital	12.2	11.3	8.8	9.4			7.5	8.0
	21.6	22.5	17.6	11.9			13.7	13.4
	-155.7	59.2	28.8	35.6			32.3	38.1
EBIT/Interest	4.9	7.5	(33) 7.7	(16) 3.9			(81) 6.8	(85) 4.5
	2.1	4.3	2.8	2.6			2.1	2.3
	1.3	-.6	1.8	1.5			1.2	1.2
Net Profit + Depr., Dep., Amort./Cur. Mat. L./T/D			(18) 13.3				(47) 8.4	(43) 4.8
			3.1				3.2	2.8
			2.2				1.1	1.3
Fixed/Worth	.3	.2	.1	.2			.1	.1
	.6	.4	.3	.3			.4	.3
	2.1	3.3	.6	.5			.8	.6
Debt/Worth	1.4	1.0	1.3	1.1			1.1	1.0
	2.0	3.2	2.4	1.8			2.1	1.9
	2.9	25.6	5.3	2.8			4.9	4.5
% Profit Before Taxes/Tangible Net Worth	(10) 64.7	(17) 58.5	36.1	15.6			(83) 25.7	(89) 19.8
	28.2	13.4	24.7	10.1			15.4	10.6
	-.6	-9.9	10.3	6.3			2.8	2.5
% Profit Before Taxes/Total Assets	14.8	7.6	12.2	5.0			9.5	7.2
	4.2	4.2	5.6	4.0			4.3	2.6
	.4	-6.5	3.0	1.4			.7	.7
Sales/Net Fixed Assets	32.7	123.8	222.5	125.8			130.9	143.7
	21.7	55.0	44.7	39.4			37.7	44.0
	15.5	26.8	21.6	24.1			16.4	20.3
Sales/Total Assets	5.9	6.0	4.5	4.5			4.6	4.9
	4.0	4.0	3.5	3.9			3.6	3.8
	2.7	2.6	2.8	3.5			2.7	2.7
% Depr., Dep., Amort./Sales		(18) .2	(33) .2	(13) .2			(77) .3	(72) .2
		.4	.5	.4			.5	.4
		1.0	1.1	.7			1.0	.8
% Officers', Directors', Owners' Comp/Sales		(12) 2.2	(12) 1.1				(35) 1.4	(39) 2.1
		3.2	3.0				2.6	3.9
		4.8	9.0				5.1	6.7
Net Sales ($)	13147M	92091M	628107M	1803424M		876403M	3221443M	4748157M
Total Assets ($)	3479M	21637M	176853M	413842M		242815M	863717M	1285706M

M = $ thousand   MM = $ million
See Pages 1 through 15 for Explanation of Ratios and Data

Comparative Historical Data | Current Data Sorted By Sales

1	5	3		0-1MM	1-3MM	3-5MM	5-10MM	10-25MM	25MM & OVER
			# Postretirement Benefits					1	2
			Type of Statement						
26	17	25	Unqualified	1	4	3	2	10	13
28	20	21	Reviewed				6	5	2
15	14	19	Compiled	3	7	4	1	3	1
1		1	Tax Returns						
22	23	21	Other	2	2		3	5	9
4/1/92-3/31/93	4/1/93-3/31/94	4/1/94-3/31/95		30 (4/1-9/30/94)			56 (10/1/94-3/31/95)		
ALL	ALL	ALL							
92	75	86	**NUMBER OF STATEMENTS**	6	13	7	12	23	25
%	%	%	**ASSETS**	%	%	%	%	%	%
7.2	6.3	4.4	Cash & Equivalents		6.7		7.6	2.8	2.2
42.1	45.0	47.6	Trade Receivables - (net)		44.9		49.9	50.1	52.6
25.4	27.0	27.3	Inventory		25.1		20.2	30.5	28.5
2.0	1.9	.9	All Other Current		.8		.7	.7	1.2
76.8	80.2	80.3	Total Current		77.6		78.4	84.1	84.4
13.7	13.6	13.1	Fixed Assets (net)		14.9		14.2	10.1	9.9
2.6	1.3	1.3	Intangibles (net)		1.2		2.6	.5	.6
6.9	4.8	5.2	All Other Non-Current		6.3		4.8	5.3	5.0
100.0	100.0	100.0	Total		100.0		100.0	100.0	100.0
			LIABILITIES						
16.8	16.5	20.4	Notes Payable-Short Term		11.6		20.7	19.6	24.8
2.7	2.8	1.9	Cur. Mat.-L/T/D		5.3		1.3	1.3	.9
21.6	23.2	26.8	Trade Payables		29.2		22.8	28.7	26.8
.3	1.1	.4	Income Taxes Payable		.2		.1	.4	.2
8.1	6.1	6.5	All Other Current		9.1		6.8	8.5	4.2
49.6	49.7	56.1	Total Current		55.3		51.7	58.4	57.0
11.8	10.9	8.1	Long Term Debt		16.1		5.5	3.4	6.8
.3	.4	.3	Deferred Taxes		.1		.7	.3	.1
1.7	2.3	4.6	All Other-Non-Current		10.6		4.7	3.9	2.9
36.6	36.8	30.9	Net Worth		17.9		37.4	34.0	33.2
100.0	100.0	100.0	Total Liabilities & Net Worth		100.0		100.0	100.0	100.0
			INCOME DATA						
100.0	100.0	100.0	Net Sales		100.0		100.0	100.0	100.0
23.3	23.0	22.6	Gross Profit		32.3		30.6	15.8	13.3
20.1	21.6	20.5	Operating Expenses		30.1		27.3	13.2	13.7
3.2	1.4	2.1	Operating Profit		2.3		3.3	2.6	-.4
.7	.2	.9	All Other Expenses (net)		1.5		.4	.4	.3
2.5	1.2	1.3	Profit Before Taxes		.8		2.8	2.2	-.8
			RATIOS						
2.2	2.2	1.8	Current		1.9		2.0	1.7	1.8
1.6	1.6	1.5			1.5		1.3	1.5	1.6
1.2	1.2	1.2			1.0		1.2	1.2	1.2
1.6	1.5	1.2	Quick		1.2		1.4	1.4	1.2
1.0	1.0	.9			1.0		1.1	1.0	1.0
.7	.7	.8			.7		.9	.7	.8
33 11.1	37 9.9	37 9.8	Sales/Receivables	27 13.3		42 8.7		37 9.9	41 9.0
41 8.8	44 8.3	46 8.0		41 9.0		50 7.3		46 8.0	46 8.0
49 7.4	53 6.9	55 6.6		64 5.7		62 5.9		54 6.8	51 7.1
15 23.7	20 18.4	20 18.2	Cost of Sales/Inventory	11 33.4		6 64.9		16 22.4	23 16.1
30 12.3	34 10.7	33 11.2		30 12.3		32 11.4		31 11.7	29 12.5
61 6.0	58 6.3	52 7.0		49 7.4		72 5.1		51 7.1	45 8.2
15 24.1	17 21.1	20 18.7	Cost of Sales/Payables	15 25.0		27 13.7		18 20.8	20 18.0
23 16.2	25 14.7	28 12.9		41 9.0		36 10.2		23 16.1	29 13.6
38 9.5	37 9.9	42 8.7		69 5.3		39 9.4		31 11.7	29 12.4
8.2	7.6	9.9	Sales/Working Capital	8.6		6.6		9.7	10.4
14.2	14.6	16.8		16.1		16.2		18.1	13.0
37.2	28.1	30.2		NM		28.5		26.8	29.5
(82) 6.2	(69) 8.6	(82) 5.6	EBIT/Interest	5.8		(11) 7.5		(21) 9.2	(24) 3.0
2.9	2.9	2.7		1.3		4.7		4.7	2.3
1.2	.7	1.3		-1.1		3.2		1.9	1.6
(45) 6.1	(33) 9.3	(34) 10.1	Net Profit + Depr., Dep., Amort./Cur. Mat. L/T/D						(13) 7.3
2.7	2.3	2.9							3.4
.7	.3	.9							2.2
.1	.1	.1	Fixed/Worth		.1		.2	.1	.2
.3	.3	.3			.6		.3	.2	.3
.9	.7	.7			10.2		.5	.5	.5
.8	.8	1.3	Debt/Worth		1.2		.8	1.2	1.3
2.0	2.0	2.3			2.3		2.7	2.0	1.9
5.0	4.4	5.3			31.4		5.4	5.3	4.7
(85) 33.3	(74) 33.3	(82) 40.9	% Profit Before Taxes/Tangible Net Worth	(11) 115.8		40.0		43.1	24.1
19.2	9.5	18.6		13.5		26.2		22.2	10.1
4.6	-.3	3.6		-12.0		17.0		10.2	6.3
11.8	7.6	10.7	% Profit Before Taxes/Total Assets	7.7		12.7		12.2	5.0
5.6	3.6	4.5		3.8		7.9		6.1	3.8
1.3	-.4	1.0		-6.5		4.7		3.0	1.4
105.7	95.8	138.0	Sales/Net Fixed Assets	78.8		112.0		322.8	125.8
38.1	48.2	39.4		32.7		29.7		87.5	39.4
19.1	20.3	22.1		20.4		15.3		25.5	24.1
4.7	4.7	4.6	Sales/Total Assets	4.9		4.2		6.4	4.5
3.9	3.8	3.8		3.9		2.9		4.3	3.8
2.7	2.9	2.8		2.4		2.4		2.8	3.3
(82) .2	(65) .3	(74) .3	% Depr., Dep., Amort./Sales	(11) .3		(11) .2		(21) .1	(20) .3
.7	.6	.5		.6		.5		.3	.4
1.1	1.1	1.1		1.3		1.6		.6	.7
(33) 1.6	(33) 1.6	(35) 1.5	% Officers', Directors', Owners' Comp/Sales						
3.4	2.6	3.1							
6.0	6.7	6.6							
3167356M	2921055M	3413172M	Net Sales ($)	3139M	25594M	28819M	81893M	421604M	2852123M
882940M	733572M	858626M	Total Assets ($)	2200M	8436M	7344M	26939M	111087M	702620M

M = $ thousand   MM = $ million
See Pages 1 through 15 for Explanation of Ratios and Data

Current Data Sorted By Assets   Comparative Historical Data

	0-500M	500M-2MM	2-10MM	10-50MM	50-100MM	100-250MM		4/1/90-3/31/91 ALL	4/1/91-3/31/92 ALL
# Postretirement Benefits	2	6	1	2					
Type of Statement									
Unqualified		3	14	8	1	2		33	22
Reviewed	6	25	22	2				55	55
Compiled	27	31	7	1		1		65	64
Tax Returns	4	2						2	4
Other	13	18	6	2				39	48
		75 (4/1-9/30/94)		120 (10/1/94-3/31/95)					
NUMBER OF STATEMENTS	50	79	49	13	2	2		194	193
	%	%	%	%	%	%		%	%
ASSETS									
Cash & Equivalents	6.5	5.3	5.5	5.1				4.9	6.7
Trade Receivables - (net)	44.2	45.9	41.8	38.5				40.7	40.9
Inventory	20.8	25.9	26.4	23.8				29.9	27.8
All Other Current	3.9	1.2	1.2	2.2				2.3	2.2
Total Current	75.4	78.4	74.8	69.5				77.7	77.7
Fixed Assets (net)	17.0	12.6	17.8	19.6				14.7	14.4
Intangibles (net)	3.9	2.3	1.5	2.6				1.1	1.5
All Other Non-Current	3.7	6.7	5.9	8.2				6.5	6.4
Total	100.0	100.0	100.0	100.0				100.0	100.0
LIABILITIES									
Notes Payable-Short Term	16.3	13.6	14.9	19.4				15.5	16.1
Cur. Mat. -L/T/D	4.4	2.9	2.3	2.5				4.0	3.6
Trade Payables	25.2	26.5	20.5	17.8				22.9	24.8
Income Taxes Payable	.1	.3	.3	.1				.5	.5
All Other Current	7.5	8.5	10.1	6.6				7.3	8.2
Total Current	53.6	51.8	48.1	46.3				50.2	53.3
Long Term Debt	10.6	10.2	11.4	13.0				11.0	11.5
Deferred Taxes	.1	.1	.3	1.8				.2	.2
All Other-Non-Current	2.9	4.5	3.4	1.2				2.2	2.0
Net Worth	32.7	33.5	36.8	37.8				36.4	32.9
Total Liabilities & Net Worth	100.0	100.0	100.0	100.0				100.0	100.0
INCOME DATA									
Net Sales	100.0	100.0	100.0	100.0				100.0	100.0
Gross Profit	36.7	31.2	30.4	32.6				31.4	32.0
Operating Expenses	34.1	29.0	28.0	28.4				29.6	29.5
Operating Profit	2.6	2.3	2.4	4.2				1.9	2.5
All Other Expenses (net)	.4	.5	.5	.8				.7	.7
Profit Before Taxes	2.2	1.8	1.8	3.4				1.2	1.8
RATIOS									
Current	2.0	2.2	2.0	2.0				2.3	2.0
	1.4	1.5	1.5	1.5				1.6	1.5
	1.1	1.2	1.3	1.2				1.2	1.1
Quick	1.5	1.3	1.3	1.1				1.3	1.3
	1.0	1.0	1.1	.8				.9	.9
	.6	.8	.8	.7				.6	.6
Sales/Receivables	29 12.8	33 11.1	38 9.6	45 8.2				34 10.7	31 11.6
	38 9.6	41 8.8	46 7.9	50 7.3				41 8.9	40 9.1
	46 8.0	49 7.5	56 6.5	61 6.0				49 7.4	49 7.5
Cost of Sales/Inventory	3 136.6	17 21.4	25 14.7	28 12.9				24 15.4	16 22.4
	21 17.2	32 11.4	42 8.7	42 8.6				43 8.4	37 10.0
	61 6.0	55 6.6	65 5.6	68 5.4				76 4.8	70 5.2
Cost of Sales/Payables	18 19.9	22 16.5	22 16.9	23 15.6				20 17.9	20 18.5
	33 11.1	31 11.6	33 10.9	37 9.9				32 11.3	34 10.8
	49 7.4	47 7.8	43 8.5	42 8.6				47 7.8	50 7.3
Sales/Working Capital	10.1	8.0	6.9	7.8				7.7	8.9
	21.3	14.5	13.0	12.5				13.1	14.8
	88.3	25.1	24.2	24.9				31.9	47.7
EBIT/Interest	(42) 8.3	(76) 7.7	(46) 6.3	(12) 5.5				(174) 4.7	(181) 5.5
	2.9	3.5	2.5	3.5				2.0	2.2
	1.1	1.9	1.6	2.1				1.2	1.3
Net Profit + Depr., Dep., Amort./Cur. Mat. L /T/D	(11) 2.2	(32) 3.5	(28) 4.0					(103) 4.9	(78) 5.8
	.7	2.0	2.2					1.9	1.9
	.5	1.3	1.0					.7	.7
Fixed/Worth	.2	.2	.2	.2				.1	.2
	.6	.3	.5	.5				.3	.4
	3.5	1.0	.7	.8				.8	1.0
Debt/Worth	1.0	1.2	1.3	1.3				.9	1.0
	2.1	2.0	2.0	2.0				1.8	2.2
	13.1	5.0	3.5	2.5				4.2	4.8
% Profit Before Taxes/Tangible Net Worth	(40) 47.2	(71) 31.5	31.0	25.6				(180) 30.0	(173) 32.0
	26.8	16.6	15.8	24.4				13.3	16.2
	2.2	8.1	7.0	16.1				2.0	3.4
% Profit Before Taxes/Total Assets	19.1	8.0	9.7	10.7				9.8	10.4
	9.3	4.9	3.9	6.9				3.7	4.4
	.3	2.1	2.0	4.1				.5	1.1
Sales/Net Fixed Assets	75.4	85.8	50.3	41.4				85.1	75.2
	44.1	46.7	30.2	21.2				34.0	35.6
	23.1	26.9	15.0	9.6				15.2	19.4
Sales/Total Assets	6.1	4.7	4.1	3.0				4.7	4.7
	4.5	4.1	3.1	2.7				3.6	3.7
	3.0	3.4	2.5	2.4				2.5	2.7
% Depr., Dep., Amort./Sales	(45) .4	(73) .4	(43) .5	(11) .7				(164) .5	(172) .5
	.7	.8	1.0	1.5				.8	.8
	1.5	1.1	1.3	2.7				1.3	1.5
% Officers', Directors', Owners' Comp/Sales	(26) 4.0	(47) 2.0	(16) 1.5					(92) 2.2	(104) 2.9
	7.7	4.5	2.5					4.4	4.7
	13.5	6.9	4.4					9.9	8.3
Net Sales ($)	71870M	334153M	683014M	696667M	115903M	826893M		1680510M	1840273M
Total Assets ($)	15362M	84401M	218900M	264668M	150432M	292976M		641265M	632702M

M = $ thousand   MM = $ million
See Pages 1 through 15 for Explanation of Ratios and Data

Comparative Historical Data				Current Data Sorted By Sales					
5	11	11	**# Postretirement Benefits**	1	1	2	4	1	2
			Type of Statement						
32	27	28	Unqualified		1	3	1	13	10
51	47	55	Reviewed	3	9	9	18	10	6
83	69	67	Compiled	9	28	9	15	4	2
7	9	6	Tax Returns	3	3				
33	42	39	Other	3	13	12	6	3	2
4/1/92-3/31/93 ALL	4/1/93-3/31/94 ALL	4/1/94-3/31/95 ALL		75 (4/1-9/30/94)			120 (10/1/94-3/31/95)		
				0-1MM	1-3MM	3-5MM	5-10MM	10-25MM	25MM & OVER
206	194	195	**NUMBER OF STATEMENTS**	18	54	33	40	30	20
%	%	%	**ASSETS**	%	%	%	%	%	%
6.0	6.4	5.6	Cash & Equivalents	7.4	5.8	4.7	6.4	4.6	4.9
42.5	44.4	43.4	Trade Receivables - (net)	34.0	45.4	43.7	47.7	40.7	41.7
26.8	25.6	24.4	Inventory	25.3	22.3	24.0	24.5	28.8	23.5
2.1	2.0	2.0	All Other Current	2.5	3.2	1.3	1.2	1.3	2.2
77.4	78.4	75.5	Total Current	69.2	76.7	73.7	79.8	75.4	72.3
14.1	15.1	15.5	Fixed Assets (net)	22.2	15.1	15.3	13.3	16.3	14.3
2.1	1.5	2.8	Intangibles (net)	6.1	2.9	2.2	2.0	1.0	4.9
6.4	5.0	6.2	All Other Non-Current	2.6	5.2	8.8	5.0	7.3	8.6
100.0	100.0	100.0	Total	100.0	100.0	100.0	100.0	100.0	100.0
			LIABILITIES						
16.0	13.7	14.9	Notes Payable-Short Term	14.2	14.5	13.5	13.5	19.1	15.6
3.6	2.9	3.1	Cur. Mat.-L /T/D	6.6	3.2	3.5	2.6	1.9	1.8
25.6	23.4	23.8	Trade Payables	25.9	25.1	25.1	25.6	18.9	20.1
.3	2.2	.3	Income Taxes Payable	.4	.1	.2	.5	.3	.5
8.2	8.1	8.5	All Other Current	2.9	8.3	8.8	8.8	10.8	9.7
53.7	50.4	50.6	Total Current	50.0	51.2	51.2	50.9	51.0	47.7
11.5	9.2	11.2	Long Term Debt	14.1	11.1	13.5	8.4	9.6	13.0
.2	.4	.3	Deferred Taxes	.4	.0	.1	.2	.9	.2
2.8	2.6	3.7	All Other-Non-Current	5.1	4.0	3.6	3.8	2.2	4.1
31.9	37.3	34.2	Net Worth	30.4	33.7	31.6	36.7	36.4	35.1
100.0	100.0	100.0	Total Liabilities & Net Worth	100.0	100.0	100.0	100.0	100.0	100.0
			INCOME DATA						
100.0	100.0	100.0	Net Sales	100.0	100.0	100.0	100.0	100.0	100.0
32.6	32.3	32.6	Gross Profit	39.3	36.1	29.8	28.4	32.4	30.4
30.5	30.3	30.0	Operating Expenses	35.6	33.8	27.8	26.4	29.3	26.7
2.1	2.0	2.6	Operating Profit	3.7	2.4	2.0	2.0	3.1	3.7
.5	.2	.5	All Other Expenses (net)	.3	.4	.5	.4	1.2	.4
1.6	1.8	2.1	Profit Before Taxes	3.4	2.0	1.5	1.6	1.9	3.3
			RATIOS						
1.9	2.1	2.1	Current	2.1	2.3	2.0	2.1	1.9	1.9
1.5	1.6	1.5		1.4	1.5	1.4	1.6	1.4	1.5
1.1	1.2	1.2		1.1	1.1	1.1	1.3	1.2	1.2
1.3	1.4	1.3	Quick	1.3	1.5	1.4	1.3	1.2	1.2
.9	1.0	1.0		.9	1.1	1.0	1.0	.9	.9
.7	.7	.7		.5	.7	.6	.9	.6	.7
33 11.1	34 10.7	33 11.1	Sales/Receivables	29 12.8	32 11.5	32 11.5	35 10.3	38 9.6	45 8.2
40 9.1	42 8.7	42 8.7		39 9.4	39 9.4	41 8.8	43 8.4	45 8.1	48 7.6
49 7.5	51 7.2	51 7.2		47 7.7	48 7.6	48 7.6	51 7.1	56 6.5	57 6.4
19 19.1	17 21.6	16 22.5	Cost of Sales/Inventory	6 57.7	7 51.5	17 20.9	14 25.5	31 11.7	23 16.0
37 9.9	33 11.1	36 10.2		54 6.8	30 12.0	29 12.6	31 11.9	53 6.9	40 9.2
68 5.4	60 6.1	61 6.0		111 3.3	60 6.1	49 7.4	49 7.5	68 5.4	58 6.3
23 16.1	20 17.9	22 16.9	Cost of Sales/Payables	23 15.7	19 19.3	20 18.3	22 16.7	20 17.9	26 14.3
37 10.0	31 11.9	33 11.1		42 8.6	31 11.6	33 11.2	31 11.9	31 11.9	34 10.8
49 7.5	47 7.8	46 8.0		74 4.9	49 7.5	49 7.5	42 8.7	41 8.9	42 8.7
8.6	8.1	8.6	Sales/Working Capital	6.0	9.8	7.9	9.4	7.4	8.2
15.9	13.6	15.6		17.6	16.1	19.0	14.1	14.4	14.3
37.2	28.8	33.0		80.6	43.2	304.3	22.1	29.9	23.7
(191) 4.9	(174) 7.1	(180) 7.4	EBIT/Interest	(14) 6.9	(50) 10.9	(31) 7.2	(39) 7.7	(27) 5.9	(19) 6.8
2.6	3.3	3.2		3.0	2.1	3.5	3.6	2.3	3.8
1.1	1.5	1.7		-.2	1.1	1.6	2.2	1.6	2.2
(87) 3.7	(79) 4.9	(78) 4.0	Net Profit + Depr., Dep., Amort./Cur. Mat. L/T/D		(15) 3.3	(14) 2.3	(19) 5.1	(19) 5.3	
1.4	2.0	2.1			1.2	1.8	2.3	2.2	
.3	.6	1.0			.5	1.3	1.2	1.1	
.2	.2	.2	Fixed/Worth	.3	.1	.2	.2	.2	.3
.4	.4	.4		.8	.3	.4	.3	.4	.5
1.0	.7	.9		2.5	2.1	1.6	.8	.7	.7
1.1	.8	1.1	Debt/Worth	1.5	.9	1.4	.9	1.4	1.5
2.2	1.9	2.0		2.5	1.8	2.2	1.9	2.1	2.0
5.6	3.8	4.8		10.0	10.0	9.7	3.5	3.5	2.9
(183) 30.9	(184) 31.9	(176) 33.0	% Profit Before Taxes/Tangible Net Worth	(15) 70.0	(43) 40.3	(30) 35.9	(39) 33.8	28.9	(19) 25.7
13.9	14.5	18.2		14.7	23.2	18.4	15.8	14.2	23.0
2.0	4.1	7.6		-2.8	4.9	8.3	8.4	6.9	16.6
10.3	10.1	12.4	% Profit Before Taxes/Total Assets	24.2	15.4	7.9	7.5	8.2	11.0
4.6	5.2	5.3		5.9	5.2	4.9	4.9	3.7	7.5
.3	1.3	2.1		-.6	.4	2.2	3.0	2.4	4.6
80.9	66.2	68.0	Sales/Net Fixed Assets	60.7	93.2	65.2	110.7	56.4	41.7
37.5	35.4	37.6		30.3	44.1	47.3	41.9	30.0	25.2
20.0	19.4	20.5		8.0	23.2	26.4	27.5	14.2	10.1
4.8	4.7	4.6	Sales/Total Assets	4.3	5.0	5.1	4.7	4.2	4.0
3.8	3.9	3.9		3.0	4.1	4.0	4.2	2.9	2.9
2.8	2.7	2.8		2.2	3.1	3.2	3.3	2.5	2.7
(192) .5	(169) .5	(175) .5	% Depr., Dep., Amort./Sales	(15) .5	(51) .3	(28) .5	(39) .4	(25) .5	(17) .7
.8	.8	.9		1.0	.7	.9	.9	.9	1.0
1.4	1.4	1.3		1.7	1.2	1.3	1.1	1.1	1.7
(92) 2.1	(80) 2.2	(92) 2.2	% Officers', Directors', Owners' Comp/Sales		(27) 4.0	(20) 1.9	(23) 1.8		
4.2	4.7	4.4			6.1	3.4	4.4		
6.8	7.7	7.4			9.6	7.1	6.7		
1780898M	2085927M	2728500M	Net Sales ($)	12052M	102126M	132414M	274948M	421467M	1785493M
618507M	654661M	1026739M	Total Assets ($)	6224M	26394M	38750M	75269M	161348M	718754M

M = $ thousand   MM = $ million
See Pages 1 through 15 for Explanation of Ratios and Data

Current Data Sorted By Assets   **Comparative Historical Data**

						# Postretirement Benefits		
5	10	29	11	2	6	**Type of Statement**		
4	5	49	39	8	6	Unqualified	82	97
9	42	126	12		1	Reviewed	135	151
27	87	71	9	1		Compiled	153	193
2	2	3				Tax Returns	2	6
10	29	71	24	3	4	Other	88	86
	311 (4/1-9/30/94)		332 (10/1/94-3/31/95)				4/1/90- 3/31/91 ALL	4/1/91- 3/31/92 ALL
0-500M	**500M-2MM**	**2-10MM**	**10-50MM**	**50-100MM**	**100-250MM**			
52	165	320	84	12	10	**NUMBER OF STATEMENTS**	460	533
%	%	%	%	%	%	**ASSETS**	%	%
9.4	11.2	8.8	6.5	4.7	3.6	Cash & Equivalents	8.1	8.9
38.7	33.3	27.6	22.7	30.7	24.4	Trade Receivables - (net)	31.3	29.2
19.3	14.4	13.4	11.7	11.2	14.4	Inventory	15.9	15.7
2.2	1.3	2.3	2.2	2.2	2.2	All Other Current	2.7	1.9
69.6	60.2	52.1	43.1	48.8	44.6	Total Current	58.0	55.8
21.9	30.0	37.2	44.5	41.7	46.1	Fixed Assets (net)	32.4	35.0
1.8	1.8	2.1	1.8	3.4	1.0	Intangibles (net)	1.6	1.9
6.7	8.0	8.6	10.6	6.1	8.3	All Other Non-Current	8.1	7.4
100.0	100.0	100.0	100.0	100.0	100.0	Total	100.0	100.0
						LIABILITIES		
9.5	7.2	6.7	7.9	9.8	9.0	Notes Payable-Short Term	11.1	9.6
5.1	4.0	4.0	3.8	2.1	4.8	Cur. Mat.-L/T/D	4.5	4.4
21.7	24.7	24.6	19.1	24.2	22.6	Trade Payables	22.8	21.1
.3	.6	.8	.3	.3	.1	Income Taxes Payable	1.0	.8
8.0	7.9	8.4	8.8	5.8	5.1	All Other Current	7.2	7.4
44.6	44.5	44.5	39.9	42.3	41.6	Total Current	46.6	43.4
17.0	14.2	16.9	21.6	20.2	14.6	Long Term Debt	18.1	19.9
.1	.3	.8	1.3	3.6	3.0	Deferred Taxes	.6	.5
3.0	2.2	2.6	3.3	3.5	1.2	All Other-Non-Current	1.9	1.9
35.2	38.8	35.3	33.9	30.4	39.6	Net Worth	32.8	34.3
100.0	100.0	100.0	100.0	100.0	100.0	Total Liabilities & Net Worth	100.0	100.0
						INCOME DATA		
100.0	100.0	100.0	100.0	100.0	100.0	Net Sales	100.0	100.0
25.2	16.9	15.1	15.6	22.6	18.2	Gross Profit	15.1	15.7
24.7	15.7	13.5	13.4	20.3	13.8	Operating Expenses	14.0	14.3
.5	1.2	1.6	2.2	2.3	4.3	Operating Profit	1.1	1.3
-.5	-.2	.0	.4	1.1	.4	All Other Expenses (net)	.1	.2
1.0	1.3	1.7	1.8	1.2	4.0	Profit Before Taxes	1.0	1.1
						RATIOS		
2.4	1.8	1.5	1.4	1.2	1.3		1.6	1.7
1.5	1.4	1.2	1.0	1.1	1.1	Current	1.2	1.2
1.1	1.0	.9	.8	.9	1.0		1.0	1.0
2.0	1.4	1.1	1.0	1.0	1.0		1.2	1.2
1.0	1.0	.8	.7	.7	.8	Quick	.8	.8
.6	.7	.6	.5	.6	.4		.5	.6
18 19.8	12 30.1	11 33.6	10 36.4	22 16.9	22 16.6		13 28.8	12 30.5
31 11.6	22 16.5	19 19.7	17 20.9	31 11.8	40 9.2	Sales/Receivables	21 17.8	19 18.9
38 9.7	31 11.9	30 12.2	31 11.7	49 7.5	54 6.7		30 12.1	30 12.1
6 61.7	5 80.6	5 72.0	8 46.8	6 62.2	1 368.5		5 67.1	6 63.4
15 23.7	10 37.1	10 37.0	11 34.6	18 20.2	9 41.1	Cost of Sales/Inventory	11 33.2	11 34.0
41 8.8	17 21.2	18 20.7	18 20.3	33 10.9	66 5.5		20 18.5	19 19.5
10 37.0	12 30.7	14 26.6	15 24.8	17 21.8	19 18.9		11 32.3	10 34.9
17 21.3	16 22.2	19 19.5	19 19.1	23 16.0	43 8.4	Cost of Sales/Payables	17 22.1	15 23.8
39 9.4	24 15.4	29 12.8	24 14.9	44 8.3	64 5.7		24 15.3	23 16.1
9.2	17.5	24.0	32.9	67.1	36.1		19.5	20.1
18.3	34.8	83.1	999.8	168.7	67.0	Sales/Working Capital	60.1	50.0
103.2	-999.8	-138.3	-53.2	-83.1	NM		-250.9	-411.1
(41) 8.7	(154) 7.1	(297) 6.4	(82) 6.5	(11) 4.1	14.5		(426) 4.0	(500) 4.2
2.0	3.4	3.2	3.4	2.4	3.6	EBIT/Interest	2.1	2.0
.8	1.8	1.8	2.2	1.0	2.4		1.1	1.1
	(68) 4.1	(167) 4.0	(44) 4.2				(267) 3.8	(279) 3.4
	2.6	2.2	2.2			Net Profit + Depr., Dep., Amort./Cur. Mat. L./T/D	2.0	1.8
	1.4	1.4	1.6				1.0	.9
.2	.4	.6	.9	.8	.5		.5	.6
.5	.8	1.2	1.4	1.6	1.2	Fixed/Worth	1.1	1.1
3.3	1.3	1.9	2.4	2.2	1.6		2.0	2.0
.8	1.0	1.2	1.4	1.7	1.3		1.2	1.2
1.8	1.8	2.2	2.2	2.4	1.5	Debt/Worth	2.2	2.0
11.6	3.6	3.7	3.5	3.8	2.2		4.6	4.5
(46) 47.3	(161) 36.0	(312) 29.5	(82) 35.0	23.9	28.7		(432) 26.4	(498) 25.9
12.8	16.4	16.8	20.7	14.1	15.3	% Profit Before Taxes/Tangible Net Worth	12.7	10.9
-1.5	5.9	8.2	13.6	-.1	6.0		2.8	1.6
12.6	10.6	8.9	9.7	7.5	12.6		8.1	7.8
4.6	5.4	5.0	6.1	4.1	4.4	% Profit Before Taxes/Total Assets	3.9	3.2
-.8	2.0	2.2	3.4	-.0	2.2		.3	.2
78.4	47.5	26.3	15.7	30.9	18.4		40.3	31.5
24.6	20.0	13.7	9.2	8.9	4.1	Sales/Net Fixed Assets	16.3	15.1
12.5	10.8	8.1	4.6	2.6	2.2		9.2	8.5
6.5	7.6	6.6	5.7	6.2	3.4		7.0	6.7
4.7	5.2	4.9	3.6	3.2	2.2	Sales/Total Assets	4.9	4.9
3.6	4.0	3.5	2.7	1.3	1.4		3.3	3.6
(41) .7	(160) .6	(305) .7	(79) .9	(10) .7			(424) .6	(502) .7
1.6	1.1	1.3	1.5	1.9		% Depr., Dep., Amort./Sales	1.1	1.2
2.4	1.6	1.8	2.2	3.9			1.9	1.9
(22) 1.4	(100) 1.0	(149) .6	(22) .4				(202) .6	(226) .8
2.8	1.7	1.1	1.0			% Officers', Directors', Owners' Comp/Sales	1.2	1.4
4.5	2.0	2.0					2.6	2.3
92807M	1137104M	7366516M	7087917M	3324979M	5335028M	Net Sales ($)	16407455M	23032604M
16718M	195006M	1446724M	1725695M	806128M	1595317M	Total Assets ($)	2980088M	3952534M

© Robert Morris Associates 1995

M = $ thousand   MM = $ million

See Pages 1 through 15 for Explanation of Ratios and Data

Comparative Historical Data				Current Data Sorted By Sales					
4	16	57	# Postretirement Benefits Type of Statement	2	5	3	14	16	17
91	82	111	Unqualified	2	3	1	10	21	74
151	158	189	Reviewed	1	14	17	33	74	50
144	155	195	Compiled	6	33	21	46	54	35
7	11	7	Tax Returns	2	1		1	2	1
73	107	141	Other	4	8	10	26	42	51
4/1/92- 3/31/93	4/1/93- 3/31/94	4/1/94- 3/31/95		311 (4/1-9/30/94)			332 (10/1/94-3/31/95)		
ALL	ALL	ALL		0-1MM	1-3MM	3-5MM	5-10MM	10-25MM	25MM & OVER
466	513	643	NUMBER OF STATEMENTS	15	59	49	116	193	211
%	%	%	ASSETS	%	%	%	%	%	%
8.5	9.9	9.0	Cash & Equivalents	9.7	9.0	9.9	9.3	9.4	8.3
29.2	30.7	29.3	Trade Receivables - (net)	26.1	36.0	29.3	31.4	27.0	28.7
14.7	14.1	13.9	Inventory	20.7	19.0	13.4	14.3	13.5	12.2
2.3	2.1	2.0	All Other Current	2.5	1.3	1.4	2.0	1.7	2.6
54.7	56.9	54.2	Total Current	58.9	65.3	53.9	57.0	51.5	51.9
35.3	33.3	35.3	Fixed Assets (net)	30.0	25.9	32.5	33.4	37.4	38.1
2.2	2.1	2.0	Intangibles (net)	2.0	2.5	2.8	1.5	2.0	1.8
7.8	7.8	8.5	All Other Non-Current	9.0	6.3	10.7	8.1	9.1	8.3
100.0	100.0	100.0	Total	100.0	100.0	100.0	100.0	100.0	100.0
			LIABILITIES						
9.1	7.2	7.3	Notes Payable-Short Term	9.6	9.7	10.6	7.0	6.3	6.7
4.5	3.9	4.1	Cur. Mat.-L /T/D	6.0	4.5	4.9	4.3	4.2	3.3
22.6	22.4	23.7	Trade Payables	14.6	21.5	19.1	22.7	23.6	26.5
.8	2.1	.6	Income Taxes Payable	.5	.3	.5	.7	.7	.6
8.1	9.0	8.2	All Other Current	6.3	7.9	6.6	7.0	8.7	9.0
45.1	44.7	43.8	Total Current	37.0	43.9	41.7	41.7	43.6	46.1
19.0	16.7	16.8	Long Term Debt	23.0	16.1	16.1	16.3	17.4	16.5
.6	.5	.8	Deferred Taxes	.0	.3	.8	.6	.7	1.1
2.2	2.4	2.6	All Other-Non-Current	5.2	1.8	2.9	2.9	3.0	2.1
33.1	35.7	36.0	Net Worth	34.8	38.0	38.5	38.5	35.3	34.1
100.0	100.0	100.0	Total Liabilities & Net Worth	100.0	100.0	100.0	100.0	100.0	100.0
			INCOME DATA						
100.0	100.0	100.0	Net Sales	100.0	100.0	100.0	100.0	100.0	100.0
15.3	15.6	16.7	Gross Profit	36.4	26.9	19.7	17.4	14.2	13.5
14.1	14.2	15.1	Operating Expenses	37.7	24.7	18.2	15.3	12.8	12.1
1.2	1.3	1.6	Operating Profit	-1.3	2.2	1.5	2.1	1.4	1.5
-.1	.0	.0	All Other Expenses (net)	-1.7	-.1	-.1	.3	-.1	.0
1.3	1.3	1.6	Profit Before Taxes	.4	2.3	1.7	1.8	1.5	1.5
			RATIOS						
1.6	1.6	1.6	Current	3.3	2.2	1.9	1.9	1.5	1.4
1.2	1.2	1.2		1.8	1.4	1.3	1.4	1.2	1.1
.9	1.0	.9		1.0	1.2	.9	1.0	.9	.9
1.1	1.2	1.2	Quick	2.9	1.6	1.4	1.4	1.1	1.0
.8	.8	.8		.9	1.0	.8	.9	.8	.8
.6	.6	.6		.5	.7	.7	.7	.6	.6
12 30.6	12 30.3	11 31.8	Sales/Receivables	16 23.5	22 16.3	17 22.0	14 26.3	10 36.6	11 34.6
20 18.2	21 17.8	21 17.5		31 11.8	32 11.3	23 16.2	26 14.1	17 21.4	18 20.5
32 11.5	31 11.7	32 11.3		54 6.7	40 9.1	37 9.8	38 9.5	27 13.3	28 13.1
6 63.6	5 72.7	5 67.6	Cost of Sales/Inventory	8 44.7	10 38.3	5 73.6	6 60.5	5 71.2	4 88.5
10 35.3	10 37.0	10 35.2		44 8.3	21 17.1	14 26.3	12 30.9	9 38.4	9 41.2
18 20.6	18 20.1	18 19.9		61 6.0	47 7.8	24 15.0	21 17.7	16 23.0	15 24.9
12 30.2	11 33.9	13 27.6	Cost of Sales/Payables	9 38.5	12 30.0	10 36.5	13 28.1	13 27.9	14 25.7
17 21.5	17 21.6	18 19.9		21 17.5	25 14.7	16 22.4	19 19.5	17 21.3	19 19.7
25 14.8	25 14.4	28 13.0		56 6.5	46 8.0	33 11.0	32 11.4	24 15.3	24 15.3
20.7	20.0	19.8	Sales/Working Capital	6.0	9.6	16.3	15.5	25.3	38.3
69.9	57.0	60.0		7.4	18.1	52.5	30.3	88.9	143.9
-167.2	-222.9	-159.6		150.3	59.8	-88.9	198.0	-121.9	-109.8
(435) 4.7	(455) 5.3	(595) 6.7	EBIT/Interest	(11) 5.9	(50) 6.1	(46) 8.5	(112) 6.3	(175) 5.2	(201) 7.8
2.0	2.5	3.2		1.3	2.3	3.4	3.1	3.0	3.7
1.1	1.6	1.8		-.8	1.0	1.5	1.7	1.8	2.2
(246) 3.3	(232) 4.2	(301) 4.0	Net Profit + Depr., Dep., Amort./Cur. Mat. L/T/D		(11) 2.4	(21) 3.2	(55) 5.7	(106) 3.9	(106) 4.3
1.7	1.9	2.2			1.1	1.9	2.2	2.1	2.3
1.0	1.2	1.4			.2	1.0	1.4	1.3	1.6
.6	.5	.5	Fixed/Worth	.2	.3	.6	.5	.6	.7
1.1	1.0	1.1		.5	.5	.9	.9	1.1	1.2
2.1	1.9	1.9		14.0	2.8	1.5	1.7	2.1	1.9
1.2	1.0	1.1	Debt/Worth	.4	.8	1.0	1.0	1.2	1.4
2.3	2.1	2.0		1.9	1.9	1.4	1.9	2.2	2.2
4.6	4.0	3.7		24.3	8.9	3.5	3.3	4.0	3.6
(434) 22.7	(489) 26.6	(623) 32.3	% Profit Before Taxes/Tangible Net Worth	(12) 42.9	(54) 44.2	(48) 35.2	(111) 25.3	(190) 28.6	(208) 36.3
10.6	13.5	16.9		8.0	15.4	18.3	11.8	16.9	19.9
2.2	4.9	7.7		-19.4	.2	5.7	6.6	8.6	10.4
7.0	8.7	9.7	% Profit Before Taxes/Total Assets	10.9	13.1	10.9	9.2	8.9	10.3
3.0	3.9	5.2		1.8	4.9	6.0	4.7	4.7	6.0
.4	1.6	2.2		-8.8	.0	1.7	1.7	2.3	3.2
29.7	36.7	32.9	Sales/Net Fixed Assets	19.9	47.0	26.4	45.6	27.3	32.8
14.8	16.6	14.9		11.0	21.3	15.6	14.2	14.9	14.1
8.5	8.6	8.2		3.0	9.4	8.2	7.6	8.3	8.0
6.4	6.6	6.6	Sales/Total Assets	4.1	5.0	5.7	6.0	6.9	7.5
4.7	4.8	4.8		2.2	4.1	4.6	4.5	5.0	5.4
3.3	3.2	3.3		1.2	2.9	3.1	3.0	3.8	3.6
(438) .7	(485) .7	(603) .7	% Depr., Dep., Amort./Sales	(12) 1.1	(51) .8	(46) .9	(115) .6	(184) .7	(195) .5
1.2	1.2	1.2		2.8	1.6	1.5	1.3	1.2	1.1
2.0	1.8	1.9		4.8	3.5	2.1	2.1	1.7	1.7
(201) .7	(213) .8	(294) .8	% Officers', Directors', Owners' Comp/Sales		(31) 1.5	(27) 1.5	(64) .8	(97) .7	(69) .4
1.4	1.5	1.4			3.0	2.4	1.4	1.1	.9
2.4	2.8	2.4			4.1	3.4	2.5	1.8	1.4
17772161M	20945701M	24344351M	Net Sales ($)	9634M	110679M	194787M	873655M	3112192M	20043404M
3663787M	4451654M	5785588M	Total Assets ($)	5764M	38064M	57367M	272762M	742642M	4668989M

M = $ thousand   MM = $ million
See Pages 1 through 15 for Explanation of Ratios and Data

WHOLESALERS—PETROLEUM BULK STATIONS & TERMINALS. SIC# 5171

Current Data Sorted By Assets   **Comparative Historical Data**

Postretirement Benefits — Type of Statement

	2	11					Type of Statement		
1	3	16	25	1	3		Unqualified	73	45
4	23	64	8				Reviewed	90	84
14	49	33		1			Compiled	132	103
	2	2					Tax Returns	2	
4	26	30	9				Other	64	58

	153 (4/1-9/30/94)		165 (10/1/94-3/31/95)					4/1/90-3/31/91	4/1/91-3/31/92
0-500M	500M-2MM	2-10MM	10-50MM	50-100MM	100-250MM			ALL	ALL
23	103	145	42	2	3		**NUMBER OF STATEMENTS**	361	290

	0-500M %	500M-2MM %	2-10MM %	10-50MM %	50-100MM %	100-250MM %		Hist ALL %	Hist ALL %
							ASSETS		
Cash & Equivalents	9.7	9.0	9.6	7.1				7.6	7.9
Trade Receivables - (net)	34.6	33.0	23.9	20.7				29.3	26.9
Inventory	25.2	15.6	13.2	12.1				16.1	14.9
All Other Current	.7	2.7	2.4	2.8				2.0	2.2
Total Current	70.2	60.2	49.1	42.7				55.0	52.0
Fixed Assets (net)	24.9	30.4	41.3	46.5				35.7	38.1
Intangibles (net)	2.9	1.5	1.7	1.6				1.6	1.8
All Other Non-Current	1.9	8.0	7.9	9.1				7.7	8.1
Total	100.0	100.0	100.0	100.0				100.0	100.0
							LIABILITIES		
Notes Payable-Short Term	13.6	7.7	6.2	4.8				8.8	8.8
Cur. Mat. -L/T/D	2.8	4.5	4.5	3.9				4.3	4.4
Trade Payables	21.5	23.1	23.3	22.7				22.4	21.3
Income Taxes Payable	.1	.4	.4	.2				.8	.6
All Other Current	7.9	11.1	8.6	6.5				7.5	8.3
Total Current	46.0	46.8	43.0	38.0				43.9	43.4
Long Term Debt	23.0	15.6	20.1	22.5				20.4	20.2
Deferred Taxes	.0	.2	.6	1.3				.7	.7
All Other-Non-Current	4.6	1.3	1.7	1.8				1.7	2.1
Net Worth	26.4	36.1	34.6	36.3				33.3	33.6
Total Liabilities & Net Worth	100.0	100.0	100.0	100.0				100.0	100.0
							INCOME DATA		
Net Sales	100.0	100.0	100.0	100.0				100.0	100.0
Gross Profit	15.2	14.9	14.6	16.4				14.2	13.9
Operating Expenses	15.7	13.9	13.5	13.9				13.2	13.1
Operating Profit	-.5	1.0	1.1	2.5				1.1	.8
All Other Expenses (net)	.3	.0	-.2	.0				.1	.1
Profit Before Taxes	-.8	1.0	1.3	2.5				1.0	.7

RATIOS

Ratio	0-500M	500M-2MM	2-10MM	10-50MM	Hist ALL	Hist ALL
Current	2.1 / 1.6 / 1.1	1.8 / 1.3 / 1.0	1.5 / 1.2 / .9	1.5 / 1.1 / .9	1.6 / 1.3 / 1.0	1.5 / 1.2 / .9
Quick	1.3 / .9 / .7	1.3 / .9 / .7	1.1 / .8 / .6	.9 / .8 / .5	1.2 / .8 / .6	1.1 / .8 / .5
Sales/Receivables	11 / 34.6 — 22 / 16.7 — 31 / 11.8	15 / 24.3 — 23 / 15.8 — 31 / 11.9	9 / 41.3 — 15 / 25.1 — 25 / 14.6	11 / 33.2 — 15 / 24.4 — 24 / 14.9	12 / 31.2 — 20 / 18.3 — 29 / 12.7	11 / 33.4 — 17 / 21.6 — 26 / 14.3
Cost of Sales/Inventory	10 / 37.3 — 15 / 23.8 — 24 / 15.2	6 / 56.2 — 11 / 33.7 — 18 / 20.3	7 / 52.0 — 10 / 34.8 — 17 / 21.8	7 / 55.2 — 10 / 35.8 — 18 / 20.7	8 / 47.7 — 13 / 29.0 — 19 / 19.5	7 / 55.0 — 10 / 35.1 — 16 / 23.4
Cost of Sales/Payables	5 / 73.6 — 14 / 26.7 — 30 / 12.0	12 / 30.5 — 17 / 21.9 — 24 / 15.1	14 / 25.8 — 18 / 20.6 — 26 / 14.3	16 / 22.8 — 21 / 17.0 — 30 / 12.3	12 / 30.1 — 17 / 21.4 — 24 / 15.3	11 / 32.6 — 15 / 24.2 — 21 / 17.5
Sales/Working Capital	18.4 / 28.0 / 82.6	20.4 / 41.2 / 999.8	29.8 / 87.1 / -186.3	30.6 / 126.3 / -98.5	21.2 / 52.6 / -622.3	28.5 / 68.4 / -213.0
EBIT/Interest	(20) 3.7 / 2.9 / 1.2	(97) 5.9 / 3.1 / 1.3	(138) 5.9 / 3.4 / 1.8	8.9 / 4.7 / 2.1	(343) 4.0 / 2.0 / 1.3	(269) 3.1 / 1.7 / .9
Net Profit + Depr., Dep., Amort./Cur. Mat. L/T/D		(43) 3.5 / 1.9 / 1.0	(78) 4.1 / 2.3 / 1.1	(20) 8.7 / 1.8 / 1.2	(222) 3.5 / 2.2 / 1.3	(168) 2.6 / 1.7 / .9
Fixed/Worth	.2 / 1.0 / 2.0	.4 / .9 / 1.7	.8 / 1.2 / 2.0	.9 / 1.4 / 2.2	.6 / 1.1 / 2.0	.6 / 1.2 / 2.2
Debt/Worth	1.6 / 3.6 / 4.5	.9 / 2.0 / 3.9	1.2 / 2.1 / 3.3	1.1 / 1.9 / 3.2	1.2 / 2.2 / 4.5	1.1 / 2.2 / 4.1
% Profit Before Taxes/Tangible Net Worth	(19) 48.7 / 28.7 / 14.1	(97) 24.5 / 12.3 / 3.1	(141) 30.0 / 15.7 / 7.5	(41) 31.2 / 17.4 / 11.2	(345) 23.2 / 12.8 / 3.3	(271) 17.4 / 9.0 / .0
% Profit Before Taxes/Total Assets	11.4 / 7.1 / 3.8	6.8 / 4.0 / 1.1	9.1 / 5.6 / 2.4	11.0 / 6.8 / 3.3	7.4 / 3.8 / 1.0	5.6 / 2.8 / -.5
Sales/Net Fixed Assets	67.4 / 26.6 / 16.2	35.8 / 19.1 / 11.4	20.6 / 12.1 / 7.8	13.4 / 7.9 / 4.8	28.1 / 15.1 / 9.0	28.7 / 14.3 / 8.1
Sales/Total Assets	8.3 / 6.1 / 3.6	7.1 / 5.0 / 3.8	6.1 / 4.9 / 3.6	5.2 / 3.6 / 2.7	6.3 / 5.1 / 3.6	6.9 / 5.1 / 3.5
% Depr., Dep., Amort./Sales	(20) .4 / .8 / 1.1	(101) .6 / 1.1 / 1.7	(140) .8 / 1.3 / 1.8	.9 / 1.6 / 2.4	(340) .8 / 1.2 / 1.9	(282) .7 / 1.2 / 1.9
% Officers', Directors', Owners' Comp/Sales		(63) .8 / 1.5 / 3.1	(68) .5 / 1.4 / 2.0		(146) .7 / 1.2 / 2.2	(126) .6 / 1.1 / 1.9

	0-500M	500M-2MM	2-10MM	10-50MM	50-100MM	100-250MM		Hist ALL	Hist ALL
Net Sales ($)	59435M	683741M	3185785M	3519438M	589797M	3523294M		12388653M	7887096M
Total Assets ($)	8262M	123567M	633053M	831612M	170993M	505388M		2947897M	1730241M

M = $ thousand   MM = $ million
See Pages 1 through 15 for Explanation of Ratios and Data

Comparative Historical Data / Current Data Sorted By Sales

Reference column numbers: Comparative = 2, 8, 13 | Current = 1 … 7 … 5

Type of Statement (# Postretirement Benefits)

Type of Statement	2	8	13	0-1MM	1-3MM	3-5MM	5-10MM	10-25MM	25MM & OVER
Unqualified	64	68	49			3	4	6	36
Reviewed	99	91	99	2	2	4	21	42	28
Compiled	123	105	97	3	14	18	24	28	10
Tax Returns	3	7	4		2		1	1	
Other	57	65	69	2	11	4	15	21	16

Comparative periods: 4/1/92-3/31/93 ALL (346); 4/1/93-3/31/94 ALL (336); 4/1/94-3/31/95 ALL (318)
Current periods: 153 (4/1-9/30/94); 165 (10/1/94-3/31/95)

Main Data

2 (92-93)	8 (93-94)	13 (94-95)	Item	0-1MM	1-3MM	3-5MM	5-10MM	10-25MM	25MM & OVER
346	336	318	**NUMBER OF STATEMENTS**	7	29	29	65	98	90
%	%	%	**ASSETS**	%	%	%	%	%	%
8.7	9.3	9.0	Cash & Equivalents		6.8	10.0	9.0	9.3	9.0
27.3	27.1	27.3	Trade Receivables - (net)		31.0	35.3	29.9	24.5	24.9
14.5	14.1	14.7	Inventory		20.2	17.0	15.1	14.0	12.7
2.4	1.7	2.4	All Other Current		4.9	1.2	1.2	2.8	2.5
52.9	52.2	53.5	Total Current		62.9	63.6	55.2	50.7	49.0
37.4	38.7	37.2	Fixed Assets (net)		28.3	26.3	34.5	42.2	40.1
1.5	1.9	1.7	Intangibles (net)		.3	2.2	1.8	1.5	1.6
8.2	7.2	7.6	All Other Non-Current		8.5	7.9	8.5	5.6	9.2
100.0	100.0	100.0	Total		100.0	100.0	100.0	100.0	100.0
			LIABILITIES						
7.9	6.7	7.2	Notes Payable-Short Term		14.0	7.2	7.7	5.8	6.0
4.2	4.5	4.3	Cur. Mat.-L /T/D		2.7	7.1	3.9	4.3	4.2
21.1	20.3	23.0	Trade Payables		16.6	23.3	22.6	22.4	26.4
.5	1.4	.3	Income Taxes Payable		.4	.1	.4	.4	.3
9.3	9.1	9.0	All Other Current		8.6	8.3	10.0	9.3	8.6
43.0	41.9	43.8	Total Current		42.4	45.9	44.5	42.4	45.4
18.5	20.0	19.2	Long Term Debt		18.8	13.6	19.1	20.0	19.4
.6	.7	.6	Deferred Taxes		.1	.3	.2	.4	1.3
1.6	1.4	1.9	All Other-Non-Current		.2	3.7	1.1	2.0	2.1
36.3	36.0	34.5	Net Worth		38.5	36.5	35.2	35.2	31.9
100.0	100.0	100.0	Total Liabilities & Net Worth		100.0	100.0	100.0	100.0	100.0
			INCOME DATA						
100.0	100.0	100.0	Net Sales		100.0	100.0	100.0	100.0	100.0
15.0	15.6	14.8	Gross Profit		17.9	15.6	15.4	14.4	13.2
14.0	14.3	13.7	Operating Expenses		16.4	14.7	14.3	13.1	11.8
.9	1.3	1.1	Operating Profit		1.5	1.0	1.1	1.4	1.3
-.1	.2	-.1	All Other Expenses (net)		-.2	-.1	.1	-.1	-.2
1.0	1.2	1.2	Profit Before Taxes		1.7	1.1	1.0	1.4	1.5
			RATIOS						
1.6 / 1.2 / .9	1.7 / 1.2 / 1.0	1.6 / 1.2 / 1.0	Current		2.6 / 1.6 / 1.1	1.8 / 1.5 / 1.1	1.7 / 1.3 / 1.0	1.6 / 1.2 / 1.0	1.3 / 1.1 / .9
1.1 / .8 / .5	1.2 / .8 / .6	1.1 / .8 / .6	Quick		1.8 / 1.0 / .6	1.4 / 1.0 / .7	1.2 / .9 / .6	1.1 / .8 / .5	1.0 / .8 / .5
11 33.7 / 18 20.8 / 27 13.6	11 34.1 / 18 20.0 / 28 12.9	11 34.0 / 18 20.6 / 28 13.0	Sales/Receivables		23 15.7 / 31 11.9 / 41 9.0	16 23.0 / 26 14.3 / 35 10.3	14 26.4 / 21 17.7 / 28 12.9	9 41.3 / 16 23.4 / 24 15.0	10 37.5 / 14 26.3 / 24 15.3
7 56.1 / 11 32.8 / 18 20.5	7 54.8 / 11 33.9 / 18 20.7	7 54.0 / 11 33.5 / 17 21.1	Cost of Sales/Inventory		10 35.6 / 19 19.5 / 32 11.4	8 43.5 / 15 24.3 / 25 14.7	7 52.9 / 12 31.2 / 19 19.0	6 56.8 / 10 36.6 / 15 23.9	6 60.6 / 10 37.8 / 15 24.7
13 29.2 / 16 22.6 / 22 16.7	11 32.1 / 16 23.2 / 22 16.3	13 28.1 / 18 20.7 / 26 14.1	Cost of Sales/Payables		11 33.6 / 17 21.6 / 35 10.5	9 40.6 / 20 18.0 / 35 10.5	13 27.1 / 17 20.9 / 26 14.2	13 27.8 / 17 21.6 / 21 17.8	14 25.7 / 19 19.0 / 26 14.2
23.0 / 62.2 / -145.9	22.5 / 67.0 / -405.9	23.1 / 53.5 / -250.7	Sales/Working Capital		7.8 / 19.4 / 68.6	13.3 / 28.9 / 80.5	23.4 / 46.9 / -232.8	27.2 / 73.3 / -329.0	37.5 / 184.6 / -134.6
(319) 3.5 / 2.1 / 1.2	(318) 5.0 / 2.5 / 1.6	(302) 5.9 / 3.3 / 1.7	EBIT/Interest		(25) 6.5 / 3.1 / 1.5	(28) 4.7 / 1.8 / .2	(62) 5.2 / 2.8 / 1.7	(93) 5.4 / 3.4 / 2.0	(88) 7.3 / 4.5 / 2.2
(178) 3.3 / 1.7 / 1.0	(159) 3.7 / 1.8 / 1.2	(149) 3.9 / 2.0 / 1.1	Net Profit + Depr., Dep., Amort./Cur. Mat. L/T/D			(13) 4.0 / 1.9 / 1.2	(28) 3.2 / 1.4 / .9	(54) 4.8 / 2.5 / 1.2	(46) 4.5 / 1.9 / 1.1
.6 / 1.1 / 2.1	.6 / 1.2 / 2.0	.6 / 1.1 / 2.1	Fixed/Worth		.3 / .7 / 1.6	.4 / .7 / 1.2	.6 / 1.1 / 2.0	.7 / 1.2 / 2.0	.8 / 1.2 / 2.0
1.1 / 2.0 / 3.7	1.1 / 2.0 / 3.5	1.1 / 2.1 / 3.8	Debt/Worth		.6 / 2.0 / 3.8	.8 / 1.7 / 3.9	1.1 / 2.1 / 4.0	1.0 / 2.1 / 3.3	1.4 / 2.3 / 3.8
(331) 18.9 / 10.0 / 2.4	(319) 28.1 / 14.1 / 5.0	(303) 28.7 / 15.5 / 7.2	% Profit Before Taxes/Tangible Net Worth		(27) 31.2 / 14.7 / 6.5	(27) 22.1 / 8.4 / -1.5	(62) 24.9 / 9.6 / 5.8	(97) 27.2 / 15.4 / 7.2	(86) 33.4 / 20.6 / 12.5
6.0 / 3.1 / .6	8.1 / 4.5 / 1.8	9.1 / 5.3 / 2.1	% Profit Before Taxes/Total Assets		9.6 / 5.8 / 1.8	7.6 / 2.7 / -.6	7.3 / 4.3 / 2.0	8.5 / 5.7 / 2.2	10.8 / 6.8 / 3.3
26.3 / 13.4 / 7.9	23.3 / 12.5 / 8.2	26.7 / 13.8 / 7.9	Sales/Net Fixed Assets		29.2 / 16.0 / 6.9	40.7 / 21.5 / 10.2	28.2 / 14.9 / 8.4	21.4 / 12.2 / 8.1	24.3 / 12.2 / 7.2
6.8 / 4.9 / 3.4	6.5 / 4.7 / 3.5	6.6 / 4.8 / 3.4	Sales/Total Assets		4.6 / 3.6 / 2.2	6.6 / 4.6 / 3.5	6.6 / 4.7 / 3.4	6.6 / 5.1 / 3.8	7.6 / 5.1 / 3.5
(323) .7 / 1.2 / 1.9	(322) .7 / 1.2 / 1.9	(308) .7 / 1.2 / 1.8	% Depr., Dep., Amort./Sales		(27) .8 / 1.2 / 2.1	(27) .5 / 1.2 / 1.8	(63) .8 / 1.2 / 1.8	(95) .8 / 1.2 / 1.7	(89) .6 / 1.2 / 1.9
(139) .6 / 1.2 / 2.0	(156) .6 / 1.2 / 2.1	(140) .8 / 1.4 / 2.2	% Officers', Directors', Owners' Comp/Sales		(13) 2.2 / 3.6 / 4.7	(14) 1.1 / 1.5 / 2.0	(40) .8 / 1.5 / 2.9	(46) .7 / 1.1 / 1.9	(25) .4 / .8 / 1.9
9826037M	11723060M	11561490M	Net Sales ($)	4638M	57313M	114687M	486064M	1624047M	9274741M
2432234M	2268702M	2272875M	Total Assets ($)	2323M	25785M	30452M	114186M	365591M	1734538M

M = $ thousand   MM = $ million
See Pages 1 through 15 for Explanation of Ratios and Data

WHOLESALERS—PHOTOGRAPHIC EQUIPMENT & SUPPLIES. SIC# 5043

Current Data Sorted By Assets | | | | | | Comparative Historical Data

0-500M	500M-2MM	2-10MM	10-50MM	50-100MM	100-250MM	# Postretirement Benefits / Type of Statement	4/1/90-3/31/91 ALL	4/1/91-3/31/92 ALL
		6	2		1	Unqualified	11	9
	8	9				Reviewed	11	15
2	2	6	1			Compiled	10	6
1						Tax Returns	1	
	4	2	1			Other	6	5
	19 (4/1-9/30/94)		26 (10/1/94-3/31/95)					
3	14	23	4		1	NUMBER OF STATEMENTS	39	35

0-500M %	500M-2MM %	2-10MM %	10-50MM %	50-100MM %	100-250MM %	ASSETS	ALL %	ALL %
	9.2	3.8				Cash & Equivalents	4.9	4.2
	30.7	39.8				Trade Receivables - (net)	34.8	33.1
	33.1	33.4				Inventory	30.9	38.9
	.9	1.2				All Other Current	1.8	1.9
	73.8	78.0				Total Current	72.4	78.2
	13.3	16.2				Fixed Assets (net)	16.7	15.8
	3.4	2.1				Intangibles (net)	2.2	1.1
	9.4	3.6				All Other Non-Current	8.7	4.9
	100.0	100.0				Total	100.0	100.0

	500M-2MM	2-10MM				LIABILITIES	ALL	ALL
	15.1	18.5				Notes Payable-Short Term	17.7	13.7
	3.1	2.8				Cur. Mat. -L/T/D	4.1	4.5
	22.2	23.0				Trade Payables	23.8	22.5
	.0	.5				Income Taxes Payable	.3	.5
	7.9	8.2				All Other Current	9.1	9.8
	48.3	53.1				Total Current	55.0	51.0
	5.4	9.2				Long Term Debt	11.7	11.3
	.0	.4				Deferred Taxes	.2	.3
	8.6	2.8				All Other-Non-Current	.7	3.5
	37.7	34.5				Net Worth	32.4	33.9
	100.0	100.0				Total Liabilities & Net Worth	100.0	100.0

	500M-2MM	2-10MM				INCOME DATA	ALL	ALL
	100.0	100.0				Net Sales	100.0	100.0
	29.4	26.9				Gross Profit	33.0	30.2
	28.1	24.0				Operating Expenses	31.3	27.3
	1.3	2.9				Operating Profit	1.7	2.9
	.3	.7				All Other Expenses (net)	1.0	1.5
	1.0	2.2				Profit Before Taxes	.7	1.4

RATIOS

	500M-2MM	2-10MM				Ratio	ALL	ALL
	1.8	1.9				Current	2.1	1.9
	1.6	1.3					1.4	1.4
	1.3	1.2					1.0	1.2
	1.1	1.1				Quick	1.1	1.0
	.7	.8					.7	.7
	.5	.6					.5	.6
25 14.6		36 10.2				Sales/Receivables	31 11.8	32 11.3
38 9.6		45 8.1					40 9.1	41 8.8
53 6.9		58 6.3					52 7.0	51 7.1
31 11.9		28 13.1				Cost of Sales/Inventory	28 13.2	34 10.6
51 7.1		51 7.2					54 6.7	68 5.4
94 3.9		69 5.3					87 4.2	122 3.0
12 29.9		20 18.1				Cost of Sales/Payables	22 16.3	29 12.6
28 13.2		31 11.6					34 10.6	34 10.7
54 6.8		56 6.5					64 5.7	55 6.6
	6.2	6.8				Sales/Working Capital	8.3	6.9
	12.1	14.3					16.7	11.6
	18.3	29.0					153.4	20.9
	5.8	16.0				EBIT/Interest	(38) 3.9	(34) 3.9
(13)	2.6	4.1					2.2	2.0
	1.0	1.8					1.6	1.0
		9.2				Net Profit + Depr., Dep., Amort./Cur. Mat. L /T/D	(16) 4.4	(15) 10.5
	(13)	4.2					2.2	2.5
		1.5					.4	.4
	.1	.2				Fixed/Worth	.1	.1
	.4	.4					.3	.3
	.7	.8					1.7	1.2
	.9	1.5				Debt/Worth	.9	1.4
	2.2	1.9					2.5	2.1
	4.8	4.6					11.0	3.5
	20.2	45.5				% Profit Before Taxes/Tangible Net Worth	(37) 26.0	(34) 23.4
(13)	10.4	21.4					13.3	9.2
	1.5	6.3					4.1	-1.1
	5.7	19.8				% Profit Before Taxes/Total Assets	7.2	7.6
	3.3	6.0					4.0	2.7
	.0	.9					1.2	.3
	137.5	69.7				Sales/Net Fixed Assets	71.7	53.8
	41.8	35.5					24.5	38.1
	16.7	12.2					10.4	13.1
	4.0	3.7				Sales/Total Assets	3.9	3.6
	3.3	3.0					3.2	2.8
	2.2	2.1					1.9	2.0
	.3	.4				% Depr., Dep., Amort./Sales	(35) .4	(31) .5
(13)	.5	.8					.8	.9
	1.2	1.9					1.9	1.5
						% Officers', Directors', Owners' Comp/Sales	(16) 2.1	(15) 1.8
							3.0	2.7
							6.1	3.8

0-500M	500M-2MM	2-10MM	10-50MM	50-100MM	100-250MM		Hist	Hist
3753M	57851M	324179M	247592M		238154M	Net Sales ($)	656778M	433858M
853M	18726M	102971M	83623M		120760M	Total Assets ($)	258837M	172159M

M = $ thousand   MM = $ million
See Pages 1 through 15 for Explanation of Ratios and Data

Comparative Historical Data				Current Data Sorted By Sales					
1	1	1	# Postretirement Benefits				1		
			Type of Statement						
16	19	9	Unqualified				1	4	4
18	19	17	Reviewed		1	4	10	2	
14	10	11	Compiled	1	1	1	3	2	3
1	1	1	Tax Returns		1				
10	6	7	Other	2	1	1	1	1	1
4/1/92-3/31/93	4/1/93-3/31/94	4/1/94-3/31/95		19 (4/1-9/30/94)			26 (10/1/94-3/31/95)		
ALL	ALL	ALL		0-1MM	1-3MM	3-5MM	5-10MM	10-25MM	25MM & OVER
59	55	45	NUMBER OF STATEMENTS	3	4	6	15	9	8
%	%	%	ASSETS	%	%	%	%	%	%
6.8	5.6	5.6	Cash & Equivalents				2.9		
33.1	36.0	37.1	Trade Receivables - (net)				37.3		
38.6	36.7	33.0	Inventory				31.2		
1.2	2.3	1.0	All Other Current				.6		
79.7	80.5	76.7	Total Current				72.0		
13.8	10.9	14.3	Fixed Assets (net)				19.4		
1.4	2.5	3.2	Intangibles (net)				2.6		
5.0	6.0	5.8	All Other Non-Current				6.0		
100.0	100.0	100.0	Total				100.0		
			LIABILITIES						
11.7	12.3	15.5	Notes Payable-Short Term				18.0		
4.9	2.5	3.0	Cur. Mat.-L /T/D				3.8		
20.9	22.0	24.6	Trade Payables				21.7		
.4	.9	.3	Income Taxes Payable				.3		
10.7	10.1	7.9	All Other Current				10.3		
48.6	47.9	51.3	Total Current				54.2		
11.0	7.9	10.3	Long Term Debt				9.7		
.1	.4	.3	Deferred Taxes				.4		
3.7	1.8	5.2	All Other-Non-Current				4.4		
36.5	41.9	33.0	Net Worth				31.4		
100.0	100.0	100.0	Total Liabilities & Net Worth				100.0		
			INCOME DATA						
100.0	100.0	100.0	Net Sales				100.0		
30.1	28.4	27.4	Gross Profit				27.7		
27.5	25.8	25.4	Operating Expenses				27.0		
2.6	2.6	2.0	Operating Profit				.6		
.4	.3	.6	All Other Expenses (net)				.9		
2.1	2.3	1.5	Profit Before Taxes				−.2		
			RATIOS						
2.3	2.5	2.0					1.7		
1.5	1.7	1.5	Current				1.2		
1.2	1.3	1.2					1.1		
1.1	1.3	1.2					1.1		
.8	.8	.9	Quick				.8		
.6	.7	.5					.6		
31 11.6	31 11.7	33 11.1					36 10.2		
39 9.4	42 8.6	46 8.0	Sales/Receivables				45 8.1		
49 7.5	58 6.3	57 6.4					54 6.7		
46 7.9	40 9.1	31 11.8					31 11.9		
66 5.5	60 6.1	51 7.2	Cost of Sales/Inventory				41 8.9		
111 3.3	96 3.8	72 5.1					64 5.7		
19 19.0	15 24.5	21 17.8					14 25.9		
32 11.5	34 10.8	33 11.1	Cost of Sales/Payables				29 12.6		
44 8.3	49 7.5	55 6.6					45 8.2		
5.7	6.0	6.4					6.8		
10.0	9.6	12.6	Sales/Working Capital				20.8		
25.1	23.5	24.2					52.4		
5.7	22.5	10.6					5.6		
(55) 3.5	6.0	(44) 3.8	EBIT/Interest				2.2		
1.6	2.2	1.2					1.0		
3.4	11.9	9.1							
(26) 1.6	(22) 3.9	(25) 3.7	Net Profit + Depr., Dep., Amort./Cur. Mat. L/T/D						
.8	1.9	1.5							
.1	.1	.2					.4		
.2	.2	.4	Fixed/Worth				.5		
1.0	.6	.7					1.4		
1.1	.6	1.3					1.5		
2.2	1.6	2.8	Debt/Worth				2.8		
3.6	3.5	4.7					5.2		
32.4	40.0	34.4					37.7		
(56) 17.2	(53) 24.0	(41) 17.4	% Profit Before Taxes/Tangible Net Worth			(14) 12.1			
7.7	13.7	5.6					.1		
9.5	15.0	8.9					6.0		
5.1	7.4	4.3	% Profit Before Taxes/Total Assets				3.3		
1.8	4.0	.8					−.1		
83.1	122.2	74.8					46.1		
41.0	48.1	39.8	Sales/Net Fixed Assets				20.8		
15.7	18.8	18.5					11.7		
3.8	4.1	4.1					3.8		
2.9	3.2	3.0	Sales/Total Assets				3.3		
2.1	2.1	2.2					3.0		
.4	.3	.3					.5		
(51) .8	(49) .6	(44) .7	% Depr., Dep., Amort./Sales				1.1		
1.2	1.3	1.8					2.0		
1.2	1.9	2.2							
(29) 2.5	(22) 2.5	(11) 3.9	% Officers', Directors', Owners' Comp/Sales						
5.0	3.8	4.8							
643477M	854948M	871529M	Net Sales ($)	918M	8650M	24689M	109289M	142924M	
223657M	286877M	326933M	Total Assets ($)	1510M	3621M	9431M	36959M	50518M	

© Robert Morris Associates 1995

M = $ thousand   MM = $ million
See Pages 1 through 15 for Explanation of Ratios and Data

Current Data Sorted By Assets | **Comparative Historical Data**

Type of Statement

4	5	2	1			# Postretirement Benefits / Type of Statement		
				6	3			
10	5	20	19			Unqualified	41	30
13	28	29	1			Reviewed	43	62
13	29	20				Compiled	62	50
6	6	1				Tax Returns	2	2
13	13	15	5			Other	39	34

60 (4/1-9/30/94)   182 (10/1/94-3/31/95)   4/1/90-3/31/91 ALL   4/1/91-3/31/92 ALL

0-500M	500M-2MM	2-10MM	10-50MM	50-100MM	100-250MM		4/1/90-3/31/91 ALL	4/1/91-3/31/92 ALL
42	81	85	25	6	3	**NUMBER OF STATEMENTS**	187	178
%	%	%	%	%	%	**ASSETS**	%	%
13.3	8.2	6.5	5.1			Cash & Equivalents	6.1	7.2
22.7	24.3	28.2	34.0			Trade Receivables - (net)	24.8	24.0
43.2	50.1	47.0	42.9			Inventory	47.8	49.4
1.0	1.4	1.1	3.7			All Other Current	1.9	1.2
80.2	84.0	82.7	85.7			Total Current	80.7	81.7
12.5	10.4	10.9	9.3			Fixed Assets (net)	11.7	11.8
3.1	1.4	1.1	1.7			Intangibles (net)	1.6	1.4
4.2	4.1	5.3	3.3			All Other Non-Current	6.0	5.1
100.0	100.0	100.0	100.0			Total	100.0	100.0
						LIABILITIES		
14.8	15.9	17.9	29.4			Notes Payable-Short Term	15.8	17.2
3.1	2.6	1.1	2.8			Cur. Mat. -L/T/D	3.7	3.7
23.2	17.7	20.1	20.3			Trade Payables	21.0	18.5
.1	.4	.2	1.2			Income Taxes Payable	.5	.4
11.9	6.7	7.6	10.0			All Other Current	7.1	6.3
53.1	43.3	47.0	63.7			Total Current	48.1	46.1
11.5	10.3	9.5	5.8			Long Term Debt	10.3	9.8
.0	.1	.1	.2			Deferred Taxes	.2	.1
3.9	4.3	5.3	1.0			All Other-Non-Current	4.1	3.3
31.4	42.0	38.1	29.4			Net Worth	37.4	40.7
100.0	100.0	100.0	100.0			Total Liabilities & Net Worth	100.0	100.0
						INCOME DATA		
100.0	100.0	100.0	100.0			Net Sales	100.0	100.0
34.8	29.8	26.4	26.0			Gross Profit	29.4	29.7
33.0	26.8	22.9	21.4			Operating Expenses	25.3	25.6
1.8	3.0	3.5	4.6			Operating Profit	4.1	4.1
1.1	1.1	.9	1.2			All Other Expenses (net)	1.4	1.1
.7	1.8	2.6	3.4			Profit Before Taxes	2.7	3.0
						RATIOS		
2.5	2.7	2.5	1.8			Current	2.4	2.6
1.6	2.0	1.7	1.3				1.6	1.8
1.1	1.4	1.3	1.1				1.3	1.4
1.2	1.2	1.2	.9			Quick	1.0	1.1
.7	.7	.7	.5				.6	.6
.3	.5	.4	.5				.4	.4
7 52.1	18 20.8	24 15.1	32 11.3			Sales/Receivables	20 18.5	16 22.8
27 13.6	30 12.2	37 9.9	57 6.4				33 10.9	33 10.9
38 9.5	42 8.7	57 6.4	73 5.0				51 7.1	51 7.1
45 8.2	57 6.4	64 5.7	73 5.0			Cost of Sales/Inventory	64 5.7	65 5.6
73 5.0	94 3.9	94 3.9	89 4.1				101 3.6	99 3.7
152 2.4	146 2.5	140 2.6	130 2.8				152 2.4	146 2.5
12 31.5	11 32.8	19 19.7	16 22.4			Cost of Sales/Payables	15 24.6	14 25.7
27 13.6	23 15.9	35 10.5	29 12.7				34 10.6	30 12.1
65 5.6	49 7.5	49 7.4	57 6.4				58 6.3	58 6.3
5.0	4.3	4.5	6.4			Sales/Working Capital	5.1	4.4
16.1	7.9	7.6	9.1				8.5	7.5
146.7	13.0	14.0	32.7				16.0	14.1
(35) 15.0	(78) 5.2	(78) 6.5	5.1			EBIT/Interest	(171) 5.0	(163) 6.7
3.0	3.0	2.5	3.6				2.3	2.6
.3	1.4	1.5	2.1				1.4	1.3
	(28) 3.6	(30) 7.3				Net Profit + Depr., Dep., Amort./Cur. Mat. L /T/D	(82) 9.7	(62) 5.0
	1.4	2.3					2.5	1.9
	.6	.7					.9	.5
.1	.1	.1	.2			Fixed/Worth	.1	.1
.3	.2	.2	.3				.2	.2
1.6	.5	.5	.6				.6	.5
.8	.8	.9	1.4			Debt/Worth	.9	.8
1.5	1.4	2.1	3.0				1.9	1.6
14.8	2.9	3.6	7.4				5.0	3.4
(34) 85.1	(78) 26.4	(81) 42.1	46.3			% Profit Before Taxes/Tangible Net Worth	(177) 37.8	(170) 30.8
22.1	13.6	15.7	28.6				15.7	15.6
1.1	2.7	4.7	14.6				5.2	4.3
27.4	10.6	12.3	12.7			% Profit Before Taxes/Total Assets	12.3	13.4
5.2	5.5	6.1	5.6				5.6	5.8
-2.7	1.3	1.5	2.5				1.4	1.5
109.0	90.5	104.8	74.5			Sales/Net Fixed Assets	75.2	98.5
47.8	46.2	44.3	38.4				36.3	43.9
18.1	20.8	14.8	14.0				14.0	16.6
4.9	3.6	3.5	2.7			Sales/Total Assets	3.4	3.3
3.2	2.8	2.4	2.3				2.4	2.5
1.9	1.8	1.9	1.7				1.8	1.9
(30) .5	(73) .4	(80) .3	(24) .3			% Depr., Dep., Amort./Sales	(155) .5	(155) .3
1.0	.8	.5	.6				.7	.6
2.7	1.2	1.2	.9				1.2	1.2
(23) 2.4	(48) 2.3	(43) 1.8				% Officers', Directors', Owners' Comp/Sales	(76) 2.2	(82) 1.6
4.4	3.8	2.8					3.9	3.2
6.9	6.7	5.6					7.4	5.5
51912M	286169M	1004316M	1199535M	905268M	653624M	Net Sales ($)	2214975M	2236238M
12245M	88212M	374751M	506911M	405148M	524523M	Total Assets ($)	1161325M	1022206M

Comparative Historical Data				Current Data Sorted By Sales					
2	8	12	# Postretirement Benefits		3	1	1	4	3
			Type of Statement						
36	38	53	Unqualified		2	4	5	14	28
50	55	68	Reviewed	8	16	14	15	12	3
64	62	62	Compiled	6	23	9	15	9	
5	7	13	Tax Returns	4	5	1	3		
52	46	46	Other	11	11	4	8	6	6
4/1/92-3/31/93	4/1/93-3/31/94	4/1/94-3/31/95		**60 (4/1-9/30/94)**			**182 (10/1/94-3/31/95)**		
ALL	ALL	ALL		0-1MM	1-3MM	3-5MM	5-10MM	10-25MM	25MM & OVER
207	208	242	**NUMBER OF STATEMENTS**	29	57	32	46	41	37
%	%	%	**ASSETS**	%	%	%	%	%	%
6.5	7.8	8.0	Cash & Equivalents	9.3	10.5	7.9	7.6	7.2	4.3
23.8	26.3	26.3	Trade Receivables - (net)	20.7	22.6	28.5	23.1	32.9	31.2
50.9	46.5	46.7	Inventory	50.7	48.1	43.7	49.1	46.3	41.6
1.8	1.3	1.5	All Other Current	.9	.9	1.1	1.9	.7	3.4
83.0	81.8	82.4	Total Current	81.6	82.1	81.1	81.6	87.1	80.5
10.4	11.1	10.9	Fixed Assets (net)	12.1	11.5	12.5	12.3	6.8	10.6
1.2	1.9	2.0	Intangibles (net)	3.2	1.8	1.3	.9	1.6	4.1
5.4	5.2	4.6	All Other Non-Current	3.2	4.6	5.1	5.2	4.5	4.7
100.0	100.0	100.0	Total	100.0	100.0	100.0	100.0	100.0	100.0
			LIABILITIES						
17.4	17.8	17.9	Notes Payable-Short Term	17.8	16.3	16.4	13.5	20.2	24.5
3.6	2.0	2.2	Cur. Mat.-L /T/D	3.6	2.7	2.4	1.4	1.0	2.4
20.7	18.4	19.6	Trade Payables	20.2	18.2	17.0	22.0	20.5	19.6
.4	1.5	.3	Income Taxes Payable	.2	.1	.6	.2	.3	.8
7.9	7.7	8.3	All Other Current	12.3	6.3	9.9	6.7	7.4	9.5
50.0	47.3	48.3	Total Current	54.0	43.6	46.3	43.9	49.3	56.8
8.4	8.8	9.7	Long Term Debt	14.1	12.6	8.9	8.8	6.3	7.1
.1	.1	.1	Deferred Taxes	.0	.0	.1	.1	.2	.4
2.8	2.6	4.1	All Other-Non-Current	4.2	2.3	5.2	7.7	5.2	.4
38.6	41.1	37.8	Net Worth	27.7	41.4	39.6	39.6	38.9	35.3
100.0	100.0	100.0	Total Liabilities & Net Worth	100.0	100.0	100.0	100.0	100.0	100.0
			INCOME DATA						
100.0	100.0	100.0	Net Sales	100.0	100.0	100.0	100.0	100.0	100.0
29.1	27.8	29.0	Gross Profit	36.5	32.3	30.5	25.6	25.1	25.0
25.2	24.1	25.7	Operating Expenses	36.2	28.2	26.8	23.2	22.1	19.5
3.9	3.7	3.3	Operating Profit	.3	4.1	3.7	2.4	3.1	5.5
.8	.8	1.1	All Other Expenses (net)	1.6	.7	1.3	1.2	.9	1.2
3.1	2.8	2.2	Profit Before Taxes	-1.3	3.4	2.5	1.2	2.2	4.3
			RATIOS						
2.3	2.5	2.6		2.6	2.6	2.3	3.9	2.4	2.0
1.7	1.7	1.7	Current	1.9	1.9	1.8	1.7	1.7	1.4
1.3	1.3	1.3		1.1	1.3	1.5	1.3	1.3	1.1
1.0	1.1	1.2		1.1	1.1	1.3	1.2	1.3	1.2
.5	.7	.7	Quick	.5	.7	.7	.6	.7	.5
.3	.5	.4		.3	.3	.7	.5	.3	.4
16 23.0	15 24.6	19 19.6		8 43.4	16 23.0	21 17.2	14 26.7	25 14.7	23 15.9
32 11.4	36 10.2	34 10.6	Sales/Receivables	36 10.2	29 12.8	36 10.2	29 12.7	38 9.6	49 7.4
54 6.8	56 6.5	55 6.6		60 6.1	41 9.0	61 6.0	41 8.9	56 6.5	69 5.3
66 5.5	59 6.2	59 6.2		68 5.4	58 6.3	43 8.5	59 6.2	52 7.0	69 5.3
104 3.5	96 3.8	94 3.9	Cost of Sales/Inventory	146 2.5	101 3.6	91 4.0	79 4.6	73 5.0	81 4.5
159 2.3	140 2.6	140 2.6		281 1.3	159 2.3	146 2.5	130 2.8	111 3.3	130 2.8
16 22.8	11 32.2	15 24.6		13 28.1	12 30.5	14 26.6	15 23.6	14 25.5	17 21.1
35 10.5	26 14.0	30 12.0	Cost of Sales/Payables	42 8.6	24 15.1	26 13.9	35 10.3	31 11.6	30 12.1
63 5.8	52 7.0	50 7.3		99 3.7	49 7.4	46 7.9	54 6.8	49 7.5	49 7.5
4.8	4.9	4.5		2.8	3.7	4.5	5.0	6.7	5.7
8.5	7.9	8.0	Sales/Working Capital	5.1	6.9	7.0	8.9	9.0	11.4
16.4	15.5	18.4		358.7	15.5	19.2	15.2	13.3	33.9
(192) 6.7	(194) 8.4	(225) 6.2		(25) 8.9	(53) 6.8	(31) 4.1	(42) 5.9	(37) 7.3	7.2
2.7	3.7	3.0	EBIT/Interest	1.2	3.3	2.9	2.4	3.0	4.1
1.3	1.5	1.5		-1.8	1.5	1.6	1.2	2.0	2.3
(66) 14.6	(64) 7.0	(76) 6.3	Net Profit + Depr., Dep.,		(15) 3.7	(13) 8.9	(15) 9.6	(13) 6.4	(13) 21.6
2.7	3.0	1.8	Amort./Cur. Mat. L/T/D		.9	1.8	3.3	2.1	2.9
.5	.6	.6			.4	.9	.4	.9	1.2
.1	.1	.1		.1	.1	.1	.1	.1	.2
.2	.2	.2	Fixed/Worth	.2	.2	.2	.2	.1	.2
.5	.4	.6		NM	.7	.8	.5	.3	.5
.8	.7	.9		.8	.8	1.0	.8	.9	1.2
1.9	1.7	1.8	Debt/Worth	2.7	1.4	1.6	1.8	1.9	2.0
3.9	3.6	4.0		NM	3.6	2.5	3.0	4.8	6.5
(198) 32.1	(197) 36.4	(227) 36.8	% Profit Before Taxes/Tangible	(22) 68.9	(54) 37.5	(31) 21.5	(44) 28.7	(39) 41.6	45.7
17.2	17.4	16.7	Net Worth	3.9	14.8	14.2	13.7	19.9	28.6
5.9	5.2	4.7		-6.0	2.4	6.6	2.7	10.8	14.6
11.8	12.1	12.7	% Profit Before Taxes/Total	18.4	13.8	8.6	10.1	12.8	13.1
5.6	5.9	6.1	Assets	.6	6.3	5.3	3.7	7.1	8.6
1.3	1.6	1.4		-11.3	1.4	2.0	.9	2.6	2.8
110.4	103.1	89.7		76.0	89.7	61.9	104.1	114.2	74.5
45.0	40.4	40.9	Sales/Net Fixed Assets	28.5	41.4	22.3	50.5	71.0	31.1
20.1	19.9	16.3		12.0	19.7	13.7	15.7	35.3	13.8
3.3	3.5	3.5		3.0	3.7	3.5	3.7	4.0	3.1
2.5	2.6	2.6	Sales/Total Assets	1.9	2.6	2.9	2.7	3.0	2.3
1.8	1.9	1.8		1.2	1.8	1.8	2.0	2.2	1.8
(180) .3	(183) .3	(215) .4		(21) .7	(50) .5	(30) .6	(41) .3	(38) .2	(35) .3
.6	.6	.7	% Depr., Dep., Amort./Sales	1.1	.7	.8	.7	.4	.6
1.1	1.1	1.3		3.0	1.3	1.5	1.1	.7	1.4
(98) 2.0	(93) 1.8	(117) 1.9	% Officers', Directors',	(14) 3.1	(36) 2.5	(19) 2.4	(22) 2.0	(20) 1.5	
3.7	3.6	3.5	Owners' Comp/Sales	4.7	4.6	3.2	3.6	2.5	
5.8	6.3	6.6		11.2	6.7	7.3	5.8	5.1	
2907791M	3286965M	4100824M	Net Sales ($)	17218M	106969M	122841M	320842M	631576M	2901378M
1267890M	1388876M	1911790M	Total Assets ($)	11335M	44636M	52465M	125962M	224940M	1452452M

See Pages 1 through 15 for Explanation of Ratios and Data

WHOLESALERS—FOOTWEAR. SIC# 5139

Current Data Sorted By Assets						# Postretirement Benefits	Comparative Historical Data	
	1	2	4	2		**Type of Statement**		
	2	5	6	1	1	Unqualified	16	15
	15	4	2			Reviewed	14	17
3	2	2				Compiled	17	10
						Tax Returns	1	
	2	1	7	2		Other	7	12
	13 (4/1-9/30/94)		42 (10/1/94-3/31/95)				4/1/90-3/31/91	4/1/91-3/31/92
0-500M	500M-2MM	2-10MM	10-50MM	50-100MM	100-250MM		ALL	ALL
3	21	12	15	3	1	**NUMBER OF STATEMENTS**	55	54
%	%	%	%	%	%	**ASSETS**	%	%
	8.5	5.4	6.1			Cash & Equivalents	10.2	8.3
	35.1	36.7	30.1			Trade Receivables - (net)	33.1	34.5
	41.8	47.2	44.6			Inventory	41.3	41.9
	.4	1.6	3.5			All Other Current	1.8	2.0
	85.8	91.0	84.4			Total Current	86.4	86.7
	5.6	4.2	5.6			Fixed Assets (net)	6.7	5.3
	.6	.3	4.0			Intangibles (net)	1.2	1.5
	8.0	4.5	6.0			All Other Non-Current	5.7	6.5
	100.0	100.0	100.0			Total	100.0	100.0
						LIABILITIES		
	22.1	20.9	15.2			Notes Payable-Short Term	23.0	22.9
	.8	.7	5.2			Cur. Mat. -L/T/D	1.1	1.0
	15.4	25.1	15.6			Trade Payables	18.3	16.9
	.0	.8	1.2			Income Taxes Payable	.3	.3
	4.5	6.3	8.7			All Other Current	9.3	10.3
	42.9	53.8	45.9			Total Current	52.0	51.5
	6.2	5.2	5.1			Long Term Debt	5.1	4.4
	.0	.0	.9			Deferred Taxes	.1	.0
	6.6	8.3	7.2			All Other-Non-Current	4.2	2.0
	44.3	32.7	40.8			Net Worth	38.5	42.2
	100.0	100.0	100.0			Total Liabilities & Net Worth	100.0	100.0
						INCOME DATA		
	100.0	100.0	100.0			Net Sales	100.0	100.0
	31.9	25.4	26.5			Gross Profit	24.8	25.7
	29.3	21.0	23.8			Operating Expenses	22.0	22.7
	2.6	4.4	2.7			Operating Profit	2.8	3.1
	1.1	.9	1.8			All Other Expenses (net)	1.1	1.2
	1.6	3.5	.9			Profit Before Taxes	1.7	1.9
						RATIOS		
	3.3	2.1	2.5				2.6	2.3
	2.1	1.6	1.8			Current	1.6	1.8
	1.4	1.4	1.6				1.3	1.3
	1.4	1.3	1.2				1.2	1.1
	1.2	.8	.7			Quick	.8	.9
	.6	.5	.4				.5	.5
	40 9.2	21 17.3	27 13.7				29 12.4	33 11.2
	51 7.1	55 6.6	43 8.5			Sales/Receivables	46 7.9	47 7.8
	78 4.7	122 3.0	59 6.2				78 4.7	78 4.7
	42 8.7	44 8.3	68 5.4				43 8.5	54 6.7
	104 3.5	101 3.6	87 4.2			Cost of Sales/Inventory	81 4.5	81 4.5
	146 2.5	159 2.3	174 2.1				152 2.4	130 2.8
	6 57.5	16 23.0	8 47.5				13 28.9	14 26.3
	33 11.2	35 10.5	32 11.5			Cost of Sales/Payables	24 15.1	26 14.1
	47 7.8	49 7.5	49 7.5				53 6.9	52 7.0
	3.5	3.1	3.1				4.1	4.3
	5.0	5.6	7.6			Sales/Working Capital	6.5	6.3
	14.4	13.9	12.3				16.8	16.8
	3.0	5.7	8.5				5.0	5.1
	(17) 2.0	4.2	(14) 3.7			EBIT/Interest	(50) 1.8	(44) 2.4
	1.4	2.6	.4				1.2	1.2
						Net Profit + Depr., Dep.,		10.3
						Amort./Cur. Mat. L /T/D	(14) 3.9	
								1.5
	.0	.0	.0				.0	.0
	.1	.1	.1			Fixed/Worth	.1	.1
	.3	.4	.2				.3	.4
	.5	1.1	.7				.7	.7
	1.6	2.2	1.6			Debt/Worth	1.9	1.3
	3.5	4.6	2.1				4.0	4.1
	18.3	65.5	39.5				28.3	31.9
	(20) 10.0	18.5	(14) 16.2			% Profit Before Taxes/Tangible	(52) 17.4	(53) 15.4
	1.4	7.4	7.9			Net Worth	3.3	2.3
	6.5	9.4	18.0				11.1	10.1
	3.5	7.4	8.7			% Profit Before Taxes/Total	3.9	4.8
	.5	3.3	1.5			Assets	.9	1.1
	464.5	280.9	95.6				148.5	225.0
	157.1	108.5	56.4			Sales/Net Fixed Assets	79.1	84.8
	33.0	49.4	36.6				32.8	33.3
	3.0	4.5	3.2				3.7	3.2
	2.3	2.2	2.4			Sales/Total Assets	2.1	2.2
	1.7	1.4	1.5				1.5	1.8
	.1	.2	.2				.3	.2
	(18) .4	(11) .3	(13) .4			% Depr., Dep., Amort./Sales	(46) .4	(42) .4
	.8	.6	.6				.6	.7
	2.4						1.2	2.1
	(13) 4.0					% Officers', Directors',	(22) 3.8	(23) 4.4
	7.3					Owners' Comp/Sales	6.2	8.4
13595M	73806M	138176M	818814M	373210M	154935M	Net Sales ($)	1039669M	1242046M
1188M	30000M	58516M	334304M	237211M	100324M	Total Assets ($)	540533M	566306M

© Robert Morris Associates 1995

M = $ thousand   MM = $ million
See Pages 1 through 15 for Explanation of Ratios and Data

Comparative Historical Data				Current Data Sorted By Sales					
	5	9	# Postretirement Benefits		1			2	6
			Type of Statement						
17	19	15	Unqualified		1	1	2	3	8
22	22	21	Reviewed	7	7	3	2	2	
13	11	7	Compiled	1	3	3			
			Tax Returns						
14	13	12	Other		1	2	1	8	
4/1/92-3/31/93	4/1/93-3/31/94	4/1/94-3/31/95			13 (4/1-9/30/94)			42 (10/1/94-3/31/95)	
ALL	ALL	ALL		0-1MM	1-3MM	3-5MM	5-10MM	10-25MM	25MM & OVER
66	65	55	NUMBER OF STATEMENTS	1	8	12	7	9	18

93 ALL %	94 ALL %	95 ALL %		0-1MM %	1-3MM %	3-5MM %	5-10MM %	10-25MM %	25MM & OVER %
			ASSETS						
7.7	9.8	10.6	Cash & Equivalents			7.5			12.3
33.9	34.6	32.5	Trade Receivables - (net)			37.5			28.8
42.1	40.3	42.2	Inventory			36.5			42.6
1.9	1.8	1.5	All Other Current			.6			2.9
85.5	86.5	86.9	Total Current			82.2			86.7
6.3	6.0	5.3	Fixed Assets (net)			6.6			6.1
2.5	.8	1.7	Intangibles (net)			.6			1.3
5.7	6.7	6.1	All Other Non-Current			10.6			6.0
100.0	100.0	100.0	Total			100.0			100.0
			LIABILITIES						
21.8	21.1	18.9	Notes Payable-Short Term			23.9			10.5
2.4	.6	1.9	Cur. Mat.-L /T/D			.9			3.9
17.2	16.8	17.2	Trade Payables			12.6			17.8
.6	1.1	.5	Income Taxes Payable			.0			1.1
9.8	7.2	6.3	All Other Current			4.9			7.7
51.8	46.9	44.9	Total Current			42.3			41.0
6.3	4.2	5.1	Long Term Debt			4.7			4.1
.3	.3	.3	Deferred Taxes			.0			1.0
4.9	2.9	6.9	All Other-Non-Current			11.4			2.9
36.7	45.7	42.8	Net Worth			41.6			51.1
100.0	100.0	100.0	Total Liabilities & Net Worth			100.0			100.0
			INCOME DATA						
100.0	100.0	100.0	Net Sales			100.0			100.0
30.3	29.6	29.0	Gross Profit			36.8			30.5
26.0	25.4	26.0	Operating Expenses			33.4			23.0
4.2	4.3	3.0	Operating Profit			3.4			7.5
1.2	.5	1.1	All Other Expenses (net)			1.5			.9
3.0	3.8	1.9	Profit Before Taxes			1.9			6.6
			RATIOS						
2.4	2.4	2.7				3.5			4.7
1.7	1.7	1.8	Current			2.1			2.0
1.3	1.4	1.4				1.3			1.6
1.1	1.4	1.6				1.4			2.5
.8	1.1	1.0	Quick			1.1			.9
.4	.6	.6				.7			.4
30 12.0	28 13.0	27 13.4				22 16.3			24 14.9
47 7.7	42 8.6	48 7.6	Sales/Receivables			50 7.3			43 8.4
64 5.7	66 5.5	76 4.8				81 4.5			58 6.3
39 9.3	35 10.5	46 7.9				32 11.5			62 5.9
73 5.0	79 4.6	87 4.2	Cost of Sales/Inventory			91 4.0			81 4.5
146 2.5	135 2.7	152 2.4				107 3.4			135 2.7
15 24.8	13 27.4	8 45.5				3 125.8			18 20.0
29 12.4	26 14.1	32 11.5	Cost of Sales/Payables			15 25.1			29 12.5
56 6.5	42 8.7	49 7.5				41 8.8			49 7.4
4.1	3.9	3.1				4.0			2.6
7.8	7.0	5.7	Sales/Working Capital			9.4			7.0
16.2	13.3	13.7				14.9			10.5
8.3	10.1	8.1				4.4			10.6
(62) 3.3	(58) 3.4	(48) 2.7	EBIT/Interest		(11) 2.0			(16) 7.4	
1.5	1.4	1.4				1.2			2.3
11.5	61.2	19.3							
(22) 2.6	(12) 5.0	(20) 7.3	Net Profit + Depr., Dep., Amort./Cur. Mat. L/T/D						
1.4	.4	1.8							
.1	.0	.0				.0			.0
.1	.1	.1	Fixed/Worth			.1			.1
.4	.3	.2				.3			.2
.9	.7	.7				.6			.3
1.7	1.4	1.6	Debt/Worth			1.2			1.4
4.7	2.3	3.4				4.7			2.0
48.9	32.5	28.5				21.8			39.5
(59) 23.8	(64) 17.6	(53) 15.3	% Profit Before Taxes/Tangible Net Worth		(11) 5.1				19.3
5.9	4.4	4.1				4.1			13.2
15.5	15.1	13.8				12.7			18.6
8.1	6.8	5.9	% Profit Before Taxes/Total Assets			3.4			14.4
2.0	1.8	.8				1.2			3.5
133.5	237.4	292.1				398.8			90.4
70.0	80.3	80.5	Sales/Net Fixed Assets			107.4			44.2
32.9	26.7	36.6				40.7			27.6
3.6	3.6	3.0				4.5			3.3
2.3	2.3	2.3	Sales/Total Assets			2.5			2.4
1.9	1.8	1.5				2.1			1.6
.2	.3	.2				.1			.3
(56) .6	(49) .5	(47) .4	% Depr., Dep., Amort./Sales		(11) .3			(16) .6	
.9	.8	.8				.8			1.0
1.9	1.9	2.1							
(23) 3.2	(24) 3.7	(28) 3.6	% Officers', Directors', Owners' Comp/Sales						
9.4	8.4	7.7							
1398803M	1302628M	1572536M	Net Sales ($)	391M	15202M	47021M	47189M	122480M	1340253M
580093M	627085M	761543M	Total Assets ($)	398M	10302M	17472M	21622M	63835M	647914M

M = $ thousand   MM = $ million
See Pages 1 through 15 for Explanation of Ratios and Data

	Current Data Sorted By Assets							Comparative Historical Data	
	2	3	6	1			# Postretirement Benefits		
							Type of Statement		
	1	1	10	12	2	4	Unqualified	32	32
	6	16	14	1			Reviewed	34	54
	9	14	7				Compiled	19	22
		1	1				Tax Returns		
	7	8	14	3	2	1	Other	21	21
		30 (4/1-9/30/94)		104 (10/1/94-3/31/95)				4/1/90-3/31/91	4/1/91-3/31/92
	0-500M	500M-2MM	2-10MM	10-50MM	50-100MM	100-250MM		ALL	ALL
	23	40	46	16	4	5	**NUMBER OF STATEMENTS**	106	129
	%	%	%	%	%	%	**ASSETS**	%	%
	7.6	9.3	6.4	1.7			Cash & Equivalents	7.5	9.2
	34.1	28.0	28.8	23.6			Trade Receivables - (net)	25.9	25.6
	41.3	40.5	47.9	58.4			Inventory	45.5	47.4
	.1	1.7	2.6	1.2			All Other Current	3.2	1.4
	83.2	79.5	85.7	84.8			Total Current	82.0	83.6
	10.6	9.6	8.0	10.5			Fixed Assets (net)	11.3	8.5
	1.8	.2	1.1	2.6			Intangibles (net)	1.2	1.8
	4.4	10.7	5.1	2.1			All Other Non-Current	5.5	6.1
	100.0	100.0	100.0	100.0			Total	100.0	100.0
							LIABILITIES		
	19.5	15.6	17.2	26.9			Notes Payable-Short Term	18.0	20.1
	1.8	2.1	1.7	2.0			Cur. Mat. -L/T/D	3.0	2.8
	18.1	20.1	20.9	21.6			Trade Payables	19.9	20.0
	.0	1.0	.7	.3			Income Taxes Payable	.7	.4
	7.9	6.0	6.0	5.6			All Other Current	8.9	8.4
	47.3	44.7	46.5	56.4			Total Current	50.6	51.6
	12.3	7.0	6.7	6.8			Long Term Debt	10.7	7.5
	.0	.1	.2	.1			Deferred Taxes	.1	.1
	11.7	5.8	3.2	2.9			All Other-Non-Current	4.1	4.5
	28.8	42.5	43.4	33.8			Net Worth	34.5	36.3
	100.0	100.0	100.0	100.0			Total Liabilities & Net Worth	100.0	100.0
							INCOME DATA		
	100.0	100.0	100.0	100.0			Net Sales	100.0	100.0
	30.5	33.9	26.0	21.8			Gross Profit	27.9	27.3
	26.0	30.0	22.5	16.9			Operating Expenses	24.2	23.5
	4.5	3.9	3.6	4.9			Operating Profit	3.7	3.9
	1.6	.6	.6	1.4			All Other Expenses (net)	1.0	1.2
	2.9	3.3	3.0	3.5			Profit Before Taxes	2.7	2.6
							RATIOS		
	3.9	2.8	2.7	1.8				2.3	2.4
	2.0	1.7	1.8	1.4			Current	1.6	1.6
	1.3	1.3	1.3	1.3				1.3	1.3
	2.0	1.4	1.1	.7				1.0	1.1
(22)	1.0	.9	.7	.5			Quick	.6	.7
	.5	.5	.4	.3				.4	.4
	18 19.9	19 19.2	22 16.3	25 14.5				19 19.0	17 21.2
	49 7.5	38 9.7	38 9.7	32 11.5			Sales/Receivables	36 10.1	34 10.8
	63 5.8	51 7.1	54 6.7	45 8.1				54 6.7	49 7.5
	28 13.1	52 7.0	54 6.8	74 4.9				54 6.8	54 6.8
	48 7.6	81 4.5	85 4.3	91 4.0			Cost of Sales/Inventory	94 3.9	87 4.2
	130 2.8	130 2.8	122 3.0	152 2.4				135 2.7	135 2.7
	2 220.6	10 36.0	21 17.1	24 15.0				14 26.4	14 25.2
	34 10.7	29 12.6	35 10.4	34 10.8			Cost of Sales/Payables	32 11.4	33 11.2
	57 6.4	51 7.2	60 6.1	43 8.5				61 6.0	47 7.7
	4.2	5.5	4.6	6.1				5.0	5.7
	12.8	8.4	8.4	9.8			Sales/Working Capital	9.5	9.4
	27.6	18.6	14.6	18.1				18.0	20.3
	6.2	6.4	7.2	7.1				6.3	5.5
(20)	3.1	(33) 2.5	(40) 3.4	3.5			EBIT/Interest	(94) 2.1	(113) 2.6
	.2	1.4	1.8	1.4				1.2	1.3
		4.3	17.6					16.4	8.3
	(11) 2.8	(10) 4.8				Net Profit + Depr., Dep.,	(38) 2.6	(43) 3.6
		.5	1.3				Amort./Cur. Mat. L /T/D	.8	1.3
	.1	.1	.0	.1				.1	.1
	.4	.1	.1	.2			Fixed/Worth	.2	.2
	–3.9	.4	.4	.4				.8	.5
	.8	.8	.8	1.2				1.1	.9
	1.4	1.4	1.4	1.9			Debt/Worth	2.1	2.3
	–36.8	2.9	3.1	4.0				4.8	4.5
	118.2	37.9	28.6	32.6			% Profit Before Taxes/Tangible	45.8	44.8
(17)	40.7	16.9	17.1	(15) 21.8			Net Worth	(101) 17.5	(123) 22.8
	6.3	4.9	6.2	4.1				4.2	5.9
	33.3	17.0	13.0	12.3			% Profit Before Taxes/Total	12.9	14.2
	12.9	6.1	4.8	7.7			Assets	5.1	6.2
	–2.4	2.0	2.3	1.3				.6	1.7
	113.6	231.3	237.4	100.7				181.0	146.9
	45.4	52.8	74.2	49.9			Sales/Net Fixed Assets	35.8	54.7
	25.1	17.0	19.9	17.1				14.7	21.5
	6.5	4.3	3.4	3.2				3.4	3.8
	3.0	2.5	2.7	2.6			Sales/Total Assets	2.5	2.7
	2.0	2.0	2.0	2.1				1.9	1.9
	.4	.2	.2	.3				.2	.2
(13)	.7	(33) .8	(39) .5	(15) .5			% Depr., Dep., Amort./Sales	(86) .5	(105) .5
	1.5	2.3	1.0	.9				1.1	1.0
	2.5	4.0	1.1					1.9	2.0
(10)	4.4	(27) 5.8	(22) 2.8				% Officers', Directors',	(51) 3.1	(56) 3.4
	5.8	8.8	4.2				Owners' Comp/Sales	6.3	7.4
	27337M	125122M	627296M	930358M	472700M	1107138M	Net Sales ($)	1872925M	2068193M
	6279M	42678M	217255M	341300M	248325M	753657M	Total Assets ($)	964681M	874165M

M = $ thousand   MM = $ million
See Pages 1 through 15 for Explanation of Ratios and Data

Comparative Historical Data				Current Data Sorted By Sales					
	6	12		1	1	2	3	4	1
			# Postretirement Benefits						
			Type of Statement						
49	33	30	Unqualified		1	1	5	5	18
30	37	37	Reviewed	4	10	8	5	8	2
18	29	30	Compiled	8	9	7	4	2	
1	4	2	Tax Returns				2		
20	23	35	Other	4	6	6	2	9	8
4/1/92-3/31/93 ALL	4/1/93-3/31/94 ALL	4/1/94-3/31/95 ALL		30 (4/1-9/30/94)			104 (10/1/94-3/31/95)		
				0-1MM	1-3MM	3-5MM	5-10MM	10-25MM	25MM & OVER
118	126	134	**NUMBER OF STATEMENTS**	16	26	22	18	24	28
%	%	%	**ASSETS**	%	%	%	%	%	%
8.3	6.5	6.6	Cash & Equivalents	7.3	7.1	10.8	9.0	3.4	3.5
28.6	31.0	28.6	Trade Receivables - (net)	31.4	28.9	26.9	33.0	28.7	25.2
46.0	43.3	45.6	Inventory	43.8	41.5	43.8	42.9	46.9	52.7
1.7	1.4	1.9	All Other Current	.5	1.9	.6	2.5	3.1	2.4
84.6	82.2	82.7	Total Current	83.0	79.4	82.1	87.4	82.1	83.8
9.4	11.4	9.8	Fixed Assets (net)	8.6	12.4	7.6	7.6	9.1	11.8
1.0	1.0	1.2	Intangibles (net)	.0	1.6	.5	.7	2.9	.7
4.9	5.3	6.3	All Other Non-Current	8.3	6.7	9.8	4.3	5.9	3.7
100.0	100.0	100.0	Total	100.0	100.0	100.0	100.0	100.0	100.0
			LIABILITIES						
20.9	18.3	18.0	Notes Payable-Short Term	24.6	17.9	11.9	16.5	15.6	22.1
1.8	2.3	1.8	Cur. Mat.-L /T/D	1.6	2.8	1.7	1.6	1.8	1.3
21.0	19.7	20.2	Trade Payables	15.1	19.4	19.3	18.9	24.3	21.7
.6	1.6	.6	Income Taxes Payable	.0	.5	1.3	.2	1.2	.2
7.6	7.1	6.6	All Other Current	8.4	4.4	7.7	4.0	8.5	7.0
51.9	49.0	47.2	Total Current	49.7	44.9	41.8	41.2	51.4	52.2
6.8	8.3	8.0	Long Term Debt	16.1	7.0	6.3	5.7	7.1	7.7
.0	.2	.2	Deferred Taxes	.0	.1	.0	.4	.2	.5
3.4	4.2	5.3	All Other-Non-Current	18.0	4.4	5.9	1.2	3.4	2.6
37.9	38.4	39.4	Net Worth	16.2	43.6	46.0	51.5	37.8	37.0
100.0	100.0	100.0	Total Liabilities & Net Worth	100.0	100.0	100.0	100.0	100.0	100.0
			INCOME DATA						
100.0	100.0	100.0	Net Sales	100.0	100.0	100.0	100.0	100.0	100.0
25.8	29.6	28.7	Gross Profit	39.9	31.2	28.8	30.1	24.2	22.9
21.5	24.9	24.5	Operating Expenses	35.4	25.9	26.6	26.8	20.2	17.8
4.3	4.7	4.2	Operating Profit	4.5	5.4	2.2	3.3	4.0	5.1
.9	1.0	.9	All Other Expenses (net)	2.3	.6	.3	.5	1.0	1.1
3.4	3.6	3.2	Profit Before Taxes	2.2	4.7	1.9	2.9	3.0	4.0
			RATIOS						
2.3	2.4	2.6		3.2	3.0	2.8	3.7	2.0	2.2
1.6	1.7	1.7	Current	1.9	1.6	2.3	2.0	1.7	1.6
1.2	1.3	1.3		1.1	1.3	1.4	1.6	1.2	1.3
1.1	1.2	1.1		1.5	1.4	1.4	2.0	.9	.9
.7 (125)	.8 (133)	.7	Quick	.8	.8 (21)	.9	1.0	.7	.5
.4	.5	.4		.3	.4	.6	.7	.3	.3
19 18.8	27 13.4	22 16.4		19 19.1	12 29.4	18 20.0	26 13.9	22 16.5	23 15.7
33 10.9	41 9.0	37 9.8	Sales/Receivables	61 6.0	35 10.3	35 10.5	42 8.7	34 10.8	32 11.5
57 6.4	55 6.6	54 6.7		107 3.4	56 6.5	44 8.3	56 6.5	51 7.2	52 7.0
47 7.7	43 8.4	51 7.2		55 6.6	32 11.3	25 14.4	59 6.2	53 6.9	73 5.0
81 4.5	81 4.5	87 4.2	Cost of Sales/Inventory	135 2.7	85 4.3	78 4.7	81 4.5	74 4.9	96 3.8
122 3.0	130 2.8	130 2.8		281 1.3	152 3.0	122 2.4	122 3.0	107 3.4	152 2.4
11 32.6	16 22.2	16 22.7		6 57.2	9 40.1	10 38.2	12 31.0	25 14.8	23 15.8
33 11.2	30 12.2	34 10.7	Cost of Sales/Payables	39 9.4	33 11.1	26 13.9	28 13.1	37 9.8	38 9.5
58 6.3	55 6.6	55 6.6		69 5.3	50 7.3	63 5.8	46 7.9	62 5.9	56 6.5
5.7	5.6	4.9		2.3	6.0	4.8	3.8	7.5	4.6
9.7	8.0	8.5	Sales/Working Capital	3.7	10.9	7.6	6.5	11.6	8.4
20.0	19.3	16.9		43.3	17.6	16.8	15.5	25.8	15.8
5.6	10.2	6.8		5.3	6.3	7.5	6.0	7.1	9.3
(103) 2.8	(117) 3.0	(117) 3.2	EBIT/Interest	(15) 2.4	(23) 2.8	(16) 4.1	(15) 2.8	(21) 3.7	(27) 4.5
1.5	1.7	1.4		.2	1.9	.7	1.1	1.7	1.8
17.6	9.8	8.8	Net Profit + Depr., Dep.,						
(39) 4.3	(37) 2.9	(32) 3.0	Amort./Cur. Mat. L/T/D						
1.3	.9	1.1							
.1	.1	.1		.1	.1	.0	.0	.1	.1
.2	.2	.2	Fixed/Worth	.3	.2	.1	.1	.3	.2
.4	.6	.4		NM	1.4	.3	.3	.4	.4
1.1	.9	.9		1.1	.5	.8	.4	1.1	1.2
1.9	1.9	1.4	Debt/Worth	3.1	1.3	1.3	1.1	1.7	1.5
3.8	3.3	3.5		NM	6.9	2.3	2.0	5.3	3.3
45.7	55.8	40.7	% Profit Before Taxes/Tangible	58.3	54.9	38.4	30.1	28.8	45.0
(114) 21.3	(120) 24.9	(127) 18.4	Net Worth	(12) 13.1	(24) 29.2	15.9	8.3	(23) 23.2	21.9
6.2	7.1	5.9		4.6	7.6	1.0	3.2	8.4	5.7
15.5	18.6	16.8	% Profit Before Taxes/Total	17.6	20.1	15.3	16.9	12.9	17.2
7.3	6.7	6.1	Assets	4.1	8.4	6.4	3.9	7.5	7.7
1.4	1.9	2.1		-3.5	2.6	.6	.8	2.4	3.0
170.3	124.1	127.3		84.5	130.5	348.2	278.2	124.3	97.9
56.7	41.8	50.4	Sales/Net Fixed Assets	30.2	35.9	69.3	68.3	58.9	30.9
19.9	17.7	17.0		9.5	17.4	42.1	19.2	18.2	13.9
3.6	3.5	3.5		2.3	3.2	5.9	3.8	3.7	3.2
2.8	2.7	2.6	Sales/Total Assets	1.8	2.5	2.7	2.9	3.1	2.4
2.0	2.1	1.9		1.1	2.1	1.8	2.0	2.5	1.9
.3	.3	.3			.3	.3	.1	.2	.3
(98) .5	(106) .6	(106) .6	% Depr., Dep., Amort./Sales		(21) .8	(17) .6	(16) .7	(21) .5	(23) .6
.9	1.2	1.4			2.4	1.1	1.3	.8	1.7
1.2	2.6	2.1			2.4	4.9	1.5	1.6	
(50) 3.2	(55) 4.4	(63) 4.1	% Officers', Directors', Owners' Comp/Sales		(16) 4.1	(13) 5.2	(10) 3.1	(10) 3.0	
5.2	8.8	6.9			8.0	9.5	6.4	4.3	
3077984M	3100169M	3289951M	Net Sales ($)	7342M	48295M	86930M	130711M	385489M	2631184M
1235924M	1272291M	1609494M	Total Assets ($)	6201M	19510M	33223M	52489M	134605M	1363466M

M = $ thousand   MM = $ million
See Pages 1 through 15 for Explanation of Ratios and Data

	Current Data Sorted By Assets						# Postretirement Benefits	Comparative Historical Data	
	1	1	2	4			**Type of Statement**		
	2	4	14	10			Unqualified	23	35
	3	10	30	4			Reviewed	33	39
	7	21	6				Compiled	43	30
			1				Tax Returns		
	4	12	14	3			Other	14	15
		51 (4/1-9/30/94)		94 (10/1/94-3/31/95)				4/1/90-3/31/91	4/1/91-3/31/92
	0-500M	500M-2MM	2-10MM	10-50MM	50-100MM	100-250MM		ALL	ALL
	16	47	65	17			**NUMBER OF STATEMENTS**	113	119
	%	%	%	%	%	%	**ASSETS**	%	%
	16.0	8.5	9.4	4.0			Cash & Equivalents	6.9	6.3
	28.4	30.9	32.3	29.6			Trade Receivables - (net)	34.6	29.5
	30.1	42.0	37.5	47.3			Inventory	41.1	47.6
	4.1	1.5	1.2	2.2			All Other Current	2.8	3.0
	78.5	82.9	80.4	83.1			Total Current	85.5	86.4
	13.3	8.4	11.3	11.0			Fixed Assets (net)	8.9	7.6
	.6	2.6	1.8	1.0			Intangibles (net)	.5	.9
	7.6	6.0	6.5	5.0			All Other Non-Current	5.1	5.1
	100.0	100.0	100.0	100.0			Total	100.0	100.0
							LIABILITIES		
	8.3	12.2	15.8	22.0			Notes Payable-Short Term	13.9	15.7
	5.3	2.3	1.3	2.0			Cur. Mat. -L/T/D	2.5	2.4
	19.5	25.3	24.5	18.7			Trade Payables	22.5	22.5
	.5	.2	.2	.3			Income Taxes Payable	.8	.7
	13.1	8.7	9.2	4.1			All Other Current	8.3	7.2
	46.6	48.6	51.0	47.2			Total Current	48.0	48.5
	11.2	6.5	6.1	11.7			Long Term Debt	8.9	6.4
	.8	.1	.3	.7			Deferred Taxes	.2	.1
	5.3	6.7	2.2	2.8			All Other-Non-Current	.9	2.0
	36.0	38.1	40.5	37.7			Net Worth	41.9	43.0
	100.0	100.0	100.0	100.0			Total Liabilities & Net Worth	100.0	100.0
							INCOME DATA		
	100.0	100.0	100.0	100.0			Net Sales	100.0	100.0
	38.0	26.8	25.0	19.9			Gross Profit	26.5	28.0
	33.4	23.7	22.5	18.5			Operating Expenses	22.5	24.3
	4.5	3.2	2.5	1.4			Operating Profit	4.0	3.8
	1.3	.5	.7	1.6			All Other Expenses (net)	.9	.8
	3.2	2.7	1.8	-.2			Profit Before Taxes	3.1	3.0
							RATIOS		
	3.6	2.2	2.3	2.5			Current	2.7	2.7
	1.8	1.8	1.5	1.7				1.8	1.7
	1.0	1.4	1.2	1.4				1.4	1.5
	1.7	1.2	1.2	.9			Quick	1.3	1.2
	1.0	.8	.7	.7				.9	.7
	.5	.5	.6	.5				.5	.5
	11 32.0	27 13.3	34 10.7	38 9.5			Sales/Receivables	26 13.8	26 14.3
	29 12.6	39 9.4	47 7.8	53 6.9				42 8.7	41 8.9
	46 7.9	50 7.3	66 5.5	62 5.9				63 5.8	60 6.1
	9 40.6	37 9.9	39 9.4	76 4.8			Cost of Sales/Inventory	41 8.8	60 6.1
	47 7.8	85 4.3	70 5.2	89 4.1				76 4.8	91 4.0
	87 4.2	122 3.0	140 2.6	140 2.6				126 2.9	146 2.5
	0 UND	19 18.8	29 12.5	25 14.7			Cost of Sales/Payables	22 16.9	24 15.4
	15 23.8	43 8.4	49 7.5	39 9.4				33 10.9	38 9.5
	46 8.0	70 5.2	64 5.7	57 6.4				63 5.8	62 5.9
	6.9	5.0	5.4	4.2			Sales/Working Capital	4.4	4.2
	9.9	7.7	9.4	7.6				7.2	6.9
	NM	13.8	18.6	13.0				13.5	12.0
	7.6	8.5	5.4	5.1			EBIT/Interest	5.7	5.7
	(12) 4.8	(39) 2.5	(57) 2.4	2.6				(101) 2.5	(107) 2.7
	2.0	1.3	1.3	1.2				1.4	1.3
		(10) 9.0	(22) 5.1	(10) 4.1			Net Profit + Depr., Dep.,	(35) 4.1	(45) 9.1
		4.1	2.5	2.2			Amort./Cur. Mat. L./T/D	1.4	3.4
		.3	.7	1.5				.6	.5
	.0	.0	.1	.0			Fixed/Worth	.0	.1
	.2	.1	.2	.1				.1	.1
	.7	.4	.5	.4				.4	.3
	.6	.9	.8	1.2			Debt/Worth	.7	.7
	1.5	1.6	2.0	1.8				1.4	1.5
	6.3	5.1	3.6	4.1				2.8	2.3
	96.7	41.5	34.4	28.8			% Profit Before Taxes/Tangible	34.7	34.2
	(14) 51.6	(45) 15.2	11.6	15.6			Net Worth	(110) 16.0	(117) 13.9
	17.3	2.3	2.9	4.0				4.5	4.2
	24.9	9.8	9.3	8.9			% Profit Before Taxes/Total	14.0	10.8
	16.7	3.7	4.0	4.9			Assets	5.3	5.7
	8.0	.7	1.1	.8				1.8	1.4
	UND	276.7	161.6	195.1			Sales/Net Fixed Assets	182.4	151.1
	77.7	81.0	39.2	92.6				67.7	58.7
	35.5	26.4	16.2	9.2				22.4	28.1
	5.6	3.5	2.9	2.8			Sales/Total Assets	3.6	3.4
	4.0	2.8	2.4	2.3				2.7	2.5
	2.6	2.1	1.9	1.7				2.0	2.0
		(35) .3	(58) .3	(16) .1			% Depr., Dep., Amort./Sales	(99) .2	(108) .2
		.5	.7	.3				.5	.4
		1.1	1.1	3.1				.9	.8
		(30) 2.8	(33) 1.4				% Officers', Directors',	(54) 1.8	(61) 1.6
		5.1	2.9				Owners' Comp/Sales	3.2	3.2
		8.3	6.6					6.6	5.6
	19304M	161351M	765583M	963261M			Net Sales ($)	1513035M	1775756M
	3640M	57538M	297571M	407590M			Total Assets ($)	592274M	742406M

M = $ thousand   MM = $ million
See Pages 1 through 15 for Explanation of Ratios and Data

Comparative Historical Data				Current Data Sorted By Sales					
4	10	8	# Postretirement Benefits		2		2		4
			Type of Statement						
24	38	30	Unqualified	1	4	1	6	9	9
54	50	47	Reviewed	2	8	4	20	10	3
33	34	34	Compiled	5	9	11	7	2	
5	4	1	Tax Returns					1	
20	20	33	Other	2	9	6	5	7	4
4/1/92-3/31/93	4/1/93-3/31/94	4/1/94-3/31/95		51 (4/1-9/30/94)			94 (10/1/94-3/31/95)		
ALL	ALL	ALL		0-1MM	1-3MM	3-5MM	5-10MM	10-25MM	25MM & OVER
136	146	145	**NUMBER OF STATEMENTS**	10	30	22	39	28	16
%	%	%	**ASSETS**	%	%	%	%	%	%
7.1	6.0	9.2	Cash & Equivalents	11.6	10.1	10.3	9.6	9.5	2.9
33.4	32.0	31.1	Trade Receivables - (net)	30.3	25.0	34.2	31.5	35.5	30.0
43.0	44.0	39.3	Inventory	30.9	39.2	40.1	39.0	35.0	51.6
3.1	1.7	1.7	All Other Current	6.3	.9	.6	2.2	1.0	2.3
86.6	83.7	81.3	Total Current	79.0	75.3	85.2	82.3	81.0	86.7
8.2	9.0	10.5	Fixed Assets (net)	12.6	11.7	6.6	11.2	12.5	7.3
.6	1.2	1.9	Intangibles (net)	.8	3.4	1.7	.8	2.5	1.0
4.5	6.1	6.3	All Other Non-Current	7.6	9.6	6.4	5.6	4.0	4.9
100.0	100.0	100.0	Total	100.0	100.0	100.0	100.0	100.0	100.0
			LIABILITIES						
15.9	16.3	14.5	Notes Payable-Short Term	10.6	9.7	13.4	16.0	14.8	23.4
1.6	1.4	2.1	Cur. Mat.-L /T/D	2.4	4.7	1.4	.8	1.7	2.0
22.0	21.0	23.5	Trade Payables	13.6	23.7	25.0	24.4	25.3	21.6
.3	1.0	.2	Income Taxes Payable	.6	.1	.2	.3	.2	.3
8.3	7.1	8.9	All Other Current	13.9	8.7	7.6	9.2	10.5	4.3
48.2	46.8	49.3	Total Current	41.1	46.9	47.7	50.7	52.5	51.5
6.8	7.8	7.5	Long Term Debt	7.2	11.7	2.6	5.9	6.3	12.1
.3	.3	.3	Deferred Taxes	.2	.4	.0	.6	.2	.6
3.7	3.2	4.1	All Other-Non-Current	6.6	7.6	5.5	2.3	1.3	3.0
41.1	41.9	38.9	Net Worth	44.9	33.4	44.3	40.4	39.7	32.9
100.0	100.0	100.0	Total Liabilities & Net Worth	100.0	100.0	100.0	100.0	100.0	100.0
			INCOME DATA						
100.0	100.0	100.0	Net Sales	100.0	100.0	100.0	100.0	100.0	100.0
25.4	25.5	26.4	Gross Profit	41.3	29.3	27.3	24.9	24.6	17.5
21.7	23.8	23.6	Operating Expenses	36.2	26.1	25.0	23.0	20.3	16.6
3.7	1.7	2.8	Operating Profit	5.2	3.2	2.3	2.0	4.3	.9
1.2	.7	.8	All Other Expenses (net)	.8	.6	.2	.8	1.0	1.8
2.5	1.0	2.0	Profit Before Taxes	4.3	2.6	2.1	1.2	3.3	-.9
			RATIOS						
2.8	2.5	2.3	Current	4.7	2.5	2.3	2.1	2.2	2.5
1.8	1.7	1.7		2.0	1.7	1.8	1.6	1.4	1.6
1.4	1.4	1.3		1.2	1.3	1.3	1.2	1.2	1.3
1.4	1.3	1.2	Quick	2.4	1.1	1.8	1.2	1.0	.8
(135) .8	.8	.8		1.0	.8	.8	.7	.8	.7
.5	.5	.5		.5	.5	.4	.6	.6	.5
26 13.8	31 11.7	30 12.3	Sales/Receivables	14 25.2	15 24.8	30 12.3	27 13.3	35 10.3	33 11.2
45 8.2	42 8.6	43 8.5		41 9.0	36 10.1	42 8.7	47 7.8	45 8.2	47 7.7
62 5.9	59 6.2	62 5.9		54 6.7	51 7.1	68 5.4	65 5.6	57 6.4	61 6.0
47 7.8	45 8.1	42 8.6	Cost of Sales/Inventory	17 21.4	56 6.5	35 10.3	48 7.6	33 10.9	63 5.8
74 4.9	76 4.8	78 4.7		47 7.8	85 4.3	65 5.6	72 5.1	56 6.5	87 4.2
118 3.1	130 2.8	122 3.0		166 2.2	126 2.9	126 2.6	140 2.6	111 3.3	140 2.6
23 16.1	23 15.6	23 15.9	Cost of Sales/Payables	0 UND	13 27.5	9 40.7	32 11.3	25 14.8	22 16.9
37 9.9	35 10.5	43 8.5		14 25.2	44 8.3	52 7.0	43 8.5	43 8.5	38 9.5
59 6.2	54 6.8	63 5.8		49 7.4	74 4.9	69 5.3	62 5.9	66 5.5	51 7.2
4.5	4.2	5.1	Sales/Working Capital	3.4	5.1	5.0	5.7	7.0	4.5
7.4	7.0	8.6		8.0	8.4	6.8	8.0	11.8	8.6
14.7	14.2	16.5		NM	20.6	18.4	15.8	19.3	14.4
8.1	6.7	6.5	EBIT/Interest		(26) 4.3	(18) 10.1	(35) 7.4	(24) 7.9	4.5
(120) 3.0	(128) 2.6	(125) 2.6			2.1	4.4	1.9	3.1	1.9
1.4	1.4	1.3			1.1	1.6	1.3	2.3	1.2
6.5	5.9	5.3	Net Profit + Depr., Dep., Amort./Cur. Mat. L/T/D				(13) 10.3		
(38) 2.0	(38) 3.8	(47) 2.3					2.8		
.5	.5	1.0					1.0		
.0	.0	.0	Fixed/Worth	.0	.0	.0	.1	.1	.0
.1	.1	.1		.0	.2	.1	.2	.3	.1
.3	.3	.5		.6	.7	.2	.5	.7	.3
.7	.8	.9	Debt/Worth	.3	.9	.6	.9	1.1	1.4
1.6	1.5	1.8		1.3	2.3	1.5	1.8	2.0	2.2
3.3	3.3	3.9		3.2	10.9	3.7	3.5	3.2	4.4
27.2	32.3	41.7	% Profit Before Taxes/Tangible Net Worth		(27) 60.0	30.1	39.2	57.2	35.4
(130) 11.8	(143) 11.9	(141) 14.6			13.9	10.0	12.5	17.5	16.4
4.0	3.3	3.9			1.5	2.6	2.7	7.8	4.5
10.7	10.2	10.8	% Profit Before Taxes/Total Assets	22.1	9.8	10.6	9.8	12.4	7.5
4.4	4.3	4.3		14.9	3.5	3.4	4.2	6.6	4.5
1.7	1.1	1.1		3.3	.6	1.1	.8	2.8	.8
260.6	155.3	191.8	Sales/Net Fixed Assets	UND	352.5	160.5	166.5	91.2	361.8
67.7	59.0	55.8		UND	57.9	76.0	48.7	31.9	93.1
30.3	20.8	19.0		16.3	15.6	41.9	16.2	16.7	27.8
3.7	3.3	3.4	Sales/Total Assets	3.7	3.6	3.5	3.3	3.4	3.0
2.7	2.5	2.6		2.7	2.3	2.8	2.5	2.7	2.6
2.1	1.9	1.9		1.7	1.7	2.1	1.9	2.1	1.8
.2	.2	.3	% Depr., Dep., Amort./Sales		(20) .3	(17) .3	(36) .2	(25) .3	(14) .1
(109) .4	(129) .5	(117) .6			.8	.6	.6	.8	.3
.7	.9	1.2			2.0	.9	1.0	1.2	1.7
1.8	1.7	2.0	% Officers', Directors', Owners' Comp/Sales		(17) 4.4	(17) 2.3	(16) 1.7	1.0	
(77) 3.3	(80) 3.5	(78) 3.8			5.6	3.1	3.3	2.5	
6.9	6.0	7.3			9.7	7.7	6.6	7.0	
2067093M	2459050M	1909499M	Net Sales ($)	5605M	61188M	90500M	289592M	466958M	995656M
826907M	1115203M	766339M	Total Assets ($)	2244M	28653M	36015M	127855M	185136M	386436M

M = $ thousand   MM = $ million
See Pages 1 through 15 for Explanation of Ratios and Data

Current Data Sorted By Assets | Comparative Historical Data

Type of Statement	0-500M	500M-2MM	2-10MM	10-50MM	50-100MM	100-250MM	# Postretirement Benefits	4/1/90-3/31/91 ALL	4/1/91-3/31/92 ALL
		1	4	5	2	1			
Unqualified	1	2	10	14	2			21	26
Reviewed	6	6	13	2				18	26
Compiled	2	8	4			1		28	22
Tax Returns	1	1							
Other	3	3	8	5	1			15	16
Period		20 (4/1-9/30/94)		73 (10/1/94-3/31/95)					
NUMBER OF STATEMENTS	13	20	35	21	3	1		82	90

ASSETS

	0-500M %	500M-2MM %	2-10MM %	10-50MM %	50-100MM %	100-250MM %		90-91 %	91-92 %
Cash & Equivalents	21.9	9.5	9.6	2.7				8.5	9.9
Trade Receivables - (net)	20.0	31.9	28.8	36.4				33.0	32.2
Inventory	45.8	39.2	45.4	45.2				38.8	41.2
All Other Current	.1	1.1	1.1	1.2				2.3	2.8
Total Current	87.9	81.6	84.9	85.6				82.6	86.2
Fixed Assets (net)	6.8	7.7	7.1	7.9				11.4	9.1
Intangibles (net)	1.0	4.4	1.7	.4				.6	.3
All Other Non-Current	4.3	6.2	6.3	6.1				5.4	4.4
Total	100.0	100.0	100.0	100.0				100.0	100.0

LIABILITIES

	0-500M	500M-2MM	2-10MM	10-50MM	50-100MM	100-250MM		90-91	91-92
Notes Payable-Short Term	7.3	18.4	24.1	19.9				20.4	18.7
Cur. Mat. -L/T/D	4.5	1.2	2.3	1.4				1.8	1.7
Trade Payables	16.6	20.9	17.6	16.5				19.9	19.7
Income Taxes Payable	.0	.2	.2	.7				.3	.5
All Other Current	9.2	9.5	8.0	9.9				8.9	6.9
Total Current	37.6	50.1	52.2	48.4				51.3	47.6
Long Term Debt	20.4	5.1	4.5	4.2				5.4	3.8
Deferred Taxes	.0	.9	.2	.1				.0	.1
All Other-Non-Current	4.0	2.8	5.6	2.2				2.6	4.1
Net Worth	38.0	41.1	37.6	45.0				40.7	44.4
Total Liabilities & Net Worth	100.0	100.0	100.0	100.0				100.0	100.0

INCOME DATA

	0-500M	500M-2MM	2-10MM	10-50MM	50-100MM	100-250MM		90-91	91-92
Net Sales	100.0	100.0	100.0	100.0				100.0	100.0
Gross Profit	37.7	34.7	27.4	26.1				29.9	29.8
Operating Expenses	36.3	32.0	24.8	22.3				26.7	25.9
Operating Profit	1.4	2.7	2.6	3.8				3.2	3.9
All Other Expenses (net)	1.0	1.0	.8	.3				1.4	1.3
Profit Before Taxes	.4	1.8	1.8	3.4				1.8	2.6

RATIOS

	0-500M	500M-2MM	2-10MM	10-50MM	50-100MM	100-250MM		90-91	91-92
Current	4.4	2.3	2.5	2.9				2.7	2.6
	2.5	1.4	1.8	1.8				1.6	1.8
	1.6	1.2	1.3	1.3				1.2	1.4
Quick	1.7	1.4	1.1	1.5				1.2	1.5
	1.1	.9	.7	.8				.8	1.0
	.8	.2	.5	.5				.5	.5
Sales/Receivables	0 UND	11 34.4	24 14.9	33 11.2				25 14.4	18 20.8
	19 19.4	29 12.5	35 10.5	48 7.6				40 9.2	35 10.4
	38 9.6	60 6.1	51 7.2	72 5.1				60 6.1	57 6.4
Cost of Sales/Inventory	35 10.3	13 27.2	63 5.8	62 5.9				40 9.1	35 10.3
	83 4.4	87 4.2	96 3.8	104 3.5				69 5.3	64 5.7
	228 1.6	104 3.5	130 2.8	146 2.5				101 3.6	122 3.0
Cost of Sales/Payables	0 UND	3 122.8	19 18.9	11 34.3				17 21.7	12 30.4
	15 24.6	28 13.0	28 13.2	22 16.7				28 12.9	28 13.2
	70 5.2	73 5.0	47 7.7	44 8.3				49 7.4	50 7.3
Sales/Working Capital	2.1	6.3	4.7	4.8				5.1	4.9
	5.0	11.4	7.6	8.1				10.1	8.0
	15.5	22.9	13.6	16.3				27.5	14.4
EBIT/Interest		(16) 3.9	(33) 4.8	(18) 8.4				(69) 4.6	(75) 6.5
		2.3	2.4	3.9				2.0	3.1
		1.0	1.2	2.3				.9	1.6
Net Profit + Depr., Dep., Amort./Cur. Mat. L./T/D								(26) 21.0	(15) 6.0
								5.3	2.0
								.6	1.4
Fixed/Worth	.0	.0	.0	.1				.1	.0
	.1	.1	.1	.1				.2	.1
	1.2	.6	.5	.2				.5	.3
Debt/Worth	.6	.7	.8	.6				.6	.7
	.9	2.0	1.5	1.3				1.5	1.2
	17.7	3.9	4.7	2.7				3.2	2.5
% Profit Before Taxes/Tangible Net Worth	31.0	44.6	35.2	27.3				34.6	36.7
	(11) 6.2	(18) 9.7	(33) 20.6	15.1				(79) 14.3	(88) 16.4
	-24.0	1.1	1.8	2.2				.8	5.6
% Profit Before Taxes/Total Assets	10.4	9.0	15.3	11.3				12.2	14.6
	1.7	3.6	4.6	6.0				4.4	8.0
	-7.9	1.1	1.8	.2				.2	2.6
Sales/Net Fixed Assets	687.4	797.4	202.3	131.8				142.1	260.5
	68.4	89.3	109.1	91.2				43.4	76.4
	29.7	21.2	21.3	24.0				17.7	25.4
Sales/Total Assets	5.7	4.5	3.4	3.1				3.6	4.0
	2.1	3.0	2.4	2.4				2.8	3.1
	1.4	2.3	1.8	2.1				2.2	2.2
% Depr., Dep., Amort./Sales		(13) .3	(25) .2	(18) .2				(68) .2	(73) .2
		.7	.4	.3				.4	.3
		1.7	.8	.9				1.3	.8
% Officers', Directors', Owners' Comp/Sales	(10) 4.1	(11) 3.9	(17) 1.7					(37) 1.9	(49) 1.9
	5.7	6.4	3.5					3.2	4.0
	9.7	10.5	8.7					6.9	6.9
Net Sales ($)	13076M	80965M	406200M	1295274M	385916M	428870M		1580701M	1876972M
Total Assets ($)	3801M	18052M	149603M	506789M	180082M	134592M		583577M	718106M

M = $ thousand   MM = $ million

See Pages 1 through 15 for Explanation of Ratios and Data

Comparative Historical Data | **Current Data Sorted By Sales**

1	6	11	# Postretirement Benefits / Type of Statement	1		2		4	6
35	33	29	Unqualified	1	2		2	6	18
43	33	27	Reviewed	4	6	4	7	5	1
36	18	15	Compiled	2	6	2	2	2	1
2	4	2	Tax Returns	1	1				
15	15	20	Other	3	2	1	2	6	6
4/1/92-3/31/93 ALL	4/1/93-3/31/94 ALL	4/1/94-3/31/95 ALL		**20 (4/1-9/30/94)**			**73 (10/1/94-3/31/95)**		
				0-1MM	1-3MM	3-5MM	5-10MM	10-25MM	25MM & OVER
131	103	93	NUMBER OF STATEMENTS	11	15	9	13	19	26
%	%	%	**ASSETS**	%	%	%	%	%	%
10.9	9.6	9.8	Cash & Equivalents	18.5	12.2		8.0	10.6	4.8
25.7	31.1	30.1	Trade Receivables - (net)	19.7	24.1		25.4	35.8	34.4
40.5	42.1	44.0	Inventory	48.6	42.7		40.1	44.2	45.0
4.1	1.5	.9	All Other Current	.2	1.1		.5	.9	1.1
81.3	84.4	84.8	Total Current	87.1	80.1		74.0	91.5	85.3
12.4	9.0	7.4	Fixed Assets (net)	4.4	9.4		12.1	4.2	8.3
.7	1.1	1.8	Intangibles (net)	1.6	5.5		4.5	.1	.3
5.7	5.5	5.9	All Other Non-Current	7.0	5.1		9.5	4.2	6.1
100.0	100.0	100.0	Total	100.0	100.0		100.0	100.0	100.0
			LIABILITIES						
18.8	17.5	19.4	Notes Payable-Short Term	13.5	18.0		23.5	22.7	19.0
1.6	2.6	2.1	Cur. Mat.-L/T/D	3.2	3.0		1.0	3.4	1.3
19.3	14.3	17.7	Trade Payables	10.2	23.9		16.3	21.8	13.9
.7	1.2	.3	Income Taxes Payable	.1	.2		.3	.2	.5
7.9	9.1	9.1	All Other Current	10.2	9.0		12.8	6.0	10.0
48.3	44.7	48.6	Total Current	37.2	54.2		53.8	54.1	44.7
6.1	5.7	6.6	Long Term Debt	16.8	11.1		6.9	1.8	3.7
.1	.2	.3	Deferred Taxes	.0	1.2		.3	.1	.1
4.4	7.6	3.8	All Other-Non-Current	4.1	3.1		5.8	5.5	1.8
41.1	41.8	40.8	Net Worth	41.9	30.4		33.1	38.6	49.7
100.0	100.0	100.0	Total Liabilities & Net Worth	100.0	100.0		100.0	100.0	100.0
			INCOME DATA						
100.0	100.0	100.0	Net Sales	100.0	100.0		100.0	100.0	100.0
29.3	29.6	30.3	Gross Profit	43.4	33.7		32.2	21.4	27.2
24.9	26.0	27.4	Operating Expenses	44.9	29.1		28.5	18.5	23.6
4.4	3.6	2.9	Operating Profit	-1.5	4.6		3.7	2.9	3.6
1.1	.9	.7	All Other Expenses (net)	1.1	.9		1.0	.8	.2
3.4	2.7	2.2	Profit Before Taxes	-2.6	3.7		2.7	2.1	3.4
			RATIOS						
2.7	2.8	2.7	Current	4.1	2.4		2.2	2.9	3.3
1.8	1.9	1.8		2.3	1.3		1.6	1.8	1.8
1.3	1.4	1.3		1.8	1.2		1.0	1.3	1.4
1.3	1.6	1.3	Quick	1.6	1.3		.9	1.9	1.5
.8	.9	.8		1.1	.6		.7	.8	.8
.4	.5	.5		.4	.2		.3	.4	.5
12 · 30.0	27 · 13.3	21 · 17.1	Sales/Receivables	17 · 21.1	0 · UND		23 · 16.1	24 · 15.5	28 · 13.2
30 · 12.1	45 · 8.1	37 · 9.9		38 · 9.6	16 · 23.4		35 · 10.5	30 · 12.2	46 · 8.0
53 · 6.9	68 · 5.4	61 · 6.0		41 · 8.8	45 · 8.1		81 · 4.5	40 · 9.1	73 · 5.0
38 · 9.7	49 · 7.4	57 · 6.4	Cost of Sales/Inventory	83 · 4.4	29 · 12.7		43 · 8.4	18 · 20.5	68 · 5.4
64 · 5.7	79 · 4.6	94 · 3.9		140 · 2.6	85 · 4.3		96 · 3.8	69 · 5.3	96 · 3.8
122 · 3.0	140 · 2.6	130 · 2.8		304 · 1.2	96 · 3.8		159 · 2.3	104 · 3.5	126 · 2.9
13 · 27.9	10 · 35.8	12 · 30.5	Cost of Sales/Payables	3 · 138.7	5 · 70.2		25 · 14.5	8 · 44.5	11 · 33.3
26 · 14.2	25 · 14.8	27 · 13.6		14 · 26.7	28 · 13.2		30 · 12.3	21 · 17.3	23 · 15.7
45 · 8.1	40 · 9.1	54 · 6.7		96 · 3.8	72 · 5.1		49 · 7.4	44 · 8.3	41 · 8.8
5.3	4.3	4.8	Sales/Working Capital	2.0	8.7		4.8	6.7	5.0
8.7	7.4	7.8		3.6	15.6		10.3	9.3	6.1
16.3	12.9	15.6		5.0	69.4		NM	15.1	11.7
(115) 8.8	(94) 9.2	(79) 5.2	EBIT/Interest		(14) 3.6		(12) 4.3	(16) 5.9	(23) 9.4
3.4	3.5	2.9			2.8		1.7	4.2	4.2
1.7	1.6	1.7			1.1		1.3	1.3	2.5
(27) 10.6	(17) 3.6	(17) 10.1	Net Profit + Depr., Dep., Amort./Cur. Mat. L/T/D						(10) 10.5
6.0	1.9	2.8							4.3
1.1	.8	1.0							.9
.1	.0	.0	Fixed/Worth	.0	.0		.1	.0	.1
.1	.1	.1		.1	.4		.2	.1	.1
.4	.3	.4		.2	1.1		1.1	.2	.2
.7	.8	.7	Debt/Worth	.6	1.1		1.1	.5	.5
1.5	1.6	1.5		.9	3.3		2.9	1.5	1.1
2.8	3.3	3.2		11.2	10.9		15.0	2.8	2.2
(126) 54.3	(101) 39.7	(87) 32.3	% Profit Before Taxes/Tangible Net Worth	(10) 12.8	(12) 76.8		(12) 32.9	(18) 44.7	28.5
26.2	15.8	14.1		-15.6	37.0		21.7	22.0	14.6
7.5	4.2	1.9		-33.6	5.3		3.3	1.8	4.9
17.7	14.5	11.9	% Profit Before Taxes/Total Assets	6.6	12.0		12.5	15.4	13.1
7.8	6.5	4.7		-4.9	4.6		2.9	9.4	6.1
2.3	1.7	.7		-10.8	1.0		1.1	.8	2.9
128.6	225.6	193.1	Sales/Net Fixed Assets	104.7	375.0		190.8	767.6	119.5
62.6	71.9	89.4		48.5	89.3		104.6	167.4	65.1
24.4	20.7	21.5		21.1	17.7		15.6	55.8	21.6
4.2	3.4	3.4	Sales/Total Assets	2.1	4.3		2.5	5.2	3.2
2.8	2.6	2.5		1.5	3.0		2.2	3.3	2.7
1.9	1.8	1.8		1.3	2.5		1.8	2.5	2.1
(107) .2	(84) .2	(67) .2	% Depr., Dep., Amort./Sales		(10) .4		(10) .3	(10) .1	(22) .2
.5	.4	.5			1.0		.4	.3	.4
1.0	1.0	.9			2.4		1.0	.6	1.0
(65) 1.7	(48) 1.7	(49) 2.4	% Officers', Directors', Owners' Comp/Sales						(13) 2.7
4.4	4.4	4.8							4.7
8.2	7.2	8.8							10.8
2162718M	2224003M	2610301M	Net Sales ($)	6792M	29258M	34368M	87574M	300380M	2151929M
760494M	1099253M	992919M	Total Assets ($)	3837M	9331M	15824M	45966M	89697M	828264M

M = $ thousand   MM = $ million
See Pages 1 through 15 for Explanation of Ratios and Data

WHOLESALERS—TEXTILE WASTE. SIC# 5093

Current Data Sorted By Assets / Comparative Historical Data

0-500M	500M-2MM	2-10MM	10-50MM	50-100MM	100-250MM		4/1/90-3/31/91 ALL	4/1/91-3/31/92 ALL
						# Postretirement Benefits		
						Type of Statement		
			4	3	2	Unqualified	29	19
	5	13	9			Reviewed	45	49
8	14	7				Compiled	45	35
	1	1				Tax Returns		
	5	18	8	2		Other	17	15
							4/1/90-3/31/91	4/1/91-3/31/92
26 (4/1-9/30/94)			75 (10/1/94-3/31/95)				ALL	ALL
8	25	43	20	4	1	**NUMBER OF STATEMENTS**	136	118
%	%	%	%	%	%	**ASSETS**	%	%
	4.5	4.5	5.1			Cash & Equivalents	10.2	10.8
	42.6	34.6	37.5			Trade Receivables - (net)	27.5	25.3
	17.2	20.6	23.2			Inventory	21.2	21.5
	2.0	2.4	.9			All Other Current	1.7	1.3
	66.3	62.1	66.8			Total Current	60.6	58.9
	29.3	27.4	21.4			Fixed Assets (net)	28.3	32.2
	.2	1.9	1.4			Intangibles (net)	1.2	1.2
	4.2	8.6	10.4			All Other Non-Current	9.8	7.7
	100.0	100.0	100.0			Total	100.0	100.0
						LIABILITIES		
	12.7	15.9	15.6			Notes Payable-Short Term	13.1	13.1
	3.6	3.1	2.6			Cur. Mat. -L/T/D	3.4	3.6
	27.7	20.6	21.7			Trade Payables	16.8	15.4
	.7	.3	.4			Income Taxes Payable	.6	.5
	7.7	7.9	10.3			All Other Current	6.0	6.8
	52.4	47.8	50.5			Total Current	39.8	39.5
	11.7	11.8	9.8			Long Term Debt	12.9	12.0
	.3	.6	.2			Deferred Taxes	.5	.3
	3.3	4.8	2.8			All Other-Non-Current	1.4	3.5
	32.2	35.1	36.7			Net Worth	45.4	44.7
	100.0	100.0	100.0			Total Liabilities & Net Worth	100.0	100.0
						INCOME DATA		
	100.0	100.0	100.0			Net Sales	100.0	100.0
	25.5	26.5	18.8			Gross Profit	24.4	24.0
	21.7	21.7	14.6			Operating Expenses	21.8	22.7
	3.9	4.9	4.2			Operating Profit	2.7	1.3
	.9	.8	-.4			All Other Expenses (net)	.7	.6
	3.0	4.1	4.5			Profit Before Taxes	2.0	.7
						RATIOS		
	1.8 / 1.3 / 1.0	1.9 / 1.2 / 1.0	1.7 / 1.2 / 1.0			Current	2.5 / 1.6 / 1.1	2.8 / 1.4 / 1.0
	1.2 / .9 / .6	1.1 / .7 / .6	1.1 / .9 / .5			Quick	1.5 / 1.0 / .6	1.6 / .8 / .5
	25 14.5 / 32 11.5 / 54 6.7	36 10.2 / 44 8.3 / 57 6.4	38 9.6 / 49 7.4 / 54 6.8			Sales/Receivables	19 18.8 / 31 11.9 / 46 8.0	18 20.0 / 29 12.7 / 40 9.1
	6 65.8 / 20 17.9 / 40 9.2	11 34.4 / 40 9.2 / 73 5.0	14 26.4 / 41 8.9 / 76 4.8			Cost of Sales/Inventory	12 29.8 / 29 12.8 / 64 5.7	13 27.7 / 30 12.0 / 53 6.9
	16 22.5 / 25 14.4 / 42 8.7	17 20.9 / 29 12.4 / 57 6.4	20 18.6 / 33 10.9 / 49 7.5			Cost of Sales/Payables	9 40.0 / 23 15.9 / 34 10.6	11 34.1 / 21 17.5 / 34 10.8
	11.3 / 32.8 / NM	10.1 / 23.7 / -120.3	9.9 / 23.4 / NM			Sales/Working Capital	7.3 / 17.0 / 105.4	7.1 / 22.9 / -172.3
	(24) 9.9 / 4.1 / 1.5	(41) 12.5 / 3.5 / 2.4	(17) 13.2 / 6.1 / 3.2			EBIT/Interest	(117) 5.7 / 2.5 / 1.3	(104) 4.6 / 2.0 / .9
		(19) 7.6 / 4.1 / 1.5				Net Profit + Depr., Dep., Amort./Cur. Mat. L /T/D	(69) 7.2 / 2.8 / 1.4	(56) 5.3 / 2.0 / .6
	.3 / .8 / 1.8	.3 / .7 / 1.8	.2 / .6 / 1.2			Fixed/Worth	.3 / .5 / 1.3	.3 / .7 / 1.5
	1.0 / 2.2 / 4.7	.8 / 2.4 / 4.9	1.2 / 1.8 / 3.3			Debt/Worth	.6 / 1.4 / 3.0	.5 / 1.5 / 3.3
	(24) 45.0 / 28.2 / 5.0	(41) 58.0 / 23.6 / 8.9	49.0 / 23.9 / 11.4			% Profit Before Taxes/Tangible Net Worth	(131) 32.4 / 14.4 / 3.6	(111) 15.0 / 6.1 / -.6
	13.4 / 6.6 / 2.1	14.5 / 8.1 / 3.0	14.7 / 8.6 / 3.6			% Profit Before Taxes/Total Assets	12.7 / 5.5 / 1.1	5.9 / 2.1 / -.7
	62.8 / 15.8 / 6.6	19.4 / 12.0 / 6.5	26.6 / 13.1 / 6.3			Sales/Net Fixed Assets	29.1 / 13.6 / 6.5	25.1 / 9.9 / 5.1
	6.2 / 3.8 / 2.7	3.5 / 2.6 / 2.1	3.6 / 2.5 / 1.7			Sales/Total Assets	4.1 / 2.8 / 2.1	4.2 / 3.0 / 2.0
	(23) .7 / 1.7 / 3.1	(39) .9 / 1.8 / 2.4	(18) 1.0 / 1.5 / 2.4			% Depr., Dep., Amort./Sales	(126) .9 / 2.0 / 3.2	(112) .9 / 1.9 / 3.6
	(13) 2.9 / 4.2 / 11.8	(22) .9 / 3.0 / 5.1				% Officers', Directors', Owners' Comp/Sales	(64) 1.8 / 2.8 / 5.2	(58) 1.5 / 2.8 / 5.7
11446M	123004M	571970M	1189820M	783764M	420649M	Net Sales ($)	3255577M	2773916M
2637M	30979M	212825M	426916M	302256M	168378M	Total Assets ($)	960176M	1035735M

© Robert Morris Associates 1995

M = $ thousand   MM = $ million

See Pages 1 through 15 for Explanation of Ratios and Data

Comparative Historical Data / Current Data Sorted By Sales

	Comparative Historical Data 4/1/92-3/31/93 ALL	4/1/93-3/31/94 ALL	4/1/94-3/31/95 ALL	Current Data Sorted By Sales 0-1MM	1-3MM	3-5MM	5-10MM	10-25MM	25MM & OVER
# Postretirement Benefits	3		7	1	1			1	4
Type of Statement									
Unqualified	10	7	10				1	2	7
Reviewed	44	20	27	1	2	2	3	12	7
Compiled	23	20	29	2	9	4	9	4	1
Tax Returns		1	2			1	1		
Other	10	17	33		2		11	9	10
				26 (4/1-9/30/94)			75 (10/1/94-3/31/95)		
NUMBER OF STATEMENTS	87	65	101	3	13	8	25	27	25
ASSETS	%	%	%	%	%	%	%	%	%
Cash & Equivalents	9.1	8.4	5.7		9.0		6.5	3.9	3.8
Trade Receivables - (net)	28.7	31.3	36.3		33.7		32.9	43.3	37.7
Inventory	19.9	17.5	19.8		15.6		22.0	16.5	23.7
All Other Current	2.2	1.7	1.9		2.8		1.3	2.6	1.3
Total Current	59.8	59.0	63.8		61.0		62.7	66.3	66.5
Fixed Assets (net)	28.0	29.9	27.4		32.3		28.5	21.7	25.0
Intangibles (net)	2.0	.4	1.2		.2		1.4	1.8	1.4
All Other Non-Current	10.2	10.7	7.6		6.5		7.5	10.2	7.0
Total	100.0	100.0	100.0		100.0		100.0	100.0	100.0
LIABILITIES									
Notes Payable-Short Term	13.0	12.9	14.0		5.9		16.6	16.0	14.5
Cur. Mat.-L /T/D	5.3	3.4	3.4		5.1		2.3	2.2	3.6
Trade Payables	17.2	15.8	22.0		15.4		23.1	24.1	23.2
Income Taxes Payable	.4	1.9	.4		.0		.5	.6	.4
All Other Current	6.0	7.0	8.4		10.3		9.0	6.8	9.2
Total Current	41.8	41.0	48.2		36.7		51.5	49.7	50.9
Long Term Debt	10.8	14.2	12.0		15.6		15.1	5.5	12.0
Deferred Taxes	.3	.3	.4		.4		.3	.8	.5
All Other-Non-Current	2.0	2.4	3.5		4.4		2.9	5.2	1.6
Net Worth	45.0	42.2	35.8		42.9		30.2	38.9	35.0
Total Liabilities & Net Worth	100.0	100.0	100.0		100.0		100.0	100.0	100.0
INCOME DATA									
Net Sales	100.0	100.0	100.0		100.0		100.0	100.0	100.0
Gross Profit	24.1	26.1	24.3		31.8		27.6	21.2	18.6
Operating Expenses	21.9	24.8	20.0		27.9		24.4	16.7	14.1
Operating Profit	2.3	1.2	4.2		3.9		3.2	4.5	4.4
All Other Expenses (net)	.6	.2	.4		.6		1.1	.1	.0
Profit Before Taxes	1.7	1.0	3.8		3.3		2.0	4.4	4.4
RATIOS									
Current	2.4 / 1.3 / .9	2.3 / 1.4 / 1.1	1.8 / 1.3 / 1.0		2.2 / 1.5 / 1.2		1.6 / 1.3 / 1.1	2.3 / 1.2 / .9	1.6 / 1.3 / 1.0
Quick	1.4 / .9 / .6	1.6 / 1.0 / .6	1.2 / .9 / .6		1.6 / 1.3 / .7		1.2 / .7 / .6	1.7 / .9 / .6	1.0 / .9 / .6
Sales/Receivables	20 17.9 / 31 11.6 / 41 8.8	24 15.3 / 39 9.3 / 46 7.9	29 12.7 / 43 8.5 / 54 6.8		20 18.3 / 38 9.6 / 56 6.5		25 14.4 / 32 11.4 / 49 7.4	38 9.7 / 43 8.5 / 62 5.9	41 8.9 / 49 7.5 / 51 7.2
Cost of Sales/Inventory	12 29.7 / 25 14.8 / 55 6.6	12 29.9 / 28 13.2 / 47 7.8	11 32.3 / 30 12.2 / 56 6.5		8 46.8 / 17 20.9 / 33 10.9		15 25.0 / 42 8.6 / 78 4.7	5 75.5 / 22 16.8 / 38 9.5	18 20.6 / 39 9.4 / 56 6.5
Cost of Sales/Payables	11 34.1 / 18 19.9 / 44 8.3	10 35.6 / 25 14.6 / 40 9.1	17 20.9 / 29 12.4 / 45 8.2		10 36.0 / 25 14.8 / 44 8.3		11 34.2 / 31 11.8 / 51 7.2	17 21.9 / 28 12.9 / 54 6.8	25 14.4 / 34 10.6 / 43 8.5
Sales/Working Capital	8.2 / 18.1 / -89.6	8.2 / 19.0 / NM	10.1 / 24.6 / -669.1		7.3 / 15.7 / 41.5		11.1 / 28.4 / 144.1	10.1 / 23.7 / -105.9	10.0 / 24.6 / NM
EBIT/Interest	(79) 4.7 / 2.0 / 1.0	(59) 4.3 / 1.7 / 1.1	(95) 11.8 / 4.5 / 2.4		12.9 / 3.5 / 1.6		(24) 8.8 / 2.7 / 1.7	(25) 17.6 / 4.7 / 3.1	(22) 12.8 / 6.7 / 3.5
Net Profit + Depr., Dep., Amort./Cur. Mat. L/T/D	(37) 4.9 / 1.3 / .5	(19) 2.3 / 1.2 / .1	(43) 6.0 / 3.4 / 1.6					(12) 5.8 / 3.6 / 1.8	(14) 8.4 / 4.7 / 3.2
Fixed/Worth	.2 / .7 / 1.3	.3 / .6 / 1.4	.3 / .7 / 1.3		.3 / .8 / 1.2		.2 / .6 / 3.1	.2 / .6 / 1.2	.5 / .7 / 1.3
Debt/Worth	.6 / 1.6 / 3.5	.6 / 1.6 / 4.2	1.0 / 2.0 / 3.8		.6 / 2.1 / 2.3		.8 / 3.4 / 7.3	.7 / 2.3 / 4.1	1.3 / 1.9 / 2.9
% Profit Before Taxes/Tangible Net Worth	(85) 18.0 / 5.1 / -.0	(62) 23.3 / 10.2 / 1.0	(98) 49.4 / 23.5 / 9.2		32.2 / 14.6 / 3.1		(22) 35.7 / 16.9 / 1.1	46.1 / 25.3 / 9.0	52.2 / 27.6 / 16.8
% Profit Before Taxes/Total Assets	8.4 / 2.0 / -.1	8.0 / 2.6 / .2	14.7 / 8.1 / 3.2		18.9 / 4.8 / 1.1		13.4 / 6.6 / .9	20.1 / 7.7 / 3.0	15.2 / 10.2 / 5.0
Sales/Net Fixed Assets	28.8 / 12.0 / 6.5	19.1 / 11.0 / 5.7	29.7 / 12.6 / 6.4		31.5 / 9.3 / 4.7		61.0 / 8.9 / 5.8	28.0 / 14.0 / 8.4	18.3 / 13.3 / 7.6
Sales/Total Assets	4.0 / 2.9 / 2.1	4.0 / 2.9 / 2.1	4.0 / 2.9 / 2.2		4.5 / 3.7 / 1.9		4.0 / 2.7 / 2.1	4.0 / 2.8 / 2.2	3.7 / 3.0 / 2.3
% Depr., Dep., Amort./Sales	(83) .7 / 1.6 / 3.3	(61) 1.1 / 1.6 / 3.2	(92) .9 / 1.6 / 2.4	(12) .8 / 1.7 / 2.4			(23) .9 / 1.8 / 3.4	(23) .8 / 1.7 / 2.2	(23) 1.0 / 1.5 / 2.4
% Officers', Directors', Owners' Comp/Sales	(50) 1.7 / 2.9 / 6.8	(34) 1.4 / 2.8 / 8.4	(47) 1.7 / 3.3 / 5.9				(11) 2.5 / 4.2 / 5.9	(14) .9 / 1.7 / 2.9	
Net Sales ($)	1475931M	1525414M	3100653M	1924M	27119M	31792M	180842M	427919M	2431057M
Total Assets ($)	478478M	519288M	1143991M	1688M	10996M	13399M	74516M	173942M	869450M

© Robert Morris Associates 1995

M = $ thousand   MM = $ million
See Pages 1 through 15 for Explanation of Ratios and Data

WHOLESALERS—TOYS, HOBBY GOODS & SUPPLIES.   SIC# 5092

Current Data Sorted By Assets							Comparative Historical Data	
1	2	4	4	1	1	# Postretirement Benefits		
						Type of Statement		
	2	11	7			Unqualified	14	17
1	9	10	6			Reviewed	13	18
5	14	6	1			Compiled	27	25
2	4					Tax Returns		3
1	10	11	7	1	1	Other	15	17
0-500M	28 (4/1-9/30/94) 500M-2MM	2-10MM	81 (10/1/94-3/31/95) 10-50MM	50-100MM	100-250MM		4/1/90-3/31/91 ALL	4/1/91-3/31/92 ALL
9	39	38	21	1	1	**NUMBER OF STATEMENTS**	69	80
%	%	%	%	%	%	**ASSETS**	%	%
	9.4	6.3	8.2			Cash & Equivalents	5.8	7.3
	24.4	33.2	25.1			Trade Receivables - (net)	27.9	28.3
	44.4	42.6	38.9			Inventory	47.1	44.1
	2.3	.7	3.1			All Other Current	1.2	1.6
	80.5	82.7	75.3			Total Current	81.9	81.3
	14.6	9.5	13.1			Fixed Assets (net)	10.8	10.7
	1.5	2.6	1.9			Intangibles (net)	1.9	1.4
	3.3	5.1	9.7			All Other Non-Current	5.4	6.6
	100.0	100.0	100.0			Total	100.0	100.0
						LIABILITIES		
	11.8	16.4	18.8			Notes Payable-Short Term	15.9	18.6
	1.6	1.1	1.3			Cur. Mat. -L/T/D	2.2	2.4
	25.9	25.3	20.1			Trade Payables	21.4	20.9
	.9	1.2	1.8			Income Taxes Payable	.6	.4
	7.1	7.9	5.1			All Other Current	5.5	7.8
	47.3	51.9	47.1			Total Current	45.5	50.2
	10.0	5.3	5.2			Long Term Debt	10.4	9.4
	.0	.1	.1			Deferred Taxes	.0	.2
	4.9	4.3	8.3			All Other-Non-Current	3.4	3.4
	37.8	38.4	39.3			Net Worth	40.7	36.8
	100.0	100.0	100.0			Total Liabilities & Net Worth	100.0	100.0
						INCOME DATA		
	100.0	100.0	100.0			Net Sales	100.0	100.0
	34.6	33.0	37.6			Gross Profit	31.3	32.8
	30.0	30.1	29.7			Operating Expenses	25.8	29.1
	4.6	2.8	7.9			Operating Profit	5.5	3.6
	1.0	1.0	.7			All Other Expenses (net)	.9	1.3
	3.6	1.9	7.1			Profit Before Taxes	4.6	2.4
						RATIOS		
	2.4	2.1	2.3			Current	2.9	2.3
	1.6	1.6	1.3				1.9	1.6
	1.2	1.2	1.2				1.3	1.1
	.9	1.3	1.5			Quick	1.2	1.1
	.7	.8	.5				.7	.7
	.5	.5	.3				.4	.4
12	30.8	26	14.0	25	14.7	Sales/Receivables	21	17.4	17	21.5
30	12.3	41	8.8	48	7.6		39	9.3	35	10.5
42	8.7	66	5.5	66	5.5		70	5.2	64	5.7
51	7.1	47	7.8	70	5.2	Cost of Sales/Inventory	61	6.0	53	6.9
96	3.8	94	3.9	130	2.8		118	3.1	96	3.8
146	2.5	192	1.9	203	1.8		166	2.2	192	1.9
21	17.8	22	16.3	30	12.3	Cost of Sales/Payables	13	27.3	14	25.2
37	9.8	42	8.7	46	7.9		41	8.9	39	9.4
79	4.6	79	4.6	73	5.0		64	5.7	72	5.1
	5.3	3.9	3.7			Sales/Working Capital	4.0	5.1
	9.1	8.4	11.5				6.6	9.3
	30.0	22.1	17.5				13.4	31.4
	8.6	5.6	18.8			EBIT/Interest	8.3	6.5
(36)	3.3	(34) 2.5	(19) 3.6				(66) 2.2	2.9
	2.0	1.2	1.5				1.4	1.3
						Net Profit + Depr., Dep., Amort./Cur. Mat. L./T/D	8.5	7.1
							(24) 2.5	(31) 1.5
							1.7	.7
	.1	.1	.1			Fixed/Worth	.1	.1
	.2	.2	.4				.2	.2
	.7	.5	.7				.7	.6
	.9	.9	1.0			Debt/Worth	.7	1.1
	2.0	1.8	1.8				1.8	1.8
	3.3	3.7	3.3				4.5	4.8
	51.6	47.4	45.1			% Profit Before Taxes/Tangible Net Worth	42.4	33.1
(37)	25.3	(34) 27.3	(19) 22.4				(63) 20.6	(76) 21.5
	7.9	5.1	7.3				3.9	3.3
	15.8	16.5	20.7			% Profit Before Taxes/Total Assets	17.8	11.8
	9.7	4.9	7.4				7.6	7.0
	3.0	.9	1.7				1.2	.7
	107.0	101.2	25.2			Sales/Net Fixed Assets	123.9	82.0
	49.7	32.7	15.6				36.6	35.8
	13.5	15.8	9.0				12.8	18.0
	3.9	3.5	2.4			Sales/Total Assets	3.1	3.5
	2.7	2.4	1.8				2.2	2.6
	2.0	1.5	1.4				1.6	1.9
	.3	.3	.5			% Depr., Dep., Amort./Sales	.3	.4
(34)	.6	(30) .9	1.0				(56) .6	(74) .8
	1.5	1.3	1.7				1.2	1.4
	1.7	1.6				% Officers', Directors', Owners' Comp/Sales	1.7	1.9
(22)	4.2	(16) 2.6					(25) 2.7	(43) 3.0
	7.5	4.3					4.6	5.7
10761M	139371M	404521M	828629M	107099M	276256M	Net Sales ($)	779007M	1383229M
2508M	46354M	154811M	442417M	80860M	118573M	Total Assets ($)	404214M	643146M

M = $ thousand   MM = $ million
See Pages 1 through 15 for Explanation of Ratios and Data

Comparative Historical Data				Current Data Sorted By Sales					
3	7	13	# Postretirement Benefits	1	2	2	1	3	4
			Type of Statement						
22	12	20	Unqualified	1		4	6	3	6
13	11	26	Reviewed	1	3	5	6	6	5
32	25	26	Compiled	4	8	7	3	3	1
4	2	6	Tax Returns	1	2	1	2		
19	17	31	Other	1	6	4	8	4	8
4/1/92-	4/1/93-	4/1/94-			28 (4/1-9/30/94)		81 (10/1/94-3/31/95)		
3/31/93	3/31/94	3/31/95		0-1MM	1-3MM	3-5MM	5-10MM	10-25MM	25MM & OVER
ALL	ALL	ALL							
90	67	109	NUMBER OF STATEMENTS	8	19	21	25	16	20
%	%	%	ASSETS	%	%	%	%	%	%
7.5	8.9	8.0	Cash & Equivalents		10.5	6.4	7.6	6.0	9.6
26.7	25.3	26.7	Trade Receivables - (net)		23.6	27.2	30.9	33.6	26.2
46.1	47.1	44.0	Inventory		43.2	50.6	41.1	37.7	40.1
1.7	.9	1.7	All Other Current		.5	1.6	.5	4.4	.7
82.0	82.1	80.5	Total Current		77.8	85.9	80.1	81.8	76.7
12.0	11.4	12.5	Fixed Assets (net)		17.0	8.5	13.6	7.0	13.5
.9	1.8	1.9	Intangibles (net)		2.8	1.8	1.1	3.3	1.5
5.2	4.7	5.2	All Other Non-Current		2.4	3.9	5.2	7.9	8.4
100.0	100.0	100.0	Total		100.0	100.0	100.0	100.0	100.0
			LIABILITIES						
18.7	16.4	15.5	Notes Payable-Short Term		13.2	20.3	13.6	15.0	14.9
2.0	2.1	2.5	Cur. Mat.-L./T/D		3.9	1.1	1.3	1.5	1.1
22.7	16.4	24.2	Trade Payables		20.4	27.8	25.0	22.4	26.8
.4	.7	1.1	Income Taxes Payable		.7	.4	2.0	.3	2.3
6.5	8.5	6.9	All Other Current		5.7	5.7	8.6	8.1	5.8
50.3	44.1	50.3	Total Current		43.9	55.4	50.6	47.2	50.9
6.5	7.8	7.4	Long Term Debt		10.8	7.3	7.4	5.7	4.7
.1	.0	.1	Deferred Taxes		.0	.0	.1	.1	.3
4.5	5.3	4.9	All Other-Non-Current		7.0	2.8	3.1	10.5	4.4
38.5	42.7	37.3	Net Worth		38.4	34.5	38.8	36.4	39.7
100.0	100.0	100.0	Total Liabilities & Net Worth		100.0	100.0	100.0	100.0	100.0
			INCOME DATA						
100.0	100.0	100.0	Net Sales		100.0	100.0	100.0	100.0	100.0
33.0	35.0	34.3	Gross Profit		36.5	36.3	30.7	32.5	33.8
28.0	31.4	30.1	Operating Expenses		32.3	35.0	27.8	25.5	27.2
5.0	3.6	4.2	Operating Profit		4.2	1.4	3.0	7.1	6.6
.6	.9	.9	All Other Expenses (net)		.9	1.4	.6	.9	.7
4.4	2.7	3.3	Profit Before Taxes		3.2	.0	2.4	6.2	5.9
			RATIOS						
2.4	3.0	2.4			3.7	2.3	2.1	2.4	1.6
1.6	1.8	1.5	Current		2.0	1.8	1.5	1.9	1.4
1.3	1.3	1.2			1.1	1.1	1.2	1.3	1.2
1.2	1.3	1.3			1.9	.9	1.2	1.6	.9
.7	.8	.7	Quick		.8	.7	.7	.8	.5
.3	.5	.4			.4	.4	.5	.4	.4

								Sales/Receivables									
15	23.6	18	19.9	21	17.7		16	23.3	23	15.9	21	17.2	23	15.8	26	14.2
31	11.6	37	10.0	35	10.3		30	12.0	41	8.9	38	9.5	39	9.3	38	9.6
61	6.0	56	6.5	59	6.2		53	6.9	65	5.6	64	5.7	60	6.1	63	5.8

						Cost of Sales/Inventory											
63	5.8	72	5.1	51	7.1		60	6.1	69	5.3	47	7.8	33	11.0	41	8.8
99	3.7	118	3.1	99	3.7		99	3.7	130	2.8	69	5.3	76	4.8	111	3.3
174	2.1	192	1.9	159	2.3		146	2.5	203	1.8	146	2.5	159	2.3	174	2.1

						Cost of Sales/Payables											
14	25.4	6	58.2	21	17.0		8	45.1	23	16.0	22	16.5	24	15.5	28	12.9
33	11.1	26	13.9	41	9.0		38	9.5	44	8.3	35	10.5	42	8.6	53	6.9
63	5.8	51	7.1	73	5.0		87	4.2	135	2.7	70	5.2	54	6.7	78	4.7

						Sales/Working Capital						
	4.5		4.1		5.0			4.3	4.3	5.0	4.9	7.8
	9.0		7.3		9.1			10.2	7.8	8.1	9.4	13.5
	20.5		13.7		25.5			39.7	34.0	31.8	13.6	21.6

						EBIT/Interest											
	9.3		4.9		8.0			4.9		7.6		12.5		13.2		25.6
(80)	3.5	(62)	2.3	(96)	3.2		(13)	2.8		2.3	(24)	3.8	(13)	4.4	(19)	3.7
	1.6		1.4		1.5			1.7		-1.0		1.9		1.6		1.5

						Net Profit + Depr., Dep., Amort./Cur. Mat. L/T/D						
	10.1		7.8		10.3							
(29)	5.2	(23)	4.4	(25)	4.5							
	1.4		.7		1.2							

						Fixed/Worth						
	.1		.1		.1			.1	.1	.1	.1	.1
	.3		.3		.3			.3	.2	.3	.1	.4
	.6		.6		.6			1.6	.6	.6	.4	.6

						Debt/Worth						
	1.0		.5		.9			.6	.8	.9	1.2	.9
	1.8		1.6		1.9			2.0	1.6	1.6	1.8	1.9
	3.8		3.5		3.3			7.2	4.0	3.0	4.8	3.3

						% Profit Before Taxes/Tangible Net Worth											
	50.1		30.1		47.4			43.8		51.3		52.0		55.3		39.8
(89)	23.9	(63)	12.4	(98)	24.1		(16)	18.1	(18)	22.4	(24)	26.8	(15)	45.1	(19)	22.4
	7.8		4.5		7.1			8.5		-10.9		7.7		27.2		7.2

						% Profit Before Taxes/Total Assets						
	15.9		11.0		16.9			14.8	14.3	17.7	30.7	19.1
	6.6		4.3		7.8			9.7	2.7	7.9	11.4	7.6
	2.2		1.6		2.2			3.2	-8.3	2.5	2.5	2.1

						Sales/Net Fixed Assets						
	71.8		69.5		98.6			112.0	73.4	73.4	110.0	45.5
	31.9		29.4		31.3			40.8	38.5	19.4	63.0	17.7
	15.5		15.0		14.1			6.2	15.4	13.8	16.4	9.0

						Sales/Total Assets						
	3.5		3.3		3.7			3.6	3.6	4.0	3.9	3.5
	2.4		2.4		2.4			2.1	2.3	2.5	2.8	2.2
	1.8		1.8		1.8			1.8	1.8	2.1	1.6	1.6

						% Depr., Dep., Amort./Sales											
	.4		.3		.4			.4		.3		.4		.3		.4
(82)	.7	(61)	.8	(93)	.8		(16)	.6	(19)	.9	(22)	.7	(13)	1.0	(17)	1.1
	1.4		1.3		1.5			4.0		1.7		.9		1.1		1.7

						% Officers', Directors', Owners' Comp/Sales							
	2.0		2.0		1.7				2.4		1.2		
(38)	3.1	(31)	4.7	(49)	3.3		(11)	5.8		(10)	2.2		
	6.5		8.4		6.3				13.8		4.5		

1571583M	1345556M	1766637M	Net Sales ($)	5882M	38483M	84190M	174170M	266384M	1197528M
661415M	677620M	845523M	Total Assets ($)	3973M	18198M	40165M	74928M	125843M	582416M

M = $ thousand   MM = $ million
See Pages 1 through 15 for Explanation of Ratios and Data

PART III

RETAILING, SERVICE, AGRICULTURAL AND NOT ELSEWHERE CLASSIFIED INDUSTRIES

Type of Statement

Type of Statement	0-500M	500M-2MM	2-10MM	10-50MM	50-100MM	100-250MM	# Postretirement Benefits 4/1/90-3/31/91 ALL	4/1/91-3/31/92 ALL
Unqualified		1	1	4	1	2	11	7
Reviewed		1		1			5	16
Compiled	5	7	4				21	19
Tax Returns	1	4	2					3
Other	4	4	4	3			15	8
		11 (4/1-9/30/94)		38 (10/1/94-3/31/95)				
NUMBER OF STATEMENTS	10	17	11	8	1	2	52	53

Data

0-500M %	500M-2MM %	2-10MM %	10-50MM %	50-100MM %	100-250MM %		4/1/90-3/31/91 ALL %	4/1/91-3/31/92 ALL %
						ASSETS		
14.7	10.8	9.5				Cash & Equivalents	5.3	10.1
6.8	16.5	16.0				Trade Receivables - (net)	15.9	15.8
55.2	47.8	49.3				Inventory	53.2	42.7
4.3	7.2	7.4				All Other Current	1.9	4.4
81.0	82.4	82.3				Total Current	76.4	72.9
16.3	13.8	11.4				Fixed Assets (net)	17.7	21.0
.0	.2	3.0				Intangibles (net)	.1	1.6
2.8	3.7	3.3				All Other Non-Current	5.7	4.5
100.0	100.0	100.0				Total	100.0	100.0
						LIABILITIES		
29.5	33.8	33.6				Notes Payable-Short Term	38.4	28.1
2.7	1.0	.8				Cur. Mat.-L/T/D	5.0	4.0
4.7	16.4	9.5				Trade Payables	9.0	12.3
.4	.3	.4				Income Taxes Payable	.7	.2
25.6	9.3	22.4				All Other Current	5.2	11.1
62.8	60.8	66.6				Total Current	58.4	55.8
24.4	6.2	8.4				Long Term Debt	11.4	12.6
.6	.0	.1				Deferred Taxes	.3	.4
.0	5.2	1.6				All Other-Non-Current	5.3	1.6
12.2	27.7	23.4				Net Worth	24.5	29.7
100.0	100.0	100.0				Total Liabilities & Net Worth	100.0	100.0
						INCOME DATA		
100.0	100.0	100.0				Net Sales	100.0	100.0
26.8	26.1	15.3				Gross Profit	26.6	25.7
21.3	21.7	13.2				Operating Expenses	22.4	24.5
5.5	4.4	2.1				Operating Profit	4.1	1.1
1.8	1.1	1.0				All Other Expenses (net)	2.1	1.1
3.7	3.2	1.2				Profit Before Taxes	2.0	.0
						RATIOS		
1.6 / 1.3 / 1.1	2.1 / 1.2 / 1.1	1.4 / 1.2 / 1.2				Current	1.7 / 1.2 / 1.0	1.8 / 1.2 / 1.0
.6 / .3 / .1	.7 / .5 / .2	.6 / .3 / .1				Quick	(51) .7 / .3 / .1	(52) .9 / .4 / .2
0 UND / 3 125.4 / 17 21.5	0 UND / 23 15.9 / 55 6.6	6 57.6 / 13 28.5 / 30 12.0				Sales/Receivables	4 100.4 / 17 21.1 / 37 10.0	6 63.3 / 23 16.2 / 36 10.2
41 8.9 / 83 4.4 / 122 3.0	50 7.3 / 101 3.6 / 203 1.8	28 12.9 / 66 5.5 / 114 3.2				Cost of Sales/Inventory	35 10.4 / 96 3.8 / 192 1.9	39 9.3 / 72 5.1 / 114 3.2
0 UND / 0 UND / 22 16.3	1 254.9 / 17 21.6 / 74 4.9	6 60.2 / 10 37.9 / 18 20.7				Cost of Sales/Payables	3 128.5 / 12 31.7 / 29 12.7	5 72.6 / 18 20.0 / 32 11.3
7.4 / 17.7 / 92.0	5.8 / 9.4 / 107.4	10.7 / 22.8 / 40.0				Sales/Working Capital	7.2 / 24.3 / 999.8	7.0 / 16.1 / UND
	7.8 / 2.2 / 1.0	4.5 / 1.7 / 1.1				EBIT/Interest	(50) 3.3 / 1.6 / 1.0	(49) 2.9 / 1.7 / .7
						Net Profit + Depr., Dep., Amort./Cur. Mat. L /T/D	(13) 5.9 / 1.3 / .1	(17) 2.5 / .9 / .2
.2 / .3 / NM	.2 / .5 / 1.0	.2 / .3 / 1.1				Fixed/Worth	.2 / .5 / 2.8	.3 / .8 / 1.7
1.7 / 3.1 / NM	1.4 / 3.2 / 9.3	1.9 / 3.6 / 8.9				Debt/Worth	1.8 / 4.7 / 22.3	1.1 / 3.2 / 6.0
	(16) 38.2 / 29.7 / 8.0	51.3 / 14.3 / .4				% Profit Before Taxes/Tangible Net Worth	(49) 52.6 / 20.3 / 1.6	(47) 27.6 / 11.7 / -4.4
21.7 / 15.8 / 1.9	13.9 / 7.1 / .0	9.4 / 2.3 / .1				% Profit Before Taxes/Total Assets	10.1 / 3.8 / -2.6	9.1 / 2.3 / -2.1
92.0 / 22.2 / 12.1	128.0 / 27.5 / 7.3	99.8 / 49.8 / 13.7				Sales/Net Fixed Assets	112.8 / 30.7 / 8.0	58.5 / 18.0 / 6.4
4.5 / 3.3 / 2.4	3.2 / 2.1 / 1.7	4.6 / 3.3 / 1.9				Sales/Total Assets	5.0 / 2.3 / 1.6	3.9 / 2.5 / 1.8
	(14) .2 / .7 / 1.5	(10) .4 / .7 / 1.0				% Depr., Dep., Amort./Sales	(43) .2 / .9 / 1.8	(46) .3 / 1.5 / 3.7
						% Officers', Directors', Owners' Comp/Sales	(16) 1.4 / 3.3 / 4.4	(28) 1.5 / 2.6 / 6.4
10460M	47402M	151252M	446151M	53803M	400765M	Net Sales ($)	662646M	663029M
2923M	18888M	47122M	202791M	56539M	357371M	Total Assets ($)	314600M	357651M

M = $ thousand   MM = $ million
See Pages 1 through 15 for Explanation of Ratios and Data

Comparative Historical Data				Current Data Sorted By Sales					
1		2	# Postretirement Benefits	1					1
			Type of Statement						
8	3	9	Unqualified				2	2	5
5	11	5	Reviewed		1			4	
9	12	15	Compiled	4	6	2	1	1	1
1	3	5	Tax Returns	2	2	1			2
14	7	15	Other	1	6	2		2	4
4/1/92-3/31/93 ALL	4/1/93-3/31/94 ALL	4/1/94-3/31/95 ALL		0-1MM	11 (4/1-9/30/94) 1-3MM	3-5MM	5-10MM	38 (10/1/94-3/31/95) 10-25MM	25MM & OVER
37	36	49	NUMBER OF STATEMENTS	7	15	5	3	9	10
%	%	%	ASSETS	%	%	%	%	%	%
7.7	4.3	9.7	Cash & Equivalents		11.2				5.7
10.3	16.5	13.3	Trade Receivables - (net)		13.4				11.4
45.4	46.8	47.2	Inventory		59.8				44.1
2.5	1.1	7.2	All Other Current		2.1				9.8
65.8	68.6	77.3	Total Current		86.5				71.0
26.2	24.5	17.8	Fixed Assets (net)		10.2				20.7
2.0	1.1	.9	Intangibles (net)		.2				1.7
6.0	5.8	4.0	All Other Non-Current		3.1				6.6
100.0	100.0	100.0	Total		100.0				100.0
			LIABILITIES						
30.3	29.4	33.6	Notes Payable-Short Term		40.4				42.1
4.2	6.8	1.6	Cur. Mat.-L /T/D		.6				2.2
9.5	10.9	11.9	Trade Payables		13.2				14.7
.6	.7	.3	Income Taxes Payable		.4				.0
6.7	11.3	15.3	All Other Current		15.1				7.0
51.3	59.2	62.6	Total Current		69.6				66.1
15.1	17.0	10.7	Long Term Debt		5.0				7.7
.5	.4	.3	Deferred Taxes		.0				.4
2.9	4.9	2.5	All Other-Non-Current		3.8				1.4
30.2	18.5	23.9	Net Worth		21.6				24.4
100.0	100.0	100.0	Total Liabilities & Net Worth		100.0				100.0
			INCOME DATA						
100.0	100.0	100.0	Net Sales		100.0				100.0
26.5	29.2	24.7	Gross Profit		25.8				22.0
23.5	25.8	20.5	Operating Expenses		21.2				18.1
2.9	3.4	4.2	Operating Profit		4.6				3.9
1.4	1.2	1.2	All Other Expenses (net)		1.5				.7
1.6	2.1	3.0	Profit Before Taxes		3.1				3.2
			RATIOS						
1.6 1.3 1.0	1.6 1.1 1.0	1.6 1.2 1.1	Current		1.4 1.2 1.1				1.6 1.1 .9
.5 .3 .1	.6 .2 .2	.6 .3 .1	Quick		.5 .4 .1				.5 .3 .1
1 495.1 9 38.7 25 14.5	8 43.5 17 21.5 35 10.4	3 137.9 14 26.0 34 10.6	Sales/Receivables		0 UND 10 38.1 39 9.4				0 UND 22 16.6 34 10.6
35 10.3 85 4.3 183 2.0	40 9.2 83 4.4 192 1.9	43 8.4 83 4.4 140 2.6	Cost of Sales/Inventory		69 5.3 85 4.3 192 1.9				33 11.2 83 4.4 118 3.1
2 177.5 11 33.4 26 14.0	6 59.3 13 28.9 32 11.4	2 223.3 14 25.3 39 9.4	Cost of Sales/Payables		0 UND 7 55.1 58 6.3				2 211.7 23 15.6 47 7.8
5.4 16.6 NM	8.2 24.4 -324.2	7.6 16.7 114.0	Sales/Working Capital		8.1 18.7 104.9				6.9 20.0 -96.1
(35) 3.2 1.6 1.1	4.6 1.9 1.1	(47) 6.4 2.5 1.2	EBIT/Interest		(14) 3.5 2.1 1.0				8.3 6.5 2.3
(15) 2.7 2.1 .8	(17) 3.5 .9 -.0		Net Profit + Depr., Dep., Amort./Cur. Mat. L/T/D						
.3 .6 2.5	.3 .8 6.2	.2 .5 1.1	Fixed/Worth		.1 .4 1.1				.2 .7 1.8
1.6 3.1 5.3	1.7 4.1 14.7	1.6 3.2 7.6	Debt/Worth		1.9 3.2 11.1				.8 4.1 10.9
(35) 29.4 10.0 1.9	(31) 38.1 14.0 8.2	(45) 46.4 23.7 7.7	% Profit Before Taxes/Tangible Net Worth		(14) 61.4 29.7 10.6				
6.0 2.7 .3	9.2 4.7 .9	12.8 7.1 .9	% Profit Before Taxes/Total Assets		15.7 5.0 .2				11.8 8.5 5.1
34.6 15.7 4.5	80.1 21.0 4.9	94.9 24.0 8.9	Sales/Net Fixed Assets		140.4 43.8 20.4				115.3 10.9 6.4
3.5 2.2 1.5	3.7 2.3 1.5	3.5 2.3 1.7	Sales/Total Assets		3.7 2.3 1.8				3.1 2.2 1.6
(32) .8 1.5 3.4	(34) .4 1.1 2.2	(40) .4 .8 2.2	% Depr., Dep., Amort./Sales		(12) .3 .5 1.2				
(14) .8 3.2 6.2	(15) 1.8 3.9 4.5	(21) 1.0 3.6 5.7	% Officers', Directors', Owners' Comp/Sales						
538711M 359973M	429101M 272636M	1109833M 685634M	Net Sales ($) Total Assets ($)	4173M 2236M	28120M 12509M	20230M 7478M	25469M 23130M	122714M 51746M	909127M 588535M

M = $ thousand   MM = $ million
See Pages 1 through 15 for Explanation of Ratios and Data

Current Data Sorted By Assets

2	5	6	2	1	1	# Postretirement Benefits		
						Type of Statement		
	2	12	9	3	6	Unqualified	27	31
4	18	15	2	1		Reviewed	36	34
23	22	4	2			Compiled	77	71
7	3		2			Tax Returns	2	6
13	10	7	4	1	3	Other	28	37

Comparative Historical Data

	37 (4/1-9/30/94)			136 (10/1/94-3/31/95)			4/1/90-3/31/91	4/1/91-3/31/92
0-500M	500M-2MM	2-10MM	10-50MM	50-100MM	100-250MM		ALL	ALL
47	55	38	19	5	9	NUMBER OF STATEMENTS	170	179

0-500M	500M-2MM	2-10MM	10-50MM	50-100MM	100-250MM		4/1/90-3/31/91 ALL	4/1/91-3/31/92 ALL
%	%	%	%	%	%	**ASSETS**	%	%
11.8	8.5	9.0	8.0			Cash & Equivalents	8.7	8.7
5.2	8.3	6.9	13.8			Trade Receivables - (net)	10.3	10.5
57.3	57.1	48.1	44.8			Inventory	52.7	52.7
2.4	1.4	2.2	1.4			All Other Current	2.4	1.9
76.6	75.4	66.2	68.0			Total Current	74.2	73.9
17.6	18.2	24.5	20.9			Fixed Assets (net)	19.7	18.3
1.7	.3	2.5	5.5			Intangibles (net)	1.3	1.7
4.0	6.1	6.8	5.7			All Other Non-Current	4.9	6.2
100.0	100.0	100.0	100.0			Total	100.0	100.0
						LIABILITIES		
11.2	12.3	9.9	13.1			Notes Payable-Short Term	12.1	11.7
4.5	2.1	2.3	2.0			Cur. Mat. -L/T/D	2.8	2.9
13.3	17.7	18.5	17.5			Trade Payables	17.1	15.9
.1	.3	.1	.5			Income Taxes Payable	.3	.4
8.7	7.1	9.3	9.4			All Other Current	6.3	7.2
37.7	39.4	40.2	42.5			Total Current	38.7	38.1
14.8	9.5	11.0	7.7			Long Term Debt	16.5	15.5
.0	.1	.3	.0			Deferred Taxes	.4	.2
5.6	5.5	5.6	5.8			All Other-Non-Current	2.4	3.3
41.8	45.5	43.0	44.0			Net Worth	42.1	42.8
100.0	100.0	100.0	100.0			Total Liabilities & Net Worth	100.0	100.0
						INCOME DATA		
100.0	100.0	100.0	100.0			Net Sales	100.0	100.0
40.6	37.7	39.5	37.8			Gross Profit	38.7	37.9
37.2	33.7	37.5	35.7			Operating Expenses	35.9	35.7
3.4	4.0	2.0	2.0			Operating Profit	2.9	2.2
.7	.9	.5	-.1			All Other Expenses (net)	.8	.9
2.6	3.0	1.5	2.1			Profit Before Taxes	2.0	1.2
						RATIOS		
5.0	3.2	2.8	1.9			Current	3.1	3.2
2.4	2.1	1.8	1.8				2.1	2.1
1.2	1.4	1.4	1.2				1.4	1.4
.9	.8	.8	.6			Quick	.9	1.0
.4 (54)	.4 (37)	.4	.4				.4 (178)	.4
.1	.2	.1	.2				.2	.1
0 UND	0 999.8	0 999.8	3 128.0			Sales/Receivables	1 347.4	0 814.7
1 257.0	4 84.8	3 122.8	9 39.4				6 66.2	4 83.6
10 37.8	22 16.9	16 23.1	29 12.5				24 15.1	32 11.5
83 4.4	76 4.8	72 5.1	87 4.2			Cost of Sales/Inventory	85 4.3	89 4.1
146 2.5	174 2.1	99 3.7	111 3.3				140 2.6	122 3.0
215 1.7	243 1.5	135 2.7	166 2.2				192 1.9	192 1.9
4 84.0	19 19.7	20 18.0	29 12.5			Cost of Sales/Payables	19 19.3	20 18.3
23 15.7	40 9.2	37 9.8	45 8.2				37 9.9	32 11.3
41 9.0	57 6.4	57 6.4	53 6.9				58 6.3	52 7.0
3.6	3.6	7.0	5.8			Sales/Working Capital	3.8	4.0
7.0	5.8	11.1	9.1				6.5	6.7
25.7	16.6	17.3	20.4				14.2	13.9
10.2	8.9	4.1	8.4			EBIT/Interest	5.0	4.1
(38) 2.6	(52) 3.1	(34) 2.7	(18) 3.4				(157) 2.2	(159) 1.7
.1	1.0	.5	1.6				.7	.9
	3.4	2.0				Net Profit + Depr., Dep.,	6.3	7.8
	(19) 2.0	(13) 1.6				Amort./Cur. Mat. L /T/D	(69) 2.4	(62) 2.0
	1.4	-.7					.5	.4
.2	.1	.3	.2			Fixed/Worth	.1	.2
.4	.3	.4	.4				.4	.4
.9	.6	1.1	.8				1.0	1.0
.5	.5	.7	1.0			Debt/Worth	.7	.7
1.5	1.3	1.4	1.4				1.3	1.4
4.4	2.9	2.8	2.7				2.9	2.8
66.7	23.6	26.6	34.0			% Profit Before Taxes/Tangible	24.8	26.6
(43) 18.8	(36) 12.4	(18) 16.8	24.7			Net Worth	(158) 10.2	(168) 8.1
-2.3	.3	.5	7.5				.4	.2
24.9	11.9	8.8	16.9			% Profit Before Taxes/Total	10.9	10.0
6.6	4.9	4.6	4.6			Assets	4.6	2.5
-.6	.3	-.4	3.3				-1.3	-.3
55.3	41.0	29.7	35.7			Sales/Net Fixed Assets	46.4	42.0
28.6	21.0	18.3	13.8				18.2	18.5
10.4	8.3	7.6	10.1				8.0	9.2
3.5	3.6	3.5	2.6			Sales/Total Assets	3.1	3.1
2.7	2.3	3.1	2.3				2.4	2.3
2.0	1.7	2.2	1.9				1.7	1.8
.5	.5	.9	.7			% Depr., Dep., Amort./Sales	.7	.7
(36) .9	(49) 1.1	(32) 1.4	(17) 1.1				(151) 1.2	(159) 1.2
1.6	1.5	2.7	1.9				2.2	2.0
2.6	3.2	1.3				% Officers', Directors',	2.6	2.5
(22) 4.5	(29) 4.2	(15) 1.8				Owners' Comp/Sales	(77) 4.9	(94) 5.1
10.2	8.8	3.6					8.4	8.8
40284M	152251M	527839M	910916M	1087226M	3608913M	Net Sales ($)	3824583M	4168480M
13053M	58039M	182738M	385667M	365524M	1511507M	Total Assets ($)	1884618M	1832142M

M = $ thousand   MM = $ million
See Pages 1 through 15 for Explanation of Ratios and Data

Comparative Historical Data / Current Data Sorted By Sales

1	11	17	# Postretirement Benefits / Type of Statement	2	5	2		4	4
41	31	32	Unqualified	1	1			11	19
35	29	40	Reviewed	1	14	8	7	8	2
75	74	51	Compiled	24	17	4	4		2
6	10	12	Tax Returns	4	5	1	1	1	1
31	59	38	Other	13	7	3	1	1	9
4/1/92-3/31/93 ALL	4/1/93-3/31/94 ALL	4/1/94-3/31/95 ALL		37 (4/1-9/30/94)			136 (10/1/94-3/31/95)		
				0-1MM	1-3MM	3-5MM	5-10MM	10-25MM	25MM & OVER
188	203	173	NUMBER OF STATEMENTS	43	44	15	13	25	33
%	%	%	ASSETS	%	%	%	%	%	%
8.9	9.4	9.6	Cash & Equivalents	7.8	11.1	8.7	11.0	8.0	10.8
9.8	9.3	7.3	Trade Receivables - (net)	5.6	7.1	6.3	5.4	12.1	7.1
53.4	52.6	52.7	Inventory	60.1	53.5	58.1	48.4	47.8	45.0
1.3	1.0	1.9	All Other Current	2.0	2.0	.9	3.5	1.7	1.5
73.5	72.2	71.4	Total Current	75.6	73.7	73.9	68.3	69.6	64.5
19.0	20.8	21.0	Fixed Assets (net)	17.1	20.3	20.9	22.2	20.6	26.8
2.2	.8	1.9	Intangibles (net)	1.5	.6	.2	1.6	5.0	2.6
5.3	6.2	5.7	All Other Non-Current	5.8	5.4	5.1	7.9	4.7	6.1
100.0	100.0	100.0	Total	100.0	100.0	100.0	100.0	100.0	100.0
			LIABILITIES						
12.8	10.5	10.7	Notes Payable-Short Term	11.4	10.9	13.9	3.3	15.2	7.8
3.4	2.6	2.7	Cur. Mat.-L /T/D	4.5	2.3	2.5	2.0	2.8	1.2
17.0	16.8	16.5	Trade Payables	13.4	16.4	15.3	20.0	20.5	16.8
.6	1.3	.3	Income Taxes Payable	.1	.1	.8	.4	.1	.7
7.9	8.5	8.5	All Other Current	3.9	10.4	11.4	9.3	8.7	10.4
41.7	39.7	38.8	Total Current	33.3	40.1	43.8	35.0	47.2	36.9
12.7	13.0	10.9	Long Term Debt	13.9	13.7	9.3	8.3	7.1	7.8
.2	.2	.2	Deferred Taxes	.0	.1	.1	.5	.1	.4
4.2	4.5	5.3	All Other-Non-Current	7.2	3.3	6.0	8.1	7.5	2.5
41.3	42.6	44.8	Net Worth	45.6	42.9	40.9	48.1	38.0	52.3
100.0	100.0	100.0	Total Liabilities & Net Worth	100.0	100.0	100.0	100.0	100.0	100.0
			INCOME DATA						
100.0	100.0	100.0	Net Sales	100.0	100.0	100.0	100.0	100.0	100.0
37.7	39.0	38.3	Gross Profit	39.5	39.8	41.1	38.7	37.7	33.9
34.3	35.5	35.1	Operating Expenses	34.5	36.6	38.4	36.9	36.5	30.8
3.4	3.5	3.2	Operating Profit	5.0	3.1	2.7	1.8	1.2	3.1
.7	1.0	.7	All Other Expenses (net)	1.0	.8	1.0	.5	.3	.4
2.6	2.5	2.5	Profit Before Taxes	4.1	2.4	1.8	1.3	.9	2.7
			RATIOS						
2.9	2.9	3.1	Current	5.1	3.4	2.3	3.7	2.0	2.5
1.9	1.9	1.9		2.9	2.1	1.7	1.8	1.7	1.8
1.4	1.3	1.4		1.5	1.3	1.5	1.5	1.3	1.4
.9	.9	.8	Quick	1.0	.8	.7	.9	.8	.7
(186) .4	(202) .4	(171) .4		.4	(43) .3	(14) .3	.3	.4	.4
.1	.2	.2		.1	.1	.1	.1	.1	.2
0 852.4	0 999.8	0 999.8	Sales/Receivables	0 UND	0 UND	0 999.8	0 UND	0 746.6	1 486.6
4 91.8	3 118.7	3 107.8		5 68.4	2 168.7	3 129.2	4 98.9	4 82.5	3 119.3
21 17.5	21 17.0	15 24.8		14 26.5	21 17.5	29 12.7	5 72.3	19 19.2	10 36.9
85 4.3	79 4.6	76 4.8	Cost of Sales/Inventory	122 3.0	60 6.1	94 3.9	59 6.2	72 5.1	62 5.9
111 3.3	118 3.1	114 3.2		192 1.9	111 3.3	174 2.1	78 4.7	96 3.8	94 3.9
174 2.1	174 2.1	203 1.8		261 1.4	215 1.7	215 1.7	135 2.7	114 3.2	122 3.0
20 18.6	14 26.1	17 21.2	Cost of Sales/Payables	8 44.9	15 25.1	27 13.5	16 22.4	22 16.7	21 17.5
34 10.7	32 11.5	34 10.6		30 12.3	31 11.6	37 9.8	37 9.8	38 9.7	37 9.9
51 7.1	54 6.7	51 7.1		50 7.3	49 7.5	63 5.8	62 5.9	60 6.1	46 7.9
4.8	4.6	4.5	Sales/Working Capital	2.7	3.9	5.2	7.2	8.3	6.3
8.0	8.4	8.1		4.1	6.0	8.8	9.8	12.7	8.4
18.7	19.0	18.1		14.6	33.7	17.1	15.0	22.6	19.3
9.3	5.7	9.8	EBIT/Interest	6.2	11.0	6.8	8.4	4.1	17.9
(167) 2.8	(175) 2.8	(155) 3.1		(35) 2.4	(40) 3.4	(14) 2.6	(12) 2.6	(24) 2.8	(30) 6.5
1.0	1.1	1.0		.9	.6	.1	.0	1.1	2.2
3.9	4.0	4.3	Net Profit + Depr., Dep., Amort./Cur. Mat. L/T/D		3.4				64.2
(72) 1.9	(60) 1.6	(49) 2.2			(15) 2.0			(13)	5.1
.3	.4	1.2			1.4				2.6
.2	.2	.2	Fixed/Worth	.2	.1	.3	.2	.2	.3
.4	.4	.4		.3	.3	.5	.4	.4	.5
.9	1.0	.9		.9	.8	1.1	1.0	1.0	.9
.7	.7	.6	Debt/Worth	.3	.6	.7	.6	.9	.4
1.3	1.4	1.3		1.1	1.4	1.7	1.2	1.9	1.0
2.9	2.8	2.9		4.7	2.9	3.1	2.7	4.2	1.6
33.4	32.4	32.0	% Profit Before Taxes/Tangible Net Worth	48.9	40.0	31.9	24.3	41.9	30.5
(178) 17.9	(194) 13.8	(165) 14.7		(40) 14.7	(43) 13.0	9.1	13.7	(22) 21.6	(32) 20.2
2.1	1.7	2.0		.1	.0	-8.9	-.3	3.1	7.4
14.1	11.8	13.8	% Profit Before Taxes/Total Assets	13.9	16.9	12.9	7.6	9.2	17.9
6.7	5.4	5.9		5.2	7.5	3.9	3.0	4.8	9.2
.5	.5	.3		.0	-1.4	-3.2	-.4	.2	3.4
42.4	37.0	37.5	Sales/Net Fixed Assets	85.6	43.0	25.9	45.9	33.6	15.0
18.3	17.9	17.3		23.7	25.8	16.4	19.5	23.3	10.7
9.3	8.9	8.3		8.0	8.5	7.1	12.6	10.2	7.7
3.6	3.4	3.4	Sales/Total Assets	2.7	4.1	3.4	4.5	4.0	3.3
2.5	2.6	2.5		2.0	2.5	2.4	3.2	3.2	2.6
2.0	2.0	2.0		1.4	2.1	2.1	2.5	2.2	2.1
.7	.6	.7	% Depr., Dep., Amort./Sales	.7	.4	.7	.5	.8	.9
(161) 1.2	(178) 1.0	(146) 1.2		(29) 1.1	(42) 1.0	(14) 1.2	(11) 1.0	(20) 1.1	(30) 1.3
1.9	1.8	1.8		1.6	1.7	2.0	1.4	2.5	2.3
2.6	2.6	2.2	% Officers', Directors', Owners' Comp/Sales	2.7	2.7				
(81) 4.7	(97) 4.7	(69) 3.7		(16) 5.3	(24) 4.4				
9.4	9.4	8.2		11.3	8.9				
5754330M	4476086M	6327429M	Net Sales ($)	25503M	83135M	59144M	99061M	419674M	5640912M
2390457M	1806894M	2516528M	Total Assets ($)	15501M	36673M	24853M	31049M	164935M	2243517M

M = $ thousand   MM = $ million
See Pages 1 through 15 for Explanation of Ratios and Data

506

RETAILERS—FURS. SIC# 5632

Current Data Sorted By Assets						# Postretirement Benefits	Comparative Historical Data	
		1	1			**Type of Statement**		
1						Unqualified	3	2
3	2					Reviewed	5	6
5	8					Compiled	9	16
						Tax Returns	1	1
1	3					Other	3	5
	9 (4/1-9/30/94)		15 (10/1/94-3/31/95)				4/1/90-3/31/91	4/1/91-3/31/92
0-500M	500M-2MM	2-10MM	10-50MM	50-100MM	100-250MM		ALL	ALL
9	13	1	1			**NUMBER OF STATEMENTS**	21	30
%	%	%	%	%	%	**ASSETS**	%	%
	12.3					Cash & Equivalents	13.0	9.9
	12.3					Trade Receivables - (net)	15.5	13.3
	51.2					Inventory	45.1	55.6
	1.1					All Other Current	1.6	1.6
	76.9					Total Current	75.2	80.4
	14.8					Fixed Assets (net)	15.9	12.4
	.5					Intangibles (net)	.2	1.5
	7.9					All Other Non-Current	8.8	5.7
	100.0					Total	100.0	100.0
						LIABILITIES		
	14.8					Notes Payable-Short Term	10.4	20.7
	3.4					Cur. Mat. -L/T/D	8.3	2.4
	13.5					Trade Payables	18.3	19.8
	.0					Income Taxes Payable	.0	.1
	11.8					All Other Current	11.6	14.9
	43.5					Total Current	48.6	57.8
	11.1					Long Term Debt	13.4	13.4
	.0					Deferred Taxes	.0	.0
	3.8					All Other-Non-Current	2.4	3.1
	41.7					Net Worth	35.6	25.8
	100.0					Total Liabilities & Net Worth	100.0	100.0
						INCOME DATA		
	100.0					Net Sales	100.0	100.0
	53.7					Gross Profit	42.0	52.1
	50.0					Operating Expenses	42.5	50.9
	3.6					Operating Profit	-.5	1.2
	.4					All Other Expenses (net)	2.4	3.0
	3.2					Profit Before Taxes	-3.0	-1.8
						RATIOS		
	2.9						4.3	3.5
	1.6					Current	2.1	1.4
	1.2						1.0	.9
	1.1						2.0	.7
	.5					Quick	.6	.5
	.4						.3	.1
	0 UND						12 29.8	0 UND
	29 12.4					Sales/Receivables	29 12.5	22 16.3
	48 7.6						39 9.4	59 6.2
	96 3.8						69 5.3	166 2.2
	281 1.3					Cost of Sales/Inventory	183 2.0	261 1.4
	406 .9						365 1.0	406 .9
	12 29.5						14 26.5	24 14.9
	29 12.6					Cost of Sales/Payables	49 7.4	68 5.4
	57 6.4						135 2.7	192 1.9
	3.1						3.0	3.1
	4.8					Sales/Working Capital	5.1	7.0
	22.6						70.9	-41.6
	3.7						1.6	2.2
(10)	1.8					EBIT/Interest	(19) .9	(29) 1.4
	1.1						-.2	-.7
							.9	
						Net Profit + Depr., Dep.,	(12) .1	
						Amort./Cur. Mat. L /T/D	-1.9	
	.2						.1	.1
	.2					Fixed/Worth	.4	.3
	.8						1.1	3.1
	.9						.8	.8
	1.3					Debt/Worth	2.0	3.3
	3.5						6.7	16.9
	14.0						10.2	38.7
	4.4					% Profit Before Taxes/Tangible Net Worth	(19) -1.6	(25) 6.0
	.1						-23.1	-7.7
	7.1						3.3	6.0
	2.1					% Profit Before Taxes/Total Assets	-.6	1.9
	.1						-8.3	-7.7
	62.1						52.3	104.9
	17.2					Sales/Net Fixed Assets	13.7	22.1
	11.9						8.4	7.0
	3.0						2.6	1.9
	1.8					Sales/Total Assets	1.7	1.6
	1.3						1.3	1.3
	.5						.5	.7
(12)	.8					% Depr., Dep., Amort./Sales	(18) 1.5	(25) 1.1
	1.4						2.3	1.8
							4.0	3.7
						% Officers', Directors', Owners' Comp/Sales	(11) 7.2	(15) 8.1
							10.3	11.2
3122M	25335M	4986M	47842M			Net Sales ($)	69182M	78605M
1971M	11812M	4258M	12779M			Total Assets ($)	35049M	42840M

M = $ thousand   MM = $ million
See Pages 1 through 15 for Explanation of Ratios and Data

© Robert Morris Associates 1995

Comparative Historical Data							Current Data Sorted By Sales					
						# Postretirement Benefits	1					
						Type of Statement						
	3		2		2	Unqualified			1			1
	6		6		5	Reviewed	3	2				
	12		16		13	Compiled	8	4	1			
	1		1			Tax Returns						
	3		5		4	Other	1	2		1		
	4/1/92-3/31/93		4/1/93-3/31/94		4/1/94-3/31/95		0-1MM	9 (4/1-9/30/94)		15 (10/1/94-3/31/95)		
	ALL		ALL		ALL			1-3MM	3-5MM	5-10MM	10-25MM	25MM & OVER
	25		30		24	**NUMBER OF STATEMENTS**	12	8	2	1		1
	%		%		%	**ASSETS**	%	%	%	%	%	%
	9.3		12.3		12.4	Cash & Equivalents	10.0					
	17.7		20.0		15.1	Trade Receivables - (net)	15.9					
	47.7		45.4		49.6	Inventory	47.6					
	1.2		.4		.7	All Other Current	.3					
	75.8		78.2		77.7	Total Current	73.9					
	17.5		12.4		11.5	Fixed Assets (net)	9.8					
	1.4		1.0		.8	Intangibles (net)	1.0					
	5.3		8.3		9.9	All Other Non-Current	15.4					
	100.0		100.0		100.0	Total	100.0					
						LIABILITIES						
	15.3		19.3		14.7	Notes Payable-Short Term	12.0					
	2.5		3.4		3.7	Cur. Mat.-L./T/D	3.9					
	13.2		15.5		10.8	Trade Payables	6.6					
	.3		.9		.0	Income Taxes Payable	.0					
	8.3		9.0		11.3	All Other Current	9.9					
	39.5		48.2		40.5	Total Current	32.3					
	12.1		14.1		9.2	Long Term Debt	10.9					
	.0		.0		.0	Deferred Taxes	.0					
	3.0		5.1		4.3	All Other-Non-Current	5.6					
	45.4		32.7		46.0	Net Worth	51.2					
	100.0		100.0		100.0	Total Liabilities & Net Worth	100.0					
						INCOME DATA						
	100.0		100.0		100.0	Net Sales	100.0					
	50.6		51.2		51.0	Gross Profit	52.6					
	46.5		47.0		47.0	Operating Expenses	46.1					
	4.1		4.2		4.1	Operating Profit	6.5					
	2.4		2.5		.7	All Other Expenses (net)	1.8					
	1.6		1.7		3.3	Profit Before Taxes	4.7					
						RATIOS						
	4.2		3.7		4.2	Current	4.4					
	2.4		1.6		1.9		2.8					
	1.2		1.2		1.3		1.6					
	1.1		1.7		1.3	Quick	1.7					
	.6		.8		.7		.9					
	.4		.3		.4		.5					
15	24.2	17	22.1	1	713.6	Sales/Receivables	10 / 35.0					
38	9.6	41	8.8	29	12.8		34 / 10.8					
61	6.0	73	5.0	54	6.7		74 / 4.9					
99	3.7	135	2.7	104	3.5	Cost of Sales/Inventory	159 / 2.3					
159	2.3	183	2.0	215	1.7		228 / 1.6					
406	.9	456	.8	365	1.0		608 / .6					
18	20.7	13	27.9	8	43.2	Cost of Sales/Payables	0 / UND					
39	9.3	50	7.3	27	13.3		13 / 27.4					
70	5.2	130	2.8	53	6.9		56 / 6.5					
	2.7		2.8		2.8	Sales/Working Capital	2.2					
	4.4		4.0		4.2		3.9					
	20.0		12.1		17.6		6.6					
(23)	6.5	(28)	3.7	(18)	3.9	EBIT/Interest						
	2.5		2.2		1.9							
	.9		.0		1.2							
						Net Profit + Depr., Dep., Amort./Cur. Mat. L/T/D						
	.1		.1		.1	Fixed/Worth	.0					
	.2		.3		.2		.1					
	1.1		.5		.4		.3					
	.6		1.1		.5	Debt/Worth	.5					
	1.1		2.3		1.3		1.3					
	4.7		3.8		3.4		1.5					
(24)	17.5	(28)	28.5		15.0	% Profit Before Taxes/Tangible Net Worth	21.3					
	6.3		9.5		5.1		6.6					
	-2.8		-6.3		.3		1.8					
	9.0		8.3		6.9	% Profit Before Taxes/Total Assets	7.5					
	4.2		2.5		2.1		3.1					
	-.5		-2.4		.2		1.3					
	135.3		104.3		65.7	Sales/Net Fixed Assets	445.0					
	17.6		34.5		35.4		44.6					
	4.9		9.6		11.1		9.9					
	2.6		2.1		2.5	Sales/Total Assets	2.3					
	1.9		1.5		1.8		1.5					
	1.1		1.1		1.2		.8					
(19)	.8	(25)	.6	(19)	.5	% Depr., Dep., Amort./Sales						
	1.7		1.0		.7							
	2.1		1.7		1.4							
(11)	3.2	(17)	4.1	(11)	2.8	% Officers', Directors', Owners' Comp/Sales						
	8.5		5.8		6.9							
	9.5		15.4		11.3							
	89998M		42248M		81285M	Net Sales ($)	4805M	13089M	8069M	7480M		47842M
	45460M		29835M		30820M	Total Assets ($)	3967M	6405M	6005M	1664M		12779M

© Robert Morris Associates 1995

M = $ thousand   MM = $ million

See Pages 1 through 15 for Explanation of Ratios and Data

	Current Data Sorted By Assets							Comparative Historical Data	

	0-500M	500M-2MM	2-10MM	10-50MM	50-100MM	100-250MM		4/1/90-3/31/91 ALL	4/1/91-3/31/92 ALL
	4	2	2	2		1	**# Postretirement Benefits**		
							Type of Statement	22	28
Unqualified	2	6	6	6	2	1			
Reviewed	12	15	14	2				64	51
Compiled	44	22	7					111	97
Tax Returns	3	1						2	6
Other	15	11	5	2	1	1		45	32
	67 (4/1-9/30/94)			111 (10/1/94-3/31/95)					
NUMBER OF STATEMENTS	76	55	32	10	3	2		244	214
ASSETS	%	%	%	%	%	%		%	%
Cash & Equivalents	8.5	5.8	7.2	11.8				6.4	7.4
Trade Receivables - (net)	9.7	10.7	7.7	4.8				10.6	10.1
Inventory	61.0	61.0	52.1	40.4				60.0	58.1
All Other Current	1.4	1.4	1.5	1.8				1.5	1.2
Total Current	80.6	78.8	68.6	58.9				78.5	76.9
Fixed Assets (net)	12.5	13.5	22.9	26.2				14.1	14.9
Intangibles (net)	1.3	2.1	1.5	6.2				1.4	1.9
All Other Non-Current	5.6	5.5	7.1	8.7				6.0	6.3
Total	100.0	100.0	100.0	100.0				100.0	100.0
LIABILITIES									
Notes Payable-Short Term	13.3	10.7	8.8	6.6				13.6	12.6
Cur. Mat. -L/T/D	4.0	2.2	2.2	6.4				3.4	3.3
Trade Payables	18.0	20.8	20.0	17.5				17.1	17.0
Income Taxes Payable	.4	.1	.8	.6				.6	.4
All Other Current	11.0	6.3	9.3	11.0				7.2	7.7
Total Current	46.7	40.2	41.1	42.0				42.0	41.1
Long Term Debt	15.0	9.7	9.1	17.0				15.3	13.1
Deferred Taxes	.0	.1	.1	2.3				.2	.1
All Other-Non-Current	3.5	3.4	5.7	3.8				2.8	3.4
Net Worth	34.8	46.5	44.1	34.9				39.8	42.3
Total Liabilities & Net Worth	100.0	100.0	100.0	100.0				100.0	100.0
INCOME DATA									
Net Sales	100.0	100.0	100.0	100.0				100.0	100.0
Gross Profit	42.6	40.1	44.0	35.3				41.4	41.2
Operating Expenses	39.4	39.2	41.2	31.1				40.1	38.4
Operating Profit	3.2	.9	2.8	4.3				1.3	2.8
All Other Expenses (net)	.7	1.0	.3	1.5				1.0	1.4
Profit Before Taxes	2.5	-.1	2.4	2.8				.4	1.3
RATIOS									
Current	3.2 / 1.9 / 1.3	2.8 / 2.1 / 1.6	2.2 / 1.6 / 1.3	2.1 / 1.4 / 1.0				2.9 / 2.0 / 1.4	2.9 / 1.9 / 1.4
Quick	.7 / .3 / .1	.7 / .3 / .1	.7 / .4 / .1	.8 / .3 / .1				.8 / .4 / .1	.8 / .3 / .2
Sales/Receivables	1 675.0 / 7 51.5 / 21 17.8	0 999.8 / 9 38.5 / 29 12.6	0 999.8 / 2 156.7 / 24 15.3	1 365.4 / 4 86.8 / 13 28.9				2 201.2 / 9 39.7 / 30 12.3	2 226.9 / 8 45.7 / 31 11.9
Cost of Sales/Inventory	99 3.7 / 146 2.5 / 215 1.7	130 2.8 / 183 2.0 / 243 1.5	101 3.6 / 152 2.4 / 228 1.6	63 5.8 / 89 4.1 / 122 3.0				111 3.3 / 166 2.2 / 243 1.5	114 3.2 / 174 2.1 / 228 1.6
Cost of Sales/Payables	17 22.0 / 32 11.4 / 62 5.9	30 12.2 / 52 7.0 / 81 4.5	21 17.3 / 43 8.4 / 87 4.2	27 13.3 / 32 11.3 / 50 7.3				22 16.6 / 42 8.6 / 69 5.3	21 17.1 / 39 9.4 / 73 5.0
Sales/Working Capital	4.5 / 8.8 / 17.9	3.9 / 5.5 / 9.7	4.4 / 9.2 / 18.5	6.4 / 19.6 / -569.1				3.6 / 6.5 / 12.1	3.6 / 6.0 / 11.4
EBIT/Interest	(68) 4.3 / 2.3 / .9	(54) 4.4 / 2.8 / .5	(28) 5.5 / 3.3 / 1.7	15.8 / 6.1 / .6				(236) 3.3 / 1.6 / .0	(193) 3.7 / 1.6 / .4
Net Profit + Depr., Dep., Amort./Cur. Mat. L /T/D	(15) 3.7 / .9 / .5	(14) 4.2 / 1.5 / -.8						(98) 2.8 / 1.1 / .3	(70) 4.2 / .9 / -.0
Fixed/Worth	.1 / .2 / .8	.1 / .2 / .5	.3 / .5 / .9	.3 / .9 / 2.1				.1 / .3 / .6	.1 / .3 / .7
Debt/Worth	.8 / 1.8 / 5.3	.6 / 1.3 / 2.1	.6 / 1.7 / 3.5	1.0 / 2.1 / 6.5				.8 / 1.5 / 3.3	.7 / 1.5 / 2.7
% Profit Before Taxes/Tangible Net Worth	(68) 44.8 / 15.2 / .8	(54) 21.4 / 5.6 / -2.1	31.5 / 10.7 / 2.1					(231) 17.6 / 5.5 / -5.5	(205) 21.6 / 4.7 / -3.9
% Profit Before Taxes/Total Assets	13.0 / 4.9 / .1	8.8 / 3.1 / -.9	10.9 / 5.1 / 1.4	18.2 / 8.0 / -3.4				7.2 / 2.2 / -3.2	9.0 / 2.3 / -2.0
Sales/Net Fixed Assets	97.5 / 52.1 / 16.1	74.0 / 20.2 / 9.2	20.6 / 14.3 / 7.3	28.1 / 10.9 / 6.6				62.2 / 24.1 / 11.0	53.5 / 24.3 / 10.2
Sales/Total Assets	3.3 / 2.6 / 2.0	2.8 / 2.0 / 1.6	3.0 / 2.2 / 1.7	2.6 / 2.2 / 1.9				3.0 / 2.2 / 1.7	2.7 / 2.2 / 1.6
% Depr., Dep., Amort./Sales	(62) .3 / .6 / 1.2	(45) .5 / 1.1 / 1.7	(29) .8 / 1.5 / 1.8	1.0 / 1.8 / 2.3				(198) .7 / 1.1 / 1.7	(177) .6 / 1.0 / 1.7
% Officers', Directors', Owners' Comp/Sales	(40) 4.2 / 6.4 / 9.3	(28) 2.6 / 4.4 / 6.9	(13) 2.1 / 4.6 / 12.1					(116) 3.4 / 6.0 / 9.0	(97) 3.0 / 5.3 / 10.5
Net Sales ($)	64331M	181684M	302500M	435407M	496381M	574665M		1923228M	2366846M
Total Assets ($)	20559M	61941M	126880M	204831M	242029M	405512M		888764M	1151769M

© Robert Morris Associates 1995

M = $ thousand   MM = $ million
See Pages 1 through 15 for Explanation of Ratios and Data

Comparative Historical Data | Current Data Sorted By Sales

1	5	11	# Postretirement Benefits / Type of Statement	2	3	1	1	1	3
19	20	23	Unqualified	2	5	2		5	9
57	40	43	Reviewed	6	14	4	11	5	3
82	74	73	Compiled	42	19	6	6		
7	5	4	Tax Returns	3	1				
26	27	35	Other	13	9	5	2	1	5

1	5	11		67 (4/1-9/30/94)		111 (10/1/94-3/31/95)			
4/1/92-3/31/93 ALL	4/1/93-3/31/94 ALL	4/1/94-3/31/95 ALL		0-1MM	1-3MM	3-5MM	5-10MM	10-25MM	25MM & OVER
191	166	178	**NUMBER OF STATEMENTS**	66	48	17	19	11	17

ASSETS

1	5	11		0-1MM	1-3MM	3-5MM	5-10MM	10-25MM	25MM & OVER
%	%	%		%	%	%	%	%	%
8.3	8.1	7.4	Cash & Equivalents	4.8	9.7	4.5	11.8	9.4	7.7
11.4	8.6	9.3	Trade Receivables - (net)	9.4	9.9	10.6	8.8	10.4	5.6
56.8	59.5	57.9	Inventory	65.3	54.8	61.0	56.9	42.7	46.2
1.5	1.0	1.5	All Other Current	1.0	1.2	3.2	.8	3.2	2.1
78.0	77.2	76.1	Total Current	80.4	75.6	79.3	78.4	65.6	61.6
14.2	14.8	16.0	Fixed Assets (net)	13.2	16.5	11.4	15.9	22.4	25.7
1.7	2.6	1.8	Intangibles (net)	1.2	2.1	2.5	.0	3.8	3.7
6.1	5.5	6.1	All Other Non-Current	5.3	5.8	6.8	5.8	8.2	9.0
100.0	100.0	100.0	Total	100.0	100.0	100.0	100.0	100.0	100.0

LIABILITIES

1	5	11		0-1MM	1-3MM	3-5MM	5-10MM	10-25MM	25MM & OVER
10.0	11.3	11.0	Notes Payable-Short Term	12.9	11.6	12.5	8.8	7.8	4.6
3.0	2.9	3.2	Cur. Mat.-L /T/D	3.8	3.4	1.1	.9	4.2	4.3
19.7	16.7	19.1	Trade Payables	16.6	17.3	27.8	22.8	23.8	18.2
.4	1.9	.4	Income Taxes Payable	.3	.3	.6	.2	1.3	.9
7.7	8.2	9.1	All Other Current	8.7	8.3	8.1	13.2	10.4	8.8
40.8	41.0	42.9	Total Current	42.2	40.9	50.1	46.0	47.5	36.8
11.7	12.6	12.2	Long Term Debt	15.5	13.5	5.0	5.5	9.1	13.1
.1	.1	.2	Deferred Taxes	.0	.1	.0	.2	.0	1.8
3.3	3.8	3.8	All Other-Non-Current	2.8	4.7	2.6	4.5	7.8	2.8
44.0	42.5	40.9	Net Worth	39.4	40.7	42.2	43.9	35.6	45.6
100.0	100.0	100.0	Total Liabilities & Net Worth	100.0	100.0	100.0	100.0	100.0	100.0

INCOME DATA

1	5	11		0-1MM	1-3MM	3-5MM	5-10MM	10-25MM	25MM & OVER
100.0	100.0	100.0	Net Sales	100.0	100.0	100.0	100.0	100.0	100.0
41.9	41.7	41.5	Gross Profit	41.6	41.2	44.8	41.6	50.5	32.7
38.5	39.5	39.0	Operating Expenses	37.7	41.3	41.7	39.9	47.1	28.3
3.5	2.2	2.5	Operating Profit	3.9	-.1	3.1	1.7	3.3	4.5
.7	1.0	.8	All Other Expenses (net)	1.1	.3	.7	.3	.9	1.1
2.7	1.2	1.8	Profit Before Taxes	2.8	-.5	2.4	1.4	2.5	3.4

RATIOS

1	5	11		0-1MM	1-3MM	3-5MM	5-10MM	10-25MM	25MM & OVER
3.5 / 1.9 / 1.4	3.0 / 1.9 / 1.4	2.8 / 1.9 / 1.3	Current	3.5 / 2.0 / 1.4	2.9 / 1.9 / 1.5	2.3 / 1.6 / 1.2	3.2 / 2.0 / 1.3	1.7 / 1.3 / 1.1	2.3 / 1.8 / 1.3
(189) 1.0 / .4 / .2	(165) .9 / .3 / .1	.7 / .3 / .1	Quick	.7 / .3 / .1	.9 / .3 / .1	.5 / .4 / .1	1.1 / .5 / .1	.6 / .5 / .1	.7 / .2 / .1
2 178.0 / 9 41.0 / 33 11.2	0 839.5 / 6 57.6 / 21 17.5	1 728.3 / 6 56.2 / 21 17.2	Sales/Receivables	2 189.5 / 10 37.4 / 22 16.7	0 UND / 7 49.0 / 24 15.1	2 152.1 / 4 88.4 / 28 13.0	1 363.4 / 4 82.0 / 15 24.1	0 UND / 2 168.9 / 43 8.4	1 437.6 / 3 122.7 / 10 38.0
107 3.4 / 166 2.2 / 228 1.6	111 3.3 / 159 2.3 / 228 1.6	101 3.6 / 159 2.3 / 228 1.6	Cost of Sales/Inventory	111 3.3 / 174 2.1 / 281 1.3	94 3.9 / 152 2.4 / 215 1.7	130 2.8 / 174 2.1 / 203 1.8	101 3.6 / 159 2.3 / 243 1.5	73 5.0 / 104 3.5 / 130 2.8	74 4.9 / 96 3.8 / 159 2.3
23 16.1 / 44 8.3 / 76 4.8	18 19.9 / 38 9.5 / 70 5.2	21 17.0 / 38 9.5 / 70 5.2	Cost of Sales/Payables	18 20.4 / 35 10.3 / 63 5.8	13 27.2 / 35 10.3 / 68 5.4	40 9.1 / 61 6.0 / 96 3.8	21 17.0 / 40 9.2 / 57 4.0	21 17.4 / 40 6.4 / 89 4.1	28 13.2 / 38 9.7 / 52 7.0
3.6 / 6.7 / 11.9	4.1 / 6.4 / 13.1	4.4 / 7.8 / 16.1	Sales/Working Capital	3.8 / 6.3 / 12.0	3.9 / 7.0 / 14.8	5.2 / 8.3 / 21.8	3.7 / 7.5 / 15.3	11.6 / 22.2 / 46.8	6.3 / 9.8 / 34.7
(170) 5.5 / 2.3 / 1.1	(155) 5.4 / 2.1 / 1.0	(165) 5.4 / 2.7 / .9	EBIT/Interest	(60) 4.0 / 2.4 / .4	(46) 4.1 / 1.8 / .1	(16) 6.0 / 3.6 / 1.9	(17) 11.2 / 3.5 / 1.5		11.1 / 6.5 / 3.7
(66) 4.4 / 1.4 / .7	(61) 3.1 / 1.2 / .0	(46) 5.8 / 2.1 / .4	Net Profit + Depr., Dep., Amort./Cur. Mat. L/T/D	(10) 1.9 / .8 / .3	(18) 5.2 / 1.6 / -.1			(10) 22.2 / 3.1 / .2	
.1 / .3 / .5	.1 / .3 / .7	.1 / .3 / .7	Fixed/Worth	.1 / .2 / .5	.2 / .3 / .9	.2 / .3 / .5	.1 / .4 / .7	.6 / .8 / 1.1	.3 / .5 / 1.2
.6 / 1.2 / 2.8	.7 / 1.4 / 3.7	.7 / 1.5 / 3.3	Debt/Worth	.7 / 1.6 / 3.9	.6 / 1.4 / 3.4	.7 / 1.8 / 2.6	.3 / 1.3 / 3.8	1.0 / 2.9 / 3.6	.7 / 1.0 / 2.9
(181) 26.8 / 9.4 / 1.2	(161) 22.7 / 8.2 / .5	(168) 31.5 / 11.0 / .7	% Profit Before Taxes/Tangible Net Worth	(62) 42.4 / 13.4 / .4	(44) 21.6 / 5.8 / -6.4	(18) 34.0 / 9.4 / 4.3	23.8 / 9.0 / 2.7	56.5 / 13.4 / 3.5	(16) 30.9 / 17.8 / 8.2
11.2 / 3.9 / .4	8.4 / 3.2 / -.1	10.8 / 4.4 / -.1	% Profit Before Taxes/Total Assets	11.4 / 4.7 / -.9	9.7 / 2.5 / -3.1	12.2 / 3.7 / 1.6	9.0 / 5.7 / .7	17.4 / 5.0 / 1.7	14.4 / 7.6 / 3.7
48.2 / 23.2 / 11.4	49.7 / 20.2 / 9.6	74.1 / 20.9 / 9.3	Sales/Net Fixed Assets	94.4 / 44.5 / 11.8	78.0 / 22.2 / 8.6	39.1 / 21.4 / 14.6	31.4 / 18.4 / 12.4	18.3 / 13.3 / 8.3	28.5 / 9.1 / 7.0
3.0 / 2.3 / 1.8	2.9 / 2.3 / 1.7	3.1 / 2.4 / 1.8	Sales/Total Assets	3.1 / 2.3 / 1.6	3.2 / 2.4 / 1.6	3.1 / 2.3 / 1.8	3.3 / 2.5 / 1.8	3.6 / 3.0 / 2.4	2.7 / 2.1 / 1.8
(163) .7 / 1.0 / 1.7	(147) .6 / 1.0 / 1.8	(151) .5 / 1.0 / 1.7	% Depr., Dep., Amort./Sales	(52) .4 / .8 / 1.5	(43) .5 / .9 / 1.8	(13) .5 / 1.2 / 1.7	(17) .5 / 1.1 / 1.6		1.0 / 1.7 / 2.1
(98) 4.2 / 6.6 / 9.4	(81) 3.2 / 5.4 / 9.4	(83) 3.1 / 5.4 / 9.0	% Officers', Directors', Owners' Comp/Sales	(32) 4.1 / 6.8 / 10.1	(29) 3.5 / 5.4 / 8.8				
1147176M	1905159M	2054968M	Net Sales ($)	38841M	85366M	63493M	127251M	156913M	1583104M
542044M	860763M	1061752M	Total Assets ($)	18858M	41950M	27349M	53611M	58314M	861670M

M = $ thousand   MM = $ million
See Pages 1 through 15 for Explanation of Ratios and Data

Current Data Sorted By Assets   Comparative Historical Data

	0-500M	500M-2MM	2-10MM	10-50MM	50-100MM	100-250MM		4/1/90-3/31/91 ALL	4/1/91-3/31/92 ALL
	3	2		1		2	# Postretirement Benefits		
							Type of Statement		
	2	2	5	4	4	2	Unqualified	25	33
	6	6	6	1			Reviewed	33	26
	21	20	4				Compiled	85	60
	6	3					Tax Returns		1
	8	8	4	4		2	Other	35	40
	31 (4/1-9/30/94)			83 (10/1/94-3/31/95)					
NUMBER OF STATEMENTS	43	39	15	9	4	4		178	160
	%	%	%	%	%	%	**ASSETS**	%	%
Cash & Equivalents	6.3	8.1	4.0					5.1	5.3
Trade Receivables - (net)	3.9	10.4	4.8					5.0	5.2
Inventory	68.7	66.1	69.4					68.9	66.2
All Other Current	.7	.3	.7					.7	1.0
Total Current	79.6	84.9	78.9					79.7	77.6
Fixed Assets (net)	14.4	9.4	14.0					12.4	15.3
Intangibles (net)	2.0	1.5	4.1					1.9	2.1
All Other Non-Current	4.0	4.2	3.1					6.0	5.1
Total	100.0	100.0	100.0					100.0	100.0
							LIABILITIES		
Notes Payable-Short Term	7.5	14.0	17.5					11.7	10.3
Cur. Mat. -L/T/D	4.2	4.0	2.6					3.4	3.9
Trade Payables	26.7	22.2	16.9					24.6	23.7
Income Taxes Payable	.1	.2	.3					.4	.5
All Other Current	8.8	7.0	4.0					8.1	6.8
Total Current	47.4	47.5	41.3					48.3	45.2
Long Term Debt	19.5	9.1	8.8					14.8	17.3
Deferred Taxes	.1	.0	.2					.2	.1
All Other-Non-Current	1.1	.4	2.6					3.0	3.0
Net Worth	31.9	43.0	47.1					33.8	34.3
Total Liabilities & Net Worth	100.0	100.0	100.0					100.0	100.0
							INCOME DATA		
Net Sales	100.0	100.0	100.0					100.0	100.0
Gross Profit	39.1	38.9	39.0					40.7	41.4
Operating Expenses	35.2	34.5	36.3					38.0	37.9
Operating Profit	3.9	4.3	2.7					2.7	3.5
All Other Expenses (net)	.7	1.0	.9					1.3	1.4
Profit Before Taxes	3.2	3.4	1.7					1.5	2.1
							RATIOS		
Current	2.9	2.8	2.6					2.4	2.6
	1.8	1.8	1.9					1.7	1.8
	1.1	1.3	1.5					1.4	1.3
Quick	.4	.6	.4					.3	.4
	(42) .2	.2	.2				(176) / (158)	.2	.2
	.1	.1	.0					.1	.1
Sales/Receivables	0 UND	0 UND	0 UND					0 UND	0 UND
	1 342.0	2 176.7	2 150.5					3 141.0	2 203.3
	5 76.7	23 15.6	8 44.9					6 57.9	8 45.8
Cost of Sales/Inventory	126 2.9	89 4.1	107 3.4					135 2.7	135 2.7
	159 2.3	203 1.8	174 2.1					183 2.0	174 2.1
	243 1.5	281 1.3	215 1.7					243 1.5	228 1.6
Cost of Sales/Payables	25 14.7	25 14.4	23 15.6					31 11.6	30 12.0
	57 6.4	48 7.6	35 10.5					56 6.5	49 7.5
	91 4.0	85 4.3	51 7.2					83 4.4	85 4.3
Sales/Working Capital	4.4	3.6	5.7					4.7	4.6
	7.7	6.7	7.9					7.5	7.8
	52.3	13.4	12.3					14.9	13.8
EBIT/Interest	9.6	9.4	7.0					4.4	5.8
	(39) 3.0	2.7	4.3				(169) / (150)	1.9	2.2
	1.0	1.3	1.4					.5	.7
Net Profit + Depr., Dep., Amort./Cur. Mat. L /T/D	1.4	2.8						3.5	3.2
	(10) .5	(19) .8					(74) / (60)	1.3	1.2
	.1	.1						.2	.2
Fixed/Worth	.1	.1	.2					.1	.2
	.3	.2	.3					.3	.4
	1.4	.4	.5					.9	1.2
Debt/Worth	1.0	.6	.7					1.0	.9
	2.3	1.6	1.3					2.0	2.1
	13.9	2.5	2.0					5.3	5.6
% Profit Before Taxes/Tangible Net Worth	74.3	28.2	35.1					26.1	29.9
	(37) 23.1	(38) 8.5	13.1				(160) / (147)	10.9	14.2
	3.4	3.0	4.2					.0	2.1
% Profit Before Taxes/Total Assets	16.5	10.9	11.5					9.4	10.0
	6.3	3.3	6.8					3.3	4.5
	.0	.9	1.5					-1.4	.3
Sales/Net Fixed Assets	92.7	54.4	34.3					50.8	38.7
	25.8	41.2	17.1					22.0	20.2
	11.4	24.1	12.7					13.3	10.7
Sales/Total Assets	3.4	2.7	3.3					2.9	3.0
	2.5	2.2	2.9					2.4	2.4
	2.1	1.9	2.0					1.8	1.9
% Depr., Dep., Amort./Sales	.5	.4	1.0					.6	.7
	(34) .9	(35) .8	(14) 1.3				(154) / (136)	1.1	1.1
	1.6	1.1	1.6					1.7	1.8
% Officers', Directors', Owners' Comp/Sales	4.0	3.1						2.7	3.6
	(22) 6.3	(16) 4.0					(91) / (71)	4.5	4.8
	8.2	5.2						6.9	7.8
Net Sales ($)	30453M	110456M	206464M	384382M	615026M	1039695M		1940458M	4024090M
Total Assets ($)	10747M	41950M	71148M	158142M	354990M	542181M		881504M	1851496M

M = $ thousand   MM = $ million

See Pages 1 through 15 for Explanation of Ratios and Data

RETAILERS—SHOES. SIC# 5661

511

Comparative Historical Data					Current Data Sorted By Sales					
2	4	8	# Postretirement Benefits	3		2				3
			Type of Statement							
22	14	19	Unqualified	1	2	1	2	4		9
23	14	18	Reviewed	5	2	4	3	3		1
68	51	46	Compiled	22	14	6	1	3		
5	8	9	Tax Returns	6	2	1				
37	32	22	Other	4	9	3				6
4/1/92-3/31/93	4/1/93-3/31/94	4/1/94-3/31/95		31 (4/1-9/30/94)			83 (10/1/94-3/31/95)			
ALL	ALL	ALL		0-1MM	1-3MM	3-5MM	5-10MM	10-25MM		25MM & OVER
155	119	114	**NUMBER OF STATEMENTS**	38	29	15	6	10		16
%	%	%	**ASSETS**	%	%	%	%	%		%
6.9	7.5	6.8	Cash & Equivalents	5.3	9.1	7.9		5.3		6.9
5.1	5.0	6.8	Trade Receivables - (net)	3.3	4.1	16.5		14.7		6.6
64.4	65.9	66.4	Inventory	71.0	68.4	60.2		60.6		60.8
2.1	1.0	.6	All Other Current	.7	.3	.5		.6		1.2
78.5	79.5	80.6	Total Current	80.4	81.8	85.2		81.2		75.5
14.2	14.7	13.4	Fixed Assets (net)	12.7	13.8	8.5		13.4		18.9
2.6	1.6	1.9	Intangibles (net)	1.6	2.6	.5		2.4		.8
4.7	4.3	4.1	All Other Non-Current	5.3	1.8	5.9		3.0		4.8
100.0	100.0	100.0	Total	100.0	100.0	100.0		100.0		100.0
			LIABILITIES							
11.6	11.6	11.4	Notes Payable-Short Term	8.6	11.8	10.8		17.4		11.1
4.4	2.7	3.5	Cur. Mat.-L /T/D	4.6	2.5	6.0		2.0		1.7
23.8	20.4	22.4	Trade Payables	22.7	26.0	26.3		21.5		16.6
.4	3.1	.2	Income Taxes Payable	.2	.0	.5		.3		.3
6.7	6.8	7.1	All Other Current	8.5	8.7	3.9		5.5		5.4
47.0	44.6	44.7	Total Current	44.6	49.1	47.5		46.7		35.0
15.6	13.0	13.5	Long Term Debt	21.6	9.1	8.6		8.7		11.9
.0	.1	.2	Deferred Taxes	.1	.0	.1		.1		1.1
3.3	2.6	1.3	All Other-Non-Current	1.3	.0	1.5		4.9		1.9
34.1	39.7	40.3	Net Worth	32.5	41.8	42.3		39.6		50.2
100.0	100.0	100.0	Total Liabilities & Net Worth	100.0	100.0	100.0		100.0		100.0
			INCOME DATA							
100.0	100.0	100.0	Net Sales	100.0	100.0	100.0		100.0		100.0
39.6	39.0	38.5	Gross Profit	39.6	39.9	38.1		32.6		35.9
36.5	36.3	34.4	Operating Expenses	35.6	36.0	34.2		29.3		30.3
3.0	2.7	4.1	Operating Profit	4.0	4.0	3.9		3.2		5.6
1.2	.9	1.0	All Other Expenses (net)	1.1	.6	.7		1.0		1.7
1.8	1.8	3.1	Profit Before Taxes	3.0	3.3	3.2		2.3		3.9
			RATIOS							
2.5	2.9	2.8		3.2	2.7	3.0		2.6		4.5
1.7	2.0	1.9	Current	1.9	1.8	1.8		1.6		1.9
1.3	1.3	1.4		1.4	1.2	1.3		1.4		1.7
.4	.4	.5		.4	.4	1.2		.9		.9
(117) .2	(112) .2	.2	Quick	(37) .2	.2	.2		.2 (15)		.2
.1	.1	.1		.0	.0	.1		.1		.1
0 UND	0 UND	0 UND		0 UND	0 UND	1 494.2		0 UND		2 179.6
1 280.0	2 216.9	2 181.9	Sales/Receivables	1 336.0	0 999.8	5 76.0		5 78.8		3 123.9
7 52.4	6 61.5	7 49.8		5 68.1	5 75.6	23 15.6		20 18.0		15 23.7
114 3.2	118 3.1	114 3.2		130 2.8	111 3.3	76 4.8		69 5.3		122 3.0
159 2.3	166 2.2	174 2.1	Cost of Sales/Inventory	174 2.1	203 1.8	192 1.9		107 3.4		159 2.3
215 1.7	228 1.6	243 1.5		261 1.4	261 1.4	215 1.7		183 2.0		183 2.0
31 11.9	17 21.5	25 14.7		24 15.3	29 12.8	26 14.0		15 24.7		24 14.9
48 7.6	41 8.9	47 7.7	Cost of Sales/Payables	62 5.9	49 7.4	45 8.1		26 14.2		43 8.5
73 5.0	70 5.2	81 4.5		91 4.0	101 3.6	72 5.1		48 7.6		57 6.4
5.2	4.1	3.8		3.8	3.7	4.6		7.3		3.5
8.5	6.6	6.8	Sales/Working Capital	5.4	7.3	9.2		10.5		6.4
15.7	17.3	13.4		12.6	34.0	17.8		23.1		7.2
5.1	6.7	9.5		4.5	12.2	15.4		7.3		12.8
(144) 2.5	(113) 3.7	(110) 3.5	EBIT/Interest	(34) 2.3	4.0	4.9		6.7		6.4
1.0	1.1	1.3		1.0	1.1	1.3		2.2		3.0
4.8	3.7	5.6		1.2						12.0
(54) 2.1	(32) 1.4	(42) 1.4	Net Profit + Depr., Dep., Amort./Cur. Mat. L/T/D	(12) .4					(10)	7.7
.7	-.3	.2		.1						4.7
.1	.1	.1		.1	.1	.1		.1		.3
.4	.3	.3	Fixed/Worth	.3	.3	.2		.3		.4
.9	.6	.7		1.9	1.1	.4		.7		.5
.8	.7	.7		1.0	.6	.5		1.0		.6
1.9	1.3	1.5	Debt/Worth	1.5	1.6	2.0		1.8		1.1
5.9	3.8	3.1		12.0	2.5	2.8		3.2		1.7
28.5	30.0	42.1		59.5	31.4	47.8		44.8		41.9
(138) 13.8	(109) 13.7	(107) 14.6	% Profit Before Taxes/Tangible Net Worth	(33) 14.1	(27) 8.3	14.7		30.0		18.3
3.5	1.5	3.4		3.3	2.0	3.1		6.8		3.7
10.2	12.0	15.2		11.0	15.7	15.1		17.0		17.5
5.0	5.0	5.1	% Profit Before Taxes/Total Assets	3.3	2.2	4.8		7.7		8.5
.2	.0	1.2		.0	.4	.9		2.3		1.8
46.5	69.2	55.1		77.8	59.3	54.4		108.0		20.4
21.7	26.9	24.8	Sales/Net Fixed Assets	26.0	34.3	44.3		29.9		13.7
12.9	10.6	12.7		11.3	12.1	24.7		15.9		7.5
3.2	3.3	3.0		3.1	3.1	5.0		4.3		2.9
2.6	2.5	2.4	Sales/Total Assets	2.3	2.3	2.5		2.9		2.2
2.1	2.0	2.0		1.9	1.9	2.2		2.5		2.0
.6	.5	.5		.5	.4	.6				1.1
(134) 1.1	(99) 1.1	(96) .9	% Depr., Dep., Amort./Sales	(30) .8	(26) .8	(14) .9		(13)		1.3
1.7	1.6	1.5		1.6	1.4	1.1				1.6
3.2	2.9	3.1		4.0	3.5					
(78) 4.8	(57) 4.3	(45) 4.6	% Officers', Directors', Owners' Comp/Sales	(21) 6.4	(13) 4.0					
8.6	7.1	7.3		7.9	5.1					
3045890M	2480556M	2386476M	Net Sales ($)	20565M	47368M	57159M	44830M	190453M		2026101M
1346632M	1134574M	1179158M	Total Assets ($)	10757M	22126M	20901M	18938M	62756M		1043680M

© Robert Morris Associates 1995

M = $ thousand   MM = $ million
See Pages 1 through 15 for Explanation of Ratios and Data

RETAILERS—WOMEN'S READY-TO-WEAR. SIC# 5621

Current Data Sorted By Assets							Comparative Historical Data	
1	4		1		1	**# Postretirement Benefits**		
						Type of Statement		
2	5	5	9	3	4	Unqualified	27	33
4	16	12	2			Reviewed	57	41
58	22	7				Compiled	115	97
6	4					Tax Returns	5	3
26	10	3	2	2	2	Other	54	59
	63 (4/1-9/30/94)		141 (10/1/94-3/31/95)				4/1/90-3/31/91	4/1/91-3/31/92
0-500M	500M-2MM	2-10MM	10-50MM	50-100MM	100-250MM		ALL	ALL
96	57	27	13	5	6	NUMBER OF STATEMENTS	258	233
%	%	%	%	%	%	**ASSETS**	%	%
10.6	10.6	8.5	8.4			Cash & Equivalents	9.4	9.9
8.6	10.2	15.1	7.9			Trade Receivables - (net)	12.2	11.0
59.4	53.1	42.5	41.5			Inventory	51.0	50.9
1.1	.5	3.4	2.3			All Other Current	1.5	1.0
79.7	74.4	69.5	60.2			Total Current	74.1	72.8
14.2	18.3	17.0	29.1			Fixed Assets (net)	19.3	19.0
1.8	2.2	4.2	3.4			Intangibles (net)	1.6	1.4
4.4	5.1	9.3	7.4			All Other Non-Current	5.0	6.7
100.0	100.0	100.0	100.0			Total	100.0	100.0
						LIABILITIES		
12.5	10.8	10.9	5.1			Notes Payable-Short Term	13.5	11.3
4.0	3.4	2.5	1.6			Cur. Mat. -L/T/D	3.7	3.5
16.4	20.3	20.3	20.1			Trade Payables	14.5	15.3
.4	.3	.7	.1			Income Taxes Payable	.5	.4
10.8	8.8	6.7	7.8			All Other Current	9.5	8.5
44.1	43.6	41.0	34.8			Total Current	41.7	39.0
11.3	11.0	8.6	18.7			Long Term Debt	13.2	12.2
.0	.1	.1	.4			Deferred Taxes	.3	.3
5.2	3.0	4.6	2.8			All Other-Non-Current	3.0	3.5
39.3	42.2	45.6	43.3			Net Worth	41.8	45.0
100.0	100.0	100.0	100.0			Total Liabilities & Net Worth	100.0	100.0
						INCOME DATA		
100.0	100.0	100.0	100.0			Net Sales	100.0	100.0
39.5	43.1	35.8	39.3			Gross Profit	40.5	39.9
37.8	41.8	35.9	37.1			Operating Expenses	38.5	37.7
1.6	1.3	-.1	2.3			Operating Profit	2.0	2.2
.6	1.0	.4	.6			All Other Expenses (net)	1.2	.8
1.1	.2	-.5	1.7			Profit Before Taxes	.8	1.4
						RATIOS		
3.4	2.9	2.3	2.3			Current	2.8	3.0
1.9	1.9	1.8	1.7				1.9	2.0
1.4	1.3	1.3	1.4				1.4	1.3
.9	.9	.8	1.1			Quick	1.0	1.1
.4	.3	.5	.4		(257)		.5	.5
.1	.1	.2	.1				.2	.2
0 UND	1 323.8	1 399.9	0 778.5			Sales/Receivables	1 483.3	1 383.8
3 131.5	5 79.6	9 42.8	2 221.9				6 59.6	5 72.4
18 20.3	28 13.2	41 8.8	12 31.2				27 13.5	24 15.0
74 4.9	81 4.5	54 6.8	36 10.1			Cost of Sales/Inventory	70 5.2	70 5.2
118 3.1	135 2.7	70 5.2	78 4.7				107 3.4	101 3.6
174 2.1	192 1.9	118 3.1	96 3.8				152 2.4	152 2.4
14 25.7	20 18.2	20 18.6	15 24.9			Cost of Sales/Payables	15 24.3	15 23.8
27 13.5	39 9.3	37 9.9	38 9.7				31 11.8	29 12.5
41 8.8	66 5.5	53 6.9	51 7.2				45 8.1	46 8.0
4.5	4.4	7.5	11.0			Sales/Working Capital	4.8	4.7
8.0	7.9	10.3	14.7				9.3	8.6
18.0	26.7	26.3	26.1				18.4	19.2
5.7	3.6	4.7	19.6			EBIT/Interest	4.3	5.9
(77) 2.0	(50) 1.9	(21) 1.9	(12) 4.9				(232) 2.0	(205) 1.8
-.4	.5	-.1	1.1				-.5	-.3
3.8	2.0					Net Profit + Depr., Dep.,	2.4	3.0
(11) 2.4	(18) 1.3					Amort./Cur. Mat. L /T/D	(98) .7	(74) .8
.3	.7						-1.1	-.4
.1	.2	.1	.5			Fixed/Worth	.2	.2
.3	.4	.4	.7				.4	.4
.7	.9	.8	.9				1.0	.8
.7	.7	.7	1.0			Debt/Worth	.6	.6
1.4	1.5	1.2	1.2				1.4	1.2
3.3	3.0	3.1	3.2				3.5	2.6
41.0	16.4	24.7	38.9			% Profit Before Taxes/Tangible	24.0	22.8
(86) 11.4	(54) 7.5	(25) 3.9	16.4			Net Worth	(235) 8.1	(221) 7.8
-10.7	-2.8	-5.3	.5				-8.4	-6.6
16.8	7.9	6.4	14.7			% Profit Before Taxes/Total	9.8	11.8
3.9	2.8	1.4	4.5			Assets	3.6	3.0
-7.1	-.7	-3.1	.3				-6.9	-3.5
66.4	37.7	41.8	16.3			Sales/Net Fixed Assets	49.6	38.7
31.1	22.6	17.3	12.9				20.4	18.3
16.5	10.2	13.4	8.8				10.3	10.1
4.2	3.4	4.2	4.8			Sales/Total Assets	3.8	3.7
3.0	2.5	3.2	3.8				2.8	2.7
2.2	1.8	2.2	2.6				2.0	2.1
.6	.6	.6	1.2			% Depr., Dep., Amort./Sales	.7	.6
(73) .9	(53) .9	(22) 1.1	1.5				(222) 1.3	(204) 1.2
1.3	1.6	1.7	2.2				2.1	2.1
4.6	2.8	2.0				% Officers', Directors',	2.6	2.8
(54) 7.3	(29) 5.2	(11) 2.4				Owners' Comp/Sales	(110) 4.7	(94) 4.9
10.6	8.2	3.5					9.1	8.5
61202M	161921M	328812M	891381M	939300M	1918032M	Net Sales ($)	3259309M	3682901M
20413M	56949M	100635M	258589M	326153M	863198M	Total Assets ($)	1306963M	1491938M

M = $ thousand   MM = $ million
See Pages 1 through 15 for Explanation of Ratios and Data

Comparative Historical Data | Current Data Sorted By Sales

				# Postretirement Benefits	1	3	1			2
	5		7	**Type of Statement**						
	35	20	28	Unqualified	2	4	2	1	2	17
	37	38	34	Reviewed	2	8	5	8	10	1
	99	85	87	Compiled	44	30	6	3	3	1
	7	8	10	Tax Returns	7	3				
	41	36	45	Other	26	7	4	2		6
	4/1/92-3/31/93	4/1/93-3/31/94	4/1/94-3/31/95		63 (4/1-9/30/94)			141 (10/1/94-3/31/95)		
	ALL	ALL	ALL		0-1MM	1-3MM	3-5MM	5-10MM	10-25MM	25MM & OVER
	219	187	204	**NUMBER OF STATEMENTS**	81	52	17	14	15	25
	%	%	%	**ASSETS**	%	%	%	%	%	%
	10.5	11.1	10.7	Cash & Equivalents	11.9	6.8	10.8	10.0	13.1	13.8
	10.1	10.3	9.8	Trade Receivables - (net)	8.8	10.7	9.0	21.5	7.1	6.6
	51.0	52.3	52.8	Inventory	58.3	55.3	56.0	39.8	46.2	38.5
	1.4	1.0	1.3	All Other Current	1.0	.6	.9	2.4	4.0	2.2
	72.9	74.7	74.6	Total Current	80.1	73.4	76.7	73.7	70.4	61.1
	18.8	18.1	17.3	Fixed Assets (net)	13.5	18.1	17.7	15.5	18.9	27.9
	1.8	2.0	2.5	Intangibles (net)	1.9	3.2	3.2	.8	1.7	3.8
	6.4	5.2	5.6	All Other Non-Current	4.5	5.3	2.4	10.0	9.0	7.1
	100.0	100.0	100.0	Total	100.0	100.0	100.0	100.0	100.0	100.0
				LIABILITIES						
	9.2	11.3	10.7	Notes Payable-Short Term	12.5	12.1	13.7	5.9	9.0	3.2
	3.1	3.2	3.3	Cur. Mat.-L /T/D	4.3	3.2	3.1	3.5	2.7	1.0
	16.6	16.0	18.2	Trade Payables	16.0	18.0	18.8	28.2	19.4	19.0
	.6	2.5	.4	Income Taxes Payable	.4	.2	.0	.5	1.6	.2
	9.7	7.5	9.4	All Other Current	9.9	11.4	7.1	7.4	5.9	8.2
	39.1	40.5	42.0	Total Current	43.3	44.8	42.7	45.4	38.5	31.6
	11.8	13.0	11.2	Long Term Debt	12.4	10.9	6.9	10.1	7.4	13.3
	.1	.1	.2	Deferred Taxes	.0	.1	.0	.2	.1	.7
	3.6	4.9	4.2	All Other-Non-Current	5.8	2.4	4.6	4.0	4.6	2.6
	45.4	41.5	42.5	Net Worth	38.5	41.7	45.7	40.3	49.5	51.8
	100.0	100.0	100.0	Total Liabilities & Net Worth	100.0	100.0	100.0	100.0	100.0	100.0
				INCOME DATA						
	100.0	100.0	100.0	Net Sales	100.0	100.0	100.0	100.0	100.0	100.0
	40.4	40.1	39.7	Gross Profit	39.6	42.2	41.5	39.0	36.2	36.3
	38.2	38.0	38.5	Operating Expenses	37.4	42.4	40.3	37.7	34.7	35.1
	2.1	2.2	1.3	Operating Profit	2.2	-.2	1.3	1.3	1.4	1.2
	.7	.7	.6	All Other Expenses (net)	.5	.4	1.2	.3	2.5	.0
	1.5	1.4	.7	Profit Before Taxes	1.7	-.6	.1	1.0	-1.1	1.3
				RATIOS						
	3.0	2.9	2.9		3.7	2.5	3.0	2.1	2.6	2.7
	2.0	1.8	1.9	Current	2.1	1.8	1.8	1.7	1.8	1.8
	1.4	1.3	1.4		1.3	1.3	1.3	1.2	1.4	1.5
	1.0	1.1	.9		1.1	.7	1.5	1.2	.7	1.2
(217)	.5	(186) .4	.4	Quick	.4	.4	.3	.7	.5	.7
	.2	.2	.1		.1	.1	.1	.2	.3	.2
0	735.4	0 UND	0 740.5		0 UND	0 UND	2 163.2	2 210.8	0 999.8	1 480.2
4	86.4	4 85.0	4 94.6	Sales/Receivables	3 107.3	6 66.3	5 80.0	15 24.0	2 180.3	2 221.9
26	14.3	23 15.9	21 17.5		21 17.1	27 13.5	27 13.6	62 5.9	13 28.7	8 43.3
65	5.6	63 5.8	65 5.6		74 4.9	87 4.2	85 4.3	51 7.2	47 7.8	55 6.6
104	3.5	111 3.3	107 3.4	Cost of Sales/Inventory	122 3.0	130 2.8	140 2.6	61 6.0	70 5.2	72 5.1
159	2.3	166 2.2	166 2.2		192 1.9	166 2.2	183 2.0	79 4.6	118 3.1	83 4.4
18	20.0	14 26.4	17 21.7		13 28.0	20 18.6	18 20.7	30 12.1	16 22.3	19 18.9
31	11.7	28 12.9	33 11.1	Cost of Sales/Payables	27 13.6	33 11.2	39 9.3	48 7.6	35 10.5	37 9.8
49	7.5	49 7.5	51 7.2		45 8.1	52 7.0	73 5.0	66 5.5	48 7.6	51 7.1
	4.8	4.6	5.0		4.1	5.1	5.6	6.3	8.0	6.0
	9.2	10.0	9.2	Sales/Working Capital	6.3	9.9	7.9	12.9	10.9	14.2
	17.1	19.9	18.7		17.0	20.8	21.4	28.1	28.3	17.5
	7.6	7.6	5.6		5.3	4.0	5.6	7.7	13.0	20.7
(192)	2.4	(160) 3.0	(168) 2.2	EBIT/Interest	(64) 2.0	(47) 2.3	(15) 1.4	(11) 2.1	(10) 1.6	(21) 6.4
	.3	1.1	.5		.7	-2.5	-1.1	-.4	-.9	1.5
	4.9	3.4	3.6	Net Profit + Depr., Dep.,		3.6				
(53)	1.7	(47) 1.4	(40) 1.7	Amort./Cur. Mat. L/T/D		(16) 1.6				
	1.0	.4	.7			.3				
	.2	.2	.2		.1	.2	.1	.1	.2	.4
	.4	.4	.4	Fixed/Worth	.3	.4	.4	.3	.4	.7
	.7	.9	.8		.7	.9	.7	.7	.8	.8
	.6	.6	.6		.6	.8	.6	.7	.5	.5
	1.1	1.5	1.3	Debt/Worth	1.5	1.3	1.8	1.2	1.1	1.1
	2.5	3.2	3.1		3.7	3.0	3.1	3.3	2.4	2.0
	29.7	30.2	28.1	% Profit Before Taxes/Tangible	36.2	23.4	19.4	26.3	24.2	31.3
(210)	11.9	(172) 11.9	(189) 8.3	Net Worth	(71) 11.4	(49) 7.9	4.9	(12) 11.3	3.5	16.1
	.0	1.1	-3.7		.0	-17.9	-7.0	-2.4	-6.0	.7
	11.8	11.8	11.7	% Profit Before Taxes/Total	15.5	8.5	8.2	11.6	9.7	12.9
	4.3	5.5	3.4	Assets	3.6	2.6	1.5	3.5	.9	6.3
	-2.0	.0	-2.0		-1.4	-9.7	-2.1	-4.2	-2.6	.3
	51.1	52.8	46.7		72.2	37.4	80.8	41.0	41.8	15.8
	19.6	23.2	23.3	Sales/Net Fixed Assets	31.9	23.0	25.7	24.4	17.3	10.1
	10.2	11.0	11.8		16.0	11.1	7.4	14.4	12.9	8.1
	3.9	4.0	3.9		3.9	3.7	3.4	4.5	4.5	4.3
	2.8	2.9	2.8	Sales/Total Assets	2.7	2.7	2.8	3.1	3.8	3.1
	2.1	2.1	2.1		1.8	2.2	1.8	2.4	2.6	2.2
	.6	.6	.6		.6	.6	.6	.4	.6	1.3
(187)	1.1	(153) 1.1	(170) 1.0	% Depr., Dep., Amort./Sales	(60) .9	(48) 1.0	(14) .9	(12) .9	(13) 1.1	(23) 1.8
	1.9	1.9	1.6		1.3	1.6	1.5	1.2	1.8	2.3
	2.3	1.9	2.9	% Officers', Directors',	4.8	4.1				
(95)	5.0	(87) 4.9	(98) 5.4	Owners' Comp/Sales	(47) 8.4	(24) 6.2				
	8.1	9.6	9.3		11.6	8.0				
	4122715M	2966656M	4300648M	Net Sales ($)	38887M	87185M	62594M	106261M	222607M	3783114M
	1579465M	1105719M	1625937M	Total Assets ($)	16609M	34106M	25639M	34558M	66327M	1448698M

Current Data Sorted By Assets **Comparative Historical Data**

5	19	73	16	3		# Postretirement Benefits / Type of Statement		
7	7	67	52	6	1	Unqualified	147	130
7	46	241	54	1	.	Reviewed	260	255
27	73	178	18	1	1	Compiled	256	233
10	19	38	1			Tax Returns	16	24
16	320	1403	241	5	1	Other	1430	1323

	236 (4/1-9/30/94)		2604 (10/1/94-3/31/95)				4/1/90-3/31/91	4/1/91-3/31/92
0-500M	500M-2MM	2-10MM	10-50MM	50-100MM	100-250MM		ALL	ALL
67	465	1927	366	12	3	**NUMBER OF STATEMENTS**	2109	1965
%	%	%	%	%	%	**ASSETS**	%	%
9.0	6.0	4.9	5.5	7.7		Cash & Equivalents	5.0	4.7
12.4	7.1	7.5	10.3	8.2		Trade Receivables - (net)	8.6	8.8
59.3	72.6	68.6	57.2	47.8		Inventory	66.2	65.6
2.9	3.2	3.6	4.2	6.3		All Other Current	2.9	3.0
83.6	88.9	84.7	77.2	69.9		Total Current	82.7	82.1
10.2	7.0	9.4	13.5	21.9		Fixed Assets (net)	10.0	10.9
1.4	.9	.8	1.2	.8		Intangibles (net)	.9	.9
4.8	3.2	5.1	8.1	7.4		All Other Non-Current	6.4	6.1
100.0	100.0	100.0	100.0	100.0		Total	100.0	100.0
						LIABILITIES		
34.6	53.6	57.6	54.4	50.3		Notes Payable-Short Term	55.0	55.1
1.8	.9	1.1	1.1	.7		Cur. Mat. -L/T/D	1.3	1.7
7.7	4.8	4.6	5.4	4.5		Trade Payables	5.5	4.6
.5	.3	.3	.2	.4		Income Taxes Payable	.3	.2
9.4	5.9	6.4	6.8	8.8		All Other Current	6.4	6.3
54.0	65.4	69.9	67.8	64.8		Total Current	68.4	67.9
7.0	6.6	7.5	9.5	15.5		Long Term Debt	9.0	9.5
.0	.0	.1	.2	.1		Deferred Taxes	.1	.1
4.3	1.7	1.6	1.3	3.9		All Other-Non-Current	1.4	1.5
34.7	26.3	20.8	21.1	15.7		Net Worth	21.1	21.0
100.0	100.0	100.0	100.0	100.0		Total Liabilities & Net Worth	100.0	100.0
						INCOME DATA		
100.0	100.0	100.0	100.0	100.0		Net Sales	100.0	100.0
20.7	13.0	12.2	12.0	17.3		Gross Profit	13.8	13.8
17.3	11.4	10.9	10.3	16.0		Operating Expenses	13.0	13.1
3.4	1.6	1.3	1.7	1.3		Operating Profit	.9	.7
.2	.1	.0	–.1	.4		All Other Expenses (net)	.3	.3
3.2	1.5	1.4	1.8	.9		Profit Before Taxes	.6	.5
						RATIOS		
2.8	1.6	1.4	1.3	1.1		Current	1.4	1.4
1.5	1.3	1.2	1.1	1.1			1.2	1.2
1.1	1.2	1.1	1.0	1.0			1.1	1.1
.8	.3	.3	.3	.5		Quick	.3	.3
(66) .3	.2	(1920) .2	.2	.2			(2095) .2	(1954) .2
.1	.1	.1	.1	.1			.1	.1
0 UND	2 180.3	3 126.6	5 77.0	5 79.5		Sales/Receivables	4 99.8	4 99.0
4 98.0	4 92.1	5 75.2	8 44.8	6 58.5			6 60.3	6 58.2
16 23.4	7 49.9	8 46.2	12 31.3	11 34.2			10 36.8	10 35.9
24 15.0	54 6.8	49 7.4	43 8.5	43 8.4		Cost of Sales/Inventory	52 7.0	52 7.0
54 6.7	70 5.2	62 5.9	53 6.9	54 6.7			66 5.5	68 5.4
81 4.5	89 4.1	78 4.7	66 5.5	74 4.9			87 4.2	87 4.2
0 UND	1 313.9	2 217.3	2 167.0	4 103.4		Cost of Sales/Payables	2 187.3	2 183.7
2 195.0	2 171.7	3 136.8	3 107.7	5 77.2			3 113.3	3 112.7
10 36.3	4 87.3	4 89.3	5 71.8	5 67.7			5 69.3	5 70.9
6.9	13.0	19.8	24.0	42.2		Sales/Working Capital	17.9	17.3
18.3	21.8	33.6	51.6	101.0			31.3	31.6
102.4	37.4	80.0	470.8	-334.4			100.1	100.2
5.2	4.8	6.3	7.7	4.7		EBIT/Interest	2.4	2.5
(50) 2.1	(397) 2.6	(1638) 2.9	(308) 3.7	(10) 1.8			(1948) 1.4	(1853) 1.4
1.1	1.4	1.7	2.1	.4			.8	.8
	5.4	6.6	8.0			Net Profit + Depr., Dep., Amort./Cur. Mat. L./T/D	5.2	3.8
	(44) 2.9	(208) 2.5	(58) 2.7				(537) 1.7	(420) 1.0
	.9	1.0	1.3				.2	-.2
.0	.1	.2	.3	.4		Fixed/Worth	.2	.2
.2	.2	.4	.5	1.0			.4	.4
1.3	.5	.9	1.3	1.9			1.1	1.3
.6	1.8	2.6	2.7	3.8		Debt/Worth	2.3	2.3
1.9	3.2	4.4	4.7	5.3			4.4	4.4
15.1	5.7	8.3	8.2	11.8			9.5	9.8
65.8	41.0	53.1	58.3	50.8		% Profit Before Taxes/Tangible Net Worth	28.1	26.2
(56) 22.8	(438) 20.2	(1814) 30.4	(351) 34.5	33.5			(1910) 11.0	(1749) 9.9
5.8	8.3	14.0	20.7	-16.2			-.9	-1.0
18.0	9.2	10.0	11.6	7.3		% Profit Before Taxes/Total Assets	5.8	5.2
8.7	5.2	5.4	7.0	4.1			2.1	1.7
.9	1.7	2.2	3.4	-1.3			-.7	-1.1
254.3	204.9	148.2	107.2	83.5		Sales/Net Fixed Assets	139.7	134.2
95.0	101.2	77.7	50.0	30.0			68.0	62.8
40.6	46.5	40.3	20.7	10.0			32.2	28.4
7.0	5.5	5.5	5.4	4.5		Sales/Total Assets	5.1	5.0
4.7	4.4	4.6	4.3	3.9			4.1	4.1
3.0	3.5	3.8	3.5	3.0			3.4	3.3
.2	.1	.1	.2	.2		% Depr., Dep., Amort./Sales	.2	.2
(42) .3	(371) .2	(1759) .2	(347) .3	.4			(1858) .3	(1775) .3
.7	.4	.4	.4	.6			.5	.5
1.6	.5	.3	.2			% Officers', Directors', Owners' Comp/Sales	.4	.4
(29) 2.3	(316) .8	(1414) .5	(245) .3				(1409) .6	(1295) .7
4.2	1.4	.9	.6				1.2	1.2
96135M	3226084M	43326667M	26529647M	2731469M	2292494M	Net Sales ($)	41200172M	38697683M
17953M	639183M	9119151M	6098606M	734759M	603620M	Total Assets ($)	10067696M	9698554M

M = $ thousand   MM = $ million
See Pages 1 through 15 for Explanation of Ratios and Data

Comparative Historical Data				Current Data Sorted By Sales					
24	100	116	# Postretirement Benefits	1	4	6	11	49	45
			Type of Statement						
143	195	140	Unqualified	5	3	1	6	33	92
262	329	349	Reviewed	2	7	13	48	140	139
191	203	297	Compiled	15	28	18	52	108	76
30	53	68	Tax Returns	5	6	9	15	21	12
1384	1464	1986	Other	7	51	83	310	815	720
4/1/92-3/31/93	4/1/93-3/31/94	4/1/94-3/31/95		236 (4/1-9/30/94)		2604 (10/1/94-3/31/95)			
ALL	ALL	ALL		0-1MM	1-3MM	3-5MM	5-10MM	10-25MM	25MM & OVER
2010	2244	2840	**NUMBER OF STATEMENTS**	34	95	124	431	1117	1039
%	%	%	**ASSETS**	%	%	%	%	%	%
5.0	5.0	5.3	Cash & Equivalents	7.6	8.2	6.5	5.2	4.9	5.3
8.0	8.5	7.9	Trade Receivables - (net)	10.6	12.7	6.6	6.3	7.0	9.2
65.8	66.4	67.5	Inventory	60.9	58.6	72.0	72.9	70.2	62.8
3.7	3.3	3.6	All Other Current	1.5	3.5	2.6	3.3	3.5	4.0
82.6	83.3	84.3	Total Current	80.5	83.1	87.8	87.7	85.6	81.3
10.7	10.2	9.6	Fixed Assets (net)	11.8	10.6	7.9	8.1	8.7	11.2
.9	.8	.9	Intangibles (net)	2.3	.4	1.0	.9	.7	1.0
5.9	5.7	5.2	All Other Non-Current	5.3	5.8	3.2	3.2	4.9	6.4
100.0	100.0	100.0	Total	100.0	100.0	100.0	100.0	100.0	100.0
			LIABILITIES						
55.7	54.7	55.9	Notes Payable-Short Term	29.4	40.1	51.7	55.6	58.7	56.0
1.5	1.4	1.1	Cur. Mat.-L /T/D	1.0	3.0	1.3	.8	.9	1.2
4.5	5.7	4.8	Trade Payables	9.6	6.6	5.2	4.2	4.4	5.1
.2	.4	.3	Income Taxes Payable	.7	.3	.1	.3	.3	.3
6.5	6.4	6.4	All Other Current	7.2	8.2	5.5	5.9	5.8	7.2
68.4	68.5	68.5	Total Current	47.8	58.2	63.8	66.8	70.1	69.8
9.1	8.4	7.7	Long Term Debt	8.5	7.3	7.8	7.1	7.6	7.9
.1	.1	.1	Deferred Taxes	.0	.0	.0	.1	.1	.1
1.5	1.8	1.7	All Other-Non-Current	2.7	4.7	1.4	1.9	1.6	1.4
21.0	21.2	22.1	Net Worth	41.0	29.7	27.0	24.1	20.6	20.9
100.0	100.0	100.0	Total Liabilities & Net Worth	100.0	100.0	100.0	100.0	100.0	100.0
			INCOME DATA						
100.0	100.0	100.0	Net Sales	100.0	100.0	100.0	100.0	100.0	100.0
13.6	13.0	12.5	Gross Profit	30.8	16.9	13.8	12.2	12.2	11.9
12.4	11.7	11.1	Operating Expenses	25.3	14.6	12.2	10.8	11.0	10.4
1.2	1.3	1.5	Operating Profit	5.5	2.3	1.6	1.4	1.2	1.5
.2	.1	.0	All Other Expenses (net)	.3	.3	.2	.1	.0	-.1
1.0	1.2	1.5	Profit Before Taxes	5.2	2.0	1.4	1.3	1.3	1.6
			RATIOS						
1.4	1.4	1.4	Current	3.2	2.1	1.7	1.5	1.4	1.3
1.2	1.2	1.2		1.9	1.4	1.3	1.3	1.2	1.1
1.1	1.1	1.1		1.0	1.1	1.2	1.2	1.1	1.0
.3	.3	.3	Quick	.8	.7	.3	.2	.2	.3
(2005) .2	(2239) .2	(2832) .2		.3	(94) .2	.2	(430) .1	(1115) .1	(1035) .2
.1	.1	.1		.1	.1	.1	.1	.1	.1
3 122.1	3 121.3	3 130.7	Sales/Receivables	0 UND	2 158.8	2 163.5	2 169.1	3 139.9	3 107.0
5 68.7	6 65.7	5 72.9		8 47.1	6 58.1	5 79.3	4 85.6	4 82.0	6 62.3
9 40.2	9 41.8	9 42.7		18 20.8	20 17.9	9 40.8	7 50.8	8 48.1	9 39.0
51 7.1	49 7.5	48 7.6	Cost of Sales/Inventory	41 8.8	55 6.6	64 5.7	61 6.0	53 6.9	41 8.8
66 5.5	62 5.9	62 5.9		87 4.2	79 4.6	87 4.2	76 4.8	65 5.6	51 7.2
83 4.4	78 4.7	78 4.7		192 1.9	111 3.3	101 3.6	94 3.9	79 4.6	64 5.7
2 195.9	2 211.2	2 225.9	Cost of Sales/Payables	0 UND	1 580.0	1 317.3	1 274.2	2 225.7	2 198.4
3 118.7	3 124.1	3 134.9		3 142.1	4 97.2	3 143.0	2 146.4	3 140.4	3 127.6
5 76.2	5 77.0	4 88.4		21 17.0	11 34.0	5 70.0	4 83.4	4 90.2	4 85.4
17.8	18.3	18.5	Sales/Working Capital	4.6	6.2	11.7	13.1	19.3	25.7
30.7	33.1	32.2		7.1	14.3	18.0	21.3	31.0	49.9
91.5	94.9	78.5		UND	45.6	33.2	35.6	64.6	210.4
4.1	5.3	6.2	EBIT/Interest	10.2	4.5	3.9	5.0	5.8	7.8
(1830) 2.1	(2025) 2.5	(2406) 2.9		(23) 3.0	(80) 1.8	(108) 2.2	(372) 2.6	(954) 2.7	(869) 3.7
1.2	1.5	1.7		1.2	1.1	1.4	1.4	1.6	2.0
6.1	5.3	6.2	Net Profit + Depr., Dep., Amort./Cur. Mat. L/T/D		2.5		5.5	5.6	8.3
(316) 1.9	(309) 2.2	(320) 2.5			(11) 1.2		(52) 3.3	(123) 2.3	(124) 3.0
.6	.7	1.0			.0		1.9	.7	1.3
.2	.2	.2	Fixed/Worth	.0	.1	.1	.1	.2	.2
.4	.4	.4		.2	.2	.2	.2	.3	.5
1.1	1.1	.9		1.0	.9	.8	.7	.9	1.1
2.5	2.5	2.4	Debt/Worth	.5	1.1	1.6	2.1	2.6	2.7
4.4	4.4	4.2		1.6	2.4	3.3	3.6	4.3	4.6
9.0	8.5	8.0		12.7	11.0	8.2	6.5	8.1	8.3
38.2	44.4	52.1	% Profit Before Taxes/Tangible Net Worth	47.6	30.3	34.2	40.5	47.7	63.7
(1842) 18.6	(2074) 23.1	(2674) 29.2		(29) 21.8	(85) 12.5	(116) 18.0	(406) 20.6	(1046) 27.7	(992) 37.7
4.8	10.3	13.4		10.5	2.8	7.3	8.4	12.6	22.0
7.1	8.5	10.3	% Profit Before Taxes/Total Assets	21.2	11.1	8.1	8.0	9.4	12.2
3.5	4.5	5.6		11.6	2.5	4.1	4.7	4.8	7.0
.7	1.5	2.2		1.0	.4	1.3	1.8	1.9	3.6
131.9	138.1	151.1	Sales/Net Fixed Assets	UND	171.8	196.5	163.3	156.1	139.8
68.3	69.2	77.6		55.7	47.8	101.3	79.3	80.8	73.8
29.3	32.3	37.5		18.4	21.8	34.7	39.2	43.8	31.8
5.1	5.5	5.5	Sales/Total Assets	4.5	4.6	4.8	4.8	5.3	6.0
4.1	4.5	4.5		2.8	3.1	3.7	3.9	4.5	5.0
3.3	3.6	3.7		1.6	2.3	2.9	3.4	3.8	4.1
.2	.2	.1	% Depr., Dep., Amort./Sales	.2	.2	.1	.1	.1	.1
(1792) .3	(2005) .3	(2533) .2		(20) .7	(71) .4	(91) .2	(362) .3	(1013) .2	(976) .2
.5	.4	.4		2.7	.8	.5	.4	.4	.4
.4	.3	.3	% Officers', Directors', Owners' Comp/Sales	2.8	.9	.6	.5	.3	.2
(1352) .7	(1513) .6	(2009) .5		(13) 4.6	(49) 1.6	(84) 1.0	(313) .7	(814) .6	(736) .4
1.2	1.1	1.0		5.9	2.4	1.6	1.2	.9	.7
44868336M	54559346M	78202496M	Net Sales ($)	16906M	194755M	507763M	3265754M	18531900M	55685418M
10825901M	12825195M	17213272M	Total Assets ($)	12365M	83086M	157902M	863666M	4293090M	11803163M

© Robert Morris Associates 1995

M = $ thousand   MM = $ million
See Pages 1 through 15 for Explanation of Ratios and Data

Current Data Sorted By Assets   Comparative Historical Data

						# Postretirement Benefits		
						Type of Statement		
7	7							
4	4	1	4			Unqualified	8	6
9	19	9				Reviewed	23	31
77	60	12		1		Compiled	137	125
26	12					Tax Returns	6	10
39	30	18	2			Other	74	74
	79 (4/1-9/30/94)		248 (10/1/94-3/31/95)				4/1/90-3/31/91	4/1/91-3/31/92
0-500M	500M-2MM	2-10MM	10-50MM	50-100MM	100-250MM		ALL	ALL
155	125	40	6	1		NUMBER OF STATEMENTS	248	246
%	%	%	%	%	%	**ASSETS**	%	%
9.8	6.1	5.1				Cash & Equivalents	6.9	6.7
10.4	12.7	19.0				Trade Receivables - (net)	14.3	14.2
61.9	57.7	51.7				Inventory	54.8	56.5
1.3	3.1	1.4				All Other Current	2.2	2.3
83.4	79.6	77.2				Total Current	78.2	79.6
13.4	12.6	16.1				Fixed Assets (net)	16.8	14.4
.8	.8	.2				Intangibles (net)	.5	.8
2.3	7.0	6.6				All Other Non-Current	4.4	5.1
100.0	100.0	100.0				Total	100.0	100.0
						LIABILITIES		
37.5	37.5	33.0				Notes Payable-Short Term	36.9	38.2
1.9	1.6	1.2				Cur. Mat. -L/T/D	2.7	2.2
5.6	4.2	7.0				Trade Payables	4.4	4.1
.4	.3	.1				Income Taxes Payable	.6	.4
8.1	5.9	10.3				All Other Current	7.6	7.0
53.6	49.6	51.6				Total Current	52.3	52.0
10.6	9.7	18.7				Long Term Debt	13.0	11.2
.0	.1	.0				Deferred Taxes	.2	.3
4.7	3.3	5.5				All Other-Non-Current	3.4	3.3
31.1	37.3	24.2				Net Worth	31.2	33.2
100.0	100.0	100.0				Total Liabilities & Net Worth	100.0	100.0
						INCOME DATA		
100.0	100.0	100.0				Net Sales	100.0	100.0
19.9	16.6	20.4				Gross Profit	20.6	19.8
15.9	13.5	17.4				Operating Expenses	17.4	17.1
3.9	3.1	3.0				Operating Profit	3.2	2.6
1.0	.3	-.3				All Other Expenses (net)	.7	.3
2.9	2.8	3.3				Profit Before Taxes	2.4	2.4
						RATIOS		
2.7 / 1.4 / 1.1	2.4 / 1.5 / 1.2	2.4 / 1.3 / 1.1				Current	2.3 / 1.5 / 1.1	2.4 / 1.4 / 1.1
(152) .8 / .2 / .1	(123) .7 / .2 / .1	.8 / .3 / .1				Quick	(245) 1.0 / .2 / .1	(242) .7 / .3 / .1
(0) UND / (1) 272.7 / (8) 46.1	(0) 985.7 / (3) 106.1 / (13) 29.1	(3) 138.1 / (7) 50.2 / (22) 16.8				Sales/Receivables	(0) UND / (2) 155.3 / (14) 26.2	(0) UND / (3) 123.4 / (14) 25.7
(37) 9.9 / (52) 7.0 / (72) 5.1	(36) 10.2 / (55) 6.6 / (78) 4.7	(35) 10.3 / (60) 6.1 / (94) 3.9				Cost of Sales/Inventory	(36) 10.1 / (55) 6.6 / (83) 4.4	(36) 10.2 / (53) 6.9 / (83) 4.4
(0) UND / (1) 442.8 / (4) 103.8	(0) UND / (2) 193.7 / (5) 71.5	(2) 232.7 / (4) 82.6 / (11) 32.2				Cost of Sales/Payables	(0) UND / (2) 203.0 / (6) 63.6	(0) UND / (1) 251.7 / (5) 76.3
8.4 / 24.1 / 89.3	8.2 / 16.6 / 49.2	8.8 / 20.3 / 51.3				Sales/Working Capital	8.5 / 18.3 / 65.4	8.8 / 20.2 / 101.3
(138) 5.4 / 2.5 / 1.2	(119) 5.7 / 3.1 / 1.7	(38) 5.1 / 2.6 / 1.6				EBIT/Interest	(231) 3.5 / 1.9 / 1.1	(224) 4.4 / 2.1 / 1.1
(13) 14.6 / 4.9 / -1.4	(21) 11.0 / 3.0 / .9	(10) 16.9 / 5.0 / 1.3				Net Profit + Depr., Dep., Amort./Cur. Mat. L /T/D	(46) 6.5 / 1.8 / .1	(22) 7.4 / 2.4 / .6
.0 / .2 / 1.3	.1 / .2 / .8	.1 / .5 / 1.3				Fixed/Worth	.1 / .4 / 1.3	.1 / .3 / 1.4
1.0 / 2.6 / 7.8	.8 / 1.9 / 3.9	1.9 / 4.5 / 8.2				Debt/Worth	1.1 / 2.6 / 7.9	.8 / 2.5 / 6.7
(137) 69.5 / 33.8 / 12.1	(119) 46.7 / 26.6 / 13.4	88.0 / 40.6 / 18.4				% Profit Before Taxes/Tangible Net Worth	(226) 47.0 / 19.9 / 5.5	(223) 46.4 / 21.1 / 6.8
22.0 / 9.2 / 2.1	16.4 / 8.3 / 3.1	12.8 / 6.3 / 2.7				% Profit Before Taxes/Total Assets	13.5 / 5.0 / .5	15.2 / 6.3 / .7
706.0 / 104.3 / 22.8	298.4 / 67.8 / 18.7	94.9 / 56.2 / 11.8				Sales/Net Fixed Assets	265.0 / 46.0 / 13.8	417.1 / 69.0 / 16.2
7.2 / 5.3 / 3.6	6.1 / 4.3 / 2.8	5.5 / 3.4 / 1.9				Sales/Total Assets	6.2 / 4.0 / 2.5	6.7 / 4.4 / 2.4
(92) .1 / .4 / .7	(97) .1 / .3 / .8	(37) .2 / .3 / .7				% Depr., Dep., Amort./Sales	(183) .2 / .4 / .9	(162) .2 / .4 / 1.0
(73) 1.3 / 2.7 / 4.5	(66) .7 / 1.6 / 3.0	(25) .7 / 1.1 / 2.1				% Officers', Directors', Owners' Comp/Sales	(127) 1.4 / 2.6 / 4.8	(119) 1.2 / 2.5 / 4.3
272425M	597533M	659177M	178320M	601079M		Net Sales ($)	935978M	875607M
43616M	116855M	155760M	137238M	99262M		Total Assets ($)	452852M	222728M

M = $ thousand   MM = $ million
See Pages 1 through 15 for Explanation of Ratios and Data

Comparative Historical Data / Current Data Sorted By Sales

# Postretirement Benefits Type of Statement	1	4	14	4	6	1	2	1	
Unqualified	10	5	13	3	3	1	1	1	4
Reviewed	24	23	37	1	8	8	15	4	1
Compiled	148	129	150	31	61	27	20	8	3
Tax Returns	19	32	38	12	16	5	5		
Other	72	86	89	18	32	10	11	13	5

	4/1/92-3/31/93 ALL	4/1/93-3/31/94 ALL	4/1/94-3/31/95 ALL	79 (4/1-9/30/94)		248 (10/1/94-3/31/95)			
				0-1MM	1-3MM	3-5MM	5-10MM	10-25MM	25MM & OVER
NUMBER OF STATEMENTS	273	275	327	65	120	51	52	26	13
ASSETS	%	%	%	%	%	%	%	%	%
Cash & Equivalents	7.0	7.0	7.7	11.3	7.8	5.7	5.6	8.2	3.9
Trade Receivables - (net)	13.5	12.5	13.2	16.0	10.7	11.2	12.6	13.0	31.2
Inventory	56.4	59.0	58.1	50.5	59.5	62.6	63.2	59.7	43.8
All Other Current	3.1	1.2	2.2	1.0	1.9	3.0	1.9	3.3	5.3
Total Current	80.0	79.8	81.2	78.9	80.0	82.4	83.3	84.2	84.2
Fixed Assets (net)	14.0	15.5	13.3	18.2	13.5	11.6	11.7	8.4	10.3
Intangibles (net)	.9	.8	.7	1.0	.8	1.1	.4	.0	.0
All Other Non-Current	5.0	3.9	4.8	1.9	5.8	4.9	4.6	7.4	5.6
Total	100.0	100.0	100.0	100.0	100.0	100.0	100.0	100.0	100.0
LIABILITIES									
Notes Payable-Short Term	38.6	37.5	36.5	38.0	36.5	33.7	38.0	37.2	32.9
Cur. Mat.-L /T/D	2.1	2.0	1.9	1.7	1.6	1.7	2.4	.7	6.5
Trade Payables	4.6	4.0	5.2	3.7	4.9	6.3	6.0	3.2	12.8
Income Taxes Payable	.4	.6	.4	.5	.2	.6	.2	.3	1.0
All Other Current	7.2	6.6	7.5	7.4	8.0	7.1	7.3	8.2	4.4
Total Current	52.8	50.8	51.5	51.2	51.1	49.4	54.0	49.5	57.7
Long Term Debt	12.3	12.1	11.2	12.9	11.2	10.3	10.9	11.3	8.6
Deferred Taxes	.1	.1	.1	.0	.0	.1	.1	.0	.2
All Other-Non-Current	4.3	4.0	4.3	5.5	3.9	2.2	4.8	6.7	4.6
Net Worth	30.5	32.9	32.9	30.4	33.8	38.0	30.2	32.4	28.9
Total Liabilities & Net Worth	100.0	100.0	100.0	100.0	100.0	100.0	100.0	100.0	100.0
INCOME DATA									
Net Sales	100.0	100.0	100.0	100.0	100.0	100.0	100.0	100.0	100.0
Gross Profit	19.1	17.8	19.0	25.4	19.4	17.5	14.4	13.0	18.4
Operating Expenses	16.1	15.0	15.4	19.9	15.9	14.0	12.2	11.1	14.2
Operating Profit	3.0	2.8	3.6	5.5	3.5	3.4	2.2	1.9	4.2
All Other Expenses (net)	.1	.4	.5	1.1	.6	.5	.5	-.5	-.9
Profit Before Taxes	2.9	2.4	3.1	4.4	2.9	2.9	1.7	2.4	5.1
RATIOS									
Current	2.2	2.5	2.5	2.6	3.2	2.4	2.3	2.5	2.6
	1.5	1.5	1.5	1.4	1.4	1.7	1.5	1.4	1.3
	1.1	1.1	1.1	1.1	1.1	1.2	1.2	1.3	1.0
Quick	.7	.7	.8	1.0	.9	.6	.5	.8	2.0
	(271) .2	(268) .3	(322) .3	(63) .4	.2	(48) .2	.2	.2	.3
	.1	.1	.1	.1	.1	.1	.1	.1	.2
Sales/Receivables	0 UND	0 999.8	0 UND	0 UND	0 UND	1 682.5	2 215.3	0 999.8	5 78.2
	2 154.6	4 102.1	3 134.7	2 179.0	2 210.4	3 118.5	5 74.6	3 128.9	15 24.4
	10 34.9	12 31.4	11 31.8	26 14.2	9 42.8	14 26.4	10 36.3	10 35.8	53 6.9
Cost of Sales/Inventory	33 11.1	35 10.3	37 10.0	44 8.3	44 8.3	35 10.4	28 13.1	18 19.9	23 15.7
	49 7.4	53 6.9	54 6.8	66 5.5	55 6.6	49 7.5	47 7.8	46 8.0	32 11.4
	76 4.8	81 4.5	78 4.7	118 3.1	78 4.7	72 5.1	61 6.0	66 5.5	64 5.7
Cost of Sales/Payables	0 UND	0 UND	0 UND	0 UND	0 UND	1 713.0	1 556.2	0 999.8	6 57.1
	2 216.7	1 294.8	2 220.3	0 UND	2 228.8	3 122.6	2 200.3	1 297.0	11 34.6
	7 51.6	5 66.4	6 58.7	3 114.4	4 90.0	8 43.4	8 48.6	4 91.1	15 23.9
Sales/Working Capital	8.7	8.8	8.1	5.4	7.4	11.2	11.0	15.7	3.1
	21.7	19.4	21.0	10.7	21.1	16.6	28.0	27.2	21.7
	63.7	55.8	63.4	72.8	97.6	37.8	48.7	69.4	179.5
EBIT/Interest	4.6	4.8	5.6	5.2	5.8	7.8	5.4	4.4	7.2
	(254) 2.6	(257) 2.7	(302) 2.8	(57) 2.5	(109) 2.5	(50) 3.4	(50) 2.8	(23) 3.2	3.9
	1.3	1.5	1.5	1.2	1.4	1.6	1.7	2.0	2.2
Net Profit + Depr., Dep., Amort./Cur. Mat. L/T/D	4.0	3.5	13.3		14.0		17.2		
	(27) 1.1	(35) 1.9	(47) 3.8		(13) 3.8		(12) 4.0		
	.2	.6	1.0		.9		1.7		
Fixed/Worth	.1	.1	.1	.1	.1	.1	.1	.1	.2
	.3	.3	.2	.4	.3	.2	.2	.1	.2
	1.3	1.1	.9	1.9	1.2	.7	.8	.5	.7
Debt/Worth	1.2	1.0	1.0	.9	.8	.9	1.3	1.4	1.3
	2.9	2.4	2.4	2.8	2.3	1.4	3.0	2.2	4.1
	7.6	5.8	6.1	9.3	7.3	5.5	5.8	4.0	6.2
% Profit Before Taxes/Tangible Net Worth	55.9	54.9	62.5	64.5	65.5	57.4	48.8	55.9	87.0
	(247) 26.6	(253) 25.9	(303) 30.6	(58) 30.1	(106) 30.2	(49) 30.3	(51) 30.4	32.3	32.9
	7.8	9.3	13.4	13.1	13.1	9.7	13.8	13.6	22.4
% Profit Before Taxes/Total Assets	15.5	14.7	18.0	19.0	20.3	18.0	15.1	12.6	18.3
	7.2	7.2	8.3	10.7	8.6	8.3	6.5	8.3	7.5
	1.3	2.5	2.5	3.0	1.4	3.3	2.1	3.7	4.0
Sales/Net Fixed Assets	378.2	262.0	346.9	307.5	419.1	406.4	330.5	664.8	160.9
	79.1	66.0	69.4	43.8	55.6	131.8	108.6	152.3	63.7
	20.4	17.4	20.5	9.6	18.6	19.1	37.8	42.8	18.1
Sales/Total Assets	6.9	6.6	6.7	5.1	6.1	6.9	8.6	13.6	7.9
	4.5	4.7	4.6	3.2	4.5	5.1	5.7	6.9	4.8
	2.8	2.9	2.8	2.0	3.0	3.4	3.7	3.7	1.5
% Depr., Dep., Amort./Sales	.1	.1	.1	.3	.2	.1	.1	.0	.1
	(194) .3	(207) .3	(231) .3	(36) .6	(79) .4	(39) .3	(44) .2	(21) .2	(12) .3
	.8	.8	.7	1.5	.8	.8	.4	.3	.5
% Officers', Directors', Owners' Comp/Sales	1.1	1.0	.9	2.2	1.5	1.0	.6	.4	
	(140) 2.2	(137) 2.2	(167) 2.0	(26) 3.8	(58) 2.6	(33) 1.5	(28) 1.2	(14) .7	
	4.5	3.9	3.7	7.8	4.4	2.7	2.4	1.2	
Net Sales ($)	1003321M	1895069M	2308534M	42458M	223502M	191102M	368371M	398705M	1084396M
Total Assets ($)	253456M	560508M	552731M	15694M	61237M	46150M	80366M	80796M	268488M

M = $ thousand   MM = $ million
See Pages 1 through 15 for Explanation of Ratios and Data

	Current Data Sorted By Assets							Comparative Historical Data	
	8	21	5	2		1	# Postretirement Benefits		
							Type of Statement		
	6	11	15	5	3	5	Unqualified	29	25
	7	42	27	4			Reviewed	93	77
	102	113	23	2		1	Compiled	231	203
	28	15					Tax Returns	7	15
	44	41	26	8	2	2	Other	110	93
		179 (4/1-9/30/94)		353 (10/1/94-3/31/95)				4/1/90-3/31/91	4/1/91-3/31/92
	0-500M	500M-2MM	2-10MM	10-50MM	50-100MM	100-250MM		ALL	ALL
	187	222	91	19	5	8	NUMBER OF STATEMENTS	470	413
	%	%	%	%	%	%	ASSETS	%	%
	8.2	7.5	4.8	3.7			Cash & Equivalents	6.2	5.3
	18.3	20.3	18.2	15.3			Trade Receivables - (net)	19.1	18.9
	47.7	46.3	49.8	42.5			Inventory	48.8	47.8
	1.4	1.4	1.1	1.3			All Other Current	1.3	1.3
	75.5	75.5	74.0	62.7			Total Current	75.4	73.3
	19.5	18.2	19.8	25.8			Fixed Assets (net)	19.1	19.8
	1.3	1.4	1.6	4.1			Intangibles (net)	1.1	1.6
	3.7	4.9	4.5	7.4			All Other Non-Current	4.4	5.3
	100.0	100.0	100.0	100.0			Total	100.0	100.0
							LIABILITIES		
	8.1	7.3	10.0	6.3			Notes Payable-Short Term	8.2	9.6
	4.7	3.3	2.9	2.3			Cur. Mat. -L/T/D	4.3	4.7
	21.6	23.2	26.5	26.5			Trade Payables	23.9	23.3
	.3	.3	.4	.2			Income Taxes Payable	.5	.4
	9.6	6.9	5.9	7.5			All Other Current	6.2	6.3
	44.4	40.9	45.7	42.9			Total Current	43.1	44.2
	19.2	13.9	13.5	13.8			Long Term Debt	18.9	20.7
	.1	.2	.1	.3			Deferred Taxes	.2	.2
	4.9	2.1	1.5	3.7			All Other-Non-Current	2.3	2.5
	31.5	42.9	39.2	39.3			Net Worth	35.6	32.5
	100.0	100.0	100.0	100.0			Total Liabilities & Net Worth	100.0	100.0
							INCOME DATA		
	100.0	100.0	100.0	100.0			Net Sales	100.0	100.0
	37.6	33.3	33.7	36.2			Gross Profit	35.3	35.9
	34.6	30.8	31.9	33.0			Operating Expenses	32.5	33.5
	3.0	2.5	1.8	3.2			Operating Profit	2.8	2.5
	.7	.2	.3	-.2			All Other Expenses (net)	.7	1.0
	2.4	2.3	1.5	3.4			Profit Before Taxes	2.1	1.4
							RATIOS		
	3.1	3.0	2.3	1.9				2.6	2.8
	1.9	2.0	1.6	1.5			Current	1.8	1.7
	1.3	1.4	1.2	1.2				1.4	1.2
	1.0	1.1	.7	.7				.9	.9
	.6	.7	.5	.3			Quick	.6 (411)	.6
	.3	.4	.3	.2				.4	.3
	11 33.5	17 21.4	9 41.7	6 59.6				12 30.7	12 30.7
	21 17.1	27 13.4	25 14.4	30 12.2			Sales/Receivables	25 14.6	23 15.9
	28 13.2	35 10.3	37 9.9	38 9.6				36 10.2	35 10.5
	50 7.3	64 5.7	65 5.6	70 5.2				65 5.6	63 5.8
	89 4.1	96 3.8	101 3.6	99 3.7			Cost of Sales/Inventory	96 3.8	101 3.6
	146 2.5	135 2.7	140 2.6	135 2.7				140 2.6	140 2.6
	21 17.1	27 13.6	32 11.4	44 8.3				28 13.1	27 13.3
	35 10.4	42 8.7	50 7.3	64 5.7			Cost of Sales/Payables	42 8.6	40 9.1
	55 6.6	62 5.9	70 5.2	69 5.3				63 5.8	62 5.9
	5.1	4.3	6.4	6.7				4.9	5.1
	9.7	7.5	10.8	13.0			Sales/Working Capital	9.2	9.5
	25.9	18.5	21.4	39.6				17.4	26.0
	7.0	6.4	9.4	11.4				4.6	3.9
(168)	2.5	(209) 3.4	(87) 3.4	4.2			EBIT/Interest	(435) 2.3	(386) 1.9
	1.2	1.7	1.8	3.1				1.2	1.0
	3.8	4.8	3.1				Net Profit + Depr., Dep.,	3.4	3.0
(45)	1.7	(93) 2.6	(40) 2.2				Amort./Cur. Mat. L./T/D	(216) 1.5	(154) 1.5
	.6	.9	1.2					.7	.5
	.2	.2	.3	.4				.2	.2
	.5	.4	.5	.6			Fixed/Worth	.5	.5
	2.0	.8	1.0	1.1				1.1	1.7
	1.0	.7	.9	1.1				1.0	1.0
	2.1	1.5	1.8	1.7			Debt/Worth	1.8	2.1
	7.9	3.1	3.7	2.5				4.1	6.4
	39.8	26.5	27.3	39.0			% Profit Before Taxes/Tangible	28.3	26.0
(162)	19.1	(217) 13.1	(89) 13.4	25.7			Net Worth	(431) 12.3	(360) 10.7
	2.9	5.8	6.0	12.0				4.0	1.6
	13.3	9.3	10.8	11.5			% Profit Before Taxes/Total	9.4	8.5
	5.9	5.1	4.1	7.9			Assets	4.6	3.4
	.6	2.3	1.3	5.8				.8	.0
	52.4	43.0	25.9	16.9				42.2	40.1
	22.0	20.9	17.7	12.7			Sales/Net Fixed Assets	20.3	20.8
	11.9	11.1	11.3	6.9				9.6	9.7
	4.1	3.4	3.4	3.3				3.6	3.6
	3.1	2.6	2.8	2.3			Sales/Total Assets	2.7	2.7
	2.2	2.0	2.2	1.9				2.1	2.1
	.8	.8	.9	1.0				.8	.8
(156)	1.3	(208) 1.1	(87) 1.3	(18) 1.5			% Depr., Dep., Amort./Sales	(430) 1.4	(379) 1.4
	2.1	1.7	1.7	1.8				2.1	2.0
	3.4	2.1	1.1				% Officers', Directors',	2.7	2.4
(89)	5.2	(119) 3.4	(41) 2.2				Owners' Comp/Sales	(218) 4.3	(191) 4.0
	8.3	4.5	3.4					6.5	6.6
	165636M	612264M	1098627M	936908M	996960M	2462109M	Net Sales ($)	3699935M	4759620M
	51937M	224743M	375662M	362387M	388776M	1352602M	Total Assets ($)	1692983M	2020146M

M = $ thousand   MM = $ million
See Pages 1 through 15 for Explanation of Ratios and Data

	Comparative Historical Data			# Postretirement Benefits	Current Data Sorted By Sales					
	8	29	37		5	13	9	4	2	4
				Type of Statement						
	40	50	45	Unqualified	7	7	3	6	8	14
	81	78	80	Reviewed	8	23	15	19	9	6
	228	247	241	Compiled	78	101	33	19	8	2
	17	36	43	Tax Returns	21	16	5	1		
	104	117	123	Other	30	39	12	13	15	14
	4/1/92-3/31/93	4/1/93-3/31/94	4/1/94-3/31/95		179 (4/1-9/30/94)			353 (10/1/94-3/31/95)		
	ALL	ALL	ALL		0-1MM	1-3MM	3-5MM	5-10MM	10-25MM	25MM & OVER
NUMBER OF STATEMENTS	470	528	532		144	186	68	58	40	36
	%	%	%	**ASSETS**	%	%	%	%	%	%
	6.2	7.1	7.1	Cash & Equivalents	7.4	8.4	6.6	5.8	4.7	4.9
	19.1	20.8	18.8	Trade Receivables - (net)	16.4	18.9	22.8	24.5	17.1	13.0
	48.3	47.0	47.1	Inventory	47.0	48.2	45.8	45.8	51.2	41.9
	1.1	.9	1.4	All Other Current	1.4	1.3	1.3	1.4	1.6	1.5
	74.8	75.8	74.3	Total Current	72.1	76.7	76.6	77.4	74.6	61.3
	18.8	17.7	19.5	Fixed Assets (net)	22.8	18.0	15.6	16.0	19.1	26.9
	1.2	1.4	1.7	Intangibles (net)	1.4	1.0	2.4	1.3	1.5	5.7
	5.2	5.1	4.5	All Other Non-Current	3.6	4.3	5.4	5.2	4.9	6.1
	100.0	100.0	100.0	Total	100.0	100.0	100.0	100.0	100.0	100.0
				LIABILITIES						
	9.5	8.0	7.8	Notes Payable-Short Term	8.2	7.1	7.4	9.0	12.8	3.6
	4.5	3.5	3.6	Cur. Mat.-L /T/D	5.2	3.6	2.6	2.6	2.7	2.5
	23.4	23.2	23.4	Trade Payables	17.9	23.0	25.6	32.6	23.2	29.1
	.4	1.8	.3	Income Taxes Payable	.3	.2	.4	.4	.2	.4
	7.0	8.3	7.8	All Other Current	10.3	6.5	7.2	7.2	6.1	8.3
	44.8	44.9	43.0	Total Current	41.9	40.4	43.2	51.8	45.0	43.9
	17.2	15.8	15.7	Long Term Debt	22.8	14.4	12.7	10.0	10.3	15.4
	.1	.1	.1	Deferred Taxes	.1	.2	.0	.0	.2	.5
	2.7	1.8	3.2	All Other-Non-Current	2.5	4.8	1.3	1.9	2.2	5.4
	35.2	37.4	37.9	Net Worth	32.8	40.3	42.8	36.3	42.3	34.8
	100.0	100.0	100.0	Total Liabilities & Net Worth	100.0	100.0	100.0	100.0	100.0	100.0
				INCOME DATA						
	100.0	100.0	100.0	Net Sales	100.0	100.0	100.0	100.0	100.0	100.0
	35.6	35.6	35.0	Gross Profit	38.0	35.1	32.1	33.2	31.6	34.7
	33.2	33.3	32.3	Operating Expenses	34.2	32.5	30.4	31.2	30.5	30.8
	2.4	2.3	2.7	Operating Profit	3.8	2.6	1.7	1.9	1.2	3.9
	.6	.3	.4	All Other Expenses (net)	.9	.3	.2	.2	-.1	.5
	1.8	2.0	2.3	Profit Before Taxes	2.9	2.3	1.5	1.7	1.3	3.4

RATIOS

Ratio	Hist. 8	Hist. 29	Hist. 37	0-1MM	1-3MM	3-5MM	5-10MM	10-25MM	25MM & OVER
Current	2.7 / 1.7 / 1.3	2.6 / 1.7 / 1.2	2.7 / 1.8 / 1.3	3.3 / 1.9 / 1.2	3.2 / 2.1 / 1.4	2.7 / 1.7 / 1.3	2.3 / 1.5 / 1.2	2.3 / 1.6 / 1.1	1.9 / 1.3 / 1.1
Quick	(469) .9 / .6 / .3	1.0 / .6 / .4	1.0 / .6 / .4	.9 / .5 / .3	1.2 / .7 / .4	1.0 / .7 / .5	.8 / .6 / .3	.6 / .5 / .3	.7 / .3 / .2
Sales/Receivables	12 29.6 / 24 15.4 / 34 10.7	13 27.6 / 24 14.9 / 36 10.2	12 29.8 / 24 15.3 / 34 10.8	10 37.1 / 22 16.6 / 32 11.4	14 25.9 / 24 15.0 / 32 11.3	20 18.1 / 29 12.8 / 37 9.9	13 29.2 / 28 13.0 / 43 8.5	9 40.9 / 21 17.1 / 33 11.0	2 151.6 / 10 37.7 / 32 11.3
Cost of Sales/Inventory	62 5.9 / 99 3.7 / 140 2.6	59 6.2 / 85 4.3 / 130 2.8	62 5.9 / 94 3.9 / 140 2.6	63 5.8 / 118 3.1 / 174 2.1	66 5.5 / 94 3.9 / 130 2.8	48 7.6 / 91 4.0 / 130 2.8	51 7.1 / 79 4.6 / 118 3.1	61 6.0 / 85 4.3 / 130 2.8	64 5.7 / 91 4.0 / 140 2.6
Cost of Sales/Payables	27 13.5 / 41 9.0 / 61 6.0	25 14.7 / 39 9.3 / 59 6.2	27 13.4 / 43 8.5 / 64 5.7	19 19.6 / 34 10.6 / 54 6.8	27 13.7 / 40 9.1 / 58 6.3	31 11.9 / 48 7.6 / 66 5.5	36 10.1 / 57 6.4 / 73 5.0	18 20.1 / 42 8.6 / 55 6.6	48 7.6 / 63 5.8 / 74 4.9
Sales/Working Capital	4.9 / 9.7 / 25.2	5.2 / 10.0 / 26.7	4.8 / 8.8 / 21.2	4.3 / 7.7 / 29.4	4.5 / 7.5 / 16.0	5.2 / 8.7 / 19.1	7.7 / 13.9 / 29.3	7.5 / 9.0 / 17.3	6.3 / 15.9 / 104.9
EBIT/Interest	(430) 5.2 / 2.4 / 1.2	(473) 6.5 / 3.0 / 1.5	(495) 7.0 / 3.4 / 1.6	(127) 6.5 / 2.4 / 1.2	(174) 7.4 / 3.5 / 1.8	(65) 5.5 / 3.2 / 1.8	(55) 6.7 / 3.0 / 1.5	(39) 11.0 / 3.9 / 2.2	(35) 11.4 / 5.4 / 2.4
Net Profit + Depr., Dep., Amort./Cur. Mat. L/T/D	(196) 3.3 / 1.6 / .6	(178) 3.5 / 1.7 / .7	(191) 4.4 / 2.1 / 1.0	(34) 3.6 / 1.5 / .5	(68) 5.0 / 2.3 / .9	(29) 4.6 / 2.6 / 1.0	(27) 4.2 / 2.2 / 1.2	(18) 4.0 / 2.3 / 1.1	(15) 7.4 / 3.3 / 1.7
Fixed/Worth	.2 / .5 / 1.3	.2 / .4 / 1.0	.2 / .4 / 1.1	.2 / .6 / 2.7	.2 / .4 / .9	.2 / .3 / .7	.2 / .4 / .9	.3 / .5 / .7	.5 / 1.1 / 1.8
Debt/Worth	.8 / 1.9 / 4.6	.8 / 1.9 / 4.1	.8 / 1.7 / 3.9	.8 / 2.2 / 10.1	.7 / 1.6 / 3.2	.8 / 1.6 / 2.9	.9 / 2.0 / 4.0	.8 / 1.3 / 2.5	1.4 / 2.2 / 3.8
% Profit Before Taxes/Tangible Net Worth	(422) 26.8 / 13.3 / 2.6	(498) 32.1 / 15.0 / 4.9	(499) 32.0 / 15.6 / 5.5	(122) 32.6 / 16.9 / 3.6	(178) 33.9 / 15.2 / 5.6	28.8 / 11.7 / 5.3	(57) 29.3 / 14.1 / 6.5	(39) 22.6 / 12.8 / 3.9	(35) 41.2 / 26.0 / 14.5
% Profit Before Taxes/Total Assets	9.7 / 4.3 / .6	10.1 / 5.6 / 1.3	10.9 / 5.4 / 1.7	11.7 / 5.8 / .7	10.9 / 5.3 / 1.9	8.5 / 4.1 / 2.3	10.7 / 4.6 / 1.3	10.1 / 4.4 / 2.2	12.7 / 9.6 / 4.1
Sales/Net Fixed Assets	39.3 / 20.1 / 11.8	44.9 / 23.1 / 12.1	39.6 / 19.6 / 10.9	43.3 / 17.0 / 7.5	43.0 / 21.7 / 11.5	41.7 / 23.7 / 13.6	47.6 / 23.7 / 17.2	23.5 / 16.0 / 11.4	17.1 / 11.7 / 8.2
Sales/Total Assets	3.6 / 2.8 / 2.2	3.7 / 2.9 / 2.2	3.5 / 2.8 / 2.1	3.4 / 2.4 / 1.8	3.6 / 2.8 / 2.2	3.5 / 2.8 / 2.2	3.7 / 3.2 / 2.6	3.5 / 2.9 / 2.5	3.7 / 2.5 / 2.1
% Depr., Dep., Amort./Sales	(445) .9 / 1.3 / 1.8	(484) .8 / 1.2 / 1.9	(480) .8 / 1.2 / 1.8	(118) .9 / 1.5 / 2.5	(173) .8 / 1.1 / 1.8	(62) .8 / 1.2 / 1.5	(56) .8 / 1.1 / 1.5	(38) 1.0 / 1.4 / 1.6	(33) .9 / 1.6 / 2.0
% Officers', Directors', Owners' Comp/Sales	(228) 2.2 / 4.1 / 6.2	(247) 2.6 / 4.2 / 6.8	(258) 2.2 / 3.7 / 6.0	(64) 4.1 / 6.4 / 9.6	(96) 2.2 / 3.2 / 5.1	(42) 1.9 / 3.4 / 4.6	(28) 1.4 / 2.5 / 4.2	(21) .8 / 2.2 / 6.9	
Net Sales ($)	5060616M	5673414M	6272504M	90143M	336583M	255871M	413160M	611203M	4565544M
Total Assets ($)	1976128M	2369814M	2756107M	42124M	129587M	98556M	138906M	220611M	2126323M

M = $ thousand   MM = $ million
See Pages 1 through 15 for Explanation of Ratios and Data

Current Data Sorted By Assets							Comparative Historical Data	
8	4	12	11		1	**# Postretirement Benefits**		
						Type of Statement		
3	3	22	43	9	8	Unqualified	63	57
6	24	41	14			Reviewed	77	82
109	55	32	4			Compiled	139	156
29	9	5			1	Tax Returns	10	9
44	57	46	20	3	2	Other	115	94
213 (4/1-9/30/94)			**376 (10/1/94-3/31/95)**				4/1/90-3/31/91	4/1/91-3/31/92
0-500M	500M-2MM	2-10MM	10-50MM	50-100MM	100-250MM		ALL	ALL
191	148	146	81	12	11	**NUMBER OF STATEMENTS**	404	398
%	%	%	%	%	%	**ASSETS**	%	%
14.1	10.0	11.2	8.7	8.9	8.9	Cash & Equivalents	9.9	9.5
10.8	10.3	10.2	9.3	5.9	6.3	Trade Receivables - (net)	14.0	11.1
22.5	16.2	12.9	11.1	11.5	9.2	Inventory	19.3	18.2
2.6	1.7	2.5	1.7	1.2	1.4	All Other Current	2.2	2.0
50.0	38.2	36.8	30.8	27.5	25.7	Total Current	45.4	40.9
39.3	51.4	53.1	59.0	62.8	63.1	Fixed Assets (net)	44.6	48.4
4.4	3.4	2.0	2.4	2.2	1.1	Intangibles (net)	2.2	2.1
6.4	7.1	8.1	7.7	7.5	10.0	All Other Non-Current	7.8	8.6
100.0	100.0	100.0	100.0	100.0	100.0	Total	100.0	100.0
						LIABILITIES		
6.0	5.2	3.7	4.3	9.0	1.3	Notes Payable-Short Term	5.3	6.7
4.1	4.6	4.3	3.8	3.4	2.4	Cur. Mat. -L/T/D	4.4	4.3
14.6	16.3	18.2	15.7	10.3	14.1	Trade Payables	19.2	16.9
.4	.4	.2	.6	.0	.4	Income Taxes Payable	.7	.5
11.5	7.5	9.0	8.4	10.0	8.4	All Other Current	8.5	9.0
36.6	34.1	35.4	32.7	32.7	26.7	Total Current	38.1	37.4
29.3	33.0	25.3	25.5	24.4	33.8	Long Term Debt	26.7	26.7
.1	.1	.7	1.1	1.2	1.2	Deferred Taxes	.4	.4
5.9	4.1	2.2	2.6	4.3	1.8	All Other-Non-Current	2.1	2.0
28.2	28.7	36.4	38.1	37.3	36.5	Net Worth	32.6	33.5
100.0	100.0	100.0	100.0	100.0	100.0	Total Liabilities & Net Worth	100.0	100.0
						INCOME DATA		
100.0	100.0	100.0	100.0	100.0	100.0	Net Sales	100.0	100.0
23.2	19.9	18.9	17.0	19.8	17.5	Gross Profit	19.6	18.3
21.0	17.9	16.5	14.9	17.3	14.8	Operating Expenses	18.0	16.9
2.2	2.0	2.5	2.1	2.5	2.7	Operating Profit	1.6	1.4
.3	.5	.2	-.2	.5	.7	All Other Expenses (net)	.3	.4
1.9	1.5	2.3	2.3	1.9	2.0	Profit Before Taxes	1.3	1.0
						RATIOS		
2.6	1.7	1.4	1.1	1.2	1.3		1.7	1.7
1.6	1.1	1.0	1.0	.9	.9	Current	1.2	1.1
.9	.8	.8	.7	.5	.9		.8	.8
1.4	1.0	.9	.7	.8	.7		.9	.9
(190) .7	(147) .6	.5	.5	.4	.6	Quick	(403) .6	(396) .5
.3	.3	.3	.3	.3	.4		.4	.3
1 477.6	1 283.2	3 138.3	3 126.3	3 118.2	1 306.0		3 138.4	2 199.9
3 133.3	3 113.9	6 65.9	6 58.5	5 69.6	7 50.9	Sales/Receivables	6 59.6	5 78.6
7 52.6	9 42.0	12 31.7	12 30.8	10 38.2	21 17.1		13 27.7	10 35.7
7 51.1	7 52.8	8 46.1	8 47.0	9 39.8	7 48.8		8 45.9	7 53.6
11 33.8	11 33.4	12 31.6	12 31.7	12 31.6	12 30.0	Cost of Sales/Inventory	12 30.7	11 34.7
19 19.5	17 21.9	17 21.3	15 23.7	19 19.2	17 22.1		18 19.9	17 21.5
2 170.7	4 83.4	12 30.9	13 28.1	10 38.3	16 22.8		7 52.5	6 61.1
6 57.0	11 34.4	17 21.2	17 21.4	12 30.2	19 19.5	Cost of Sales/Payables	14 25.2	12 31.1
14 26.8	17 21.6	22 16.6	22 16.6	20 18.4	23 16.2		21 17.5	18 20.7
25.6	37.4	52.8	108.0	103.9	89.0		32.9	36.4
59.4	131.7	NM	-299.7	-77.8	-238.5	Sales/Working Capital	101.2	190.0
-196.0	-65.0	-62.6	-38.7	-21.2	-45.4		-78.1	-68.6
9.4	6.0	8.0	8.0	6.6	10.9		4.9	4.0
(161) 3.5	(134) 2.8	(136) 3.2	(79) 4.1	3.8	(10) 4.8	EBIT/Interest	(353) 2.2	(357) 1.8
1.6	1.4	1.8	2.2	3.2	1.5		1.2	.9
3.6	3.7	4.4	5.6				4.4	3.5
(29) 1.8	(41) 2.3	(75) 2.4	(41) 2.9			Net Profit + Depr., Dep., Amort./Cur. Mat. L./T/D	(197) 2.3	(165) 1.7
.9	1.1	1.3	1.7				1.2	.8
.5	.9	1.0	1.2	1.4	1.3		.7	.8
1.7	2.2	1.7	1.9	1.9	1.6	Fixed/Worth	1.6	1.7
13.0	5.7	3.0	2.6	2.1	2.6		3.4	3.7
.8	1.4	1.0	1.3	1.4	1.0		1.1	1.0
2.7	3.1	2.2	1.9	2.1	1.6	Debt/Worth	2.3	2.3
34.5	8.2	4.0	3.3	2.7	3.3		5.2	5.6
91.1	54.1	33.8	36.7	31.6	35.3		35.9	30.3
(152) 35.9	(128) 21.9	(142) 20.3	(79) 21.0	19.0	(10) 16.2	% Profit Before Taxes/Tangible Net Worth	(358) 16.5	(356) 11.9
14.7	8.6	9.6	12.3	14.6	5.7		3.7	.9
25.0	13.8	11.1	13.4	8.9	12.4		11.6	9.3
11.2	6.3	6.4	7.8	7.1	6.3	% Profit Before Taxes/Total Assets	5.0	3.5
2.2	1.7	2.8	3.8	4.7	4.1		1.0	-.7
71.5	24.1	14.8	9.7	6.4	7.7		32.6	30.5
22.2	10.3	8.4	7.0	5.3	5.5	Sales/Net Fixed Assets	12.3	11.5
8.5	4.9	5.7	4.6	4.0	3.0		6.7	6.6
12.7	7.7	5.9	5.2	3.8	4.8		8.3	8.5
7.5	5.3	4.5	3.8	3.6	3.3	Sales/Total Assets	5.4	5.5
4.5	3.1	3.4	2.9	2.8	1.7		3.7	3.9
.5	.8	1.1	1.3	1.6			.7	.7
(168) 1.1	(136) 1.4	(139) 1.5	(80) 1.8	1.7		% Depr., Dep., Amort./Sales	(374) 1.1	(372) 1.2
2.0	2.4	2.0	2.2	2.6			1.9	1.9
1.4	1.1	.7	.5				.8	.7
(102) 2.7	(72) 1.8	(54) 1.0	(15) 1.0			% Officers', Directors', Owners' Comp/Sales	(150) 1.8	(155) 1.6
4.1	3.2	1.8	2.7				3.9	3.3
379352M	929132M	3431941M	6569449M	3229316M	7118081M	Net Sales ($)	12994441M	15844627M
48175M	158338M	733832M	1682442M	942493M	1759755M	Total Assets ($)	3187036M	3050357M

M = $ thousand   MM = $ million
See Pages 1 through 15 for Explanation of Ratios and Data

Comparative Historical Data				Current Data Sorted By Sales					
5	21	36	# Postretirement Benefits	4	2	5	4	6	15
			Type of Statement						
55	69	88	Unqualified	2	2		2	10	72
84	79	85	Reviewed	3	5	6	15	28	28
175	161	200	Compiled	29	79	32	20	28	12
28	30	44	Tax Returns	7	25	3	4	3	2
125	121	172	Other	8	46	19	26	32	41
4/1/92-3/31/93	4/1/93-3/31/94	4/1/94-3/31/95		213 (4/1-9/30/94)			376 (10/1/94-3/31/95)		
ALL	ALL	ALL		0-1MM	1-3MM	3-5MM	5-10MM	10-25MM	25MM & OVER
467	460	589	**NUMBER OF STATEMENTS**	49	157	60	67	101	155
%	%	%	**ASSETS**	%	%	%	%	%	%
10.5	11.3	11.4	Cash & Equivalents	8.8	12.4	11.7	12.7	12.6	9.7
11.1	10.7	10.1	Trade Receivables - (net)	10.2	9.9	7.6	11.2	12.9	9.1
17.9	17.0	16.5	Inventory	20.3	18.9	19.0	17.5	16.1	11.7
1.8	1.9	2.2	All Other Current	3.7	1.9	1.3	2.6	2.1	2.2
41.3	41.0	40.2	Total Current	43.0	43.1	39.5	44.1	43.7	32.6
48.1	48.5	49.4	Fixed Assets (net)	47.2	46.6	50.0	43.4	46.1	57.4
2.9	2.4	3.2	Intangibles (net)	2.4	4.6	4.4	4.5	1.7	1.9
7.6	8.1	7.3	All Other Non-Current	7.3	5.8	6.1	8.0	8.5	8.1
100.0	100.0	100.0	Total	100.0	100.0	100.0	100.0	100.0	100.0
			LIABILITIES						
5.5	5.7	5.0	Notes Payable-Short Term	7.1	6.4	4.1	4.3	3.9	4.2
4.7	4.5	4.2	Cur. Mat.-L /T/D	4.6	4.6	4.6	3.8	4.3	3.7
16.6	15.0	16.0	Trade Payables	14.0	11.9	14.3	18.7	20.0	17.5
.3	1.5	.4	Income Taxes Payable	.1	.3	.8	.3	.3	.4
9.0	9.5	9.3	All Other Current	10.1	10.1	6.7	9.0	9.7	9.3
36.2	36.2	34.9	Total Current	35.9	33.3	30.4	36.1	38.3	35.2
27.9	26.8	28.7	Long Term Debt	33.6	36.1	29.7	25.9	23.4	23.9
.5	.5	.4	Deferred Taxes	.0	.1	.1	.2	.5	1.1
3.4	2.9	4.0	All Other-Non-Current	4.4	4.7	7.9	3.6	2.7	2.5
32.0	33.7	32.1	Net Worth	26.1	25.8	31.9	34.1	35.2	37.3
100.0	100.0	100.0	Total Liabilities & Net Worth	100.0	100.0	100.0	100.0	100.0	100.0
			INCOME DATA						
100.0	100.0	100.0	Net Sales	100.0	100.0	100.0	100.0	100.0	100.0
19.7	19.9	20.3	Gross Profit	34.8	21.9	20.6	17.6	18.0	16.6
18.2	17.9	18.1	Operating Expenses	32.8	18.9	18.0	16.0	16.2	14.7
1.5	2.0	2.2	Operating Profit	2.0	3.0	2.7	1.5	1.7	1.9
.4	.2	.2	All Other Expenses (net)	.7	.7	.3	.0	.0	-.1
1.2	1.8	2.0	Profit Before Taxes	1.3	2.3	2.4	1.5	1.8	2.0
			RATIOS						
1.8	1.7	1.7	Current	2.4	2.4	2.1	1.6	1.6	1.1
1.1	1.1	1.1		1.4	1.4	1.2	1.2	1.1	.9
.9	.8	.8		.8	.9	.8	.9	.8	.7
.9	1.0	1.0	Quick	1.3	1.4	1.1	1.0	1.0	.8
(466) .6	.6	(587) .6		.6	(155) .6	.6	.7	.6	.5
.3	.3	.3		.2	.3	.3	.4	.4	.3
1 269.4	2 213.0	1 255.5	Sales/Receivables	1 487.3	1 423.9	1 434.5	1 412.5	2 177.1	3 124.2
4 88.6	5 76.1	4 85.1		5 73.4	3 132.6	3 140.1	3 118.6	6 62.9	6 64.3
10 35.5	11 32.9	10 38.0		11 34.6	7 54.1	7 49.8	9 41.7	11 32.6	11 34.7
7 49.3	7 49.3	8 48.4	Cost of Sales/Inventory	13 29.0	8 47.6	8 48.3	6 60.5	8 45.5	7 49.0
11 32.9	11 33.8	11 32.3		21 17.1	10 33.5	10 36.3	11 34.6	11 32.0	11 33.7
17 21.8	17 20.9	17 21.4		49 7.5	17 22.0	15 25.0	18 20.7	16 22.9	15 23.6
6 60.7	5 78.7	6 63.5	Cost of Sales/Payables	2 183.2	2 166.8	3 122.1	7 56.1	10 34.8	13 28.2
12 30.7	12 31.3	13 28.2		14 26.4	6 60.5	8 47.1	13 28.7	15 24.5	17 21.7
18 20.8	18 20.1	20 18.6		29 12.5	13 28.3	14 25.7	17 21.0	21 17.8	22 16.9
33.7	32.3	36.6	Sales/Working Capital	16.9	25.2	42.9	39.4	49.6	99.3
219.9	190.8	153.3		44.3	67.6	117.4	97.0	117.2	-186.9
-64.0	-65.0	-70.2		-56.2	-110.2	-68.7	-79.3	-79.7	-42.9
5.1	7.2	7.9	EBIT/Interest	5.2	6.8	9.0	8.0	8.8	8.1
(420) 2.4	(414) 3.3	(532) 3.3		(41) 3.0	(139) 2.9	(48) 3.0	(64) 3.0	(92) 3.6	(148) 3.8
1.1	1.9	1.7		.2	1.4	1.4	1.4	1.9	2.2
2.9	4.2	4.1	Net Profit + Depr., Dep., Amort./Cur. Mat. L/T/D		3.1	3.6	3.9	4.9	5.5
(171) 1.7	(148) 1.9	(195) 2.3			(21) 1.6	(17) 2.3	(26) 2.5	(44) 2.1	(79) 2.8
.9	1.1	1.3			.7	1.0	1.2	1.3	1.6
.8	.8	.8	Fixed/Worth	.6	.6	.8	.7	.8	1.2
1.7	1.5	1.9		1.9	2.4	2.2	1.4	1.5	1.8
3.7	3.3	4.0		10.8	16.8	8.2	4.2	2.7	2.6
1.0	1.0	1.1	Debt/Worth	.9	1.1	.9	1.2	1.0	1.2
2.4	2.2	2.4		2.9	3.4	2.7	2.4	2.3	2.0
6.1	5.3	5.7		20.1	35.5	14.0	5.8	4.6	3.3
34.0	49.7	47.1	% Profit Before Taxes/Tangible Net Worth	62.1	82.5	50.0	60.8	39.7	32.6
(403) 15.2	(422) 23.5	(523) 24.2		(40) 17.5	(124) 39.0	(51) 26.8	(62) 24.8	(96) 20.3	(150) 20.0
2.8	10.9	10.3		.4	14.8	13.4	8.4	9.6	11.5
11.1	14.5	15.2	% Profit Before Taxes/Total Assets	20.0	20.9	16.6	17.6	11.9	11.5
4.8	7.0	7.8		7.4	9.5	8.0	8.1	6.8	7.2
.4	2.8	2.7		-2.9	2.4	2.0	1.8	3.4	3.9
28.9	25.7	22.0	Sales/Net Fixed Assets	23.9	50.6	41.7	38.2	21.7	10.9
11.4	10.1	9.8		7.1	12.8	11.9	13.2	12.7	7.7
6.5	6.0	5.5		3.1	5.5	4.9	7.2	7.4	5.2
8.4	8.0	7.7	Sales/Total Assets	5.8	9.7	9.4	10.0	8.2	5.6
5.4	5.2	5.0		3.2	6.0	5.6	6.1	5.5	4.3
3.9	3.6	3.4		1.8	3.4	4.0	4.3	3.6	3.4
.8	.8	.9	% Depr., Dep., Amort./Sales	1.0	.7	.7	.8	.7	1.2
(443) 1.3	(417) 1.3	(542) 1.4		(41) 1.9	(139) 1.4	(57) 1.3	(63) 1.2	(95) 1.3	(147) 1.7
1.8	2.0	2.0		4.0	2.2	2.2	1.9	1.7	2.1
.9	.9	.9	% Officers', Directors', Owners' Comp/Sales	2.8	1.4	1.2	.9	.7	.5
(204) 1.8	(204) 1.6	(244) 1.8		(25) 3.8	(83) 2.7	(27) 2.0	(32) 1.4	(44) 1.0	(33) 1.0
3.4	3.1	3.4		11.4	4.2	3.2	2.6	1.6	2.3
11722701M	14033029M	21657271M	Net Sales ($)	30255M	285108M	230666M	516296M	1659321M	18935625M
2890057M	3082042M	5325035M	Total Assets ($)	16215M	64464M	56108M	98729M	356296M	4733223M

M = $ thousand   MM = $ million
See Pages 1 through 15 for Explanation of Ratios and Data

Current Data Sorted By Assets   Comparative Historical Data

Type of Statement

0-500M	500M-2MM	2-10MM	10-50MM	50-100MM	100-250MM		4/1/90-3/31/91 ALL	4/1/91-3/31/92 ALL
2	1	1				# Postretirement Benefits		
1		5	1			Unqualified	8	7
3	26	10				Reviewed	38	41
21	56	18	1			Compiled	94	94
9	7	1				Tax Returns	1	2
4	20	8	2			Other	35	21

57 (4/1-9/30/94)   136 (10/1/94-3/31/95)

0-500M	500M-2MM	2-10MM	10-50MM	50-100MM	100-250MM	NUMBER OF STATEMENTS	4/1/90-3/31/91 ALL 176	4/1/91-3/31/92 ALL 165
38	109	42	4				176	165
%	%	%	%	%	%	**ASSETS**	%	%
12.6	10.4	7.7				Cash & Equivalents	7.8	7.9
7.7	5.4	7.5				Trade Receivables - (net)	7.6	7.2
53.9	63.5	50.4				Inventory	56.4	54.4
.7	2.6	3.7				All Other Current	2.3	1.9
75.0	81.8	69.4				Total Current	74.1	71.5
18.4	11.9	22.2				Fixed Assets (net)	17.0	18.7
1.5	.8	.1				Intangibles (net)	.5	.4
5.1	5.5	8.3				All Other Non-Current	8.3	9.5
100.0	100.0	100.0				Total	100.0	100.0
						LIABILITIES		
28.4	41.4	36.4				Notes Payable-Short Term	40.7	39.1
3.0	3.4	2.1				Cur. Mat. -L/T/D	2.0	3.2
6.5	5.7	8.9				Trade Payables	5.4	4.4
.0	.5	.2				Income Taxes Payable	.3	.3
8.3	12.8	9.9				All Other Current	10.1	8.1
46.2	63.9	57.5				Total Current	58.5	55.0
13.8	6.7	10.3				Long Term Debt	12.4	11.8
.0	.1	.1				Deferred Taxes	.2	.1
3.0	2.4	3.6				All Other-Non-Current	2.7	4.2
37.0	26.9	28.5				Net Worth	26.2	28.8
100.0	100.0	100.0				Total Liabilities & Net Worth	100.0	100.0
						INCOME DATA		
100.0	100.0	100.0				Net Sales	100.0	100.0
31.4	22.4	26.1				Gross Profit	24.5	26.4
21.7	19.4	21.5				Operating Expenses	22.4	24.5
9.7	3.1	4.7				Operating Profit	2.0	1.8
3.5	-.1	.6				All Other Expenses (net)	.8	.3
6.2	3.2	4.1				Profit Before Taxes	1.3	1.6
						RATIOS		
2.9	1.6	1.4					1.6	1.6
1.4	1.2	1.2				Current	1.2	1.2
1.1	1.1	1.0					1.0	1.0
1.3	.4	.4					.4	.4
.3	.2	(41) .3				Quick	(175) .2	.2
.2	.1	.1					.1	.1
0 UND	1 492.4	1 487.9					0 799.4	1 291.4
3 123.1	3 119.2	5 75.0				Sales/Receivables	4 89.6	7 55.1
16 22.3	11 32.4	15 23.7					16 23.1	16 22.5
57 6.4	73 5.0	70 5.2					76 4.8	81 4.5
89 4.1	111 3.3	96 3.8				Cost of Sales/Inventory	104 3.5	111 3.3
126 2.9	140 2.6	130 2.8					159 2.3	152 2.4
0 UND	1 376.8	3 122.7					1 402.5	1 304.4
2 169.7	4 94.6	7 52.7				Cost of Sales/Payables	4 93.6	4 90.3
18 20.6	8 43.1	27 13.3					12 31.7	12 31.3
5.6	9.4	12.0					8.1	7.8
16.0	18.4	23.7				Sales/Working Capital	19.1	19.2
38.6	50.9	582.1					246.2	94.4
7.2	4.9	5.5					2.4	2.9
(35) 3.2	(103) 2.4	(41) 2.6				EBIT/Interest	(160) 1.4	(156) 1.4
2.0	1.5	1.4					.9	.9
	11.1	8.5					3.4	4.9
	(28) 3.3	(12) 3.0				Net Profit + Depr., Dep., Amort./Cur. Mat. L /T/D	(62) 1.5	(53) 2.0
	.6	1.1					.5	.1
.1	.2	.3					.2	.2
.5	.4	.7				Fixed/Worth	.5	.5
1.1	.8	1.1					1.5	1.3
.7	1.6	1.5					1.7	1.4
2.3	3.1	3.6				Debt/Worth	3.6	3.1
6.1	7.0	8.5					9.0	7.5
116.9	65.4	53.6					26.4	31.3
(37) 54.8	(104) 29.0	(41) 21.9				% Profit Before Taxes/Tangible Net Worth	(160) 8.8	(155) 11.4
14.2	10.9	10.6					-1.4	1.0
33.5	14.3	12.5					6.5	8.8
11.9	6.9	3.8				% Profit Before Taxes/Total Assets	2.5	2.6
6.6	2.7	2.0					-.5	-.4
117.7	67.0	50.6					63.5	57.3
27.2	34.7	18.9				Sales/Net Fixed Assets	26.1	27.3
10.4	16.9	9.8					10.6	8.9
4.2	3.7	3.6					3.4	3.1
3.4	2.8	2.6				Sales/Total Assets	2.4	2.3
2.3	2.1	1.8					1.8	1.6
.5	.4	.4					.4	.4
(29) 1.3	(101) .6	(40) .9				% Depr., Dep., Amort./Sales	(155) .7	(145) .8
2.3	1.1	2.1					1.5	1.5
1.4	1.3	.7					2.1	1.6
(22) 3.0	(64) 2.1	(21) 1.7				% Officers', Directors', Owners' Comp/Sales	(88) 3.7	(78) 2.9
7.1	3.6	3.7					6.0	5.1
39367M	354857M	476206M	107202M			Net Sales ($)	667315M	677426M
12078M	121969M	184963M	58451M			Total Assets ($)	322833M	353545M

M = $ thousand   MM = $ million
See Pages 1 through 15 for Explanation of Ratios and Data

Comparative Historical Data				Current Data Sorted By Sales					
1	6	4	# Postretirement Benefits	1	1	1	1		
			Type of Statement						
7	5	7	Unqualified	1	1		2	2	1
30	28	39	Reviewed	4	15	11	7	2	
81	90	96	Compiled	17	36	20	15	7	1
4	10	17	Tax Returns	5	6	4	1	1	
24	22	34	Other	3	10	8	5	5	3
4/1/92-3/31/93 ALL	4/1/93-3/31/94 ALL	4/1/94-3/31/95 ALL		57 (4/1-9/30/94)			136 (10/1/94-3/31/95)		
				0-1MM	1-3MM	3-5MM	5-10MM	10-25MM	25MM & OVER
146	155	193	**NUMBER OF STATEMENTS**	30	68	43	30	17	5
%	%	%	**ASSETS**	%	%	%	%	%	%
7.8	10.8	10.1	Cash & Equivalents	9.9	10.4	12.4	8.8	6.5	
8.4	8.3	6.5	Trade Receivables - (net)	7.2	5.3	5.9	7.4	9.5	
53.2	56.0	58.3	Inventory	49.3	60.4	59.9	59.7	58.2	
1.9	2.3	2.5	All Other Current	2.0	1.5	4.6	1.0	3.6	
71.4	77.3	77.3	Total Current	68.4	77.6	82.8	76.8	77.7	
19.0	15.2	15.4	Fixed Assets (net)	17.0	17.2	11.9	12.9	19.0	
1.2	.4	.8	Intangibles (net)	3.2	.2	.4	.6	.0	
8.4	7.2	6.5	All Other Non-Current	11.4	4.9	5.0	9.6	3.3	
100.0	100.0	100.0	Total	100.0	100.0	100.0	100.0	100.0	
			LIABILITIES						
38.1	39.1	37.6	Notes Payable-Short Term	28.2	37.8	42.6	34.8	40.4	
1.8	2.1	3.0	Cur. Mat.-L/T/D	1.2	3.3	3.6	4.5	1.6	
5.8	6.6	6.4	Trade Payables	2.7	6.8	6.0	8.2	8.4	
.3	.6	.3	Income Taxes Payable	.0	.2	.7	.6	.3	
9.4	8.0	11.3	All Other Current	10.5	10.3	13.2	10.7	15.3	
55.3	56.4	58.7	Total Current	42.6	58.4	66.1	58.8	65.9	
10.5	8.9	9.5	Long Term Debt	13.1	10.3	5.1	12.4	7.1	
.2	.3	.1	Deferred Taxes	.0	.1	.0	.2	.1	
3.4	2.9	2.8	All Other-Non-Current	5.3	3.2	1.4	2.4	1.1	
30.6	31.6	29.0	Net Worth	39.0	28.0	27.3	26.3	25.7	
100.0	100.0	100.0	Total Liabilities & Net Worth	100.0	100.0	100.0	100.0	100.0	
			INCOME DATA						
100.0	100.0	100.0	Net Sales	100.0	100.0	100.0	100.0	100.0	
25.9	23.9	24.9	Gross Profit	36.1	26.7	21.8	18.5	20.3	
22.7	20.8	20.2	Operating Expenses	27.0	21.9	18.3	15.7	17.1	
3.2	3.1	4.7	Operating Profit	9.1	4.8	3.5	2.8	3.2	
.3	.0	.8	All Other Expenses (net)	4.0	.4	−.5	.3	.6	
2.9	3.1	3.9	Profit Before Taxes	5.1	4.4	4.1	2.6	2.6	
			RATIOS						
1.7	1.8	1.6		2.9	1.8	1.4	1.5	1.4	
1.2	1.3	1.2	Current	1.5	1.2	1.2	1.2	1.2	
1.0	1.1	1.1		1.1	1.1	1.1	1.1	1.1	
.5	.5	.4		1.2	.4	.4	.4	.4	
.2	.3 (192)	.2	Quick	.2	.2	.2	.3	.3 (16)	
.1	.2	.1		.1	.1	.2	.2	.1	
1 446.6	1 668.0	0 792.7		0 UND	1 494.3	0 841.0	1 495.7	1 434.0	
7 50.7	5 71.1	3 106.5	Sales/Receivables	3 108.8	3 145.8	3 127.0	5 80.7	8 47.9	
16 23.4	15 25.1	12 30.1		19 18.9	14 26.4	10 35.1	12 31.3	16 22.7	
74 4.9	73 5.0	70 5.2		76 4.8	91 4.0	65 5.6	57 6.4	53 6.9	
101 3.6	107 3.4	101 3.6	Cost of Sales/Inventory	122 3.0	122 3.0	85 4.3	76 4.8	83 4.4	
146 2.5	146 2.5	135 2.7		228 1.6	159 2.3	126 2.9	126 2.9	104 3.5	
2 231.9	1 355.1	1 335.0		0 UND	0 942.5	2 199.4	2 208.5	2 157.9	
5 71.3	5 81.1	4 87.9	Cost of Sales/Payables	1 248.0	4 85.5	4 84.6	5 76.4	5 70.3	
15 24.2	11 32.9	12 29.8		16 23.4	11 33.4	9 42.6	15 23.6	26 14.2	
7.5	7.5	9.1		3.9	8.6	10.9	12.3	16.9	
25.7	16.9	19.2	Sales/Working Capital	8.6	17.0	20.6	23.3	24.7	
104.8	43.7	58.4		48.4	37.5	77.8	105.3	299.8	
	4.7		4.2		5.5		7.0		5.0		5.6		5.3		4.9	
(142) 2.0	(144) 2.3	(181) 2.6	EBIT/Interest	(29) 3.0	(62) 2.6	(42) 3.1	(28) 2.1	(16) 2.5	
1.2	1.5	1.5		1.4	1.4	1.4	1.4	1.4	
5.8	5.4	8.6	Net Profit + Depr., Dep.,		8.2	22.2	9.3		
(37) 2.8	(40) 2.2	(49) 3.2	Amort./Cur. Mat. L/T/D	(17) 3.2	(10) 2.3	(11) 4.0			
1.1	.8	.7		.4	.2	.4			
.2	.2	.2		.1	.2	.2	.3	.3	
.6	.4	.5	Fixed/Worth	.3	.5	.4	.5	.7	
1.0	.8	1.0		1.1	1.0	.9	1.0	1.5	
1.4	1.4	1.5		1.0	1.2	1.5	1.8	1.8	
2.5	2.8	3.1	Debt/Worth	2.2	3.1	3.1	3.7	3.6	
6.0	5.7	7.0		5.1	8.2	7.9	9.4	6.3	
48.3	52.3	67.3	% Profit Before Taxes/Tangible	69.7	64.3	71.3	68.8	51.2	
(137) 21.6	(150) 19.9	(185) 31.2	Net Worth	(29) 15.5	(64) 32.1	(42) 30.7	(28) 35.0	37.9	
5.8	8.7	12.1		5.9	8.9	16.7	20.6	14.8	
9.8	12.6	15.5	% Profit Before Taxes/Total	23.1	14.0	19.6	16.4	14.2	
5.3	6.6	7.1	Assets	7.2	7.4	7.6	5.6	5.3	
1.1	2.1	2.8		2.1	2.3	3.5	2.9	2.3	
49.0	66.1	67.3		109.3	61.8	71.5	73.8	46.7	
25.7	29.3	28.4	Sales/Net Fixed Assets	19.1	25.3	44.7	39.9	19.8	
8.3	12.9	13.3		4.9	12.2	23.6	15.0	11.4	
3.4	3.6	3.7		3.5	3.4	3.8	4.6	4.1	
2.4	2.5	2.8	Sales/Total Assets	1.9	2.6	3.3	3.5	2.9	
1.7	1.9	2.1		1.1	2.0	2.4	2.5	2.6	
.4	.4	.4		1.0	.5	.3	.3	.5	
(128) .8	(136) .7	(174) .8	% Depr., Dep., Amort./Sales	(22) 1.7	(61) .9	(42) .6	(28) .5	(16) .9	
1.5	1.2	1.4		3.2	1.7	.9	1.0	1.8	
1.8	1.5	1.2	% Officers', Directors',	1.8	1.4	1.2	1.1		
(70) 3.4	(77) 2.8	(109) 2.1	Owners' Comp/Sales	(17) 3.0	(40) 2.5	(26) 1.8	(15) 2.5		
5.9	5.2	3.8		7.4	3.8	2.4	5.4		
504184M	761565M	977632M	Net Sales ($)	20074M	138744M	161698M	202857M	277613M	176646M
224037M	277100M	377461M	Total Assets ($)	13983M	70982M	61557M	86332M	96301M	48306M

© Robert Morris Associates 1995   M = $ thousand   MM = $ million

See Pages 1 through 15 for Explanation of Ratios and Data

RETAILERS—MOTORCYCLES. SIC# 5571

Current Data Sorted By Assets							Comparative Historical Data	
3	5	2				**# Postretirement Benefits**		
						Type of Statement		
1		1				Unqualified	3	1
	17	6				Reviewed	16	21
26	61	4				Compiled	77	66
4	5	1				Tax Returns	3	7
8	34	10	1			Other	35	29
	42 (4/1-9/30/94)		137 (10/1/94-3/31/95)				4/1/90-3/31/91	4/1/91-3/31/92
0-500M	500M-2MM	2-10MM	10-50MM	50-100MM	100-250MM		ALL	ALL
39	117	22	1			**NUMBER OF STATEMENTS**	134	124
%	%	%	%	%	%	**ASSETS**	%	%
9.9	10.0	6.0				Cash & Equivalents	6.4	5.9
3.0	4.2	4.8				Trade Receivables - (net)	3.9	3.9
72.0	69.9	67.3				Inventory	71.8	73.6
.2	1.2	1.3				All Other Current	1.5	1.4
85.0	85.2	79.4				Total Current	83.6	84.8
12.7	11.2	15.1				Fixed Assets (net)	12.1	11.4
1.0	1.1	1.5				Intangibles (net)	1.2	1.2
1.3	2.5	3.9				All Other Non-Current	3.0	2.6
100.0	100.0	100.0				Total	100.0	100.0
						LIABILITIES		
31.9	32.4	28.4				Notes Payable-Short Term	38.7	40.2
1.1	2.8	3.6				Cur. Mat. -L/T/D	2.7	1.8
12.8	10.8	13.9				Trade Payables	9.4	8.9
.2	.3	.1				Income Taxes Payable	.3	.3
7.8	9.1	8.6				All Other Current	7.8	8.5
53.8	55.3	54.6				Total Current	58.9	59.8
8.9	8.4	13.3				Long Term Debt	10.2	9.3
.0	.1	.1				Deferred Taxes	.0	.0
2.6	1.9	2.1				All Other-Non-Current	1.2	1.7
34.7	34.3	29.9				Net Worth	29.6	29.2
100.0	100.0	100.0				Total Liabilities & Net Worth	100.0	100.0
						INCOME DATA		
100.0	100.0	100.0				Net Sales	100.0	100.0
22.7	21.5	21.1				Gross Profit	23.2	22.4
18.9	18.6	18.0				Operating Expenses	20.0	19.6
3.8	2.9	3.1				Operating Profit	3.1	2.9
.7	.2	.2				All Other Expenses (net)	1.2	1.0
3.1	2.7	2.9				Profit Before Taxes	1.9	1.9
						RATIOS		
2.2	2.0	1.7					1.7	1.8
1.6	1.4	1.4				Current	1.4	1.4
1.3	1.2	1.2					1.1	1.2
.7	.5	.3					.3	.3
.1	.2	.2				Quick	.1	.1
.0	.1	.1					.1	.1
0 UND	1 485.8	2 229.9					1 272.1	1 458.0
1 270.7	3 122.8	4 87.7				Sales/Receivables	3 114.1	3 132.9
4 81.6	6 57.4	6 61.6					7 54.9	6 56.8
69 5.3	78 4.7	70 5.2					96 3.8	96 3.8
118 3.1	111 3.3	118 3.1				Cost of Sales/Inventory	140 2.6	135 2.7
183 2.0	159 2.3	135 2.7					183 2.0	192 1.9
4 94.1	4 81.3	5 77.1					3 108.1	4 95.1
10 35.4	9 39.8	10 38.2				Cost of Sales/Payables	8 46.7	7 54.6
29 12.5	18 20.5	23 15.6					16 22.3	13 27.6
7.7	6.8	8.0					7.4	7.0
9.1	11.9	13.4				Sales/Working Capital	11.2	11.1
16.2	17.7	34.2					20.6	19.5
8.7	6.4	7.8					3.3	3.7
(37) 2.6	(110) 2.9	(20) 3.2				EBIT/Interest	(124) 1.8	(121) 2.0
1.4	1.8	1.6					1.1	1.2
	8.0						6.1	7.9
	(18) 3.6					Net Profit + Depr., Dep., Amort./Cur. Mat. L /T/D	(36) 2.6	(29) 3.0
	.9						.5	.7
.1	.1	.2					.1	.1
.3	.3	.4				Fixed/Worth	.3	.3
.7	.6	1.0					1.1	.9
1.0	1.1	1.6					1.3	1.3
1.8	2.2	2.8				Debt/Worth	2.3	2.7
5.2	4.7	4.2					6.2	6.4
46.9	39.2	32.6					29.2	35.8
(37) 27.9	(115) 22.8	(20) 23.1				% Profit Before Taxes/Tangible Net Worth	(123) 15.2	(111) 18.0
7.2	11.7	11.0					3.5	5.5
15.2	13.5	10.2					9.5	10.0
9.1	7.5	7.1				% Profit Before Taxes/Total Assets	3.8	5.1
1.5	3.2	2.3					.3	.8
164.3	87.7	53.3					81.2	89.9
47.9	35.0	43.8				Sales/Net Fixed Assets	34.7	40.3
16.6	19.0	16.4					16.5	18.4
4.0	3.8	3.4					3.1	3.2
3.2	2.9	2.7				Sales/Total Assets	2.5	2.6
2.1	2.4	2.3					2.0	2.0
.3	.4	.3					.4	.4
(31) .9	(98) .7	(18) .5				% Depr., Dep., Amort./Sales	(123) .7	(111) .7
2.1	1.1	.9					1.2	1.1
2.2	1.4	.8					1.5	1.5
(23) 2.8	(72) 2.7	(11) 1.4				% Officers', Directors', Owners' Comp/Sales	(70) 2.5	(69) 2.6
3.9	4.9	4.3					4.3	5.4
45813M	718876M	178078M	13133M			Net Sales ($)	626667M	599808M
14319M	125518M	58987M	10727M			Total Assets ($)	203967M	192936M

M = $ thousand   MM = $ million
See Pages 1 through 15 for Explanation of Ratios and Data

Comparative Historical Data			# Postretirement Benefits	Current Data Sorted By Sales					
2	3	10		1	4	1	3	1	
			Type of Statement						
3	4	2	Unqualified		1		1		
16	15	23	Reviewed		7	8	6	2	
63	60	91	Compiled	11	43	26	10	1	
6	3	10	Tax Returns	1	6	1	2		
28	30	53	Other	4	23	12	10	3	1
4/1/92- 3/31/93	4/1/93- 3/31/94	4/1/94- 3/31/95		0-1MM	42 (4/1-9/30/94) 1-3MM	3-5MM	137 (10/1/94-3/31/95) 5-10MM	10-25MM	25MM & OVER
ALL	ALL	ALL							
116	112	179	**NUMBER OF STATEMENTS**	16	80	47	29	6	1
%	%	%	**ASSETS**	%	%	%	%	%	%
7.9	10.4	9.7	Cash & Equivalents	5.4	9.4	12.7	7.4		
3.3	2.7	4.0	Trade Receivables - (net)	1.3	3.9	4.2	5.2		
74.5	69.6	69.7	Inventory	75.9	71.1	67.3	70.1		
.7	.9	1.0	All Other Current	.3	.9	1.3	1.0		
86.4	83.5	84.4	Total Current	82.8	85.3	85.6	83.7		
10.1	13.5	12.0	Fixed Assets (net)	14.1	11.3	11.1	12.4		
1.1	1.0	1.1	Intangibles (net)	1.5	1.1	.9	1.1		
2.4	2.0	2.4	All Other Non-Current	1.6	2.2	2.4	2.8		
100.0	100.0	100.0	Total	100.0	100.0	100.0	100.0		
			LIABILITIES						
31.7	28.5	31.6	Notes Payable-Short Term	38.4	34.0	29.2	25.6		
1.7	2.2	2.5	Cur. Mat.-L ./T/D	2.0	2.2	2.6	4.0		
11.4	12.2	11.6	Trade Payables	13.0	10.7	9.3	17.0		
.4	1.3	.3	Income Taxes Payable	.1	.3	.2	.3		
9.9	10.4	8.7	All Other Current	5.1	6.7	11.1	12.1		
55.1	54.6	54.7	Total Current	58.6	54.0	52.4	59.0		
9.0	9.1	9.0	Long Term Debt	10.7	9.7	6.8	10.3		
.0	.0	.1	Deferred Taxes	.0	.1	.1	.0		
1.7	2.1	2.0	All Other-Non-Current	3.5	1.5	2.6	2.3		
34.1	34.2	34.2	Net Worth	27.3	34.7	38.1	28.4		
100.0	100.0	100.0	Total Liabilities & Net Worth	100.0	100.0	100.0	100.0		
			INCOME DATA						
100.0	100.0	100.0	Net Sales	100.0	100.0	100.0	100.0		
23.2	22.0	21.7	Gross Profit	25.9	21.9	21.3	20.2		
20.0	18.3	18.6	Operating Expenses	21.6	19.0	18.0	17.4		
3.3	3.7	3.1	Operating Profit	4.3	3.0	3.3	2.8		
.6	.4	.3	All Other Expenses (net)	1.1	.5	-.2	.1		
2.7	3.2	2.8	Profit Before Taxes	3.1	2.4	3.5	2.7		
			RATIOS						
2.0	2.1	2.0		1.7	2.1	2.3	1.7		
1.6	1.4	1.5	Current	1.5	1.5	1.5	1.4		
1.3	1.2	1.2		1.2	1.2	1.3	1.1		
.3	.4	.5		.3	.5	.6	.4		
.2	.2	.2	Quick	.1	.1	.2	.2		
.1	.1	.1		.0	.1	.1	.1		
1 313.7	1 463.0	1 491.2		0 UND	1 524.8	1 434.6	1 378.8		
3 122.6	3 118.7	3 136.2	Sales/Receivables	1 246.0	2 175.4	3 115.9	4 91.8		
5 69.6	5 68.5	6 62.9		4 87.6	6 63.5	6 62.9	9 39.9		
89 4.1	79 4.6	76 4.8		146 2.5	85 4.3	65 5.6	65 5.6		
126 2.9	118 3.1	114 3.2	Cost of Sales/Inventory	203 1.8	122 3.0	99 3.7	104 3.5		
174 2.1	152 2.4	159 2.3		261 1.4	174 2.1	130 2.8	130 2.8		
4 89.1	3 111.1	5 80.9		4 93.2	4 88.6	5 78.8	5 73.7		
8 48.5	9 40.3	10 37.9	Cost of Sales/Payables	18 20.1	9 40.0	9 40.6	10 36.4		
16 22.3	19 19.3	19 19.0		66 5.5	20 18.2	13 29.0	26 14.1		
6.7	7.1	7.0		5.5	6.7	6.5	8.9		
10.3	11.7	11.6	Sales/Working Capital	8.0	10.1	12.1	16.3		
16.1	17.9	17.7		14.2	15.1	17.1	35.3		
5.9	9.1	7.1		5.1	5.3	18.7	8.4		
(110) 2.8	(107) 3.7	(167) 2.9	EBIT/Interest	(76) 2.8	2.3	(43) 4.0	(27) 3.3		
1.6	1.8	1.8		1.1	1.8	1.9	1.7		
6.3	8.1	7.7	Net Profit + Depr., Dep.,			10.3			
(30) 2.4	(18) 3.5	(31) 3.8	Amort./Cur. Mat. L/T/D			(10) 2.8			
.5		1.4 .8				1.1			
.1	.1	.1		.1	.1	.1	.2		
.2	.3	.3	Fixed/Worth	.3	.3	.2	.5		
.6	.9	.6		1.2	.6	.4	.8		
1.1	1.0	1.1		1.5	1.0	1.0	1.6		
2.1	2.5	2.2	Debt/Worth	3.3	2.6	1.8	3.0		
4.6	5.8	4.5		5.5	4.8	4.1	4.4		
44.2	52.4	40.1	% Profit Before Taxes/Tangible	42.9	40.9	40.4	40.0		
(111) 20.1	(108) 23.0	(173) 22.8	Net Worth	(15) 14.7	(79) 22.8	(46) 24.9	(27) 23.3		
9.4	13.1	10.8		.9	10.7	18.3	15.5		
12.1	15.9	13.5	% Profit Before Taxes/Total	10.1	13.9	16.1	10.6		
5.9	7.5	7.5	Assets	6.6	7.0	9.5	6.8		
2.4	3.0	3.0		.2	2.8	4.6	3.3		
104.4	79.5	90.5		370.7	90.7	93.6	60.9		
45.5	35.3	37.7	Sales/Net Fixed Assets	25.4	33.2	37.7	45.5		
22.5	18.4	17.3		7.8	15.1	21.6	18.3		
3.6	3.4	3.8		2.5	3.4	4.0	4.0		
2.8	2.9	2.9	Sales/Total Assets	1.7	2.7	3.1	3.1		
2.3	2.4	2.3		1.4	2.2	2.6	2.7		
.3	.4	.4		.3	.4	.4	.3		
(101) .6	(95) .7	(148) .7	% Depr., Dep., Amort./Sales	(12) 1.0	(65) .9	(40) .6	(24) .6		
1.0	1.1	1.2		2.3	1.5	.9	1.0		
1.7	1.6	1.4	% Officers', Directors',		1.8	1.4	1.3		
(73) 3.0	(58) 2.9	(106) 2.7	Owners' Comp/Sales	(49) 3.0	(28) 2.1	(17) 2.4			
4.5	4.7	4.8			4.7	3.8	7.0		
282202M	355153M	955900M	Net Sales ($)	9871M	150939M	173264M	187338M	80858M	353630M
96289M	123253M	209551M	Total Assets ($)	5623M	61056M	55223M	59342M	27381M	926M

© Robert Morris Associates 1995   M = $ thousand   MM = $ million
See Pages 1 through 15 for Explanation of Ratios and Data

Current Data Sorted By Assets							Comparative Historical Data	

0-500M	500M-2MM	2-10MM	10-50MM	50-100MM	100-250MM	# Postretirement Benefits / Type of Statement	4/1/90-3/31/91 ALL	4/1/91-3/31/92 ALL
2	1	2	1			# Postretirement Benefits		
						Type of Statement		
	1	3			1	Unqualified	8	7
3	12	14	2			Reviewed	34	33
24	54	17	1			Compiled	70	76
5	7	4				Tax Returns		5
11	19	29	1			Other	44	44
43 (4/1-9/30/94)			165 (10/1/94-3/31/95)					
43	93	67	4		1	**NUMBER OF STATEMENTS**	156	165
%	%	%	%	%	%	**ASSETS**	%	%
8.7	5.9	5.0				Cash & Equivalents	5.1	5.6
5.1	1.7	3.9				Trade Receivables - (net)	3.7	3.3
66.6	78.2	74.2				Inventory	74.2	72.5
.5	2.0	3.0				All Other Current	1.2	.7
80.8	87.8	86.1				Total Current	84.1	82.1
15.8	8.9	11.2				Fixed Assets (net)	12.2	13.8
.6	.6	.3				Intangibles (net)	.7	.7
2.8	2.7	2.5				All Other Non-Current	2.9	3.3
100.0	100.0	100.0				Total	100.0	100.0
						LIABILITIES		
38.3	48.4	53.0				Notes Payable-Short Term	46.7	46.8
3.2	1.8	3.5				Cur. Mat. -L/T/D	2.6	2.5
9.3	2.2	4.0				Trade Payables	5.5	5.6
.3	.2	.5				Income Taxes Payable	.3	.2
5.8	8.8	7.9				All Other Current	7.4	6.2
56.9	61.4	68.8				Total Current	62.4	61.4
15.4	8.3	8.6				Long Term Debt	8.3	9.4
.1	.1	.4				Deferred Taxes	.0	.1
5.9	2.4	.8				All Other-Non-Current	2.1	2.7
21.8	27.8	21.4				Net Worth	27.1	26.4
100.0	100.0	100.0				Total Liabilities & Net Worth	100.0	100.0
						INCOME DATA		
100.0	100.0	100.0				Net Sales	100.0	100.0
23.4	20.0	17.0				Gross Profit	20.4	21.0
18.7	16.8	14.3				Operating Expenses	18.2	18.0
4.6	3.2	2.7				Operating Profit	2.1	3.0
1.7	.8	.6				All Other Expenses (net)	1.6	1.8
3.0	2.4	2.1				Profit Before Taxes	.5	1.2
						RATIOS		
2.1	1.7	1.4					1.6	1.6
1.4	1.3	1.2				Current	1.3	1.3
1.1	1.2	1.1					1.1	1.1
.6	.2	.2					.2	.2
.2	.1	.1				Quick	(154) .1	(163) .1
.1	.0	.0					.0	.0
0 UND	0 UND	1 356.7					0 904.5	0 999.8
1 478.5	1 443.4	3 119.0				Sales/Receivables	2 242.6	1 255.4
8 45.2	3 137.9	5 68.4					7 53.8	5 72.2
68 5.4	99 3.7	89 4.1					91 4.0	94 3.9
91 4.0	130 2.8	107 3.4				Cost of Sales/Inventory	118 3.1	126 2.9
140 2.6	159 2.3	135 2.7					166 2.2	166 2.2
0 UND	0 UND	2 212.2					1 400.8	1 428.8
2 159.0	1 306.9	3 106.8				Cost of Sales/Payables	3 114.4	3 125.0
17 21.9	4 89.8	6 57.7					7 50.5	9 41.4
7.8	8.4	13.0					8.5	7.6
18.5	13.7	22.1				Sales/Working Capital	15.5	16.4
73.1	23.1	34.4					36.8	62.5
4.8	3.4	3.1					1.9	2.3
(41) 2.5	(89) 2.0	(65) 1.9				EBIT/Interest	(150) 1.2	(157) 1.3
1.5	1.4	1.5					.8	1.0
	6.8	7.5					3.1	3.6
	(17) 3.0	(16) 3.6				Net Profit + Depr., Dep., Amort./Cur. Mat. L./T/D	(49) 1.6	(41) 1.6
	.9	2.2					-.1	.3
.2	.1	.2					.1	.1
.7	.2	.4				Fixed/Worth	.3	.4
1.7	.5	.8					1.1	1.3
1.4	1.8	2.5					1.7	1.5
3.1	3.2	4.5				Debt/Worth	3.3	3.3
13.5	5.4	7.5					8.1	9.1
71.5	35.3	43.4					21.5	32.4
(37) 36.3	20.6	(64) 26.4				% Profit Before Taxes/Tangible Net Worth	(143) 6.2	(151) 11.6
17.3	6.8	15.7					-4.2	1.1
17.0	8.7	8.5					5.2	7.0
7.8	4.5	4.6				% Profit Before Taxes/Total Assets	1.6	2.4
2.2	1.8	2.5					-1.3	.1
77.8	226.0	188.3					140.2	101.8
34.0	75.1	50.6				Sales/Net Fixed Assets	50.5	40.3
14.4	25.7	17.7					19.5	12.2
4.6	3.4	3.6					3.7	3.6
3.1	2.7	3.0				Sales/Total Assets	2.7	2.7
2.1	2.2	2.5					2.1	2.0
.4	.2	.1					.2	.3
(31) .6	(77) .4	(59) .3				% Depr., Dep., Amort./Sales	(137) .5	(137) .5
1.2	.9	.6					.9	1.1
2.4	1.5	.6					1.0	1.3
(16) 3.1	(57) 2.5	(33) 1.2				% Officers', Directors', Owners' Comp/Sales	(80) 1.9	(88) 2.0
5.0	4.5	2.1					3.5	3.7
52493M	317396M	762675M	276643M		452116M	Net Sales ($)	2146839M	930088M
13215M	106376M	249246M	71086M		183959M	Total Assets ($)	592433M	391077M

M = $ thousand   MM = $ million
See Pages 1 through 15 for Explanation of Ratios and Data

Comparative Historical Data				Current Data Sorted By Sales					
1	6	6	# Postretirement Benefits Type of Statement	2	1		1	1	1
4	9	5	Unqualified				2	2	1
35	32	31	Reviewed	1	6	6	10	6	2
68	71	96	Compiled	15	40	16	17	7	1
5	9	16	Tax Returns	4	5	2	2	3	
31	40	60	Other	6	16	7	14	14	3
4/1/92- 3/31/93 ALL	4/1/93- 3/31/94 ALL	4/1/94- 3/31/95 ALL		43 (4/1-9/30/94)			165 (10/1/94-3/31/95)		
				0-1MM	1-3MM	3-5MM	5-10MM	10-25MM	25MM & OVER
143	161	208	**NUMBER OF STATEMENTS**	26	67	31	45	32	7
%	%	%	**ASSETS**	%	%	%	%	%	%
5.7	6.4	6.1	Cash & Equivalents	9.2	6.4	6.0	5.7	4.6	
3.0	4.2	3.2	Trade Receivables - (net)	5.9	2.3	1.8	2.7	4.5	
74.6	72.0	74.3	Inventory	59.6	77.2	75.9	77.3	75.2	
.8	.9	2.0	All Other Current	.3	1.0	1.3	3.5	3.4	
84.1	83.5	85.7	Total Current	74.9	86.9	84.9	89.2	87.6	
11.8	12.8	11.1	Fixed Assets (net)	19.9	10.9	11.1	7.9	9.3	
.6	1.0	.5	Intangibles (net)	.4	.3	1.2	.6	.1	
3.6	2.7	2.7	All Other Non-Current	4.9	1.8	2.8	2.3	3.0	
100.0	100.0	100.0	Total	100.0	100.0	100.0	100.0	100.0	
			LIABILITIES						
50.1	47.0	47.3	Notes Payable-Short Term	33.2	46.4	55.3	49.9	51.4	
2.6	1.5	2.6	Cur. Mat.-L /T/D	2.4	2.3	3.0	1.5	5.2	
4.4	6.7	5.1	Trade Payables	10.7	3.0	2.9	4.1	3.2	
.2	.5	.3	Income Taxes Payable	.0	.2	.2	.2	.7	
7.9	5.8	7.8	All Other Current	3.7	8.8	4.2	10.2	9.9	
65.2	61.6	63.1	Total Current	50.0	60.8	65.6	65.9	70.4	
6.8	9.6	9.7	Long Term Debt	20.3	8.8	8.5	9.5	5.7	
.1	.0	.2	Deferred Taxes	.0	.2	.0	.0	.7	
1.6	2.7	2.7	All Other-Non-Current	6.4	3.5	1.6	1.2	.8	
26.4	26.1	24.3	Net Worth	23.3	26.7	24.3	23.4	22.3	
100.0	100.0	100.0	Total Liabilities & Net Worth	100.0	100.0	100.0	100.0	100.0	
			INCOME DATA						
100.0	100.0	100.0	Net Sales	100.0	100.0	100.0	100.0	100.0	
19.7	19.6	19.6	Gross Profit	28.9	20.3	19.9	17.5	14.7	
16.9	17.0	16.3	Operating Expenses	22.9	16.6	17.0	15.3	12.1	
2.8	2.6	3.3	Operating Profit	6.0	3.7	2.9	2.2	2.6	
1.1	.9	.9	All Other Expenses (net)	2.1	1.2	.5	.3	.7	
1.7	1.7	2.4	Profit Before Taxes	3.9	2.5	2.4	1.9	1.9	
			RATIOS						
1.5	1.6	1.6		3.8	1.7	1.5	1.5	1.4	
1.2	1.3	1.3	Current	1.4	1.3	1.2	1.2	1.2	
1.1	1.1	1.1		1.1	1.2	1.1	1.1	1.1	
.2	.3	.2		1.1	.2	.2	.2	.2	
.1	(158) .1	.1	Quick	.2	.1	.1	.1	.1	
.0	.1	.0		.1	.0	.0	.0	.0	
0 999.8	1 684.2	0 999.8		0 UND	0 UND	0 779.3	0 999.8	1 347.0	
1 249.5	2 179.5	1 287.4	Sales/Receivables	1 710.8	1 405.2	1 345.6	2 193.9	2 151.1	
5 76.8	7 55.8	5 80.1		12 31.6	3 144.8	3 113.2	5 78.6	5 72.8	
91 4.0	85 4.3	85 4.3		69 5.3	96 3.8	104 3.5	81 4.5	72 5.1	
111 3.3	118 3.1	114 3.2	Cost of Sales/Inventory	104 3.5	130 2.8	122 3.0	111 3.3	96 3.8	
159 2.3	146 2.5	146 2.5		183 2.0	174 2.1	146 2.5	135 2.7	114 3.2	
1 458.4	1 482.9	0 999.8		0 UND	0 UND	0 UND	1 504.0	2 212.1	
3 130.0	3 121.3	2 151.4	Cost of Sales/Payables	0 UND	1 246.7	3 112.4	3 121.2	3 121.0	
7 52.7	10 35.8	6 57.0		29 12.8	5 72.8	8 48.0	5 71.3	5 66.5	
9.5	9.7	9.1		4.6	7.6	10.7	9.3	14.6	
20.5	15.3	18.3	Sales/Working Capital	16.4	12.8	20.9	22.1	22.2	
47.6	35.3	33.4		68.3	22.9	37.1	34.8	34.5	
2.6	3.6	3.6		5.3	3.7	2.9	3.2	3.0	
(135) 1.7	(153) 1.8	(200) 2.1	EBIT/Interest	(25) 2.5	(63) 2.2	(30) 2.1	(44) 2.1	(31) 1.9	
1.2	1.3	1.4		.9	1.4	1.5	1.4	1.4	
7.7	6.1	6.0			9.8			9.9	
(29) 3.0	(38) 1.9	(37) 3.0	Net Profit + Depr., Dep., Amort./Cur. Mat. L/T/D		(11) 3.0			(11) 3.5	
1.2	.8	1.2			1.3			.8	
.1	.2	.1		.3	.1	.1	.1	.1	
.3	.3	.3	Fixed/Worth	.8	.3	.3	.2	.3	
1.0	1.1	.8		3.5	.6	.7	.5	.9	
1.9	1.9	2.0		1.2	1.7	2.4	2.4	2.4	
3.7	3.5	3.6	Debt/Worth	3.1	3.1	3.9	3.8	4.4	
7.7	7.4	6.6		27.3	6.3	5.5	7.8	6.5	
38.8	50.0	44.3		75.3	36.0	49.7	43.5	42.8	
(139) 15.7	(151) 18.5	(199) 24.5	% Profit Before Taxes/Tangible Net Worth	(22) 35.0	(65) 22.9	24.3	(43) 27.4	(31) 24.5	
4.7	7.5	11.6		4.4	6.9	12.6	14.9	14.6	
6.9	8.7	10.3		17.2	10.4	8.5	9.2	8.4	
3.6	3.7	5.1	% Profit Before Taxes/Total Assets	8.0	5.5	4.7	5.1	4.4	
1.1	1.5	2.2		−.9	1.9	3.3	2.6	1.8	
154.0	89.6	191.7		48.5	130.8	211.3	172.1	205.9	
45.3	41.6	57.9	Sales/Net Fixed Assets	20.2	55.0	72.0	67.2	65.9	
15.6	15.7	17.9		9.0	18.4	19.2	44.2	29.9	
3.8	3.9	3.7		3.4	3.4	3.7	4.2	3.9	
2.8	2.8	2.9	Sales/Total Assets	2.2	2.7	2.7	3.1	3.4	
2.1	2.2	2.3		1.7	2.2	2.2	2.8	2.7	
.2	.2	.2		.4	.2	.1	.2	.1	
(122) .4	(139) .4	(171) .4	% Depr., Dep., Amort./Sales	(17) .6	(53) .5	(27) .4	(40) .3	(29) .2	
.9	.7	.8		1.5	1.0	1.0	.6	.5	
1.2	1.0	1.0		3.0	1.7	.9	.6	.9	
(81) 2.4	(88) 1.6	(109) 1.9	% Officers', Directors', Owners' Comp/Sales	(10) 4.8	(38) 2.9	(18) 1.6	(21) 1.4	(17) 1.3	
4.1	3.4	3.7		9.3	4.5	2.1	2.6	2.1	
735873M	1649686M	1861323M	Net Sales ($)	15655M	129712M	121730M	336602M	475737M	781887M
239616M	571116M	623882M	Total Assets ($)	6566M	51127M	46367M	104995M	146633M	268194M

M = $ thousand   MM = $ million
See Pages 1 through 15 for Explanation of Ratios and Data

RETAILERS—TRUCKS– NEW & USED. SIC# 5511

Current Data Sorted By Assets

# Postretirement Benefits / Type of Statement	0-500M	500M-2MM	2-10MM	10-50MM	50-100MM	100-250MM	Comparative Historical Data 4/1/90-3/31/91 ALL	4/1/91-3/31/92 ALL
# Postretirement Benefits		3	16	6				
Unqualified	1	2	30	18	2		67	82
Reviewed	6	17	44	16			115	120
Compiled		27	19	2			92	95
Tax Returns		2					6	5
Other	13	63	295	42	1		298	355
		87 (4/1-9/30/94)		513 (10/1/94-3/31/95)				
NUMBER OF STATEMENTS	20	111	388	78	3		578	657

	0-500M %	500M-2MM %	2-10MM %	10-50MM %	50-100MM %	100-250MM %	ALL %	ALL %
ASSETS								
Cash & Equivalents	10.6	6.9	7.5	5.1			5.4	5.6
Trade Receivables - (net)	14.5	10.4	9.1	13.8			9.9	10.7
Inventory	60.8	62.7	63.5	54.6			62.9	61.9
All Other Current	3.1	5.0	5.5	4.3			3.1	3.0
Total Current	89.1	85.0	85.6	77.8			81.4	81.1
Fixed Assets (net)	7.4	10.3	9.1	16.0			12.4	11.8
Intangibles (net)	.7	.6	.3	.4			.8	.9
All Other Non-Current	2.8	4.1	5.0	5.8			5.4	6.1
Total	100.0	100.0	100.0	100.0			100.0	100.0
LIABILITIES								
Notes Payable-Short Term	22.9	41.0	48.1	46.2			52.2	51.7
Cur. Mat. -L/T/D	7.2	1.6	2.1	2.1			2.0	2.3
Trade Payables	9.5	7.4	6.0	7.6			5.8	5.8
Income Taxes Payable	.5	.3	.3	.5			.3	.2
All Other Current	8.1	9.1	11.3	11.5			6.7	6.4
Total Current	48.1	59.3	67.7	68.0			67.0	66.5
Long Term Debt	8.6	7.8	7.7	11.7			10.0	10.0
Deferred Taxes	.0	.1	.2	.3			.1	.1
All Other-Non-Current	3.3	1.5	.8	1.3			1.1	1.4
Net Worth	40.0	31.4	23.6	18.7			21.8	22.0
Total Liabilities & Net Worth	100.0	100.0	100.0	100.0			100.0	100.0
INCOME DATA								
Net Sales	100.0	100.0	100.0	100.0			100.0	100.0
Gross Profit	20.2	15.1	12.1	13.4			14.5	14.4
Operating Expenses	17.9	12.9	10.7	11.7			13.5	13.5
Operating Profit	2.3	2.2	1.5	1.8			1.1	.9
All Other Expenses (net)	.1	.1	-.1	.0			.4	.5
Profit Before Taxes	2.1	2.1	1.6	1.8			.7	.4
RATIOS								
Current	3.2 / 1.8 / 1.3	1.7 / 1.4 / 1.2	1.4 / 1.2 / 1.1	1.2 / 1.1 / 1.0			1.4 / 1.2 / 1.0	1.4 / 1.2 / 1.1
Quick	1.1 / .6 / .1	.5 / .3 / .1	.4 / .2 / .1	.4 / .3 / .2			.3 / .2 / .1	.4 / .2 / .1
Sales/Receivables	0 UND / 5 73.2 / 24 15.0	2 201.1 / 5 77.4 / 14 25.7	3 132.8 / 5 68.9 / 11 33.5	6 64.5 / 12 31.4 / 21 17.5			4 98.1 / 7 52.7 / 13 27.5	4 84.8 / 8 47.0 / 14 25.2
Cost of Sales/Inventory	38 9.7 / 54 6.8 / 74 4.9	43 8.5 / 58 6.3 / 79 4.6	43 8.4 / 58 6.3 / 74 4.9	42 8.6 / 57 6.4 / 68 5.4			52 7.0 / 66 5.5 / 85 4.3	52 7.0 / 68 5.4 / 87 4.2
Cost of Sales/Payables	0 UND / 2 229.0 / 12 30.3	1 260.7 / 3 110.0 / 10 35.3	2 199.5 / 3 119.6 / 7 55.4	3 124.0 / 5 81.0 / 12 29.3			2 179.1 / 4 99.4 / 7 53.9	2 160.8 / 4 93.4 / 8 46.1
Sales/Working Capital	9.3 / 13.3 / 31.4	11.7 / 20.4 / 34.5	17.3 / 28.5 / 61.2	28.1 / 56.8 / 162.1			16.5 / 31.8 / 134.6	16.6 / 30.7 / 89.5
EBIT/Interest	(19) 18.8 / 3.1 / 1.1	(94) 7.3 / 2.8 / 1.7	(336) 7.8 / 3.7 / 1.9	(68) 6.7 / 3.2 / 1.8			(535) 2.5 / 1.4 / .9	(624) 2.2 / 1.3 / .7
Net Profit + Depr., Dep., Amort./Cur. Mat. L /T/D		(35) 7.8 / 2.8 / 1.2	(87) 6.3 / 1.9 / 1.0	(31) 13.7 / 2.0 / 1.3			(166) 4.0 / 1.3 / .4	(177) 2.6 / .9 / .1
Fixed/Worth	.0 / .1 / .3	.1 / .2 / .6	.2 / .3 / .6	.3 / .8 / 1.9			.2 / .5 / 1.4	.2 / .5 / 1.2
Debt/Worth	.7 / 2.0 / 3.3	1.3 / 2.8 / 4.9	2.2 / 3.7 / 6.8	3.5 / 5.3 / 9.0			2.2 / 4.6 / 10.8	2.2 / 4.6 / 9.5
% Profit Before Taxes/Tangible Net Worth	76.0 / 26.8 / 2.3	(109) 45.5 / 22.1 / 8.2	(380) 54.2 / 33.0 / 13.7	55.7 / 31.1 / 19.8			(520) 28.3 / 11.9 / .6	(608) 23.6 / 8.4 / -3.6
% Profit Before Taxes/Total Assets	16.7 / 9.7 / .1	10.1 / 5.8 / 2.9	11.7 / 6.4 / 3.0	9.8 / 5.0 / 3.0			5.8 / 2.1 / -.6	4.8 / 1.4 / -1.4
Sales/Net Fixed Assets	812.8 / 155.3 / 54.1	189.6 / 93.5 / 35.5	173.7 / 82.8 / 38.7	98.4 / 36.9 / 12.3			117.0 / 55.3 / 24.0	115.6 / 54.2 / 22.8
Sales/Total Assets	7.3 / 5.6 / 4.2	6.0 / 4.5 / 3.1	5.9 / 4.7 / 3.6	5.5 / 4.1 / 2.9			5.2 / 4.0 / 3.2	4.8 / 3.8 / 2.9
% Depr., Dep., Amort./Sales	(12) .2 / .4 / 1.5	(94) .2 / .3 / .6	(349) .2 / .2 / .4	(72) .2 / .3 / .7			(505) .2 / .4 / .6	(587) .2 / .3 / .6
% Officers', Directors', Owners' Comp/Sales	(10) .8 / 3.7 / 5.0	(71) .6 / 1.1 / 2.1	(244) .3 / .6 / 1.1	(43) .2 / .3 / .9			(330) .5 / .8 / 1.9	(395) .4 / .7 / 1.3
Net Sales ($)	31417M	711436M	9036450M	5395123M	254004M		10794058M	11156256M
Total Assets ($)	5933M	149433M	1899890M	1282982M	205021M		2894623M	2994398M

M = $ thousand   MM = $ million
See Pages 1 through 15 for Explanation of Ratios and Data

Comparative Historical Data / Current Data Sorted By Sales

2	11	25	# Postretirement Benefits / Type of Statement	0-1MM	1-3MM	3-5MM	5-10MM	10-25MM	25MM & OVER
66	43	53	Unqualified		2	1	4	17	29
111	67	77	Reviewed	1	3	3	13	32	25
77	38	54	Compiled	6	6	12	14	12	4
6	2	2	Tax Returns				1	1	
275	385	414	Other	5	22	18	53	150	166
4/1/92-3/31/93 ALL	4/1/93-3/31/94 ALL	4/1/94-3/31/95 ALL		87 (4/1-9/30/94)		513 (10/1/94-3/31/95)			
535	535	600	**NUMBER OF STATEMENTS**	12	33	34	85	212	224
%	%	%	**ASSETS**	%	%	%	%	%	%
5.3	6.8	7.2	Cash & Equivalents	9.6	6.6	6.9	6.8	7.4	7.1
10.6	10.5	10.2	Trade Receivables - (net)	15.3	9.5	9.1	9.8	9.0	11.5
61.9	61.8	62.0	Inventory	31.5	55.2	56.1	66.1	64.3	61.7
2.7	3.7	5.2	All Other Current	15.6	13.0	12.1	3.3	3.8	4.3
80.4	82.7	84.5	Total Current	72.0	84.3	84.2	85.9	84.5	84.7
11.6	11.1	10.3	Fixed Assets (net)	20.4	11.3	11.4	9.5	10.1	9.8
1.2	.9	.4	Intangibles (net)	2.9	.6	.7	.2	.3	.4
6.8	5.4	4.8	All Other Non-Current	4.6	3.8	3.7	4.4	5.1	5.1
100.0	100.0	100.0	Total	100.0	100.0	100.0	100.0	100.0	100.0
			LIABILITIES						
49.4	47.3	45.5	Notes Payable-Short Term	22.1	17.5	29.2	46.4	47.8	50.8
2.2	1.5	2.2	Cur. Mat.-L/T/D	4.6	6.3	3.9	2.2	1.6	1.8
6.3	4.8	6.5	Trade Payables	7.5	8.8	6.2	7.3	6.0	6.4
.4	2.3	.3	Income Taxes Payable	.3	.1	.6	.1	.4	.4
7.4	8.4	10.9	All Other Current	8.4	19.7	17.4	8.5	10.4	10.0
65.7	64.3	65.4	Total Current	42.9	52.4	57.3	64.5	66.2	69.4
9.3	8.5	8.3	Long Term Debt	5.0	12.8	6.5	6.3	8.9	8.3
.2	.2	.2	Deferred Taxes	.3	.0	.2	.0	.1	.3
1.8	1.3	1.1	All Other-Non-Current	.5	3.3	.7	1.5	1.2	.6
23.0	25.8	25.0	Net Worth	51.3	31.4	35.3	27.7	23.5	21.4
100.0	100.0	100.0	Total Liabilities & Net Worth	100.0	100.0	100.0	100.0	100.0	100.0
			INCOME DATA						
100.0	100.0	100.0	Net Sales	100.0	100.0	100.0	100.0	100.0	100.0
14.3	13.7	13.3	Gross Profit	31.8	18.4	15.4	12.8	12.6	12.0
13.2	12.0	11.6	Operating Expenses	25.2	16.8	13.5	11.0	11.1	10.4
1.1	1.6	1.7	Operating Profit	6.6	1.6	1.9	1.8	1.4	1.6
.1	.1	−.1	All Other Expenses (net)	−.7	.3	.0	.1	−.2	−.1
1.0	1.5	1.7	Profit Before Taxes	7.3	1.3	1.9	1.7	1.6	1.7
			RATIOS						
1.4 / 1.2 / 1.1	1.4 / 1.3 / 1.1	1.5 / 1.2 / 1.1	Current	2.6 / 1.7 / 1.3	2.1 / 1.5 / 1.2	1.7 / 1.4 / 1.2	1.6 / 1.3 / 1.1	1.5 / 1.3 / 1.1	1.4 / 1.2 / 1.1
.4 / .2 / .1 (534)	.4 / .2 / .1	.4 / .2 / .1	Quick	1.1 / .6 / .2	.9 / .2 / .1	.5 / .2 / .1	.4 / .2 / .1	.4 / .2 / .1	.4 / .3 / .2
3 106.5 / 7 53.9 / 14 26.1	3 127.5 / 6 62.2 / 13 28.6	3 129.4 / 6 63.8 / 14 26.4	Sales/Receivables	7 55.0 / 24 15.3 / 52 7.0	4 98.3 / 14 26.7 / 24 15.3	2 153.3 / 7 51.7 / 15 23.8	2 181.9 / 5 71.9 / 15 24.5	2 158.2 / 5 80.3 / 11 33.1	4 104.2 / 6 63.6 / 12 30.9
49 7.5 / 68 5.4 / 85 4.3	46 8.0 / 58 6.3 / 78 4.7	43 8.5 / 58 6.3 / 73 5.0	Cost of Sales/Inventory	0 UND / 28 12.9 / 101 3.6	44 8.3 / 70 5.2 / 192 1.9	48 7.6 / 69 5.3 / 91 4.0	51 7.2 / 70 5.2 / 94 3.9	47 7.7 / 60 6.1 / 76 4.8	38 9.7 / 49 7.4 / 62 5.9
2 168.9 / 4 91.5 / 9 40.5	0 UND / 0 UND / 6 57.8	2 202.7 / 3 107.8 / 8 45.4	Cost of Sales/Payables	0 UND / 8 47.6 / 20 18.0	2 229.0 / 10 35.1 / 25 14.5	1 245.6 / 6 64.2 / 14 26.4	2 236.7 / 3 110.0 / 10 36.9	2 217.2 / 3 116.2 / 7 55.4	2 181.9 / 3 111.5 / 6 62.9
16.2 / 32.8 / 93.0	15.7 / 27.9 / 53.2	15.5 / 28.0 / 59.6	Sales/Working Capital	1.6 / 14.3 / 49.4	5.8 / 9.4 / 13.6	7.8 / 12.8 / 21.9	12.7 / 22.0 / 40.1	16.7 / 27.7 / 55.3	22.8 / 39.0 / 82.4
3.5 / 2.0 / 1.2 (476)	6.3 / 3.2 / 1.9 (482)	7.3 / 3.3 / 1.9 (520)	EBIT/Interest	14.2 / 2.1 / 1.0 (11)	5.5 / 2.5 / 1.2 (29)	6.4 / 3.0 / 1.7 (31)	6.7 / 3.3 / 1.8 (74)	6.0 / 3.3 / 1.8 (185)	9.2 / 4.0 / 2.2 (190)
3.9 / 1.9 / .8 (144)	4.1 / 1.8 / 1.0 (85)	6.4 / 2.0 / 1.1 (158)	Net Profit + Depr., Dep., Amort./Cur. Mat. L/T/D		1.7 / .2 / −.1 (13)	7.4 / 2.2 / .5 (14)	4.6 / 2.0 / 1.5 (20)	7.8 / 2.1 / 1.2 (51)	13.4 / 2.1 / 1.3 (57)
.2 / .4 / 1.0	.1 / .3 / .7	.1 / .3 / .7	Fixed/Worth	.0 / .2 / .7	.1 / .2 / .7	.1 / .3 / .6	.1 / .3 / .6	.1 / .3 / .6	.2 / .3 / .9
2.1 / 4.1 / 8.8	2.1 / 3.5 / 5.9	2.2 / 3.6 / 6.7	Debt/Worth	.4 / 1.1 / 2.5	1.1 / 2.6 / 5.2	1.3 / 2.3 / 3.4	1.8 / 3.4 / 6.6	2.4 / 3.6 / 6.3	2.4 / 4.5 / 7.6
34.3 / 17.8 / 5.2 (491)	47.1 / 24.8 / 11.8 (526)	53.3 / 29.7 / 13.6 (590)	% Profit Before Taxes/Tangible Net Worth	76.9 / 13.1 / .0	29.1 / 8.6 / 2.6 (32)	35.1 / 15.3 / 5.2 (83)	42.8 / 23.0 / 11.4 (208)	51.6 / 28.4 / 13.8 (221)	61.4 / 38.9 / 22.0
6.5 / 3.1 / .8	9.7 / 5.8 / 2.5	11.3 / 6.1 / 2.8	% Profit Before Taxes/Total Assets	17.4 / 6.0 / .0	8.5 / 3.1 / .2	8.7 / 4.2 / 1.6	9.4 / 5.8 / 2.0	10.9 / 6.1 / 2.7	12.7 / 7.2 / 3.7
131.8 / 56.8 / 25.5	141.5 / 76.1 / 31.2	169.8 / 76.4 / 31.4	Sales/Net Fixed Assets	UND / 25.3 / 3.3	155.3 / 45.4 / 8.4	185.2 / 31.3 / 16.4	154.3 / 75.4 / 43.2	172.0 / 78.8 / 35.1	173.7 / 97.2 / 37.5
5.0 / 3.9 / 3.1	5.5 / 4.4 / 3.3	5.9 / 4.6 / 3.5	Sales/Total Assets	6.8 / 2.1 / .4	5.0 / 2.8 / .9	4.4 / 3.1 / 2.4	5.0 / 4.0 / 3.0	5.6 / 4.5 / 3.5	6.5 / 5.2 / 4.2
.2 / .3 / .6 (449)	.2 / .3 / .5 (468)	.2 / .3 / .5 (529)	% Depr., Dep., Amort./Sales		.2 / .4 / 1.0 (26)	.2 / .3 / .7 (30)	.2 / .3 / .6 (75)	.2 / .2 / .4 (189)	.1 / .2 / .4 (203)
.4 / .7 / 1.4 (299)	.4 / .6 / 1.2 (334)	.3 / .6 / 1.2 (368)	% Officers', Directors', Owners' Comp/Sales		.6 / .9 / 3.1 (20)	.4 / 1.1 / 4.2 (22)	.5 / 1.1 / 1.6 (50)	.4 / .7 / 1.1 (134)	.2 / .4 / .9 (137)
10809960M	11036184M	15428430M	Net Sales ($)	7612M	65290M	135006M	627826M	3550657M	11042039M
2824563M	2602558M	3543259M	Total Assets ($)	8860M	53712M	57095M	174499M	884399M	2364694M

© Robert Morris Associates 1995

M = $ thousand   MM = $ million
See Pages 1 through 15 for Explanation of Ratios and Data

Current Data Sorted By Assets

Comparative Historical Data

# Postretirement Benefits / Type of Statement	0-500M	500M-2MM	2-10MM	10-50MM	50-100MM	100-250MM	4/1/90-3/31/91 ALL	4/1/91-3/31/92 ALL
(Postretirement Benefits)		7	1					
Unqualified	1	2	3	1	1		6	13
Reviewed	4	24	12	1			62	58
Compiled	22	70	20	1			140	130
Tax Returns	4	5	2				6	5
Other	12	36	32	3		1	60	39

62 (4/1-9/30/94)   195 (10/1/94-3/31/95)

	0-500M	500M-2MM	2-10MM	10-50MM	50-100MM	100-250MM	4/1/90-3/31/91 ALL	4/1/91-3/31/92 ALL
NUMBER OF STATEMENTS	43	137	69	6	2		274	245
	%	%	%	%	%	%	%	%
ASSETS								
Cash & Equivalents	8.0	5.7	6.3				4.5	6.1
Trade Receivables - (net)	4.0	4.8	4.0				4.6	5.3
Inventory	68.2	72.8	69.1				71.1	65.4
All Other Current	.9	1.0	.5				.8	.8
Total Current	81.1	84.3	79.9				81.0	77.7
Fixed Assets (net)	17.0	12.3	15.5				15.9	18.1
Intangibles (net)	.3	.6	.5				.4	.7
All Other Non-Current	1.7	2.8	4.2				2.7	3.6
Total	100.0	100.0	100.0				100.0	100.0
LIABILITIES								
Notes Payable-Short Term	36.0	40.9	43.3				41.7	37.0
Cur. Mat. -L/T/D	1.2	2.5	1.5				4.4	3.1
Trade Payables	11.5	7.6	6.9				7.5	8.6
Income Taxes Payable	.1	.6	.5				.3	.2
All Other Current	11.6	8.2	10.0				7.6	7.1
Total Current	60.5	59.8	62.3				61.4	56.0
Long Term Debt	9.9	10.1	9.5				12.6	13.0
Deferred Taxes	.0	.0	.1				.0	.2
All Other-Non-Current	2.0	3.8	2.6				3.3	2.5
Net Worth	27.6	26.4	25.5				22.7	28.2
Total Liabilities & Net Worth	100.0	100.0	100.0				100.0	100.0
INCOME DATA								
Net Sales	100.0	100.0	100.0				100.0	100.0
Gross Profit	25.9	23.5	21.8				24.9	26.4
Operating Expenses	23.6	20.7	18.7				22.3	23.7
Operating Profit	2.2	2.8	3.2				2.6	2.7
All Other Expenses (net)	.5	1.3	.2				2.4	2.1
Profit Before Taxes	1.7	1.5	2.9				.1	.6

RATIOS

Ratio	0-500M	500M-2MM	2-10MM	4/1/90-3/31/91 ALL	4/1/91-3/31/92 ALL
Current	1.8	1.7	1.5	1.6	1.9
	1.4	1.3	1.2	1.3	1.4
	1.1	1.1	1.1	1.1	1.1
Quick	.4	.3	.3	.3	.4
	.1 (136)	.1 (68)	.1	.1 (272)	.2 (244)
	.1	.0	.1	.1	.1
Sales/Receivables	0 UND	1 654.3	2 161.4	1 268.9	1 345.3
	2 202.3	4 100.6	5 73.2	5 76.9	5 69.8
	10 35.5	9 38.6	9 39.4	12 31.4	13 29.0
Cost of Sales/Inventory	70 5.2	118 3.1	107 3.4	107 3.4	114 3.2
	126 2.9	166 2.2	146 2.5	166 2.2	174 2.1
	203 1.8	228 1.6	192 1.9	228 1.6	228 1.6
Cost of Sales/Payables	1 723.0	2 224.6	2 176.0	2 154.4	3 120.4
	9 39.7	6 64.2	5 67.0	7 52.0	8 43.9
	30 12.2	19 19.5	13 28.9	18 20.5	21 17.1
Sales/Working Capital	7.2	5.5	7.6	6.3	5.5
	15.9	10.1	15.5	12.6	10.1
	28.0	24.6	64.9	29.1	27.0
EBIT/Interest	(39) 3.4	(131) 3.0	(63) 5.0	(258) 2.0	(237) 2.1
	2.0	1.8	2.7	1.2	1.3
	1.3	1.2	1.8	.7	.8
Net Profit + Depr., Dep., Amort./Cur. Mat. L./T/D	(13) 7.0	(45) 4.4	(17) 6.5	(104) 3.4	(81) 4.6
	1.9	2.1	3.3	.8	1.5
	.5	.7	.7	-.0	.3
Fixed/Worth	.2	.2	.2	.2	.2
	.5	.4	.6	.6	.5
	1.3	1.3	1.1	1.5	1.7
Debt/Worth	1.4	1.6	1.6	1.9	1.3
	2.4	3.8	3.5	4.1	3.2
	5.6	11.0	8.1	14.0	7.4
% Profit Before Taxes/Tangible Net Worth	(38) 32.9	(133) 44.4	(67) 58.1	(243) 21.7	(226) 19.1
	13.5	16.7	24.0	6.6	7.0
	4.2	6.9	11.7	-8.1	-1.5
% Profit Before Taxes/Total Assets	11.8	6.2	10.2	5.7	5.2
	3.1	3.4	4.8	.9	1.4
	.9	.8	2.7	-2.1	-.8
Sales/Net Fixed Assets	72.6	86.5	51.0	62.1	51.5
	33.0	28.9	24.1	23.5	18.8
	7.8	13.4	9.7	9.1	6.9
Sales/Total Assets	4.0	2.7	2.8	2.7	2.5
	2.5	2.2	2.1	2.0	1.9
	1.8	1.6	1.6	1.5	1.4
% Depr., Dep., Amort./Sales	(39) .5	(121) .4	(62) .5	(243) .5	(232) .5
	.8	.8	.7	.8	1.0
	1.8	1.2	1.0	1.6	1.8
% Officers', Directors', Owners' Comp/Sales	(14) 1.5	(65) 1.6	(37) 1.0	(144) 1.5	(137) 1.6
	3.6	2.8	1.7	2.7	2.8
	5.6	5.7	3.5	4.9	4.8

	0-500M	500M-2MM	2-10MM	10-50MM	50-100MM	4/1/90-3/31/91 ALL	4/1/91-3/31/92 ALL
Net Sales ($)	49081M	349472M	542416M	366167M	221566M	1061308M	982941M
Total Assets ($)	15055M	148315M	246361M	143584M	158616M	486996M	451430M

© Robert Morris Associates 1995

M = $ thousand   MM = $ million
See Pages 1 through 15 for Explanation of Ratios and Data

Comparative Historical Data | Current Data Sorted By Sales

	93	94	95		0-1MM	1-3MM	3-5MM	5-10MM	10-25MM	25MM & OVER
# Postretirement Benefits	3	3	8		2	3	1	2		
Type of Statement										
Unqualified	12	8	8		1	2	1	1	1	2
Reviewed	38	42	41		8	14	4	13	1	1
Compiled	113	110	113		20	55	17	19	1	1
Tax Returns	5	9	11		2	4	2	2	1	
Other	45	54	84		11	27	16	17	8	5
	4/1/92-3/31/93 ALL	4/1/93-3/31/94 ALL	4/1/94-3/31/95 ALL		62 (4/1-9/30/94)			195 (10/1/94-3/31/95)		
NUMBER OF STATEMENTS	213	223	257		42	102	40	52	12	9
	%	%	%		%	%	%	%	%	%
ASSETS										
Cash & Equivalents	6.1	6.3	6.2		5.4	6.8	6.0	5.6	9.2	
Trade Receivables - (net)	4.9	5.3	4.4		4.0	5.0	3.5	4.6	3.7	
Inventory	68.8	67.5	70.7		68.4	72.2	70.6	71.8	68.7	
All Other Current	.7	1.4	.8		1.0	.9	.8	.5	.4	
Total Current	80.6	80.5	82.2		78.8	84.9	81.0	82.5	82.0	
Fixed Assets (net)	15.5	15.5	14.0		18.5	12.0	14.6	14.1	11.5	
Intangibles (net)	.7	.6	.5		.5	.3	.9	.6	.0	
All Other Non-Current	3.2	3.3	3.3		2.2	2.8	3.5	2.7	6.5	
Total	100.0	100.0	100.0		100.0	100.0	100.0	100.0	100.0	
LIABILITIES										
Notes Payable-Short Term	38.4	34.7	40.6		38.6	40.2	36.2	46.3	43.7	
Cur. Mat.-L /T/D	3.3	3.0	2.0		1.2	2.6	1.9	1.7	.8	
Trade Payables	8.5	8.8	8.0		6.9	9.7	5.6	8.1	7.4	
Income Taxes Payable	.2	.8	.5		.1	.2	1.2	.6	.7	
All Other Current	8.9	8.7	9.3		11.5	8.7	9.6	8.0	11.6	
Total Current	59.3	56.1	60.4		58.3	61.4	54.5	64.7	64.2	
Long Term Debt	12.5	11.5	9.9		12.8	8.2	11.8	8.2	14.0	
Deferred Taxes	.1	.1	.0		.0	.0	.0	.1	.2	
All Other-Non-Current	2.7	3.4	3.4		1.6	4.3	3.8	2.2	1.3	
Net Worth	25.3	28.9	26.3		27.3	26.0	29.9	24.9	20.3	
Total Liabilities & Net Worth	100.0	100.0	100.0		100.0	100.0	100.0	100.0	100.0	
INCOME DATA										
Net Sales	100.0	100.0	100.0		100.0	100.0	100.0	100.0	100.0	
Gross Profit	25.3	24.4	23.6		28.8	24.2	19.7	21.5	19.4	
Operating Expenses	23.7	21.7	20.7		26.4	21.3	17.2	19.0	14.5	
Operating Profit	1.6	2.7	2.9		2.4	3.0	2.5	2.4	5.0	
All Other Expenses (net)	1.0	1.0	.9		1.5	1.3	.3	–.1	1.0	
Profit Before Taxes	.6	1.7	2.0		.9	1.7	2.2	2.5	3.9	
RATIOS										
Current	1.9 / 1.3 / 1.1	1.8 / 1.4 / 1.1	1.7 / 1.3 / 1.1		1.7 / 1.4 / 1.1	1.6 / 1.3 / 1.1	2.1 / 1.3 / 1.1	1.6 / 1.2 / 1.1	1.7 / 1.2 / 1.0	
Quick	.3 / .2 / .1 (210)	.4 / .2 / .1	.3 / .1 / .1 (255)		.2 / .1 / .1	.4 / .1 / .0	.3 / .1 / .0 (50)	.3 / .2 / .1	.5 / .1 / .1	
Sales/Receivables	268.0 (1) / 71.8 (5) / 33.4 (11)	189.9 (2) / 69.1 (5) / 35.6 (10)	432.0 (1) / 93.5 (4) / 40.0 (9)		386.5 (1) / 48.4 (8) / 28.8 (13)	690.3 (1) / 117.1 (3) / 35.4 (10)	448.2 (1) / 119.7 (3) / 55.2 (7)	162.1 (2) / 76.8 (5) / 40.1 (9)	844.6 (0) / 97.4 (4) / 42.8 (9)	
Cost of Sales/Inventory	3.1 (118) / 2.2 (166) / 1.5 (243)	3.6 (101) / 2.4 (152) / 1.6 (228)	3.3 (111) / 2.4 (152) / 1.7 (215)		2.6 (140) / 1.7 (215) / 1.3 (281)	3.1 (118) / 2.2 (166) / 1.6 (228)	4.1 (89) / 2.7 (135) / 2.2 (166)	4.3 (85) / 2.8 (130) / 2.0 (183)	4.2 (87) / 3.5 (104) / 2.2 (166)	
Cost of Sales/Payables	163.5 (2) / 44.3 (8) / 16.8 (22)	166.3 (2) / 61.5 (6) / 18.6 (20)	224.6 (2) / 61.0 (6) / 21.5 (17)		404.0 (1) / 42.9 (9) / 19.9 (18)	224.7 (2) / 55.3 (7) / 13.6 (27)	312.5 (1) / 79.3 (5) / 32.0 (11)	178.8 (2) / 66.8 (5) / 28.9 (13)	166.2 (2) / 72.1 (5) / 21.8 (17)	
Sales/Working Capital	6.1 / 10.6 / 31.5	5.7 / 10.3 / 24.3	6.7 / 12.1 / 28.4		4.1 / 8.7 / 19.2	5.9 / 10.5 / 24.1	5.8 / 14.1 / 28.9	9.4 / 15.9 / 44.5	10.2 / 18.3 / NM	
EBIT/Interest	2.6 / 1.5 / .8 (209)	3.1 / 1.8 / 1.2 (210)	3.8 / 2.1 / 1.3 (241)		2.2 / 1.6 / 1.1 (36)	3.7 / 2.1 / 1.2 (98)	3.8 / 1.9 / 1.3 (37)	4.3 / 2.3 / 1.5 (49)	5.5 / 3.9 / 2.8	
Net Profit + Depr., Dep., Amort./Cur. Mat. L/T/D	3.8 / 1.7 / .5 (51)	5.8 / 3.3 / .7 (47)	5.2 / 2.2 / .7 (80)		6.1 / 2.5 / .7 (14)	4.5 / 2.1 / .7 (39)		5.6 / 2.5 / 1.1 (13)		
Fixed/Worth	.2 / .5 / 1.8	.2 / .4 / 1.3	.2 / .5 / 1.3		.2 / .5 / 1.6	.2 / .4 / 1.1	.2 / .5 / 1.4	.3 / .5 / 1.0	.2 / .5 / 1.4	
Debt/Worth	1.5 / 3.8 / 10.7	1.2 / 3.1 / 8.9	1.6 / 3.5 / 9.5		1.4 / 3.8 / 10.0	1.7 / 3.2 / 10.9	1.1 / 3.1 / 10.2	1.8 / 3.6 / 6.8	1.6 / 5.9 / 16.0	
% Profit Before Taxes/Tangible Net Worth	22.9 / 7.3 / .1 (190)	31.3 / 12.9 / 3.5 (205)	45.9 / 19.4 / 7.7 (246)		22.2 / 9.6 / 2.3 (39)	46.9 / 19.4 / 7.0 (98)	33.2 / 19.7 / 8.2 (38)	57.1 / 21.4 / 9.9 (51)	86.9 / 58.1 / 23.3 (11)	
% Profit Before Taxes/Total Assets	6.3 / 1.7 / –.8	6.7 / 3.1 / .6	7.6 / 3.9 / 1.4		3.7 / 2.3 / .2	7.2 / 3.9 / .8	7.6 / 3.5 / 1.2	9.0 / 4.4 / 2.3	17.9 / 8.7 / 5.9	
Sales/Net Fixed Assets	57.2 / 21.4 / 8.8	77.9 / 24.1 / 9.0	70.0 / 25.3 / 10.8		33.9 / 13.4 / 4.1	78.5 / 32.3 / 15.3	86.4 / 29.0 / 11.2	83.2 / 27.1 / 12.1	64.7 / 36.2 / 11.0	
Sales/Total Assets	2.8 / 2.0 / 1.5	3.0 / 2.2 / 1.6	2.9 / 2.2 / 1.6		2.1 / 1.5 / 1.2	2.8 / 2.1 / 1.7	3.0 / 2.5 / 1.9	3.4 / 2.5 / 1.9	3.3 / 2.7 / 2.2	
% Depr., Dep., Amort./Sales	.5 / .8 / 1.5 (192)	.4 / .8 / 1.4 (200)	.4 / .8 / 1.3 (230)		.8 / 1.5 / 2.1 (39)	.4 / .7 / 1.3 (89)	.5 / .7 / 1.0 (34)	.4 / .6 / .9 (49)	.4 / .5 / .8 (11)	
% Officers', Directors', Owners' Comp/Sales	1.4 / 3.2 / 6.5 (113)	1.5 / 2.8 / 5.2 (113)	1.3 / 2.5 / 4.8 (117)		4.3 / 5.0 / 7.6 (11)	1.5 / 2.6 / 6.0 (46)	1.3 / 2.3 / 3.1 (23)	1.1 / 1.8 / 3.6 (30)		
Net Sales ($)	933233M	1015179M	1528702M		27707M	196027M	154677M	361570M	173109M	615612M
Total Assets ($)	416669M	463712M	711931M		23895M	96173M	67866M	147106M	64942M	311949M

© Robert Morris Associates 1995

M = $ thousand   MM = $ million
See Pages 1 through 15 for Explanation of Ratios and Data

RETAILERS—BOOKS. SIC# 5942

Current Data Sorted By Assets | Comparative Historical Data

0-500M	500M-2MM	2-10MM	10-50MM	50-100MM	100-250MM	# Postretirement Benefits / Type of Statement	4/1/90-3/31/91 ALL	4/1/91-3/31/92 ALL
2		2						
1	6		2	1	2	Unqualified	21	10
5	8		1			Reviewed	12	15
12	11	6				Compiled	33	33
6	1	2				Tax Returns	4	7
10	14	5	2		1	Other	7	23
35 (4/1-9/30/94)			61 (10/1/94-3/31/95)					
28	32	27	5	1	3	NUMBER OF STATEMENTS	77	88
%	%	%	%	%	%	**ASSETS**	%	%
7.0	5.4	8.9				Cash & Equivalents	10.0	8.9
3.9	8.1	8.0				Trade Receivables - (net)	10.9	12.6
63.8	63.4	53.5				Inventory	50.8	50.9
.5	1.3	2.8				All Other Current	1.7	.7
75.1	78.1	73.2				Total Current	73.3	73.1
18.1	15.9	20.2				Fixed Assets (net)	18.6	20.4
1.5	1.7	1.4				Intangibles (net)	2.2	1.7
5.3	4.3	5.2				All Other Non-Current	5.9	4.8
100.0	100.0	100.0				Total	100.0	100.0
						LIABILITIES		
12.9	11.0	6.8				Notes Payable-Short Term	8.6	9.3
5.4	3.5	2.3				Cur. Mat. -L/T/D	2.8	3.6
27.3	25.2	28.3				Trade Payables	27.8	25.2
.5	.7	.4				Income Taxes Payable	.4	.3
9.1	9.4	9.2				All Other Current	6.5	6.9
55.1	49.8	47.0				Total Current	46.2	45.3
14.3	11.8	13.5				Long Term Debt	16.0	16.9
.1	.1	.1				Deferred Taxes	.3	.0
3.0	4.3	1.6				All Other-Non-Current	2.5	2.6
27.5	34.1	37.8				Net Worth	35.0	35.2
100.0	100.0	100.0				Total Liabilities & Net Worth	100.0	100.0
						INCOME DATA		
100.0	100.0	100.0				Net Sales	100.0	100.0
37.9	38.8	34.9				Gross Profit	36.4	39.2
33.2	35.8	32.3				Operating Expenses	32.3	35.5
4.6	3.0	2.7				Operating Profit	4.1	3.7
.8	.9	1.0				All Other Expenses (net)	.9	.6
3.9	2.1	1.7				Profit Before Taxes	3.2	3.1
						RATIOS		
2.5	2.7	2.6				Current	2.3	2.6
1.5	1.5	1.5					1.6	1.8
.9	1.1	1.1					1.2	1.3
.5	.6	.6				Quick	.8	.9
.1	.2	.2					.4	.4
.1	.1	.1					.2	.2
0 948.3	2 202.6	2 204.5				Sales/Receivables	2 189.1	1 256.8
2 198.9	7 51.2	6 59.3					7 49.0	8 45.2
6 65.6	14 26.0	22 16.4					19 19.5	31 11.6
65 5.6	114 3.2	78 4.7				Cost of Sales/Inventory	72 5.1	76 4.8
114 3.2	166 2.2	111 3.3					101 3.6	107 3.4
140 2.6	261 1.4	140 2.6					130 2.8	152 2.4
16 23.0	31 11.8	25 14.8				Cost of Sales/Payables	27 13.3	22 16.6
34 10.7	72 5.1	50 7.3					51 7.2	46 8.0
69 5.3	101 3.6	107 3.4					85 4.3	79 4.6
7.2	4.0	5.1				Sales/Working Capital	6.2	5.6
16.2	8.4	11.9					8.8	9.1
−39.5	34.1	25.3					40.1	27.8
12.6	(30) 8.2	(26) 6.6				EBIT/Interest	(71) 7.9	(82) 9.5
5.1	2.7	4.3					3.7	4.4
1.7	1.3	1.5					1.7	1.5
		(14) 4.7				Net Profit + Depr., Dep., Amort./Cur. Mat. L /T/D	(35) 7.4	(28) 4.0
		2.5					3.0	1.7
		.2					1.2	1.0
.2	.1	.2				Fixed/Worth	.2	.2
.7	.5	.5					.5	.6
5.4	1.5	1.1					1.3	1.6
.9	1.1	.9				Debt/Worth	.9	.7
4.4	2.5	2.3					1.9	1.6
14.3	4.7	3.8					5.9	6.0
(23) 91.3	(29) 34.9	47.8				% Profit Before Taxes/Tangible Net Worth	(67) 46.2	(77) 37.3
45.5	17.1	14.5					15.5	22.2
15.5	1.7	5.1					7.3	5.1
25.9	11.7	12.3				% Profit Before Taxes/Total Assets	13.6	17.8
12.3	4.1	6.8					7.4	9.0
2.4	.6	1.6					2.3	.9
41.6	35.4	26.5				Sales/Net Fixed Assets	50.6	45.9
26.6	20.1	15.2					20.4	18.0
16.8	8.5	8.6					9.5	8.1
5.1	2.9	3.3				Sales/Total Assets	3.5	3.4
3.8	2.2	2.6					2.9	2.8
2.8	1.6	2.1					2.0	2.0
(25) .5	(27) .6	(26) .8				% Depr., Dep., Amort./Sales	(71) .7	(79) .7
1.1	1.1	1.2					1.2	1.3
2.2	2.1	1.5					1.6	1.9
(15) 3.9	(14) 1.9	(11) 1.2				% Officers', Directors', Owners' Comp/Sales	(26) 2.2	(38) 1.7
6.0	3.5	2.0					3.8	4.7
8.6	10.1	8.7					7.7	8.8
25928M	75966M	331678M	193053M	79068M	931366M	Net Sales ($)	964347M	1096751M
6473M	33559M	126647M	77178M	67735M	538874M	Total Assets ($)	332367M	459770M

M = $ thousand   MM = $ million
See Pages 1 through 15 for Explanation of Ratios and Data

Comparative Historical Data / Current Data Sorted By Sales

4/1/92-3/31/93 ALL	4/1/93-3/31/94 ALL	4/1/94-3/31/95 ALL		0-1MM	1-3MM	3-5MM	5-10MM	10-25MM	25MM & OVER
				35 (4/1-9/30/94)			61 (10/1/94-3/31/95)		
3	4	4	# Postretirement Benefits	1		1		2	
			Type of Statement						
8	14	12	Unqualified			3		3	6
13	12	14	Reviewed	2		2	2	6	2
29	27	29	Compiled	9	11	5	2	2	
2	5	9	Tax Returns	4	2	1	1	1	
30	21	32	Other	10	10	4		3	3
82	79	96	**NUMBER OF STATEMENTS**	25	23	15	7	15	11
%	%	%	**ASSETS**	%	%	%	%	%	%
9.5	9.0	7.5	Cash & Equivalents	4.8	6.6	7.9		11.3	9.9
8.6	8.9	7.3	Trade Receivables - (net)	3.7	8.0	8.4		9.7	12.2
53.9	53.6	58.1	Inventory	65.8	69.3	43.3		51.7	39.3
.9	.8	1.4	All Other Current	.5	.3	3.3		3.2	1.1
72.9	72.4	74.3	Total Current	74.8	84.2	62.9		75.9	62.6
20.1	20.5	18.6	Fixed Assets (net)	18.8	13.7	22.8		18.6	24.4
1.5	1.1	1.5	Intangibles (net)	1.9	.4	2.5		1.0	1.1
5.4	6.0	5.6	All Other Non-Current	4.5	1.7	11.8		4.6	12.0
100.0	100.0	100.0	Total	100.0	100.0	100.0		100.0	100.0
			LIABILITIES						
7.5	7.9	9.8	Notes Payable-Short Term	11.1	14.5	8.3		7.7	4.7
3.1	2.6	3.5	Cur. Mat.-L /T/D	5.7	3.6	3.2		2.4	1.1
27.7	23.0	26.6	Trade Payables	21.2	32.4	23.1		29.1	24.1
.5	2.5	.5	Income Taxes Payable	.4	.7	.8		.2	.5
8.1	8.2	9.0	All Other Current	6.8	11.2	9.3		11.1	7.6
46.9	44.1	49.4	Total Current	45.2	62.4	44.8		50.5	38.1
16.9	14.6	12.9	Long Term Debt	16.7	12.2	14.5		9.7	11.2
.1	.1	.1	Deferred Taxes	.1	.0	.2		.1	.2
1.2	1.6	3.0	All Other-Non-Current	3.4	4.4	2.2		2.6	2.5
35.0	39.6	34.6	Net Worth	34.5	21.0	38.3		37.2	48.1
100.0	100.0	100.0	Total Liabilities & Net Worth	100.0	100.0	100.0		100.0	100.0
			INCOME DATA						
100.0	100.0	100.0	Net Sales	100.0	100.0	100.0		100.0	100.0
37.5	37.1	37.0	Gross Profit	40.8	35.4	41.0		34.3	35.4
32.6	34.0	33.9	Operating Expenses	35.1	32.5	38.3		30.7	34.9
4.9	3.1	3.1	Operating Profit	5.7	2.9	2.7		3.6	.5
.7	.6	.8	All Other Expenses (net)	1.4	.4	1.1		.8	.4
4.2	2.4	2.3	Profit Before Taxes	4.3	2.5	1.7		2.8	.1
			RATIOS						
2.4	2.9	2.6	Current	2.9	2.4	2.3		2.3	3.0
1.7	1.7	1.5		1.7	1.4	1.4		1.5	1.6
1.1	1.2	1.1		1.1	1.0	1.0		1.1	1.2
.8	.9	.6	Quick	.5	.5	.6		.7	1.4
(80) .3	(77) .4	.2		.1	.2	.2		.3	.4
.1	.2	.1		.1	.1	.1		.2	.2
1 380.0	2 167.9	1 284.5	Sales/Receivables	1 413.3	2 204.8	1 680.0		2 204.5	6 62.4
4 102.0	8 43.6	6 64.0		3 134.3	6 59.7	2 159.4		6 59.3	11 32.4
12 31.1	21 17.1	12 29.5		8 43.9	12 30.5	21 17.3		23 15.9	43 8.4
74 4.9	78 4.7	81 4.5	Cost of Sales/Inventory	104 3.5	99 3.7	72 5.1		72 5.1	70 5.2
107 3.4	130 2.8	122 3.0		135 2.7	140 2.6	91 4.0		111 3.3	78 4.7
159 2.3	159 2.3	166 2.2		261 1.4	203 1.8	140 2.6		135 2.7	140 2.6
30 12.3	22 16.4	20 18.6	Cost of Sales/Payables	16 22.8	25 14.5	15 23.8		20 18.0	26 13.8
48 7.6	44 8.3	54 6.7		46 8.0	51 7.1	63 5.8		44 8.3	54 6.7
85 4.3	87 4.2	91 4.0		94 3.9	107 3.4	99 3.7		73 5.0	85 4.3
5.8	4.5	5.2	Sales/Working Capital	4.3	5.4	4.2		7.1	4.8
11.1	8.8	10.8		8.9	11.9	11.5		14.7	7.2
43.1	23.9	38.5		38.3	-317.6	-310.1		27.9	30.9
14.0	12.6	9.2	EBIT/Interest	12.3	8.0	7.4		7.1	10.7
(71) 3.9	(67) 3.4	(93) 4.0		4.0	(22) 3.8	(14) 3.3		3.2	5.1
1.6	1.1	1.3		1.6	1.3	1.0		1.6	.4
3.6	12.8	4.7	Net Profit + Depr., Dep., Amort./Cur. Mat. L/T/D						
(29) 2.6	(23) 2.9	(30) 1.8							
1.1	1.0	.3							
.3	.2	.2	Fixed/Worth	.2	.1	.2		.3	.4
.5	.5	.6		.6	1.1	.8		.5	.6
1.4	1.2	1.4		2.3	5.7	1.7		1.1	.8
.8	.6	.8	Debt/Worth	.8	1.3	.8		.9	.6
1.7	1.4	2.4		1.9	4.3	2.0		2.3	.9
4.6	4.6	4.9		9.9	26.9	3.8		4.4	3.4
50.2	36.7	47.2	% Profit Before Taxes/Tangible Net Worth	89.6	57.1	35.5		35.1	34.1
(75) 23.2	(74) 13.3	(88) 18.8		(23) 24.7	(18) 34.9	(14) 15.8		11.4	15.8
5.2	3.7	2.3		2.9	3.3	.4		6.4	-4.7
17.9	12.0	13.7	% Profit Before Taxes/Total Assets	24.0	13.5	10.9		17.5	11.3
7.6	5.8	7.0		8.7	7.0	4.1		4.3	8.2
1.0	.6	.9		2.1	1.2	-.3		1.6	-1.0
37.3	31.6	36.0	Sales/Net Fixed Assets	39.3	56.9	27.5		27.0	16.1
21.1	15.0	18.1		19.7	31.5	13.0		16.4	8.4
9.2	8.1	8.8		11.0	15.1	4.2		9.5	7.2
3.6	3.3	3.5	Sales/Total Assets	3.9	3.9	2.9		3.3	3.5
3.0	2.6	2.7		2.8	3.1	2.1		2.6	2.7
2.1	1.9	2.0		1.4	2.2	1.7		2.4	1.2
.7	.8	.7	% Depr., Dep., Amort./Sales	1.0	.6	.6		.8	.9
(70) 1.2	(73) 1.2	(87) 1.2		(21) 1.6	(19) .8	1.2		1.0	1.8
1.5	1.9	2.1		2.9	1.9	1.5		1.6	2.6
1.2	2.5	1.9	% Officers', Directors', Owners' Comp/Sales	3.9					
(39) 3.1	(29) 4.8	(41) 4.3		(14) 7.0					
6.1	10.6	8.7		10.8					
1363220M	1601088M	1637059M	Net Sales ($)	16296M	39210M	57619M	49142M	215380M	1259412M
685349M	909113M	850466M	Total Assets ($)	8071M	14554M	31568M	19286M	77885M	699102M

M = $ thousand   MM = $ million
See Pages 1 through 15 for Explanation of Ratios and Data

Current Data Sorted By Assets							Comparative Historical Data	
4	7	5				**# Postretirement Benefits**		
						Type of Statement		
	5	5	1		2	Unqualified	21	13
2	23	11		1		Reviewed	54	45
43	28	5				Compiled	97	86
3	3					Tax Returns		1
11	17	10	2			Other	47	37
0-500M	500M-2MM	2-10MM	10-50MM	50-100MM	100-250MM		4/1/90-3/31/91 ALL	4/1/91-3/31/92 ALL
62 (4/1-9/30/94)			110 (10/1/94-3/31/95)					
59	76	31	3	1	2	**NUMBER OF STATEMENTS**	219	182
%	%	%	%	%	%	**ASSETS**	%	%
7.2	6.4	6.3				Cash & Equivalents	6.7	6.7
34.7	36.1	39.6				Trade Receivables - (net)	29.0	27.8
34.3	33.5	33.5				Inventory	40.8	39.0
.8	1.5	2.2				All Other Current	1.7	1.5
77.0	77.5	81.7				Total Current	78.2	75.0
16.1	15.6	12.4				Fixed Assets (net)	15.1	17.8
3.2	1.5	1.0				Intangibles (net)	1.6	1.7
3.7	5.4	4.9				All Other Non-Current	5.1	5.5
100.0	100.0	100.0				Total	100.0	100.0
						LIABILITIES		
10.6	9.6	13.8				Notes Payable-Short Term	9.9	10.7
4.3	7.1	2.7				Cur. Mat. -L/T/D	4.5	5.5
26.2	22.8	19.5				Trade Payables	20.8	20.5
.7	.4	.4				Income Taxes Payable	.6	.4
9.6	7.7	10.6				All Other Current	8.0	8.0
51.4	47.6	47.0				Total Current	43.8	45.0
18.1	13.0	10.9				Long Term Debt	15.7	15.2
.0	.2	.1				Deferred Taxes	.1	.2
5.6	3.8	1.7				All Other-Non-Current	1.9	2.7
24.8	35.3	40.2				Net Worth	38.5	37.0
100.0	100.0	100.0				Total Liabilities & Net Worth	100.0	100.0
						INCOME DATA		
100.0	100.0	100.0				Net Sales	100.0	100.0
35.2	34.6	31.1				Gross Profit	36.3	36.4
31.8	32.0	29.9				Operating Expenses	34.1	35.1
3.4	2.6	1.1				Operating Profit	2.3	1.4
.9	.2	.0				All Other Expenses (net)	.6	.5
2.6	2.4	1.1				Profit Before Taxes	1.7	.8
						RATIOS		
2.3	2.3	2.4					2.8	2.6
1.5	1.6	1.6				Current	1.8	1.8
1.2	1.3	1.4					1.4	1.2
1.1	1.4	1.2					1.3	1.2
.8	.9	1.0				Quick	.9	.8
.6	.6	.8					.5	.5
(21) 17.8	(31) 11.8	(34) 10.7					(22) 16.6	(22) 16.8
(32) 11.5	(40) 9.2	(41) 8.8				Sales/Receivables	(32) 11.3	(32) 11.3
(41) 8.8	(47) 7.8	(48) 7.6					(42) 8.7	(41) 9.0
(26) 13.8	(32) 11.5	(30) 12.3					(45) 8.2	(37) 9.9
(52) 7.0	(61) 6.0	(47) 7.7				Cost of Sales/Inventory	(70) 5.2	(65) 5.6
(94) 3.9	(104) 3.5	(81) 4.5					(118) 3.1	(111) 3.3
(23) 15.9	(24) 15.5	(22) 16.5					(21) 17.4	(21) 17.1
(35) 10.3	(34) 10.6	(30) 12.2				Cost of Sales/Payables	(33) 11.0	(31) 11.8
(52) 7.0	(51) 7.1	(43) 8.5					(53) 6.9	(47) 7.7
8.3	6.9	6.7					5.8	6.4
14.6	12.3	12.1				Sales/Working Capital	9.4	11.1
29.2	22.2	16.1					17.3	25.0
(58) 9.9	(69) 5.6	(28) 11.1					(207) 6.0	(176) 3.9
4.4	3.0	3.5				EBIT/Interest	2.5	1.7
.7	1.5	1.3					1.2	.2
(17) 4.6	(39) 5.5	(19) 3.2				Net Profit + Depr., Dep.,	(105) 3.8	(94) 2.8
2.1	1.7	2.3				Amort./Cur. Mat. L /T/D	1.5	1.2
-.3	.3	1.1					.7	.3
.2	.2	.1					.2	.2
.9	.4	.3				Fixed/Worth	.4	.5
-7.2	1.0	.5					.8	.9
1.3	1.0	1.2					.7	.8
3.2	2.2	1.9				Debt/Worth	1.8	1.9
-31.0	5.2	2.4					3.7	4.5
(44) 53.7	(75) 38.1	30.8				% Profit Before Taxes/Tangible	(201) 29.3	(167) 26.5
28.3	14.2	14.0				Net Worth	15.5	6.3
1.6	4.4	.7					3.7	-3.6
15.4	10.2	11.0				% Profit Before Taxes/Total	11.5	7.6
5.1	5.2	5.8				Assets	5.4	2.5
-1.7	1.7	.3					.8	-2.4
96.8	50.3	58.9					50.5	43.8
30.2	29.1	33.4				Sales/Net Fixed Assets	27.7	24.6
17.6	14.9	15.2					14.8	12.2
4.8	4.4	4.1					4.2	4.2
3.7	3.1	3.6				Sales/Total Assets	3.2	3.1
2.8	2.3	2.9					2.3	2.3
(51) .5	(69) .7	(30) .6				% Depr., Dep., Amort./Sales	(195) .7	(166) .8
1.0	1.0	.8					1.2	1.2
1.7	1.5	1.4					1.7	1.7
(29) 4.1	(38) 2.1	(19) .8				% Officers', Directors',	(120) 2.8	(100) 3.0
6.0	3.3	3.5				Owners' Comp/Sales	5.2	4.7
10.1	5.8	12.1					7.8	7.6
53968M	263677M	413014M	213441M	248456M	779924M	Net Sales ($)	2263648M	1263679M
15113M	80089M	120914M	77073M	78661M	377651M	Total Assets ($)	800745M	555672M

M = $ thousand   MM = $ million
See Pages 1 through 15 for Explanation of Ratios and Data

	Comparative Historical Data				Current Data Sorted By Sales					
	1	6	16	# Postretirement Benefits		6	3	4	1	2
				Type of Statement						
	13	6	13	Unqualified		2	2	2	4	3
	48	47	37	Reviewed	1	12	7	10	6	1
	83	80	76	Compiled	22	35	12	5	2	
	7	7	6	Tax Returns	2	2	1	1		
	27	35	40	Other	10	8	8	6	3	5
	4/1/92- 3/31/93	4/1/93- 3/31/94	4/1/94- 3/31/95		62 (4/1-9/30/94)			110 (10/1/94-3/31/95)		
	ALL	ALL	ALL		0-1MM	1-3MM	3-5MM	5-10MM	10-25MM	25MM & OVER
	178	175	172	NUMBER OF STATEMENTS	35	59	30	24	15	9
	%	%	%	ASSETS	%	%	%	%	%	%
	7.4	7.7	6.7	Cash & Equivalents	7.4	7.1	5.3	7.0	6.2	
	31.2	34.1	36.1	Trade Receivables - (net)	28.9	33.1	39.6	43.1	43.7	
	38.6	36.4	33.6	Inventory	33.9	37.9	33.2	27.5	29.6	
	1.2	1.1	1.4	All Other Current	.5	1.6	1.3	2.6	1.4	
	78.3	79.2	77.8	Total Current	70.7	79.6	79.3	80.2	80.9	
	14.9	13.9	15.2	Fixed Assets (net)	20.9	13.6	13.4	15.9	13.7	
	1.6	.8	2.4	Intangibles (net)	4.1	1.7	1.8	.4	1.3	
	5.2	6.1	4.6	All Other Non-Current	4.3	5.0	5.4	3.5	4.1	
	100.0	100.0	100.0	Total	100.0	100.0	100.0	100.0	100.0	
				LIABILITIES						
	12.1	9.2	10.6	Notes Payable-Short Term	10.0	9.6	9.5	13.7	11.2	
	4.8	3.9	5.1	Cur. Mat.-L./T/D	7.8	5.0	6.1	3.5	2.5	
	21.1	20.6	23.3	Trade Payables	23.5	23.3	25.9	21.3	20.2	
	.3	1.2	.6	Income Taxes Payable	.9	.4	.7	.3	.4	
	7.9	7.9	8.7	All Other Current	8.5	8.6	6.8	11.1	11.9	
	46.2	42.9	48.4	Total Current	50.7	46.8	48.9	49.8	46.2	
	12.4	14.1	14.4	Long Term Debt	24.5	13.0	12.4	11.1	11.6	
	.1	.1	.1	Deferred Taxes	.0	.2	.1	.0	.2	
	2.6	2.6	4.1	All Other-Non-Current	6.2	4.9	2.4	3.5	.6	
	38.7	40.3	33.0	Net Worth	18.6	35.0	36.2	35.6	41.4	
	100.0	100.0	100.0	Total Liabilities & Net Worth	100.0	100.0	100.0	100.0	100.0	
				INCOME DATA						
	100.0	100.0	100.0	Net Sales	100.0	100.0	100.0	100.0	100.0	
	35.9	35.7	34.0	Gross Profit	36.2	37.7	31.1	31.2	28.5	
	33.8	32.8	31.3	Operating Expenses	31.5	35.1	29.0	30.8	25.2	
	2.1	2.9	2.7	Operating Profit	4.7	2.6	2.0	.4	3.3	
	.4	.9	.4	All Other Expenses (net)	1.4	.5	.0	-.2	.1	
	1.7	2.0	2.3	Profit Before Taxes	3.3	2.1	2.1	.6	3.2	
				RATIOS						
	2.6	3.1	2.3		2.2	2.6	2.3	2.1	2.4	
	1.8	1.9	1.6	Current	1.5	1.7	1.6	1.5	1.6	
	1.3	1.4	1.3		1.1	1.3	1.3	1.3	1.5	
	1.4	1.5	1.2		1.0	1.3	1.4	1.1	1.3	
	.9	.9	.9	Quick	.7	.8	1.0	.9	1.0	
	.5	.7	.7		.6	.6	.6	.6	.9	
25	14.7	27 13.6	29 12.8		19 19.1	29 12.8	30 12.0	30 12.2	34 10.7	
34	10.8	35 10.5	38 9.5	Sales/Receivables	31 11.7	38 9.5	37 9.8	41 8.9	41 8.8	
43	8.5	43 8.5	46 7.9		44 8.3	47 7.8	45 8.1	47 7.8	48 7.6	
35	10.4	31 11.8	31 11.6		34 10.6	45 8.1	29 12.4	23 16.0	29 12.6	
64	5.7	58 6.3	55 6.6	Cost of Sales/Inventory	68 5.4	76 4.8	47 7.8	37 10.0	45 8.2	
107	3.4	99 3.7	91 4.0		118 3.1	118 3.1	81 4.5	66 5.5	65 5.6	
19	19.0	20 18.5	23 15.7		23 15.9	30 12.3	23 16.1	20 18.2	22 16.5	
30	12.1	30 12.0	34 10.6	Cost of Sales/Payables	34 10.6	40 9.2	31 11.6	25 14.4	30 12.2	
43	8.5	43 8.4	49 7.4		63 5.8	54 6.8	43 8.5	35 10.3	39 9.4	
	6.1	6.1	6.8		5.9	5.5	8.4	10.5	6.7	
	10.9	10.1	12.3	Sales/Working Capital	16.8	10.9	13.7	13.1	12.5	
	20.3	18.5	23.0		43.7	20.2	23.1	20.5	16.1	
	5.7	5.4	8.3		7.0	7.0	10.1	7.9	12.3	
(160)	2.5	(157) 2.6	(161) 3.5	EBIT/Interest	2.9 (53)	1.9 (28)	3.8 (23)	3.8 (14)	5.9	
	1.1	1.3	1.2		.9	.6	2.6	1.1	3.4	
	3.1	3.0	5.3			3.9	7.7	3.1		
(79)	1.4	(69) 1.3	(78) 2.0	Net Profit + Depr., Dep., Amort./Cur. Mat. L/T/D	(29) .9	(16) 2.7	(12) 2.0			
	.5	.6	.7		.1	.8	1.2			
	.2	.1	.2		.3	.1	.2	.3	.1	
	.4	.3	.4	Fixed/Worth	1.5	.4	.4	.4	.3	
	.8	.7	1.2		-3.0	1.4	.9	.8	.5	
	.8	.7	1.1		1.5	1.0	.8	1.1	1.1	
	1.7	1.7	2.3	Debt/Worth	3.9	2.2	2.3	2.2	1.6	
	3.1	3.5	5.5		-14.0	6.7	5.4	2.7	2.8	
	28.3	29.6	44.1		54.3	32.5	59.8	47.4	56.7	
(167)	10.6	(166) 13.4	(156) 16.4	% Profit Before Taxes/Tangible Net Worth	(25) 28.2	(53) 9.9	16.3	11.8	24.3	
	1.2	3.3	4.0		-1.2	1.7	7.5	1.4	14.0	
	9.7	9.8	11.2		12.5	10.8	11.4	9.6	14.6	
	4.0	4.4	5.3	% Profit Before Taxes/Total Assets	4.4	3.6	7.7	5.3	7.4	
	.4	1.3	.6		-1.1	-1.0	3.5	.4	5.8	
	52.6	69.9	56.8		43.6	76.4	53.0	53.6	69.8	
	31.0	31.2	29.2	Sales/Net Fixed Assets	20.8	34.5	26.7	31.3	48.8	
	15.6	17.3	15.2		10.8	14.9	18.5	13.3	16.3	
	4.3	4.4	4.4		4.2	4.5	4.8	5.1	4.4	
	3.2	3.3	3.3	Sales/Total Assets	3.2	3.0	3.6	3.9	3.6	
	2.5	2.7	2.6		2.0	2.3	3.0	2.9	3.1	
	.6	.6	.6		1.0	.5	.5	.5	.6	
(161)	1.0	(155) 1.0	(154) 1.0	% Depr., Dep., Amort./Sales	(30) 1.5	(54) .9	(27) .9	(22) .9	(14) .8	
	1.6	1.5	1.5		2.3	1.5	1.4	1.5	1.3	
	2.4	2.6	2.3		3.6	3.2	1.8	2.3		
(98)	4.1	(89) 4.7	(88) 4.1	% Officers', Directors', Owners' Comp/Sales	(15) 5.9	(33) 5.2	(14) 4.0	(16) 3.3		
	6.4	7.5	7.3		11.3	7.1	7.8	7.1		
	1022052M	787567M	1972500M	Net Sales ($)	20770M	104927M	112979M	175016M	216260M	1342548M
	355909M	226280M	749501M	Total Assets ($)	8248M	39965M	32671M	50267M	65291M	553059M

M = $ thousand   MM = $ million
See Pages 1 through 15 for Explanation of Ratios and Data

RETAILERS—BUILDING MATERIALS. SIC# 5211

	Current Data Sorted By Assets										Comparative Historical Data		
		6		6		3			1	# Postretirement Benefits			
										Type of Statement			
2		7		10		12	1		2	Unqualified		32	41
1		27		41		5				Reviewed		79	80
14		45		22		1				Compiled		90	98
4		8		1						Tax Returns		3	6
7		19		19		4				Other		45	40

	58 (4/1-9/30/94)				194 (10/1/94-3/31/95)							4/1/90-3/31/91	4/1/91-3/31/92
	0-500M	500M-2MM		2-10MM		10-50MM		50-100MM	100-250MM			ALL	ALL
	28	106		93		22		1	2	NUMBER OF STATEMENTS		249	265

ASSETS

	0-500M	500M-2MM	2-10MM	10-50MM	50-100MM	100-250MM	Item	4/1/90-3/31/91 ALL	4/1/91-3/31/92 ALL
	%	%	%	%	%	%		%	%
	8.0	3.7	5.1	4.5			Cash & Equivalents	6.4	6.0
	32.0	30.6	30.5	30.6			Trade Receivables - (net)	26.9	27.3
	35.0	40.7	34.0	30.7			Inventory	36.8	36.4
	.7	2.0	.9	3.3			All Other Current	2.0	2.1
	75.7	76.9	70.6	69.0			Total Current	72.1	71.8
	16.3	16.3	18.2	18.9			Fixed Assets (net)	21.3	19.5
	2.9	.8	.7	.8			Intangibles (net)	.5	.4
	5.1	6.0	10.5	11.2			All Other Non-Current	6.1	7.9
	100.0	100.0	100.0	100.0			Total	100.0	100.0

LIABILITIES

	0-500M	500M-2MM	2-10MM	10-50MM	50-100MM	100-250MM	Item	4/1/90-3/31/91 ALL	4/1/91-3/31/92 ALL
	8.5	11.5	12.9	12.2			Notes Payable-Short Term	12.4	12.3
	4.5	3.6	2.7	2.8			Cur. Mat. -L/T/D	4.8	3.6
	22.7	19.6	18.6	12.6			Trade Payables	16.4	17.3
	.5	.4	.5	.6			Income Taxes Payable	.6	.4
	9.2	6.8	6.1	13.3			All Other Current	7.2	7.2
	45.3	42.0	40.7	41.4			Total Current	41.4	40.8
	17.7	14.1	12.2	13.0			Long Term Debt	15.6	16.1
	.2	.1	.2	.4			Deferred Taxes	.2	.4
	.7	3.5	1.7	2.8			All Other-Non-Current	1.7	2.6
	36.2	40.3	45.2	42.3			Net Worth	41.2	40.1
	100.0	100.0	100.0	100.0			Total Liabilities & Net Worth	100.0	100.0

INCOME DATA

	0-500M	500M-2MM	2-10MM	10-50MM	50-100MM	100-250MM	Item	4/1/90-3/31/91 ALL	4/1/91-3/31/92 ALL
	100.0	100.0	100.0	100.0			Net Sales	100.0	100.0
	28.8	23.9	23.7	24.1			Gross Profit	28.2	27.2
	26.3	21.2	20.9	19.2			Operating Expenses	25.6	24.6
	2.4	2.7	2.9	4.9			Operating Profit	2.6	2.6
	–.3	.3	–.2	–.1			All Other Expenses (net)	.6	.5
	2.8	2.3	3.0	5.0			Profit Before Taxes	2.0	2.1

RATIOS

n	0-500M	n	500M-2MM	n	2-10MM	n	10-50MM	50-100MM	100-250MM	Item	nH	4/1/90-3/31/91 ALL	nH	4/1/91-3/31/92 ALL
	2.6		2.7		2.5		2.5			Current		3.0		2.9
	1.6		1.9		1.8		1.5					1.8		1.9
	1.1		1.4		1.3		1.2					1.3		1.3
	1.5		1.2		1.3		1.2			Quick		1.3		1.4
	.9		.8		.9		.9					.8		.8
	.6		.6		.6		.6					.6		.5
15	25.1	24	15.0	31	11.9	31	11.8			Sales/Receivables	23	15.9	25	14.5
33	11.2	38	9.7	37	9.9	39	9.4				33	11.0	35	10.4
57	6.4	46	7.9	46	7.9	49	7.4				45	8.2	46	7.9
31	11.8	44	8.3	42	8.7	41	9.0			Cost of Sales/Inventory	45	8.2	42	8.6
54	6.7	64	5.7	56	6.5	54	6.7				64	5.7	68	5.4
101	3.6	85	4.3	78	4.7	85	4.3				89	4.1	96	3.8
16	23.2	16	22.3	20	18.7	12	30.7			Cost of Sales/Payables	16	23.0	18	20.6
30	12.1	29	12.6	26	14.1	19	19.0				24	15.0	26	13.8
69	5.3	41	9.0	38	9.5	30	12.1				35	10.3	38	9.5
	6.8		6.0		6.3		5.1			Sales/Working Capital		5.7		5.1
	12.8		9.9		9.5		9.4					9.4		8.3
	42.2		13.1		19.0		22.5					18.9		17.2
(23)	7.8	(101)	6.2	(90)	9.6	(20)	9.6			EBIT/Interest	(226)	3.9	(249)	4.2
	4.3		3.2		3.9		4.4					2.0		1.8
	1.6		2.0		2.1		2.6					1.1		1.0
		(48)	3.1	(42)	5.3	(10)	7.6			Net Profit + Depr., Dep.,	(140)	4.3	(125)	5.6
			2.1		2.2		3.9			Amort./Cur. Mat. L /T/D		1.6		1.6
			.8		1.2		1.7					.6		.4
	.2		.2		.2		.2			Fixed/Worth		.2		.2
	.4		.3		.4		.5					.4		.5
	.9		.8		.7		.8					1.0		1.0
	1.4		.8		.7		1.0			Debt/Worth		.7		.7
	2.4		1.6		1.1		1.7					1.5		1.7
	3.2		3.2		2.2		2.5					2.9		3.5
(26)	64.3	(103)	32.4	(90)	26.1		34.2			% Profit Before Taxes/Tangible	(233)	25.7	(253)	23.9
	33.3		15.1		14.2		22.0			Net Worth		10.2		8.4
	5.6		8.0		8.2		16.9					2.9		.8
	22.7		10.8		12.2		13.7			% Profit Before Taxes/Total		10.0		9.1
	9.5		6.1		6.3		9.3			Assets		4.2		3.2
	.9		2.9		2.8		4.9					.4		.2
	62.1		46.8		34.4		34.2			Sales/Net Fixed Assets		35.4		34.2
	29.9		25.1		18.2		12.7					18.3		17.2
	12.9		13.5		10.6		8.6					8.8		9.2
	4.8		3.9		3.6		3.6			Sales/Total Assets		3.6		3.3
	3.4		3.0		2.9		2.6					2.8		2.7
	2.1		2.6		2.3		1.7					2.3		2.0
(21)	.5	(101)	.6	(90)	.6	(20)	.7			% Depr., Dep., Amort./Sales	(231)	.8	(247)	.7
	.9		.9		.9		1.0					1.2		1.0
	1.5		1.3		1.3		1.3					1.8		1.7
(11)	2.1	(49)	1.7	(42)	1.3					% Officers', Directors',	(130)	1.9	(118)	1.4
	4.0		2.5		2.4					Owners' Comp/Sales		2.9		3.0
	5.5		3.7		3.7							5.2		5.3

0-500M	500M-2MM	2-10MM	10-50MM	50-100MM	100-250MM	Item	4/1/90-3/31/91 ALL	4/1/91-3/31/92 ALL
28118M	392326M	1190672M	1077589M	30258M	1195104M	Net Sales ($)	1852197M	2444481M
8035M	123292M	406783M	376041M	75046M	417116M	Total Assets ($)	696561M	986248M

M = $ thousand   MM = $ million
See Pages 1 through 15 for Explanation of Ratios and Data

Comparative Historical Data | Current Data Sorted By Sales

10	6	16	# Postretirement Benefits / Type of Statement	2	3	4	4	3	
36	24	34	Unqualified	2	4	3	2	9	14
82	72	74	Reviewed	1	11	8	26	21	7
101	81	82	Compiled	9	25	15	22	9	2
8	9	13	Tax Returns	1	9	2	1		
43	39	49	Other	6	7	12	13	8	3
4/1/92-3/31/93 ALL	4/1/93-3/31/94 ALL	4/1/94-3/31/95 ALL		58 (4/1-9/30/94)			194 (10/1/94-3/31/95)		
				0-1MM	1-3MM	3-5MM	5-10MM	10-25MM	25MM & OVER
270	225	252	**NUMBER OF STATEMENTS**	19	56	40	64	47	26
%	%	%	**ASSETS**	%	%	%	%	%	%
5.5	6.2	4.8	Cash & Equivalents	8.2	4.6	2.9	4.1	4.9	6.9
28.9	29.2	30.5	Trade Receivables - (net)	30.7	25.5	31.5	32.2	34.3	28.4
36.8	35.6	36.7	Inventory	39.6	40.3	36.8	35.6	35.0	32.5
2.1	1.3	1.6	All Other Current	.1	1.9	2.2	1.3	1.8	1.1
73.2	72.3	73.6	Total Current	78.7	72.3	73.4	73.2	76.0	68.9
18.4	20.0	17.5	Fixed Assets (net)	17.2	17.9	17.4	16.0	17.0	21.3
1.1	.9	1.0	Intangibles (net)	1.0	2.4	.4	.3	.9	.7
7.3	6.8	8.0	All Other Non-Current	3.1	7.4	8.7	10.4	6.0	9.0
100.0	100.0	100.0	Total	100.0	100.0	100.0	100.0	100.0	100.0
			LIABILITIES						
12.4	11.6	11.6	Notes Payable-Short Term	9.1	12.0	13.6	9.9	15.2	7.4
3.4	3.1	3.2	Cur. Mat.-L /T/D	4.2	4.4	3.8	2.9	1.7	2.9
17.9	17.7	18.9	Trade Payables	20.3	18.8	20.9	19.6	16.6	17.6
.4	.6	.4	Income Taxes Payable	.4	.4	.6	.2	.8	.3
6.8	7.6	7.4	All Other Current	7.3	6.8	7.8	5.8	8.0	11.4
40.9	40.6	41.7	Total Current	41.3	42.3	46.7	38.4	42.3	39.6
13.4	13.0	13.8	Long Term Debt	19.2	15.8	14.3	11.3	11.9	14.6
.3	.2	.2	Deferred Taxes	.2	.1	.1	.3	.2	.3
2.9	3.7	2.4	All Other-Non-Current	5.8	2.6	2.8	1.7	1.7	2.1
42.5	42.5	41.9	Net Worth	33.5	39.1	36.1	48.3	44.0	43.5
100.0	100.0	100.0	Total Liabilities & Net Worth	100.0	100.0	100.0	100.0	100.0	100.0
			INCOME DATA						
100.0	100.0	100.0	Net Sales	100.0	100.0	100.0	100.0	100.0	100.0
27.8	26.8	24.4	Gross Profit	29.8	26.2	24.2	22.8	23.7	22.2
25.3	23.9	21.5	Operating Expenses	27.6	23.5	21.4	19.5	20.8	18.9
2.5	3.0	2.9	Operating Profit	2.2	2.7	2.8	3.2	2.9	3.3
.3	.3	.0	All Other Expenses (net)	−.8	.4	.2	−.1	−.1	.3
2.2	2.7	2.9	Profit Before Taxes	3.0	2.3	2.6	3.4	3.1	3.0
			RATIOS						
2.9 / 1.8 / 1.3	2.6 / 1.8 / 1.4	2.6 / 1.8 / 1.3	Current	3.6 / 2.0 / 1.3	2.5 / 1.8 / 1.4	2.1 / 1.5 / 1.3	2.7 / 1.9 / 1.4	2.8 / 1.8 / 1.4	2.5 / 1.9 / 1.3
1.4 / .8 / .5	1.3 / .9 / .6	1.3 / .9 / .6	Quick	1.6 / 1.2 / .6	1.1 / .7 / .7	1.0 / .7 / .6	1.3 / .9 / .7	1.3 / .9 / .7	1.2 / .9 / .7
24 15.0 / 37 10.0 / 50 7.3	26 14.1 / 37 9.8 / 47 7.7	27 13.5 / 37 9.8 / 47 7.8	Sales/Receivables	14 26.8 / 43 8.4 / 63 5.8	23 16.0 / 35 10.4 / 45 8.2	27 13.4 / 40 9.1 / 49 7.5	28 12.9 / 37 9.9 / 45 8.1	31 11.9 / 38 9.7 / 50 7.3	26 13.9 / 35 10.5 / 40 9.2
45 8.2 / 65 5.6 / 99 3.7	36 10.2 / 59 6.2 / 94 3.9	41 8.8 / 58 6.3 / 83 4.4	Cost of Sales/Inventory	42 8.7 / 91 4.0 / 107 3.4	56 6.5 / 73 5.0 / 94 3.9	44 8.3 / 58 6.3 / 83 4.4	32 11.3 / 52 7.0 / 68 5.4	43 8.4 / 54 6.8 / 73 5.0	34 10.8 / 46 7.9 / 74 4.9
17 20.9 / 26 14.2 / 40 9.2	19 19.1 / 27 13.4 / 39 9.3	16 22.2 / 26 13.8 / 40 9.2	Cost of Sales/Payables	16 23.3 / 33 11.0 / 64 5.7	17 21.7 / 31 11.7 / 55 6.6	17 21.7 / 31 11.7 / 47 7.7	19 19.2 / 25 14.6 / 37 10.0	15 23.9 / 24 15.5 / 33 11.0	14 25.6 / 20 17.9 / 37 9.9
5.2 / 9.2 / 16.1	5.8 / 9.1 / 18.2	6.2 / 9.6 / 17.0	Sales/Working Capital	3.2 / 7.8 / 21.7	5.6 / 8.9 / 16.0	6.9 / 11.2 / 17.5	6.6 / 9.6 / 17.8	5.8 / 9.3 / 15.5	7.1 / 10.6 / 21.4
(248) 7.5 / 2.8 / 1.3	(206) 8.2 / 3.1 / 1.8	(237) 8.3 / 3.7 / 2.1	EBIT/Interest	(15) 6.8 / 4.3 / 1.7	(53) 7.3 / 2.9 / 1.5	(39) 5.1 / 3.0 / 1.4	(61) 11.6 / 4.4 / 2.2	(44) 8.1 / 3.9 / 2.3	(25) 9.5 / 5.4 / 3.2
(114) 6.9 / 2.2 / 1.0	(80) 4.7 / 1.9 / .7	(104) 4.4 / 2.3 / 1.2	Net Profit + Depr., Dep., Amort./Cur. Mat. L/T/D		(22) 2.7 / 2.1 / .7	(19) 3.8 / 1.6 / .6	(25) 5.9 / 1.9 / 1.2	(22) 5.1 / 3.6 / 1.9	(14) 11.3 / 4.1 / 1.7
.2 / .4 / .8	.2 / .4 / .9	.2 / .4 / .7	Fixed/Worth	.2 / .5 / 1.0	.2 / .4 / 1.0	.2 / .4 / .7	.1 / .3 / .7	.2 / .3 / .5	.3 / .6 / .8
.6 / 1.4 / 2.6	.7 / 1.5 / 2.6	.8 / 1.5 / 2.9	Debt/Worth	1.1 / 2.7 / 3.5	.9 / 1.8 / 3.1	.9 / 2.0 / 3.6	.5 / 1.3 / 2.3	.7 / 1.2 / 2.3	1.0 / 1.2 / 2.0
(251) 28.8 / 13.3 / 4.2	(213) 31.8 / 14.5 / 5.7	(244) 30.8 / 17.1 / 8.2	% Profit Before Taxes/Tangible Net Worth	(18) 64.3 / 27.7 / 7.6	(53) 40.3 / 17.1 / 6.0	(39) 30.6 / 17.2 / 6.4	(44) 27.8 / 13.3 / 8.6	24.4 / 17.4 / 11.5	34.1 / 20.0 / 12.7
11.3 / 5.0 / 1.3	12.8 / 6.2 / 2.3	12.2 / 6.6 / 3.0	% Profit Before Taxes/Total Assets	16.1 / 6.4 / .7	11.7 / 6.1 / 1.9	10.5 / 5.5 / 1.3	11.9 / 6.5 / 3.4	13.4 / 8.0 / 3.1	13.0 / 9.3 / 5.7
37.6 / 21.2 / 10.2	37.3 / 19.0 / 10.2	39.9 / 21.6 / 11.6	Sales/Net Fixed Assets	76.7 / 21.5 / 7.6	49.6 / 21.8 / 10.7	34.9 / 20.4 / 12.1	46.1 / 23.9 / 13.3	36.9 / 20.9 / 12.3	38.0 / 15.3 / 8.6
3.5 / 2.8 / 2.1	3.6 / 2.9 / 2.2	3.8 / 2.9 / 2.4	Sales/Total Assets	4.2 / 2.2 / 1.6	3.3 / 2.8 / 2.2	3.4 / 2.8 / 2.5	4.1 / 3.3 / 2.6	3.8 / 2.9 / 2.3	4.0 / 3.1 / 2.5
(249) .7 / 1.0 / 1.4	(211) .6 / .9 / 1.5	(235) .6 / .9 / 1.3	% Depr., Dep., Amort./Sales	(13) .7 / 1.1 / 2.3	(53) .7 / 1.0 / 1.8	(39) .5 / 1.0 / 1.3	(60) .6 / .9 / 1.3	(45) .5 / .7 / 1.0	(25) .7 / 1.0 / 1.3
(116) 1.5 / 3.0 / 5.3	(115) 1.5 / 2.9 / 4.8	(107) 1.7 / 2.5 / 3.9	% Officers', Directors', Owners' Comp/Sales		(28) 2.0 / 2.6 / 4.0	(19) 1.7 / 3.2 / 4.8	(29) 1.4 / 2.5 / 3.4	(18) 1.2 / 2.2 / 4.7	
3963326M	3037699M	3914067M	Net Sales ($)	13494M	110158M	156555M	455033M	738967M	2439860M
1688230M	1214517M	1406313M	Total Assets ($)	5816M	45458M	60403M	161732M	277521M	855383M

© Robert Morris Associates 1995

M = $ thousand   MM = $ million
See Pages 1 through 15 for Explanation of Ratios and Data

Current Data Sorted By Assets

Comparative Historical Data

0-500M	500M-2MM	2-10MM	10-50MM	50-100MM	100-250MM	# Postretirement Benefits / Type of Statement	4/1/90-3/31/91 ALL	4/1/91-3/31/92 ALL
4	10	3		1				
	9	9	5	3	3	Unqualified	24	22
8	38	23				Reviewed	67	67
68	61	16				Compiled	169	173
18	11	1				Tax Returns	10	12
31	32	19	1			Other	86	68
	104 (4/1-9/30/94)		252 (10/1/94-3/31/95)					
125	151	68	6	3	3	NUMBER OF STATEMENTS	356	342
%	%	%	%	%	%	**ASSETS**	%	%
5.4	5.3	4.6				Cash & Equivalents	5.5	4.5
11.2	15.0	14.0				Trade Receivables - (net)	10.9	12.7
57.5	51.1	48.8				Inventory	54.7	53.7
1.1	.8	1.6				All Other Current	1.6	1.2
75.2	72.2	69.0				Total Current	72.6	72.2
12.8	15.0	19.8				Fixed Assets (net)	15.8	15.2
1.1	1.4	1.3				Intangibles (net)	.7	1.4
10.9	11.4	9.9				All Other Non-Current	10.8	11.2
100.0	100.0	100.0				Total	100.0	100.0
						LIABILITIES		
8.7	7.5	10.9				Notes Payable-Short Term	9.6	10.5
3.9	4.1	3.6				Cur. Mat. -L/T/D	3.9	3.8
14.5	16.9	19.1				Trade Payables	15.1	15.8
.4	.2	.5				Income Taxes Payable	.3	.4
5.7	8.1	5.6				All Other Current	8.0	7.3
33.3	36.9	39.8				Total Current	36.9	37.7
25.7	19.7	12.9				Long Term Debt	23.0	21.3
.1	.1	.1				Deferred Taxes	.2	.1
4.7	5.4	3.8				All Other-Non-Current	4.1	4.0
36.2	37.9	43.4				Net Worth	35.7	36.8
100.0	100.0	100.0				Total Liabilities & Net Worth	100.0	100.0
						INCOME DATA		
100.0	100.0	100.0				Net Sales	100.0	100.0
34.7	33.5	33.1				Gross Profit	34.6	34.5
32.1	31.2	30.7				Operating Expenses	31.6	32.2
2.6	2.3	2.4				Operating Profit	3.0	2.3
.5	.6	-.1				All Other Expenses (net)	1.2	.7
2.1	1.7	2.5				Profit Before Taxes	1.8	1.6
						RATIOS		
4.3	3.1	2.4					3.3	3.2
2.7	2.0	1.7				Current	2.1	2.1
1.7	1.5	1.3					1.4	1.4
.9	1.0	.8					.8	.8
.5	.5	.4				Quick	.4 (341)	.5
.2	.2	.2					.2	.2
8 45.4	8 44.2	8 47.5					6 57.6	8 47.8
13 27.1	16 22.7	17 21.9				Sales/Receivables	13 28.5	15 24.6
22 16.8	32 11.5	29 12.4					25 14.8	28 13.1
91 4.0	89 4.1	81 4.5					99 3.7	96 3.8
146 2.5	122 3.0	118 3.1				Cost of Sales/Inventory	140 2.6	140 2.6
192 1.9	174 2.1	159 2.3					183 2.0	192 1.9
13 28.6	20 18.0	25 14.8					18 20.2	19 18.8
27 13.7	34 10.8	38 9.6				Cost of Sales/Payables	31 11.6	32 11.3
45 8.2	53 6.9	56 6.5					51 7.1	48 7.6
3.7	4.3	5.1					4.1	4.1
5.2	6.8	8.8				Sales/Working Capital	6.4	6.5
9.5	10.8	15.4					12.2	12.9
(111) 5.8	(143) 4.6	(63) 7.2					(336) 4.4	(326) 4.2
3.0	2.0	2.8				EBIT/Interest	2.0	1.9
1.1	1.1	1.5					.8	.9
(30) 2.6	(53) 3.2	(29) 5.7					(157) 4.1	(125) 2.8
1.7	1.6	1.4				Net Profit + Depr., Dep., Amort./Cur. Mat. L/T/D	1.3	1.4
.5	.5	.7					.4	.3
.1	.1	.2					.1	.1
.3	.3	.4				Fixed/Worth	.4	.3
1.2	1.2	.8					1.2	1.1
.6	.8	.8					.8	.7
1.8	1.8	1.4				Debt/Worth	1.9	1.7
8.4	4.2	2.9					5.1	4.9
(109) 37.8	(139) 24.6	(66) 22.3					(328) 28.1	(302) 26.5
13.3	10.2	11.1				% Profit Before Taxes/Tangible Net Worth	11.8	9.0
2.6	1.4	3.6					.6	1.9
12.0	8.1	10.3					9.4	8.8
4.7	3.3	4.7				% Profit Before Taxes/Total Assets	3.9	3.5
.2	.4	1.6					-.7	-.2
57.2	57.6	33.4					56.5	54.3
25.1	26.2	17.5				Sales/Net Fixed Assets	21.9	24.2
14.7	8.9	7.7					9.1	10.2
3.0	3.0	2.9					2.8	2.8
2.3	2.3	2.4				Sales/Total Assets	2.3	2.2
1.9	1.7	1.8					1.7	1.7
(103) .8	(143) .5	(65) .6					(306) .7	(311) .6
1.2	1.0	1.0				% Depr., Dep., Amort./Sales	1.1	1.0
1.8	2.0	1.4					1.9	1.7
(61) 3.1	(88) 1.8	(35) 1.4					(193) 2.5	(177) 2.6
4.7	3.3	2.7				% Officers', Directors', Owners' Comp/Sales	4.3	4.5
7.5	5.4	4.8					6.9	7.2
96992M	379275M	650818M	307049M	598781M	946254M	Net Sales ($)	2132647M	2039729M
39760M	157368M	255585M	153703M	196196M	374895M	Total Assets ($)	818793M	973376M

M = $ thousand   MM = $ million
See Pages 1 through 15 for Explanation of Ratios and Data

RETAILERS—HARDWARE. SIC# 5251

Comparative Historical Data				Current Data Sorted By Sales					
4	9	18	**# Postretirement Benefits / Type of Statement**	4	7	2	4		1
17	31	29	Unqualified		9	3	3	4	10
58	62	69	Reviewed	5	21	16	19	7	1
162	133	145	Compiled	60	53	19	10	3	
14	16	30	Tax Returns	18	9	2	1		
77	73	83	Other	31	28	5	12	4	3
4/1/92-3/31/93 ALL	4/1/93-3/31/94 ALL	4/1/94-3/31/95 ALL		104 (4/1-9/30/94)			252 (10/1/94-3/31/95)		
				0-1MM	1-3MM	3-5MM	5-10MM	10-25MM	25MM & OVER
328	315	356	**NUMBER OF STATEMENTS**	114	120	45	45	18	14
%	%	%	**ASSETS**	%	%	%	%	%	%
4.7	4.5	5.1	Cash & Equivalents	5.8	5.2	4.0	5.4	4.8	2.7
12.8	13.5	13.3	Trade Receivables - (net)	9.2	13.0	17.7	17.9	18.2	15.5
54.1	53.0	52.9	Inventory	57.8	51.7	51.4	48.3	48.8	48.7
1.4	1.5	1.1	All Other Current	1.0	1.0	1.0	1.6	1.4	1.3
72.9	72.5	72.5	Total Current	73.8	70.8	74.1	73.2	73.2	68.2
15.8	15.5	15.4	Fixed Assets (net)	14.5	15.7	13.1	16.9	15.7	21.0
.9	1.4	1.4	Intangibles (net)	1.1	1.5	2.1	.4	1.2	4.6
10.4	10.5	10.7	All Other Non-Current	10.6	11.9	10.7	9.5	9.9	6.2
100.0	100.0	100.0	Total	100.0	100.0	100.0	100.0	100.0	100.0
			LIABILITIES						
9.3	8.4	8.8	Notes Payable-Short Term	9.3	6.7	8.9	9.4	16.0	12.7
4.0	3.5	3.9	Cur. Mat.-L./T/D	3.8	4.4	3.7	3.4	4.0	2.1
16.2	16.2	16.7	Trade Payables	13.0	15.8	19.8	21.0	18.5	28.0
.3	1.0	.4	Income Taxes Payable	.4	.2	.3	.4	.8	.3
7.1	7.9	6.8	All Other Current	6.6	7.0	6.8	6.2	6.1	8.9
36.9	37.0	36.5	Total Current	33.1	34.1	39.6	40.4	45.4	52.0
18.4	19.4	20.3	Long Term Debt	27.7	20.6	16.9	13.4	5.0	9.5
.1	.2	.1	Deferred Taxes	.1	.1	.1	.1	.3	1.2
4.4	4.6	4.7	All Other-Non-Current	5.3	4.9	4.6	3.4	5.6	2.0
40.3	38.8	38.3	Net Worth	33.8	40.4	38.8	42.8	43.7	35.2
100.0	100.0	100.0	Total Liabilities & Net Worth	100.0	100.0	100.0	100.0	100.0	100.0
			INCOME DATA						
100.0	100.0	100.0	Net Sales	100.0	100.0	100.0	100.0	100.0	100.0
34.9	34.5	33.7	Gross Profit	35.0	33.7	32.1	33.7	33.4	29.2
32.9	32.4	31.2	Operating Expenses	32.6	31.7	29.6	30.0	31.5	25.4
2.0	2.1	2.5	Operating Profit	2.5	1.9	2.5	3.7	2.0	3.7
.4	.5	.4	All Other Expenses (net)	.8	.3	.8	-.1	-.1	.6
1.6	1.6	2.0	Profit Before Taxes	1.7	1.7	1.7	3.8	2.1	3.1
			RATIOS						
3.3	3.4	3.5		4.2	3.5	2.3	2.7	2.4	1.7
2.2	2.0	2.0	Current	2.7	2.1	1.9	1.7	1.6	1.3
1.4	1.5	1.5		1.6	1.6	1.6	1.4	1.2	1.1
.9	.8	.9		.8	.9	1.1	.9	.9	.5
.4	(314) .5	.4	Quick	.4	.5	.5	.4	.5	.3
.2	.2	.2		.2	.2	.2	.3	.2	.2
8 47.9	7 49.2	8 47.0		7 50.8	9 41.4	7 52.8	9 38.9	8 46.6	4 81.6
14 26.1	14 25.3	15 25.0	Sales/Receivables	13 28.6	14 25.2	17 21.1	19 19.7	24 15.2	7 48.9
29 12.6	30 12.3	28 13.0		21 17.2	29 12.4	33 11.2	33 11.0	44 8.3	34 10.7
96 3.8	89 4.1	89 4.1		114 3.2	91 4.0	64 5.7	81 4.5	78 4.7	64 5.7
135 2.7	130 2.8	130 2.8	Cost of Sales/Inventory	174 2.1	126 2.9	94 3.9	104 3.5	96 3.8	89 4.1
183 2.0	174 2.1	174 2.1		228 1.6	159 2.3	152 2.4	146 2.5	126 2.9	126 2.9
20 18.4	17 21.2	18 20.0		13 28.4	18 20.0	20 17.9	24 15.1	27 13.7	28 13.1
32 11.4	36 10.2	32 11.3	Cost of Sales/Payables	29 12.6	31 11.9	36 10.1	36 10.2	38 9.7	47 7.7
51 7.1	53 6.9	53 6.9		50 7.3	55 6.6	52 7.0	54 6.8	47 7.7	78 4.7
4.2	4.1	4.2		3.2	4.3	4.9	5.3	5.6	8.3
6.3	6.3	6.6	Sales/Working Capital	4.7	6.4	9.0	9.0	10.2	17.6
12.2	11.8	11.5		7.9	9.7	12.5	14.6	17.9	34.6
(304) 4.3	(285) 5.0	(328) 5.5		(100) 5.0	(114) 4.8	(42) 5.3	(43) 6.6	(16) 11.5	(13) 10.5
1.9	2.2	2.4	EBIT/Interest	2.0	2.0	2.9	2.8	5.3	5.4
1.0	1.0	1.2		.9	1.0	1.3	1.5	2.0	2.6
(130) 3.1	(114) 4.0	(118) 3.8		(21) 2.7	(40) 2.4	(23) 5.3	(20) 3.6		
1.2	1.7	1.6	Net Profit + Depr., Dep., Amort./Cur. Mat. L/T/D	1.7	1.3	2.0	1.2		
.4	.5	.6		.3	.3	.8	.7		
.1	.1	.1		.1	.1	.1	.2	.2	.4
.3	.4	.3	Fixed/Worth	.3	.3	.3	.4	.3	.6
.9	1.0	1.1		2.9	1.1	.7	1.0	.5	1.1
.6	.7	.8		.8	.6	.9	.8	.7	1.2
1.6	1.6	1.7	Debt/Worth	1.9	1.6	1.8	1.3	1.5	2.6
3.8	4.1	4.0		12.2	4.2	3.4	3.0	2.5	3.6
(304) 19.3	(288) 25.6	(325) 28.8		(96) 33.0	(114) 27.3	(41) 25.6	(44) 23.7	(17) 26.1	(13) 41.9
8.1	11.6	12.8	% Profit Before Taxes/Tangible Net Worth	11.2	11.3	14.0	14.0	14.7	23.3
.7	2.9	2.4		.2	1.3	5.6	6.9	6.8	12.5
7.5	9.5	9.8		10.4	8.7	9.1	13.3	11.0	10.6
2.9	4.5	4.2	% Profit Before Taxes/Total Assets	3.7	3.3	4.6	5.8	4.9	8.3
.0	.2	.6		-1.1	.3	1.7	1.9	2.2	4.9
44.0	49.7	51.1		54.4	51.9	62.3	52.1	41.8	34.5
20.4	23.2	23.1	Sales/Net Fixed Assets	19.5	26.3	25.9	19.7	20.6	16.1
10.6	11.8	10.9		10.6	9.1	12.4	11.1	13.3	8.1
2.9	2.9	3.0		2.5	2.9	3.6	3.2	3.1	3.8
2.3	2.4	2.3	Sales/Total Assets	2.0	2.3	2.9	2.5	2.6	3.1
1.8	1.7	1.8		1.6	1.8	2.2	1.9	2.1	1.9
(296) .7	(276) .6	(321) .6		(93) .8	(113) .5	(42) .7	(16) .5	(12) .6	.5
1.1	1.0	1.0	% Depr., Dep., Amort./Sales	1.4	1.0	.9	.9	.9	.9
1.7	1.7	1.7		1.9	1.9	1.6	1.4	1.2	1.3
(169) 2.4	(170) 2.2	(184) 2.0		(59) 3.2	(65) 1.8	(27) 1.7	(24) 1.4		
4.3	4.0	3.5	% Officers', Directors', Owners' Comp/Sales	5.2	3.3	3.3	2.9		
7.4	6.6	5.9		8.0	5.1	4.3	5.9		
2686580M	4765100M	2979169M	Net Sales ($)	73276M	214058M	176298M	312449M	270282M	1932806M
1204365M	1985064M	1177507M	Total Assets ($)	40524M	105914M	69759M	127704M	110956M	722650M

M = $ thousand   MM = $ million
See Pages 1 through 15 for Explanation of Ratios and Data

Current Data Sorted By Assets / Comparative Historical Data

						# Postretirement Benefits Type of Statement		
4	17	22	7	1	1			
	9	41	42	6	5	Unqualified	96	83
12	75	105	19			Reviewed	198	192
33	115	48	4			Compiled	221	201
8	10	1				Tax Returns	4	14
10	58	50	12		2	Other	109	96
	128 (4/1-9/30/94)		537 (10/1/94-3/31/95)				4/1/90-3/31/91 ALL	4/1/91-3/31/92 ALL
0-500M	500M-2MM	2-10MM	10-50MM	50-100MM	100-250MM			
63	267	245	77	6	7	NUMBER OF STATEMENTS	628	586

ASSETS

0-500M	500M-2MM	2-10MM	10-50MM	50-100MM	100-250MM		Hist. ALL 4/1/90-3/31/91	Hist. ALL 4/1/91-3/31/92
%	%	%	%	%	%	**ASSETS**	%	%
8.1	4.7	5.4	4.7			Cash & Equivalents	4.8	5.6
23.1	30.0	32.1	28.9			Trade Receivables - (net)	28.1	27.1
40.0	38.4	35.0	31.8			Inventory	37.0	36.5
.4	1.0	1.9	2.6			All Other Current	2.3	1.8
71.7	74.1	74.4	68.0			Total Current	72.3	71.0
21.8	17.4	17.6	23.4			Fixed Assets (net)	19.5	19.8
1.7	1.0	.7	.8			Intangibles (net)	.6	.8
4.8	7.5	7.4	7.8			All Other Non-Current	7.6	8.4
100.0	100.0	100.0	100.0			Total	100.0	100.0

LIABILITIES

0-500M	500M-2MM	2-10MM	10-50MM	50-100MM	100-250MM		Hist. 1	Hist. 2
8.4	12.1	16.3	15.4			Notes Payable-Short Term	13.3	12.7
4.6	3.0	2.6	3.1			Cur. Mat. -L/T/D	3.2	3.5
19.6	18.0	15.8	12.3			Trade Payables	15.6	15.1
.4	.3	.5	.4			Income Taxes Payable	.5	.4
8.4	7.3	6.9	7.8			All Other Current	6.8	6.9
41.3	40.7	42.0	38.9			Total Current	39.4	38.7
18.1	12.8	10.8	13.2			Long Term Debt	14.3	13.8
.0	.1	.3	.6			Deferred Taxes	.3	.2
6.6	4.3	3.0	2.2			All Other-Non-Current	2.4	3.0
34.0	42.1	43.8	45.1			Net Worth	43.6	44.3
100.0	100.0	100.0	100.0			Total Liabilities & Net Worth	100.0	100.0

INCOME DATA

0-500M	500M-2MM	2-10MM	10-50MM	50-100MM	100-250MM		Hist. 1	Hist. 2
100.0	100.0	100.0	100.0			Net Sales	100.0	100.0
28.4	25.1	23.5	23.4			Gross Profit	25.2	26.3
25.9	22.4	21.0	19.1			Operating Expenses	23.4	24.9
2.5	2.7	2.4	4.3			Operating Profit	1.8	1.4
.5	.3	.2	.6			All Other Expenses (net)	.4	.5
2.1	2.4	2.2	3.7			Profit Before Taxes	1.4	1.0

RATIOS

0-500M	500M-2MM	2-10MM	10-50MM	50-100MM	100-250MM		Hist. 1	Hist. 2
3.1	2.8	2.5	2.5			Current	3.0	2.9
2.0	1.9	1.7	1.8				1.9	1.9
1.3	1.4	1.4	1.3				1.4	1.4
1.4	1.3	1.3	1.2			Quick	1.3	1.4
.8	.9	.9	.8				.8	.9
.4	.6	.6	.6				.5	.5
8 43.2	26 14.3	30 12.0	28 13.2			Sales/Receivables	24 15.0	25 14.8
23 16.0	35 10.4	39 9.3	39 9.4				36 10.2	37 10.0
38 9.6	43 8.4	51 7.1	48 7.6				47 7.7	49 7.5
30 12.0	41 8.8	40 9.2	44 8.3			Cost of Sales/Inventory	46 8.0	46 7.9
64 5.7	63 5.8	59 6.2	59 6.2				68 5.4	70 5.2
99 3.7	91 4.0	78 4.7	76 4.8				91 4.0	94 3.9
11 32.2	17 21.7	16 22.6	15 24.8			Cost of Sales/Payables	15 24.4	15 24.3
28 13.1	26 13.9	23 15.6	19 19.5				23 15.7	23 15.6
46 8.0	37 9.8	34 10.6	28 13.1				35 10.4	35 10.4
5.6	5.8	6.3	6.4			Sales/Working Capital	5.2	5.1
10.5	9.2	9.1	9.4				8.6	8.3
45.3	16.4	17.2	16.5				16.1	14.8
(54) 6.0	(249) 6.7	(229) 6.8	(75) 8.1			EBIT/Interest	(579) 4.4	(544) 4.1
2.1	2.7	2.9	4.1				2.0	1.8
1.3	1.5	1.6	2.2				1.0	.8
(15) 4.6	(82) 3.8	(107) 5.0	(43) 8.8			Net Profit + Depr., Dep., Amort./Cur. Mat. L /T/D	(331) 4.8	(284) 3.5
1.1	1.7	2.3	3.3				1.9	1.3
.3	1.0	1.1	1.4				.7	.3
.2	.2	.2	.3			Fixed/Worth	.2	.2
.7	.4	.4	.5				.4	.4
2.4	.9	.7	1.0				.8	.8
.8	.7	.7	.7			Debt/Worth	.7	.6
2.0	1.3	1.4	1.5				1.3	1.2
5.7	3.1	2.4	2.2				2.6	2.6
(53) 58.7	(253) 32.1	(240) 27.3	(76) 31.1			% Profit Before Taxes/Tangible Net Worth	(592) 20.0	(556) 16.8
18.9	11.7	13.5	20.8				8.8	6.8
4.5	3.7	6.0	11.0				.8	-1.0
14.2	12.7	11.8	15.1			% Profit Before Taxes/Total Assets	8.5	7.5
4.8	5.1	6.2	8.8				3.8	2.7
1.4	1.4	2.0	4.1				.1	-1.0
50.2	41.9	33.6	22.3			Sales/Net Fixed Assets	34.0	31.3
23.7	23.9	20.6	15.3				17.9	17.2
10.5	11.6	11.0	7.4				9.1	8.8
5.1	3.8	3.5	3.2			Sales/Total Assets	3.5	3.2
3.6	3.0	2.8	2.8				2.6	2.6
2.3	2.3	2.3	2.1				2.1	2.0
(56) .6	(239) .6	(233) .6	(72) .7			% Depr., Dep., Amort./Sales	(587) .7	(559) .7
1.2	.9	.8	1.0				1.0	1.1
1.5	1.4	1.1	1.5				1.6	1.6
(29) 2.6	(132) 1.9	(108) 1.1	(24) .9			% Officers', Directors', Owners' Comp/Sales	(296) 1.6	(290) 1.9
4.6	2.9	2.0	1.5				3.2	3.3
6.6	4.8	3.2	3.2				5.4	5.4
76507M	925994M	3122171M	4337445M	1130439M	3429408M	Net Sales ($)	7654678M	7547329M
20490M	295961M	1085249M	1641110M	453792M	1257177M	Total Assets ($)	3389058M	3012902M

M = $ thousand   MM = $ million
See Pages 1 through 15 for Explanation of Ratios and Data

Comparative Historical Data / Current Data Sorted By Sales

	17	29	52	# Postretirement Benefits / Type of Statement	2	8	9	12	9	12
	100	94	103	Unqualified		4	4	12	27	56
	228	207	211	Reviewed	8	32	39	64	41	27
	219	217	200	Compiled	20	76	42	34	23	5
	11	12	19	Tax Returns	2	12	3	2		
	101	123	132	Other	7	30	22	26	29	18
	4/1/92-3/31/93 ALL	4/1/93-3/31/94 ALL	4/1/94-3/31/95 ALL		128 (4/1-9/30/94) 0-1MM	1-3MM	3-5MM	537 (10/1/94-3/31/95) 5-10MM	10-25MM	25MM & OVER
	659	653	665	NUMBER OF STATEMENTS	37	154	110	138	120	106
	%	%	%	**ASSETS**	%	%	%	%	%	%
	4.5	5.0	5.3	Cash & Equivalents	8.5	5.6	5.1	5.4	4.2	5.1
	28.4	29.8	29.6	Trade Receivables - (net)	18.3	25.3	31.0	34.1	33.3	28.2
	37.4	36.7	36.6	Inventory	36.7	41.3	38.3	32.7	35.2	34.7
	1.7	1.6	1.6	All Other Current	.3	.7	1.7	2.1	1.5	2.6
	72.0	73.1	73.1	Total Current	63.8	72.9	76.1	74.4	74.2	70.7
	19.2	18.9	18.7	Fixed Assets (net)	31.9	18.6	15.6	16.1	18.2	21.2
	.7	.5	.9	Intangibles (net)	.4	1.7	.8	.3	1.0	.9
	8.0	7.5	7.3	All Other Non-Current	3.9	6.7	7.5	9.3	6.6	7.2
	100.0	100.0	100.0	Total	100.0	100.0	100.0	100.0	100.0	100.0
				LIABILITIES						
	12.8	12.7	13.7	Notes Payable-Short Term	9.9	12.4	12.3	13.1	16.3	16.1
	3.8	2.7	3.0	Cur. Mat.-L/T/D	4.0	3.5	2.7	3.3	2.2	2.6
	16.6	15.8	16.7	Trade Payables	13.2	17.1	17.4	18.5	16.5	14.3
	.4	1.6	.4	Income Taxes Payable	.6	.2	.2	.4	.5	.4
	7.1	7.6	7.3	All Other Current	7.1	6.4	7.9	8.6	6.6	7.5
	40.8	40.4	41.0	Total Current	34.8	39.5	40.5	43.9	42.0	40.9
	13.8	14.0	12.7	Long Term Debt	22.7	15.4	11.2	11.3	9.7	11.7
	.2	.3	.2	Deferred Taxes	.0	.0	.2	.2	.4	.6
	2.9	2.7	3.7	All Other-Non-Current	4.6	5.8	4.0	3.4	2.5	1.9
	42.3	42.6	42.3	Net Worth	37.8	39.2	44.0	41.2	45.4	44.8
	100.0	100.0	100.0	Total Liabilities & Net Worth	100.0	100.0	100.0	100.0	100.0	100.0
				INCOME DATA						
	100.0	100.0	100.0	Net Sales	100.0	100.0	100.0	100.0	100.0	100.0
	25.3	25.0	24.6	Gross Profit	30.3	27.1	24.0	23.5	23.1	22.8
	23.3	22.5	21.8	Operating Expenses	27.1	24.5	21.6	21.2	20.0	19.1
	2.0	2.5	2.8	Operating Profit	3.2	2.5	2.4	2.3	3.1	3.6
	.3	.2	.3	All Other Expenses (net)	.6	.6	.1	.1	.2	.5
	1.8	2.3	2.5	Profit Before Taxes	2.6	1.9	2.4	2.1	2.9	3.1
				RATIOS						
	2.7	2.7	2.7	Current	3.2	3.1	3.0	2.4	2.5	2.5
	1.9	1.8	1.8		2.0	1.9	1.9	1.7	1.8	1.7
	1.4	1.4	1.4		1.4	1.4	1.5	1.4	1.3	1.3
	1.3	1.3	1.3	Quick	1.5	1.3	1.3	1.3	1.2	1.1
(658)	.8	.9	.9		.7	.8	.9	.9	.8	.8
	.6	.6	.6		.3	.5	.6	.6	.6	.6
	26 14.3	27 13.7	26 14.1	Sales/Receivables	16 22.2	21 17.8	26 13.9	30 12.2	29 12.5	26 14.3
	36 10.1	38 9.7	37 10.0		24 15.2	33 11.1	36 10.2	39 9.3	38 9.6	37 10.0
	48 7.6	49 7.4	46 7.9		52 7.0	43 8.4	44 8.3	51 7.1	46 8.0	46 8.0
	46 7.9	45 8.2	41 9.0	Cost of Sales/Inventory	63 5.8	49 7.4	41 9.0	33 11.2	39 9.4	42 8.7
	66 5.5	64 5.7	60 6.1		91 4.0	73 5.0	58 6.3	52 7.0	58 6.3	56 6.5
	89 4.1	85 4.4	83 4.4		159 2.3	104 3.5	87 4.2	69 5.3	74 4.9	73 5.0
	17 21.8	15 24.7	16 23.2	Cost of Sales/Payables	11 34.0	16 23.2	15 24.9	18 20.3	15 24.1	15 24.6
	25 14.5	24 15.2	24 15.4		28 12.9	27 13.4	23 16.0	24 15.1	23 16.2	20 18.6
	37 9.8	35 10.4	36 10.2		64 5.7	43 8.4	33 10.9	35 10.4	33 11.2	32 11.4
	5.6	5.5	6.2	Sales/Working Capital	3.2	4.9	6.0	6.8	6.8	6.9
	8.7	8.6	9.3		7.0	8.7	8.9	10.0	9.2	10.1
	16.9	16.0	17.1		21.6	15.1	14.9	17.2	19.5	17.5
	5.5	6.1	7.0	EBIT/Interest	4.8	5.8	8.0	6.7	8.3	9.2
(617) / (607) / (620)	2.6	3.0	3.0		(33) 1.9	(139) 2.6	(102) 2.7	(131) 2.7	(114) 4.2	(101) 4.3
	1.3	1.6	1.6		.0	1.2	1.6	1.6	2.5	2.4
	4.9	5.6	5.0	Net Profit + Depr., Dep., Amort./Cur. Mat. L/T/D	2.2	5.4	3.0	4.4	5.7	9.9
(289) / (290) / (257)	1.9	2.3	2.4		(11) .4	(39) 1.9	(41) 1.5	(56) 2.3	(48) 2.5	(62) 3.5
	.9	1.0	1.1		.1	.9	.7	1.1	1.7	1.4
	.2	.2	.2	Fixed/Worth	.2	.2	.2	.2	.2	.3
	.4	.4	.4		.8	.4	.3	.3	.4	.4
	.8	.8	.8		4.4	1.2	.6	.8	.7	.8
	.7	.7	.7	Debt/Worth	.7	.8	.5	.7	.6	.7
	1.4	1.3	1.4		1.1	1.5	1.3	1.3	1.3	1.5
	2.7	2.7	2.8		5.5	4.0	2.9	2.9	2.3	2.2
	22.1	27.2	30.9	% Profit Before Taxes/Tangible Net Worth	60.5	33.0	28.9	24.1	31.3	31.5
(623) / (630) / (635)	11.5	13.9	15.3		(31) 9.7	(143) 9.7	(104) 11.8	(133) 11.6	(119) 21.0	(105) 20.5
	3.2	4.4	5.7		1.4	1.9	4.8	5.2	10.0	10.9
	9.1	10.2	12.6	% Profit Before Taxes/Total Assets	10.9	11.5	12.3	10.7	14.1	15.1
	4.5	5.3	5.8		3.1	3.6	4.9	5.0	8.0	8.7
	1.0	1.5	1.9		-.8	.6	1.8	1.9	4.1	4.2
	35.7	34.9	36.6	Sales/Net Fixed Assets	22.4	40.0	44.0	42.6	34.5	25.3
	18.6	18.7	20.8		7.7	22.0	23.4	24.0	20.7	18.1
	9.6	10.2	10.7		3.7	10.3	12.7	12.3	11.9	9.5
	3.5	3.6	3.7	Sales/Total Assets	3.3	3.6	3.7	3.8	3.8	3.3
	2.7	2.8	2.9		1.9	2.8	3.1	3.0	3.0	3.0
	2.1	2.2	2.3		1.1	2.1	2.4	2.5	2.5	2.3
	.7	.7	.6	% Depr., Dep., Amort./Sales	1.0	.6	.6	.6	.6	.6
(620) / (614) / (612)	1.0	1.0	.9		(33) 1.3	(137) .9	(101) .9	(129) .8	(114) .9	(98) .9
	1.5	1.3	1.3		2.5	1.5	1.3	1.2	1.1	1.2
	1.5	1.4	1.4	% Officers', Directors', Owners' Comp/Sales	1.1	2.3	1.7	1.3	.8	.8
(315) / (313) / (294)	3.0	2.7	2.6		(12) 6.1	(75) 4.1	(61) 2.8	(66) 2.3	(47) 1.7	(33) 1.4
	5.3	5.0	4.6		8.6	5.6	4.2	4.1	3.3	3.1
	10974445M	13217382M	13021964M	Net Sales ($)	24122M	302032M	431410M	987557M	1833407M	9443436M
	4149658M	4890024M	4753779M	Total Assets ($)	17446M	124540M	159261M	360420M	640605M	3451507M

M = $ thousand   MM = $ million
See Pages 1 through 15 for Explanation of Ratios and Data

Current Data Sorted By Assets / Comparative Historical Data

0-500M	500M-2MM	2-10MM	10-50MM	50-100MM	100-250MM	# Postretirement Benefits / Type of Statement	4/1/90-3/31/91 ALL	4/1/91-3/31/92 ALL
2	3							
	3	2	1			Unqualified	7	14
4	11	7	1			Reviewed	18	17
25	15		1			Compiled	48	34
8	1					Tax Returns	5	2
9	9	2				Other	28	21
	18 (4/1-9/30/94)		81 (10/1/94-3/31/95)					
46	39	11	3			**NUMBER OF STATEMENTS**	106	88
%	%	%	%	%	%	**ASSETS**	%	%
8.9	7.1	4.2				Cash & Equivalents	7.6	7.6
25.4	23.5	25.8				Trade Receivables - (net)	28.1	25.3
33.9	38.9	44.9				Inventory	37.5	37.9
1.8	2.8	.3				All Other Current	2.0	1.7
69.9	72.3	75.2				Total Current	75.3	72.4
18.1	16.8	13.9				Fixed Assets (net)	18.3	16.6
3.2	2.2	2.8				Intangibles (net)	1.2	1.9
8.7	8.6	8.1				All Other Non-Current	5.2	9.1
100.0	100.0	100.0				Total	100.0	100.0
						LIABILITIES		
9.0	8.2	11.1				Notes Payable-Short Term	12.8	10.0
4.5	4.6	4.5				Cur. Mat. -L/T/D	3.4	3.6
26.5	27.2	31.2				Trade Payables	20.8	19.2
.2	.2	.4				Income Taxes Payable	.4	.5
6.9	6.5	5.1				All Other Current	7.6	8.0
47.0	46.7	52.2				Total Current	45.0	41.3
20.4	12.9	10.0				Long Term Debt	13.5	13.6
.0	.2	.1				Deferred Taxes	.4	1.0
1.4	2.8	2.5				All Other-Non-Current	1.7	3.3
31.2	37.4	35.2				Net Worth	39.4	40.7
100.0	100.0	100.0				Total Liabilities & Net Worth	100.0	100.0
						INCOME DATA		
100.0	100.0	100.0				Net Sales	100.0	100.0
38.1	36.5	31.7				Gross Profit	37.2	37.6
34.3	33.9	28.0				Operating Expenses	33.8	35.4
3.9	2.6	3.7				Operating Profit	3.4	2.2
.5	.7	.4				All Other Expenses (net)	.9	.2
3.4	1.9	3.3				Profit Before Taxes	2.5	2.0
						RATIOS		
2.6	2.6	2.0				Current	2.8	2.9
1.7	1.9	1.4					1.8	1.8
1.0	1.1	1.1					1.2	1.4
1.3	1.3	.9				Quick	1.4	1.4
.8	.8	.5					.8	.8
.4	.4	.3					.5	.5
17 22.1	24 15.4	7 49.7				Sales/Receivables	23 16.1	19 19.3
26 14.2	31 11.9	30 12.1					33 10.9	28 12.9
41 9.0	43 8.4	45 8.2					52 7.0	42 8.6
30 12.3	54 6.7	50 7.3				Cost of Sales/Inventory	47 7.7	55 6.6
60 6.1	83 4.4	54 6.7					74 4.9	83 4.4
101 3.6	130 2.8	107 3.4					114 3.2	114 3.2
24 15.2	37 9.9	35 10.5				Cost of Sales/Payables	20 18.0	22 16.9
47 7.7	53 6.9	56 6.5					35 10.5	33 11.0
73 5.0	73 5.0	64 5.7					51 7.2	59 6.2
6.8	5.2	8.4				Sales/Working Capital	5.5	5.6
13.5	8.8	11.2					9.0	9.0
234.1	22.4	50.5					20.0	15.0
(42) 5.9	(37) 16.1	7.7				EBIT/Interest	(95) 6.5	(82) 6.1
3.4	3.1	6.7					3.5	3.1
1.6	1.1	1.2					1.1	1.1
	(15) 2.6					Net Profit + Depr., Dep., Amort./Cur. Mat. L /T/D	(49) 6.4	(37) 4.3
	2.0						1.7	2.0
	.3						.5	1.0
.1	.2	.2				Fixed/Worth	.2	.2
.4	.4	.3					.4	.4
3.1	1.5	.8					1.0	.8
.7	.7	1.5				Debt/Worth	.8	.6
2.6	1.4	2.2					1.4	1.5
8.8	6.7	2.8					3.2	2.9
(38) 42.3	(34) 21.9	58.3				% Profit Before Taxes/Tangible Net Worth	(97) 36.0	(79) 29.0
21.0	10.8	25.8					14.5	12.4
2.5	1.9	3.0					1.5	3.1
15.0	8.0	13.1				% Profit Before Taxes/Total Assets	14.2	10.9
5.8	3.9	9.0					5.9	5.4
1.3	.3	1.1					.5	.5
73.6	30.5	64.2				Sales/Net Fixed Assets	40.4	52.3
35.8	19.4	29.3					24.1	20.2
12.5	9.8	15.4					12.6	11.5
4.0	3.3	3.7				Sales/Total Assets	3.6	3.4
3.3	2.3	3.4					2.8	2.7
2.5	1.9	2.5					2.3	2.2
(36) .6	(37) .7	.4				% Depr., Dep., Amort./Sales	(94) 1.0	(81) .8
1.1	1.1	.7					1.3	1.3
2.2	1.8	1.0					2.1	1.9
(25) 4.4	(28) 2.7					% Officers', Directors', Owners' Comp/Sales	(51) 3.8	(37) 2.7
7.0	4.3						5.4	4.0
11.5	6.0						9.9	6.4
33727M	97896M	141501M	139385M			Net Sales ($)	329549M	457678M
10667M	39568M	45176M	54964M			Total Assets ($)	113344M	174271M

M = $ thousand   MM = $ million
See Pages 1 through 15 for Explanation of Ratios and Data

Comparative Historical Data | Current Data Sorted By Sales

2	2	5	# Postretirement Benefits	3	1	1			
			Type of Statement						
9	7	6	Unqualified			3	1	1	1
24	15	23	Reviewed	3	9	2	3	5	1
48	53	41	Compiled	19	17	4		1	
2	6	9	Tax Returns	7	2				
13	19	20	Other	7	9	1	1	2	
4/1/92-3/31/93 ALL	4/1/93-3/31/94 ALL	4/1/94-3/31/95 ALL		18 (4/1-9/30/94) 0-1MM	1-3MM	3-5MM	81 (10/1/94-3/31/95) 5-10MM	10-25MM	25MM & OVER
96	100	99	**NUMBER OF STATEMENTS**	36	37	10	5	9	2
%	%	%	**ASSETS**	%	%	%	%	%	%
7.5	6.5	7.7	Cash & Equivalents	6.6	10.5	4.8			
24.8	25.1	24.5	Trade Receivables - (net)	20.8	26.9	24.7			
37.1	37.7	37.2	Inventory	35.5	37.2	35.8			
1.6	.9	2.0	All Other Current	1.6	1.5	7.4			
71.0	70.2	71.4	Total Current	64.6	76.0	72.7			
19.7	18.2	17.4	Fixed Assets (net)	21.1	14.3	18.7			
2.4	2.4	2.7	Intangibles (net)	4.0	1.7	3.0			
6.9	9.2	8.5	All Other Non-Current	10.3	8.0	5.6			
100.0	100.0	100.0	Total	100.0	100.0	100.0			
			LIABILITIES						
9.8	7.2	9.1	Notes Payable-Short Term	9.1	9.3	5.5			
4.1	3.6	4.5	Cur. Mat.-L./T/D	4.6	5.4	1.6			
20.3	25.9	26.9	Trade Payables	27.9	23.8	35.2			
.3	1.2	.2	Income Taxes Payable	.1	.2	.2			
7.8	8.6	6.4	All Other Current	6.1	7.3	7.9			
42.3	46.5	47.1	Total Current	47.9	45.8	50.4			
14.8	12.5	16.0	Long Term Debt	25.5	12.3	5.4			
.2	.1	.1	Deferred Taxes	.0	.2	.1			
2.6	4.7	2.1	All Other-Non-Current	1.7	2.2	3.4			
40.2	36.2	34.7	Net Worth	24.9	39.5	40.8			
100.0	100.0	100.0	Total Liabilities & Net Worth	100.0	100.0	100.0			
			INCOME DATA						
100.0	100.0	100.0	Net Sales	100.0	100.0	100.0			
37.8	36.3	36.5	Gross Profit	39.3	36.8	31.8			
35.0	34.4	33.3	Operating Expenses	35.3	34.1	29.6			
2.8	1.9	3.3	Operating Profit	4.0	2.7	2.2			
.3	.4	.5	All Other Expenses (net)	.8	.6	.0			
2.4	1.5	2.7	Profit Before Taxes	3.2	2.1	2.2			
			RATIOS						
2.8	2.8	2.5		2.4	2.7	3.0			
1.8	1.8	1.7	Current	1.5	2.0	1.9			
1.2	1.1	1.1		.9	1.2	1.0			
1.4	1.5	1.3		1.2	1.6	1.3			
.8	.8	.8	Quick	.7	1.0	.9			
.4	.3	.4		.3	.4	.3			
20 18.3	19 19.3	19 19.2		13 29.0	24 15.3	18 20.7			
31 11.8	32 11.4	30 12.3	Sales/Receivables	25 14.6	30 12.1	34 10.7			
41 9.0	41 8.8	42 8.7		37 9.8	45 8.1	39 9.3			
51 7.2	46 7.9	46 7.9		41 8.8	47 7.8	41 8.9			
76 4.8	81 4.5	68 5.4	Cost of Sales/Inventory	81 4.5	65 5.6	60 6.1			
114 3.2	107 3.4	118 3.1		107 3.4	126 2.9	126 2.9			
22 16.9	25 14.7	28 13.1		28 13.1	24 15.5	36 10.2			
36 10.2	41 9.0	50 7.3	Cost of Sales/Payables	58 6.3	47 7.8	57 6.4			
55 6.6	74 4.9	72 5.1		81 4.5	72 5.1	81 4.5			
5.8	5.2	6.2		7.3	5.6	4.9			
8.6	8.5	11.2	Sales/Working Capital	13.8	7.4	10.7			
24.3	39.4	65.0		−103.7	20.0	117.6			
(83) 7.6	(88) 6.1	(93) 9.6		(32) 3.9	(36) 13.8				
2.8	2.9	3.2	EBIT/Interest	2.0	3.3				
1.2	1.0	1.5		1.0	1.8				
(30) 3.2	(28) 3.5	(32) 4.0			(13) 3.4				
1.3	1.6	2.0	Net Profit + Depr., Dep., Amort./Cur. Mat. L/T/D		2.0				
.9	.5	.4			.6				
.2	.2	.2		.1	.2	.3			
.4	.5	.4	Fixed/Worth	.9	.4	.5			
1.2	1.0	1.6		3.9	1.2	1.0			
.6	.8	.8		.8	.6	.8			
1.5	1.8	2.1	Debt/Worth	3.7	1.4	1.1			
3.3	5.3	5.9		104.4	4.6	8.3			
29.8	29.8	34.1		67.9	25.6				
(88) 11.3	(88) 10.4	(86) 13.9	% Profit Before Taxes/Tangible Net Worth	(28) 11.3	(33) 13.6				
2.8	1.1	2.9		−1.2	3.2				
13.4	9.0	11.7		12.5	11.5	10.3			
4.5	3.5	5.3	% Profit Before Taxes/Total Assets	3.9	5.3	5.8			
.6	.1	1.1		−.2	1.7	.5			
41.4	41.2	49.5		67.0	45.5	29.1			
22.6	24.8	23.4	Sales/Net Fixed Assets	21.2	27.1	18.9			
10.7	11.4	11.6		8.3	14.2	7.5			
3.8	3.6	3.7		3.7	3.5	4.0			
2.8	2.9	2.8	Sales/Total Assets	2.7	2.8	2.6			
2.2	2.3	2.1		2.0	2.1	2.0			
(88) .7	(89) .7	(87) .6		(29) .7	(32) .6	.8			
1.2	1.1	1.1	% Depr., Dep., Amort./Sales	1.1	1.2	1.1			
1.8	2.0	1.8		2.2	1.8	1.9			
(43) 3.4	(56) 3.6	(56) 3.4		(21) 3.9	(25) 4.0				
5.5	5.4	4.8	% Officers', Directors', Owners' Comp/Sales	7.1	4.8				
8.5	7.5	7.8		10.6	6.9				
1427446M	625621M	412509M	Net Sales ($)	18481M	65852M	36195M	32604M	139950M	119427M
455073M	292796M	150375M	Total Assets ($)	7519M	25911M	13941M	9546M	49175M	44283M

M = $ thousand   MM = $ million
See Pages 1 through 15 for Explanation of Ratios and Data

Current Data Sorted By Assets   Comparative Historical Data

	2	5	8	6	1	1	# Postretirement Benefits		
							Type of Statement		
	5	17	31	26	3	1	Unqualified	83	78
	8	54	78	5			Reviewed	119	129
	25	63	35	3			Compiled	145	142
	5	6					Tax Returns	2	1
	10	24	34				Other	61	51
		104 (4/1-9/30/94)		334 (10/1/94-3/31/95)				4/1/90-3/31/91	4/1/91-3/31/92
	0-500M	500M-2MM	2-10MM	10-50MM	50-100MM	100-250MM		ALL	ALL
	53	164	178	39	3	1	**NUMBER OF STATEMENTS**	410	401
	%	%	%	%	%	%	**ASSETS**	%	%
	11.3	7.2	3.9	2.8			Cash & Equivalents	5.5	5.3
	27.7	36.1	33.0	35.8			Trade Receivables - (net)	31.8	33.0
	38.5	38.8	43.1	44.0			Inventory	41.0	39.7
	3.2	.9	1.5	1.0			All Other Current	1.8	1.5
	80.7	83.0	81.6	83.6			Total Current	80.1	79.5
	13.3	11.9	12.7	10.9			Fixed Assets (net)	13.8	13.3
	.4	.9	.8	.5			Intangibles (net)	1.1	1.2
	5.6	4.1	4.9	4.9			All Other Non-Current	4.9	6.0
	100.0	100.0	100.0	100.0			Total	100.0	100.0
							LIABILITIES		
	11.2	11.5	16.0	15.3			Notes Payable-Short Term	14.5	14.2
	1.7	2.8	2.2	1.7			Cur. Mat. -L/T/D	3.1	3.0
	26.2	25.6	22.0	22.1			Trade Payables	20.9	20.4
	.7	.7	.3	.4			Income Taxes Payable	.6	.3
	7.9	7.6	6.7	7.4			All Other Current	6.5	6.9
	47.6	48.1	47.3	47.0			Total Current	45.6	44.8
	13.7	6.4	7.3	12.5			Long Term Debt	10.8	10.3
	.0	.1	.2	.2			Deferred Taxes	.2	.2
	3.0	4.6	2.8	2.1			All Other-Non-Current	1.8	2.4
	35.7	40.8	42.4	38.1			Net Worth	41.6	42.3
	100.0	100.0	100.0	100.0			Total Liabilities & Net Worth	100.0	100.0
							INCOME DATA		
	100.0	100.0	100.0	100.0			Net Sales	100.0	100.0
	33.8	27.3	25.0	23.8			Gross Profit	28.2	28.4
	31.1	24.9	22.5	20.3			Operating Expenses	25.8	26.5
	2.7	2.4	2.5	3.5			Operating Profit	2.4	1.9
	.6	.4	.2	.5			All Other Expenses (net)	.8	.4
	2.1	1.9	2.3	3.0			Profit Before Taxes	1.7	1.5
							RATIOS		
	2.6	2.2	2.1	2.4				2.7	2.6
	1.7	1.8	1.8	1.8			Current	1.8	1.8
	1.3	1.4	1.4	1.4				1.4	1.4
	1.3	1.2	1.1	1.3				1.2	1.3
	.9	.9	.7	.7			Quick	.8	.8
	.5	.7	.6	.6				.6	.6
16	22.4	34	10.8	35	10.3	40	9.1	Sales/Receivables	34	10.7	36	10.1
35	10.5	42	8.6	43	8.4	44	8.3		42	8.6	43	8.4
42	8.7	51	7.2	54	6.8	53	6.9		50	7.3	55	6.6

Sales/Receivables (with divisor counts):

n	0-500M	n	500M-2MM	n	2-10MM	n	10-50MM	Ratio	n	4/1/90-3/31/91	n	4/1/91-3/31/92
16	22.4	34	10.8	35	10.3	40	9.1	Sales/Receivables	34	10.7	36	10.1
35	10.5	42	8.6	43	8.4	44	8.3		42	8.6	43	8.4
42	8.7	51	7.2	54	6.8	53	6.9		50	7.3	55	6.6
20	18.5	41	8.8	56	6.5	59	6.2	Cost of Sales/Inventory	50	7.3	49	7.4
62	5.9	63	5.8	78	4.7	73	5.0		79	4.6	78	4.7
126	2.9	94	3.9	104	3.5	94	3.9		107	3.4	118	3.1
22	16.9	26	14.1	27	13.4	25	14.8	Cost of Sales/Payables	26	14.2	24	15.0
41	9.0	39	9.3	36	10.2	36	10.1		35	10.5	36	10.2
58	6.3	56	6.5	47	7.7	49	7.5		49	7.5	49	7.4

	0-500M	500M-2MM	2-10MM	10-50MM	Ratio	4/1/90-3/31/91	4/1/91-3/31/92
	6.6	5.9	5.5	5.8	Sales/Working Capital	5.1	5.0
	10.1	8.8	8.0	8.2		8.0	7.6
	31.3	14.9	13.1	11.3		13.6	14.6
(42)	8.5	(154) 6.8	(168) 6.6	(38) 7.9	EBIT/Interest	(374) 5.9	(377) 4.5
	4.2	3.3	3.2	5.0		2.1	2.0
	1.5	1.6	1.8	2.1		1.1	.9
(11)	7.9	(75) 5.9	(88) 7.4	(22) 9.2	Net Profit + Depr., Dep., Amort./Cur. Mat. L /T/D	(226) 5.2	(189) 5.4
	2.8	2.1	2.7	3.6		2.2	1.8
	.2	.7	1.3	2.0		.7	.4
	.1	.1	.1	.2	Fixed/Worth	.1	.1
	.3	.2	.3	.2		.3	.3
	.8	.5	.5	.5		.6	.7
	1.0	.8	.8	1.0	Debt/Worth	.7	.7
	1.4	1.6	1.4	1.6		1.5	1.5
	4.1	3.1	2.5	2.5		2.9	3.1
(49)	56.5	(157) 32.3	(175) 22.6	(38) 29.0	% Profit Before Taxes/Tangible Net Worth	(396) 23.0	(386) 18.2
	27.9	12.9	11.9	18.5		9.6	7.2
	6.0	4.1	5.4	9.3		1.1	.0
	15.1	10.0	8.7	12.2	% Profit Before Taxes/Total Assets	9.9	7.4
	7.4	4.6	4.5	7.2		3.6	2.8
	1.6	1.5	2.1	3.7		.3	-.4
	123.4	81.0	59.4	54.8	Sales/Net Fixed Assets	55.6	65.4
	33.5	42.3	29.5	42.8		29.7	29.2
	17.3	18.9	15.4	16.2		15.0	14.3
	4.6	3.7	3.3	3.5	Sales/Total Assets	3.4	3.3
	3.5	3.1	2.7	3.0		2.7	2.6
	2.6	2.4	2.1	2.2		2.2	2.0
(42)	.3	(158) .5	(171) .5	(37) .4	% Depr., Dep., Amort./Sales	(382) .5	(373) .5
	.7	.7	.7	.6		.9	.8
	1.6	1.1	1.0	.8		1.3	1.4
(24)	5.7	(80) 3.0	(76) 1.7		% Officers', Directors', Owners' Comp/Sales	(189) 2.2	(170) 1.9
	7.2	4.9	2.7			3.8	3.8
	13.2	7.5	4.4			7.3	6.2

	0-500M	500M-2MM	2-10MM	10-50MM	50-100MM	100-250MM		4/1/90-3/31/91	4/1/91-3/31/92
	58993M	563797M	2124158M	2485211M	488988M	440202M	Net Sales ($)	6489010M	5750691M
	16287M	186650M	792281M	873291M	190424M	208623M	Total Assets ($)	2450128M	2187221M

M = $ thousand   MM = $ million
See Pages 1 through 15 for Explanation of Ratios and Data

Comparative Historical Data				Current Data Sorted By Sales					
9	24	23	# Postretirement Benefits / Type of Statement	1	1	3	5	4	9
83	90	83	Unqualified	2	9	9	7	25	31
149	136	145	Reviewed	1	25	28	54	30	7
140	115	126	Compiled	13	48	24	29	8	4
6	7	11	Tax Returns	3	5	3			
63	72	73	Other	7	14	11	18	17	6
4/1/92-3/31/93 ALL	4/1/93-3/31/94 ALL	4/1/94-3/31/95 ALL		104 (4/1-9/30/94) 0-1MM	1-3MM	334 (10/1/94-3/31/95) 3-5MM	5-10MM	10-25MM	25MM & OVER
441	420	438	NUMBER OF STATEMENTS	26	101	75	108	80	48
%	%	%	ASSETS	%	%	%	%	%	%
5.4	5.6	5.9	Cash & Equivalents	9.6	10.5	5.9	4.7	2.7	2.7
33.4	35.1	33.8	Trade Receivables - (net)	21.0	31.2	38.4	33.5	35.3	37.4
41.2	39.4	40.9	Inventory	43.6	37.5	38.4	42.0	43.4	44.1
1.8	1.6	1.4	All Other Current	.9	2.2	1.5	1.5	.9	.9
81.7	81.8	82.1	Total Current	75.2	81.4	84.1	81.8	82.2	85.0
12.1	11.9	12.4	Fixed Assets (net)	17.0	12.8	10.8	13.0	12.6	9.6
1.1	.9	.8	Intangibles (net)	.5	1.1	.9	.9	.4	.6
5.1	5.4	4.7	All Other Non-Current	7.4	4.8	4.2	4.3	4.8	4.8
100.0	100.0	100.0	Total	100.0	100.0	100.0	100.0	100.0	100.0
			LIABILITIES						
12.7	12.6	13.6	Notes Payable-Short Term	17.3	10.1	10.0	14.0	19.0	14.7
2.7	2.3	2.3	Cur. Mat.-L /T/D	2.6	2.6	2.2	2.4	2.2	1.6
23.2	23.7	23.9	Trade Payables	19.5	24.5	26.1	22.7	23.8	24.4
.4	1.6	.5	Income Taxes Payable	.7	.5	.5	.6	.3	.5
7.6	7.3	7.3	All Other Current	6.0	6.6	10.4	6.1	7.0	7.7
46.7	47.5	47.6	Total Current	46.2	44.3	49.2	45.8	52.4	48.9
8.7	8.1	8.3	Long Term Debt	16.0	8.3	5.9	8.7	6.4	10.2
.1	.3	.1	Deferred Taxes	.0	.0	.1	.2	.2	.3
2.3	2.7	3.4	All Other-Non-Current	4.9	4.2	3.8	2.9	3.1	1.8
42.2	41.4	40.6	Net Worth	32.9	43.2	41.0	42.4	37.9	38.8
100.0	100.0	100.0	Total Liabilities & Net Worth	100.0	100.0	100.0	100.0	100.0	100.0
			INCOME DATA						
100.0	100.0	100.0	Net Sales	100.0	100.0	100.0	100.0	100.0	100.0
27.6	26.5	26.7	Gross Profit	35.2	30.8	26.0	25.7	23.8	22.1
25.4	24.5	24.2	Operating Expenses	33.0	28.0	23.6	23.2	21.2	19.4
2.2	2.0	2.5	Operating Profit	2.2	2.8	2.4	2.5	2.5	2.7
.3	.2	.4	All Other Expenses (net)	1.1	.5	.1	.2	.5	.3
1.9	1.8	2.2	Profit Before Taxes	1.1	2.3	2.3	2.3	2.0	2.3
			RATIOS						
2.6 / 1.7 / 1.3	2.3 / 1.7 / 1.4	2.2 / 1.8 / 1.4	Current	3.5 / 1.7 / 1.1	2.9 / 1.9 / 1.4	2.4 / 1.8 / 1.4	2.2 / 1.8 / 1.5	1.9 / 1.6 / 1.3	2.2 / 1.8 / 1.4
1.2 / .8 / .6	1.2 / .8 / .6	1.2 / .8 / .6	Quick	1.2 / .7 / .4	1.4 / .9 / .7	1.2 / .9 / .7	1.1 / .8 / .6	.9 / .7 / .6	1.2 / .7 / .6
(34) 10.7 / (43) 8.5 / (52) 7.0	(37) 9.9 / (43) 8.4 / (54) 6.7	(34) 10.8 / (42) 8.6 / (51) 7.1	Sales/Receivables	(13) 28.5 / (39) 9.4 / (50) 7.3	(31) 11.9 / (40) 9.2 / (50) 7.3	(36) 10.2 / (42) 8.7 / (50) 7.3	(33) 11.2 / (43) 8.5 / (54) 6.8	(36) 10.2 / (43) 8.5 / (54) 6.8	(40) 9.2 / (44) 8.3 / (53) 6.9
(50) 7.3 / (74) 4.9 / (107) 3.4	(47) 7.8 / (70) 5.2 / (101) 3.6	(47) 7.7 / (70) 5.2 / (104) 3.5	Cost of Sales/Inventory	(43) 8.4 / (122) 3.0 / (203) 1.8	(39) 9.3 / (70) 5.2 / (111) 3.3	(33) 11.2 / (60) 6.1 / (101) 3.6	(52) 7.0 / (74) 4.9 / (104) 3.5	(54) 6.7 / (72) 5.1 / (94) 3.9	(57) 6.4 / (68) 5.4 / (85) 4.3
(27) 13.5 / (38) 9.6 / (53) 6.9	(26) 14.2 / (39) 9.3 / (54) 6.8	(26) 14.0 / (38) 9.7 / (51) 7.1	Cost of Sales/Payables	(23) 15.9 / (43) 8.4 / (70) 5.2	(24) 15.4 / (41) 9.0 / (58) 6.3	(25) 14.4 / (37) 9.9 / (55) 6.6	(27) 13.6 / (36) 10.2 / (50) 7.3	(27) 13.7 / (37) 9.9 / (47) 7.8	(29) 12.8 / (37) 10.0 / (48) 7.6
4.8 / 8.0 / 15.3	5.5 / 8.7 / 15.0	5.9 / 8.5 / 14.1	Sales/Working Capital	3.2 / 7.6 / NM	5.2 / 8.1 / 14.6	5.9 / 8.6 / 19.2	5.6 / 8.0 / 12.2	6.7 / 9.3 / 15.6	6.7 / 8.5 / 11.3
(410) 6.7 / 2.9 / 1.4	(385) 7.0 / 3.0 / 1.5	(406) 7.0 / 3.4 / 1.7	EBIT/Interest	(19) 6.0 / 1.8 / .5	(92) 11.5 / 3.9 / 1.4	(70) 11.6 / 3.4 / 1.6	(99) 5.7 / 3.3 / 2.0	(46) 5.8 / 3.0 / 1.5	8.3 / 5.5 / 2.7
(199) 5.3 / 2.4 / 1.0	(184) 6.1 / 2.4 / 1.2	(200) 6.5 / 2.7 / 1.3	Net Profit + Depr., Dep., Amort./Cur. Mat. L/T/D		(33) 6.4 / 1.9 / -.2	(33) 5.9 / 2.0 / .8	(63) 5.5 / 2.1 / 1.4	(37) 9.0 / 3.5 / 1.5	(28) 9.6 / 4.2 / 2.1
.1 / .2 / .5	.1 / .2 / .5	.1 / .2 / .5	Fixed/Worth	.1 / .4 / 2.7	.1 / .2 / .5	.1 / .2 / .5	.1 / .3 / .5	.2 / .3 / .6	.1 / .2 / .4
.7 / 1.5 / 3.0	.8 / 1.5 / 3.0	.8 / 1.5 / 2.9	Debt/Worth	1.0 / 1.5 / 9.4	.5 / 1.3 / 2.9	.8 / 1.5 / 3.1	.8 / 1.5 / 2.5	1.0 / 1.7 / 3.0	1.0 / 1.7 / 2.5
(429) 23.4 / 11.1 / 4.1	(413) 27.1 / 12.7 / 3.2	(423) 28.3 / 14.0 / 5.5	% Profit Before Taxes/Tangible Net Worth	(23) 52.2 / 8.5 / -.5	(95) 36.6 / 15.4 / 4.1	(73) 30.8 / 16.5 / 3.3	(107) 22.4 / 11.3 / 5.8	(78) 23.0 / 12.5 / 5.2	(47) 28.5 / 21.4 / 12.0
9.3 / 4.3 / 1.4	9.3 / 4.3 / 1.2	10.1 / 4.9 / 2.0	% Profit Before Taxes/Total Assets	9.8 / 4.4 / -3.2	12.8 / 6.2 / 1.8	10.2 / 4.8 / 1.1	8.9 / 4.1 / 2.3	7.7 / 4.3 / 2.0	12.5 / 7.6 / 4.3
66.5 / 33.4 / 16.9	66.4 / 35.9 / 18.1	66.0 / 34.3 / 17.0	Sales/Net Fixed Assets	94.0 / 20.3 / 11.6	78.5 / 37.3 / 18.5	96.2 / 39.0 / 18.1	58.9 / 29.3 / 15.6	62.4 / 33.6 / 16.9	60.3 / 43.7 / 19.5
3.4 / 2.8 / 2.2	3.5 / 2.8 / 2.2	3.5 / 2.9 / 2.2	Sales/Total Assets	3.5 / 2.4 / 1.4	3.7 / 2.9 / 2.0	3.9 / 3.1 / 2.5	3.4 / 2.8 / 2.2	3.4 / 2.9 / 2.3	3.6 / 3.1 / 2.6
(410) .5 / .7 / 1.2	(392) .5 / .7 / 1.2	(412) .5 / .7 / 1.1	% Depr., Dep., Amort./Sales	(20) .4 / .7 / 2.3	(94) .5 / .7 / 1.3	(71) .4 / .7 / 1.1	(106) .5 / .7 / 1.0	(75) .5 / .6 / 1.0	(46) .4 / .5 / .7
(226) 2.0 / 3.8 / 6.7	(203) 2.1 / 3.7 / 5.9	(189) 2.2 / 3.7 / 6.6	% Officers', Directors', Owners' Comp/Sales		(49) 3.9 / 6.2 / 9.0	(40) 2.9 / 4.7 / 7.1	(50) 1.7 / 3.0 / 4.6	(31) 1.1 / 2.5 / 3.6	(11) 1.1 / 2.1 / 3.1
6403255M / 2452030M	5837462M / 2255024M	6161349M / 2267556M	Net Sales ($) / Total Assets ($)	16080M / 7681M	195611M / 76335M	294761M / 109223M	773152M / 307000M	1270620M / 472875M	3611125M / 1294442M

M = $ thousand   MM = $ million
See Pages 1 through 15 for Explanation of Ratios and Data

Current Data Sorted By Assets | # Postretirement Benefits | **Comparative Historical Data**

0-500M	500M-2MM	2-10MM	10-50MM	50-100MM	100-250MM	Type of Statement	4/1/90-3/31/91 ALL	4/1/91-3/31/92 ALL
					1	Unqualified	7	5
4	2	6			1	Reviewed	13	13
11	10					Compiled	23	24
		2	1			Tax Returns	2	3
3	4	2	1		1	Other	15	17
	24 (4/1-9/30/94)			25 (10/1/94-3/31/95)				
19	16	10	2		2	**NUMBER OF STATEMENTS**	60	62
%	%	%	%	%	%	**ASSETS**	%	%
9.1	9.9	12.5				Cash & Equivalents	9.3	10.0
8.4	16.1	19.3				Trade Receivables - (net)	16.7	15.7
56.9	49.6	42.6				Inventory	42.0	44.1
.6	.7	1.6				All Other Current	2.8	1.7
75.0	76.4	76.0				Total Current	70.7	71.5
18.6	16.2	18.0				Fixed Assets (net)	22.3	20.8
1.7	3.1	1.4				Intangibles (net)	1.7	1.5
4.7	4.3	4.6				All Other Non-Current	5.2	6.3
100.0	100.0	100.0				Total	100.0	100.0
						LIABILITIES		
5.1	9.0	11.1				Notes Payable-Short Term	8.8	6.8
3.6	3.2	1.8				Cur. Mat. -L/T/D	4.8	5.5
20.3	26.6	30.0				Trade Payables	23.6	23.7
.1	.2	.0				Income Taxes Payable	.2	.4
7.6	6.8	7.0				All Other Current	8.1	9.9
36.7	45.8	49.9				Total Current	45.6	46.4
14.3	8.8	4.2				Long Term Debt	15.4	12.9
.0	.1	.1				Deferred Taxes	.1	.1
9.2	4.4	1.5				All Other-Non-Current	3.0	4.5
39.7	40.9	44.3				Net Worth	36.0	36.0
100.0	100.0	100.0				Total Liabilities & Net Worth	100.0	100.0
						INCOME DATA		
100.0	100.0	100.0				Net Sales	100.0	100.0
40.0	30.7	31.2				Gross Profit	35.7	34.6
38.8	30.6	25.1				Operating Expenses	33.3	31.7
1.2	.1	6.0				Operating Profit	2.4	3.0
.2	.2	3.2				All Other Expenses (net)	.6	.5
.9	-.1	2.8				Profit Before Taxes	1.8	2.5
						RATIOS		
3.9	2.5	2.8					2.1	2.2
2.0	1.6	1.4				Current	1.5	1.6
1.3	1.3	1.0					1.3	1.2
.8	1.2	1.9					.8	.9
.5	.5	.6				Quick	.5	.5
.3	.2	.2					.4	.3
0 UND	12 30.2	4 87.5					9 40.8	7 49.1
8 44.6	18 20.7	11 32.4				Sales/Receivables	18 20.6	14 26.0
17 21.1	25 14.8	49 7.4					35 10.5	27 13.3
65 5.6	58 6.3	36 10.1					61 6.0	55 6.6
91 4.0	89 4.1	59 6.2				Cost of Sales/Inventory	76 4.8	74 4.9
159 2.3	140 2.6	101 3.6					118 3.1	118 3.1
9 39.2	26 14.2	20 18.3					35 10.5	25 14.4
32 11.5	54 6.8	43 8.5				Cost of Sales/Payables	45 8.2	41 9.0
61 6.0	72 5.1	73 5.0					65 5.6	61 6.0
7.0	5.2	5.7					6.7	7.1
9.2	11.5	13.5				Sales/Working Capital	11.7	13.8
23.8	22.2	NM					23.0	28.9
2.6	7.1						5.4	6.4
(14) 1.7	(15) 2.6					EBIT/Interest	(55) 2.0	(56) 2.9
.4	1.0						1.1	1.2
							5.9	3.4
						Net Profit + Depr., Dep., Amort./Cur. Mat. L /T/D	(32) 2.1	(26) 2.0
							.9	.7
.2	.2	.1					.2	.2
.3	.4	.4				Fixed/Worth	.5	.5
4.7	.8	.6					1.2	1.1
.5	.9	.4					1.0	1.1
1.2	1.8	2.4				Debt/Worth	2.1	1.8
7.7	4.1	5.7					3.6	3.9
17.3	34.3	17.8					26.8	34.2
(17) 1.3	(15) 12.9	12.8				% Profit Before Taxes/Tangible Net Worth	(58) 15.6	(57) 15.1
-2.4	1.4	2.7					2.0	3.2
6.9	12.1	12.0					10.4	10.8
.4	3.2	3.4				% Profit Before Taxes/Total Assets	6.3	5.0
-2.7	.4	.6					.6	.3
52.3	31.9	138.3					43.2	49.7
28.1	20.0	26.4				Sales/Net Fixed Assets	16.8	26.3
18.1	12.4	9.2					7.3	8.9
5.1	3.7	3.7					3.7	4.1
3.6	2.7	2.9				Sales/Total Assets	2.8	3.0
2.2	2.5	2.5					2.1	2.4
.9	1.0						.8	.7
(15) 1.2	1.4					% Depr., Dep., Amort./Sales	(53) 1.8	(54) 1.2
3.1	2.0						2.8	2.4
	3.0						2.6	2.8
	(10) 4.7					% Officers', Directors', Owners' Comp/Sales	(26) 4.3	(23) 5.7
	9.1						8.1	7.4
20154M	57015M	108682M	99370M		1024639M	Net Sales ($)	559636M	449100M
5410M	18854M	33503M	23674M		295086M	Total Assets ($)	231431M	158923M

M = $ thousand   MM = $ million
See Pages 1 through 15 for Explanation of Ratios and Data

Comparative Historical Data / Current Data Sorted By Sales

			# Postretirement Benefits	1					
1		1		1					

Type of Statement

Hist 1	Hist 2	Hist 3	Type of Statement	0-1MM	1-3MM	3-5MM	5-10MM	10-25MM	25MM & OVER
5	4	2	Unqualified		1				1
8	13	12	Reviewed	1	4	2	3	1	1
20	16	21	Compiled	7	11	1	2		1
	1	3	Tax Returns				2	1	1
10	18	11	Other	2	2	2	2	1	2
4/1/92-3/31/93 ALL	4/1/93-3/31/94 ALL	4/1/94-3/31/95 ALL		24 (4/1-9/30/94)			25 (10/1/94-3/31/95)		
43	52	49	**NUMBER OF STATEMENTS**	10	18	5	9	2	5

ASSETS

Hist 1 %	Hist 2 %	Hist 3 %		0-1MM %	1-3MM %	3-5MM %	5-10MM %	10-25MM %	25MM & OVER %
7.2	8.6	9.8	Cash & Equivalents	10.0	11.6				
13.7	14.3	13.1	Trade Receivables - (net)	5.1	11.1				
50.8	42.2	52.0	Inventory	64.2	50.7				
1.0	1.0	.9	All Other Current	.2	.8				
72.7	66.1	75.9	Total Current	79.5	74.2				
20.7	27.5	17.7	Fixed Assets (net)	16.6	19.2				
1.9	1.5	2.0	Intangibles (net)	.5	1.6				
4.7	4.9	4.4	All Other Non-Current	3.4	5.1				
100.0	100.0	100.0	Total	100.0	100.0				

LIABILITIES

Hist 1	Hist 2	Hist 3		0-1MM	1-3MM				
7.8	10.0	8.9	Notes Payable-Short Term	.9	7.5				
2.9	3.7	2.9	Cur. Mat.-L /T/D	3.0	3.7				
24.4	21.1	25.9	Trade Payables	25.6	18.6				
.3	2.6	.2	Income Taxes Payable	.2	.1				
6.9	5.5	7.1	All Other Current	7.0	6.8				
42.2	42.8	45.0	Total Current	36.7	36.7				
12.6	14.4	10.0	Long Term Debt	11.4	13.8				
.1	.1	.1	Deferred Taxes	.0	.1				
5.9	3.7	5.5	All Other-Non-Current	10.8	4.7				
39.1	39.0	39.5	Net Worth	41.0	44.7				
100.0	100.0	100.0	Total Liabilities & Net Worth	100.0	100.0				

INCOME DATA

Hist 1	Hist 2	Hist 3		0-1MM	1-3MM				
100.0	100.0	100.0	Net Sales	100.0	100.0				
31.5	35.4	34.8	Gross Profit	44.3	32.3				
29.0	32.7	33.5	Operating Expenses	42.7	32.0				
2.5	2.7	1.3	Operating Profit	1.6	.2				
.6	1.1	.8	All Other Expenses (net)	.1	.4				
1.8	1.6	.5	Profit Before Taxes	1.5	−.2				

RATIOS

Hist 1	Hist 2	Hist 3		0-1MM	1-3MM				
2.6	2.3	2.6	Current	4.4	3.4				
1.7	1.7	1.5		2.2	2.1				
1.3	1.1	1.2		1.4	1.4				
.9	.9	.9	Quick	.8	1.3				
.4	.5	.5		.5	.5				
.3	.3	.2		.2	.3				
7 52.7	9 40.0	4 96.3	Sales/Receivables	0 UND	4 97.0				
12 29.3	13 27.4	13 27.8		4 81.4	15 25.1				
18 20.4	20 18.1	19 19.3		16 23.5	19 19.3				
53 6.9	57 6.4	57 6.4	Cost of Sales/Inventory	83 4.4	55 6.6				
70 5.2	76 4.8	87 4.2		135 2.7	83 4.4				
101 3.6	114 3.2	126 2.9		183 2.0	126 2.9				
27 13.5	24 15.3	22 16.3	Cost of Sales/Payables	14 26.5	7 52.5				
40 9.2	40 9.1	41 8.8		43 8.5	34 10.8				
49 7.4	57 6.4	72 5.1		91 4.0	53 6.9				
7.0	6.8	6.9	Sales/Working Capital	4.6	5.3				
12.4	10.9	12.4		8.3	7.6				
24.2	52.1	31.6		17.0	19.5				
(38) 5.7	(47) 12.4	(39) 5.9	EBIT/Interest		(16) 3.4				
1.9	2.6	2.0			2.6				
.3	1.1	.9			1.4				
(16) 5.0	(18) 9.8	(14) 3.7	Net Profit + Depr., Dep., Amort./Cur. Mat. L/T/D						
2.1	2.0	1.7							
1.0	.4	.4							
.2	.3	.2	Fixed/Worth	.1	.2				
.4	.7	.4		.2	.4				
1.0	1.5	1.1		NM	.7				
.8	.7	.6	Debt/Worth	.3	.5				
1.8	1.6	2.1		1.1	1.3				
4.0	3.4	6.2		NM	3.3				
(40) 24.4	(47) 23.6	(46) 22.6	% Profit Before Taxes/Tangible Net Worth		17.9				
11.4	12.9	10.7			8.6				
−1.2	2.0	.8			.1				
7.5	11.7	9.2	% Profit Before Taxes/Total Assets	9.4	6.9				
3.6	4.5	2.4		.0	3.8				
−1.1	.6	.0		−7.3	−.3				
39.3	30.8	49.0	Sales/Net Fixed Assets	UND	33.3				
26.0	14.8	24.0		30.7	20.7				
13.9	7.1	11.7		6.4	12.7				
4.5	3.7	4.2	Sales/Total Assets	5.5	4.2				
3.4	3.0	3.5		2.9	3.5				
2.6	2.2	2.5		1.9	2.6				
(41) .8	(49) .9	(41) .9	% Depr., Dep., Amort./Sales		.9				
1.3	1.5	1.3			1.1				
1.9	2.6	2.0			2.1				
(21) 1.9	(26) 1.9	(25) 2.3	% Officers', Directors', Owners' Comp/Sales		(10) 4.1				
3.3	4.0	4.3			7.3				
9.2	7.8	7.4			11.9				
449123M	1179426M	1309860M	Net Sales ($)	5094M	36245M	20231M	63495M	28902M	1155893M
128177M	403652M	376527M	Total Assets ($)	1871M	12195M	8116M	19948M	7540M	326857M

M = $ thousand   MM = $ million
See Pages 1 through 15 for Explanation of Ratios and Data

RETAILERS—CATALOG & MAIL-ORDER HOUSES. SIC# 5961

Current Data Sorted By Assets							Comparative Historical Data	
1	3	4	2		1	**# Postretirement Benefits** **Type of Statement**		
	5	19	16	4	10	Unqualified	45	35
1	4	7	3	1		Reviewed	12	23
12	12	4				Compiled	10	20
	2	1				Tax Returns		2
2	10	16	7	2	2	Other	23	25
	56 (4/1-9/30/94)			84 (10/1/94-3/31/95)			4/1/90- 3/31/91 ALL	4/1/91- 3/31/92 ALL
0-500M	500M-2MM	2-10MM	10-50MM	50-100MM	100-250MM			
15	33	47	26	7	12	**NUMBER OF STATEMENTS**	90	105
%	%	%	%	%	%	**ASSETS**	%	%
12.1	12.5	7.3	8.3		9.6	Cash & Equivalents	6.7	10.6
24.6	15.1	17.5	15.4		22.7	Trade Receivables - (net)	14.1	15.4
36.6	48.3	40.3	39.9		31.2	Inventory	41.3	42.2
1.8	2.3	3.2	4.4		4.5	All Other Current	4.2	3.6
75.2	78.2	68.4	68.0		68.1	Total Current	66.3	71.7
13.1	15.3	17.3	19.1		19.6	Fixed Assets (net)	20.1	16.7
2.6	1.3	5.4	4.7		5.0	Intangibles (net)	3.0	3.0
9.0	5.2	8.8	8.1		7.3	All Other Non-Current	10.6	8.7
100.0	100.0	100.0	100.0		100.0	Total	100.0	100.0
						LIABILITIES		
11.7	8.0	10.7	11.4		7.9	Notes Payable-Short Term	11.2	11.0
2.7	2.0	2.5	2.0		1.9	Cur. Mat. -L/T/D	1.9	2.6
22.5	25.8	29.6	25.6		18.0	Trade Payables	23.1	22.6
.3	.1	.4	.4		2.6	Income Taxes Payable	.6	.5
9.5	14.4	8.8	10.2		14.5	All Other Current	7.9	9.4
46.8	50.3	52.0	49.6		44.9	Total Current	44.7	46.1
8.2	10.2	13.3	6.8		4.5	Long Term Debt	13.1	11.8
.2	.3	.1	.5		.7	Deferred Taxes	.1	.3
2.8	2.4	4.3	4.7		2.5	All Other-Non-Current	3.7	3.5
42.1	36.9	30.2	38.4		47.4	Net Worth	38.3	38.3
100.0	100.0	100.0	100.0		100.0	Total Liabilities & Net Worth	100.0	100.0
						INCOME DATA		
100.0	100.0	100.0	100.0		100.0	Net Sales	100.0	100.0
40.1	42.1	42.1	39.6		32.5	Gross Profit	38.5	42.2
37.9	40.7	39.1	36.4		26.7	Operating Expenses	35.6	38.5
2.2	1.4	3.0	3.1		5.8	Operating Profit	2.9	3.7
–.6	.2	.8	–.1		.4	All Other Expenses (net)	.4	.4
2.8	1.2	2.2	3.2		5.5	Profit Before Taxes	2.5	3.3
						RATIOS		
2.4	2.6	1.9	2.1		2.1		2.4	2.4
1.7	1.4	1.4	1.4		1.4	Current	1.5	1.6
1.4	1.1	1.0	1.0		1.3		1.1	1.2
1.7	1.0	.9	.8		1.5		.9	1.0
.7	.5	.4	.4		.7	Quick (89)	.5	.5
.5	.2	.2	.2		.3		.2	.2
5 74.9	3 124.4	4 83.8	4 92.2		12 30.3		3 104.5	3 123.7
18 20.0	8 44.1	10 35.3	8 48.5		31 11.6	Sales/Receivables	11 33.9	8 44.7
42 8.7	29 12.8	33 11.2	26 13.9		47 7.7		23 15.8	33 11.1
27 13.4	40 9.1	54 6.8	41 8.9		42 8.7		40 9.2	49 7.5
56 6.5	79 4.6	70 5.2	81 4.5		63 5.8	Cost of Sales/Inventory	81 4.5	74 4.9
122 3.0	135 2.7	107 3.4	114 3.2		122 3.0		126 2.9	130 2.8
7 48.8	22 16.8	29 12.7	25 14.7		19 19.3		22 16.9	27 13.7
15 24.0	41 8.8	46 7.9	49 7.4		37 9.9	Cost of Sales/Payables	38 9.7	41 8.8
47 7.8	55 6.6	69 5.3	73 5.0		60 6.1		61 6.0	62 5.9
6.6	6.2	6.6	8.0		5.8		8.7	7.1
15.7	15.2	19.0	23.9		15.8	Sales/Working Capital	14.5	12.3
88.5	69.5	999.8	106.2		17.7		54.0	31.9
(13) 17.3	(25) 6.6	(42) 13.7	(21) 10.9		139.0		(79) 8.5	(94) 10.2
3.8	3.4	5.6	4.2		(11) 26.5	EBIT/Interest	3.2	4.9
2.2	1.3	1.5	1.6		3.6		1.1	1.9
	(10) 8.6	(13) 20.3	(12) 14.3				(38) 8.8	(40) 11.5
	3.3	3.3	8.7			Net Profit + Depr., Dep., Amort./Cur. Mat. L /T/D	2.3	3.1
	.4	1.2	2.9				1.3	1.3
.1	.1	.2	.3		.3		.2	.2
.2	.3	.6	.7		.5	Fixed/Worth	.5	.4
.7	1.3	1.5	1.1		.8		.9	.9
.6	.6	1.0	.8		.7		.6	.8
1.5	1.7	1.8	1.9		1.2	Debt/Worth	1.6	1.7
5.5	4.3	6.2	7.1		2.1		4.4	3.9
(14) 59.3	(30) 42.6	(39) 68.5	49.1		(11) 39.6		(76) 46.5	(93) 57.1
37.5	21.3	31.3	29.1		20.0	% Profit Before Taxes/Tangible Net Worth	19.6	24.9
10.1	1.9	14.9	5.1		12.8		4.3	10.3
20.0	13.5	19.9	16.9		18.2		13.5	16.4
9.6	7.8	11.6	8.0		10.2	% Profit Before Taxes/Total Assets	7.1	9.4
4.4	.7	2.4	2.1		4.4		.5	3.6
178.0	87.1	48.2	30.4		23.2		44.8	49.2
43.7	39.8	28.8	17.1		14.6	Sales/Net Fixed Assets	20.0	24.9
20.9	17.5	14.2	11.7		7.7		10.1	13.4
6.2	5.5	4.9	4.2		3.4		4.7	4.1
4.5	3.8	3.3	3.1		2.5	Sales/Total Assets	3.1	3.1
3.5	2.8	2.4	2.3		1.8		2.2	2.3
(11) .5	(29) .5	(40) .6	(23) .8				(78) .7	(92) .6
1.0	.8	.9	1.2			% Depr., Dep., Amort./Sales	1.1	.9
1.4	1.5	1.6	1.4				1.5	1.3
(11) 4.2	(19) 3.5	(15) 3.2					(27) 1.7	(36) 2.2
4.9	6.2	4.3				% Officers', Directors', Owners' Comp/Sales	2.8	3.3
17.1	12.3	6.0					4.8	6.4
19472M	139929M	846604M	1881901M	1203616M	4910984M	Net Sales ($)	5376935M	6157523M
3873M	35836M	239334M	542043M	424689M	1902342M	Total Assets ($)	1951992M	2341360M

© Robert Morris Associates 1995

M = $ thousand   MM = $ million
See Pages 1 through 15 for Explanation of Ratios and Data

Comparative Historical Data				Current Data Sorted By Sales					
2	5	11		3	1		2	5	
			# Postretirement Benefits						
			Type of Statement						
50	38	54	Unqualified	1	5	4	9	35	
23	14	16	Reviewed	1	3	4	3	5	
21	22	28	Compiled	6	11	4	4	3	
4	5	3	Tax Returns		1	1	1		
27	35	39	Other		4	5	5	8	17
4/1/92- 3/31/93 ALL	4/1/93- 3/31/94 ALL	4/1/94- 3/31/95 ALL		56 (4/1-9/30/94)			84 (10/1/94-3/31/95)		
				0-1MM	1-3MM	3-5MM	5-10MM	10-25MM	25MM & OVER
125	114	140	**NUMBER OF STATEMENTS**	7	17	18	17	24	57
%	%	%	**ASSETS**	%	%	%	%	%	%
11.3	12.5	10.3	Cash & Equivalents		9.6	10.1	13.8	6.0	10.7
16.1	14.1	17.8	Trade Receivables - (net)		17.5	21.9	12.3	16.1	18.1
38.8	35.6	40.1	Inventory		47.4	37.5	49.9	42.9	35.8
4.2	3.0	3.1	All Other Current		2.7	.4	4.4	2.3	4.0
70.4	68.2	71.3	Total Current		77.2	69.9	80.4	67.4	68.5
17.7	17.0	16.9	Fixed Assets (net)		13.6	19.6	13.7	16.1	19.2
2.8	4.8	3.8	Intangibles (net)		3.7	3.5	.0	4.8	4.5
9.2	10.0	7.9	All Other Non-Current		5.5	6.9	5.8	11.7	7.8
100.0	100.0	100.0	Total		100.0	100.0	100.0	100.0	100.0
			LIABILITIES						
9.7	7.8	9.7	Notes Payable-Short Term		12.2	8.2	6.8	13.6	9.1
2.6	2.3	2.2	Cur. Mat.-L./T/D		2.0	4.0	2.0	1.7	1.7
23.9	24.1	25.7	Trade Payables		18.3	25.9	21.8	31.4	26.7
.4	1.9	.5	Income Taxes Payable		.3	.1	.6	.2	.8
12.4	10.9	10.9	All Other Current		10.8	13.1	9.4	8.8	12.0
48.9	47.0	49.0	Total Current		43.6	51.2	40.6	55.8	50.4
9.3	9.1	9.8	Long Term Debt		9.0	13.6	10.9	8.8	8.8
.5	.4	.3	Deferred Taxes		.4	.2	.1	.1	.6
3.8	2.4	3.5	All Other-Non-Current		4.0	2.7	2.7	2.9	3.8
37.5	41.2	37.4	Net Worth		42.9	32.3	45.7	32.4	36.5
100.0	100.0	100.0	Total Liabilities & Net Worth		100.0	100.0	100.0	100.0	100.0
			INCOME DATA						
100.0	100.0	100.0	Net Sales		100.0	100.0	100.0	100.0	100.0
42.9	42.4	40.3	Gross Profit		36.1	44.4	45.5	40.7	37.7
39.7	38.2	37.4	Operating Expenses		34.1	44.7	41.3	36.6	34.3
3.1	4.2	2.9	Operating Profit		2.0	−.3	4.2	4.1	3.4
.4	.1	.3	All Other Expenses (net)		.8	.4	.0	.9	.1
2.8	4.2	2.6	Profit Before Taxes		1.2	−.7	4.2	3.2	3.4
			RATIOS						
2.4	2.4	2.2			3.4	1.8	3.4	1.5	2.1
1.4	1.5	1.5	Current		2.0	1.3	1.9	1.1	1.5
1.1	1.2	1.1			1.3	1.1	1.3	1.0	1.1
1.0	1.1	1.0			1.4	.8	1.3	.8	1.1
.5	.6	.5	Quick		.5	.7	.8	.3	.5
.2	.2	.2			.3	.4	.1	.1	.3
4 90.7	4 99.8	4 82.4		6 58.0	5 68.0	1 595.3	4 91.2	5 78.0	
9 38.9	10 37.2	11 34.2	Sales/Receivables	15 24.6	13 28.0	6 58.9	7 51.6	11 34.7	
31 11.6	22 16.7	33 11.2		27 13.4	43 8.5	15 24.4	43 8.5	32 11.4	
40 9.2	44 8.3	41 9.0		29 12.6	38 9.7	58 6.3	44 8.3	37 10.0	
73 5.0	74 4.9	73 5.0	Cost of Sales/Inventory	126 2.9	59 6.2	111 3.3	72 5.1	65 5.6	
114 3.2	118 3.1	114 3.2		166 2.2	104 3.5	166 2.2	140 2.6	91 4.0	
25 14.5	25 14.8	23 15.9		9 42.4	28 13.2	24 15.4	35 10.4	24 15.5	
43 8.5	42 8.6	41 8.9	Cost of Sales/Payables	18 20.5	38 9.5	37 10.0	49 7.4	38 9.5	
64 5.7	64 5.7	62 5.9		46 7.9	54 6.7	61 6.0	94 3.9	62 5.9	
6.7	6.5	6.7		4.3	9.8	5.7	11.2	8.0	
16.0	16.4	16.4	Sales/Working Capital	6.6	27.3	7.5	58.2	17.0	
53.7	45.0	79.2		240.1	80.6	27.9	NM	63.1	
	12.0		17.7		13.1		11.5		6.1		12.5		42.4		24.2
(113) 4.5	(101) 6.6	(118) 4.7	EBIT/Interest	(15) 4.1	(15) 3.2	(13) 5.0	(21) 4.4	(48) 6.3	
1.6	2.6	1.8		1.5	−.1	2.0	1.6	2.5	
	8.7		10.1		12.9	Net Profit + Depr., Dep.,									22.3
(41) 2.9	(35) 5.2	(48) 4.1	Amort./Cur. Mat. L/T/D					(22) 8.7	
2.2	1.3	2.2						2.8	
.2	.2	.2		.1	.2	.1	.2	.2	
.5	.4	.5	Fixed/Worth	.3	.6	.2	.7	.6	
1.0	1.0	1.1		.6	1.5	.7	1.0	1.3	
.7	.7	.8		.5	1.1	.4	1.4	.8	
1.8	1.6	1.7	Debt/Worth	1.1	2.2	1.5	2.4	1.5	
4.0	3.8	5.0		5.8	6.4	3.4	7.2	4.9	
45.2	55.7	51.7	% Profit Before Taxes/Tangible	57.2	30.1	43.4	74.3	48.0	
(113) 24.0	(101) 25.4	(126) 28.2	Net Worth	(16) 20.5	(15) 21.4	(15) 18.0	(22) 34.5	(52) 29.8	
7.2	13.2	9.0		2.6	−41.1	6.3	14.6	13.3	
16.4	19.1	16.9	% Profit Before Taxes/Total	14.4	12.6	28.4	17.2	19.5	
6.8	10.1	9.2	Assets	7.0	4.7	11.6	8.9	12.7	
1.9	3.1	2.5		1.0	−6.8	3.7	2.4	3.8	
44.3	48.5	50.7		77.6	70.1	142.1	49.7	38.8	
23.0	24.6	27.3	Sales/Net Fixed Assets	33.0	28.6	34.5	28.4	20.7	
13.2	12.6	13.5		15.0	20.4	10.4	11.4	11.8	
4.3	4.4	4.8		5.2	5.4	4.0	4.7	4.7	
3.1	3.3	3.4	Sales/Total Assets	3.5	3.8	3.2	3.2	3.1	
2.2	2.2	2.4		1.8	3.3	1.7	2.2	2.8	
.7	.6	.6		.5	.6	.5	.6	.6	
(108) 1.0	(100) 1.1	(118) .9	% Depr., Dep., Amort./Sales	(14) 1.0	(15) .8	(15) 1.3	(22) .8	(47) .9	
1.5	1.7	1.5		1.6	2.3	2.4	1.6	1.3	
2.0	2.4	2.8		4.3		3.0		1.9	
(44) 4.3	(33) 4.6	(54) 4.7	% Officers', Directors', Owners' Comp/Sales	(12) 4.8	(10) 4.4		(10) 2.7	
9.2	7.7	7.1		11.0	8.0		6.2	
8726067M	9380927M	9002506M	Net Sales ($)	3342M	35879M	65772M	112796M	389600M	8395117M
3204383M	3229785M	3148117M	Total Assets ($)	1270M	15018M	17966M	47380M	142258M	2924225M

M = $ thousand   MM = $ million
See Pages 1 through 15 for Explanation of Ratios and Data

Current Data Sorted By Assets   Comparative Historical Data

	0-500M	500M-2MM	2-10MM	10-50MM	50-100MM	100-250MM	# Postretirement Benefits / Type of Statement	4/1/90-3/31/91 ALL	4/1/91-3/31/92 ALL
	2	7	2	2					
	6	18	6	4	4		Unqualified	32	37
	6	27	16				Reviewed	69	55
	42	31	11				Compiled	85	70
	16	3					Tax Returns	5	4
	22	44	15	3	1		Other	72	80
	86 (4/1-9/30/94)			189 (10/1/94-3/31/95)					
NUMBER OF STATEMENTS	86	111	60	9	5	4		263	246

ASSETS

Item	0-500M %	500M-2MM %	2-10MM %	10-50MM %	50-100MM %	100-250MM %	4/1/90-3/31/91 ALL %	4/1/91-3/31/92 ALL %
Cash & Equivalents	10.8	7.2	8.3				7.2	7.1
Trade Receivables - (net)	41.6	42.6	49.3				36.9	38.0
Inventory	26.7	28.7	22.8				35.1	33.6
All Other Current	1.2	2.2	.9				1.6	1.6
Total Current	80.3	80.6	81.3				80.8	80.3
Fixed Assets (net)	13.2	13.1	12.1				12.0	13.2
Intangibles (net)	2.5	2.0	1.3				1.9	1.8
All Other Non-Current	4.0	4.3	5.2				5.2	4.7
Total	100.0	100.0	100.0				100.0	100.0

LIABILITIES

Item	0-500M	500M-2MM	2-10MM				4/1/90-3/31/91	4/1/91-3/31/92
Notes Payable-Short Term	14.0	16.5	13.0				17.3	15.5
Cur. Mat. -L/T/D	4.2	2.4	3.0				3.8	3.5
Trade Payables	22.2	25.7	29.1				25.2	25.7
Income Taxes Payable	.6	1.0	.4				1.0	.7
All Other Current	10.1	11.4	12.3				11.4	11.3
Total Current	51.1	56.9	57.8				58.6	56.7
Long Term Debt	14.3	8.2	6.8				11.3	11.0
Deferred Taxes	.1	.3	.2				.3	.3
All Other-Non-Current	5.5	4.4	4.9				3.1	3.3
Net Worth	29.0	30.2	30.2				26.6	28.7
Total Liabilities & Net Worth	100.0	100.0	100.0				100.0	100.0

INCOME DATA

Item	0-500M	500M-2MM	2-10MM				4/1/90-3/31/91	4/1/91-3/31/92
Net Sales	100.0	100.0	100.0				100.0	100.0
Gross Profit	36.0	31.8	31.3				33.7	31.2
Operating Expenses	33.1	29.2	27.4				30.5	29.1
Operating Profit	2.8	2.6	3.9				3.2	2.2
All Other Expenses (net)	.5	.4	1.1				1.0	.5
Profit Before Taxes	2.3	2.2	2.8				2.2	1.6

RATIOS

Ratio	0-500M	500M-2MM	2-10MM				4/1/90-3/31/91	4/1/91-3/31/92
Current	2.2 / 1.6 / 1.3	1.8 / 1.5 / 1.1	1.7 / 1.3 / 1.2				1.9 / 1.4 / 1.1	1.9 / 1.4 / 1.2
Quick	1.7 / 1.0 / .7	(110) 1.3 / .9 / .6	1.3 / .9 / .8				1.1 / .7 / .5	(245) 1.1 / .8 / .6
Sales/Receivables	(22) 16.4 / (32) 11.4 / (47) 7.8	(29) 12.7 / (38) 9.5 / (55) 6.6	(38) 9.5 / (46) 8.0 / (60) 6.1				(24) 15.1 / (35) 10.5 / (54) 6.7	(24) 15.2 / (35) 10.3 / (50) 7.3
Cost of Sales/Inventory	(13) 28.1 / (30) 12.3 / (51) 7.1	(18) 20.4 / (34) 10.7 / (62) 5.9	(13) 27.5 / (25) 14.8 / (44) 8.3				(26) 14.2 / (47) 7.8 / (83) 4.4	(23) 15.8 / (43) 8.5 / (69) 5.3
Cost of Sales/Payables	(12) 31.7 / (25) 14.6 / (44) 8.3	(16) 22.4 / (29) 12.7 / (52) 7.0	(21) 17.2 / (38) 9.5 / (53) 6.9				(19) 19.3 / (33) 11.1 / (55) 6.6	(18) 20.6 / (32) 11.4 / (50) 7.3
Sales/Working Capital	9.4 / 15.4 / 29.2	8.9 / 14.9 / 52.1	8.9 / 14.2 / 30.9				9.0 / 16.9 / 58.4	10.0 / 16.6 / 36.1
EBIT/Interest	(72) 10.8 / 3.3 / .8	(103) 8.6 / 3.0 / 1.1	(54) 9.8 / 3.4 / 1.9				(248) 6.1 / 2.5 / 1.1	(230) 7.6 / 2.9 / 1.1
Net Profit + Depr., Dep., Amort./Cur. Mat. L/T/D	(14) 3.8 / 1.2 / -.5	(38) 6.8 / 2.1 / .9	(17) 8.2 / 1.7 / 1.2				(123) 7.2 / 2.3 / .7	(91) 7.1 / 1.7 / .6
Fixed/Worth	.2 / .4 / 1.0	.1 / .4 / 1.0	.1 / .3 / .9				.2 / .3 / .9	.2 / .3 / .8
Debt/Worth	.9 / 3.1 / 10.9	1.5 / 2.8 / 5.4	1.5 / 2.7 / 5.4				1.5 / 3.0 / 6.9	1.5 / 2.6 / 5.5
% Profit Before Taxes/Tangible Net Worth	(76) 85.7 / 30.9 / 2.2	(102) 47.6 / 22.1 / 5.9	(57) 45.3 / 26.7 / 15.6				(241) 46.5 / 23.2 / 3.0	(225) 45.9 / 20.9 / 6.7
% Profit Before Taxes/Total Assets	22.2 / 6.5 / -.7	11.2 / 5.5 / .5	12.4 / 6.2 / 2.5				11.9 / 5.7 / .4	12.8 / 5.6 / .8
Sales/Net Fixed Assets	120.7 / 47.0 / 22.0	131.4 / 38.2 / 18.3	139.4 / 53.0 / 17.4				105.6 / 46.0 / 20.3	105.5 / 49.3 / 20.7
Sales/Total Assets	5.9 / 4.3 / 3.4	5.0 / 3.8 / 2.5	4.9 / 3.7 / 2.5				4.9 / 3.6 / 2.7	4.9 / 3.8 / 2.7
% Depr., Dep., Amort./Sales	(57) .4 / .8 / 1.7	(89) .2 / .7 / 1.4	(51) .3 / .6 / 1.6				(223) .4 / .7 / 1.5	(215) .4 / .7 / 1.4
% Officers', Directors', Owners' Comp/Sales	(43) 3.2 / 6.2 / 9.9	(46) 1.9 / 3.7 / 7.4	(16) .9 / 2.4 / 3.8				(101) 2.0 / 3.6 / 6.9	(100) 1.7 / 3.4 / 7.5

Item	0-500M	500M-2MM	2-10MM	10-50MM	50-100MM	100-250MM	4/1/90-3/31/91	4/1/91-3/31/92
Net Sales ($)	102531M	456500M	835161M	662897M	877360M	819185M	3665420M	3853272M
Total Assets ($)	21224M	112191M	231141M	232443M	393077M	632446M	1276501M	1158115M

M = $ thousand   MM = $ million
See Pages 1 through 15 for Explanation of Ratios and Data

Comparative Historical Data				Current Data Sorted By Sales					
4	15	13	# Postretirement Benefits	1	6	1	1	2	2
			Type of Statement						
24	36	38	Unqualified		5	5	3	7	18
48	63	49	Reviewed	4	12	9	12	11	1
83	79	84	Compiled	21	29	11	17	6	
6	14	19	Tax Returns	9	9	1			
63	75	85	Other	11	32	11	14	12	5
4/1/92-3/31/93 ALL	4/1/93-3/31/94 ALL	4/1/94-3/31/95 ALL		86 (4/1-9/30/94)			189 (10/1/94-3/31/95)		
				0-1MM	1-3MM	3-5MM	5-10MM	10-25MM	25MM & OVER
224	267	275	**NUMBER OF STATEMENTS**	45	87	36	47	36	24
%	%	%	**ASSETS**	%	%	%	%	%	%
9.3	7.7	8.7	Cash & Equivalents	11.6	8.8	11.2	5.4	7.2	8.3
37.4	43.6	43.0	Trade Receivables - (net)	41.7	39.4	40.1	47.3	52.9	39.3
30.9	27.8	26.3	Inventory	20.3	29.2	30.4	28.1	24.3	20.6
1.0	1.6	1.9	All Other Current	1.0	2.2	1.5	1.5	.9	5.1
78.5	80.6	79.9	Total Current	74.6	79.6	83.2	82.4	85.3	73.3
13.4	12.6	12.8	Fixed Assets (net)	15.8	14.8	11.6	10.3	9.9	10.6
2.9	2.4	2.2	Intangibles (net)	5.1	1.7	.8	1.5	1.0	4.3
5.2	4.3	5.0	All Other Non-Current	4.5	3.9	4.3	5.8	3.8	11.8
100.0	100.0	100.0	Total	100.0	100.0	100.0	100.0	100.0	100.0
			LIABILITIES						
13.5	14.9	14.5	Notes Payable-Short Term	15.2	14.9	13.6	14.6	15.6	11.6
3.8	3.4	3.1	Cur. Mat.-L /T/D	3.5	4.0	4.5	1.9	1.3	2.4
23.3	25.3	25.2	Trade Payables	18.1	23.3	25.4	28.0	33.6	26.6
.7	1.2	.7	Income Taxes Payable	.3	1.1	.7	.8	.3	.7
11.2	10.5	11.6	All Other Current	11.0	10.5	9.3	13.3	12.0	17.0
52.5	55.2	55.2	Total Current	48.1	53.8	53.5	58.6	62.8	58.3
10.5	9.5	9.9	Long Term Debt	14.8	12.0	8.0	7.5	4.9	7.8
.4	.4	.3	Deferred Taxes	.2	.3	.2	.1	.3	.8
5.4	4.2	4.8	All Other-Non-Current	4.5	5.7	4.0	5.6	3.5	3.4
31.2	30.7	29.9	Net Worth	32.4	28.2	34.3	28.2	28.5	29.7
100.0	100.0	100.0	Total Liabilities & Net Worth	100.0	100.0	100.0	100.0	100.0	100.0
			INCOME DATA						
100.0	100.0	100.0	Net Sales	100.0	100.0	100.0	100.0	100.0	100.0
34.6	32.1	32.8	Gross Profit	42.7	36.6	30.5	25.7	27.0	26.6
31.2	28.8	29.6	Operating Expenses	39.8	33.0	27.6	24.7	22.9	20.8
3.5	3.2	3.2	Operating Profit	2.9	3.6	2.9	1.0	4.1	5.8
.8	.5	.7	All Other Expenses (net)	.8	.7	.2	.5	.7	1.3
2.7	2.7	2.6	Profit Before Taxes	2.1	2.9	2.7	.5	3.4	4.5
			RATIOS						
2.0	2.0	1.9	Current	2.2	2.0	1.9	2.0	1.7	1.5
1.5	1.4	1.5		1.6	1.5	1.6	1.4	1.3	1.3
1.2	1.2	1.2		1.3	1.2	1.3	1.1	1.1	1.1
1.3	1.3	1.3	Quick	1.7	1.2	1.3	1.3	1.2	1.2
.9	.9 (274)	.9		1.1	.9	.9 (46)	.9	.9	.8
.6	.7	.7		.8	.6	.7	.7	.8	.4
24 15.2	27 13.3	29 12.7	Sales/Receivables	30 12.1	27 13.7	24 15.2	31 11.9	37 9.9	33 11.0
36 10.2	38 9.6	41 8.9		45 8.2	35 10.3	33 11.1	43 8.5	43 8.4	50 7.3
51 7.2	54 6.8	54 6.7		56 6.5	53 6.9	47 7.7	54 6.7	56 6.5	59 6.2
22 16.8	14 26.6	16 22.8	Cost of Sales/Inventory	9 42.8	18 20.7	21 17.4	14 26.7	15 24.3	13 27.2
39 9.3	33 11.1	31 11.9		31 11.6	40 9.2	32 11.5	26 14.1	24 15.4	27 13.5
76 4.8	58 6.3	55 6.6		59 6.2	68 5.4	49 7.5	48 7.6	31 11.6	53 6.9
18 20.3	16 23.4	17 22.1	Cost of Sales/Payables	5 68.6	16 23.3	17 22.1	20 18.3	19 19.0	20 18.3
33 11.2	32 11.5	31 11.6		27 13.7	31 11.7	28 12.9	26 13.8	36 10.1	42 8.7
49 7.4	49 7.4	51 7.1		53 6.9	53 6.9	40 9.1	46 7.9	52 7.0	63 5.8
8.1	9.6	9.2	Sales/Working Capital	8.4	8.7	9.6	9.2	10.5	11.2
15.2	17.1	15.3		13.9	14.5	14.4	17.6	22.4	19.6
32.9	41.3	37.8		26.1	30.0	24.9	76.2	44.7	27.8
(206) 7.0	(240) 9.3	(244) 9.3	EBIT/Interest	(36) 8.2	(79) 11.3	(33) 9.9	(43) 7.8	(32) 10.1	(21) 14.2
2.6	3.3	3.2		2.3	3.0	3.1	2.6	3.4	5.0
1.2	1.4	1.1		-1.5	1.1	1.8	.6	2.0	2.1
(71) 6.8	(69) 6.3	(80) 6.6	Net Profit + Depr., Dep., Amort./Cur. Mat. L/T/D		(28) 3.9	(14) 5.1	(15) 10.7		(11) 83.8
1.5	1.7	2.1			2.0	1.8	1.8		7.0
.5	.5	.9			.5	.9	1.4		3.6
.2	.2	.1	Fixed/Worth	.2	.2	.1	.2	.1	.2
.4	.3	.4		.6	.4	.2	.4	.2	.3
1.0	.8	1.0		2.7	1.2	.9	1.0	.8	.7
1.3	1.5	1.3	Debt/Worth	.8	1.2	1.2	1.6	1.4	2.2
2.9	2.9	2.9		3.2	2.9	2.1	3.1	2.9	2.9
6.6	5.7	6.1		19.5	8.9	4.2	6.0	7.1	5.7
(203) 57.0	(251) 59.5	(252) 53.6	% Profit Before Taxes/Tangible Net Worth	(39) 85.0	(77) 70.8	(35) 47.4	(44) 34.9	(34) 46.1	(23) 56.8
21.1	26.7	26.6		14.8	29.2	18.5	21.3	26.6	42.4
4.8	7.6	6.9		-44.2	5.4	7.4	.8	19.0	20.3
14.6	14.0	15.3	% Profit Before Taxes/Total Assets	21.6	16.6	11.7	10.1	19.6	14.2
4.9	6.1	6.1		5.6	6.8	5.9	3.9	7.0	9.0
.7	1.7	.8		-7.3	.6	2.0	-.1	2.7	3.5
89.0	125.2	130.3	Sales/Net Fixed Assets	65.5	110.0	143.0	156.5	288.0	92.1
39.1	43.8	39.6		27.1	35.8	52.2	46.0	110.0	47.6
16.7	20.2	19.0		16.3	14.8	21.2	27.2	24.9	9.1
4.9	5.4	5.2	Sales/Total Assets	4.2	5.3	5.3	5.2	5.6	4.7
3.8	4.0	3.9		3.4	3.9	4.3	4.4	4.4	3.0
2.7	2.8	2.6		2.3	2.4	3.1	3.2	3.0	1.3
(187) .4	(215) .3	(212) .3	% Depr., Dep., Amort./Sales	(30) .6	(66) .3	(25) .4	(40) .2	(30) .2	(21) .3
.7	.8	.7		1.3	.8	.8	.7	.4	.6
1.8	1.6	1.6		2.7	1.7	1.0	1.3	.8	3.7
(103) 2.1	(123) 1.8	(105) 2.1	% Officers', Directors', Owners' Comp/Sales	(20) 5.1	(46) 2.3	(13) 1.9	(15) 1.8		
3.8	3.6	4.5		6.9	5.0	3.0	3.2		
7.0	6.4	7.3		10.2	7.9	6.2	3.9		
3446689M	3859744M	3753634M	Net Sales ($)	28406M	165356M	139225M	324120M	547468M	2549059M
1114970M	1114532M	1622522M	Total Assets ($)	9711M	52768M	40610M	89505M	136571M	1293357M

M = $ thousand   MM = $ million
See Pages 1 through 15 for Explanation of Ratios and Data

Current Data Sorted By Assets						# Postretirement Benefits	Comparative Historical Data	
1		3			2	**Type of Statement**		
2	2	5	10	3	7	Unqualified	37	46
	2	4	4			Reviewed	16	25
2	2	6				Compiled	22	17
2	1					Tax Returns	1	4
3	2	7		5	4	Other	24	27
10 (4/1-9/30/94)		61 (10/1/94-3/31/95)					4/1/90-3/31/91	4/1/91-3/31/92
0-500M	500M-2MM	2-10MM	10-50MM	50-100MM	100-250MM		ALL	ALL
7	9	22	14	8	11	**NUMBER OF STATEMENTS**	100	119
%	%	%	%	%	%	**ASSETS**	%	%
		4.9	4.9		3.6	Cash & Equivalents	5.1	7.5
		14.8	10.9		12.1	Trade Receivables - (net)	15.1	13.7
		50.4	49.4		43.6	Inventory	47.3	46.3
		1.2	1.1		1.9	All Other Current	1.7	1.5
		71.4	66.3		61.2	Total Current	69.3	69.0
		19.5	27.7		31.1	Fixed Assets (net)	23.4	24.7
		1.0	.7		2.4	Intangibles (net)	1.5	.8
		8.2	5.3		5.3	All Other Non-Current	5.8	5.5
		100.0	100.0		100.0	Total	100.0	100.0
						LIABILITIES		
		5.0	9.8		4.1	Notes Payable-Short Term	11.9	7.3
		4.2	1.7		1.6	Cur. Mat. -L/T/D	3.2	3.1
		18.5	13.4		15.3	Trade Payables	15.1	14.3
		.4	.5		1.5	Income Taxes Payable	1.1	.6
		5.6	5.7		7.8	All Other Current	6.6	7.2
		33.7	31.1		30.1	Total Current	37.8	32.6
		8.9	21.3		16.4	Long Term Debt	19.0	18.9
		.2	1.0		.8	Deferred Taxes	.7	.6
		.7	3.6		2.2	All Other-Non-Current	2.8	4.2
		56.5	43.0		50.5	Net Worth	39.8	43.7
		100.0	100.0		100.0	Total Liabilities & Net Worth	100.0	100.0
						INCOME DATA		
		100.0	100.0		100.0	Net Sales	100.0	100.0
		32.5	33.6		31.9	Gross Profit	34.1	33.8
		32.3	28.8		29.8	Operating Expenses	32.8	32.3
		.2	4.8		2.0	Operating Profit	1.3	1.5
		-.2	1.6		-.2	All Other Expenses (net)	.8	.5
		.4	3.2		2.3	Profit Before Taxes	.5	1.0
						RATIOS		
		2.9	4.3		2.6		2.8	3.1
		2.2	1.8		2.3	Current	1.9	2.3
		1.7	1.5		1.4		1.3	1.6
		1.0	1.3		1.0		1.2	1.3
		.4	.5		.6	Quick (99)	.5	.6
		.1	.1		.2		.1	.2
		2 167.0	1 617.3		3 114.1		1 282.2	3 145.1
		6 65.2	16 22.2		14 25.9	Sales/Receivables	10 36.5	10 36.0
		34 10.7	34 10.7		57 6.4		60 6.1	49 7.5
		85 4.3	74 4.9		91 4.0		83 4.4	81 4.5
		101 3.6	114 3.2		104 3.5	Cost of Sales/Inventory	107 3.4	104 3.5
		126 2.9	146 2.5		114 3.2		135 2.7	130 2.8
		16 22.8	17 21.2		20 18.3		17 20.9	18 20.8
		28 13.2	32 11.3		29 12.7	Cost of Sales/Payables	31 11.6	29 12.4
		45 8.1	54 6.7		47 7.8		43 8.4	41 9.0
		4.0	3.6		4.1		4.1	3.8
		7.5	6.5		6.5	Sales/Working Capital	6.7	6.1
		12.8	11.2		17.5		15.6	14.1
		7.0	4.7		19.0		3.4	3.6
	(20)	2.1	2.1	(10)	3.9	EBIT/Interest (95)	1.7	(106) 1.6
		-2.4	1.4		2.3		.8	1.0
		4.2					3.9	6.5
	(10)	2.0				Net Profit + Depr., Dep., Amort./Cur. Mat. L./T/D (50)	1.6	(66) 2.1
		-.9					.7	.6
		.1	.3		.5		.3	.3
		.3	.6		.7	Fixed/Worth	.6	.5
		.5	1.4		.8		1.2	1.2
		.4	.8		.8		.9	.8
		.7	1.6		.9	Debt/Worth	1.8	1.3
		1.5	2.6		1.4		2.8	2.5
		17.1	28.0		24.6		19.8	14.7
	(21)	3.9	13.5		11.1	% Profit Before Taxes/Tangible Net Worth (96)	5.7	(117) 6.4
		-9.3	3.5		5.1		-.9	.1
		8.8	10.6		13.1		6.5	8.3
		2.0	2.4		5.5	% Profit Before Taxes/Total Assets	2.3	2.4
		-6.4	1.7		2.5		-1.2	.0
		42.2	14.3		10.7		27.8	23.6
		22.8	7.3		8.9	Sales/Net Fixed Assets	12.1	10.0
		7.9	5.5		6.4		6.3	6.3
		4.3	2.8		2.8		3.0	3.2
		2.9	2.0		2.7	Sales/Total Assets	2.4	2.5
		1.7	1.4		1.7		1.7	1.7
		.5	.8		1.2		.8	.9
	(21)	1.0	(12) 1.5	(10)	2.0	% Depr., Dep., Amort./Sales (86)	1.5	(111) 1.5
		1.4	2.3		3.0		2.2	2.3
							1.1	.7
						% Officers', Directors', Owners' Comp/Sales (28)	3.3	(29) 2.9
							7.3	7.3
3384M	20953M	278860M	777620M	1136705M	3709095M	Net Sales ($)	6848931M	11344570M
1559M	9711M	98770M	368189M	584472M	1579547M	Total Assets ($)	3287216M	4893875M

M = $ thousand   MM = $ million
See Pages 1 through 15 for Explanation of Ratios and Data

Comparative Historical Data / Current Data Sorted By Sales

	4/1/92-3/31/93 ALL	4/1/93-3/31/94 ALL	4/1/94-3/31/95 ALL		0-1MM	1-3MM	3-5MM	5-10MM	10-25MM	25MM & OVER
# Postretirement Benefits	2	2	6			1			1	2 / 2
Type of Statement										
Unqualified	41	33	29		1	3			8	17
Reviewed	18	13	10		1	1	1	1	2	4
Compiled	10	8	10		2	1	2	1	4	
Tax Returns	3	1	1			1				
Other	18	16	21		3	2		4	3	9
					10 (4/1-9/30/94)			61 (10/1/94-3/31/95)		
NUMBER OF STATEMENTS	90	71	71		7	8	3	6	17	30
ASSETS	%	%	%		%	%	%	%	%	%
Cash & Equivalents	7.6	5.7	4.5						5.3	3.9
Trade Receivables - (net)	14.3	12.1	13.7						11.9	13.7
Inventory	45.4	48.8	51.1						47.0	50.3
All Other Current	1.0	1.6	1.7						1.1	1.4
Total Current	68.3	68.3	70.9						65.2	69.3
Fixed Assets (net)	22.7	23.6	21.9						25.5	24.5
Intangibles (net)	1.8	1.5	1.7						1.0	1.4
All Other Non-Current	7.2	6.7	5.4						8.2	4.8
Total	100.0	100.0	100.0						100.0	100.0
LIABILITIES										
Notes Payable-Short Term	5.8	6.1	6.2						4.5	9.0
Cur. Mat.-L /T/D	2.3	3.1	2.8						3.7	2.1
Trade Payables	15.9	15.9	16.1						17.7	14.7
Income Taxes Payable	.6	1.3	.7						.6	1.0
All Other Current	8.5	8.1	6.6						6.2	6.7
Total Current	33.1	34.4	32.4						32.7	33.6
Long Term Debt	20.8	18.9	15.8						13.5	18.9
Deferred Taxes	.6	.7	.6						.9	.4
All Other-Non-Current	3.5	2.8	3.0						2.0	2.4
Net Worth	41.9	43.1	48.2						50.9	44.6
Total Liabilities & Net Worth	100.0	100.0	100.0						100.0	100.0
INCOME DATA										
Net Sales	100.0	100.0	100.0						100.0	100.0
Gross Profit	31.2	33.6	32.9						32.3	31.6
Operating Expenses	29.9	31.7	30.5						29.5	29.0
Operating Profit	1.3	2.0	2.4						2.8	2.6
All Other Expenses (net)	.8	.2	.4						.8	.5
Profit Before Taxes	.6	1.8	2.0						1.9	2.1
RATIOS										
Current	3.9 / 2.2 / 1.7	2.8 / 2.2 / 1.6	3.2 / 2.3 / 1.6						2.5 / 2.1 / 1.4	2.9 / 2.1 / 1.5
Quick	1.5 / .6 / .3	(70) .9 / .5 / .1	(70) 1.0 / .4 / .2						1.1 / .6 / .2	1.0 / .4 / .2
Sales/Receivables	2 204.8 / 13 28.3 / 58 6.3	2 220.8 / 9 40.4 / 41 8.8	2 168.3 / 10 37.0 / 40 9.1						1 294.8 / 10 36.2 / 31 11.7	2 185.5 / 8 46.8 / 59 6.2
Cost of Sales/Inventory	78 4.7 / 107 3.4 / 140 2.6	87 4.2 / 111 3.3 / 159 2.3	89 4.1 / 111 3.3 / 146 2.5						56 6.5 / 87 4.2 / 126 2.9	99 3.7 / 111 3.3 / 135 2.7
Cost of Sales/Payables	22 16.7 / 33 11.1 / 46 8.0	20 18.5 / 34 10.7 / 58 6.3	20 18.3 / 33 11.0 / 47 7.8						15 24.9 / 30 12.2 / 55 6.6	20 18.3 / 32 11.4 / 43 8.5
Sales/Working Capital	3.7 / 5.7 / 12.8	4.3 / 6.2 / 12.8	3.9 / 5.6 / 10.6						4.2 / 8.9 / 14.5	4.1 / 6.5 / 10.2
EBIT/Interest	(83) 4.3 / 2.1 / .0	(68) 5.3 / 2.3 / 1.0	(66) 6.5 / 2.4 / 1.3						7.1 / 2.4 / -.4	(29) 5.1 / 2.4 / 1.5
Net Profit + Depr., Dep., Amort./Cur. Mat. L/T/D	(42) 5.5 / 2.2 / .7	(40) 4.5 / 1.8 / .5	(32) 6.9 / 2.9 / 1.2							(15) 8.7 / 3.8 / 2.4
Fixed/Worth	.3 / .6 / 1.0	.3 / .5 / 1.0	.2 / .4 / .8						.2 / .4 / .9	.4 / .6 / .8
Debt/Worth	.7 / 1.5 / 2.4	.9 / 1.4 / 2.3	.6 / 1.1 / 1.9						.5 / 1.0 / 1.9	.9 / 1.2 / 1.9
% Profit Before Taxes/Tangible Net Worth	(86) 19.1 / 7.8 / -.0	(70) 20.6 / 6.5 / .3	(68) 21.3 / 11.0 / 2.3						23.9 / 7.2 / -6.0	20.4 / 10.8 / 5.0
% Profit Before Taxes/Total Assets	8.0 / 3.2 / -1.4	9.7 / 2.5 / .1	9.3 / 4.4 / .9						10.2 / 2.5 / -2.1	8.7 / 4.2 / 1.9
Sales/Net Fixed Assets	28.4 / 11.4 / 6.7	21.6 / 11.0 / 6.7	27.7 / 12.3 / 6.6						26.3 / 18.8 / 5.5	16.2 / 9.5 / 6.6
Sales/Total Assets	3.1 / 2.3 / 1.9	2.8 / 2.2 / 1.6	3.0 / 2.3 / 1.7						4.3 / 2.8 / 1.5	2.8 / 2.4 / 1.9
% Depr., Dep., Amort./Sales	(82) .8 / 1.4 / 2.1	(65) 1.0 / 1.4 / 2.2	(63) .9 / 1.4 / 2.1						.6 / 1.1 / 1.6	(27) 1.0 / 1.5 / 2.3
% Officers', Directors', Owners' Comp/Sales	(21) .7 / 3.9 / 7.7	(15) 1.0 / 5.6 / 9.3	(14) .8 / 3.1 / 9.3							
Net Sales ($)	8321531M	7222475M	5926617M		2857M	15453M	11690M	43483M	265507M	5587627M
Total Assets ($)	3797244M	3304030M	2642248M		2148M	10655M	5421M	20355M	153286M	2450383M

© Robert Morris Associates 1995

M = $ thousand   MM = $ million
See Pages 1 through 15 for Explanation of Ratios and Data

554 RETAILERS—DRY GOODS & GENERAL MERCHANDISE. SIC# 5399

Current Data Sorted By Assets

Type of Statement	0-500M	500M-2MM	2-10MM	10-50MM	50-100MM	100-250MM
		1		1		
		6	8	5	2	
		2	2	1		
	9	13	6	2		1
	2	1				
	6		3	3		

	35 (4/1-9/30/94)			41 (10/1/94-3/31/95)		
	0-500M	500M-2MM	2-10MM	10-50MM	50-100MM	100-250MM
NUMBER OF STATEMENTS	15	28	19	11	2	1

Comparative Historical Data

# Postretirement Benefits / Type of Statement	4/1/90-3/31/91 ALL	4/1/91-3/31/92 ALL
Unqualified	28	19
Reviewed	23	22
Compiled	32	28
Tax Returns		
Other	13	20
NUMBER OF STATEMENTS	96	89

Main Data

0-500M	500M-2MM	2-10MM	10-50MM	50-100MM	100-250MM		4/1/90-3/31/91 ALL	4/1/91-3/31/92 ALL
%	%	%	%	%	%	**ASSETS**	%	%
11.8	12.6	6.3	7.2			Cash & Equivalents	8.3	8.5
16.7	7.9	9.3	6.0			Trade Receivables - (net)	11.8	8.5
51.3	47.6	52.0	46.7			Inventory	47.3	48.6
.6	1.3	1.2	.5			All Other Current	2.5	1.9
80.4	69.5	68.8	60.5			Total Current	69.9	67.5
14.9	22.6	17.8	30.5			Fixed Assets (net)	22.4	23.0
1.5	.1	.6	5.0			Intangibles (net)	1.2	1.6
3.1	7.8	12.9	4.1			All Other Non-Current	6.5	7.9
100.0	100.0	100.0	100.0			Total	100.0	100.0
						LIABILITIES		
8.9	8.5	8.3	10.0			Notes Payable-Short Term	9.2	10.4
4.3	1.9	2.9	2.6			Cur. Mat. -L/T/D	3.9	3.8
15.6	15.6	23.1	17.0			Trade Payables	20.3	16.7
.9	.4	.1	.3			Income Taxes Payable	.6	.6
11.0	10.3	7.9	8.7			All Other Current	6.3	6.9
40.7	36.7	42.2	38.6			Total Current	40.2	38.5
16.7	10.2	10.9	12.5			Long Term Debt	17.4	18.1
.0	.1	.0	.3			Deferred Taxes	.2	.1
1.7	2.1	4.8	2.5			All Other-Non-Current	2.3	3.4
40.9	50.9	42.1	46.1			Net Worth	40.0	39.9
100.0	100.0	100.0	100.0			Total Liabilities & Net Worth	100.0	100.0
						INCOME DATA		
100.0	100.0	100.0	100.0			Net Sales	100.0	100.0
42.8	33.7	33.1	38.0			Gross Profit	35.6	34.4
38.4	31.6	31.5	32.8			Operating Expenses	32.4	32.4
4.3	2.1	1.6	5.3			Operating Profit	3.3	2.0
-.2	-.5	.6	1.5			All Other Expenses (net)	.2	.9
4.5	2.5	1.0	3.8			Profit Before Taxes	3.0	1.1
						RATIOS		
10.9	2.7	2.2	1.9			Current	3.0	2.8
3.0	2.0	1.6	1.6				1.8	1.9
1.2	1.3	1.2	1.5				1.3	1.2
2.5	.9	.7	.5			Quick	1.0	.8
.9	.4	.3	.3				.3	.3
.3	.2	.1	.1				.1	.1
0 UND	0 UND	0 999.8	1 249.7			Sales/Receivables	1 498.5	0 992.6
6 62.0	0 UND	4 82.0	3 133.4				5 73.4	3 106.5
28 13.1	5 66.6	31 11.7	14 25.7				26 14.2	13 27.8
39 9.4	29 12.8	49 7.4	104 3.5			Cost of Sales/Inventory	64 5.7	52 7.0
99 3.7	79 4.6	114 3.2	118 3.1				114 3.2	111 3.3
130 2.8	104 3.5	203 1.8	146 2.5				166 2.2	166 2.2
3 113.8	2 231.1	32 11.5	22 16.6			Cost of Sales/Payables	23 15.8	14 25.4
17 22.0	21 17.2	45 8.1	30 12.2				40 9.2	32 11.4
57 6.4	35 10.5	79 4.6	62 5.9				64 5.7	51 7.1
5.0	7.1	5.4	8.3			Sales/Working Capital	4.8	4.8
5.4	15.1	12.6	8.8				8.1	8.3
24.6	31.2	23.1	11.2				18.3	34.1
6.2	6.4	9.4				EBIT/Interest	5.6	4.4
(12) 3.6	(24) 2.9	(17) 1.9					(85) 2.1	(80) 1.9
1.5	1.2	.9					1.2	1.0
						Net Profit + Depr., Dep.,	6.9	5.8
						Amort./Cur. Mat. L/T/D	(52) 1.9	(40) 2.2
							.7	.4
.1	.1	.2	.4			Fixed/Worth	.2	.2
.3	.3	.4	.5				.5	.4
1.3	.7	.9	1.7				1.2	1.3
.3	.3	.9	.8			Debt/Worth	.7	.8
1.2	1.0	1.5	1.1				1.6	1.7
6.1	2.7	2.9	2.3				3.4	3.7
68.0	27.4	19.7	25.3			% Profit Before Taxes/Tangible	28.9	23.0
(13) 16.0	14.1	(18) 7.3	(10) 6.2			Net Worth	(90) 13.1	(83) 8.7
10.1	2.0	-.1	-5.5				3.1	2.0
17.0	9.6	5.3	15.4			% Profit Before Taxes/Total	11.0	8.9
8.4	5.1	2.3	2.3			Assets	4.3	3.6
4.2	1.1	-.2	-2.1				1.1	.4
252.6	89.1	31.1	27.1			Sales/Net Fixed Assets	38.9	38.8
25.0	25.0	15.5	10.0				13.6	14.1
16.5	9.2	8.3	5.4				5.8	6.5
4.9	5.7	2.8	2.9			Sales/Total Assets	3.2	3.2
3.8	4.0	2.2	2.1				2.4	2.5
2.1	2.1	1.9	1.8				1.6	1.7
.2	.4	.7	.9			% Depr., Dep., Amort./Sales	.6	.6
(12) .9	(25) .7	(18) 1.0	(10) 1.4				(85) 1.1	(81) 1.1
2.1	1.6	1.3	2.0				2.2	2.4
	2.4					% Officers', Directors',	2.8	1.4
	(15) 3.6					Owners' Comp/Sales	(37) 6.1	(38) 3.3
	7.8						8.4	6.3
16757M	135767M	212618M	522645M	344395M	380702M	Net Sales ($)	3098036M	3465866M
4486M	31916M	84476M	202002M	175824M	151585M	Total Assets ($)	1231259M	1258796M

© Robert Morris Associates 1995

M = $ thousand   MM = $ million

See Pages 1 through 15 for Explanation of Ratios and Data

Comparative Historical Data / Current Data Sorted By Sales

	1	2	# Postretirement Benefits / Type of Statement		35 (4/1-9/30/94)		41 (10/1/94-3/31/95)	2	
15	16	21	Unqualified		1	1	8	5	6
14	17	5	Reviewed	1	1	1		1	1
29	25	31	Compiled	4	12	5	5	3	2
4	3	3	Tax Returns	1	1			1	
17	18	16	Other	4	1	2	4	3	2
4/1/92-3/31/93 ALL	4/1/93-3/31/94 ALL	4/1/94-3/31/95 ALL		0-1MM	1-3MM	3-5MM	5-10MM	10-25MM	25MM & OVER
79	79	76	NUMBER OF STATEMENTS	10	16	9	17	13	11
%	%	%	**ASSETS**	%	%	%	%	%	%
9.0	5.3	9.8	Cash & Equivalents	10.9	12.0		10.0	8.3	5.5
11.2	7.4	9.5	Trade Receivables - (net)	10.5	13.4		8.7	4.7	10.5
48.4	54.9	49.6	Inventory	45.8	51.3		47.8	54.6	51.1
1.3	1.9	1.0	All Other Current	.0	2.6		1.0	1.1	.5
70.0	69.4	69.9	Total Current	67.1	79.3		67.4	68.8	67.7
20.4	20.6	21.4	Fixed Assets (net)	26.1	15.3		24.3	18.5	25.5
2.9	1.4	1.2	Intangibles (net)	2.3	.1		.5	3.5	1.1
6.8	8.5	7.5	All Other Non-Current	4.6	5.3		7.8	9.2	5.8
100.0	100.0	100.0	Total	100.0	100.0		100.0	100.0	100.0
			LIABILITIES						
11.9	10.9	8.5	Notes Payable-Short Term	7.8	9.0		9.1	9.2	8.7
5.2	2.4	2.8	Cur. Mat.-L/T/D	5.8	2.2		2.5	3.4	2.0
17.0	15.8	17.7	Trade Payables	10.6	15.2		16.7	19.8	22.1
.6	2.1	.4	Income Taxes Payable	.5	.6		.3	.3	.4
8.7	9.9	9.4	All Other Current	10.9	7.6		10.3	8.1	9.7
43.5	41.1	38.7	Total Current	35.6	34.5		38.9	40.8	42.9
11.3	14.7	12.3	Long Term Debt	24.7	12.0		8.0	11.8	11.1
.4	.3	.1	Deferred Taxes	.0	.0		.1	.2	.1
3.9	4.3	2.7	All Other-Non-Current	1.1	1.4		7.0	1.1	1.4
40.9	39.6	46.2	Net Worth	38.6	52.1		46.0	46.0	44.5
100.0	100.0	100.0	Total Liabilities & Net Worth	100.0	100.0		100.0	100.0	100.0
			INCOME DATA						
100.0	100.0	100.0	Net Sales	100.0	100.0		100.0	100.0	100.0
34.7	33.8	35.7	Gross Profit	45.4	40.4		35.3	29.4	32.5
31.5	33.0	32.8	Operating Expenses	40.2	36.2		33.1	27.5	30.6
3.2	.8	2.9	Operating Profit	5.2	4.1		2.3	1.8	1.9
.6	.5	.2	All Other Expenses (net)	-.1	-.1		.7	.6	.1
2.6	.2	2.7	Profit Before Taxes	5.3	4.2		1.6	1.2	1.8
			RATIOS						
2.6	2.9	2.9		11.4	5.8		2.2	2.3	2.3
1.7	1.8	1.8	Current	2.0	2.8		1.6	1.6	1.6
1.2	1.3	1.3		1.6	1.3		1.2	1.4	1.5
1.0	.5	.9		3.4	2.5		.7	.9	.5
.3	.2	.4	Quick	.7	.6		.4	.2	.3
.1	.1	.2		.1	.3		.2	.1	.2
0 UND	0 UND	0 UND		0 UND	0 UND		0 UND	0 UND	2 162.8
3 105.0	3 135.8	4 100.0	Sales/Receivables	2 151.0	4 88.1		3 137.7	1 249.7	6 58.9
24 15.1	10 38.0	20 18.3		57 6.4	26 14.3		11 32.8	12 30.6	16 23.4
41 8.9	64 5.7	45 8.1		62 5.9	43 8.4		32 11.5	49 7.5	94 3.9
107 3.4	111 3.3	101 3.6	Cost of Sales/Inventory	146 2.5	87 4.2		79 4.6	104 3.5	107 3.4
152 2.4	174 2.1	140 2.6		304 1.2	126 2.9		107 3.4	159 2.5	146 2.5
17 21.5	9 42.8	9 40.0		0 UND	1 403.5		17 21.2	14 26.7	27 13.6
28 13.0	27 13.4	30 12.1	Cost of Sales/Payables	11 32.9	9 41.7		27 13.3	33 11.0	41 8.9
49 7.5	43 8.4	49 7.4		61 6.0	41 9.0		41 8.9	47 7.7	69 5.3
5.3	4.9	5.4		4.5	4.7		9.7	5.4	8.7
10.0	10.0	9.3	Sales/Working Capital	5.1	7.9		17.4	8.3	8.9
37.8	24.9	24.2		17.4	19.8		46.5	22.6	11.2
8.3	6.1	6.2		5.1	8.6		2.8	12.1	
(75) 2.8	(73) 3.1	(64) 2.4	EBIT/Interest	3.3	(13) 3.6	(14)	1.6	(11) 2.0	
1.1	1.2	1.0		-1.0	1.4		.8	-.8	
9.8	7.3	5.9							
(32) 2.6	(33) 2.1	(27) 1.9	Net Profit + Depr., Dep., Amort./Cur. Mat. L/T/D						
1.3	.7	.7							
.1	.2	.2		.2	.1		.2	.3	.3
.4	.4	.4	Fixed/Worth	1.1	.2		.5	.4	.5
1.1	1.2	.9		NM	.7		.9	.9	.7
.9	.7	.5		.5	.2		.8	.6	.9
1.5	1.7	1.2	Debt/Worth	1.2	.7		1.2	1.6	1.3
2.8	3.5	3.0		NM	3.4		1.9	3.6	1.9
28.4	29.8	25.5			30.9		26.4	20.8	28.5
(74) 11.4	(75) 12.2	(72) 11.1	% Profit Before Taxes/Tangible Net Worth	(15)	13.0		6.8	(12) 8.3	7.7
1.2	1.0	1.4			4.7		-.5	-6.2	-.2
11.4	9.7	9.6		13.9	21.3		7.4	12.4	8.6
4.6	4.9	4.5	% Profit Before Taxes/Total Assets	7.8	7.0		2.3	2.5	2.3
.3	.2	.8		-2.3	4.1		-.3	-2.4	-.1
53.6	46.8	44.5		24.0	251.2		81.2	42.7	27.1
23.5	23.1	21.7	Sales/Net Fixed Assets	12.9	51.1		28.0	25.7	10.0
7.8	8.4	8.6		2.2	11.4		7.0	8.8	6.2
3.6	3.9	4.2		3.1	4.9		5.6	3.9	3.1
2.8	2.8	2.9	Sales/Total Assets	2.0	3.9		3.6	2.6	2.7
1.9	1.9	2.0		1.0	2.4		2.0	1.9	2.1
.5	.6	.6			.2		.6	.6	.9
(69) .8	(69) .7	(68) 1.0	% Depr., Dep., Amort./Sales	(13) .5		(15)	1.0	(12) 1.0	(10) 1.4
1.9	1.5	1.5			1.2		1.5	1.3	1.4
1.5	1.1	1.6			2.4				
(27) 3.5	(31) 4.1	(30) 3.3	% Officers', Directors', Owners' Comp/Sales	(12)	5.7				
5.6	7.7	7.2			9.1				
1985981M	1801617M	1612884M	Net Sales ($)	6615M	27672M	38516M	121616M	211993M	1206472M
927821M	647905M	650289M	Total Assets ($)	6632M	8072M	15092M	47241M	86756M	486496M

© Robert Morris Associates 1995 M = $ thousand MM = $ million
See Pages 1 through 15 for Explanation of Ratios and Data

Current Data Sorted By Assets						# Postretirement Benefits Type of Statement	Comparative Historical Data	
1	3		1					
1	2	4	8	1	1	Unqualified	24	11
	3	8	2			Reviewed	13	12
16	13	2				Compiled	32	34
6	2					Tax Returns	1	4
7	6	1	3	2	2	Other	21	13
0-500M	500M-2MM	2-10MM	10-50MM	50-100MM	100-250MM		4/1/90-3/31/91 ALL	4/1/91-3/31/92 ALL
	23 (4/1-9/30/94)		65 (10/1/94-3/31/95)					
30	26	15	11	3	3	**NUMBER OF STATEMENTS**	91	74
%	%	%	%	%	%	**ASSETS**	%	%
7.0	11.3	6.6	4.1			Cash & Equivalents	6.7	9.7
2.7	3.8	2.9	4.7			Trade Receivables - (net)	4.2	4.0
61.4	57.1	58.8	44.8			Inventory	58.7	55.1
3.3	.5	1.0	4.6			All Other Current	2.0	1.5
74.4	72.7	69.4	58.2			Total Current	71.5	70.3
16.3	20.0	21.2	30.0			Fixed Assets (net)	18.2	20.2
3.5	2.1	.9	2.0			Intangibles (net)	2.9	2.4
5.8	5.1	8.6	9.8			All Other Non-Current	7.4	7.1
100.0	100.0	100.0	100.0			Total	100.0	100.0
						LIABILITIES		
11.9	6.1	8.6	6.8			Notes Payable-Short Term	8.8	9.8
4.0	3.6	5.2	1.5			Cur. Mat. -L/T/D	3.1	3.4
16.3	17.5	16.1	20.1			Trade Payables	16.9	14.2
.6	.1	.5	.7			Income Taxes Payable	.8	.9
7.2	6.7	14.5	9.5			All Other Current	8.2	8.0
40.0	34.0	44.8	38.8			Total Current	37.8	36.3
28.6	15.2	11.9	19.0			Long Term Debt	22.6	19.3
.0	.0	.2	.4			Deferred Taxes	.3	.3
4.3	6.3	8.4	5.6			All Other-Non-Current	4.2	3.6
27.1	44.5	34.7	36.2			Net Worth	35.2	40.4
100.0	100.0	100.0	100.0			Total Liabilities & Net Worth	100.0	100.0
						INCOME DATA		
100.0	100.0	100.0	100.0			Net Sales	100.0	100.0
41.6	34.1	41.9	38.4			Gross Profit	36.2	37.4
41.4	30.4	38.9	35.2			Operating Expenses	33.1	32.9
.2	3.7	3.1	3.2			Operating Profit	3.0	4.4
.4	1.0	.5	1.0			All Other Expenses (net)	1.7	.8
-.3	2.7	2.5	2.3			Profit Before Taxes	1.3	3.6
						RATIOS		
3.6	3.8	1.9	1.8				2.9	3.3
2.0	2.1	1.6	1.5			Current	2.0	2.1
1.4	1.4	1.2	1.0				1.3	1.3
.4	.7	.3	.3				.5	.7
.3	.3	.2	.2			Quick (86) (70)	.2	.3
.0	.1	.1	.1				.1	.1
0 UND	0 UND	0 999.8	1 300.3				0 UND	0 UND
0 UND	1 262.7	2 184.2	3 118.5			Sales/Receivables	1 405.0	0 882.7
2 156.3	5 70.5	5 80.7	14 25.9				5 80.9	4 87.6
59 6.2	83 4.4	104 3.5	65 5.6				79 4.6	53 6.9
130 2.8	126 2.9	152 2.4	111 3.3			Cost of Sales/Inventory	130 2.8	122 3.0
243 1.5	183 2.0	159 2.3	146 2.5				203 1.8	166 2.2
8 43.8	13 28.7	12 29.9	41 8.9				14 26.0	9 39.9
24 14.9	27 13.5	30 12.3	49 7.4			Cost of Sales/Payables	29 12.4	22 16.3
34 10.6	47 7.7	65 5.6	62 5.9				56 6.5	47 7.7
3.9	4.2	7.6	8.3				4.6	5.0
10.0	7.3	13.0	13.6			Sales/Working Capital	8.4	8.4
24.8	22.4	25.6	47.6				16.9	19.2
(29) 7.3	(20) 4.9	7.9	(10) 7.2				(85) 4.8	(65) 5.8
3.6	2.4	5.2	3.2			EBIT/Interest	2.6	3.4
-.5	1.5	.8	2.0				.9	1.8
						Net Profit + Depr., Dep., Amort./Cur. Mat. L /T/D	(38) 6.8	(21) 4.2
							2.3	2.3
							.4	1.0
.1	.1	.3	.4				.2	.1
.5	.4	.6	.7			Fixed/Worth	.5	.4
2.3	.8	1.3	1.7				1.7	1.5
.9	.5	1.3	1.2				.8	.7
2.6	1.6	1.7	1.9			Debt/Worth	2.2	1.5
15.2	2.3	2.3	2.9				7.3	4.6
(24) 78.5	(24) 26.4	(13) 46.9	29.5			% Profit Before Taxes/Tangible Net Worth	(84) 39.4	(65) 50.2
26.3	10.8	16.3	11.5				10.8	16.8
-.6	5.5	6.5	5.7				2.1	7.0
18.5	9.9	13.7	13.0			% Profit Before Taxes/Total Assets	12.9	15.8
7.2	4.5	4.0	5.3				4.8	6.7
-4.9	1.5	-.4	2.2				.0	2.1
55.7	69.1	29.8	19.1				44.6	58.4
38.1	19.1	17.7	9.2			Sales/Net Fixed Assets	20.6	21.5
17.4	9.3	9.6	5.0				9.2	8.9
5.4	3.6	3.5	2.5				3.5	3.7
2.9	2.7	2.6	2.0			Sales/Total Assets	2.6	2.9
2.0	1.8	2.3	1.7				1.9	2.0
.7	.4	.4					.5	.4
(24) 1.1	(25) .8	1.0				% Depr., Dep., Amort./Sales	(80) 1.0	(60) .9
1.4	1.8	2.2					1.7	2.3
2.7	2.2						1.9	4.0
(20) 4.8	(12) 4.0					% Officers', Directors', Owners' Comp/Sales	(38) 3.7	(34) 5.6
8.4	8.0						5.7	9.2
27260M	79033M	207589M	548795M	595003M	857292M	Net Sales ($)	2470401M	1966518M
7441M	25845M	68287M	241783M	220872M	428882M	Total Assets ($)	999604M	739013M

M = $ thousand   MM = $ million
See Pages 1 through 15 for Explanation of Ratios and Data

Comparative Historical Data / Current Data Sorted By Sales

Hist 1	Hist 2	Hist 3	# Postretirement Benefits	0-1MM	1-3MM	3-5MM	5-10MM	10-25MM	25MM & OVER
2	12	5	# Postretirement Benefits	1	3				1
			Type of Statement						
18	22	17	Unqualified	1	1	1	2	3	9
10	10	11	Reviewed		1	1	2	5	1
35	30	31	Compiled	13	12	3	3		
3	7	8	Tax Returns	4	3	1			
24	18	21	Other	6	4	2	1	1	7
4/1/92-3/31/93 ALL	4/1/93-3/31/94 ALL	4/1/94-3/31/95 ALL		23 (4/1-9/30/94)			65 (10/1/94-3/31/95)		
90	87	88	**NUMBER OF STATEMENTS**	24	22	8	8	9	17
%	%	%	**ASSETS**	%	%	%	%	%	%
7.3	6.5	8.0	Cash & Equivalents	10.7	6.3				5.9
4.1	4.7	3.3	Trade Receivables - (net)	3.2	2.1				2.9
59.3	57.0	56.7	Inventory	55.7	64.0				50.8
2.9	.7	2.1	All Other Current	1.9	2.7				3.4
73.5	68.8	70.0	Total Current	71.6	75.1				62.9
20.3	21.8	20.6	Fixed Assets (net)	18.5	18.1				23.9
1.6	2.9	3.1	Intangibles (net)	2.1	3.7				5.8
4.6	6.4	6.4	All Other Non-Current	7.8	3.0				7.3
100.0	100.0	100.0	Total	100.0	100.0				100.0
			LIABILITIES						
10.9	6.5	8.2	Notes Payable-Short Term	11.6	8.3				6.1
3.6	3.8	3.5	Cur. Mat.-L /T/D	5.4	3.5				3.0
16.7	16.2	17.0	Trade Payables	12.6	16.9				17.6
.7	1.2	.6	Income Taxes Payable	.6	.3				1.5
8.1	8.7	8.6	All Other Current	7.4	7.1				7.5
39.9	36.6	37.8	Total Current	37.5	36.0				35.7
18.6	20.1	20.0	Long Term Debt	28.7	19.9				14.9
.1	.2	.2	Deferred Taxes	.0	.0				.4
4.2	6.3	6.2	All Other-Non-Current	3.3	8.1				7.4
37.2	36.9	35.8	Net Worth	30.5	36.0				41.5
100.0	100.0	100.0	Total Liabilities & Net Worth	100.0	100.0				100.0
			INCOME DATA						
100.0	100.0	100.0	Net Sales	100.0	100.0				100.0
38.0	36.2	38.2	Gross Profit	42.1	38.2				35.7
34.3	32.7	35.9	Operating Expenses	41.3	35.3				32.9
3.7	3.5	2.3	Operating Profit	.9	2.9				2.8
1.4	1.7	.7	All Other Expenses (net)	.4	1.4				.5
2.3	1.8	1.6	Profit Before Taxes	.4	1.5				2.4
			RATIOS						
2.9	3.5	2.8	Current	4.4	3.7				2.6
2.0	2.1	1.9		2.2	2.3				1.8
1.3	1.2	1.4		1.5	1.4				1.4
.5	.6	.5	Quick	.7	.4				.4
(87) .2	(85) .2	.2		.3	.1				.2
.1	.1	.1		.2	.0				.1
0 UND	0 UND	0 UND	Sales/Receivables	0 UND	0 UND				1 470.1
1 266.9	1 433.9	1 300.4		1 478.5	0 UND				3 145.2
4 83.3	4 82.4	5 75.9		7 52.5	2 207.3				5 70.2
89 4.1	69 5.3	72 5.1	Cost of Sales/Inventory	59 6.2	101 3.6				78 4.7
130 2.8	122 3.0	122 3.0		152 2.4	135 2.7				111 3.3
192 1.9	174 2.1	174 2.1		281 1.3	192 1.9				152 2.4
15 24.8	14 27.0	17 21.4	Cost of Sales/Payables	3 120.2	16 23.0				22 16.7
26 13.8	31 11.6	30 12.2		23 15.7	27 13.5				41 8.9
47 7.8	50 7.3	49 7.5		37 9.8	43 8.5				55 6.6
4.5	4.8	4.8	Sales/Working Capital	2.9	4.0				5.7
7.6	8.2	9.0		8.7	6.3				8.5
26.0	21.2	22.8		14.5	22.1				19.4
7.0	9.5	6.8	EBIT/Interest	7.0	4.9				21.3
(86) 3.0	(82) 3.0	(79) 3.6		(22) 3.9	(20) 2.3			(15)	5.3
1.2	1.1	1.1		–.2	1.0				2.1
5.6	13.3	8.3	Net Profit + Depr., Dep., Amort./Cur. Mat. L/T/D						42.0
(31) 1.9	(33) 3.0	(32) 4.1						(11)	9.0
.8	1.1	.7							.9
.2	.3	.3	Fixed/Worth	.1	.2				.4
.5	.6	.6		.4	.4				.7
1.7	1.3	1.2		31.7	.9				1.0
.9	.9	.9	Debt/Worth	.6	1.1				.9
1.5	1.7	1.8		1.5	2.0				1.7
4.9	4.5	4.6		37.5	4.4				3.4
36.6	38.1	43.7	% Profit Before Taxes/Tangible Net Worth	52.9	66.3				35.5
(80) 18.2	(79) 19.3	(76) 15.6		(19) 14.4	(20) 12.3			(15)	11.5
4.2	2.7	5.5		2.8	1.8				5.1
14.6	13.6	13.0	% Profit Before Taxes/Total Assets	13.9	12.7				13.0
4.6	6.6	5.5		7.0	3.5				3.4
.5	.0	1.0		–3.4	.3				2.4
48.2	34.4	45.5	Sales/Net Fixed Assets	46.5	57.4				18.4
22.1	17.6	18.6		29.9	19.3				12.4
9.9	7.9	9.4		14.5	9.5				6.8
3.6	3.8	3.6	Sales/Total Assets	3.5	3.5				3.3
2.7	2.6	2.5		2.2	2.7				2.3
2.0	2.0	2.0		1.6	2.2				1.9
.5	.7	.6	% Depr., Dep., Amort./Sales	.7	.5				1.0
(80) 1.1	(73) 1.0	(79) 1.1		(20) 1.0	(20) 1.0			(15)	1.6
2.1	2.2	1.8		1.4	2.3				2.0
1.5	1.0	2.2	% Officers', Directors', Owners' Comp/Sales	2.2	2.6				
(40) 3.9	(31) 4.2	(42) 4.6		(16) 4.8	(10) 3.9				
5.4	9.8	8.2		10.6	6.6				
2327276M	3720000M	2314972M	Net Sales ($)	13434M	39824M	32239M	57559M	151462M	2020454M
803028M	1590146M	993110M	Total Assets ($)	8108M	15620M	11867M	17286M	59893M	880336M

© Robert Morris Associates 1995

M = $ thousand   MM = $ million

See Pages 1 through 15 for Explanation of Ratios and Data

Current Data Sorted By Assets							Comparative Historical Data	
6	7	5	2	1	1	**# Postretirement Benefits**		
						Type of Statement		
4	3	12	9	3	7	Unqualified	41	39
10	22	12	1			Reviewed	63	47
70	43	5	1			Compiled	160	156
24	10					Tax Returns	12	18
24	22	8	6	2		Other	78	47
	131 (4/1-9/30/94)		167 (10/1/94-3/31/95)				4/1/90-3/31/91	4/1/91-3/31/92
0-500M	500M-2MM	2-10MM	10-50MM	50-100MM	100-250MM		ALL	ALL
132	100	37	17	5	7	**NUMBER OF STATEMENTS**	354	307
%	%	%	%	%	%	**ASSETS**	%	%
7.0	7.3	5.1	9.0			Cash & Equivalents	6.7	6.5
17.4	25.2	23.6	11.4			Trade Receivables - (net)	19.9	20.9
52.4	43.1	41.8	51.4			Inventory	47.1	47.1
1.7	1.4	1.9	1.2			All Other Current	1.6	1.6
78.5	77.1	72.5	73.0			Total Current	75.2	76.1
12.4	16.5	18.7	16.0			Fixed Assets (net)	15.8	14.6
4.0	1.5	2.1	.7			Intangibles (net)	2.8	3.3
5.0	4.8	6.7	10.3			All Other Non-Current	6.2	6.0
100.0	100.0	100.0	100.0			Total	100.0	100.0
						LIABILITIES		
6.3	5.3	10.0	4.2			Notes Payable-Short Term	7.0	6.6
5.3	4.3	4.1	3.7			Cur. Mat. -L/T/D	4.3	3.9
20.7	20.9	25.8	23.9			Trade Payables	21.3	19.3
.5	.6	.7	.6			Income Taxes Payable	.6	.7
6.5	7.6	6.6	5.6			All Other Current	7.3	7.3
39.2	38.7	47.3	37.9			Total Current	40.4	37.8
21.2	16.4	16.6	12.9			Long Term Debt	20.4	17.9
.0	.1	.4	.3			Deferred Taxes	.2	.2
3.6	2.1	5.7	4.0			All Other-Non-Current	3.2	4.0
36.0	42.8	30.0	44.9			Net Worth	35.8	40.1
100.0	100.0	100.0	100.0			Total Liabilities & Net Worth	100.0	100.0
						INCOME DATA		
100.0	100.0	100.0	100.0			Net Sales	100.0	100.0
28.8	30.8	29.0	22.0			Gross Profit	30.4	29.9
26.0	28.7	28.8	24.2			Operating Expenses	28.2	26.8
2.8	2.1	.1	-2.1			Operating Profit	2.2	3.1
.6	-.1	.2	.2			All Other Expenses (net)	.3	.3
2.1	2.1	-.1	-2.3			Profit Before Taxes	1.9	2.9
						RATIOS		
3.9	3.3	1.9	3.0				3.0	3.2
2.4	2.1	1.6	2.1			Current	2.0	2.1
1.4	1.4	1.3	1.6				1.4	1.5
1.2	1.3	.8	.9				1.2	1.2
.7	.9	.6	.4			Quick	(353) .7	(306) .7
.3	.4	.3	.2				.3	.4
7 52.3	11 32.3	7 49.9	3 105.1				8 45.1	8 46.7
14 25.7	20 18.2	16 22.5	9 42.4			Sales/Receivables	16 22.8	15 23.9
20 18.3	35 10.5	48 7.6	16 22.9				28 13.1	31 11.8
45 8.1	47 7.8	38 9.6	33 11.1				47 7.7	48 7.6
57 6.4	60 6.1	73 5.0	65 5.6			Cost of Sales/Inventory	64 5.7	65 5.6
85 4.3	78 4.7	91 4.0	94 3.9				85 4.3	85 4.3
13 27.7	18 20.3	26 13.9	21 17.0				18 19.9	18 20.5
20 18.0	24 14.9	30 12.2	27 13.6			Cost of Sales/Payables	26 14.0	24 15.0
32 11.3	37 9.8	46 8.0	36 10.1				39 9.3	37 9.8
6.7	6.6	9.4	7.6				7.0	6.7
9.9	10.1	14.3	8.9			Sales/Working Capital	10.2	9.5
22.9	17.7	22.4	17.2				19.3	16.2
8.0	6.4	4.2	4.7				5.6	6.2
(111) 3.5	(92) 3.3	(33) 2.1	(14) 1.3			EBIT/Interest	(318) 2.6	(273) 3.1
1.3	1.2	1.2	-1.2				1.3	1.6
5.7	7.0	1.9	2.7				4.6	4.5
(29) 1.4	(40) 1.7	(14) .6	(10) 1.5			Net Profit + Depr., Dep., Amort./Cur. Mat. L/T/D	(163) 1.6	(120) 2.1
.5	.7	.0	-7.3				.7	1.0
.1	.1	.4	.2				.1	.1
.3	.3	.6	.3			Fixed/Worth	.4	.3
1.2	.8	1.1	.9				1.1	.9
.6	.6	1.2	.4				.7	.7
1.9	1.4	2.3	1.3			Debt/Worth	1.7	1.6
8.5	3.4	5.2	3.3				6.0	4.6
47.4	33.1	31.2	14.6				42.1	45.3
(108) 18.1	(94) 13.6	(32) 11.4	(16) 4.7			% Profit Before Taxes/Tangible Net Worth	(307) 16.8	(278) 20.3
6.3	1.7	2.4	-24.9				4.8	5.6
15.5	12.2	7.1	7.4				12.5	14.1
7.7	5.5	1.9	1.2			% Profit Before Taxes/Total Assets	6.5	7.7
1.4	.4	.2	-20.3				1.1	2.4
148.6	69.1	38.9	52.8				71.6	74.6
53.5	31.4	23.6	24.9			Sales/Net Fixed Assets	33.9	32.4
24.6	17.5	10.1	17.7				16.7	17.3
5.4	4.6	4.3	4.2				4.7	4.5
4.3	3.9	3.2	3.8			Sales/Total Assets	3.8	3.8
3.4	3.0	2.6	2.8				3.0	2.8
.4	.4	.5	.5				.6	.6
(101) .7	(93) .8	(35) .9	(16) .7			% Depr., Dep., Amort./Sales	(301) 1.1	(258) .9
1.3	1.4	1.6	.9				1.6	1.4
3.2	1.9	2.1					2.8	2.9
(80) 5.3	(60) 3.7	(10) 2.7				% Officers', Directors', Owners' Comp/Sales	(169) 4.9	(150) 4.6
7.4	6.1	3.3					8.4	7.3
160349M	377369M	526594M	1327558M	700494M	3161343M	Net Sales ($)	6902975M	6746648M
37238M	98169M	145558M	375600M	319164M	1325438M	Total Assets ($)	2363512M	2258525M

M = $ thousand   MM = $ million
See Pages 1 through 15 for Explanation of Ratios and Data

Comparative Historical Data | Current Data Sorted By Sales

	1	12	22	# Postretirement Benefits / Type of Statement	4	5	1	4	1	7
	32	48	38	Unqualified	2	3	1	5	3	24
	39	35	45	Reviewed	1	19	5	14	5	1
	147	138	119	Compiled	30	55	18	12	3	1
	33	23	34	Tax Returns	13	16	4	1		1
	57	45	62	Other	11	24	8	6	5	8
	4/1/92-3/31/93 ALL	4/1/93-3/31/94 ALL	4/1/94-3/31/95 ALL		131 (4/1-9/30/94) 0-1MM	1-3MM	1-3MM / 167 (10/1/94-3/31/95) 3-5MM	5-10MM	10-25MM	25MM & OVER
	308	289	298	NUMBER OF STATEMENTS	57	117	36	38	16	34
	%	%	%	ASSETS	%	%	%	%	%	%
	7.5	7.1	7.4	Cash & Equivalents	6.8	7.9	4.9	4.8	9.8	11.3
	19.2	20.8	20.2	Trade Receivables - (net)	14.9	18.9	27.6	30.2	24.7	12.8
	47.4	46.2	47.0	Inventory	51.9	48.1	48.2	41.4	39.8	43.3
	1.3	1.5	1.6	All Other Current	2.0	1.6	1.5	2.1	.3	1.3
	75.4	75.6	76.3	Total Current	75.7	76.5	82.2	78.4	74.6	68.7
	14.6	14.5	15.1	Fixed Assets (net)	16.4	13.6	13.7	15.2	19.5	17.3
	3.5	3.3	3.0	Intangibles (net)	3.9	3.3	2.4	1.5	.9	3.9
	6.4	6.7	5.6	All Other Non-Current	4.0	6.6	1.7	4.8	4.9	10.1
	100.0	100.0	100.0	Total	100.0	100.0	100.0	100.0	100.0	100.0
				LIABILITIES						
	6.6	6.3	6.1	Notes Payable-Short Term	6.7	5.4	5.9	8.9	10.4	2.9
	4.9	4.4	4.5	Cur. Mat.-L /T/D	4.5	5.5	3.2	4.4	5.3	2.3
	21.2	19.9	21.4	Trade Payables	21.6	19.3	21.6	23.6	28.3	22.3
	.6	1.3	.6	Income Taxes Payable	.7	.5	.4	.4	1.0	.8
	7.5	7.8	6.8	All Other Current	7.9	5.7	8.6	8.1	6.7	5.6
	40.7	39.7	39.4	Total Current	41.3	36.4	39.6	45.4	51.8	33.9
	17.2	18.6	18.2	Long Term Debt	25.7	18.8	13.7	14.9	18.4	11.8
	.1	.1	.2	Deferred Taxes	.1	.1	.0	.3	.4	.4
	2.7	2.5	3.3	All Other-Non-Current	4.4	2.0	5.0	3.2	.9	5.5
	39.3	39.1	38.9	Net Worth	28.5	42.7	41.7	36.2	28.4	48.5
	100.0	100.0	100.0	Total Liabilities & Net Worth	100.0	100.0	100.0	100.0	100.0	100.0
				INCOME DATA						
	100.0	100.0	100.0	Net Sales	100.0	100.0	100.0	100.0	100.0	100.0
	29.9	29.3	29.2	Gross Profit	31.4	28.7	30.5	30.7	29.9	23.7
	27.1	27.0	27.1	Operating Expenses	27.1	26.3	28.9	30.2	27.7	24.4
	2.8	2.3	2.0	Operating Profit	4.2	2.4	1.6	.4	2.1	-.7
	.3	.3	.3	All Other Expenses (net)	1.1	.1	.1	.0	.5	.3
	2.5	2.0	1.7	Profit Before Taxes	3.2	2.3	1.5	.5	1.6	-.9
				RATIOS						
	2.7	3.0	3.2	Current	4.0	3.6	3.1	2.5	1.9	3.0
	2.0	2.0	2.1		2.2	2.4	2.1	1.6	1.4	2.0
	1.5	1.5	1.4		1.2	1.5	1.5	1.3	1.2	1.7
	1.1	1.1	1.2	Quick	1.2	1.3	1.3	1.1	1.1	1.0
	.7	.7	.7		.6	.7	.9	.7	.6	.7
	.3	.4	.3		.2	.4	.4	.4	.2	.4
	7 49.7	8 44.5	8 48.3	Sales/Receivables	3 143.7	10 36.4	13 29.2	10 36.2	4 83.9	5 79.5
	15 24.6	16 23.4	15 23.9		16 22.9	14 25.7	22 16.4	23 16.0	22 16.8	10 34.8
	28 13.2	28 13.1	27 13.7		22 16.6	21 17.5	37 9.9	47 7.8	40 9.2	17 22.1
	46 7.9	42 8.6	45 8.1	Cost of Sales/Inventory	49 7.4	45 8.2	47 7.7	32 11.5	13 28.2	32 11.3
	63 5.8	64 5.7	62 5.9		74 4.9	57 6.4	63 5.8	58 6.3	73 5.0	61 6.0
	83 4.4	81 4.5	83 4.4		96 3.8	78 4.7	81 4.5	78 4.7	81 4.5	85 4.3
	19 19.4	17 21.4	17 21.2	Cost of Sales/Payables	15 23.8	14 26.4	18 20.1	22 16.6	22 16.5	21 17.1
	24 15.0	25 14.7	24 14.9		23 15.7	21 17.6	26 13.9	29 12.5	30 12.3	24 13.0
	36 10.1	35 10.4	38 9.7		45 8.1	31 11.8	34 10.6	41 9.0	59 6.2	38 9.6
	7.2	6.7	7.0	Sales/Working Capital	5.6	7.2	6.6	7.9	11.9	7.3
	10.1	10.5	10.2		8.9	10.1	9.9	11.7	17.3	9.3
	19.0	18.9	19.0		46.4	16.0	15.8	24.4	40.8	17.8
	(271) 7.8	(254) 6.7	(261) 7.2	EBIT/Interest	(43) 5.8	(108) 10.3	(31) 4.7	(35) 5.1	7.9	(28) 18.6
	2.9	2.6	3.1		2.1	4.4	3.4	2.6	2.0	3.2
	1.4	1.3	1.3		1.0	1.6	1.5	1.3	.9	1.0
	(110) 4.0	(114) 4.1	(100) 4.5	Net Profit + Depr., Dep., Amort./Cur. Mat. L/T/D		(39) 6.8	(12) 28.4	(12) 1.9	(10) 8.2	(19) 15.2
	1.4	1.4	1.6			1.7	1.5	1.1	.6	2.2
	.7	.5	.5			.7	.6	.7	.3	-28.1
	.1	.1	.1	Fixed/Worth	.1	.1	.1	.2	.3	.2
	.3	.3	.4		.5	.3	.4	.5	.5	.3
	.9	.9	1.0		-4.6	.9	.8	.8	1.0	.8
	.7	.8	.6	Debt/Worth	.8	.5	.6	.9	1.2	.5
	1.5	1.6	1.6		2.4	1.4	1.4	2.0	2.2	1.0
	4.2	4.2	4.2		-19.2	3.6	3.3	3.8	5.2	2.8
	(276) 40.4	(260) 32.3	(262) 35.2	% Profit Before Taxes/Tangible Net Worth	(41) 47.2	(106) 37.1	(33) 30.7	(36) 31.2	(14) 44.5	(32) 23.0
	17.7	15.5	14.1		17.7	19.7	9.4	11.5	11.6	10.1
	5.3	4.0	2.7		1.2	6.2	2.4	2.4	2.3	-24.9
	13.6	13.6	12.9	% Profit Before Taxes/Total Assets	14.7	15.9	9.1	9.4	8.0	10.0
	6.9	5.4	5.6		5.2	7.7	4.7	3.1	2.2	2.7
	1.5	1.4	.4		.0	2.0	1.1	.5	.0	-30.6
	77.1	77.0	83.6	Sales/Net Fixed Assets	113.5	133.8	73.6	54.5	68.7	35.4
	35.0	37.2	32.0		41.8	42.1	34.6	28.9	27.5	22.4
	18.2	18.0	17.9		17.9	20.8	21.5	16.9	11.0	11.9
	4.7	4.8	4.9	Sales/Total Assets	4.8	5.2	4.7	5.0	5.0	4.4
	3.7	3.8	3.9		3.7	4.0	4.0	3.7	3.8	3.5
	3.1	3.0	3.0		2.8	3.2	3.3	2.9	2.9	2.6
	(266) .5	(247) .5	(255) .5	% Depr., Dep., Amort./Sales	(40) .6	(100) .4	(32) .3	(37) .5	(15) .7	(31) .6
	.8	.8	.8		.9	.7	.7	.8	.9	.9
	1.3	1.4	1.4		1.8	1.4	1.4	1.3	1.8	1.1
	(160) 3.0	(144) 2.8	(150) 2.6	% Officers', Directors', Owners' Comp/Sales	(31) 4.4	(73) 2.7	(20) 1.9	(22) 1.7		
	4.9	4.4	4.3		6.4	4.4	3.1	2.8		
	7.6	7.5	6.8		8.4	6.3	5.6	7.1		
	5856106M	7511583M	6253707M	Net Sales ($)	38170M	213992M	138992M	258312M	223863M	5380378M
	2088933M	2819086M	2301167M	Total Assets ($)	12099M	56336M	37670M	73080M	66158M	2055824M

M = $ thousand   MM = $ million
See Pages 1 through 15 for Explanation of Ratios and Data

Current Data Sorted By Assets								Comparative Historical Data	
2	8	14	3	1		# Postretirement Benefits			
						Type of Statement			
2	10	42	13	3	3	Unqualified		59	62
4	21	65	11			Reviewed		115	119
27	90	63	3			Compiled		176	166
5	9	11				Tax Returns		3	6
12	41	42	8		1	Other		80	97
	103 (4/1-9/30/94)			383 (10/1/94-3/31/95)				4/1/90-3/31/91	4/1/91-3/31/92
0-500M	500M-2MM	2-10MM	10-50MM	50-100MM	100-250MM	NUMBER OF STATEMENTS		ALL	ALL
50	171	223	35	3	4			433	450
%	%	%	%	%	%	**ASSETS**		%	%
4.8	6.4	4.3	2.4			Cash & Equivalents		4.7	4.7
15.7	14.6	14.6	19.3			Trade Receivables - (net)		14.5	15.5
58.7	60.5	65.5	57.1			Inventory		64.5	63.0
1.3	1.9	1.7	1.3			All Other Current		1.4	1.5
80.5	83.4	86.1	80.1			Total Current		85.1	84.6
15.3	12.4	9.7	14.5			Fixed Assets (net)		10.6	10.4
.9	.2	.4	.8			Intangibles (net)		.4	.6
3.3	3.9	3.8	4.6			All Other Non-Current		3.9	4.4
100.0	100.0	100.0	100.0			Total		100.0	100.0
						LIABILITIES			
17.8	21.1	29.4	28.5			Notes Payable-Short Term		27.2	27.1
5.6	3.3	2.1	3.7			Cur. Mat. -L/T/D		2.9	2.5
23.1	20.3	23.6	20.4			Trade Payables		23.8	25.4
.2	.3	.3	.4			Income Taxes Payable		.3	.3
4.9	7.0	6.3	7.9			All Other Current		5.9	5.0
51.6	52.0	61.7	60.9			Total Current		60.1	60.3
18.9	9.1	7.4	8.4			Long Term Debt		9.3	8.0
.0	.1	.2	.0			Deferred Taxes		.1	.1
4.9	1.1	1.7	2.5			All Other-Non-Current		1.7	1.7
24.7	37.8	29.1	28.2			Net Worth		28.8	29.9
100.0	100.0	100.0	100.0			Total Liabilities & Net Worth		100.0	100.0
						INCOME DATA			
100.0	100.0	100.0	100.0			Net Sales		100.0	100.0
27.6	22.2	18.5	22.1			Gross Profit		21.5	21.9
24.6	19.8	16.7	18.8			Operating Expenses		19.3	20.5
3.0	2.4	1.8	3.3			Operating Profit		2.1	1.4
.7	.0	.0	.4			All Other Expenses (net)		.6	.4
2.3	2.5	1.8	2.9			Profit Before Taxes		1.5	1.1
						RATIOS			
2.4	2.1	1.6	1.5					1.7	1.7
1.4	1.6	1.3	1.3			Current		1.3	1.3
1.2	1.3	1.2	1.1					1.2	1.2
.8	.7	.5	.6					.5	.6
(49) .4	.3	.2	.3			Quick		(449) .3	.3
.2	.2	.1	.2					.1	.1
4 95.2	9 41.5	9 41.4	16 23.5					11 34.2	10 38.4
11 33.4	19 19.5	18 20.1	29 12.7			Sales/Receivables		20 18.0	20 18.3
29 12.5	31 11.7	33 11.2	40 9.1					35 10.5	37 10.0
46 8.0	70 5.2	99 3.7	83 4.4					104 3.5	96 3.8
114 3.2	118 3.1	140 2.6	122 3.0			Cost of Sales/Inventory		152 2.4	152 2.4
174 2.1	183 2.0	174 2.1	174 2.1					228 1.6	215 1.7
8 46.1	8 45.1	8 43.5	14 26.5					10 37.5	11 32.7
23 15.8	23 15.9	31 11.7	23 16.2			Cost of Sales/Payables		26 14.3	35 10.5
69 5.3	55 6.6	81 4.5	70 5.2					101 3.6	96 3.8
5.9	5.1	6.3	8.7					5.7	5.5
10.3	9.3	10.5	10.9			Sales/Working Capital		8.9	9.7
41.5	14.2	17.2	25.9					17.1	19.9
7.0	6.3	5.5	5.0					3.6	3.3
(48) 2.6	(163) 3.0	(215) 2.8	(33) 3.2			EBIT/Interest		(413) 1.9	(425) 1.8
1.4	1.5	1.7	2.2					1.2	1.0
5.1	4.0	5.7	8.0					4.6	4.1
(13) 1.8	(57) 2.3	(99) 2.8	(15) 1.7			Net Profit + Depr., Dep., Amort./Cur. Mat. L./T/D		(212) 2.0	(172) 1.5
.1	.6	.9	.9					.7	.4
.1	.1	.1	.2					.2	.1
.4	.3	.3	.4			Fixed/Worth		.3	.3
1.5	.6	.6	.9					.7	.7
1.3	.9	1.6	1.7					1.5	1.5
3.0	1.8	2.9	2.9			Debt/Worth		3.2	2.9
11.5	4.3	5.0	5.7					6.3	5.9
50.8	27.6	26.6	39.6					24.7	21.6
(41) 26.3	(164) 12.4	(220) 14.3	19.1			% Profit Before Taxes/Tangible Net Worth		(423) 10.3	(437) 8.7
5.1	3.7	7.7	10.4					2.6	.6
14.3	8.0	7.0	8.8					5.5	5.4
5.8	4.8	3.5	5.3			% Profit Before Taxes/Total Assets		2.6	2.1
1.0	1.1	1.8	2.9					.7	.0
99.7	71.6	66.7	49.0					62.0	62.1
36.6	34.6	32.7	24.6			Sales/Net Fixed Assets		31.1	32.0
15.0	15.0	17.4	9.5					14.2	15.8
3.9	3.2	2.7	2.5					2.5	2.6
3.0	2.3	2.2	1.9			Sales/Total Assets		1.9	2.0
2.1	1.8	1.9	1.7					1.5	1.5
.5	.5	.4	.5					.5	.5
(41) 1.0	(150) .9	(204) .6	(32) .8			% Depr., Dep., Amort./Sales		(397) .8	(405) .8
1.7	1.5	1.0	1.8					1.3	1.3
2.6	1.6	.9	1.0					1.2	1.2
(29) 5.1	(87) 2.9	(116) 1.5	(14) 1.6			% Officers', Directors', Owners' Comp/Sales		(192) 2.2	(222) 2.3
9.1	5.5	2.9	3.5					4.0	4.3
54218M	552530M	2146835M	1270428M	423377M	1528042M	Net Sales ($)		3386768M	3619185M
14618M	213174M	940907M	592792M	243560M	610709M	Total Assets ($)		1847373M	1781490M

M = $ thousand   MM = $ million
See Pages 1 through 15 for Explanation of Ratios and Data

Comparative Historical Data   Current Data Sorted By Sales

7	31	28	# Postretirement Benefits	3	2	5	8	8	2
			Type of Statement						
68	73	73	Unqualified	2	3	5	20	24	19
98	103	101	Reviewed	5	6	19	34	29	8
157	170	183	Compiled	23	54	47	40	16	3
10	22	25	Tax Returns	3	6	4	8	4	
88	109	104	Other	10	25	18	26	18	7
4/1/92-3/31/93 ALL	4/1/93-3/31/94 ALL	4/1/94-3/31/95 ALL		103 (4/1-9/30/94) 0-1MM	1-3MM	3-5MM	383 (10/1/94-3/31/95) 5-10MM	10-25MM	25MM & OVER
421	477	486	**NUMBER OF STATEMENTS**	43	94	93	128	91	37
%	%	%	**ASSETS**	%	%	%	%	%	%
4.9	5.0	4.9	Cash & Equivalents	6.2	8.0	5.4	3.5	3.9	2.3
14.9	15.7	15.2	Trade Receivables - (net)	12.8	14.1	13.9	12.9	20.0	19.8
63.0	61.6	62.2	Inventory	58.4	60.7	62.4	68.2	58.2	58.6
1.5	1.6	1.7	All Other Current	.9	2.1	1.8	1.6	1.8	1.3
84.3	83.9	84.0	Total Current	78.3	84.8	83.4	86.2	83.8	82.1
10.6	11.0	11.7	Fixed Assets (net)	18.6	11.5	12.3	9.1	11.7	12.1
.8	.8	.4	Intangibles (net)	.5	.4	.2	.5	.4	1.0
4.3	4.3	3.9	All Other Non-Current	2.6	3.3	4.1	4.2	4.1	4.8
100.0	100.0	100.0	Total	100.0	100.0	100.0	100.0	100.0	100.0
			LIABILITIES						
26.2	23.2	25.1	Notes Payable-Short Term	14.2	24.3	22.1	30.3	25.7	27.3
2.8	2.9	3.0	Cur. Mat.-L /T/D	5.8	3.4	2.9	2.6	1.8	2.9
21.6	23.4	22.2	Trade Payables	20.5	18.1	25.2	22.2	24.2	22.9
.2	.8	.3	Income Taxes Payable	.1	.1	.3	.2	.5	.5
5.8	6.2	6.5	All Other Current	4.3	6.5	6.4	5.9	8.0	8.5
56.6	56.6	57.1	Total Current	45.0	52.3	57.0	61.2	60.1	62.0
9.1	9.3	9.3	Long Term Debt	21.1	9.9	9.6	7.2	6.2	8.5
.2	.1	.1	Deferred Taxes	.0	.1	.1	.2	.1	.1
2.3	2.3	1.8	All Other-Non-Current	1.9	2.2	1.7	1.5	1.7	2.9
31.8	31.7	31.6	Net Worth	32.0	35.4	31.6	30.0	31.9	26.5
100.0	100.0	100.0	Total Liabilities & Net Worth	100.0	100.0	100.0	100.0	100.0	100.0
			INCOME DATA						
100.0	100.0	100.0	Net Sales	100.0	100.0	100.0	100.0	100.0	100.0
22.2	21.6	21.0	Gross Profit	33.5	22.8	19.8	18.1	18.6	21.5
20.3	19.5	18.7	Operating Expenses	28.3	20.7	17.9	16.4	16.8	17.7
1.9	2.1	2.3	Operating Profit	5.3	2.1	1.9	1.6	1.8	3.7
.3	.1	.1	All Other Expenses (net)	1.0	-.1	.0	.0	-.1	.6
1.6	2.0	2.2	Profit Before Taxes	4.3	2.2	1.9	1.7	1.9	3.1
			RATIOS						
1.9 / 1.4 / 1.2	1.8 / 1.4 / 1.2	1.8 / 1.4 / 1.2	Current	2.8 / 1.6 / 1.2	2.4 / 1.6 / 1.2	1.8 / 1.5 / 1.2	1.6 / 1.4 / 1.2	1.7 / 1.4 / 1.2	1.5 / 1.3 / 1.1
(420) .6 / .3 / .1	(476) .6 / .3 / .1	(485) .6 / .3 / .1	Quick	.7 / .3 / .1	.7 / .4 / .2	.6 / .3 / .1	(127) .4 / .2 / .1	.7 / .4 / .2	.6 / .3 / .1
9 39.5 / 18 20.3 / 34 10.8	10 37.8 / 19 19.3 / 36 10.2	9 41.7 / 19 19.4 / 33 11.2	Sales/Receivables	2 197.2 / 12 30.5 / 29 12.5	10 36.7 / 19 18.9 / 34 10.8	9 42.8 / 16 22.4 / 28 13.0	8 47.1 / 13 29.0 / 26 13.9	15 25.1 / 26 13.8 / 38 9.5	15 24.4 / 30 12.1 / 45 8.1
89 4.1 / 140 2.6 / 203 1.8	87 4.2 / 130 2.8 / 183 2.0	83 4.4 / 130 2.8 / 174 2.1	Cost of Sales/Inventory	79 4.6 / 174 2.1 / 243 1.5	83 4.4 / 140 2.6 / 203 1.8	83 4.4 / 130 2.8 / 174 2.1	94 3.9 / 135 2.7 / 166 2.2	66 5.5 / 104 3.5 / 152 2.4	81 4.5 / 104 3.5 / 174 2.1
9 39.3 / 24 15.0 / 74 4.9	11 33.4 / 27 13.4 / 81 4.5	9 42.1 / 26 14.0 / 70 5.2	Cost of Sales/Payables	7 51.9 / 21 17.2 / 81 4.5	7 49.3 / 19 19.6 / 50 7.3	14 26.2 / 29 12.6 / 83 4.4	7 51.5 / 21 17.5 / 73 5.0	11 32.9 / 32 11.4 / 70 5.2	18 20.7 / 34 10.8 / 73 5.0
5.3 / 8.9 / 17.1	6.0 / 9.4 / 16.2	6.0 / 10.4 / 17.4	Sales/Working Capital	2.8 / 7.1 / 19.3	4.5 / 7.5 / 11.3	5.7 / 11.4 / 18.4	7.2 / 10.7 / 16.5	7.3 / 12.7 / 20.4	8.4 / 12.1 / 25.4
(394) 4.2 / 2.3 / 1.2	(446) 5.2 / 2.8 / 1.6	(466) 5.6 / 2.9 / 1.7	EBIT/Interest	(40) 7.6 / 2.5 / 1.2	(87) 7.1 / 3.2 / 1.4	(91) 5.1 / 2.4 / 1.3	(123) 5.8 / 2.8 / 1.7	(90) 5.6 / 3.4 / 2.0	(35) 5.3 / 3.6 / 2.3
(164) 3.8 / 1.8 / .8	(179) 3.8 / 2.0 / .8	(187) 5.3 / 2.4 / .8	Net Profit + Depr., Dep., Amort./Cur. Mat. L/T/D	(10) 3.7 / 1.5 / .3	(28) 4.0 / 2.6 / .1	(35) 5.0 / 2.3 / .8	(55) 5.7 / 2.4 / .7	(42) 7.4 / 3.2 / 1.5	(17) 8.2 / 3.4 / 1.3
.1 / .3 / .6	.1 / .3 / .6	.1 / .3 / .6	Fixed/Worth	.1 / .6 / 1.4	.1 / .2 / .5	.2 / .3 / .8	.1 / .2 / .5	.2 / .4 / .6	.2 / .4 / .6
1.2 / 2.7 / 5.6	1.3 / 2.4 / 5.1	1.2 / 2.6 / 5.0	Debt/Worth	.5 / 2.4 / 7.3	.9 / 2.0 / 5.5	1.2 / 2.8 / 4.7	1.5 / 2.8 / 5.0	1.2 / 2.5 / 4.8	1.8 / 3.5 / 5.0
(408) 24.9 / 10.3 / 3.2	(458) 28.7 / 14.1 / 5.6	(467) 28.9 / 14.5 / 6.9	% Profit Before Taxes/Tangible Net Worth	(36) 28.1 / 11.3 / 2.1	(88) 29.3 / 12.7 / 3.5	(89) 27.7 / 10.9 / 3.6	(126) 26.6 / 16.8 / 8.6	26.6 / 15.3 / 8.5	50.0 / 28.8 / 13.4
6.4 / 2.6 / .8	7.1 / 3.9 / 1.5	8.0 / 4.1 / 1.6	% Profit Before Taxes/Total Assets	13.5 / 4.7 / .2	7.6 / 4.8 / 1.0	7.0 / 2.9 / .9	6.4 / 3.6 / 1.9	8.4 / 4.5 / 2.2	11.1 / 6.0 / 3.4
64.6 / 32.1 / 16.9	67.1 / 33.1 / 16.1	65.0 / 32.4 / 16.4	Sales/Net Fixed Assets	78.1 / 22.6 / 8.4	61.1 / 29.1 / 18.3	62.1 / 32.3 / 13.5	74.7 / 39.1 / 21.8	60.9 / 28.2 / 16.8	50.9 / 33.8 / 19.2
2.8 / 2.1 / 1.6	2.9 / 2.2 / 1.7	2.9 / 2.3 / 1.8	Sales/Total Assets	2.8 / 2.0 / 1.4	3.0 / 2.0 / 1.6	2.8 / 2.3 / 1.9	2.9 / 2.4 / 1.9	3.0 / 2.5 / 2.0	3.2 / 2.3 / 1.8
(382) .5 / .8 / 1.2	(432) .5 / .8 / 1.3	(432) .5 / .7 / 1.2	% Depr., Dep., Amort./Sales	(34) .6 / 1.0 / 1.8	(81) .6 / 1.1 / 1.6	(81) .5 / .8 / 1.2	(118) .4 / .6 / 1.0	(86) .4 / .6 / 1.1	(32) .5 / .7 / 1.2
(207) 1.1 / 2.3 / 5.3	(235) 1.3 / 2.0 / 4.1	(247) 1.2 / 2.2 / 4.3	% Officers', Directors', Owners' Comp/Sales	(22) 5.0 / 7.4 / 11.1	(47) 2.1 / 3.0 / 5.8	(46) 1.1 / 1.8 / 3.1	(76) .9 / 1.7 / 3.3	(46) .9 / 1.6 / 3.1	(10) .8 / 1.5 / 2.5
3484525M	4571697M	5975430M	Net Sales ($)	25643M	181922M	377909M	884466M	1367000M	3138490M
1665226M	2150980M	2615760M	Total Assets ($)	16502M	88412M	174682M	386874M	580777M	1368513M

M = $ thousand   MM = $ million
See Pages 1 through 15 for Explanation of Ratios and Data

	Current Data Sorted By Assets							Comparative Historical Data	
	3	3	2	2		1	# Postretirement Benefits		
							Type of Statement		
	1	1	6	6		2	Unqualified	24	27
	7	22	18	1			Reviewed	53	73
	65	54	11				Compiled	125	114
	16	4					Tax Returns	7	7
	25	20	9	2	2		Other	62	58
		75 (4/1-9/30/94)		197 (10/1/94-3/31/95)				4/1/90-3/31/91	4/1/91-3/31/92
	0-500M	500M-2MM	2-10MM	10-50MM	50-100MM	100-250MM		ALL	ALL
	114	101	44	9	2	2	NUMBER OF STATEMENTS	271	279
	%	%	%	%	%	%	ASSETS	%	%
	9.6	8.2	5.4				Cash & Equivalents	7.2	7.3
	10.9	16.3	18.1				Trade Receivables - (net)	16.5	13.3
	35.7	38.5	37.2				Inventory	38.7	39.7
	1.4	1.2	1.6				All Other Current	1.8	1.6
	57.5	64.2	62.3				Total Current	64.2	61.9
	34.7	28.5	29.4				Fixed Assets (net)	29.6	31.3
	1.5	1.7	1.9				Intangibles (net)	.8	1.5
	6.2	5.6	6.4				All Other Non-Current	5.4	5.3
	100.0	100.0	100.0				Total	100.0	100.0
							LIABILITIES		
	12.1	12.1	10.9				Notes Payable-Short Term	14.1	15.0
	6.0	3.7	3.5				Cur. Mat. -L/T/D	3.7	4.5
	13.7	16.3	17.2				Trade Payables	16.7	17.0
	.2	.4	.2				Income Taxes Payable	.6	.5
	7.8	8.6	7.7				All Other Current	7.7	8.8
	39.7	41.2	39.5				Total Current	42.9	45.8
	22.7	16.3	15.8				Long Term Debt	19.9	19.0
	.1	.5	.7				Deferred Taxes	.4	.3
	3.1	3.5	6.6				All Other-Non-Current	2.7	3.0
	34.5	38.5	37.3				Net Worth	34.1	31.8
	100.0	100.0	100.0				Total Liabilities & Net Worth	100.0	100.0
							INCOME DATA		
	100.0	100.0	100.0				Net Sales	100.0	100.0
	40.3	36.5	33.7				Gross Profit	35.8	36.9
	36.7	33.0	29.5				Operating Expenses	32.5	34.0
	3.6	3.5	4.2				Operating Profit	3.3	2.8
	1.4	.7	.4				All Other Expenses (net)	1.2	1.3
	2.3	2.8	3.8				Profit Before Taxes	2.1	1.5
							RATIOS		
	2.6	2.8	2.0					2.6	2.3
	1.5	1.6	1.5				Current	1.6	1.4
	1.0	1.2	1.1					1.1	1.0
	1.2	1.1	.9					1.1	.9
	.4	.6	.6				Quick (270)	.5	.4
	.2	.2	.3					.2	.1
	2 196.2	5 68.0	10 35.2					5 67.8	3 109.2
	7 52.3	17 22.0	30 12.0				Sales/Receivables	16 22.7	13 29.2
	16 22.8	31 11.8	49 7.4					32 11.3	29 12.6
	32 11.5	42 8.7	48 7.6					39 9.3	41 8.8
	58 6.3	74 4.9	72 5.1				Cost of Sales/Inventory	78 4.7	79 4.6
	99 3.7	122 3.0	135 2.7					126 2.9	126 2.9
	5 75.2	12 31.5	16 23.5					11 31.9	11 32.6
	14 26.1	24 14.9	32 11.5				Cost of Sales/Payables	24 14.9	26 14.1
	36 10.1	47 7.8	64 5.7					51 7.1	53 6.9
	10.4	6.7	5.8					6.8	6.6
	20.3	12.5	11.7				Sales/Working Capital	12.8	15.1
	-429.9	31.8	37.4					65.8	-203.4
	6.0	6.1	4.9					4.0	3.3
	(103) 2.7	(96) 3.5	(39) 2.1				EBIT/Interest (247)	1.8	(267) 1.7
	1.2	1.8	1.4					1.1	1.0
	4.5	6.8	2.5					4.5	4.1
	(15) 1.6	(43) 2.9	(19) 1.8				Net Profit + Depr., Dep., Amort./Cur. Mat. L /T/D (112)	2.1	(112) 1.7
	.5	1.4	.9					.8	.8
	.3	.3	.4					.3	.4
	1.0	.7	.8				Fixed/Worth	.8	.9
	4.9	1.8	2.1					2.0	3.1
	.6	.8	.9					.8	.9
	1.8	1.7	1.7				Debt/Worth	2.0	2.3
	15.2	5.2	3.9					5.6	7.2
	44.7	27.7	24.5					31.7	26.8
	(94) 15.6	(93) 17.0	(41) 10.5				% Profit Before Taxes/Tangible Net Worth (241)	16.2	(239) 12.5
	2.3	6.7	3.8					4.9	1.0
	14.5	10.4	7.8					10.0	10.0
	7.3	5.7	3.6				% Profit Before Taxes/Total Assets	5.0	3.3
	.7	2.4	1.0					.9	.0
	31.8	25.7	19.8					29.4	22.8
	13.1	13.4	9.9				Sales/Net Fixed Assets	12.4	11.0
	5.3	5.6	5.1					5.6	5.1
	4.7	3.6	3.2					3.6	3.7
	3.5	2.7	2.2				Sales/Total Assets	2.7	2.7
	2.2	1.9	1.5					1.9	1.7
	.9	.9	1.0					.9	1.0
	(98) 1.9	(92) 1.5	(42) 1.9				% Depr., Dep., Amort./Sales (247)	1.7	(259) 1.9
	3.5	2.4	2.7					3.0	3.0
	3.0	2.6	.5					2.5	2.8
	(53) 4.9	(55) 4.2	(15) 2.9				% Officers', Directors', Owners' Comp/Sales (136)	4.4	(121) 4.9
	8.0	7.1	9.9					7.9	7.8
	102213M	275041M	397590M	341108M	180976M	784961M	Net Sales ($)	1711478M	1778721M
	29136M	99170M	172995M	171179M	125803M	335920M	Total Assets ($)	771118M	803445M

© Robert Morris Associates 1995

M = $ thousand   MM = $ million
See Pages 1 through 15 for Explanation of Ratios and Data

Comparative Historical Data				Current Data Sorted By Sales					
5	7	11	# Postretirement Benefits	2	2	1	2	2	2
			Type of Statement						
18	19	16	Unqualified	1	3		2	5	5
53	41	48	Reviewed	1	18	11	11	6	1
110	94	130	Compiled	49	56	13	7	5	
10	9	20	Tax Returns	13	4		7		
53	45	58	Other	17	24	7	2	4	4
4/1/92-3/31/93 ALL	4/1/93-3/31/94 ALL	4/1/94-3/31/95 ALL		75 (4/1-9/30/94)			197 (10/1/94-3/31/95)		
				0-1MM	1-3MM	3-5MM	5-10MM	10-25MM	25MM & OVER
244	208	272	**NUMBER OF STATEMENTS**	81	105	31	25	20	10
%	%	%	**ASSETS**	%	%	%	%	%	%
7.9	8.1	8.2	Cash & Equivalents	8.6	8.5	9.6	5.1	8.7	3.2
13.6	13.2	14.3	Trade Receivables - (net)	9.9	13.7	19.8	18.7	20.7	14.2
39.6	37.7	37.3	Inventory	31.0	41.7	37.1	38.5	36.9	41.0
1.5	1.5	1.5	All Other Current	1.3	1.4	1.3	1.1	1.5	4.2
62.5	60.5	61.2	Total Current	50.9	65.3	67.8	63.4	67.8	62.7
29.7	32.2	30.9	Fixed Assets (net)	39.2	28.6	24.0	29.0	26.5	23.5
1.1	1.7	1.8	Intangibles (net)	2.4	1.8	.0	1.4	.2	4.8
6.7	5.6	6.1	All Other Non-Current	7.4	4.2	8.1	6.3	5.5	9.0
100.0	100.0	100.0	Total	100.0	100.0	100.0	100.0	100.0	100.0
			LIABILITIES						
12.6	13.0	11.9	Notes Payable-Short Term	10.8	11.7	14.6	10.6	13.9	13.5
4.6	3.4	4.6	Cur. Mat.-L/T/D	6.4	4.5	1.7	3.0	4.4	4.7
17.2	15.8	15.4	Trade Payables	11.4	14.5	17.8	25.0	18.8	19.7
.3	.9	.3	Income Taxes Payable	.2	.3	.2	.3	.3	.0
8.7	8.1	8.1	All Other Current	7.1	8.6	10.7	6.3	7.2	8.1
43.3	41.2	40.2	Total Current	35.9	39.6	45.0	45.2	44.6	46.1
16.4	18.3	18.9	Long Term Debt	27.2	17.9	10.8	13.3	11.3	17.3
.6	.3	.5	Deferred Taxes	.0	.5	.4	.7	2.3	.7
2.6	4.5	3.8	All Other-Non-Current	2.4	4.2	2.7	8.0	4.9	2.4
37.1	35.6	36.6	Net Worth	34.6	37.9	41.1	32.8	37.0	33.6
100.0	100.0	100.0	Total Liabilities & Net Worth	100.0	100.0	100.0	100.0	100.0	100.0
			INCOME DATA						
100.0	100.0	100.0	Net Sales	100.0	100.0	100.0	100.0	100.0	100.0
38.2	37.9	37.4	Gross Profit	40.9	37.9	33.7	34.3	33.4	29.7
35.2	35.2	33.7	Operating Expenses	36.9	33.7	30.9	31.6	30.5	29.7
3.0	2.7	3.6	Operating Profit	4.1	4.3	2.8	2.7	2.9	.0
.9	.8	1.0	All Other Expenses (net)	1.4	1.3	-.1	.1	.5	1.8
2.1	1.9	2.6	Profit Before Taxes	2.7	3.0	2.9	2.6	2.4	-1.8
			RATIOS						
2.5	2.7	2.6	Current	2.7	2.9	2.2	1.8	3.0	1.9
1.4	1.6	1.5		1.5	1.6	1.4	1.5	1.5	1.5
1.1	1.0	1.1		.9	1.2	1.1	1.1	1.1	1.1
.9	1.0	1.0	Quick	1.5	1.0	1.0	.9	1.0	.5
.5 (207)	.6	.5		.4	.6	.6	.5	.7	.4
.2	.2	.2		.2	.2	.2	.2	.4	.1
4 90.1	3 123.8	3 129.4	Sales/Receivables	2 212.6	4 94.3	3 133.7	5 74.3	5 68.7	1 500.5
12 29.6	12 30.2	12 30.5		7 49.0	12 30.1	22 16.7	21 17.5	27 13.7	14 26.8
28 13.2	27 13.6	30 12.2		18 20.3	29 12.7	37 9.9	37 10.0	52 7.0	52 7.0
38 9.6	38 9.5	38 9.7	Cost of Sales/Inventory	30 12.2	42 8.6	36 10.1	51 7.2	39 9.4	59 6.2
76 4.8	72 5.1	68 5.4		56 6.5	78 4.7	69 5.3	66 5.5	60 6.1	73 5.0
126 2.9	118 3.1	114 3.2		104 3.5	126 2.9	107 3.4	111 3.3	111 3.3	228 1.6
9 39.8	10 35.5	10 36.1	Cost of Sales/Payables	0 UND	10 35.9	15 24.2	15 23.9	13 27.4	36 10.2
23 15.8	24 15.0	22 16.3		13 27.8	22 16.8	29 12.4	33 10.9	31 11.9	51 7.1
54 6.8	50 7.3	47 7.7		37 9.9	46 8.0	47 7.8	68 5.4	53 6.9	69 5.3
7.2	7.1	8.0	Sales/Working Capital	10.0	7.1	6.8	8.9	4.8	5.8
15.2	15.7	14.0		19.7	12.5	13.0	15.9	13.7	10.0
66.3	813.0	68.3		-144.8	33.1	42.4	87.8	37.4	271.1
6.0	6.8	5.7	EBIT/Interest	5.5	6.9	6.6	5.1	8.5	
(229) 2.8	(196) 2.5	(250) 2.7		(73) 2.7	(98) 3.2	(29) 3.6	(22) 2.7	(19) 2.0	
1.2	1.2	1.4		1.1	1.8	1.6	1.6	1.2	
5.5	5.4	5.2	Net Profit + Depr., Dep., Amort./Cur. Mat. L/T/D	2.6	6.2	10.8	13.7	2.8	
(92) 2.2	(72) 1.8	(82) 2.3		(12) 1.3	(33) 2.6	(12) 3.1	(10) 2.6	(11) 2.0	
.6	.4	1.0		.2	1.3	1.5	.5	.9	
.3	.4	.3	Fixed/Worth	.4	.3	.2	.4	.3	.4
.8	.9	.7		1.4	.7	.5	.7	.7	.9
1.6	2.2	2.4		8.9	2.5	1.4	2.2	1.6	1.7
.7	.7	.7	Debt/Worth	.5	.7	.8	1.1	.8	1.6
1.7	1.8	1.8		2.0	1.6	1.7	2.0	1.7	2.9
4.2	5.3	5.4		18.8	5.6	3.4	6.6	3.7	5.5
26.9	37.5	28.5	% Profit Before Taxes/Tangible Net Worth	41.5	30.1	29.2	26.0	18.4	22.4
(216) 13.2	(179) 14.3	(241) 15.5		(65) 13.1	(95) 16.9	(30) 17.4	(22) 17.1	(19) 7.5	12.5
3.1	3.4	4.7		1.1	6.2	4.8	8.7	1.8	-13.5
12.5	10.4	12.1	% Profit Before Taxes/Total Assets	14.4	12.2	13.7	8.6	8.6	4.4
5.4	4.7	5.3		6.1	6.6	5.6	4.9	3.1	1.3
.7	.6	1.4		.2	1.9	1.6	2.6	.5	-7.1
26.4	22.1	26.3	Sales/Net Fixed Assets	24.0	29.4	39.8	27.0	24.7	16.7
12.8	11.6	11.8		8.0	13.1	17.8	13.5	11.1	7.2
6.1	6.0	5.3		3.8	6.5	7.1	6.0	5.9	6.0
3.8	3.8	4.0	Sales/Total Assets	4.2	4.0	4.2	4.3	3.5	2.7
2.8	2.8	2.8		2.5	3.0	3.0	3.2	2.8	2.2
2.0	2.0	1.9		1.6	2.0	1.7	1.9	1.8	1.8
1.0	1.0	.9	% Depr., Dep., Amort./Sales	1.1	.8	.8	1.0	.8	
(231) 1.5	(200) 1.7	(242) 1.7		(69) 2.5	(96) 1.5	(28) 1.6	(22) 1.6	1.5	
2.6	3.1	2.8		4.5	2.5	2.5	2.4	2.7	
2.5	2.8	2.7	% Officers', Directors', Owners' Comp/Sales	4.0	2.7	1.9	1.7		
(125) 4.2	(96) 4.1	(124) 4.4		(35) 6.7	(52) 4.1	(16) 3.0	(13) 4.4		
7.1	6.6	7.6		8.5	7.0	5.8	9.1		
1687074M	1977519M	2081889M	Net Sales ($)	46468M	187437M	115095M	174112M	310292M	1248485M
696490M	857195M	934203M	Total Assets ($)	22043M	81339M	45450M	65523M	138829M	581019M

© Robert Morris Associates 1995

M = $ thousand   MM = $ million
See Pages 1 through 15 for Explanation of Ratios and Data

Current Data Sorted By Assets

Comparative Historical Data

							# Postretirement Benefits Type of Statement		
2		2	1						
		2	2				Unqualified	7	4
5	4	2	2				Reviewed	20	15
28	13	3					Compiled	52	56
16	1						Tax Returns	3	6
19	5	2	2				Other	23	19
	48 (4/1-9/30/94)		56 (10/1/94-3/31/95)					4/1/90-3/31/91	4/1/91-3/31/92
0-500M	500M-2MM	2-10MM	10-50MM	50-100MM	100-250MM			ALL	ALL
68	23	9	4				NUMBER OF STATEMENTS	105	100
%	%	%	%	%	%		ASSETS	%	%
10.3	8.8						Cash & Equivalents	6.6	6.5
20.6	22.7						Trade Receivables - (net)	22.8	19.0
22.0	22.4						Inventory	21.9	21.2
1.6	.5						All Other Current	2.0	1.7
54.5	54.4						Total Current	53.2	48.5
36.1	34.6						Fixed Assets (net)	35.4	39.0
4.1	1.5						Intangibles (net)	4.5	4.8
5.4	9.4						All Other Non-Current	6.9	7.8
100.0	100.0						Total	100.0	100.0
							LIABILITIES		
6.7	10.5						Notes Payable-Short Term	6.5	9.8
6.7	6.6						Cur. Mat. -L/T/D	5.2	4.8
15.5	15.5						Trade Payables	16.7	16.7
.3	.2						Income Taxes Payable	.7	.9
9.3	5.9						All Other Current	7.6	9.0
38.5	38.7						Total Current	36.8	41.1
27.1	14.3						Long Term Debt	27.7	31.6
.1	.0						Deferred Taxes	.3	.3
5.2	8.8						All Other-Non-Current	2.1	2.4
29.2	38.2						Net Worth	33.1	24.5
100.0	100.0						Total Liabilities & Net Worth	100.0	100.0
							INCOME DATA		
100.0	100.0						Net Sales	100.0	100.0
50.4	49.9						Gross Profit	53.3	54.0
47.4	48.0						Operating Expenses	49.4	49.7
3.1	1.9						Operating Profit	4.0	4.3
.0	1.1						All Other Expenses (net)	1.2	1.4
3.0	.8						Profit Before Taxes	2.8	2.9
							RATIOS		
2.3	2.5							2.6	2.3
1.5	1.4						Current	1.6	1.3
1.0	1.0							1.0	.8
1.4	1.5							1.4	1.4
(67) .8	.7						Quick	.8	.6
.4	.5							.4	.4
11 32.0	14 25.9							16 22.5	12 30.0
22 16.6	23 16.0						Sales/Receivables	23 15.6	22 16.9
29 12.4	33 10.9							32 11.5	31 11.9
19 19.4	25 14.5							27 13.3	28 13.2
44 8.3	48 7.6						Cost of Sales/Inventory	49 7.4	49 7.5
78 4.7	111 3.3							79 4.6	81 4.5
10 37.8	24 15.0							22 16.9	18 19.8
26 13.8	34 10.6						Cost of Sales/Payables	37 9.8	33 11.0
58 6.3	49 7.4							58 6.3	62 5.9
10.6	11.1							7.5	10.4
21.4	20.8						Sales/Working Capital	19.5	27.2
NM	94.6							279.8	-33.6
4.9	2.3							5.7	3.9
(58) 2.2	(18) 1.1						EBIT/Interest	(98) 2.3	(96) 2.2
1.0	-.1							.9	1.0
3.1							Net Profit + Depr., Dep.,	3.6	2.3
(19) 1.5							Amort./Cur. Mat. L./T/D	(53) 1.9	(26) 1.3
.5								.9	.4
.5	.4							.5	.6
1.2	.7						Fixed/Worth	.9	1.6
12.2	2.4							5.7	13.4
.6	.7							.7	1.0
2.6	1.6						Debt/Worth	2.2	2.8
36.0	4.3							10.6	45.7
55.5	13.0						% Profit Before Taxes/Tangible	55.3	42.3
(53) 18.2	(21) 1.9						Net Worth	(86) 12.7	(78) 15.2
3.2	-6.5							-1.4	.2
16.9	8.3						% Profit Before Taxes/Total	14.4	14.6
4.8	.6						Assets	5.8	5.0
.5	-1.1							-.9	.2
25.8	19.8							24.8	23.2
13.4	9.3						Sales/Net Fixed Assets	10.8	9.6
7.5	5.1							4.3	3.5
4.9	3.5							4.6	4.0
3.7	2.8						Sales/Total Assets	2.8	2.6
2.2	2.1							1.9	2.0
1.2	1.2							1.5	1.5
(62) 1.9	(21) 2.0						% Depr., Dep., Amort./Sales	(93) 2.4	(89) 2.3
2.6	3.6							3.5	3.6
3.1	2.1						% Officers', Directors',	4.3	3.6
(41) 6.2	(14) 3.3						Owners' Comp/Sales	(48) 6.1	(49) 5.4
9.6	5.5							11.4	11.0
50788M	73471M	98249M	178809M				Net Sales ($)	403794M	215463M
15182M	23865M	36325M	73417M				Total Assets ($)	179287M	74914M

© Robert Morris Associates 1995

M = $ thousand   MM = $ million
See Pages 1 through 15 for Explanation of Ratios and Data

Comparative Historical Data				Current Data Sorted By Sales					
	1	5	# Postretirement Benefits	1	1		2 (5-10MM)	1 (10-25MM)	2 (25MM&OVER)
			Type of Statement						
2	3	4	Unqualified					1	2
19	9	11	Reviewed	3	4	2	1	2	
61	60	44	Compiled	24	12	4	3	1	
7	12	17	Tax Returns	12	5				
19	25	28	Other	12	8	2	2	2	2
4/1/92-3/31/93	4/1/93-3/31/94	4/1/94-3/31/95		48 (4/1-9/30/94)		56 (10/1/94-3/31/95)			
ALL	ALL	ALL		0-1MM	1-3MM	3-5MM	5-10MM	10-25MM	25MM & OVER
108	109	104	**NUMBER OF STATEMENTS**	51	29	8	6	6	4
%	%	%	**ASSETS**	%	%	%	%	%	%
8.7	6.8	9.6	Cash & Equivalents	10.0	7.1				
17.0	19.4	20.6	Trade Receivables - (net)	18.4	24.7				
21.6	24.3	23.3	Inventory	22.5	23.8				
1.6	1.5	1.3	All Other Current	1.6	.9				
48.9	52.1	54.8	Total Current	52.5	56.5				
38.0	35.0	35.2	Fixed Assets (net)	37.9	34.7				
4.7	4.0	3.1	Intangibles (net)	4.5	2.4				
8.4	8.9	6.9	All Other Non-Current	5.0	6.4				
100.0	100.0	100.0	Total	100.0	100.0				
			LIABILITIES						
7.9	9.8	8.6	Notes Payable-Short Term	5.4	13.0				
5.2	5.8	6.4	Cur. Mat.-L /T/D	7.0	6.7				
13.2	15.8	15.9	Trade Payables	15.1	16.1				
.7	1.4	.4	Income Taxes Payable	.4	.0				
8.8	8.5	8.2	All Other Current	7.9	10.7				
35.8	41.4	39.5	Total Current	35.9	46.5				
28.4	22.5	22.2	Long Term Debt	29.2	17.1				
.2	.5	.2	Deferred Taxes	.1	.0				
3.0	3.5	5.9	All Other-Non-Current	4.8	6.0				
32.6	32.0	32.3	Net Worth	30.1	30.4				
100.0	100.0	100.0	Total Liabilities & Net Worth	100.0	100.0				
			INCOME DATA						
100.0	100.0	100.0	Net Sales	100.0	100.0				
51.8	54.2	49.4	Gross Profit	51.4	52.0				
48.3	51.6	46.8	Operating Expenses	47.8	50.2				
3.5	2.6	2.6	Operating Profit	3.5	1.8				
.4	.2	.4	All Other Expenses (net)	.2	−.2				
3.1	2.4	2.2	Profit Before Taxes	3.3	2.0				
			RATIOS						
2.3 1.4 1.0	2.3 1.3 .9	2.3 1.4 1.0	Current	2.4 1.6 1.0	1.6 1.3 .9				
1.3 .7 .4	1.1 .7 .4	(103) 1.3 .7 .4	Quick	(50) 1.5 .8 .4	1.1 .7 .4				
8 44.6 19 19.2 30 12.0	11 33.3 23 15.8 34 10.6	12 31.3 22 16.5 31 11.9	Sales/Receivables	10 35.3 18 20.1 29 12.5	14 25.5 24 15.1 37 9.9				
26 14.3 47 7.8 89 4.1	27 13.7 49 7.4 101 3.6	21 17.8 48 7.6 87 4.2	Cost of Sales/Inventory	19 19.0 50 7.3 85 4.3	26 14.3 41 9.0 87 4.2				
9 40.0 30 12.3 50 7.3	20 18.1 37 9.9 65 5.6	13 27.7 33 11.2 54 6.7	Cost of Sales/Payables	9 41.5 27 13.6 58 6.3	19 19.3 37 10.0 51 7.2				
9.5 20.7 432.8	8.6 27.0 -40.6	10.4 20.8 798.9	Sales/Working Capital	8.8 18.6 -212.0	14.0 28.2 NM				
(96) 6.5 2.9 1.0	(105) 6.0 2.0 .4	(87) 4.2 1.8 .7	EBIT/Interest	(43) 4.5 2.3 1.1	(26) 5.2 1.3 .3				
(36) 3.7 1.6 .5	(39) 6.3 1.4 .5	(31) 3.1 1.5 .5	Net Profit + Depr., Dep., Amort./Cur. Mat. L/T/D	(12) 2.8 1.6 .5					
.6 1.1 3.3	.4 1.1 4.0	.5 1.1 4.8	Fixed/Worth	.4 1.2 7.3	.6 1.1 4.2				
1.0 2.3 7.2	1.2 2.2 7.1	.6 2.1 10.7	Debt/Worth	.6 2.7 28.0	.8 2.5 12.0				
(90) 49.5 14.4 .9	(92) 38.7 12.3 -5.2	(87) 35.8 11.7 .7	% Profit Before Taxes/Tangible Net Worth	(41) 55.5 14.1 2.0	(24) 27.2 13.0 -1.3				
14.0 6.5 .3	14.7 4.2 -1.5	12.8 3.9 -.5	% Profit Before Taxes/Total Assets	16.8 5.6 .7	9.6 2.7 -1.8				
20.3 9.9 4.2	21.7 11.6 6.0	23.6 12.0 5.3	Sales/Net Fixed Assets	25.6 13.4 4.0	19.0 12.7 8.1				
4.1 2.8 2.0	4.4 3.0 2.1	4.2 3.2 2.1	Sales/Total Assets	4.9 2.7 2.0	4.1 3.6 2.7				
(97) 1.4 2.0 3.5	(102) 1.4 1.8 2.7	(95) 1.2 1.9 2.7	% Depr., Dep., Amort./Sales	(45) 1.2 1.9 2.8	(28) 1.3 2.0 2.8				
(60) 4.0 5.5 9.1	(59) 4.7 6.8 10.1	(58) 2.8 5.5 9.0	% Officers', Directors', Owners' Comp/Sales	(29) 5.2 7.4 11.3	(18) 3.0 4.5 7.0				
271663M	228667M	401317M	Net Sales ($)	24209M	47305M	30406M	35421M	85167M	178809M
106943M	110178M	148789M	Total Assets ($)	9412M	15709M	11944M	14725M	23582M	73417M

M = $ thousand   MM = $ million
See Pages 1 through 15 for Explanation of Ratios and Data

RETAILERS—BAKERIES. SIC# 5461

Current Data Sorted By Assets | **Comparative Historical Data**

	0-500M	500M-2MM	2-10MM	10-50MM	50-100MM	100-250MM		4/1/90-3/31/91 ALL	4/1/91-3/31/92 ALL
	16 (4/1-9/30/94)			49 (10/1/94-3/31/95)					
# Postretirement Benefits	1	3	1	1		1			
Type of Statement									
Unqualified			2	1		2		6	8
Reviewed	2	4	2					8	3
Compiled	16	8	2	1				21	19
Tax Returns	8	2	2					2	3
Other	7	3	4	1		1		16	10
NUMBER OF STATEMENTS	33	17	10	3		2		53	43
ASSETS	%	%	%	%	%	%		%	%
Cash & Equivalents	14.2	9.5	5.3					8.4	11.9
Trade Receivables - (net)	4.7	8.0	14.6					9.7	8.6
Inventory	8.0	7.4	9.8					9.6	10.1
All Other Current	.7	4.4	.7					2.3	1.7
Total Current	27.5	29.3	30.3					29.9	32.2
Fixed Assets (net)	53.4	49.6	58.4					51.9	48.6
Intangibles (net)	6.6	8.1	6.4					7.8	10.0
All Other Non-Current	12.5	12.9	4.9					10.3	9.2
Total	100.0	100.0	100.0					100.0	100.0
LIABILITIES									
Notes Payable-Short Term	5.5	4.9	2.2					6.8	5.5
Cur. Mat. -L/T/D	4.6	6.2	5.6					5.2	8.6
Trade Payables	10.8	10.0	15.4					11.5	11.6
Income Taxes Payable	.2	.6	.1					.7	.8
All Other Current	15.4	14.5	4.9					10.8	13.9
Total Current	36.5	36.3	28.3					35.0	40.4
Long Term Debt	36.0	23.5	23.8					33.9	28.9
Deferred Taxes	.0	.4	.5					.2	.5
All Other-Non-Current	1.0	5.6	11.9					5.6	3.8
Net Worth	26.4	34.2	35.5					25.3	26.4
Total Liabilities & Net Worth	100.0	100.0	100.0					100.0	100.0
INCOME DATA									
Net Sales	100.0	100.0	100.0					100.0	100.0
Gross Profit	58.6	54.7	50.3					50.6	52.6
Operating Expenses	52.9	52.5	45.4					48.1	46.9
Operating Profit	5.7	2.2	4.9					2.5	5.7
All Other Expenses (net)	1.0	-.6	1.8					1.6	2.5
Profit Before Taxes	4.7	2.8	3.1					.9	3.2
RATIOS									
Current	2.8 / .8 / .3	1.3 / .8 / .4	1.6 / .9 / .5					1.7 / 1.0 / .5	1.2 / .8 / .4
Quick	2.2 / .4 / .1	(16) .9 / .5 / .2	1.1 / .6 / .3					1.1 / .5 / .2	.9 / .5 / .2
Sales/Receivables	0 UND / 0 999.8 / 5 78.7	0 UND / 3 116.0 / 22 16.8	2 218.3 / 14 26.0 / 35 10.3					0 UND / 5 80.9 / 16 22.6	0 UND / 1 283.0 / 20 18.1
Cost of Sales/Inventory	6 58.8 / 13 29.0 / 22 16.5	7 51.5 / 16 23.4 / 25 14.8	7 56.0 / 37 9.9 / 56 6.5					8 44.2 / 18 20.8 / 33 10.9	5 66.4 / 12 29.8 / 33 11.2
Cost of Sales/Payables	0 UND / 14 25.2 / 30 12.3	8 47.3 / 26 14.1 / 39 9.4	24 15.4 / 35 10.3 / 146 2.5					7 49.3 / 26 13.8 / 47 7.7	7 54.6 / 20 18.2 / 41 8.8
Sales/Working Capital	25.7 / -256.0 / -16.2	35.1 / -24.5 / -12.4	26.1 / -150.0 / -18.4					22.2 / -294.5 / -16.0	39.8 / -81.4 / -12.9
EBIT/Interest	(28) 10.3 / 4.6 / 1.6	(16) 13.5 / 2.8 / 1.2						(47) 4.3 / 2.0 / 1.1	(40) 4.7 / 2.7 / 1.2
Net Profit + Depr., Dep., Amort./Cur. Mat. L /T/D								(20) 3.8 / 2.1 / 1.0	(21) 2.8 / 1.6 / 1.0
Fixed/Worth	.9 / 2.7 / NM	1.3 / 2.1 / 7.0	1.2 / 2.3 / 3.8					1.1 / 4.0 / -46.6	.9 / 3.7 / -12.5
Debt/Worth	1.0 / 3.5 / NM	1.1 / 3.4 / 9.2	1.1 / 2.1 / 3.7					1.6 / 4.4 / -67.1	1.2 / 4.8 / -17.7
% Profit Before Taxes/Tangible Net Worth	(25) 124.6 / 65.5 / 20.8	(15) 46.4 / 17.9 / 3.2						(39) 87.3 / 32.1 / 7.1	(28) 68.2 / 37.6 / 17.9
% Profit Before Taxes/Total Assets	27.7 / 15.8 / 2.4	11.6 / 6.0 / 1.4	18.4 / 8.9 / -1.6					13.4 / 4.5 / .1	19.3 / 10.3 / 1.5
Sales/Net Fixed Assets	16.7 / 6.7 / 3.6	7.7 / 6.4 / 3.9	10.9 / 4.0 / 2.1					10.6 / 5.8 / 3.3	12.4 / 7.6 / 4.8
Sales/Total Assets	6.4 / 4.1 / 2.1	3.8 / 3.0 / 2.0	3.2 / 2.3 / 1.4					3.8 / 2.8 / 2.1	4.5 / 3.5 / 2.4
% Depr., Dep., Amort./Sales	(30) 1.9 / 2.6 / 4.4	(15) 2.5 / 3.6 / 4.3	2.9 / 4.2 / 4.4					(46) 2.6 / 4.1 / 6.1	(39) 1.8 / 3.2 / 4.3
% Officers', Directors', Owners' Comp/Sales	(16) 2.3 / 7.8 / 12.0							(20) 2.0 / 5.6 / 8.9	(19) 2.6 / 5.7 / 10.0
Net Sales ($)	33698M	47585M	73712M	53621M		382468M		308288M	592567M
Total Assets ($)	7590M	16117M	31483M	35240M		285641M		183088M	271575M

M = $ thousand   MM = $ million
See Pages 1 through 15 for Explanation of Ratios and Data

Comparative Historical Data   Current Data Sorted By Sales

# Postretirement Benefits / Type of Statement	92-93	93-94	94-95	0-1MM	1-3MM	3-5MM	5-10MM	10-25MM	25MM & OVER
# Postretirement Benefits		4	7	1	3			1	2
Unqualified	3	2	5					3	2
Reviewed	14	13	8		2	3	3		
Compiled	35	28	27	13	7	3	3		1
Tax Returns	3	11	10	5	4	1			
Other	11	13	15	6	5	1	1	2	

Periods: 4/1/92-3/31/93 ALL · 4/1/93-3/31/94 ALL · 4/1/94-3/31/95 ALL
Current: 16 (4/1-9/30/94) [0-1MM, 1-3MM] · 49 (10/1/94-3/31/95) [3-5MM, 5-10MM, 10-25MM, 25MM & OVER]

NUMBER OF STATEMENTS	66	67	65	24	18	8	7	5	3
ASSETS	%	%	%	%	%	%	%	%	%
Cash & Equivalents	13.9	15.5	10.9	12.6	12.5				
Trade Receivables - (net)	6.5	7.1	7.2	3.5	7.4				
Inventory	7.9	6.6	7.8	5.7	9.7				
All Other Current	1.7	.7	1.6	.4	4.6				
Total Current	29.9	30.0	27.4	22.2	34.2				
Fixed Assets (net)	46.8	52.4	54.2	57.9	46.0				
Intangibles (net)	9.6	8.5	7.3	5.6	11.3				
All Other Non-Current	13.7	9.1	11.1	14.3	8.5				
Total	100.0	100.0	100.0	100.0	100.0				
LIABILITIES									
Notes Payable-Short Term	4.7	6.3	4.4	5.7	4.3				
Cur. Mat.-L /T/D	7.4	5.5	5.1	4.7	5.3				
Trade Payables	13.8	11.5	11.4	8.0	11.7				
Income Taxes Payable	.3	1.2	.3	.2	.2				
All Other Current	11.6	11.4	12.7	15.4	14.9				
Total Current	37.8	36.0	33.9	33.9	36.4				
Long Term Debt	26.9	24.4	30.8	40.5	28.9				
Deferred Taxes	.6	.2	.4	.0	.4				
All Other-Non-Current	1.9	7.2	4.7	.4	3.4				
Net Worth	32.7	32.2	30.2	25.2	30.8				
Total Liabilities & Net Worth	100.0	100.0	100.0	100.0	100.0				
INCOME DATA									
Net Sales	100.0	100.0	100.0	100.0	100.0				
Gross Profit	55.2	53.7	55.6	62.0	52.0				
Operating Expenses	51.2	47.5	51.1	55.2	49.9				
Operating Profit	4.1	6.2	4.5	6.8	2.0				
All Other Expenses (net)	.7	1.0	.8	1.7	-.1				
Profit Before Taxes	3.4	5.2	3.7	5.1	2.1				

RATIOS

Ratio	92-93	93-94	94-95	0-1MM	1-3MM
Current	1.2 / .9 / .5	1.3 / .8 / .4	1.6 / .8 / .4	3.6 / .7 / .2	1.5 / 1.0 / .5
Quick	.9 / .6 / .3	1.0 / .5 / .3	1.2 / (64) .5 / .2	3.3 / .4 / .1	1.2 / (17) .4 / .2
Sales/Receivables	0 UND / 2 158.8 / 12 30.7	0 UND / 2 178.0 / 11 32.9	0 UND / 2 186.3 / 15 24.2	0 UND / 0 UND / 3 104.3	0 UND / 2 236.3 / 20 18.1
Cost of Sales/Inventory	8 43.9 / 14 25.5 / 24 15.4	6 56.5 / 11 33.6 / 19 19.3	7 50.9 / 14 26.5 / 29 12.8	8 44.5 / 12 30.5 / 17 20.9	4 101.8 / 19 18.9 / 33 11.0
Cost of Sales/Payables	8 46.4 / 25 14.8 / 46 7.9	14 25.3 / 22 16.8 / 30 12.3	4 95.2 / 23 15.6 / 40 9.1	0 UND / 6 56.2 / 26 14.1	3 128.6 / 25 14.4 / 41 8.9
Sales/Working Capital	66.1 / -85.3 / -22.0	63.4 / -60.7 / -15.6	30.7 / -68.5 / -16.2	14.7 / -182.6 / -10.5	34.0 / NM / -21.4
EBIT/Interest	(57) 9.0 / 2.8 / 1.3	(57) 9.6 / 4.9 / 1.7	(57) 8.4 / 3.6 / 1.5	(18) 8.3 / 4.1 / 1.7	8.4 / 3.3 / 1.3
Net Profit + Depr., Dep., Amort./Cur. Mat. L/T/D	(24) 4.4 / 2.0 / 1.1	(16) 2.3 / 1.4 / .9	(18) 2.9 / 1.5 / 1.1		
Fixed/Worth	1.0 / 2.0 / 9.5	1.0 / 2.0 / 5.7	1.3 / 2.2 / 8.9	1.1 / 2.8 / NM	1.3 / 2.4 / 8.9
Debt/Worth	1.0 / 3.0 / 25.4	1.1 / 2.1 / 10.2	1.2 / 3.2 / 12.5	1.1 / 3.4 / NM	1.0 / 4.6 / 12.3
% Profit Before Taxes/Tangible Net Worth	(51) 84.0 / 28.3 / 12.1	(53) 128.1 / 51.3 / 11.7	(53) 84.1 / 40.4 / 7.7	(18) 125.5 / 63.2 / 14.2	(15) 108.2 / 41.1 / -.7
% Profit Before Taxes/Total Assets	21.4 / 8.5 / 1.5	34.8 / 13.5 / 2.2	21.9 / 8.5 / 1.6	27.9 / 13.1 / 1.5	22.1 / 6.4 / 1.9
Sales/Net Fixed Assets	16.6 / 6.9 / 4.4	12.8 / 6.3 / 4.2	11.4 / 6.0 / 2.9	8.8 / 5.1 / 2.3	16.1 / 6.7 / 5.0
Sales/Total Assets	4.5 / 3.4 / 2.3	4.7 / 3.5 / 2.3	4.5 / 2.9 / 1.9	4.6 / 2.5 / 1.6	4.6 / 3.8 / 2.1
% Depr., Dep., Amort./Sales	(59) 1.7 / 2.7 / 3.9	(64) 2.2 / 3.6 / 5.0	(59) 2.2 / 3.4 / 4.5	(21) 2.4 / 3.3 / 5.1	(16) 1.6 / 2.5 / 4.6
% Officers', Directors', Owners' Comp/Sales	(37) 3.9 / 6.3 / 10.3	(36) 3.9 / 6.3 / 10.9	(29) 3.2 / 6.6 / 11.1		(14) 1.9 / 5.6 / 10.9

	92-93	93-94	94-95	0-1MM	1-3MM	3-5MM	5-10MM	10-25MM	25MM & OVER
Net Sales ($)	279930M	239291M	591084M	11446M	32221M	30307M	44989M	64191M	407930M
Total Assets ($)	127069M	85382M	376071M	4976M	11361M	9434M	18699M	34270M	297331M

M = $ thousand   MM = $ million
See Pages 1 through 15 for Explanation of Ratios and Data

Current Data Sorted By Assets							Comparative Historical Data	
0-500M	18 (4/1-9/30/94) 500M-2MM	2-10MM	10-50MM	13 (10/1/94-3/31/95) 50-100MM	100-250MM		5 4/1/90- 3/31/91 ALL	6 4/1/91- 3/31/92 ALL
3					1	# Postretirement Benefits		
						Type of Statement		
1		1			1	Unqualified		
	2	3				Reviewed	2	2
6	4	1				Compiled	2	5
	1					Tax Returns	1	1
7	4					Other	5	6
14	11	5			1	**NUMBER OF STATEMENTS**	10	14
%	%	%	%	%	%	**ASSETS**	%	%
14.6	14.4					Cash & Equivalents	13.2	18.1
10.9	14.7					Trade Receivables - (net)	13.0	16.2
25.6	21.9					Inventory	18.6	29.0
2.2	.1					All Other Current	1.2	.8
53.3	51.1					Total Current	45.9	64.1
29.9	39.4					Fixed Assets (net)	38.8	26.8
11.6	2.1					Intangibles (net)	2.4	1.8
5.2	7.5					All Other Non-Current	12.9	7.3
100.0	100.0					Total	100.0	100.0
						LIABILITIES		
17.3	2.3					Notes Payable-Short Term	4.0	16.7
5.7	5.0					Cur. Mat. -L/T/D	4.3	8.2
12.3	12.5					Trade Payables	11.4	20.7
.3	.3					Income Taxes Payable	.5	1.5
7.5	8.9					All Other Current	6.9	6.5
43.2	29.0					Total Current	27.0	53.4
15.6	30.3					Long Term Debt	15.3	14.9
.0	.1					Deferred Taxes	.2	.0
.8	3.6					All Other-Non-Current	2.4	1.8
40.4	37.1					Net Worth	55.1	29.8
100.0	100.0					Total Liabilities & Net Worth	100.0	100.0
						INCOME DATA		
100.0	100.0					Net Sales	100.0	100.0
47.0	44.1					Gross Profit	42.9	43.9
42.8	39.0					Operating Expenses	38.4	39.6
4.1	5.1					Operating Profit	4.5	4.3
.8	1.4					All Other Expenses (net)	.4	-.2
3.3	3.7					Profit Before Taxes	4.1	4.6
						RATIOS		
2.2	2.6					Current	3.5	1.7
1.7	2.3						1.7	1.1
.8	1.1						.6	.8
1.7	1.6					Quick	1.7	1.1
.9	.9						.6	.6
.1	.5						.3	.4
0 UND	2 213.3					Sales/Receivables	0 UND	0 UND
0 UND	14 26.4						4 91.1	7 51.4
20 18.1	27 13.5						35 10.5	36 10.2
20 18.5	26 14.2					Cost of Sales/Inventory	6 57.2	17 21.3
33 10.9	38 9.6						13 27.3	37 9.9
85 4.3	72 5.1						76 4.8	96 3.8
3 110.0	4 81.7					Cost of Sales/Payables	4 91.0	8 43.9
12 31.0	17 21.5						14 26.5	18 20.8
26 14.0	58 6.3						55 6.6	48 7.6
9.4	10.7					Sales/Working Capital	7.0	19.8
22.8	19.6						22.5	47.2
-53.0	58.8						-52.4	-49.9
10.8						EBIT/Interest		11.0
(13) 4.6							(11)	3.8
2.9								2.1
						Net Profit + Depr., Dep., Amort./Cur. Mat. L./T/D		
.5	.3					Fixed/Worth	.3	.6
1.0	1.0						.8	.9
3.2	-712.0						1.6	NM
1.1	.3					Debt/Worth	.4	.6
2.0	2.0						.7	2.3
5.3	-835.5						1.8	NM
84.6						% Profit Before Taxes/Tangible	49.7	88.7
(12) 51.7						Net Worth	(11) 24.1	25.3
16.1							-1.2	13.8
23.1	18.5					% Profit Before Taxes/Total	28.1	51.4
13.8	7.7					Assets	14.8	8.4
5.6	-1.3						-1.0	2.4
27.4	11.4					Sales/Net Fixed Assets	18.7	33.3
17.1	9.1						9.5	18.2
8.1	3.6						5.3	7.8
5.4	4.5					Sales/Total Assets	3.7	5.9
3.4	2.6						3.1	3.7
2.4	1.7						2.1	2.5
1.2						% Depr., Dep., Amort./Sales	.9	.8
(12) 2.3							1.4	(12) 1.8
4.2							1.9	3.4
						% Officers', Directors', Owners' Comp/Sales		
15760M	44994M	59130M			284923M	Net Sales ($)	118802M	309550M
3666M	13023M	18762M			231421M	Total Assets ($)	42000M	113351M

M = $ thousand   MM = $ million
See Pages 1 through 15 for Explanation of Ratios and Data

Comparative Historical Data / Current Data Sorted By Sales

					Current Data Sorted By Sales					
1	2	4	# Postretirement Benefits		2	1				1
			Type of Statement							
	4	3	Unqualified	1		1				1
2	3	5	Reviewed		1	1	2	1		
8	10	11	Compiled	2	7		1	1		
	3	1	Tax Returns		1					
10	8	11	Other	5	3	1	1		1	
					18 (4/1-9/30/94)			13 (10/1/94-3/31/95)		
4/1/92-3/31/93	4/1/93-3/31/94	4/1/94-3/31/95		0-1MM	1-3MM	3-5MM	5-10MM	10-25MM	25MM & OVER	
ALL	ALL	ALL								
20	28	31	**NUMBER OF STATEMENTS**	8	12	2	5	3	1	
%	%	%	**ASSETS**	%	%	%	%	%	%	
14.2	13.9	12.5	Cash & Equivalents		12.3					
10.6	7.0	12.4	Trade Receivables - (net)		13.6					
23.8	23.0	25.1	Inventory		26.2					
1.6	1.4	1.1	All Other Current		.1					
50.2	45.3	51.1	Total Current		52.3					
40.7	46.6	36.3	Fixed Assets (net)		39.1					
4.9	3.5	6.2	Intangibles (net)		1.3					
4.2	4.6	6.4	All Other Non-Current		7.3					
100.0	100.0	100.0	Total		100.0					
			LIABILITIES							
9.6	7.4	11.4	Notes Payable-Short Term		8.5					
3.1	3.4	5.2	Cur. Mat.-L /T/D		5.4					
6.3	10.2	12.3	Trade Payables		13.6					
1.1	.5	.3	Income Taxes Payable		.2					
8.9	6.4	7.7	All Other Current		6.0					
29.0	27.9	36.9	Total Current		33.7					
36.9	23.5	21.2	Long Term Debt		24.3					
.0	.0	.3	Deferred Taxes		.1					
7.9	8.1	3.2	All Other-Non-Current		3.5					
26.2	40.5	38.5	Net Worth		38.4					
100.0	100.0	100.0	Total Liabilities & Net Worth		100.0					
			INCOME DATA							
100.0	100.0	100.0	Net Sales		100.0					
47.3	53.8	44.9	Gross Profit		40.6					
42.7	48.5	40.4	Operating Expenses		35.2					
4.6	5.3	4.6	Operating Profit		5.4					
2.3	1.1	1.1	All Other Expenses (net)		1.3					
2.3	4.2	3.5	Profit Before Taxes		4.1					
			RATIOS							
3.5	3.7	2.3			3.0					
2.0	1.6	1.7	Current		1.4					
1.2	1.0	.9			.9					
2.1	2.2	1.6			1.8					
.6	.6	.9	Quick		.7					
.4	.3	.1			.2					
1 557.9	0 UND	0 UND			0 911.1					
4 100.9	0 985.1	5 75.9	Sales/Receivables		7 51.1					
15 24.9	5 73.0	21 17.3			31 11.9					
24 15.1	28 13.1	26 14.2			30 12.3					
54 6.8	49 7.5	39 9.4	Cost of Sales/Inventory		52 7.0					
101 3.6	96 3.8	78 4.7			78 4.7					
2 238.4	6 58.0	4 81.7			5 69.3					
11 33.9	19 19.5	17 21.2	Cost of Sales/Payables		15 23.8					
24 15.4	34 10.8	32 11.5			54 6.7					
5.8	6.9	9.9			8.6					
11.4	24.4	19.6	Sales/Working Capital		24.5					
49.7	NM	-83.2			NM					
7.1	9.6	11.3			17.5					
1.7	(26) 4.0	(28) 4.1	EBIT/Interest		3.3					
.0	.8	2.4			1.4					
		1.6								
		(10) 1.3	Net Profit + Depr., Dep., Amort./Cur. Mat. L/T/D							
		.5								
1.1	.7	.6			.3					
1.7	1.0	1.0	Fixed/Worth		1.0					
NM	3.2	3.0			NM					
1.5	.7	.9			.5					
3.1	1.5	1.9	Debt/Worth		1.8					
NM	4.8	11.3			NM					
71.1	92.5	67.8								
(15) 18.1	(24) 24.1	(26) 26.0	% Profit Before Taxes/Tangible Net Worth							
-2.3	3.6	14.3								
10.8	18.4	19.2			16.9					
2.7	10.7	10.2	% Profit Before Taxes/Total Assets		10.7					
-3.1	.0	1.7			.6					
10.6	8.2	21.2			20.1					
5.6	4.9	10.2	Sales/Net Fixed Assets		9.0					
3.9	3.1	5.5			4.0					
3.4	3.6	4.9			4.7					
2.6	2.4	3.0	Sales/Total Assets		2.8					
1.5	1.7	2.3			1.8					
2.0	1.8	1.1			.9					
(18) 3.7	(26) 3.0	(26) 2.2	% Depr., Dep., Amort./Sales	(10)	2.3					
7.3	4.1	4.0			4.2					
2.6	3.9	3.1								
(11) 8.6	(12) 6.7	(18) 5.2	% Officers', Directors', Owners' Comp/Sales							
9.6	12.4	10.6								
245883M	331976M	404807M	Net Sales ($)	3918M	23361M	8208M	40162M	44235M	284923M	
86676M	196437M	266872M	Total Assets ($)	1334M	9793M	2130M	11514M	10680M	231421M	

M = $ thousand   MM = $ million
See Pages 1 through 15 for Explanation of Ratios and Data

RETAILERS—CONVENIENCE FOOD STORES. SIC# 5411

Current Data Sorted By Assets						# Postretirement Benefits / Type of Statement	Comparative Historical Data	
4	6	9	7	1	3			
1	11	17	38	6	11	Unqualified	80	75
7	10	22	5			Reviewed	48	36
31	48	22	6			Compiled	112	96
20	5	1				Tax Returns	8	11
28	28	29	16	4	5	Other	103	85
	135 (4/1-9/30/94)			236 (10/1/94-3/31/95)			4/1/90-3/31/91	4/1/91-3/31/92
0-500M	500M-2MM	2-10MM	10-50MM	50-100MM	100-250MM		ALL	ALL
87	102	91	65	10	16	NUMBER OF STATEMENTS	351	303
%	%	%	%	%	%	ASSETS	%	%
13.2	11.5	12.6	8.6	11.6	8.1	Cash & Equivalents	8.7	8.6
5.7	5.2	5.8	6.4	4.0	3.4	Trade Receivables - (net)	5.1	4.9
31.4	23.9	21.1	17.2	14.9	18.9	Inventory	27.3	27.7
1.0	1.7	1.8	2.1	1.6	3.3	All Other Current	2.1	1.8
51.4	42.3	41.2	34.2	32.1	33.7	Total Current	43.2	43.1
39.8	48.1	49.9	55.6	55.1	52.6	Fixed Assets (net)	46.6	45.1
1.7	2.6	1.5	1.5	3.3	7.1	Intangibles (net)	2.0	2.8
7.1	7.0	7.3	8.7	9.5	6.5	All Other Non-Current	8.2	9.0
100.0	100.0	100.0	100.0	100.0	100.0	Total	100.0	100.0
						LIABILITIES		
6.9	3.6	2.3	4.4	.9	1.9	Notes Payable-Short Term	5.4	4.8
5.4	4.9	4.4	5.1	4.1	1.4	Cur. Mat. -L/T/D	4.7	5.3
14.3	19.9	17.5	17.8	12.2	17.3	Trade Payables	19.6	19.4
.5	.6	.5	.1	.7	.2	Income Taxes Payable	1.0	.5
9.1	9.7	9.6	9.7	9.9	10.6	All Other Current	7.6	7.9
36.2	38.8	34.4	37.0	27.7	31.4	Total Current	38.2	37.9
32.9	31.0	26.2	26.0	30.4	27.4	Long Term Debt	30.9	28.9
.1	.2	.8	1.2	1.2	1.9	Deferred Taxes	.7	.7
5.8	3.3	2.3	3.3	6.0	3.9	All Other-Non-Current	2.3	3.2
25.0	26.8	36.3	32.5	34.7	35.4	Net Worth	27.8	29.2
100.0	100.0	100.0	100.0	100.0	100.0	Total Liabilities & Net Worth	100.0	100.0
						INCOME DATA		
100.0	100.0	100.0	100.0	100.0	100.0	Net Sales	100.0	100.0
22.5	22.5	22.1	23.8	24.7	23.9	Gross Profit	22.4	22.1
20.6	20.8	20.1	20.8	22.7	21.2	Operating Expenses	20.9	21.0
1.9	1.7	2.0	3.0	2.0	2.7	Operating Profit	1.5	1.1
.5	.3	.2	.4	.5	.8	All Other Expenses (net)	.4	.2
1.4	1.4	1.8	2.6	1.5	1.9	Profit Before Taxes	1.1	.9
						RATIOS		
3.4	1.8	1.6	1.1	1.4	1.2	Current	1.7	1.7
1.8	1.2	1.2	1.0	1.0	1.2		1.1	1.1
1.0	.7	.9	.7	.9	.8		.8	.8
1.5	.9	.8	.6	.8	.7	Quick	.6	.6
(86) .5	(100) .4	.5	.4	.4	.3		(344) .3	(301) .3
.2	.2	.3	.2	.3	.2		.1	.2
0 UND	0 880.0	1 486.0	2 190.4	2 203.8	2 173.3	Sales/Receivables	1 669.0	1 531.3
1 566.3	1 313.6	4 136.5	3 111.4	3 116.0	3 127.4		2 224.2	2 182.2
3 105.9	4 94.7	5 78.0	6 62.0	5 71.9	4 85.9		4 91.4	4 81.5
11 33.4	11 33.9	12 31.7	12 31.4	17 21.6	15 24.5	Cost of Sales/Inventory	14 26.0	14 25.9
17 21.1	16 22.7	18 20.5	17 22.0	22 16.9	19 18.8		20 18.3	20 18.7
26 13.9	28 13.0	25 14.8	22 16.4	23 15.6	38 9.7		28 13.2	28 13.0
0 UND	6 62.7	11 32.7	14 26.6	12 30.1	17 21.7	Cost of Sales/Payables	9 41.7	9 38.6
5 69.7	14 26.6	15 23.7	19 19.1	17 21.1	21 17.2		16 23.5	15 25.0
14 25.9	21 17.1	20 18.1	24 14.9	22 16.9	31 11.7		21 17.1	21 17.0
19.6	35.3	27.6	103.6	30.2	51.8	Sales/Working Capital	33.7	32.3
37.1	76.3	95.6	-246.6	NM	75.5		120.1	126.8
999.8	-65.4	-145.4	-46.1	-157.9	-82.1		-70.3	-63.7
8.8	5.6	6.2	5.4	4.8	10.8	EBIT/Interest	4.0	4.0
(68) 2.5	(91) 2.8	(85) 3.3	(59) 2.8	2.7	(14) 5.0		(315) 1.8	(286) 2.1
1.2	1.2	2.1	1.8	1.7	1.3		1.0	.9
3.1	5.2	4.0	3.4			Net Profit + Depr., Dep., Amort./Cur. Mat. L./T/D	3.5	3.3
(17) 1.2	(29) 2.5	(44) 2.3	(35) 1.9				(170) 1.8	(149) 1.8
.3	.9	1.3	1.4				.8	.8
.4	.7	.9	1.3	1.2	1.2	Fixed/Worth	.9	.8
1.4	2.1	1.7	1.7	2.1	1.5		2.1	1.8
25.1	14.4	2.8	2.9	3.0	3.2		5.8	4.2
.9	1.2	1.0	1.3	1.1	1.1	Debt/Worth	1.3	1.2
3.6	3.3	2.1	2.1	2.8	1.9		2.8	2.7
82.3	16.2	4.2	3.7	4.2	4.0		11.0	7.0
81.0	63.2	38.0	30.3	32.4	29.2	% Profit Before Taxes/Tangible Net Worth	41.5	36.2
(69) 37.9	(85) 25.9	(89) 21.9	(62) 20.4	17.7	(14) 19.5		(295) 18.7	(258) 17.7
16.5	8.8	11.1	10.6	11.3	9.8		3.5	5.4
18.8	14.1	12.3	10.0	8.4	10.8	% Profit Before Taxes/Total Assets	11.2	9.3
9.5	7.2	7.7	6.1	5.8	7.1		4.1	4.6
2.3	1.2	3.6	3.0	2.3	1.8		.1	-.2
66.1	28.0	16.9	11.6	9.6	7.6	Sales/Net Fixed Assets	28.0	28.0
18.0	10.5	9.9	8.1	7.2	6.4		11.8	12.6
8.3	4.8	6.5	5.2	3.6	5.6		5.9	6.6
11.0	8.4	6.7	5.7	4.9	5.1	Sales/Total Assets	7.6	7.8
6.6	4.7	4.9	4.5	3.1	3.3		5.2	5.3
4.5	3.3	3.9	2.9	2.6	2.2		3.5	3.4
.6	.8	1.0	1.2	1.3		% Depr., Dep., Amort./Sales	.8	.8
(79) 1.0	(92) 1.3	(90) 1.4	(64) 1.6	1.6			(322) 1.3	(282) 1.2
2.0	2.1	1.9	2.1	1.9			2.1	1.9
1.4	1.1	.8				% Officers', Directors', Owners' Comp/Sales	.6	.9
(55) 3.0	(59) 2.0	(34) 1.4					(108) 1.4	(94) 1.5
4.7	4.2	5.5					2.7	2.9
155511M	609097M	2122134M	6434976M	2746123M	8908181M	Net Sales ($)	17422363M	19487769M
20077M	104747M	409098M	1474365M	775620M	2546770M	Total Assets ($)	4187133M	4393464M

M = $ thousand   MM = $ million
See Pages 1 through 15 for Explanation of Ratios and Data

Comparative Historical Data				Current Data Sorted By Sales					
8	14	30	# Postretirement Benefits	1	4	3	2	7	13
			Type of Statement						
63	61	84	Unqualified	1	3	3	7	11	59
41	37	44	Reviewed	3	6	3	9	10	13
133	100	107	Compiled	8	34	12	16	20	17
28	27	26	Tax Returns	5	15	4	1	1	
65	76	110	Other	8	25	13	11	18	35
4/1/92-3/31/93	4/1/93-3/31/94	4/1/94-3/31/95				135 (4/1-9/30/94)		236 (10/1/94-3/31/95)	
ALL	ALL	ALL		0-1MM	1-3MM	3-5MM	5-10MM	10-25MM	25MM & OVER
330	301	371	NUMBER OF STATEMENTS	25	83	35	44	60	124
%	%	%	ASSETS	%	%	%	%	%	%
10.3	10.7	11.5	Cash & Equivalents	7.6	13.5	8.3	11.3	15.0	10.3
5.2	5.6	5.6	Trade Receivables - (net)	3.6	5.5	5.3	7.6	5.7	5.4
26.4	24.3	23.3	Inventory	30.1	23.0	23.8	27.9	23.8	20.2
1.5	1.7	1.7	All Other Current	1.1	.9	1.6	1.9	1.9	2.2
43.5	42.2	42.1	Total Current	42.4	42.9	39.0	48.6	46.4	38.1
45.6	47.2	48.3	Fixed Assets (net)	51.0	48.4	50.5	40.7	45.0	51.4
2.3	2.5	2.1	Intangibles (net)	2.9	1.9	2.9	1.7	1.9	2.1
8.6	8.1	7.5	All Other Non-Current	3.7	6.8	7.6	8.9	6.8	8.5
100.0	100.0	100.0	Total	100.0	100.0	100.0	100.0	100.0	100.0
			LIABILITIES						
3.9	4.9	4.0	Notes Payable-Short Term	6.9	5.3	5.7	3.7	1.9	3.3
5.0	4.9	4.8	Cur. Mat.-L /T/D	6.0	5.9	3.5	3.5	5.4	4.2
17.6	16.6	17.3	Trade Payables	8.4	12.8	17.9	22.6	20.5	18.6
.5	1.8	.4	Income Taxes Payable	.2	.5	.6	.4	.8	.2
9.1	9.6	9.6	All Other Current	10.5	6.8	11.9	11.1	9.4	10.2
36.2	37.7	36.2	Total Current	32.0	31.3	39.9	41.4	37.9	36.5
29.5	28.9	29.2	Long Term Debt	47.0	36.8	29.1	25.9	25.0	23.8
.5	.6	.6	Deferred Taxes	.3	.0	.1	.3	.6	1.2
1.7	3.1	3.7	All Other-Non-Current	12.5	3.3	5.2	3.9	1.2	3.0
32.2	29.7	30.3	Net Worth	8.2	28.6	25.7	28.6	35.2	35.5
100.0	100.0	100.0	Total Liabilities & Net Worth	100.0	100.0	100.0	100.0	100.0	100.0
			INCOME DATA						
100.0	100.0	100.0	Net Sales	100.0	100.0	100.0	100.0	100.0	100.0
21.7	21.9	22.7	Gross Profit	32.9	22.2	21.8	22.8	20.9	22.2
20.2	20.3	20.6	Operating Expenses	28.3	19.6	20.1	21.3	19.2	20.4
1.5	1.6	2.1	Operating Profit	4.5	2.6	1.6	1.5	1.8	1.8
.3	.2	.4	All Other Expenses (net)	1.3	.9	-.4	.2	.2	.2
1.2	1.4	1.7	Profit Before Taxes	3.3	1.7	2.1	1.3	1.6	1.6
			RATIOS						
1.8	1.5	1.8		3.2	3.1	1.8	1.8	1.5	1.3
1.1	1.1	1.2	Current	1.8	1.3	1.1	1.3	1.2	1.0
.8	.8	.8		.9	.9	.7	1.0	.9	.8
.8	.7	.8		1.0	1.6	.7	.9	.9	.6
(328) .4	(299) .4	(368) .4	Quick	.3 (81) .6	.3	.4	(59) .5	.4	
.2	.2	.2		.1	.2	.1	.1	.3	.2
0 741.2	1 490.5	1 707.4		0 UND	0 UND	1 707.4	1 690.4	1 622.1	2 208.0
2 201.8	2 174.5	2 161.6	Sales/Receivables	0 UND	1 289.1	2 231.0	1 257.4	3 143.5	3 123.8
4 83.8	4 85.0	5 80.1		1 339.9	4 96.1	4 89.9	5 79.6	5 72.1	5 74.1
13 28.7	12 30.6	12 31.7		16 23.4	10 35.0	10 37.5	13 28.4	11 33.8	13 28.3
18 19.9	17 21.1	17 21.1	Cost of Sales/Inventory	28 13.1	14 26.5	18 20.7	19 19.3	16 22.8	17 21.0
28 13.2	25 14.7	25 14.6		42 8.6	22 16.7	29 12.6	29 12.8	22 16.5	23 15.7
8 46.4	7 52.2	8 48.5		0 UND	1 371.3	6 63.9	7 55.9	11 33.6	13 28.0
14 25.4	13 28.3	15 25.0	Cost of Sales/Payables	4 83.3	7 51.6	14 25.9	13 28.8	15 23.6	17 21.3
20 18.4	21 17.7	21 17.0		21 17.1	17 22.0	23 16.0	23 16.0	20 18.1	23 16.2
31.0	35.8	29.0		18.0	20.6	32.8	28.5	38.0	52.4
100.6	151.0	99.2	Sales/Working Capital	26.3	60.4	144.2	52.7	101.4	999.8
-75.1	-59.3	-84.2		NM	-132.7	-29.2	-187.4	-175.9	-53.3
4.4	5.9	6.0		2.8	5.2	6.4	5.7	9.0	7.5
(295) 2.5	(277) 2.9	(327) 3.0	EBIT/Interest	(22) 2.0	(66) 2.5	(31) 2.8	(39) 2.8	(55) 3.7	(114) 3.3
1.3	1.3	1.6		1.2	1.0	1.1	1.4	2.0	1.9
2.6	3.8	4.1			3.4	6.6	5.0	2.9	6.3
(132) 1.5	(103) 1.8	(141) 2.2	Net Profit + Depr., Dep.,		(19) 1.4	(12) 1.9	(13) 1.9	(27) 1.8	(67) 2.4
1.0	1.0	1.2	Amort./Cur. Mat. L/T/D		.9	.0	1.3	1.1	1.4
.7	.9	.8		.7	.7	.7	.5	.6	1.1
1.6	1.8	1.7	Fixed/Worth	14.5	2.3	2.5	1.9	1.4	1.6
4.3	4.6	4.7		-2.7	10.7	22.9	6.4	3.2	2.5
1.0	1.3	1.2		2.0	.9	1.2	1.3	1.0	1.2
2.2	2.5	2.4	Debt/Worth	15.0	3.6	5.2	2.7	2.1	2.0
7.0	6.5	6.5		-4.2	28.1	37.3	8.3	4.5	3.3
39.1	44.5	43.4		73.2	67.6	93.1	50.2	37.2	32.3
(282) 18.8	(258) 26.8	(329) 24.0	% Profit Before Taxes/Tangible Net Worth	(17) 37.5	(68) 27.5	(29) 41.0	(39) 25.0	(56) 21.0	(120) 20.7
5.2	10.9	11.4		15.1	9.5	20.1	6.3	11.7	11.1
11.2	13.0	12.6		9.0	17.5	19.5	13.9	12.9	10.8
5.2	7.5	7.0	% Profit Before Taxes/Total Assets	3.7	8.9	9.8	6.9	7.2	6.7
1.3	2.1	2.4		2.3	.9	.5	1.9	3.6	3.0
29.6	25.6	23.3		26.0	45.5	20.4	43.1	27.4	12.7
10.8	10.6	9.7	Sales/Net Fixed Assets	8.3	12.4	8.5	17.1	11.4	8.6
6.5	5.9	6.0		3.4	4.7	4.8	5.9	8.1	6.1
7.5	7.7	7.2		6.7	7.8	6.1	9.1	8.4	6.3
5.1	5.1	4.9	Sales/Total Assets	3.3	5.6	4.2	5.3	5.3	4.8
3.6	3.3	3.4		2.5	3.3	3.3	3.9	4.2	3.3
.8	.8	.9		1.3	.7	.9	.7	.9	1.1
(302) 1.4	(278) 1.4	(343) 1.5	% Depr., Dep., Amort./Sales	(24) 2.0	(78) 1.4	(30) 1.5	(39) 1.1	(58) 1.3	(114) 1.5
2.0	1.9	2.0		3.4	2.3	2.1	1.8	1.9	1.9
1.0	.9	1.1		2.8	1.5	1.0	1.0	.7	.7
(140) 1.7	(117) 1.6	(156) 2.0	% Officers', Directors', Owners' Comp/Sales	(17) 4.0	(50) 3.1	(20) 2.4	(26) 1.6	(21) 1.1	(22) 1.1
5.1	3.1	4.6		8.0	4.5	5.1	3.7	1.8	7.0
16813241M	15599511M	20976022M	Net Sales ($)	15627M	151237M	132146M	322619M	964557M	19389836M
4006910M	3645013M	5330677M	Total Assets ($)	14864M	38540M	36076M	64788M	214876M	4961533M

M = $ thousand   MM = $ million
See Pages 1 through 15 for Explanation of Ratios and Data

RETAILERS—DRINKING PLACES. SIC# 5813

| Current Data Sorted By Assets | | | | | | | Comparative Historical Data | |

Postretirement Benefits

						Type of Statement		
1	1	1	1			Unqualified	4	3
1	2	1				Reviewed	4	5
39	8	2				Compiled	41	32
13	2					Tax Returns	5	8
9	1		1			Other	16	23

0-500M	18 (4/1-9/30/94) 500M-2MM	2-10MM	65 (10/1/94-3/31/95) 10-50MM	50-100MM	100-250MM		4/1/90- 3/31/91 ALL	4/1/91- 3/31/92 ALL
63	14	5	1			NUMBER OF STATEMENTS	70	71
%	%	%	%	%	%	ASSETS	%	%
9.1	8.9					Cash & Equivalents	10.3	11.3
1.3	7.9					Trade Receivables - (net)	3.5	2.7
8.9	12.5					Inventory	10.2	9.0
.8	.1					All Other Current	2.2	1.3
20.0	29.4					Total Current	26.2	24.3
59.2	59.0					Fixed Assets (net)	49.4	55.1
10.6	4.7					Intangibles (net)	11.6	10.9
10.2	6.9					All Other Non-Current	12.8	9.6
100.0	100.0					Total	100.0	100.0
						LIABILITIES		
8.7	8.9					Notes Payable-Short Term	4.8	2.0
6.4	3.9					Cur. Mat. -L/T/D	4.8	5.9
6.5	8.4					Trade Payables	6.9	8.0
.4	.6					Income Taxes Payable	.6	.6
12.3	10.7					All Other Current	9.9	9.7
34.2	32.6					Total Current	27.0	26.1
30.0	20.8					Long Term Debt	39.1	33.1
.0	.0					Deferred Taxes	.3	.1
7.6	3.4					All Other-Non-Current	2.6	5.5
28.1	43.2					Net Worth	30.9	35.3
100.0	100.0					Total Liabilities & Net Worth	100.0	100.0
						INCOME DATA		
100.0	100.0					Net Sales	100.0	100.0
61.7	64.0					Gross Profit	59.9	57.3
59.2	52.3					Operating Expenses	56.0	50.3
2.5	11.7					Operating Profit	3.9	6.9
.8	1.3					All Other Expenses (net)	.8	1.7
1.7	10.4					Profit Before Taxes	3.1	5.2
						RATIOS		
1.4	2.8					Current	1.7	1.9
.7	.7						1.0	1.1
.3	.5						.4	.6
(62) .9	1.8					Quick	(68) 1.0	1.2
.3	.5						.4	.5
.1	.1						.1	.1
0 UND	0 UND					Sales/Receivables	0 UND	0 UND
0 UND	0 997.9						0 UND	0 UND
0 999.8	6 59.9						2 190.8	2 217.0
10 35.7	15 24.8					Cost of Sales/Inventory	13 28.0	11 32.5
22 16.6	17 21.1						19 19.6	16 22.7
30 12.3	32 11.3						41 8.9	29 12.8
0 UND	5 66.4					Cost of Sales/Payables	0 UND	0 UND
11 31.8	13 28.6						14 25.4	10 36.5
25 14.6	46 7.9						38 9.5	30 12.2
84.9	11.0					Sales/Working Capital	26.0	27.0
-45.7	-39.5						NM	870.0
-11.6	-10.8						-15.7	-25.1
6.1	25.5					EBIT/Interest	5.8	6.1
(53) 2.9	(13) 4.6						(62) 2.3	(60) 2.4
.5	2.6						.6	1.5
2.8						Net Profit + Depr., Dep., Amort./Cur. Mat. L /T/D	4.5	2.9
(11) 1.3							(20) 3.2	(22) 1.4
-.1							-.1	.4
1.2	.7					Fixed/Worth	.9	.9
2.6	1.3						2.0	2.2
UND	NM						UND	17.4
1.4	.6					Debt/Worth	.9	.8
3.1	1.3						2.3	2.3
-93.0	NM						NM	21.8
70.3	64.6					% Profit Before Taxes/Tangible Net Worth	61.2	72.7
(47) 11.8	(11) 32.0						(53) 24.4	(57) 32.0
-11.9	23.2						.2	7.0
18.8	29.1					% Profit Before Taxes/Total Assets	20.5	20.2
5.0	10.3						6.5	9.2
-4.0	6.4						-4.3	2.3
10.1	7.0					Sales/Net Fixed Assets	18.2	15.2
5.7	4.0						6.4	5.5
2.9	1.4						2.7	2.8
5.1	3.1					Sales/Total Assets	5.3	5.1
3.1	2.3						2.9	3.0
1.8	1.0						1.6	1.9
2.3	2.0					% Depr., Dep., Amort./Sales	1.8	1.6
(58) 3.7	3.5						(63) 3.2	(65) 3.1
5.1	5.4						5.2	4.5
2.6						% Officers', Directors', Owners' Comp/Sales	3.8	4.1
(35) 5.9							(31) 5.7	(35) 8.5
9.9							10.7	11.4
45571M	42912M	65471M	12193M			Net Sales ($)	91787M	153737M
12892M	15925M	27982M	10344M			Total Assets ($)	38531M	53877M

M = $ thousand   MM = $ million
See Pages 1 through 15 for Explanation of Ratios and Data

Comparative Historical Data | | | **Current Data Sorted By Sales**

# Postretirement Benefits / Type of Statement	4/1/92-3/31/93	4/1/93-3/31/94	4/1/94-3/31/95	0-1MM	1-3MM	3-5MM	5-10MM	10-25MM	25MM & OVER
Unqualified	3		4	1				3	
Reviewed	4	5	4		2	1		1	
Compiled	34	40	49	29	16	3	1		
Tax Returns	12	11	15	11	4				
Other	18	15	11	6	4			1	

Comparative Historical: 4/1/92-3/31/93 ALL; 4/1/93-3/31/94 ALL; 4/1/94-3/31/95 ALL
Current Data: 18 (4/1-9/30/94) covers 0-1MM and 1-3MM; 65 (10/1/94-3/31/95) covers 3-5MM, 5-10MM, 10-25MM, 25MM & OVER

	4/1/92-3/31/93 ALL		4/1/93-3/31/94 ALL		4/1/94-3/31/95 ALL		0-1MM		1-3MM	3-5MM	5-10MM	10-25MM	25MM & OVER
NUMBER OF STATEMENTS	71		71		83		47		26	4	1	5	
	%		%		%	**ASSETS**	%		%	%	%	%	%
Cash & Equivalents	12.9		7.8		9.2		8.8		10.2				
Trade Receivables - (net)	1.9		3.6		2.6		.6		3.1				
Inventory	7.2		8.6		9.8		8.0		9.8				
All Other Current	1.9		.4		.6		.4		1.1				
Total Current	23.8		20.5		22.3		17.9		24.2				
Fixed Assets (net)	56.4		53.7		59.2		63.8		54.7				
Intangibles (net)	10.0		10.5		9.0		10.4		8.3				
All Other Non-Current	9.8		15.3		9.6		8.0		12.8				
Total	100.0		100.0		100.0		100.0		100.0				
						LIABILITIES							
Notes Payable-Short Term	3.6		6.3		8.7		11.3		4.9				
Cur. Mat.-L /T/D	5.5		5.9		5.7		6.9		4.8				
Trade Payables	6.5		9.2		6.9		4.0		10.9				
Income Taxes Payable	.7		1.3		.4		.3		.6				
All Other Current	10.3		13.2		11.9		10.6		12.1				
Total Current	26.6		35.9		33.6		33.0		33.4				
Long Term Debt	28.4		30.3		28.3		31.5		28.0				
Deferred Taxes	.0		.1		.0		.0		.0				
All Other-Non-Current	6.7		5.9		7.2		9.8		2.3				
Net Worth	38.3		27.8		30.9		25.7		36.3				
Total Liabilities & Net Worth	100.0		100.0		100.0		100.0		100.0				
						INCOME DATA							
Net Sales	100.0		100.0		100.0		100.0		100.0				
Gross Profit	60.8		61.6		62.4		61.5		64.3				
Operating Expenses	54.1		57.2		58.1		58.4		57.8				
Operating Profit	6.7		4.4		4.3		3.1		6.5				
All Other Expenses (net)	.7		1.7		1.0		1.1		1.3				
Profit Before Taxes	5.9		2.6		3.3		2.0		5.2				

RATIOS

Ratio	4/1/92-3/31/93	4/1/93-3/31/94	4/1/94-3/31/95	0-1MM	1-3MM	3-5MM	5-10MM	10-25MM	25MM & OVER
Current	2.3 / 1.2 / .4	1.3 / .5 / .2	1.5 / .7 / .4	1.5 / .7 / .2	1.3 / .7 / .4				
Quick	(68) 1.7 / .7 / .1	(70) .8 / .2 / .1	(82) .9 / .3 / .1	1.0 / .3 / .1	(25) .7 / .4 / .2				
Sales/Receivables	0 UND / 0 UND / 1 451.5	0 UND / 0 UND / 2 159.7	0 UND / 0 UND / 2 174.0	0 UND / 0 UND / 0 UND	0 UND / 0 999.8 / 3 107.8				
Cost of Sales/Inventory	10 34.8 / 16 23.4 / 26 13.8	10 36.3 / 17 21.8 / 26 14.2	15 25.1 / 22 16.8 / 30 12.1	16 22.5 / 23 16.1 / 30 12.0	10 36.1 / 17 21.2 / 26 14.0				
Cost of Sales/Payables	0 UND / 10 38.3 / 29 12.5	3 119.0 / 20 18.5 / 43 8.4	0 UND / 15 24.4 / 30 12.0	0 UND / 5 75.0 / 20 18.3	8 45.4 / 24 15.1 / 36 10.2				
Sales/Working Capital	27.4 / 143.0 / -15.7	77.1 / -26.9 / -8.3	54.1 / -45.7 / -11.6	42.2 / -39.3 / -7.9	106.0 / -44.8 / -12.1				
EBIT/Interest	(59) 9.5 / 4.0 / 1.5	(61) 5.4 / 2.6 / 1.0	(71) 7.4 / 3.0 / .8	(40) 4.2 / 1.6 / .1	(22) 10.6 / 4.4 / 2.2				
Net Profit + Depr., Dep., Amort./Cur. Mat. L/T/D	(11) 4.4 / 1.4 / .4	(13) 2.0 / 1.1 / .7	(16) 4.2 / 2.4 / .1						
Fixed/Worth	1.0 / 1.8 / 6.0	.9 / 3.3 / -2.8	1.1 / 2.5 / 29.1	1.7 / 3.3 / -88.5	.8 / 1.4 / 5.1				
Debt/Worth	.9 / 2.2 / 7.1	1.1 / 3.7 / -4.9	1.1 / 2.8 / 46.3	1.8 / 3.3 / -93.0	.6 / 1.7 / NM				
% Profit Before Taxes/Tangible Net Worth	(60) 122.3 / 44.4 / 10.1	(48) 49.3 / 19.3 / .4	(64) 68.7 / 23.5 / .2	(35) 77.8 / 9.7 / -15.7	(20) 62.6 / 27.3 / 9.7				
% Profit Before Taxes/Total Assets	31.5 / 12.9 / 2.0	18.4 / 5.4 / -.9	20.5 / 6.9 / -.8	14.8 / 1.5 / -7.1	26.5 / 10.1 / 4.8				
Sales/Net Fixed Assets	12.7 / 6.9 / 2.7	18.3 / 6.6 / 3.3	9.6 / 5.3 / 2.4	7.2 / 3.5 / 1.9	14.4 / 7.6 / 3.6				
Sales/Total Assets	5.2 / 3.3 / 1.8	5.6 / 3.1 / 2.2	4.8 / 2.8 / 1.7	3.9 / 2.2 / 1.3	5.9 / 4.6 / 2.4				
% Depr., Dep., Amort./Sales	(66) 1.3 / 2.8 / 4.1	(66) 1.3 / 3.2 / 5.2	(78) 2.3 / 3.6 / 5.3	(44) 2.5 / 4.1 / 6.5	(24) 2.0 / 2.6 / 4.9				
% Officers', Directors', Owners' Comp/Sales	(36) 2.8 / 5.7 / 10.5	(32) 4.0 / 6.7 / 9.5	(42) 3.0 / 6.1 / 9.5	(24) 3.3 / 7.5 / 11.6	(16) 2.7 / 4.9 / 7.7				
Net Sales ($)	85913M	332733M	166147M	19730M	41996M	15149M	8132M	81140M	
Total Assets ($)	30354M	99373M	67143M	9625M	16015M	4498M	3941M	33064M	

M = $ thousand   MM = $ million
See Pages 1 through 15 for Explanation of Ratios and Data

Current Data Sorted By Assets / Comparative Historical Data

0-500M	500M-2MM	2-10MM	10-50MM	50-100MM	100-250MM		4/1/90-3/31/91 ALL	4/1/91-3/31/92 ALL
4	5	11	6	4	1	# Postretirement Benefits Type of Statement		
2	13	25	40	8	13	Unqualified	71	74
7	32	56	8	4		Reviewed	78	97
55	78	54	9	1		Compiled	178	165
11	11	5				Tax Returns	4	9
34	70	38	21	11	3	Other	144	129
	207 (4/1-9/30/94)		402 (10/1/94-3/31/95)					
109	204	178	78	24	16	**NUMBER OF STATEMENTS**	475	474
%	%	%	%	%	%	**ASSETS**	%	%
7.8	10.6	13.9	9.6	7.0	9.5	Cash & Equivalents	9.5	9.0
4.7	4.6	5.7	5.7	5.2	3.7	Trade Receivables - (net)	5.5	4.9
40.8	34.7	28.0	27.5	23.1	22.5	Inventory	33.5	33.5
1.1	2.2	2.5	2.8	1.6	1.6	All Other Current	1.9	2.3
54.5	52.1	50.0	45.6	37.0	37.2	Total Current	50.5	49.7
34.7	32.9	37.0	42.6	51.9	54.5	Fixed Assets (net)	37.9	37.5
3.2	3.4	2.4	2.8	4.4	3.4	Intangibles (net)	2.5	2.5
7.7	11.7	10.6	9.0	6.7	5.0	All Other Non-Current	9.2	10.3
100.0	100.0	100.0	100.0	100.0	100.0	Total	100.0	100.0
						LIABILITIES		
9.9	4.6	3.9	3.1	3.0	.8	Notes Payable-Short Term	5.3	5.8
4.2	4.4	4.8	4.2	3.4	1.7	Cur. Mat. -L/T/D	4.7	5.3
16.6	20.5	20.7	22.5	20.0	14.2	Trade Payables	20.7	18.7
.3	.4	.4	.7	.2	.1	Income Taxes Payable	.6	.5
9.1	9.0	9.2	9.5	7.5	9.9	All Other Current	8.9	9.8
40.1	38.8	39.0	40.0	34.0	26.7	Total Current	40.2	40.0
32.8	22.5	22.5	21.4	24.0	25.7	Long Term Debt	27.3	24.7
.1	.1	.4	1.1	1.2	1.8	Deferred Taxes	.4	.5
3.5	3.6	2.7	3.6	4.8	1.7	All Other-Non-Current	2.0	2.9
23.5	34.9	35.4	33.9	36.0	44.1	Net Worth	30.2	31.9
100.0	100.0	100.0	100.0	100.0	100.0	Total Liabilities & Net Worth	100.0	100.0
						INCOME DATA		
100.0	100.0	100.0	100.0	100.0	100.0	Net Sales	100.0	100.0
24.0	22.8	22.4	22.7	22.6	25.0	Gross Profit	22.3	22.5
22.0	21.5	21.3	21.5	21.3	22.1	Operating Expenses	21.2	21.2
2.0	1.2	1.1	1.2	1.3	2.9	Operating Profit	1.1	1.3
.1	.0	-.3	.1	.5	.5	All Other Expenses (net)	.2	.0
1.9	1.3	1.4	1.1	.7	2.4	Profit Before Taxes	1.0	1.2
						RATIOS		
2.7	2.2	1.9	1.6	1.4	1.9	Current	1.9	1.9
1.5	1.4	1.3	1.1	1.0	1.3		1.3	1.3
.9	1.0	.9	.9	.8	1.0		.9	.9
(106) .7	(201) .8	(177) .9	(77) .6	.6	.9	Quick	(467) .7	(465) .6
.3	.3	.5	.3	.3	.4		.3	.3
.1	.1	.2	.2	.2	.2		.2	.2
0 999.8	0 879.1	1 536.8	1 318.0	1 490.5	2 165.0	Sales/Receivables	1 718.7	1 599.1
1 339.9	1 298.7	2 228.0	3 143.4	3 126.0	3 106.2		1 264.7	1 243.7
3 135.8	3 129.1	3 124.8	4 88.0	4 89.2	5 75.8		3 107.2	3 105.3
20 18.0	18 20.5	16 23.0	16 22.3	18 20.6	20 18.3	Cost of Sales/Inventory	17 20.9	17 20.9
27 13.6	23 15.7	21 17.8	21 17.8	22 16.7	31 11.9		23 15.6	23 15.8
37 9.8	31 11.8	26 14.2	27 13.4	31 11.6	47 7.7		30 12.3	31 11.8
4 102.3	7 51.4	9 38.9	13 28.1	17 21.9	14 25.2	Cost of Sales/Payables	8 43.4	7 51.7
9 40.9	12 31.5	14 26.7	17 21.8	20 18.4	20 18.2		14 26.0	12 30.4
16 22.8	18 20.1	20 18.1	24 15.2	30 12.2	26 13.9		21 17.7	19 19.5
19.7	21.1	21.2	36.2	31.2	19.4	Sales/Working Capital	23.7	26.2
42.4	51.7	56.5	175.7	404.8	40.6		61.9	64.4
-167.9	-999.8	-174.7	-147.4	-82.9	NM		-112.9	-167.3
(97) 10.2	(177) 7.1	(165) 10.1	(73) 7.0	(19) 6.9	(14) 5.7	EBIT/Interest	(438) 5.4	(440) 5.5
3.8	2.7	3.9	3.1	2.1	3.8		2.2	2.7
1.0	1.4	1.8	1.7	1.5	2.4		1.0	1.3
(10) 1.7	(59) 2.6	(67) 4.1	(42) 4.1	(16) 3.4		Net Profit + Depr., Dep., Amort./Cur. Mat. L /T/D	(234) 4.1	(203) 3.6
1.1	1.6	2.3	2.0	2.4			2.2	1.9
.0	.9	1.4	1.3	1.5			1.1	1.0
.5	.4	.6	.9	1.1	1.1	Fixed/Worth	.6	.6
1.6	.9	1.1	1.5	1.7	1.4		1.4	1.4
NM	2.6	2.7	2.7	3.4	1.9		3.5	3.4
1.0	.8	.9	1.1	1.3	.8	Debt/Worth	1.1	1.0
4.0	2.0	2.1	2.2	2.1	1.5		2.3	2.2
-25.4	7.2	4.4	4.7	5.2	2.6		7.5	6.9
(81) 80.9	(178) 42.3	(161) 45.1	(72) 28.1	(23) 28.9	27.5	% Profit Before Taxes/Tangible Net Worth	(409) 34.0	(409) 37.0
38.3	18.8	20.1	18.8	13.4	17.9		17.0	18.3
15.0	5.0	9.2	7.9	2.9	11.4		3.4	5.9
17.7	13.3	14.4	9.7	6.7	9.7	% Profit Before Taxes/Total Assets	11.5	12.4
9.2	5.7	7.0	5.3	2.4	7.6		4.9	5.8
.9	1.5	2.3	2.1	.8	4.9		.2	1.0
65.0	54.2	30.8	19.3	11.2	7.4	Sales/Net Fixed Assets	36.5	35.9
23.0	24.3	17.2	13.7	8.9	6.4		18.3	17.5
9.0	11.5	10.7	8.4	6.4	5.6		9.3	9.7
9.5	8.9	7.9	7.0	5.6	4.2	Sales/Total Assets	8.7	8.4
6.3	6.6	6.0	5.6	4.1	3.6		6.1	6.2
3.8	4.7	4.5	4.6	3.8	3.0		4.4	4.4
(89) .5	(189) .6	(171) .8	(72) .9	(23) 1.2		% Depr., Dep., Amort./Sales	(437) .7	(442) .6
1.0	.9	1.1	1.3	1.5			1.1	1.0
1.7	1.4	1.5	1.6	1.9			1.5	1.5
(45) 1.5	(102) .9	(69) .7	(11) .2			% Officers', Directors', Owners' Comp/Sales	(192) .8	(195) .7
2.2	1.4	1.0	.9				1.4	1.5
4.3	2.7	2.2	1.1				2.6	2.8
225553M	1554699M	5088656M	9663604M	7126789M	8410372M	Net Sales ($)	23736953M	28032825M
32188M	226209M	801899M	1795820M	1681075M	2475956M	Total Assets ($)	4860586M	5613146M

© Robert Morris Associates 1995

M = $ thousand   MM = $ million

See Pages 1 through 15 for Explanation of Ratios and Data

Comparative Historical Data				Current Data Sorted By Sales					
10	36	31	# Postretirement Benefits	5	1	3	7	15	
			Type of Statement						
111	105	101	Unqualified		6	3	8	9	75
96	109	107	Reviewed		7	7	17	34	42
171	195	197	Compiled	14	42	22	44	40	35
23	41	27	Tax Returns	4	5	4	8	4	2
143	173	177	Other	6	33	24	32	36	46
4/1/92-3/31/93	4/1/93-3/31/94	4/1/94-3/31/95		207 (4/1-9/30/94)		402 (10/1/94-3/31/95)			
ALL	ALL	ALL		0-1MM	1-3MM	3-5MM	5-10MM	10-25MM	25MM & OVER
544	623	609	NUMBER OF STATEMENTS	24	93	60	109	123	200
%	%	%	ASSETS	%	%	%	%	%	%
9.7	10.6	10.8	Cash & Equivalents	4.9	8.7	10.0	11.3	13.4	10.7
4.9	5.4	5.1	Trade Receivables - (net)	4.6	4.8	4.6	3.9	5.4	5.8
33.7	32.1	32.1	Inventory	32.6	33.4	35.7	37.4	30.5	28.6
2.4	2.0	2.1	All Other Current	1.5	1.2	.8	3.1	2.6	2.3
50.7	50.1	50.1	Total Current	43.6	48.2	51.1	55.6	51.8	47.4
36.3	36.9	37.0	Fixed Assets (net)	44.8	39.1	32.9	30.5	34.9	41.0
2.4	2.6	3.0	Intangibles (net)	8.2	2.5	4.1	2.5	2.9	2.6
10.6	10.4	9.9	All Other Non-Current	3.4	10.2	11.9	11.4	10.3	9.0
100.0	100.0	100.0	Total	100.0	100.0	100.0	100.0	100.0	100.0
			LIABILITIES						
4.9	5.0	5.0	Notes Payable-Short Term	14.2	5.9	7.2	4.7	4.7	3.1
4.8	4.9	4.4	Cur. Mat.-L /T/D	2.2	4.1	4.9	4.2	5.2	4.2
20.8	19.6	19.9	Trade Payables	8.6	14.1	16.0	21.0	22.7	22.8
.4	.9	.4	Income Taxes Payable	.3	.4	.1	.3	.2	.6
9.1	10.1	9.1	All Other Current	6.0	7.0	12.9	9.5	8.1	9.7
40.0	40.4	38.7	Total Current	31.4	31.4	41.1	39.6	41.0	40.5
25.7	24.4	24.4	Long Term Debt	22.7	36.4	33.4	16.6	22.9	21.4
.5	.4	.4	Deferred Taxes	.4	.2	.0	.2	.2	.9
2.9	3.3	3.3	All Other-Non-Current	5.2	2.5	3.6	3.8	3.9	2.8
31.0	31.4	33.2	Net Worth	40.4	29.5	21.9	39.9	32.1	34.4
100.0	100.0	100.0	Total Liabilities & Net Worth	100.0	100.0	100.0	100.0	100.0	100.0
			INCOME DATA						
100.0	100.0	100.0	Net Sales	100.0	100.0	100.0	100.0	100.0	100.0
22.9	23.4	22.9	Gross Profit	26.9	25.0	22.4	22.8	21.8	22.4
21.9	22.2	21.6	Operating Expenses	23.2	22.6	21.5	21.8	20.8	21.2
1.0	1.2	1.4	Operating Profit	3.7	2.4	.9	.9	1.1	1.2
-.1	-.1	-.1	All Other Expenses (net)	.8	.1	.0	-.3	-.3	.0
1.1	1.2	1.4	Profit Before Taxes	2.9	2.3	.9	1.2	1.4	1.2
			RATIOS						
1.9	1.9	2.0	Current	4.7	2.8	2.3	2.3	1.9	1.6
1.3	1.3	1.3		1.5	1.7	1.5	1.5	1.3	1.1
.9	.9	1.0		.6	1.0	.9	1.0	1.0	.9
.6	.7	.7	Quick	.6	.9	.9	.9	.8	.6
(533) .3	(618) .4	(601) .4		.2	(91) .4	(58) .3	(107) .4	.5	(198) .3
.2	.2	.2		.0	.1	.1	.2	.2	.2
1 666.6	1 665.6	1 634.8	Sales/Receivables	0 UND	0 999.8	0 961.3	0 999.8	1 553.2	1 409.6
1 249.0	2 233.5	2 230.3		1 565.0	1 285.7	1 377.8	1 352.8	2 225.7	2 161.0
3 112.5	4 101.6	3 113.5		3 120.0	4 97.4	3 116.7	2 151.9	3 117.6	4 98.5
18 20.2	16 22.2	17 21.0	Cost of Sales/Inventory	17 21.3	22 16.8	21 17.7	18 20.2	15 24.8	16 22.3
24 15.5	23 15.7	23 16.2		28 13.0	30 12.0	26 13.9	24 15.2	20 18.5	20 18.1
31 11.6	31 11.9	31 11.8		45 8.1	41 9.0	33 11.2	30 12.0	26 14.2	27 13.7
9 41.8	8 46.4	8 46.9	Cost of Sales/Payables	0 UND	5 68.7	6 58.2	7 53.3	9 39.1	12 29.8
14 25.2	14 26.9	14 26.6		7 50.7	10 37.4	10 36.9	12 31.5	13 29.2	17 22.0
21 17.0	21 17.7	20 18.1		27 13.4	19 18.8	14 25.2	19 19.3	20 18.2	22 16.8
22.8	25.9	22.4	Sales/Working Capital	11.6	15.3	22.5	17.9	24.8	29.5
63.1	52.7	54.8		63.7	31.2	36.2	43.9	65.2	101.9
-169.0	-213.4	-229.3		-24.0	391.9	-248.9	-613.3	999.8	-166.7
5.6	6.8	7.9	EBIT/Interest	(19) 12.0	(86) 8.7	(56) 5.7	(91) 12.1	(108) 7.2	(185) 7.5
(493) 2.7	(563) 3.0	(545) 3.3		3.1	3.3	1.9	3.7	3.7	3.2
1.1	1.1	1.6		1.2	1.4	1.2	1.4	1.8	1.8
4.3	3.4	4.0	Net Profit + Depr., Dep., Amort./Cur. Mat. L/T/D		(17) 2.9	(16) 1.9	(32) 3.4	(40) 3.4	(94) 4.5
(206) 1.9	(234) 1.9	(200) 1.9			1.3	1.4	1.7	1.9	2.4
1.0	.8	1.2			-.0	.7	1.1	1.1	1.5
.6	.6	.6	Fixed/Worth	.4	.4	.6	.3	.6	.8
1.4	1.4	1.2		1.2	1.5	1.9	.7	1.1	1.3
3.4	3.2	3.1		11.6	15.0	8.9	1.9	3.1	2.6
1.1	1.0	1.0	Debt/Worth	.3	.9	1.4	.6	1.0	1.1
2.3	2.3	2.1		1.2	2.0	3.9	1.4	2.3	2.1
7.2	6.6	6.6		119.9	25.6	16.5	3.7	6.2	4.3
37.2	37.3	43.9	% Profit Before Taxes/Tangible Net Worth	(19) 79.0	(75) 65.4	(50) 52.1	(95) 33.7	(105) 58.7	(187) 32.8
(467) 17.2	(541) 18.2	(531) 20.3		27.5	30.8	20.1	15.7	26.8	18.8
4.2	5.5	8.4		12.3	13.4	4.7	4.8	10.3	9.2
11.8	12.6	13.4	% Profit Before Taxes/Total Assets	17.2	17.1	7.9	13.0	16.0	10.9
5.3	5.4	6.2		9.9	7.8	3.9	6.1	8.4	5.4
.3	.7	1.7		1.9	2.0	.3	.9	2.5	2.2
36.7	38.5	36.0	Sales/Net Fixed Assets	30.4	34.8	56.4	63.3	35.6	26.4
18.3	17.1	17.0		8.1	15.5	22.4	24.6	18.1	16.0
9.4	9.4	9.3		3.4	6.2	9.3	12.0	11.8	8.6
8.4	8.3	8.1	Sales/Total Assets	5.7	6.7	8.2	9.1	9.0	7.7
5.9	5.9	5.8		3.4	4.8	5.6	6.4	6.5	5.8
4.4	4.2	4.1		2.1	3.2	3.9	4.6	5.0	4.6
.7	.7	.7	% Depr., Dep., Amort./Sales	(18) .7	(80) .7	(52) .6	(103) .5	(118) .7	(182) .8
(500) 1.1	(579) 1.1	(553) 1.1		1.8	1.2	1.0	.8	1.1	1.2
1.5	1.6	1.6		3.8	2.1	1.4	1.3	1.5	1.5
.8	.8	.9	% Officers', Directors', Owners' Comp/Sales		(38) 1.5	(27) 1.1	(57) .8	(52) .6	(47) .7
(214) 1.4	(257) 1.4	(230) 1.4			2.6	2.1	1.3	1.2	.9
3.0	3.0	2.7			5.4	3.0	2.5	1.6	2.2
31564719M	38476971M	32069673M	Net Sales ($)	13981M	169416M	239747M	801614M	1930893M	28914022M
7208512M	8646989M	7013147M	Total Assets ($)	98773M	43319M	49527M	147430M	339375M	6334723M

© Robert Morris Associates 1995

M = $ thousand   MM = $ million

See Pages 1 through 15 for Explanation of Ratios and Data

Current Data Sorted By Assets							Comparative Historical Data	
1				3	1	# Postretirement Benefits		
		4			2	Type of Statement		
2	4	3				Unqualified	6	3
4	2	1			1	Reviewed	5	8
6	2					Compiled	13	17
2		1	2			Tax Returns	1	
						Other	8	10
	9 (4/1-9/30/94)		31 (10/1/94-3/31/95)				4/1/90-3/31/91	4/1/91-3/31/92
0-500M	500M-2MM	2-10MM	10-50MM	50-100MM	100-250MM		ALL	ALL
14	9	9	5		3	**NUMBER OF STATEMENTS**	33	38
%	%	%	%	%	%	**ASSETS**	%	%
14.7						Cash & Equivalents	7.6	10.2
4.0						Trade Receivables - (net)	10.5	8.4
39.5						Inventory	26.5	29.4
.8						All Other Current	3.1	3.3
59.0						Total Current	47.7	51.2
31.1						Fixed Assets (net)	38.9	40.8
5.6						Intangibles (net)	2.8	2.8
4.3						All Other Non-Current	10.6	5.2
100.0						Total	100.0	100.0
						LIABILITIES		
2.5						Notes Payable-Short Term	6.2	9.6
2.8						Cur. Mat. -L/T/D	5.8	5.5
9.3						Trade Payables	17.4	19.2
.8						Income Taxes Payable	1.2	.5
13.5						All Other Current	9.7	10.5
28.9						Total Current	40.3	45.3
15.6						Long Term Debt	27.9	19.5
.0						Deferred Taxes	.5	.5
3.2						All Other-Non-Current	2.6	3.9
52.4						Net Worth	28.7	30.8
100.0						Total Liabilities & Net Worth	100.0	100.0
						INCOME DATA		
100.0						Net Sales	100.0	100.0
43.7						Gross Profit	42.4	40.1
34.2						Operating Expenses	39.7	35.5
9.5						Operating Profit	2.7	4.6
1.9						All Other Expenses (net)	.9	1.5
7.5						Profit Before Taxes	1.7	3.0
						RATIOS		
4.2							1.6	1.5
2.3						Current	1.1	1.2
1.1							.8	.8
1.6							.7	.9
.9						Quick	.3	.4
.2							.2	.2
0 UND							1 579.8	0 UND
0 UND						Sales/Receivables	3 138.5	1 588.7
1 358.4							21 17.5	13 27.1
21 17.4							16 23.0	26 14.1
38 9.6						Cost of Sales/Inventory	44 8.3	39 9.3
72 5.1							94 3.9	78 4.7
0 UND							14 26.9	11 34.2
8 47.3						Cost of Sales/Payables	30 12.2	18 19.8
21 17.0							49 7.4	38 9.5
7.2							13.1	19.0
24.5						Sales/Working Capital	81.6	74.7
109.4							-60.1	-36.8
30.8							(30) 3.8	(36) 8.6
(12) 16.0						EBIT/Interest	1.5	3.5
3.5							.7	1.2
							(16) 5.3	(21) 8.3
						Net Profit + Depr., Dep., Amort./Cur. Mat. L /T/D	2.1	3.0
							1.4	1.7
.2							.5	.5
.5						Fixed/Worth	1.6	1.5
1.3							4.1	3.3
.3							1.7	1.3
1.2						Debt/Worth	3.3	2.2
3.0							7.4	5.5
165.4							(28) 36.2	(33) 63.0
66.3						% Profit Before Taxes/Tangible Net Worth	9.0	21.5
22.5							-5.7	2.3
44.2							9.6	18.6
28.0						% Profit Before Taxes/Total Assets	1.5	9.2
6.0							-2.0	.7
65.5							16.2	27.5
18.9						Sales/Net Fixed Assets	10.4	11.5
6.8							5.3	5.0
7.4							4.4	5.9
6.4						Sales/Total Assets	3.0	3.8
2.7							2.4	2.4
.8							(31) 1.3	1.2
(11) 1.1						% Depr., Dep., Amort./Sales	1.8	2.2
2.9							4.1	3.5
							(11) .7	(15) 1.7
						% Officers', Directors', Owners' Comp/Sales	1.7	3.5
							4.3	4.6
19460M	25243M	120418M	246466M		1724474M	Net Sales ($)	282157M	507560M
3376M	9424M	41452M	111239M		398020M	Total Assets ($)	110955M	160415M

© Robert Morris Associates 1995

M = $ thousand   MM = $ million

See Pages 1 through 15 for Explanation of Ratios and Data

Comparative Historical Data — Current Data Sorted By Sales

	4/1/92-3/31/93 ALL	4/1/93-3/31/94 ALL	4/1/94-3/31/95 ALL	0-1MM	1-3MM	3-5MM	5-10MM	10-25MM	25MM & OVER
# Postretirement Benefits				1					1
Type of Statement									
Unqualified	6	6	9				2	2	5
Reviewed	3	1	9		5		4		
Compiled	7	6	8	2	4			1	1
Tax Returns	3	2	8	5	3				
Other	7	9	6	1	2		2		1
			9 (4/1-9/30/94)				*31 (10/1/94-3/31/95)*		
NUMBER OF STATEMENTS	26	24	40	8	14		8	3	7
ASSETS	%	%	%	%	%	%	%	%	%
Cash & Equivalents	9.4	9.8	11.0		8.9				
Trade Receivables - (net)	9.2	6.6	9.1		7.5				
Inventory	25.7	31.7	30.8		33.2				
All Other Current	.6	.3	1.7		2.5				
Total Current	44.7	48.3	52.6		52.0				
Fixed Assets (net)	35.9	41.1	35.6		37.9				
Intangibles (net)	7.1	3.7	5.0		4.4				
All Other Non-Current	12.3	6.9	6.8		5.7				
Total	100.0	100.0	100.0		100.0				
LIABILITIES									
Notes Payable-Short Term	2.7	9.6	4.4		4.9				
Cur. Mat.-L /T/D	5.6	3.2	3.8		3.8				
Trade Payables	20.2	17.0	12.8		12.6				
Income Taxes Payable	.4	1.3	.5		.4				
All Other Current	11.4	15.4	10.6		6.1				
Total Current	40.4	46.4	32.2		27.7				
Long Term Debt	22.6	22.6	18.4		21.4				
Deferred Taxes	.3	.3	.2		.1				
All Other-Non-Current	3.8	4.5	3.3		3.2				
Net Worth	32.9	26.2	45.9		47.6				
Total Liabilities & Net Worth	100.0	100.0	100.0		100.0				
INCOME DATA									
Net Sales	100.0	100.0	100.0		100.0				
Gross Profit	39.1	40.4	40.1		41.0				
Operating Expenses	36.8	35.0	35.1		36.7				
Operating Profit	2.3	5.4	5.0		4.3				
All Other Expenses (net)	.7	1.9	1.1		1.2				
Profit Before Taxes	1.7	3.5	3.9		3.0				
RATIOS									
Current	1.7	1.6	3.0		4.0				
	1.1	1.1	1.4		1.6				
	.8	.7	1.1		1.1				
Quick	.9	.9	1.2		1.2				
	.4	.3	.6		.3				
	.1	.1	.2		.1				
Sales/Receivables	0 UND	0 UND	0 UND		0 UND				
	0 999.8	0 UND	1 286.5		1 649.6				
	18 20.0	8 47.0	31 11.6		32 11.4				
Cost of Sales/Inventory	20 18.4	29 12.4	16 22.7		14 26.8				
	37 9.9	51 7.2	38 9.6		33 11.1				
	85 4.3	79 4.6	111 3.3		72 5.1				
Cost of Sales/Payables	13 27.9	11 33.5	6 56.2		3 105.0				
	26 14.3	30 12.2	17 21.2		11 33.2				
	61 6.0	45 8.2	35 10.4		37 9.8				
Sales/Working Capital	16.5	14.2	7.1		7.3				
	119.3	265.7	24.5		43.9				
	-33.2	-20.8	361.3		174.2				
EBIT/Interest	(23) 4.8	(22) 12.3	(34) 26.1		(10) 30.8				
	2.2	4.2	6.3		13.8				
	1.1	1.1	2.1		.1				
Net Profit + Depr., Dep., Amort./Cur. Mat. L/T/D	(11) 5.3		(14) 12.3						
	2.3		4.5						
	1.3		.8						
Fixed/Worth	.8	.8	.4		.3				
	1.8	1.7	.7		.8				
	8.4	10.8	1.9		1.8				
Debt/Worth	1.2	1.4	.6		.5				
	4.1	2.4	1.3		1.2				
	40.8	17.6	2.4		2.5				
% Profit Before Taxes/Tangible Net Worth	(21) 69.5	(19) 142.7	(38) 42.8		(13) 72.3				
	23.2	33.8	22.9		19.4				
	6.8	14.4	13.7		-2.2				
% Profit Before Taxes/Total Assets	11.1	22.6	20.6		22.3				
	3.9	9.6	9.8		6.0				
	.4	1.4	3.8		-2.7				
Sales/Net Fixed Assets	56.8	19.3	23.2		47.3				
	8.3	9.8	9.8		12.5				
	5.3	4.5	5.3		4.5				
Sales/Total Assets	5.1	6.1	5.6		6.4				
	3.0	3.3	3.3		3.6				
	2.2	2.3	2.2		1.5				
% Depr., Dep., Amort./Sales	(25) .7	(22) 1.4	(34) 1.0		(13) .6				
	1.5	1.9	1.4		1.3				
	3.0	3.8	3.1		4.9				
% Officers', Directors', Owners' Comp/Sales		(11) 1.9	(15) 4.0						
		3.6	5.2						
		5.6	8.3						
Net Sales ($)	880984M	718869M	2136061M	4236M	29420M		54900M	64862M	1982643M
Total Assets ($)	216553M	276455M	563511M	1373M	11863M		35987M	22031M	492257M

M = $ thousand   MM = $ million
See Pages 1 through 15 for Explanation of Ratios and Data

Current Data Sorted By Assets   Comparative Historical Data

						# Postretirement Benefits		
						Type of Statement		
3	1					Unqualified	3	6
2	1					Reviewed	3	2
8	3					Compiled	10	13
5						Tax Returns	1	1
4						Other	8	8
	6 (4/1-9/30/94)		21 (10/1/94-3/31/95)				4/1/90-3/31/91	4/1/91-3/31/92
0-500M	500M-2MM	2-10MM	10-50MM	50-100MM	100-250MM		ALL	ALL
22	5					**NUMBER OF STATEMENTS**	25	30
%	%	%	%	%	%	**ASSETS**	%	%
13.7						Cash & Equivalents	9.2	12.7
2.4						Trade Receivables - (net)	8.4	3.4
7.9						Inventory	7.8	7.9
2.6						All Other Current	1.3	1.4
26.5						Total Current	26.7	25.4
52.2						Fixed Assets (net)	55.9	57.0
9.4						Intangibles (net)	7.3	7.5
12.0						All Other Non-Current	10.1	10.2
100.0						Total	100.0	100.0
						LIABILITIES		
10.9						Notes Payable-Short Term	.8	2.8
7.2						Cur. Mat. -L/T/D	10.1	9.4
9.6						Trade Payables	10.1	13.2
.5						Income Taxes Payable	.6	.3
18.2						All Other Current	14.7	13.8
46.4						Total Current	36.2	39.5
30.7						Long Term Debt	41.4	30.5
.0						Deferred Taxes	.1	.3
2.0						All Other-Non-Current	5.4	.5
20.9						Net Worth	16.8	29.3
100.0						Total Liabilities & Net Worth	100.0	100.0
						INCOME DATA		
100.0						Net Sales	100.0	100.0
64.0						Gross Profit	52.0	60.0
60.9						Operating Expenses	48.4	54.8
3.1						Operating Profit	3.6	5.2
1.9						All Other Expenses (net)	3.6	4.1
1.2						Profit Before Taxes	.1	1.1
						RATIOS		
1.6							1.7	1.1
.9						Current	.6	.6
.2							.2	.2
1.2							1.0	.6
.4						Quick	.3	.2
.1							.1	.1
0 UND							0 UND	0 UND
0 UND						Sales/Receivables	3 144.3	1 394.3
3 135.7							12 31.3	6 57.3
11 32.1							6 65.8	8 47.1
15 24.6						Cost of Sales/Inventory	22 16.3	15 25.0
25 14.7							33 11.2	32 11.3
0 UND							9 42.0	15 23.9
15 24.0						Cost of Sales/Payables	26 14.2	36 10.1
36 10.2							72 5.1	83 4.4
22.0							28.8	84.0
-99.1						Sales/Working Capital	-22.0	-15.7
-7.1							-8.3	-6.5
13.1							3.6	8.2
(18) 2.2						EBIT/Interest	(21) 1.3	(26) 1.8
.5							.6	.8
						Net Profit + Depr., Dep.,	7.4	4.9
						Amort./Cur. Mat. L /T/D	(11) 1.0 (10) 2.7	
							.5	1.5
1.0							1.0	.9
2.9						Fixed/Worth	4.9	3.1
-3.3							-4.1	19.2
1.2							1.4	1.0
6.1						Debt/Worth	15.0	3.3
-5.9							-5.4	19.5
60.5						% Profit Before Taxes/Tangible	28.3	70.5
(14) 29.9						Net Worth	(13) 11.9	(24) 17.0
-13.1							.7	-1.4
26.6						% Profit Before Taxes/Total	8.4	11.1
5.7						Assets	3.3	4.6
-11.4							-3.0	-2.8
14.6							10.4	11.4
9.8						Sales/Net Fixed Assets	3.2	3.8
4.5							2.2	1.6
5.6							3.3	3.3
4.3						Sales/Total Assets	2.0	2.5
2.0							1.5	1.2
1.4							2.2	2.4
(21) 2.9						% Depr., Dep., Amort./Sales	(24) 4.3	(27) 4.0
5.8							6.4	5.5
4.8						% Officers', Directors',	3.0	1.7
(12) 9.4						Owners' Comp/Sales	(11) 4.0	(10) 3.4
14.9							6.8	6.4
20076M	12541M					Net Sales ($)	110870M	430488M
4604M	5570M					Total Assets ($)	64725M	148486M

M = $ thousand   MM = $ million
See Pages 1 through 15 for Explanation of Ratios and Data

Comparative Historical Data

Current Data Sorted By Sales

Postretirement Benefits

Type of Statement	92-93	93-94	94-95	0-1MM	1-3MM	3-5MM
Unqualified	3	2	4	1	3	
Reviewed	4	1	3	2		1
Compiled	19	9	11	5	6	
Tax Returns	1	5	5	5		
Other	17	4	4	2	2	

	4/1/92-3/31/93 ALL	4/1/93-3/31/94 ALL	4/1/94-3/31/95 ALL		6 (4/1-9/30/94)		21 (10/1/94-3/31/95)			
					0-1MM	1-3MM	3-5MM	5-10MM	10-25MM	25MM & OVER
NUMBER OF STATEMENTS	44	21	27		15	11	1			
ASSETS	%	%	%		%	%	%	%	%	%
Cash & Equivalents	8.0	8.2	11.5		11.1	13.0				
Trade Receivables - (net)	1.9	5.7	2.8		1.5	2.7				
Inventory	7.6	8.8	7.5		6.9	7.0				
All Other Current	.8	.8	2.1		3.3	.6				
Total Current	18.3	23.6	23.9		22.9	23.3				
Fixed Assets (net)	63.6	54.7	56.0		54.8	57.9				
Intangibles (net)	10.5	8.7	8.1		11.0	4.8				
All Other Non-Current	7.5	13.0	12.0		11.3	14.0				
Total	100.0	100.0	100.0		100.0	100.0				
LIABILITIES										
Notes Payable-Short Term	7.1	9.8	9.3		12.6	5.4				
Cur. Mat.-L/T/D	6.3	5.5	7.2		9.0	4.7				
Trade Payables	8.0	11.1	9.4		6.9	11.8				
Income Taxes Payable	.2	.1	.4		.1	.9				
All Other Current	10.9	9.4	16.2		18.4	14.5				
Total Current	32.5	35.8	42.6		46.9	37.3				
Long Term Debt	31.8	35.0	34.1		40.6	26.4				
Deferred Taxes	.2	.3	.0		.0	.0				
All Other-Non-Current	2.9	1.3	1.7		2.6	.6				
Net Worth	32.6	27.5	21.6		9.8	35.7				
Total Liabilities & Net Worth	100.0	100.0	100.0		100.0	100.0				
INCOME DATA										
Net Sales	100.0	100.0	100.0		100.0	100.0				
Gross Profit	61.4	62.7	61.0		64.2	59.8				
Operating Expenses	55.1	61.8	57.6		61.2	55.9				
Operating Profit	6.4	.9	3.3		3.1	3.9				
All Other Expenses (net)	2.3	1.2	1.8		2.4	1.1				
Profit Before Taxes	4.0	-.3	1.6		.7	2.8				
RATIOS										
Current	1.2 / .6 / .3	1.3 / .8 / .2	1.4 / .8 / .2		1.4 / .4 / .1	1.4 / .8 / .2				
Quick	.5 / .2 / .1	.9 / .2 / .1	.8 / .3 / .1		1.2 / .1 / .1	.8 / .4 / .1				
Sales/Receivables	0 UND / 0 UND / 2 205.7	0 UND / 0 UND / 1 566.2	0 UND / 0 999.8 / 3 131.6		0 UND / 0 UND / 2 197.8	0 UND / 0 999.8 / 3 131.6				
Cost of Sales/Inventory	9 39.8 / 18 20.4 / 42 8.7	13 28.8 / 18 20.8 / 34 10.6	11 34.0 / 14 25.2 / 24 15.3		12 31.5 / 20 18.2 / 35 10.3	7 50.1 / 13 29.1 / 15 24.0				
Cost of Sales/Payables	5 73.1 / 22 16.3 / 42 8.6	4 99.7 / 21 17.4 / 62 5.9	1 302.0 / 16 22.5 / 39 9.4		0 UND / 20 18.6 / 35 10.5	3 123.0 / 15 23.6 / 43 8.4				
Sales/Working Capital	101.5 / -26.2 / -9.5	36.1 / -65.3 / -9.0	25.6 / -87.0 / -7.2		21.8 / -14.9 / -5.4	91.9 / -89.3 / -12.1				
EBIT/Interest	(40) 4.5 / 2.6 / 1.3	(19) 3.0 / 1.9 / 1.0	(23) 7.3 / 2.2 / .8		(13) 3.3 / 1.2 / .2					
Net Profit + Depr., Dep., Amort./Cur. Mat. L/T/D	(12) 4.9 / 2.6 / .9									
Fixed/Worth	1.3 / 3.7 / -9.1	.8 / 3.0 / 20.3	1.1 / 2.4 / -4.7		2.2 / 37.8 / -2.0	.9 / 1.6 / 8.9				
Debt/Worth	.8 / 4.0 / -10.6	1.0 / 3.5 / 23.7	1.3 / 3.7 / -7.9		3.2 / 48.8 / -3.6	.5 / 1.2 / 8.4				
% Profit Before Taxes/Tangible Net Worth	(30) 41.4 / 20.8 / 6.2	(17) 79.1 / 16.6 / -18.9	(18) 49.2 / 25.0 / 2.0							
% Profit Before Taxes/Total Assets	15.9 / 10.5 / 1.8	14.8 / 3.8 / -3.7	19.6 / 4.9 / -4.0		19.1 / 1.3 / -11.1	27.9 / 10.0 / .9				
Sales/Net Fixed Assets	8.2 / 3.3 / 2.2	19.4 / 4.6 / 2.5	13.6 / 8.0 / 2.5		12.5 / 5.2 / 2.2	14.1 / 9.9 / 2.5				
Sales/Total Assets	3.0 / 2.1 / 1.6	4.1 / 2.6 / 1.7	5.4 / 4.1 / 1.9		5.0 / 3.5 / 1.9	8.8 / 5.4 / 1.8				
% Depr., Dep., Amort./Sales	(38) 2.9 / 4.8 / 6.9	(19) 2.3 / 3.3 / 6.0	(26) 1.7 / 2.8 / 5.8		(14) 1.4 / 4.8 / 8.4	1.9 / 2.3 / 3.3				
% Officers', Directors', Owners' Comp/Sales	(15) 3.2 / 4.3 / 11.8		(16) 4.3 / 6.7 / 13.6		(10) 6.0 / 9.4 / 14.5					
Net Sales ($)	234796M	81722M	32617M		7717M	20419M	4481M			
Total Assets ($)	197298M	44235M	10174M		2783M	6653M	738M			

M = $ thousand   MM = $ million
See Pages 1 through 15 for Explanation of Ratios and Data

Current Data Sorted By Assets   Comparative Historical Data

0-500M	500M-2MM	2-10MM	10-50MM	50-100MM	100-250MM		4/1/90-3/31/91 ALL	4/1/91-3/31/92 ALL
38	23	18	9	1	2	**# Postretirement Benefits**		
						Type of Statement	138	144
7	18	58	57	15	24	Unqualified	138	144
37	59	53	9	1		Reviewed	173	168
322	143	45	4			Compiled	476	523
118	43	7			1	Tax Returns	26	55
149	129	81	33	10	6	Other	293	304
	344 (4/1-9/30/94)		1085 (10/1/94-3/31/95)					
633	392	244	103	26	31	**NUMBER OF STATEMENTS**	1106	1194
%	%	%	%	%	%	**ASSETS**	%	%
16.7	10.6	11.1	8.6	11.6	6.0	Cash & Equivalents	12.2	12.5
3.3	3.8	3.7	3.9	5.9	3.4	Trade Receivables - (net)	4.3	3.6
8.5	5.4	4.7	4.2	2.9	3.4	Inventory	6.8	6.6
2.1	2.2	2.0	2.2	1.4	2.4	All Other Current	2.1	2.0
30.6	22.1	21.5	18.9	21.8	15.3	Total Current	25.3	24.7
50.7	59.6	61.1	59.6	64.7	63.3	Fixed Assets (net)	56.1	55.2
7.5	7.1	6.7	10.6	3.8	9.7	Intangibles (net)	6.8	7.0
11.3	11.3	10.7	10.8	9.8	11.8	All Other Non-Current	11.8	13.0
100.0	100.0	100.0	100.0	100.0	100.0	Total	100.0	100.0
						LIABILITIES		
5.4	4.9	3.0	2.4	2.7	.5	Notes Payable-Short Term	6.0	5.8
4.8	5.8	5.8	5.8	2.4	2.5	Cur. Mat. -L/T/D	6.1	6.2
12.1	11.1	10.6	8.5	8.7	6.4	Trade Payables	11.2	11.0
.6	.3	.4	.3	.4	.4	Income Taxes Payable	.7	.8
16.0	11.0	12.7	8.0	8.6	11.0	All Other Current	11.9	12.3
38.9	33.1	32.5	24.9	22.8	20.9	Total Current	36.0	36.1
24.3	32.6	31.3	34.8	19.4	25.5	Long Term Debt	32.1	30.8
.0	.2	.3	.7	.8	1.6	Deferred Taxes	.4	.4
4.8	4.0	4.9	3.7	5.7	3.2	All Other-Non-Current	3.7	3.7
31.9	30.1	31.1	35.9	51.3	48.8	Net Worth	27.9	29.0
100.0	100.0	100.0	100.0	100.0	100.0	Total Liabilities & Net Worth	100.0	100.0
						INCOME DATA		
100.0	100.0	100.0	100.0	100.0	100.0	Net Sales	100.0	100.0
57.0	57.8	55.8	50.3	37.5	39.9	Gross Profit	56.3	57.4
52.4	53.8	51.5	45.7	30.7	32.1	Operating Expenses	52.0	52.7
4.6	3.9	4.3	4.6	6.8	7.8	Operating Profit	4.4	4.7
.8	1.4	1.6	1.9	1.1	1.9	All Other Expenses (net)	1.7	1.7
3.8	2.5	2.7	2.7	5.7	5.9	Profit Before Taxes	2.6	3.0
						RATIOS		
1.7	1.1	1.2	1.0	2.0	1.2	Current	1.3	1.3
.8	.6	.6	.6	.8	.7		.7	.6
.4	.3	.3	.3	.4	.4		.3	.3
1.2	.8	.8	.7	1.6	.8	Quick	.9	.9
(625) .4	(388) .3	.4	.4	.7	.4		(1094) .4	(1186) .4
.1	.1	.2	.2	.2	.2		.1	.1
0 UND	0 UND	0 999.8	1 472.7	3 107.4	2 190.7	Sales/Receivables	0 UND	0 UND
0 UND	1 639.5	1 330.5	2 178.1	6 64.3	5 66.6		1 629.4	0 736.8
2 195.0	3 127.7	5 77.8	7 53.5	17 21.8	12 29.7		4 95.7	3 111.7
6 56.9	7 54.9	7 50.7	6 59.3	5 78.7	6 63.8	Cost of Sales/Inventory	7 52.1	7 50.6
11 32.7	11 33.1	11 33.1	12 30.9	9 40.0	11 34.5		11 31.8	12 30.9
18 20.8	17 21.1	18 20.7	21 17.3	17 21.8	16 22.3		19 19.4	19 19.5
0 UND	14 26.5	17 21.8	23 16.1	19 19.5	13 27.6	Cost of Sales/Payables	9 41.3	9 39.2
13 28.2	27 13.4	30 12.3	34 10.7	27 13.6	22 16.5		24 15.2	24 15.4
30 12.3	44 8.3	51 7.2	53 6.9	48 7.6	29 12.7		43 8.5	39 9.3
36.6	104.4	71.2	-605.8	14.4	71.6	Sales/Working Capital	63.2	56.7
-71.3	-27.3	-27.3	-22.7	-32.7	-26.9		-36.1	-34.0
-18.3	-12.5	-10.8	-12.8	-16.0	-12.8		-12.7	-12.9
11.5	6.8	7.2	4.8	20.0	15.3	EBIT/Interest	5.4	6.0
(476) 3.5	(352) 2.4	(229) 3.0	(98) 2.4	(24) 4.3	(29) 4.7		(972) 2.1	(1056) 2.4
1.0	.8	1.4	1.2	2.7	1.7		.9	1.1
3.9	3.2	5.0	4.4	29.9	22.9	Net Profit + Depr., Dep., Amort./Cur. Mat. L./T/D	3.7	3.3
(95) 2.0	(92) 1.6	(89) 2.2	(64) 2.4	(19) 11.3	(11) 13.9		(451) 1.8	(377) 1.6
.5	.9	1.2	1.0	2.4	5.5		.9	.8
.8	1.3	1.3	1.3	.8	1.0	Fixed/Worth	1.1	1.0
2.1	3.0	2.8	2.5	1.5	1.6		2.7	2.5
NM	11.7	9.6	33.8	2.6	2.7		284.5	45.7
.7	1.1	1.2	1.1	.4	.5	Debt/Worth	1.1	1.0
2.9	3.3	2.9	2.4	.9	1.0		3.2	3.0
-127.0	16.7	11.2	35.8	2.9	3.2		UND	108.9
106.0	66.1	70.4	36.7	19.8	34.7	% Profit Before Taxes/Tangible Net Worth	71.9	70.4
(473) 42.9	(317) 23.6	(201) 30.0	(80) 16.4	(25) 14.8	(29) 26.9		(834) 24.8	(908) 26.4
12.6	6.3	7.8	4.6	7.6	13.4		4.6	6.3
32.7	14.6	15.5	10.4	12.4	14.9	% Profit Before Taxes/Total Assets	17.9	20.2
13.2	6.0	7.4	5.5	8.2	8.7		5.9	6.3
.4	.0	1.3	1.1	3.1	4.2		-.4	.6
23.2	10.1	7.2	5.3	3.1	2.9	Sales/Net Fixed Assets	12.5	13.3
10.8	5.6	3.9	2.8	2.2	2.1		6.1	6.3
5.1	2.6	2.4	2.0	1.5	1.6		3.0	3.1
7.4	4.6	3.4	2.4	2.0	1.7	Sales/Total Assets	4.9	5.0
4.9	3.0	2.5	1.8	1.4	1.4		3.3	3.3
3.2	1.9	1.6	1.3	1.2	1.1		2.0	2.1
1.1	1.9	2.3	3.1	3.8	3.5	% Depr., Dep., Amort./Sales	1.9	1.8
(556) 2.1	(369) 3.0	(234) 3.1	(98) 4.0	(14) 4.4	4.0		(1005) 3.0	(1104) 2.8
3.3	4.1	4.0	4.9	5.1	4.7		4.5	4.2
3.2	2.7	1.9	.8			% Officers', Directors', Owners' Comp/Sales	3.0	3.0
(351) 5.6	(188) 4.5	(75) 3.7	(12) 3.0				(425) 5.0	(529) 5.3
8.9	7.1	5.5	5.3				8.6	8.6
673147M	1322459M	3046877M	4125684M	3229061M	8498349M	Net Sales ($)	13190157M	15200072M
141091M	394508M	1119899M	2201313M	1863072M	4952098M	Total Assets ($)	6597401M	6864212M

M = $ thousand   MM = $ million

See Pages 1 through 15 for Explanation of Ratios and Data

Comparative Historical Data				Current Data Sorted By Sales					
10	38	91	# Postretirement Benefits	30	18	8	12	13	10
			Type of Statement						
163	164	179	Unqualified	4	12	9	17	52	85
174	131	159	Reviewed	21	43	24	37	25	9
468	443	514	Compiled	202	208	49	40	11	4
92	112	169	Tax Returns	78	69	16	4	1	1
322	327	408	Other	97	121	37	55	57	41
4/1/92-3/31/93	4/1/93-3/31/94	4/1/94-3/31/95		344 (4/1-9/30/94)			1085 (10/1/94-3/31/95)		
ALL	ALL	ALL		0-1MM	1-3MM	3-5MM	5-10MM	10-25MM	25MM & OVER
1219	1177	1429	**NUMBER OF STATEMENTS**	402	453	135	153	146	140
%	%	%	**ASSETS**	%	%	%	%	%	%
12.4	12.3	13.1	Cash & Equivalents	13.7	15.3	11.6	12.4	11.3	8.8
3.5	3.5	3.6	Trade Receivables - (net)	2.4	3.4	4.6	4.2	4.3	5.4
6.5	6.9	6.5	Inventory	7.1	7.1	6.9	5.2	5.9	4.4
2.0	2.0	2.1	All Other Current	2.0	2.1	2.3	2.4	2.0	1.9
24.4	24.6	25.3	Total Current	25.2	27.9	25.4	24.2	23.5	20.6
56.6	56.7	56.1	Fixed Assets (net)	57.6	52.4	55.5	57.9	59.0	59.0
6.6	7.2	7.5	Intangibles (net)	8.3	6.4	8.0	6.9	7.7	8.3
12.4	11.5	11.1	All Other Non-Current	8.9	13.3	11.2	11.0	9.9	12.1
100.0	100.0	100.0	Total	100.0	100.0	100.0	100.0	100.0	100.0
			LIABILITIES						
4.6	4.9	4.5	Notes Payable-Short Term	5.0	4.9	5.4	4.3	3.3	2.3
5.9	5.2	5.2	Cur. Mat.-L /T/D	4.7	5.1	5.2	6.0	6.2	4.8
11.6	11.0	11.1	Trade Payables	9.3	12.2	11.9	12.1	12.4	9.8
.6	1.2	.5	Income Taxes Payable	.5	.5	.3	.3	.5	.3
13.8	13.6	13.3	All Other Current	13.3	14.7	12.9	12.8	12.2	10.4
36.5	36.0	34.5	Total Current	32.8	37.5	35.6	35.5	34.7	27.6
30.3	30.4	28.5	Long Term Debt	31.7	26.0	27.1	30.8	26.4	28.0
.3	.3	.2	Deferred Taxes	.0	.1	.2	.2	.4	.9
3.2	4.3	4.5	All Other-Non-Current	4.9	4.6	3.7	3.9	5.7	3.3
29.8	29.0	32.3	Net Worth	30.6	31.7	33.3	29.5	32.9	40.3
100.0	100.0	100.0	Total Liabilities & Net Worth	100.0	100.0	100.0	100.0	100.0	100.0
			INCOME DATA						
100.0	100.0	100.0	Net Sales	100.0	100.0	100.0	100.0	100.0	100.0
57.4	56.6	55.8	Gross Profit	57.2	58.2	53.0	58.7	54.0	45.6
52.5	52.2	51.3	Operating Expenses	52.1	54.4	47.8	55.7	49.3	40.4
4.9	4.4	4.5	Operating Profit	5.2	3.8	5.2	3.1	4.6	5.3
1.4	1.2	1.2	All Other Expenses (net)	1.7	.8	.8	1.4	1.1	1.3
3.5	3.2	3.3	Profit Before Taxes	3.5	3.0	4.4	1.6	3.6	4.0
			RATIOS						
1.2	1.3	1.3		2.0	1.4	1.1	1.2	1.0	1.1
.6	.6	.7	Current	.7	.7	.7	.6	.6	.6
.3	.3	.3		.3	.3	.3	.3	.4	.4
.8	.9	.9		1.2	1.0	.9	.9	.7	.8
(1210) .4	(1167) .4	(1417) .4	Quick	(396) .4	(449) .4	(133) .4	.4	.3	.4
.1	.1	.2		.1	.1	.1	.1	.2	.2
0 UND	0 UND	0 UND		0 UND	0 UND	0 999.8	0 UND	0 925.6	1 409.6
1 684.0	1 590.0	1 646.5	Sales/Receivables	0 UND	1 716.0	1 320.4	1 651.6	2 197.1	3 121.8
3 110.8	4 102.7	3 111.8		1 253.6	3 128.1	5 79.7	3 125.8	6 63.2	10 37.8
7 50.2	8 48.2	7 55.7		7 55.9	6 56.6	6 59.2	7 50.9	8 47.4	6 58.9
11 32.3	12 30.1	11 33.0	Cost of Sales/Inventory	12 29.6	11 33.8	9 38.6	11 34.1	12 31.1	11 34.7
18 19.8	20 18.7	18 20.7		19 19.7	17 21.4	16 23.1	17 21.0	19 19.1	17 22.1
11 34.1	7 51.2	8 44.1		0 UND	7 51.9	14 26.4	16 23.3	20 18.7	17 21.3
24 15.2	23 16.0	22 16.3	Cost of Sales/Payables	11 34.2	22 16.5	23 16.0	30 12.1	33 11.2	28 13.2
41 9.0	41 9.0	41 9.0		29 12.6	41 8.9	35 10.5	49 7.4	50 7.3	48 7.6
75.9	61.1	51.5		33.6	48.6	77.1	55.7	933.9	111.4
–34.2	–35.4	–41.0	Sales/Working Capital	–57.7	–49.5	–39.7	–33.7	–26.7	–26.5
–13.1	–13.5	–13.8		–15.7	–14.0	–13.2	–10.9	–13.6	–13.6
7.3	7.3	8.1		6.9	10.0	9.3	6.2	6.4	10.3
(1050) 2.8	(1017) 2.8	(1208) 2.9	EBIT/Interest	(305) 2.3	(376) 3.0	(119) 2.9	(135) 2.5	(140) 3.2	(133) 4.1
1.1	1.1	1.1		.8	1.0	1.6	.9	1.5	1.6
4.1	3.5	4.8		3.4	4.0	5.2	3.1	5.5	13.6
(350) 1.9	(317) 1.4	(370) 2.2	Net Profit + Depr., Dep., Amort./Cur. Mat. L/T/D	(54) 1.6	(90) 2.0	(34) 2.3	(50) 1.8	(67) 2.4	(75) 3.8
1.0	.6	1.0		.1	.8	1.2	.5	1.3	1.6
1.0	1.0	1.0		1.0	.8	1.1	1.3	1.3	1.1
2.5	2.7	2.4	Fixed/Worth	2.9	2.2	2.4	2.8	2.3	1.9
19.8	26.3	16.6		–21.5	26.9	7.3	20.4	6.9	5.4
1.0	1.0	.9		.7	.9	.9	1.1	1.2	.7
2.9	3.0	2.9	Debt/Worth	3.4	2.9	2.7	3.3	2.6	1.9
31.9	54.0	24.6		–27.6	50.5	9.7	26.7	8.2	7.3
73.1	71.4	76.3		85.9	92.2	80.5	83.1	64.5	38.0
(951) 25.7	(903) 28.0	(1125) 29.8	% Profit Before Taxes/Tangible Net Worth	(293) 35.6	(357) 30.3	(112) 30.4	(121) 30.0	(124) 27.3	(118) 20.0
7.8	7.3	8.1		9.7	6.7	6.7	8.9	8.6	9.4
19.5	17.9	20.9		25.4	26.1	23.6	15.7	14.5	14.0
8.0	7.5	8.3	% Profit Before Taxes/Total Assets	9.5	8.2	7.3	7.3	7.3	8.0
1.0	.5	.8		.0	.0	1.6	.2	2.2	2.9
12.3	12.9	14.1		17.5	19.1	13.0	9.7	8.1	6.5
6.0	6.2	6.3	Sales/Net Fixed Assets	7.0	8.4	6.7	5.8	5.0	3.1
2.9	2.8	2.9		3.0	3.8	3.3	3.1	2.4	2.1
5.0	5.2	5.3		6.2	6.0	5.4	4.8	4.0	2.9
3.3	3.2	3.3	Sales/Total Assets	3.4	3.9	3.7	3.1	2.6	2.0
2.0	1.9	1.9		1.9	2.4	2.1	2.0	1.7	1.4
1.7	1.7	1.6		1.4	1.4	1.4	2.1	2.2	2.6
(1140) 2.8	(1082) 2.8	(1297) 2.8	% Depr., Dep., Amort./Sales	(349) 2.6	(412) 2.4	(131) 2.4	(144) 3.0	(143) 3.0	(118) 3.8
4.1	4.1	4.0		4.1	3.7	3.7	3.8	4.1	4.5
3.1	2.7	2.9		3.8	2.6	2.8	1.8	2.1	1.0
(524) 5.3	(557) 5.2	(629) 4.9	% Officers', Directors', Owners' Comp/Sales	(225) 6.0	(237) 4.5	(65) 4.8	(53) 3.2	(33) 3.5	(16) 2.4
8.1	9.0	7.8		9.6	7.3	7.0	5.7	4.9	6.1
13420103M	16655146M	20895577M	Net Sales ($)	239860M	802300M	525053M	1072420M	2442699M	15813245M
6701178M	9115615M	10671981M	Total Assets ($)	92444M	277978M	215804M	405808M	1126705M	8553242M

M = $ thousand   MM = $ million
See Pages 1 through 15 for Explanation of Ratios and Data

Current Data Sorted By Assets — Comparative Historical Data

	0-500M	500M-2MM	2-10MM	10-50MM	50-100MM	100-250MM	Item	4/1/90-3/31/91 ALL	4/1/91-3/31/92 ALL
# Postretirement Benefits	13	11	11	3		2			
							Type of Statement		
Unqualified	7	9	29	27	5	11		81	82
Reviewed	18	42	49	5				114	108
Compiled	126	113	49					225	280
Tax Returns	14	13	1					11	26
Other	65	51	67	17	3	2		199	180
	149 (4/1-9/30/94)			574 (10/1/94-3/31/95)					
NUMBER OF STATEMENTS	230	228	195	49	8	13		630	676

ASSETS

	0-500M %	500M-2MM %	2-10MM %	10-50MM %	50-100MM %	100-250MM %		ALL %	ALL %
Cash & Equivalents	16.8	13.4	9.9	10.7		5.2		11.2	11.6
Trade Receivables - (net)	1.1	1.1	1.4	2.1		5.7		2.2	1.8
Inventory	5.5	3.2	2.6	2.4		4.0		4.4	4.0
All Other Current	2.2	2.1	1.9	1.9		2.4		2.4	1.7
Total Current	25.5	19.8	15.8	17.1		17.3		20.1	19.1
Fixed Assets (net)	51.6	55.3	61.0	62.7		52.5		58.3	57.9
Intangibles (net)	11.0	14.5	11.2	9.0		13.5		9.3	11.4
All Other Non-Current	11.9	10.4	12.1	11.2		16.7		12.3	11.6
Total	100.0	100.0	100.0	100.0		100.0		100.0	100.0

LIABILITIES

	0-500M	500M-2MM	2-10MM	10-50MM	50-100MM	100-250MM		ALL	ALL
Notes Payable-Short Term	3.3	2.8	1.8	4.6		.2		4.2	4.9
Cur. Mat. -L/T/D	6.2	7.2	7.8	6.2		5.0		7.8	8.2
Trade Payables	9.4	8.7	9.3	8.1		7.1		9.4	8.8
Income Taxes Payable	.4	.2	.2	.3		.2		.6	.8
All Other Current	16.6	10.5	9.3	8.5		11.6		11.3	10.2
Total Current	36.0	29.4	28.4	27.8		24.1		33.2	32.9
Long Term Debt	31.8	39.6	40.4	38.7		36.5		39.5	38.5
Deferred Taxes	.4	.1	.1	.4		1.3		.2	.1
All Other-Non-Current	3.9	2.0	3.3	2.1		5.5		2.6	2.9
Net Worth	27.8	28.9	27.8	30.9		32.6		24.5	25.6
Total Liabilities & Net Worth	100.0	100.0	100.0	100.0		100.0		100.0	100.0

INCOME DATA

	0-500M	500M-2MM	2-10MM	10-50MM	50-100MM	100-250MM		ALL	ALL
Net Sales	100.0	100.0	100.0	100.0		100.0		100.0	100.0
Gross Profit	61.1	62.7	61.5	54.0		41.0		60.6	61.1
Operating Expenses	55.4	57.1	56.5	48.0		35.4		55.3	55.6
Operating Profit	5.7	5.6	5.0	6.1		5.6		5.3	5.5
All Other Expenses (net)	1.1	1.6	1.4	1.9		1.7		2.4	2.3
Profit Before Taxes	4.7	4.0	3.7	4.2		3.9		2.9	3.2

RATIOS

	0-500M	500M-2MM	2-10MM	10-50MM	50-100MM	100-250MM	Ratio	ALL	ALL
	1.5	1.1	.8	1.0		1.2	Current	1.1	1.1
	.6	.6	.5	.6		.5		.5	.5
	.3	.3	.3	.3		.3		.3	.3
	1.0	.8	.6	.8		.6	Quick	.8	.8
	(229) .4	(221) .4	.3	.5		.3		(622) .4	(673) .3
	.1	.2	.2	.2		.2		.1	.1
	0 UND	0 UND	0 UND	0 UND		1 252.4	Sales/Receivables	0 UND	0 UND
	0 UND	0 UND	0 999.8	1 281.1		6 61.3		0 UND	0 UND
	0 999.8	1 584.3	1 491.9	3 104.4		12 30.4		1 389.9	1 460.5
	6 57.7	7 50.9	6 62.9	6 59.1		7 54.7	Cost of Sales/Inventory	7 54.6	7 53.8
	9 40.2	9 39.8	8 43.4	9 41.1		12 31.3		10 38.2	10 37.4
	13 27.9	12 30.4	11 32.4	14 25.5		24 14.9		14 26.5	13 27.8
	3 109.6	14 26.8	18 20.3	17 21.2		14 26.8	Cost of Sales/Payables	11 34.4	9 42.2
	14 26.2	22 16.5	29 12.5	31 11.8		25 14.6		24 15.3	22 16.6
	30 12.0	36 10.1	45 8.1	49 7.4		46 7.9		41 9.0	39 9.3
	54.3	178.2	-69.3	NM		126.0	Sales/Working Capital	214.4	310.1
	-38.6	-27.1	-23.2	-19.8		-16.0		-27.6	-25.9
	-16.6	-15.4	-12.9	-12.0		-12.3		-12.0	-11.8
	10.2	7.9	6.3	5.1		12.3	EBIT/Interest	4.4	5.5
	(181) 4.5	(210) 3.3	(187) 3.1	(45) 2.5		4.0		(578) 2.0	(625) 2.5
	1.2	1.3	1.5	1.4		1.3		1.1	1.2
	3.7	3.5	2.3	3.7			Net Profit + Depr., Dep., Amort./Cur. Mat. L./T/D	2.9	2.5
	(25) 2.0	(39) 1.4	(50) 1.4	(26) 2.2				(250) 1.7	(172) 1.4
	.8	.9	.9	.9				.9	.8
	1.1	1.3	1.8	1.7		.8	Fixed/Worth	1.5	1.5
	2.5	4.4	4.3	2.3		1.9		4.3	4.1
	-9.4	-11.3	-216.2	13.1		NM		-12.1	-10.7
	.9	1.5	1.7	1.6		.7	Debt/Worth	1.4	1.5
	3.6	5.0	4.7	2.6		1.6		5.4	5.1
	-13.2	-13.5	-393.4	15.7		NM		-20.1	-15.5
	122.6	98.1	72.1	53.4		48.8	% Profit Before Taxes/Tangible Net Worth	81.5	94.1
	(159) 62.5	(155) 43.7	(146) 40.5	(38) 28.2		(10) 12.5		(439) 32.0	(473) 38.4
	17.2	15.6	18.6	11.2		2.5		10.0	13.6
	34.6	22.1	16.6	13.7		9.0	% Profit Before Taxes/Total Assets	17.6	19.5
	15.9	10.1	9.5	7.5		7.6		6.8	8.1
	1.6	2.0	3.2	2.3		1.0		.5	1.7
	21.8	10.9	7.3	4.6		11.7	Sales/Net Fixed Assets	10.5	10.4
	9.4	6.3	4.2	2.9		2.5		5.8	5.6
	4.1	3.0	2.7	2.0		2.0		2.8	2.8
	6.4	4.6	3.4	2.6		1.8	Sales/Total Assets	4.7	4.6
	4.3	3.2	2.6	1.8		1.5		3.1	3.0
	2.6	2.0	1.8	1.4		1.3		1.9	1.9
	1.5	2.3	2.7	3.0			% Depr., Dep., Amort./Sales	2.3	2.3
	(200) 2.5	(210) 3.4	(188) 3.5	(48) 4.4				(576) 3.5	(627) 3.5
	4.1	4.6	4.3	5.7				4.8	5.0
	3.5	2.7	1.8				% Officers', Directors', Owners' Comp/Sales	2.8	2.4
	(105) 5.7	(119) 4.3	(81) 3.0					(236) 5.1	(278) 4.3
	9.2	7.4	5.0					8.2	7.3
Net Sales ($)	238935M	837745M	2301419M	1877001M	933860M	4238903M		13883563M	6900698M
Total Assets ($)	56617M	250437M	831497M	958365M	573818M	2063232M		3822174M	3427669M

M = $ thousand   MM = $ million
See Pages 1 through 15 for Explanation of Ratios and Data

	Comparative Historical Data				**Current Data Sorted By Sales**					
	7	21	40	# Postretirement Benefits	7	6	5	10	9	3
				Type of Statement						
	92	88	88	Unqualified	1	7	7	14	22	37
	115	134	114	Reviewed	8	24	19	24	34	5
	300	276	288	Compiled	77	107	40	41	21	2
	20	43	28	Tax Returns	12	9	3	3	1	
	174	202	205	Other	46	44	23	40	37	15
	4/1/92-3/31/93 ALL	4/1/93-3/31/94 ALL	4/1/94-3/31/95 ALL		0-1MM	1-3MM	3-5MM	5-10MM	10-25MM	25MM & OVER
					149 (4/1-9/30/94)			**574 (10/1/94-3/31/95)**		
	701	743	723	**NUMBER OF STATEMENTS**	144	191	92	122	115	59
	%	%	%	**ASSETS**	%	%	%	%	%	%
	13.6	12.4	13.1	Cash & Equivalents	15.0	14.6	14.9	11.9	9.8	10.0
	1.4	1.6	1.3	Trade Receivables - (net)	.7	1.1	1.3	1.0	1.6	3.9
	4.3	3.7	3.7	Inventory	4.8	3.8	3.9	3.1	3.2	3.2
	1.6	1.9	2.1	All Other Current	1.5	2.5	2.0	1.8	2.1	2.6
	20.8	19.7	20.3	Total Current	22.0	22.0	22.0	17.9	16.7	19.7
	57.0	57.6	56.3	Fixed Assets (net)	57.2	53.6	52.3	54.2	64.2	58.0
	11.7	11.5	12.0	Intangibles (net)	10.0	13.3	13.6	14.9	9.1	9.6
	10.5	11.2	11.5	All Other Non-Current	10.9	11.1	12.1	13.0	10.0	12.7
	100.0	100.0	100.0	Total	100.0	100.0	100.0	100.0	100.0	100.0
				LIABILITIES						
	4.1	4.0	2.8	Notes Payable-Short Term	2.8	3.1	4.1	1.2	2.2	4.1
	7.4	7.4	6.9	Cur. Mat.-L/T/D	5.4	6.7	7.5	7.9	8.4	5.5
	9.5	9.5	9.0	Trade Payables	6.8	8.9	10.3	9.9	9.7	9.6
	.4	.5	.2	Income Taxes Payable	.3	.3	.1	.2	.2	.3
	11.1	11.5	12.0	All Other Current	13.2	14.4	10.7	9.7	10.6	10.3
	32.5	33.0	30.9	Total Current	28.5	33.3	32.8	29.0	31.1	29.8
	35.9	35.5	37.3	Long Term Debt	37.4	38.1	36.9	37.1	35.9	37.4
	.2	.2	.3	Deferred Taxes	.7	.0	.3	.1	.1	.6
	2.4	3.2	3.1	All Other-Non-Current	3.3	3.6	1.5	2.5	3.7	3.0
	29.0	28.1	28.5	Net Worth	30.1	24.9	28.5	31.3	29.2	29.1
	100.0	100.0	100.0	Total Liabilities & Net Worth	100.0	100.0	100.0	100.0	100.0	100.0
				INCOME DATA						
	100.0	100.0	100.0	Net Sales	100.0	100.0	100.0	100.0	100.0	100.0
	62.0	61.7	60.7	Gross Profit	60.7	62.1	62.7	63.5	60.3	48.3
	55.6	56.4	55.2	Operating Expenses	54.6	56.4	56.8	58.9	54.8	43.3
	6.4	5.3	5.5	Operating Profit	6.1	5.7	5.9	4.5	5.4	5.1
	1.9	1.7	1.4	All Other Expenses (net)	1.5	1.4	1.5	1.0	1.4	1.7
	4.5	3.6	4.1	Profit Before Taxes	4.6	4.3	4.4	3.5	4.0	3.4
				RATIOS						
	1.1	1.1	1.1	Current	1.6	1.3	1.0	1.0	.8	1.0
	.5	.6	.6		.7	.5	.6	.6	.5	.6
	.3	.3	.3		.3	.2	.3	.3	.3	.4
	.9	.8	.8	Quick	1.0	1.0	.8	.7	.5	.7
	(695) .4	(739) .4	(715) .4		(143) .5	(189) .4	(89) .5	(120) .4	.3	.5
	.1	.1	.2		.1	.1	.2	.2	.2	.2
	0 UND	0 UND	0 UND	Sales/Receivables	0 UND	0 UND	0 UND	0 UND	0 UND	0 999.8
	0 UND	0 UND	0 UND		0 UND	0 UND	0 UND	0 UND	0 999.8	2 220.2
	1 489.8	1 505.1	1 469.8		0 949.0	0 999.8	1 243.7	0 745.5	1 316.0	7 53.9
	7 51.0	7 54.8	6 56.9	Cost of Sales/Inventory	6 63.4	7 54.9	7 53.8	7 53.5	6 57.3	6 65.2
	10 37.5	9 39.4	9 40.4		9 38.7	9 40.4	9 39.0	9 40.2	9 41.9	9 41.9
	14 26.8	12 29.9	12 30.0		14 26.0	13 29.0	12 30.6	11 33.5	12 30.7	14 26.5
	11 32.9	11 33.5	12 31.0	Cost of Sales/Payables	2 167.8	11 32.5	15 23.9	16 23.5	18 20.3	18 20.6
	24 15.4	24 15.0	23 16.1		12 31.7	20 18.4	23 16.0	29 12.5	28 13.0	29 12.7
	42 8.7	40 9.1	38 9.5		32 11.5	34 10.8	37 9.9	40 9.1	45 8.2	45 8.2
	149.9	248.6	134.9	Sales/Working Capital	53.7	54.4	NM	-935.1	-54.7	999.8
	-28.5	-27.6	-27.0		-57.5	-26.1	-28.7	-30.2	-21.4	-21.5
	-11.8	-12.6	-14.8		-15.1	-13.8	-18.3	-16.3	-14.3	-13.0
	6.9	7.0	7.0	EBIT/Interest	7.5	7.4	8.8	6.7	6.8	5.9
	(623) 3.0	(665) 3.1	(644) 3.2		(123) 3.3	(158) 3.1	(84) 3.5	(112) 2.8	(110) 3.8	(57) 3.1
	1.5	1.3	1.3		1.2	1.2	1.3	1.5	1.7	1.4
	3.1	2.3	3.4	Net Profit + Depr., Dep., Amort./Cur. Mat. L/T/D	3.4	3.8	3.7	3.1	2.3	4.9
	(189) 1.8	(190) 1.3	(152) 1.6		(17) 2.0	(23) 1.2	(13) 1.6	(34) 1.4	(32) 1.5	(33) 2.5
	1.0	.7	1.0		.6	.5	1.1	1.0	.7	1.6
	1.3	1.3	1.3	Fixed/Worth	1.2	1.2	1.2	1.4	1.6	1.6
	3.4	3.7	3.4		2.7	5.0	3.2	3.4	3.5	2.5
	-76.7	-14.5	-14.6		53.8	-5.9	-4.7	-288.8	-77.0	8.2
	1.3	1.3	1.3	Debt/Worth	1.1	1.3	1.4	1.7	1.5	1.5
	4.0	4.1	4.0		3.6	5.2	5.5	3.6	3.5	2.7
	-96.5	-24.1	-20.5		NM	-7.8	-9.7	-711.9	-98.3	9.6
	99.0	79.4	89.4	% Profit Before Taxes/Tangible Net Worth	108.1	91.0	83.4	91.6	79.3	61.3
	(517) 37.7	(527) 32.4	(516) 42.1		(108) 57.0	(124) 42.6	(61) 37.8	(91) 43.7	(85) 43.6	(47) 29.1
	15.0	10.9	15.6		14.7	8.6	18.7	17.8	18.7	10.9
	21.7	18.4	22.2	% Profit Before Taxes/Total Assets	27.5	23.3	23.0	18.2	20.0	13.1
	9.8	8.4	10.4		12.5	10.1	11.4	9.6	11.5	7.8
	2.9	1.7	1.9		1.5	.9	2.3	3.0	3.8	2.0
	11.2	10.6	11.0	Sales/Net Fixed Assets	14.7	13.8	13.1	12.1	7.4	7.0
	5.3	5.7	5.5		6.3	6.7	6.4	5.7	4.5	3.4
	2.7	2.9	3.0		3.0	2.7	3.4	3.9	2.8	2.1
	4.8	4.7	4.6	Sales/Total Assets	5.3	4.9	5.1	4.5	4.3	2.7
	3.0	3.1	2.9		2.9	2.9	3.6	3.1	2.7	2.0
	1.9	2.0	1.9		1.9	1.8	2.2	2.3	2.0	1.5
	2.2	2.3	2.2	% Depr., Dep., Amort./Sales	1.6	1.8	2.2	2.5	2.6	2.8
	(647) 3.4	(703) 3.3	(660) 3.3		(129) 3.0	(168) 3.3	(88) 3.3	(112) 3.4	(112) 3.2	(51) 3.8
	4.7	4.4	4.4		4.5	4.9	4.1	4.2	4.2	4.6
	2.4	2.8	2.5	% Officers', Directors', Owners' Comp/Sales	3.4	3.5	2.5	1.9	1.5	2.5
	(269) 4.4	(306) 4.5	(318) 4.4		(65) 5.9	(87) 4.8	(49) 4.2	(61) 3.1	(44) 2.8	(12) 3.8
	8.1	7.4	7.5		9.4	8.0	6.0	6.8	4.7	20.0
	6715638M	8267500M	10427863M	Net Sales ($)	89115M	337356M	354945M	858069M	1774874M	7013504M
	3500809M	4131273M	4733966M	Total Assets ($)	33729M	145006M	136502M	308653M	706140M	3403936M

© Robert Morris Associates 1995

M = $ thousand   MM = $ million
See Pages 1 through 15 for Explanation of Ratios and Data

Current Data Sorted By Assets

2	3	9				# Postretirement Benefits		
						Type of Statement		
8	19	15	1			Unqualified	32	38
9	53	45	1			Reviewed	114	116
33	43	13	1			Compiled	90	81
2	4	2				Tax Returns		3
12	13	11	1	1		Other	40	36

0-500M	500M-2MM	2-10MM	10-50MM	50-100MM	100-250MM		4/1/90-3/31/91 ALL	4/1/91-3/31/92 ALL
	184 (4/1-9/30/94)		103 (10/1/94-3/31/95)					
56	121	90	18	2		**NUMBER OF STATEMENTS**	276	274
%	%	%	%	%	%	**ASSETS**	%	%
7.1	9.8	7.9	3.4			Cash & Equivalents	9.5	9.9
29.9	26.8	24.8	20.4			Trade Receivables - (net)	27.6	27.9
12.2	11.7	11.7	11.8			Inventory	12.6	12.3
1.2	1.0	1.5	1.4			All Other Current	2.4	2.0
50.4	49.3	45.9	37.0			Total Current	52.1	52.1
30.1	31.8	39.2	39.7			Fixed Assets (net)	33.1	32.7
4.7	6.9	4.5	12.2			Intangibles (net)	5.3	5.2
14.9	12.0	10.4	11.2			All Other Non-Current	9.5	10.0
100.0	100.0	100.0	100.0			Total	100.0	100.0
						LIABILITIES		
9.7	6.3	7.2	11.1			Notes Payable-Short Term	10.6	9.1
6.5	5.3	5.4	7.1			Cur. Mat.-L/T/D	4.8	5.0
14.8	15.9	16.3	14.9			Trade Payables	15.0	14.6
.4	.4	.4	.2			Income Taxes Payable	.7	.8
11.0	12.2	10.8	9.1			All Other Current	9.5	9.9
42.4	40.2	40.2	42.4			Total Current	40.5	39.4
20.9	17.0	18.4	27.3			Long Term Debt	18.0	17.2
.0	.5	.6	1.4			Deferred Taxes	.4	.5
3.2	3.3	4.1	2.8			All Other-Non-Current	1.8	2.3
33.5	39.1	36.7	26.2			Net Worth	39.3	40.6
100.0	100.0	100.0	100.0			Total Liabilities & Net Worth	100.0	100.0
						INCOME DATA		
100.0	100.0	100.0	100.0			Net Sales	100.0	100.0
26.7	25.0	21.9	25.2			Gross Profit	22.0	22.1
24.9	23.6	19.5	22.2			Operating Expenses	20.8	21.1
1.8	1.5	2.4	3.0			Operating Profit	1.2	1.0
.4	.2	.5	.8			All Other Expenses (net)	.2	.1
1.3	1.3	1.9	2.2			Profit Before Taxes	1.0	.9
						RATIOS		
2.1	1.9	1.6	1.1				1.9	1.9
1.4	1.3	1.2	.8			Current	1.3	1.3
.8	1.0	.9	.6				.9	.9
1.5	1.4	1.2	.7				1.3	1.4
1.1	1.0	.8	.6			Quick	.9	.9
.5	.6	.5	.4				.6	.6
13 28.6	15 24.9	13 28.7	14 26.3				15 24.7	15 24.9
22 16.3	23 15.7	21 17.0	21 17.1			Sales/Receivables	22 16.7	22 16.6
33 11.0	34 10.6	32 11.5	29 12.7				32 11.4	30 12.0
2 160.1	6 65.4	8 45.9	12 31.1				7 55.7	6 65.6
8 44.9	11 32.4	14 26.7	15 23.6			Cost of Sales/Inventory	11 32.0	11 33.2
19 19.3	18 20.4	19 19.6	20 18.7				19 18.8	18 20.4
4 85.3	9 39.2	13 28.3	17 21.0				9 40.6	8 47.8
12 31.7	17 22.0	18 19.8	22 16.8			Cost of Sales/Payables	14 25.4	13 27.3
17 21.1	25 14.5	24 15.0	27 13.5				21 17.1	19 19.2
14.3	15.7	23.4	107.7				17.4	15.2
48.0	44.7	64.4	-52.7			Sales/Working Capital	44.6	41.4
-43.2	-191.5	-54.1	-22.2				-151.3	-137.2
5.3	5.8	4.5	3.9				3.6	3.7
(53) 2.1	(116) 2.7	(83) 2.7	2.2			EBIT/Interest	(246) 1.8	(251) 1.8
.6	1.2	1.8	1.7				1.1	.7
5.2	3.2	4.6	2.3				3.7	3.5
(16) 2.0	(64) 2.3	(47) 2.3	(11) 1.6			Net Profit + Depr., Dep., Amort./Cur. Mat. L /T/D	(166) 1.9	(141) 1.9
1.0	1.3	1.4	1.1				1.1	.9
.3	.5	.7	1.4				.5	.4
1.0	.9	1.2	2.4			Fixed/Worth	1.1	1.0
2.0	2.2	2.2	-1.5				2.7	2.2
.8	.9	1.1	1.8				.8	.8
2.4	1.7	2.2	4.1			Debt/Worth	2.1	1.8
4.9	4.7	4.1	-11.0				5.6	3.9
44.8	24.5	26.8	38.5				20.4	22.8
(49) 13.9	(105) 11.9	(86) 15.4	(13) 24.5			% Profit Before Taxes/Tangible Net Worth	(251) 9.3	(246) 9.7
1.6	3.2	10.3	11.2				1.1	-.2
12.1	8.8	8.2	7.9				7.7	9.0
4.8	4.6	5.3	4.2			% Profit Before Taxes/Total Assets	2.8	3.2
-.6	.8	2.8	2.7				.3	-1.6
35.1	25.4	17.2	15.2				24.3	23.7
21.9	15.6	10.1	10.6			Sales/Net Fixed Assets	14.4	14.2
9.6	8.6	6.1	5.2				8.5	9.0
7.4	5.5	5.1	4.2				5.4	5.8
4.7	4.0	3.7	3.2			Sales/Total Assets	4.1	4.0
3.0	3.0	2.7	2.2				3.0	3.1
.9	1.0	1.1	1.4				1.1	1.0
(49) 1.7	(111) 1.7	(82) 1.7	(15) 1.8			% Depr., Dep., Amort./Sales	(262) 1.7	(262) 1.6
2.6	2.4	2.8	2.3				2.4	2.6
3.6	1.5	.9					1.3	1.3
(34) 4.8	(70) 2.8	(40) 2.0				% Officers', Directors', Owners' Comp/Sales	(137) 2.5	(141) 2.7
7.5	5.7	3.8					4.1	4.9
94890M	600074M	1445518M	1415686M	375017M		Net Sales ($)	3145864M	3864040M
16888M	134950M	369358M	422173M	120773M		Total Assets ($)	791724M	964089M

M = $ thousand   MM = $ million
See Pages 1 through 15 for Explanation of Ratios and Data

Comparative Historical Data				Current Data Sorted By Sales					
1	9	14	# Postretirement Benefits	2	1	2	1	6	2
			Type of Statement						
39	49	43	Unqualified		4	3	4	13	19
112	104	108	Reviewed	4	20	18	31	27	8
79	98	90	Compiled	13	30	18	18	8	3
3	7	8	Tax Returns		2	1	3	1	1
35	37	38	Other	4	9	4	8	10	3
4/1/92-3/31/93 ALL	4/1/93-3/31/94 ALL	4/1/94-3/31/95 ALL		184 (4/1-9/30/94)			103 (10/1/94-3/31/95)		
				0-1MM	1-3MM	3-5MM	5-10MM	10-25MM	25MM & OVER
268	295	287	**NUMBER OF STATEMENTS**	21	65	44	64	59	34
%	%	%	**ASSETS**	%	%	%	%	%	%
10.3	9.4	8.2	Cash & Equivalents	7.5	8.5	9.9	8.9	8.1	5.1
25.5	26.5	26.3	Trade Receivables - (net)	18.1	28.3	29.0	27.2	25.4	23.9
12.9	11.6	11.8	Inventory	9.9	12.2	11.2	9.8	14.5	12.1
1.6	2.0	1.2	All Other Current	1.9	1.1	1.0	.8	1.3	1.7
50.2	49.6	47.5	Total Current	37.4	50.1	51.0	46.6	49.4	42.7
33.8	33.3	34.4	Fixed Assets (net)	32.2	30.4	28.6	36.2	38.3	40.5
4.9	5.5	6.2	Intangibles (net)	8.1	5.5	7.8	6.9	3.1	8.1
11.1	11.7	12.0	All Other Non-Current	22.2	14.0	12.6	10.2	9.3	8.6
100.0	100.0	100.0	Total	100.0	100.0	100.0	100.0	100.0	100.0
			LIABILITIES						
8.3	10.3	7.6	Notes Payable-Short Term	11.0	7.0	7.9	7.0	6.6	8.7
5.0	4.7	5.7	Cur. Mat.-L /T/D	5.7	5.0	7.1	6.0	5.0	6.1
14.8	14.4	15.7	Trade Payables	5.6	14.7	13.9	17.4	18.6	18.1
.5	1.4	.4	Income Taxes Payable	.3	.5	.2	.4	.6	.3
10.6	11.0	11.3	All Other Current	12.2	13.5	10.5	10.7	11.1	9.2
39.1	41.8	40.7	Total Current	34.8	40.8	39.5	41.5	42.0	42.5
16.1	18.1	19.0	Long Term Debt	29.1	17.7	17.9	18.2	16.6	22.2
.5	.7	.5	Deferred Taxes	.0	.2	.4	.5	.7	1.1
2.5	3.4	3.5	All Other-Non-Current	.8	4.4	2.9	2.8	4.2	4.4
41.8	36.0	36.3	Net Worth	35.4	37.0	39.2	37.1	36.5	29.8
100.0	100.0	100.0	Total Liabilities & Net Worth	100.0	100.0	100.0	100.0	100.0	100.0
			INCOME DATA						
100.0	100.0	100.0	Net Sales	100.0	100.0	100.0	100.0	100.0	100.0
22.9	23.9	24.4	Gross Profit	34.9	28.8	27.1	21.7	19.1	20.2
21.7	22.3	22.4	Operating Expenses	30.3	26.9	25.7	20.0	17.5	17.9
1.2	1.6	2.0	Operating Profit	4.6	1.9	1.4	1.7	1.5	2.3
.1	.3	.4	All Other Expenses (net)	2.7	.3	.2	.2	.1	.5
1.1	1.3	1.6	Profit Before Taxes	1.9	1.6	1.2	1.6	1.5	1.8
			RATIOS						
2.0	1.8	1.8	Current	3.1	2.1	1.9	1.6	1.6	1.3
1.3	1.2	1.2		1.3	1.4	1.4	1.2	1.2	.9
.9	.8	.8		.4	.9	1.0	.9	.8	.7
1.5	1.3	1.3	Quick	2.3	1.6	1.4	1.2	1.3	.9
.9	.8	.9		.9	1.1	1.1	1.0	.7	.6
.6	.5	.5		.3	.5	.6	.6	.5	.4
13 28.2	14 25.8	14 26.3	Sales/Receivables	8 48.2	15 24.1	18 20.5	13 27.1	10 37.7	13 27.5
21 17.7	22 16.3	22 16.3		26 13.8	28 12.9	24 15.5	23 15.8	16 22.9	18 20.5
31 11.6	31 11.8	33 11.2		40 9.2	37 9.9	34 10.7	31 11.9	29 12.8	26 14.2
6 58.5	6 65.7	6 63.3	Cost of Sales/Inventory	0 UND	6 58.8	6 59.9	4 87.5	6 62.0	9 41.9
12 31.6	11 32.0	12 30.5		6 62.4	13 27.7	11 32.9	10 34.8	13 28.3	13 28.7
19 19.3	19 19.7	19 19.7		23 15.7	22 16.3	19 18.8	18 20.3	16 22.4	17 21.6
9 41.0	8 43.1	10 37.2	Cost of Sales/Payables	1 325.8	9 42.9	10 37.3	11 33.1	10 35.4	15 24.0
14 25.4	15 24.9	17 22.0		7 49.9	16 22.7	14 25.2	18 20.0	17 21.9	20 18.3
21 17.6	22 16.5	24 15.5		16 22.7	30 12.1	23 15.9	23 15.8	22 16.6	26 14.3
14.3	17.6	18.5	Sales/Working Capital	10.0	12.7	13.2	23.5	24.5	35.4
39.4	67.5	61.6		51.1	32.5	25.2	65.0	89.5	-272.4
-92.8	-46.7	-52.6		-10.3	-36.9	NM	-155.5	-52.6	-25.2
4.5	4.5	4.8	EBIT/Interest	4.8	8.0	4.8	5.5	4.2	3.9
(249) 2.0	(270) 2.3	(272) 2.6		(18) 2.4	(63) 2.2	(43) 2.7	(62) 2.7	(53) 2.7	(33) 2.6
.9	1.4	1.4		.3	.6	1.3	1.3	1.5	1.8
3.3	3.7	4.1	Net Profit + Depr., Dep., Amort./Cur. Mat. L/T/D		4.0	3.0	3.7	5.1	3.1
(130) 1.8	(132) 2.0	(140) 2.1			(24) 2.1	(24) 1.9	(33) 2.3	(36) 2.1	(20) 1.8
1.0	1.2	1.3			1.0	1.2	1.2	1.4	1.1
.4	.5	.6	Fixed/Worth	.1	.4	.4	.7	.6	.9
.9	1.1	1.1		1.0	.8	1.1	1.2	1.2	1.8
1.9	2.9	2.3		2.0	2.0	2.3	2.0	2.3	4.0
.7	.9	1.0	Debt/Worth	.5	.7	.9	1.1	1.0	1.4
1.6	2.2	2.0		2.0	1.7	1.8	2.0	2.0	2.6
3.6	6.6	4.9		9.3	4.7	5.5	3.9	4.0	6.8
19.9	25.4	27.6	% Profit Before Taxes/Tangible Net Worth	49.4	24.7	29.2	27.6	26.4	35.4
(244) 7.6	(257) 11.6	(254) 14.3		(17) 12.4	(54) 12.7	(39) 16.1	(59) 12.8	(56) 15.4	(29) 17.6
.4	4.3	5.8		4.0	1.5	2.6	6.3	7.6	13.1
7.4	7.8	8.8	% Profit Before Taxes/Total Assets	9.1	13.2	8.8	8.5	8.1	8.7
2.5	3.9	5.0		3.1	4.6	5.5	4.6	5.0	5.4
-.2	1.5	1.4		-1.3	-.5	1.2	1.2	1.7	3.4
23.3	26.5	23.8	Sales/Net Fixed Assets	53.9	26.0	28.1	18.0	23.3	18.1
14.0	13.9	13.5		8.3	16.0	18.7	12.0	13.7	10.7
9.0	8.4	7.4		4.9	7.4	9.3	8.2	6.9	5.4
5.7	5.6	5.4	Sales/Total Assets	4.3	5.0	5.3	5.9	5.9	5.2
4.0	4.1	3.9		2.7	3.5	4.1	3.8	4.7	4.1
3.0	2.9	2.8		1.7	2.4	3.1	2.8	3.6	3.1
1.0	1.0	1.1	% Depr., Dep., Amort./Sales	1.8	1.1	1.2	1.0	1.0	1.0
(252) 1.6	(271) 1.7	(259) 1.7		(15) 3.2	(60) 1.8	(39) 2.0	(62) 1.7	(53) 1.3	(30) 1.7
2.4	2.4	2.6		5.3	2.5	2.9	2.8	1.9	2.2
1.4	1.3	1.4	% Officers', Directors', Owners' Comp/Sales	6.1	3.2	2.3	1.4	.6	.5
(144) 2.8	(150) 2.7	(150) 3.1		(10) 8.0	(37) 4.6	(30) 3.7	(41) 2.6	(22) 1.0	(10) .9
5.2	5.1	5.6		15.2	7.1	5.7	3.5	1.8	1.4
5088911M	4581258M	3931185M	Net Sales ($)	12464M	125711M	172168M	459048M	918414M	2243380M
1034913M	1191624M	1064142M	Total Assets ($)	8667M	40072M	45640M	128940M	215924M	624899M

M = $ thousand   MM = $ million
See Pages 1 through 15 for Explanation of Ratios and Data

RETAILERS—LIQUEFIED PETROLEUM GAS (BOTTLED GAS). SIC# 5984

Current Data Sorted By Assets / Comparative Historical Data

Type of Statement

0-500M	500M-2MM	2-10MM	10-50MM	50-100MM	100-250MM		4/1/90-3/31/91 ALL	4/1/91-3/31/92 ALL
	4	1	1		1	# Postretirement Benefits		
						Type of Statement		
		6	6	3	2	Unqualified	17	15
1	9	6	1			Reviewed	17	14
7	20	4				Compiled	31	28
		1				Tax Returns	1	2
1	6	5	2			Other	8	12
	42 (4/1-9/30/94)			38 (10/1/94-3/31/95)				
9	35	22	9	3	2	NUMBER OF STATEMENTS	74	71

Main Data

0-500M %	500M-2MM %	2-10MM %	10-50MM %	50-100MM %	100-250MM %		4/1/90-3/31/91 ALL %	4/1/91-3/31/92 ALL %
						ASSETS		
	7.5	10.0				Cash & Equivalents	8.4	9.0
	17.7	16.7				Trade Receivables - (net)	22.4	19.1
	11.6	14.3				Inventory	13.0	10.1
	3.8	2.5				All Other Current	3.8	1.9
	40.6	43.5				Total Current	47.5	40.1
	46.3	44.9				Fixed Assets (net)	43.3	46.7
	5.8	3.4				Intangibles (net)	1.6	3.7
	7.3	8.2				All Other Non-Current	7.6	9.5
	100.0	100.0				Total	100.0	100.0
						LIABILITIES		
	5.9	7.7				Notes Payable-Short Term	8.5	5.2
	7.3	5.4				Cur. Mat. -L/T/D	5.1	5.8
	10.2	14.1				Trade Payables	13.0	12.9
	.2	.3				Income Taxes Payable	.8	.5
	8.3	9.5				All Other Current	5.7	5.5
	31.9	37.0				Total Current	33.0	30.0
	22.2	23.2				Long Term Debt	19.8	22.6
	.5	1.1				Deferred Taxes	.7	1.2
	2.8	.2				All Other-Non-Current	2.4	5.2
	42.6	38.5				Net Worth	44.0	41.1
	100.0	100.0				Total Liabilities & Net Worth	100.0	100.0
						INCOME DATA		
	100.0	100.0				Net Sales	100.0	100.0
	40.6	38.3				Gross Profit	39.5	41.3
	37.6	35.1				Operating Expenses	35.4	37.8
	3.0	3.2				Operating Profit	4.1	3.5
	.6	-.4				All Other Expenses (net)	.5	1.3
	2.4	3.7				Profit Before Taxes	3.6	2.3
						RATIOS		
	1.7	1.8				Current	2.4	1.9
	1.2	1.2					1.3	1.2
	.8	.7					1.0	.9
	1.1	1.3				Quick	1.5	1.4
	.8	.7					.9	.9
	.5	.4					.6	.6
	20 18.3	14 27.0				Sales/Receivables	19 19.6	19 19.0
	29 12.5	21 17.3					29 12.7	32 11.5
	39 9.3	41 8.9					47 7.8	42 8.7
	16 23.3	15 23.7				Cost of Sales/Inventory	14 26.7	15 24.7
	28 13.2	27 13.5					30 12.0	24 15.1
	49 7.5	51 7.2					48 7.6	42 8.7
	16 22.6	19 19.2				Cost of Sales/Payables	16 22.7	14 26.0
	27 13.3	23 16.2					29 12.7	34 10.6
	44 8.3	33 11.1					46 7.9	51 7.1
	12.7	11.9				Sales/Working Capital	7.4	9.2
	33.9	47.9					24.3	46.5
	-46.5	-18.3					-110.2	-51.8
	4.7	(19) 11.2				EBIT/Interest	4.9	5.1
	(31) 2.1	2.0					(67) 2.7	(67) 2.2
	1.0	1.5					1.5	1.1
	4.8					Net Profit + Depr., Dep.,	3.7	3.0
	(18) 2.2					Amort./Cur. Mat. L/T/D	(36) 2.1	(33) 1.4
	1.7						1.6	.6
	.7	.5				Fixed/Worth	.6	.7
	1.2	1.4					1.1	1.4
	3.9	4.5					2.0	2.6
	.7	.7				Debt/Worth	.5	.5
	1.3	2.2					1.8	1.7
	5.8	4.8					3.2	4.4
	25.7	31.8				% Profit Before Taxes/Tangible	33.5	32.3
	(31) 6.9	(20) 22.1				Net Worth	(70) 17.0	(65) 13.4
	.1	6.4					4.9	3.6
	11.1	15.5				% Profit Before Taxes/Total	12.5	14.7
	3.6	5.2				Assets	6.6	4.2
	.1	2.2					1.7	.9
	7.2	10.1				Sales/Net Fixed Assets	9.6	8.1
	5.8	5.5					5.6	4.5
	2.9	3.4					4.0	3.3
	2.8	2.9				Sales/Total Assets	3.0	2.9
	2.0	2.1					2.2	2.0
	1.6	1.8					1.7	1.5
	2.8	2.1				% Depr., Dep., Amort./Sales	3.1	3.3
	4.6	(20) 3.6					(67) 4.4	(65) 5.4
	6.3	5.7					5.6	6.2
	4.0					% Officers', Directors',	2.3	2.9
	(18) 6.9					Owners' Comp/Sales	(37) 4.9	(34) 6.1
	7.9						7.5	8.1
7557M	83180M	273659M	821347M	469797M	227423M	Net Sales ($)	1111065M	1481742M
2924M	39762M	107270M	183464M	195516M	230427M	Total Assets ($)	466992M	955872M

M = $ thousand   MM = $ million

See Pages 1 through 15 for Explanation of Ratios and Data

Comparative Historical Data				Current Data Sorted By Sales					
	3	7	# Postretirement Benefits		2	1	1	2	1
			Type of Statement						
16	18	17	Unqualified				1	5	11
12	10	17	Reviewed	1	6	3	2	4	1
37	25	31	Compiled	6	18	3	2	2	
1	1	1	Tax Returns			1			
12	15	14	Other		5	3		5	1
4/1/92-3/31/93 ALL	4/1/93-3/31/94 ALL	4/1/94-3/31/95 ALL		0-1MM	1-3MM	3-5MM	5-10MM	10-25MM	25MM & OVER
					42 (4/1-9/30/94)		38 (10/1/94-3/31/95)		
78	69	80	NUMBER OF STATEMENTS	7	29	9	6	16	13
%	%	%	ASSETS	%	%	%	%	%	%
8.8	6.5	7.9	Cash & Equivalents		8.8			8.2	7.3
18.0	17.6	18.3	Trade Receivables - (net)		17.4			15.8	21.7
11.2	10.4	12.4	Inventory		9.9			13.8	11.7
3.6	1.9	3.3	All Other Current		3.8			1.7	4.6
41.6	36.4	41.9	Total Current		39.9			39.5	45.3
49.5	53.8	47.6	Fixed Assets (net)		47.3			51.2	45.3
2.1	3.2	4.1	Intangibles (net)		7.0			2.1	3.7
6.8	6.6	6.4	All Other Non-Current		5.9			7.2	5.7
100.0	100.0	100.0	Total		100.0			100.0	100.0
			LIABILITIES						
7.3	5.3	6.7	Notes Payable-Short Term		7.5			7.5	2.8
6.1	6.8	5.4	Cur. Mat.-L /T/D		5.5			5.2	3.8
11.5	10.7	12.1	Trade Payables		7.7			14.2	20.5
.6	1.7	.3	Income Taxes Payable		.2			.3	.2
6.6	8.2	7.9	All Other Current		8.6			10.4	7.8
32.1	32.7	32.4	Total Current		29.6			37.5	35.0
25.5	23.9	21.1	Long Term Debt		19.9			25.2	21.6
1.5	1.6	1.3	Deferred Taxes		.3			1.2	4.6
2.8	2.5	2.4	All Other-Non-Current		3.1			.1	3.3
38.1	39.3	42.8	Net Worth		47.0			35.9	35.6
100.0	100.0	100.0	Total Liabilities & Net Worth		100.0			100.0	100.0
			INCOME DATA						
100.0	100.0	100.0	Net Sales		100.0			100.0	100.0
43.1	40.7	38.6	Gross Profit		44.6			35.5	27.1
37.8	37.2	35.0	Operating Expenses		39.5			31.1	21.7
5.4	3.5	3.6	Operating Profit		5.2			4.4	5.5
1.5	1.0	.2	All Other Expenses (net)		.5			-.1	.8
3.9	2.5	3.4	Profit Before Taxes		4.7			4.5	4.6
			RATIOS						
2.1	1.7	1.8	Current		2.2			1.7	1.8
1.3	1.1	1.2			1.2			1.2	1.2
.9	.7	.8			.8			.8	.9
1.4	1.3	1.2	Quick		1.5			1.1	1.1
.8	.8	.8			.8			.7	.8
.4	.4	.5			.5			.4	.5
17　21.2	18　20.5	19　19.5	Sales/Receivables	20　18.7			9　42.7	15　23.8	
30　12.3	28　12.9	28　13.0		29　12.6			21　17.3	24　15.4	
46　7.9	38　9.6	40　9.1		35　10.4			38　9.6	39　9.4	
15　25.0	13　27.7	15　23.6	Cost of Sales/Inventory	11　31.8			16　23.0	9　41.0	
29　12.8	26　14.2	28　12.9		24　14.9			23　16.2	16　22.7	
46　7.9	39　9.4	50　7.3		49　7.4			49　7.4	46　7.9	
14　25.3	13　27.3	16　23.2	Cost of Sales/Payables	16　23.5			15　24.7	18　20.6	
27　13.7	24　15.3	24　14.9		26　14.0			23　16.2	26　14.3	
48　7.6	35　10.5	37　9.8		32　11.5			31　11.8	48　7.6	
7.3	11.7	12.4	Sales/Working Capital		7.9			13.0	13.9
27.4	57.3	40.6			83.2			47.9	42.3
-36.1	-18.5	-39.4			-35.3			-23.3	-40.0
(73) 6.2	(62) 4.5	(73) 6.3	EBIT/Interest	(27) 4.7			(13) 12.1	15.9	
2.4	2.7	2.6		2.2			2.7	3.6	
1.2	1.5	1.4		1.7			1.4	2.8	
(34) 4.7	(26) 3.5	(37) 5.0	Net Profit + Depr., Dep., Amort./Cur. Mat. L/T/D	(12) 8.4					
1.6	2.1	2.2		2.2					
.7	1.0	1.7		1.8					
.6	.8	.7	Fixed/Worth		.6			.8	.6
1.4	1.5	1.2			1.3			1.4	1.2
3.2	2.7	3.0			3.7			4.1	2.2
.8	.9	.7	Debt/Worth		.6			.8	1.0
1.9	1.8	1.6			1.6			2.2	1.6
4.2	4.2	4.3			4.7			4.9	3.6
(71) 44.9	(64) 36.1	(72) 30.8	% Profit Before Taxes/Tangible Net Worth	(26) 33.3			(15) 32.3	(11) 36.4	
20.8	18.9	16.1		14.1			22.2	24.1	
7.1	7.6	3.0		3.6			5.9	9.7	
13.5	10.0	13.0	% Profit Before Taxes/Total Assets		15.2			15.6	14.5
5.5	5.0	4.4			4.1			7.1	10.3
1.2	2.0	1.6			2.3			2.4	5.0
7.3	7.0	8.0	Sales/Net Fixed Assets		6.6			9.7	18.6
4.1	3.9	5.5			5.2			5.5	5.6
2.6	2.3	2.9			3.2			2.9	1.8
2.9	2.8	2.9	Sales/Total Assets		2.8			3.0	5.3
1.9	2.0	2.1			2.1			2.4	3.0
1.3	1.5	1.6			1.6			1.9	1.1
(75) 3.2	(65) 2.7	(78) 2.6	% Depr., Dep., Amort./Sales	(28) 3.9			(15) 2.5	.7	
5.2	5.1	4.5		5.1			4.1	3.0	
7.0	6.9	6.1		6.2			5.8	6.8	
(37) 2.7	(23) 2.5	(31) 2.6	% Officers', Directors', Owners' Comp/Sales	(18) 4.1					
6.5	4.0	6.3		7.1					
9.5	5.4	7.7		7.9					
1449337M	1455502M	1882963M	Net Sales ($)	4112M	54510M	33829M	35702M	244692M	1510118M
772917M	669079M	759363M	Total Assets ($)	2556M	28764M	17848M	16937M	110728M	582530M

M = $ thousand　　MM = $ million
See Pages 1 through 15 for Explanation of Ratios and Data

Current Data Sorted By Assets — Comparative Historical Data

	0-500M	500M-2MM	2-10MM	10-50MM	50-100MM	100-250MM		4/1/90-3/31/91 ALL	4/1/91-3/31/92 ALL
# Postretirement Benefits	5	4	7						
Type of Statement									
Unqualified	1	6	6					19	16
Reviewed	9	21	25	2				65	76
Compiled	58	58	6					120	122
Tax Returns	14	3	1					2	1
Other	25	30	6	1				46	43
	98 (4/1-9/30/94)			174 (10/1/94-3/31/95)					
NUMBER OF STATEMENTS	107	118	44	3				252	258
ASSETS	%	%	%	%	%	%		%	%
Cash & Equivalents	8.0	6.7	4.9					7.2	6.4
Trade Receivables - (net)	30.4	32.1	31.4					31.1	28.8
Inventory	35.0	37.1	36.8					36.5	38.4
All Other Current	1.8	2.0	3.5					2.6	2.1
Total Current	75.3	77.9	76.6					77.4	75.8
Fixed Assets (net)	16.0	14.7	17.2					15.1	16.9
Intangibles (net)	2.2	1.2	.4					1.0	1.4
All Other Non-Current	6.5	6.1	5.9					6.4	5.9
Total	100.0	100.0	100.0					100.0	100.0
LIABILITIES									
Notes Payable-Short Term	9.1	12.7	14.1					13.5	10.9
Cur. Mat. -L/T/D	4.0	2.9	2.4					3.3	3.6
Trade Payables	19.2	18.6	19.4					20.1	22.1
Income Taxes Payable	.3	.3	.5					.9	.5
All Other Current	12.7	10.9	11.0					12.5	10.8
Total Current	45.3	45.3	47.5					50.3	47.9
Long Term Debt	12.5	10.1	10.1					10.7	13.0
Deferred Taxes	.1	.5	.5					.2	.4
All Other-Non-Current	3.0	2.8	3.2					2.2	2.4
Net Worth	39.1	41.2	38.7					36.7	36.3
Total Liabilities & Net Worth	100.0	100.0	100.0					100.0	100.0
INCOME DATA									
Net Sales	100.0	100.0	100.0					100.0	100.0
Gross Profit	34.5	32.8	30.9					31.8	32.6
Operating Expenses	31.8	30.3	29.4					29.4	30.9
Operating Profit	2.7	2.4	1.5					2.4	1.7
All Other Expenses (net)	.5	.2	.2					.4	.6
Profit Before Taxes	2.2	2.2	1.3					2.0	1.1
RATIOS									
Current	2.8 / 1.6 / 1.3	2.3 / 1.7 / 1.4	2.1 / 1.6 / 1.3					2.4 / 1.6 / 1.2	2.4 / 1.6 / 1.3
Quick	1.4 / .8 / .5	1.2 / .9 / .5	1.1 / .7 / .4					1.2 / .8 / .5	1.2 / .8 / .4
Sales/Receivables	9 39.9 / 23 16.0 / 38 9.5	19 19.7 / 33 11.2 / 47 7.8	15 24.2 / 37 9.9 / 49 7.4					15 23.9 / 29 12.7 / 43 8.4	14 25.3 / 28 13.2 / 42 8.6
Cost of Sales/Inventory	19 19.3 / 37 9.8 / 55 6.6	26 14.2 / 56 6.5 / 85 4.3	33 11.0 / 59 6.2 / 81 4.5					26 14.1 / 44 8.3 / 81 4.5	30 12.0 / 53 6.9 / 89 4.1
Cost of Sales/Payables	10 36.3 / 22 16.8 / 38 9.5	14 25.9 / 25 14.7 / 38 9.6	17 21.7 / 34 10.7 / 52 7.0					16 23.3 / 25 14.4 / 37 9.8	18 20.1 / 30 12.1 / 46 7.9
Sales/Working Capital	8.4 / 15.2 / 34.2	6.7 / 11.5 / 20.0	7.0 / 10.3 / 19.1					7.4 / 13.2 / 32.9	7.7 / 11.9 / 29.0
EBIT/Interest	(90) 10.1 / 4.2 / -.1	(110) 7.9 / 3.6 / 1.9	(42) 5.1 / 2.8 / 2.0					(234) 7.1 / 2.2 / 1.0	(236) 5.2 / 2.1 / .7
Net Profit + Depr., Dep., Amort./Cur. Mat. L./T/D	(21) 2.4 / 1.1 / -.9	(42) 4.3 / 1.8 / 1.0	(22) 7.6 / 1.6 / .7					(118) 6.0 / 2.0 / .5	(103) 3.1 / .9 / .1
Fixed/Worth	.1 / .4 / .8	.2 / .3 / .6	.1 / .3 / .6					.1 / .3 / .9	.2 / .4 / 1.2
Debt/Worth	.6 / 1.7 / 3.9	.8 / 1.5 / 2.5	1.1 / 1.7 / 3.3					.8 / 1.9 / 4.4	.9 / 1.9 / 4.1
% Profit Before Taxes/Tangible Net Worth	(96) 69.2 / 25.1 / .0	(113) 35.1 / 17.7 / 5.0	30.6 / 15.1 / 8.5					(231) 36.6 / 13.2 / 1.3	(239) 27.4 / 8.9 / -.8
% Profit Before Taxes/Total Assets	21.2 / 7.4 / -2.1	13.6 / 5.5 / 1.9	9.2 / 5.5 / 3.0					13.3 / 4.2 / .1	10.3 / 3.1 / -1.3
Sales/Net Fixed Assets	90.5 / 44.7 / 18.4	67.2 / 38.3 / 18.1	62.7 / 26.4 / 10.8					69.3 / 36.7 / 18.1	66.7 / 30.9 / 17.1
Sales/Total Assets	5.8 / 4.3 / 3.3	4.3 / 3.6 / 2.7	3.8 / 2.9 / 2.4					4.9 / 3.8 / 2.7	4.6 / 3.5 / 2.7
% Depr., Dep., Amort./Sales	(90) .4 / .8 / 1.2	(107) .4 / .7 / 1.1	(43) .5 / .6 / 1.0					(226) .5 / .8 / 1.2	(232) .5 / .8 / 1.1
% Officers', Directors', Owners' Comp/Sales	(62) 3.5 / 6.5 / 9.3	(69) 2.0 / 3.9 / 6.8	(25) 1.5 / 2.7 / 6.7					(121) 2.6 / 4.5 / 8.7	(139) 2.3 / 4.5 / 6.6
Net Sales ($)	122024M	416958M	542430M	100205M				883405M	977789M
Total Assets ($)	28333M	117710M	177791M	33876M				278801M	302130M

M = $ thousand　　MM = $ million
See Pages 1 through 15 for Explanation of Ratios and Data

Comparative Historical Data | | | Current Data Sorted By Sales

	1		6		16	# Postretirement Benefits		4		3		1		2		6	
						Type of Statement										
	16		18		13	Unqualified		2		1				3		6	1
	72		71		57	Reviewed		4		16		8		13		12	4
	126		138		122	Compiled		31		55		21		13		1	1
	8		7		18	Tax Returns		10		5		3					
	41		46		62	Other		12		29		10		7		3	1
	4/1/92-3/31/93		4/1/93-3/31/94		4/1/94-3/31/95			98 (4/1-9/30/94)						174 (10/1/94-3/31/95)			
	ALL		ALL		ALL			0-1MM		1-3MM		3-5MM		5-10MM		10-25MM	25MM & OVER
	263		280		272	**NUMBER OF STATEMENTS**		59		106		42		36		22	7
	%		%		%	**ASSETS**		%		%		%		%		%	%
	7.2		6.6		6.9	Cash & Equivalents		6.0		8.8		6.6		5.1		5.1	
	28.9		30.0		31.3	Trade Receivables - (net)		23.3		32.5		32.3		36.1		36.3	
	38.4		37.3		36.3	Inventory		37.0		36.8		36.2		34.8		31.6	
	1.4		1.9		2.2	All Other Current		1.9		1.9		1.7		2.9		3.8	
	76.0		75.7		76.7	Total Current		68.2		80.0		76.8		78.8		76.9	
	15.9		16.6		15.6	Fixed Assets (net)		20.5		14.0		14.9		13.1		17.4	
	1.3		1.2		1.5	Intangibles (net)		3.3		1.2		.5		1.5		.1	
	6.9		6.5		6.2	All Other Non-Current		8.0		4.8		7.8		6.5		5.6	
	100.0		100.0		100.0	Total		100.0		100.0		100.0		100.0		100.0	
						LIABILITIES											
	12.4		11.3		11.5	Notes Payable-Short Term		10.1		10.4		11.2		15.6		13.2	
	3.5		3.3		3.2	Cur. Mat.-L /T/D		4.7		3.3		2.5		2.2		2.7	
	21.5		20.1		18.9	Trade Payables		17.4		18.6		19.0		20.9		20.1	
	.7		1.4		.4	Income Taxes Payable		.2		.3		.3		.5		.6	
	10.3		10.2		11.7	All Other Current		12.5		10.2		13.2		10.6		14.8	
	48.4		46.3		45.8	Total Current		44.9		43.0		46.3		49.7		51.4	
	10.6		12.8		11.0	Long Term Debt		15.2		11.9		8.8		7.2		8.5	
	.2		.2		.3	Deferred Taxes		.2		.3		1.1		.1		.3	
	2.6		2.8		2.9	All Other-Non-Current		3.1		2.9		2.0		3.6		3.3	
	38.2		38.0		40.0	Net Worth		36.7		41.9		41.9		39.4		36.5	
	100.0		100.0		100.0	Total Liabilities & Net Worth		100.0		100.0		100.0		100.0		100.0	
						INCOME DATA											
	100.0		100.0		100.0	Net Sales		100.0		100.0		100.0		100.0		100.0	
	33.1		33.0		33.0	Gross Profit		39.1		31.6		33.3		29.1		31.8	
	30.7		30.5		30.6	Operating Expenses		36.0		28.8		31.9		27.7		29.9	
	2.3		2.5		2.4	Operating Profit		3.1		2.9		1.5		1.4		1.9	
	.6		.4		.3	All Other Expenses (net)		1.3		.2		-.3		.3		-.2	
	1.7		2.2		2.1	Profit Before Taxes		1.9		2.6		1.7		1.1		2.0	
						RATIOS											
	2.5		2.4		2.4			2.7		2.8		2.0		1.9		2.0	
	1.6		1.8		1.7	Current		1.6		1.9		1.6		1.6		1.4	
	1.2		1.3		1.3			1.1		1.5		1.4		1.3		1.1	
	1.2		1.2		1.3			1.2		1.5		1.2		1.1		1.1	
(262)	.8		.8		.8	Quick		.6		.9		.8		.9		.8	
	.4		.5		.5			.3		.6		.5		.6		.6	
14	27.0	17	21.8	15	24.2		6	61.3	16	23.2	19	19.7	26	14.1	10	36.6	
27	13.4	30	12.0	30	12.0	Sales/Receivables	19	19.5	31	11.9	31	11.8	34	10.7	44	8.3	
41	8.8	45	8.1	43	8.4		40	9.1	44	8.3	39	9.4	42	8.7	57	6.4	
30	12.0	32	11.4	23	15.7		22	16.4	22	16.4	27	13.7	21	17.7	24	15.2	
51	7.2	51	7.1	47	7.8	Cost of Sales/Inventory	41	8.9	46	7.9	53	7.6	48	7.6	41	8.9	
87	4.2	83	4.4	78	4.7		96	3.8	79	4.6	85	4.3	76	4.8	74	4.9	
17	21.5	16	22.8	13	28.6		9	40.2	11	34.0	12	29.3	17	21.3	16	23.0	
29	12.8	27	13.6	25	14.7	Cost of Sales/Payables	25	14.4	23	15.7	25	14.8	24	14.9	30	12.2	
45	8.2	42	8.7	39	9.3		41	9.0	39	9.3	39	9.4	37	9.9	44	8.3	
	7.4		7.0		7.0			6.7		6.6		6.9		8.8		10.2	
	12.7		11.6		12.4	Sales/Working Capital		14.0		9.8		12.8		13.0		13.7	
	28.5		23.7		23.6			61.0		20.9		20.9		23.5		58.0	
	7.1		6.3		8.3			9.2		8.7		10.6		6.6		6.4	
(236)	3.0	(256)	3.0	(245)	3.6	EBIT/Interest	(51)	4.2	(94)	3.2	(39)	4.5	(33)	4.2	(21)	3.8	
	1.2		1.3		1.7			.3		1.1		2.0		2.2		2.1	
	4.1		4.6		4.1	Net Profit + Depr., Dep.,				4.4		3.9		8.3		4.0	
(97)	1.5	(92)	2.0	(86)	1.6	Amort./Cur. Mat. L/T/D			(31)	1.4	(16)	1.5	(15)	2.3	(12)	2.0	
	.5		.7		.7					.3		.5		1.4		1.1	
	.1		.1		.1			.2		.1		.1		.2		.2	
	.3		.4		.3	Fixed/Worth		.4		.3		.3		.3		.3	
	.8		.8		.7			1.0		.6		.6		.5		.8	
	.8		.7		.7			.6		.7		.7		1.1		1.0	
	1.8		1.6		1.7	Debt/Worth		2.0		1.4		1.7		1.6		1.7	
	3.7		3.6		3.3			4.3		2.5		2.7		4.1		3.5	
	35.6		31.2		38.8	% Profit Before Taxes/Tangible		74.2		34.6		33.3		44.2		32.4	
(250)	13.2	(255)	13.7	(256)	16.7	Net Worth	(52)	25.1	(99)	16.7	(40)	14.2		22.8		15.6	
	2.0		1.8		5.1			6.3		1.6		3.8		7.3		10.2	
	11.2		11.4		14.9	% Profit Before Taxes/Total		19.5		16.7		14.9		11.2		9.7	
	5.4		5.0		5.9	Assets		9.4		5.3		4.6		7.5		6.1	
	.6		1.0		1.5			-1.0		.4		1.7		3.5		3.5	
	69.5		69.6		73.3			65.9		82.2		72.5		72.6		69.2	
	37.1		33.1		38.6	Sales/Net Fixed Assets		27.0		42.4		33.2		39.5		44.3	
	15.9		14.4		17.2			12.6		19.3		15.9		19.3		14.4	
	4.7		4.5		4.8			5.6		4.8		4.8		4.7		4.3	
	3.5		3.5		3.7	Sales/Total Assets		3.8		3.7		3.6		3.9		3.5	
	2.6		2.5		2.7			2.3		2.8		2.6		3.1		2.7	
	.5		.5		.4			.6		.4		.4		.5		.4	
(235)	.8	(251)	.8	(243)	.7	% Depr., Dep., Amort./Sales	(48)	1.0	(94)	.7	(40)	.6	(33)	.7	(21)	.6	
	1.3		1.2		1.1			1.4		1.2		.9		.9		1.1	
	2.7		2.9		2.3			5.9		2.4		2.3		1.4		1.2	
(141)	4.8	(150)	4.6	(157)	4.6	% Officers', Directors',	(32)	8.0	(59)	4.1	(33)	4.9	(19)	2.8	(12)	2.3	
	7.7		8.2		7.9	Owners' Comp/Sales		11.5		7.2		8.0		5.3		3.0	
	1130163M		1037410M		1181617M	Net Sales ($)		37780M		195755M		161111M		253985M		311271M	221715M
	368294M		321264M		357710M	Total Assets ($)		13330M		59136M		52733M		71984M		95161M	65366M

© Robert Morris Associates 1995   M = $ thousand   MM = $ million

See Pages 1 through 15 for Explanation of Ratios and Data

RETAILERS—FURNITURE. SIC# 5712

	Current Data Sorted By Assets							Comparative Historical Data	
	5	14	9	2	1		# Postretirement Benefits		
							Type of Statement		
	2	9	20	24	9	5	Unqualified	59	67
	10	53	51	5			Reviewed	169	154
	75	129	35	2			Compiled	272	241
	23	12	7				Tax Returns	6	15
	31	43	38	4	3	3	Other	113	98
	222 (4/1-9/30/94)			371 (10/1/94-3/31/95)				4/1/90-3/31/91	4/1/91-3/31/92
	0-500M	500M-2MM	2-10MM	10-50MM	50-100MM	100-250MM		ALL	ALL
	141	246	151	35	12	8	NUMBER OF STATEMENTS	619	575
	%	%	%	%	%	%	ASSETS	%	%
Cash & Equivalents	8.5	7.0	6.3	6.8	7.8			6.6	6.4
Trade Receivables - (net)	14.0	13.2	20.9	17.9	26.3			19.4	17.7
Inventory	57.8	55.7	46.1	41.1	31.7			51.8	51.6
All Other Current	.5	1.2	2.5	1.2	2.6			1.5	1.3
Total Current	80.7	77.2	75.8	67.0	68.4			79.3	77.0
Fixed Assets (net)	14.5	16.9	18.0	25.3	24.5			14.8	16.8
Intangibles (net)	1.7	1.0	.6	.4	2.0			1.0	.9
All Other Non-Current	3.2	4.9	5.5	7.3	5.1			4.9	5.3
Total	100.0	100.0	100.0	100.0	100.0			100.0	100.0
							LIABILITIES		
Notes Payable-Short Term	9.5	8.4	10.0	10.5	14.4			12.4	12.4
Cur. Mat. -L/T/D	4.0	2.6	2.4	2.5	1.7			3.8	3.6
Trade Payables	20.8	18.3	19.5	16.0	9.0			17.9	17.7
Income Taxes Payable	.2	.4	.6	.5	.0			.6	.5
All Other Current	15.7	15.3	14.0	14.6	11.7			12.0	12.1
Total Current	50.3	44.9	46.6	44.1	36.9			46.8	46.3
Long Term Debt	14.3	13.3	11.3	15.6	17.4			14.1	15.0
Deferred Taxes	.0	.2	.4	.1	.3			.2	.2
All Other-Non-Current	3.8	3.2	4.0	1.5	3.0			3.5	2.8
Net Worth	31.6	38.3	37.6	38.7	42.5			35.4	35.7
Total Liabilities & Net Worth	100.0	100.0	100.0	100.0	100.0			100.0	100.0
							INCOME DATA		
Net Sales	100.0	100.0	100.0	100.0	100.0			100.0	100.0
Gross Profit	40.6	39.4	38.4	41.1	36.6			40.2	39.9
Operating Expenses	37.6	36.6	36.0	36.5	36.1			38.1	37.8
Operating Profit	3.0	2.7	2.4	4.6	.5			2.1	2.2
All Other Expenses (net)	.7	.2	.2	.8	-3.3			.7	.7
Profit Before Taxes	2.4	2.5	2.1	3.7	3.8			1.4	1.5
							RATIOS		
Current	2.7	3.0	2.2	2.6	3.0			2.7	2.6
	1.8	1.7	1.5	1.4	1.8			1.8	1.7
	1.2	1.2	1.3	1.1	1.3			1.3	1.2
Quick	.9	.9	1.2	1.0	1.8			1.0	.9
	.4	(245) .3	.4	.3	1.0			(617) .5	(574) .4
	.2	.1	.2	.2	.4			.2	.2
Sales/Receivables	0 UND	2 157.5	3 129.5	3 109.7	4 100.3			3 129.5	2 151.6
	8 44.8	9 38.7	15 24.7	8 46.3	72 5.1			16 22.2	14 25.4
	25 14.6	27 13.4	55 6.6	42 8.7	126 2.9			42 8.6	40 9.1
Cost of Sales/Inventory	63 5.8	87 4.2	79 4.6	85 4.3	114 3.2			89 4.1	81 4.5
	111 3.3	130 2.8	114 3.2	107 3.4	122 3.0			130 2.8	126 2.9
	166 2.2	174 2.1	159 2.3	174 2.1	146 2.5			174 2.1	192 1.9
Cost of Sales/Payables	17 21.4	21 17.2	29 12.7	21 17.1	25 14.6			22 16.6	21 17.3
	33 11.0	37 9.9	41 8.8	40 9.1	34 10.7			38 9.7	37 9.9
	51 7.2	53 6.9	60 6.1	69 5.3	46 8.0			59 6.2	55 6.6
Sales/Working Capital	5.1	4.3	5.0	3.5	2.1			4.3	4.3
	10.0	8.1	10.2	9.9	4.9			8.3	8.5
	28.4	26.8	20.3	47.0	13.4			20.0	24.0
EBIT/Interest	(120) 10.0	6.9	8.8	9.5	5.3			(551) 4.9	(537) 3.6
	2.9	(213) 3.1	(137) 2.9	(32) 4.6	2.8			1.9	1.8
	.8	1.6	1.3	1.8	1.8			.8	.8
Net Profit + Depr., Dep., Amort./Cur. Mat. L /T/D	(31) 3.2	3.2	6.7	30.8				(273) 4.1	(230) 3.6
	1.4	(91) 1.7	(54) 2.2	(14) 8.5				1.5	1.5
	.6	.7	.9	2.6				.2	.2
Fixed/Worth	.1	.2	.2	.3	.3			.1	.2
	.3	.3	.4	.8	.6			.3	.4
	1.6	1.0	.9	1.2	1.1			.9	1.1
Debt/Worth	.9	.8	1.0	1.0	.7			.8	.8
	1.9	1.6	1.9	1.7	1.6			1.9	1.9
	7.4	4.2	2.9	3.4	2.8			4.7	4.3
% Profit Before Taxes/Tangible Net Worth	(120) 57.2	29.6	30.9	37.0	29.3			(567) 24.9	(534) 23.7
	17.3	(227) 13.5	(146) 14.7	(34) 19.7	16.6			9.3	8.1
	1.1	4.5	3.6	7.4	3.5			.2	.3
% Profit Before Taxes/Total Assets	16.0	10.5	10.9	14.3	9.2			9.0	8.2
	6.3	4.7	5.2	7.5	5.4			3.2	2.8
	-1.0	1.5	1.3	2.1	1.9			-.7	-.6
Sales/Net Fixed Assets	84.5	57.2	33.5	19.5	11.0			53.6	45.2
	30.4	25.5	19.0	9.7	6.8			26.5	22.3
	14.4	11.3	10.2	6.5	4.6			12.1	10.0
Sales/Total Assets	4.5	3.3	3.3	3.0	2.3			3.3	3.3
	3.3	2.6	2.6	2.1	1.4			2.5	2.5
	2.3	1.9	1.6	1.4	1.1			1.7	1.7
% Depr., Dep., Amort./Sales	(112) .4	.5	.6	.8	1.1			(553) .6	(524) .6
	1.0	(220) .8	(143) .9	(33) 1.2	(10) 1.6			.9	1.0
	1.8	1.3	1.3	1.9	2.2			1.5	1.5
% Officers', Directors', Owners' Comp/Sales	(83) 3.1	2.4	1.8					(306) 2.7	(291) 2.7
	4.6	(129) 4.3	(76) 2.7					4.8	4.5
	6.9	6.4	5.6					7.5	6.8
Net Sales ($)	140460M	728179M	1539433M	1774687M	1240364M	1761161M		4402965M	5608844M
Total Assets ($)	40820M	267685M	583919M	838740M	779067M	1240901M		2444149M	3213247M

© Robert Morris Associates 1995

M = $ thousand   MM = $ million
See Pages 1 through 15 for Explanation of Ratios and Data

Comparative Historical Data | Current Data Sorted By Sales

8	14	31	# Postretirement Benefits	3	12	4	7	2	3
			Type of Statement						
65	55	69	Unqualified	1	8	3	11	9	37
130	145	119	Reviewed	7	35	13	37	23	4
251	258	241	Compiled	56	106	47	20	11	1
27	32	42	Tax Returns	12	18	5	5	2	
119	131	122	Other	21	33	22	24	9	13
4/1/92-3/31/93	4/1/93-3/31/94	4/1/94-3/31/95		222 (4/1-9/30/94)			371 (10/1/94-3/31/95)		
ALL	ALL	ALL		0-1MM	1-3MM	3-5MM	5-10MM	10-25MM	25MM & OVER
592	621	593	**NUMBER OF STATEMENTS**	97	200	90	97	54	55
%	%	%	**ASSETS**	%	%	%	%	%	%
6.7	6.9	7.2	Cash & Equivalents	7.7	7.5	7.0	6.4	6.6	7.2
18.8	19.0	16.1	Trade Receivables - (net)	16.3	14.6	15.0	17.8	16.6	19.7
50.5	48.9	52.0	Inventory	53.9	53.4	57.0	50.2	49.0	41.2
1.1	1.1	1.4	All Other Current	.4	1.1	1.0	2.4	3.3	1.5
77.1	75.9	76.7	Total Current	78.3	76.7	80.0	76.8	75.6	69.7
16.4	17.5	17.4	Fixed Assets (net)	17.1	17.8	14.0	16.8	17.1	23.5
1.1	1.0	1.0	Intangibles (net)	1.7	1.1	.9	.8	.5	.7
5.4	5.5	4.9	All Other Non-Current	2.8	4.4	5.1	5.7	6.8	6.1
100.0	100.0	100.0	Total	100.0	100.0	100.0	100.0	100.0	100.0
			LIABILITIES						
10.1	10.0	9.2	Notes Payable-Short Term	11.9	7.6	9.3	9.5	9.8	9.0
3.1	3.3	2.9	Cur. Mat.-L /T/D	4.2	2.7	2.6	2.7	2.5	1.9
18.8	17.5	18.7	Trade Payables	16.2	18.3	19.3	21.3	22.0	16.1
.4	1.5	.4	Income Taxes Payable	.3	.3	.3	.6	.8	.3
13.2	13.4	14.9	All Other Current	15.1	13.0	17.3	15.3	15.4	16.3
45.5	45.6	46.1	Total Current	47.7	41.9	48.8	49.4	50.5	43.7
14.3	13.4	13.4	Long Term Debt	18.1	13.8	11.7	10.9	8.9	15.4
.2	.2	.2	Deferred Taxes	.0	.1	.4	.5	.3	.1
3.2	4.2	3.4	All Other-Non-Current	4.2	2.6	4.4	3.9	3.1	2.8
36.8	36.6	36.9	Net Worth	29.9	41.6	34.7	35.3	37.3	37.9
100.0	100.0	100.0	Total Liabilities & Net Worth	100.0	100.0	100.0	100.0	100.0	100.0
			INCOME DATA						
100.0	100.0	100.0	Net Sales	100.0	100.0	100.0	100.0	100.0	100.0
39.6	39.4	39.4	Gross Profit	42.5	39.3	39.3	37.8	37.3	39.5
37.3	36.8	36.6	Operating Expenses	38.8	35.9	36.9	37.0	34.5	36.0
2.3	2.6	2.8	Operating Profit	3.7	3.4	2.4	.9	2.8	3.6
.5	.3	.3	All Other Expenses (net)	1.2	.3	.3	.1	.1	-.6
1.9	2.3	2.5	Profit Before Taxes	2.6	3.1	2.1	.8	2.7	4.1
			RATIOS						
2.8	2.7	2.7	Current	3.2	3.0	2.6	2.0	1.9	2.8
1.8	1.7	1.7		1.9	2.0	1.6	1.5	1.5	1.6
1.3	1.3	1.2		1.2	1.3	1.2	1.2	1.2	1.2
1.0	1.1	1.0	Quick	1.0	1.1	.9	.8	.9	1.4
(589) .5	(617) .5	(592) .4		.4	.4	.3	.4	(53) .3	.7
.2	.2	.2		.2	.2	.1	.1	.1	.1
3 131.1	3 140.2	2 181.1	Sales/Receivables	0 834.0	2 177.8	2 166.5	3 117.7	2 214.9	3 125.7
15 24.6	14 26.0	10 36.5		12 29.9	11 32.5	9 39.5	13 27.3	7 53.9	7 53.1
42 8.6	43 8.4	36 10.2		36 10.1	31 11.9	29 12.8	43 8.4	37 9.8	89 4.1
83 4.4	76 4.8	79 4.6	Cost of Sales/Inventory	81 4.5	85 4.3	101 3.6	74 4.9	54 6.7	78 4.7
122 3.0	122 3.0	118 3.1		135 2.7	122 3.0	130 2.8	114 3.2	96 3.8	114 3.2
183 2.0	166 2.2	166 2.2		203 1.8	174 2.1	174 2.1	152 2.4	130 2.8	146 2.5
22 16.6	19 18.9	22 16.8	Cost of Sales/Payables	20 18.6	19 19.1	23 16.1	25 14.4	22 16.7	24 15.5
38 9.7	35 10.5	38 9.6		34 10.7	35 10.3	39 9.4	41 9.0	35 10.3	38 9.5
59 6.2	59 6.2	55 6.6		56 6.5	54 6.7	51 7.2	58 6.3	62 5.9	54 6.7
4.0	4.4	4.5	Sales/Working Capital	3.4	4.2	5.5	5.8	8.7	3.3
7.2	8.8	8.9		6.8	7.1	10.2	11.5	14.7	8.4
22.4	22.5	23.0		23.2	17.1	27.1	24.0	27.9	43.4
5.3	8.3	7.9	EBIT/Interest	7.2	9.1	7.0	4.8	10.0	10.0
(531) 2.3	(563) 3.1	(522) 3.1		(79) 2.0	(177) 3.4	(82) 3.2	(83) 2.5	(51) 5.6	(50) 4.2
1.2	1.3	1.4		.1	1.6	1.3	1.2	2.5	2.0
4.9	4.7	5.1	Net Profit + Depr., Dep., Amort./Cur. Mat. L/T/D	2.0	3.9	2.3	6.8	7.4	33.5
(218) 2.0	(208) 1.6	(199) 2.0		(18) .9	(69) 1.9	(34) 1.5	(35) 1.7	(20) 2.6	(23) 9.9
.6	.7	.8		-.4	.7	.8	1.0	.6	5.8
.1	.2	.2	Fixed/Worth	.1	.1	.2	.2	.2	.3
.4	.4	.4		.5	.3	.4	.4	.4	.6
1.0	1.1	1.0		2.9	.9	1.0	1.0	.8	1.2
.8	.8	.9	Debt/Worth	.9	.6	.9	.9	1.0	.8
1.7	1.8	1.8		2.1	1.4	2.3	1.9	2.0	1.7
4.0	4.1	3.7		14.9	3.3	4.7	3.4	2.8	3.4
26.6	36.0	34.3	% Profit Before Taxes/Tangible Net Worth	47.0	33.2	29.6	29.0	45.6	34.9
(546) 11.2	(575) 15.7	(547) 14.9		(80) 12.2	(185) 15.0	(81) 11.4	(95) 12.3	(52) 19.1	(54) 22.6
2.4	4.6	4.3		-3.8	5.3	3.9	2.7	7.2	10.1
8.9	12.2	11.8	% Profit Before Taxes/Total Assets	15.4	13.1	10.2	7.8	14.5	12.5
3.9	4.9	5.4		3.9	5.6	4.1	4.5	7.2	8.2
.5	1.3	1.0		-4.1	1.8	.8	1.1	3.1	3.5
51.1	49.6	45.3	Sales/Net Fixed Assets	70.8	42.5	66.3	45.2	43.3	14.5
24.1	22.7	22.0		21.9	23.2	24.5	26.8	22.7	8.9
10.4	10.0	10.1		9.6	10.0	13.5	11.5	14.7	6.4
3.4	3.5	3.5	Sales/Total Assets	3.5	3.4	3.6	3.6	4.1	3.3
2.5	2.6	2.7		2.4	2.6	2.7	2.9	3.1	2.3
1.7	1.8	1.8		1.5	1.8	2.0	2.0	2.5	1.4
.6	.6	.5	% Depr., Dep., Amort./Sales	.5	.5	.6	.5	.5	.8
(538) .9	(569) .9	(525) .9		(73) 1.2	(182) .9	(79) .8	(90) .9	(51) .8	(50) 1.3
1.4	1.4	1.4		2.0	1.4	1.2	1.2	1.0	2.0
2.6	2.5	2.3	% Officers', Directors', Owners' Comp/Sales	3.3	3.0	2.0	1.8	1.2	
(287) 4.4	(277) 4.1	(295) 4.0		(52) 5.1	(109) 4.4	(47) 4.0	(49) 2.7	(30) 2.4	
7.3	7.4	6.4		8.0	6.6	6.0	4.7	4.9	
6129816M	6813492M	7184284M	Net Sales ($)	58456M	366802M	345636M	681605M	821814M	4909971M
3341580M	3591163M	3751132M	Total Assets ($)	29903M	180500M	138704M	287789M	328019M	2786217M

M = $ thousand   MM = $ million
See Pages 1 through 15 for Explanation of Ratios and Data

Current Data Sorted By Assets / # Postretirement Benefits / Comparative Historical Data

	1	3		1	2		Type of Statement	11	13
	1	3	4	1	2	4	Unqualified	11	13
	4	13	13	1			Reviewed	22	24
	20	26	6	1		1	Compiled	77	73
	5	3					Tax Returns	2	5
	13	7	6	1			Other	38	33

	0-500M	500M-2MM	2-10MM	10-50MM	50-100MM	100-250MM		4/1/90-3/31/91 ALL	4/1/91-3/31/92 ALL
	\[50 (4/1-9/30/94)\]			\[85 (10/1/94-3/31/95)\]					
NUMBER OF STATEMENTS	43	52	29	4	2	5		150	148
	%	%	%	%	%	%	**ASSETS**	%	%
	8.7	8.5	7.8				Cash & Equivalents	8.2	8.1
	13.3	19.0	23.5				Trade Receivables - (net)	14.9	14.6
	51.5	48.6	43.1				Inventory	50.5	50.7
	1.0	1.7	1.4				All Other Current	1.9	1.6
	74.5	77.8	75.7				Total Current	75.5	75.0
	18.9	16.3	17.4				Fixed Assets (net)	18.6	19.3
	3.2	1.4	2.8				Intangibles (net)	1.6	1.3
	3.4	4.4	4.1				All Other Non-Current	4.3	4.3
	100.0	100.0	100.0				Total	100.0	100.0
							LIABILITIES		
	16.4	16.3	22.6				Notes Payable-Short Term	20.8	17.0
	2.6	3.2	1.6				Cur. Mat. -L/T/D	3.1	3.8
	20.5	21.4	17.3				Trade Payables	20.3	25.0
	.3	.6	.4				Income Taxes Payable	.5	.2
	11.9	8.5	11.3				All Other Current	8.7	9.4
	51.6	49.8	53.3				Total Current	53.4	55.4
	19.6	9.5	8.1				Long Term Debt	14.5	14.6
	.1	.1	.1				Deferred Taxes	.2	.1
	4.5	3.9	1.0				All Other-Non-Current	3.4	2.1
	24.3	36.6	37.5				Net Worth	28.5	27.8
	100.0	100.0	100.0				Total Liabilities & Net Worth	100.0	100.0
							INCOME DATA		
	100.0	100.0	100.0				Net Sales	100.0	100.0
	32.5	30.8	30.8				Gross Profit	31.2	30.8
	29.3	29.0	27.5				Operating Expenses	28.6	29.1
	3.2	1.8	3.3				Operating Profit	2.6	1.7
	.8	.0	–.3				All Other Expenses (net)	.6	.6
	2.4	1.9	3.6				Profit Before Taxes	2.0	1.2
							RATIOS		
	2.6	1.9	2.0				Current	2.1	2.0
	1.6	1.6	1.4					1.4	1.4
	1.0	1.3	1.1					1.1	1.1
	.8	.9	1.0				Quick	.8	.6
	.4	.4	.7				(147)	.4	.4
	.2	.3	.3					.2	.2
	3 108.8	9 40.4	10 35.1				Sales/Receivables	8 45.9	5 71.0
	9 39.7	17 22.0	22 16.7					16 22.5	14 27.0
	19 19.0	31 11.6	51 7.1					28 12.9	25 14.8
	47 7.7	60 6.1	62 5.9				Cost of Sales/Inventory	69 5.3	63 5.8
	81 4.5	83 4.4	79 4.6					96 3.8	87 4.2
	122 3.0	111 3.3	94 3.9					140 2.6	122 3.0
	6 58.8	16 23.4	16 22.3				Cost of Sales/Payables	13 28.2	16 22.8
	18 20.3	30 12.0	27 13.7					32 11.3	36 10.1
	52 7.0	56 6.5	59 6.2					59 6.2	62 5.9
	6.9	6.5	6.3				Sales/Working Capital	5.7	7.6
	20.1	12.5	10.2					12.1	13.9
	–229.0	20.0	43.2					47.5	68.9
(34)	7.0	(51) 6.5	(26) 5.9				EBIT/Interest	(126) 4.0	(133) 3.1
	3.3	2.9	4.0					2.0	1.7
	1.1	1.6	1.8					.8	.9
		(14) 3.1	(10) 4.4				Net Profit + Depr., Dep., Amort./Cur. Mat. L /T/D	(51) 3.3	(57) 3.5
		1.8	3.4					1.8	1.4
		.4	1.7					.2	.0
	.3	.2	.3				Fixed/Worth	.2	.3
	.7	.4	.4					.6	.6
	6.5	.7	.9					1.9	1.9
	1.0	1.1	1.0				Debt/Worth	1.2	1.2
	3.8	2.1	2.3					3.0	2.7
	68.8	3.5	4.4					7.6	7.4
(34)	32.5	(50) 23.2	(28) 44.3				% Profit Before Taxes/Tangible Net Worth	(129) 29.3	(128) 24.6
	11.4	13.1	17.2					11.6	9.4
	1.1	5.9	8.7					.0	.3
	17.1	8.9	12.1				% Profit Before Taxes/Total Assets	8.4	7.1
	7.8	4.6	7.1					3.3	2.8
	.7	1.7	2.2					–1.1	–.8
	68.5	59.4	56.3				Sales/Net Fixed Assets	64.6	48.6
	29.9	28.9	24.3					22.9	24.8
	14.6	17.0	8.0					9.3	10.7
	4.4	4.2	3.8				Sales/Total Assets	3.5	3.7
	3.4	3.4	3.1					2.7	3.0
	2.5	2.1	1.7					2.0	2.3
(34)	.8	(47) .5	(27) .4				% Depr., Dep., Amort./Sales	(125) .6	(130) .6
	1.2	.9	.9					1.0	1.0
	2.2	1.6	1.6					1.7	1.7
(17)	2.8	(24) 2.3	(17) 1.3				% Officers', Directors', Owners' Comp/Sales	(60) 1.8	(70) 2.2
	3.4	3.9	1.8					3.6	3.7
	4.6	6.4	4.4					8.6	6.1
	37383M	171079M	406130M	314551M	218358M	1566218M	Net Sales ($)	1201858M	1446624M
	10814M	54009M	128860M	101511M	121912M	716974M	Total Assets ($)	532814M	533440M

M = $ thousand   MM = $ million
See Pages 1 through 15 for Explanation of Ratios and Data

Comparative Historical Data				Current Data Sorted By Sales					
			# Postretirement Benefits	1		1	2		2
			Type of Statement						
9	14	15	Unqualified	1		4		1	9
18	30	31	Reviewed	2	8	6	7	7	1
69	62	54	Compiled	12	24	7	5	4	2
7	6	8	Tax Returns	4	2	1	1		
19	21	27	Other	10	8	2	4	1	2
4/1/92-3/31/93 ALL	4/1/93-3/31/94 ALL	4/1/94-3/31/95 ALL		50 (4/1-9/30/94)			85 (10/1/94-3/31/95)		
				0-1MM	1-3MM	3-5MM	5-10MM	10-25MM	25MM & OVER
122	133	135	**NUMBER OF STATEMENTS**	29	42	20	17	13	14
%	%	%	**ASSETS**	%	%	%	%	%	%
8.3	9.2	8.1	Cash & Equivalents	10.2	7.8	6.9	9.3	7.5	5.5
16.4	16.7	17.9	Trade Receivables - (net)	13.1	16.7	23.6	21.2	22.8	14.8
49.0	48.9	48.3	Inventory	50.8	48.4	44.7	46.6	47.8	50.5
1.5	1.5	1.5	All Other Current	1.1	1.0	3.2	.3	1.7	2.6
75.2	76.2	75.7	Total Current	75.1	73.9	78.3	77.4	79.7	73.3
17.9	17.4	17.8	Fixed Assets (net)	18.4	20.2	15.7	14.7	13.4	19.9
1.2	1.9	2.4	Intangibles (net)	4.0	1.4	2.1	3.3	1.2	2.2
5.6	4.4	4.1	All Other Non-Current	2.5	4.4	3.9	4.7	5.7	4.6
100.0	100.0	100.0	Total	100.0	100.0	100.0	100.0	100.0	100.0
			LIABILITIES						
19.8	17.5	16.8	Notes Payable-Short Term	17.0	17.9	19.9	11.0	22.7	9.9
3.2	2.9	2.5	Cur. Mat.-L/T/D	3.1	2.5	3.3	2.1	1.7	1.4
20.3	19.4	20.1	Trade Payables	21.8	16.9	17.5	29.2	17.6	20.9
.7	1.6	.5	Income Taxes Payable	.3	.5	.4	.4	.6	.6
9.3	12.1	10.5	All Other Current	8.1	11.9	8.1	10.5	12.6	12.2
53.3	53.5	50.3	Total Current	50.4	49.7	49.4	53.1	55.2	45.1
10.9	12.0	13.3	Long Term Debt	22.5	11.2	10.1	8.9	7.2	16.2
.4	.1	.1	Deferred Taxes	.0	.2	.1	.2	.0	.3
2.7	5.0	3.5	All Other-Non-Current	6.0	1.9	5.5	2.3	1.3	4.0
32.7	29.4	32.8	Net Worth	21.2	37.0	34.9	35.5	36.3	34.4
100.0	100.0	100.0	Total Liabilities & Net Worth	100.0	100.0	100.0	100.0	100.0	100.0
			INCOME DATA						
100.0	100.0	100.0	Net Sales	100.0	100.0	100.0	100.0	100.0	100.0
32.0	30.5	31.0	Gross Profit	31.8	34.5	33.3	26.2	27.2	25.3
29.5	28.7	28.3	Operating Expenses	27.6	32.6	30.7	24.5	24.6	21.6
2.6	1.8	2.7	Operating Profit	4.2	1.9	2.6	1.7	2.7	3.7
.4	.3	.2	All Other Expenses (net)	.9	.1	–.4	–.1	.0	.4
2.2	1.5	2.5	Profit Before Taxes	3.3	1.8	3.1	1.8	2.7	3.3
			RATIOS						
2.4 / 1.5 / 1.1	2.1 / 1.4 / 1.1	2.2 / 1.6 / 1.2	Current	2.8 / 1.6 / 1.0	2.1 / 1.6 / 1.2	2.3 / 1.8 / 1.3	1.6 / 1.4 / 1.2	2.2 / 1.3 / 1.1	2.5 / 1.6 / 1.2
(121) .8 / .4 / .2	.9 / .5 / .2	.9 / .4 / .2	Quick	.8 / .4 / .2	.7 / .5 / .3	1.0 / .7 / .3	1.1 / .5 / .3	.9 / .4 / .2	.8 / .3 / .2
4 87.8 / 12 29.9 / 26 13.8	6 65.5 / 12 29.9 / 29 12.7	7 54.2 / 14 26.6 / 31 11.9	Sales/Receivables	4 90.7 / 10 37.1 / 22 16.9	8 47.0 / 14 25.7 / 21 17.3	9 39.8 / 28 13.2 / 50 7.3	7 49.4 / 17 21.5 / 30 12.0	8 44.7 / 13 28.4 / 45 8.1	2 182.7 / 12 31.2 / 33 10.9
54 6.8 / 89 4.1 / 126 2.9	55 6.6 / 81 4.5 / 111 3.3	61 6.0 / 81 4.5 / 107 3.4	Cost of Sales/Inventory	52 7.0 / 101 3.6 / 135 2.7	58 6.3 / 83 4.4 / 122 3.0	73 5.0 / 89 4.1 / 107 3.4	41 8.9 / 65 5.6 / 91 4.0	58 6.3 / 74 4.9 / 87 4.2	63 5.8 / 76 4.8 / 146 2.5
13 28.4 / 27 13.3 / 51 7.1	9 39.5 / 26 14.1 / 54 6.8	15 25.0 / 29 12.7 / 56 6.5	Cost of Sales/Payables	6 65.8 / 28 12.9 / 66 5.5	12 29.4 / 30 12.0 / 50 7.3	11 33.0 / 28 13.0 / 66 5.5	25 14.7 / 35 10.3 / 62 5.9	8 47.0 / 23 15.7 / 42 8.6	22 16.9 / 26 14.2 / 49 7.4
7.3 / 13.8 / 55.4	7.2 / 13.1 / 38.9	6.4 / 12.4 / 37.8	Sales/Working Capital	4.7 / 16.5 / -312.8	6.8 / 11.7 / 25.0	4.8 / 7.6 / 19.5	9.4 / 15.3 / 39.6	7.1 / 13.6 / 137.5	4.9 / 12.5 / 28.4
(112) 6.5 / 2.3 / 1.1	(121) 6.1 / 2.6 / 1.3	(121) 7.1 / 3.3 / 1.6	EBIT/Interest	(23) 7.2 / 3.6 / 1.6	(39) 6.3 / 2.8 / 1.4	(19) 6.5 / 2.4 / 1.2	(11) 4.9 / 4.2 / 2.2	(12) 8.5 / 3.3 / 1.8	11.6 / 6.5 / 2.5
(27) 3.9 / 1.2 / .6	(40) 5.2 / 1.6 / .5	(35) 4.4 / 2.5 / .8	Net Profit + Depr., Dep., Amort./Cur. Mat. L/T/D						
.2 / .4 / 1.2	.2 / .5 / 1.8	.2 / .5 / 1.0	Fixed/Worth	.3 / .7 / -9.6	.2 / .4 / .9	.2 / .4 / .9	.2 / .5 / .8	.2 / .3 / .9	.3 / .5 / 1.0
1.0 / 2.2 / 6.9	1.0 / 2.4 / 6.4	1.0 / 2.5 / 4.8	Debt/Worth	1.4 / 3.7 / -39.3	.8 / 1.9 / 3.7	1.0 / 3.0 / 4.3	1.2 / 2.8 / 4.2	.7 / 2.0 / 6.0	1.3 / 2.6 / 4.1
(110) 33.8 / 9.5 / 1.6	(117) 29.0 / 14.3 / 3.8	(123) 27.9 / 14.4 / 6.3	% Profit Before Taxes/Tangible Net Worth	(21) 81.8 / 20.8 / 1.6	(41) 21.9 / 10.7 / 6.8	(19) 30.5 / 19.6 / 3.6	(16) 23.9 / 13.9 / 7.3	(12) 26.7 / 15.3 / 9.4	57.8 / 24.9 / 14.5
11.0 / 3.5 / .4	10.0 / 4.0 / 1.1	12.4 / 5.8 / 1.9	% Profit Before Taxes/Total Assets	23.3 / 13.2 / 1.7	7.9 / 4.8 / 1.6	11.4 / 4.3 / .8	10.7 / 4.7 / 2.5	13.9 / 6.3 / 1.6	20.5 / 9.4 / 3.3
54.0 / 28.0 / 12.4	58.7 / 28.1 / 11.9	53.9 / 27.5 / 12.0	Sales/Net Fixed Assets	69.3 / 29.9 / 15.0	60.1 / 25.2 / 10.3	39.8 / 24.3 / 10.6	49.0 / 36.1 / 19.5	72.2 / 45.3 / 12.1	37.9 / 18.1 / 10.0
4.0 / 3.2 / 2.3	3.9 / 3.1 / 2.3	4.2 / 3.2 / 2.2	Sales/Total Assets	3.8 / 2.8 / 2.2	4.3 / 3.5 / 2.0	3.7 / 2.7 / 1.7	4.9 / 3.9 / 3.0	3.8 / 3.5 / 2.5	4.5 / 3.0 / 2.0
(109) .5 / .9 / 1.4	(116) .5 / .8 / 1.6	(118) .6 / 1.0 / 1.6	% Depr., Dep., Amort./Sales	(22) 1.0 / 1.3 / 2.4	(38) .6 / 1.0 / 1.9	(18) .5 / .9 / 1.5	(15) .5 / .9 / 1.2	(12) .4 / .7 / 1.2	(13) .4 / .7 / 1.6
(59) 2.0 / 3.5 / 5.3	(64) 1.8 / 3.6 / 7.4	(60) 1.7 / 3.0 / 4.7	% Officers', Directors', Owners' Comp/Sales		(19) 2.8 / 3.8 / 5.0	(12) 2.1 / 2.4 / 5.5			
1112857M / 444845M	2242680M / 877230M	2713719M / 1134080M	Net Sales ($) / Total Assets ($)	18267M / 7033M	72296M / 27813M	78624M / 34225M	110976M / 33850M	212265M / 75798M	2221291M / 955361M

M = $ thousand   MM = $ million
See Pages 1 through 15 for Explanation of Ratios and Data

	Current Data Sorted By Assets							Comparative Historical Data	
# Postretirement Benefits	3	3	3	2		1			
Type of Statement									
Unqualified	3	1	6	9	4	2		15	11
Reviewed	4	9	9	1				27	33
Compiled	42	17	7					66	65
Tax Returns	9	2	1	1				7	6
Other	20	14	4	3		4		47	26
	52 (4/1-9/30/94)			120 (10/1/94-3/31/95)				4/1/90-3/31/91	4/1/91-3/31/92
	0-500M	500M-2MM	2-10MM	10-50MM	50-100MM	100-250MM		ALL	ALL
NUMBER OF STATEMENTS	78	43	27	14	4	6		162	141
	%	%	%	%	%	%	**ASSETS**	%	%
Cash & Equivalents	8.2	7.5	3.8	7.2				6.8	7.9
Trade Receivables - (net)	13.2	14.4	15.7	22.9				14.7	11.7
Inventory	53.0	56.0	42.3	40.1				53.1	53.1
All Other Current	.8	.7	1.3	2.2				1.9	.7
Total Current	75.2	78.5	63.1	72.3				76.4	73.5
Fixed Assets (net)	18.2	16.3	27.8	19.5				16.5	18.0
Intangibles (net)	1.7	1.5	.6	5.0				2.3	2.5
All Other Non-Current	4.9	3.6	8.5	3.2				4.8	6.1
Total	100.0	100.0	100.0	100.0				100.0	100.0
							LIABILITIES		
Notes Payable-Short Term	9.9	8.5	14.7	5.7				11.6	10.6
Cur. Mat. -L/T/D	4.7	2.0	1.7	1.5				3.8	3.9
Trade Payables	21.0	19.9	16.5	16.8				20.1	15.9
Income Taxes Payable	.6	.3	.8	.1				.7	.6
All Other Current	10.8	12.1	6.8	7.0				9.3	10.0
Total Current	47.0	42.8	40.6	31.1				45.5	41.0
Long Term Debt	17.3	10.9	16.3	16.7				15.5	17.7
Deferred Taxes	.0	.0	.0	.1				.3	.1
All Other-Non-Current	2.3	3.3	5.3	1.6				2.5	4.3
Net Worth	33.4	43.0	37.8	50.5				36.3	36.8
Total Liabilities & Net Worth	100.0	100.0	100.0	100.0				100.0	100.0
							INCOME DATA		
Net Sales	100.0	100.0	100.0	100.0				100.0	100.0
Gross Profit	39.2	39.6	41.6	40.7				40.0	42.7
Operating Expenses	34.8	36.1	35.6	33.4				37.2	39.9
Operating Profit	4.4	3.5	6.0	7.3				2.8	2.9
All Other Expenses (net)	.8	.7	1.1	1.0				1.1	1.1
Profit Before Taxes	3.6	2.8	5.0	6.4				1.7	1.7
							RATIOS		
Current	3.1	2.4	1.9	3.8				2.7	3.0
	1.6	1.9	1.5	3.0				1.7	1.8
	1.2	1.5	1.2	1.4				1.3	1.4
Quick	.8	.9	.8	2.0				.8	.9
(76)	.5	.5	.4	.9				.4	.5
	.2	.2	.2	.4				.2	.2
Sales/Receivables	0 UND	0 UND	3 126.5	0 UND				1 334.0	0 877.3
	10 37.4	14 26.4	21 17.4	5 66.9				13 28.2	8 47.0
	24 14.9	33 11.2	52 7.0	56 6.5				33 10.9	28 13.1
Cost of Sales/Inventory	54 6.8	85 4.3	99 3.7	51 7.1				85 4.3	101 3.6
	107 3.4	122 3.0	122 3.0	87 4.2				130 2.8	146 2.5
	166 2.2	174 2.1	146 2.5	166 2.2				192 1.9	192 1.9
Cost of Sales/Payables	15 24.0	21 17.2	29 12.7	16 23.5				21 17.6	19 19.7
	34 10.6	44 8.3	47 7.7	41 8.9				36 10.1	32 11.5
	70 5.2	57 6.4	78 4.7	70 5.2				66 5.5	55 6.6
Sales/Working Capital	5.6	5.7	6.0	3.3				4.9	4.9
	10.0	7.3	9.8	4.9				8.5	7.3
	31.7	14.8	28.6	NM				19.3	14.3
EBIT/Interest	12.2	8.1	14.7	11.4				5.6	4.9
(64) (41) (26) (12) [(144) (126)]	4.4	3.5	3.6	6.4				2.2	2.2
	1.8	1.5	2.2	.9				.8	.9
Net Profit + Depr., Dep., Amort./Cur. Mat. L/T/D	3.8							3.9	4.3
(12) [(77) (57)]	1.4							1.7	1.5
	.1							.3	.6
Fixed/Worth	.1	.2	.3	.3				.1	.2
	.5	.3	.4	.6				.4	.5
	3.4	.6	1.6	1.0				.9	1.3
Debt/Worth	.9	.8	.9	.5				.8	.8
	1.6	1.3	1.6	1.3				1.8	1.7
	8.6	2.1	5.0	2.8				4.1	6.2
% Profit Before Taxes/Tangible Net Worth	61.3	37.5	49.8	50.0				32.8	35.2
(65) (42) (26) [(145) (121)]	26.3	13.2	28.6	28.3				11.4	13.3
	8.1	2.8	7.0	4.0				.2	3.6
% Profit Before Taxes/Total Assets	21.5	14.2	18.3	27.7				10.9	11.2
	11.7	5.2	9.1	10.5				4.4	4.3
	2.0	1.2	2.4	1.4				-.6	-.3
Sales/Net Fixed Assets	71.9	47.8	29.6	21.5				50.8	43.6
	38.7	26.7	11.7	12.8				25.5	20.7
	12.1	11.8	5.8	8.6				12.6	8.3
Sales/Total Assets	4.2	3.7	3.0	2.9				3.5	3.3
	3.1	3.0	1.9	2.3				2.6	2.5
	2.3	2.0	1.2	1.8				1.9	1.9
% Depr., Dep., Amort./Sales	.5	.6	.8	.6				.7	.7
(57) (38) (25) (12) [(146) (128)]	1.1	1.0	1.3	1.0				1.2	1.2
	1.9	1.6	2.1	1.6				2.0	2.1
% Officers', Directors', Owners' Comp/Sales	4.0	1.9	2.4					3.7	3.8
(40) (25) (12) [(88) (74)]	6.3	3.4	3.6					5.5	5.4
	10.4	6.8	4.8					8.2	10.0
Net Sales ($)	67386M	129730M	243528M	837190M	542759M	1421502M		1449380M	1063300M
Total Assets ($)	20549M	44660M	115888M	326436M	271767M	819975M		670105M	555550M

M = $ thousand   MM = $ million
See Pages 1 through 15 for Explanation of Ratios and Data

Comparative Historical Data				Current Data Sorted By Sales					
	6	12	# Postretirement Benefits	1	4	2	1	1	3
			Type of Statement						
17	18	25	Unqualified	3	1	2	3		16
28	27	23	Reviewed	4	5	4	5	4	1
59	53	66	Compiled	32	20	10	3	1	
9	16	13	Tax Returns	5	5	2			1
23	38	45	Other	16	14	2	4	1	8
4/1/92-3/31/93 ALL	4/1/93-3/31/94 ALL	4/1/94-3/31/95 ALL		52 (4/1-9/30/94) 0-1MM	1-3MM	3-5MM	120 (10/1/94-3/31/95) 5-10MM	10-25MM	25MM & OVER
136	152	172	**NUMBER OF STATEMENTS**	60	45	20	15	6	26
%	%	%	**ASSETS**	%	%	%	%	%	%
8.4	8.5	7.2	Cash & Equivalents	8.0	7.7	6.9	5.5		7.1
13.9	14.1	14.7	Trade Receivables - (net)	10.7	17.1	16.2	12.2		16.0
54.3	50.6	50.6	Inventory	54.1	50.9	48.6	49.2		45.6
1.4	2.0	1.1	All Other Current	.7	1.0	1.2	.5		2.3
77.9	75.2	73.5	Total Current	73.5	76.6	72.8	67.4		70.9
15.3	19.1	19.1	Fixed Assets (net)	19.6	17.3	19.6	27.1		18.3
1.8	1.8	2.1	Intangibles (net)	2.1	1.2	1.6	.2		5.8
4.9	3.9	5.2	All Other Non-Current	4.9	4.8	6.0	5.3		5.0
100.0	100.0	100.0	Total	100.0	100.0	100.0	100.0		100.0
			LIABILITIES						
12.1	12.1	9.6	Notes Payable-Short Term	7.7	12.0	11.8	11.8		6.1
3.8	3.8	3.1	Cur. Mat.-L /T/D	5.1	2.5	2.2	1.8		1.0
18.7	17.9	19.3	Trade Payables	19.1	21.5	19.5	18.5		16.4
.6	1.6	.5	Income Taxes Payable	.2	.7	1.1	.9		.4
10.1	10.0	10.1	All Other Current	11.5	10.0	6.8	13.1		9.0
45.3	45.4	42.5	Total Current	43.5	46.7	41.4	46.1		32.9
14.3	11.8	14.9	Long Term Debt	19.1	12.0	14.5	13.0		13.4
.1	.1	.0	Deferred Taxes	.0	.0	.1	.0		.2
3.8	5.3	2.9	All Other-Non-Current	2.8	3.2	4.2	2.2		1.9
36.5	37.4	39.6	Net Worth	34.5	38.1	39.9	38.7		51.6
100.0	100.0	100.0	Total Liabilities & Net Worth	100.0	100.0	100.0	100.0		100.0
			INCOME DATA						
100.0	100.0	100.0	Net Sales	100.0	100.0	100.0	100.0		100.0
39.6	39.9	39.6	Gross Profit	40.4	38.8	35.6	43.0		38.3
37.3	36.4	34.8	Operating Expenses	35.6	35.1	32.3	36.7		31.8
2.4	3.6	4.8	Operating Profit	4.8	3.7	3.4	6.3		6.5
.8	.7	.8	All Other Expenses (net)	1.1	.7	-.1	2.1		.8
1.5	2.9	3.9	Profit Before Taxes	3.7	3.1	3.4	4.3		5.7
			RATIOS						
2.6 / 1.7 / 1.3	2.8 / 1.8 / 1.2	3.0 / 1.8 / 1.3	Current	3.3 / 1.6 / 1.2	2.5 / 1.8 / 1.3	2.3 / 1.9 / 1.5	1.6 / 1.4 / 1.1		3.8 / 2.6 / 1.5
.8 / .4 / .2	.9 / .5 / .2	(170) .9 / .5 / .2	Quick	(58) .7 / .4 / .2	1.0 / .5 / .3	1.1 / .5 / .3	.6 / .4 / .3		1.5 / .6 / .2
1 341.1 / 11 31.9 / 33 11.0	0 979.7 / 13 27.1 / 35 10.5	0 916.1 / 12 30.3 / 32 11.4	Sales/Receivables	0 UND / 5 75.7 / 24 15.1	2 231.5 / 18 20.5 / 31 11.7	0 801.6 / 27 13.7 / 34 10.8	1 258.0 / 9 42.3 / 29 12.5		0 UND / 3 112.7 / 49 7.5
79 4.6 / 118 3.1 / 174 2.1	73 5.0 / 118 3.1 / 174 2.1	68 5.4 / 118 3.1 / 166 2.2	Cost of Sales/Inventory	83 4.4 / 146 2.5 / 215 1.7	61 6.0 / 111 3.3 / 146 2.5	65 5.6 / 107 3.4 / 146 2.5	68 5.4 / 114 3.2 / 146 2.5		74 4.9 / 122 3.0 / 159 2.3
20 18.3 / 37 10.0 / 64 5.7	20 18.6 / 33 10.9 / 54 6.8	20 18.6 / 40 9.2 / 65 5.6	Cost of Sales/Payables	17 21.1 / 40 9.1 / 73 5.0	16 22.6 / 40 9.1 / 61 6.0	21 17.3 / 34 10.8 / 54 6.7	16 23.2 / 42 8.7 / 78 4.7		26 13.9 / 39 9.3 / 63 5.8
5.5 / 8.4 / 17.3	5.3 / 8.9 / 21.0	5.1 / 8.2 / 20.9	Sales/Working Capital	4.9 / 8.2 / 24.1	5.8 / 9.4 / 21.9	6.2 / 8.7 / 15.1	7.3 / 18.0 / 39.9		3.6 / 5.1 / 10.3
(118) 6.3 / 2.6 / .9	(127) 6.7 / 2.9 / 1.2	(149) 12.1 / 4.1 / 1.7	EBIT/Interest	(47) 9.3 / 3.8 / 1.7	(42) 10.9 / 4.1 / 1.4	13.4 / 3.8 / 1.2	17.3 / 5.2 / 2.3	(19)	7.7 / 5.7 / .6
(50) 3.8 / 2.1 / .8	(47) 3.8 / .9 / .2	(36) 3.9 / 1.9 / .7	Net Profit + Depr., Dep., Amort./Cur. Mat. L/T/D		(11) 3.5 / 2.5 / .2			(10)	18.1 / 5.7 / 1.7
.2 / .4 / .9	.2 / .4 / 1.1	.2 / .4 / .9	Fixed/Worth	.1 / .4 / 3.7	.1 / .4 / 1.1	.2 / .5 / .9	.2 / .4 / .9		.2 / .4 / .7
.8 / 1.6 / 3.5	.7 / 1.6 / 4.2	.7 / 1.4 / 3.9	Debt/Worth	.7 / 1.7 / 7.3	.9 / 1.3 / 3.1	.9 / 1.4 / 3.5	1.0 / 1.8 / 2.4		.5 / 1.3 / 2.2
(122) 40.8 / 15.4 / 5.2	(135) 40.6 / 16.9 / 3.0	(157) 45.3 / 22.4 / 7.0	% Profit Before Taxes/Tangible Net Worth	(50) 52.7 / 20.7 / 3.2	(41) 39.7 / 17.6 / 9.6	(19) 53.1 / 18.6 / 1.2	41.8 / 25.0 / 10.5		48.2 / 28.4 / 8.5
11.8 / 5.2 / .0	12.7 / 5.4 / .4	17.3 / 9.3 / 2.3	% Profit Before Taxes/Total Assets	20.1 / 9.4 / 1.5	16.9 / 8.6 / 1.6	16.8 / 7.7 / .5	15.2 / 8.9 / 3.8		20.2 / 11.0 / 3.3
55.0 / 25.2 / 15.0	40.2 / 19.8 / 10.5	49.5 / 22.8 / 9.2	Sales/Net Fixed Assets	67.5 / 30.9 / 8.8	124.3 / 39.2 / 11.9	36.0 / 19.3 / 7.6	36.9 / 20.3 / 12.0		30.3 / 12.8 / 8.6
3.7 / 2.9 / 2.0	3.5 / 2.7 / 1.8	3.7 / 2.7 / 1.8	Sales/Total Assets	3.5 / 2.8 / 1.9	4.5 / 3.2 / 1.9	3.9 / 2.8 / 1.9	3.6 / 3.0 / 1.5		2.9 / 2.3 / 1.6
(116) .6 / 1.0 / 1.8	(144) .5 / 1.0 / 1.8	(139) .6 / 1.2 / 1.8	% Depr., Dep., Amort./Sales	(40) .8 / 1.4 / 2.3	(39) .5 / .7 / 1.4	.9 / 1.3 / 1.6	(14) .6 / 1.4 / 2.0	(21)	.8 / 1.4 / 2.0
(68) 2.6 / 4.5 / 7.9	(74) 2.3 / 5.0 / 9.8	(81) 2.8 / 5.0 / 8.6	% Officers', Directors', Owners' Comp/Sales	(30) 4.1 / 6.7 / 10.6	(25) 2.5 / 3.9 / 8.0	(13) 1.4 / 2.5 / 4.9			
1879117M	1638964M	3242095M	Net Sales ($)	37062M	83633M	72365M	101370M	91580M	2856085M
726810M	830059M	1599275M	Total Assets ($)	15441M	34008M	29187M	52374M	42945M	1425320M

M = $ thousand   MM = $ million
See Pages 1 through 15 for Explanation of Ratios and Data

Current Data Sorted By Assets | **Comparative Historical Data**

	0-500M	500M-2MM	2-10MM	10-50MM	50-100MM	100-250MM		4/1/90-3/31/91 ALL	4/1/91-3/31/92 ALL
	2	1	1	1	1		# Postretirement Benefits		
							Type of Statement		
Unqualified	4	4	8	7	2	1		26	19
Reviewed	2	17	9	1				33	26
Compiled	31	24	6	1				59	69
Tax Returns	5	2	1					4	8
Other	12	13	4	5	4			39	36
		69 (4/1-9/30/94)		93 (10/1/94-3/31/95)					
NUMBER OF STATEMENTS	54	60	28	13	6	1		161	158
	%	%	%	%	%	%	**ASSETS**	%	%
	9.1	6.1	5.2	1.5			Cash & Equivalents	7.5	7.5
	13.8	18.6	22.2	17.9			Trade Receivables - (net)	15.2	16.1
	47.7	49.3	53.1	52.2			Inventory	48.4	48.5
	.8	.9	.8	.6			All Other Current	1.6	1.5
	71.5	74.9	81.3	72.1			Total Current	72.7	73.6
	23.0	16.2	14.1	18.7			Fixed Assets (net)	19.9	18.9
	1.5	2.1	.4	4.6			Intangibles (net)	2.3	1.0
	4.0	6.9	4.2	4.7			All Other Non-Current	5.2	6.5
	100.0	100.0	100.0	100.0			Total	100.0	100.0
							LIABILITIES		
	13.8	11.6	17.9	15.2			Notes Payable-Short Term	15.4	14.9
	5.1	3.2	2.2	1.5			Cur. Mat. -L/T/D	3.0	3.1
	19.7	23.1	26.4	30.0			Trade Payables	23.5	21.9
	.2	.3	.5	.2			Income Taxes Payable	.6	.5
	8.9	10.3	12.7	9.2			All Other Current	8.2	9.7
	47.7	48.6	59.6	56.1			Total Current	50.8	50.0
	23.0	11.5	6.4	15.9			Long Term Debt	15.9	12.7
	.0	.0	.1	.3			Deferred Taxes	.3	.2
	4.2	2.7	3.8	2.3			All Other-Non-Current	3.8	2.9
	25.1	37.1	30.1	25.5			Net Worth	29.1	34.2
	100.0	100.0	100.0	100.0			Total Liabilities & Net Worth	100.0	100.0
							INCOME DATA		
	100.0	100.0	100.0	100.0			Net Sales	100.0	100.0
	38.8	32.9	26.4	26.8			Gross Profit	36.7	36.1
	35.8	30.2	26.1	23.7			Operating Expenses	34.0	33.0
	3.0	2.7	.4	3.1			Operating Profit	2.7	3.1
	.9	.3	.4	.4			All Other Expenses (net)	1.0	.6
	2.1	2.4	.0	2.6			Profit Before Taxes	1.7	2.6
							RATIOS		
	2.3	2.1	1.7	1.8				2.1	2.1
	1.5	1.5	1.4	1.2			Current	1.5	1.4
	1.0	1.2	1.2	1.0				1.1	1.1
	1.0	.9	.7	.5				.8	.9
(53)	.4	.4	.4	.4			Quick	(157) .4	.4
	.2	.2	.3	.1				.2	.2
2	171.1	6 63.9	7 53.9	7 51.8				4 86.8	5 71.6
8	45.1	16 22.7	18 20.4	14 27.0			Sales/Receivables	10 35.3	12 31.2
21	17.2	37 9.8	42 8.6	25 14.7				31 11.8	28 13.0
36	10.1	61 6.0	60 6.1	59 6.2				56 6.5	61 6.0
87	4.2	91 4.0	87 4.2	78 4.7			Cost of Sales/Inventory	85 4.3	94 3.9
130	2.8	146 2.5	118 3.1	94 3.9				122 3.0	135 2.7
11	33.8	21 17.1	21 17.8	28 13.0				22 16.9	14 25.5
26	14.2	35 10.4	38 9.5	40 9.1			Cost of Sales/Payables	42 8.6	41 9.0
49	7.5	59 6.2	51 7.1	52 7.0				61 6.0	64 5.7
	6.7	6.9	8.7	11.0				8.0	7.6
	14.0	12.4	16.1	24.8			Sales/Working Capital	15.2	14.2
	NM	28.6	38.7	165.3				77.2	66.4
	5.2	6.4	6.8	8.7				4.8	5.6
(49)	1.9	(57) 2.6	(25) 3.7	6.5			EBIT/Interest	(143) 2.5	(137) 2.2
	.3	1.6	1.8	4.1				1.1	.7
		4.2	6.5				Net Profit + Depr., Dep.,	6.4	7.3
		(18) 2.5	(14) 3.3				Amort./Cur. Mat. L./T/D	(67) 3.0	(48) 2.4
		1.3	1.6					.7	.8
	.2	.2	.2	.5				.2	.2
	.7	.4	.5	.9			Fixed/Worth	.5	.6
	6.2	.7	1.0	1.1				3.1	1.4
	1.4	1.0	1.4	2.3				1.1	1.0
	3.1	1.6	3.0	3.0			Debt/Worth	2.6	2.2
	19.9	3.3	5.6	6.0				9.7	6.3
	81.9	28.4	34.2	46.8			% Profit Before Taxes/Tangible	41.3	32.6
(47)	18.4	(57) 12.9	(27) 22.6	(11) 35.2			Net Worth	(141) 19.5	(142) 16.1
	-6.1	5.7	4.5	25.6				4.3	2.3
	17.5	9.6	10.6	12.1			% Profit Before Taxes/Total	12.5	9.1
	5.2	4.5	4.5	8.4			Assets	5.3	5.1
	-2.5	2.1	1.1	6.9				.4	.0
	65.5	64.1	64.2	28.9				57.3	50.7
	24.2	26.8	36.0	18.8			Sales/Net Fixed Assets	23.6	23.0
	9.7	12.1	11.1	15.6				10.3	9.2
	4.9	3.7	4.3	4.1				3.9	3.8
	3.3	2.9	3.1	3.3			Sales/Total Assets	3.1	2.8
	2.2	2.2	2.4	2.8				2.3	2.1
	.5	.6	.4	.6				.6	.5
(42)	1.3	(50) 1.0	(26) .7	(12) 1.1			% Depr., Dep., Amort./Sales	(135) 1.1	(136) 1.0
	2.5	1.7	1.0	1.3				1.7	2.1
	2.8	2.2	1.1					2.2	2.3
(33)	6.1	(37) 3.2	(16) 1.9				% Officers', Directors', Owners' Comp/Sales	(68) 4.0	(86) 4.3
	10.0	6.3	4.9					7.0	7.9
	51599M	181661M	418547M	906039M	953541M	724713M	Net Sales ($)	2761576M	2483588M
	14592M	62151M	124478M	236003M	433524M	188712M	Total Assets ($)	1129249M	921228M

M = $ thousand   MM = $ million
See Pages 1 through 15 for Explanation of Ratios and Data

Comparative Historical Data / Current Data Sorted By Sales

3	2	6	# Postretirement Benefits Type of Statement	1	2			1	2
22	20	26	Unqualified	3	4	1	3	3	12
30	28	29	Reviewed	1	9	4	7	6	2
66	63	61	Compiled	21	26	5	7	1	1
12	11	8	Tax Returns	5	1		1	1	
30	44	38	Other	7	14	4		4	9
4/1/92-3/31/93 ALL	4/1/93-3/31/94 ALL	4/1/94-3/31/95 ALL		0-1MM	1-3MM	3-5MM	5-10MM	10-25MM	25MM & OVER
				69 (4/1-9/30/94)			93 (10/1/94-3/31/95)		
160	166	162	**NUMBER OF STATEMENTS**	37	54	14	18	15	24
%	%	%	**ASSETS**	%	%	%	%	%	%
8.1	8.4	6.4	Cash & Equivalents	8.8	6.7	7.8	6.0	5.5	2.2
17.9	17.1	17.5	Trade Receivables - (net)	13.6	16.9	24.2	18.0	20.4	19.0
48.5	46.5	49.5	Inventory	41.7	49.9	50.9	58.9	52.7	50.5
.9	.9	.9	All Other Current	.6	1.2	.2	1.0	1.1	1.0
75.3	72.9	74.3	Total Current	64.7	74.7	83.2	83.8	79.7	72.7
17.3	20.4	18.7	Fixed Assets (net)	26.7	17.4	15.0	9.4	16.4	19.7
1.5	1.4	1.9	Intangibles (net)	1.6	2.6	.2	.4	.4	3.9
5.9	5.3	5.1	All Other Non-Current	7.0	5.4	1.7	6.3	3.6	3.7
100.0	100.0	100.0	Total	100.0	100.0	100.0	100.0	100.0	100.0
			LIABILITIES						
11.6	12.2	13.8	Notes Payable-Short Term	18.2	7.8	14.1	19.0	18.3	13.4
3.1	3.2	3.5	Cur. Mat.-L./T/D	5.8	3.6	2.5	2.2	2.8	1.3
24.3	21.3	23.2	Trade Payables	15.1	22.6	29.8	27.2	23.2	29.9
.5	1.1	.3	Income Taxes Payable	.2	.4	.2	.1	.6	.2
8.8	9.4	10.2	All Other Current	12.0	8.1	8.4	9.2	16.2	10.0
48.3	47.3	50.9	Total Current	51.4	42.5	55.0	57.7	61.0	54.9
13.9	12.7	14.7	Long Term Debt	25.4	15.0	8.6	6.7	6.5	11.9
.2	.2	.1	Deferred Taxes	.0	.0	.1	.0	.2	.5
3.9	3.8	3.4	All Other-Non-Current	3.8	3.2	1.6	5.0	3.1	3.4
33.7	36.1	31.0	Net Worth	19.4	39.3	34.7	30.6	29.2	29.3
100.0	100.0	100.0	Total Liabilities & Net Worth	100.0	100.0	100.0	100.0	100.0	100.0
			INCOME DATA						
100.0	100.0	100.0	Net Sales	100.0	100.0	100.0	100.0	100.0	100.0
35.4	33.9	33.2	Gross Profit	41.9	34.9	28.3	28.2	27.4	26.3
32.6	31.2	30.7	Operating Expenses	37.6	32.6	26.0	25.9	26.8	24.6
2.8	2.8	2.5	Operating Profit	4.3	2.3	2.2	2.3	.6	1.7
.5	1.0	.5	All Other Expenses (net)	1.3	.1	.6	.2	.5	.4
2.3	1.7	2.0	Profit Before Taxes	3.0	2.2	1.6	2.1	.1	1.3
			RATIOS						
2.5	2.4	2.0		2.1	2.5	1.9	1.8	1.5	1.6
1.5	1.6	1.5	Current	1.3	1.7	1.5	1.4	1.3	1.4
1.2	1.2	1.1		1.0	1.3	1.1	1.3	1.0	1.1
1.0	.9	.8		.8	1.0	1.0	.7	.7	.5
(159) .5	.5	(161) .4	Quick	(36) .4	.5	.5	.4	.3	.3
.2	.2	.2		.1	.3	.3	.2	.2	.2
5 73.1	5 69.4	5 67.4		2 217.0	5 79.3	6 59.4	4 97.0	6 61.9	7 53.3
13 28.4	13 27.3	14 27.0	Sales/Receivables	8 45.0	15 23.9	16 22.5	17 21.5	17 22.1	13 27.3
31 11.7	28 12.9	29 12.5		24 15.4	36 10.2	37 9.8	43 8.4	38 9.5	24 15.3
55 6.6	53 6.9	58 6.3		31 11.6	62 5.9	35 10.5	72 5.1	47 7.8	65 5.6
87 4.2	79 4.6	87 4.2	Cost of Sales/Inventory	89 4.1	96 3.8	73 5.0	89 4.1	85 4.3	81 4.5
122 3.0	118 3.1	130 2.8		166 2.2	146 2.5	107 3.4	130 2.8	118 3.1	94 3.9
19 19.1	19 19.6	19 19.1		11 34.3	20 18.6	21 17.4	21 17.8	17 22.0	31 11.6
40 9.1	32 11.3	34 10.6	Cost of Sales/Payables	24 15.4	36 10.2	40 9.2	44 8.3	27 13.6	41 9.0
61 6.0	49 7.4	55 6.6		38 9.7	59 6.2	64 5.7	61 6.0	48 7.6	57 6.4
7.5	7.0	7.4		5.5	6.2	8.0	8.8	7.9	11.0
12.8	12.2	14.4	Sales/Working Capital	31.9	9.1	16.8	14.3	22.3	17.4
34.5	24.9	42.7		−127.5	26.6	44.8	19.2	320.4	45.1
6.0	7.3	7.0		4.4	7.8	4.3	6.6	6.9	10.9
(143) 2.5	(150) 3.0	(151) 3.0	EBIT/Interest	(35) 2.0	(48) 2.6	2.6	3.6	(12) 3.2	6.4
1.4	1.4	1.5		.1	1.4	1.6	1.5	1.4	2.9
4.6	5.0	8.3	Net Profit + Depr., Dep.,		6.6		8.3		18.9
(56) 1.8	(54) 2.4	(51) 3.5	Amort./Cur. Mat. L/T/D		(13) 2.8		(11) 3.5		(14) 9.9
.7	.5	1.5			1.3		1.5		4.6
.2	.2	.2		.3	.1	.3	.2	.3	.4
.5	.5	.5	Fixed/Worth	1.0	.4	.4	.2	.8	.7
1.1	1.2	1.1		UND	1.0	.7	.5	1.1	1.0
1.0	.9	1.3		1.2	.9	1.4	1.4	1.3	1.7
2.5	2.0	2.4	Debt/Worth	4.2	1.7	1.8	2.9	3.6	2.9
5.2	4.2	5.0		UND	3.7	3.2	3.4	8.2	4.1
31.3	36.3	40.5	% Profit Before Taxes/Tangible	110.2	35.7	24.2	34.3	40.9	45.7
(143) 18.5	(157) 18.5	(149) 18.4	Net Worth	(29) 15.2	(52) 14.4	13.0	23.3	(14) 16.4	(22) 26.2
4.8	6.7	6.0		−.9	4.1	6.3	6.3	1.8	19.0
11.0	13.4	11.1	% Profit Before Taxes/Total	15.0	11.1	7.1	11.1	12.4	11.1
5.3	5.8	5.2	Assets	3.5	5.6	4.6	5.4	4.5	7.8
1.3	1.3	1.4		−3.1	1.4	2.1	2.1	.4	4.0
56.4	47.1	56.9		53.6	69.7	56.3	84.5	54.4	31.2
30.2	23.4	24.3	Sales/Net Fixed Assets	20.1	25.6	30.7	49.0	35.4	17.0
13.3	11.5	11.6		4.4	12.2	17.9	36.1	10.2	11.9
4.1	4.2	3.9		4.2	3.6	4.7	4.1	4.3	4.2
3.0	3.1	3.1	Sales/Total Assets	2.3	2.9	3.8	3.3	3.6	3.1
2.3	2.3	2.3		1.6	2.3	2.9	2.7	2.3	2.4
.5	.6	.6		.8	.6	.7	.4	.3	.6
(143) .9	(144) 1.0	(136) 1.0	% Depr., Dep., Amort./Sales	(28) 1.8	(42) 1.1	(13) 1.0	.7	(13) .6	(22) 1.1
1.6	1.7	1.7		3.9	2.0	1.3	.9	.9	1.6
1.7	1.8	2.0	% Officers', Directors',	3.7	2.5		1.0	1.0	
(83) 3.7	(84) 3.7	(88) 3.7	Owners' Comp/Sales	(23) 7.4	(33) 4.0	(11) 2.2	(10) 1.6		
6.3	6.6	6.8		13.0	6.1		3.8	3.1	
2870217M	3849923M	3236100M	Net Sales ($)	19929M	98600M	56425M	129269M	220511M	2711366M
916150M	1314651M	1059460M	Total Assets ($)	9581M	37359M	15391M	41624M	70683M	884822M

M = $ thousand   MM = $ million
See Pages 1 through 15 for Explanation of Ratios and Data

Current Data Sorted By Assets   **Comparative Historical Data**

Type of Statement

	0-500M	500M-2MM	2-10MM	10-50MM	50-100MM	100-250MM	# Postretirement Benefits / Type of Statement	4/1/90-3/31/91 ALL	4/1/91-3/31/92 ALL
			3	2		1			
Unqualified	3	1	3	2		2	Unqualified	8	10
Reviewed		6					Reviewed	10	10
Compiled	15	7	2				Compiled	26	23
Tax Returns	5						Tax Returns	1	4
Other	4	7	4	3			Other	25	19
	23 (4/1-9/30/94)		**41 (10/1/94-3/31/95)**						
NUMBER OF STATEMENTS	27	21	9	5		2	NUMBER OF STATEMENTS	70	66

Main Data

0-500M %	500M-2MM %	2-10MM %	10-50MM %	50-100MM %	100-250MM %		4/1/90-3/31/91 %	4/1/91-3/31/92 %
						ASSETS		
12.1	6.8					Cash & Equivalents	7.6	7.4
3.5	11.9					Trade Receivables - (net)	8.9	5.5
58.3	55.7					Inventory	60.1	61.8
.9	1.3					All Other Current	1.5	1.5
74.8	75.7					Total Current	78.1	76.2
20.9	15.1					Fixed Assets (net)	15.6	17.0
2.2	1.2					Intangibles (net)	1.7	1.4
2.2	8.0					All Other Non-Current	4.6	5.4
100.0	100.0					Total	100.0	100.0
						LIABILITIES		
12.8	12.5					Notes Payable-Short Term	8.4	9.7
4.7	4.0					Cur. Mat. -L/T/D	4.3	4.2
16.0	11.6					Trade Payables	25.7	19.0
.1	.7					Income Taxes Payable	.5	.5
5.3	5.1					All Other Current	6.9	7.7
38.9	33.9					Total Current	45.8	41.1
23.8	13.1					Long Term Debt	17.3	14.1
.0	.1					Deferred Taxes	.7	.3
1.6	7.2					All Other-Non-Current	4.8	2.7
35.7	45.7					Net Worth	31.4	41.8
100.0	100.0					Total Liabilities & Net Worth	100.0	100.0
						INCOME DATA		
100.0	100.0					Net Sales	100.0	100.0
39.2	41.3					Gross Profit	37.1	36.9
36.4	38.0					Operating Expenses	33.9	33.2
2.8	3.3					Operating Profit	3.2	3.6
1.2	.8					All Other Expenses (net)	1.1	.8
1.5	2.5					Profit Before Taxes	2.1	2.9
						RATIOS		
4.0	4.4						3.4	3.1
2.1	2.2					Current	1.7	1.9
1.3	1.5						1.2	1.4
.9	1.2						.7	.8
.4	.5					Quick	(69) .3	.3
.1	.3						.1	.1
0 UND	2 192.8						0 UND	0 UND
0 999.8	19 18.8					Sales/Receivables	2 152.8	2 215.4
6 62.4	46 8.0						16 22.4	7 54.5
78 4.7	135 2.7						85 4.3	96 3.8
135 2.7	159 2.3					Cost of Sales/Inventory	126 2.9	135 2.7
192 1.9	215 1.7						174 2.1	192 1.9
0 UND	12 30.0						24 15.5	18 20.6
27 13.3	32 11.4					Cost of Sales/Payables	45 8.1	33 11.0
46 8.0	49 7.4						69 5.3	58 6.3
5.0	3.4						4.6	4.5
8.8	5.8					Sales/Working Capital	9.4	7.5
22.6	7.7						30.6	17.9
3.6	4.0						4.3	7.9
(25) 2.2	(20) 2.4					EBIT/Interest	(64) 1.8	(60) 3.5
.8	.5						1.0	1.8
							4.9	8.3
						Net Profit + Depr., Dep., Amort./Cur. Mat. L /T/D	(30) 1.4	(24) 2.5
							.7	.8
.2	.1						.2	.2
.6	.3					Fixed/Worth	.5	.4
3.4	.6						1.2	.7
1.2	.6						1.2	.6
2.3	1.2					Debt/Worth	2.6	1.4
4.9	2.2						6.3	4.1
44.4	25.3						40.4	39.5
(23) 15.0	(20) 10.9					% Profit Before Taxes/Tangible Net Worth	(62) 20.3	(63) 19.6
5.2	1.2						.6	6.8
11.6	9.9						12.9	16.2
6.0	5.4					% Profit Before Taxes/Total Assets	4.5	8.6
−.9	−.9						.0	2.7
34.4	33.5						75.3	39.5
16.8	17.0					Sales/Net Fixed Assets	25.6	20.0
8.1	12.9						11.7	11.0
3.3	2.6						3.5	3.4
2.3	2.0					Sales/Total Assets	2.7	2.7
1.8	1.4						2.2	2.2
1.0	.8						.7	.6
(22) 1.7	(19) 1.3					% Depr., Dep., Amort./Sales	(57) 1.2	(59) 1.4
2.1	2.5						1.9	2.0
	2.3						2.1	1.7
	(10) 4.1					% Officers', Directors', Owners' Comp/Sales	(26) 5.5	(25) 3.2
	11.0						8.3	6.9
17367M	40371M	92060M	345885M		491125M	Net Sales ($)	913655M	1113443M
6055M	20509M	47665M	147014M		269004M	Total Assets ($)	421803M	560433M

M = $ thousand   MM = $ million
See Pages 1 through 15 for Explanation of Ratios and Data

Comparative Historical Data | Current Data Sorted By Sales

					0-1MM	1-3MM	3-5MM	5-10MM	10-25MM	25MM & OVER
3	3	6	# Postretirement Benefits			2	1	1	1	1
			Type of Statement							
7	9	8	Unqualified		1		1	2		4
9	15	9	Reviewed		2	4	3	1		
29	28	24	Compiled		11	10	1	1	1	1
4	4	5	Tax Returns		4	1				
18	26	18	Other		4	7		1	3	3
4/1/92-3/31/93 ALL	4/1/93-3/31/94 ALL	4/1/94-3/31/95 ALL			23 (4/1-9/30/94)		41 (10/1/94-3/31/95)			
67	82	64	**NUMBER OF STATEMENTS**		22	22	5	4	4	7
%	%	%	**ASSETS**		%	%	%	%	%	%
8.6	9.1	11.2	Cash & Equivalents		9.8	10.3				
6.1	9.9	8.5	Trade Receivables - (net)		3.1	10.2				
62.0	53.4	56.2	Inventory		60.0	53.4				
.8	.8	1.2	All Other Current		.6	1.3				
77.5	73.2	77.1	Total Current		73.4	75.2				
17.0	16.3	16.6	Fixed Assets (net)		23.7	14.2				
.8	3.5	1.9	Intangibles (net)		2.0	1.6				
4.7	7.1	4.4	All Other Non-Current		.9	9.0				
100.0	100.0	100.0	Total		100.0	100.0				
			LIABILITIES							
10.0	12.0	12.7	Notes Payable-Short Term		14.8	10.1				
3.1	3.3	3.9	Cur. Mat.-L /T/D		4.7	4.4				
19.3	16.0	15.3	Trade Payables		12.1	16.2				
.2	.7	.3	Income Taxes Payable		.1	.6				
7.0	7.9	5.7	All Other Current		4.6	5.5				
39.6	40.0	37.8	Total Current		36.4	36.7				
17.6	14.1	16.2	Long Term Debt		27.0	13.5				
.3	.2	.1	Deferred Taxes		.0	.1				
2.5	2.9	4.4	All Other-Non-Current		2.5	4.8				
40.0	42.8	41.5	Net Worth		34.1	44.9				
100.0	100.0	100.0	Total Liabilities & Net Worth		100.0	100.0				
			INCOME DATA							
100.0	100.0	100.0	Net Sales		100.0	100.0				
39.6	42.0	39.4	Gross Profit		41.4	39.9				
35.4	36.8	36.8	Operating Expenses		37.5	37.7				
4.3	5.2	2.7	Operating Profit		3.9	2.2				
1.2	1.3	.8	All Other Expenses (net)		1.7	.3				
3.1	3.9	1.9	Profit Before Taxes		2.2	1.9				
			RATIOS							
4.0 / 2.0 / 1.3	3.5 / 2.0 / 1.3	4.1 / 2.1 / 1.4	Current		4.2 / 2.1 / 1.3	4.3 / 2.2 / 1.4				
.7 / .3 / .1	.9 / (81) .4 / .1	1.0 / .4 / .2	Quick		.9 / .4 / .1	1.1 / .5 / .2				
0 UND / 1 301.0 / 7 54.0	0 995.5 / 4 97.8 / 19 19.0	0 UND / 3 141.9 / 23 15.6	Sales/Receivables		0 UND / 0 UND / 5 66.7	1 658.2 / 6 61.6 / 31 11.8				
89 4.1 / 140 2.6 / 183 2.0	89 4.1 / 130 2.8 / 228 1.6	111 3.3 / 152 2.4 / 192 1.9	Cost of Sales/Inventory		114 3.2 / 166 2.2 / 304 1.2	104 3.5 / 140 2.6 / 183 2.0				
16 23.1 / 30 12.1 / 63 5.8	12 30.5 / 29 12.4 / 50 7.3	13 28.1 / 33 11.2 / 50 7.3	Cost of Sales/Payables		0 UND / 19 19.1 / 48 7.6	12 29.3 / 30 12.1 / 49 7.5				
4.2 / 7.3 / 17.0	5.0 / 7.8 / 20.4	3.7 / 6.6 / 10.8	Sales/Working Capital		3.9 / 7.7 / 10.5	4.3 / 6.7 / 17.7				
(60) 8.3 / 3.7 / 1.7	(73) 9.8 / 2.5 / .3	(60) 5.6 / 2.7 / .9	EBIT/Interest		(20) 3.1 / 1.9 / .8	(21) 5.3 / 3.5 / 1.1				
(22) 8.3 / 2.2 / 1.0	(24) 6.1 / 1.2 / –.2	(19) 3.1 / 1.9 / .3	Net Profit + Depr., Dep., Amort./Cur. Mat. L/T/D							
.2 / .4 / .8	.2 / .4 / .8	.2 / .3 / .9	Fixed/Worth		.2 / .7 / 4.1	.1 / .2 / .7				
.7 / 1.7 / 3.8	.6 / 1.5 / 3.9	.6 / 1.7 / 3.6	Debt/Worth		1.3 / 2.6 / 6.8	.6 / 1.2 / 2.8				
(62) 48.9 / 25.0 / 8.1	(75) 37.9 / 15.9 / .0	(59) 44.2 / 14.0 / 3.3	% Profit Before Taxes/Tangible Net Worth		(19) 50.0 / 17.2 / 3.3	(20) 25.3 / 14.5 / 2.5				
16.8 / 8.8 / 2.3	17.2 / 5.6 / –2.1	11.4 / 6.0 / .6	% Profit Before Taxes/Total Assets		8.8 / 6.0 / –1.4	10.6 / 5.6 / .6				
39.6 / 20.8 / 12.6	45.7 / 19.0 / 10.4	35.5 / 16.8 / 10.5	Sales/Net Fixed Assets		27.1 / 15.8 / 5.7	117.2 / 24.1 / 13.5				
3.3 / 2.7 / 2.2	3.5 / 2.5 / 1.8	2.8 / 2.3 / 1.5	Sales/Total Assets		2.5 / 2.0 / 1.4	3.1 / 2.5 / 1.7				
(63) .5 / 1.0 / 1.7	(71) .7 / 1.2 / 2.0	(56) .9 / 1.4 / 2.1	% Depr., Dep., Amort./Sales		(19) 1.2 / 2.1 / 2.3	(18) .7 / 1.2 / 2.3				
(28) 2.5 / 4.6 / 8.1	(35) 2.4 / 4.4 / 7.6	(22) 2.3 / 4.4 / 8.2	% Officers', Directors', Owners' Comp/Sales			(10) 4.2 / 5.9 / 11.0				
472333M	940924M	986808M	Net Sales ($)		9650M	33482M	18069M	27145M	61452M	837010M
173994M	425531M	490247M	Total Assets ($)		5145M	15257M	15626M	16335M	21866M	416018M

RETAILERS—JEWELRY. SIC# 5944

	Current Data Sorted By Assets							Comparative Historical Data	
	2	3	4		1	3	**# Postretirement Benefits**		
							Type of Statement	19	26
	3	5	7	3	3	3	Unqualified	59	74
	4	16	28	4	3	3	Reviewed	181	156
	66	68	11				Compiled	9	19
	6	11	1				Tax Returns	60	65
	24	20	18	3	2	2	Other		
	130 (4/1-9/30/94)			178 (10/1/94-3/31/95)				4/1/90-3/31/91	4/1/91-3/31/92
	0-500M	500M-2MM	2-10MM	10-50MM	50-100MM	100-250MM		ALL	ALL
	103	120	65	10	5	5	**NUMBER OF STATEMENTS**	328	340
	%	%	%	%	%	%	**ASSETS**	%	%
	7.5	6.3	6.6	2.5			Cash & Equivalents	6.6	6.7
	9.7	12.6	13.5	14.1			Trade Receivables - (net)	11.9	11.8
	66.1	66.2	60.6	56.1			Inventory	66.7	64.8
	.6	1.9	1.1	4.5			All Other Current	1.6	.9
	83.9	87.0	81.9	77.2			Total Current	86.7	84.2
	9.4	7.7	11.0	15.6			Fixed Assets (net)	9.2	11.0
	1.8	1.9	2.5	1.9			Intangibles (net)	.7	.9
	4.9	3.4	4.6	5.3			All Other Non-Current	3.3	3.9
	100.0	100.0	100.0	100.0			Total	100.0	100.0
							LIABILITIES		
	9.1	13.1	10.3	13.8			Notes Payable-Short Term	13.5	11.8
	2.7	2.2	3.7	1.7			Cur. Mat. -L/T/D	3.4	3.7
	18.4	19.7	21.3	21.0			Trade Payables	19.6	18.7
	.2	.5	.5	.1			Income Taxes Payable	.7	.4
	10.9	7.0	9.4	7.4			All Other Current	6.8	7.2
	41.4	42.5	45.2	44.0			Total Current	43.9	41.9
	14.5	10.1	10.5	7.6			Long Term Debt	13.4	12.6
	.0	.0	.1	1.1			Deferred Taxes	.1	.1
	5.0	4.8	3.3	4.7			All Other-Non-Current	3.4	4.6
	39.1	42.6	40.9	42.7			Net Worth	39.2	40.9
	100.0	100.0	100.0	100.0			Total Liabilities & Net Worth	100.0	100.0
							INCOME DATA		
	100.0	100.0	100.0	100.0			Net Sales	100.0	100.0
	46.8	44.3	43.1	51.4			Gross Profit	46.2	45.2
	40.2	40.0	39.7	48.1			Operating Expenses	41.4	40.8
	6.6	4.3	3.4	3.3			Operating Profit	4.7	4.4
	1.3	.7	.5	-.1			All Other Expenses (net)	1.8	1.3
	5.4	3.6	2.9	3.4			Profit Before Taxes	3.0	3.1
							RATIOS		
	4.0	3.2	2.6	2.4			Current	3.1	3.3
	2.4	2.1	1.9	2.0				2.0	2.1
	1.5	1.6	1.5	1.6				1.5	1.5
	.8	.9	.9	.7			Quick	.8	.8
	.3	.4	.4	.3			(325)	.4	.4
	.2	.1	.1	.2				.2	.2
	0 UND	5 79.0	4 90.3	5 73.9			Sales/Receivables	4 92.4	4 98.5
	10 37.6	17 21.0	13 27.8	26 14.2				18 20.5	16 22.8
	27 13.7	41 8.9	51 7.2	64 5.7				44 8.3	38 9.7
	166 2.2	192 1.9	159 2.3	215 1.7			Cost of Sales/Inventory	203 1.8	183 2.0
	261 1.4	261 1.4	228 1.6	304 1.2				281 1.3	281 1.3
	365 1.0	365 1.0	304 1.2	365 1.0				365 1.0	365 1.0
	17 21.6	37 9.9	39 9.3	74 4.9			Cost of Sales/Payables	43 8.5	34 10.6
	64 5.7	68 5.4	69 5.3	94 3.9				70 5.2	66 5.5
	107 3.4	101 3.6	101 3.6	107 3.4				114 3.2	107 3.4
	2.4	2.4	3.2	2.9			Sales/Working Capital	2.4	2.6
	3.6	3.7	4.7	3.8				3.7	3.9
	8.4	6.2	8.7	8.5				6.9	7.3
	6.6	6.4	7.0	6.3			EBIT/Interest	4.6	4.8
	(90) 3.4	(107) 2.7	(62) 2.5	3.0				(305) 2.1	(318) 2.2
	1.5	1.1	1.3	.9				1.2	1.1
	3.0	2.5	2.6				Net Profit + Depr., Dep.,	2.9	3.0
	(23) 1.1	(34) 1.3	(26) .9				Amort./Cur. Mat. L /T/D	(127) 1.2	(134) 1.0
	.4	.5	.4					.4	.1
	.1	.1	.1	.2			Fixed/Worth	.1	.1
	.2	.2	.2	.4				.2	.2
	.5	.4	.5	.9				.5	.5
	.6	.7	.9	.7			Debt/Worth	.8	.7
	1.7	1.4	1.8	1.2				1.5	1.5
	3.3	3.1	2.7	2.1				3.4	3.5
	46.1	25.9	23.8				% Profit Before Taxes/Tangible	24.3	25.1
	(93) 24.6	(111) 11.6	(63) 8.1				Net Worth	(313) 11.0	(324) 10.3
	4.2	2.9	3.4					2.3	1.8
	16.1	9.8	8.8	10.5			% Profit Before Taxes/Total	8.9	9.3
	7.3	4.6	2.8	3.2			Assets	4.0	4.0
	1.2	.5	1.0	-.5				.6	.3
	87.8	82.6	61.3	19.7			Sales/Net Fixed Assets	70.1	64.3
	30.5	29.3	16.7	12.9				26.3	21.8
	13.9	16.3	11.2	5.7				12.2	10.1
	2.3	2.1	2.1	1.8			Sales/Total Assets	2.0	2.1
	1.8	1.6	1.6	1.4				1.6	1.6
	1.3	1.2	1.4	1.1				1.2	1.2
	.4	.5	.6	.9			% Depr., Dep., Amort./Sales	.7	.6
	(78) .9	(105) .8	(56) 1.1	1.7				(267) 1.2	(280) 1.0
	1.8	1.5	1.6	2.8				1.8	2.0
	4.4	4.2	2.0				% Officers', Directors',	4.7	4.2
	(63) 8.1	(72) 6.9	(32) 4.6				Owners' Comp/Sales	(180) 7.6	(166) 7.0
	12.6	9.7	7.1					11.0	11.4
	54853M	219814M	518683M	305679M	439492M	990003M	Net Sales ($)	1593533M	1443297M
	30079M	120260M	276713M	162258M	345134M	742726M	Total Assets ($)	989039M	901698M

© Robert Morris Associates 1995

M = $ thousand   MM = $ million
See Pages 1 through 15 for Explanation of Ratios and Data

Comparative Historical Data				Current Data Sorted By Sales					
2	**8**	**13**	# Postretirement Benefits	**3**	**2**	**1**	**2**	**1**	**4**
			Type of Statement						
22	23	24	Unqualified	3	4	3	1	5	8
63	50	52	Reviewed	6	15	11	10	10	
161	142	145	Compiled	80	46	15	4		
16	22	18	Tax Returns	8	9		1		
40	50	69	Other	26	15	6	9	8	5
4/1/92-3/31/93 ALL	4/1/93-3/31/94 ALL	4/1/94-3/31/95 ALL		130 (4/1-9/30/94)			178 (10/1/94-3/31/95)		
				0-1MM	**1-3MM**	**3-5MM**	**5-10MM**	**10-25MM**	**25MM & OVER**
302	287	308	**NUMBER OF STATEMENTS**	123	89	35	25	23	13
%	%	%	**ASSETS**	%	%	%	%	%	%
6.1	7.0	6.7	Cash & Equivalents	6.5	6.6	8.8	6.2	5.2	6.7
12.5	11.9	12.3	Trade Receivables - (net)	10.3	12.5	13.9	16.2	10.7	22.2
64.5	65.7	63.8	Inventory	66.2	67.1	61.5	55.7	61.4	45.3
.9	1.1	1.3	All Other Current	.9	1.7	1.6	1.3	2.2	.6
84.0	85.7	84.2	Total Current	84.0	87.9	85.8	79.5	79.5	74.8
10.7	9.8	9.5	Fixed Assets (net)	8.9	7.6	7.1	15.0	13.6	17.6
.8	.8	2.1	Intangibles (net)	2.4	1.5	2.9	.4	1.5	4.7
4.5	3.7	4.2	All Other Non-Current	4.7	3.1	4.1	5.1	5.4	2.9
100.0	100.0	100.0	Total	100.0	100.0	100.0	100.0	100.0	100.0
			LIABILITIES						
11.7	9.7	10.9	Notes Payable-Short Term	10.8	11.7	12.7	10.7	9.7	3.3
3.9	3.5	2.7	Cur. Mat.-L /T/D	2.4	2.7	3.4	3.1	2.5	2.5
19.4	18.4	19.4	Trade Payables	17.4	19.1	23.6	24.1	23.2	13.9
.3	1.6	.4	Income Taxes Payable	.2	.6	.3	.2	.4	1.3
7.6	8.7	8.9	All Other Current	9.6	8.0	7.1	11.8	8.6	9.0
42.9	41.9	42.3	Total Current	40.4	42.0	47.1	49.9	44.3	30.0
11.6	12.7	12.0	Long Term Debt	13.8	10.9	9.0	9.2	8.5	22.1
.1	.0	.1	Deferred Taxes	.0	.0	.1	.0	.6	.5
5.3	4.8	4.7	All Other-Non-Current	6.2	3.4	3.1	3.7	3.2	8.3
40.2	40.5	40.9	Net Worth	39.6	43.6	40.7	37.3	43.4	39.1
100.0	100.0	100.0	Total Liabilities & Net Worth	100.0	100.0	100.0	100.0	100.0	100.0
			INCOME DATA						
100.0	100.0	100.0	Net Sales	100.0	100.0	100.0	100.0	100.0	100.0
45.8	44.2	45.3	Gross Profit	47.1	44.8	41.9	42.1	45.3	46.5
41.0	39.6	40.2	Operating Expenses	40.9	40.4	37.4	39.7	42.2	37.9
4.8	4.6	5.0	Operating Profit	6.2	4.4	4.5	2.4	3.2	8.6
1.3	1.1	.9	All Other Expenses (net)	1.0	1.0	.5	.2	.3	3.2
3.5	3.5	4.1	Profit Before Taxes	5.2	3.4	4.0	2.2	2.8	5.4
			RATIOS						
3.1	3.4	3.2	Current	4.0	3.1	2.7	2.0	2.5	3.8
2.1	2.2	2.1		2.4	2.0	2.0	1.6	2.0	2.3
1.5	1.6	1.6		1.6	1.6	1.5	1.3	1.7	1.8
.8	.9	.9	Quick	.9	.8	1.0	1.0	.7	2.0
(301) .3	.4	.4		.4	.4	.4	.4	.3	1.0
.2	.2	.1		.2	.1	.1	.1	.1	.1
4 92.2	2 181.6	3 126.3	Sales/Receivables	1 517.0	2 156.0	6 59.9	3 129.6	5 74.8	2 180.5
15 24.3	15 24.0	14 26.9		11 33.1	15 24.6	18 20.5	15 23.8	13 27.8	69 5.3
44 8.3	43 8.5	42 8.6		33 11.1	41 8.9	50 7.3	54 6.8	34 10.8	118 3.1
192 1.9	174 2.1	174 2.1	Cost of Sales/Inventory	192 1.9	192 1.9	166 2.2	83 4.4	192 1.9	118 3.1
281 1.3	261 1.4	261 1.4		304 1.2	261 1.4	228 1.6	159 2.3	228 1.6	203 1.8
365 1.0	365 1.0	365 1.0		406 .9	365 1.0	304 1.2	304 1.2	304 1.2	243 1.5
41 8.9	29 12.5	32 11.4	Cost of Sales/Payables	21 17.4	38 9.7	48 7.6	31 11.9	44 8.3	23 15.6
66 5.5	64 5.7	66 5.5		69 5.3	61 6.0	72 5.1	60 6.1	83 4.4	54 6.7
111 3.3	107 3.4	101 3.6		107 3.4	104 3.5	107 3.4	101 3.6	101 3.6	85 4.3
2.5	2.4	2.5	Sales/Working Capital	2.2	2.6	2.9	4.5	3.4	2.0
3.8	3.8	3.9		3.2	4.0	4.1	6.9	4.4	3.2
6.9	7.1	6.8		6.2	5.9	7.7	15.0	6.4	8.3
5.3	7.0	6.5	EBIT/Interest	5.9	6.2	10.0	8.4	8.2	5.8
(286) 2.5	(269) 3.1	(279) 2.9		(108) 2.9	(77) 2.8	(34) 3.1	3.4	(22) 2.2	3.4
1.3	1.3	1.3		1.3	1.3	1.5	1.6	1.1	1.4
2.3	2.6	2.9	Net Profit + Depr., Dep.,	3.0	2.0	1.4		3.8	
(97) 1.0	(80) 1.3	(94) 1.1	Amort./Cur. Mat. L/T/D	(28) 1.5	(28) .9	(11) .9		(11) 1.3	
.3	.4	.5		.5	.2	.4		.8	
.1	.1	.1	Fixed/Worth	.1	.1	.0	.1	.2	.4
.2	.2	.2		.2	.2	.1	.4	.3	.5
.5	.5	.5		.5	.3	.3	.7	.5	.8
.7	.6	.7	Debt/Worth	.6	.7	.7	1.1	.7	.7
1.4	1.4	1.6		1.6	1.4	1.5	1.9	1.1	2.2
3.4	3.2	3.1		3.6	3.1	3.1	2.7	2.2	3.2
24.5	29.1	32.1	% Profit Before Taxes/Tangible	42.0	26.6	32.8	33.2	17.8	48.3
(283) 12.0	(266) 12.2	(285) 13.3	Net Worth	(109) 18.5	(84) 13.0	(34) 11.1	19.3	(21) 7.3	(12) 20.1
2.4	2.6	3.5		3.5	2.9	3.6	4.3	2.3	9.0
9.6	10.7	12.1	% Profit Before Taxes/Total	14.3	10.9	11.8	9.7	8.6	15.1
4.7	5.1	4.8	Assets	5.0	5.5	3.2	4.6	2.3	8.4
.9	.9	.9		.7	.9	1.1	1.8	.6	1.7
61.8	87.4	65.9	Sales/Net Fixed Assets	84.5	92.1	195.6	35.6	23.4	11.9
23.8	29.3	24.3		28.9	29.7	34.6	15.2	14.0	9.0
11.2	12.4	12.2		13.2	16.5	14.7	11.0	10.5	7.0
2.0	2.2	2.2	Sales/Total Assets	2.1	2.3	1.9	3.1	2.1	2.6
1.6	1.7	1.6		1.6	1.7	1.6	2.1	1.7	1.4
1.3	1.3	1.2		1.1	1.3	1.4	1.5	1.5	1.2
.5	.5	.5	% Depr., Dep., Amort./Sales	.5	.4	.3	.5	1.0	2.0
(255) 1.1	(233) 1.0	(259) 1.0		(94) .9	(81) .8	(30) .9	(20) 1.0	(22) 1.3	(12) 2.5
1.6	1.7	1.7		1.8	1.4	1.5	1.5	1.9	2.5
4.8	4.0	4.0	% Officers', Directors',	4.5	4.5	2.2	2.3		
(167) 7.9	(140) 6.6	(170) 6.5	Owners' Comp/Sales	(76) 7.8	(52) 6.8	(24) 5.1	(11) 3.8		
12.3	12.0	9.9		11.9	9.6	9.5	6.7		
1900638M	2300865M	2528524M	Net Sales ($)	65682M	152559M	131732M	187746M	345709M	1645096M
1088708M	1445211M	1677170M	Total Assets ($)	45281M	91975M	87223M	97486M	204360M	1150845M

Current Data Sorted By Assets / Comparative Historical Data

0-500M	500M-2MM	2-10MM	10-50MM	50-100MM	100-250MM		4/1/90-3/31/91 ALL	4/1/91-3/31/92 ALL
2	3	2	1	1		**# Postretirement Benefits**		
						Type of Statement		
2	2	2	2	3	1	Unqualified	9	6
2	5	7				Reviewed	13	26
41	30	4				Compiled	53	62
12	5	5				Tax Returns	1	7
11	8	5				Other	46	20
	54 (4/1-9/30/94)			88 (10/1/94-3/31/95)				
68	50	18	2	3	1	**NUMBER OF STATEMENTS**	122	121
%	%	%	%	%	%	**ASSETS**	%	%
10.7	9.0	8.0				Cash & Equivalents	7.4	11.4
.7	3.4	4.3				Trade Receivables - (net)	4.0	2.9
50.0	47.0	58.8				Inventory	41.0	48.4
2.3	1.0	.5				All Other Current	1.4	1.7
63.7	60.3	71.6				Total Current	53.7	64.4
19.5	25.0	19.0				Fixed Assets (net)	26.3	20.5
10.4	5.0	4.9				Intangibles (net)	9.8	7.4
6.4	9.6	4.6				All Other Non-Current	10.1	7.7
100.0	100.0	100.0				Total	100.0	100.0
						LIABILITIES		
8.3	8.4	13.3				Notes Payable-Short Term	13.6	11.7
4.1	5.0	3.0				Cur. Mat. -L/T/D	4.6	4.3
13.2	22.8	22.7				Trade Payables	17.1	19.1
.3	.6	.4				Income Taxes Payable	.7	.4
12.7	7.4	9.3				All Other Current	9.0	11.0
38.6	44.2	48.8				Total Current	45.0	46.5
23.9	22.7	10.3				Long Term Debt	24.3	20.8
.0	.1	.0				Deferred Taxes	.0	.1
7.9	4.8	6.1				All Other-Non-Current	1.5	4.5
29.6	28.1	34.8				Net Worth	29.2	28.1
100.0	100.0	100.0				Total Liabilities & Net Worth	100.0	100.0
						INCOME DATA		
100.0	100.0	100.0				Net Sales	100.0	100.0
22.5	20.7	22.1				Gross Profit	23.9	22.4
21.0	18.8	19.8				Operating Expenses	21.2	20.5
1.5	1.9	2.3				Operating Profit	2.8	1.9
.5	.7	.4				All Other Expenses (net)	.5	.5
1.0	1.3	1.9				Profit Before Taxes	2.3	1.3
						RATIOS		
3.0	2.0	2.0				Current	2.4	2.4
2.0	1.3	1.4					1.4	1.5
1.0	1.1	1.2					.8	1.0
.6	.4	.5				Quick	(120) .6	(119) .6
.2	.2	.2					.2	.2
.1	.1	.1					.1	.1
0 UND	0 UND	0 UND				Sales/Receivables	0 UND	0 UND
0 UND	1 711.7	1 434.8					0 968.4	1 693.7
0 UND	3 129.6	4 101.2					3 118.2	2 194.3
29 12.7	37 9.9	45 8.2				Cost of Sales/Inventory	31 11.6	39 9.3
45 8.2	52 7.0	74 4.9					51 7.2	47 7.7
56 6.5	78 4.7	111 3.3					72 5.1	68 5.4
0 UND	8 48.3	13 28.5				Cost of Sales/Payables	8 43.3	7 51.5
8 47.7	19 19.3	23 16.2					18 20.6	16 22.4
20 18.1	31 11.7	37 9.9					30 12.1	37 10.0
10.5	10.5	10.0				Sales/Working Capital	12.0	10.0
15.7	20.9	21.7					24.1	23.2
608.2	189.4	48.3					-57.1	661.2
(60) 5.0	(44) 6.7	10.8				EBIT/Interest	(109) 3.8	(103) 3.5
2.4	2.7	2.5					1.9	1.8
.3	1.6	1.5					1.1	.7
	(11) 3.9					Net Profit + Depr., Dep., Amort./Cur. Mat. L./T/D	(41) 6.1	(32) 3.3
	1.9						1.4	1.3
	.5						.4	.3
.2	.4	.3				Fixed/Worth	.3	.2
.8	1.0	.7					1.2	.7
-4.0	3.6	1.5					19.8	12.8
1.0	1.1	.9				Debt/Worth	1.2	1.0
3.8	3.4	1.9					3.2	3.5
-15.9	14.0	5.4					UND	159.8
(45) 63.0	(41) 41.5	(15) 33.6				% Profit Before Taxes/Tangible Net Worth	(93) 61.8	(93) 64.0
25.8	21.0	18.7					18.5	18.9
2.6	9.1	8.3					5.3	3.6
17.0	13.3	11.0				% Profit Before Taxes/Total Assets	12.5	10.6
5.6	5.6	5.7					4.1	3.7
-1.4	1.7	1.8					.9	-1.3
101.9	78.9	46.5				Sales/Net Fixed Assets	56.4	83.3
48.5	21.9	29.5					18.2	31.6
14.7	8.0	11.0					6.5	14.1
7.6	5.0	4.8				Sales/Total Assets	5.5	5.7
5.2	3.8	3.7					3.8	4.3
3.5	2.9	2.9					2.5	2.9
(58) .3	(44) .5	(16) .3				% Depr., Dep., Amort./Sales	(101) .5	(104) .3
.6	1.0	.6					1.2	.7
1.5	1.8	1.3					1.9	1.5
(38) 3.1	(29) 1.3					% Officers', Directors', Owners' Comp/Sales	(61) 1.9	(68) 2.0
5.2	2.3						3.1	3.6
6.2	4.2						5.0	6.2
80771M	211846M	291642M	56860M	527340M	245381M	Net Sales ($)	1332141M	1221518M
14838M	49533M	73079M	24367M	241296M	125817M	Total Assets ($)	532244M	283462M

M = $ thousand   MM = $ million
See Pages 1 through 15 for Explanation of Ratios and Data

Comparative Historical Data				Current Data Sorted By Sales					
1	6	9	# Postretirement Benefits	1	4		2	2	
			Type of Statement						
6	6	12	Unqualified	2	1		1	2	6
21	20	14	Reviewed		2	2	6	4	
50	58	75	Compiled	21	32	7	12	2	1
14	19	17	Tax Returns	7	7	3			
31	22	24	Other	8	6	3	2	4	1
4/1/92-3/31/93 ALL	4/1/93-3/31/94 ALL	4/1/94-3/31/95 ALL		54 (4/1-9/30/94)			88 (10/1/94-3/31/95)		
				0-1MM	1-3MM	3-5MM	5-10MM	10-25MM	25MM & OVER
122	125	142	**NUMBER OF STATEMENTS**	38	48	15	21	12	8
%	%	%	**ASSETS**	%	%	%	%	%	%
8.2	8.5	9.7	Cash & Equivalents	10.7	9.4	7.6	10.2	9.1	
2.9	2.9	2.4	Trade Receivables - (net)	.2	1.5	1.9	8.1	1.4	
49.9	51.2	49.2	Inventory	45.2	49.3	51.3	54.8	57.3	
.6	1.2	1.6	All Other Current	1.7	2.0	1.5	1.1	.3	
61.7	63.7	63.0	Total Current	57.8	62.1	62.4	74.2	68.0	
21.6	23.0	21.9	Fixed Assets (net)	24.2	19.9	27.0	16.1	20.9	
9.2	7.5	7.8	Intangibles (net)	11.9	8.8	2.0	3.7	6.3	
7.5	5.8	7.4	All Other Non-Current	6.1	9.2	8.6	6.1	4.7	
100.0	100.0	100.0	Total	100.0	100.0	100.0	100.0	100.0	
			LIABILITIES						
10.2	8.8	8.8	Notes Payable-Short Term	10.2	6.3	8.7	11.4	12.3	
4.3	4.9	4.3	Cur. Mat.-L /T/D	5.2	3.2	4.3	6.6	2.5	
18.9	21.2	18.0	Trade Payables	10.2	16.0	24.1	25.8	27.0	
.3	.5	.4	Income Taxes Payable	.1	.5	.5	.5	.9	
10.3	7.1	10.1	All Other Current	12.7	10.8	10.5	7.2	5.8	
44.0	42.4	41.6	Total Current	38.5	36.8	48.1	51.6	48.5	
24.4	27.9	21.5	Long Term Debt	30.4	22.0	16.2	15.0	13.7	
.0	.1	.1	Deferred Taxes	.0	.0	.2	.1	.0	
4.3	4.8	6.4	All Other-Non-Current	5.8	6.1	4.1	13.2	1.5	
27.2	24.8	30.3	Net Worth	25.3	35.0	31.3	20.1	36.3	
100.0	100.0	100.0	Total Liabilities & Net Worth	100.0	100.0	100.0	100.0	100.0	
			INCOME DATA						
100.0	100.0	100.0	Net Sales	100.0	100.0	100.0	100.0	100.0	
21.4	21.4	21.9	Gross Profit	24.6	21.5	21.2	19.0	21.6	
19.9	19.1	20.1	Operating Expenses	23.0	19.3	17.8	18.9	20.2	
1.5	2.3	1.8	Operating Profit	1.7	2.2	3.4	.1	1.4	
.2	.6	.5	All Other Expenses (net)	.8	.6	.8	.0	.5	
1.3	1.7	1.3	Profit Before Taxes	.9	1.6	2.6	.0	.9	
			RATIOS						
2.5 / 1.5 / 1.1	2.7 / 1.5 / 1.0	2.5 / 1.6 / 1.1	Current	2.8 / 1.9 / .9	3.6 / 1.8 / 1.1	2.0 / 1.3 / 1.0	2.2 / 1.4 / 1.1	1.7 / 1.4 / 1.1	
(119) .5 / .2 / .1	(122) .6 / .2 / .1	.5 / .2 / .1	Quick	.6 / .2 / .1	.6 / .2 / .1	.3 / .2 / .1	.6 / .3 / .1	.4 / .1 / .1	
0 UND / 0 999.8 / 2 194.6	0 UND / 0 UND / 2 207.2	0 UND / 0 UND / 1 265.7	Sales/Receivables	0 UND / 0 UND / 0 UND	0 UND / 0 UND / 2 234.6	0 UND / 0 999.8 / 2 209.7	0 999.8 / 1 274.4 / 9 40.7	0 UND / 1 345.3 / 2 172.6	
40 9.1 / 49 7.5 / 69 5.3	40 9.1 / 55 6.6 / 74 4.9	33 11.0 / 49 7.5 / 73 5.0	Cost of Sales/Inventory	30 12.2 / 46 8.0 / 70 5.2	31 11.6 / 49 7.4 / 65 5.6	45 8.2 / 50 7.3 / 79 4.6	33 11.1 / 41 8.9 / 83 4.4	39 9.3 / 55 6.6 / 114 3.2	
5 68.6 / 18 20.7 / 38 9.6	8 44.7 / 21 17.6 / 35 10.3	4 85.9 / 15 25.1 / 27 13.4	Cost of Sales/Payables	0 UND / 5 68.8 / 17 20.9	2 182.9 / 15 23.8 / 26 13.8	5 67.0 / 24 15.3 / 38 9.6	9 40.8 / 22 16.4 / 30 12.1	14 26.9 / 24 15.3 / 51 7.2	
10.4 / 20.3 / 174.3	9.2 / 20.2 / UND	10.5 / 19.7 / 120.3	Sales/Working Capital	8.8 / 18.0 / -61.0	10.3 / 15.7 / 46.2	10.2 / 35.9 / 786.5	12.4 / 24.1 / 109.3	11.2 / 25.0 / 120.4	
(104) 4.5 / 2.1 / .7	(109) 5.1 / 2.1 / 1.0	(127) 6.1 / 2.4 / 1.2	EBIT/Interest	(34) 4.5 / 1.6 / -.5	(43) 7.0 / 2.7 / 1.1	(13) 7.1 / 3.7 / 2.4	(19) 8.1 / 1.7 / 1.0	(10) 6.7 / 2.3 / 1.5	
(31) 2.1 / 1.8 / 1.0	(37) 2.5 / 1.2 / .9	(25) 3.1 / 1.8 / .4	Net Profit + Depr., Dep., Amort./Cur. Mat. L/T/D						
.3 / 1.0 / UND	.3 / 1.3 / -5.3	.2 / .8 / -21.3	Fixed/Worth	.4 / 1.3 / -4.1	.2 / .8 / -14.8	.2 / 1.2 / 2.0	.4 / .5 / NM	.3 / .7 / 2.1	
1.1 / 3.5 / -36.1	1.4 / 4.6 / -15.3	1.1 / 3.4 / -229.8	Debt/Worth	1.1 / 4.8 / -7.4	.8 / 2.8 / -31.6	1.6 / 2.4 / 5.2	1.1 / 5.3 / NM	1.0 / 1.6 / 4.3	
(91) 49.6 / 16.4 / 3.3	(88) 33.7 / 17.3 / 6.4	(106) 45.5 / 21.2 / 7.1	% Profit Before Taxes/Tangible Net Worth	(25) 67.1 / 25.8 / -11.9	(33) 47.8 / 27.9 / 3.9	62.3 / 30.7 / 16.9	(16) 24.4 / 12.6 / 3.7	(10) 20.7 / 12.3 / 8.3	
11.8 / 4.0 / -1.2	10.4 / 5.1 / .5	14.2 / 5.6 / .6	% Profit Before Taxes/Total Assets	14.7 / 4.6 / -5.4	17.3 / 6.9 / .6	15.5 / 8.6 / 5.4	11.5 / 3.9 / .3	9.5 / 4.0 / 2.1	
80.9 / 26.3 / 10.8	64.4 / 26.2 / 10.0	79.6 / 31.8 / 10.9	Sales/Net Fixed Assets	87.5 / 28.7 / 9.6	80.1 / 43.1 / 10.9	87.4 / 24.9 / 6.5	77.8 / 45.6 / 18.9	107.6 / 23.3 / 10.6	
5.5 / 3.9 / 2.9	5.5 / 3.8 / 2.8	6.0 / 4.2 / 3.0	Sales/Total Assets	6.1 / 4.3 / 2.6	6.4 / 4.2 / 3.4	4.8 / 3.8 / 3.3	6.7 / 4.9 / 3.2	5.1 / 4.2 / 2.9	
(101) .4 / .8 / 1.3	(111) .4 / .9 / 1.4	(124) .4 / .9 / 1.6	% Depr., Dep., Amort./Sales	(30) .4 / 1.0 / 2.2	(44) .4 / .7 / 1.7	(11) .5 / .8 / 1.4	(20) .4 / .8 / 1.2	.3 / .7 / 1.3	
(64) 2.4 / 4.0 / 6.1	(68) 1.2 / 2.5 / 4.6	(75) 2.1 / 4.0 / 5.9	% Officers', Directors', Owners' Comp/Sales	(20) 3.5 / 5.7 / 8.6	(32) 1.4 / 4.1 / 5.4				
911722M	1123558M	1413840M	Net Sales ($)	22448M	90827M	56931M	149156M	179146M	915332M
323043M	328093M	528930M	Total Assets ($)	6146M	22107M	15338M	33267M	56082M	395990M

Current Data Sorted By Assets | Comparative Historical Data

0-500M	500M-2MM	2-10MM	10-50MM	50-100MM	100-250MM		# Postretirement Benefits Type of Statement	4/1/90-3/31/91 ALL	4/1/91-3/31/92 ALL
3	3	2	2						
1	1	7	7	2			Unqualified	8	15
7	11	13	1				Reviewed	33	21
40	27	7	1				Compiled	82	91
19	4						Tax Returns	6	15
19	20	13	4	1			Other	41	39
69 (4/1-9/30/94)			136 (10/1/94-3/31/95)						
86	63	40	13	3			NUMBER OF STATEMENTS	170	181
%	%	%	%	%	%		**ASSETS**	%	%
13.6	10.2	6.6	9.0				Cash & Equivalents	9.3	10.2
3.8	8.2	12.7	7.4				Trade Receivables - (net)	6.3	4.2
58.8	55.6	46.7	48.1				Inventory	57.8	59.9
1.5	.3	.8	1.5				All Other Current	1.0	1.1
77.7	74.3	66.8	66.0				Total Current	74.3	75.4
17.5	19.7	22.0	23.8				Fixed Assets (net)	18.6	18.5
1.8	2.1	1.3	4.9				Intangibles (net)	1.6	1.3
3.0	3.8	9.9	5.2				All Other Non-Current	5.5	4.8
100.0	100.0	100.0	100.0				Total	100.0	100.0
							LIABILITIES		
8.3	9.0	9.8	7.9				Notes Payable-Short Term	11.8	12.2
3.5	3.2	2.8	2.3				Cur. Mat. -L/T/D	4.6	3.7
17.4	20.4	21.6	18.5				Trade Payables	18.3	18.4
.5	.2	.3	.3				Income Taxes Payable	.7	.4
12.2	7.5	6.0	10.3				All Other Current	9.5	7.8
41.9	40.3	40.3	39.3				Total Current	44.9	42.5
19.0	20.4	13.3	15.4				Long Term Debt	19.2	16.4
.3	.0	.2	.0				Deferred Taxes	.1	.3
6.6	3.6	6.2	6.6				All Other-Non-Current	2.9	4.4
32.2	35.7	40.0	38.7				Net Worth	33.0	36.5
100.0	100.0	100.0	100.0				Total Liabilities & Net Worth	100.0	100.0
							INCOME DATA		
100.0	100.0	100.0	100.0				Net Sales	100.0	100.0
43.6	45.2	47.0	43.0				Gross Profit	45.2	45.2
38.9	41.4	41.4	38.2				Operating Expenses	41.4	41.7
4.7	3.8	5.7	4.8				Operating Profit	3.9	3.5
1.5	1.4	1.2	.2				All Other Expenses (net)	1.4	1.6
3.1	2.4	4.5	4.6				Profit Before Taxes	2.4	1.9
							RATIOS		
3.5	2.6	2.1	3.1				Current	2.7	2.9
1.8	2.0	1.6	1.6					1.6	1.8
1.3	1.3	1.2	1.2					1.2	1.3
.8	.9	.7	.8				Quick	(167) .6	(179) .6
.4	.4	(39) .3	.6					.3	.3
.1	.1	.2	.1					.1	.1
0 UND	0 999.8	0 999.8	0 UND				Sales/Receivables	0 UND	0 UND
0 UND	2 224.4	4 100.6	2 218.4					1 387.7	0 777.0
4 98.5	16 23.4	33 10.9	9 40.3					8 44.9	6 60.6
104 3.5	101 3.6	81 4.5	99 3.7				Cost of Sales/Inventory	111 3.3	111 3.3
146 2.5	174 2.1	140 2.6	126 2.9					166 2.2	159 2.3
215 1.7	243 1.5	203 1.8	261 1.4					243 1.5	215 1.7
5 69.8	19 18.8	37 9.9	11 32.4				Cost of Sales/Payables	17 22.1	16 23.1
28 13.1	53 6.9	49 7.4	59 6.2					45 8.2	45 8.2
70 5.2	81 4.5	107 3.4	85 4.3					79 4.6	76 4.8
4.5	4.1	6.2	5.1				Sales/Working Capital	4.6	4.8
6.7	8.0	9.5	9.8					8.5	7.7
19.3	17.8	28.3	21.1					35.7	15.0
(73) 9.9	(56) 4.4	(39) 9.0	(11) 9.9				EBIT/Interest	(157) 4.7	(167) 5.1
2.8	2.5	3.6	4.2					2.0	2.1
1.2	1.0	1.4	1.5					1.0	.7
(11) 2.5	(16) 2.6	(14) 5.0					Net Profit + Depr., Dep., Amort./Cur. Mat. L /T/D	(65) 3.2	(55) 2.9
2.2	1.8	3.1						1.5	1.4
.4	.4	1.9						.7	.2
.1	.3	.2	.5				Fixed/Worth	.2	.2
.5	.6	.5	.9					.5	.5
3.4	1.9	1.1	1.2					2.0	1.4
.8	.9	.7	.7				Debt/Worth	.8	.8
2.3	2.1	1.8	1.7					2.3	1.8
21.3	7.2	3.4	4.7					6.4	4.6
(72) 56.3	(56) 40.4	38.7	(11) 39.9				% Profit Before Taxes/Tangible Net Worth	(150) 45.3	(164) 34.7
29.2	17.8	19.2	17.8					19.2	13.9
5.8	5.3	5.2	13.6					1.2	.1
19.8	9.9	13.2	12.3				% Profit Before Taxes/Total Assets	12.3	12.4
8.2	5.0	5.9	9.3					5.4	5.1
1.1	.1	1.7	2.7					-.3	-.7
69.5	33.8	42.3	15.8				Sales/Net Fixed Assets	37.6	36.4
20.4	14.4	15.9	8.7					15.4	16.6
8.4	9.6	8.4	6.7					8.4	9.0
3.6	3.1	3.2	3.3				Sales/Total Assets	2.9	3.1
2.6	2.3	2.4	2.1					2.4	2.3
1.7	1.7	1.7	1.4					1.8	1.9
(66) .8	(56) .8	(36) .7	(12) 1.8				% Depr., Dep., Amort./Sales	(149) .9	(152) .9
1.4	1.4	1.6	2.7					1.8	1.5
2.4	2.5	2.1	3.1					2.8	2.5
(45) 4.3	(38) 3.0	(15) 1.3					% Officers', Directors', Owners' Comp/Sales	(78) 2.9	(81) 3.2
6.5	5.2	2.6						5.3	5.1
9.7	7.4	12.0						8.9	9.3
56867M	169079M	413500M	717068M	459349M			Net Sales ($)	834635M	1263399M
21398M	66324M	161032M	316142M	248596M			Total Assets ($)	355554M	714206M

M = $ thousand MM = $ million
See Pages 1 through 15 for Explanation of Ratios and Data

Comparative Historical Data				Current Data Sorted By Sales					
	8	10	# Postretirement Benefits	3	1	2	2	2	2
			Type of Statement						
14	18	18	Unqualified	2	1	1	2	3	9
18	26	32	Reviewed	2	7	7	10	5	1
100	80	75	Compiled	44	15	8	4	3	1
8	20	23	Tax Returns	15	7	1			
65	53	57	Other	19	16	4	5	8	5
4/1/92-3/31/93	4/1/93-3/31/94	4/1/94-3/31/95		69 (4/1-9/30/94)			136 (10/1/94-3/31/95)		
ALL	ALL	ALL		0-1MM	1-3MM	3-5MM	5-10MM	10-25MM	25MM & OVER
205	197	205	**NUMBER OF STATEMENTS**	82	46	20	22	19	16
%	%	%	**ASSETS**	%	%	%	%	%	%
10.3	10.6	10.9	Cash & Equivalents	13.4	8.6	13.2	5.7	8.7	12.0
6.3	5.1	7.1	Trade Receivables - (net)	2.5	9.5	10.0	6.6	17.2	8.4
58.8	58.3	54.4	Inventory	60.4	52.4	51.7	57.4	42.7	41.5
.7	1.0	1.0	All Other Current	1.3	.8	.5	.4	1.0	1.4
76.1	74.9	73.4	Total Current	77.7	71.3	75.4	70.1	69.6	63.3
16.5	18.4	19.8	Fixed Assets (net)	17.5	21.3	18.5	22.7	18.8	26.0
2.2	1.9	2.0	Intangibles (net)	2.0	1.9	1.8	.6	2.0	3.8
5.2	4.7	4.9	All Other Non-Current	2.8	5.4	4.2	6.7	9.5	6.9
100.0	100.0	100.0	Total	100.0	100.0	100.0	100.0	100.0	100.0
			LIABILITIES						
12.8	11.1	8.6	Notes Payable-Short Term	7.6	12.1	7.3	9.6	8.0	5.1
4.3	2.9	3.2	Cur. Mat.-L /T/D	4.0	2.4	2.7	3.3	2.6	2.3
18.9	16.8	19.1	Trade Payables	14.9	21.7	24.4	22.0	23.6	16.8
.4	.9	.4	Income Taxes Payable	.3	.5	.3	.0	.5	1.0
9.9	11.7	9.4	All Other Current	12.5	7.2	5.6	6.0	8.7	9.5
46.4	43.3	40.6	Total Current	39.3	43.7	40.3	41.1	43.4	34.6
17.1	17.4	18.1	Long Term Debt	21.8	18.6	13.3	14.3	8.0	20.3
.0	.1	.2	Deferred Taxes	.3	.0	.0	.0	.4	.0
3.7	4.1	5.5	All Other-Non-Current	7.1	5.0	5.5	3.1	3.0	5.6
32.8	35.1	35.6	Net Worth	31.5	32.6	40.9	41.5	45.3	39.5
100.0	100.0	100.0	Total Liabilities & Net Worth	100.0	100.0	100.0	100.0	100.0	100.0
			INCOME DATA						
100.0	100.0	100.0	Net Sales	100.0	100.0	100.0	100.0	100.0	100.0
44.4	43.6	44.7	Gross Profit	44.4	46.4	41.7	48.2	40.7	45.7
39.8	39.8	40.1	Operating Expenses	38.9	44.5	37.6	44.6	34.6	36.9
4.6	3.8	4.7	Operating Profit	5.5	1.9	4.1	3.5	6.1	8.8
1.2	1.2	1.3	All Other Expenses (net)	2.2	.9	−.1	1.0	1.4	.2
3.4	2.6	3.3	Profit Before Taxes	3.3	.9	4.3	2.5	4.6	8.6
			RATIOS						
2.5	3.0	2.7	Current	3.8	2.3	2.8	2.1	2.1	3.1
1.7	1.9	1.8		2.0	1.6	2.1	1.5	1.7	2.0
1.2	1.3	1.3		1.4	1.2	1.4	1.3	1.1	1.3
.7	.8	.8	Quick	.9	.7	1.0	.4	.8	1.0
(201) .3	(194) .3	(204) .4		.4	.3	.6	(21) .3	.6	.6
.1	.1	.1		.1	.1	.2	.1	.3	.1
0 UND	0 UND	0 UND	Sales/Receivables	0 UND	0 UND	0 900.8	0 999.8	0 999.8	0 930.8
0 860.0	0 999.8	1 388.2		0 UND	1 540.4	2 159.4	2 205.1	4 93.8	1 370.8
7 52.1	4 96.4	6 57.2		4 93.3	11 34.6	30 12.3	9 41.3	41 8.9	4 81.3
118 3.1	99 3.7	101 3.6	Cost of Sales/Inventory	118 3.1	96 3.8	78 4.7	111 3.3	47 7.7	91 4.0
166 2.2	152 2.4	140 2.6		166 2.2	135 2.7	126 2.9	152 2.4	107 3.4	111 3.3
228 1.6	228 1.6	228 1.6		281 1.3	203 1.8	183 2.0	261 1.4	152 2.4	146 2.5
16 22.5	11 33.4	18 20.4	Cost of Sales/Payables	6 59.3	21 17.5	26 14.0	38 9.6	24 15.4	15 24.7
38 9.5	33 11.0	41 8.8		29 12.5	46 7.9	47 7.7	59 6.2	41 8.9	35 10.3
81 4.5	68 5.4	81 4.5		89 4.1	79 4.6	79 4.6	107 3.4	72 5.1	78 4.7
5.0	4.7	4.8	Sales/Working Capital	3.6	5.7	5.5	5.9	7.0	5.9
7.8	7.9	8.1		5.6	10.9	8.2	9.0	11.0	8.9
23.2	18.2	19.2		12.5	38.2	11.1	20.5	29.1	20.0
6.1	9.4	8.2	EBIT/Interest	6.4	5.3	8.5	8.6	14.2	16.9
(185) 2.8	(181) 3.7	(182) 2.9		(68) 2.2	(44) 2.6	(18) 4.0	(19) 3.3	5.1	(14) 5.7
1.2	1.1	1.3		.7	1.3	1.2	1.3	2.4	2.0
3.1	5.3	3.5	Net Profit + Depr., Dep.,	2.4					
(45) 1.8	(44) 2.9	(49) 2.2	Amort./Cur. Mat. L/T/D	(10) 1.4					
.3	.6	1.3		.1					
.1	.2	.2	Fixed/Worth	.1	.3	.3	.1	.3	.5
.5	.5	.6		.5	.8	.5	.6	.4	.9
1.7	1.4	1.6		5.5	2.9	1.4	1.0	.6	1.2
.9	.8	.8	Debt/Worth	.9	.8	.5	.9	.7	.7
2.2	1.7	2.0		2.4	2.5	2.0	1.7	1.4	1.7
8.5	7.0	5.9		34.0	12.8	5.8	3.0	2.1	4.7
48.1	40.0	44.5	% Profit Before Taxes/Tangible	57.0	29.1	55.0	36.0	47.0	43.8
(175) 21.8	(174) 22.6	(182) 21.6	Net Worth	(67) 29.2	(40) 14.8	24.9	10.6	27.4	(14) 27.8
6.0	4.5	5.9		3.9	4.5	7.7	4.4	9.7	13.8
14.1	16.8	14.5	% Profit Before Taxes/Total	18.5	11.5	14.9	11.7	17.3	17.8
5.7	7.0	6.4	Assets	6.6	4.9	9.3	4.3	9.5	9.5
.7	.3	1.6		−.2	.8	1.6	1.2	3.3	3.9
45.8	40.4	45.8	Sales/Net Fixed Assets	70.3	46.1	46.4	38.1	38.1	16.8
20.5	16.9	14.8		16.3	14.8	17.4	15.6	16.3	9.2
10.7	8.7	8.4		7.0	10.5	10.8	6.5	10.0	5.2
3.0	3.3	3.4	Sales/Total Assets	3.0	3.6	3.3	3.4	3.6	3.6
2.3	2.5	2.4		2.0	2.7	2.7	2.4	3.0	2.2
1.9	1.8	1.7		1.4	1.9	2.0	1.9	2.4	1.7
.8	.7	.8	% Depr., Dep., Amort./Sales	1.0	.7	.7	.9	.5	1.7
(167) 1.4	(164) 1.6	(173) 1.6		(61) 1.8	(42) 1.3	(16) 1.0	(21) 1.7	(18) 1.2	(15) 2.6
2.3	2.5	2.5		2.7	2.4	2.1	2.5	1.8	3.1
2.4	2.6	2.9	% Officers', Directors',	4.4	4.0	2.8	1.1		
(100) 4.2	(106) 4.8	(101) 5.7	Owners' Comp/Sales	(41) 6.6	(27) 4.9	(11) 5.5	(16) 2.6		
8.7	10.7	7.9		9.5	7.7	7.4	8.2		
948077M	1649483M	1815863M	Net Sales ($)	45197M	81372M	74888M	158174M	255624M	1200608M
396885M	752482M	813492M	Total Assets ($)	24432M	37697M	30222M	67926M	90018M	563197M

M = $ thousand   MM = $ million
See Pages 1 through 15 for Explanation of Ratios and Data

Current Data Sorted By Assets

Comparative Historical Data

							# Postretirement Benefits		
		3		1		1	**Type of Statement**		
		1		4	5	1	Unqualified	15	11
	1	7		12	2		Reviewed	18	23
	26	31		4			Compiled	46	55
		3					Tax Returns	1	6
	6	6		7			Other	30	24
		66 (4/1-9/30/94)			50 (10/1/94-3/31/95)			4/1/90-3/31/91	4/1/91-3/31/92
	0-500M	500M-2MM	2-10MM	10-50MM	50-100MM	100-250MM		ALL	ALL
	33	48	27	7	1		**NUMBER OF STATEMENTS**	110	119
	%	%	%	%	%	%	**ASSETS**	%	%
	8.8	5.5	4.4				Cash & Equivalents	6.6	4.8
	9.0	15.5	16.7				Trade Receivables - (net)	16.9	17.1
	61.3	53.5	53.4				Inventory	56.9	59.0
	1.2	.8	1.8				All Other Current	2.3	1.7
	80.2	75.4	76.3				Total Current	82.8	82.6
	15.5	17.7	18.7				Fixed Assets (net)	11.3	12.0
	.8	1.2	1.6				Intangibles (net)	.7	.5
	3.5	5.7	3.5				All Other Non-Current	5.2	4.9
	100.0	100.0	100.0				Total	100.0	100.0
							LIABILITIES		
	16.7	16.8	16.6				Notes Payable-Short Term	19.3	18.7
	3.1	3.8	4.5				Cur. Mat. -L/T/D	3.2	3.0
	11.1	16.7	21.9				Trade Payables	20.3	19.5
	.1	.3	.3				Income Taxes Payable	.5	.5
	12.6	7.5	7.7				All Other Current	5.9	6.0
	43.5	45.2	50.9				Total Current	49.2	47.6
	7.9	7.9	14.8				Long Term Debt	11.1	10.4
	.0	.4	.2				Deferred Taxes	.2	.1
	2.9	5.3	3.1				All Other-Non-Current	2.5	4.2
	45.7	41.2	31.0				Net Worth	37.0	37.8
	100.0	100.0	100.0				Total Liabilities & Net Worth	100.0	100.0
							INCOME DATA		
	100.0	100.0	100.0				Net Sales	100.0	100.0
	43.7	41.7	39.0				Gross Profit	41.6	42.3
	35.8	39.1	36.7				Operating Expenses	38.0	39.5
	7.9	2.6	2.3				Operating Profit	3.6	2.8
	1.0	−.2	.9				All Other Expenses (net)	.7	.2
	6.9	2.9	1.4				Profit Before Taxes	2.9	2.6
							RATIOS		
	3.5	2.8	1.9					2.7	2.5
	2.0	1.7	1.5				Current	1.6	1.7
	1.3	1.2	1.1					1.2	1.3
	1.0	.6	.7					.9	.8
	.3	.3	.3				Quick	.4	.4
	.2	.2	.2					.2	.2
	2 170.5	5 80.8	13 27.6					6 57.8	9 42.9
	6 56.8	13 28.9	23 16.1				Sales/Receivables	21 17.6	25 14.5
	19 19.7	42 8.6	43 8.4					47 7.8	46 7.9
	122 3.0	135 2.7	96 3.8					111 3.3	140 2.6
	192 1.9	183 2.0	135 2.7				Cost of Sales/Inventory	174 2.1	183 2.0
	281 1.3	228 1.6	281 1.3					261 1.4	281 1.3
	10 38.0	15 23.6	27 13.3					24 15.4	21 17.4
	21 17.1	51 7.1	60 6.1				Cost of Sales/Payables	41 8.8	49 7.5
	59 6.2	85 4.3	101 3.6					99 3.7	104 3.5
	3.6	3.9	4.5					3.6	3.3
	5.4	7.9	6.9				Sales/Working Capital	6.7	6.0
	11.1	13.8	50.4					17.3	13.9
	8.5	4.7	3.4					3.9	3.9
(31)	5.8	(47) 2.4	1.8				EBIT/Interest	(104) 2.0	(116) 2.0
	2.8	1.2	1.0					1.2	1.1
		9.1	7.4					5.0	3.8
	(17)	1.5 (18)	1.5				Net Profit + Depr., Dep., Amort./Cur. Mat. L /T/D	(55) 2.3	(52) 1.4
		.6	.5					.6	.5
	.1	.1	.1					.1	.1
	.2	.2	.4				Fixed/Worth	.3	.2
	.5	.9	1.3					.6	.5
	.3	.8	1.2					1.0	.9
	1.4	1.6	2.5				Debt/Worth	2.0	1.6
	2.5	2.9	4.3					4.0	3.3
	48.7	21.3	35.5					27.1	21.7
(31)	23.1	(47) 13.1	(26) 15.0				% Profit Before Taxes/Tangible Net Worth	(108) 13.2	(114) 11.1
	13.4	.9	3.9					4.6	2.5
	16.9	9.0	8.9					10.0	7.8
	12.2	4.5	3.4				% Profit Before Taxes/Total Assets	5.1	3.8
	6.4	.3	.3					1.1	.6
	131.8	65.2	66.1					54.4	72.0
	43.5	25.2	25.6				Sales/Net Fixed Assets	25.0	33.3
	11.2	6.6	5.5					12.3	12.7
	3.0	2.4	3.1					2.7	2.5
	2.4	1.8	1.9				Sales/Total Assets	2.0	1.9
	1.5	1.4	1.3					1.4	1.4
	.4	.5	.7					.8	.5
(25)	.8	(42) 1.1	(26) .8				% Depr., Dep., Amort./Sales	(93) 1.1	(98) 1.0
	2.7	1.7	1.3					1.9	2.0
	4.3	3.2	.7					2.8	2.9
(18)	7.7	(25) 6.2	(13) 1.8				% Officers', Directors', Owners' Comp/Sales	(47) 4.9	(51) 5.0
	14.9	7.9	2.6					8.2	9.9
	19823M	98127M	250317M	314460M	122347M		Net Sales ($)	775598M	518241M
	8856M	48761M	105925M	148032M	97460M		Total Assets ($)	397795M	260457M

M = $ thousand   MM = $ million
See Pages 1 through 15 for Explanation of Ratios and Data

Comparative Historical Data				Current Data Sorted By Sales					
			# Postretirement Benefits		2		2		1
			Type of Statement						
9	11	11	Unqualified		1	1		3	6
14	17	22	Reviewed	2	6	5	7	1	1
57	56	61	Compiled	30	21	6	3	1	
7	7	3	Tax Returns		2	1			
19	30	19	Other	5	6	3	2	3	
4/1/92-3/31/93 ALL	4/1/93-3/31/94 ALL	4/1/94-3/31/95 ALL		66 (4/1-9/30/94)			50 (10/1/94-3/31/95)		
				0-1MM	1-3MM	3-5MM	5-10MM	10-25MM	25MM & OVER
106	121	116	NUMBER OF STATEMENTS	37	36	16	12	8	7
%	%	%	ASSETS	%	%	%	%	%	%
5.2	6.2	6.0	Cash & Equivalents	8.0	5.8	3.4	6.1		
15.8	14.7	14.7	Trade Receivables - (net)	10.6	16.6	10.4	15.5		
57.5	55.1	55.1	Inventory	57.4	53.3	63.4	46.3		
1.1	2.4	1.7	All Other Current	.6	1.5	.4	5.3		
79.6	78.4	77.5	Total Current	76.7	77.3	77.6	73.3		
13.5	16.1	16.8	Fixed Assets (net)	18.1	17.0	17.6	19.8		
.4	1.0	1.1	Intangibles (net)	.6	1.8	.5	2.7		
6.5	4.5	4.5	All Other Non-Current	4.6	3.9	4.3	4.3		
100.0	100.0	100.0	Total	100.0	100.0	100.0	100.0		
			LIABILITIES						
18.1	15.2	17.2	Notes Payable-Short Term	20.4	12.6	18.4	16.4		
3.3	2.6	3.5	Cur. Mat.-L /T/D	3.2	4.1	3.5	5.5		
18.0	15.8	16.4	Trade Payables	11.6	15.6	22.8	17.4		
.3	1.4	.3	Income Taxes Payable	.1	.3	.4	.2		
7.1	8.4	9.0	All Other Current	10.6	7.2	8.1	11.4		
46.8	43.3	46.4	Total Current	45.9	39.8	53.2	50.8		
10.8	12.2	10.3	Long Term Debt	7.5	10.1	12.2	13.6		
.2	.3	.3	Deferred Taxes	.4	.1	.0	.3		
3.6	3.5	3.9	All Other-Non-Current	4.2	4.8	2.3	5.4		
38.6	40.6	39.2	Net Worth	41.9	45.2	32.3	29.9		
100.0	100.0	100.0	Total Liabilities & Net Worth	100.0	100.0	100.0	100.0		
			INCOME DATA						
100.0	100.0	100.0	Net Sales	100.0	100.0	100.0	100.0		
42.4	41.1	41.3	Gross Profit	44.3	42.2	40.0	43.8		
39.0	37.6	37.1	Operating Expenses	37.7	39.0	36.8	40.5		
3.3	3.5	4.1	Operating Profit	6.5	3.2	3.2	3.3		
.3	.3	.4	All Other Expenses (net)	.6	–.4	1.1	.3		
3.0	3.2	3.8	Profit Before Taxes	5.9	3.6	2.0	3.0		
			RATIOS						
2.5 / 1.7 / 1.3	2.8 / 1.8 / 1.3	2.4 / 1.7 / 1.2	Current	3.4 / 1.7 / 1.3	3.0 / 1.9 / 1.4	1.8 / 1.4 / 1.1	2.2 / 1.4 / 1.1		
.9 / .4 / .1	.7 / .4 / .2	.7 / .3 / .2	Quick	.8 / .3 / .1	.8 / .4 / .2	.3 / .2 / .1	.9 / .3 / .2		
8 46.2 / 18 20.6 / 37 10.0	6 64.4 / 18 20.6 / 33 11.2	5 70.7 / 14 26.5 / 39 9.4	Sales/Receivables	2 183.3 / 6 56.8 / 33 11.2	6 61.7 / 18 20.5 / 49 7.4	5 74.2 / 15 24.4 / 27 13.6	9 40.3 / 24 15.4 / 40 9.1		
126 2.9 / 192 1.9 / 281 1.3	126 2.9 / 183 2.0 / 243 1.5	118 3.1 / 174 2.1 / 243 1.5	Cost of Sales/Inventory	140 2.6 / 203 1.8 / 304 1.2	126 2.9 / 192 1.9 / 228 1.6	122 3.0 / 192 1.9 / 332 1.1	99 3.7 / 135 2.7 / 243 1.5		
18 20.1 / 43 8.5 / 91 4.0	16 22.5 / 38 9.6 / 74 4.9	18 20.3 / 43 8.5 / 79 4.6	Cost of Sales/Payables	12 30.0 / 30 12.2 / 70 5.2	17 21.9 / 44 8.3 / 85 4.3	34 10.7 / 69 5.3 / 130 2.8	18 20.4 / 44 8.3 / 140 2.6		
3.6 / 6.4 / 14.9	3.7 / 6.9 / 10.3	3.9 / 6.6 / 14.7	Sales/Working Capital	3.2 / 5.4 / 16.4	3.6 / 5.8 / 8.5	4.5 / 7.2 / 104.4	6.2 / 7.6 / 41.3		
(103) 4.7 / 2.1 / 1.3	(113) 6.3 / 2.8 / 1.5	(113) 6.8 / 2.8 / 1.4	EBIT/Interest	(34) 7.9 / 4.3 / 1.2	7.4 / 3.3 / 2.1	2.4 / 1.7 / 1.1	5.1 / 2.0 / 1.0		
(45) 5.4 / 2.2 / 1.0	(41) 5.6 / 2.3 / .9	(45) 8.2 / 2.1 / .6	Net Profit + Depr., Dep., Amort./Cur. Mat. L/T/D		(11) 3.9 / 1.5 / .6	(10) 21.7 / 1.2 / .5			
.1 / .3 / .7	.1 / .3 / .8	.1 / .3 / .9	Fixed/Worth	.0 / .2 / .8	.1 / .2 / .7	.1 / .4 / 1.2	.1 / .7 / 1.7		
.7 / 1.9 / 4.4	.7 / 1.7 / 3.3	.9 / 1.9 / 3.4	Debt/Worth	.6 / 1.4 / 3.0	.7 / 1.3 / 2.6	1.4 / 2.4 / 4.5	1.3 / 3.3 / 5.4		
(104) 25.5 / 12.4 / 5.0	(115) 33.3 / 16.0 / 6.7	(112) 33.8 / 15.8 / 6.2	% Profit Before Taxes/Tangible Net Worth	(34) 45.5 / 19.0 / 5.9	28.5 / 15.2 / 10.3	19.8 / 12.0 / 3.8	(11) 45.3 / 21.3 / .4		
9.6 / 4.4 / 1.3	11.4 / 5.7 / 1.8	12.0 / 5.5 / 1.2	% Profit Before Taxes/Total Assets	15.6 / 9.0 / 1.3	12.8 / 6.3 / 3.9	5.8 / 2.3 / .5	10.3 / 3.6 / –.9		
53.5 / 27.5 / 12.4	50.9 / 20.9 / 9.1	68.6 / 26.6 / 7.8	Sales/Net Fixed Assets	131.8 / 25.4 / 6.9	64.3 / 36.6 / 7.9	100.9 / 25.4 / 6.0	65.8 / 12.0 / 4.8		
2.8 / 2.0 / 1.4	2.7 / 2.0 / 1.5	2.8 / 1.9 / 1.4	Sales/Total Assets	2.8 / 1.6 / 1.3	2.5 / 1.9 / 1.4	2.2 / 1.9 / 1.6	3.0 / 2.0 / 1.8		
(96) .6 / 1.0 / 1.8	(100) .7 / 1.2 / 2.2	(101) .5 / 1.0 / 1.9	% Depr., Dep., Amort./Sales	(27) .4 / .7 / 2.7	(33) .7 / 1.2 / 1.7	.4 / .8 / 3.9	(11) .7 / 1.0 / 1.2		
(51) 2.6 / 4.5 / 7.2	(53) 3.3 / 6.0 / 7.6	(58) 2.5 / 5.6 / 8.5	% Officers', Directors', Owners' Comp/Sales	(17) 5.9 / 9.1 / 15.2	(21) 3.2 / 4.3 / 7.0				
402093M	848890M	805074M	Net Sales ($)	21603M	61303M	57899M	79318M	145879M	439072M
190937M	431367M	409034M	Total Assets ($)	13244M	36168M	33769M	47260M	50196M	228397M

M = $ thousand   MM = $ million
See Pages 1 through 15 for Explanation of Ratios and Data

Current Data Sorted By Assets   Comparative Historical Data

						# Postretirement Benefits Type of Statement		
1	1	1	2		1			
	1	1	1	1	1	Unqualified	4	4
2	4	4				Reviewed	7	4
15	10	1				Compiled	26	17
9	3	1				Tax Returns	1	7
6	4	5	3	1		Other	16	18
0-500M	21 (4/1-9/30/94) 500M-2MM	2-10MM	10-50MM	51 (10/1/94-3/31/95) 50-100MM	100-250MM		4/1/90-3/31/91 ALL	4/1/91-3/31/92 ALL
32	21	12	4	2	1	NUMBER OF STATEMENTS	54	50
%	%	%	%	%	%	ASSETS	%	%
13.6	7.1	5.0				Cash & Equivalents	8.9	11.6
10.2	14.9	16.2				Trade Receivables - (net)	20.0	15.5
35.2	38.7	34.5				Inventory	32.1	35.0
1.1	1.4	.9				All Other Current	.9	1.2
60.0	62.1	56.6				Total Current	61.8	63.3
25.5	21.5	27.4				Fixed Assets (net)	25.7	23.7
6.2	6.4	10.2				Intangibles (net)	3.1	3.7
8.3	10.0	5.8				All Other Non-Current	9.4	9.3
100.0	100.0	100.0				Total	100.0	100.0
						LIABILITIES		
12.3	11.3	7.6				Notes Payable-Short Term	11.7	9.3
8.1	5.2	3.6				Cur. Mat. -L/T/D	5.2	4.1
21.2	22.3	23.5				Trade Payables	20.5	13.8
.1	.1	.0				Income Taxes Payable	.8	.2
12.2	8.7	9.2				All Other Current	7.9	13.9
53.9	47.7	43.9				Total Current	46.0	41.4
21.8	12.7	20.6				Long Term Debt	14.2	16.7
.1	.0	.3				Deferred Taxes	.2	.2
7.2	3.7	8.0				All Other-Non-Current	1.9	1.1
17.1	35.8	27.2				Net Worth	37.7	40.7
100.0	100.0	100.0				Total Liabilities & Net Worth	100.0	100.0
						INCOME DATA		
100.0	100.0	100.0				Net Sales	100.0	100.0
52.6	49.5	51.7				Gross Profit	52.9	53.1
46.8	46.0	51.3				Operating Expenses	49.7	49.9
5.9	3.5	.4				Operating Profit	3.2	3.2
.8	.9	2.2				All Other Expenses (net)	.8	.4
5.1	2.6	-1.7				Profit Before Taxes	2.5	2.9
						RATIOS		
2.2	2.0	1.9					1.9	2.5
1.3	1.4	1.0				Current	1.6	1.5
.8	.9	.8					.9	1.1
1.0	1.1	1.0					1.2	1.1
.5	.5	(11) .3				Quick	(53) .6	.5
.2	.2	.1					.3	.3
0 UND	1 294.0	6 58.9					4 101.7	2 189.9
3 116.3	18 19.9	9 38.5				Sales/Receivables	16 23.1	10 37.9
11 34.4	32 11.3	38 9.7					38 9.7	29 12.8
42 8.7	56 6.5	47 7.8					49 7.5	54 6.7
69 5.3	83 4.4	83 4.4				Cost of Sales/Inventory	74 4.9	81 4.5
114 3.2	130 2.8	174 2.1					159 2.3	140 2.6
15 25.1	32 11.3	29 12.8					28 13.2	18 20.5
23 15.9	41 8.8	76 4.8				Cost of Sales/Payables	68 5.4	37 10.0
78 4.7	73 5.0	114 3.2					89 4.1	60 6.1
8.9	8.6	12.4					7.8	6.9
57.5	18.3	NM				Sales/Working Capital	13.3	13.5
-26.7	-186.6	-17.6					-101.6	92.0
(23) 9.0	(20) 6.9	7.9					(50) 6.9	(41) 4.5
4.5	2.7	3.8				EBIT/Interest	2.8	2.3
2.1	1.6	1.0					.9	.1
						Net Profit + Depr., Dep., Amort./Cur. Mat. L /T/D	(23) 7.1	(15) 4.4
							2.4	1.0
							.7	.7
.5	.2	.2					.2	.3
1.8	.6	2.0				Fixed/Worth	.5	.5
-1.4	1.2	5.8					2.2	1.5
1.0	1.1	1.4					.9	.8
5.1	2.2	5.9				Debt/Worth	1.6	1.5
-5.1	9.2	28.9					3.0	4.1
111.6	36.0	95.4					40.6	51.0
(21) 23.3	(18) 23.0	(11) 29.3				% Profit Before Taxes/Tangible Net Worth	(49) 17.3	(44) 9.3
.5	10.1	.0					-1.4	-4.4
37.4	13.9	15.8					14.5	11.8
11.5	4.3	6.3				% Profit Before Taxes/Total Assets	7.1	4.6
.7	2.1	.3					-2.3	-2.1
61.7	46.4	57.8					53.7	46.4
17.9	19.5	14.3				Sales/Net Fixed Assets	22.0	16.7
9.2	9.5	5.6					5.6	7.5
5.1	3.6	4.2					4.1	3.9
3.3	3.0	2.6				Sales/Total Assets	2.9	2.9
2.5	2.4	1.6					1.9	2.4
(22) .7	(19) .6	(11) .6					(48) .7	(45) .7
2.0	1.4	1.3				% Depr., Dep., Amort./Sales	1.7	1.6
4.2	2.1	3.2					4.1	2.5
(17) 3.1	(15) 2.6						(30) 3.3	(26) 4.5
6.3	5.7					% Officers', Directors', Owners' Comp/Sales	6.1	7.6
7.2	8.9						11.8	11.3
23806M	75155M	123935M	193837M	245192M	195931M	Net Sales ($)	188502M	155254M
6539M	24485M	43892M	84044M	162863M	140269M	Total Assets ($)	94225M	47285M

M = $ thousand   MM = $ million
See Pages 1 through 15 for Explanation of Ratios and Data

Comparative Historical Data / Current Data Sorted By Sales

	4/1/92-3/31/93 ALL	4/1/93-3/31/94 ALL	4/1/94-3/31/95 ALL	21 (4/1-9/30/94) 0-1MM	1-3MM	51 (10/1/94-3/31/95) 3-5MM	5-10MM	10-25MM	25MM & OVER
# Postretirement Benefits			6			1	1	1	3
Type of Statement									
Unqualified								1	3
Reviewed	3	3	4	1	2	3	4		
Compiled	5	6	10	11	9	3	3		
Tax Returns	26	21	26	7	3	1	2		
Other	11	9	13	6	1	4	1	4	3
	15	12	19						
NUMBER OF STATEMENTS	60	51	72	25	15	11	10	5	6

	%	%	%	%	%	%	%	%	%
ASSETS									
Cash & Equivalents	7.9	8.1	10.4	13.7	9.1	7.3	3.2		
Trade Receivables - (net)	12.5	12.9	13.0	12.2	9.4	12.3	15.9		
Inventory	33.8	31.0	34.8	36.3	35.0	34.5	40.9		
All Other Current	.5	1.8	1.1	1.3	1.4	.3	1.0		
Total Current	54.7	53.9	59.3	63.4	54.8	54.4	61.0		
Fixed Assets (net)	33.1	32.2	26.2	22.3	26.1	30.4	25.4		
Intangibles (net)	5.6	4.9	6.4	7.8	.4	12.5	9.9		
All Other Non-Current	6.6	9.0	8.0	6.5	18.7	2.7	3.7		
Total	100.0	100.0	100.0	100.0	100.0	100.0	100.0		
LIABILITIES									
Notes Payable-Short Term	8.7	10.7	10.2	9.7	15.3	11.7	6.8		
Cur. Mat.-L/T/D	6.9	6.0	5.8	10.0	3.4	5.9	4.4		
Trade Payables	15.9	15.1	20.7	21.5	21.0	20.6	24.3		
Income Taxes Payable	.1	1.4	.1	.0	.1	.2	.0		
All Other Current	7.7	11.5	10.4	13.5	7.6	10.8	7.7		
Total Current	39.3	44.8	47.1	54.6	47.3	49.3	43.2		
Long Term Debt	28.2	19.4	18.2	25.1	11.3	15.0	19.8		
Deferred Taxes	.1	.0	.1	.1	.0	.0	.4		
All Other-Non-Current	2.6	5.1	6.9	8.4	3.5	5.3	5.5		
Net Worth	29.7	30.7	27.7	11.8	38.0	30.4	31.0		
Total Liabilities & Net Worth	100.0	100.0	100.0	100.0	100.0	100.0	100.0		
INCOME DATA									
Net Sales	100.0	100.0	100.0	100.0	100.0	100.0	100.0		
Gross Profit	56.8	57.1	52.1	50.3	55.9	52.9	47.9		
Operating Expenses	53.2	52.7	47.6	44.9	51.0	50.1	46.6		
Operating Profit	3.6	4.3	4.5	5.4	5.0	2.8	1.2		
All Other Expenses (net)	.7	.8	1.0	.7	.7	1.6	2.5		
Profit Before Taxes	2.9	3.5	3.5	4.7	4.2	1.2	-1.3		
RATIOS									
Current	2.1	2.0	2.1	2.7	1.9	2.2	2.6		
	1.4	1.3	1.4	1.5	1.4	1.0	1.1		
	1.1	.8	.9	.7	.9	.7	.8		
Quick	.9	.8	1.0	1.2	.7	1.4	1.1		
	.4	.4	(71) .5	.5	.4	(10) .4	.2		
	.2	.2	.2	.2	.3	.1	.1		
Sales/Receivables	1 549.7	2 214.1	1 369.3	0 UND	0 UND	1 331.6	2 223.8		
	10 35.6	8 46.7	9 42.6	6 60.0	10 38.0	6 59.2	9 38.5		
	25 14.5	23 15.7	21 17.4	12 31.0	20 18.5	34 10.7	45 8.1		
Cost of Sales/Inventory	62 5.9	58 6.3	51 7.2	42 8.7	54 6.8	52 7.0	65 5.6		
	91 4.0	81 4.5	79 4.6	70 5.2	73 5.0	83 4.4	96 3.8		
	159 2.3	126 2.9	126 2.9	122 3.0	126 2.9	107 3.4	166 2.2		
Cost of Sales/Payables	26 14.0	21 17.8	21 17.7	15 24.6	20 18.6	29 12.5	33 11.1		
	39 9.4	32 11.4	39 9.4	29 12.6	41 8.8	35 10.4	76 4.8		
	68 5.4	74 4.9	85 4.3	76 4.8	81 4.5	89 4.1	114 3.2		
Sales/Working Capital	8.2	8.5	8.6	7.3	11.8	12.7	6.0		
	21.5	20.4	22.9	25.0	26.7	-340.1	109.1		
	96.6	-32.8	-43.8	-22.0	-161.5	-13.2	-26.2		
EBIT/Interest	(55) 5.3	(46) 7.8	(60) 8.2	(16) 8.3	7.4	(10) 4.5	9.0		
	2.3	3.0	3.3	4.2	2.6	3.2	2.4		
	1.0	1.4	1.4	2.2	1.4	1.0	1.1		
Net Profit + Depr., Dep., Amort./Cur. Mat. L/T/D	(14) 3.7	(15) 2.9	(15) 16.0						
	1.8	1.3	2.4						
	1.2	.7	1.0						
Fixed/Worth	.4	.3	.3	.5	.1	.5	.3		
	1.0	1.0	1.0	2.3	.8	1.3	.7		
	3.0	2.5	6.4	-1.1	1.2	-54.1	2.7		
Debt/Worth	1.2	1.1	1.0	1.4	.4	1.0	1.2		
	2.1	2.0	2.7	7.7	1.8	5.3	2.7		
	5.0	3.9	31.0	-4.9	3.5	-99.7	8.9		
% Profit Before Taxes/Tangible Net Worth	43.3	38.1	67.8	(15) 123.7	(14) 49.8				
	(50) 11.2	(41) 14.6	(57) 23.3	23.3	18.8				
	.9	4.5	2.8	-14.3	3.4				
% Profit Before Taxes/Total Assets	13.9	16.9	18.2	28.6	17.5	10.6	16.5		
	4.5	6.0	6.9	12.1	5.2	4.3	5.5		
	-.3	1.9	1.2	-2.2	1.3	.0	.8		
Sales/Net Fixed Assets	21.3	27.6	45.4	54.9	60.4	53.3	38.9		
	10.8	14.6	16.7	16.5	18.8	13.3	14.2		
	5.2	4.6	7.5	9.4	8.0	4.3	6.9		
Sales/Total Assets	3.6	4.1	4.1	4.5	5.2	3.7	3.3		
	2.9	2.4	3.0	3.1	3.3	3.1	2.6		
	1.9	2.0	2.4	2.5	2.3	2.4	1.7		
% Depr., Dep., Amort./Sales	.9	.9	.7	(16) .8	(12) .6	.6			
	(56) 2.3	(45) 2.2	(59) 1.8	2.2	1.7	1.4			
	4.0	3.6	3.5	4.7	3.0	4.1			
% Officers', Directors', Owners' Comp/Sales	3.1	2.6	2.7	(13) 2.8					
	(26) 9.9	(29) 6.4	(37) 6.1	6.2					
	14.4	11.5	8.1	6.9					
Net Sales ($)	777325M	383649M	857856M	12889M	27120M	42787M	70841M	89553M	614666M
Total Assets ($)	369108M	177177M	462092M	4427M	8465M	15156M	33308M	26448M	374288M

M = $ thousand   MM = $ million
See Pages 1 through 15 for Explanation of Ratios and Data

Current Data Sorted By Assets — Comparative Historical Data

	0-500M	500M-2MM	2-10MM	10-50MM	50-100MM	100-250MM		4/1/90-3/31/91 ALL	4/1/91-3/31/92 ALL
# Postretirement Benefits	3	3	5	3	4	2			
Type of Statement									
Unqualified	3	2	31	34	14	19		118	98
Reviewed	2	24	31	6				80	70
Compiled	6	16	10					80	61
Tax Returns		3							3
Other	5	15	24	13	4	6		69	59
		64 (4/1-9/30/94)		204 (10/1/94-3/31/95)					
NUMBER OF STATEMENTS	16	60	96	53	18	25		347	291
ASSETS	%	%	%	%	%	%		%	%
Cash & Equivalents	10.7	10.7	4.7	3.2	1.3	1.2		5.1	5.5
Trade Receivables - (net)	28.2	22.7	22.5	18.4	21.4	16.6		20.2	19.9
Inventory	44.1	45.3	51.3	54.9	49.6	54.9		47.7	48.9
All Other Current	3.1	1.2	.9	2.7	3.9	2.8		2.3	1.7
Total Current	86.1	79.8	79.4	79.2	76.3	75.4		75.3	75.9
Fixed Assets (net)	10.7	16.8	16.5	14.8	17.3	16.0		18.7	17.5
Intangibles (net)	.6	.5	.3	.9	.5	.5		.4	.5
All Other Non-Current	2.6	2.9	3.7	5.1	5.9	8.1		5.7	6.0
Total	100.0	100.0	100.0	100.0	100.0	100.0		100.0	100.0
LIABILITIES									
Notes Payable-Short Term	17.6	21.3	26.0	28.0	24.7	17.0		25.5	22.6
Cur. Mat. -L/T/D	3.1	3.5	4.4	4.6	4.9	1.7		6.9	5.7
Trade Payables	16.2	17.8	18.4	19.3	20.7	24.2		14.8	14.9
Income Taxes Payable	.2	.4	.4	.3	.3	.1		.4	.3
All Other Current	11.1	9.5	7.6	6.0	5.2	7.8		6.0	7.8
Total Current	48.3	52.6	56.8	58.2	55.9	50.8		53.6	51.3
Long Term Debt	15.0	10.0	10.5	10.1	13.3	17.7		13.0	13.2
Deferred Taxes	.1	.1	.5	.3	.7	.5		.5	.4
All Other-Non-Current	2.4	4.1	1.8	1.7	1.6	1.5		2.3	1.7
Net Worth	34.2	33.3	30.4	29.7	28.5	29.4		30.6	33.4
Total Liabilities & Net Worth	100.0	100.0	100.0	100.0	100.0	100.0		100.0	100.0
INCOME DATA									
Net Sales	100.0	100.0	100.0	100.0	100.0	100.0		100.0	100.0
Gross Profit	22.5	29.2	25.1	23.0	22.5	20.5		27.1	27.5
Operating Expenses	19.7	24.9	20.8	18.1	18.0	15.9		23.5	24.7
Operating Profit	2.8	4.3	4.3	4.9	4.5	4.6		3.6	2.8
All Other Expenses (net)	.2	.7	.6	.7	.2	.4		1.6	1.4
Profit Before Taxes	2.6	3.6	3.7	4.2	4.3	4.2		2.0	1.3
RATIOS									
Current	4.9	2.1	1.6	1.6	1.9	2.0		2.0	2.1
	1.7	1.5	1.3	1.3	1.3	1.5		1.3	1.4
	1.1	1.2	1.2	1.2	1.0	1.1		1.1	1.1
Quick	1.5	1.0	.6	.5	.6	.5		.8	.8
	.7	.7	.5	.4	.4	.3		.4	.5
	.5	.3	.3	.2	.3	.3		.3	.3
Sales/Receivables	4 81.6	20 18.1	24 15.4	27 13.7	38 9.7	33 11.0		24 15.1	25 14.5
	23 16.2	32 11.5	35 10.3	37 9.9	47 7.8	43 8.5		35 10.3	37 10.0
	43 8.5	43 8.5	50 7.3	43 8.5	64 5.7	57 6.4		47 7.8	49 7.4
Cost of Sales/Inventory	17 21.3	42 8.6	64 5.7	111 3.3	104 3.5	140 2.6		66 5.5	78 4.7
	42 8.7	85 4.3	118 3.1	152 2.4	159 2.3	203 1.8		126 2.9	135 2.7
	140 2.6	135 2.7	159 2.3	174 2.1	174 2.1	228 1.6		192 1.7	215 1.7
Cost of Sales/Payables	0 UND	12 31.7	12 30.0	16 22.5	28 13.2	53 6.9		11 33.0	12 29.4
	8 43.3	26 13.8	30 12.3	33 10.9	70 5.2	81 4.5		26 13.9	28 12.9
	29 12.6	49 7.5	54 6.8	78 4.7	85 4.3	104 3.5		57 6.4	57 6.4
Sales/Working Capital	4.0	6.4	7.0	5.2	4.2	3.9		5.0	4.5
	13.7	11.7	11.2	10.1	7.5	6.1		10.8	8.4
	33.1	21.5	20.1	16.1	60.4	13.7		33.5	19.5
EBIT/Interest	(15) 5.9	(58) 6.9	(94) 5.6	(52) 5.3	(17) 5.2	(24) 7.6		(328) 3.1	(269) 2.7
	3.0	3.6	2.7	3.2	4.6	4.5		1.7	1.6
	2.2	1.6	1.8	2.3	2.9	3.1		1.1	.8
Net Profit + Depr., Dep., Amort./Cur. Mat. L /T/D		(16) 6.1	(46) 4.8	(25) 11.7				(198) 4.6	(136) 3.3
		2.6	2.1	3.8				1.3	1.3
		.6	.9	1.4				.5	.3
Fixed/Worth	.0	.2	.2	.1	.2	.3		.2	.2
	.2	.3	.4	.3	.4	.4		.5	.4
	4.5	1.2	.9	.9	1.0	.5		1.1	.9
Debt/Worth	.7	1.3	1.5	1.7	2.1	1.6		1.4	1.2
	2.3	2.5	2.6	2.9	2.6	2.7		2.8	2.4
	NM	4.3	4.4	4.4	3.0	4.0		4.9	4.4
% Profit Before Taxes/Tangible Net Worth	(12) 49.9	(56) 39.6	(94) 32.0	(17) 40.4	39.1	35.8		(333) 25.0	(287) 18.8
	14.8	19.6	17.5	24.3	28.2	24.5		11.3	7.4
	1.5	9.9	10.2	16.1	16.6	15.7		3.3	-1.4
% Profit Before Taxes/Total Assets	14.7	14.0	9.1	9.8	10.6	10.1		7.1	5.4
	8.3	6.3	4.9	6.6	7.8	7.3		3.1	2.1
	1.1	2.7	2.6	4.5	4.3	4.4		.6	-.6
Sales/Net Fixed Assets	396.4	60.7	52.1	51.0	30.6	24.0		40.1	41.2
	92.9	32.2	26.2	27.3	12.8	11.2		15.5	16.9
	22.9	13.9	10.4	10.4	5.6	6.3		7.2	7.0
Sales/Total Assets	6.2	3.5	2.7	2.3	1.7	1.6		2.5	2.3
	3.9	2.6	2.1	1.8	1.5	1.5		1.7	1.7
	2.4	1.9	1.6	1.5	1.3	1.3		1.4	1.3
% Depr., Dep., Amort./Sales	(10) .4	(53) .5	(90) .4	(48) .6	(14) .6	(19) .6		(300) .7	(252) .7
	1.1	1.0	.8	.8	.9	1.0		1.2	1.2
	2.4	2.7	2.3	2.2	2.6	1.5		3.1	3.2
% Officers', Directors', Owners' Comp/Sales		(33) 2.5	(41) 1.3					(110) 1.9	(100) 1.9
		4.1	2.3					3.6	3.8
		6.3	4.6					6.5	7.9
Net Sales ($)	16970M	169647M	988325M	2160388M	2008105M	4876139M		7997882M	6928751M
Total Assets ($)	4377M	63223M	445007M	1202725M	1325826M	3577095M		5136931M	4883390M

M = $ thousand　　MM = $ million
See Pages 1 through 15 for Explanation of Ratios and Data

Comparative Historical Data				Current Data Sorted By Sales					
4	20	17	# Postretirement Benefits	1	5	1	1	9	

Type of Statement

					0-1MM	1-3MM	3-5MM	5-10MM	10-25MM	25MM & OVER
109	106	103	Unqualified		2	2	3	14	21	61
68	74	63	Reviewed		4	8	15	17	15	4
59	51	32	Compiled		4	14	5	6	3	
2	3	3	Tax Returns			3				
52	68	67	Other		3	14	9	12		20
4/1/92-3/31/93 ALL	4/1/93-3/31/94 ALL	4/1/94-3/31/95 ALL		64 (4/1-9/30/94)			204 (10/1/94-3/31/95)			
290	302	268	**NUMBER OF STATEMENTS**	13	41	32	49	48	85

%	%	%	**ASSETS**	%	%	%	%	%	%
5.0	5.4	5.5	Cash & Equivalents	12.9	10.8	9.0	4.6	3.3	2.4
20.2	20.9	21.5	Trade Receivables - (net)	18.0	24.7	23.2	20.4	23.9	19.0
48.4	50.0	50.5	Inventory	49.7	41.3	40.6	57.0	52.7	53.6
2.1	1.8	1.8	All Other Current	.0	1.7	1.5	1.1	2.3	2.5
75.7	77.9	79.3	Total Current	80.6	78.5	74.4	83.1	82.2	77.5
18.3	16.7	15.9	Fixed Assets (net)	15.8	19.3	20.6	13.2	12.9	15.8
.6	.4	.5	Intangibles (net)	.6	.1	.9	.2	1.2	.3
5.4	4.9	4.3	All Other Non-Current	3.0	2.1	4.1	3.6	3.7	6.4
100.0	100.0	100.0	Total	100.0	100.0	100.0	100.0	100.0	100.0

			LIABILITIES						
22.7	24.3	23.9	Notes Payable-Short Term	22.8	16.7	25.1	26.2	30.6	22.1
5.2	4.7	4.0	Cur. Mat.-L./T/D	3.7	3.8	5.5	3.6	3.5	4.0
15.5	17.0	19.0	Trade Payables	6.2	20.2	15.2	17.9	19.7	22.0
.3	.8	.3	Income Taxes Payable	.2	.3	.6	.1	.6	.2
7.2	6.9	7.8	All Other Current	9.1	9.8	8.4	8.2	7.1	6.5
51.0	53.6	55.0	Total Current	41.9	50.8	54.8	56.0	61.5	54.9
12.5	10.8	11.4	Long Term Debt	17.6	12.6	11.1	9.5	8.0	13.1
.4	.4	.4	Deferred Taxes	.1	.1	.7	.3	.4	.4
1.9	2.6	2.3	All Other-Non-Current	1.0	4.8	2.9	2.5	1.1	1.6
34.2	32.6	30.9	Net Worth	39.4	31.6	30.5	31.6	29.1	30.0
100.0	100.0	100.0	Total Liabilities & Net Worth	100.0	100.0	100.0	100.0	100.0	100.0

			INCOME DATA						
100.0	100.0	100.0	Net Sales	100.0	100.0	100.0	100.0	100.0	100.0
28.0	26.0	24.8	Gross Profit	28.1	32.9	27.7	23.5	22.6	21.5
24.5	22.4	20.5	Operating Expenses	23.9	27.8	23.4	19.7	18.9	16.7
3.5	3.7	4.4	Operating Profit	4.2	5.1	4.2	3.8	3.7	4.8
1.0	.6	.6	All Other Expenses (net)	-.6	.7	.3	.9	1.0	.3
2.5	3.1	3.8	Profit Before Taxes	4.8	4.4	3.9	2.9	2.7	4.4

			RATIOS						
2.1	1.9	1.7	Current	6.1	2.4	1.6	1.8	1.6	1.8
1.4	1.4	1.4		2.6	1.5	1.4	1.4	1.3	1.4
1.2	1.2	1.2		1.0	1.2	1.2	1.2	1.2	1.2
.7	.7	.7	Quick	2.9	1.2	1.0	.6	.6	.5
.4	.4	.5		.6	.7	.7	.4	.4	.4
.3	.3	.3		.1	.4	.4	.3	.3	.3
25 14.5	24 15.1	26 14.2	Sales/Receivables	0 UND	21 17.0	17 21.3	23 16.1	28 12.9	30 12.1
37 9.8	35 10.3	35 10.3		32 11.4	30 12.0	32 11.3	31 11.6	35 10.3	40 9.2
51 7.2	49 7.5	48 7.6		59 6.2	46 8.0	59 6.2	45 8.2	51 7.2	51 7.1
73 5.0	76 4.8	66 5.5	Cost of Sales/Inventory	35 10.5	40 9.1	34 10.6	66 5.5	74 4.9	104 3.5
135 2.7	126 2.9	122 3.0		130 2.8	74 4.9	89 4.1	114 3.2	122 3.0	152 2.4
203 2.0	183 2.0	174 2.1		215 1.7	146 2.5	126 2.9	183 2.0	166 2.2	203 1.8
13 28.9	13 27.8	15 24.0	Cost of Sales/Payables	0 UND	19 19.0	8 45.1	11 32.1	16 22.7	22 16.7
29 12.4	27 13.3	33 10.9		8 45.5	33 11.2	21 17.3	29 12.6	37 9.8	60 6.1
61 6.0	64 5.7	66 5.5		24 15.0	56 6.5	43 8.4	49 7.4	61 6.0	87 4.2
4.7	4.9	6.0	Sales/Working Capital	3.2	5.9	7.4	6.5	7.9	4.6
8.1	9.5	10.7		4.5	11.7	12.6	11.2	11.2	8.7
17.9	20.1	20.1		NM	22.1	24.3	18.8	15.2	19.0
(273) 4.0	(294) 4.8	(260) 6.1	EBIT/Interest	(12) 6.1	(40) 7.0	(31) 5.8	(46) 4.9	(82) 3.9	6.9
2.1	2.9	3.4		3.0	3.5	3.0	2.7	2.4	4.2
1.3	1.7	2.0		1.7	1.5	1.6	2.0	1.7	3.0
(128) 4.3	(115) 5.0	(104) 7.0	Net Profit + Depr., Dep., Amort./Cur. Mat. L/T/D			(15) 4.9	(23) 4.7	(22) 4.0	(36) 19.4
1.5	2.1	2.6				2.1	1.8	2.5	5.5
.6	.8	1.1				.5	.6	1.3	1.4
.2	.2	.2	Fixed/Worth	.0	.1	.2	.2	.1	.2
.4	.4	.3		.2	.3	.4	.3	.3	.3
.8	.9	1.0		NM	1.4	1.2	.6	.8	.9
1.3	1.3	1.5	Debt/Worth	.2	1.1	1.5	1.4	1.8	1.7
2.3	2.4	2.7		2.3	2.6	2.7	2.4	3.0	2.7
4.1	3.8	4.4		NM	5.1	3.7	4.7	4.5	3.9
(283) 23.1	(289) 30.8	(257) 37.8	% Profit Before Taxes/Tangible Net Worth	(10) 49.9	(37) 45.3	(30) 30.9	(48) 26.1	38.7	(84) 39.2
11.6	16.8	21.0		15.8	17.3	19.3	17.3	19.0	27.1
3.2	7.4	11.6		8.0	9.3	10.0	8.5	9.2	17.8
7.5	9.2	10.4	% Profit Before Taxes/Total Assets	13.6	14.7	14.1	8.5	8.9	10.4
3.1	4.9	6.4		7.1	6.6	5.4	4.8	3.8	7.3
.8	2.2	3.1		-.6	2.8	2.6	2.3	2.5	5.1
34.5	43.0	51.9	Sales/Net Fixed Assets	186.4	76.4	43.3	70.1	51.5	35.1
16.8	20.5	25.0		27.6	30.1	26.5	29.8	28.4	19.1
7.5	8.7	10.2		14.7	6.6	6.1	13.2	13.5	8.1
2.3	2.4	2.6	Sales/Total Assets	2.8	3.4	3.4	2.9	2.5	2.1
1.7	1.9	2.0		2.0	2.5	2.3	2.1	2.2	1.6
1.3	1.5	1.5		1.0	1.9	1.6	1.6	1.8	1.4
(255) .8	(259) .6	(234) .5	% Depr., Dep., Amort./Sales	(11) .7	(31) .5	(30) .5	(45) .5	(47) .4	(70) .6
1.2	1.0	.8		1.6	1.0	1.0	.7	.7	.8
3.4	2.5	2.3		7.3	6.0	2.9	1.6	1.7	1.8
(100) 1.7	(112) 1.8	(88) 1.7	% Officers', Directors', Owners' Comp/Sales		(21) 3.0	(17) 2.3	(21) 1.4	(15) 1.2	(11) .8
3.6	3.0	2.8			5.1	3.2	2.3	1.9	2.1
7.1	4.9	5.7			7.4	6.0	4.6	2.8	6.4
7198933M	7873740M	10219574M	Net Sales ($)	7548M	83033M	128645M	369950M	761387M	8869011M
4855746M	4987418M	6618253M	Total Assets ($)	5915M	35631M	64158M	181826M	389682M	5941041M

M = $ thousand   MM = $ million
See Pages 1 through 15 for Explanation of Ratios and Data

Current Data Sorted By Assets							Comparative Historical Data	
3	6	3	1				# Postretirement Benefits	
							Type of Statement	
	2	9	4	4	3		Unqualified	27	19
11	23	21	3				Reviewed	72	67
93	75	19					Compiled	172	182
28	18	3					Tax Returns	7	7
31	45	12	2	2	2		Other	75	77
	132 (4/1-9/30/94)			278 (10/1/94-3/31/95)				4/1/90-3/31/91	4/1/91-3/31/92
0-500M	500M-2MM	2-10MM	10-50MM	50-100MM	100-250MM			ALL	ALL
163	163	64	9	6	5		**NUMBER OF STATEMENTS**	353	352
%	%	%	%	%	%		**ASSETS**	%	%
7.6	6.5	5.7					Cash & Equivalents	6.2	6.4
5.6	8.9	7.4					Trade Receivables - (net)	6.6	8.3
63.7	61.9	61.2					Inventory	64.0	63.6
.6	1.2	1.7					All Other Current	1.1	1.1
77.5	78.4	76.0					Total Current	77.9	79.5
15.7	16.5	17.2					Fixed Assets (net)	15.1	14.2
2.9	1.5	1.4					Intangibles (net)	2.1	2.5
3.9	3.5	5.4					All Other Non-Current	4.9	3.8
100.0	100.0	100.0					Total	100.0	100.0
							LIABILITIES		
11.6	11.4	10.6					Notes Payable-Short Term	14.4	13.1
4.0	2.7	2.4					Cur. Mat. -L/T/D	3.5	3.7
22.7	24.7	25.2					Trade Payables	24.7	25.2
.4	.4	.3					Income Taxes Payable	.4	.4
8.9	7.2	8.0					All Other Current	7.7	7.8
47.7	46.3	46.4					Total Current	50.7	50.2
19.9	11.3	9.9					Long Term Debt	14.7	14.8
.3	.2	.2					Deferred Taxes	.1	.2
3.3	4.0	5.0					All Other-Non-Current	1.9	3.3
28.8	38.2	38.5					Net Worth	32.6	31.4
100.0	100.0	100.0					Total Liabilities & Net Worth	100.0	100.0
							INCOME DATA		
100.0	100.0	100.0					Net Sales	100.0	100.0
36.0	33.9	35.1					Gross Profit	35.2	34.6
32.7	30.7	31.4					Operating Expenses	32.3	32.0
3.3	3.2	3.7					Operating Profit	2.8	2.7
1.3	.7	.6					All Other Expenses (net)	1.0	.8
2.0	2.5	3.0					Profit Before Taxes	1.8	1.8
							RATIOS		
2.8	2.3	2.4						2.3	2.4
1.8	1.6	1.6					Current	1.6	1.6
1.2	1.3	1.2						1.2	1.2
.5	.6	.6						.4	.6
(161) .2	.2	.2					Quick	(351) .2	(345) .2
.1	.1	.1						.1	.1
0 UND	0 925.5	1 509.7						0 929.4	0 887.6
1 258.5	4 81.8	4 97.2					Sales/Receivables	4 100.3	4 99.0
8 48.5	19 19.6	18 20.2						13 27.6	16 22.6
91 4.0	91 4.0	107 3.4						111 3.3	96 3.8
135 2.7	130 2.8	130 2.8					Cost of Sales/Inventory	146 2.5	135 2.7
183 2.0	174 2.1	174 2.1						203 1.8	192 1.9
19 19.3	28 13.2	23 15.6						28 13.0	26 13.8
40 9.2	47 7.7	51 7.1					Cost of Sales/Payables	51 7.2	49 7.5
72 5.1	72 5.1	91 4.0						85 4.3	74 4.9
5.5	5.3	5.3						5.5	5.0
8.4	7.8	9.8					Sales/Working Capital	9.6	8.7
24.6	17.8	18.0						20.9	25.5
6.5	6.9	8.1						5.0	4.7
(147) 2.7	(146) 2.9	(60) 4.2					EBIT/Interest	(336) 2.1	(331) 2.2
1.1	1.3	1.8						1.0	1.1
2.9	5.1	4.3					Net Profit + Depr., Dep.,	4.5	3.4
(21) .9	(47) 2.2	(26) 2.9					Amort./Cur. Mat. L /T/D	(126) 1.5	(107) 1.3
.2	.9	1.3						.4	.3
.1	.1	.2						.1	.1
.6	.3	.4					Fixed/Worth	.4	.4
3.7	1.0	1.0						1.2	1.3
1.2	.8	.9						1.0	1.0
2.8	1.7	1.7					Debt/Worth	2.2	2.6
17.5	3.7	3.2						6.2	7.1
59.1	28.2	36.9					% Profit Before Taxes/Tangible	34.5	34.9
(132) 22.2	(151) 14.6	(63) 16.0					Net Worth	(312) 13.9	(320) 12.6
6.1	4.5	7.4						2.2	2.6
15.6	9.9	12.1					% Profit Before Taxes/Total	9.5	9.8
5.8	4.8	5.5					Assets	3.9	4.0
.7	1.2	2.0						.0	.2
80.2	61.1	33.5						56.3	65.3
34.8	30.3	16.9					Sales/Net Fixed Assets	26.2	30.6
12.8	10.6	10.0						12.5	15.9
3.5	3.3	3.0						3.2	3.4
2.8	2.7	2.5					Sales/Total Assets	2.5	2.6
2.0	2.0	2.1						1.8	1.9
.4	.5	.6						.6	.5
(133) .9	(144) .9	(62) 1.1					% Depr., Dep., Amort./Sales	(305) 1.1	(317) .9
2.1	1.6	1.8						1.7	1.7
3.4	2.3	1.7						2.5	2.6
(83) 4.8	(91) 3.8	(28) 3.3					% Officers', Directors',	(155) 3.9	(182) 4.5
8.2	5.6	6.7					Owners' Comp/Sales	6.4	7.6
130657M	460092M	637246M	590096M	704265M	1333037M		Net Sales ($)	2321929M	1922584M
45541M	166958M	247759M	188070M	509457M	797338M		Total Assets ($)	1007163M	829658M

M = $ thousand　　MM = $ million
See Pages 1 through 15 for Explanation of Ratios and Data

Comparative Historical Data				Current Data Sorted By Sales					
2	9	13	**# Postretirement Benefits**	2	4	2	4		1
			Type of Statement						
21	16	22	Unqualified	1	1		4	6	10
63	72	58	Reviewed	8	11	12	12	13	2
179	181	187	Compiled	75	69	18	20	5	
24	33	49	Tax Returns	23	16	7	3		
78	77	94	Other	27	34	15	9	4	5
4/1/92-3/31/93 ALL	4/1/93-3/31/94 ALL	4/1/94-3/31/95 ALL		132 (4/1-9/30/94) 0-1MM	1-3MM	3-5MM	278 (10/1/94-3/31/95) 5-10MM	10-25MM	25MM & OVER
365	379	410	**NUMBER OF STATEMENTS**	134	131	52	48	28	17
%	%	%	**ASSETS**	%	%	%	%	%	%
5.8	7.1	6.8	Cash & Equivalents	7.4	6.8	5.9	6.3	6.4	6.2
7.0	7.4	7.4	Trade Receivables - (net)	4.2	9.2	10.2	8.0	6.1	11.2
65.3	61.8	62.3	Inventory	61.7	63.1	61.8	62.8	66.3	54.0
1.6	.9	1.0	All Other Current	.4	1.0	2.2	1.0	1.1	2.5
79.7	77.2	77.5	Total Current	73.7	80.1	80.0	78.1	79.9	73.9
14.5	16.5	16.3	Fixed Assets (net)	18.4	15.2	15.0	15.8	13.2	16.9
2.1	1.7	2.3	Intangibles (net)	3.1	1.8	1.9	.9	1.7	5.6
3.7	4.5	4.0	All Other Non-Current	4.8	2.9	3.1	5.2	5.2	3.7
100.0	100.0	100.0	Total	100.0	100.0	100.0	100.0	100.0	100.0
			LIABILITIES						
13.1	10.5	11.5	Notes Payable-Short Term	11.4	13.3	9.8	7.1	11.9	16.8
2.6	3.2	3.1	Cur. Mat.-L /T/D	4.3	2.8	2.4	2.8	1.9	1.5
23.9	23.1	23.8	Trade Payables	21.1	22.2	28.7	29.3	29.5	17.4
.5	1.5	.4	Income Taxes Payable	.5	.3	.6	.4	.2	.9
8.2	8.1	8.1	All Other Current	7.9	8.1	8.3	7.8	8.5	9.5
48.3	46.5	47.0	Total Current	45.0	46.7	49.8	47.4	52.0	46.1
13.4	15.2	14.3	Long Term Debt	23.2	11.6	8.7	10.5	6.9	5.2
.1	.3	.3	Deferred Taxes	.3	.1	.3	.1	.0	1.4
3.1	4.7	4.0	All Other-Non-Current	2.5	4.7	6.3	2.9	4.7	4.2
35.1	33.2	34.5	Net Worth	28.9	36.8	34.8	39.1	36.4	43.2
100.0	100.0	100.0	Total Liabilities & Net Worth	100.0	100.0	100.0	100.0	100.0	100.0
			INCOME DATA						
100.0	100.0	100.0	Net Sales	100.0	100.0	100.0	100.0	100.0	100.0
34.5	35.6	34.8	Gross Profit	38.1	33.1	33.1	33.1	36.5	30.4
31.4	32.8	31.6	Operating Expenses	33.4	30.6	30.3	30.8	33.4	28.3
3.1	2.9	3.2	Operating Profit	4.6	2.4	2.8	2.3	3.1	2.1
1.1	1.0	.9	All Other Expenses (net)	1.8	.5	.6	.5	.3	1.0
2.0	1.9	2.3	Profit Before Taxes	2.8	2.0	2.2	1.8	2.7	1.1
			RATIOS						
2.6	2.5	2.5		3.0	2.5	2.1	2.3	2.4	2.3
1.7	1.7	1.7	Current	1.8	1.9	1.6	1.6	1.4	1.5
1.2	1.2	1.3		1.2	1.3	1.3	1.3	1.2	1.2
.5	.5	.6		.5	.7	.6	.5	.5	.7
(360) .2	(377) .2	(408) .2	Quick	(133) .2	(130) .2	.2	.2	.2	.2
.1	.1	.1		.1	.1	.1	.1	.1	.1
0 999.8	0 811.0	0 999.8		0 UND	0 999.8	0 952.8	1 655.3	2 243.3	4 101.4
3 107.8	3 116.3	3 115.1	Sales/Receivables	2 241.5	3 105.7	4 84.3	3 135.0	4 87.2	8 48.6
12 30.1	12 29.3	12 29.4		8 46.2	18 19.9	19 19.2	10 36.1	15 23.8	15 24.6
101 3.6	96 3.8	94 3.9		114 3.2	89 4.1	78 4.7	79 4.6	107 3.4	85 4.3
140 2.6	140 2.6	135 2.7	Cost of Sales/Inventory	166 2.2	130 2.8	126 2.9	111 3.3	135 2.7	114 3.2
203 1.8	192 1.9	174 2.1		228 1.6	174 2.1	166 2.2	146 2.5	174 2.1	192 1.9
25 14.8	22 16.8	23 15.8		21 17.7	18 19.8	30 12.2	29 12.8	27 13.5	24 15.3
48 7.6	47 7.7	47 7.8	Cost of Sales/Payables	49 7.5	37 9.8	52 7.0	46 7.9	55 6.6	43 8.5
73 5.0	76 4.8	74 4.9		81 4.5	66 5.5	85 4.3	74 4.9	91 4.0	54 6.7
4.9	5.0	5.4		4.6	5.3	6.1	6.9	6.5	5.7
8.3	8.4	8.5	Sales/Working Capital	7.1	7.7	8.6	10.2	12.3	10.5
20.5	20.3	18.6		23.1	18.5	17.0	19.7	21.9	14.6
6.4	6.4	7.1		6.1	5.6	7.6	10.2	15.2	11.7
(336) 2.4	(346) 2.7	(373) 3.0	EBIT/Interest	(116) 2.6	(122) 2.7	(48) 3.0	(46) 4.5	(25) 4.9	(16) 4.4
1.0	1.2	1.4		1.1	1.1	1.5	1.9	2.3	2.4
5.6	4.1	4.7		3.3	2.8	11.9	3.9	5.9	16.9
(97) 2.1	(108) 1.6	(105) 2.3	Net Profit + Depr., Dep., Amort./Cur. Mat. L/T/D	(16) 1.2	(28) 2.0	(19) 2.5	(19) 1.3	(12) 3.7	(11) 5.5
.7	.3	.9		.3	.8	1.2	.7	2.2	2.3
.1	.1	.1		.2	.1	.1	.2	.2	.2
.3	.4	.4	Fixed/Worth	.6	.3	.3	.4	.4	.4
1.0	1.3	1.2		5.4	1.1	1.0	.7	.7	.8
1.0	1.0	.9		1.2	.9	1.0	1.0	.9	.9
2.0	2.2	2.0	Debt/Worth	3.0	1.9	1.7	1.6	1.8	1.7
5.2	5.2	5.7		19.4	4.6	3.4	3.2	4.7	2.4
35.6	36.0	36.8		62.7	28.1	28.5	32.2	60.7	36.7
(327) 14.6	(338) 15.2	(364) 17.4	% Profit Before Taxes/Tangible Net Worth	(108) 23.1	(119) 13.4	(47) 12.1	(47) 16.3	(27) 24.4	(16) 19.9
2.3	4.8	5.5		5.3	3.7	6.7	6.8	7.7	7.9
11.3	11.1	12.1		15.3	11.0	8.8	12.1	14.4	15.1
4.8	4.2	5.4	% Profit Before Taxes/Total Assets	6.0	4.8	4.0	7.0	5.5	6.3
.3	.7	1.2		.6	.9	1.4	2.3	1.8	2.5
63.0	57.3	61.2		54.4	86.7	65.9	42.4	71.2	28.5
33.0	27.4	26.8	Sales/Net Fixed Assets	23.4	37.4	29.4	25.3	23.6	13.7
13.8	11.2	11.2		7.6	15.1	13.0	14.1	13.6	7.4
3.3	3.4	3.3		3.1	3.4	3.4	4.0	3.2	3.4
2.6	2.6	2.7	Sales/Total Assets	2.3	2.9	2.7	3.0	2.7	2.1
2.0	2.0	2.0		1.6	2.2	2.2	2.5	2.4	1.7
.5	.5	.5		.5	.5	.5	.6	.5	.9
(310) .9	(334) .9	(357) 1.0	% Depr., Dep., Amort./Sales	(111) 1.0	(114) 1.0	(47) 1.1	(43) .9	(26) .9	(16) 1.5
1.5	1.6	1.8		2.5	1.7	1.5	1.5	1.4	1.5
2.5	2.7	2.5		3.2	2.7	2.0		1.4	
(176) 4.2	(204) 4.5	(203) 4.2	% Officers', Directors', Owners' Comp/Sales	(66) 4.8	(68) 4.3	(32) 3.7	(25) 2.9	(11) 4.7	
6.5	7.6	7.0		8.3	6.4	5.6	4.2	12.6	
2830348M	3173177M	3855393M	Net Sales ($)	77042M	233553M	202558M	327877M	421995M	2592368M
1197651M	1479345M	1955123M	Total Assets ($)	40492M	93548M	82844M	112980M	242539M	1382720M

M = $ thousand   MM = $ million
See Pages 1 through 15 for Explanation of Ratios and Data

Current Data Sorted By Assets   Comparative Historical Data

0-500M	500M-2MM	2-10MM	10-50MM	50-100MM	100-250MM		4/1/90-3/31/91 ALL	4/1/91-3/31/92 ALL
						# Postretirement Benefits		
						Type of Statement		
		4			1	Unqualified	4	6
	7	5	3		1	Reviewed	14	10
15	13	2				Compiled	29	32
7	5					Tax Returns	3	1
11	4	4	1			Other	13	10
30 (4/1-9/30/94)			**53 (10/1/94-3/31/95)**					
33	29	15	4		2	**NUMBER OF STATEMENTS**	63	59
%	%	%	%	%	%	**ASSETS**	%	%
3.4	6.6	5.5				Cash & Equivalents	6.4	7.6
10.2	19.5	22.4				Trade Receivables - (net)	13.8	16.5
60.1	58.4	46.3				Inventory	58.3	44.3
.6	2.1	1.2				All Other Current	1.2	4.9
74.4	86.6	75.4				Total Current	79.7	73.4
17.8	9.0	16.0				Fixed Assets (net)	14.2	18.1
1.8	.6	.8				Intangibles (net)	1.6	1.7
6.1	3.9	7.7				All Other Non-Current	4.5	6.9
100.0	100.0	100.0				Total	100.0	100.0
						LIABILITIES		
15.0	18.6	24.0				Notes Payable-Short Term	16.2	18.9
5.0	3.7	.9				Cur. Mat. -L/T/D	3.6	3.7
5.9	7.9	7.4				Trade Payables	7.3	7.0
.4	.4	.2				Income Taxes Payable	.7	.2
9.9	9.5	4.4				All Other Current	11.3	8.2
36.1	40.1	37.0				Total Current	39.2	37.9
21.9	9.4	13.2				Long Term Debt	11.9	9.8
.0	.0	.1				Deferred Taxes	.0	.0
3.7	2.9	4.6				All Other-Non-Current	4.7	3.2
38.3	47.7	45.2				Net Worth	44.2	49.1
100.0	100.0	100.0				Total Liabilities & Net Worth	100.0	100.0
						INCOME DATA		
100.0	100.0	100.0				Net Sales	100.0	100.0
43.7	38.5	43.2				Gross Profit	43.7	47.1
35.6	32.4	36.6				Operating Expenses	37.1	40.6
8.1	6.1	6.7				Operating Profit	6.6	6.6
2.2	1.2	2.4				All Other Expenses (net)	2.6	1.5
5.8	4.8	4.3				Profit Before Taxes	4.0	5.1
						RATIOS		
4.4	3.6	3.2					3.7	4.0
2.6	2.0	2.3				Current	2.2	2.1
1.5	1.7	1.5					1.4	1.3
1.2	1.4	1.4					1.0	1.3
(30) .4	(28) .5	1.1				Quick	.5	.5
.2	.3	.2					.2	.2
0 UND	4 82.3	5 73.0					3 105.2	1 381.7
7 55.4	22 16.8	26 13.8				Sales/Receivables	19 19.2	13 29.0
18 20.0	54 6.7	91 4.0					40 9.2	38 9.5
73 5.0	76 4.8	118 3.1					81 4.5	57 6.4
159 2.3	146 2.5	183 2.0				Cost of Sales/Inventory	192 1.9	140 2.6
281 1.3	332 1.1	203 1.8					332 1.1	243 1.5
0 UND	1 498.1	4 82.7					3 106.5	2 147.0
6 57.1	9 41.4	20 18.6				Cost of Sales/Payables	16 22.9	12 30.4
17 21.9	33 11.1	52 7.0					35 10.4	25 14.4
3.5	2.1	2.5					2.5	2.5
8.8	5.0	4.0				Sales/Working Capital	4.9	6.4
18.9	10.2	8.2					12.3	18.0
8.3	8.0	6.3					6.5	7.1
(29) 3.2	(28) 3.2	(14) 4.5				EBIT/Interest	(56) 3.0	(57) 2.7
1.4	1.7	1.6					1.3	1.4
	6.6						6.1	7.1
	(12) 2.5					Net Profit + Depr., Dep., Amort./Cur. Mat. L /T/D	(22) 1.3	(20) 2.8
	.9						.6	.9
.1	.1	.1					.1	.1
.4	.1	.2				Fixed/Worth	.2	.3
1.3	.3	.3					.8	.6
.8	.5	.6					.5	.4
1.4	1.2	1.8				Debt/Worth	1.3	1.0
5.7	2.0	2.6					4.0	2.1
46.3	37.1	26.2					36.6	32.1
(28) 31.8	13.0	(14) 17.1				% Profit Before Taxes/Tangible Net Worth	(58) 15.4	(55) 17.0
14.2	4.6	4.3					3.2	2.8
21.4	15.2	9.9					14.0	13.4
12.2	6.2	6.3				% Profit Before Taxes/Total Assets	7.7	7.9
3.2	1.5	.2					1.7	.9
90.8	127.0	48.6					58.5	57.8
32.6	51.8	25.6				Sales/Net Fixed Assets	24.7	23.5
7.2	13.9	8.6					11.9	6.5
4.6	3.7	2.4					3.8	3.8
2.2	2.0	1.7				Sales/Total Assets	1.7	2.0
1.6	1.3	1.0					1.1	1.3
.6	.3	.4					.6	.5
(28) 1.4	(24) .6	.7				% Depr., Dep., Amort./Sales	(51) .9	(48) .9
2.0	1.2	2.1					1.8	2.5
4.7	3.0						3.7	4.7
(15) 8.3	(17) 4.6					% Officers', Directors', Owners' Comp/Sales	(29) 7.9	(26) 7.6
12.1	7.3						12.8	14.1
25374M	80394M	109454M	116535M		272717M	Net Sales ($)	602220M	392202M
9091M	29675M	61724M	80491M		350448M	Total Assets ($)	466197M	369732M

M = $ thousand   MM = $ million
See Pages 1 through 15 for Explanation of Ratios and Data

Comparative Historical Data / Current Data Sorted By Sales

	1	2	3	# Postretirement Benefits / Type of Statement	0-1MM	1-3MM	3-5MM	5-10MM	10-25MM	25MM & OVER
				# Postretirement Benefits	1	1				1
				Type of Statement						
				Unqualified				3	3	2
	5	8	8	Reviewed		2	2	7	1	
	12	11	12	Compiled	12	11		2		1
	41	33	31	Tax Returns	8	4	5			
	8	12	12	Other	11	6		2	1	
	17	17	20							
	4/1/92-3/31/93 ALL	4/1/93-3/31/94 ALL	4/1/94-3/31/95 ALL		30 (4/1-9/30/94)			53 (10/1/94-3/31/95)		
	83	81	83	**NUMBER OF STATEMENTS**	31	23	7	14	5	3
	%	%	%	**ASSETS**	%	%	%	%	%	%
	7.1	8.8	5.2	Cash & Equivalents	3.2	7.1		4.0		
	16.9	18.7	16.5	Trade Receivables - (net)	11.8	17.3		24.2		
	46.8	47.4	54.1	Inventory	57.9	54.8		56.8		
	3.6	1.8	1.4	All Other Current	.2	.7		1.2		
	74.5	76.7	77.2	Total Current	73.1	79.8		86.2		
	15.8	15.8	15.1	Fixed Assets (net)	20.5	10.0		8.8		
	2.2	2.0	2.0	Intangibles (net)	1.4	1.3		1.4		
	7.5	5.4	5.7	All Other Non-Current	5.1	8.9		3.6		
	100.0	100.0	100.0	Total	100.0	100.0		100.0		
				LIABILITIES						
	17.9	15.7	17.3	Notes Payable-Short Term	17.2	9.9		28.3		
	3.9	2.1	3.6	Cur. Mat.-L /T/D	5.0	2.8		1.9		
	6.3	8.1	6.8	Trade Payables	4.5	6.2		7.6		
	.3	.8	.4	Income Taxes Payable	.4	.5		.2		
	8.2	9.3	8.8	All Other Current	11.5	8.2		6.7		
	36.6	36.0	36.9	Total Current	38.5	27.5		44.8		
	13.4	13.7	15.0	Long Term Debt	24.5	14.9		4.0		
	.0	.0	.1	Deferred Taxes	.0	.0		.1		
	7.4	4.3	3.8	All Other-Non-Current	3.8	2.6		6.3		
	42.7	46.0	44.3	Net Worth	33.2	55.1		44.8		
	100.0	100.0	100.0	Total Liabilities & Net Worth	100.0	100.0		100.0		
				INCOME DATA						
	100.0	100.0	100.0	Net Sales	100.0	100.0		100.0		
	44.6	48.0	41.5	Gross Profit	46.7	42.0		38.0		
	38.5	41.4	34.6	Operating Expenses	38.1	34.2		34.3		
	6.2	6.5	6.9	Operating Profit	8.6	7.9		3.6		
	2.0	2.0	1.8	All Other Expenses (net)	3.2	1.3		.6		
	4.1	4.5	5.1	Profit Before Taxes	5.4	6.6		3.0		
				RATIOS						
	3.9	3.5	3.9	Current	4.2	4.1		2.7		
	2.1	2.1	2.2		2.1	3.0		1.8		
	1.3	1.6	1.6		1.2	2.2		1.4		
	1.2	1.5	1.4	Quick	1.2	2.4		1.2		
	.6	.7	(79) .6		(29) .4	(22) 1.2		.5		
	.2	.3	.3		.2	.4		.2		
1	317.3	3 112.3	2 243.3	Sales/Receivables	1 604.0	1 322.3		6 57.7		
16	22.4	22 16.8	14 25.8		7 53.4	15 23.9		23 15.7		
40	9.2	58 6.3	54 6.8		47 7.7	49 7.5		96 3.8		
66	5.5	89 4.1	76 4.8	Cost of Sales/Inventory	140 2.6	76 4.8		76 4.8		
140	2.6	166 2.2	166 2.2		203 1.8	152 2.4		174 2.1		
243	1.5	281 1.3	261 1.4		304 1.2	261 1.4		228 1.6		
0	UND	0 UND	0 835.5	Cost of Sales/Payables	0 UND	1 279.5		6 58.5		
9	40.3	11 34.7	9 41.4		1 481.0	9 41.4		14 26.1		
31	11.9	33 10.9	27 13.5		27 13.5	25 14.5		54 6.8		
	2.7	2.3	2.7	Sales/Working Capital	2.4	2.5		3.0		
	5.9	5.2	5.8		6.3	4.5		5.3		
	15.1	11.0	12.3		20.3	6.5		13.3		
	5.5	6.4	7.5	EBIT/Interest	7.4	10.1		6.5		
	(77) 3.0	(73) 2.9	(77) 3.6		(26) 2.1	5.5		2.7		
	1.5	1.7	1.6		1.3	2.0		1.7		
	3.8	5.4	13.5	Net Profit + Depr., Dep., Amort./Cur. Mat. L/T/D		9.0				
	(24) 2.1	(26) 2.4	(25) 3.0			(10) 3.4				
	.4	.8	1.6			1.8				
	.1	.1	.1	Fixed/Worth	.1	.0		.1		
	.2	.2	.2		.6	.1		.2		
	.7	.5	.7		2.8	.2		.3		
	.6	.6	.6	Debt/Worth	1.0	.4		.6		
	1.4	1.3	1.2		2.5	.8		2.0		
	3.3	2.7	3.2		8.7	1.3		3.1		
	43.9	30.1	41.3	% Profit Before Taxes/Tangible Net Worth	56.3	29.2		24.1		
	(76) 15.4	(80) 15.0	(77) 18.1		(26) 26.0	(22) 15.9		10.7		
	6.7	5.9	5.2		2.3	12.2		4.6		
	15.4	12.5	18.3	% Profit Before Taxes/Total Assets	20.7	15.3		9.6		
	6.9	6.2	7.7		7.3	8.9		4.3		
	1.5	2.3	1.6		.2	5.9		1.6		
	73.9	43.7	85.0	Sales/Net Fixed Assets	75.1	192.3		95.4		
	26.1	22.9	28.4		17.9	40.3		27.4		
	8.4	8.6	8.6		5.7	13.9		16.1		
	3.0	3.1	3.6	Sales/Total Assets	2.3	3.0		3.8		
	2.0	2.0	2.0		1.7	2.0		2.0		
	1.2	1.0	1.3		1.2	1.4		1.4		
	.7	.6	.4	% Depr., Dep., Amort./Sales	.8	.3		.5		
	(67) 1.3	(69) 1.2	(72) .9		(25) 1.6	(20) .6		(13) .7		
	2.1	2.0	2.0		2.1	1.9		1.3		
	4.1	4.1	3.7	% Officers', Directors', Owners' Comp/Sales	4.8	3.7				
	(47) 6.9	(34) 8.0	(40) 5.4		(14) 8.3	(12) 4.6				
	13.4	17.6	11.4		19.4	11.3				
	390476M	604414M	604474M	Net Sales ($)	16301M	38955M	25136M	101281M	75240M	347561M
	351917M	562898M	531429M	Total Assets ($)	14770M	23311M	6452M	59088M	58815M	368993M

M = $ thousand   MM = $ million
See Pages 1 through 15 for Explanation of Ratios and Data

Current Data Sorted By Assets / Comparative Historical Data

# Postretirement Benefits / Type of Statement	0-500M	500M-2MM	2-10MM	10-50MM	50-100MM	100-250MM	4/1/90-3/31/91 ALL	4/1/91-3/31/92 ALL
Unqualified	5	1	8	6	1		19	14
Reviewed	4	17	9	2			32	25
Compiled	27	27	4	1			69	59
Tax Returns	3	2						2
Other	6	14	12	2		1	24	28
	65 (4/1-9/30/94)			82 (10/1/94-3/31/95)				
NUMBER OF STATEMENTS	40	61	33	11	1	1	144	128

	0-500M	500M-2MM	2-10MM	10-50MM	50-100MM	100-250MM		4/1/90-3/31/91	4/1/91-3/31/92
	%	%	%	%	%	%	**ASSETS**	%	%
	10.1	8.9	9.2	6.3			Cash & Equivalents	9.0	8.4
	4.0	6.5	10.0	15.3			Trade Receivables - (net)	8.3	7.1
	16.3	14.3	19.2	18.5			Inventory	19.1	17.9
	1.2	1.0	1.0	1.8			All Other Current	1.6	1.4
	31.5	30.7	39.4	42.0			Total Current	38.0	34.8
	60.9	60.3	51.3	44.1			Fixed Assets (net)	54.2	56.0
	2.1	2.7	2.3	5.6			Intangibles (net)	2.3	2.2
	5.5	6.2	7.0	8.3			All Other Non-Current	5.5	6.9
	100.0	100.0	100.0	100.0			Total	100.0	100.0
							LIABILITIES		
	9.3	5.1	9.5	9.8			Notes Payable-Short Term	5.5	8.1
	8.9	10.9	8.4	5.6			Cur. Mat. -L/T/D	10.7	8.6
	11.2	13.7	17.0	16.6			Trade Payables	14.3	14.9
	.2	.1	.3	.1			Income Taxes Payable	.5	.4
	9.3	6.1	8.7	6.0			All Other Current	7.0	8.9
	38.9	35.9	43.8	38.2			Total Current	38.0	41.0
	26.7	24.7	18.2	23.8			Long Term Debt	25.0	24.2
	.0	.3	.5	.4			Deferred Taxes	.7	.7
	3.8	5.0	3.0	1.3			All Other-Non-Current	3.3	2.9
	30.6	34.1	34.5	36.3			Net Worth	33.0	31.1
	100.0	100.0	100.0	100.0			Total Liabilities & Net Worth	100.0	100.0
							INCOME DATA		
	100.0	100.0	100.0	100.0			Net Sales	100.0	100.0
	50.8	47.3	47.2	37.4			Gross Profit	42.2	45.6
	46.9	45.5	45.3	35.0			Operating Expenses	39.9	43.0
	3.9	1.8	1.8	2.4			Operating Profit	2.2	2.6
	1.0	.7	.2	.3			All Other Expenses (net)	1.0	1.1
	2.9	1.1	1.6	2.2			Profit Before Taxes	1.2	1.5
							RATIOS		
	1.5	1.1	1.3	1.5				1.6	1.3
	.8	.9	1.0	1.2			Current	1.0	.8
	.5	.7	.6	.7				.6	.5
	.9	.7	.7	.8				.8	.6
(39)	.3	.4	.4	.5			Quick	(143) .4	.3
	.1	.2	.2	.2				.2	.2
0	UND	1 718.3	3 107.0	3 141.5				0 760.8	0 999.8
0	UND	3 120.8	6 62.6	12 29.6			Sales/Receivables	4 100.6	3 125.8
4	87.8	7 49.0	17 21.3	36 10.1				12 30.4	9 40.2
10	36.4	24 15.2	27 13.3	29 12.8				21 17.8	24 15.5
27	13.7	31 11.7	36 10.1	47 7.8			Cost of Sales/Inventory	32 11.3	32 11.5
45	8.2	45 8.2	56 6.5	65 5.6				48 7.6	45 8.1
0	UND	14 26.2	24 15.2	25 14.6				13 27.3	16 23.4
13	28.5	29 12.8	35 10.5	41 9.0			Cost of Sales/Payables	25 14.8	26 13.9
33	10.9	45 8.2	51 7.2	64 5.7				41 9.0	44 8.3
	33.3	77.7	23.0	12.5				21.8	37.9
	-80.7	-123.7	-429.9	21.6			Sales/Working Capital	-345.3	-37.5
	-23.5	-22.5	-18.9	-22.8				-19.1	-14.8
	4.7	3.5	5.4	6.1				3.9	2.7
(36)	2.6	(59) 2.4	(30) 2.7	2.1			EBIT/Interest	(137) 1.8	(120) 1.7
	.7	.4	1.2	1.8				1.0	.7
	3.1	2.9	3.5					2.7	3.5
(11)	1.6	(31) 1.8	(13) 1.6				Net Profit + Depr., Dep., Amort./Cur. Mat. L./T/D	(85) 1.7	(55) 1.7
	1.0	1.2	1.2					1.1	1.3
	1.1	1.3	.8	.6				.9	1.0
	1.9	1.8	1.8	1.2			Fixed/Worth	1.7	2.0
	11.1	3.1	7.0	3.2				4.5	4.6
	.9	.9	.8	1.7				.9	1.1
	1.9	1.7	2.5	2.2			Debt/Worth	1.9	2.5
	12.5	3.7	18.4	3.2				6.1	6.5
	69.4	22.7	41.9	26.3				24.0	33.4
(34)	17.7	(55) 11.2	(29) 20.1	16.5			% Profit Before Taxes/Tangible Net Worth	(123) 12.7	(114) 11.6
	-2.8	.3	4.0	7.5				2.4	-2.7
	13.9	8.0	12.5	9.2				9.5	8.3
	6.2	3.9	5.2	3.9			% Profit Before Taxes/Total Assets	3.1	3.2
	-2.4	-3.0	.6	2.6				.0	-1.6
	12.0	6.9	8.2	12.3				8.5	8.0
	6.7	4.6	6.1	5.4			Sales/Net Fixed Assets	5.7	5.6
	2.5	3.0	4.2	3.5				4.1	3.8
	5.3	3.7	3.7	2.7				4.3	4.2
	3.4	2.7	3.0	2.4			Sales/Total Assets	3.2	3.0
	2.2	2.1	2.4	1.9				2.3	2.2
	4.4	4.7	3.2	1.5				3.6	4.2
(37)	6.7	(58) 6.5	(32) 4.8	5.2			% Depr., Dep., Amort./Sales	(137) 5.3	(126) 5.4
	11.6	8.7	6.7	6.1				7.2	6.9
	3.7	2.4						2.2	2.2
(20)	6.0	(36) 3.9					% Officers', Directors', Owners' Comp/Sales	(75) 3.9	(70) 4.1
	10.6	8.2						6.6	5.9
	40961M	187009M	496584M	371612M	158864M	84493M	Net Sales ($)	1385515M	1009204M
	10804M	60873M	153675M	159623M	84392M	118082M	Total Assets ($)	493967M	360644M

M = $ thousand   MM = $ million
See Pages 1 through 15 for Explanation of Ratios and Data

Comparative Historical Data				Current Data Sorted By Sales					
1	**6**	**6**	**# Postretirement Benefits**	3	2				1
			Type of Statement						
18	18	16	Unqualified		1	1	2	4	8
31	32	32	Reviewed	2	13	5	6	4	2
65	51	59	Compiled	16	31	5	3	3	1
6	6	5	Tax Returns	3	2				
22	28	35	Other	3	7	6	9	6	4
4/1/92-3/31/93 ALL	4/1/93-3/31/94 ALL	4/1/94-3/31/95 ALL		65 (4/1-9/30/94)		82 (10/1/94-3/31/95)			
				0-1MM	1-3MM	3-5MM	5-10MM	10-25MM	25MM & OVER
142	135	147	**NUMBER OF STATEMENTS**	24	54	17	20	17	15
%	**%**	**%**	**ASSETS**	**%**	**%**	**%**	**%**	**%**	**%**
8.3	8.5	9.0	Cash & Equivalents	7.5	9.6	9.5	8.2	10.7	8.0
7.5	6.6	7.4	Trade Receivables - (net)	3.2	5.6	4.1	12.9	12.4	11.5
15.8	15.0	16.2	Inventory	12.2	16.3	14.7	19.7	19.4	15.7
1.2	1.1	1.2	All Other Current	1.5	.9	1.0	.6	1.5	2.6
32.7	31.2	33.8	Total Current	24.3	32.4	29.3	41.4	44.1	37.7
56.9	59.8	56.7	Fixed Assets (net)	67.8	58.7	61.5	49.4	46.6	47.3
2.5	3.6	3.0	Intangibles (net)	1.7	3.2	1.3	2.7	3.0	6.2
7.8	5.5	6.5	All Other Non-Current	6.1	5.7	8.0	6.5	6.4	8.9
100.0	100.0	100.0	Total	100.0	100.0	100.0	100.0	100.0	100.0
			LIABILITIES						
7.7	6.2	7.5	Notes Payable-Short Term	8.2	7.0	6.9	4.4	13.3	6.4
10.8	8.2	9.3	Cur. Mat.-L /T/D	7.4	11.2	11.1	10.0	6.3	5.6
13.0	11.9	14.0	Trade Payables	6.0	13.9	13.3	19.5	18.4	16.0
.3	.7	.2	Income Taxes Payable	.2	.1	.2	.3	.2	.2
7.9	7.6	7.5	All Other Current	6.3	7.8	5.2	10.0	7.1	8.1
39.7	34.6	38.5	Total Current	28.2	40.0	36.6	44.0	45.4	36.3
21.7	25.9	23.8	Long Term Debt	35.1	24.1	22.9	18.8	12.3	25.5
.6	.5	.3	Deferred Taxes	.0	.1	.3	.7	.2	.7
4.5	3.2	3.9	All Other-Non-Current	3.8	3.7	11.2	1.0	3.3	1.4
33.4	35.7	33.6	Net Worth	33.0	32.2	28.9	35.5	38.8	36.1
100.0	100.0	100.0	Total Liabilities & Net Worth	100.0	100.0	100.0	100.0	100.0	100.0
			INCOME DATA						
100.0	100.0	100.0	Net Sales	100.0	100.0	100.0	100.0	100.0	100.0
47.1	45.2	47.1	Gross Profit	52.2	48.0	50.7	44.1	44.0	39.3
43.7	42.9	44.6	Operating Expenses	47.1	46.0	48.9	42.5	42.8	35.2
3.4	2.3	2.6	Operating Profit	5.1	2.0	1.9	1.6	1.2	4.1
.7	.7	.6	All Other Expenses (net)	1.6	.7	.7	.2	-.2	.4
2.7	1.6	1.9	Profit Before Taxes	3.6	1.3	1.2	1.4	1.4	3.7
			RATIOS						
1.4 .8 .5	1.4 .8 .6	1.4 1.0 .6	Current	1.5 1.1 .5	1.3 .9 .6	1.1 .8 .5	1.2 1.0 .6	1.6 1.1 .7	1.5 1.0 .7
.7 .3 (133) .1	.7 .4 (146) .2	.8 .4 .2	Quick	1.1 .3 (53) .0	.7 .4 .2	.6 .3 .2	.7 .5 .3	1.1 .6 .2	.9 .5 .3
1 450.4 3 130.8 10 35.7	1 253.8 3 110.1 9 41.8	0 857.0 3 107.9 9 40.4	Sales/Receivables	0 UND 0 UND 6 61.2	0 UND 2 167.8 6 56.6	1 279.1 3 120.8 7 55.0	4 97.8 7 52.4 16 23.0	3 125.1 6 64.0 24 14.9	2 180.7 12 29.6 30 12.3
20 18.1 31 11.8 48 7.6	20 18.1 31 11.9 42 8.6	23 16.0 32 11.3 47 7.7	Cost of Sales/Inventory	7 55.3 26 14.0 47 7.7	21 17.0 33 10.9 47 7.8	24 15.5 26 14.3 44 8.3	26 14.1 35 10.3 47 7.8	24 14.9 40 9.1 59 6.2	24 15.5 31 11.8 47 7.8
13 28.8 26 13.9 46 7.9	10 35.0 24 14.9 41 8.8	13 28.2 29 12.8 46 7.9	Cost of Sales/Payables	0 UND 12 31.0 35 10.5	11 32.7 21 17.7 50 7.3	14 27.0 33 11.2 38 9.6	24 15.0 33 10.9 50 7.3	24 15.0 39 9.4 54 6.7	16 23.0 29 12.8 59 6.2
32.0 -49.4 -13.0	31.4 -46.9 -20.9	25.6 -160.7 -22.1	Sales/Working Capital	25.3 151.4 -12.0	48.4 -125.7 -22.5	132.8 -61.2 -18.4	36.9 -352.8 -23.7	17.3 44.1 -21.8	12.5 -263.6 -25.4
(135) 4.7 2.4 1.1	(129) 4.3 2.2 1.2	(137) 4.7 2.4 1.1	EBIT/Interest	(20) 4.0 2.1 .4	(53) 4.4 2.4 .3	(16) 3.2 1.5 1.1	(19) 6.4 2.9 1.5	(15) 5.1 2.9 -.1	(14) 7.4 2.5 1.8
(64) 3.7 1.8 1.1	(52) 2.7 1.7 1.0	(62) 3.3 1.9 1.1	Net Profit + Depr., Dep., Amort./Cur. Mat. L/T/D		(25) 3.7 2.5 1.2		(11) 2.9 2.2 1.4		
1.0 2.0 6.6	1.1 2.0 4.0	1.0 1.8 3.8	Fixed/Worth	1.5 2.0 5.2	1.1 1.8 5.0	1.2 1.8 4.2	.9 1.4 3.6	.7 1.0 3.1	.9 2.2 3.7
1.0 2.2 8.0	1.0 2.0 5.3	1.0 1.9 4.4	Debt/Worth	1.2 1.8 5.4	.8 1.7 9.1	1.1 2.0 5.1	.9 2.1 4.9	.6 2.5 3.5	1.6 2.0 4.5
(124) 37.6 14.3 3.3	(119) 34.3 14.1 3.9	(130) 31.2 15.1 3.7	% Profit Before Taxes/Tangible Net Worth	(23) 74.1 26.7 -3.9	(45) 23.9 11.2 -7.3	(14) 20.8 9.1 -1.2	(19) 64.8 19.3 3.6	(16) 37.6 16.9 4.1	(13) 31.9 20.1 13.7
10.9 5.1 .6	9.5 4.2 .6	11.3 4.6 -1.4	% Profit Before Taxes/Total Assets	13.6 5.1 -4.8	9.2 4.5 -3.7	7.2 2.4 -.7	12.3 3.4 1.5	13.3 4.8 -1.8	11.7 6.6 3.4
8.0 5.3 3.8	7.1 5.1 3.3	7.9 5.5 3.2	Sales/Net Fixed Assets	6.8 2.6 1.9	7.5 5.1 3.2	7.6 4.6 3.2	12.4 7.3 5.0	11.1 6.1 4.5	7.3 6.1 4.4
3.9 3.0 2.2	3.9 3.1 2.2	3.8 2.9 2.1	Sales/Total Assets	3.5 2.1 1.4	3.8 2.8 2.2	3.9 2.9 2.2	4.1 3.7 3.0	3.6 2.9 2.2	3.6 2.7 1.9
(138) 4.3 5.5 7.3	(131) 3.7 5.6 7.9	(139) 4.3 6.0 8.4	% Depr., Dep., Amort./Sales	(22) 5.5 10.9 14.6	(53) 5.1 6.9 8.9	(14) 4.3 4.8 7.3	2.6 5.0 6.4	(16) 1.7 3.9 6.5	(14) 3.6 5.1 6.0
(61) 2.3 4.0 6.5	(69) 2.3 3.5 6.1	(66) 2.4 4.5 8.4	% Officers', Directors', Owners' Comp/Sales	(12) 4.8 6.9 12.1	(32) 2.3 3.7 6.1				
1106916M 459859M	906817M 331716M	1339523M 587449M	Net Sales ($) Total Assets ($)	12142M 5954M	98205M 34843M	66234M 23883M	142933M 48554M	263575M 99263M	756434M 374952M

M = $ thousand   MM = $ million
See Pages 1 through 15 for Explanation of Ratios and Data

Current Data Sorted By Assets / Comparative Historical Data

0-500M	500M-2MM	2-10MM	10-50MM	50-100MM	100-250MM		4/1/90-3/31/91 ALL	4/1/91-3/31/92 ALL
21	12	7	1			**# Postretirement Benefits**		
						Type of Statement		
6	6	6	1			Unqualified	30	23
2	5	5				Reviewed	9	16
89	51	21		1		Compiled	158	161
21	3					Tax Returns	3	12
125	116	46	8	3		Other	309	280
193 (4/1-9/30/94)			322 (10/1/94-3/31/95)					
243	181	78	9	4		**NUMBER OF STATEMENTS**	509	492
%	%	%	%	%	%	**ASSETS**	%	%
12.2	8.9	9.8				Cash & Equivalents	8.7	8.3
35.8	48.8	48.2				Trade Receivables - (net)	43.8	46.0
3.1	6.7	4.4				Inventory	4.2	3.9
6.1	6.6	6.5				All Other Current	5.7	5.8
57.2	71.0	69.0				Total Current	62.5	64.1
24.2	14.6	17.5				Fixed Assets (net)	20.8	19.5
5.9	4.0	4.0				Intangibles (net)	5.5	5.5
12.7	10.5	9.5				All Other Non-Current	11.2	10.9
100.0	100.0	100.0				Total	100.0	100.0
						LIABILITIES		
15.7	10.2	11.1				Notes Payable-Short Term	14.8	14.5
5.7	3.3	2.9				Cur. Mat. -L/T/D	4.9	5.4
2.7	2.3	4.3				Trade Payables	3.2	3.3
.2	.3	.6				Income Taxes Payable	.7	.5
15.2	12.2	10.4				All Other Current	9.4	9.3
39.6	28.2	29.4				Total Current	32.9	33.0
16.3	9.7	10.9				Long Term Debt	16.8	15.1
.6	.7	.7				Deferred Taxes	.7	.7
2.6	6.3	6.2				All Other-Non-Current	3.4	4.1
41.0	55.1	52.8				Net Worth	46.2	47.3
100.0	100.0	100.0				Total Liabilities & Net Worth	100.0	100.0
						INCOME DATA		
100.0	100.0	100.0				Net Sales	100.0	100.0
						Gross Profit		
86.9	86.9	83.7				Operating Expenses	85.0	84.6
13.1	13.1	16.3				Operating Profit	15.0	15.4
1.5	2.1	2.5				All Other Expenses (net)	2.8	2.5
11.6	11.0	13.8				Profit Before Taxes	12.2	12.9
						RATIOS		
3.5	5.0	4.5					4.0	4.1
1.6	2.7	2.3				Current	2.1	2.2
.9	1.8	1.7					1.3	1.3
2.9	4.2	3.6					3.2	3.5
1.4	2.1	2.1				Quick	1.7	1.9
.7	1.3	1.4					1.0	1.0
0 UND	51 7.1	58 6.3					42 8.6	47 7.8
49 7.4	74 4.9	89 4.1				Sales/Receivables	70 5.2	73 5.0
72 5.1	104 3.5	118 3.1					99 3.7	101 3.6
						Cost of Sales/Inventory		
						Cost of Sales/Payables		
5.8	3.6	3.1					4.3	4.1
13.7	5.5	5.1				Sales/Working Capital	7.3	7.1
-77.1	9.4	8.5					23.2	23.8
21.4	22.4	27.7					17.3	18.2
(196) 6.2	(157) 5.2	(67) 7.5				EBIT/Interest	(441) 4.7	(441) 5.4
1.5	1.4	2.2					1.4	1.7
2.9	3.8	6.7					4.2	3.7
(23) 1.5	(21) 1.4	(10) 2.6				Net Profit + Depr., Dep., Amort./Cur. Mat. L /T/D	(89) 1.6	(70) 1.9
.4	.7	.1					.7	.6
.2	.1	.1					.2	.2
.4	.3	.3				Fixed/Worth	.4	.4
2.4	.5	.6					1.3	1.1
.5	.4	.4					.5	.5
1.4	.8	1.0				Debt/Worth	1.2	1.1
6.1	1.9	2.0					3.8	3.4
103.9	77.1	87.2					109.3	109.9
(203) 39.9	(174) 20.2	35.6				% Profit Before Taxes/Tangible Net Worth	(451) 39.8	(440) 37.5
8.0	2.6	4.0					5.3	7.9
49.8	42.0	35.9					50.2	53.1
13.5	10.2	11.8				% Profit Before Taxes/Total Assets	14.8	14.4
2.5	1.3	2.0					1.6	2.8
37.4	30.8	29.0					30.5	31.5
22.4	19.2	16.2				Sales/Net Fixed Assets	16.5	17.6
11.2	12.9	9.9					9.8	10.6
4.8	2.9	2.3					3.2	3.1
3.1	2.4	1.9				Sales/Total Assets	2.4	2.4
2.3	1.8	1.5					1.8	1.8
1.5	1.4	1.6					1.5	1.5
(180) 2.2	(144) 2.1	(71) 2.0				% Depr., Dep., Amort./Sales	(414) 2.2	(410) 2.1
3.1	2.7	2.8					3.1	2.8
20.7	20.3	13.4					19.2	17.0
(126) 26.5	(110) 27.2	(39) 22.5				% Officers', Directors', Owners' Comp/Sales	(261) 25.1	(261) 25.4
35.6	32.6	30.6					32.3	33.9
211793M	477005M	587625M	283892M	766245M		Net Sales ($)	1551155M	2024798M
59727M	192554M	309209M	149969M	332574M		Total Assets ($)	817826M	1070299M

M = $ thousand   MM = $ million
See Pages 1 through 15 for Explanation of Ratios and Data

Comparative Historical Data				Current Data Sorted By Sales					
16	23	41	# Postretirement Benefits	13	19	2	6	1	
			Type of Statement						
18	27	19	Unqualified	6	6	2	3	2	
12	11	12	Reviewed	3	3	3	3		
188	160	162	Compiled	67	65	12	12	5	1
10	21	24	Tax Returns	14	10				
293	310	298	Other	92	112	42	27	18	7
4/1/92-3/31/93 ALL	4/1/93-3/31/94 ALL	4/1/94-3/31/95 ALL		193 (4/1-9/30/94)			322 (10/1/94-3/31/95)		
				0-1MM	1-3MM	3-5MM	5-10MM	10-25MM	25MM & OVER
521	529	515	**NUMBER OF STATEMENTS**	182	196	59	45	25	8
%	%	%	**ASSETS**	%	%	%	%	%	%
8.9	8.8	10.7	Cash & Equivalents	10.5	10.6	9.8	11.2	12.7	
44.2	44.4	42.5	Trade Receivables - (net)	36.0	43.7	54.0	45.7	47.2	
4.1	4.2	4.5	Inventory	2.6	5.7	6.5	5.9	2.1	
6.4	6.1	6.4	All Other Current	6.0	6.9	5.3	6.8	6.7	
63.5	63.6	64.1	Total Current	55.0	67.0	75.7	69.5	68.7	
18.7	19.4	19.5	Fixed Assets (net)	24.2	17.9	14.2	19.4	12.0	
6.0	4.8	4.9	Intangibles (net)	7.7	3.8	2.7	2.5	3.4	
11.8	12.2	11.5	All Other Non-Current	13.1	11.4	7.4	8.5	15.9	
100.0	100.0	100.0	Total	100.0	100.0	100.0	100.0	100.0	
			LIABILITIES						
12.7	13.0	12.8	Notes Payable-Short Term	17.5	11.6	9.7	8.7	5.9	
5.0	4.1	4.4	Cur. Mat.-L./T/D	5.2	4.5	3.1	3.8	2.1	
3.0	3.4	2.9	Trade Payables	3.0	2.3	2.9	2.8	5.4	
.3	.3	.3	Income Taxes Payable	.2	.2	.2	.7	.4	
10.7	12.1	13.3	All Other Current	13.6	13.8	11.8	11.6	14.0	
31.6	32.9	33.6	Total Current	39.5	32.5	27.7	27.5	27.8	
14.5	12.1	13.0	Long Term Debt	18.7	11.3	6.8	9.2	7.5	
.9	.9	.6	Deferred Taxes	.6	.6	1.3	.4	.0	
4.8	3.8	4.4	All Other-Non-Current	2.0	5.6	5.2	7.7	5.0	
48.2	50.2	48.4	Net Worth	39.1	50.0	59.0	55.2	59.8	
100.0	100.0	100.0	Total Liabilities & Net Worth	100.0	100.0	100.0	100.0	100.0	
			INCOME DATA						
100.0	100.0	100.0	Net Sales	100.0	100.0	100.0	100.0	100.0	
			Gross Profit						
85.2	86.2	86.1	Operating Expenses	84.9	87.8	85.1	87.4	85.8	
14.8	13.8	13.9	Operating Profit	15.1	12.2	14.9	12.6	14.2	
2.2	1.3	1.8	All Other Expenses (net)	2.2	1.9	.9	2.5	.6	
12.6	12.5	12.1	Profit Before Taxes	12.9	10.3	14.0	10.1	13.6	
			RATIOS						
4.7	4.2	4.4	Current	3.4	4.4	6.1	4.9	4.7	
2.4	2.2	2.2		1.6	2.3	2.9	2.5	2.8	
1.3	1.3	1.3		.9	1.5	1.8	2.0	1.7	
3.8	3.5	3.5	Quick	2.7	3.5	6.0	3.8	4.5	
(520) 1.9	1.8	1.8		1.4	1.8	2.4	2.2	2.3	
1.1	1.1	1.1		.6	1.1	1.4	1.6	1.4	
41 8.8	41 8.9	39 9.4	Sales/Receivables	0 UND	43 8.4	53 6.9	42 8.7	46 7.9	
68 5.4	66 5.5	62 5.9		54 6.8	63 5.8	94 3.9	62 5.9	79 4.6	
96 3.8	94 3.9	94 3.9		87 4.2	85 4.3	118 3.1	91 4.0	111 3.3	
			Cost of Sales/Inventory						
			Cost of Sales/Payables						
4.2	4.3	4.2	Sales/Working Capital	4.6	4.5	3.2	4.2	2.9	
6.7	7.1	7.0		12.6	7.0	4.9	5.7	5.3	
22.5	22.3	23.4		-56.0	15.4	8.4	9.8	13.5	
(457) 21.4	(453) 25.3	(429) 22.8	EBIT/Interest	(147) 15.0	(166) 23.0	(50) 35.8	(38) 18.9	(23) 42.6	
5.9	5.8	6.6		6.2	4.8	12.1	4.9	13.0	
1.8	1.8	1.7		1.5	1.4	3.4	1.2	6.1	
(57) 6.9	(52) 3.1	(55) 4.1	Net Profit + Depr., Dep., Amort./Cur. Mat. L/T/D	(15) 2.8	(26) 3.7				
1.8	1.7	1.7		1.5	1.6				
1.1	.4	.4		.4	.4				
.2	.2	.2	Fixed/Worth	.2	.2	.1	.2	.1	
.4	.3	.3		.5	.3	.2	.3	.2	
.9	.8	.9		3.8	.6	.5	.6	.4	
.5	.4	.4	Debt/Worth	.6	.4	.3	.4	.3	
1.1	1.0	1.0		1.9	1.0	.7	1.0	.7	
3.3	2.4	2.8		14.7	2.3	1.9	1.7	1.2	
(478) 104.9	(485) 93.9	(468) 93.2	% Profit Before Taxes/Tangible Net Worth	(150) 95.1	(181) 93.9	98.4	70.9	67.2	
33.4	34.3	32.5		38.0	27.0	27.6	12.1	36.6	
6.3	5.4	5.4		9.0	2.1	9.3	1.6	11.2	
48.9	51.9	46.0	% Profit Before Taxes/Total Assets	43.9	38.5	60.8	40.8	40.9	
13.1	11.1	12.9		13.4	11.6	12.9	5.8	24.7	
2.5	1.9	2.1		3.6	1.1	3.7	.5	5.3	
32.2	29.5	32.6	Sales/Net Fixed Assets	34.1	34.0	32.0	29.8	33.1	
17.8	17.6	20.0		17.2	21.4	19.8	19.3	22.1	
11.1	11.0	12.1		8.8	14.5	12.7	12.4	13.3	
3.3	3.3	3.5	Sales/Total Assets	3.9	3.6	3.0	3.3	2.7	
2.5	2.4	2.5		2.5	2.7	2.3	2.5	1.9	
1.9	1.8	1.9		1.6	2.1	1.9	2.0	1.6	
(432) 1.4	(427) 1.5	(405) 1.5	% Depr., Dep., Amort./Sales	(134) 1.6	(153) 1.3	(51) 1.6	(39) 1.5	(21) 1.1	
2.1	2.2	2.1		2.4	2.0	2.0	2.1	1.9	
3.0	3.0	2.9		3.7	2.7	2.4	2.7	2.4	
(301) 19.0	(278) 19.9	(277) 19.4	% Officers', Directors', Owners' Comp/Sales	(96) 18.6	(118) 21.4	(25) 21.6	(25) 12.4	(12) 2.4	
26.4	27.5	26.0		25.5	27.8	26.9	23.8	18.4	
34.1	35.5	33.2		33.1	35.1	34.3	32.3	20.9	
2051133M	2802912M	2326560M	Net Sales ($)	96109M	352831M	230403M	298706M	398563M	949948M
1145954M	1574321M	1044033M	Total Assets ($)	53944M	151538M	109291M	123150M	189976M	416134M

Current Data Sorted By Assets   Comparative Historical Data

								4/1/90-3/31/91 ALL	4/1/91-3/31/92 ALL
2	2	2	1			# Postretirement Benefits / Type of Statement			
2	1	7	6		1	Unqualified			9
2	2	5	2			Reviewed			5
13	8	3				Compiled			11
2	1					Tax Returns			1
4	5	5			2	Other			11
0-500M	**500M-2MM**	**2-10MM**	**10-50MM**	**50-100MM**	**100-250MM**				
27 (4/1-9/30/94)			44 (10/1/94-3/31/95)						
23	17	20	8		3	NUMBER OF STATEMENTS			37
%	%	%	%	%	%	**ASSETS**		%	%
36.0	30.9	18.2				Cash & Equivalents	D		24.5
14.1	24.9	27.3				Trade Receivables - (net)	A		21.3
.0	.3	.1				Inventory	T		.1
.5	4.9	19.0				All Other Current	A		5.5
50.6	60.9	64.5				Total Current			51.4
36.0	26.0	18.5				Fixed Assets (net)	N		32.4
8.3	1.5	3.1				Intangibles (net)	O		3.2
5.1	11.5	13.9				All Other Non-Current	T		13.0
100.0	100.0	100.0				Total			100.0
						LIABILITIES	A		
13.0	10.4	18.0				Notes Payable-Short Term	V		6.8
6.9	3.3	2.1				Cur. Mat. -L/T/D	A		4.6
11.2	10.9	8.8				Trade Payables	I		9.8
1.3	1.4	.3				Income Taxes Payable	L		1.1
16.9	10.6	15.3				All Other Current	A		20.5
49.3	36.6	44.6				Total Current	B		42.8
18.8	12.4	13.4				Long Term Debt	L		15.4
.1	.1	1.0				Deferred Taxes	E		.4
1.1	4.7	2.3				All Other-Non-Current			4.3
30.7	46.1	38.7				Net Worth			37.2
100.0	100.0	100.0				Total Liabilities & Net Worth			100.0
						INCOME DATA			
100.0	100.0	100.0				Net Sales			100.0
						Gross Profit			
94.6	88.5	89.0				Operating Expenses			94.0
5.4	11.5	11.0				Operating Profit			6.0
.3	3.2	4.4				All Other Expenses (net)			.4
5.1	8.3	6.6				Profit Before Taxes			5.5
						RATIOS			
2.5	4.3	1.9				Current			1.9
1.0	1.5	1.4							1.3
.4	.9	1.0							.7
2.5	4.2	1.7				Quick			1.9
1.0	1.5	1.0							1.2
.4	.7	.5							.6
0 UND	0 UND	16 22.6				Sales/Receivables		3	111.6
6 58.2	26 13.8	36 10.1						23	15.8
18 20.7	53 6.9	52 7.0						35	10.3
						Cost of Sales/Inventory			
						Cost of Sales/Payables			
10.3	2.1	3.3				Sales/Working Capital			9.3
UND	14.9	10.7							38.7
-29.3	NM	101.9							-40.3
22.6	6.7	14.3				EBIT/Interest			25.4
(17) 4.0	(10) 3.1	(17) 3.2						(34)	5.6
1.2	2.1	2.2							2.3
						Net Profit + Depr., Dep., Amort./Cur. Mat. L /T/D			8.3
								(18)	3.3
									1.5
.4	.1	.3				Fixed/Worth			.4
1.3	.4	.5							1.0
UND	1.2	1.0							1.9
1.1	.4	.8				Debt/Worth			1.0
3.7	1.5	2.1							2.3
UND	3.1	4.1							3.9
167.2	69.8	46.8				% Profit Before Taxes/Tangible Net Worth			58.1
(18) 42.9	27.2	31.1						(34)	26.0
13.8	1.4	18.5							16.0
46.5	26.1	15.8				% Profit Before Taxes/Total Assets			19.8
12.9	11.3	8.5							10.4
1.3	.5	4.5							6.6
58.8	67.6	19.8				Sales/Net Fixed Assets			29.5
16.1	18.3	12.3							12.6
8.6	6.5	6.4							6.5
9.1	4.3	3.1				Sales/Total Assets			4.6
4.3	1.9	2.0							2.9
2.3	1.2	.8							2.2
2.2	.7	1.3				% Depr., Dep., Amort./Sales			1.3
(18) 2.8	(13) 3.0	(17) 2.5						(35)	2.1
4.4	4.5	4.0							3.3
8.1						% Officers', Directors', Owners' Comp/Sales			5.2
(12) 19.1								(18)	11.8
31.4									22.1
28661M	47914M	177624M	260570M		195897M	Net Sales ($)			344928M
5596M	18880M	89227M	232314M		416652M	Total Assets ($)			223506M

Comparative Historical Data				Current Data Sorted By Sales					
			# Postretirement Benefits	1		3		3	
			Type of Statement						
13	14	17	Unqualified	1	2	3	4	4	3
9	7	11	Reviewed		3	4	1	1	2
14	18	24	Compiled	8	10	3	3		
2	1	3	Tax Returns	2	1				
13	12	16	Other	4	5		2	4	1
4/1/92- 3/31/93 ALL	4/1/93- 3/31/94 ALL	4/1/94- 3/31/95 ALL		27 (4/1-9/30/94)			44 (10/1/94-3/31/95)		
				0-1MM	1-3MM	3-5MM	5-10MM	10-25MM	25MM & OVER
51	52	71	NUMBER OF STATEMENTS	15	21	10	10	9	6
%	%	%	**ASSETS**	%	%	%	%	%	%
23.3	25.6	27.6	Cash & Equivalents	43.3	26.1	23.5	21.4		
25.8	22.2	24.5	Trade Receivables - (net)	15.5	21.2	39.8	24.2		
1.3	.8	.1	Inventory	.0	.2	.0	.0		
8.2	6.0	7.7	All Other Current	2.3	11.4	6.9	3.2		
58.6	54.6	59.9	Total Current	61.1	58.9	70.2	48.9		
26.1	27.9	24.5	Fixed Assets (net)	27.5	26.5	20.5	27.9		
1.9	7.5	5.8	Intangibles (net)	6.1	2.8	4.5	7.8		
13.4	10.0	9.8	All Other Non-Current	5.3	11.7	4.8	15.4		
100.0	100.0	100.0	Total	100.0	100.0	100.0	100.0		
			LIABILITIES						
9.7	10.0	14.9	Notes Payable-Short Term	8.2	16.5	24.4	17.4		
5.0	3.9	3.8	Cur. Mat.-L /T/D	7.6	2.0	1.9	5.8		
10.8	12.3	10.0	Trade Payables	5.8	15.4	8.5	7.8		
.6	.8	.9	Income Taxes Payable	2.4	.9	.0	.3		
23.4	17.6	15.0	All Other Current	17.3	11.8	23.0	12.9		
49.5	44.7	44.6	Total Current	41.2	46.6	57.9	44.1		
11.9	13.3	14.9	Long Term Debt	21.6	12.3	9.6	14.4		
.2	.7	.3	Deferred Taxes	.2	.2	.3	1.3		
3.3	5.7	4.2	All Other-Non-Current	1.5	4.3	.7	1.1		
35.1	35.7	36.0	Net Worth	35.4	36.6	31.5	39.1		
100.0	100.0	100.0	Total Liabilities & Net Worth	100.0	100.0	100.0	100.0		
			INCOME DATA						
100.0	100.0	100.0	Net Sales	100.0	100.0	100.0	100.0		
			Gross Profit						
91.6	94.4	88.6	Operating Expenses	90.6	88.5	85.5	93.8		
8.4	5.6	11.4	Operating Profit	9.4	11.5	14.5	6.2		
1.9	1.1	4.8	All Other Expenses (net)	2.4	3.7	7.2	1.6		
6.5	4.5	6.6	Profit Before Taxes	6.9	7.8	7.2	4.6		
			RATIOS						
1.7	2.2	2.5		4.7	1.9	2.1	2.0		
1.2	1.4	1.3	Current	1.3	1.3	1.2	1.2		
.9	.9	.9		.6	.8	1.0	.6		
1.4	1.7	2.4		4.7	1.8	2.0	2.0		
1.1	1.2	1.3	Quick	1.3	.9	1.2	1.1		
.6	.7	.7		.6	.4	.8	.5		
1 365.0	6 59.7	2 163.4		0 UND	3 143.1	1 535.1	10 35.4		
29 12.7	25 14.4	25 14.5	Sales/Receivables	6 58.2	15 25.1	34 10.8	33 11.2		
51 7.2	45 8.1	46 8.0		26 13.8	44 8.3	1217 .3	51 7.2		
			Cost of Sales/Inventory						
			Cost of Sales/Payables						
7.9	7.7	3.6		3.0	2.4	7.4	9.0		
26.1	19.0	10.8	Sales/Working Capital	10.3	17.2	23.2	38.4		
-63.1	-73.2	-78.4		-31.8	-27.3	NM	-26.8		
18.3	12.1	11.8			8.1		34.0		
(43) 5.8	(42) 4.1	(51) 3.7	EBIT/Interest	(17) 4.0			7.8		
1.3	.6	1.9			1.4		.0		
7.0	9.3	13.4							
(22) 3.5	(15) 5.1	(18) 3.8	Net Profit + Depr., Dep.,						
.9	1.5	2.0	Amort./Cur. Mat. L/T/D						
.3	.4	.2		.0	.2	.1	.4		
.7	.8	.5	Fixed/Worth	.4	.5	.5	1.0		
1.6	2.7	1.9		24.3	1.9	1.5	1.7		
.9	.9	.9		1.1	1.0	2.0	.5		
1.8	1.9	2.7	Debt/Worth	3.5	2.7	4.1	2.6		
4.6	8.9	6.5		59.3	4.0	12.3	6.5		
47.1	74.2	69.8		112.9	94.6				
(47) 21.9	(45) 19.6	(65) 32.6	% Profit Before Taxes/Tangible	(13) 40.5	(20) 31.6				
3.1	2.9	5.6	Net Worth	10.6	3.6				
20.8	18.5	19.8		55.3	26.9	22.2	21.9		
6.6	5.7	6.9	% Profit Before Taxes/Total	9.5	12.9	10.4	7.2		
.5	.5	1.6	Assets	1.6	.6	.5	-5.2		
25.9	28.2	36.6		UND	19.1	26.0	20.1		
15.7	13.7	15.4	Sales/Net Fixed Assets	23.2	14.2	17.5	12.3		
8.9	7.0	8.4		5.7	5.7	15.1	6.8		
4.3	4.2	4.1		6.4	3.6	6.0	3.6		
2.9	2.7	2.2	Sales/Total Assets	2.2	1.9	3.4	2.9		
1.7	1.7	1.3		1.6	.6	.3	1.9		
1.3	1.7	1.6			1.5				
(47) 1.6	(42) 2.6	(57) 2.8	% Depr., Dep., Amort./Sales	(20) 3.1					
3.5	4.0	4.4			4.3				
7.8	7.1	6.7							
(20) 17.4	(25) 10.4	(28) 12.7	% Officers', Directors',						
28.1	16.8	25.1	Owners' Comp/Sales						
457424M	656102M	710666M	Net Sales ($)	6790M	33277M	41530M	82262M	129611M	417196M
301091M	554104M	762669M	Total Assets ($)	5073M	36989M	105278M	33463M	240082M	341784M

M = $ thousand   MM = $ million
See Pages 1 through 15 for Explanation of Ratios and Data

Current Data Sorted By Assets | Comparative Historical Data

						# Postretirement Benefits Type of Statement		
5	8	9	4					
7	6	20	13	1	2	Unqualified	28	34
13	41	29	5	2		Reviewed	113	102
52	38	16	1			Compiled	127	131
10	9	1				Tax Returns	4	7
29	40	23	9	1	1	Other	95	94
100 (4/1-9/30/94)			269 (10/1/94-3/31/95)				4/1/90- 3/31/91	4/1/91- 3/31/92
0-500M	500M-2MM	2-10MM	10-50MM	50-100MM	100-250MM		ALL	ALL
111	134	89	28	4	3	**NUMBER OF STATEMENTS**	367	368
%	%	%	%	%	%	**ASSETS**	%	%
11.8	9.7	14.5	11.6			Cash & Equivalents	12.4	10.5
52.2	55.4	55.7	55.5			Trade Receivables - (net)	51.7	53.0
4.0	5.3	3.3	2.9			Inventory	4.4	4.1
3.5	2.7	4.2	5.7			All Other Current	3.8	3.7
71.4	73.1	77.6	75.7			Total Current	72.3	71.2
21.1	16.9	14.1	14.8			Fixed Assets (net)	17.9	17.5
1.5	1.6	2.0	2.8			Intangibles (net)	2.1	2.7
5.9	8.4	6.2	6.7			All Other Non-Current	7.7	8.6
100.0	100.0	100.0	100.0			Total	100.0	100.0
						LIABILITIES		
13.0	7.6	5.8	1.7			Notes Payable-Short Term	8.9	9.0
4.6	3.3	2.5	1.2			Cur. Mat. -L/T/D	3.4	3.4
26.1	38.2	41.0	53.7			Trade Payables	35.5	36.1
.6	.9	.4	.5			Income Taxes Payable	.7	.7
13.7	14.5	18.5	13.9			All Other Current	13.1	12.8
58.1	64.5	68.2	70.9			Total Current	61.5	62.0
11.8	7.9	7.6	7.1			Long Term Debt	10.5	9.0
.5	.9	.4	.2			Deferred Taxes	.5	1.1
2.6	2.3	3.8	3.9			All Other-Non-Current	2.5	2.9
27.0	24.4	20.0	17.8			Net Worth	25.0	25.0
100.0	100.0	100.0	100.0			Total Liabilities & Net Worth	100.0	100.0
						INCOME DATA		
100.0	100.0	100.0	100.0			Net Sales	100.0	100.0
						Gross Profit		
96.6	96.8	97.0	96.9			Operating Expenses	97.4	97.6
3.4	3.2	3.0	3.1			Operating Profit	2.6	2.4
.8	.6	.5	1.7			All Other Expenses (net)	.8	.5
2.6	2.6	2.6	1.4			Profit Before Taxes	1.8	1.9
						RATIOS		
1.8	1.5	1.4	1.2				1.6	1.5
1.4	1.1	1.1	1.1			Current	1.2	1.2
.9	.9	1.0	1.0				1.0	.9
1.7	1.3	1.2	1.1				1.4	1.4
1.2	1.0	1.0	.9			Quick	1.1	1.0
.8	.8	.9	.8				.8	.8
27 13.5	41 8.8	44 8.3	46 8.0				38 9.7	38 9.6
42 8.7	54 6.8	60 6.1	111 3.3			Sales/Receivables	54 6.8	53 6.9
69 5.3	74 4.9	104 3.5	215 1.7				72 5.1	83 4.4
						Cost of Sales/Inventory		
						Cost of Sales/Payables		
13.5	13.9	14.5	15.3				12.1	12.5
27.4	58.8	37.8	41.3			Sales/Working Capital	37.7	40.0
-131.3	-47.8	NM	-169.8				-137.4	-60.4
11.4	12.8	21.1	34.1				10.2	8.3
(84) 3.5	(122) 5.1	(74) 5.2	(23) 5.9			EBIT/Interest	(322) 3.9	(320) 3.0
.8	1.4	1.9	2.1				1.0	.6
7.6	4.8	9.7	15.7				5.8	4.3
(19) 2.5	(45) 2.7	(34) 4.3	(13) 4.3			Net Profit + Depr., Dep., Amort./Cur. Mat. L /T/D	(159) 2.6	(150) 1.9
.7	1.1	2.1	2.4				.5	.4
.3	.3	.3	.3				.3	.3
.6	.6	.6	.7			Fixed/Worth	.6	.6
3.6	2.3	1.7	1.4				1.9	2.6
1.0	1.9	2.3	2.7				1.4	1.5
2.2	3.8	4.5	5.1			Debt/Worth	3.8	3.4
28.3	12.4	10.5	10.7				11.5	16.1
85.6	67.2	55.0	43.0				49.0	56.9
(88) 34.0	(117) 29.7	(80) 19.2	(26) 32.7			% Profit Before Taxes/Tangible Net Worth	(316) 20.6	(311) 21.8
8.9	5.6	3.6	9.5				3.2	1.6
25.2	12.8	7.3	6.7				11.6	12.7
7.8	5.4	3.1	3.9			% Profit Before Taxes/Total Assets	5.0	4.2
.0	.9	.6	.9				.1	-.9
56.9	55.8	68.3	57.4				61.7	54.4
31.1	27.9	28.6	13.1			Sales/Net Fixed Assets	28.0	25.7
17.3	16.3	12.7	8.1				13.5	13.2
6.6	4.6	4.6	3.6				4.9	5.1
4.3	3.7	3.1	2.1			Sales/Total Assets	3.7	3.6
3.2	2.6	1.5	.9				2.4	2.1
.6	.6	.5	.5				.6	.7
(88) 1.2	(120) 1.0	(79) 1.1	(24) 1.3			% Depr., Dep., Amort./Sales	(321) 1.3	(322) 1.2
2.4	1.9	2.3	3.4				2.3	2.4
5.9	3.6	2.8					4.6	4.3
(57) 9.7	(70) 6.2	(34) 5.7				% Officers', Directors', Owners' Comp/Sales	(156) 7.4	(162) 6.9
16.2	13.0	10.0					11.7	12.8
145284M	543434M	1054912M	1218616M	281176M	461004M	Net Sales ($)	2747012M	3023959M
29249M	148260M	336813M	519276M	305486M	428627M	Total Assets ($)	1175695M	1693002M

M = $ thousand   MM = $ million
See Pages 1 through 15 for Explanation of Ratios and Data

Comparative Historical Data				Current Data Sorted By Sales					
9	13	26	# Postretirement Benefits	5	2	9	3	4	3
			Type of Statement						
42	33	49	Unqualified	4	12	2	6	9	16
86	78	90	Reviewed	4	25	21	17	16	7
118	108	107	Compiled	28	39	19	14	5	2
11	22	20	Tax Returns	5	9	4	1	1	
89	104	103	Other	15	28	18	20	13	9
4/1/92-3/31/93 ALL	4/1/93-3/31/94 ALL	4/1/94-3/31/95 ALL		0-1MM 100 (4/1-9/30/94)	1-3MM	3-5MM	5-10MM 269 (10/1/94-3/31/95)	10-25MM	25MM & OVER
346	345	369	**NUMBER OF STATEMENTS**	56	113	64	58	44	34
%	%	%	**ASSETS**	%	%	%	%	%	%
11.8	12.9	11.7	Cash & Equivalents	10.3	11.5	9.5	11.8	16.6	12.7
51.7	50.6	54.2	Trade Receivables - (net)	51.5	52.2	55.7	57.0	58.0	53.0
3.7	4.7	4.2	Inventory	4.2	4.9	4.7	3.4	3.6	3.5
4.4	4.7	3.6	All Other Current	3.4	2.6	4.1	3.2	4.3	6.1
71.5	72.8	73.8	Total Current	69.4	71.2	74.0	75.5	82.5	75.3
18.1	17.0	17.2	Fixed Assets (net)	22.5	19.5	16.5	15.4	10.5	14.1
2.1	2.2	1.8	Intangibles (net)	2.3	1.9	.7	1.5	2.2	2.1
8.3	7.9	7.2	All Other Non-Current	5.9	7.4	8.8	7.6	4.8	8.6
100.0	100.0	100.0	Total	100.0	100.0	100.0	100.0	100.0	100.0
			LIABILITIES						
9.0	8.3	8.3	Notes Payable-Short Term	15.6	9.8	7.8	5.0	4.6	3.0
3.2	3.6	3.3	Cur. Mat.-L /T/D	5.2	3.3	4.8	1.6	2.3	1.6
35.6	32.7	36.6	Trade Payables	26.5	28.9	37.1	42.8	48.6	51.9
.7	1.5	.7	Income Taxes Payable	.2	1.3	.4	.4	.5	.7
13.4	13.6	15.3	All Other Current	14.2	13.3	16.4	17.8	16.4	15.7
61.9	59.8	64.2	Total Current	61.7	56.4	66.6	67.6	72.4	72.9
9.6	8.0	8.9	Long Term Debt	14.7	10.8	6.5	5.9	5.9	6.6
.7	.8	.6	Deferred Taxes	.4	.5	1.6	.6	.2	.3
2.5	2.7	2.9	All Other-Non-Current	3.0	2.4	2.0	2.1	6.2	2.5
25.3	28.7	23.4	Net Worth	20.2	29.8	23.3	23.9	15.2	17.7
100.0	100.0	100.0	Total Liabilities & Net Worth	100.0	100.0	100.0	100.0	100.0	100.0
			INCOME DATA						
100.0	100.0	100.0	Net Sales	100.0	100.0	100.0	100.0	100.0	100.0
			Gross Profit						
95.9	97.0	96.7	Operating Expenses	95.6	95.8	97.7	98.4	96.4	97.1
4.1	3.0	3.3	Operating Profit	4.4	4.2	2.3	1.6	3.6	2.9
.9	.6	.7	All Other Expenses (net)	1.2	.7	.6	.7	.8	.5
3.2	2.4	2.6	Profit Before Taxes	3.1	3.6	1.7	.9	2.7	2.4
			RATIOS						
1.5	1.6	1.5	Current	1.8	1.7	1.4	1.4	1.4	1.2
1.1	1.2	1.1		1.3	1.3	1.1	1.1	1.1	1.1
.9	1.0	1.0		.8	1.0	.9	.9	1.0	1.0
1.4	1.5	1.4	Quick	1.7	1.5	1.2	1.3	1.2	1.0
1.0	1.1	1.0		1.0	1.1	1.0	1.0	1.0	.9
.8	.8	.8		.7	.9	.8	.8	.9	.8
36 10.1	35 10.4	38 9.6	Sales/Receivables	30 12.1	38 9.6	39 9.4	46 7.9	38 9.6	42 8.6
54 6.7	53 6.9	52 7.0		48 7.6	53 6.9	53 6.9	56 6.5	47 7.7	53 6.9
78 4.7	76 4.8	81 4.5		87 4.2	83 4.4	79 4.6	73 5.0	73 5.0	126 2.9
			Cost of Sales/Inventory						
			Cost of Sales/Payables						
12.7	11.1	14.3	Sales/Working Capital	11.4	11.1	17.4	14.8	17.9	20.7
44.2	29.9	34.7		28.9	22.1	46.0	35.5	88.5	80.9
-82.6	-101.8	-92.7		-25.2	-168.4	-82.8	-45.7	899.2	-234.6
(300) 15.8	(296) 14.0	(310) 13.2	EBIT/Interest	(41) 9.6	(97) 13.1	(55) 11.2	(48) 15.5	(41) 46.5	(28) 36.6
5.0	5.0	4.9		3.0	4.1	3.6	6.6	7.0	7.5
1.7	1.4	1.5		.5	1.5	1.3	1.3	3.0	2.8
(114) 7.7	(114) 6.2	(114) 6.2	Net Profit + Depr., Dep., Amort./Cur. Mat. L/T/D		(29) 5.4	(21) 5.1	(24) 8.1	(14) 11.7	(17) 16.6
2.9	2.5	3.3			2.8	2.0	3.9	3.4	4.7
1.4	1.0	1.5			1.4	1.0	2.6	1.6	3.0
.3	.3	.3	Fixed/Worth	.3	.3	.3	.3	.3	.3
.7	.6	.6		.8	.6	.6	.6	.6	.6
1.9	1.3	2.0		NM	2.2	1.5	1.9	1.7	1.4
1.6	1.4	1.6	Debt/Worth	1.0	1.3	1.7	2.0	3.1	2.7
3.4	3.2	3.9		2.7	2.8	3.5	4.4	6.6	5.0
10.6	7.5	11.3		-22.3	7.5	8.5	11.5	14.6	11.3
(299) 71.0	(313) 64.2	(318) 64.0	% Profit Before Taxes/Tangible Net Worth	(40) 84.0	(99) 68.2	(59) 59.4	(50) 70.7	(37) 64.2	(33) 48.7
28.3	26.1	29.7		36.2	29.7	20.1	23.5	32.2	31.3
6.1	6.1	6.3		13.9	7.9	3.1	1.2	10.3	17.7
15.4	13.8	12.3	% Profit Before Taxes/Total Assets	28.0	16.5	12.0	8.7	8.8	7.0
6.1	5.2	4.7		7.8	7.0	4.6	3.7	4.6	3.8
.9	.8	.7		.0	.6	.3	.4	.7	1.4
52.5	59.9	57.9	Sales/Net Fixed Assets	41.4	54.0	54.2	50.4	104.3	93.6
27.0	29.0	28.0		22.4	26.3	28.1	27.4	45.7	31.4
13.3	13.9	13.8		11.5	12.2	20.1	17.8	18.5	9.2
4.8	4.9	4.8	Sales/Total Assets	5.7	4.6	4.6	4.8	5.7	4.7
3.6	3.5	3.6		3.4	3.5	3.8	3.5	4.2	3.3
2.4	2.3	2.3		2.2	2.2	2.2	2.7	3.0	1.7
(302) .6	(303) .6	(318) .6	% Depr., Dep., Amort./Sales	(43) .7	(97) .8	(55) .7	(52) .7	(39) .5	(32) .3
1.2	1.1	1.2		1.6	1.5	1.1	1.0	.8	.9
2.3	2.3	2.3		3.1	2.6	1.7	1.9	1.2	2.4
(158) 4.4	(166) 3.7	(166) 3.9	% Officers', Directors', Owners' Comp/Sales	(25) 6.0	(57) 5.3	(30) 4.1	(32) 3.1	(15) 2.8	
7.3	7.4	7.6		9.7	9.3	8.3	5.7	3.5	
13.1	12.7	13.8		16.7	16.5	16.5	13.2	6.4	
2921069M	2711862M	3704426M	Net Sales ($)	32631M	226741M	238731M	406409M	645938M	2153976M
1222889M	940839M	1767711M	Total Assets ($)	11659M	98637M	90232M	145850M	246123M	1175210M

M = $ thousand   MM = $ million
See Pages 1 through 15 for Explanation of Ratios and Data

Current Data Sorted By Assets | Comparative Historical Data

						# Postretirement Benefits		
2	3	1			1	**Type of Statement**	9	8
1	1	2	4	1	2	Unqualified	9	8
1	6	1				Reviewed	7	9
7	12	3				Compiled	13	15
3	1					Tax Returns		1
3	4	5	2			Other	11	9
	7 (4/1-9/30/94)		51 (10/1/94-3/31/95)				4/1/90-3/31/91 ALL	4/1/91-3/31/92 ALL
0-500M	500M-2MM	2-10MM	10-50MM	50-100MM	100-250MM			
14	24	11	6	1	2	**NUMBER OF STATEMENTS**	40	42
%	%	%	%	%	%	**ASSETS**	%	%
12.6	5.5	6.6				Cash & Equivalents	5.5	5.1
18.0	19.4	10.5				Trade Receivables - (net)	16.7	15.4
3.8	3.3	5.2				Inventory	4.0	4.8
5.2	.4	.2				All Other Current	2.3	1.1
39.6	28.5	22.5				Total Current	28.4	26.5
50.6	53.7	59.9				Fixed Assets (net)	60.5	60.3
5.3	5.8	4.9				Intangibles (net)	5.5	5.0
4.5	12.0	12.7				All Other Non-Current	5.6	8.2
100.0	100.0	100.0				Total	100.0	100.0
						LIABILITIES		
10.3	2.1	1.9				Notes Payable-Short Term	10.3	13.5
4.2	14.1	5.3				Cur. Mat. -L/T/D	8.7	11.0
8.8	9.0	2.1				Trade Payables	4.2	8.4
.0	.1	.0				Income Taxes Payable	.5	.4
15.0	6.5	4.2				All Other Current	7.2	6.2
38.5	31.8	13.4				Total Current	30.9	39.4
30.0	28.9	35.7				Long Term Debt	33.4	33.0
.0	.9	.1				Deferred Taxes	.1	.2
3.1	1.7	12.1				All Other-Non-Current	4.8	4.8
28.5	36.6	38.6				Net Worth	30.8	22.6
100.0	100.0	100.0				Total Liabilities & Net Worth	100.0	100.0
						INCOME DATA		
100.0	100.0	100.0				Net Sales	100.0	100.0
						Gross Profit		
90.7	84.8	78.2				Operating Expenses	86.6	92.7
9.3	15.2	21.8				Operating Profit	13.4	7.3
1.5	2.2	5.0				All Other Expenses (net)	9.8	5.1
7.8	13.0	16.7				Profit Before Taxes	3.6	2.2
						RATIOS		
2.4	1.9	2.9				Current	1.7	1.3
1.1	1.2	1.5					.9	.7
.2	.5	1.0					.5	.3
2.4	1.8	2.0				Quick	1.2	1.0
.9	1.0	1.1					.7	.5
.2	.5	.8					.3	.3
0 UND	24 14.9	20 18.5				Sales/Receivables	26 13.9	20 17.9
16 23.3	32 11.4	47 7.8					42 8.6	37 9.9
40 9.2	49 7.4	61 6.0					61 6.0	52 7.0
						Cost of Sales/Inventory		
						Cost of Sales/Payables		
13.1	15.0	8.3				Sales/Working Capital	14.7	13.9
232.8	199.3	12.0					-48.6	-29.6
-17.3	-14.6	UND					-6.6	-4.3
8.0	10.4	14.4				EBIT/Interest	6.0	4.1
(11) 3.6	(22) 3.9	(10) 4.2					(29) 3.3	(38) 1.6
2.0	2.2	2.6					1.2	.6
						Net Profit + Depr., Dep.,	4.3	12.7
						Amort./Cur. Mat. L /T/D	(16) 1.4	(16) 1.5
							.7	1.1
.7	.7	.9				Fixed/Worth	1.0	1.2
2.1	1.5	1.9					2.4	3.0
7.4	2.7	11.1					20.3	-9.1
1.2	1.0	.7				Debt/Worth	1.0	1.3
3.5	2.4	1.5					2.4	4.2
13.9	5.3	14.8					22.0	-10.5
282.5	81.0					% Profit Before Taxes/Tangible	46.8	41.8
(13) 97.1	(22) 37.5					Net Worth	(32) 31.6	(30) 17.1
19.6	12.2						9.9	4.9
29.0	21.9	20.3				% Profit Before Taxes/Total	16.6	9.5
13.6	13.2	11.6				Assets	7.9	2.4
.8	6.1	4.0					-.5	-5.5
39.0	7.3	1.6				Sales/Net Fixed Assets	4.9	7.1
6.7	2.6	1.3					1.4	1.7
2.0	1.5	.9					.7	1.0
6.9	2.6	.9				Sales/Total Assets	2.0	2.3
2.2	1.5	.7					.9	1.1
1.6	1.0	.5					.6	.7
2.6	1.9	5.6				% Depr., Dep., Amort./Sales	3.6	2.4
(11) 7.6	(22) 5.4	6.5					(34) 7.9	(40) 8.8
10.1	7.7	10.0					15.4	14.1
	5.8					% Officers', Directors',	3.9	5.0
	(12) 8.2					Owners' Comp/Sales	(18) 5.7	(22) 9.1
	10.6						13.2	12.5
11312M	48393M	46141M	130293M	153626M	215067M	Net Sales ($)	295890M	187420M
3415M	26380M	59182M	142773M	53082M	379746M	Total Assets ($)	526776M	180965M

M = $ thousand MM = $ million
See Pages 1 through 15 for Explanation of Ratios and Data

Comparative Historical Data   **Current Data Sorted By Sales**

	4/1/92-3/31/93 ALL	4/1/93-3/31/94 ALL	4/1/94-3/31/95 ALL	0-1MM	1-3MM	3-5MM	5-10MM	10-25MM	25MM & OVER
# Postretirement Benefits				3	1	1	1		1
Type of Statement									
Unqualified	9	12	10	1	1		2	1	5
Reviewed	11	9	8		4	4			
Compiled	10	15	22	12	7	2	1		
Tax Returns		2	4	3		1			
Other	9	13	14	3	5		3	3	
				7 (4/1-9/30/94)		51 (10/1/94-3/31/95)			
NUMBER OF STATEMENTS	39	51	58	19	17	7	6	4	5
ASSETS	%	%	%	%	%	%	%	%	%
Cash & Equivalents	7.0	6.1	7.2	11.1	7.0				
Trade Receivables - (net)	15.8	18.0	17.6	9.1	17.1				
Inventory	2.5	6.4	3.3	1.3	6.8				
All Other Current	4.4	1.5	1.9	4.0	.2				
Total Current	29.6	32.0	30.0	25.4	31.1				
Fixed Assets (net)	52.7	51.1	53.9	57.3	55.1				
Intangibles (net)	6.3	9.1	6.2	10.7	.9				
All Other Non-Current	11.4	7.8	10.0	6.5	12.9				
Total	100.0	100.0	100.0	100.0	100.0				
LIABILITIES									
Notes Payable-Short Term	9.2	6.1	3.7	6.3	1.9				
Cur. Mat.-L/T/D	10.0	8.7	8.5	6.6	14.7				
Trade Payables	5.4	7.6	7.3	3.0	8.0				
Income Taxes Payable	.1	1.1	.2	.1	.1				
All Other Current	9.9	7.8	8.3	11.5	6.6				
Total Current	34.6	31.3	27.9	27.5	31.3				
Long Term Debt	29.2	35.5	34.6	34.4	24.9				
Deferred Taxes	.6	.5	.7	.0	.2				
All Other-Non-Current	6.5	5.1	5.5	3.9	4.0				
Net Worth	29.0	27.6	31.3	34.2	39.6				
Total Liabilities & Net Worth	100.0	100.0	100.0	100.0	100.0				
INCOME DATA									
Net Sales	100.0	100.0	100.0	100.0	100.0				
Gross Profit									
Operating Expenses	88.9	87.3	85.3	81.5	87.6				
Operating Profit	11.1	12.7	14.7	18.5	12.4				
All Other Expenses (net)	4.3	4.9	4.0	2.7	2.5				
Profit Before Taxes	6.8	7.8	10.6	15.8	10.0				
RATIOS									
Current	2.2	2.2	2.1	2.3	1.9				
Current	.9	1.2	1.2	.9	1.3				
Current	.4	.6	.8	.2	.8				
Quick	1.7	1.4	2.0	2.3	1.6				
Quick	(38) .7	.8	1.0	.8	1.1				
Quick	.3	.5	.6	.2	.7				
Sales/Receivables	20 18.7	22 16.3	19 19.0	0 UND	10 35.4				
Sales/Receivables	32 11.5	38 9.6	38 9.5	20 18.5	34 10.8				
Sales/Receivables	51 7.1	52 7.0	54 6.8	46 7.9	46 7.9				
Cost of Sales/Inventory									
Cost of Sales/Payables									
Sales/Working Capital	7.7	9.3	12.1	13.3	12.6				
Sales/Working Capital	-33.7	28.8	33.3	-88.4	24.3				
Sales/Working Capital	-5.4	-10.4	-22.3	-12.4	-70.3				
EBIT/Interest	(37) 7.1	(44) 6.1	(49) 8.6	(14) 15.1	(16) 6.1				
EBIT/Interest	2.9	3.3	3.9	3.9	3.6				
EBIT/Interest	1.1	1.5	2.2	1.9	2.1				
Net Profit + Depr., Dep., Amort./Cur. Mat. L/T/D	(11) 3.5	(17) 4.0	(17) 3.4						
Net Profit + Depr., Dep., Amort./Cur. Mat. L/T/D	1.4	2.2	1.4						
Net Profit + Depr., Dep., Amort./Cur. Mat. L/T/D	.9	1.4	.8						
Fixed/Worth	1.0	.9	.8	1.0	.7				
Fixed/Worth	2.2	2.1	1.9	1.9	1.1				
Fixed/Worth	-16.9	-5.3	6.9	4.2	4.1				
Debt/Worth	.9	1.3	1.0	1.1	.7				
Debt/Worth	3.3	2.9	2.8	1.7	2.3				
Debt/Worth	-20.9	-7.3	11.9	13.3	5.0				
% Profit Before Taxes/Tangible Net Worth	(28) 70.7	(37) 66.6	(49) 96.6	(17) 202.5	(16) 78.2				
% Profit Before Taxes/Tangible Net Worth	30.9	27.8	55.1	68.6	14.7				
% Profit Before Taxes/Tangible Net Worth	8.8	9.2	13.0	18.2	7.1				
% Profit Before Taxes/Total Assets	19.8	16.5	22.0	30.2	15.5				
% Profit Before Taxes/Total Assets	7.2	7.4	11.9	16.3	10.2				
% Profit Before Taxes/Total Assets	-.3	2.1	2.8	1.5	3.3				
Sales/Net Fixed Assets	7.0	7.7	8.4	12.0	4.3				
Sales/Net Fixed Assets	2.3	2.4	2.2	2.7	1.5				
Sales/Net Fixed Assets	1.1	1.1	1.3	1.5	1.4				
Sales/Total Assets	2.1	2.3	2.4	2.6	1.9				
Sales/Total Assets	1.0	1.3	1.4	1.6	1.3				
Sales/Total Assets	.7	.7	.7	.6	1.0				
% Depr., Dep., Amort./Sales	(34) 3.7	(45) 2.8	(51) 2.6	(14) 7.3	1.9				
% Depr., Dep., Amort./Sales	6.6	6.4	6.7	8.4	5.8				
% Depr., Dep., Amort./Sales	12.8	12.7	8.6	13.5	7.7				
% Officers', Directors', Owners' Comp/Sales	(18) 5.5	(23) 2.0	(25) 5.8						
% Officers', Directors', Owners' Comp/Sales	9.8	6.9	8.4						
% Officers', Directors', Owners' Comp/Sales	20.5	11.3	11.0						
Net Sales ($)	229512M	472892M	604832M	10490M	28914M	25547M	38112M	52098M	449671M
Total Assets ($)	397849M	678425M	664578M	13778M	24167M	16450M	41674M	57874M	510635M

M = $ thousand   MM = $ million
See Pages 1 through 15 for Explanation of Ratios and Data

Current Data Sorted By Assets   Comparative Historical Data

						# Postretirement Benefits Type of Statement		
1	1	1	2	2	4	Unqualified	11	16
1	6	2				Reviewed	6	13
2	3		1			Compiled	11	6
1	1					Tax Returns		1
2	2	4		3	1	Other	12	14
	11 (4/1-9/30/94)			29 (10/1/94-3/31/95)			4/1/90- 3/31/91	4/1/91- 3/31/92
0-500M	500M-2MM	2-10MM	10-50MM	50-100MM	100-250MM		ALL	ALL
7	13	7	3	5	5	NUMBER OF STATEMENTS	40	50
%	%	%	%	%	%	**ASSETS**	%	%
	5.2					Cash & Equivalents	7.0	7.0
	28.8					Trade Receivables - (net)	15.5	15.4
	10.2					Inventory	14.8	7.8
	3.8					All Other Current	2.7	1.9
	48.0					Total Current	40.1	32.1
	40.9					Fixed Assets (net)	44.3	51.7
	1.5					Intangibles (net)	6.5	3.9
	9.6					All Other Non-Current	9.1	12.2
	100.0					Total	100.0	100.0
						LIABILITIES		
	4.4					Notes Payable-Short Term	8.3	9.5
	10.1					Cur. Mat. -L/T/D	7.5	6.1
	16.0					Trade Payables	12.4	9.3
	.6					Income Taxes Payable	.5	.5
	10.0					All Other Current	7.9	7.8
	41.1					Total Current	36.6	33.2
	22.1					Long Term Debt	30.8	32.1
	.3					Deferred Taxes	.5	1.3
	6.5					All Other-Non-Current	2.8	2.3
	30.0					Net Worth	29.3	31.0
	100.0					Total Liabilities & Net Worth	100.0	100.0
						INCOME DATA		
	100.0					Net Sales	100.0	100.0
						Gross Profit		
	94.1					Operating Expenses	95.4	92.2
	5.9					Operating Profit	4.6	7.8
	4.9					All Other Expenses (net)	4.1	3.0
	1.0					Profit Before Taxes	.5	4.9
						RATIOS		
	1.9						1.6	1.9
	1.1					Current	1.0	1.1
	.7						.5	.5
	1.2						1.0	1.3
	.8					Quick	.5	.7
	.4						.2	.4
	8 45.0						11 32.8	10 35.8
	37 9.8					Sales/Receivables	20 18.0	31 11.7
	43 8.5						38 9.6	53 6.9
						Cost of Sales/Inventory		
						Cost of Sales/Payables		
	12.9						9.6	9.7
	77.6					Sales/Working Capital	106.4	79.3
	-53.5						-7.3	-11.1
	11.6						3.2	4.2
	(11) 2.4					EBIT/Interest	(36) 1.4	(46) 1.8
	1.4						-.1	1.0
							3.5	2.3
						Net Profit + Depr., Dep., Amort./Cur. Mat. L /T/D	(21) 1.9	(20) 1.5
							.4	1.1
	.6						.6	.8
	1.0					Fixed/Worth	1.6	2.3
	6.2						14.9	5.9
	1.0						1.0	1.2
	2.6					Debt/Worth	3.9	3.2
	7.5						17.3	8.7
	41.0					% Profit Before Taxes/Tangible	35.4	38.2
	(11) 19.7					Net Worth	(31) 13.1	(44) 20.3
	-1.1						-15.9	1.3
	12.2					% Profit Before Taxes/Total	7.9	13.8
	4.3					Assets	2.0	4.7
	-2.7						-7.5	-.1
	30.2						14.4	7.3
	5.5					Sales/Net Fixed Assets	4.0	2.1
	2.4						1.5	1.4
	5.3						2.8	2.0
	2.6					Sales/Total Assets	1.3	1.2
	1.2						.8	.8
	.7						2.2	4.1
	3.0					% Depr., Dep., Amort./Sales	(33) 5.9	(43) 7.2
	8.1						11.3	10.5
						% Officers', Directors', Owners' Comp/Sales		(10) 2.3 5.2 11.4
8155M	50682M	64640M	173091M	257785M	644126M	Net Sales ($)	532653M	1586788M
2031M	15844M	34350M	87468M	338651M	701309M	Total Assets ($)	504401M	1217093M

M = $ thousand   MM = $ million
See Pages 1 through 15 for Explanation of Ratios and Data

Comparative Historical Data / Current Data Sorted By Sales

2	3		# Postretirement Benefits Type of Statement	0-1MM	1-3MM	3-5MM	5-10MM	10-25MM	25MM & OVER
18	7	11	Unqualified	1		1		1	8
11	11	9	Reviewed	1	5		2	1	
10	11	6	Compiled	2	3			1	
2	2	2	Tax Returns	1	1				
7	17	12	Other		4		1	3	4
4/1/92-3/31/93 ALL	4/1/93-3/31/94 ALL	4/1/94-3/31/95 ALL			11 (4/1-9/30/94)		29 (10/1/94-3/31/95)		
48	48	40	**NUMBER OF STATEMENTS**	5	13	1	3	6	12
%	%	%	**ASSETS**	%	%	%	%	%	%
7.1	11.2	7.4	Cash & Equivalents		7.0				12.1
18.1	18.6	23.4	Trade Receivables - (net)		23.4				13.7
9.4	7.3	8.0	Inventory		10.6				9.2
1.5	1.1	3.3	All Other Current		4.3				3.0
36.1	38.2	42.1	Total Current		45.3				38.1
51.1	48.9	46.9	Fixed Assets (net)		44.4				53.8
3.1	3.4	3.7	Intangibles (net)		1.2				2.4
9.7	9.5	7.2	All Other Non-Current		9.2				5.8
100.0	100.0	100.0	Total		100.0				100.0
			LIABILITIES						
5.5	5.4	4.7	Notes Payable-Short Term		3.7				2.9
8.7	6.6	6.6	Cur. Mat.-L /T/D		9.5				6.8
9.6	12.7	14.3	Trade Payables		16.2				8.5
.4	.5	.4	Income Taxes Payable		.7				.0
8.2	8.5	10.0	All Other Current		7.4				8.8
32.5	33.6	36.0	Total Current		37.4				27.1
29.5	27.9	25.7	Long Term Debt		26.7				26.0
1.3	1.1	1.3	Deferred Taxes		.3				3.6
2.1	3.0	4.8	All Other-Non-Current		3.5				2.6
34.6	34.5	32.1	Net Worth		32.0				40.7
100.0	100.0	100.0	Total Liabilities & Net Worth		100.0				100.0
			INCOME DATA						
100.0	100.0	100.0	Net Sales		100.0				100.0
			Gross Profit						
93.4	93.5	91.9	Operating Expenses		92.2				92.1
6.6	6.5	8.1	Operating Profit		7.8				7.9
1.9	.0	2.8	All Other Expenses (net)		2.0				2.6
4.8	6.5	5.3	Profit Before Taxes		5.8				5.3
			RATIOS						
1.9	2.2	2.0			2.0				2.5
1.1	1.2	1.1	Current		1.1				1.8
.6	.8	.6			.7				.8
1.0	1.5	1.2			1.5				1.9
.6	.9	.8	Quick		.8				.8
.4	.4	.5			.4				.4
14 26.8	16 23.1	18 19.8			8 43.5				20 18.1
38 9.5	30 12.1	38 9.6	Sales/Receivables		37 9.8				48 7.6
48 7.6	47 7.8	49 7.4			40 9.1				58 6.3
			Cost of Sales/Inventory						
			Cost of Sales/Payables						
10.2	7.3	7.5			10.7				4.2
55.3	49.1	73.5	Sales/Working Capital		27.9				6.6
-10.3	-20.9	-14.2			-53.5				-16.4
(43) 6.9	(42) 8.4	(36) 11.5			(12) 13.1				(11) 18.7
1.9	3.5	3.1	EBIT/Interest		3.1				2.8
1.3	.7	.8			1.5				-4.7
(14) 4.9	(23) 3.7	(15) 3.6	Net Profit + Depr., Dep.,						
1.3	1.5	1.6	Amort./Cur. Mat. L/T/D						
.3	.6	.1							
.8	.7	.6			.6				.6
2.1	1.2	1.6	Fixed/Worth		1.6				1.5
3.5	5.0	23.1			6.2				29.0
.9	.9	.9			.7				.3
2.8	2.0	2.9	Debt/Worth		1.9				1.4
5.2	6.1	33.5			9.1				33.5
(44) 38.9	(42) 55.3	(33) 65.5	% Profit Before Taxes/Tangible		(11) 53.7				(10) 42.3
15.6	21.4	24.6	Net Worth		27.0				18.8
5.7	5.3	3.1			3.9				-4.5
11.4	16.0	14.0	% Profit Before Taxes/Total		14.9				19.9
4.4	8.5	6.0	Assets		7.4				3.7
1.2	-.2	-1.3			1.4				-3.7
9.3	12.8	15.5			17.6				4.4
1.8	3.4	3.0	Sales/Net Fixed Assets		5.5				2.0
1.4	1.5	1.8			2.4				.9
1.9	3.0	4.1			4.3				1.5
1.2	1.9	1.6	Sales/Total Assets		2.6				1.1
.8	.9	.9			1.2				.6
(37) 2.3	(47) 2.7	(36) 1.1			(12) .9				(11) 2.4
6.2	4.7	4.0	% Depr., Dep., Amort./Sales		3.6				3.9
9.8	8.3	7.2			7.0				6.0
(12) 1.6	(15) 2.6	(10) 3.2	% Officers', Directors',						
7.0	3.6	4.8	Owners' Comp/Sales						
20.5	9.0	7.5							
1232805M	860270M	1198479M	Net Sales ($)	2259M	24014M	3337M	19913M	85634M	1063322M
1069464M	890301M	1179653M	Total Assets ($)	5488M	12119M	2120M	10328M	96313M	1053285M

© Robert Morris Associates 1995

M = $ thousand   MM = $ million
See Pages 1 through 15 for Explanation of Ratios and Data

Current Data Sorted By Assets   Comparative Historical Data

0-500M	500M-2MM	2-10MM	10-50MM	50-100MM	100-250MM	# Postretirement Benefits / Type of Statement	4/1/90-3/31/91 ALL	4/1/91-3/31/92 ALL
		2	8	1	2	Unqualified	14	8
1	1	3	1			Reviewed	5	5
		6			1	Compiled	9	6
	1					Tax Returns	1	
1	5	2	6	2	3	Other	12	16
	16 (4/1-9/30/94)		30 (10/1/94-3/31/95)					
2	7	13	15	3	6	NUMBER OF STATEMENTS	41	35

0-500M %	500M-2MM %	2-10MM %	10-50MM %	50-100MM %	100-250MM %		%	%
						ASSETS		
		11.3	10.8			Cash & Equivalents	8.9	12.4
		25.7	16.9			Trade Receivables - (net)	21.5	27.3
		3.4	6.4			Inventory	12.9	5.6
		1.1	1.8			All Other Current	3.1	4.3
		41.6	36.0			Total Current	46.4	49.6
		50.9	49.4			Fixed Assets (net)	43.5	37.2
		1.3	2.5			Intangibles (net)	1.3	1.5
		6.1	12.1			All Other Non-Current	8.8	11.7
		100.0	100.0			Total	100.0	100.0
						LIABILITIES		
		6.2	1.6			Notes Payable-Short Term	8.0	6.2
		4.8	4.8			Cur. Mat. -L/T/D	4.6	6.2
		16.2	16.8			Trade Payables	11.8	13.5
		.3	.8			Income Taxes Payable	.6	1.2
		7.0	20.1			All Other Current	12.2	15.2
		34.4	44.0			Total Current	37.2	42.3
		25.2	29.3			Long Term Debt	23.0	20.8
		2.3	3.1			Deferred Taxes	1.6	1.0
		1.4	4.9			All Other-Non-Current	6.7	7.4
		36.7	18.6			Net Worth	31.5	28.5
		100.0	100.0			Total Liabilities & Net Worth	100.0	100.0
						INCOME DATA		
		100.0	100.0			Net Sales	100.0	100.0
						Gross Profit		
		91.5	94.8			Operating Expenses	94.4	94.1
		8.5	5.2			Operating Profit	5.6	5.9
		1.2	2.7			All Other Expenses (net)	1.2	1.2
		7.3	2.5			Profit Before Taxes	4.4	4.7
						RATIOS		
		1.7	1.0				2.2	1.9
		1.2	.8			Current	1.2	1.2
		.7	.7				.6	.9
		1.6	.8				1.4	1.6
		1.2	.7			Quick	.7	1.0
		.6	.4				.4	.6
		14 25.2	23 15.7				15 23.9	12 29.5
		37 9.9	31 11.6			Sales/Receivables	33 11.2	37 10.0
		62 5.9	52 7.0				58 6.3	49 7.4
						Cost of Sales/Inventory		
						Cost of Sales/Payables		
		8.9	-111.3				5.9	11.1
		26.3	-23.0			Sales/Working Capital	28.0	28.9
		-41.6	-17.2				-18.4	-28.3
		6.2	4.5				(36) 3.6	(31) 6.9
		3.8	(12) 1.5			EBIT/Interest	2.0	2.2
		1.3	-1.3				-.9	1.4
						Net Profit + Depr., Dep., Amort./Cur. Mat. L /T/D	(21) 4.2 / 1.9 / -.3	(19) 4.1 / 1.8 / 1.5
		.4	.9				.6	.8
		1.2	3.2			Fixed/Worth	1.4	1.4
		5.7	7.5				3.4	2.8
		.7	2.6				1.1	1.2
		3.0	5.5			Debt/Worth	2.5	3.3
		6.1	21.1				5.4	6.4
		(12) 34.9	(13) 66.0			% Profit Before Taxes/Tangible Net Worth	(38) 52.8	(31) 65.1
		22.7	34.0				22.7	24.7
		8.3	-1.4				-4.2	8.9
		15.8	12.7			% Profit Before Taxes/Total Assets	17.2	15.0
		5.8	2.9				6.5	8.1
		1.8	1.3				-2.3	.7
		12.5	11.3			Sales/Net Fixed Assets	10.7	23.9
		5.1	2.8				5.2	5.2
		2.1	1.9				1.9	2.7
		3.5	2.5			Sales/Total Assets	3.2	5.0
		2.0	1.5				1.7	2.0
		1.4	1.0				1.1	1.3
		1.6	1.9			% Depr., Dep., Amort./Sales	(38) 1.9	(33) 1.5
		3.6	5.2				3.5	3.1
		5.7	7.1				9.2	7.2
						% Officers', Directors', Owners' Comp/Sales	(12) 2.8 / 4.6 / 6.4	
444M	23971M	91766M	751314M	491459M	780684M	Net Sales ($)	905572M	1129850M
408M	6985M	45860M	343630M	191455M	966877M	Total Assets ($)	548898M	633194M

M = $ thousand   MM = $ million
See Pages 1 through 15 for Explanation of Ratios and Data

Comparative Historical Data / Current Data Sorted By Sales

	2		2	**# Postretirement Benefits**					1		1
				Type of Statement							
	20	9	13	Unqualified					3		9
	2	2	6	Reviewed	1		1	2	1		
	4	6	7	Compiled			2	3	1		1
		3	1	Tax Returns		1					
	17	13	19	Other	1	4	1	2	3		8
	4/1/92-	4/1/93-	4/1/94-				16 (4/1-9/30/94)		30 (10/1/94-3/31/95)		
	3/31/93	3/31/94	3/31/95		0-1MM	1-3MM	3-5MM	5-10MM	10-25MM		25MM & OVER
	ALL	ALL	ALL								
	43	33	46	**NUMBER OF STATEMENTS**	2	5	5	8	8		18
	%	%	%	**ASSETS**	%	%	%	%	%		%
	14.6	10.7	11.5	Cash & Equivalents							16.9
	19.4	26.7	25.2	Trade Receivables - (net)							17.8
	3.9	5.1	4.8	Inventory							5.3
	1.5	3.1	1.4	All Other Current							1.1
	39.4	45.7	43.0	Total Current							41.1
	49.7	41.9	44.8	Fixed Assets (net)							44.0
	2.3	2.9	2.1	Intangibles (net)							1.6
	8.6	9.5	10.1	All Other Non-Current							13.4
	100.0	100.0	100.0	Total							100.0
				LIABILITIES							
	3.9	2.5	5.7	Notes Payable-Short Term							1.4
	4.5	5.2	4.6	Cur. Mat.-L /T/D							5.5
	11.8	13.4	14.9	Trade Payables							13.4
	.6	.7	.4	Income Taxes Payable							.8
	15.0	13.7	16.2	All Other Current							20.6
	35.8	35.5	41.8	Total Current							41.7
	29.2	22.3	24.9	Long Term Debt							24.3
	2.3	1.2	2.2	Deferred Taxes							3.5
	5.6	2.9	3.0	All Other-Non-Current							1.8
	27.2	38.2	28.1	Net Worth							28.7
	100.0	100.0	100.0	Total Liabilities & Net Worth							100.0
				INCOME DATA							
	100.0	100.0	100.0	Net Sales							100.0
				Gross Profit							
	95.4	93.4	91.7	Operating Expenses							94.0
	4.6	6.6	8.3	Operating Profit							6.0
	2.2	1.6	3.8	All Other Expenses (net)							1.9
	2.4	5.0	4.4	Profit Before Taxes							4.1
				RATIOS							
	1.5	2.4	1.5								1.5
	1.1	1.1	1.0	Current							.9
	.6	.8	.7								.7
	1.3	2.3	1.3								1.2
	.8	.9	.8	Quick							.8
	.5	.5	.5								.6
17	21.3	19	19.0	25	14.4	Sales/Receivables				26	14.1
33	11.2	33	11.0	34	10.8					33	10.9
43	8.4	59	6.2	53	6.9					42	8.6
				Cost of Sales/Inventory							
				Cost of Sales/Payables							
	12.2	7.6	11.0								12.8
	57.7	92.2	-115.2	Sales/Working Capital							-96.7
	-12.0	-31.9	-19.0								-20.3
	5.1	5.7	7.3								15.1
(37)	1.8	(26) 3.0	(40) 3.2	EBIT/Interest					(15)		3.5
	.8	.7	1.2								1.0
	3.9	1.9	2.5	Net Profit + Depr., Dep.,							3.0
(20)	1.9	(13) 1.0	(24) 1.5	Amort./Cur. Mat. L/T/D					(12)		1.5
	1.0	-.3	.8								.6
	1.3	.5	.8								.8
	2.3	1.2	1.6	Fixed/Worth							2.1
	5.6	2.6	7.2								3.9
	1.6	.8	1.8								1.8
	3.6	2.3	3.4	Debt/Worth							3.2
	6.9	3.4	10.0								7.6
	53.1	38.7	41.1	% Profit Before Taxes/Tangible							65.1
(37)	17.2	(30) 17.3	(40) 27.0	Net Worth					(17)		36.1
	3.3	-.4	7.1								8.1
	11.3	12.8	15.4	% Profit Before Taxes/Total							16.0
	4.7	7.3	5.4	Assets							8.5
	-1.1	-1.2	1.0								.6
	7.0	11.2	12.1								11.7
	2.9	7.7	5.1	Sales/Net Fixed Assets							7.0
	2.2	2.3	1.9								1.9
	2.3	3.2	3.1								2.7
	1.8	2.4	1.8	Sales/Total Assets							1.7
	1.3	1.5	1.1								1.2
	2.4	2.1	1.7								1.6
(36)	4.9	(27) 3.1	(41) 3.6	% Depr., Dep., Amort./Sales					(16)		2.6
	8.4	6.5	6.6								6.2
		2.1	1.4	% Officers', Directors',							
		(10) 3.4	(12) 2.4	Owners' Comp/Sales							
		11.7	6.4								
	2829668M	2498078M	2139638M	Net Sales ($)	444M	9651M	22743M	61462M	122755M		1922583M
	1713525M	1128103M	1555215M	Total Assets ($)	408M	6935M	15991M	22330M	291910M		1217641M

M = $ thousand   MM = $ million
See Pages 1 through 15 for Explanation of Ratios and Data

Current Data Sorted By Assets | Comparative Historical Data

# Postretirement Benefits — Type of Statement	0-500M	500M-2MM	2-10MM	10-50MM	50-100MM	100-250MM		4/1/90-3/31/91 ALL	4/1/91-3/31/92 ALL
Unqualified		3	3	1				18	20
Reviewed		5	3	1				6	9
Compiled	5	12	10	12	4	4		15	28
Tax Returns	1	1	1						
Other	5	6	9	5	1			9	16
		41 (4/1-9/30/94)		51 (10/1/94-3/31/95)					
NUMBER OF STATEMENTS	11	27	26	19	5	4		48	73
ASSETS %	%	%	%	%	%	%		%	%
Cash & Equivalents	9.9	7.8	7.1	6.3				5.9	7.2
Trade Receivables - (net)	17.5	14.7	16.7	15.2				17.8	16.9
Inventory	29.4	14.9	15.6	21.0				19.1	20.5
All Other Current	1.7	1.1	.7	1.1				2.4	2.2
Total Current	58.5	38.5	40.1	43.6				45.2	46.8
Fixed Assets (net)	37.3	52.7	47.3	46.6				47.6	46.1
Intangibles (net)	.1	2.8	2.7	2.6				1.7	1.6
All Other Non-Current	4.2	6.1	9.8	7.1				5.5	5.5
Total	100.0	100.0	100.0	100.0				100.0	100.0
LIABILITIES									
Notes Payable-Short Term	12.4	7.1	4.9	12.6				12.8	10.1
Cur. Mat. -L/T/D	3.1	9.1	8.4	3.4				3.8	7.0
Trade Payables	17.3	8.6	9.1	8.1				10.8	9.5
Income Taxes Payable	.2	.6	.3	.2				.7	.4
All Other Current	13.0	8.6	9.2	6.1				5.2	9.4
Total Current	45.9	33.9	31.9	30.4				33.3	36.5
Long Term Debt	25.1	29.6	24.1	14.8				28.9	27.8
Deferred Taxes	.0	.1	1.2	1.7				.7	.5
All Other-Non-Current	4.8	3.7	3.4	1.5				4.4	3.2
Net Worth	24.1	32.8	39.4	51.6				32.8	32.0
Total Liabilities & Net Worth	100.0	100.0	100.0	100.0				100.0	100.0
INCOME DATA									
Net Sales	100.0	100.0	100.0	100.0				100.0	100.0
Gross Profit									
Operating Expenses	95.9	92.4	92.1	95.5				97.5	95.5
Operating Profit	4.1	7.6	7.9	4.5				2.5	4.5
All Other Expenses (net)	.7	3.9	2.0	1.7				2.9	1.6
Profit Before Taxes	3.4	3.7	5.9	2.7				-.4	2.8
RATIOS									
Current	2.8	1.9	2.3	2.2				2.3	2.1
	1.7	1.1	1.2	1.4				1.4	1.4
	.7	.7	.9	1.0				1.0	1.0
Quick	1.2	1.4	1.2	1.4				1.3	1.4
	1.0	.6	.7	.6				.7	.7
	.3	.3	.5	.5				.6	.3
Sales/Receivables	10 37.0	13 28.1	17 21.9	31 11.7				22 16.8	18 20.4
	15 25.0	21 17.1	23 15.7	49 7.5				35 10.5	28 13.0
	28 13.0	49 7.4	30 12.2	81 4.5				48 7.6	41 8.9
Cost of Sales/Inventory									
Cost of Sales/Payables									
Sales/Working Capital	5.4	9.2	7.7	4.6				6.5	7.0
	9.9	22.9	40.7	8.1				14.6	19.1
	-34.3	-13.1	-98.9	-142.0				157.7	NM
EBIT/Interest		2.9	6.8	8.2				2.0	3.6
		(24) 1.7	(24) 4.5	(18) 2.7				(41) 1.3	(66) 1.9
		.2	1.8	.7				.6	.8
Net Profit + Depr., Dep., Amort./Cur. Mat. L /T/D		3.3	4.8	25.6				2.6	3.9
		(12) .8	(14) 2.7	(10) 2.9				(27) 1.6	(30) 2.1
		-.1	1.7	1.1				.9	.8
Fixed/Worth	.5	.7	.5	.5				.8	.7
	1.5	1.7	1.2	1.0				1.7	1.4
	-48.5	-137.0	3.5	1.4				5.7	3.0
Debt/Worth	.9	.8	.7	.4				1.0	1.2
	2.7	1.7	1.3	.9				2.3	2.2
	-89.3	-172.7	6.1	3.1				9.8	6.5
% Profit Before Taxes/Tangible Net Worth		38.5	35.2	21.0				22.5	34.9
		(20) 11.2	(24) 17.6	12.2				(41) 6.9	(65) 13.5
		-2.3	7.2	-1.0				-.0	1.7
% Profit Before Taxes/Total Assets	17.0	21.2	15.7	10.5				5.3	8.6
	10.8	2.6	8.5	4.0				1.9	4.2
	-4.1	-2.0	3.3	-.4				-1.2	-1.4
Sales/Net Fixed Assets	14.4	8.7	12.2	8.0				11.1	11.0
	8.2	3.0	4.3	3.3				3.8	4.8
	6.7	1.4	1.8	.9				1.5	2.2
Sales/Total Assets	3.8	2.2	2.4	1.5				2.7	2.9
	3.0	1.4	1.9	1.2				1.6	1.9
	2.5	.8	1.1	.6				1.0	1.1
% Depr., Dep., Amort./Sales	1.6	2.1	1.5	2.7				2.0	1.6
	3.1	4.8	(23) 3.7	(17) 3.9				(46) 4.4	(69) 3.5
	4.3	7.4	8.4	7.9				8.2	7.5
% Officers', Directors', Owners' Comp/Sales								1.8	2.3
								(13) 3.4	(24) 2.8
								8.0	4.2
Net Sales ($)	10225M	58485M	200723M	347102M	177511M	89908M		1313234M	899165M
Total Assets ($)	3356M	31968M	98952M	374822M	374604M	722965M		612292M	691930M

© Robert Morris Associates 1995

M = $ thousand   MM = $ million
See Pages 1 through 15 for Explanation of Ratios and Data

Comparative Historical Data				Current Data Sorted By Sales					
	5	4	**# Postretirement Benefits**	1	1	1	1		
			Type of Statement						
24	24	26	Unqualified	1	3	3	7	8	4
10	14	16	Reviewed	2	1	4	6	3	
13	14	22	Compiled	7	10	1	3	1	
1	3	2	Tax Returns		2				
13	21	26	Other	6	5	5	1	7	2
4/1/92-3/31/93	4/1/93-3/31/94	4/1/94-3/31/95		41 (4/1-9/30/94)			51 (10/1/94-3/31/95)		
ALL	ALL	ALL		0-1MM	1-3MM	3-5MM	5-10MM	10-25MM	25MM & OVER
61	76	92	**NUMBER OF STATEMENTS**	16	21	13	17	19	6
%	%	%	**ASSETS**	%	%	%	%	%	%
8.2	5.9	7.6	Cash & Equivalents	5.4	6.8	11.6	6.7	9.5	
17.5	18.7	14.5	Trade Receivables - (net)	10.6	15.0	7.3	15.4	22.5	
15.7	15.0	16.6	Inventory	16.4	19.3	13.1	15.2	16.9	
2.6	1.7	1.2	All Other Current	1.1	1.5	1.2	.6	.8	
44.1	41.2	40.0	Total Current	33.4	42.6	33.3	37.9	49.6	
45.6	49.3	50.3	Fixed Assets (net)	63.7	44.3	63.4	50.6	35.5	
2.6	1.5	2.2	Intangibles (net)	.6	5.0	.3	2.6	1.9	
7.8	8.0	7.5	All Other Non-Current	2.3	8.1	3.0	8.9	13.0	
100.0	100.0	100.0	Total	100.0	100.0	100.0	100.0	100.0	
			LIABILITIES						
8.2	11.5	7.5	Notes Payable-Short Term	8.7	7.6	1.0	9.2	10.2	
5.9	4.3	6.2	Cur. Mat.-L /T/D	4.4	9.7	9.7	5.7	3.7	
10.6	10.3	9.0	Trade Payables	9.4	11.1	6.1	6.7	10.7	
.2	1.2	.3	Income Taxes Payable	.1	.2	.8	.2	.5	
10.5	8.6	8.4	All Other Current	11.6	7.5	4.1	5.0	12.8	
35.5	35.9	31.5	Total Current	34.3	36.1	21.8	26.7	37.8	
21.2	24.6	24.7	Long Term Debt	26.4	35.5	18.7	23.8	13.3	
.7	.7	.7	Deferred Taxes	.5	.1	.5	1.7	.8	
5.3	4.6	3.0	All Other-Non-Current	6.0	2.7	4.6	2.6	.7	
37.2	34.3	40.1	Net Worth	32.8	25.6	54.4	45.1	47.4	
100.0	100.0	100.0	Total Liabilities & Net Worth	100.0	100.0	100.0	100.0	100.0	
			INCOME DATA						
100.0	100.0	100.0	Net Sales	100.0	100.0	100.0	100.0	100.0	
			Gross Profit						
98.0	94.6	93.6	Operating Expenses	84.8	97.8	96.2	96.1	93.4	
2.0	5.4	6.4	Operating Profit	15.2	2.2	3.8	3.9	6.6	
2.7	3.0	3.0	All Other Expenses (net)	5.2	2.1	1.7	3.2	2.1	
-.7	2.4	3.4	Profit Before Taxes	10.0	.1	2.2	.7	4.5	
			RATIOS						
1.7	1.9	2.2		2.6	1.9	2.5	3.0	2.7	
1.2	1.2	1.4	Current	1.0	1.1	1.9	1.1	1.4	
.9	.8	.9		.2	.8	1.1	1.0	1.0	
1.4	1.2	1.4		1.1	1.2	1.5	1.1	2.1	
.7	.7	.7	Quick	.4	.7	1.1	.7	1.0	
.4	.4	.4		.1	.4	.6	.4	.5	
23 16.1	23 15.6	17 22.0		7 52.2	13 29.1	14 27.0	20 17.9	22 16.6	
31 11.7	33 11.0	26 14.0	Sales/Receivables	15 23.7	26 14.1	19 19.0	29 12.4	38 9.5	
49 7.5	46 7.9	47 7.8		35 10.4	49 7.4	26 14.0	55 6.6	56 6.5	
			Cost of Sales/Inventory						
			Cost of Sales/Payables						
8.1	7.4	5.6		4.8	9.3	4.7	6.1	4.2	
20.2	25.9	17.0	Sales/Working Capital	NM	21.4	11.7	54.0	9.0	
-73.5	-16.9	-54.9		-2.9	-14.8	NM	NM	-118.6	
(52) 3.4	(70) 4.3	(80) 6.7		(13) 7.4	(19) 2.9	8.4	(14) 5.1	(17) 12.0	
1.2	2.2	2.6	EBIT/Interest	2.6	1.5	4.8	1.4	4.2	
.2	.8	.8		.2	-.2	1.8	.0	2.0	
(24) 3.2	(31) 2.9	(38) 4.7					(11) 2.8	(11) 28.1	
1.2	1.4	2.3	Net Profit + Depr., Dep., Amort./Cur. Mat. L/T/D				1.9	4.1	
.6	.6	.8					.8	1.8	
.8	.8	.7		1.0	1.2	.7	.6	.3	
1.2	1.4	1.3	Fixed/Worth	1.8	4.3	1.1	1.1	1.0	
2.6	3.4	2.8		NM	-7.0	1.5	2.2	1.4	
.8	1.0	.7		.7	.9	.4	.7	.4	
1.8	2.5	1.3	Debt/Worth	2.2	7.0	.7	1.2	1.4	
4.9	5.2	4.6		NM	-41.3	1.5	3.6	2.3	
(55) 18.3	(68) 23.9	(80) 33.9	% Profit Before Taxes/Tangible Net Worth	(12) 71.2	(14) 62.7	(12) 36.7	17.6	33.2	
3.6	7.9	15.2		11.4	12.2	21.1	7.5	21.0	
-3.2	-3.1	.5		-2.7	-.4	7.2	-2.2	.8	
5.7	8.1	12.1	% Profit Before Taxes/Total Assets	11.8	11.4	25.1	8.9	15.7	
1.0	2.5	4.1		2.3	2.6	8.8	1.8	9.3	
-2.7	-1.0	-.4		-3.3	-4.8	3.8	-1.7	.7	
10.5	7.4	8.9		7.9	13.1	6.3	6.6	18.2	
4.9	3.6	3.6	Sales/Net Fixed Assets	1.4	6.7	2.7	3.2	8.0	
1.5	1.5	1.3		.3	1.7	.9	.8	2.3	
2.5	2.3	2.3		2.6	3.0	2.1	2.2	3.3	
1.8	1.5	1.6	Sales/Total Assets	.8	1.7	1.7	1.3	1.5	
.8	.9	.8		.3	1.2	.8	.6	1.0	
(56) 2.2	(71) 2.2	(87) 2.5		(15) 2.9	(20) 1.8	(11) 3.4	(16) 2.6	1.2	
4.3	4.2	4.3	% Depr., Dep., Amort./Sales	7.1	4.7	9.2	4.0	3.3	
6.3	6.5	9.2		15.0	6.5	15.9	11.0	6.5	
(13) 2.8	(21) 1.8	(24) 2.7	% Officers', Directors', Owners' Comp/Sales						
4.2	3.4	4.6							
8.1	5.9	6.2							
918931M	1182169M	883954M	Net Sales ($)	9860M	34409M	52720M	127541M	325355M	334069M
993104M	1314710M	1606667M	Total Assets ($)	59847M	21496M	130370M	274501M	598745M	521708M

© Robert Morris Associates 1995   M = $ thousand   MM = $ million
See Pages 1 through 15 for Explanation of Ratios and Data

Current Data Sorted By Assets							Comparative Historical Data	
3	1	3				# Postretirement Benefits		
						Type of Statement		
1	6	3	4			Unqualified	12	20
3	10	8				Reviewed	23	30
17	10	5	1			Compiled	40	50
3	2					Tax Returns	1	2
11	7	5	3	1	1	Other	24	22
	41 (4/1-9/30/94)			60 (10/1/94-3/31/95)			4/1/90-3/31/91	4/1/91-3/31/92
0-500M	500M-2MM	2-10MM	10-50MM	50-100MM	100-250MM		ALL	ALL
35	35	21	8	1	1	NUMBER OF STATEMENTS	100	124
%	%	%	%	%	%	ASSETS	%	%
10.2	10.8	7.4				Cash & Equivalents	7.4	10.7
27.2	36.6	25.9				Trade Receivables - (net)	28.0	27.3
.2	1.6	1.5				Inventory	3.0	1.3
2.8	2.2	1.6				All Other Current	2.5	2.4
40.4	51.2	36.4				Total Current	40.9	41.6
48.6	39.2	49.5				Fixed Assets (net)	42.4	45.9
1.9	1.6	4.5				Intangibles (net)	3.6	2.8
9.2	8.1	9.6				All Other Non-Current	13.0	9.6
100.0	100.0	100.0				Total	100.0	100.0
						LIABILITIES		
17.0	5.9	2.2				Notes Payable-Short Term	9.9	8.0
8.6	8.3	7.2				Cur. Mat. -L/T/D	9.9	9.7
8.1	7.1	6.7				Trade Payables	5.9	5.8
.0	1.7	1.3				Income Taxes Payable	.8	.6
9.9	11.6	6.3				All Other Current	9.4	10.5
43.8	34.6	23.6				Total Current	35.9	34.6
22.8	17.2	22.7				Long Term Debt	24.4	22.7
.0	2.5	1.9				Deferred Taxes	1.5	1.3
2.3	2.8	3.6				All Other-Non-Current	1.8	3.1
31.1	42.9	48.2				Net Worth	36.4	38.4
100.0	100.0	100.0				Total Liabilities & Net Worth	100.0	100.0
						INCOME DATA		
100.0	100.0	100.0				Net Sales	100.0	100.0
						Gross Profit		
94.6	94.0	93.0				Operating Expenses	93.5	94.5
5.4	6.0	7.0				Operating Profit	6.5	5.5
.7	.8	2.2				All Other Expenses (net)	1.6	2.0
4.7	5.1	4.8				Profit Before Taxes	4.9	3.5
						RATIOS		
1.7	2.9	2.7					2.1	2.9
.9	1.5	1.7				Current	1.1	1.2
.4	1.0	.8					.6	.6
1.7	2.0	2.5					1.8	2.7
.9	1.4	1.5				Quick	.9	1.2
.4	.8	.8					.4	.5
3 123.0	31 11.6	30 12.2					14 25.7	14 26.5
24 14.9	54 6.8	38 9.6				Sales/Receivables	37 10.0	35 10.3
55 6.6	74 4.9	64 5.7					68 5.4	62 5.9
						Cost of Sales/Inventory		
						Cost of Sales/Payables		
13.1	6.5	6.4					8.3	7.7
-521.8	11.1	15.4				Sales/Working Capital	118.5	31.3
-10.8	-96.8	-40.6					-17.6	-15.6
(28) 5.9	(31) 10.0	(20) 10.6					(93) 5.1	(118) 5.9
2.7	4.8	3.8				EBIT/Interest	2.5	3.0
1.3	1.9	1.2					1.2	1.2
	(16) 9.6	(11) 4.3					(52) 3.5	(63) 3.5
	3.8	2.3				Net Profit + Depr., Dep., Amort./Cur. Mat. L./T/D	1.4	1.8
	1.2	1.9					1.0	.9
.8	.5	.6					.6	.6
2.0	1.1	.9				Fixed/Worth	1.3	1.2
3.5	1.8	2.2					2.8	2.7
1.1	.6	.5					1.0	.8
2.2	1.3	1.1				Debt/Worth	1.8	1.8
5.0	4.3	2.1					3.6	5.1
(31) 71.7	(33) 49.0	(19) 23.7				% Profit Before Taxes/Tangible Net Worth	(90) 49.6	(114) 46.8
27.3	25.0	15.8					22.6	21.0
-3.0	14.2	4.2					4.8	3.9
17.8	21.7	14.2				% Profit Before Taxes/Total Assets	16.2	17.3
7.1	12.2	7.0					7.4	7.3
-.8	3.7	.7					.8	.6
15.8	15.0	7.2				Sales/Net Fixed Assets	10.5	9.6
7.6	6.4	5.8					5.7	5.6
3.1	4.1	2.3					2.9	3.4
4.3	3.3	2.8				Sales/Total Assets	3.0	3.3
2.6	2.6	1.8					2.1	2.4
1.9	2.2	1.5					1.6	1.6
(28) 3.0	(34) 2.8	3.6				% Depr., Dep., Amort./Sales	(89) 3.2	(118) 3.6
5.2	4.8	4.8					5.5	5.4
8.8	8.1	6.6					9.9	8.0
(16) 3.5	(15) 2.7					% Officers', Directors', Owners' Comp/Sales	(47) 4.0	(57) 3.7
6.7	6.6						6.1	5.9
11.7	13.6						10.2	10.2
36006M	100991M	160583M	298333M	104364M	311727M	Net Sales ($)	350399M	661803M
9425M	36078M	84019M	166738M	90041M	233195M	Total Assets ($)	173077M	446839M

© Robert Morris Associates 1995

M = $ thousand　　MM = $ million

See Pages 1 through 15 for Explanation of Ratios and Data

Comparative Historical Data				Current Data Sorted By Sales					
1	6	7	# Postretirement Benefits	2	2		1	2	
			Type of Statement						
15	11	14	Unqualified	1	3	4	1	3	2
28	17	21	Reviewed	3	4	4	8	2	
35	38	33	Compiled	9	15	4	3	1	1
4	7	5	Tax Returns	2	3				
27	24	28	Other	12	7		3	1	5
4/1/92-3/31/93	4/1/93-3/31/94	4/1/94-3/31/95		41 (4/1-9/30/94)			60 (10/1/94-3/31/95)		
ALL	ALL	ALL		0-1MM	1-3MM	3-5MM	5-10MM	10-25MM	25MM & OVER
109	97	101	NUMBER OF STATEMENTS	27	32	12	15	7	8
%	%	%	ASSETS	%	%	%	%	%	%
7.2	9.6	9.5	Cash & Equivalents	9.1	12.6	10.1	6.5		
27.4	25.2	30.4	Trade Receivables - (net)	21.9	35.7	34.9	35.1		
.8	.8	1.0	Inventory	.2	.5	1.1	4.0		
2.7	2.5	2.6	All Other Current	4.5	1.3	1.3	2.0		
38.0	38.1	43.5	Total Current	35.7	50.1	47.4	47.7		
48.8	47.4	43.8	Fixed Assets (net)	53.7	39.3	44.3	40.6		
5.2	3.7	4.2	Intangibles (net)	2.0	1.9	1.2	.3		
8.0	10.7	8.5	All Other Non-Current	8.6	8.8	7.2	11.4		
100.0	100.0	100.0	Total	100.0	100.0	100.0	100.0		
			LIABILITIES						
6.7	6.3	8.9	Notes Payable-Short Term	13.2	10.1	2.8	7.4		
9.6	9.3	8.3	Cur. Mat.-L./T/D	9.2	6.8	8.0	8.8		
5.6	7.1	7.6	Trade Payables	5.6	8.5	6.2	8.9		
.7	.7	.9	Income Taxes Payable	.0	1.2	1.8	1.7		
7.6	9.2	9.3	All Other Current	9.6	9.7	13.9	8.0		
30.3	32.6	34.9	Total Current	37.6	36.4	32.7	34.7		
23.7	21.3	20.7	Long Term Debt	27.6	17.4	14.7	17.9		
1.9	1.6	1.5	Deferred Taxes	.0	1.2	2.4	3.6		
4.6	5.2	2.8	All Other-Non-Current	1.2	2.9	.4	3.4		
39.4	39.4	40.1	Net Worth	33.6	42.0	49.8	40.4		
100.0	100.0	100.0	Total Liabilities & Net Worth	100.0	100.0	100.0	100.0		
			INCOME DATA						
100.0	100.0	100.0	Net Sales	100.0	100.0	100.0	100.0		
			Gross Profit						
92.9	93.8	93.8	Operating Expenses	90.4	95.1	97.7	93.9		
7.1	6.2	6.2	Operating Profit	9.6	4.9	2.3	6.1		
2.3	1.3	1.2	All Other Expenses (net)	3.0	.8	–.8	.1		
4.8	4.9	4.9	Profit Before Taxes	6.6	4.1	3.1	6.0		
			RATIOS						
2.2	2.2	2.3		1.8	2.9	2.9	2.1		
1.3	1.2	1.3	Current	.9	1.7	1.5	1.3		
.7	.6	.7		.3	1.0	.7	1.0		
2.1	2.1	2.0		1.8	2.8	2.8	2.0		
1.2	1.1	1.2	Quick	.9	1.6	1.5	1.3		
.6	.5	.6		.3	.9	.7	.8		
16 22.3	10 35.9	21 17.1		0 UND	26 13.8	30 12.1	32 11.4		
40 9.1	35 10.5	46 8.0	Sales/Receivables	24 14.9	52 7.0	47 7.8	46 7.9		
66 5.5	63 5.8	70 5.2		72 5.1	66 5.5	78 4.7	74 4.9		
			Cost of Sales/Inventory						
			Cost of Sales/Payables						
8.1	9.2	7.0		6.5	7.4	5.5	8.6		
32.3	45.4	29.4	Sales/Working Capital	–73.0	12.1	14.5	23.1		
–31.9	–22.1	–27.8		–10.5	–257.7	–21.9	–974.6		
7.1	6.6	9.8		8.8	7.5	11.6	12.2		
(101) 3.2	(90) 2.5	(88) 4.1	EBIT/Interest	(21) 3.1	(26) 4.1	3.2	4.8		
1.4	1.0	1.7		1.7	1.5	1.3	2.3		
4.1	5.2	5.0			10.7				
(64) 2.1	(41) 1.7	(40) 2.6	Net Profit + Depr., Dep.,		(15) 3.1				
1.2	1.1	1.2	Amort./Cur. Mat. L/T/D		1.2				
.7	.8	.6		.8	.5	.5	.5		
1.4	1.2	1.3	Fixed/Worth	2.0	1.0	1.1	.8		
3.3	2.5	2.4		3.5	1.9	1.5	2.0		
.8	.8	.8		1.1	.4	.8	.6		
1.9	1.5	1.6	Debt/Worth	2.2	1.5	1.1	1.1		
4.1	4.6	4.1		3.2	3.2	1.5	4.8		
54.3	44.8	55.3	% Profit Before Taxes/Tangible	82.9	42.1	26.6	46.6		
(100) 23.6	(85) 16.8	(92) 23.7	Net Worth	(25) 28.9	(28) 21.6	15.3	20.8		
6.6	2.0	8.6		2.7	6.0	2.5	15.0		
18.3	17.4	17.3	% Profit Before Taxes/Total	29.3	16.4	12.5	14.6		
8.9	5.4	8.5	Assets	9.3	10.0	6.1	7.5		
2.6	.4	2.0		1.0	–1.4	1.0	5.0		
8.9	9.2	10.4		8.0	19.6	9.3	12.3		
5.6	5.7	6.3	Sales/Net Fixed Assets	4.3	7.4	5.3	7.5		
3.6	3.4	3.3		2.3	4.4	3.1	6.0		
3.3	3.3	3.3		3.4	3.6	3.0	3.9		
2.4	2.4	2.3	Sales/Total Assets	2.1	2.6	2.4	2.8		
1.5	1.5	1.8		1.6	2.2	1.6	1.6		
3.4	3.6	3.3		4.4	1.7	3.9	2.0		
(106) 5.0	(90) 5.0	(92) 5.0	% Depr., Dep., Amort./Sales	(21) 7.8	(31) 4.1	(11) 4.7	3.4		
7.4	8.5	7.7		11.2	7.6	7.3	5.8		
2.9	4.0	3.1		4.2	3.4				
(50) 5.9	(41) 6.5	(38) 6.6	% Officers', Directors',	(13) 8.0	(13) 6.5				
10.1	11.2	12.3	Owners' Comp/Sales	12.6	10.6				
657373M	480259M	1012004M	Net Sales ($)	15455M	58761M	49621M	114454M	89041M	684672M
407507M	238499M	619496M	Total Assets ($)	13026M	21819M	23057M	46890M	62248M	452456M

© Robert Morris Associates 1995

M = $ thousand   MM = $ million

See Pages 1 through 15 for Explanation of Ratios and Data

Current Data Sorted By Assets

Comparative Historical Data

0-500M	500M-2MM	2-10MM	10-50MM	50-100MM	100-250MM	# Postretirement Benefits / Type of Statement	4/1/90-3/31/91 ALL	4/1/91-3/31/92 ALL
	2	5	13	3	1	Unqualified	11	13
1	3	10	2			Reviewed	11	15
6	9	4				Compiled	9	13
2		2				Tax Returns		
2	5	5	7	3	1	Other	5	16
	18 (4/1-9/30/94)		68 (10/1/94-3/31/95)					
11	19	26	22	6	2	**NUMBER OF STATEMENTS**	36	57
%	%	%	%	%	%	**ASSETS**	%	%
10.4	6.6	7.9	5.8			Cash & Equivalents	6.8	10.2
1.2	4.0	.8	2.2			Trade Receivables - (net)	1.7	2.8
5.1	5.1	2.3	3.3			Inventory	4.3	3.2
.4	.5	1.0	2.4			All Other Current	1.1	1.3
17.1	16.2	12.1	13.7			Total Current	13.9	17.5
71.5	71.2	79.5	65.9			Fixed Assets (net)	73.0	69.5
.4	1.2	1.1	4.9			Intangibles (net)	2.9	2.2
10.9	11.4	7.3	15.4			All Other Non-Current	10.1	10.8
100.0	100.0	100.0	100.0			Total	100.0	100.0
						LIABILITIES		
5.1	5.5	3.5	4.5			Notes Payable-Short Term	9.1	5.7
3.8	5.0	4.9	4.2			Cur. Mat. -L/T/D	6.5	8.3
5.2	8.5	4.4	5.9			Trade Payables	2.7	3.5
.0	.7	.1	.2			Income Taxes Payable	.3	.5
14.7	9.9	6.1	7.1			All Other Current	6.9	7.4
28.8	29.7	19.0	22.0			Total Current	25.5	25.3
15.2	28.2	49.4	36.5			Long Term Debt	39.2	35.4
.0	.0	1.3	1.6			Deferred Taxes	.4	.5
.0	5.0	5.8	5.2			All Other-Non-Current	8.1	4.9
56.0	37.1	24.5	34.8			Net Worth	26.8	33.8
100.0	100.0	100.0	100.0			Total Liabilities & Net Worth	100.0	100.0
						INCOME DATA		
100.0	100.0	100.0	100.0			Net Sales	100.0	100.0
						Gross Profit		
97.9	89.6	93.7	88.3			Operating Expenses	90.2	89.9
2.1	10.4	6.3	11.7			Operating Profit	9.8	10.1
.0	2.2	6.9	4.0			All Other Expenses (net)	5.4	4.3
2.1	8.2	-.6	7.7			Profit Before Taxes	4.4	5.8
						RATIOS		
3.1	1.1	1.2	1.0			Current	1.2	1.3
1.0	.5	.5	.4				.5	.7
.4	.3	.2	.2				.2	.2
2.8	1.0	.8	.5			Quick	.6	1.1
.9	.4	.3	.2				.3	.5
.2	.2	.1	.1				.1	.1
0 UND	0 UND	0 UND	0 854.9			Sales/Receivables	0 UND	0 UND
0 UND	2 193.8	1 689.6	3 123.0				2 197.8	2 201.2
1 521.7	6 58.7	5 70.0	7 51.6				7 54.0	6 63.1
						Cost of Sales/Inventory		
						Cost of Sales/Payables		
16.5	24.3	32.9	NM			Sales/Working Capital	61.3	34.6
-107.3	-11.1	-12.4	-9.0				-11.6	-23.0
-11.3	-6.8	-4.7	-4.6				-4.0	-5.4
8.7	13.5	2.7	5.2			EBIT/Interest	4.0	5.1
2.2	(16) 2.7	(25) 1.4	(20) 3.1				(34) 2.0	(52) 2.2
-5.0	1.3	.3	1.3				.8	1.0
						Net Profit + Depr., Dep., Amort./Cur. Mat. L /T/D	5.7	4.0
							(17) 2.6	(27) 2.7
							.8	1.0
.8	1.2	1.8	1.1			Fixed/Worth	1.5	1.3
1.1	1.9	4.3	2.1				3.2	2.4
5.2	5.0	NM	5.0				6.1	5.8
.2	.6	1.3	.8			Debt/Worth	1.0	.9
.5	2.4	3.7	1.9				3.4	2.8
4.9	6.5	NM	4.6				6.7	5.7
153.3	121.0	23.5	36.0			% Profit Before Taxes/Tangible Net Worth	54.8	42.6
3.3	(17) 45.6	(20) 16.3	(19) 29.4				(30) 23.8	(50) 20.1
-3.7	7.0	-.1	4.2				5.3	3.4
25.8	29.4	6.4	14.8			% Profit Before Taxes/Total Assets	13.5	14.0
3.3	9.2	1.7	6.2				6.9	4.6
-2.8	1.9	-4.1	2.3				-1.1	-.0
3.6	4.0	1.4	2.5			Sales/Net Fixed Assets	2.9	2.8
2.7	2.0	.8	1.6				1.5	1.5
1.5	.8	.7	.8				1.1	.9
2.5	2.3	1.0	1.4			Sales/Total Assets	1.8	1.8
1.3	1.5	.7	.8				1.1	.9
1.1	.6	.5	.7				.8	.6
4.0	5.9	8.9	6.3			% Depr., Dep., Amort./Sales	7.8	6.5
6.8	10.2	(23) 12.9	(21) 8.6				(35) 9.2	(52) 9.2
9.1	13.3	18.5	12.6				12.3	14.4
		3.6				% Officers', Directors', Owners' Comp/Sales	2.6	2.8
	(11)	5.3					(18) 5.9	(25) 6.9
		9.5					13.3	12.2
6892M	36507M	112209M	434023M	434802M	330877M	Net Sales ($)	597481M	848059M
3358M	19621M	122060M	430856M	460020M	378494M	Total Assets ($)	753024M	982742M

M = $ thousand   MM = $ million

See Pages 1 through 15 for Explanation of Ratios and Data

Comparative Historical Data / Current Data Sorted By Sales

			# Postretirement Benefits					1	1
1	2	2	**Type of Statement**	0-1MM	1-3MM	3-5MM	5-10MM	10-25MM	25MM & OVER
17	23	24	Unqualified		2		7	9	6
19	19	16	Reviewed	3	6	4		3	
1	11	19	Compiled	10	6	2	1		
1	2	4	Tax Returns	3	1				
15	18	23	Other	3	6		4	4	6
4/1/92-3/31/93	4/1/93-3/31/94	4/1/94-3/31/95		18 (4/1-9/30/94)			68 (10/1/94-3/31/95)		
ALL	ALL	ALL							
64	73	86	**NUMBER OF STATEMENTS**	19	21	6	12	16	12
%	%	%	**ASSETS**	%	%	%	%	%	%
10.0	7.5	7.2	Cash & Equivalents	7.4	7.4		8.6	6.3	4.4
2.9	2.6	2.1	Trade Receivables - (net)	2.3	1.7		.7	2.8	3.7
3.6	4.6	3.8	Inventory	3.2	3.3		2.4	5.9	5.3
1.4	2.0	1.3	All Other Current	.4	.7		.5	3.0	1.5
17.8	16.8	14.4	Total Current	13.2	13.2		12.1	18.0	14.9
68.5	71.9	72.2	Fixed Assets (net)	78.1	74.3		76.8	60.8	66.9
2.5	2.5	2.2	Intangibles (net)	1.0	1.3		.8	6.0	2.5
11.1	8.7	11.2	All Other Non-Current	7.7	11.2		10.3	15.3	15.7
100.0	100.0	100.0	Total	100.0	100.0		100.0	100.0	100.0
			LIABILITIES						
9.8	6.6	4.4	Notes Payable-Short Term	2.4	7.9		1.7	6.4	3.3
7.1	6.6	4.5	Cur. Mat.-L /T/D	5.3	3.8		5.1	4.7	2.5
4.2	3.7	5.7	Trade Payables	3.9	6.5		7.8	6.1	5.1
.2	.4	.3	Income Taxes Payable	.1	.6		.0	.1	.5
11.8	11.5	8.6	All Other Current	4.5	13.0		7.7	8.9	9.3
33.1	28.7	23.5	Total Current	16.2	31.7		22.3	26.2	20.7
25.9	26.3	35.1	Long Term Debt	35.3	34.1		42.5	36.5	25.2
.7	.8	.9	Deferred Taxes	.0	.8		1.5	1.0	.9
4.2	8.2	5.4	All Other-Non-Current	4.5	3.1		8.6	6.1	8.6
36.1	36.0	35.1	Net Worth	44.0	30.3		25.1	30.1	44.5
100.0	100.0	100.0	Total Liabilities & Net Worth	100.0	100.0		100.0	100.0	100.0
			INCOME DATA						
100.0	100.0	100.0	Net Sales	100.0	100.0		100.0	100.0	100.0
			Gross Profit						
89.3	90.2	91.1	Operating Expenses	95.8	89.7		96.5	86.1	85.8
10.7	9.8	8.9	Operating Profit	4.2	10.3		3.5	13.9	14.2
2.9	2.7	3.9	All Other Expenses (net)	3.4	5.1		3.6	4.3	2.5
7.8	7.1	5.0	Profit Before Taxes	.8	5.2		-.1	9.5	11.6
			RATIOS						
1.2	1.2	1.3		2.8	1.1		.8	1.2	1.3
.5	.5	.5	Current	1.0	.4		.5	.5	.6
.2	.1	.2		.3	.2		.2	.2	.4
.9	.8	.8		1.5	.8		.8	.5	.5
.3	.2	.3	Quick	.9	.3		.3	.2	.4
.1	.1	.1		.2	.1		.1	.1	.3
0 UND	0 UND	0 UND		0 UND	0 UND		0 UND	1 243.5	3 138.3
2 187.3	1 250.7	2 202.1	Sales/Receivables	0 UND	1 521.7		1 587.0	5 77.1	7 54.7
5 66.7	6 61.3	6 65.4		0 UND	2 150.4		2 173.4	6 58.2	19 19.4
			Cost of Sales/Inventory						
			Cost of Sales/Payables						
36.8	41.6	27.8		16.5	91.3		-82.2	91.4	36.8
-12.7	-15.8	-12.7	Sales/Working Capital	-107.3	-11.1		-11.3	-8.9	-19.3
-5.5	-3.2	-5.1		-7.4	-4.3		-5.1	-4.4	-7.2
(62) 8.3	(67) 7.5	(79) 4.4		(17) 4.2	(19) 11.3		(11) 3.7	5.0	(10) 13.5
2.6	2.8	2.5	EBIT/Interest	1.0	2.6		2.2	3.2	4.4
1.1	1.1	1.0		-.3	1.2		.2	1.6	2.8
(26) 8.9	(28) 3.0	(24) 3.4	Net Profit + Depr., Dep.,						
3.1	1.8	1.9	Amort./Cur. Mat. L/T/D						
1.0	.5	.8							
1.1	1.3	1.2		1.1	1.6		2.0	1.1	1.2
2.1	2.1	2.1	Fixed/Worth	1.5	2.2		4.0	2.2	1.3
8.7	5.5	7.2		15.8	23.0		9.3	13.1	2.3
.6	.7	.9		.3	1.0		1.6	.9	.6
1.9	1.7	1.8	Debt/Worth	1.0	3.0		3.5	2.5	1.0
11.5	5.8	7.7		15.5	28.0		10.5	13.4	2.2
(52) 37.8	(61) 36.3	(74) 57.9	% Profit Before Taxes/Tangible	(15) 31.6	(19) 220.8		(10) 38.9	(13) 54.4	(11) 58.6
21.0	18.9	20.3	Net Worth	3.3	45.3		21.3	30.8	20.3
4.9	5.1	3.5		-3.3	6.1		6.4	8.6	8.7
13.5	13.9	13.8	% Profit Before Taxes/Total	7.4	22.2		8.7	15.8	17.0
7.5	5.9	5.6	Assets	1.6	6.0		5.6	7.3	12.6
.1	.4	.3		-2.8	1.6		-4.1	2.9	5.1
4.4	3.0	3.1		2.0	3.5		3.5	3.5	2.9
2.1	1.4	1.4	Sales/Net Fixed Assets	1.3	1.9		.8	1.7	1.6
1.0	.8	.8		.6	.8		.8	.9	.9
2.3	1.7	1.7		1.2	2.4		2.2	1.5	1.9
1.1	1.0	.9	Sales/Total Assets	1.1	1.3		.7	.9	1.1
.8	.7	.6		.5	.7		.7	.7	.6
(61) 4.8	(66) 6.1	(80) 6.2	% Depr., Dep., Amort./Sales	5.6	(19) 6.2		(11) 7.7	(15) 6.1	(10) 4.7
6.4	8.9	9.3		9.7	9.8		12.3	8.7	6.6
11.4	13.3	13.3		17.9	16.0		14.0	12.3	7.5
(27) 4.6	(27) 1.9	(28) 3.2	% Officers', Directors',		(11) 3.8				
7.7	5.4	5.2	Owners' Comp/Sales		6.4				
12.1	10.1	9.4			11.6				
1003980M	1228876M	1355310M	Net Sales ($)	9811M	39037M	24066M	85834M	256497M	940065M
935857M	1167316M	1414409M	Total Assets ($)	15381M	38075M	37286M	98075M	299405M	926187M

© Robert Morris Associates 1995

M = $ thousand   MM = $ million

See Pages 1 through 15 for Explanation of Ratios and Data

Current Data Sorted By Assets   Comparative Historical Data

2	8	5	1	3	1	# Postretirement Benefits Type of Statement		
2	1	5	10	4	1	Unqualified	18	22
6	22	17	4			Reviewed	30	35
14	29	9		1		Compiled	31	40
4	1	1				Tax Returns	1	
11	15	17	7	2	2	Other	19	30

	54 (4/1-9/30/94)		131 (10/1/94-3/31/95)				4/1/90-3/31/91 ALL	4/1/91-3/31/92 ALL
0-500M	500M-2MM	2-10MM	10-50MM	50-100MM	100-250MM			
37	68	49	21	7	3	NUMBER OF STATEMENTS	99	127
%	%	%	%	%	%	**ASSETS**	%	%
15.7	8.7	9.4	4.2			Cash & Equivalents	10.1	10.8
40.5	51.2	52.1	49.5			Trade Receivables - (net)	50.3	50.3
1.1	2.8	2.2	8.0			Inventory	1.1	1.7
2.2	4.2	4.4	2.9			All Other Current	3.3	2.9
59.6	66.9	68.1	64.6			Total Current	64.9	65.7
26.7	23.6	24.9	26.1			Fixed Assets (net)	22.1	22.8
.7	1.2	1.5	1.3			Intangibles (net)	2.5	2.0
13.1	8.3	5.5	8.0			All Other Non-Current	10.5	9.6
100.0	100.0	100.0	100.0			Total	100.0	100.0
						LIABILITIES		
11.2	12.5	10.9	14.4			Notes Payable-Short Term	11.7	8.2
2.8	3.8	3.8	4.5			Cur. Mat. -L/T/D	4.9	4.5
19.6	23.7	26.2	28.9			Trade Payables	26.8	29.8
.9	1.6	.3	.5			Income Taxes Payable	.7	.7
10.7	11.2	9.0	10.1			All Other Current	12.1	11.5
45.1	53.5	50.1	58.4			Total Current	56.2	54.8
12.2	10.7	13.0	10.5			Long Term Debt	11.3	11.0
.3	.7	1.4	1.1			Deferred Taxes	1.6	.8
4.0	2.3	3.3	3.0			All Other-Non-Current	2.4	2.1
38.4	32.7	32.2	26.9			Net Worth	28.5	31.3
100.0	100.0	100.0	100.0			Total Liabilities & Net Worth	100.0	100.0
						INCOME DATA		
100.0	100.0	100.0	100.0			Net Sales	100.0	100.0
						Gross Profit		
96.1	95.2	95.9	92.4			Operating Expenses	96.6	95.5
3.9	4.8	4.1	7.6			Operating Profit	3.4	4.5
.6	1.0	.3	1.5			All Other Expenses (net)	.8	.7
3.2	3.7	3.8	6.1			Profit Before Taxes	2.6	3.9
						RATIOS		
3.0	1.8	1.9	1.3				1.5	1.6
1.4	1.3	1.3	1.1			Current	1.2	1.2
.9	.9	1.1	.9				.9	.9
3.0	1.7	1.6	1.2				1.4	1.5
1.3	1.1	1.3	1.0			Quick	1.1	1.1
.7	.8	.9	.6				.8	.9
10 38.3	28 13.0	31 11.8	32 11.5			Sales/Receivables	28 12.9	28 13.0
27 13.4	39 9.3	40 9.1	50 7.3				43 8.5	41 8.8
45 8.1	61 6.0	56 6.5	122 3.0				83 4.4	76 4.8
						Cost of Sales/Inventory		
						Cost of Sales/Payables		
13.1	11.9	8.2	14.7			Sales/Working Capital	12.3	13.9
44.6	31.7	23.9	73.1				50.5	41.0
-123.6	-56.9	116.1	-150.3				-82.4	-77.3
(28) 13.4	(61) 15.7	(44) 27.4	(17) 11.6			EBIT/Interest	(77) 7.2	(106) 8.1
3.4	5.7	4.5	4.1				2.8	3.2
1.2	1.9	1.8	2.2				1.2	1.9
	(31) 6.2	(17) 10.5				Net Profit + Depr., Dep., Amort./Cur. Mat. L /T/D	(48) 4.4	(55) 6.9
	2.4	4.3					2.1	2.6
	1.1	1.1					.8	1.0
.1	.2	.2	.4			Fixed/Worth	.2	.3
.5	.5	.6	.8				.8	.6
2.7	1.9	1.9	1.6				2.1	2.2
.6	1.3	1.1	1.8			Debt/Worth	1.4	1.2
1.7	2.6	2.4	3.9				3.1	2.6
3.6	4.7	6.4	7.5				9.4	7.3
(33) 75.4	(65) 60.4	(47) 84.6	(19) 42.7			% Profit Before Taxes/Tangible Net Worth	(86) 54.0	(116) 51.1
28.2	28.9	28.7	21.4				28.3	24.2
4.2	9.4	12.9	8.7				3.2	7.2
24.1	16.1	15.0	8.1			% Profit Before Taxes/Total Assets	20.1	13.0
6.9	6.7	6.5	4.8				4.3	6.1
.5	2.7	2.7	2.8				.3	1.9
133.2	127.4	177.0	61.2			Sales/Net Fixed Assets	75.1	93.8
45.7	32.0	22.8	17.1				19.6	23.8
10.3	8.5	6.6	3.0				7.5	9.3
9.5	6.1	6.3	6.4			Sales/Total Assets	7.1	6.2
4.8	4.4	3.7	2.3				3.3	3.6
3.2	2.1	1.8	.8				1.5	1.5
(27) .3	(61) .3	(39) .3	(20) .3			% Depr., Dep., Amort./Sales	(81) .6	(111) .4
1.3	.7	1.3	1.0				2.1	1.2
6.0	2.6	4.3	4.1				4.1	3.0
(19) 4.4	(36) 1.6	(17) .7				% Officers', Directors', Owners' Comp/Sales	(37) 1.7	(51) 2.0
8.5	4.8	4.8					4.1	4.0
23.1	10.1	6.7					13.6	12.1
62200M	320931M	915694M	1858356M	1259501M	964795M	Net Sales ($)	1340111M	2829633M
10549M	76138M	203363M	475127M	456537M	432842M	Total Assets ($)	675211M	1206204M

M = $ thousand   MM = $ million
See Pages 1 through 15 for Explanation of Ratios and Data

Comparative Historical Data				Current Data Sorted By Sales					
3	5	20	# Postretirement Benefits	1	3	4	3	3	6
			Type of Statement						
23	20	23	Unqualified		3	2	2	2	14
32	36	49	Reviewed	1	9	11	13	7	8
52	47	53	Compiled	8	17	14	8	5	1
5	6	6	Tax Returns	3	2	1			
37	30	54	Other	7	10	5	9	6	17
4/1/92-3/31/93	4/1/93-3/31/94	4/1/94-3/31/95		54 (4/1-9/30/94)			131 (10/1/94-3/31/95)		
ALL	ALL	ALL		0-1MM	1-3MM	3-5MM	5-10MM	10-25MM	25MM & OVER
149	139	185	**NUMBER OF STATEMENTS**	19	41	33	32	20	40
%	%	%	**ASSETS**	%	%	%	%	%	%
11.4	8.4	9.6	Cash & Equivalents	18.6	13.5	9.3	5.4	9.1	5.3
51.1	49.4	48.4	Trade Receivables - (net)	17.3	50.9	47.7	52.0	60.6	52.4
1.2	1.8	2.8	Inventory	1.7	3.2	3.1	2.1	.4	4.2
2.7	2.8	3.6	All Other Current	4.3	1.0	5.3	4.2	4.9	3.5
66.5	62.4	64.5	Total Current	41.9	68.5	65.4	63.7	75.1	65.5
23.9	22.6	25.9	Fixed Assets (net)	47.1	22.8	24.2	25.2	16.2	25.7
1.7	2.8	1.4	Intangibles (net)	.5	1.8	1.0	.4	1.2	2.6
7.9	12.2	8.3	All Other Non-Current	10.5	6.8	9.3	10.7	7.6	6.3
100.0	100.0	100.0	Total	100.0	100.0	100.0	100.0	100.0	100.0
			LIABILITIES						
8.4	9.0	11.9	Notes Payable-Short Term	8.8	12.6	9.4	13.2	15.1	12.2
3.8	4.3	4.1	Cur. Mat.-L./T/D	5.0	3.1	4.5	4.2	3.2	4.6
31.3	27.8	23.9	Trade Payables	5.9	18.4	26.0	25.2	35.5	29.3
.7	2.0	.9	Income Taxes Payable	.2	.8	2.8	.4	.4	.4
10.5	9.6	10.5	All Other Current	9.4	11.8	8.5	13.1	8.8	10.3
54.7	52.7	51.3	Total Current	29.3	46.7	51.2	56.1	63.0	56.8
8.8	11.0	12.6	Long Term Debt	23.6	9.2	10.5	13.9	5.8	14.9
.8	1.0	.9	Deferred Taxes	.4	.5	1.8	.7	1.1	.8
1.2	2.2	3.1	All Other-Non-Current	2.2	3.7	3.3	2.5	1.4	3.9
34.6	33.1	32.2	Net Worth	44.5	39.9	33.2	26.9	28.8	23.5
100.0	100.0	100.0	Total Liabilities & Net Worth	100.0	100.0	100.0	100.0	100.0	100.0
			INCOME DATA						
100.0	100.0	100.0	Net Sales	100.0	100.0	100.0	100.0	100.0	100.0
			Gross Profit						
96.9	96.9	95.2	Operating Expenses	88.8	95.1	96.1	95.7	96.3	96.5
3.1	3.1	4.8	Operating Profit	11.2	4.9	3.9	4.3	3.7	3.5
.5	.3	.8	All Other Expenses (net)	2.1	.8	.5	1.6	-.3	.5
2.5	2.8	4.0	Profit Before Taxes	9.1	4.1	3.4	2.7	4.1	2.9
			RATIOS						
1.6	1.6	1.9		5.4	2.3	1.9	1.6	1.9	1.6
1.2	1.2	1.3	Current	1.2	1.5	1.3	1.3	1.1	1.1
1.0	1.0	.9		.4	1.1	.9	.8	.9	1.0
1.5	1.5	1.7		4.3	2.2	1.6	1.4	1.5	1.5
1.1	1.1	1.1	Quick	1.1	1.4	1.2	1.1	1.1	1.1
.9	.9	.8		.4	1.0	.8	.8	.9	.8
27 13.6	23 15.7	26 13.8		0 UND	27 13.7	23 16.2	29 12.5	26 13.8	32 11.4
38 9.6	36 10.1	39 9.4	Sales/Receivables	33 10.9	41 9.0	37 9.8	40 9.2	39 9.3	41 8.9
61 6.0	64 5.7	57 6.4		60 6.1	118 3.1	54 6.7	54 6.7	52 7.0	53 6.9
			Cost of Sales/Inventory						
			Cost of Sales/Payables						
18.8	16.1	12.7		8.2	6.2	12.4	18.9	16.3	21.9
56.3	46.7	35.1	Sales/Working Capital	44.6	12.1	34.1	30.5	37.8	65.8
-82.8	-172.6	-153.9		-7.0	115.4	-80.4	-37.0	-211.5	-267.7
15.4	16.5	14.6		(14) 14.9	(35) 12.5	(27) 13.3	(29) 16.2	(19) 30.4	(35) 25.0
(128) 4.3	(120) 4.2	(159) 4.7	EBIT/Interest	5.3	3.3	5.7	2.8	6.6	4.7
1.5	1.8	1.9		1.3	1.6	2.9	1.6	4.3	2.2
6.5	6.4	6.4			11.9	7.5	4.3		8.5
(46) 3.0	(57) 2.0	(63) 2.0	Net Profit + Depr., Dep.,	(14) 2.6	(14) 3.1	(12) 2.4	(17) 1.2
1.6	1.0	1.0	Amort./Cur. Mat. L/T/D		1.9	1.0	.4		.5
.2	.3	.2		.2	.2	.2	.2	.1	.4
.5	.5	.6	Fixed/Worth	1.4	.5	.5	.5	.4	.8
1.4	1.3	2.0		3.0	1.6	2.0	1.9	3.4	1.7
1.0	1.3	1.1		.2	.7	1.2	1.5	1.0	1.5
2.5	2.5	2.3	Debt/Worth	2.0	1.8	2.4	2.8	3.9	3.9
5.9	5.7	5.5		4.9	4.1	4.5	5.2	10.4	7.7
60.9	47.5	64.2	% Profit Before Taxes/Tangible	(18) 75.2	(39) 50.2	(31) 71.1	(29) 52.2	(18) 101.4	(38) 58.9
(142) 23.8	(127) 25.3	(173) 27.1	Net Worth	23.9	15.4	37.3	18.0	57.0	26.6
7.7	7.5	11.4		3.8	5.7	12.9	8.7	17.3	17.9
13.3	12.3	14.5	% Profit Before Taxes/Total	23.1	12.6	17.6	15.4	23.9	14.0
6.5	6.4	6.7	Assets	8.3	5.0	9.2	5.5	9.2	7.5
1.5	1.7	2.6		.6	1.3	3.9	2.0	3.9	2.2
100.2	96.0	91.6		18.4	64.9	145.8	69.8	374.6	116.9
25.1	27.0	23.2	Sales/Net Fixed Assets	6.4	19.0	45.9	32.0	56.5	23.8
8.4	7.5	6.8		1.2	4.9	9.1	9.3	13.4	8.7
7.1	7.3	6.6		4.0	5.0	7.1	6.1	7.8	7.5
4.5	4.5	4.0	Sales/Total Assets	2.1	2.5	4.7	4.8	5.4	4.3
2.2	1.8	2.0		.8	1.2	2.3	3.3	3.3	2.0
.4	.3	.3		(17) 1.0	(35) .5	(28) .2	(25) .4	(16) .2	(34) .3
(123) 1.2	(119) 1.1	(155) 1.1	% Depr., Dep., Amort./Sales	2.9	2.1	.6	1.1	.4	.7
3.1	3.5	3.3		10.9	6.6	4.6	2.3	3.1	1.6
1.3	1.3	1.6		(10) 11.3	(21) 4.0	(19) 1.6	(11) 1.7		
(56) 2.8	(53) 3.2	(76) 5.2	% Officers', Directors',	15.6	15.6	3.6	3.9		
6.8	8.2	12.0	Owners' Comp/Sales	27.3	15.6	6.4	6.4		
4314456M	3377543M	5381477M	Net Sales ($)	11718M	72376M	132333M	226320M	321461M	4617269M
1466202M	1282990M	1654556M	Total Assets ($)	9141M	58569M	39606M	104121M	88839M	1354280M

M = $ thousand   MM = $ million
See Pages 1 through 15 for Explanation of Ratios and Data

SERVICES—ART & GRAPHIC DESIGN – COMMERCIAL. SIC# 7336

Current Data Sorted By Assets							Comparative Historical Data	
4	2	1				# Postretirement Benefits		
						Type of Statement		
2			2	1		Unqualified	2	5
4	15	9				Reviewed	11	16
25	33	8				Compiled	14	30
7	3	1				Tax Returns	1	
17	15	5	2			Other	15	9
52 (4/1-9/30/94)			97 (10/1/94-3/31/95)				4/1/90-3/31/91	4/1/91-3/31/92
0-500M	500M-2MM	2-10MM	10-50MM	50-100MM	100-250MM		ALL	ALL
55	66	25	3			NUMBER OF STATEMENTS	43	60
%	%	%	%	%	%		%	%
						ASSETS		
11.6	7.8	6.5				Cash & Equivalents	10.1	9.4
36.8	39.2	32.0				Trade Receivables - (net)	37.0	38.7
8.1	11.5	10.4				Inventory	9.4	9.0
2.6	1.6	1.3				All Other Current	.8	1.4
59.1	60.0	50.2				Total Current	57.3	58.5
32.8	32.9	43.6				Fixed Assets (net)	30.6	27.2
1.9	1.7	1.6				Intangibles (net)	2.0	2.4
6.2	5.4	4.6				All Other Non-Current	10.2	11.9
100.0	100.0	100.0				Total	100.0	100.0
						LIABILITIES		
7.4	6.1	8.7				Notes Payable-Short Term	10.2	10.5
7.3	5.1	8.7				Cur. Mat. -L/T/D	6.3	6.8
14.4	14.5	14.4				Trade Payables	18.2	16.7
1.0	.8	1.0				Income Taxes Payable	1.2	.6
7.7	11.0	10.6				All Other Current	10.3	10.0
37.8	37.6	43.3				Total Current	46.2	44.6
17.7	17.0	20.3				Long Term Debt	18.9	20.4
1.1	1.6	.9				Deferred Taxes	.8	1.1
1.4	2.9	4.3				All Other-Non-Current	3.5	2.2
42.0	40.9	31.2				Net Worth	30.6	31.7
100.0	100.0	100.0				Total Liabilities & Net Worth	100.0	100.0
						INCOME DATA		
100.0	100.0	100.0				Net Sales	100.0	100.0
						Gross Profit		
91.3	94.0	96.1				Operating Expenses	98.5	96.7
8.7	6.0	3.9				Operating Profit	1.5	3.3
1.8	1.4	1.8				All Other Expenses (net)	1.3	1.2
6.9	4.5	2.2				Profit Before Taxes	.2	2.1
						RATIOS		
2.9	2.5	1.9					1.7	2.0
1.8	1.5	1.2				Current	1.4	1.5
1.2	1.2	.9					.9	1.0
2.1	2.2	1.5					1.5	1.8
1.4	1.2	.9				Quick	1.0	1.3
.8	.8	.6					.7	.7
26 13.8	41 9.0	36 10.2					38 9.7	32 11.5
48 7.6	56 6.5	56 6.5				Sales/Receivables	54 6.8	54 6.7
65 5.6	70 5.2	66 5.5					72 5.1	70 5.2
						Cost of Sales/Inventory		
						Cost of Sales/Payables		
6.9	7.7	8.6					8.3	7.5
13.8	12.1	38.1				Sales/Working Capital	17.3	14.1
93.7	40.0	-41.1					-83.4	-96.5
16.1	11.7	4.8					5.4	4.8
(44) 5.6	(58) 3.1	(23) 2.3				EBIT/Interest	(39) 1.9	(55) 2.2
1.7	.6	1.0					.0	.0
3.2	4.9	5.8					4.6	3.9
(15) 2.8	(33) 2.3	(12) 1.6				Net Profit + Depr., Dep., Amort./Cur. Mat. L /T/D	(19) 1.0	(30) 1.6
1.8	1.1	1.0					.1	.5
.3	.4	.7					.4	.3
.7	.7	1.1				Fixed/Worth	.9	.9
1.6	1.7	4.2					2.2	2.9
.6	.7	1.1					1.0	.9
1.1	1.7	1.8				Debt/Worth	1.8	2.3
3.1	3.0	4.9					5.0	8.5
64.7	56.0	35.1					35.2	44.0
(50) 18.6	(63) 23.1	(23) 13.0				% Profit Before Taxes/Tangible Net Worth	(35) 16.5	(51) 19.7
6.0	2.0	-.9					2.6	.0
27.9	22.9	15.4					11.6	14.0
8.9	7.4	6.2				% Profit Before Taxes/Total Assets	3.6	4.7
1.6	-.2	-.9					-4.0	-2.5
28.6	20.7	9.8					16.8	27.5
9.8	8.7	4.5				Sales/Net Fixed Assets	10.3	10.6
4.8	4.8	3.2					5.9	6.7
4.0	3.4	2.8					3.8	3.6
2.5	2.6	2.0				Sales/Total Assets	2.5	2.5
2.0	2.1	1.7					1.9	1.9
1.8	1.9	2.3					1.7	1.6
(47) 3.6	(59) 3.1	5.1				% Depr., Dep., Amort./Sales	(38) 2.9	(54) 2.7
5.9	5.4	7.3					4.7	4.3
6.2	3.7	3.0					5.0	4.4
(35) 9.4	(38) 7.0	(12) 4.5				% Officers', Directors', Owners' Comp/Sales	(15) 9.3	(30) 6.8
18.5	12.0	16.4					16.2	13.3
40954M	166992M	195213M	95190M			Net Sales ($)	122136M	941214M
14052M	62963M	89299M	65373M			Total Assets ($)	54043M	169754M

M = $ thousand   MM = $ million
See Pages 1 through 15 for Explanation of Ratios and Data

Comparative Historical Data				Current Data Sorted By Sales					
1	5	7	# Postretirement Benefits	4	2			1	
			Type of Statement						
9	6	5	Unqualified	2			1	2	
29	33	28	Reviewed	5	10	5	5	3	
47	42	66	Compiled	19	30	10	7		
3	2	11	Tax Returns	5	5	1			
27	26	39	Other	17	13	3	3	1	2
4/1/92-	4/1/93-	4/1/94-		52 (4/1-9/30/94)			97 (10/1/94-3/31/95)		
3/31/93	3/31/94	3/31/95		0-1MM	1-3MM	3-5MM	5-10MM	10-25MM	25MM & OVER
ALL	ALL	ALL							
115	109	149	NUMBER OF STATEMENTS	48	58	19	16	6	2
%	%	%	ASSETS	%	%	%	%	%	%
7.4	11.1	8.8	Cash & Equivalents	12.1	7.9	6.7	7.0		
40.0	33.2	37.4	Trade Receivables - (net)	32.0	39.5	43.2	38.4		
7.9	11.7	10.0	Inventory	8.9	9.5	10.8	10.5		
2.3	1.6	2.0	All Other Current	2.3	1.8	2.2	2.1		
57.6	57.7	58.3	Total Current	55.4	58.7	62.9	58.0		
31.5	33.9	34.4	Fixed Assets (net)	35.9	35.0	28.5	36.2		
2.0	2.3	1.8	Intangibles (net)	2.2	1.7	1.4	1.0		
8.9	6.1	5.6	All Other Non-Current	6.4	4.7	7.2	4.9		
100.0	100.0	100.0	Total	100.0	100.0	100.0	100.0		
			LIABILITIES						
8.6	10.4	7.5	Notes Payable-Short Term	6.7	6.5	11.1	5.5		
6.6	6.9	6.5	Cur. Mat.-L /T/D	7.6	5.2	7.3	7.1		
16.7	12.4	14.6	Trade Payables	10.4	16.5	16.8	15.1		
.8	2.6	1.0	Income Taxes Payable	.9	1.0	.9	1.2		
9.6	9.0	9.7	All Other Current	7.9	9.1	9.9	18.5		
42.3	41.3	39.3	Total Current	33.5	38.1	45.9	47.5		
16.4	19.3	17.7	Long Term Debt	21.6	16.6	15.0	14.4		
1.0	1.0	1.3	Deferred Taxes	1.0	1.4	2.3	1.0		
4.7	1.6	2.5	All Other-Non-Current	1.8	2.2	3.8	4.7		
35.6	36.8	39.2	Net Worth	42.1	41.8	32.9	32.4		
100.0	100.0	100.0	Total Liabilities & Net Worth	100.0	100.0	100.0	100.0		
			INCOME DATA						
100.0	100.0	100.0	Net Sales	100.0	100.0	100.0	100.0		
			Gross Profit						
96.2	94.3	93.4	Operating Expenses	90.8	94.1	94.8	96.0		
3.8	5.7	6.6	Operating Profit	9.2	5.9	5.2	4.0		
1.1	1.2	1.6	All Other Expenses (net)	2.7	1.0	.8	2.2		
2.7	4.5	5.0	Profit Before Taxes	6.5	4.9	4.4	1.8		
			RATIOS						
2.1	2.3	2.4		3.0	2.5	2.2	1.8		
1.4	1.5	1.5	Current	1.8	1.6	1.5	1.3		
1.0	1.0	1.1		1.1	1.1	1.0	1.0		
1.7	1.9	1.9		2.3	2.1	1.8	1.6		
1.2	1.2	1.3	Quick	1.5	1.2	1.2	.9		
.7	.7	.7		.7	.9	.7	.8		
41 8.9	29 12.5	37 10.0		25 14.7	40 9.2	45 8.2	39 9.3		
58 6.3	49 7.4	54 6.8	Sales/Receivables	48 7.6	56 6.5	57 6.4	53 6.9		
74 4.9	64 5.7	66 5.5		74 4.9	68 5.4	65 5.6	70 5.2		
			Cost of Sales/Inventory						
			Cost of Sales/Payables						
7.2	6.2	7.2		6.3	7.9	7.4	8.3		
18.1	13.9	13.1	Sales/Working Capital	12.1	12.7	15.5	15.1		
−731.3	NM	87.0		138.5	59.4	−180.5	769.0		
7.7	10.2	12.4		13.8	17.0	12.6	4.8		
(104) 2.5	(99) 3.2	(128) 3.1	EBIT/Interest	(37) 2.6	(52) 4.2	(17) 5.0	(15) 2.6		
1.0	1.5	1.3		1.2	1.1	1.6	1.4		
3.0	3.1	4.4		3.1	4.7		3.4		
(49) 1.6	(39) 1.7	(63) 2.3	Net Profit + Depr., Dep.,	(11) 2.0	(29) 2.7		(11) 1.8		
.8	.9	1.1	Amort./Cur. Mat. L/T/D	1.7	1.2		1.6		
.4	.4	.4		.3	.4	.2	.5		
1.0	.9	.8	Fixed/Worth	.8	.9	.6	.7		
2.2	2.0	1.8		2.0	1.7	4.2	2.5		
.8	.8	.7		.5	.8	.7	1.1		
1.8	1.8	1.5	Debt/Worth	1.1	1.5	2.2	2.2		
5.3	4.4	3.9		3.4	2.6	5.0	4.0		
37.8	47.8	61.4	% Profit Before Taxes/Tangible	50.3	59.3	116.9	33.9		
(104) 14.8	(99) 22.2	(139) 19.0	Net Worth	(42) 13.4	(57) 23.8	(17) 28.2	(15) 11.4		
1.2	6.1	3.8		2.3	1.0	7.2	4.6		
14.7	17.6	21.7	% Profit Before Taxes/Total	25.3	25.1	20.9	12.2		
4.5	8.7	7.3	Assets	5.7	8.9	8.9	4.0		
.4	2.1	1.0		1.0	.6	2.0	−.0		
23.7	18.4	19.7		26.7	18.1	36.0	14.0		
9.2	8.3	8.1	Sales/Net Fixed Assets	6.4	8.4	20.3	8.0		
5.3	4.4	4.3		3.4	5.0	3.5	4.0		
3.6	3.4	3.4		3.2	3.6	3.7	3.6		
2.6	2.4	2.5	Sales/Total Assets	2.3	2.7	2.6	2.3		
1.8	1.9	1.9		1.5	2.2	1.8	1.7		
1.4	2.0	1.9		2.3	2.1	1.0	.9		
(102) 2.9	(97) 3.1	(134) 3.5	% Depr., Dep., Amort./Sales	(38) 3.8	(54) 3.5	(18) 2.4	3.8		
5.2	5.0	5.7		6.7	5.3	7.2	6.4		
4.7	3.5	3.9		8.3	3.7				
(57) 8.2	(57) 6.5	(86) 8.0	% Officers', Directors',	(26) 10.3	(38) 6.9				
12.8	11.6	15.6	Owners' Comp/Sales	18.6	12.8				
829453M	821453M	498349M	Net Sales ($)	25806M	113469M	72966M	112106M	87428M	86574M
416097M	412177M	231687M	Total Assets ($)	12848M	47144M	30304M	53810M	34796M	52785M

M = $ thousand   MM = $ million
See Pages 1 through 15 for Explanation of Ratios and Data

Current Data Sorted By Assets

0-500M	500M-2MM	2-10MM	10-50MM	50-100MM	100-250MM		4/1/90-3/31/91 ALL	4/1/91-3/31/92 ALL
						# Postretirement Benefits		
1	1	4	1		1	**Type of Statement**		
1	12	17	6	1	1	Unqualified		
	4	2				Reviewed		
1	3	1				Compiled		
2	2					Tax Returns		
3	7	5		1		Other		
	44 (4/1-9/30/94)			25 (10/1/94-3/31/95)				
7	28	25	7	1	1	**NUMBER OF STATEMENTS**		
%	%	%	%	%	%	**ASSETS**	%	%
	16.2	7.6				Cash & Equivalents	D	D
	6.3	9.4				Trade Receivables - (net)	A	A
	2.5	.9				Inventory	T	T
	3.9	3.0				All Other Current	A	A
	28.9	20.9				Total Current		
	64.4	58.1				Fixed Assets (net)	N	N
	.2	.4				Intangibles (net)	O	O
	6.5	20.6				All Other Non-Current	T	T
	100.0	100.0				Total		
						LIABILITIES	A	A
	4.3	3.1				Notes Payable-Short Term	V	V
	2.5	1.8				Cur. Mat. -L/T/D	A	A
	4.1	4.7				Trade Payables	I	I
	.0	.0				Income Taxes Payable	L	L
	7.6	6.3				All Other Current	A	A
	18.6	16.0				Total Current	B	B
	22.8	19.5				Long Term Debt	L	L
	.0	.0				Deferred Taxes	E	E
	8.1	4.8				All Other-Non-Current		
	50.5	59.8				Net Worth		
	100.0	100.0				Total Liabilities & Net Worth		
						INCOME DATA		
	100.0	100.0				Net Sales		
						Gross Profit		
	85.1	95.6				Operating Expenses		
	14.9	4.4				Operating Profit		
	7.6	1.5				All Other Expenses (net)		
	7.3	2.9				Profit Before Taxes		
						RATIOS		
	4.7	2.7				Current		
	1.8	1.2						
	.8	.8						
	3.3	2.5				Quick		
	1.3	1.0						
	.6	.7						
0	UND	2 185.3				Sales/Receivables		
6	60.7	29 12.6						
40	9.2	64 5.7						
						Cost of Sales/Inventory		
						Cost of Sales/Payables		
	2.5	5.3				Sales/Working Capital		
	15.0	20.3						
	-32.9	-18.7						
	6.0	5.5				EBIT/Interest		
(14)	2.2	(16) 2.5						
	-.7	1.2						
						Net Profit + Depr., Dep., Amort./Cur. Mat. L /T/D		
	.8	.8				Fixed/Worth		
	1.1	1.0						
	3.9	1.5						
	.3	.3				Debt/Worth		
	.7	.6						
	3.0	1.3						
	14.2	6.2				% Profit Before Taxes/Tangible Net Worth		
(26)	6.6	4.0						
	-2.5	-.5						
	7.6	4.6				% Profit Before Taxes/Total Assets		
	2.0	1.8						
	-1.5	-.1						
	2.7	3.0				Sales/Net Fixed Assets		
	1.4	1.0						
	.3	.6						
	1.3	.9				Sales/Total Assets		
	.9	.6						
	.2	.4						
	3.0	3.3				% Depr., Dep., Amort./Sales		
(24)	5.8	(22) 6.6						
	12.2	10.9						
						% Officers', Directors', Owners' Comp/Sales		
4887M	32517M	64745M	415658M	42436M	88622M	Net Sales ($)		
1321M	31606M	103785M	127566M	62728M	196126M	Total Assets ($)		

Comparative Historical Data

© Robert Morris Associates 1995

M = $ thousand   MM = $ million

See Pages 1 through 15 for Explanation of Ratios and Data

Comparative Historical Data					Current Data Sorted By Sales					
			# Postretirement Benefits		1	2	3	1		1
			Type of Statement							
		8								
		38	Unqualified		7	17	7	4		3
		6	Reviewed		3	1	2			
		5	Compiled		5					
		4	Tax Returns		4					
		16	Other		9	3	2	1	1	
4/1/92-3/31/93 ALL	4/1/93-3/31/94 ALL	4/1/94-3/31/95 ALL			44 (4/1-9/30/94)			25 (10/1/94-3/31/95)		
					0-1MM	1-3MM	3-5MM	5-10MM	10-25MM	25MM & OVER
		69	NUMBER OF STATEMENTS		28	21	11	5	1	3
%	%	%	ASSETS		%	%	%	%	%	%
D	D	14.1	Cash & Equivalents		18.2	9.3	12.6			
A	A	7.2	Trade Receivables - (net)		2.4	7.8	10.8			
T	T	1.5	Inventory		1.6	1.9	1.2			
A	A	3.2	All Other Current		3.9	3.3	2.4			
		26.0	Total Current		26.0	22.3	27.0			
N	N	60.0	Fixed Assets (net)		62.7	64.4	58.6			
O	O	.5	Intangibles (net)		.3	1.2	.0			
T	T	13.6	All Other Non-Current		10.9	12.1	14.4			
		100.0	Total		100.0	100.0	100.0			
A	A		LIABILITIES							
V	V	3.0	Notes Payable-Short Term		4.7	2.0	.7			
A	A	2.9	Cur. Mat.-L /T/D		3.5	3.2	1.6			
I	I	4.2	Trade Payables		2.7	3.9	4.2			
L	L	.0	Income Taxes Payable		.0	.0	.0			
A	A	8.3	All Other Current		6.8	7.6	10.2			
B	B	18.4	Total Current		17.7	16.7	16.6			
L	L	20.6	Long Term Debt		28.3	19.8	12.8			
E	E	.1	Deferred Taxes		.0	.0	.0			
		6.2	All Other-Non-Current		8.7	3.4	5.1			
		54.6	Net Worth		45.3	60.0	65.5			
		100.0	Total Liabilities & Net Worth		100.0	100.0	100.0			
			INCOME DATA							
		100.0	Net Sales		100.0	100.0	100.0			
			Gross Profit							
		90.4	Operating Expenses		86.3	92.8	98.1			
		9.6	Operating Profit		13.7	7.2	1.9			
		5.8	All Other Expenses (net)		9.6	1.5	-.3			
		3.9	Profit Before Taxes		4.1	5.7	2.3			
			RATIOS							
		3.1			9.5	1.9	3.1			
		1.4	Current		2.4	1.1	1.3			
		.8			.5	.8	.8			
		2.6			4.9	1.6	2.5			
		1.2	Quick		1.9	.8	1.2			
		.6			.4	.6	.7			
	1	331.5		0 UND	6 63.9	4 99.4				
	8	44.5	Sales/Receivables	2 242.4	29 12.6	17 21.6				
	41	8.8		12 30.1	58 6.3	51 7.1				
			Cost of Sales/Inventory							
			Cost of Sales/Payables							
		4.4			2.2	5.6	12.4			
		20.3	Sales/Working Capital		9.5	40.2	32.9			
		-23.3			-7.8	-13.9	-25.1			
		5.3			6.7	4.9				
	(38)	1.6	EBIT/Interest	(11)	2.7	(16) 1.7				
		.7			.4	.8				
		3.1	Net Profit + Depr., Dep.,							
	(12)	1.7	Amort./Cur. Mat. L/T/D							
		1.4								
		.8			.5	.8	.7			
		1.1	Fixed/Worth		1.7	1.1	1.0			
		2.0			6.2	2.3	1.2			
		.3			.4	.2	.3			
		.6	Debt/Worth		1.0	.6	.5			
		1.9			6.1	1.5	.6			
		8.2	% Profit Before Taxes/Tangible		13.9	10.7	5.1			
	(66)	3.6	Net Worth	(25)	.8	4.9	4.0			
		-2.5			-9.8	-1.5	.2			
		5.4	% Profit Before Taxes/Total		7.6	6.1	3.7			
		1.6	Assets		.7	2.3	2.3			
		-1.3			-1.8	-.1	.2			
		3.0			3.1	2.0	7.1			
		1.4	Sales/Net Fixed Assets		1.1	1.1	1.4			
		.6			.2	.6	.8			
		1.2			1.1	1.0	1.8			
		.7	Sales/Total Assets		.5	.6	1.0			
		.4			.2	.4	.6			
		2.8			2.7	5.1				
	(59)	5.8	% Depr., Dep., Amort./Sales	(23)	6.8	(19) 6.9				
		11.7			19.2	9.7				
			% Officers', Directors', Owners' Comp/Sales							
		648865M	Net Sales ($)		12653M	39821M	40206M	31488M	11256M	513441M
		523132M	Total Assets ($)		37339M	89797M	49084M	40455M	12530M	293927M

M = $ thousand   MM = $ million
See Pages 1 through 15 for Explanation of Ratios and Data

Current Data Sorted By Assets   Comparative Historical Data

0-500M	500M-2MM 13 (4/1-9/30/94)	2-10MM	10-50MM 33 (10/1/94-3/31/95)	50-100MM	100-250MM	# Postretirement Benefits / Type of Statement	4/1/90-3/31/91 ALL	4/1/91-3/31/92 ALL
1	3					Unqualified	1	2
	4					Reviewed	3	7
19	10	2	1			Compiled	13	21
3	1					Tax Returns		1
1		1	1			Other	7	7
23	18	3	2			**NUMBER OF STATEMENTS**	24	38
%	%	%	%	%	%	**ASSETS**	%	%
19.4	18.3					Cash & Equivalents	14.5	9.8
5.3	3.9					Trade Receivables - (net)	10.0	4.4
19.1	21.9					Inventory	21.9	28.0
.3	1.7					All Other Current	1.0	2.0
44.1	45.8					Total Current	47.4	44.1
37.4	37.3					Fixed Assets (net)	29.8	31.3
15.2	10.5					Intangibles (net)	9.9	11.6
3.3	6.5					All Other Non-Current	12.9	12.9
100.0	100.0					Total	100.0	100.0
						LIABILITIES		
9.3	8.3					Notes Payable-Short Term	5.3	5.3
4.1	5.9					Cur. Mat. -L/T/D	6.6	7.2
11.8	9.6					Trade Payables	7.7	11.4
.3	.5					Income Taxes Payable	.2	.9
7.3	10.2					All Other Current	9.6	13.3
32.9	34.5					Total Current	29.4	38.1
28.4	25.7					Long Term Debt	30.5	29.3
4.0	.1					Deferred Taxes	.0	.1
6.5	8.0					All Other-Non-Current	2.1	2.8
28.3	31.7					Net Worth	38.0	29.7
100.0	100.0					Total Liabilities & Net Worth	100.0	100.0
						INCOME DATA		
100.0	100.0					Net Sales	100.0	100.0
						Gross Profit		
92.7	95.5					Operating Expenses	91.6	95.4
7.3	4.5					Operating Profit	8.4	4.6
2.3	1.4					All Other Expenses (net)	1.9	1.6
5.0	3.1					Profit Before Taxes	6.5	3.1
						RATIOS		
3.3 / 1.7 / .9	2.1 / 1.2 / 1.0					Current	2.5 / 1.9 / 1.1	1.7 / 1.0 / .8
(22) 1.8 / .8 / .3	1.1 / .5 / .3					Quick	(23) 1.3 / .8 / .3	.6 / .4 / .1
2 200.6 / 3 108.5 / 8 43.0	0 UND / 2 186.2 / 4 90.6					Sales/Receivables	2 200.5 / 3 122.4 / 18 20.5	1 265.0 / 2 150.2 / 5 67.6
						Cost of Sales/Inventory		
						Cost of Sales/Payables		
8.5 / 28.2 / -66.8	6.3 / 35.2 / NM					Sales/Working Capital	9.0 / 17.2 / 89.0	14.8 / 532.2 / -31.7
(20) 4.6 / 3.7 / 2.0	9.5 / 1.9 / 1.4					EBIT/Interest	(20) 7.2 / 2.9 / 1.0	(32) 5.4 / 2.7 / .8
						Net Profit + Depr., Dep., Amort./Cur. Mat. L /T/D		(17) 3.6 / .7 / .2
.5 / 4.5 / -3.7	.7 / 1.7 / 5.8					Fixed/Worth	.2 / .8 / 5.6	.3 / 2.5 / NM
1.6 / 4.9 / -7.6	1.8 / 3.5 / 10.2					Debt/Worth	.9 / 1.9 / 9.3	1.2 / 6.5 / NM
(15) 241.2 / 50.8 / 35.6	(16) 66.7 / 20.2 / 11.0					% Profit Before Taxes/Tangible Net Worth	(21) 129.2 / 28.6 / 10.0	(29) 85.0 / 26.0 / 4.6
20.5 / 12.7 / 5.2	14.0 / 5.5 / 1.4					% Profit Before Taxes/Total Assets	24.2 / 9.3 / 2.1	15.5 / 6.8 / .0
25.1 / 12.9 / 3.5	12.2 / 6.9 / 2.7					Sales/Net Fixed Assets	46.3 / 14.9 / 5.2	30.1 / 14.5 / 4.0
3.9 / 3.2 / 2.0	4.0 / 2.4 / 1.4					Sales/Total Assets	4.3 / 2.9 / 1.8	4.4 / 2.3 / 1.7
(17) 1.5 / 2.9 / 4.0	1.7 / 2.3 / 4.4					% Depr., Dep., Amort./Sales	(20) 1.5 / 2.2 / 3.4	(36) 1.4 / 2.0 / 3.5
(15) 6.2 / 8.0 / 12.2	(11) 2.5 / 5.2 / 7.4					% Officers', Directors', Owners' Comp/Sales	(12) 2.6 / 4.2 / 8.5	(23) 2.8 / 3.9 / 9.2
14823M	53366M	16556M	44750M			Net Sales ($)	108932M	167200M
4928M	17968M	6645M	22556M			Total Assets ($)	49318M	66647M

M = $ thousand   MM = $ million
See Pages 1 through 15 for Explanation of Ratios and Data

Comparative Historical Data						Current Data Sorted By Sales					
1		2		1	# Postretirement Benefits	1					
					Type of Statement						
2		2		3	Unqualified	2	1				
9		9		5	Reviewed		2	1	1	1	
21		25		32	Compiled	17	8	4	2	1	
5		3		4	Tax Returns	3	1		1		
5		5		2	Other		1		1		
4/1/92-3/31/93 ALL		4/1/93-3/31/94 ALL		4/1/94-3/31/95 ALL		13 (4/1-9/30/94)		33 (10/1/94-3/31/95)			
						0-1MM	1-3MM	3-5MM	5-10MM	10-25MM	25MM & OVER
37		44		46	NUMBER OF STATEMENTS	22	12	5	5	2	
%		%		%	ASSETS	%	%	%	%	%	%
10.2		10.6		18.5	Cash & Equivalents	18.1	16.5				
4.8		5.7		4.6	Trade Receivables - (net)	5.4	5.1				
25.7		26.1		20.6	Inventory	21.9	15.6				
1.7		1.8		.8	All Other Current	.3	.3				
42.4		44.2		44.5	Total Current	45.8	37.5				
35.1		34.3		36.8	Fixed Assets (net)	38.9	40.7				
9.1		7.4		13.7	Intangibles (net)	12.8	16.4				
13.4		14.2		5.0	All Other Non-Current	2.5	5.4				
100.0		100.0		100.0	Total	100.0	100.0				
					LIABILITIES						
5.6		3.0		8.9	Notes Payable-Short Term	9.0	3.2				
6.0		5.6		4.8	Cur. Mat.-L /T/D	3.3	8.8				
10.9		13.2		10.8	Trade Payables	11.1	9.7				
.5		2.4		.4	Income Taxes Payable	.2	.5				
11.4		10.2		8.2	All Other Current	7.0	6.5				
34.4		34.4		33.2	Total Current	30.7	28.7				
34.4		28.7		26.8	Long Term Debt	26.8	37.3				
.2		.1		2.2	Deferred Taxes	4.2	.1				
6.2		2.7		7.0	All Other-Non-Current	7.8	8.9				
24.8		34.0		30.8	Net Worth	30.5	25.0				
100.0		100.0		100.0	Total Liabilities & Net Worth	100.0	100.0				
					INCOME DATA						
100.0		100.0		100.0	Net Sales	100.0	100.0				
					Gross Profit						
95.7		94.7		94.0	Operating Expenses	93.7	92.7				
4.3		5.3		6.0	Operating Profit	6.3	7.3				
2.3		1.7		1.8	All Other Expenses (net)	2.1	2.2				
2.1		3.6		4.2	Profit Before Taxes	4.2	5.0				
					RATIOS						
2.0		2.0		2.9		3.7	1.8				
1.3		1.1		1.3	Current	2.7	1.3				
.8		.8		1.0		.9	1.0				
.7		.8		1.3		2.3	.9				
.4	(43)	.5	(45)	.6	Quick	(21) 1.1	.8				
.2		.2		.3		.3	.5				
1 354.8		2 203.5		2 213.5		2 181.1	1 282.7				
3 114.9		3 123.0		3 125.5	Sales/Receivables	4 98.8	2 162.8				
6 65.4		7 49.8		7 53.4		9 39.5	4 83.6				
					Cost of Sales/Inventory						
					Cost of Sales/Payables						
11.1		12.7		8.3		5.5	17.6				
48.5		54.0		30.5	Sales/Working Capital	8.7	32.6				
-23.0		-60.6		-225.7		-118.8	NM				
3.6		6.7		5.4		4.9	4.6				
(36) 1.4	(39)	2.5	(43)	2.4	EBIT/Interest	(19) 2.4	2.5				
.6		1.3		1.8		1.5	1.5				
3.3		5.5		3.7	Net Profit + Depr., Dep.,						
(11) 1.6	(14)	2.2	(16)	1.9	Amort./Cur. Mat. L/T/D						
.8		.7		1.0							
.7		.3		.7		.4	1.3				
1.4		1.3		3.1	Fixed/Worth	4.5	3.1				
-6.2		-49.4		NM		-4.5	11.9				
1.1		.8		1.7		.7	2.0				
5.1		2.4		4.8	Debt/Worth	4.8	5.5				
-11.4		-82.4		NM		-9.5	28.8				
51.8		56.3		123.0	% Profit Before Taxes/Tangible	123.0	270.8				
(27) 12.2	(32)	16.9	(35)	40.0	Net Worth	(15) 43.9	(10) 39.5				
1.1		2.0		15.6		13.2	19.3				
10.6		15.1		17.0	% Profit Before Taxes/Total	18.4	27.1				
3.0		7.1		8.1	Assets	8.1	8.5				
-3.8		.6		3.2		1.7	2.4				
24.2		39.4		17.5		18.9	22.5				
8.9		11.0		8.7	Sales/Net Fixed Assets	6.1	7.3				
2.9		4.2		2.9		2.6	3.0				
3.3		4.1		3.9		3.9	3.9				
2.2		2.6		2.8	Sales/Total Assets	2.3	2.8				
1.5		1.8		1.8		1.4	1.9				
1.4		1.2		1.7		2.0	1.9				
(33) 2.7	(40)	2.4	(40)	2.5	% Depr., Dep., Amort./Sales	(17) 2.9	(11) 3.7				
4.8		4.1		4.1		4.2	5.6				
3.2		4.0		4.4		7.6	2.1				
(19) 7.3	(22)	5.4	(27)	7.2	% Officers', Directors',	(12) 8.6	(10) 4.8				
12.9		6.2		8.9	Owners' Comp/Sales	24.9	7.3				
124330M		75247M		129495M	Net Sales ($)	11161M	21439M	19757M	32388M	44750M	
56231M		30944M		52097M	Total Assets ($)	5694M	8888M	7629M	7330M	22556M	

Current Data Sorted By Assets

22	4			
5	2	9	2	
16	22	4	1	
131	36	5		
50	3			
64	20	2	4	

Comparative Historical Data

 # Postretirement Benefits — Type of Statement

Type of Statement	4/1/90-3/31/91 ALL	4/1/91-3/31/92 ALL
Unqualified	12	8
Reviewed	40	32
Compiled	144	144
Tax Returns	12	14
Other	68	81

	0-500M	500M-2MM	2-10MM	10-50MM	50-100MM	100-250MM		4/1/90-3/31/91 ALL	4/1/91-3/31/92 ALL
	118 (4/1-9/30/94)			258 (10/1/94-3/31/95)					
NUMBER OF STATEMENTS	266	83	20	7				276	279
ASSETS	%	%	%	%	%	%		%	%
Cash & Equivalents	11.9	9.3	5.3					9.7	9.0
Trade Receivables - (net)	14.4	16.0	20.4					16.1	15.7
Inventory	23.6	25.2	27.0					26.5	22.9
All Other Current	1.3	1.3	2.3					2.5	1.7
Total Current	51.2	51.8	55.0					54.7	49.3
Fixed Assets (net)	38.8	36.4	32.8					35.0	38.6
Intangibles (net)	2.9	2.0	3.3					2.6	3.3
All Other Non-Current	7.1	9.8	8.9					7.7	8.8
Total	100.0	100.0	100.0					100.0	100.0
LIABILITIES									
Notes Payable-Short Term	8.3	8.3	12.6					10.7	9.3
Cur. Mat. -L/T/D	5.5	3.6	6.2					5.4	5.2
Trade Payables	14.9	13.2	16.7					13.9	12.9
Income Taxes Payable	.8	.4	.7					.8	.4
All Other Current	9.9	6.2	8.4					8.6	8.5
Total Current	39.4	31.8	44.4					39.4	36.3
Long Term Debt	26.3	24.4	18.1					24.8	25.5
Deferred Taxes	.1	.2	.4					.3	.3
All Other-Non-Current	2.8	3.0	2.7					2.5	1.3
Net Worth	31.5	40.7	34.3					32.9	36.5
Total Liabilities & Net Worth	100.0	100.0	100.0					100.0	100.0
INCOME DATA									
Net Sales	100.0	100.0	100.0					100.0	100.0
Gross Profit									
Operating Expenses	94.8	95.2	94.7					95.3	95.4
Operating Profit	5.2	4.8	5.3					4.7	4.6
All Other Expenses (net)	1.2	.9	1.0					1.3	1.6
Profit Before Taxes	4.0	4.0	4.3					3.5	3.0
RATIOS									
Current	2.3 / 1.4 / .8	3.0 / 1.7 / 1.0	2.1 / 1.2 / 1.0					2.3 / 1.4 / .9	2.3 / 1.4 / .8
Quick	1.2 / .7 / .3	1.7 / .8 / .4	.9 / .6 / .4					1.1 / .6 / .3 (276)	1.3 / .7 / .3
Sales/Receivables	2 166.7 / 9 38.8 / 22 16.7	5 74.4 / 20 18.6 / 35 10.3	15 23.8 / 37 9.8 / 54 6.8					3 129.0 / 12 30.8 / 29 12.4	3 111.0 / 13 28.6 / 29 12.4
Cost of Sales/Inventory									
Cost of Sales/Payables									
Sales/Working Capital	10.5 / 38.5 / -79.2	6.0 / 12.9 / 260.5	6.8 / 15.8 / -411.5					9.1 / 23.1 / -107.2	8.7 / 26.9 / -48.1
EBIT/Interest	(219) 6.7 / 3.2 / 1.3	(76) 11.2 / 3.0 / 1.5	(19) 10.7 / 3.4 / 1.9					(245) 6.0 / 2.7 / 1.2	(241) 6.0 / 2.3 / 1.0
Net Profit + Depr., Dep., Amort./Cur. Mat. L./T/D	(47) 4.7 / 1.6 / .9	(26) 4.1 / 2.3 / 1.1						(120) 4.0 / 1.8 / .7	(88) 3.0 / 1.4 / .3
Fixed/Worth	.4 / 1.3 / 7.6	.4 / .8 / 2.1	.5 / 1.0 / 2.9					.4 / 1.0 / 3.4	.4 / 1.0 / 3.5
Debt/Worth	.8 / 2.1 / 17.4	.6 / 1.6 / 3.9	1.0 / 2.6 / 7.1					.9 / 2.1 / 7.3	.7 / 1.8 / 6.3
% Profit Before Taxes/Tangible Net Worth	(219) 94.4 / 29.0 / 7.0	(79) 39.3 / 16.0 / 3.9	(19) 77.6 / 26.3 / 8.3					(241) 60.8 / 22.0 / 5.1	(242) 44.3 / 14.7 / .0
% Profit Before Taxes/Total Assets	24.9 / 9.0 / .6	15.1 / 6.7 / 1.3	14.1 / 6.1 / 4.0					18.0 / 7.8 / 1.0	16.2 / 5.8 / -.7
Sales/Net Fixed Assets	31.2 / 14.0 / 5.6	18.6 / 9.0 / 4.4	15.6 / 8.0 / 4.7					28.0 / 14.8 / 5.4	26.4 / 10.5 / 4.2
Sales/Total Assets	6.0 / 3.8 / 2.5	3.7 / 2.6 / 1.9	2.9 / 2.3 / 1.5					4.7 / 3.2 / 2.3	4.3 / 2.9 / 1.9
% Depr., Dep., Amort./Sales	(223) 1.0 / 1.9 / 3.3	(75) 1.2 / 2.1 / 3.2	(19) 1.0 / 1.7 / 3.0					(249) 1.1 / 2.0 / 3.1	(253) 1.1 / 2.0 / 3.2
% Officers', Directors', Owners' Comp/Sales	(151) 4.8 / 7.7 / 12.4	(48) 3.0 / 4.1 / 7.0	(10) 1.2 / 2.4 / 5.2					(143) 3.8 / 6.5 / 10.2	(158) 3.3 / 6.4 / 10.1
Net Sales ($)	200970M	213366M	186452M	247032M				1537876M	555970M
Total Assets ($)	56090M	77348M	85005M	130231M				365028M	312975M

M = $ thousand   MM = $ million
See Pages 1 through 15 for Explanation of Ratios and Data

Comparative Historical Data / Current Data Sorted By Sales

	4/1/92-3/31/93 ALL	4/1/93-3/31/94 ALL	4/1/94-3/31/95 ALL	118 (4/1-9/30/94) 0-1MM	1-3MM	258 (10/1/94-3/31/95) 3-5MM	5-10MM	10-25MM	25MM & OVER
# Postretirement Benefits				13	13				
Type of Statement									
Unqualified	14	16	18	5	2	5	5		1
Reviewed	45	33	43	11	21	4	4	2	1
Compiled	151	174	172	107	53	7	4	1	
Tax Returns	37	44	53	43	9		1		
Other	73	80	90	50	29	1	6		4
NUMBER OF STATEMENTS	320	347	376	216	112	14	20	8	6
ASSETS	%	%	%	%	%	%	%	%	%
Cash & Equivalents	9.5	11.0	10.8	11.7	10.3	10.4	7.8		
Trade Receivables - (net)	16.7	15.8	15.2	12.4	18.9	20.5	17.8		
Inventory	27.5	24.4	24.2	22.3	26.8	18.6	28.9		
All Other Current	2.1	1.7	1.4	1.3	1.4	.6	1.9		
Total Current	55.8	52.9	51.5	47.8	57.5	50.1	56.4		
Fixed Assets (net)	34.8	36.4	37.6	42.1	32.0	37.5	30.3		
Intangibles (net)	2.2	2.8	3.1	2.9	2.1	3.2	2.4		
All Other Non-Current	7.2	7.8	7.8	7.2	8.4	9.1	10.9		
Total	100.0	100.0	100.0	100.0	100.0	100.0	100.0		
LIABILITIES									
Notes Payable-Short Term	10.2	8.3	8.6	8.0	8.1	12.9	12.0		
Cur. Mat.-L /T/D	4.3	4.2	5.1	5.4	4.7	3.2	6.3		
Trade Payables	14.1	14.2	14.7	12.9	17.2	17.3	15.8		
Income Taxes Payable	.5	1.7	.7	.9	.3	1.0	.7		
All Other Current	9.3	9.4	8.9	9.6	7.8	9.8	8.8		
Total Current	38.4	37.7	38.1	36.8	38.1	44.3	43.5		
Long Term Debt	24.2	21.2	25.3	28.1	23.4	9.6	21.2		
Deferred Taxes	.1	.1	.1	.0	.2	.2	.8		
All Other-Non-Current	3.3	3.1	2.8	2.5	3.1	2.5	4.1		
Net Worth	34.0	37.8	33.7	32.6	35.3	43.4	30.3		
Total Liabilities & Net Worth	100.0	100.0	100.0	100.0	100.0	100.0	100.0		
INCOME DATA									
Net Sales	100.0	100.0	100.0	100.0	100.0	100.0	100.0		
Gross Profit									
Operating Expenses	95.5	95.4	94.8	94.3	95.8	93.7	95.5		
Operating Profit	4.5	4.6	5.2	5.7	4.2	6.3	4.5		
All Other Expenses (net)	1.5	.9	1.1	1.4	.8	.5	.6		
Profit Before Taxes	3.0	3.7	4.0	4.3	3.4	5.8	4.0		
RATIOS									
Current	2.6 / 1.5 / 1.0	2.6 / 1.5 / .9	2.4 / 1.4 / .9	2.3 / 1.4 / .8	3.0 / 1.6 / 1.0	2.0 / 1.4 / .9	2.1 / 1.3 / .7		
Quick	(318) 1.2 / .7 / .3	1.3 / .7 / .4	1.2 / .7 / .3	1.2 / .6 / .3	1.5 / .8 / .4	1.3 / .9 / .3	.9 / .6 / .4		
Sales/Receivables	4 96.5 / 15 24.9 / 33 10.9	3 112.7 / 11 34.0 / 29 12.8	3 124.1 / 12 29.5 / 29 12.8	2 197.8 / 9 40.2 / 22 16.9	7 51.7 / 18 20.7 / 33 11.2	4 102.7 / 29 12.8 / 37 9.8	4 98.8 / 18 20.1 / 38 9.5		
Cost of Sales/Inventory									
Cost of Sales/Payables									
Sales/Working Capital	8.3 / 19.7 / -477.0	8.3 / 25.2 / -95.9	8.9 / 31.2 / -88.4	10.2 / 40.7 / -65.8	7.0 / 15.9 / NM	9.1 / 21.1 / NM	7.5 / 34.9 / -35.6		
EBIT/Interest	(270) 6.0 / 2.3 / 1.0	(283) 7.6 / 3.0 / 1.2	(320) 7.5 / 3.1 / 1.4	(172) 6.1 / 3.1 / 1.1	(103) 10.6 / 2.9 / 1.4	24.1 / 9.2 / 4.1	(19) 10.7 / 2.5 / 1.8		
Net Profit + Depr., Dep., Amort./Cur. Mat. L/T/D	(85) 2.8 / 1.5 / .4	(81) 3.9 / 1.4 / .4	(85) 4.5 / 1.8 / 1.0	(33) 2.3 / 1.4 / .8	(34) 4.7 / 2.4 / 1.0				
Fixed/Worth	.3 / .9 / 3.0	.4 / 1.0 / 3.2	.4 / 1.1 / 4.2	.5 / 1.4 / 5.1	.4 / .8 / 3.2	.4 / .7 / 3.0	.2 / .6 / 4.2		
Debt/Worth	.8 / 2.0 / 6.7	.6 / 1.5 / 5.4	.8 / 2.1 / 10.7	.8 / 2.2 / 14.0	.7 / 1.8 / 6.3	.7 / 1.3 / 3.7	.9 / 2.1 / 10.0		
% Profit Before Taxes/Tangible Net Worth	(279) 43.9 / 17.9 / 1.5	(297) 53.7 / 19.8 / 2.5	(322) 69.8 / 23.5 / 5.8	(180) 79.4 / 29.5 / 6.0	(100) 62.1 / 16.4 / 3.9	116.3 / 40.7 / 22.2	(17) 38.7 / 20.7 / 8.0		
% Profit Before Taxes/Total Assets	17.6 / 6.2 / .2	19.5 / 8.2 / .8	19.9 / 8.0 / 1.4	23.9 / 8.4 / .5	17.3 / 7.3 / 1.2	25.2 / 12.1 / 7.6	22.5 / 6.0 / 3.2		
Sales/Net Fixed Assets	31.2 / 12.3 / 5.3	29.9 / 13.5 / 5.4	28.0 / 12.3 / 5.3	27.7 / 11.8 / 4.3	30.4 / 13.0 / 6.2	15.8 / 10.4 / 5.6	36.9 / 16.9 / 5.2		
Sales/Total Assets	4.5 / 3.2 / 1.9	5.3 / 3.4 / 2.2	5.0 / 3.3 / 2.2	5.6 / 3.5 / 1.9	4.7 / 3.3 / 2.5	4.4 / 2.6 / 2.2	4.7 / 3.3 / 2.6		
% Depr., Dep., Amort./Sales	(276) 1.0 / 1.7 / 2.9	(304) 1.0 / 1.8 / 3.1	(322) 1.0 / 1.9 / 3.3	(180) 1.1 / 2.1 / 3.7	(98) 1.0 / 1.8 / 2.9	1.8 / 2.1 / 3.1	(18) .6 / 1.1 / 2.4		
% Officers', Directors', Owners' Comp/Sales	(175) 3.6 / 5.9 / 9.4	(185) 4.0 / 7.0 / 12.3	(210) 4.0 / 6.3 / 10.1	(117) 5.9 / 8.6 / 13.6	(68) 3.5 / 5.1 / 7.4		(14) 1.1 / 2.5 / 4.5		
Net Sales ($)	1287427M	901237M	847820M	115839M	190553M	51706M	137176M	126720M	225826M
Total Assets ($)	539858M	328176M	348674M	42458M	64813M	19534M	48466M	85151M	88252M

© Robert Morris Associates 1995

M = $ thousand   MM = $ million
See Pages 1 through 15 for Explanation of Ratios and Data

Current Data Sorted By Assets   Comparative Historical Data

	2	1	1				# Postretirement Benefits Type of Statement		
	1	4	3	1			Unqualified	9	9
	12	13		1			Reviewed	23	19
	80	23	5			1	Compiled	88	102
	29	2					Tax Returns	3	9
	25	16	2				Other	42	37
		73 (4/1-9/30/94)		145 (10/1/94-3/31/95)				4/1/90-3/31/91 ALL	4/1/91-3/31/92 ALL
	0-500M	500M-2MM	2-10MM	10-50MM	50-100MM	100-250MM	NUMBER OF STATEMENTS	165	176
	147	58	10	2		1			
	%	%	%	%	%	%	**ASSETS**	%	%
	15.9	10.1	11.3				Cash & Equivalents	11.5	11.0
	14.2	22.7	18.1				Trade Receivables - (net)	13.7	17.4
	15.5	18.5	30.4				Inventory	17.2	17.4
	1.5	1.3	2.0				All Other Current	2.6	2.4
	47.1	52.6	61.8				Total Current	44.9	48.2
	44.9	35.2	29.8				Fixed Assets (net)	45.9	41.8
	2.6	4.3	1.7				Intangibles (net)	1.7	2.2
	5.5	7.8	6.7				All Other Non-Current	7.5	7.8
	100.0	100.0	100.0				Total	100.0	100.0
							LIABILITIES		
	9.0	7.5	10.3				Notes Payable-Short Term	10.7	11.9
	5.2	3.4	3.9				Cur. Mat. -L/T/D	5.3	5.9
	15.8	18.6	16.4				Trade Payables	13.9	14.8
	.7	.4	.4				Income Taxes Payable	.8	.9
	9.7	8.5	14.4				All Other Current	8.7	10.5
	40.4	38.4	45.3				Total Current	39.4	44.1
	24.3	17.9	17.0				Long Term Debt	27.0	25.8
	.1	.2	.1				Deferred Taxes	.2	.2
	4.1	4.0	4.7				All Other-Non-Current	2.5	1.7
	31.1	39.5	33.0				Net Worth	30.9	28.2
	100.0	100.0	100.0				Total Liabilities & Net Worth	100.0	100.0
							INCOME DATA		
	100.0	100.0	100.0				Net Sales	100.0	100.0
							Gross Profit		
	95.6	96.6	94.6				Operating Expenses	94.8	97.1
	4.4	3.4	5.4				Operating Profit	5.2	2.9
	.7	.4	.9				All Other Expenses (net)	1.8	1.1
	3.8	3.1	4.5				Profit Before Taxes	3.4	1.7
							RATIOS		
	2.2	2.1	2.2					2.2	1.8
	1.1	1.4	1.5				Current	1.2	1.2
	.7	.9	1.0					.7	.8
	1.5	1.4	1.3					1.4	1.1
(146)	.7	.9	.8				Quick	.6	.7
	.4	.5	.4					.3	.4
1	485.0	9 40.3	15 24.3					4 91.7	5 75.5
8	47.0	20 18.1	19 19.4				Sales/Receivables	9 40.8	13 27.8
17	21.8	39 9.4	43 8.4					18 19.8	26 14.3
							Cost of Sales/Inventory		
							Cost of Sales/Payables		
	16.7	9.4	9.1					13.8	14.1
	82.6	22.4	22.6				Sales/Working Capital	76.7	61.9
	-42.5	-250.5	NM					-30.4	-33.9
	9.7	7.7	13.9					7.2	5.5
(124)	4.1	(52) 3.8	7.5				EBIT/Interest	(149) 2.9	(163) 2.2
	1.4	1.7	3.7					1.2	.6
	5.6	5.6						5.0	4.5
(17)	3.6	(29) 2.9					Net Profit + Depr., Dep., Amort./Cur. Mat. L /T/D	(60) 2.1	(66) 1.6
	1.3	1.5						.9	.7
	.6	.4	.3					.6	.5
	1.4	.8	.8				Fixed/Worth	1.7	1.4
	7.8	2.7	2.3					5.5	7.7
	.8	.8	.8					.9	1.0
	2.3	1.8	2.3				Debt/Worth	2.6	2.4
	14.6	4.0	5.3					11.6	12.1
	89.0	50.0						80.1	65.0
(122)	37.7	(54) 20.0					% Profit Before Taxes/Tangible Net Worth	(142) 25.0	(147) 22.5
	7.1	5.2						6.0	3.1
	24.9	17.2	20.5					21.6	16.8
	12.1	7.1	10.2				% Profit Before Taxes/Total Assets	6.7	6.0
	1.1	1.9	3.5					.8	-2.0
	26.4	29.5	23.1					21.4	24.9
	11.1	12.8	9.7				Sales/Net Fixed Assets	9.5	11.9
	5.8	4.9	6.3					3.6	5.0
	6.8	4.3	4.5					5.2	5.5
	4.7	3.2	2.8				Sales/Total Assets	3.3	3.6
	3.2	2.3	1.5					2.2	2.3
	1.1	.9						1.1	1.3
(131)	2.0	(57) 1.7					% Depr., Dep., Amort./Sales	(147) 1.9	(159) 2.0
	3.6	3.1						2.9	3.3
	3.6	4.0						3.4	3.9
(93)	6.5	(35) 5.9					% Officers', Directors', Owners' Comp/Sales	(94) 6.4	(102) 5.7
	11.2	8.8						9.3	10.0
	150433M	205892M	101162M	72147M		1321562M	Net Sales ($)	481305M	367799M
	32268M	56387M	33694M	48932M		188093M	Total Assets ($)	194166M	153792M

M = $ thousand   MM = $ million
See Pages 1 through 15 for Explanation of Ratios and Data

Comparative Historical Data				**Current Data Sorted By Sales**					
4	6	4	# Postretirement Benefits	1	1	1	1		
			Type of Statement						
2	5	9	Unqualified	1	2	2	1	1	2
21	28	26	Reviewed	5	15	2	3	1	
92	95	109	Compiled	53	42	3	9		2
9	25	31	Tax Returns	19	9	3	3		
36	33	43	Other	18	16	6	1	2	
4/1/92-3/31/93	4/1/93-3/31/94	4/1/94-3/31/95		73 (4/1-9/30/94)		145 (10/1/94-3/31/95)			
ALL	ALL	ALL		0-1MM	1-3MM	3-5MM	5-10MM	10-25MM	25MM & OVER
160	186	218	**NUMBER OF STATEMENTS**	96	84	16	14	4	4
%	%	%	**ASSETS**	%	%	%	%	%	%
12.7	14.1	14.1	Cash & Equivalents	14.4	14.8	14.2	12.1		
14.6	16.0	16.6	Trade Receivables - (net)	12.5	18.7	19.5	23.7		
16.8	15.2	16.9	Inventory	16.5	14.4	15.1	35.4		
2.4	2.2	1.5	All Other Current	1.8	1.3	.8	.4		
46.5	47.5	49.0	Total Current	45.2	49.2	49.6	71.6		
44.2	41.4	41.6	Fixed Assets (net)	47.9	38.4	42.1	23.8		
2.3	2.4	3.0	Intangibles (net)	2.6	3.8	2.4	1.2		
7.0	8.7	6.3	All Other Non-Current	4.3	8.6	5.9	3.5		
100.0	100.0	100.0	Total	100.0	100.0	100.0	100.0		
			LIABILITIES						
10.7	7.5	8.5	Notes Payable-Short Term	10.1	7.3	8.8	5.3		
5.3	4.7	4.7	Cur. Mat.-L /T/D	5.4	4.0	4.5	4.7		
17.9	16.3	16.5	Trade Payables	12.7	17.7	18.5	28.4		
1.2	1.8	.6	Income Taxes Payable	.8	.4	.6	.1		
9.6	8.8	9.6	All Other Current	9.9	8.9	7.5	12.8		
44.7	39.0	39.8	Total Current	38.9	38.3	40.0	51.3		
21.8	22.1	22.0	Long Term Debt	29.8	18.4	15.5	5.8		
.2	.1	.1	Deferred Taxes	.1	.2	.2	.0		
3.0	3.5	4.1	All Other-Non-Current	2.6	5.7	5.0	4.6		
30.3	35.4	33.9	Net Worth	28.6	37.4	39.3	38.4		
100.0	100.0	100.0	Total Liabilities & Net Worth	100.0	100.0	100.0	100.0		
			INCOME DATA						
100.0	100.0	100.0	Net Sales	100.0	100.0	100.0	100.0		
			Gross Profit						
95.5	95.8	95.9	Operating Expenses	94.8	96.4	96.2	98.9		
4.5	4.2	4.1	Operating Profit	5.2	3.6	3.8	1.1		
.9	.7	.6	All Other Expenses (net)	.8	.4	.2	.3		
3.6	3.5	3.5	Profit Before Taxes	4.4	3.2	3.6	.7		
			RATIOS						
2.0	2.2	2.1	Current	2.4	2.2	1.9	1.8		
1.2	1.2	1.3		1.1	1.4	1.4	1.5		
.7	.7	.8		.6	.9	.8	1.1		
1.2	1.5	1.4	Quick	1.4	1.6	1.5	1.1		
(185) .7	(217) .7	.8		(95) .6	.9	1.1	.6		
.3	.4	.4		.2	.5	.5	.5		
3 / 113.2	3 / 115.0	4 / 101.4	Sales/Receivables	1 / 320.3	5 / 76.3	4 / 92.8	14 / 26.4		
10 / 36.1	11 / 34.3	11 / 32.5		8 / 47.8	11 / 32.0	13 / 27.6	19 / 18.9		
19 / 19.7	23 / 16.0	23 / 15.7		18 / 20.1	26 / 14.3	42 / 8.6	31 / 11.7		
			Cost of Sales/Inventory						
			Cost of Sales/Payables						
14.8	13.0	13.6	Sales/Working Capital	12.9	14.7	10.7	12.0		
76.1	68.4	47.8		208.1	43.6	38.3	19.6		
-35.2	-48.0	-48.1		-19.6	-147.8	-38.5	NM		
(129) 7.7	(163) 9.4	(188) 9.2	EBIT/Interest	(82) 7.6	(73) 9.9	(14) 15.3	(12) 7.0		
3.3	4.0	4.0		4.1	4.3	4.5	2.9		
1.5	2.0	1.5		1.5	1.5	1.8	.4		
(40) 4.8	(47) 5.5	(52) 5.7	Net Profit + Depr., Dep., Amort./Cur. Mat. L/T/D	(10) 7.7	(26) 5.3				
2.4	2.2	3.1		3.4	2.9				
.9	.9	1.9		1.4	1.7				
.6	.4	.5	Fixed/Worth	.7	.5	.4	.2		
1.3	1.2	1.2		1.7	1.1	1.1	.5		
4.7	4.0	4.5		25.7	3.8	2.6	1.2		
.8	.7	.8	Debt/Worth	1.1	.7	.9	.8		
2.2	2.0	2.1		2.7	1.9	1.7	1.7		
6.2	5.6	6.2		36.7	5.3	3.4	2.3		
(135) 70.3	(166) 65.0	(188) 60.8	% Profit Before Taxes/Tangible Net Worth	(75) 95.9	(78) 57.9	(15) 45.0	(13) 28.3		
27.4	29.7	32.0		39.6	34.7	23.1	13.6		
8.6	6.4	5.5		10.2	2.9	3.6	4.3		
18.9	23.0	20.6	% Profit Before Taxes/Total Assets	24.8	20.1	13.9	14.6		
9.4	9.4	9.2		11.5	11.1	3.9	4.8		
2.0	2.1	1.7		2.8	.8	-.3	1.1		
29.9	27.2	27.5	Sales/Net Fixed Assets	18.8	28.4	23.3	43.3		
11.9	13.3	11.3		8.1	14.8	13.8	27.4		
4.6	5.0	5.5		3.7	8.0	5.2	10.0		
6.5	6.0	6.0	Sales/Total Assets	5.8	6.3	6.6	5.9		
4.0	3.9	4.1		3.9	4.4	3.8	4.2		
2.4	2.5	2.7		2.2	2.8	2.7	3.0		
(151) .9	(173) .9	(199) 1.1	% Depr., Dep., Amort./Sales	(82) 1.5	(81) 1.0	1.3	(13) .7		
1.8	1.8	1.9		2.8	1.7	1.8	1.0		
2.9	3.2	3.3		4.3	3.1	2.6	1.6		
(86) 3.2	(119) 3.5	(133) 3.8	% Officers', Directors', Owners' Comp/Sales	(52) 3.9	(60) 4.0		(11) 2.1		
6.1	5.4	6.3		7.3	6.6		4.4		
9.4	9.3	10.4		13.6	9.6		5.9		
226296M	500242M	1851196M	Net Sales ($)	55469M	151888M	60367M	90644M	72478M	1420350M
64211M	178717M	359374M	Total Assets ($)	19900M	40310M	18600M	23818M	25192M	231554M

M = $ thousand   MM = $ million
See Pages 1 through 15 for Explanation of Ratios and Data

Current Data Sorted By Assets **Comparative Historical Data**

0-500M	500M-2MM	2-10MM	10-50MM	50-100MM	100-250MM	# Postretirement Benefits / Type of Statement	4/1/90-3/31/91 ALL	4/1/91-3/31/92 ALL
2	1							
1		1	2			Unqualified	9	11
4	11	2				Reviewed	18	16
33	30	7				Compiled	62	86
7		1				Tax Returns	3	5
13	11	6	1			Other	24	28
	51 (4/1-9/30/94)			79 (10/1/94-3/31/95)				
58	52	17	3			NUMBER OF STATEMENTS	116	146
%	%	%	%	%	%	**ASSETS**	%	%
13.4	7.1	5.3				Cash & Equivalents	8.6	8.4
3.1	1.2	1.1				Trade Receivables - (net)	.8	.9
5.4	3.0	5.0				Inventory	4.0	5.3
1.5	1.2	.6				All Other Current	2.4	1.9
23.3	12.5	12.0				Total Current	15.9	16.4
60.0	72.3	76.8				Fixed Assets (net)	68.9	67.0
6.8	1.6	2.1				Intangibles (net)	2.0	3.1
9.8	13.6	9.1				All Other Non-Current	13.2	13.5
100.0	100.0	100.0				Total	100.0	100.0
						LIABILITIES		
8.3	4.8	5.9				Notes Payable-Short Term	7.0	6.7
7.5	8.1	5.6				Cur. Mat. -L/T/D	7.3	7.5
6.0	2.9	2.4				Trade Payables	4.6	5.2
.4	.2	.0				Income Taxes Payable	.8	.7
9.6	7.3	6.4				All Other Current	5.6	9.1
31.8	23.3	20.3				Total Current	25.3	29.0
34.5	53.2	62.5				Long Term Debt	45.2	44.5
.0	.2	.0				Deferred Taxes	.3	.2
4.8	6.8	5.6				All Other-Non-Current	4.0	1.8
28.8	16.4	11.6				Net Worth	25.2	24.5
100.0	100.0	100.0				Total Liabilities & Net Worth	100.0	100.0
						INCOME DATA		
100.0	100.0	100.0				Net Sales	100.0	100.0
						Gross Profit		
95.5	90.5	93.7				Operating Expenses	90.8	90.6
4.5	9.5	6.3				Operating Profit	9.2	9.4
2.4	4.9	9.0				All Other Expenses (net)	6.2	6.0
2.1	4.6	-2.7				Profit Before Taxes	3.0	3.4
						RATIOS		
1.9	1.2	1.5					1.3	1.1
.5	.5	.7				Current	.5	.4
.2	.2	.1					.3	.2
1.2	.9	.6					.7	.6
.4	.3	.3				Quick	.3 (144)	.2
.1	.1	.1					.1	.1
0 UND	0 UND	0 UND					0 UND	0 UND
0 UND	0 UND	1 323.0				Sales/Receivables	0 UND	0 UND
2 202.2	1 449.6	4 92.5					1 254.7	1 348.1
						Cost of Sales/Inventory		
						Cost of Sales/Payables		
19.4	101.1	297.3					74.9	83.7
-21.0	-12.7	-14.6				Sales/Working Capital	-14.7	-10.3
-7.4	-5.5	-4.7					-6.5	-6.0
(51) 4.5	(49) 3.5	(13) 1.7					(98) 3.0	(120) 2.9
1.4	1.9	1.2				EBIT/Interest	1.6	1.8
.4	1.1	.0					.9	1.0
(18) 1.5	(15) 3.0						(57) 2.2	(53) 2.7
1.0	1.3					Net Profit + Depr., Dep., Amort./Cur. Mat. L./T/D	1.2	1.2
.4	.6						.6	.7
.9	2.1	2.5					1.4	1.4
3.4	4.7	5.0				Fixed/Worth	3.5	4.3
-9.3	NM	-6.9					23.6	34.0
.5	1.9	2.7					1.3	1.4
4.4	6.1	9.7				Debt/Worth	4.0	4.2
-13.8	NM	-8.4					23.1	43.9
(38) 38.4	(39) 83.4	(12) 20.4					(91) 58.1	(116) 52.8
10.5	26.6	6.5				% Profit Before Taxes/Tangible Net Worth	15.9	17.9
.0	5.4	-97.2					-1.9	4.2
10.2	10.4	4.2					10.4	10.3
3.2	4.4	-1.1				% Profit Before Taxes/Total Assets	3.2	4.6
-2.9	.2	-8.9					-2.1	-1.5
10.1	2.4	1.5					3.5	3.4
4.3	1.6	.8				Sales/Net Fixed Assets	1.6	1.7
2.1	.9	.5					1.0	1.0
3.9	1.5	1.0					2.0	1.9
2.2	1.1	.7				Sales/Total Assets	1.1	1.1
1.4	.7	.4					.8	.7
(52) 2.7	(48) 6.1	7.6					(111) 4.3	(142) 3.9
5.0	8.2	11.7				% Depr., Dep., Amort./Sales	7.3	6.7
8.7	11.8	16.6					11.3	10.0
(23) 4.7	(23) 3.4						(46) 4.4	(55) 3.9
8.5	4.9					% Officers', Directors', Owners' Comp/Sales	7.2	6.0
11.5	11.7						12.9	9.8
32671M	57945M	43100M	30518M			Net Sales ($)	561938M	433344M
14341M	53577M	54125M	42942M			Total Assets ($)	711191M	562002M

M = $ thousand   MM = $ million
See Pages 1 through 15 for Explanation of Ratios and Data

Comparative Historical Data				Current Data Sorted By Sales					
2	3	3	# Postretirement Benefits	3					
			Type of Statement						
3	9	4	Unqualified	1	1		1	1	
19	23	17	Reviewed	8	6	2	1		
65	61	70	Compiled	47	22	1			
5	9	8	Tax Returns	6	2				
19	23	31	Other	18	10	1	2		
4/1/92- 3/31/93	4/1/93- 3/31/94	4/1/94- 3/31/95		51 (4/1-9/30/94)		79 (10/1/94-3/31/95)			
ALL	ALL	ALL		0-1MM	1-3MM	3-5MM	5-10MM	10-25MM	25MM & OVER
111	125	130	NUMBER OF STATEMENTS	80	41	4	4	1	
%	%	%	ASSETS	%	%	%	%	%	%
10.4	8.5	9.6	Cash & Equivalents	11.3	7.2				
1.0	2.2	2.0	Trade Receivables - (net)	2.2	1.5				
4.2	6.5	4.3	Inventory	3.9	4.0				
2.6	3.4	1.2	All Other Current	1.4	1.1				
18.2	20.6	17.1	Total Current	18.8	13.8				
63.0	65.7	67.7	Fixed Assets (net)	63.0	76.2				
2.8	4.7	4.0	Intangibles (net)	5.1	2.0				
16.1	9.0	11.2	All Other Non-Current	13.1	8.0				
100.0	100.0	100.0	Total	100.0	100.0				
			LIABILITIES						
5.2	4.9	6.4	Notes Payable-Short Term	7.4	5.0				
9.2	8.0	7.4	Cur. Mat.-L /T/D	7.8	7.1				
6.0	5.3	4.3	Trade Payables	4.4	3.6				
.4	.2	.3	Income Taxes Payable	.2	.4				
8.5	9.4	8.1	All Other Current	7.3	8.9				
29.3	27.8	26.5	Total Current	27.1	25.0				
41.2	45.2	46.3	Long Term Debt	44.8	48.5				
1.3	1.1	.1	Deferred Taxes	.0	.1				
3.6	3.5	5.6	All Other-Non-Current	7.1	3.8				
24.5	22.5	21.4	Net Worth	21.0	22.6				
100.0	100.0	100.0	Total Liabilities & Net Worth	100.0	100.0				
			INCOME DATA						
100.0	100.0	100.0	Net Sales	100.0	100.0				
			Gross Profit						
92.7	93.4	93.1	Operating Expenses	93.6	91.3				
7.3	6.6	6.9	Operating Profit	6.4	8.7				
4.7	3.5	4.4	All Other Expenses (net)	4.3	5.0				
2.6	3.1	2.5	Profit Before Taxes	2.1	3.7				
			RATIOS						
1.2	1.1	1.4		1.7	1.2				
.6	.5	.5	Current	.5	.5				
.2	.3	.2		.2	.2				
.7	.7	.9		1.0	1.0				
(110) .3	.3	.3	Quick	.4	.3				
.1	.1	.1		.1	.1				
0 UND	0 UND	0 UND		0 UND	0 UND				
0 UND	0 UND	0 UND	Sales/Receivables	0 UND	0 999.8				
1 281.0	1 254.8	1 263.4		1 283.4	1 299.3				
			Cost of Sales/Inventory						
			Cost of Sales/Payables						
32.2	112.2	25.8		18.9	62.1				
-17.6	-15.0	-15.3	Sales/Working Capital	-14.7	-14.6				
-7.2	-6.1	-6.0		-5.9	-5.9				
3.1	3.1	3.2		2.9	3.5				
(98) 1.4	(106) 1.7	(116) 1.5	EBIT/Interest	(68) 1.4	(39) 2.3				
.5	.8	.9		.6	1.0				
3.0	2.1	1.8	Net Profit + Depr., Dep.,	1.6	1.9				
(51) 1.2	(49) 1.2	(40) 1.2	Amort./Cur. Mat. L/T/D	(24) 1.0	(11) 1.3				
.1	.5	.4		.3	.6				
1.3	1.6	1.4		1.2	2.0				
3.2	3.8	4.2	Fixed/Worth	7.6	3.0				
123.4	UND	-16.4		-12.8	NM				
1.3	1.2	1.4		1.2	1.4				
3.8	3.6	5.0	Debt/Worth	10.1	3.1				
-122.3	UND	-19.9		-16.1	NM				
30.4	57.5	39.2	% Profit Before Taxes/Tangible	58.5	34.4				
(82) 13.7	(96) 15.5	(92) 13.9	Net Worth	(52) 12.2	(31) 24.5				
-3.5	-.2	3.4		.8	5.0				
10.3	9.9	9.3	% Profit Before Taxes/Total	7.2	11.3				
2.6	4.2	2.7	Assets	2.4	7.3				
-2.5	-1.2	-1.7		-2.5	-.5				
4.2	4.3	4.6		5.3	3.1				
2.0	1.7	2.0	Sales/Net Fixed Assets	2.2	1.7				
1.0	.9	1.0		1.0	.9				
2.3	2.2	2.2		2.6	1.8				
1.1	1.2	1.3	Sales/Total Assets	1.3	1.4				
.7	.7	.8		.7	.8				
3.6	4.3	4.1		3.8	4.3				
(107) 6.7	(119) 6.7	(120) 7.5	% Depr., Dep., Amort./Sales	(72) 8.0	(39) 7.3				
10.0	10.6	10.8		10.8	11.1				
4.5	3.8	3.4		4.1	2.7				
(49) 7.8	(53) 7.1	(53) 6.8	% Officers', Directors', Owners' Comp/Sales	(34) 7.6	(15) 6.4				
14.1	11.2	11.5		12.9	10.7				
186315M	696103M	164234M	Net Sales ($)	43378M	61631M	16394M	30424M	12407M	
199311M	638963M	164985M	Total Assets ($)	43572M	58184M	11049M	38333M	13847M	

© Robert Morris Associates 1995   M = $ thousand   MM = $ million
See Pages 1 through 15 for Explanation of Ratios and Data

Current Data Sorted By Assets   **Comparative Historical Data**

0-500M	500M-2MM	2-10MM	10-50MM	50-100MM	100-250MM	# Postretirement Benefits / Type of Statement	4/1/90-3/31/91 ALL	4/1/91-3/31/92 ALL
		1	1			# Postretirement Benefits		
	1	1	3			Unqualified		2
2	9	12	1			Reviewed		9
2	14	3	1			Compiled		13
1	2	1				Tax Returns		
1		8				Other		1
6	27	25	4			**NUMBER OF STATEMENTS**		25

0-500M	500M-2MM	2-10MM	10-50MM	50-100MM	100-250MM		4/1/90-3/31/91 ALL	4/1/91-3/31/92 ALL
%	%	%	%	%	%	**ASSETS**	%	%
	15.6	8.7				Cash & Equivalents		12.9
	8.1	7.1				Trade Receivables - (net)	D	8.0
	1.6	2.1				Inventory	A	2.1
	3.8	1.8				All Other Current	T	1.0
	29.0	19.6				Total Current	A	23.9
	62.9	73.1				Fixed Assets (net)		63.6
	1.9	.6				Intangibles (net)	N	2.4
	6.1	6.8				All Other Non-Current	O	10.1
	100.0	100.0				Total	T	100.0
						LIABILITIES	A	
	2.6	.8				Notes Payable-Short Term	V	5.5
	9.8	10.3				Cur. Mat. -L/T/D	A	16.7
	3.0	3.4				Trade Payables	I	4.3
	.1	.1				Income Taxes Payable	L	.3
	6.1	4.3				All Other Current	A	2.8
	21.5	18.8				Total Current	B	29.7
	36.6	38.2				Long Term Debt	L	37.6
	1.5	3.3				Deferred Taxes	E	1.0
	2.7	2.6				All Other-Non-Current		1.2
	37.7	37.2				Net Worth		30.6
	100.0	100.0				Total Liabilities & Net Worth		100.0
						INCOME DATA		
	100.0	100.0				Net Sales		100.0
						Gross Profit		
	90.0	95.3				Operating Expenses		96.7
	10.0	4.7				Operating Profit		3.3
	3.1	2.4				All Other Expenses (net)		2.6
	6.9	2.3				Profit Before Taxes		.7
						RATIOS		
	3.0 / 1.1 / .5	1.6 / 1.2 / .6				Current		1.4 / .7 / .4
	2.8 / .9 / .4	1.4 / .8 / .4				Quick		1.2 / .5 / .3
3 124.5 / 10 38.0 / 28 13.2		8 45.5 / 16 23.4 / 34 10.8				Sales/Receivables		2 185.4 / 10 36.4 / 26 14.2
						Cost of Sales/Inventory		
						Cost of Sales/Payables		
	6.7 / 100.6 / -9.9	13.0 / 48.6 / -13.2				Sales/Working Capital		14.3 / -16.9 / -6.7
	(22) 5.7 / 3.0 / 1.3	3.2 / 1.4 / 1.1				EBIT/Interest		(24) 2.9 / 1.6 / .3
	(10) 3.6 / 1.3 / 1.0	(11) 2.0 / 1.6 / 1.2				Net Profit + Depr., Dep., Amort./Cur. Mat. L /T/D		(15) 1.5 / 1.3 / .8
	.9 / 2.5 / 4.6	1.3 / 2.2 / 3.7				Fixed/Worth		1.0 / 1.9 / 25.6
	.7 / 3.0 / 5.5	.9 / 2.1 / 4.2				Debt/Worth		.8 / 2.4 / 29.1
	(26) 59.5 / 24.1 / 11.0	11.5 / 6.6 / 1.2				% Profit Before Taxes/Tangible Net Worth		(20) 29.8 / 10.0 / -3.2
	15.7 / 5.5 / 2.8	4.5 / 2.1 / .4				% Profit Before Taxes/Total Assets		7.1 / 3.1 / -5.7
	4.2 / 3.0 / 1.5	2.0 / 1.8 / 1.0				Sales/Net Fixed Assets		4.4 / 2.3 / 1.7
	2.4 / 1.8 / 1.1	1.5 / 1.2 / .8				Sales/Total Assets		2.1 / 1.6 / 1.2
	4.6 / 8.6 / 12.3	(24) 8.8 / 11.5 / 13.8				% Depr., Dep., Amort./Sales		(23) 6.8 / 10.0 / 16.6
	(12) 3.9 / 5.0 / 8.8	(13) 1.3 / 1.8 / 3.0				% Officers', Directors', Owners' Comp/Sales		(15) 3.8 / 6.3 / 11.5
1496M	49978M	128110M	81021M			Net Sales ($)		72159M
1142M	27605M	107148M	62776M			Total Assets ($)		50607M

M = $ thousand   MM = $ million
See Pages 1 through 15 for Explanation of Ratios and Data

	Comparative Historical Data				Current Data Sorted By Sales					
	1		2	# Postretirement Benefits			1			1
				Type of Statement						
	1	5	5	Unqualified			1	1	2	1
	10	7	24	Reviewed	4	9	6	3	2	
	16	13	19	Compiled	7	9	3			
	2	1	4	Tax Returns	1	1	1	1		
	7	8	10	Other	1	3	2	3	1	
	4/1/92-3/31/93 ALL	4/1/93-3/31/94 ALL	4/1/94-3/31/95 ALL		18 (4/1-9/30/94) 0-1MM	1-3MM	3-5MM	44 (10/1/94-3/31/95) 5-10MM	10-25MM	25MM & OVER
	36	34	62	**NUMBER OF STATEMENTS**	13	22	13	8	5	1
	%	%	%	**ASSETS**	%	%	%	%	%	%
	12.7	9.4	11.6	Cash & Equivalents	7.7	13.4	14.0			
	6.4	10.7	7.4	Trade Receivables - (net)	4.8	6.1	10.2			
	4.3	2.4	1.8	Inventory	.5	1.4	2.6			
	2.0	1.8	2.6	All Other Current	4.6	2.1	2.1			
	25.3	24.2	23.4	Total Current	17.6	22.9	29.0			
	67.3	60.0	69.0	Fixed Assets (net)	78.5	68.7	64.0			
	1.4	2.7	1.2	Intangibles (net)	.3	2.4	.9			
	6.0	13.1	6.5	All Other Non-Current	3.7	6.0	6.1			
	100.0	100.0	100.0	Total	100.0	100.0	100.0			
				LIABILITIES						
	7.8	3.8	1.9	Notes Payable-Short Term	3.8	2.5	.7			
	10.2	11.4	10.4	Cur. Mat.-L /T/D	12.8	11.3	8.2			
	4.9	9.1	3.6	Trade Payables	4.0	2.4	4.9			
	.3	.6	.1	Income Taxes Payable	.1	.1	.1			
	8.3	11.2	6.3	All Other Current	7.4	5.0	7.3			
	31.5	36.1	22.2	Total Current	28.1	21.2	21.1			
	30.0	26.2	35.8	Long Term Debt	40.9	37.7	29.3			
	1.2	2.0	2.3	Deferred Taxes	1.4	2.3	2.5			
	.9	2.8	3.6	All Other-Non-Current	5.8	3.5	2.2			
	36.5	32.9	36.1	Net Worth	23.8	35.3	45.0			
	100.0	100.0	100.0	Total Liabilities & Net Worth	100.0	100.0	100.0			
				INCOME DATA						
	100.0	100.0	100.0	Net Sales	100.0	100.0	100.0			
				Gross Profit						
	94.0	96.1	92.5	Operating Expenses	83.2	96.0	92.7			
	6.0	3.9	7.5	Operating Profit	16.8	4.0	7.3			
	.2	.4	3.0	All Other Expenses (net)	9.8	.6	1.0			
	5.8	3.5	4.5	Profit Before Taxes	7.0	3.3	6.3			
				RATIOS						
	1.6	1.2	1.9		.9	2.2	3.2			
	.8	.6	1.0	Current	.5	1.0	1.5			
	.4	.3	.5		.2	.4	.7			
	1.3	1.0	1.5		.7	1.7	2.7			
	.5	.5	.8	Quick	.4	.8	1.1			
	.3	.2	.4		.2	.3	.5			
	4 93.9	5 76.8	4 81.7		0 UND	3 136.4	7 50.2			
	7 51.1	15 25.0	13 27.4	Sales/Receivables	10 38.1	10 35.6	12 31.6			
	14 25.3	22 16.7	26 13.8		29 12.4	25 14.5	25 14.4			
				Cost of Sales/Inventory						
				Cost of Sales/Payables						
	20.3	42.4	13.2		NM	10.1	9.1			
	-34.3	-18.0	NM	Sales/Working Capital	-8.9	-132.9	15.7			
	-9.3	-8.6	-9.9		-3.7	-9.1	-15.5			
	(34) 7.8	(31) 6.0	(57) 4.2		(11) 3.4	(20) 4.9	(12) 6.3			
	2.3	2.9	2.2	EBIT/Interest	1.7	1.7	3.2			
	1.3	1.8	1.2		1.2	.2	2.2			
	(13) 2.4	(15) 7.6	(25) 2.2			(10) 3.6				
	1.4	1.9	1.6	Net Profit + Depr., Dep., Amort./Cur. Mat. L/T/D		1.4				
	1.0	1.1	1.1			.8				
	1.0	1.0	1.2		2.9	.9	.9			
	1.9	2.0	2.3	Fixed/Worth	4.4	3.3	1.9			
	8.2	13.8	4.4		8.0	6.6	2.8			
	.5	.6	.8		2.0	.8	.6			
	1.5	1.9	2.2	Debt/Worth	4.6	3.1	1.5			
	11.8	25.6	4.8		8.0	7.2	2.3			
	(31) 26.5	(27) 30.4	(60) 28.4		(12) 53.1	(21) 26.7	48.5			
	17.7	15.7	13.1	% Profit Before Taxes/Tangible Net Worth	27.8	14.3	14.9			
	6.1	5.4	4.6		12.7	-10.6	6.6			
	13.6	10.4	8.3		11.1	11.5	12.6			
	5.4	6.1	4.0	% Profit Before Taxes/Total Assets	3.6	3.4	5.5			
	1.4	2.8	1.1		1.8	-3.1	3.1			
	4.8	5.2	2.9		1.6	3.9	3.9			
	2.8	2.8	1.9	Sales/Net Fixed Assets	1.4	1.9	2.0			
	2.1	1.7	1.4		.8	1.2	1.5			
	2.6	2.7	1.8		1.3	2.2	2.8			
	1.9	1.8	1.3	Sales/Total Assets	1.1	1.4	1.4			
	1.5	1.3	1.0		.7	1.0	.9			
	(34) 4.0	(33) 5.3	(61) 7.3		8.6	7.1	3.1			
	7.4	8.2	9.3	% Depr., Dep., Amort./Sales	18.1	9.2	9.4			
	12.8	10.7	13.0		27.6	11.8	12.8			
	(23) 1.8	(16) 1.3	(27) 1.7			(12) 1.5				
	4.1	3.0	3.2	% Officers', Directors', Owners' Comp/Sales		4.1				
	6.0	5.6	5.3			5.2				
	130564M	189933M	260605M	Net Sales ($)	6473M	41024M	50942M	58658M	73699M	29809M
	69011M	83898M	198671M	Total Assets ($)	7192M	33357M	40585M	39316M	55356M	22865M

© Robert Morris Associates 1995

M = $ thousand   MM = $ million
See Pages 1 through 15 for Explanation of Ratios and Data

Current Data Sorted By Assets

Comparative Historical Data

0-500M	500M-2MM	2-10MM	10-50MM	50-100MM	100-250MM	# Postretirement Benefits / Type of Statement	4/1/90-3/31/91 ALL	4/1/91-3/31/92 ALL
		2						
1	2	4	3	1		Unqualified	5	11
	2	3				Reviewed	6	8
1	4	7	1			Compiled	5	7
						Tax Returns		
1	3	1	5			Other	5	4
	15 (4/1-9/30/94)			24 (10/1/94-3/31/95)				
3	11	15	9	1		**NUMBER OF STATEMENTS**	21	30
%	%	%	%	%	%	**ASSETS**	%	%
	15.9	5.3				Cash & Equivalents	5.7	7.3
	11.3	8.8				Trade Receivables - (net)	14.4	21.7
	.3	1.9				Inventory	3.5	3.6
	.8	2.5				All Other Current	3.8	2.4
	28.3	18.4				Total Current	27.4	35.0
	67.9	69.4				Fixed Assets (net)	63.2	55.2
	.2	3.7				Intangibles (net)	1.7	1.7
	3.6	8.5				All Other Non-Current	7.7	8.1
	100.0	100.0				Total	100.0	100.0
						LIABILITIES		
	6.7	2.6				Notes Payable-Short Term	3.3	4.0
	11.6	10.5				Cur. Mat. -L/T/D	11.0	10.6
	3.6	4.1				Trade Payables	6.7	10.9
	.1	.5				Income Taxes Payable	.2	.2
	5.9	5.9				All Other Current	8.4	4.9
	27.9	23.7				Total Current	29.6	30.6
	32.7	35.0				Long Term Debt	31.7	32.4
	2.6	2.2				Deferred Taxes	1.2	.9
	2.1	1.3				All Other-Non-Current	2.1	1.6
	34.7	37.8				Net Worth	35.3	34.7
	100.0	100.0				Total Liabilities & Net Worth	100.0	100.0
						INCOME DATA		
	100.0	100.0				Net Sales	100.0	100.0
						Gross Profit		
	94.1	93.8				Operating Expenses	98.8	95.0
	5.9	6.2				Operating Profit	1.2	5.0
	–.2	2.7				All Other Expenses (net)	.8	2.1
	6.2	3.5				Profit Before Taxes	.4	2.9
						RATIOS		
	2.6	1.3					1.2	2.0
	1.0	.9				Current	.9	.9
	.5	.4					.7	.5
	2.5	1.1					.8	1.6
	.9	.7				Quick	.6	.7
	.5	.3					.5	.4
	9 40.6	15 24.2					12 30.9	10 38.3
	12 31.4	35 10.5				Sales/Receivables	22 16.5	24 15.3
	24 15.2	41 8.9					34 10.8	53 6.9
						Cost of Sales/Inventory		
						Cost of Sales/Payables		
	13.1	27.1					34.4	6.3
	371.0	–70.8				Sales/Working Capital	–69.4	–45.2
	–10.3	–5.8					–24.2	–13.4
		3.6					3.1	2.5
	(13)	2.1				EBIT/Interest	1.3	(24) 1.4
		1.3					.7	.6
		2.4					2.1	1.6
	(12)	1.3				Net Profit + Depr., Dep., Amort./Cur. Mat. L /T/D	(14) 1.2	(14) 1.1
		1.0					.8	.8
	1.1	1.1					1.1	.8
	2.4	2.7				Fixed/Worth	2.0	2.6
	4.5	5.0					3.4	5.1
	.7	.8					.9	.6
	1.8	2.4				Debt/Worth	2.2	2.3
	6.7	5.9					4.9	5.9
	71.8	31.4					15.0	37.4
	28.9 (14)	20.9				% Profit Before Taxes/Tangible Net Worth	(19) 7.9	(26) 14.0
	22.8	6.2					–6.9	–5.8
	14.2	7.9					6.5	8.7
	9.4	5.4				% Profit Before Taxes/Total Assets	2.1	3.1
	6.7	1.5					–1.7	–4.4
	4.2	2.7					4.3	7.0
	2.5	1.9				Sales/Net Fixed Assets	2.9	3.6
	1.8	1.3					1.7	1.7
	3.2	1.6					2.2	2.8
	2.0	1.3				Sales/Total Assets	1.6	1.7
	1.4	.9					1.3	1.1
	3.6	8.1					6.5	3.5
	7.9 (14)	9.4				% Depr., Dep., Amort./Sales	7.6	(29) 5.3
	14.0	11.6					13.9	12.9
								3.2
						% Officers', Directors', Owners' Comp/Sales	(19)	4.5
								7.5
1076M	28101M	84085M	151794M	29131M		Net Sales ($)	122872M	131742M
817M	13121M	69523M	163039M	85470M		Total Assets ($)	83555M	116809M

© Robert Morris Associates 1995

M = $ thousand　　MM = $ million
See Pages 1 through 15 for Explanation of Ratios and Data

Comparative Historical Data | Current Data Sorted By Sales

4/1/92-3/31/93 ALL	4/1/93-3/31/94 ALL	4/1/94-3/31/95 ALL	# Postretirement Benefits / Type of Statement	0-1MM	1-3MM	3-5MM	5-10MM	10-25MM	25MM & OVER
		2	# Postretirement Benefits		1		1		
			Type of Statement						
11	5	11	Unqualified	1	2	3	2	2	1
8	6	5	Reviewed	2		1	1	1	
14	11	13	Compiled	1	5	2	5		
			Tax Returns						
3	2	10	Other	1	2	1	1		2

				15 (4/1-9/30/94)			24 (10/1/94-3/31/95)		
36	24	39	NUMBER OF STATEMENTS	5	9	7	9	6	3
%	%	%	ASSETS	%	%	%	%	%	%
6.2	5.6	8.4	Cash & Equivalents						
9.9	10.1	10.0	Trade Receivables - (net)						
4.5	4.6	1.4	Inventory						
5.8	6.9	1.5	All Other Current						
26.3	27.3	21.2	Total Current						
62.4	63.3	67.5	Fixed Assets (net)						
2.3	1.8	2.0	Intangibles (net)						
9.0	7.6	9.2	All Other Non-Current						
100.0	100.0	100.0	Total						
			LIABILITIES						
7.6	2.1	4.2	Notes Payable-Short Term						
11.6	9.8	8.7	Cur. Mat.-L /T/D						
7.0	7.0	3.8	Trade Payables						
.4	.7	.3	Income Taxes Payable						
9.2	5.1	7.0	All Other Current						
35.8	24.7	24.1	Total Current						
33.6	31.8	31.1	Long Term Debt						
.9	1.7	1.9	Deferred Taxes						
4.1	3.0	1.3	All Other-Non-Current						
25.5	38.7	41.7	Net Worth						
100.0	100.0	100.0	Total Liabilities & Net Worth						
			INCOME DATA						
100.0	100.0	100.0	Net Sales						
			Gross Profit						
94.8	94.3	93.9	Operating Expenses						
5.2	5.7	6.1	Operating Profit						
2.7	2.5	1.7	All Other Expenses (net)						
2.6	3.2	4.4	Profit Before Taxes						

RATIOS

4/1/92-3/31/93	4/1/93-3/31/94	4/1/94-3/31/95	Ratio
1.1 / .8 / .4	1.6 / 1.0 / .8	1.7 / 1.1 / .5	Current
.8 / .5 / .2	1.0 / .7 / .4	1.3 / .9 / .4	Quick
9 38.5 / 16 23.0 / 27 13.3	14 25.9 / 21 17.3 / 34 10.6	10 35.4 / 20 18.0 / 41 8.9	Sales/Receivables
			Cost of Sales/Inventory
			Cost of Sales/Payables
32.5 / -27.9 / -8.0	12.7 / NM / -29.7	12.3 / 114.9 / -11.9	Sales/Working Capital
2.9 / (34) 1.4 / .9	3.9 / (23) 2.7 / 1.2	4.9 / (31) 2.9 / 1.6	EBIT/Interest
1.7 / (19) 1.3 / .9	1.4 / (13) 1.3 / .9	2.4 / (22) 1.4 / 1.1	Net Profit + Depr., Dep., Amort./Cur. Mat. L/T/D
1.3 / 2.7 / 7.1	1.0 / 2.1 / 3.7	1.1 / 1.6 / 3.6	Fixed/Worth
1.3 / 2.9 / 9.1	.8 / 2.1 / 4.5	.7 / 1.6 / 3.9	Debt/Worth
18.0 / (29) 12.0 / .2	21.5 / 13.6 / 2.2	37.8 / (37) 21.6 / 6.1	% Profit Before Taxes/Tangible Net Worth
5.9 / 2.3 / -.2	8.3 / 5.5 / 1.0	10.6 / 5.5 / 1.7	% Profit Before Taxes/Total Assets
4.1 / 2.7 / 1.8	3.3 / 2.3 / 1.5	3.0 / 2.0 / 1.3	Sales/Net Fixed Assets
2.2 / 1.6 / 1.2	1.9 / 1.4 / 1.0	1.9 / 1.4 / .9	Sales/Total Assets
4.8 / (34) 7.3 / 11.4	5.0 / (22) 7.8 / 11.0	6.0 / (35) 9.4 / 14.0	% Depr., Dep., Amort./Sales
2.1 / (14) 3.5 / 7.5	1.4 / (10) 3.0 / 4.5	3.3 / (13) 4.4 / 8.3	% Officers', Directors', Owners' Comp/Sales

4/1/92-3/31/93	4/1/93-3/31/94	4/1/94-3/31/95		0-1MM	1-3MM	3-5MM	5-10MM	10-25MM	25MM & OVER
224477M	150138M	294187M	Net Sales ($)	2672M	18613M	28028M	60644M	98677M	85553M
236724M	113366M	331970M	Total Assets ($)	1982M	40883M	20272M	52195M	90749M	125889M

© Robert Morris Associates 1995

M = $ thousand   MM = $ million

See Pages 1 through 15 for Explanation of Ratios and Data

SERVICES—BUSES – SCHOOL. SIC# 4151

Current Data Sorted By Assets   Comparative Historical Data

Postretirement Benefits

Type of Statement	0-500M	500M-2MM	2-10MM	10-50MM	50-100MM	100-250MM		4/1/90-3/31/91 ALL	4/1/91-3/31/92 ALL
Unqualified		3	7	4				10	13
Reviewed	2	13	12	1				14	23
Compiled	10	17	3		1			29	23
Tax Returns	3	3							1
Other	1	3	1	2				8	8
		48 (4/1-9/30/94)		38 (10/1/94-3/31/95)					
NUMBER OF STATEMENTS	16	39	23	7	1			61	68
ASSETS	%	%	%	%	%	%		%	%
Cash & Equivalents	13.1	11.2	9.3					10.9	12.0
Trade Receivables - (net)	2.9	9.7	7.8					9.6	8.5
Inventory	7.3	1.9	5.1					3.7	2.5
All Other Current	8.5	3.4	2.2					3.2	1.6
Total Current	31.8	26.1	24.4					27.4	24.5
Fixed Assets (net)	58.5	60.7	64.7					61.4	64.5
Intangibles (net)	1.6	3.7	1.0					1.8	3.2
All Other Non-Current	8.0	9.4	9.8					9.4	7.9
Total	100.0	100.0	100.0					100.0	100.0
LIABILITIES									
Notes Payable-Short Term	12.0	6.8	8.0					6.5	4.2
Cur. Mat. -L/T/D	16.1	11.3	12.6					13.3	12.7
Trade Payables	4.2	4.1	3.9					4.4	3.8
Income Taxes Payable	.2	.1	.3					.7	.2
All Other Current	8.0	6.3	6.3					4.8	5.3
Total Current	40.5	28.6	31.2					29.6	26.2
Long Term Debt	28.4	25.0	28.6					31.7	28.3
Deferred Taxes	.5	1.4	2.7					1.1	.9
All Other-Non-Current	.0	.8	1.3					1.5	1.8
Net Worth	30.6	44.2	36.3					36.2	42.8
Total Liabilities & Net Worth	100.0	100.0	100.0					100.0	100.0
INCOME DATA									
Net Sales	100.0	100.0	100.0					100.0	100.0
Gross Profit									
Operating Expenses	95.9	95.0	93.3					91.9	92.5
Operating Profit	4.1	5.0	6.7					8.1	7.5
All Other Expenses (net)	1.2	2.2	2.0					1.9	2.1
Profit Before Taxes	2.9	2.8	4.7					6.1	5.4
RATIOS									
Current	1.4 / .7 / .3	1.6 / .8 / .4	1.2 / .7 / .5					1.6 / .9 / .4	1.4 / .9 / .6
Quick	(15) .8 / .4 / .1	1.4 / .7 / .4	.9 / .6 / .4					1.5 / .6 / .3	1.2 / .8 / .5
Sales/Receivables	0 UND / 0 UND / 3 135.3	4 95.0 / 13 28.1 / 27 13.6	7 56.1 / 19 19.6 / 23 16.1					1 373.6 / 11 33.5 / 30 12.2	4 99.9 / 16 22.3 / 30 12.1
Cost of Sales/Inventory									
Cost of Sales/Payables									
Sales/Working Capital	45.5 / -45.5 / -11.6	14.3 / -33.7 / -9.3	24.6 / -22.6 / -8.5					13.8 / -85.5 / -10.7	22.0 / -67.2 / -16.4
EBIT/Interest	5.7 / 2.4 / .7	(38) 3.1 / 2.1 / 1.0	4.8 / 2.1 / 1.2					(59) 4.5 / 2.1 / 1.3	(63) 3.6 / 2.2 / 1.6
Net Profit + Depr., Dep., Amort./Cur. Mat. L /T/D		(20) 1.8 / 1.5 / .9	(16) 2.2 / 1.3 / .9					(33) 2.7 / 1.7 / 1.2	(37) 2.1 / 1.5 / 1.2
Fixed/Worth	.9 / 1.8 / NM	.9 / 1.4 / 3.3	1.3 / 1.9 / 2.6					1.0 / 1.9 / 3.3	1.1 / 1.5 / 2.8
Debt/Worth	.7 / 1.7 / NM	.6 / 1.1 / 3.5	1.2 / 1.7 / 3.1					.9 / 1.8 / 3.8	.8 / 1.2 / 3.0
% Profit Before Taxes/Tangible Net Worth	(12) 44.5 / 20.6 / 2.3	(33) 22.9 / 9.0 / 3.0	37.7 / 17.9 / 6.4					(54) 41.0 / 22.4 / 6.7	(63) 28.9 / 15.1 / 8.2
% Profit Before Taxes/Total Assets	20.7 / 5.3 / -1.5	8.3 / 3.7 / .0	11.8 / 5.1 / 1.1					15.3 / 6.5 / 1.2	11.7 / 6.3 / 2.0
Sales/Net Fixed Assets	8.3 / 4.6 / 3.1	4.2 / 2.9 / 1.8	3.0 / 2.0 / 1.7					4.2 / 2.4 / 1.7	3.9 / 2.4 / 1.8
Sales/Total Assets	4.9 / 2.4 / 2.0	2.5 / 1.6 / 1.1	2.0 / 1.4 / 1.2					2.2 / 1.7 / 1.2	2.1 / 1.6 / 1.2
% Depr., Dep., Amort./Sales	(15) 7.0 / 13.0 / 14.5	8.4 / 12.0 / 14.9	6.0 / 10.6 / 13.1					(56) 7.0 / 11.0 / 15.1	(62) 7.4 / 10.2 / 14.3
% Officers', Directors', Owners' Comp/Sales	(10) 5.0 / 8.9 / 13.5	(26) 4.8 / 8.4 / 11.7	(13) 1.3 / 3.9 / 5.4					(34) 3.8 / 6.8 / 9.5	(38) 3.3 / 5.0 / 8.5
Net Sales ($)	16428M	80608M	186868M	205711M	63582M			485320M	386778M
Total Assets ($)	4329M	43526M	112142M	158757M	60275M			316406M	274179M

© Robert Morris Associates 1995

M = $ thousand   MM = $ million
See Pages 1 through 15 for Explanation of Ratios and Data

Comparative Historical Data				Current Data Sorted By Sales					
4	1		# Postretirement Benefits						
			Type of Statement						
23	22	14	Unqualified	1		4	2	5	2
30	31	28	Reviewed	3	12	2	6	5	
36	32	31	Compiled	10	17	2	1		1
	4	6	Tax Returns	2	3		1		
17	8	7	Other	1	3	1	1		
4/1/92-3/31/93	4/1/93-3/31/94	4/1/94-3/31/95		48 (4/1-9/30/94)			38 (10/1/94-3/31/95)		
ALL	ALL	ALL		0-1MM	1-3MM	3-5MM	5-10MM	10-25MM	25MM & OVER
106	97	86	NUMBER OF STATEMENTS	17	35	9	11	11	3
%	%	%	ASSETS	%	%	%	%	%	%
11.1	10.2	11.1	Cash & Equivalents	11.5	11.8		10.3	8.3	
13.0	9.0	7.7	Trade Receivables - (net)	4.5	6.7		9.1	10.0	
2.4	1.8	3.8	Inventory	1.6	3.3		4.2	9.4	
1.8	1.7	4.0	All Other Current	4.9	3.8		5.8	2.8	
28.3	22.7	26.6	Total Current	22.5	25.5		29.5	30.5	
60.1	64.7	61.3	Fixed Assets (net)	65.5	61.1		59.7	57.2	
3.1	3.3	2.5	Intangibles (net)	4.5	2.6		1.4	2.6	
8.5	9.3	9.6	All Other Non-Current	7.5	10.7		9.4	9.7	
100.0	100.0	100.0	Total	100.0	100.0		100.0	100.0	
			LIABILITIES						
3.9	2.7	7.8	Notes Payable-Short Term	9.3	7.5		4.8	16.9	
13.9	12.9	12.0	Cur. Mat.-L /T/D	14.9	12.3		13.1	8.2	
4.9	4.9	4.3	Trade Payables	2.4	4.3		5.4	8.3	
.3	.7	.1	Income Taxes Payable	.2	.1		.3	.0	
5.9	7.8	6.6	All Other Current	5.7	5.3		7.5	7.2	
28.8	29.1	31.0	Total Current	32.5	29.4		31.0	40.6	
27.8	31.4	26.7	Long Term Debt	29.3	26.9		23.4	26.6	
1.2	1.5	1.6	Deferred Taxes	.6	1.6		2.9	1.8	
1.2	2.3	1.2	All Other-Non-Current	1.1	.6		.5	2.0	
41.0	35.7	39.5	Net Worth	36.5	41.5		42.0	29.0	
100.0	100.0	100.0	Total Liabilities & Net Worth	100.0	100.0		100.0	100.0	
			INCOME DATA						
100.0	100.0	100.0	Net Sales	100.0	100.0		100.0	100.0	
			Gross Profit						
91.8	94.3	94.3	Operating Expenses	95.2	94.5		94.7	94.6	
8.2	5.7	5.7	Operating Profit	4.8	5.5		5.3	5.4	
2.3	1.4	1.9	All Other Expenses (net)	1.7	2.2		.9	1.6	
5.9	4.3	3.8	Profit Before Taxes	3.1	3.4		4.3	3.9	
			RATIOS						
1.6	1.3	1.4		1.0	1.5		2.0	1.2	
.8	.7	.8	Current	.7	.8		.7	.7	
.4	.4	.5		.4	.4		.5	.4	
1.3	1.1	1.1		1.0	1.1		.9	.8	
.6	.6	(85) .6	Quick	(16) .6	.6		.6	.5	
.3	.3	.4		.1	.3		.4	.3	
5 67.5	6 57.3	2 181.0		0 UND	0 999.8		4 95.2	12 30.1	
16 22.2	13 27.5	12 31.5	Sales/Receivables	3 124.0	11 31.9		11 34.0	18 19.9	
35 10.4	26 14.0	23 15.9		17 21.5	23 16.0		26 13.8	24 15.5	
			Cost of Sales/Inventory						
			Cost of Sales/Payables						
16.9	32.0	14.7		NM	13.1		25.4	24.6	
-29.4	-26.9	-32.0	Sales/Working Capital	-26.1	-34.9		-23.7	-26.5	
-8.0	-8.0	-10.6		-11.8	-8.9		-11.3	-6.9	
4.6	5.1	4.4		3.4	3.3		5.3	4.3	
(97) 2.4	(93) 2.3	(84) 2.1	EBIT/Interest	2.0	(34) 2.1		(10) 3.0	1.7	
1.5	1.4	1.1		.9	.9		1.6	1.2	
2.1	2.1	2.1			1.8				
(49) 1.5	(49) 1.5	(47) 1.5	Net Profit + Depr., Dep., Amort./Cur. Mat. L/T/D		(18) 1.3				
.8	1.0	1.0			.9				
.9	1.2	1.0		1.2	.9		.7	1.2	
1.7	2.0	1.8	Fixed/Worth	1.6	1.7		1.8	2.2	
3.9	7.1	3.2		-32.7	2.7		3.1	4.1	
.7	.9	.9		.7	.6		.9	1.6	
1.6	1.7	1.5	Debt/Worth	1.2	1.5		1.5	2.0	
4.9	8.3	3.7		-39.2	3.5		2.5	5.6	
38.6	32.9	34.5		39.4	25.5		43.8	37.0	
(98) 18.7	(81) 17.4	(75) 12.2	% Profit Before Taxes/Tangible Net Worth	(12) 9.4	(31) 9.6		(10) 27.0	(10) 22.8	
6.4	5.1	4.7		1.6	2.5		10.6	5.5	
13.0	11.9	11.9		16.2	8.3		12.7	13.3	
5.9	6.0	5.0	% Profit Before Taxes/Total Assets	4.3	3.9		9.8	2.3	
2.4	1.4	.3		-.4	.0		5.1	.8	
4.4	3.9	4.4		5.1	3.8		6.7	4.3	
2.4	2.5	2.9	Sales/Net Fixed Assets	3.3	2.7		3.0	3.0	
1.7	1.7	1.7		2.2	1.6		2.1	1.9	
2.1	2.2	2.4		3.4	2.1		3.1	2.2	
1.5	1.6	1.6	Sales/Total Assets	1.9	1.6		2.1	1.6	
1.1	1.3	1.2		1.3	1.1		1.5	1.4	
6.0	7.9	7.3		7.7	9.1		4.6	3.5	
(100) 9.8	(94) 10.0	(84) 11.1	% Depr., Dep., Amort./Sales	13.3	(34) 12.4		7.6	6.8	
14.1	13.8	13.7		16.6	15.9		12.1	11.0	
2.9	3.2	3.1		5.0	6.5				
(69) 6.1	(59) 6.1	(51) 6.7	% Officers', Directors', Owners' Comp/Sales	(13) 6.9	(20) 9.3				
11.0	9.4	11.0		14.4	12.0				
676917M	760399M	553197M	Net Sales ($)	10549M	62035M	37387M	75717M	183803M	183706M
456037M	503232M	379029M	Total Assets ($)	6567M	44083M	25591M	41910M	105578M	155300M

M = $ thousand   MM = $ million
See Pages 1 through 15 for Explanation of Ratios and Data

	Current Data Sorted By Assets							Comparative Historical Data	
# Postretirement Benefits	1	2	2	1					
Type of Statement									
Unqualified	3	3	24	12	11	8		25	27
Reviewed		2	7					10	12
Compiled	3	10	4	2				10	8
Tax Returns	1	1						1	
Other	3	5	6	9	1	2		18	20
	23 (4/1-9/30/94)			94 (10/1/94-3/31/95)				4/1/90-3/31/91 ALL	4/1/91-3/31/92 ALL
	0-500M	500M-2MM	2-10MM	10-50MM	50-100MM	100-250MM			
NUMBER OF STATEMENTS	10	21	41	23	12	10		64	67
ASSETS	%	%	%	%	%	%		%	%
Cash & Equivalents	6.4	6.8	8.6	9.2	3.7	8.9		4.4	5.3
Trade Receivables - (net)	22.8	23.9	8.0	10.1	4.1	4.7		12.3	11.1
Inventory	2.3	8.7	4.7	2.4	.1	.7		2.8	3.0
All Other Current	3.9	.4	2.9	.6	.2	2.1		1.9	2.0
Total Current	35.4	39.8	24.3	22.3	8.0	16.4		21.4	21.4
Fixed Assets (net)	50.2	48.1	53.1	47.7	49.2	39.8		57.3	54.7
Intangibles (net)	7.0	3.0	14.0	20.2	39.2	35.4		12.5	14.6
All Other Non-Current	7.4	9.0	8.6	9.8	3.6	8.4		8.7	9.3
Total	100.0	100.0	100.0	100.0	100.0	100.0		100.0	100.0
LIABILITIES									
Notes Payable-Short Term	19.8	7.9	3.8	3.1	11.5	.0		7.2	7.2
Cur. Mat. -L/T/D	1.8	7.3	6.1	3.1	2.5	2.0		5.2	8.4
Trade Payables	14.5	9.5	7.8	6.6	2.4	3.8		7.2	6.4
Income Taxes Payable	.6	.5	.6	1.0	.0	.1		.4	.4
All Other Current	8.6	9.7	8.1	4.9	6.1	17.3		7.0	9.7
Total Current	45.3	34.9	26.3	18.6	22.6	23.1		26.8	32.2
Long Term Debt	20.8	22.7	42.2	33.4	52.8	40.1		42.4	34.9
Deferred Taxes	1.4	.0	2.5	1.0	3.3	1.4		1.0	1.0
All Other-Non-Current	.0	4.3	7.6	6.0	8.4	10.3		3.3	3.6
Net Worth	32.5	38.1	21.3	41.0	12.9	25.1		26.4	28.4
Total Liabilities & Net Worth	100.0	100.0	100.0	100.0	100.0	100.0		100.0	100.0
INCOME DATA									
Net Sales	100.0	100.0	100.0	100.0	100.0	100.0		100.0	100.0
Gross Profit									
Operating Expenses	91.2	91.1	87.4	86.8	89.5	76.0		84.7	90.4
Operating Profit	8.8	8.9	12.6	13.2	10.5	24.0		15.3	9.6
All Other Expenses (net)	3.7	4.1	14.1	9.4	22.8	13.1		14.0	13.2
Profit Before Taxes	5.0	4.7	−1.4	3.8	−12.3	10.9		1.3	−3.6
RATIOS									
Current	1.6	1.7	1.2	2.2	1.6	1.1		1.4	1.4
	.5	1.2	.8	1.1	.7	.7		.5	.5
	.3	.3	.4	.6	.1	.2		.2	.2
Quick	1.0	1.5	.9	1.6	1.6	.9		1.1	1.1
	.4	.8	.6	1.1	.7	.7		.4	.3
	.3	.3	.2	.5	.2	.2		.2	.2
Sales/Receivables	0 UND	14 26.1	7 51.5	10 35.0	8 46.8	12 30.0		7 50.7	7 49.3
	31 11.6	36 10.2	14 25.7	22 16.6	12 30.3	17 21.9		23 15.6	16 22.9
	60 6.1	50 7.3	34 10.6	52 7.0	26 14.1	30 12.1		45 8.1	40 9.1
Cost of Sales/Inventory									
Cost of Sales/Payables									
Sales/Working Capital	14.9	9.6	19.6	5.8	10.8	25.2		23.1	14.9
	−30.1	201.0	−16.6	36.8	−18.5	−19.7		−11.5	−9.0
	−6.2	−6.7	−4.9	−8.7	−3.1	−5.8		−3.5	−3.4
EBIT/Interest		(15) 25.3	(32) 5.6	(21) 6.9	(10) 1.9			(47) 3.2	(45) 3.2
		5.3	2.5	1.9	−.3			2.0	1.4
		1.7	.6	.4	−2.5			1.0	.4
Net Profit + Depr., Dep., Amort./Cur. Mat. L./T/D			(13) 9.4					(22) 6.3	(21) 10.3
			2.4					2.2	2.8
			1.4					.9	.4
Fixed/Worth	.6	.2	1.4	.7	NM	3.5		1.5	.9
	2.1	1.9	4.8	2.6	−2.6	−4.7		3.5	4.3
	NM	5.3	−6.8	−3.2	−.5	−1.0		−6.1	−2.9
Debt/Worth	.9	.4	1.0	.7	NM	4.7		1.7	1.0
	2.4	1.8	6.8	3.0	−3.7	−6.8		4.8	4.9
	NM	8.9	−9.2	−7.0	−1.8	−2.2		−8.1	−4.9
% Profit Before Taxes/Tangible Net Worth		(18) 97.8	(27) 42.9	(16) 30.9				(44) 41.7	(41) 37.4
		29.6	9.6	8.6				16.1	5.6
		10.0	−21.2	−3.3				5.0	−5.9
% Profit Before Taxes/Total Assets	11.8	27.7	8.4	10.5	4.5	17.6		12.6	5.8
	2.2	13.2	1.9	2.3	−5.7	9.2		2.9	.1
	−1.8	1.3	−4.6	−3.7	−11.9	−.3		−3.0	−5.8
Sales/Net Fixed Assets	19.6	43.8	3.0	7.5	2.2	2.9		4.7	3.8
	1.8	3.7	1.1	1.1	.9	1.2		1.1	1.2
	1.4	.9	.7	.6	.6	.9		.5	.6
Sales/Total Assets	4.0	3.7	1.2	1.0	.8	.9		1.4	1.5
	1.4	2.3	.6	.7	.4	.6		.7	.6
	.6	.7	.4	.3	.4	.4		.4	.3
% Depr., Dep., Amort./Sales	2.4	(18) 1.0	(33) 7.0	(20) 3.6				(57) 6.1	(60) 7.2
	9.3	9.3	16.5	18.2				17.1	19.1
	27.9	17.7	27.4	28.5				27.8	33.2
% Officers', Directors', Owners' Comp/Sales								(13) 3.5	(14) 6.1
								5.6	10.2
								18.2	14.7
Net Sales ($)	7842M	65907M	221456M	458638M	436435M	933549M		589379M	916653M
Total Assets ($)	2924M	27159M	203838M	585476M	787544M	1615543M		1225215M	1690587M

M = $ thousand   MM = $ million
See Pages 1 through 15 for Explanation of Ratios and Data

Comparative Historical Data				Current Data Sorted By Sales					
1	6	6	# Postretirement Benefits	1	3	1	1		
			Type of Statement						
37	55	61	Unqualified	4	15	5	8	7	22
5	12	9	Reviewed		3	3	3		
15	20	19	Compiled	6	5	2	5	1	
1	5	2	Tax Returns	2					
31	16	26	Other	3	8	2	2	2	3
4/1/92-3/31/93 ALL	4/1/93-3/31/94 ALL	4/1/94-3/31/95 ALL		23 (4/1-9/30/94) 0-1MM	1-3MM	3-5MM	94 (10/1/94-3/31/95) 5-10MM	10-25MM	25MM & OVER
89	108	117	NUMBER OF STATEMENTS	15	31	12	18	16	25
%	%	%	ASSETS	%	%	%	%	%	%
8.1	8.2	7.8	Cash & Equivalents	4.1	6.4	15.2	9.0	7.6	7.3
10.6	14.0	11.8	Trade Receivables - (net)	10.4	9.5	14.9	11.0	19.1	10.2
4.0	4.7	4.0	Inventory	1.6	2.7	3.7	7.5	6.1	3.1
1.1	2.0	1.7	All Other Current	8.6	.4	.6	.4	1.1	1.2
23.7	28.8	25.3	Total Current	24.7	18.9	34.4	27.9	33.9	21.8
51.5	47.8	49.4	Fixed Assets (net)	61.2	59.3	38.4	49.8	36.8	42.9
14.9	13.7	17.0	Intangibles (net)	12.7	12.1	14.1	11.2	20.6	29.2
9.9	9.7	8.3	All Other Non-Current	1.4	9.7	13.1	11.1	8.8	6.0
100.0	100.0	100.0	Total	100.0	100.0	100.0	100.0	100.0	100.0
			LIABILITIES						
6.8	6.4	6.2	Notes Payable-Short Term	17.0	3.3	1.9	7.4	13.0	.3
6.6	6.6	4.6	Cur. Mat.-L /T/D	4.8	4.6	8.9	4.6	3.8	3.1
7.5	8.9	7.5	Trade Payables	6.0	8.7	6.8	7.0	9.6	6.6
.3	.3	.5	Income Taxes Payable	.4	.6	.0	.2	1.7	.2
7.7	8.0	8.4	All Other Current	4.5	9.0	9.7	6.5	3.4	13.9
29.0	30.1	27.3	Total Current	32.7	26.2	27.3	25.7	31.4	24.1
39.6	35.7	36.1	Long Term Debt	30.8	36.8	36.8	40.9	27.5	40.0
1.4	1.6	1.6	Deferred Taxes	.9	1.6	4.1	.4	2.2	1.6
4.4	5.4	6.3	All Other-Non-Current	.2	7.3	13.5	5.6	4.9	6.9
25.6	27.1	28.6	Net Worth	35.3	28.2	18.3	27.5	34.0	27.5
100.0	100.0	100.0	Total Liabilities & Net Worth	100.0	100.0	100.0	100.0	100.0	100.0
			INCOME DATA						
100.0	100.0	100.0	Net Sales	100.0	100.0	100.0	100.0	100.0	100.0
			Gross Profit						
84.8	83.4	87.5	Operating Expenses	90.0	93.9	80.6	84.5	85.9	84.6
15.2	16.6	12.5	Operating Profit	10.0	6.1	19.4	15.5	14.1	15.4
15.2	11.9	11.3	All Other Expenses (net)	12.2	11.2	14.7	10.0	10.3	10.8
.0	4.7	1.2	Profit Before Taxes	-2.2	-5.1	4.7	5.5	3.8	4.6
			RATIOS						
1.6	1.8	1.5	Current	1.7	1.1	2.2	1.6	2.5	1.6
.6	.8	.8		.5	.5	1.1	.8	1.1	.8
.3	.3	.3		.2	.3	.8	.4	.3	.5
1.2	1.2	1.1	Quick	.9	.9	1.9	1.3	2.5	1.3
.5	.6	.7		.3	.5	.9	.6	.8	.7
.2	.3	.3		.1	.2	.8	.2	.3	.5
5 67.8	9 42.4	9 39.5	Sales/Receivables	11 32.4	6 64.5	7 54.9	8 47.1	8 46.0	13 28.1
15 23.7	21 17.7	18 20.3		18 20.7	18 20.3	13 29.2	22 16.7	23 16.1	20 18.7
35 10.4	37 9.8	40 9.1		49 7.5	37 10.0	45 8.2	39 9.4	70 5.2	48 7.6
			Cost of Sales/Inventory						
			Cost of Sales/Payables						
12.3	8.8	12.1	Sales/Working Capital	5.7	60.0	5.2	7.7	6.4	9.4
-19.1	-19.1	-29.6		-14.7	-12.5	NM	-128.8	29.4	-30.4
-4.2	-5.4	-5.4		-3.1	-4.3	-30.1	-4.8	-4.6	-10.8
4.2	7.5	5.6	EBIT/Interest	4.0	6.3		17.0	6.0	6.2
(65) 2.3	(90) 2.6	(96) 2.3		(10) 1.8	(24) 1.4		(17) 2.2	(14) 3.5	(22) 3.0
1.0	.8	.5		-1.5	-.8		.7	-.1	1.2
7.2	10.4	9.0	Net Profit + Depr., Dep., Amort./Cur. Mat. L/T/D						
(19) 3.3	(29) 3.2	(31) 2.4							
1.7	1.2	1.4							
.9	.6	1.0	Fixed/Worth	.9	1.3	.6	.7	.8	1.5
3.2	2.8	4.6		4.7	4.4	15.0	2.6	4.9	18.4
-2.9	-3.7	-3.2		-1.9	-4.5	-2.5	-8.5	-2.3	-.9
1.4	1.0	1.0	Debt/Worth	.6	1.1	.6	1.2	.9	2.2
4.5	4.4	6.8		3.9	7.5	79.8	3.1	6.1	64.5
-5.3	-5.5	-4.8		-4.3	-7.2	-4.8	-15.7	-3.4	-3.2
34.1	68.2	55.7	% Profit Before Taxes/Tangible Net Worth	42.9	26.7		59.9	65.8	84.6
(54) 14.8	(69) 27.5	(76) 14.9		(11) 1.0	(23) 8.6		(12) 37.0	(10) 40.1	(13) 29.5
1.2	5.0	-1.9		-13.8	-20.6		-2.3	26.8	8.6
10.3	14.7	10.9	% Profit Before Taxes/Total Assets	6.6	6.3	18.5	22.0	16.2	10.1
3.2	4.4	3.4		-1.4	1.1	3.7	3.9	8.0	7.0
-5.3	-3.0	-3.2		-3.9	-6.4	-.5	-2.1	-3.1	-1.7
3.6	6.2	4.6	Sales/Net Fixed Assets	1.5	3.3	6.4	11.3	13.8	4.8
1.3	1.3	1.3		.8	1.0	2.4	1.7	2.4	1.7
.7	.8	.8		.6	.6	1.0	.8	.8	1.0
1.3	1.7	1.3	Sales/Total Assets	.9	1.5	2.2	2.3	2.0	1.0
.7	.7	.7		.5	.7	.8	.9	.9	.8
.4	.4	.4		.3	.4	.5	.4	.4	.6
6.4	4.8	4.1	% Depr., Dep., Amort./Sales	9.6	8.9		2.6	2.9	3.7
(67) 17.8	(87) 16.3	(91) 15.3		(14) 24.7	(27) 15.4		(17) 11.2	(12) 12.7	(13) 15.3
25.3	27.1	26.8		33.2	35.2		22.7	37.5	24.4
3.6	3.7	3.2	% Officers', Directors', Owners' Comp/Sales						
(14) 7.1	(25) 6.9	(23) 5.9							
12.2	13.5	13.2							
1316959M	1687160M	2123827M	Net Sales ($)	7731M	60390M	48628M	116610M	256821M	1633647M
2532453M	3062777M	3222484M	Total Assets ($)	18231M	136989M	77290M	174513M	626140M	2189321M

M = $ thousand   MM = $ million
See Pages 1 through 15 for Explanation of Ratios and Data

SERVICES—CAR WASHES. SIC# 7542

	Current Data Sorted By Assets							Comparative Historical Data	
	2	1	1				# Postretirement Benefits		
							Type of Statement		
1	1	2	1				Unqualified	6	6
3	8	1	1				Reviewed	12	20
25	18	3					Compiled	43	56
10	3						Tax Returns	5	5
17	16	5	2				Other	32	25
	17 (4/1-9/30/94)			100 (10/1/94-3/31/95)				4/1/90-3/31/91	4/1/91-3/31/92
0-500M	**500M-2MM**	**2-10MM**	**10-50MM**	**50-100MM**	**100-250MM**			**ALL**	**ALL**
56	46	11	4				NUMBER OF STATEMENTS	98	112
%	%	%	%	%	%			%	%
							ASSETS		
16.6	7.2	6.7					Cash & Equivalents	7.4	8.0
3.5	2.4	2.2					Trade Receivables - (net)	5.1	4.1
5.1	3.5	8.4					Inventory	3.6	3.2
2.0	2.3	1.0					All Other Current	1.8	2.5
27.2	15.3	18.2					Total Current	17.8	17.7
58.2	71.4	67.3					Fixed Assets (net)	68.1	68.9
5.2	3.5	6.5					Intangibles (net)	3.4	3.0
9.4	9.8	8.0					All Other Non-Current	10.7	10.4
100.0	100.0	100.0					Total	100.0	100.0
							LIABILITIES		
4.3	3.5	8.9					Notes Payable-Short Term	6.4	3.8
5.8	4.7	7.0					Cur. Mat. -L/T/D	6.6	6.2
4.6	4.5	5.2					Trade Payables	6.2	4.6
.5	.0	.0					Income Taxes Payable	.2	.5
11.9	7.3	2.9					All Other Current	11.8	6.4
27.0	20.1	24.1					Total Current	31.2	21.4
36.9	54.8	38.5					Long Term Debt	47.6	47.8
.1	.0	.1					Deferred Taxes	.3	.7
3.3	5.2	3.6					All Other-Non-Current	2.6	4.9
32.8	19.9	33.7					Net Worth	18.3	25.2
100.0	100.0	100.0					Total Liabilities & Net Worth	100.0	100.0
							INCOME DATA		
100.0	100.0	100.0					Net Sales	100.0	100.0
							Gross Profit		
87.8	89.1	88.8					Operating Expenses	92.3	87.6
12.2	10.9	11.2					Operating Profit	7.7	12.4
6.2	6.4	3.1					All Other Expenses (net)	9.7	8.7
6.0	4.5	8.1					Profit Before Taxes	-2.0	3.6
							RATIOS		
2.1	1.4	1.3						1.2	1.4
1.0	.7	.5					Current	.6	.8
.2	.3	.5						.2	.3
1.5	1.0	.7						.8	1.0
(55) .8	.4	.4					Quick	(110) .3	.4
.1	.2	.2						.1	.2
0 UND	0 742.0	0 UND						0 UND	0 UND
0 UND	2 183.2	3 112.9					Sales/Receivables	3 135.0	1 275.8
3 117.8	7 55.8	9 38.8						7 49.3	6 59.9
							Cost of Sales/Inventory		
							Cost of Sales/Payables		
19.1	42.0	19.5						90.3	42.6
UND	-38.3	-21.8					Sales/Working Capital	-24.6	-67.1
-7.0	-8.6	-8.9						-4.3	-5.7
8.8	4.3	5.5						2.5	4.3
(38) 3.0	(41) 2.1	(10) 2.2					EBIT/Interest	(69) 1.2	(79) 2.0
1.7	.9	.9						.2	1.1
	6.2							3.7	1.9
	(13) 2.9						Net Profit + Depr., Dep., Amort./Cur. Mat. L /T/D	(36) 1.1	(28) 1.4
	1.3							.4	.7
.7	1.6	1.1						1.5	1.3
1.9	5.0	2.7					Fixed/Worth	5.4	4.8
9.1	NM	87.5						-12.4	58.5
.7	1.6	.9						1.7	1.2
2.0	4.5	2.5					Debt/Worth	6.4	4.9
20.7	NM	117.5						-26.0	68.6
68.7	53.1							30.8	53.4
(44) 33.5	(35) 18.3						% Profit Before Taxes/Tangible Net Worth	(69) 6.2	(86) 18.4
8.7	-4.2							-25.6	-3.3
23.6	11.3	13.7						8.0	12.2
9.8	4.8	6.7					% Profit Before Taxes/Total Assets	-.2	4.6
1.9	-.9	-.2						-7.8	-2.4
20.6	3.7	4.4						5.2	4.9
3.5	1.5	1.9					Sales/Net Fixed Assets	1.7	1.7
.8	.7	.7						.6	.6
4.3	1.9	2.5						2.4	2.5
1.7	1.1	1.4					Sales/Total Assets	1.3	.9
.7	.6	.6						.5	.5
2.9	3.5	2.5						3.5	3.5
(50) 7.4	(45) 5.9	(10) 4.7					% Depr., Dep., Amort./Sales	(87) 7.1	(104) 7.8
13.4	9.6	9.1						16.4	13.8
6.1	2.6							2.7	2.4
(22) 10.3	(15) 5.5						% Officers', Directors', Owners' Comp/Sales	(37) 4.8	(45) 6.0
15.6	8.5							8.9	15.0
31534M	80351M	82058M	166481M				Net Sales ($)	253159M	292797M
13149M	44670M	43078M	76797M				Total Assets ($)	166846M	227582M

M = $ thousand   MM = $ million
See Pages 1 through 15 for Explanation of Ratios and Data

Comparative Historical Data				Current Data Sorted By Sales					
1	2	4	# Postretirement Benefits	2		1			1
			Type of Statement						
5	2	5	Unqualified	1	2	1			1
14	15	13	Reviewed	5	4	1		2	1
53	49	46	Compiled	34	7	2	1	2	
3	10	13	Tax Returns	11	1	1			
21	31	40	Other	21	13	3		1	2
4/1/92-3/31/93 ALL	4/1/93-3/31/94 ALL	4/1/94-3/31/95 ALL		17 (4/1-9/30/94)		100 (10/1/94-3/31/95)			
				0-1MM	1-3MM	3-5MM	5-10MM	10-25MM	25MM & OVER
96	107	117	**NUMBER OF STATEMENTS**	72	27	8	1	5	4
%	%	%	**ASSETS**	%	%	%	%	%	%
11.5	7.9	11.5	Cash & Equivalents	10.7	14.3				
3.9	4.2	3.4	Trade Receivables - (net)	2.2	4.2				
3.2	3.7	4.7	Inventory	2.2	7.9				
1.2	2.9	2.0	All Other Current	1.9	3.0				
19.9	18.7	21.6	Total Current	17.1	29.4				
68.7	68.9	64.2	Fixed Assets (net)	71.9	47.4				
3.9	4.6	4.5	Intangibles (net)	3.7	7.3				
7.5	7.8	9.7	All Other Non-Current	7.3	15.9				
100.0	100.0	100.0	Total	100.0	100.0				
			LIABILITIES						
4.4	7.3	4.3	Notes Payable-Short Term	5.1	.8				
5.0	7.1	5.6	Cur. Mat.-L /T/D	5.1	5.8				
4.8	5.3	5.2	Trade Payables	3.2	5.8				
.2	.4	.2	Income Taxes Payable	.3	.0				
9.7	8.4	9.2	All Other Current	9.5	9.3				
24.2	28.5	24.5	Total Current	23.2	21.8				
41.8	46.2	43.9	Long Term Debt	49.3	35.3				
.3	.1	.1	Deferred Taxes	.0	.1				
6.4	5.1	4.3	All Other-Non-Current	3.5	6.7				
27.4	20.1	27.2	Net Worth	24.1	36.1				
100.0	100.0	100.0	Total Liabilities & Net Worth	100.0	100.0				
			INCOME DATA						
100.0	100.0	100.0	Net Sales	100.0	100.0				
			Gross Profit						
88.9	88.7	88.6	Operating Expenses	85.2	92.9				
11.1	11.3	11.4	Operating Profit	14.8	7.1				
7.4	7.4	5.9	All Other Expenses (net)	8.6	1.7				
3.6	4.0	5.5	Profit Before Taxes	6.2	5.4				
			RATIOS						
1.4	1.4	1.7	Current	1.6	2.6				
.6	.5	.8		.7	1.4				
.2	.2	.3		.2	.5				
1.1	.9	1.3	Quick	1.3	1.6				
(105) .4	(116) .3	.6		(71) .4	.8				
.1	.1	.1		.1	.3				
0 UND	0 UND	0 UND	Sales/Receivables	0 UND	1 577.0				
2 218.5	1 298.5	1 314.0		0 UND	3 111.2				
5 74.9	4 82.5	5 66.9		3 104.9	8 46.3				
			Cost of Sales/Inventory						
			Cost of Sales/Payables						
35.7	30.1	22.9	Sales/Working Capital	37.4	11.1				
-23.1	-22.5	-48.3		-25.4	44.4				
-5.8	-5.6	-8.6		-4.5	-13.4				
5.4	4.7	5.9	EBIT/Interest	5.9	6.2				
(75) 2.4	(84) 2.0	(93) 2.5		(53) 2.3	(23) 2.5				
1.1	1.0	1.3		1.2	1.4				
1.6	2.2	5.0	Net Profit + Depr., Dep., Amort./Cur. Mat. L/T/D						
(23) 1.1	(27) 1.1	(23) 2.9							
.3	.3	.8							
1.3	1.5	1.2	Fixed/Worth	1.6	.5				
3.6	4.8	2.9		3.4	1.8				
40.3	-39.3	29.3		11.1	-92.1				
.9	1.6	1.2	Debt/Worth	1.3	.5				
3.4	5.7	2.9		3.4	2.6				
41.5	-43.6	35.6		20.7	-102.9				
60.0	55.5	54.6	% Profit Before Taxes/Tangible Net Worth	54.1	60.0				
(75) 28.1	(77) 29.8	(91) 29.4		(57) 30.3	(20) 25.7				
9.2	5.0	7.4		6.0	8.0				
13.8	14.2	17.1	% Profit Before Taxes/Total Assets	19.0	18.3				
5.9	4.6	7.4		7.2	6.7				
-.4	-.3	.8		-.5	1.9				
5.5	5.0	7.5	Sales/Net Fixed Assets	3.9	23.9				
2.0	1.6	2.0		1.1	3.7				
.6	.7	.8		.6	1.8				
2.8	2.5	3.0	Sales/Total Assets	1.9	3.5				
1.4	1.2	1.4		.9	1.8				
.5	.6	.6		.5	1.1				
2.9	3.9	3.1	% Depr., Dep., Amort./Sales	4.9	2.2				
(94) 6.6	(100) 6.9	(108) 5.6		(66) 9.8	(25) 3.2				
15.7	13.7	10.7		13.7	5.9				
2.9	3.8	3.7	% Officers', Directors', Owners' Comp/Sales	5.4					
(42) 7.6	(35) 8.4	(42) 7.2		(26) 8.4					
10.8	15.8	12.2		13.6					
195822M	227723M	360424M	Net Sales ($)	29562M	46068M	32033M	9203M	77077M	166481M
118783M	131638M	177694M	Total Assets ($)	32165M	32665M	13170M	636M	22261M	76797M

M = $ thousand   MM = $ million
See Pages 1 through 15 for Explanation of Ratios and Data

	Current Data Sorted By Assets							Comparative Historical Data	
		1	5	1			# Postretirement Benefits		
							Type of Statement		
	12	27	40	14		1	Unqualified		30
		1	1				Reviewed		3
	4	3					Compiled		4
	2	2					Tax Returns		
	8	11	11	7	1	1	Other		8
		102 (4/1-9/30/94)		44 (10/1/94-3/31/95)				4/1/90-3/31/91	4/1/91-3/31/92
	0-500M	500M-2MM	2-10MM	10-50MM	50-100MM	100-250MM		ALL	ALL
	26	44	52	21		2	**NUMBER OF STATEMENTS**		45
	%	%	%	%	%	%	**ASSETS**	%	%
	16.4	19.3	13.7	12.8			Cash & Equivalents		10.6
	34.1	28.1	21.7	10.9			Trade Receivables - (net)		18.8
	.2	2.0	.4	.3			Inventory		.4
	2.6	1.0	1.6	4.8			All Other Current		1.5
	53.4	50.4	37.4	28.7			Total Current		31.3
	38.7	41.2	51.6	53.8			Fixed Assets (net)		56.2
	.5	2.1	1.9	2.5			Intangibles (net)		.9
	7.5	6.3	9.1	15.0			All Other Non-Current		11.7
	100.0	100.0	100.0	100.0			Total		100.0
							LIABILITIES		
	7.6	7.6	4.2	2.3			Notes Payable-Short Term		6.3
	1.9	1.9	3.0	1.4			Cur. Mat. -L/T/D		2.5
	13.7	10.1	7.8	3.6			Trade Payables		5.8
	.5	.1	.2	.0			Income Taxes Payable		.5
	18.4	12.4	11.1	5.5			All Other Current		11.6
	42.2	32.1	26.2	12.8			Total Current		26.6
	11.6	24.0	26.8	32.8			Long Term Debt		30.1
	.0	.0	.0	.0			Deferred Taxes		.1
	3.0	5.9	1.6	7.7			All Other-Non-Current		8.5
	43.2	38.0	45.3	46.7			Net Worth		34.7
	100.0	100.0	100.0	100.0			Total Liabilities & Net Worth		100.0
							INCOME DATA		
	100.0	100.0	100.0	100.0			Net Sales		100.0
							Gross Profit		
	99.2	93.9	96.6	96.1			Operating Expenses		94.7
	.8	6.1	3.4	3.9			Operating Profit		5.3
	–.2	2.3	.5	.5			All Other Expenses (net)		4.2
	1.0	3.8	2.9	3.4			Profit Before Taxes		1.1
							RATIOS		
	2.0	3.0	2.5	4.0					2.0
	1.3	1.5	1.3	2.0			Current		1.3
	.9	1.0	.9	1.5					.8
	1.8	2.7	2.2	3.8					1.9
	1.2	1.4	1.3	1.6			Quick		1.1
	.8	1.0	.9	.9					.8
	9 40.0	5 68.8	30 12.3	27 13.4				16 22.8	
	29 12.7	29 12.6	38 9.5	41 9.0			Sales/Receivables	30 12.1	
	53 6.9	51 7.1	49 7.4	55 6.6				47 7.7	
							Cost of Sales/Inventory		
							Cost of Sales/Payables		
	13.8	5.4	7.5	3.1					13.3
	45.3	13.6	19.2	6.3			Sales/Working Capital		35.6
	–266.7	UND	–107.8	16.6					–26.2
	6.1	6.0	10.0	4.7					4.3
	(12) –.2	(32) 2.5	(44) 3.1	(16) 2.1			EBIT/Interest	(37) 1.4	
	–6.0	1.3	1.5	1.1					.0
			3.7						4.5
			(12) 3.2				Net Profit + Depr., Dep.,	(14) 1.1	
			1.4				Amort./Cur. Mat. L /T/D		–.2
	.3	.3	.7	.6					.8
	.7	1.0	1.3	1.4			Fixed/Worth		1.9
	1.5	3.5	2.2	3.2					7.9
	.4	.6	.6	.4					.8
	1.0	2.0	1.7	1.3			Debt/Worth		2.2
	4.4	4.7	2.8	3.4					9.3
	54.6	25.7	24.5	12.6			% Profit Before Taxes/Tangible		30.5
	(23) 1.6	(39) 8.0	(51) 11.1	(18) 5.6			Net Worth	(40) 3.0	
	–15.2	1.4	3.3	2.8					–13.0
	11.3	10.4	7.9	4.0					9.0
	2.6	3.3	5.1	2.2			% Profit Before Taxes/Total Assets		.9
	–5.9	.5	.9	.4					–4.1
	66.0	40.7	6.9	2.2					5.3
	14.5	7.5	2.8	1.7			Sales/Net Fixed Assets		2.6
	3.9	1.4	1.6	.6					1.4
	6.4	3.8	2.8	1.2					2.9
	4.4	2.1	1.8	.6			Sales/Total Assets		1.4
	2.1	1.0	1.0	.4					.9
	.8	1.0	1.5	3.0					1.8
	(19) 1.6	(35) 3.1	(49) 2.8	(19) 4.0			% Depr., Dep., Amort./Sales	(42) 2.9	
	4.8	4.9	4.2	7.1					4.9
							% Officers', Directors', Owners' Comp/Sales		
	30619M	125440M	434389M	356647M	98839M	179971M	Net Sales ($)		310595M
	5908M	51521M	232203M	460033M	50738M	317253M	Total Assets ($)		368572M

(Comparative Historical Data column 4/1/90-3/31/91 ALL: DATA NOT AVAILABLE)

M = $ thousand   MM = $ million
See Pages 1 through 15 for Explanation of Ratios and Data

Comparative Historical Data				Current Data Sorted By Sales					
	7	7	# Postretirement Benefits	1		2	2	1	1
			Type of Statement						
37	58	94	Unqualified	14	18	17	23	16	6
3	6	2	Reviewed		1	1			
6	12	7	Compiled	3	4				
		4	Tax Returns	4					
26	26	39	Other	7	10	4	8	7	3
4/1/92-3/31/93 ALL	4/1/93-3/31/94 ALL	4/1/94-3/31/95 ALL		102 (4/1-9/30/94)			44 (10/1/94-3/31/95)		
				0-1MM	1-3MM	3-5MM	5-10MM	10-25MM	25MM & OVER
72	102	146	NUMBER OF STATEMENTS	28	33	22	31	23	9
%	%	%	ASSETS	%	%	%	%	%	%
16.3	12.1	15.6	Cash & Equivalents	13.4	21.9	11.7	13.8	15.3	
20.7	22.9	24.1	Trade Receivables - (net)	20.6	21.9	27.0	26.7	27.0	
.3	.2	.8	Inventory	3.1	.2	.4	.3	.1	
2.8	2.7	2.1	All Other Current	2.2	2.1	.8	3.0	2.3	
40.1	37.8	42.7	Total Current	39.2	46.0	39.9	43.7	44.7	
50.2	50.5	46.7	Fixed Assets (net)	53.7	45.2	49.3	43.4	44.8	
1.5	1.2	1.8	Intangibles (net)	.3	1.7	.8	2.8	2.7	
8.2	10.5	8.8	All Other Non-Current	6.8	7.1	9.9	10.0	7.8	
100.0	100.0	100.0	Total	100.0	100.0	100.0	100.0	100.0	
			LIABILITIES						
6.6	6.3	5.6	Notes Payable-Short Term	4.6	6.0	7.8	3.7	6.1	
5.3	2.7	2.2	Cur. Mat.-L /T/D	2.2	2.0	2.5	2.5	1.8	
6.0	6.8	8.8	Trade Payables	9.0	7.0	7.1	11.8	10.4	
.1	.7	.2	Income Taxes Payable	.4	.2	.2	.1	.3	
15.8	12.2	11.9	All Other Current	7.5	16.4	9.6	11.1	14.5	
33.8	28.6	28.7	Total Current	23.6	31.5	27.1	29.2	33.2	
25.0	28.1	24.3	Long Term Debt	27.4	24.3	19.4	21.4	29.7	
.1	.1	.0	Deferred Taxes	.0	.0	.0	.0	.1	
3.9	4.8	4.6	All Other-Non-Current	3.2	3.4	2.6	8.4	4.1	
37.2	38.4	42.4	Net Worth	45.8	40.8	50.9	41.0	33.0	
100.0	100.0	100.0	Total Liabilities & Net Worth	100.0	100.0	100.0	100.0	100.0	
			INCOME DATA						
100.0	100.0	100.0	Net Sales	100.0	100.0	100.0	100.0	100.0	
			Gross Profit						
94.4	91.8	96.2	Operating Expenses	95.7	94.4	96.4	97.6	96.4	
5.6	8.2	3.8	Operating Profit	4.3	5.6	3.6	2.4	3.6	
1.8	3.3	.9	All Other Expenses (net)	2.7	1.0	.4	.5	.5	
3.8	4.9	3.0	Profit Before Taxes	1.6	4.5	3.2	1.9	3.1	
			RATIOS						
2.4	2.3	2.9	Current	4.0	2.9	2.5	3.0	2.4	
1.3	1.3	1.5		1.6	1.5	1.5	1.5	1.3	
.9	.9	1.0		.8	1.0	1.1	1.0	1.0	
2.2	2.1	2.3	Quick	2.5	2.4	2.4	2.6	1.9	
1.2	1.2	1.4		1.6	1.3	1.4	1.4	1.2	
.8	.8	.9		.5	.9	1.0	1.0	1.0	
24 15.3	10 38.0	19 19.5	Sales/Receivables	1 280.7	5 75.4	37 10.0	29 12.8	33 10.9	
32 11.5	36 10.2	36 10.1		20 18.1	26 13.8	46 8.0	38 9.7	40 9.2	
45 8.1	53 6.9	51 7.2		37 9.9	50 7.3	53 6.9	50 7.3	51 7.1	
			Cost of Sales/Inventory						
			Cost of Sales/Payables						
6.7	7.6	6.3	Sales/Working Capital	4.8	6.7	6.2	4.8	7.5	
32.8	26.7	18.9		17.5	20.3	16.4	16.2	21.9	
-36.2	-38.9	UND		-58.8	NM	71.9	-475.9	318.1	
(56) 4.3	(78) 7.0	(107) 6.4	EBIT/Interest	(14) 3.8	(26) 7.3	(17) 4.7	(23) 7.8	(20) 14.3	
2.0	2.7	2.4		1.5	2.6	2.1	2.3	2.8	
1.2	1.4	1.3		.1	1.2	.1	.7	1.6	
(16) 5.9	(16) 6.1	(26) 3.8	Net Profit + Depr., Dep., Amort./Cur. Mat. L/T/D						
3.3	2.0	2.5							
1.6	.7	1.5							
.6	.7	.5	Fixed/Worth	.4	.3	.5	.6	.9	
1.3	1.2	1.1		.9	1.0	1.0	1.2	1.8	
3.7	3.6	2.3		2.4	2.5	2.2	1.9	2.7	
.8	.7	.5	Debt/Worth	.4	.5	.2	.6	1.5	
2.1	1.8	1.8		1.0	2.2	.9	1.7	2.7	
4.6	5.2	3.5		3.8	5.0	2.6	3.2	3.6	
(67) 26.3	(93) 31.1	(134) 24.5	% Profit Before Taxes/Tangible Net Worth	(27) 27.4	(29) 45.3	(20) 12.0	(27) 20.4	(22) 31.6	
13.0	12.3	8.1		6.3	7.4	5.0	7.9	16.6	
3.3	2.4	1.3		-7.0	2.6	-5.5	1.9	4.4	
9.1	9.5	8.9	% Profit Before Taxes/Total Assets	9.8	11.1	4.9	7.6	9.7	
3.9	5.0	3.4		1.9	3.7	2.6	4.0	3.3	
1.1	.5	.5		-2.3	.8	-2.9	.5	1.1	
12.0	13.1	14.9	Sales/Net Fixed Assets	23.6	24.9	8.1	13.2	12.1	
3.0	3.1	3.2		2.1	6.4	2.7	3.7	5.8	
1.7	1.3	1.5		.8	1.2	1.9	1.4	1.7	
3.1	3.0	3.3	Sales/Total Assets	4.5	3.9	2.6	3.9	3.0	
1.7	1.7	1.8		1.3	1.6	1.7	2.0	2.3	
1.1	.7	.9		.7	.8	1.2	.7	1.2	
(65) 1.7	(85) 1.6	(125) 1.5	% Depr., Dep., Amort./Sales	(24) 1.3	(26) .9	(20) 2.0	(25) 1.8	(22) 1.3	
3.0	2.8	3.1		4.8	2.9	3.3	2.6	2.1	
4.7	5.2	4.8		7.3	4.4	4.2	4.6	3.8	
	(10) 3.3	(14) 2.8	% Officers', Directors', Owners' Comp/Sales						
	5.5	5.9							
	7.3	8.2							
422634M	1320600M	1225905M	Net Sales ($)	14324M	63459M	83992M	226987M	364875M	472268M
350436M	742468M	1117656M	Total Assets ($)	16998M	47166M	67619M	208354M	393788M	383731M

© Robert Morris Associates 1995   M = $ thousand   MM = $ million
See Pages 1 through 15 for Explanation of Ratios and Data

Current Data Sorted By Assets   **Comparative Historical Data**

0-500M	500M-2MM	2-10MM	10-50MM	50-100MM	100-250MM	# Postretirement Benefits / Type of Statement	12 / 4/1/90-3/31/91 / ALL	7 / 4/1/91-3/31/92 / ALL
		8	2	2	1	Unqualified	19	19
		4			1	Reviewed	5	7
1						Compiled	8	6
						Tax Returns		
	1					Other	12	7
1	2	3	2	1	2			
13 (4/1-9/30/94)			17 (10/1/94-3/31/95)					
1	3	15	5	3	3	NUMBER OF STATEMENTS	44	39
%	%	%	%	%	%	**ASSETS**	%	%
		7.8				Cash & Equivalents	10.4	10.5
		31.0				Trade Receivables - (net)	24.2	28.9
		.8				Inventory	2.0	4.9
		1.0				All Other Current	1.8	1.2
		40.7				Total Current	38.4	45.5
		50.3				Fixed Assets (net)	48.2	46.4
		2.4				Intangibles (net)	.1	1.0
		6.7				All Other Non-Current	13.3	7.2
		100.0				Total	100.0	100.0
						LIABILITIES		
		5.4				Notes Payable-Short Term	6.8	11.6
		6.7				Cur. Mat. -L/T/D	5.9	6.0
		11.9				Trade Payables	10.4	10.5
		.1				Income Taxes Payable	1.9	1.1
		10.1				All Other Current	9.3	9.6
		34.2				Total Current	34.3	38.9
		19.3				Long Term Debt	26.1	21.3
		.5				Deferred Taxes	2.6	1.4
		3.4				All Other-Non-Current	2.4	2.5
		42.7				Net Worth	34.6	35.9
		100.0				Total Liabilities & Net Worth	100.0	100.0
						INCOME DATA		
		100.0				Net Sales	100.0	100.0
						Gross Profit		
		89.6				Operating Expenses	91.7	90.5
		10.4				Operating Profit	8.3	9.5
		3.0				All Other Expenses (net)	2.3	3.2
		7.4				Profit Before Taxes	6.0	6.3
						RATIOS		
		1.8					1.7	1.8
		1.1				Current	1.4	1.1
		.6					.8	.9
		1.8					1.6	1.5
		1.1				Quick	1.2	1.0
		.6					.6	.7
		38 9.7					26 14.3	34 10.6
		49 7.4				Sales/Receivables	49 7.5	57 6.4
		85 4.3					68 5.4	74 4.9
						Cost of Sales/Inventory		
						Cost of Sales/Payables		
		4.9					8.1	9.0
		72.0				Sales/Working Capital	18.9	58.2
		-8.3					-17.5	-28.2
		25.6					(32) 8.9	(34) 10.4
		(14) 4.5				EBIT/Interest	3.6	4.0
		1.0					1.3	1.6
						Net Profit + Depr., Dep.,	(26) 5.0	(22) 3.3
						Amort./Cur. Mat. L./T/D	1.8	2.1
							.6	1.4
		.5					.6	.9
		1.2				Fixed/Worth	1.3	1.5
		4.1					2.9	2.3
		.5					.8	1.0
		1.0				Debt/Worth	1.9	2.1
		5.6					5.4	4.0
		44.5				% Profit Before Taxes/Tangible	(39) 57.2	(36) 54.5
		(14) 13.7				Net Worth	12.4	28.4
		-4.1					2.8	6.8
		14.4				% Profit Before Taxes/Total	15.7	15.3
		7.3				Assets	5.5	7.8
		-1.0					.6	2.1
		15.4					10.2	9.7
		2.2				Sales/Net Fixed Assets	4.5	3.9
		1.0					1.1	1.4
		3.6					2.5	3.0
		1.3				Sales/Total Assets	1.5	1.5
		.8					.7	.9
		2.3					(39) 2.2	(37) 1.6
		(14) 6.1				% Depr., Dep., Amort./Sales	4.1	3.0
		12.8					8.0	9.4
						% Officers', Directors',	(10) 3.0	
						Owners' Comp/Sales	5.8	
							20.8	
904M	8433M	156173M	169781M	225930M	777059M	Net Sales ($)	1028323M	1299179M
213M	3694M	78722M	153316M	245732M	390738M	Total Assets ($)	932530M	1163462M

M = $ thousand   MM = $ million
See Pages 1 through 15 for Explanation of Ratios and Data

Comparative Historical Data				Current Data Sorted By Sales					
	2	3	# Postretirement Benefits		1		1		1
			Type of Statement						
12	14	13	Unqualified	2		2	1	4	4
8	6	4	Reviewed		1		1	2	
3	3	2	Compiled		2				
			Tax Returns						
			Other	1		2	2	1	4
9	13	11		1	13 (4/1-9/30/94)		17 (10/1/94-3/31/95)		
4/1/92-	4/1/93-	4/1/94-							
3/31/93	3/31/94	3/31/95							
ALL	ALL	ALL		0-1MM	1-3MM	3-5MM	5-10MM	10-25MM	25MM & OVER
32	36	30	NUMBER OF STATEMENTS	3	4	4	4	7	8
%	%	%	ASSETS	%	%	%	%	%	%
8.8	4.9	11.3	Cash & Equivalents						
24.5	25.0	27.1	Trade Receivables - (net)						
4.4	6.3	2.8	Inventory						
1.8	2.2	1.1	All Other Current						
39.4	38.5	42.3	Total Current						
43.4	50.2	48.7	Fixed Assets (net)						
.4	1.0	2.2	Intangibles (net)						
16.8	10.3	6.8	All Other Non-Current						
100.0	100.0	100.0	Total						
			LIABILITIES						
5.8	12.0	4.6	Notes Payable-Short Term						
8.0	6.2	5.2	Cur. Mat.-L /T/D						
13.4	9.7	13.6	Trade Payables						
.5	.5	.3	Income Taxes Payable						
10.3	9.3	8.9	All Other Current						
38.0	37.7	32.6	Total Current						
14.0	25.7	17.7	Long Term Debt						
1.5	1.2	1.7	Deferred Taxes						
4.3	3.4	3.3	All Other-Non-Current						
42.3	31.9	44.6	Net Worth						
100.0	100.0	100.0	Total Liabilities & Net Worth						
			INCOME DATA						
100.0	100.0	100.0	Net Sales						
			Gross Profit						
91.7	92.7	90.2	Operating Expenses						
8.3	7.3	9.8	Operating Profit						
1.3	2.4	2.0	All Other Expenses (net)						
7.1	4.9	7.8	Profit Before Taxes						
			RATIOS						
1.5	1.7	1.9							
1.1	1.1	1.4	Current						
.6	.7	.7							
1.4	1.4	1.8							
.9	.9	1.2	Quick						
.4	.5	.7							
20 18.1	37 10.0	40 9.2							
47 7.7	51 7.2	53 6.9	Sales/Receivables						
56 6.5	74 4.9	78 4.7							
			Cost of Sales/Inventory						
			Cost of Sales/Payables						
17.1	9.3	6.4							
392.4	58.9	17.2	Sales/Working Capital						
−7.4	−14.2	−18.5							
5.6	8.3	23.2							
(29) 4.0	(35) 2.1	(27) 4.5	EBIT/Interest						
1.5	1.0	1.7							
4.5	1.8	5.0	Net Profit + Depr., Dep.,						
(12) 1.7	(12) 1.6	(13) 1.7	Amort./Cur. Mat. L/T/D						
.4	.6	.6							
.3	.7	.6							
1.1	1.4	1.2	Fixed/Worth						
2.0	3.7	1.8							
.7	.9	.6							
1.4	2.3	1.2	Debt/Worth						
3.6	6.1	4.3							
36.8	29.1	34.8	% Profit Before Taxes/Tangible						
23.3	(33) 19.7	(29) 16.7	Net Worth						
5.7	.5	2.3							
14.2	10.6	13.9	% Profit Before Taxes/Total						
5.3	5.2	7.4	Assets						
2.4	.1	.7							
30.4	15.8	14.8							
4.0	2.6	2.7	Sales/Net Fixed Assets						
1.8	1.0	1.1							
3.3	3.1	2.6							
1.9	1.5	1.6	Sales/Total Assets						
.8	.7	.8							
2.0	2.8	2.7							
(25) 3.9	(28) 4.5	(26) 6.3	% Depr., Dep., Amort./Sales						
11.4	9.3	12.7							
	2.3		% Officers', Directors',						
	(10) 4.3		Owners' Comp/Sales						
	9.3								
539069M	1745392M	1338280M	Net Sales ($)	2367M	8367M	18171M	31726M	112523M	1165126M
829544M	1428127M	872415M	Total Assets ($)	9760M	16314M	13328M	26788M	159462M	646763M

M = $ thousand   MM = $ million
See Pages 1 through 15 for Explanation of Ratios and Data

SERVICES—CHIROPRACTORS. SIC# 8041

								4/1/90-3/31/91 ALL	4/1/91-3/31/92 ALL
3	1					# Postretirement Benefits			
						Type of Statement			
						Unqualified			1
1						Reviewed			
21	4					Compiled			18
6	1					Tax Returns			2
6	1					Other			9
	7 (4/1-9/30/94)			33 (10/1/94-3/31/95)					
0-500M	500M-2MM	2-10MM	10-50MM	50-100MM	100-250MM				
34	6					**NUMBER OF STATEMENTS**			30
%	%	%	%	%	%	**ASSETS**	%	%
10.5						Cash & Equivalents		11.3
26.2						Trade Receivables - (net)	D	14.9
.9						Inventory	A	.4
1.7						All Other Current	T	3.5
39.3						Total Current	A	30.2
46.9						Fixed Assets (net)		56.0
6.7						Intangibles (net)	N	5.3
7.1						All Other Non-Current	O	8.6
100.0						Total	T	100.0
						LIABILITIES	A	
10.9						Notes Payable-Short Term	V	5.4
3.7						Cur. Mat. -L/T/D	A	5.7
.7						Trade Payables	I	.5
.8						Income Taxes Payable	L	.1
9.6						All Other Current	A	10.7
25.7						Total Current	B	22.4
27.2						Long Term Debt	L	41.7
.8						Deferred Taxes	E	.5
3.3						All Other-Non-Current		1.2
43.1						Net Worth		34.2
100.0						Total Liabilities & Net Worth		100.0
						INCOME DATA		
100.0						Net Sales		100.0
						Gross Profit		
90.4						Operating Expenses		79.6
9.6						Operating Profit		20.4
.9						All Other Expenses (net)		1.8
8.7						Profit Before Taxes		18.6
						RATIOS		
5.0								5.8
1.9						Current		1.1
.6								.2
4.6								5.6
1.8						Quick		.8
.6								.1
0 UND							0 UND	
0 UND						Sales/Receivables	0 UND	
126 2.9							76 4.8	
						Cost of Sales/Inventory		
						Cost of Sales/Payables		
4.4								6.8
32.9						Sales/Working Capital		UND
−39.5								−21.7
10.5								14.8
(26) 2.4						EBIT/Interest	(26)	6.3
1.2								1.0
						Net Profit + Depr., Dep., Amort./Cur. Mat. L /T/D		
.4								.5
1.7						Fixed/Worth		2.0
3.7								22.0
.5								1.1
2.0						Debt/Worth		2.2
6.3								27.2
81.8								227.9
(27) 30.8						% Profit Before Taxes/Tangible Net Worth	(25)	110.0
2.6								2.7
30.3								73.6
9.2						% Profit Before Taxes/Total Assets		30.5
.7								−.2
13.4								13.0
8.9						Sales/Net Fixed Assets		5.0
4.4								3.2
5.5								4.7
2.1						Sales/Total Assets		3.1
1.3								1.5
2.1								2.8
(30) 3.9						% Depr., Dep., Amort./Sales	(23)	4.5
5.4								6.9
15.5								14.4
(21) 29.3						% Officers', Directors', Owners' Comp/Sales	(23)	24.0
40.4								28.8
16123M	10436M					Net Sales ($)		25094M
6318M	4874M					Total Assets ($)		9866M

© Robert Morris Associates 1995

M = $ thousand   MM = $ million
See Pages 1 through 15 for Explanation of Ratios and Data

Comparative Historical Data							Current Data Sorted By Sales					
	2		1		4	# Postretirement Benefits	3		1			
						Type of Statement						
	2		1			Unqualified						
	2				1	Reviewed	1					
	13		22		25	Compiled	23	1		1		
	1		8		7	Tax Returns	5	2				
	5		9		7	Other	6	1				
	4/1/92-3/31/93 ALL		4/1/93-3/31/94 ALL		4/1/94-3/31/95 ALL			7 (4/1-9/30/94)		33 (10/1/94-3/31/95)		
							0-1MM	1-3MM	3-5MM	5-10MM	10-25MM	25MM & OVER
	23		40		40	NUMBER OF STATEMENTS	35	4		1		
	%		%		%	ASSETS	%	%	%	%	%	%
	13.3		18.7		9.9	Cash & Equivalents	9.4					
	23.0		19.5		28.4	Trade Receivables - (net)	31.8					
	.1		.5		.8	Inventory	.9					
	2.0		.2		1.7	All Other Current	1.5					
	38.5		38.8		40.8	Total Current	43.7					
	53.9		49.4		44.4	Fixed Assets (net)	45.2					
	2.6		3.5		5.7	Intangibles (net)	6.4					
	5.0		8.3		9.1	All Other Non-Current	4.7					
	100.0		100.0		100.0	Total	100.0					
						LIABILITIES						
	9.1		9.6		12.1	Notes Payable-Short Term	10.3					
	8.7		5.8		3.6	Cur. Mat.-L./T/D	3.8					
	.2		1.4		.7	Trade Payables	.7					
	.8		.2		.8	Income Taxes Payable	.7					
	10.2		11.0		9.8	All Other Current	10.1					
	29.1		28.0		26.9	Total Current	25.7					
	31.3		27.4		25.8	Long Term Debt	27.2					
	.0		.1		.7	Deferred Taxes	.8					
	5.5		2.0		4.6	All Other-Non-Current	5.0					
	34.2		42.5		42.0	Net Worth	41.3					
	100.0		100.0		100.0	Total Liabilities & Net Worth	100.0					
						INCOME DATA						
	100.0		100.0		100.0	Net Sales	100.0					
						Gross Profit						
	83.5		81.3		89.3	Operating Expenses	88.5					
	16.5		18.7		10.7	Operating Profit	11.5					
	1.2		1.2		.8	All Other Expenses (net)	1.0					
	15.3		17.5		10.0	Profit Before Taxes	10.5					
						RATIOS						
	3.5		7.0		5.3		5.5					
	1.2		1.6		1.9	Current	2.0					
	.5		.4		.6		.7					
	3.3		7.0		4.7		4.8					
	1.2		1.6		1.8	Quick	2.0					
	.4		.4		.5		.7					
0	UND	0	UND	0	UND		0	UND				
0	UND	0	UND	3	106.2	Sales/Receivables	63	5.8				
87	4.2	79	4.6	146	2.5		146	2.5				
						Cost of Sales/Inventory						
						Cost of Sales/Payables						
	3.9		4.8		3.9		3.5					
	113.8		64.1		32.9	Sales/Working Capital	13.7					
	-21.2		-30.4		-38.9		-86.8					
(21)	9.8	(34)	14.8	(31)	11.9		(26)	10.5				
	6.7		5.5		2.4	EBIT/Interest		3.5				
	2.9		1.5		1.2			1.2				
						Net Profit + Depr., Dep., Amort./Cur. Mat. L/T/D						
	.5		.4		.3		.3					
	2.5		1.6		1.5	Fixed/Worth	1.5					
	4.6		9.4		3.7		4.2					
	.9		.3		.5		.6					
	2.5		2.1		2.0	Debt/Worth	2.1					
	6.1		19.0		8.1		9.1					
(20)	158.9	(34)	203.8	(33)	83.6	% Profit Before Taxes/Tangible	(28)	83.3				
	55.0		53.6		31.9	Net Worth		32.9				
	26.3		7.1		4.4			4.0				
	41.4		60.9		31.6	% Profit Before Taxes/Total	31.2					
	18.0		19.9		9.9	Assets	10.5					
	10.4		1.8		1.0		1.0					
	18.5		18.2		13.7		13.1					
	6.7		6.9		8.9	Sales/Net Fixed Assets	8.8					
	2.0		2.5		4.8		3.2					
	5.2		7.8		5.3		4.8					
	1.8		2.2		1.9	Sales/Total Assets	1.7					
	1.2		1.3		1.3		1.2					
(20)	1.4	(33)	2.1	(36)	2.1	% Depr., Dep., Amort./Sales	(32)	2.2				
	3.1		3.7		3.7			3.9				
	5.7		5.6		5.3			5.3				
(13)	19.5	(24)	14.3	(25)	15.5	% Officers', Directors',	(22)	14.5				
	27.4		22.4		27.2	Owners' Comp/Sales		27.2				
	38.1		33.6		40.4			39.6				
	13468M		29891M		26559M	Net Sales ($)	15647M	5227M		5685M		
	6776M		15647M		11192M	Total Assets ($)	8913M	1132M		1147M		

M = $ thousand   MM = $ million
See Pages 1 through 15 for Explanation of Ratios and Data

Current Data Sorted By Assets   **Comparative Historical Data**

						# Postretirement Benefits / Type of Statement		
3	6	3	1					
5	14		6		1	Unqualified	25	29
16	29	14				Reviewed	51	46
41	26	1				Compiled	52	64
14	5	1				Tax Returns	2	1
24	27	20	2			Other	31	57

	71 (4/1-9/30/94)		175 (10/1/94-3/31/95)				4/1/90-3/31/91 ALL	4/1/91-3/31/92 ALL
0-500M	500M-2MM	2-10MM	10-50MM	50-100MM	100-250MM			
95	92	50	8	1		**NUMBER OF STATEMENTS**	161	197
%	%	%	%	%	%	**ASSETS**	%	%
10.4	8.1	8.6				Cash & Equivalents	10.7	9.5
34.7	46.3	48.1				Trade Receivables - (net)	40.8	42.3
2.4	4.6	3.8				Inventory	4.8	4.2
1.5	1.7	3.3				All Other Current	4.3	3.7
49.0	60.7	63.7				Total Current	60.5	59.8
36.2	25.2	21.1				Fixed Assets (net)	24.9	26.2
5.0	4.7	3.9				Intangibles (net)	5.1	4.8
9.8	9.4	11.3				All Other Non-Current	9.5	9.2
100.0	100.0	100.0				Total	100.0	100.0
						LIABILITIES		
12.6	10.4	11.6				Notes Payable-Short Term	11.5	10.3
6.8	4.4	3.2				Cur. Mat. -L/T/D	5.7	5.6
10.1	12.1	11.5				Trade Payables	9.6	10.6
1.3	.8	.8				Income Taxes Payable	1.8	1.1
13.5	15.7	16.5				All Other Current	12.8	16.9
44.2	43.4	43.6				Total Current	41.4	44.4
19.6	13.1	11.7				Long Term Debt	18.4	16.2
.2	1.2	.5				Deferred Taxes	.9	.7
3.1	3.6	2.3				All Other-Non-Current	2.4	3.0
32.9	38.7	42.0				Net Worth	36.9	35.7
100.0	100.0	100.0				Total Liabilities & Net Worth	100.0	100.0
						INCOME DATA		
100.0	100.0	100.0				Net Sales	100.0	100.0
						Gross Profit		
95.5	95.8	95.7				Operating Expenses	95.1	96.0
4.5	4.2	4.3				Operating Profit	4.9	4.0
1.4	.8	1.1				All Other Expenses (net)	1.5	1.1
3.2	3.4	3.3				Profit Before Taxes	3.3	2.9
						RATIOS		
1.8	1.9	2.1					2.2	2.3
1.2	1.4	1.4				Current	1.5	1.3
.8	1.1	1.1					1.0	.9
1.7	1.8	2.0					1.9	2.0
1.1	1.3	1.3				Quick	1.3	1.2
.7	.8	1.0					.8	.8
12 30.8	31 11.8	31 11.7					26 14.2	27 13.6
27 13.4	43 8.4	43 8.4				Sales/Receivables	35 10.4	36 10.2
41 8.9	59 6.2	58 6.3					47 7.7	51 7.1
						Cost of Sales/Inventory		
						Cost of Sales/Payables		
20.2	12.0	10.1					10.7	11.4
56.9	23.7	25.7				Sales/Working Capital	19.2	25.7
-44.7	134.0	62.4					217.6	-132.8
8.1	11.9	14.6					7.5	9.5
(80) 3.9	(85) 4.2	(45) 4.8				EBIT/Interest	(149) 3.5	(175) 3.2
1.3	1.5	2.6					1.5	1.1
4.0	7.8	8.6				Net Profit + Depr., Dep.,	6.6	5.7
(24) 2.8	(48) 3.0	(22) 4.0				Amort./Cur. Mat. L /T/D	(88) 3.0	(75) 2.5
.8	1.1	1.7					1.4	.8
.6	.3	.3					.3	.3
1.2	.6	.5				Fixed/Worth	.7	.7
3.5	1.5	1.1					2.2	2.2
1.0	.9	.9					.8	.8
1.8	1.8	1.9				Debt/Worth	1.9	1.9
8.4	4.0	2.7					5.7	6.2
78.6	49.2	40.3				% Profit Before Taxes/Tangible	56.8	64.7
(81) 31.8	(87) 29.2	(46) 22.2				Net Worth	(137) 24.7	(172) 24.7
5.5	6.1	11.2					7.0	2.7
23.1	18.0	14.1				% Profit Before Taxes/Total	20.0	19.2
11.4	7.6	8.4				Assets	9.5	8.3
1.3	2.6	3.7					2.2	.2
27.9	42.4	39.8					36.7	34.3
17.0	19.7	26.7				Sales/Net Fixed Assets	23.0	20.8
8.0	9.8	14.3					9.6	10.3
6.5	5.4	5.2					5.3	5.6
4.9	4.0	4.1				Sales/Total Assets	4.0	4.1
3.3	2.7	2.9					2.6	2.9
1.1	.8	.6					.9	1.0
(80) 1.8	(86) 1.5	(44) 1.0				% Depr., Dep., Amort./Sales	(138) 1.7	(176) 1.7
4.1	2.3	1.7					3.1	2.8
5.4	3.0	2.0				% Officers', Directors',	4.1	3.5
(50) 7.8	(51) 5.3	(19) 3.1				Owners' Comp/Sales	(79) 6.3	(92) 6.2
11.5	7.5	4.8					12.5	10.8
120608M	363977M	933126M	418703M	136414M		Net Sales ($)	1402351M	2297474M
22609M	92503M	226249M	103902M	75815M		Total Assets ($)	411619M	881932M

M = $ thousand   MM = $ million
See Pages 1 through 15 for Explanation of Ratios and Data

Comparative Historical Data				Current Data Sorted By Sales					
	5	13	# Postretirement Benefits	2	3	2	2	3	1
			Type of Statement						
29	29	26	Unqualified	1		2	5	8	10
40	44	59	Reviewed	5	15	12	14	12	1
69	56	68	Compiled	20	27	13	7	1	
4	8	20	Tax Returns	11	5	2	2		
48	58	73	Other	12	28	7	10	9	7
4/1/92- 3/31/93 ALL	4/1/93- 3/31/94 ALL	4/1/94- 3/31/95 ALL		71 (4/1-9/30/94)			175 (10/1/94-3/31/95)		
				0-1MM	1-3MM	3-5MM	5-10MM	10-25MM	25MM & OVER
190	195	246	NUMBER OF STATEMENTS	49	75	36	38	30	18
%	%	%	ASSETS	%	%	%	%	%	%
8.7	9.3	9.1	Cash & Equivalents	9.8	8.7	8.1	11.9	7.1	7.9
39.6	41.0	41.7	Trade Receivables - (net)	27.2	39.6	49.5	48.2	49.6	47.0
4.0	4.5	3.6	Inventory	2.6	4.7	3.1	2.8	4.8	3.0
3.1	3.5	2.1	All Other Current	2.1	1.2	1.8	2.5	3.8	2.7
55.4	58.3	56.5	Total Current	41.8	54.1	62.5	65.5	65.3	60.6
28.4	25.9	28.2	Fixed Assets (net)	40.2	33.5	22.6	21.1	18.5	16.4
4.9	4.9	4.9	Intangibles (net)	7.6	4.6	1.2	4.0	4.6	8.6
11.3	10.9	10.4	All Other Non-Current	10.4	7.8	13.7	9.5	11.6	14.4
100.0	100.0	100.0	Total	100.0	100.0	100.0	100.0	100.0	100.0
			LIABILITIES						
13.5	12.6	11.3	Notes Payable-Short Term	12.0	11.6	10.2	10.6	11.4	11.3
5.8	5.1	5.1	Cur. Mat.-L /T/D	6.5	6.2	4.0	3.6	4.5	2.8
9.9	11.0	11.2	Trade Payables	8.3	10.9	15.0	11.8	12.3	9.1
.7	1.3	1.0	Income Taxes Payable	1.9	.6	.5	1.2	1.2	.5
14.8	15.6	15.1	All Other Current	9.4	14.6	18.1	15.9	16.6	22.3
44.8	45.6	43.6	Total Current	38.1	43.8	47.8	43.1	45.9	46.1
14.2	13.3	15.1	Long Term Debt	27.9	16.1	8.6	9.3	9.8	10.7
.9	.5	.7	Deferred Taxes	.0	.3	.8	2.0	.5	1.1
2.8	1.9	3.3	All Other-Non-Current	4.9	2.2	2.0	5.1	1.8	4.9
37.3	38.7	37.3	Net Worth	29.0	37.6	40.9	40.5	42.1	37.1
100.0	100.0	100.0	Total Liabilities & Net Worth	100.0	100.0	100.0	100.0	100.0	100.0
			INCOME DATA						
100.0	100.0	100.0	Net Sales	100.0	100.0	100.0	100.0	100.0	100.0
			Gross Profit						
96.8	96.7	95.6	Operating Expenses	93.8	94.7	97.0	97.0	96.2	97.0
3.2	3.3	4.4	Operating Profit	6.2	5.3	3.0	3.0	3.8	3.0
.9	.5	1.0	All Other Expenses (net)	2.5	1.3	.3	.3	.1	.4
2.4	2.8	3.4	Profit Before Taxes	3.7	4.0	2.6	2.7	3.7	2.6
			RATIOS						
2.0	2.2	1.9		2.0	1.9	1.9	2.0	2.1	1.7
1.3	1.4	1.3	Current	1.3	1.3	1.3	1.5	1.5	1.3
.9	1.0	1.0		.7	.9	1.0	1.1	1.1	1.0
1.8	1.8	1.7		1.7	1.7	1.8	1.9	1.7	1.4
1.1	1.2	1.2	Quick	1.1	1.1	1.3	1.4	1.2	1.2
.7	.8	.8		.6	.7	.8	1.0	.9	.8
23 16.0	26 13.9	23 15.6		5 80.6	23 15.6	27 13.6	29 12.8	30 12.3	23 15.8
32 11.4	35 10.4	36 10.2	Sales/Receivables	27 13.5	37 9.9	41 8.8	39 9.4	43 8.4	35 10.4
47 7.8	49 7.4	50 7.3		43 8.4	51 7.2	63 5.8	50 7.3	57 6.4	47 7.8
			Cost of Sales/Inventory						
			Cost of Sales/Payables						
13.4	11.4	15.5		18.2	16.0	12.3	16.4	10.9	22.7
37.7	24.8	29.1	Sales/Working Capital	31.3	46.3	20.1	27.6	20.9	33.5
-47.5	-396.8	-626.1		-43.4	-57.4	NM	90.6	214.0	-922.0
8.2	9.1	11.8		4.1	11.7	13.1	21.9	14.6	14.3
(172) 3.3	(174) 3.8	(218) 4.3	EBIT/Interest	(41) 1.6	(63) 5.6	(34) 3.7	(37) 6.0	(27) 5.3	(16) 4.8
1.3	2.0	1.8		-.3	2.9	.4	2.6	2.6	3.0
5.2	4.8	6.5			7.4	12.3	6.4	5.8	
(80) 2.2	(71) 2.2	(100) 3.1	Net Profit + Depr., Dep., Amort./Cur. Mat. L/T/D		(30) 3.1	(17) 3.0	(19) 3.7	(17) 3.4	
.7	.9	1.3			1.6	.8	1.7	1.6	
.3	.3	.4		.8	.5	.2	.4	.3	.2
.8	.7	.8	Fixed/Worth	1.8	.9	.5	.5	.5	.6
2.1	1.5	2.0		NM	2.6	1.0	1.1	1.1	NM
.8	.7	.9		1.1	.9	.9	.9	.7	1.3
1.7	1.7	1.8	Debt/Worth	2.7	1.8	1.7	1.6	1.9	1.9
5.2	4.5	4.2		NM	4.4	2.6	2.8	2.5	NM
53.1	54.2	55.9		100.0	69.9	40.2	55.3	38.6	52.8
(169) 21.2	(171) 20.5	(221) 30.1	% Profit Before Taxes/Tangible Net Worth	(37) 20.0	(71) 42.4	(35) 21.2	(36) 21.4	(28) 28.2	(14) 35.1
5.8	7.0	7.6		-7.3	12.0	1.1	7.5	12.0	19.9
14.3	18.1	18.6		22.3	20.7	17.3	18.9	14.7	15.0
7.6	7.5	9.2	% Profit Before Taxes/Total Assets	4.0	12.8	7.0	6.8	8.7	12.3
2.2	2.4	2.5		-4.1	5.2	-1.2	3.3	4.8	6.6
39.9	43.8	36.3		22.6	31.7	41.2	59.1	42.3	58.5
21.6	20.7	19.8	Sales/Net Fixed Assets	11.5	15.5	22.1	28.2	26.7	29.9
10.2	10.7	9.8		4.3	8.4	11.6	14.8	13.8	22.1
5.8	5.4	5.7		5.8	5.7	5.5	6.5	5.3	6.1
4.5	4.1	4.3	Sales/Total Assets	3.4	4.3	4.0	4.2	4.1	4.9
3.0	2.9	2.9		2.0	2.8	2.9	3.4	3.1	4.2
.8	.7	.8		1.4	1.1	.6	.7	.6	.5
(169) 1.6	(168) 1.4	(219) 1.5	% Depr., Dep., Amort./Sales	(39) 3.7	(68) 1.5	(34) 1.4	(36) 1.2	(26) .9	(16) 1.3
2.7	2.9	2.8		5.6	3.6	1.9	1.8	1.9	1.9
3.9	3.2	3.3		6.2	4.2	3.3	2.0	1.6	
(97) 6.6	(109) 6.4	(121) 6.0	% Officers', Directors', Owners' Comp/Sales	(23) 9.9	(43) 6.9	(20) 4.7	(19) 3.5	(13) 2.6	
10.1	10.7	8.7		15.6	9.9	7.4	6.6	5.1	
2050640M 668748M	1521661M 483495M	1972828M 521078M	Net Sales ($) Total Assets ($)	26275M 10724M	135644M 41703M	138266M 39726M	252283M 59136M	484872M 136466M	935488M 233323M

M = $ thousand   MM = $ million
See Pages 1 through 15 for Explanation of Ratios and Data

Current Data Sorted By Assets   Comparative Historical Data

	1	6	13				# Postretirement Benefits		
							Type of Statement		
	3	31	128	17	3	2	Unqualified	126	153
	5	21	31	1			Reviewed	38	48
	21	46	25	3			Compiled	70	108
	5	6	2				Tax Returns	5	3
	21	43	81	14	1	2	Other	81	96
		159 (4/1-9/30/94)		353 (10/1/94-3/31/95)					
	0-500M	500M-2MM	2-10MM	10-50MM	50-100MM	100-250MM		4/1/90-3/31/91 ALL	4/1/91-3/31/92 ALL
	55	147	267	35	4	4	**NUMBER OF STATEMENTS**	320	408
	%	%	%	%	%	%	**ASSETS**	%	%
	11.6	8.2	5.8	7.2			Cash & Equivalents	7.1	6.4
	7.6	8.1	7.2	8.8			Trade Receivables - (net)	8.3	7.1
	3.0	2.2	1.5	1.0			Inventory	2.5	2.0
	.6	.8	1.0	1.5			All Other Current	1.4	1.0
	22.7	19.3	15.5	18.6			Total Current	19.4	16.4
	67.7	75.6	79.6	75.1			Fixed Assets (net)	74.6	77.9
	1.1	.7	.6	.7			Intangibles (net)	.3	.7
	8.5	4.4	4.2	5.6			All Other Non-Current	5.6	5.0
	100.0	100.0	100.0	100.0			Total	100.0	100.0
							LIABILITIES		
	3.2	4.0	1.8	1.4			Notes Payable-Short Term	4.4	4.1
	4.6	4.4	2.6	3.0			Cur. Mat. -L/T/D	3.0	3.6
	4.3	3.6	3.5	3.3			Trade Payables	4.3	3.8
	.0	.2	.1	.1			Income Taxes Payable	.2	.2
	13.1	6.7	6.9	8.5			All Other Current	7.8	6.4
	25.3	19.0	14.8	16.4			Total Current	19.8	18.0
	36.6	30.7	28.9	19.8			Long Term Debt	25.9	30.9
	.2	.3	.1	1.1			Deferred Taxes	.2	.3
	4.8	4.5	4.4	3.9			All Other-Non-Current	4.2	3.6
	33.1	45.5	51.8	58.8			Net Worth	49.9	47.2
	100.0	100.0	100.0	100.0			Total Liabilities & Net Worth	100.0	100.0
							INCOME DATA		
	100.0	100.0	100.0	100.0			Net Sales	100.0	100.0
							Gross Profit		
	92.5	94.5	96.8	98.1			Operating Expenses	94.9	95.3
	7.5	5.5	3.2	1.9			Operating Profit	5.1	4.7
	2.6	2.5	2.3	2.2			All Other Expenses (net)	3.6	4.0
	4.9	3.0	.9	-.2			Profit Before Taxes	1.6	.7
							RATIOS		
	2.0	2.0	1.7	2.3				1.8	1.7
	1.0	1.2	1.1	1.2			Current	1.0	1.1
	.6	.6	.8	.7				.6	.6
	1.5	1.6	1.5	2.1				1.4	1.5
	.8	.9	1.0	1.0			Quick	.8 (407)	.8
	.3	.4	.6	.6				.5	.4
0	UND	3 134.8	23 16.2	17 21.3				15 24.9	13 28.5
5	79.2	21 17.0	35 10.4	39 9.3			Sales/Receivables	33 11.1	31 11.7
20	18.0	40 9.1	47 7.7	69 5.3				49 7.4	47 7.7
							Cost of Sales/Inventory		
							Cost of Sales/Payables		
	11.9	10.4	9.6	7.0				10.2	12.0
	179.0	38.4	41.7	25.4			Sales/Working Capital	194.2	129.7
	-13.2	-14.8	-17.4	-14.8				-9.8	-9.4
	(45) 6.6	(128) 4.8	(212) 2.8	(29) 1.7				(253) 3.3	(338) 2.7
	2.6	1.9	1.3	.1			EBIT/Interest	1.3	1.4
	.8	.6	.2	-3.4				.3	.5
		(42) 4.2	(56) 4.9					(132) 5.9	(134) 4.2
		2.1	1.7				Net Profit + Depr., Dep.,	2.6	2.0
		1.1	.7				Amort./Cur. Mat. L /T/D	1.3	.9
	1.0	1.1	1.1	1.0				1.0	1.1
	2.2	1.5	1.5	1.3			Fixed/Worth	1.5	1.6
	7.7	2.8	2.4	1.7				2.4	3.0
	.9	.6	.4	.2				.4	.4
	2.6	1.0	.8	.5			Debt/Worth	.9	1.0
	12.2	3.0	2.2	1.0				2.1	2.6
	(50) 48.1	(137) 18.2	(257) 6.6	(33) 3.0			% Profit Before Taxes/Tangible	(304) 9.4	(382) 11.0
	7.2	4.4	.8	-2.7			Net Worth	2.2	2.8
	-10.3	-2.1	-4.3	-5.3				-4.6	-4.4
	14.7	7.6	3.4	1.8			% Profit Before Taxes/Total	5.0	5.0
	2.7	2.2	.3	-1.2			Assets	.7	1.4
	-2.5	-1.1	-2.1	-3.5				-2.4	-2.2
	6.2	1.7	1.1	1.0				1.5	1.4
	1.7	1.2	.8	.6			Sales/Net Fixed Assets	.9	.9
	1.1	.7	.6	.4				.6	.6
	2.5	1.3	.8	.7				1.1	1.0
	1.3	.9	.6	.5			Sales/Total Assets	.8	.7
	1.0	.6	.5	.3				.5	.5
	(48) 4.1	(135) 6.0	(237) 7.5	(29) 8.0			% Depr., Dep., Amort./Sales	(294) 6.3	(363) 6.9
	6.7	8.1	9.3	10.3				9.1	8.9
	9.3	10.7	11.7	13.0				11.5	11.9
	(13) 5.1	(20) 3.4	(32) 2.9				% Officers', Directors',	(48) 4.1	(75) 4.8
	12.1	5.4	5.5				Owners' Comp/Sales	9.9	8.9
	24.1	20.7	11.2					24.8	23.5
	28078M	170697M	761842M	295889M	177817M	174692M	Net Sales ($)	743183M	1052193M
	17649M	172501M	1215040M	529253M	329056M	594255M	Total Assets ($)	1034378M	1721925M

M = $ thousand   MM = $ million
See Pages 1 through 15 for Explanation of Ratios and Data

Comparative Historical Data | | | | **Current Data Sorted By Sales** | | | | | |

1	11	20		4	11	5			
			# Postretirement Benefits						
			Type of Statement						
138	164	184	Unqualified	16	87	52	19	6	4
53	61	58	Reviewed	14	33	10	1		
92	99	95	Compiled	48	38	8		1	
6	9	13	Tax Returns	10	3				
108	148	162	Other	44	76	26	11	2	3
4/1/92-3/31/93 ALL	4/1/93-3/31/94 ALL	4/1/94-3/31/95 ALL		159 (4/1-9/30/94)		353 (10/1/94-3/31/95)			
				0-1MM	1-3MM	3-5MM	5-10MM	10-25MM	25MM & OVER
397	481	512	**NUMBER OF STATEMENTS**	132	237	96	31	9	7
%	%	%	**ASSETS**	%	%	%	%	%	%
6.8	7.5	7.2	Cash & Equivalents	8.9	6.5	6.5	8.4		
7.0	6.8	7.6	Trade Receivables - (net)	4.7	8.2	8.9	7.7		
1.9	2.6	1.8	Inventory	1.9	1.8	1.8	1.9		
.7	.8	.9	All Other Current	.7	1.1	.9	.9		
16.4	17.7	17.5	Total Current	16.1	17.5	18.0	19.0		
78.3	76.8	76.6	Fixed Assets (net)	77.8	77.4	77.1	72.0		
.7	.9	.9	Intangibles (net)	.6	.7	.7	1.1		
4.6	4.6	5.0	All Other Non-Current	5.5	4.4	4.2	7.9		
100.0	100.0	100.0	Total	100.0	100.0	100.0	100.0		
			LIABILITIES						
3.2	2.7	2.5	Notes Payable-Short Term	3.4	2.1	2.4	2.7		
4.1	3.0	3.4	Cur. Mat.-L /T/D	5.0	3.1	2.0	3.5		
3.4	3.7	3.6	Trade Payables	2.5	3.7	3.8	6.1		
.2	.3	.1	Income Taxes Payable	.0	.2	.1	.1		
6.2	7.5	7.6	All Other Current	7.8	7.2	7.1	11.5		
17.2	17.1	17.2	Total Current	18.8	16.3	15.4	23.8		
28.4	29.0	29.8	Long Term Debt	36.1	30.7	22.5	18.8		
.3	.2	.3	Deferred Taxes	.1	.2	.1	.2		
3.6	4.5	4.5	All Other-Non-Current	3.9	4.4	6.0	1.4		
50.5	49.1	48.2	Net Worth	41.1	48.3	56.0	55.8		
100.0	100.0	100.0	Total Liabilities & Net Worth	100.0	100.0	100.0	100.0		
			INCOME DATA						
100.0	100.0	100.0	Net Sales	100.0	100.0	100.0	100.0		
			Gross Profit						
95.8	96.4	95.7	Operating Expenses	91.9	96.1	100.2	97.4		
4.2	3.6	4.3	Operating Profit	8.1	3.9	-.2	2.6		
2.8	2.4	2.4	All Other Expenses (net)	4.3	2.3	.6	.6		
1.5	1.2	1.8	Profit Before Taxes	3.7	1.6	-.9	2.0		
			RATIOS						
1.9 / 1.1 / .6	1.8 / 1.1 / .7	1.8 / 1.1 / .7	Current	2.0 / 1.1 / .6	1.7 / 1.1 / .7	1.8 / 1.2 / .8	2.0 / 1.3 / .6		
1.6 / .9 / .5	1.6 / .9 / .5	1.5 / .9 / .5	Quick	1.6 / .9 / .3	1.5 / 1.0 / .6	1.6 / 1.0 / .7	1.7 / 1.1 / .5		
13 29.1 / 30 12.0 / 45 8.1	10 36.0 / 28 13.0 / 43 8.5	12 29.6 / 30 12.3 / 45 8.1	Sales/Receivables	0 UND / 6 63.0 / 34 10.6	18 19.9 / 32 11.3 / 46 7.9	27 13.3 / 35 10.4 / 46 8.0	19 18.8 / 38 9.6 / 49 7.4		
			Cost of Sales/Inventory						
			Cost of Sales/Payables						
10.2 / 57.9 / -12.2	9.1 / 75.8 / -11.6	9.8 / 46.8 / -15.3	Sales/Working Capital	10.4 / 76.2 / -11.0	9.8 / 41.1 / -18.0	10.4 / 38.5 / -19.3	7.6 / 21.4 / -8.5		
(318) 2.9 / 1.5 / .4	(396) 3.0 / 1.2 / .2	(419) 3.4 / 1.5 / .2	EBIT/Interest	(108) 4.8 / 1.8 / .7	(202) 3.4 / 1.4 / .1	(75) 2.5 / 1.0 / -.3	(22) 3.3 / 1.3 / -.8		
(132) 3.7 / 2.0 / 1.1	(137) 3.6 / 1.7 / .5	(115) 4.4 / 1.8 / .9	Net Profit + Depr., Dep., Amort./Cur. Mat. L/T/D	(23) 4.4 / 1.5 / .7	(64) 4.8 / 2.0 / 1.1	(18) 4.4 / 1.4 / .4			
1.1 / 1.5 / 2.5	1.1 / 1.5 / 2.7	1.1 / 1.5 / 2.8	Fixed/Worth	1.2 / 1.9 / 4.5	1.1 / 1.5 / 2.7	1.0 / 1.3 / 2.0	.9 / 1.2 / 1.8		
.4 / .9 / 2.1	.4 / .9 / 2.5	.5 / .9 / 2.8	Debt/Worth	.7 / 1.4 / 4.4	.5 / .9 / 2.4	.3 / .7 / 1.7	.3 / .6 / 1.5		
(376) 9.3 / 2.8 / -3.9	(456) 10.4 / 1.6 / -5.1	(483) 10.0 / 1.7 / -3.9	% Profit Before Taxes/Tangible Net Worth	(123) 18.7 / 5.8 / -2.6	(224) 9.7 / 1.4 / -5.3	(93) 4.7 / .0 / -3.9	(29) 7.8 / 1.8 / -2.0		
5.1 / 1.4 / -2.2	4.5 / .7 / -2.5	4.7 / .9 / -2.1	% Profit Before Taxes/Total Assets	8.2 / 2.0 / -1.2	4.4 / .8 / -2.7	2.9 / .0 / -2.2	4.6 / .4 / -1.5		
1.3 / .9 / .6	1.3 / .9 / .6	1.4 / .9 / .6	Sales/Net Fixed Assets	1.6 / .9 / .5	1.3 / .9 / .6	1.4 / .9 / .7	1.6 / 1.0 / .7		
1.0 / .7 / .6	1.0 / .7 / .6	1.0 / .7 / .5	Sales/Total Assets	1.1 / .8 / .4	1.0 / .7 / .5	1.0 / .7 / .6	1.1 / .7 / .6		
(367) 6.9 / 8.8 / 12.0	(447) 6.8 / 8.8 / 11.4	(455) 6.7 / 8.8 / 11.4	% Depr., Dep., Amort./Sales	(117) 5.9 / 8.8 / 13.5	(212) 7.0 / 8.8 / 11.0	(87) 7.4 / 9.0 / 11.1	(26) 6.7 / 8.6 / 11.9		
(65) 3.5 / 6.4 / 15.5	(82) 4.9 / 8.8 / 22.0	(70) 3.6 / 5.6 / 18.8	% Officers', Directors', Owners' Comp/Sales	(18) 4.4 / 5.6 / 19.2	(32) 2.8 / 5.5 / 20.7	(14) 4.8 / 6.7 / 15.5			
900722M	1281460M	1609015M	Net Sales ($)	72978M	446020M	368239M	199301M	147323M	375154M
1247217M	2116683M	2857754M	Total Assets ($)	296294M	785385M	565700M	268806M	294075M	647494M

M = $ thousand   MM = $ million
See Pages 1 through 15 for Explanation of Ratios and Data

Current Data Sorted By Assets | **Comparative Historical Data**

	0-500M	500M-2MM	2-10MM	10-50MM	50-100MM	100-250MM		4/1/90-3/31/91 ALL	4/1/91-3/31/92 ALL
	4	6	6	4	1	1	**# Postretirement Benefits**		
							Type of Statement		
	4	6	43	23	9	7	Unqualified	14	59
	8	24	18	1			Reviewed	5	27
	24	23	2				Compiled	6	20
	5				1		Tax Returns		2
	20	32	38	17	3	5	Other	10	38
	\<— 105 (4/1-9/30/94) —\>		\<— 208 (10/1/94-3/31/95) —\>						
	61	85	101	41	13	12	**NUMBER OF STATEMENTS**	35	146
	%	%	%	%	%	%	**ASSETS**	%	%
	12.3	9.7	13.5	16.9	9.6	17.3	Cash & Equivalents	9.4	12.7
	46.2	48.2	50.1	46.5	46.4	27.1	Trade Receivables - (net)	49.9	44.0
	10.4	12.5	5.7	7.2	8.3	3.0	Inventory	11.3	9.4
	2.4	3.7	4.3	5.0	5.8	4.1	All Other Current	3.0	3.1
	71.3	74.0	73.7	75.6	70.1	51.4	Total Current	73.6	69.1
	19.6	14.7	12.5	11.1	14.2	18.9	Fixed Assets (net)	18.1	17.2
	1.5	4.9	6.6	6.3	7.6	13.9	Intangibles (net)	3.2	4.1
	7.6	6.3	7.2	6.9	8.1	15.9	All Other Non-Current	5.1	9.6
	100.0	100.0	100.0	100.0	100.0	100.0	Total	100.0	100.0
							LIABILITIES		
	15.3	11.1	8.3	9.4	2.0	1.3	Notes Payable-Short Term	10.6	8.8
	2.1	3.2	2.0	1.3	3.0	1.6	Cur. Mat. -L/T/D	3.5	1.5
	16.7	21.5	18.3	12.9	12.8	4.1	Trade Payables	15.2	16.3
	2.4	.9	1.4	1.0	.4	.4	Income Taxes Payable	2.2	.8
	13.3	17.3	18.3	21.5	18.1	19.6	All Other Current	14.0	13.9
	49.7	53.9	48.3	46.0	36.2	27.0	Total Current	45.4	43.1
	8.8	6.5	6.9	5.1	6.1	16.4	Long Term Debt	10.8	11.7
	.5	.6	1.4	1.6	.4	2.8	Deferred Taxes	3.3	1.5
	4.9	5.9	4.7	2.5	4.5	4.1	All Other-Non-Current	2.4	3.7
	36.1	33.1	38.7	44.8	52.8	49.6	Net Worth	38.1	40.1
	100.0	100.0	100.0	100.0	100.0	100.0	Total Liabilities & Net Worth	100.0	100.0
							INCOME DATA		
	100.0	100.0	100.0	100.0	100.0	100.0	Net Sales	100.0	100.0
							Gross Profit		
	96.9	94.0	93.4	94.4	98.4	94.7	Operating Expenses	95.8	95.8
	3.1	6.0	6.6	5.6	1.6	5.3	Operating Profit	4.2	4.2
	.5	1.1	1.1	.4	-.4	2.2	All Other Expenses (net)	2.8	.7
	2.6	4.9	5.5	5.2	2.0	3.1	Profit Before Taxes	1.3	3.6
							RATIOS		
	2.4	1.9	2.1	2.8	2.4	2.7	Current	2.4	2.7
	1.6	1.4	1.5	1.5	2.0	2.1		1.6	1.6
	1.1	1.1	1.2	1.3	1.6	1.2		1.2	1.1
	2.1	1.7	1.9	2.6	2.1	2.2	Quick	2.2	2.2
	1.3	1.1	1.2	1.3	1.7	1.8		1.4	1.3
	.9	.7	1.0	.9	1.3	1.0		1.0	.9
	22 16.5	38 9.6	54 6.7	60 6.1	68 5.4	49 7.5	Sales/Receivables	49 7.5	47 7.8
	38 9.5	61 6.0	74 4.9	96 3.8	91 4.0	78 4.7		72 5.1	69 5.3
	72 5.1	79 4.6	96 3.8	118 3.1	107 3.4	89 4.1		107 3.4	96 3.8
							Cost of Sales/Inventory		
							Cost of Sales/Payables		
	8.0	7.8	5.3	3.0	3.3	2.9	Sales/Working Capital	5.1	5.2
	20.3	15.7	10.5	6.4	5.5	6.4		9.6	9.6
	109.8	64.8	24.6	17.1	8.4	269.1		41.3	35.1
	(52) 17.9	(78) 16.6	(85) 30.0	(30) 57.2	(12) 30.9		EBIT/Interest	(29) 7.4	(127) 13.9
	4.9	6.3	8.4	10.9	12.5			2.3	3.8
	1.5	2.4	2.7	3.8	-5.9			-1.6	1.5
		(23) 8.5	(38) 10.9	(17) 20.1			Net Profit + Depr., Dep., Amort./Cur. Mat. L /T/D	(15) 2.8	(62) 9.6
		4.9	3.1	4.6				1.9	2.9
		.4	1.1	.9				-.4	1.4
	.2	.2	.1	.1	.2	.2	Fixed/Worth	.3	.2
	.5	.4	.4	.3	.3	.6		.4	.4
	1.0	1.6	.9	.5	.4	1.9		.8	1.0
	.7	1.3	.9	.5	.5	.3	Debt/Worth	1.0	.7
	1.7	2.6	2.0	1.5	1.0	1.5		2.0	1.9
	5.0	5.8	5.3	4.5	2.2	8.7		4.5	4.4
	(54) 79.7	(78) 85.8	(90) 57.7	(40) 42.5	(12) 31.5	(11) 38.9	% Profit Before Taxes/Tangible Net Worth	(33) 40.8	(136) 44.2
	44.4	44.3	31.5	26.5	20.7	6.4		16.2	23.1
	5.6	18.2	15.0	7.5	11.7	-5.1		-17.6	7.5
	24.8	21.6	20.2	17.1	14.6	12.5	% Profit Before Taxes/Total Assets	13.7	15.8
	11.0	9.7	9.9	7.7	9.5	3.9		6.1	6.7
	1.0	3.0	4.0	3.3	1.2	-4.0		-5.6	1.5
	87.5	56.3	50.4	39.6	24.2	11.9	Sales/Net Fixed Assets	26.6	39.3
	34.7	30.7	25.7	21.5	15.4	8.1		21.3	17.8
	16.5	13.8	13.1	11.3	10.1	5.5		7.3	9.7
	6.4	4.0	3.3	2.3	2.6	1.4	Sales/Total Assets	3.5	3.2
	4.4	3.2	2.4	1.8	1.7	1.2		2.7	2.5
	3.1	2.2	1.7	1.3	1.6	1.1		1.6	1.5
	(46) .7	(73) .5	(77) .7	(35) 1.1	(11) 1.8		% Depr., Dep., Amort./Sales	(24) 1.5	(117) 1.0
	1.3	1.2	1.7	2.6	2.5			2.6	2.0
	2.6	2.1	2.8	4.0	3.1			4.1	3.4
	(27) 6.5	(35) 3.8	(23) 1.3				% Officers', Directors', Owners' Comp/Sales		(27) 3.8
	9.3	5.8	3.5						8.1
	19.1	11.3	6.4						18.3
	79283M	294375M	1115735M	1767720M	1813353M	3070565M	Net Sales ($)	1432551M	3812209M
	16346M	93262M	450275M	945591M	924226M	2059451M	Total Assets ($)	901293M	2190050M

© Robert Morris Associates 1995

M = $ thousand MM = $ million
See Pages 1 through 15 for Explanation of Ratios and Data

	Comparative Historical Data				**Current Data Sorted By Sales**					
	5	11	22	**# Postretirement Benefits**	4	1	4	5	3	5
				Type of Statement						
	63	60	92	Unqualified	2	7	4	19	24	36
	36	31	51	Reviewed	3	14	7	19	7	1
	32	39	49	Compiled	13	27	6	3		
	3	2	6	Tax Returns	1	4				1
	45	61	115	Other	13	31	9	22	18	22
	4/1/92-3/31/93 ALL	4/1/93-3/31/94 ALL	4/1/94-3/31/95 ALL		105 (4/1-9/30/94) 0-1MM	1-3MM	3-5MM	208 (10/1/94-3/31/95) 5-10MM	10-25MM	25MM & OVER
	179	193	313	**NUMBER OF STATEMENTS**	32	83	26	63	49	60
	%	%	%	**ASSETS**	%	%	%	%	%	%
	12.4	12.1	12.7	Cash & Equivalents	10.0	11.4	11.2	15.7	11.1	14.7
	43.6	44.9	47.3	Trade Receivables - (net)	40.7	46.0	52.7	46.5	53.2	46.3
	10.8	9.3	8.7	Inventory	10.3	10.5	8.8	8.8	6.6	6.8
	3.1	3.9	3.9	All Other Current	3.7	3.8	1.7	2.8	5.1	5.2
	70.0	70.2	72.6	Total Current	64.8	71.8	74.4	73.8	76.0	72.9
	16.3	16.5	14.6	Fixed Assets (net)	20.9	16.4	16.0	11.9	12.6	12.9
	5.2	5.0	5.4	Intangibles (net)	1.6	6.0	4.5	7.0	4.9	5.9
	8.6	8.4	7.4	All Other Non-Current	12.7	5.9	5.1	7.4	6.4	8.4
	100.0	100.0	100.0	Total	100.0	100.0	100.0	100.0	100.0	100.0
				LIABILITIES						
	10.9	11.1	10.0	Notes Payable-Short Term	20.2	10.2	10.3	7.8	8.3	7.9
	2.8	2.6	2.3	Cur. Mat.-L /T/D	1.8	3.4	2.3	2.1	1.6	1.6
	17.0	17.5	17.4	Trade Payables	14.7	19.8	16.7	19.1	19.3	12.2
	1.2	1.7	1.3	Income Taxes Payable	1.0	1.9	1.0	1.6	1.0	.8
	15.9	16.1	17.5	All Other Current	11.6	17.1	15.0	18.3	18.4	20.7
	47.8	49.1	48.5	Total Current	49.2	52.4	45.4	49.0	48.7	43.2
	8.0	8.3	7.3	Long Term Debt	8.2	7.9	7.5	4.9	9.3	6.7
	1.1	.9	1.1	Deferred Taxes	.9	.4	.8	1.1	1.6	1.7
	5.3	5.1	4.7	All Other-Non-Current	6.2	5.1	3.4	6.9	2.9	3.1
	37.7	36.7	38.5	Net Worth	35.4	34.2	42.9	38.1	37.5	45.2
	100.0	100.0	100.0	Total Liabilities & Net Worth	100.0	100.0	100.0	100.0	100.0	100.0
				INCOME DATA						
	100.0	100.0	100.0	Net Sales	100.0	100.0	100.0	100.0	100.0	100.0
				Gross Profit						
	95.9	95.9	94.6	Operating Expenses	97.3	94.1	96.3	92.8	94.4	95.4
	4.1	4.1	5.4	Operating Profit	2.7	5.9	3.7	7.2	5.6	4.6
	1.1	1.2	.9	All Other Expenses (net)	.8	1.2	.2	1.0	1.1	.4
	3.0	3.0	4.5	Profit Before Taxes	1.9	4.7	3.4	6.2	4.5	4.2
				RATIOS						
	2.4	2.2	2.2	Current	2.4	2.2	2.8	2.0	2.1	2.6
	1.5	1.5	1.5		1.5	1.4	1.5	1.6	1.4	1.8
	1.1	1.1	1.1		1.0	1.1	1.1	1.2	1.2	1.3
	2.1	1.8	1.9	Quick	1.8	1.7	2.5	1.7	1.9	2.1
	(178) 1.3	1.2	1.2		1.2	1.1	1.1	1.3	1.2	1.5
	.8	.9	.9		.5	.8	.9	1.0	1.0	1.1
	42 8.6	40 9.2	42 8.6	Sales/Receivables	26 14.0	30 12.1	45 8.2	39 9.4	54 6.7	61 6.0
	63 5.8	60 6.1	68 5.4		50 7.3	57 6.4	63 5.8	61 6.0	78 4.7	83 4.4
	83 4.4	81 4.5	91 4.0		83 4.4	83 4.4	79 4.6	91 4.0	99 3.7	107 3.4
				Cost of Sales/Inventory						
				Cost of Sales/Payables						
	5.4	6.0	5.7	Sales/Working Capital	5.7	7.0	6.7	6.9	4.6	3.2
	9.8	12.2	11.8		16.7	18.3	15.5	10.6	10.8	7.9
	35.7	43.4	37.1		NM	101.9	50.8	21.2	24.6	18.4
	18.5	18.2	21.4	EBIT/Interest	7.5	18.7	21.8	31.9	15.5	32.8
	(148) 4.7	(158) 4.0	(264) 7.4		(27) 3.0	(72) 6.9	(23) 7.7	(54) 10.9	(42) 6.9	(46) 9.4
	1.2	1.1	1.1		.3	2.0	3.3	3.9	2.3	3.2
	7.4	7.7	11.7	Net Profit + Depr., Dep., Amort./Cur. Mat. L/T/D		6.9		20.7	10.4	16.3
	(61) 2.4	(65) 2.5	(94) 3.6			(20) 2.7		(14) 2.2	(26) 3.4	(24) 5.0
	.3	.5	1.1			.3		.7	1.5	1.4
	.2	.2	.2	Fixed/Worth	.1	.2	.2	.1	.2	.1
	.3	.4	.4		.4	.6	.3	.3	.4	.3
	1.0	1.3	.9		3.0	1.2	1.3	.9	.8	.5
	.8	.9	.8	Debt/Worth	.6	1.1	.5	1.1	.8	.5
	1.7	1.9	2.0		1.9	2.3	1.7	1.9	2.0	1.4
	5.1	4.6	5.2		11.7	5.8	3.7	5.3	5.3	4.2
	63.6	55.7	62.8	% Profit Before Taxes/Tangible Net Worth	98.3	79.7	67.4	72.2	62.2	40.0
	(154) 25.7	(178) 23.9	(285) 31.6		(27) 16.5	(75) 43.9	(24) 43.4	(57) 35.6	(45) 31.2	(57) 25.9
	4.3	2.6	12.1		-3.3	15.6	19.9	18.7	14.6	6.1
	18.4	17.7	19.0	% Profit Before Taxes/Total Assets	18.8	21.4	23.3	25.2	15.8	15.7
	8.4	8.3	9.5		4.7	9.7	14.1	11.0	7.7	8.6
	.6	.2	3.2		-2.1	2.3	3.0	5.5	4.1	2.2
	46.3	41.2	53.1	Sales/Net Fixed Assets	66.0	50.9	55.8	78.5	50.4	37.7
	18.8	20.8	24.6		25.9	24.7	20.0	33.8	25.0	20.1
	11.0	10.8	12.2		8.5	13.0	12.5	15.8	13.2	10.0
	3.6	3.6	3.8	Sales/Total Assets	5.2	4.5	4.1	3.8	3.4	2.9
	2.7	2.7	2.7		3.4	3.2	3.0	2.7	2.5	1.8
	1.6	1.7	1.7		1.8	1.9	2.3	2.1	1.7	1.4
	.8	.8	.7	% Depr., Dep., Amort./Sales	.9	.6	.7	.6	.7	1.0
	(146) 1.7	(150) 1.6	(246) 1.6		(24) 2.4	(67) 1.3	(24) 1.5	(47) 1.7	(40) 1.6	(44) 2.3
	3.6	3.3	3.0		4.3	2.2	2.4	2.4	2.9	3.4
	4.0	4.2	3.4	% Officers', Directors', Owners' Comp/Sales	8.2	4.4	2.4	3.2		
	(52) 6.5	(52) 7.7	(88) 6.4		(13) 13.8	(31) 8.1	(12) 5.8	(21) 4.4		
	11.1	12.7	11.6		20.7	11.3	12.5	7.4		
	3309504M	3439155M	8141031M	Net Sales ($)	19206M	167454M	100654M	462782M	771735M	6619200M
	1980519M	2085498M	4489151M	Total Assets ($)	8624M	70768M	39550M	189244M	374308M	3806657M

© Robert Morris Associates 1995

M = $ thousand   MM = $ million

See Pages 1 through 15 for Explanation of Ratios and Data

Current Data Sorted By Assets   Comparative Historical Data

0-500M	500M-2MM	2-10MM	10-50MM	50-100MM	100-250MM		4/1/90-3/31/91 ALL	4/1/91-3/31/92 ALL
		2				# Postretirement Benefits		
						Type of Statement		
		2				Unqualified		
3	4	2				Reviewed		
5	4	1				Compiled		
2	4	3				Tax Returns		
						Other		
14 (4/1-9/30/94)		16 (10/1/94-3/31/95)						
10	12	8				**NUMBER OF STATEMENTS**		
%	%	%	%	%	%	**ASSETS**	%	%
9.1	14.8					Cash & Equivalents	D	D
36.0	36.8					Trade Receivables - (net)	A	A
29.5	22.9					Inventory	T	T
.8	1.4					All Other Current	A	A
75.4	75.9					Total Current		
17.5	14.2					Fixed Assets (net)	N	N
4.2	1.2					Intangibles (net)	O	O
2.9	8.7					All Other Non-Current	T	T
100.0	100.0					Total		
						LIABILITIES	A	A
11.7	7.5					Notes Payable-Short Term	V	V
14.7	1.3					Cur. Mat. -L/T/D	A	A
11.4	16.5					Trade Payables	I	I
.4	.1					Income Taxes Payable	L	L
11.1	17.6					All Other Current	A	A
49.3	43.1					Total Current	B	B
9.5	5.6					Long Term Debt	L	L
.0	.2					Deferred Taxes	E	E
7.2	13.2					All Other-Non-Current		
34.1	37.8					Net Worth		
100.0	100.0					Total Liabilities & Net Worth		
						INCOME DATA		
100.0	100.0					Net Sales		
47.5	48.9					Gross Profit		
42.1	45.6					Operating Expenses		
5.3	3.3					Operating Profit		
2.6	.6					All Other Expenses (net)		
2.7	2.7					Profit Before Taxes		
						RATIOS		
7.2	3.2							
1.6	1.8					Current		
.8	1.2							
3.4	2.1							
.8	1.1					Quick		
.5	.9							
15 23.6	33 10.9							
28 13.1	49 7.5					Sales/Receivables		
48 7.6	60 6.1							
32 11.3	17 21.7							
56 6.5	50 7.3					Cost of Sales/Inventory		
228 1.6	159 2.3							
0 UND	24 15.1							
21 17.7	34 10.7					Cost of Sales/Payables		
34 10.7	69 5.3							
4.9	4.5							
13.8	8.5					Sales/Working Capital		
-64.8	23.7							
						EBIT/Interest		
						Net Profit + Depr., Dep., Amort./Cur. Mat. L /T/D		
.1	.2							
.8	.5					Fixed/Worth		
NM	.8							
.2	.8							
2.1	1.9					Debt/Worth		
NM	6.2							
	57.7					% Profit Before Taxes/Tangible		
	7.5					Net Worth		
	4.9							
25.5	9.9					% Profit Before Taxes/Total		
5.1	3.3					Assets		
-12.9	1.2							
79.9	34.1							
34.0	21.7					Sales/Net Fixed Assets		
15.8	11.4							
4.9	3.7							
3.0	2.7					Sales/Total Assets		
1.9	2.2							
	1.0							
(10)	1.7					% Depr., Dep., Amort./Sales		
	2.6							
						% Officers', Directors', Owners' Comp/Sales		
8199M	36492M	81339M				Net Sales ($)		
2392M	13368M	34182M				Total Assets ($)		

M = $ thousand   MM = $ million
See Pages 1 through 15 for Explanation of Ratios and Data

Comparative Historical Data | Current Data Sorted By Sales

				# Postretirement Benefits				2	
		2							

Type of Statement

				Type of Statement	0-1MM	1-3MM	3-5MM	5-10MM	10-25MM	25MM & OVER
		2		Unqualified				1	1	
		9		Reviewed	1	4	2	2		
		10		Compiled	4	4	1		1	
				Tax Returns						
		9		Other	2	1	3	1	2	

4/1/92-3/31/93 ALL	4/1/93-3/31/94 ALL	4/1/94-3/31/95 ALL			14 (4/1-9/30/94)			16 (10/1/94-3/31/95)		
		30		NUMBER OF STATEMENTS	7	9	6	4	4	
%	%	%		ASSETS	%	%	%	%	%	%
D	D	10.3		Cash & Equivalents						
A	A	36.5		Trade Receivables - (net)						
T	T	24.1		Inventory						
A	A	1.8		All Other Current						
		72.7		Total Current						
N	N	17.8		Fixed Assets (net)						
O	O	2.3		Intangibles (net)						
T	T	7.2		All Other Non-Current						
		100.0		Total						
A	A			LIABILITIES						
V	V	12.6		Notes Payable-Short Term						
A	A	6.2		Cur. Mat.-L /T/D						
I	I	13.6		Trade Payables						
L	L	.2		Income Taxes Payable						
A	A	14.4		All Other Current						
B	B	47.1		Total Current						
L	L	9.8		Long Term Debt						
E	E	.2		Deferred Taxes						
		8.1		All Other-Non-Current						
		34.8		Net Worth						
		100.0		Total Liabilities & Net Worth						
				INCOME DATA						
		100.0		Net Sales						
		46.3		Gross Profit						
		41.8		Operating Expenses						
		4.5		Operating Profit						
		1.2		All Other Expenses (net)						
		3.4		Profit Before Taxes						
				RATIOS						
		2.7								
		1.4		Current						
		1.1								
		1.8								
		1.0		Quick						
		.6								
	31	11.6								
	45	8.2		Sales/Receivables						
	58	6.3								
	27	13.4								
	47	7.7		Cost of Sales/Inventory						
	152	2.4								
	19	19.5								
	29	12.8		Cost of Sales/Payables						
	62	5.9								
		5.5								
		12.0		Sales/Working Capital						
		70.0								
		6.0								
	(23)	3.1		EBIT/Interest						
		1.8								
				Net Profit + Depr., Dep., Amort./Cur. Mat. L/T/D						
		.2								
		.6		Fixed/Worth						
		.9								
		.9								
		2.2		Debt/Worth						
		6.7								
		50.8		% Profit Before Taxes/Tangible Net Worth						
	(28)	21.3								
		4.9								
		14.6		% Profit Before Taxes/Total Assets						
		5.7								
		1.3								
		45.4								
		24.8		Sales/Net Fixed Assets						
		10.7								
		3.9								
		2.6		Sales/Total Assets						
		2.1								
		1.0								
	(24)	1.6		% Depr., Dep., Amort./Sales						
		2.7								
		2.1		% Officers', Directors', Owners' Comp/Sales						
	(11)	4.1								
		12.4								
		126030M		Net Sales ($)	3327M	16058M	25306M	30611M	50728M	
		49942M		Total Assets ($)	1371M	5860M	8529M	12238M	21944M	

M = $ thousand   MM = $ million
See Pages 1 through 15 for Explanation of Ratios and Data

Current Data Sorted By Assets **Comparative Historical Data**

0-500M	500M-2MM	2-10MM	10-50MM	50-100MM	100-250MM		4/1/90-3/31/91 ALL	4/1/91-3/31/92 ALL
4	6	6	4	2	1	**# Postretirement Benefits**		
						Type of Statement		
5	12	25	11	5	6	Unqualified	47	48
2	14	7			1	Reviewed	15	23
13	14	2				Compiled	22	19
4						Tax Returns		
11	15	21	10	1	1	Other	41	46
	56 (4/1-9/30/94)		124 (10/1/94-3/31/95)					
35	55	55	21	6	8	**NUMBER OF STATEMENTS**	125	136
%	%	%	%	%	%	**ASSETS**	%	%
18.2	12.8	13.3	12.0			Cash & Equivalents	12.0	13.1
35.3	38.7	37.7	26.9			Trade Receivables - (net)	36.0	35.5
9.2	2.3	1.7	3.1			Inventory	4.6	4.1
2.0	3.7	2.4	7.2			All Other Current	2.2	2.9
64.6	57.5	55.1	49.2			Total Current	54.7	55.6
22.4	30.1	31.1	27.0			Fixed Assets (net)	29.2	28.2
5.6	3.4	4.8	10.6			Intangibles (net)	4.8	6.2
7.3	9.0	9.0	13.1			All Other Non-Current	11.3	10.0
100.0	100.0	100.0	100.0			Total	100.0	100.0
						LIABILITIES		
14.7	7.2	8.1	6.1			Notes Payable-Short Term	10.0	7.0
6.0	5.7	5.7	2.5			Cur. Mat. -L/T/D	6.0	6.7
15.5	9.6	10.9	12.3			Trade Payables	10.3	10.7
.1	.1	1.0	.8			Income Taxes Payable	1.4	.9
15.2	19.2	14.3	11.0			All Other Current	12.2	14.6
51.5	41.8	40.1	32.7			Total Current	39.9	40.0
14.9	16.7	14.4	12.3			Long Term Debt	15.7	15.1
.6	1.1	2.0	1.5			Deferred Taxes	.9	1.2
10.6	3.2	3.1	6.7			All Other-Non-Current	3.2	2.8
22.3	37.2	40.4	46.7			Net Worth	40.4	40.9
100.0	100.0	100.0	100.0			Total Liabilities & Net Worth	100.0	100.0
						INCOME DATA		
100.0	100.0	100.0	100.0			Net Sales	100.0	100.0
						Gross Profit		
97.4	95.9	91.7	95.8			Operating Expenses	94.2	95.4
2.6	4.1	8.3	4.2			Operating Profit	5.8	4.6
.5	1.2	2.0	1.0			All Other Expenses (net)	1.0	1.1
2.0	2.9	6.3	3.2			Profit Before Taxes	4.8	3.5
						RATIOS		
2.4	1.8	2.1	2.5				2.4	2.2
1.5	1.2	1.4	1.4			Current	1.3	1.4
.9	1.1	1.0	1.1				1.0	1.1
2.1	1.6	2.0	1.8				1.9	2.0
1.1	1.1	1.2	1.2			Quick	1.2	1.2
.7	.9	1.0	.8				.8	.9
13 28.9	37 10.0	42 8.6	46 8.0				34 10.6	34 10.8
29 12.4	43 8.4	59 6.2	70 5.2			Sales/Receivables	49 7.4	49 7.5
54 6.8	68 5.4	81 4.5	85 4.3				74 4.9	72 5.1
						Cost of Sales/Inventory		
						Cost of Sales/Payables		
11.3	8.8	7.5	4.4				6.7	7.5
21.5	24.3	16.3	10.3			Sales/Working Capital	18.7	17.8
-24.9	87.1	274.4	86.6				-120.6	76.5
(33) 10.0	(50) 6.8	(50) 12.3	(20) 24.1				(110) 8.0	(122) 7.7
5.5	4.1	6.1	6.0			EBIT/Interest	2.9	3.2
-.9	1.6	1.8	.9				1.2	1.1
	(22) 4.8	(28) 12.8	(10) 10.5				(57) 8.2	(61) 6.1
	2.5	3.6	5.6			Net Profit + Depr., Dep., Amort./Cur. Mat. L /T/D	3.1	2.0
	1.3	1.5	2.9				1.5	1.2
.5	.4	.3	.3				.3	.3
.8	.9	.8	.6			Fixed/Worth	.8	.8
-1.3	1.8	1.2	1.2				2.1	1.4
.8	.9	.8	.4				.7	.7
3.6	2.3	1.5	1.2			Debt/Worth	1.7	1.7
-4.9	5.8	4.5	4.1				5.6	4.2
(24) 141.4	(52) 50.9	(50) 53.7	(20) 35.0				(111) 48.3	(127) 46.8
40.5	26.0	28.8	17.5			% Profit Before Taxes/Tangible Net Worth	21.1	22.2
13.5	2.6	11.2	4.9				2.9	1.5
22.7	12.6	17.9	12.2				16.4	17.3
15.4	7.6	7.5	6.4			% Profit Before Taxes/Total Assets	7.5	8.0
-8.2	1.4	2.7	-.1				1.1	1.0
45.1	19.1	16.4	13.0				20.4	22.9
26.9	9.4	6.7	5.8			Sales/Net Fixed Assets	8.9	9.8
11.4	5.8	3.9	4.2				4.2	4.6
5.9	3.8	2.9	2.0				3.4	3.6
4.1	2.7	2.0	1.4			Sales/Total Assets	2.2	2.4
2.8	1.9	1.4	.7				1.5	1.7
(26) .8	(49) 1.6	(50) 2.1	(15) 3.7				(100) 2.1	(115) 2.2
1.5	3.3	4.2	6.9			% Depr., Dep., Amort./Sales	4.4	4.0
4.0	5.7	6.3	7.7				7.6	7.1
(16) 5.0	(21) 5.3	(11) 4.5					(30) 5.3	(41) 3.4
10.3	9.6	6.7				% Officers', Directors', Owners' Comp/Sales	12.2	9.4
18.9	14.1	13.5					17.2	16.4
41247M	164286M	654184M	627647M	10417404M	1757244M	Net Sales ($)	1809165M	2074800M
9164M	58911M	265800M	448575M	434139M	1348163M	Total Assets ($)	1352486M	1496502M

M = $ thousand   MM = $ million
See Pages 1 through 15 for Explanation of Ratios and Data

Comparative Historical Data   Current Data Sorted By Sales

2	6	23	# Postretirement Benefits	2	5	5	3	4	4
			Type of Statement						
44	54	64	Unqualified	6	6	7	11	16	18
29	32	24	Reviewed	2	9	5	6	1	1
35	23	29	Compiled	9	13	5	1	1	
3	4	4	Tax Returns	2	2				
45	54	59	Other	7	12	9	11	15	5
4/1/92-3/31/93 ALL	4/1/93-3/31/94 ALL	4/1/94-3/31/95 ALL		56 (4/1-9/30/94) → 0-1MM	1-3MM	3-5MM	124 (10/1/94-3/31/95) → 5-10MM	10-25MM	25MM & OVER
156	167	180	**NUMBER OF STATEMENTS**	26	42	26	29	33	24
%	%	%	**ASSETS**	%	%	%	%	%	%
13.2	15.6	14.4	Cash & Equivalents	24.2	11.9	11.0	15.0	8.6	19.5
37.0	37.1	35.3	Trade Receivables - (net)	27.0	39.7	33.7	36.5	41.3	28.2
4.8	4.2	3.6	Inventory	6.4	5.8	1.4	2.7	1.8	2.8
2.4	2.2	3.4	All Other Current	4.8	2.8	2.1	3.8	3.4	4.2
57.3	59.1	56.8	Total Current	62.4	60.2	48.3	58.0	55.1	54.6
28.5	27.6	27.9	Fixed Assets (net)	26.3	26.9	38.8	24.2	29.1	22.1
5.0	3.5	6.1	Intangibles (net)	4.1	3.7	5.0	6.6	5.8	13.3
9.1	9.7	9.3	All Other Non-Current	7.2	9.2	7.9	11.2	10.0	10.0
100.0	100.0	100.0	Total	100.0	100.0	100.0	100.0	100.0	100.0
			LIABILITIES						
9.3	8.6	8.3	Notes Payable-Short Term	11.2	10.4	3.6	11.0	8.1	3.5
6.0	3.9	5.1	Cur. Mat.-L./T/D	5.0	6.6	6.4	4.8	4.7	1.9
10.6	11.9	11.2	Trade Payables	8.8	13.7	9.5	10.3	12.1	10.7
.8	1.1	.6	Income Taxes Payable	.1	.2	.4	.4	1.1	1.5
14.6	14.5	15.8	All Other Current	18.4	18.8	9.8	15.7	14.1	16.6
41.4	40.1	40.9	Total Current	43.5	49.7	29.8	42.2	40.2	34.2
13.2	11.6	14.5	Long Term Debt	14.2	18.9	18.4	11.9	13.4	8.0
1.1	1.6	1.5	Deferred Taxes	.1	1.1	2.5	1.9	1.3	2.0
4.1	3.2	5.1	All Other-Non-Current	10.9	4.7	2.5	4.0	5.6	3.0
40.1	43.6	38.0	Net Worth	31.2	25.6	46.8	40.1	39.4	52.7
100.0	100.0	100.0	Total Liabilities & Net Worth	100.0	100.0	100.0	100.0	100.0	100.0
			INCOME DATA						
100.0	100.0	100.0	Net Sales	100.0	100.0	100.0	100.0	100.0	100.0
			Gross Profit						
94.6	95.6	94.3	Operating Expenses	99.2	93.1	94.7	95.2	93.5	90.3
5.4	4.4	5.7	Operating Profit	.8	6.9	5.3	4.8	6.5	9.7
1.2	.5	1.2	All Other Expenses (net)	.0	1.5	1.0	1.6	2.5	.1
4.2	3.9	4.5	Profit Before Taxes	.7	5.4	4.4	3.2	4.0	9.5
			RATIOS						
2.3	2.4	2.1		2.6	1.6	2.9	2.7	2.0	2.1
1.5	1.5	1.4	Current	1.6	1.1	1.5	1.5	1.4	1.5
1.0	1.0	1.1		1.0	.9	.9	1.0	1.1	1.2
2.2	2.2	1.8		2.4	1.5	2.1	2.4	1.7	2.0
1.3	1.3	1.2	Quick	1.5	1.0	1.3	1.2	1.3	1.4
.9	.9	.9		.7	.8	.9	.9	1.0	1.1
(29) 12.4	(38) 9.5	(36) 10.2		(16) 23.0	(27) 13.4	(29) 12.5	(39) 9.4	(51) 7.1	(40) 9.1
(47) 7.7	(49) 7.4	(52) 7.0	Sales/Receivables	(39) 9.4	(46) 7.9	(38) 9.5	(63) 5.8	(61) 6.0	(54) 6.7
(68) 5.4	(66) 5.5	(74) 4.9		(76) 4.8	(69) 5.3	(54) 6.7	(87) 4.2	(78) 4.7	(85) 4.3
			Cost of Sales/Inventory						
			Cost of Sales/Payables						
7.1	6.8	7.5		7.8	13.9	8.7	5.5	7.6	4.7
16.0	14.7	17.2	Sales/Working Capital	12.9	32.2	22.0	11.8	15.4	8.0
-542.7	130.0	104.7		NM	-112.2	-109.1	186.7	38.9	48.4
(135) 11.1	(139) 11.3	(165) 13.0		(23) 7.5	(40) 8.8	(23) 11.4	(27) 15.2	(31) 11.6	(21) 49.1
3.8	4.6	5.4	EBIT/Interest	3.4	4.6	4.1	6.4	4.9	25.3
1.4	1.2	1.5		-1.9	1.4	1.5	2.8	.1	10.8
(51) 5.5	(59) 7.8	(71) 6.8			(18) 8.7		(11) 24.9	(20) 6.4	
2.6	2.7	3.1	Net Profit + Depr., Dep., Amort./Cur. Mat. L/T/D		2.2		4.3	3.6	
.9	1.0	1.5			1.1		1.6	1.7	
.3	.2	.4		.4	.4	.4	.2	.4	.4
.7	.6	.8	Fixed/Worth	.8	1.0	1.0	.6	.7	.5
2.2	1.4	1.9		UND	8.6	1.8	1.4	1.2	.9
.6	.6	.8		.7	1.0	.6	.7	.9	.5
1.4	1.3	1.9	Debt/Worth	2.3	3.5	1.6	1.2	1.8	1.1
4.1	3.0	6.3		UND	15.0	3.6	5.3	3.9	4.9
(135) 48.7	(153) 50.1	(158) 52.6		(21) 122.9	(34) 79.9	(25) 50.1	(26) 48.6	(30) 47.9	(22) 55.6
20.5	20.4	29.9	% Profit Before Taxes/Tangible Net Worth	32.8	33.5	24.8	24.9	24.4	35.8
5.1	3.3	7.5		.0	5.1	6.9	8.5	6.3	22.7
18.2	19.6	17.9		16.5	20.1	13.8	21.7	16.4	22.0
7.6	7.3	9.0	% Profit Before Taxes/Total Assets	3.7	10.9	7.1	9.2	6.7	13.1
.6	.7	1.8		-8.1	1.9	2.2	2.7	-1.6	9.1
27.3	29.8	28.3		29.0	40.3	22.3	30.4	15.4	22.6
12.6	9.5	9.3	Sales/Net Fixed Assets	11.6	12.3	6.8	10.7	6.8	9.1
6.1	5.5	5.2		5.9	5.7	4.5	4.7	5.1	5.2
4.1	3.9	3.6		3.7	4.5	4.2	3.2	3.2	2.3
2.7	2.5	2.2	Sales/Total Assets	2.7	2.5	3.0	2.1	1.9	1.6
1.7	1.4	1.5		1.3	1.8	1.6	1.4	1.4	1.2
(129) 1.3	(143) 1.4	(148) 1.5		(21) 1.3	(33) 1.3	1.3	(26) 1.4	(27) 3.1	(15) 1.9
2.9	3.1	3.6	% Depr., Dep., Amort./Sales	3.3	2.2	3.9	2.8	3.8	4.0
6.0	6.2	6.1		7.5	5.0	6.6	5.1	7.1	7.6
(45) 4.9	(48) 4.7	(52) 4.7			(16) 4.5	(12) 6.7			
8.2	8.4	7.6	% Officers', Directors', Owners' Comp/Sales		7.6	10.0			
17.8	17.8	13.7			12.7	14.6			
1979871M	2917428M	13662012M	Net Sales ($)	16005M	80006M	107518M	204486M	524498M	12729499M
1150268M	2030375M	2564752M	Total Assets ($)	10326M	34856M	47846M	117654M	346299M	2007771M

© Robert Morris Associates 1995

M = $ thousand   MM = $ million
See Pages 1 through 15 for Explanation of Ratios and Data

Current Data Sorted By Assets

Comparative Historical Data

	2	3	8	2					
		14	26	10	6	2	# Postretirement Benefits / Type of Statement		
	9	13	15				Unqualified	62	53
	18	14	6				Reviewed	43	48
	6	1					Compiled	49	32
	19	30	18	8		1	Tax Returns	2	7
							Other	64	44

	0-500M	56 (4/1-9/30/94) 500M-2MM	2-10MM	160 (10/1/94-3/31/95) 10-50MM	50-100MM	100-250MM		4/1/90-3/31/91 ALL	4/1/91-3/31/92 ALL
NUMBER OF STATEMENTS	52	72	65	18	6	3		220	184
	%	%	%	%	%	%	**ASSETS**	%	%
	14.0	11.7	13.3	19.2			Cash & Equivalents	13.0	11.1
	41.6	47.6	47.3	40.8			Trade Receivables - (net)	41.0	41.5
	6.0	5.2	4.5	3.3			Inventory	8.0	7.3
	2.7	4.1	5.6	4.1			All Other Current	3.6	3.6
	64.3	68.6	70.7	67.4			Total Current	65.6	63.5
	22.0	18.4	15.4	16.1			Fixed Assets (net)	21.6	20.8
	3.3	5.8	4.1	11.0			Intangibles (net)	4.6	7.5
	10.4	7.2	9.9	5.5			All Other Non-Current	8.2	8.2
	100.0	100.0	100.0	100.0			Total	100.0	100.0
							LIABILITIES		
	14.0	13.6	8.3	4.4			Notes Payable-Short Term	10.4	12.2
	5.3	2.6	2.3	1.9			Cur. Mat. -L/T/D	4.0	4.9
	11.1	11.3	12.8	10.7			Trade Payables	13.0	11.4
	.6	.7	.8	1.3			Income Taxes Payable	1.7	.9
	15.9	21.6	18.8	19.3			All Other Current	15.8	16.0
	46.9	49.9	43.1	37.7			Total Current	44.9	45.3
	11.3	7.0	6.1	4.3			Long Term Debt	11.5	10.3
	.9	1.3	1.3	.9			Deferred Taxes	1.5	1.9
	4.4	5.7	4.3	8.5			All Other-Non-Current	4.4	3.4
	36.5	36.1	45.2	48.5			Net Worth	37.7	39.0
	100.0	100.0	100.0	100.0			Total Liabilities & Net Worth	100.0	100.0
							INCOME DATA		
	100.0	100.0	100.0	100.0			Net Sales	100.0	100.0
							Gross Profit		
	94.2	93.6	90.8	91.5			Operating Expenses	94.8	95.0
	5.8	6.4	9.2	8.5			Operating Profit	5.2	5.0
	1.1	.9	.5	.3			All Other Expenses (net)	1.0	.9
	4.7	5.5	8.7	8.2			Profit Before Taxes	4.3	4.0
							RATIOS		
	3.2	2.3	2.5	3.1				2.2	2.2
	1.4	1.4	1.8	1.8			Current	1.5	1.5
	1.0	1.0	1.2	1.3				1.1	1.1
	2.8	2.1	2.3	3.0				1.9	1.9
	1.2	1.2	1.4	1.5			Quick	1.2	1.3
	.8	.8	.9	1.1				.8	.8
	19 18.8	38 9.6	50 7.3	61 6.0				34 10.6	40 9.1
	33 11.0	57 6.4	66 5.5	85 4.3			Sales/Receivables	58 6.3	60 6.1
	76 4.8	81 4.5	96 3.8	101 3.6				79 4.6	83 4.4
							Cost of Sales/Inventory		
							Cost of Sales/Payables		
	8.4	6.5	5.7	3.8				6.9	6.0
	19.7	14.1	9.5	5.8			Sales/Working Capital	13.2	13.0
	-162.0	-191.3	29.2	15.6				46.0	73.7
	15.0	30.4	48.4	28.7				13.1	12.1
	(43) 7.0	(65) 7.1	(54) 17.4	(14) 16.3			EBIT/Interest	(180) 4.5	(150) 4.1
	2.6	1.7	4.3	2.8				1.6	1.0
		20.8	19.8				Net Profit + Depr., Dep.,	8.3	8.3
		(15) 4.0	(21) 8.9				Amort./Cur. Mat. L /T/D	(92) 3.8	(63) 3.2
		2.0	2.4					1.1	1.1
	.2	.2	.1	.1				.2	.2
	.5	.4	.3	.3			Fixed/Worth	.5	.5
	2.4	1.5	.8	1.0				1.5	2.2
	.5	.8	.6	.9				.9	.7
	2.3	1.7	1.6	1.2			Debt/Worth	1.8	1.6
	29.8	5.3	3.6	3.0				4.5	7.1
	106.9	76.6	72.2	89.4			% Profit Before Taxes/Tangible	57.8	61.5
	(42) 37.1	(61) 35.1	(63) 44.6	(16) 53.5			Net Worth	(193) 31.2	(160) 31.0
	12.7	17.1	27.1	15.8				10.1	3.5
	29.2	23.5	26.5	30.4				20.3	20.7
	14.1	11.1	18.0	15.6			% Profit Before Taxes/Total Assets	9.9	9.7
	3.5	3.6	9.7	5.2				1.5	.2
	61.1	36.2	48.6	52.8				35.3	29.4
	26.5	19.7	24.0	15.4			Sales/Net Fixed Assets	15.1	15.3
	13.4	12.9	12.7	5.5				8.1	9.3
	6.0	3.8	3.3	2.3				3.6	3.6
	4.0	2.8	2.5	1.8			Sales/Total Assets	2.7	2.7
	2.5	2.1	1.7	1.3				1.8	1.8
	.6	.9	.7	.9				1.2	1.3
	(40) 1.7	(61) 1.7	(53) 1.7	(12) 3.1			% Depr., Dep., Amort./Sales	(165) 2.2	(149) 2.5
	2.7	3.1	3.2	4.0				4.2	4.3
	8.5	4.4	2.2				% Officers', Directors',	3.0	4.7
	(29) 12.0	(16) 7.9	(13) 3.2				Owners' Comp/Sales	(63) 6.2	(42) 8.4
	19.2	10.4	8.4					11.7	15.8
	56455M	245618M	757612M	680233M	828251M	700975M	Net Sales ($)	3080896M	2894880M
	13222M	80988M	290844M	366458M	416955M	578432M	Total Assets ($)	1700275M	1511405M

© Robert Morris Associates 1995

M = $ thousand   MM = $ million
See Pages 1 through 15 for Explanation of Ratios and Data

Comparative Historical Data				Current Data Sorted By Sales					
3	12	15	# Postretirement Benefits / Type of Statement	2	2	1	2	6	2
48	47	58	Unqualified	1	4	7	11	17	18
41	32	37	Reviewed	5	14	3	11	4	
34	31	38	Compiled	10	20	3	1	4	
4	1	7	Tax Returns	2	4	1			
39	69	76	Other	13	23	10	11	12	7
4/1/92-3/31/93 ALL	4/1/93-3/31/94 ALL	4/1/94-3/31/95 ALL		56 (4/1-9/30/94)			160 (10/1/94-3/31/95)		
				0-1MM	1-3MM	3-5MM	5-10MM	10-25MM	25MM & OVER
166	180	216	**NUMBER OF STATEMENTS**	31	65	24	34	37	25
%	%	%	**ASSETS**	%	%	%	%	%	%
12.5	14.9	13.4	Cash & Equivalents	17.2	9.4	16.8	10.4	15.5	17.3
42.8	44.4	44.8	Trade Receivables - (net)	31.0	46.0	41.6	55.5	50.2	39.2
5.4	5.1	4.9	Inventory	5.6	5.7	6.7	4.8	3.1	3.4
4.4	3.7	4.4	All Other Current	4.9	2.4	7.0	2.1	6.7	6.0
65.2	68.1	67.6	Total Current	58.7	63.5	72.1	72.9	75.5	65.9
20.8	18.0	18.5	Fixed Assets (net)	24.4	21.1	14.8	14.9	14.3	18.7
6.9	5.6	5.3	Intangibles (net)	4.6	5.7	5.3	3.9	4.9	7.7
7.1	8.2	8.7	All Other Non-Current	12.3	9.8	7.9	8.4	5.4	7.7
100.0	100.0	100.0	Total	100.0	100.0	100.0	100.0	100.0	100.0
			LIABILITIES						
9.6	9.2	10.9	Notes Payable-Short Term	10.4	15.6	12.4	8.6	8.2	5.1
3.2	2.8	3.1	Cur. Mat.-L/T/D	5.3	3.9	1.2	2.3	2.5	1.6
10.5	11.5	11.7	Trade Payables	8.4	11.0	10.1	16.0	12.9	11.2
.9	1.9	.8	Income Taxes Payable	.9	.4	1.1	1.0	.5	1.4
17.8	17.0	18.9	All Other Current	18.0	19.5	13.3	20.8	21.5	17.0
42.0	42.4	45.3	Total Current	42.9	50.5	38.2	48.6	45.7	36.3
10.0	9.6	7.4	Long Term Debt	14.5	7.7	4.7	6.6	6.3	3.2
1.8	1.3	1.2	Deferred Taxes	.2	1.7	1.3	1.6	.9	.6
4.0	3.8	5.2	All Other-Non-Current	6.1	5.3	7.4	4.1	3.9	5.2
42.2	42.8	40.9	Net Worth	36.2	34.8	48.4	39.1	43.3	54.8
100.0	100.0	100.0	Total Liabilities & Net Worth	100.0	100.0	100.0	100.0	100.0	100.0
			INCOME DATA						
100.0	100.0	100.0	Net Sales	100.0	100.0	100.0	100.0	100.0	100.0
			Gross Profit						
93.1	94.9	92.9	Operating Expenses	92.2	93.6	93.7	91.1	93.0	93.5
6.9	5.1	7.1	Operating Profit	7.8	6.4	6.3	8.9	7.0	6.5
1.1	.4	.7	All Other Expenses (net)	1.2	1.0	.3	1.0	.3	.0
5.8	4.7	6.4	Profit Before Taxes	6.6	5.4	6.0	7.9	6.7	6.5
			RATIOS						
2.6 / 1.6 / 1.1	2.5 / 1.7 / 1.1	2.6 / 1.5 / 1.1	Current	3.2 / 1.4 / 1.0	2.3 / 1.3 / .8	10.4 / 2.1 / 1.1	2.4 / 1.5 / 1.1	2.4 / 1.8 / 1.2	3.1 / 1.8 / 1.3
2.2 / 1.4 / 1.0	2.4 / 1.5 / 1.0	2.3 / 1.3 / .9	Quick	2.7 / 1.3 / .8	2.1 / 1.1 / .7	6.0 / 1.5 / 1.0	2.0 / 1.3 / .9	2.2 / 1.5 / 1.0	2.9 / 1.5 / 1.0
42 8.6 / 58 6.3 / 81 4.5	38 9.6 / 58 6.3 / 78 4.7	37 10.0 / 59 6.2 / 87 4.2	Sales/Receivables	14 26.0 / 37 9.8 / 87 4.2	32 11.4 / 53 6.9 / 89 4.1	34 10.8 / 42 8.7 / 68 5.4	48 7.6 / 59 6.2 / 78 4.7	51 7.1 / 68 5.4 / 94 3.9	50 7.3 / 66 5.5 / 96 3.8
			Cost of Sales/Inventory						
			Cost of Sales/Payables						
6.2 / 10.3 / 41.3	6.3 / 11.5 / 51.2	5.9 / 11.8 / 83.2	Sales/Working Capital	5.6 / 8.7 / UND	21.2 / -42.1	4.7 / 9.5 / 43.9	7.5 / 13.2 / 64.8	5.4 / 8.3 / 23.3	3.7 / 6.6 / 17.0
(139) 20.2 / 6.0 / 2.1	(145) 21.7 / 7.3 / 1.6	(182) 27.6 / 8.3 / 2.6	EBIT/Interest	(22) 12.0 / 5.9 / 3.6	(60) 24.0 / 6.7 / 1.6	(21) 54.6 / 10.2 / 2.1	(27) 27.6 / 13.7 / 2.2	(33) 45.9 / 16.0 / 4.1	(19) 31.3 / 9.8 / 4.2
(52) 16.0 / 3.9 / 1.6	(39) 10.5 / 2.2 / .4	(49) 20.6 / 5.6 / 1.8	Net Profit + Depr., Dep., Amort./Cur. Mat. L/T/D		(10) 11.8 / 5.5 / 2.2		(13) 20.6 / 8.9 / 1.8		
.3 / .5 / 1.1	.2 / .4 / 1.1	.2 / .4 / 1.3	Fixed/Worth	.2 / .7 / -27.3	.2 / .6 / 2.4	.1 / .3 / .7	.2 / .3 / 1.1	.1 / .4 / .8	.1 / .2 / .8
.8 / 1.7 / 3.7	.6 / 1.3 / 4.3	.6 / 1.6 / 5.1	Debt/Worth	.4 / 2.1 / -35.7	.8 / 2.2 / 8.2	.3 / 1.2 / 4.8	.8 / 1.8 / 5.1	.8 / 1.6 / 3.8	.6 / .9 / 1.5
(153) 64.7 / 34.6 / 15.5	(161) 69.6 / 31.2 / 6.6	(191) 75.8 / 40.5 / 17.9	% Profit Before Taxes/Tangible Net Worth	(23) 80.7 / 27.2 / 12.6	(55) 64.0 / 33.7 / 12.8	(23) 84.4 / 38.7 / 15.3	(36) 83.5 / 52.4 / 29.3	(24) 71.7 / 47.3 / 21.8	56.3 / 30.8 / 11.8
21.7 / 12.9 / 4.1	23.3 / 11.0 / 1.7	25.4 / 14.0 / 4.7	% Profit Before Taxes/Total Assets	25.4 / 14.2 / 3.5	19.4 / 11.2 / 5.1	36.3 / 13.1 / 2.9	25.7 / 19.9 / 7.2	27.1 / 15.0 / 4.9	26.0 / 12.7 / 5.2
37.4 / 15.6 / 8.9	39.2 / 17.5 / 9.7	47.7 / 20.6 / 11.4	Sales/Net Fixed Assets	36.9 / 13.5 / 7.6	34.6 / 20.2 / 13.2	52.2 / 19.8 / 16.1	62.6 / 35.0 / 14.8	47.7 / 23.9 / 12.9	54.4 / 15.6 / 7.5
3.7 / 2.6 / 1.7	3.9 / 2.7 / 2.0	3.9 / 2.6 / 1.9	Sales/Total Assets	3.5 / 2.5 / 1.5	4.5 / 3.0 / 2.0	4.4 / 2.8 / 2.3	4.2 / 3.2 / 1.9	3.5 / 2.6 / 1.9	2.8 / 2.0 / 1.6
(126) 1.1 / 2.5 / 4.3	(137) .9 / 2.3 / 4.4	(170) .8 / 1.7 / 3.3	% Depr., Dep., Amort./Sales	(24) 1.4 / 2.3 / 6.4	(53) .9 / 1.7 / 2.6	(20) .9 / 2.2 / 4.1	(27) .5 / 1.1 / 1.7	(31) .5 / 1.8 / 3.3	(15) .9 / 2.5 / 3.6
(45) 4.5 / 8.5 / 20.8	(55) 2.6 / 6.5 / 16.1	(60) 4.0 / 9.2 / 13.8	% Officers', Directors', Owners' Comp/Sales	(13) 9.5 / 12.9 / 18.5	(25) 7.0 / 11.1 / 20.1				
2530161M	3155559M	3269144M	Net Sales ($)	17546M	127981M	94024M	241084M	554555M	2233954M
1494592M	1653202M	1746899M	Total Assets ($)	8887M	53899M	33658M	89772M	236980M	1323703M

							Comparative Historical Data	
Current Data Sorted By Assets								
1	1	3	1		1	# Postretirement Benefits		
						Type of Statement		
		13	2	2	3	Unqualified	26	19
1	2	3	4			Reviewed	7	15
2	4	2	1			Compiled	9	9
1						Tax Returns		
2	5	4	5		1	Other	11	10
	19 (4/1-9/30/94)		38 (10/1/94-3/31/95)				4/1/90-3/31/91	4/1/91-3/31/92
0-500M	500M-2MM	2-10MM	10-50MM	50-100MM	100-250MM		ALL	ALL
6	11	22	12	2	4	NUMBER OF STATEMENTS	53	53
%	%	%	%	%	%	**ASSETS**	%	%
	6.0	5.9	2.8			Cash & Equivalents	4.6	5.7
	20.9	30.4	14.6			Trade Receivables - (net)	18.6	15.5
	9.0	9.7	15.2			Inventory	13.1	13.9
	2.6	10.5	18.4			All Other Current	4.1	2.6
	38.4	56.5	50.9			Total Current	40.4	37.7
	43.3	35.2	35.7			Fixed Assets (net)	35.2	41.0
	.5	1.0	.1			Intangibles (net)	1.1	1.3
	17.8	7.3	13.2			All Other Non-Current	23.3	20.0
	100.0	100.0	100.0			Total	100.0	100.0
						LIABILITIES		
	15.1	11.0	15.2			Notes Payable-Short Term	14.1	12.2
	12.6	12.6	13.9			Cur. Mat. -L/T/D	12.3	13.3
	8.0	13.3	9.4			Trade Payables	9.1	8.8
	.3	.9	.1			Income Taxes Payable	.4	.3
	11.4	5.5	9.5			All Other Current	6.1	5.4
	47.4	43.3	48.1			Total Current	41.9	40.2
	19.0	19.3	26.3			Long Term Debt	24.1	23.1
	1.2	3.3	1.2			Deferred Taxes	1.8	1.7
	3.0	1.6	6.9			All Other-Non-Current	8.6	6.8
	29.4	32.5	17.6			Net Worth	23.6	28.3
	100.0	100.0	100.0			Total Liabilities & Net Worth	100.0	100.0
						INCOME DATA		
	100.0	100.0	100.0			Net Sales	100.0	100.0
						Gross Profit		
	96.9	86.3	85.4			Operating Expenses	84.5	89.9
	3.1	13.7	14.6			Operating Profit	15.5	10.1
	1.7	5.4	6.9			All Other Expenses (net)	7.5	6.4
	1.4	8.4	7.7			Profit Before Taxes	7.9	3.7
						RATIOS		
	1.0	1.9	1.5				1.7	1.6
	.6	1.2	1.0			Current	.8	.8
	.5	.8	.2				.3	.3
	.9	1.2	.7				1.1	.9
	.6	.8	.2			Quick	.5	.5
	.3	.4	.1				.2	.2
4 89.5		23 15.8	3 106.7				18 20.6	14 25.2
28 13.0		42 8.7	27 13.7			Sales/Receivables	30 12.2	30 12.3
58 6.3		63 5.8	48 7.6				54 6.8	47 7.8
						Cost of Sales/Inventory		
						Cost of Sales/Payables		
	-999.8	6.2	11.4				8.7	10.2
	-7.9	36.2	-41.2			Sales/Working Capital	-90.0	-26.6
	-5.7	-5.4	-2.1				-2.7	-4.0
	3.0	(17) 7.2	(10) 3.8				(44) 2.6	(48) 2.3
	2.0	2.8	1.9			EBIT/Interest	1.6	1.6
	1.2	1.9	1.4				1.3	1.1
		(12) 2.1					(17) 2.4	(20) 5.1
		1.2				Net Profit + Depr., Dep., Amort./Cur. Mat. L /T/D	1.0	.8
		.9					.3	.3
	.5	.2	.3				.2	.3
	1.3	.9	.9			Fixed/Worth	.6	1.5
	2.6	2.5	4.7				3.6	4.6
	1.5	1.9	3.0				1.7	1.4
	2.4	3.3	6.2			Debt/Worth	4.2	3.7
	4.4	5.5	8.5				11.5	8.5
	40.4	43.1	61.1				60.2	34.8
	(10) 22.7	29.7	26.0			% Profit Before Taxes/Tangible Net Worth	(50) 32.8	(51) 18.5
	-3.5	23.5	20.7				10.7	2.5
	7.6	15.3	10.6				11.4	6.9
	6.1	7.6	4.1			% Profit Before Taxes/Total Assets	4.5	3.6
	.8	3.6	2.6				1.3	.6
	37.1	58.1	31.9				50.9	38.5
	5.6	6.1	9.6			Sales/Net Fixed Assets	10.3	5.4
	2.3	1.3	.7				1.3	1.4
	2.5	3.1	1.8				3.0	2.3
	2.0	1.5	.8			Sales/Total Assets	1.1	1.0
	1.4	.7	.4				.6	.5
	.6	.8					1.1	2.6
	(10) 6.4	(19) 10.3				% Depr., Dep., Amort./Sales	(32) 14.0	(43) 7.4
	15.4	39.1					28.7	23.1
							(14) 1.6	
						% Officers', Directors', Owners' Comp/Sales	3.0	
							6.3	
3891M	34764M	215955M	520777M	91907M	324750M	Net Sales ($)	1232591M	1198924M
1613M	11286M	118526M	285895M	170891M	795932M	Total Assets ($)	1292548M	1400444M

Comparative Historical Data | Current Data Sorted By Sales

1	2	7	# Postretirement Benefits / Type of Statement	0-1MM	1-3MM	3-5MM	5-10MM	10-25MM	25MM & OVER
			(# Postretirement Benefits)	1	1			4	1
23	16	20	Unqualified		2	4	4	3	7
7	13	10	Reviewed		4	1	2	3	
9	9	9	Compiled	3	2	1	1	1	1
1		1	Tax Returns	1					
14	14	17	Other	2	5		2	4	4
4/1/92-3/31/93 ALL	4/1/93-3/31/94 ALL	4/1/94-3/31/95 ALL			19 (4/1-9/30/94)			38 (10/1/94-3/31/95)	
54	52	57	NUMBER OF STATEMENTS	6	13	6	9	11	12
%	%	%	ASSETS	%	%	%	%	%	%
7.0	7.1	5.1	Cash & Equivalents		3.5			6.8	3.3
19.8	19.2	20.5	Trade Receivables - (net)		27.1			20.3	20.4
14.0	13.1	10.7	Inventory		9.3			12.0	13.9
2.3	5.4	11.8	All Other Current		2.0			18.0	16.0
43.1	44.7	48.0	Total Current		41.9			57.0	53.4
42.9	36.1	35.2	Fixed Assets (net)		43.7			20.4	21.2
.6	2.7	.8	Intangibles (net)		.4			1.1	.3
13.4	16.4	16.0	All Other Non-Current		14.1			21.5	25.0
100.0	100.0	100.0	Total		100.0			100.0	100.0
			LIABILITIES						
13.2	13.1	11.9	Notes Payable-Short Term		14.8			13.7	11.9
11.7	11.9	13.4	Cur. Mat.-L /T/D		11.4			8.5	12.3
6.8	8.2	9.4	Trade Payables		11.3			10.0	12.3
.3	.2	.4	Income Taxes Payable		.2			1.8	.0
7.6	9.3	8.1	All Other Current		9.1			14.2	6.2
39.6	42.8	43.2	Total Current		46.8			48.3	42.8
27.9	22.1	22.4	Long Term Debt		22.9			25.1	23.4
1.1	1.1	2.5	Deferred Taxes		1.4			8.3	1.6
7.5	7.3	5.7	All Other-Non-Current		5.5			1.6	10.6
23.9	26.7	26.2	Net Worth		23.4			16.6	21.7
100.0	100.0	100.0	Total Liabilities & Net Worth		100.0			100.0	100.0
			INCOME DATA						
100.0	100.0	100.0	Net Sales		100.0			100.0	100.0
			Gross Profit						
85.6	87.1	86.5	Operating Expenses		89.4			83.9	89.8
14.4	12.9	13.5	Operating Profit		10.6			16.1	10.2
7.8	5.9	5.4	All Other Expenses (net)		6.5			5.4	4.1
6.6	7.0	8.1	Profit Before Taxes		4.2			10.7	6.2
			RATIOS						
1.6	1.8	1.6			1.3			1.2	1.8
1.0	.9	1.0	Current		.7			1.0	1.4
.4	.5	.5			.5			.3	.5
1.0	.9	.9			1.1			.9	.9
.5	.6	.6	Quick		.6			.3	.5
.3	.2	.3			.3			.0	.3
10 34.9	9 40.6	5 70.8		22 16.4				0 UND	13 29.2
33 11.0	31 11.9	33 11.2	Sales/Receivables	36 10.1				43 8.5	25 14.6
51 7.1	53 6.9	54 6.8		76 4.8				51 7.1	57 6.4
			Cost of Sales/Inventory						
			Cost of Sales/Payables						
9.0	8.8	10.4			6.3			27.0	9.3
NM	-79.1	-149.8	Sales/Working Capital		-21.7			-999.8	22.4
-4.3	-5.3	-5.1			-5.8			-5.0	-15.0
4.3	4.8	3.4			2.2				17.9
(49) 1.8	(48) 2.2	(48) 2.3	EBIT/Interest	(12) 1.6				(10) 2.4	
1.4	1.1	1.6			.4				1.6
2.1	7.3	2.1							
(13) 1.0	(10) .5	(24) 1.1	Net Profit + Depr., Dep., Amort./Cur. Mat. L/T/D						
.4	.3	.8							
.3	.3	.3			.8			.3	.1
1.4	1.4	1.1	Fixed/Worth		2.2			.9	.3
4.3	3.8	2.7			3.6			1.3	1.7
1.5	1.6	2.1			1.6			4.6	2.7
3.8	4.2	4.0	Debt/Worth		3.8			5.8	5.5
7.7	9.6	6.2			5.5			7.1	8.9
41.3	57.1	41.5			31.3			68.7	83.2
(49) 19.7	(48) 29.5	(55) 29.8	% Profit Before Taxes/Tangible Net Worth	(11) 22.8				38.2	30.7
5.3	9.2	21.0			-12.4			22.1	25.6
10.1	10.5	10.7			6.9			9.4	11.8
4.5	4.3	6.4	% Profit Before Taxes/Total Assets		5.0			5.1	7.6
2.1	.4	2.9			-1.5			2.7	2.8
19.6	22.2	40.4			21.8			47.1	126.0
3.4	5.6	5.6	Sales/Net Fixed Assets		3.1			23.9	20.0
.9	1.4	1.6			1.8			2.2	3.1
2.5	2.2	2.5			2.2			4.2	3.3
1.0	1.1	1.4	Sales/Total Assets		1.6			1.1	1.7
.5	.5	.5			1.1			.4	.5
2.6	3.7	1.0			1.2				
(38) 11.0	(40) 11.0	(45) 10.4	% Depr., Dep., Amort./Sales	(12) 10.3					
40.3	35.9	36.1			27.4				
3.4	2.5	1.0							
(15) 7.5	(22) 4.4	(17) 3.2	% Officers', Directors', Owners' Comp/Sales						
10.0	11.3	8.0							
690421M	949634M	1192044M	Net Sales ($)	3361M	22883M	22141M	64666M	173937M	905056M
922418M	1207203M	1384143M	Total Assets ($)	5831M	25508M	38370M	72101M	355355M	886978M

M = $ thousand   MM = $ million
See Pages 1 through 15 for Explanation of Ratios and Data

Current Data Sorted By Assets / Comparative Historical Data

						# Postretirement Benefits Type of Statement		
7	6	9	2					
6	21	53	23	4	4	Unqualified	62	66
27	47	37	3		1	Reviewed	63	61
43	27	12				Compiled	68	63
18	4	2				Tax Returns	2	5
44	37	47	13	3	4	Other	74	74
	144 (4/1-9/30/94)		336 (10/1/94-3/31/95)				4/1/90-3/31/91	4/1/91-3/31/92
0-500M	500M-2MM	2-10MM	10-50MM	50-100MM	100-250MM		ALL	ALL
138	136	151	39	7	9	NUMBER OF STATEMENTS	269	269
%	%	%	%	%	%	ASSETS	%	%
19.8	14.1	12.0	12.2			Cash & Equivalents	13.5	15.1
37.7	47.5	48.0	34.9			Trade Receivables - (net)	37.1	38.6
2.7	2.0	3.3	5.3			Inventory	4.1	3.9
3.4	5.1	5.4	7.2			All Other Current	4.3	3.8
63.6	68.8	68.6	59.5			Total Current	59.1	61.4
23.4	19.1	18.1	22.5			Fixed Assets (net)	23.5	22.1
3.1	2.7	2.3	7.9			Intangibles (net)	2.5	3.6
9.8	9.3	11.0	10.2			All Other Non-Current	14.9	12.9
100.0	100.0	100.0	100.0			Total	100.0	100.0
						LIABILITIES		
11.6	10.2	11.4	7.0			Notes Payable-Short Term	14.5	12.3
6.2	3.0	2.8	2.5			Cur. Mat. -L/T/D	3.4	3.4
11.7	13.1	14.0	11.5			Trade Payables	13.0	11.8
1.0	1.6	.9	.3			Income Taxes Payable	1.0	1.0
16.0	18.8	18.1	16.9			All Other Current	14.9	15.9
46.6	46.7	47.2	38.2			Total Current	46.7	44.4
11.0	9.2	8.0	13.0			Long Term Debt	11.6	11.6
.4	1.6	1.8	1.9			Deferred Taxes	1.1	1.5
3.2	2.7	5.0	2.8			All Other-Non-Current	4.3	2.8
38.8	39.8	38.0	44.0			Net Worth	36.3	39.7
100.0	100.0	100.0	100.0			Total Liabilities & Net Worth	100.0	100.0
						INCOME DATA		
100.0	100.0	100.0	100.0			Net Sales	100.0	100.0
						Gross Profit		
93.2	95.1	92.8	89.3			Operating Expenses	92.6	94.1
6.8	4.9	7.2	10.7			Operating Profit	7.4	5.9
1.2	1.0	1.3	1.5			All Other Expenses (net)	2.7	1.2
5.5	3.9	5.9	9.3			Profit Before Taxes	4.8	4.6
						RATIOS		
3.1	2.4	2.3	2.2			Current	2.0	2.4
1.3	1.5	1.5	1.6				1.4	1.4
1.0	1.0	1.1	1.2				.9	.9
3.0	2.3	2.0	1.7			Quick	1.7	2.1
1.2	1.4	1.3	1.4				1.1	1.3
.7	.9	.9	.9				.8	.8

Sales/Receivables

4	88.3	32	11.5	48	7.6	40	9.1			23	16.0	23	15.6
39	9.3	59	6.2	66	5.5	62	5.9			49	7.4	49	7.4
63	5.8	83	4.4	99	3.7	91	4.0			79	4.6	85	4.3

Cost of Sales/Inventory

Cost of Sales/Payables

0-500M	500M-2MM	2-10MM	10-50MM				4/1/90-3/31/91	4/1/91-3/31/92
9.5	7.0	6.6	6.7			Sales/Working Capital	8.0	6.8
26.3	12.5	11.7	9.8				21.2	16.0
NM	95.3	73.1	20.1				-115.3	-92.2

EBIT/Interest

	22.7		13.9		28.4		31.7				9.7		10.6
(99)	6.0	(112)	4.1	(134)	6.3	(32)	7.1			(208)	3.4	(225)	3.9
	1.5		.9		2.2		3.9				1.3		1.3

Net Profit + Depr., Dep., Amort./Cur. Mat. L /T/D

	4.9		6.9		8.6		17.3				4.9		5.8
(18)	1.6	(37)	2.0	(55)	3.3	(20)	5.0			(102)	1.9	(90)	2.2
	.3		.9		1.0		2.2				.9		.6

0-500M	500M-2MM	2-10MM	10-50MM				4/1/90-3/31/91	4/1/91-3/31/92
.1	.2	.2	.2			Fixed/Worth	.2	.2
.4	.4	.4	.5				.6	.4
1.5	1.2	1.1	1.2				1.6	1.4
.6	.7	.9	.7			Debt/Worth	.9	.7
1.6	1.5	1.9	2.2				2.1	1.8
4.7	4.2	4.3	3.5				5.4	5.0

% Profit Before Taxes/Tangible Net Worth

	100.0		43.1		60.8		50.5				56.3		52.4
(119)	40.0	(123)	20.0	(142)	33.7	(36)	28.9			(243)	17.7	(245)	23.0
	12.7		2.5		11.9		13.1				3.7		4.7

0-500M	500M-2MM	2-10MM	10-50MM				4/1/90-3/31/91	4/1/91-3/31/92
37.1	13.9	20.2	17.2			% Profit Before Taxes/Total Assets	15.4	20.4
11.9	6.7	9.4	8.3				5.8	7.4
2.0	.4	3.1	4.5				.4	1.0
62.9	42.9	42.6	17.4			Sales/Net Fixed Assets	39.4	49.4
22.2	22.9	23.1	12.0				17.7	20.3
12.6	13.1	11.8	7.6				7.9	7.7
6.4	4.3	3.4	2.6			Sales/Total Assets	4.0	3.8
4.0	2.9	2.4	2.0				2.7	2.8
2.7		1.6	1.1				1.6	1.7

% Depr., Dep., Amort./Sales

	.9		1.0		.8		1.4				.9		.7
(92)	1.6	(114)	1.6	(133)	1.5	(32)	2.3			(227)	1.7	(231)	1.5
	2.7		2.9		2.8		3.3				3.2		3.1

% Officers', Directors', Owners' Comp/Sales

	8.0		4.9		4.5						5.6		9.4
(66)	16.4	(43)	8.8	(29)	8.4					(88)	13.9	(83)	14.2
	23.6		16.5		12.9						23.1		25.7

129496M	476339M	1558038M	1594879M	438041M	1597857M	Net Sales ($)	3130189M	4419384M
30591M	142121M	644323M	906894M	438613M	1349589M	Total Assets ($)	1833916M	2508300M

M = $ thousand   MM = $ million
See Pages 1 through 15 for Explanation of Ratios and Data

Comparative Historical Data				Current Data Sorted By Sales					
10	10	24	# Postretirement Benefits	6	9	1	4	3	1
			Type of Statement						
58	78	111	Unqualified	10	12	10	21	31	27
84	68	115	Reviewed	16	35	19	30	12	3
69	61	82	Compiled	25	36	7	8	6	
9	12	24	Tax Returns	12	9	2		1	
75	97	148	Other	31	36	14	27	25	15
4/1/92-3/31/93 ALL	4/1/93-3/31/94 ALL	4/1/94-3/31/95 ALL		144 (4/1-9/30/94)			336 (10/1/94-3/31/95)		
				0-1MM	1-3MM	3-5MM	5-10MM	10-25MM	25MM & OVER
295	316	480	**NUMBER OF STATEMENTS**	94	128	52	86	75	45
%	%	%	**ASSETS**	%	%	%	%	%	%
14.1	14.2	14.9	Cash & Equivalents	19.6	17.3	11.2	12.3	10.4	14.5
41.3	41.9	42.9	Trade Receivables - (net)	30.3	42.1	53.3	52.0	46.1	36.4
2.8	3.6	3.1	Inventory	2.3	2.5	1.9	3.1	4.1	5.9
4.3	5.5	5.0	All Other Current	4.8	4.3	6.9	4.3	4.8	6.5
62.5	65.2	65.8	Total Current	57.0	66.2	73.3	71.7	65.4	63.3
21.3	20.5	20.3	Fixed Assets (net)	26.5	21.5	16.5	15.9	18.5	20.0
2.4	3.1	3.3	Intangibles (net)	4.4	2.6	3.0	1.2	3.7	6.9
13.8	11.2	10.6	All Other Non-Current	12.1	9.7	7.3	11.2	12.4	9.8
100.0	100.0	100.0	Total	100.0	100.0	100.0	100.0	100.0	100.0
			LIABILITIES						
10.3	10.0	10.8	Notes Payable-Short Term	10.7	10.9	15.0	8.2	13.1	6.6
3.6	3.3	3.8	Cur. Mat.-L /T/D	5.7	4.4	3.0	3.3	2.1	3.2
12.6	13.1	12.7	Trade Payables	11.3	10.1	14.7	13.0	17.7	11.5
1.0	1.0	1.1	Income Taxes Payable	1.9	1.2	.6	.6	.7	1.3
17.3	17.8	17.4	All Other Current	14.7	17.3	17.6	17.3	19.7	19.7
44.9	45.2	45.8	Total Current	44.3	44.0	50.7	42.3	53.4	42.3
11.7	9.5	9.8	Long Term Debt	12.6	10.1	10.4	7.1	7.0	11.8
1.7	1.5	1.4	Deferred Taxes	.4	.5	3.0	2.2	1.0	2.5
3.6	4.4	3.8	All Other-Non-Current	3.4	2.0	4.3	4.7	5.8	4.0
38.2	39.4	39.3	Net Worth	39.3	43.3	31.5	43.6	32.8	39.4
100.0	100.0	100.0	Total Liabilities & Net Worth	100.0	100.0	100.0	100.0	100.0	100.0
			INCOME DATA						
100.0	100.0	100.0	Net Sales	100.0	100.0	100.0	100.0	100.0	100.0
			Gross Profit						
94.4	92.3	92.8	Operating Expenses	91.3	93.6	92.7	93.1	92.1	94.7
5.6	7.7	7.2	Operating Profit	8.7	6.4	7.3	6.9	7.9	5.3
1.5	1.5	1.5	All Other Expenses (net)	1.7	1.3	2.0	1.1	2.2	.9
4.0	6.1	5.7	Profit Before Taxes	7.1	5.2	5.3	5.8	5.7	4.5
			RATIOS						
2.3	2.5	2.4	Current	2.7	3.0	2.3	2.6	2.0	2.1
1.5	1.5	1.5		1.2	1.5	1.5	1.7	1.3	1.5
1.0	1.0	1.1		.7	1.1	1.1	1.2	.9	1.2
2.0	2.2	2.2	Quick	2.4	2.6	2.0	2.5	1.9	1.7
1.4	1.3	1.3		1.1	1.4	1.3	1.6	1.1	1.3
.8	.8	.8		.6	.9	.9	1.0	.7	.8
24 15.3	30 12.2	29 12.4	Sales/Receivables	0 UND	18 20.2	45 8.1	51 7.2	29 12.7	38 9.6
49 7.4	57 6.4	57 6.4		38 9.6	52 7.0	73 5.0	61 6.0	62 5.9	61 6.0
79 4.6	85 4.3	83 4.4		63 5.8	81 4.5	96 3.8	89 4.1	87 4.2	83 4.4
			Cost of Sales/Inventory						
			Cost of Sales/Payables						
6.8	5.8	7.0	Sales/Working Capital	8.8	6.9	6.7	6.1	7.9	7.5
16.2	13.5	13.6		30.0	13.6	13.3	9.1	20.4	11.2
−150.5	103.4	127.7		−16.7	108.8	60.7	25.9	−119.1	24.4
(233) 14.2	(251) 16.2	(389) 18.6	EBIT/Interest	(61) 16.9	(106) 17.2	(43) 13.9	(75) 32.3	(62) 18.0	(42) 22.5
5.0	5.7	5.7		4.0	5.2	4.5	6.8	6.2	6.5
1.8	1.5	1.6		1.4	1.3	1.4	1.8	2.3	2.5
(99) 7.8	(90) 11.3	(136) 8.8	Net Profit + Depr., Dep., Amort./Cur. Mat. L/T/D	(10) 11.3	(31) 4.7	(16) 7.9	(33) 14.3	(21) 8.0	(25) 25.5
2.5	3.1	2.9		2.4	2.0	2.9	2.4	3.6	4.4
.8	.6	1.1		.6	.8	.7	1.1	.7	2.4
.2	.2	.2	Fixed/Worth	.1	.1	.2	.2	.2	.3
.5	.4	.4		.6	.4	.4	.3	.5	.6
1.6	1.1	1.2		2.2	.9	1.4	.6	1.6	1.1
.7	.7	.7	Debt/Worth	.6	.6	.9	.9	1.3	.9
1.6	1.6	1.6		1.5	1.4	2.0	1.4	2.4	1.6
4.9	4.3	4.3		7.3	3.7	7.1	2.3	6.4	4.2
(265) 50.8	(285) 56.0	(433) 60.6	% Profit Before Taxes/Tangible Net Worth	(80) 100.0	(116) 50.8	(45) 53.4	(83) 52.2	(70) 66.6	(39) 44.9
21.6	25.2	27.3		39.7	24.2	27.4	27.0	36.1	27.1
5.4	6.3	8.3		6.7	8.8	5.1	8.3	11.2	14.3
17.3	19.8	21.3	% Profit Before Taxes/Total Assets	36.1	21.7	21.1	26.3	20.0	17.6
6.8	8.3	8.7		8.0	9.9	7.2	9.2	9.2	8.3
1.5	1.4	2.1		1.3	1.3	1.4	2.6	2.3	3.2
49.5	48.0	44.1	Sales/Net Fixed Assets	51.4	49.4	40.3	42.9	48.7	20.1
21.5	18.6	21.2		17.5	24.3	21.1	25.2	27.3	12.5
10.0	9.4	10.7		8.8	12.0	14.3	13.6	12.1	8.7
4.3	3.9	4.1	Sales/Total Assets	4.6	4.8	4.3	3.6	3.9	3.0
3.0	2.6	2.8		2.7	3.1	2.8	2.7	3.0	2.3
2.1	1.7	2.0		1.5	2.4	2.1	2.1	2.1	1.3
(255) .8	(260) .9	(381) .9	% Depr., Dep., Amort./Sales	(58) 1.4	(106) .9	(44) 1.2	(72) .9	(61) .5	(40) 1.3
1.7	1.9	1.7		2.1	1.6	2.0	1.4	1.2	2.1
2.9	3.1	2.9		4.7	2.8	3.1	2.4	2.2	3.0
(101) 7.1	(115) 5.2	(145) 5.6	% Officers', Directors', Owners' Comp/Sales	(45) 9.4	(46) 5.9	(10) 5.0	(22) 3.6	(15) 5.0	
15.0	11.6	11.0		17.0	9.1	8.5	7.3	11.9	
23.5	22.7	22.9		26.3	19.5	30.8	10.6	32.3	
3162961M	4035784M	5794650M	Net Sales ($)	43873M	232519M	203796M	609509M	1120352M	3584601M
1560559M	2646357M	3512131M	Total Assets ($)	34633M	110753M	180031M	333141M	718992M	2134581M

M = $ thousand   MM = $ million
See Pages 1 through 15 for Explanation of Ratios and Data

Current Data Sorted By Assets   Comparative Historical Data

	0-500M	500M-2MM	2-10MM	10-50MM	50-100MM	100-250MM		4/1/90-3/31/91 ALL	4/1/91-3/31/92 ALL
	3	2					# Postretirement Benefits		
							Type of Statement		
	9	12	10	1		1	Unqualified	23	20
	2	2	2				Reviewed	9	7
	32	11	1				Compiled	19	36
	11	3					Tax Returns	4	7
	26	12	1	3		1	Other	16	27
	65 (4/1-9/30/94)			75 (10/1/94-3/31/95)					
NUMBER OF STATEMENTS	80	40	14	4	1	1		71	97
	%	%	%	%	%	%		%	%
							ASSETS		
	19.8	12.9	12.8				Cash & Equivalents	13.9	16.9
	9.4	10.6	20.4				Trade Receivables - (net)	11.5	11.4
	.1	.1	.2				Inventory	.5	.6
	.9	1.3	4.3				All Other Current	1.0	2.2
	30.2	25.0	37.6				Total Current	26.9	31.1
	51.4	65.7	47.3				Fixed Assets (net)	60.2	58.2
	4.4	2.9	2.6				Intangibles (net)	3.0	2.5
	14.1	6.4	12.5				All Other Non-Current	9.9	8.2
	100.0	100.0	100.0				Total	100.0	100.0
							LIABILITIES		
	5.3	4.4	6.7				Notes Payable-Short Term	7.1	7.7
	4.5	3.1	3.8				Cur. Mat. -L/T/D	5.2	6.0
	5.9	6.5	8.6				Trade Payables	5.4	8.2
	.3	.2	.0				Income Taxes Payable	.6	1.1
	14.6	11.0	13.6				All Other Current	10.5	15.5
	30.6	25.2	32.7				Total Current	28.7	38.4
	24.1	35.5	35.0				Long Term Debt	33.1	29.0
	.2	.0	2.0				Deferred Taxes	.1	.1
	4.9	2.5	1.2				All Other-Non-Current	5.5	3.0
	40.2	36.8	29.1				Net Worth	32.5	29.5
	100.0	100.0	100.0				Total Liabilities & Net Worth	100.0	100.0
							INCOME DATA		
	100.0	100.0	100.0				Net Sales	100.0	100.0
							Gross Profit		
	93.0	91.6	96.0				Operating Expenses	92.3	94.1
	7.0	8.4	4.0				Operating Profit	7.7	5.9
	1.3	4.3	2.1				All Other Expenses (net)	3.8	3.1
	5.7	4.2	1.9				Profit Before Taxes	4.0	2.9
							RATIOS		
	2.6	2.0	2.4				Current	1.6	1.5
	1.1	.9	.9					.8	.7
	.3	.3	.6					.4	.3
	2.6	1.9	2.3				Quick	1.6	1.3
	1.1	.7	.8					.7 (96)	.6
	.3	.3	.6					.3	.3
	0 UND	0 UND	8 44.7				Sales/Receivables	0 UND	0 UND
	1 578.8	6 66.2	19 19.3					5 78.7	5 78.7
	12 31.0	14 26.4	34 10.7					26 14.1	18 19.9
							Cost of Sales/Inventory		
							Cost of Sales/Payables		
	21.6	17.5	14.8				Sales/Working Capital	19.2	29.0
	323.3	-76.4	-66.9					-183.0	-38.0
	-15.5	-13.8	-21.7					-15.1	-13.4
	(52) 9.4	(34) 3.8	(12) 5.8				EBIT/Interest	(57) 5.1	(73) 3.5
	3.9	2.3	2.5					2.0	1.5
	1.1	.8	1.6					1.1	.0
		(10) 3.4					Net Profit + Depr., Dep.,	(26) 4.2	(26) 3.2
		1.6					Amort./Cur. Mat. L /T/D	2.1	1.0
		-.0						.8	.3
	.6	1.1	.7				Fixed/Worth	1.0	.7
	1.7	1.9	2.1					2.1	2.2
	5.0	5.8	12.8					9.3	12.5
	.7	.6	1.4				Debt/Worth	.9	.9
	1.5	2.7	3.4					2.7	3.2
	6.0	5.6	19.1					10.3	19.8
	(72) 102.3	(35) 39.0	(12) 55.1				% Profit Before Taxes/Tangible	(62) 77.0	(80) 49.6
	32.3	13.6	16.6				Net Worth	18.5	18.9
	11.3	-1.4	2.3					2.3	-4.7
	36.8	14.1	8.2				% Profit Before Taxes/Total	12.5	15.5
	12.4	7.3	4.9				Assets	4.1	3.4
	3.6	-.7	.7					.4	-2.7
	20.2	8.2	18.7				Sales/Net Fixed Assets	11.1	16.8
	10.3	2.5	5.0					3.4	6.1
	3.2	1.1	1.5					1.4	1.6
	6.5	3.8	4.3				Sales/Total Assets	3.3	5.7
	4.1	1.7	2.5					1.8	2.6
	2.2	.9	1.0					1.1	1.3
	(64) 1.4	(37) 1.8	(12) 1.3				% Depr., Dep., Amort./Sales	(62) 2.1	(86) 1.8
	2.7	3.9	1.9					3.7	3.3
	4.2	6.0	4.4					5.3	4.4
	(38) 3.9	(12) 3.2					% Officers', Directors',	(15) 5.6	(30) 4.0
	6.3	5.0					Owners' Comp/Sales	8.8	6.7
	10.2	10.7						13.1	14.4
	62522M	102400M	144370M	94802M	55323M	249452M	Net Sales ($)	371362M	399267M
	15716M	40316M	58247M	73325M	64691M	169503M	Total Assets ($)	265693M	249382M

M = $ thousand   MM = $ million
See Pages 1 through 15 for Explanation of Ratios and Data

Comparative Historical Data				Current Data Sorted By Sales					
1	6	5							
			# Postretirement Benefits	3	2				
			Type of Statement						
19	29	33	Unqualified	9	8	6	3	5	2
5	5	6	Reviewed	2	2	1	1		
36	46	44	Compiled	31	9	2	2		
16	13	14	Tax Returns	10	4				
31	27	43	Other	24	8	3	3	3	2
4/1/92- 3/31/93	4/1/93- 3/31/94	4/1/94- 3/31/95		65 (4/1-9/30/94)			75 (10/1/94-3/31/95)		
ALL	ALL	ALL		0-1MM	1-3MM	3-5MM	5-10MM	10-25MM	25MM & OVER
107	120	140	NUMBER OF STATEMENTS	76	31	12	9	8	4
%	%	%	ASSETS	%	%	%	%	%	%
16.6	16.9	16.9	Cash & Equivalents	17.6	15.7	20.0			
5.6	8.3	10.6	Trade Receivables - (net)	6.8	10.2	14.4			
.3	.3	.1	Inventory	.1	.1	.3			
2.0	2.9	1.3	All Other Current	.5	1.8	2.5			
24.5	28.4	29.0	Total Current	25.0	27.7	37.2			
60.7	56.4	54.4	Fixed Assets (net)	58.2	57.6	47.8			
5.3	6.0	4.2	Intangibles (net)	4.7	1.6	3.5			
9.5	9.2	12.3	All Other Non-Current	12.1	13.1	11.5			
100.0	100.0	100.0	Total	100.0	100.0	100.0			
			LIABILITIES						
6.2	4.6	5.0	Notes Payable-Short Term	4.7	5.3	5.3			
5.6	5.4	4.0	Cur. Mat.-L /T/D	4.4	2.9	2.8			
4.4	5.0	6.4	Trade Payables	4.9	5.0	6.7			
.5	1.3	.2	Income Taxes Payable	.3	.1	.4			
14.4	12.5	13.7	All Other Current	11.9	13.4	15.6			
31.1	28.7	29.2	Total Current	26.1	26.7	30.9			
31.1	28.6	28.5	Long Term Debt	33.8	21.7	26.1			
.1	.6	.4	Deferred Taxes	.2	.6	.1			
4.9	5.4	3.9	All Other-Non-Current	4.2	5.0	.2			
32.8	36.6	38.0	Net Worth	35.6	46.0	42.8			
100.0	100.0	100.0	Total Liabilities & Net Worth	100.0	100.0	100.0			
			INCOME DATA						
100.0	100.0	100.0	Net Sales	100.0	100.0	100.0			
			Gross Profit						
94.0	93.0	93.0	Operating Expenses	90.5	94.8	97.1			
6.0	7.0	7.0	Operating Profit	9.5	5.2	2.9			
2.5	2.0	2.3	All Other Expenses (net)	3.1	1.3	.4			
3.5	5.0	4.8	Profit Before Taxes	6.3	3.9	2.6			
			RATIOS						
2.0	2.0	2.5		2.7	2.6	2.0			
.7	.9	1.0	Current	1.0	1.0	1.0			
.2	.3	.4		.3	.3	.7			
1.9	1.8	2.3		2.6	2.0	1.8			
.5	.8	1.0	Quick	1.0	1.0	1.0			
.2	.3	.3		.3	.3	.6			
0 UND	0 UND	0 UND		0 UND	0 UND	5 77.4			
0 UND	2 148.3	5 69.1	Sales/Receivables	0 UND	2 183.1	9 41.1			
9 40.8	13 27.8	15 23.7		11 32.9	13 28.1	33 11.2			
			Cost of Sales/Inventory						
			Cost of Sales/Payables						
21.0	29.4	18.2		11.8	27.7	22.1			
-63.9	-135.3	NM	Sales/Working Capital	UND	244.4	-553.0			
-10.3	-18.2	-15.6		-12.2	-20.9	-28.4			
3.6	6.8	6.7		8.2	8.6				
(80) 1.4	(82) 2.2	(103) 2.6	EBIT/Interest	(55) 2.3	(23) 3.0				
.5	1.3	1.0		.9	1.0				
4.9	3.5	3.5							
(27) 1.2	(20) 1.2	(25) 2.0	Net Profit + Depr., Dep., Amort./Cur. Mat. L/T/D						
.7	.7	1.3							
.9	.8	.8		.9	.6	.5			
2.1	2.0	1.7	Fixed/Worth	2.2	1.2	1.0			
20.7	5.6	5.3		6.8	3.2	NM			
.7	.6	.7		.8	.5	.5			
3.0	2.7	1.9	Debt/Worth	2.1	1.2	1.1			
25.3	6.5	6.6		10.9	3.7	NM			
83.3	68.6	80.8		114.1	50.5				
(85) 21.4	(100) 31.0	(123) 23.5	% Profit Before Taxes/Tangible Net Worth	(67) 29.7	(29) 33.3				
.0	9.8	3.3		2.7	12.3				
19.7	22.8	17.4		31.3	21.3	15.1			
3.9	6.9	8.3	% Profit Before Taxes/Total Assets	9.2	9.8	7.0			
-.6	2.1	.6		.6	3.2	.7			
14.3	14.4	16.8		17.3	17.4	15.2			
4.5	5.8	6.0	Sales/Net Fixed Assets	3.9	6.3	6.5			
2.0	2.3	1.9		1.4	2.8	2.1			
6.1	6.0	5.1		4.7	8.3	4.8			
2.6	2.9	2.7	Sales/Total Assets	2.3	4.1	3.3			
1.1	1.4	1.3		1.1	1.8	1.3			
1.6	1.8	1.5		1.8	1.2	1.5			
(93) 3.4	(102) 3.3	(117) 3.0	% Depr., Dep., Amort./Sales	(62) 3.5	(29) 2.8	(10) 2.9			
4.6	4.4	4.6		5.1	4.5	4.1			
3.7	4.6	3.7		4.1	3.8				
(36) 7.3	(49) 7.2	(51) 5.8	% Officers', Directors', Owners' Comp/Sales	(31) 6.6	(16) 5.1				
8.9	13.5	10.0		10.8	9.5				
674767M	638242M	708869M	Net Sales ($)	35181M	56551M	48400M	62261M	136661M	369815M
431868M	416968M	421798M	Total Assets ($)	22046M	23110M	24081M	36624M	48042M	267895M

M = $ thousand   MM = $ million
See Pages 1 through 15 for Explanation of Ratios and Data

SERVICES—DENTAL LABORATORIES. SIC# 8072

Current Data Sorted By Assets							Comparative Historical Data	
		1	1			# Postretirement Benefits Type of Statement		
2	4					Unqualified	2	2
3	6					Reviewed	2	4
3						Compiled	15	15
5	2					Tax Returns		3
						Other	8	7
	12 (4/1-9/30/94)		15 (10/1/94-3/31/95)				4/1/90-3/31/91	4/1/91-3/31/92
0-500M	500M-2MM	2-10MM	10-50MM	50-100MM	100-250MM		ALL	ALL
13	12	1	1			NUMBER OF STATEMENTS	27	31
%	%	%	%	%	%	ASSETS	%	%
11.0	6.1					Cash & Equivalents	8.1	9.0
37.3	35.0					Trade Receivables - (net)	37.2	39.1
9.0	24.3					Inventory	8.2	5.3
1.6	1.2					All Other Current	2.2	1.5
58.8	66.6					Total Current	55.8	54.9
29.4	24.3					Fixed Assets (net)	28.1	24.6
2.5	1.1					Intangibles (net)	2.2	1.8
9.3	8.1					All Other Non-Current	13.8	18.6
100.0	100.0					Total	100.0	100.0
						LIABILITIES		
8.5	11.1					Notes Payable-Short Term	8.2	4.6
7.4	4.5					Cur. Mat. -L/T/D	3.2	7.4
12.0	12.9					Trade Payables	6.4	11.5
.2	.3					Income Taxes Payable	1.7	.9
6.5	8.5					All Other Current	10.9	10.1
34.7	37.4					Total Current	30.5	34.4
15.4	14.0					Long Term Debt	23.5	25.1
.0	.8					Deferred Taxes	1.3	.9
.0	2.6					All Other-Non-Current	1.8	1.4
49.9	45.2					Net Worth	42.9	38.2
100.0	100.0					Total Liabilities & Net Worth	100.0	100.0
						INCOME DATA		
100.0	100.0					Net Sales	100.0	100.0
49.9	39.2					Gross Profit	49.0	49.7
46.1	35.2					Operating Expenses	46.1	41.7
3.8	4.0					Operating Profit	3.0	8.0
.9	1.1					All Other Expenses (net)	.9	1.5
3.0	2.9					Profit Before Taxes	2.1	6.5
						RATIOS		
6.6	2.9					Current	2.5	3.1
2.7	1.7						1.9	1.5
1.1	1.1						1.2	1.2
6.2	2.1					Quick	1.8	2.8
2.3	1.0						1.5	1.4
.9	.7						.8	.9
0 UND	41 9.0					Sales/Receivables	36 10.1	31 11.9
40 9.1	46 8.0						42 8.7	42 8.7
45 8.1	51 7.1						55 6.6	45 8.1
0 UND	13 28.2					Cost of Sales/Inventory	6 63.0	0 UND
8 45.6	30 12.3						24 15.5	5 66.6
20 18.6	140 2.6						33 11.2	20 18.2
0 UND	16 23.1					Cost of Sales/Payables	4 103.6	6 57.7
13 28.1	20 18.3						15 24.1	16 23.3
31 11.8	52 7.0						41 9.0	35 10.4
7.8	6.0					Sales/Working Capital	7.2	9.7
30.2	8.4						11.5	15.3
NM	89.4						32.5	107.0
13.5	6.4					EBIT/Interest	6.5	11.0
(12) 6.3	(11) 4.3						3.1	(29) 4.0
1.3	.6						.7	1.4
						Net Profit + Depr., Dep., Amort./Cur. Mat. L/T/D	11.1	10.0
							(11) 1.8	(16) 3.3
							.4	.4
.4	.1					Fixed/Worth	.3	.2
.6	.5						.7	.7
1.7	1.5						1.0	1.4
.2	.4					Debt/Worth	.6	.7
.6	1.5						1.2	1.6
7.9	2.5						3.3	8.4
46.1	29.7					% Profit Before Taxes/Tangible Net Worth	35.0	51.2
(11) 17.7	19.0						(24) 21.6	(29) 25.0
12.8	1.5						6.5	6.4
22.2	13.1					% Profit Before Taxes/Total Assets	16.6	17.1
12.0	6.7						8.7	9.0
2.6	1.0						−1.9	1.5
23.7	56.3					Sales/Net Fixed Assets	23.1	34.2
16.1	18.3						10.8	20.0
10.2	6.7						5.8	9.4
5.7	3.4					Sales/Total Assets	3.7	4.7
4.7	2.8						2.9	4.0
2.9	1.8						1.9	2.8
1.8						% Depr., Dep., Amort./Sales	1.3	1.1
(11) 2.9							(23) 2.4	(24) 2.2
3.3							3.4	3.2
6.8						% Officers', Directors', Owners' Comp/Sales		9.0
(10) 10.7								(17) 13.1
18.6								24.4
13095M	27265M	10960M	43493M			Net Sales ($)	54244M	57067M
3064M	10387M	4116M	13975M			Total Assets ($)	22908M	22281M

M = $ thousand   MM = $ million
See Pages 1 through 15 for Explanation of Ratios and Data

Comparative Historical Data / Current Data Sorted By Sales

	4/1/92-3/31/93 ALL	4/1/93-3/31/94 ALL	4/1/94-3/31/95 ALL	# Postretirement Benefits / Type of Statement	0-1MM	1-3MM	3-5MM	5-10MM	10-25MM	25MM & OVER
				# Postretirement Benefits		1				
	1	2	2	Unqualified					1	1
	5	4	6	Reviewed		5	1			
	14	10	9	Compiled	3	4	2			
	2	8	3	Tax Returns	3					
	8	4	7	Other	3	4				
					12 (4/1-9/30/94)			15 (10/1/94-3/31/95)		
NUMBER OF STATEMENTS	30	28	27		9	13	3		1	1
	%	%	%	ASSETS	%	%	%	%	%	%
Cash & Equivalents	8.6	10.9	8.1			5.1				
Trade Receivables - (net)	38.2	40.9	36.3			40.3				
Inventory	10.9	10.0	16.0			17.4				
All Other Current	1.3	3.8	1.4			.9				
Total Current	58.9	65.7	61.8			63.7				
Fixed Assets (net)	29.8	22.9	26.8			24.7				
Intangibles (net)	1.8	2.3	2.2			.9				
All Other Non-Current	9.5	9.1	9.2			10.8				
Total	100.0	100.0	100.0			100.0				
				LIABILITIES						
Notes Payable-Short Term	9.3	8.4	9.4			10.5				
Cur. Mat.-L /T/D	7.1	3.4	6.0			4.3				
Trade Payables	12.9	11.4	12.3			13.3				
Income Taxes Payable	.9	1.0	.3			.2				
All Other Current	11.2	10.4	8.3			7.3				
Total Current	41.4	34.5	36.2			35.7				
Long Term Debt	23.6	13.4	15.3			11.3				
Deferred Taxes	.6	.6	.3			.7				
All Other-Non-Current	.7	1.9	2.9			2.4				
Net Worth	33.8	49.5	45.2			49.9				
Total Liabilities & Net Worth	100.0	100.0	100.0			100.0				
				INCOME DATA						
Net Sales	100.0	100.0	100.0			100.0				
Gross Profit	44.7	50.6	44.4			42.5				
Operating Expenses	40.0	44.7	40.7			38.5				
Operating Profit	4.7	5.9	3.8			3.9				
All Other Expenses (net)	.8	.0	1.0			.4				
Profit Before Taxes	4.0	5.9	2.7			3.5				
				RATIOS						
Current	3.0 / 1.5 / 1.1	2.9 / 1.9 / 1.4	4.4 / 1.8 / 1.2			3.2 / 2.4 / 1.2				
Quick	2.2 / 1.3 / .9	2.4 / 1.4 / 1.1	2.9 / 1.2 / .8			2.6 / 1.2 / .8				
Sales/Receivables	30 12.1 / 41 9.0 / 49 7.4	38 9.5 / 46 8.0 / 54 6.7	33 10.9 / 45 8.1 / 49 7.5			37 10.0 / 46 8.0 / 54 6.8				
Cost of Sales/Inventory	8 43.4 / 17 21.4 / 27 13.5	0 UND / 14 25.5 / 28 12.9	5 76.4 / 17 21.3 / 54 6.7			6 57.5 / 19 18.8 / 52 7.0				
Cost of Sales/Payables	10 36.2 / 19 19.7 / 39 9.4	10 35.6 / 21 17.6 / 28 12.9	10 36.5 / 19 19.5 / 42 8.6			14 26.6 / 19 19.1 / 45 8.2				
Sales/Working Capital	7.9 / 17.9 / 55.2	6.7 / 12.9 / 21.8	6.1 / 17.3 / 58.9			6.1 / 9.1 / 52.4				
EBIT/Interest	(27) 5.3 / 2.7 / 1.3	(25) 11.2 / 6.3 / 2.8	(25) 8.5 / 4.3 / .9			8.5 / 5.8 / 3.8				
Net Profit + Depr., Dep., Amort./Cur. Mat. L/T/D	(18) 5.0 / 2.3 / .7	(11) 12.3 / 2.6 / .7	(13) 2.9 / 1.1 / .4							
Fixed/Worth	.5 / .7 / 2.2	.2 / .4 / .7	.3 / .6 / 1.6			.2 / .6 / 1.4				
Debt/Worth	.7 / 1.5 / 5.5	.4 / 1.0 / 1.9	.3 / 1.2 / 2.7			.4 / 1.2 / 2.3				
% Profit Before Taxes/Tangible Net Worth	(24) 27.4 / 13.1 / 5.8	(25) 65.9 / 20.9 / 2.8	(24) 38.4 / 17.4 / 3.7			35.8 / 21.8 / 12.8				
% Profit Before Taxes/Total Assets	10.1 / 6.6 / 1.8	25.9 / 9.2 / 1.5	14.0 / 7.1 / .8			15.0 / 12.3 / 6.0				
Sales/Net Fixed Assets	20.1 / 12.8 / 7.3	27.1 / 14.4 / 9.5	26.1 / 16.5 / 8.7			37.7 / 21.3 / 10.4				
Sales/Total Assets	4.3 / 3.4 / 2.3	4.1 / 3.2 / 2.3	4.7 / 3.1 / 2.7			5.2 / 2.8 / 2.2				
% Depr., Dep., Amort./Sales	(26) 1.3 / 2.0 / 2.7	(24) 1.1 / 1.7 / 3.0	(22) 1.6 / 2.5 / 3.3			(11) 1.5 / 2.0 / 2.4				
% Officers', Directors', Owners' Comp/Sales	(18) 8.4 / 13.4 / 17.6	(15) 7.8 / 12.0 / 15.9	(13) 7.6 / 10.6 / 18.6							
Net Sales ($)	67570M	84627M	94813M		6700M	23661M	9999M		10960M	43493M
Total Assets ($)	24712M	29144M	31542M		2453M	8018M	2980M		4116M	13975M

M = $ thousand   MM = $ million
See Pages 1 through 15 for Explanation of Ratios and Data

Current Data Sorted By Assets   Comparative Historical Data

# Postretirement Benefits / Type of Statement	0-500M	500M-2MM	2-10MM	10-50MM	50-100MM	100-250MM	4/1/90-3/31/91 ALL	4/1/91-3/31/92 ALL
(13)								
Unqualified		1	3	1			5	8
Reviewed	5	3	2				12	7
Compiled	93	19	2			1	120	133
Tax Returns	48	3					15	22
Other	44	6	3				38	45
	47 (4/1-9/30/94)			187 (10/1/94-3/31/95)				
NUMBER OF STATEMENTS	190	32	10	1		1	190	215

ASSETS	0-500M %	500M-2MM %	2-10MM %	10-50MM %	50-100MM %	100-250MM %	ALL %	ALL %
Cash & Equivalents	19.7	8.9	9.2				17.2	16.8
Trade Receivables - (net)	14.3	36.5	38.1				19.5	19.5
Inventory	.5	.9	6.5				1.1	1.1
All Other Current	2.1	2.0	4.3				2.0	1.6
Total Current	36.6	48.2	58.1				39.8	39.0
Fixed Assets (net)	47.0	33.7	31.9				42.2	45.3
Intangibles (net)	7.9	6.8	4.8				5.1	5.2
All Other Non-Current	8.5	11.3	5.3				12.9	10.5
Total	100.0	100.0	100.0				100.0	100.0
LIABILITIES								
Notes Payable-Short Term	10.1	9.1	7.5				10.7	11.6
Cur. Mat. -L/T/D	8.8	6.8	3.5				8.4	8.4
Trade Payables	1.7	2.5	4.9				2.2	2.2
Income Taxes Payable	.3	1.6	3.4				.9	.6
All Other Current	14.0	8.8	9.3				11.3	12.0
Total Current	34.9	28.8	28.7				33.4	34.8
Long Term Debt	27.3	25.4	20.9				31.2	28.9
Deferred Taxes	.2	1.2	.1				.6	.7
All Other-Non-Current	5.1	8.5	13.1				4.0	4.0
Net Worth	32.6	36.2	37.2				30.7	31.6
Total Liabilities & Net Worth	100.0	100.0	100.0				100.0	100.0
INCOME DATA								
Net Sales	100.0	100.0	100.0				100.0	100.0
Gross Profit								
Operating Expenses	87.7	90.1	86.6				88.9	87.8
Operating Profit	12.3	9.9	13.4				11.1	12.2
All Other Expenses (net)	1.5	1.0	1.7				2.5	1.8
Profit Before Taxes	10.8	8.9	11.7				8.6	10.4

RATIOS	0-500M	500M-2MM	2-10MM	10-50MM	50-100MM	100-250MM	ALL	ALL
Current	3.0	3.8	3.0				3.5	2.8
	1.1	2.2	2.4				1.1	1.2
	.3	1.0	1.0				.4	.5
Quick	2.8	3.2	3.0				3.3	2.5
	1.1	2.1	2.1				1.0	1.1
	.2	.8	.8				.4	.5
Sales/Receivables	0 UND	11 31.8	24 14.9				0 UND	0 UND
	0 UND	54 6.8	51 7.1				0 UND	0 UND
	37 9.8	87 4.2	130 2.8				46 7.9	51 7.2
Cost of Sales/Inventory								
Cost of Sales/Payables								
Sales/Working Capital	12.1	5.8	3.0				10.7	12.4
	133.7	9.5	6.8				144.1	103.3
	-28.9	-97.2	NM				-24.1	-27.3
EBIT/Interest	(146) 12.5	(31) 9.7					(163) 6.8	(190) 9.4
	4.6	4.1					2.1	3.3
	1.1	1.2					.9	1.1
Net Profit + Depr., Dep., Amort./Cur. Mat. L./T/D	(22) 3.6	(11) 4.0					(47) 2.0	(34) 2.4
	1.4	1.2					1.2	1.0
	.8	.6					.2	.1
Fixed/Worth	.5	.3	.3				.6	.6
	2.1	1.4	.6				1.7	1.9
	28.4	6.8	NM				12.7	15.0
Debt/Worth	.6	.6	.5				.9	.9
	2.7	2.4	1.8				2.7	2.9
	75.2	10.1	NM				24.1	37.7
% Profit Before Taxes/Tangible Net Worth	(147) 254.2	(25) 74.1					(153) 139.3	(169) 173.4
	78.6	35.7					25.5	30.6
	5.3	1.3					.0	3.5
% Profit Before Taxes/Total Assets	60.9	20.7	35.5				34.5	36.5
	17.5	6.5	9.0				7.6	9.7
	.7	.3	-2.7				-.0	.0
Sales/Net Fixed Assets	27.8	20.2	22.4				28.7	25.1
	12.4	13.1	8.1				10.5	9.9
	6.3	4.5	3.0				5.9	4.6
Sales/Total Assets	8.6	3.9	2.5				6.6	6.2
	4.7	2.7	2.0				4.0	3.2
	2.8	1.4	1.4				2.3	2.0
% Depr., Dep., Amort./Sales	(156) 1.4	(28) 1.3	1.3				(158) 1.5	(188) 1.5
	2.5	1.9	1.9				2.7	2.8
	4.2	4.8	3.0				4.7	4.3
% Officers', Directors', Owners' Comp/Sales	(117) 20.4	(15) 14.8					(110) 19.0	(128) 19.0
	27.4	23.6					25.8	27.5
	33.8	34.3					33.4	32.9
Net Sales ($)	151551M	75911M	102610M	53746M		351433M	229463M	247831M
Total Assets ($)	30009M	28416M	59363M	31913M		154917M	68522M	75050M

M = $ thousand   MM = $ million
See Pages 1 through 15 for Explanation of Ratios and Data

Comparative Historical Data

Current Data Sorted By Sales

2	6	13	**# Postretirement Benefits**		8	5				
			Type of Statement							
5	3	5	Unqualified				1	1	2	1
14	11	10	Reviewed		4	4		1	1	
146	115	115	Compiled		77	32	4		1	1
45	38	51	Tax Returns		38	11	1	1		
44	48	53	Other		31	13	6	3		
4/1/92-3/31/93	4/1/93-3/31/94	4/1/94-3/31/95			47 (4/1-9/30/94)			187 (10/1/94-3/31/95)		
ALL	ALL	ALL			0-1MM	1-3MM	3-5MM	5-10MM	10-25MM	25MM & OVER
254	215	234	**NUMBER OF STATEMENTS**		150	60	12	6	4	2
%	%	%	**ASSETS**		%	%	%	%	%	%
16.3	17.2	17.6	Cash & Equivalents		19.8	15.6	9.9			
18.7	18.2	18.4	Trade Receivables - (net)		14.7	22.1	37.4			
.9	1.5	1.1	Inventory		.6	.3	1.3			
2.5	2.3	2.2	All Other Current		2.0	2.4	1.3			
38.3	39.2	39.3	Total Current		37.1	40.4	49.9			
46.2	44.4	44.4	Fixed Assets (net)		46.9	43.3	30.8			
6.4	6.8	7.6	Intangibles (net)		8.2	6.1	6.3			
9.1	9.6	8.7	All Other Non-Current		7.8	10.2	13.0			
100.0	100.0	100.0	Total		100.0	100.0	100.0			
			LIABILITIES							
8.9	7.3	9.9	Notes Payable-Short Term		11.5	6.9	6.0			
8.4	8.0	8.2	Cur. Mat.-L /T/D		7.7	11.2	4.8			
1.8	2.9	2.1	Trade Payables		1.7	2.1	2.8			
.4	.9	.6	Income Taxes Payable		.2	1.2	2.5			
12.2	13.5	13.1	All Other Current		12.9	13.6	11.5			
31.7	32.6	34.0	Total Current		34.1	35.0	27.5			
32.0	29.1	26.9	Long Term Debt		26.6	29.5	16.4			
.4	.9	.3	Deferred Taxes		.2	.3	1.5			
5.2	5.5	5.8	All Other-Non-Current		3.4	8.6	12.1			
30.7	31.9	33.0	Net Worth		35.7	26.6	42.4			
100.0	100.0	100.0	Total Liabilities & Net Worth		100.0	100.0	100.0			
			INCOME DATA							
100.0	100.0	100.0	Net Sales		100.0	100.0	100.0			
			Gross Profit							
87.6	87.9	87.9	Operating Expenses		85.9	91.2	94.2			
12.4	12.1	12.1	Operating Profit		14.1	8.8	5.8			
1.9	1.4	1.4	All Other Expenses (net)		1.4	1.9	.2			
10.5	10.7	10.7	Profit Before Taxes		12.7	7.0	5.5			
			RATIOS							
3.0	3.1	3.0			3.4	2.5	3.1			
1.2	1.2	1.4	Current		1.2	1.6	2.2			
.5	.4	.4			.3	.4	.8			
2.6	2.8	2.8			3.0	2.5	2.6			
(253) 1.1	(213) 1.0	1.2	Quick		1.1	1.4	2.1			
.4	.4	.3			.3	.3	.7			
0 UND	0 UND	0 UND			0 UND	0 UND	0 UND			
0 UND	0 UND	0 UND	Sales/Receivables		0 UND	0 UND	32 11.5			
51 7.1	49 7.5	45 8.1			41 8.9	48 7.6	70 5.2			
			Cost of Sales/Inventory							
			Cost of Sales/Payables							
11.4	9.8	9.6			10.5	8.8	7.3			
132.7	240.8	54.4	Sales/Working Capital		81.6	85.4	13.4			
-28.4	-33.0	-31.6			-25.2	-52.2	-81.2			
8.9	12.0	11.9			14.0	9.8	9.9			
(215) 3.0	(177) 4.0	(188) 4.1	EBIT/Interest	(117)	5.5	(48) 3.5	4.2			
.9	1.3	1.2			1.2	1.0	1.2			
2.1	2.4	3.7			4.8	2.2				
(30) 1.6	(28) 1.0	(35) 1.3	Net Profit + Depr., Dep., Amort./Cur. Mat. L/T/D	(13)	1.7	(16) 1.1				
.5	.4	.7			.9	.5				
.6	.5	.4			.5	.5	.2			
1.8	2.2	1.6	Fixed/Worth		1.6	2.4	1.0			
32.6	27.6	21.6			14.1	-45.1	2.3			
.8	.8	.6			.5	.9	.7			
2.4	2.9	2.7	Debt/Worth		2.6	3.1	1.6			
NM	56.2	65.1			38.1	-57.2	2.7			
160.0	166.4	193.6			226.9	229.7	39.6			
(191) 31.5	(166) 49.6	(181) 58.5	% Profit Before Taxes/Tangible Net Worth	(119)	80.0	(43) 58.5	(11) 29.5			
.0	4.6	5.1			5.0	8.1	1.0			
54.3	44.7	52.0			66.9	38.2	19.0			
9.4	10.4	14.7	% Profit Before Taxes/Total Assets		19.5	12.9	8.7			
-.5	.9	.6			.9	.0	.6			
24.5	27.3	24.7			21.7	27.0	65.9			
9.5	13.0	11.9	Sales/Net Fixed Assets		9.9	15.9	23.7			
4.9	6.3	6.1			4.6	9.5	10.5			
6.2	7.0	7.4			7.0	8.6	4.7			
3.5	3.5	4.0	Sales/Total Assets		4.0	4.9	3.6			
2.4	2.4	2.5			2.4	3.5	2.7			
1.5	1.6	1.4			1.5	1.3	.7			
(218) 2.9	(178) 2.6	(195) 2.4	% Depr., Dep., Amort./Sales	(124)	3.1	(51) 1.9	(10) 1.8			
4.7	4.3	4.1			5.2	3.1	3.1			
16.9	19.7	19.0			20.2	17.2				
(151) 25.0	(129) 27.4	(137) 26.0	% Officers', Directors', Owners' Comp/Sales	(87)	26.8	(37) 29.3				
32.4	33.3	33.6			34.8	32.9				
335003M	297492M	735251M	Net Sales ($)		75593M	101123M	46825M	42108M	64423M	405179M
113021M	114033M	304618M	Total Assets ($)		25212M	23201M	18291M	20982M	30102M	186830M

M = $ thousand   MM = $ million
See Pages 1 through 15 for Explanation of Ratios and Data

Current Data Sorted By Assets | **Comparative Historical Data**

Date groupings for current data: 28 (4/1-9/30/94) applies to the 500M-2MM column; 45 (10/1/94-3/31/95) applies to the 10-50MM column.

	0-500M	500M-2MM	2-10MM	10-50MM	50-100MM	100-250MM		4/1/90-3/31/91 ALL	4/1/91-3/31/92 ALL
# Postretirement Benefits	1	3	1						
Type of Statement									
Unqualified		5	5	6		2		16	11
Reviewed	2	6	5					14	13
Compiled	12	12	1					15	17
Tax Returns	1							1	
Other	3	5	7	1				5	10
NUMBER OF STATEMENTS	18	28	18	7		2		51	51
ASSETS	%	%	%	%	%	%		%	%
Cash & Equivalents	13.7	9.3	6.6					10.9	6.9
Trade Receivables - (net)	43.5	47.8	52.1					45.7	45.0
Inventory	.2	2.1	2.3					1.3	1.1
All Other Current	3.6	2.6	1.5					3.1	3.0
Total Current	60.9	61.9	62.5					61.0	56.0
Fixed Assets (net)	23.7	20.7	21.3					21.7	24.2
Intangibles (net)	4.3	4.1	2.1					4.0	5.7
All Other Non-Current	11.1	13.3	14.1					13.2	14.0
Total	100.0	100.0	100.0					100.0	100.0
LIABILITIES									
Notes Payable-Short Term	21.0	14.5	24.1					11.7	11.2
Cur. Mat.-L/T/D	4.6	3.3	4.0					5.1	5.8
Trade Payables	5.7	7.9	8.6					8.0	8.0
Income Taxes Payable	.7	1.0	.2					1.5	1.3
All Other Current	13.6	15.3	16.4					15.4	19.8
Total Current	45.6	42.0	53.2					41.7	46.1
Long Term Debt	18.2	9.2	5.2					15.3	15.3
Deferred Taxes	.0	1.4	.1					1.1	1.8
All Other-Non-Current	6.2	5.5	3.7					4.3	5.1
Net Worth	30.0	41.9	37.8					37.6	31.6
Total Liabilities & Net Worth	100.0	100.0	100.0					100.0	100.0
INCOME DATA									
Net Sales	100.0	100.0	100.0					100.0	100.0
Gross Profit									
Operating Expenses	98.3	97.0	96.1					95.8	95.7
Operating Profit	1.7	3.0	3.9					4.2	4.3
All Other Expenses (net)	.3	.3	1.0					1.1	1.1
Profit Before Taxes	1.4	2.7	2.8					3.2	3.3
RATIOS									
Current	2.3	2.0	1.6					2.1	1.6
	1.2	1.3	1.2					1.3	1.2
	.9	1.1	.8					1.1	.9
Quick	2.2	1.8	1.5					2.1	1.5
	1.1	1.3	1.1					1.2	1.2
	.7	1.0	.8					1.0	.8
Sales/Receivables	0 UND	35 10.4	34 10.6					33 10.9	36 10.2
	34 10.8	45 8.1	45 8.1					41 8.8	41 9.0
	45 8.2	54 6.7	65 5.6					50 7.3	46 8.0
Cost of Sales/Inventory									
Cost of Sales/Payables									
Sales/Working Capital	12.2	14.0	18.5					12.1	17.4
	41.8	26.5	46.2					32.2	39.8
	-69.5	81.7	-24.5					78.0	-70.3
EBIT/Interest	(16) 6.1	(25) 7.5	14.9					(43) 5.2	(49) 9.6
	2.3	3.2	3.4					2.5	2.9
	-1.0	2.1	2.1					1.2	1.3
Net Profit + Depr., Dep., Amort./Cur. Mat. L./T/D		(12) 3.5						(26) 2.9	(26) 5.7
		1.7						2.1	2.3
		.8						1.0	.6
Fixed/Worth	.3	.2	.1					.2	.2
	1.0	.5	.4					.6	.7
	NM	1.6	2.8					1.6	3.3
Debt/Worth	.8	.9	.6					.9	1.0
	3.9	2.0	2.2					2.0	2.6
	NM	3.7	4.1					4.6	8.5
% Profit Before Taxes/Tangible Net Worth	(14) 33.1	51.0	(16) 39.5					(46) 62.9	(45) 64.2
	17.8	24.0	29.3					29.9	25.2
	-16.6	8.5	11.3					6.0	5.8
% Profit Before Taxes/Total Assets	16.4	17.9	19.5					18.8	18.0
	8.0	5.3	7.6					6.9	7.1
	-4.4	2.9	2.7					1.3	1.5
Sales/Net Fixed Assets	50.8	64.8	84.6					57.7	65.7
	33.7	34.3	28.3					24.9	23.5
	12.5	11.2	9.3					13.1	10.8
Sales/Total Assets	6.6	5.1	5.1					5.5	5.4
	5.2	4.4	4.0					4.2	3.9
	3.0	3.3	2.6					2.9	2.9
% Depr., Dep., Amort./Sales	(13) .9	(26) .7	(16) .5					(44) .6	(45) .8
	2.0	1.1	.9					1.3	1.3
	4.7	2.3	4.1					2.7	3.4
% Officers', Directors', Owners' Comp/Sales		(13) 1.5						(22) 2.6	(21) 3.3
		4.9						4.8	4.5
		9.6						12.8	9.1
Net Sales ($)	24580M	126734M	311718M	527878M		951209M		580690M	1134492M
Total Assets ($)	4834M	31426M	78139M	132864M		318637M		168854M	312528M

M = $ thousand   MM = $ million
See Pages 1 through 15 for Explanation of Ratios and Data

Comparative Historical Data | **Current Data Sorted By Sales**

	1	3	5	# Postretirement Benefits		2	1	1	1		9
Type of Statement					0-1MM	1-3MM	3-5MM	5-10MM	10-25MM	25MM & OVER	
Unqualified	14	17	18			1	1	2	5	9	
Reviewed	17	14	13		1	2	4	2	4		
Compiled	15	17	25		5	9	7	3		1	
Tax Returns	1		1		1						
Other	14	12	16		2	5	2	3	1	3	

Periods:
- Historical: 1 = 4/1/92-3/31/93 ALL; 3 = 4/1/93-3/31/94 ALL; 5 = 4/1/94-3/31/95 ALL
- Current: 28 (4/1-9/30/94); 45 (10/1/94-3/31/95)

	Hist 1	Hist 3	Hist 5	0-1MM	1-3MM	3-5MM	5-10MM	10-25MM	25MM & OVER
NUMBER OF STATEMENTS	61	60	73	9	17	14	10	10	13
	%	%	%	%	%	%	%	%	%
ASSETS									
Cash & Equivalents	6.3	9.4	9.0		10.1	10.9	8.5	5.3	4.9
Trade Receivables - (net)	47.5	49.4	47.7		41.8	37.8	60.1	57.3	50.5
Inventory	1.2	.6	1.6		3.4	.9	2.3	1.0	.9
All Other Current	3.3	3.6	2.6		1.5	3.6	1.2	2.1	2.1
Total Current	58.4	63.0	60.8		56.8	53.3	72.0	65.8	58.3
Fixed Assets (net)	23.7	19.3	22.1		20.8	29.8	15.3	20.7	19.7
Intangibles (net)	4.5	6.0	3.6		5.4	6.9	.7	.8	2.9
All Other Non-Current	13.4	11.7	13.5		17.1	10.0	12.0	12.8	19.1
Total	100.0	100.0	100.0		100.0	100.0	100.0	100.0	100.0
LIABILITIES									
Notes Payable-Short Term	17.0	15.9	17.4		11.0	15.4	24.3	26.1	11.0
Cur. Mat.-L /T/D	5.5	5.0	4.1		5.7	3.5	4.7	2.1	4.4
Trade Payables	5.6	6.8	7.8		8.8	8.1	10.4	4.3	10.0
Income Taxes Payable	.9	1.2	.7		.9	1.7	.1	.3	.4
All Other Current	17.9	21.3	15.4		10.9	14.3	16.7	20.2	18.0
Total Current	46.8	50.2	45.4		37.3	43.0	56.1	53.0	43.8
Long Term Debt	12.7	12.8	12.2		11.8	11.2	6.9	6.1	16.4
Deferred Taxes	1.2	1.2	.7		.1	1.7	1.4	.1	.8
All Other-Non-Current	6.6	3.4	5.2		7.7	9.0	.8	1.0	4.0
Net Worth	32.8	32.5	36.5		43.2	35.1	34.8	39.8	35.0
Total Liabilities & Net Worth	100.0	100.0	100.0		100.0	100.0	100.0	100.0	100.0
INCOME DATA									
Net Sales	100.0	100.0	100.0		100.0	100.0	100.0	100.0	100.0
Gross Profit									
Operating Expenses	95.7	97.1	97.1		96.2	97.7	98.2	95.7	96.7
Operating Profit	4.3	2.9	2.9		3.8	2.3	1.8	4.3	3.3
All Other Expenses (net)	.8	1.1	.6		.8	.5	.3	.5	.8
Profit Before Taxes	3.5	1.8	2.4		3.1	1.8	1.5	3.8	2.5
RATIOS									
Current	1.7 / 1.3 / .9	1.6 / 1.1 / 1.0	1.9 / 1.3 / 1.0		2.4 / 1.9 / .9	1.7 / 1.2 / 1.0	1.8 / 1.2 / 1.1	1.6 / 1.3 / .9	1.6 / 1.4 / 1.0
Quick	1.6 / 1.1 / .8	1.6 / 1.1 / .9	1.7 / 1.2 / .9		2.1 / 1.5 / .9	1.6 / 1.1 / .9	1.8 / 1.2 / 1.0	1.4 / 1.2 / .8	1.5 / 1.3 / .9
Sales/Receivables	32 11.5 / 41 8.9 / 53 6.9	30 12.3 / 41 8.8 / 54 6.8	33 11.0 / 43 8.5 / 54 6.7		28 13.0 / 34 10.6 / 54 6.7	19 18.8 / 39 9.3 / 53 6.9	37 9.8 / 48 7.6 / 63 5.8	35 10.3 / 43 8.4 / 59 6.2	37 9.8 / 43 8.4 / 52 7.0
Cost of Sales/Inventory									
Cost of Sales/Payables									
Sales/Working Capital	15.3 / 34.3 / -98.4	14.4 / 58.2 / 861.4	15.4 / 32.3 / 242.5		11.5 / 16.6 / -537.4	19.2 / 48.3 / NM	18.9 / 44.3 / 82.0	18.1 / 41.3 / -67.4	18.6 / 27.1 / NM
EBIT/Interest	(56) 6.0 / 3.9 / 2.3	(54) 7.5 / 3.6 / 1.0	(68) 6.9 / 3.2 / 1.9		(14) 5.4 / 2.8 / 1.5	(13) 11.8 / 5.9 / 1.7	4.2 / 3.0 / 2.2	17.8 / 4.4 / 2.6	8.8 / 3.7 / 2.7
Net Profit + Depr., Dep., Amort./Cur. Mat. L/T/D	(32) 10.6 / 3.2 / 1.3	(24) 5.0 / 1.9 / 1.0	(30) 5.1 / 1.8 / 1.3						
Fixed/Worth	.3 / .7 / 2.1	.3 / .6 / 1.6	.2 / .5 / 2.5		.1 / .5 / 3.8	.3 / .7 / 3.3	.2 / .5 / .6	.1 / .4 / 1.2	.2 / .5 / 1.6
Debt/Worth	1.1 / 2.5 / 5.8	1.0 / 2.9 / 7.4	1.0 / 2.1 / 4.4		.8 / 1.3 / 6.2	1.1 / 2.5 / 4.9	1.3 / 2.2 / 4.0	1.0 / 2.1 / 3.5	1.2 / 2.0 / 3.8
% Profit Before Taxes/Tangible Net Worth	(55) 58.1 / 36.0 / 16.7	(53) 44.4 / 27.0 / -1.4	(66) 40.6 / 24.0 / 10.8		(16) 63.9 / 18.4 / 4.7	(13) 54.9 / 26.1 / 9.4	29.6 / 19.8 / 10.9	54.2 / 37.0 / 25.3	(11) 30.4 / 24.5 / 19.6
% Profit Before Taxes/Total Assets	16.6 / 9.2 / 4.7	12.4 / 7.1 / -1.2	15.0 / 7.5 / 3.5		17.0 / 7.6 / 2.4	18.0 / 7.4 / .1	6.1 / 4.6 / 3.7	24.8 / 9.8 / 5.2	10.3 / 8.2 / 6.1
Sales/Net Fixed Assets	61.8 / 23.9 / 10.4	50.1 / 29.4 / 16.0	58.2 / 28.8 / 11.3		62.6 / 36.7 / 11.5	51.5 / 21.0 / 5.7	64.3 / 43.9 / 12.8	97.1 / 35.4 / 14.8	82.1 / 24.1 / 14.6
Sales/Total Assets	5.2 / 4.2 / 3.0	5.6 / 4.2 / 3.1	5.3 / 4.3 / 3.0		6.2 / 3.5 / 2.3	5.5 / 4.8 / 2.7	5.1 / 4.4 / 3.9	5.8 / 4.7 / 3.3	5.2 / 3.5 / 3.0
% Depr., Dep., Amort./Sales	(58) .7 / 1.2 / 3.3	(52) .7 / 1.3 / 2.0	(63) .6 / 1.4 / 2.7		(13) .6 / 2.1 / 2.9	.9 / 1.7 / 4.6	.5 / .9 / 1.9	.4 / .7 / 1.8	(10) .5 / 1.2 / 5.0
% Officers', Directors', Owners' Comp/Sales	(26) 1.6 / 5.6 / 8.2	(15) 2.0 / 5.8 / 8.1	(27) 1.9 / 4.9 / 10.2						
Net Sales ($)	1097331M	1657099M	1942119M	5574M	37541M	54076M	74182M	165188M	1605558M
Total Assets ($)	306703M	524957M	565900M	1721M	12445M	14749M	17432M	41724M	477829M

M = $ thousand   MM = $ million
See Pages 1 through 15 for Explanation of Ratios and Data

SERVICES—DIRECT MAIL ADVERTISING. SIC# 7331

Current Data Sorted By Assets								Comparative Historical Data	
3	2	3			1	**# Postretirement Benefits**			
						Type of Statement			
1	3	14	7	2	3	Unqualified		22	18
1	11	12	2			Reviewed		27	30
8	13	7	1			Compiled		23	29
6						Tax Returns		1	2
8	10	8	6			Other		19	25
	43 (4/1-9/30/94)		80 (10/1/94-3/31/95)					4/1/90-3/31/91	4/1/91-3/31/92
0-500M	500M-2MM	2-10MM	10-50MM	50-100MM	100-250MM			ALL	ALL
24	37	41	16	2	3	**NUMBER OF STATEMENTS**		92	104
%	%	%	%	%	%	**ASSETS**		%	%
16.6	11.5	9.2	10.5			Cash & Equivalents		10.0	10.9
34.0	40.6	37.7	38.5			Trade Receivables - (net)		37.7	38.5
2.5	4.7	3.7	5.0			Inventory		5.7	5.1
3.9	1.1	2.1	2.9			All Other Current		3.5	2.7
57.0	57.9	52.7	56.9			Total Current		56.8	57.2
32.8	27.4	35.8	28.5			Fixed Assets (net)		32.5	31.9
1.7	2.3	3.3	2.2			Intangibles (net)		2.5	2.3
8.5	12.5	8.2	12.4			All Other Non-Current		8.2	8.6
100.0	100.0	100.0	100.0			Total		100.0	100.0
						LIABILITIES			
9.5	6.5	4.4	6.5			Notes Payable-Short Term		9.2	7.8
5.2	6.3	6.6	4.3			Cur. Mat. -L/T/D		6.7	5.5
9.7	14.1	12.7	19.3			Trade Payables		16.5	15.2
.2	1.1	.7	1.4			Income Taxes Payable		1.0	.6
13.8	15.0	16.4	14.8			All Other Current		13.0	15.7
38.3	42.9	40.7	46.3			Total Current		46.4	44.8
19.0	14.8	18.8	16.9			Long Term Debt		19.0	17.4
.0	.5	.7	1.8			Deferred Taxes		1.1	.6
9.8	3.9	3.8	.6			All Other-Non-Current		2.7	2.9
33.0	37.9	36.0	34.3			Net Worth		30.8	34.3
100.0	100.0	100.0	100.0			Total Liabilities & Net Worth		100.0	100.0
						INCOME DATA			
100.0	100.0	100.0	100.0			Net Sales		100.0	100.0
						Gross Profit			
95.7	94.8	93.1	91.7			Operating Expenses		94.2	95.7
4.3	5.2	6.9	8.3			Operating Profit		5.8	4.3
.9	.4	1.1	1.9			All Other Expenses (net)		1.7	2.0
3.4	4.8	5.8	6.4			Profit Before Taxes		4.1	2.3
						RATIOS			
2.8	2.2	1.6	2.0			Current		1.8	1.8
1.9	1.4	1.2	1.2					1.2	1.2
1.0	1.1	1.0	.9					.9	1.0
2.3	2.1	1.6	1.7			Quick		1.5	1.6
1.3	1.4	1.1	1.0					1.0	(103) 1.1
.8	.9	.8	.8					.7	.8
13 27.2	28 13.2	51 7.1	55 6.6			Sales/Receivables		31 11.9	34 10.7
27 13.7	51 7.1	66 5.5	81 4.5					48 7.6	54 6.7
42 8.7	73 5.0	81 4.5	104 3.5					72 5.1	74 4.9
						Cost of Sales/Inventory			
						Cost of Sales/Payables			
10.3	9.1	10.9	5.8			Sales/Working Capital		9.0	10.8
22.8	17.8	27.3	19.1					26.8	24.1
UND	53.8	NM	NM					-52.9	-360.9
9.0	10.3	12.0	10.7			EBIT/Interest		(85) 6.1	(95) 6.6
(23) 3.2	(35) 6.8	(39) 6.1	3.6					3.1	2.8
2.0	3.8	2.5	2.3					1.5	1.0
	6.3	4.4	6.3			Net Profit + Depr., Dep.,		(52) 5.0	(54) 3.7
	(17) 3.3	(19) 2.6	(11) 2.1			Amort./Cur. Mat. L./T/D		2.7	2.2
	2.3	1.0	1.6					1.3	1.0
.5	.4	.6	.4			Fixed/Worth		.5	.5
1.0	.7	1.0	.8					1.0	1.0
3.3	1.7	2.4	3.1					2.4	2.6
.9	.8	1.0	1.6			Debt/Worth		1.0	.8
1.9	2.2	1.8	2.0					2.0	1.9
23.4	5.1	4.4	4.9					8.5	5.7
171.8	61.6	54.9	43.1			% Profit Before Taxes/Tangible		(76) 49.4	(96) 51.2
(22) 43.3	(35) 42.4	(36) 35.8	(15) 27.7			Net Worth		23.5	18.5
10.1	13.0	15.5	18.3					3.8	.9
26.4	20.0	20.2	15.7			% Profit Before Taxes/Total		17.6	13.4
9.2	9.9	8.6	7.1			Assets		6.7	5.0
2.4	5.7	5.4	4.7					1.3	.1
46.3	29.7	10.7	12.0			Sales/Net Fixed Assets		17.4	18.0
13.6	12.4	5.8	7.9					9.2	9.2
7.4	7.5	4.1	4.1					4.5	4.9
5.5	3.8	2.8	2.0			Sales/Total Assets		3.8	3.3
3.7	3.1	2.1	1.7					2.6	2.4
2.9	2.3	1.6	1.3					1.9	1.8
1.4	1.6	2.6	2.3			% Depr., Dep., Amort./Sales		1.6	1.7
(19) 3.0	(34) 2.6	(40) 3.6	(15) 3.0					(81) 3.4	(96) 3.0
3.8	4.0	5.4	4.4					5.2	4.8
2.9	3.6	2.0				% Officers', Directors',		2.6	3.7
(14) 6.4	(20) 6.4	(15) 5.4				Owners' Comp/Sales		(40) 5.0	(42) 7.1
8.7	12.1	10.2						9.2	13.6
30881M	122897M	368379M	487776M	158938M	2266181M	Net Sales ($)		1394076M	1845212M
5650M	39003M	174447M	287030M	125435M	628619M	Total Assets ($)		468971M	652497M

M = $ thousand   MM = $ million
See Pages 1 through 15 for Explanation of Ratios and Data

Comparative Historical Data				Current Data Sorted By Sales					
2	5	9	# Postretirement Benefits		3	1	4		1
			Type of Statement						
21	23	30	Unqualified	1	1	3	6	10	9
27	26	26	Reviewed	1	6	5	7	6	1
29	37	29	Compiled	1	13	7	5	1	2
5	4	6	Tax Returns	4	1		1		
28	40	32	Other	7	4	7	8	4	2
4/1/92-	4/1/93-	4/1/94-			43 (4/1-9/30/94)		80 (10/1/94-3/31/95)		
3/31/93	3/31/94	3/31/95							
ALL	ALL	ALL		0-1MM	1-3MM	3-5MM	5-10MM	10-25MM	25MM & OVER
110	130	123	NUMBER OF STATEMENTS	14	25	22	27	21	14
%	%	%	ASSETS	%	%	%	%	%	%
12.0	11.8	11.8	Cash & Equivalents	15.7	10.1	10.2	12.7	11.8	12.1
37.8	36.8	37.4	Trade Receivables - (net)	27.7	41.1	39.9	35.0	41.4	34.9
3.9	4.5	4.1	Inventory	2.4	3.7	4.2	2.9	5.1	6.9
3.2	2.5	2.3	All Other Current	6.8	.7	1.2	2.3	1.4	4.0
56.9	55.6	55.6	Total Current	52.6	55.7	55.5	52.9	59.6	58.0
31.9	32.0	31.1	Fixed Assets (net)	33.1	31.5	31.9	32.2	30.2	26.6
2.5	3.9	3.2	Intangibles (net)	1.8	2.2	2.2	4.7	.9	8.6
8.6	8.5	10.0	All Other Non-Current	12.5	10.7	10.4	10.1	9.3	6.9
100.0	100.0	100.0	Total	100.0	100.0	100.0	100.0	100.0	100.0
			LIABILITIES						
7.9	9.2	6.1	Notes Payable-Short Term	5.9	8.8	6.3	4.9	4.2	6.3
5.6	4.9	5.8	Cur. Mat.-L /T/D	1.8	7.3	7.6	7.1	4.1	4.9
15.3	14.3	13.3	Trade Payables	7.3	12.3	14.2	12.0	17.6	15.5
.5	.9	.8	Income Taxes Payable	.1	.4	1.0	.6	1.9	.6
16.5	15.0	15.5	All Other Current	10.1	19.6	14.0	13.1	18.6	16.3
45.8	44.3	41.5	Total Current	25.2	48.3	43.1	37.6	46.4	43.6
16.5	16.0	17.3	Long Term Debt	25.5	15.7	16.2	19.2	13.6	15.5
.6	.6	.7	Deferred Taxes	.2	.5	.2	.6	1.6	1.0
3.4	3.3	4.6	All Other-Non-Current	16.6	5.1	.9	3.5	3.4	1.7
33.8	35.8	35.9	Net Worth	32.5	30.4	39.6	39.0	34.9	38.2
100.0	100.0	100.0	Total Liabilities & Net Worth	100.0	100.0	100.0	100.0	100.0	100.0
			INCOME DATA						
100.0	100.0	100.0	Net Sales	100.0	100.0	100.0	100.0	100.0	100.0
			Gross Profit						
94.4	94.7	93.7	Operating Expenses	96.1	94.4	94.9	92.6	93.3	91.2
5.6	5.3	6.3	Operating Profit	3.9	5.6	5.1	7.4	6.7	8.8
1.0	1.0	1.0	All Other Expenses (net)	1.3	.8	.4	1.1	1.2	1.2
4.6	4.4	5.3	Profit Before Taxes	2.6	4.8	4.7	6.3	5.5	7.5
			RATIOS						
1.8	2.0	2.2		3.0	2.0	1.7	3.1	1.7	1.9
1.2	1.3	1.3	Current	2.3	1.2	1.2	1.2	1.2	1.2
.9	.8	1.0		1.6	1.0	1.1	1.0	1.1	1.0
1.6	1.9	1.9		2.7	1.7	1.5	2.4	1.7	1.4
1.1	1.1	1.2	Quick	2.0	1.2	1.1	1.2	1.1	1.0
.8	.7	.9		1.1	.7	.9	.8	.9	.7
32 11.3	30 12.1	29 12.6		12 30.2	22 16.5	31 11.7	43 8.4	42 8.6	32 11.5
55 6.6	53 6.9	53 6.9	Sales/Receivables	31 11.6	42 8.7	51 7.1	62 5.9	68 5.4	63 5.8
72 5.1	73 5.0	78 4.7		69 5.3	69 5.3	76 4.8	73 5.0	94 3.9	91 4.0
			Cost of Sales/Inventory						
			Cost of Sales/Payables						
10.7	9.5	9.9		6.6	11.8	14.0	11.0	9.3	6.0
23.7	28.7	21.6	Sales/Working Capital	9.5	26.3	22.2	42.2	28.9	20.0
-50.3	-33.6	192.3		21.7	NM	67.6	-117.4	81.2	NM
11.4	11.3	10.7		5.3	10.1	11.2	11.9	11.7	16.2
(102) 4.6	(118) 4.3	(116) 5.4	EBIT/Interest	(12) 3.3	(24) 6.1	(21) 6.8	(26) 4.7	6.0	(12) 7.1
1.4	1.6	2.5		1.7	2.6	2.4	2.5	2.8	1.9
4.8	5.7	5.8	Net Profit + Depr., Dep.,			4.2		5.3	
(51) 2.6	(52) 2.4	(54) 2.8	Amort./Cur. Mat. L/T/D		(12) 2.4	(12) 2.4		2.4	
1.4	1.2	1.6				1.8		1.6	
.5	.5	.5		.3	.5	.6	.4	.5	.5
1.0	1.0	.9	Fixed/Worth	1.3	1.0	.8	1.0	.9	.6
2.8	2.7	2.7		28.4	2.9	1.6	2.5	1.6	4.3
.9	1.0	.9		.8	1.3	1.0	.8	.9	1.1
2.1	2.1	2.0	Debt/Worth	2.2	2.3	2.0	2.3	1.7	2.0
6.3	6.1	6.1		56.8	11.3	3.3	4.4	4.6	7.3
57.4	58.4	59.3	% Profit Before Taxes/Tangible	319.0	101.0	63.6	63.3	36.7	44.9
(97) 28.0	(115) 22.2	(111) 36.6	Net Worth	(13) 19.2	(22) 36.6	(21) 44.9	(25) 43.2	(18) 23.0	(12) 36.6
7.3	7.0	15.8		5.5	13.6	13.9	23.8	15.3	25.3
16.6	20.0	19.4	% Profit Before Taxes/Total	13.4	20.8	25.9	26.1	16.6	21.1
7.6	7.9	9.5	Assets	8.2	9.8	9.4	11.6	8.0	10.6
1.8	2.1	5.2		-1.4	4.5	4.7	5.2	5.8	5.3
19.3	15.4	17.3		25.7	25.1	21.3	16.6	12.9	13.3
9.6	10.0	9.1	Sales/Net Fixed Assets	9.0	9.9	11.2	7.9	8.2	8.8
5.2	5.5	5.0		4.8	7.1	4.9	4.4	4.4	6.3
3.4	3.5	3.5		3.5	4.7	3.7	3.2	2.9	2.9
2.4	2.5	2.5	Sales/Total Assets	2.4	3.3	2.9	2.1	2.0	2.0
1.7	1.9	1.7		1.5	2.3	2.0	1.7	1.4	1.5
1.6	1.6	2.1		1.9	2.0	1.7	1.7	2.6	2.3
(104) 3.2	(117) 3.0	(110) 3.0	% Depr., Dep., Amort./Sales	(12) 3.2	(22) 3.2	(20) 2.8	(25) 3.5	(20) 2.8	(11) 2.6
5.0	4.7	4.4		6.2	4.1	5.2	5.2	4.3	4.6
4.5	2.8	2.9	% Officers', Directors',		3.6	3.0			
(49) 7.4	(55) 5.6	(52) 5.4	Owners' Comp/Sales		(22) 6.9	(10) 4.4			
14.0	12.1	10.4			11.8	5.6			
1741998M	2444366M	3435052M	Net Sales ($)	8011M	43646M	84951M	183639M	312690M	2802115M
692798M	1191386M	1260184M	Total Assets ($)	4065M	15233M	31979M	93374M	174098M	941435M

M = $ thousand   MM = $ million
See Pages 1 through 15 for Explanation of Ratios and Data

Current Data Sorted By Assets							Comparative Historical Data	
	1					# Postretirement Benefits		
						Type of Statement		
		1	3			Unqualified	3	5
	3	2				Reviewed	7	13
15	6	1				Compiled	19	21
1						Tax Returns		2
7	3	2	1			Other	14	11
11 (4/1-9/30/94)			34 (10/1/94-3/31/95)				4/1/90-3/31/91	4/1/91-3/31/92
0-500M	500M-2MM	2-10MM	10-50MM	50-100MM	100-250MM		ALL	ALL
23	12	6	4			NUMBER OF STATEMENTS	43	52
%	%	%	%	%	%	**ASSETS**	%	%
14.1	20.1					Cash & Equivalents	13.2	15.2
22.3	20.0					Trade Receivables - (net)	26.1	23.7
4.5	4.8					Inventory	4.1	4.0
2.1	2.4					All Other Current	2.3	1.3
43.1	47.3					Total Current	45.7	44.1
41.8	33.4					Fixed Assets (net)	31.4	35.3
3.0	1.1					Intangibles (net)	6.0	7.9
12.1	18.2					All Other Non-Current	16.9	12.7
100.0	100.0					Total	100.0	100.0
						LIABILITIES		
5.1	2.5					Notes Payable-Short Term	6.9	5.9
10.9	5.5					Cur. Mat. -L/T/D	8.1	8.0
6.4	8.3					Trade Payables	11.8	8.9
.4	.8					Income Taxes Payable	.6	.4
8.1	9.8					All Other Current	10.5	12.9
30.9	26.9					Total Current	37.9	36.1
23.3	18.4					Long Term Debt	16.9	20.9
.3	3.8					Deferred Taxes	.8	1.5
1.1	.1					All Other-Non-Current	3.0	2.5
44.3	50.7					Net Worth	41.5	39.0
100.0	100.0					Total Liabilities & Net Worth	100.0	100.0
						INCOME DATA		
100.0	100.0					Net Sales	100.0	100.0
						Gross Profit		
96.4	96.0					Operating Expenses	95.8	95.6
3.6	4.0					Operating Profit	4.2	4.4
.9	.3					All Other Expenses (net)	.7	.8
2.7	3.6					Profit Before Taxes	3.5	3.6
						RATIOS		
2.4	2.7						2.4	2.7
1.8	1.8					Current	1.3	1.3
.7	.9						.7	.8
2.3	2.6						2.3	2.3
1.4	1.6					Quick	1.1	1.1
.5	.7						.6	.7
17 21.4	**7** 52.9						**16** 22.2	**18** 20.3
25 14.4	**23** 16.0					Sales/Receivables	**27** 13.4	**26** 14.0
32 11.4	**33** 10.9						**39** 9.4	**33** 11.1
						Cost of Sales/Inventory		
						Cost of Sales/Payables		
12.3	11.8						12.0	11.0
21.8	16.1					Sales/Working Capital	27.8	35.7
−76.0	−262.8						−19.1	−41.7
7.5	8.1						11.2	10.4
(19) 2.7	(11) 4.0					EBIT/Interest	(39) 2.4	(47) 2.9
.8	.8						1.5	1.3
							9.7	5.3
						Net Profit + Depr., Dep., Amort./Cur. Mat. L /T/D	(22) 2.0	(25) 2.2
							.8	.9
.5	.2						.5	.7
.9	.6					Fixed/Worth	1.0	1.2
12.5	1.7						1.9	3.4
.4	.3						.6	1.0
.9	.5					Debt/Worth	1.4	1.7
26.1	2.3						6.1	9.2
27.5	46.0						53.2	60.9
(19) 15.4	(10) 15.7					% Profit Before Taxes/Tangible Net Worth	(36) 23.5	(45) 26.8
−3.5	−1.4						5.5	8.7
15.8	15.2						20.0	23.0
5.8	8.8					% Profit Before Taxes/Total Assets	9.8	8.5
−1.5	1.5						2.3	1.8
17.3	18.3						21.5	16.6
9.4	10.2					Sales/Net Fixed Assets	12.2	10.6
5.5	6.3						7.3	7.0
4.9	4.3						4.1	4.5
3.4	3.6					Sales/Total Assets	3.3	3.4
2.5	2.3						2.5	2.8
2.9	2.4						1.4	2.1
(20) 4.0	(10) 2.7					% Depr., Dep., Amort./Sales	(37) 2.8	(50) 3.3
5.6	3.7						4.3	4.0
8.2							6.3	6.2
(15) 10.4						% Officers', Directors', Owners' Comp/Sales	(22) 10.3	(25) 11.8
15.9							19.9	24.3
16818M	**47374M**	**78098M**	**179363M**			Net Sales ($)	**197602M**	**335838M**
4986M	**12432M**	**24616M**	**60197M**			Total Assets ($)	**69048M**	**95870M**

© Robert Morris Associates 1995

M = $ thousand MM = $ million

See Pages 1 through 15 for Explanation of Ratios and Data

Comparative Historical Data				Current Data Sorted By Sales					
	3	1	# Postretirement Benefits		1				
			Type of Statement						
4	6	4	Unqualified				1		3
14	8	5	Reviewed		1	1	1	2	
25	29	22	Compiled	9	10	2		1	
1	4	1	Tax Returns	1					
13	11	13	Other	6	1		5		1
4/1/92-3/31/93	4/1/93-3/31/94	4/1/94-3/31/95		0-1MM	11 (4/1-9/30/94) 1-3MM	3-5MM	34 (10/1/94-3/31/95) 5-10MM	10-25MM	25MM & OVER
ALL	ALL	ALL							
57	58	45	**NUMBER OF STATEMENTS**	16	12	3	7	3	4
%	%	%	**ASSETS**	%	%	%	%	%	%
14.3	15.5	17.1	Cash & Equivalents	15.9	15.7				
25.6	22.8	21.4	Trade Receivables - (net)	19.9	23.9				
4.8	3.9	4.3	Inventory	2.2	8.2				
3.5	1.6	1.8	All Other Current	2.5	.9				
48.2	43.7	44.6	Total Current	40.6	48.7				
30.1	34.8	38.7	Fixed Assets (net)	44.6	33.3				
5.0	8.1	3.3	Intangibles (net)	2.8	2.1				
16.7	13.4	13.3	All Other Non-Current	12.0	15.9				
100.0	100.0	100.0	Total	100.0	100.0				
			LIABILITIES						
6.4	5.2	3.9	Notes Payable-Short Term	7.1	2.5				
7.1	7.5	8.9	Cur. Mat.-L /T/D	7.3	13.1				
10.0	7.6	7.7	Trade Payables	3.1	11.2				
.4	2.2	.5	Income Taxes Payable	.5	.8				
11.9	15.1	10.4	All Other Current	8.1	7.9				
35.7	37.6	31.4	Total Current	26.0	35.5				
15.7	17.9	21.2	Long Term Debt	20.5	28.7				
1.9	.9	1.2	Deferred Taxes	.5	.0				
2.6	3.3	.9	All Other-Non-Current	.0	2.2				
44.1	40.4	45.3	Net Worth	53.0	33.6				
100.0	100.0	100.0	Total Liabilities & Net Worth	100.0	100.0				
			INCOME DATA						
100.0	100.0	100.0	Net Sales	100.0	100.0				
			Gross Profit						
95.9	95.2	95.7	Operating Expenses	96.0	96.6				
4.1	4.8	4.3	Operating Profit	4.0	3.4				
.7	1.1	.7	All Other Expenses (net)	.9	.9				
3.5	3.7	3.6	Profit Before Taxes	3.0	2.6				
			RATIOS						
2.6	1.8	2.3		4.2	2.2				
1.4	1.2	1.4	Current	1.6	1.8				
.9	.8	.9		.8	.8				
2.0	1.6	2.1		4.0	2.2				
1.1	1.1	1.3	Quick	1.5	1.2				
.7	.7	.7		.6	.6				
17 22.0	15 24.4	17 21.9		16 22.7	18 20.5				
27 13.6	26 14.3	25 14.5	Sales/Receivables	27 13.6	26 14.1				
38 9.6	34 10.6	32 11.4		34 10.8	33 10.9				
			Cost of Sales/Inventory						
			Cost of Sales/Payables						
9.6	15.2	12.3		7.3	11.2				
25.2	49.9	21.8	Sales/Working Capital	26.3	15.7				
-82.6	-41.9	-89.8		NM	-36.0				
11.6	11.1	8.5		8.5	8.1				
(51) 2.3	(52) 3.2	(40) 4.0	EBIT/Interest	(13) 1.1	(11) 2.7				
1.0	.7	.9		.8	.1				
3.2	3.7	4.4							
(22) 1.6	(20) 1.3	(20) 2.0	Net Profit + Depr., Dep., Amort./Cur. Mat. L/T/D						
.7	.9	1.3							
.3	.5	.5		.5	.4				
.7	1.1	.8	Fixed/Worth	1.1	.6				
1.6	3.4	2.6		5.5	-7.7				
.6	.7	.5		.3	.6				
1.2	2.0	1.0	Debt/Worth	.8	.8				
2.8	5.0	4.6		9.2	-13.3				
47.8	66.2	45.2		39.9					
(52) 17.9	(52) 27.9	(39) 23.3	% Profit Before Taxes/Tangible Net Worth	(15) 11.6					
2.9	6.4	.0		-3.5					
19.4	18.5	16.4		15.0	16.8				
7.1	8.2	9.0	% Profit Before Taxes/Total Assets	.2	7.7				
.7	1.1	-.3		-1.3	-4.5				
21.8	14.6	17.2		16.6	18.4				
12.1	11.2	8.9	Sales/Net Fixed Assets	7.8	12.2				
6.8	7.8	6.1		4.7	6.2				
4.2	4.2	4.4		4.8	4.4				
3.2	3.3	3.5	Sales/Total Assets	2.8	3.4				
2.4	2.2	2.5		1.9	2.3				
1.7	2.4	2.5		3.4	2.4				
(53) 3.2	(52) 3.4	(39) 3.5	% Depr., Dep., Amort./Sales	(13) 4.7	2.8				
4.6	4.8	5.0		6.4	3.8				
7.5	6.3	4.6			7.4				
(26) 9.6	(32) 9.7	(28) 8.7	% Officers', Directors', Owners' Comp/Sales		(10) 10.0				
20.1	14.0	12.0			12.2				
797090M	358839M	321653M	Net Sales ($)	7708M	18097M	11178M	48278M	57029M	179363M
320866M	121446M	102231M	Total Assets ($)	2760M	5842M	2583M	13445M	17404M	60197M

M = $ thousand   MM = $ million
See Pages 1 through 15 for Explanation of Ratios and Data

SERVICES—EMPLOYMENT AGENCIES.   SIC# 7361

Current Data Sorted By Assets							Comparative Historical Data	
3	8	3	1	2		**# Postretirement Benefits** **Type of Statement**		
2	9	20	5	3	1	Unqualified	20	23
3	21	10				Reviewed	41	24
28	30	5			1	Compiled	43	48
8						Tax Returns	3	3
19	23	14	2	1		Other	38	38
	47 (4/1-9/30/94)		158 (10/1/94-3/31/95)				4/1/90- 3/31/91	4/1/91- 3/31/92
0-500M	**500M-2MM**	**2-10MM**	**10-50MM**	**50-100MM**	**100-250MM**	**NUMBER OF STATEMENTS**	**ALL**	**ALL**
60	83	49	7	4	2		145	136
%	%	%	%	%	%	**ASSETS**	%	%
15.1	7.6	12.9				Cash & Equivalents	13.4	11.3
53.9	61.4	61.6				Trade Receivables - (net)	51.0	54.8
.0	.4	.3				Inventory	.5	.5
4.3	4.5	2.8				All Other Current	3.0	2.8
73.4	74.0	77.5				Total Current	67.8	69.3
14.9	9.8	12.1				Fixed Assets (net)	17.7	14.1
1.3	4.0	3.4				Intangibles (net)	2.4	3.3
10.3	12.2	6.9				All Other Non-Current	12.1	13.3
100.0	100.0	100.0				Total	100.0	100.0
						LIABILITIES		
16.2	17.4	17.4				Notes Payable-Short Term	17.3	19.0
1.0	1.8	1.1				Cur. Mat. -L/T/D	4.6	3.5
2.9	4.0	6.2				Trade Payables	7.5	4.5
1.1	.9	.9				Income Taxes Payable	.7	.7
23.3	23.9	20.2				All Other Current	16.5	19.3
44.4	48.0	45.7				Total Current	46.6	47.0
8.0	5.0	4.0				Long Term Debt	10.5	8.1
.8	1.7	.9				Deferred Taxes	1.7	1.2
2.4	5.4	8.6				All Other-Non-Current	3.9	3.2
44.3	40.0	40.8				Net Worth	37.3	40.4
100.0	100.0	100.0				Total Liabilities & Net Worth	100.0	100.0
						INCOME DATA		
100.0	100.0	100.0				Net Sales	100.0	100.0
						Gross Profit		
94.4	96.0	94.9				Operating Expenses	96.2	96.9
5.6	4.0	5.1				Operating Profit	3.8	3.1
.3	1.1	.5				All Other Expenses (net)	.9	.5
5.3	2.9	4.6				Profit Before Taxes	3.0	2.6
						RATIOS		
2.9 1.8 1.2	2.3 1.5 1.1	3.1 1.6 1.2				Current	2.7 1.6 1.0	2.4 1.6 1.1
(59) 2.9 1.8 1.0	2.2 1.5 1.0	3.1 1.5 1.2				Quick	(144) 2.5 1.6 1.0	2.4 1.5 1.0
16 23.2 37 9.9 54 6.8	33 11.0 42 8.7 55 6.6	37 9.8 49 7.5 69 5.3				Sales/Receivables	25 14.6 41 8.9 57 6.4	31 11.9 39 9.3 50 7.3
						Cost of Sales/Inventory		
						Cost of Sales/Payables		
8.9 18.9 220.2	9.5 20.6 105.0	7.0 17.3 31.5				Sales/Working Capital	10.2 23.0 NM	11.1 20.3 186.7
18.1 (44) 7.3 1.5	15.5 (74) 5.9 2.4	23.2 (39) 4.5 1.3				EBIT/Interest	10.6 (122) 2.9 .5	12.6 (116) 3.5 1.5
	7.8 (17) 3.8 2.0	12.3 (12) 6.7 1.8				Net Profit + Depr., Dep., Amort./Cur. Mat. L /T/D	3.5 (42) 1.3 −.3	5.0 (24) 3.0 1.3
.1 .2 .9	.1 .3 .6	.1 .3 .6				Fixed/Worth	.2 .4 1.3	.2 .3 .9
.5 1.2 3.4	.8 1.4 5.2	.6 2.2 4.9				Debt/Worth	.7 1.6 5.0	.7 1.6 4.5
83.8 (58) 37.3 9.2	69.9 (73) 25.6 9.6	64.9 (48) 35.0 11.1				% Profit Before Taxes/Tangible Net Worth	51.6 (126) 20.2 .3	75.3 (121) 21.8 3.5
33.7 17.4 1.9	27.4 10.8 2.3	24.3 10.8 2.2				% Profit Before Taxes/Total Assets	20.3 6.6 −2.1	21.3 8.5 1.0
199.2 67.2 32.9	161.5 66.7 36.1	99.5 57.0 33.6				Sales/Net Fixed Assets	92.7 38.9 19.2	100.9 43.3 26.4
8.6 6.5 4.0	6.8 5.1 3.4	5.5 4.2 2.9				Sales/Total Assets	6.5 4.8 3.0	6.8 5.3 3.4
.4 (40) .7 1.0	.3 (67) .5 .8	.5 (43) .8 1.2				% Depr., Dep., Amort./Sales	.4 (112) .9 1.7	.4 (110) .7 1.6
3.6 (28) 6.7 14.6	2.0 (42) 3.6 6.2	2.2 (14) 5.1 6.9				% Officers', Directors', Owners' Comp/Sales	3.4 (63) 6.9 11.5	2.6 (60) 6.0 8.4
101775M	503522M	874780M	443387M	750165M	2173328M	Net Sales ($)	1597430M	2468782M
14693M	83517M	202272M	176302M	333590M	400761M	Total Assets ($)	448335M	780169M

© Robert Morris Associates 1995

M = $ thousand   MM = $ million
See Pages 1 through 15 for Explanation of Ratios and Data

Comparative Historical Data / Current Data Sorted By Sales

Postretirement Benefits — Type of Statement

Type of Statement	1	5	17	2	4	2	3	1	5
Unqualified	15	23	40		7	2	5	11	15
Reviewed	33	24	34	1	10	5	9	7	2
Compiled	43	37	64	11	15	15	15	7	1
Tax Returns	4	3	8	4	3		1		
Other	37	40	59	9	18	6	9	10	7

Dates / Ranges:

	4/1/92-3/31/93 ALL	4/1/93-3/31/94 ALL	4/1/94-3/31/95 ALL	47 (4/1-9/30/94)		158 (10/1/94-3/31/95)			
				0-1MM	1-3MM	3-5MM	5-10MM	10-25MM	25MM & OVER
NUMBER OF STATEMENTS	132	127	205	25	53	28	39	35	25

ASSETS (%)

	1	5	17	0-1MM	1-3MM	3-5MM	5-10MM	10-25MM	25MM & OVER
Cash & Equivalents	10.6	8.4	11.2	25.3	10.4	5.7	10.0	10.0	8.9
Trade Receivables - (net)	58.8	60.9	58.1	39.3	54.5	64.4	61.1	68.5	57.8
Inventory	.1	.6	.5	.0	.4	.0	.4	1.5	.5
All Other Current	3.0	2.7	4.1	4.3	4.5	7.8	2.2	2.1	4.3
Total Current	72.5	72.5	73.9	68.9	69.8	78.0	73.7	82.2	71.5
Fixed Assets (net)	14.0	14.7	12.0	19.3	11.5	11.5	11.9	8.8	11.5
Intangibles (net)	3.0	2.5	3.9	3.3	3.4	1.1	4.6	2.7	9.0
All Other Non-Current	10.4	10.3	10.2	8.5	15.3	9.4	9.8	6.4	8.0
Total	100.0	100.0	100.0	100.0	100.0	100.0	100.0	100.0	100.0

LIABILITIES

	1	5	17	0-1MM	1-3MM	3-5MM	5-10MM	10-25MM	25MM & OVER
Notes Payable-Short Term	21.3	18.0	16.5	14.8	15.0	21.1	14.3	20.3	14.5
Cur. Mat.-L /T/D	2.1	2.6	1.5	.4	1.7	1.0	2.0	.8	3.0
Trade Payables	5.8	7.2	4.5	3.0	3.0	3.8	4.5	3.1	11.9
Income Taxes Payable	.5	1.2	1.0	.8	.9	1.6	.8	.9	.8
All Other Current	19.7	17.6	22.6	23.3	22.0	20.3	22.4	27.9	18.9
Total Current	49.4	46.5	46.1	42.2	42.5	47.8	44.0	53.1	49.0
Long Term Debt	7.4	6.7	6.0	4.2	6.1	7.1	7.2	3.3	8.0
Deferred Taxes	1.3	1.1	1.2	.1	2.0	2.1	.4	.9	1.5
All Other-Non-Current	4.4	4.9	5.2	2.3	4.7	4.2	7.3	7.6	3.6
Net Worth	37.5	40.7	41.5	51.2	44.7	38.8	41.1	35.2	37.9
Total Liabilities & Net Worth	100.0	100.0	100.0	100.0	100.0	100.0	100.0	100.0	100.0

INCOME DATA

	1	5	17	0-1MM	1-3MM	3-5MM	5-10MM	10-25MM	25MM & OVER
Net Sales	100.0	100.0	100.0	100.0	100.0	100.0	100.0	100.0	100.0
Gross Profit									
Operating Expenses	96.9	95.1	95.1	88.3	95.7	96.1	96.0	96.8	95.9
Operating Profit	3.1	4.9	4.9	11.7	4.3	3.9	4.0	3.2	4.1
All Other Expenses (net)	.3	.6	.7	.5	1.3	.4	.5	.7	.4
Profit Before Taxes	2.8	4.3	4.2	11.2	3.1	3.5	3.5	2.5	3.6

RATIOS

	1	5	17	0-1MM	1-3MM	3-5MM	5-10MM	10-25MM	25MM & OVER
Current	2.4	2.8	2.6	3.0	2.9	2.6	2.6	2.8	1.8
	1.4	1.6	1.6	2.0	1.7	1.5	1.5	1.5	1.4
	1.1	1.1	1.1	1.2	1.0	1.1	1.1	1.2	1.1
Quick	2.4	2.7	(204) 2.6	2.8	(52) 2.8	2.2	2.6	2.8	1.8
	1.4	1.5	1.5	2.0	1.7	1.5	1.5	1.5	1.4
	1.0	1.1	1.0	1.0	1.0	1.0	1.0	1.1	1.1
Sales/Receivables	32 11.4	36 10.2	31 11.6	0 UND	29 12.5	34 10.8	33 10.9	33 10.9	38 9.6
	44 8.3	45 8.2	42 8.6	33 11.1	41 9.0	43 8.4	41 8.8	40 9.1	51 7.2
	53 6.9	61 6.0	60 6.1	73 5.0	57 6.4	63 5.8	54 6.8	59 6.2	63 5.8
Cost of Sales/Inventory									
Cost of Sales/Payables									
Sales/Working Capital	11.2	9.9	8.6	6.2	8.4	9.8	8.8	9.4	12.8
	21.8	21.3	19.1	9.4	17.6	17.4	19.4	20.1	26.6
	93.4	54.8	56.5	44.3	NM	56.6	37.3	52.3	54.4
EBIT/Interest	(112) 15.3	(112) 21.5	(170) 17.9	(15) 24.7	(43) 13.3	(26) 18.2	(34) 15.5	(28) 20.8	(24) 26.3
	3.5	6.7	6.0	12.3	4.6	6.1	5.4	5.9	7.5
	1.1	1.9	2.0	6.2	1.4	2.0	1.0	2.1	3.9
Net Profit + Depr., Dep., Amort./Cur. Mat. L/T/D	(27) 8.9	(27) 7.3	(42) 9.4		(10) 3.5			(10) 10.3	
	3.1	2.6	5.3		3.1			6.2	
	.9	.8	1.3		.1			1.6	
Fixed/Worth	.1	.1	.1	.1	.1	.1	.1	.1	.2
	.3	.2	.3	.3	.2	.2	.2	.3	.3
	.8	.8	.6	.7	.7	.6	.8	.5	.6
Debt/Worth	.8	.8	.6	.3	.5	.8	.6	1.0	1.3
	1.8	1.6	1.6	.9	1.4	1.5	1.5	2.4	2.2
	4.6	3.7	4.5	1.9	4.1	3.5	5.8	5.8	3.9
% Profit Before Taxes/Tangible Net Worth	(117) 64.4	(116) 70.8	(191) 68.6	(23) 96.8	(50) 70.6	(26) 87.4	(36) 63.8	(32) 63.3	(24) 83.2
	23.2	34.4	33.9	48.0	25.8	32.2	27.8	35.0	44.2
	2.8	9.3	11.2	13.3	5.3	6.0	5.4	13.3	30.2
% Profit Before Taxes/Total Assets	21.6	29.2	27.5	49.3	26.7	28.5	29.4	20.2	23.1
	8.9	10.2	11.3	21.1	7.9	11.5	10.5	9.9	11.1
	.1	2.3	2.4	5.5	1.7	2.8	.3	4.1	8.3
Sales/Net Fixed Assets	121.1	134.4	139.5	81.6	189.8	196.2	138.3	111.2	126.4
	55.6	55.1	63.5	31.7	72.0	67.3	63.4	69.0	47.2
	26.2	20.5	31.9	12.2	36.6	31.8	32.9	44.9	23.0
Sales/Total Assets	6.9	6.6	6.8	6.2	6.9	7.2	6.8	8.2	6.0
	5.3	4.7	5.0	2.7	5.1	5.5	4.7	5.5	4.2
	3.6	3.3	3.2	1.7	2.9	4.2	3.4	4.2	2.7
% Depr., Dep., Amort./Sales	(105) .3	(98) .3	(162) .3	(14) .8	(41) .4	(23) .2	(34) .3	(31) .4	(19) .5
	.7	.7	.6	1.0	.7	.4	.4	.5	.7
	1.4	1.3	1.1	2.4	1.1	1.0	.9	.9	1.5
% Officers', Directors', Owners' Comp/Sales	(72) 2.2	(54) 2.2	(84) 2.4		(28) 3.4	(14) 2.2	(19) 1.8		
	5.5	4.4	4.6		5.3	3.6	3.5		
	10.5	8.6	8.4		9.0	6.2	5.4		
Net Sales ($)	1342458M	1725080M	4846957M	12596M	103956M	106209M	255842M	539848M	3828506M
Total Assets ($)	356242M	529680M	1211135M	8920M	29340M	23045M	59692M	138296M	951842M

M = $ thousand   MM = $ million
See Pages 1 through 15 for Explanation of Ratios and Data

Current Data Sorted By Assets							Comparative Historical Data	
15	34	36	11	2	7	**# Postretirement Benefits** **Type of Statement**		
2	29	85	61	16	17	Unqualified	157	208
35	169	125	10			Reviewed	306	316
143	149	38	4			Compiled	307	331
41	7	2				Tax Returns	9	22
86	102	100	17	4	5	Other	248	273
	303 (4/1-9/30/94)		944 (10/1/94-3/31/95)				4/1/90-3/31/91	4/1/91-3/31/92
0-500M	500M-2MM	2-10MM	10-50MM	50-100MM	100-250MM		ALL	ALL
307	456	350	92	20	22	**NUMBER OF STATEMENTS**	1027	1150
%	%	%	%	%	%	**ASSETS**	%	%
13.8	7.6	6.9	6.7	16.0	7.5	Cash & Equivalents	8.7	8.9
40.8	55.1	53.7	48.7	41.0	42.5	Trade Receivables - (net)	48.4	48.0
3.2	4.2	4.8	4.4	1.9	8.1	Inventory	3.8	3.7
3.7	4.7	7.5	11.8	7.7	4.8	All Other Current	5.6	5.8
61.4	71.7	72.9	71.8	66.6	62.8	Total Current	66.6	66.5
26.9	18.9	16.5	16.3	17.3	17.7	Fixed Assets (net)	21.7	22.0
2.0	1.2	1.5	2.8	6.6	8.9	Intangibles (net)	1.6	1.7
9.7	8.2	9.1	9.2	9.5	10.5	All Other Non-Current	10.1	9.8
100.0	100.0	100.0	100.0	100.0	100.0	Total	100.0	100.0
						LIABILITIES		
16.1	12.6	11.6	9.4	.9	4.3	Notes Payable-Short Term	13.0	13.0
5.0	3.8	3.0	3.0	1.0	2.4	Cur. Mat. -L/T/D	4.5	4.4
9.4	12.5	12.9	12.9	11.0	9.7	Trade Payables	11.0	10.5
.8	1.3	1.3	1.6	.6	.5	Income Taxes Payable	1.7	1.2
12.6	13.5	16.8	18.7	18.7	19.1	All Other Current	13.1	13.4
43.9	43.6	45.5	45.7	32.2	36.1	Total Current	43.3	42.5
12.7	9.3	7.0	7.9	9.4	14.0	Long Term Debt	11.6	10.3
1.5	3.8	4.4	5.0	1.9	1.1	Deferred Taxes	3.5	3.7
1.6	2.8	4.1	4.6	3.4	8.5	All Other-Non-Current	2.8	2.4
40.3	40.4	39.0	36.8	53.1	40.3	Net Worth	38.9	41.2
100.0	100.0	100.0	100.0	100.0	100.0	Total Liabilities & Net Worth	100.0	100.0
						INCOME DATA		
100.0	100.0	100.0	100.0	100.0	100.0	Net Sales	100.0	100.0
						Gross Profit		
93.7	94.5	95.3	95.9	93.9	93.0	Operating Expenses	95.0	96.2
6.3	5.5	4.7	4.1	6.1	7.0	Operating Profit	5.0	3.8
1.2	.9	.6	1.2	.6	1.3	All Other Expenses (net)	1.4	1.2
5.1	4.6	4.1	2.9	5.5	5.6	Profit Before Taxes	3.6	2.6
						RATIOS		
2.6	2.7	2.3	2.0	3.1	2.5	Current	2.6	2.5
1.5	1.7	1.6	1.6	2.1	1.7		1.6	1.6
.9	1.2	1.2	1.3	1.6	1.4		1.2	1.2
2.4	2.4	1.9	1.7	2.9	1.6	Quick	2.3	2.2
(306) 1.4	1.5	1.3	1.3	1.7	1.3		1.4	1.4
.8	1.0	1.0	.9	1.1	1.1		.9	.9
0 UND	53 6.9	57 6.4	54 6.7	73 5.0	49 7.5	Sales/Receivables	46 8.0	45 8.1
47 7.8	78 4.7	83 4.4	76 4.8	87 4.2	87 4.2		72 5.1	72 5.1
76 4.8	104 3.5	107 3.4	96 3.8	107 3.4	114 3.2		99 3.7	99 3.7
						Cost of Sales/Inventory		
						Cost of Sales/Payables		
7.4	5.4	5.2	6.2	3.0	3.8	Sales/Working Capital	5.5	5.5
17.1	8.9	9.1	8.9	5.3	7.8		10.7	10.0
-124.5	23.9	21.2	13.8	9.8	17.2		37.8	38.1
15.1	15.8	17.4	12.8	17.6	14.8	EBIT/Interest	9.9	8.4
(258) 4.7	(412) 5.6	(317) 5.3	(83) 6.0	(15) 8.3	(19) 5.0		(921) 3.6	(1020) 2.9
1.0	1.7	1.9	1.8	1.4	2.6		1.0	.5
4.4	5.9	6.9	12.3	18.0	5.5	Net Profit + Depr., Dep.,	6.5	4.7
(61) 1.9	(168) 2.8	(162) 2.5	(59) 3.9	(12) 6.7	(13) 2.4	Amort./Cur. Mat. L./T/D	(500) 2.7	(500) 1.8
-.8	1.1	1.3	1.5	1.5	1.9		.9	.6
.2	.2	.2	.2	.2	.4	Fixed/Worth	.2	.2
.5	.4	.4	.4	.4	.5		.5	.4
1.4	.8	.7	.9	.7	1.0		1.0	.9
.6	.8	.9	1.1	.6	.8	Debt/Worth	.8	.7
1.5	1.5	1.7	1.8	1.0	1.8		1.6	1.5
4.5	3.1	3.3	3.4	2.5	5.2		3.6	3.1
81.5	49.7	42.2	36.9	26.7	30.4	% Profit Before Taxes/Tangible	50.3	40.3
(267) 32.4	(430) 22.4	(338) 21.4	(88) 20.4	(19) 18.1	(20) 19.7	Net Worth	(965) 21.0	(1089) 16.8
5.6	4.6	6.4	6.7	7.3	6.3		1.7	-2.3
33.2	19.8	14.7	12.1	12.4	9.2	% Profit Before Taxes/Total	18.1	15.6
12.5	8.6	7.2	6.9	8.2	8.0	Assets	7.3	5.7
.3	1.7	1.9	2.0	2.6	2.3		.2	-1.5
38.7	33.2	33.2	31.1	21.1	23.7	Sales/Net Fixed Assets	30.9	28.5
21.2	18.7	18.8	17.1	14.1	11.1		16.7	16.3
11.7	11.0	10.5	11.2	6.1	6.4		9.8	9.7
5.9	3.4	3.0	2.8	2.5	2.9	Sales/Total Assets	3.5	3.5
3.6	2.6	2.4	2.3	1.7	1.9		2.6	2.6
2.6	2.1	1.8	2.0	1.3	1.1		2.0	1.9
1.1	1.2	1.1	1.1	1.1	1.0	% Depr., Dep., Amort./Sales	1.2	1.2
(246) 1.8	(422) 1.9	(313) 1.8	(83) 1.9	(19) 2.0	(15) 2.0		(935) 2.0	(1036) 2.1
2.9	2.8	2.6	2.8	3.6	4.1		3.0	3.1
8.1	5.1	2.8	.7			% Officers', Directors',	5.3	5.2
(138) 13.3	(180) 8.7	(89) 6.1	(14) 2.2			Owners' Comp/Sales	(364) 9.8	(391) 10.2
23.1	13.9	12.2	10.7				18.0	17.8
305953M	1451865M	3778288M	4487386M	2497153M	7478648M	Net Sales ($)	10286934M	14702791M
76417M	526011M	1523376M	1786747M	1444262M	3593879M	Total Assets ($)	4669718M	6684509M

M = $ thousand   MM = $ million
See Pages 1 through 15 for Explanation of Ratios and Data

Comparative Historical Data / Current Data Sorted By Sales

	26	63	105	# Postretirement Benefits / Type of Statement	9	23	20	17	14	22
	207	180	210	Unqualified	3	9	17	35	53	93
	323	293	339	Reviewed	24	98	77	84	48	8
	312	345	334	Compiled	87	141	57	42	5	2
	23	43	50	Tax Returns	34	13		2	1	
	311	293	314	Other	63	80	53	52	34	32
	4/1/92-3/31/93 ALL	4/1/93-3/31/94 ALL	4/1/94-3/31/95 ALL		303 (4/1-9/30/94) 0-1MM	1-3MM	3-5MM	944 (10/1/94-3/31/95) 5-10MM	10-25MM	25MM & OVER
	1176	1154	1247	**NUMBER OF STATEMENTS**	211	341	204	215	141	135
	%	%	%	**ASSETS**	%	%	%	%	%	%
	8.7	9.6	9.0	Cash & Equivalents	13.2	9.3	7.3	7.1	6.8	9.3
	48.1	48.9	50.3	Trade Receivables - (net)	37.7	53.0	54.0	53.8	54.6	47.2
	3.9	3.5	4.2	Inventory	3.4	3.6	5.8	4.1	4.8	4.2
	5.8	6.1	5.8	All Other Current	3.7	4.2	5.8	6.6	8.2	9.6
	66.5	68.1	69.3	Total Current	57.9	70.1	72.8	71.6	74.5	70.3
	21.3	20.4	20.0	Fixed Assets (net)	29.1	20.1	17.8	17.5	16.6	16.0
	1.9	1.6	1.8	Intangibles (net)	2.8	1.0	1.2	2.0	1.0	4.1
	10.3	9.9	8.9	All Other Non-Current	10.2	8.8	8.3	8.9	8.0	9.6
	100.0	100.0	100.0	Total	100.0	100.0	100.0	100.0	100.0	100.0
				LIABILITIES						
	13.4	13.0	12.6	Notes Payable-Short Term	14.6	14.3	13.7	10.5	11.7	7.7
	3.7	3.6	3.7	Cur. Mat.-L /T/D	5.2	3.9	3.6	3.5	2.6	2.6
	11.0	11.1	11.8	Trade Payables	8.4	11.7	13.6	12.1	14.2	11.7
	1.2	1.4	1.2	Income Taxes Payable	.7	1.1	1.4	1.0	1.9	1.0
	14.3	14.1	14.8	All Other Current	11.3	12.9	13.9	16.5	17.5	20.6
	43.7	43.2	44.1	Total Current	40.3	44.0	46.2	43.6	47.9	43.6
	9.6	9.1	9.5	Long Term Debt	15.5	9.1	8.5	6.9	7.7	8.5
	3.0	3.5	3.4	Deferred Taxes	1.0	3.2	4.7	4.9	4.0	2.9
	2.6	2.9	3.1	All Other-Non-Current	1.9	2.2	2.3	4.7	4.0	5.1
	41.1	41.2	39.9	Net Worth	41.3	41.5	38.3	39.8	36.5	40.0
	100.0	100.0	100.0	Total Liabilities & Net Worth	100.0	100.0	100.0	100.0	100.0	100.0
				INCOME DATA						
	100.0	100.0	100.0	Net Sales	100.0	100.0	100.0	100.0	100.0	100.0
				Gross Profit						
	96.2	95.5	94.6	Operating Expenses	91.7	94.7	95.1	95.9	95.9	94.5
	3.8	4.5	5.4	Operating Profit	8.3	5.3	4.9	4.1	4.1	5.5
	.9	.8	.9	All Other Expenses (net)	1.7	.8	.7	.6	.6	1.1
	2.9	3.7	4.5	Profit Before Taxes	6.6	4.4	4.2	3.6	3.6	4.4
				RATIOS						
	2.4	2.5	2.5	Current	2.8	2.7	2.6	2.5	2.1	2.3
	1.6	1.6	1.6		1.5	1.7	1.7	1.6	1.6	1.7
	1.2	1.2	1.2		.8	1.2	1.2	1.2	1.2	1.3
	2.2	2.2	2.2	Quick	2.5	2.4	2.3	2.0	1.8	1.8
	1.3	1.4 (1246)	1.4		1.3 (340)	1.5	1.4	1.3	1.3	1.3
	.9	.9	1.0		.7	1.0	1.0	1.0	1.0	1.0
45 / 68 / 96	8.1 / 5.4 / 3.8	45 / 72 / 101 8.2 / 5.1 / 3.6	47 / 73 / 101 7.7 / 5.0 / 3.6	Sales/Receivables	0 / 52 / 99 UND / 7.0 / 3.7	47 / 74 / 107 7.8 / 4.9 / 3.4	51 / 79 / 111 7.1 / 4.6 / 3.3	51 / 74 / 96 7.1 / 4.9 / 3.8	57 / 83 / 101 6.4 / 4.4 / 3.6	45 / 72 / 91 8.1 / 5.1 / 4.0
				Cost of Sales/Inventory						
				Cost of Sales/Payables						
	5.9	5.4	5.7	Sales/Working Capital	5.4	5.4	5.3	5.9	6.4	6.1
	11.4	10.2	10.0		12.9	9.8	8.6	10.4	9.7	9.4
	40.7	35.7	28.7		-87.0	33.8	24.5	25.2	18.9	17.0
(1037)	11.1 / 3.7 / 1.0	(1012) 13.0 / 4.5 / 1.3	(1104) 15.3 / 5.3 / 1.6	EBIT/Interest	(175) 15.0 / 5.0 / 1.0	(306) 14.5 / 4.6 / 1.1	(180) 16.8 / 5.7 / 1.7	(201) 16.1 / 5.7 / 2.0	(122) 17.0 / 5.4 / 2.2	(120) 17.3 / 7.2 / 2.0
(481)	4.4 / 2.1 / .8	(435) 5.3 / 2.3 / .7	(475) 6.8 / 2.7 / 1.2	Net Profit + Depr., Dep., Amort./Cur. Mat. L/T/D	(36) 6.0 / 1.9 / -.2	(116) 5.0 / 2.3 / .6	(83) 5.6 / 2.9 / 1.3	(91) 5.5 / 2.3 / 1.0	(70) 9.3 / 3.6 / 1.5	(79) 12.3 / 3.9 / 1.5
	.2 / .4 / 1.0	.2 / .4 / .9	.2 / .4 / .9	Fixed/Worth	.2 / .6 / 2.0	.2 / .4 / .9	.2 / .4 / .8	.2 / .4 / .7	.2 / .4 / .8	.2 / .4 / .8
	.7 / 1.5 / 3.0	.7 / 1.5 / 3.2	.8 / 1.5 / 3.4	Debt/Worth	.5 / 1.4 / 5.2	.7 / 1.5 / 3.0	.8 / 1.7 / 3.2	.9 / 1.5 / 3.3	1.1 / 1.9 / 3.4	.9 / 1.6 / 3.6
(1101)	45.3 / 18.1 / 1.6	(1085) 44.6 / 19.0 / 2.5	(1162) 50.6 / 22.9 / 6.0	% Profit Before Taxes/Tangible Net Worth	(189) 80.6 / 29.6 / 3.3	(315) 54.1 / 24.7 / 3.8	(187) 44.3 / 22.7 / 6.3	(205) 50.7 / 22.9 / 6.7	(139) 37.1 / 22.1 / 8.8	(127) 37.1 / 21.6 / 7.3
	16.1 / 6.4 / .1	17.2 / 7.4 / .5	19.5 / 8.3 / 1.7	% Profit Before Taxes/Total Assets	30.3 / 11.1 / .3	23.6 / 8.0 / 1.0	17.3 / 8.8 / 2.1	17.9 / 7.6 / 2.1	12.6 / 7.3 / 2.4	12.8 / 8.5 / 2.3
	32.1 / 18.1 / 10.3	33.2 / 18.8 / 10.5	33.8 / 18.9 / 10.9	Sales/Net Fixed Assets	32.6 / 14.2 / 7.4	32.4 / 19.7 / 11.7	35.6 / 18.5 / 12.0	34.3 / 20.6 / 11.7	36.1 / 19.8 / 10.9	35.0 / 17.4 / 10.6
	3.5 / 2.6 / 2.0	3.5 / 2.6 / 2.0	3.5 / 2.6 / 2.0	Sales/Total Assets	4.1 / 2.8 / 1.9	3.7 / 2.8 / 2.1	3.2 / 2.5 / 2.0	3.5 / 2.8 / 2.1	3.0 / 2.4 / 2.1	3.2 / 2.5 / 1.9
(1057)	1.2 / 1.9 / 3.0	(1022) 1.2 / 1.9 / 2.8	(1098) 1.2 / 1.8 / 2.8	% Depr., Dep., Amort./Sales	(163) 1.3 / 2.2 / 4.6	(310) 1.2 / 1.8 / 2.9	(182) 1.2 / 1.8 / 2.6	(202) 1.1 / 1.9 / 2.8	(125) 1.1 / 1.7 / 2.4	(116) 1.0 / 1.8 / 2.7
(413)	4.7 / 10.7 / 18.8	(427) 5.3 / 10.2 / 18.7	(422) 4.8 / 9.5 / 16.3	% Officers', Directors', Owners' Comp/Sales	(99) 9.3 / 15.0 / 23.7	(144) 5.9 / 10.1 / 16.7	(72) 3.1 / 6.6 / 13.1	(62) 3.6 / 6.9 / 11.8	(29) 1.7 / 5.4 / 14.3	(16) .6 / 2.2 / 5.6
	16558202M	16369489M	19999293M	Net Sales ($)	124014M	639971M	795291M	1526838M	2199104M	14714075M
	7327194M	6686436M	8950692M	Total Assets ($)	59071M	256810M	346525M	610317M	932264M	6745705M

M = $ thousand   MM = $ million
See Pages 1 through 15 for Explanation of Ratios and Data

Current Data Sorted By Assets   **Comparative Historical Data**

	0-500M	500M-2MM	2-10MM	10-50MM	50-100MM	100-250MM		4/1/90-3/31/91 ALL	4/1/91-3/31/92 ALL
	1	2	4	1		2	# Postretirement Benefits		
							Type of Statement		
	1	8	18	14	1	4	Unqualified		8
	4	13	31	5			Reviewed		14
	6	20	11	1		1	Compiled		13
	2	3	3	3			Tax Returns		2
	5	14	17	8	1	2	Other		10
		58 (4/1-9/30/94)		135 (10/1/94-3/31/95)					
	18	58	80	28	2	7	**NUMBER OF STATEMENTS**		47
	%	%	%	%	%	%	**ASSETS**	%	%
	12.8	6.6	5.7	3.6			Cash & Equivalents		7.8
	20.1	19.3	20.4	20.3			Trade Receivables - (net)	D	15.1
	3.9	9.3	13.0	19.5			Inventory	A	7.0
	1.7	3.3	1.4	3.7			All Other Current	T	3.5
	38.4	38.4	40.5	47.0			Total Current	A	33.3
	52.0	54.7	52.8	44.9			Fixed Assets (net)		55.8
	3.2	.5	.4	.2			Intangibles (net)	N	.5
	6.3	6.5	6.3	7.9			All Other Non-Current	O	10.4
	100.0	100.0	100.0	100.0			Total	T	100.0
							LIABILITIES	A	
	3.5	9.6	10.7	14.7			Notes Payable-Short Term	V	7.2
	12.9	10.6	8.9	11.0			Cur. Mat. -L/T/D	A	14.8
	3.9	6.8	9.3	7.5			Trade Payables	I	5.4
	.5	.6	.4	.5			Income Taxes Payable	L	.7
	8.5	8.0	4.6	5.1			All Other Current	A	6.4
	29.3	35.7	33.9	38.7			Total Current	B	34.5
	22.7	25.3	22.5	29.8			Long Term Debt	L	24.9
	.0	.6	1.7	2.5			Deferred Taxes	E	1.6
	9.3	3.5	2.7	1.1			All Other-Non-Current		3.5
	38.8	34.9	39.2	28.0			Net Worth		35.5
	100.0	100.0	100.0	100.0			Total Liabilities & Net Worth		100.0
							INCOME DATA		
	100.0	100.0	100.0	100.0			Net Sales		100.0
							Gross Profit		
	92.1	92.1	90.1	89.8			Operating Expenses		92.8
	7.9	7.9	9.9	10.2			Operating Profit		7.2
	6.6	3.2	2.0	3.2			All Other Expenses (net)		3.3
	1.3	4.6	7.9	7.1			Profit Before Taxes		3.9
							RATIOS		
	3.1	1.7	1.9	1.5					1.7
	1.2	1.2	1.2	1.2			Current		1.1
	.5	.5	.8	.8					.7
	1.9	1.4	1.5	1.1					1.1
	1.0	.8	.8	.5			Quick		.7
	.5	.3	.4	.3					.4
	0 UND	20 18.4	33 11.2	38 9.7					33 11.0
	18 19.9	43 8.4	51 7.2	59 6.2			Sales/Receivables		46 7.9
	44 8.3	57 6.4	63 5.8	76 4.8					64 5.7
							Cost of Sales/Inventory		
							Cost of Sales/Payables		
	6.2	7.6	6.9	6.9					6.2
	61.3	23.7	25.9	17.6			Sales/Working Capital		35.4
	-12.1	-6.7	-13.5	-14.6					-9.2
	4.1	4.9	5.8	4.5					3.1
	(14) 2.0	(55) 2.6	(75) 3.4	(26) 2.7			EBIT/Interest		(45) 1.5
	.9	1.2	2.2	1.8					1.0
		4.0	6.0	5.0			Net Profit + Depr., Dep.,		4.0
		(18) 1.4	(37) 2.8	(18) 1.9			Amort./Cur. Mat. L./T/D		(26) 2.1
		.8	1.2	1.0					.8
	.5	.8	.8	.7					1.0
	1.8	1.5	1.2	1.3			Fixed/Worth		1.8
	13.8	4.1	2.5	2.7					2.4
	.5	.9	.9	1.7					1.0
	2.7	2.1	2.0	3.0			Debt/Worth		1.7
	18.3	4.8	3.3	4.7					3.6
	58.9	46.1	36.2	41.3			% Profit Before Taxes/Tangible		29.3
	(15) 12.8	(55) 16.2	(77) 20.3	21.0			Net Worth		(44) 6.8
	.0	2.7	8.3	12.0					.1
	11.3	12.4	12.7	9.8			% Profit Before Taxes/Total		8.2
	6.6	7.0	6.9	5.3			Assets		2.5
	-1.0	.7	3.9	3.0					-.1
	12.9	6.6	5.2	10.0					3.0
	2.8	2.3	2.5	2.1			Sales/Net Fixed Assets		2.0
	1.6	1.2	1.5	1.2					1.3
	3.3	2.1	1.9	1.7					1.6
	1.6	1.3	1.3	1.2			Sales/Total Assets		1.1
	1.0	.8	1.0	.6					.7
	7.4	5.8	4.8	4.3			% Depr., Dep., Amort./Sales		7.9
	(13) 12.4	(55) 12.5	(76) 9.8	(26) 9.5					(46) 13.6
	60.4	24.8	17.7	13.9					21.4
		4.0	2.3				% Officers', Directors',		6.5
		(24) 7.6	(34) 3.8				Owners' Comp/Sales		(18) 10.5
		15.2	6.4						15.6
	8958M	127698M	505215M	632851M	96701M	1160246M	Net Sales ($)		231048M
	4682M	62596M	364187M	541400M	140803M	1087057M	Total Assets ($)		242752M

Comparative Historical Data / Current Data Sorted By Sales

			# Postretirement Benefits — Type of Statement	2	1		4	3
19	24	46	Unqualified	7	5	5	6	10	13
23	39	53	Reviewed	8	10	9	18	6	2
36	51	39	Compiled	11	15	8	2	2	1
4	6	8	Tax Returns	5	1		1		1
17	21	47	Other	10	10	7	9	6	5

4/1/92-3/31/93 ALL	4/1/93-3/31/94 ALL	4/1/94-3/31/95 ALL		58 (4/1-9/30/94)			135 (10/1/94-3/31/95)		
				0-1MM	1-3MM	3-5MM	5-10MM	10-25MM	25MM & OVER
99	141	193	NUMBER OF STATEMENTS	41	41	29	36	24	22

ASSETS (%)

Yr1	Yr2	Yr3		0-1MM	1-3MM	3-5MM	5-10MM	10-25MM	25MM&OVER
7.5	6.8	6.1	Cash & Equivalents	6.6	8.3	6.2	6.5	3.8	3.1
16.2	16.1	19.6	Trade Receivables - (net)	13.9	23.0	23.1	16.2	24.2	19.4
11.9	11.3	13.2	Inventory	3.4	5.2	16.0	18.7	10.6	36.7
1.0	2.3	2.5	All Other Current	3.2	1.5	4.2	2.0	2.4	1.4
36.6	36.5	41.4	Total Current	27.2	38.0	49.5	43.3	40.9	60.5
55.4	55.3	51.0	Fixed Assets (net)	61.7	58.1	44.0	48.5	49.0	33.4
.7	.5	.6	Intangibles (net)	1.4	.3	.9	.4	.3	.3
7.3	7.6	7.0	All Other Non-Current	9.7	3.6	5.6	7.8	9.8	5.7
100.0	100.0	100.0	Total	100.0	100.0	100.0	100.0	100.0	100.0

LIABILITIES

Yr1	Yr2	Yr3		0-1MM	1-3MM	3-5MM	5-10MM	10-25MM	25MM&OVER
8.0	7.3	10.7	Notes Payable-Short Term	5.5	8.5	13.5	9.8	11.9	21.0
13.0	11.3	9.8	Cur. Mat.-L /T/D	15.4	8.1	7.8	10.2	8.3	6.2
6.8	7.8	8.3	Trade Payables	3.1	6.7	9.5	8.7	11.3	15.2
.9	.5	.5	Income Taxes Payable	.5	.6	.4	.4	.6	.2
4.3	6.2	6.1	All Other Current	5.7	7.3	6.8	3.9	6.7	6.2
33.0	33.1	35.3	Total Current	30.0	31.3	37.9	33.1	38.8	48.9
29.7	26.4	24.0	Long Term Debt	30.0	24.4	20.5	25.8	20.7	17.4
1.6	1.1	1.2	Deferred Taxes	.7	1.1	1.7	1.5	2.0	.8
1.3	4.5	3.7	All Other-Non-Current	6.3	4.6	2.3	2.9	2.1	2.3
34.3	34.8	35.7	Net Worth	33.0	38.5	37.7	36.8	36.4	30.5
100.0	100.0	100.0	Total Liabilities & Net Worth	100.0	100.0	100.0	100.0	100.0	100.0

INCOME DATA

Yr1	Yr2	Yr3		0-1MM	1-3MM	3-5MM	5-10MM	10-25MM	25MM&OVER
100.0	100.0	100.0	Net Sales	100.0	100.0	100.0	100.0	100.0	100.0
			Gross Profit						
91.8	91.7	90.7	Operating Expenses	88.0	91.0	91.4	91.0	91.0	93.2
8.2	8.3	9.3	Operating Profit	12.0	9.0	8.6	9.0	9.0	6.8
3.8	3.1	3.1	All Other Expenses (net)	5.8	3.8	2.2	2.1	1.1	1.8
4.4	5.2	6.2	Profit Before Taxes	6.2	5.2	6.4	6.9	7.9	5.0

RATIOS

Yr1	Yr2	Yr3		0-1MM	1-3MM	3-5MM	5-10MM	10-25MM	25MM&OVER
1.7 / 1.3 / .7	1.5 / 1.0 / .6	1.8 / 1.2 / .7	Current	1.4 / .7 / .2	2.4 / 1.5 / .5	1.8 / 1.4 / 1.1	2.1 / 1.2 / .9	1.6 / 1.1 / .6	1.7 / 1.3 / 1.1
1.3 / .7 / .4	1.1 / .7 / .4	1.4 / .8 / .3	Quick	1.0 / .5 / .2	1.8 / 1.2 / .4	1.5 / .9 / .5	1.6 / .8 / .4	1.1 / .6 / .4	1.0 / .3 / .3
29 12.7 / 41 8.8 / 63 5.8	27 13.3 / 42 8.6 / 58 6.3	27 13.4 / 46 7.9 / 62 5.9	Sales/Receivables	0 UND / 22 16.8 / 48 7.6	28 13.0 / 50 7.3 / 70 5.2	36 10.1 / 54 6.8 / 70 5.2	28 13.0 / 49 7.4 / 62 5.9	43 8.4 / 54 6.7 / 61 6.0	29 12.6 / 45 8.1 / 56 6.5
			Cost of Sales/Inventory						
			Cost of Sales/Payables						
6.0 / 21.9 / -13.9	8.0 / 136.3 / -8.4	6.8 / 21.4 / -11.4	Sales/Working Capital	7.5 / -15.2 / -2.7	6.3 / 12.3 / -6.4	6.0 / 12.7 / 73.8	6.4 / 21.2 / -28.3	11.4 / 43.4 / -9.3	7.1 / 15.8 / 68.5
(96) 3.2 / 1.6 / .9	(130) 4.4 / 2.3 / 1.1	(178) 5.2 / 2.9 / 1.6	EBIT/Interest	(34) 4.8 / 2.3 / 1.2	(39) 4.9 / 2.6 / 1.0	(25) 5.9 / 2.2 / 1.6	(34) 4.4 / 3.2 / 2.2	9.4 / 4.0 / 2.0	6.0 / 3.2 / 2.0
(49) 3.0 / 1.4 / .8	(64) 3.2 / 1.5 / .8	(76) 5.1 / 2.1 / 1.0	Net Profit + Depr., Dep., Amort./Cur. Mat. L/T/D	(12) 2.1 / 1.2 / .8	(16) 7.1 / 2.8 / .9	(11) 4.4 / 2.1 / 1.2	(14) 4.5 / 1.7 / 1.1	(16) 7.2 / 4.0 / 1.0	
.9 / 1.6 / 2.9	.9 / 1.6 / 3.8	.7 / 1.4 / 3.0	Fixed/Worth	.7 / 2.5 / 8.3	.8 / 1.5 / 3.1	.8 / 1.1 / 2.4	.7 / 1.3 / 2.5	.6 / 1.1 / 3.1	.3 / .8 / 1.6
1.1 / 2.0 / 3.8	.9 / 2.3 / 4.7	.9 / 2.2 / 4.4	Debt/Worth	.9 / 2.8 / 10.5	.9 / 1.9 / 3.3	.9 / 2.0 / 4.4	1.0 / 2.3 / 3.7	.9 / 2.3 / 3.7	1.5 / 2.5 / 4.8
(96) 34.6 / 11.2 / .1	(130) 31.5 / 15.3 / 3.8	(184) 39.3 / 19.2 / 8.2	% Profit Before Taxes/Tangible Net Worth	(38) 66.2 / 15.9 / 8.4	(38) 32.1 / 14.1 / -1.9	(26) 24.2 / 18.5 / 8.0	41.7 / 24.5 / 9.1	49.1 / 30.5 / 8.2	29.0 / 20.6 / 16.1
8.7 / 3.1 / -.1	10.4 / 5.1 / .3	11.3 / 6.2 / 2.4	% Profit Before Taxes/Total Assets	10.4 / 6.0 / .8	13.2 / 7.1 / .0	10.9 / 4.5 / 2.1	11.0 / 7.2 / 4.0	19.5 / 9.3 / 2.6	9.0 / 6.3 / 3.6
4.8 / 2.4 / 1.2	5.3 / 2.4 / 1.2	7.0 / 2.4 / 1.4	Sales/Net Fixed Assets	3.5 / 1.2 / .6	4.0 / 2.2 / 1.5	6.5 / 3.2 / 1.9	8.2 / 2.7 / 1.5	8.3 / 2.8 / 1.5	22.6 / 9.3 / 2.0
1.9 / 1.3 / .7	1.9 / 1.3 / .8	1.9 / 1.3 / .9	Sales/Total Assets	1.3 / .8 / .4	2.0 / 1.3 / 1.0	2.0 / 1.5 / 1.1	1.9 / 1.4 / .9	2.1 / 1.3 / 1.1	2.0 / 1.4 / 1.1
(97) 6.1 / 12.2 / 22.3	(123) 6.5 / 10.8 / 18.7	(173) 4.8 / 10.9 / 18.2	% Depr., Dep., Amort./Sales	(38) 9.9 / 23.0 / 60.2	(37) 9.7 / 13.8 / 18.8	(27) 4.0 / 7.7 / 15.6	(33) 4.5 / 9.0 / 14.5	(22) 4.3 / 8.3 / 12.9	(16) .9 / 2.4 / 6.1
(40) 3.4 / 5.5 / 10.3	(52) 4.0 / 7.4 / 13.2	(73) 2.5 / 4.3 / 9.3	% Officers', Directors', Owners' Comp/Sales	(14) 4.2 / 12.6 / 15.7	(17) 3.8 / 7.7 / 14.8		(21) 2.2 / 3.7 / 4.6		
1034099M / 822057M	803502M / 817917M	2531669M / 2200725M	Net Sales ($) / Total Assets ($)	22217M / 38233M	73199M / 75944M	115538M / 119090M	232218M / 233906M	335744M / 269971M	1752753M / 1463581M

M = $ thousand   MM = $ million
See Pages 1 through 15 for Explanation of Ratios and Data

Current Data Sorted By Assets | **Comparative Historical Data**

6	7	9	3	1	2	# Postretirement Benefits Type of Statement		
3	8	20	25	4	2	Unqualified	67	58
17	39	34	7		2	Reviewed	120	105
50	79	24	2			Compiled	157	167
13	7					Tax Returns	8	15
40	33	42	12	2	3	Other	108	95
123 (4/1-9/30/94)			343 (10/1/94-3/31/95)				4/1/90-3/31/91	4/1/91-3/31/92
0-500M	500M-2MM	2-10MM	10-50MM	50-100MM	100-250MM		ALL	ALL
123	166	120	46	6	5	**NUMBER OF STATEMENTS**	460	440
%	%	%	%	%	%	**ASSETS**	%	%
7.9	7.2	5.7	4.2			Cash & Equivalents	6.5	6.6
8.2	11.8	13.3	12.2			Trade Receivables - (net)	12.9	12.6
7.5	6.9	9.1	7.2			Inventory	6.8	7.0
2.0	1.9	1.2	3.3			All Other Current	1.9	2.2
25.6	27.7	29.3	26.9			Total Current	28.1	28.4
67.8	66.0	62.0	65.0			Fixed Assets (net)	63.7	62.9
1.9	1.4	2.0	2.4			Intangibles (net)	.9	1.3
4.8	5.0	6.8	5.7			All Other Non-Current	7.3	7.4
100.0	100.0	100.0	100.0			Total	100.0	100.0
						LIABILITIES		
5.6	7.5	9.9	8.8			Notes Payable-Short Term	10.3	9.4
11.0	9.7	9.5	10.5			Cur. Mat. -L/T/D	10.9	10.4
4.7	7.2	7.6	5.6			Trade Payables	5.7	6.1
.2	.7	.4	.2			Income Taxes Payable	.5	.5
7.7	6.5	5.7	4.5			All Other Current	5.7	6.0
29.2	31.6	33.1	29.6			Total Current	33.1	32.3
31.6	25.6	25.3	34.2			Long Term Debt	28.6	28.4
.2	.5	1.0	3.0			Deferred Taxes	1.0	.9
4.6	2.9	4.3	1.9			All Other-Non-Current	2.4	3.4
34.3	39.4	36.2	31.2			Net Worth	34.8	35.0
100.0	100.0	100.0	100.0			Total Liabilities & Net Worth	100.0	100.0
						INCOME DATA		
100.0	100.0	100.0	100.0			Net Sales	100.0	100.0
						Gross Profit		
85.0	86.8	87.2	85.8			Operating Expenses	86.7	87.4
15.0	13.2	12.8	14.2			Operating Profit	13.3	12.6
5.7	4.1	3.7	5.4			All Other Expenses (net)	5.6	5.5
9.3	9.1	9.1	8.9			Profit Before Taxes	7.7	7.1
						RATIOS		
2.2	1.5	1.6	1.4			Current	1.6	1.8
1.0	.9	1.1	.9				.9	1.0
.4	.4	.4	.5				.4	.4
1.3	1.0	1.1	.9			Quick	1.2	1.3
.6	.7	.6	.6				.6	.7
.2	.2	.2	.3				.2	.2
0 UND	2 155.1	12 30.3	39 9.3			Sales/Receivables	7 55.6	5 69.5
12 30.7	23 16.1	34 10.7	58 6.3				34 10.7	29 12.8
29 12.4	42 8.7	51 7.2	70 5.2				52 7.0	49 7.4
						Cost of Sales/Inventory		
						Cost of Sales/Payables		
12.9	16.4	9.6	7.4			Sales/Working Capital	10.7	9.6
-657.0	-36.0	57.9	-24.0				-58.3	-126.9
-6.7	-6.8	-4.7	-5.8				-4.5	-5.8
(109) 7.0	(150) 6.3	(113) 6.0	(40) 4.6			EBIT/Interest	(395) 4.3	(380) 3.9
3.2	3.2	2.9	2.5				2.1	1.8
1.1	1.7	1.6	1.4				1.2	.9
(22) 4.3	(61) 3.8	(52) 3.9	(25) 1.7			Net Profit + Depr., Dep., Amort./Cur. Mat. L /T/D	(229) 2.9	(181) 2.4
2.4	2.0	2.2	1.4				1.6	1.4
1.2	1.4	1.1	.9				1.0	.9
1.0	1.0	1.1	1.5			Fixed/Worth	1.1	1.0
2.3	1.8	1.9	2.6				2.2	1.9
10.0	3.2	3.3	5.6				4.3	4.0
.7	.7	.9	1.4			Debt/Worth	.9	.8
2.0	1.8	2.1	2.7				2.2	2.0
11.1	3.6	4.4	5.7				4.8	5.2
(102) 60.5	(156) 36.9	(113) 33.0	(45) 38.0			% Profit Before Taxes/Tangible Net Worth	(425) 40.8	(395) 36.4
24.2	19.3	20.3	22.0				17.6	15.4
5.9	8.2	11.8	8.5				4.2	1.4
20.5	13.6	12.0	11.4			% Profit Before Taxes/Total Assets	12.9	11.8
8.3	7.4	5.9	4.3				5.2	4.1
.7	2.6	2.7	1.4				.9	-.3
3.9	3.6	3.9	1.9			Sales/Net Fixed Assets	3.2	3.6
2.5	2.3	2.0	1.0				1.9	2.0
1.0	.7	.7	.7				1.0	.9
2.3	2.1	1.7	1.0			Sales/Total Assets	1.8	1.9
1.5	1.5	1.2	.7				1.2	1.2
.8	.6	.5	.5				.7	.7
(117) 8.3	(160) 6.9	(116) 6.7	(43) 9.0			% Depr., Dep., Amort./Sales	(435) 8.0	(413) 7.1
16.0	11.1	14.4	15.2				14.0	13.3
37.0	23.7	25.8	20.6				27.8	26.4
(54) 7.0	(70) 4.7	(41) 2.5				% Officers', Directors', Owners' Comp/Sales	(150) 3.4	(160) 3.7
10.6	7.1	5.9					6.9	7.3
15.1	12.7	12.0					13.6	12.9
55223M	240156M	635347M	825791M	343469M	736254M	Net Sales ($)	2821685M	2518782M
33211M	166399M	497565M	996490M	395616M	710530M	Total Assets ($)	2676722M	2868167M

M = $ thousand   MM = $ million
See Pages 1 through 15 for Explanation of Ratios and Data

Comparative Historical Data				Current Data Sorted By Sales					
9	12	28	# Postretirement Benefits	11	5	4	2	3	3
			Type of Statement						
67	53	62	Unqualified	11	5	7	14	14	11
100	100	97	Reviewed	31	30	15	12	8	1
157	160	155	Compiled	79	57	12	5	2	
23	21	20	Tax Returns	18	2				
88	106	132	Other	55	26	15	15	15	6
4/1/92-	4/1/93-	4/1/94-		123 (4/1-9/30/94)			343 (10/1/94-3/31/95)		
3/31/93	3/31/94	3/31/95							
ALL	ALL	ALL		0-1MM	1-3MM	3-5MM	5-10MM	10-25MM	25MM & OVER
435	440	466	NUMBER OF STATEMENTS	194	120	49	46	39	18
%	%	%	ASSETS	%	%	%	%	%	%
6.5	7.2	6.6	Cash & Equivalents	7.1	6.9	8.7	4.2	4.0	5.7
10.8	12.0	11.3	Trade Receivables - (net)	7.3	12.0	15.6	15.9	16.1	15.9
6.4	6.4	7.5	Inventory	4.9	7.9	11.1	12.2	9.1	8.2
1.7	2.1	1.9	All Other Current	1.8	1.5	3.1	2.1	1.6	1.3
25.5	27.6	27.4	Total Current	21.3	28.2	38.6	34.4	30.9	31.1
66.2	63.7	65.3	Fixed Assets (net)	71.9	65.3	50.7	59.3	60.8	59.6
1.4	1.5	1.8	Intangibles (net)	1.9	1.3	2.0	1.3	3.1	1.5
6.9	7.2	5.6	All Other Non-Current	5.0	5.2	8.7	5.0	5.3	7.8
100.0	100.0	100.0	Total	100.0	100.0	100.0	100.0	100.0	100.0
			LIABILITIES						
10.0	9.0	7.7	Notes Payable-Short Term	7.9	6.7	7.5	10.9	7.6	5.3
10.7	9.9	9.9	Cur. Mat.-L /T/D	10.8	10.3	9.0	9.5	7.8	7.0
5.4	6.1	6.5	Trade Payables	3.9	7.5	9.8	10.2	7.0	8.5
.4	.6	.5	Income Taxes Payable	.4	.5	.5	.6	.3	.4
5.7	6.0	6.4	All Other Current	7.0	5.5	7.8	5.1	5.4	5.7
32.1	31.7	31.0	Total Current	30.0	30.6	34.5	36.2	28.5	26.8
27.8	27.5	27.9	Long Term Debt	31.2	26.3	23.4	25.4	26.8	25.2
.9	.7	.9	Deferred Taxes	.4	.6	1.8	1.8	2.3	3.9
3.9	3.0	3.6	All Other-Non-Current	3.3	3.1	6.2	2.3	5.6	1.3
35.2	37.1	36.6	Net Worth	35.2	39.4	35.1	34.3	36.8	42.8
100.0	100.0	100.0	Total Liabilities & Net Worth	100.0	100.0	100.0	100.0	100.0	100.0
			INCOME DATA						
100.0	100.0	100.0	Net Sales	100.0	100.0	100.0	100.0	100.0	100.0
			Gross Profit						
86.2	86.7	86.3	Operating Expenses	81.7	87.8	93.6	89.5	90.4	89.4
13.8	13.3	13.7	Operating Profit	18.3	12.2	6.4	10.5	9.6	10.6
5.7	4.2	4.5	All Other Expenses (net)	7.1	3.4	1.4	3.1	2.0	2.2
8.1	9.0	9.2	Profit Before Taxes	11.3	8.8	5.1	7.4	7.5	8.4
			RATIOS						
1.6	1.6	1.6		1.6	1.6	1.8	1.4	1.6	1.9
.9	.9	1.0	Current	.7	.9	1.1	1.0	1.1	1.1
.3	.5	.4		.2	.5	.8	.6	.8	.7
1.1	1.2	1.1		1.1	1.1	1.0	1.0	1.2	1.5
.5	.6	.6	Quick	.5	.7	.7	.6	.8	.7
.2	.3	.2		.1	.3	.4	.3	.4	.5
1 249.2	4 93.0	1 311.5		0 UND	7 50.7	18 20.1	27 13.6	29 12.5	41 8.9
23 15.8	29 12.8	26 13.9	Sales/Receivables	12 30.0	25 14.4	38 9.7	45 8.2	48 7.6	51 7.1
47 7.7	50 7.3	49 7.5		33 11.2	41 8.8	49 7.4	63 5.8	68 5.4	68 5.4
			Cost of Sales/Inventory						
			Cost of Sales/Payables						
14.2	10.8	10.8		15.7	11.0	7.7	11.5	7.8	5.0
-34.5	-60.2	-96.4	Sales/Working Capital	-16.1	-83.1	52.6	50.9	39.7	150.4
-4.3	-6.0	-6.0		-2.4	-9.9	-26.5	-7.6	-15.7	-10.6
	4.7		5.7		6.1		15.7		11.0		7.7		11.5		7.8		5.0
(372) 2.3	(404) 2.7	(422) 3.0	EBIT/Interest	(164) 2.8	(112) 3.1	(48) 3.0	2.8	(37) 3.9	(15) 2.6
1.2	1.5	1.6		1.3	1.6	1.7	1.6	1.7	2.1
2.8	3.5	3.7		3.0	3.9	4.7	2.5	5.4	
(174) 1.5	(148) 2.0	(162) 1.9	Net Profit + Depr., Dep.,	(38) 2.1	(48) 1.8	(24) 2.6	(26) 1.5	(19) 1.9	
1.0	1.1	1.2	Amort./Cur. Mat. L/T/D	1.2	1.2	1.5	.8	1.2	
1.2	1.1	1.1		1.1	1.0	.9	1.2	1.1	1.2
2.0	1.8	2.0	Fixed/Worth	2.5	1.8	1.3	2.1	1.8	1.7
4.7	3.8	4.5		8.2	3.0	2.5	3.3	4.4	2.7
.9	.8	.8		.7	.7	1.0	1.2	1.0	.8
1.9	1.7	2.0	Debt/Worth	2.0	1.8	1.8	2.6	2.4	1.6
5.1	4.7	5.3		8.1	3.0	3.9	5.2	5.2	2.8
38.6	44.6	39.7	% Profit Before Taxes/Tangible	47.6	42.2	30.8	38.5	44.7	27.7
(394) 16.3	(406) 20.8	(427) 20.8	Net Worth	(169) 19.0	(113) 22.3	(44) 18.3	(45) 21.9	(38) 27.2	21.5
3.7	7.5	8.8		5.8	10.8	11.4	9.2	13.1	15.1
12.1	14.2	14.3	% Profit Before Taxes/Total	15.6	16.1	11.5	11.2	14.4	12.2
5.3	6.3	6.9	Assets	5.8	7.7	5.5	6.3	7.1	7.4
.9	2.0	1.9		1.0	2.9	3.5	1.4	2.3	4.2
3.6	3.5	3.6		2.9	4.0	5.3	4.0	4.0	4.4
2.1	1.9	2.0	Sales/Net Fixed Assets	1.1	2.5	3.4	2.1	2.2	1.5
.8	.9	.8		.5	1.4	1.6	1.4	1.1	.9
2.0	2.0	2.0		1.8	2.2	2.2	2.0	2.2	1.7
1.3	1.2	1.3	Sales/Total Assets	.9	1.6	1.5	1.3	1.3	1.0
.6	.6	.6		.4	.9	1.0	.7	.7	.7
7.9	7.8	7.4		10.3	7.3	5.1	5.6	6.7	4.0
(413) 13.5	(415) 13.8	(441) 13.1	% Depr., Dep., Amort./Sales	(186) 20.2	(118) 10.1	(47) 8.8	(43) 12.7	(36) 12.5	(11) 8.1
25.4	27.8	27.2		51.3	18.4	19.8	18.1	19.2	11.7
4.4	3.1	4.4		7.1	3.5	4.0	1.2		
(154) 7.5	(175) 6.5	(172) 7.5	% Officers', Directors',	(68) 10.9	(54) 6.8	(27) 6.4	(16) 3.4		
13.8	11.0	12.9	Owners' Comp/Sales	15.8	11.3	12.0	10.0		
2617032M	2443485M	2836240M	Net Sales ($)	86239M	208726M	186926M	326261M	645825M	1382263M
2886624M	2555773M	2799811M	Total Assets ($)	125386M	210149M	157041M	348893M	675310M	1283032M

M = $ thousand   MM = $ million
See Pages 1 through 15 for Explanation of Ratios and Data

Current Data Sorted By Assets

							# Postretirement Benefits	Comparative Historical Data	
8	5	2					**Type of Statement**		
	2	3	1	2			Unqualified	13	8
11	22	13					Reviewed	45	44
54	61	12	1	1			Compiled	116	135
18	5	1					Tax Returns	6	9
19	36	8	2				Other	44	57

0-500M	100 (4/1-9/30/94) 500M-2MM	2-10MM	172 (10/1/94-3/31/95) 10-50MM	50-100MM	100-250MM			4/1/90-3/31/91 ALL	4/1/91-3/31/92 ALL
102	126	37	4	3			**NUMBER OF STATEMENTS**	224	253
%	%	%	%	%	%		**ASSETS**	%	%
12.2	9.8	13.4					Cash & Equivalents	11.5	9.5
17.0	16.2	10.8					Trade Receivables - (net)	19.5	20.3
7.8	5.8	5.5					Inventory	6.1	7.1
3.0	2.2	1.7					All Other Current	2.7	3.1
39.9	34.1	31.3					Total Current	39.7	40.1
46.7	43.9	38.0					Fixed Assets (net)	39.7	40.0
6.0	5.4	5.8					Intangibles (net)	4.5	3.6
7.5	16.7	24.9					All Other Non-Current	16.1	16.3
100.0	100.0	100.0					Total	100.0	100.0
							LIABILITIES		
5.8	2.6	4.8					Notes Payable-Short Term	5.1	3.6
4.9	3.1	2.5					Cur. Mat. -L/T/D	5.0	4.4
6.8	4.6	2.6					Trade Payables	4.9	6.6
.6	.3	.2					Income Taxes Payable	.5	.5
8.1	8.8	5.1					All Other Current	9.0	9.8
26.2	19.4	15.2					Total Current	24.5	24.8
27.8	34.9	25.8					Long Term Debt	28.2	30.3
.0	.3	.2					Deferred Taxes	.5	.4
5.7	7.5	14.2					All Other-Non-Current	9.1	7.6
40.3	37.9	44.6					Net Worth	37.7	36.9
100.0	100.0	100.0					Total Liabilities & Net Worth	100.0	100.0
							INCOME DATA		
100.0	100.0	100.0					Net Sales	100.0	100.0
							Gross Profit		
90.8	91.3	89.0					Operating Expenses	91.4	92.6
9.2	8.7	11.0					Operating Profit	8.6	7.4
2.0	1.3	-.3					All Other Expenses (net)	2.3	1.2
7.2	7.3	11.3					Profit Before Taxes	6.4	6.3
							RATIOS		
3.1	3.3	4.7						3.2	3.4
1.6	1.9	2.8					Current	1.8	1.8
1.0	1.1	1.2						1.1	1.1
2.0	2.8	3.4						2.5	2.6
1.1	(125) 1.4	1.7					Quick	1.5	(252) 1.3
.7	.7	.9						.8	.8
12 30.7	29 12.6	29 12.5						35 10.5	33 11.1
35 10.5	41 9.0	45 8.2					Sales/Receivables	49 7.5	46 8.0
53 6.9	59 6.2	66 5.5						70 5.2	69 5.3
							Cost of Sales/Inventory		
							Cost of Sales/Payables		
6.1	4.4	2.6						4.4	4.8
12.6	8.9	6.3					Sales/Working Capital	8.0	8.8
-228.0	118.5	34.8						44.9	52.7
7.4	6.5	8.0						5.1	6.2
(88) 3.7	(116) 2.6	(32) 4.5					EBIT/Interest	(199) 2.3	(226) 2.3
1.4	1.2	2.1						1.3	1.3
4.5	3.9	10.0					Net Profit + Depr., Dep.,	4.2	3.3
(32) 2.1	(55) 1.8	(14) 3.5					Amort./Cur. Mat. L /T/D	(116) 1.9	(106) 1.9
.9	.7	2.2						1.1	.8
.7	.6	.4						.6	.6
1.3	1.4	.9					Fixed/Worth	1.2	1.1
3.5	4.4	2.0						3.3	2.6
.7	.7	.6						.7	.7
2.0	2.1	1.0					Debt/Worth	1.8	1.9
5.2	9.4	4.5						7.4	5.7
64.0	44.4	35.6					% Profit Before Taxes/Tangible	33.2	34.9
(85) 21.9	(109) 15.8	(32) 15.8					Net Worth	(191) 14.3	(219) 17.0
4.0	5.0	6.7						3.7	4.8
21.7	12.0	13.5					% Profit Before Taxes/Total	12.0	12.1
9.3	5.9	7.3					Assets	5.2	5.5
1.7	.8	3.1						.8	1.1
8.9	6.0	4.5						7.6	7.8
5.2	3.0	2.1					Sales/Net Fixed Assets	3.3	3.8
2.3	1.4	1.5						1.8	1.8
2.9	1.6	1.0						1.8	2.0
2.0	1.0	.8					Sales/Total Assets	1.2	1.3
1.2	.7	.5						.8	.8
2.5	2.9	2.6						2.7	2.9
(94) 4.2	(121) 4.1	(36) 4.3					% Depr., Dep., Amort./Sales	(212) 4.2	(239) 4.2
6.5	6.2	5.7						6.0	6.1
9.7	10.4	8.5					% Officers', Directors',	8.7	9.0
(63) 14.8	(77) 13.5	(19) 13.1					Owners' Comp/Sales	(132) 13.8	(142) 13.2
19.5	18.7	15.7						19.2	20.4
53241M	150129M	97326M	49824M	53845M			Net Sales ($)	499531M	430133M
27302M	134034M	133639M	84591M	210222M			Total Assets ($)	737558M	533333M

M = $ thousand   MM = $ million
See Pages 1 through 15 for Explanation of Ratios and Data

Comparative Historical Data

	3	10	15

Current Data Sorted By Sales

	8	6	1

	3	10	15		8	6	1			
# Postretirement Benefits					8	6	1			
Type of Statement										
Unqualified	8	9	8		2	3			3	
Reviewed	52	43	46		20	16	8	2		
Compiled	118	139	129		79	46	2	1	1	
Tax Returns	19	24	24		21	3		1		
Other	52	59	65		36	22	5	1	1	

	4/1/92-3/31/93 ALL	4/1/93-3/31/94 ALL	4/1/94-3/31/95 ALL		100 (4/1-9/30/94) 0-1MM	1-3MM	3-5MM	172 (10/1/94-3/31/95) 5-10MM	10-25MM	25MM & OVER
NUMBER OF STATEMENTS	249	274	272		158	90	15	4	5	
ASSETS	%	%	%		%	%	%	%	%	%
Cash & Equivalents	10.9	10.2	11.0		11.3	11.4	9.4			
Trade Receivables - (net)	18.5	17.7	15.5		14.7	17.6	16.1			
Inventory	6.2	6.5	6.4		6.9	6.0	5.8			
All Other Current	2.5	2.8	2.5		2.9	1.5	2.6			
Total Current	38.1	37.2	35.5		35.9	36.4	33.8			
Fixed Assets (net)	43.8	44.2	44.0		45.2	41.3	47.5			
Intangibles (net)	3.7	3.1	5.7		5.8	5.7	4.1			
All Other Non-Current	14.3	15.5	14.7		13.1	16.7	14.6			
Total	100.0	100.0	100.0		100.0	100.0	100.0			
LIABILITIES										
Notes Payable-Short Term	4.3	3.7	4.0		3.9	4.3	4.7			
Cur. Mat.-L /T/D	3.9	3.5	3.7		3.7	4.1	2.7			
Trade Payables	6.7	5.3	5.1		5.7	4.2	4.5			
Income Taxes Payable	.5	.6	.4		.3	.7	.0			
All Other Current	7.7	8.5	8.0		8.6	7.8	4.3			
Total Current	23.1	21.7	21.2		22.0	21.1	16.4			
Long Term Debt	29.6	29.4	30.6		34.7	24.5	27.9			
Deferred Taxes	.5	.7	.2		.1	.3	.4			
All Other-Non-Current	7.0	8.6	7.9		8.2	8.3	.0			
Net Worth	39.7	39.6	40.1		34.8	45.8	55.4			
Total Liabilities & Net Worth	100.0	100.0	100.0		100.0	100.0	100.0			
INCOME DATA										
Net Sales	100.0	100.0	100.0		100.0	100.0	100.0			
Gross Profit										
Operating Expenses	91.0	90.7	90.5		90.3	91.7	90.1			
Operating Profit	9.0	9.3	9.5		9.7	8.3	9.9			
All Other Expenses (net)	1.6	1.6	1.4		2.3	–.2	.5			
Profit Before Taxes	7.4	7.7	8.0		7.4	8.5	9.4			
RATIOS										
Current	3.7	3.8	3.3		3.3	3.6	4.1			
	1.9	2.0	1.8		1.7	2.0	1.7			
	1.1	1.1	1.1		1.0	1.1	1.4			
Quick	2.7	2.9	2.6		2.4	2.9	3.0			
	1.5	1.4 (271)	1.3		1.2 (89)	1.5	1.4			
	.8	.8	.7		.6	.8	1.0			
Sales/Receivables	29 12.5	29 12.6	23 15.7		22 16.8	30 12.2	32 11.3			
	46 8.0	42 8.6	39 9.3		38 9.6	41 9.0	47 7.8			
	64 5.7	60 6.1	57 6.4		58 6.3	56 6.5	58 6.3			
Cost of Sales/Inventory										
Cost of Sales/Payables										
Sales/Working Capital	4.6	4.4	4.7		4.6	5.0	4.1			
	8.9	9.4	9.3		9.9	9.0	10.1			
	37.9	48.9	100.4		–165.4	66.0	16.2			
EBIT/Interest	(224) 5.9	(243) 6.9	(242) 7.2		(137) 5.4	(83) 12.5	(14) 7.9			
	2.8	3.3	3.6		2.7	4.2	5.8			
	1.4	1.8	1.4		1.1	2.1	2.8			
Net Profit + Depr., Dep., Amort./Cur. Mat. L/T/D	(104) 3.9	(95) 4.0	(105) 4.0		(49) 3.6	(45) 4.7				
	2.1	2.3	2.2		1.7	2.7				
	1.3	1.2	1.0		.5	1.3				
Fixed/Worth	.6	.6	.6		.8	.4	.6			
	1.3	1.2	1.3		1.6	.9	1.1			
	3.2	2.9	3.7		5.8	2.3	1.4			
Debt/Worth	.7	.6	.7		.7	.5	.4			
	1.5	1.6	1.9		2.5	1.2	.8			
	6.5	5.6	6.4		14.4	3.9	1.9			
% Profit Before Taxes/Tangible Net Worth	(222) 38.9	(237) 41.4	(232) 44.5		(128) 44.4	(81) 47.4	29.5			
	18.1	19.6	17.8		18.4	16.7	16.1			
	7.3	9.1	5.2		3.3	6.7	11.6			
% Profit Before Taxes/Total Assets	12.6	14.3	14.5		15.3	13.8	17.5			
	6.7	7.9	7.1		5.4	7.8	9.0			
	1.9	3.1	1.3		.4	3.2	5.4			
Sales/Net Fixed Assets	7.0	6.3	6.6		6.9	6.8	5.3			
	3.1	3.3	3.3		3.2	3.7	2.4			
	1.6	1.7	1.6		1.4	1.8	1.5			
Sales/Total Assets	1.9	2.0	2.0		2.1	2.1	1.7			
	1.2	1.2	1.2		1.1	1.3	1.2			
	.8	.8	.7		.6	.9	1.0			
% Depr., Dep., Amort./Sales	(238) 2.6	(256) 2.7	(258) 2.8		(146) 2.9	(88) 2.5	3.5			
	4.1	4.5	4.2		4.3	3.9	4.9			
	6.3	6.2	6.3		7.2	5.1	5.7			
% Officers', Directors', Owners' Comp/Sales	(147) 8.9	(170) 7.7	(161) 9.2		(89) 10.1	(59) 10.7				
	13.1	13.7	13.7		14.0	13.8				
	18.8	19.3	18.7		18.9	19.2				
Net Sales ($)	379770M	562373M	404365M		82157M	150560M	55721M	28653M	87274M	
Total Assets ($)	479767M	841720M	589788M		92519M	147101M	47441M	33210M	269517M	

M = $ thousand   MM = $ million
See Pages 1 through 15 for Explanation of Ratios and Data

Current Data Sorted By Assets / Comparative Historical Data

Type of Statement

0-500M	500M-2MM	2-10MM	10-50MM	50-100MM	100-250MM		4/1/90-3/31/91 ALL	4/1/91-3/31/92 ALL
		1	3	1		# Postretirement Benefits		
						Type of Statement		
	2	12	4	2	2	Unqualified	8	6
1	9	7				Reviewed	11	16
10	39	14				Compiled	29	25
4	6	5				Tax Returns		3
5	18	16	7	1		Other	14	16
20	74	54	11	3	2	**NUMBER OF STATEMENTS**	62	66

Date ranges: 500M-2MM span labeled **25 (4/1-9/30/94)**; 2-10MM through 100-250MM span labeled **139 (10/1/94-3/31/95)**.

0-500M	500M-2MM	2-10MM	10-50MM	50-100MM	100-250MM		4/1/90-3/31/91 ALL	4/1/91-3/31/92 ALL
%	%	%	%	%	%	**ASSETS**	%	%
13.2	6.7	5.3	3.8			Cash & Equivalents	10.7	6.8
7.0	1.3	2.4	2.5			Trade Receivables - (net)	4.6	3.1
6.6	4.8	5.2	1.5			Inventory	6.6	2.2
2.8	1.7	.3	1.1			All Other Current	.6	.5
29.7	14.5	13.2	8.8			Total Current	22.6	12.6
56.3	79.8	76.4	86.4			Fixed Assets (net)	68.7	77.6
4.8	1.1	4.0	1.4			Intangibles (net)	.7	.7
9.2	4.6	6.4	3.4			All Other Non-Current	7.9	9.1
100.0	100.0	100.0	100.0			Total	100.0	100.0
						LIABILITIES		
9.5	3.8	4.2	1.0			Notes Payable-Short Term	4.6	4.5
3.7	5.1	3.0	4.3			Cur. Mat. -L/T/D	6.3	7.7
5.5	3.0	2.7	2.1			Trade Payables	7.0	1.7
.1	.1	.4	.0			Income Taxes Payable	.4	.6
14.0	6.5	6.6	12.4			All Other Current	7.6	6.0
32.7	18.5	16.9	19.9			Total Current	26.1	20.4
29.9	41.1	48.7	23.7			Long Term Debt	36.0	41.4
.0	.2	.2	.1			Deferred Taxes	1.2	.1
11.3	6.0	3.0	3.3			All Other-Non-Current	4.7	4.5
26.2	34.2	31.1	53.0			Net Worth	32.1	33.6
100.0	100.0	100.0	100.0			Total Liabilities & Net Worth	100.0	100.0
						INCOME DATA		
100.0	100.0	100.0	100.0			Net Sales	100.0	100.0
						Gross Profit		
90.8	86.7	89.6	94.0			Operating Expenses	89.4	86.6
9.2	13.3	10.4	6.0			Operating Profit	10.6	13.4
3.1	7.1	9.7	4.0			All Other Expenses (net)	7.2	9.3
6.1	6.2	.7	2.0			Profit Before Taxes	3.5	4.1
						RATIOS		
2.1	1.9	1.5	1.1			Current	1.9	1.4
.8	.9	.6	.7				1.0	.5
.4	.2	.2	.1				.4	.2
1.0	1.3	1.1	.8			Quick	1.4	1.1
.6	(73) .3	.3	.3				.6	.4
.1	.2	.1	.1				.2	.1
0 UND	0 UND	0 999.8	2 196.0			Sales/Receivables	0 UND	0 UND
0 UND	1 667.5	4 90.0	12 31.1				3 139.9	0 UND
3 118.1	6 61.6	13 27.9	27 13.4				15 24.3	13 29.2
						Cost of Sales/Inventory		
						Cost of Sales/Payables		
21.3	11.5	19.1	47.5			Sales/Working Capital	13.6	20.7
-62.1	-83.8	-12.3	-10.5				-161.3	-15.8
-12.1	-5.9	-3.5	-1.1				-6.1	-4.1
(16) 6.1	(68) 4.0	(42) 3.2	(10) 1.7			EBIT/Interest	(51) 4.2	(53) 4.7
2.4	1.7	1.6	1.0				1.7	2.1
1.3	1.0	.7	-1.4				1.0	1.2
	(23) 4.6					Net Profit + Depr., Dep., Amort./Cur. Mat. L /T/D	(29) 4.8	(23) 4.0
	1.7						2.1	1.8
	1.1						.8	1.1
1.0	1.2	1.5	1.1			Fixed/Worth	1.1	1.2
4.6	2.5	3.0	1.5				2.0	2.3
NM	13.3	19.0	3.2				8.2	8.7
.7	.7	1.1	.2			Debt/Worth	.8	.7
4.8	2.0	2.7	.9				2.0	2.2
NM	14.5	24.0	2.7				10.2	9.1
(15) 80.9	(60) 33.2	(46) 35.6				% Profit Before Taxes/Tangible Net Worth	(53) 31.1	(56) 37.3
34.8	13.6	9.5					15.2	13.8
7.4	.1	-8.2					2.6	-2.7
39.0	10.4	6.4	1.3			% Profit Before Taxes/Total Assets	9.1	11.0
8.6	3.7	2.5	.2				2.7	4.5
1.8	-.0	-3.5	-2.8				-.0	-1.2
13.4	1.4	1.0	.7			Sales/Net Fixed Assets	3.5	1.2
5.0	.9	.7	.5				1.2	.8
1.9	.6	.4	.3				.6	.6
4.5	1.0	.9	.5			Sales/Total Assets	1.7	1.0
2.4	.8	.5	.4				.8	.5
1.3	.6	.4	.3				.5	.5
(19) 1.7	(69) 6.7	(51) 7.1				% Depr., Dep., Amort./Sales	(57) 5.8	(63) 6.0
3.0	9.2	9.8					8.2	10.2
6.5	13.1	13.7					12.1	13.4
(10) 6.1	(20) 4.7	(12) 2.1				% Officers', Directors', Owners' Comp/Sales	(18) 4.2	(27) 4.0
8.2	6.2	5.6					8.5	6.8
16.3	9.5	9.5					11.3	12.4
14055M	67767M	121072M	85548M	102444M	397480M	Net Sales ($)	139613M	92589M
5076M	80671M	197189M	236723M	270710M	257421M	Total Assets ($)	160102M	142893M

M = $ thousand   MM = $ million
See Pages 1 through 15 for Explanation of Ratios and Data

Comparative Historical Data | Current Data Sorted By Sales

4	6	5	# Postretirement Benefits	2	2	1			
			Type of Statement						
7	21	22	Unqualified	2	7	3	5	2	3
17	13	17	Reviewed	8	7	1	1		
54	55	63	Compiled	39	21	1	2		
5	6	15	Tax Returns	7	6	1	1		
26	25	47	Other	22	16	3	5		1
4/1/92-3/31/93	4/1/93-3/31/94	4/1/94-3/31/95		25 (4/1-9/30/94)			139 (10/1/94-3/31/95)		
ALL	ALL	ALL		0-1MM	1-3MM	3-5MM	5-10MM	10-25MM	25MM & OVER
109	120	164	**NUMBER OF STATEMENTS**	78	57	9	14	2	4
%	%	%	**ASSETS**	%	%	%	%	%	%
4.3	6.5	6.7	Cash & Equivalents	6.3	8.5		4.6		
2.0	2.5	2.5	Trade Receivables - (net)	2.2	2.6		2.4		
3.6	4.6	4.9	Inventory	2.8	4.4		18.4		
.8	1.1	1.4	All Other Current	2.3	.2		.9		
10.8	14.7	15.5	Total Current	13.7	15.7		26.3		
79.2	77.7	76.1	Fixed Assets (net)	78.2	76.6		62.3		
1.3	.9	2.6	Intangibles (net)	2.1	3.0		1.1		
8.7	6.7	5.9	All Other Non-Current	6.0	4.8		10.3		
100.0	100.0	100.0	Total	100.0	100.0		100.0		
			LIABILITIES						
6.2	5.8	4.3	Notes Payable-Short Term	4.9	3.9		3.8		
4.4	5.5	4.2	Cur. Mat.-L /T/D	4.7	4.0		4.2		
2.9	3.3	3.1	Trade Payables	2.3	3.4		6.0		
.9	.1	.2	Income Taxes Payable	.4	.1		.1		
7.2	6.6	7.8	All Other Current	5.5	9.1		10.8		
21.6	21.5	19.7	Total Current	17.8	20.5		24.9		
41.5	38.4	40.9	Long Term Debt	43.6	44.7		18.6		
.2	.1	.2	Deferred Taxes	.3	.1		.4		
5.6	10.0	5.3	All Other-Non-Current	6.5	5.6		1.8		
31.0	29.9	33.8	Net Worth	31.8	29.2		54.3		
100.0	100.0	100.0	Total Liabilities & Net Worth	100.0	100.0		100.0		
			INCOME DATA						
100.0	100.0	100.0	Net Sales	100.0	100.0		100.0		
			Gross Profit						
88.5	89.2	88.7	Operating Expenses	89.1	86.7		92.2		
11.5	10.8	11.3	Operating Profit	10.9	13.3		7.8		
8.1	7.0	7.3	All Other Expenses (net)	7.7	8.4		2.3		
3.3	3.8	4.1	Profit Before Taxes	3.2	4.9		5.6		
			RATIOS						
1.2 / .5 / .2	1.6 / .7 / .3	1.6 / .8 / .3	Current	2.0 / .5 / .2	1.3 / .8 / .3		1.4 / .9 / .4		
.7 / .3 / .1	(119) 1.2 / .4 / .1	(163) 1.1 / .4 / .1	Quick	(77) 1.0 / .2 / .1	1.2 / .4 / .1		.8 / .2 / .1		
0 UND / 0 813.0 / 8 43.4	0 UND / 2 242.1 / 15 23.7	0 UND / 1 287.3 / 11 34.3	Sales/Receivables	0 UND / 0 UND / 7 55.4	0 UND / 2 171.3 / 9 39.8		1 637.5 / 2 161.3 / 24 15.1		
			Cost of Sales/Inventory						
			Cost of Sales/Payables						
84.4 / -10.9 / -3.0	17.0 / -18.8 / -5.3	18.5 / -26.9 / -5.2	Sales/Working Capital	16.7 / -18.9 / -4.5	21.6 / -36.6 / -6.7		14.3 / NM / -7.6		
(86) 3.4 / 1.6 / .8	(100) 3.3 / 1.6 / 1.0	(141) 3.8 / 1.6 / .9	EBIT/Interest	(66) 3.1 / 1.5 / .7	(48) 4.0 / 1.8 / 1.2		(13) 6.6 / 1.8 / 1.0		
(26) 2.4 / 1.1 / .7	(29) 3.4 / 1.8 / .5	(40) 4.2 / 1.4 / .5	Net Profit + Depr., Dep., Amort./Cur. Mat. L/T/D	(22) 4.0 / 1.4 / .9					
1.4 / 3.0 / 9.2	1.4 / 2.8 / 22.6	1.2 / 2.8 / 10.1	Fixed/Worth	1.4 / 3.0 / 13.3	1.2 / 3.6 / 36.7		.8 / 1.1 / 1.6		
.8 / 2.6 / 10.7	.7 / 2.4 / 29.2	.8 / 2.2 / 13.6	Debt/Worth	.8 / 2.2 / 14.5	1.0 / 3.6 / 45.9		.2 / .9 / 1.8		
(86) 29.7 / 12.5 / .7	(95) 31.8 / 11.4 / .6	(135) 33.6 / 11.6 / -.2	% Profit Before Taxes/Tangible Net Worth	(62) 31.9 / 11.4 / -1.4	(47) 64.2 / 14.3 / .8		(13) 24.2 / 7.3 / .3		
8.7 / 2.7 / -1.6	7.9 / 3.1 / -.3	10.2 / 3.2 / -.9	% Profit Before Taxes/Total Assets	10.2 / 2.4 / -1.0	10.0 / 4.4 / .2		7.6 / 2.4 / .2		
1.6 / .7 / .5	1.8 / .8 / .6	1.5 / .8 / .5	Sales/Net Fixed Assets	1.3 / .8 / .5	1.7 / .9 / .5		40.4 / .7 / .4		
1.1 / .6 / .4	1.2 / .7 / .5	1.1 / .7 / .4	Sales/Total Assets	1.0 / .7 / .4	1.2 / .7 / .4		2.0 / .5 / .4		
(108) 6.1 / 9.4 / 13.2	(113) 6.3 / 9.6 / 12.9	(153) 6.1 / 9.2 / 13.1	% Depr., Dep., Amort./Sales	(72) 6.1 / 9.9 / 13.3	(54) 6.4 / 9.3 / 13.1		(13) .8 / 7.0 / 11.9		
(33) 5.8 / 8.3 / 24.1	(42) 4.5 / 8.4 / 14.4	(45) 4.0 / 6.8 / 10.8	% Officers', Directors', Owners' Comp/Sales	(24) 4.7 / 6.5 / 9.5	(14) 4.1 / 6.9 / 10.5				
164228M	320082M	788366M	Net Sales ($)	46500M	93474M	34899M	96789M	41673M	475031M
285157M	492581M	1047790M	Total Assets ($)	88270M	137957M	61608M	204677M	113244M	442034M

M = $ thousand   MM = $ million
See Pages 1 through 15 for Explanation of Ratios and Data

	Current Data Sorted By Assets						Comparative Historical Data	
		30 (4/1-9/30/94)		46 (10/1/94-3/31/95)			4/1/90-3/31/91	4/1/91-3/31/92
	0-500M	500M-2MM	2-10MM	10-50MM	50-100MM	100-250MM	ALL	ALL
# Postretirement Benefits / Type of Statement								
# Postretirement Benefits	3		2	1				
Unqualified		2	3	1	1	1	6	6
Reviewed	4	3	1				7	4
Compiled	22	1	2	1			30	23
Tax Returns	12							3
Other	16	2	5				17	20
NUMBER OF STATEMENTS	54	8	11	1	1	1	60	56
	%	%	%	%	%	%	%	%
ASSETS								
Cash & Equivalents	16.7		24.0				12.6	12.0
Trade Receivables - (net)	7.2		8.7				6.9	6.0
Inventory	10.8		10.7				9.4	12.2
All Other Current	2.7		5.0				2.6	2.4
Total Current	37.3		48.4				31.6	32.7
Fixed Assets (net)	48.7		34.5				50.7	49.9
Intangibles (net)	8.1		3.2				8.3	7.2
All Other Non-Current	5.8		13.8				9.5	10.2
Total	100.0		100.0				100.0	100.0
LIABILITIES								
Notes Payable-Short Term	7.3		10.2				11.3	8.9
Cur. Mat. -L/T/D	4.2		1.7				7.9	7.6
Trade Payables	9.0		8.0				5.3	10.8
Income Taxes Payable	.4		.6				.9	.4
All Other Current	13.8		25.0				10.5	18.6
Total Current	34.8		45.5				35.9	46.4
Long Term Debt	23.3		5.2				19.8	29.2
Deferred Taxes	.6		.4				.7	.2
All Other-Non-Current	4.3		2.4				4.6	2.9
Net Worth	37.0		46.5				38.9	21.3
Total Liabilities & Net Worth	100.0		100.0				100.0	100.0
INCOME DATA								
Net Sales	100.0		100.0				100.0	100.0
Gross Profit								
Operating Expenses	94.4		91.6				94.4	93.0
Operating Profit	5.6		8.4				5.6	7.0
All Other Expenses (net)	1.2		.6				.9	1.3
Profit Before Taxes	4.4		7.8				4.6	5.7
RATIOS								
Current	2.2		2.0				2.2	1.3
	1.2		1.5				.9	.7
	.6		.6				.4	.4
Quick	2.1		1.7				1.2	.7
	(53) .5		.7				(59) .5	(55) .3
	.2		.3				.2	.1
Sales/Receivables	0 UND		0 UND				0 UND	0 UND
	0 UND		13 28.9				0 UND	0 UND
	3 109.6		16 22.5				2 211.1	3 120.5
Cost of Sales/Inventory								
Cost of Sales/Payables								
Sales/Working Capital	19.6		6.9				21.9	58.4
	152.4		16.3				-159.4	-59.6
	-25.8		-13.9				-18.9	-13.1
EBIT/Interest	14.9						6.8	5.6
	(40) 4.7						(50) 3.2	(49) 3.3
	1.2						1.4	1.0
Net Profit + Depr., Dep., Amort./Cur. Mat. L /T/D							3.9	3.9
							(19) 2.7	(17) 1.7
							.5	1.0
Fixed/Worth	.7		.3				.9	1.0
	1.7		.7				1.6	3.1
	13.4		1.2				11.4	-14.5
Debt/Worth	.8		.8				.8	1.5
	1.9		1.3				1.6	6.4
	32.8		2.3				75.1	-13.3
% Profit Before Taxes/Tangible Net Worth	98.8		61.8				85.0	122.9
	(43) 41.0		35.7				(47) 24.9	(37) 38.5
	4.4		15.5				-1.7	3.3
% Profit Before Taxes/Total Assets	31.4		27.6				26.0	28.0
	16.1		13.1				11.1	11.6
	1.6		5.5				.1	-.4
Sales/Net Fixed Assets	22.8		20.3				15.0	15.9
	11.9		11.1				9.6	9.3
	5.1		6.2				5.5	5.4
Sales/Total Assets	7.5		3.0				5.4	6.2
	4.8		2.5				4.2	4.3
	3.5		2.2				2.7	2.7
% Depr., Dep., Amort./Sales	1.2						1.7	1.6
	(44) 1.9						(55) 2.8	(49) 2.1
	3.2						3.6	3.4
% Officers', Directors', Owners' Comp/Sales	6.3						4.9	5.9
	(25) 8.7						(36) 9.4	(21) 9.7
	12.3						17.8	15.7
Net Sales ($)	47937M	25923M	135238M	124168M	130816M	308080M	270490M	402778M
Total Assets ($)	10838M	6601M	48411M	24891M	96172M	176032M	79443M	159982M

© Robert Morris Associates 1995

M = $ thousand   MM = $ million
See Pages 1 through 15 for Explanation of Ratios and Data

Comparative Historical Data				Current Data Sorted By Sales					
	2	6	# Postretirement Benefits	2	1		1	1	1
			Type of Statement						
8	7	7	Unqualified	1	1		2	1	2
4	7	8	Reviewed		4	2	1	1	
22	28	26	Compiled	14	10		1		1
6	10	12	Tax Returns	11	1				
25	24	23	Other	8	9	1	2	2	1
4/1/92- 3/31/93 ALL	4/1/93- 3/31/94 ALL	4/1/94- 3/31/95 ALL		30 (4/1-9/30/94)		46 (10/1/94-3/31/95)			
				0-1MM	1-3MM	3-5MM	5-10MM	10-25MM	25MM & OVER
65	76	76	**NUMBER OF STATEMENTS**	34	25	3	6	4	4
%	%	%	**ASSETS**	%	%	%	%	%	%
14.5	13.7	16.3	Cash & Equivalents	14.7	17.7				
7.5	4.8	6.7	Trade Receivables - (net)	4.1	10.3				
10.9	13.6	10.7	Inventory	9.6	11.6				
2.6	1.1	2.8	All Other Current	2.7	2.9				
35.6	33.2	36.5	Total Current	31.1	42.5				
47.2	45.5	47.7	Fixed Assets (net)	56.2	41.9				
6.9	10.0	7.9	Intangibles (net)	6.7	10.0				
10.3	11.3	7.9	All Other Non-Current	6.0	5.6				
100.0	100.0	100.0	Total	100.0	100.0				
			LIABILITIES						
3.8	5.5	7.4	Notes Payable-Short Term	7.6	8.9				
5.2	4.8	4.0	Cur. Mat.-L /T/D	3.6	4.7				
7.9	5.3	8.9	Trade Payables	8.5	8.5				
.5	1.4	.4	Income Taxes Payable	.1	.7				
15.6	15.1	15.6	All Other Current	12.8	13.8				
33.0	32.1	36.3	Total Current	32.7	36.5				
26.2	27.2	20.9	Long Term Debt	29.6	13.9				
.1	.3	.6	Deferred Taxes	1.0	.0				
2.2	3.1	3.9	All Other-Non-Current	3.0	6.1				
38.5	37.3	38.3	Net Worth	33.8	43.5				
100.0	100.0	100.0	Total Liabilities & Net Worth	100.0	100.0				
			INCOME DATA						
100.0	100.0	100.0	Net Sales	100.0	100.0				
			Gross Profit						
95.0	94.4	93.9	Operating Expenses	92.8	96.5				
5.0	5.6	6.1	Operating Profit	7.2	3.5				
1.8	.6	1.0	All Other Expenses (net)	1.7	.9				
3.3	5.1	5.1	Profit Before Taxes	5.5	2.5				
			RATIOS						
1.6	2.2	2.0		2.2	1.9				
1.1	1.0	1.1	Current	1.2	1.1				
.7	.6	.6		.6	.6				
1.3	1.4	1.5		2.2	1.4				
.6	.6	(74) .6	Quick	(33) .5	.7				
.2	.2	.2		.2	.2				
0 UND	0 UND	0 UND		0 UND	0 UND				
0 UND	0 UND	0 UND	Sales/Receivables	0 UND	0 UND				
8 47.8	2 170.3	9 40.0		2 153.8	7 49.3				
			Cost of Sales/Inventory						
			Cost of Sales/Payables						
25.8	24.7	16.1		16.9	18.8				
247.3	UND	236.8	Sales/Working Capital	235.6	153.6				
-50.3	-34.6	-22.6		-20.1	-41.4				
(53) 8.3	(58) 8.4	(60) 14.5		(22) 15.2	(23) 14.8				
3.8	3.9	6.1	EBIT/Interest	3.9	3.2				
1.6	1.3	1.2		1.2	.8				
(18) 2.2	(18) 4.3	(19) 8.9	Net Profit + Depr., Dep.,						
1.7	1.3	3.3	Amort./Cur. Mat. L/T/D						
1.2	.8	1.9							
.7	.8	.7		.8	.7				
1.8	1.9	1.5	Fixed/Worth	1.8	1.5				
4.2	12.9	4.2		6.3	29.0				
1.0	.9	.8		.8	.6				
1.7	2.2	1.7	Debt/Worth	2.0	1.5				
6.9	17.2	4.3		6.3	190.0				
(58) 103.4	(61) 141.3	(63) 76.9	% Profit Before Taxes/Tangible	(28) 99.7	(20) 36.7				
32.8	33.3	35.7	Net Worth	47.0	16.3				
7.6	12.2	6.4		7.9	-.6				
25.7	28.4	27.9	% Profit Before Taxes/Total	47.2	19.4				
9.5	14.2	15.9	Assets	20.2	14.2				
2.0	2.7	1.8		2.0	.1				
20.9	26.6	20.4		17.3	26.8				
9.1	8.8	10.3	Sales/Net Fixed Assets	8.7	14.0				
5.3	4.7	4.9		3.9	5.4				
6.8	7.1	6.4		8.2	6.2				
4.7	4.7	4.3	Sales/Total Assets	4.8	4.3				
2.3	2.2	2.6		2.1	3.8				
(56) 1.4	(63) 1.3	(61) 1.4		(26) 1.5	(22) 1.1				
2.1	2.6	2.1	% Depr., Dep., Amort./Sales	1.9	2.2				
3.0	3.7	3.5		4.6	3.5				
(34) 5.5	(36) 5.2	(31) 5.9	% Officers', Directors',	(16) 7.0	(12) 4.6				
10.1	8.5	8.5	Owners' Comp/Sales	9.9	7.1				
15.9	14.0	11.2		13.0	9.7				
427120M	819544M	772162M	Net Sales ($)	12520M	44393M	10697M	47989M	49175M	607388M
160607M	352069M	362945M	Total Assets ($)	4185M	12860M	2514M	16082M	21437M	305867M

© Robert Morris Associates 1995   M = $ thousand   MM = $ million
See Pages 1 through 15 for Explanation of Ratios and Data

	Current Data Sorted By Assets							Comparative Historical Data	
		6	3	1	1		# Postretirement Benefits Type of Statement		
Unqualified	3	28	32	12	7	4		33	51
Reviewed	8	8	5					13	8
Compiled	15	17	3					15	23
Tax Returns	3	2	1						
Other	10	26	16	12	1	4		28	41
		83 (4/1-9/30/94)		134 (10/1/94-3/31/95)				4/1/90- 3/31/91 ALL	4/1/91- 3/31/92 ALL
	0-500M	500M-2MM	2-10MM	10-50MM	50-100MM	100-250MM	NUMBER OF STATEMENTS		
NUMBER OF STATEMENTS	39	81	57	24	8	8		89	123
	%	%	%	%	%	%	ASSETS	%	%
Cash & Equivalents	14.2	11.6	13.9	12.9			Cash & Equivalents	12.4	13.5
Trade Receivables - (net)	49.6	56.5	43.1	35.5			Trade Receivables - (net)	43.4	47.0
Inventory	2.8	1.4	2.5	3.3			Inventory	2.6	2.7
All Other Current	4.8	3.6	3.9	4.1			All Other Current	3.4	2.5
Total Current	71.4	73.2	63.4	55.7			Total Current	61.7	65.7
Fixed Assets (net)	23.7	16.2	22.8	29.3			Fixed Assets (net)	27.5	21.2
Intangibles (net)	1.1	1.4	2.8	7.9			Intangibles (net)	3.6	3.1
All Other Non-Current	3.9	9.3	11.0	7.1			All Other Non-Current	7.2	10.1
Total	100.0	100.0	100.0	100.0			Total	100.0	100.0
							LIABILITIES		
Notes Payable-Short Term	15.8	9.3	6.3	7.1			Notes Payable-Short Term	10.3	8.4
Cur. Mat. -L/T/D	5.0	4.3	3.4	2.2			Cur. Mat. -L/T/D	3.9	3.8
Trade Payables	10.4	10.8	12.3	13.2			Trade Payables	9.9	10.8
Income Taxes Payable	.3	.3	.6	.2			Income Taxes Payable	1.4	.6
All Other Current	17.5	24.5	18.1	13.5			All Other Current	14.9	16.4
Total Current	49.0	49.2	40.7	36.1			Total Current	40.4	40.0
Long Term Debt	6.5	8.9	17.4	17.2			Long Term Debt	16.1	12.2
Deferred Taxes	1.2	.7	1.3	.3			Deferred Taxes	1.0	1.1
All Other-Non-Current	1.8	5.2	2.9	4.4			All Other-Non-Current	2.0	2.0
Net Worth	41.5	35.9	37.7	42.1			Net Worth	40.5	44.8
Total Liabilities & Net Worth	100.0	100.0	100.0	100.0			Total Liabilities & Net Worth	100.0	100.0
							INCOME DATA		
Net Sales	100.0	100.0	100.0	100.0			Net Sales	100.0	100.0
Gross Profit							Gross Profit		
Operating Expenses	97.3	96.5	95.4	94.9			Operating Expenses	91.8	93.9
Operating Profit	2.7	3.5	4.6	5.1			Operating Profit	8.2	6.1
All Other Expenses (net)	-.6	.9	.3	1.7			All Other Expenses (net)	1.5	.8
Profit Before Taxes	3.3	2.6	4.3	3.5			Profit Before Taxes	6.8	5.3
							RATIOS		
Current	2.9	2.2	2.5	2.4			Current	2.3	2.9
	1.6	1.5	1.6	1.4				1.6	1.9
	.9	1.1	1.1	1.1				1.0	1.1
Quick	2.8	2.2	2.4	2.1			Quick	2.1	2.6
	1.3	1.4	1.5	1.2				1.4	1.7
	.7	1.0	1.0	.9				.8	1.1
Sales/Receivables	17 21.8	42 8.6	44 8.3	33 11.1			Sales/Receivables	38 9.6	41 8.8
	54 6.8	60 6.1	64 5.7	58 6.3				56 6.5	60 6.1
	73 5.0	79 4.6	96 3.8	81 4.5				94 3.9	91 4.0
Cost of Sales/Inventory							Cost of Sales/Inventory		
Cost of Sales/Payables							Cost of Sales/Payables		
Sales/Working Capital	7.9	8.1	4.4	5.5			Sales/Working Capital	5.8	4.6
	23.6	13.2	11.4	12.3				13.0	10.0
	-66.3	155.2	59.0	68.8				-251.8	47.1
EBIT/Interest	(28) 12.6	(65) 10.3	(47) 16.1	(19) 4.7			EBIT/Interest	(75) 10.4	(101) 17.3
	3.6	3.2	5.2	1.8				2.7	5.0
	-.8	1.2	1.1	1.2				1.2	1.7
Net Profit + Depr., Dep., Amort./Cur. Mat. L /T/D		3.7	2.9				Net Profit + Depr., Dep., Amort./Cur. Mat. L /T/D	(29) 8.0	(43) 9.8
		(15) .8	(16) 1.4					3.3	3.2
		.0	.0					.7	1.8
Fixed/Worth	.1	.1	.2	.2			Fixed/Worth	.3	.2
	.7	.4	.6	.6				.6	.4
	4.0	1.4	2.1	2.8				2.5	1.2
Debt/Worth	.4	.8	.7	.6			Debt/Worth	.6	.5
	1.3	1.7	1.8	1.6				1.4	1.1
	11.8	7.9	5.1	7.0				4.9	3.2
% Profit Before Taxes/Tangible Net Worth	(32) 64.3	(71) 34.1	(49) 54.2	(22) 36.9			% Profit Before Taxes/Tangible Net Worth	(78) 69.3	(110) 48.8
	29.6	12.3	24.3	13.4				24.6	24.1
	-11.8	4.1	9.8	2.6				8.1	10.2
% Profit Before Taxes/Total Assets	27.4	12.5	15.2	13.7			% Profit Before Taxes/Total Assets	23.8	20.3
	10.2	5.4	8.6	2.8				6.3	8.9
	-3.1	.5	-.5	.9				1.2	2.0
Sales/Net Fixed Assets	104.9	117.4	37.5	20.6			Sales/Net Fixed Assets	58.2	51.7
	38.3	41.7	13.6	9.4				14.2	18.2
	13.3	12.5	5.2	3.6				3.6	8.0
Sales/Total Assets	6.7	4.9	3.2	2.4			Sales/Total Assets	4.0	3.6
	4.1	3.6	2.3	1.8				2.5	2.6
	2.5	2.1	1.5	1.1				1.4	1.8
% Depr., Dep., Amort./Sales	(34) .4	(69) .4	(51) .7	(22) 1.6			% Depr., Dep., Amort./Sales	(75) .8	(103) .7
	1.5	.7	1.4	2.7				1.7	1.1
	3.8	1.7	4.0	4.1				3.5	3.1
% Officers', Directors', Owners' Comp/Sales	(14) 3.6	(13) 4.8	(13) 2.5				% Officers', Directors', Owners' Comp/Sales	(17) 4.5	(21) 4.1
	6.7	7.4	4.5					9.1	7.7
	10.1	15.8	14.5					15.5	14.7
Net Sales ($)	47921M	303201M	692781M	1002040M	489258M	1677834M	Net Sales ($)	1217904M	2074388M
Total Assets ($)	10257M	84441M	251979M	577045M	498180M	1240398M	Total Assets ($)	908071M	1373253M

M = $ thousand MM = $ million
See Pages 1 through 15 for Explanation of Ratios and Data

Comparative Historical Data				Current Data Sorted By Sales					
2	4	11	# Postretirement Benefits	2	2	4	2	1	
			Type of Statement						
76	79	86	Unqualified	4	8	15	25	15	19
15	21	21	Reviewed	4	6	4	5	1	1
31	23	35	Compiled	8	16	5	4	1	1
1	5	6	Tax Returns	3	2				1
44	53	69	Other	9	18	8	9	10	15
4/1/92-3/31/93 ALL	4/1/93-3/31/94 ALL	4/1/94-3/31/95 ALL		0-1MM 28	1-3MM 50	3-5MM 32	5-10MM 43	10-25MM 27	25MM & OVER 37
				83 (4/1-9/30/94)		134 (10/1/94-3/31/95)			
167	181	217	**NUMBER OF STATEMENTS**	28	50	32	43	27	37
%	%	%	**ASSETS**	%	%	%	%	%	%
11.4	13.1	12.7	Cash & Equivalents	20.5	10.8	9.3	10.2	13.8	14.1
44.1	46.3	46.9	Trade Receivables - (net)	40.2	53.7	50.3	53.2	43.0	35.6
4.1	2.7	2.2	Inventory	3.8	1.2	3.2	1.2	2.3	2.7
3.1	2.6	3.9	All Other Current	3.5	3.1	7.7	3.2	2.4	4.0
62.7	64.6	65.8	Total Current	68.1	68.7	70.6	67.9	61.5	56.5
22.1	21.0	21.8	Fixed Assets (net)	27.5	18.9	19.2	20.2	23.2	24.7
4.5	5.2	3.6	Intangibles (net)	1.8	1.6	1.9	2.0	3.8	10.7
10.7	9.2	8.8	All Other Non-Current	2.5	10.8	8.3	9.9	11.5	8.2
100.0	100.0	100.0	Total	100.0	100.0	100.0	100.0	100.0	100.0
			LIABILITIES						
8.4	7.7	8.9	Notes Payable-Short Term	9.8	13.3	6.7	8.7	9.5	4.0
3.0	2.9	3.8	Cur. Mat.-L /T/D	5.5	4.4	4.7	3.8	2.2	1.9
10.2	9.1	11.1	Trade Payables	10.2	10.9	9.8	9.6	10.9	15.2
.5	.6	.4	Income Taxes Payable	.3	.2	.4	.3	.9	.5
17.9	19.7	19.3	All Other Current	14.5	18.3	22.3	23.6	14.5	20.4
40.0	40.2	43.5	Total Current	40.2	47.1	44.0	46.0	38.1	42.1
15.4	13.6	12.9	Long Term Debt	11.8	9.5	14.5	11.9	15.4	16.1
.8	.5	.9	Deferred Taxes	.1	1.3	.2	.6	3.0	.5
5.1	4.0	3.7	All Other-Non-Current	3.2	4.9	5.5	2.9	3.5	2.1
38.7	41.7	39.0	Net Worth	44.7	37.3	35.9	38.7	40.0	39.2
100.0	100.0	100.0	Total Liabilities & Net Worth	100.0	100.0	100.0	100.0	100.0	100.0
			INCOME DATA						
100.0	100.0	100.0	Net Sales	100.0	100.0	100.0	100.0	100.0	100.0
			Gross Profit						
94.4	94.1	95.8	Operating Expenses	93.1	95.9	98.2	97.0	96.4	94.0
5.6	5.9	4.2	Operating Profit	6.9	4.1	1.8	3.0	3.6	6.0
1.1	.7	.6	All Other Expenses (net)	1.7	.4	.8	–.1	.0	1.3
4.6	5.2	3.6	Profit Before Taxes	5.2	3.7	1.0	3.2	3.6	4.7
			RATIOS						
2.5	3.0	2.5	Current	5.8	3.5	2.4	2.2	2.4	2.2
1.7	1.7	1.5		1.7	1.7	1.7	1.5	1.5	1.3
1.2	1.1	1.0		.8	.9	1.2	1.1	1.1	1.0
2.2	2.6	2.4	Quick	5.8	3.2	2.0	1.9	2.4	1.8
1.5	1.5	1.4		1.4	1.7	1.4	1.5	1.4	1.1
.9	1.0	.9		.7	.8	.9	1.0	.9	.9
38 9.6	38 9.5	40 9.1	Sales/Receivables	23 16.1	47 7.8	39 9.4	44 8.3	42 8.6	37 9.8
61 6.0	57 6.4	59 6.2		60 6.1	66 5.5	56 6.5	58 6.3	45 8.1	59 6.2
89 4.1	85 4.3	79 4.6		104 3.5	87 4.2	79 4.6	78 4.7	72 5.1	87 4.2
			Cost of Sales/Inventory						
			Cost of Sales/Payables						
5.4	5.9	6.7	Sales/Working Capital	5.2	6.0	6.5	7.8	7.6	5.7
11.7	11.2	13.2		9.9	10.3	13.2	18.5	16.4	16.3
44.5	59.1	203.4		–24.5	–44.6	38.7	37.6	52.5	335.8
(143) 11.9	(148) 12.1	(174) 10.2	EBIT/Interest	(20) 12.6	(40) 11.6	(26) 9.5	(33) 9.4	(25) 9.3	(30) 14.6
4.1	4.1	3.6		5.1	2.8	3.2	3.6	4.2	4.3
1.2	1.4	1.1		–.1	.5	1.7	.4	.9	1.7
(55) 7.0	(51) 6.5	(54) 5.1	Net Profit + Depr., Dep., Amort./Cur. Mat. L/T/D		(10) 9.2			(13) 7.3	
3.1	2.8	1.7			2.8			4.7	
1.1	1.4	.2			.2			1.3	
.2	.2	.2	Fixed/Worth	.1	.1	.1	.2	.2	.3
.5	.5	.6		.7	.6	.6	.3	.6	.8
1.6	1.6	2.0		3.6	4.7	1.6	1.0	1.5	2.6
.7	.6	.7	Debt/Worth	.3	.5	1.2	1.0	.7	.8
1.6	1.7	1.7		1.0	1.7	1.7	1.5	1.8	2.4
4.9	3.8	6.0		22.1	13.9	5.2	3.1	3.2	8.5
(143) 50.9	(157) 45.0	(189) 43.7	% Profit Before Taxes/Tangible Net Worth	(24) 45.2	(42) 48.7	(28) 33.8	(37) 38.1	(25) 51.6	(33) 41.9
26.4	23.3	19.2		20.6	18.1	15.0	17.0	22.1	21.1
6.6	6.9	2.8		–11.8	1.0	6.2	.7	–.9	5.7
15.9	16.1	14.2	% Profit Before Taxes/Total Assets	24.9	19.9	10.5	12.7	21.4	13.4
7.5	8.1	6.8		7.1	6.3	6.4	4.7	7.9	4.5
.3	1.8	.1		–2.2	–1.0	1.5	–.7	–.1	1.4
48.8	60.7	62.4	Sales/Net Fixed Assets	59.8	79.6	77.0	69.6	39.9	37.5
21.7	23.2	20.5		13.5	33.3	33.1	24.2	18.3	10.6
7.6	7.6	6.9		5.8	8.1	7.0	6.9	8.7	3.5
4.1	4.5	4.5	Sales/Total Assets	4.3	4.1	5.0	5.0	4.1	3.2
2.6	2.8	2.7		2.4	3.2	3.5	3.3	2.7	1.8
1.6	1.7	1.6		1.0	2.0	1.8	1.8	1.7	1.7
(142) .7	(157) .6	(190) .5	% Depr., Dep., Amort./Sales	(24) 1.1	(43) .4	(30) .5	(35) .4	(25) .6	(33) 1.0
1.6	1.3	1.4		3.1	.8	1.0	1.1	1.3	2.3
3.4	2.6	3.1		9.5	1.8	2.5	2.9	3.5	4.1
(40) 4.6	(41) 4.0	(47) 3.6	% Officers', Directors', Owners' Comp/Sales		(15) 3.8				
6.9	5.6	6.0			7.4				
15.6	13.9	15.5			15.2				
3029292M	3241281M	4213035M	Net Sales ($)	15096M	98388M	125709M	301115M	428395M	3244332M
2056891M	2235194M	2662300M	Total Assets ($)	11920M	47381M	65653M	140205M	244698M	2152443M

© Robert Morris Associates 1995   M = $ thousand   MM = $ million
See Pages 1 through 15 for Explanation of Ratios and Data

Current Data Sorted By Assets							Comparative Historical Data	
2	5	4	1		1	# Postretirement Benefits		
						Type of Statement		
1	10	20	12	1	4	Unqualified	27	34
8	23	11				Reviewed	27	34
20	26	7				Compiled	39	37
4	3					Tax Returns	1	
17	22	27	6	1	2	Other	33	44
	54 (4/1-9/30/94)		171 (10/1/94-3/31/95)				4/1/90-3/31/91	4/1/91-3/31/92
0-500M	500M-2MM	2-10MM	10-50MM	50-100MM	100-250MM		ALL	ALL
50	84	65	18	2	6	NUMBER OF STATEMENTS	127	149
%	%	%	%	%	%	ASSETS	%	%
15.0	9.0	9.6	15.7			Cash & Equivalents	10.8	11.3
59.4	63.9	59.4	47.5			Trade Receivables - (net)	57.3	59.8
.4	.9	.5	2.0			Inventory	1.4	1.5
3.6	2.5	4.8	2.2			All Other Current	2.6	2.6
78.4	76.4	74.3	67.4			Total Current	72.2	75.2
8.5	10.7	13.0	14.0			Fixed Assets (net)	14.8	12.1
3.0	3.4	3.1	6.0			Intangibles (net)	2.2	2.8
10.1	9.4	9.6	12.6			All Other Non-Current	10.8	9.9
100.0	100.0	100.0	100.0			Total	100.0	100.0
						LIABILITIES		
14.5	19.8	17.9	12.1			Notes Payable-Short Term	15.4	15.7
3.6	3.3	1.9	3.0			Cur. Mat. -L/T/D	3.7	3.8
5.8	5.2	5.5	6.4			Trade Payables	6.2	5.4
1.0	.6	1.2	.6			Income Taxes Payable	1.0	1.2
21.8	16.4	26.5	18.6			All Other Current	19.9	19.0
46.6	45.3	53.1	40.7			Total Current	46.1	45.2
7.6	6.1	7.1	8.4			Long Term Debt	10.2	7.7
.4	.9	.5	.0			Deferred Taxes	1.6	1.3
3.0	5.0	4.3	1.7			All Other-Non-Current	2.3	3.6
42.4	42.7	35.1	49.1			Net Worth	39.8	42.3
100.0	100.0	100.0	100.0			Total Liabilities & Net Worth	100.0	100.0
						INCOME DATA		
100.0	100.0	100.0	100.0			Net Sales	100.0	100.0
						Gross Profit		
96.7	97.2	96.2	95.2			Operating Expenses	97.4	97.7
3.3	2.8	3.8	4.8			Operating Profit	2.6	2.3
.3	.3	-.1	1.4			All Other Expenses (net)	.7	.5
3.1	2.5	3.9	3.4			Profit Before Taxes	1.9	1.8
						RATIOS		
3.4	2.9	1.8	2.5				2.5	2.8
1.8	1.6	1.4	1.6			Current	1.6	1.6
1.3	1.2	1.0	1.0				1.1	1.2
3.1	2.7	1.7	2.3				2.5	2.6
1.7	1.5	1.3	1.4			Quick	1.5	1.5
1.2	1.1	1.0	.9				1.1	1.2
21 17.3	33 11.0	33 10.9	26 13.8				28 13.1	32 11.5
29 12.6	40 9.1	45 8.1	57 6.4			Sales/Receivables	37 10.0	43 8.5
41 9.0	55 6.6	62 5.9	76 4.8				46 8.0	54 6.7
						Cost of Sales/Inventory		
						Cost of Sales/Payables		
12.9	10.8	12.9	5.7				12.7	10.7
19.9	21.7	26.6	20.0			Sales/Working Capital	20.0	19.9
63.9	52.1	143.6	-378.5				52.7	43.5
(34) 17.6	(74) 12.5	(59) 13.7	(14) 195.0				(107) 9.7	(128) 10.1
7.1	4.7	5.0	17.1			EBIT/Interest	2.9	3.7
3.1	1.5	2.2	3.5				.8	1.2
(10) 15.8	(10) 12.1	(26) 23.5					(52) 7.0	(49) 7.5
5.2	3.8	5.9				Net Profit + Depr., Dep., Amort./Cur. Mat. L./T/D	2.3	2.3
2.4	1.0	2.8					.5	.5
.0	.1	.1	.1				.2	.1
.1	.2	.3	.2			Fixed/Worth	.3	.3
.4	.6	.8	.4				.7	.7
.6	.8	1.2	.6				.7	.7
1.4	1.7	2.3	1.4			Debt/Worth	1.5	1.6
4.1	3.2	5.0	3.3				3.5	3.5
(44) 81.5	(81) 59.7	(61) 68.8	62.3				(112) 44.0	(138) 50.9
42.6	27.0	32.1	38.2			% Profit Before Taxes/Tangible Net Worth	22.0	26.2
19.9	6.4	12.6	22.9				4.4	5.6
43.2	21.5	20.4	23.5				19.6	18.8
17.9	10.3	10.7	14.2			% Profit Before Taxes/Total Assets	7.9	8.8
5.8	2.2	3.9	10.1				.3	.9
686.5	195.4	86.9	96.0				123.2	149.7
173.0	79.3	47.5	53.6			Sales/Net Fixed Assets	53.9	64.3
58.1	42.3	26.1	26.6				30.9	29.7
9.7	7.0	6.5	5.9				7.5	7.1
7.6	5.8	4.6	3.6			Sales/Total Assets	5.7	5.2
5.6	4.6	3.1	1.8				4.0	3.7
(35) .1	(69) .2	(62) .3	(17) .2				(115) .3	(128) .3
.3	.5	.5	.5			% Depr., Dep., Amort./Sales	.6	.6
.7	.9	1.0	1.1				1.1	1.0
(22) 2.7	(46) 2.1	(27) .9					(54) 2.2	(63) 1.9
5.5	3.2	2.4				% Officers', Directors', Owners' Comp/Sales	3.9	3.1
9.4	5.4	4.4					5.9	5.9
110161M	508053M	1589146M	1836696M	357813M	3577339M	Net Sales ($)	1811083M	4674931M
13080M	91824M	292809M	399779M	144625M	953025M	Total Assets ($)	396724M	1243575M

M = $ thousand   MM = $ million
See Pages 1 through 15 for Explanation of Ratios and Data

Comparative Historical Data				Current Data Sorted By Sales					
1	11	13	# Postretirement Benefits / Type of Statement	1	1	2	4	2	3
40	40	48	Unqualified	1	3	4	8	7	25
41	44	42	Reviewed	2	4	7	18	8	3
53	59	53	Compiled	6	16	11	17	3	
3	4	7	Tax Returns	1	2	1	3		
54	63	75	Other	3	15	10	11	19	17
4/1/92-3/31/93 ALL	4/1/93-3/31/94 ALL	4/1/94-3/31/95 ALL		54 (4/1-9/30/94)			171 (10/1/94-3/31/95)		
				0-1MM	1-3MM	3-5MM	5-10MM	10-25MM	25MM & OVER
191	210	225	NUMBER OF STATEMENTS	13	40	33	57	37	45
%	%	%	ASSETS	%	%	%	%	%	%
10.1	10.4	10.9	Cash & Equivalents	17.8	12.8	9.8	10.3	8.3	10.9
64.9	63.0	59.7	Trade Receivables - (net)	44.1	53.2	71.1	61.8	62.0	57.1
.8	.6	.8	Inventory	1.3	.0	.6	1.2	1.2	.7
1.4	2.6	3.8	All Other Current	3.8	4.6	2.7	3.4	3.3	4.6
77.3	76.6	75.1	Total Current	67.0	70.6	84.2	76.6	74.7	73.3
11.6	11.1	11.2	Fixed Assets (net)	13.0	13.6	7.8	10.6	13.4	9.9
2.9	2.8	3.8	Intangibles (net)	7.9	2.9	1.2	3.3	3.3	6.4
8.3	9.5	9.9	All Other Non-Current	12.0	13.0	6.8	9.5	8.6	10.4
100.0	100.0	100.0	Total	100.0	100.0	100.0	100.0	100.0	100.0
			LIABILITIES						
18.8	17.0	16.8	Notes Payable-Short Term	10.9	20.5	16.4	15.6	20.0	14.4
1.6	2.2	2.8	Cur. Mat.-L /T/D	6.0	2.4	1.4	4.7	1.9	1.8
5.4	4.9	5.7	Trade Payables	4.7	5.4	6.5	5.9	4.3	6.5
.8	.9	.8	Income Taxes Payable	.6	.4	1.3	.8	.7	1.1
19.5	19.4	20.8	All Other Current	19.1	21.0	18.9	18.3	21.3	25.5
46.1	44.4	47.0	Total Current	41.4	49.6	44.5	45.3	48.2	49.3
7.2	7.0	7.3	Long Term Debt	6.9	8.6	8.7	6.3	4.4	8.8
.5	1.0	.6	Deferred Taxes	.6	1.1	.5	.6	.4	.3
3.5	4.9	4.0	All Other-Non-Current	.0	5.7	6.6	3.3	3.6	3.0
42.7	42.6	41.1	Net Worth	51.1	35.0	39.7	44.6	43.3	38.6
100.0	100.0	100.0	Total Liabilities & Net Worth	100.0	100.0	100.0	100.0	100.0	100.0
			INCOME DATA						
100.0	100.0	100.0	Net Sales	100.0	100.0	100.0	100.0	100.0	100.0
			Gross Profit						
96.5	96.7	96.6	Operating Expenses	94.9	96.8	96.7	96.8	96.9	96.5
3.5	3.3	3.4	Operating Profit	5.1	3.2	3.3	3.2	3.1	3.5
.3	.7	.3	All Other Expenses (net)	.3	.0	.3	.1	.8	.3
3.1	2.6	3.1	Profit Before Taxes	4.7	3.3	3.0	3.1	2.3	3.2
			RATIOS						
2.8	3.0	2.5	Current	3.4	2.9	3.3	3.0	1.9	2.2
1.7	1.7	1.5		2.0	1.4	1.9	1.6	1.4	1.5
1.2	1.2	1.2		1.1	1.1	1.4	1.1	1.2	1.0
2.8	2.8	2.4	Quick	3.4	2.3	3.3	2.8	1.9	2.2
1.6	1.7	1.4		1.7	1.3	1.7	1.4	1.4	1.3
1.2	1.2	1.1		.9	1.1	1.3	1.1	1.1	1.0
(33) 11.2	(33) 11.0	(29) 12.4	Sales/Receivables	(28) 13.2	(24) 15.4	(28) 13.0	(32) 11.4	(33) 10.9	(28) 13.0
(43) 8.5	(43) 8.5	(40) 9.1		(37) 9.8	(34) 10.8	(38) 9.6	(41) 8.9	(47) 7.7	(41) 8.8
(55) 6.6	(55) 6.6	(56) 6.5		(69) 5.3	(63) 5.8	(50) 7.3	(54) 6.7	(62) 5.9	(54) 6.8
			Cost of Sales/Inventory						
			Cost of Sales/Payables						
10.2	9.6	11.4	Sales/Working Capital	11.4	12.2	12.5	10.0	14.0	11.4
18.9	18.9	21.3		16.6	26.8	16.8	21.3	20.7	30.6
42.7	46.1	63.3		NM	69.3	31.8	114.6	43.2	463.1
17.0	16.9	15.5	EBIT/Interest		14.4	10.1	16.1	18.3	53.6
(167) 4.6	(180) 5.8	(187) 5.2		(34) 4.9	(27) 5.2	(49) 4.6	(33) 5.6	(39) 9.9	
1.8	1.8	2.2			2.1	2.4	1.9	2.0	3.5
7.0	7.7	20.4	Net Profit + Depr., Dep., Amort./Cur. Mat. L/T/D				27.3	26.6	
(44) 3.6	(32) 3.3	(57) 4.8					(15) 6.1	(18) 5.2	
1.7	1.9	1.7					1.1	1.8	
.1	.1	.1	Fixed/Worth	.1	.0	.1	.1	.1	.1
.2	.2	.2		.2	.2	.2	.2	.3	.3
.5	.5	.6		.7	.9	.5	.6	.6	.5
.7	.6	.8	Debt/Worth	.3	.8	.7	.6	.9	1.1
1.4	1.5	1.8		2.1	1.9	1.7	1.6	1.7	2.0
3.5	3.4	3.8		3.6	5.7	3.8	2.8	2.9	4.8
65.3	61.4	64.3	% Profit Before Taxes/Tangible Net Worth	(12) 72.1	(36) 81.5	(30) 63.8	(54) 55.1	(43) 60.8	66.9
(177) 26.9	(197) 29.1	(212) 31.5		47.5	30.9	32.0	28.6	27.0	42.9
7.3	8.7	11.9		12.3	5.9	4.8	11.7	11.0	23.3
26.5	23.6	23.6	% Profit Before Taxes/Total Assets	47.3	31.0	36.5	22.1	21.2	21.5
9.5	11.2	11.4		9.9	11.4	11.3	10.6	11.0	13.3
2.9	2.3	3.8		.9	1.7	4.1	3.4	3.5	6.9
156.9	167.7	188.2	Sales/Net Fixed Assets	189.5	594.4	354.0	210.4	78.6	115.6
75.5	76.2	73.2		58.1	76.4	155.8	83.2	46.3	73.3
37.6	42.1	35.8		28.3	22.1	49.3	37.2	33.4	32.5
7.3	7.4	7.3	Sales/Total Assets	7.4	7.7	8.9	7.0	6.6	6.9
5.5	5.7	5.6		4.5	5.5	6.9	5.7	5.0	5.1
4.3	4.0	3.7		2.9	3.1	5.2	4.2	3.6	3.6
.3	.3	.2	% Depr., Dep., Amort./Sales	(10) .2	(27) .2	(28) .1	(47) .1	(34) .4	(41) .2
(162) .5	(164) .5	(187) .5		.7	.6	.3	.5	.5	.4
.8	.9	1.0		1.9	1.6	.7	1.0	1.0	.7
1.6	2.1	1.8	% Officers', Directors', Owners' Comp/Sales		(15) 2.3	(13) 2.5	(38) 1.9	(15) 1.8	(11) .7
(76) 3.0	(76) 3.7	(98) 3.3			5.4	3.3	3.2	3.3	.9
5.7	6.5	5.7			12.7	6.6	5.0	3.7	1.4
5699684M	5376475M	7979208M	Net Sales ($)	8201M	76695M	129615M	419186M	602227M	6743284M
1284618M	1647280M	1895142M	Total Assets ($)	3403M	22071M	24585M	96760M	178537M	1569786M

M = $ thousand   MM = $ million
See Pages 1 through 15 for Explanation of Ratios and Data

Current Data Sorted By Assets							Comparative Historical Data	
13	19	17	5		3	# Postretirement Benefits		
						Type of Statement		
2	21	41	34	13	15	Unqualified	87	119
29	61	55	4		1	Reviewed	160	188
84	77	28				Compiled	215	209
44	16	3				Tax Returns	17	16
51	72	56	23	2	6	Other	161	176
221 (4/1-9/30/94)			517 (10/1/94-3/31/95)				4/1/90-3/31/91	4/1/91-3/31/92
0-500M	500M-2MM	2-10MM	10-50MM	50-100MM	100-250MM		ALL	ALL
210	247	183	61	15	22	NUMBER OF STATEMENTS	640	708
%	%	%	%	%	%	ASSETS	%	%
20.1	23.1	27.1	27.2	14.2	37.2	Cash & Equivalents	21.7	23.9
21.8	30.9	34.4	24.9	19.3	18.5	Trade Receivables - (net)	32.0	31.9
.6	.5	.9	.3	5.8	.2	Inventory	.5	.9
3.6	2.9	2.5	8.8	20.1	12.3	All Other Current	4.2	4.3
46.1	57.4	65.0	61.1	59.4	68.2	Total Current	58.4	61.0
21.3	16.9	11.2	11.0	8.7	4.6	Fixed Assets (net)	16.2	14.6
15.0	10.3	7.0	5.8	11.5	5.1	Intangibles (net)	11.4	9.8
17.6	15.4	16.8	22.0	20.4	22.1	All Other Non-Current	14.0	14.7
100.0	100.0	100.0	100.0	100.0	100.0	Total	100.0	100.0
						LIABILITIES		
11.8	7.6	7.0	9.2	5.3	5.1	Notes Payable-Short Term	8.8	8.8
5.8	3.8	2.1	1.7	1.1	.6	Cur. Mat. -L/T/D	4.6	3.6
25.2	36.6	36.1	21.1	11.4	16.4	Trade Payables	35.6	36.0
.5	.3	.4	.9	.3	2.0	Income Taxes Payable	.5	.3
12.9	12.7	16.9	18.1	19.0	31.1	All Other Current	13.0	12.9
56.1	61.0	62.5	51.0	37.2	55.1	Total Current	62.5	61.6
17.4	14.0	11.6	6.8	10.9	4.3	Long Term Debt	16.5	13.8
.1	.2	.5	.3	1.0	1.0	Deferred Taxes	.2	.3
4.2	2.8	3.8	5.7	16.5	14.3	All Other-Non-Current	2.2	3.2
22.2	22.0	21.5	36.1	34.4	25.4	Net Worth	18.6	21.1
100.0	100.0	100.0	100.0	100.0	100.0	Total Liabilities & Net Worth	100.0	100.0
						INCOME DATA		
100.0	100.0	100.0	100.0	100.0	100.0	Net Sales	100.0	100.0
						Gross Profit		
91.9	93.4	91.9	86.8	89.9	90.1	Operating Expenses	94.0	94.6
8.1	6.6	8.1	13.2	10.1	9.9	Operating Profit	6.0	5.4
1.3	1.1	1.4	3.3	2.4	.2	All Other Expenses (net)	1.2	1.4
6.8	5.6	6.7	9.9	7.7	9.7	Profit Before Taxes	4.8	4.0
						RATIOS		
1.4	1.2	1.2	1.9	3.0	1.5		1.2	1.3
.8	1.0	1.0	1.2	1.5	1.1	Current	1.0	1.0
.4	.7	.8	1.0	1.1	1.0		.7	.7
1.2	1.1	1.2	1.7	2.4	1.3		1.1	1.2
.8	.9	1.0	1.1	1.0	1.0	Quick (638)	.9	.9
.4	.7	.8	.7	.8	.6		.6	.6
0 UND	25 14.8	51 7.1	31 11.9	21 17.5	0 UND		26 14.0	28 13.1
19 19.4	73 5.0	111 3.3	73 5.0	49 7.4	41 8.9	Sales/Receivables	79 4.6	85 4.3
57 6.4	140 2.6	203 1.8	152 2.4	166 2.2	107 3.4		159 2.3	166 2.2
						Cost of Sales/Inventory		
						Cost of Sales/Payables		
21.6	11.1	8.2	2.1	2.2	1.9		11.1	9.1
-37.7	-78.0	-330.5	9.5	5.3	7.4	Sales/Working Capital	-52.3	-85.5
-7.3	-7.0	-8.6	-48.4	6.8	-63.1		-6.8	-8.2
11.0	6.8	11.0	17.9		16.5		6.4	7.0
(175) 3.4	(201) 3.0	(139) 3.8	(39) 7.1		(11) 10.4	EBIT/Interest (528) (565)	2.4	2.4
1.3	1.6	1.8	2.3		2.3		1.0	1.0
4.1	2.7	4.4	8.6				4.1	3.9
(41) 2.0	(68) 1.4	(54) 1.7	(23) 3.2			Net Profit + Depr., Dep., Amort./Cur. Mat. L /T/D (244) (235)	1.7	1.9
.5	.8	.8	1.2				.5	.7
.3	.3	.2	.1	.2	.0		.3	.2
1.4	1.0	.7	.3	.2	.1	Fixed/Worth	1.5	.9
-1.0	-2.4	3.2	.7	.4	.5		-1.4	-2.1
1.4	2.0	2.4	1.1	1.3	2.1		2.2	2.1
7.0	6.4	5.5	2.8	2.9	4.4	Debt/Worth	8.0	6.6
-5.0	-16.1	30.2	6.1	16.6	9.1		-9.3	-14.9
109.7	59.3	48.2	38.5	35.4	65.7		60.5	45.2
(124) 22.1	(168) 20.7	(151) 21.5	(57) 17.9	(14) 16.4	(21) 22.6	% Profit Before Taxes/Tangible Net Worth (425) (488)	20.4	15.2
.1	4.4	6.2	7.0	11.8	6.8		2.7	3.2
24.3	10.7	7.5	8.1	9.4	9.2		10.2	8.3
8.0	3.6	3.4	4.5	4.3	5.1	% Profit Before Taxes/Total Assets	3.5	3.0
.9	.9	1.1	1.7	1.5	1.3		.1	.0
41.5	26.8	31.5	43.8	26.3	259.5		28.3	29.5
17.5	13.6	14.3	15.7	9.1	19.2	Sales/Net Fixed Assets	13.2	14.4
10.2	6.9	7.2	7.3	7.5	10.7		6.8	7.9
3.9	1.8	1.3	1.2	.7	1.1		1.9	1.8
2.2	1.2	.9	.7	.6	.5	Sales/Total Assets	1.1	1.1
1.5	.8	.6	.4	.4	.3		.8	.7
1.4	1.4	1.5	1.8	1.9			1.7	1.5
(145) 2.1	(197) 2.8	(145) 2.7	(42) 3.1	(10) 2.6		% Depr., Dep., Amort./Sales (499) (541)	3.0	2.7
3.8	4.3	4.1	5.1	5.2			4.6	4.2
11.0	10.4	7.7					11.3	12.4
(117) 19.3	(123) 15.7	(78) 15.3				% Officers', Directors', Owners' Comp/Sales (327) (326)	19.8	20.1
30.1	25.2	22.8					27.7	28.2
148973M	441371M	961145M	1201960M	792965M	2832736M	Net Sales ($)	3871877M	4606889M
52216M	266529M	836242M	1413175M	1068488M	3492590M	Total Assets ($)	3199407M	4588550M

M = $ thousand   MM = $ million
See Pages 1 through 15 for Explanation of Ratios and Data

Comparative Historical Data				Current Data Sorted By Sales					
11	32	57	# Postretirement Benefits	17	21	7	6	3	3
			Type of Statement						
103	95	126	Unqualified	12	20	18	23	22	31
149	170	150	Reviewed	48	58	21	17	4	2
195	179	189	Compiled	109	55	14	10		1
31	31	63	Tax Returns	48	10	3	2		
149	194	210	Other	69	64	22	22	15	18
4/1/92-3/31/93 ALL	4/1/93-3/31/94 ALL	4/1/94-3/31/95 ALL		221 (4/1-9/30/94)			517 (10/1/94-3/31/95)		
				0-1MM	1-3MM	3-5MM	5-10MM	10-25MM	25MM & OVER
627	669	738	**NUMBER OF STATEMENTS**	286	207	78	74	41	52
%	%	%	**ASSETS**	%	%	%	%	%	%
23.3	23.9	23.8	Cash & Equivalents	19.9	24.1	24.4	30.1	28.1	30.8
31.0	28.7	28.1	Trade Receivables - (net)	26.9	30.5	31.2	31.0	24.1	19.0
.4	.6	.7	Inventory	.5	1.0	.5	.6	.2	2.0
4.1	4.8	4.1	All Other Current	3.0	2.3	4.8	4.0	10.5	11.6
58.8	58.0	56.7	Total Current	50.3	58.0	60.9	65.6	62.8	63.4
15.0	16.0	15.7	Fixed Assets (net)	19.4	13.6	16.0	13.3	12.9	8.9
11.3	9.2	10.3	Intangibles (net)	14.0	10.1	6.0	5.2	9.1	5.9
14.9	16.8	17.2	All Other Non-Current	16.3	18.3	17.0	15.9	15.2	21.9
100.0	100.0	100.0	Total	100.0	100.0	100.0	100.0	100.0	100.0
			LIABILITIES						
7.6	8.0	8.7	Notes Payable-Short Term	11.0	8.2	7.4	7.2	5.9	3.7
4.3	3.5	3.6	Cur. Mat.-L /T/D	4.9	3.4	3.1	2.5	2.0	1.4
35.6	32.8	30.8	Trade Payables	28.5	36.8	34.5	31.8	22.7	19.5
.3	2.0	.5	Income Taxes Payable	.4	.2	.7	.7	.3	1.1
13.3	14.7	14.9	All Other Current	11.4	15.0	18.5	15.8	19.0	24.2
61.1	61.0	58.5	Total Current	56.2	63.6	64.2	58.0	49.8	49.9
14.3	13.6	13.4	Long Term Debt	17.8	11.2	13.4	9.9	9.2	6.5
.3	.3	.3	Deferred Taxes	.1	.3	.3	.7	.4	.7
2.5	4.0	4.3	All Other-Non-Current	3.8	3.6	3.4	4.0	7.7	9.3
21.7	21.2	23.5	Net Worth	22.1	21.3	18.8	27.5	32.9	33.6
100.0	100.0	100.0	Total Liabilities & Net Worth	100.0	100.0	100.0	100.0	100.0	100.0
			INCOME DATA						
100.0	100.0	100.0	Net Sales	100.0	100.0	100.0	100.0	100.0	100.0
			Gross Profit						
94.9	93.1	91.9	Operating Expenses	89.8	93.5	93.4	94.1	90.7	91.6
5.1	6.9	8.1	Operating Profit	10.2	6.5	6.6	5.9	9.3	8.4
.8	.8	1.4	All Other Expenses (net)	2.5	.5	1.9	.0	1.5	.1
4.3	6.1	6.7	Profit Before Taxes	7.7	5.9	4.7	5.8	7.8	8.2
			RATIOS						
1.3	1.3	1.3		1.3	1.2	1.1	1.5	1.8	2.1
1.0	1.0	1.0	Current	.9	.9	1.0	1.1	1.1	1.2
.7	.7	.7		.5	.7	.8	.9	1.0	1.0
1.2	1.2	1.2		1.2	1.1	1.1	1.5	1.3	1.6
.9	.9	.9	Quick	.9	.9	.9	1.0	1.0	1.0
.6	.6	.6		.5	.6	.7	.8	.7	.7
27 13.4	22 16.5	15 23.9		4 92.8	29 12.5	42 8.7	12 30.0	28 13.0	7 49.5
81 4.5	73 5.0	60 6.1	Sales/Receivables	41 8.8	73 5.0	94 3.9	58 6.3	54 6.8	37 10.0
159 2.3	146 2.5	135 2.7		122 3.0	135 2.7	192 1.9	135 2.7	130 2.8	94 3.9
			Cost of Sales/Inventory						
			Cost of Sales/Payables						
9.4	9.5	9.0		9.3	16.8	9.7	8.0	3.7	3.5
-72.8	-85.7	-119.4	Sales/Working Capital	-35.1	-39.8	-58.7	40.8	22.3	9.0
-7.1	-7.3	-7.7		-6.5	-7.1	-6.5	-18.7	-104.2	-130.7
6.6	9.3	10.6		8.8	6.3	10.2	28.0	22.3	14.8
(524) 2.6	(534) 3.4	(574) 3.5	EBIT/Interest	(234) 3.3	(163) 2.9	(62) 3.1	(53) 5.3	(29) 7.1	(33) 7.0
1.0	1.6	1.6		1.5	1.3	1.6	2.4	3.0	4.4
4.2	3.4	4.3		4.1	2.5	5.9	7.3	7.8	11.7
(191) 1.9	(170) 1.6	(195) 1.7	Net Profit + Depr., Dep., Amort./Cur. Mat. L/T/D	(59) 1.5	(54) 1.3	(26) 2.5	(24) 1.4	(13) 3.2	(19) 4.4
.6	.8	.8		.6	.6	1.2	.8	1.9	1.6
.3	.3	.2		.3	.3	.3	.2	.2	.1
1.0	.9	.8	Fixed/Worth	1.2	.9	1.0	.5	.4	.2
-2.1	-4.5	-9.8		-1.2	-1.8	19.2	1.9	1.2	.5
2.0	1.9	1.9		1.8	2.3	2.5	1.5	1.3	1.3
6.7	6.1	5.4	Debt/Worth	6.9	7.0	7.3	4.0	3.1	3.2
-15.5	-28.6	-36.3		-6.2	-16.1	122.9	18.1	14.6	5.6
47.3	55.7	58.8		72.1	59.8	45.2	60.6	51.2	49.0
(441) 16.4	(475) 23.3	(535) 20.5	% Profit Before Taxes/Tangible Net Worth	(181) 17.8	(144) 19.5	(60) 19.4	(64) 31.1	(36) 23.1	(50) 20.6
1.5	6.9	5.5		4.2	3.0	5.8	6.7	12.9	9.3
9.2	11.4	11.8		14.5	11.8	6.1	14.6	12.1	9.8
3.0	4.9	4.1	% Profit Before Taxes/Total Assets	5.1	3.4	2.8	4.9	6.6	5.1
.0	1.2	1.1		1.3	.7	1.0	1.1	2.2	2.8
31.6	29.6	33.2		33.6	29.7	28.3	41.8	26.5	48.3
13.1	13.5	15.4	Sales/Net Fixed Assets	15.7	14.4	14.5	18.5	12.1	18.5
7.2	7.3	7.9		5.7	8.6	7.3	10.4	7.9	8.6
1.9	1.8	2.1		2.2	1.9	1.6	3.4	1.5	2.1
1.1	1.1	1.2	Sales/Total Assets	1.4	1.1	1.0	1.3	1.1	.8
.8	.8	.7		.8	.8	.6	.8	.6	.5
1.5	1.5	1.5		1.5	1.4	1.8	.8	1.3	1.4
(478) 2.6	(527) 2.6	(546) 2.6	% Depr., Dep., Amort./Sales	(203) 2.8	(161) 2.4	(63) 3.2	(61) 2.1	(28) 2.7	(30) 2.5
4.2	4.0	4.2		4.9	3.6	4.3	3.3	5.0	5.0
10.6	10.8	9.9		11.7	10.6	6.9	3.1		
(316) 18.9	(325) 18.5	(327) 16.4	% Officers', Directors', Owners' Comp/Sales	(152) 20.9	(105) 17.1	(32) 17.1	(26) 8.8		
27.8	27.2	26.5		30.3	23.5	22.2	13.7		
5765299M	6149989M	6379150M	Net Sales ($)	151825M	374933M	301682M	487437M	654562M	4408711M
5330236M	6348197M	7129240M	Total Assets ($)	153709M	431448M	385081M	464233M	1002264M	4692505M

© Robert Morris Associates 1995   M = $ thousand   MM = $ million
See Pages 1 through 15 for Explanation of Ratios and Data

SERVICES—KIDNEY DIALYSIS CENTERS. SIC# 8092

Current Data Sorted By Assets						# Postretirement Benefits Type of Statement	Comparative Historical Data	
	1	4			2	Unqualified		
		2				Reviewed		
1	3					Compiled		
1						Tax Returns		
3	7	5	1			Other	4/1/90- 3/31/91 ALL	4/1/91- 3/31/92 ALL
0-500M	7 (4/1-9/30/94) 500M-2MM	2-10MM	23 (10/1/94-3/31/95) 10-50MM	50-100MM	100-250MM			
5	11	11	1		2	NUMBER OF STATEMENTS		
%	%	%	%	%	%		%	%
	14.7	17.6				**ASSETS** Cash & Equivalents		
	47.8	35.3				Trade Receivables - (net)	D	D
	7.0	2.2				Inventory	A	A
	.3	.5				All Other Current	T	T
	69.8	55.6				Total Current	A	A
	18.0	34.4				Fixed Assets (net)		
	.2	5.8				Intangibles (net)	N	N
	11.9	4.3				All Other Non-Current	O	O
	100.0	100.0				Total	T	T
	9.8	.1				**LIABILITIES** Notes Payable-Short Term	A	A
	.2	5.3				Cur. Mat. -L/T/D	V	V
	14.9	5.9				Trade Payables	A	A
	.1	.0				Income Taxes Payable	I	I
	12.5	10.4				All Other Current	L	L
	37.5	21.8				Total Current	A	A
	4.0	25.9				Long Term Debt	B	B
	.0	.0				Deferred Taxes	L	L
	.4	.0				All Other-Non-Current	E	E
	58.1	52.2				Net Worth		
	100.0	100.0				Total Liabilities & Net Worth		
	100.0	100.0				**INCOME DATA** Net Sales		
						Gross Profit		
	88.2	91.8				Operating Expenses		
	11.8	8.2				Operating Profit		
	−3.0	.4				All Other Expenses (net)		
	14.8	7.8				Profit Before Taxes		
	6.2	4.3				**RATIOS**		
	3.4	2.2				Current		
	1.0	1.8						
	6.1	3.8						
	3.1	2.0				Quick		
	.8	1.6						
70	5.2	63 5.8						
76	4.8	81 4.5				Sales/Receivables		
91	4.0	91 4.0						
						Cost of Sales/Inventory		
						Cost of Sales/Payables		
	3.1	4.5						
	4.0	5.9				Sales/Working Capital		
	482.8	8.1						
						EBIT/Interest		
						Net Profit + Depr., Dep., Amort./Cur. Mat. L /T/D		
	.1	.2						
	.2	.8				Fixed/Worth		
	.7	5.0						
	.2	.5						
	.3	1.2				Debt/Worth		
	2.7	5.6						
	65.0					% Profit Before Taxes/Tangible Net Worth		
	54.0							
	49.7							
	50.0	23.3				% Profit Before Taxes/Total Assets		
	45.1	16.5						
	13.9	8.8						
	35.8	8.9						
	22.5	3.7				Sales/Net Fixed Assets		
	9.6	2.3						
	2.6	2.5						
	2.2	1.6				Sales/Total Assets		
	1.9	1.2						
		2.8						
		3.4				% Depr., Dep., Amort./Sales		
		5.1						
						% Officers', Directors', Owners' Comp/Sales		
5468M	20622M	89298M	48879M		263343M	Net Sales ($)		
1744M	9553M	56962M	35422M		300396M	Total Assets ($)		

M = $ thousand   MM = $ million
See Pages 1 through 15 for Explanation of Ratios and Data

Comparative Historical Data | **Current Data Sorted By Sales**

			# Postretirement Benefits / Type of Statement	0-1MM	1-3MM	3-5MM	5-10MM	10-25MM	25MM & OVER
		7	Unqualified			2	1	2	2
		2	Reviewed				1	1	
		4	Compiled	1	3				
		1	Tax Returns	1					
		16	Other	1	10	1	3		1

4/1/92-3/31/93 ALL	4/1/93-3/31/94 ALL	4/1/94-3/31/95 ALL		7 (4/1-9/30/94)		23 (10/1/94-3/31/95)			
			NUMBER OF STATEMENTS	0-1MM	1-3MM	3-5MM	5-10MM	10-25MM	25MM & OVER
%	%	30 %		3 %	13 %	3 %	5 %	3 %	3 %
			ASSETS						
D A T A N O T A V A I L A B L E	D A T A N O T A V A I L A B L E	18.6	Cash & Equivalents		21.8				
		39.0	Trade Receivables - (net)		46.0				
		4.4	Inventory		5.0				
		1.0	All Other Current		.3				
		63.1	Total Current		73.1				
		26.0	Fixed Assets (net)		12.5				
		4.1	Intangibles (net)		1.5				
		6.8	All Other Non-Current		12.9				
		100.0	Total		100.0				
			LIABILITIES						
		3.7	Notes Payable-Short Term		7.8				
		3.7	Cur. Mat.-L /T/D		.7				
		9.3	Trade Payables		9.0				
		.1	Income Taxes Payable		.0				
		10.5	All Other Current		10.2				
		27.2	Total Current		27.7				
		14.7	Long Term Debt		8.6				
		.3	Deferred Taxes		.0				
		1.1	All Other-Non-Current		.4				
		56.7	Net Worth		63.3				
		100.0	Total Liabilities & Net Worth		100.0				
			INCOME DATA						
		100.0	Net Sales		100.0				
			Gross Profit						
		90.8	Operating Expenses		89.0				
		9.2	Operating Profit		11.0				
		–.8	All Other Expenses (net)		–3.0				
		10.0	Profit Before Taxes		14.0				
			RATIOS						
		5.5			6.5				
		2.2	Current		4.2				
		1.7			1.7				
		5.0			6.2				
		2.2	Quick		4.0				
		1.5			1.7				
	63	5.8		64	5.7				
	76	4.8	Sales/Receivables	76	4.8				
	89	4.1		96	3.8				
			Cost of Sales/Inventory						
			Cost of Sales/Payables						
		3.6			3.3				
		4.9	Sales/Working Capital		4.0				
		8.5			9.0				
		13.7							
	(17)	4.2	EBIT/Interest						
		1.9							
			Net Profit + Depr., Dep., Amort./Cur. Mat. L/T/D						
		.1			.1				
		.5	Fixed/Worth		.2				
		1.2			.6				
		.2			.2				
		.6	Debt/Worth		.2				
		3.0			2.5				
		62.0			64.2				
	(27)	49.7	% Profit Before Taxes/Tangible Net Worth	(12)	55.8				
		10.3			50.0				
		46.7			55.0				
		16.9	% Profit Before Taxes/Total Assets		46.0				
		9.5			22.2				
		25.2			109.4				
		9.3	Sales/Net Fixed Assets		23.6				
		3.3			12.0				
		2.6			3.0				
		2.0	Sales/Total Assets		2.2				
		1.3			2.0				
		1.3			.5				
	(26)	2.2	% Depr., Dep., Amort./Sales	(11)	1.4				
		4.1			2.2				
			% Officers', Directors', Owners' Comp/Sales						
		427610M	Net Sales ($)	1282M	24306M	11211M	37332M	41257M	312222M
		404077M	Total Assets ($)	1104M	14412M	11227M	20628M	20888M	335818M

© Robert Morris Associates 1995

M = $ thousand   MM = $ million
See Pages 1 through 15 for Explanation of Ratios and Data

SERVICES—LAUNDRIES & DRYCLEANERS. SIC# 7211 (16)

	Current Data Sorted By Assets							Comparative Historical Data	
	5	4	2	1		1	# Postretirement Benefits		
							Type of Statement		
	1	1	5		1		Unqualified	14	8
	3	12	12	1			Reviewed	30	26
	54	29	3	1			Compiled	67	83
	12	4					Tax Returns	1	8
	21	9	3	1	1		Other	35	33
		46 (4/1-9/30/94)		128 (10/1/94-3/31/95)				4/1/90-3/31/91	4/1/91-3/31/92
	0-500M	500M-2MM	2-10MM	10-50MM	50-100MM	100-250MM		ALL	ALL
	91	55	23	3	2		NUMBER OF STATEMENTS	147	158
	%	%	%	%	%	%	**ASSETS**	%	%
	14.7	8.2	9.0				Cash & Equivalents	11.3	11.3
	8.9	11.9	13.6				Trade Receivables - (net)	11.0	10.2
	1.7	6.6	10.7				Inventory	5.7	4.6
	2.2	2.1	2.5				All Other Current	3.1	1.6
	27.3	28.9	35.8				Total Current	31.0	27.7
	53.3	54.0	51.5				Fixed Assets (net)	51.3	53.8
	10.9	3.6	4.4				Intangibles (net)	6.3	7.3
	8.4	13.5	8.3				All Other Non-Current	11.4	11.3
	100.0	100.0	100.0				Total	100.0	100.0
							LIABILITIES		
	4.3	4.2	4.7				Notes Payable-Short Term	6.4	5.4
	10.0	6.7	5.3				Cur. Mat. -L/T/D	7.0	8.5
	6.8	7.1	10.1				Trade Payables	6.3	6.8
	.3	.2	.3				Income Taxes Payable	.7	.4
	9.6	7.3	4.8				All Other Current	7.7	7.4
	31.0	25.5	25.2				Total Current	28.1	28.6
	40.5	28.1	27.9				Long Term Debt	29.9	31.8
	.1	.3	.9				Deferred Taxes	.5	.9
	4.4	7.4	2.7				All Other-Non-Current	4.3	4.8
	24.0	38.8	43.3				Net Worth	37.1	34.0
	100.0	100.0	100.0				Total Liabilities & Net Worth	100.0	100.0
							INCOME DATA		
	100.0	100.0	100.0				Net Sales	100.0	100.0
							Gross Profit		
	93.0	95.2	94.1				Operating Expenses	93.2	93.1
	7.0	4.8	5.9				Operating Profit	6.8	6.9
	3.0	1.6	2.1				All Other Expenses (net)	2.8	2.3
	4.0	3.2	3.8				Profit Before Taxes	3.9	4.6
							RATIOS		
	2.3	1.9	2.1					2.2	2.3
	.6	1.2	1.4				Current	1.1	1.1
	.3	.6	1.0					.7	.4
	1.9	1.6	1.2					1.6	1.7
	.5	.7	1.0				Quick	.8 (157)	.8
	.2	.4	.4					.4	.3
	0 UND	4 89.2	10 37.2					0 UND	0 UND
	4 84.2	11 33.3	27 13.5				Sales/Receivables	10 35.2	9 41.5
	12 30.4	33 10.9	39 9.4					31 11.7	25 14.4
							Cost of Sales/Inventory		
							Cost of Sales/Payables		
	16.0	16.2	8.5					13.2	15.5
	-27.5	77.7	17.8				Sales/Working Capital	161.6	119.9
	-8.6	-18.3	-796.6					-19.4	-13.4
	5.0	7.0	6.6					4.5	5.3
	(79) 2.2	(48) 3.4	(22) 3.0				EBIT/Interest	(127) 2.0	(144) 2.4
	.8	1.2	1.6					.9	1.2
	5.0	3.8					Net Profit + Depr., Dep.,	4.1	3.4
	(19) 1.3	(17) 1.7					Amort./Cur. Mat. L /T/D	(67) 1.9	(53) 1.7
	1.0	.7						1.0	.5
	.9	.8	.7					.8	.9
	7.1	1.4	1.4				Fixed/Worth	1.4	2.0
	-4.3	4.0	2.1					9.9	8.5
	1.2	.7	.6					.6	.7
	10.2	1.1	1.6				Debt/Worth	1.8	2.4
	-7.8	4.3	2.7					17.7	22.6
	103.8	46.7	36.4				% Profit Before Taxes/Tangible	42.2	44.2
	(52) 43.1	(47) 16.1	(21) 17.4				Net Worth	(118) 15.1	(122) 20.7
	6.3	8.1	7.1					2.3	5.0
	25.0	16.2	14.4				% Profit Before Taxes/Total	17.1	18.1
	7.3	7.4	5.3				Assets	5.1	6.9
	-2.2	1.2	1.9					.2	1.0
	12.2	7.3	6.1					8.3	8.4
	6.6	4.2	4.5				Sales/Net Fixed Assets	4.6	4.7
	2.6	3.1	2.4					3.0	2.8
	4.3	2.8	2.5					3.5	3.3
	2.7	2.2	2.2				Sales/Total Assets	2.3	2.4
	1.7	1.9	1.4					1.7	1.8
	3.3	3.2	3.7					2.8	2.8
	(81) 5.6	(51) 5.1	(21) 5.4				% Depr., Dep., Amort./Sales	(136) 4.8	(147) 4.6
	8.7	6.9	8.0					7.4	7.0
	6.1	2.9					% Officers', Directors',	3.4	4.1
	(47) 8.3	(38) 5.7					Owners' Comp/Sales	(78) 6.3	(82) 7.4
	13.0	10.5						9.9	15.7
	56854M	141884M	182377M	74238M	237017M		Net Sales ($)	560642M	529119M
	18611M	60466M	87968M	42282M	193856M		Total Assets ($)	417091M	354836M

M = $ thousand   MM = $ million
See Pages 1 through 15 for Explanation of Ratios and Data

Comparative Historical Data				Current Data Sorted By Sales					
1	5	12		3	4	1	3	1	
			# Postretirement Benefits						
			Type of Statement						
13	16	8	Unqualified		1	2	3	1	1
20	18	28	Reviewed	4	6	2	15	1	
78	67	87	Compiled	51	26	5	4	1	
13	7	16	Tax Returns	14	1	1			
47	36	35	Other	14	14	3	1		3
4/1/92- 3/31/93	4/1/93- 3/31/94	4/1/94- 3/31/95		46 (4/1-9/30/94)		128 (10/1/94-3/31/95)			
ALL	ALL	ALL		0-1MM	1-3MM	3-5MM	5-10MM	10-25MM	25MM & OVER
171	144	174	**NUMBER OF STATEMENTS**	83	48	13	23	3	4
%	%	%	**ASSETS**	%	%	%	%	%	%
9.7	10.2	11.5	Cash & Equivalents	13.8	10.3	9.6	8.4		
9.2	9.5	10.5	Trade Receivables - (net)	6.0	15.4	10.0	15.0		
4.5	3.9	4.8	Inventory	1.6	5.6	9.9	9.6		
2.0	2.8	2.3	All Other Current	3.2	.9	.3	2.6		
25.4	26.4	29.1	Total Current	24.6	32.2	29.7	35.6		
57.3	58.0	52.9	Fixed Assets (net)	55.2	51.3	56.6	51.2		
7.1	5.8	7.7	Intangibles (net)	11.0	5.3	1.9	4.5		
10.2	9.8	10.2	All Other Non-Current	9.2	11.2	11.8	8.6		
100.0	100.0	100.0	Total	100.0	100.0	100.0	100.0		
			LIABILITIES						
4.6	4.2	4.3	Notes Payable-Short Term	4.6	3.6	8.9	2.6		
7.4	8.5	8.2	Cur. Mat.-L /T/D	10.7	6.6	4.3	6.0		
6.2	7.4	7.4	Trade Payables	4.6	10.3	5.9	9.9		
.4	.5	.3	Income Taxes Payable	.4	.1	.0	.3		
6.1	5.7	8.2	All Other Current	8.2	10.6	3.7	6.0		
24.7	26.2	28.4	Total Current	28.5	31.2	22.8	24.8		
36.5	32.5	34.3	Long Term Debt	44.1	28.2	21.4	24.8		
.4	.3	.3	Deferred Taxes	.1	.1	1.5	.1		
3.1	4.2	5.5	All Other-Non-Current	6.2	4.8	2.5	3.8		
35.4	36.9	31.5	Net Worth	21.1	35.7	51.8	46.5		
100.0	100.0	100.0	Total Liabilities & Net Worth	100.0	100.0	100.0	100.0		
			INCOME DATA						
100.0	100.0	100.0	Net Sales	100.0	100.0	100.0	100.0		
			Gross Profit						
91.4	93.7	93.8	Operating Expenses	92.1	96.6	92.8	95.2		
8.6	6.3	6.2	Operating Profit	7.9	3.4	7.2	4.8		
2.6	2.1	2.4	All Other Expenses (net)	3.9	.8	1.6	1.3		
6.0	4.2	3.7	Profit Before Taxes	4.0	2.6	5.6	3.5		
			RATIOS						
1.9	2.0	2.0		2.7	1.9	3.1	2.1		
1.0	1.0	1.0	Current	.6	1.1	1.4	1.3		
.5	.4	.4		.3	.5	.9	.9		
1.4	1.4	1.5		1.9	1.5	2.3	1.2		
.8	.7	.6	Quick	.4	.7	1.0	.9		
.4	.3	.3		.2	.4	.5	.4		
0 UND	0 UND	0 UND		0 UND	5 68.7	4 83.8	8 47.6		
8 48.5	10 36.8	9 42.6	Sales/Receivables	2 230.0	11 31.9	9 41.8	21 17.3		
26 13.8	25 14.4	28 13.2		12 30.4	34 10.6	30 12.3	42 8.6		
			Cost of Sales/Inventory						
			Cost of Sales/Payables						
17.3	16.9	14.0		15.5	13.3	16.9	9.0		
-811.0	443.0	NM	Sales/Working Capital	-27.1	112.6	29.7	20.6		
-17.0	-14.1	-14.2		-8.1	-15.1	NM	-122.6		
(155) 7.1	(137) 6.0	(154) 5.7		(73) 4.8	(44) 6.7		8.7		
3.2	2.6	2.6	EBIT/Interest	2.1	3.2		3.5		
1.6	1.0	1.1		.7	.6		1.6		
(43) 5.5	(48) 2.9	(48) 4.2		(15) 5.0	(18) 3.3				
2.3	1.5	1.5	Net Profit + Depr., Dep.,	1.4	1.4				
1.3	.6	1.0	Amort./Cur. Mat. L/T/D	1.1	.6				
1.0	1.1	.8		1.3	.8	.5	.8		
2.1	2.0	2.1	Fixed/Worth	9.2	1.6	1.2	1.3		
11.0	5.6	-27.0		-3.6	4.7	3.1	1.9		
.9	.9	.8		1.3	.8	.2	.6		
2.4	2.1	2.9	Debt/Worth	24.1	2.0	.7	1.4		
18.8	8.1	-23.3		-5.7	5.0	5.0	1.8		
(140) 63.9	(123) 57.2	(124) 58.9	% Profit Before Taxes/Tangible	(45) 118.0	(40) 50.0	(11) 59.0	(22) 34.4		
27.4	23.3	22.2	Net Worth	41.7	15.2	14.5	16.1		
9.4	2.7	7.1		6.3	5.2	7.2	6.9		
19.1	17.2	19.5	% Profit Before Taxes/Total	25.0	16.0	24.6	14.4		
9.8	6.1	7.1	Assets	7.5	6.5	7.4	8.7		
2.7	.0	.9		-2.2	-.9	4.0	1.9		
8.3	6.1	9.0		10.7	8.1	7.4	6.3		
4.5	3.8	4.7	Sales/Net Fixed Assets	4.3	6.4	3.4	5.1		
2.5	2.5	2.9		2.0	3.4	2.8	4.0		
3.4	3.1	3.5		3.7	4.1	2.9	3.0		
2.4	2.1	2.4	Sales/Total Assets	2.4	2.5	2.2	2.4		
1.6	1.5	1.6		1.3	2.1	1.8	1.8		
(157) 3.1	(134) 3.4	(157) 3.3		(74) 4.3	(45) 2.6	(10) 3.9	(22) 2.9		
4.6	5.3	5.2	% Depr., Dep., Amort./Sales	6.4	4.5	5.5	4.7		
7.5	8.0	8.1		9.6	6.3	8.7	6.3		
(83) 3.1	(68) 4.8	(93) 4.8	% Officers', Directors',	(40) 5.8	(33) 3.7		(12) 2.1		
6.7	7.2	7.8	Owners' Comp/Sales	9.7	7.6		5.7		
10.8	11.5	11.7		13.0	11.7		7.4		
916177M	703283M	692370M	Net Sales ($)	37216M	91387M	47785M	150071M	41559M	324352M
568060M	409951M	403183M	Total Assets ($)	20294M	39215M	25402M	71333M	26690M	220249M

M = $ thousand   MM = $ million
See Pages 1 through 15 for Explanation of Ratios and Data

Current Data Sorted By Assets   **Comparative Historical Data**

	0-500M	500M-2MM	2-10MM	10-50MM	50-100MM	100-250MM		4/1/90-3/31/91 ALL	4/1/91-3/31/92 ALL
# Postretirement Benefits	1	5	3	2	2	2			
Type of Statement									
Unqualified		1	6	16	7	6		33	32
Reviewed	2	4	15	12	1			37	43
Compiled	17	14	13	3				47	43
Tax Returns		4						4	7
Other	6	11	23	17	2			54	53
		63 (4/1-9/30/94)		117 (10/1/94-3/31/95)					
NUMBER OF STATEMENTS	25	34	57	48	10	6		175	178
	%	%	%	%	%	%	**ASSETS**	%	%
	21.1	6.3	3.6	4.5	4.4		Cash & Equivalents	5.2	5.4
	11.7	15.8	7.5	7.0	21.6		Trade Receivables - (net)	7.2	7.4
	2.7	1.4	16.7	8.1	11.3		Inventory	13.3	12.3
	4.6	4.4	5.4	4.3	8.6		All Other Current	3.1	3.5
	40.1	27.9	33.2	23.9	46.0		Total Current	28.8	28.5
	53.9	65.7	59.0	55.8	40.2		Fixed Assets (net)	60.1	61.3
	.5	1.4	.4	1.1	1.6		Intangibles (net)	2.0	1.1
	5.6	5.0	7.3	19.2	12.2		All Other Non-Current	9.0	9.1
	100.0	100.0	100.0	100.0	100.0		Total	100.0	100.0
							LIABILITIES		
	7.4	22.1	31.1	21.3	52.1		Notes Payable-Short Term	27.3	28.9
	10.3	7.4	10.5	10.1	7.4		Cur. Mat.-L/T/D	10.5	11.6
	5.9	7.4	1.9	1.6	3.3		Trade Payables	2.8	3.0
	1.4	.2	.1	.4	.0		Income Taxes Payable	.2	.2
	13.0	5.9	4.6	6.3	4.5		All Other Current	6.2	6.0
	38.0	43.0	48.1	39.7	67.2		Total Current	47.0	49.6
	31.8	37.6	32.3	38.2	8.4		Long Term Debt	32.4	31.2
	.0	.2	1.6	1.8	1.0		Deferred Taxes	.7	.8
	1.7	5.3	1.7	3.5	11.4		All Other-Non-Current	2.8	1.5
	28.5	13.8	16.2	16.8	12.0		Net Worth	17.1	16.8
	100.0	100.0	100.0	100.0	100.0		Total Liabilities & Net Worth	100.0	100.0
							INCOME DATA		
	100.0	100.0	100.0	100.0	100.0		Net Sales	100.0	100.0
							Gross Profit		
	91.7	94.0	86.0	85.1	88.4		Operating Expenses	88.8	87.2
	8.3	6.0	14.0	14.9	11.6		Operating Profit	11.2	12.8
	2.5	5.5	9.4	8.7	4.9		All Other Expenses (net)	7.0	8.8
	5.8	.5	4.6	6.1	6.7		Profit Before Taxes	4.2	3.9
							RATIOS		
	2.6	1.5	1.2	1.4	1.0			1.1	1.1
	.9	.7	.9	.6	.8		Current	.6	.5
	.5	.2	.2	.1	.3			.2	.2
	2.0	1.1	.6	1.0	1.0			.6	.6
	.9	.5	.2	.1	.2		Quick (174)	.2	.2
	.3	.2	.1	.1	.1			.1	.1
	0 UND	7 53.1	5 66.8	8 46.3	13 28.1			8 46.4	7 49.2
	2 164.4	17 21.4	13 29.2	15 24.5	18 19.8		Sales/Receivables	17 22.0	18 20.4
	19 19.1	55 6.6	29 12.5	36 10.2	61 6.0			35 10.5	38 9.5
							Cost of Sales/Inventory		
							Cost of Sales/Payables		
	23.8	22.1	8.9	8.6	NM			18.8	22.2
	-275.5	-6.7	-17.8	-14.8	-10.6		Sales/Working Capital	-7.0	-4.7
	-6.1	-1.9	-1.7	-1.2	-3.9			-1.6	-1.6
	(19) 14.4	(28) 2.1	(48) 1.7	(36) 1.9				(130) 1.9	(136) 1.8
	4.4	1.2	1.3	1.4			EBIT/Interest	1.4	1.3
	.6	.6	1.1	1.3				1.1	1.1
		(10) 2.4	(10) 1.7	(13) 3.0				(55) 2.6	(38) 1.9
		1.2	1.0	.8			Net Profit + Depr., Dep., Amort./Cur. Mat. L/T/D	1.1	1.2
		.8	.5	.3				.8	.8
	.4	1.7	.5	.7	1.0			1.3	1.2
	3.1	6.0	4.1	4.6	3.7		Fixed/Worth	3.4	4.6
	21.4	40.2	8.5	9.8	5.3			9.1	16.7
	.7	1.9	3.2	3.5	5.5			2.6	3.2
	4.0	6.1	6.6	6.8	7.7		Debt/Worth	6.2	6.7
	NM	72.8	10.5	12.7	80.1			20.0	21.6
	(19) 97.1	(28) 23.4	(54) 38.5	(47) 24.0	245.2			(150) 30.8	(152) 31.6
	44.8	11.1	15.9	17.0	45.0		% Profit Before Taxes/Tangible Net Worth	14.3	14.9
	18.8	-5.8	6.1	11.0	31.5			4.3	4.6
	40.8	4.4	4.1	3.9	6.1			4.4	4.6
	8.3	1.1	1.4	2.3	3.8		% Profit Before Taxes/Total Assets	1.9	1.7
	-2.4	-3.2	.5	1.2	2.4			.2	.4
	87.1	2.8	22.2	12.2	26.8			4.1	4.2
	2.7	.9	.9	.7	3.2		Sales/Net Fixed Assets	1.0	1.1
	.8	.6	.6	.5	1.2			.6	.7
	8.1	1.1	.8	.6	2.4			.9	1.0
	2.2	.6	.6	.4	.7		Sales/Total Assets	.6	.7
	.6	.4	.4	.3	.3			.5	.5
	(17) 3.6	(32) 11.0	(45) 11.4	(34) 11.3				(144) 13.2	(142) 16.8
	39.1	34.2	33.7	30.8			% Depr., Dep., Amort./Sales	30.2	31.7
	67.4	67.6	45.6	65.0				51.3	54.0
	(10) 5.2	(10) 6.5	(24) 1.0	(16) .9				(58) 1.9	(60) 1.7
	10.1	10.2	2.4	4.0			% Officers', Directors', Owners' Comp/Sales	4.4	4.0
	12.7	16.0	4.2	6.1				8.8	10.6
	38841M	39649M	309707M	554304M	693181M	378176M	Net Sales ($)	1086945M	1372199M
	6827M	42003M	290346M	982120M	671574M	912452M	Total Assets ($)	1346027M	1924123M

M = $ thousand   MM = $ million
See Pages 1 through 15 for Explanation of Ratios and Data

Comparative Historical Data / Current Data Sorted By Sales

6	9	15	# Postretirement Benefits / Type of Statement	3	4	1	1	2	4
25	30	36	Unqualified		5	5	6	9	11
41	27	34	Reviewed	5	11	5	4	7	2
42	30	47	Compiled	22	13	4	5	1	2
1	1	4	Tax Returns	4					
50	29	59	Other	15	13	8	13	7	3
4/1/92-3/31/93 ALL	4/1/93-3/31/94 ALL	4/1/94-3/31/95 ALL		63 (4/1-9/30/94)		117 (10/1/94-3/31/95)			
				0-1MM	1-3MM	3-5MM	5-10MM	10-25MM	25MM & OVER
159	117	180	**NUMBER OF STATEMENTS**	46	42	22	28	24	18
%	%	%	**ASSETS**	%	%	%	%	%	%
4.9	5.2	6.8	Cash & Equivalents	11.1	5.5	5.1	5.2	5.1	5.4
10.3	8.0	10.7	Trade Receivables - (net)	11.5	12.8	9.0	4.4	16.1	8.2
9.8	9.1	8.8	Inventory	.5	8.4	14.7	11.5	9.5	18.2
5.9	6.7	5.5	All Other Current	6.2	3.0	5.9	3.1	10.0	6.5
30.9	29.1	31.7	Total Current	29.3	29.7	34.7	24.2	40.7	38.2
59.0	58.1	57.6	Fixed Assets (net)	60.8	63.0	59.7	56.3	46.2	51.9
1.0	.4	.8	Intangibles (net)	1.3	.5	.2	1.0	1.0	.7
9.1	12.4	9.9	All Other Non-Current	8.7	6.8	5.4	18.5	12.1	9.2
100.0	100.0	100.0	Total	100.0	100.0	100.0	100.0	100.0	100.0
			LIABILITIES						
29.9	21.4	25.7	Notes Payable-Short Term	21.5	27.0	24.5	13.9	34.8	41.2
9.7	11.6	9.3	Cur. Mat.-L /T/D	10.1	11.9	8.3	7.8	7.6	7.0
2.7	2.8	3.5	Trade Payables	3.6	5.1	1.6	2.7	2.6	3.9
.2	.2	.4	Income Taxes Payable	.6	.5	.1	.3	.2	.4
4.9	5.1	6.4	All Other Current	5.4	5.6	3.5	8.1	4.6	13.9
47.4	41.2	45.2	Total Current	41.1	50.0	38.0	32.8	49.8	66.3
31.7	35.4	33.1	Long Term Debt	34.2	32.5	40.5	43.5	29.9	11.1
.9	1.0	1.1	Deferred Taxes	.1	1.7	1.2	1.7	1.0	1.5
2.2	3.7	3.4	All Other-Non-Current	1.8	4.5	2.6	4.7	5.4	1.3
17.9	18.7	17.1	Net Worth	22.8	11.3	17.7	17.2	13.8	19.8
100.0	100.0	100.0	Total Liabilities & Net Worth	100.0	100.0	100.0	100.0	100.0	100.0
			INCOME DATA						
100.0	100.0	100.0	Net Sales	100.0	100.0	100.0	100.0	100.0	100.0
			Gross Profit						
85.6	87.5	87.9	Operating Expenses	86.2	89.4	88.0	86.5	86.8	92.3
14.4	12.5	12.1	Operating Profit	13.8	10.6	12.0	13.5	13.2	7.7
9.2	6.7	7.4	All Other Expenses (net)	8.2	7.0	8.7	8.6	7.0	2.9
5.2	5.8	4.7	Profit Before Taxes	5.6	3.6	3.3	4.9	6.2	4.8
			RATIOS						
1.2 / .6 / .2	1.3 / .7 / .2	1.3 / .7 / .2	Current	1.5 / .7 / .2	1.1 / .5 / .1	1.9 / 1.0 / .2	1.2 / 1.0 / .3	1.7 / 1.0 / .1	1.1 / .4 / .2
.6 / .2 / .1	.7 / .2 / .1	1.0 / .2 / .1	Quick	1.2 / .5 / .1	.8 / .2 / .1	1.4 / .4 / .1	1.1 / .3 / .1	.9 / .1 / .1	.3 / .1 / .1
8 47.4 / 20 18.5 / 48 7.6	5 77.7 / 12 31.0 / 33 11.0	6 62.1 / 14 26.3 / 35 10.4	Sales/Receivables	0 UND / 11 33.7 / 49 7.5	7 49.0 / 15 24.0 / 43 8.4	12 30.7 / 19 19.5 / 36 10.2	6 56.8 / 13 27.5 / 27 13.6	4 100.9 / 11 32.8 / 26 14.2	10 36.2 / 17 21.8 / 22 16.6
			Cost of Sales/Inventory						
			Cost of Sales/Payables						
10.7 / -7.7 / -1.6	11.8 / -16.6 / -1.8	13.2 / -16.4 / -1.7	Sales/Working Capital	5.0 / -7.0 / -1.7	32.1 / -7.4 / -1.4	5.9 / 44.6 / -3.2	15.0 / -171.5 / -2.8	7.0 / -197.8 / -1.7	72.6 / -7.2 / -1.2
(125) 2.1 / 1.5 / 1.2	(95) 2.5 / 1.7 / 1.3	(143) 2.2 / 1.4 / 1.1	EBIT/Interest	(35) 4.3 / 1.6 / .7	(31) 1.7 / 1.3 / .8	(18) 1.6 / 1.3 / 1.0	(23) 1.9 / 1.4 / 1.1	(18) 1.7 / 1.4 / 1.3	3.9 / 2.2 / 1.7
(34) 3.2 / 1.1 / .9	(25) 2.3 / .8 / .4	(39) 1.8 / 1.1 / .4	Net Profit + Depr., Dep., Amort./Cur. Mat. L/T/D	(11) 2.3 / 1.2 / .9	(10) 5.8 / 1.0 / .5				
1.0 / 3.9 / 8.6	.5 / 3.1 / 7.7	.8 / 4.2 / 9.8	Fixed/Worth	.8 / 4.0 / 21.9	1.5 / 5.4 / 12.9	1.1 / 4.5 / 10.2	.8 / 3.8 / 9.8	.3 / 2.2 / 11.5	.6 / 3.5 / 5.8
3.2 / 6.5 / 14.7	2.9 / 6.2 / 11.0	2.9 / 6.7 / 16.1	Debt/Worth	1.9 / 5.3 / 27.2	3.2 / 6.8 / 88.7	3.5 / 6.8 / 13.6	3.5 / 6.7 / 10.6	5.5 / 10.5 / 16.4	2.6 / 4.5 / 7.6
(146) 34.1 / 16.6 / 6.8	(107) 32.5 / 17.5 / 8.2	(164) 39.5 / 19.0 / 8.9	% Profit Before Taxes/Tangible Net Worth	(39) 52.9 / 19.1 / -6.3	(34) 45.4 / 13.9 / 8.3	21.0 / 16.1 / 4.4	(27) 25.9 / 20.9 / 8.9	49.3 / 21.6 / 12.6	66.4 / 33.5 / 16.6
4.6 / 2.3 / .7	4.5 / 2.9 / 1.1	5.0 / 2.1 / .6	% Profit Before Taxes/Total Assets	8.4 / 3.7 / -1.6	4.3 / 1.5 / -.6	2.3 / 1.2 / .3	3.7 / 2.3 / .6	4.5 / 1.9 / 1.5	7.3 / 4.8 / 2.6
7.6 / .9 / .6	14.1 / .9 / .6	16.9 / .9 / .6	Sales/Net Fixed Assets	4.7 / .8 / .5	10.0 / 1.0 / .6	9.3 / .6 / .5	22.6 / .9 / .5	42.3 / 2.3 / .8	20.0 / 3.2 / .8
.7 / .5 / .4	.7 / .6 / .4	.9 / .6 / .4	Sales/Total Assets	.7 / .5 / .3	1.2 / .6 / .4	.7 / .5 / .3	.7 / .5 / .4	.8 / .5 / .5	2.5 / .9 / .6
(125) 18.2 / 32.7 / 60.1	(86) 15.6 / 33.8 / 58.2	(138) 6.0 / 31.2 / 59.4	% Depr., Dep., Amort./Sales	(39) 25.2 / 51.0 / 72.0	(33) 13.0 / 36.7 / 45.3	(17) 27.8 / 38.4 / 61.9	(20) .9 / 26.1 / 56.7	(16) 2.7 / 20.2 / 50.3	(13) .4 / 4.9 / 12.1
(60) 2.0 / 4.1 / 10.3	(40) 1.7 / 3.0 / 6.6	(60) 1.8 / 3.7 / 9.3	% Officers', Directors', Owners' Comp/Sales	(15) 7.6 / 10.4 / 13.2	(10) 1.7 / 4.0 / 8.9	(13) 1.8 / 3.5 / 5.4	(11) .9 / 3.1 / 3.6		
1186386M / 1985236M	912171M / 1666865M	2013858M / 2905322M	Net Sales ($) / Total Assets ($)	20949M / 49399M	75639M / 143501M	84837M / 191647M	192991M / 378017M	368495M / 952488M	1270947M / 1190270M

M = $ thousand   MM = $ million
See Pages 1 through 15 for Explanation of Ratios and Data

SERVICES—LEGAL SERVICES. SIC# 8111

Current Data Sorted By Assets						# Postretirement Benefits / Type of Statement	Comparative Historical Data	
25	26	11	10	1				
6	8	16	28	1	2	Unqualified	43	54
19	41	55	20	1		Reviewed	129	156
98	77	34	3			Compiled	232	270
60	18	7		1		Tax Returns	17	46
104	99	89	44	3	3	Other	315	341
	102 (4/1-9/30/94)		735 (10/1/94-3/31/95)				4/1/90-3/31/91 ALL	4/1/91-3/31/92 ALL
0-500M	500M-2MM	2-10MM	10-50MM	50-100MM	100-250MM	NUMBER OF STATEMENTS		
287	243	201	95	6	5		736	867
%	%	%	%	%	%	ASSETS	%	%
28.0	20.6	19.9	22.6			Cash & Equivalents	21.8	22.5
12.2	27.2	32.2	29.4			Trade Receivables - (net)	22.0	21.9
.4	1.1	2.6	1.1			Inventory	1.7	1.3
7.1	9.3	8.5	8.0			All Other Current	8.5	8.1
47.7	58.2	63.1	61.1			Total Current	53.9	53.8
34.5	27.9	23.5	25.5			Fixed Assets (net)	32.7	32.0
2.5	2.0	1.0	3.4			Intangibles (net)	1.7	1.8
15.4	11.8	12.4	10.1			All Other Non-Current	11.8	12.4
100.0	100.0	100.0	100.0			Total	100.0	100.0
						LIABILITIES		
22.4	14.9	8.5	5.3			Notes Payable-Short Term	13.7	15.3
6.7	4.2	5.0	3.4			Cur. Mat. -L/T/D	4.8	4.1
2.9	3.5	2.6	1.5			Trade Payables	2.1	2.6
.7	1.0	1.3	.4			Income Taxes Payable	.9	.9
25.9	19.0	19.5	10.6			All Other Current	17.2	18.8
58.6	42.5	36.8	21.2			Total Current	38.8	41.7
13.1	14.2	12.7	10.9			Long Term Debt	15.6	15.5
.4	1.0	1.7	.2			Deferred Taxes	.6	.8
3.6	4.8	6.6	7.9			All Other-Non-Current	4.4	3.4
24.3	37.5	42.2	59.9			Net Worth	40.6	38.5
100.0	100.0	100.0	100.0			Total Liabilities & Net Worth	100.0	100.0
						INCOME DATA		
100.0	100.0	100.0	100.0			Net Sales	100.0	100.0
						Gross Profit		
87.5	85.5	82.2	67.5			Operating Expenses	80.6	81.3
12.5	14.5	17.8	32.5			Operating Profit	19.4	18.7
.2	.3	.9	3.5			All Other Expenses (net)	1.7	1.6
12.4	14.2	16.9	29.1			Profit Before Taxes	17.8	17.1
						RATIOS		
1.7	3.3	4.6	7.6				3.5	3.5
.8	1.4	2.0	3.7			Current	1.5	1.4
.4	.8	1.0	1.8				.8	.8
1.4	3.0	3.6	6.9				2.9	2.9
(286) .7	1.3	1.4	3.4			Quick	1.2	(865) 1.2
.3	.6	.8	1.5				.6	.5
0 UND	0 UND	1 392.7	4 97.0				0 UND	0 UND
0 UND	9 38.9	40 9.1	21 17.2			Sales/Receivables	7 48.7	2 152.4
7 56.0	65 5.6	89 4.1	101 3.6				62 5.9	58 6.3
						Cost of Sales/Inventory		
						Cost of Sales/Payables		
27.6	6.6	4.1	3.6				6.7	7.2
-83.3	24.7	11.0	6.7			Sales/Working Capital	28.8	38.8
-21.0	-48.6	475.2	16.1				-51.9	-41.1
25.2	51.8	58.3	108.2				42.9	41.8
(231) 3.2	(206) 6.6	(163) 9.4	(79) 51.6			EBIT/Interest	(645) 9.2	(753) 7.8
.1	1.0	1.2	16.6				1.3	1.1
4.8	3.6	2.5					3.7	3.6
(24) 1.1	(27) 1.5	(28) 1.4				Net Profit + Depr., Dep., Amort./Cur. Mat. L /T/D	(97) 1.6	(106) 1.6
.6	.8	.6					.7	.5
.5	.2	.2	.2				.3	.3
1.6	.7	.6	.4			Fixed/Worth	.8	.8
-8.6	3.3	1.3	.7				2.3	3.0
1.0	.6	.5	.2				.5	.6
3.1	1.7	1.4	.6			Debt/Worth	1.4	1.7
-21.5	8.3	4.3	1.4				5.3	7.2
367.1	276.3	203.5	268.5				287.4	305.2
(210) 67.1	(210) 33.0	(192) 50.6	(91) 177.3			% Profit Before Taxes/Tangible Net Worth	(656) 72.5	(764) 71.6
.0	2.0	3.8	59.0				6.4	4.5
115.4	114.8	97.7	149.3				133.2	128.0
16.3	11.2	17.5	90.1			% Profit Before Taxes/Total Assets	24.4	20.1
-1.8	.0	.5	36.0				.8	.4
49.7	38.0	27.5	17.8				28.2	29.5
26.6	21.3	17.2	12.9			Sales/Net Fixed Assets	16.6	17.4
14.8	13.6	11.1	9.4				9.9	10.4
12.1	7.0	4.3	3.9				6.6	7.2
7.2	4.2	2.7	2.8			Sales/Total Assets	4.0	4.1
4.1	2.4	1.8	1.8				2.3	2.3
1.1	1.2	1.3	1.5				1.4	1.2
(211) 1.6	(210) 1.6	(181) 1.9	(84) 2.0			% Depr., Dep., Amort./Sales	(632) 2.0	(758) 1.8
2.3	2.1	2.5	2.6				2.7	2.6
18.5	15.0	15.6	11.2				17.6	18.7
(169) 30.9	(126) 29.0	(85) 27.3	(20) 27.7			% Officers', Directors', Owners' Comp/Sales	(347) 29.1	(415) 29.0
38.9	38.0	36.2	37.4				37.4	36.9
516866M	1248534M	2890303M	5795246M	8333386M	1403831M	Net Sales ($)	11429199M	13188206M
64939M	252405M	876602M	2041949M	447734M	728887M	Total Assets ($)	3553897M	3626588M

M = $ thousand   MM = $ million
See Pages 1 through 15 for Explanation of Ratios and Data

Comparative Historical Data				Current Data Sorted By Sales					
22	39	73	# Postretirement Benefits	13	20	11	10	7	12
			Type of Statement						
69	48	61	Unqualified	2	6	7	2	10	34
152	140	136	Reviewed	6	17	17	39	33	24
256	217	212	Compiled	41	80	38	36	10	7
70	94	86	Tax Returns	32	30	11	7	5	1
341	351	342	Other	39	83	49	56	58	57
4/1/92-3/31/93 ALL	4/1/93-3/31/94 ALL	4/1/94-3/31/95 ALL		102 (4/1-9/30/94)		735 (10/1/94-3/31/95)			
				0-1MM	1-3MM	3-5MM	5-10MM	10-25MM	25MM & OVER
888	850	837	**NUMBER OF STATEMENTS**	120	216	122	140	116	123
%	%	%	**ASSETS**	%	%	%	%	%	%
23.1	24.3	23.3	Cash & Equivalents	25.3	24.8	22.8	20.0	21.5	24.4
22.3	22.1	23.3	Trade Receivables - (net)	18.0	22.2	19.7	26.7	30.3	23.6
1.2	.9	1.2	Inventory	.0	2.0	2.0	1.5	1.0	.2
8.7	7.9	8.3	All Other Current	6.7	8.0	11.6	8.2	8.3	6.9
55.3	55.3	56.1	Total Current	50.0	57.0	56.0	56.4	61.2	55.1
31.3	29.9	28.9	Fixed Assets (net)	31.5	26.6	27.6	29.4	28.9	31.0
1.6	2.0	2.1	Intangibles (net)	2.5	2.3	2.0	1.5	.8	3.0
11.9	12.7	13.0	All Other Non-Current	16.0	14.0	14.3	12.8	9.1	10.9
100.0	100.0	100.0	Total	100.0	100.0	100.0	100.0	100.0	100.0
			LIABILITIES						
14.1	13.4	14.7	Notes Payable-Short Term	19.1	19.4	15.8	16.4	8.5	4.8
4.8	4.4	5.1	Cur. Mat.-L /T/D	4.1	5.3	5.3	5.7	5.3	4.9
2.7	2.4	2.8	Trade Payables	4.6	2.7	2.1	2.5	3.5	1.4
.7	.6	.9	Income Taxes Payable	.8	.7	1.8	.2	1.5	.3
19.0	21.1	20.5	All Other Current	21.7	24.2	20.5	21.8	18.7	12.9
41.4	42.0	43.9	Total Current	50.3	52.3	45.5	46.7	37.6	24.3
14.6	13.7	13.1	Long Term Debt	13.8	13.3	11.2	12.8	14.7	13.1
.9	.9	.8	Deferred Taxes	.5	.9	.9	1.4	1.1	.2
4.0	4.3	5.1	All Other-Non-Current	3.8	3.8	4.2	8.2	6.1	5.1
39.2	39.1	37.0	Net Worth	31.5	29.7	38.3	30.9	40.6	57.3
100.0	100.0	100.0	Total Liabilities & Net Worth	100.0	100.0	100.0	100.0	100.0	100.0
			INCOME DATA						
100.0	100.0	100.0	Net Sales	100.0	100.0	100.0	100.0	100.0	100.0
			Gross Profit						
81.8	81.2	83.0	Operating Expenses	86.6	88.1	83.9	85.7	79.8	69.4
18.2	18.8	17.0	Operating Profit	13.4	11.9	16.1	14.3	20.2	30.6
1.2	1.1	.8	All Other Expenses (net)	.5	.1	−.1	.7	1.5	2.8
17.0	17.7	16.2	Profit Before Taxes	12.9	11.8	16.2	13.6	18.6	27.8
			RATIOS						
3.3	3.8	3.5		2.2	2.5	2.9	3.1	4.9	5.9
1.5	1.6	1.4	Current	1.0	1.1	1.3	1.3	1.7	3.4
.8	.7	.7		.4	.6	.7	.7	.9	1.4
2.8	3.2	3.0		2.1	1.9	2.2	2.6	3.7	5.0
1.2 (845)	1.2 (836)	1.1	Quick	.9	.9 (121)	1.0	1.1	1.3	2.8
.5	.6	.6		.3	.4	.3	.6	.8	1.1
0 UND	0 UND	0 UND		0 UND	0 UND	0 UND	0 UND	0 UND	0 UND
3 105.4	4 83.7	6 59.3	Sales/Receivables	0 UND	0 UND	0 UND	13 27.2	14 25.5	14 26.9
59 6.2	58 ·6.3	61 6.0		38 9.6	60 6.1	54 6.7	68 5.4	76 4.8	64 5.7
			Cost of Sales/Inventory						
			Cost of Sales/Payables						
6.8	7.0	6.6		10.2	6.9	7.5	6.3	4.8	4.7
32.5	28.8	28.9	Sales/Working Capital	UND	191.8	36.2	26.7	23.9	11.0
−57.2	−47.7	−42.8		−13.4	−27.6	−41.4	−40.2	−171.7	36.9
56.8	65.9	54.4		16.0	28.7	51.5	52.8	71.0	113.3
10.0 (755)	11.4 (714)	8.0 (688)	EBIT/Interest	3.7 (88)	6.1 (182)	5.6 (101)	5.1 (116)	15.0 (99)	43.1 (102)
1.2	1.5	1.0		−.2	.8	.8	1.0	1.1	14.0
3.4	2.5	3.5			4.4	4.6	2.1		
1.8 (100)	1.4 (88)	1.4 (80)	Net Profit + Depr., Dep., Amort./Cur. Mat. L/T/D		1.5 (19)	1.4 (19)	1.0 (21)		
.6	.6	.7			.8	.3	.5		
.3	.3	.3		.3	.3	.2	.3	.3	.3
.7	.7	.8	Fixed/Worth	1.0	.9	.7	1.1	.9	.5
2.5	2.4	2.9		9.8	10.0	2.6	4.0	2.3	.9
.5	.6	.6		.6	.8	.5	.8	.5	.3
1.6	1.4	1.7	Debt/Worth	2.1	2.5	1.7	2.2	1.4	.7
5.9	6.4	10.3		34.3	26.5	10.3	16.6	4.6	1.4
278.2	291.9	254.5		185.0	260.9	309.7	164.9	279.3	267.8
67.3 (783)	78.1 (738)	65.1 (713)	% Profit Before Taxes/Tangible Net Worth	77.4 (94)	35.1 (172)	50.1 (106)	40.7 (116)	87.0 (108)	179.9 (117)
6.3	7.4	3.8		.7	.0	2.8	2.3	3.9	28.7
120.7	132.4	115.1		63.2	51.8	107.7	93.1	125.5	149.3
21.1	24.2	19.7	% Profit Before Taxes/Total Assets	11.2	14.8	11.5	9.1	42.2	99.8
.8	.9	.2		−1.3	−.6	−.1	−.0	.3	8.6
33.5	35.4	35.9		39.7	46.4	38.6	36.3	28.1	20.0
18.6	19.7	20.4	Sales/Net Fixed Assets	17.4	26.7	23.1	21.1	19.2	13.0
11.4	11.8	12.4		8.7	15.1	14.4	13.0	13.2	9.3
7.4	7.4	7.3		7.1	8.6	7.7	8.3	6.9	5.0
4.0	4.1	4.1	Sales/Total Assets	3.8	4.6	4.4	4.3	3.8	3.2
2.5	2.4	2.4		2.1	2.7	2.1	2.4	2.5	2.4
1.1	1.1	1.2		1.2	1.1	1.1	1.3	1.2	1.5
1.7 (767)	1.7 (717)	1.7 (693)	% Depr., Dep., Amort./Sales	1.8 (79)	1.7 (166)	1.5 (112)	1.7 (127)	1.5 (103)	2.1 (106)
2.4	2.4	2.4		3.0	2.5	2.1	2.1	2.1	2.6
17.8	20.4	16.2		19.9	16.3	14.5	11.4	17.8	17.7
29.7 (434)	29.9 (410)	29.1 (404)	% Officers', Directors', Owners' Comp/Sales	32.9 (67)	28.5 (126)	28.0 (64)	29.5 (65)	29.0 (49)	28.9 (33)
37.6	39.1	38.4		40.7	36.0	37.8	39.7	40.6	38.7
12299200M	11723035M	20188166M	Net Sales ($)	67081M	409442M	481704M	989723M	1833530M	16406686M
3745224M	3794322M	4412516M	Total Assets ($)	28267M	128519M	179953M	304611M	573526M	3197640M

M = $ thousand   MM = $ million
See Pages 1 through 15 for Explanation of Ratios and Data

Current Data Sorted By Assets							Comparative Historical Data	
	1	3		1	3	# Postretirement Benefits		
						Type of Statement		
	1	7	5	2	4	Unqualified	22	19
	2	4				Reviewed	18	18
5	5	2				Compiled	14	21
	2					Tax Returns		3
3	4	8				Other	13	7
	21 (4/1-9/30/94)		33 (10/1/94-3/31/95)				4/1/90-3/31/91	4/1/91-3/31/92
0-500M	500M-2MM	2-10MM	10-50MM	50-100MM	100-250MM		ALL	ALL
8	14	21	5	2	4	NUMBER OF STATEMENTS	67	68
%	%	%	%	%	%	ASSETS	%	%
	11.2	6.1				Cash & Equivalents	5.9	6.8
	26.8	18.8				Trade Receivables - (net)	18.8	19.0
	10.7	11.7				Inventory	14.1	13.5
	1.2	3.8				All Other Current	2.5	3.3
	49.9	40.4				Total Current	41.4	42.7
	41.9	41.9				Fixed Assets (net)	40.9	43.4
	1.5	5.7				Intangibles (net)	6.4	4.9
	6.7	12.0				All Other Non-Current	11.3	9.0
	100.0	100.0				Total	100.0	100.0
						LIABILITIES		
	4.1	4.7				Notes Payable-Short Term	7.3	6.8
	4.7	5.9				Cur. Mat. -L/T/D	5.1	6.3
	12.0	9.1				Trade Payables	11.4	11.5
	.1	.0				Income Taxes Payable	1.3	.2
	7.5	12.6				All Other Current	7.7	9.6
	28.4	32.3				Total Current	32.8	34.4
	16.7	23.4				Long Term Debt	22.7	25.2
	.0	2.0				Deferred Taxes	1.1	.9
	1.8	1.6				All Other-Non-Current	1.8	2.5
	53.1	40.8				Net Worth	41.5	37.0
	100.0	100.0				Total Liabilities & Net Worth	100.0	100.0
						INCOME DATA		
	100.0	100.0				Net Sales	100.0	100.0
						Gross Profit		
	94.6	92.3				Operating Expenses	93.6	95.4
	5.4	7.7				Operating Profit	6.4	4.6
	.7	1.6				All Other Expenses (net)	1.6	1.5
	4.7	6.2				Profit Before Taxes	4.9	3.1
						RATIOS		
	2.8	2.2					1.9	2.1
	1.5	1.3				Current	1.2	1.2
	1.0	1.0					.9	.8
	2.7	1.4					1.1	1.3
	1.2	.7				Quick	.8 (67)	.8
	.7	.5					.5	.5
28	13.1	30 12.1					25 14.7	26 14.2
30	12.2	36 10.1				Sales/Receivables	33 11.2	33 10.9
45	8.1	41 8.8					39 9.4	39 9.3
						Cost of Sales/Inventory		
						Cost of Sales/Payables		
	6.4	7.9					7.7	10.3
	13.6	23.9				Sales/Working Capital	30.0	43.8
	NM	-84.0					-37.7	-31.2
	26.9	6.9					6.3	6.1
	3.7	(20) 3.6				EBIT/Interest	(63) 3.3	(64) 2.4
	1.5	2.4					1.6	1.3
							5.4	4.1
						Net Profit + Depr., Dep., Amort./Cur. Mat. L /T/D	(42) 2.5	(28) 2.8
							1.6	1.2
	.3	.6					.6	.7
	.7	1.3				Fixed/Worth	1.1	1.3
	1.8	4.2					1.9	4.5
	.4	.7					.8	.8
	.9	2.3				Debt/Worth	1.5	1.8
	2.7	5.2					3.0	6.2
	38.0	43.2					34.6	31.7
	25.0	(18) 20.9				% Profit Before Taxes/Tangible Net Worth	(59) 15.5	(61) 21.9
	5.8	9.1					4.6	3.6
	21.4	12.3					12.7	13.6
	7.2	7.3				% Profit Before Taxes/Total Assets	6.7	6.8
	2.6	2.8					2.5	1.6
	16.1	8.7					9.7	9.9
	6.3	4.9				Sales/Net Fixed Assets	6.0	5.3
	4.0	3.2					2.9	3.2
	3.5	2.4					2.5	2.9
	2.8	2.0				Sales/Total Assets	1.9	1.9
	1.5	1.6					1.5	1.5
	1.5	2.0					2.5	2.3
(13)	2.6	(18) 4.7				% Depr., Dep., Amort./Sales	(61) 4.2	(64) 3.8
	6.8	7.2					5.6	6.0
							2.7	2.8
						% Officers', Directors', Owners' Comp/Sales	(23) 4.6	(27) 5.1
							6.9	7.7
7983M	40411M	198130M	146150M	290162M	847429M	Net Sales ($)	708288M	744684M
2091M	16802M	105583M	89290M	182609M	666188M	Total Assets ($)	387035M	389397M

M = $ thousand   MM = $ million
See Pages 1 through 15 for Explanation of Ratios and Data

Comparative Historical Data | Current Data Sorted By Sales

	3		5		8	# Postretirement Benefits	1	2	1	4		
						Type of Statement						
	12		16		19	Unqualified	1	2	3	4	9	
	22		17		6	Reviewed	1	1	1	3		
	15		10		12	Compiled	2	5	2	3		
	3		2		2	Tax Returns	1	1				
	9		10		15	Other	3	4		5	1	
	4/1/92- 3/31/93		4/1/93- 3/31/94		4/1/94- 3/31/95		21 (4/1-9/30/94)			33 (10/1/94-3/31/95)		
	ALL		ALL		ALL		0-1MM	1-3MM	3-5MM	5-10MM	10-25MM	25MM & OVER
	61		55		54	**NUMBER OF STATEMENTS**	5	12	8	12	8	9
	%		%		%	**ASSETS**	%	%	%	%	%	%
	6.3		6.7		6.7	Cash & Equivalents		8.1		4.4		
	23.8		20.5		21.9	Trade Receivables - (net)		30.9		20.4		
	14.1		13.1		11.9	Inventory		6.8		10.2		
	2.0		2.2		2.7	All Other Current		1.0		6.2		
	46.2		42.6		43.1	Total Current		46.8		41.3		
	39.3		39.2		42.0	Fixed Assets (net)		41.1		39.4		
	6.0		6.0		4.8	Intangibles (net)		5.4		4.8		
	8.5		12.2		10.1	All Other Non-Current		6.7		14.5		
	100.0		100.0		100.0	Total		100.0		100.0		
						LIABILITIES						
	6.4		7.6		4.4	Notes Payable-Short Term		8.2		4.9		
	7.1		5.3		6.2	Cur. Mat.-L /T/D		10.2		6.9		
	12.4		13.4		11.0	Trade Payables		16.9		9.7		
	.6		.8		.2	Income Taxes Payable		.0		.1		
	7.0		9.0		9.6	All Other Current		8.6		16.0		
	33.5		36.2		31.4	Total Current		43.9		37.7		
	23.2		23.7		24.2	Long Term Debt		25.1		22.2		
	1.5		1.4		1.2	Deferred Taxes		.0		2.0		
	4.2		3.6		1.5	All Other-Non-Current		1.0		.5		
	37.6		35.0		41.8	Net Worth		30.0		37.7		
	100.0		100.0		100.0	Total Liabilities & Net Worth		100.0		100.0		
						INCOME DATA						
	100.0		100.0		100.0	Net Sales		100.0		100.0		
						Gross Profit						
	95.7		95.3		93.5	Operating Expenses		95.5		96.0		
	4.3		4.7		6.5	Operating Profit		4.5		4.0		
	1.6		1.5		1.6	All Other Expenses (net)		1.5		.6		
	2.7		3.2		4.9	Profit Before Taxes		3.1		3.4		
						RATIOS						
	2.4		1.7		2.4	Current		1.5		1.9		
	1.5		1.3		1.4			1.1		1.2		
	1.0		.9		1.0			.6		.8		
	1.2		1.1		1.4	Quick		1.2		1.0		
(60)	.9		.7		.9			.8		.7		
	.6		.5		.6			.5		.3		
30	12.1	29	12.4	28	12.9	Sales/Receivables	27	13.3	21	17.8		
35	10.4	34	10.6	35	10.5		30	12.2	35	10.3		
40	9.1	41	9.0	43	8.5		45	8.2	40	9.2		
						Cost of Sales/Inventory						
						Cost of Sales/Payables						
	8.1		10.5		7.3	Sales/Working Capital		11.1		12.0		
	13.5		21.9		17.7			157.8		42.5		
	NM		-45.5		-100.6			-23.0		-39.7		
	5.2		4.9		7.4	EBIT/Interest		5.6		9.5		
(56)	2.6	(45)	2.9	(53)	3.4			2.1	(11)	2.9		
	1.2		1.6		2.1			.0		2.3		
	8.1		4.0		6.0	Net Profit + Depr., Dep., Amort./Cur. Mat. L/T/D						
(34)	2.6	(23)	1.6	(22)	3.1							
	.8		.9		1.2							
	.7		.6		.6	Fixed/Worth		.6		.4		
	1.1		1.1		1.2			1.4		1.4		
	3.3		2.3		2.5			5.0		5.9		
	.9		1.0		.6	Debt/Worth		.8		.8		
	1.9		1.8		1.7			2.9		2.4		
	5.0		5.5		4.4			5.5		7.8		
	41.8		36.6		33.1	% Profit Before Taxes/Tangible Net Worth		38.0		51.5		
(56)	14.7	(48)	17.2	(49)	21.1		(10)	22.0	(10)	31.4		
	7.4		8.3		9.0			-11.1		8.6		
	11.6		13.6		12.4	% Profit Before Taxes/Total Assets		16.6		13.0		
	5.3		5.8		7.2			6.9		7.2		
	1.2		2.5		2.6			-3.4		.2		
	11.9		9.0		10.1	Sales/Net Fixed Assets		23.1		12.3		
	5.4		5.4		5.0			11.0		6.3		
	3.9		3.5		3.1			2.5		3.5		
	3.2		2.6		2.7	Sales/Total Assets		4.7		2.6		
	2.1		2.0		2.0			3.2		2.1		
	1.6		1.5		1.4			1.5		1.8		
	2.5		2.2		2.0	% Depr., Dep., Amort./Sales		1.7				
(54)	3.7	(49)	4.0	(45)	3.8		(11)	2.6				
	5.6		5.2		5.9			7.5				
	2.8		3.3		3.6	% Officers', Directors', Owners' Comp/Sales						
(23)	5.8	(23)	5.6	(25)	5.0							
	7.5		9.1		7.5							
	892639M		1596162M		1530265M	Net Sales ($)	3147M	24164M	27454M	94718M	139492M	1241290M
	514264M		1054567M		1062563M	Total Assets ($)	1311M	10456M	20596M	44936M	77646M	907618M

M = $ thousand   MM = $ million
See Pages 1 through 15 for Explanation of Ratios and Data

Current Data Sorted By Assets							Comparative Historical Data	
3	4	2	4			**# Postretirement Benefits**		
						Type of Statement		
5	15	24	23	7	3	Unqualified		14
6	14	10	2			Reviewed		8
12	9	4		1		Compiled		4
6	8	1				Tax Returns		
6	19	18	5	4	3	Other		8
63 (4/1-9/30/94)			142 (10/1/94-3/31/95)				4/1/90-3/31/91 ALL	4/1/91-3/31/92 ALL
0-500M	500M-2MM	2-10MM	10-50MM	50-100MM	100-250MM			
35	65	57	30	12	6	**NUMBER OF STATEMENTS**		34
%	%	%	%	%	%	**ASSETS**	%	%
23.7	13.1	14.3	19.5	13.3		Cash & Equivalents	D	17.0
27.9	25.0	25.9	22.6	25.2		Trade Receivables - (net)	A	25.7
.5	4.7	7.4	7.9	3.7		Inventory	T	4.7
7.4	4.4	5.2	3.3	3.2		All Other Current	A	6.0
59.4	47.2	52.7	53.3	45.4		Total Current		53.4
20.4	27.8	22.6	28.8	27.7		Fixed Assets (net)	N	25.9
4.0	3.4	6.9	11.1	8.0		Intangibles (net)	O	7.7
16.2	21.7	17.8	6.9	19.0		All Other Non-Current	T	12.9
100.0	100.0	100.0	100.0	100.0		Total		100.0
						LIABILITIES	A	
8.4	7.7	8.6	9.1	4.5		Notes Payable-Short Term	V	7.0
3.2	4.0	3.0	3.6	.8		Cur. Mat. -L/T/D	A	5.9
12.4	9.7	14.6	12.4	12.4		Trade Payables	I	11.1
.5	.8	.2	.8	.5		Income Taxes Payable	L	2.3
19.5	15.5	14.2	13.2	9.9		All Other Current	A	18.2
44.0	37.6	40.6	39.0	28.2		Total Current	B	44.6
14.6	21.5	14.3	17.0	27.5		Long Term Debt	L	14.2
.7	1.3	1.2	.8	.1		Deferred Taxes	E	1.1
3.6	5.1	4.2	2.8	3.2		All Other-Non-Current		2.9
37.2	34.4	39.6	40.3	41.0		Net Worth		37.2
100.0	100.0	100.0	100.0	100.0		Total Liabilities & Net Worth		100.0
						INCOME DATA		
100.0	100.0	100.0	100.0	100.0		Net Sales		100.0
						Gross Profit		
84.4	85.4	87.4	92.8	84.4		Operating Expenses		88.9
15.6	14.6	12.6	7.2	15.6		Operating Profit		11.1
2.3	2.4	2.2	1.7	9.5		All Other Expenses (net)		.9
13.2	12.2	10.4	5.4	6.1		Profit Before Taxes		10.2
						RATIOS		
2.8	2.1	2.8	2.2	3.2				2.7
1.7	1.1	1.2	1.4	1.5		Current		1.2
1.0	.6	.8	1.0	1.2				.6
2.5	1.7	1.7	1.5	2.9				1.9
1.5	.9	.9	1.1	1.3		Quick		.8
.6	.4	.4	.6	.9				.5
0 UND	0 UND	1 292.9	16 23.0	28 13.1			6 64.0	
17 21.6	26 13.9	33 11.1	48 7.6	66 5.5		Sales/Receivables	28 12.9	
76 4.8	78 4.7	65 5.6	76 4.8	126 2.9			61 6.0	
						Cost of Sales/Inventory		
						Cost of Sales/Payables		
6.3	5.6	6.3	3.1	2.7				5.5
18.9	58.0	24.7	10.7	4.6		Sales/Working Capital		21.4
-117.3	-13.9	-22.6	NM	26.5				-32.5
(18) 18.4	(45) 13.0	(41) 25.5	(27) 20.1				(29) 17.5	
6.0	3.8	4.3	3.7			EBIT/Interest		8.0
2.1	1.7	1.9	2.1					1.2
	(14) 5.5	(12) 5.2	(14) 4.1				(14) 8.9	
	2.5	2.4	2.2			Net Profit + Depr., Dep.,		2.6
	.9	.7	1.0			Amort./Cur. Mat. L /T/D		1.7
.1	.1	.1	.2	.1				.2
.3	.6	.5	.9	1.2		Fixed/Worth		.9
19.0	8.9	1.8	2.1	1.9				2.9
.6	.7	.7	1.1	1.1				.8
1.3	1.9	2.1	2.1	1.8		Debt/Worth		2.0
24.0	10.7	5.6	6.4	3.5				11.1
(28) 107.9	(52) 63.9	(52) 68.9	(26) 42.2	20.0		% Profit Before Taxes/Tangible	(28) 62.3	
52.8	33.5	27.2	18.0	12.0		Net Worth		28.1
6.4	12.6	9.2	3.9	-.5				1.6
46.2	20.6	12.9	15.4	6.3		% Profit Before Taxes/Total		30.9
9.1	8.5	7.0	5.8	5.6		Assets		11.2
.0	1.8	1.7	1.9	.2				.4
130.3	69.9	66.9	25.9	22.5				32.1
29.7	14.3	13.8	8.2	3.8		Sales/Net Fixed Assets		13.2
9.2	2.0	3.1	2.5	1.5				6.0
5.6	2.8	3.1	2.2	1.3				5.0
3.4	1.5	2.1	1.3	.8		Sales/Total Assets		2.3
1.9	.8	.6	.4	.7				.8
(24) .5	(53) .8	(44) .9	(27) 1.5	1.1			(29) .6	
1.1	2.5	2.2	3.7	2.1		% Depr., Dep., Amort./Sales		1.8
3.5	4.3	5.4	7.2	5.5				4.6
(10) 5.3	(17) 3.6	(13) 2.1				% Officers', Directors',	(11) 19.3	
12.0	8.9	4.3				Owners' Comp/Sales		21.6
26.7	23.1	14.2						25.2
31330M	134247M	477939M	1539589M	925054M	1468983M	Net Sales ($)		393504M
8344M	68413M	253083M	686838M	852353M	1165200M	Total Assets ($)		406551M

M = $ thousand   MM = $ million
See Pages 1 through 15 for Explanation of Ratios and Data

Comparative Historical Data				Current Data Sorted By Sales					
4	3	13	# Postretirement Benefits	4	4		2		3
			Type of Statement						
38	32	77	Unqualified	10	14	8	12	13	20
28	21	32	Reviewed	9	9	2	5	6	1
18	33	26	Compiled	14	7	3	1	1	
4	9	15	Tax Returns	9	3	1	1	1	
36	44	55	Other	10	17	3	5	10	10
4/1/92-3/31/93 ALL	4/1/93-3/31/94 ALL	4/1/94-3/31/95 ALL		63 (4/1-9/30/94)			142 (10/1/94-3/31/95)		
				0-1MM	1-3MM	3-5MM	5-10MM	10-25MM	25MM & OVER
124	139	205	NUMBER OF STATEMENTS	52	50	17	24	31	31
%	%	%	ASSETS	%	%	%	%	%	%
13.5	13.9	16.2	Cash & Equivalents	14.0	17.3	18.9	12.7	20.9	14.4
24.8	24.0	25.0	Trade Receivables - (net)	16.7	24.8	21.7	32.9	35.1	24.7
4.3	5.0	5.1	Inventory	3.7	1.9	4.7	8.1	8.7	7.0
5.3	4.6	5.0	All Other Current	4.6	6.6	1.9	4.3	5.3	5.1
47.9	47.5	51.3	Total Current	39.0	50.6	47.2	58.0	70.0	51.3
30.8	29.0	25.4	Fixed Assets (net)	36.2	23.7	18.5	20.1	17.8	25.7
5.6	3.5	6.0	Intangibles (net)	5.6	4.9	3.9	7.5	3.9	10.5
15.8	20.0	17.3	All Other Non-Current	19.2	20.8	30.5	14.3	8.3	12.5
100.0	100.0	100.0	Total	100.0	100.0	100.0	100.0	100.0	100.0
			LIABILITIES						
11.6	7.5	7.9	Notes Payable-Short Term	7.2	6.9	12.7	12.9	7.4	4.4
4.5	5.2	3.3	Cur. Mat.-L./T/D	4.9	2.4	4.7	2.4	2.2	2.9
9.1	10.1	12.1	Trade Payables	6.5	9.9	15.0	15.1	19.4	13.8
.9	1.5	.5	Income Taxes Payable	.3	.4	2.0	.0	.3	1.0
15.0	16.6	15.1	All Other Current	10.5	15.8	30.1	15.6	14.5	13.6
41.0	40.8	38.8	Total Current	29.3	35.4	64.4	46.0	43.8	35.7
19.2	17.1	18.0	Long Term Debt	29.5	12.4	21.0	12.2	9.1	19.8
1.1	.8	1.0	Deferred Taxes	1.1	.8	1.5	.9	1.8	.3
4.6	6.0	4.1	All Other-Non-Current	6.8	3.1	1.2	5.3	3.0	2.8
34.0	35.3	38.0	Net Worth	33.2	48.3	11.9	35.6	42.2	41.4
100.0	100.0	100.0	Total Liabilities & Net Worth	100.0	100.0	100.0	100.0	100.0	100.0
			INCOME DATA						
100.0	100.0	100.0	Net Sales	100.0	100.0	100.0	100.0	100.0	100.0
			Gross Profit						
90.0	90.9	86.9	Operating Expenses	75.7	85.9	92.2	93.9	94.0	91.8
10.0	9.1	13.1	Operating Profit	24.3	14.1	7.8	6.1	6.0	8.2
2.9	2.6	2.7	All Other Expenses (net)	6.7	.7	4.8	1.9	.4	1.0
7.1	6.5	10.4	Profit Before Taxes	17.6	13.4	3.0	4.3	5.6	7.2
			RATIOS						
2.0	1.8	2.5		2.8	2.8	1.2	1.7	2.5	2.2
1.2	1.2	1.3	Current	1.4	1.4	.9	1.2	1.5	1.5
.6	.6	.8		.6	.7	.4	.9	1.1	1.0
1.7	1.5	1.9		2.3	2.4	1.0	1.5	2.2	1.8
1.0	1.0	1.0	Quick	1.0	1.0	.6	1.1	1.2	1.0
.4	.3	.5		.4	.4	.3	.6	.9	.7
4 98.7	1 483.0	1 322.9		0 UND	0 UND	0 UND	19 19.7	23 15.6	8 44.6
37 9.9	27 13.5	32 11.5	Sales/Receivables	17 21.5	21 17.6	8 45.8	56 6.5	49 7.5	33 10.9
69 5.3	62 5.9	76 4.8		76 4.8	78 4.7	63 5.8	73 5.0	81 4.5	81 4.5
			Cost of Sales/Inventory						
			Cost of Sales/Payables						
5.9	9.0	5.0		3.9	5.8	79.2	7.3	4.7	4.5
28.5	32.1	15.3	Sales/Working Capital	19.1	16.1	-15.8	13.2	12.7	10.5
-13.9	-22.3	-27.1		-14.4	-18.4	-8.2	-68.2	101.5	-999.8
10.0	11.1	14.5		11.7	31.2	5.2	24.3	24.6	10.7
(96) 3.9	(112) 3.5	(144) 4.7	EBIT/Interest	(30) 5.0	(32) 6.4	(14) 3.3	(19) 3.8	(23) 5.4	(26) 5.3
1.5	1.4	2.0		2.1	1.9	1.0	1.3	1.9	2.6
10.3	3.2	5.1			7.2			6.1	20.2
(31) 2.9	(39) 1.3	(48) 2.5	Net Profit + Depr., Dep., Amort./Cur. Mat. L/T/D		(10) 2.8		(10) 2.8	(13) 2.8	2.8
1.2	.6	1.0			1.8			1.6	1.1
.3	.2	.1		.1	.1	.3	.2	.1	.2
.9	.7	.6	Fixed/Worth	1.1	.5	2.4	.5	.2	1.2
5.0	1.8	2.6		27.4	1.6	-1.8	1.8	1.2	1.8
.9	.8	.8		.8	.4	1.5	.7	1.0	
3.0	2.1	1.9	Debt/Worth	2.1	1.2	8.7	3.2	1.2	1.9
10.7	6.7	6.3		121.0	4.1	-5.8	6.1	3.3	3.7
69.3	47.5	64.8		94.6	82.1	52.9	61.0	46.8	32.0
(107) 27.5	(121) 21.5	(175) 24.0	% Profit Before Taxes/Tangible Net Worth	(41) 33.9	(44) 32.9	(11) 20.1	(23) 25.8	(29) 22.4	(27) 19.8
8.9	7.2	8.0		7.0	4.7	3.9	4.5	9.5	11.5
17.5	15.6	18.2		30.1	31.1	8.6	10.7	16.4	14.8
6.4	5.9	6.9	% Profit Before Taxes/Total Assets	7.4	11.6	2.1	6.3	7.7	6.1
1.3	1.7	1.4		.5	.8	.0	2.0	1.8	3.5
26.6	29.9	62.7		31.9	94.2	64.3	62.1	84.1	30.4
9.6	13.1	12.8	Sales/Net Fixed Assets	4.7	17.6	29.4	10.2	25.7	8.7
3.1	3.6	3.0		1.3	2.2	12.6	3.0	8.5	2.8
3.1	3.5	3.0		2.4	3.2	4.5	3.1	3.6	2.9
1.9	2.2	1.7	Sales/Total Assets	.9	1.8	2.7	2.5	2.4	1.4
.7	1.0	.7		.3	.7	1.0	.8	1.8	.7
1.3	1.3	.9		.9	1.0	.8	.2	.5	1.1
(104) 2.9	(116) 2.6	(163) 2.2	% Depr., Dep., Amort./Sales	(39) 3.7	(38) 2.3	(15) 1.2	(23) 2.4	(21) 1.5	(27) 1.9
6.2	4.9	4.4		9.0	5.1	3.0	3.7	3.9	4.2
3.2	4.8	3.2		5.1	5.6				
(36) 7.0	(37) 10.4	(45) 7.9	% Officers', Directors', Owners' Comp/Sales	(11) 12.7	(13) 17.0				
15.6	25.0	17.6		22.9	24.0				
2439068M	2331069M	4577142M	Net Sales ($)	26418M	89966M	63025M	173554M	455743M	3768436M
1830481M	1594414M	3034231M	Total Assets ($)	47261M	132116M	93365M	220477M	262734M	2278278M

© Robert Morris Associates 1995

M = $ thousand   MM = $ million
See Pages 1 through 15 for Explanation of Ratios and Data

Current Data Sorted By Assets | Comparative Historical Data

0-500M	500M-2MM	2-10MM	10-50MM	50-100MM	100-250MM	# Postretirement Benefits / Type of Statement	4/1/90-3/31/91 ALL	4/1/91-3/31/92 ALL
	4	1	1			Unqualified	7	4
	7	6				Reviewed	8	11
11	19	4				Compiled	35	28
5	3	1				Tax Returns		3
2	5	9	1		1	Other	14	14
	19 (4/1-9/30/94)			61 (10/1/94-3/31/95)				
18	38	21	2	1		NUMBER OF STATEMENTS	64	60
%	%	%	%	%	%	**ASSETS**	%	%
9.3	4.5	4.9				Cash & Equivalents	6.4	6.5
14.3	4.6	10.3				Trade Receivables - (net)	11.4	9.5
28.0	21.2	18.0				Inventory	28.8	22.7
4.4	1.4	1.3				All Other Current	1.6	1.6
56.0	31.7	34.5				Total Current	48.3	40.4
36.8	61.1	55.4				Fixed Assets (net)	43.3	51.9
1.6	3.3	2.4				Intangibles (net)	.5	.8
5.6	3.9	7.6				All Other Non-Current	7.9	7.0
100.0	100.0	100.0				Total	100.0	100.0
						LIABILITIES		
10.3	10.8	9.6				Notes Payable-Short Term	16.8	11.8
3.3	6.9	7.8				Cur. Mat. -L/T/D	3.0	5.7
7.5	4.8	4.2				Trade Payables	5.3	4.8
.1	.3	.1				Income Taxes Payable	.6	1.1
9.9	8.2	6.3				All Other Current	11.8	10.1
31.1	31.0	28.0				Total Current	37.5	33.5
34.1	40.4	31.6				Long Term Debt	30.3	32.3
.0	.0	.3				Deferred Taxes	.0	.2
3.7	6.3	13.3				All Other-Non-Current	2.8	6.7
31.1	22.2	26.8				Net Worth	29.4	27.3
100.0	100.0	100.0				Total Liabilities & Net Worth	100.0	100.0
						INCOME DATA		
100.0	100.0	100.0				Net Sales	100.0	100.0
55.2	45.0	40.1				Gross Profit	48.1	50.0
50.3	39.7	30.9				Operating Expenses	42.7	42.6
4.9	5.4	9.2				Operating Profit	5.4	7.5
2.1	6.3	4.2				All Other Expenses (net)	3.5	4.5
2.8	-.9	4.9				Profit Before Taxes	1.9	3.0
						RATIOS		
4.4	1.4	1.8					2.7	1.7
1.6	.9	1.2				Current	1.2	1.2
1.1	.5	.8					.8	.8
1.6	.5	1.2					(63) .9	.7
.9	.2	.4				Quick	.4	.4
.4	.1	.2					.2	.1
6 57.7	3 118.6	5 69.4					7 49.0	5 74.3
19 18.9	12 30.2	17 21.9				Sales/Receivables	23 16.1	14 26.9
29 12.6	27 13.5	43 8.4					47 7.7	31 11.8
37 9.9	15 25.1	7 49.0					28 13.0	28 13.1
55 6.6	87 4.2	61 6.0				Cost of Sales/Inventory	89 4.1	76 4.8
192 1.9	183 2.0	146 2.5					215 1.7	152 2.4
0 UND	5 76.2	4 83.8					6 61.2	4 86.1
17 21.8	21 17.8	19 19.2				Cost of Sales/Payables	12 29.9	20 17.9
37 10.0	41 8.9	37 9.8					30 12.2	35 10.3
7.4	10.3	6.6					4.6	8.0
12.5	-206.4	15.0				Sales/Working Capital	19.6	24.8
46.6	-8.3	-21.2					-14.4	-15.0
2.1	1.9	2.2					3.1	3.3
(14) 1.7	(37) 1.3	(20) 1.3				EBIT/Interest	(57) 1.3	(55) 1.4
1.1	.6	.9					.7	1.0
	2.5						9.2	2.6
	(10) 1.1					Net Profit + Depr., Dep., Amort./Cur. Mat. L /T/D	(22) 1.7	(25) 1.7
	.1						.2	1.1
.5	2.2	1.1					.4	.9
1.7	4.3	1.9				Fixed/Worth	1.4	1.9
NM	6.8	15.7					7.6	23.7
1.1	2.6	1.7					1.0	1.1
3.2	5.0	3.5				Debt/Worth	3.2	3.2
NM	9.3	19.4					9.8	25.8
46.0	30.0	22.6					32.6	49.3
(14) 10.2	(35) 10.4	(17) 9.0				% Profit Before Taxes/Tangible Net Worth	(55) 7.0	(50) 16.8
1.4	-16.2	.1					-3.8	1.6
7.8	4.3	5.4					9.3	10.0
3.1	1.7	2.1				% Profit Before Taxes/Total Assets	1.5	2.7
.4	-2.0	-.0					-2.2	-.1
14.7	6.2	5.8					11.4	6.3
9.2	1.6	1.5				Sales/Net Fixed Assets	3.2	3.3
3.2	.8	.7					1.3	1.1
3.5	2.3	1.4					1.9	2.0
2.1	1.2	.9				Sales/Total Assets	1.3	1.2
1.1	.6	.6					.7	.8
1.4	2.5	2.5					1.9	2.4
(16) 2.7	(36) 5.9	(17) 5.9				% Depr., Dep., Amort./Sales	(58) 4.1	(59) 4.5
6.5	9.8	8.8					8.3	7.9
	2.0						2.4	2.0
	(17) 4.7					% Officers', Directors', Owners' Comp/Sales	(28) 6.2	(30) 4.2
	8.0						9.0	9.7
10588M	49809M	66489M	116628M	32425M		Net Sales ($)	123270M	136965M
4521M	39706M	64629M	63210M	82350M		Total Assets ($)	101929M	108207M

M = $ thousand   MM = $ million
See Pages 1 through 15 for Explanation of Ratios and Data

Comparative Historical Data   Current Data Sorted By Sales

1	1	2	# Postretirement Benefits	1	1				
			Type of Statement						
6	6	6	Unqualified	1	2	2			1
10	19	13	Reviewed	2	8	2	1		
26	33	34	Compiled	20	13		1		
6	7	9	Tax Returns	5	3	1			
15	13	18	Other	3	8	2	3	1	1
4/1/92-3/31/93	4/1/93-3/31/94	4/1/94-3/31/95		19 (4/1-9/30/94)		61 (10/1/94-3/31/95)			
ALL	ALL	ALL		0-1MM	1-3MM	3-5MM	5-10MM	10-25MM	25MM & OVER
63	78	80	**NUMBER OF STATEMENTS**	31	34	7	5	1	2
%	%	%	**ASSETS**	%	%	%	%	%	%
5.7	4.3	5.8	Cash & Equivalents	4.1	6.6				
8.6	9.2	8.6	Trade Receivables - (net)	8.4	6.4				
24.0	21.7	21.7	Inventory	18.9	22.6				
.4	2.6	2.0	All Other Current	3.0	1.9				
38.7	37.8	38.0	Total Current	34.4	37.5				
51.6	51.3	53.8	Fixed Assets (net)	58.1	54.3				
2.7	3.1	2.6	Intangibles (net)	2.5	1.7				
7.0	7.8	5.6	All Other Non-Current	5.1	6.5				
100.0	100.0	100.0	Total	100.0	100.0				
			LIABILITIES						
12.5	13.4	10.0	Notes Payable-Short Term	7.5	11.9				
6.1	5.4	6.5	Cur. Mat.-L /T/D	6.2	6.5				
3.8	4.5	5.1	Trade Payables	4.2	5.8				
.1	.4	.2	Income Taxes Payable	.2	.3				
10.3	11.3	8.1	All Other Current	7.3	6.6				
32.9	35.0	29.9	Total Current	25.3	31.0				
38.2	32.2	36.3	Long Term Debt	39.5	40.6				
.2	.2	.1	Deferred Taxes	.0	.1				
7.1	6.4	8.0	All Other-Non-Current	7.4	6.5				
21.6	26.2	25.7	Net Worth	27.7	21.8				
100.0	100.0	100.0	Total Liabilities & Net Worth	100.0	100.0				
			INCOME DATA						
100.0	100.0	100.0	Net Sales	100.0	100.0				
47.5	46.2	45.5	Gross Profit	58.8	42.5				
40.7	40.9	39.0	Operating Expenses	48.2	38.9				
6.8	5.3	6.5	Operating Profit	10.6	3.6				
4.3	4.7	4.8	All Other Expenses (net)	6.8	3.9				
2.5	.5	1.8	Profit Before Taxes	3.8	−.3				
			RATIOS						
2.0	1.7	1.8		1.8	1.5				
1.1	1.1	1.1	Current	1.1	1.1				
.6	.6	.7		.7	.8				
1.2	.7	.9		.9	.6				
.3	.3	.4	Quick	.4	.3				
.1	.1	.2		.2	.1				
3 120.5	4 81.8	4 84.5		4 87.3	5 79.7				
11 33.6	16 22.8	16 23.2	Sales/Receivables	26 14.2	10 34.9				
33 11.1	37 9.8	34 10.7		42 8.6	23 16.0				
34 10.7	38 9.7	24 15.1		37 10.0	21 17.4				
89 4.1	81 4.5	64 5.7	Cost of Sales/Inventory	65 5.6	63 5.8				
183 2.0	140 2.6	166 2.2		215 1.7	152 2.4				
4 95.8	4 89.4	5 74.6		8 47.0	4 93.7				
11 33.5	12 30.7	17 21.2	Cost of Sales/Payables	23 15.9	14 26.6				
31 11.7	24 15.4	40 9.1		66 5.5	40 9.1				
6.5	6.9	8.5		7.6	9.8				
28.5	42.5	41.1	Sales/Working Capital	46.6	66.0				
−7.6	−7.8	−20.9		−8.4	−21.4				
2.7	2.2	2.0		2.0	1.6				
(59) 1.4	(66) 1.3	(72) 1.3	EBIT/Interest	(26) 1.3	(33) 1.3				
.8	.5	.9		.9	.9				
3.0	2.0	2.2	Net Profit + Depr., Dep.,						
(20) 1.8	(23) 1.1	(16) 1.1	Amort./Cur. Mat. L/T/D						
.6	.3	.2							
.9	.7	1.1		1.2	1.5				
3.4	2.4	3.6	Fixed/Worth	3.8	3.6				
20.3	19.9	9.3		11.6	14.8				
1.5	1.4	1.9		1.9	2.3				
4.4	3.7	4.3	Debt/Worth	4.3	4.7				
20.6	25.4	14.9		16.8	25.6				
27.9	29.2	28.0	% Profit Before Taxes/Tangible	20.0	29.0				
(49) 9.5	(63) 3.8	(68) 9.7	Net Worth	(26) 7.1	(29) 12.8				
−2.6	−7.8	−.7		−4.0	−.5				
6.4	5.0	5.1	% Profit Before Taxes/Total	5.9	4.3				
1.7	.8	1.9	Assets	1.8	1.9				
−1.3	−2.9	−.6		−1.6	−.4				
7.2	6.8	8.8		8.9	8.6				
1.8	2.5	2.4	Sales/Net Fixed Assets	1.0	2.4				
.9	.9	.9		.4	1.1				
1.8	1.7	2.2		2.0	2.5				
1.1	1.2	1.2	Sales/Total Assets	.8	1.2				
.6	.7	.6		.4	.7				
2.0	2.2	2.3		2.9	2.4				
(60) 5.3	(73) 4.7	(71) 5.2	% Depr., Dep., Amort./Sales	(29) 6.4	(29) 5.8				
12.0	9.8	9.4		15.7	8.7				
2.2	2.1	2.3	% Officers', Directors',	2.4	2.8				
(27) 6.1	(30) 4.0	(29) 4.6	Owners' Comp/Sales	(13) 4.6	(12) 5.6				
9.1	9.1	8.9		12.7	7.1				
161542M	162709M	275939M	Net Sales ($)	15513M	53841M	24728M	32804M	23491M	125562M
175220M	150991M	254416M	Total Assets ($)	23308M	49008M	14918M	21622M	17074M	128486M

M = $ thousand   MM = $ million
See Pages 1 through 15 for Explanation of Ratios and Data

Current Data Sorted By Assets / Comparative Historical Data

0-500M	500M-2MM	2-10MM	10-50MM	50-100MM	100-250MM	# Postretirement Benefits / Type of Statement	4/1/90-3/31/91 ALL	4/1/91-3/31/92 ALL
	2	1	1			# Postretirement Benefits		
		6	6		1	Unqualified	12	12
2	14	7	1			Reviewed	12	16
8	7	2				Compiled	13	22
1	1					Tax Returns		2
3	6	6	2		1	Other	6	11
	30 (4/1-9/30/94)		44 (10/1/94-3/31/95)					
14	28	21	9		2	NUMBER OF STATEMENTS	43	63
%	%	%	%	%	%	**ASSETS**	%	%
8.9	6.0	1.5				Cash & Equivalents	7.2	6.7
31.3	36.7	35.4				Trade Receivables - (net)	33.4	36.2
16.8	15.6	11.4				Inventory	10.2	13.1
.0	.7	.9				All Other Current	1.1	.8
56.9	58.9	49.2				Total Current	52.0	56.8
32.8	33.5	38.2				Fixed Assets (net)	37.5	33.9
3.1	3.8	1.0				Intangibles (net)	2.1	1.5
7.1	3.9	11.5				All Other Non-Current	8.3	7.9
100.0	100.0	100.0				Total	100.0	100.0
						LIABILITIES		
22.4	6.3	12.1				Notes Payable-Short Term	9.9	9.0
4.7	9.0	6.4				Cur. Mat. -L/T/D	7.9	8.0
7.9	14.1	12.9				Trade Payables	9.0	10.4
.1	.2	.1				Income Taxes Payable	1.3	.7
11.0	4.3	8.3				All Other Current	8.2	7.9
46.0	33.9	39.9				Total Current	36.4	36.0
18.3	26.4	20.3				Long Term Debt	20.4	18.4
.1	1.2	1.6				Deferred Taxes	1.7	.8
3.6	2.8	4.7				All Other-Non-Current	1.4	1.1
32.0	35.8	33.4				Net Worth	40.2	43.7
100.0	100.0	100.0				Total Liabilities & Net Worth	100.0	100.0
						INCOME DATA		
100.0	100.0	100.0				Net Sales	100.0	100.0
71.3	67.1	60.1				Gross Profit	67.4	66.5
67.7	60.2	52.0				Operating Expenses	56.3	57.2
3.6	7.0	8.2				Operating Profit	11.0	9.4
2.8	2.2	1.2				All Other Expenses (net)	2.2	2.6
.9	4.7	6.9				Profit Before Taxes	8.9	6.7
						RATIOS		
2.7	2.3	1.8					3.4	2.8
1.5	1.7	1.2				Current	1.4	1.7
.7	1.4	.9					1.0	1.2
2.0	1.8	1.1					2.2	2.4
1.3	1.3	.9				Quick	1.1	1.3
.5	.9	.8					.8	.7
0 UND	59 6.2	68 5.4					42 8.6	43 8.5
51 7.1	69 5.3	91 4.0				Sales/Receivables	79 4.6	68 5.4
81 4.5	89 4.1	122 3.0					114 3.2	96 3.8
35 10.5	40 9.1	0 UND					30 12.1	17 21.5
63 5.8	70 5.2	74 4.9				Cost of Sales/Inventory	63 5.8	68 5.4
130 2.8	130 2.8	126 2.9					104 3.5	126 2.9
0 UND	32 11.5	49 7.4					37 9.9	26 14.0
3 126.2	62 5.9	81 4.5				Cost of Sales/Payables	46 7.9	51 7.1
56 6.5	130 2.8	130 2.8					111 3.3	99 3.7
4.4	4.4	7.7					4.3	4.4
13.4	9.3	11.7				Sales/Working Capital	11.4	8.8
-51.1	14.2	-76.1					-372.0	22.1
(11) 2.4	(27) 8.7	(20) 6.7					(37) 8.9	(58) 9.3
1.2	2.7	3.3				EBIT/Interest	3.4	3.1
-1.1	1.9	1.5					1.4	1.4
	(15) 3.3	(13) 2.9				Net Profit + Depr., Dep.,	(21) 4.5	(32) 3.9
	1.4	1.7				Amort./Cur. Mat. L /T/D	1.8	1.7
	.9	1.1					1.0	1.0
.2	.5	.7					.5	.3
.7	.9	1.2				Fixed/Worth	1.1	.7
-3.5	4.1	1.8					2.2	2.0
.5	.8	1.5					.6	.4
1.7	2.1	2.6				Debt/Worth	2.3	1.8
-9.3	7.5	3.2					4.5	4.4
(10) 76.2	(22) 39.8	37.1				% Profit Before Taxes/Tangible	(41) 50.8	(60) 44.4
5.2	22.3	20.9				Net Worth	24.9	20.7
-17.0	10.5	13.2					11.7	9.4
17.7	13.6	13.2				% Profit Before Taxes/Total	21.7	17.5
2.3	7.1	7.9				Assets	12.5	8.1
-6.7	3.5	2.0					2.7	2.7
13.6	10.8	7.2					8.9	10.9
9.0	6.2	4.5				Sales/Net Fixed Assets	4.7	5.4
4.0	3.5	2.1					3.0	3.3
2.8	2.3	1.8					2.1	2.2
2.4	1.9	1.5				Sales/Total Assets	1.7	1.8
1.6	1.5	.9					1.2	1.3
(12) 3.6	2.4	3.1				% Depr., Dep., Amort./Sales	(39) 4.0	(56) 2.2
5.3	5.6	5.7					6.8	5.4
8.9	8.0	10.1					10.5	9.1
	(11) 3.5					% Officers', Directors',	(17) 4.5	(24) 1.9
	5.2					Owners' Comp/Sales	13.7	7.3
	10.3						24.9	14.7
8920M	52432M	122548M	169592M		149888M	Net Sales ($)	237127M	513992M
4039M	28427M	92587M	165593M		415185M	Total Assets ($)	275152M	339630M

M = $ thousand   MM = $ million
See Pages 1 through 15 for Explanation of Ratios and Data

Comparative Historical Data			# Postretirement Benefits	Current Data Sorted By Sales					
	8	4	Type of Statement	2		1	1		
14	12	13	Unqualified			1	4	5	3
21	22	24	Reviewed	4	11	5	4		
21	18	17	Compiled	7	9	1			
7	3	2	Tax Returns	2					
18	13	18	Other	4	5	4	1	3	1
4/1/92-3/31/93 ALL	4/1/93-3/31/94 ALL	4/1/94-3/31/95 ALL		30 (4/1-9/30/94)			44 (10/1/94-3/31/95)		
				0-1MM	1-3MM	3-5MM	5-10MM	10-25MM	25MM & OVER
81	68	74	NUMBER OF STATEMENTS	17	25	11	9	8	4

ASSETS

%	%	%		%	%	%	%	%	%
6.0	7.4	4.7	Cash & Equivalents	8.9	5.4	1.6			
34.2	35.9	32.9	Trade Receivables - (net)	29.0	35.7	37.8			
12.9	13.5	13.4	Inventory	16.0	14.2	11.8			
2.2	1.3	.7	All Other Current	.2	.6	.6			
55.2	58.1	51.6	Total Current	54.1	56.0	51.9			
36.0	30.4	38.1	Fixed Assets (net)	36.1	34.8	35.2			
1.5	1.6	3.5	Intangibles (net)	2.2	4.6	.1			
7.3	9.9	6.8	All Other Non-Current	7.5	4.5	12.7			
100.0	100.0	100.0	Total	100.0	100.0	100.0			

LIABILITIES

9.8	9.3	11.0	Notes Payable-Short Term	20.0	7.4	6.8			
8.3	7.2	7.2	Cur. Mat.-L /T/D	5.0	8.9	7.1			
8.5	12.3	11.7	Trade Payables	7.4	12.6	18.6			
.3	.6	.1	Income Taxes Payable	.1	.2	.0			
9.0	4.4	7.2	All Other Current	9.0	4.5	8.6			
35.9	33.8	37.3	Total Current	41.5	33.6	41.1			
19.4	20.6	25.4	Long Term Debt	21.6	25.9	21.6			
1.7	2.1	1.3	Deferred Taxes	.1	1.4	2.4			
3.0	3.1	3.1	All Other-Non-Current	2.7	3.1	7.9			
40.0	40.4	32.8	Net Worth	34.1	36.0	27.0			
100.0	100.0	100.0	Total Liabilities & Net Worth	100.0	100.0	100.0			

INCOME DATA

100.0	100.0	100.0	Net Sales	100.0	100.0	100.0			
64.3	65.1	64.9	Gross Profit	73.1	69.0	53.3			
52.8	58.2	58.2	Operating Expenses	66.3	63.5	44.5			
11.5	6.9	6.8	Operating Profit	6.8	5.6	8.8			
2.4	1.6	2.5	All Other Expenses (net)	3.3	2.1	.7			
9.2	5.4	4.3	Profit Before Taxes	3.5	3.5	8.1			

RATIOS

2.3	2.6	2.0	Current	2.8	2.3	1.8			
1.4	1.7	1.4		1.5	1.8	1.3			
1.1	1.2	1.0		.6	1.4	.9			
1.6	2.1	1.5	Quick	2.1	1.8	1.1			
1.1	1.2	1.1		1.1	1.4	.9			
.8	.9	.7		.3	1.0	.8			

Sales/Receivables												
33	11.0	46	8.0	57	6.4	33	11.2	57	6.4	68	5.4
69	5.3	74	4.9	73	5.0	57	6.4	66	5.5	81	4.5
99	3.7	96	3.8	96	3.8	85	4.3	89	4.1	135	2.7

Cost of Sales/Inventory												
4	89.8	16	22.9	35	10.5	34	10.6	38	9.5	0	UND
53	6.9	57	6.4	70	5.2	63	5.8	68	5.4	41	8.8
96	3.8	114	3.2	118	3.1	192	1.9	122	3.0	83	4.4

Cost of Sales/Payables												
8	44.6	34	10.8	29	12.6	0	UND	30	12.0	46	7.9
42	8.7	56	6.5	58	6.3	32	11.5	59	6.2	81	4.5
79	4.6	101	3.6	118	3.1	174	2.1	126	2.9	130	2.8

5.1	5.4	5.4	Sales/Working Capital	3.8	4.5	7.9			
13.0	8.8	11.7		12.5	9.4	14.3			
68.9	30.5	78.9		-38.9	14.3	-33.9			

	7.7		8.0		4.7	EBIT/Interest		3.1		7.9		8.4
(72)	4.3	(61)	3.4	(69)	2.7		(14)	1.4	(24)	2.7	(10)	3.4
	2.0		1.4		1.4			-.8		1.5		1.8

	3.6		2.9		3.4	Net Profit + Depr., Dep., Amort./Cur. Mat. L/T/D				3.6		
(42)	1.7	(30)	1.7	(36)	1.7				(11)	1.7		
	.9		.5		1.1					.9		

.4	.4	.6	Fixed/Worth	.2	.6	.8			
1.0	.9	1.1		.7	.9	1.5			
1.8	1.5	4.3		8.2	NM	2.3			

.8	.8	1.0	Debt/Worth	.6	.8	1.4			
1.7	1.6	2.3		2.0	2.1	3.0			
3.8	3.0	6.7		15.1	NM	5.2			

	73.9		41.5		41.0	% Profit Before Taxes/Tangible Net Worth		63.7		27.5		48.4
(79)	31.8	(63)	22.7	(61)	21.4		(14)	21.3	(19)	14.1	(10)	30.6
	11.2		8.4		10.1			-1.5		7.2		17.0

27.8	20.7	12.4	% Profit Before Taxes/Total Assets	21.7	13.2	13.8			
11.6	8.1	6.8		4.6	6.8	11.2			
4.7	2.0	1.9		-4.5	2.3	3.6			

14.6	15.6	9.5	Sales/Net Fixed Assets	13.2	9.6	10.6			
5.7	6.1	5.3		7.7	6.1	4.5			
3.0	3.2	2.3		2.9	3.6	2.1			

2.4	2.4	2.3	Sales/Total Assets	2.6	2.5	2.0			
1.9	1.8	1.7		1.7	1.9	1.5			
1.3	1.3	1.1		1.2	1.6	1.0			

	2.6		2.1		2.7	% Depr., Dep., Amort./Sales		3.6		2.6		1.0
(72)	5.4	(64)	4.7	(70)	6.0		(16)	5.7	(24)	5.9		4.6
	9.1		8.7		8.8			9.6		7.8		10.3

	4.5		5.5		3.7	% Officers', Directors', Owners' Comp/Sales				4.1		
(43)	10.7	(38)	9.5	(21)	5.2				(10)	8.6		
	17.4		15.3		11.0					12.0		

492515M	503624M	503380M	Net Sales ($)	10229M	45015M	45343M	69410M	115662M	217721M
253374M	238280M	705831M	Total Assets ($)	7950M	25405M	38041M	59415M	114355M	460665M

M = $ thousand   MM = $ million
See Pages 1 through 15 for Explanation of Ratios and Data

	Current Data Sorted By Assets							Comparative Historical Data	
	5	2	7	3	1		# Postretirement Benefits		
							Type of Statement		
	3	8	29	18	4	4	Unqualified	44	48
	5	15	11	1			Reviewed	30	32
	16	16	7				Compiled	64	44
	7	4					Tax Returns		2
	12	19	23	6	3	1	Other	41	45
	73 (4/1-9/30/94)			139 (10/1/94-3/31/95)				4/1/90-3/31/91 ALL	4/1/91-3/31/92 ALL
	0-500M	500M-2MM	2-10MM	10-50MM	50-100MM	100-250MM			
NUMBER OF STATEMENTS	43	62	70	25	7	5		179	171
ASSETS	%	%	%	%	%	%		%	%
Cash & Equivalents	16.3	10.4	11.8	18.3				12.5	13.8
Trade Receivables - (net)	19.0	29.8	27.4	18.5				28.8	29.1
Inventory	4.5	1.6	3.8	1.7				3.4	2.5
All Other Current	2.9	3.5	2.6	4.0				2.2	2.9
Total Current	42.7	45.3	45.6	42.5				46.9	48.2
Fixed Assets (net)	40.8	42.5	41.0	32.6				41.1	37.8
Intangibles (net)	5.1	4.7	3.2	13.6				3.8	4.1
All Other Non-Current	11.3	7.6	10.3	11.4				8.2	9.8
Total	100.0	100.0	100.0	100.0				100.0	100.0
LIABILITIES									
Notes Payable-Short Term	17.7	7.3	4.3	1.3				9.9	7.1
Cur. Mat. -L/T/D	10.1	7.5	7.5	6.6				7.7	6.9
Trade Payables	4.8	8.8	9.9	6.2				7.4	8.1
Income Taxes Payable	.9	.2	1.3	.2				.7	.8
All Other Current	12.1	11.3	10.2	12.5				11.1	13.0
Total Current	45.5	35.0	33.2	26.8				36.9	35.8
Long Term Debt	14.4	25.3	22.8	24.5				23.4	21.9
Deferred Taxes	.0	1.3	1.7	.7				.8	1.0
All Other-Non-Current	3.3	2.1	1.4	4.5				3.2	3.7
Net Worth	36.7	36.3	40.8	43.5				35.7	37.5
Total Liabilities & Net Worth	100.0	100.0	100.0	100.0				100.0	100.0
INCOME DATA									
Net Sales	100.0	100.0	100.0	100.0				100.0	100.0
Gross Profit									
Operating Expenses	96.8	90.4	89.3	92.6				89.7	88.8
Operating Profit	3.2	9.6	10.7	7.4				10.3	11.2
All Other Expenses (net)	1.2	2.2	2.4	3.7				2.3	2.8
Profit Before Taxes	2.1	7.4	8.3	3.7				8.1	8.5
RATIOS									
Current	1.9	2.9	2.6	2.2				2.4	2.6
	1.1	1.2	1.6	1.4				1.4	1.5
	.6	.7	.9	1.0				.8	.9
Quick	1.5	2.7	2.0	1.8				2.2	2.5
	(42) .9	1.2	1.3	1.2				1.2	1.3
	.5	.6	.7	.8				.7	.8
Sales/Receivables	0 UND	0 UND	40 9.1	27 13.7				26 14.3	34 10.6
	0 UND	47 7.8	50 7.3	42 8.7				53 6.9	53 6.9
	50 7.3	66 5.5	65 5.6	69 5.3				70 5.2	73 5.0
Cost of Sales/Inventory									
Cost of Sales/Payables									
Sales/Working Capital	12.4	6.8	5.2	4.4				6.4	6.0
	999.8	35.0	14.2	7.3				21.5	18.7
	-23.7	-21.4	-35.1	NM				-53.0	-49.6
EBIT/Interest	(38) 8.9	(55) 13.7	(63) 13.3	(17) 9.0				(159) 9.9	(147) 11.4
	3.2	4.3	4.6	3.9				3.9	4.6
	.6	1.5	2.0	1.4				1.1	1.2
Net Profit + Depr., Dep., Amort./Cur. Mat. L /T/D		(10) 13.4	(26) 4.0	(16) 4.1				(78) 6.5	(64) 5.5
		1.1	2.5	1.7				2.8	1.6
		.7	1.3	.5				1.3	.7
Fixed/Worth	.4	.5	.5	.4				.5	.4
	1.1	1.3	.9	.9				1.2	1.1
	-23.0	8.6	2.6	NM				3.4	3.2
Debt/Worth	.5	.6	.7	.6				1.0	.7
	1.6	2.2	1.4	1.7				1.9	1.9
	-34.2	8.4	3.5	NM				5.9	7.9
% Profit Before Taxes/Tangible Net Worth	(32) 49.6	(53) 70.1	(60) 56.9	(19) 24.3				(157) 79.9	(148) 72.8
	16.2	27.2	28.1	13.6				33.5	27.8
	-2.1	8.8	10.3	.0				3.9	4.8
% Profit Before Taxes/Total Assets	25.5	21.0	20.3	9.7				30.2	24.7
	8.0	12.1	8.9	7.5				9.5	8.1
	-1.6	1.6	3.4	-.2				.0	.8
Sales/Net Fixed Assets	23.1	21.0	12.1	9.5				17.3	18.6
	15.9	9.2	4.7	5.3				6.7	6.6
	6.2	3.3	2.3	2.1				3.2	3.0
Sales/Total Assets	8.1	3.7	2.7	1.8				3.8	3.1
	3.6	2.8	1.8	1.1				2.2	2.3
	2.5	1.6	1.1	.7				1.3	1.2
% Depr., Dep., Amort./Sales	(39) 1.3	(57) 2.2	(65) 3.0	(22) 2.8				(160) 1.8	(147) 2.4
	2.6	3.7	4.3	5.7				4.0	3.9
	6.5	4.6	11.1	10.6				6.9	7.4
% Officers', Directors', Owners' Comp/Sales	(22) 5.2	(27) 5.2	(16) 3.6					(58) 7.8	(41) 5.8
	16.1	12.0	7.2					14.4	12.1
	24.1	19.6	17.2					28.2	23.6
Net Sales ($)	61614M	211728M	698116M	666504M	545758M	782056M		1940917M	2646969M
Total Assets ($)	10238M	70153M	320501M	546044M	463798M	951472M		1515278M	2285072M

© Robert Morris Associates 1995

M = $ thousand   MM = $ million
See Pages 1 through 15 for Explanation of Ratios and Data

Comparative Historical Data				Current Data Sorted By Sales					
6	9	18	# Postretirement Benefits	1	5	3	1	4	4
			Type of Statement						
64	52	66	Unqualified	2	12	2	15	17	18
23	23	32	Reviewed	5	8	7	6	6	
44	39	39	Compiled	9	18	3	6	3	
4	6	11	Tax Returns	4	4		2	1	
53	53	64	Other	8	17	12	9	9	9
4/1/92-3/31/93 ALL	4/1/93-3/31/94 ALL	4/1/94-3/31/95 ALL		73 (4/1-9/30/94)			139 (10/1/94-3/31/95)		
				0-1MM	1-3MM	3-5MM	5-10MM	10-25MM	25MM & OVER
188	173	212	NUMBER OF STATEMENTS	28	59	24	38	36	27
%	%	%	ASSETS	%	%	%	%	%	%
12.5	11.9	13.0	Cash & Equivalents	10.1	12.1	11.1	15.1	16.0	12.6
27.9	29.6	25.1	Trade Receivables - (net)	27.2	20.0	26.3	30.7	25.9	23.7
4.7	3.8	3.1	Inventory	5.3	1.9	2.0	1.5	4.5	5.0
2.4	2.9	3.1	All Other Current	2.3	2.1	1.3	3.4	4.3	5.7
47.4	48.1	44.3	Total Current	44.9	36.0	40.7	50.8	50.7	47.0
36.9	37.2	40.4	Fixed Assets (net)	40.2	51.2	41.8	37.2	29.3	35.2
5.2	4.5	5.3	Intangibles (net)	6.3	2.5	6.9	2.2	10.2	7.2
10.5	10.2	9.9	All Other Non-Current	8.6	10.2	10.6	9.8	9.8	10.5
100.0	100.0	100.0	Total	100.0	100.0	100.0	100.0	100.0	100.0
			LIABILITIES						
6.4	6.8	7.4	Notes Payable-Short Term	19.0	5.0	10.7	6.7	4.2	2.8
6.5	7.9	7.5	Cur. Mat.-L./T/D	5.6	10.2	10.4	6.7	7.1	2.9
9.8	8.9	7.8	Trade Payables	5.5	5.7	7.8	7.0	11.0	11.2
.8	.8	.8	Income Taxes Payable	.6	.6	.2	1.1	1.2	.9
13.5	11.1	11.1	All Other Current	6.3	8.7	16.1	13.0	12.9	11.9
37.0	35.4	34.6	Total Current	37.0	30.3	45.1	34.6	36.4	29.7
20.7	19.2	21.9	Long Term Debt	17.3	29.4	19.9	22.5	17.0	17.6
1.1	1.4	1.1	Deferred Taxes	.0	.3	1.7	2.3	1.7	1.2
2.9	3.2	2.5	All Other-Non-Current	3.8	.7	2.9	2.4	4.2	2.5
38.4	40.9	39.9	Net Worth	42.0	39.3	30.4	38.2	40.7	48.9
100.0	100.0	100.0	Total Liabilities & Net Worth	100.0	100.0	100.0	100.0	100.0	100.0
			INCOME DATA						
100.0	100.0	100.0	Net Sales	100.0	100.0	100.0	100.0	100.0	100.0
			Gross Profit						
91.3	91.8	91.9	Operating Expenses	94.6	88.0	92.5	91.4	93.5	95.5
8.7	8.2	8.1	Operating Profit	5.4	12.1	7.5	8.6	6.5	4.5
1.6	1.2	2.1	All Other Expenses (net)	4.1	3.1	.6	2.9	.8	-.1
7.2	6.9	6.0	Profit Before Taxes	1.3	9.0	6.9	5.7	5.8	4.6
			RATIOS						
2.2	2.6	2.4		2.5	2.8	1.5	2.2	2.5	2.4
1.3	1.5	1.3	Current	1.1	1.2	1.1	1.5	1.5	1.7
.8	.9	.8		.7	.6	.5	.9	.9	1.1
2.0	2.2	2.0		1.7	2.7	1.5	2.0	1.9	1.9
(187) 1.1	(172) 1.3	(211) 1.2	Quick	.8	(58) 1.1	1.0	1.4	1.2	1.3
.7	.8	.7		.6	.5	.5	.9	.7	.9
27 13.4	38 9.6	23 15.9		0 UND	0 UND	0 UND	36 10.2	32 11.3	33 11.1
51 7.1	53 6.9	47 7.8	Sales/Receivables	44 8.3	45 8.2	49 7.4	49 7.5	44 8.3	55 6.6
72 5.1	73 5.0	66 5.5		74 4.9	69 5.3	64 5.7	78 4.7	52 7.0	74 4.9
			Cost of Sales/Inventory						
			Cost of Sales/Payables						
7.1	5.9	5.6		8.6	5.1	12.6	5.7	5.5	4.8
20.2	16.1	26.7	Sales/Working Capital	57.1	33.1	190.1	14.7	15.7	9.0
-53.8	-49.0	-30.9		-17.2	-18.4	-24.0	-168.6	-35.0	39.0
9.7	16.7	12.0		6.0	12.4	12.6	13.6	19.4	9.9
(157) 3.4	(149) 4.4	(183) 4.1	EBIT/Interest	(25) 2.7	(56) 3.6	(20) 6.1	(31) 4.4	(31) 4.7	(20) 4.5
1.4	1.1	1.4		-1.5	1.1	1.9	1.1	2.5	1.4
4.4	4.8	4.3	Net Profit + Depr., Dep.,				3.0	3.8	5.6
(74) 1.8	(41) 1.4	(61) 1.7	Amort./Cur. Mat. L/T/D			(15) 1.6	(15) 1.6	(13) 3.5	
1.1	.2	.9					-.1	1.3	1.4
.6	.4	.5		.4	.5	.7	.5	.4	.5
1.0	1.0	1.0	Fixed/Worth	1.2	1.4	1.2	.8	.7	.8
2.6	2.4	4.2		NM	4.8	4.2	2.1	UND	2.3
.8	.6	.6		.4	.5	.8	.7	.8	.4
1.7	1.4	1.6	Debt/Worth	1.3	1.9	2.0	1.4	1.8	1.4
5.3	5.3	5.8		NM	6.9	6.6	4.0	UND	3.8
63.0	60.6	49.6	% Profit Before Taxes/Tangible	32.7	65.8	149.0	44.5	72.1	31.3
(163) 29.6	(148) 22.5	(176) 23.2	Net Worth	(21) 11.8	(50) 23.9	(19) 43.6	(34) 21.5	(28) 26.5	(24) 12.4
6.8	2.8	5.5		-13.9	8.5	12.8	1.8	10.1	2.7
21.8	22.1	19.9	% Profit Before Taxes/Total	20.9	21.0	34.9	20.2	18.5	10.1
8.4	7.0	8.4	Assets	4.8	11.8	15.3	5.6	8.5	6.6
1.8	.3	.7		-3.9	.3	3.0	.4	3.3	.2
16.4	16.0	16.5		20.3	12.9	20.4	18.4	16.0	10.2
6.9	6.5	6.7	Sales/Net Fixed Assets	9.1	4.5	8.1	7.0	9.8	3.6
2.9	3.0	2.8		2.6	2.2	4.2	3.2	5.3	2.1
3.4	3.1	3.4		3.6	3.5	3.9	3.5	3.5	2.2
2.2	1.9	2.2	Sales/Total Assets	2.5	2.1	3.0	2.3	2.4	1.2
1.2	1.1	1.2		1.1	1.0	1.8	1.5	1.5	.9
1.7	1.9	2.3		1.3	2.9	1.7	2.3	2.2	3.5
(167) 3.8	(144) 3.8	(192) 4.0	% Depr., Dep., Amort./Sales	(26) 3.3	(56) 4.2	(23) 4.1	(33) 3.2	(33) 3.6	(21) 4.8
6.6	6.4	7.4		8.2	11.8	7.1	6.8	4.4	7.1
5.8	4.7	5.0	% Officers', Directors',	6.9	5.2				
(54) 15.1	(56) 10.9	(68) 12.5	Owners' Comp/Sales	(16) 16.9	(26) 12.0				
31.4	21.9	20.9		20.9	20.3				
2850287M	2638891M	2965776M	Net Sales ($)	16427M	106803M	98735M	255663M	586733M	1901415M
2619902M	2169124M	2362206M	Total Assets ($)	9792M	79988M	45170M	161930M	327764M	1737562M

M = $ thousand   MM = $ million
See Pages 1 through 15 for Explanation of Ratios and Data

Current Data Sorted By Assets   Comparative Historical Data

0-500M	500M-2MM	2-10MM	10-50MM	50-100MM	100-250MM		4/1/90-3/31/91 ALL	4/1/91-3/31/92 ALL
						# Postretirement Benefits		
		1				Type of Statement		
2	2	13	2	1	1	Unqualified		
1	1	1				Reviewed		
						Compiled		
						Tax Returns		
	5	3	2		1	Other		
	28 (4/1-9/30/94)			7 (10/1/94-3/31/95)				
3	8	17	4	1	2	NUMBER OF STATEMENTS		
%	%	%	%	%	%	**ASSETS**	%	%
		33.8				Cash & Equivalents	D	D
		9.1				Trade Receivables - (net)	A	A
		1.2				Inventory	T	T
		.5				All Other Current	A	A
		44.5				Total Current		
		31.4				Fixed Assets (net)	N	N
		.3				Intangibles (net)	O	O
		23.8				All Other Non-Current	T	T
		100.0				Total		
						LIABILITIES	A	A
		1.4				Notes Payable-Short Term	V	V
		1.6				Cur. Mat. -L/T/D	A	A
		5.3				Trade Payables	I	I
		.0				Income Taxes Payable	L	L
		22.1				All Other Current	A	A
		30.4				Total Current	B	B
		6.3				Long Term Debt	L	L
		.0				Deferred Taxes	E	E
		9.1				All Other-Non-Current		
		54.2				Net Worth		
		100.0				Total Liabilities & Net Worth		
						INCOME DATA		
		100.0				Net Sales		
						Gross Profit		
		94.7				Operating Expenses		
		5.3				Operating Profit		
		.1				All Other Expenses (net)		
		5.1				Profit Before Taxes		
						RATIOS		
		3.4						
		1.7				Current		
		1.1						
		3.1						
		1.7				Quick		
		1.1						
		5 72.9						
		11 34.6				Sales/Receivables		
		24 15.1						
						Cost of Sales/Inventory		
						Cost of Sales/Payables		
		4.1						
		8.9				Sales/Working Capital		
		NM						
						EBIT/Interest		
						Net Profit + Depr., Dep., Amort./Cur. Mat. L /T/D		
		.4						
		.5				Fixed/Worth		
		1.1						
		.3						
		.8				Debt/Worth		
		2.3						
		15.3						
		5.8				% Profit Before Taxes/Tangible Net Worth		
		.6						
		8.3						
		3.3				% Profit Before Taxes/Total Assets		
		.2						
		9.1						
		2.5				Sales/Net Fixed Assets		
		2.0						
		1.5						
		1.1				Sales/Total Assets		
		.8						
		2.3						
	(15)	3.5				% Depr., Dep., Amort./Sales		
		4.1						
						% Officers', Directors', Owners' Comp/Sales		
3124M	16040M	141697M	56896M	53676M	73248M	Net Sales ($)		
1019M	11204M	107387M	65009M	66986M	274516M	Total Assets ($)		

M = $ thousand   MM = $ million
See Pages 1 through 15 for Explanation of Ratios and Data

Comparative Historical Data				Current Data Sorted By Sales					
		1	# Postretirement Benefits				1		
			Type of Statement						
		21	Unqualified		5	4	5	5	2
		3	Reviewed	1	1	1			
			Compiled						
			Tax Returns						
		11	Other		5	1	1	4	
4/1/92-3/31/93 ALL	4/1/93-3/31/94 ALL	4/1/94-3/31/95 ALL			28 (4/1-9/30/94)			7 (10/1/94-3/31/95)	
				0-1MM	1-3MM	3-5MM	5-10MM	10-25MM	25MM & OVER
		35	**NUMBER OF STATEMENTS**	1	11	6	6	9	2
%	%	%	**ASSETS**	%	%	%	%	%	%
		33.5	Cash & Equivalents		37.4				
D	D	9.0	Trade Receivables - (net)		10.9				
A	A	.9	Inventory		.7				
T	T	2.5	All Other Current		1.9				
A	A	45.8	Total Current		50.9				
		31.4	Fixed Assets (net)		30.1				
N	N	.2	Intangibles (net)		.0				
O	O	22.6	All Other Non-Current		19.0				
T	T	100.0	Total		100.0				
A	A		**LIABILITIES**						
V	V	.7	Notes Payable-Short Term		.0				
A	A	1.2	Cur. Mat.-L /T/D		.9				
I	I	4.7	Trade Payables		3.1				
L	L	.3	Income Taxes Payable		.6				
A	A	23.5	All Other Current		26.4				
B	B	30.4	Total Current		31.0				
L	L	9.4	Long Term Debt		9.8				
E	E	.0	Deferred Taxes		.0				
		7.1	All Other-Non-Current		4.0				
		53.1	Net Worth		55.3				
		100.0	Total Liabilities & Net Worth		100.0				
			INCOME DATA						
		100.0	Net Sales		100.0				
			Gross Profit						
		95.5	Operating Expenses		96.1				
		4.5	Operating Profit		3.9				
		–.3	All Other Expenses (net)		–1.3				
		4.8	Profit Before Taxes		5.2				
			RATIOS						
		3.9			7.2				
		1.7	Current		3.2				
		.8			.8				
		3.4			6.3				
		1.5	Quick		2.0				
		.8			.8				
	8	46.5		14	25.8				
	15	24.1	Sales/Receivables	15	24.2				
	27	13.5		28	13.2				
			Cost of Sales/Inventory						
			Cost of Sales/Payables						
		3.2			3.1				
		6.7	Sales/Working Capital		5.3				
		–15.5			–15.5				
		30.2							
	(13)	2.6	EBIT/Interest						
		–1.0							
			Net Profit + Depr., Dep., Amort./Cur. Mat. L/T/D						
		.3			.2				
		.6	Fixed/Worth		.6				
		1.2			1.6				
		.3			.1				
		.8	Debt/Worth		.7				
		2.2			3.2				
		19.5	% Profit Before Taxes/Tangible Net Worth		27.6				
	(34)	6.1		(10)	14.8				
		–.8			–25.9				
		11.6	% Profit Before Taxes/Total Assets		16.6				
		3.4			10.7				
		–.5			–5.6				
		9.5			20.8				
		3.2	Sales/Net Fixed Assets		7.4				
		1.9			2.3				
		1.5			2.4				
		1.1	Sales/Total Assets		1.5				
		.8			1.2				
		2.0							
	(29)	2.6	% Depr., Dep., Amort./Sales						
		4.0							
		1.8							
	(10)	8.1	% Officers', Directors', Owners' Comp/Sales						
		18.7							
		344681M	Net Sales ($)	244M	21032M	25120M	47432M	137956M	112897M
		526121M	Total Assets ($)	182M	15405M	32301M	41846M	254914M	181473M

M = $ thousand   MM = $ million
See Pages 1 through 15 for Explanation of Ratios and Data

Current Data Sorted By Assets   Comparative Historical Data

	0-500M	500M-2MM	2-10MM	10-50MM	50-100MM	100-250MM		4/1/90-3/31/91 ALL	4/1/91-3/31/92 ALL
# Postretirement Benefits	7	15	9	3	1	2	**# Postretirement Benefits**		
							Type of Statement		
	1	22	61	53	18	21	Unqualified	92	101
	6	35	52	11	1		Reviewed	86	102
	51	122	73	8	2		Compiled	178	206
	28	40	8	1			Tax Returns	9	17
	25	79	100	45	9	7	Other	153	174
		164 (4/1-9/30/94)		715 (10/1/94-3/31/95)					
NUMBER OF STATEMENTS	111	298	294	118	30	28	**NUMBER OF STATEMENTS**	518	600
ASSETS	%	%	%	%	%	%	**ASSETS**	%	%
Cash & Equivalents	19.4	8.0	6.8	7.1	7.7	5.6	Cash & Equivalents	6.5	6.4
Trade Receivables - (net)	4.9	2.4	2.4	2.6	5.4	1.8	Trade Receivables - (net)	3.3	3.0
Inventory	2.2	1.3	.9	1.1	1.7	.9	Inventory	1.6	1.5
All Other Current	2.1	1.1	.9	1.3	2.5	1.5	All Other Current	1.7	1.6
Total Current	28.5	12.7	11.0	12.1	17.3	9.8	Total Current	13.1	12.5
Fixed Assets (net)	62.6	79.4	78.1	74.2	64.7	71.7	Fixed Assets (net)	73.8	76.5
Intangibles (net)	2.5	2.3	2.3	1.3	3.4	3.4	Intangibles (net)	2.7	2.3
All Other Non-Current	6.5	5.6	8.6	12.4	14.6	15.1	All Other Non-Current	10.4	8.7
Total	100.0	100.0	100.0	100.0	100.0	100.0	Total	100.0	100.0
LIABILITIES							**LIABILITIES**		
Notes Payable-Short Term	5.6	3.0	3.5	1.7	.9	.5	Notes Payable-Short Term	3.8	4.1
Cur. Mat. -L/T/D	3.5	5.1	5.1	6.7	4.7	2.5	Cur. Mat. -L/T/D	4.2	5.5
Trade Payables	6.4	2.7	2.9	4.0	4.2	3.1	Trade Payables	3.8	3.3
Income Taxes Payable	.1	.1	.1	.3	.2	.1	Income Taxes Payable	.2	.1
All Other Current	12.6	5.9	6.1	8.4	6.4	5.0	All Other Current	8.0	7.4
Total Current	28.2	16.8	17.7	21.2	16.4	11.2	Total Current	19.9	20.4
Long Term Debt	29.4	58.3	58.1	46.0	44.2	49.2	Long Term Debt	56.1	54.4
Deferred Taxes	.0	.1	.1	.8	1.9	2.2	Deferred Taxes	.5	.4
All Other-Non-Current	5.8	3.8	4.4	2.6	2.3	6.9	All Other-Non-Current	2.9	4.8
Net Worth	36.5	21.0	19.7	29.4	35.3	30.5	Net Worth	20.6	20.0
Total Liabilities & Net Worth	100.0	100.0	100.0	100.0	100.0	100.0	Total Liabilities & Net Worth	100.0	100.0
INCOME DATA							**INCOME DATA**		
Net Sales	100.0	100.0	100.0	100.0	100.0	100.0	Net Sales	100.0	100.0
Gross Profit							Gross Profit		
Operating Expenses	87.5	82.8	83.8	86.6	84.1	83.9	Operating Expenses	85.9	84.6
Operating Profit	12.5	17.2	16.2	13.4	15.9	16.1	Operating Profit	14.1	15.4
All Other Expenses (net)	3.9	9.1	9.2	7.0	6.5	5.4	All Other Expenses (net)	11.6	12.0
Profit Before Taxes	8.6	8.1	7.1	6.4	9.4	10.6	Profit Before Taxes	2.6	3.5
RATIOS							**RATIOS**		
Current	2.4	1.9	1.2	1.2	2.1	1.2	Current	1.4	1.4
	.8	.8	.6	.6	1.0	.9		.6	.6
	.3	.3	.3	.3	.6	.4		.3	.3
Quick	2.3	1.7	1.1	.9	1.5	.9	Quick	1.1	1.2
	.7	.7	.5	.5	.8	.6		.4 (599)	.4
	.2	.2	.2	.2	.5	.2		.2	.2
Sales/Receivables	0 UND	1 678.0	3 109.3	3 124.9	2 158.9	2 164.3	Sales/Receivables	2 185.0	2 193.3
	0 954.0	4 88.2	8 47.5	9 42.5	10 38.2	7 54.0		8 46.6	7 56.1
	7 53.9	9 40.0	14 26.6	15 23.9	30 12.0	18 20.6		14 26.3	12 30.1
Cost of Sales/Inventory							Cost of Sales/Inventory		
Cost of Sales/Payables							Cost of Sales/Payables		
Sales/Working Capital	14.0	14.9	35.2	41.5	7.8	27.2	Sales/Working Capital	30.4	29.6
	-77.3	-64.0	-17.6	-16.6	NM	-57.4		-18.3	-20.0
	-10.5	-8.0	-5.6	-5.1	-6.5	-9.8		-5.9	-5.7
EBIT/Interest	(76) 5.0	(249) 3.5	(246) 3.0	(109) 4.3	(27) 6.0	5.0	EBIT/Interest	(361) 2.6	(426) 2.6
	2.4	1.8	1.8	2.3	2.3	3.4		1.5	1.6
	1.5	1.1	1.1	1.2	1.2	1.4		.7	.9
Net Profit + Depr., Dep., Amort./Cur. Mat. L./T/D	(10) 4.0	(50) 2.8	(56) 5.1	(39) 6.6	(16) 6.0	(15) 4.5	Net Profit + Depr., Dep., Amort./Cur. Mat. L./T/D	(197) 4.0	(174) 3.2
	2.6	1.8	2.6	2.8	2.8	3.2		1.9	1.8
	.6	.7	.9	1.2	1.2	2.6		1.0	.8
Fixed/Worth	.7	2.3	2.3	1.6	1.3	1.7	Fixed/Worth	1.9	2.1
	1.8	5.6	5.5	2.5	2.2	2.3		5.9	5.0
	8.2	105.6	-282.6	9.7	3.8	7.1		-542.8	41.2
Debt/Worth	.6	1.9	2.1	1.1	1.1	1.1	Debt/Worth	1.9	1.9
	1.8	5.4	5.6	2.4	2.6	2.4		6.3	5.3
	13.1	116.1	-301.7	10.5	5.0	8.3		-291.0	58.8
% Profit Before Taxes/Tangible Net Worth	(91) 63.8	(231) 64.7	(219) 51.9	(99) 44.3	(27) 31.4	(23) 43.1	% Profit Before Taxes/Tangible Net Worth	(384) 40.0	(466) 44.2
	25.0	23.3	22.4	19.2	10.9	18.7		11.8	15.2
	7.0	3.7	4.1	2.2	4.5	6.2		-4.6	-1.1
% Profit Before Taxes/Total Assets	20.5	11.1	9.4	8.4	10.0	11.2	% Profit Before Taxes/Total Assets	8.0	8.0
	8.2	4.6	3.8	5.0	2.9	6.7		1.7	2.7
	1.1	.2	.2	.3	1.1	1.6		-2.4	-1.8
Sales/Net Fixed Assets	11.0	1.6	1.3	1.5	1.7	1.4	Sales/Net Fixed Assets	1.7	1.4
	3.4	.8	.8	1.0	.9	1.0		.9	.8
	1.2	.5	.5	.6	.5	.7		.5	.5
Sales/Total Assets	4.0	1.1	1.0	1.1	.9	.9	Sales/Total Assets	1.1	1.0
	2.1	.7	.6	.7	.7	.7		.7	.6
	.9	.5	.4	.5	.4	.5		.4	.4
% Depr., Dep., Amort./Sales	(101) 2.5	(286) 6.7	(283) 6.9	(117) 6.5	(21) 5.1	5.7	% Depr., Dep., Amort./Sales	(483) 6.3	(558) 6.8
	6.2	9.7	9.3	8.0	7.7	6.6		10.1	10.2
	11.2	13.5	12.4	11.4	11.6	8.6		14.4	13.5
% Officers', Directors', Owners' Comp/Sales	(43) 2.0	(79) 4.1	(86) 2.9	(18) 2.0			% Officers', Directors', Owners' Comp/Sales	(154) 3.4	(173) 3.9
	6.5	7.4	5.4	3.4				6.3	6.9
	11.3	13.1	12.2	10.1				13.6	12.5
Net Sales ($)	69849M	330479M	1062000M	2336959M	1456622M	3097600M	Net Sales ($)	2940277M	3878545M
Total Assets ($)	29104M	361143M	1337711M	2604492M	2108116M	4453776M	Total Assets ($)	4226242M	5993167M

M = $ thousand   MM = $ million
See Pages 1 through 15 for Explanation of Ratios and Data

Comparative Historical Data				Current Data Sorted By Sales					
4	23	37	# Postretirement Benefits	14	13	1	2	4	3
			Type of Statement						
128	129	176	Unqualified	13	30	19	33	28	53
101	103	105	Reviewed	22	44	12	21	6	
220	211	256	Compiled	130	87	20	13	4	2
51	54	77	Tax Returns	61	14	2			
140	174	265	Other	79	74	39	23	20	30
4/1/92-3/31/93 ALL	4/1/93-3/31/94 ALL	4/1/94-3/31/95 ALL		164 (4/1-9/30/94)			715 (10/1/94-3/31/95)		
				0-1MM	1-3MM	3-5MM	5-10MM	10-25MM	25MM & OVER
640	671	879	**NUMBER OF STATEMENTS**	305	249	92	90	58	85
%	%	%	**ASSETS**	%	%	%	%	%	%
7.0	9.0	8.8	Cash & Equivalents	9.0	9.4	7.8	9.2	6.6	8.8
3.0	2.5	2.8	Trade Receivables - (net)	1.5	3.4	3.5	3.4	2.8	4.1
1.5	1.2	1.3	Inventory	1.0	1.2	1.5	1.7	1.1	1.6
1.1	1.4	1.2	All Other Current	.8	1.5	.9	1.7	1.2	2.0
12.6	14.1	14.1	Total Current	12.3	15.6	13.7	16.1	11.7	16.5
76.5	75.1	75.4	Fixed Assets (net)	80.9	73.6	75.3	71.5	72.8	66.7
2.4	2.5	2.3	Intangibles (net)	1.9	2.6	2.8	1.6	1.6	3.0
8.5	8.3	8.2	All Other Non-Current	4.9	8.2	8.2	10.8	13.9	13.8
100.0	100.0	100.0	Total	100.0	100.0	100.0	100.0	100.0	100.0
			LIABILITIES						
3.4	3.4	3.2	Notes Payable-Short Term	3.6	3.7	4.4	2.2	1.0	1.2
5.1	5.6	5.0	Cur. Mat.-L /T/D	4.5	5.4	4.0	6.5	6.9	3.7
3.5	3.1	3.5	Trade Payables	2.0	3.7	4.7	5.4	3.6	4.8
.2	.4	.1	Income Taxes Payable	.1	.1	.2	.2	.4	.2
8.2	8.2	7.1	All Other Current	6.4	6.9	7.3	8.7	7.5	8.5
20.4	20.6	18.9	Total Current	16.6	19.8	20.5	23.0	19.4	18.4
53.1	50.1	52.2	Long Term Debt	55.7	53.6	50.7	50.9	45.8	42.6
.6	.4	.3	Deferred Taxes	.0	.1	.2	.4	.8	1.6
3.9	4.0	4.1	All Other-Non-Current	3.8	5.1	3.4	4.9	3.0	3.6
21.9	24.8	24.5	Net Worth	23.9	21.5	25.2	20.9	31.0	33.7
100.0	100.0	100.0	Total Liabilities & Net Worth	100.0	100.0	100.0	100.0	100.0	100.0
			INCOME DATA						
100.0	100.0	100.0	Net Sales	100.0	100.0	100.0	100.0	100.0	100.0
			Gross Profit						
85.4	84.5	84.3	Operating Expenses	81.7	84.4	88.1	85.5	86.2	86.9
14.6	15.5	15.7	Operating Profit	18.3	15.6	11.9	14.5	13.8	13.1
10.0	8.1	8.0	All Other Expenses (net)	10.2	8.1	6.2	6.9	5.8	4.4
4.6	7.3	7.7	Profit Before Taxes	8.1	7.6	5.7	7.6	8.0	8.7
			RATIOS						
1.3	1.5	1.6		2.0	1.5	1.2	1.4	1.4	1.3
.6	.7	.7	Current	.7	.7	.8	.7	.7	.8
.2	.3	.3		.2	.3	.3	.3	.3	.5
1.1	1.2	1.4		1.9	1.3	1.1	1.1	1.1	1.0
(637) .5	(670) .5	.6	Quick	.6	.6	.5	.5	.5	.6
.2	.2	.2		.2	.2	.3	.2	.2	.3
2 194.1	1 280.0	2 238.8		0 UND	3 121.7	4 93.5	4 94.4	2 154.7	2 159.0
7 53.8	6 64.2	6 61.0	Sales/Receivables	2 157.6	7 51.9	9 41.8	8 45.7	8 47.1	7 53.4
13 29.1	11 33.1	12 30.8		7 52.7	12 30.7	15 24.7	14 26.6	14 25.6	18 20.6
			Cost of Sales/Inventory						
			Cost of Sales/Payables						
33.9	20.3	18.6		14.0	20.1	46.2	29.4	22.7	23.8
-16.8	-27.5	-28.3	Sales/Working Capital	-34.0	-24.3	-28.3	-20.1	-27.5	-42.2
-5.4	-6.1	-6.6		-6.4	-6.1	-6.1	-5.8	-7.9	-9.6
2.7	3.5	3.6		3.1	3.5	3.0	3.5	4.9	6.2
(513) 1.6	(564) 2.0	(735) 1.9	EBIT/Interest	(232) 1.9	(202) 1.8	(82) 1.7	(82) 1.8	(54) 2.7	(83) 3.0
1.0	1.2	1.2		1.2	1.2	1.0	1.0	1.5	1.2
3.7	4.3	4.9		2.7	4.9	3.8	6.0	7.2	6.0
(173) 2.1	(153) 2.1	(186) 2.4	Net Profit + Depr., Dep., Amort./Cur. Mat. L/T/D	(37) 1.4	(42) 1.8	(19) 2.6	(22) 2.3	(22) 4.4	(44) 2.8
1.1	.8	1.1		.4	.8	1.7	1.2	2.0	1.3
2.1	1.7	1.8		2.1	2.1	1.7	1.9	1.5	1.5
5.0	4.2	4.2	Fixed/Worth	5.2	5.5	3.4	3.8	2.3	2.1
45.4	21.0	30.6		30.6	106.5	NM	NM	10.0	5.3
1.7	1.5	1.5		1.7	1.9	1.5	1.4	.8	1.1
5.3	4.3	4.3	Debt/Worth	5.1	5.3	3.7	4.3	2.1	2.2
55.5	23.7	36.9		36.9	123.0	NM	NM	10.5	6.2
49.2	50.0	52.9		51.5	73.3	45.2	44.6	42.6	43.7
(499) 17.9	(538) 19.3	(690) 21.1	% Profit Before Taxes/Tangible Net Worth	(240) 18.5	(191) 26.1	(69) 16.9	(68) 25.3	(48) 21.7	(74) 17.7
.6	5.0	4.4		3.6	4.2	-.6	1.7	9.4	6.1
9.0	10.1	10.9		10.7	10.5	12.6	11.0	9.4	12.7
3.0	4.3	4.5	% Profit Before Taxes/Total Assets	4.3	4.3	3.8	4.6	6.7	6.0
-1.0	.5	.4		-.2	.3	-.5	.2	2.4	1.1
1.5	1.6	1.7		1.2	2.0	1.8	1.8	1.6	1.9
.9	.9	.9	Sales/Net Fixed Assets	.6	1.0	1.1	1.2	1.0	1.3
.5	.5	.6		.4	.6	.8	.8	.7	.9
1.1	1.2	1.2		.9	1.3	1.4	1.3	1.0	1.2
.7	.7	.7	Sales/Total Assets	.6	.9	.9	.9	.8	.9
.5	.5	.5		.4	.5	.6	.6	.5	.7
6.7	6.3	6.2		7.7	6.1	6.0	5.7	6.4	5.1
(609) 9.8	(638) 9.2	(838) 8.8	% Depr., Dep., Amort./Sales	(292) 11.3	(238) 8.4	(85) 8.2	(89) 7.4	(57) 8.0	(77) 6.5
13.4	12.6	12.4		15.3	11.3	11.1	10.9	11.3	7.7
3.6	3.6	3.0		4.3	3.3	2.1	1.9	1.7	
(193) 6.5	(203) 6.4	(231) 5.6	% Officers', Directors', Owners' Comp/Sales	(94) 7.9	(73) 6.0	(31) 4.6	(16) 3.3	(10) 3.2	
13.7	13.6	11.5		13.4	10.9	7.6	6.0	10.4	
3642193M	4161146M	8353509M	Net Sales ($)	163679M	447128M	353520M	636544M	904101M	5848537M
5323715M	6016809M	10894342M	Total Assets ($)	314806M	683110M	460148M	977771M	1361428M	7097079M

M = $ thousand   MM = $ million
See Pages 1 through 15 for Explanation of Ratios and Data

Current Data Sorted By Assets   Comparative Historical Data

0-500M	500M-2MM	2-10MM	10-50MM	50-100MM	100-250MM		4/1/90-3/31/91 ALL	4/1/91-3/31/92 ALL
2	3	3	4	1		**# Postretirement Benefits**		
						Type of Statement		
2	2	12	16		1	Unqualified	11	19
3	21	11	1			Reviewed	28	28
10	16	3				Compiled	27	35
7	2					Tax Returns		
9	17	6	5	2		Other	34	46
	48 (4/1-9/30/94)		98 (10/1/94-3/31/95)					
31	58	32	22	2	1	**NUMBER OF STATEMENTS**	100	128
%	%	%	%	%	%	**ASSETS**	%	%
14.8	7.4	11.6	9.2			Cash & Equivalents	9.9	9.4
30.5	29.9	19.2	22.4			Trade Receivables - (net)	29.0	28.8
1.6	6.7	5.9	11.6			Inventory	3.9	6.0
3.2	3.5	5.4	2.0			All Other Current	2.3	3.9
50.1	47.5	42.1	45.2			Total Current	45.0	48.1
42.4	42.3	42.5	26.7			Fixed Assets (net)	44.5	39.1
.6	3.9	4.6	9.1			Intangibles (net)	2.7	3.5
6.9	6.3	10.8	19.0			All Other Non-Current	7.7	9.3
100.0	100.0	100.0	100.0			Total	100.0	100.0
						LIABILITIES		
4.5	7.4	6.3	7.3			Notes Payable-Short Term	9.7	11.9
7.8	8.7	8.2	3.9			Cur. Mat. -L/T/D	7.4	6.4
17.6	12.9	11.8	12.7			Trade Payables	13.2	12.7
.0	.4	1.0	.5			Income Taxes Payable	1.0	.3
10.2	12.7	11.6	15.5			All Other Current	10.3	12.8
40.2	42.0	38.9	40.0			Total Current	41.7	44.0
21.8	19.2	15.6	14.0			Long Term Debt	21.1	18.5
.6	.4	.6	1.7			Deferred Taxes	.9	.5
6.9	3.0	3.9	2.4			All Other-Non-Current	2.7	3.3
30.4	35.5	40.9	42.0			Net Worth	33.5	33.6
100.0	100.0	100.0	100.0			Total Liabilities & Net Worth	100.0	100.0
						INCOME DATA		
100.0	100.0	100.0	100.0			Net Sales	100.0	100.0
						Gross Profit		
92.7	95.9	91.8	93.7			Operating Expenses	93.8	96.2
7.3	4.1	8.2	6.3			Operating Profit	6.2	3.8
1.3	1.0	2.0	2.4			All Other Expenses (net)	2.3	1.9
6.1	3.1	6.2	4.0			Profit Before Taxes	4.0	1.9
						RATIOS		
2.6	1.7	1.7	1.5			Current	1.7	1.8
1.3	1.0	1.2	1.1				1.1	1.3
1.0	.8	.8	.8				.8	.8
2.0	1.3	1.5	1.3			Quick	1.6	1.4
(29) 1.1	.9	.9	(21) .8				1.0	1.0
.8	.6	.5	.5				.6	.5
9 39.9	31 11.7	25 14.6	31 11.9			Sales/Receivables	26 13.9	28 13.0
45 8.2	49 7.5	46 8.0	64 5.7				45 8.1	46 7.9
62 5.9	69 5.3	64 5.7	104 3.5				61 6.0	62 5.9
						Cost of Sales/Inventory		
						Cost of Sales/Payables		
9.0	10.0	9.7	6.3			Sales/Working Capital	9.0	9.7
29.2	152.5	33.1	65.5				53.3	27.6
-109.8	-29.1	-25.6	-11.8				-22.8	-19.0
(26) 9.7	(55) 8.0	(29) 7.5	(18) 9.0			EBIT/Interest	(89) 9.4	(118) 4.2
2.2	3.0	4.2	2.6				2.7	1.8
-1.0	.4	1.5	.8				.9	-.1
	(22) 6.7	(13) 3.9				Net Profit + Depr., Dep.,	(55) 5.3	(49) 4.8
	1.6	1.9				Amort./Cur. Mat. L /T/D	2.7	1.7
	.9	-.5					1.3	1.0
.2	.6	.6	.2			Fixed/Worth	.7	.6
1.5	1.4	1.1	.8				1.2	1.2
4.5	2.7	2.2	1.6				3.6	3.2
.7	1.1	.8	.9			Debt/Worth	.8	.9
2.5	1.7	1.5	1.4				1.9	2.3
18.8	4.0	4.8	4.6				5.3	6.5
(27) 75.5	(53) 43.8	(30) 55.1	(20) 38.3			% Profit Before Taxes/Tangible	(85) 49.3	(113) 45.5
37.9	19.4	22.8	21.6			Net Worth	25.5	15.0
-7.3	3.0	4.0	-.5				2.4	-3.1
28.8	13.1	19.1	13.4			% Profit Before Taxes/Total	16.6	9.8
5.7	5.7	11.7	6.7			Assets	4.4	4.6
-2.3	-1.2	2.2	-.5				-.6	-4.3
48.1	12.8	11.0	23.4			Sales/Net Fixed Assets	10.5	19.1
5.3	5.0	2.7	7.2				4.8	7.5
3.0	2.6	1.9	1.7				2.8	2.6
3.5	2.8	2.0	1.9			Sales/Total Assets	3.3	3.3
2.2	2.2	1.4	1.1				2.1	2.0
1.7	1.5	1.1	.6				1.4	1.4
(25) 2.7	(49) 3.2	(26) 3.9	(16) 2.8			% Depr., Dep., Amort./Sales	(85) 2.4	(103) 2.2
7.5	6.6	6.8	6.1				7.0	5.2
10.9	10.1	13.2	10.0				9.9	10.3
(17) 9.5	(26) 4.6					% Officers', Directors',	(45) 6.1	(60) 4.0
16.0	8.0					Owners' Comp/Sales	11.7	7.2
23.5	10.9						17.4	14.9
20301M	143250M	249630M	502233M	177674M	214809M	Net Sales ($)	492001M	847258M
7099M	65747M	156278M	411944M	122995M	121518M	Total Assets ($)	365787M	530806M

M = $ thousand   MM = $ million
See Pages 1 through 15 for Explanation of Ratios and Data

Comparative Historical Data / Current Data Sorted By Sales

1	4	13	# Postretirement Benefits	2	3	4	2	2
			Type of Statement					
21	22	33	Unqualified	2	1	6	8	12	4
30	24	36	Reviewed	3	13	9	8	3	
32	40	29	Compiled	8	18	1	1	1	
1	9	9	Tax Returns	6	3				
34	21	39	Other	10	9	6	5	3	6

				48 (4/1-9/30/94)			98 (10/1/94-3/31/95)		
4/1/92-3/31/93 ALL	4/1/93-3/31/94 ALL	4/1/94-3/31/95 ALL		0-1MM	1-3MM	3-5MM	5-10MM	10-25MM	25MM & OVER
118	116	146	**NUMBER OF STATEMENTS**	29	44	22	22	19	10
%	%	%	**ASSETS**	%	%	%	%	%	%
9.0	10.6	10.1	Cash & Equivalents	11.0	11.4	8.1	10.7	9.1	6.9
25.5	26.2	26.3	Trade Receivables - (net)	26.2	29.1	32.1	18.0	22.0	28.8
6.7	5.8	6.1	Inventory	2.6	5.7	4.2	6.3	10.0	14.1
2.2	3.3	3.6	All Other Current	7.8	1.0	2.7	2.9	5.4	2.3
43.5	46.0	46.1	Total Current	47.6	47.2	47.1	37.9	46.5	52.1
43.9	40.5	40.2	Fixed Assets (net)	45.6	43.8	41.2	40.2	30.5	23.9
3.9	5.3	4.1	Intangibles (net)	1.9	1.8	5.7	4.6	9.0	6.8
8.7	8.1	9.7	All Other Non-Current	4.9	7.2	6.0	17.3	14.0	17.2
100.0	100.0	100.0	Total	100.0	100.0	100.0	100.0	100.0	100.0
			LIABILITIES						
7.7	6.7	6.6	Notes Payable-Short Term	5.5	4.3	9.7	8.2	7.8	6.6
7.1	6.7	7.6	Cur. Mat.-L/T/D	7.8	8.7	10.3	7.3	5.1	1.3
11.6	12.6	13.5	Trade Payables	15.6	12.5	13.6	11.1	13.1	18.1
.4	1.2	.4	Income Taxes Payable	.0	.3	.4	.4	1.6	.2
9.2	13.1	12.5	All Other Current	11.0	7.5	18.3	11.7	14.5	23.5
36.0	40.3	40.6	Total Current	39.9	33.3	52.4	38.7	42.2	49.7
22.6	17.9	18.1	Long Term Debt	25.9	19.9	16.3	14.3	14.4	6.5
.6	.7	.7	Deferred Taxes	.3	.8	.1	1.3	1.1	.3
2.4	3.6	4.1	All Other-Non-Current	6.4	4.0	4.4	1.8	2.8	4.2
38.3	37.5	36.6	Net Worth	27.6	42.0	26.9	43.8	39.6	39.3
100.0	100.0	100.0	Total Liabilities & Net Worth	100.0	100.0	100.0	100.0	100.0	100.0
			INCOME DATA						
100.0	100.0	100.0	Net Sales	100.0	100.0	100.0	100.0	100.0	100.0
			Gross Profit						
93.9	94.1	93.8	Operating Expenses	94.2	95.0	93.1	93.0	92.4	93.4
6.1	5.9	6.2	Operating Profit	5.8	5.0	6.9	7.0	7.6	6.6
1.3	1.7	1.5	All Other Expenses (net)	1.2	1.2	1.8	1.7	2.3	.9
4.7	4.3	4.7	Profit Before Taxes	4.6	3.8	5.1	5.3	5.2	5.7
			RATIOS						
2.0	2.1	1.7		2.2	2.8	1.2	1.5	1.6	2.0
1.2	1.1	1.1	Current	1.3	1.2	1.0	1.0	1.1	1.1
.8	.8	.8		1.0	.8	.8	.7	.9	.7
1.6	1.7	1.5		1.8	1.9	1.0	1.4	1.1	
1.0	1.0 (143)	.9	Quick (27)	1.0	1.0	.9	.7	.8	
.6	.6	.6		.8	.8	.7	.5	.5	
25 14.7	27 13.7	29 12.6		22 16.4	32 11.4	38 9.6	29 12.4	12 29.3	33 11.0
46 7.9	43 8.4	49 7.5	Sales/Receivables	42 8.6	46 7.9	50 7.3	47 7.8	61 6.0	41 8.8
68 5.4	66 5.5	69 5.3		65 5.6	68 5.4	70 5.2	66 5.5	79 4.6	62 5.9
			Cost of Sales/Inventory						
			Cost of Sales/Payables						
8.3	8.6	9.5		7.7	8.7	28.1	12.2	11.8	6.0
30.9	43.3	55.8	Sales/Working Capital	16.4	30.2	292.7	-152.5	75.9	40.9
-22.4	-29.4	-26.2		-85.6	-31.6	-19.3	-10.9	-14.5	-5.5
(106) 7.9	(103) 9.1	(131) 8.0		(25) 5.8	(41) 9.3	(20) 8.8	(20) 7.2	(18) 15.3	
2.8	3.8	3.0	EBIT/Interest	1.6	3.0	4.6	3.3	5.5	
1.3	1.3	.7		-1.3	1.4	.6	-.8	1.6	
(43) 6.1	(48) 4.8	(50) 4.9			(16) 12.4	(12) 3.8			
1.9	2.3	1.8	Net Profit + Depr., Dep., Amort./Cur. Mat. L/T/D		1.5	2.2			
1.2	1.6	.9			1.0	.8			
.6	.6	.5		.5	.4	.8	.5	.3	.1
1.1	1.3	1.2	Fixed/Worth	1.8	1.3	1.6	.9	.9	.4
2.8	2.6	2.6		4.6	2.6	3.0	2.1	1.5	3.1
.8	.8	.9		1.0	.7	1.2	.6	1.0	1.2
2.0	2.0	1.7	Debt/Worth	2.8	1.3	2.5	1.3	1.4	1.5
3.7	4.0	5.1		12.4	3.4	10.9	5.6	4.5	6.0
(109) 52.9	(106) 48.3	(133) 51.5		(25) 44.0	(42) 56.5	(18) 52.3	(21) 39.4	(18) 72.2	
18.8	24.3	21.4	% Profit Before Taxes/Tangible Net Worth	13.3	22.2	21.0	14.5	29.7	
4.2	4.8	3.7		-15.1	9.4	3.6	-39.2	4.8	
14.7	14.8	16.1		18.5	15.2	18.1	16.0	16.3	18.2
6.0	7.5	6.5	% Profit Before Taxes/Total Assets	3.6	6.9	8.6	3.3	11.5	9.1
1.1	.4	.2		-9.9	3.1	-.5	-6.9	2.8	1.2
9.6	18.0	13.0		12.6	12.2	16.3	9.9	25.5	46.4
4.8	6.8	4.9	Sales/Net Fixed Assets	4.4	4.6	5.3	2.8	7.3	15.3
2.7	2.8	2.4		2.4	2.3	2.4	2.2	1.6	5.9
2.6	3.4	2.7		2.4	2.9	2.8	1.9	2.2	2.7
1.8	2.1	1.8	Sales/Total Assets	2.0	1.9	2.3	1.4	1.3	1.9
1.3	1.4	1.3		1.2	1.5	1.5	1.0	1.0	1.4
(102) 3.2	(102) 1.8	(117) 3.2		(23) 4.9	(39) 2.9	(19) 3.2	(19) 2.7	(12) 4.2	
6.7	4.6	6.8	% Depr., Dep., Amort./Sales	10.1	6.3	5.0	6.3	7.1	
10.9	9.7	10.6		11.4	10.2	8.1	12.8	10.2	
(45) 5.3	(53) 6.1	(52) 5.4		(16) 9.7	(19) 6.1				
7.1	10.5	9.7	% Officers', Directors', Owners' Comp/Sales	16.6	9.4				
13.3	16.6	15.9		23.8	13.7				
1077598M	828512M	1307897M	Net Sales ($)	14284M	79487M	84479M	148804M	296496M	684347M
937281M	546365M	885581M	Total Assets ($)	8691M	48767M	48176M	146376M	226031M	407540M

M = $ thousand   MM = $ million
See Pages 1 through 15 for Explanation of Ratios and Data

SERVICES—NURSING, CONVALESCENT & REST HOMES. SIC# 8051 (59)

	Current Data Sorted By Assets						Comparative Historical Data	
# Postretirement Benefits	6	11	32	21		2		
Type of Statement								
Unqualified	11	51	175	100	14	11	247	289
Reviewed	8	39	27	3	1		52	62
Compiled	33	70	46	1			110	135
Tax Returns	10	15	2				9	4
Other	24	71	67	40	8	5	136	168
	353 (4/1-9/30/94)			479 (10/1/94-3/31/95)			4/1/90-3/31/91 ALL	4/1/91-3/31/92 ALL
	0-500M	500M-2MM	2-10MM	10-50MM	50-100MM	100-250MM		
NUMBER OF STATEMENTS	86	246	317	144	23	16	554	658
ASSETS	%	%	%	%	%	%	%	%
Cash & Equivalents	19.0	10.5	8.2	8.6	6.1	7.5	8.4	7.9
Trade Receivables - (net)	25.1	25.6	15.4	10.3	7.7	13.8	17.5	20.8
Inventory	.6	.8	.7	.5	1.2	1.0	.6	.9
All Other Current	2.2	1.9	2.8	2.8	1.7	4.6	2.7	2.0
Total Current	46.9	38.8	27.0	22.3	16.7	26.9	29.2	31.6
Fixed Assets (net)	38.3	47.4	60.0	59.0	64.5	52.2	55.3	54.1
Intangibles (net)	3.4	3.0	2.1	3.1	1.6	4.8	1.8	2.5
All Other Non-Current	11.4	10.8	10.9	15.6	17.2	16.0	13.7	11.8
Total	100.0	100.0	100.0	100.0	100.0	100.0	100.0	100.0
LIABILITIES								
Notes Payable-Short Term	11.5	3.6	2.8	1.6	.2	.9	6.3	5.9
Cur. Mat. -L/T/D	3.7	4.7	3.5	2.5	3.4	3.8	4.1	5.1
Trade Payables	9.1	8.7	6.8	4.8	3.8	6.1	7.0	7.4
Income Taxes Payable	.2	.2	.1	.2	.0	.3	.5	.3
All Other Current	20.3	16.5	10.9	8.9	7.4	7.4	12.0	14.2
Total Current	44.7	33.8	24.1	18.1	14.8	18.5	29.9	32.9
Long Term Debt	19.4	33.7	46.0	46.2	47.6	42.7	42.4	40.9
Deferred Taxes	.1	.2	.4	.7	.7	.8	.5	.4
All Other-Non-Current	4.0	3.7	4.1	9.9	15.9	6.2	4.8	5.0
Net Worth	31.8	28.7	25.4	25.2	21.0	31.8	22.3	20.8
Total Liabilities & Net Worth	100.0	100.0	100.0	100.0	100.0	100.0	100.0	100.0
INCOME DATA								
Net Sales	100.0	100.0	100.0	100.0	100.0	100.0	100.0	100.0
Gross Profit								
Operating Expenses	91.3	91.0	91.7	90.4	90.9	91.1	92.5	90.6
Operating Profit	8.7	9.0	8.3	9.6	9.1	8.9	7.5	9.4
All Other Expenses (net)	3.0	3.5	3.5	4.4	3.7	3.4	4.3	5.0
Profit Before Taxes	5.8	5.5	4.7	5.1	5.4	5.5	3.2	4.3
RATIOS								
Current	2.4	2.1	1.8	2.1	1.6	2.6	1.6	1.7
	1.1	1.2	1.1	1.3	1.0	1.4	1.0	1.0
	.6	.7	.7	.8	.8	1.1	.6	.6
Quick	2.4	1.9	1.6	1.8	1.4	2.0	1.5	1.5
	1.0	1.1	1.0	1.1	1.0	1.1	.9	.9
	.6	.6	.6	.6	.6	.8	.5	.5
Sales/Receivables	0 UND	15 24.7	20 18.4	17 20.9	10 36.8	37 10.0	16 22.7	18 19.9
	16 23.2	29 12.8	31 11.6	32 11.4	36 10.1	50 7.3	29 12.7	31 11.6
	37 9.9	46 7.9	47 7.8	47 7.7	49 7.4	72 5.1	43 8.4	52 7.0
Cost of Sales/Inventory								
Cost of Sales/Payables								
Sales/Working Capital	16.9	10.9	10.6	6.3	9.8	5.6	13.4	12.8
	140.8	51.3	60.6	22.2	414.1	13.5	200.4	175.3
	-19.8	-18.0	-19.6	-27.4	-17.2	43.3	-12.8	-14.0
EBIT/Interest	6.9	8.7	3.9	3.6	3.3	6.4	3.0	3.8
	(55) 3.6	(205) 2.9	(282) 2.1	(121) 2.0	(21) 2.0	2.8	(467) 1.6	(570) 1.8
	1.1	1.4	1.1	1.2	1.0	1.3	.9	1.1
Net Profit + Depr., Dep., Amort./Cur. Mat. L /T/D	3.0	5.2	4.7	4.9		5.9	5.2	4.3
	(14) 1.9	(47) 2.5	(84) 2.2	(35) 2.4	(11) 3.0		(236) 2.1	(199) 2.1
	.7	1.3	.9	1.4	1.4		.9	.7
Fixed/Worth	.2	.7	1.2	1.3	2.2	1.0	1.0	1.1
	1.3	1.9	2.8	2.9	3.1	1.5	3.5	3.5
	10.1	15.8	36.2	18.0	7.5	9.1	36.0	192.7
Debt/Worth	.7	1.0	1.4	1.5	2.1	1.2	1.6	1.7
	2.2	3.0	3.9	5.0	3.4	1.9	4.7	5.1
	20.7	28.6	53.6	25.7	10.6	15.5	57.6	327.2
% Profit Before Taxes/Tangible Net Worth	85.6	76.2	36.3	32.9	38.8	24.3	46.0	70.3
	(69) 31.5	(193) 39.3	(249) 16.6	(116) 14.4	(20) 19.9	(14) 17.6	(430) 15.9	(499) 24.5
	8.1	11.4	4.2	4.3	1.8	11.6	.2	4.8
% Profit Before Taxes/Total Assets	23.7	18.3	9.2	6.9	5.9	8.1	8.8	11.2
	10.9	7.2	4.0	2.9	2.9	5.7	3.0	4.1
	.5	1.6	.6	.8	.5	1.9	-.6	.5
Sales/Net Fixed Assets	52.0	18.9	3.6	2.4	2.2	2.4	9.0	11.1
	16.2	4.8	1.8	1.0	.8	1.9	1.9	2.1
	3.5	1.8	1.1	.6	.3	1.4	1.0	1.0
Sales/Total Assets	6.5	3.4	1.7	1.2	1.2	1.2	2.4	2.7
	4.2	2.1	1.1	.6	.6	1.0	1.1	1.3
	1.7	1.3	.8	.4	.2	.8	.7	.8
% Depr., Dep., Amort./Sales	.7	1.3	2.4	3.3	3.2	2.5	2.1	1.9
	(69) 1.6	(226) 2.3	(302) 3.7	(137) 5.2	7.3	3.6	(508) 4.1	(624) 3.6
	4.0	4.2	5.3	8.3	13.8	5.9	5.9	5.8
% Officers', Directors', Owners' Comp/Sales	5.6	2.9	2.9	3.9			2.9	3.4
	(37) 8.0	(64) 4.9	(66) 6.9	(33) 9.2			(136) 5.8	(166) 6.8
	18.6	9.1	14.0	23.7			12.7	11.3
Net Sales ($)	98063M	682332M	1948152M	3043155M	1156303M	2090683M	4963473M	7104168M
Total Assets ($)	22710M	291412M	1409166M	3206889M	1550400M	2095119M	5680050M	7008566M

M = $ thousand   MM = $ million
See Pages 1 through 15 for Explanation of Ratios and Data

Comparative Historical Data				Current Data Sorted By Sales					
14	48	72	# Postretirement Benefits	4	18	15	17	8	10
			Type of Statement						
282	280	362	Unqualified	20	60	71	103	66	42
74	75	78	Reviewed	10	31	15	15	5	2
123	136	150	Compiled	30	68	30	19	2	1
6	18	27	Tax Returns	11	10	4	2		
196	209	215	Other	22	66	36	38	26	27
4/1/92-	4/1/93-	4/1/94-		353 (4/1-9/30/94)			479 (10/1/94-3/31/95)		
3/31/93	3/31/94	3/31/95		0-1MM	1-3MM	3-5MM	5-10MM	10-25MM	25MM & OVER
ALL	ALL	ALL							
681	718	832	NUMBER OF STATEMENTS	93	235	156	177	99	72
%	%	%	ASSETS	%	%	%	%	%	%
8.9	9.5	10.0	Cash & Equivalents	11.8	9.7	10.6	9.9	9.1	9.1
19.5	19.2	18.3	Trade Receivables - (net)	12.6	17.4	20.6	18.9	19.9	19.5
.7	.6	.7	Inventory	.2	.8	.4	1.0	.5	1.3
2.4	2.5	2.5	All Other Current	2.0	1.7	2.2	2.4	4.0	4.6
31.6	31.9	31.4	Total Current	26.6	29.5	33.7	32.2	33.5	34.4
54.7	53.9	53.8	Fixed Assets (net)	61.5	56.0	52.7	53.7	49.8	45.2
2.2	2.1	2.7	Intangibles (net)	3.0	3.4	1.8	1.7	2.9	4.1
11.5	12.2	12.0	All Other Non-Current	8.9	11.1	11.8	12.4	13.8	16.3
100.0	100.0	100.0	Total	100.0	100.0	100.0	100.0	100.0	100.0
			LIABILITIES						
4.6	3.8	3.6	Notes Payable-Short Term	7.3	3.8	3.7	2.2	3.9	1.4
4.6	4.1	3.7	Cur. Mat.-L /T/D	4.1	4.8	3.6	2.8	2.5	3.7
7.3	7.3	7.1	Trade Payables	4.0	6.1	7.1	9.4	7.4	9.1
.4	.8	.2	Income Taxes Payable	.1	.2	.2	.1	.1	.5
13.2	13.8	13.0	All Other Current	11.4	13.0	13.2	13.2	12.7	14.7
30.1	29.9	27.7	Total Current	27.0	27.7	27.8	27.7	26.5	29.4
41.1	41.0	39.6	Long Term Debt	42.0	42.1	38.9	38.1	34.2	41.1
.7	.6	.4	Deferred Taxes	.5	.1	.3	.6	.2	.9
4.3	5.7	5.4	All Other-Non-Current	4.9	4.7	3.5	6.4	8.8	5.0
23.8	22.9	27.0	Net Worth	25.6	25.4	29.5	27.3	30.3	23.5
100.0	100.0	100.0	Total Liabilities & Net Worth	100.0	100.0	100.0	100.0	100.0	100.0
			INCOME DATA						
100.0	100.0	100.0	Net Sales	100.0	100.0	100.0	100.0	100.0	100.0
			Gross Profit						
90.9	91.4	91.2	Operating Expenses	82.7	90.4	94.0	92.2	93.5	93.2
9.1	8.6	8.8	Operating Profit	17.3	9.6	6.0	7.8	6.5	6.8
4.2	4.2	3.6	All Other Expenses (net)	8.9	4.4	1.8	2.9	1.8	2.2
4.9	4.4	5.2	Profit Before Taxes	8.5	5.2	4.1	4.9	4.7	4.5
			RATIOS						
1.8	1.8	2.0		2.0	1.9	2.3	1.8	2.1	1.7
1.1	1.1	1.2	Current	.8	1.1	1.2	1.2	1.4	1.2
.7	.7	.7		.4	.6	.8	.8	1.0	1.0
1.6	1.6	1.7		1.9	1.7	1.9	1.7	1.8	1.6
(680) 1.0	1.0	1.0	Quick	.8	1.0	1.2	1.0	1.2	1.0
.6	.6	.6		.3	.5	.7	.7	.8	.7
17 21.7	16 22.4	16 23.4		0 UND	12 30.7	20 18.0	22 16.5	22 16.3	31 11.8
30 12.2	30 12.0	30 12.0	Sales/Receivables	3 104.9	24 14.9	33 11.0	33 11.0	34 10.7	41 9.0
45 8.2	46 7.9	47 7.8		37 9.8	42 8.6	46 7.9	47 7.7	49 7.5	51 7.2
			Cost of Sales/Inventory						
			Cost of Sales/Payables						
11.8	12.0	9.8		10.1	10.5	9.0	10.4	8.1	9.5
67.2	62.4	46.4	Sales/Working Capital	-93.3	93.7	40.8	34.6	22.6	42.3
-22.0	-20.1	-19.4		-7.4	-14.9	-23.3	-29.0	-88.8	-114.8
4.8	3.9	5.2		4.5	5.8	5.0	4.9	5.6	5.0
(585) 2.2	(614) 2.0	(700) 2.3	EBIT/Interest	(62) 2.5	(201) 2.2	(134) 2.4	(146) 2.3	(89) 2.0	(68) 2.4
1.2	1.2	1.2		1.0	1.2	1.1	1.2	1.4	1.3
5.1	3.6	4.8	Net Profit + Depr., Dep.,	2.7	3.8	4.0	5.6	10.9	5.2
(217) 2.3	(168) 1.8	(200) 2.3	Amort./Cur. Mat. L/T/D	(14) 1.9	(52) 2.1	(37) 2.3	(34) 2.6	(25) 2.2	(38) 2.6
1.1	.7	1.1		1.0	1.3	1.1	.5	1.3	1.3
1.1	1.0	1.0		1.2	1.0	.9	1.1	.8	.9
2.9	2.9	2.5	Fixed/Worth	3.4	3.4	2.2	2.5	2.2	2.0
31.2	33.3	18.1		39.7	-79.3	12.0	14.6	8.4	8.5
1.5	1.5	1.2		1.6	1.2	.9	1.2	1.2	1.7
3.9	4.0	3.4	Debt/Worth	4.4	4.2	2.7	3.2	2.7	5.5
44.9	59.0	30.0		52.1	-91.2	15.8	22.9	10.4	18.2
66.7	56.0	51.6	% Profit Before Taxes/Tangible	62.7	59.6	51.7	46.6	40.4	50.8
(533) 27.7	(557) 23.7	(661) 20.6	Net Worth	(75) 21.0	(170) 23.1	(127) 19.3	(144) 15.3	(84) 19.0	(61) 25.1
6.8	5.7	5.7		3.9	8.9	3.4	3.9	8.6	14.8
12.7	11.4	12.1	% Profit Before Taxes/Total	14.5	14.5	12.8	9.9	10.4	10.3
5.2	4.5	4.7	Assets	6.2	5.4	4.6	4.1	4.4	6.0
1.1	.9	.8		.0	.7	.6	.9	1.7	1.6
9.0	9.6	9.0		9.2	8.2	8.2	9.0	11.4	10.0
2.3	2.3	2.2	Sales/Net Fixed Assets	1.6	2.2	2.5	2.0	2.4	2.5
1.2	1.1	1.1		.5	1.2	1.4	1.0	1.1	1.8
2.7	2.8	2.5		2.1	2.6	2.7	2.6	2.5	2.2
1.3	1.4	1.3	Sales/Total Assets	.9	1.4	1.5	1.3	1.2	1.4
.8	.8	.8		.4	.8	.9	.7	.6	1.0
1.7	1.8	1.7		2.9	1.7	1.7	1.7	1.6	1.4
(639) 3.4	(681) 3.5	(773) 3.5	% Depr., Dep., Amort./Sales	(79) 5.5	(220) 3.6	(145) 3.1	(164) 3.4	(95) 3.8	(70) 2.9
5.3	5.6	5.6		11.5	5.6	4.5	5.8	5.6	4.2
3.7	2.9	3.7	% Officers', Directors',	8.3	3.8	2.9	3.5	2.0	4.0
(186) 6.6	(176) 6.1	(203) 6.9	Owners' Comp/Sales	(24) 14.2	(56) 5.6	(50) 5.3	(42) 7.8	(20) 6.1	(11) 13.0
12.0	12.2	14.6		24.0	8.7	13.3	12.5	23.3	20.0
8387279M	9166133M	9018688M	Net Sales ($)	49941M	472083M	604613M	1204401M	1513562M	5174088M
7221644M	8131154M	8575696M	Total Assets ($)	88449M	471275M	588921M	1512680M	1713039M	4201332M

M = $ thousand   MM = $ million
See Pages 1 through 15 for Explanation of Ratios and Data

Current Data Sorted By Assets   **Comparative Historical Data**

0-500M	500M-2MM	2-10MM	10-50MM	50-100MM	100-250MM	# Postretirement Benefits / Type of Statement	4/1/90-3/31/91 ALL	4/1/91-3/31/92 ALL
	2	1			1	Unqualified		1
2	4					Reviewed		4
6	4					Compiled		9
7	1					Tax Returns		
4	3	1				Other		4
	9 (4/1-9/30/94)		23 (10/1/94-3/31/95)					
19	10	2			1	NUMBER OF STATEMENTS		18
%	%	%	%	%	%	**ASSETS**	%	%
17.1	4.1					Cash & Equivalents		11.1
7.0	26.3					Trade Receivables - (net)	D	22.9
4.5	3.4					Inventory	A	8.1
1.3	7.7					All Other Current	T	5.1
29.9	41.4					Total Current	A	47.2
53.7	51.4					Fixed Assets (net)		41.6
1.7	.9					Intangibles (net)	N	2.1
14.6	6.3					All Other Non-Current	O	9.1
100.0	100.0					Total	T	100.0
						LIABILITIES	A	
17.1	4.8					Notes Payable-Short Term	V	11.5
7.1	2.5					Cur. Mat. -L/T/D	A	10.4
1.9	2.2					Trade Payables	I	5.1
.3	.3					Income Taxes Payable	L	.0
15.8	2.9					All Other Current	A	13.2
42.3	12.8					Total Current	B	40.2
22.2	36.6					Long Term Debt	L	26.8
.0	.0					Deferred Taxes	E	.4
.1	10.8					All Other-Non-Current		5.3
35.5	39.8					Net Worth		27.3
100.0	100.0					Total Liabilities & Net Worth		100.0
						INCOME DATA		
100.0	100.0					Net Sales		100.0
						Gross Profit		
93.7	90.4					Operating Expenses		92.1
6.3	9.6					Operating Profit		7.9
.4	1.8					All Other Expenses (net)		1.3
5.9	7.8					Profit Before Taxes		6.6
						RATIOS		

	0-500M	500M-2MM	2-10MM	10-50MM	50-100MM	100-250MM		4/1/90-3/31/91 ALL	4/1/91-3/31/92 ALL
	1.4	10.5					Current		2.0
	.7	5.1							1.1
	.2	.3							.5
(18)	1.5	9.6					Quick		1.5
	.6	3.7							.8
	.2	.2							.4
0	UND	0 UND					Sales/Receivables	0	UND
0	UND	51 7.1						35	10.3
0	999.8	104 3.5						54	6.8
							Cost of Sales/Inventory		
							Cost of Sales/Payables		
	30.8	3.6					Sales/Working Capital		9.0
	-84.1	4.4							41.5
	-18.5	-123.6							-23.9
(15)	7.0						EBIT/Interest	(16)	4.5
	1.0								1.9
	-1.5								.8
							Net Profit + Depr., Dep., Amort./Cur. Mat. L /T/D		
	.8	.6					Fixed/Worth		.6
	1.7	1.5							1.4
	4.0	2.3							39.8
	1.2	.6					Debt/Worth		1.2
	2.0	1.7							2.2
	3.6	4.1							63.6
	338.8	62.3					% Profit Before Taxes/Tangible Net Worth		63.0
	7.3	29.4						(15)	9.0
	-5.1	-8.3							-10.0
	21.1	22.8					% Profit Before Taxes/Total Assets		11.7
	2.4	8.4							4.7
	-1.7	-2.0							-1.9
	28.5	14.2					Sales/Net Fixed Assets		17.0
	16.6	4.3							10.8
	10.4	2.0							4.3
	11.0	2.7					Sales/Total Assets		4.4
	7.2	2.0							2.9
	5.6	1.2							1.5
(18)	1.4						% Depr., Dep., Amort./Sales	(16)	1.3
	2.3								2.9
	3.9								4.9
(13)	24.1						% Officers', Directors', Owners' Comp/Sales		
	31.6								
	37.5								
	35046M	23445M	24010M			104720M	Net Sales ($)		96754M
	4545M	9782M	8069M			174239M	Total Assets ($)		55114M

© Robert Morris Associates 1995

M = $ thousand   MM = $ million

See Pages 1 through 15 for Explanation of Ratios and Data

Comparative Historical Data				Current Data Sorted By Sales					
			# Postretirement Benefits						
			Type of Statement						
2	1	3	Unqualified	2					1
5	2	3	Reviewed		1		1	1	
9	16	10	Compiled	2	7	1			
2	4	8	Tax Returns	4	3	1			
2	7	8	Other	2	1	1	3		
4/1/92-3/31/93	4/1/93-3/31/94	4/1/94-3/31/95			9 (4/1-9/30/94)		23 (10/1/94-3/31/95)		
ALL	ALL	ALL		0-1MM	1-3MM	3-5MM	5-10MM	10-25MM	25MM & OVER
20	30	32	NUMBER OF STATEMENTS	10	13	3	4	1	1
%	%	%	ASSETS	%	%	%	%	%	%
14.2	18.1	12.6	Cash & Equivalents	14.9	11.5				
20.5	9.8	15.3	Trade Receivables - (net)	10.3	16.5				
3.9	4.6	3.8	Inventory	.6	6.9				
.8	3.5	3.3	All Other Current	.3	6.4				
39.5	35.9	35.0	Total Current	26.1	41.3				
50.9	44.4	51.4	Fixed Assets (net)	60.2	45.5				
3.3	6.9	1.6	Intangibles (net)	.6	2.8				
6.3	12.8	12.1	All Other Non-Current	13.1	10.4				
100.0	100.0	100.0	Total	100.0	100.0				
			LIABILITIES						
15.1	7.9	11.8	Notes Payable-Short Term	1.1	18.2				
4.6	6.8	5.4	Cur. Mat.-L /T/D	8.4	3.2				
5.2	2.6	2.7	Trade Payables	1.9	2.3				
.8	.2	.3	Income Taxes Payable	.0	.3				
15.9	16.9	10.9	All Other Current	13.8	9.3				
41.6	34.4	31.1	Total Current	25.2	33.3				
18.6	25.7	26.4	Long Term Debt	35.3	26.8				
2.8	.1	.0	Deferred Taxes	.0	.0				
.6	7.4	3.6	All Other-Non-Current	.0	3.1				
36.5	32.4	38.8	Net Worth	39.5	36.9				
100.0	100.0	100.0	Total Liabilities & Net Worth	100.0	100.0				
			INCOME DATA						
100.0	100.0	100.0	Net Sales	100.0	100.0				
			Gross Profit						
97.1	93.0	93.0	Operating Expenses	87.1	92.4				
2.9	7.0	7.0	Operating Profit	12.9	7.6				
.6	2.9	.9	All Other Expenses (net)	2.9	.4				
2.3	4.1	6.1	Profit Before Taxes	10.0	7.2				
			RATIOS						
2.5	4.1	5.4		5.8	13.6				
.9	.9	1.2	Current	1.1	2.7				
.3	.4	.4		.3	.3				
2.5	2.1	4.4		5.8	12.7				
.9	.7 (31)	1.0	Quick	1.1	1.0				
.3	.4	.2		.2	.2				
0 UND	0 UND	0 UND		0 UND	0 UND				
4 88.2	0 UND	0 UND	Sales/Receivables	0 UND	1 272.0				
66 5.5	32 11.3	57 6.4		0 UND	51 7.1				
			Cost of Sales/Inventory						
			Cost of Sales/Payables						
9.7	20.8	4.6		19.4	4.1				
−558.6	NM	259.6	Sales/Working Capital	NM	25.0				
−19.2	−11.1	−25.5		−18.5	−16.7				
4.7	8.2	7.4			9.3				
(14) 2.1	(27) 1.7	(26) 1.5	EBIT/Interest	(12) 5.5					
−1.7	−1.3	.0			.9				
			Net Profit + Depr., Dep., Amort./Cur. Mat. L/T/D						
.6	.7	.7		.7	1.0				
1.1	1.6	1.5	Fixed/Worth	1.9	1.6				
5.8	−52.8	2.5		6.2	2.2				
.9	.8	.9		.5	.9				
1.8	2.8	1.9	Debt/Worth	2.0	2.5				
7.2	−59.4	3.5		6.3	3.5				
45.3	61.9	83.6	% Profit Before Taxes/Tangible Net Worth	94.9	244.6				
(19) 5.3	(22) 9.1	10.5		33.6	27.7				
−52.3	−4.9	−4.6		2.9	−1.6				
22.1	16.0	19.2	% Profit Before Taxes/Total Assets	15.4	71.1				
1.3	.9	3.2		7.9	8.5				
−9.7	−9.3	−1.4		1.0	−.4				
21.9	23.3	22.9	Sales/Net Fixed Assets	23.7	22.7				
12.6	8.7	11.7		10.5	12.0				
6.3	4.3	4.0		1.1	4.3				
10.6	5.8	9.7	Sales/Total Assets	7.2	8.5				
4.2	3.0	5.3		4.1	5.0				
2.3	2.0	2.0		.9	2.0				
1.5	2.3	1.6	% Depr., Dep., Amort./Sales		2.0				
(18) 2.0	(24) 3.6	(29) 2.7		(12) 3.2					
3.5	7.9	4.2			4.1				
11.5	19.3	21.7	% Officers', Directors', Owners' Comp/Sales						
(13) 31.0	(20) 26.1	(19) 31.6							
37.3	41.0	39.3							
86667M	151397M	187221M	Net Sales ($)	5553M	23376M	12111M	25342M	16119M	104720M
27672M	113850M	196635M	Total Assets ($)	3616M	6636M	1075M	7218M	3851M	174239M

M = $ thousand   MM = $ million
See Pages 1 through 15 for Explanation of Ratios and Data

	Current Data Sorted By Assets						# Postretirement Benefits	Comparative Historical Data	
3	1						**Type of Statement**		
		1		1			Unqualified	1	1
							Reviewed	3	7
29	13						Compiled	24	31
9	1						Tax Returns	3	8
9	6	2		1			Other	13	15
	12 (4/1-9/30/94)			60 (10/1/94-3/31/95)				4/1/90-3/31/91	4/1/91-3/31/92
0-500M	500M-2MM	2-10MM	10-50MM	50-100MM	100-250MM			ALL	ALL
47	20	3	2				**NUMBER OF STATEMENTS**	44	62
%	%	%	%	%	%		**ASSETS**	%	%
18.2	14.2						Cash & Equivalents	13.3	14.8
10.1	20.6						Trade Receivables - (net)	15.2	10.6
16.0	11.8						Inventory	11.9	15.7
2.6	.5						All Other Current	1.3	.4
47.0	47.1						Total Current	41.7	41.5
44.9	42.6						Fixed Assets (net)	38.0	41.3
1.4	5.5						Intangibles (net)	6.6	7.8
6.7	4.8						All Other Non-Current	13.8	9.4
100.0	100.0						Total	100.0	100.0
							LIABILITIES		
10.2	4.7						Notes Payable-Short Term	7.4	10.8
12.8	6.8						Cur. Mat. -L/T/D	8.6	8.4
6.2	5.1						Trade Payables	9.7	9.3
.1	.0						Income Taxes Payable	.6	.4
9.7	6.5						All Other Current	10.5	9.9
39.0	23.2						Total Current	36.8	38.9
27.3	23.9						Long Term Debt	30.6	33.5
.0	1.4						Deferred Taxes	1.0	.0
1.4	3.7						All Other-Non-Current	3.8	3.6
32.3	47.9						Net Worth	27.8	24.0
100.0	100.0						Total Liabilities & Net Worth	100.0	100.0
							INCOME DATA		
100.0	100.0						Net Sales	100.0	100.0
							Gross Profit		
90.5	85.1						Operating Expenses	92.1	94.2
9.5	14.9						Operating Profit	7.9	5.8
1.8	2.4						All Other Expenses (net)	.8	1.4
7.7	12.4						Profit Before Taxes	7.1	4.3
							RATIOS		
3.0	4.9							2.2	2.4
1.6	1.9						Current	1.2	1.1
.8	1.0							.5	.6
1.8	4.2							1.5	1.9
.9	1.1						Quick	.8	(61)	.8
.5	.3							.3	.3
0 UND	2 200.6							0 UND	0 UND
2 165.0	13 28.1						Sales/Receivables	5 67.8	3 136.8
20 18.0	46 7.9							29 12.8	23 16.1
							Cost of Sales/Inventory		
							Cost of Sales/Payables		
12.3	5.5							12.9	13.0
42.4	13.7						Sales/Working Capital	53.9	87.5
−52.4	374.4							−53.6	−31.1
	9.4		21.5						7.8		7.8
(39) 4.0	(15) 6.3						EBIT/Interest	(36) 2.8	(55) 2.2
	1.0		2.7						.5		.8
									4.1		2.7
							Net Profit + Depr., Dep., Amort./Cur. Mat. L /T/D	(12) 1.7	(19) 1.4
									1.2		.8
.7	.6							.6	.9
1.5	1.3						Fixed/Worth	1.5	2.1
5.2	2.1							14.4	21.8
.7	.7							1.4	1.3
2.9	1.4						Debt/Worth	3.9	4.1
6.0	3.1							17.8	58.8
	160.0		92.7				% Profit Before Taxes/Tangible Net Worth		92.6		130.1
(41) 36.0	44.5							(37) 12.8	(49) 30.8
	4.4		15.1						−5.9		1.8
36.6	27.1							34.6	27.0
10.1	11.5						% Profit Before Taxes/Total Assets	7.1	5.2
.0	5.3							−1.5	.0
20.6	15.3							20.9	16.1
13.4	8.8						Sales/Net Fixed Assets	12.3	10.1
5.8	3.5							7.7	6.1
7.1	3.9							6.6	5.9
4.4	2.4						Sales/Total Assets	3.9	3.5
2.7	1.6							2.9	2.5
	1.8		2.1						2.2		1.9
(43) 3.2	(18) 2.7						% Depr., Dep., Amort./Sales	(35) 3.8	(56) 3.2
	4.3		5.6						5.2		3.8
	13.9		9.1						11.5		13.8
(32) 20.9	(14) 20.3						% Officers', Directors', Owners' Comp/Sales	(20) 20.6	(32) 23.6
	30.6		32.8						30.5		33.3
43834M	53762M	41442M	103655M				Net Sales ($)	109214M	218148M
9106M	20552M	12668M	40955M				Total Assets ($)	34330M	69109M

M = $ thousand　　MM = $ million
See Pages 1 through 15 for Explanation of Ratios and Data

Comparative Historical Data				Current Data Sorted By Sales					
2	5	4	# Postretirement Benefits	1	3				
			Type of Statement						
2	1	2	Unqualified				1		1
7	3		Reviewed						
36	29	42	Compiled	24	10	8			
9	15	10	Tax Returns	7	3				
26	10	18	Other	8	4	2	2	2	
4/1/92-3/31/93	4/1/93-3/31/94	4/1/94-3/31/95		12 (4/1-9/30/94)			60 (10/1/94-3/31/95)		
ALL	ALL	ALL		0-1MM	1-3MM	3-5MM	5-10MM	10-25MM	25MM & OVER
80	58	72	NUMBER OF STATEMENTS	39	17	10	3	2	1
%	%	%	ASSETS	%	%	%	%	%	%
13.6	11.7	16.3	Cash & Equivalents	16.2	14.6	25.0			
13.7	12.3	13.6	Trade Receivables - (net)	12.1	16.4	13.5			
16.2	17.8	15.2	Inventory	18.0	9.2	12.3			
1.0	.9	1.9	All Other Current	2.6	.6	2.3			
44.4	42.7	47.0	Total Current	48.8	40.8	53.1			
40.7	42.5	43.2	Fixed Assets (net)	41.1	52.3	39.1			
5.9	2.9	3.5	Intangibles (net)	3.6	1.1	1.9			
9.0	11.9	6.3	All Other Non-Current	6.5	5.7	5.9			
100.0	100.0	100.0	Total	100.0	100.0	100.0			
			LIABILITIES						
12.3	8.1	8.2	Notes Payable-Short Term	7.8	10.0	4.1			
7.0	7.8	10.7	Cur. Mat.-L /T/D	12.4	9.3	9.8			
10.8	8.5	6.5	Trade Payables	6.7	4.3	5.9			
.3	.8	.0	Income Taxes Payable	.1	.0	.0			
11.0	10.4	8.6	All Other Current	6.8	10.8	13.6			
41.4	35.6	34.1	Total Current	33.7	34.4	33.4			
23.9	29.4	26.3	Long Term Debt	28.4	24.0	24.7			
.2	.4	.4	Deferred Taxes	.0	1.0	1.2			
4.6	4.0	2.0	All Other-Non-Current	2.1	3.4	.0			
29.9	30.7	37.2	Net Worth	35.9	37.3	40.7			
100.0	100.0	100.0	Total Liabilities & Net Worth	100.0	100.0	100.0			
			INCOME DATA						
100.0	100.0	100.0	Net Sales	100.0	100.0	100.0			
			Gross Profit						
91.6	91.9	88.9	Operating Expenses	88.5	86.7	94.1			
8.4	8.1	11.1	Operating Profit	11.5	13.3	5.9			
1.7	1.0	1.9	All Other Expenses (net)	2.0	2.8	.3			
6.8	7.1	9.2	Profit Before Taxes	9.5	10.5	5.6			
			RATIOS						
2.3	2.2	3.2		3.4	4.2	2.8			
1.3	1.3	1.6	Current	1.6	1.1	1.8			
.6	.8	.9		.9	.6	.9			
1.5	1.2	2.1		1.8	3.3	2.1			
(79) .7	(57) .6	1.0	Quick	1.0	.9	1.0			
.3	.3	.4		.5	.3	.6			
0 UND	0 UND	0 UND		0 UND	0 UND	0 UND			
6 58.4	6 60.4	9 41.5	Sales/Receivables	10 37.6	5 73.4	2 183.4			
23 15.6	25 14.4	23 16.1		23 16.1	30 12.2	24 15.1			
			Cost of Sales/Inventory						
			Cost of Sales/Payables						
16.3	11.3	8.8		8.2	9.5	10.6			
42.0	47.2	33.5	Sales/Working Capital	23.6	55.0	29.3			
−22.1	−47.8	−128.8		−116.7	−20.8	NM			
11.5	9.8	14.5		14.0	6.0				
(72) 2.4	(51) 3.0	(59) 5.2	EBIT/Interest	(31) 5.5	(13) 1.3				
.7	1.0	1.1		2.2	.3				
3.3	2.2	1.6							
(21) 1.8	(10) .7	(12) .9	Net Profit + Depr., Dep., Amort./Cur. Mat. L/T/D						
.5	.3	.5							
.7	.7	.6		.5	.8	.6			
1.6	1.5	1.4	Fixed/Worth	1.4	1.7	.7			
−25.3	4.7	3.4		3.4	4.3	19.8			
1.1	1.2	.8		.7	.8	.6			
3.1	2.4	2.2	Debt/Worth	2.4	2.9	1.4			
−44.3	8.6	5.7		5.2	5.9	42.8			
142.1	134.8	148.6		148.6	86.1				
(59) 28.4	(50) 24.5	(66) 38.5	% Profit Before Taxes/Tangible Net Worth	(34) 54.9	31.9				
.0	.9	9.8		13.2	−5.7				
33.8	41.8	36.3		35.3	35.1	88.6			
5.6	4.4	10.4	% Profit Before Taxes/Total Assets	15.5	7.7	4.2			
−1.3	.0	1.4		3.4	−1.3	−1.0			
22.7	18.8	18.2		27.0	15.2	20.4			
13.4	10.1	11.0	Sales/Net Fixed Assets	8.9	8.7	16.9			
6.6	6.3	5.0		4.9	3.7	11.2			
6.6	6.8	5.6		4.9	8.1	8.5			
4.3	3.6	3.5	Sales/Total Assets	3.4	3.2	4.4			
3.0	2.6	2.2		1.7	1.9	3.6			
1.7	2.1	2.0		1.7	2.1	1.2			
(74) 2.4	(52) 3.1	(66) 3.2	% Depr., Dep., Amort./Sales	(34) 3.3	(16) 3.1	2.1			
3.7	4.3	4.4		4.9	5.1	2.6			
11.4	11.3	12.9		12.5	18.8				
(48) 18.8	(34) 19.2	(47) 20.6	% Officers', Directors', Owners' Comp/Sales	(23) 17.2	(14) 23.6				
27.6	34.5	31.8		22.1	32.0				
259956M	203889M	242693M	Net Sales ($)	21824M	30340M	36819M	25229M	48627M	79854M
76529M	60687M	83281M	Total Assets ($)	9893M	10480M	7855M	6587M	20282M	28184M

M = $ thousand   MM = $ million
See Pages 1 through 15 for Explanation of Ratios and Data

Current Data Sorted By Assets / Comparative Historical Data

						# Postretirement Benefits / Type of Statement		
2	3	1	1					
	1	3	3			Unqualified	7	5
1	7	5	1			Reviewed	11	17
11	15	10				Compiled	29	31
7	2					Tax Returns		2
11	11	1	2	2		Other	17	15
26 (4/1-9/30/94)			67 (10/1/94-3/31/95)				4/1/90-3/31/91	4/1/91-3/31/92
0-500M	500M-2MM	2-10MM	10-50MM	50-100MM	100-250MM		ALL	ALL
30	36	19	6	2		NUMBER OF STATEMENTS	64	70
%	%	%	%	%	%	ASSETS	%	%
16.4	6.8	6.5				Cash & Equivalents	7.6	10.8
29.1	30.0	27.1				Trade Receivables - (net)	28.7	26.6
8.6	10.8	8.5				Inventory	12.0	11.1
.2	.9	1.2				All Other Current	1.5	1.3
54.4	48.5	43.2				Total Current	49.7	49.8
37.1	43.2	47.8				Fixed Assets (net)	39.9	36.5
2.0	3.7	4.7				Intangibles (net)	3.2	5.7
6.5	4.6	4.3				All Other Non-Current	7.2	8.0
100.0	100.0	100.0				Total	100.0	100.0
						LIABILITIES		
7.2	4.8	9.5				Notes Payable-Short Term	8.0	7.7
6.5	8.8	9.3				Cur. Mat. -L/T/D	8.9	7.5
12.2	12.0	13.5				Trade Payables	14.1	10.6
.4	.3	.4				Income Taxes Payable	1.1	.1
9.5	7.8	7.5				All Other Current	8.4	7.4
35.8	33.8	40.3				Total Current	40.5	33.3
20.6	21.9	24.3				Long Term Debt	26.8	23.6
.5	2.1	1.1				Deferred Taxes	.6	1.1
4.3	5.2	2.0				All Other-Non-Current	2.2	.5
38.9	37.1	32.3				Net Worth	29.8	41.6
100.0	100.0	100.0				Total Liabilities & Net Worth	100.0	100.0
						INCOME DATA		
100.0	100.0	100.0				Net Sales	100.0	100.0
51.8	51.2	39.9				Gross Profit	47.9	48.0
45.0	47.9	35.6				Operating Expenses	45.6	42.3
6.9	3.3	4.2				Operating Profit	2.4	5.7
1.0	1.1	.9				All Other Expenses (net)	.7	1.7
5.9	2.2	3.3				Profit Before Taxes	1.6	4.0
						RATIOS		
3.0	2.0	1.9					2.3	3.5
1.6	1.5	1.0				Current	1.5	1.4
.9	1.1	.8					.9	1.0
2.3	1.7	1.4					1.6	2.5
1.4	1.0	.8				Quick	1.0	1.1
.7	.7	.5					.6	.7
21 17.1	30 12.0	34 10.7					29 12.7	27 13.7
28 13.0	42 8.7	47 7.7				Sales/Receivables	44 8.3	40 9.2
34 10.7	62 5.9	52 7.0					57 6.4	51 7.2
3 109.2	13 29.0	16 22.7					11 32.1	8 43.9
13 29.1	26 13.8	21 17.4				Cost of Sales/Inventory	25 14.4	24 15.1
31 11.8	61 6.0	32 11.5					45 8.1	45 8.2
8 46.9	22 16.6	15 23.7					21 17.3	15 24.0
27 13.6	36 10.1	36 10.2				Cost of Sales/Payables	36 10.1	26 14.3
47 7.7	51 7.1	46 8.0					51 7.2	38 9.5
10.4	7.2	9.0					7.5	8.5
19.3	18.2	-157.9				Sales/Working Capital	14.8	17.2
-306.6	81.2	-26.4					-69.7	NM
8.8	4.4	6.2					4.0	7.0
(23) 5.6	(32) 1.8	(18) 2.7				EBIT/Interest	(61) 1.6	(63) 2.9
3.0	1.0	1.5					.7	1.1
	1.8	3.3					3.7	4.5
	(15) 1.1	(12) 1.8				Net Profit + Depr., Dep., Amort./Cur. Mat. L./T/D	(45) 1.5	(35) 1.8
	.5	1.0					.8	1.1
.4	.8	1.0					.6	.5
1.1	1.2	1.8				Fixed/Worth	1.4	1.0
3.3	2.1	4.3					4.0	2.6
.9	1.2	1.2					1.1	.8
1.5	1.8	2.4				Debt/Worth	2.0	1.6
6.9	3.7	5.6					6.9	4.3
114.3	31.3	50.6					42.5	56.7
(27) 42.5	(34) 16.3	(16) 16.7				% Profit Before Taxes/Tangible Net Worth	(55) 11.8	(65) 21.3
25.6	2.3	8.1					-3.9	7.9
37.4	10.5	10.9					11.8	19.1
21.1	5.9	5.0				% Profit Before Taxes/Total Assets	2.4	6.7
6.2	.6	3.2					-1.9	.8
27.6	7.6	7.5					12.3	14.4
10.9	5.2	5.4				Sales/Net Fixed Assets	6.3	6.8
4.4	3.5	3.6					4.4	4.0
5.2	3.2	3.1					3.4	3.5
3.6	2.2	2.4				Sales/Total Assets	2.6	2.5
2.7	1.6	1.6					1.9	1.8
.8	2.5	3.2					2.4	2.4
(23) 3.3	(34) 4.4	4.5				% Depr., Dep., Amort./Sales	(58) 4.2	(65) 3.6
5.1	5.8	5.3					5.5	5.8
5.1	4.0	.8					4.4	2.3
(23) 8.0	(22) 8.6	(11) 2.1				% Officers', Directors', Owners' Comp/Sales	(25) 6.9	(35) 5.0
15.7	11.2	4.4					10.5	13.0
24986M	90778M	193569M	297629M	218020M		Net Sales ($)	424229M	387787M
5856M	37572M	79730M	115933M	127508M		Total Assets ($)	241170M	252817M

© Robert Morris Associates 1995

M = $ thousand　　MM = $ million
See Pages 1 through 15 for Explanation of Ratios and Data

Comparative Historical Data				Current Data Sorted By Sales					
2	4	7		2	3			1	1

Hist 2	Hist 4	Hist 7	# Postretirement Benefits / Type of Statement	0-1MM	1-3MM	3-5MM	5-10MM	10-25MM	25MM & OVER
10	7	7	Unqualified		1		2	2	2
18	15	14	Reviewed		7		5	1	1
38	41	36	Compiled	10	14	3	5	3	1
4	6	9	Tax Returns	4	4	1			
22	19	27	Other	10	8	2	2	1	4
4/1/92-3/31/93 ALL	4/1/93-3/31/94 ALL	4/1/94-3/31/95 ALL		26 (4/1-9/30/94)			67 (10/1/94-3/31/95)		
92	88	93	NUMBER OF STATEMENTS	24	34	6	14	7	8
%	%	%	**ASSETS**	%	%	%	%	%	%
9.4	6.7	10.2	Cash & Equivalents	11.2	12.6		7.1		
28.7	26.9	28.8	Trade Receivables - (net)	28.2	29.5		32.1		
10.2	12.8	9.7	Inventory	10.2	9.4		7.4		
1.1	1.4	1.4	All Other Current	.1	.5		2.2		
49.4	47.7	50.1	Total Current	49.7	52.0		48.8		
39.6	40.6	41.1	Fixed Assets (net)	43.8	41.3		40.7		
2.6	5.2	3.3	Intangibles (net)	1.6	2.5		7.0		
8.4	6.4	5.5	All Other Non-Current	4.8	4.2		3.5		
100.0	100.0	100.0	Total	100.0	100.0		100.0		
			LIABILITIES						
6.7	5.8	6.8	Notes Payable-Short Term	6.4	3.6		10.3		
7.3	7.9	8.1	Cur. Mat.-L /T/D	7.0	8.2		9.3		
13.1	12.8	12.9	Trade Payables	13.4	11.0		14.0		
.6	.9	.4	Income Taxes Payable	.3	.2		.4		
8.4	9.0	8.7	All Other Current	10.2	7.0		7.8		
36.1	36.4	36.9	Total Current	37.3	30.0		41.7		
21.8	26.4	21.2	Long Term Debt	26.7	19.0		23.8		
.8	.4	1.3	Deferred Taxes	.6	1.5		1.5		
3.3	2.3	4.1	All Other-Non-Current	4.8	5.0		2.5		
37.9	34.5	36.4	Net Worth	30.6	44.5		30.4		
100.0	100.0	100.0	Total Liabilities & Net Worth	100.0	100.0		100.0		
			INCOME DATA						
100.0	100.0	100.0	Net Sales	100.0	100.0		100.0		
49.8	50.0	47.8	Gross Profit	55.8	51.7		33.9		
43.8	45.0	42.9	Operating Expenses	49.5	47.1		31.6		
6.0	5.1	4.9	Operating Profit	6.3	4.6		2.3		
1.4	1.1	1.0	All Other Expenses (net)	1.3	.9		.9		
4.6	4.0	3.9	Profit Before Taxes	5.0	3.8		1.5		
			RATIOS						
2.3	2.0	2.2	Current	2.6	2.5		2.0		
1.5	1.2	1.4		1.5	1.7		1.0		
1.0	.9	.9		1.0	1.2		.9		
1.8	1.5	1.7	Quick	1.8	2.2		1.7		
1.2	.9	1.0		1.0	1.2		.8		
.7	.6	.6		.6	.8		.6		
28 13.2	27 13.3	25 14.4	Sales/Receivables	21 17.0	30 12.0		36 10.1		
40 9.1	39 9.3	38 9.7		29 12.8	41 9.0		48 7.6		
52 7.0	52 7.0	52 7.0		38 9.5	62 5.9		52 7.0		
10 35.3	11 34.1	10 34.9	Cost of Sales/Inventory	10 38.0	7 50.5		9 40.6		
20 18.2	26 14.0	21 17.4		20 17.9	19 19.0		19 19.6		
33 11.2	51 7.2	36 10.1		46 8.0	42 8.7		24 15.5		
20 18.5	20 18.7	17 21.0	Cost of Sales/Payables	20 18.7	15 23.7		14 25.7		
30 12.2	35 10.5	34 10.8		35 10.4	35 10.3		32 11.3		
49 7.4	53 6.9	47 7.8		51 7.2	57 6.4		39 9.4		
10.0	10.1	8.8	Sales/Working Capital	10.6	7.5		8.9		
17.8	26.3	22.2		22.8	13.1		-119.3		
-999.8	-120.2	-65.9		NM	30.0		-59.5		
(85) 8.9	(84) 11.0	(81) 6.8	EBIT/Interest	(19) 7.4	(28) 6.3		(13) 2.5		
4.2	3.5	3.1		4.7	2.6		1.9		
1.3	1.3	1.5		1.6	1.5		.3		
(32) 3.4	(42) 3.8	(40) 2.4	Net Profit + Depr., Dep., Amort./Cur. Mat. L/T/D		(12) 2.0				
2.1	1.6	1.8			1.0				
1.4	.9	1.0			.5				
.6	.8	.8	Fixed/Worth	.8	.6		.7		
1.0	1.3	1.4		2.0	1.0		1.8		
2.3	3.4	2.6		6.1	1.6		-36.2		
.7	1.2	1.2	Debt/Worth	1.1	.9		1.4		
1.4	2.2	1.9		2.2	1.4		2.5		
3.4	6.4	4.6		15.0	2.3		-74.6		
(83) 52.3	(79) 69.9	(85) 57.9	% Profit Before Taxes/Tangible Net Worth	(21) 91.9	42.3		(10) 15.9		
20.9	26.5	26.8		28.2	24.2		9.9		
5.3	10.8	7.7		10.3	3.8		-3.5		
18.8	16.7	20.3	% Profit Before Taxes/Total Assets	29.4	21.1		5.3		
9.1	7.2	8.4		11.9	7.7		3.9		
1.5	1.6	2.2		1.6	1.2		-1.1		
13.3	10.4	12.9	Sales/Net Fixed Assets	13.4	9.4		10.8		
7.1	6.7	6.2		8.3	5.4		5.8		
4.2	4.1	4.0		3.6	3.8		3.9		
3.5	3.1	3.6	Sales/Total Assets	4.5	3.3		3.1		
2.5	2.5	2.6		3.1	2.4		2.4		
2.0	1.9	1.9		2.1	1.7		1.6		
(87) 2.3	(81) 2.3	(83) 2.3	% Depr., Dep., Amort./Sales	(17) 2.5	(33) 2.4		(13) 2.8		
3.9	4.4	3.7		3.7	3.6		4.5		
6.0	7.1	5.4		5.6	6.0		5.4		
(51) 3.0	(45) 2.8	(56) 3.0	% Officers', Directors', Owners' Comp/Sales	(17) 4.2	(22) 6.2				
6.4	5.6	6.7		6.5	8.8				
11.6	9.4	11.7		17.2	13.8				
477491M	866690M	824982M	Net Sales ($)	12118M	64714M	20167M	97684M	104505M	525794M
219793M	354051M	366599M	Total Assets ($)	4732M	30863M	6728M	44823M	44548M	234905M

M = $ thousand   MM = $ million
See Pages 1 through 15 for Explanation of Ratios and Data

Current Data Sorted By Assets   Comparative Historical Data

		1		4			# Postretirement Benefits		

Type of Statement

0-500M	500M-2MM	2-10MM	10-50MM	50-100MM	100-250MM	Type of Statement	4/1/90-3/31/91 ALL	4/1/91-3/31/92 ALL
1	2	4	3			Unqualified	4	9
4	11	7				Reviewed	16	23
12	11	1				Compiled	26	34
1	1	1				Tax Returns	1	4
9	14	7				Other	25	21
25 (4/1-9/30/94)			64 (10/1/94-3/31/95)					
27	39	20	3			**NUMBER OF STATEMENTS**	72	91
%	%	%	%	%	%	**ASSETS**	%	%
14.9	11.8	8.1				Cash & Equivalents	9.6	10.8
20.0	24.3	25.6				Trade Receivables - (net)	23.2	20.3
7.6	7.9	10.0				Inventory	12.4	11.4
.4	1.4	.8				All Other Current	1.4	1.3
42.9	45.4	44.5				Total Current	46.6	43.8
47.4	43.5	45.2				Fixed Assets (net)	44.5	45.5
2.9	3.3	2.3				Intangibles (net)	3.2	3.4
6.8	7.9	7.9				All Other Non-Current	5.7	7.3
100.0	100.0	100.0				Total	100.0	100.0
						LIABILITIES		
6.8	6.2	7.5				Notes Payable-Short Term	6.8	9.1
6.2	12.3	10.4				Cur. Mat. -L/T/D	9.3	8.2
10.6	11.7	11.8				Trade Payables	13.3	12.8
.2	.2	.6				Income Taxes Payable	.7	.6
6.9	7.8	10.2				All Other Current	7.3	10.5
30.7	38.2	40.5				Total Current	37.3	41.2
38.1	25.1	15.3				Long Term Debt	30.5	28.2
.1	.5	1.0				Deferred Taxes	.5	.6
5.6	2.6	3.3				All Other-Non-Current	2.7	2.8
25.5	33.6	39.9				Net Worth	29.0	27.3
100.0	100.0	100.0				Total Liabilities & Net Worth	100.0	100.0
						INCOME DATA		
100.0	100.0	100.0				Net Sales	100.0	100.0
59.2	48.7	40.5				Gross Profit	48.5	49.8
52.1	42.7	35.6				Operating Expenses	44.8	45.5
7.1	6.0	4.9				Operating Profit	3.8	4.2
2.6	1.5	.9				All Other Expenses (net)	2.0	1.4
4.6	4.5	4.0				Profit Before Taxes	1.8	2.8
						RATIOS		
5.0	1.8	1.6					1.9	1.8
1.5	1.1	1.1				Current	1.3	1.2
.8	.8	.8					.9	.8
3.8	1.6	1.3					1.4	1.4
1.1	.9	.8				Quick	.8	.8
.5	.6	.6					.6	.4
10 35.4	24 15.2	30 12.3					16 22.3	14 26.4
20 18.7	38 9.7	41 8.8				Sales/Receivables	39 9.4	30 12.1
41 9.0	51 7.1	61 6.0					51 7.1	50 7.3
5 68.9	8 46.4	12 29.9					14 26.6	11 34.0
18 20.0	22 16.4	20 18.6				Cost of Sales/Inventory	26 13.9	25 14.6
63 5.8	37 9.8	30 12.0					51 7.2	42 8.7
0 UND	13 28.8	16 23.0					19 19.1	20 18.6
26 13.9	24 15.0	28 13.2				Cost of Sales/Payables	33 11.1	30 12.0
60 6.1	54 6.7	41 9.0					64 5.7	56 6.5
7.3	9.8	10.5					9.8	11.1
19.1	74.6	59.5				Sales/Working Capital	26.1	43.4
−45.6	−22.2	−34.7					−37.5	−24.2
5.5	6.2	8.3					3.8	4.5
(22) 2.7	(35) 2.4	(19) 3.8				EBIT/Interest	(67) 2.0	(84) 2.3
.3	1.6	1.8					.7	1.3
	2.7	3.2					3.1	2.4
	(18) 1.5	(14) 2.3				Net Profit + Depr., Dep., Amort./Cur. Mat. L./T/D	(45) 1.6	(38) 1.7
	.9	1.2					.6	.9
1.3	.6	.8					.8	.8
2.9	1.4	1.4				Fixed/Worth	1.5	1.6
−15.3	4.0	2.0					5.1	11.1
1.3	1.0	1.0					1.1	1.1
3.3	1.8	1.7				Debt/Worth	2.6	2.5
−19.3	6.0	2.4					12.5	23.1
63.1	56.2	33.2					36.9	49.8
(18) 34.4	(33) 17.3	(19) 16.9				% Profit Before Taxes/Tangible Net Worth	(57) 17.8	(73) 20.3
1.5	11.2	9.0					.8	7.4
29.1	12.9	12.6					12.0	14.3
13.5	6.9	10.0				% Profit Before Taxes/Total Assets	5.3	7.5
−3.6	2.9	3.1					−1.3	1.2
8.6	9.3	7.8					9.6	9.5
6.0	4.8	4.2				Sales/Net Fixed Assets	5.3	5.5
2.9	3.7	3.1					3.2	3.3
3.5	2.8	2.5					3.0	3.1
2.5	2.4	2.0				Sales/Total Assets	2.3	2.3
1.6	1.9	1.7					1.8	1.8
4.5	2.8	2.4					3.0	2.9
(22) 6.7	(38) 5.3	(19) 3.9				% Depr., Dep., Amort./Sales	(65) 5.0	(85) 4.5
10.3	7.6	5.4					7.4	6.3
5.1	2.8	3.0					5.1	3.8
(10) 6.3	(20) 5.6	(10) 3.6				% Officers', Directors', Owners' Comp/Sales	(28) 7.5	(43) 7.4
8.9	10.9	5.1					9.5	13.7
16551M	104924M	175210M	114411M			Net Sales ($)	232827M	380364M
6019M	41019M	75631M	74089M			Total Assets ($)	102506M	247371M

© Robert Morris Associates 1995

M = $ thousand   MM = $ million
See Pages 1 through 15 for Explanation of Ratios and Data

	Comparative Historical Data				Current Data Sorted By Sales					
	1	5	5	# Postretirement Benefits		1		2	2	
				Type of Statement						
	6	7	10	Unqualified	1		3	2	1	3
	18	17	22	Reviewed	4	9	4	5		
	24	21	24	Compiled	11	10	2	1		
	3	10	3	Tax Returns	1	1		1		
	12	15	30	Other	8	12	2	4	4	
	4/1/92-	4/1/93-	4/1/94-			25 (4/1-9/30/94)			64 (10/1/94-3/31/95)		
	3/31/93	3/31/94	3/31/95		0-1MM	1-3MM	3-5MM	5-10MM	10-25MM	25MM & OVER
	ALL	ALL	ALL							
	63	70	89	NUMBER OF STATEMENTS	25	32	11	13	5	3
	%	%	%	ASSETS	%	%	%	%	%	%
	12.9	11.9	11.8	Cash & Equivalents	12.0	14.3	8.3	10.5		
	21.0	21.0	22.9	Trade Receivables - (net)	17.4	24.4	34.8	25.3		
	10.6	11.5	8.2	Inventory	7.3	7.7	7.9	6.6		
	1.9	1.2	1.2	All Other Current	.4	.9	1.9	.6		
	46.4	45.6	44.0	Total Current	37.1	47.4	52.8	43.0		
	43.6	45.6	45.5	Fixed Assets (net)	50.7	43.1	38.2	46.7		
	3.6	3.4	3.0	Intangibles (net)	4.6	1.4	4.2	3.1		
	6.4	5.5	7.5	All Other Non-Current	7.6	8.1	4.8	7.2		
	100.0	100.0	100.0	Total	100.0	100.0	100.0	100.0		
				LIABILITIES						
	7.8	6.1	6.6	Notes Payable-Short Term	7.1	3.3	14.7	8.8		
	10.6	8.3	9.8	Cur. Mat.-L /T/D	5.6	14.7	8.4	8.5		
	10.9	13.1	11.3	Trade Payables	10.6	10.6	12.0	9.2		
	.5	.6	.4	Income Taxes Payable	.3	.2	.9	.4		
	6.5	7.3	8.1	All Other Current	7.8	7.2	7.6	8.4		
	36.2	35.5	36.2	Total Current	31.4	35.9	43.6	35.2		
	27.6	28.7	26.9	Long Term Debt	41.5	26.2	13.0	16.7		
	1.2	.6	.7	Deferred Taxes	.1	.5	.9	.5		
	1.3	3.0	3.6	All Other-Non-Current	6.0	3.2	.9	4.1		
	33.6	32.2	32.7	Net Worth	20.9	34.1	41.6	43.5		
	100.0	100.0	100.0	Total Liabilities & Net Worth	100.0	100.0	100.0	100.0		
				INCOME DATA						
	100.0	100.0	100.0	Net Sales	100.0	100.0	100.0	100.0		
	49.9	52.3	49.6	Gross Profit	61.8	46.9	47.6	42.3		
	43.8	47.1	43.3	Operating Expenses	55.0	40.8	41.5	37.2		
	6.1	5.1	6.3	Operating Profit	6.8	6.1	6.0	5.1		
	1.4	1.5	1.6	All Other Expenses (net)	2.5	1.5	1.4	1.3		
	4.7	3.7	4.7	Profit Before Taxes	4.3	4.6	4.6	3.9		
				RATIOS						
	2.4	1.9	2.0		3.3	2.1	1.7	1.5		
	1.3	1.3	1.2	Current	1.2	1.4	1.0	1.1		
	.9	.9	.8		.7	.8	.9	.8		
	1.9	1.6	1.7		3.1	1.7	1.6	1.3		
	1.0	1.0	.9	Quick	1.0	1.0	.8	.9		
	.7	.6	.6		.5	.7	.7	.6		
	21 17.6	14 25.2	18 20.0		8 45.4	26 14.2	29 12.7	27 13.4		
	37 9.9	36 10.2	34 10.7	Sales/Receivables	20 18.7	39 9.3	45 8.2	41 9.0		
	49 7.5	49 7.4	50 7.3		38 9.6	50 7.3	54 6.8	59 6.2		
	13 28.6	14 25.4	8 44.3		9 40.0	6 56.5	12 31.1	11 32.2		
	24 15.2	26 13.9	20 18.7	Cost of Sales/Inventory	25 14.7	18 20.5	20 18.4	20 18.7		
	53 6.9	51 7.1	46 8.0		60 6.1	42 8.7	51 7.0	30 12.1		
	17 21.9	18 20.3	12 30.0		0 UND	9 40.3	18 20.1	15 24.0		
	31 11.9	33 11.2	26 13.9	Cost of Sales/Payables	35 10.4	23 15.9	42 8.6	26 14.0		
	47 7.7	52 7.0	54 6.8		83 4.4	47 7.7	54 6.7	43 8.5		
	10.2	9.4	9.0		7.3	8.4	5.6	11.4		
	22.1	26.7	46.9	Sales/Working Capital	22.1	20.4	173.2	65.9		
	−67.8	−107.2	−24.6		−19.4	−27.9	−55.0	−21.0		
	5.9	5.9	6.3		5.5	3.3	20.9	5.7		
	(57) 2.5	(65) 2.4	(79) 3.0	EBIT/Interest	(22) 2.7	(27) 2.3	(10) 3.6	(12) 2.8		
	1.4	.7	1.7		1.3	1.4	1.0	1.3		
	2.7	2.2	2.9			2.8		3.2		
	(26) 1.9	(29) 1.3	(37) 1.5	Net Profit + Depr., Dep., Amort./Cur. Mat. L/T/D		(13) 1.5		(10) 1.7		
	1.2	.6	.9			.9		.9		
	.7	.9	.8		1.4	.6	.4	.9		
	1.6	1.4	1.6	Fixed/Worth	3.3	1.4	1.1	1.4		
	4.5	4.4	4.8		−7.0	5.9	2.9	1.9		
	.9	1.0	1.0		1.3	.9	1.0	1.0		
	1.9	1.9	2.1	Debt/Worth	4.2	1.8	1.2	1.7		
	8.0	6.0	6.6		−16.6	9.6	6.0	2.2		
	45.5	40.0	54.0		56.5	57.2	50.0	37.0		
	(52) 22.7	(59) 14.0	(73) 24.6	% Profit Before Taxes/Tangible Net Worth	(16) 30.2	(26) 20.7	(10) 18.7	16.4		
	5.5	−3.3	9.5		4.4	10.0	5.0	5.8		
	20.0	16.1	15.8		22.2	12.9	14.6	13.6		
	6.8	5.2	8.6	% Profit Before Taxes/Total Assets	7.5	7.4	6.4	8.6		
	2.3	−1.4	2.6		−1.3	2.7	1.7	1.7		
	9.9	9.3	8.6		8.2	9.1	13.8	7.0		
	5.6	5.3	4.8	Sales/Net Fixed Assets	4.7	4.7	6.6	3.9		
	3.6	3.2	3.3		2.7	3.7	4.8	3.0		
	3.0	3.1	3.0		3.1	2.8	3.2	2.5		
	2.3	2.2	2.3	Sales/Total Assets	2.4	2.3	2.4	2.0		
	1.8	1.7	1.7		1.4	1.7	2.1	1.6		
	2.4	3.5	3.5		4.6	4.0	2.3	2.1		
	(60) 4.5	(65) 4.7	(83) 5.0	% Depr., Dep., Amort./Sales	(23) 6.6	(28) 6.2	4.4	3.8		
	7.4	6.8	7.8		9.2	9.5	5.1	5.5		
	4.3	3.5	3.3		5.1	3.4				
	(23) 7.7	(32) 6.2	(41) 5.1	% Officers', Directors', Owners' Comp/Sales	(11) 6.2	(13) 7.1				
	12.7	8.4	7.9		8.7	11.6				
	294119M	415101M	411096M	Net Sales ($)	11639M	64390M	41236M	88238M	91182M	114411M
	103618M	202233M	196758M	Total Assets ($)	5694M	30728M	17255M	44978M	24014M	74089M

M = $ thousand   MM = $ million
See Pages 1 through 15 for Explanation of Ratios and Data

Comparative / Current Data

Current Data Sorted By Assets | **Comparative Historical Data**

Type of Statement counts

0-500M	500M-2MM	2-10MM	10-50MM	50-100MM	100-250MM		4/1/90-3/31/91 ALL	4/1/91-3/31/92 ALL
3	2	2				# Postretirement Benefits		
						Type of Statement		
	2	1	2	1	2	Unqualified	6	6
3	11	6				Reviewed	24	17
34	9	2				Compiled	37	41
9	3					Tax Returns	1	2
8	3	3	1			Other	19	21
| 38 (4/1-9/30/94)			62 (10/1/94-3/31/95)					
54	28	12	3	1	2	NUMBER OF STATEMENTS	87	87

Common-Size & Ratios

0-500M %	500M-2MM %	2-10MM %	10-50MM %	50-100MM %	100-250MM %	Item	ALL %	ALL %
						ASSETS		
15.1	8.1	6.7				Cash & Equivalents	10.7	12.1
18.0	23.5	32.5				Trade Receivables - (net)	29.9	23.4
6.3	8.8	8.3				Inventory	9.0	8.8
3.9	1.4	6.0				All Other Current	1.2	2.0
43.3	41.9	53.5				Total Current	50.8	46.2
44.1	42.6	41.5				Fixed Assets (net)	39.2	39.8
4.5	5.0	.7				Intangibles (net)	3.4	3.9
8.1	10.5	4.3				All Other Non-Current	6.6	10.1
100.0	100.0	100.0				Total	100.0	100.0
						LIABILITIES		
13.7	7.4	8.0				Notes Payable-Short Term	10.0	7.2
5.8	6.2	5.6				Cur. Mat. -L/T/D	7.5	6.3
8.4	11.8	7.2				Trade Payables	13.5	13.0
.3	1.2	.0				Income Taxes Payable	1.0	.4
15.5	11.6	12.8				All Other Current	10.2	11.3
43.8	38.0	33.6				Total Current	42.1	38.1
21.0	20.4	18.8				Long Term Debt	18.9	20.2
.5	.3	.7				Deferred Taxes	1.2	1.1
3.7	4.9	1.4				All Other-Non-Current	2.5	2.2
30.9	36.5	45.5				Net Worth	35.3	38.4
100.0	100.0	100.0				Total Liabilities & Net Worth	100.0	100.0
						INCOME DATA		
100.0	100.0	100.0				Net Sales	100.0	100.0
						Gross Profit		
93.7	92.8	91.2				Operating Expenses	96.3	96.1
6.3	7.2	8.8				Operating Profit	3.7	3.9
1.4	3.3	.3				All Other Expenses (net)	1.7	1.1
4.9	3.9	8.5				Profit Before Taxes	2.0	2.8
						RATIOS		
2.5	1.9	2.3				Current	2.0	2.4
1.2	1.3	1.6					1.2	1.3
.6	.6	.8					.8	.9
2.0	1.6	2.1				Quick	1.7	1.8
.7	.9	1.1					1.1	1.0
.5	.5	.7					.6	.5

Sales/Receivables (days / times)

0-500M	500M-2MM	2-10MM	Item	ALL	ALL
0 UND	2 158.5	53 6.9	Sales/Receivables	11 31.8 / 6 57.0	
15 25.0	40 9.2	78 4.7		38 9.7 / 36 10.2	
48 7.6	58 6.3	89 4.1		73 5.0 / 60 6.1	
			Cost of Sales/Inventory		
			Cost of Sales/Payables		

Additional Ratios

0-500M	500M-2MM	2-10MM	Item	ALL	ALL
9.8	9.2	3.6	Sales/Working Capital	10.6	10.1
50.0	57.7	7.0		38.8	32.5
-12.7	-13.8	NM		-22.1	-31.9
(49) 7.4	(26) 7.0	(11) 9.6	EBIT/Interest	(76) 5.6	(78) 6.9
3.3	3.6	5.5		2.0	2.8
-.1	.3	2.6		.6	.9
(13) 7.1	(14) 4.4		Net Profit + Depr., Dep., Amort./Cur. Mat. L /T/D	(44) 4.2	(31) 4.0
2.0	2.1			1.6	1.2
-.2	.5			.1	.3
.7	.6	.5	Fixed/Worth	.5	.5
2.2	1.6	.8		1.2	1.0
53.8	NM	1.4		3.0	3.1
.8	.7	.5	Debt/Worth	.8	.7
3.1	1.7	1.4		2.4	1.3
97.6	NM	2.7		6.5	6.6
(43) 83.5	(21) 48.8	56.4	% Profit Before Taxes/Tangible Net Worth	(74) 43.5	(75) 36.5
29.8	14.0	35.7		17.1	15.6
.0	-12.6	11.8		-5.4	1.3
21.6	16.5	17.5	% Profit Before Taxes/Total Assets	13.6	15.1
8.4	8.7	11.1		5.1	5.9
-4.5	-4.3	4.9		-2.9	-2.1
12.6	14.8	9.0	Sales/Net Fixed Assets	17.9	17.6
7.7	6.5	5.0		7.5	8.5
4.2	2.9	2.5		4.6	4.4
4.5	3.4	2.0	Sales/Total Assets	3.8	3.6
2.9	2.3	1.7		2.7	2.7
2.1	1.4	1.3		1.8	1.7
(44) 2.3	(27) 2.1	2.4	% Depr., Dep., Amort./Sales	(76) 1.9	(84) 1.8
3.7	2.9	4.8		3.5	3.5
5.6	5.9	7.7		5.5	5.5
(33) 9.6	(12) 6.3		% Officers', Directors', Owners' Comp/Sales	(41) 5.0	(48) 3.9
15.7	10.8			9.1	8.1
22.1	15.8			15.2	15.1

Dollar Totals

0-500M	500M-2MM	2-10MM	10-50MM	50-100MM	100-250MM	Item	ALL	ALL
31757M	91380M	79893M	306136M	144880M	583922M	Net Sales ($)	962345M	221071M
9943M	31956M	38646M	91795M	59557M	391779M	Total Assets ($)	433672M	114652M

M = $ thousand   MM = $ million
See Pages 1 through 15 for Explanation of Ratios and Data

Comparative Historical Data / Current Data Sorted By Sales

1	4	7		4	2			1	
			# Postretirement Benefits						
			Type of Statement						
3	4	8	Unqualified	1		1		1	5
17	14	20	Reviewed	5	4	5	4	2	
39	44	45	Compiled	30	11	3	1		
4	9	12	Tax Returns	9	3				
21	17	15	Other	7	3	3		1	1
4/1/92- 3/31/93	4/1/93- 3/31/94	4/1/94- 3/31/95		38 (4/1-9/30/94)			62 (10/1/94-3/31/95)		
ALL	ALL	ALL		0-1MM	1-3MM	3-5MM	5-10MM	10-25MM	25MM & OVER
84	88	100	**NUMBER OF STATEMENTS**	52	21	12	5	4	6
%	%	%	**ASSETS**	%	%	%	%	%	%
12.9	10.9	12.7	Cash & Equivalents	15.2	7.3	7.9			
21.4	22.2	20.7	Trade Receivables - (net)	17.6	25.0	34.0			
7.2	8.4	7.0	Inventory	5.9	6.3	7.8			
1.0	1.6	3.4	All Other Current	3.6	3.3	2.3			
42.4	43.2	43.8	Total Current	42.3	42.0	52.0			
46.1	42.7	43.9	Fixed Assets (net)	46.1	42.0	37.4			
3.6	5.0	4.1	Intangibles (net)	4.2	5.4	2.6			
7.9	9.2	8.3	All Other Non-Current	7.4	10.7	8.0			
100.0	100.0	100.0	Total	100.0	100.0	100.0			
			LIABILITIES						
7.5	5.8	11.0	Notes Payable-Short Term	11.9	11.0	8.4			
6.7	5.2	5.6	Cur. Mat.-L/T/D	5.3	8.0	5.7			
8.2	10.3	9.1	Trade Payables	6.9	13.8	9.7			
.6	.7	.6	Income Taxes Payable	.3	1.5	.1			
10.3	11.0	14.2	All Other Current	12.8	12.2	13.0			
33.2	33.0	40.5	Total Current	37.2	46.6	37.0			
22.5	22.1	19.5	Long Term Debt	24.4	19.4	11.2			
1.6	1.0	.5	Deferred Taxes	.6	.1	.5			
2.6	5.5	3.7	All Other-Non-Current	3.5	3.9	1.5			
40.1	38.5	35.8	Net Worth	34.3	30.0	49.7			
100.0	100.0	100.0	Total Liabilities & Net Worth	100.0	100.0	100.0			
			INCOME DATA						
100.0	100.0	100.0	Net Sales	100.0	100.0	100.0			
			Gross Profit						
93.5	93.5	92.9	Operating Expenses	91.7	96.6	91.9			
6.5	6.5	7.1	Operating Profit	8.3	3.4	8.1			
1.5	1.1	1.8	All Other Expenses (net)	2.6	.7	.6			
5.0	5.4	5.3	Profit Before Taxes	5.7	2.7	7.5			
			RATIOS						
2.1	3.3	2.2		2.8	1.8	2.2			
1.4	1.2	1.2	Current	1.4	.9	1.5			
.8	.7	.6		.7	.6	.9			
1.9	2.0	1.8		2.4	1.6	1.7			
1.2	1.2	.9	Quick	1.1	.7	1.2			
.6	.5	.5		.5	.2	.7			
1 249.2	9 42.5	0 897.5		0 UND	4 84.4	25 14.5			
22 16.5	33 11.0	24 15.4	Sales/Receivables	20 18.5	43 8.5	38 9.7			
59 6.2	58 6.3	54 6.7		53 6.9	59 6.2	89 4.1			
			Cost of Sales/Inventory						
			Cost of Sales/Payables						
9.4	6.6	9.1		9.0	9.2	4.1			
23.1	30.4	34.8	Sales/Working Capital	25.2	-47.7	20.6			
-61.6	-24.3	-15.4		-13.4	-11.2	-68.9			
(70) 9.4	(77) 11.1	(92) 9.3		(45) 6.2	6.7	(11) 46.5			
4.5	5.4	4.0	EBIT/Interest	3.0	3.3	7.5			
1.7	1.1	.4		-.2	.9	2.4			
(31) 4.6	(29) 3.3	(37) 6.5	Net Profit + Depr., Dep.,	(16) 5.1					
2.1	1.6	2.1	Amort./Cur. Mat. L/T/D	1.9					
1.1	.9	.8		.4					
.6	.6	.6		.6	.9	.5			
1.3	1.3	1.6	Fixed/Worth	1.9	1.9	.7			
3.1	4.0	8.9		43.9	-14.7	1.5			
.7	.7	.7		.6	1.2	.4			
1.3	1.6	2.0	Debt/Worth	2.5	2.6	.9			
5.9	16.4	20.4		79.9	-102.4	3.1			
(72) 60.8	(71) 63.9	(82) 57.4	% Profit Before Taxes/Tangible	(42) 69.2	(15) 38.6	64.9			
23.9	27.1	28.6	Net Worth	29.0	15.8	40.4			
4.5	7.4	1.5		-8.4	6.0	13.5			
22.4	24.4	19.6	% Profit Before Taxes/Total	21.7	12.0	27.2			
7.3	10.7	9.4	Assets	6.6	9.5	15.9			
2.0	.1	-2.2		-5.5	-.1	7.6			
13.2	13.7	12.8		11.5	13.7	18.9			
7.2	6.6	6.2	Sales/Net Fixed Assets	5.9	8.3	6.5			
3.5	3.6	3.8		3.5	3.9	4.0			
4.1	3.6	3.6		3.5	3.6	4.4			
2.7	2.3	2.4	Sales/Total Assets	2.3	2.6	1.9			
1.8	1.6	1.7		1.4	1.8	1.7			
(78) 2.1	(79) 2.3	(87) 2.3		(42) 2.8	(20) 1.6	1.4			
3.6	3.7	3.8	% Depr., Dep., Amort./Sales	4.2	2.7	4.7			
6.5	5.7	5.6		6.8	4.5	5.6			
(47) 4.4	(43) 5.9	(51) 7.9	% Officers', Directors',	(29) 10.2	(13) 6.4				
9.4	10.6	13.5	Owners' Comp/Sales	15.7	16.1				
12.9	18.6	18.5		22.1	16.1				
518153M	768607M	1237968M	Net Sales ($)	20510M	41441M	48783M	33709M	58587M	1034938M
227619M	318537M	623676M	Total Assets ($)	12465M	18040M	22254M	15361M	12425M	543131M

M = $ thousand   MM = $ million
See Pages 1 through 15 for Explanation of Ratios and Data

Current Data Sorted By Assets   Comparative Historical Data

0-500M	500M-2MM	2-10MM	10-50MM	50-100MM	100-250MM		4/1/90-3/31/91 ALL	4/1/91-3/31/92 ALL
						# Postretirement Benefits		
						Type of Statement =		
2	1	5				Unqualified	11	15
1	4	1	2			Reviewed	8	9
14	12	4				Compiled	28	28
1	3					Tax Returns	2	4
5	14	9	1	1		Other	27	28
17 (4/1-9/30/94)			63 (10/1/94-3/31/95)					
23	34	19	3	1		**NUMBER OF STATEMENTS**	76	84
%	%	%	%	%	%	**ASSETS**	%	%
17.4	3.0	9.9				Cash & Equivalents	7.3	9.0
3.1	10.5	9.0				Trade Receivables - (net)	10.0	10.2
1.7	3.5	.5				Inventory	4.2	3.8
1.9	2.1	4.5				All Other Current	1.9	2.3
24.0	19.2	24.0				Total Current	23.4	25.3
56.8	72.8	65.4				Fixed Assets (net)	63.5	64.0
7.2	3.8	2.4				Intangibles (net)	1.7	1.8
12.0	4.2	8.2				All Other Non-Current	11.4	8.9
100.0	100.0	100.0				Total	100.0	100.0
						LIABILITIES		
10.8	7.8	1.2				Notes Payable-Short Term	4.4	5.7
6.5	7.7	5.6				Cur. Mat. -L/T/D	2.7	4.4
4.4	3.1	3.4				Trade Payables	5.1	4.5
.4	.2	.2				Income Taxes Payable	.6	.3
8.1	7.0	6.9				All Other Current	11.0	11.1
30.2	25.8	17.3				Total Current	23.7	26.0
30.9	36.1	36.7				Long Term Debt	34.6	35.3
.3	2.8	.1				Deferred Taxes	.4	.4
6.7	7.9	7.0				All Other-Non-Current	8.8	6.7
31.9	27.4	38.9				Net Worth	32.6	31.5
100.0	100.0	100.0				Total Liabilities & Net Worth	100.0	100.0
						INCOME DATA		
100.0	100.0	100.0				Net Sales	100.0	100.0
						Gross Profit		
93.9	92.4	89.5				Operating Expenses	91.1	91.1
6.1	7.6	10.5				Operating Profit	8.9	8.9
3.0	3.4	5.4				All Other Expenses (net)	5.3	4.3
3.1	4.2	5.1				Profit Before Taxes	3.6	4.6
						RATIOS		
5.4	1.4	2.6					2.0	2.1
.4	.6	1.6				Current	.9	1.0
.3	.3	.8					.4	.5
3.6	.9	2.0					1.3	1.8
.3	.5	.9				Quick	.6	.8
.2	.1	.3					.2	.3
0 UND	0 UND	1 377.0					0 963.9	0 UND
0 UND	8 46.9	7 53.1				Sales/Receivables	9 39.2	9 38.7
12 31.5	36 10.1	37 9.8					35 10.3	33 11.2
						Cost of Sales/Inventory		
						Cost of Sales/Payables		
22.2	23.4	6.3					12.6	9.3
-13.2	-15.2	10.1				Sales/Working Capital	-259.5	-255.3
-9.9	-4.9	-31.8					-10.3	-10.3
5.2	5.3	6.4					3.4	4.7
(19) 2.1	(31) 2.0	(16) 2.9				EBIT/Interest	(63) 1.8	(75) 2.3
.3	.9	1.7					.8	1.2
							4.4	3.5
						Net Profit + Depr., Dep., Amort./Cur. Mat. L/T/D	(19) 2.0	(18) 1.0
							1.3	.2
.9	1.5	.8					1.0	1.2
4.5	3.4	2.5				Fixed/Worth	1.9	2.0
27.0	166.2	5.4					45.0	5.6
1.0	1.5	.5					.7	.9
4.8	2.8	2.6				Debt/Worth	2.1	2.2
49.5	173.5	5.6					99.7	8.1
42.4	49.1	65.6				% Profit Before Taxes/Tangible	35.7	31.4
(19) 12.8	(27) 21.9	31.2				Net Worth	(60) 11.1	(71) 16.3
-20.6	10.2	-.8					-5.7	3.1
21.2	13.5	13.6				% Profit Before Taxes/Total	11.3	12.8
8.4	6.0	5.8				Assets	3.8	5.8
-4.0	-.2	-.7					-2.4	.7
9.9	3.1	4.2					5.1	5.9
3.5	1.6	1.7				Sales/Net Fixed Assets	1.9	1.8
1.5	.9	.8					.7	.8
3.4	1.8	1.6					2.0	2.8
2.1	1.1	.9				Sales/Total Assets	1.2	1.2
1.0	.7	.7					.6	.7
5.3	3.7	3.5					3.8	4.1
(22) 6.6	(33) 6.6	(17) 5.7				% Depr., Dep., Amort./Sales	(70) 6.5	(76) 6.0
12.0	10.3	7.9					9.4	9.0
	3.1						3.0	3.2
	(15) 7.1					% Officers', Directors', Owners' Comp/Sales	(26) 6.6	(25) 5.7
	16.6						21.8	10.9
15595M	50575M	83883M	35839M	36994M		Net Sales ($)	1251449M	985875M
6092M	37188M	82694M	32273M	84775M		Total Assets ($)	603071M	701391M

Comparative Historical Data				Current Data Sorted By Sales					
1	5	4	**# Postretirement Benefits**	1	1	2			
			Type of Statement						
17	8	8	Unqualified	3	2	1	1	1	
2	13	8	Reviewed	2	3	1	1	1	
31	34	30	Compiled	19	7	3	1		
5	6	4	Tax Returns	2	2				
23	30	30	Other	8	13	4	3	1	1
4/1/92-3/31/93	4/1/93-3/31/94	4/1/94-3/31/95		17 (4/1-9/30/94)		63 (10/1/94-3/31/95)			
ALL	ALL	ALL		0-1MM	1-3MM	3-5MM	5-10MM	10-25MM	25MM & OVER
78	91	80	**NUMBER OF STATEMENTS**	34	27	9	6	3	1
%	%	%	**ASSETS**	%	%	%	%	%	%
6.9	9.7	8.9	Cash & Equivalents	8.4	6.0				
11.6	11.1	8.0	Trade Receivables - (net)	5.7	7.1				
2.6	2.5	2.3	Inventory	.8	1.2				
3.1	2.0	2.8	All Other Current	2.7	3.0				
24.2	25.4	22.1	Total Current	17.6	17.3				
62.8	63.7	65.8	Fixed Assets (net)	67.6	72.2				
2.0	2.9	4.5	Intangibles (net)	5.0	4.5				
10.9	7.9	7.6	All Other Non-Current	9.8	6.0				
100.0	100.0	100.0	Total	100.0	100.0				
			LIABILITIES						
3.4	4.0	7.1	Notes Payable-Short Term	6.5	5.3				
5.5	5.3	6.6	Cur. Mat.-L /T/D	6.9	8.5				
3.7	5.1	3.8	Trade Payables	2.9	2.9				
.1	.4	.3	Income Taxes Payable	.3	.1				
10.1	12.6	7.3	All Other Current	7.7	6.6				
22.8	27.4	25.0	Total Current	24.3	23.3				
30.2	30.9	35.7	Long Term Debt	37.9	33.6				
1.3	.7	1.3	Deferred Taxes	2.4	.8				
7.1	8.9	7.3	All Other-Non-Current	9.6	7.2				
38.5	32.2	30.7	Net Worth	25.8	35.1				
100.0	100.0	100.0	Total Liabilities & Net Worth	100.0	100.0				
			INCOME DATA						
100.0	100.0	100.0	Net Sales	100.0	100.0				
			Gross Profit						
89.7	91.0	91.7	Operating Expenses	96.1	88.2				
10.3	9.0	8.3	Operating Profit	3.9	11.8				
3.8	4.7	4.2	All Other Expenses (net)	3.2	4.2				
6.4	4.3	4.2	Profit Before Taxes	.7	7.6				
			RATIOS						
2.2	2.6	2.2		2.1	2.7				
1.0	1.2	.8	Current	.5	.8				
.3	.4	.3		.2	.3				
1.8	2.2	1.6		1.2	1.7				
(77) .8	1.0	.6	Quick	.4	.5				
.2	.2	.2		.2	.1				
0 UND	1 558.0	0 UND		0 UND	0 UND				
8 43.4	8 46.7	5 68.8	Sales/Receivables	3 139.2	3 108.4				
32 11.4	50 7.3	25 14.5		24 15.4	20 18.1				
			Cost of Sales/Inventory						
			Cost of Sales/Payables						
10.4	8.3	8.9		27.4	8.1				
NM	34.8	-39.7	Sales/Working Capital	-13.1	-94.9				
-10.9	-8.5	-6.9		-5.3	-5.2				
6.3	6.3	5.2		3.4	7.1				
(66) 3.0	(80) 2.6	(70) 2.2	EBIT/Interest	(30) 2.0	(23) 3.0				
1.6	1.1	.8		-.1	1.6				
2.0	3.7	2.9	Net Profit + Depr., Dep.,						
(11) 1.4	(21) 1.0	(25) 1.4	Amort./Cur. Mat. L/T/D						
.7	.6	.1							
.9	.9	1.1		1.6	1.0				
1.6	2.0	3.2	Fixed/Worth	4.8	2.9				
3.7	14.8	7.3		-19.0	5.9				
.7	.5	1.3		1.5	1.0				
2.0	1.7	3.7	Debt/Worth	4.5	2.8				
5.6	33.4	8.9		-20.6	8.5				
78.8	46.7	49.0	% Profit Before Taxes/Tangible	34.4	89.8				
(73) 17.1	(71) 21.8	(68) 20.6	Net Worth	(25) 11.9	(25) 22.3				
4.0	7.3	-.5		-13.9	8.3				
14.8	11.9	13.5	% Profit Before Taxes/Total	10.4	20.8				
6.0	6.0	6.0	Assets	4.4	9.9				
1.4	.6	-1.0		-5.0	1.5				
7.5	6.6	5.7		6.1	3.7				
2.3	1.5	1.9	Sales/Net Fixed Assets	1.9	1.6				
.8	.8	.9		.9	1.0				
2.3	2.3	2.3		2.2	2.1				
1.1	1.2	1.1	Sales/Total Assets	1.0	1.0				
.6	.6	.7		.7	.8				
3.7	3.7	3.9		5.2	3.9				
(71) 5.2	(86) 6.9	(76) 6.4	% Depr., Dep., Amort./Sales	(33) 8.5	(26) 6.2				
8.3	10.8	10.2		12.2	8.6				
3.6	3.8	3.2	% Officers', Directors',	5.1					
(22) 7.6	(32) 8.6	(25) 8.1	Owners' Comp/Sales	(13) 8.3					
11.7	23.5	18.9		26.3					
960203M	631551M	222886M	Net Sales ($)	19310M	47219M	35693M	38384M	45286M	36994M
702993M	545494M	243022M	Total Assets ($)	20454M	45656M	28244M	32853M	31040M	84775M

M = $ thousand   MM = $ million
See Pages 1 through 15 for Explanation of Ratios and Data

SERVICES—PHYSICAL THERAPISTS. SIC# 8049

Current Data Sorted By Assets | Comparative Historical Data

Type of Statement counts

0-500M	500M-2MM	2-10MM	10-50MM	50-100MM	100-250MM	# Postretirement Benefits / Type of Statement
1	3		1			
2	1	6	2			Unqualified
5	4	1				Reviewed
12	9	2				Compiled
6	2		2			Tax Returns
10	4	2	2			Other
17 (4/1-9/30/94)		53 (10/1/94-3/31/95)				

Main data

0-500M	500M-2MM	2-10MM	10-50MM	50-100MM	100-250MM		4/1/90-3/31/91 ALL	4/1/91-3/31/92 ALL
35	20	11	4			NUMBER OF STATEMENTS		
%	%	%	%	%	%	**ASSETS**	%	%
20.3	8.1	5.9				Cash & Equivalents	D	D
26.4	49.0	40.2				Trade Receivables - (net)	A	A
.2	.2	.0				Inventory	T	T
1.1	3.8	3.5				All Other Current	A	A
48.0	61.2	49.6				Total Current		
37.8	26.7	38.1				Fixed Assets (net)	N	N
2.8	2.8	.4				Intangibles (net)	O	O
11.3	9.4	11.9				All Other Non-Current	T	T
100.0	100.0	100.0				Total		
						LIABILITIES	A	A
10.1	3.3	1.0				Notes Payable-Short Term	V	V
11.0	6.2	3.9				Cur. Mat. -L/T/D	A	A
1.9	1.9	11.2				Trade Payables	I	I
.0	1.0	1.5				Income Taxes Payable	L	L
16.8	12.2	12.9				All Other Current	A	A
39.8	24.7	30.6				Total Current	B	B
13.1	21.1	26.4				Long Term Debt	L	L
.6	3.6	1.9				Deferred Taxes	E	E
6.0	3.7	1.1				All Other-Non-Current		
40.5	46.9	40.0				Net Worth		
100.0	100.0	100.0				Total Liabilities & Net Worth		
						INCOME DATA		
100.0	100.0	100.0				Net Sales		
						Gross Profit		
92.2	92.5	86.2				Operating Expenses		
7.8	7.5	13.8				Operating Profit		
.2	1.1	-.1				All Other Expenses (net)		
7.6	6.4	13.9				Profit Before Taxes		
						RATIOS		
4.7	4.7	5.7				Current		
1.3	3.2	2.0						
.5	1.4	1.3						
4.7	4.7	5.7				Quick		
1.2	3.1	1.8						
.4	1.4	.6						
0 UND	65 5.6	32 11.5				Sales/Receivables		
0 UND	87 4.2	68 5.4						
69 5.3	126 2.9	87 4.2						
						Cost of Sales/Inventory		
						Cost of Sales/Payables		
5.9	3.7	5.4				Sales/Working Capital		
74.7	6.0	12.1						
-22.5	14.5	106.0						
(28) 18.5	(17) 22.8					EBIT/Interest		
3.7	4.4							
.8	-.4							
						Net Profit + Depr., Dep., Amort./Cur. Mat. L /T/D		
.2	.2	.2				Fixed/Worth		
1.0	.5	1.1						
2.0	1.1	3.7						
.3	.4	.8				Debt/Worth		
1.9	1.2	1.0						
5.0	2.2	18.6						
(31) 112.0	(18) 31.3	89.0				% Profit Before Taxes/Tangible Net Worth		
29.8	15.9	42.9						
1.0	7.0	9.1						
30.3	14.1	33.2				% Profit Before Taxes/Total Assets		
15.5	7.3	12.7						
.0	1.7	1.1						
32.7	29.1	23.2				Sales/Net Fixed Assets		
19.8	11.0	6.7						
5.9	3.2	1.6						
8.3	3.2	3.2				Sales/Total Assets		
4.4	2.3	1.6						
2.2	1.4	.9						
(25) 1.5	(15) 1.0	.6				% Depr., Dep., Amort./Sales		
2.3	2.0	2.1						
5.3	4.0	3.5						
(17) 13.6	(10) 12.4					% Officers', Directors', Owners' Comp/Sales		
19.3	15.8							
23.4	20.2							
45580M	48308M	92425M	94822M			Net Sales ($)		
8387M	20898M	47127M	88959M			Total Assets ($)		

M = $ thousand   MM = $ million
See Pages 1 through 15 for Explanation of Ratios and Data

Comparative Historical Data				Current Data Sorted By Sales					
		3	5	# Postretirement Benefits	1	2	1		1	
				Type of Statement						
		2	11	Unqualified		3		4	4	
		3	10	Reviewed	2	5	2		1	
		18	23	Compiled	10	7	5	1		
		2	8	Tax Returns	5	2	1			
		5	18	Other	9	4	2		2	1
						17 (4/1-9/30/94)			53 (10/1/94-3/31/95)	
	4/1/92-3/31/93 ALL	4/1/93-3/31/94 ALL	4/1/94-3/31/95 ALL		0-1MM	1-3MM	3-5MM	5-10MM	10-25MM	25MM & OVER
		30	70	NUMBER OF STATEMENTS	26	21	10	5	7	1
	%	%	%	ASSETS	%	%	%	%	%	%
	DATA NOT AVAILABLE	11.4	13.5	Cash & Equivalents	16.6	13.0	15.0			
		42.9	34.8	Trade Receivables - (net)	27.3	38.0	49.7			
		.3	.5	Inventory	.1	.5	.0			
		1.6	2.3	All Other Current	1.1	2.8	1.2			
		56.2	51.0	Total Current	45.1	54.3	65.9			
		31.9	35.4	Fixed Assets (net)	44.2	30.3	24.6			
		5.1	3.1	Intangibles (net)	4.0	.5	4.1			
		6.8	10.5	All Other Non-Current	6.8	14.9	5.5			
		100.0	100.0	Total	100.0	100.0	100.0			
				LIABILITIES						
		5.7	6.4	Notes Payable-Short Term	9.8	5.9	4.5			
		7.4	8.3	Cur. Mat.-L/T/D	7.1	13.7	4.4			
		1.8	3.5	Trade Payables	1.0	3.0	1.5			
		.0	.6	Income Taxes Payable	.3	.6	.1			
		11.4	14.2	All Other Current	13.8	10.4	18.8			
		26.3	33.0	Total Current	32.0	33.6	29.4			
		19.8	18.0	Long Term Debt	19.4	14.8	16.1			
		1.8	1.6	Deferred Taxes	1.6	.5	5.0			
		1.6	4.2	All Other-Non-Current	3.9	8.2	1.5			
		50.6	43.2	Net Worth	43.0	42.9	48.0			
		100.0	100.0	Total Liabilities & Net Worth	100.0	100.0	100.0			
				INCOME DATA						
		100.0	100.0	Net Sales	100.0	100.0	100.0			
				Gross Profit						
		89.3	91.4	Operating Expenses	87.4	92.7	96.9			
		10.7	8.6	Operating Profit	12.6	7.3	3.1			
		1.1	.5	All Other Expenses (net)	.7	.4	.0			
		9.6	8.1	Profit Before Taxes	11.9	6.9	3.1			
				RATIOS						
		4.8	4.5		7.4	4.4	4.9			
		2.8	1.7	Current	1.8	1.7	3.6			
		1.2	.8		.5	.5	1.4			
		4.8	4.5		7.2	4.4	4.9			
		2.8	1.7	Quick	1.5	1.7	3.5			
		1.2	.5		.5	.5	1.4			
		0 UND	**0** UND		**0** UND	**0** UND	**0** UND			
		69 5.3	**60** 6.1	Sales/Receivables	**0** UND	**64** 5.7	**74** 4.9			
		111 3.3	**99** 3.7		**126** 2.9	**81** 4.5	**99** 3.7			
				Cost of Sales/Inventory						
				Cost of Sales/Payables						
		4.3	5.3		3.7	5.6	4.9			
		6.7	12.5	Sales/Working Capital	22.9	12.8	6.0			
		21.1	−151.4		−37.6	−24.6	30.1			
		19.9	17.0		18.5	18.5				
		(29) 7.7	(55) 4.4	EBIT/Interest	(20) 5.3	(17) 4.4				
		1.1	1.3		1.3	.9				
			3.2							
			(17) 1.2	Net Profit + Depr., Dep., Amort./Cur. Mat. L/T/D						
			.3							
		.3	.2		.2	.2	.1			
		.8	1.0	Fixed/Worth	1.1	1.0	.3			
		1.4	1.7		2.5	1.6	.5			
		.5	.5		.3	.3	.5			
		1.2	1.2	Debt/Worth	1.3	2.0	.9			
		3.0	3.2		3.2	4.4	1.6			
		73.4	63.4		63.2	128.7				
		(29) 21.9	(63) 19.8	% Profit Before Taxes/Tangible Net Worth	(23) 26.0	(19) 26.1				
		4.6	5.8		15.3	13.1				
		32.0	26.6		36.8	25.8	9.1			
		14.9	8.8	% Profit Before Taxes/Total Assets	13.8	12.8	1.2			
		1.5	1.2		4.6	4.0	−9.8			
		19.0	27.8		20.9	57.2	66.6			
		10.1	12.4	Sales/Net Fixed Assets	10.5	16.0	28.5			
		5.3	3.4		2.6	5.7	7.4			
		3.5	4.7		5.5	6.3	4.0			
		2.6	2.7	Sales/Total Assets	2.3	3.3	3.1			
		1.8	1.6		1.3	2.0	2.4			
		1.5	1.3		2.0	1.2	.6			
		(27) 2.4	(55) 2.2	% Depr., Dep., Amort./Sales	(20) 3.9	(12) 2.8	1.6			
		3.7	4.2		9.5	4.1	2.4			
		10.9	11.2		16.7					
		(15) 19.1	(30) 17.7	% Officers', Directors', Owners' Comp/Sales	(15) 19.3					
		24.1	22.7		23.8					
		69541M	281135M	Net Sales ($)	15744M	33515M	38677M	38234M	117692M	37273M
		43311M	165371M	Total Assets ($)	10059M	13091M	14850M	22848M	77969M	26554M

M = $ thousand MM = $ million

See Pages 1 through 15 for Explanation of Ratios and Data

SERVICES—PHYSICIANS. SIC# 8011

Current Data Sorted By Assets							Comparative Historical Data	
37	8	11	3	2	3	# Postretirement Benefits		
						Type of Statement		
4	17	45	33	15	15	Unqualified	102	105
32	37	30	1			Reviewed	106	116
234	107	28	3			Compiled	399	440
102	18	5				Tax Returns	23	61
121	75	70	25	4	8	Other	250	250
	313 (4/1-9/30/94)		716 (10/1/94-3/31/95)				4/1/90-3/31/91	4/1/91-3/31/92
0-500M	500M-2MM	2-10MM	10-50MM	50-100MM	100-250MM		ALL	ALL
493	254	178	62	19	23	NUMBER OF STATEMENTS	880	972
%	%	%	%	%	%	**ASSETS**	%	%
24.7	14.5	11.3	14.3	13.6	10.3	Cash & Equivalents	18.1	18.5
9.3	26.9	30.7	29.4	20.6	15.8	Trade Receivables - (net)	20.0	20.7
.5	1.3	1.5	3.4	1.2	.9	Inventory	.8	.9
2.0	2.4	3.2	4.0	1.0	2.2	All Other Current	3.2	2.3
36.5	45.1	46.7	51.0	36.4	29.2	Total Current	42.1	42.4
46.2	41.8	43.1	31.5	42.7	44.9	Fixed Assets (net)	42.3	43.0
3.8	2.6	2.7	6.3	4.2	5.7	Intangibles (net)	2.5	2.9
13.5	10.5	7.5	11.3	16.7	20.3	All Other Non-Current	13.1	11.8
100.0	100.0	100.0	100.0	100.0	100.0	Total	100.0	100.0
						LIABILITIES		
16.4	10.5	5.3	3.2	.5	.2	Notes Payable-Short Term	11.8	12.5
8.9	7.1	4.6	3.1	1.9	2.4	Cur. Mat. -L/T/D	7.0	6.2
2.7	4.4	5.1	8.8	5.2	5.0	Trade Payables	3.5	3.6
.5	.4	.6	.6	.1	.1	Income Taxes Payable	1.5	.8
23.4	17.2	16.1	12.0	13.5	9.1	All Other Current	18.0	18.6
51.8	39.7	31.8	27.7	21.2	17.0	Total Current	41.7	41.8
18.3	23.6	28.3	19.6	29.1	37.0	Long Term Debt	21.9	20.4
.3	1.2	1.2	1.9	.3	.4	Deferred Taxes	1.1	.9
3.3	4.7	6.6	3.8	5.3	4.0	All Other-Non-Current	3.5	4.1
26.3	30.8	32.1	47.0	44.1	41.7	Net Worth	31.8	32.8
100.0	100.0	100.0	100.0	100.0	100.0	Total Liabilities & Net Worth	100.0	100.0
						INCOME DATA		
100.0	100.0	100.0	100.0	100.0	100.0	Net Sales	100.0	100.0
						Gross Profit		
94.0	90.9	87.8	90.4	89.0	94.2	Operating Expenses	91.5	92.2
6.0	9.1	12.2	9.6	11.0	5.8	Operating Profit	8.5	7.8
1.0	2.3	4.0	3.0	5.6	2.3	All Other Expenses (net)	2.0	2.1
5.0	6.8	8.2	6.7	5.3	3.5	Profit Before Taxes	6.5	5.7
						RATIOS		
1.4	2.8	2.8	3.3	2.3	2.4		2.5	2.3
.6	1.1	1.5	1.9	1.9	1.5	Current	1.1	1.0
.3	.4	.8	1.4	1.3	1.2		.4	.4
1.3	2.4	2.6	2.9	2.1	2.2		2.3	2.2
(490) .6	(253) 1.0	1.3	1.7	1.7	1.3	Quick	(879) .9	(971) 1.0
.2	.4	.7	1.1	1.2	1.1		.3	.4
0 UND	0 UND	0 UND	45 8.2	41 8.9	57 6.4		0 UND	0 UND
0 UND	13 28.5	49 7.4	60 6.1	63 5.8	62 5.9	Sales/Receivables	0 UND	0 999.8
0 UND	72 5.1	74 4.9	78 4.7	76 4.8	73 5.0		60 6.1	61 6.0
						Cost of Sales/Inventory		
						Cost of Sales/Payables		
77.0	8.0	5.7	4.8	5.3	4.4		9.7	10.6
-81.1	145.8	14.5	7.6	9.3	9.9	Sales/Working Capital	271.5	999.8
-21.0	-20.0	-38.7	16.8	17.0	22.6		-21.2	-24.0
7.8	10.2	14.3	16.7	7.3	4.3		8.7	7.8
(386) 2.1	(214) 2.4	(145) 3.8	(51) 4.9	(18) 3.6	(21) 1.8	EBIT/Interest	(708) 2.5	(777) 2.4
.2	.7	1.2	1.7	1.4	1.2		.6	.8
3.2	2.5	6.5	11.2				4.2	4.5
(65) 1.4	(45) 1.1	(44) 1.9	(21) 2.5			Net Profit + Depr., Dep., Amort./Cur. Mat. L/T/D	(234) 1.7	(206) 1.5
.6	.8	1.1	.7				.8	.6
.7	.4	.6	.3	.5	.8		.5	.6
2.1	1.3	1.4	.7	1.1	1.3	Fixed/Worth	1.4	1.5
-167.5	6.9	5.1	1.5	2.7	1.7		6.1	6.3
1.0	.9	.9	.5	.4	1.3		.9	.9
3.4	2.8	2.5	1.4	1.3	1.5	Debt/Worth	2.4	2.3
-128.2	13.1	9.5	3.1	4.6	2.1		11.6	12.5
109.0	66.1	61.4	43.5	16.3	18.1		76.0	66.9
(366) 19.7	(208) 15.4	(152) 23.1	(59) 20.7	(18) 9.4	(21) 6.7	% Profit Before Taxes/Tangible Net Worth	(744) 18.0	(809) 16.1
-3.3	-3.8	4.4	4.2	6.9	2.6		-.7	-.8
26.3	18.3	20.5	14.6	7.8	6.2		24.4	21.0
4.2	3.6	5.9	5.9	5.5	3.1	% Profit Before Taxes/Total Assets	5.2	4.3
-3.0	-1.3	.3	1.5	1.4	.7		-1.3	-1.1
45.8	34.3	17.3	18.9	5.9	2.8		30.8	32.0
23.2	12.7	5.4	5.8	2.3	1.7	Sales/Net Fixed Assets	13.5	15.2
13.0	5.7	2.8	2.8	1.5	1.5		6.0	6.7
14.4	6.5	3.3	2.4	1.7	1.1		8.0	9.0
8.9	3.4	2.2	1.7	1.2	.9	Sales/Total Assets	4.0	4.3
4.9	2.0	1.3	1.1	.8	.7		2.2	2.2
1.0	1.2	1.6	1.4	1.9	3.3		1.2	1.1
(403) 1.7	(217) 2.1	(158) 3.0	(55) 2.8	(17) 4.5	5.0	% Depr., Dep., Amort./Sales	(769) 2.2	(852) 2.0
2.7	3.8	6.7	4.7	6.1	6.4		4.2	3.5
24.7	13.1	9.4	5.3				19.1	19.9
(289) 34.0	(114) 24.5	(55) 22.3	(10) 21.9			% Officers', Directors', Owners' Comp/Sales	(376) 30.3	(438) 32.0
40.5	39.9	36.3	36.7				40.9	40.4
970974M	1219852M	1944437M	2735983M	1667316M	3401697M	Net Sales ($)	7762169M	9353780M
101839M	264681M	757157M	1438060M	1351922M	3744050M	Total Assets ($)	3839723M	4520019M

M = $ thousand   MM = $ million
See Pages 1 through 15 for Explanation of Ratios and Data

Comparative Historical Data   **Current Data Sorted By Sales**

28	49	64	# Postretirement Benefits / Type of Statement	8	25	7	9	5	10
106	90	129	Unqualified	5	13	9	13	29	60
110	73	100	Reviewed	8	37	15	16	21	3
434	377	372	Compiled	106	138	64	47	14	3
84	96	125	Tax Returns	51	55	8	9	2	3
255	248	303	Other	37	96	51	47	40	32
4/1/92-3/31/93 ALL	4/1/93-3/31/94 ALL	4/1/94-3/31/95 ALL		313 (4/1-9/30/94) 0-1MM	1-3MM	3-5MM	716 (10/1/94-3/31/95) 5-10MM	10-25MM	25MM & OVER
989	884	1029	**NUMBER OF STATEMENTS**	207	339	147	132	106	98
%	%	%	**ASSETS**	%	%	%	%	%	%
19.3	19.4	18.7	Cash & Equivalents	18.0	21.6	20.3	17.7	14.0	14.0
18.8	18.3	18.9	Trade Receivables - (net)	12.5	17.3	18.6	23.0	26.7	24.4
.7	1.0	1.1	Inventory	.4	1.0	.6	1.1	1.6	2.6
2.1	2.3	2.4	All Other Current	3.0	1.3	2.2	3.9	2.6	3.2
40.9	41.0	41.1	Total Current	33.8	41.3	41.7	45.8	44.8	44.2
44.3	43.8	43.6	Fixed Assets (net)	50.2	43.2	43.1	44.6	37.0	37.6
2.5	2.7	3.5	Intangibles (net)	4.6	2.9	2.2	3.0	5.6	3.6
12.4	12.4	11.8	All Other Non-Current	11.3	12.6	12.9	6.7	12.6	14.6
100.0	100.0	100.0	Total	100.0	100.0	100.0	100.0	100.0	100.0
			LIABILITIES						
11.0	12.1	11.6	Notes Payable-Short Term	11.7	13.9	15.0	9.8	9.4	2.7
6.4	6.8	7.1	Cur. Mat.-L /T/D	9.0	7.7	7.1	7.4	4.7	3.1
3.2	3.5	4.0	Trade Payables	2.6	3.0	3.6	6.0	5.2	7.0
.7	.9	.5	Income Taxes Payable	.4	.5	.6	.3	.3	.7
20.4	21.0	19.4	All Other Current	15.2	21.5	22.1	20.0	20.0	15.8
41.7	44.2	42.5	Total Current	38.9	46.6	48.3	43.6	39.6	29.4
21.7	21.5	22.0	Long Term Debt	26.7	20.4	17.4	23.2	19.5	25.9
.9	.8	.8	Deferred Taxes	.3	.7	.4	.9	1.6	1.6
4.1	3.5	4.3	All Other-Non-Current	5.7	3.3	4.4	4.6	5.5	3.0
31.7	30.0	30.4	Net Worth	28.3	29.1	29.4	27.8	33.8	40.1
100.0	100.0	100.0	Total Liabilities & Net Worth	100.0	100.0	100.0	100.0	100.0	100.0
			INCOME DATA						
100.0	100.0	100.0	Net Sales	100.0	100.0	100.0	100.0	100.0	100.0
			Gross Profit						
92.0	92.6	91.8	Operating Expenses	83.6	93.7	94.8	94.3	93.7	93.1
8.0	7.4	8.2	Operating Profit	16.4	6.3	5.2	5.7	6.3	6.9
2.0	2.0	2.1	All Other Expenses (net)	5.6	1.2	.9	1.0	.7	2.5
6.0	5.4	6.1	Profit Before Taxes	10.9	5.1	4.4	4.7	5.6	4.4
			RATIOS						
2.1	2.2	2.3	Current	2.5	2.1	1.9	2.4	2.4	2.4
1.0	1.0	1.1		.9	.9	1.0	1.1	1.2	1.6
.4	.4	.4		.3	.4	.4	.5	.6	1.2
1.9	2.0	2.0	Quick	2.4	1.9	1.7	2.2	2.1	2.2
(987) .9	(883) .9	(1025) 1.0		(204) .7	.8	.8	(131) 1.0	1.0	1.4
.3	.3	.4		.2	.3	.3	.4	.6	1.0
0 UND	0 UND	0 UND	Sales/Receivables	0 UND	0 UND	0 UND	0 UND	0 UND	34 10.7
0 UND	0 UND	0 UND		0 UND	0 UND	0 UND	2 195.4	39 9.3	59 6.2
58 6.3	55 6.6	57 6.4		15 24.0	40 9.1	54 6.8	64 5.7	64 5.7	72 5.1
			Cost of Sales/Inventory						
			Cost of Sales/Payables						
12.5	12.1	10.7	Sales/Working Capital	14.4	14.3	15.2	8.3	8.8	6.2
-999.8	-891.4	453.1		-113.0	-190.0	-999.8	199.4	113.8	12.7
-24.5	-23.1	-26.8		-11.9	-25.4	-30.8	-33.6	-50.5	36.9
8.1	9.0	10.0	EBIT/Interest	12.5	8.7	8.1	10.4	10.4	7.9
(786) 2.2	(718) 2.3	(835) 2.7		(140) 3.0	(280) 2.8	(128) 2.2	(108) 2.2	(93) 3.0	(86) 3.0
.5	.4	.7		1.0	.4	.2	.3	1.1	1.4
3.4	3.3	3.5	Net Profit + Depr., Dep., Amort./Cur. Mat. L/T/D	2.7	2.7	3.2	3.2	8.9	4.8
(186) 1.6	(186) 1.2	(187) 1.7		(23) 1.0	(44) 1.4	(27) 1.9	(27) 1.3	(34) 2.2	(32) 2.5
.5	.3	.9		.1	.6	1.0	.4	1.3	.9
.5	.6	.6	Fixed/Worth	.6	.5	.6	.6	.5	.6
1.5	1.5	1.6		2.2	1.7	1.4	1.6	1.3	1.1
7.7	10.0	9.9		UND	12.0	8.5	19.8	5.5	1.8
.8	.9	.9	Debt/Worth	.9	.9	.9	1.0	.9	.9
2.4	2.7	2.7		3.2	2.6	2.8	2.9	2.7	1.8
15.4	21.9	24.1		UND	38.8	22.4	55.9	9.5	3.7
64.0	61.7	71.5	% Profit Before Taxes/Tangible Net Worth	117.0	80.6	67.2	82.7	44.1	29.0
(820) 14.8	(713) 13.0	(824) 18.7		(156) 27.7	(264) 20.7	(119) 12.3	(103) 20.3	(88) 12.8	(94) 11.9
-2.7	-3.2	.0		.0	-1.7	-7.1	-1.2	.5	3.9
17.9	18.2	20.3	% Profit Before Taxes/Total Assets	33.3	22.5	18.9	18.6	14.8	8.7
3.9	3.3	4.5		5.8	4.0	3.0	3.9	4.5	5.4
-1.5	-2.4	-1.1		-.4	-2.2	-3.2	-1.8	.2	1.0
33.6	34.8	35.1	Sales/Net Fixed Assets	30.6	42.3	39.6	35.2	31.2	18.2
15.0	15.0	15.6		11.4	19.0	18.7	14.3	13.9	5.2
6.2	6.1	5.4		3.1	9.4	10.0	5.1	5.4	2.1
9.8	9.5	9.7	Sales/Total Assets	7.2	12.2	11.5	9.9	7.2	3.5
4.6	4.5	4.4		3.9	6.1	7.3	4.4	3.4	1.7
2.3	2.3	2.0		1.4	2.6	3.1	2.2	2.0	1.0
1.1	1.2	1.2	% Depr., Dep., Amort./Sales	1.5	1.1	1.1	1.2	1.2	1.4
(861) 2.0	(772) 1.9	(869) 2.0		(167) 3.2	(286) 1.8	(124) 1.5	(117) 2.0	(90) 2.1	(85) 2.4
3.6	3.6	3.8		7.0	3.0	2.8	3.4	3.4	4.9
18.9	19.4	19.7	% Officers', Directors', Owners' Comp/Sales	20.9	21.2	23.9	12.7	9.5	8.8
(456) 30.8	(408) 32.1	(474) 30.5		(100) 29.5	(191) 33.1	(72) 35.2	(58) 24.7	(33) 29.2	(20) 22.0
40.4	40.3	40.0		35.5	40.4	42.2	40.8	38.9	41.9
10832733M	8358741M	11940259M	Net Sales ($)	117726M	634163M	567910M	933777M	1624121M	8062562M
6036018M	4931693M	7657709M	Total Assets ($)	102703M	197985M	139715M	363777M	660415M	6193114M

M = $ thousand   MM = $ million
See Pages 1 through 15 for Explanation of Ratios and Data

SERVICES—PUBLIC RELATIONS SERVICES. SIC# 8743

Current Data Sorted By Assets							Comparative Historical Data	
						# Postretirement Benefits		
1	2					**Type of Statement**		
1	2	2		1	1	Unqualified		
	1	1				Reviewed		
6	3	1				Compiled		
1					1	Tax Returns		
2	7	2			1	Other		
5 (4/1-9/30/94)			28 (10/1/94-3/31/95)				4/1/90-3/31/91 ALL	4/1/91-3/31/92 ALL
0-500M	500M-2MM	2-10MM	10-50MM	50-100MM	100-250MM			
10	13	6		1	3	**NUMBER OF STATEMENTS**		
%	%	%	%	%	%	**ASSETS**	%	%
7.9	13.5					Cash & Equivalents	D	D
55.8	51.1					Trade Receivables - (net)	A	A
3.5	1.5					Inventory	T	T
1.0	1.8					All Other Current	A	A
68.2	67.9					Total Current		
22.5	14.1					Fixed Assets (net)	N	N
.8	5.7					Intangibles (net)	O	O
8.4	12.3					All Other Non-Current	T	T
100.0	100.0					Total		
						LIABILITIES	A	A
14.3	17.6					Notes Payable-Short Term	V	V
8.7	2.8					Cur. Mat. -L/T/D	A	A
23.7	22.2					Trade Payables	I	I
5.2	1.4					Income Taxes Payable	L	L
15.1	15.1					All Other Current	A	A
67.0	59.2					Total Current	B	B
7.2	9.2					Long Term Debt	L	L
.0	1.1					Deferred Taxes	E	E
.0	3.7					All Other-Non-Current		
25.8	26.9					Net Worth		
100.0	100.0					Total Liabilities & Net Worth		
						INCOME DATA		
100.0	100.0					Net Sales		
						Gross Profit		
101.8	92.8					Operating Expenses		
-1.8	7.2					Operating Profit		
-.2	3.0					All Other Expenses (net)		
-1.7	4.3					Profit Before Taxes		
						RATIOS		
1.9	1.8							
1.0	1.2					Current		
.7	.9							
1.6	1.8							
.9	1.1					Quick		
.7	.7							
30 12.1	29 12.7							
49 7.4	62 5.9					Sales/Receivables		
66 5.5	118 3.1							
						Cost of Sales/Inventory		
						Cost of Sales/Payables		
13.8	7.0							
NM	44.7					Sales/Working Capital		
-21.4	-35.8							
						EBIT/Interest		
						Net Profit + Depr., Dep., Amort./Cur. Mat. L /T/D		
.2	.1							
.7	.8					Fixed/Worth		
NM	2.9							
1.2	1.1							
3.1	2.7					Debt/Worth		
NM	25.8							
	167.1							
(11)	51.6					% Profit Before Taxes/Tangible Net Worth		
	1.5							
12.2	30.0							
4.4	8.0					% Profit Before Taxes/Total Assets		
-4.0	-.9							
87.2	33.7							
26.8	25.5					Sales/Net Fixed Assets		
16.9	17.4							
5.5	5.4							
4.5	2.6					Sales/Total Assets		
3.9	1.8							
.6	.8							
1.2	(11) 1.2					% Depr., Dep., Amort./Sales		
1.8	1.6							
						% Officers', Directors', Owners' Comp/Sales		
9391M	54585M	53763M		64052M	1619938M	Net Sales ($)		
2145M	15141M	16656M		81091M	498282M	Total Assets ($)		

M = $ thousand   MM = $ million
See Pages 1 through 15 for Explanation of Ratios and Data

Comparative Historical Data | Current Data Sorted By Sales

	4/1/92-3/31/93 ALL	4/1/93-3/31/94 ALL	4/1/94-3/31/95 ALL		0-1MM	1-3MM	3-5MM	5-10MM	10-25MM	25MM & OVER
# Postretirement Benefits			3			2		1		
Type of Statement										
Unqualified			7		1	1		3		2
Reviewed			2				1	1		
Compiled			10		4	3	1	2		
Tax Returns			2		1					
Other			12			5	3	2	1	1
					5 (4/1-9/30/94)			28 (10/1/94-3/31/95)		
NUMBER OF STATEMENTS			33		6	9	5	8	1	4
	%	%	%		%	%	%	%	%	%
ASSETS										
Cash & Equivalents	D	D	12.6							
Trade Receivables - (net)	A	A	48.2							
Inventory	T	T	3.0							
All Other Current	A	A	1.3							
Total Current			65.1							
Fixed Assets (net)	N	N	18.2							
Intangibles (net)	O	O	3.9							
All Other Non-Current	T	T	12.8							
Total			100.0							
LIABILITIES	A	A								
Notes Payable-Short Term	V	V	16.5							
Cur. Mat.-L./T/D	A	A	4.2							
Trade Payables	I	I	22.7							
Income Taxes Payable	L	L	2.2							
All Other Current	A	A	15.6							
Total Current	B	B	61.1							
Long Term Debt	L	L	7.9							
Deferred Taxes	E	E	.6							
All Other-Non-Current			4.1							
Net Worth			26.3							
Total Liabilities & Net Worth			100.0							
INCOME DATA										
Net Sales			100.0							
Gross Profit										
Operating Expenses			96.6							
Operating Profit			3.4							
All Other Expenses (net)			1.1							
Profit Before Taxes			2.3							
RATIOS										
Current			1.5 / 1.1 / .9							
Quick			1.4 / 1.0 / .8							
Sales/Receivables			31 11.7 / 60 6.1 / 101 3.6							
Cost of Sales/Inventory										
Cost of Sales/Payables										
Sales/Working Capital			11.4 / 70.2 / −35.8							
EBIT/Interest			(26) 9.0 / 3.1 / −.0							
Net Profit + Depr., Dep., Amort./Cur. Mat. L/T/D			(10) 5.4 / 2.2 / .7							
Fixed/Worth			.2 / .9 / 2.9							
Debt/Worth			1.2 / 2.7 / 25.9							
% Profit Before Taxes/Tangible Net Worth			(28) 56.3 / 23.1 / 3.2							
% Profit Before Taxes/Total Assets			11.4 / 4.7 / −.3							
Sales/Net Fixed Assets			40.4 / 25.4 / 14.3							
Sales/Total Assets			5.0 / 3.8 / 2.0							
% Depr., Dep., Amort./Sales			(30) .8 / 1.2 / 2.2							
% Officers', Directors', Owners' Comp/Sales										
Net Sales ($)			1801729M		3438M	15143M	17608M	61472M	20078M	1683990M
Total Assets ($)			613315M		741M	7208M	5536M	15480M	4977M	579373M

© Robert Morris Associates 1995

M = $ thousand   MM = $ million
See Pages 1 through 15 for Explanation of Ratios and Data

Current Data Sorted By Assets							Comparative Historical Data	
1	1	1	1	1		# Postretirement Benefits		
						Type of Statement		
		7	10	4		Unqualified	11	19
		1	1			Reviewed	2	
4	2		2			Compiled	5	4
1						Tax Returns		
1	1	6	7	1		Other	11	7
	8 (4/1-9/30/94)		40 (10/1/94-3/31/95)				4/1/90-3/31/91	4/1/91-3/31/92
0-500M	500M-2MM	2-10MM	10-50MM	50-100MM	100-250MM		ALL	ALL
6	3	14	20	5		NUMBER OF STATEMENTS	29	30
%	%	%	%	%	%		%	%
						ASSETS		
		14.6	18.4			Cash & Equivalents	17.0	14.2
		5.6	2.8			Trade Receivables - (net)	4.7	4.9
		1.0	.2			Inventory	.9	1.1
		.4	3.1			All Other Current	2.4	3.9
		21.6	24.5			Total Current	25.1	24.1
		64.2	65.8			Fixed Assets (net)	60.0	62.4
		3.9	2.2			Intangibles (net)	3.5	5.2
		10.3	7.4			All Other Non-Current	11.5	8.3
		100.0	100.0			Total	100.0	100.0
						LIABILITIES		
		.1	.7			Notes Payable-Short Term	3.0	1.7
		6.2	6.3			Cur. Mat. -L/T/D	8.7	7.0
		7.9	10.4			Trade Payables	10.3	7.1
		.4	.3			Income Taxes Payable	.4	.6
		8.4	13.3			All Other Current	11.5	10.7
		23.0	31.0			Total Current	33.8	27.2
		31.6	33.9			Long Term Debt	24.0	32.5
		.8	2.9			Deferred Taxes	.7	.1
		7.3	3.2			All Other-Non-Current	5.2	4.8
		37.4	29.0			Net Worth	36.3	35.4
		100.0	100.0			Total Liabilities & Net Worth	100.0	100.0
						INCOME DATA		
		100.0	100.0			Net Sales	100.0	100.0
						Gross Profit		
		95.2	89.2			Operating Expenses	92.7	91.8
		4.8	10.8			Operating Profit	7.3	8.2
		2.1	5.6			All Other Expenses (net)	2.0	2.3
		2.7	5.2			Profit Before Taxes	5.3	5.8
						RATIOS		
		1.4	1.5				1.6	2.2
		1.3	.8			Current	.9	.9
		.7	.3				.1	.3
		1.4	1.4				1.3	1.4
		1.1	.7			Quick	.6	.6
		.7	.2				.1	.3
		1 320.3	4 91.9				0 999.8	1 729.0
		4 89.4	6 64.3			Sales/Receivables	2 223.9	3 113.7
		18 19.9	16 23.1				14 25.9	14 26.3
						Cost of Sales/Inventory		
						Cost of Sales/Payables		
		17.7	12.7				22.5	22.6
		51.0	-21.4			Sales/Working Capital	-88.0	-521.2
		-48.4	-5.5				-5.1	-9.4
		4.9	13.2				7.9	13.2
	(11)	2.4	(17) 5.1			EBIT/Interest	(24) 3.0	(27) 2.5
		1.1	.9				.5	1.0
							5.6	9.2
						Net Profit + Depr., Dep., Amort./Cur. Mat. L /T/D	(16) 1.8	(10) 1.6
							.6	.3
		1.3	1.0				1.0	1.2
		1.6	2.5			Fixed/Worth	1.8	2.3
		3.8	NM				6.3	31.6
		.7	1.1				.8	1.0
		1.1	2.7			Debt/Worth	1.3	2.1
		4.2	NM				7.2	43.9
		20.5	57.4				39.8	41.8
	(13)	11.1	(15) 45.5			% Profit Before Taxes/Tangible Net Worth	(24) 20.5	(25) 13.3
		.7	-.5				12.3	2.2
		7.6	18.0				19.5	14.0
		3.8	7.9			% Profit Before Taxes/Total Assets	8.7	4.7
		.2	-1.9				-1.7	-1.4
		11.5	2.4				5.2	4.8
		1.9	1.5			Sales/Net Fixed Assets	2.7	2.1
		1.1	1.0				1.2	1.5
		3.9	1.6				3.2	2.5
		1.2	1.0			Sales/Total Assets	2.2	1.5
		1.0	.7				.9	1.0
		.9	2.8				2.1	2.8
	(13)	3.9	(19) 6.1			% Depr., Dep., Amort./Sales	(26) 3.8	(26) 5.0
		8.8	8.3				7.6	6.6
								.4
						% Officers', Directors', Owners' Comp/Sales		(11) 2.3
								10.2
9335M	12417M	141130M	488520M	226360M		Net Sales ($)	580928M	718594M
1811M	2592M	69095M	422395M	395608M		Total Assets ($)	409048M	498146M

M = $ thousand   MM = $ million
See Pages 1 through 15 for Explanation of Ratios and Data

Comparative Historical Data | **Current Data Sorted By Sales**

93	94	95	Type of Statement	0-1MM	1-3MM	3-5MM	5-10MM	10-25MM	25MM & OVER
2		5	# Postretirement Benefits		1	1	1	1	1
21	18	21	Unqualified		1	1	3	7	9
1		2	Reviewed			1		1	
	5	8	Compiled	1	4	2	1	1	
1	1	1	Tax Returns		1				
9	17	16	Other	1	1		5	7	2

4/1/92-3/31/93 ALL	4/1/93-3/31/94 ALL	4/1/94-3/31/95 ALL		8 (4/1-9/30/94)			40 (10/1/94-3/31/95)		
32	**41**	**48**	**NUMBER OF STATEMENTS**	**2**	**7**	**4**	**8**	**16**	**11**
%	%	%	**ASSETS**	%	%	%	%	%	%
13.8	12.3	15.4	Cash & Equivalents					15.5	24.1
5.0	3.4	5.0	Trade Receivables - (net)					4.7	3.2
.6	.8	2.5	Inventory					.8	.3
.8	1.1	1.6	All Other Current					2.1	2.0
20.2	17.7	24.5	Total Current					23.1	29.6
70.1	71.7	63.2	Fixed Assets (net)					66.4	60.1
2.2	3.4	2.3	Intangibles (net)					3.0	1.4
7.4	7.2	10.1	All Other Non-Current					7.5	8.9
100.0	100.0	100.0	Total					100.0	100.0
			LIABILITIES						
1.0	2.6	3.2	Notes Payable-Short Term					.9	.0
6.6	3.6	4.8	Cur. Mat.-L /T/D					10.0	2.0
7.4	6.9	10.0	Trade Payables					6.7	15.7
.6	.5	.3	Income Taxes Payable					.1	.5
11.4	9.7	10.4	All Other Current					11.8	9.5
26.9	23.4	28.7	Total Current					29.6	27.7
30.3	28.4	30.0	Long Term Debt					35.0	22.2
1.3	2.3	1.7	Deferred Taxes					2.7	2.4
4.8	5.9	5.2	All Other-Non-Current					5.3	3.4
36.7	40.0	34.4	Net Worth					27.5	44.2
100.0	100.0	100.0	Total Liabilities & Net Worth					100.0	100.0
			INCOME DATA						
100.0	100.0	100.0	Net Sales					100.0	100.0
			Gross Profit						
91.1	89.1	92.1	Operating Expenses					88.7	89.6
8.9	10.9	7.9	Operating Profit					11.3	10.4
4.0	3.0	3.0	All Other Expenses (net)					5.3	-.2
4.9	7.9	4.9	Profit Before Taxes					6.0	10.6
			RATIOS						
1.4 .8 .2	1.3 .5 .2	1.5 .9 .4	Current					1.5 .8 .2	5.3 1.2 .5
1.3 .7 .1	1.3 .5 .1	1.4 .8 .2	Quick					1.3 .7 .2	5.1 1.1 .5
(3) 137.3 (8) 44.7 (15) 24.6	(1) 548.8 (3) 122.1 (10) 37.1	(2) 156.9 (5) 73.7 (13) 27.6	Sales/Receivables					(3) 112.7 (5) 69.0 (17) 20.9	(4) 81.8 (9) 38.7 (13) 29.0
			Cost of Sales/Inventory						
			Cost of Sales/Payables						
21.1 -24.9 -5.7	22.1 -12.6 -6.4	15.5 -195.1 -9.7	Sales/Working Capital					12.7 -44.3 -5.5	2.5 31.0 -9.5
(30) 4.1 1.9 .8	(36) 6.9 3.4 1.0	(40) 10.1 3.4 .8	EBIT/Interest					(13) 8.7 3.3 .9	
(13) 6.0 1.5 1.0	(16) 13.8 1.1 .8	(19) 13.5 4.6 .9	Net Profit + Depr., Dep., Amort./Cur. Mat. L/T/D						
1.0 2.0 8.2	1.0 2.0 7.1	1.0 1.8 4.4	Fixed/Worth					.9 2.4 NM	.9 1.5 3.8
.8 2.6 8.2	.6 1.7 6.4	.7 1.8 7.9	Debt/Worth					.8 2.7 NM	.4 1.6 21.3
(30) 23.2 9.4 -3.7	(37) 36.5 17.7 3.3	(40) 50.7 15.1 -.3	% Profit Before Taxes/Tangible Net Worth					(12) 53.1 24.3 1.6	(10) 75.7 27.3 -7.6
7.5 2.5 -1.6	13.6 3.5 -.1	14.6 6.1 -.7	% Profit Before Taxes/Total Assets					12.7 6.6 -.2	24.1 9.5 3.4
2.2 1.3 .8	3.3 1.5 .9	5.8 2.0 1.1	Sales/Net Fixed Assets					3.2 1.5 1.1	3.7 2.1 .9
1.3 1.0 .6	2.1 1.2 .6	3.0 1.1 .7	Sales/Total Assets					2.4 1.0 .7	2.1 1.1 .7
4.2 (38) 6.1 9.1	3.0 (46) 5.6 8.5	1.5 4.9 7.7	% Depr., Dep., Amort./Sales					2.5 (15) 4.4 8.3	1.5 4.7 6.6
		(12) 2.6 9.4 18.4	% Officers', Directors', Owners' Comp/Sales						
633387M	736154M	877762M	Net Sales ($)	1548M	14889M	13845M	65403M	269669M	512408M
879903M	798275M	891501M	Total Assets ($)	533M	8889M	19935M	50961M	296642M	514541M

M = $ thousand   MM = $ million
See Pages 1 through 15 for Explanation of Ratios and Data

	Current Data Sorted By Assets						Comparative Historical Data	
	1	3	2			1	# Postretirement Benefits	
							Type of Statement	
Unqualified	1	4	10	9	2	6	26	24
Reviewed	1	8	8	2		1	11	19
Compiled	12	20	8	1			30	38
Tax Returns	3	1	1	1			1	1
Other	5	13	17	6	1	1	47	42
		28 (4/1-9/30/94)		113 (10/1/94-3/31/95)			4/1/90-3/31/91	4/1/91-3/31/92
	0-500M	500M-2MM	2-10MM	10-50MM	50-100MM	100-250MM	ALL	ALL
NUMBER OF STATEMENTS	22	46	44	18	3	8	115	124
	%	%	%	%	%	%	%	%
ASSETS								
Cash & Equivalents	11.4	5.8	7.1	3.5			6.8	5.1
Trade Receivables - (net)	21.9	22.2	18.9	12.9			18.2	20.6
Inventory	.0	.4	.1	.1			.6	.7
All Other Current	.9	2.1	1.8	1.5			1.8	.6
Total Current	34.3	30.4	27.9	18.1			27.4	27.0
Fixed Assets (net)	35.1	37.0	30.7	28.3			35.5	32.8
Intangibles (net)	21.6	23.2	29.3	40.8			20.9	25.6
All Other Non-Current	9.0	9.4	12.1	12.8			16.2	14.6
Total	100.0	100.0	100.0	100.0			100.0	100.0
LIABILITIES								
Notes Payable-Short Term	7.2	4.6	2.4	1.2			7.7	6.6
Cur. Mat.-L/T/D	6.7	8.0	10.2	8.1			9.8	10.1
Trade Payables	3.8	3.7	2.9	2.9			5.1	5.0
Income Taxes Payable	.2	.2	.3	.2			.2	.2
All Other Current	4.8	13.3	6.4	5.0			7.4	9.3
Total Current	22.5	29.9	22.1	17.4			30.2	31.2
Long Term Debt	59.1	44.8	42.0	41.9			45.3	40.3
Deferred Taxes	.0	.0	1.1	1.4			.2	.2
All Other-Non-Current	10.7	7.7	9.6	3.3			4.7	7.7
Net Worth	7.6	17.6	25.2	36.0			19.5	20.7
Total Liabilities & Net Worth	100.0	100.0	100.0	100.0			100.0	100.0
INCOME DATA								
Net Sales	100.0	100.0	100.0	100.0			100.0	100.0
Gross Profit								
Operating Expenses	88.8	93.2	89.1	90.9			91.9	93.4
Operating Profit	11.2	6.8	10.9	9.1			8.1	6.6
All Other Expenses (net)	4.5	4.1	5.1	4.4			10.1	9.4
Profit Before Taxes	6.7	2.7	5.8	4.7			-2.0	-2.8
RATIOS								
Current	5.6	2.2	2.9	1.5			2.3	2.3
	1.9	1.2	1.4	1.2			1.0	1.2
	.9	.5	.8	.8			.5	.5
Quick	5.0	1.8	2.6	1.4			2.2	2.0
	1.9	1.1	1.3	1.1			1.0	1.1
	.9	.5	.8	.7			.5	.5
Sales/Receivables	31 11.7	43 8.4	56 6.5	52 7.0			47 7.8	50 7.3
	51 7.2	62 5.9	64 5.7	64 5.7			58 6.3	60 6.1
	70 5.2	76 4.8	76 4.8	87 4.2			72 5.1	78 4.7
Cost of Sales/Inventory								
Cost of Sales/Payables								
Sales/Working Capital	4.4	8.8	6.4	10.3			6.6	7.5
	12.9	30.3	13.5	28.2			128.6	42.5
	NM	-6.8	-20.6	-20.2			-7.1	-6.4
EBIT/Interest	(21) 4.0	(43) 3.5	(42) 4.6	(15) 5.8			(95) 2.6	(101) 3.9
	2.7	1.7	2.1	2.3			1.1	1.3
	1.6	.5	1.0	.8			.1	.2
Net Profit + Depr., Dep., Amort./Cur. Mat. L /T/D		(13) 2.9	(15) 4.0				(47) 2.2	(46) 2.3
		1.2	2.4				1.0	1.0
		.6	.7				.1	-.0
Fixed/Worth	4.1	1.6	1.1	8.3			1.2	.9
	-2.7	-5.3	-5.6	-4.3			22.5	-13.6
	-.7	-.9	-.6	-.6			-1.0	-.7
Debt/Worth	7.2	2.1	1.3	10.5			2.1	1.1
	-5.7	-8.3	-19.9	-8.2			40.0	-25.5
	-3.5	-2.9	-2.4	-2.1			-2.9	-2.5
% Profit Before Taxes/Tangible Net Worth		(22) 90.2	(21) 99.5				(61) 72.7	(59) 28.6
		22.5	32.3				16.1	11.7
		-7.4	13.6				2.4	-15.9
% Profit Before Taxes/Total Assets	21.1	15.8	13.5	11.9			9.2	7.5
	9.0	4.1	7.6	4.1			.4	-.2
	1.6	-2.7	.5	.5			-9.0	-10.3
Sales/Net Fixed Assets	8.7	8.9	6.5	5.2			6.5	8.0
	5.1	4.0	3.7	3.2			2.8	3.9
	2.8	1.7	2.4	1.8			1.8	2.1
Sales/Total Assets	1.8	1.7	1.2	1.1			1.5	1.6
	1.5	1.2	1.0	.8			.9	.9
	1.2	.7	.8	.4			.6	.6
% Depr., Dep., Amort./Sales	(20) 1.9	(41) 4.5	(39) 4.0	(16) 6.0			(100) 4.1	(102) 3.3
	5.1	7.4	7.2	7.5			6.4	7.5
	11.6	12.4	11.1	11.3			13.4	13.5
% Officers', Directors', Owners' Comp/Sales	(12) 8.5	(16) 3.9	(10) 8.6				(31) 6.0	(27) 6.9
	11.4	7.6	13.7				11.7	8.8
	16.1	8.9	22.3				26.4	16.9
Net Sales ($)	11362M	54273M	186028M	288577M	136471M	409029M	863755M	891777M
Total Assets ($)	6841M	45690M	186883M	411600M	220915M	1236489M	1178079M	1222490M

M = $ thousand   MM = $ million
See Pages 1 through 15 for Explanation of Ratios and Data

Comparative Historical Data			# Postretirement Benefits	Current Data Sorted By Sales					
5	15	7		4	1		1		1
			Type of Statement						
30	37	32	Unqualified		8	3	6	6	9
23	17	20	Reviewed	6	5	5	2	1	1
21	35	41	Compiled	23	14		3	1	
2	1	5	Tax Returns	4			1		
41	48	43	Other	9	13	9	6	2	4
4/1/92-3/31/93 ALL	4/1/93-3/31/94 ALL	4/1/94-3/31/95 ALL		28 (4/1-9/30/94)			113 (10/1/94-3/31/95)		
				0-1MM	1-3MM	3-5MM	5-10MM	10-25MM	25MM & OVER
117	138	141	NUMBER OF STATEMENTS	42	40	17	18	10	14
%	%	%	ASSETS	%	%	%	%	%	%
7.0	6.3	6.7	Cash & Equivalents	7.5	7.4	5.2	8.0	3.9	5.0
18.1	18.9	18.9	Trade Receivables - (net)	18.3	21.8	19.4	22.0	14.5	10.5
1.0	.5	.2	Inventory	.0	.4	.1	.2	.0	.2
2.5	1.3	1.7	All Other Current	.6	3.7	.8	.9	.8	2.6
28.7	26.9	27.5	Total Current	26.4	33.3	25.5	31.2	19.3	18.3
32.8	31.3	32.3	Fixed Assets (net)	37.0	33.0	33.0	28.9	32.0	20.0
24.3	30.5	29.9	Intangibles (net)	29.3	22.1	29.1	23.7	43.4	53.3
14.3	11.2	10.3	All Other Non-Current	7.3	11.6	12.5	16.2	5.3	8.4
100.0	100.0	100.0	Total	100.0	100.0	100.0	100.0	100.0	100.0
			LIABILITIES						
10.5	5.2	3.6	Notes Payable-Short Term	4.7	5.0	3.0	2.6	.0	.5
7.5	7.8	8.4	Cur. Mat.-L /T/D	7.2	7.3	19.2	5.9	6.5	6.8
3.9	3.6	3.3	Trade Payables	3.2	3.4	3.9	2.8	2.8	3.4
.2	.5	.3	Income Taxes Payable	.3	.1	.2	.3	.3	.9
8.3	9.3	7.9	All Other Current	9.3	9.5	6.4	7.3	5.3	3.8
30.4	26.4	23.5	Total Current	24.7	25.2	32.7	18.8	14.9	15.4
39.1	42.3	46.2	Long Term Debt	51.7	49.6	37.9	31.8	50.8	45.7
.3	.9	.6	Deferred Taxes	.0	.1	2.0	1.1	.6	1.2
4.5	7.0	7.8	All Other-Non-Current	6.1	11.5	11.4	6.3	4.2	2.3
25.8	23.4	22.0	Net Worth	17.5	13.5	16.0	42.0	29.5	35.4
100.0	100.0	100.0	Total Liabilities & Net Worth	100.0	100.0	100.0	100.0	100.0	100.0
			INCOME DATA						
100.0	100.0	100.0	Net Sales	100.0	100.0	100.0	100.0	100.0	100.0
			Gross Profit						
92.3	90.0	90.2	Operating Expenses	94.0	90.1	85.3	89.7	90.6	85.7
7.7	10.0	9.8	Operating Profit	6.0	9.9	14.7	10.3	9.4	14.3
6.7	7.9	4.9	All Other Expenses (net)	4.7	4.6	6.2	2.8	5.1	7.5
1.0	2.1	4.9	Profit Before Taxes	1.4	5.3	8.5	7.5	4.3	6.8
			RATIOS						
2.0	2.2	2.7	Current	3.6	2.6	1.4	4.1	1.7	3.0
1.2	1.2	1.3		1.2	1.4	1.0	1.5	1.4	1.5
.5	.8	.8		.6	1.0	.5	.4	1.1	.8
1.7	2.2	2.4	Quick	3.6	2.3	1.4	3.8	1.5	2.8
1.1	1.1	1.2		1.1	1.2	1.0	1.5	1.3	1.1
.5	.7	.7		.6	.9	.5	.4	1.1	.8
41 9.0	47 7.7	49 7.5	Sales/Receivables	40 9.2	54 6.8	52 7.0	55 6.6	37 9.8	64 5.7
57 6.4	62 5.9	62 5.9		56 6.5	62 5.9	60 6.1	69 5.3	57 6.4	81 4.5
70 5.2	76 4.8	76 4.8		73 5.0	78 4.7	69 5.3	79 4.6	70 5.2	111 3.3
			Cost of Sales/Inventory						
			Cost of Sales/Payables						
8.8	7.8	6.7	Sales/Working Capital	7.1	6.5	12.7	4.8	10.8	3.2
34.4	21.6	18.4		39.1	11.6	157.0	10.8	20.0	8.4
-7.3	-13.5	-15.2		-9.7	-191.9	-4.5	-13.1	NM	-8.2
(105) 3.3	(124) 4.0	(132) 3.9	EBIT/Interest	(40) 3.2	(39) 3.4	(16) 5.8	(16) 9.1		(13) 2.7
1.5	1.9	2.2		1.6	2.0	2.3	3.7		2.3
.2	.5	1.0		.5	1.0	1.1	2.1		1.3
(28) 3.0	(51) 2.7	(44) 3.0	Net Profit + Depr., Dep., Amort./Cur. Mat. L/T/D	(12) 3.4					
1.5	1.4	1.7		1.6					
.0	.4	.8		.6					
.8	1.5	1.6	Fixed/Worth	11.1	1.0	7.5	.7	10.1	NM
6.9	-3.8	-3.5		-2.7	50.7	-2.2	1.5	-4.3	-.4
-1.0	-.5	-.6		-.9	-.6	-.3	-3.5	-.5	-.2
1.2	2.1	2.9	Debt/Worth	15.2	2.0	9.0	.8	16.6	NM
17.0	-8.7	-6.9		-5.9	293.9	-6.0	3.7	-8.2	-2.8
-2.9	-2.5	-2.6		-3.2	-2.4	-1.8	-10.2	-2.1	-1.6
(63) 36.7	(59) 43.9	(59) 103.5	% Profit Before Taxes/Tangible Net Worth	(14) 116.7	(21) 68.9		(12) 100.6		
12.8	14.5	30.2		33.7	22.3		35.6		
.5	-1.3	5.5		-31.2	2.4		14.4		
9.2	12.3	13.4	% Profit Before Taxes/Total Assets	11.0	14.2	16.6	15.5	14.6	6.6
2.5	3.9	5.0		3.4	5.2	7.8	10.3	6.8	4.5
-4.9	-3.2	.2		-3.3	.4	1.3	5.9	-3.2	.8
7.5	7.4	6.6	Sales/Net Fixed Assets	6.1	7.6	8.1	7.3	5.9	4.6
4.1	3.9	3.9		3.9	3.8	4.1	4.9	3.2	3.7
1.9	1.9	2.3		2.3	2.2	2.2	2.3	2.6	1.5
1.6	1.5	1.4	Sales/Total Assets	1.6	1.7	1.2	1.5	1.3	.7
1.0	1.0	1.0		1.2	1.0	1.1	1.0	.9	.5
.6	.6	.7		.7	.8	.9	.8	.5	.3
(98) 3.9	(113) 3.4	(124) 4.2	% Depr., Dep., Amort./Sales	(38) 4.7	(36) 3.6	(15) 4.0	(16) 2.6		(11) 4.1
6.2	6.3	7.1		8.2	6.9	7.4	5.8		7.0
11.3	11.0	11.6		12.7	12.0	9.2	9.8		13.0
(35) 4.4	(39) 5.4	(43) 6.6	% Officers', Directors', Owners' Comp/Sales	(18) 7.5	(13) 3.7				
8.8	9.9	9.4		10.5	8.0				
14.5	13.1	14.1		13.0	12.8				
779282M	1512923M	1085740M	Net Sales ($)	23890M	69553M	63394M	125227M	156283M	647393M
1065112M	2461705M	2108418M	Total Assets ($)	24125M	79579M	69696M	174271M	187434M	1573313M

Current Data Sorted By Assets							Comparative Historical Data	
1		7	6	1	2	# Postretirement Benefits		
						Type of Statement		
1	2	10	9	6	3	Unqualified		
1	3	3				Reviewed		
	1	1	1			Compiled		
						Tax Returns		
	2	7	4	2	2	Other		
	8 (4/1-9/30/94)		50 (10/1/94-3/31/95)				4/1/90-3/31/91 ALL	4/1/91-3/31/92 ALL
0-500M	500M-2MM	2-10MM	10-50MM	50-100MM	100-250MM	NUMBER OF STATEMENTS		
2	8	21	14	8	5			
%	%	%	%	%	%	ASSETS	%	%
		5.2	7.0			Cash & Equivalents	D	D
		12.5	13.1			Trade Receivables - (net)	A	A
		1.4	5.8			Inventory	T	T
		1.6	1.3			All Other Current	A	A
		20.7	27.2			Total Current		
		69.7	63.3			Fixed Assets (net)	N	N
		2.8	1.8			Intangibles (net)	O	O
		6.8	7.7			All Other Non-Current	T	T
		100.0	100.0			Total		
						LIABILITIES	A	A
		4.7	1.2			Notes Payable-Short Term	V	V
		5.0	2.6			Cur. Mat. -L/T/D	A	A
		11.1	12.4			Trade Payables	I	I
		1.2	.3			Income Taxes Payable	L	L
		9.2	8.3			All Other Current	A	A
		31.2	24.7			Total Current	B	B
		25.0	27.2			Long Term Debt	L	L
		7.7	9.7			Deferred Taxes	E	E
		5.8	3.1			All Other-Non-Current		
		30.3	35.3			Net Worth		
		100.0	100.0			Total Liabilities & Net Worth		
						INCOME DATA		
		100.0	100.0			Net Sales		
						Gross Profit		
		82.5	81.3			Operating Expenses		
		17.5	18.7			Operating Profit		
		4.8	3.8			All Other Expenses (net)		
		12.7	14.8			Profit Before Taxes		
						RATIOS		
		.9	1.2					
		.7	.9			Current		
		.6	.6					
		.9	.9					
		.6	.7			Quick		
		.4	.5					
		25 14.4	30 12.1					
		51 7.2	64 5.7			Sales/Receivables		
		70 5.2	89 4.1					
						Cost of Sales/Inventory		
						Cost of Sales/Payables		
		-60.3	7.6					
		-11.5	-29.5			Sales/Working Capital		
		-6.4	-9.4					
		6.9	8.6					
		(18) 4.1	(13) 3.8			EBIT/Interest		
		2.3	2.8					
		8.4				Net Profit + Depr., Dep.,		
		(14) 4.4				Amort./Cur. Mat. L./T/D		
		1.4						
		1.9	1.4					
		2.3	2.6			Fixed/Worth		
		5.3	3.2					
		1.6	1.5					
		2.1	2.5			Debt/Worth		
		5.6	3.4					
		53.0	45.3			% Profit Before Taxes/Tangible		
		(20) 40.2	30.4			Net Worth		
		22.2	16.4					
		16.7	10.3			% Profit Before Taxes/Total		
		7.9	7.8			Assets		
		5.9	5.9					
		2.2	1.5					
		.9	1.1			Sales/Net Fixed Assets		
		.7	.7					
		1.2	1.0					
		.7	.6			Sales/Total Assets		
		.5	.5					
		5.3	6.1					
		7.2	(12) 7.7			% Depr., Dep., Amort./Sales		
		8.0	10.6					
						% Officers', Directors', Owners' Comp/Sales		
1328M	14433M	130843M	216070M	309862M	487433M	Net Sales ($)		
260M	11200M	138611M	284223M	571059M	665955M	Total Assets ($)		

© Robert Morris Associates 1995

M = $ thousand   MM = $ million
See Pages 1 through 15 for Explanation of Ratios and Data

Comparative Historical Data / Current Data Sorted By Sales

Comparative Historical Data			# Postretirement Benefits	Current Data Sorted By Sales					
1	3	17	Type of Statement		3	5	2	4	3
18	19	31	Unqualified	2	2	6	3	8	10
3	5	7	Reviewed	1	3	2	1		
1	2	3	Compiled	1	1		1		
			Tax Returns						
			Other		3	3	3	3	5
11	8	17							
4/1/92-3/31/93	4/1/93-3/31/94	4/1/94-3/31/95			8 (4/1-9/30/94)		50 (10/1/94-3/31/95)		
ALL	ALL	ALL		0-1MM	1-3MM	3-5MM	5-10MM	10-25MM	25MM & OVER
33	34	58	NUMBER OF STATEMENTS	4	9	11	8	11	15

ASSETS (%)

1	3	17	Assets	0-1MM	1-3MM	3-5MM	5-10MM	10-25MM	25MM & OVER
5.3	4.9	6.0	Cash & Equivalents			4.0		9.3	3.4
10.6	11.8	12.5	Trade Receivables - (net)			7.8		15.0	12.9
1.6	3.9	2.3	Inventory			1.0		3.8	4.4
.9	4.9	1.5	All Other Current			1.9		2.1	.7
18.4	25.5	22.2	Total Current			14.7		30.2	21.3
68.8	66.3	68.4	Fixed Assets (net)			75.6		62.3	72.1
5.9	3.0	1.6	Intangibles (net)			4.1		1.9	.8
6.9	5.2	7.7	All Other Non-Current			5.5		5.5	5.7
100.0	100.0	100.0	Total			100.0		100.0	100.0

LIABILITIES

1	3	17	Liabilities	0-1MM	1-3MM	3-5MM	5-10MM	10-25MM	25MM & OVER
3.5	9.4	2.8	Notes Payable-Short Term			.7		4.0	1.7
4.9	3.6	4.6	Cur. Mat.-L /T/D			3.8		5.7	3.2
11.0	10.0	10.5	Trade Payables			8.5		14.2	9.7
.7	.4	.6	Income Taxes Payable			1.8		.2	.3
7.1	9.0	8.9	All Other Current			6.9		8.3	8.5
27.1	32.4	27.4	Total Current			21.7		32.5	23.4
33.4	21.9	27.9	Long Term Debt			24.0		23.1	35.8
7.3	4.4	7.7	Deferred Taxes			11.6		6.9	9.5
4.2	4.1	4.8	All Other-Non-Current			11.3		1.4	3.7
27.9	37.2	32.3	Net Worth			31.4		36.2	27.5
100.0	100.0	100.0	Total Liabilities & Net Worth			100.0		100.0	100.0

INCOME DATA

1	3	17	Income Data	0-1MM	1-3MM	3-5MM	5-10MM	10-25MM	25MM & OVER
100.0	100.0	100.0	Net Sales			100.0		100.0	100.0
			Gross Profit						
83.6	88.4	86.0	Operating Expenses			82.7		85.1	91.3
16.4	11.6	14.0	Operating Profit			17.3		14.9	8.7
7.6	3.6	3.7	All Other Expenses (net)			2.9		3.6	2.8
8.8	8.0	10.3	Profit Before Taxes			14.4		11.4	5.9

RATIOS

1	3	17	Ratio	0-1MM	1-3MM	3-5MM	5-10MM	10-25MM	25MM & OVER
.9 / .7 / .5	1.3 / .9 / .4	1.1 / .8 / .6	Current			.9 / .7 / .6		1.3 / .9 / .8	1.1 / .9 / .6
.8 / .6 / .4	.9 / .6 / .3	.9 / .7 / .4	Quick			.8 / .5 / .4		.9 / .7 / .4	.9 / .7 / .6
(23) 16.0 / (52) 7.0 / (78) 4.7	(14) 25.8 / 52 7.0 / 64 5.7	(27) 13.6 / 58 6.3 / 74 4.9	Sales/Receivables			13 29.1 / 51 7.1 / 66 5.5		27 13.7 / 55 6.6 / 78 4.7	58 6.3 / 68 5.4 / 74 4.9
			Cost of Sales/Inventory						
			Cost of Sales/Payables						
-49.5 / -7.4 / -3.9	15.4 / -21.3 / -2.4	56.7 / -16.8 / -6.9	Sales/Working Capital			-48.9 / -8.5 / -6.5		10.4 / -45.6 / -14.8	51.7 / -21.8 / -5.5
(30) 5.0 / 2.4 / 1.3	(28) 9.0 / 3.3 / .8	(50) 5.0 / 3.7 / 2.4	EBIT/Interest			10.7 / 4.1 / 2.6		(10) 4.8 / 3.6 / 2.6	4.4 / 2.7 / .0
(23) 3.6 / 1.4 / .7	(18) 6.4 / 1.6 / .7	(36) 4.6 / 3.3 / 1.5	Net Profit + Depr., Dep., Amort./Cur. Mat. L/T/D					(12) 3.4 / 2.2 / 1.5	
1.9 / 2.9 / 36.3	1.1 / 2.2 / 5.7	1.5 / 2.2 / 3.7	Fixed/Worth			2.0 / 2.3 / 4.6		1.5 / 1.8 / 3.0	1.6 / 3.7 / 4.4
1.6 / 2.8 / NM	1.1 / 2.3 / 6.7	1.4 / 2.0 / 3.8	Debt/Worth			1.5 / 1.9 / 5.1		1.5 / 2.1 / 3.3	1.3 / 3.6 / 4.8
(25) 48.9 / 19.1 / 7.0	(30) 41.7 / 18.8 / -.1	(54) 45.9 / 29.0 / 16.6	% Profit Before Taxes/Tangible Net Worth		(10) 56.8 / 23.2 / 17.7			41.2 / 35.6 / 15.1	(13) 45.7 / 22.4 / 13.3
13.2 / 4.9 / 1.2	12.2 / 5.8 / -1.6	10.2 / 7.4 / 4.7	% Profit Before Taxes/Total Assets			10.9 / 7.1 / 5.6		14.1 / 7.6 / 4.9	8.2 / 6.1 / -2.8
1.0 / .7 / .6	1.9 / .9 / .6	2.0 / .9 / .7	Sales/Net Fixed Assets			1.7 / .8 / .6		2.4 / 1.6 / .8	1.5 / .7 / .6
.7 / .5 / .4	.8 / .7 / .4	1.2 / .7 / .5	Sales/Total Assets			.8 / .7 / .5		1.5 / .8 / .6	1.0 / .6 / .5
(30) 5.2 / 6.9 / 12.0	(31) 4.5 / 6.4 / 10.1	(55) 5.9 / 7.5 / 9.6	% Depr., Dep., Amort./Sales			6.0 / 7.3 / 7.6		(10) 4.8 / 6.1 / 8.6 (14)	7.2 / 8.4 / 9.6
			% Officers', Directors', Owners' Comp/Sales						
646863M / 1298662M	370435M / 639009M	1159969M / 1671308M	Net Sales ($) / Total Assets ($)	1580M / 3110M	19262M / 21114M	44823M / 74302M	58387M / 89407M	155712M / 210405M	880205M / 1272970M

M = $ thousand   MM = $ million
See Pages 1 through 15 for Explanation of Ratios and Data

Current Data Sorted By Assets   Comparative Historical Data

	0-500M	500M-2MM	2-10MM	10-50MM	50-100MM	100-250MM	Item	4/1/90-3/31/91 ALL	4/1/91-3/31/92 ALL
	12	8	12	5	1	2	# Postretirement Benefits		
							Type of Statement		
	8	16	35	34	5	9	Unqualified	60	55
	19	35	34	13	2		Reviewed	80	63
	56	98	59	11			Compiled	180	161
	66	61	15	1		1	Tax Returns	13	38
	60	77	63	22	3	4	Other	160	141
	168 (4/1-9/30/94)			639 (10/1/94-3/31/95)					
NUMBER OF STATEMENTS	209	287	206	81	10	14		493	458
	%	%	%	%	%	%	ASSETS	%	%
	21.2	9.8	8.9	7.9	5.0	8.5	Cash & Equivalents	15.5	14.4
	8.6	7.4	6.6	11.7	1.8	10.1	Trade Receivables - (net)	9.5	10.2
	3.1	4.7	3.9	7.9	8.3	2.2	Inventory	4.1	3.6
	3.6	4.3	4.4	1.5	7.1	1.3	All Other Current	6.5	5.1
	36.6	26.2	23.7	29.0	22.1	22.1	Total Current	35.6	33.3
	44.7	58.2	53.8	44.7	68.6	39.7	Fixed Assets (net)	42.7	44.3
	2.7	2.2	2.1	4.1	2.4	3.4	Intangibles (net)	1.8	2.5
	16.0	13.4	20.4	22.2	6.9	34.8	All Other Non-Current	19.9	19.9
	100.0	100.0	100.0	100.0	100.0	100.0	Total	100.0	100.0
							LIABILITIES		
	12.1	10.2	7.1	9.2	17.6	7.5	Notes Payable-Short Term	13.3	14.0
	5.3	3.9	4.8	4.4	7.2	3.9	Cur. Mat. -L/T/D	4.2	5.3
	5.2	3.4	3.3	5.2	2.1	3.6	Trade Payables	4.6	4.3
	.2	.2	.2	.1	.2	.4	Income Taxes Payable	.3	.3
	13.6	9.5	10.4	8.7	3.3	11.4	All Other Current	13.7	12.2
	36.4	27.2	25.9	27.7	30.4	26.8	Total Current	36.2	36.0
	24.3	37.8	39.1	38.2	37.9	28.4	Long Term Debt	30.8	29.4
	.1	.4	.4	1.1	2.2	.5	Deferred Taxes	.6	.5
	2.7	3.5	3.9	2.9	1.3	10.4	All Other-Non-Current	3.8	4.1
	36.5	31.1	30.7	30.1	28.1	33.9	Net Worth	28.5	30.1
	100.0	100.0	100.0	100.0	100.0	100.0	Total Liabilities & Net Worth	100.0	100.0
							INCOME DATA		
	100.0	100.0	100.0	100.0	100.0	100.0	Net Sales	100.0	100.0
							Gross Profit		
	82.3	70.7	73.0	77.9	69.5	71.1	Operating Expenses	84.4	82.4
	17.7	29.3	27.0	22.1	30.5	28.9	Operating Profit	15.6	17.6
	7.4	14.6	15.1	10.0	23.0	12.9	All Other Expenses (net)	10.0	10.8
	10.4	14.7	11.9	12.0	7.5	16.0	Profit Before Taxes	5.6	6.8
							RATIOS		
	2.2	1.6	1.6	1.6	1.8	1.8	Current	1.7	1.6
	1.0	.8	.9	1.0	.6	.9		.9	.9
	.4	.2	.3	.4	.0	.3		.4	.4
	1.8	1.2	1.2	1.2	.8	1.6	Quick	1.2	1.3
	.8	(286) .5	.5	.6	.1	.8		.6	.6
	.2	.1	.1	.2	.0	.3		.1	.2
	0 UND	0 UND	0 UND	4 100.8	0 UND	18 20.1	Sales/Receivables	0 UND	0 UND
	0 UND	0 UND	3 132.3	17 21.1	0 999.8	41 8.8		3 145.4	3 142.8
	7 54.8	14 25.7	28 13.0	58 6.3	12 31.2	64 5.7		23 15.9	29 12.4
							Cost of Sales/Inventory		
							Cost of Sales/Payables		
	15.8	10.2	9.5	5.2	15.6	8.1	Sales/Working Capital	9.4	11.2
	-486.0	-25.0	-32.6	-999.8	-10.4	-43.6		-105.2	-50.6
	-12.1	-3.5	-2.9	-3.8	-.6	-1.1		-5.1	-4.9
	12.0	8.3	11.8	7.4			EBIT/Interest	5.4	5.6
	(137) 3.8	(152) 3.6	(110) 4.2	(54) 3.5				(322) 1.7	(299) 2.0
	1.0	1.9	1.4	1.5				.0	.7
	4.6	4.0	2.8	5.8			Net Profit + Depr., Dep., Amort./Cur. Mat. L /T/D	2.8	3.1
	(35) 1.4	(53) 1.5	(49) 1.5	(28) 1.9				(151) 1.1	(119) 1.1
	.4	.9	.4	.7				.2	.2
	.3	.6	.6	.4	1.1	.0	Fixed/Worth	.4	.4
	1.3	2.3	2.1	1.1	6.8	.8		1.6	1.4
	5.2	8.5	7.5	7.6	NM	3.5		10.2	8.3
	.6	1.1	1.0	1.2	.9	.8	Debt/Worth	1.0	1.1
	2.0	3.2	3.3	3.0	6.2	2.6		3.1	2.9
	9.3	10.7	11.5	8.5	NM	6.9		18.1	14.5
	74.9	53.0	48.0	39.4		35.4	% Profit Before Taxes/Tangible Net Worth	39.0	33.3
	(178) 29.2	(254) 20.8	(180) 19.5	(70) 20.9		15.6		(414) 11.3	(381) 13.1
	5.2	5.4	2.4	8.4		5.1		-3.0	-1.4
	22.5	11.4	10.6	9.3	6.5	8.7	% Profit Before Taxes/Total Assets	10.1	10.8
	8.5	5.3	4.0	4.4	3.2	3.0		1.8	3.0
	.0	1.0	.3	1.3	-.7	2.0		-1.9	-.9
	45.9	13.0	14.5	20.5	15.9	UND	Sales/Net Fixed Assets	24.5	22.4
	13.9	.6	.7	2.6	.2	4.6		7.8	5.7
	.7	.2	.2	.3	.1	.3		.5	.4
	7.7	2.0	1.3	1.3	.9	1.0	Sales/Total Assets	3.3	3.1
	3.1	.4	.3	.4	.2	.4		1.1	.9
	.4	.2	.2	.2	.1	.1		.3	.3
	1.0	2.3	1.9	1.6		2.8	% Depr., Dep., Amort./Sales	1.4	1.3
	(163) 2.6	(247) 11.3	(184) 9.0	(71) 6.9		(10) 6.3		(420) 3.2	(411) 3.2
	11.8	20.4	21.3	16.2		16.7		14.6	14.1
	5.7	4.6	3.5	2.6			% Officers', Directors', Owners' Comp/Sales	4.8	3.6
	(77) 10.7	(63) 9.2	(45) 6.7	(12) 5.4				(153) 9.5	(151) 8.6
	17.1	18.4	12.1	15.3				17.8	16.5
	192999M	555517M	941663M	1718273M	474402M	1249050M	Net Sales ($)	3303827M	1916469M
	50898M	292923M	935382M	1819583M	657858M	2306250M	Total Assets ($)	2975216M	2470683M

M = $thousand   MM = $ million
See Pages 1 through 15 for Explanation of Ratios and Data

Comparative Historical Data				Current Data Sorted By Sales					
8	23	40	**# Postretirement Benefits**	14	9	5	4	5	3
			Type of Statement						
70	84	107	Unqualified	26	22	11	16	13	19
99	85	103	Reviewed	43	23	6	12	11	8
172	189	224	Compiled	132	55	13	14	7	3
81	107	144	Tax Returns	117	20	2	2	2	1
163	164	229	Other	100	53	24	24	18	10
4/1/92-3/31/93	4/1/93-3/31/94	4/1/94-3/31/95		168 (4/1-9/30/94)			639 (10/1/94-3/31/95)		
ALL	ALL	ALL		0-1MM	1-3MM	3-5MM	5-10MM	10-25MM	25MM & OVER
585	629	807	**NUMBER OF STATEMENTS**	418	173	56	68	51	41
%	%	%	**ASSETS**	%	%	%	%	%	%
12.2	14.8	12.3	Cash & Equivalents	9.4	15.7	16.7	15.4	16.4	10.1
9.7	9.3	7.9	Trade Receivables - (net)	5.0	9.4	9.2	11.3	10.2	20.9
3.8	4.3	4.4	Inventory	3.6	4.0	.8	9.3	8.3	6.5
5.2	3.9	3.8	All Other Current	2.1	6.6	5.3	4.0	7.9	2.6
30.9	32.2	28.4	Total Current	20.1	35.7	32.0	40.1	42.8	40.0
49.5	50.5	52.0	Fixed Assets (net)	64.9	42.7	39.7	35.9	32.9	27.6
2.1	2.0	2.5	Intangibles (net)	1.5	3.1	3.7	4.5	3.1	5.2
17.4	15.3	17.0	All Other Non-Current	13.5	18.5	24.7	19.5	21.2	27.3
100.0	100.0	100.0	Total	100.0	100.0	100.0	100.0	100.0	100.0
			LIABILITIES						
9.9	8.9	9.9	Notes Payable-Short Term	9.3	11.0	9.1	11.0	10.5	9.2
5.9	5.1	4.6	Cur. Mat.-L /T/D	5.1	3.1	4.2	5.3	6.4	3.2
4.4	4.6	4.0	Trade Payables	1.8	5.6	5.8	6.3	8.0	9.0
.2	.4	.2	Income Taxes Payable	.1	.3	.3	.2	.4	.3
12.0	11.4	10.7	All Other Current	7.1	14.6	16.1	12.1	15.5	14.3
32.5	30.3	29.3	Total Current	23.4	34.7	35.5	34.8	40.8	36.0
33.3	34.7	34.5	Long Term Debt	42.8	26.8	29.4	24.0	22.7	21.8
.5	.4	.4	Deferred Taxes	.2	.5	.7	.4	.8	1.3
3.4	3.6	3.4	All Other-Non-Current	2.8	2.9	3.4	6.2	5.5	4.6
30.4	31.1	32.3	Net Worth	30.8	35.2	31.1	34.6	30.3	36.4
100.0	100.0	100.0	Total Liabilities & Net Worth	100.0	100.0	100.0	100.0	100.0	100.0
			INCOME DATA						
100.0	100.0	100.0	Net Sales	100.0	100.0	100.0	100.0	100.0	100.0
			Gross Profit						
77.8	77.1	75.0	Operating Expenses	64.9	85.0	86.4	86.7	84.0	89.6
22.2	22.9	25.0	Operating Profit	35.1	15.0	13.6	13.3	16.0	10.4
12.5	11.2	12.5	All Other Expenses (net)	18.8	6.0	3.1	6.3	7.4	4.1
9.7	11.7	12.6	Profit Before Taxes	16.3	9.0	10.5	7.0	8.6	6.3
			RATIOS						
1.7	2.0	1.7		1.7	1.7	1.5	1.9	1.5	1.8
1.0	1.0	.9	Current	.6	1.0	.9	1.2	1.0	1.1
.3	.3	.3		.2	.5	.3	.5	.6	.7
1.4	1.6	1.3		1.4	1.3	1.2	1.6	1.0	1.3
.6	.6	(806) .6	Quick	(417) .5	.7	.7	.6	.6	1.0
.2	.2	.2		.1	.2	.2	.2	.2	.5
0 UND	0 UND	0 UND		0 UND	0 UND	0 751.4	0 999.8	0 UND	16 22.4
2 184.7	1 305.0	1 383.0	Sales/Receivables	0 UND	3 118.1	5 69.3	9 42.9	7 51.1	40 9.1
26 14.2	23 15.7	23 16.2		6 60.1	26 14.2	21 17.3	31 11.7	30 12.2	64 5.7
			Cost of Sales/Inventory						
			Cost of Sales/Payables						
10.9	8.6	11.2		10.0	11.2	16.7	7.9	12.6	10.8
-103.8	-361.9	-57.2	Sales/Working Capital	-13.3	743.3	-536.3	49.5	150.4	104.8
-4.7	-4.6	-4.2		-2.5	-9.5	-9.1	-8.8	-11.6	-26.9
(341) 8.8	(389) 8.8	(467) 10.2		(175) 7.2	(119) 8.8	(43) 11.8	(53) 13.4	(41) 16.6	(36) 19.5
3.5	3.8	3.8	EBIT/Interest	3.4	3.1	3.9	4.4	6.5	6.2
1.5	1.5	1.6		1.5	1.0	1.7	1.5	2.7	2.7
(128) 3.2	(128) 3.3	(171) 4.4	Net Profit + Depr., Dep.,	(54) 2.0	(45) 4.7	(13) 15.4	(22) 5.4	(20) 14.7	(17) 10.4
1.3	1.6	1.5	Amort./Cur. Mat. L/T/D	1.2	1.6	2.5	1.4	1.9	4.4
.4	.5	.7		.5	.2	.5	.7	.5	1.6
.5	.5	.4		.9	.4	.3	.2	.3	.4
1.7	1.7	1.8	Fixed/Worth	2.8	1.4	1.2	.7	.9	.6
7.1	6.8	6.9		11.1	5.2	6.2	3.5	3.5	1.6
1.1	1.0	1.0		1.0	.8	1.1	.7	1.3	.9
2.7	3.0	2.9	Debt/Worth	3.3	2.7	2.7	2.9	2.7	1.9
10.7	11.6	10.6		12.5	7.0	12.1	12.6	7.4	5.3
(498) 49.2	(545) 51.6	(704) 54.8	% Profit Before Taxes/Tangible	(356) 44.8	(158) 56.7	(49) 69.6	(58) 52.1	(45) 65.0	(38) 45.2
19.2	21.1	21.0	Net Worth	15.1	23.7	34.7	20.8	45.2	25.8
4.4	4.8	5.1		2.7	5.0	17.2	7.3	20.8	12.3
13.3	13.5	13.3	% Profit Before Taxes/Total	9.9	13.8	18.9	17.7	19.7	17.1
4.6	4.8	5.3	Assets	3.7	5.6	6.5	6.5	10.9	8.1
.6	1.1	.7		.3	.5	2.5	1.2	3.4	3.2
20.1	21.3	21.4		5.5	21.7	32.9	37.8	42.4	40.2
3.4	3.1	2.2	Sales/Net Fixed Assets	.3	8.9	18.6	19.0	16.5	13.7
.3	.3	.3		.2	.8	1.5	2.0	2.8	6.4
2.8	2.8	2.5		.6	3.4	5.3	4.2	4.3	3.4
.7	.6	.5	Sales/Total Assets	.2	1.8	2.3	1.6	2.6	1.7
.2	.2	.2		.2	.4	.5	.5	.5	1.1
(521) 1.4	(536) 1.5	(683) 1.6	% Depr., Dep., Amort./Sales	(350) 6.8	(155) 1.3	(45) 1.1	(57) .9	(45) .8	(31) 1.1
4.2	5.1	7.7		16.5	2.6	1.8	1.9	1.3	1.9
18.0	17.6	19.2		23.7	10.9	7.4	7.8	5.7	3.2
(187) 4.0	(202) 3.9	(199) 4.5	% Officers', Directors',	(80) 7.1	(56) 5.5	(18) 3.6	(24) 2.4	(14) 1.9	
9.0	8.8	9.1	Owners' Comp/Sales	13.9	8.3	6.4	4.1	5.0	
15.6	17.6	15.1		24.2	12.3	11.2	9.4	9.1	
2959484M	2732455M	5131904M	Net Sales ($)	150009M	306461M	221527M	473782M	819796M	3160329M
3071158M	4041737M	6062894M	Total Assets ($)	534402M	567716M	362934M	841181M	1259275M	2497386M

M = $ thousand   MM = $ million
See Pages 1 through 15 for Explanation of Ratios and Data

SERVICES—REAL ESTATE HOLDING COMPANIES. SIC# 6719

	Current Data Sorted By Assets							Comparative Historical Data	
	12	16	21	12	4	3	# Postretirement Benefits Type of Statement		
	6	36	63	66	19	18	Unqualified	116	103
	14	37	52	21	1	1	Reviewed	77	89
	43	121	74	13	1		Compiled	190	198
	52	59	28	2			Tax Returns	21	40
	29	78	90	46	7	5	Other	182	175
	210 (4/1-9/30/94)			771 (10/1/94-3/31/95)				4/1/90-3/31/91 ALL	4/1/91-3/31/92 ALL
	0-500M	500M-2MM	2-10MM	10-50MM	50-100MM	100-250MM	NUMBER OF STATEMENTS		
	144	331	307	148	28	23		586	605
	%	%	%	%	%	%	ASSETS	%	%
	9.9	5.3	4.8	6.6	12.1	4.9	Cash & Equivalents	5.5	5.9
	3.3	3.9	3.6	9.5	15.4	16.7	Trade Receivables - (net)	4.5	4.9
	1.1	2.6	6.1	9.7	11.8	12.3	Inventory	4.0	3.8
	.6	2.2	2.2	5.2	1.6	3.7	All Other Current	3.2	2.5
	14.8	14.0	16.7	31.0	40.9	37.5	Total Current	17.3	17.1
	74.0	75.5	67.9	49.2	35.6	38.4	Fixed Assets (net)	68.7	68.8
	1.9	1.6	1.0	2.3	6.7	5.4	Intangibles (net)	1.8	1.9
	9.3	9.0	14.4	17.5	16.8	18.6	All Other Non-Current	12.3	12.2
	100.0	100.0	100.0	100.0	100.0	100.0	Total	100.0	100.0
							LIABILITIES		
	4.0	4.8	7.4	8.9	11.7	11.8	Notes Payable-Short Term	7.5	9.5
	6.1	5.1	4.2	4.0	3.1	2.5	Cur. Mat. -L/T/D	5.4	4.9
	2.5	1.5	2.6	4.8	6.9	8.1	Trade Payables	2.8	2.5
	.1	.2	.3	.2	.8	.8	Income Taxes Payable	.2	.2
	8.9	5.3	5.4	7.2	8.0	6.7	All Other Current	4.7	6.2
	21.6	16.9	19.9	25.2	30.6	29.9	Total Current	20.7	23.3
	47.0	50.1	51.3	33.1	23.0	29.0	Long Term Debt	48.9	46.2
	.1	.2	.9	1.1	2.4	1.4	Deferred Taxes	.4	.5
	3.2	3.5	2.9	4.0	1.6	7.1	All Other-Non-Current	3.8	3.3
	28.1	29.3	25.0	36.6	42.5	32.7	Net Worth	26.2	26.7
	100.0	100.0	100.0	100.0	100.0	100.0	Total Liabilities & Net Worth	100.0	100.0
							INCOME DATA		
	100.0	100.0	100.0	100.0	100.0	100.0	Net Sales	100.0	100.0
							Gross Profit		
	56.8	58.6	61.6	74.7	87.4	81.3	Operating Expenses	62.0	63.1
	43.2	41.4	38.4	25.3	12.6	18.7	Operating Profit	38.0	36.9
	21.3	22.3	22.9	14.7	6.4	7.0	All Other Expenses (net)	25.5	24.8
	21.9	19.1	15.5	10.7	6.2	11.7	Profit Before Taxes	12.5	12.1
							RATIOS		
	1.1	1.6	1.4	2.3	2.1	1.6	Current	1.5	1.4
	.4	.5	.5	1.1	1.2	1.0		.6	.6
	.1	.1	.1	.3	.9	.3		.2	.1
	(143) 1.1	(330) 1.3	(306) .9	1.4	1.3	1.0	Quick	(585) 1.0	1.0
	.4	.4	.3	.6	.9	.4		.3	.3
	.1	.1	.1	.2	.4	.2		.1	.1
	0 UND	0 UND	0 UND	2 224.0	9 41.9	8 44.2	Sales/Receivables	0 UND	0 UND
	0 UND	0 UND	0 UND	18 20.1	43 8.4	46 8.0		0 UND	0 UND
	0 UND	12 29.3	18 20.4	45 8.1	66 5.5	65 5.6		18 19.8	20 18.1
							Cost of Sales/Inventory		
							Cost of Sales/Payables		
	47.1	12.4	12.6	4.5	4.1	4.7	Sales/Working Capital	11.6	10.2
	-8.0	-8.2	-7.6	40.9	17.8	-76.7		-10.7	-7.9
	-2.0	-2.0	-1.8	-3.1	-42.6	-3.7		-2.4	-1.9
	(55) 9.4	(137) 6.9	(111) 5.7	(88) 8.0	(23) 4.6	(16) 11.8	EBIT/Interest	(202) 5.7	(199) 4.9
	4.3	3.8	2.9	3.9	3.0	2.7		2.8	2.5
	2.2	1.7	1.7	1.9	2.4	1.3		1.2	1.2
	(18) 2.7	(48) 3.2	(72) 2.7	(55) 3.4	(13) 4.4		Net Profit + Depr., Dep., Amort./Cur. Mat. L./T/D	(173) 2.9	(156) 2.7
	1.3	1.2	1.5	1.6	2.0			1.6	1.4
	.3	.5	.8	.9	1.1			.8	.6
	1.1	1.4	1.4	.4	.3	.2	Fixed/Worth	1.1	1.2
	4.2	3.5	3.6	1.4	1.0	1.5		3.9	3.5
	14.6	15.8	10.4	3.6	2.9	3.6		19.0	13.2
	1.2	1.2	1.5	.9	.8	.9	Debt/Worth	1.3	1.3
	4.9	3.3	3.6	2.4	1.7	1.8		4.5	4.1
	30.2	15.7	14.0	5.0	6.7	7.6		24.8	15.9
	(114) 59.0	(283) 43.1	(262) 30.3	(138) 28.9	(25) 28.5	(19) 20.4	% Profit Before Taxes/Tangible Net Worth	(485) 41.5	(509) 33.4
	27.8	16.7	14.5	13.2	10.9	8.4		13.3	10.1
	11.7	5.8	4.4	3.7	2.7	3.7		1.8	.6
	12.1	9.1	6.8	7.5	8.6	7.9	% Profit Before Taxes/Total Assets	7.7	6.8
	6.3	3.9	3.0	3.8	3.9	3.2		2.7	2.4
	1.5	1.1	.5	1.1	1.3	.8		.0	-.3
	.9	.5	1.3	7.8	16.9	18.3	Sales/Net Fixed Assets	1.4	1.1
	.3	.3	.3	.9	4.5	3.5		.3	.3
	.2	.2	.2	.2	1.3	.7		.2	.2
	.6	.4	.4	1.2	1.5	1.2	Sales/Total Assets	.5	.4
	.3	.2	.2	.3	.8	.8		.2	.2
	.2	.2	.2	.1	.2	.2		.2	.2
	(125) 10.5	(305) 11.3	(281) 7.4	(123) 2.7	(22) 2.1	(12) 2.7	% Depr., Dep., Amort./Sales	(521) 8.3	(533) 8.4
	15.7	17.2	16.4	8.4	4.7	7.2		17.8	18.0
	24.1	24.3	22.7	21.7	9.7	17.8		27.5	24.9
	(16) 5.1	(48) 2.8	(62) 2.7	(20) 2.8			% Officers', Directors', Owners' Comp/Sales	(90) 3.9	(110) 3.4
	9.6	6.3	6.3	7.5				7.9	8.5
	26.4	11.8	17.0	9.1				14.4	16.6
	33990M	189422M	678031M	2743447M	2009396M	2826788M	Net Sales ($)	4741675M	4063429M
	43065M	383512M	1387885M	3283796M	2051146M	3592755M	Total Assets ($)	5065717M	5580521M

© Robert Morris Associates 1995

M = $ thousand   MM = $ million
See Pages 1 through 15 for Explanation of Ratios and Data

Comparative Historical Data				Current Data Sorted By Sales					
3	45	68	# Postretirement Benefits	41	10	2	7	3	5
			Type of Statement						
136	148	208	Unqualified	67	41	9	22	24	45
114	106	125	Reviewed	72	24	7	11	5	6
221	227	252	Compiled	192	40	7	8	3	2
77	99	141	Tax Returns	132	7		1	1	
154	195	255	Other	156	42	11	16	10	20
4/1/92-3/31/93 ALL	4/1/93-3/31/94 ALL	4/1/94-3/31/95 ALL		210 (4/1-9/30/94) 0-1MM	1-3MM	3-5MM	771 (10/1/94-3/31/95) 5-10MM	10-25MM	25MM & OVER
702	775	981	**NUMBER OF STATEMENTS**	619	154	34	58	43	73
%	%	%	**ASSETS**	%	%	%	%	%	%
5.4	5.2	6.2	Cash & Equivalents	5.0	7.0	10.6	10.1	8.0	8.6
3.9	4.5	5.2	Trade Receivables - (net)	1.3	8.1	5.3	11.5	14.8	21.2
3.6	2.6	5.0	Inventory	1.4	5.8	12.2	7.8	18.5	20.4
1.6	2.6	2.4	All Other Current	1.8	1.9	6.1	6.1	2.2	3.8
14.5	14.9	18.8	Total Current	9.6	22.8	34.3	35.5	43.6	53.9
72.7	71.9	67.0	Fixed Assets (net)	79.5	59.0	43.1	36.0	38.6	29.6
1.8	1.8	1.8	Intangibles (net)	1.1	2.4	2.9	2.2	2.2	5.5
10.9	11.4	12.4	All Other Non-Current	9.9	15.8	19.7	26.3	15.7	11.0
100.0	100.0	100.0	Total	100.0	100.0	100.0	100.0	100.0	100.0
			LIABILITIES						
7.3	5.8	6.5	Notes Payable-Short Term	4.5	8.6	9.4	11.5	10.1	11.0
5.4	5.0	4.7	Cur. Mat.-L /T/D	5.1	4.0	4.2	3.4	3.8	4.4
2.6	2.7	2.8	Trade Payables	1.0	3.1	3.7	5.6	5.9	12.6
.1	.3	.2	Income Taxes Payable	.1	.3	.3	.4	.5	.7
6.0	6.8	6.3	All Other Current	5.3	5.4	9.7	11.2	7.1	9.9
21.5	20.6	20.4	Total Current	16.1	21.4	27.2	32.0	27.5	38.6
48.7	48.1	46.2	Long Term Debt	53.8	43.2	33.7	24.8	28.8	21.5
.6	.4	.6	Deferred Taxes	.2	.7	1.0	2.6	1.9	1.4
3.7	3.5	3.4	All Other-Non-Current	3.1	3.1	3.3	4.2	4.4	5.0
25.5	27.4	29.3	Net Worth	26.8	31.6	34.8	36.3	37.5	33.5
100.0	100.0	100.0	Total Liabilities & Net Worth	100.0	100.0	100.0	100.0	100.0	100.0
			INCOME DATA						
100.0	100.0	100.0	Net Sales	100.0	100.0	100.0	100.0	100.0	100.0
			Gross Profit						
61.0	61.2	63.1	Operating Expenses	53.8	68.9	78.9	83.1	84.0	93.8
39.0	38.8	36.9	Operating Profit	46.2	31.1	21.1	16.9	16.0	6.2
22.9	21.5	20.4	All Other Expenses (net)	26.2	17.4	9.2	6.8	6.4	1.6
16.1	17.3	16.6	Profit Before Taxes	20.0	13.7	11.9	10.1	9.6	4.6
			RATIOS						
1.4	1.5	1.6		1.3	2.0	2.8	1.8	1.9	2.1
.5	.5	.6	Current	.4	.7	1.3	1.0	1.2	1.4
.1	.1	.2		.1	.2	.4	.4	.8	1.0
1.0	1.1	1.1		1.0	1.3	1.2	1.4	1.4	1.3
(701) .3	1.1 .3	(978) .4	Quick	(616) .3	.5	.6	.7	.9	.8
.1	.1	.1		.1	.1	.1	.3	.4	.4
0 UND	0 UND	0 UND		0 UND	0 UND	1 355.8	5 71.7	8 44.8	29 12.7
0 UND	0 UND	0 UND	Sales/Receivables	0 UND	3 118.9	10 37.2	15 24.9	24 15.0	45 8.2
14 26.9	15 23.8	23 15.8		4 99.3	32 11.3	21 17.5	49 7.4	54 6.8	61 6.0
			Cost of Sales/Inventory						
			Cost of Sales/Payables						
13.7	12.3	9.6		21.0	8.1	2.9	6.3	4.3	5.1
-7.7	-7.3	-10.8	Sales/Working Capital	-5.2	-16.6	21.2	NM	31.5	13.5
-1.8	-1.8	-2.1		-1.6	-2.8	-3.4	-4.7	-18.6	-125.2
5.6	6.0	6.9		6.0	6.9	10.6	6.5	9.2	7.8
(280) 2.8	(336) 3.1	(430) 3.4	EBIT/Interest	(193) 3.8	(71) 2.9	(24) 2.9	(41) 2.7	(33) 3.2	(68) 3.7
1.6	1.4	1.7		2.1	1.1	.9	1.4	2.2	2.1
3.3	2.5	3.1		2.4	2.5	4.6	3.3	6.8	5.1
(171) 1.5	(164) 1.4	(211) 1.5	Net Profit + Depr., Dep., Amort./Cur. Mat. L/T/D	• (81) 1.1	(42) 1.1	(11) 2.4	(23) 2.1	(22) 2.1	(32) 1.8
.7	.6	.7		.4	.4	1.7	.9	1.5	.9
1.4	1.3	1.0		1.7	.7	.3	.1	.2	.4
3.8	3.8	3.0	Fixed/Worth	4.1	2.7	1.3	.9	1.0	.9
16.3	11.8	10.8		15.0	8.5	6.1	3.1	2.6	1.9
1.4	1.3	1.2		1.4	1.1	.9	.6	.9	1.2
4.1	3.7	3.2	Debt/Worth	3.9	2.8	2.7	2.4	2.0	2.5
22.2	14.3	13.4		17.2	15.5	6.8	6.9	4.1	5.9
45.2	42.9	39.5		41.6	41.0	23.7	27.8	51.8	40.9
(578) 16.0	(666) 18.8	(841) 16.6	% Profit Before Taxes/Tangible Net Worth	(520) 16.6	(131) 15.2	(31) 11.9	(53) 13.6	(41) 17.4	(65) 23.4
3.3	3.9	4.6		4.5	1.6	1.1	5.9	4.9	11.5
8.2	9.0	8.4		8.1	7.5	7.2	7.9	8.8	10.2
3.4	3.5	3.8	% Profit Before Taxes/Total Assets	3.6	3.2	3.9	4.2	5.3	7.9
.3	.2	.9		.7	.2	.5	1.8	2.3	3.3
.8	.8	2.3		.4	5.5	23.3	29.5	16.3	16.8
.3	.3	.3	Sales/Net Fixed Assets	.2	.4	.9	3.8	5.2	7.1
.2	.2	.2		.2	.2	.5	.7	.8	3.7
.4	.4	.5		.3	.7	1.9	1.9	1.7	2.2
.2	.2	.2	Sales/Total Assets	.2	.2	.4	.5	.8	1.6
.2	.2	.2		.1	.2	.2	.2	.3	1.1
9.5	9.6	6.9		13.1	3.8	1.0	1.5	1.5	1.4
(646) 17.3	(703) 17.4	(868) 16.0	% Depr., Dep., Amort./Sales	(569) 18.6	(129) 13.8	(31) 6.7	(47) 5.3	(35) 3.5	(57) 2.4
24.3	24.3	23.0		24.7	22.5	15.0	10.3	10.8	4.9
2.6	2.7	3.3		3.6	2.8		1.0		
(107) 6.9	(109) 6.4	(152) 6.7	% Officers', Directors', Owners' Comp/Sales	(80) 8.6	(39) 5.7		(10) 3.8		
13.3	11.9	13.4		17.8	13.9		5.8		
4855624M	5285427M	8481074M	Net Sales ($)	213082M	273420M	131385M	413366M	704069M	6745752M
7247117M	8067639M	10742159M	Total Assets ($)	1146730M	1240417M	455952M	1206983M	1756561M	4935516M

M = $ thousand   MM = $ million
See Pages 1 through 15 for Explanation of Ratios and Data

Current Data Sorted By Assets | | **Comparative Historical Data**

	0-500M	500M-2MM	2-10MM	10-50MM	50-100MM	100-250MM		4/1/90-3/31/91 ALL	4/1/91-3/31/92 ALL
	1						# Postretirement Benefits		
							Type of Statement		
	1	1	2			1	Unqualified	5	7
	2	15	5				Reviewed	18	22
	14	8	1			1	Compiled	26	37
	2						Tax Returns		4
	5	5	3	2			Other	8	17
		24 (4/1-9/30/94)		44 (10/1/94-3/31/95)					
NUMBER OF STATEMENTS	24	29	11	2		2		57	87
	%	%	%	%	%	%	**ASSETS**	%	%
	6.3	8.1	12.7				Cash & Equivalents	12.4	12.4
	41.0	34.3	42.6				Trade Receivables - (net)	37.3	38.5
	13.4	19.1	17.4				Inventory	17.2	18.9
	2.2	4.7	3.9				All Other Current	3.2	2.3
	63.0	66.3	76.6				Total Current	70.0	72.0
	33.1	21.5	12.9				Fixed Assets (net)	23.8	21.2
	.4	1.6	.0				Intangibles (net)	2.0	1.3
	3.6	10.6	10.4				All Other Non-Current	4.2	5.4
	100.0	100.0	100.0				Total	100.0	100.0
							LIABILITIES		
	9.1	10.0	4.6				Notes Payable-Short Term	7.4	8.2
	7.0	4.7	2.4				Cur. Mat. -L/T/D	5.6	4.2
	20.3	18.2	22.3				Trade Payables	16.5	20.3
	.4	.8	.5				Income Taxes Payable	.9	.4
	7.8	8.8	13.0				All Other Current	10.3	7.4
	44.6	42.6	42.8				Total Current	40.5	40.6
	17.8	10.0	7.3				Long Term Debt	10.9	10.7
	.5	.2	.9				Deferred Taxes	.3	.5
	3.2	2.2	3.6				All Other-Non-Current	5.0	2.2
	33.9	45.0	45.4				Net Worth	43.3	46.0
	100.0	100.0	100.0				Total Liabilities & Net Worth	100.0	100.0
							INCOME DATA		
	100.0	100.0	100.0				Net Sales	100.0	100.0
							Gross Profit		
	95.1	98.9	96.2				Operating Expenses	97.1	96.7
	4.9	1.1	3.8				Operating Profit	2.9	3.3
	1.6	.5	-.4				All Other Expenses (net)	.2	1.0
	3.4	.6	4.3				Profit Before Taxes	2.7	2.3
							RATIOS		
	2.3	3.5	2.7				Current	3.0	2.8
	1.6	1.5	2.0					1.9	1.8
	1.1	1.2	1.4					1.4	1.3
	1.6	1.8	2.1				Quick	2.2	1.9
	1.2	1.0	1.4					1.3	1.3
	.8	.7	1.0					.9	.9
	39 9.4	31 11.8	41 8.9				Sales/Receivables	23 15.6	25 14.7
	46 8.0	44 8.3	48 7.6					38 9.5	39 9.4
	61 6.0	60 6.1	60 6.1					57 6.4	61 6.0
							Cost of Sales/Inventory		
							Cost of Sales/Payables		
	8.0	4.7	5.8				Sales/Working Capital	6.2	6.5
	18.0	13.7	9.7					10.2	12.0
	138.6	41.4	16.1					21.2	21.2
	9.8	10.2					EBIT/Interest	8.8	10.3
	(23) 2.5	3.3						(50) 3.5	(77) 3.4
	1.3	-.4						1.3	1.1
		3.9					Net Profit + Depr., Dep., Amort./Cur. Mat. L./T/D	4.0	5.2
		(12) 2.5						(32) 2.2	(35) 1.7
		.5						1.5	-.1
	.4	.2	.1				Fixed/Worth	.2	.2
	.9	.5	.3					.4	.4
	3.8	.9	.7					1.3	.8
	.7	.8	.5				Debt/Worth	.6	.5
	2.0	1.7	1.1					1.2	1.2
	5.4	3.0	2.0					3.2	2.7
	60.2	25.2	40.7				% Profit Before Taxes/Tangible Net Worth	46.4	32.4
	(20) 15.7	(28) 14.7	22.9					(54) 15.8	(85) 11.9
	.8	-.1	4.6					5.1	1.0
	18.2	8.6	20.0				% Profit Before Taxes/Total Assets	15.7	11.5
	5.3	5.4	8.1					6.0	4.8
	.1	-2.1	1.9					2.0	.6
	24.1	36.7	61.1				Sales/Net Fixed Assets	30.3	30.7
	10.4	18.5	38.4					18.7	19.3
	6.9	7.9	12.3					10.3	12.7
	4.4	3.7	3.7				Sales/Total Assets	4.1	4.3
	3.3	3.0	2.8					3.2	3.3
	2.3	2.0	2.4					2.5	2.6
	1.3	1.2					% Depr., Dep., Amort./Sales	.9	1.1
	(22) 2.6	(27) 1.6						(54) 1.4	(81) 1.6
	4.0	2.5						2.3	2.5
	6.9	2.8					% Officers', Directors', Owners' Comp/Sales	3.8	3.7
	(11) 10.4	(16) 3.9						(33) 5.7	(50) 6.4
	12.2	6.8						8.3	8.5
	21037M	88431M	113797M	109737M		514254M	Net Sales ($)	180724M	196694M
	6391M	31087M	37907M	40510M		347399M	Total Assets ($)	118310M	60331M

M = $ thousand   MM = $ million
See Pages 1 through 15 for Explanation of Ratios and Data

Comparative Historical Data				Current Data Sorted By Sales					
1	**2**	**1**	# Postretirement Benefits		**1**				
			Type of Statement	0-1MM	1-3MM	3-5MM	5-10MM	10-25MM	25MM & OVER
3	7	5	Unqualified	1	1		1	1	1
26	32	22	Reviewed	3	7	4	7	1	
29	32	24	Compiled	10	10	3			1
2	3	2	Tax Returns	1	1				
25	16	15	Other	4	4	1	2	2	2
4/1/92-3/31/93 ALL	4/1/93-3/31/94 ALL	4/1/94-3/31/95 ALL			24 (4/1-9/30/94)		44 (10/1/94-3/31/95)		
85	90	68	**NUMBER OF STATEMENTS**	19	23	8	10	4	4
%	%	%	**ASSETS**	%	%	%	%	%	%
9.5	9.6	8.3	Cash & Equivalents	7.0	8.9		8.3		
37.8	40.6	38.1	Trade Receivables - (net)	36.7	38.1		41.8		
17.3	15.7	16.4	Inventory	18.1	12.5		18.0		
3.4	3.3	3.7	All Other Current	2.5	3.5		5.6		
67.9	69.2	66.5	Total Current	64.4	63.0		73.7		
22.7	20.8	23.9	Fixed Assets (net)	32.1	27.3		14.9		
1.9	1.1	1.3	Intangibles (net)	.7	.0		.1		
7.4	8.9	8.4	All Other Non-Current	2.9	9.7		11.3		
100.0	100.0	100.0	Total	100.0	100.0		100.0		
			LIABILITIES						
10.1	10.0	9.2	Notes Payable-Short Term	9.3	7.9		9.0		
6.8	4.5	5.0	Cur. Mat.-L /T/D	7.5	5.0		2.9		
20.1	18.2	19.5	Trade Payables	20.5	15.1		23.2		
.4	1.0	.6	Income Taxes Payable	.4	.7		.6		
8.1	9.2	9.2	All Other Current	5.9	8.9		13.9		
45.5	43.0	43.5	Total Current	43.6	37.6		49.6		
11.6	10.0	12.4	Long Term Debt	16.3	15.0		4.9		
.2	.8	.4	Deferred Taxes	.7	.0		1.0		
3.5	2.4	2.8	All Other-Non-Current	1.5	3.9		2.9		
39.3	43.8	40.8	Net Worth	37.9	43.4		41.6		
100.0	100.0	100.0	Total Liabilities & Net Worth	100.0	100.0		100.0		
			INCOME DATA						
100.0	100.0	100.0	Net Sales	100.0	100.0		100.0		
			Gross Profit						
96.5	96.8	97.2	Operating Expenses	95.7	96.8		98.5		
3.5	3.2	2.8	Operating Profit	4.3	3.2		1.5		
.0	.2	.7	All Other Expenses (net)	.3	2.2		-.3		
3.6	3.1	2.1	Profit Before Taxes	4.0	1.0		1.8		
			RATIOS						
2.6	2.6	2.6		3.5	3.3		2.2		
1.5	1.6	1.5	Current	1.7	1.6		1.5		
1.1	1.3	1.2		1.1	1.3		1.1		
1.7	1.8	1.7		1.6	2.3		1.8		
1.0	1.2	1.2	Quick	1.2	1.2		1.0		
.8	.8	.8		.8	.9		.7		
29 12.5	33 11.1	35 10.4		39 9.4	40 9.2		31 11.6		
45 8.2	47 7.7	46 8.0	Sales/Receivables	48 7.6	46 7.9		45 8.2		
55 6.6	66 5.5	62 5.9		69 5.3	55 6.6		61 6.0		
			Cost of Sales/Inventory						
			Cost of Sales/Payables						
7.9	6.2	6.4		4.3	4.8		6.9		
15.4	11.2	12.4	Sales/Working Capital	10.6	12.8		14.9		
72.2	25.4	34.8		169.2	27.7		88.4		
(71) 9.0	(78) 8.5	(64) 9.0		(18) 5.4	10.0				
3.4	3.5	2.7	EBIT/Interest	2.8	2.2				
1.4	1.5	1.2		1.4	-.4				
(33) 2.4	(32) 2.3	(23) 4.2							
1.5	1.5	2.5	Net Profit + Depr., Dep., Amort./Cur. Mat. L/T/D						
.5	.6	1.5							
.3	.2	.3		.3	.3		.1		
.5	.4	.5	Fixed/Worth	.8	.5		.4		
1.2	.8	1.2		2.2	.9		.7		
.7	.8	.7		.4	.7		.7		
1.8	1.3	1.6	Debt/Worth	1.5	1.2		1.5		
3.8	2.6	3.3		3.6	2.9		3.2		
(80) 51.9	(88) 48.9	(63) 30.7	% Profit Before Taxes/Tangible Net Worth	(17) 58.1	(21) 29.0		29.4		
20.2	14.5	14.9		15.1	14.6		14.0		
6.1	4.6	.7		.7	-.8		4.2		
17.6	16.4	12.2	% Profit Before Taxes/Total Assets	7.8	13.5		10.1		
7.4	6.4	5.1		5.3	4.4		4.9		
1.7	1.5	.1		.5	-3.5		1.8		
28.6	32.7	37.9		17.6	26.1		55.4		
17.7	18.9	17.8	Sales/Net Fixed Assets	9.9	17.3		35.1		
11.5	11.0	8.5		5.3	7.5		16.6		
4.0	3.8	3.8		4.0	3.7		4.1		
3.2	2.8	3.0	Sales/Total Assets	2.8	3.0		3.7		
2.5	2.3	2.2		2.2	2.1		2.4		
(77) 1.0	(81) 1.1	(62) 1.0	% Depr., Dep., Amort./Sales	(17) 1.5	(22) 1.2				
1.6	1.7	1.7		2.7	1.9				
2.6	2.6	2.8		4.5	2.9				
(48) 3.5	(59) 2.8	(34) 3.1	% Officers', Directors', Owners' Comp/Sales		(12) 3.2				
6.3	4.9	5.5			5.6				
9.0	9.7	9.9			9.4				
248308M	308379M	847256M	Net Sales ($)	11788M	43583M	31162M	69951M	66781M	623991M
90328M	115322M	463294M	Total Assets ($)	6136M	16598M	10177M	22120M	20354M	387909M

M = $ thousand   MM = $ million
See Pages 1 through 15 for Explanation of Ratios and Data

SERVICES—REFUSE SYSTEMS. SIC# 4953

	Current Data Sorted By Assets							Comparative Historical Data	
3	4	8	3	1	1	# Postretirement Benefits			
						Type of Statement			
2	8	28	23	5	7	Unqualified		58	70
3	31	27	4			Reviewed		61	52
27	31	15				Compiled		72	87
5	5	3				Tax Returns		3	5
10	17	22	20	2	5	Other		32	54
	94 (4/1-9/30/94)		206 (10/1/94-3/31/95)					4/1/90-3/31/91	4/1/91-3/31/92
0-500M	500M-2MM	2-10MM	10-50MM	50-100MM	100-250MM			ALL	ALL
47	92	95	47	7	12	NUMBER OF STATEMENTS		226	268
%	%	%	%	%	%	ASSETS		%	%
10.8	9.0	9.8	7.7		5.8	Cash & Equivalents		11.1	8.2
21.9	23.9	22.4	17.9		12.4	Trade Receivables - (net)		22.1	22.7
2.4	2.3	2.0	2.0		2.6	Inventory		1.6	1.4
2.0	1.8	2.7	2.8		1.1	All Other Current		2.8	2.2
37.1	36.9	36.9	30.5		21.8	Total Current		37.6	34.6
50.2	51.0	50.8	50.9		61.6	Fixed Assets (net)		48.2	50.4
3.7	4.2	3.7	6.9		8.9	Intangibles (net)		5.2	4.9
9.0	7.9	8.6	11.6		7.7	All Other Non-Current		9.0	10.2
100.0	100.0	100.0	100.0		100.0	Total		100.0	100.0
						LIABILITIES			
7.5	6.3	4.4	3.3		.2	Notes Payable-Short Term		5.7	5.1
9.9	9.2	8.0	6.6		4.0	Cur. Mat. -L/T/D		8.5	8.4
8.8	11.1	12.2	8.7		5.6	Trade Payables		9.8	11.2
.6	.2	.6	.3		.0	Income Taxes Payable		.7	.6
9.9	10.3	9.0	7.5		4.4	All Other Current		9.2	7.8
36.6	37.1	34.2	26.3		14.3	Total Current		33.9	33.3
21.9	25.4	22.6	25.2		33.1	Long Term Debt		22.9	25.3
1.0	.4	1.4	2.0		2.9	Deferred Taxes		.8	1.3
7.0	5.6	5.3	7.0		3.5	All Other-Non-Current		4.4	4.8
33.5	31.5	36.5	39.5		46.2	Net Worth		38.0	35.4
100.0	100.0	100.0	100.0		100.0	Total Liabilities & Net Worth		100.0	100.0
						INCOME DATA			
100.0	100.0	100.0	100.0		100.0	Net Sales		100.0	100.0
						Gross Profit			
87.5	91.7	90.5	94.1		85.7	Operating Expenses		91.4	92.4
12.5	8.3	9.5	5.9		14.3	Operating Profit		8.6	7.6
3.5	1.9	1.3	1.5		5.4	All Other Expenses (net)		1.8	2.3
9.0	6.5	8.2	4.4		8.9	Profit Before Taxes		6.8	5.2
						RATIOS			
1.8	1.7	1.5	1.6		1.8			1.8	1.7
1.2	.9	1.1	1.2		1.4	Current		1.1	1.0
.5	.6	.8	.9		.9			.6	.6
1.8	1.5	1.4	1.4		1.7			1.6	1.6
1.0	.8	.9	.9		1.1	Quick		1.0	.9
.4	.5	.6	.7		.7			.6	.5
1 576.0	20 18.4	35 10.4	40 9.2		49 7.4			28 13.2	29 12.8
18 20.0	39 9.3	46 8.0	58 6.3		57 6.4	Sales/Receivables		41 8.8	43 8.5
49 7.4	60 6.1	69 5.3	73 5.0		81 4.5			54 6.8	61 6.0
						Cost of Sales/Inventory			
						Cost of Sales/Payables			
17.6	12.6	13.4	8.6		5.3			10.5	11.6
65.0	−66.2	72.2	32.2		14.0	Sales/Working Capital		58.9	220.4
−18.1	−12.2	−19.1	−33.7		NM			−17.0	−11.8
13.1	9.2	8.6	7.3		6.4			8.5	6.2
(41) 6.4	(83) 3.8	(84) 4.4	3.6		(11) 4.6	EBIT/Interest		(209) 3.4	(253) 2.9
2.0	2.1	2.2	.8		3.5			1.5	1.1
7.1	5.1	5.0	3.5			Net Profit + Depr., Dep.,		4.4	3.9
(12) 2.2	(26) 2.5	(41) 2.6	(24) 1.8			Amort./Cur. Mat. L /T/D		(134) 1.8	(128) 1.9
1.2	1.3	1.6	1.2					1.1	1.0
.7	.7	1.0	.9		1.1			.9	.9
1.6	2.0	1.6	1.5		1.8	Fixed/Worth		1.6	1.7
4.4	13.8	3.4	3.7		7.6			3.4	3.9
.7	1.1	1.1	.9		.6			.9	.9
1.6	2.3	2.2	1.9		1.4	Debt/Worth		1.8	2.1
4.4	21.0	4.1	5.9		9.4			4.6	6.7
98.8	68.1	52.3	38.2		31.7	% Profit Before Taxes/Tangible		62.1	54.9
(39) 42.0	(75) 33.8	(90) 30.6	(43) 17.8		(11) 11.1	Net Worth		(203) 28.0	(234) 24.8
21.4	11.8	12.1	−2.8		4.7			12.2	6.4
36.2	20.4	14.7	12.9		8.7	% Profit Before Taxes/Total		18.0	15.2
15.3	9.4	8.5	5.3		5.3	Assets		9.0	7.4
6.7	3.5	3.6	−1.1		.7			2.5	.5
14.9	7.0	5.7	3.6		1.8			6.5	6.1
5.6	4.5	3.4	2.5		1.0	Sales/Net Fixed Assets		4.1	3.5
3.6	2.8	1.9	1.5		.6			2.5	2.2
3.6	2.9	2.3	1.7		.8			2.6	2.5
2.5	2.2	1.7	1.2		.6	Sales/Total Assets		1.8	1.8
1.9	1.4	1.0	.8		.4			1.3	1.2
2.7	4.0	4.0	6.0					3.7	3.9
(43) 5.0	(85) 6.8	(88) 6.3	(44) 9.0			% Depr., Dep., Amort./Sales		(212) 6.6	(248) 6.8
8.5	10.2	9.5	13.0					9.7	9.5
5.2	3.1	2.4				% Officers', Directors',		3.0	2.9
(22) 7.6	(51) 5.8	(37) 4.2				Owners' Comp/Sales		(105) 6.0	(114) 5.4
10.2	8.9	8.4						10.3	9.1
39372M	246848M	701272M	1183313M	540954M	1137466M	Net Sales ($)		2715099M	3550720M
13247M	108795M	420515M	1041681M	577718M	1842030M	Total Assets ($)		2421638M	3339492M

M = $ thousand   MM = $ million
See Pages 1 through 15 for Explanation of Ratios and Data

Comparative Historical Data / Current Data Sorted By Sales

	Comparative Historical Data			Current Data Sorted By Sales					
# Postretirement Benefits	7	17	20	3	5	2	4	3	3
Type of Statement									
Unqualified	71	84	73	2	6	8	15	20	22
Reviewed	76	69	65	6	22	11	18	6	2
Compiled	65	90	73	25	24	15	6	3	
Tax Returns	7	6	13	5	6	1	1		
Other	47	64	76	8	21	9	12	13	13
	4/1/92-3/31/93 ALL	4/1/93-3/31/94 ALL	4/1/94-3/31/95 ALL	94 (4/1-9/30/94)			206 (10/1/94-3/31/95)		
				0-1MM	1-3MM	3-5MM	5-10MM	10-25MM	25MM & OVER
NUMBER OF STATEMENTS	266	313	300	46	79	44	51	43	37
ASSETS	%	%	%	%	%	%	%	%	%
Cash & Equivalents	7.9	8.2	9.1	10.0	9.5	10.0	9.0	8.5	6.9
Trade Receivables - (net)	20.5	22.8	21.5	17.5	23.6	21.6	25.1	19.7	18.7
Inventory	1.2	2.2	2.2	1.1	2.6	1.2	2.0	3.8	2.7
All Other Current	3.0	2.4	2.2	1.9	2.1	1.4	3.4	2.5	2.1
Total Current	32.5	35.6	35.0	30.5	37.7	34.2	39.5	34.4	30.5
Fixed Assets (net)	50.7	48.7	51.4	57.4	49.6	54.7	47.9	47.7	53.0
Intangibles (net)	6.1	6.8	4.7	2.3	4.3	5.1	3.2	6.5	8.2
All Other Non-Current	10.7	9.0	8.8	9.8	8.3	6.0	9.4	11.3	8.3
Total	100.0	100.0	100.0	100.0	100.0	100.0	100.0	100.0	100.0
LIABILITIES									
Notes Payable-Short Term	6.7	5.7	5.0	4.0	7.2	4.4	5.8	3.7	2.9
Cur. Mat.-L /T/D	7.7	8.2	8.2	10.6	8.1	9.2	8.2	7.4	5.0
Trade Payables	10.4	11.1	10.3	8.3	8.3	10.4	13.6	14.4	7.6
Income Taxes Payable	.4	.7	.4	.6	.3	.5	.6	.3	.2
All Other Current	7.9	8.7	9.1	9.1	9.9	5.8	10.9	10.2	7.4
Total Current	33.1	34.5	33.0	32.6	33.8	30.3	39.1	36.1	23.1
Long Term Debt	23.4	24.2	24.5	27.7	24.4	26.7	18.8	22.8	28.1
Deferred Taxes	1.0	1.1	1.2	.7	.9	1.5	1.0	1.4	2.5
All Other-Non-Current	6.5	5.3	5.9	5.4	8.2	5.6	4.8	5.6	3.9
Net Worth	36.1	35.0	35.4	33.6	32.8	36.1	36.4	34.2	42.5
Total Liabilities & Net Worth	100.0	100.0	100.0	100.0	100.0	100.0	100.0	100.0	100.0
INCOME DATA									
Net Sales	100.0	100.0	100.0	100.0	100.0	100.0	100.0	100.0	100.0
Gross Profit									
Operating Expenses	92.7	92.7	90.7	84.5	91.2	88.4	94.2	95.3	90.1
Operating Profit	7.3	7.3	9.3	15.5	8.8	11.6	5.8	4.7	9.9
All Other Expenses (net)	1.9	2.2	2.2	5.7	1.1	1.3	.8	1.4	3.7
Profit Before Taxes	5.4	5.2	7.1	9.7	7.7	10.4	5.0	3.2	6.3
RATIOS									
Current	1.6	1.6	1.6	1.6	2.0	2.2	1.5	1.3	1.8
	1.0	1.0	1.1	.8	1.1	1.0	1.0	1.1	1.3
	.7	.7	.7	.4	.6	.7	.7	.8	1.0
Quick	1.4	1.5	1.5	1.6	2.0	2.0	1.2	1.2	1.5
	.9	.9	.9	.7	.9	.9	.8	.8	1.1
	.5	.6	.6	.4	.5	.7	.5	.6	.8
Sales/Receivables	29 12.7	29 12.8	29 12.5	9 40.1	27 13.4	24 15.5	34 10.8	35 10.4	42 8.7
	43 8.5	43 8.5	42 8.6	26 14.2	42 8.7	41 9.0	44 8.3	46 7.9	59 6.2
	61 6.0	59 6.2	68 5.4	57 6.4	72 5.1	63 5.8	66 5.5	61 6.0	72 5.1
Cost of Sales/Inventory									
Cost of Sales/Payables									
Sales/Working Capital	13.0	11.4	10.5	19.5	6.7	6.9	18.0	20.3	6.8
	243.7	−685.8	70.1	−27.2	41.0	190.1	−413.2	67.9	20.7
	−12.6	−15.8	−18.1	−8.0	−20.1	−19.0	−19.1	−16.1	NM
EBIT/Interest	(253) 6.3	(287) 6.4	(272) 8.8	(38) 11.0	(69) 10.6	(42) 10.3	(48) 6.8	(40) 8.4	(35) 8.6
	3.0	2.9	4.3	4.9	4.9	4.5	3.8	2.8	4.6
	1.5	1.4	1.9	2.1	2.1	2.4	1.4	.8	2.3
Net Profit + Depr., Dep., Amort./Cur. Mat. L/T/D	(135) 4.2	(130) 3.0	(113) 5.4	(13) 5.7	(24) 8.4	(17) 4.8	(18) 4.7	(22) 4.0	(19) 6.5
	2.1	1.9	2.3	2.2	2.9	2.2	2.1	2.1	2.9
	1.2	1.0	1.4	1.0	1.6	1.3	1.2	1.4	1.5
Fixed/Worth	.9	.9	.8	.8	.6	1.1	.9	1.1	.9
	1.7	1.8	1.7	2.0	1.7	1.8	1.4	1.9	1.5
	4.7	5.2	4.4	7.7	13.6	3.5	2.9	6.8	2.6
Debt/Worth	1.0	1.0	.9	.8	.8	1.0	1.2	1.0	.7
	2.1	2.5	2.1	2.0	2.3	2.0	2.0	2.6	1.9
	7.0	7.5	6.8	13.1	20.9	4.8	3.8	10.2	3.2
% Profit Before Taxes/Tangible Net Worth	(233) 48.4	(263) 48.2	(264) 56.0	(38) 76.4	(66) 88.5	(39) 64.0	(49) 43.5	(39) 45.7	(33) 35.8
	23.2	19.9	28.7	43.6	37.1	34.9	21.2	17.8	22.1
	9.8	4.4	11.1	20.5	12.2	15.2	9.4	−2.1	8.9
% Profit Before Taxes/Total Assets	13.2	14.1	17.0	20.0	21.1	19.5	14.5	12.3	12.9
	6.7	6.1	8.4	11.8	9.6	10.2	8.5	5.3	7.0
	1.8	.9	2.8	4.5	3.6	4.2	2.7	−.8	2.9
Sales/Net Fixed Assets	6.8	6.8	6.0	6.3	8.3	5.4	7.4	6.6	3.3
	3.5	4.1	3.6	3.5	4.4	3.1	4.3	3.7	2.3
	1.9	2.2	2.0	1.6	2.4	1.7	2.8	2.1	1.2
Sales/Total Assets	2.5	2.7	2.5	2.5	3.0	2.6	2.4	2.7	1.8
	1.7	1.9	1.8	1.8	2.1	1.8	1.9	1.8	1.2
	1.1	1.1	1.2	1.1	1.3	1.0	1.4	1.0	.7
% Depr., Dep., Amort./Sales	(245) 4.2	(291) 4.2	(274) 4.0	(44) 4.6	(72) 3.6	(39) 4.5	(48) 3.5	(40) 4.0	(31) 5.6
	7.1	6.7	6.9	7.1	6.7	7.7	5.7	6.4	8.4
	9.8	9.5	10.2	10.8	9.6	11.6	8.9	11.3	10.4
% Officers', Directors', Owners' Comp/Sales	(114) 3.3	(140) 3.2	(118) 2.9	(19) 4.0	(41) 3.5	(18) 2.6	(22) 1.8	(15) 2.5	
	5.6	6.0	5.8	7.3	6.5	3.8	4.8	6.2	
	10.4	10.0	9.1	9.5	9.1	6.7	9.8	9.7	
Net Sales ($)	3053505M	3121872M	3849225M	26121M	154156M	171002M	365188M	691865M	2440893M
Total Assets ($)	3135484M	2965113M	4003986M	22518M	137309M	183363M	220691M	567211M	2872894M

Current Data Sorted By Assets   **Comparative Historical Data**

							# Postretirement Benefits		
3	4	12					**Type of Statement**		
2	4	14	12	3	2		Unqualified		
	5	5	1				Reviewed		
2	10	11	1				Compiled		
							Tax Returns		
11	29	41	8	2			Other		
	66 (4/1-9/30/94)		97 (10/1/94-3/31/95)					4/1/90-3/31/91 ALL	4/1/91-3/31/92 ALL
0-500M	500M-2MM	2-10MM	10-50MM	50-100MM	100-250MM				
15	48	71	22	5	2		**NUMBER OF STATEMENTS**		
%	%	%	%	%	%		**ASSETS**	%	%
43.1	15.3	6.3	15.4				Cash & Equivalents	D	D
.4	.5	2.7	4.3				Trade Receivables - (net)	A	A
.8	.7	.4	.5				Inventory	T	T
1.5	1.1	2.2	2.8				All Other Current	A	A
45.8	17.5	11.5	23.0				Total Current		
27.7	79.4	77.7	61.4				Fixed Assets (net)	N	N
.0	.1	.3	.9				Intangibles (net)	O	O
26.5	3.0	10.5	14.8				All Other Non-Current	T	T
100.0	100.0	100.0	100.0				Total		
							LIABILITIES	A	A
1.5	5.0	5.4	2.8				Notes Payable-Short Term	V	V
1.9	2.2	1.2	.9				Cur. Mat. -L/T/D	A	A
2.1	.7	2.0	4.6				Trade Payables	I	I
.0	.0	.0	.0				Income Taxes Payable	L	L
13.5	1.3	5.1	7.6				All Other Current	A	A
19.0	9.3	13.6	15.8				Total Current	B	B
26.9	19.4	20.9	15.0				Long Term Debt	L	L
.0	.0	.0	.0				Deferred Taxes	E	E
2.5	1.0	.9	6.6				All Other-Non-Current		
51.7	70.3	64.6	62.6				Net Worth		
100.0	100.0	100.0	100.0				Total Liabilities & Net Worth		
							INCOME DATA		
100.0	100.0	100.0	100.0				Net Sales		
							Gross Profit		
89.2	88.9	89.5	92.5				Operating Expenses		
10.8	11.1	10.5	7.5				Operating Profit		
4.2	3.5	3.7	1.2				All Other Expenses (net)		
6.6	7.6	6.8	6.3				Profit Before Taxes		
							RATIOS		
10.8	14.8	2.4	2.9						
2.0	1.9	1.1	1.7				Current		
1.5	.3	.7	.8						
10.8	14.8	2.0	2.9						
2.0	1.4	1.0	1.5				Quick		
.8	.2	.5	.6						
0 UND	0 UND	0 UND	0 UND						
0 UND	0 UND	0 UND	1 313.1				Sales/Receivables		
0 UND	0 UND	8 48.6	28 13.1						
							Cost of Sales/Inventory		
							Cost of Sales/Payables		
4.8	2.2	9.9	2.9						
9.6	9.1	155.7	11.3				Sales/Working Capital		
174.6	-7.1	-30.0	-27.6						
	4.2	4.8	6.8						
	(26) 1.4	(41) 2.2	(12) 1.3				EBIT/Interest		
	.9	1.0	-1.4						
							Net Profit + Depr., Dep., Amort./Cur. Mat. L /T/D		
.0	.8	.9	.3						
.2	1.2	1.2	.9				Fixed/Worth		
1.4	1.6	1.8	1.6						
.1	.1	.2	.1						
.9	.4	.5	.7				Debt/Worth		
1.8	.7	1.2	2.0						
56.9	7.1	10.5	11.0				% Profit Before Taxes/Tangible		
(14) 15.9	2.1	1.2	2.3				Net Worth		
3.8	-.3	-.4	-3.2						
23.1	4.4	4.8	5.9				% Profit Before Taxes/Total		
3.7	1.4	.8	1.8				Assets		
.6	-.1	-.3	-1.1						
UND	1.0	.7	2.2						
UND	.5	.4	.8				Sales/Net Fixed Assets		
.5	.3	.2	.4						
3.5	.8	.5	.7						
2.4	.4	.3	.4				Sales/Total Assets		
.4	.3	.2	.3						
	1.7	2.3	1.4						
	(24) 6.1	(31) 5.3	(13) 3.0				% Depr., Dep., Amort./Sales		
	9.7	8.0	5.7						
		7.3					% Officers', Directors',		
		(14) 19.5					Owners' Comp/Sales		
		32.8							
9985M	33135M	175004M	274761M	58678M	35646M		Net Sales ($)		
4756M	61132M	333553M	463103M	354010M	234447M		Total Assets ($)		

M = $ thousand   MM = $ million
See Pages 1 through 15 for Explanation of Ratios and Data

Comparative Historical Data   **Current Data Sorted By Sales**

4/1/92-3/31/93 ALL	4/1/93-3/31/94 ALL	4/1/94-3/31/95 ALL		0-1MM	1-3MM	3-5MM	5-10MM	10-25MM	25MM & OVER
		19	# Postretirement Benefits	12	6	1			
			Type of Statement						
		37	Unqualified	3	8	7	6	10	3
		11	Reviewed	7	2		1	1	
		24	Compiled	12	10	1	1		
			Tax Returns						
		91	Other	51	29	6	3	2	
					66 (4/1-9/30/94)		97 (10/1/94-3/31/95)		
163			**NUMBER OF STATEMENTS**	73	49	14	11	13	3
%	%	%	**ASSETS**	%	%	%	%	%	%
D	D	13.8	Cash & Equivalents	14.4	12.7	10.8	16.0	18.1	
A	A	2.0	Trade Receivables - (net)	.2	1.2	6.4	1.9	10.9	
T	T	.5	Inventory	.3	.6	.1	.6	1.6	
A	A	2.6	All Other Current	1.5	1.6	4.9	2.5	8.9	
		18.9	Total Current	16.3	16.1	22.2	21.0	39.5	
N	N	69.2	Fixed Assets (net)	75.6	73.5	64.5	63.2	29.5	
O	O	.3	Intangibles (net)	.1	.2	.1	1.0	1.2	
T	T	11.6	All Other Non-Current	8.0	10.2	13.2	14.7	29.7	
		100.0	Total	100.0	100.0	100.0	100.0	100.0	
A	A		**LIABILITIES**						
V	V	4.4	Notes Payable-Short Term	5.0	5.2	2.0	1.0	4.0	
A	A	1.7	Cur. Mat.-L /T/D	1.9	1.3	1.0	4.6	.4	
I	I	2.4	Trade Payables	.2	1.7	4.4	3.4	14.2	
L	L	.0	Income Taxes Payable	.0	.0	.0	.0	.1	
A	A	5.8	All Other Current	3.1	3.6	9.8	8.6	19.9	
B	B	14.3	Total Current	10.2	11.8	17.2	17.6	38.6	
L	L	19.6	Long Term Debt	18.5	26.4	13.7	28.2	3.4	
E	E	.0	Deferred Taxes	.0	.0	.0	.0	.0	
		1.8	All Other-Non-Current	.6	1.9	5.6	.5	6.2	
		64.2	Net Worth	70.7	59.8	63.5	53.7	51.8	
		100.0	Total Liabilities & Net Worth	100.0	100.0	100.0	100.0	100.0	
			INCOME DATA						
		100.0	Net Sales	100.0	100.0	100.0	100.0	100.0	
			Gross Profit						
		89.7	Operating Expenses	89.0	87.9	90.9	81.1	104.3	
		10.3	Operating Profit	11.0	12.1	9.1	18.9	-4.3	
		3.6	All Other Expenses (net)	3.9	4.1	1.5	10.0	-1.8	
		6.6	Profit Before Taxes	7.1	8.0	7.6	8.9	-2.5	
			RATIOS						
		3.4		9.2	2.8	8.3	2.5	2.3	
		1.3	Current	1.6	1.0	2.8	.9	1.3	
		.6		.4	.7	1.0	.3	.6	
		3.0		8.7	2.2	8.2	2.5	1.5	
		1.1	Quick	1.3	1.0	2.8	.7	1.3	
		.4		.3	.5	1.0	.3	.4	
0 UND	0 UND	0 UND		0 UND	0 UND	0 UND	0 UND	9 39.2	
0 UND	0 UND		Sales/Receivables	0 UND	0 UND	0 999.8	7 49.8	28 13.1	
		7 49.8		0 UND	8 47.6	16 23.4	20 18.2	114 3.2	
			Cost of Sales/Inventory						
			Cost of Sales/Payables						
		5.3		3.6	9.1	3.5	6.0	3.6	
		43.3	Sales/Working Capital	37.9	413.0	11.3	-22.6	15.4	
		-13.3		-10.6	-32.8	NM	-4.1	-15.0	
		4.2		3.4	6.9				
	(88)	1.9	EBIT/Interest	(36) 1.4	(29) 2.7				
		.8		.7	1.1				
			Net Profit + Depr., Dep., Amort./Cur. Mat. L/T/D						
		.8		.8	.8	.7	.6	.1	
		1.1	Fixed/Worth	1.2	1.3	1.0	.8	.3	
		1.6		1.6	2.0	1.6	2.6	1.0	
		.2		.1	.4	.0	.4	.2	
		.5	Debt/Worth	.3	.6	.6	.7	.8	
		1.2		.8	1.3	2.5	2.4	2.9	
		10.5	% Profit Before Taxes/Tangible	6.6	11.6	16.2	15.2	13.7	
	(162)	2.3	Net Worth	(72) 1.1	3.8	4.1	6.6	-.9	
		-.5		-.4	-.1	.1	-.5	-5.8	
		5.4	% Profit Before Taxes/Total	4.0	7.3	6.1	7.4	3.5	
		1.0	Assets	.8	2.1	3.6	2.2	-.3	
		-.3		-.3	-.0	-.1	-.4	-2.7	
		1.1		.6	1.0	2.5	3.2	104.8	
		.6	Sales/Net Fixed Assets	.4	.6	.9	.7	2.5	
		.3		.2	.4	.5	.4	.9	
		.7		.4	.8	.6	1.0	1.8	
		.4	Sales/Total Assets	.3	.5	.5	.4	.6	
		.2		.2	.3	.3	.2	.3	
		1.6		1.5	2.4	2.0	1.9		
	(77)	4.6	% Depr., Dep., Amort./Sales	(24) 5.5	(21) 6.4	(11) 6.4	(10) 4.8		
		7.8		10.5	8.1	8.2	6.1		
		7.4	% Officers', Directors',	11.1					
	(24)	16.1	Owners' Comp/Sales	(13) 20.5					
		28.1		29.0					
		587209M	Net Sales ($)	37298M	84060M	57443M	78303M	214577M	115528M
		1451001M	Total Assets ($)	127218M	210977M	126853M	289569M	494758M	201626M

M = $ thousand   MM = $ million
See Pages 1 through 15 for Explanation of Ratios and Data

Current Data Sorted By Assets | Comparative Historical Data

	0-500M	500M-2MM	2-10MM	10-50MM	50-100MM	100-250MM
# Postretirement Benefits		1	1			
Type of Statement						
Unqualified		5	12	7	4	2
Reviewed	2	8	10	6	3	
Compiled	8	15	5	3	1	
Tax Returns	3		1			
Other	8	10	20	10	2	
	0-500M	43 (4/1-9/30/94) 500M-2MM	2-10MM	98 (10/1/94-3/31/95) 10-50MM	50-100MM	100-250MM
NUMBER OF STATEMENTS	21	38	48	26	6	2

Comparative Historical Data columns: **4/1/90-3/31/91 ALL** and **4/1/91-3/31/92 ALL** — both marked "DATA NOT AVAILABLE".

	0-500M	500M-2MM	2-10MM	10-50MM	50-100MM	100-250MM		4/1/90-3/31/91 ALL	4/1/91-3/31/92 ALL
	%	%	%	%	%	%	**ASSETS**	%	%
	7.8	7.5	3.4	3.4			Cash & Equivalents	D	D
	5.9	5.4	5.2	7.2			Trade Receivables - (net)	A	A
	9.0	5.2	8.8	23.3			Inventory	T	T
	1.7	.9	7.8	10.1			All Other Current	A	A
	24.4	19.0	25.2	43.9			Total Current		
	67.0	74.1	61.3	52.0			Fixed Assets (net)	N	N
	6.5	2.0	2.1	.7			Intangibles (net)	O	O
	2.1	4.8	11.3	3.4			All Other Non-Current	T	T
	100.0	100.0	100.0	100.0			Total		
							LIABILITIES	A	A
	28.4	19.1	31.2	36.5			Notes Payable-Short Term	V	V
	5.6	10.4	5.8	5.8			Cur. Mat. -L/T/D	A	A
	6.0	3.3	3.5	5.3			Trade Payables	I	I
	.3	.2	.2	.1			Income Taxes Payable	L	L
	10.8	4.8	6.1	5.6			All Other Current	A	A
	51.1	37.8	46.8	53.3			Total Current	B	B
	16.7	37.0	30.6	30.0			Long Term Debt	L	L
	.0	.9	.9	1.2			Deferred Taxes	E	E
	6.4	4.3	2.1	.2			All Other-Non-Current		
	25.7	19.9	19.5	15.3			Net Worth		
	100.0	100.0	100.0	100.0			Total Liabilities & Net Worth		
							INCOME DATA		
	100.0	100.0	100.0	100.0			Net Sales		
							Gross Profit		
	95.4	87.0	91.1	85.0			Operating Expenses		
	4.6	13.0	8.9	15.0			Operating Profit		
	.9	6.3	5.4	10.2			All Other Expenses (net)		
	3.6	6.7	3.6	4.8			Profit Before Taxes		
							RATIOS		
	1.0	1.1	1.1	1.3					
	.3	.5	.5	1.0			Current		
	.1	.2	.2	.2					
	.6	1.0	.5	.6					
	.2	.5	.2	.2			Quick		
	.1	.1	.1	.1					
	1 501.3	5 72.3	8 46.5	8 46.5					
	5 68.3	21 17.8	15 24.0	22 16.9			Sales/Receivables		
	24 15.3	28 12.9	28 13.0	43 8.5					
							Cost of Sales/Inventory		
							Cost of Sales/Payables		
	NM	55.8	50.0	10.0					
	-7.8	-7.2	-11.5	23.5			Sales/Working Capital		
	-2.6	-3.5	-1.1	-1.5					
	2.7	2.5	2.2	2.3					
	(19) 2.0	(34) 1.5	(41) 1.3	(24) 1.4			EBIT/Interest		
	1.2	1.2	.9	1.2					
			41.4						
		(10)	1.8				Net Profit + Depr., Dep., Amort./Cur. Mat. L./T/D		
			.4						
	1.9	1.8	1.0	.4					
	6.0	4.2	4.7	3.5			Fixed/Worth		
	25.9	15.7	9.9	6.3					
	2.1	2.2	2.8	4.5					
	7.7	6.6	6.5	6.9			Debt/Worth		
	28.3	16.8	16.1	12.8					
	58.5	41.6	36.9	32.1			% Profit Before Taxes/Tangible		
	(17) 17.4	(32) 26.6	(43) 12.9	20.3			Net Worth		
	1.9	7.9	1.0	6.4					
	11.1	6.8	5.3	4.0			% Profit Before Taxes/Total		
	4.6	2.6	1.9	2.3			Assets		
	.7	1.3	-.4	1.1					
	5.9	1.6	4.7	25.3					
	1.6	.9	1.0	1.0			Sales/Net Fixed Assets		
	1.2	.6	.6	.5					
	2.5	1.2	.8	.7					
	1.4	.6	.6	.5			Sales/Total Assets		
	.9	.5	.5	.4					
	11.8	13.3	7.0	12.5			% Depr., Dep., Amort./Sales		
	(19) 20.8	(35) 25.2	(42) 24.7	(15) 29.0					
	33.3	35.4	31.6	39.2					
		2.8	1.7	2.3			% Officers', Directors',		
	(12)	6.9	(18) 5.8	(11) 3.3			Owners' Comp/Sales		
		15.0	13.7	12.8					
	11327M	38799M	203818M	338491M	459034M	807300M	Net Sales ($)		
	5739M	40708M	258449M	611833M	361321M	288423M	Total Assets ($)		

M = $ thousand   MM = $ million
See Pages 1 through 15 for Explanation of Ratios and Data

	Comparative Historical Data				Current Data Sorted By Sales					
	4	6	2	# Postretirement Benefits	1	1				
				Type of Statement						
	11	20	30	Unqualified	3	4	7	4	5	7
	15	15	26	Reviewed	6	6	7	1	6	
	19	21	31	Compiled	17	8	4	1	1	
	2	1	4	Tax Returns	3	1				
	21	36	50	Other	14	15	6	6	7	2
	4/1/92-	4/1/93-	4/1/94-		43 (4/1-9/30/94)			98 (10/1/94-3/31/95)		
	3/31/93	3/31/94	3/31/95							
	ALL	ALL	ALL		0-1MM	1-3MM	3-5MM	5-10MM	10-25MM	25MM & OVER
	68	93	141	**NUMBER OF STATEMENTS**	43	33	25	12	19	9
	%	%	%	**ASSETS**	%	%	%	%	%	%
	6.7	5.1	5.4	Cash & Equivalents	6.6	5.4	4.6	4.4	3.7	
	7.9	4.2	6.0	Trade Receivables - (net)	4.1	4.6	10.1	5.8	5.7	
	16.9	13.5	12.0	Inventory	6.1	12.5	7.7	3.0	22.8	
	3.1	3.8	5.6	All Other Current	1.2	1.9	9.5	14.3	9.5	
	34.6	26.7	29.0	Total Current	17.9	24.4	31.9	27.5	41.7	
	56.8	63.5	62.2	Fixed Assets (net)	75.3	66.3	49.3	68.5	54.4	
	2.4	3.3	2.5	Intangibles (net)	2.5	3.5	3.2	1.5	.7	
	6.2	6.5	6.3	All Other Non-Current	4.3	5.8	15.5	2.5	3.3	
	100.0	100.0	100.0	Total	100.0	100.0	100.0	100.0	100.0	
				LIABILITIES						
	37.3	44.8	29.8	Notes Payable-Short Term	23.7	25.8	35.0	24.7	33.8	
	7.6	5.6	6.7	Cur. Mat.-L /T/D	9.2	5.5	9.3	5.9	3.4	
	4.2	2.9	4.2	Trade Payables	2.4	5.5	3.4	3.4	7.4	
	.3	.2	.2	Income Taxes Payable	.2	.2	.4	.0	.1	
	6.1	4.2	6.7	All Other Current	4.9	5.9	11.7	6.9	3.6	
	55.4	57.6	47.6	Total Current	40.3	43.0	59.8	40.9	48.3	
	22.8	22.8	29.1	Long Term Debt	32.4	35.2	12.8	40.5	34.0	
	1.3	.6	.8	Deferred Taxes	.4	.9	1.1	.9	1.3	
	1.0	1.1	3.0	All Other-Non-Current	6.7	2.2	1.0	1.5	.1	
	19.5	17.9	19.5	Net Worth	20.1	18.8	25.3	16.2	16.2	
	100.0	100.0	100.0	Total Liabilities & Net Worth	100.0	100.0	100.0	100.0	100.0	
				INCOME DATA						
	100.0	100.0	100.0	Net Sales	100.0	100.0	100.0	100.0	100.0	
				Gross Profit						
	91.9	90.9	89.3	Operating Expenses	88.8	89.3	88.4	91.8	90.5	
	8.1	9.1	10.7	Operating Profit	11.2	10.7	11.6	8.2	9.5	
	4.1	4.4	6.0	All Other Expenses (net)	5.7	5.9	7.4	5.1	5.0	
	4.0	4.7	4.6	Profit Before Taxes	5.6	4.7	4.3	3.1	4.4	
				RATIOS						
	1.3	1.1	1.1		1.1	1.2	1.0	1.0	1.6	
	.6	.3	.6	Current	.4	.7	.4	.5	1.1	
	.2	.1	.2		.2	.2	.1	.2	.3	
	.7	.4	.7		.8	.8	.4	.6	.8	
	.2	.2	.2	Quick	.3	.2	.2	.2	.3	
	.1		.1		.1	.1	.1	.2	.1	
	9 39.3	7 56.0	6 60.1		3 109.5	5 75.1	9 41.3	9 41.4	7 52.2	
	18 20.1	17 21.7	17 21.0	Sales/Receivables	20 18.7	12 29.5	21 17.8	19 19.3	17 21.6	
	29 12.8	27 13.3	29 12.5		28 13.1	24 15.0	35 10.4	31 11.6	36 10.2	
				Cost of Sales/Inventory						
				Cost of Sales/Payables						
	12.8	27.2	19.0		22.6	22.2	57.1	168.7	10.3	
	-12.2	-4.9	-12.8	Sales/Working Capital	-6.1	-13.3	-5.2	-24.8	20.1	
	-1.7	-1.0	-2.3		-2.3	-3.2	-.9	-2.5	-3.5	
	3.0	2.1	2.3		2.6	2.4	1.8	2.7	2.6	
(62)	1.5	(85) 1.6	(125) 1.5	EBIT/Interest	(39) 1.5	(28) 1.7	(22) 1.1	(10) 1.3	(18) 1.7	
	1.1	1.2	1.1		1.2	1.2	.9	.9	1.3	
	5.5	2.4	2.8							
(20)	1.6	(13) 1.3	(23) 1.3	Net Profit + Depr., Dep.,						
	1.3	.5	.8	Amort./Cur. Mat. L/T/D						
	.9	1.5	1.0		2.4	2.1	.3	2.1	.4	
	3.9	5.8	4.5	Fixed/Worth	6.2	4.5	2.1	5.6	4.3	
	14.3	10.8	9.2		15.6	11.2	9.7	6.5	6.3	
	3.4	3.7	3.1		2.5	2.9	2.4	4.5	3.9	
	7.2	6.8	6.9	Debt/Worth	8.2	5.8	6.4	6.0	6.1	
	21.9	15.7	15.2		16.8	18.3	20.2	13.9	12.5	
	47.9	40.2	40.9	% Profit Before Taxes/Tangible	44.0	70.4	27.6	29.0	36.9	
(56)	14.9	(84) 19.3	(126) 21.1	Net Worth	(35) 26.2	(30) 23.5	(22) 7.1	(11) 13.6	22.7	
	8.5	10.3	5.5		5.3	11.6	-1.5	1.0	11.7	
	6.4	5.6	5.7	% Profit Before Taxes/Total	7.3	6.9	3.7	6.1	5.5	
	2.9	2.9	2.5	Assets	2.6	3.1	1.1	1.9	2.5	
	.7	1.4	.4		.3	1.3	-.5	-.6	1.5	
	19.1	4.2	6.4		1.6	3.0	25.5	5.9	19.7	
	1.2	1.0	1.2	Sales/Net Fixed Assets	.9	1.2	2.3	1.6	1.6	
	.8	.7	.6		.6	.6	.6	.6	.7	
	1.2	.9	1.2		1.2	1.3	.8	1.8	1.1	
	.8	.6	.7	Sales/Total Assets	.6	.7	.6	.7	.7	
	.6	.5	.5		.5	.5	.5	.5	.5	
	14.6	13.5	9.8		18.2	7.1	4.2	7.2	4.0	
(53)	28.4	(74) 28.0	(115) 24.2	% Depr., Dep., Amort./Sales	(40) 30.3	(30) 23.8	(19) 24.9	(10) 20.2	(12) 20.4	
	32.8	34.9	33.7		38.0	29.0	31.1	35.0	28.6	
	1.8	3.1	2.3		2.7	2.9				
(36)	4.5	(24) 7.6	(49) 4.8	% Officers', Directors',	(14) 6.9	(13) 8.2				
	9.7	12.6	13.4	Owners' Comp/Sales	14.8	16.7				
	530399M	915566M	1858769M	Net Sales ($)	20904M	58423M	96223M	86369M	274933M	1321917M
	616664M	1264580M	1566473M	Total Assets ($)	30865M	114185M	190665M	101119M	433943M	695696M

M = $ thousand   MM = $ million
See Pages 1 through 15 for Explanation of Ratios and Data

Current Data Sorted By Assets **Comparative Historical Data**

0-500M	500M-2MM	2-10MM	10-50MM	50-100MM	100-250MM		4/1/90-3/31/91 ALL	4/1/91-3/31/92 ALL
	24 (4/1-9/30/94)		50 (10/1/94-3/31/95)					
1	3	1			1	# Postretirement Benefits		
						Type of Statement		
2	4	6	5	1	2	Unqualified		
3	14	3				Reviewed		
6	8					Compiled		
1						Tax Returns		
5	8	3	2	1		Other		
17	34	12	7	2	2	**NUMBER OF STATEMENTS**		
%	%	%	%	%	%		%	%
						ASSETS		
8.4	11.2	14.1				Cash & Equivalents	D	D
40.2	48.5	48.7				Trade Receivables - (net)	A	A
.6	3.1	.3				Inventory	T	T
5.7	5.4	7.9				All Other Current	A	A
54.9	68.2	70.9				Total Current		
29.4	21.4	17.3				Fixed Assets (net)	N	N
3.2	.5	4.0				Intangibles (net)	O	O
12.4	9.9	7.7				All Other Non-Current	T	T
100.0	100.0	100.0				Total		
						LIABILITIES	A	A
7.5	9.2	12.5				Notes Payable-Short Term	V	V
3.8	2.7	2.4				Cur. Mat. -L/T/D	A	A
16.0	13.3	10.1				Trade Payables	I	I
1.0	.8	1.3				Income Taxes Payable	L	L
20.3	20.5	21.6				All Other Current	A	A
48.6	46.5	48.0				Total Current	B	B
11.4	4.9	7.9				Long Term Debt	L	L
.3	1.3	1.6				Deferred Taxes	E	E
1.3	2.8	5.0				All Other-Non-Current		
38.3	44.4	37.6				Net Worth		
100.0	100.0	100.0				Total Liabilities & Net Worth		
						INCOME DATA		
100.0	100.0	100.0				Net Sales		
						Gross Profit		
94.5	96.8	96.5				Operating Expenses		
5.5	3.2	3.5				Operating Profit		
3.4	.1	.3				All Other Expenses (net)		
2.0	3.1	3.2				Profit Before Taxes		
						RATIOS		
4.4	2.4	2.4						
1.3	1.3	1.4				Current		
.8	1.1	1.2						
4.4	2.1	2.0						
1.3	1.2	1.3				Quick		
.5	.8	1.1						
17 21.3	41 9.0	54 6.7						
33 11.2	55 6.6	87 4.2				Sales/Receivables		
79 4.6	81 4.5	114 3.2						
						Cost of Sales/Inventory		
						Cost of Sales/Payables		
13.0	6.4	5.4						
35.1	19.4	11.4				Sales/Working Capital		
-26.0	117.0	17.1						
7.1	11.2	15.6						
(12) 1.7	(30) 7.2	(10) 7.0				EBIT/Interest		
-.7	1.5	1.3						
	8.4					Net Profit + Depr., Dep.,		
	(14) 3.7					Amort./Cur. Mat. L /T/D		
	1.3							
.2	.3	.3						
.9	.4	.6				Fixed/Worth		
NM	.8	.7						
.9	.6	1.4						
1.5	1.3	2.3				Debt/Worth		
NM	2.8	3.8						
54.7	47.3	55.7				% Profit Before Taxes/Tangible		
(13) 16.0	22.2	16.4				Net Worth		
-10.3	3.8	2.2						
30.7	17.6	14.1				% Profit Before Taxes/Total		
8.5	8.4	7.2				Assets		
-3.4	1.7	.6						
48.8	34.4	24.7						
16.9	17.1	18.0				Sales/Net Fixed Assets		
12.1	12.5	7.0						
5.7	3.8	2.8						
4.4	3.1	2.0				Sales/Total Assets		
2.1	2.5	1.6						
.9	1.1	1.3						
(14) 2.5	(31) 1.8	(11) 1.8				% Depr., Dep., Amort./Sales		
3.7	2.8	3.2						
	3.2					% Officers', Directors',		
	(16) 5.7					Owners' Comp/Sales		
	12.0							
16442M	124516M	134261M	348223M	166153M	311473M	Net Sales ($)		
3962M	41026M	63694M	172255M	151627M	298899M	Total Assets ($)		

M = $ thousand   MM = $ million
See Pages 1 through 15 for Explanation of Ratios and Data

Comparative Historical Data — **Current Data Sorted By Sales**

		3	6		1	2	2		1
				# Postretirement Benefits					
				Type of Statement					
	8	10	20	Unqualified	2	3	1	2	4	8
	10	10	20	Reviewed	2	7	5	5	1	
	13	13	14	Compiled	1	8	3	2		
		1	1	Tax Returns	1					
	4	9	19	Other	4	5	2	4	2	2
	4/1/92-3/31/93 ALL	4/1/93-3/31/94 ALL	4/1/94-3/31/95 ALL		24 (4/1-9/30/94)			50 (10/1/94-3/31/95)		
					0-1MM	1-3MM	3-5MM	5-10MM	10-25MM	25MM & OVER
	35	43	74	**NUMBER OF STATEMENTS**	10	23	11	13	7	10
	%	%	%	**ASSETS**	%	%	%	%	%	%
	7.6	10.9	11.1	Cash & Equivalents	4.7	8.2	20.8	12.0		10.2
	54.1	51.2	45.3	Trade Receivables - (net)	31.8	49.8	43.5	51.4		42.4
	4.7	3.4	1.7	Inventory	1.0	2.9	1.1	2.0		.2
	5.6	2.8	6.1	All Other Current	8.2	2.9	9.5	5.5		7.1
	71.9	68.3	64.2	Total Current	45.6	63.8	74.9	70.9		59.9
	20.4	22.2	22.7	Fixed Assets (net)	34.7	25.0	17.3	14.8		19.9
	.8	1.9	2.2	Intangibles (net)	5.5	.8	.0	1.8		4.2
	6.9	7.5	10.9	All Other Non-Current	14.2	10.4	7.8	12.5		16.0
	100.0	100.0	100.0	Total	100.0	100.0	100.0	100.0		100.0
				LIABILITIES						
	10.9	11.3	8.7	Notes Payable-Short Term	10.5	8.5	8.9	9.7		8.8
	5.1	3.0	2.7	Cur. Mat.-L /T/D	1.6	4.2	2.8	1.6		1.3
	15.9	13.7	12.9	Trade Payables	14.5	15.1	11.8	12.3		10.8
	1.6	1.4	.8	Income Taxes Payable	.9	1.3	.5	.5		.2
	17.4	21.4	20.7	All Other Current	17.1	20.3	19.7	25.8		14.1
	50.9	50.9	45.9	Total Current	44.6	49.3	43.7	49.9		35.2
	7.0	8.2	6.9	Long Term Debt	12.5	6.3	5.0	5.9		2.7
	2.1	1.4	1.0	Deferred Taxes	.3	1.3	1.5	1.0		.6
	4.7	4.0	2.6	All Other-Non-Current	.0	2.9	3.6	2.3		1.6
	35.3	35.5	43.6	Net Worth	42.6	40.0	46.2	40.9		60.0
	100.0	100.0	100.0	Total Liabilities & Net Worth	100.0	100.0	100.0	100.0		100.0
				INCOME DATA						
	100.0	100.0	100.0	Net Sales	100.0	100.0	100.0	100.0		100.0
				Gross Profit						
	95.4	95.3	96.1	Operating Expenses	95.0	97.0	97.4	94.9		95.0
	4.6	4.7	3.9	Operating Profit	5.0	3.0	2.6	5.1		5.0
	.9	1.5	.9	All Other Expenses (net)	4.2	.6	-.3	.7		.1
	3.6	3.2	3.0	Profit Before Taxes	.8	2.4	3.0	4.4		4.9
				RATIOS						
	2.2	2.0	2.5	Current	4.1	2.4	2.6	1.9		3.1
	1.4	1.4	1.3		1.2	1.2	1.9	1.3		1.8
	1.1	1.0	1.1		.7	.9	1.3	1.2		1.2
	2.1	2.0	2.1	Quick	4.1	2.1	2.4	1.7		2.1
	1.3	1.2	1.2		1.2	1.2	1.3	1.3		1.7
	.9	.9	.9		.4	.8	.9	.9		1.1
	51 7.2	47 7.7	38 9.7	Sales/Receivables	0 UND	28 13.0	38 9.7	41 8.8		59 6.2
	69 5.3	68 5.4	63 5.8		42 8.7	54 6.7	52 7.0	72 5.1		85 4.3
	78 4.7	85 4.3	89 4.1		101 3.6	87 4.2	79 4.6	91 4.0		96 3.8
				Cost of Sales/Inventory						
				Cost of Sales/Payables						
	6.4	8.9	6.4	Sales/Working Capital	14.2	7.9	6.3	9.2		4.0
	15.4	15.0	17.6		62.2	21.4	9.0	17.7		8.8
	45.8	-364.5	65.7		-12.4	-40.3	24.2	61.6		25.6
	11.9	15.7	11.2	EBIT/Interest		7.2		28.6		
	(32) 5.0	(35) 5.2	(62) 6.9			(19) 2.3		(11) 10.6		
	2.1	1.6	1.3			-1.0		3.4		
	6.8	3.4	8.0	Net Profit + Depr., Dep., Amort./Cur. Mat. L/T/D						
	(16) 2.4	(11) 2.7	(30) 3.5							
	1.2	1.2	1.5							
	.2	.3	.3	Fixed/Worth	.3	.3	.3	.3		.2
	.4	.6	.5		1.1	.6	.4	.4		.3
	1.0	1.7	.9		-3.0	1.0	.6	.6		.7
	1.0	1.0	.6	Debt/Worth	.7	1.0	.6	.6		.4
	1.6	2.0	1.5		1.2	1.5	1.3	2.2		.5
	2.9	4.2	3.3		-23.8	3.4	2.7	3.7		2.1
	50.5	58.6	41.6	% Profit Before Taxes/Tangible Net Worth		40.7	47.4	62.2		37.6
	(33) 27.1	(39) 28.3	(70) 18.0			(22) 22.2	16.9	30.3		17.7
	13.0	8.3	3.6			-.7	-.4	9.8		3.6
	16.1	23.6	15.3	% Profit Before Taxes/Total Assets	19.8	16.8	13.2	23.5		13.4
	8.2	8.0	7.8		7.7	7.9	4.6	13.2		10.3
	5.8	1.9	1.0		-4.4	-.3	-.2	4.7		2.6
	34.2	34.6	26.7	Sales/Net Fixed Assets	25.4	20.8	40.7	31.6		17.6
	16.9	15.8	16.7		15.6	14.2	20.4	19.4		11.2
	10.6	10.0	10.7		4.7	10.8	16.7	16.4		4.0
	3.8	3.8	3.9	Sales/Total Assets	4.6	5.1	4.1	3.6		3.0
	3.1	3.1	2.9		2.1	3.4	3.1	3.1		1.8
	2.4	2.1	1.9		1.6	2.3	2.5	2.1		1.1
	1.3	1.0	1.2	% Depr., Dep., Amort./Sales		1.7	.8	1.2		
	(31) 2.0	(39) 1.7	(66) 2.0			(20) 2.6	(10) 1.4	(11) 1.5		
	2.7	3.1	3.3			3.5	2.3	1.8		
	2.5	4.7	3.5	% Officers', Directors', Owners' Comp/Sales						
	(11) 11.9	(15) 10.8	(26) 7.6							
	13.7	14.5	13.4							
	448994M	518863M	1101068M	Net Sales ($)	5393M	45189M	42938M	87498M	96443M	823607M
	169073M	211533M	731463M	Total Assets ($)	3596M	20281M	13522M	34089M	52953M	607022M

M = $ thousand   MM = $ million
See Pages 1 through 15 for Explanation of Ratios and Data

SERVICES—RESEARCH – COMMERCIAL (PHYSICAL & BIOLOGICAL). SIC# 8731

Current Data Sorted By Assets							Comparative Historical Data	
1	2	4	1		1	**# Postretirement Benefits** **Type of Statement**		
2	5	12	12	4	3	Unqualified	24	28
1	7	6				Reviewed	10	20
7	6					Compiled	14	17
2	1					Tax Returns		
4	13	9	5		3	Other	13	13
	42 (4/1-9/30/94)		60 (10/1/94-3/31/95)				4/1/90- 3/31/91	4/1/91- 3/31/92
0-500M	500M-2MM	2-10MM	10-50MM	50-100MM	100-250MM		ALL	ALL
16	32	27	17	7	3	**NUMBER OF STATEMENTS**	61	78
%	%	%	%	%	%	**ASSETS**	%	%
14.0	10.8	17.4	21.7			Cash & Equivalents	11.3	11.2
44.0	36.4	33.3	24.8			Trade Receivables - (net)	37.4	36.3
.9	2.2	7.4	3.1			Inventory	6.8	5.3
3.5	4.7	3.0	8.2			All Other Current	6.4	7.1
62.4	54.1	61.1	57.9			Total Current	62.0	59.9
30.4	35.2	26.9	29.5			Fixed Assets (net)	28.5	30.4
2.8	1.6	2.0	3.5			Intangibles (net)	2.4	3.8
4.4	9.0	10.0	9.1			All Other Non-Current	7.1	5.8
100.0	100.0	100.0	100.0			Total	100.0	100.0
						LIABILITIES		
5.0	7.6	7.8	4.0			Notes Payable-Short Term	8.9	7.9
4.5	3.5	2.9	2.1			Cur. Mat. -L/T/D	4.7	4.7
8.3	13.1	7.9	11.0			Trade Payables	11.3	10.4
.0	1.3	1.3	.3			Income Taxes Payable	1.8	.7
17.5	11.2	15.7	14.1			All Other Current	13.4	15.5
35.3	36.7	35.7	31.5			Total Current	40.1	37.9
21.0	17.0	12.5	15.9			Long Term Debt	9.6	11.5
.1	.8	2.3	1.6			Deferred Taxes	1.9	1.6
.9	4.5	1.9	2.2			All Other-Non-Current	4.1	3.6
42.7	41.0	47.7	48.8			Net Worth	44.3	45.5
100.0	100.0	100.0	100.0			Total Liabilities & Net Worth	100.0	100.0
						INCOME DATA		
100.0	100.0	100.0	100.0			Net Sales	100.0	100.0
						Gross Profit		
96.3	93.0	96.7	103.3			Operating Expenses	95.5	96.6
3.7	7.0	3.3	-3.3			Operating Profit	4.5	3.4
.3	1.0	1.3	-.1			All Other Expenses (net)	1.1	1.8
3.4	6.1	2.0	-3.2			Profit Before Taxes	3.4	1.6
						RATIOS		
3.8	2.0	2.4	2.8				2.4	2.9
2.2	1.4	1.9	1.5			Current	1.5	1.6
1.2	1.1	1.2	1.1				1.1	1.1
2.9	1.6	2.3	2.4				2.2	2.0
2.1	1.4	1.3	1.2			Quick	1.4	1.3
1.2	.9	1.1	.8				.8	.8
26 14.0	30 12.3	39 9.4	46 8.0				42 8.6	46 7.9
43 8.4	49 7.4	62 5.9	76 4.8			Sales/Receivables	65 5.6	60 6.1
87 4.2	78 4.7	89 4.1	104 3.5				89 4.1	74 4.9
						Cost of Sales/Inventory		
						Cost of Sales/Payables		
5.9	7.9	4.2	3.2				5.3	5.6
14.6	16.4	6.8	7.6			Sales/Working Capital	12.0	11.0
31.5	107.5	22.7	104.0				38.3	69.9
(10) 8.7	(26) 13.1	(23) 13.1	(12) 8.7				(49) 11.3	(70) 8.9
2.2	8.8	4.6	2.5			EBIT/Interest	3.4	3.5
-.9	1.8	1.4	-14.2				.9	1.3
		(14) 8.7					(33) 8.0	(30) 7.4
		2.7				Net Profit + Depr., Dep., Amort./Cur. Mat. L./T/D	2.3	3.9
		.9					1.3	1.5
.2	.4	.3	.3				.2	.3
.4	.9	.5	.7			Fixed/Worth	.6	.7
6.7	1.8	1.0	1.1				1.4	1.4
.5	.6	.6	.6				.7	.7
1.3	1.6	1.2	1.5			Debt/Worth	1.4	1.5
9.5	2.7	2.0	2.5				2.6	3.6
(15) 79.4	(30) 64.8	38.3	21.1				(58) 40.0	(74) 44.5
21.2	36.3	14.4	6.9			% Profit Before Taxes/Tangible Net Worth	17.9	15.7
14.1	19.2	.7	-25.3				4.2	1.6
31.8	26.4	16.3	13.0				14.9	15.8
9.3	15.2	6.9	2.0			% Profit Before Taxes/Total Assets	7.1	5.8
-9.6	6.4	.5	-9.4				1.4	.3
50.1	23.6	19.6	16.4				26.5	19.9
20.4	7.1	6.0	4.0			Sales/Net Fixed Assets	9.9	9.3
6.1	3.8	3.5	2.1				4.7	3.8
4.2	3.4	2.3	1.9				3.0	3.1
3.6	2.3	1.7	1.4			Sales/Total Assets	2.3	2.2
2.6	1.7	1.2	.6				1.5	1.4
(12) .7	(25) 1.9	(23) 1.6	(12) 1.2				(54) 1.4	(68) 1.5
2.6	3.0	2.9	4.5			% Depr., Dep., Amort./Sales	2.8	3.2
5.1	5.2	5.9	7.1				5.0	5.1
							(15) 6.2	(19) 4.7
						% Officers', Directors', Owners' Comp/Sales	10.2	6.4
							15.7	14.4
18474M	96284M	213357M	496308M	743585M	370076M	Net Sales ($)	1224078M	1030543M
4402M	37859M	123920M	375850M	505307M	488451M	Total Assets ($)	562482M	670464M

M = $ thousand   MM = $ million
See Pages 1 through 15 for Explanation of Ratios and Data

Comparative Historical Data				Current Data Sorted By Sales					
3	6	9	# Postretirement Benefits	1		1	5	1	1
			Type of Statement						
43	31	38	Unqualified	2	3	5	7	8	13
11	19	14	Reviewed		3	7	4		
14	21	13	Compiled	5	6	2			
3	5	3	Tax Returns		1	1	1		
17	28	34	Other	4	12	4	4	5	5
4/1/92-3/31/93 ALL	4/1/93-3/31/94 ALL	4/1/94-3/31/95 ALL		42 (4/1-9/30/94) 0-1MM	1-3MM	3-5MM	60 (10/1/94-3/31/95) 5-10MM	10-25MM	25MM & OVER
88	104	102	NUMBER OF STATEMENTS	11	25	19	16	13	18
%	%	%	ASSETS	%	%	%	%	%	%
15.0	14.2	15.2	Cash & Equivalents	11.0	12.8	17.3	16.1	16.6	17.2
33.6	33.4	33.3	Trade Receivables - (net)	50.0	33.8	28.2	36.7	35.6	23.3
4.5	4.4	3.8	Inventory	1.2	2.2	4.8	5.6	5.1	3.8
3.8	3.2	4.9	All Other Current	5.0	2.5	5.3	1.2	6.2	9.9
56.9	55.3	57.2	Total Current	67.2	51.3	55.6	59.6	63.5	54.2
32.8	34.1	31.4	Fixed Assets (net)	27.3	38.3	35.7	26.5	19.8	32.8
2.6	2.4	2.7	Intangibles (net)	1.3	3.4	1.0	1.4	3.7	4.5
7.7	8.2	8.7	All Other Non-Current	4.2	6.9	7.7	12.5	13.0	8.5
100.0	100.0	100.0	Total	100.0	100.0	100.0	100.0	100.0	100.0
			LIABILITIES						
8.0	6.8	5.9	Notes Payable-Short Term	3.5	5.6	8.0	9.4	5.6	2.7
3.1	4.5	3.0	Cur. Mat.-L /T/D	4.2	3.7	3.9	3.0	1.4	1.7
11.5	10.5	10.1	Trade Payables	11.0	10.3	9.8	8.8	11.0	10.0
.8	1.0	.8	Income Taxes Payable	.0	.3	1.8	1.8	.6	.2
11.3	14.5	14.5	All Other Current	17.8	9.9	10.8	17.1	17.9	17.9
34.6	37.3	34.3	Total Current	36.5	29.8	34.3	40.1	36.5	32.4
14.6	14.3	16.2	Long Term Debt	18.2	17.8	23.0	10.4	9.7	15.4
1.3	1.2	1.2	Deferred Taxes	.0	1.2	1.0	1.0	4.0	.4
3.1	3.8	2.8	All Other-Non-Current	3.5	1.9	2.2	2.0	4.6	3.5
46.5	43.4	45.6	Net Worth	41.8	49.3	39.5	46.6	45.2	48.4
100.0	100.0	100.0	Total Liabilities & Net Worth	100.0	100.0	100.0	100.0	100.0	100.0
			INCOME DATA						
100.0	100.0	100.0	Net Sales	100.0	100.0	100.0	100.0	100.0	100.0
			Gross Profit						
97.9	94.4	96.3	Operating Expenses	97.9	93.5	95.4	100.1	98.6	95.2
2.1	5.6	3.7	Operating Profit	2.1	6.5	4.6	-.1	1.4	4.8
.7	.5	.7	All Other Expenses (net)	.6	1.0	1.6	-.6	.7	.6
1.3	5.2	3.0	Profit Before Taxes	1.5	5.5	3.0	.4	.7	4.2
			RATIOS						
2.7	2.7	2.5	Current	4.0	3.2	2.7	2.2	2.5	2.4
1.7	1.7	1.6		2.2	1.7	1.3	1.4	1.7	1.7
1.2	1.1	1.2		1.1	1.3	1.0	1.2	1.0	1.2
2.3	2.2	2.2	Quick	3.1	3.0	2.2	2.1	1.5	2.0
1.3	1.4	1.4		2.0	1.5	1.2	1.2	1.3	1.2
1.0	.9	1.0		1.1	1.2	.8	1.0	1.0	1.0
41 8.9	38 9.7	38 9.5	Sales/Receivables	38 9.6	26 13.8	19 19.4	37 10.0	52 7.0	43 8.4
55 6.6	55 6.6	56 6.5		61 6.0	53 6.9	41 9.0	65 5.6	76 4.8	49 7.5
74 4.9	81 4.5	91 4.0		101 3.6	85 4.3	66 5.5	99 3.7	104 3.5	83 4.4
			Cost of Sales/Inventory						
			Cost of Sales/Payables						
4.5	4.9	5.4	Sales/Working Capital	5.8	5.9	4.2	5.9	3.7	4.5
9.9	11.9	11.2		10.0	11.5	27.8	14.5	6.1	7.2
38.7	46.9	33.5		34.6	26.6	780.3	26.5	472.3	21.0
(74) 15.6	(91) 15.1	(79) 11.6	EBIT/Interest		(19) 18.9	(17) 9.9	(15) 13.6		(15) 9.6
3.3	4.9	4.8			7.0	4.4	5.6		5.3
-.2	1.6	1.6			-1.1	1.8	1.4		2.2
(42) 11.8	(43) 6.7	(31) 8.3	Net Profit + Depr., Dep., Amort./Cur. Mat. L/T/D			(10) 7.5			
3.2	2.9	2.5				2.1			
.6	1.3	1.1				.7			
.3	.4	.3	Fixed/Worth	.2	.3	.4	.3	.1	.4
.7	.8	.6		.3	.8	1.2	.4	.6	.7
1.2	1.8	1.4		4.9	1.6	1.8	1.0	.9	1.3
.5	.5	.6	Debt/Worth	.3	.5	1.0	.4	.8	.6
1.2	1.4	1.3		1.5	.8	1.9	1.4	1.5	1.0
2.3	3.0	2.5		14.8	2.4	2.7	2.4	2.5	2.2
(83) 45.1	(94) 50.8	(98) 43.3	% Profit Before Taxes/Tangible Net Worth	54.6	68.3	57.1	39.6	35.8	25.3
24.4	21.8	18.8		19.6	(17) 34.9	29.1	(12) 17.4	(17) 13.5	10.8
.0	4.6	3.6		-25.0	12.5	9.8	2.3	-16.6	-2.1
19.6	17.1	17.0	% Profit Before Taxes/Total Assets	16.1	32.7	20.6	15.6	17.2	12.9
8.6	8.4	7.7		8.2	13.0	6.9	7.5	8.9	5.6
-1.9	1.9	1.1		-4.2	3.4	3.3	.9	-4.3	.6
17.5	15.4	20.6	Sales/Net Fixed Assets	22.6	25.3	20.1	27.0	24.0	14.3
8.4	7.6	6.3		6.9	6.5	5.2	11.1	7.6	4.0
3.3	3.4	3.1		6.0	2.6	3.8	3.3	3.9	2.3
3.0	2.6	3.0	Sales/Total Assets	3.8	3.3	3.4	3.1	2.3	2.1
2.3	2.2	1.8		2.8	2.0	2.1	2.1	1.7	1.4
1.3	1.4	1.3		1.2	1.5	1.5	1.2	.8	1.2
(74) 2.2	(91) 2.1	(80) 1.6	% Depr., Dep., Amort./Sales		(19) 1.7	(18) 1.1	(13) 1.3		(14) 1.5
3.7	3.4	3.3			4.1	2.6	4.0		4.1
6.0	6.4	5.6			6.3	4.6	5.2		5.8
(22) 3.8	(25) 3.3	(22) 3.2	% Officers', Directors', Owners' Comp/Sales						
9.7	6.3	6.1							
18.8	13.0	12.7							
1597402M	1728048M	1938084M	Net Sales ($)	6354M	50744M	73454M	120226M	219060M	1468246M
1177215M	1308269M	1535789M	Total Assets ($)	2827M	27360M	46585M	80261M	214266M	1164490M

M = $ thousand   MM = $ million
See Pages 1 through 15 for Explanation of Ratios and Data

Current Data Sorted By Assets							Comparative Historical Data	
		1	1					
1	6	4	5	1		# Postretirement Benefits		
						Type of Statement		
1	6	4	5	1		Unqualified		
2	3	1				Reviewed		
1	3					Compiled		
2						Tax Returns		
6	6	2	1			Other		
	27 (4/1-9/30/94)		17 (10/1/94-3/31/95)				4/1/90-3/31/91	4/1/91-3/31/92
0-500M	500M-2MM	2-10MM	10-50MM	50-100MM	100-250MM		ALL	ALL
12	18	7	6	1		NUMBER OF STATEMENTS		
%	%	%	%	%	%	ASSETS	%	%
15.8	22.9					Cash & Equivalents	D	D
21.0	17.8					Trade Receivables - (net)	A	A
1.9	3.0					Inventory	T	T
.2	.4					All Other Current	A	A
38.9	44.1					Total Current		
34.1	44.6					Fixed Assets (net)	N	N
.8	2.4					Intangibles (net)	O	O
26.2	8.9					All Other Non-Current	T	T
100.0	100.0					Total		
						LIABILITIES	A	A
12.1	2.8					Notes Payable-Short Term	V	V
3.8	1.2					Cur. Mat. -L/T/D	A	A
4.9	6.9					Trade Payables	I	I
.6	.0					Income Taxes Payable	L	L
14.3	14.3					All Other Current	A	A
35.7	25.2					Total Current	B	B
21.4	10.9					Long Term Debt	L	L
.0	.0					Deferred Taxes	E	E
3.5	3.2					All Other-Non-Current		
39.4	60.8					Net Worth		
100.0	100.0					Total Liabilities & Net Worth		
						INCOME DATA		
100.0	100.0					Net Sales		
						Gross Profit		
90.2	94.3					Operating Expenses		
9.8	5.7					Operating Profit		
4.9	−.2					All Other Expenses (net)		
4.9	5.9					Profit Before Taxes		
						RATIOS		
3.2	4.5							
1.2	1.6					Current		
.4	.9							
3.2	3.7							
.9	1.4					Quick		
.4	.6							
0　UND	0　UND							
5　67.8	24　15.5					Sales/Receivables		
53　6.9	45　8.1							
						Cost of Sales/Inventory		
						Cost of Sales/Payables		
9.6	6.1							
72.5	14.1					Sales/Working Capital		
−29.8	−27.8							
	22.5							
	(10) 3.3					EBIT/Interest		
	−4.7							
						Net Profit + Depr., Dep., Amort./Cur. Mat. L /T/D		
.2	.3							
.7	.8					Fixed/Worth		
2.4	1.4							
.8	.2							
1.5	.6					Debt/Worth		
1.8	1.4							
79.2	35.1							
(11) 45.8	(17) 15.3					% Profit Before Taxes/Tangible Net Worth		
17.7	−.3							
31.7	17.6							
16.6	5.2					% Profit Before Taxes/Total Assets		
9.3	−1.9							
41.0	25.0							
19.9	7.8					Sales/Net Fixed Assets		
5.4	1.2							
6.0	3.1							
3.0	2.0					Sales/Total Assets		
1.9	.9							
1.0	1.3							
(10) 1.3	(14) 2.4					% Depr., Dep., Amort./Sales		
3.1	6.2							
						% Officers', Directors', Owners' Comp/Sales		
8691M	42854M	27406M	58472M	217232M		Net Sales ($)		
2229M	20156M	23942M	123555M	90352M		Total Assets ($)		

© Robert Morris Associates 1995

M = $ thousand　　MM = $ million
See Pages 1 through 15 for Explanation of Ratios and Data

Comparative Historical Data				Current Data Sorted By Sales					

			# Postretirement Benefits			1		1	
		2	**Type of Statement**						
		17	Unqualified	2	5	4	2	3	1
		6	Reviewed	1	3		1	1	
		4	Compiled	2	1	1			
		2	Tax Returns	1	1				
		15	Other	6	4	4	1		
4/1/92-3/31/93 ALL	4/1/93-3/31/94 ALL	4/1/94-3/31/95 ALL		27 (4/1-9/30/94)			17 (10/1/94-3/31/95)		
				0-1MM	1-3MM	3-5MM	5-10MM	10-25MM	25MM & OVER
		44	NUMBER OF STATEMENTS	12	14	9	4	4	1
%	%	%	**ASSETS**	%	%	%	%	%	%
		19.6	Cash & Equivalents	11.1	16.8				
D	D	15.5	Trade Receivables - (net)	13.4	22.7				
A	A	2.0	Inventory	2.6	1.3				
T	T	1.5	All Other Current	.3	.4				
A	A	38.6	Total Current	27.5	41.2				
		42.8	Fixed Assets (net)	55.2	40.9				
N	N	1.2	Intangibles (net)	.8	.2				
O	O	17.4	All Other Non-Current	16.6	17.7				
T	T	100.0	Total	100.0	100.0				
A	A		**LIABILITIES**						
V	V	5.1	Notes Payable-Short Term	10.6	6.4				
A	A	2.1	Cur. Mat.-L /T/D	4.2	1.3				
I	I	6.6	Trade Payables	4.4	7.5				
L	L	.2	Income Taxes Payable	.6	.0				
A	A	13.9	All Other Current	8.4	14.0				
B	B	27.8	Total Current	28.1	29.1				
L	L	14.5	Long Term Debt	18.3	15.8				
E	E	.0	Deferred Taxes	.0	.0				
		3.7	All Other-Non-Current	2.2	1.8				
		53.9	Net Worth	51.4	53.2				
		100.0	Total Liabilities & Net Worth	100.0	100.0				
			INCOME DATA						
		100.0	Net Sales	100.0	100.0				
			Gross Profit						
		94.9	Operating Expenses	91.6	93.3				
		5.1	Operating Profit	8.4	6.7				
		1.0	All Other Expenses (net)	5.4	.1				
		4.0	Profit Before Taxes	3.0	6.6				
			RATIOS						
		4.7		3.2	3.2				
		1.4	Current	.9	1.3				
		.8		.3	.9				
		3.8		1.8	3.2				
		1.1	Quick	.7	1.2				
		.6		.2	.8				
	1	345.2		0 UND	5 72.8				
	19	18.9	Sales/Receivables	0 UND	32 11.5				
	49	7.5		63 5.8	64 5.7				
			Cost of Sales/Inventory						
			Cost of Sales/Payables						
		4.1		4.7	10.7				
		18.8	Sales/Working Capital	−31.6	43.1				
		−23.1		−10.4	−64.5				
		6.2							
	(25)	3.1	EBIT/Interest						
		−1.3							
			Net Profit + Depr., Dep., Amort./Cur. Mat. L/T/D						
		.3		.4	.3				
		.8	Fixed/Worth	1.1	.8				
		1.3		1.9	1.5				
		.3		.4	.2				
		.8	Debt/Worth	1.1	.7				
		1.8		1.7	1.8				
		42.8		79.2	44.7				
	(41)	15.3	% Profit Before Taxes/Tangible Net Worth	20.3 (13)	15.3				
		.6		−5.4	3.4				
		18.4		26.3	25.5				
		5.5	% Profit Before Taxes/Total Assets	11.0	6.9				
		−.9		−4.3	1.7				
		19.7		20.7	37.0				
		5.1	Sales/Net Fixed Assets	3.8	8.1				
		1.1		.8	1.6				
		3.1		2.8	4.4				
		1.6	Sales/Total Assets	1.3	1.8				
		.7		.5	1.1				
		1.2			.8				
	(34)	2.7	% Depr., Dep., Amort./Sales	(13)	1.8				
		5.7			4.4				
			% Officers', Directors', Owners' Comp/Sales						
		354655M	Net Sales ($)	4464M	24683M	32129M	26587M	49560M	217232M
		260234M	Total Assets ($)	5661M	14659M	39088M	40118M	70356M	90352M

M = $ thousand   MM = $ million
See Pages 1 through 15 for Explanation of Ratios and Data

Current Data Sorted By Assets   **Comparative Historical Data**

0-500M	500M-2MM	2-10MM	10-50MM	50-100MM	100-250MM		4/1/90-3/31/91 ALL	4/1/91-3/31/92 ALL
1	2	2				# Postretirement Benefits		
						Type of Statement		
1	14	48	17	3	3	Unqualified		
2	3	1	1			Reviewed		
1	5	6	5			Compiled		
		1	1			Tax Returns		
2	5	13	11		2	Other		
	139 (4/1-9/30/94)		6 (10/1/94-3/31/95)					
6	28	68	35	3	5	**NUMBER OF STATEMENTS**		
%	%	%	%	%	%	**ASSETS**	%	%
	15.6	18.2	18.8			Cash & Equivalents	D	D
	20.1	5.2	5.7			Trade Receivables - (net)	A	A
	.2	.6	.6			Inventory	T	T
	3.5	2.7	6.9			All Other Current	A	A
	39.5	26.7	31.9			Total Current		
	49.5	61.1	41.4			Fixed Assets (net)	N	N
	.1	.7	1.1			Intangibles (net)	O	O
	10.9	11.5	25.6			All Other Non-Current	T	T
	100.0	100.0	100.0			Total		
						LIABILITIES	A	A
	7.3	4.4	2.4			Notes Payable-Short Term	V	V
	3.8	2.5	.5			Cur. Mat. -L/T/D	A	A
	7.0	3.2	3.8			Trade Payables	I	I
	.1	.0	.1			Income Taxes Payable	L	L
	21.5	15.2	9.3			All Other Current	A	A
	39.7	25.4	16.0			Total Current	B	B
	20.5	17.8	13.9			Long Term Debt	L	L
	.1	.1	.0			Deferred Taxes	E	E
	5.6	4.7	8.3			All Other-Non-Current		
	34.0	52.0	61.7			Net Worth		
	100.0	100.0	100.0			Total Liabilities & Net Worth		
						INCOME DATA		
	100.0	100.0	100.0			Net Sales		
						Gross Profit		
	98.1	95.9	97.7			Operating Expenses		
	1.9	4.1	2.3			Operating Profit		
	−.4	−.3	2.1			All Other Expenses (net)		
	2.2	4.4	.3			Profit Before Taxes		
						RATIOS		
	1.3	1.7	4.1					
	.9	1.0	1.7			Current		
	.6	.6	.7					
	1.3	1.6	3.2					
	.8	.9	1.0			Quick		
	.6	.4	.5					
	5 80.3	3 145.1	4 91.0					
	13 27.9	7 54.8	11 32.3			Sales/Receivables		
	37 9.8	21 17.6	20 18.2					
						Cost of Sales/Inventory		
						Cost of Sales/Payables		
	13.8	10.2	2.1					
	−63.3	255.6	12.3			Sales/Working Capital		
	−11.6	−9.5	−15.8					
	4.9	6.4	5.4					
	(18) 3.1	(44) 3.0	(18) 1.6			EBIT/Interest		
	1.8	1.3	−1.1					
						Net Profit + Depr., Dep., Amort./Cur. Mat. L /T/D		
	.9	.8	.0					
	1.3	1.2	.7			Fixed/Worth		
	4.2	1.7	1.0					
	1.0	.4	.2					
	1.6	.9	.5			Debt/Worth		
	6.6	1.9	1.5					
	33.3	12.9	8.4					
	(26) 15.7	(66) 6.3	(34) .6			% Profit Before Taxes/Tangible Net Worth		
	.2	.4	−4.3					
	11.2	6.7	4.5					
	4.6	3.9	.6			% Profit Before Taxes/Total Assets		
	.3	.4	−2.5					
	11.5	2.1	999.8					
	5.2	1.4	1.0			Sales/Net Fixed Assets		
	1.8	1.0	.6					
	3.0	1.2	1.1					
	2.2	.9	.6			Sales/Total Assets		
	1.3	.7	.4					
	1.1	3.0	1.9					
	(23) 2.2	(49) 4.7	(13) 4.9			% Depr., Dep., Amort./Sales		
	4.6	6.2	8.2					
						% Officers', Directors', Owners' Comp/Sales		
7383M	70516M	346362M	615600M	169434M	880998M	Net Sales ($)		
1788M	31634M	329839M	731184M	173465M	775932M	Total Assets ($)		

M = $ thousand   MM = $ million
See Pages 1 through 15 for Explanation of Ratios and Data

Comparative Historical Data				Current Data Sorted By Sales					
4/1/92-3/31/93 ALL	4/1/93-3/31/94 ALL	4/1/94-3/31/95 ALL							
		5	# Postretirement Benefits	1	2	1	1		
			Type of Statement						
		86	Unqualified	3	15	31	20	8	9
		7	Reviewed	3	2		2		
		17	Compiled	1	7	4	1	1	3
		2	Tax Returns	1		1			
		33	Other	1	9	5	6	9	3
				139 (4/1-9/30/94)			6 (10/1/94-3/31/95)		
				0-1MM	1-3MM	3-5MM	5-10MM	10-25MM	25MM & OVER
ALL	ALL	145	**NUMBER OF STATEMENTS**	9	33	41	29	18	15
%	%	%	**ASSETS**	%	%	%	%	%	%
D A T A N O T A V A I L A B L E	D A T A N O T A V A I L A B L E	18.5	Cash & Equivalents		17.0	14.4	15.7	21.9	28.6
		8.5	Trade Receivables - (net)		5.5	10.1	9.1	6.8	9.7
		.7	Inventory		.3	.6	.3	.7	1.4
		3.9	All Other Current		3.1	2.3	1.8	10.2	6.9
		31.6	Total Current		25.9	27.4	26.8	39.7	46.6
		51.8	Fixed Assets (net)		67.3	60.1	55.1	27.3	23.7
		.6	Intangibles (net)		.2	.4	.1	1.5	2.7
		16.0	All Other Non-Current		6.5	12.2	17.9	31.5	27.0
		100.0	Total		100.0	100.0	100.0	100.0	100.0
			LIABILITIES						
		4.1	Notes Payable-Short Term		3.8	5.4	6.2	3.1	.4
		2.1	Cur. Mat.-L /T/D		1.7	2.0	.5	3.6	1.1
		4.2	Trade Payables		3.5	4.3	3.3	3.2	8.0
		.0	Income Taxes Payable		.0	.1	.0	.0	.2
		14.7	All Other Current		14.0	16.9	10.6	17.5	12.5
		25.1	Total Current		23.0	28.7	20.6	27.4	22.1
		16.9	Long Term Debt		20.2	14.7	13.0	18.9	17.9
		.1	Deferred Taxes		.1	.1	.0	.2	.0
		5.9	All Other-Non-Current		4.9	4.5	7.2	3.7	11.7
		52.0	Net Worth		51.8	52.0	59.2	49.8	48.3
		100.0	Total Liabilities & Net Worth		100.0	100.0	100.0	100.0	100.0
			INCOME DATA						
		100.0	Net Sales		100.0	100.0	100.0	100.0	100.0
			Gross Profit						
		97.2	Operating Expenses		93.8	98.3	98.7	99.4	93.2
		2.8	Operating Profit		6.2	1.7	1.3	.6	6.8
		.3	All Other Expenses (net)		-.4	-.4	.4	2.4	1.4
		2.5	Profit Before Taxes		6.6	2.1	.9	-1.8	5.4
			RATIOS						
		2.5			1.4	1.8	3.7	3.3	3.2
		1.1	Current		1.1	.9	1.0	1.3	2.6
		.6			.5	.5	.6	.8	.8
		1.9			1.3	1.8	2.9	1.6	2.9
		1.0	Quick		.9	.8	1.0	1.0	1.8
		.5			.5	.4	.5	.4	.8
	3	107.4			3 114.9	3 114.4	2 203.3	3 127.9	8 43.3
	8	43.3	Sales/Receivables		8 45.8	7 52.4	8 43.4	10 35.2	15 24.1
	24	15.4			21 17.7	28 13.0	41 9.0	19 19.3	26 14.1
			Cost of Sales/Inventory						
			Cost of Sales/Payables						
		6.1			9.8	12.6	3.6	6.1	4.6
		53.3	Sales/Working Capital		43.2	-49.5	-365.7	28.2	6.0
		-11.3			-7.7	-9.6	-11.2	-28.5	-29.1
		6.0			(22) 6.4	(30) 4.2	(16) 3.3		
	(86)	2.6	EBIT/Interest		4.6	2.6	1.8		
		1.2			1.6	1.5	-.4		
			Net Profit + Depr., Dep., Amort./Cur. Mat. L/T/D						
		.6			.9	.8	.6	.0	.0
		1.0	Fixed/Worth		1.3	1.2	1.0	.3	.0
		1.5			2.2	1.7	1.1	1.0	.8
		.4			.3	.5	.2	.2	.4
		.9	Debt/Worth		1.2	.9	.6	1.2	1.4
		2.2			1.8	1.6	1.4	2.9	2.9
		16.1			28.7	10.5	9.9	11.3	18.0
	(140)	5.7	% Profit Before Taxes/Tangible Net Worth		13.3	(39) 7.4	(28) 1.6	(17) -1.5	(14) 9.2
		-1.4			.6	2.4	-2.5	-20.6	-.3
		7.7			11.4	5.5	5.3	6.4	8.1
		2.8	% Profit Before Taxes/Total Assets		6.0	3.9	1.0	-.4	2.5
		-.6			.2	1.2	-1.6	-5.6	-.1
		7.9			2.3	4.2	1.7	UND	UND
		1.6	Sales/Net Fixed Assets		1.2	1.5	1.0	3.6	UND
		.9			1.0	1.0	.6	.9	1.5
		1.8			1.7	1.7	1.0	2.4	2.1
		1.0	Sales/Total Assets		1.0	1.0	.6	.9	1.3
		.6			.7	.7	.4	.5	.7
		2.0			2.1	2.4	1.5		
	(92)	4.1	% Depr., Dep., Amort./Sales		(25) 4.6	(33) 4.7	(16) 4.0		
		5.9			5.3	6.4	5.8		
		4.4							
	(14)	6.5	% Officers', Directors', Owners' Comp/Sales						
		9.4							
		2090293M	Net Sales ($)	6328M	70118M	166174M	197438M	276881M	1373354M
		2043842M	Total Assets ($)	6052M	86671M	184294M	347513M	548084M	871228M

© Robert Morris Associates 1995

M = $ thousand   MM = $ million
See Pages 1 through 15 for Explanation of Ratios and Data

Current Data Sorted By Assets   Comparative Historical Data

	0-500M	500M-2MM	2-10MM	10-50MM	50-100MM	100-250MM		4/1/90-3/31/91 ALL	4/1/91-3/31/92 ALL
# Postretirement Benefits	1	3	1	6	1				
Type of Statement									
Unqualified	1	6	7	6				6	9
Reviewed	6	21	8	1				12	17
Compiled	9	8	2					19	27
Tax Returns	7	3						1	1
Other	12	8	8	3	2			13	20
	44 (4/1-9/30/94)			74 (10/1/94-3/31/95)					
NUMBER OF STATEMENTS	35	46	25	10	2			51	74
	%	%	%	%	%	%	**ASSETS**	%	%
Cash & Equivalents	12.3	5.5	7.9	3.8				6.8	8.0
Trade Receivables - (net)	29.9	40.8	35.9	15.3				32.4	30.4
Inventory	12.9	12.2	12.0	11.2				12.0	10.5
All Other Current	3.1	2.6	8.2	1.0				3.9	1.9
Total Current	58.2	61.1	64.1	31.3				55.1	50.8
Fixed Assets (net)	27.3	21.1	15.1	28.0				26.7	27.0
Intangibles (net)	7.8	5.1	12.7	32.8				5.9	11.5
All Other Non-Current	6.6	12.7	8.1	7.8				12.3	10.7
Total	100.0	100.0	100.0	100.0				100.0	100.0
							LIABILITIES		
Notes Payable-Short Term	6.4	11.8	6.7	.7				11.6	13.6
Cur. Mat. -L/T/D	7.0	5.5	3.5	5.6				6.6	6.8
Trade Payables	20.1	12.8	20.4	7.6				12.8	11.9
Income Taxes Payable	.3	.5	.9	.6				1.1	.2
All Other Current	14.6	17.9	12.2	10.9				15.4	12.7
Total Current	48.4	48.5	43.7	25.4				47.6	45.1
Long Term Debt	17.4	13.6	16.5	24.9				21.8	19.5
Deferred Taxes	.0	.6	2.7	1.2				1.2	.4
All Other-Non-Current	6.5	5.3	8.6	7.1				5.8	5.3
Net Worth	27.7	32.1	28.5	41.3				23.6	29.6
Total Liabilities & Net Worth	100.0	100.0	100.0	100.0				100.0	100.0
							INCOME DATA		
Net Sales	100.0	100.0	100.0	100.0				100.0	100.0
Gross Profit									
Operating Expenses	96.8	95.6	94.6	94.3				94.8	96.8
Operating Profit	3.2	4.4	5.4	5.7				5.2	3.2
All Other Expenses (net)	.5	1.3	1.7	5.4				2.3	2.3
Profit Before Taxes	2.6	3.1	3.7	.3				2.9	.8
							RATIOS		
Current	2.8 / 1.3 / .9	1.7 / 1.3 / .8	2.0 / 1.3 / 1.0	1.8 / 1.5 / .6				1.6 / 1.2 / .9	2.0 / 1.2 / .8
Quick	2.5 / .8 / .6	1.3 / 1.0 / .6	1.3 / 1.0 / .5	1.1 / .9 / .5			(50)	1.1 / .9 / .6	1.3 / .9 / .6
Sales/Receivables	18 19.8 / 27 13.5 / 49 7.4	36 10.2 / 46 8.0 / 60 6.1	32 11.4 / 58 6.3 / 89 4.1	34 10.8 / 46 8.0 / 59 6.2				27 13.6 / 42 8.7 / 59 6.2	25 14.8 / 36 10.2 / 58 6.3
Cost of Sales/Inventory									
Cost of Sales/Payables									
Sales/Working Capital	9.6 / 46.2 / -46.7	10.5 / 21.0 / -49.3	5.5 / 15.3 / NM	8.5 / 14.8 / -8.2				11.2 / 29.8 / -27.8	10.2 / 31.0 / -24.0
EBIT/Interest	(29) 7.9 / 2.9 / 1.1	7.4 / 3.0 / 1.5	(24) 13.6 / 3.5 / .8	5.4 / 3.2 / -.9			(46)	5.0 / 2.9 / 1.2	(64) 3.8 / 2.2 / .2
Net Profit + Depr., Dep., Amort./Cur. Mat. L /T/D	(10) 3.6 / 1.8 / 1.3	(24) 5.1 / 1.9 / .8	(10) 9.8 / 5.3 / 1.2				(21)	5.7 / 2.7 / .8	(28) 4.8 / 2.8 / .5
Fixed/Worth	.5 / 1.7 / 40.5	.3 / .6 / 1.6	.1 / .4 / 166.1	.9 / 3.8 / -3.7				.5 / 1.1 / -118.3	.4 / 1.0 / 7.9
Debt/Worth	1.6 / 4.6 / -65.3	1.0 / 2.4 / 6.9	1.1 / 2.1 / 356.4	1.4 / 4.6 / -12.5				1.5 / 2.8 / -406.9	1.0 / 3.7 / 14.9
% Profit Before Taxes/Tangible Net Worth	(26) 116.9 / 43.2 / 5.5	(39) 36.9 / 20.8 / 7.0	(20) 62.0 / 30.1 / 14.9				(38)	66.5 / 27.9 / 14.1	(60) 34.6 / 13.9 / -1.1
% Profit Before Taxes/Total Assets	16.5 / 8.6 / .7	13.4 / 5.5 / 1.7	18.6 / 5.3 / -1.3	9.9 / 6.5 / -3.4				16.0 / 6.8 / 1.4	9.2 / 4.1 / -2.1
Sales/Net Fixed Assets	31.8 / 13.4 / 8.0	38.7 / 22.2 / 9.6	61.2 / 23.7 / 7.3	8.1 / 4.4 / 3.1				21.7 / 14.8 / 7.6	28.1 / 13.9 / 6.6
Sales/Total Assets	4.6 / 3.5 / 2.5	4.5 / 2.5 / 1.9	2.9 / 1.8 / 1.3	1.6 / 1.1 / .8				3.4 / 2.7 / 1.9	4.2 / 3.0 / 1.9
% Depr., Dep., Amort./Sales	(26) 1.4 / 2.5 / 2.9	(41) .9 / 2.0 / 4.1	(21) .5 / .8 / 8.3				(42)	1.6 / 2.9 / 4.9	(64) 1.2 / 2.8 / 5.4
% Officers', Directors', Owners' Comp/Sales	(15) 3.3 / 6.4 / 13.5	(22) 2.5 / 4.3 / 6.0					(24)	5.1 / 7.5 / 11.6	(35) 3.3 / 6.1 / 9.9
Net Sales ($)	30384M	153676M	202119M	235278M	198542M			934445M	634909M
Total Assets ($)	8636M	50832M	97895M	206311M	165940M			524730M	451551M

M = $ thousand   MM = $ million
See Pages 1 through 15 for Explanation of Ratios and Data

Comparative Historical Data				Current Data Sorted By Sales					
2	7	5	# Postretirement Benefits	1		1	1	3	
			Type of Statement						
14	16	20	Unqualified	1	4	3	3	8	1
26	31	36	Reviewed	4	12	10	6	3	1
29	28	19	Compiled	7	6	4	2		
1	6	10	Tax Returns	3	6	1			
17	19	33	Other	9	8	5	3	5	3
4/1/92-3/31/93	4/1/93-3/31/94	4/1/94-3/31/95		44 (4/1-9/30/94)			74 (10/1/94-3/31/95)		
ALL	ALL	ALL		0-1MM	1-3MM	3-5MM	5-10MM	10-25MM	25MM & OVER
87	100	118	NUMBER OF STATEMENTS	24	36	23	14	16	5
%	%	%	ASSETS	%	%	%	%	%	%
9.3	8.2	7.8	Cash & Equivalents	12.9	8.2	6.7	4.4	6.1	
35.2	38.3	33.9	Trade Receivables - (net)	26.5	30.4	38.2	49.7	37.9	
12.6	11.8	12.4	Inventory	15.2	14.2	8.3	10.9	9.2	
3.5	2.8	3.8	All Other Current	2.5	4.2	3.8	1.3	7.8	
60.6	61.1	58.0	Total Current	57.1	56.9	57.1	66.3	61.0	
22.7	20.8	22.6	Fixed Assets (net)	25.1	23.1	24.9	13.8	16.6	
6.8	7.7	10.1	Intangibles (net)	10.2	6.9	8.5	12.1	17.3	
9.9	10.4	9.3	All Other Non-Current	7.6	13.1	9.6	7.8	5.1	
100.0	100.0	100.0	Total	100.0	100.0	100.0	100.0	100.0	
			LIABILITIES						
9.2	8.9	8.0	Notes Payable-Short Term	8.9	7.9	6.9	12.1	6.8	
5.3	5.4	5.5	Cur. Mat.-L./T/D	3.8	8.3	5.2	4.8	3.2	
12.6	14.6	16.1	Trade Payables	16.1	18.6	13.1	17.6	15.9	
.8	1.5	.5	Income Taxes Payable	.1	.6	.4	.7	1.1	
12.9	12.2	14.9	All Other Current	13.5	13.2	19.3	17.5	14.1	
40.8	42.5	45.0	Total Current	42.5	48.6	44.9	52.7	41.1	
15.5	14.1	16.4	Long Term Debt	19.6	16.4	14.0	17.1	11.7	
.8	.9	1.0	Deferred Taxes	.0	.6	2.8	.0	1.3	
5.5	5.0	6.5	All Other-Non-Current	6.1	5.5	6.1	6.4	10.0	
37.4	37.5	31.0	Net Worth	31.8	28.9	32.2	23.7	35.9	
100.0	100.0	100.0	Total Liabilities & Net Worth	100.0	100.0	100.0	100.0	100.0	
			INCOME DATA						
100.0	100.0	100.0	Net Sales	100.0	100.0	100.0	100.0	100.0	
			Gross Profit						
96.8	96.2	95.7	Operating Expenses	95.6	94.9	95.5	98.5	95.8	
3.2	3.8	4.3	Operating Profit	4.4	5.1	4.5	1.5	4.2	
1.5	1.1	1.5	All Other Expenses (net)	.6	1.7	2.6	.8	1.1	
1.8	2.7	2.8	Profit Before Taxes	3.7	3.3	1.9	.7	3.1	
			RATIOS						
2.2	2.5	1.9		4.4	1.6	2.0	1.5	2.0	
1.4	1.4	1.3	Current	1.3	1.2	1.3	1.2	1.5	
1.1	1.0	.9		.9	.8	.7	.9	1.1	
1.6	1.7	1.3		3.7	1.1	1.3	1.4	1.4	
1.0	1.1	.9	Quick	.9	.7	1.0	1.1	1.0	
.7	.7	.6		.7	.5	.5	.5	.7	
27 13.3	31 11.8	27 13.6		18 20.1	28 13.0	31 11.9	30 12.0	41 8.8	
37 10.0	41 9.0	45 8.2	Sales/Receivables	23 16.1	42 8.6	49 7.5	46 7.9	56 6.5	
53 6.9	65 5.6	60 6.1		56 6.5	51 7.2	68 5.4	62 5.9	81 4.5	
			Cost of Sales/Inventory						
			Cost of Sales/Payables						
8.2	8.6	8.8		7.1	9.5	7.5	14.5	6.2	
16.8	15.5	19.9	Sales/Working Capital	26.1	34.6	21.1	29.7	12.7	
171.4	349.8	-62.4		-65.1	-20.7	-22.8	-72.5	60.9	
7.8	(91) 9.5	(111) 7.4		(20) 8.7	(34) 5.1	7.4	9.2	(15) 12.4	
(80) 3.0	4.2	2.9	EBIT/Interest	3.2	2.6	3.2	2.0	3.4	
.5	1.7	1.3		1.3	1.3	1.2	.8	1.3	
4.9	(44) 9.1	(51) 5.2			(16) 2.4	(10) 8.1			
(35) 1.8	3.2	2.2	Net Profit + Depr., Dep.,		.9	2.4			
.8	1.5	1.0	Amort./Cur. Mat. L/T/D		.6	1.2			
.3	.3	.3		.2	.4	.2	.3	.3	
.5	.7	.8	Fixed/Worth	.9	1.0	.6	.5	.6	
1.9	2.0	6.6		NM	5.4	6.9	-20.8	18.2	
.9	.8	1.2		1.3	.9	.8	1.7	1.3	
2.0	1.7	2.7	Debt/Worth	3.2	4.5	1.9	3.0	2.4	
5.7	7.6	20.6		-26.9	15.3	18.6	-44.1	30.2	
(78) 43.5	(84) 53.6	(94) 53.7		(17) 82.9	(30) 52.1	(19) 33.9	(10) 44.2	(13) 64.9	
23.4	27.4	24.8	% Profit Before Taxes/Tangible	47.1	25.3	18.2	25.3	43.8	
1.5	7.1	6.7	Net Worth	8.6	4.1	9.6	1.4	19.9	
13.6	16.8	14.2		15.9	14.0	11.4	11.3	21.5	
6.1	9.2	6.1	% Profit Before Taxes/Total	7.9	6.4	5.1	3.8	7.1	
-.7	2.0	1.0	Assets	1.0	1.8	.6	-.5	1.3	
29.9	36.5	37.4		31.4	33.2	38.0	55.4	58.4	
17.8	17.5	14.5	Sales/Net Fixed Assets	13.7	12.7	17.6	33.3	14.5	
9.5	9.7	7.4		7.2	9.9	5.5	17.5	5.4	
4.4	3.9	3.8		3.9	3.2	4.5	4.8	3.6	
3.0	3.0	2.5	Sales/Total Assets	3.0	2.5	2.5	4.1	2.1	
2.1	2.2	1.7		1.9	1.8	1.7	2.1	1.1	
(76) 1.1	(87) .9	(96) .9		(17) 1.4	(30) 1.6	(21) .6	(12) .6	(12) .5	
1.9	1.8	2.2	% Depr., Dep., Amort./Sales	2.2	2.7	2.2	.9	1.1	
3.2	3.7	4.9		2.7	4.4	6.4	1.8	10.5	
(37) 3.2	(48) 3.6	(44) 3.0			(19) 3.9				
7.8	6.9	4.6	% Officers', Directors',		5.8				
10.6	10.9	6.5	Owners' Comp/Sales		9.5				
633694M	789906M	819999M	Net Sales ($)	14045M	59597M	88478M	97981M	236376M	323522M
290013M	313450M	529614M	Total Assets ($)	7078M	28384M	58189M	36537M	159805M	239621M

M = $ thousand   MM = $ million
See Pages 1 through 15 for Explanation of Ratios and Data

Current Data Sorted By Assets   **Comparative Historical Data**

0-500M	500M-2MM	2-10MM	10-50MM	50-100MM	100-250MM		4/1/90-3/31/91 ALL	4/1/91-3/31/92 ALL
						# Postretirement Benefits		
1	1	1	1			**Type of Statement**		
	1	1	3		2	Unqualified	14	22
3	5	2				Reviewed	10	7
6	10	4				Compiled	16	16
3						Tax Returns	1	2
6	4	3	2			Other	8	11
18 (4/1-9/30/94)			37 (10/1/94-3/31/95)					
18	20	10	5		2	**NUMBER OF STATEMENTS**	49	58
%	%	%	%	%	%		%	%
12.3	13.4	6.1				**ASSETS** Cash & Equivalents	11.5	10.0
2.7	1.3	4.0				Trade Receivables - (net)	7.4	10.2
24.5	3.1	7.2				Inventory	6.0	4.4
.7	.7	2.8				All Other Current	4.1	2.2
40.2	18.5	20.2				Total Current	28.9	26.9
51.9	73.8	69.4				Fixed Assets (net)	60.1	57.8
1.5	3.2	.9				Intangibles (net)	2.8	2.4
6.3	4.4	9.6				All Other Non-Current	8.2	12.9
100.0	100.0	100.0				Total	100.0	100.0
4.3	5.0	11.7				**LIABILITIES** Notes Payable-Short Term	3.2	6.0
3.3	5.7	2.8				Cur. Mat. -L/T/D	5.5	5.6
6.7	2.7	13.6				Trade Payables	5.9	6.6
.0	.4	.1				Income Taxes Payable	1.1	.5
7.2	4.7	11.4				All Other Current	14.1	14.5
21.5	18.6	39.6				Total Current	29.7	33.2
25.9	38.3	18.4				Long Term Debt	29.7	28.6
.2	.5	.2				Deferred Taxes	.2	.8
8.8	2.6	7.8				All Other-Non-Current	5.8	3.6
43.7	40.1	34.1				Net Worth	34.6	33.7
100.0	100.0	100.0				Total Liabilities & Net Worth	100.0	100.0
100.0	100.0	100.0				**INCOME DATA** Net Sales	100.0	100.0
						Gross Profit		
90.8	84.8	99.5				Operating Expenses	91.7	91.0
9.2	15.2	.5				Operating Profit	8.3	9.0
2.5	5.8	2.3				All Other Expenses (net)	3.5	3.7
6.7	9.4	-1.9				Profit Before Taxes	4.9	5.3
						RATIOS		
3.1	2.0	1.2					1.6	1.5
1.9	1.0	.7				Current	1.0	.8
1.1	.2	.2					.4	.5
1.5	1.9	.5					1.3	1.1
.8	.5	.3				Quick	.6	.6
.1	.1	.1					.1	.2
0 UND	0 UND	0 UND					0 UND	0 UND
0 UND	0 UND	1 445.1				Sales/Receivables	3 144.0	3 106.7
0 UND	3 120.7	3 107.1					18 20.6	14 25.2
						Cost of Sales/Inventory		
						Cost of Sales/Payables		
6.4	11.6	41.8					18.9	36.4
11.5	NM	-13.6				Sales/Working Capital	-735.0	-32.2
UND	-7.1	-4.5					-9.4	-5.2
(13) 21.3	(17) 4.8						7.4	9.2
2.2	3.2					EBIT/Interest	(41) 2.1	(47) 3.3
.5	1.1						1.1	-.2
							8.7	3.8
						Net Profit + Depr., Dep., Amort./Cur. Mat. L /T/D	(18) 2.3	(20) 1.6
							1.0	.0
.5	1.2	1.2					1.1	.9
1.3	1.6	1.9				Fixed/Worth	1.8	1.6
4.2	10.5	NM					11.7	6.4
.3	.7	.9					.6	.7
1.8	1.6	1.7				Debt/Worth	2.8	2.0
9.7	10.4	NM					19.2	10.6
(16) 65.7	55.3					% Profit Before Taxes/Tangible	52.2	70.8
23.4	17.6					Net Worth	(42) 16.3	(51) 24.6
-1.6	6.0						1.5	-.7
29.3	11.8	8.0				% Profit Before Taxes/Total	13.9	17.2
9.1	6.8	-.0				Assets	4.3	7.3
-1.8	.7	-8.0					.0	-1.7
17.1	2.1	4.7					8.4	14.0
6.0	.9	1.9				Sales/Net Fixed Assets	2.0	2.3
1.0	.6	.9					1.0	.8
4.0	1.5	2.1					2.9	2.4
2.0	.8	1.4				Sales/Total Assets	1.3	1.2
.9	.5	.8					.7	.7
(15) 1.6	(19) 8.2					% Depr., Dep., Amort./Sales	3.3	1.7
5.3	10.0						(45) 4.7	(56) 6.2
8.2	12.2						10.8	11.4
	(10) 1.8					% Officers', Directors',	3.6	4.4
	3.4					Owners' Comp/Sales	(15) 7.0	(22) 7.4
	9.2						10.5	12.1
8317M	22940M	56236M	71102M		248438M	Net Sales ($)	275252M	669200M
4465M	22652M	36365M	92054M		406991M	Total Assets ($)	382014M	654488M

© Robert Morris Associates 1995

M = $ thousand   MM = $ million
See Pages 1 through 15 for Explanation of Ratios and Data

Comparative Historical Data					Current Data Sorted By Sales					
	2		**4**	# Postretirement Benefits	**2**				**1**	**1**
				Type of Statement						
18	8		7	Unqualified			1	1	3	2
10	8		10	Reviewed	6	2	1	1		
24	11		20	Compiled	12	5	2	1		
1	1		3	Tax Returns	3					
12	9		15	Other	8	3	3			1
4/1/92-3/31/93	4/1/93-3/31/94		4/1/94-3/31/95		**18 (4/1-9/30/94)**			**37 (10/1/94-3/31/95)**		
ALL	ALL		ALL		0-1MM	1-3MM	3-5MM	5-10MM	10-25MM	25MM & OVER
65	37		55	**NUMBER OF STATEMENTS**	29	10	7	3	3	3
%	%		%	**ASSETS**	%	%	%	%	%	%
10.8	16.8		10.7	Cash & Equivalents	12.0	11.0				
5.7	7.2		2.3	Trade Receivables - (net)	2.1	.1				
4.7	3.9		10.7	Inventory	14.7	5.1				
1.5	.3		1.3	All Other Current	.4	1.6				
22.6	28.2		25.0	Total Current	29.1	17.8				
60.0	61.4		65.9	Fixed Assets (net)	64.8	74.7				
5.4	1.4		2.0	Intangibles (net)	1.1	.9				
12.0	9.0		7.1	All Other Non-Current	5.0	6.6				
100.0	100.0		100.0	Total	100.0	100.0				
				LIABILITIES						
7.6	3.6		5.4	Notes Payable-Short Term	4.1	1.6				
5.1	4.5		4.0	Cur. Mat.-L /T/D	4.5	5.0				
6.9	3.8		6.1	Trade Payables	5.0	1.8				
.1	1.9		.2	Income Taxes Payable	.0	.7				
10.1	11.6		6.7	All Other Current	4.5	14.0				
29.9	25.5		22.4	Total Current	18.1	23.1				
26.1	31.0		29.2	Long Term Debt	34.1	31.5				
.5	.3		.4	Deferred Taxes	.1	.9				
6.1	4.0		6.0	All Other-Non-Current	7.2	.1				
37.5	39.1		41.9	Net Worth	40.4	44.5				
100.0	100.0		100.0	Total Liabilities & Net Worth	100.0	100.0				
				INCOME DATA						
100.0	100.0		100.0	Net Sales	100.0	100.0				
				Gross Profit						
91.1	87.9		90.8	Operating Expenses	87.0	94.1				
8.9	12.1		9.2	Operating Profit	13.0	5.9				
4.7	5.7		3.7	All Other Expenses (net)	4.7	4.0				
4.1	6.3		5.5	Profit Before Taxes	8.3	1.9				
				RATIOS						
1.5	1.5		2.0		2.6	2.2				
.6	1.1		1.2	Current	1.7	.5				
.2	.3		.5		.6	.2				
1.0	1.4		1.3		1.6	1.0				
.4	.4		.5	Quick	.8	.4				
.1	.2		.1		.1	.1				
0 UND	0 UND		0 UND		0 UND	0 UND				
2 182.4	0 UND		0 UND	Sales/Receivables	0 UND	0 UND				
10 34.8	10 35.7		2 151.3		0 UND	1 645.4				
				Cost of Sales/Inventory						
				Cost of Sales/Payables						
21.5	11.2		11.5		7.4	21.6				
-21.8	420.0		44.4	Sales/Working Capital	13.1	-13.6				
-5.5	-10.2		-9.3		-8.3	-5.7				
7.4	4.9		5.1		6.8					
(55) 3.0	(30) 2.3	(46)	2.4	EBIT/Interest	(22) 2.4					
1.2	.6		.7		1.1					
5.2			2.7	Net Profit + Depr., Dep.,						
(18) 1.8		(14)	2.0	Amort./Cur. Mat. L/T/D						
.9			1.6							
1.0	.7		1.0		.7	1.0				
1.8	1.5		1.6	Fixed/Worth	1.7	1.5				
5.7	2.8		3.8		7.7	10.4				
.6	.9		.6		.6	.4				
1.7	1.4		1.5	Debt/Worth	1.7	.9				
14.5	3.3		6.1		12.0	11.2				
57.0	46.2		38.8	% Profit Before Taxes/Tangible	65.2					
(58) 22.8	(34) 20.8	(51)	18.3	Net Worth	(27) 19.2					
4.5	2.5		.0		.4					
13.5	17.3		13.9	% Profit Before Taxes/Total	15.8	12.3				
5.7	6.8		6.1	Assets	6.5	5.3				
.9	.0		-.8		.1	-1.2				
6.4	5.5		5.1		7.0	2.8				
1.9	2.0		1.6	Sales/Net Fixed Assets	.9	1.5				
.8	.9		.7		.6	.8				
2.2	2.5		2.1		2.5	1.7				
1.1	1.1		.9	Sales/Total Assets	.8	1.2				
.7	.7		.6		.6	.8				
4.2	4.2		5.1		2.9					
(59) 7.9	(34) 6.3	(49)	8.2	% Depr., Dep., Amort./Sales	(26) 8.2					
10.9	12.6		10.9		10.8					
3.4	2.5		2.8	% Officers', Directors',						
(18) 5.6	(10) 3.7	(18)	5.0	Owners' Comp/Sales						
9.3	10.5		11.7							
969523M	210046M		407033M	Net Sales ($)	14070M	16629M	26254M	26442M	48300M	275338M
689666M	276910M		562527M	Total Assets ($)	17222M	26858M	20781M	21590M	46008M	430068M

M = $ thousand   MM = $ million
See Pages 1 through 15 for Explanation of Ratios and Data

Current Data Sorted By Assets						# Postretirement Benefits / Type of Statement	Comparative Historical Data	
4	6	11	5		1			
25	77	98	16	2	1	Unqualified	23	86
5	3	4	1			Reviewed	1	3
7	4	2				Compiled	7	13
3	2	1				Tax Returns		1
18	23	44	5		1	Other	7	27
	261 (4/1-9/30/94)			81 (10/1/94-3/31/95)			4/1/90-3/31/91 ALL	4/1/91-3/31/92 ALL
0-500M	500M-2MM	2-10MM	10-50MM	50-100MM	100-250MM			
58	109	149	22	3	1	NUMBER OF STATEMENTS	38	130
%	%	%	%	%	%	**ASSETS**	%	%
22.3	14.4	16.1	13.3			Cash & Equivalents	15.5	15.6
22.0	29.3	23.0	13.6			Trade Receivables - (net)	22.4	23.8
.3	1.5	.9	.9			Inventory	2.9	1.1
5.1	2.7	4.6	2.2			All Other Current	4.8	4.6
49.8	47.9	44.5	30.0			Total Current	45.6	45.0
44.2	44.4	46.0	54.6			Fixed Assets (net)	41.3	42.3
1.2	.6	.6	.4			Intangibles (net)	.7	1.1
4.7	7.1	9.0	15.0			All Other Non-Current	12.3	11.6
100.0	100.0	100.0	100.0			Total	100.0	100.0
						LIABILITIES		
6.5	6.4	4.5	3.4			Notes Payable-Short Term	4.4	7.2
3.8	1.8	1.3	3.0			Cur. Mat. -L/T/D	1.4	1.8
11.6	8.4	8.1	5.8			Trade Payables	6.6	8.5
.1	.2	.0	.0			Income Taxes Payable	.7	.4
15.6	14.8	13.5	8.6			All Other Current	13.8	14.4
37.5	31.5	27.4	20.8			Total Current	26.8	32.3
13.7	16.4	18.7	36.1			Long Term Debt	17.7	15.4
.6	.1	.0	.0			Deferred Taxes	.1	.2
5.5	4.0	3.3	7.8			All Other-Non-Current	6.6	3.2
42.7	47.9	50.6	35.3			Net Worth	48.8	48.9
100.0	100.0	100.0	100.0			Total Liabilities & Net Worth	100.0	100.0
						INCOME DATA		
100.0	100.0	100.0	100.0			Net Sales	100.0	100.0
						Gross Profit		
95.8	95.3	94.7	90.9			Operating Expenses	92.8	96.6
4.2	4.7	5.3	9.1			Operating Profit	7.2	3.4
1.0	1.1	.7	2.1			All Other Expenses (net)	4.0	.8
3.2	3.6	4.6	6.9			Profit Before Taxes	3.2	2.7
						RATIOS		
6.8	2.9	2.8	2.8			Current	3.7	2.4
1.4	1.6	1.8	1.6				1.9	1.5
.7	1.0	1.1	.8				.9	.9
6.8	2.6	2.4	2.2			Quick	3.1	2.2
1.4	1.5	1.5	1.5				1.7	1.3
.5	.9	.9	.9				.8	.8
0 UND	23 15.7	13 27.8	10 34.9			Sales/Receivables	16 22.9	17 20.9
18 19.9	41 8.9	41 8.9	39 9.4				30 12.0	31 11.7
35 10.3	56 6.5	65 5.6	69 5.3				42 8.6	51 7.1
						Cost of Sales/Inventory		
						Cost of Sales/Payables		
8.9	7.2	4.9	4.1			Sales/Working Capital	6.5	7.7
30.1	16.2	11.2	12.0				13.1	19.6
-36.7	639.9	100.6	-26.1				-756.5	-64.3
(28) 18.8	(69) 8.3	(92) 7.0	(17) 5.9			EBIT/Interest	(24) 8.5	(80) 9.0
1.7	1.8	3.8	2.0				1.8	2.1
-3.7	.1	1.1	1.2				-4.5	.2
		(14) 29.7				Net Profit + Depr., Dep., Amort./Cur. Mat. L /T/D	(10) 12.6	(19) 3.9
		9.8					2.1	1.9
		1.5					-4.6	-.1
.3	.4	.5	1.0			Fixed/Worth	.3	.4
.8	.9	.9	1.6				.8	.8
3.8	1.6	1.6	4.6				2.0	1.5
.4	.5	.4	.9			Debt/Worth	.4	.5
1.4	1.0	1.0	2.2				1.0	1.0
6.8	2.4	2.3	6.2				2.1	2.0
(52) 44.2	(104) 26.5	(145) 18.4	(20) 21.3			% Profit Before Taxes/Tangible Net Worth	(37) 18.1	(123) 25.5
5.7	7.6	8.3	10.9				8.1	6.1
-18.0	-1.4	1.0	4.3				-11.8	-3.2
14.6	11.8	8.5	6.1			% Profit Before Taxes/Total Assets	7.2	11.5
4.0	2.8	3.4	3.4				3.0	2.5
-5.1	-1.6	.3	1.0				-5.3	-1.9
28.2	21.7	8.0	3.4			Sales/Net Fixed Assets	38.4	19.0
9.3	4.6	3.4	2.0				6.9	5.7
2.8	1.8	1.6	1.2				1.6	1.8
4.9	3.1	2.3	1.5			Sales/Total Assets	3.8	3.8
2.9	1.9	1.5	1.1				2.2	2.1
1.5	1.1	.9	.5				1.0	.9
(42) 1.3	(87) 1.3	(125) 1.0	(18) 2.5			% Depr., Dep., Amort./Sales	(30) .8	(97) 1.4
2.3	2.5	2.1	3.3				1.9	2.1
3.9	3.5	4.0	5.0				3.8	4.1
(14) 8.0		(21) 3.2				% Officers', Directors', Owners' Comp/Sales		(17) 8.8
16.5		9.3						15.3
24.5		19.2						22.9
46111M	300038M	1038560M	474067M	219522M	158455M	Net Sales ($)	177003M	746802M
15158M	125195M	629141M	457889M	196266M	136457M	Total Assets ($)	113538M	464270M

M = $ thousand   MM = $ million
See Pages 1 through 15 for Explanation of Ratios and Data

Comparative Historical Data / Current Data Sorted By Sales

	4/1/92-3/31/93 ALL	4/1/93-3/31/94 ALL	4/1/94-3/31/95 ALL		0-1MM	1-3MM	3-5MM	5-10MM	10-25MM	25MM & OVER
# Postretirement Benefits		7	27		6	3	2	9	4	3
Type of Statement										
Unqualified	76	117	219		38	55	38	46	31	11
Reviewed	4	7	13		5	4		1	3	
Compiled	12	15	13		7	4	2			
Tax Returns	1	3	6		3	2		1		
Other	45	60	91		24	22	13	19	8	5
				261 (4/1-9/30/94)			81 (10/1/94-3/31/95)			
NUMBER OF STATEMENTS	138	202	342		77	87	53	67	42	16
ASSETS	%	%	%		%	%	%	%	%	%
Cash & Equivalents	17.0	17.8	16.4		16.5	18.0	16.1	16.2	14.7	12.8
Trade Receivables - (net)	20.3	20.2	24.1		17.3	20.9	26.5	27.9	36.8	16.8
Inventory	.9	1.0	1.0		.4	1.2	1.5	.7	.5	3.9
All Other Current	6.0	5.6	3.9		2.4	3.8	6.2	5.2	2.7	1.1
Total Current	44.1	44.7	45.3		36.6	43.8	50.3	50.0	54.7	34.5
Fixed Assets (net)	45.0	46.1	45.9		55.7	47.8	40.7	40.4	37.4	51.4
Intangibles (net)	.7	.8	.7		.5	.8	.7	1.1	.5	.7
All Other Non-Current	10.2	8.4	8.1		7.3	7.6	8.3	8.5	7.4	13.4
Total	100.0	100.0	100.0		100.0	100.0	100.0	100.0	100.0	100.0
LIABILITIES										
Notes Payable-Short Term	7.3	4.4	5.4		5.1	7.0	6.1	3.2	5.4	4.0
Cur. Mat.-L /T/D	2.8	2.4	2.0		2.6	2.2	1.1	2.3	1.1	1.8
Trade Payables	8.4	7.1	8.6		9.4	5.3	8.8	9.1	12.3	9.1
Income Taxes Payable	.1	.4	.1		.1	.0	.3	.0	.0	.2
All Other Current	15.3	11.9	13.9		7.2	16.0	14.1	16.6	18.9	9.7
Total Current	34.0	26.1	29.9		24.5	30.6	30.5	31.2	37.7	24.7
Long Term Debt	17.8	18.5	18.5		21.9	15.6	12.0	17.2	23.1	32.3
Deferred Taxes	.2	.3	.2		.5	.0	.0	.2	.0	.2
All Other-Non-Current	4.3	5.3	4.2		4.2	5.3	3.3	5.0	1.1	5.5
Net Worth	43.8	49.8	47.3		48.9	48.4	54.2	46.5	38.1	37.2
Total Liabilities & Net Worth	100.0	100.0	100.0		100.0	100.0	100.0	100.0	100.0	100.0
INCOME DATA										
Net Sales	100.0	100.0	100.0		100.0	100.0	100.0	100.0	100.0	100.0
Gross Profit										
Operating Expenses	95.2	95.7	94.8		91.2	93.4	97.8	97.0	96.7	95.6
Operating Profit	4.8	4.3	5.2		8.8	6.6	2.2	3.0	3.3	4.4
All Other Expenses (net)	1.4	1.1	1.0		3.4	.5	.1	–.3	.9	1.0
Profit Before Taxes	3.3	3.2	4.2		5.4	6.1	2.1	3.3	2.5	3.4
RATIOS										
Current	2.6	3.1	2.9		6.1	3.2	2.9	2.5	2.2	2.1
	1.2	1.8	1.6		1.7	1.7	1.6	1.9	1.4	1.5
	.8	1.1	1.0		.8	.9	1.2	1.2	1.0	.8
Quick	2.1	2.7	2.5		5.8	2.8	2.7	2.3	2.0	2.1
	1.0	1.5	1.5		1.5	1.4	1.5	1.6	1.4	1.3
	.6	.9	.9		.7	.8	.9	1.0	.9	.8
Sales/Receivables	6 61.3	11 34.0	13 27.1		3 114.2	10 37.8	15 24.9	21 17.1	33 11.2	17 21.6
	26 14.1	29 12.7	37 10.0		20 18.3	35 10.3	38 9.6	39 9.3	46 8.0	39 9.3
	44 8.3	49 7.5	58 6.3		57 6.4	60 6.1	64 5.7	56 6.5	63 5.8	53 6.9
Cost of Sales/Inventory										
Cost of Sales/Payables										
Sales/Working Capital	8.1	6.0	5.6		5.1	5.1	5.2	5.5	9.9	7.8
	31.2	12.8	14.0		16.2	13.1	15.5	10.9	15.2	14.7
	-33.1	105.2	-365.0		-34.4	-74.3	44.5	66.8	NM	-52.9
EBIT/Interest	5.5	5.8	7.3		8.1	5.3	16.8	9.2	6.7	3.9
	(86) 2.1	(127) 2.7	(209) 2.9		(38) 1.1	(56) 3.0	(30) 3.8	(45) 4.5	(28) 2.6	(12) 1.9
	.8	.4	.9		-1.0	.9	-.0	1.3	1.0	1.3
Net Profit + Depr., Dep., Amort./Cur. Mat. L/T/D	4.1	2.5	11.8							
	(17) .8	(37) 1.0	(29) 2.8							
	.2	.3	1.0							
Fixed/Worth	.4	.5	.5		.6	.5	.4	.4	.4	1.0
	.9	.9	.9		1.1	.9	.8	.8	.9	1.5
	1.7	1.7	1.8		2.4	1.9	1.1	1.3	3.0	2.3
Debt/Worth	.5	.5	.4		.2	.4	.4	.7	.7	.8
	1.3	1.1	1.1		.9	1.0	.7	1.1	2.0	1.9
	3.6	2.5	2.7		3.6	2.6	1.6	1.8	4.2	2.5
% Profit Before Taxes/Tangible Net Worth	24.2	19.5	21.8		13.8	28.5	19.4	21.9	28.7	25.4
	(129) 8.8	(196) 6.9	(325) 7.7		(71) 4.6	(83) 6.5	(52) 6.6	(65) 12.0	(38) 11.3	13.0
	-1.3	-2.3	-.7		-3.8	-1.2	-2.5	1.2	.5	4.6
% Profit Before Taxes/Total Assets	9.4	8.4	9.2		8.8	10.2	10.3	9.2	8.8	6.9
	3.0	3.3	3.4		1.5	3.8	2.5	4.7	3.3	3.8
	-1.0	-1.2	-.4		-2.2	-1.0	-2.1	.4	.1	1.7
Sales/Net Fixed Assets	18.4	16.7	13.1		10.1	14.2	18.5	11.5	36.3	4.5
	5.1	3.9	3.5		1.9	2.8	3.9	4.9	5.6	2.7
	1.9	1.7	1.7		.9	1.5	2.4	2.7	3.3	1.8
Sales/Total Assets	3.2	3.1	2.8		2.6	2.5	3.0	3.1	3.5	2.1
	1.7	2.0	1.6		1.1	1.4	1.8	2.1	2.3	1.4
	.9	1.1	1.0		.3	1.0	1.0	1.3	1.7	1.0
% Depr., Dep., Amort./Sales	1.5	1.4	1.2		2.0	1.5	1.1	.9	.9	1.9
	(108) 2.4	(166) 2.5	(276) 2.5		(57) 3.6	(70) 3.0	(42) 2.4	(56) 1.6	(37) 1.4	(14) 3.3
	4.6	4.1	3.9		6.4	4.6	3.6	2.9	2.5	4.3
% Officers', Directors', Owners' Comp/Sales	7.4	3.6	4.4		8.8			3.0		
	(20) 11.6	(22) 11.4	(45) 9.3		(15) 20.8			(13) 6.8		
	35.8	22.9	21.5		30.0			15.6		
Net Sales ($)	707072M	1449270M	2236753M		40805M	161964M	210803M	490629M	571732M	760820M
Total Assets ($)	616830M	1051013M	1560106M		61614M	140532M	152071M	325640M	292320M	587929M

Current Data Sorted By Assets						# Postretirement Benefits / Type of Statement	Comparative Historical Data	
1	3	2	1		1			
4	28	37	19		8	Unqualified	47	91
6	6	10				Reviewed	35	29
12	11	5			1	Compiled	21	14
						Tax Returns		
10	19	21	9	3	6	Other	43	45
	90 (4/1-9/30/94)		125 (10/1/94-3/31/95)				4/1/90-3/31/91 ALL	4/1/91-3/31/92 ALL
0-500M	500M-2MM	2-10MM	10-50MM	50-100MM	100-250MM			
28	40	64	46	22	15	NUMBER OF STATEMENTS	146	179
%	%	%	%	%	%	ASSETS	%	%
12.8	8.6	17.9	30.8	41.6	30.6	Cash & Equivalents	16.1	18.4
39.4	43.4	42.4	31.8	25.9	28.0	Trade Receivables - (net)	41.5	35.9
8.6	8.0	5.4	4.1	3.6	2.3	Inventory	8.1	7.6
3.4	3.0	3.7	3.9	4.3	3.9	All Other Current	3.6	3.6
64.2	62.9	69.4	70.6	75.3	64.7	Total Current	69.3	65.4
23.3	15.4	14.9	12.7	8.6	12.5	Fixed Assets (net)	17.6	15.6
4.1	10.2	7.0	5.9	3.8	11.3	Intangibles (net)	5.7	9.1
8.4	11.5	8.7	10.8	12.2	11.6	All Other Non-Current	7.4	9.9
100.0	100.0	100.0	100.0	100.0	100.0	Total	100.0	100.0
						LIABILITIES		
13.4	12.6	6.4	3.5	2.6	.0	Notes Payable-Short Term	10.2	6.7
2.7	3.1	3.1	1.8	1.2	1.4	Cur. Mat. -L/T/D	3.5	3.0
13.6	17.5	13.1	8.1	10.7	5.8	Trade Payables	13.7	13.2
.3	1.2	1.6	1.2	.8	1.6	Income Taxes Payable	1.5	1.1
18.6	19.5	22.2	21.8	22.4	25.5	All Other Current	16.4	18.5
48.6	53.8	46.4	36.4	37.7	34.3	Total Current	45.3	42.4
8.5	11.6	5.0	3.4	3.1	4.6	Long Term Debt	9.8	8.4
.5	.6	2.2	1.3	.5	1.3	Deferred Taxes	1.6	1.3
5.0	9.0	6.1	5.1	2.3	9.3	All Other-Non-Current	3.2	5.1
37.4	25.0	40.3	53.9	56.3	50.5	Net Worth	40.1	42.8
100.0	100.0	100.0	100.0	100.0	100.0	Total Liabilities & Net Worth	100.0	100.0
						INCOME DATA		
100.0	100.0	100.0	100.0	100.0	100.0	Net Sales	100.0	100.0
58.0	57.3	64.3	61.8	66.8	69.8	Gross Profit	58.5	60.6
52.0	54.3	56.1	56.7	56.3	58.7	Operating Expenses	52.6	55.4
6.0	3.0	8.2	5.1	10.4	11.1	Operating Profit	5.9	5.2
1.0	1.3	.2	1.2	4.4	.9	All Other Expenses (net)	.9	.8
5.0	1.8	7.9	3.9	6.0	10.2	Profit Before Taxes	5.0	4.4
						RATIOS		
2.9	1.9	2.6	3.9	5.4	3.8	Current	2.5	2.6
1.3	1.3	1.4	1.9	2.4	1.5		1.5	1.7
.9	.8	1.2	1.4	1.1	1.1		1.2	1.2
2.7	1.6	2.1	3.6	4.8	3.8	Quick	2.1	2.2
1.1	1.1	1.2	1.6	2.1	1.4		1.3	1.4
.5	.6	1.0	1.1	1.0	1.0		.8	.8
18 20.5	33 11.2	53 6.9	60 6.1	47 7.8	74 4.9	Sales/Receivables	41 9.0	39 9.4
41 9.0	56 6.5	68 5.4	83 4.4	74 4.9	89 4.1		64 5.7	64 5.7
65 5.6	76 4.8	87 4.2	114 3.2	114 3.2	114 3.2		89 4.1	101 3.6
0 UND	2 190.2	0 UND	0 UND	0 UND	0 UND	Cost of Sales/Inventory	0 UND	0 UND
9 40.2	19 19.4	10 34.8	12 31.1	17 21.3	0 UND		16 22.9	20 18.1
118 3.1	56 6.5	46 8.0	40 9.2	63 5.8	55 6.6		61 6.0	60 6.1
1 362.9	20 18.0	25 14.5	30 12.2	64 5.7	35 10.3	Cost of Sales/Payables	21 17.1	31 11.9
29 12.7	51 7.2	66 5.5	62 5.9	85 4.3	78 4.7		44 8.3	60 6.1
81 4.5	118 3.1	118 3.1	101 3.6	140 2.6	107 3.4		94 3.9	114 3.2
8.6	10.1	5.2	1.9	1.4	1.6	Sales/Working Capital	5.2	3.9
29.8	23.3	9.5	4.2	2.1	6.1		10.6	10.3
-80.3	-16.6	24.1	11.1	40.2	35.5		36.3	40.0
(21) 9.5	(34) 18.5	(56) 53.2	(36) 43.2	(12) 162.5		EBIT/Interest	(111) 13.4	(148) 16.6
3.4	4.7	17.8	13.5	4.7			3.8	4.8
1.1	1.0	3.7	1.3	-6.3			1.2	1.4
		(22) 11.4	(22) 11.1			Net Profit + Depr., Dep., Amort./Cur. Mat. L /T/D	(52) 9.4	(67) 16.1
		4.9	4.9				3.4	3.9
		2.7	.6				1.3	1.6
.2	.3	.2	.1	.1	.2	Fixed/Worth	.2	.2
.7	.7	.4	.2	.2	.2		.5	.4
1.9	-7.6	1.0	.5	.5	.9		1.3	1.3
.7	1.5	.8	.4	.2	.6	Debt/Worth	.7	.7
1.9	5.0	1.9	1.0	.7	1.0		1.9	1.5
8.3	-88.1	4.1	1.9	4.1	4.2		4.1	6.1
(23) 91.2	(29) 109.7	(58) 92.0	(44) 28.4	(20) 27.6	(12) 42.4	% Profit Before Taxes/Tangible Net Worth	(130) 59.2	(152) 45.7
32.9	38.7	43.7	18.6	18.5	24.5		31.7	24.1
7.4	17.7	15.4	-.3	7.9	20.3		5.8	6.2
28.6	17.7	25.6	14.6	16.0	16.3	% Profit Before Taxes/Total Assets	20.4	18.0
7.7	8.6	13.5	8.1	9.2	12.0		9.3	7.9
1.0	1.5	4.6	-1.4	1.1	-3.2		1.0	1.4
47.8	43.3	34.4	20.1	18.2	14.0	Sales/Net Fixed Assets	28.2	24.8
19.8	27.3	16.6	11.0	12.1	11.4		15.1	14.9
8.1	13.4	10.9	7.7	9.0	5.8		9.1	9.3
7.5	4.0	2.8	1.6	1.2	1.3	Sales/Total Assets	3.2	2.9
3.4	3.0	2.1	1.3	1.1	1.1		2.3	1.9
1.6	1.8	1.7	.9	.8	.9		1.5	1.1
(21) 1.0	(24) 1.1	(52) 1.1	(42) 2.3	(19) 1.9		% Depr., Dep., Amort./Sales	(115) 1.0	(134) 1.5
1.8	1.6	2.5	3.6	3.3			2.4	2.9
2.5	3.3	4.2	6.0	4.1			4.2	5.0
(12) 5.6	(15) 2.2	(10) 1.9				% Officers', Directors', Owners' Comp/Sales	(34) 4.8	(39) 2.8
10.1	12.0	4.9					8.7	8.0
19.9	17.1	14.2					14.6	16.1
31721M	124828M	682841M	1347832M	1923637M	2799725M	Net Sales ($)	2675950M	5544444M
8216M	43268M	315804M	1052998M	1646709M	2480441M	Total Assets ($)	1910562M	4166540M

M = $ thousand   MM = $ million
See Pages 1 through 15 for Explanation of Ratios and Data

Comparative Historical Data				Current Data Sorted By Sales					
3	9	8	# Postretirement Benefits	1	3		2		2
			Type of Statement						
87	90	96	Unqualified	2	1	1	12	33	47
27	19	22	Reviewed	4	5	2	9	2	
24	25	29	Compiled	8	10	6	2	2	1
	8		Tax Returns						
56	48	68	Other	7	13	9	11	15	13
				90 (4/1-9/30/94)			125 (10/1/94-3/31/95)		
4/1/92-3/31/93 ALL	4/1/93-3/31/94 ALL	4/1/94-3/31/95 ALL		0-1MM	1-3MM	3-5MM	5-10MM	10-25MM	25MM & OVER
194	190	215	NUMBER OF STATEMENTS	21	29	18	34	52	61
%	%	%	ASSETS	%	%	%	%	%	%
20.8	23.3	21.6	Cash & Equivalents	10.4	13.0	11.1	16.1	25.5	32.3
36.4	36.0	37.2	Trade Receivables - (net)	35.9	37.6	47.2	44.9	38.6	29.1
5.7	6.5	5.6	Inventory	7.4	7.0	6.2	6.4	4.6	4.6
3.5	3.2	3.7	All Other Current	5.4	2.8	.7	2.0	5.0	4.2
66.5	68.9	68.1	Total Current	59.1	60.4	65.1	69.5	73.7	70.1
16.0	14.9	14.8	Fixed Assets (net)	23.9	15.6	13.5	14.6	13.9	12.5
8.1	7.0	7.0	Intangibles (net)	6.4	12.6	8.6	7.1	4.4	6.1
9.4	9.2	10.2	All Other Non-Current	10.6	11.3	12.8	8.8	8.0	11.3
100.0	100.0	100.0	Total	100.0	100.0	100.0	100.0	100.0	100.0
			LIABILITIES						
7.4	6.3	7.0	Notes Payable-Short Term	14.2	15.7	7.6	6.6	3.3	3.6
2.8	2.1	2.4	Cur. Mat.-L/T/D	3.4	2.7	4.6	3.5	1.1	1.9
12.1	11.9	12.2	Trade Payables	13.0	13.9	15.2	15.8	10.0	10.0
1.1	1.1	1.2	Income Taxes Payable	.5	.9	1.6	1.7	1.5	1.0
17.6	19.1	21.4	All Other Current	15.2	20.7	13.6	22.1	24.8	22.8
41.1	40.6	44.2	Total Current	46.3	53.9	42.6	49.7	40.7	39.2
7.3	6.7	6.1	Long Term Debt	10.9	10.5	13.2	3.4	3.5	4.1
1.6	1.2	1.2	Deferred Taxes	.0	.1	1.6	3.2	1.2	1.0
4.5	4.0	6.1	All Other-Non-Current	4.4	7.5	10.5	7.3	5.5	4.6
45.6	47.5	42.3	Net Worth	38.3	28.0	32.1	36.4	49.2	51.0
100.0	100.0	100.0	Total Liabilities & Net Worth	100.0	100.0	100.0	100.0	100.0	100.0
			INCOME DATA						
100.0	100.0	100.0	Net Sales	100.0	100.0	100.0	100.0	100.0	100.0
61.8	60.9	62.3	Gross Profit	60.3	63.8	56.1	57.0	66.5	63.4
54.7	54.4	55.6	Operating Expenses	53.9	60.8	49.3	50.8	57.7	56.3
7.1	6.5	6.7	Operating Profit	6.4	3.0	6.8	6.2	8.8	7.2
1.1	.8	1.2	All Other Expenses (net)	2.1	1.1	.4	-.1	.9	2.3
6.1	5.6	5.5	Profit Before Taxes	4.4	1.9	6.4	6.3	7.9	4.9
			RATIOS						
2.9	3.2	2.8		3.2	2.0	2.8	2.4	3.0	3.7
1.8	1.7	1.5	Current	1.4	1.2	1.5	1.3	1.9	1.7
1.1	1.2	1.1		.8	.8	1.0	1.0	1.2	1.2
2.6	2.8	2.5		2.4	1.6	2.2	1.8	2.7	3.2
1.6	1.5	1.3	Quick	1.0	1.1	1.3	1.2	1.6	1.5
.9	.9	.9		.5	.7	.9	.9	1.1	1.0
43 8.4	47 7.8	48 7.6		36 10.1	21 17.0	34 10.8	52 7.0	59 6.2	58 6.3
65 5.6	65 5.6	66 5.5	Sales/Receivables	58 6.3	45 8.2	58 6.3	63 5.8	74 4.9	76 4.8
96 3.8	96 3.8	94 3.9		99 3.7	74 4.9	76 4.8	96 3.8	96 3.8	114 3.2
0 UND	0 UND	0 UND		0 UND	0 UND	0 UND	0 UND	0 UND	0 UND
12 30.8	15 24.5	12 30.0	Cost of Sales/Inventory	10 37.4	17 21.5	12 30.1	7 49.6	11 33.4	11 32.2
47 7.8	46 8.0	53 6.9		146 2.5	63 5.8	42 8.6	31 11.6	35 10.4	59 6.2
27 13.6	24 15.1	28 13.2		1 245.6	17 20.9	7 56.1	21 17.2	30 12.3	43 8.5
64 5.7	52 7.0	62 5.9	Cost of Sales/Payables	41 8.8	51 7.2	28 12.9	63 5.8	63 5.8	78 4.7
126 2.9	96 3.8	107 3.4		118 3.1	118 3.1	69 5.3	118 3.1	107 3.4	107 3.4
3.6	2.6	3.7		3.8	8.8	7.9	5.8	3.4	1.6
7.9	7.6	9.5	Sales/Working Capital	11.3	33.5	14.1	16.6	6.3	5.1
51.4	32.7	48.4		-37.7	-17.1	NM	NM	16.5	26.4
28.1	39.4	27.8		13.2	9.8	17.9	34.9	145.7	25.3
(153) 6.2	(139) 9.1	(165) 9.5	EBIT/Interest	(17) 2.2	(23) 4.8	(15) 6.8	(29) 17.1	(42) 27.5	(39) 5.1
1.3	1.7	1.6		.9	.5	1.8	3.5	6.2	-2.6
17.5	30.0	11.0					8.4	13.4	14.1
(68) 5.1	(62) 7.0	(61) 4.1	Net Profit + Depr., Dep., Amort./Cur. Mat. L/T/D				(12) 3.8	(20) 6.3	(20) 5.4
2.3	1.3	.2					.9	3.4	-.9
.2	.1	.2		.1	.3	.3	.2	.1	.1
.3	.3	.4	Fixed/Worth	.7	.6	.8	.4	.3	.2
1.1	.9	1.0		UND	NM	NM	2.1	.6	.6
.5	.4	.6		.6	1.1	.8	1.3	.5	.5
1.3	1.1	1.6	Debt/Worth	2.0	2.4	4.2	2.6	1.1	1.0
4.1	4.0	4.9		UND	-51.8	NM	6.9	2.8	3.3
51.7	46.5	57.8		47.9	126.2	114.3	87.2	56.8	26.9
(172) 26.7	(166) 23.2	(186) 26.5	% Profit Before Taxes/Tangible Net Worth	(17) 15.0	(21) 41.7	(14) 56.7	(30) 46.0	(50) 29.6	(54) 20.4
9.6	5.6	11.5		6.2	18.4	22.7	14.6	11.3	7.3
19.4	17.7	18.9		18.0	24.4	15.9	25.1	24.1	15.2
9.7	8.2	10.0	% Profit Before Taxes/Total Assets	5.5	9.6	7.4	16.0	12.5	8.5
1.9	1.2	2.0		.5	1.5	2.6	2.1	5.3	-2.3
27.6	24.1	28.6		35.1	34.7	58.8	29.7	24.9	16.5
14.5	14.5	14.4	Sales/Net Fixed Assets	13.0	23.0	34.2	16.9	13.6	11.7
9.1	9.5	9.0		3.7	12.7	20.5	12.0	8.3	8.4
2.7	2.7	2.9		2.4	4.1	5.1	3.1	2.5	1.4
1.9	1.8	1.8	Sales/Total Assets	1.6	2.9	3.6	2.4	1.7	1.2
1.3	1.1	1.2		1.0	1.8	1.7	1.9	1.3	.9
1.4	1.4	1.3		1.8	1.1	1.1	1.2	1.3	1.9
(151) 2.8	(151) 2.6	(165) 2.7	% Depr., Dep., Amort./Sales	(15) 2.5	(18) 2.0	(12) 1.3	(26) 2.1	(47) 3.1	(47) 3.5
4.2	4.2	4.3		5.5	2.9	2.4	3.2	5.2	5.0
4.1	4.1	2.3			4.0				
(40) 7.6	(42) 10.4	(39) 6.9	% Officers', Directors', Owners' Comp/Sales		(13) 12.0				
13.9	17.7	16.6			16.6				
5966724M	5908813M	6910584M	Net Sales ($)	11779M	56314M	68993M	237640M	840472M	5695386M
4541061M	4689406M	5547436M	Total Assets ($)	8242M	25572M	29361M	119991M	567912M	4796358M

M = $ thousand MM = $ million

See Pages 1 through 15 for Explanation of Ratios and Data

SERVICES—TELEPHONE COMMUNICATIONS. SIC# 4812 (13)

Current Data Sorted By Assets | Comparative Historical Data

	1	6	4	10	4	1	# Postretirement Benefits Type of Statement		
	2	10	24	31	11	12	Unqualified	46	69
	2	22	16	4			Reviewed	22	33
	19	26	5	1	1		Compiled	46	30
	7	3	1				Tax Returns	1	3
	12	26	18	20	7	4	Other	43	40
		71 (4/1-9/30/94)		213 (10/1/94-3/31/95)				4/1/90-3/31/91	4/1/91-3/31/92
	0-500M	500M-2MM	2-10MM	10-50MM	50-100MM	100-250MM		ALL	ALL
	42	87	64	56	19	16	NUMBER OF STATEMENTS	158	175
	%	%	%	%	%	%	ASSETS	%	%
	8.1	7.4	9.0	6.1	6.2	5.3	Cash & Equivalents	8.0	6.9
	27.5	33.2	26.2	19.8	20.5	14.3	Trade Receivables - (net)	22.8	22.8
	16.7	12.7	9.9	3.7	4.9	3.1	Inventory	9.2	8.9
	2.4	1.3	2.5	2.1	1.4	2.4	All Other Current	3.4	2.1
	54.8	54.6	47.6	31.7	32.9	25.1	Total Current	43.2	40.7
	34.8	36.7	40.7	52.0	43.4	53.1	Fixed Assets (net)	42.9	45.1
	3.4	3.4	2.9	7.4	14.2	8.4	Intangibles (net)	4.8	3.4
	7.1	5.4	8.8	8.9	9.4	13.4	All Other Non-Current	9.1	10.8
	100.0	100.0	100.0	100.0	100.0	100.0	Total	100.0	100.0
							LIABILITIES		
	9.7	8.7	5.9	5.5	4.2	2.3	Notes Payable-Short Term	8.2	7.9
	3.2	6.8	6.5	5.0	1.7	4.2	Cur. Mat. -L/T/D	5.3	5.7
	15.2	15.3	17.2	13.7	9.3	8.3	Trade Payables	12.5	12.7
	.3	.3	.4	.5	1.6	.2	Income Taxes Payable	.7	.9
	14.4	10.5	8.4	9.1	8.6	7.5	All Other Current	7.5	8.6
	42.9	41.6	38.4	33.8	25.4	22.5	Total Current	34.2	35.8
	19.2	20.6	21.0	20.2	19.3	30.6	Long Term Debt	23.1	22.3
	.3	1.4	1.1	3.9	2.9	5.2	Deferred Taxes	2.1	2.7
	7.6	3.6	4.2	3.0	2.4	4.9	All Other-Non-Current	4.4	3.5
	30.0	32.8	35.2	39.1	50.0	36.7	Net Worth	36.2	35.7
	100.0	100.0	100.0	100.0	100.0	100.0	Total Liabilities & Net Worth	100.0	100.0
							INCOME DATA		
	100.0	100.0	100.0	100.0	100.0	100.0	Net Sales	100.0	100.0
							Gross Profit		
	96.5	93.2	89.0	87.2	86.9	87.9	Operating Expenses	88.6	89.1
	3.5	6.8	11.0	12.8	13.1	12.1	Operating Profit	11.4	10.9
	1.3	1.1	2.4	2.8	2.3	3.2	All Other Expenses (net)	2.5	2.5
	2.3	5.6	8.6	10.0	10.8	8.9	Profit Before Taxes	8.9	8.3
							RATIOS		
	2.3	2.1	2.1	1.7	1.7	1.6		2.1	1.8
	1.6	1.4	1.2	.9	1.3	1.2	Current	1.3	1.2
	1.0	1.0	.8	.6	.8	.6		.7	.7
	1.5	1.5	1.6	1.4	1.5	1.2		1.4	1.3
	1.0	1.0	.9	.7	.9	.9	Quick	.9	.8
	.5	.7	.5	.4	.6	.6		.5	.5
10	36.0	29	12.6	35	10.4	43	8.5	46	7.9	44	8.3		33	11.1	31	11.7

							Sales/Receivables				

Sales/Receivables:

size col	v1	size2	v2	size3	v3	size4	v4	size5	v5	size6	v6	label	h1n	h1v	h2n	h2v
10	36.0	29	12.6	35	10.4	43	8.5	46	7.9	44	8.3	Sales/Receivables	33	11.1	31	11.7
34	10.7	44	8.3	47	7.8	55	6.6	58	6.3	56	6.5		43	8.4	45	8.1
48	7.6	62	5.9	62	5.9	68	5.4	104	3.5	76	4.8		59	6.2	61	6.0

Cost of Sales/Inventory

Cost of Sales/Payables

	9.1	8.8	7.2	7.6	5.7	6.5		6.7	7.5
	15.6	18.5	18.6	-55.7	18.6	19.9	Sales/Working Capital	18.7	34.3
	-221.3	-295.3	-16.2	-6.8	-12.5	-8.6		-13.0	-15.3

												EBIT/Interest				
(35)	9.7	(82)	6.5	(59)	13.6	(50)	12.0	(15)	11.1		7.6	EBIT/Interest	(143)	7.4	(163)	6.6
	4.4		3.4		6.0		6.1		5.3		4.2			3.5		3.1
	-.2		2.1		1.4		1.7		-.2		1.0			1.5		1.5

												Net Profit + Depr., Dep., Amort./Cur. Mat. L /T/D				
		(34)	3.3	(26)	5.7	(30)	18.7	(10)	37.5			Net Profit + Depr., Dep., Amort./Cur. Mat. L /T/D	(83)	10.3	(83)	8.2
			2.4		1.8		9.5		4.3					3.2		2.6
			1.2		.7		1.9		1.9					1.1		1.0

	.6	.5	.5	1.1	.6	.8		.6	.6
	.8	1.2	1.3	1.7	1.4	1.7	Fixed/Worth	1.4	1.4
	5.1	2.5	3.7	2.9	1.9	5.4		2.5	3.2

	1.2	1.3	.9	.9	.5	1.0		1.0	1.1
	2.3	2.2	2.1	1.7	1.2	1.9	Debt/Worth	1.9	1.9
	17.2	4.0	6.6	5.3	3.0	6.1		5.7	5.2

												% Profit Before Taxes/Tangible Net Worth				
(36)	90.8	(81)	62.3	(55)	54.0	(50)	41.9	(17)	34.7	(14)	42.4	% Profit Before Taxes/Tangible Net Worth	(134)	52.9	(156)	43.0
	31.1		29.5		30.2		28.2		19.9		24.9			24.1		22.7
	7.6		8.8		5.1		15.8		1.4		14.7			10.0		9.8

	25.0	13.8	17.2	15.4	14.2	12.3		15.7	13.8
	9.9	6.9	10.6	9.1	9.5	6.7	% Profit Before Taxes/Total Assets	8.3	7.1
	-.8	2.9	1.4	2.8	-1.5	.3		2.3	2.2

	36.7	24.4	15.3	9.3	3.7	3.3		19.4	14.0
	15.4	7.0	3.7	1.5	1.6	1.1	Sales/Net Fixed Assets	5.1	4.2
	5.0	3.4	1.6	.7	1.2	.6		1.0	.8

	5.1	3.4	2.8	1.8	1.3	1.1		2.7	2.8
	3.4	2.5	1.8	.9	1.0	.6	Sales/Total Assets	1.8	1.6
	2.2	1.7	.9	.4	.5	.3		.6	.6

												% Depr., Dep., Amort./Sales				
(34)	1.1	(79)	1.4	(63)	1.8	(51)	4.4	(16)	3.8			% Depr., Dep., Amort./Sales	(137)	2.1	(149)	2.2
	1.9		3.6		4.8		11.2		7.8					5.6		5.4
	6.1		8.7		13.2		17.5		16.3					15.5		14.5

												% Officers', Directors', Owners' Comp/Sales				
(23)	3.5	(35)	3.6	(15)	2.4							% Officers', Directors', Owners' Comp/Sales	(45)	3.5	(47)	5.2
	7.8		5.5		3.3									7.3		8.3
	16.6		8.0		5.3									11.2		13.7

	38035M	257969M	587782M	1571003M	1229832M	1898610M	Net Sales ($)	1723389M	2932899M
	10459M	98484M	325410M	1281301M	1268158M	2663911M	Total Assets ($)	2041138M	3695321M

M = $ thousand   MM = $ million
See Pages 1 through 15 for Explanation of Ratios and Data

Comparative Historical Data				Current Data Sorted By Sales					
12	21	26	# Postretirement Benefits / Type of Statement	1	5	4	4	7	5
78	65	90	Unqualified	5	7	7	16	22	33
23	28	44	Reviewed		16	9	10	6	3
	33	52	Compiled	15	22	6	4	4	1
1	6	11	Tax Returns	8	2		1		
52	59	87	Other	11	22	10	12	11	21
4/1/92-3/31/93 ALL	4/1/93-3/31/94 ALL	4/1/94-3/31/95 ALL		71 (4/1-9/30/94) 0-1MM	1-3MM	3-5MM	213 (10/1/94-3/31/95) 5-10MM	10-25MM	25MM & OVER
196	191	284	NUMBER OF STATEMENTS	39	69	32	43	43	58
%	%	%	ASSETS	%	%	%	%	%	%
7.9	10.5	7.4	Cash & Equivalents	8.3	6.5	8.0	7.3	8.1	7.1
24.3	24.7	26.2	Trade Receivables - (net)	22.3	27.3	28.1	31.2	19.2	27.9
8.8	7.8	9.8	Inventory	13.0	13.5	11.0	11.0	6.4	4.5
2.6	2.0	2.0	All Other Current	1.8	1.7	2.4	1.2	2.0	2.6
43.5	45.0	45.4	Total Current	45.4	49.0	49.6	50.7	35.7	42.1
42.5	42.0	41.7	Fixed Assets (net)	41.4	41.3	37.2	38.8	49.8	41.0
5.3	4.8	5.1	Intangibles (net)	5.7	2.1	6.7	2.0	6.4	8.6
8.7	8.1	7.8	All Other Non-Current	7.5	7.5	6.6	8.5	8.1	8.3
100.0	100.0	100.0	Total	100.0	100.0	100.0	100.0	100.0	100.0
			LIABILITIES						
7.9	5.6	6.9	Notes Payable-Short Term	11.2	7.5	6.4	7.2	4.6	5.2
4.5	4.4	5.4	Cur. Mat.-L /T/D	3.2	6.2	7.3	7.6	5.6	3.0
13.5	13.8	14.6	Trade Payables	10.6	13.2	14.1	17.8	14.9	16.5
.9	.9	.5	Income Taxes Payable	.3	.2	.1	.7	.3	1.0
8.0	10.3	10.0	All Other Current	7.3	11.6	10.8	8.1	9.9	11.1
34.9	35.1	37.4	Total Current	32.5	38.7	38.7	41.5	35.2	36.8
20.8	21.9	20.9	Long Term Debt	29.9	21.2	22.9	15.5	19.9	18.1
3.6	2.5	2.0	Deferred Taxes	.4	1.8	2.2	1.8	2.8	2.7
4.2	3.4	4.2	All Other-Non-Current	6.3	5.1	3.6	4.9	2.6	2.8
36.6	37.1	35.5	Net Worth	30.9	33.2	32.7	36.3	39.5	39.5
100.0	100.0	100.0	Total Liabilities & Net Worth	100.0	100.0	100.0	100.0	100.0	100.0
			INCOME DATA						
100.0	100.0	100.0	Net Sales	100.0	100.0	100.0	100.0	100.0	100.0
			Gross Profit						
87.8	87.8	90.9	Operating Expenses	94.8	89.4	94.8	90.0	88.1	90.3
12.2	12.2	9.1	Operating Profit	5.2	10.6	5.2	10.0	11.9	9.7
1.9	2.7	1.9	All Other Expenses (net)	2.3	1.2	2.6	2.0	2.1	2.0
10.3	9.5	7.2	Profit Before Taxes	2.8	9.3	2.6	8.0	9.8	7.7
			RATIOS						
2.0	2.1	2.0	Current	3.0	2.3	1.8	2.0	1.8	1.6
1.2	1.3	1.3		1.8	1.4	1.3	1.3	.9	1.1
.8	.8	.8		1.0	.9	.8	.7	.5	.8
1.6	1.7	1.5	Quick	2.1	1.5	1.5	1.5	1.5	1.4
.9	1.0	.9		1.1	1.0	.7	1.0	.6	.9
.5	.6	.5		.5	.6	.5	.6	.4	.6
34 10.7	34 10.6	32 11.3	Sales/Receivables	16 22.3	29 12.6	28 13.1	37 9.9	35 10.4	44 8.3
46 7.9	47 7.8	46 7.9		39 9.4	42 8.7	44 8.3	49 7.5	49 7.4	55 6.6
62 5.9	62 5.9	63 5.8		56 6.5	63 5.8	61 6.0	60 6.1	62 5.9	70 5.2
			Cost of Sales/Inventory						
			Cost of Sales/Payables						
6.7	6.9	7.9	Sales/Working Capital	5.9	8.4	9.2	7.6	7.8	7.5
23.3	16.5	20.0		10.8	14.6	20.2	20.5	-29.1	49.0
-20.4	-22.3	-21.9		-295.3	-85.3	-72.9	-14.0	-6.2	-16.2
(187) 9.3	(165) 11.2	(257) 8.8	EBIT/Interest	(35) 6.0	(64) 7.8	(27) 7.8	(42) 9.2	(39) 15.7	(50) 13.4
4.5	5.2	4.2		2.2	3.6	3.8	5.1	6.1	6.5
2.0	1.9	1.7		-.5	2.1	1.3	3.0	1.5	1.8
(90) 10.8	(87) 13.8	(112) 9.1	Net Profit + Depr., Dep., Amort./Cur. Mat. L/T/D		(32) 4.9		(20) 9.1	(19) 11.5	(24) 18.8
4.4	4.5	2.8			2.4		3.3	4.1	4.3
1.5	1.7	1.2			1.3		.9	1.2	1.4
.6	.5	.6	Fixed/Worth	.7	.5	.5	.5	.5	.6
1.3	1.3	1.3		1.3	1.2	1.8	1.0	1.6	1.2
3.1	2.8	2.9		4.2	2.9	10.0	1.7	4.1	2.3
1.0	.8	1.0	Debt/Worth	1.4	.9	1.4	.9	.9	.8
1.8	1.6	2.1		2.3	2.1	2.2	1.8	1.7	1.8
5.4	5.9	5.1		10.7	5.0	21.3	4.0	5.6	5.5
(171) 57.1	(165) 52.8	(253) 58.3	% Profit Before Taxes/Tangible Net Worth	(35) 81.8	(62) 62.9	(26) 59.3	(39) 41.2	(39) 40.1	(52) 56.9
28.3	26.1	28.3		22.3	29.2	30.4	28.9	21.6	31.5
14.3	14.7	9.5		2.7	12.5	.7	11.8	6.9	17.7
16.0	17.8	15.4	% Profit Before Taxes/Total Assets	17.6	14.9	14.6	15.2	13.6	18.4
8.8	10.6	8.8		5.8	9.9	7.7	9.9	8.2	10.5
4.1	3.2	2.3		-5.0	3.5	-.2	4.4	.5	2.7
16.2	17.7	17.6	Sales/Net Fixed Assets	10.5	25.2	22.4	22.4	10.5	11.1
4.6	4.6	4.6		5.3	6.7	5.7	5.3	1.6	3.0
.8	.8	1.5		2.0	2.0	2.4	2.2	.7	1.5
2.7	3.2	3.1	Sales/Total Assets	2.9	3.4	3.4	3.4	2.5	2.4
1.7	1.8	1.8		1.7	2.3	2.5	2.4	1.0	1.3
.6	.5	.9		1.1	1.2	1.0	.8	.5	.8
(167) 2.2	(164) 2.0	(248) 1.8	% Depr., Dep., Amort./Sales	(35) 1.7	(62) 1.5	(29) 1.6	(42) 2.0	(37) 2.5	(43) 2.5
5.9	5.7	4.8		5.4	4.7	3.9	4.1	11.0	4.4
13.7	14.6	12.2		9.1	12.8	11.2	10.6	18.6	8.6
(55) 4.3	(49) 5.0	(81) 3.4	% Officers', Directors', Owners' Comp/Sales	(16) 2.9	(33) 3.6	(10) 3.8	(12) 3.3		
7.2	7.9	5.8		9.1	6.4	5.9	3.5		
11.3	12.6	10.5		18.3	10.8	8.0	4.8		
3839942M	3125542M	5583231M	Net Sales ($)	22151M	133591M	121983M	305224M	629328M	4370954M
4278831M	3652936M	5647723M	Total Assets ($)	17788M	113652M	94130M	290059M	902389M	4229705M

M = $ thousand   MM = $ million
See Pages 1 through 15 for Explanation of Ratios and Data

Current Data Sorted By Assets | Comparative Historical Data

0-500M	500M-2MM	2-10MM	10-50MM	50-100MM	100-250MM	# Postretirement Benefits / Type of Statement	4/1/90-3/31/91 ALL	4/1/91-3/31/92 ALL
1		3	3		1	# Postretirement Benefits		
						Type of Statement		
1	3	11	15	6	6	Unqualified	36	37
	3	1	1			Reviewed	5	8
3						Compiled	4	3
2						Tax Returns		
	1	8	9	1	2	Other	12	13
		30 (4/1-9/30/94)	43 (10/1/94-3/31/95)				12	13
6	7	20	25	7	8	**NUMBER OF STATEMENTS**	57	61
%	%	%	%	%	%	**ASSETS**	%	%
		16.2	7.5			Cash & Equivalents	8.2	9.6
		14.5	17.2			Trade Receivables - (net)	15.3	14.5
		.5	1.9			Inventory	2.5	1.8
		3.6	5.4			All Other Current	4.8	5.9
		34.8	32.0			Total Current	30.8	31.8
		51.5	31.9			Fixed Assets (net)	38.4	45.0
		4.2	19.3			Intangibles (net)	14.7	10.9
		9.5	16.8			All Other Non-Current	16.1	12.3
		100.0	100.0			Total	100.0	100.0
						LIABILITIES		
		1.7	3.8			Notes Payable-Short Term	2.7	4.9
		5.9	9.1			Cur. Mat. -L/T/D	6.7	6.3
		6.1	5.4			Trade Payables	5.6	6.2
		.5	.1			Income Taxes Payable	.6	.8
		11.1	9.9			All Other Current	9.4	11.1
		25.3	28.3			Total Current	25.0	29.3
		29.9	34.7			Long Term Debt	26.5	27.3
		.2	1.2			Deferred Taxes	1.1	1.0
		3.5	9.1			All Other-Non-Current	6.0	4.2
		41.1	26.8			Net Worth	41.4	38.1
		100.0	100.0			Total Liabilities & Net Worth	100.0	100.0
						INCOME DATA		
		100.0	100.0			Net Sales	100.0	100.0
						Gross Profit		
		93.1	88.9			Operating Expenses	92.6	92.1
		6.9	11.1			Operating Profit	7.4	7.9
		1.3	4.6			All Other Expenses (net)	4.2	8.6
		5.6	6.5			Profit Before Taxes	3.2	-.8
						RATIOS		
		2.2	2.4				1.9	1.9
		1.3	1.2			Current	1.4	1.1
		.7	.9				.9	.7
		1.9	1.8				1.7	1.5
		1.2	1.0			Quick	.9	.8
		.6	.6				.6	.5
		15 24.9	52 7.0				23 15.9	13 28.7
		57 6.4	63 5.8			Sales/Receivables	58 6.3	47 7.8
		72 5.1	76 4.8				68 5.4	70 5.2
						Cost of Sales/Inventory		
						Cost of Sales/Payables		
		5.5	5.5				7.2	9.4
		12.4	23.7			Sales/Working Capital	12.3	50.3
		-16.7	-113.8				-79.8	-14.6
		7.6	9.4				(45) 5.8	(42) 2.8
		(16) 3.5	(23) 3.1			EBIT/Interest	1.7	1.2
		2.0	1.0				-.1	-.2
						Net Profit + Depr., Dep.,	(26) 4.0	(21) 3.3
						Amort./Cur. Mat. L /T/D	1.9	1.2
							.8	.5
		1.0	.8				.7	.9
		1.4	2.2			Fixed/Worth	1.2	1.3
		4.0	-.8				22.8	NM
		.5	.9				.5	.5
		1.8	4.2			Debt/Worth	1.8	2.0
		7.9	-3.0				51.1	NM
		112.7	72.8			% Profit Before Taxes/Tangible	38.2	14.2
		(18) 8.4	(15) 42.6			Net Worth	(44) 14.1	(46) 2.7
		-11.2	5.2				-.8	-8.6
		21.8	17.2			% Profit Before Taxes/Total	10.9	5.3
		4.5	4.9			Assets	4.8	.3
		-4.0	.0				-2.3	-3.9
		3.9	5.7				5.0	4.8
		2.1	3.2			Sales/Net Fixed Assets	2.8	2.5
		1.6	2.4				2.0	1.5
		1.7	1.4				1.4	1.7
		1.1	1.0			Sales/Total Assets	.9	.9
		.9	.6				.7	.7
		4.1	3.5				(53) 6.5	(50) 3.8
		9.2	(22) 8.2			% Depr., Dep., Amort./Sales	9.5	8.2
		14.0	12.7				13.5	12.2
						% Officers', Directors',	(13) 4.2	(11) 7.6
						Owners' Comp/Sales	8.2	9.7
							22.6	25.7
3542M	6216M	122296M	571696M	354300M	566873M	Net Sales ($)	936569M	1137447M
1531M	5531M	101811M	593133M	455738M	1363155M	Total Assets ($)	1206080M	1483984M

M = $ thousand   MM = $ million
See Pages 1 through 15 for Explanation of Ratios and Data

Comparative Historical Data				Current Data Sorted By Sales					
3	7	8	# Postretirement Benefits	1		1	2	1	3
			Type of Statement						
40	41	42	Unqualified	3	2	3	7	8	19
6	4	5	Reviewed	1	3			1	
2	4	3	Compiled	2	1				
		2	Tax Returns	2					
20	26	21	Other	1	1	1	8	6	4
4/1/92-3/31/93 ALL	4/1/93-3/31/94 ALL	4/1/94-3/31/95 ALL		30 (4/1-9/30/94) 0-1MM	1-3MM	3-5MM	43 (10/1/94-3/31/95) 5-10MM	10-25MM	25MM & OVER
68	75	73	**NUMBER OF STATEMENTS**	9	7	4	15	15	23
%	%	%	**ASSETS**	%	%	%	%	%	%
8.8	8.8	10.4	Cash & Equivalents				11.2	7.6	7.5
15.0	12.5	14.2	Trade Receivables - (net)				11.9	15.5	15.5
1.2	1.2	1.6	Inventory				.4	.6	4.0
4.6	4.8	5.3	All Other Current				5.3	3.3	3.3
29.6	27.3	31.6	Total Current				28.8	27.0	30.3
38.7	37.8	39.2	Fixed Assets (net)				44.3	32.8	30.0
16.8	14.6	17.0	Intangibles (net)				13.3	24.7	28.0
14.9	20.2	12.3	All Other Non-Current				13.6	15.5	11.6
100.0	100.0	100.0	Total				100.0	100.0	100.0
			LIABILITIES						
2.1	2.3	4.5	Notes Payable-Short Term				2.3	1.6	2.2
7.6	8.4	8.1	Cur. Mat.-L /T/D				10.2	7.6	7.1
7.6	6.8	5.6	Trade Payables				4.3	4.5	6.5
.2	1.1	.4	Income Taxes Payable				.0	.5	.4
7.3	7.1	8.6	All Other Current				8.6	9.5	9.9
24.8	25.8	27.2	Total Current				25.4	23.6	26.3
36.8	28.8	32.7	Long Term Debt				41.5	37.1	30.8
.7	1.2	.9	Deferred Taxes				.0	.4	2.5
7.2	4.9	7.5	All Other-Non-Current				3.6	5.3	11.5
30.6	39.4	31.6	Net Worth				29.4	33.6	28.9
100.0	100.0	100.0	Total Liabilities & Net Worth				100.0	100.0	100.0
			INCOME DATA						
100.0	100.0	100.0	Net Sales				100.0	100.0	100.0
			Gross Profit						
92.1	88.2	89.4	Operating Expenses				91.6	86.0	87.8
7.9	11.8	10.6	Operating Profit				8.4	14.0	12.2
8.6	5.3	4.3	All Other Expenses (net)				4.2	5.8	5.6
–.7	6.5	6.3	Profit Before Taxes				4.2	8.2	6.6
			RATIOS						
1.9	2.0	2.2					1.9	2.3	1.6
1.2	1.3	1.2	Current				1.2	1.3	1.2
.8	.8	.8					.7	.6	1.0
1.6	1.5	1.7					1.9	1.9	1.2
1.0	1.1	1.0	Quick				1.1	1.1	1.0
.6	.5	.6					.5	.5	.7
27 13.6	21 17.8	26 14.1					22 16.5	30 12.2	54 6.7
58 6.3	58 6.3	61 6.0	Sales/Receivables				63 5.8	72 5.1	69 5.3
73 5.0	76 4.8	76 4.8					74 4.9	79 4.6	81 4.5
			Cost of Sales/Inventory						
			Cost of Sales/Payables						
7.4	6.4	5.4					4.8	6.7	5.1
29.2	21.4	23.7	Sales/Working Capital				23.7	15.6	27.2
–21.1	–19.0	–18.3					–12.1	–5.1	–206.0
5.0	8.2	6.5					3.5	17.7	5.4
(52) 1.4	(60) 2.7	(63) 2.3	EBIT/Interest	(12) 1.8		(14) 6.3		(20) 2.7	
–.0	1.0	1.0					.7	–.5	1.5
2.9	2.0	4.0							4.3
(19) 1.4	(18) 1.1	(24) 2.2	Net Profit + Depr., Dep., Amort./Cur. Mat. L/T/D					(14) 2.8	
.6	.2	1.5							1.6
.8	.6	.9					1.1	.7	.9
2.4	1.3	2.1	Fixed/Worth				1.5	3.3	3.9
–1.9	–13.2	–1.3					–1.2	–.7	–.5
.7	.5	.8					.9	.7	1.7
6.8	2.3	2.7	Debt/Worth				2.7	3.8	9.7
–4.5	–27.7	–3.9					–3.5	–2.0	–2.2
30.7	34.8	72.2					57.9		73.4
(46) 8.8	(55) 6.4	(50) 18.6	% Profit Before Taxes/Tangible Net Worth	(10) 8.4				(14) 28.7	
–3.2	–4.1	–2.7					–3.7		4.0
8.0	10.0	17.7					10.3	23.7	13.3
.9	4.7	3.9	% Profit Before Taxes/Total Assets				2.7	4.9	6.6
–4.8	–2.1	–.4					–1.1	–3.6	1.8
5.0	5.0	4.7					4.0	4.5	5.9
2.8	2.7	2.6	Sales/Net Fixed Assets				2.1	3.3	2.7
1.6	1.7	1.6					1.5	1.9	1.5
1.4	1.3	1.5					1.2	1.4	1.4
.9	.9	1.0	Sales/Total Assets				.8	1.0	.7
.6	.5	.5					.6	.4	.5
6.1	5.7	3.7					5.4	5.7	2.8
(55) 8.9	(61) 8.0	(62) 8.5	% Depr., Dep., Amort./Sales	(13) 9.4		(13) 8.7		(18) 6.9	
14.2	12.1	12.3					14.0	14.8	11.2
	3.4	4.6							
(11) 5.8	(10) 9.9		% Officers', Directors', Owners' Comp/Sales						
13.8	19.6								
1707755M	2136029M	1624923M	Net Sales ($)	3860M	13186M	16250M	95151M	248871M	1247605M
2770126M	3057024M	2520899M	Total Assets ($)	4945M	11828M	11990M	121275M	356878M	2013983M

M = $ thousand   MM = $ million
See Pages 1 through 15 for Explanation of Ratios and Data

Current Data Sorted By Assets						# Postretirement Benefits	Comparative Historical Data	
2	2	4			1	**Type of Statement**		
	6	19	5	1	3	Unqualified	18	28
4	13	15				Reviewed	21	36
21	22	3	1			Compiled	29	32
7	2	2				Tax Returns	2	1
10	17	12	4			Other	24	26
	45 (4/1-9/30/94)		122 (10/1/94-3/31/95)				4/1/90-3/31/91	4/1/91-3/31/92
0-500M	500M-2MM	2-10MM	10-50MM	50-100MM	100-250MM		ALL	ALL
42	60	51	10	1	3	**NUMBER OF STATEMENTS**	94	123
%	%	%	%	%	%	**ASSETS**	%	%
11.5	7.2	8.1	6.2			Cash & Equivalents	9.3	9.1
37.3	40.3	34.5	21.2			Trade Receivables - (net)	34.4	33.6
4.6	3.6	4.2	1.6			Inventory	4.5	4.5
.9	2.0	1.8	5.1			All Other Current	3.7	2.4
54.2	53.1	48.6	34.1			Total Current	52.0	49.6
34.4	37.7	42.3	51.4			Fixed Assets (net)	39.1	41.4
3.3	1.6	2.0	6.1			Intangibles (net)	1.8	2.3
8.1	7.6	7.1	8.4			All Other Non-Current	7.1	6.8
100.0	100.0	100.0	100.0			Total	100.0	100.0
						LIABILITIES		
7.5	8.5	7.3	2.8			Notes Payable-Short Term	11.8	9.5
4.8	5.6	5.8	5.2			Cur. Mat. -L/T/D	5.7	5.8
7.5	9.4	8.2	6.2			Trade Payables	10.6	9.2
1.3	.5	.6	.9			Income Taxes Payable	1.2	1.1
7.1	9.8	7.9	11.2			All Other Current	8.6	9.3
28.2	33.8	29.9	26.3			Total Current	37.9	34.8
20.9	15.2	16.0	26.9			Long Term Debt	20.0	19.1
.5	2.1	2.0	1.8			Deferred Taxes	1.2	1.3
6.6	1.8	3.9	4.3			All Other-Non-Current	2.4	2.9
43.8	47.0	48.2	40.6			Net Worth	38.6	41.9
100.0	100.0	100.0	100.0			Total Liabilities & Net Worth	100.0	100.0
						INCOME DATA		
100.0	100.0	100.0	100.0			Net Sales	100.0	100.0
						Gross Profit		
93.1	94.6	92.1	90.7			Operating Expenses	93.8	93.6
6.9	5.4	7.9	9.3			Operating Profit	6.2	6.4
1.7	.2	1.4	4.3			All Other Expenses (net)	1.5	2.4
5.2	5.2	6.5	5.0			Profit Before Taxes	4.7	4.1
						RATIOS		
3.8	2.2	2.7	2.0				2.2	2.3
2.2	1.6	1.6	1.1			Current	1.4	1.5
1.2	1.2	1.1	.7				1.1	1.0
3.6	2.2	2.1	1.5				2.0	2.0
1.9	1.4	1.4	.9			Quick	1.1	1.3
1.1	1.0	1.0	.5				.8	.8
33 11.0	51 7.2	50 7.3	48 7.6				42 8.6	42 8.6
51 7.1	62 5.9	62 5.9	68 5.4			Sales/Receivables	63 5.8	58 6.3
76 4.8	83 4.4	83 4.4	85 4.3				85 4.3	83 4.4
						Cost of Sales/Inventory		
						Cost of Sales/Payables		
5.1	6.6	5.7	7.1				6.9	5.9
11.4	11.7	12.0	30.7			Sales/Working Capital	16.6	12.4
42.8	27.6	33.6	-12.4				88.5	140.0
13.0	10.9	14.6					7.5	7.5
(39) 4.8	(54) 3.3	(49) 5.1				EBIT/Interest	(85) 3.1	(115) 2.5
.8	1.3	1.6					1.0	.7
5.6	3.7	7.7				Net Profit + Depr., Dep.,	4.7	5.0
(11) 2.2	(22) 2.1	(23) 2.7				Amort./Cur. Mat. L /T/D	(56) 2.5	(70) 2.4
1.0	1.2	1.3					1.3	1.2
.3	.4	.4	.7				.5	.5
.9	.9	1.0	1.5			Fixed/Worth	1.1	1.1
2.0	1.4	1.6	4.0				2.0	2.1
.6	.6	.6	.7				.6	.7
1.1	1.2	1.2	2.1			Debt/Worth	1.5	1.4
3.6	2.3	2.2	3.7				3.9	3.0
78.4	45.6	40.1				% Profit Before Taxes/Tangible	47.8	40.6
(38) 30.7	(58) 18.5	22.5				Net Worth	(87) 21.7	(112) 22.0
1.6	1.4	6.3					1.8	2.9
29.6	16.9	21.0	13.5			% Profit Before Taxes/Total	16.0	17.6
17.1	7.8	10.2	1.3			Assets	8.5	8.2
.1	-.0	2.1	-3.0				-.1	-1.3
16.4	12.2	7.5	3.4				9.3	7.6
7.7	6.0	4.5	2.7			Sales/Net Fixed Assets	5.5	5.0
5.0	3.7	2.2	1.3				3.3	3.1
3.5	2.8	2.3	1.4				2.6	2.7
2.6	2.1	1.8	1.1			Sales/Total Assets	1.9	1.9
1.8	1.6	1.2	.8				1.5	1.4
2.7	2.3	3.2	5.9				3.0	3.1
(34) 4.9	(57) 3.8	(49) 5.5	7.0			% Depr., Dep., Amort./Sales	(82) 5.0	(113) 5.2
7.0	6.8	8.3	10.8				7.0	7.0
9.3	3.7						3.5	5.2
(25) 12.4	(23) 10.1					% Officers', Directors',	(26) 7.2	(40) 9.6
16.7	14.2					Owners' Comp/Sales	10.5	16.2
36756M	131790M	393127M	190800M	24768M	599177M	Net Sales ($)	981177M	965095M
12487M	61775M	209254M	183886M	53861M	493070M	Total Assets ($)	687897M	703994M

© Robert Morris Associates 1995

M = $ thousand   MM = $ million
See Pages 1 through 15 for Explanation of Ratios and Data

Comparative Historical Data | Current Data Sorted By Sales

# Postretirement Benefits	2	7	9		4	3	1	1	1	6

Type of Statement

Type of Statement	92-93	93-94	94-95	0-1MM	1-3MM	3-5MM	5-10MM	10-25MM	25MM & OVER
Unqualified	29	28	34		4	9	4	11	6
Reviewed	29	27	32	3	14	6	7	2	
Compiled	36	44	47	16	19	8	2	2	
Tax Returns	3	4	11	6	4	1			
Other	29	31	43	15	14	4	6	3	1
	4/1/92-3/31/93 ALL	4/1/93-3/31/94 ALL	4/1/94-3/31/95 ALL	45 (4/1-9/30/94)			122 (10/1/94-3/31/95)		
NUMBER OF STATEMENTS	126	134	167	40	55	28	19	18	7

	%	%	%	0-1MM %	1-3MM %	3-5MM %	5-10MM %	10-25MM %	25MM & OVER %
ASSETS									
Cash & Equivalents	9.2	9.5	8.6	9.4	9.8	7.8	7.8	4.8	
Trade Receivables - (net)	34.3	34.3	36.2	32.7	39.3	36.6	34.3	38.1	
Inventory	4.5	2.8	3.8	3.6	4.7	4.7	3.5	2.1	
All Other Current	2.9	2.7	1.9	.9	1.9	.7	1.3	4.1	
Total Current	50.9	49.3	50.6	46.5	55.7	49.8	46.9	49.0	
Fixed Assets (net)	38.7	41.3	38.7	39.8	37.5	38.5	45.7	37.3	
Intangibles (net)	3.6	3.1	2.9	3.9	1.8	1.0	.8	6.4	
All Other Non-Current	6.7	6.3	7.7	9.7	4.9	10.8	6.5	7.3	
Total	100.0	100.0	100.0	100.0	100.0	100.0	100.0	100.0	
LIABILITIES									
Notes Payable-Short Term	8.4	7.5	7.4	8.8	6.9	9.0	9.4	3.7	
Cur. Mat.-L./T/D	5.9	7.1	5.4	5.7	4.8	6.1	6.2	5.3	
Trade Payables	8.6	8.1	8.3	9.4	7.1	8.3	7.7	9.3	
Income Taxes Payable	.9	.5	.8	.6	1.1	.3	.2	1.5	
All Other Current	9.5	8.9	8.7	4.0	10.6	10.1	8.9	8.0	
Total Current	33.4	32.2	30.6	28.4	30.5	33.7	32.4	27.7	
Long Term Debt	17.5	19.0	17.7	25.4	13.3	15.5	17.5	17.0	
Deferred Taxes	1.8	1.0	1.7	.8	2.3	1.0	2.1	1.8	
All Other-Non-Current	1.8	2.0	4.1	7.4	3.2	3.1	1.7	2.3	
Net Worth	45.6	45.8	46.0	37.9	50.6	46.7	46.4	51.3	
Total Liabilities & Net Worth	100.0	100.0	100.0	100.0	100.0	100.0	100.0	100.0	
INCOME DATA									
Net Sales	100.0	100.0	100.0	100.0	100.0	100.0	100.0	100.0	
Gross Profit									
Operating Expenses	92.4	93.5	93.2	94.6	93.7	92.1	90.0	93.9	
Operating Profit	7.6	6.5	6.8	5.4	6.3	7.9	10.0	6.1	
All Other Expenses (net)	1.4	1.3	1.2	2.0	.8	.5	2.1	1.0	
Profit Before Taxes	6.2	5.2	5.7	3.4	5.5	7.4	7.9	5.1	
RATIOS									
Current	2.5 / 1.6 / 1.0	2.6 / 1.4 / 1.1	2.6 / 1.6 / 1.1	2.7 / 1.6 / 1.0	2.9 / 1.9 / 1.2	2.6 / 1.6 / 1.2	2.0 / 1.2 / .9	2.4 / 1.6 / 1.3	
Quick	2.1 / 1.4 / .9	2.6 / 1.3 / .8	2.3 / 1.5 / 1.0	2.6 / 1.5 / .8	2.6 / 1.7 / 1.1	2.3 / 1.4 / 1.1	1.7 / 1.1 / .8	2.0 / 1.4 / 1.1	
Sales/Receivables	41 8.8 / 60 6.1 / 79 4.6	41 8.8 / 58 6.3 / 78 4.7	47 7.7 / 61 6.0 / 81 4.5	45 8.2 / 63 5.8 / 94 3.9	47 7.8 / 59 6.2 / 79 4.6	53 6.9 / 65 5.6 / 83 4.4	34 10.8 / 59 6.2 / 79 4.6	50 7.3 / 69 5.3 / 87 4.2	
Cost of Sales/Inventory									
Cost of Sales/Payables									
Sales/Working Capital	5.7 / 11.3 / 253.9	6.4 / 16.7 / 115.8	6.0 / 11.7 / 33.6	5.4 / 11.4 / NM	5.8 / 9.9 / 28.8	6.0 / 12.6 / 27.3	6.3 / 28.7 / -72.2	4.9 / 13.0 / 22.3	
EBIT/Interest	(112) 9.5 / 3.8 / 1.3	(116) 8.8 / 2.7 / 1.1	(155) 12.0 / 4.2 / 1.3	(38) 6.3 / 2.8 / -.5	(49) 20.4 / 4.4 / 1.1	(25) 11.0 / 4.0 / 1.5	17.8 / 4.6 / 1.8	19.7 / 6.6 / 2.0	
Net Profit + Depr., Dep., Amort./Cur. Mat. L/T/D	(62) 5.0 / 2.4 / 1.4	(53) 3.0 / 1.8 / .7	(63) 5.6 / 2.3 / 1.2	(12) 3.6 / 1.5 / .5	(17) 6.1 / 3.4 / 1.9	(12) 3.0 / 1.9 / 1.3		(12) 9.7 / 3.2 / 1.9	
Fixed/Worth	.4 / 1.0 / 1.7	.5 / 1.0 / 2.0	.4 / 1.0 / 1.6	.5 / 1.2 / 2.7	.4 / .9 / 1.3	.5 / 1.0 / 1.6	.4 / 1.0 / 1.7	.4 / .8 / 1.6	
Debt/Worth	.6 / 1.2 / 3.0	.6 / 1.3 / 2.7	.6 / 1.3 / 2.9	.7 / 1.6 / 3.9	.5 / 1.0 / 2.4	.6 / 1.1 / 2.1	.6 / 1.3 / 3.0	.7 / 1.0 / 2.1	
% Profit Before Taxes/Tangible Net Worth	(118) 41.2 / 18.7 / 3.2	(130) 40.1 / 15.0 / 1.4	(160) 46.5 / 21.0 / 3.1	(34) 48.4 / 26.3 / -5.9	52.9 / 18.4 / -.3	46.5 / 24.4 / 9.8	48.2 / 30.3 / 13.0	(17) 39.4 / 15.5 / 7.5	
% Profit Before Taxes/Total Assets	19.5 / 7.8 / .9	17.4 / 5.4 / .8	21.8 / 9.7 / .7	22.1 / 8.9 / -2.7	22.0 / 10.5 / -.2	24.5 / 10.3 / 2.6	26.5 / 12.1 / 3.3	18.4 / 8.1 / 2.0	
Sales/Net Fixed Assets	10.3 / 6.0 / 3.4	12.7 / 5.5 / 3.3	10.7 / 5.5 / 2.8	10.0 / 4.3 / 2.2	15.4 / 6.6 / 4.0	9.2 / 4.9 / 3.0	8.9 / 4.3 / 2.8	7.5 / 5.3 / 2.9	
Sales/Total Assets	2.7 / 2.2 / 1.5	2.9 / 2.2 / 1.4	2.8 / 2.0 / 1.4	2.7 / 1.7 / 1.1	3.1 / 2.3 / 1.7	2.7 / 2.0 / 1.6	2.6 / 2.1 / 1.4	2.4 / 1.8 / 1.2	
% Depr., Dep., Amort./Sales	(113) 2.4 / 4.2 / 6.5	(120) 2.7 / 5.3 / 7.6	(152) 2.8 / 5.2 / 7.8	(35) 4.6 / 6.5 / 9.7	(50) 2.0 / 3.5 / 6.4	(26) 3.0 / 5.0 / 8.1	(18) 2.4 / 3.8 / 8.8	4.9 / 6.2 / 7.8	
% Officers', Directors', Owners' Comp/Sales	(51) 5.4 / 8.4 / 14.9	(49) 6.2 / 9.3 / 16.4	(58) 4.9 / 10.3 / 14.7	(18) 8.4 / 12.0 / 17.9	(29) 5.7 / 10.5 / 15.0				
Net Sales ($)	1075563M	902927M	1376418M	24009M	104643M	108163M	127839M	278026M	733738M
Total Assets ($)	898167M	765552M	1014333M	19806M	53404M	65241M	87816M	189472M	598594M

M = $ thousand   MM = $ million
See Pages 1 through 15 for Explanation of Ratios and Data

Current Data Sorted By Assets   # Postretirement Benefits   Comparative Historical Data

0-500M	500M-2MM	2-10MM	10-50MM	50-100MM	100-250MM		4/1/90-3/31/91 ALL	4/1/91-3/31/92 ALL
		1	4	1		# Postretirement Benefits		
						Type of Statement		
2		1	7	3	2	Unqualified	8	16
	1	8	3			Reviewed	7	6
4	3	1				Compiled	10	12
1		1				Tax Returns	1	1
4	3	4	4	1	1	Other	9	11
	16 (4/1-9/30/94)		38 (10/1/94-3/31/95)					
11	7	15	14	4	3	**NUMBER OF STATEMENTS**	35	46
%	%	%	%	%	%	**ASSETS**	%	%
15.6		11.0	20.3			Cash & Equivalents	10.4	11.8
2.0		1.0	3.5			Trade Receivables - (net)	3.8	3.4
2.8		.8	.9			Inventory	3.4	2.0
4.5		.4	1.2			All Other Current	3.2	1.3
24.9		13.2	25.9			Total Current	20.8	18.5
67.1		68.3	67.2			Fixed Assets (net)	71.1	68.2
3.1		12.4	.7			Intangibles (net)	1.2	3.5
4.9		6.2	6.2			All Other Non-Current	6.8	9.9
100.0		100.0	100.0			Total	100.0	100.0
						LIABILITIES		
4.2		3.7	5.2			Notes Payable-Short Term	9.2	6.6
9.1		4.8	3.6			Cur. Mat.-L/T/D	3.3	5.4
3.8		7.1	7.6			Trade Payables	8.0	8.7
.1		.0	.1			Income Taxes Payable	.8	.4
17.5		7.3	5.1			All Other Current	7.0	8.1
34.6		22.9	21.6			Total Current	28.3	29.1
22.4		46.3	27.6			Long Term Debt	27.4	37.4
.3		.8	.8			Deferred Taxes	.7	.7
17.2		1.0	1.3			All Other-Non-Current	4.4	4.3
25.5		29.1	48.7			Net Worth	39.2	28.5
100.0		100.0	100.0			Total Liabilities & Net Worth	100.0	100.0
						INCOME DATA		
100.0		100.0	100.0			Net Sales	100.0	100.0
						Gross Profit		
92.3		89.4	88.8			Operating Expenses	90.5	92.7
7.8		10.6	11.2			Operating Profit	9.5	7.3
.2		4.4	1.7			All Other Expenses (net)	2.4	5.1
7.6		6.2	9.5			Profit Before Taxes	7.1	2.2
						RATIOS		
2.0		.8	1.8				2.1	1.5
.8		.6	.9			Current	.5	.5
.4		.1	.4				.3	.2
1.8		.8	1.7				1.3	1.2
.8		.5	.8			Quick (33)	.4	.4
.4		.1	.3				.1	.1
0 UND		0 UND	0 999.8				0 UND	0 UND
0 UND		1 645.4	1 383.3			Sales/Receivables	1 658.0	1 411.4
3 132.0		2 201.8	8 44.8				3 133.9	3 114.4
						Cost of Sales/Inventory		
						Cost of Sales/Payables		
16.0		-39.0	5.7				12.0	28.4
-262.0		-15.2	-106.1			Sales/Working Capital	-13.3	-12.2
-13.5		-5.2	-10.0				-8.3	-5.6
		3.2	10.6				3.9	4.8
		2.1	(13) 3.6			EBIT/Interest (30) (39)	2.6	2.2
		1.4	2.5				1.8	1.4
							4.8	5.0
						Net Profit + Depr., Dep., Amort./Cur. Mat. L /T/D (15) (18)	2.8	2.1
							1.8	.3
1.0		1.8	.6				1.3	1.2
3.5		3.6	1.9			Fixed/Worth	1.6	3.3
-3.4		-14.7	2.4				3.2	10.6
.4		1.6	.5				.7	.9
3.0		3.5	1.3			Debt/Worth	1.4	2.4
-6.3		-19.3	2.1				2.8	11.0
		56.5	42.4				29.5	28.4
	(11)	29.9	23.6			% Profit Before Taxes/Tangible Net Worth (32) (36)	17.9	14.2
		11.3	14.7				7.1	5.1
36.2		12.9	15.5				10.6	10.7
13.3		4.5	9.9			% Profit Before Taxes/Total Assets	6.2	5.2
3.0		3.1	6.3				3.8	1.0
8.2		3.6	2.8				3.1	3.8
5.5		2.1	1.6			Sales/Net Fixed Assets	1.8	1.9
2.5		.8	1.3				1.0	.9
4.3		1.7	1.7				1.9	2.5
4.0		1.1	1.2			Sales/Total Assets	1.3	1.4
2.3		.6	.7				.6	.7
1.2		5.2	4.2				3.9	4.3
(10) 2.8		8.3	(13) 4.9			% Depr., Dep., Amort./Sales (43)	6.1	5.4
5.4		12.5	6.1				9.8	7.9
							4.4	3.5
(12)						% Officers', Directors', Owners' Comp/Sales (16)	5.7	5.4
							10.4	11.3
5458M	10451M	77300M	361632M	320092M	430180M	Net Sales ($)	381411M	1037294M
1831M	6698M	70212M	284525M	254276M	443326M	Total Assets ($)	405687M	935723M

M = $ thousand   MM = $ million
See Pages 1 through 15 for Explanation of Ratios and Data

Comparative Historical Data				Current Data Sorted By Sales					
		6	# Postretirement Benefits			1		1	4
			Type of Statement						
12	20	15	Unqualified	2		1	1	3	8
13	9	12	Reviewed	1		3	6	1	1
17	14	8	Compiled	6		2			
1	1	2	Tax Returns	1				1	
13	18	17	Other	5	3	3	1	1	4
4/1/92-3/31/93	4/1/93-3/31/94	4/1/94-3/31/95			16 (4/1-9/30/94)		38 (10/1/94-3/31/95)		
ALL	ALL	ALL		0-1MM	1-3MM	3-5MM	5-10MM	10-25MM	25MM & OVER
56	62	54	**NUMBER OF STATEMENTS**	15	3	9	8	6	13
%	%	%	**ASSETS**	%	%	%	%	%	%
12.2	9.6	13.9	Cash & Equivalents	13.1					13.2
4.4	2.3	2.5	Trade Receivables - (net)	1.5					4.1
.9	.9	1.1	Inventory	2.1					.8
1.9	1.3	1.5	All Other Current	3.3					.7
19.3	14.1	19.0	Total Current	20.0					18.8
68.2	69.5	69.1	Fixed Assets (net)	72.1					67.9
2.4	6.1	5.9	Intangibles (net)	2.4					7.1
10.1	10.3	6.0	All Other Non-Current	5.5					6.2
100.0	100.0	100.0	Total	100.0					100.0
			LIABILITIES						
4.0	2.9	3.9	Notes Payable-Short Term	3.1					3.5
4.7	5.0	5.4	Cur. Mat.-L./T/D	7.3					4.7
7.2	7.0	6.5	Trade Payables	4.0					8.6
.4	.6	.1	Income Taxes Payable	.1					.4
9.3	8.4	9.1	All Other Current	13.1					9.3
25.7	23.9	25.0	Total Current	27.5					26.5
39.2	41.8	37.1	Long Term Debt	32.8					36.5
.3	.4	.8	Deferred Taxes	.2					1.9
2.4	2.0	4.2	All Other-Non-Current	12.6					1.3
32.4	31.8	32.8	Net Worth	26.8					33.8
100.0	100.0	100.0	Total Liabilities & Net Worth	100.0					100.0
			INCOME DATA						
100.0	100.0	100.0	Net Sales	100.0					100.0
			Gross Profit						
87.9	87.8	89.4	Operating Expenses	90.0					90.1
12.1	12.2	10.6	Operating Profit	10.1					9.9
5.0	5.1	2.9	All Other Expenses (net)	3.0					1.6
7.1	7.1	7.7	Profit Before Taxes	7.0					8.3
			RATIOS						
1.3	1.1	1.3		2.0					1.2
.8	.6	.7	Current	.8					.5
.2	.2	.2		.4					.2
1.0	.9	1.3		1.8					1.1
.6	.5	.6	Quick	.8					.4
.1	.1	.2		.4					.1
0 UND	0 UND	0 UND		0 UND					0 UND
0 UND	0 856.4	0 965.9	Sales/Receivables	0 UND					0 999.8
3 130.9	2 174.2	3 124.7		2 188.0					4 85.2
			Cost of Sales/Inventory						
			Cost of Sales/Payables						
31.2	114.4	35.0		16.0					82.5
-54.0	-20.4	-17.9	Sales/Working Capital	-262.0					-13.9
-7.8	-7.2	-6.3		-13.5					-4.9
(48) 6.8	(57) 6.2	(48) 6.6		(11) 8.2					(12) 6.6
2.4	2.0	2.8	EBIT/Interest	3.0					3.6
1.4	1.3	2.1		1.5					2.4
(16) 2.5	6.8	4.0	Net Profit + Depr., Dep.,						
1.3	(17) 2.7	(17) 1.8	Amort./Cur. Mat. L/T/D						
1.1	1.1	1.1							
1.4	1.4	1.4		1.4					1.3
2.5	3.1	2.8	Fixed/Worth	3.5					2.0
6.7	5.8	6.6		-5.5					6.8
1.0	1.4	1.1		.6					1.0
2.3	3.8	2.4	Debt/Worth	3.0					1.7
7.2	6.8	7.3		-7.7					7.3
(50) 66.4	(53) 65.6	(44) 55.6	% Profit Before Taxes/Tangible	(11) 130.8					(11) 44.3
23.7	25.0	28.4	Net Worth	25.3					41.0
10.8	13.4	11.3		7.4					15.5
14.3	13.7	15.5	% Profit Before Taxes/Total	25.4					14.9
5.6	5.8	7.7	Assets	8.3					7.0
1.7	1.5	4.4		3.0					5.2
4.5	3.5	3.9		6.9					3.2
1.7	1.7	1.8	Sales/Net Fixed Assets	3.5					1.7
1.0	1.2	1.2		1.2					1.5
2.4	1.9	2.5		4.3					2.0
1.3	1.2	1.2	Sales/Total Assets	3.1					1.4
.8	.9	.9		.8					1.0
(52) 3.4	(59) 4.2	(51) 4.1	% Depr., Dep., Amort./Sales	(13) 1.6					(12) 4.1
5.6	6.1	5.2		4.5					4.4
8.7	9.0	8.3		8.1					4.9
(22) 2.2	(22) 2.4	(18) 3.0	% Officers', Directors',						
5.6	4.4	5.3	Owners' Comp/Sales						
11.3	7.8	15.1							
934598M	900812M	1205113M	Net Sales ($)	7333M	4891M	34642M	59712M	119292M	979243M
803268M	710855M	1060868M	Total Assets ($)	4892M	13771M	29873M	67576M	119212M	825544M

M = $ thousand   MM = $ million
See Pages 1 through 15 for Explanation of Ratios and Data

	Current Data Sorted By Assets						# Postretirement Benefits Type of Statement	Comparative Historical Data	
	1	2							
1	4	12	5				Unqualified	8	17
2	4	1					Reviewed	7	6
5	6	1					Compiled	7	4
2							Tax Returns	1	1
6	6	3	1				Other	9	8
	45 (4/1-9/30/94)		14 (10/1/94-3/31/95)					4/1/90-3/31/91	4/1/91-3/31/92
0-500M	500M-2MM	2-10MM	10-50MM	50-100MM	100-250MM			ALL	ALL
16	20	17	6				**NUMBER OF STATEMENTS**	32	36
%	%	%	%	%	%		**ASSETS**	%	%
24.8	11.9	17.2					Cash & Equivalents	17.8	13.2
21.0	19.0	11.1					Trade Receivables - (net)	14.0	20.1
2.8	5.9	.7					Inventory	6.1	4.5
2.5	1.9	1.7					All Other Current	6.3	4.7
51.1	38.6	30.7					Total Current	44.3	42.6
28.2	42.9	52.4					Fixed Assets (net)	42.5	40.9
.7	3.6	1.1					Intangibles (net)	.7	4.6
20.0	14.9	15.8					All Other Non-Current	12.5	11.9
100.0	100.0	100.0					Total	100.0	100.0
							LIABILITIES		
5.6	6.2	3.8					Notes Payable-Short Term	5.8	9.8
4.3	8.8	3.4					Cur. Mat. -L/T/D	4.2	2.8
9.6	17.8	5.9					Trade Payables	14.9	10.4
1.7	.1	.6					Income Taxes Payable	1.3	1.0
20.4	16.4	21.0					All Other Current	16.1	22.5
41.6	49.4	34.9					Total Current	42.3	46.4
6.8	18.0	15.4					Long Term Debt	19.6	16.3
.0	3.5	.0					Deferred Taxes	.1	.4
5.6	5.6	8.9					All Other-Non-Current	6.5	5.0
46.1	23.5	40.9					Net Worth	31.5	31.9
100.0	100.0	100.0					Total Liabilities & Net Worth	100.0	100.0
							INCOME DATA		
100.0	100.0	100.0					Net Sales	100.0	100.0
							Gross Profit		
93.2	96.0	93.7					Operating Expenses	94.4	95.4
6.8	4.0	6.3					Operating Profit	5.6	4.6
.1	1.5	.7					All Other Expenses (net)	1.2	.0
6.6	2.5	5.6					Profit Before Taxes	4.5	4.5
							RATIOS		
3.4	2.4	1.8						1.7	1.6
1.3	.8	.8					Current	.9	.9
.6	.3	.4						.6	.4
3.0	2.2	1.7						1.4	1.6
1.2	.6	.7					Quick	.6	.6
.4	.2	.3						.3	.3
0 UND	2 240.0	7 50.1						1 404.6	2 181.7
2 181.7	20 18.4	17 20.9					Sales/Receivables	10 36.8	9 40.0
61 6.0	33 10.9	57 6.4						30 12.3	65 5.6
							Cost of Sales/Inventory		
							Cost of Sales/Payables		
11.3	15.6	3.6						12.0	8.1
54.7	−26.5	−40.9					Sales/Working Capital	−68.7	−71.6
−171.5	−6.1	−4.0						−13.5	−8.4
	(18) 6.8	(13) 9.5						(25) 8.4	(29) 4.8
	1.3	3.9					EBIT/Interest	2.8	1.8
	.3	−.4						−.2	−.3
							Net Profit + Depr., Dep., Amort./Cur. Mat. L /T/D		
.3	.8	.7						.6	.6
.7	2.1	1.3					Fixed/Worth	1.1	1.2
1.1	8.4	2.6						2.3	5.8
.6	.9	.7						1.1	.9
1.0	2.9	1.5					Debt/Worth	2.0	2.3
3.5	13.2	3.2						6.3	9.0
65.0	(17) 115.1	(16) 44.2					% Profit Before Taxes/Tangible	(27) 78.6	(29) 47.2
31.7	9.7	2.9					Net Worth	24.2	17.5
5.8	−2.3	−14.8						7.8	.5
27.0	13.3	17.5					% Profit Before Taxes/Total	23.5	13.8
16.3	1.3	1.6					Assets	8.1	3.7
1.5	−2.0	−2.7						−1.4	−3.6
60.8	25.3	2.8						21.0	23.4
19.2	11.7	1.5					Sales/Net Fixed Assets	10.4	12.3
6.7	1.7	.8						2.4	1.5
10.2	3.2	1.4						4.8	3.2
4.2	2.3	.8					Sales/Total Assets	2.4	2.0
2.7	.9	.4						1.2	.7
(11) .5	(19) .8	(16) 3.4						(31) 1.1	(32) .8
3.1	2.8	6.9					% Depr., Dep., Amort./Sales	1.9	1.6
3.8	8.4	9.1						6.4	4.4
									(10) 2.6
							% Officers', Directors',		4.7
							Owners' Comp/Sales		12.1
14677M	69686M	85793M	78184M				Net Sales ($)	163282M	251515M
3289M	20701M	86128M	151405M				Total Assets ($)	71629M	182794M

M = $ thousand   MM = $ million
See Pages 1 through 15 for Explanation of Ratios and Data

Comparative Historical Data				Current Data Sorted By Sales					
1	4	3	**# Postretirement Benefits** / Type of Statement			3			
16	20	22	Unqualified	3	7	5	4	2	1
4	7	7	Reviewed	2	3		1		1
11	13	12	Compiled	5	3	2	1	1	
2	1	2	Tax Returns	1	1				
10	14	16	Other	5	6	2	2	1	
4/1/92-3/31/93 ALL	4/1/93-3/31/94 ALL	4/1/94-3/31/95 ALL		45 (4/1-9/30/94)			14 (10/1/94-3/31/95)		
				0-1MM	1-3MM	3-5MM	5-10MM	10-25MM	25MM & OVER
43	55	59	**NUMBER OF STATEMENTS**	16	20	9	8	4	2
%	%	%	**ASSETS**	%	%	%	%	%	%
14.0	22.8	18.0	Cash & Equivalents	15.2	19.7				
14.2	14.1	15.5	Trade Receivables - (net)	16.6	13.7				
1.8	4.4	3.0	Inventory	.0	8.2				
1.6	2.7	3.4	All Other Current	2.6	.9				
31.6	44.0	39.8	Total Current	34.5	42.5				
46.2	42.1	41.3	Fixed Assets (net)	49.5	39.2				
1.7	1.4	1.8	Intangibles (net)	3.8	1.2				
20.5	12.5	17.1	All Other Non-Current	12.2	17.1				
100.0	100.0	100.0	Total	100.0	100.0				
			LIABILITIES						
10.6	7.4	4.8	Notes Payable-Short Term	4.4	3.2				
4.7	2.9	5.2	Cur. Mat.-L./T/D	5.4	3.5				
9.4	9.9	10.5	Trade Payables	7.0	10.6				
.1	1.0	.7	Income Taxes Payable	1.7	.1				
14.7	15.5	19.3	All Other Current	13.0	19.4				
39.5	36.7	40.4	Total Current	31.5	36.9				
15.7	12.4	12.9	Long Term Debt	20.0	13.6				
2.3	.9	1.3	Deferred Taxes	.0	.1				
10.3	7.1	6.0	All Other-Non-Current	7.5	1.3				
32.1	42.9	39.5	Net Worth	41.0	48.1				
100.0	100.0	100.0	Total Liabilities & Net Worth	100.0	100.0				
			INCOME DATA						
100.0	100.0	100.0	Net Sales	100.0	100.0				
			Gross Profit						
93.7	94.0	95.8	Operating Expenses	91.9	93.2				
6.3	6.1	4.2	Operating Profit	8.1	6.8				
.3	.8	.2	All Other Expenses (net)	2.8	.9				
6.0	5.3	4.0	Profit Before Taxes	5.3	5.9				
			RATIOS						
1.8	3.6	2.0		1.7	1.9				
.6	1.1	1.0	Current	1.1	1.1				
.2	.6	.5		.2	.6				
1.8	3.5	1.7		1.7	1.8				
.6	.9	.8	Quick	.9	.8				
.1	.5	.4		.2	.4				
1 656.5	1 545.0	1 401.8		0 UND	0 UND				
10 36.4	9 42.1	14 25.9	Sales/Receivables	3 125.1	16 23.4				
47 7.8	41 9.0	39 9.4		52 7.0	28 13.2				
			Cost of Sales/Inventory						
			Cost of Sales/Payables						
15.4	6.3	6.5		10.7	5.5				
-29.5	28.7	UND	Sales/Working Capital	92.3	236.2				
-6.2	-15.4	-9.3		-11.1	-9.4				
(33) 6.8	(39) 10.0	(42) 8.8		(11) 6.5	(15) 10.5				
2.5	2.8	1.9	EBIT/Interest	1.1	6.3				
1.2	1.1	.3		.6	1.0				
(12) 1.7	(14) 22.6	(16) 6.0							
1.3	4.3	1.3	Net Profit + Depr., Dep., Amort./Cur. Mat. L/T/D						
-1.1	1.9	.5							
.4	.4	.5		.7	.4				
1.4	1.1	1.0	Fixed/Worth	1.5	.9				
3.2	1.6	2.5		2.5	1.4				
1.0	.4	.5		.7	.4				
2.0	1.3	1.3	Debt/Worth	1.3	1.2				
6.9	3.8	4.3		4.4	3.6				
(38) 39.8	(50) 50.2	(55) 53.3		(15) 67.4	44.4				
13.5	9.9	5.7	% Profit Before Taxes/Tangible Net Worth	23.5	8.2				
.0	.6	-1.5		-4.3	.0				
9.7	16.0	17.7		22.7	15.9				
3.7	5.1	2.2	% Profit Before Taxes/Total Assets	3.4	2.9				
.0	.2	-1.1		-2.0	-.1				
23.0	39.4	22.9		46.6	24.1				
5.0	4.5	6.5	Sales/Net Fixed Assets	6.6	6.0				
2.3	1.6	1.1		.5	.8				
3.3	4.0	3.7		4.3	3.6				
1.9	1.8	1.9	Sales/Total Assets	1.6	1.3				
.7	.7	.6		.4	.4				
(39) 1.0	(42) 1.3	(52) 1.3		(12) 3.1	(19) 1.2				
2.7	3.8	3.3	% Depr., Dep., Amort./Sales	6.5	3.1				
5.5	9.1	8.1		11.4	8.4				
(14) 4.7	(13) 3.2	(15) 4.2							
7.2	7.3	8.3	% Officers', Directors', Owners' Comp/Sales						
21.4	23.0	29.9							
276160M	496320M	248340M	Net Sales ($)	8311M	35102M	32389M	51212M	60412M	60914M
272209M	497829M	261523M	Total Assets ($)	8804M	68641M	15240M	75658M	79191M	13989M

M = $ thousand   MM = $ million
See Pages 1 through 15 for Explanation of Ratios and Data

Current Data Sorted By Assets							# Postretirement Benefits	Comparative Historical Data	
1			4	1			**Type of Statement**		
	1			2			Unqualified	1	4
1	6		4	2			Reviewed	2	9
5	18		4				Compiled	14	15
	2						Tax Returns		
5	4		2				Other	3	3
	23 (4/1-9/30/94)			33 (10/1/94-3/31/95)				4/1/90-3/31/91 ALL	4/1/91-3/31/92 ALL
0-500M	500M-2MM	2-10MM	10-50MM	50-100MM	100-250MM				
11	31	10	4				NUMBER OF STATEMENTS	20	31
%	%	%	%	%	%		**ASSETS**	%	%
10.2	7.4	10.4					Cash & Equivalents	7.0	6.0
16.7	26.4	29.9					Trade Receivables - (net)	31.1	29.2
31.5	29.3	27.4					Inventory	30.3	29.9
1.2	.6	.7					All Other Current	1.2	1.2
59.6	63.6	68.4					Total Current	69.6	66.3
33.4	29.4	25.0					Fixed Assets (net)	20.6	24.4
.3	1.5	.2					Intangibles (net)	4.2	.8
6.8	5.5	6.4					All Other Non-Current	5.6	8.5
100.0	100.0	100.0					Total	100.0	100.0
							LIABILITIES		
10.8	3.8	3.9					Notes Payable-Short Term	5.4	6.4
4.1	3.9	2.6					Cur. Mat. -L/T/D	3.5	5.8
19.0	26.3	27.6					Trade Payables	31.6	31.6
.9	.8	.5					Income Taxes Payable	.4	1.8
8.7	5.7	7.2					All Other Current	10.0	4.1
43.5	40.4	41.7					Total Current	50.9	49.7
24.2	18.2	11.6					Long Term Debt	18.9	21.8
.0	.2	.1					Deferred Taxes	.1	.0
.8	4.6	4.3					All Other-Non-Current	.0	2.0
31.6	36.6	42.3					Net Worth	30.0	26.6
100.0	100.0	100.0					Total Liabilities & Net Worth	100.0	100.0
							INCOME DATA		
100.0	100.0	100.0					Net Sales	100.0	100.0
							Gross Profit		
96.3	98.1	97.7					Operating Expenses	98.6	98.1
3.7	1.9	2.3					Operating Profit	1.4	1.9
.6	-.1	-.3					All Other Expenses (net)	.2	.7
3.2	2.0	2.6					Profit Before Taxes	1.2	1.1
							RATIOS		
2.0 / 1.9 / .7	2.1 / 1.6 / 1.3	1.9 / 1.7 / 1.3					Current	1.8 / 1.5 / 1.2	1.9 / 1.4 / 1.2
1.2 / .6 / .4	1.3 / .8 / .5	1.4 / 1.0 / .8					Quick	1.0 / .8 / .5	1.0 / .7 / .5
4　83.6 / 19　18.8 / 48　7.6	31　11.9 / 39　9.4 / 51　7.2	25　14.7 / 41　9.0 / 57　6.4					Sales/Receivables	27　13.7 / 35　10.3 / 54　6.7	36　10.1 / 43　8.4 / 59　6.2
							Cost of Sales/Inventory		
							Cost of Sales/Payables		
10.5 / 15.3 / -41.5	6.8 / 11.9 / 19.8	7.4 / 10.3 / 18.8					Sales/Working Capital	9.4 / 12.2 / 30.1	7.5 / 12.0 / 28.5
	(30) 6.4 / 3.2 / .8	12.7 / 4.1 / 2.3					EBIT/Interest	(19) 5.2 / 2.6 / .9	(29) 3.0 / 1.6 / .3
	(12) 3.7 / 1.6 / 1.3						Net Profit + Depr., Dep., Amort./Cur. Mat. L./T/D	(12) 8.0 / 2.3 / 1.0	(16) 2.4 / .8 / .2
.3 / 1.2 / 2.1	.4 / .8 / 1.6	.2 / .6 / 1.0					Fixed/Worth	.3 / .7 / 2.4	.4 / .6 / 2.3
.7 / 2.6 / 4.5	1.0 / 2.0 / 4.1	.8 / 1.3 / 2.8					Debt/Worth	1.2 / 2.3 / 7.0	1.2 / 2.3 / 8.2
	(29) 30.2 / 7.8 / 1.3	31.3 / 14.8 / 5.8					% Profit Before Taxes/Tangible Net Worth	(16) 32.4 / 16.0 / 7.4	(27) 17.4 / 6.4 / -6.7
17.9 / 11.6 / 4.3	8.4 / 3.4 / .0	9.3 / 4.4 / 2.5					% Profit Before Taxes/Total Assets	9.3 / 5.7 / -.4	6.3 / 2.4 / -3.0
30.4 / 15.3 / 6.0	16.8 / 10.7 / 6.1	22.8 / 19.7 / 6.6					Sales/Net Fixed Assets	25.1 / 14.3 / 8.5	21.8 / 13.9 / 6.1
4.8 / 3.7 / 2.2	2.9 / 2.4 / 2.0	3.4 / 2.7 / 2.0					Sales/Total Assets	3.5 / 2.8 / 1.9	3.0 / 2.3 / 1.7
.8 / 1.4 / 5.3	(27) 1.4 / 2.2 / 2.6						% Depr., Dep., Amort./Sales	(19) 1.1 / 1.5 / 2.2	1.2 / 2.0 / 2.7
	(18) 2.6 / 4.0 / 7.2						% Officers', Directors', Owners' Comp/Sales		(15) 2.7 / 4.7 / 7.3
10260M	81151M	103567M	293017M				Net Sales ($)	59577M	276507M
3120M	34082M	39168M	112730M				Total Assets ($)	23784M	147950M

M = $ thousand　　MM = $ million
See Pages 1 through 15 for Explanation of Ratios and Data

Comparative Historical Data				Current Data Sorted By Sales					
1	1	6	# Postretirement Benefits		1		1	3	1
			Type of Statement						
			Unqualified		1				
2	6	3	Reviewed	1	5	1	2	2	2
5	6	13	Compiled	3	14	5	2	3	2
18	16	27	Tax Returns		2				
1	3	2	Other	3	5	2	1		
6	6	11							
4/1/92-3/31/93 ALL	4/1/93-3/31/94 ALL	4/1/94-3/31/95 ALL		23 (4/1-9/30/94)		33 (10/1/94-3/31/95)			
				0-1MM	1-3MM	3-5MM	5-10MM	10-25MM	25MM & OVER
32	37	56	**NUMBER OF STATEMENTS**	7	27	8	5	5	4
%	%	%	**ASSETS**	%	%	%	%	%	%
6.2	7.5	8.5	Cash & Equivalents		8.4				
27.4	29.0	25.5	Trade Receivables - (net)		24.3				
30.6	30.5	29.9	Inventory		28.6				
1.5	1.1	.7	All Other Current		.4				
65.7	68.1	64.6	Total Current		61.7				
28.8	23.9	28.6	Fixed Assets (net)		30.2				
1.4	2.0	1.1	Intangibles (net)		1.8				
4.2	6.0	5.8	All Other Non-Current		6.3				
100.0	100.0	100.0	Total		100.0				
			LIABILITIES						
4.2	5.5	5.5	Notes Payable-Short Term		2.8				
6.0	3.8	3.6	Cur. Mat.-L /T/D		4.3				
28.0	28.7	25.6	Trade Payables		27.0				
.6	1.5	.7	Income Taxes Payable		1.2				
5.7	5.2	6.5	All Other Current		5.5				
44.5	44.6	42.0	Total Current		40.8				
20.9	16.2	17.7	Long Term Debt		17.1				
.4	.2	.2	Deferred Taxes		.2				
.9	2.2	3.5	All Other-Non-Current		4.6				
33.3	36.8	36.7	Net Worth		37.4				
100.0	100.0	100.0	Total Liabilities & Net Worth		100.0				
			INCOME DATA						
100.0	100.0	100.0	Net Sales		100.0				
			Gross Profit						
97.2	97.7	97.6	Operating Expenses		98.3				
2.8	2.3	2.4	Operating Profit		1.7				
.5	.4	.0	All Other Expenses (net)		−.2				
2.2	1.9	2.4	Profit Before Taxes		1.9				
			RATIOS						
2.2	2.0	2.0			2.0				
1.6	1.6	1.6	Current		1.4				
1.1	1.2	1.3			1.1				
1.1	1.1	1.3			1.1				
.8	.8	.8	Quick		.7				
.6	.8	.5			.5				
23 16.2	31 11.7	26 14.2			26 13.8				
35 10.5	41 8.8	38 9.7	Sales/Receivables		36 10.2				
57 6.4	49 7.4	51 7.2			52 7.0				
			Cost of Sales/Inventory						
			Cost of Sales/Payables						
6.5	6.9	7.0			6.8				
9.8	11.2	12.1	Sales/Working Capital		12.7				
71.0	26.9	19.6			29.6				
5.4	7.2	9.5			9.5				
2.6	(34) 3.5	(53) 3.9	EBIT/Interest		(25) 3.4				
1.1	1.6	1.8			.6				
3.4	3.1	3.8			2.9				
(17) 1.0	(17) 1.7	(23) 2.0	Net Profit + Depr., Dep., Amort./Cur. Mat. L/T/D		(13) 1.6				
.5	1.0	1.4			1.2				
.4	.4	.4			.3				
.7	.6	.8	Fixed/Worth		.9				
1.7	1.3	1.6			2.3				
.9	1.2	.9			.8				
1.9	1.9	2.0	Debt/Worth		2.0				
3.8	3.4	3.7			4.5				
32.1	27.8	31.9			38.0				
(30) 8.2	12.5	(52) 17.5	% Profit Before Taxes/Tangible Net Worth		(25) 8.9				
.9	6.1	4.6			1.3				
7.9	8.9	9.6			8.5				
4.0	4.5	5.8	% Profit Before Taxes/Total Assets		3.4				
.1	1.4	1.6			.0				
17.4	23.2	19.8			17.5				
9.6	14.5	12.8	Sales/Net Fixed Assets		10.7				
6.4	8.1	6.3			6.0				
3.3	3.1	3.2			3.1				
2.5	2.6	2.6	Sales/Total Assets		2.6				
2.1	2.1	2.1			2.0				
1.2	1.3	1.2			1.2				
(31) 1.9	(35) 1.9	(50) 1.9	% Depr., Dep., Amort./Sales		(25) 1.9				
2.7	2.4	2.5			2.9				
2.8	2.3	2.7			3.2				
(17) 4.0	(17) 3.1	(32) 3.9	% Officers', Directors', Owners' Comp/Sales		(14) 4.1				
4.8	4.0	6.7			7.1				
386638M	461205M	487995M	Net Sales ($)	3694M	55974M	29831M	35643M	69836M	293017M
184394M	170691M	189100M	Total Assets ($)	1634M	24243M	12145M	12614M	25734M	112730M

M = $ thousand   MM = $ million
See Pages 1 through 15 for Explanation of Ratios and Data

Current Data Sorted By Assets   Comparative Historical Data

		2		3		2		1	# Postretirement Benefits		

Type of Statement

0-500M	500M-2MM	2-10MM	10-50MM	50-100MM	100-250MM		4/1/90-3/31/91 ALL	4/1/91-3/31/92 ALL
1		2	10	2	1	Unqualified	11	7
2	4	1	1			Reviewed	8	11
3	7	4				Compiled	13	22
8	3	1				Tax Returns	1	2
	5	2	5			Other	11	6

Date ranges: **13 (4/1-9/30/94)**   **49 (10/1/94-3/31/95)**

0-500M	500M-2MM	2-10MM	10-50MM	50-100MM	100-250MM		4/1/90-3/31/91 ALL	4/1/91-3/31/92 ALL
14	19	10	16	2	1	**NUMBER OF STATEMENTS**	44	48
%	%	%	%	%	%	**ASSETS**	%	%
18.8	6.5	9.6	4.9			Cash & Equivalents	9.7	7.9
17.5	24.6	27.1	14.1			Trade Receivables - (net)	20.1	18.9
.9	.1	.4	.5			Inventory	2.0	1.7
5.9	.8	1.3	2.0			All Other Current	1.9	.6
43.2	32.0	38.3	21.5			Total Current	33.7	29.2
30.3	53.7	39.4	67.9			Fixed Assets (net)	53.9	55.9
6.6	.0	4.4	1.2			Intangibles (net)	.9	.8
19.9	14.2	17.9	9.4			All Other Non-Current	11.5	14.1
100.0	100.0	100.0	100.0			Total	100.0	100.0
						LIABILITIES		
4.4	13.5	2.2	.9			Notes Payable-Short Term	6.5	9.1
9.9	10.0	6.1	6.6			Cur. Mat. -L/T/D	7.2	8.9
6.6	10.3	11.3	8.7			Trade Payables	9.8	6.2
.4	.6	2.5	.4			Income Taxes Payable	.4	1.0
10.1	9.7	13.1	7.2			All Other Current	9.9	8.5
31.4	44.2	35.1	23.7			Total Current	33.8	33.7
20.4	25.9	19.7	34.8			Long Term Debt	31.9	31.7
.0	1.0	2.0	3.4			Deferred Taxes	1.6	.8
7.2	2.3	.2	2.7			All Other-Non-Current	1.3	4.6
40.9	26.7	42.9	35.5			Net Worth	31.4	29.3
100.0	100.0	100.0	100.0			Total Liabilities & Net Worth	100.0	100.0
						INCOME DATA		
100.0	100.0	100.0	100.0			Net Sales	100.0	100.0
						Gross Profit		
88.5	89.4	95.0	88.2			Operating Expenses	88.6	85.4
11.5	10.6	5.0	11.8			Operating Profit	11.4	14.6
.6	2.3	-2.1	2.7			All Other Expenses (net)	3.0	5.2
10.9	8.4	7.1	9.2			Profit Before Taxes	8.4	9.4
						RATIOS		
7.9	1.2	2.2	1.4				1.7	1.4
2.2	.9	1.2	1.1			Current	1.0	.8
.8	.4	.9	.7				.5	.5
7.7	1.2	2.0	1.3				1.5	1.4
2.2	.9	1.1	1.0			Quick	.8	.7
.5	.3	.7	.6				.4	.5
0 UND	24 15.1	41 8.9	45 8.2				20 17.9	24 15.1
0 UND	45 8.2	60 6.1	49 7.4			Sales/Receivables	39 9.3	40 9.1
30 12.1	66 5.5	79 4.6	57 6.4				60 6.1	59 6.2
						Cost of Sales/Inventory		
						Cost of Sales/Payables		
7.8	55.9	6.0	12.6				12.0	19.0
19.7	-41.0	NM	76.8			Sales/Working Capital	NM	-25.0
-57.1	-5.1	-30.9	-12.0				-10.2	-9.4
(11) 28.0	(16) 7.4		5.8				(43) 5.1	(43) 6.8
14.8	1.9		4.1			EBIT/Interest	3.2	3.0
3.2	.2		1.7				1.6	1.7
			(11) 2.7			Net Profit + Depr., Dep.,	(26) 3.6	(22) 4.6
			2.2			Amort./Cur. Mat. L /T/D	2.3	1.9
			1.6				1.2	1.1
.2	1.3	.5	1.7				1.0	1.1
.3	2.3	.8	2.1			Fixed/Worth	1.7	2.1
2.0	4.0	2.0	2.5				5.2	4.7
.3	1.4	.7	1.2				1.0	1.5
1.8	3.2	1.4	1.8			Debt/Worth	2.0	3.2
4.3	5.8	2.7	2.6				5.3	5.2
(12) 180.5	(18) 47.4		29.6			% Profit Before Taxes/Tangible	(40) 63.7	(42) 58.1
35.7	14.4		21.8			Net Worth	31.6	36.5
19.2	-20.4		8.1				6.1	22.0
49.5	18.9	18.5	13.9			% Profit Before Taxes/Total	20.3	22.2
16.1	5.3	9.1	9.5			Assets	10.5	10.8
6.5	-5.2	3.3	2.6				2.5	4.1
307.0	6.1	7.5	1.9				7.9	6.6
13.4	2.9	4.1	1.6			Sales/Net Fixed Assets	2.6	2.4
5.2	1.1	2.9	1.3				1.4	1.3
5.3	2.2	2.0	1.1				2.7	2.3
3.0	1.7	1.5	1.0			Sales/Total Assets	1.4	1.4
2.2	.9	1.2	.9				.9	.9
(10) .9	(17) 2.6		5.4			% Depr., Dep., Amort./Sales	(41) 2.2	(45) 3.6
2.0	4.7		8.9				5.3	6.5
4.0	12.3		10.6				8.6	10.8
	(10) 2.8					% Officers', Directors',		(10) 3.2
	7.4					Owners' Comp/Sales		7.8
	24.1							13.0
13060M	35379M	65191M	376959M	102476M	132956M	Net Sales ($)	799855M	305781M
3484M	21930M	39237M	356852M	126790M	111007M	Total Assets ($)	480345M	277395M

M = $ thousand   MM = $ million
See Pages 1 through 15 for Explanation of Ratios and Data

Comparative Historical Data / Current Data Sorted By Sales

3	2	8	# Postretirement Benefits	1	1	1	2	2	1
			Type of Statement						
14	17	16	Unqualified		1	1		7	7
13	10	8	Reviewed		5	2	1		
15	11	14	Compiled	3	7	3	1		
3	10	12	Tax Returns	11		1			
11	13	12	Other	2	3		1	3	3
4/1/92-3/31/93 ALL	4/1/93-3/31/94 ALL	4/1/94-3/31/95 ALL		13 (4/1-9/30/94)		49 (10/1/94-3/31/95)			
				0-1MM	1-3MM	3-5MM	5-10MM	10-25MM	25MM & OVER
56	61	62	**NUMBER OF STATEMENTS**	16	16	6	4	10	10
%	%	%	**ASSETS**	%	%	%	%	%	%
8.6	9.6	9.2	Cash & Equivalents	16.9	6.8			5.9	4.3
17.5	15.7	20.1	Trade Receivables - (net)	14.3	22.3			17.1	12.7
.6	1.8	.5	Inventory	.8	.1			.2	1.0
3.1	2.0	2.3	All Other Current	1.1	4.8			2.3	.9
29.9	29.1	32.1	Total Current	33.2	34.0			25.6	18.9
54.7	53.6	50.9	Fixed Assets (net)	44.0	50.4			65.6	67.9
1.5	2.1	2.5	Intangibles (net)	5.8	.0			.6	1.2
13.9	15.3	14.5	All Other Non-Current	17.0	15.6			8.2	12.1
100.0	100.0	100.0	Total	100.0	100.0			100.0	100.0
			LIABILITIES						
9.1	5.5	5.7	Notes Payable-Short Term	5.7	8.3			1.4	1.0
7.5	7.6	8.3	Cur. Mat.-L /T/D	7.2	13.5			7.0	5.2
7.3	8.1	9.1	Trade Payables	3.1	11.1			9.0	9.6
.5	.9	.8	Income Taxes Payable	.4	.9			.9	.6
7.6	7.1	9.4	All Other Current	6.1	18.4			7.5	7.0
32.0	29.2	33.3	Total Current	22.4	52.2			25.7	23.3
31.9	23.4	26.2	Long Term Debt	28.4	20.3			34.1	31.4
1.1	1.9	1.7	Deferred Taxes	.1	1.0			2.7	3.6
1.0	4.2	3.2	All Other-Non-Current	6.9	2.1			.8	4.3
34.0	41.2	35.7	Net Worth	42.1	24.5			36.7	37.4
100.0	100.0	100.0	Total Liabilities & Net Worth	100.0	100.0			100.0	100.0
			INCOME DATA						
100.0	100.0	100.0	Net Sales	100.0	100.0			100.0	100.0
			Gross Profit						
91.2	91.0	89.8	Operating Expenses	84.4	92.9			87.4	92.7
8.8	9.0	10.2	Operating Profit	15.6	7.1			12.6	7.3
3.9	.9	1.4	All Other Expenses (net)	3.0	.9			3.3	1.8
4.8	8.1	8.8	Profit Before Taxes	12.6	6.1			9.3	5.6
			RATIOS						
1.8 / 1.0 / .5	1.7 / .9 / .6	1.7 / 1.1 / .7	Current	6.5 / 1.9 / .7	1.1 / .7 / .2			1.4 / 1.1 / .9	1.3 / .9 / .6
1.5 / .9 / .4	1.6 / .7 / .5	1.5 / 1.0 / .5	Quick	6.5 / 1.9 / .6	1.0 / .5 / .2			1.3 / 1.0 / .7	1.2 / .8 / .5
21 17.3 / 43 8.4 / 69 5.3	6 63.2 / 41 8.9 / 56 6.5	25 14.8 / 46 7.9 / 60 6.1	Sales/Receivables	0 UND / 0 UND / 81 4.5	20 18.0 / 33 11.2 / 50 7.3			41 9.0 / 51 7.2 / 61 6.0	40 9.2 / 48 7.6 / 51 7.2
			Cost of Sales/Inventory						
			Cost of Sales/Payables						
11.8 / -248.0 / -7.6	13.5 / -58.4 / -11.1	10.2 / 100.6 / -13.2	Sales/Working Capital	5.7 / 17.5 / -34.5	70.8 / -28.1 / -6.0			10.1 / NM / -51.7	27.4 / NM / -8.6
(49) 6.3 / 2.0 / .5	(56) 10.9 / 3.4 / 2.0	(55) 8.8 / 4.1 / 1.2	EBIT/Interest	(12) 26.3 / 7.1 / 1.2	(14) 8.3 / 1.9 / .4			6.2 / 3.2 / 1.6	6.2 / 3.3 / .9
(25) 2.1 / 1.3 / .7	(28) 3.1 / 2.2 / 1.0	(28) 3.9 / 2.0 / .9	Net Profit + Depr., Dep., Amort./Cur. Mat. L/T/D						
1.0 / 2.0 / 5.1	.8 / 1.4 / 3.5	.7 / 1.8 / 2.8	Fixed/Worth	.3 / 1.0 / 3.7	1.3 / 2.4 / 3.2			1.5 / 1.9 / 2.8	1.2 / 2.2 / 2.8
.9 / 1.7 / 5.8	.6 / 1.3 / 3.9	1.0 / 1.9 / 4.2	Debt/Worth	.4 / 1.6 / 6.1	1.6 / 3.2 / 4.7			1.1 / 1.6 / 3.5	1.1 / 1.9 / 2.9
(48) 35.6 / 16.3 / 4.1	(55) 42.7 / 24.8 / 10.9	(58) 41.0 / 24.2 / 5.8	% Profit Before Taxes/Tangible Net Worth	(15) 82.1 / 24.4 / 7.7	(14) 68.4 / 14.4 / -20.4			33.2 / 20.0 / 5.8	26.7 / 19.4 / -5.2
11.6 / 4.3 / -1.3	19.8 / 7.6 / 3.4	18.4 / 8.8 / .9	% Profit Before Taxes/Total Assets	32.6 / 14.5 / .8	16.3 / 5.5 / -4.4			15.1 / 7.2 / 1.9	11.5 / 7.4 / -.6
6.3 / 2.4 / 1.4	6.6 / 2.9 / 1.4	7.8 / 3.0 / 1.6	Sales/Net Fixed Assets	13.4 / 5.0 / .9	9.4 / 4.0 / 2.1			3.0 / 1.8 / .9	1.8 / 1.6 / 1.3
2.2 / 1.4 / .9	2.7 / 1.4 / 1.0	2.5 / 1.6 / 1.1	Sales/Total Assets	2.9 / 2.0 / .6	4.0 / 2.0 / 1.6			1.8 / 1.1 / .7	1.2 / 1.1 / 1.0
(53) 2.3 / 5.4 / 8.0	(58) 3.1 / 5.2 / 8.7	(55) 2.5 / 4.8 / 10.0	% Depr., Dep., Amort./Sales	(13) 1.7 / 3.5 / 16.3	(14) 2.3 / 4.6 / 7.3			4.5 / 7.0 / 12.2	5.0 / 8.9 / 10.6
(20) 3.6 / 5.7 / 10.9	(22) 4.3 / 5.4 / 11.1	(27) 3.6 / 5.4 / 19.5	% Officers', Directors', Owners' Comp/Sales		(10) 3.3 / 10.1 / 26.3				
488340M	662179M	726021M	Net Sales ($)	9571M	33705M	23912M	30011M	155794M	473028M
402714M	563259M	659300M	Total Assets ($)	9117M	16823M	15785M	22143M	178033M	417399M

M = $ thousand   MM = $ million
See Pages 1 through 15 for Explanation of Ratios and Data

	Current Data Sorted By Assets							Comparative Historical Data	
			3	4		1	# Postretirement Benefits / Type of Statement		
	9	24	21	6		1	Unqualified		15
	1	2	1	1			Reviewed		2
	3	2	1				Compiled		2
	1	1					Tax Returns		
	4	8	13	4			Other		6
	65 (4/1-9/30/94)			38 (10/1/94-3/31/95)				4/1/90-3/31/91 ALL	4/1/91-3/31/92 ALL
	0-500M	500M-2MM	2-10MM	10-50MM	50-100MM	100-250MM			
	18	37	36	11		1	NUMBER OF STATEMENTS		25
	%	%	%	%	%	%	ASSETS	%	%
	17.3	13.2	13.4	8.3			Cash & Equivalents		9.6
	24.2	26.3	24.6	24.1			Trade Receivables - (net)	D A T A	28.9
	3.7	3.6	2.6	2.2			Inventory		4.3
	7.4	3.1	2.3	5.1			All Other Current		2.9
	52.6	46.3	43.0	39.8			Total Current		45.7
	34.2	44.3	46.7	42.0			Fixed Assets (net)	N O T	40.3
	.8	1.3	1.1	.7			Intangibles (net)		2.4
	12.3	8.1	9.2	17.5			All Other Non-Current		11.6
	100.0	100.0	100.0	100.0			Total	A V A I L A B L E	100.0
							LIABILITIES		
	8.6	3.7	4.0	2.7			Notes Payable-Short Term		6.7
	2.6	2.6	2.4	1.7			Cur. Mat. -L/T/D		2.9
	2.6	9.4	8.4	5.5			Trade Payables		8.3
	.4	.3	.3	.1			Income Taxes Payable		1.1
	31.7	15.1	11.0	20.8			All Other Current		13.9
	45.9	31.1	26.2	30.8			Total Current		32.7
	14.3	15.3	18.2	18.1			Long Term Debt		19.2
	.3	.0	.0	.0			Deferred Taxes		.1
	3.7	4.2	3.4	4.0			All Other-Non-Current		8.1
	35.8	49.4	52.2	47.0			Net Worth		39.8
	100.0	100.0	100.0	100.0			Total Liabilities & Net Worth		100.0
							INCOME DATA		
	100.0	100.0	100.0	100.0			Net Sales		100.0
							Gross Profit		
	99.0	95.7	98.1	95.0			Operating Expenses		96.7
	1.0	4.3	1.9	5.0			Operating Profit		3.3
	.1	.5	−.3	−.3			All Other Expenses (net)		.6
	.9	3.8	2.2	5.3			Profit Before Taxes		2.7
							RATIOS		
	3.0	2.5	2.3	2.0					3.0
	1.2	1.4	1.9	1.7			Current		1.4
	.8	.9	1.1	.8					1.0
	2.3	2.0	2.1	1.7					2.4
	1.2	1.2	1.5	1.3			Quick		1.1
	.6	.8	1.0	.4					.7
	11 34.3	26 14.0	35 10.5	20 18.3				27 13.5	
	21 17.8	42 8.7	44 8.3	43 8.4			Sales/Receivables	41 9.0	
	33 11.1	66 5.5	55 6.6	74 4.9				66 5.5	
							Cost of Sales/Inventory		
							Cost of Sales/Payables		
	8.8	7.0	7.0	7.7					7.7
	51.0	15.3	10.8	15.3			Sales/Working Capital		16.4
	−45.1	−96.7	57.0	−24.4					NM
	4.8	9.6	7.4						3.5
	(11) 2.0	(30) 2.4	(33) 2.2				EBIT/Interest	(18) 2.1	
	−.3	.9	.5						.8
							Net Profit + Depr., Dep., Amort./Cur. Mat. L /T/D		
	.4	.5	.7	.5					.5
	.9	.9	.9	.8			Fixed/Worth		1.0
	UND	1.8	1.3	1.6					3.2
	.3	.4	.5	.6					.5
	1.2	1.0	.9	1.3			Debt/Worth		2.9
	UND	2.4	2.1	2.4					7.6
	30.6	27.8	20.2	34.2			% Profit Before Taxes/Tangible Net Worth		37.8
	(15) 1.4	(35) 7.5	4.6	11.4					6.1
	−19.3	−1.7	−.9	5.9					−1.6
	13.3	13.0	6.3	14.5			% Profit Before Taxes/Total Assets		9.0
	1.4	3.4	2.2	7.0					2.6
	−14.0	−.7	−.5	1.9					−1.1
	44.7	9.8	6.4	13.2					27.5
	12.6	4.5	4.1	1.8			Sales/Net Fixed Assets		5.0
	5.7	2.8	2.2	1.3					2.3
	6.3	2.5	2.3	2.5					3.1
	4.3	1.8	1.7	1.3			Sales/Total Assets		1.8
	2.1	1.5	1.2	.7					1.2
	1.0	1.7	1.8						1.5
	(11) 2.0	(36) 2.5	(35) 2.6				% Depr., Dep., Amort./Sales	(22) 2.5	
	4.3	3.7	3.4						3.7
							% Officers', Directors', Owners' Comp/Sales		
	14989M	86464M	282934M	360312M		126787M	Net Sales ($)		257143M
	4058M	43066M	162316M	184369M		146494M	Total Assets ($)		123445M

M = $ thousand   MM = $ million
See Pages 1 through 15 for Explanation of Ratios and Data

Comparative Historical Data				Current Data Sorted By Sales					
	4	7	# Postretirement Benefits	1	1	2	1	2	
			Type of Statement						
18	45	61	Unqualified	12	15	9	14	7	4
5	6	5	Reviewed	1	2			2	
3	1	6	Compiled	2	3	1			
1	1	2	Tax Returns	1	1				
16	23	29	Other	3	9	5	6	5	1
4/1/92-3/31/93 ALL	4/1/93-3/31/94 ALL	4/1/94-3/31/95 ALL		65 (4/1-9/30/94) 0-1MM	1-3MM	3-5MM	38 (10/1/94-3/31/95) 5-10MM	10-25MM	25MM & OVER
43	76	103	NUMBER OF STATEMENTS	19	30	14	21	14	5
%	%	%	ASSETS	%	%	%	%	%	%
15.3	14.0	13.4	Cash & Equivalents	15.7	13.0	13.0	16.9	7.6	
26.3	24.5	25.1	Trade Receivables - (net)	21.5	23.1	23.9	22.7	34.4	
3.5	2.4	3.1	Inventory	1.3	5.8	1.9	2.7	1.3	
1.9	5.3	3.8	All Other Current	6.4	3.0	1.2	4.9	3.8	
47.0	46.0	45.4	Total Current	45.1	44.9	39.9	47.2	47.1	
44.0	43.5	43.1	Fixed Assets (net)	41.1	46.8	44.1	45.3	42.2	
.6	.8	1.2	Intangibles (net)	.7	1.7	.1	.9	1.8	
8.4	9.6	10.2	All Other Non-Current	13.2	6.7	15.9	6.6	8.8	
100.0	100.0	100.0	Total	100.0	100.0	100.0	100.0	100.0	
			LIABILITIES						
3.6	5.4	4.5	Notes Payable-Short Term	5.6	4.7	3.5	5.7	3.3	
3.2	1.9	2.4	Cur. Mat.-L /T/D	2.1	3.6	2.5	1.8	1.8	
8.2	6.5	7.4	Trade Payables	3.7	5.7	9.8	8.4	11.6	
.2	1.3	.3	Income Taxes Payable	.3	.3	.8	.0	.0	
13.5	14.2	17.1	All Other Current	26.4	16.4	10.7	11.5	16.6	
28.8	29.3	31.7	Total Current	38.1	30.7	27.3	27.3	33.4	
21.6	18.5	16.6	Long Term Debt	16.8	14.4	16.2	21.0	16.1	
.0	.6	.1	Deferred Taxes	.1	.1	.1	.0	.0	
1.9	2.7	3.8	All Other-Non-Current	.8	5.4	3.9	1.5	7.7	
47.7	48.9	47.8	Net Worth	44.2	49.4	52.5	50.1	42.8	
100.0	100.0	100.0	Total Liabilities & Net Worth	100.0	100.0	100.0	100.0	100.0	
			INCOME DATA						
100.0	100.0	100.0	Net Sales	100.0	100.0	100.0	100.0	100.0	
			Gross Profit						
93.9	95.5	97.0	Operating Expenses	95.2	98.6	95.8	97.7	97.8	
6.1	4.5	3.0	Operating Profit	4.8	1.4	4.2	2.3	2.2	
1.2	.1	.1	All Other Expenses (net)	.9	.1	-1.0	.3	-.3	
4.9	4.4	2.9	Profit Before Taxes	4.0	1.4	5.2	2.0	2.5	
			RATIOS						
3.3	3.2	2.4		2.3	2.7	2.0	3.1	1.9	
1.7	1.6	1.6	Current	1.3	1.3	1.5	2.2	1.3	
1.1	1.1	1.0		.8	.9	1.2	1.1	1.1	
2.8	2.4	2.1		2.1	2.4	1.8	3.1	1.8	
1.4	1.4	1.3	Quick	1.2	1.1	1.3	1.8	1.2	
.8	.8	.8		.6	.8	1.2	.9	.7	
23 16.1	22 16.3	22 16.4		12 29.4	22 16.6	19 18.9	29 12.6	36 10.2	
34 10.7	39 9.4	41 8.8	Sales/Receivables	24 15.2	37 10.0	41 8.8	45 8.2	46 8.0	
57 6.4	58 6.3	56 6.5		56 6.5	51 7.1	51 7.1	57 6.4	63 5.8	
			Cost of Sales/Inventory						
			Cost of Sales/Payables						
7.3	4.7	7.7		7.2	8.3	10.6	3.7	10.2	
13.4	13.9	14.4	Sales/Working Capital	54.8	27.3	16.5	8.2	14.7	
81.4	84.5	552.0		-33.0	-73.9	34.4	87.3	NM	
(35) 13.3	(56) 9.4	(83) 8.2		(12) 5.1	(22) 4.6	(13) 12.7	(20) 3.8	(12) 6.3	
5.2	3.2	2.6	EBIT/Interest	2.1	1.9	8.7	2.1	2.4	
2.8	1.0	1.0		-1.5	-.4	2.6	.6	.6	
	(17) 6.4	(22) 6.5	Net Profit + Depr., Dep., Amort./Cur. Mat. L/T/D						
	.6	2.9							
	-.3	.7							
.4	.4	.5		.6	.5	.6	.5	.8	
1.0	.9	.9	Fixed/Worth	.9	1.0	.9	.9	1.0	
2.1	1.8	1.7		4.4	2.4	1.4	1.8	1.7	
.5	.5	.4		.4	.3	.4	.6	.7	
.9	1.0	1.0	Debt/Worth	1.0	.7	.7	.9	1.5	
3.1	2.0	2.5		4.9	3.1	1.8	2.3	3.1	
(40) 39.6	(71) 25.5	(98) 25.1	% Profit Before Taxes/Tangible Net Worth	(17) 31.3	(27) 15.8	48.7	25.2	14.8	
23.6	9.5	5.8		3.6	.8	18.5	3.3	7.4	
5.0	.7	-1.8		-8.9	-8.7	4.0	-1.5	-4.0	
19.2	13.5	10.2	% Profit Before Taxes/Total Assets	14.3	6.7	20.1	6.4	5.8	
5.6	4.4	2.5		1.9	1.4	11.1	2.0	3.0	
2.6	.1	-1.2		-5.5	-2.7	2.3	-.9	-1.8	
10.8	13.6	10.0		33.0	11.6	7.3	7.7	14.6	
3.8	4.4	4.8	Sales/Net Fixed Assets	5.9	4.6	3.8	4.3	5.6	
2.6	2.0	2.7		2.9	2.8	2.8	1.9	1.8	
3.1	2.7	2.6		4.7	2.7	2.6	2.2	2.7	
2.0	1.8	1.8	Sales/Total Assets	2.0	1.8	1.9	1.7	2.1	
1.4	1.2	1.3		.9	1.5	1.2	1.2	1.1	
(40) 1.5	(69) 1.7	(92) 1.8	% Depr., Dep., Amort./Sales	(14) 1.8	(28) 1.8	(12) 1.1	(20) 1.8	1.6	
2.7	2.8	2.5		3.3	2.5	2.3	2.8	2.4	
3.5	3.8	3.7		5.5	3.7	3.3	3.5	4.0	
	(15) 3.6	(16) 7.5	% Officers', Directors', Owners' Comp/Sales						
	6.1	10.0							
	20.9	14.2							
240445M	498144M	871486M	Net Sales ($)	11618M	59025M	57718M	149282M	203843M	390000M
144185M	259939M	540303M	Total Assets ($)	8562M	33082M	34369M	105502M	127078M	231710M

SERVICES—TRAVEL AGENCIES. SIC# 4724

	Current Data Sorted By Assets							Comparative Historical Data	
	5	1	3	3	1		# Postretirement Benefits		
							Type of Statement		
	2	3	10	5			Unqualified	15	13
	10	13	12	3	1		Reviewed	31	33
	48	18	6	1			Compiled	93	80
	18		2				Tax Returns	4	5
	20	8	5	1	1		Other	52	50
		58 (4/1-9/30/94)		129 (10/1/94-3/31/95)				4/1/90-3/31/91 ALL	4/1/91-3/31/92 ALL
	0-500M	500M-2MM	2-10MM	10-50MM	50-100MM	100-250MM	NUMBER OF STATEMENTS		
	98	42	35	10	2			195	181
	%	%	%	%	%	%	**ASSETS**	%	%
	30.1	19.1	22.0	32.3			Cash & Equivalents	22.9	23.2
	29.9	29.0	23.0	14.2			Trade Receivables - (net)	35.2	31.7
	.7	1.5	1.7	2.1			Inventory	.8	.4
	2.4	3.7	7.5	6.8			All Other Current	3.8	4.1
	63.1	53.4	54.2	55.4			Total Current	62.8	59.4
	17.2	22.2	23.9	17.4			Fixed Assets (net)	19.0	21.7
	7.2	9.3	6.5	.8			Intangibles (net)	6.1	5.8
	12.5	15.2	15.5	26.4			All Other Non-Current	12.2	13.1
	100.0	100.0	100.0	100.0			Total	100.0	100.0
							LIABILITIES		
	14.9	9.2	4.9	.9			Notes Payable-Short Term	12.9	13.9
	5.7	4.1	3.9	6.2			Cur. Mat. -L/T/D	3.3	3.2
	13.3	15.9	14.8	16.7			Trade Payables	16.3	16.2
	.5	.5	.4	.6			Income Taxes Payable	.7	.3
	16.2	18.5	27.4	38.1			All Other Current	18.5	18.2
	50.6	48.3	51.4	62.4			Total Current	51.8	51.7
	9.7	13.7	11.6	8.4			Long Term Debt	12.9	16.0
	.2	.2	.5	.6			Deferred Taxes	.2	.2
	1.8	3.4	4.5	1.3			All Other-Non-Current	3.8	3.8
	37.8	34.5	32.0	27.4			Net Worth	31.3	28.3
	100.0	100.0	100.0	100.0			Total Liabilities & Net Worth	100.0	100.0
							INCOME DATA		
	100.0	100.0	100.0	100.0			Net Sales	100.0	100.0
							Gross Profit		
	97.0	96.7	96.9	92.9			Operating Expenses	97.2	97.8
	3.0	3.3	3.1	7.1			Operating Profit	2.8	2.2
	.3	.7	-.1	-1.8			All Other Expenses (net)	.2	.4
	2.6	2.6	3.2	8.9			Profit Before Taxes	2.7	1.8
							RATIOS		
	2.5	1.5	1.5	1.4				2.2	2.0
	1.4	1.1	1.0	1.0			Current	1.2	1.2
	.8	.8	.7	.6				.9	.8
	2.3	1.3	1.2	1.2				2.0	1.8
	1.3	1.0	.8	.7		(194)	Quick	1.1	1.1
	.7	.7	.5	.4				.8	.7
1	278.8	5 75.9	4 82.0	3 139.3				6 59.9	6 62.6
8	45.5	12 29.5	29 12.8	10 35.7			Sales/Receivables	13 28.3	18 20.6
23	16.0	33 11.0	40 9.1	31 11.7				59 6.2	47 7.8
							Cost of Sales/Inventory		
							Cost of Sales/Payables		
	23.9	22.5	28.7	9.9				10.0	15.4
	123.0	230.3	-221.2	NM			Sales/Working Capital	81.3	135.8
	-166.0	-127.7	-21.6	-7.2				-128.9	-51.0
	12.0	10.3	15.8					8.1	6.9
(74)	4.7	(39) 4.8	(25) 5.0				EBIT/Interest	(156) 3.1	(148) 2.5
	1.3	1.7	1.6					1.2	.5
	2.8	5.4	11.3				Net Profit + Depr., Dep.,	6.6	3.9
(18)	1.6	(14) 2.3	(11) 2.3				Amort./Cur. Mat. L /T/D	(59) 2.6	(50) 1.9
	1.0	1.3	.6					1.2	.2
	.1	.3	.3	.2				.2	.2
	.4	.7	.9	.6			Fixed/Worth	.5	.7
	2.9	1.9	2.9	1.6				6.7	4.6
	.5	1.7	1.1	1.6				.8	1.1
	1.7	2.7	3.6	2.6			Debt/Worth	2.1	2.9
	10.4	5.4	18.4	6.4				30.3	30.5
	66.8	50.3	33.6	73.3			% Profit Before Taxes/Tangible	57.1	53.2
(81)	29.3	(40) 32.1	(30) 17.9	22.9			Net Worth	(155) 25.6	(145) 17.3
	6.3	6.0	10.3	5.7				5.1	.2
	28.1	16.2	9.7	21.1			% Profit Before Taxes/Total	20.3	14.4
	9.7	9.5	6.0	4.8			Assets	7.4	4.4
	1.4	2.3	2.5	1.9				1.3	-2.4
	381.1	125.4	119.8	53.7				136.8	148.1
	105.2	47.9	18.7	19.1			Sales/Net Fixed Assets	39.7	28.5
	28.4	13.6	8.5	4.9				11.5	11.9
	26.8	17.3	9.8	3.9				15.2	12.9
	11.4	4.8	3.0	1.2			Sales/Total Assets	4.1	3.7
	3.1	2.4	1.7	.8				2.0	2.1
	.2	.2	.2					.3	.3
(72)	.4	(35) .9	(33) 1.0				% Depr., Dep., Amort./Sales	(159) 1.0	(150) 1.0
	1.2	2.5	3.1					2.5	2.4
	1.5	1.5						1.1	1.6
(47)	5.4	(12) 3.2					% Officers', Directors',	(68) 3.7	(65) 6.3
	10.6	10.3					Owners' Comp/Sales	14.0	12.7
	308471M	374775M	912625M	768629M	404844M		Net Sales ($)	3740236M	1800057M
	21524M	40315M	147900M	205717M	114408M		Total Assets ($)	699238M	282316M

M = $ thousand   MM = $ million
See Pages 1 through 15 for Explanation of Ratios and Data

	Comparative Historical Data				Current Data Sorted By Sales					
# Postretirement Benefits	3	9	13		1	3	1	1	2	5
Type of Statement										
Unqualified	9	16	20			2	3	2	6	7
Reviewed	24	28	39		5	7	3	9	6	9
Compiled	68	73	73		18	25	7	12	10	1
Tax Returns	7	14	20		8	8	1	1	2	
Other	47	45	35		5	10	3	8	6	3
	4/1/92-3/31/93	4/1/93-3/31/94	4/1/94-3/31/95			58 (4/1-9/30/94)		129 (10/1/94-3/31/95)		
	ALL	ALL	ALL		0-1MM	1-3MM	3-5MM	5-10MM	10-25MM	25MM & OVER
NUMBER OF STATEMENTS	155	176	187		36	52	17	32	30	20
ASSETS	%	%	%		%	%	%	%	%	%
Cash & Equivalents	23.5	26.6	26.2		34.1	25.5	27.2	18.7	22.1	31.3
Trade Receivables - (net)	33.7	27.1	27.6		24.7	27.8	25.7	31.7	30.9	22.2
Inventory	1.6	1.7	1.1		.0	.4	2.7	2.7	1.7	.3
All Other Current	2.9	4.2	4.0		1.0	3.3	1.2	7.8	5.6	5.2
Total Current	61.8	59.6	59.0		59.8	57.1	56.8	60.9	60.4	58.9
Fixed Assets (net)	18.7	20.4	19.5		13.6	25.7	22.1	16.5	18.6	18.0
Intangibles (net)	6.9	7.9	7.1		8.2	5.5	5.8	8.2	9.6	5.1
All Other Non-Current	12.6	12.1	14.4		18.4	11.6	15.3	14.3	11.4	17.9
Total	100.0	100.0	100.0		100.0	100.0	100.0	100.0	100.0	100.0
LIABILITIES										
Notes Payable-Short Term	12.1	10.3	10.8		13.6	15.0	16.5	6.2	6.5	3.9
Cur. Mat.-L/T/D	3.4	3.1	5.0		2.0	8.6	5.6	5.4	3.1	2.7
Trade Payables	19.5	14.5	14.4		9.0	14.4	11.8	16.7	17.9	17.5
Income Taxes Payable	.9	1.4	.5		.4	.6	.3	.3	.5	.6
All Other Current	18.2	17.9	20.4		14.2	20.3	8.7	26.4	18.3	35.2
Total Current	54.0	47.3	51.1		39.3	59.0	43.0	54.9	46.4	59.9
Long Term Debt	10.4	12.0	10.9		12.3	11.7	16.1	7.3	8.0	12.1
Deferred Taxes	.2	.2	.3		.1	.0	.7	.2	.5	.6
All Other-Non-Current	4.0	4.1	2.6		.2	3.7	5.8	2.0	2.8	2.2
Net Worth	31.5	36.4	35.1		48.2	25.6	34.4	35.6	42.4	25.3
Total Liabilities & Net Worth	100.0	100.0	100.0		100.0	100.0	100.0	100.0	100.0	100.0
INCOME DATA										
Net Sales	100.0	100.0	100.0		100.0	100.0	100.0	100.0	100.0	100.0
Gross Profit										
Operating Expenses	97.4	96.7	96.7		94.1	96.8	97.6	97.1	97.8	98.5
Operating Profit	2.6	3.3	3.3		5.9	3.2	2.4	2.9	2.2	1.5
All Other Expenses (net)	.2	.7	.2		.9	.3	-.2	.0	-.2	-.1
Profit Before Taxes	2.4	2.6	3.0		5.0	2.9	2.6	2.9	2.3	1.6
RATIOS										
Current	2.0	2.2	1.9		3.6	1.6	3.1	1.8	1.9	1.3
	1.2	1.3	1.2		1.6	1.0	1.3	1.1	1.2	1.0
	.8	.9	.8		1.0	.5	.8	.8	.9	.7
Quick	1.9	2.0	1.7		3.5	1.5	2.5	1.7	1.6	1.2
	1.1	(175) 1.1	1.1		1.6	.8	1.2	1.1	1.1	.9
	.7	.7	.7		.9	.5	.7	.7	.8	.7
Sales/Receivables	7 55.8	3 110.2	4 101.3		7 49.6	2 233.1	3 115.8	4 87.4	3 111.3	4 100.3
	19 19.1	12 31.4	11 33.6		34 10.8	12 31.1	31 11.9	9 40.7	7 54.5	6 61.5
	58 6.3	43 8.4	32 11.4		72 5.1	25 14.8	45 8.2	35 10.3	23 16.1	10 37.3
Cost of Sales/Inventory										
Cost of Sales/Payables										
Sales/Working Capital	17.2	18.0	23.7		4.1	28.2	25.1	54.8	35.8	69.3
	106.6	78.3	146.1		14.7	-765.1	66.8	232.0	150.9	NM
	-45.7	-75.5	-51.7		UND	-26.5	-91.3	-42.8	-406.7	-35.9
EBIT/Interest	(122) 10.9	(126) 14.5	(144) 11.7		(25) 13.7	(44) 12.6	(15) 8.3	(27) 12.4	(21) 23.8	(12) 9.2
	2.9	5.0	4.8		3.0	5.5	3.9	5.0	6.6	4.7
	.3	1.7	1.6		1.1	1.5	1.3	2.2	2.4	1.8
Net Profit + Depr., Dep., Amort./Cur. Mat. L/T/D	(41) 10.1	(36) 8.0	(46) 4.9					(13) 11.1		
	3.4	2.1	1.8					2.2		
	1.2	1.0	.8					1.5		
Fixed/Worth	.2	.2	.2		.0	.2	.1	.3	.2	.4
	.6	.5	.6		.2	1.5	.5	.6	.4	1.5
	6.6	2.4	2.4		1.0	10.6	2.9	1.5	1.6	2.1
Debt/Worth	.8	.7	.8		.3	1.0	1.0	1.2	1.0	2.5
	2.7	2.0	2.5		.7	2.9	2.8	2.4	2.0	3.9
	77.2	10.5	6.9		5.9	15.1	22.9	6.7	4.7	18.8
% Profit Before Taxes/Tangible Net Worth	(120) 56.2	(145) 52.9	(163) 52.9		(31) 45.2	(41) 51.9	(15) 47.4	(30) 62.8	(28) 85.1	(18) 52.0
	18.1	28.0	22.2		17.2	34.9	12.1	24.5	23.1	21.0
	3.7	8.5	7.4		1.2	13.3	5.2	10.7	4.4	12.8
% Profit Before Taxes/Total Assets	16.3	20.1	19.7		28.2	26.5	19.1	13.5	19.9	7.8
	6.1	8.1	8.1		8.1	9.9	6.0	8.6	9.5	4.4
	-1.2	2.2	2.3		.7	3.5	1.7	1.7	1.8	2.5
Sales/Net Fixed Assets	115.8	161.9	189.8		143.4	182.0	196.4	279.4	243.3	162.6
	37.0	37.2	58.6		33.3	47.8	53.2	69.1	116.5	107.0
	13.9	13.3	15.9		16.1	13.2	4.4	13.5	18.3	29.2
Sales/Total Assets	15.3	16.0	20.9		4.0	18.1	28.2	23.3	29.9	17.8
	3.8	4.5	5.8		2.4	9.3	4.4	7.9	19.9	12.0
	2.2	2.4	2.4		1.6	3.0	1.8	2.5	3.2	5.2
% Depr., Dep., Amort./Sales	(128) .2	(139) .2	(151) .2		(24) .9	(42) .3	(13) .2	(27) .1	(26) .2	(19) .2
	.8	.8	.6		1.4	.7	1.4	.4	.3	.2
	2.3	2.0	2.0		2.0	2.5	4.9	1.1	1.9	.6
% Officers', Directors', Owners' Comp/Sales	(66) 2.3	(61) 1.8	(67) 1.5		(18) 5.9	(24) 1.8		(12) 1.1		
	6.9	3.4	4.9		8.9	4.7		1.5		
	12.1	8.7	9.3		23.0	11.0		4.2		
Net Sales ($)	1064165M	1699119M	2769344M		18214M	105063M	66097M	223014M	507656M	1849300M
Total Assets ($)	207751M	294800M	529864M		8502M	21470M	21793M	74190M	122384M	281525M

M = $ thousand   MM = $ million
See Pages 1 through 15 for Explanation of Ratios and Data

Current Data Sorted By Assets / Comparative Historical Data

Postretirement Benefits — Type of Statement

Type of Statement	0-500M	500M-2MM	2-10MM	10-50MM	50-100MM	100-250MM	4/1/90-3/31/91 ALL	4/1/91-3/31/92 ALL
Unqualified		1	7	4			39	30
Reviewed	5	2	9	19	5	4	39	41
Compiled	8	8	21	10			31	38
Tax Returns	4	15	12					2
Other	6	16	14	13	4		31	22

Period headers: 46 (4/1-9/30/94) covers 0-500M & 500M-2MM; 130 (10/1/94-3/31/95) covers 2-10MM through 100-250MM.

	0-500M	500M-2MM	2-10MM	10-50MM	50-100MM	100-250MM	4/1/90-3/31/91 ALL	4/1/91-3/31/92 ALL
NUMBER OF STATEMENTS	23	42	56	42	9	4	140	133
ASSETS	%	%	%	%	%	%	%	%
Cash & Equivalents	8.5	4.5	5.5	5.0			7.0	7.3
Trade Receivables - (net)	22.3	9.8	10.3	8.5			13.3	11.8
Inventory	.4	8.4	4.1	7.6			6.0	5.4
All Other Current	2.1	.7	3.6	1.0			2.3	2.7
Total Current	33.4	23.4	23.4	22.1			28.5	27.2
Fixed Assets (net)	59.8	63.0	63.3	64.9			61.2	61.3
Intangibles (net)	.3	2.2	.5	1.7			1.0	.9
All Other Non-Current	6.5	11.5	12.8	11.3			9.3	10.6
Total	100.0	100.0	100.0	100.0			100.0	100.0
LIABILITIES								
Notes Payable-Short Term	19.3	5.5	6.9	9.1			7.5	6.2
Cur. Mat. -L/T/D	7.9	13.7	13.6	13.4			12.5	13.5
Trade Payables	9.6	5.1	4.4	4.9			6.8	4.9
Income Taxes Payable	.1	.3	.3	.3			.3	.3
All Other Current	10.1	4.4	5.9	3.1			5.3	7.5
Total Current	46.9	29.0	31.2	30.8			32.5	32.4
Long Term Debt	23.4	33.0	30.7	40.7			34.5	33.7
Deferred Taxes	.0	.4	2.0	2.3			1.5	1.3
All Other-Non-Current	2.3	5.6	4.2	1.8			2.8	2.1
Net Worth	27.4	31.9	32.0	24.4			28.8	30.5
Total Liabilities & Net Worth	100.0	100.0	100.0	100.0			100.0	100.0
INCOME DATA								
Net Sales	100.0	100.0	100.0	100.0			100.0	100.0
Gross Profit								
Operating Expenses	92.8	87.1	88.9	89.7			90.1	89.2
Operating Profit	7.2	12.9	11.1	10.3			9.9	10.8
All Other Expenses (net)	3.2	2.9	3.2	4.1			5.2	5.6
Profit Before Taxes	4.0	10.0	7.9	6.2			4.7	5.1
RATIOS								
Current	1.6	1.3	1.1	1.0			1.4	1.3
	.5	.7	.6	.8			.8	.8
	.2	.3	.3	.5			.4	.4
Quick	1.6	.9	.9	.8			.9	1.0
	.5	.4	.5	.6			.5	.6
	.2	.2	.2	.3			.3	.3
Sales/Receivables	10 35.5	1 297.4	14 25.9	27 13.6			19 18.9	17 21.7
	24 14.9	28 13.0	33 11.2	38 9.7			36 10.2	37 10.0
	39 9.4	47 7.8	49 7.4	42 8.6			51 7.2	52 7.0
Cost of Sales/Inventory								
Cost of Sales/Payables								
Sales/Working Capital	25.0	23.4	50.8	NM			21.0	18.7
	-7.4	-8.1	-7.9	-13.4			-18.9	-15.7
	-3.0	-3.2	-3.1	-7.0			-5.6	-5.5
EBIT/Interest	(18) 6.7	(41) 7.0	(54) 3.9	(39) 2.7			(116) 2.4	(114) 2.4
	4.2	2.8	2.1	2.0			1.5	1.3
	.7	1.4	1.5	1.6			1.1	1.1
Net Profit + Depr., Dep., Amort./Cur. Mat. L/T/D		(11) 3.7	(26) 2.2	(21) 1.6			(86) 1.8	(63) 1.9
		1.7	1.3	1.2			1.2	1.2
		1.2	1.0	1.1			.9	.9
Fixed/Worth	1.0	.9	1.0	1.8			1.2	1.0
	1.9	1.8	2.4	3.8			2.3	2.6
	-23.4	7.1	4.1	5.9			5.9	4.9
Debt/Worth	.8	1.1	1.2	2.4			1.4	1.2
	2.5	2.1	2.8	4.2			3.4	3.0
	-26.7	10.3	4.5	7.1			7.7	6.4
% Profit Before Taxes/Tangible Net Worth	(17) 60.1	(37) 58.8	(53) 23.9	(40) 37.5			(133) 24.2	(120) 26.1
	31.0	29.8	16.2	21.9			11.9	9.5
	15.1	9.9	8.4	13.8			3.4	2.1
% Profit Before Taxes/Total Assets	27.5	15.2	7.7	7.1			6.7	6.9
	9.3	5.6	4.2	4.5			2.6	2.3
	-4.1	1.8	2.0	3.0			.7	.3
Sales/Net Fixed Assets	10.3	3.4	2.0	2.4			3.9	3.1
	2.2	1.2	1.0	1.2			1.5	1.3
	.8	.8	.7	.7			.9	.9
Sales/Total Assets	5.3	1.3	1.2	1.1			1.5	1.5
	1.6	.8	.7	.8			.9	.8
	.7	.6	.5	.6			.6	.6
% Depr., Dep., Amort./Sales	4.5	8.8	11.6	14.2			7.4	9.5
	18.1	(39) 24.8	(52) 23.7	(36) 19.8			(127) 19.7	(117) 19.8
	45.5	42.7	34.2	22.7			30.6	32.7
% Officers', Directors', Owners' Comp/Sales		(13) 2.0	(20) 1.7				(49) 2.7	(36) 2.5
		6.8	3.5				4.4	4.6
		14.1	5.3				9.1	7.0
Net Sales ($)	15000M	57016M	264169M	931491M	352569M	797824M	1374934M	1131428M
Total Assets ($)	6547M	48220M	257900M	984539M	606974M	784042M	1431324M	1519440M

M = $ thousand   MM = $ million
See Pages 1 through 15 for Explanation of Ratios and Data

Comparative Historical Data				Current Data Sorted By Sales			
1	9	12	# Postretirement Benefits	4	5	2	1

Type of Statement

1	9	12		0-1MM	1-3MM	3-5MM	5-10MM	10-25MM	25MM & OVER
40	41	39	Unqualified	1	3	3	6	10	16
45	38	44	Reviewed	9	10	5	8	11	1
40	36	35	Compiled	17	11	5	1	1	
2	1	5	Tax Returns	3	2				
34	49	53	Other	16	12	5	8	5	7
4/1/92-3/31/93	4/1/93-3/31/94	4/1/94-3/31/95		46 (4/1-9/30/94)		130 (10/1/94-3/31/95)			
ALL	ALL	ALL							
161	165	176	NUMBER OF STATEMENTS	46	38	18	23	27	24
%	%	%	**ASSETS**	%	%	%	%	%	%
7.0	6.1	5.4	Cash & Equivalents	6.1	4.5	5.3	7.1	4.5	5.2
12.2	13.2	11.7	Trade Receivables - (net)	10.9	11.2	11.8	14.9	11.6	10.7
4.7	3.8	5.8	Inventory	3.3	2.8	1.4	10.8	9.9	8.9
1.7	2.6	1.9	All Other Current	1.6	1.9	2.1	3.6	1.1	1.9
25.7	25.7	24.8	Total Current	21.8	20.4	20.7	36.4	27.1	26.6
61.4	60.7	61.8	Fixed Assets (net)	67.1	67.1	63.5	52.2	58.3	55.0
.7	.7	1.1	Intangibles (net)	2.0	.3	.4	2.2	.6	1.0
12.1	13.0	12.3	All Other Non-Current	9.0	12.3	15.5	9.2	14.0	17.4
100.0	100.0	100.0	Total	100.0	100.0	100.0	100.0	100.0	100.0
			LIABILITIES						
7.3	7.6	9.3	Notes Payable-Short Term	8.8	6.3	8.1	10.8	15.1	8.3
14.0	12.0	12.7	Cur. Mat.-L /T/D	15.0	12.8	9.0	11.0	13.2	11.8
4.4	5.2	5.3	Trade Payables	3.7	5.7	5.8	6.0	5.6	6.5
.3	.9	.3	Income Taxes Payable	.2	.2	.4	.3	.5	.3
5.9	5.2	5.2	All Other Current	7.9	5.0	3.5	5.9	2.4	3.9
32.0	30.9	32.8	Total Current	35.6	30.0	26.8	34.0	36.7	30.8
32.2	30.6	33.4	Long Term Debt	35.1	30.6	27.2	26.3	35.3	43.9
1.9	1.8	1.7	Deferred Taxes	.2	1.1	2.5	1.7	1.6	4.6
1.4	3.1	3.5	All Other-Non-Current	4.5	4.2	8.1	2.8	.6	.8
32.5	33.6	28.7	Net Worth	24.6	34.1	35.5	35.3	25.8	19.9
100.0	100.0	100.0	Total Liabilities & Net Worth	100.0	100.0	100.0	100.0	100.0	100.0
			INCOME DATA						
100.0	100.0	100.0	Net Sales	100.0	100.0	100.0	100.0	100.0	100.0
			Gross Profit						
86.9	88.0	88.3	Operating Expenses	86.9	87.8	89.3	89.4	87.6	90.8
13.1	12.0	11.7	Operating Profit	13.1	12.2	10.7	10.6	12.4	9.2
5.0	2.9	4.0	All Other Expenses (net)	3.4	4.0	2.7	5.1	4.8	4.1
8.1	9.1	7.7	Profit Before Taxes	9.7	8.3	8.0	5.5	7.6	5.0
			RATIOS						
1.5	1.5	1.2		.9	1.0	2.2	1.4	1.2	1.2
.8	.8	.7	Current	.5	.4	.7	1.0	.8	.9
.4	.3	.3		.2	.2	.4	.7	.3	.6
1.1	1.2	.9		.8	.9	1.5	1.2	.8	.8
.6	.6	.5	Quick	.4	.3	.6	.6	.5	.6
.3	.2	.2		.2	.1	.3	.2	.2	.3
17 21.4	15 24.3	14 25.9		5 78.2	7 50.6	15 24.5	27 13.5	21 17.3	27 13.6
33 10.9	33 11.1	32 11.4	Sales/Receivables	29 12.7	26 13.8	28 12.9	41 8.8	34 10.7	33 10.9
50 7.3	45 8.1	46 8.0		54 6.7	39 9.4	43 8.4	53 6.9	40 9.1	42 8.6
			Cost of Sales/Inventory						
			Cost of Sales/Payables						
15.1	15.5	35.0		-47.1	NM	19.4	20.6	32.7	46.9
-27.0	-17.2	-10.9	Sales/Working Capital	-5.2	-5.4	-13.5	-49.4	-12.3	-63.1
-3.9	-4.0	-3.7		-2.3	-3.0	-5.2	-9.5	-3.4	-10.1
(129) 2.9	(142) 5.5	(161) 4.2		(41) 6.3	(37) 6.3	(16) 3.7	(21) 5.6	(24) 2.6	(22) 3.0
1.8	2.1	2.2	EBIT/Interest	2.4	2.6	2.3	2.0	1.8	2.2
1.3	1.5	1.5		1.1	1.3	1.5	1.6	1.6	1.8
(75) 1.8	(71) 2.2	(67) 2.1		(12) 2.8	(14) 3.1		(11) 1.8	(13) 1.6	
1.2	1.2	1.2	Net Profit + Depr., Dep., Amort./Cur. Mat. L/T/D	1.8	1.3		1.2	1.1	
1.0	1.0	1.0		.8	1.0		1.0	1.0	
.8	.8	1.1		1.3	1.2	1.0	.5	1.0	1.1
2.3	2.0	2.4	Fixed/Worth	3.0	2.4	1.7	1.6	2.4	3.1
4.3	4.2	5.2		-29.6	3.8	4.2	4.2	5.9	4.6
1.2	.8	1.3		1.1	1.0	1.0	1.0	2.1	3.1
2.9	2.8	3.2	Debt/Worth	3.2	2.8	2.1	2.1	3.8	3.7
5.7	5.2	6.8		-52.3	4.1	4.6	4.5	5.7	6.7
(154) 29.7	(155) 30.9	(160) 38.6	% Profit Before Taxes/Tangible Net Worth	(34) 62.0	(37) 46.2	(17) 31.7	24.9	(26) 30.8	(23) 38.1
17.4	18.4	20.7		25.0	17.9	18.1	18.2	16.1	25.9
7.4	8.4	10.5		10.5	5.8	11.0	6.7	13.1	16.1
7.9	9.4	8.8	% Profit Before Taxes/Total Assets	16.9	13.7	8.6	7.0	5.9	7.6
3.7	4.7	4.5		4.4	5.3	5.7	3.8	4.3	5.2
1.5	2.3	2.0		.4	1.4	2.0	3.0	2.9	2.9
3.9	4.7	4.3		2.0	4.8	2.0	32.2	7.3	8.3
1.2	1.3	1.2	Sales/Net Fixed Assets	.9	1.1	1.2	1.6	1.4	1.5
.7	.8	.7		.6	.7	.9	1.0	.7	.9
1.4	1.6	1.4		1.0	1.6	1.3	1.6	1.4	1.6
.8	.9	.8	Sales/Total Assets	.7	.8	.8	.9	.8	1.0
.5	.5	.5		.4	.5	.6	.6	.5	.7
(142) 9.8	(145) 8.6	(157) 10.2	% Depr., Dep., Amort./Sales	(44) 18.6	(36) 8.1	(17) 14.2	(20) 6.3	(22) 7.5	(18) 2.1
22.3	20.0	20.8		36.7	21.7	23.4	17.4	19.4	11.1
37.4	30.7	33.5		53.2	32.7	29.2	29.5	22.1	20.5
(31) 2.0	(40) 2.9	(48) 2.1	% Officers', Directors', Owners' Comp/Sales	(16) 2.1					
4.6	6.5	4.2		4.4					
6.9	13.7	7.5		8.4					
1762120M	2449588M	2418069M	Net Sales ($)	23607M	66415M	68291M	158788M	411511M	1689457M
2301336M	2605987M	2688222M	Total Assets ($)	41722M	94217M	90046M	235421M	604720M	1622096M

M = $ thousand   MM = $ million
See Pages 1 through 15 for Explanation of Ratios and Data

Current Data Sorted By Assets							Comparative Historical Data	
2	18	23	11	4	5	**# Postretirement Benefits**		
						Type of Statement		
3	7	50	122	19	26	Unqualified	189	208
16	70	163	32		1	Reviewed	194	202
59	159	82	11	1		Compiled	263	305
9	14	1				Tax Returns	6	8
22	73	87	63	14	10	Other	217	198
	259 (4/1-9/30/94)			855 (10/1/94-3/31/95)			4/1/90-3/31/91	4/1/91-3/31/92
0-500M	500M-2MM	2-10MM	10-50MM	50-100MM	100-250MM		ALL	ALL
109	323	383	228	34	37	**NUMBER OF STATEMENTS**	869	921
%	%	%	%	%	%	**ASSETS**	%	%
10.9	7.8	6.3	5.4	5.4	3.4	Cash & Equivalents	6.6	6.9
27.5	29.1	27.2	19.6	18.1	21.4	Trade Receivables - (net)	26.0	27.0
1.7	1.8	1.2	1.9	.9	2.1	Inventory	2.0	2.0
2.0	2.1	2.6	2.7	2.8	2.3	All Other Current	3.3	2.9
42.2	40.7	37.3	29.6	27.2	29.2	Total Current	37.9	38.8
45.9	47.3	52.8	61.2	66.2	61.5	Fixed Assets (net)	50.6	48.5
2.6	1.8	1.2	1.6	1.0	3.0	Intangibles (net)	1.8	2.1
9.3	10.2	8.6	7.5	5.5	6.3	All Other Non-Current	9.7	10.7
100.0	100.0	100.0	100.0	100.0	100.0	Total	100.0	100.0
						LIABILITIES		
7.9	7.0	5.3	3.6	2.1	.6	Notes Payable-Short Term	7.2	7.7
11.3	10.3	12.1	11.9	9.3	7.5	Cur. Mat. -L/T/D	10.7	11.3
10.9	11.3	10.4	7.1	6.0	8.0	Trade Payables	9.8	10.5
.6	.4	.5	.4	.2	.5	Income Taxes Payable	.5	.4
8.4	7.5	7.6	8.3	8.9	10.6	All Other Current	9.2	9.2
39.2	36.4	36.0	31.4	26.6	27.2	Total Current	37.4	39.1
23.5	26.4	25.5	31.1	34.1	30.1	Long Term Debt	25.5	24.5
.4	.8	2.1	3.6	3.2	5.3	Deferred Taxes	1.5	1.5
4.0	2.9	2.3	1.8	2.6	2.4	All Other-Non-Current	2.1	2.0
32.9	33.5	34.1	32.1	33.4	34.9	Net Worth	33.4	32.9
100.0	100.0	100.0	100.0	100.0	100.0	Total Liabilities & Net Worth	100.0	100.0
						INCOME DATA		
100.0	100.0	100.0	100.0	100.0	100.0	Net Sales	100.0	100.0
						Gross Profit		
95.9	95.5	94.7	92.3	93.3	91.0	Operating Expenses	96.8	96.5
4.1	4.5	5.3	7.7	6.7	9.0	Operating Profit	3.2	3.5
.4	1.1	1.1	2.2	1.8	2.0	All Other Expenses (net)	1.5	1.6
3.7	3.4	4.3	5.5	4.9	7.0	Profit Before Taxes	1.7	1.9
						RATIOS		
1.9	1.8	1.4	1.3	1.3	1.4		1.5	1.5
1.1	1.1	1.0	.9	.9	1.1	Current	1.0	1.0
.6	.7	.7	.7	.7	.8		.7	.7
1.7	1.6	1.3	1.1	1.1	1.1		1.3	1.3
(108) .9	1.0	.9	(227) .8	.8	.9	Quick	.8	.9
.5	.6	.6	.5	.5	.7		.5	.5
6 62.6	**20** 18.5	**26** 13.8	**30** 12.0	**33** 10.9	**37** 10.0		**23** 15.6	**24** 15.0
21 17.5	**31** 11.9	**33** 11.0	**36** 10.2	**37** 9.8	**43** 8.5	Sales/Receivables	**32** 11.5	**32** 11.3
33 11.0	**40** 9.2	**42** 8.7	**41** 8.8	**43** 8.5	**48** 7.6		**42** 8.7	**42** 8.6
						Cost of Sales/Inventory		
						Cost of Sales/Payables		
17.6	17.8	23.5	29.3	34.2	26.7		20.9	20.7
542.5	87.3	709.1	-82.1	-32.9	80.2	Sales/Working Capital	999.8	-999.8
-18.7	-24.2	-20.9	-14.2	-15.2	-21.1		-17.7	-16.6
6.2	6.5	5.9	5.6	5.7	10.2		3.2	3.4
(93) 3.0	(302) 3.1	(370) 3.4	(218) 3.5	(32) 3.2	5.1	EBIT/Interest	(796) 1.7	(855) 1.9
1.2	1.5	2.1	2.2	1.5	2.7		.9	.9
3.6	2.8	2.9	1.9	5.3	39.0		2.2	2.1
(26) 2.1	(124) 1.9	(216) 1.6	(153) 1.3	(16) 1.4	(10) 2.7	Net Profit + Depr., Dep., Amort./Cur. Mat. L./T/D	(523) 1.3	(515) 1.3
1.3	1.1	1.1	1.0	.7	2.0		.9	.8
.5	.7	.9	1.3	1.4	1.4		.9	.8
1.7	1.4	1.7	2.3	2.1	1.9	Fixed/Worth	1.8	1.6
4.4	3.4	3.2	3.6	4.0	3.0		3.4	3.4
1.1	1.0	1.2	1.5	1.2	1.2		1.1	1.1
2.3	2.0	2.2	2.5	2.2	1.9	Debt/Worth	2.3	2.3
7.2	4.9	4.5	4.3	4.5	5.1		5.0	5.4
77.1	52.1	49.8	45.9	31.0	40.3		30.4	32.4
(94) 28.1	(290) 27.6	(375) 29.6	(222) 31.3	(33) 18.3	(36) 32.4	% Profit Before Taxes/Tangible Net Worth	(793) 13.6	(846) 14.6
4.9	9.8	13.6	19.6	11.4	21.0		1.9	1.1
20.2	16.4	15.0	12.4	10.4	14.8		9.1	9.5
6.9	7.9	8.1	8.3	6.6	10.4	% Profit Before Taxes/Total Assets	3.8	3.9
.5	2.4	4.0	5.1	2.8	8.2		-.0	-.5
28.6	15.1	8.7	4.8	3.2	3.3		10.1	11.5
8.2	6.5	4.4	2.8	2.3	2.7	Sales/Net Fixed Assets	4.8	5.2
4.2	3.6	2.8	1.9	1.6	1.8		2.9	2.9
6.4	4.6	3.4	2.5	2.0	2.1		3.6	3.7
3.8	3.1	2.5	1.7	1.5	1.7	Sales/Total Assets	2.5	2.6
2.4	2.2	1.8	1.3	1.2	1.3		1.8	1.8
2.4	2.3	2.8	3.8	3.9	1.4		2.9	2.6
(88) 5.7	(301) 5.1	(369) 5.2	(226) 6.3	(28) 6.6	(12) 3.9	% Depr., Dep., Amort./Sales	(785) 5.4	(841) 5.2
10.2	8.0	8.5	9.8	9.4	5.1		8.4	8.3
2.6	2.1	1.3	1.6		6.1		1.7	1.7
(49) 4.6	(157) 3.5	(154) 2.8	(67) 2.9		(11) 11.2	% Officers', Directors', Owners' Comp/Sales	(340) 3.5	(358) 3.4
10.3	6.1	5.6	8.1		22.9		7.2	7.3
146891M	1291934M	4669035M	9342174M	3855093M	9797290M	Net Sales ($)	18821081M	19061871M
31925M	369578M	1714232M	4899928M	2383937M	5108288M	Total Assets ($)	8860516M	9717796M

M = $ thousand   MM = $ million
See Pages 1 through 15 for Explanation of Ratios and Data

Comparative Historical Data				Current Data Sorted By Sales					
15	38	63		10	8	11	12	22	
			# Postretirement Benefits						
			Type of Statement						
195	187	227	Unqualified	1	6	7	17	50	146
215	225	282	Reviewed	11	34	40	73	91	33
317	308	312	Compiled	38	99	60	69	38	8
22	21	24	Tax Returns	5	11	7	1		
209	271	269	Other	11	39	31	49	61	78
4/1/92-3/31/93	4/1/93-3/31/94	4/1/94-3/31/95		259 (4/1-9/30/94)		855 (10/1/94-3/31/95)			
ALL	ALL	ALL		0-1MM	1-3MM	3-5MM	5-10MM	10-25MM	25MM & OVER
958	1012	1114	**NUMBER OF STATEMENTS**	66	189	145	209	240	265
%	%	%	**ASSETS**	%	%	%	%	%	%
7.4	7.3	6.9	Cash & Equivalents	10.3	8.7	7.2	5.9	7.0	5.2
25.8	26.5	25.8	Trade Receivables - (net)	15.2	24.1	27.9	29.8	26.3	24.7
2.1	1.7	1.6	Inventory	.6	1.7	1.8	1.4	1.4	1.9
2.7	2.4	2.4	All Other Current	2.5	2.3	1.9	2.4	2.3	2.9
38.0	37.9	36.6	Total Current	28.6	36.8	38.9	39.6	37.0	34.6
49.7	51.2	53.0	Fixed Assets (net)	60.8	50.3	51.4	49.3	53.3	56.3
1.9	1.7	1.7	Intangibles (net)	1.5	2.2	1.4	1.7	1.1	2.0
10.4	9.2	8.7	All Other Non-Current	9.1	10.8	8.4	9.4	8.6	7.0
100.0	100.0	100.0	Total	100.0	100.0	100.0	100.0	100.0	100.0
			LIABILITIES						
5.9	6.3	5.4	Notes Payable-Short Term	5.1	6.6	6.4	6.1	5.2	3.8
11.2	10.6	11.2	Cur. Mat.-L /T/D	12.6	10.3	12.5	11.5	11.9	10.1
10.3	9.7	9.8	Trade Payables	6.7	10.1	10.5	11.4	9.5	9.2
.5	.9	.5	Income Taxes Payable	.3	.4	.4	.5	.6	.5
8.6	8.7	7.9	All Other Current	8.7	6.3	7.3	6.7	8.5	9.8
36.6	36.2	34.9	Total Current	33.4	33.7	37.1	36.2	35.6	33.4
24.3	25.5	27.1	Long Term Debt	31.5	26.2	27.8	26.9	25.6	27.8
1.7	1.7	2.0	Deferred Taxes	.8	.8	1.2	1.6	2.4	3.6
2.2	2.1	2.6	All Other-Non-Current	2.8	3.2	3.6	2.2	2.5	1.8
35.1	34.6	33.4	Net Worth	31.6	36.1	30.3	33.0	33.9	33.4
100.0	100.0	100.0	Total Liabilities & Net Worth	100.0	100.0	100.0	100.0	100.0	100.0
			INCOME DATA						
100.0	100.0	100.0	Net Sales	100.0	100.0	100.0	100.0	100.0	100.0
			Gross Profit						
95.4	95.4	94.4	Operating Expenses	89.7	95.2	95.2	95.9	94.4	93.3
4.6	4.6	5.6	Operating Profit	10.3	4.8	4.8	4.1	5.6	6.7
1.2	.9	1.3	All Other Expenses (net)	3.6	.5	1.2	.7	1.4	1.6
3.4	3.7	4.3	Profit Before Taxes	6.8	4.3	3.6	3.3	4.2	5.1
			RATIOS						
1.5	1.6	1.5		1.4	1.8	1.6	1.5	1.4	1.3
1.0	1.0	1.0	Current	.7	1.1	1.1	1.0	1.0	1.0
.7	.7	.7		.4	.7	.8	.7	.7	.7
1.4	1.4	1.3		1.2	1.6	1.4	1.3	1.3	1.1
.9 (1011)	.9 (1112)	.9	Quick	.6 (188)	.9	1.0	.9 (239)	.9	.8
.6	.6	.6		.3	.6	.6	.6	.6	.6
23 15.8	24 15.3	25 14.8		0 UND	15 24.0	24 15.0	25 14.8	26 14.3	31 11.6
32 11.4	32 11.3	33 11.0	Sales/Receivables	16 22.7	30 12.2	33 11.1	33 11.2	33 11.2	37 9.8
40 9.2	41 8.9	41 8.8		40 9.1	40 9.1	41 8.8	40 9.1	41 9.0	44 8.3
			Cost of Sales/Inventory						
			Cost of Sales/Payables						
19.5	19.7	22.2		18.8	15.9	19.0	22.1	27.0	27.6
419.7	405.4	984.2	Sales/Working Capital	-16.2	158.3	109.9	269.1	597.3	-134.8
-18.9	-20.2	-19.8		-7.1	-21.2	-25.0	-20.8	-20.8	-19.4
5.0	5.9	6.0		5.7	6.7	5.0	5.5	6.0	6.7
(887) 2.5	(956) 3.0	(1052) 3.3	EBIT/Interest	(56) 3.1	(167) 3.2	(139) 2.6	(202) 3.0	(232) 3.5	(256) 4.0
1.4	1.7	1.9		1.1	1.6	1.6	1.6	2.1	2.4
2.5	2.2	2.6		2.3	2.9	2.6	2.9	2.8	2.5
(460) 1.4	(464) 1.4	(545) 1.6	Net Profit + Depr., Dep.,	(23) 1.4	(66) 1.9	(64) 1.4	(95) 1.7	(140) 1.5	(157) 1.5
.9	1.0	1.1	Amort./Cur. Mat. L/T/D	.5	1.1	1.0	1.1	1.0	1.1
.8	.8	.9		1.1	.7	.9	.8	1.0	1.2
1.6	1.7	1.8	Fixed/Worth	2.3	1.6	1.8	1.5	1.9	1.9
3.3	3.4	3.4		5.7	3.2	4.0	3.3	3.1	3.3
1.1	1.0	1.2		1.3	.9	1.2	1.1	1.3	1.4
2.1	2.2	2.2	Debt/Worth	2.1	1.8	2.2	2.2	2.4	2.3
4.5	4.9	4.7		7.2	5.0	5.3	4.9	4.4	4.2
40.1	44.2	49.8	% Profit Before Taxes/Tangible	63.0	61.0	49.9	45.7	49.5	49.2
(888) 20.5	(958) 24.5	(1050) 29.1	Net Worth	(57) 17.5	(171) 27.0	(133) 31.7	(196) 24.4	(235) 30.9	(258) 31.4
7.6	10.7	13.3		4.7	8.6	10.4	9.8	16.4	19.6
12.0	13.5	14.8	% Profit Before Taxes/Total	15.7	17.7	14.2	14.8	14.9	13.7
6.6	7.2	8.1	Assets	4.9	8.1	7.1	7.2	8.5	9.6
2.1	3.3	3.5		.2	2.3	2.6	2.8	4.4	5.8
10.6	10.3	9.3		5.5	10.2	10.4	11.3	9.7	6.3
5.3	4.9	4.5	Sales/Net Fixed Assets	2.8	5.2	5.5	5.9	4.2	3.3
3.1	2.9	2.6		1.5	2.9	3.1	3.2	2.5	2.0
3.7	3.8	3.6		2.8	3.8	3.9	4.2	3.6	2.8
2.6	2.5	2.5	Sales/Total Assets	1.6	2.8	2.9	2.8	2.5	2.0
1.9	1.8	1.7		.7	1.9	1.9	2.1	1.7	1.4
2.8	2.9	2.9		6.5	2.9	3.2	2.7	2.4	2.9
(874) 5.1	(926) 5.3	(1024) 5.3	% Depr., Dep., Amort./Sales	(61) 11.6	(170) 5.5	(138) 5.3	(193) 5.1	(232) 5.3	(230) 4.9
8.0	8.6	8.7		17.3	8.9	8.5	8.0	8.4	7.8
1.8	1.8	1.9		3.8	2.5	2.0	1.2	1.1	1.5
(404) 3.8	(415) 3.3	(442) 3.4	% Officers', Directors',	(27) 6.5	(89) 4.2	(76) 3.0	(90) 2.5	(85) 3.0	(75) 2.9
9.3	7.1	6.7	Owners' Comp/Sales	18.7	7.1	4.6	4.9	6.1	10.4
21949511M	23523573M	29102417M	Net Sales ($)	36745M	372862M	584130M	1514022M	3772478M	22822180M
10517822M	11777735M	14507888M	Total Assets ($)	47970M	160806M	268214M	616908M	1727203M	11686787M

Current Data Sorted By Assets | # Postretirement Benefits — Type of Statement | Comparative Historical Data

	0-500M	500M-2MM	2-10MM	10-50MM	50-100MM	100-250MM		ALL 4/1/90-3/31/91	ALL 4/1/91-3/31/92
	5	6	5	2			# Postretirement Benefits — Type of Statement		
	1	10	13	10	7		Unqualified	36	50
	14	35	52	2			Reviewed	80	79
	53	85	42	2	1		Compiled	151	136
	21	5	2				Tax Returns	7	5
	36	35	17	8			Other	75	66
	\<103 (4/1-9/30/94)\>			\<348 (10/1/94-3/31/95)\>					
NUMBER OF STATEMENTS	125	170	126	22	8		NUMBER OF STATEMENTS	349	336
	%	%	%	%	%	%	ASSETS	%	%
Cash & Equivalents	12.1	8.0	7.9	6.7			Cash & Equivalents	9.6	8.6
Trade Receivables - (net)	27.0	28.7	26.5	15.4			Trade Receivables - (net)	26.3	26.2
Inventory	1.0	2.1	1.1	4.2			Inventory	1.4	2.1
All Other Current	2.1	3.0	3.3	4.6			All Other Current	2.7	2.8
Total Current	42.2	41.8	38.7	30.8			Total Current	39.9	39.6
Fixed Assets (net)	48.1	48.6	50.7	57.7			Fixed Assets (net)	48.2	48.1
Intangibles (net)	1.5	1.4	1.5	1.4			Intangibles (net)	2.8	2.9
All Other Non-Current	8.2	8.2	9.1	10.2			All Other Non-Current	9.1	9.3
Total	100.0	100.0	100.0	100.0			Total	100.0	100.0
							LIABILITIES		
Notes Payable-Short Term	7.9	6.2	6.5	5.7			Notes Payable-Short Term	8.4	7.2
Cur. Mat. -L/T/D	10.3	10.2	11.1	10.5			Cur. Mat. -L/T/D	10.3	10.4
Trade Payables	13.2	11.3	11.4	6.7			Trade Payables	11.1	11.5
Income Taxes Payable	.5	.5	.4	.4			Income Taxes Payable	.6	.5
All Other Current	8.2	6.8	7.6	7.6			All Other Current	7.7	7.7
Total Current	40.1	35.1	36.9	30.9			Total Current	38.1	37.3
Long Term Debt	25.3	22.6	23.6	28.1			Long Term Debt	22.2	22.4
Deferred Taxes	.2	1.0	1.5	3.7			Deferred Taxes	1.0	1.0
All Other-Non-Current	2.0	2.0	1.8	.7			All Other-Non-Current	2.7	1.9
Net Worth	32.4	39.3	36.2	36.6			Net Worth	36.1	37.3
Total Liabilities & Net Worth	100.0	100.0	100.0	100.0			Total Liabilities & Net Worth	100.0	100.0
							INCOME DATA		
Net Sales	100.0	100.0	100.0	100.0			Net Sales	100.0	100.0
Gross Profit							Gross Profit		
Operating Expenses	93.3	96.2	95.2	91.1			Operating Expenses	95.4	96.1
Operating Profit	6.7	3.8	4.8	8.9			Operating Profit	4.6	3.9
All Other Expenses (net)	1.0	.5	1.2	2.4			All Other Expenses (net)	1.5	1.7
Profit Before Taxes	5.7	3.2	3.6	6.5			Profit Before Taxes	3.2	2.3
							RATIOS		
Current	2.0	2.0	1.6	1.4			Current	1.7	1.8
	1.1	1.2	1.0	.8				1.1	1.1
	.5	.8	.7	.5				.7	.7
Quick	1.8	1.7	1.4	1.2			Quick	1.5	1.6
	1.0	1.0	.9	.6				1.0 (335)	.9
	.4	.6	.6	.4				.6	.6
Sales/Receivables	0 UND	19 19.0	28 12.9	29 12.8			Sales/Receivables	20 18.5	19 19.0
	24 15.4	32 11.3	33 10.9	40 9.2				31 11.7	31 11.9
	38 9.5	45 8.2	47 7.7	47 7.8				46 8.0	42 8.6
Cost of Sales/Inventory							Cost of Sales/Inventory		
Cost of Sales/Payables							Cost of Sales/Payables		
Sales/Working Capital	15.0	14.0	17.7	14.7			Sales/Working Capital	15.9	14.2
	155.2	46.9	-167.3	-20.6				164.9	115.8
	-21.7	-28.4	-15.7	-9.6				-19.5	-21.6
EBIT/Interest	(107) 9.0	(161) 7.2	(117) 6.3	(21) 5.6			EBIT/Interest	(324) 5.1	(301) 4.6
	3.7	3.2	2.6	3.0				2.3	2.1
	1.8	1.2	1.5	1.6				1.1	1.1
Net Profit + Depr., Dep., Amort./Cur. Mat. L /T/D	(26) 3.1	(71) 3.0	(71) 2.8	(18) 2.8			Net Profit + Depr., Dep., Amort./Cur. Mat. L /T/D	(190) 2.8	(163) 2.7
	1.4	1.6	1.5	1.5				1.7	1.4
	.7	.9	1.0	1.2				.8	.9
Fixed/Worth	.7	.7	.7	1.0			Fixed/Worth	.8	.7
	1.4	1.3	1.5	1.8				1.4	1.4
	5.1	2.4	3.2	3.3				3.4	2.7
Debt/Worth	1.1	.8	.9	1.0			Debt/Worth	.9	.9
	2.1	1.6	2.0	1.7				2.0	1.9
	10.7	3.8	4.6	3.1				4.7	4.3
% Profit Before Taxes/Tangible Net Worth	(107) 81.7	(162) 48.3	(120) 35.0	37.0			% Profit Before Taxes/Tangible Net Worth	(322) 43.8	(317) 36.7
	37.6	24.3	17.2	26.1				18.4	13.3
	10.2	4.3	6.6	12.7				3.5	1.7
% Profit Before Taxes/Total Assets	22.4	15.7	12.5	14.8			% Profit Before Taxes/Total Assets	14.0	10.5
	11.2	7.0	5.8	7.8				5.6	4.3
	3.5	.8	2.0	3.1				.3	.2
Sales/Net Fixed Assets	17.1	9.6	9.1	4.3			Sales/Net Fixed Assets	11.6	11.0
	8.5	6.0	4.4	2.5				6.4	5.6
	4.8	3.5	2.7	1.6				3.2	3.1
Sales/Total Assets	5.5	4.0	3.2	2.0			Sales/Total Assets	4.0	3.9
	3.5	2.9	2.4	1.3				2.7	2.7
	2.2	2.0	1.6	1.2				1.8	1.8
% Depr., Dep., Amort./Sales	(111) 2.3	(162) 3.0	(125) 2.9	5.2			% Depr., Dep., Amort./Sales	(324) 2.8	(320) 2.7
	4.6	5.3	5.7	6.8				5.4	5.5
	8.7	8.3	8.3	10.6				8.6	9.2
% Officers', Directors', Owners' Comp/Sales	(56) 2.3	(95) 1.9	(52) 1.5				% Officers', Directors', Owners' Comp/Sales	(144) 2.1	(149) 2.2
	3.9	4.2	2.7					4.1	4.2
	7.9	7.1	6.3					7.6	8.5
Net Sales ($)	146057M	583839M	1247953M	696493M	920988M		Net Sales ($)	2397506M	2275399M
Total Assets ($)	37636M	194014M	525853M	453738M	568809M		Total Assets ($)	1307511M	1033493M

M = $ thousand　　MM = $ million
See Pages 1 through 15 for Explanation of Ratios and Data

Comparative Historical Data			# Postretirement Benefits	Current Data Sorted By Sales					
1	10	18	Type of Statement	3	5	2	3	5	
36	52	41	Unqualified		8	2	6	10	15
78	87	103	Reviewed	9	27	11	37	18	1
143	172	183	Compiled	29	72	31	33	16	2
13	15	28	Tax Returns	12	13	1	1	1	
52	68	96	Other	17	30	18	12	16	3
4/1/92-3/31/93 ALL	4/1/93-3/31/94 ALL	4/1/94-3/31/95 ALL		103 (4/1-9/30/94)			348 (10/1/94-3/31/95)		
				0-1MM	1-3MM	3-5MM	5-10MM	10-25MM	25MM & OVER
322	394	451	**NUMBER OF STATEMENTS**	67	150	63	89	61	21
%	%	%	**ASSETS**	%	%	%	%	%	%
9.1	9.0	9.0	Cash & Equivalents	14.1	9.1	6.8	8.3	7.3	6.0
25.9	26.6	26.8	Trade Receivables - (net)	20.3	24.7	29.2	30.7	32.5	21.9
1.7	1.3	1.6	Inventory	.6	1.6	2.0	1.7	.9	4.1
2.1	2.7	2.9	All Other Current	2.5	2.7	3.4	1.9	4.9	1.2
38.8	39.6	40.2	Total Current	37.6	38.2	41.4	42.6	45.6	33.2
47.6	47.1	49.8	Fixed Assets (net)	51.1	52.3	50.8	47.2	42.4	57.9
2.3	2.4	1.5	Intangibles (net)	2.9	1.1	.6	1.2	2.1	1.3
11.3	10.9	8.5	All Other Non-Current	8.4	8.5	7.2	8.9	9.8	7.6
100.0	100.0	100.0	Total	100.0	100.0	100.0	100.0	100.0	100.0
			LIABILITIES						
6.6	6.6	6.7	Notes Payable-Short Term	8.2	6.0	7.3	6.2	7.0	5.5
10.3	9.2	10.5	Cur. Mat.-L /T/D	10.6	10.5	11.2	11.6	8.5	9.2
11.4	11.2	11.5	Trade Payables	9.7	11.3	10.9	13.6	13.5	6.7
.7	1.0	.5	Income Taxes Payable	.5	.4	.4	.7	.4	.5
8.3	7.7	7.4	All Other Current	7.0	6.9	6.5	5.3	12.3	9.8
37.4	35.7	36.6	Total Current	36.1	35.1	36.3	37.4	41.8	31.7
21.4	21.9	24.2	Long Term Debt	29.2	25.3	21.8	21.4	20.7	29.4
1.1	1.1	1.1	Deferred Taxes	.2	.8	.9	2.0	1.2	3.2
3.3	1.9	1.9	All Other-Non-Current	1.2	2.0	2.5	1.9	2.0	.8
36.8	39.4	36.2	Net Worth	33.4	36.8	38.5	37.4	34.3	35.0
100.0	100.0	100.0	Total Liabilities & Net Worth	100.0	100.0	100.0	100.0	100.0	100.0
			INCOME DATA						
100.0	100.0	100.0	Net Sales	100.0	100.0	100.0	100.0	100.0	100.0
			Gross Profit						
95.3	95.2	94.8	Operating Expenses	89.9	95.8	95.2	96.8	95.3	93.0
4.7	4.8	5.2	Operating Profit	10.1	4.2	4.8	3.2	4.7	7.0
.9	.8	1.0	All Other Expenses (net)	2.7	.5	.7	.6	.7	1.6
3.8	3.9	4.2	Profit Before Taxes	7.4	3.7	4.1	2.6	4.0	5.4
			RATIOS						
1.6 1.0 .7	1.8 1.0 .7	1.7 1.1 .7	Current	2.0 .9 .4	2.0 1.2 .7	1.7 1.0 .7	1.8 1.0 .7	1.6 1.1 .7	1.5 1.1 .6
1.5 .9 .6	1.5 1.0 .6	1.6 .9 .6	Quick	1.9 .8 .3	1.7 1.1 .5	1.5 .9 .6	1.6 1.0 .6	1.5 .9 .6	1.4 .8 .6
18 19.9 30 12.3 44 8.3	19 19.6 32 11.3 44 8.3	20 18.6 32 11.4 44 8.3	Sales/Receivables	0 UND 19 19.1 43 8.5	13 27.8 28 12.9 38 9.5	17 21.8 36 10.2 49 7.4	26 14.0 33 11.2 41 8.9	29 12.7 37 9.9 47 7.7	35 10.5 41 8.9 48 7.6
			Cost of Sales/Inventory						
			Cost of Sales/Payables						
20.3 218.6 -20.6	16.3 155.7 -22.3	14.5 140.0 -19.9	Sales/Working Capital	6.7 -94.3 -12.3	14.5 54.6 -23.5	14.4 395.6 -23.6	14.3 238.1 -23.8	17.8 140.0 -15.3	15.7 108.9 -13.9
(281) 6.0 2.8 1.3	(357) 6.7 3.4 1.6	(414) 7.2 3.1 1.5	EBIT/Interest	(55) 7.3 2.8 1.0	(140) 7.9 3.2 1.2	(61) 7.2 3.5 1.9	(80) 6.1 2.6 1.2	(57) 6.8 2.8 1.8	8.2 5.0 2.1
(130) 3.2 1.7 1.1	(161) 2.9 1.7 1.0	(191) 2.9 1.5 1.0	Net Profit + Depr., Dep., Amort./Cur. Mat. L/T/D		(58) 3.1 1.4 .9	(24) 3.2 1.9 1.2	(51) 2.4 1.4 .9	(32) 3.0 1.4 1.2	(17) 5.1 1.8 1.1
.7 1.4 3.0	.7 1.3 2.6	.7 1.4 3.0	Fixed/Worth	.7 1.9 17.0	.8 1.4 2.8	.7 1.3 2.3	.7 1.3 3.0	.5 1.2 3.7	1.2 1.7 3.5
.9 1.9 4.3	.8 1.8 4.0	.9 1.8 4.5	Debt/Worth	1.0 2.5 17.8	.8 1.5 4.3	.9 1.7 3.3	.8 1.7 3.9	1.1 2.1 5.4	1.2 1.6 3.8
(303) 46.9 22.8 7.3	(370) 52.4 21.1 7.3	(419) 49.5 25.6 8.0	% Profit Before Taxes/Tangible Net Worth	(57) 100.2 27.9 5.1	(136) 51.0 28.3 7.0	(62) 47.5 23.8 9.1	(83) 36.4 19.1 3.9	(60) 67.9 30.5 12.0	41.0 24.1 14.7
13.9 7.2 1.4	15.2 7.9 1.9	16.5 7.5 2.0	% Profit Before Taxes/Total Assets	26.5 8.1 .0	18.6 8.1 .9	16.1 7.2 3.3	13.6 6.5 .9	15.0 7.8 3.1	14.6 7.8 4.2
12.1 6.4 3.4	12.0 5.6 3.3	10.8 5.5 3.2	Sales/Net Fixed Assets	9.5 5.0 2.1	10.2 5.8 3.5	10.8 5.8 3.2	10.7 5.5 3.4	16.0 6.5 3.1	4.6 3.2 1.9
4.1 2.9 2.0	4.0 2.6 1.8	4.0 2.7 1.8	Sales/Total Assets	3.5 2.0 1.3	4.5 3.1 2.0	3.8 2.9 2.1	3.8 2.8 2.1	4.4 2.9 1.9	2.5 1.8 1.3
(298) 2.8 5.2 9.4	(363) 3.1 5.4 9.1	(428) 2.9 5.5 8.5	% Depr., Dep., Amort./Sales	(58) 3.6 7.6 12.2	(140) 3.4 5.6 8.9	(61) 2.9 5.1 8.9	(87) 2.5 5.2 7.9	1.4 3.9 6.3	3.6 6.2 8.3
(147) 2.8 5.1 8.8	(183) 2.4 4.3 7.9	(209) 1.9 3.7 7.0	% Officers', Directors', Owners' Comp/Sales	(26) 2.6 5.4 9.6	(77) 2.1 4.7 7.9	(38) 1.7 3.0 5.7	(40) 1.9 2.9 6.3	(22) 1.3 2.8 4.3	
2699079M 1288449M	2922603M 1424089M	3595330M 1780050M	Net Sales ($) Total Assets ($)	38027M 22367M	286679M 126690M	239087M 100970M	610499M 254701M	923747M 390808M	1497291M 884514M

M = $ thousand   MM = $ million
See Pages 1 through 15 for Explanation of Ratios and Data

SERVICES—TRUCKING & STORAGE, LOCAL – INCLUDING HOUSEHOLD GOODS. SIC# 4214

Current Data Sorted By Assets							Comparative Historical Data	
3	2	7	1		1	# Postretirement Benefits		
						Type of Statement		
1	3	8	10			Unqualified	23	21
11	39	31	2			Reviewed	42	59
43	35	16				Compiled	81	73
8	4					Tax Returns		5
11	21	16	2	1	2	Other	47	53
	39 (4/1-9/30/94)		225 (10/1/94-3/31/95)				4/1/90-3/31/91	4/1/91-3/31/92
0-500M	500M-2MM	2-10MM	10-50MM	50-100MM	100-250MM		ALL	ALL
74	102	71	14	1	2	**NUMBER OF STATEMENTS**	193	211
%	%	%	%	%	%	**ASSETS**	%	%
11.4	8.7	7.6	4.6			Cash & Equivalents	8.3	9.1
35.3	35.8	32.2	21.5			Trade Receivables - (net)	30.3	31.1
.8	1.5	2.1	.5			Inventory	1.4	1.3
2.0	2.2	1.5	1.3			All Other Current	3.5	1.5
49.6	48.2	43.4	28.0			Total Current	43.5	43.0
35.3	37.7	41.3	63.3			Fixed Assets (net)	41.3	41.6
2.4	2.1	1.8	.6			Intangibles (net)	1.7	2.8
12.7	12.0	13.5	8.1			All Other Non-Current	13.6	12.6
100.0	100.0	100.0	100.0			Total	100.0	100.0
						LIABILITIES		
6.9	5.9	6.3	3.7			Notes Payable-Short Term	8.4	7.0
7.3	6.5	6.3	11.0			Cur. Mat. -L/T/D	7.3	7.3
14.4	10.1	10.8	7.0			Trade Payables	10.2	10.1
.4	.7	.5	.5			Income Taxes Payable	.4	.5
10.7	8.9	8.1	8.2			All Other Current	8.2	8.9
39.7	32.0	32.1	30.5			Total Current	34.5	33.9
21.5	20.7	23.4	35.7			Long Term Debt	22.3	23.5
.3	1.3	1.3	1.0			Deferred Taxes	.6	.9
2.9	2.0	4.4	.7			All Other-Non-Current	3.1	2.4
35.7	44.0	38.9	32.1			Net Worth	39.4	39.2
100.0	100.0	100.0	100.0			Total Liabilities & Net Worth	100.0	100.0
						INCOME DATA		
100.0	100.0	100.0	100.0			Net Sales	100.0	100.0
						Gross Profit		
96.8	96.4	93.3	92.2			Operating Expenses	96.3	95.5
3.2	3.6	6.7	7.8			Operating Profit	3.7	4.5
.3	.7	2.3	1.8			All Other Expenses (net)	1.4	2.3
2.9	2.9	4.4	6.0			Profit Before Taxes	2.3	2.2
						RATIOS		
2.5	2.5	2.2	1.6			Current	2.1	2.1
1.2	1.5	1.3	1.0				1.3	1.3
.8	1.1	.9	.5				.8	.9
2.4	2.2	2.1	1.4			Quick	1.8	2.0
1.1	1.4	1.2	.9				1.2	1.3
.8	1.0	.8	.5				.7	.8
17 21.3	29 12.6	33 11.2	36 10.2			Sales/Receivables	26 14.0	30 12.3
31 11.6	43 8.5	43 8.4	40 9.2				42 8.6	40 9.2
45 8.2	57 6.4	59 6.2	43 8.4				55 6.6	58 6.3
						Cost of Sales/Inventory		
						Cost of Sales/Payables		
10.7	9.1	10.1	19.1			Sales/Working Capital	11.7	10.9
42.9	19.1	23.5	NM				30.0	31.5
-60.9	91.5	-97.0	-8.9				-28.4	-46.7
(60) 7.9	(97) 7.0	(65) 7.1	(13) 3.6			EBIT/Interest	(162) 3.5	(189) 4.7
2.9	2.9	3.0	2.2				1.7	2.1
1.3	1.8	1.6	2.2				.5	.8
(27) 3.0	(52) 3.1	(41) 4.0				Net Profit + Depr., Dep., Amort./Cur. Mat. L /T/D	(99) 2.8	(119) 2.5
1.5	2.1	1.8					1.6	1.7
.9	1.2	1.0					.7	.8
.4	.4	.5	1.4			Fixed/Worth	.5	.6
.9	.9	1.1	2.0				1.1	1.2
2.1	1.6	2.9	3.0				2.2	2.5
.8	.7	.9	1.7			Debt/Worth	.8	.8
1.8	1.3	1.9	2.2				1.7	1.8
6.4	2.9	4.3	3.1				4.0	3.8
(66) 63.4	(100) 38.6	36.7	43.9			% Profit Before Taxes/Tangible Net Worth	(180) 29.1	(196) 30.5
26.3	16.6	18.3	18.7				12.0	12.2
2.8	5.5	7.0	12.9				-6.6	-.9
22.4	13.2	10.8	14.2			% Profit Before Taxes/Total Assets	12.0	11.2
7.4	6.4	5.1	5.3				4.1	4.9
.7	2.3	2.3	3.8				-2.2	-.9
26.4	13.7	12.3	4.2			Sales/Net Fixed Assets	14.5	13.3
12.3	8.4	7.8	3.4				7.1	8.3
6.6	5.2	3.4	1.9				3.8	3.6
5.0	3.8	3.4	2.7			Sales/Total Assets	3.7	3.8
3.5	2.8	2.5	1.9				2.7	2.6
2.7	2.1	1.6	1.4				1.7	1.7
(63) 1.8	(99) 2.0	(69) 2.0	3.4			% Depr., Dep., Amort./Sales	(172) 2.0	(198) 2.2
3.1	2.9	3.4	5.2				3.7	3.6
4.8	4.4	5.2	8.6				6.0	5.6
(40) 4.0	(54) 2.4	(31) 2.7				% Officers', Directors', Owners' Comp/Sales	(79) 2.8	(112) 3.0
7.3	4.4	4.9					4.9	5.1
11.4	6.6	9.8					10.0	8.7
81701M	336620M	649894M	705693M	180921M	549839M	Net Sales ($)	1907499M	1433645M
22274M	112700M	275240M	366627M	99265M	399860M	Total Assets ($)	507592M	851010M

M = $ thousand   MM = $ million
See Pages 1 through 15 for Explanation of Ratios and Data

Comparative Historical Data				Current Data Sorted By Sales					
3	9	14	# Postretirement Benefits	4	2	3	5	6	8
			Type of Statement						
20	18	22	Unqualified	1	1	1	5	6	8
56	58	83	Reviewed	2	27	15	25	14	
69	81	94	Compiled	32	36	16	7	3	
4	10	12	Tax Returns	6	6				
52	53	53	Other	4	19	8	10	8	4
4/1/92-3/31/93 ALL	4/1/93-3/31/94 ALL	4/1/94-3/31/95 ALL		39 (4/1-9/30/94) 0-1MM	1-3MM	3-5MM	225 (10/1/94-3/31/95) 5-10MM	10-25MM	25MM & OVER
201	220	264	**NUMBER OF STATEMENTS**	45	89	40	47	31	12
%	%	%	**ASSETS**	%	%	%	%	%	%
9.7	11.2	8.9	Cash & Equivalents	11.4	9.4	9.0	8.4	6.3	3.5
31.8	31.4	33.7	Trade Receivables - (net)	22.9	38.1	31.6	37.5	37.7	23.2
1.7	1.2	1.4	Inventory	.6	1.5	1.4	2.0	2.0	.6
2.8	2.4	2.0	All Other Current	1.4	2.1	2.0	2.5	1.2	2.8
46.0	46.3	46.0	Total Current	36.3	51.1	44.0	50.5	47.1	30.1
39.5	40.1	39.7	Fixed Assets (net)	46.1	35.6	38.7	36.3	40.1	60.9
2.1	2.3	2.0	Intangibles (net)	2.3	2.7	1.8	1.7	1.0	1.8
12.4	11.3	12.3	All Other Non-Current	15.3	10.7	15.5	11.6	11.8	7.2
100.0	100.0	100.0	Total	100.0	100.0	100.0	100.0	100.0	100.0
			LIABILITIES						
5.1	6.2	6.2	Notes Payable-Short Term	6.7	6.0	4.3	7.1	7.2	5.6
7.4	6.8	6.9	Cur. Mat.-L /T/D	6.5	6.2	7.5	7.0	7.2	9.8
12.0	9.6	11.3	Trade Payables	8.9	12.5	10.0	12.2	12.4	8.4
.4	.8	.6	Income Taxes Payable	.2	.6	.5	.8	.5	.5
9.6	9.1	9.1	All Other Current	8.1	8.8	9.7	9.9	10.5	7.3
34.5	32.5	34.0	Total Current	30.4	34.1	32.1	37.1	37.7	31.6
21.5	21.4	22.4	Long Term Debt	33.3	19.9	20.7	18.7	19.2	29.4
.9	1.1	1.0	Deferred Taxes	.3	.8	1.0	1.9	1.1	1.5
2.1	2.2	2.9	All Other-Non-Current	1.1	2.7	3.1	4.7	3.4	3.0
40.9	42.9	39.6	Net Worth	34.9	42.6	43.1	37.5	38.6	34.5
100.0	100.0	100.0	Total Liabilities & Net Worth	100.0	100.0	100.0	100.0	100.0	100.0
			INCOME DATA						
100.0	100.0	100.0	Net Sales	100.0	100.0	100.0	100.0	100.0	100.0
			Gross Profit						
95.5	95.5	95.4	Operating Expenses	92.7	95.9	96.6	96.6	95.2	93.8
4.5	4.5	4.6	Operating Profit	7.3	4.1	3.4	3.4	4.8	6.2
.7	1.1	1.1	All Other Expenses (net)	2.9	.9	.6	.8	.2	1.3
3.8	3.4	3.5	Profit Before Taxes	4.4	3.2	2.8	2.6	4.6	4.9
			RATIOS						
2.2	2.6	2.2	Current	2.3	3.0	2.2	2.0	1.8	1.4
1.4	1.5	1.3		1.1	1.5	1.4	1.4	1.3	1.0
.9	.9	1.0		.6	1.0	1.0	1.0	.9	.6
2.1	2.3	2.1	Quick	2.2	3.0	2.2	1.7	1.7	1.2
1.3	1.4	1.2		1.1	1.4	1.2	1.2	1.2	.8
.7	.8	.9		.6	.9	.9	.9	.9	.5
26 13.8	27 13.5	28 13.2	Sales/Receivables	13 28.9	31 11.8	21 17.5	31 11.6	37 9.9	31 11.6
37 9.8	41 8.9	40 9.1		21 17.0	44 8.3	39 9.4	41 8.8	45 8.1	39 9.4
53 6.9	54 6.8	54 6.8		34 10.6	60 6.1	50 7.3	51 7.2	57 6.4	46 8.0
			Cost of Sales/Inventory						
			Cost of Sales/Payables						
10.2	9.0	10.3	Sales/Working Capital	10.6	7.6	9.1	13.4	12.3	22.7
27.3	20.6	26.4		70.7	18.8	26.5	22.8	23.9	NM
-87.4	-88.8	-157.0		-26.7	444.1	-156.9	263.8	-149.4	-14.1
6.4	8.0	7.0	EBIT/Interest	(34) 7.0	(80) 7.0	(37) 6.9	(46) 6.8	(30) 9.4	(11) 3.7
(182) 3.0	(197) 3.3	(238) 2.9		2.6	3.1	2.6	2.9	3.3	2.9
1.3	1.6	1.7		1.1	1.6	1.9	1.5	2.0	2.2
3.3	4.2	3.1	Net Profit + Depr., Dep., Amort./Cur. Mat. L/T/D	(13) 3.5	(41) 2.6	(25) 3.4	(28) 3.9	(16) 5.5	
(92) 1.9	(96) 2.1	(127) 1.8		1.7	1.6	2.1	2.0	2.1	
1.1	1.1	1.1		.5	1.1	1.1	1.0	1.2	
.5	.5	.5	Fixed/Worth	.6	.4	.4	.5	.5	1.2
1.0	.9	1.0		1.3	.8	1.0	.9	1.1	1.6
2.5	2.1	2.1		4.7	1.7	1.8	2.3	2.2	3.2
.6	.7	.8	Debt/Worth	.6	.7	.7	.9	.9	1.4
1.5	1.4	1.7		1.9	1.6	1.4	1.7	2.1	1.8
3.6	2.9	4.0		7.0	3.9	3.4	3.5	3.7	3.1
44.1	36.0	41.7	% Profit Before Taxes/Tangible Net Worth	(40) 62.8	(84) 42.9	35.8	36.7	50.5	48.7
(186) 18.3	(212) 16.1	(254) 18.3		28.9	16.6	12.6	16.6	18.9	25.0
4.0	3.2	5.8		1.3	5.3	4.5	9.1	7.8	13.5
14.8	13.8	13.5	% Profit Before Taxes/Total Assets	22.5	11.9	10.9	12.0	16.2	13.9
7.0	6.0	6.3		6.2	6.2	5.1	6.4	6.9	6.7
1.3	1.3	2.3		.3	2.1	2.3	2.2	3.2	3.5
15.7	15.6	15.0	Sales/Net Fixed Assets	15.9	16.4	13.0	16.8	14.5	4.8
9.2	9.0	8.4		7.3	9.0	8.4	10.7	7.8	3.0
4.2	3.7	4.1		3.1	4.6	5.3	6.7	3.7	2.0
4.2	3.9	3.9	Sales/Total Assets	4.4	3.9	3.8	3.9	3.5	3.2
2.8	2.7	2.9		2.4	2.9	2.7	3.5	2.7	1.8
1.9	1.9	2.0		1.8	2.0	2.1	2.6	2.1	1.5
2.0	2.2	2.0	% Depr., Dep., Amort./Sales	(37) 2.0	(85) 2.2	(37) 2.2	(30) 1.4	(10) 1.5	2.6
(187) 3.3	(208) 3.5	(246) 3.2		4.6	3.2	3.4	2.7	3.0	4.2
5.1	5.1	4.9		7.3	5.0	4.3	4.4	4.3	7.3
3.4	3.3	2.7	% Officers', Directors', Owners' Comp/Sales	(24) 5.3	(45) 2.6	(19) 2.9	(28) 1.8		
(110) 6.4	(101) 5.9	(128) 5.0		7.7		5.4	3.7		
9.9	10.1	9.1		11.0	9.6	12.5	6.7		
1482432M	1653943M	2504668M	Net Sales ($)	29026M	167166M	157056M	323101M	489478M	1338841M
709691M	840122M	1275966M	Total Assets ($)	20350M	77938M	62203M	124662M	208606M	782207M

© Robert Morris Associates 1995   M = $ thousand   MM = $ million
See Pages 1 through 15 for Explanation of Ratios and Data

SERVICES—VETERINARIANS. SIC# 0741 (42)

Current Data Sorted By Assets | | | | | | **Comparative Historical Data**

0-500M	20 (4/1-9/30/94) 500M-2MM	2-10MM	77 (10/1/94-3/31/95) 10-50MM	50-100MM	100-250MM	# Postretirement Benefits / Type of Statement	4/1/90-3/31/91 ALL	4/1/91-3/31/92 ALL
7		1				# Postretirement Benefits		
						Type of Statement		
						Unqualified	2	3
2	2	1				Reviewed	5	9
49	4	1				Compiled	46	49
15	1					Tax Returns	3	8
22						Other	15	26
88	**7**	**2**				**NUMBER OF STATEMENTS**	**71**	**95**
%	%	%	%	%	%	**ASSETS**	%	%
16.6						Cash & Equivalents	14.5	16.2
8.8						Trade Receivables - (net)	8.9	7.7
8.7						Inventory	10.2	9.3
.8						All Other Current	1.1	2.0
35.1						Total Current	34.6	35.2
49.4						Fixed Assets (net)	44.8	47.3
7.6						Intangibles (net)	6.0	6.8
7.9						All Other Non-Current	14.6	10.8
100.0						Total	100.0	100.0
						LIABILITIES		
6.0						Notes Payable-Short Term	7.7	6.7
4.9						Cur. Mat. -L/T/D	7.2	5.3
6.7						Trade Payables	4.5	4.6
.2						Income Taxes Payable	.3	.6
9.0						All Other Current	9.1	10.8
26.8						Total Current	28.8	28.2
27.9						Long Term Debt	33.4	38.1
.2						Deferred Taxes	.1	.0
3.5						All Other-Non-Current	4.2	1.7
41.6						Net Worth	33.6	32.1
100.0						Total Liabilities & Net Worth	100.0	100.0
						INCOME DATA		
100.0						Net Sales	100.0	100.0
						Gross Profit		
89.0						Operating Expenses	88.3	89.9
11.0						Operating Profit	11.7	10.1
1.4						All Other Expenses (net)	2.4	1.5
9.6						Profit Before Taxes	9.3	8.5
						RATIOS		
2.4 / 1.5 / .7						Current	3.6 / 1.4 / .6	4.2 / 1.4 / .7
1.8 / .8 / .3						Quick	2.6 / .9 / .3	2.3 / .8 / .4
0 UND / 2 184.1 / 11 33.7						Sales/Receivables	0 UND / 3 111.8 / 15 24.4	0 UND / 2 200.0 / 16 22.3
						Cost of Sales/Inventory		
						Cost of Sales/Payables		
19.0 / 59.8 / -44.1						Sales/Working Capital	11.0 / 39.9 / -19.3	12.9 / 68.0 / -46.3
(67) 12.8 / 5.3 / 2.3						EBIT/Interest	(63) 8.0 / 3.3 / 1.0	(82) 8.9 / 3.8 / 1.5
						Net Profit + Depr., Dep., Amort./Cur. Mat. L /T/D	(14) 5.5 / 2.5 / .5	(14) 4.4 / 2.9 / 1.3
.7 / 1.5 / 5.2						Fixed/Worth	.4 / 1.4 / 27.3	.5 / 1.7 / 9.6
.7 / 1.9 / 6.4						Debt/Worth	.6 / 2.5 / 113.8	.9 / 2.7 / 15.2
(77) 166.7 / 77.4 / 24.7						% Profit Before Taxes/Tangible Net Worth	(54) 131.2 / 44.2 / -.5	(76) 195.4 / 52.3 / 9.8
47.0 / 22.3 / 6.0						% Profit Before Taxes/Total Assets	42.4 / 13.7 / -1.4	41.6 / 14.0 / 2.2
24.7 / 10.5 / 4.0						Sales/Net Fixed Assets	20.0 / 11.0 / 3.3	24.2 / 11.6 / 3.6
6.6 / 4.2 / 2.3						Sales/Total Assets	5.0 / 3.5 / 1.9	6.3 / 3.5 / 2.2
(76) 1.2 / 2.6 / 4.4						% Depr., Dep., Amort./Sales	(60) 1.9 / 3.3 / 4.3	(87) 1.4 / 2.7 / 4.2
(59) 9.2 / 15.0 / 24.5						% Officers', Directors', Owners' Comp/Sales	(41) 10.4 / 17.1 / 23.8	(55) 12.3 / 20.8 / 27.7
55217M / 12404M / 9119M						Net Sales ($)	57539M	142331M
13846M / 5917M / 11070M						Total Assets ($)	24978M	57744M

M = $ thousand   MM = $ million
See Pages 1 through 15 for Explanation of Ratios and Data

Comparative Historical Data				Current Data Sorted By Sales					
			# Postretirement Benefits	6		1		1	
			Type of Statement						
1	4		Unqualified						
3	8	5	Reviewed	2	2		1		
49	58	54	Compiled	45	9				
15	14	16	Tax Returns	11	3	1	1		
18	15	22	Other	18	4				
4/1/92-	4/1/93-	4/1/94-		20 (4/1-9/30/94)			77 (10/1/94-3/31/95)		
3/31/93	3/31/94	3/31/95		0-1MM	1-3MM	3-5MM	5-10MM	10-25MM	25MM & OVER
ALL	ALL	ALL							
86	99	97	NUMBER OF STATEMENTS	76	18	1	2		
%	%	%	ASSETS	%	%	%	%	%	%
14.9	15.3	15.6	Cash & Equivalents	16.0	15.0				
10.0	10.5	8.4	Trade Receivables - (net)	8.6	8.4				
9.3	10.9	8.2	Inventory	8.1	9.3				
1.9	.8	1.1	All Other Current	.9	.4				
36.1	37.6	33.3	Total Current	33.6	33.1				
46.0	48.3	51.3	Fixed Assets (net)	51.8	47.1				
7.3	6.5	7.6	Intangibles (net)	7.6	8.3				
10.6	7.6	7.8	All Other Non-Current	7.1	11.5				
100.0	100.0	100.0	Total	100.0	100.0				
			LIABILITIES						
7.3	5.7	6.1	Notes Payable-Short Term	4.3	9.2				
5.7	4.0	4.7	Cur. Mat.-L /T/D	5.3	3.0				
4.8	5.5	6.3	Trade Payables	5.9	8.5				
.5	.6	.2	Income Taxes Payable	.2	.4				
8.9	9.8	8.5	All Other Current	8.3	10.0				
27.2	25.6	25.8	Total Current	24.1	31.1				
34.1	31.7	28.6	Long Term Debt	29.0	28.6				
.0	.4	.2	Deferred Taxes	.2	.1				
2.7	1.5	4.0	All Other-Non-Current	4.9	.6				
36.0	40.7	41.4	Net Worth	41.7	39.5				
100.0	100.0	100.0	Total Liabilities & Net Worth	100.0	100.0				
			INCOME DATA						
100.0	100.0	100.0	Net Sales	100.0	100.0				
			Gross Profit						
89.6	90.7	89.0	Operating Expenses	88.0	93.1				
10.4	9.3	11.0	Operating Profit	12.0	6.9				
2.6	1.5	1.6	All Other Expenses (net)	1.6	1.4				
7.8	7.9	9.4	Profit Before Taxes	10.4	5.6				
			RATIOS						
3.9	3.3	2.4		2.5	1.8				
1.3	1.4	1.3	Current	1.6	1.1				
.5	.8	.7		.7	.5				
2.3	2.0	1.8		2.1	1.5				
.7	1.0	.8	Quick	.8	.7				
.3	.5	.3		.3	.4				
0 UND	0 UND	0 UND		0 UND	0 UND				
2 203.2	3 130.3	2 170.0	Sales/Receivables	2 242.0	4 85.7				
15 25.0	12 29.8	11 34.1		11 33.7	11 32.1				
			Cost of Sales/Inventory						
			Cost of Sales/Payables						
9.8	12.4	19.3		19.9	17.7				
54.6	29.8	81.9	Sales/Working Capital	59.8	118.2				
-22.2	-80.2	-47.1		-44.1	-48.0				
6.7	8.4	12.4		16.2	8.6				
(78) 3.2	(86) 3.6	(76) 4.3	EBIT/Interest	(57) 5.1	(16) 4.0				
1.0	1.4	2.1		2.2	1.0				
3.3	2.5								
(10) 1.7	(13) 2.1		Net Profit + Depr., Dep.,						
.4	1.2		Amort./Cur. Mat. L/T/D						
.5	.6	.7		.7	.7				
1.1	1.2	1.6	Fixed/Worth	1.5	2.1				
18.8	8.4	4.8		6.0	3.8				
.6	.5	.7		.6	1.0				
2.2	1.5	2.0	Debt/Worth	1.9	2.3				
26.1	20.4	5.9		6.8	6.1				
147.9	126.7	165.2	% Profit Before Taxes/Tangible	164.4	225.8				
(70) 26.0	(82) 29.1	(85) 71.1	Net Worth	(66) 78.5	(16) 60.9				
.0	1.1	16.9		26.4	1.9				
33.5	33.3	45.3	% Profit Before Taxes/Total	47.0	26.2				
7.8	9.0	21.7	Assets	22.3	16.0				
.0	-.1	4.8		7.4	-.3				
29.7	23.3	24.4		20.9	34.1				
10.0	8.5	9.6	Sales/Net Fixed Assets	9.2	17.5				
3.5	3.9	3.5		3.6	2.8				
5.8	6.4	6.3		6.4	7.1				
3.1	3.4	3.8	Sales/Total Assets	3.6	4.4				
2.0	1.9	2.1		2.0	2.1				
1.5	1.2	1.3		1.3	1.2				
(78) 2.7	(88) 2.2	(84) 2.8	% Depr., Dep., Amort./Sales	(66) 3.4	(15) 2.0				
4.2	4.6	4.4		4.7	3.9				
10.4	10.6	8.0		9.3	7.2				
(57) 18.1	(66) 15.5	(63) 15.0	% Officers', Directors',	(50) 15.5	(12) 10.8				
26.4	26.5	24.5	Owners' Comp/Sales	23.2	24.6				
74648M	116158M	76740M	Net Sales ($)	34124M	24273M	3641M	14702M		
23923M	48037M	30833M	Total Assets ($)	11449M	13376M	794M	5214M		

© Robert Morris Associates 1995

M = $ thousand   MM = $ million
See Pages 1 through 15 for Explanation of Ratios and Data

SERVICES—VIDEO TAPE RENTALS. SIC# 7841

Current Data Sorted By Assets / Comparative Historical Data

Postretirement Benefits — Type of Statement

Type of Statement	0-500M	500M-2MM	2-10MM	10-50MM	50-100MM	100-250MM	4/1/90-3/31/91 ALL	4/1/91-3/31/92 ALL
Unqualified		1	7	1		1	10	8
Reviewed		6	2				10	11
Compiled	16	14	3				35	33
Tax Returns	3	6						4
Other	10	6	7	1			24	15

Date groups: 25 (4/1-9/30/94) 59 (10/1/94-3/31/95)

	0-500M	500M-2MM	2-10MM	10-50MM	50-100MM	100-250MM		4/1/90-3/31/91 ALL	4/1/91-3/31/92 ALL
NUMBER OF STATEMENTS	29	33	19	2		1		79	71
	%	%	%	%	%	%		%	%
ASSETS									
Cash & Equivalents	11.9	8.1	11.2					9.3	11.0
Trade Receivables - (net)	2.3	4.6	3.3					5.5	5.8
Inventory	21.1	14.9	15.6					14.1	15.4
All Other Current	.8	2.4	5.9					2.6	1.7
Total Current	36.1	30.1	36.0					31.6	33.9
Fixed Assets (net)	54.8	59.4	49.1					58.1	54.6
Intangibles (net)	2.3	4.1	5.8					3.4	4.8
All Other Non-Current	6.8	6.4	9.1					6.9	6.8
Total	100.0	100.0	100.0					100.0	100.0
LIABILITIES									
Notes Payable-Short Term	6.0	5.2	4.4					10.7	8.4
Cur. Mat. -L/T/D	4.6	5.6	6.5					6.6	7.1
Trade Payables	5.7	19.3	16.4					11.8	10.1
Income Taxes Payable	.1	.1	.7					.6	.4
All Other Current	8.1	8.1	8.2					6.2	7.3
Total Current	24.4	38.2	36.2					36.0	33.2
Long Term Debt	25.5	21.0	23.6					28.6	26.8
Deferred Taxes	.0	.5	1.6					.3	1.3
All Other-Non-Current	14.6	6.5	5.0					6.4	3.4
Net Worth	35.5	33.8	33.6					28.7	35.2
Total Liabilities & Net Worth	100.0	100.0	100.0					100.0	100.0
INCOME DATA									
Net Sales	100.0	100.0	100.0					100.0	100.0
Gross Profit									
Operating Expenses	90.3	94.2	96.5					91.7	93.8
Operating Profit	9.7	5.8	3.5					8.3	6.2
All Other Expenses (net)	1.8	1.4	2.1					3.0	2.2
Profit Before Taxes	7.9	4.4	1.4					5.3	4.1
RATIOS									
Current	5.1	1.5	1.8					2.0	2.7
	1.7	.6	1.0					.7	1.0
	.5	.4	.4					.2	.3
Quick	1.6	(32) .5	.8				(78)	1.2	1.2
	.5	.3	.2					.3	.4
	.1	.2	.0					.1	.1
Sales/Receivables	0 UND	0 UND	0 999.8					0 UND	0 UND
	0 UND	0 UND	2 234.5					0 UND	1 311.0
	5 80.8	3 117.4	7 51.4					3 110.6	6 56.6
Cost of Sales/Inventory									
Cost of Sales/Payables									
Sales/Working Capital	3.1	25.9	7.7					18.2	11.7
	14.7	-19.6	107.1					-29.5	-556.0
	-21.3	-11.4	-7.1					-7.4	-7.2
EBIT/Interest	(27) 7.6	(29) 10.1	(17) 5.2				(71)	4.9	(61) 6.1
	5.0	2.7	4.5					2.4	2.7
	2.3	1.5	3.2					.8	.8
Net Profit + Depr., Dep., Amort./Cur. Mat. L /T/D							(17)	3.9	(10) 9.7
								2.3	2.4
								1.4	1.0
Fixed/Worth	.5	1.3	1.1					1.0	.8
	1.4	1.8	2.1					3.1	1.9
	3.2	5.5	3.5					30.4	14.9
Debt/Worth	.7	1.0	1.5					1.0	1.0
	1.1	1.6	2.7					2.7	2.3
	10.1	10.9	4.3					36.4	35.4
% Profit Before Taxes/Tangible Net Worth	(24) 52.5	(28) 74.5	(18) 60.6				(62)	60.7	(56) 51.5
	31.5	25.0	35.3					23.6	23.4
	8.3	8.4	7.7					-2.5	5.4
% Profit Before Taxes/Total Assets	23.7	18.2	16.4					18.3	16.0
	13.6	7.9	9.1					6.8	8.7
	2.7	1.1	2.7					-1.2	-.9
Sales/Net Fixed Assets	6.6	9.3	7.8					8.1	9.4
	3.4	4.2	3.5					3.5	3.6
	2.3	2.6	1.7					2.0	2.0
Sales/Total Assets	2.5	3.1	2.0					2.9	3.4
	1.8	2.3	1.5					2.2	2.0
	1.2	1.8	.9					1.4	1.4
% Depr., Dep., Amort./Sales	(20) 3.8	(20) 2.4	(13) 8.6				(54)	3.5	(48) 2.7
	18.2	5.9	21.3					10.0	6.4
	26.1	17.0	26.2					23.6	21.1
% Officers', Directors', Owners' Comp/Sales	(13) 5.2	(18) 3.0					(31)	4.5	(34) 4.2
	10.0	5.3						7.3	5.9
	19.7	13.0						10.4	10.5
Net Sales ($)	14622M	76211M	121200M	55266M		73288M		517987M	582179M
Total Assets ($)	7136M	30028M	83204M	29618M		142861M		379324M	406072M

M = $ thousand   MM = $ million
See Pages 1 through 15 for Explanation of Ratios and Data

Comparative Historical Data				Current Data Sorted By Sales					
1	1	4	# Postretirement Benefits			3			1
			Type of Statement						
6	10	10	Unqualified		2	2	4		2
5	5	8	Reviewed	2	1	3	2		
25	28	33	Compiled	15	13	3	2		
2	8	9	Tax Returns	3	4	2			
21	20	24	Other	10	7		4	2	1
4/1/92-3/31/93	4/1/93-3/31/94	4/1/94-3/31/95		25 (4/1-9/30/94)			59 (10/1/94-3/31/95)		
ALL	ALL	ALL		0-1MM	1-3MM	3-5MM	5-10MM	10-25MM	25MM & OVER
59	71	84	**NUMBER OF STATEMENTS**	30	27	10	12	2	3
%	%	%	**ASSETS**	%	%	%	%	%	%
9.2	10.1	10.4	Cash & Equivalents	10.9	10.4	11.2	8.3		
6.4	6.0	3.4	Trade Receivables - (net)	1.8	6.1	1.4	3.8		
16.0	13.1	16.8	Inventory	22.3	13.5	21.2	10.9		
1.1	1.4	2.6	All Other Current	.8	3.1	1.1	8.2		
32.7	30.5	33.3	Total Current	35.8	33.1	34.9	31.1		
54.6	56.7	54.9	Fixed Assets (net)	56.4	53.6	49.9	59.2		
5.7	5.5	4.1	Intangibles (net)	2.5	4.8	5.7	3.9		
7.1	7.3	7.8	All Other Non-Current	5.4	8.5	9.5	5.7		
100.0	100.0	100.0	Total	100.0	100.0	100.0	100.0		
			LIABILITIES						
7.1	5.3	5.1	Notes Payable-Short Term	7.3	2.6	6.1	5.0		
	4.7	5.3	Cur. Mat.-L /T/D	3.9	6.4	3.8	8.1		
13.2	14.4	13.7	Trade Payables	4.6	15.4	26.8	20.9		
.5	.6	.2	Income Taxes Payable	.1	.1	.2	.8		
12.7	9.8	7.9	All Other Current	7.3	8.6	7.8	8.8		
41.0	34.9	32.2	Total Current	23.2	33.1	44.6	43.6		
20.4	20.7	23.0	Long Term Debt	25.9	25.0	20.4	14.7		
.2	.3	.6	Deferred Taxes	.1	.6	2.1	.3		
3.5	1.7	8.8	All Other-Non-Current	11.4	10.9	2.1	6.5		
35.0	42.5	35.4	Net Worth	39.4	30.4	30.8	34.9		
100.0	100.0	100.0	Total Liabilities & Net Worth	100.0	100.0	100.0	100.0		
			INCOME DATA						
100.0	100.0	100.0	Net Sales	100.0	100.0	100.0	100.0		
			Gross Profit						
92.3	90.7	93.0	Operating Expenses	90.0	99.1	90.0	92.3		
7.7	9.3	7.0	Operating Profit	10.0	.9	10.0	7.7		
2.0	1.6	1.8	All Other Expenses (net)	2.0	1.2	1.8	1.9		
5.7	7.7	5.2	Profit Before Taxes	8.0	-.3	8.3	5.8		
			RATIOS						
1.5	1.7	2.2		6.6	1.7	1.3	1.3		
.6	.8	1.0	Current	1.9	1.0	.8	.7		
.3	.4	.4		.6	.4	.4	.2		
.7	.8	.8		1.5	.8	.5	.7		
.3	.5	(83) .4	Quick	.5	(26) .3	.3	.3		
.1	.1	.2		.1	.2	.1	.0		
0 UND	0 UND	0 UND		0 UND	0 UND	0 UND	0 UND		
2 190.6	2 234.5	0 UND	Sales/Receivables	0 UND	0 UND	1 483.2	1 415.6		
11 33.1	9 38.9	5 68.8		6 59.7	3 133.2	5 66.8	5 75.8		
			Cost of Sales/Inventory						
			Cost of Sales/Payables						
16.2	21.8	7.9		2.9	11.6	23.4	23.1		
-21.0	-36.1	-416.7	Sales/Working Capital	15.0	-657.3	-50.8	-26.9		
-6.4	-8.6	-12.0		-25.7	-11.5	-11.5	-5.7		
7.4	16.0	8.8		9.9	7.7		8.8		
(54) 3.3	(67) 5.2	(76) 4.5	EBIT/Interest	(27) 4.6	(24) 2.5		(11) 5.4		
1.0	2.4	2.0		2.3	.1		4.0		
3.4	8.7	6.0							
(12) 2.4	(14) 4.8	(15) 3.8	Net Profit + Depr., Dep., Amort./Cur. Mat. L/T/D						
1.0	2.7	2.2							
1.1	.9	.9		.5	.9	1.3	1.1		
1.9	1.6	1.6	Fixed/Worth	1.5	1.8	1.6	2.0		
4.1	3.5	3.4		3.1	-58.8	3.2	3.3		
.8	.5	.9		.7	.7	1.2	1.5		
2.3	1.6	1.6	Debt/Worth	1.1	1.9	2.1	1.7		
6.2	4.0	4.7		5.4	-65.7	9.4	3.6		
66.7	60.4	58.9		45.7	38.0		62.6		
(51) 29.4	(63) 41.6	(73) 28.6	% Profit Before Taxes/Tangible Net Worth	(27) 30.3	(20) 21.2		46.8		
8.1	10.4	9.1		8.1	-5.7		21.4		
20.5	23.1	19.3		22.8	15.8	37.7	21.2		
9.1	12.8	10.6	% Profit Before Taxes/Total Assets	10.6	6.7	13.9	12.7		
.5	4.0	2.6		3.3	-3.7	2.9	7.8		
10.0	7.0	7.2		5.4	9.8	9.8	8.1		
3.6	3.6	3.8	Sales/Net Fixed Assets	2.6	4.5	5.5	3.5		
2.0	1.9	2.1		1.4	2.3	3.9	2.1		
2.8	3.1	2.7		2.0	3.1	3.4	3.4		
2.0	2.0	1.9	Sales/Total Assets	1.4	2.3	2.5	1.9		
1.5	1.3	1.4		.8	1.9	1.8	1.5		
3.7	3.8	3.6		3.6	3.2		3.2		
(45) 10.8	(55) 12.2	(54) 13.8	% Depr., Dep., Amort./Sales	(23) 18.0	(16) 11.7		(10) 14.9		
23.2	23.2	24.2		27.3	20.0		26.1		
5.8	3.4	3.1		6.6	3.6				
(20) 8.5	(27) 6.5	(39) 6.6	% Officers', Directors', Owners' Comp/Sales	(11) 12.2	(18) 6.4				
12.7	11.8	14.2		19.6	14.0				
185996M	710090M	340587M	Net Sales ($)	13174M	48170M	39007M	85763M	25919M	128554M
137439M	344398M	292847M	Total Assets ($)	10373M	27355M	17587M	47287M	17766M	172479M

M = $ thousand   MM = $ million
See Pages 1 through 15 for Explanation of Ratios and Data

Current Data Sorted By Assets   Comparative Historical Data

0-500M	500M-2MM	2-10MM	10-50MM	50-100MM	100-250MM		4/1/90-3/31/91 ALL	4/1/91-3/31/92 ALL
	2		1		2	# Postretirement Benefits / Type of Statement		
	5	16	10		2	Unqualified	16	20
3	15	8	2			Reviewed	9	17
3	5	4	1			Compiled	15	8
3						Tax Returns		1
5	3	5	5			Other	7	5
	72 (4/1-9/30/94)		20 (10/1/94-3/31/95)					
11	28	33	18		2	NUMBER OF STATEMENTS	47	51
%	%	%	%	%	%	**ASSETS**	%	%
25.7	12.3	11.9	13.3			Cash & Equivalents	10.3	8.5
6.9	16.2	21.4	15.3			Trade Receivables - (net)	15.7	14.8
10.3	14.0	17.2	18.6			Inventory	14.9	12.4
4.5	3.9	4.4	7.1			All Other Current	6.2	6.4
47.4	46.4	54.8	54.3			Total Current	47.1	42.0
42.3	43.9	36.9	37.3			Fixed Assets (net)	42.1	43.7
.0	.3	.8	.3			Intangibles (net)	1.0	1.8
10.3	9.4	7.5	8.1			All Other Non-Current	9.8	12.5
100.0	100.0	100.0	100.0			Total	100.0	100.0
						LIABILITIES		
11.3	12.6	11.1	15.3			Notes Payable-Short Term	14.2	9.9
7.6	2.3	3.8	2.7			Cur. Mat. -L/T/D	3.0	5.3
13.1	10.4	13.9	9.1			Trade Payables	11.2	9.3
.2	.0	.2	1.2			Income Taxes Payable	.2	.4
17.8	7.0	7.5	11.1			All Other Current	7.0	7.8
50.0	32.3	36.6	39.2			Total Current	35.5	32.6
21.3	20.6	18.4	22.7			Long Term Debt	22.4	18.4
.1	1.1	1.4	1.9			Deferred Taxes	.9	.8
.0	.8	3.4	1.2			All Other-Non-Current	4.6	3.4
28.6	45.1	40.0	35.0			Net Worth	36.5	44.7
100.0	100.0	100.0	100.0			Total Liabilities & Net Worth	100.0	100.0
						INCOME DATA		
100.0	100.0	100.0	100.0			Net Sales	100.0	100.0
						Gross Profit		
88.6	94.9	95.1	85.6			Operating Expenses	91.6	92.3
11.4	5.1	4.9	14.4			Operating Profit	8.4	7.7
4.4	3.0	.8	3.1			All Other Expenses (net)	4.0	4.8
7.0	2.1	4.1	11.3			Profit Before Taxes	4.4	2.9
						RATIOS		
1.7	3.8	2.0	1.7			Current	1.7	1.9
1.1	1.5	1.4	1.3				1.2	1.2
.3	.9	1.2	1.1				.8	.7
1.0	2.0	1.7	1.5			Quick	1.3	1.2
.5	1.0	.8	.8				(46) .6	(50) .6
.3	.5	.4	.3				.3	.3
0 UND	5 71.9	10 35.6	7 49.9			Sales/Receivables	7 51.2	6 57.4
1 537.0	13 27.3	28 12.9	22 16.3				20 18.4	18 20.5
17 21.1	34 10.6	60 6.1	43 8.5				41 8.9	37 10.0
						Cost of Sales/Inventory		
						Cost of Sales/Payables		
13.9	6.5	4.3	6.2			Sales/Working Capital	7.4	8.3
58.7	37.6	16.3	16.8				28.1	37.2
-8.0	NM	48.9	81.8				-25.0	-15.5
	3.8	5.6	4.7			EBIT/Interest	4.6	3.5
	(24) 2.3	(32) 2.7	(15) 2.2				(40) 1.8	(45) 1.8
	1.2	1.2	1.8				1.1	.6
	18.0	5.5	3.0			Net Profit + Depr., Dep., Amort./Cur. Mat. L /T/D	7.4	3.9
	(10) 2.4	(16) 2.6	(11) 1.4				(21) 1.7	(24) .9
	1.2	1.5	1.0				.9	.3
.2	.5	.6	.5			Fixed/Worth	.5	.5
1.2	1.2	.8	.8				1.3	1.0
4.0	1.9	1.7	1.9				2.9	1.9
.8	.4	.7	1.2			Debt/Worth	1.0	.8
3.8	1.8	2.0	2.2				1.8	1.2
6.8	3.4	3.0	5.6				5.3	2.6
	21.7	18.7	23.6			% Profit Before Taxes/Tangible Net Worth	20.0	19.2
	(32) 9.4	(16) 9.8	12.0				(43) 6.3	6.3
	.7	2.5	8.4				2.2	-1.7
16.3	7.6	8.6	12.0			% Profit Before Taxes/Total Assets	8.5	7.6
4.0	3.3	3.2	4.9				1.6	2.5
.2	.5	.8	3.1				.4	-1.2
76.9	18.3	12.1	11.0			Sales/Net Fixed Assets	15.5	9.2
7.2	8.6	6.3	4.6				6.0	5.0
.5	2.8	2.5	1.2				2.0	1.2
7.2	5.4	4.0	2.7			Sales/Total Assets	3.9	3.6
3.0	2.9	2.0	1.2				1.8	1.9
.5	1.5	.9	.6				.7	.6
	.7	1.2	.9			% Depr., Dep., Amort./Sales	1.3	1.6
	(27) 1.7	(31) 2.4	(17) 2.2				(45) 1.9	(49) 3.6
	2.6	4.9	5.1				4.7	6.8
		.7				% Officers', Directors', Owners' Comp/Sales	2.3	1.6
		(10) 1.4					(16) 6.1	(21) 3.3
		12.8					14.5	7.7
8123M	104951M	330366M	683713M		807616M	Net Sales ($)	290664M	1089327M
2907M	31581M	146320M	433155M		332760M	Total Assets ($)	178434M	495238M

© Robert Morris Associates 1995

M = $ thousand   MM = $ million

See Pages 1 through 15 for Explanation of Ratios and Data

SERVICES—WAREHOUSING & STORAGE – FARM PRODUCT. SIC# 4221

823

Comparative Historical Data / Current Data Sorted By Sales

	1		5	# Postretirement Benefits	1	1				3
				Type of Statement						
	27	23	33	Unqualified		2	4	7	10	10
	19	21	28	Reviewed	3	9	5	7	2	2
	7	11	10	Compiled	2	2	3	1		2
	1	5	3	Tax Returns	3					
	9	10	18	Other	4	6	3	1	1	3
	4/1/92-3/31/93	4/1/93-3/31/94	4/1/94-3/31/95		72 (4/1-9/30/94)			20 (10/1/94-3/31/95)		
	ALL	ALL	ALL		0-1MM	1-3MM	3-5MM	5-10MM	10-25MM	25MM & OVER
	63	70	92	**NUMBER OF STATEMENTS**	12	19	15	16	15	15
	%	%	%	**ASSETS**	%	%	%	%	%	%
	7.5	9.7	13.7	Cash & Equivalents	23.4	14.3	11.0	11.9	12.0	11.7
	14.6	12.7	16.8	Trade Receivables - (net)	5.9	13.8	24.3	15.1	26.8	13.6
	15.9	16.3	16.2	Inventory	3.7	12.7	14.1	18.8	16.1	30.1
	6.2	6.4	4.8	All Other Current	4.9	7.1	3.5	3.8	1.8	7.1
	44.2	45.1	51.5	Total Current	38.0	47.9	52.9	49.6	56.7	62.5
	45.7	47.3	39.4	Fixed Assets (net)	52.8	37.0	39.7	44.5	33.9	31.5
	.9	1.3	.4	Intangibles (net)	.6	1.0	.2	.3	.4	.1
	9.2	6.3	8.6	All Other Non-Current	8.7	14.1	7.2	5.6	9.0	5.9
	100.0	100.0	100.0	Total	100.0	100.0	100.0	100.0	100.0	100.0
				LIABILITIES						
	8.9	10.7	12.7	Notes Payable-Short Term	11.3	13.4	13.8	6.7	10.3	20.7
	4.6	3.6	3.5	Cur. Mat.-L/T/D	7.9	3.0	2.3	4.6	3.2	1.3
	9.7	7.8	11.6	Trade Payables	11.6	9.6	7.4	12.1	17.2	12.0
	.2	1.5	.4	Income Taxes Payable	.2	.0	.3	.2	.3	1.1
	8.4	8.6	9.9	All Other Current	16.2	5.4	6.7	11.2	6.2	16.0
	31.8	32.3	38.1	Total Current	47.2	31.4	30.5	34.7	37.1	51.2
	18.2	20.3	20.2	Long Term Debt	26.0	23.5	17.5	24.5	19.3	10.3
	1.0	1.0	1.2	Deferred Taxes	.2	1.4	1.2	1.0	1.6	1.8
	1.0	1.6	1.7	All Other-Non-Current	1.8	.2	.0	7.1	.4	.9
	48.0	44.8	38.8	Net Worth	24.8	43.5	50.7	32.6	41.7	35.8
	100.0	100.0	100.0	Total Liabilities & Net Worth	100.0	100.0	100.0	100.0	100.0	100.0
				INCOME DATA						
	100.0	100.0	100.0	Net Sales	100.0	100.0	100.0	100.0	100.0	100.0
				Gross Profit						
	91.2	89.7	92.4	Operating Expenses	81.8	96.6	93.1	90.0	94.0	95.8
	8.8	10.3	7.6	Operating Profit	18.2	3.4	6.9	10.0	6.0	4.2
	2.7	4.2	2.4	All Other Expenses (net)	10.5	-.6	.9	4.5	.4	.8
	6.2	6.1	5.2	Profit Before Taxes	7.7	4.0	6.0	5.5	5.5	3.5
				RATIOS						
	2.0	2.2	1.9		1.3	4.1	4.8	1.6	2.0	1.4
	1.4	1.3	1.4	Current	.8	1.7	1.6	1.3	1.6	1.2
	.9	.9	1.0		.3	.9	1.1	1.2	1.3	1.1
	1.2	1.5	1.5		1.1	2.8	4.2	1.1	1.5	.7
	.8	.6	.7	Quick	.5	.6	1.6	.7	1.0	.4
	.4	.3	.4		.3	.3	.5	.6	.6	.3
	6 61.5	5 75.1	7 53.8		0 UND	17 21.6	11 33.2	7 54.3	11 33.0	7 54.3
	16 23.5	12 30.8	19 19.6	Sales/Receivables	0 UND	25 14.6	46 8.0	16 23.5	25 14.8	18 20.7
	37 10.0	33 10.9	42 8.6		30 12.1	42 8.6	65 5.6	25 14.8	78 4.7	30 12.0
				Cost of Sales/Inventory						
				Cost of Sales/Payables						
	10.0	8.5	6.3		13.5	4.3	2.9	13.1	11.5	13.2
	27.4	24.6	20.0	Sales/Working Capital	-12.8	7.7	9.2	27.8	16.8	20.3
	-104.2	-99.5	123.6		-1.4	-52.8	501.4	66.8	41.3	119.2
	3.7	8.6	4.3			3.7	4.7	9.0	4.3	2.7
(60)	2.1	(63) 3.9	(80) 2.2	EBIT/Interest	(17) 1.9	(13) 4.2	2.6	2.1	(12) 2.2
	1.0	2.0	1.2			.8	2.1	2.1	1.4	1.2
	4.8	4.2	5.2				13.3			
(28)	1.5	(26) 1.8	(40) 2.0	Net Profit + Depr., Dep.,		(10) 2.4			
	.9	1.0	1.3	Amort./Cur. Mat. L/T/D			1.0			
	.5	.6	.5		.4	.3	.5	.7	.5	.5
	.9	1.0	1.0	Fixed/Worth	2.2	1.2	.6	1.2	.7	.8
	1.8	1.8	1.9		6.3	2.2	1.7	2.8	1.3	1.7
	.5	.5	.7		.9	.3	.4	1.4	.5	1.4
	1.2	1.5	2.0	Debt/Worth	5.0	1.8	1.3	2.4	1.7	2.7
	2.3	3.6	3.8		13.1	3.6	2.5	4.0	3.4	3.9
	23.1	28.5	24.5		80.8	24.5	23.0	36.9	15.0	20.1
	9.5	(68) 13.0	(87) 11.4	% Profit Before Taxes/Tangible	(10) 28.6	2.5	11.0	(14) 13.2	(14) 7.9	11.7
	1.0	5.7	2.5	Net Worth	10.6	-2.0	4.0	5.6	2.5	7.7
	9.2	10.8	9.0		10.1	10.6	9.3	12.3	6.7	8.4
	3.5	5.2	3.5	% Profit Before Taxes/Total	5.3	2.1	4.7	5.8	2.6	3.4
	.4	2.1	1.1	Assets	.1	-.4	2.7	2.5	.6	1.6
	14.1	13.0	14.4		59.4	12.6	13.4	17.7	20.4	25.9
	6.1	5.1	7.0	Sales/Net Fixed Assets	.9	4.6	6.8	7.0	10.3	10.6
	2.4	1.8	2.1		.5	2.1	1.5	3.9	4.3	5.2
	4.4	3.8	4.0		2.9	3.0	3.4	5.3	5.3	4.5
	2.8	2.1	2.3	Sales/Total Assets	.5	1.4	2.6	2.3	3.2	2.7
	1.1	.9	.7		.3	.6	1.5	1.2	1.7	1.4
	1.0	1.0	.9			1.1	1.5	.7	.4	.7
(57)	2.4	3.2	(85) 1.8	% Depr., Dep., Amort./Sales	(18) 2.2	1.8	(15) 1.5	(14) 1.5	(14) 1.1
	5.0	6.3	5.1			5.8	4.9	3.1	3.5	2.7
	2.3	1.5	.7							
(21)	4.2	(25) 4.7	(26) 2.8	% Officers', Directors',						
	15.1	15.1	8.4	Owners' Comp/Sales						
	739617M	801684M	1934769M	Net Sales ($)	4719M	41003M	58383M	122843M	238478M	1469343M
	343941M	488266M	946723M	Total Assets ($)	6690M	43679M	54106M	83737M	148256M	610255M

M = $ thousand   MM = $ million
See Pages 1 through 15 for Explanation of Ratios and Data

Current Data Sorted By Assets / Comparative Historical Data

	0-500M	500M-2MM	2-10MM	10-50MM	50-100MM	100-250MM	# Postretirement Benefits / Type of Statement	4/1/90-3/31/91 ALL	4/1/91-3/31/92 ALL
	3	3	4	2					
	1	7	10	12	5	2	Unqualified	27	35
	3	18	21	5			Reviewed	28	40
	15	27	18	2			Compiled	52	40
	7	3	2				Tax Returns	2	4
	6	25	21	5			Other	34	46
		40 (4/1-9/30/94)		175 (10/1/94-3/31/95)					
NUMBER OF STATEMENTS	32	80	72	24	5	2		143	165
	%	%	%	%	%	%	**ASSETS**	%	%
Cash & Equivalents	11.5	7.0	7.8	7.7				7.6	8.1
Trade Receivables - (net)	12.6	17.3	16.5	17.2				18.4	18.5
Inventory	3.5	2.6	1.4	6.0				3.3	3.3
All Other Current	1.1	2.0	1.7	.7				2.0	2.4
Total Current	28.8	28.9	27.4	31.7				31.3	32.3
Fixed Assets (net)	55.2	61.7	61.2	57.6				57.3	57.6
Intangibles (net)	.7	.9	1.9	1.7				2.5	1.3
All Other Non-Current	15.3	8.5	9.5	9.0				8.9	8.8
Total	100.0	100.0	100.0	100.0				100.0	100.0
							LIABILITIES		
Notes Payable-Short Term	4.3	4.2	6.4	6.2				6.8	6.4
Cur. Mat. -L/T/D	5.3	5.5	4.9	4.8				5.5	5.8
Trade Payables	6.7	5.9	5.9	7.9				7.7	8.0
Income Taxes Payable	.3	.4	.5	.2				.4	.5
All Other Current	17.6	10.5	7.5	9.6				6.5	10.1
Total Current	34.2	26.6	25.2	28.8				27.0	30.8
Long Term Debt	36.1	41.2	33.6	36.9				36.7	35.0
Deferred Taxes	.1	1.2	.7	1.0				.6	.4
All Other-Non-Current	3.0	3.3	4.4	.8				2.8	2.4
Net Worth	26.7	27.7	36.0	32.5				33.0	31.3
Total Liabilities & Net Worth	100.0	100.0	100.0	100.0				100.0	100.0
							INCOME DATA		
Net Sales	100.0	100.0	100.0	100.0				100.0	100.0
Gross Profit									
Operating Expenses	74.1	79.1	84.2	87.6				84.6	84.3
Operating Profit	25.9	20.9	15.8	12.4				15.4	15.7
All Other Expenses (net)	9.7	9.8	5.4	3.8				9.3	9.4
Profit Before Taxes	16.2	11.1	10.4	8.6				6.1	6.3
							RATIOS		
Current	1.7	2.1	1.7	1.8				2.0	1.9
	.7	1.0	1.1	1.1				1.2	1.1
	.2	.3	.6	.8				.6	.6
Quick	1.5	1.6	1.5	1.7				1.8	1.6
	.6	.8	1.0	.9				.9	.9
	.2	.2	.5	.5				.5	.5
Sales/Receivables	0 UND	0 UND	22 16.5	20 17.9				20 18.0	14 25.5
	0 UND	24 15.0	35 10.3	38 9.7				33 11.2	33 11.2
	38 9.7	41 9.0	45 8.2	48 7.6				53 6.9	47 7.7
Cost of Sales/Inventory									
Cost of Sales/Payables									
Sales/Working Capital	11.4	10.1	14.0	8.3				6.6	8.8
	-26.0	NM	120.8	150.8				38.0	75.9
	-2.1	-6.8	-7.1	-54.1				-9.2	-9.6
EBIT/Interest	8.7	6.9	7.8	5.5				6.0	7.0
	(20) 3.2	(56) 3.5	(60) 3.6	(21) 2.7				(107) 2.0	(125) 2.6
	2.0	1.3	2.0	1.7				1.3	1.5
Net Profit + Depr., Dep., Amort./Cur. Mat. L/T/D		3.7	3.6	2.5				3.4	2.9
		(27) 1.8	(30) 1.9	(14) 1.6				(68) 1.9	(59) 1.6
		1.2	1.2	.7				.8	.7
Fixed/Worth	.4	.9	.9	.8				.8	.7
	2.0	2.9	1.9	2.0				1.9	1.7
	NM	8.7	4.4	9.8				6.3	6.6
Debt/Worth	1.0	1.0	1.0	1.2				.9	1.1
	2.4	3.1	1.9	2.2				2.3	2.3
	NM	9.0	4.9	10.4				6.8	8.3
% Profit Before Taxes/Tangible Net Worth	109.0	49.5	44.3	43.7				30.1	37.1
	(24) 40.9	(69) 19.5	(65) 25.3	(21) 22.3				(126) 11.4	(142) 16.5
	27.3	6.0	10.7	8.9				2.2	6.1
% Profit Before Taxes/Total Assets	19.8	12.3	14.5	12.0				8.6	10.4
	11.4	7.1	8.0	5.9				3.3	5.5
	2.7	.9	3.1	3.4				.1	.1
Sales/Net Fixed Assets	30.7	8.0	6.7	4.5				6.9	7.9
	1.3	1.9	1.6	1.3				1.4	2.0
	.5	.3	.5	.9				.5	.5
Sales/Total Assets	3.6	2.7	2.3	1.7				2.2	2.6
	.9	1.0	1.0	1.0				.9	1.0
	.3	.3	.5	.7				.3	.4
% Depr., Dep., Amort./Sales	2.3	2.9	3.2	1.8				4.6	2.5
	(28) 12.1	(74) 6.7	(66) 5.1	5.2				(130) 7.9	(153) 5.6
	18.6	12.9	9.1	7.5				14.1	13.7
% Officers', Directors', Owners' Comp/Sales		3.2	2.6					3.4	4.3
		(29) 5.0	(27) 3.8					(41) 6.4	(55) 7.6
		12.7	6.5					11.6	11.2
Net Sales ($)	14825M	145659M	404840M	1038323M	504578M	175188M		712225M	1069696M
Total Assets ($)	8781M	91841M	289498M	532641M	332172M	305472M		844239M	1083135M

M = $ thousand   MM = $ million
See Pages 1 through 15 for Explanation of Ratios and Data

Comparative Historical Data				Current Data Sorted By Sales					
12	6	12	# Postretirement Benefits	3	4	1	2	1	1
			Type of Statement						
39	30	37	Unqualified	4	3	4	8	3	15
51	49	47	Reviewed	3	18	7	12	6	1
49	47	62	Compiled	35	17	4	2	4	
5	9	12	Tax Returns	11	1				
47	52	57	Other	21	13	7	11	4	1
4/1/92-3/31/93	4/1/93-3/31/94	4/1/94-3/31/95		40 (4/1-9/30/94)			175 (10/1/94-3/31/95)		
ALL	ALL	ALL		0-1MM	1-3MM	3-5MM	5-10MM	10-25MM	25MM & OVER
191	187	215	NUMBER OF STATEMENTS	74	52	22	33	17	17
%	%	%	ASSETS	%	%	%	%	%	%
8.1	7.4	7.9	Cash & Equivalents	6.8	7.7	8.3	9.4	11.0	7.0
17.2	17.0	16.3	Trade Receivables - (net)	4.2	17.4	28.9	25.7	25.8	21.6
3.3	3.0	2.9	Inventory	1.5	2.5	2.5	3.5	5.1	7.0
2.7	1.3	1.6	All Other Current	1.2	2.0	2.5	1.8	1.3	1.2
31.3	28.7	28.7	Total Current	13.6	29.6	42.2	40.5	43.2	36.8
58.5	60.3	59.9	Fixed Assets (net)	75.5	60.9	43.7	46.8	46.1	49.7
1.2	2.3	1.5	Intangibles (net)	.7	.8	1.8	3.0	1.4	4.0
8.9	8.7	9.9	All Other Non-Current	10.3	8.7	12.2	9.8	9.2	9.5
100.0	100.0	100.0	Total	100.0	100.0	100.0	100.0	100.0	100.0
			LIABILITIES						
5.3	6.0	5.3	Notes Payable-Short Term	3.0	3.2	9.7	10.0	4.7	7.7
6.5	5.0	5.2	Cur. Mat.-L /T/D	5.4	5.0	4.6	5.4	5.4	4.9
6.8	6.9	6.3	Trade Payables	2.9	6.1	9.5	9.1	8.5	9.8
.5	.6	.4	Income Taxes Payable	.3	.1	.7	.3	1.5	.3
9.2	9.5	10.4	All Other Current	9.5	10.2	10.4	11.2	10.0	13.6
28.2	28.0	27.5	Total Current	21.1	24.6	34.8	35.9	30.1	36.3
33.9	36.8	37.4	Long Term Debt	51.8	34.1	33.6	22.1	27.1	29.4
.5	1.0	.8	Deferred Taxes	.3	1.8	.0	.6	1.5	.9
3.5	2.6	3.5	All Other-Non-Current	2.0	4.6	6.0	1.8	6.3	3.7
34.0	31.6	30.8	Net Worth	24.8	34.9	25.5	39.6	35.0	29.7
100.0	100.0	100.0	Total Liabilities & Net Worth	100.0	100.0	100.0	100.0	100.0	100.0
			INCOME DATA						
100.0	100.0	100.0	Net Sales	100.0	100.0	100.0	100.0	100.0	100.0
			Gross Profit						
83.6	82.9	81.4	Operating Expenses	65.4	85.5	92.7	91.0	95.0	92.2
16.4	17.1	18.6	Operating Profit	34.6	14.5	7.3	9.0	5.0	7.8
8.6	7.1	7.4	All Other Expenses (net)	16.6	4.1	2.2	1.7	1.8	1.6
7.8	10.1	11.1	Profit Before Taxes	18.0	10.4	5.1	7.3	3.2	6.1
			RATIOS						
1.9	1.8	1.7		1.5	1.7	3.1	1.6	2.1	1.3
1.0	1.1	1.0	Current	.4	1.0	1.1	1.1	1.8	1.0
.5	.6	.4		.1	.6	.7	.8	1.1	.7
1.6	1.7	1.5		1.2	1.7	3.1	1.4	2.0	1.1
.9	.9	.9	Quick	.3	1.0	1.0	1.0	1.3	.8
.4	.5	.3		.1	.5	.7	.7	.8	.6
16 23.5	12 30.2	2 227.0		0 UND	14 26.5	30 12.3	29 12.7	34 10.8	28 13.2
30 12.0	33 11.0	31 11.7	Sales/Receivables	0 UND	32 11.3	40 9.1	38 9.5	40 9.2	45 8.1
48 7.6	46 7.9	45 8.2		12 30.4	44 8.3	50 7.3	48 7.6	47 7.8	56 6.5
			Cost of Sales/Inventory						
			Cost of Sales/Payables						
10.4	12.8	11.5		13.0	12.7	7.3	13.6	9.6	17.6
125.0	148.5	UND	Sales/Working Capital	-7.8	194.1	56.9	41.5	14.8	-98.9
-7.4	-11.0	-7.0		-2.1	-10.6	-24.3	-22.2	NM	-17.6
(137) 6.9	(146) 5.9	(164) 6.3		(38) 4.6	(46) 6.4	(18) 8.1	(31) 11.3	(15) 5.0	(16) 5.6
2.8	3.1	3.3	EBIT/Interest	3.3	2.7	3.5	4.2	2.7	3.1
1.6	1.8	1.7		1.9	1.4	1.3	2.2	1.9	1.5
(77) 3.4	(63) 3.1	(81) 3.1		(13) 1.9	(25) 4.4		(15) 3.8		(12) 2.8
1.8	1.7	1.9	Net Profit + Depr., Dep.,	1.5	2.0		2.3		2.1
.9	1.1	1.1	Amort./Cur. Mat. L/T/D	.9	1.1		1.7		.9
.8	.9	.9		1.5	1.0	.7	.6	.7	.7
1.8	2.4	2.2	Fixed/Worth	3.7	1.9	2.9	1.3	1.3	2.3
5.7	6.1	5.9		36.3	4.9	7.1	3.2	3.2	NM
1.0	1.2	1.0		1.1	.8	1.1	.9	1.1	1.6
2.5	2.7	2.3	Debt/Worth	4.1	1.6	3.8	1.7	2.0	2.4
6.9	6.9	8.0		45.0	5.4	11.9	3.7	3.9	NM
(172) 39.8	(167) 43.7	(184) 47.6	% Profit Before Taxes/Tangible	(58) 67.2	(48) 41.1	(19) 53.8	(31) 60.2	(15) 23.0	(13) 41.9
15.8	21.2	25.7	Net Worth	29.0	21.7	12.3	33.3	12.8	27.5
6.7	6.2	10.0		11.7	5.4	-7.1	18.4	4.9	18.1
11.7	12.4	13.7	% Profit Before Taxes/Total	13.4	14.5	9.6	21.7	9.0	12.8
5.3	5.8	7.6	Assets	6.2	8.3	5.0	10.6	7.0	7.9
1.6	2.1	2.5		1.7	1.7	-2.4	4.5	2.5	2.8
7.4	7.7	7.3		1.0	8.0	10.9	16.3	12.5	10.8
1.5	1.6	1.5	Sales/Net Fixed Assets	.4	1.7	6.0	4.3	4.3	2.2
.5	.6	.5		.3	.7	1.7	1.6	1.5	1.2
2.5	2.4	2.5		.6	2.8	3.3	3.0	3.7	2.6
1.0	1.1	.9	Sales/Total Assets	.3	1.1	2.2	2.0	1.9	1.4
.4	.5	.4		.2	.6	1.0	1.1	1.0	.8
(173) 3.2	(174) 3.4	(199) 2.9		(69) 8.4	(46) 2.9	(19) 2.7	(32) 2.0	(16) 2.1	.9
5.8	6.1	5.9	% Depr., Dep., Amort./Sales	12.8	5.9	4.1	3.4	3.7	4.3
13.9	11.7	12.1		20.7	9.1	5.4	5.0	6.7	6.9
(61) 4.1	(62) 3.4	(70) 2.7	% Officers', Directors',	(14) 3.9	(25) 3.7		(15) 2.0		
6.3	5.5	4.9	Owners' Comp/Sales	6.3	6.2		3.1		
11.7	10.0	10.3		13.5	14.0		5.9		
1201246M	1464642M	2283413M	Net Sales ($)	26726M	109707M	90913M	229312M	267155M	1559600M
979732M	1172065M	1560405M	Total Assets ($)	72264M	151929M	77812M	151911M	177974M	928515M

M = $ thousand   MM = $ million
See Pages 1 through 15 for Explanation of Ratios and Data

Current Data Sorted By Assets   **Comparative Historical Data**

Comparative Historical Data periods: 19 (4/1-9/30/94) — current ; 62 (10/1/94-3/31/95) — current ; 4/1/90-3/31/91 ALL (61) ; 4/1/91-3/31/92 ALL (66)

Postretirement Benefits — Type of Statement

	0-500M	500M-2MM	2-10MM	10-50MM	50-100MM	100-250MM	4/1/90-3/31/91 ALL	4/1/91-3/31/92 ALL
# Postretirement Benefits			1	2	1			
Unqualified	2		5	15	1	3	25	23
Reviewed	2	3	12	1			12	16
Compiled	3	4	6	1			15	16
Tax Returns	1	1						1
Other		3	12	6			9	10
NUMBER OF STATEMENTS	8	11	35	23	1	3	61	66

Financial Data (percent of totals / ratios)

0-500M	500M-2MM	2-10MM	10-50MM	50-100MM	100-250MM		4/1/90-3/31/91 ALL	4/1/91-3/31/92 ALL
%	%	%	%	%	%	**ASSETS**	%	%
	13.6	5.2	6.9			Cash & Equivalents	7.4	8.3
	11.4	7.1	7.0			Trade Receivables - (net)	13.9	12.3
	.5	4.0	.3			Inventory	3.1	3.5
	.2	.9	2.2			All Other Current	3.0	4.1
	25.8	17.2	16.3			Total Current	27.4	28.3
	54.2	70.6	76.5			Fixed Assets (net)	63.8	60.1
	2.5	.9	3.2			Intangibles (net)	1.7	2.1
	17.5	11.3	3.9			All Other Non-Current	7.2	9.5
	100.0	100.0	100.0			Total	100.0	100.0
						LIABILITIES		
	1.4	4.3	.2			Notes Payable-Short Term	4.0	3.9
	6.1	6.5	4.0			Cur. Mat. -L/T/D	4.9	3.3
	2.2	2.4	5.3			Trade Payables	4.6	7.0
	.0	.5	.0			Income Taxes Payable	.4	.5
	7.0	3.9	3.8			All Other Current	6.4	6.4
	16.8	17.6	13.4			Total Current	20.3	21.0
	17.1	47.8	45.5			Long Term Debt	42.4	37.1
	.0	.4	2.3			Deferred Taxes	.7	.5
	.3	2.5	2.6			All Other-Non-Current	5.8	6.0
	65.7	31.6	36.2			Net Worth	30.8	35.3
	100.0	100.0	100.0			Total Liabilities & Net Worth	100.0	100.0
						INCOME DATA		
	100.0	100.0	100.0			Net Sales	100.0	100.0
						Gross Profit		
	81.6	82.6	77.3			Operating Expenses	87.5	87.1
	18.4	17.4	22.7			Operating Profit	12.5	12.9
	2.4	8.1	7.5			All Other Expenses (net)	7.0	6.0
	16.0	9.3	15.2			Profit Before Taxes	5.5	6.9
						RATIOS		
	2.3	1.7	1.9				2.0	1.9
	1.3	.9	1.0			Current	1.2	1.2
	.6	.5	.8				.7	.8
	2.3	1.3	1.9				1.9	1.7
	1.3	.7	.9			Quick	1.0	1.0
	.6	.3	.7				.5	.6
	9 38.8	27 13.5	35 10.5				24 14.9	23 15.8
	22 16.8	33 11.2	43 8.4			Sales/Receivables	41 9.0	36 10.2
	53 6.9	46 7.9	51 7.1				57 6.4	51 7.2
						Cost of Sales/Inventory		
						Cost of Sales/Payables		
	8.0	10.4	5.6				6.3	7.9
	46.8	-43.9	955.3			Sales/Working Capital	25.4	24.9
	-46.2	-5.1	-30.4				-19.5	-29.5
	19.1	3.1	4.9				3.5	3.8
	7.9	(33) 1.9	(22) 3.1			EBIT/Interest	(50) 1.9	(56) 2.1
	5.0	1.1	1.6				1.2	1.3
			3.5				4.2	4.4
		(12) 2.5				Net Profit + Depr., Dep., Amort./Cur. Mat. L./T/D	(31) 2.1	(21) 1.7
		1.9					1.4	1.1
	.6	1.4	1.7				1.4	.9
	.7	2.8	2.6			Fixed/Worth	2.5	2.2
	1.2	6.0	3.3				5.9	5.0
	.3	1.0	1.6				1.2	.9
	.6	3.4	2.4			Debt/Worth	2.5	2.7
	.8	5.3	3.1				8.6	5.5
	53.5	29.5	41.4				37.0	31.5
	39.0 (33)	13.8	33.6			% Profit Before Taxes/Tangible Net Worth	(56) 16.4	(59) 17.7
	11.8	5.8	16.7				4.7	6.2
	26.7	8.1	13.9				10.1	10.8
	21.1	3.9	9.7			% Profit Before Taxes/Total Assets	4.4	5.2
	7.6	1.4	2.8				.5	1.6
	8.9	1.4	1.3				3.2	3.9
	2.5	.9	.7			Sales/Net Fixed Assets	1.0	1.1
	1.0	.5	.5				.6	.7
	2.5	.8	.8				1.5	1.5
	1.2	.6	.6			Sales/Total Assets	.8	.7
	.7	.4	.4				.5	.5
	2.5	7.8	7.6				5.4	5.0
	6.5 (32)	12.4 (22)	10.5			% Depr., Dep., Amort./Sales	(59) 10.6	(60) 8.0
	11.6	15.7	14.6				14.4	13.7
			2.4				2.2	4.0
		(10)	4.9			% Officers', Directors', Owners' Comp/Sales	(18) 3.7	(24) 8.1
			15.9				5.8	13.7
7184M	23164M	127561M	290163M	86795M	438061M	Net Sales ($)	437120M	774562M
2069M	16147M	176024M	489137M	59235M	425513M	Total Assets ($)	512448M	767964M

Comparative Historical Data

Current Data Sorted By Sales

						19 (4/1-9/30/94)			62 (10/1/94-3/31/95)			
1		1		4	**# Postretirement Benefits**	1		1		1		1
					Type of Statement							
21		29		26	Unqualified	3		2	5	3	9	4
11		14		18	Reviewed	4		9	2	1	2	
17		8		14	Compiled	4		8	1		1	
				1	Tax Returns			1		1		
				2	Other	1		6	3	5	6	
16		13		21								
4/1/92-		4/1/93-		4/1/94-								
3/31/93		3/31/94		3/31/95				0-1MM	1-3MM	3-5MM	5-10MM	10-25MM
ALL		ALL		ALL								25MM & OVER
65		65		81	**NUMBER OF STATEMENTS**	12		26	11	10	18	4
%		%		%	**ASSETS**	%		%	%	%	%	%
9.3		9.1		7.5	Cash & Equivalents	5.7		11.0	6.6	7.8	5.3	
14.0		10.6		10.0	Trade Receivables - (net)	4.3		12.6	9.1	10.5	8.7	
2.8		3.1		2.6	Inventory	1.5		3.0	.8	3.6	1.3	
1.7		1.6		1.5	All Other Current	.3		1.4	3.6	.4	1.0	
27.9		24.3		21.7	Total Current	11.8		28.0	20.1	22.2	16.3	
63.6		68.3		66.8	Fixed Assets (net)	62.5		63.2	68.4	66.6	76.6	
1.6		1.1		1.7	Intangibles (net)	.6		.9	2.6	.4	3.9	
6.9		6.3		9.9	All Other Non-Current	25.1		7.9	8.9	10.8	3.3	
100.0		100.0		100.0	Total	100.0		100.0	100.0	100.0	100.0	
					LIABILITIES							
3.3		5.4		3.6	Notes Payable-Short Term	2.8		8.1	.1	2.6	.3	
4.8		6.2		5.4	Cur. Mat.-L /T/D	3.0		6.7	5.3	6.2	5.1	
7.8		4.8		4.7	Trade Payables	1.7		6.3	7.2	2.5	3.7	
.1		.3		.2	Income Taxes Payable	.1		.5	.0	.0	.3	
7.9		7.0		5.3	All Other Current	1.7		6.7	6.0	3.8	3.4	
23.9		23.7		19.2	Total Current	9.3		28.4	18.7	15.1	12.7	
41.0		37.3		40.3	Long Term Debt	37.2		30.7	54.5	48.1	45.8	
.3		.6		.9	Deferred Taxes	.1		.3	.0	1.6	2.4	
4.4		3.2		2.0	All Other-Non-Current	.9		.8	.7	2.1	5.1	
30.5		35.1		37.6	Net Worth	52.5		39.9	26.1	33.1	34.1	
100.0		100.0		100.0	Total Liabilities & Net Worth	100.0		100.0	100.0	100.0	100.0	
					INCOME DATA							
100.0		100.0		100.0	Net Sales	100.0		100.0	100.0	100.0	100.0	
					Gross Profit							
86.5		85.5		81.1	Operating Expenses	71.5		85.5	84.2	83.3	78.7	
13.5		14.5		18.9	Operating Profit	28.5		14.5	15.8	16.7	21.3	
5.7		4.9		6.5	All Other Expenses (net)	9.3		4.7	8.3	6.2	7.0	
7.8		9.5		12.4	Profit Before Taxes	19.2		9.8	7.5	10.5	14.3	
					RATIOS							
1.8		1.7		1.9		2.1		2.3	2.2	2.5	1.8	
1.2		1.1		1.0	Current	.9		.9	1.1	1.4	.9	
.8		.6		.7		.5		.6	.7	.7	.8	
1.8		1.6		1.5		1.6		2.0	1.9	2.5	1.3	
1.0		.9		.8	Quick	.9		.7	.9	1.1	.9	
.5		.4		.5		.4		.3	.5	.6	.7	
21 17.5	24 15.3		25 14.7			0 UND		20 18.2	30 12.0	31 11.8	27 13.3	
37 10.0	37 10.0		36 10.1	Sales/Receivables	27 13.5		31 11.6	43 8.5	42 8.7	41 8.8	
60 6.1	47 7.7		49 7.5		79 4.6		38 9.7	50 7.3	48 7.6	46 7.9	
					Cost of Sales/Inventory							
					Cost of Sales/Payables							
7.4		8.7		9.1		4.5		13.3	9.2	3.4	9.3	
54.9		46.5		-214.0	Sales/Working Capital	NM		-46.2	61.2	29.0	-101.0	
-9.1		-9.4		-17.7		-4.5		-9.2	-14.5	-17.2	-30.9	
	5.2		5.8		5.3			5.3		13.4	4.2	4.9		4.2
(55) 3.0	(62) 2.7		(77) 2.8	EBIT/Interest	(10) 2.1		(25) 2.5	1.6	2.7	(17) 3.1	
	1.4		1.6		1.4			-1.4		1.4	1.1	1.8		1.6
	4.7		5.4		3.2								
(21) 2.4	(19) 2.9		(26) 2.5	Net Profit + Depr., Dep., Amort./Cur. Mat. L/T/D							
	1.1		1.9		1.3								
1.2		1.4		1.1		.7		.7	1.3	1.3	2.2	
2.0		2.3		2.4	Fixed/Worth	1.4		2.1	2.7	2.1	2.7	
4.5		3.4		4.0		3.0		4.8	11.1	3.4	3.4	
1.2		1.1		.8		.3		.6	2.1	1.2	1.7	
2.5		2.4		2.4	Debt/Worth	.8		2.5	2.9	2.5	2.5	
5.1		4.1		4.1		3.0		7.0	13.0	3.0	3.6	
	41.3		38.5		40.7			11.2		55.1	42.8			42.8
(59) 19.2	(60) 24.5		(78) 23.5	% Profit Before Taxes/Tangible Net Worth	5.8		(25) 29.6	(10) 12.8		36.3	
	5.8		8.3		7.5			-3.5		7.2	6.3			21.0
12.4		11.8		13.9		8.7		23.3	10.7	15.7	13.9	
6.4		7.2		7.6	% Profit Before Taxes/Total Assets	3.7		7.6	2.5	8.4	10.5	
-.0		3.1		2.0		-1.2		1.7	.4	5.0	2.8	
3.0		2.0		1.8		1.3		4.2	1.3	2.8	1.4	
1.0		.9		1.0	Sales/Net Fixed Assets	.6		1.4	1.0	.8	.8	
.6		.6		.6		.3		.6	.4	.7	.6	
1.3		1.4		1.0		.5		1.9	.8	1.7	1.0	
.7		.6		.7	Sales/Total Assets	.3		.8	.6	.7	.7	
.5		.5		.4		.1		.5	.4	.5	.5	
	5.1		4.8		6.4					3.5	6.5			7.0
(61) 9.0	(57) 10.3		(73) 10.2	% Depr., Dep., Amort./Sales			(25) 8.2	12.2		(17) 9.3	
	14.8		14.6		14.4					15.8	14.4			14.0
	1.6		2.5		3.1								
(24) 4.7	(21) 4.4		(28) 6.4	% Officers', Directors', Owners' Comp/Sales							
	13.6		12.6		10.5								
809260M		1284004M		972928M	Net Sales ($)	5909M		48222M	44146M	63412M	286383M	524856M
680858M		1262084M		1168125M	Total Assets ($)	33168M		65319M	79861M	94019M	411010M	484748M

M = $ thousand   MM = $ million
See Pages 1 through 15 for Explanation of Ratios and Data

SERVICES—WATER SUPPLY. SIC# 4941

Current Data Sorted By Assets | Comparative Historical Data

						# Postretirement Benefits		
		1	4		1	**Type of Statement**		
	2	9	9	6	7	Unqualified	10	16
	2	4				Reviewed	10	4
2	2	5				Compiled	6	2
1	1	1				Tax Returns		
1	2	9	7	2	2	Other	2	1
		19 (4/1-9/30/94)	55 (10/1/94-3/31/95)				4/1/90-3/31/91	4/1/91-3/31/92
0-500M	500M-2MM	2-10MM	10-50MM	50-100MM	100-250MM		ALL	ALL
4	9	28	16	8	9	**NUMBER OF STATEMENTS**	28	23
%	%	%	%	%	%	**ASSETS**	%	%
		6.9	5.2			Cash & Equivalents	8.5	8.1
		9.6	2.5			Trade Receivables - (net)	15.9	15.8
		4.3	.4			Inventory	6.3	7.3
		.6	1.4			All Other Current	1.1	3.3
		21.4	9.5			Total Current	31.9	34.5
		67.5	81.7			Fixed Assets (net)	55.4	58.0
		2.4	.3			Intangibles (net)	1.0	1.1
		8.7	8.4			All Other Non-Current	11.7	6.4
		100.0	100.0			Total	100.0	100.0
						LIABILITIES		
		3.6	2.3			Notes Payable-Short Term	3.6	8.0
		2.2	1.5			Cur. Mat. -L/T/D	3.7	2.4
		4.9	1.4			Trade Payables	6.4	8.6
		.7	.0			Income Taxes Payable	1.0	.2
		4.1	2.5			All Other Current	10.5	5.6
		15.4	7.8			Total Current	25.3	24.8
		31.2	29.1			Long Term Debt	22.4	15.1
		1.0	1.6			Deferred Taxes	.6	5.2
		4.6	20.6			All Other-Non-Current	5.4	7.1
		47.8	40.9			Net Worth	46.3	47.8
		100.0	100.0			Total Liabilities & Net Worth	100.0	100.0
						INCOME DATA		
		100.0	100.0			Net Sales	100.0	100.0
						Gross Profit	48.3	41.1
		86.7	73.7			Operating Expenses	38.9	27.8
		13.3	26.3			Operating Profit	9.4	13.3
		7.0	7.3			All Other Expenses (net)	5.2	3.1
		6.4	19.0			Profit Before Taxes	4.2	10.3
						RATIOS		
		2.2	3.2			Current	1.5	2.2
		1.4	1.2				1.2	1.1
		.7	.5				.9	.6
		2.0	2.5			Quick	1.4	1.3
		.9	1.1				.9	.7
		.5	.2				.5	.4
		25 14.7	22 16.7			Sales/Receivables	20 18.6	37 9.8
		38 9.6	38 9.7				42 8.6	44 8.3
		53 6.9	55 6.6				62 5.9	57 6.4
						Cost of Sales/Inventory	0 UND	4 101.2
							16 23.2	18 20.3
							52 7.0	47 7.7
						Cost of Sales/Payables	21 17.6	16 23.1
							32 11.5	35 10.5
							83 4.4	54 6.7
		4.1	2.9			Sales/Working Capital	6.1	4.3
		11.1	20.2				31.6	36.0
		-11.5	-6.1				-33.0	-6.3
		5.2	5.6			EBIT/Interest	11.9	5.9
		(23) 2.8	(15) 2.8				(24) 3.1	(20) 2.8
		1.3	1.4				1.0	1.2
						Net Profit + Depr., Dep.,	4.4	5.8
						Amort./Cur. Mat. L./T/D	(11) 1.8	(12) 3.9
							.9	1.3
		.8	1.3			Fixed/Worth	.7	.3
		1.5	2.4				1.3	1.1
		2.7	3.2				1.8	2.4
		.4	.7			Debt/Worth	.4	.4
		1.3	2.0				1.1	1.6
		2.8	2.6				2.4	2.5
		20.9	19.8			% Profit Before Taxes/Tangible	23.1	18.9
		(26) 5.1	8.8			Net Worth	(25) 6.0	(22) 9.1
		.0	2.5				1.1	5.0
		6.2	5.5			% Profit Before Taxes/Total	9.9	6.1
		3.3	3.7			Assets	2.9	4.9
		.0	1.2				.0	1.0
		3.2	.3			Sales/Net Fixed Assets	9.1	22.4
		.3	.2				1.6	.5
		.2	.1				.3	.3
		1.2	.2			Sales/Total Assets	2.1	1.3
		.3	.2				.8	.4
		.2	.1				.2	.2
		6.1	8.4			% Depr., Dep., Amort./Sales	2.5	2.4
		(26) 12.8	(15) 10.1				6.7	(21) 7.8
		20.6	17.8				17.8	9.8
						% Officers', Directors', Owners' Comp/Sales		
3946M	4519M	79580M	88988M	164304M	327484M	Net Sales ($)	321631M	503974M
1404M	10028M	128667M	410589M	651352M	1337420M	Total Assets ($)	424473M	845571M

© Robert Morris Associates 1995

M = $ thousand   MM = $ million
See Pages 1 through 15 for Explanation of Ratios and Data

Comparative Historical Data				Current Data Sorted By Sales					
	5	6	# Postretirement Benefits	4	1			1	
			Type of Statement						
	20	33	Unqualified	8	8	1	3	7	6
	7	6	Reviewed	2	2		1	1	
	5	9	Compiled	2	5		2		
		3	Tax Returns	2			1		
	8	23	Other	8	5		3	6	1
4/1/92-3/31/93 ALL	4/1/93-3/31/94 ALL	4/1/94-3/31/95 ALL		19 (4/1-9/30/94)			55 (10/1/94-3/31/95)		
				0-1MM	1-3MM	3-5MM	5-10MM	10-25MM	25MM & OVER
(DATA NOT AVAILABLE)	40	74	**NUMBER OF STATEMENTS**	22	20	1	10	14	7
%	%	%	**ASSETS**	%	%	%	%	%	%
	6.4	6.1	Cash & Equivalents	9.2	4.3		9.0	3.7	
	3.4	5.9	Trade Receivables - (net)	2.3	5.0		16.8	6.5	
	1.0	2.2	Inventory	.6	1.7		6.9	2.9	
	1.5	.9	All Other Current	.9	.5		1.6	1.2	
	12.2	15.0	Total Current	13.0	11.5		34.3	14.3	
	80.5	74.2	Fixed Assets (net)	75.8	77.6		57.0	74.1	
	.8	2.5	Intangibles (net)	4.5	3.1		1.3	.4	
	6.6	8.3	All Other Non-Current	6.7	7.8		7.4	11.2	
	100.0	100.0	Total	100.0	100.0		100.0	100.0	
			LIABILITIES						
	1.4	3.1	Notes Payable-Short Term	2.4	3.0		4.4	4.4	
	4.6	1.8	Cur. Mat.-L /T/D	2.2	2.1		2.1	1.0	
	2.3	3.0	Trade Payables	1.4	2.3		7.6	4.0	
	.3	.4	Income Taxes Payable	.0	.2		1.1	.4	
	3.0	3.7	All Other Current	2.5	3.0		7.7	3.5	
	11.6	12.0	Total Current	8.5	10.5		23.1	13.4	
	30.0	32.6	Long Term Debt	33.9	33.9		36.1	24.0	
	1.7	1.6	Deferred Taxes	.2	1.3		1.3	2.9	
	8.0	11.3	All Other-Non-Current	4.5	13.6		3.7	20.6	
	48.7	42.5	Net Worth	52.8	40.6		35.9	39.2	
	100.0	100.0	Total Liabilities & Net Worth	100.0	100.0		100.0	100.0	
			INCOME DATA						
	100.0	100.0	Net Sales	100.0	100.0		100.0	100.0	
			Gross Profit						
	80.7	80.2	Operating Expenses	81.1	82.8		84.2	75.2	
	19.3	19.8	Operating Profit	18.9	17.2		15.8	24.8	
	9.0	7.4	All Other Expenses (net)	9.1	6.2		7.2	5.4	
	10.3	12.4	Profit Before Taxes	9.9	11.0		8.6	19.4	
			RATIOS						
	3.0	2.3		2.4	2.2		3.8	1.5	
	1.2	1.2	Current	1.8	1.0		1.6	.5	
	.4	.5		.7	.4		1.0	.4	
	2.8	2.1		2.4	2.1		2.7	1.3	
	.9	.9	Quick	1.5	.6		1.2	.4	
	.3	.4		.5	.2		.8	.3	
29 12.8	24 15.1		Sales/Receivables	19 19.1	22 16.9		28 13.1	32 11.4	
34 10.7	33 10.9			26 14.0	33 11.1		44 8.3	49 7.4	
43 8.5	54 6.8			45 8.1	52 7.0		61 6.0	59 6.2	
			Cost of Sales/Inventory						
			Cost of Sales/Payables						
	3.2	3.8		2.1	4.8		3.2	7.3	
	27.1	37.8	Sales/Working Capital	4.8	NM		11.1	-6.3	
	-4.7	-6.7		-13.9	-6.1		518.9	-3.5	
	3.9	4.9		5.1	3.8			6.0	
(31) 3.0	(65) 2.8		EBIT/Interest	(17) 2.1	2.1		(13) 4.3		
	1.8	1.6		1.3	1.2		2.1		
	14.0	10.0		Net Profit + Depr., Dep.,						
(15) 3.3	(23) 3.9		Amort./Cur. Mat. L/T/D						
	1.0	2.2							
	1.2	1.3		1.1	1.4		.9	1.0	
	1.9	2.0	Fixed/Worth	1.8	2.2		1.5	2.6	
	3.3	3.2		2.2	5.9		2.5	3.6	
	.4	.7		.5	.7		1.1	.7	
	1.3	1.7	Debt/Worth	1.0	1.9		1.7	2.4	
	2.7	2.8		1.9	6.8		3.0	3.1	
	16.9	20.8	% Profit Before Taxes/Tangible	9.6	16.0			25.5	
(39) 7.2	(70) 8.7		Net Worth	(21) 4.9	(18) 6.5		18.6		
	3.2	2.2		.0	1.7		9.0		
	5.4	6.2	% Profit Before Taxes/Total	5.9	4.5		10.3	8.2	
	2.7	3.8	Assets	2.3	3.3		5.8	4.9	
	1.2	1.2		.0	.4		.7	2.9	
	.5	.5		.4	1.1		5.2	.4	
	.3	.3	Sales/Net Fixed Assets	.3	.3		2.1	.3	
	.2	.2		.2	.1		.3	.2	
	.4	.4		.3	.8		2.3	.4	
	.2	.2	Sales/Total Assets	.2	.2		1.0	.2	
	.2	.2		.2	.1		.2	.2	
	8.1	7.5		9.7	7.8		2.8	8.4	
(38) 10.6	(71) 9.8		% Depr., Dep., Amort./Sales	(21) 16.5	(19) 9.0		(13) 7.0	10.1	
	16.2	17.1		21.3	18.4		15.4	11.8	
		2.0	% Officers', Directors',						
	(17)	3.1	Owners' Comp/Sales						
		13.8							
	206198M	668821M	Net Sales ($)	12118M	36397M	3682M	65855M	239357M	311412M
	795351M	2539460M	Total Assets ($)	58467M	205360M	11378M	218785M	1023328M	1022142M

M = $ thousand   MM = $ million
See Pages 1 through 15 for Explanation of Ratios and Data

Current Data Sorted By Assets | **Comparative Historical Data**

0-500M	500M-2MM	2-10MM	10-50MM	50-100MM	100-250MM		4/1/90-3/31/91 ALL	4/1/91-3/31/92 ALL
						# Postretirement Benefits		
						Type of Statement		
	1	1	5	4	5	Unqualified	15	20
3		1				Reviewed	4	5
1	6	3				Compiled	10	9
1	1	3	2			Tax Returns		1
3	3	9	5	1	3	Other	9	6
	13 (4/1-9/30/94)		48 (10/1/94-3/31/95)				4/1/90-3/31/91 ALL	4/1/91-3/31/92 ALL
8	11	17	12	5	8	**NUMBER OF STATEMENTS**	38	41
%	%	%	%	%	%	**ASSETS**	%	%
	6.4	5.7	10.9			Cash & Equivalents	9.0	10.3
	16.0	12.4	12.1			Trade Receivables - (net)	16.1	16.2
	11.8	4.2	1.1			Inventory	5.6	2.4
	.8	.7	1.5			All Other Current	4.2	6.6
	35.0	22.9	25.6			Total Current	34.9	35.5
	53.1	69.6	58.4			Fixed Assets (net)	55.1	52.7
	.2	.7	2.1			Intangibles (net)	1.1	1.7
	11.7	6.8	13.9			All Other Non-Current	8.9	10.2
	100.0	100.0	100.0			Total	100.0	100.0
						LIABILITIES		
	17.2	6.4	3.1			Notes Payable-Short Term	8.4	5.2
	6.7	4.7	10.1			Cur. Mat. -L/T/D	7.1	6.6
	6.4	5.1	8.6			Trade Payables	9.1	8.4
	.8	.0	.4			Income Taxes Payable	.3	.4
	5.7	6.2	6.6			All Other Current	10.0	8.5
	36.9	22.5	28.8			Total Current	35.0	29.1
	24.1	36.6	20.3			Long Term Debt	27.7	23.8
	.9	.6	2.6			Deferred Taxes	2.0	2.7
	10.7	1.8	2.7			All Other-Non-Current	1.6	3.5
	27.4	38.5	45.6			Net Worth	33.7	40.9
	100.0	100.0	100.0			Total Liabilities & Net Worth	100.0	100.0
						INCOME DATA		
	100.0	100.0	100.0			Net Sales	100.0	100.0
						Gross Profit		
	97.1	93.7	95.7			Operating Expenses	90.4	90.3
	2.9	6.3	4.3			Operating Profit	9.6	9.7
	1.1	4.3	-1.9			All Other Expenses (net)	3.7	2.1
	1.9	2.0	6.2			Profit Before Taxes	5.9	7.6
						RATIOS		
	1.7	1.7	1.4			Current	1.7	1.9
	1.0	1.0	1.1				1.0	1.2
	.2	.3	.6				.7	.7
	1.2	1.6	1.3			Quick	1.4	1.7
	1.0	.9	.9				.8	.9
	.1	.3	.5				.3	.4
0 UND	3 106.8	20 18.0				Sales/Receivables	16 23.1	8 46.8
10 37.3	20 18.4	36 10.1					32 11.3	33 11.1
50 7.3	37 9.8	60 6.1					47 7.7	52 7.0
						Cost of Sales/Inventory		
						Cost of Sales/Payables		
	20.3	16.7	13.2			Sales/Working Capital	7.6	8.4
	77.4	-162.7	44.7				NM	25.8
	-8.1	-6.5	-8.4				-12.2	-15.8
	3.7	7.0	7.9			EBIT/Interest	5.5	5.6
	1.8	1.0	2.5				(32) 2.5	(35) 3.0
	1.0	.8	1.2				.8	1.8
						Net Profit + Depr., Dep., Amort./Cur. Mat. L /T/D	2.6	2.7
							(18) 2.1	(25) 2.0
							.6	1.1
	.7	.9	.9			Fixed/Worth	.7	.8
	1.7	2.3	1.3				1.7	1.4
	20.3	6.4	2.0				4.4	2.7
	1.3	.6	.8			Debt/Worth	.9	.9
	2.0	1.9	1.2				1.9	1.3
	19.6	7.1	2.4				7.0	3.6
		21.0	42.6			% Profit Before Taxes/Tangible Net Worth	20.6	40.1
		2.2	17.2				(36) 15.9	(39) 21.2
		-9.6	.5				-.0	7.8
	5.9	9.9	13.0			% Profit Before Taxes/Total Assets	9.3	11.1
	5.2	.2	5.0				5.8	7.0
	-.1	-1.5	.3				-.7	3.7
	20.5	3.8	2.3			Sales/Net Fixed Assets	4.7	5.3
	2.1	1.3	1.6				1.8	1.9
	1.8	.9	1.2				.9	1.2
	7.2	1.8	1.3			Sales/Total Assets	2.1	2.1
	1.5	1.1	1.0				1.1	1.2
	1.2	.7	.8				.7	.9
	1.5	3.7	3.2			% Depr., Dep., Amort./Sales	2.4	3.1
	(10) 8.8	7.9	6.2				(35) 6.0	(34) 7.0
	13.7	10.7	10.3				12.6	9.3
						% Officers', Directors', Owners' Comp/Sales		
10726M	43611M	101051M	321197M	269879M	1027053M	Net Sales ($)	682413M	1306496M
2293M	11776M	77338M	255178M	369145M	1093841M	Total Assets ($)	640055M	1124526M

M = $ thousand   MM = $ million
See Pages 1 through 15 for Explanation of Ratios and Data

Comparative Historical Data / Current Data Sorted By Sales

2	4	4	# Postretirement Benefits Type of Statement		2		1		1
23	18	17	Unqualified		1		2	2	12
9	5	10	Reviewed	1	4		4	1	
11	8	7	Compiled	1	4		1	1	
	2	3	Tax Returns	2	1				
13	24	24	Other	1	6	2	4	5	6
4/1/92-3/31/93 ALL	4/1/93-3/31/94 ALL	4/1/94-3/31/95 ALL		13 (4/1-9/30/94)			48 (10/1/94-3/31/95)		
				0-1MM	1-3MM	3-5MM	5-10MM	10-25MM	25MM & OVER
56	57	61	NUMBER OF STATEMENTS	5	16	2	11	9	18
%	%	%	**ASSETS**	%	%	%	%	%	%
9.5	9.9	7.2	Cash & Equivalents		6.6		3.8		10.9
14.2	11.9	15.6	Trade Receivables - (net)		14.3		17.0		15.9
4.4	3.1	4.3	Inventory		2.0		9.2		1.9
2.4	4.3	1.6	All Other Current		.2		.7		1.5
30.5	29.2	28.7	Total Current		23.1		30.7		30.1
58.2	56.7	59.4	Fixed Assets (net)		65.1		54.0		59.6
1.3	3.4	1.3	Intangibles (net)		.5		.5		3.2
10.1	10.7	10.7	All Other Non-Current		11.4		14.8		7.0
100.0	100.0	100.0	Total		100.0		100.0		100.0
			LIABILITIES						
4.3	5.0	7.2	Notes Payable-Short Term		13.0		1.9		2.2
7.1	5.6	7.6	Cur. Mat.-L /T/D		6.3		10.7		5.8
10.1	10.9	7.4	Trade Payables		7.8		6.3		8.9
.5	.6	.4	Income Taxes Payable		.4		.2		.8
7.0	8.9	10.4	All Other Current		13.5		11.5		8.3
29.1	31.0	33.0	Total Current		41.0		30.6		26.1
25.7	27.3	27.1	Long Term Debt		38.7		18.8		27.7
2.3	1.6	1.9	Deferred Taxes		.9		.3		4.6
3.7	4.2	3.1	All Other-Non-Current		1.9		2.4		.7
39.3	35.9	34.9	Net Worth		17.4		47.9		40.9
100.0	100.0	100.0	Total Liabilities & Net Worth		100.0		100.0		100.0
			INCOME DATA						
100.0	100.0	100.0	Net Sales		100.0		100.0		100.0
			Gross Profit						
91.6	90.6	93.2	Operating Expenses		96.8		94.8		91.7
8.4	9.4	6.8	Operating Profit		3.2		5.2		8.3
1.8	2.4	2.1	All Other Expenses (net)		4.4		−.3		1.7
6.6	6.9	4.8	Profit Before Taxes		−1.2		5.5		6.6
			RATIOS						
1.6 1.0 .7	1.4 1.0 .7	1.6 1.0 .5	Current		1.1 .4 .1		1.6 1.0 .6		1.5 1.2 .8
1.5 .8 .3	1.1 .8 .3	1.4 .9 .4	Quick		1.1 .4 .1		1.4 .6 .5		1.4 1.0 .7
10 35.0 39 9.4 49 7.4	4 92.9 28 12.9 45 8.2	3 110.6 30 12.0 57 6.4	Sales/Receivables		0 UND 1 336.5 49 7.4		15 24.6 27 13.3 40 9.1		34 10.7 54 6.8 91 4.0
			Cost of Sales/Inventory						
			Cost of Sales/Payables						
9.4 163.9 −10.4	14.7 −999.8 −10.9	11.8 86.3 −8.2	Sales/Working Capital		86.5 −12.0 −5.5		23.3 −162.7 −9.3		8.5 27.7 −18.4
(51) 5.7 3.5 1.2	(54) 7.1 2.3 1.0	(60) 5.5 2.5 1.0	EBIT/Interest		(15) 2.5 1.0 .6		7.7 3.2 1.0		8.3 2.9 1.5
(31) 2.9 1.4 .7	(21) 3.1 1.9 .5	(25) 1.9 1.1 .7	Net Profit + Depr., Dep., Amort./Cur. Mat. L/T/D					(10)	2.1 1.1 .9
1.0 1.7 2.6	.8 1.5 3.4	1.0 1.5 4.4	Fixed/Worth		1.4 4.3 13.8		.8 1.1 1.8		1.3 1.4 2.5
.8 1.6 4.5	.9 2.0 5.0	1.1 1.9 5.7	Debt/Worth		2.7 7.2 16.1		.5 1.3 2.2		1.0 1.5 2.6
(53) 33.1 17.2 4.5	(53) 24.1 9.8 .6	(58) 32.1 13.6 .4	% Profit Before Taxes/Tangible Net Worth		(15) 61.5 9.5 −9.4		34.2 12.8 .0		21.7 14.4 10.2
11.6 5.8 1.0	9.6 3.2 −.1	11.1 4.6 .0	% Profit Before Taxes/Total Assets		5.8 1.7 −2.1		12.8 9.2 .0		7.5 4.7 1.7
4.3 1.5 1.0	5.7 2.0 1.0	4.8 1.7 1.1	Sales/Net Fixed Assets		4.0 1.9 .8		13.7 2.0 1.3		2.2 1.5 1.1
1.6 1.0 .8	1.8 1.1 .8	2.2 1.1 .8	Sales/Total Assets		2.7 1.3 .6		2.5 1.4 1.0		1.2 .9 .8
(50) 3.0 6.5 10.4	(48) 3.4 6.9 10.4	(54) 3.5 7.5 10.5	% Depr., Dep., Amort./Sales		(14) 5.0 10.7 12.9		1.0 5.8 8.1		(14) 4.1 6.3 9.1
(17) 4.6 7.6 15.2	(16) 2.4 5.1 10.5	(15) 2.8 4.0 11.1	% Officers', Directors', Owners' Comp/Sales						
1734802M 1874970M	1458702M 1394607M	1773517M 1809571M	Net Sales ($) Total Assets ($)	1458M 1517M	30154M 31866M	8528M 4245M	79829M 65266M	132862M 208270M	1520686M 1498407M

Current Data Sorted By Assets   **Comparative Historical Data**

	0-500M	500M-2MM	2-10MM	10-50MM	50-100MM	100-250MM	# Postretirement Benefits / Type of Statement	4/1/90-3/31/91 ALL	4/1/91-3/31/92 ALL
		1		1					
	2	2	1				Unqualified	3	3
	3	9	4				Reviewed	19	15
	16	8					Compiled	27	23
	3	1					Tax Returns		1
	8	5	1	1			Other	9	9
		17 (4/1-9/30/94)		47 (10/1/94-3/31/95)					
NUMBER OF STATEMENTS	32	25	6	1				58	51
ASSETS	%	%	%	%	%	%		%	%
Cash & Equivalents	14.7	9.9						9.0	7.7
Trade Receivables - (net)	32.5	37.0						32.2	30.4
Inventory	13.3	9.1						14.5	17.6
All Other Current	4.1	2.6						1.5	1.1
Total Current	64.7	58.7						57.2	56.8
Fixed Assets (net)	28.0	33.7						32.4	34.4
Intangibles (net)	1.9	2.5						1.3	2.0
All Other Non-Current	5.4	5.1						9.1	6.8
Total	100.0	100.0						100.0	100.0
LIABILITIES									
Notes Payable-Short Term	12.3	6.2						14.6	7.3
Cur. Mat. -L/T/D	3.6	4.9						4.7	4.6
Trade Payables	13.6	15.5						12.0	14.7
Income Taxes Payable	.3	.5						1.3	.2
All Other Current	7.4	5.9						7.0	9.9
Total Current	37.3	33.1						39.6	36.7
Long Term Debt	16.2	12.2						14.9	17.3
Deferred Taxes	.3	1.5						.2	.3
All Other-Non-Current	1.8	3.1						1.8	1.4
Net Worth	44.4	50.2						43.5	44.4
Total Liabilities & Net Worth	100.0	100.0						100.0	100.0
INCOME DATA									
Net Sales	100.0	100.0						100.0	100.0
Gross Profit									
Operating Expenses	93.0	93.9						93.4	95.7
Operating Profit	7.0	6.1						6.6	4.3
All Other Expenses (net)	1.2	.9						1.5	1.6
Profit Before Taxes	5.8	5.2						5.1	2.7
RATIOS									
Current	3.5 / 1.7 / 1.2	2.6 / 2.0 / 1.3						2.8 / 1.5 / 1.1	2.6 / 1.6 / 1.1
Quick	2.8 / 1.2 / .8	2.3 / 1.5 / 1.2						(56) 2.0 / 1.1 / .6	2.1 / 1.2 / .7
Sales/Receivables	24 15.3 / 40 9.1 / 58 6.3	39 9.3 / 51 7.1 / 66 5.5						27 13.7 / 41 8.8 / 57 6.4	29 12.6 / 45 8.2 / 62 5.9
Cost of Sales/Inventory									
Cost of Sales/Payables									
Sales/Working Capital	7.6 / 13.4 / 36.0	6.2 / 9.6 / 22.2						7.0 / 13.2 / 40.3	7.0 / 10.3 / 89.4
EBIT/Interest	(28) 6.8 / 3.8 / 1.2	(24) 13.5 / 4.9 / 2.2						(48) 11.6 / 3.4 / 1.8	(48) 8.3 / 2.7 / .8
Net Profit + Depr., Dep., Amort./Cur. Mat. L /T/D								(34) 7.1 / 1.9 / .7	(19) 6.8 / 1.5 / .1
Fixed/Worth	.2 / .6 / 1.8	.5 / .7 / 1.0						.4 / .6 / 1.6	.5 / .7 / 1.6
Debt/Worth	.6 / 1.6 / 3.7	.5 / .8 / 2.1						.5 / 1.1 / 4.3	.5 / 1.0 / 3.3
% Profit Before Taxes/Tangible Net Worth	(31) 83.3 / 32.3 / 2.0	(24) 46.4 / 17.1 / 5.5						(52) 40.2 / 22.5 / 6.4	(46) 39.7 / 14.7 / -.3
% Profit Before Taxes/Total Assets	30.2 / 10.2 / 1.3	21.2 / 6.6 / 2.8						19.4 / 9.4 / 1.2	16.6 / 6.1 / -1.0
Sales/Net Fixed Assets	37.3 / 13.5 / 7.1	13.9 / 7.6 / 4.6						17.4 / 9.8 / 6.2	16.5 / 7.3 / 5.1
Sales/Total Assets	4.2 / 2.9 / 1.8	2.9 / 2.3 / 1.9						3.6 / 2.7 / 2.1	3.5 / 2.3 / 2.0
% Depr., Dep., Amort./Sales	(23) .9 / 2.0 / 5.1	(23) 1.1 / 2.2 / 3.8						(51) 1.6 / 2.5 / 3.4	(47) 1.9 / 3.8 / 5.0
% Officers', Directors', Owners' Comp/Sales	(16) 3.9 / 6.4 / 15.0	(11) 4.1 / 4.6 / 5.8						(30) 3.6 / 9.0 / 14.2	(31) 5.1 / 7.4 / 11.1
Net Sales ($)	24164M	69189M	49367M	17590M				206797M	195572M
Total Assets ($)	8794M	25123M	24059M	16194M				80763M	92223M

M = $ thousand   MM = $ million
See Pages 1 through 15 for Explanation of Ratios and Data

Comparative Historical Data / Current Data Sorted By Sales

4/1/92-3/31/93 ALL	4/1/93-3/31/94 ALL	4/1/94-3/31/95 ALL		0-1MM	1-3MM	3-5MM	5-10MM	10-25MM	25MM & OVER
			# Postretirement Benefits			1		1	
			Type of Statement						
3	5	5	Unqualified	2	2	1			
17	15	16	Reviewed	2	8	3	3		
22	27	24	Compiled	14	9	1			
1	1	4	Tax Returns	2	1	1			
9	10	15	Other	7	4	1		3	
				17 (4/1-9/30/94)			47 (10/1/94-3/31/95)		
52	58	64	**NUMBER OF STATEMENTS**	27	24	7	3	3	
%	%	%	**ASSETS**	%	%	%	%	%	%
12.9	8.8	13.0	Cash & Equivalents	16.6	9.8				
30.4	31.8	34.2	Trade Receivables - (net)	31.0	34.9				
11.6	14.7	12.1	Inventory	11.2	12.9				
2.4	3.0	3.5	All Other Current	4.9	1.4				
57.3	58.3	62.8	Total Current	63.6	59.1				
32.6	30.4	29.9	Fixed Assets (net)	28.6	32.9				
1.7	3.4	2.0	Intangibles (net)	1.4	3.6				
8.5	7.9	5.3	All Other Non-Current	6.5	4.4				
100.0	100.0	100.0	Total	100.0	100.0				
			LIABILITIES						
9.7	10.9	9.1	Notes Payable-Short Term	10.7	9.7				
6.9	5.4	4.3	Cur. Mat.-L /T/D	3.8	4.9				
11.3	15.7	14.5	Trade Payables	13.9	13.2				
.8	2.0	.5	Income Taxes Payable	.3	.5				
8.1	11.8	6.9	All Other Current	8.1	4.0				
36.7	45.8	35.2	Total Current	36.8	32.3				
19.5	16.8	13.6	Long Term Debt	17.5	11.7				
.3	1.2	.8	Deferred Taxes	.7	.4				
1.1	4.1	2.2	All Other-Non-Current	1.4	3.9				
42.3	32.0	48.2	Net Worth	43.7	51.7				
100.0	100.0	100.0	Total Liabilities & Net Worth	100.0	100.0				
			INCOME DATA						
100.0	100.0	100.0	Net Sales	100.0	100.0				
			Gross Profit						
93.8	96.1	93.5	Operating Expenses	93.3	94.1				
6.2	3.9	6.5	Operating Profit	6.7	5.9				
2.7	1.9	1.1	All Other Expenses (net)	1.0	1.1				
3.5	2.0	5.5	Profit Before Taxes	5.7	4.8				
			RATIOS						
2.9 1.6 1.2	2.6 1.4 1.0	2.9 2.0 1.3	Current	4.6 1.8 1.1	2.8 2.0 1.4				
2.3 1.3 .7	1.7 .9 .5	2.4 1.5 1.0	Quick	2.1 1.0 .8	2.4 1.5 1.1				
28 13.2 45 8.2 55 6.6	25 14.8 45 8.2 62 5.9	35 10.5 47 7.8 63 5.8	Sales/Receivables	24 15.3 47 7.8 69 5.3	36 10.2 46 8.0 55 6.6				
			Cost of Sales/Inventory						
			Cost of Sales/Payables						
5.6 11.8 70.0	6.7 16.6 -129.5	6.0 10.0 24.6	Sales/Working Capital	5.0 13.1 38.4	7.3 10.0 15.1				
(47) 7.0 2.9 1.1	(51) 7.4 2.9 -1.7	(56) 8.7 4.5 1.9	EBIT/Interest	(23) 6.0 2.8 1.0	(23) 9.2 4.5 2.3				
(21) 3.0 1.4 .6	(19) 2.9 1.4 -.3	(15) 4.7 2.9 1.6	Net Profit + Depr., Dep., Amort./Cur. Mat. L/T/D						
.4 .7 2.1	.4 .7 3.2	.2 .7 1.2	Fixed/Worth	.2 .6 2.2	.3 .7 .9				
.5 1.5 4.1	.7 2.4 9.8	.5 1.1 3.1	Debt/Worth	.4 1.7 3.9	.5 .8 1.9				
(48) 27.9 13.7 -3.3	(46) 40.8 18.8 1.4	(62) 53.2 22.9 5.1	% Profit Before Taxes/Tangible Net Worth	(26) 85.3 12.3 .6	(23) 42.8 17.1 6.8				
14.5 5.5 -2.9	13.7 6.6 -4.7	21.4 8.5 2.3	% Profit Before Taxes/Total Assets	32.4 6.2 .5	20.3 7.0 4.0				
19.8 9.1 4.6	31.1 11.7 5.8	26.9 9.8 5.2	Sales/Net Fixed Assets	33.4 11.9 4.2	23.1 8.1 5.4				
3.6 2.3 1.9	4.1 2.5 1.8	3.5 2.3 1.8	Sales/Total Assets	4.1 2.3 1.6	3.5 2.6 2.2				
(47) 1.4 2.6 3.9	(50) 1.3 2.4 4.4	(53) 1.1 2.1 4.0	% Depr., Dep., Amort./Sales	(20) .9 2.3 6.0	(21) 1.2 2.2 4.0				
(26) 5.5 8.3 12.4	(31) 5.9 7.7 11.1	(27) 4.1 5.0 12.9	% Officers', Directors', Owners' Comp/Sales	(11) 4.5 9.8 16.0	(15) 3.7 4.8 5.8				
147620M 75151M	123464M 63070M	160310M 74170M	Net Sales ($) Total Assets ($)	15105M 6982M	42827M 16871M	29915M 13780M	24981M 10579M	47482M 25958M	

M = $ thousand   MM = $ million
See Pages 1 through 15 for Explanation of Ratios and Data

Current Data Sorted By Assets   **Comparative Historical Data**

Type of Statement

0-500M	500M-2MM	2-10MM	10-50MM	50-100MM	100-250MM	# Postretirement Benefits / Type of Statement	4/1/90-3/31/91 ALL	4/1/91-3/31/92 ALL
		1	1		1	# Postretirement Benefits		
						Type of Statement		
			1			Unqualified	3	4
	1	8				Reviewed	7	2
3	14	8	4			Compiled	11	6
1	5	5				Tax Returns	4	3
2	12	6	3			Other	11	11
	16 (4/1-9/30/94)		58 (10/1/94-3/31/95)					
6	32	27	8		1	**NUMBER OF STATEMENTS**	36	26

Percentages

0-500M	500M-2MM	2-10MM	10-50MM	50-100MM	100-250MM		4/1/90-3/31/91 ALL	4/1/91-3/31/92 ALL
%	%	%	%	%	%	**ASSETS**	%	%
	5.5	2.0				Cash & Equivalents	3.5	4.0
	3.2	3.0				Trade Receivables - (net)	8.0	3.5
	38.4	42.4				Inventory	41.4	32.3
	1.0	1.9				All Other Current	3.0	3.8
	48.0	49.3				Total Current	55.9	43.8
	42.2	40.3				Fixed Assets (net)	34.1	45.2
	2.3	.2				Intangibles (net)	.6	.2
	7.5	10.3				All Other Non-Current	9.4	10.9
	100.0	100.0				Total	100.0	100.0
						LIABILITIES		
	27.8	38.2				Notes Payable-Short Term	33.3	36.5
	3.5	1.9				Cur. Mat. -L/T/D	1.7	1.3
	2.5	8.8				Trade Payables	5.9	4.6
	.0	.0				Income Taxes Payable	.3	.1
	6.5	2.4				All Other Current	6.3	1.7
	40.3	51.4				Total Current	47.6	44.2
	12.6	19.9				Long Term Debt	8.0	19.5
	.0	.8				Deferred Taxes	.9	.3
	2.9	2.9				All Other-Non-Current	1.6	2.7
	44.2	25.0				Net Worth	42.0	33.3
	100.0	100.0				Total Liabilities & Net Worth	100.0	100.0
						INCOME DATA		
	100.0	100.0				Net Sales	100.0	100.0
	41.8	34.9				Gross Profit	30.9	35.6
	38.0	34.3				Operating Expenses	23.3	33.0
	3.7	.5				Operating Profit	7.6	2.6
	1.8	2.5				All Other Expenses (net)	2.5	2.8
	1.9	-2.0				Profit Before Taxes	5.1	-.2

Ratios

0-500M	500M-2MM	2-10MM	10-50MM	50-100MM	100-250MM		4/1/90-3/31/91 ALL	4/1/91-3/31/92 ALL
	2.0	1.3				Current	1.9	1.5
	1.1	1.0					1.1	1.1
	.7	.7					.7	.7
	.4	.2				Quick	.4	.4
(30)	.1	(24) .1					(25) .1	.1
	.0	.0					.0	.0
0	UND	0 UND				Sales/Receivables	0 UND	0 UND
0	UND	2 156.8					4 93.8	0 UND
6	63.5	12 31.4					19 19.4	11 32.1
114	3.2	38 9.7				Cost of Sales/Inventory	34 10.7	18 20.7
261	1.4	146 2.5					152 2.4	99 3.7
456	.8	261 1.4					304 1.2	261 1.4
0	UND	0 UND				Cost of Sales/Payables	0 UND	0 UND
0	UND	3 110.2					3 142.6	10 37.3
12	30.4	28 13.1					27 13.7	28 13.1
	2.9	8.6				Sales/Working Capital	5.4	10.8
	28.2	-60.0					49.6	30.4
	-5.9	-6.0					-18.3	-7.1
	4.5	1.7				EBIT/Interest	3.5	2.7
(30)	1.8	(26) 1.1					(33) 1.6	(21) 1.6
	.6	-.2					1.2	.2
						Net Profit + Depr., Dep.,	8.0	
						Amort./Cur. Mat. L /T/D	(11) 2.4	
							-.1	
	.4	.6				Fixed/Worth	.2	.6
	1.1	1.5					.9	1.6
	2.2	26.9					1.6	2.9
	.3	1.2				Debt/Worth	.8	.9
	1.4	5.2					1.4	2.9
	6.0	48.9					2.9	6.8
	10.4	20.8				% Profit Before Taxes/Tangible	30.6	26.1
(29)	6.5	(22) 4.9				Net Worth	(35) 10.2	(24) 3.0
	-8.6	-5.8					1.8	-13.3
	7.1	3.4				% Profit Before Taxes/Total	12.8	6.6
	3.1	.4				Assets	4.5	.8
	-.9	-3.3					.7	-4.2
	9.2	11.0				Sales/Net Fixed Assets	50.7	10.5
	2.0	4.0					8.4	2.8
	.6	1.3					2.1	.9
	1.4	2.5				Sales/Total Assets	3.0	1.8
	.7	1.3					1.6	1.1
	.3	.7					.8	.7
	1.0	.8				% Depr., Dep., Amort./Sales	.6	1.5
(28)	4.4	(26) 2.6					(28) 1.2	(20) 3.4
	9.4	4.4					3.9	8.3
	3.1					% Officers', Directors',	.3	
(10)	6.7					Owners' Comp/Sales	(13) 1.2	
	9.9						5.5	
4059M	84125M	285170M	118462M		190560M	Net Sales ($)	1021090M	560686M
1668M	36973M	115735M	194487M		146257M	Total Assets ($)	348901M	474532M

© Robert Morris Associates 1995

M = $ thousand   MM = $ million
See Pages 1 through 15 for Explanation of Ratios and Data

Comparative Historical Data | Current Data Sorted By Sales

Type of Statement

	1	3	# Postretirement Benefits / Type of Statement	0-1MM	1-3MM	3-5MM	5-10MM	10-25MM	25MM & OVER
			# Postretirement Benefits		2				1
4	3	1	Unqualified						1
6	4	10	Reviewed	1		3	2	3	1
13	12	29	Compiled	12	9	1	3	3	1
6	11	11	Tax Returns	3	4	2	3	1	
11	26	23	Other	8	7	3	3		2

4/1/92-3/31/93 ALL	4/1/93-3/31/94 ALL	4/1/94-3/31/95 ALL		16 (4/1-9/30/94)			58 (10/1/94-3/31/95)		
40	56	74	NUMBER OF STATEMENTS	24	20	9	9	7	5

ASSETS

%	%	%		%	%	%	%	%	%
3.2	3.9	4.0	Cash & Equivalents	4.0	4.4				
5.9	5.9	4.8	Trade Receivables - (net)	1.5	5.2				
34.1	34.2	37.9	Inventory	33.6	37.5				
1.4	1.7	1.7	All Other Current	1.3	.3				
44.5	45.7	48.5	Total Current	40.5	47.5				
44.0	42.8	41.5	Fixed Assets (net)	50.5	39.0				
.4	.7	1.3	Intangibles (net)	2.7	1.6				
11.1	10.9	8.6	All Other Non-Current	6.3	12.0				
100.0	100.0	100.0	Total	100.0	100.0				

LIABILITIES

36.6	25.8	29.1	Notes Payable-Short Term	21.1	33.5				
1.7	.9	2.6	Cur. Mat.-L /T/D	4.5	1.0				
2.5	2.9	6.3	Trade Payables	3.7	5.8				
.1	.0	.0	Income Taxes Payable	.1	.0				
2.3	6.6	5.2	All Other Current	9.4	3.9				
43.2	36.3	43.2	Total Current	38.7	44.2				
14.9	17.1	15.7	Long Term Debt	13.8	11.5				
.2	.2	2.0	Deferred Taxes	.0	4.7				
4.4	3.1	4.4	All Other-Non-Current	2.8	.4				
37.3	43.2	34.7	Net Worth	44.7	39.2				
100.0	100.0	100.0	Total Liabilities & Net Worth	100.0	100.0				

INCOME DATA

100.0	100.0	100.0	Net Sales	100.0	100.0				
37.8	38.0	36.9	Gross Profit	45.2	43.1				
29.5	33.6	35.8	Operating Expenses	41.7	45.9				
8.3	4.4	1.2	Operating Profit	3.4	-2.8				
2.5	1.5	2.2	All Other Expenses (net)	3.2	1.2				
5.9	3.0	-1.0	Profit Before Taxes	.2	-4.0				

RATIOS

1.9	2.4	2.0	Current	1.7	2.8				
1.1	1.2	1.2		1.0	1.0				
.6	.7	.7		.7	.7				
(38) .6	(54) .6	(69) .5	Quick	(23) .5	(19) .3				
.1	.1	.1		.0	.1				
.0	.0	.0		.0	.0				
0 UND	0 UND	0 UND	Sales/Receivables	0 UND	0 UND				
1 244.3	1 373.5	2 171.3		0 UND	1 286.2				
17 21.2	16 23.4	15 24.0		12 31.7	18 20.8				
21 17.3	45 8.1	76 4.8	Cost of Sales/Inventory	73 5.0	118 3.1				
118 3.1	183 2.0	159 2.3		406 .9	192 1.9				
261 1.4	456 .8	406 .9		1217 .3	406 .9				
0 UND	0 UND	0 UND	Cost of Sales/Payables	0 UND	0 UND				
2 238.7	0 UND	3 113.9		0 UND	14 26.5				
12 29.6	13 28.6	28 13.0		8 43.6	38 9.6				
5.7	3.5	3.8	Sales/Working Capital	2.9	2.5				
41.3	15.6	20.4		NM	NM				
-7.9	-14.5	-6.3		-4.3	-7.0				
(37) 2.9	(54) 3.7	(66) 3.2	EBIT/Interest	(21) 3.5	(16) 2.7				
1.7	1.9	1.4		1.2	1.2				
1.2	.8	-.2		-.4	-.2				
			Net Profit + Depr., Dep., Amort./Cur. Mat. L/T/D						
.5	.4	.4	Fixed/Worth	.7	.3				
1.1	.9	1.2		1.1	1.1				
2.3	1.9	4.0		1.7	3.2				
.8	.5	.7	Debt/Worth	.4	.6				
1.5	1.4	2.2		1.4	1.9				
5.4	2.9	7.5		3.6	13.3				
(39) 32.5	(49) 20.4	(63) 11.3	% Profit Before Taxes/Tangible Net Worth	(23) 7.7	(17) 14.5				
8.8	4.8	5.5		3.0	.7				
1.2	-.7	-5.5		-7.8	-12.0				
6.5	7.3	4.3	% Profit Before Taxes/Total Assets	3.3	5.1				
3.1	3.5	1.2		1.1	.6				
.8	-.5	-3.2		-2.7	-4.8				
9.6	7.0	10.0	Sales/Net Fixed Assets	4.6	8.0				
2.9	2.1	3.0		.8	2.6				
.9	1.0	.8		.4	.9				
2.0	1.4	1.8	Sales/Total Assets	.9	1.6				
1.0	.8	1.0		.4	1.0				
.6	.5	.4		.3	.5				
(35) .5	(49) .7	(65) 1.0	% Depr., Dep., Amort./Sales	(19) 4.4	(19) .9				
2.6	2.7	3.9		9.4	3.3				
5.6	6.5	8.6		11.8	5.4				
	(12) 1.6	(16) .6	% Officers', Directors', Owners' Comp/Sales						
	3.9	4.7							
	8.6	7.5							
742596M	454681M	682376M	Net Sales ($)	11086M	31684M	37251M	65820M	114481M	422054M
472197M	464648M	495120M	Total Assets ($)	26897M	63582M	33268M	98640M	46396M	226337M

M = $ thousand   MM = $ million
See Pages 1 through 15 for Explanation of Ratios and Data

Current Data Sorted By Assets   **Comparative Historical Data**

0-500M	500M-2MM	2-10MM	10-50MM	50-100MM	100-250MM		4/1/90-3/31/91 ALL	4/1/91-3/31/92 ALL
		1	1			# Postretirement Benefits		
						Type of Statement		
	3	9	10			Unqualified		
1	4	13	9		1	Reviewed		
	5	5	1			Compiled		
		1				Tax Returns		
1	3	4	6	1		Other		
	42 (4/1-9/30/94)		35 (10/1/94-3/31/95)					
2	15	32	26	1	1	**NUMBER OF STATEMENTS**		
%	%	%	%	%	%	**ASSETS**	%	%
	9.8	14.3	6.8			Cash & Equivalents	D	D
	23.3	17.7	22.7			Trade Receivables - (net)	A	A
	16.1	20.4	25.6			Inventory	T	T
	4.7	3.0	2.5			All Other Current	A	A
	53.8	55.4	57.6			Total Current		
	38.0	37.0	30.5			Fixed Assets (net)	N	N
	.5	.8	1.7			Intangibles (net)	O	O
	7.6	6.8	10.2			All Other Non-Current	T	T
	100.0	100.0	100.0			Total		
						LIABILITIES	A	A
	15.6	15.7	15.2			Notes Payable-Short Term	V	V
	4.7	2.3	2.0			Cur. Mat. -L/T/D	A	A
	16.7	17.0	15.7			Trade Payables	I	I
	.2	.8	.1			Income Taxes Payable	L	L
	6.0	12.0	9.4			All Other Current	A	A
	43.2	47.7	42.3			Total Current	B	B
	12.6	10.4	15.0			Long Term Debt	L	L
	.1	.8	1.8			Deferred Taxes	E	E
	2.2	1.2	2.9			All Other-Non-Current		
	41.9	39.9	38.0			Net Worth		
	100.0	100.0	100.0			Total Liabilities & Net Worth		
						INCOME DATA		
	100.0	100.0	100.0			Net Sales		
	38.4	25.2	24.5			Gross Profit		
	34.9	19.0	19.1			Operating Expenses		
	3.4	6.2	5.4			Operating Profit		
	1.0	.2	1.2			All Other Expenses (net)		
	2.4	6.0	4.2			Profit Before Taxes		
						RATIOS		
	2.4	1.8	2.6					
	1.3	1.1	1.3			Current		
	.8	1.0	1.0					
	1.5	1.1	1.4					
	.7	.8	.8			Quick		
	.4	.4	.3					
	15 25.0	11 34.0	26 13.9					
	27 13.5	20 18.7	38 9.6			Sales/Receivables		
	39 9.3	49 7.5	87 4.2					
	7 49.0	7 51.2	26 14.2					
	28 13.1	33 11.2	74 4.9			Cost of Sales/Inventory		
	107 3.4	65 5.6	122 3.0					
	4 81.6	5 73.2	15 24.6					
	20 18.0	19 19.7	26 13.8			Cost of Sales/Payables		
	215 1.7	36 10.1	62 5.9					
	7.6	8.7	5.0					
	14.6	59.5	15.9			Sales/Working Capital		
	-30.5	-136.7	-142.3					
	8.3	10.2	6.5					
	(13) 3.2	(31) 3.4	(25) 3.9			EBIT/Interest		
	1.4	1.0	1.2					
		4.8	8.8					
		(12) 2.5	(10) 2.3			Net Profit + Depr., Dep., Amort./Cur. Mat. L /T/D		
		-4.3	1.0					
	.3	.6	.3					
	.7	.9	1.1			Fixed/Worth		
	1.5	1.6	2.7					
	.4	.8	.7					
	1.7	1.7	2.3			Debt/Worth		
	3.8	4.2	5.6					
	34.2	53.2	32.5					
	(13) 13.9	(30) 16.6	16.6			% Profit Before Taxes/Tangible Net Worth		
	8.8	.3	3.1					
	11.5	14.6	12.5					
	5.8	5.0	4.9			% Profit Before Taxes/Total Assets		
	1.2	-.1	1.0					
	17.6	17.6	13.6					
	8.5	8.4	5.2			Sales/Net Fixed Assets		
	2.8	3.9	2.1					
	4.3	3.7	2.3					
	2.3	2.3	1.6			Sales/Total Assets		
	1.3	1.4	1.0					
	1.1	1.0	.9					
	2.1	(29) 1.9	(21) 1.5			% Depr., Dep., Amort./Sales		
	3.8	3.2	4.5					
		.8						
		(11) 4.2				% Officers', Directors', Owners' Comp/Sales		
		6.5						
2458M	50740M	340164M	874936M	35108M	224735M	Net Sales ($)		
618M	19335M	137695M	537468M	54843M	103519M	Total Assets ($)		

© Robert Morris Associates 1995

M = $ thousand   MM = $ million
See Pages 1 through 15 for Explanation of Ratios and Data

Comparative Historical Data | | | | **Current Data Sorted By Sales** | | | | |

Comparative Historical Data					Current Data Sorted By Sales				
1	1	2	# Postretirement Benefits				1	1	
			Type of Statement						
9	21	23	Unqualified	1	2	2	9	9	
4	18	27	Reviewed	6	3	7	8	3	
5	7	11	Compiled	2	3	4	1	1	
	2	1	Tax Returns				1		
8	10	15	Other	5	1	1	4	4	
4/1/92-3/31/93	4/1/93-3/31/94	4/1/94-3/31/95			42 (4/1-9/30/94)		35 (10/1/94-3/31/95)		
ALL	ALL	ALL		0-1MM	1-3MM	3-5MM	5-10MM	10-25MM	25MM & OVER
26	58	77	**NUMBER OF STATEMENTS**		14	9	14	23	17
%	%	%	**ASSETS**	%	%	%	%	%	%
7.8	5.9	10.2	Cash & Equivalents		7.2		6.2	14.7	2.3
30.3	21.3	20.7	Trade Receivables - (net)		18.1		28.9	14.9	27.6
15.8	22.4	22.1	Inventory		19.2		19.5	25.4	31.4
3.6	3.0	3.1	All Other Current		.5		4.2	1.7	3.2
57.5	52.6	56.0	Total Current		45.1		58.8	56.8	64.5
35.6	38.3	35.1	Fixed Assets (net)		50.1		35.4	34.0	25.9
.1	.7	1.0	Intangibles (net)		.9		.1	2.4	.4
6.8	8.4	7.8	All Other Non-Current		3.9		5.6	6.8	9.2
100.0	100.0	100.0	Total		100.0		100.0	100.0	100.0
			LIABILITIES						
8.1	13.0	15.6	Notes Payable-Short Term		11.7		15.4	14.8	22.4
6.0	4.7	2.8	Cur. Mat.-L /T/D		5.7		3.2	2.2	1.2
18.7	12.2	16.1	Trade Payables		15.7		17.8	13.2	15.2
.4	.2	.4	Income Taxes Payable		.1		.2	.2	.3
11.6	7.2	10.2	All Other Current		5.4		9.7	18.4	5.6
44.9	37.4	45.1	Total Current		38.5		46.3	48.8	44.8
10.8	18.1	12.4	Long Term Debt		14.7		16.1	12.7	9.2
.8	1.1	1.0	Deferred Taxes		.1		.5	1.1	1.8
4.6	4.7	1.9	All Other-Non-Current		.0		3.4	1.6	3.2
38.9	38.7	39.7	Net Worth		46.7		33.7	35.9	41.0
100.0	100.0	100.0	Total Liabilities & Net Worth		100.0		100.0	100.0	100.0
			INCOME DATA						
100.0	100.0	100.0	Net Sales		100.0		100.0	100.0	100.0
25.7	26.0	27.4	Gross Profit		39.0		27.8	26.9	15.7
20.0	22.9	21.6	Operating Expenses		32.8		23.1	20.2	9.9
5.7	3.2	5.8	Operating Profit		6.2		4.7	6.6	5.8
.7	1.6	.7	All Other Expenses (net)		1.8		1.4	.3	.9
5.0	1.6	5.1	Profit Before Taxes		4.3		3.3	6.4	4.9
			RATIOS						
2.1 / 1.2 / .9	2.2 / 1.5 / 1.0	1.9 / 1.2 / 1.0	Current		1.8 / 1.2 / .7		1.8 / 1.4 / 1.0	2.0 / 1.0 / 1.0	2.1 / 1.3 / 1.1
1.5 / .8 / .5	1.4 / .8 / .4	1.1 / .7 / .4	Quick		1.2 / .4 / .3		1.1 / .7 / .5	1.1 / .8 / .3	1.3 / .7 / .4
19 18.8 / 36 10.0 / 65 5.6	23 15.8 / 37 10.0 / 58 6.3	16 22.7 / 32 11.4 / 47 7.8	Sales/Receivables		14 26.2 / 29 12.5 / 56 6.5		24 15.1 / 40 9.1 / 96 3.8	13 28.9 / 21 17.7 / 43 8.4	35 10.5 / 38 9.5 / 45 8.1
0 UND / 30 12.3 / 76 4.8	17 21.6 / 46 7.9 / 101 3.6	11 34.6 / 39 9.4 / 104 3.5	Cost of Sales/Inventory		30 12.3 / 78 4.7 / 332 1.1		10 37.8 / 29 12.5 / 73 5.0	7 54.4 / 45 8.2 / 101 3.6	22 16.3 / 61 6.0 / 101 3.6
7 51.9 / 26 13.9 / 73 5.0	8 46.4 / 18 20.7 / 50 7.3	8 47.9 / 22 16.5 / 52 7.0	Cost of Sales/Payables		6 57.4 / 30 12.2 / 215 1.7		4 88.5 / 36 10.2 / 74 4.9	9 41.2 / 19 19.1 / 43 8.5	10 36.9 / 19 19.5 / 32 11.5
8.9 / 17.7 / -206.2	6.2 / 13.6 / 59.2	7.4 / 16.5 / -109.7	Sales/Working Capital		8.1 / 13.6 / -25.5		8.3 / 15.0 / NM	6.7 / 117.6 / -63.6	6.3 / 10.8 / 39.0
(25) 7.5 / 3.9 / 1.5	(57) 4.9 / 2.2 / 1.0	(71) 8.4 / 3.4 / 1.1	EBIT/Interest		(12) 10.6 / 2.7 / .3		6.5 / 3.3 / 1.7	(21) 7.7 / 2.1 / .4	(16) 8.2 / 4.4 / 1.2
(12) 27.6 / 8.0 / 3.6	(28) 5.5 / 2.7 / 1.2	(28) 7.6 / 3.1 / 1.0	Net Profit + Depr., Dep., Amort./Cur. Mat. L/T/D						(10) 19.8 / 2.7 / 1.1
.4 / .9 / 1.5	.4 / .8 / 2.5	.5 / .9 / 1.6	Fixed/Worth		.6 / 1.1 / 1.7		.5 / .9 / 2.0	.7 / 1.1 / 2.3	.3 / .7 / 1.2
.7 / 1.4 / 4.3	.7 / 1.5 / 4.2	.7 / 1.8 / 4.6	Debt/Worth		.4 / 1.5 / 3.2		1.2 / 1.9 / 4.4	.8 / 2.7 / 5.8	.8 / 1.7 / 4.3
(23) 43.1 / 23.4 / 6.7	(51) 24.0 / 11.7 / .9	(73) 43.3 / 16.0 / 4.1	% Profit Before Taxes/Tangible Net Worth		(13) 35.4 / 11.3 / -2.1		(13) 35.3 / 17.8 / 6.9	(21) 54.2 / 17.0 / -.4	38.3 / 17.6 / 2.5
16.7 / 11.0 / 2.3	7.6 / 3.9 / -.8	12.8 / 5.7 / .3	% Profit Before Taxes/Total Assets		13.8 / 5.2 / -3.9		19.2 / 4.7 / 1.1	12.0 / 4.3 / -.4	12.8 / 7.4 / 1.1
14.2 / 7.4 / 2.8	11.5 / 5.9 / 2.6	14.6 / 6.8 / 3.1	Sales/Net Fixed Assets		7.9 / 2.5 / 1.3		15.1 / 8.5 / 3.8	14.0 / 6.6 / 3.8	20.5 / 9.8 / 5.2
3.4 / 2.2 / 1.2	2.2 / 1.7 / 1.0	3.1 / 2.0 / 1.2	Sales/Total Assets		2.1 / 1.2 / .8		4.6 / 2.4 / .9	3.7 / 1.8 / 1.0	2.8 / 2.3 / 1.5
(25) .9 / 1.5 / 4.2	(57) 1.5 / 2.8 / 5.1	(67) 1.1 / 1.9 / 3.7	% Depr., Dep., Amort./Sales		(13) 2.1 / 3.7 / 6.6		1.8 / 2.0 / 4.0	(18) .5 / 1.6 / 3.9	(14) .8 / 1.3 / 2.7
	(20) 1.5 / 3.1 / 5.2	(22) 1.7 / 4.2 / 6.6	% Officers', Directors', Owners' Comp/Sales						
722473M / 350192M	1703211M / 1136851M	1528141M / 853478M	Net Sales ($) / Total Assets ($)		23500M / 21141M	39384M / 20299M	103189M / 80638M	373778M / 221623M	968290M / 509777M

M = $ thousand   MM = $ million
See Pages 1 through 15 for Explanation of Ratios and Data

Current Data Sorted By Assets | # Postretirement Benefits | Comparative Historical Data

0-500M	500M-2MM	2-10MM	10-50MM	50-100MM	100-250MM	Type of Statement	4/1/90-3/31/91 ALL	4/1/91-3/31/92 ALL
1				1		Unqualified		
	1			1		Reviewed		
	3	7	2			Compiled		
1	9	4				Tax Returns		
3	4					Other		
	13 (4/1-9/30/94)			22 (10/1/94-3/31/95)				
4	17	11	2	1		NUMBER OF STATEMENTS		
%	%	%	%	%	%	ASSETS	%	%
	3.5	3.4				Cash & Equivalents	D	D
	10.4	14.8				Trade Receivables - (net)	A	A
	6.5	27.7				Inventory	T	T
	.5	.9				All Other Current	A	A
	21.0	46.8				Total Current		
	60.7	42.4				Fixed Assets (net)	N	N
	.1	.1				Intangibles (net)	O	O
	18.2	10.7				All Other Non-Current	T	T
	100.0	100.0				Total		
						LIABILITIES	A	A
	17.8	21.4				Notes Payable-Short Term	V	V
	3.6	3.4				Cur. Mat. -L/T/D	A	A
	7.7	7.8				Trade Payables	I	I
	.3	1.1				Income Taxes Payable	L	L
	5.1	9.0				All Other Current	A	A
	34.5	42.7				Total Current	B	B
	16.6	17.9				Long Term Debt	L	L
	.5	3.3				Deferred Taxes	E	E
	5.9	2.1				All Other-Non-Current		
	42.4	34.0				Net Worth		
	100.0	100.0				Total Liabilities & Net Worth		
						INCOME DATA		
	100.0	100.0				Net Sales		
						Gross Profit		
	97.4	98.3				Operating Expenses		
	2.6	1.7				Operating Profit		
	4.7	2.6				All Other Expenses (net)		
	–2.0	–.9				Profit Before Taxes		
						RATIOS		
	1.5	1.8				Current		
	.8	1.1						
	.1	.9						
	1.4	1.0				Quick		
	.5	(10) .3						
	.1	.0						
0	UND	0 UND				Sales/Receivables		
6	62.9	13 28.4						
46	7.9	47 7.7						
						Cost of Sales/Inventory		
						Cost of Sales/Payables		
	5.1	3.3				Sales/Working Capital		
	–69.4	18.2						
	–5.0	–7.1						
	4.6	4.7				EBIT/Interest		
	(15) 1.4	1.7						
	–2.0	–1.2						
						Net Profit + Depr., Dep., Amort./Cur. Mat. L./T/D		
	.8	.6				Fixed/Worth		
	1.0	1.4						
	2.1	2.6						
	.3	1.2				Debt/Worth		
	1.1	2.2						
	5.5	4.4						
	9.8	20.7				% Profit Before Taxes/Tangible Net Worth		
	(15) 2.2	12.6						
	–7.1	–11.7						
	5.8	5.7				% Profit Before Taxes/Total Assets		
	–.7	3.9						
	–6.8	–3.7						
	3.2	2.2				Sales/Net Fixed Assets		
	1.8	1.5						
	.7	1.0						
	1.7	1.3				Sales/Total Assets		
	1.0	.7						
	.5	.5						
	3.5	4.6				% Depr., Dep., Amort./Sales		
	6.8	(10) 7.1						
	9.9	10.3						
						% Officers', Directors', Owners' Comp/Sales		
3462M	30328M	63807M	38385M	27690M		Net Sales ($)		
1371M	20468M	38603M	53826M	65838M		Total Assets ($)		

M = $ thousand   MM = $ million
See Pages 1 through 15 for Explanation of Ratios and Data

	Comparative Historical Data				Current Data Sorted By Sales					
			2	# Postretirement Benefits		1				1
				Type of Statement						
			2	Unqualified	1					1
		11	12	Reviewed	1	4	2	1	4	
		8	14	Compiled	4	9		1		
		5		Tax Returns						
		3	7	Other	5	1	1			
	4/1/92-3/31/93 ALL	4/1/93-3/31/94 ALL	4/1/94-3/31/95 ALL		13 (4/1-9/30/94) 0-1MM	1-3MM	3-5MM	22 (10/1/94-3/31/95) 5-10MM	10-25MM	25MM & OVER
		27	35	**NUMBER OF STATEMENTS**	11	14	3	2	4	1
	%	%	%	**ASSETS**	%	%	%	%	%	%
		8.2	3.9	Cash & Equivalents	5.3	3.9				
		14.3	11.3	Trade Receivables - (net)	7.0	6.7				
		14.1	14.3	Inventory	9.9	17.7				
		3.3	.6	All Other Current	.3	.1				
		39.8	30.2	Total Current	22.5	28.4				
		47.6	56.9	Fixed Assets (net)	63.0	58.7				
		.0	.1	Intangibles (net)	.0	.2				
		12.6	12.9	All Other Non-Current	14.5	12.7				
		100.0	100.0	Total	100.0	100.0				
				LIABILITIES						
		8.4	19.6	Notes Payable-Short Term	9.4	28.4				
		5.2	3.3	Cur. Mat.-L /T/D	2.2	3.1				
		3.6	7.3	Trade Payables	3.4	3.7				
		.2	.5	Income Taxes Payable	.4	.0				
		5.8	5.8	All Other Current	1.6	2.7				
		23.1	36.6	Total Current	17.0	38.0				
		20.3	22.6	Long Term Debt	29.2	20.9				
		.6	1.8	Deferred Taxes	.8	2.6				
		3.5	3.6	All Other-Non-Current	.1	8.6				
		52.5	35.5	Net Worth	52.9	29.8				
		100.0	100.0	Total Liabilities & Net Worth	100.0	100.0				
				INCOME DATA						
		100.0	100.0	Net Sales	100.0	100.0				
				Gross Profit						
		85.8	94.9	Operating Expenses	95.3	93.9				
		14.2	5.1	Operating Profit	4.7	6.1				
		2.8	3.4	All Other Expenses (net)	4.8	3.5				
		11.3	1.7	Profit Before Taxes	.0	2.7				
				RATIOS						
		7.6	1.8	Current	3.5	1.8				
		1.4	1.1		1.7	1.0				
		1.0	.4		.9	.1				
		2.7	1.1	Quick	2.4	.6				
		.6 (34)	.4		1.6	.2				
		.1	.1		.1	.0				
	0	UND	0 UND	Sales/Receivables	0 UND	0 UND				
	19	19.6	6 59.7		6 59.7	0 UND				
	111	3.3	47 7.7		64 5.7	39 9.3				
				Cost of Sales/Inventory						
				Cost of Sales/Payables						
		1.9	6.6	Sales/Working Capital	4.5	5.8				
		7.4	44.0		7.1	NM				
		56.8	-6.3		-7.6	-4.5				
		6.0	4.5	EBIT/Interest		5.1				
	(21)	2.0	1.8 (32)			1.4				
		.5	-.1			-2.3				
			2.2	Net Profit + Depr., Dep., Amort./Cur. Mat. L/T/D						
			1.0 (12)							
			.3							
		.5	.9	Fixed/Worth	.9	.8				
		.9	1.3		1.0	1.5				
		1.9	2.9		2.6	4.6				
		.2	.8	Debt/Worth	.2	1.0				
		1.2	2.2		1.1	1.8				
		2.5	4.5		3.1	5.3				
		20.5	21.7	% Profit Before Taxes/Tangible Net Worth	10.0	24.1				
	(26)	6.9	6.8 (32)		-.4 (10)	10.6 (12)				
		.3	-6.8		-6.3	-10.0				
		13.0	7.9	% Profit Before Taxes/Total Assets	13.9	9.9				
		3.0	1.4		1.7	2.3				
		.6	-3.7		-3.2	-11.1				
		3.5	3.0	Sales/Net Fixed Assets	1.6	3.8				
		1.8	1.7		.9	1.9				
		.9	.9		.6	1.1				
		.9	1.6	Sales/Total Assets	1.0	1.6				
		.7	.9		.6	1.1				
		.5	.5		.4	.6				
		2.9	3.7	% Depr., Dep., Amort./Sales	6.5	3.6				
	(25)	5.2	6.8 (33)		8.9	6.8 (13)				
		7.7	9.6		17.4	9.7				
			1.1	% Officers', Directors', Owners' Comp/Sales						
		(10)	2.7							
			15.3							
		72951M	163672M	Net Sales ($)	5812M	24171M	11055M	11650M	83294M	27690M
		96474M	180106M	Total Assets ($)	10766M	25989M	11714M	2587M	63212M	65838M

(Left column 4/1/92-3/31/93 ALL: DATA NOT AVAILABLE)

M = $ thousand   MM = $ million
See Pages 1 through 15 for Explanation of Ratios and Data

Current Data Sorted By Assets — **Comparative Historical Data**

	0-500M	500M-2MM	2-10MM	10-50MM	50-100MM	100-250MM		4/1/90-3/31/91 ALL	4/1/91-3/31/92 ALL
# Postretirement Benefits									
Type of Statement									
Unqualified			3	3					
Reviewed		1	4	3					
Compiled		4	3	1					
Tax Returns		1							
Other		2	6	5		1			
		13 (4/1-9/30/94)		24 (10/1/94-3/31/95)					
NUMBER OF STATEMENTS		8	16	12		1			
ASSETS	%	%	%	%	%	%		%	%
Cash & Equivalents			4.9	2.0				D	D
Trade Receivables - (net)			19.6	13.0				A	A
Inventory			21.5	15.8				T	T
All Other Current			3.1	12.4				A	A
Total Current			49.1	43.2					
Fixed Assets (net)			36.0	48.1				N	N
Intangibles (net)			.3	.9				O	O
All Other Non-Current			14.7	7.8				T	T
Total			100.0	100.0					
LIABILITIES								A	A
Notes Payable-Short Term			14.2	21.9				V	V
Cur. Mat. -L/T/D			4.4	6.3				A	A
Trade Payables			14.1	11.6				I	I
Income Taxes Payable			.1	1.0				L	L
All Other Current			4.1	7.8				A	A
Total Current			37.0	48.6				B	B
Long Term Debt			19.5	26.0				L	L
Deferred Taxes			2.0	.8				E	E
All Other-Non-Current			4.0	1.5					
Net Worth			37.5	23.1					
Total Liabilities & Net Worth			100.0	100.0					
INCOME DATA									
Net Sales			100.0	100.0					
Gross Profit			15.6	17.7					
Operating Expenses			15.7	19.8					
Operating Profit			-.1	-2.1					
All Other Expenses (net)			1.0	2.0					
Profit Before Taxes			-1.2	-4.1					
RATIOS									
Current			1.8	1.2					
			1.3	.9					
			1.0	.7					
Quick			.9	.4					
			.7	.4					
			.3	.2					
Sales/Receivables			17 20.9	17 21.9					
			22 16.7	24 15.4					
			28 13.0	30 12.3					
Cost of Sales/Inventory			15 24.2	23 16.0					
			24 15.5	36 10.1					
			58 6.3	60 6.1					
Cost of Sales/Payables			6 64.2	17 21.8					
			17 20.9	27 13.3					
			29 12.5	36 10.1					
Sales/Working Capital			13.3	41.2					
			38.3	-57.0					
			-501.9	-15.8					
EBIT/Interest			3.0	.8					
			(15) .0	-1.0					
			-1.4	-1.7					
Net Profit + Depr., Dep., Amort./Cur. Mat. L /T/D									
Fixed/Worth			.7	1.3					
			1.0	2.1					
			4.0	4.9					
Debt/Worth			.7	1.4					
			2.2	3.0					
			4.7	8.9					
% Profit Before Taxes/Tangible Net Worth			26.0	-1.1					
			(15) -4.9	(11) -12.8					
			-38.6	-69.7					
% Profit Before Taxes/Total Assets			7.3	-.7					
			-2.6	-4.3					
			-9.6	-12.6					
Sales/Net Fixed Assets			21.5	5.4					
			8.5	3.7					
			5.5	2.6					
Sales/Total Assets			5.0	2.1					
			2.3	1.7					
			1.7	1.5					
% Depr., Dep., Amort./Sales			1.3	3.6					
			(14) 2.2	(10) 7.2					
			6.0	11.9					
% Officers', Directors', Owners' Comp/Sales									
Net Sales ($)		27118M	348413M	448208M		254713M			
Total Assets ($)		7879M	109779M	257182M		146553M			

M = $ thousand   MM = $ million
See Pages 1 through 15 for Explanation of Ratios and Data

	Comparative Historical Data			# Postretirement Benefits Type of Statement	Current Data Sorted By Sales					
			6	Unqualified					2	4
			8	Reviewed	1			1	4	2
			8	Compiled		2	1	2	3	
			1	Tax Returns		1				
			14	Other		1	1	1	3	8
	4/1/92-3/31/93 ALL	4/1/93-3/31/94 ALL	4/1/94-3/31/95 ALL		13 (4/1-9/30/94)			24 (10/1/94-3/31/95)		
					0-1MM	1-3MM	3-5MM	5-10MM	10-25MM	25MM & OVER
			37	NUMBER OF STATEMENTS	1	4	2	4	12	14
	%	%	%	ASSETS	%	%	%	%	%	%
			5.2	Cash & Equivalents					2.8	5.1
	D	D	16.8	Trade Receivables - (net)					13.8	21.0
	A	A	19.3	Inventory					23.1	17.7
	T	T	6.1	All Other Current					10.8	4.8
	A	A	47.3	Total Current					50.4	48.5
			40.2	Fixed Assets (net)					36.7	40.1
	N	N	.6	Intangibles (net)					.8	.2
	O	O	11.9	All Other Non-Current					12.1	11.1
	T	T	100.0	Total					100.0	100.0
				LIABILITIES						
	A	A	15.8	Notes Payable-Short Term					16.6	17.0
	V	V	6.0	Cur. Mat.-L /T/D					5.1	5.0
	A	A	13.3	Trade Payables					10.3	17.1
	I	I	.5	Income Taxes Payable					.0	1.4
	L	L	7.9	All Other Current					5.4	6.4
	A	A	43.5	Total Current					37.4	46.8
	B	B	22.0	Long Term Debt					22.9	22.1
	L	L	1.3	Deferred Taxes					.2	3.2
	E	E	2.5	All Other-Non-Current					4.4	.3
			30.8	Net Worth					35.1	27.6
			100.0	Total Liabilities & Net Worth					100.0	100.0
				INCOME DATA						
			100.0	Net Sales					100.0	100.0
			18.9	Gross Profit					17.8	15.5
			19.9	Operating Expenses					19.3	15.9
			-1.0	Operating Profit					-1.5	-.4
			1.1	All Other Expenses (net)					1.7	1.1
			-2.1	Profit Before Taxes					-3.2	-1.5
				RATIOS						
			1.8						2.4	1.4
			1.2	Current					1.5	1.0
			.8						1.1	.8
			.8						.9	.9
			.5	Quick					.6	.4
			.3						.3	.3
	15	24.1		Sales/Receivables				16	22.3	17	21.5
	21	17.4						26	14.1	21	17.5
	28	13.1						31	11.8	27	13.6
	16	22.9		Cost of Sales/Inventory				25	14.6	14	26.5
	28	13.0						56	6.5	21	17.3
	60	6.1						72	5.1	50	7.3
	7	51.0		Cost of Sales/Payables				14	25.6	8	45.9
	22	16.7						20	18.7	24	15.2
	31	11.6						32	11.5	32	11.4
			10.5	Sales/Working Capital					4.8	40.6
			78.2						14.9	NM
			-22.0						111.0	-21.3
	(35)	1.3		EBIT/Interest				(11)	1.6	1.6
		.0							-1.3	.4
		-1.4							-1.9	-1.5
	(13)	4.8		Net Profit + Depr., Dep., Amort./Cur. Mat. L/T/D						
		.9								
		.2								
			.9	Fixed/Worth					.8	1.0
			1.3						1.1	1.7
			3.9						1.5	3.5
			1.4	Debt/Worth					.8	1.6
			2.4						1.8	2.4
			6.4						3.5	8.2
	(35)	3.5		% Profit Before Taxes/Tangible Net Worth				(10)	9.8	3.6
		-7.5							-6.0	-5.7
		-38.6							-11.8	-81.1
			1.3	% Profit Before Taxes/Total Assets					2.6	1.4
			-2.5						-3.4	-1.7
			-9.9						-9.6	-8.2
			16.1	Sales/Net Fixed Assets					8.3	25.1
			5.6						5.5	7.7
			3.0						3.6	3.1
			3.6	Sales/Total Assets					2.2	5.3
			1.9						1.8	3.1
			1.6						1.7	1.7
	(31)	1.4		% Depr., Dep., Amort./Sales				(10)	2.2	(12)	1.2
		4.0							5.0	2.5
		9.1							9.3	4.5
				% Officers', Directors', Owners' Comp/Sales						
			1078452M	Net Sales ($)	835M	7767M	8267M	28585M	223133M	809865M
			521393M	Total Assets ($)	507M	4009M	6897M	11200M	146475M	352305M

M = $ thousand   MM = $ million
See Pages 1 through 15 for Explanation of Ratios and Data

Current Data Sorted By Assets | **Comparative Historical Data**

Postretirement Benefits
Type of Statement

0-500M	500M-2MM	2-10MM	10-50MM	50-100MM	100-250MM		4/1/90-3/31/91 ALL	4/1/91-3/31/92 ALL
		2				Unqualified		
	6	31	2			Reviewed		
			3			Compiled		
1	5	6	2			Tax Returns		
	4	2						
1	2	4	2	1		Other		
	11 (4/1-9/30/94)		61 (10/1/94-3/31/95)					
2	17	43	9	1		**NUMBER OF STATEMENTS**		
%	%	%	%	%	%	**ASSETS**	%	%
	1.4	1.0				Cash & Equivalents		
	4.7	6.8				Trade Receivables - (net)		
	12.4	13.0				Inventory	DATA	DATA
	3.4	3.2				All Other Current		
	21.8	24.0				Total Current		
	66.5	58.8				Fixed Assets (net)		
	1.3	.7				Intangibles (net)	NOT	NOT
	10.3	16.5				All Other Non-Current		
	100.0	100.0				Total		
						LIABILITIES	AVAILABLE	AVAILABLE
	23.6	16.1				Notes Payable-Short Term		
	6.3	3.8				Cur. Mat. -L/T/D		
	1.7	2.6				Trade Payables		
	.0	.0				Income Taxes Payable		
	1.0	2.1				All Other Current		
	32.5	24.7				Total Current		
	34.7	29.1				Long Term Debt		
	.7	.1				Deferred Taxes		
	.3	2.4				All Other-Non-Current		
	31.8	43.6				Net Worth		
	100.0	100.0				Total Liabilities & Net Worth		
						INCOME DATA		
	100.0	100.0				Net Sales		
	43.4	49.6				Gross Profit		
	39.5	39.4				Operating Expenses		
	3.9	10.2				Operating Profit		
	1.9	5.5				All Other Expenses (net)		
	2.0	4.7				Profit Before Taxes		
						RATIOS		
	1.0	1.4						
	.7	1.0				Current		
	.2	.7						
	.3	.6						
	(16) .2	.3				Quick		
	.1	.2						
0	UND	24	15.3					
16	22.4	31	11.7			Sales/Receivables		
28	12.9	35	10.5					
0	UND	54	6.8					
56	6.5	118	3.1			Cost of Sales/Inventory		
174	2.1	228	1.6					
0	UND	2	201.1					
10	37.6	14	26.9			Cost of Sales/Payables		
21	17.3	30	12.0					
	-396.4	14.7						
	-10.2	-45.0				Sales/Working Capital		
	-6.4	-11.5						
	3.0	3.9						
	(42) 1.6	2.2				EBIT/Interest		
	.6	.6						
						Net Profit + Depr., Dep., Amort./Cur. Mat. L /T/D		
	1.1	.8						
	2.3	1.3				Fixed/Worth		
	5.3	2.3						
	.9	.6						
	3.6	1.4				Debt/Worth		
	6.7	2.8						
	16.1	19.2						
	(16) 4.2	(40) 8.7				% Profit Before Taxes/Tangible Net Worth		
	-22.4	-1.6						
	7.0	7.0						
	1.6	3.4				% Profit Before Taxes/Total Assets		
	-2.5	-1.1						
	2.3	1.8						
	2.0	1.5				Sales/Net Fixed Assets		
	1.5	1.0						
	1.3	1.1						
	1.2	.7				Sales/Total Assets		
	1.0	.6						
	3.8	4.7						
	(15) 9.4	8.5				% Depr., Dep., Amort./Sales		
	11.2	9.6						
		.9						
	(20)	2.2				% Officers', Directors', Owners' Comp/Sales		
		3.2						
741M	26458M	172208M	222302M	37597M		Net Sales ($)		
365M	22882M	201314M	178738M	51323M		Total Assets ($)		

M = $ thousand   MM = $ million
See Pages 1 through 15 for Explanation of Ratios and Data

Comparative Historical Data / Current Data Sorted By Sales

Comparative Historical Data			# Postretirement Benefits / Type of Statement	Current Data Sorted By Sales					
1	2	2			1		1		
4	5	2	Unqualified						2
13	53	40	Reviewed		23	10	6	1	
6	14	14	Compiled	2	5	1	5	1	
	4	6	Tax Returns	2	3	1			
2	11	10	Other	3	2	2	1		2

4/1/92-3/31/93 ALL	4/1/93-3/31/94 ALL	4/1/94-3/31/95 ALL		0-1MM	11 (4/1-9/30/94) 1-3MM	3-5MM	61 (10/1/94-3/31/95) 5-10MM	10-25MM	25MM & OVER
25	87	72	**NUMBER OF STATEMENTS**	7	33	14	12	2	4
%	%	%	**ASSETS**	%	%	%	%	%	%
1.3	2.1	1.4	Cash & Equivalents		1.0	1.4	1.0		
6.5	6.4	6.9	Trade Receivables - (net)		5.9	6.7	5.7		
15.8	16.2	12.7	Inventory		14.7	14.0	8.7		
1.3	4.9	3.9	All Other Current		4.6	1.0	8.3		
24.9	29.6	24.9	Total Current		26.3	23.0	23.6		
50.3	50.8	59.1	Fixed Assets (net)		57.7	64.7	55.3		
4.3	2.2	.8	Intangibles (net)		.9	.1	.2		
20.5	17.4	15.2	All Other Non-Current		15.1	12.2	20.9		
100.0	100.0	100.0	Total		100.0	100.0	100.0		
			LIABILITIES						
16.9	18.1	17.3	Notes Payable-Short Term		23.2	13.2	18.8		
6.2	5.9	5.5	Cur. Mat.-L /T/D		5.2	4.0	3.7		
4.2	3.5	3.0	Trade Payables		1.8	2.8	2.5		
.1	.2	.0	Income Taxes Payable		.0	.0	.0		
1.8	2.6	1.9	All Other Current		1.2	2.8	2.9		
29.1	30.2	27.7	Total Current		31.5	22.8	27.9		
29.5	26.9	30.8	Long Term Debt		29.7	37.7	25.3		
1.8	.3	.9	Deferred Taxes		.4	.9	2.7		
2.7	2.3	2.4	All Other-Non-Current		2.3	1.0	.7		
36.8	40.2	38.2	Net Worth		36.3	37.6	43.4		
100.0	100.0	100.0	Total Liabilities & Net Worth		100.0	100.0	100.0		
			INCOME DATA						
100.0	100.0	100.0	Net Sales		100.0	100.0	100.0		
40.8	44.9	47.2	Gross Profit		43.5	53.3	54.4		
30.7	36.1	39.1	Operating Expenses		37.2	40.0	42.3		
10.1	8.9	8.1	Operating Profit		6.4	13.4	12.1		
3.3	3.4	3.9	All Other Expenses (net)		4.1	5.3	4.8		
6.9	5.5	4.2	Profit Before Taxes		2.3	8.0	7.3		
			RATIOS						
1.3	1.4	1.4	Current		1.1	1.4	1.9		
.9	.9	.9			.8	1.0	1.2		
.6	.7	.6			.6	.7	.3		
.5	.5	.5	Quick		.4	.6	.5		
.3 (86)	.3 (71)	.3		(32) .2	.3	.3			
.1	.1	.2		.2	.2	.2			
14 25.2	17 21.6	19 18.9	Sales/Receivables	16 22.4	23 16.0	20 17.9			
28 13.1	27 13.4	29 12.4		29 12.4	31 11.8	25 14.7			
34 10.7	34 10.6	35 10.4		36 10.2	35 10.4	33 11.0			
18 19.9	45 8.1	14 25.5	Cost of Sales/Inventory	20 18.0	79 4.6	13 28.0			
114 3.2	135 2.7	104 3.5		118 3.1	114 3.2	107 3.4			
215 1.7	215 1.7	215 1.7		243 1.5	281 1.3	203 1.8			
1 505.7	0 UND	0 999.8	Cost of Sales/Payables	0 UND	0 UND	12 29.8			
7 52.2	15 24.7	13 28.6		10 37.6	11 34.6	17 21.7			
22 16.4	35 10.5	27 13.4		21 17.3	33 11.0	38 9.5			
14.3	11.7	12.9	Sales/Working Capital		22.5	10.3	7.7		
-86.1	-42.9	-40.8			-18.5	NM	31.0		
-13.2	-9.2	-8.7			-7.9	-11.0	-5.0		
5.6	4.1	3.7	EBIT/Interest		3.7	4.3	4.8		
(23) 2.8	(84) 2.3	(70) 2.0			1.7	2.9	3.0		
1.4	1.3	.6			.5	.7	1.0		
	4.0	8.0	Net Profit + Depr., Dep., Amort./Cur. Mat. L/T/D						
	(10) 1.2	(15) 2.5							
	.9	.9							
1.1	.7	1.0	Fixed/Worth		.9	1.1	.6		
1.4	1.4	1.5			1.4	2.1	1.1		
2.4	2.4	3.3			3.3	4.2	3.9		
.8	.8	.8	Debt/Worth		.9	1.0	.4		
1.7	1.7	1.7			1.7	2.2	1.7		
4.3	3.3	4.5			4.8	4.7	4.2		
23.3	22.3	18.8	% Profit Before Taxes/Tangible Net Worth	16.1	21.4	23.0			
(21) 13.2	(79) 9.9	(67) 9.1		(32) 8.7	(13) 16.7	(11) 17.1			
5.4	1.2	-1.9		-18.9	-12.3	2.6			
9.0	7.8	7.0	% Profit Before Taxes/Total Assets		7.1	8.1	7.6		
5.3	3.9	3.4			2.1	5.9	5.5		
2.0	.9	-2.0			-3.1	-1.6	.1		
3.1	2.7	2.0	Sales/Net Fixed Assets		2.1	1.8	2.1		
1.6	1.6	1.5			1.6	1.2	1.5		
1.2	1.1	1.1			1.5	.9	1.1		
1.1	1.1	1.3	Sales/Total Assets		1.2	1.1	1.2		
.7	.8	.8			.9	.8	.8		
.6	.6	.6			.7	.6	.6		
4.4	5.1	4.1	% Depr., Dep., Amort./Sales	5.7	3.2	6.1			
(24) 8.5	(82) 8.2	(69) 8.5		(31) 8.8	7.3	(11) 9.4			
12.9	10.3	10.1		10.5	9.3	12.2			
.6	1.3	1.0	% Officers', Directors', Owners' Comp/Sales	1.0					
(11) 2.5	(28) 2.6	(28) 2.4		(13) 1.9					
9.6	6.1	3.5		3.9					
556422M	703952M	459306M	Net Sales ($)	4429M	64454M	60128M	80614M	36902M	212779M
387849M	451277M	454622M	Total Assets ($)	15473M	76783M	84956M	108738M	23464M	145208M

M = $ thousand   MM = $ million
See Pages 1 through 15 for Explanation of Ratios and Data

Current Data Sorted By Assets | **Comparative Historical Data**

	1	2	3				# Postretirement Benefits / Type of Statement		
		2	3	4			Unqualified	2	5
	1	3	6	1			Reviewed	8	9
	4	17	9	4			Compiled	29	20
	5	5	1				Tax Returns	3	3
	1	9	14	5			Other	13	19

	0-500M	500M-2MM	2-10MM	10-50MM	50-100MM	100-250MM		4/1/90-3/31/91 ALL	4/1/91-3/31/92 ALL
	21 (4/1-9/30/94)		73 (10/1/94-3/31/95)						
NUMBER OF STATEMENTS	11	36	33	14				55	56
	%	%	%	%	%	%	**ASSETS**	%	%
	20.1	5.7	6.6	2.6			Cash & Equivalents	6.3	6.2
	10.7	11.5	14.7	14.4			Trade Receivables - (net)	12.8	10.9
	3.0	9.3	13.1	17.7			Inventory	8.8	9.7
	1.1	.9	4.5	1.5			All Other Current	2.3	2.6
	34.8	27.5	39.0	36.2			Total Current	30.2	29.4
	57.6	61.9	48.5	51.6			Fixed Assets (net)	58.0	55.5
	.0	.5	.3	.7			Intangibles (net)	.6	1.3
	7.6	10.1	12.2	11.5			All Other Non-Current	11.2	13.7
	100.0	100.0	100.0	100.0			Total	100.0	100.0
							LIABILITIES		
	6.9	22.1	14.4	10.8			Notes Payable-Short Term	16.2	12.9
	2.0	6.6	3.1	3.2			Cur. Mat. -L/T/D	6.2	3.9
	3.1	5.7	9.7	7.3			Trade Payables	5.8	6.2
	.0	.0	.1	.0			Income Taxes Payable	.1	.3
	6.0	10.4	4.0	10.6			All Other Current	4.6	5.5
	17.9	44.8	31.1	31.9			Total Current	33.0	28.9
	19.3	26.0	21.0	16.8			Long Term Debt	21.3	18.8
	.3	1.1	2.6	.5			Deferred Taxes	1.2	.8
	1.0	3.1	4.2	.8			All Other-Non-Current	.8	2.5
	61.5	25.0	41.2	50.0			Net Worth	43.6	49.1
	100.0	100.0	100.0	100.0			Total Liabilities & Net Worth	100.0	100.0
							INCOME DATA		
	100.0	100.0	100.0	100.0			Net Sales	100.0	100.0
							Gross Profit		
	85.7	95.8	94.8	92.2			Operating Expenses	95.2	91.8
	14.3	4.2	5.2	7.8			Operating Profit	4.8	8.2
	8.5	5.0	2.3	-.1			All Other Expenses (net)	2.8	.6
	5.9	-.8	2.9	7.9			Profit Before Taxes	2.0	7.6
							RATIOS		
	18.7	1.2	2.2	1.7			Current	1.7	2.8
	3.0	.8	1.4	1.3				.9	1.2
	1.2	.2	.8	.5				.3	.4
	3.3	.9	1.5	1.0			Quick	1.2	1.6
	1.2	.5	.7	.5				.5 (55)	.4
	.3	.1	.3	.2				.2	.1
	0 UND	0 UND	16 23.5	1 281.8			Sales/Receivables	0 UND	0 UND
	0 UND	3 133.9	31 11.8	30 12.2				13 27.9	13 27.2
	1 256.0	30 12.3	54 6.7	41 9.0				39 9.4	32 11.5
							Cost of Sales/Inventory		
							Cost of Sales/Payables		
	8.0	36.7	6.1	8.2			Sales/Working Capital	15.6	11.4
	23.6	-24.2	19.0	19.7				-49.2	524.6
	171.2	-4.6	-24.0	-16.4				-6.7	-6.9
	19.5	8.1	7.0	33.0			EBIT/Interest	3.7	7.1
	4.4	(34) 1.9	(29) 2.4	(13) 4.4				(49) 1.4	(53) 3.4
	2.5	-.8	1.4	1.3				.8	1.8
		5.1					Net Profit + Depr., Dep., Amort./Cur. Mat. L /T/D	4.2	11.8
	(11)	2.6						(24) 1.7	(17) 8.1
		1.0						.5	3.9
	.5	1.2	.7	.8			Fixed/Worth	.8	.6
	.8	2.1	1.0	1.0				1.3	1.1
	1.3	18.8	2.6	1.7				3.0	2.5
	.3	1.0	.6	.6			Debt/Worth	.4	.3
	.4	3.5	1.3	1.2				1.5	.9
	2.4	21.4	4.8	1.9				3.4	3.5
	45.0	43.8	22.2	30.5			% Profit Before Taxes/Tangible Net Worth	33.0	32.2
	25.6	(28) 14.8	(29) 10.6	13.8				(52) 10.7	(52) 19.1
	4.4	-10.9	6.4	1.9				1.3	6.3
	29.6	12.9	11.0	13.9			% Profit Before Taxes/Total Assets	9.4	17.0
	13.3	3.8	3.9	8.6				4.0	8.5
	2.0	-8.6	1.3	1.0				.3	2.0
	13.9	7.6	4.7	5.2			Sales/Net Fixed Assets	6.4	7.3
	6.2	2.4	2.0	3.3				2.7	2.5
	2.8	1.1	1.1	1.1				1.3	1.4
	5.6	2.6	1.9	2.1			Sales/Total Assets	2.2	2.3
	2.7	1.5	1.0	1.6				1.5	1.3
	2.1	.9	.6	.8				.8	.8
		2.1	3.4	2.1			% Depr., Dep., Amort./Sales	2.3	1.7
	(34)	6.5 (30)	5.9	3.7				(52) 4.1	(51) 3.9
		11.7	8.6	4.5				6.8	6.4
							% Officers', Directors', Owners' Comp/Sales	2.0	1.7
								(18) 3.9	(16) 3.0
								12.5	7.1
	14394M	80336M	196136M	650531M			Net Sales ($)	507536M	913675M
	3072M	36917M	142138M	314523M			Total Assets ($)	448628M	676587M

M = $ thousand   MM = $ million
See Pages 1 through 15 for Explanation of Ratios and Data

Comparative Historical Data				Current Data Sorted By Sales					
		6	# Postretirement Benefits	3			1	2	
			Type of Statement						
7	4	9	Unqualified			2	1	2	4
17	16	11	Reviewed	1	3	2	3	2	
34	20	34	Compiled	11	12	1	6	4	
7	5	11	Tax Returns	6	3	2			
21	18	29	Other	5	3	5	6		4
4/1/92-3/31/93	4/1/93-3/31/94	4/1/94-3/31/95		21 (4/1-9/30/94)			73 (10/1/94-3/31/95)		
ALL	ALL	ALL		0-1MM	1-3MM	3-5MM	5-10MM	10-25MM	25MM & OVER
86	63	94	**NUMBER OF STATEMENTS**	23	27	12	16	8	8
%	%	%	**ASSETS**	%	%	%	%	%	%
8.8	10.6	7.3	Cash & Equivalents	6.8	6.3	6.6	13.8		
10.3	13.2	13.0	Trade Receivables - (net)	7.0	12.1	20.9	10.7		
11.3	10.3	11.1	Inventory	3.0	8.6	19.1	15.8		
2.3	3.3	2.3	All Other Current	3.0	2.2	.4	.3		
32.8	37.4	33.7	Total Current	19.8	29.2	47.0	40.5		
55.9	49.2	55.2	Fixed Assets (net)	68.5	58.7	44.6	47.9		
.4	.8	.4	Intangibles (net)	.0	.1	.7	1.2		
10.9	12.6	10.7	All Other Non-Current	11.6	11.9	7.6	10.4		
100.0	100.0	100.0	Total	100.0	100.0	100.0	100.0		
			LIABILITIES						
14.8	12.5	15.9	Notes Payable-Short Term	14.8	17.2	30.6	11.0		
3.8	3.7	4.3	Cur. Mat.-L /T/D	9.4	2.9	2.2	1.9		
6.7	8.8	7.0	Trade Payables	1.8	6.2	13.6	5.3		
.7	.5	.0	Income Taxes Payable	.0	.0	.0	.1		
5.1	4.3	7.7	All Other Current	1.5	8.5	9.3	10.9		
31.1	29.8	34.9	Total Current	27.6	34.9	55.7	29.2		
20.7	17.2	22.1	Long Term Debt	34.0	22.1	15.0	18.0		
1.0	1.2	1.4	Deferred Taxes	2.4	.6	1.7	1.3		
3.2	3.3	2.9	All Other-Non-Current	1.6	5.2	6.4	.0		
44.0	48.7	38.7	Net Worth	34.4	37.3	21.3	51.5		
100.0	100.0	100.0	Total Liabilities & Net Worth	100.0	100.0	100.0	100.0		
			INCOME DATA						
100.0	100.0	100.0	Net Sales	100.0	100.0	100.0	100.0		
			Gross Profit						
95.2	91.5	93.7	Operating Expenses	88.8	96.1	103.0	92.4		
4.8	8.5	6.3	Operating Profit	11.2	3.9	–3.0	7.6		
1.4	1.1	3.7	All Other Expenses (net)	9.1	3.2	2.9	.7		
3.4	7.4	2.6	Profit Before Taxes	2.1	.7	–6.0	6.8		
			RATIOS						
2.1 / 1.0 / .6	2.4 / 1.5 / .8	1.7 / 1.1 / .7	Current	2.4 / .9 / .2	1.5 / 1.1 / .7	1.4 / 1.0 / .3	2.9 / 1.4 / .8		
1.5 / .7 / .2	1.7 / .7 / .3	1.2 / .6 / .2	Quick	1.0 / .2 / .1	1.1 / .6 / .3	1.2 / .2 / .2	2.4 / .8 / .4		
0 UND / 12 31.7 / 38 9.7	0 UND / 10 34.9 / 32 11.3	0 UND / 16 23.5 / 37 10.0	Sales/Receivables	0 UND / 0 UND / 4 83.3	0 999.8 / 25 14.8 / 74 4.9	9 41.6 / 23 16.2 / 76 4.8	4 91.4 / 17 21.3 / 31 11.7		
			Cost of Sales/Inventory						
			Cost of Sales/Payables						
9.8 / 534.5 / –10.3	6.5 / 24.5 / –37.1	11.3 / 88.4 / –11.5	Sales/Working Capital	8.0 / –33.8 / –4.2	16.7 / 171.2 / –6.8	12.6 / NM / –6.0	8.2 / 30.3 / –269.4		
(78) 7.2 / 2.3 / .9	(56) 14.7 / 4.7 / 1.5	(87) 8.7 / 2.5 / 1.2	EBIT/Interest	(21) 7.0 / 1.9 / –.3	7.5 / 2.1 / 1.3	(10) 5.3 / 1.2 / –3.2	(14) 13.7 / 3.3 / 1.5		
(30) 6.6 / 2.5 / 1.4	(16) 7.2 / 1.7 / 1.3	(24) 5.5 / 3.0 / 1.4	Net Profit + Depr., Dep., Amort./Cur. Mat. L/T/D						
.7 / 1.2 / 2.7	.4 / .9 / 1.9	.8 / 1.2 / 3.0	Fixed/Worth	1.0 / 2.0 / 3.3	.9 / 1.3 / 4.4	.6 / 1.7 / NM	.5 / 1.1 / 2.3		
.5 / 1.5 / 3.4	.4 / 1.1 / 2.4	.6 / 1.4 / 4.6	Debt/Worth	.9 / 2.4 / 5.8	.5 / 1.2 / 8.7	1.0 / 3.8 / NM	.3 / 1.1 / 2.3		
(81) 26.1 / 10.2 / –2.0	(60) 39.3 / 19.2 / 2.5	(82) 33.6 / 12.3 / 3.9	% Profit Before Taxes/Tangible Net Worth	(20) 41.5 / 9.1 / –2.9	(22) 22.9 / 12.1 / 7.6		(15) 37.8 / 10.6 / 5.6		
11.1 / 4.3 / –1.4	17.6 / 6.5 / 1.2	13.3 / 4.5 / .1	% Profit Before Taxes/Total Assets	13.3 / 2.0 / –8.6	9.0 / 4.1 / .7	8.3 / –1.2 / –17.2	21.4 / 6.0 / 1.9		
6.2 / 2.5 / 1.1	8.1 / 4.2 / 1.7	6.2 / 3.0 / 1.2	Sales/Net Fixed Assets	2.8 / 1.4 / .8	4.4 / 2.3 / 1.2	9.5 / 5.0 / 1.2	12.1 / 4.4 / 2.0		
2.5 / 1.3 / .7	3.0 / 1.6 / 1.0	2.4 / 1.5 / .8	Sales/Total Assets	1.9 / 1.0 / .6	2.2 / 1.2 / .7	2.7 / 1.7 / .9	3.7 / 1.9 / .9		
(82) 1.7 / 3.6 / 6.3	(57) 1.9 / 3.0 / 6.3	(87) 2.7 / 4.6 / 8.7	% Depr., Dep., Amort./Sales	(21) 6.4 / 8.8 / 12.8	(26) 3.1 / 6.2 / 10.2	(10) 1.9 / 3.7 / 5.7	(14) 2.0 / 3.0 / 4.8		
(30) 1.3 / 4.1 / 9.1	(21) 1.4 / 3.7 / 8.1	(23) 2.6 / 5.1 / 8.8	% Officers', Directors', Owners' Comp/Sales						
968021M	1254502M	941397M	Net Sales ($)	12754M	53970M	48333M	121350M	133074M	571916M
772779M	690128M	496650M	Total Assets ($)	20268M	49007M	37235M	81185M	80508M	228447M

M = $ thousand   MM = $ million
See Pages 1 through 15 for Explanation of Ratios and Data

Current Data Sorted By Assets / Comparative Historical Data

# Postretirement Benefits — Type of Statement	0-500M	500M-2MM	2-10MM	10-50MM	50-100MM	100-250MM		4/1/90-3/31/91 ALL	4/1/91-3/31/92 ALL
Unqualified	1	2	13	12	1	2		28	29
Reviewed		4	15	7	1			14	15
Compiled	2	13	15	7				20	15
Tax Returns	1	2	1	1					
Other	3	5	21	9	4	1		18	18
	56 (4/1-9/30/94)			85 (10/1/94-3/31/95)					
NUMBER OF STATEMENTS	7	26	65	35	6	2		80	77

ASSETS (%)

	0-500M	500M-2MM	2-10MM	10-50MM	50-100MM	100-250MM		4/1/90-3/31/91 ALL	4/1/91-3/31/92 ALL
Cash & Equivalents		3.2	4.2	1.3				5.3	5.1
Trade Receivables - (net)		16.6	20.6	13.2				18.4	18.2
Inventory		42.5	38.5	43.1				40.3	34.5
All Other Current		4.6	5.9	8.0				7.0	8.9
Total Current		66.9	69.3	65.6				71.0	66.7
Fixed Assets (net)		26.4	25.9	25.4				20.9	23.3
Intangibles (net)		.5	.3	.2				.7	2.0
All Other Non-Current		6.2	4.6	8.8				7.4	8.0
Total		100.0	100.0	100.0				100.0	100.0

LIABILITIES

	0-500M	500M-2MM	2-10MM	10-50MM	50-100MM	100-250MM		4/1/90-3/31/91 ALL	4/1/91-3/31/92 ALL
Notes Payable-Short Term		40.0	37.4	37.5				34.5	36.8
Cur. Mat. -L/T/D		1.5	1.2	.9				1.8	2.0
Trade Payables		6.5	8.6	5.7				10.5	9.7
Income Taxes Payable		.2	.4	.7				.2	.2
All Other Current		4.5	6.7	5.4				7.8	7.8
Total Current		52.7	54.2	50.3				54.9	56.4
Long Term Debt		7.9	8.1	9.2				10.6	9.2
Deferred Taxes		.7	.9	2.1				1.2	1.6
All Other-Non-Current		.3	3.0	1.8				.8	1.7
Net Worth		38.4	33.9	36.6				32.5	31.2
Total Liabilities & Net Worth		100.0	100.0	100.0				100.0	100.0

INCOME DATA

	0-500M	500M-2MM	2-10MM	10-50MM	50-100MM	100-250MM		4/1/90-3/31/91 ALL	4/1/91-3/31/92 ALL
Net Sales		100.0	100.0	100.0				100.0	100.0
Gross Profit		19.5	18.4	16.1				20.9	18.1
Operating Expenses		17.7	16.5	15.3				15.2	15.4
Operating Profit		1.8	1.9	.8				5.7	2.7
All Other Expenses (net)		1.1	.7	1.2				1.7	1.4
Profit Before Taxes		.7	1.2	-.4				4.0	1.3

RATIOS

	0-500M	500M-2MM	2-10MM	10-50MM	50-100MM	100-250MM		4/1/90-3/31/91 ALL	4/1/91-3/31/92 ALL
Current		1.7 1.4 1.0	1.6 1.3 1.1	1.5 1.3 1.1				1.5 1.3 1.1	1.5 1.2 1.0
Quick		.9 .2 .0	(64) .9 .4 .1	.4 .2 .1				(79) .8 .3 .1	.7 .3 .1
Sales/Receivables		0 UND 7 53.3 24 15.2	4 94.4 26 14.3 54 6.7	2 168.0 15 23.7 34 10.7				10 38.0 20 18.6 43 8.5	4 85.7 24 15.1 46 7.9
Cost of Sales/Inventory		19 18.8 85 4.3 126 2.9	25 14.5 76 4.8 130 2.8	52 7.0 118 3.1 159 2.3				34 10.7 87 4.2 159 2.3	22 16.9 72 5.1 159 2.3
Cost of Sales/Payables		0 UND 4 88.5 13 27.2	0 999.8 11 34.1 26 13.8	2 186.7 11 32.8 20 18.6				5 68.2 13 27.5 28 13.0	3 107.2 12 31.7 25 14.8
Sales/Working Capital		6.8 20.0 130.5	6.4 15.7 296.9	7.6 13.0 42.6				7.6 12.0 47.3	8.1 18.7 194.9
EBIT/Interest		(25) 4.3 1.8 .1	(64) 3.5 1.6 .3	(34) 2.1 1.1 -.4				(77) 3.4 2.5 1.7	(73) 4.0 1.7 1.0
Net Profit + Depr., Dep., Amort./Cur. Mat. L/T/D		(10) 8.5 5.3 1.9	(12) 7.5 2.8 -2.0	(11) 5.6 .4 -8.5				(37) 13.6 4.9 2.8	(27) 5.5 1.9 .4
Fixed/Worth		.1 .5 1.6	.4 .7 1.4	.4 .7 1.4				.3 .6 1.1	.3 .6 1.3
Debt/Worth		.8 1.7 4.2	1.0 1.9 5.1	1.2 1.7 3.1				1.2 2.4 4.4	1.7 2.6 4.6
% Profit Before Taxes/Tangible Net Worth		(24) 14.9 8.2 -7.3	(61) 21.7 4.6 -15.9	8.4 .6 -10.1				(77) 36.6 22.9 11.2	(74) 28.5 12.3 .2
% Profit Before Taxes/Total Assets		5.4 2.6 -5.5	6.9 2.2 -3.5	2.9 .4 -4.2				9.6 6.1 3.0	7.7 2.6 -.2
Sales/Net Fixed Assets		63.8 16.6 7.5	22.0 8.4 5.6	14.7 8.1 5.1				29.8 12.3 6.3	30.2 11.1 5.2
Sales/Total Assets		3.6 2.4 1.9	2.7 2.0 1.4	2.4 1.8 1.2				3.0 2.1 1.3	2.8 2.0 1.3
% Depr., Dep., Amort./Sales		(22) .8 1.6 2.6	(64) .7 1.6 2.1	.8 1.5 1.9				(75) .7 1.1 2.4	(71) .6 1.4 2.6
% Officers', Directors', Owners' Comp/Sales			(26) .5 1.4 2.4					(23) .6 1.3 2.5	(22) .5 1.6 3.0
Net Sales ($)	31827M	121024M	1050674M	1262383M	1400602M	1400082M		2586562M	2756759M
Total Assets ($)	1982M	33840M	322503M	710075M	448971M	293658M		1070259M	1227576M

M = $ thousand   MM = $ million
See Pages 1 through 15 for Explanation of Ratios and Data

Comparative Historical Data / Current Data Sorted By Sales

	8	6	# Postretirement Benefits	0-1MM	1-3MM	3-5MM	5-10MM (1)	10-25MM (1)	25MM & OVER (4)
			Type of Statement						
24	19	30	Unqualified	1		2	5	10	12
18	28	27	Reviewed		1	3	7	10	6
33	40	37	Compiled		9	5	9	10	4
2	3	4	Tax Returns	1	1	1		1	
28	37	43	Other	3	5	6	5	10	14
4/1/92-3/31/93 ALL	4/1/93-3/31/94 ALL	4/1/94-3/31/95 ALL		56 (4/1-9/30/94)			85 (10/1/94-3/31/95)		
105	127	141	**NUMBER OF STATEMENTS**	5	16	17	26	41	36
%	%	%	**ASSETS**	%	%	%	%	%	%
3.4	3.3	3.5	Cash & Equivalents		3.0	1.3	3.4	4.6	2.0
14.4	14.1	17.7	Trade Receivables - (net)		9.0	22.3	20.5	18.7	17.9
42.1	41.7	40.4	Inventory		40.2	41.7	34.5	41.3	42.7
6.3	6.1	5.6	All Other Current		.6	5.0	9.9	4.8	6.9
66.2	65.2	67.3	Total Current		52.8	70.3	68.2	69.5	69.5
26.3	26.9	26.0	Fixed Assets (net)		37.9	25.4	25.3	24.7	22.6
1.3	.2	.4	Intangibles (net)		.2	.9	.1	.3	.6
6.2	7.6	6.3	All Other Non-Current		9.2	3.4	6.4	5.6	7.3
100.0	100.0	100.0	Total		100.0	100.0	100.0	100.0	100.0
			LIABILITIES						
33.8	35.0	36.6	Notes Payable-Short Term		34.4	45.8	33.7	35.1	38.1
2.6	1.6	1.8	Cur. Mat.-L./T/D		4.4	1.5	1.3	.9	1.1
8.0	6.7	7.7	Trade Payables		2.7	7.7	7.0	9.1	9.4
.3	.4	.5	Income Taxes Payable		.1	.0	.4	1.0	.4
5.8	5.3	6.0	All Other Current		8.8	4.2	6.2	7.2	4.9
50.6	49.0	52.6	Total Current		50.4	59.2	48.7	53.3	53.9
10.6	9.3	8.9	Long Term Debt		7.1	11.0	9.2	8.3	9.5
1.5	1.9	1.1	Deferred Taxes		.0	.6	1.4	.9	2.1
1.4	1.3	2.6	All Other-Non-Current		.2	5.7	3.2	1.6	1.6
35.9	38.4	34.8	Net Worth		42.3	23.5	37.5	35.9	32.9
100.0	100.0	100.0	Total Liabilities & Net Worth		100.0	100.0	100.0	100.0	100.0
			INCOME DATA						
100.0	100.0	100.0	Net Sales		100.0	100.0	100.0	100.0	100.0
22.3	20.8	17.2	Gross Profit		31.9	25.0	18.7	12.8	8.8
18.4	17.5	15.7	Operating Expenses		27.5	22.7	16.2	11.4	9.1
3.9	3.3	1.5	Operating Profit		4.4	2.3	2.5	1.3	-.3
1.0	.3	.9	All Other Expenses (net)		2.1	1.9	.8	.8	.5
2.9	3.0	.6	Profit Before Taxes		2.3	.4	1.7	.5	-.8
			RATIOS						
1.7	1.7	1.6	Current		1.7	1.5	1.7	1.7	1.5
1.3	1.4	1.3			1.3	1.2	1.5	1.3	1.2
1.1	1.0	1.1			.5	1.1	1.1	1.1	1.1
.7	.7	.8	Quick		.3	.7	.9	.9	.6
(104) .2	(125) .3	(140) .3			.0	.2	.4 (40)	.4	.3
.1	.1	.1			.0	.0	.1	.2	.1
2 200.8	1 280.6	2 199.2	Sales/Receivables		0 UND	0 UND	3 112.3	5 75.8	2 149.0
16 22.2	17 21.9	18 20.5			0 UND	27 13.4	32 11.3	24 15.4	12 29.7
37 9.9	36 10.2	44 8.3			12 30.4	73 5.0	59 6.2	36 10.2	39 9.3
32 11.4	36 10.2	29 12.6	Cost of Sales/Inventory		24 15.5	29 12.4	24 15.5	33 11.2	22 16.4
107 3.4	96 3.8	83 4.4			104 3.5	114 3.2	53 6.9	83 4.4	63 5.8
228 1.6	192 1.9	135 2.7			243 1.5	203 1.8	146 2.5	122 3.0	118 3.1
0 UND	1 421.0	0 999.8	Cost of Sales/Payables		0 UND	0 UND	0 999.8	2 209.9	1 304.0
9 38.7	8 45.0	8 43.7			0 UND	18 19.9	13 28.7	10 38.2	7 49.8
28 13.1	22 16.6	22 16.8			10 36.8	38 9.7	25 14.4	25 14.8	18 20.1
5.5	6.1	7.6	Sales/Working Capital		5.8	6.4	5.6	8.5	11.5
11.6	12.4	18.1			11.9	15.3	11.0	17.7	24.3
66.0	140.8	77.9			-8.7	23.3	64.8	61.3	113.6
4.7	4.9	3.3	EBIT/Interest		2.9	3.1	5.0	5.0	1.7
(101) 1.9	(120) 2.7	(137) 1.4		(15)	1.9	1.9	(25) 1.5	1.8	(35) .5
1.2	1.4	.1			.5	.2	.1	.6	-.6
10.2	11.7	5.6	Net Profit + Depr., Dep.,						3.1
(30) 4.2	(37) 4.2	(38) 2.5	Amort./Cur. Mat. L/T/D					(13)	-1.1
1.5	1.8	-1.8							-13.6
.3	.3	.3	Fixed/Worth		.1	.4	.2	.4	.5
.7	.6	.7			.7	.7	.6	.7	.7
1.3	1.3	1.4			5.0	1.2	1.6	1.8	1.4
1.1	.9	1.0	Debt/Worth		.5	1.2	1.1	.9	1.2
2.1	2.0	1.8			1.1	3.1	2.0	1.6	2.4
4.9	3.8	4.5			9.1	6.2	3.8	5.8	4.6
24.8	30.1	16.4	% Profit Before Taxes/Tangible		26.8	16.2	31.4	21.8	7.7
(104) 12.4	(122) 13.6	(131) 4.2	Net Worth	(14)	5.5	(14) 9.0	5.2 (39)	6.9	(34) -3.6
2.2	4.5	-8.0			-2.6	-11.4	-4.6	-1.6	-41.5
9.7	10.3	5.4	% Profit Before Taxes/Total		5.1	5.6	10.7	8.7	2.5
2.8	5.5	1.7	Assets		2.9	2.4	2.3	2.1	-1.8
.9	1.4	-3.6			-1.9	-4.1	-2.0	-1.4	-8.9
24.9	26.9	24.4	Sales/Net Fixed Assets		24.6	23.0	28.0	22.0	22.9
9.0	9.7	9.5			6.9	7.4	12.9	8.4	13.6
3.8	4.0	5.8			1.7	4.1	6.0	5.9	8.2
2.5	2.7	2.8	Sales/Total Assets		2.6	2.4	3.2	2.9	4.5
1.8	1.9	2.0			1.9	1.9	1.9	2.1	2.4
1.2	1.3	1.5			1.1	1.2	1.1	1.6	1.8
.6	.6	.7	% Depr., Dep., Amort./Sales		1.8	1.6	.6	.5	.5
(100) 1.3	(115) 1.3	(135) 1.4		(14)	2.6	(15) 1.7	1.3 (40)	1.4	1.0
2.2	2.5	2.0			6.2	2.9	2.0	1.8	1.5
.4	.6	.5	% Officers', Directors',				.6		
(32) 1.0	(28) 1.1	(39) 1.3	Owners' Comp/Sales			(10)	1.5		
1.8	2.3	2.2					2.3		
3714582M	4155184M	5266592M	Net Sales ($)	2252M	29985M	66779M	185117M	641857M	4340602M
1839616M	1875253M	1811029M	Total Assets ($)	4447M	33640M	42928M	136922M	316380M	1276712M

M = $ thousand   MM = $ million
See Pages 1 through 15 for Explanation of Ratios and Data

Current Data Sorted By Assets						# Postretirement Benefits / Type of Statement	Comparative Historical Data	
	1	6	5	1	6	Unqualified	14	10
	1	5	3			Reviewed	6	5
2	7	4	1	1		Compiled	13	10
2	1	3				Tax Returns	1	2
2	3	3	5		1	Other	6	6
	33 (4/1-9/30/94)			29 (10/1/94-3/31/95)			4/1/90-3/31/91 ALL	4/1/91-3/31/92 ALL
0-500M	500M-2MM	2-10MM	10-50MM	50-100MM	100-250MM			
6	12	21	14	2	7	NUMBER OF STATEMENTS	40	33
%	%	%	%	%	%	ASSETS	%	%
	4.8	6.5	3.8			Cash & Equivalents	6.1	6.2
	15.5	7.4	7.4			Trade Receivables - (net)	8.2	5.1
	3.6	5.0	17.3			Inventory	9.0	7.5
	.4	2.4	.2			All Other Current	4.8	1.0
	24.3	21.3	28.6			Total Current	28.1	19.7
	57.5	55.6	62.1			Fixed Assets (net)	54.4	55.7
	3.3	1.7	1.0			Intangibles (net)	.5	3.0
	14.9	21.4	8.3			All Other Non-Current	17.0	21.6
	100.0	100.0	100.0			Total	100.0	100.0
						LIABILITIES		
	25.4	8.2	9.1			Notes Payable-Short Term	13.3	9.5
	3.2	7.6	4.1			Cur. Mat. -L/T/D	4.5	5.1
	8.9	8.6	3.4			Trade Payables	5.6	3.5
	.0	.0	.2			Income Taxes Payable	1.0	.2
	10.5	12.2	6.5			All Other Current	7.9	11.6
	48.2	36.6	23.4			Total Current	32.3	29.8
	34.1	31.0	42.6			Long Term Debt	25.3	31.0
	.1	.0	.8			Deferred Taxes	1.4	1.7
	3.0	.7	2.4			All Other-Non-Current	3.2	4.6
	14.7	31.7	30.9			Net Worth	37.7	32.9
	100.0	100.0	100.0			Total Liabilities & Net Worth	100.0	100.0
						INCOME DATA		
	100.0	100.0	100.0			Net Sales	100.0	100.0
						Gross Profit		
	94.9	92.9	95.7			Operating Expenses	97.1	82.1
	5.1	7.1	4.3			Operating Profit	2.9	17.9
	4.1	1.7	10.4			All Other Expenses (net)	3.3	6.3
	1.1	5.4	−6.0			Profit Before Taxes	−.4	11.6
						RATIOS		
	.9	1.3	3.5			Current	1.8	2.2
	.6	.4	1.2				.9	.8
	.2	.1	.8				.5	.2
	.7	.8	2.0			Quick	1.0	1.0
	.4	.2	.4				.3	.3
	.2	.1	.1				.1	.1
0 UND	0 UND	7 55.4				Sales/Receivables	0 UND	0 UND
16 23.2	9 42.4	24 15.0					23 16.2	12 31.6
54 6.8	28 12.9	42 8.6					41 8.9	37 9.9
						Cost of Sales/Inventory		
						Cost of Sales/Payables		
	−52.4	27.4	2.8			Sales/Working Capital	5.9	4.5
	−11.2	−4.0	17.0				−43.6	−31.0
	−4.3	−1.5	−21.4				−7.1	−2.2
	1.5	6.1	2.9			EBIT/Interest	4.6	8.5
(11)	1.1 (19)	2.1 (12)	1.6				(35) 2.1	(27) 2.3
	−1.1	.5	.1				−.4	1.0
						Net Profit + Depr., Dep., Amort./Cur. Mat. L /T/D	13.1	10.0
							(15) .9	(18) 3.2
							.1	.4
	1.0	.8	1.0			Fixed/Worth	.9	1.0
	3.0	1.3	2.6				1.5	2.1
	−8.8	6.9	7.8				4.4	6.5
	.9	.6	1.1			Debt/Worth	.6	.6
	4.3	2.7	3.0				2.0	2.7
	−10.7	18.4	13.7				5.7	11.2
		24.5	13.2			% Profit Before Taxes/Tangible Net Worth	29.9	31.3
	(18)	8.8 (13)	.5				(35) 8.0	(28) 10.3
		1.3	−31.4				−12.6	−1.9
	2.7	7.2	4.9			% Profit Before Taxes/Total Assets	11.7	10.6
	1.4	2.1	.2				3.9	5.2
	−4.5	−1.7	−5.4				−6.0	−.6
	6.7	6.3	3.1			Sales/Net Fixed Assets	3.7	5.2
	4.2	1.0	.7				1.5	1.4
	1.2	.7	.3				.8	.6
	3.1	1.3	1.2			Sales/Total Assets	1.6	1.4
	1.8	.6	.5				.9	.7
	.9	.4	.2				.6	.4
	2.0	1.3	2.4			% Depr., Dep., Amort./Sales	3.2	2.5
	(11) 3.1	(20) 4.8	8.9				(36) 4.3	(30) 4.4
	7.2	8.1	16.6				8.3	7.9
						% Officers', Directors', Owners' Comp/Sales		3.0
								(10) 7.3
								17.3
13862M	30696M	110138M	311058M	264597M	722279M	Net Sales ($)	804841M	569996M
1640M	14969M	104534M	441120M	159257M	1017357M	Total Assets ($)	877136M	948894M

M = $ thousand   MM = $ million
See Pages 1 through 15 for Explanation of Ratios and Data

	Comparative Historical Data			# Postretirement Benefits	Current Data Sorted By Sales					
		1	1	**Type of Statement**	1			1		
	13	16	19	Unqualified	1	3	1	3	1	10
	10	5	9	Reviewed			2	4	3	
	10	18	15	Compiled	5	3	2	3		2
	4	2	6	Tax Returns	2	2		2		
	12	10	13	Other	3	3		3	3	1
	4/1/92-3/31/93	4/1/93-3/31/94	4/1/94-3/31/95		33 (4/1-9/30/94)			29 (10/1/94-3/31/95)		
	ALL	ALL	ALL		0-1MM	1-3MM	3-5MM	5-10MM	10-25MM	25MM & OVER
	49	51	62	**NUMBER OF STATEMENTS**	11	11	5	15	7	13
	%	%	%	**ASSETS**	%	%	%	%	%	%
	6.3	9.7	5.1	Cash & Equivalents	5.6	2.0		6.5		4.6
	10.4	9.3	8.2	Trade Receivables - (net)	1.4	11.8		12.1		9.3
	7.1	7.9	10.0	Inventory	3.0	3.8		4.3		28.0
	1.3	1.5	1.5	All Other Current	.5	2.8		1.4		1.5
	25.1	28.3	24.9	Total Current	10.5	20.4		24.3		43.5
	58.6	59.0	57.5	Fixed Assets (net)	65.8	64.5		54.2		45.8
	.6	1.3	1.9	Intangibles (net)	.2	4.6		2.2		2.1
	15.8	11.5	15.7	All Other Non-Current	23.6	10.6		19.2		8.6
	100.0	100.0	100.0	Total	100.0	100.0		100.0		100.0
				LIABILITIES						
	7.5	10.4	13.8	Notes Payable-Short Term	12.2	11.3		11.0		16.3
	5.1	4.6	5.7	Cur. Mat.-L /T/D	3.4	5.1		9.3		4.1
	7.9	5.6	7.1	Trade Payables	5.8	2.1		12.6		9.5
	.1	.2	.1	Income Taxes Payable	.0	.1		.1		.1
	8.6	9.2	10.9	All Other Current	6.4	8.9		14.3		8.3
	29.2	30.0	37.6	Total Current	27.8	27.5		47.2		38.2
	26.3	27.3	33.0	Long Term Debt	37.4	41.9		36.5		20.3
	.9	1.6	.7	Deferred Taxes	.0	.1		.0		2.3
	3.4	4.0	1.9	All Other-Non-Current	1.6	.9		2.1		3.3
	40.2	37.1	26.8	Net Worth	33.3	29.6		14.2		35.9
	100.0	100.0	100.0	Total Liabilities & Net Worth	100.0	100.0		100.0		100.0
				INCOME DATA						
	100.0	100.0	100.0	Net Sales	100.0	100.0		100.0		100.0
				Gross Profit						
	88.5	92.6	93.8	Operating Expenses	86.6	96.6		96.0		92.1
	11.5	7.4	6.2	Operating Profit	13.4	3.4		4.0		7.9
	4.9	4.3	4.1	All Other Expenses (net)	3.7	6.5		3.9		1.2
	6.6	3.1	2.1	Profit Before Taxes	9.7	-3.1		.1		6.7
				RATIOS						
	2.2	2.1	1.5	Current	.6	1.5		1.6		2.2
	1.0	1.2	.7		.2	.6		.7		1.3
	.4	.4	.2		.1	.1		.2		.9
	1.4	1.5	.8	Quick	.6	.8		1.3		.6
	.5	.4	.3		.2	.2		.4		.3
	.1	.2	.1		.1	.1		.0		.3
	3 143.0	0 UND	0 UND	Sales/Receivables	0 UND	0 UND		0 UND		20 18.1
	17 21.6	21 17.6	13 28.9		0 UND	5 75.5		21 17.3		27 13.7
	42 8.6	43 8.5	33 11.2		12 29.3	38 9.6		63 5.8		42 8.6
				Cost of Sales/Inventory						
				Cost of Sales/Payables						
	6.0	5.8	8.2	Sales/Working Capital	-27.6	5.9		22.5		3.8
	-209.6	45.2	-23.6		-5.8	-9.0		-18.8		9.7
	-6.6	-7.4	-2.7		-2.5	-2.5		-2.5		-57.5
	(43) 5.1	(43) 7.0	(54) 4.9	EBIT/Interest		(10) 7.0		(13) 4.3		12.6
	2.3	2.4	1.9			.9		1.9		3.5
	1.1	.4	.5			-.5		.6		1.7
	(13) 11.9	(22) 14.1	(17) 3.7	Net Profit + Depr., Dep., Amort./Cur. Mat. L/T/D						
	3.0	2.9	1.0							
	.9	.3	.1							
	.8	.8	.8	Fixed/Worth	.7	.8		.9		.8
	1.6	1.4	1.8		1.3	3.3		3.7		.9
	4.2	5.0	11.3		12.1	14.7		-14.0		2.4
	.5	.5	.9	Debt/Worth	.6	.8		1.2		1.1
	1.8	1.2	2.8		1.0	3.0		4.9		2.4
	5.4	14.0	16.3		17.9	24.6		-21.0		3.2
	(46) 24.9	(42) 10.0	(51) 22.7	% Profit Before Taxes/Tangible Net Worth				(11) 20.2	(11) 23.4	
	11.8	4.3	7.7					7.7	17.2	
	.4	-6.7	.0					.0	7.4	
	9.6	7.3	6.2	% Profit Before Taxes/Total Assets	20.6	2.1		5.0		9.1
	5.0	2.3	2.0		2.5	-2.6		1.3		6.1
	-.6	-2.5	-3.5		.1	-6.3		-3.6		1.7
	5.1	5.6	5.8	Sales/Net Fixed Assets	4.6	4.9		18.6		7.1
	1.4	1.2	1.3		1.3	.7		4.6		2.9
	.5	.6	.7		.4	.5		.8		.8
	2.2	2.1	1.8	Sales/Total Assets	1.9	1.4		2.9		1.7
	.8	.8	.9		.9	.5		1.3		1.3
	.4	.4	.4		.2	.4		.6		.4
	(46) 2.3	(50) 2.9	(58) 1.8	% Depr., Dep., Amort./Sales	(10) 3.0	3.1		.7	(11) 1.2	
	5.7	5.4	4.8		6.3	6.0		2.4	2.7	
	9.5	11.2	10.2		12.2	14.8		4.8	10.4	
		.8	1.6	% Officers', Directors', Owners' Comp/Sales						
	(15) 3.6	(15) 3.3								
	6.3	9.0								
	1574690M	1115209M	1452630M	Net Sales ($)	5835M	23582M	19571M	92736M	121626M	1189280M
	1054994M	1489807M	1738877M	Total Assets ($)	13825M	52342M	20223M	159750M	255812M	1236925M

© Robert Morris Associates 1995   M = $ thousand   MM = $ million
See Pages 1 through 15 for Explanation of Ratios and Data

Current Data Sorted By Assets — Comparative Historical Data

0-500M	500M-2MM	2-10MM	10-50MM	50-100MM	100-250MM	# Postretirement Benefits / Type of Statement	4/1/90-3/31/91 ALL	4/1/91-3/31/92 ALL
1	1	3						
		4	1		1	Unqualified		
4	7	9	3			Reviewed		
12	15	20	3			Compiled		
11	6	1				Tax Returns		
7	22	12	2		1	Other		
	21 (4/1-9/30/94)		120 (10/1/94-3/31/95)					
34	50	46	8	1	2	NUMBER OF STATEMENTS		
%	%	%	%	%	%	**ASSETS**	%	%
12.0	3.3	4.1				Cash & Equivalents	D	D
8.5	7.6	9.1				Trade Receivables - (net)	A	A
16.7	21.3	16.6				Inventory	T	T
4.6	1.9	2.4				All Other Current	A	A
41.9	34.1	32.3				Total Current		
49.8	58.4	56.7				Fixed Assets (net)	N	N
.3	.4	.1				Intangibles (net)	O	O
8.0	7.1	10.9				All Other Non-Current	T	T
100.0	100.0	100.0				Total		
						LIABILITIES	A	A
18.4	18.4	14.7				Notes Payable-Short Term	V	V
7.4	2.6	4.6				Cur. Mat. -L/T/D	A	A
4.5	2.5	3.2				Trade Payables	I	I
.2	.1	.2				Income Taxes Payable	L	L
5.2	6.2	4.2				All Other Current	A	A
35.7	29.8	26.9				Total Current	B	B
22.8	20.0	26.0				Long Term Debt	L	L
.0	.3	.5				Deferred Taxes	E	E
3.9	.7	2.1				All Other-Non-Current		
37.7	49.2	44.5				Net Worth		
100.0	100.0	100.0				Total Liabilities & Net Worth		
						INCOME DATA		
100.0	100.0	100.0				Net Sales		
						Gross Profit		
90.0	90.5	89.7				Operating Expenses		
10.0	9.5	10.3				Operating Profit		
2.1	3.2	2.6				All Other Expenses (net)		
7.9	6.3	7.7				Profit Before Taxes		
						RATIOS		
3.7	1.8	1.6				Current		
1.2	1.3	1.2						
.4	.8	.7						
1.8	.6	1.1				Quick		
.3	.1	.3						
.1	.0	.1						
0 UND	0 UND	0 UND				Sales/Receivables		
0 UND	6 56.2	10 35.0						
12 29.4	24 15.3	33 11.1						
						Cost of Sales/Inventory		
						Cost of Sales/Payables		
4.9	3.6	5.5				Sales/Working Capital		
20.8	12.0	33.7						
-11.6	-17.3	-15.0						
(33) 8.5	(47) 3.7	(43) 5.2				EBIT/Interest		
4.1	2.3	2.3						
1.7	1.1	1.0						
						Net Profit + Depr., Dep., Amort./Cur. Mat. L /T/D		
.5	.8	.6				Fixed/Worth		
1.5	1.1	1.2						
4.2	1.5	1.7						
.7	.4	.5				Debt/Worth		
1.6	.9	1.0						
6.7	2.2	2.1						
(30) 113.3	(47) 15.3	(42) 23.0				% Profit Before Taxes/Tangible Net Worth		
25.1	5.4	6.1						
8.3	-.2	-.8						
27.2	6.6	11.3				% Profit Before Taxes/Total Assets		
13.3	3.2	3.6						
1.7	-.0	-.1						
7.9	3.1	2.7				Sales/Net Fixed Assets		
4.0	1.1	1.1						
1.7	.6	.6						
3.2	1.2	1.1				Sales/Total Assets		
1.9	.7	.7						
.9	.3	.4						
(29) 4.1	(45) 4.7	(44) 5.4				% Depr., Dep., Amort./Sales		
5.7	7.0	7.4						
10.0	12.4	10.3						
	(13) 3.5	(12) 1.7				% Officers', Directors', Owners' Comp/Sales		
	7.1	3.2						
	11.9	5.8						
20650M	53264M	205885M	116307M	21379M	155060M	Net Sales ($)		
9677M	52912M	208436M	160198M	54411M	316403M	Total Assets ($)		

© Robert Morris Associates 1995

M = $ thousand   MM = $ million
See Pages 1 through 15 for Explanation of Ratios and Data

Comparative Historical Data				Current Data Sorted By Sales					
	4	5	# Postretirement Benefits	1	3			1	
			Type of Statement						
	6	6	Unqualified		1		1	3	1
	7	23	Reviewed	8	5	4	3	3	
	29	50	Compiled	25	14	5	2	3	1
	12	18	Tax Returns	13	4	1			
	23	44	Other	25	11	3	3	1	1
4/1/92-3/31/93 ALL	4/1/93-3/31/94 ALL	4/1/94-3/31/95 ALL		21 (4/1-9/30/94)			120 (10/1/94-3/31/95)		
				0-1MM	1-3MM	3-5MM	5-10MM	10-25MM	25MM & OVER
	77	141	**NUMBER OF STATEMENTS**	71	35	13	9	10	3
%	%	%	**ASSETS**	%	%	%	%	%	%
	3.3	5.7	Cash & Equivalents	6.7	3.7	6.2		6.8	
	10.8	9.0	Trade Receivables - (net)	4.7	8.0	17.1		25.3	
	15.5	18.0	Inventory	16.7	21.0	20.2		17.9	
	3.6	2.8	All Other Current	3.3	1.7	2.3		2.9	
	33.2	35.5	Total Current	31.4	34.4	45.8		52.9	
	56.3	55.0	Fixed Assets (net)	59.7	56.4	47.6		36.6	
	.3	.3	Intangibles (net)	.2	.4	.1		.3	
	10.2	9.2	All Other Non-Current	8.7	8.9	6.4		10.2	
	100.0	100.0	Total	100.0	100.0	100.0		100.0	
			LIABILITIES						
	18.0	17.1	Notes Payable-Short Term	16.7	19.3	15.8		22.3	
	3.3	4.5	Cur. Mat.-L /T/D	4.5	4.1	7.0		4.4	
	4.2	3.3	Trade Payables	2.0	1.3	9.3		11.8	
	1.4	.1	Income Taxes Payable	.2	.1	.0		.2	
	5.5	5.1	All Other Current	5.1	3.6	7.5		5.3	
	32.5	30.2	Total Current	28.6	28.4	39.7		43.9	
	18.3	23.2	Long Term Debt	22.5	25.4	17.2		21.0	
	.5	.4	Deferred Taxes	.0	.4	.8		.9	
	2.5	2.2	All Other-Non-Current	1.5	2.7	3.8		3.2	
	46.3	44.0	Net Worth	47.4	43.1	38.5		31.0	
	100.0	100.0	Total Liabilities & Net Worth	100.0	100.0	100.0		100.0	
			INCOME DATA						
	100.0	100.0	Net Sales	100.0	100.0	100.0		100.0	
			Gross Profit						
	86.7	90.1	Operating Expenses	89.0	90.0	93.8		93.8	
	13.3	9.9	Operating Profit	11.0	10.0	6.2		6.2	
	3.8	2.8	All Other Expenses (net)	3.2	2.2	2.3		3.1	
	9.5	7.1	Profit Before Taxes	7.9	7.8	3.8		3.1	
			RATIOS						
	1.7	2.1	Current	2.5	2.0	1.6		1.4	
	1.1	1.3		1.2	1.3	1.0		1.2	
	.8	.8		.6	.7	.8		.9	
	.9	1.0	Quick	.8	1.1	1.0		1.0	
(76)	.3	.3		.2	.2	.5		.7	
	.1	.1		.1	.0	.1		.4	
0 UND	0 UND		Sales/Receivables	0 UND	0 UND	3 133.5		20 18.6	
20 18.0	7 52.4			0 UND	0 999.8	33 11.0		39 9.3	
63 5.8	30 12.0			15 23.9	26 14.2	69 5.3		76 4.8	
			Cost of Sales/Inventory						
			Cost of Sales/Payables						
	4.0	4.4	Sales/Working Capital	4.2	5.0	5.6		7.2	
	15.7	19.2		18.8	16.1	-55.8		27.3	
	-7.0	-15.0		-10.5	-13.7	-15.6		-22.5	
	5.2	5.3	EBIT/Interest	(68) 7.0	(31) 5.2	4.8		5.2	
(75)	2.1 (133)	2.5		2.6	2.3	1.9		2.2	
	1.2	1.2		1.2	1.0	.9		1.7	
		4.9	Net Profit + Depr., Dep.,						
	(18)	1.6	Amort./Cur. Mat. L/T/D						
		.7							
	.7	.7	Fixed/Worth	.8	.6	.4		.4	
	1.2	1.2		1.2	1.3	1.5		1.0	
	2.1	2.0		2.2	2.4	1.7		2.4	
	.5	.5	Debt/Worth	.4	.6	1.0		1.5	
	1.1	1.3		.9	1.2	1.5		2.3	
	2.7	2.4		2.4	2.9	1.8		4.2	
	27.2	26.0	% Profit Before Taxes/Tangible	(65) 29.5	(32) 24.7	(12) 22.5			
(73)	7.7 (129)	10.0	Net Worth	10.4	5.1	4.7			
	1.0	.2		.0	-2.5	-2.4			
	11.0	12.3	% Profit Before Taxes/Total	13.4	12.6	8.8		5.3	
	4.1	4.2	Assets	4.9	3.9	1.5		4.5	
	.4	.2		.0	-.6	-.4		2.0	
	2.9	4.3	Sales/Net Fixed Assets	3.4	3.6	10.8		21.6	
	1.1	1.6		1.0	1.7	2.8		4.1	
	.5	.7		.6	.7	1.0		1.7	
	1.2	1.5	Sales/Total Assets	1.3	1.6	1.8		3.0	
	.6	.7		.7	.7	.9		1.9	
	.3	.4		.3	.4	.7		.8	
	3.1	4.4	% Depr., Dep., Amort./Sales	(63) 5.1	(32) 5.0	2.0			
(70)	6.3 (127)	6.6		8.0	6.7	5.7			
	9.2	10.6		12.6	8.8	9.1			
	2.5	2.8	% Officers', Directors',	(16) 4.0	(10) 2.1				
(22)	6.5 (32)	6.4	Owners' Comp/Sales	7.3	4.7				
	18.4	8.7		9.1	8.7				
295335M	572545M		Net Sales ($)	35477M	62099M	49149M	62847M	177070M	185903M
373121M	802037M		Total Assets ($)	61160M	94842M	50228M	84141M	171104M	340562M

M = $ thousand   MM = $ million
See Pages 1 through 15 for Explanation of Ratios and Data

Current Data Sorted By Assets | Comparative Historical Data

0-500M	500M-2MM	2-10MM	10-50MM	50-100MM	100-250MM		4/1/90-3/31/91 ALL	4/1/91-3/31/92 ALL
6	5	5				# Postretirement Benefits		
						Type of Statement		
5	4	12	3	2		Unqualified	22	16
22	64	13	1			Reviewed	89	86
87	42	9				Compiled	128	103
23	7	1				Tax Returns	10	8
48	30	9	2			Other	50	56
	68 (4/1-9/30/94)		316 (10/1/94-3/31/95)					
185	147	44	6	2		NUMBER OF STATEMENTS	299	269

%	%	%	%	%	%	ASSETS	%	%
12.4	7.6	6.7				Cash & Equivalents	8.8	10.2
24.1	31.5	34.1				Trade Receivables - (net)	27.6	24.6
7.9	10.9	8.4				Inventory	11.4	11.6
1.4	2.3	6.1				All Other Current	3.0	2.8
45.7	52.4	55.2				Total Current	50.8	49.2
45.0	38.2	33.4				Fixed Assets (net)	39.0	40.5
1.9	1.7	1.9				Intangibles (net)	1.3	1.4
7.4	7.7	9.4				All Other Non-Current	8.9	8.9
100.0	100.0	100.0				Total	100.0	100.0
						LIABILITIES		
10.7	8.8	10.3				Notes Payable-Short Term	12.4	12.1
7.3	6.3	5.4				Cur. Mat. -L/T/D	8.2	7.9
12.1	12.8	12.9				Trade Payables	11.4	10.1
.3	.6	.4				Income Taxes Payable	.8	.5
8.7	7.9	8.9				All Other Current	7.2	7.5
39.1	36.4	37.9				Total Current	40.1	38.0
21.6	17.9	17.8				Long Term Debt	20.0	18.4
.4	1.7	2.6				Deferred Taxes	1.1	.8
2.6	1.4	3.6				All Other-Non-Current	2.7	2.7
36.2	42.6	38.1				Net Worth	36.1	40.1
100.0	100.0	100.0				Total Liabilities & Net Worth	100.0	100.0
						INCOME DATA		
100.0	100.0	100.0				Net Sales	100.0	100.0
						Gross Profit		
94.0	94.5	96.0				Operating Expenses	95.1	95.0
6.0	5.5	4.0				Operating Profit	4.9	5.0
.9	.7	1.2				All Other Expenses (net)	1.8	1.8
5.1	4.8	2.8				Profit Before Taxes	3.1	3.2

RATIOS

0-500M	500M-2MM	2-10MM					4/1/90-3/31/91	4/1/91-3/31/92
2.1	2.2	2.1				Current	2.1	2.3
1.2	1.4	1.3					1.3	1.3
.7	1.0	1.0					.9	.8
1.8	1.7	1.5				Quick	1.6	1.6
.9	1.1	.9				(298)	.9 (268)	1.0
.4	.6	.7					.4	.5
6 62.4	24 15.0	31 11.9				Sales/Receivables	16 22.7	14 26.3
22 16.3	41 8.8	52 7.0					34 10.8	29 12.6
42 8.7	66 5.5	79 4.6					57 6.4	53 6.9
						Cost of Sales/Inventory		
						Cost of Sales/Payables		
11.9	6.8	6.5				Sales/Working Capital	8.2	8.5
42.0	14.8	19.1					23.2	23.0
-29.8	-212.0	235.0					-44.9	-43.3
(166) 9.6	(138) 10.2	(42) 5.2				EBIT/Interest	(279) 5.9	(248) 5.4
3.8	4.1	3.3					2.6	2.2
1.5	1.8	1.5					1.2	1.0
(41) 4.4	(61) 4.2	(22) 6.1				Net Profit + Depr., Dep.,	(157) 3.4	(111) 3.5
2.4	2.1	2.1				Amort./Cur. Mat. L /T/D	1.8	1.5
1.5	1.3	1.4					.8	.7
.6	.5	.4				Fixed/Worth	.5	.6
1.3	.9	1.0					1.0	1.0
4.1	1.5	1.7					2.3	1.9
.6	.7	1.0				Debt/Worth	.7	.6
1.5	1.5	1.6					1.7	1.5
6.8	2.4	3.1					5.1	3.2
(160) 71.6	(139) 43.7	(42) 30.9				% Profit Before Taxes/Tangible	(273) 43.9	(247) 37.6
38.5	22.3	16.1				Net Worth	16.9	13.1
7.7	9.2	7.7					3.4	.0
28.5	16.6	11.4				% Profit Before Taxes/Total	15.6	16.2
11.0	7.7	4.9				Assets	6.3	5.3
2.2	2.8	2.5					.5	-.7
14.8	13.2	15.0				Sales/Net Fixed Assets	13.9	12.4
8.4	7.4	7.1					8.1	7.3
5.1	4.4	4.3					4.9	4.3
4.8	3.4	2.7				Sales/Total Assets	3.7	3.8
3.5	2.4	2.3					2.7	2.6
2.5	1.8	1.6					2.1	1.9
(160) 2.3	(136) 2.1	(39) 2.0				% Depr., Dep., Amort./Sales	(285) 2.1	(249) 2.2
3.7	3.4	3.2					3.6	3.7
6.4	4.9	4.8					5.6	5.8
(97) 4.9	(81) 3.0	(16) 2.5				% Officers', Directors',	(167) 3.7	(150) 3.1
6.9	4.7	3.8				Owners' Comp/Sales	6.4	6.0
12.0	8.2	6.0					9.8	10.2

0-500M	500M-2MM	2-10MM	10-50MM	50-100MM	100-250MM		4/1/90-3/31/91	4/1/91-3/31/92
154891M	375946M	354668M	181954M	261759M		Net Sales ($)	795768M	892297M
43195M	144384M	165054M	137135M	146830M		Total Assets ($)	368107M	383321M

© Robert Morris Associates 1995

M = $ thousand   MM = $ million
See Pages 1 through 15 for Explanation of Ratios and Data

Comparative Historical Data				Current Data Sorted By Sales					
3	11	16	# Postretirement Benefits	4	6	3	3		
			Type of Statement						
19	25	26	Unqualified	4	4	1	4	8	5
94	101	100	Reviewed	17	48	20	14	1	
122	119	138	Compiled	63	59	8	7	1	
12	31	31	Tax Returns	20	9	1	1		
77	68	89	Other	35	39	5	7	2	1
4/1/92-3/31/93 ALL	4/1/93-3/31/94 ALL	4/1/94-3/31/95 ALL		68 (4/1-9/30/94)		316 (10/1/94-3/31/95)			
				0-1MM	1-3MM	3-5MM	5-10MM	10-25MM	25MM & OVER
324	344	384	**NUMBER OF STATEMENTS**	139	159	35	33	12	6
%	%	%	**ASSETS**	%	%	%	%	%	%
9.9	10.8	9.7	Cash & Equivalents	12.9	8.1	8.7	7.7	5.7	
26.3	26.5	28.1	Trade Receivables - (net)	21.5	29.5	36.2	36.5	35.1	
10.5	10.3	9.3	Inventory	6.7	11.7	10.2	6.9	13.1	
2.6	2.3	2.3	All Other Current	1.5	2.3	2.5	4.2	2.5	
49.4	49.9	49.4	Total Current	42.7	51.7	57.6	55.3	56.5	
40.9	39.2	41.0	Fixed Assets (net)	48.0	38.4	33.1	36.0	33.3	
1.2	1.7	1.8	Intangibles (net)	2.2	1.4	1.3	2.1	3.3	
8.6	9.1	7.9	All Other Non-Current	7.2	8.5	8.0	6.6	6.9	
100.0	100.0	100.0	Total	100.0	100.0	100.0	100.0	100.0	
			LIABILITIES						
11.5	10.9	9.7	Notes Payable-Short Term	11.1	8.5	10.1	11.0	10.6	
7.0	6.1	6.6	Cur. Mat.-L /T/D	7.9	6.1	5.9	5.7	4.7	
10.7	11.0	12.5	Trade Payables	10.9	11.8	17.2	16.1	14.6	
.7	1.7	.4	Income Taxes Payable	.3	.4	.7	.5	.8	
8.3	8.0	8.5	All Other Current	7.3	9.0	8.6	9.1	12.2	
38.1	37.7	37.7	Total Current	37.5	35.8	42.4	42.4	42.8	
19.1	18.7	19.8	Long Term Debt	24.9	18.0	14.7	13.3	16.5	
1.2	.8	1.2	Deferred Taxes	.4	1.6	2.1	1.9	.3	
2.1	2.5	2.3	All Other-Non-Current	2.8	1.6	1.5	2.5	5.8	
39.4	40.2	39.0	Net Worth	34.4	43.0	39.3	39.9	34.5	
100.0	100.0	100.0	Total Liabilities & Net Worth	100.0	100.0	100.0	100.0	100.0	
			INCOME DATA						
100.0	100.0	100.0	Net Sales	100.0	100.0	100.0	100.0	100.0	
			Gross Profit						
95.6	95.3	94.5	Operating Expenses	92.8	95.1	96.4	96.2	95.8	
4.4	4.7	5.5	Operating Profit	7.2	4.9	3.6	3.8	4.2	
1.2	.9	.8	All Other Expenses (net)	1.0	.8	.3	.7	1.3	
3.2	3.9	4.7	Profit Before Taxes	6.2	4.2	3.3	3.1	2.9	
			RATIOS						
2.5	2.2	2.1		2.1	2.4	2.0	1.6	2.2	
1.4	1.4	1.4	Current	1.2	1.5	1.4	1.2	1.3	
.8	.9	.9		.6	.9	1.1	.9	1.0	
1.9	1.7	1.6		1.7	1.8	1.6	1.5	1.3	
1.0	1.0	1.0	Quick	.8	1.1	1.1	.9	1.0	
.6	.5	.6		.4	.6	.7	.7	.9	
11 33.6	11 32.9	14 25.6		6 60.3	19 19.7	25 14.7	29 12.5	29 12.7	
30 12.2	31 11.7	35 10.5	Sales/Receivables	23 15.8	36 10.2	47 7.8	44 8.3	41 8.9	
52 7.0	52 7.0	57 6.4		45 8.2	54 6.8	73 5.0	72 5.1	64 5.7	
			Cost of Sales/Inventory						
			Cost of Sales/Payables						
8.1	8.2	8.2		10.2	7.7	7.8	9.7	8.7	
22.3	23.8	23.3	Sales/Working Capital	42.0	15.6	24.3	24.5	25.9	
-61.8	-73.7	-57.6		-24.7	-138.6	73.2	-67.2	NM	
(292) 5.9	(316) 7.6	(352) 9.0		(126) 10.1	(149) 8.5	(31) 10.6	(30) 8.9	(11) 5.2	
2.6	3.5	3.8	EBIT/Interest	3.7	3.8	4.1	4.3	4.0	
1.2	1.5	1.6		1.6	1.7	1.6	1.5	1.9	
(121) 2.8	(109) 3.7	(129) 4.6	Net Profit + Depr., Dep.,	(30) 5.0	(60) 3.8	(13) 4.8	(19) 6.2		
1.8	1.7	2.2	Amort./Cur. Mat. L/T/D	3.2	2.1	2.1	2.1		
1.1	.6	1.4		1.3	1.4	1.5	1.1		
.5	.5	.5		.7	.5	.4	.5	.5	
1.0	.9	1.0	Fixed/Worth	1.4	.9	.8	1.0	1.1	
2.2	1.9	2.0		4.7	1.5	1.5	1.9	1.6	
.6	.7	.7		.7	.6	.8	.9	.6	
1.5	1.4	1.5	Debt/Worth	1.8	1.3	1.8	1.5	1.9	
3.6	3.3	3.5		7.9	2.5	2.8	4.0	2.7	
(292) 36.8	(311) 42.4	(349) 54.1	% Profit Before Taxes/Tangible	(120) 82.7	(148) 44.6	(32) 33.7	(32) 32.3	(11) 41.2	
17.8	17.3	24.5	Net Worth	41.5	23.3	14.3	18.3	30.7	
2.5	3.8	7.7		12.1	7.4	7.1	4.3	7.7	
14.7	16.7	21.4	% Profit Before Taxes/Total	31.8	17.8	13.9	12.2	13.8	
6.1	7.8	8.6	Assets	12.1	8.7	5.2	7.3	9.1	
.7	1.3	2.6		2.7	2.6	2.3	2.5	2.7	
12.7	14.1	14.3		12.2	15.0	16.4	22.0	12.5	
8.6	8.1	7.8	Sales/Net Fixed Assets	6.7	8.9	9.8	11.9	7.7	
4.8	4.8	4.5		3.9	5.1	5.5	5.1	4.6	
4.2	4.0	3.9		4.1	4.0	3.7	3.7	4.0	
2.9	2.8	2.8	Sales/Total Assets	2.9	2.8	2.7	2.9	2.5	
2.0	1.9	2.0		1.9	2.1	2.0	2.0	1.9	
(287) 2.2	(329) 2.1	(343) 2.1	% Depr., Dep., Amort./Sales	(121) 2.5	(143) 2.2	(32) 1.2	(30) 1.6	(11) 2.1	
3.4	3.5	3.5		4.9	3.3	2.6	2.7	4.0	
5.1	5.1	5.3		8.1	4.7	3.9	4.3	4.8	
(175) 3.5	(176) 4.0	(195) 3.6	% Officers', Directors',	(70) 4.9	(89) 3.6	(16) 3.3	(17) 2.4		
6.6	6.9	6.0	Owners' Comp/Sales	8.6	5.4	6.3	3.0		
10.2	9.5	10.2		13.4	8.4	8.6	4.4		
1291346M	1069048M	1329218M	Net Sales ($)	77028M	283903M	133439M	226410M	177601M	430837M
585561M	533232M	636598M	Total Assets ($)	32898M	122285M	51266M	102546M	81613M	245990M

M = $ thousand   MM = $ million
See Pages 1 through 15 for Explanation of Ratios and Data

Current Data Sorted By Assets   Comparative Historical Data

0-500M	500M-2MM	2-10MM	10-50MM	50-100MM	100-250MM	# Postretirement Benefits / Type of Statement	4/1/90-3/31/91 ALL	4/1/91-3/31/92 ALL
		7	8	1	1	Unqualified	16	10
	4	6	2			Reviewed	8	7
2	2	5	1			Compiled	8	7
1		1				Tax Returns		1
1	1	5	4			Other	5	6
	9 (4/1-9/30/94)		42 (10/1/94-3/31/95)					
3	7	24	15	1	1	**NUMBER OF STATEMENTS**	37	31
%	%	%	%	%	%	**ASSETS**	%	%
		4.5	9.9			Cash & Equivalents	9.2	8.3
		18.7	15.6			Trade Receivables - (net)	14.8	15.5
		12.4	13.0			Inventory	17.4	12.8
		1.5	.6			All Other Current	1.5	2.3
		37.1	39.1			Total Current	42.8	38.9
		55.6	49.1			Fixed Assets (net)	46.0	46.5
		1.0	1.1			Intangibles (net)	1.6	2.8
		6.4	10.7			All Other Non-Current	9.6	11.9
		100.0	100.0			Total	100.0	100.0
						LIABILITIES		
		5.2	2.4			Notes Payable-Short Term	5.6	6.1
		7.7	9.5			Cur. Mat. -L/T/D	9.2	7.3
		7.4	6.2			Trade Payables	9.2	7.3
		.5	.8			Income Taxes Payable	.4	.4
		6.5	6.2			All Other Current	7.1	3.6
		27.3	25.1			Total Current	31.5	24.8
		27.8	19.8			Long Term Debt	23.8	25.7
		.3	1.1			Deferred Taxes	.8	.7
		3.0	4.6			All Other-Non-Current	2.2	1.8
		41.6	49.5			Net Worth	41.6	46.9
		100.0	100.0			Total Liabilities & Net Worth	100.0	100.0
						INCOME DATA		
		100.0	100.0			Net Sales	100.0	100.0
		31.1	24.8			Gross Profit	31.6	30.2
		22.1	12.8			Operating Expenses	24.0	22.3
		9.1	12.0			Operating Profit	7.6	7.8
		1.4	.5			All Other Expenses (net)	1.5	1.0
		7.7	11.5			Profit Before Taxes	6.1	6.8
						RATIOS		
		2.0	3.4			Current	2.9	3.6
		1.3	1.3				1.9	1.5
		1.0	1.0				.9	1.1
		1.1	2.3			Quick	1.5	1.8
		.7	.9				.8	.8
		.5	.7				.4	.6
		35 10.5	33 11.2			Sales/Receivables	28 12.9	35 10.3
		56 6.5	49 7.4				41 9.0	44 8.3
		70 5.2	60 6.1				48 7.6	59 6.2
		17 21.3	29 12.8			Cost of Sales/Inventory	29 12.4	23 16.0
		49 7.4	45 8.1				57 6.4	42 8.6
		85 4.3	81 4.5				94 3.9	79 4.6
		16 22.5	17 22.0			Cost of Sales/Payables	16 22.7	15 23.6
		32 11.3	22 16.9				26 14.0	22 16.6
		48 7.6	33 11.0				42 8.7	35 10.4
		7.6	2.4			Sales/Working Capital	4.3	3.0
		14.1	15.2				7.3	8.4
		NM	-88.9				-28.6	42.6
		6.1	6.3			EBIT/Interest	5.7	14.8
	(23)	3.4	(13) 5.4				(33) 2.0	(28) 1.8
		2.2	2.9				1.1	1.3
		4.0	38.4			Net Profit + Depr., Dep., Amort./Cur. Mat. L./T/D	3.2	4.6
	(10)	2.7	(10) 2.2				(20) 1.8	(18) 1.5
		1.5	1.5				.9	1.0
		1.0	.7			Fixed/Worth	.6	.6
		1.4	1.3				1.2	.9
		2.1	1.9				3.0	3.0
		.7	.4			Debt/Worth	.4	.3
		1.8	1.3				1.6	.9
		3.2	2.3				6.9	2.8
		40.7	38.4			% Profit Before Taxes/Tangible Net Worth	22.5	17.7
		29.1	21.4				(32) 8.3	(26) 8.2
		8.6	14.8				3.2	4.8
		11.7	14.7			% Profit Before Taxes/Total Assets	12.0	8.4
		7.8	14.1				3.2	4.0
		3.7	6.4				.5	1.2
		3.2	3.0			Sales/Net Fixed Assets	4.3	3.6
		2.1	2.3				2.9	2.3
		1.3	1.6				1.9	1.7
		1.5	1.4			Sales/Total Assets	1.8	1.5
		1.1	1.1				1.1	1.0
		.8	.8				.9	.9
		5.4	4.6			% Depr., Dep., Amort./Sales	5.9	5.7
	(23)	7.6	(14) 8.7				(31) 7.3	(30) 9.5
		11.8	9.8				10.7	12.0
						% Officers', Directors', Owners' Comp/Sales	1.9	2.6
							(10) 11.2	(11) 3.4
							12.9	9.1
1568M	12266M	157803M	399989M	49294M	137437M	Net Sales ($)	659199M	303128M
1184M	7673M	127862M	323149M	52872M	110502M	Total Assets ($)	698140M	397497M

M = $ thousand   MM = $ million
See Pages 1 through 15 for Explanation of Ratios and Data

	Comparative Historical Data			# Postretirement Benefits	Current Data Sorted By Sales					
		2	3					1	1	1
				Type of Statement						
	11	15	17	Unqualified			2	4	6	5
	8	8	12	Reviewed	1	4	2	4	1	
	8	10	10	Compiled	3	2	1	2	2	
			1	Tax Returns	1					
	7	6	11	Other	1	3	1	2	1	3
	4/1/92-3/31/93	4/1/93-3/31/94	4/1/94-3/31/95		9 (4/1-9/30/94)			42 (10/1/94-3/31/95)		
	ALL	ALL	ALL		0-1MM	1-3MM	3-5MM	5-10MM	10-25MM	25MM & OVER
	34	39	51	**NUMBER OF STATEMENTS**	6	9	6	12	10	8
	%	%	%	**ASSETS**	%	%	%	%	%	%
	10.2	8.8	7.0	Cash & Equivalents				7.5	5.2	
	15.7	13.6	17.0	Trade Receivables - (net)				17.5	18.4	
	13.6	10.6	11.9	Inventory				13.3	16.5	
	.9	1.3	1.3	All Other Current				1.7	.4	
	40.3	34.2	37.3	Total Current				40.0	40.5	
	49.6	51.7	53.7	Fixed Assets (net)				50.3	49.5	
	1.3	1.2	.9	Intangibles (net)				.8	1.3	
	8.9	12.9	8.1	All Other Non-Current				8.8	8.7	
	100.0	100.0	100.0	Total				100.0	100.0	
				LIABILITIES						
	4.5	8.7	5.5	Notes Payable-Short Term				6.1	3.0	
	9.1	4.9	7.3	Cur. Mat.-L /T/D				4.6	13.7	
	5.5	6.0	6.7	Trade Payables				6.0	8.1	
	.2	.8	.6	Income Taxes Payable				.2	1.3	
	4.8	4.5	5.8	All Other Current				4.7	6.1	
	24.1	24.9	26.0	Total Current				21.6	32.1	
	24.0	22.6	22.2	Long Term Debt				23.0	17.7	
	.6	.9	.6	Deferred Taxes				.4	1.3	
	3.9	2.2	2.8	All Other-Non-Current				3.2	2.4	
	47.5	49.4	48.4	Net Worth				51.8	46.5	
	100.0	100.0	100.0	Total Liabilities & Net Worth				100.0	100.0	
				INCOME DATA						
	100.0	100.0	100.0	Net Sales				100.0	100.0	
	31.0	31.0	29.4	Gross Profit				35.1	27.2	
	21.1	22.3	20.3	Operating Expenses				22.7	15.6	
	9.9	8.7	9.0	Operating Profit				12.4	11.6	
	2.1	1.5	.5	All Other Expenses (net)				1.1	1.0	
	7.7	7.2	8.5	Profit Before Taxes				11.3	10.6	
				RATIOS						
	2.5	2.7	2.6					4.5	2.0	
	1.6	1.5	1.4	Current				1.8	1.4	
	1.2	.9	1.0					1.0	1.0	
	1.6	2.0	1.5					3.7	1.4	
	1.1	.9	.8	Quick				.8	.9	
	.6	.5	.5					.6	.4	
34	10.7	30	12.0	29	12.5	Sales/Receivables	38	9.7	31	11.6
45	8.2	45	8.2	51	7.1		54	6.7	46	8.0
57	6.4	58	6.3	62	5.9		61	6.0	65	5.6
6	56.7	16	23.0	13	28.8	Cost of Sales/Inventory	24	14.9	27	13.4
50	7.3	37	9.8	43	8.4		56	6.5	69	5.3
87	4.2	66	5.5	81	4.5		99	3.7	122	3.0
14	25.4	16	22.2	13	27.7	Cost of Sales/Payables	14	26.7	13	27.9
19	19.6	27	13.5	23	15.9		22	16.5	21	17.0
35	10.4	40	9.1	45	8.2		47	7.8	43	8.5
	4.8		4.5		6.1	Sales/Working Capital		4.2		5.7
	8.2		11.7		13.7			8.4		14.8
	36.1		-39.0		-81.8			473.7		-85.5
	6.7		4.7		6.2	EBIT/Interest		6.2		8.2
(32)	3.2	(36)	3.0	(44)	3.8		(11)	4.9		5.8
	1.7		1.3		2.3			2.4		1.6
	6.5		3.5		5.2	Net Profit + Depr., Dep.,				
(17)	1.5	(18)	2.7	(27)	2.8	Amort./Cur. Mat. L/T/D				
	1.2		1.4		1.7					
	.6		.6		.8	Fixed/Worth		.6		.8
	1.0		1.1		1.3			1.2		1.1
	2.5		2.3		2.0			1.5		2.1
	.3		.2		.6	Debt/Worth		.3		.6
	1.2		1.0		1.3			1.2		1.5
	2.7		2.2		2.5			2.6		3.7
	34.5		23.4		33.3	% Profit Before Taxes/Tangible		32.8		47.6
(31)	13.0	(36)	11.4		21.4	Net Worth		26.3		20.6
	4.9		6.4		9.3			18.1		3.3
	11.5		10.0		14.6	% Profit Before Taxes/Total		15.3		16.2
	6.9		7.2		8.9	Assets		9.7		14.2
	2.6		2.5		4.4			7.6		2.7
	3.9		3.4		3.3	Sales/Net Fixed Assets		3.1		3.5
	2.3		2.0		2.2			2.2		2.3
	1.7		1.5		1.5			1.9		1.4
	1.7		1.4		1.6	Sales/Total Assets		1.5		1.7
	1.2		1.1		1.2			1.2		1.1
	.9		.8		.9			.9		.8
	4.8		5.7		5.4	% Depr., Dep., Amort./Sales		5.4		
(32)	6.4		8.2	(47)	8.4			7.5		
	9.2		13.7		11.3			8.6		
	2.8				.9	% Officers', Directors',				
(12)	4.4			(13)	4.6	Owners' Comp/Sales				
	7.7				9.7					
	336683M	541167M	758357M	Net Sales ($)	4003M	19339M	22657M	91247M	153866M	467245M
	292654M	567168M	623242M	Total Assets ($)	5157M	24413M	22763M	80233M	149076M	341600M

M = $ thousand   MM = $ million
See Pages 1 through 15 for Explanation of Ratios and Data

Current Data Sorted By Assets							Comparative Historical Data	
						# Postretirement Benefits		
		1	1		2	Type of Statement		
		6	12	2	6	Unqualified	19	21
	1	4	5			Reviewed	11	17
3	5	2				Compiled	17	15
3	1	1				Tax Returns	1	
		7	7	4	4	Other	20	20
	20 (4/1-9/30/94)		53 (10/1/94-3/31/95)				4/1/90-3/31/91	4/1/91-3/31/92
0-500M	500M-2MM	2-10MM	10-50MM	50-100MM	100-250MM		ALL	ALL
6	7	20	24	6	10	**NUMBER OF STATEMENTS**	68	73
%	%	%	%	%	%	**ASSETS**	%	%
		8.3	9.1		7.3	Cash & Equivalents	12.7	9.0
		21.4	14.7		9.5	Trade Receivables - (net)	17.7	16.0
		9.2	7.4		5.7	Inventory	4.6	7.1
		2.2	2.4		2.2	All Other Current	1.8	3.8
		41.0	33.6		24.7	Total Current	36.8	36.0
		43.2	47.9		54.8	Fixed Assets (net)	43.8	45.6
		4.1	1.9		1.3	Intangibles (net)	1.9	2.8
		11.8	16.6		19.2	All Other Non-Current	17.5	15.6
		100.0	100.0		100.0	Total	100.0	100.0
						LIABILITIES		
		6.5	5.1		2.6	Notes Payable-Short Term	6.9	8.9
		7.6	8.8		2.8	Cur. Mat. -L/T/D	8.9	7.4
		17.9	10.0		7.2	Trade Payables	13.7	10.1
		.2	.3		.4	Income Taxes Payable	.3	.3
		7.4	6.8		6.1	All Other Current	8.6	9.3
		39.6	31.0		19.2	Total Current	38.5	36.2
		14.2	19.4		17.7	Long Term Debt	18.9	19.5
		.4	.9		3.7	Deferred Taxes	1.2	1.0
		5.6	9.4		12.7	All Other-Non-Current	5.0	5.6
		40.1	39.2		46.7	Net Worth	36.4	37.7
		100.0	100.0		100.0	Total Liabilities & Net Worth	100.0	100.0
						INCOME DATA		
		100.0	100.0		100.0	Net Sales	100.0	100.0
		21.4	16.7		30.3	Gross Profit	24.3	23.0
		17.8	11.7		18.0	Operating Expenses	21.2	18.6
		3.6	5.0		12.4	Operating Profit	3.1	4.3
		.4	.9		1.5	All Other Expenses (net)	.7	.7
		3.2	4.1		10.9	Profit Before Taxes	2.5	3.6
						RATIOS		
		1.8	1.8		1.8		1.6	2.0
		.9	1.1		1.2	Current	1.0	1.0
		.6	.6		.8		.6	.6
		1.4	1.3		1.1		1.3	1.4
		.5	.7		.9	Quick	.8	.6
		.3	.3		.6		.4	.3
		24 15.1	28 13.0		30 12.3		20 18.4	15 24.6
		43 8.4	37 10.0		38 9.7	Sales/Receivables	31 11.8	30 12.1
		57 6.4	44 8.3		45 8.1		40 9.1	40 9.1
		5 72.4	5 72.8		9 42.0		0 UND	0 UND
		17 21.4	17 21.4		21 17.6	Cost of Sales/Inventory	5 74.0	7 49.0
		45 8.1	26 14.1		43 8.5		20 18.1	21 17.1
		22 16.8	19 18.8		21 17.4		12 31.1	11 33.7
		39 9.4	24 14.9		33 11.1	Cost of Sales/Payables	25 14.7	19 19.5
		52 7.0	38 9.7		48 7.6		47 7.8	37 9.9
		7.2	10.1		8.4		15.0	8.6
		−82.6	81.7		510.4	Sales/Working Capital	NM	128.3
		−6.6	−13.9		−19.8		−11.4	−8.7
		19.1	(23) 5.8				(62) 6.2	(62) 5.8
	(18)	3.7	2.6			EBIT/Interest	2.5	2.5
		1.9	1.3				.4	1.1
			3.3				(29) 4.1	(23) 6.2
		(12)	2.3			Net Profit + Depr., Dep., Amort./Cur. Mat. L./T/D	1.4	1.5
			1.0				.3	.7
		.5	.8		.6		.6	.6
		1.7	1.2		1.3	Fixed/Worth	1.3	1.2
		2.4	2.7		2.3		2.6	2.8
		.9	.8		.6		.8	.8
		1.8	1.6		1.1	Debt/Worth	1.8	1.7
		3.6	3.9		2.7		3.9	3.6
		71.1	34.7				(60) 48.2	(64) 35.1
	(19)	15.1	21.6			% Profit Before Taxes/Tangible Net Worth	18.9	10.0
		2.6	2.5				.7	-.1
		13.8	12.4		14.5		13.6	12.7
		6.3	5.7		7.9	% Profit Before Taxes/Total Assets	7.9	3.9
		1.3	1.2		4.8		−.5	−.3
		8.4	4.6		2.6		8.7	7.7
		5.0	3.0		1.6	Sales/Net Fixed Assets	3.9	3.2
		1.5	2.1		1.1		2.6	2.1
		3.1	2.2		1.4		2.7	2.4
		1.6	1.4		1.0	Sales/Total Assets	2.0	1.6
		1.0	1.0		.7		1.2	1.1
		1.8	3.4				(57) 3.2	(67) 3.3
	(18)	5.2	(22) 5.4			% Depr., Dep., Amort./Sales	5.8	5.2
		9.0	7.8				8.7	8.5
							(16) 1.8	(14) 1.4
						% Officers', Directors', Owners' Comp/Sales	4.0	2.2
							12.2	3.2
5517M	45677M	250783M	810280M	549787M	1588695M	Net Sales ($)	2141332M	2481314M
1379M	8123M	122622M	558233M	453795M	1696703M	Total Assets ($)	1672710M	1742561M

M = $ thousand   MM = $ million
See Pages 1 through 15 for Explanation of Ratios and Data

Comparative Historical Data				Current Data Sorted By Sales					
3	3	4	# Postretirement Benefits			1			3
			Type of Statement						
22	25	26	Unqualified		1	1	1	7	16
10	7	10	Reviewed		1		1	3	5
13	18	10	Compiled	2	3		1	4	
	3	5	Tax Returns	1	3		1		
19	18	22	Other	1	3		2	6	13
4/1/92-3/31/93	4/1/93-3/31/94	4/1/94-3/31/95			20 (4/1-9/30/94)			53 (10/1/94-3/31/95)	
ALL	ALL	ALL		0-1MM	1-3MM	3-5MM	5-10MM	10-25MM	25MM & OVER
64	71	73	NUMBER OF STATEMENTS	3	9	1	6	20	34
%	%	%	ASSETS	%	%	%	%	%	%
9.0	12.1	8.7	Cash & Equivalents					8.1	8.9
16.8	21.9	18.3	Trade Receivables - (net)					27.9	15.6
6.0	4.6	8.0	Inventory					8.2	6.3
4.1	2.4	2.4	All Other Current					2.4	2.6
35.9	41.0	37.5	Total Current					46.6	33.4
43.7	40.9	46.2	Fixed Assets (net)					39.4	48.6
4.0	1.3	2.2	Intangibles (net)					2.8	1.4
16.4	16.8	14.1	All Other Non-Current					11.3	16.7
100.0	100.0	100.0	Total					100.0	100.0
			LIABILITIES						
6.8	9.0	6.1	Notes Payable-Short Term					7.9	4.4
8.0	6.9	7.8	Cur. Mat.-L /T/D					8.6	5.7
11.3	12.9	14.6	Trade Payables					15.9	11.0
.2	.7	.3	Income Taxes Payable					.1	.4
7.6	7.8	8.1	All Other Current					7.4	7.2
33.9	37.2	36.8	Total Current					39.8	28.7
16.5	13.6	15.4	Long Term Debt					15.0	16.4
1.5	1.0	1.4	Deferred Taxes					.2	2.3
6.9	6.1	10.3	All Other-Non-Current					8.9	10.1
41.3	42.0	36.1	Net Worth					36.1	42.4
100.0	100.0	100.0	Total Liabilities & Net Worth					100.0	100.0
			INCOME DATA						
100.0	100.0	100.0	Net Sales					100.0	100.0
21.9	20.1	23.9	Gross Profit					20.2	21.4
16.5	15.1	17.7	Operating Expenses					16.2	14.2
5.4	5.0	6.2	Operating Profit					3.9	7.2
.9	.2	1.0	All Other Expenses (net)					-.4	1.2
4.5	4.8	5.2	Profit Before Taxes					4.4	6.0
			RATIOS						
1.5	2.3	1.6						2.1	1.6
1.0	1.2	1.1	Current					1.4	1.1
.6	.7	.6						.6	.8
1.3	1.7	1.3						1.8	1.1
.7	.9	.8	Quick					1.0	.8
.4	.7	.3						.4	.5
20 18.5	20 18.4	25 14.8						34 10.7	27 13.5
33 11.0	36 10.1	37 9.8	Sales/Receivables					44 8.3	37 9.8
39 9.4	46 7.9	46 8.0						47 7.8	44 8.3
0 877.8	0 UND	4 99.0						7 48.8	5 68.3
11 33.0	8 44.8	16 22.9	Cost of Sales/Inventory					17 21.6	17 21.4
20 18.4	21 17.1	28 12.9						28 12.9	25 14.4
13 28.9	12 30.8	19 19.0						18 20.6	20 18.4
21 17.7	20 18.5	31 11.7	Cost of Sales/Payables					26 14.3	28 13.0
37 9.9	35 10.5	45 8.2						41 8.8	39 9.3
11.1	7.9	13.1						7.2	12.3
630.1	42.6	86.1	Sales/Working Capital					24.2	64.2
-10.5	-23.8	-11.0						-8.7	-21.0
6.3	8.5	7.0						10.6	7.0
(58) 3.7	(65) 3.8	(67) 3.5	EBIT/Interest				(18)	3.5	(32) 4.8
1.8	1.8	1.5						1.5	2.3
3.7	4.0	3.4							3.7
(22) 1.7	(19) 2.4	(29) 2.2	Net Profit + Depr., Dep., Amort./Cur. Mat. L/T/D						(21) 2.7
1.2	.7	1.3							1.8
.5	.5	.7						.5	.6
1.2	1.0	1.3	Fixed/Worth					1.2	1.3
2.4	1.9	2.6						2.8	2.4
.7	.5	.9						.7	.9
1.4	1.4	1.8	Debt/Worth					2.0	1.2
3.6	3.8	4.0						5.0	2.7
34.4	35.5	44.2						71.1	29.7
(60) 17.3	(65) 13.8	(67) 19.9	% Profit Before Taxes/Tangible Net Worth				(19)	19.9	(33) 20.4
8.1	5.0	7.0						4.5	7.5
12.5	12.4	13.6						16.2	13.4
7.9	6.3	6.4	% Profit Before Taxes/Total Assets					7.5	7.2
2.2	2.2	1.4						1.4	3.9
7.7	10.0	7.1						7.9	5.7
3.7	3.7	3.0	Sales/Net Fixed Assets					3.5	3.0
2.2	2.3	1.6						2.5	1.6
2.3	3.2	2.6						3.1	2.3
1.6	1.6	1.5	Sales/Total Assets					1.7	1.4
1.1	1.1	1.0						1.3	1.0
2.6	1.8	2.5						2.2	2.2
(56) 5.7	(63) 5.4	(63) 5.3	% Depr., Dep., Amort./Sales				(19)	6.3	(28) 4.1
7.3	7.8	7.8						8.0	5.8
2.0	2.0	1.3							
(11) 3.1	(13) 3.1	(12) 2.0	% Officers', Directors', Owners' Comp/Sales						
4.0	8.0	5.2							
2314502M	2398348M	3250739M	Net Sales ($)	737M	17194M	3790M	45603M	306965M	2876450M
1718728M	2067375M	2840855M	Total Assets ($)	536M	13075M	3832M	60652M	200711M	2562049M

M = $ thousand   MM = $ million
See Pages 1 through 15 for Explanation of Ratios and Data

Current Data Sorted By Assets   **Comparative Historical Data**

								4/1/90-3/31/91 ALL	4/1/91-3/31/92 ALL
	1	1	3	1	3	# Postretirement Benefits		
						Type of Statement		
1	3	6	12	2	6	Unqualified		
	2	1				Reviewed		
1	3	1				Compiled		
	2	1				Tax Returns		
1	2	3	1	2	1	Other		
0-500M	22 (4/1-9/30/94) 500M-2MM	2-10MM	29 (10/1/94-3/31/95) 10-50MM	50-100MM	100-250MM			
3	12	12	13	4	7	**NUMBER OF STATEMENTS**		
%	%	%	%	%	%	**ASSETS**	%	%
	2.5	5.9	3.1			Cash & Equivalents	D	D
	28.0	11.8	26.5			Trade Receivables - (net)	A	A
	16.3	8.2	4.9			Inventory	T	T
	.3	1.1	1.6			All Other Current	A	A
	47.1	27.0	36.1			Total Current		
	33.5	60.4	48.3			Fixed Assets (net)	N	N
	6.3	2.8	1.0			Intangibles (net)	O	O
	13.1	9.8	14.6			All Other Non-Current	T	T
	100.0	100.0	100.0			Total		
						LIABILITIES	A	A
	4.5	7.3	5.3			Notes Payable-Short Term	V	V
	4.2	3.4	1.5			Cur. Mat. -L/T/D	A	A
	15.4	12.0	29.0			Trade Payables	I	I
	.3	.2	.4			Income Taxes Payable	L	L
	7.2	9.2	4.7			All Other Current	A	A
	31.6	32.2	40.9			Total Current	B	B
	25.4	15.9	18.3			Long Term Debt	L	L
	1.2	3.8	5.3			Deferred Taxes	E	E
	3.5	2.3	2.3			All Other-Non-Current		
	38.3	45.8	33.2			Net Worth		
	100.0	100.0	100.0			Total Liabilities & Net Worth		
						INCOME DATA		
	100.0	100.0	100.0			Net Sales		
						Gross Profit		
	95.1	93.0	92.7			Operating Expenses		
	4.9	7.0	7.3			Operating Profit		
	.8	1.5	1.6			All Other Expenses (net)		
	4.1	5.5	5.7			Profit Before Taxes		
						RATIOS		
	1.6	1.1	1.0			Current		
	1.2	.8	.9					
	.8	.6	.5					
	.8	.9	.9			Quick		
	.7	.5	.6					
	.4	.4	.3					
	26 13.9	16 22.6	23 15.9			Sales/Receivables		
	37 10.0	29 12.5	29 12.4					
	62 5.9	45 8.2	45 8.1					
						Cost of Sales/Inventory		
						Cost of Sales/Payables		
	9.1	97.4	221.2			Sales/Working Capital		
	42.9	-60.0	-57.0					
	NM	-17.1	-7.4					
	8.7	5.0	16.1			EBIT/Interest		
	(11) 2.9	(11) 4.5	6.0					
	1.7	1.4	2.2					
			78.2			Net Profit + Depr., Dep., Amort./Cur. Mat. L /T/D		
			(10) 6.6					
			3.0					
	.3	1.0	.9			Fixed/Worth		
	.6	1.7	1.7					
	5.1	1.9	2.2					
	.7	.7	1.1			Debt/Worth		
	2.3	1.5	2.1					
	5.9	2.1	3.8					
	28.2	17.0	27.2			% Profit Before Taxes/Tangible Net Worth		
	(10) 17.6	12.7	19.2					
	10.8	7.8	12.7					
	8.0	7.5	9.2			% Profit Before Taxes/Total Assets		
	6.6	5.1	4.8					
	2.1	2.6	3.8					
	18.4	12.2	44.8			Sales/Net Fixed Assets		
	7.6	2.0	1.6					
	1.9	1.0	1.1					
	3.3	3.5	5.1			Sales/Total Assets		
	2.1	1.2	1.1					
	.8	.7	.8					
	.9	1.7	.9			% Depr., Dep., Amort./Sales		
	2.6	3.6	3.5					
	5.9	5.3	4.8					
						% Officers', Directors', Owners' Comp/Sales		
486M	29143M	123060M	965777M	767281M	719285M	Net Sales ($)		
1035M	15468M	62815M	401566M	342605M	1018352M	Total Assets ($)		

M = $ thousand   MM = $ million

See Pages 1 through 15 for Explanation of Ratios and Data

Comparative Historical Data				Current Data Sorted By Sales					
3	3	9	# Postretirement Benefits	1	1				7
			Type of Statement						
20	19	30	Unqualified	3	3		3	5	16
2	2	3	Reviewed		2	1			
2	4	5	Compiled	1		3			1
		3	Tax Returns		2	1			
7	12	10	Other	1	1	1	1	1	5
4/1/92-3/31/93 ALL	4/1/93-3/31/94 ALL	4/1/94-3/31/95 ALL		0-1MM	22 (4/1-9/30/94) 1-3MM	3-5MM	29 (10/1/94-3/31/95) 5-10MM	10-25MM	25MM & OVER
31	37	51	**NUMBER OF STATEMENTS**	5	8	6	4	6	22
%	%	%	**ASSETS**	%	%	%	%	%	%
7.4	6.9	3.4	Cash & Equivalents						3.5
20.4	17.0	19.8	Trade Receivables - (net)						23.0
4.5	5.2	8.7	Inventory						5.4
1.4	3.2	1.1	All Other Current						1.8
33.6	32.3	33.1	Total Current						33.6
54.9	58.7	52.4	Fixed Assets (net)						54.6
1.2	1.0	3.1	Intangibles (net)						1.9
10.3	7.9	11.4	All Other Non-Current						9.9
100.0	100.0	100.0	Total						100.0
			LIABILITIES						
6.2	5.3	4.9	Notes Payable-Short Term						3.4
1.7	2.7	2.9	Cur. Mat.-L./T/D						2.5
19.3	16.8	17.6	Trade Payables						25.9
.7	.5	.2	Income Taxes Payable						.2
6.9	7.0	6.3	All Other Current						6.2
34.7	32.4	31.9	Total Current						38.2
19.1	23.4	23.1	Long Term Debt						20.0
4.3	4.5	4.2	Deferred Taxes						4.8
3.1	3.1	3.9	All Other-Non-Current						5.6
38.7	36.6	36.9	Net Worth						31.4
100.0	100.0	100.0	Total Liabilities & Net Worth						100.0
			INCOME DATA						
100.0	100.0	100.0	Net Sales						100.0
			Gross Profit						
93.0	90.5	91.7	Operating Expenses						93.0
7.0	9.5	8.3	Operating Profit						7.0
1.2	2.1	2.4	All Other Expenses (net)						1.5
5.7	7.3	5.8	Profit Before Taxes						5.5
			RATIOS						
1.2	1.3	1.2	Current						1.0
1.0	1.0	1.0							.9
.6	.7	.7							.7
1.0	.9	.9	Quick						.9
.7	.6	.6							.6
.4	.3	.4							.4
24 15.1	23 16.0	25 14.8	Sales/Receivables						21 17.0
37 9.8	35 10.4	35 10.5							34 10.6
56 6.5	42 8.6	49 7.5							45 8.2
			Cost of Sales/Inventory						
			Cost of Sales/Payables						
20.9	15.7	28.6	Sales/Working Capital						547.3
−128.8	−74.1	−173.4							−47.9
−10.4	−10.3	−14.4							−16.9
5.7	4.8	6.0	EBIT/Interest						6.5
(26) 2.9	(35) 3.0	(48) 3.3						(21)	3.5
1.9	2.4	2.1							2.3
10.0	8.0	8.7	Net Profit + Depr., Dep.,						8.0
(18) 4.2	(22) 5.4	(31) 5.4	Amort./Cur. Mat. L/T/D					(15)	5.8
2.4	3.1	2.3							4.3
.8	.9	.8	Fixed/Worth						1.3
1.5	2.0	1.7							1.8
2.2	2.4	2.6							2.6
1.0	1.3	1.0	Debt/Worth						1.2
1.8	2.0	2.0							2.3
2.5	2.8	4.5							4.1
24.3	27.7	23.1	% Profit Before Taxes/Tangible						24.4
(29) 14.4	(36) 19.4	(49) 14.9	Net Worth						17.9
7.9	13.0	9.3							10.6
8.4	8.1	7.9	% Profit Before Taxes/Total						6.7
5.6	6.5	5.5	Assets						5.6
2.0	4.0	2.8							3.1
3.6	2.6	9.1	Sales/Net Fixed Assets						13.2
1.5	1.4	1.6							1.6
1.0	1.0	1.0							1.0
1.6	1.6	2.6	Sales/Total Assets						4.2
1.0	1.0	1.0							1.1
.7	.8	.7							.8
2.7	3.0	1.3	% Depr., Dep., Amort./Sales						1.3
(29) 3.8	(35) 3.9	(49) 3.9						(20)	3.4
6.5	5.4	5.5							4.8
			% Officers', Directors', Owners' Comp/Sales						
1685513M	2249054M	2605032M	Net Sales ($)	1923M	15424M	22670M	25625M	96611M	2442779M
1494878M	2136590M	1841841M	Total Assets ($)	3288M	16799M	16512M	19298M	111063M	1674881M

M = $ thousand   MM = $ million
See Pages 1 through 15 for Explanation of Ratios and Data

Current Data Sorted By Assets | | | | | | **Comparative Historical Data**

Postretirement Benefits (top counts): 1 | 4 | 6 | 1 | 1

0-500M	500M-2MM	2-10MM	10-50MM	50-100MM	100-250MM	Type of Statement	ALL	ALL
4	3	16	19	6	16	Unqualified	23	82
1	1	3			1	Reviewed	5	2
3	2	5	1			Compiled	6	11
1						Tax Returns		
2	11	12	16	7	4	Other	22	28

43 (4/1-9/30/94)		91 (10/1/94-3/31/95)					4/1/90-3/31/91 ALL	4/1/91-3/31/92 ALL
0-500M	500M-2MM	2-10MM	10-50MM	50-100MM	100-250MM			
11	17	36	36	13	21	**NUMBER OF STATEMENTS**	56	123
%	%	%	%	%	%	**ASSETS**	%	%
12.7	15.4	10.3	5.6	8.0	5.5	Cash & Equivalents	6.5	11.3
20.7	12.6	11.7	9.8	8.7	11.4	Trade Receivables - (net)	10.7	10.1
4.1	2.0	1.9	1.1	1.0	2.0	Inventory	5.1	3.1
5.7	1.0	1.0	1.8	2.3	1.7	All Other Current	4.1	2.6
43.2	31.0	24.8	18.3	20.0	20.7	Total Current	26.4	27.1
48.4	63.5	63.9	71.7	72.5	76.2	Fixed Assets (net)	57.6	65.7
2.7	1.5	.3	.2	.5	.1	Intangibles (net)	.3	.4
5.7	4.0	11.0	9.9	6.9	3.0	All Other Non-Current	15.6	6.8
100.0	100.0	100.0	100.0	100.0	100.0	Total	100.0	100.0
						LIABILITIES		
2.4	8.2	3.0	1.0	1.0	.7	Notes Payable-Short Term	9.0	3.9
10.5	3.1	6.6	4.2	2.7	1.3	Cur. Mat. -L/T/D	4.0	3.4
18.6	7.5	6.4	8.0	6.2	9.5	Trade Payables	12.3	10.6
.0	.1	.2	.3	1.5	.2	Income Taxes Payable	.2	.2
13.3	2.9	5.4	4.5	4.1	4.7	All Other Current	6.8	5.0
44.9	21.8	21.5	17.9	15.4	16.4	Total Current	32.4	23.1
21.1	12.3	22.6	26.4	15.5	26.3	Long Term Debt	17.7	16.3
.0	.6	1.7	3.0	4.9	6.1	Deferred Taxes	3.1	2.3
.0	3.2	4.3	4.7	10.4	3.4	All Other-Non-Current	5.3	2.8
34.0	62.2	49.9	48.0	53.8	47.8	Net Worth	41.5	55.5
100.0	100.0	100.0	100.0	100.0	100.0	Total Liabilities & Net Worth	100.0	100.0
						INCOME DATA		
100.0	100.0	100.0	100.0	100.0	100.0	Net Sales	100.0	100.0
43.0	57.1	44.8	52.2	45.3	46.9	Gross Profit	46.8	51.8
42.0	48.1	39.9	39.6	37.3	33.1	Operating Expenses	34.4	43.5
1.0	9.0	4.9	12.7	8.1	13.7	Operating Profit	12.4	8.4
.3	1.7	3.5	5.6	3.7	4.0	All Other Expenses (net)	3.4	2.6
.8	7.3	1.3	7.1	4.3	9.7	Profit Before Taxes	9.0	5.7
						RATIOS		
1.6	2.6	2.9	1.7	2.8	2.0	Current	1.4	2.5
.9	1.0	1.1	1.0	1.4	1.2		1.1	1.2
.6	.5	.6	.8	.9	1.0		.5	.8
1.3	2.4	2.4	1.5	2.5	1.3	Quick	1.1	1.8
.8	.9	1.0	.8	1.1	1.0		.6	1.0
.4	.5	.5	.5	.9	.8		.3	.5
12 30.9	30 12.2	24 14.9	42 8.6	39 9.3	45 8.2	Sales/Receivables	23 16.0	27 13.6
49 7.5	42 8.6	47 7.7	61 6.0	53 6.9	64 5.7		42 8.7	49 7.4
69 5.3	69 5.3	73 5.0	94 3.9	76 4.8	94 3.9		65 5.6	76 4.8
0 UND	0 UND	0 UND	0 UND	0 UND	0 UND	Cost of Sales/Inventory	0 UND	0 UND
0 UND	0 UND	0 UND	0 UND	0 UND	0 UND		19 18.9	0 UND
0 UND	16 23.3	15 23.7	14 25.5	0 UND	14 25.9		42 8.7	20 18.0
17 21.0	15 24.9	18 20.2	59 6.2	41 8.9	51 7.2	Cost of Sales/Payables	34 10.8	37 9.9
96 3.8	43 8.5	39 9.4	96 3.8	63 5.8	79 4.6		64 5.7	85 4.3
174 2.1	126 2.9	87 4.2	192 1.9	126 2.9	304 1.2		152 2.4	203 1.8
15.9	4.6	6.0	6.3	3.1	6.9	Sales/Working Capital	7.9	3.4
-100.3	106.2	140.2	-447.4	18.9	32.1		76.4	15.6
-10.9	-8.1	-7.2	-11.6	-96.0	NM		-5.5	-14.0
	10.0	3.2	6.9	5.2	8.0	EBIT/Interest	3.7	9.0
	(13) 4.8	(30) 1.4	(35) 2.5	(12) .5	(20) 3.0		(44) 2.4	(106) 2.9
	2.5	1.0	1.1	-1.0	2.0		1.0	1.3
		3.3	13.9			Net Profit + Depr., Dep., Amort./Cur. Mat. L./T/D	6.8	5.3
		(14) 1.3	(15) 1.9				(24) 1.7	(48) 3.3
		.2	1.1				1.2	1.2
.8	.8	.8	1.1	1.0	1.3	Fixed/Worth	.8	.9
1.8	1.0	1.2	1.6	1.3	1.5		1.5	1.2
3.7	1.5	2.4	2.2	2.1	1.9		2.7	2.0
1.0	.2	.3	.5	.4	.7	Debt/Worth	.8	.3
1.9	.4	1.1	1.2	.7	.9		1.4	.8
5.0	1.5	2.8	1.9	1.7	1.9		3.2	2.3
56.8	37.8	18.5	15.0	11.2	10.9	% Profit Before Taxes/Tangible Net Worth	25.8	20.9
(10) 27.2	16.3	(35) 5.6	8.3	1.1	9.0		(55) 12.2	(121) 8.4
-30.4	3.5	-.2	-.4	-11.1	6.3		4.1	.0
19.1	14.1	7.1	7.3	8.0	6.2	% Profit Before Taxes/Total Assets	9.5	9.0
8.0	11.9	2.1	3.5	.7	4.1		4.8	4.1
-11.8	2.1	-.1	-.1	-5.5	1.7		.7	-.1
18.9	2.1	2.2	1.1	2.3	1.0	Sales/Net Fixed Assets	3.5	1.6
2.1	1.3	.7	.7	.7	.5		1.0	.7
.9	.6	.6	.4	.3	.3		.5	.4
3.5	1.3	1.1	.7	1.1	.8	Sales/Total Assets	1.2	.8
1.3	.8	.6	.4	.5	.4		.6	.5
.7	.4	.4	.3	.3	.2		.4	.3
.4	5.6	7.2	13.7	3.5		% Depr., Dep., Amort./Sales	4.9	5.2
(10) 12.4	(16) 13.3	(34) 16.2	(34) 21.2	(10) 19.2			(42) 14.0	(106) 14.9
15.8	28.7	26.9	29.4	41.4			23.9	26.1
						% Officers', Directors', Owners' Comp/Sales		
7639M	26577M	281193M	521072M	767867M	2433485M	Net Sales ($)	2338943M	3899099M
3544M	18861M	170058M	1005108M	925858M	3186105M	Total Assets ($)	2419536M	4456345M

© Robert Morris Associates 1995

M = $ thousand   MM = $ million
See Pages 1 through 15 for Explanation of Ratios and Data

Comparative Historical Data | **Current Data Sorted By Sales**

	3	4	13	# Postretirement Benefits / Type of Statement	1	1	1		5	5
	79	60	64	Unqualified	7	11	4	4	16	22
	2	6	6	Reviewed		3		1	1	2
	8	9	11	Compiled	3	3		2	2	1
	2	3	1	Tax Returns	1					
	41	41	52	Other	12	10	3	7	11	9
	4/1/92-3/31/93 ALL	4/1/93-3/31/94 ALL	4/1/94-3/31/95 ALL		43 (4/1-9/30/94)			91 (10/1/94-3/31/95)		
					0-1MM	1-3MM	3-5MM	5-10MM	10-25MM	25MM & OVER
	132	119	134	**NUMBER OF STATEMENTS**	23	27	7	13	30	34
	%	%	%	**ASSETS**	%	%	%	%	%	%
	10.3	10.4	8.9	Cash & Equivalents	11.5	10.3		7.0	7.7	8.1
	13.5	13.7	11.7	Trade Receivables - (net)	10.1	11.6		8.9	10.9	15.5
	2.6	2.8	1.8	Inventory	.4	2.1		1.0	2.7	2.3
	1.0	1.3	.6	All Other Current	3.5	.9		2.3	1.2	1.9
	27.5	28.3	24.2	Total Current	25.5	24.9		19.2	22.4	27.8
	64.5	63.4	67.4	Fixed Assets (net)	67.5	61.1		71.0	69.5	66.5
	.9	1.1	.6	Intangibles (net)	2.2	.2		.5	.1	.4
	7.2	7.3	7.7	All Other Non-Current	4.8	13.7		9.3	8.0	5.4
	100.0	100.0	100.0	Total	100.0	100.0		100.0	100.0	100.0
				LIABILITIES						
	2.4	4.2	2.5	Notes Payable-Short Term	4.1	6.0		.3	1.0	1.0
	3.5	4.1	4.6	Cur. Mat.-L /T/D	2.5	9.7		4.4	2.6	3.2
	11.7	9.7	8.4	Trade Payables	9.7	6.0		6.9	8.4	10.7
	.2	.5	.3	Income Taxes Payable	.0	.0		.4	.2	.8
	3.6	5.2	5.3	All Other Current	2.5	7.2		5.8	3.7	7.2
	21.3	23.7	21.1	Total Current	18.8	28.9		17.7	15.9	22.8
	20.3	18.5	22.1	Long Term Debt	16.5	24.0		22.1	23.9	22.0
	3.0	2.4	2.8	Deferred Taxes	.6	1.1		1.7	3.5	5.3
	4.0	3.6	4.4	All Other-Non-Current	.8	6.0		6.6	5.7	4.2
	51.4	51.8	49.7	Net Worth	63.3	40.0		51.8	51.0	45.6
	100.0	100.0	100.0	Total Liabilities & Net Worth	100.0	100.0		100.0	100.0	100.0
				INCOME DATA						
	100.0	100.0	100.0	Net Sales	100.0	100.0		100.0	100.0	100.0
	51.1	48.1	48.6	Gross Profit	55.7	49.8		56.3	43.5	41.3
	39.7	38.5	39.7	Operating Expenses	51.9	43.7		46.4	34.5	29.0
	11.4	9.6	8.9	Operating Profit	3.8	6.2		9.9	9.0	12.3
	2.7	2.5	3.7	All Other Expenses (net)	1.8	4.0		7.7	2.4	3.8
	8.7	7.1	5.2	Profit Before Taxes	2.0	2.2		2.2	6.6	8.5
				RATIOS						
	2.2	2.0	2.1	Current	3.0	2.1		1.3	2.1	2.0
	1.3	1.2	1.1		1.0	.8		1.0	1.3	1.2
	.9	.8	.7		.5	.5		.7	.9	.9
	1.9	1.7	1.7	Quick	2.4	1.4		1.3	1.7	1.4
	1.0	1.0	1.0		.9	.7		.7	1.0	1.0
	.8	.6	.6		.4	.4		.4	.7	.8
	37 9.9	33 11.0	35 10.3	Sales/Receivables	32 11.5	41 8.8		28 13.0	42 8.7	36 10.1
	57 6.4	60 6.1	55 6.6		49 7.5	58 6.3		51 7.1	56 6.5	57 6.4
	89 4.1	87 4.2	79 4.6		81 4.5	74 4.9		114 3.2	87 4.2	81 4.5
	0 UND	0 UND	0 UND	Cost of Sales/Inventory	0 UND	0 UND		0 UND	0 UND	0 UND
	0 UND	0 UND	0 UND		0 UND	0 UND		0 UND	1 546.1	0 UND
	20 18.7	15 24.1	11 32.8		0 UND	19 19.6		14 25.9	12 30.9	17 21.5
	40 9.1	20 18.2	33 11.0	Cost of Sales/Payables	29 12.8	20 18.0		38 9.6	40 9.2	39 9.3
	83 4.4	89 4.1	74 4.9		99 3.7	41 9.0		85 4.3	76 4.8	72 5.1
	228 1.6	215 1.7	159 2.3		174 2.1	101 3.6		243 1.5	130 2.8	281 1.3
	4.2	4.5	6.1	Sales/Working Capital	2.7	9.0		11.0	5.5	7.3
	21.8	25.0	59.3		86.0	-17.0		-81.6	26.8	36.8
	-34.5	-17.9	-12.0		-7.9	-4.2		-5.4	-38.6	-65.6
	8.4	7.4	5.4	EBIT/Interest	6.0	4.6		5.9	8.6	5.5
	(115) 3.4	(101) 3.9	(119) 2.6		(16) 3.0	(24) 1.7		2.0	3.1	(32) 3.0
	1.7	1.5	1.1		-1.0	.9		-.3	.9	1.4
	8.0	6.5	8.2	Net Profit + Depr., Dep., Amort./Cur. Mat. L/T/D					11.1	11.5
	(48) 3.8	(36) 1.7	(42) 1.8						(14) 3.8	(11) 1.7
	1.5	.4	1.0						1.1	.9
	.8	.8	1.0	Fixed/Worth	.8	.8		.9	1.0	1.2
	1.3	1.2	1.4		1.2	1.2		1.4	1.3	1.5
	2.3	1.9	2.2		2.0	6.0		2.7	2.0	2.0
	.3	.4	.4	Debt/Worth	.2	.4		.4	.5	.7
	1.0	.9	1.1		.4	1.4		.8	1.0	1.3
	2.6	2.1	1.9		1.3	5.6		2.5	1.8	2.2
	30.6	23.8	18.0	% Profit Before Taxes/Tangible Net Worth	36.9	28.8		10.6	19.8	12.6
	(131) 10.8	(114) 11.7	(132) 8.7		9.3	(25) 11.5		5.0	8.3	8.9
	2.6	1.0	-.2		-11.3	-2.3		-17.5	-.3	6.0
	9.3	11.8	8.9	% Profit Before Taxes/Total Assets	14.3	8.0		5.5	12.7	6.4
	4.6	4.8	3.5		6.7	2.5		3.2	3.7	4.2
	1.4	.5	-.0		-9.3	-.2		-5.3	-.2	1.4
	2.1	2.3	1.5	Sales/Net Fixed Assets	1.4	1.9		1.1	1.2	3.1
	.8	.8	.7		.9	.7		.6	.7	.9
	.4	.4	.5		.5	.6		.4	.4	.4
	1.0	1.2	1.0	Sales/Total Assets	1.0	1.0		.7	.8	1.6
	.6	.5	.6		.6	.6		.4	.5	.6
	.3	.3	.3		.3	.4		.3	.4	.3
	6.1	5.3	7.3	% Depr., Dep., Amort./Sales	12.6	9.2		13.6	7.2	1.6
	(115) 15.3	(99) 15.6	(110) 15.4		(21) 15.0	(25) 15.4		20.6	(28) 19.4	(16) 3.5
	24.8	26.5	27.9		32.1	25.8		32.6	29.1	7.9
	.3	.3		% Officers', Directors', Owners' Comp/Sales						
	(13) 4.1	(11) 1.9								
	5.5	7.9								
	4750595M	4901190M	4037853M	Net Sales ($)	11746M	48873M	28012M	99639M	456892M	3392691M
	5737975M	5267076M	5309534M	Total Assets ($)	24302M	91495M	77715M	314602M	980833M	3820587M

M = $ thousand   MM = $ million
See Pages 1 through 15 for Explanation of Ratios and Data

NOT ELSEWHERE CLASSIFIED—SAND & GRAVEL – CONSTRUCTION. SIC# 1442

	Current Data Sorted By Assets							Comparative Historical Data	
		1	2	1			1	# Postretirement Benefits	
								Type of Statement	
		5	8	9			1	Unqualified	21	12
		10	11	1				Reviewed	18	19
	1	9	5					Compiled	19	15
	1		1					Tax Returns		1
	2	7	5	3				Other	11	12
		17 (4/1-9/30/94)		62 (10/1/94-3/31/95)					4/1/90-3/31/91 ALL	4/1/91-3/31/92 ALL
	0-500M	500M-2MM	2-10MM	10-50MM	50-100MM	100-250MM			

	0-500M	500M-2MM	2-10MM	10-50MM	50-100MM	100-250MM	4/1/90-3/31/91 ALL	4/1/91-3/31/92 ALL
NUMBER OF STATEMENTS	4	31	30	13		1	69	59
ASSETS %	%	%	%	%	%	%	%	%
Cash & Equivalents		10.5	8.2	7.5			6.3	7.6
Trade Receivables - (net)		18.6	17.3	15.3			17.1	16.5
Inventory		7.4	7.9	9.7			9.0	12.0
All Other Current		1.6	3.8	1.1			3.7	2.9
Total Current		38.2	37.2	33.5			36.0	39.1
Fixed Assets (net)		56.6	52.8	53.4			54.9	50.9
Intangibles (net)		1.2	2.5	1.0			2.2	2.5
All Other Non-Current		4.0	7.4	12.1			6.8	7.5
Total		100.0	100.0	100.0			100.0	100.0
LIABILITIES								
Notes Payable-Short Term		4.3	6.4	2.4			6.5	5.5
Cur. Mat. -L/T/D		6.5	6.9	3.7			10.7	6.6
Trade Payables		7.0	10.1	7.4			9.2	8.8
Income Taxes Payable		.2	.2	.2			.3	.3
All Other Current		4.6	5.9	3.3			4.5	4.7
Total Current		22.5	29.5	16.9			31.2	25.9
Long Term Debt		18.1	22.8	18.1			22.7	19.6
Deferred Taxes		.4	.6	.5			1.2	.9
All Other-Non-Current		3.9	2.1	6.1			2.5	3.5
Net Worth		55.1	44.9	58.3			42.4	50.0
Total Liabilities & Net Worth		100.0	100.0	100.0			100.0	100.0
INCOME DATA								
Net Sales		100.0	100.0	100.0			100.0	100.0
Gross Profit		41.8	34.0	30.2			33.4	31.8
Operating Expenses		34.5	26.5	18.4			25.2	27.1
Operating Profit		7.3	7.6	11.9			8.2	4.7
All Other Expenses (net)		-.2	1.4	1.8			2.5	1.5
Profit Before Taxes		7.5	6.2	10.1			5.7	3.2
RATIOS								
Current		2.7 / 1.8 / 1.0	2.4 / 1.3 / 1.0	3.7 / 1.7 / 1.4			1.9 / 1.2 / .8	3.1 / 1.4 / .8
Quick		2.3 / 1.6 / .8	1.6 / .9 / .6	3.0 / 1.1 / 1.0			1.3 / .8 / .3	1.7 / .8 / .5
Sales/Receivables		31 11.9 / 41 8.9 / 63 5.8	30 12.3 / 49 7.4 / 66 5.5	36 10.1 / 45 8.2 / 51 7.1			31 11.7 / 42 8.6 / 59 6.2	27 13.6 / 42 8.6 / 61 6.0
Cost of Sales/Inventory		0 UND / 15 23.6 / 72 5.1	0 UND / 23 15.8 / 55 6.6	21 17.7 / 30 12.0 / 41 8.8			1 346.7 / 34 10.6 / 68 5.4	10 37.5 / 45 8.2 / 99 3.7
Cost of Sales/Payables		11 34.1 / 19 19.2 / 39 9.4	13 28.7 / 28 13.1 / 58 6.3	21 17.0 / 29 12.4 / 36 10.2			14 25.7 / 28 13.0 / 50 7.3	13 27.3 / 24 15.5 / 53 6.9
Sales/Working Capital		5.9 / 9.8 / 139.5	7.9 / 13.4 / -352.9	4.5 / 9.4 / 16.8			6.5 / 18.5 / -20.8	4.0 / 11.7 / -33.7
EBIT/Interest		(28) 14.6 / 5.8 / 1.6	(29) 8.4 / 3.5 / 1.9	13.3 / 7.5 / 2.5			(67) 4.0 / 2.0 / 1.0	(56) 4.9 / 2.1 / .8
Net Profit + Depr., Dep., Amort./Cur. Mat. L./T/D		(12) 7.7 / 3.0 / 2.0	(11) 1.9 / 1.5 / 1.2				(47) 2.9 / 1.6 / .9	(28) 3.3 / 1.5 / .9
Fixed/Worth		.7 / 1.0 / 1.6	.8 / 1.2 / 2.8	.7 / 1.0 / 1.3			.9 / 1.3 / 2.5	.7 / 1.2 / 1.6
Debt/Worth		.4 / .6 / 1.5	.6 / 1.3 / 3.5	.5 / .7 / 1.2			.8 / 1.3 / 3.0	.4 / 1.0 / 2.3
% Profit Before Taxes/Tangible Net Worth		(30) 26.4 / 15.1 / 3.6	(28) 42.2 / 17.0 / 7.1	31.3 / 14.9 / 8.7			(67) 34.6 / 15.3 / 1.9	(54) 18.0 / 10.5 / 1.3
% Profit Before Taxes/Total Assets		14.7 / 7.5 / 1.6	11.5 / 5.2 / 3.1	18.1 / 8.4 / 4.8			9.3 / 5.1 / .2	8.9 / 4.8 / -1.1
Sales/Net Fixed Assets		4.0 / 2.3 / 1.6	3.2 / 2.3 / 1.4	3.1 / 2.5 / 1.6			3.8 / 2.2 / 1.6	3.6 / 2.3 / 1.4
Sales/Total Assets		2.0 / 1.3 / 1.0	1.8 / 1.1 / .8	1.5 / 1.2 / .9			1.8 / 1.2 / .9	1.5 / 1.1 / .8
% Depr., Dep., Amort./Sales		(29) 6.0 / 7.5 / 11.7	(29) 4.8 / 6.5 / 10.2	5.4 / 5.9 / 9.9			(65) 5.6 / 9.5 / 13.2	(52) 5.2 / 8.3 / 12.4
% Officers', Directors', Owners' Comp/Sales		(11) 2.6 / 8.1 / 12.5	(10) 2.3 / 4.0 / 6.4				(31) 3.3 / 5.4 / 9.7	(17) 2.8 / 5.4 / 9.2
Net Sales ($)	2300M	57832M	248339M	269861M		137266M	795106M	384076M
Total Assets ($)	1170M	38053M	126101M	250859M		190323M	522363M	356616M

M = $ thousand   MM = $ million
See Pages 1 through 15 for Explanation of Ratios and Data

Comparative Historical Data				Current Data Sorted By Sales					
2	3	5		2	1			1	1
			# Postretirement Benefits						
			Type of Statement						
19	16	23	Unqualified	1	4	4	5	5	4
34	23	22	Reviewed	3	8	6		4	1
18	13	15	Compiled	2	11	1		1	
4	2	2	Tax Returns		1	1			
10	22	17	Other	5	5	3		4	
4/1/92-3/31/93 ALL	4/1/93-3/31/94 ALL	4/1/94-3/31/95 ALL		17 (4/1-9/30/94) 0-1MM	1-3MM	3-5MM	62 (10/1/94-3/31/95) 5-10MM	10-25MM	25MM & OVER
85	76	79	**NUMBER OF STATEMENTS**	11	29	15	5	14	5
%	%	%	**ASSETS**	%	%	%	%	%	%
7.1	7.9	9.0	Cash & Equivalents	6.9	10.0	8.5		9.7	
17.0	19.3	17.8	Trade Receivables - (net)	13.4	18.4	18.4		18.9	
8.5	7.6	8.1	Inventory	13.6	4.6	9.0		7.9	
2.7	2.5	2.3	All Other Current	1.1	2.9	2.7		1.4	
35.3	37.3	37.1	Total Current	35.0	35.9	38.6		37.8	
54.4	54.7	54.5	Fixed Assets (net)	56.5	58.7	51.4		54.0	
2.7	1.3	1.9	Intangibles (net)	.0	1.2	3.1		.8	
7.6	6.6	6.5	All Other Non-Current	8.4	4.2	7.0		7.4	
100.0	100.0	100.0	Total	100.0	100.0	100.0		100.0	
			LIABILITIES						
3.5	5.1	4.7	Notes Payable-Short Term	3.0	4.1	7.5		3.7	
7.4	6.0	6.6	Cur. Mat.-L /T/D	8.3	7.0	6.7		5.1	
7.9	10.7	8.3	Trade Payables	5.3	6.5	9.2		11.7	
.3	.7	.2	Income Taxes Payable	.1	.2	.2		.2	
7.7	5.1	4.7	All Other Current	1.8	6.2	4.3		4.3	
26.8	27.5	24.4	Total Current	18.5	24.0	27.9		25.0	
22.2	20.7	20.8	Long Term Debt	31.9	19.2	16.1		15.9	
.5	.8	.5	Deferred Taxes	.2	.4	1.0		.2	
4.5	4.9	3.6	All Other-Non-Current	7.1	2.6	1.8		3.1	
46.1	46.1	50.7	Net Worth	42.2	53.9	53.2		55.7	
100.0	100.0	100.0	Total Liabilities & Net Worth	100.0	100.0	100.0		100.0	
			INCOME DATA						
100.0	100.0	100.0	Net Sales	100.0	100.0	100.0		100.0	
35.0	35.8	36.8	Gross Profit	50.5	38.8	36.2		36.4	
27.7	28.3	28.5	Operating Expenses	39.3	31.6	28.1		27.3	
7.3	7.6	8.3	Operating Profit	11.2	7.2	8.1		9.2	
1.2	1.3	.9	All Other Expenses (net)	−.7	1.2	.5		.7	
6.1	6.2	7.4	Profit Before Taxes	12.0	6.0	7.6		8.5	
			RATIOS						
2.5	2.6	2.7	Current	3.1	2.9	2.4		3.9	
1.6	1.4	1.6		1.6	1.6	1.2		1.5	
.8	1.0	1.1		1.0	1.1	1.0		1.4	
1.7	2.0	2.0	Quick	1.4	2.3	2.1		3.3	
1.0	1.0	1.1		.8	1.5	1.1		1.1	
.5	.6	.8		.5	.9	.5		1.0	
31 11.6	27 13.3	30 12.1	Sales/Receivables	30 12.2	31 11.8	29 12.6		37 9.9	
46 8.0	45 8.1	45 8.1		64 5.7	41 8.9	48 7.6		45 8.1	
64 5.7	62 5.9	63 5.8		96 3.8	55 6.6	66 5.5		58 6.3	
0 UND	5 68.1	0 999.8	Cost of Sales/Inventory	3 118.0	0 UND	0 UND		11 32.0	
33 11.0	26 13.8	23 16.1		74 4.9	8 43.0	31 11.9		25 14.6	
74 4.9	44 8.3	52 7.0		304 1.2	29 12.6	47 7.8		41 8.9	
11 33.6	17 21.0	16 22.9	Cost of Sales/Payables	19 19.3	11 34.4	15 23.8		23 16.0	
21 17.1	28 12.9	23 15.6		39 9.4	18 20.8	26 14.1		30 12.1	
40 9.2	60 6.1	45 8.2		130 2.8	29 12.4	49 7.5		48 7.6	
5.4	7.0	6.0	Sales/Working Capital	2.4	6.0	7.4		4.5	
10.3	13.4	11.4		7.1	11.3	14.0		11.6	
−18.8	−151.2	73.6		−286.0	UND	−383.6		16.8	
6.3	6.6	10.0	EBIT/Interest	10.3	12.3	12.3		19.1	
(82) 2.7	(72) 2.5	(75) 3.7		(10) 4.9	(27) 3.5	(14) 6.6		5.5	
1.4	1.5	1.9		2.8	1.6	3.3		1.8	
4.0	3.1	5.2	Net Profit + Depr., Dep., Amort./Cur. Mat. L/T/D		9.5				
(35) 2.0	(31) 1.8	(30) 2.0			(10) 3.2				
1.3	1.0	1.4			2.5				
.8	.8	.8	Fixed/Worth	.8	.7	.7		.7	
1.2	1.2	1.1		1.2	1.0	1.0		1.0	
2.2	2.1	1.7		3.4	1.6	2.1		1.3	
.5	.5	.5	Debt/Worth	.3	.4	.6		.4	
1.1	1.3	.8		1.3	.7	.8		.7	
2.6	3.2	2.2		5.3	1.6	2.2		1.7	
29.6	31.1	31.5	% Profit Before Taxes/Tangible Net Worth	40.4	26.2	45.3		28.9	
(78) 13.4	(74) 16.1	(76) 16.2		(10) 15.1	(27) 17.7	16.2		18.7	
4.1	7.2	5.4		4.0	3.8	7.5		7.0	
14.7	13.7	14.6	% Profit Before Taxes/Total Assets	10.6	14.8	16.7		17.5	
5.9	7.0	7.2		9.1	5.9	10.0		6.8	
1.8	2.5	2.8		3.4	1.4	4.5		2.8	
3.7	3.9	3.4	Sales/Net Fixed Assets	2.3	3.0	4.9		3.8	
2.1	2.5	2.3		1.0	2.3	2.9		2.7	
1.4	1.8	1.5		.9	1.5	1.7		1.9	
1.7	1.8	1.9	Sales/Total Assets	1.0	1.8	2.0		2.0	
1.1	1.2	1.2		.6	1.2	1.4		1.3	
.8	1.0	.9		.5	1.0	.9		1.0	
5.9	4.9	5.1	% Depr., Dep., Amort./Sales	6.7	5.8	4.3		5.1	
(79) 8.6	(72) 7.7	(75) 7.2		(10) 9.3	7.3	(13) 7.0		5.9	
12.6	11.1	10.7		13.7	11.4	8.7		8.8	
2.7	3.5	2.5	% Officers', Directors', Owners' Comp/Sales		2.5				
(29) 4.6	(26) 4.9	(25) 4.8			(12) 7.5				
7.3	11.5	10.4			12.2				
707078M	572455M	715598M	Net Sales ($)	6243M	59094M	57094M	38759M	240205M	314203M
801161M	462487M	606506M	Total Assets ($)	10249M	48610M	44845M	67306M	189233M	246263M

Current Data Sorted By Assets | # Postretirement Benefits | Comparative Historical Data

0-500M	500M-2MM	2-10MM	10-50MM	50-100MM	100-250MM	Type of Statement	4/1/90-3/31/91 ALL	4/1/91-3/31/92 ALL
3	3	2	1	1		# Postretirement Benefits		
1	4	10	9	1		Unqualified	22	26
1	11	14	3			Reviewed	34	27
4	12	15				Compiled	34	19
2	1					Tax Returns	1	1
5	7	14	4	1		Other	14	16
	62 (4/1-9/30/94)		57 (10/1/94-3/31/95)					
13	35	53	16	2		NUMBER OF STATEMENTS	105	89
%	%	%	%	%	%	ASSETS	%	%
8.3	4.2	4.2	2.9			Cash & Equivalents	7.2	5.8
16.9	13.4	18.7	17.8			Trade Receivables - (net)	18.4	18.8
19.1	22.9	37.0	27.3			Inventory	29.2	29.3
.5	3.6	2.3	1.9			All Other Current	2.5	1.1
44.8	44.1	62.1	50.0			Total Current	57.4	55.1
46.8	43.6	31.9	36.0			Fixed Assets (net)	32.8	37.2
3.2	1.7	.4	1.8			Intangibles (net)	.7	.4
5.2	10.5	5.6	12.2			All Other Non-Current	9.0	7.3
100.0	100.0	100.0	100.0			Total	100.0	100.0
						LIABILITIES		
21.1	10.3	14.5	4.4			Notes Payable-Short Term	13.5	12.2
4.9	3.0	3.6	2.1			Cur. Mat. -L/T/D	3.4	3.4
9.3	13.0	9.9	15.9			Trade Payables	11.0	12.3
.2	.4	.2	1.8			Income Taxes Payable	1.0	.8
9.9	7.0	4.6	13.6			All Other Current	6.7	6.2
45.4	33.7	32.7	37.9			Total Current	35.5	34.9
30.9	25.4	14.7	10.2			Long Term Debt	17.0	19.3
.4	.8	3.0	3.5			Deferred Taxes	1.4	1.6
14.0	8.0	4.6	1.5			All Other-Non-Current	2.2	2.5
9.3	32.1	45.1	47.0			Net Worth	43.9	41.7
100.0	100.0	100.0	100.0			Total Liabilities & Net Worth	100.0	100.0
						INCOME DATA		
100.0	100.0	100.0	100.0			Net Sales	100.0	100.0
44.2	35.2	33.8	25.7			Gross Profit	34.9	35.2
42.5	30.5	29.5	22.4			Operating Expenses	30.4	31.1
1.7	4.7	4.3	3.2			Operating Profit	4.5	4.1
2.7	.7	1.4	−.2			All Other Expenses (net)	1.1	2.1
−1.0	4.0	2.8	3.4			Profit Before Taxes	3.4	2.0
						RATIOS		
1.9	1.8	3.9	2.9				2.7	2.9
1.5	1.3	1.8	1.4			Current	1.8	1.6
.4	.9	1.2	.8				1.2	1.2
1.2	1.0	1.1	1.0				1.3	1.2
.5	.4	.6	.6			Quick	.7	.7
.2	.2	.4	.2				.4	.4
4 92.6	9 41.4	28 13.2	14 26.5				12 31.0	17 21.2
15 24.4	25 14.7	41 9.0	39 9.3			Sales/Receivables	26 13.8	32 11.5
38 9.5	39 9.4	60 6.1	60 6.1				46 8.0	51 7.1
0 UND	0 UND	68 5.4	0 UND				27 13.6	31 11.6
23 16.0	39 9.4	126 2.9	69 5.3			Cost of Sales/Inventory	68 5.4	64 5.7
140 2.6	114 3.2	243 1.5	122 3.0				130 2.8	183 2.0
0 UND	12 30.3	10 35.4	8 43.4				6 57.7	10 35.3
9 40.3	27 13.3	26 14.2	30 12.3			Cost of Sales/Payables	19 19.7	23 15.7
41 8.8	79 4.6	54 6.8	66 5.5				37 9.8	44 8.3
6.0	8.2	2.6	5.2				4.6	4.8
13.6	22.8	6.9	12.1			Sales/Working Capital	10.2	11.0
−17.4	−39.4	18.8	−15.2				33.1	37.7
3.2	4.4	5.7	7.0				6.1	3.3
1.9	(30) 2.1	(49) 2.2	(14) 4.0			EBIT/Interest	(92) 2.4	(83) 1.8
−.1	1.0	1.0	1.0				1.2	1.2
	5.3	3.2					8.5	4.1
	(11) 1.7	(31) 1.5				Net Profit + Depr., Dep., Amort./Cur. Mat. L /T/D	(44) 2.6	(39) 2.5
	1.2	.5					1.3	1.0
1.2	.5	.4	.3				.4	.4
31.5	1.5	.7	.6			Fixed/Worth	.6	.8
NM	3.5	1.4	1.6				1.4	1.5
2.0	1.1	.6	.5				.6	.7
46.8	2.3	1.5	.9			Debt/Worth	1.1	1.6
NM	4.5	2.5	3.8				3.0	3.0
999.8	55.8	21.3	23.1				26.4	23.2
(10) 146.7	(31) 10.3	7.5	(14) 12.3			% Profit Before Taxes/Tangible Net Worth	(98) 13.1	(88) 7.9
30.3	.5	.3	4.8				2.8	.9
14.7	7.6	8.3	10.4				12.6	8.5
6.5	4.2	3.0	6.1			% Profit Before Taxes/Total Assets	5.5	3.8
−4.2	.4	.1	1.0				.8	.5
13.3	11.6	12.0	28.7				18.1	12.4
5.9	7.3	4.5	3.4			Sales/Net Fixed Assets	7.0	5.6
3.8	2.0	2.0	1.7				3.2	2.1
5.4	2.9	1.9	2.8				3.0	2.9
2.5	2.0	1.3	1.5			Sales/Total Assets	2.3	1.9
1.6	1.1	1.0	.9				1.3	1.0
1.8	1.4	1.1	1.2				1.3	1.1
4.2	(29) 2.1	(51) 3.0	(14) 3.8			% Depr., Dep., Amort./Sales	(99) 2.3	(84) 2.4
7.0	3.7	5.3	6.2				4.6	5.7
	1.1	1.6					2.2	1.9
	(12) 3.1	(17) 2.2				% Officers', Directors', Owners' Comp/Sales	(41) 4.0	(30) 4.5
	7.3	4.8					6.3	7.9
9508M	81775M	359851M	565193M	866044M		Net Sales ($)	1076583M	997125M
2898M	38479M	234829M	366224M	152609M		Total Assets ($)	577012M	655645M

M = $ thousand   MM = $ million
See Pages 1 through 15 for Explanation of Ratios and Data

Comparative Historical Data				Current Data Sorted By Sales					
4	6	10	# Postretirement Benefits	4	2	1	1	1	1
			Type of Statement						
25	20	25	Unqualified	1	2	5	4	5	8
25	23	29	Reviewed	4	9	5	7	2	2
42	30	31	Compiled	3	11	10	7		
1	1	4	Tax Returns	1	2				1
16	20	30	Other	7	6	5	5	4	3
4/1/92-3/31/93	4/1/93-3/31/94	4/1/94-3/31/95		62 (4/1-9/30/94)			57 (10/1/94-3/31/95)		
ALL	ALL	ALL		0-1MM	1-3MM	3-5MM	5-10MM	10-25MM	25MM & OVER
109	94	119	**NUMBER OF STATEMENTS**	16	30	25	23	11	14
%	%	%	**ASSETS**	%	%	%	%	%	%
5.7	4.1	4.5	Cash & Equivalents	4.8	5.7	2.9	5.1	5.5	2.6
20.8	20.8	16.7	Trade Receivables - (net)	11.5	14.2	17.2	16.9	26.6	18.9
28.7	29.5	29.1	Inventory	25.5	23.5	37.9	33.2	25.9	25.1
1.8	2.7	2.6	All Other Current	4.5	1.1	1.8	1.6	6.5	3.5
57.1	57.2	52.8	Total Current	46.3	44.5	59.7	56.8	64.5	50.0
35.8	33.1	37.8	Fixed Assets (net)	40.7	47.7	32.9	34.8	21.7	39.7
.6	1.7	1.3	Intangibles (net)	2.0	2.3	.1	1.6	.2	.8
6.5	8.0	8.0	All Other Non-Current	10.9	5.5	7.2	6.8	13.6	9.5
100.0	100.0	100.0	Total	100.0	100.0	100.0	100.0	100.0	100.0
			LIABILITIES						
16.1	16.2	13.1	Notes Payable-Short Term	15.6	8.5	15.9	15.0	15.0	10.9
2.8	2.5	3.3	Cur. Mat.-L /T/D	5.2	2.5	3.5	3.5	3.5	2.3
13.8	12.0	11.5	Trade Payables	7.4	11.9	12.2	8.2	11.6	19.3
1.8	1.4	.5	Income Taxes Payable	.1	.5	.1	.2	2.8	.6
5.4	7.2	7.4	All Other Current	6.2	6.7	5.8	6.4	6.5	15.6
39.9	39.3	35.8	Total Current	34.4	30.1	37.4	33.1	39.5	48.8
16.0	18.5	18.8	Long Term Debt	41.0	20.8	12.9	17.7	8.5	9.8
1.4	1.7	2.1	Deferred Taxes	.4	1.4	1.9	3.7	3.9	1.9
2.2	3.2	6.1	All Other-Non-Current	13.7	7.4	6.7	3.3	2.2	1.5
40.4	37.3	37.1	Net Worth	10.6	40.3	41.1	42.2	45.9	38.0
100.0	100.0	100.0	Total Liabilities & Net Worth	100.0	100.0	100.0	100.0	100.0	100.0
			INCOME DATA						
100.0	100.0	100.0	Net Sales	100.0	100.0	100.0	100.0	100.0	100.0
34.3	31.4	34.1	Gross Profit	50.7	36.8	27.6	36.5	26.3	23.4
30.0	27.7	30.3	Operating Expenses	43.5	35.1	23.4	30.8	24.8	21.0
4.3	3.7	3.8	Operating Profit	7.1	1.7	4.2	5.7	1.5	2.4
1.6	1.3	1.1	All Other Expenses (net)	2.3	1.4	.6	.9	2.0	-.3
2.7	2.5	2.7	Profit Before Taxes	4.8	.3	3.7	4.9	-.5	2.6
			RATIOS						
2.4	2.2	2.5		1.9	3.9	2.5	3.6	3.4	1.9
1.5	1.5	1.5	Current	1.6	1.5	1.6	1.6	1.5	1.3
1.0	1.0	1.0		.5	.9	1.1	1.0	1.2	.5
1.1	1.1	1.0		1.0	1.6	1.0	.9	1.5	1.0
.7	.6	.6	Quick	.4	.6	.6	.6	.9	.6
.3	.4	.3		.1	.3	.3	.3	.5	.2
12 29.5	22 16.9	14 26.6		3 105.1	11 34.7	22 16.8	26 14.3	21 17.1	0 UND
35 10.5	39 9.4	34 10.8	Sales/Receivables	30 12.1	30 12.1	32 11.4	37 9.8	45 8.2	30 12.1
56 6.5	62 5.9	52 7.0		48 7.6	44 8.3	56 6.5	55 6.6	87 4.2	54 6.7
28 13.2	25 14.4	29 12.8		0 UND	2 146.4	46 8.0	74 4.9	29 12.5	0 UND
87 4.2	78 4.7	79 4.6	Cost of Sales/Inventory	72 5.1	50 7.3	111 3.3	114 3.2	54 6.8	54 6.7
174 2.1	146 2.5	174 2.1		332 1.1	203 1.8	203 1.8	228 1.6	87 4.2	83 4.4
8 45.9	11 31.9	9 42.7		3 108.8	2 155.2	13 28.2	7 55.2	7 50.6	0 UND
24 14.9	25 14.7	25 14.7	Cost of Sales/Payables	21 17.2	24 15.3	32 11.5	26 14.2	18 20.5	30 12.3
49 7.4	50 7.3	55 6.6		107 3.4	56 6.5	53 6.9	53 6.9	54 6.8	61 6.0
6.0	5.1	4.1		4.4	3.5	3.3	3.3	5.0	6.4
11.9	10.0	11.3	Sales/Working Capital	8.3	17.9	8.1	8.7	7.9	25.3
240.1	307.4	357.0		NM	-27.4	89.2	82.2	16.6	-9.8
(98) 4.8	(90) 4.5	(108) 5.5		(15) 2.6	(26) 6.2	(23) 4.4	5.4		(12) 8.5
2.8	2.6	2.2	EBIT/Interest	2.3	1.6	2.2	2.2		5.7
1.4	.6	1.0		1.1	-.3	1.2	1.0		2.6
(40) 5.3	(46) 6.1	(55) 4.0				(14) 6.1	(14) 6.3		
3.0	3.2	1.7	Net Profit + Depr., Dep., Amort./Cur. Mat. L/T/D			1.7	2.2		
1.6	1.0	.6				1.0	1.0		
.4	.4	.4		.9	.5	.3	.4	.3	.3
.8	.8	.9	Fixed/Worth	9.7	1.3	.7	.7	.4	.9
1.6	1.8	2.3		NM	3.8	1.5	2.2	.9	1.7
.8	.8	.8		2.4	.4	.6	.7	.8	.7
1.4	2.0	1.7	Debt/Worth	14.4	1.7	1.7	1.6	1.0	1.2
3.2	3.9	3.7		NM	4.3	3.3	3.6	2.2	6.1
(102) 31.5	(88) 29.5	(109) 31.7		(12) 381.3	(27) 29.2	26.6	(22) 31.6	13.7	(12) 34.5
12.8	14.1	10.9	% Profit Before Taxes/Tangible Net Worth	72.4	7.5	10.9	8.7	-.2	14.8
1.4	-.7	2.6		11.5	-1.7	3.8	.8	-7.0	10.4
9.8	9.2	8.9		11.9	7.8	7.7	10.6	11.1	12.6
5.6	4.4	4.2	% Profit Before Taxes/Total Assets	6.7	3.9	4.8	3.5	-.1	6.3
1.0	-.9	.1		.9	-3.2	.9	.0	-2.6	3.8
19.1	14.2	11.9		11.3	8.4	12.8	7.9	18.1	84.7
6.8	5.9	4.9	Sales/Net Fixed Assets	5.0	3.4	7.3	4.3	11.6	7.5
2.6	3.0	2.2		3.0	1.6	3.2	2.1	4.4	2.0
3.3	2.9	2.7		2.3	2.6	2.7	2.1	3.6	3.3
1.7	1.9	1.6	Sales/Total Assets	1.2	1.6	1.7	1.3	2.3	2.1
1.2	1.1	1.0		.8	.9	1.1	1.1	1.5	1.3
(100) 1.2	(88) 1.5	(108) 1.5		(14) 1.3	(27) 1.8	(24) 1.2	(21) 2.0	(10) .9	(12) .7
2.5	2.9	3.0	% Depr., Dep., Amort./Sales	3.1	3.9	2.2	3.3	1.8	3.0
4.8	4.9	5.4		7.3	7.3	3.2	5.5	4.5	5.5
(34) 2.6	(33) 2.1	(38) 1.7			(13) 1.4	(10) 1.4			
5.3	3.8	3.2	% Officers', Directors', Owners' Comp/Sales		5.8	3.1			
7.3	6.4	7.4			9.1	4.2			
1197371M	1476163M	1882371M	Net Sales ($)	7019M	57507M	102047M	165284M	151738M	1398776M
775536M	981043M	795039M	Total Assets ($)	6436M	47824M	71756M	129382M	98691M	440950M

M = $ thousand   MM = $ million
See Pages 1 through 15 for Explanation of Ratios and Data

PART IV

CONTRACTOR INDUSTRIES

As in previous editions, this section
contains data sorted only by revenue.

Current Data Sorted By Revenue | **Comparative Historical Data**

Postretirement Benefits

	0-1MM	1-10MM	10-50MM	50 & OVER	ALL	Type of Statement	4/1/90-3/31/91 ALL	4/1/91-3/31/92 ALL	4/1/92-3/31/93 ALL	4/1/93-3/31/94 ALL	4/1/94-3/31/95 ALL
			2		2	(# Postretirement Benefits)			2	5	2
	2	19	21	7	49	Unqualified	63	59	53	54	49
	2	16	1		19	Reviewed	18	17	19	10	19
	1				1	Compiled	8	1	3		1
		2			2	Tax Returns					2
	1	7	1	2	11	Other	13	6	6	7	11

23 (4/1-9/30/94)   59 (10/1/94-3/31/95)

	0-1MM	1-10MM	10-50MM	50 & OVER	ALL		4/1/90-3/31/91 ALL	4/1/91-3/31/92 ALL	4/1/92-3/31/93 ALL	4/1/93-3/31/94 ALL	4/1/94-3/31/95 ALL
NUMBER OF STATEMENTS	6	44	23	9	82		102	83	81	71	82
ASSETS	%	%	%	%	%		%	%	%	%	%
Cash & Equivalents		17.6	17.5		18.6		18.2	17.7	18.8	18.8	18.6
A/R - Progress Billings		33.8	26.4		30.4		26.5	26.9	28.3	31.0	30.4
A/R - Current Retention		3.8	5.0		4.4		5.1	5.4	4.5	5.5	4.4
Inventory		2.6	2.5		2.3		5.5	3.0	1.6	2.6	2.3
Cost & Est. Earnings In Excess of Billings		2.6	4.2		2.9		2.7	4.8	4.3	4.6	2.9
All Other Current		3.7	4.0		3.8		4.0	3.6	4.4	4.9	3.8
Total Current		64.1	59.6		62.5		61.9	61.4	61.9	67.3	62.5
Fixed Assets (net)		28.0	33.4		29.2		29.8	30.1	28.7	24.8	29.2
Joint Ventures & Investments		.8	.8		1.1		1.2	1.3	1.7	1.3	1.1
Intangibles (net)		.9	.4		.7		.3	.3	1.1	.2	.7
All Other Non-Current		6.2	5.8		6.5		6.8	6.9	6.5	6.4	6.5
Total		100.0	100.0		100.0		100.0	100.0	100.0	100.0	100.0
LIABILITIES											
Notes Payable - Short Term		5.2	2.8		3.8		5.8	4.5	4.7	5.8	3.8
A/P - Trade		18.1	19.7		18.3		17.0	16.3	18.1	21.4	18.3
A/P - Retention		.4	2.1		1.3		1.0	1.2	1.0	2.3	1.3
Billings in Excess of Costs & Est. Earnings		2.9	4.4		3.8		3.9	3.7	4.3	3.6	3.8
Income Taxes Payable		.3	.2		.3		.7	.6	.6	.7	.3
Cur. Mat. - L/T/D		4.7	4.0		4.2		4.6	4.9	4.3	3.1	4.2
All Other Current		6.3	6.5		6.0		7.2	5.5	5.5	4.9	6.0
Total Current		38.0	39.7		37.7		40.2	36.6	38.5	41.8	37.7
Long Term Debt		12.7	12.8		12.5		10.5	11.5	11.0	11.3	12.5
Deferred Taxes		1.5	1.6		1.4		1.8	1.7	1.6	1.7	1.4
All Other Non-Current		1.8	2.1		1.7		1.7	1.5	2.1	.9	1.7
Net Worth		46.0	43.8		46.6		45.9	48.6	46.7	44.3	46.6
Total Liabilities & Net Worth		100.0	100.0		100.0		100.0	100.0	100.0	100.0	100.0
INCOME DATA											
Contract Revenues		100.0	100.0		100.0		100.0	100.0	100.0	100.0	100.0
Gross Profit		18.4	12.6		16.0		15.3	15.3	18.0	13.9	16.0
Operating Expenses		16.0	9.6		13.4		13.0	13.1	16.8	12.8	13.4
Operating Profit		2.5	3.0		2.6		2.3	2.1	1.2	1.1	2.6
All Other Expenses (net)		.1	.4		.1		-.1	-.4	-.1	-.6	.1
Profit Before Taxes		2.4	2.6		2.4		2.4	2.5	1.4	1.7	2.4
RATIOS											
Current		2.2	1.7		2.2		2.3	2.6	2.3	2.1	2.2
		1.7	1.5		1.6		1.5	1.6	1.5	1.6	1.6
		1.3	1.2		1.2		1.3	1.2	1.2	1.2	1.2
Receivables/Payables		3.5	2.1		3.0		2.9	3.3	2.7	2.8	3.0
	(43)	2.2	1.7	(80)	1.8		1.8	2.1	1.8	1.6	(80) 1.8
		1.5	1.0		1.2		1.4	1.4	1.2	1.0	1.2
Revenues/Receivables	39 9.4		31 11.9		37 9.9		35 10.5	35 10.4	38 9.5	42 8.6	37 9.9
	54 6.8		45 8.1		51 7.2		51 7.2	47 7.8	53 6.9	57 6.4	51 7.2
	85 4.3		62 5.9		74 4.9		65 5.6	64 5.7	65 5.6	74 4.9	74 4.9
Cost of Revenues/Payables	17 21.6		16 22.5		17 21.5		19 19.1	19 19.7	22 16.7	26 14.0	17 21.5
	34 10.8		33 11.2		33 11.0		28 13.1	27 13.5	34 10.6	39 9.3	33 11.0
	55 6.6		50 7.3		51 7.2		40 9.2	41 8.9	54 6.7	66 5.5	51 7.2
Revenues/Working Capital		4.8	9.8		5.8		6.7	5.9	5.8	5.8	5.8
		9.1	14.3		10.4		12.1	9.8	12.0	11.1	10.4
		17.3	29.5		22.1		26.9	27.2	32.6	20.0	22.1
EBIT/Interest		8.3	12.1		8.6		9.9	9.5	9.7	12.4	8.6
	(39)	2.7	6.3	(77)	4.8	(91)	3.4	(76) 3.7	(71) 3.8	(66) 4.3	(77) 4.8
		1.0	1.8		1.5		1.5	1.5	1.0	1.2	1.5
Net Profit + Depr., Dep., Amort./Cur. Mat. L /T/D		4.4	5.6		5.3		6.4	3.5	4.0	10.4	5.3
	(24)	1.8	(15) 2.6	(47)	2.4	(57)	2.2	(52) 1.8	(51) 1.6	(35) 3.8	(47) 2.4
		.8	1.5		1.2		1.0	.9	.8	1.2	1.2
Fixed/Worth		.3	.5		.4		.4	.4	.4	.4	.4
		.6	.8		.6		.7	.6	.6	.6	.6
		1.0	1.2		1.0		1.0	1.0	1.1	.8	1.0
Debt/Worth		.7	.8		.7		.6	.6	.8	.7	.7
		1.2	1.6		1.3		1.3	1.2	1.3	1.4	1.3
		2.5	2.2		2.2		2.1	2.0	2.1	2.2	2.2
% Profit Before Taxes/Tangible Net Worth		18.8	30.3		24.1		23.2	29.9	21.7	21.5	24.1
	(43)	11.2	14.5	(81)	11.9	(101)	10.8	15.2	(79) 7.4	(70) 8.7	(81) 11.9
		.6	3.8		2.4		2.0	1.9	-.3	1.0	2.4
% Profit Before Taxes/Total Assets		8.3	9.9		9.4		10.6	13.6	9.7	9.0	9.4
		3.9	5.7		5.1		4.7	6.3	3.9	3.8	5.1
		.1	1.7		1.1		.9	1.1	-.3	.5	1.1
% Depr., Dep., Amort./Revenues		1.8	1.7		1.7		1.4	.9	1.4	1.4	1.7
	(43)	3.0	2.6	(79)	3.0	(89)	2.5	(76) 2.3	(76) 2.5	(65) 2.6	(79) 3.0
		4.9	3.8		4.3		4.2	3.8	4.4	3.6	4.3
% Officers', Directors', Owners' Comp/Revenues		2.1	.9		1.8		2.0	2.1	2.3	1.8	1.8
	(29)	3.2	(11) 1.9	(42)	2.5	(48)	3.4	(33) 3.1	(36) 3.6	(28) 2.6	(42) 2.5
					3.9		6.4	5.3	5.6	5.2	3.9
Contract Revenues ($)	4035M	209916M	491213M	1008337M	1713501M		4218198M	1812640M	1716306M	2219162M	1713501M
Total Assets ($)	3439M	103494M	214522M	428228M	749683M		1960980M	625944M	876394M	928438M	749683M

M = $ thousand   MM = $ million
See Pages 1 through 15 for Explanation of Ratios and Data

Type of Statement

	Current Data Sorted By Revenue						Comparative Historical Data				
	1	2		1	4				1	1	4
# Postretirement Benefits		1	2	1	1	4					
Unqualified							3	6	3	2	4
Reviewed	2	14			17		15	8	17	17	17
Compiled	6	14			20		18	14	13	15	20
Tax Returns	1	1			2		.	.	1	1	2
Other	1.	5			6		9	1	8	5	6

11 (4/1-9/30/94) 38 (10/1/94-3/31/95)

Financial Data

	0-1MM	1-10MM	10-50MM	50 & OVER	ALL		4/1/90-3/31/91 ALL	4/1/91-3/31/92 ALL	4/1/92-3/31/93 ALL	4/1/93-3/31/94 ALL	4/1/94-3/31/95 ALL
NUMBER OF STATEMENTS	10	35	3	1	49		45	30	42	41	49
ASSETS	%	%	%	%	%		%	%	%	%	%
Cash & Equivalents	11.7	7.2			9.0		10.2	8.9	12.6	13.7	9.0
A/R - Progress Billings	28.4	44.7			42.2		32.9	35.0	35.9	32.7	42.2
A/R - Current Retention	.0	.6			.6		3.2	2.3	3.6	3.3	.6
Inventory	13.5	12.2			12.0		10.5	13.4	11.7	8.6	12.0
Cost & Est. Earnings In Excess of Billings	.0	2.7			2.2		1.4	.8	2.4	3.2	2.2
All Other Current	.9	5.7			4.5		6.6	4.7	3.5	5.7	4.5
Total Current	54.5	73.1			70.5		64.9	65.1	69.9	67.2	70.5
Fixed Assets (net)	37.0	14.7			18.3		22.1	22.5	18.4	21.3	18.3
Joint Ventures & Investments	.0	1.1			.8		.6	.5	.3	.6	.8
Intangibles (net)	.0	2.3			1.7		2.0	.4	1.3	1.5	1.7
All Other Non-Current	8.5	8.9			8.7		10.5	11.5	10.1	9.5	8.7
Total	100.0	100.0			100.0		100.0	100.0	100.0	100.0	100.0
LIABILITIES											
Notes Payable - Short Term	12.9	10.9			11.1		13.7	15.0	14.1	16.4	11.1
A/P - Trade	27.3	24.2			24.9		20.0	19.7	21.5	20.7	24.9
A/P - Retention	.0	.5			.6		.0	.7	.1	.0	.6
Billings in Excess of Costs & Est. Earnings	.4	2.5			2.4		2.2	2.6	2.1	1.6	2.4
Income Taxes Payable	3.4	.4			1.0		.4	.7	.9	1.0	1.0
Cur. Mat. - L/T/D	3.0	1.7			1.9		3.5	3.2	3.6	2.6	1.9
All Other Current	13.5	12.4			14.1		9.1	11.3	7.8	7.3	14.1
Total Current	60.5	52.5			56.0		49.0	53.2	50.1	49.5	56.0
Long Term Debt	32.5	8.6			12.9		15.2	13.0	7.5	12.8	12.9
Deferred Taxes	.0	.6			.5		.6	1.1	1.0	.4	.5
All Other Non-Current	.4	2.7			2.0		4.2	3.9	2.3	4.5	2.0
Net Worth	6.6	35.5			28.6		31.1	28.8	39.0	32.8	28.6
Total Liabilities & Net Worth	100.0	100.0			100.0		100.0	100.0	100.0	100.0	100.0
INCOME DATA											
Contract Revenues	100.0	100.0			100.0		100.0	100.0	100.0	100.0	100.0
Gross Profit	31.3	26.1			26.0		25.2	24.5	24.1	26.7	26.0
Operating Expenses	28.5	21.9			22.2		22.8	22.5	21.2	23.0	22.2
Operating Profit	2.8	4.3			3.8		2.4	1.9	2.9	3.7	3.8
All Other Expenses (net)	3.2	.5			1.0		.9	.9	.4	1.1	1.0
Profit Before Taxes	-.4	3.7			2.7		1.5	1.0	2.5	2.6	2.7
RATIOS											
Current	2.4	1.9			1.9		2.3	1.9	1.9	1.9	1.9
	1.0	1.4			1.3		1.5	1.4	1.4	1.3	1.3
	.5	1.0			1.0		1.0	1.0	1.1	1.1	1.0
Receivables/Payables	1.7	3.4			3.2		3.3	2.9	3.7	4.7	3.2
	1.3	1.9			1.8		(39) 1.8	1.7	1.8	(39) 1.6	1.8
	.2	1.1			1.1		1.3	.8	1.1	.9	1.1
Revenues/Receivables	(0) UND	(33) 11.2			(27) 13.3		(14) 25.3	(16) 22.9	(21) 17.0	(15) 24.2	(27) 13.3
	(23) 15.6	(49) 7.5			(45) 8.2		(33) 11.0	(45) 8.1	(42) 8.7	(36) 10.1	(45) 8.2
	(46) 8.0	(65) 5.6			(64) 5.7		(60) 6.1	(73) 5.0	(58) 6.3	(60) 6.1	(64) 5.7
Cost of Revenues/Payables	(13) 27.9	(19) 19.2			(16) 22.9		(7) 50.3	(19) 18.9	(13) 29.1	(8) 46.5	(16) 22.9
	(41) 8.9	(27) 13.7			(31) 11.8		(24) 15.0	(29) 12.8	(20) 18.4	(27) 13.5	(31) 11.8
	(55) 6.6	(49) 7.5			(51) 7.2		(40) 9.2	(44) 8.3	(45) 8.2	(39) 9.4	(51) 7.2
Revenues/Working Capital	8.9	7.8			8.2		10.7	8.7	10.7	9.6	8.2
	255.7	19.5			21.2		24.7	18.0	15.0	19.1	21.2
	-9.8	167.0			271.8		147.7	NM	87.0	71.0	271.8
EBIT/Interest	(31) 19.6			(43) 16.4			(39) 8.2	(28) 8.4	(34) 10.5	(38) 9.1	(43) 16.4
	4.5			5.4			2.9	1.9	3.5	3.4	5.4
	1.5			1.9			.6	1.0	1.2	1.5	1.9
Net Profit + Depr., Dep., Amort./Cur. Mat. L/T/D	(19)						(19) 3.8	(11) 3.4	(20) 4.9	(17) 6.2	
							2.3	1.3	2.0	4.7	
							-.1	.3	.7	1.6	
Fixed/Worth	.7	.1			.1		.2	.1	.2	.2	.1
	2.9	.4			.5		.6	.5	.4	.4	.5
	-.9	1.2			2.9		1.2	1.4	.8	1.2	2.9
Debt/Worth	2.3	.8			1.1		.9	1.0	.7	.6	1.1
	3.6	2.0			2.6		2.3	2.4	1.8	2.2	2.6
	-5.3	5.7			17.7		13.1	3.9	3.6	4.8	17.7
% Profit Before Taxes/Tangible Net Worth	(32) 74.1			(43) 76.3			(38) 59.2	(26) 18.6	(40) 40.9	(37) 57.0	(43) 76.3
	41.5			40.6			18.8	10.6	16.2	16.2	40.6
	10.4			9.9			4.5	-.4	5.8	5.4	9.9
% Profit Before Taxes/Total Assets	32.1	20.7			22.3		18.8	8.7	12.6	14.6	22.3
	18.9	6.5			7.7		5.5	3.8	5.4	6.1	7.7
	-7.1	1.2			1.7		-.9	-.1	1.8	1.0	1.7
% Depr., Dep., Amort./Revenues	(31) .5			(43) .5			(38) .6	(28) .5	(37) .4	(35) .5	(43) .5
	.8			.9			1.4	1.0	.8	.9	.9
	1.2			1.3			2.2	2.4	1.3	1.8	1.3
% Officers', Directors', Owners' Comp/Revenues	(19) 2.3			(25) 2.2			(20) 2.6	(15) 4.0	(25) 4.4	(22) 2.5	(25) 2.2
	3.6			3.6			4.4	6.2	5.7	4.5	3.6
	5.3			6.0			8.3	10.1	8.9	6.7	6.0
Contract Revenues ($)	5432M	144498M	44522M	121864M	316316M		168665M	150398M	147081M	145756M	316316M
Total Assets ($)	1472M	45108M	14029M	21920M	82529M		56969M	70545M	51131M	44260M	82529M

M = $ thousand   MM = $ million
See Pages 1 through 15 for Explanation of Ratios and Data

CONTRACTORS—CONCRETE WORK. SIC# 1771

Current Data Sorted By Revenue						Comparative Historical Data				
1	7	2		10	# Postretirement Benefits / Type of Statement			4	4	10
1	22	10	1	34	Unqualified	41	40	32	41	34
7	49	9		65	Reviewed	56	54	53	72	65
20	32			52	Compiled	42	36	45	52	52
2	1			3	Tax Returns	2	4	5	3	3
3	19	1	1	24	Other	20	16	18	19	24
45 (4/1-9/30/94)			133 (10/1/94-3/31/95)			4/1/90-3/31/91	4/1/91-3/31/92	4/1/92-3/31/93	4/1/93-3/31/94	4/1/94-3/31/95
0-1MM	1-10MM	10-50MM	50 & OVER	ALL		ALL	ALL	ALL	ALL	ALL
33	123	20	2	178	NUMBER OF STATEMENTS	161	150	153	187	178
%	%	%	%	%	**ASSETS**	%	%	%	%	%
13.6	11.1	10.8		11.4	Cash & Equivalents	9.7	10.5	10.8	11.8	11.4
30.3	41.0	45.7		39.5	A/R - Progress Billings	38.3	39.7	35.4	39.4	39.5
2.2	3.7	7.8		3.8	A/R - Current Retention	5.9	4.0	3.7	4.4	3.8
1.0	2.3	2.3		2.2	Inventory	3.2	2.9	2.9	2.7	2.2
.4	1.5	1.8		1.3	Cost & Est. Earnings In Excess of Billings	2.7	2.7	1.4	1.6	1.3
3.1	3.0	.5		2.8	All Other Current	3.2	3.4	3.6	2.9	2.8
50.5	62.6	68.9		61.0	Total Current	62.9	63.2	57.8	62.9	61.0
38.7	29.6	22.3		30.4	Fixed Assets (net)	29.4	29.6	34.2	28.4	30.4
.9	.6	2.7		.9	Joint Ventures & Investments	1.2	1.0	1.4	1.3	.9
2.7	1.1	.6		1.5	Intangibles (net)	1.0	.7	.7	1.0	1.5
7.2	6.1	5.5		6.3	All Other Non-Current	5.5	5.5	5.9	6.4	6.3
100.0	100.0	100.0		100.0	Total	100.0	100.0	100.0	100.0	100.0
					LIABILITIES					
6.3	7.9	6.6		7.5	Notes Payable - Short Term	10.4	11.1	7.9	7.7	7.5
12.0	20.1	23.9		19.1	A/P - Trade	20.2	20.0	19.4	18.6	19.1
.0	.4	.7		.3	A/P - Retention	.4	.4	.2	.2	.3
.5	2.3	3.8		2.1	Billings in Excess of Costs & Est. Earnings	1.8	1.4	1.5	1.6	2.1
.5	.8	1.2		.8	Income Taxes Payable	1.0	.8	.6	1.1	.8
6.1	5.3	4.5		5.3	Cur. Mat. - L/T/D	6.0	5.7	5.3	4.7	5.3
5.9	6.9	12.1		7.4	All Other Current	6.9	7.4	5.4	7.0	7.4
31.3	43.6	52.8		42.5	Total Current	46.6	46.9	40.3	41.0	42.5
15.5	11.7	11.7		12.4	Long Term Debt	12.0	13.0	14.2	11.4	12.4
.7	1.5	.9		1.2	Deferred Taxes	1.6	1.1	1.2	1.6	1.2
2.7	1.4	.2		1.5	All Other Non-Current	1.0	2.2	1.0	2.8	1.5
49.7	41.8	34.4		42.3	Net Worth	38.8	36.9	43.3	43.2	42.3
100.0	100.0	100.0		100.0	Total Liabilities & Net Worth	100.0	100.0	100.0	100.0	100.0
					INCOME DATA					
100.0	100.0	100.0		100.0	Contract Revenues	100.0	100.0	100.0	100.0	100.0
34.3	26.0	15.1		26.2	Gross Profit	24.5	23.5	27.5	25.5	26.2
28.5	22.0	10.7		21.8	Operating Expenses	21.9	22.2	24.5	21.5	21.8
5.8	4.0	4.4		4.4	Operating Profit	2.7	1.3	3.0	4.0	4.4
1.3	.4	-.1		.5	All Other Expenses (net)	.5	.8	.3	.7	.5
4.5	3.6	4.5		3.8	Profit Before Taxes	2.1	.5	2.7	3.3	3.8
					RATIOS					
3.4	1.9	1.9		2.1	Current	1.9	2.1	2.3	2.4	2.1
1.7	1.4	1.4		1.4		1.4	1.5	1.5	1.6	1.4
1.0	1.1	1.0		1.1		1.0	1.0	1.1	1.1	1.1
(32) 7.7	(120) 4.1	3.3		(174) 4.1	Receivables/Payables	(159) 4.0	(149) 4.5	(150) 3.6	(182) 4.3	(174) 4.1
3.3	2.1	2.6		2.4		2.2	2.4	2.1	2.5	2.4
2.3	1.5	1.5		1.6		1.5	1.3	1.4	1.6	1.6
18 19.9	39 9.3	47 7.8		35 10.5	Revenues/Receivables	37 9.9	38 9.6	33 10.9	36 10.1	35 10.5
33 10.9	58 6.3	68 5.4		52 7.0		59 6.2	56 6.5	46 7.9	66 5.5	52 7.0
68 5.4	76 4.8	91 4.0		74 4.9		78 4.7	81 4.5	74 4.9	81 4.5	74 4.9
3 106.0	15 23.6	20 18.0		14 27.0	Cost of Revenues/Payables	17 21.1	17 21.4	15 24.9	15 24.3	14 27.0
15 24.3	31 11.9	33 10.9		29 12.4		31 11.9	32 11.4	30 12.3	31 11.9	29 12.4
40 9.2	52 7.0	49 7.4		47 7.8		47 7.8	51 7.2	51 7.1	52 7.0	47 7.8
5.9	9.0	8.4		8.4	Revenues/Working Capital	9.0	7.7	8.6	6.9	8.4
18.5	15.3	19.0		16.2		16.5	13.0	15.3	12.3	16.2
NM	49.5	-108.4		64.2		915.9	265.7	81.2	52.4	64.2
(29) 20.7	(115) 10.9	(19) 15.1		(165) 12.4	EBIT/Interest	(148) 7.2	(139) 6.2	(138) 10.7	(170) 9.0	(165) 12.4
5.3	4.7	10.1		4.9		3.1	2.4	3.0	3.6	4.9
1.7	2.0	2.2		2.1		1.2	.0	1.5	1.5	2.1
(10) 5.6	(59) 4.1	(10) 5.2		(81) 4.2	Net Profit + Depr., Dep., Amort./Cur. Mat. L./T/D	(87) 5.4	(74) 3.9	(66) 5.0	(102) 4.7	(81) 4.2
2.7	2.2	2.4		2.3		2.1	2.0	1.9	2.1	2.3
.5	1.4	.8		1.3		1.1	.4	1.0	1.1	1.3
.3	.4	.3		.4	Fixed/Worth	.3	.4	.3	.3	.4
.8	.7	.6		.7		.7	.7	.7	.6	.7
3.0	1.2	1.7		1.3		1.3	1.7	1.3	1.3	1.3
.4	.8	.9		.7	Debt/Worth	.8	.8	.6	.7	.7
.7	1.5	2.2		1.4		1.5	1.7	1.2	1.5	1.4
4.8	2.4	7.3		3.0		3.0	4.1	3.1	2.6	3.0
(30) 39.2	(121) 52.0	57.1		(173) 51.7	% Profit Before Taxes/Tangible Net Worth	(156) 39.0	(139) 30.7	(143) 33.2	(181) 38.3	(173) 51.7
24.2	25.4	33.3		25.7		18.0	7.6	12.7	13.6	25.7
10.4	7.8	15.6		9.3		2.5	-4.6	1.5	2.6	9.3
21.1	18.6	25.7		18.8	% Profit Before Taxes/Total Assets	13.1	11.2	14.3	15.7	18.8
9.5	9.1	10.0		9.1		4.9	2.9	5.1	5.7	9.1
3.4	2.8	4.0		3.2		.6	-3.1	.7	1.2	3.2
(28) 2.3	(118) 1.5	1.2		(168) 1.5	% Depr., Dep., Amort./Revenues	(148) 1.2	(141) 1.1	(142) 1.4	(165) 1.6	(168) 1.5
3.4	2.4	1.5		2.5		2.5	2.5	2.9	2.5	2.5
4.9	3.7	2.2		3.8		4.3	3.6	5.3	4.5	3.8
(18) 6.3	(84) 2.5			(108) 2.9	% Officers', Directors', Owners' Comp/Revenues	(87) 2.1	(81) 2.0	(91) 2.9	(105) 2.1	(108) 2.9
9.9	4.5			4.8		4.4	4.3	4.8	4.7	4.8
11.1	8.0			8.5		7.4	6.6	7.4	8.0	8.5
19913M	464465M	352245M	262461M	1099084M	Contract Revenues ($)	970627M	717873M	693291M	1083401M	1099084M
10496M	172186M	144442M	111249M	438373M	Total Assets ($)	427188M	291039M	300434M	449962M	438373M

M = $ thousand   MM = $ million
See Pages 1 through 15 for Explanation of Ratios and Data

Current Data Sorted By Revenue / Comparative Historical Data

10	33	11	5	59	# Postretirement Benefits			11	28	59
					Type of Statement					
2	61	39	3	105	Unqualified			184	147	116	101	105
34	210	25		269	Reviewed	277	256	240	259	269
35	77	3		115	Compiled	128	118	111	97	115
4	9			13	Tax Returns	4	7	6	10	13
11	45	14	4	74	Other	73	68	54	79	74

222 (4/1-9/30/94)   354 (10/1/94-3/31/95)

0-1MM	1-10MM	10-50MM	50 & OVER	ALL		4/1/90-3/31/91 ALL	4/1/91-3/31/92 ALL	4/1/92-3/31/93 ALL	4/1/93-3/31/94 ALL	4/1/94-3/31/95 ALL
86	402	81	7	576	**NUMBER OF STATEMENTS**	666	596	527	546	576
%	%	%	%	%	**ASSETS**	%	%	%	%	%
15.9	12.2	9.1		12.3	Cash & Equivalents	13.5	12.8	12.5	12.5	12.3
36.1	46.6	52.5		45.8	A/R - Progress Billings	43.0	42.5	44.1	42.6	45.8
2.1	4.1	6.4		4.1	A/R - Current Retention	5.5	4.9	4.0	5.8	4.1
11.0	8.3	3.2		8.0	Inventory	8.3	8.2	8.1	8.2	8.0
2.3	4.4	6.8		4.5	Cost & Est. Earnings In Excess of Billings	4.5	4.7	4.7	4.7	4.5
2.3	3.7	4.0		3.5	All Other Current	3.5	3.8	3.9	3.9	3.5
69.7	79.4	82.0		78.2	Total Current	78.3	76.7	77.4	77.7	78.2
21.1	14.3	11.7		15.0	Fixed Assets (net)	15.3	15.8	15.5	15.5	15.0
.9	.8	1.1		.9	Joint Ventures & Investments	.6	.9	.8	.5	.9
.2	.5	1.6		.7	Intangibles (net)	.4	.6	.7	.5	.7
8.2	4.9	3.6		5.3	All Other Non-Current	5.4	5.9	5.6	5.7	5.3
100.0	100.0	100.0		100.0	Total	100.0	100.0	100.0	100.0	100.0
					LIABILITIES					
12.2	9.5	9.1		9.9	Notes Payable - Short Term	9.6	8.9	9.9	10.1	9.9
15.3	20.1	23.0		19.7	A/P - Trade	19.4	19.4	19.9	19.7	19.7
.0	.2	.0		.2	A/P - Retention	.2	.2	.1	.1	.2
2.0	4.1	6.5		4.2	Billings in Excess of Costs & Est. Earnings	4.1	3.6	3.7	3.4	4.2
.5	.7	1.3		.7	Income Taxes Payable	1.3	.9	1.0	.8	.7
4.2	3.0	2.3		3.1	Cur. Mat. - L/T/D	3.4	3.3	3.1	3.3	3.1
9.1	10.5	11.3		10.5	All Other Current	8.2	8.4	8.2	9.6	10.5
43.4	48.2	53.5		48.2	Total Current	46.2	44.6	45.9	46.9	48.2
11.8	6.7	5.5		7.3	Long Term Debt	7.8	7.7	8.0	7.1	7.3
.6	1.2	.8		1.1	Deferred Taxes	1.0	1.0	1.4	1.1	1.1
2.6	2.1	1.1		2.0	All Other Non-Current	1.3	1.7	1.6	2.2	2.0
41.5	41.8	39.1		41.3	Net Worth	43.7	44.9	43.1	42.7	41.3
100.0	100.0	100.0		100.0	Total Liabilities & Net Worth	100.0	100.0	100.0	100.0	100.0
					INCOME DATA					
100.0	100.0	100.0		100.0	Contract Revenues	100.0	100.0	100.0	100.0	100.0
37.0	23.3	16.4		24.3	Gross Profit	24.4	24.0	23.4	23.9	24.3
33.4	20.5	13.1		21.3	Operating Expenses	21.2	22.2	21.8	21.2	21.3
3.6	2.8	3.4		3.0	Operating Profit	3.2	1.8	1.7	2.6	3.0
.8	.4	.5		.5	All Other Expenses (net)	.4	.3	.3	.3	.5
2.7	2.4	2.9		2.5	Profit Before Taxes	2.9	1.5	1.4	2.3	2.5
					RATIOS					
2.7	2.5	1.9		2.4	Current	2.4	2.6	2.6	2.4	2.4
1.8	1.7	1.5		1.7		1.7	1.7	1.7	1.7	1.7
1.2	1.3	1.3		1.3		1.3	1.3	1.3	1.3	1.3
5.7	4.5	3.9		4.5	Receivables/Payables	4.1	4.3	4.1	4.3	4.5
(79) 2.7	(398) 2.6	2.6		(565) 2.6		(657) 2.6	(590) 2.7	(524) 2.6	(535) 2.8	(565) 2.6
1.5	1.9	1.8		1.8		1.9	1.8	1.7	1.7	1.8
24 15.2	44 8.3	56 6.5		43 8.5	Revenues/Receivables	41 8.8	41 8.9	42 8.7	44 8.3	43 8.5
44 8.3	62 5.9	68 5.4		62 5.9		56 6.5	54 6.7	58 6.3	59 6.2	62 5.9
74 4.9	79 4.6	83 4.4		81 4.5		74 4.9	73 5.0	76 4.8	76 4.8	81 4.5
10 38.4	17 21.3	20 18.6		17 22.0	Cost of Revenues/Payables	16 22.3	16 22.2	18 20.6	16 22.9	17 22.0
24 15.1	29 12.5	30 12.3		28 12.9		27 13.7	26 14.2	13.1	28 13.0	28 12.9
38 9.5	44 8.3	40 9.1		42 8.7		42 8.6	42 8.7	43 8.4	46 7.9	42 8.7
4.9	6.3	8.0		6.5	Revenues/Working Capital	6.3	6.1	5.8	6.2	6.5
9.3	9.9	12.0		10.2		10.3	9.6	10.1	9.7	10.2
49.4	17.9	18.1		18.4		17.7	17.7	18.2	20.8	18.4
8.0	15.0	25.1		13.7	EBIT/Interest	12.3	10.1	10.7	12.0	13.7
(72) 3.0	(353) 5.6	(74) 7.3		(505) 5.0		(585) 4.2	(537) 3.1	(471) 3.4	(475) 4.1	(505) 5.0
-.3	1.5	2.8		1.6		1.6	.9	.8	1.0	1.6
5.7	5.6	7.9		6.0	Net Profit + Depr., Dep., Amort./Cur. Mat. L./T/D	7.2	5.5	5.8	6.2	6.0
(19) 3.2	(179) 2.5	(39) 5.3		(239) 2.8		(322) 2.9	(284) 2.3	(242) 2.4	(285) 2.2	(239) 2.8
.2	.6	1.8		.8		1.0	.8	.2	.4	.8
.2	.2	.1		.2	Fixed/Worth	.2	.2	.2	.2	.2
.4	.3	.3		.3		.3	.3	.3	.3	.3
1.0	.6	.5		.6		.6	.6	.6	.6	.6
.6	.7	.9		.7	Debt/Worth	.7	.6	.6	.7	.7
1.3	1.4	1.7		1.5		1.3	1.2	1.4	1.4	1.5
3.3	2.8	3.2		2.9		2.4	2.6	2.7	2.8	2.9
42.7	36.3	42.4		37.8	% Profit Before Taxes/Tangible Net Worth	35.0	27.5	29.3	36.4	37.8
(77) 13.3	(385) 15.2	(79) 21.1		(548) 15.9		(648) 19.1	(568) 11.3	(503) 11.2	(529) 13.4	(548) 15.9
-.3	3.7	12.5		4.3		4.8	-.6	.0	1.0	4.3
19.3	13.6	13.3		13.7	% Profit Before Taxes/Total Assets	15.4	11.7	12.8	13.2	13.7
6.1	5.8	8.3		6.2		7.1	4.5	4.8	5.4	6.2
-5.2	1.1	3.6		1.1		1.8	-.9	-.4	.0	1.1
1.0	.6	.5		.6	% Depr., Dep., Amort./Revenues	.7	.7	.7	.7	.6
(75) 1.8	(390) 1.1	(77) .7		(546) 1.1		(621) 1.1	(556) 1.1	(485) 1.1	(501) 1.1	(546) 1.1
2.6	1.6	1.2		1.7		1.8	1.7	1.9	1.8	1.7
4.4	2.6	.8		2.4	% Officers', Directors', Owners' Comp/Revenues	3.0	2.8	2.9	2.5	2.4
(49) 7.4	(233) 4.6	(35) 1.4		(318) 4.5		(347) 4.6	(343) 4.5	(312) 4.8	(298) 4.7	(318) 4.5
9.9	6.8	3.1		7.0		7.8	7.6	8.1	7.3	7.0
51439M	1538267M	1662909M	921385M	4174000M	Contract Revenues ($)	4152465M	4525712M	5868502M	4656384M	4174000M
20455M	542262M	575800M	650370M	1788887M	Total Assets ($)	1486082M	1584178M	1882767M	1833190M	1788887M

M = $ thousand   MM = $ million
See Pages 1 through 15 for Explanation of Ratios and Data

CONTRACTORS—EXCAVATING & FOUNDATION WORK. SIC# 1794

Current Data Sorted By Revenue | Comparative Historical Data

	1	11			12	# Postretirement Benefits / Type of Statement		9	18	12
	3	42	24	5	74	Unqualified	98	84	79	81	74
	15	79	8	1	103	Reviewed	115	110	96	101	103
	17	24	1		42	Compiled	46	48	27	41	42
	16	1			17	Tax Returns	2	5	6	10	17
	2	18	4		24	Other	27	28	29	33	24

68 (4/1-9/30/94)   192 (10/1/94-3/31/95)

	0-1MM	1-10MM	10-50MM	50 & OVER	ALL		4/1/90-3/31/91	4/1/91-3/31/92	4/1/92-3/31/93	4/1/93-3/31/94	4/1/94-3/31/95
NUMBER OF STATEMENTS	53	164	37	6	260		ALL 288	ALL 275	ALL 237	ALL 266	ALL 260
	%	%	%	%	%	**ASSETS**	%	%	%	%	%
	12.5	10.1	12.9		10.8	Cash & Equivalents	11.2	11.6	11.4	10.7	10.8
	18.9	31.8	34.6		29.5	A/R - Progress Billings	28.4	27.8	26.3	30.2	29.5
	.4	3.3	6.3		3.1	A/R - Current Retention	3.5	3.4	3.0	3.6	3.1
	2.7	1.5	1.3		1.8	Inventory	1.9	2.2	1.7	2.1	1.8
	.3	2.3	3.4		2.0	Cost & Est. Earnings In Excess of Billings	2.8	2.7	3.5	2.8	2.0
	4.0	2.4	3.9		2.9	All Other Current	3.1	3.2	3.2	2.3	2.9
	38.8	51.3	62.3		50.1	Total Current	50.8	51.0	49.1	51.6	50.1
	54.5	41.5	29.1		42.4	Fixed Assets (net)	41.4	40.8	43.1	40.2	42.4
	.2	.9	1.2		.8	Joint Ventures & Investments	1.2	.8	.7	.7	.8
	.9	1.1	.1		.9	Intangibles (net)	.3	1.0	1.1	.9	.9
	5.7	5.1	7.2		5.6	All Other Non-Current	6.2	6.4	5.9	6.5	5.6
	100.0	100.0	100.0		100.0	Total	100.0	100.0	100.0	100.0	100.0
						LIABILITIES					
	6.5	5.2	5.3		5.4	Notes Payable - Short Term	6.9	7.0	6.8	6.4	5.4
	7.3	14.2	17.6		13.3	A/P - Trade	14.0	14.7	14.4	15.1	13.3
	.2	.1	.6		.2	A/P - Retention	.1	.1	.2	.4	.2
	.6	2.3	3.6		2.1	Billings in Excess of Costs & Est. Earnings	1.9	1.6	1.7	1.6	2.1
	.3	.6	.8		.6	Income Taxes Payable	.8	.9	.5	.5	.6
	9.3	7.6	5.5		7.8	Cur. Mat. - L/T/D	8.2	8.1	7.8	7.0	7.8
	8.1	6.1	7.2		6.6	All Other Current	5.6	4.4	4.9	5.2	6.6
	32.4	36.1	40.6		36.0	Total Current	37.6	36.8	36.3	36.2	36.0
	24.9	16.5	11.7		17.6	Long Term Debt	15.6	15.5	16.0	15.9	17.6
	1.6	1.8	1.6		1.8	Deferred Taxes	1.7	1.5	1.8	1.9	1.8
	2.1	.7	1.6		1.1	All Other Non-Current	1.8	2.2	2.2	2.1	1.1
	39.0	44.8	44.4		43.5	Net Worth	43.3	44.1	43.6	44.0	43.5
	100.0	100.0	100.0		100.0	Total Liabilities & Net Worth	100.0	100.0	100.0	100.0	100.0
						INCOME DATA					
	100.0	100.0	100.0		100.0	Contract Revenues	100.0	100.0	100.0	100.0	100.0
	45.0	23.1	14.3		26.2	Gross Profit	25.5	25.4	24.2	25.7	26.2
	39.2	18.3	9.8		21.1	Operating Expenses	21.6	22.7	21.2	21.2	21.1
	5.8	4.8	4.5		5.0	Operating Profit	3.9	2.7	3.0	4.5	5.0
	1.2	.4	-.6		.4	All Other Expenses (net)	.7	.8	.8	.7	.4
	4.6	4.4	5.1		4.6	Profit Before Taxes	3.2	1.9	2.2	3.8	4.6
						RATIOS					
	2.4	2.1	2.2		2.2	Current	2.0	2.1	2.0	2.0	2.2
	1.5	1.4	1.5		1.4		1.4	1.4	1.4	1.4	1.4
	.6	1.1	1.2		1.1		1.0	1.0	1.0	1.0	1.1
(42)	7.9	(162) 6.2	2.8	(247) 5.8		Receivables/Payables	(284) 4.5	(272) 3.9	(229) 3.7	(257) 4.1	(247) 5.8
	2.9	2.5	2.3		2.5		2.4	2.3	2.1	2.4	2.5
	1.4	1.6	1.8		1.6		1.7	1.5	1.4	1.5	1.6
0	UND	44 8.3	51 7.1	38 9.5		Revenues/Receivables	37 9.9	37 10.0	35 10.3	38 9.6	38 9.5
30	12.1	63 5.8	68 5.4	62 5.9			62 5.9	57 6.4	54 6.8	63 5.8	62 5.9
68	5.4	89 4.1	87 4.2	87 4.2			79 4.6	79 4.6	72 5.1	83 4.4	87 4.2
0	UND	14 25.4	25 14.4	11 34.2		Cost of Revenues/Payables	15 23.8	15 24.8	15 24.1	16 22.4	11 34.2
14	26.4	27 13.3	35 10.3	27 13.5			30 12.1	32 11.5	29 12.8	34 10.8	27 13.5
34	10.6	49 7.5	41 9.0	46 8.0			46 8.0	50 7.3	48 7.6	56 6.5	46 8.0
	6.0	6.9	6.5		6.9	Revenues/Working Capital	7.2	6.7	7.2	6.7	6.9
	14.6	13.4	13.9		14.1		13.9	13.2	14.9	13.9	14.1
	-25.7	98.3	21.2		98.3		195.0	154.0	-514.6	172.0	98.3
(47)	8.8	(156) 8.6	(36) 20.5	(245) 9.7		EBIT/Interest	(267) 6.3	(258) 6.1	(222) 5.9	(251) 7.5	(245) 9.7
	3.6	4.1	6.1		4.2		2.5	2.4	2.4	3.4	4.2
	.0	1.9	2.7		1.9		1.0	.1	1.1	1.0	1.9
(18)	4.3	(84) 3.7	(23) 6.9	(127) 3.8		Net Profit + Depr., Dep., Amort./Cur. Mat. L/T/D	(151) 2.9	(148) 3.5	(122) 3.3	(148) 3.3	(127) 3.8
	1.3	1.9	1.8		1.8		1.7	1.7	1.7	1.8	1.8
	.7	1.3	1.2		1.2		1.0	.9	1.0	1.0	1.2
	.8	.6	.5		.6	Fixed/Worth	.5	.5	.6	.6	.6
	1.3	1.0	.6		1.0		.9	1.0	1.0	1.0	1.0
	2.3	1.6	1.1		1.6		1.5	1.6	1.7	1.5	1.6
	.7	.7	.8		.7	Debt/Worth	.8	.6	.7	.7	.7
	1.3	1.3	1.4		1.3		1.4	1.3	1.4	1.4	1.3
	3.3	2.7	2.3		2.6		2.3	2.6	2.5	2.7	2.6
(48)	68.5	(162) 38.0	43.3	(253) 42.0		% Profit Before Taxes/Tangible Net Worth	(282) 29.5	(266) 28.4	(232) 25.5	(258) 36.7	(253) 42.0
	26.4	15.9	20.8		17.9		14.6	10.8	11.4	15.4	17.9
	2.7	6.6	8.2		6.8		.3	-5.3	.7	1.1	6.8
	22.9	13.7	17.2		14.8	% Profit Before Taxes/Total Assets	13.4	12.2	11.5	13.8	14.8
	10.2	7.6	9.0		8.2		5.7	4.4	4.0	6.4	8.2
	-2.8	3.1	3.8		3.0		.0	-3.1	.3	.2	3.0
(49)	5.6	(157) 3.0	1.9	(248) 3.1		% Depr., Dep., Amort./Revenues	(277) 3.1	(260) 3.3	(223) 3.4	(254) 3.0	(248) 3.1
	7.3	4.9	3.4		4.9		5.6	6.1	5.3	5.3	4.9
	11.7	7.3	4.4		7.4		9.0	9.7	8.6	8.5	7.4
(31)	4.5	(94) 2.1	(19) .9	(146) 2.0		% Officers', Directors', Owners' Comp/Revenues	(142) 2.3	(141) 2.2	(126) 2.3	(146) 2.3	(146) 2.0
	6.4	4.2	1.5		4.2		4.4	4.5	3.5	4.2	4.2
	9.3	6.6	2.7		6.7		8.0	7.4	6.5	7.1	6.7
	33746M	623176M	674367M	3467863M	4799152M	Contract Revenues ($)	2056154M	1788515M	6243076M	4402443M	4799152M
	19479M	340804M	337289M	3661049M	4358621M	Total Assets ($)	1045991M	931887M	4059881M	4191998M	4358621M

M = $ thousand   MM = $ million
See Pages 1 through 15 for Explanation of Ratios and Data

Current Data Sorted By Revenue | **Comparative Historical Data**

Type of Statement

0-1MM	1-10MM	10-50MM	50 & OVER	ALL	# Postretirement Benefits / Type of Statement	4/1/90-3/31/91	4/1/91-3/31/92	4/1/92-3/31/93	4/1/93-3/31/94	4/1/94-3/31/95
	2	1		3	# Postretirement Benefits			1	4	3
	4			4	Unqualified	4	4	4	5	4
1	22	4		27	Reviewed	36	31	17	25	27
3	8	1		12	Compiled	18	15	15	16	12
	1		1	2	Tax Returns	2		1	2	2
1	8			9	Other	4	5	5	1	9

18 (4/1-9/30/94) · 36 (10/1/94-3/31/95)

0-1MM	1-10MM	10-50MM	50 & OVER	ALL		4/1/90-3/31/91 ALL	4/1/91-3/31/92 ALL	4/1/92-3/31/93 ALL	4/1/93-3/31/94 ALL	4/1/94-3/31/95 ALL
5	43	5	1	54	**NUMBER OF STATEMENTS**	64	55	42	49	54
%	%	%	%	%	**ASSETS**	%	%	%	%	%
	7.3			7.6	Cash & Equivalents	6.6	6.8	5.8	9.0	7.6
	53.1			52.2	A/R - Progress Billings	48.8	53.8	45.4	50.2	52.2
	2.4			3.0	A/R - Current Retention	6.3	3.6	.7	3.3	3.0
	10.5			11.0	Inventory	14.1	12.1	14.7	11.8	11.0
	1.4			1.6	Cost & Est. Earnings In Excess of Billings	1.8	2.4	2.9	1.6	1.6
	2.9			2.8	All Other Current	4.0	3.6	3.9	2.8	2.8
	77.5			78.2	Total Current	81.6	82.3	73.4	78.8	78.2
	12.6			12.9	Fixed Assets (net)	11.3	11.5	15.9	11.3	12.9
	1.0			.8	Joint Ventures & Investments	.3	.0	.1	.6	.8
	1.6			1.5	Intangibles (net)	.7	.7	1.4	2.1	1.5
	7.2			6.7	All Other Non-Current	6.1	5.3	9.2	7.3	6.7
	100.0			100.0	Total	100.0	100.0	100.0	100.0	100.0
					LIABILITIES					
	9.3			10.8	Notes Payable - Short Term	16.4	14.0	17.3	12.5	10.8
	21.0			22.2	A/P - Trade	21.6	22.9	21.6	21.9	22.2
	.0			.0	A/P - Retention	.0	.0	.5	.0	.0
	1.5			1.6	Billings in Excess of Costs & Est. Earnings	.8	2.4	2.2	2.5	1.6
	.7			.7	Income Taxes Payable	1.7	.5	.3	.1	.7
	3.6			3.8	Cur. Mat. - L/T/D	2.9	3.3	4.0	2.8	3.8
	10.0			9.1	All Other Current	8.5	9.5	4.6	10.2	9.1
	46.0			48.1	Total Current	51.9	52.6	50.5	50.2	48.1
	9.1			10.4	Long Term Debt	7.4	6.6	7.9	8.1	10.4
	.8			.6	Deferred Taxes	1.5	.6	.5	.4	.6
	.9			1.4	All Other Non-Current	1.8	1.8	1.3	.8	1.4
	43.2			39.4	Net Worth	37.4	38.4	39.8	40.5	39.4
	100.0			100.0	Total Liabilities & Net Worth	100.0	100.0	100.0	100.0	100.0
					INCOME DATA					
	100.0			100.0	Contract Revenues	100.0	100.0	100.0	100.0	100.0
	23.6			23.8	Gross Profit	24.2	23.8	27.3	23.7	23.8
	20.5			20.7	Operating Expenses	20.9	22.6	25.7	21.3	20.7
	3.0			3.0	Operating Profit	3.3	1.3	1.6	2.4	3.0
	.6			.7	All Other Expenses (net)	.6	.7	.4	.2	.7
	2.4			2.3	Profit Before Taxes	2.6	.6	1.1	2.2	2.3
					RATIOS					
	2.2			2.1	Current	2.1	2.1	2.0	2.4	2.1
	1.7			1.6		1.6	1.6	1.5	1.5	1.6
	1.4			1.3		1.3	1.3	1.2	1.2	1.3
	6.2			6.3	Receivables/Payables	5.8	4.7	3.7	4.8	6.3
	3.0			2.8		3.2	3.1 (39)	2.7 (48)	2.5	2.8
	1.9			1.6		1.9	2.0	1.6	1.8	1.6
	39 9.3		39 9.4		Revenues/Receivables	41 8.9	47 7.7	35 10.4	38 9.6	39 9.4
	57 6.4		60 6.1			55 6.6	58 6.3	57 6.4	55 6.6	60 6.1
	74 4.9		76 4.8			73 5.0	78 4.7	76 4.8	73 5.0	76 4.8
	12 31.2		11 31.9		Cost of Revenues/Payables	13 28.7	16 22.9	16 23.1	14 27.0	11 31.9
	25 14.7		26 14.3			24 15.4	24 14.9	27 13.4	25 14.5	26 14.3
	41 8.8		42 8.7			46 8.0	45 8.1	46 8.0	46 7.9	42 8.7
	8.0			8.4	Revenues/Working Capital	7.8	7.8	8.5	7.5	8.4
	13.3			13.9		11.8	11.1	13.2	14.3	13.9
	20.8			20.9		27.6	24.8	28.9	21.5	20.9
	9.1			8.9	EBIT/Interest	(61) 6.5	(50) 4.4	(41) 4.3	(45) 9.5	(50) 8.9
	(39) 3.9		(50) 3.8			2.7	2.1	2.3	3.5	3.8
	1.9			1.9		1.2	.2	.6	1.4	1.9
	3.2			3.2	Net Profit + Depr., Dep., Amort./Cur. Mat. L./T/D	(30) 4.5	(23) 4.3	(16) 2.8	(24) 4.5	(18) 3.2
	(18) 1.5		(18) 1.5			2.5	1.3	1.3	2.0	1.5
	.6			.6		1.1	-.7	-.5	1.3	.6
	.1			.1	Fixed/Worth	.1	.2	.2	.1	.1
	.3			.3		.3	.3	.3	.3	.3
	.6			.6		.4	.7	.6	.5	.6
	.8			.9	Debt/Worth	1.0	.9	.8	.9	.9
	1.7			1.9		1.8	1.9	1.7	1.7	1.9
	2.4			2.9		3.7	3.1	3.9	3.1	2.9
	51.3			52.7	% Profit Before Taxes/Tangible Net Worth	(62) 35.8	(52) 27.2	(41) 29.5	(47) 38.7	(53) 52.7
	(42) 19.4		(53) 18.9			19.5	7.0	7.7	14.1	18.9
	8.2			8.1		5.4	-5.8	-4.4	4.4	8.1
	13.9			14.5	% Profit Before Taxes/Total Assets	15.8	11.8	8.9	12.8	14.5
	10.0			8.6		6.3	3.0	3.0	6.4	8.6
	3.0			2.6		.6	-1.4	-1.0	1.8	2.6
	.4			.4	% Depr., Dep., Amort./Revenues	(55) .5	(50) .4	(40) .5	(44) .4	(49) .4
	(38) .6		(49) .7			.8	.7	1.0	.8	.7
	1.1			1.0		1.1	1.3	1.4	1.2	1.0
	3.1			2.5	% Officers', Directors', Owners' Comp/Revenues	(33) 3.4	(36) 3.0	(25) 2.8	(25) 2.9	(29) 2.5
	(23) 3.5		(29) 3.5			5.7	4.8	4.7	4.3	3.5
	7.4			6.8		6.7	8.1	7.2	8.7	6.8
2693M	153021M	68120M	804585M	1028419M	Contract Revenues ($)	307576M	202751M	158001M	209116M	1028419M
1021M	48422M	17297M	147665M	214405M	Total Assets ($)	89250M	59708M	50350M	67463M	214405M

M = $ thousand   MM = $ million
See Pages 1 through 15 for Explanation of Ratios and Data

Current Data Sorted By Revenue | **Comparative Historical Data**

	8	43	8	11	70	# Postretirement Benefits / Type of Statement		9	31	70
	6	61	54	35	156	Unqualified		108	86	94	121	156
	26	188	42	1	257	Reviewed		227	239	222	216	257
	50	181	20	4	255	Compiled		279	246	262	261	255
	40	87	4		131	Tax Returns		20	49	85	96	131
	32	114	35	13	194	Other		149	120	143	157	194

291 (4/1-9/30/94) 702 (10/1/94-3/31/95)

0-1MM 154	1-10MM 631	10-50MM 155	50 & OVER 53	ALL 993	NUMBER OF STATEMENTS	4/1/90-3/31/91 ALL 783	4/1/91-3/31/92 ALL 740	4/1/92-3/31/93 ALL 806	4/1/93-3/31/94 ALL 851	4/1/94-3/31/95 ALL 993
%	%	%	%	%	**ASSETS**	%	%	%	%	%
9.9	10.6	9.0	9.0	10.2	Cash & Equivalents	11.4	11.3	11.5	10.7	10.2
14.3	15.7	14.8	12.3	15.2	A/R - Progress Billings	17.8	16.0	13.6	15.2	15.2
.9	1.6	2.0	1.5	1.6	A/R - Current Retention	2.5	1.8	1.8	2.1	1.6
29.8	36.7	46.4	56.1	38.1	Inventory	30.8	33.0	36.5	36.1	38.1
3.4	6.2	4.5	2.1	5.3	Cost & Est. Earnings In Excess of Billings	4.9	5.4	6.1	4.9	5.3
6.4	6.6	5.1	3.9	6.2	All Other Current	6.3	5.6	6.0	6.3	6.2
64.6	77.4	81.8	84.9	76.5	Total Current	73.6	73.1	75.5	75.2	76.5
19.2	13.1	7.8	6.3	12.8	Fixed Assets (net)	13.6	13.7	12.6	13.2	12.8
3.6	3.0	3.1	.4	3.0	Joint Ventures & Investments	3.4	3.6	3.2	3.6	3.0
1.2	.7	.6	.5	.8	Intangibles (net)	.5	.6	.6	.6	.8
11.4	5.7	6.7	7.9	6.9	All Other Non-Current	8.9	8.9	8.1	7.3	6.9
100.0	100.0	100.0	100.0	100.0	Total	100.0	100.0	100.0	100.0	100.0
					LIABILITIES					
23.5	26.9	31.4	23.7	26.9	Notes Payable - Short Term	27.4	27.6	29.1	27.2	26.9
9.5	14.1	19.2	15.8	14.3	A/P - Trade	14.2	13.7	13.1	15.0	14.3
.1	.6	1.0	.8	.6	A/P - Retention	.8	.6	.6	.8	.6
1.9	3.1	2.9	.5	2.8	Billings in Excess of Costs & Est. Earnings	2.8	2.4	2.8	2.1	2.8
.5	.5	.2	.2	.4	Income Taxes Payable	.6	.5	.4	.6	.4
4.2	3.1	2.2	2.1	3.1	Cur. Mat. - L/T/D	2.8	3.1	3.3	3.4	3.1
10.6	10.0	7.8	8.8	9.7	All Other Current	9.5	9.9	9.5	9.2	9.7
50.2	58.3	64.7	51.8	57.7	Total Current	58.1	57.8	58.8	58.3	57.7
16.3	8.6	8.2	15.3	10.1	Long Term Debt	10.7	9.9	9.5	9.7	10.1
.2	.6	.4	.4	.5	Deferred Taxes	.7	.5	.5	.4	.5
3.0	2.4	2.9	4.9	2.7	All Other Non-Current	1.9	1.9	2.1	3.0	2.7
30.3	30.2	23.7	27.6	29.1	Net Worth	28.6	29.8	29.2	28.6	29.1
100.0	100.0	100.0	100.0	100.0	Total Liabilities & Net Worth	100.0	100.0	100.0	100.0	100.0
					INCOME DATA					
100.0	100.0	100.0	100.0	100.0	Contract Revenues	100.0	100.0	100.0	100.0	100.0
25.4	16.0	14.4	14.2	17.1	Gross Profit	17.2	17.8	16.7	17.7	17.1
19.2	12.3	10.6	9.7	13.0	Operating Expenses	14.3	14.6	13.5	13.8	13.0
6.1	3.7	3.8	4.5	4.1	Operating Profit	2.9	3.2	3.2	3.9	4.1
1.3	.1	.7	.9	.4	All Other Expenses (net)	.8	.8	.5	.8	.4
4.9	3.6	3.1	3.6	3.7	Profit Before Taxes	2.1	2.4	2.7	3.1	3.7
					RATIOS					
2.3	1.8	1.6	3.5	1.9	Current	1.8	1.8	1.7	1.8	1.9
1.2	1.3	1.3	1.5	1.3		1.3	1.2	1.3	1.3	1.3
1.0	1.0	1.0	1.2	1.0		1.0	1.0	1.0	1.0	1.0
(110) 5.8	(570) 2.2	(153) 1.2	(52) 1.0	(885) 2.0	Receivables/Payables	(711) 2.0	(678) 2.1	(732) 1.9	(773) 1.8	(885) 2.0
1.2	.7	.2	.2	.5		.9	.7	.5	.5	.5
.0	.0	.0	.0	.0		.0	.0	.0	.0	.0
0 UND	0 UND	0 736.1	0 999.8	0 UND	Revenues/Receivables	0 UND	0 UND	0 UND	0 UND	0 UND
3 123.4	4 95.9	5 78.2	2 177.6	4 97.4		9 42.2	6 65.6	3 132.3	4 104.2	4 97.4
42 8.7	35 10.4	37 9.9	37 9.8	37 9.9		45 8.1	36 10.1	36 10.2	38 9.7	37 9.9
0 UND	4 89.1	16 22.9	15 24.6	5 74.2	Cost of Revenues/Payables	6 57.6	5 66.7	4 91.1	5 70.0	5 74.2
8 44.8	18 19.9	28 13.0	25 14.7	19 19.2		18 19.8	20 18.6	18 20.0	21 17.8	19 19.2
32 11.4	34 10.8	47 7.8	51 7.1	37 9.8		39 9.3	37 10.0	36 10.2	38 9.7	37 9.8
5.1	7.3	6.5	2.3	6.6	Revenues/Working Capital	7.4	6.9	7.4	7.0	6.6
16.2	16.4	15.4	8.5	15.6		18.1	19.3	17.8	17.6	15.6
-53.8	126.0	61.1	18.8	128.5		271.3	-999.8	237.3	243.3	128.5
(112) 9.4	(512) 11.8	(125) 14.5	(44) 20.6	(793) 12.1	EBIT/Interest	(650) 7.5	(625) 9.0	(644) 11.8	(681) 11.6	(793) 12.1
3.3	3.9	4.6	5.2	3.9		2.8	2.5	3.5	3.2	3.9
1.1	1.5	1.7	2.7	1.5		1.1	1.0	1.3	1.4	1.5
(20) 2.5	(151) 6.9	(33) 14.3		(211) 7.5	Net Profit + Depr., Dep., Amort./Cur. Mat. L./T/D	(266) 8.4	(223) 6.0	(211) 7.7	(251) 7.8	(211) 7.5
1.2	2.7	2.4		2.3		2.5	2.1	2.2	2.6	2.3
-.9	.7	.2		.4		.5	.2	.3	.5	.4
.0	.1	.1	.1	.1	Fixed/Worth	.1	.1	.1	.1	.1
.3	.3	.2	.1	.3		.3	.3	.2	.3	.3
1.5	.8	.5	.3	.8		.9	.9	.8	.9	.8
1.0	1.2	2.3	2.0	1.3	Debt/Worth	1.2	1.2	1.3	1.3	1.3
3.1	2.7	3.6	2.6	3.0		2.9	3.0	3.0	2.9	3.0
10.6	7.7	8.1	4.5	8.1		9.2	8.4	8.2	8.9	8.1
(134) 74.0	(598) 58.3	(147) 56.3	47.0	(932) 59.4	% Profit Before Taxes/Tangible Net Worth	(723) 45.6	(687) 47.5	(746) 52.8	(782) 57.3	(932) 59.4
24.3	24.6	25.2	23.7	24.7		19.9	18.3	22.4	23.9	24.7
1.8	6.5	11.2	13.3	7.1		2.6	2.5	5.0	7.2	7.1
17.4	13.3	10.3	10.2	12.8	% Profit Before Taxes/Total Assets	11.8	11.2	11.8	12.9	12.8
4.5	5.5	5.1	7.0	5.5		4.2	4.1	5.0	5.5	5.5
.2	1.2	2.0	2.4	1.4		.2	.2	.8	1.1	1.4
(95) .6	(521) .3	(119) -.2	(36) .1	(771) .2	% Depr., Dep., Amort./Revenues	(639) .3	(595) .3	(636) .3	(670) .2	(771) .2
1.4	.5	.3	.3	.5		.6	.6	.5	.5	.5
3.1	1.1	.6	.6	1.2		1.4	1.2	1.0	1.2	1.2
(56) 3.5	(338) 1.8	(65) .9	(13) .5	(472) 1.6	% Officers', Directors', Owners' Comp/Revenues	(387) 2.1	(369) 1.9	(416) 2.1	(430) 1.7	(472) 1.6
5.5	3.0	1.7	1.2	2.9		3.5	3.8	4.0	3.3	2.9
9.8	5.6	3.1	2.2	5.6		5.9	6.6	6.6	5.4	5.6
83674M	2317647M	3350770M	15878308M	21630399M	Contract Revenues ($)	6083390M	5126295M	6830304M	9529415M	21630399M
104571M	1182645M	1890289M	9324600M	12502105M	Total Assets ($)	4129573M	3016066M	3913850M	5786349M	12502105M

M = $ thousand MM = $ million
See Pages 1 through 15 for Explanation of Ratios and Data

Current Data Sorted By Revenue / Comparative Historical Data

# Postretirement Benefits / Type of Statement	0-1MM	1-10MM	10-50MM	50 & OVER	ALL			37	49	83
(Postretirement Benefits counts)	2	37	33	11	83					
Unqualified	17	172	242	58	489		597	522	474	455	489
Reviewed	27	313	62	7	409		401	409	411	403	409
Compiled	15	59	8	1	83		96	97	79	79	83
Tax Returns	6	12	1		19		4	13	13	10	19
Other	12	63	43	11	129		107	115	96	121	129

369 (4/1-9/30/94)   760 (10/1/94-3/31/95)

	0-1MM	1-10MM	10-50MM	50 & OVER	ALL	4/1/90-3/31/91 ALL	4/1/91-3/31/92 ALL	4/1/92-3/31/93 ALL	4/1/93-3/31/94 ALL	4/1/94-3/31/95 ALL
NUMBER OF STATEMENTS	77	619	356	77	1129	1205	1156	1073	1068	1129
ASSETS	%	%	%	%	%	%	%	%	%	%
Cash & Equivalents	23.6	18.5	18.9	16.2	18.8	20.7	21.4	21.6	18.9	18.8
A/R - Progress Billings	24.0	41.8	47.0	41.9	42.3	41.0	39.0	37.9	40.9	42.3
A/R - Current Retention	4.1	4.1	7.2	10.5	5.5	6.7	6.2	6.2	5.7	5.5
Inventory	3.1	3.4	1.6	3.5	2.8	2.3	2.5	2.4	2.4	2.8
Cost & Est. Earnings In Excess of Billings	4.3	4.8	4.7	4.0	4.7	4.2	4.1	4.4	4.4	4.7
All Other Current	6.5	3.9	4.3	3.0	4.1	3.5	3.8	4.2	4.1	4.1
Total Current	65.5	76.5	83.8	79.1	78.2	78.4	77.1	76.6	76.4	78.2
Fixed Assets (net)	22.0	15.2	9.3	10.4	13.5	13.7	13.7	13.7	14.4	13.5
Joint Ventures & Investments	1.8	1.3	1.0	2.7	1.4	1.4	1.8	1.8	1.8	1.4
Intangibles (net)	2.8	1.0	.7	1.7	1.1	.3	.6	.8	.6	1.1
All Other Non-Current	7.9	5.9	5.2	6.0	5.8	6.1	6.8	7.1	6.9	5.8
Total	100.0	100.0	100.0	100.0	100.0	100.0	100.0	100.0	100.0	100.0
LIABILITIES										
Notes Payable - Short Term	10.7	6.1	3.6	2.9	5.4	5.7	5.5	5.4	6.0	5.4
A/P - Trade	14.0	28.2	37.3	35.2	30.6	30.1	29.3	30.0	30.9	30.6
A/P - Retention	.1	1.7	4.4	6.2	2.7	2.9	2.9	2.6	2.5	2.7
Billings in Excess of Costs & Est. Earnings	2.0	5.0	6.8	9.1	5.6	5.8	5.1	5.3	5.2	5.6
Income Taxes Payable	.6	.8	.5	.5	.7	1.1	.8	.7	.6	.7
Cur. Mat. - L/T/D	2.9	2.5	1.1	1.8	2.0	2.4	1.9	2.1	1.9	2.0
All Other Current	8.2	7.9	7.6	8.3	7.8	6.3	6.2	6.1	7.2	7.8
Total Current	38.5	52.2	61.2	64.0	54.9	54.2	51.8	52.3	54.2	54.9
Long Term Debt	10.7	6.2	4.3	6.3	5.9	6.5	6.1	6.0	6.4	5.9
Deferred Taxes	.3	1.3	.6	1.0	1.0	1.2	1.1	.9	.9	1.0
All Other Non-Current	2.5	1.5	1.5	1.5	1.6	1.0	1.1	1.4	1.1	1.6
Net Worth	48.1	38.7	32.4	27.2	36.6	37.1	39.8	39.4	37.3	36.6
Total Liabilities & Net Worth	100.0	100.0	100.0	100.0	100.0	100.0	100.0	100.0	100.0	100.0
INCOME DATA										
Contract Revenues	100.0	100.0	100.0	100.0	100.0	100.0	100.0	100.0	100.0	100.0
Gross Profit	25.7	15.9	8.7	8.6	13.8	13.6	14.3	13.6	13.5	13.8
Operating Expenses	23.4	13.2	7.4	6.8	11.6	11.8	13.2	12.4	11.8	11.6
Operating Profit	2.3	2.7	1.3	1.8	2.2	1.9	1.2	1.1	1.7	2.2
All Other Expenses (net)	-.5	-.1	-.2	.2	-.1	-.2	-.3	-.1	-.1	-.1
Profit Before Taxes	2.8	2.8	1.5	1.6	2.3	2.1	1.4	1.2	1.8	2.3
RATIOS										
Current	3.0 / 1.7 / 1.1	1.9 / 1.5 / 1.2	1.6 / 1.3 / 1.2	1.4 / 1.2 / 1.1	1.8 / 1.4 / 1.2	1.8 / 1.4 / 1.2	1.9 / 1.5 / 1.2	1.9 / 1.5 / 1.2	1.8 / 1.4 / 1.2	1.8 / 1.4 / 1.2
Receivables/Payables	(70) 5.7 / 2.5 / 1.2	(615) 2.3 / 1.5 / 1.1	1.6 / 1.3 / 1.0	1.6 / 1.2 / 1.0	(1118) 2.1 / 1.4 / 1.1	(1201) 2.0 / 1.4 / 1.2	(1149) 2.0 / 1.4 / 1.1	(1066) 1.9 / 1.3 / 1.0	(1058) 2.0 / 1.4 / 1.1	(1118) 2.1 / 1.4 / 1.1
Revenues/Receivables	16 23.2 / 37 9.8 / 73 5.0	32 11.3 / 52 7.0 / 72 5.1	46 7.9 / 58 6.3 / 74 4.9	47 7.8 / 58 6.3 / 72 5.1	37 9.9 / 54 6.7 / 72 5.1	37 9.8 / 51 7.1 / 69 5.3	35 10.5 / 49 7.4 / 68 5.4	33 11.0 / 49 7.4 / 68 5.4	37 9.8 / 54 6.7 / 73 5.0	37 9.9 / 54 6.7 / 72 5.1
Cost of Revenues/Payables	6 65.3 / 25 14.7 / 46 8.0	22 16.6 / 36 10.1 / 54 6.7	36 10.1 / 48 7.6 / 62 5.9	38 9.7 / 51 7.1 / 63 6.3	25 14.5 / 41 8.8 / 58 6.3	24 14.9 / 39 9.3 / 57 6.4	25 14.5 / 39 9.3 / 57 6.4	25 14.8 / 41 9.0 / 57 6.4	27 13.5 / 43 8.5 / 59 6.2	25 14.5 / 41 8.8 / 58 6.3
Revenues/Working Capital	4.1 / 11.7 / 59.9	7.9 / 14.5 / 28.1	10.2 / 17.4 / 28.0	14.2 / 22.8 / 37.3	8.6 / 15.9 / 30.0	8.6 / 14.6 / 27.2	8.1 / 13.4 / 26.9	8.0 / 13.9 / 29.5	8.9 / 15.2 / 28.5	8.6 / 15.9 / 30.0
EBIT/Interest	(54) 9.9 / 3.0 / -2.4	(508) 24.9 / 7.5 / 1.8	(278) 29.2 / 8.7 / 2.3	(63) 23.4 / 7.2 / 2.3	(903) 26.0 / 7.5 / 1.8	(1000) 20.9 / 5.7 / 1.6	(937) 17.1 / 4.5 / 1.1	(856) 17.1 / 4.9 / 1.3	(852) 16.1 / 4.6 / 1.1	(903) 26.0 / 7.5 / 1.8
Net Profit + Depr., Dep., Amort./Cur. Mat. L./T/D	(19) 5.0 / 2.3 / -2.9	(246) 8.1 / 3.1 / 1.0	(133) 10.9 / 4.4 / 1.7	(37) 5.6 / 2.7 / 1.4	(435) 8.8 / 3.4 / 1.3	(605) 10.7 / 3.7 / 1.0	(498) 7.2 / 2.7 / .5	(425) 6.9 / 2.7 / .8	(501) 8.4 / 3.1 / .8	(435) 8.8 / 3.4 / 1.3
Fixed/Worth	.1 / .4 / 1.0	.1 / .3 / .6	.1 / .2 / .4	.1 / .3 / .6	.1 / .3 / .6	.1 / .3 / .6	.1 / .2 / .5	.1 / .2 / .5	.1 / .3 / .6	.1 / .3 / .6
Debt/Worth	.4 / 1.0 / 4.1	.9 / 1.7 / 3.2	1.4 / 2.4 / 3.8	2.3 / 3.4 / 4.9	1.0 / 2.0 / 3.6	1.0 / 1.9 / 3.1	.9 / 1.7 / 3.0	.9 / 1.7 / 2.9	1.0 / 1.9 / 3.2	1.0 / 2.0 / 3.6
% Profit Before Taxes/Tangible Net Worth	(72) 50.0 / 18.4 / .0	(603) 40.7 / 17.5 / 4.3	(348) 29.8 / 14.3 / 4.5	(76) 30.6 / 14.7 / 4.0	(1099) 36.3 / 16.8 / 4.1	(1170) 34.7 / 16.7 / 4.4	(1121) 28.8 / 12.2 / 1.2	(1041) 27.8 / 11.2 / 1.4	(1042) 27.7 / 11.2 / 1.1	(1099) 36.3 / 16.8 / 4.1
% Profit Before Taxes/Total Assets	21.6 / 5.3 / -2.4	14.7 / 6.5 / 1.3	9.2 / 4.3 / 1.3	7.0 / 3.2 / .9	12.2 / 5.4 / 1.1	11.7 / 5.4 / 1.2	10.3 / 4.2 / .2	9.4 / 3.8 / .4	9.9 / 3.7 / .3	12.2 / 5.4 / 1.1
% Depr., Dep., Amort./Revenues	(62) 1.0 / 2.2 / 3.9	(564) .3 / .7 / 1.4	(332) .2 / .4 / .8	(68) .2 / .4 / .7	(1026) .3 / .6 / 1.3	(1127) .3 / .6 / 1.3	(1076) .4 / .7 / 1.4	(1010) .3 / .7 / 1.3	(997) .3 / .6 / 1.3	(1026) .3 / .6 / 1.3
% Officers', Directors', Owners' Comp/Revenues	(26) 2.7 / 6.0 / 8.6	(320) 1.6 / 2.7 / 4.9	(148) 1.5 / 1.5 / 2.4	(18) .9 / .9 / 1.4	(512) 1.3 / 2.3 / 4.0	(559) 1.4 / 2.6 / 4.5	(544) 1.5 / 2.7 / 4.5	(513) 1.4 / 2.5 / 4.7	(534) 1.3 / 2.4 / 4.4	(512) 1.3 / 2.3 / 4.0
Contract Revenues ($)	47864M	2818108M	7663105M	21249081M	31778158M	25339235M	19872558M	19765406M	16458361M	31778158M
Total Assets ($)	33514M	1065593M	2553207M	10267650M	13919964M	8644043M	6577664M	6853982M	5680896M	13919964M

M = $ thousand   MM = $ million
See Pages 1 through 15 for Explanation of Ratios and Data

Current Data Sorted By Revenue   Comparative Historical Data

0-1MM	1-10MM	10-50MM	50 & OVER	ALL	# Postretirement Benefits / Type of Statement	4/1/90-3/31/91 ALL	4/1/91-3/31/92 ALL	4/1/92-3/31/93 ALL	4/1/93-3/31/94 ALL	4/1/94-3/31/95 ALL
	3	1		4	# Postretirement Benefits			3	4	4
	3	2		5	Unqualified	9	9	9	4	5
	15	1		16	Reviewed	21	21	20	15	16
4	10	1		15	Compiled	15	16	9	10	15
					Tax Returns	1			3	
2	5	1		8	Other	5	5	7	8	8
16 (4/1-9/30/94)			28 (10/1/94-3/31/95)							
6	33	5		44	NUMBER OF STATEMENTS	51	51	45	40	44
%	%	%	%	%	**ASSETS**	%	%	%	%	%
	9.0			9.3	Cash & Equivalents	10.0	12.8	13.4	8.6	9.3
	48.4			49.6	A/R - Progress Billings	39.0	39.4	37.0	46.3	49.6
	7.1			6.3	A/R - Current Retention	7.6	8.5	5.6	3.1	6.3
	12.5			11.8	Inventory	15.5	13.1	13.5	14.9	11.8
	1.5			1.3	Cost & Est. Earnings In Excess of Billings	2.5	1.6	1.9	3.8	1.3
	2.3			2.0	All Other Current	3.1	2.7	4.3	2.0	2.0
	80.8			80.4	Total Current	77.7	78.2	75.7	79.1	80.4
	11.8			13.0	Fixed Assets (net)	16.3	13.6	15.3	12.7	13.0
	.1			.3	Joint Ventures & Investments	.0	.0	2.5	.3	.3
	.6			.9	Intangibles (net)	.2	.8	.5	1.6	.9
	6.7			5.5	All Other Non-Current	5.8	7.4	5.9	6.4	5.5
	100.0			100.0	Total	100.0	100.0	100.0	100.0	100.0
					LIABILITIES					
	5.8			8.0	Notes Payable - Short Term	10.5	11.3	11.7	10.0	8.0
	26.9			28.1	A/P - Trade	19.8	24.1	21.6	26.1	28.1
	.1			.1	A/P - Retention	.0	.3	.0	.0	.1
	.9			1.2	Billings in Excess of Costs & Est. Earnings	1.9	.7	1.4	2.3	1.2
	.9			.9	Income Taxes Payable	1.4	1.4	.8	.7	.9
	3.1			3.4	Cur. Mat. - L/T/D	4.5	3.2	2.5	3.5	3.4
	9.9			9.8	All Other Current	7.8	7.2	8.8	8.6	9.8
	47.7			51.6	Total Current	45.9	48.1	46.9	51.2	51.6
	9.6			9.9	Long Term Debt	9.1	6.8	8.1	8.7	9.9
	.3			.3	Deferred Taxes	1.0	.7	1.1	.5	.3
	1.8			1.6	All Other Non-Current	1.2	2.3	1.4	2.0	1.6
	40.6			36.6	Net Worth	42.8	42.1	42.6	37.5	36.6
	100.0			100.0	Total Liabilities & Net Worth	100.0	100.0	100.0	100.0	100.0
					INCOME DATA					
	100.0			100.0	Contract Revenues	100.0	100.0	100.0	100.0	100.0
	27.2			28.0	Gross Profit	31.4	29.6	26.8	28.4	28.0
	24.8			25.4	Operating Expenses	29.1	28.0	27.5	27.0	25.4
	2.4			2.6	Operating Profit	2.3	1.6	-.7	1.4	2.6
	.1			.1	All Other Expenses (net)	.5	.0	.3	.2	.1
	2.3			2.5	Profit Before Taxes	1.7	1.6	-1.0	1.2	2.5
					RATIOS					
	2.5			2.5	Current	2.5	2.4	2.5	2.5	2.5
	1.9			1.6		1.7	1.6	1.6	1.7	1.6
	1.2			1.1		1.4	1.2	1.3	1.1	1.1
	3.3			3.3	Receivables/Payables	3.7	4.7	3.7	3.1	3.3
	2.2			2.1		2.4	1.9	2.3	2.0	2.1
	1.6			1.7		1.7	1.4	1.5	1.4	1.7
	45 8.2		49 7.4		Revenues/Receivables	36 10.2	37 9.9	42 8.7	43 8.4	49 7.4
	62 5.9		60 6.1			55 6.6	61 6.0	57 6.4	62 5.9	60 6.1
	91 4.0		96 3.8			78 4.7	83 4.7	76 4.8	81 4.5	96 3.8
	23 16.0		25 14.8		Cost of Revenues/Payables	20 18.3	21 17.1	18 20.3	26 14.2	25 14.8
	42 8.7		43 8.4			35 10.4	35 10.3	36 10.2	45 8.2	43 8.4
	66 5.5		70 5.2			51 7.2	52 7.0	61 6.0	62 5.9	70 5.2
	6.9			7.0	Revenues/Working Capital	6.8	6.4	5.7	5.7	7.0
	8.5			9.2		9.1	10.8	9.9	9.3	9.2
	28.2			30.7		22.3	17.4	23.7	31.9	30.7
	9.5			9.3	EBIT/Interest	8.5	5.7	4.4	6.8	9.3
	(30) 3.5		(39) 3.8			(46) 2.3	(40) 2.4	(39) 1.1	(36) 2.1	(39) 3.8
	2.2			2.4		-.0	1.0	-6.2	1.0	2.4
	2.8			3.3	Net Profit + Depr., Dep., Amort./Cur. Mat. L./T/D	3.4	3.3	3.9	7.7	3.3
	(13) 2.2		(16) 2.3			(25) 1.7	(22) 2.4	(24) 1.3	(24) 1.9	(16) 2.3
	.6			.9		-.5	.8	-1.4	.3	.9
	.1			.1	Fixed/Worth	.2	.1	.1	.1	.1
	.3			.3		.3	.2	.3	.3	.3
	.5			.7		.8	.7	.7	.9	.7
	.8			.8	Debt/Worth	.6	.7	.7	.9	.8
	1.4			1.6		1.6	1.6	1.3	1.8	1.6
	4.4			4.3		2.9	3.5	2.7	5.1	4.3
	49.8			56.7	% Profit Before Taxes/Tangible Net Worth	29.2	18.5	17.0	19.8	56.7
	(32) 15.8		(41) 19.7			(49) 13.7	(50) 4.7	(43) .5	(38) 8.2	(41) 19.7
	6.2			6.5		-3.0	-6.1	-25.2	2.7	6.5
	10.2			15.6	% Profit Before Taxes/Total Assets	14.9	8.8	6.4	6.4	15.6
	4.7			4.9		4.4	2.1	-.4	2.7	4.9
	2.9			2.9		-2.3	-1.5	-12.8	.2	2.9
	.5			.6	% Depr., Dep., Amort./Revenues	.7	.6	.6	.5	.6
	(31) .8		(40) .9			(49) 1.1	(47) .9	(41) .9	(38) .9	(40) .9
	1.5			1.5		1.7	1.5	1.6	1.4	1.5
	2.5			2.4	% Officers', Directors', Owners' Comp/Revenues	3.4	3.7	2.9	2.8	2.4
	(21) 3.7		(27) 3.4			(27) 6.0	(30) 5.8	(23) 6.1	(26) 6.7	(27) 3.4
	6.0			6.1		9.6	10.1	8.9	8.8	6.1
2686M	88350M	70828M		161864M	Contract Revenues ($)	174545M	153620M	144408M	163996M	161864M
809M	32225M	30621M		63655M	Total Assets ($)	68843M	60326M	57451M	58007M	63655M

M = $ thousand   MM = $ million
See Pages 1 through 15 for Explanation of Ratios and Data

Current Data Sorted By Revenue | **Comparative Historical Data**

2	15	15	4	36	# Postretirement Benefits / Type of Statement			11	18	36
5	98	117	23	243	Unqualified	257	246	250	243	243
13	93	12	1	119	Reviewed	125	111	106	100	119
14	9	4	1	28	Compiled	35	39	30	38	28
2	4			6	Tax Returns	3	2	3	2	6
2	30	16	7	55	Other	41	36	50	40	55

123 (4/1-9/30/94)   328 (10/1/94-3/31/95)

0-1MM **36**	1-10MM **234**	10-50MM **149**	50 & OVER **32**	ALL **451**		4/1/90-3/31/91 ALL **461**	4/1/91-3/31/92 ALL **434**	4/1/92-3/31/93 ALL **439**	4/1/93-3/31/94 ALL **423**	4/1/94-3/31/95 ALL **451**
%	%	%	%	%	**NUMBER OF STATEMENTS** / **ASSETS**	%	%	%	%	%
16.0	14.7	16.0	11.8	15.0	Cash & Equivalents	13.9	15.0	15.6	15.0	15.0
25.7	29.9	29.5	23.5	29.0	A/R - Progress Billings	28.5	27.3	26.4	27.9	29.0
1.3	4.3	5.1	4.4	4.3	A/R - Current Retention	3.8	3.6	4.4	3.8	4.3
2.9	3.0	3.3	4.1	3.2	Inventory	3.5	3.3	3.4	3.5	3.2
1.4	2.9	2.5	3.3	2.7	Cost & Est. Earnings In Excess of Billings	3.0	2.3	2.6	2.8	2.7
2.4	3.1	3.2	7.1	3.3	All Other Current	3.5	3.7	3.3	3.3	3.3
49.8	57.9	59.6	54.2	57.5	Total Current	56.2	55.2	55.7	56.3	57.5
41.3	33.8	34.0	40.4	35.0	Fixed Assets (net)	35.6	35.9	35.8	35.5	35.0
.1	.9	1.1	1.0	.9	Joint Ventures & Investments	1.6	1.8	1.5	1.6	.9
.2	1.7	.9	.4	1.2	Intangibles (net)	.7	1.1	.8	.8	1.2
8.7	5.8	4.4	3.9	5.4	All Other Non-Current	5.9	6.0	6.1	5.8	5.4
100.0	100.0	100.0	100.0	100.0	Total	100.0	100.0	100.0	100.0	100.0
					LIABILITIES					
5.4	4.8	3.8	4.0	4.4	Notes Payable - Short Term	5.4	5.5	4.9	4.7	4.4
12.5	16.8	18.1	13.9	16.7	A/P - Trade	16.7	15.0	16.1	16.9	16.7
.0	.5	1.1	1.2	.7	A/P - Retention	.6	.7	.7	.6	.7
.7	1.9	3.7	4.4	2.6	Billings in Excess of Costs & Est. Earnings	2.2	1.9	2.4	2.0	2.6
2.1	.9	.8	.6	.9	Income Taxes Payable	1.0	.7	.8	.8	.9
9.4	5.6	5.4	4.4	5.8	Cur. Mat. - L/T/D	6.2	6.1	5.7	5.8	5.8
8.8	5.0	5.0	6.3	5.4	All Other Current	4.9	5.5	5.4	5.1	5.4
39.0	35.5	37.8	34.9	36.5	Total Current	37.0	35.3	36.1	36.0	36.5
18.5	12.5	12.9	18.4	13.5	Long Term Debt	14.5	15.0	14.5	13.9	13.5
.3	1.7	1.7	1.9	1.6	Deferred Taxes	2.0	2.0	1.8	1.7	1.6
3.0	1.4	1.4	2.3	1.6	All Other Non-Current	1.1	1.4	1.3	1.6	1.6
39.1	49.0	46.2	42.5	46.8	Net Worth	45.4	46.3	46.3	46.8	46.8
100.0	100.0	100.0	100.0	100.0	Total Liabilities & Net Worth	100.0	100.0	100.0	100.0	100.0
					INCOME DATA					
100.0	100.0	100.0	100.0	100.0	Contract Revenues	100.0	100.0	100.0	100.0	100.0
42.4	20.3	14.0	11.6	19.4	Gross Profit	18.5	18.7	19.0	18.8	19.4
35.2	16.0	10.1	8.1	15.0	Operating Expenses	15.2	16.5	16.2	15.0	15.0
7.2	4.3	3.9	3.4	4.3	Operating Profit	3.2	2.2	2.8	3.8	4.3
1.1	.1	.1	.3	.2	All Other Expenses (net)	.4	.4	.2	.1	.2
6.1	4.2	3.8	3.2	4.2	Profit Before Taxes	2.8	1.8	2.5	3.7	4.2
					RATIOS					
2.4	2.4	2.1	1.8	2.3	Current	2.2	2.3	2.3	2.3	2.3
1.1	1.7	1.5	1.5	1.5		1.5	1.6	1.5	1.6	1.5
.9	1.2	1.2	1.3	1.2		1.2	1.2	1.2	1.2	1.2
(33) 7.2	(233) 3.8	2.7	2.7	(447) 3.3	Receivables/Payables	(455) 3.1	(429) 3.6	(435) 3.2	(419) 3.0	(447) 3.3
2.5	2.1	1.8	2.0	2.0		1.9	2.1	2.0	1.8	2.0
1.4	1.4	1.4	1.6	1.4		1.4	1.4	1.4	1.4	1.4
16 22.3	37 10.0	35 10.3	30 12.3	33 10.9	Revenues/Receivables	33 10.9	32 11.5	29 12.4	31 11.8	33 10.9
40 9.1	56 6.5	51 7.1	53 6.9	53 6.9		51 7.1	49 7.4	46 7.9	51 7.1	53 6.9
85 4.3	78 4.7	73 5.0	66 5.5	74 4.9		72 5.1	70 5.2	73 5.0	72 5.1	74 4.9
5 80.0	16 23.4	20 18.2	17 21.8	17 21.2	Cost of Revenues/Payables	17 22.1	15 25.0	15 24.6	17 21.8	17 21.2
29 12.8	29 12.8	31 11.7	25 14.4	29 12.5		30 12.2	27 13.4	28 12.9	30 12.5	29 12.5
70 5.2	51 7.2	45 8.1	35 10.5	49 7.5		47 7.7	46 8.0	48 7.6	51 7.1	49 7.5
9.1	5.8	8.2	8.2	6.8	Revenues/Working Capital	7.1	6.7	6.6	6.6	6.8
29.2	10.6	13.7	11.0	12.4		12.7	12.7	12.9	12.2	12.4
NM	24.8	21.8	20.2	27.2		29.0	28.2	32.9	26.3	27.2
(28) 7.1	(211) 16.6	(144) 11.6	(31) 21.0	(414) 14.0	EBIT/Interest	(425) 6.4	(401) 5.5	(404) 7.7	(388) 9.7	(414) 14.0
2.9	4.9	4.9	5.0	4.8		2.8	2.4	3.2	4.0	4.8
1.3	1.9	2.1	1.5	1.8		1.2	.9	1.3	1.7	1.8
(12) 3.9	(114) 4.4	(80) 3.1	(17) 4.6	(223) 3.9	Net Profit + Depr., Dep., Amort./Cur. Mat. L/T/D	(274) 3.4	(262) 3.4	(249) 4.2	(283) 4.1	(223) 3.9
2.2	2.4	2.0	2.7	2.3		1.7	1.7	2.1	2.0	2.3
1.3	1.7	1.3	1.0	1.4		.9	.9	1.3	1.3	1.4
.6	.4	.5	.6	.4	Fixed/Worth	.5	.5	.5	.5	.4
1.2	.7	.8	1.0	.8		.8	.8	.8	.8	.8
2.2	1.2	1.1	1.1	1.3		1.3	1.3	1.2	1.2	1.2
.5	.5	.7	1.0	.6	Debt/Worth	.7	.6	.6	.6	.6
1.6	1.2	1.3	1.4	1.3		1.3	1.2	1.3	1.2	1.3
3.7	2.1	2.1	2.8	2.2		2.3	2.2	2.2	2.4	2.2
(34) 65.6	(229) 34.0	30.8	28.2	(444) 32.8	% Profit Before Taxes/Tangible Net Worth	(454) 24.0	(423) 22.7	(429) 26.2	(418) 28.9	(444) 32.8
24.9	17.0	16.2	21.6	17.3		11.7	9.9	11.0	14.8	17.3
5.7	4.3	5.9	3.5	5.0		1.7	.5	1.8	4.7	5.0
15.7	16.2	13.6	15.2	14.9	% Profit Before Taxes/Total Assets	10.2	10.4	10.9	12.5	14.9
8.8	7.0	7.4	8.5	7.4		5.1	4.2	4.7	5.8	7.4
2.1	2.0	2.5	1.1	2.2		.6	.1	.6	2.0	2.2
(34) 2.7	(218) 2.3	(143) 1.7	(27) 2.4	(422) 2.2	% Depr., Dep., Amort./Revenues	(434) 2.2	(409) 2.2	(424) 2.1	(393) 1.8	(422) 2.2
5.8	3.8	3.1	3.2	3.6		3.7	3.7	3.6	3.5	3.6
8.4	5.5	4.9	4.5	5.4		5.5	5.6	5.9	5.1	5.4
(20) 5.4	(128) 1.9	(67) .9		(218) 1.6	% Officers', Directors', Owners' Comp/Revenues	(198) 1.6	(186) 1.8	(206) 1.8	(193) 1.5	(218) 1.6
8.3	3.2	1.7		2.8		2.9	3.3	3.3	2.8	2.8
12.5	5.3	2.4		5.0		6.3	5.9	6.6	5.0	5.0
21177M	1082932M	3332693M	6574098M	11010900M	Contract Revenues ($)	7488612M	7324181M	6767540M	6064532M	11010900M
16860M	552380M	1605482M	3743229M	5917951M	Total Assets ($)	3711311M	3481231M	3293730M	3033464M	5917951M

M = $ thousand   MM = $ million
See Pages 1 through 15 for Explanation of Ratios and Data

Current Data Sorted By Revenue | Comparative Historical Data

	1	9	1		11	# Postretirement Benefits / Type of Statement			3	4	11
	2	8	7		17	Unqualified	30	17	20	12	17
	4	47	3		54	Reviewed	44	50	38	41	54
	7	14			21	Compiled	26	14	15	12	21
	3	1			4	Tax Returns	4			2	4
	4	9		2	15	Other	7	6	5	12	15

24 (4/1-9/30/94)			87 (10/1/94-3/31/95)				4/1/90-3/31/91	4/1/91-3/31/92	4/1/92-3/31/93	4/1/93-3/31/94	4/1/94-3/31/95
0-1MM	1-10MM	10-50MM	50 & OVER	ALL			ALL	ALL	ALL	ALL	ALL
20	79	12		111		NUMBER OF STATEMENTS	111	87	78	79	111
%	%	%	%	%		ASSETS	%	%	%	%	%
15.6	13.4	13.7		13.9		Cash & Equivalents	12.0	11.7	12.3	13.2	13.9
35.5	46.0	50.2		44.6		A/R - Progress Billings	40.9	44.1	41.1	41.4	44.6
4.2	6.0	5.6		5.6		A/R - Current Retention	6.2	7.0	5.3	6.6	5.6
4.5	3.9	2.9		3.9		Inventory	4.8	2.5	2.5	2.3	3.9
.9	3.2	5.6		3.0		Cost & Est. Earnings In Excess of Billings	2.9	2.3	2.9	3.4	3.0
2.0	2.9	4.8		2.9		All Other Current	2.8	3.8	5.2	4.3	2.9
62.8	75.4	82.9		74.0		Total Current	69.6	71.4	69.3	71.3	74.0
30.2	18.0	9.8		19.4		Fixed Assets (net)	20.4	18.6	20.6	20.5	19.4
.5	.9	.1		.8		Joint Ventures & investments	1.5	1.4	1.7	1.2	.8
2.6	.9	.3		1.2		Intangibles (net)	.8	.7	.8	.7	1.2
3.9	4.6	6.9		4.7		All Other Non-Current	7.6	8.0	7.6	6.3	4.7
100.0	100.0	100.0		100.0		Total	100.0	100.0	100.0	100.0	100.0
						LIABILITIES					
8.7	10.5	5.2		9.6		Notes Payable - Short Term	12.6	9.8	10.9	10.2	9.6
11.5	16.9	16.6		15.9		A/P - Trade	15.3	15.3	15.1	16.1	15.9
.0	.1	2.8		.4		A/P - Retention	.0	.1	.0	.6	.4
1.3	5.0	4.5		4.3		Billings in Excess of Costs & Est. Earnings	3.7	3.4	4.0	4.2	4.3
.2	1.1	1.0		.9		Income Taxes Payable	.6	1.1	.7	.8	.9
2.7	2.3	.6		2.2		Cur. Mat. - L/T/D	4.6	3.0	3.4	2.7	2.2
12.0	8.3	15.3		9.7		All Other Current	6.9	7.8	7.1	8.5	9.7
36.5	44.3	46.0		43.0		Total Current	43.7	40.5	41.2	43.2	43.0
11.7	5.9	2.2		6.6		Long Term Debt	8.6	6.0	8.7	9.2	6.6
1.3	2.2	.0		1.8		Deferred Taxes	1.5	1.9	1.0	1.1	1.8
4.5	1.4	2.4		2.1		All Other Non-Current	1.0	2.5	2.1	2.2	2.1
46.0	46.2	49.5		46.5		Net Worth	45.3	49.1	46.9	44.3	46.5
100.0	100.0	100.0		100.0		Total Liabilities & Net Worth	100.0	100.0	100.0	100.0	100.0
						INCOME DATA					
100.0	100.0	100.0		100.0		Contract Revenues	100.0	100.0	100.0	100.0	100.0
32.5	21.0	15.6		22.5		Gross Profit	22.8	21.2	21.1	20.9	22.5
30.8	17.2	12.6		19.2		Operating Expenses	20.5	19.4	19.9	18.7	19.2
1.7	3.7	3.0		3.3		Operating Profit	2.3	1.8	1.2	2.3	3.3
–.6	.1	.3		.0		All Other Expenses (net)	.1	.2	.3	.3	.0
2.3	3.6	2.8		3.3		Profit Before Taxes	2.2	1.6	.9	2.0	3.3
						RATIOS					
3.2	2.7	2.0		2.7	Current	2.8	2.7	2.8	2.6	2.7
1.9	1.8	1.8		1.8		1.5	1.7	1.7	1.7	1.8
1.3	1.2	1.5		1.2		1.2	1.2	1.2	1.2	1.2
14.0	5.6	4.3		5.4	Receivables/Payables	6.4	6.4	6.2	5.1	5.4
4.2 (78)	3.6	3.0 (110)		3.6	(110) / (86) / (76) / (110)	3.7	3.9	4.2	3.2	3.6
2.4	2.4	2.5		2.4		2.2	2.4	2.2	1.9	2.4
(18) 20.4	(47) 7.8	(55) 6.6	(42) 8.7	8.7	Revenues/Receivables	(46) 8.0	(52) 7.0	(46) 7.9	(47) 7.8	(42) 8.7
(47) 7.8	(62) 5.9	(74) 4.9	(62) 5.9	5.9		(60) 6.1	(68) 5.4	(61) 6.0	(68) 5.4	(62) 5.9
(91) 4.0	(79) 4.6	(96) 3.8	(83) 3.8	4.4		(81) 4.5	(85) 4.3	(79) 4.6	(94) 3.9	(83) 4.4
(6) 56.5	(14) 26.7	(20) 18.6	(14) 27.0	27.0	Cost of Revenues/Payables	(12) 30.3	(12) 29.9	(12) 31.3	(12) 30.0	(14) 27.0
(14) 27.0	(23) 16.1	(26) 14.3	(23) 16.2	16.2		(20) 18.6	(21) 17.3	(19) 18.9	(27) 13.6	(23) 16.2
(43) 8.5	(37) 10.0	(36) 10.2	(37) 10.2	10.0		(37) 10.0	(38) 9.5	(36) 10.2	(43) 8.4	(37) 10.0
5.5	5.5	5.8		5.5	Revenues/Working Capital	5.8	5.3	5.5	5.2	5.5
14.4	11.6	8.4		10.9		12.3	10.1	8.9	8.3	10.9
60.3	26.4	9.2		24.8		40.1	29.0	28.1	29.2	24.8
22.0	20.6	105.8		22.0	EBIT/Interest	10.7	8.5	7.5	10.9	22.0
(19) 10.0	(64) 7.3	(10) 4.9	(93) 7.5	7.5	(97) / (75) / (65) / (67) / (93)	3.1	2.8	2.4	4.7	7.5
1.0	2.0	1.5		1.9		1.2	1.0	.1	1.2	1.9
	10.4			10.9	Net Profit + Depr., Dep., Amort./Cur. Mat. L/T/D	5.7	7.8	6.7	8.3	10.9
(30)	6.0		(44)	6.0	(55) / (45) / (35) / (36) / (44)	3.0	3.4	3.2	2.8	6.0
	2.5			2.4		.7	.9	.7	1.2	2.4
.2	.2	.1		.2	Fixed/Worth	.2	.2	.2	.2	.2
.5	.4	.2		.4		.4	.3	.4	.4	.4
1.1	.8	.3		.8		.9	.7	.7	1.0	.8
.4	.6	.7		.6	Debt/Worth	.5	.5	.4	.5	.6
.9	1.2	.9		1.0		1.2	1.1	1.1	1.1	1.0
3.2	2.3	1.6		2.3		2.9	2.1	2.7	2.6	2.3
71.1	45.4	34.1		48.2	% Profit Before Taxes/Tangible Net Worth	38.7	28.4	24.1	29.7	48.2
(18) 33.1	(78) 19.5	7.5	(108) 18.8	18.8	(108) / (84) / (75) / (74) / (108)	15.2	11.5	7.8	14.0	18.8
–4.6	6.1	2.1		4.7		3.6	.5	–6.3	1.6	4.7
25.3	18.4	19.5		20.0	% Profit Before Taxes/Total Assets	15.5	11.8	10.9	13.8	20.0
14.5	9.0	3.8		8.9		6.0	5.8	3.5	6.2	8.9
–5.8	2.9	1.9		1.9		.9	.1	–4.3	.9	1.9
1.0	1.0	.4		.8	% Depr., Dep., Amort./Revenues	1.1	1.0	1.0	.9	.8
(18) 2.5	(78) 1.4	.5	(108) 1.4	1.4	(102) / (81) / (72) / (75) / (108)	2.1	1.9	1.7	1.5	1.4
4.5	2.1	.8		2.2		3.1	2.8	3.0	2.4	2.2
3.6	1.9			2.1	% Officers', Directors', Owners' Comp/Revenues	2.7	2.3	3.0	2.2	2.1
(12) 10.2	(54) 3.3		(74) 3.5	3.5	(61) / (53) / (52) / (51) / (74)	4.8	4.4	5.6	4.1	3.5
18.9	5.2			5.9		7.7	8.3	9.6	9.7	5.9
10442M	288743M	201889M		501074M	Contract Revenues ($)	584898M	395245M	393449M	316379M	501074M
6864M	104112M	69013M		179989M	Total Assets ($)	240663M	180111M	156141M	126641M	179989M

M = $ thousand   MM = $ million
See Pages 1 through 15 for Explanation of Ratios and Data

Current Data Sorted By Revenue						Comparative Historical Data				
2	7	4	4	17	**# Postretirement Benefits** **Type of Statement**				1	1	17
	4	6	4	14	Unqualified	13	7	7	6	14
1	5	2		8	Reviewed	7	8	9	11	8
8	12	1		21	Compiled	31	21	23	17	21
1	1			2	Tax Returns		2	2	6	2
2	13	4	2	21	Other	12	10	15	14	21

	23 (4/1-9/30/94)			43 (10/1/94-3/31/95)			4/1/90- 3/31/91	4/1/91- 3/31/92	4/1/92- 3/31/93	4/1/93- 3/31/94	4/1/94- 3/31/95
	0-1MM	1-10MM	10-50MM	50 & OVER	ALL		ALL	ALL	ALL	ALL	ALL
	12	35	13	6	66	NUMBER OF STATEMENTS	63	48	56	54	66
	%	%	%	%	%	**ASSETS**	%	%	%	%	%
	10.0	6.2	1.7		6.4	Cash & Equivalents	8.3	9.0	8.7	8.0	6.4
	14.8	32.6	35.4		29.5	A/R - Progress Billings	38.2	32.7	30.7	32.0	29.5
	.0	2.3	.1		1.2	A/R - Current Retention	1.9	.2	1.6	1.6	1.2
	6.2	3.1	6.4		4.9	Inventory	5.4	6.3	8.7	6.4	4.9
	.3	.0	.9		.3	Cost & Est. Earnings In Excess of Billings	1.0	.3	.7	.1	.3
	5.2	2.3	4.0		3.4	All Other Current	2.8	3.2	3.6	3.3	3.4
	36.5	46.5	48.6		45.7	Total Current	57.5	51.7	54.1	51.5	45.7
	54.4	41.4	33.5		41.6	Fixed Assets (net)	33.3	40.1	35.3	34.0	41.6
	.0	1.4	.2		.9	Joint Ventures & Investments	1.3	.6	1.3	1.3	.9
	.1	.7	7.9		2.5	Intangibles (net)	1.8	.2	1.3	2.7	2.5
	9.0	10.0	9.8		9.3	All Other Non-Current	6.0	7.4	8.1	10.6	9.3
	100.0	100.0	100.0		100.0	Total	100.0	100.0	100.0	100.0	100.0
						LIABILITIES					
	10.1	8.3	8.8		8.1	Notes Payable - Short Term	11.9	11.5	9.5	9.7	8.1
	13.8	14.9	10.5		13.5	A/P - Trade	13.1	12.3	13.5	12.1	13.5
	.0	.0	.0		.0	A/P - Retention	.4	.4	.9	.7	.0
	.0	.2	.1		.2	Billings in Excess of Costs & Est. Earnings	.1	.1	.0	.0	.2
	.1	1.5	1.2		1.1	Income Taxes Payable	2.0	1.0	.5	.5	1.1
	5.1	6.5	5.6		5.7	Cur. Mat. - L/T/D	7.4	11.3	7.5	5.7	5.7
	5.7	6.2	6.2		6.7	All Other Current	5.8	6.8	9.2	8.5	6.7
	34.9	37.6	32.5		35.3	Total Current	40.7	43.3	41.2	37.2	35.3
	28.6	19.7	17.8		20.8	Long Term Debt	19.3	20.4	15.5	14.4	20.8
	.4	.7	1.5		.8	Deferred Taxes	1.7	.9	1.4	.9	.8
	.2	5.9	1.1		3.9	All Other Non-Current	.9	1.4	2.6	2.0	3.9
	35.9	36.1	47.0		39.2	Net Worth	37.4	33.9	39.3	45.6	39.2
	100.0	100.0	100.0		100.0	Total Liabilities & Net Worth	100.0	100.0	100.0	100.0	100.0
						INCOME DATA					
	100.0	100.0	100.0		100.0	Contract Revenues	100.0	100.0	100.0	100.0	100.0
						Gross Profit					
	91.5	93.6	90.8		92.6	Operating Expenses	92.9	94.9	97.1	95.1	92.6
	8.5	6.4	9.2		7.4	Operating Profit	7.1	5.1	2.9	4.9	7.4
	2.4	3.0	2.3		2.6	All Other Expenses (net)	1.4	1.9	.7	1.8	2.6
	6.2	3.5	6.8		4.8	Profit Before Taxes	5.8	3.2	2.2	3.1	4.8
						RATIOS					
	3.4	1.8	2.0		2.0	Current	2.3	1.8	2.2	2.1	2.0
	1.2	1.3	1.6		1.4		1.4	1.3	1.4	1.3	1.4
	.6	1.0	1.1		1.0		1.1	.8	.9	1.1	1.0
(10)	UND	4.3	6.7		4.8	Receivables/Payables	5.2	4.4	5.7	4.4	4.8
	1.4	2.9	4.3	(64) 2.8	2.8		(47) 3.6	(55) 3.1	(53) 2.6	(64) 2.9	2.8
	.5	1.3	1.7		1.3		2.3	1.6	1.5	1.4	1.3
14	26.6	35 10.4	41 8.9	35 10.4	10.4	Revenues/Receivables	49 7.4	34 10.6	36 10.2	40 9.2	35 10.4
34	10.6	51 7.1	60 6.1	52 7.0	7.0		60 6.1	46 7.9	53 6.9	51 7.1	52 7.0
111	3.3	69 5.3	83 4.4	83 4.4	4.4		78 4.7	60 6.1	70 5.2	76 4.8	83 4.4
						Cost of Revenues/Payables					
	5.8	9.6	8.6		7.7	Revenues/Working Capital	6.7	8.0	7.4	6.9	7.7
	NM	30.1	16.6		17.9		15.6	23.5	12.8	14.8	17.9
	-5.5	-406.7	46.9		NM		70.0	-23.9	-37.2	71.8	NM
(10)	3.9	(31) 10.4	(12) 14.1	(59) 7.2	7.2	EBIT/Interest	(56) 8.6	(44) 7.6	(50) 5.6	(50) 6.1	(59) 7.2
	1.5	2.5	3.9	2.5	2.5		3.9	2.8	3.4	2.8	2.5
	-.3	.5	1.4	1.1	1.1		2.0	.7	.6	1.3	1.1
		(21) 3.5		(28) 3.7	3.7	Net Profit + Depr., Dep., Amort./Cur. Mat. L./T/D	(38) 5.5	(24) 2.4	(27) 3.3	(28) 3.8	3.7
		2.0		1.9	1.9		2.4	1.4	1.9	2.0	1.9
		.9		.9	.9		1.1	.4	.6	.9	.9
	.9	.6	.3		.6	Fixed/Worth	.5	.6	.5	.4	.6
	1.7	1.0	1.0		1.0		.9	1.0	.9	.9	1.0
	5.4	1.9	1.5		1.8		1.8	3.1	1.8	1.5	1.8
	.8	.9	.9		.9	Debt/Worth	.7	.8	.7	.6	.9
	1.6	1.5	1.4		1.5		1.8	1.8	1.5	1.2	1.5
	7.2	2.5	2.1		2.3		3.8	7.0	3.0	2.2	2.3
(10)	34.5	(31) 47.9	(12) 45.4	(59) 35.4	35.4	% Profit Before Taxes/Tangible Net Worth	(57) 78.9	(43) 48.8	(49) 32.8	(51) 31.6	(59) 35.4
	5.7	11.6	14.0	11.6	11.6		28.8	26.1	13.9	12.7	11.6
	-11.6	-2.5	3.5	2.5	2.5		10.9	7.2	-.2	2.3	2.5
	6.1	16.6	19.5		14.5	% Profit Before Taxes/Total Assets	24.0	16.3	12.8	11.7	14.5
	2.1	4.3	6.0		4.8		10.3	8.8	4.7	4.6	4.8
	-2.6	-1.6	1.5		-.1		4.6	-1.4	-1.0	.7	-.1
	3.2	(30) 2.3	(10) .9	(55) 2.7	2.7	% Depr., Dep., Amort./Revenues	(58) 2.0	(44) 2.2	(51) 2.7	(49) 2.1	(55) 2.7
	8.1	5.8	3.1	5.7	5.7		3.4	3.6	4.5	3.8	5.7
	19.5	6.6	9.5	7.2	7.2		5.6	6.4	6.2	6.1	7.2
		(11) 2.2		(22) 2.2	2.2	% Officers', Directors', Owners' Comp/Revenues	(22) 2.9	(18) 3.1	(26) 3.5	(24) 2.8	(22) 2.2
		2.8		3.3	3.3		7.2	7.0	5.0	4.9	3.3
		4.8		5.7	5.7		8.7	9.8	8.0	6.1	5.7
	6466M	129347M	273279M	3664022M	4073114M	Contract Revenues ($)	977383M	531176M	345242M	2937880M	4073114M
	8209M	107141M	333858M	3658909M	4108117M	Total Assets ($)	701300M	402151M	136350M	2728582M	4108117M

© Robert Morris Associates 1995

M = $ thousand   MM = $ million
See Pages 1 through 15 for Explanation of Ratios and Data

Current Data Sorted By Revenue | **Comparative Historical Data**

Type of Statement

0-1MM	1-10MM	10-50MM	50 & OVER	ALL	Type of Statement	4/1/90-3/31/91	4/1/91-3/31/92	4/1/92-3/31/93	4/1/93-3/31/94	4/1/94-3/31/95
	1		4	5	Unqualified	6	6	3	5	5
	5			5	Reviewed	4	2	3	1	5
1	5			6	Compiled	5	10	8	5	6
1	1			2	Tax Returns			1		2
3	3	3	1	10	Other	5	4	2	4	10

9 (4/1-9/30/94)   19 (10/1/94-3/31/95)

0-1MM	1-10MM	10-50MM	50 & OVER	ALL	NUMBER OF STATEMENTS	ALL	ALL	ALL	ALL	ALL
5	15	3	5	28		20	23	16	15	28
%	%	%	%	%	**ASSETS**	%	%	%	%	%
	9.2			9.0	Cash & Equivalents	10.1	8.5	8.5	3.7	9.0
	29.1			23.3	A/R - Progress Billings	29.4	25.9	27.9	30.0	23.3
	.0			2.8	A/R - Current Retention	1.6	3.7	7.3	.0	2.8
	4.4			3.5	Inventory	4.3	1.9	3.0	2.0	3.5
	.0			.0	Cost & Est. Earnings In Excess of Billings	1.1	.9	1.5	.9	.0
	2.1			2.0	All Other Current	1.7	4.6	5.9	3.7	2.0
	44.8			40.6	Total Current	48.2	45.6	54.2	40.3	40.6
	45.2			49.9	Fixed Assets (net)	44.5	44.9	31.9	41.6	49.9
	3.2			2.3	Joint Ventures & Investments	2.7	1.2	6.9	1.6	2.3
	.1			.6	Intangibles (net)	.2	.3	.0	1.9	.6
	6.8			6.7	All Other Non-Current	4.3	8.0	6.9	14.6	6.7
	100.0			100.0	Total	100.0	100.0	100.0	100.0	100.0
					LIABILITIES					
	8.2			5.0	Notes Payable - Short Term	4.7	7.5	5.6	6.8	5.0
	13.8			12.4	A/P - Trade	18.8	13.4	16.7	18.6	12.4
	.0			.0	A/P - Retention	.0	.0	.0	.0	.0
	.0			.2	Billings in Excess of Costs & Est. Earnings	.6	.0	.6	.4	.2
	.2			.5	Income Taxes Payable	1.5	2.2	1.4	.3	.5
	6.1			3.9	Cur. Mat. - L/T/D	6.9	4.3	6.6	7.5	3.9
	4.8			6.3	All Other Current	7.8	6.0	4.4	5.4	6.3
	33.1			28.3	Total Current	40.2	33.4	35.3	39.0	28.3
	15.7			17.8	Long Term Debt	27.4	19.2	8.2	22.2	17.8
	1.5			1.1	Deferred Taxes	2.1	1.2	1.2	.6	1.1
	1.8			7.1	All Other Non-Current	5.5	5.8	.2	10.5	7.1
	48.0			45.8	Net Worth	24.7	40.3	55.1	27.6	45.8
	100.0			100.0	Total Liabilities & Net Worth	100.0	100.0	100.0	100.0	100.0
					INCOME DATA					
	100.0			100.0	Contract Revenues	100.0	100.0	100.0	100.0	100.0
					Gross Profit					
	97.0			96.7	Operating Expenses	95.2	90.8	98.3	96.1	96.7
	3.0			3.3	Operating Profit	4.8	9.2	1.7	3.9	3.3
	.4			.4	All Other Expenses (net)	-.3	1.7	.3	.0	.4
	2.6			3.0	Profit Before Taxes	5.1	7.4	1.4	3.9	3.0
					RATIOS					
	2.1			2.9	Current	1.8	2.3	2.2	1.9	2.9
	1.5			1.5		1.1	1.4	1.5	1.0	1.5
	.9			1.1		.8	1.0	1.0	.7	1.1
	10.1			10.1	Receivables/Payables	4.5	4.8	4.4	3.2	10.1
	(14) 3.0			(26) 2.4		1.7	(21) 2.5	1.9	1.6	(26) 2.4
	1.5			1.2		1.1	1.5	1.3	1.2	1.2
	19 19.1			21 17.2	Revenues/Receivables	38 9.7	40 9.1	37 9.9	37 10.0	21 17.2
	50 7.3			55 6.6		51 7.2	54 6.7	49 7.4	57 6.4	55 6.6
	63 5.8			74 4.9		70 5.2	94 3.9	101 3.6	78 4.7	74 4.9
					Cost of Revenues/Payables					
	9.0			5.5	Revenues/Working Capital	5.9	6.5	8.1	11.9	5.5
	11.9			11.5		196.0	12.4	14.6	UND	11.5
	-76.9			64.4		-26.4	-171.9	NM	-10.1	64.4
	8.0			7.8	EBIT/Interest	9.2	17.7	6.4	6.6	7.8
	(14) 3.1			(27) 2.6		(20) 3.7	(13) 3.9	(14) 2.5	(14) 1.5	(27) 2.6
	1.3			1.2		1.5	1.5	-2.3	.5	1.2
					Net Profit + Depr., Dep., Amort./Cur. Mat. L/T/D	13.0	5.9		4.8	
						(14) 2.6	(14) 3.3		(10) 1.9	
						1.7	1.1		1.0	
	.6			.6	Fixed/Worth	.7	.5	.2	.5	.6
	.8			.8		1.9	1.0	.7	1.0	.8
	1.8			1.6		51.4	1.7	1.0	11.5	1.6
	.6			.5	Debt/Worth	1.0	.5	.4	.7	.5
	.8			.8		2.5	1.2	.6	1.9	.8
	2.4			2.1		292.6	2.4	1.6	17.6	2.1
	31.9			28.2	% Profit Before Taxes/ Tangible Net Worth	60.9	24.0	17.9	30.0	28.2
	(14) 11.4			(26) 6.1		(16) 36.4	(20) 10.4	(12) 8.9	10.5	(26) 6.1
	-2.8			.3		-1.5	6.3	-19.8	-.5	.3
	18.6			15.5	% Profit Before Taxes/ Total Assets	27.1	14.2	10.0	14.3	15.5
	3.0			2.9		7.6	5.7	4.4	1.5	2.9
	-.2			.4		-3.0	3.3	-6.9	-1.1	.4
	2.9			2.7	% Depr., Dep., Amort./ Revenues	4.8	3.6	4.4	2.3	2.7
	(12) 4.2			(17) 4.5		6.3	(21) 5.1	(13) 5.7	(13) 4.7	(17) 4.5
	5.9			6.2		8.1	6.6	6.8	7.5	6.2
					% Officers', Directors', Owners' Comp/Revenues					3.6
										(11) 5.3
										21.2
2618M	48532M	106908M	2594765M	2752823M	Contract Revenues ($)	398060M	274184M	92513M	608996M	2752823M
7418M	27826M	31652M	5773995M	5840891M	Total Assets ($)	433809M	442427M	54594M	593570M	5840891M

M = $ thousand   MM = $ million
See Pages 1 through 15 for Explanation of Ratios and Data

Current Data Sorted By Revenue   **Comparative Historical Data**

	2	1	3		# Postretirement Benefits Type of Statement				1	3
	3	10	3	16	Unqualified	21	20	22	15	16
	2	45	3	50	Reviewed	55	62	42	48	50
	11	7		18	Compiled	34	17	21	21	18
	4	2		6	Tax Returns			2	2	6
		10		10	Other	14	20	7	17	10

39 (4/1-9/30/94)   61 (10/1/94-3/31/95)

Historical periods: 4/1/90-3/31/91 · 4/1/91-3/31/92 · 4/1/92-3/31/93 · 4/1/93-3/31/94 · 4/1/94-3/31/95

0-1MM	1-10MM	10-50MM	50 & OVER	ALL		91	92	93	94	95
20	74	6		100	NUMBER OF STATEMENTS	124	119	94	103	100
%	%	%	%	%	**ASSETS**	%	%	%	%	%
16.1	14.4			14.2	Cash & Equivalents	14.4	16.8	13.9	14.3	14.2
29.2	43.2			40.7	A/R - Progress Billings	40.8	39.1	40.4	42.0	40.7
4.4	2.3			2.9	A/R - Current Retention	4.4	4.0	4.6	2.0	2.9
2.2	3.8			3.5	Inventory	3.8	4.1	3.3	3.2	3.5
.4	4.2			3.9	Cost & Est. Earnings In Excess of Billings	3.0	4.1	3.6	4.7	3.9
5.5	3.5			3.8	All Other Current	4.1	2.4	3.4	2.3	3.8
57.8	71.4			69.0	Total Current	70.4	70.5	69.2	68.5	69.0
33.2	18.8			21.5	Fixed Assets (net)	19.1	19.4	20.8	20.5	21.5
.1	.9			.7	Joint Ventures & Investments	.4	.7	1.7	1.0	.7
3.8	.9			1.4	Intangibles (net)	1.2	1.3	.6	1.7	1.4
5.1	8.0			7.4	All Other Non-Current	9.0	8.0	7.6	8.3	7.4
100.0	100.0			100.0	Total	100.0	100.0	100.0	100.0	100.0
					LIABILITIES					
8.6	9.3			9.6	Notes Payable - Short Term	9.4	10.0	11.0	9.7	9.6
12.8	12.2			13.0	A/P - Trade	14.1	12.5	13.3	15.1	13.0
.0	.3			.2	A/P - Retention	.3	.6	.0	.0	.2
.0	1.8			1.8	Billings in Excess of Costs & Est. Earnings	1.9	1.6	2.1	1.6	1.8
1.1	1.2			1.2	Income Taxes Payable	1.2	1.2	.9	1.0	1.2
8.6	3.6			4.5	Cur. Mat. - L/T/D	3.3	4.6	3.3	4.0	4.5
6.1	10.0			9.0	All Other Current	8.9	7.2	8.6	9.3	9.0
37.2	38.4			39.3	Total Current	39.1	37.7	39.3	40.6	39.3
17.1	6.3			8.6	Long Term Debt	10.2	11.0	9.6	10.3	8.6
.0	1.7			1.3	Deferred Taxes	1.5	1.0	1.0	1.9	1.3
5.8	3.2			3.6	All Other Non-Current	2.1	1.0	1.5	2.8	3.6
39.9	50.4			47.2	Net Worth	47.1	49.1	48.6	44.3	47.2
100.0	100.0			100.0	Total Liabilities & Net Worth	100.0	100.0	100.0	100.0	100.0
					INCOME DATA					
100.0	100.0			100.0	Contract Revenues	100.0	100.0	100.0	100.0	100.0
35.4	29.6			30.2	Gross Profit	26.8	28.7	28.7	28.0	30.2
31.8	24.1			25.2	Operating Expenses	22.7	24.9	26.0	25.8	25.2
3.6	5.4			5.0	Operating Profit	4.1	3.7	2.7	2.2	5.0
.2	.4			.4	All Other Expenses (net)	.5	.5	.5	.5	.4
3.4	5.0			4.5	Profit Before Taxes	3.6	3.3	2.2	1.7	4.5
					RATIOS					
4.7	3.0			2.9	Current	3.3	3.9	3.5	2.7	2.9
1.4	2.0			1.9		1.9	2.0	1.9	1.8	1.9
1.0	1.4			1.2		1.3	1.3	1.3	1.2	1.2
(19) 9.8	(73) 9.2		(98)	9.2	Receivables/Payables	(122) 7.8	(118) 7.9	(92) 7.1	(101) 8.0	(98) 9.2
3.2	3.6			3.6		3.4	4.0	5.0	3.3	3.6
1.8	2.5			2.3		2.3	2.7	2.2	1.9	2.3
24 15.2	45 8.2		38	9.6	Revenues/Receivables	42 8.7	44 8.3	41 8.8	37 9.8	38 9.6
34 10.6	69 5.3		58	6.3		61 6.0	58 6.3	58 6.3	65 5.6	58 6.3
49 7.4	85 4.3		81	4.5		74 4.9	76 4.8	79 4.6	79 4.6	81 4.5
5 68.8	12 31.6		11	32.2	Cost of Revenues/Payables	8 48.5	9 41.8	9 41.5	10 37.7	11 32.2
14 26.0	20 18.2		19	19.5		19 18.8	19 19.3	15 24.5	21 17.2	19 19.5
38 9.6	32 11.4		33	10.9		35 10.4	31 11.6	34 10.6	38 9.7	33 10.9
9.5	4.4			4.7	Revenues/Working Capital	5.3	4.6	5.5	5.1	4.7
18.8	8.1			9.6		9.2	8.4	9.2	9.9	9.6
UND	17.0			23.5		18.6	19.4	23.8	31.5	23.5
(17) 30.4	(61) 12.6		(84)	13.9	EBIT/Interest	(112) 13.4	(102) 9.0	(85) 10.8	(88) 8.6	(84) 13.9
1.1	3.3			3.1		4.6	3.6	2.8	3.4	3.1
-2.1	1.0			.4		1.1	1.5	.1	.1	.4
	(30) 5.3		(39)	5.3	Net Profit + Depr., Dep., Amort./Cur. Mat. L./T/D	(65) 9.7	(55) 5.0	(38) 3.4	(50) 3.5	(39) 5.3
	2.0			2.1		3.5	2.0	1.4	1.1	2.1
	.5			.6		1.2	1.2	.5	.0	.6
.3	.1			.2	Fixed/Worth	.2	.2	.2	.2	.2
.8	.4			.4		.4	.3	.3	.4	.4
2.3	.7			.8		.8	.8	.7	1.1	.8
.4	.5			.5	Debt/Worth	.5	.5	.4	.5	.5
1.3	.9			1.0		1.1	1.0	1.0	1.2	1.0
4.6	2.0			2.4		2.2	2.4	2.4	3.1	2.4
(17) 45.1	(70) 39.4		(92)	39.5	% Profit Before Taxes/Tangible Net Worth	(119) 36.5	(114) 29.7	(90) 26.9	(94) 29.6	(92) 39.5
.0	11.7			10.2		16.4	13.9	10.2	11.3	10.2
-33.3	1.7			-.3		2.6	4.8	-.4	-3.9	-.3
35.1	21.0			21.3	% Profit Before Taxes/Total Assets	19.2	14.5	14.1	14.9	21.3
.0	4.8			4.6		7.9	7.3	4.5	4.9	4.6
-12.0	1.2			-.2		.7	1.2	-.8	-3.0	-.2
(15) 1.6	(70) .9		(90)	.9	% Depr., Dep., Amort./Revenues	(119) .7	(108) .8	(87) .9	(92) 1.1	(90) .9
2.1	1.8			1.8		1.4	1.5	1.4	1.8	1.8
3.3	2.5			2.5		2.2	2.8	2.5	2.7	2.5
(12) 2.6	(44) 3.0		(57)	2.8	% Officers', Directors', Owners' Comp/Revenues	(71) 3.3	(63) 3.5	(51) 2.8	(63) 3.0	(57) 2.8
7.3	5.1			5.3		6.4	6.0	5.9	6.3	5.3
12.0	7.5			7.9		10.3	12.5	10.1	10.9	7.9
13118M	246942M	84827M		344887M	Contract Revenues ($)	481587M	400826M	348809M	358648M	344887M
5977M	107669M	28226M		141872M	Total Assets ($)	180358M	173765M	140531M	140707M	141872M

M = $ thousand   MM = $ million
See Pages 1 through 15 for Explanation of Ratios and Data

Current Data Sorted By Revenue   Comparative Historical Data

Postretirement Benefits / Type of Statement

0-1MM	1-10MM	10-50MM	50 & OVER	ALL	Type of Statement	4/1/90-3/31/91	4/1/91-3/31/92	4/1/92-3/31/93	4/1/93-3/31/94	4/1/94-3/31/95
2	10			12	# Postretirement Benefits			4	9	12
2	21	6	4	33	Unqualified	56	46	40	46	33
1	77	5		83	Reviewed	106	84	80	72	83
4	29	1		34	Compiled	55	46	41	42	34
1	5			6	Tax Returns	2	4	5	7	6
7	13	3	1	24	Other	23	11	16	22	24

67 (4/1-9/30/94)   113 (10/1/94-3/31/95)

0-1MM	1-10MM	10-50MM	50 & OVER	ALL		4/1/90-3/31/91 ALL	4/1/91-3/31/92 ALL	4/1/92-3/31/93 ALL	4/1/93-3/31/94 ALL	4/1/94-3/31/95 ALL
15	145	15	5	180	**NUMBER OF STATEMENTS**	242	191	182	189	180
%	%	%	%	%	**ASSETS**	%	%	%	%	%
5.4	10.3	4.9		9.2	Cash & Equivalents	12.2	13.2	11.3	11.3	9.2
51.2	48.3	54.4		49.3	A/R - Progress Billings	48.3	44.4	43.8	43.8	49.3
4.1	6.5	2.7		5.8	A/R - Current Retention	3.4	3.8	4.5	7.3	5.8
11.7	6.4	6.5		6.9	Inventory	6.5	7.9	7.4	6.2	6.9
.0	3.5	4.7		3.3	Cost & Est. Earnings In Excess of Billings	3.3	3.6	3.5	3.2	3.3
3.6	4.0	4.9		4.1	All Other Current	3.6	3.2	4.1	4.3	4.1
76.1	78.9	78.1		78.7	Total Current	77.2	76.0	74.7	76.2	78.7
16.1	12.5	15.6		13.1	Fixed Assets (net)	13.7	13.8	14.8	13.2	13.1
.0	1.6	.3		1.4	Joint Ventures & Investments	1.3	.9	1.0	1.2	1.4
3.5	.7	.1		.9	Intangibles (net)	1.0	1.1	1.2	1.0	.9
4.3	6.3	5.9		6.0	All Other Non-Current	6.7	8.1	8.3	8.4	6.0
100.0	100.0	100.0		100.0	Total	100.0	100.0	100.0	100.0	100.0
					LIABILITIES					
18.0	10.4	13.0		11.1	Notes Payable - Short Term	10.3	11.6	12.1	11.9	11.1
20.8	20.2	26.5		20.6	A/P - Trade	19.2	16.6	17.1	18.4	20.6
.0	.4	.0		.3	A/P - Retention	.3	.0	.0	.3	.3
.7	3.8	3.0		3.5	Billings in Excess of Costs & Est. Earnings	5.1	3.6	3.5	2.9	3.5
.4	1.1	.9		1.0	Income Taxes Payable	1.1	.9	.7	.6	1.0
1.1	2.0	1.2		1.8	Cur. Mat. - L/T/D	3.3	2.7	2.7	2.1	1.8
13.4	9.1	10.0		9.8	All Other Current	10.4	9.1	7.4	9.1	9.8
54.4	46.9	54.6		48.1	Total Current	49.6	44.4	43.5	45.3	48.1
13.6	6.8	8.7		7.9	Long Term Debt	8.0	6.5	7.4	8.7	7.9
.8	1.5	.3		1.3	Deferred Taxes	1.1	1.6	1.0	1.0	1.3
2.7	2.2	.7		2.3	All Other Non-Current	1.1	1.0	2.5	1.6	2.3
28.4	42.5	35.8		40.4	Net Worth	40.2	46.5	45.6	43.4	40.4
100.0	100.0	100.0		100.0	Total Liabilities & Net Worth	100.0	100.0	100.0	100.0	100.0
					INCOME DATA					
100.0	100.0	100.0		100.0	Contract Revenues	100.0	100.0	100.0	100.0	100.0
25.9	20.2	14.9		20.1	Gross Profit	22.4	22.6	22.5	22.4	20.1
26.8	17.5	12.8		17.8	Operating Expenses	19.9	21.1	20.7	20.9	17.8
-.9	2.7	2.1		2.3	Operating Profit	2.5	1.5	1.8	1.5	2.3
.2	.1	.3		.1	All Other Expenses (net)	.2	.2	.3	.0	.1
-1.0	2.6	1.8		2.2	Profit Before Taxes	2.3	1.3	1.5	1.4	2.2
					RATIOS					
2.3	2.5	1.8		2.3	Current	2.3	2.7	2.5	2.5	2.3
1.6	1.7	1.5		1.7		1.6	1.8	1.7	1.7	1.7
1.1	1.3	1.1		1.3		1.2	1.3	1.3	1.3	1.3
UND	5.7	4.1		5.6	Receivables/Payables	5.9	6.0	5.7	5.2	5.6
(14) 4.8	(142) 3.2	2.6	(176) 3.1			(239) 3.1	(189) 3.5	(180) 3.3	(186) 3.2	(176) 3.1
1.7	1.9	1.4		1.8		1.9	2.0	1.9	1.9	1.8
30 12.2	45 8.1	54 6.7		46 8.0	Revenues/Receivables	44 8.3	41 8.8	43 8.4	47 7.8	46 8.0
66 5.5	63 5.8	62 5.9		64 5.7		57 6.4	56 6.5	57 6.4	62 5.9	64 5.7
243 1.5	81 4.5	79 4.6		81 4.5		79 4.6	72 5.1	76 4.8	76 4.8	81 4.5
0 UND	13 27.9	20 18.1		13 27.3	Cost of Revenues/Payables	12 29.9	12 31.1	13 28.5	14 25.3	13 27.3
23 16.1	26 14.2	33 11.0		26 14.1		23 16.0	21 17.5	22 16.8	23 15.7	26 14.1
57 6.4	38 9.5	49 7.4		39 9.4		40 9.2	33 11.0	39 9.4	39 9.4	39 9.4
4.9	6.6	8.5		6.6	Revenues/Working Capital	6.8	6.1	6.2	5.8	6.6
10.7	11.6	12.1		11.3		11.6	10.5	10.0	11.1	11.3
61.7	19.0	70.1		19.8		29.3	21.7	21.1	24.1	19.8
4.7	14.3	11.5		11.4	EBIT/Interest	13.5	9.4	10.8	9.1	11.4
(10) -.4	(126) 5.1	2.7	(156) 4.4			(212) 3.9	(175) 2.5	(167) 3.1	(165) 2.7	(156) 4.4
-7.1	1.8	1.2		1.2		1.1	-.1	-.1	-.0	1.2
	7.5			7.5	Net Profit + Depr., Dep., Amort./Cur. Mat. L /T/D	7.7	8.8	4.2	4.4	7.5
	(57) 3.0		(73) 2.7			(129) 2.1	(95) 2.5	(94) 1.8	(88) 1.6	(73) 2.7
	1.1			1.2		.4	.2	-.2	-.7	1.2
.2	.1	.2		.1	Fixed/Worth	.1	.1	.1	.1	.1
.9	.3	.2		.3		.3	.3	.3	.2	.3
-19.3	.5	.5		.6		.7	.5	.6	.5	.6
.9	.7	.9		.8	Debt/Worth	.7	.6	.6	.6	.8
2.3	1.5	2.3		1.5		1.6	1.2	1.3	1.4	1.5
-21.3	2.6	3.3		3.1		3.3	2.5	2.9	2.8	3.1
65.6	44.6	21.7		43.0	% Profit Before Taxes/ Tangible Net Worth	37.9	26.1	28.7	30.1	43.0
(11) 13.2	(141) 18.2	11.0	(172) 16.3			(229) 18.0	(182) 9.1	(176) 9.3	(180) 7.9	(172) 16.3
-13.4	1.6	2.3		1.7		3.3	-2.6	-4.3	-1.4	1.7
11.1	15.3	8.3		14.2	% Profit Before Taxes/ Total Assets	12.9	11.7	12.6	10.5	14.2
1.5	6.4	3.7		5.6		6.8	3.4	4.0	3.0	5.6
-11.7	.8	.7		.6		.4	-1.9	-2.7	-1.3	.6
.5	.4	.4		.4	% Depr., Dep., Amort./ Revenues	.5	.6	.6	.5	.4
(11) .8	(136) .7	.7	(167) .7			(218) .8	(180) 1.0	(170) 1.0	(168) .8	(167) .7
1.8	1.2	.9		1.2		1.4	1.5	1.5	1.3	1.2
	2.7			2.7	% Officers', Directors', Owners' Comp/Revenues	2.3	2.7	2.9	2.8	2.7
	(94) 4.3		(109) 4.1			(141) 4.1	(105) 4.9	(102) 5.1	(102) 4.5	(109) 4.1
	6.6			6.6		7.7	9.0	7.1	7.2	6.6
7785M	542445M	275322M	724999M	1550551M	Contract Revenues ($)	1723061M	1518181M	2425385M	1318700M	1550551M
3874M	177953M	92720M	254033M	528580M	Total Assets ($)	562340M	509080M	647730M	465072M	528580M

M = $ thousand   MM = $ million
See Pages 1 through 15 for Explanation of Ratios and Data

Current Data Sorted By Revenue						Comparative Historical Data				
4	32	16		52	**# Postretirement Benefits** **Type of Statement**			21	31	52
4	59	58	8	129	Unqualified	148	163	142	108	129
17	242	22		281	Reviewed	298	323	271	269	281
37	85	1	1	124	Compiled	163	151	134	120	124
14	7	2		23	Tax Returns	7	6	9	17	23
18	75	18	1	112	Other	70	60	71	67	112
241 (4/1-9/30/94)			428 (10/1/94-3/31/95)			4/1/90-3/31/91	4/1/91-3/31/92	4/1/92-3/31/93	4/1/93-3/31/94	4/1/94-3/31/95
0-1MM	1-10MM	10-50MM	50 & OVER	ALL		ALL	ALL	ALL	ALL	ALL
90	468	101	10	669	**NUMBER OF STATEMENTS**	686	703	627	581	669
%	%	%	%	%	**ASSETS**	%	%	%	%	%
13.0	10.8	9.3	9.4	10.9	Cash & Equivalents	11.2	12.1	11.1	12.2	10.9
29.6	44.4	48.8	56.7	43.3	A/R - Progress Billings	42.8	42.7	42.7	42.2	43.3
2.6	4.9	8.0	8.6	5.1	A/R - Current Retention	5.6	5.7	4.8	5.3	5.1
15.0	9.5	4.7	2.7	9.4	Inventory	10.2	8.6	9.9	9.0	9.4
.9	4.2	4.8	3.4	3.9	Cost & Est. Earnings In Excess of Billings	3.4	3.9	4.2	4.3	3.9
2.4	3.4	6.0	6.4	3.7	All Other Current	3.5	3.7	3.5	3.3	3.7
63.6	77.3	81.5	87.3	76.3	Total Current	76.6	76.7	76.4	76.2	76.3
28.0	16.1	10.7	8.1	16.8	Fixed Assets (net)	16.8	16.7	16.3	16.3	16.8
.1	.8	1.5	.3	.8	Joint Ventures & Investments	.4	.4	.6	.5	.8
2.0	.7	.7	.0	.9	Intangibles (net)	.7	.6	.9	1.1	.9
6.3	5.1	5.7	4.3	5.3	All Other Non-Current	5.5	5.5	5.8	5.7	5.3
100.0	100.0	100.0	100.0	100.0	Total	100.0	100.0	100.0	100.0	100.0
					LIABILITIES					
11.7	8.1	8.7	1.4	8.6	Notes Payable - Short Term	9.1	8.0	8.2	7.7	8.6
15.0	24.1	26.6	30.5	23.4	A/P - Trade	23.0	23.8	23.7	23.9	23.4
.0	.4	1.0	2.9	.5	A/P - Retention	.6	.5	.6	.5	.5
1.1	3.7	6.7	8.3	3.9	Billings in Excess of Costs & Est. Earnings	3.7	3.7	3.6	3.9	3.9
.7	.8	1.1	.1	.8	Income Taxes Payable	1.0	.8	.8	.8	.8
5.5	3.4	1.8	.7	3.4	Cur. Mat. - L/T/D	3.9	3.5	3.7	3.5	3.4
8.3	9.8	11.4	14.5	9.9	All Other Current	8.6	7.5	8.3	8.6	9.9
42.4	50.3	57.3	58.5	50.4	Total Current	50.0	47.8	48.8	48.9	50.4
16.0	8.6	5.4	9.9	9.2	Long Term Debt	9.0	8.7	8.3	9.1	9.2
.5	1.0	.6	.1	.8	Deferred Taxes	.9	1.1	1.1	1.0	.8
2.2	1.5	1.8	1.1	1.6	All Other Non-Current	1.5	1.5	1.8	2.1	1.6
38.9	38.6	34.8	30.3	38.0	Net Worth	38.6	40.8	40.0	38.9	38.0
100.0	100.0	100.0	100.0	100.0	Total Liabilities & Net Worth	100.0	100.0	100.0	100.0	100.0
					INCOME DATA					
100.0	100.0	100.0	100.0	100.0	Contract Revenues	100.0	100.0	100.0	100.0	100.0
38.0	24.5	16.1	11.9	24.9	Gross Profit	25.1	23.8	24.2	24.0	24.9
33.4	21.8	14.1	9.1	22.0	Operating Expenses	22.7	22.0	22.5	21.8	22.0
4.6	2.8	2.1	2.8	2.9	Operating Profit	2.4	1.8	1.7	2.2	2.9
.6	.3	.2	.0	.4	All Other Expenses (net)	.5	.4	.4	.2	.4
4.0	2.4	1.9	2.8	2.5	Profit Before Taxes	1.9	1.4	1.3	2.0	2.5
					RATIOS					
2.6	2.2	1.6	1.9	2.1	Current	2.1	2.3	2.3	2.2	2.1
1.6	1.5	1.4	1.5	1.5		1.6	1.6	1.6	1.6	1.5
1.1	1.2	1.2	1.3	1.2		1.2	1.3	1.3	1.3	1.2
(82) 4.3	(466) 3.4	2.8	3.0	(659) 3.4	Receivables/Payables	(679) 3.2	(701) 3.3	(622) 3.2	(573) 3.1	(659) 3.4
2.1	2.1	2.0	1.9	2.1		2.1	2.2	2.2	2.0	2.1
1.3	1.5	1.6	1.5	1.5		1.6	1.5	1.4	1.4	1.5
24 15.3	40 9.1	54 6.8	58 6.3	40 9.2	Revenues/Receivables	37 9.8	39 9.3	38 9.6	38 9.6	40 9.2
40 9.2	56 6.5	68 5.4	74 4.9	56 6.5		56 6.5	57 6.4	55 6.6	55 6.6	56 6.5
57 6.4	74 4.9	81 4.5	94 3.9	74 4.9		73 5.0	74 4.9	72 5.1	74 4.9	74 4.9
11 32.8	23 16.2	26 13.9	30 12.1	21 17.0	Cost of Revenues/Payables	20 17.9	20 18.6	20 18.4	21 17.0	21 17.0
24 14.9	33 10.9	37 10.0	42 8.7	33 10.9		32 11.4	33 10.9	32 11.4	34 10.8	33 10.9
44 8.3	49 7.5	51 7.1	57 6.4	49 7.4		48 7.6	50 7.3	50 7.3	48 7.6	49 7.4
6.5	7.0	9.3	7.4	7.3	Revenues/Working Capital	7.6	6.8	7.2	7.0	7.3
13.1	12.3	14.5	10.2	12.6		11.9	10.8	11.5	11.6	12.6
59.3	24.9	20.6	18.9	23.9		23.7	20.4	21.9	21.6	23.9
(75) 9.0	(413) 9.9	(95) 12.9		(591) 10.4	EBIT/Interest	(609) 9.0	(611) 8.8	(544) 9.1	(516) 11.6	(591) 10.4
5.0	4.0	5.8		4.2		3.3	2.8	2.9	4.3	4.2
1.8	1.6	1.8		1.8		1.2	.6	.9	1.4	1.8
(25) 7.6	(234) 5.3	(47) 6.4		(309) 5.9	Net Profit + Depr., Dep., Amort./Cur. Mat. L./T/D	(368) 6.8	(347) 5.0	(299) 6.1	(307) 5.5	(309) 5.9
2.2	2.5	3.1		2.6		2.5	1.9	2.1	2.7	2.6
.5	1.0	2.0		1.1		1.0	.4	.6	.9	1.1
.3	.2	.2	.2	.2	Fixed/Worth	.2	.2	.2	.2	.2
.8	.4	.3	.2	.4		.4	.3	.3	.3	.4
1.9	.7	.5	.3	.8		.8	.7	.7	.8	.8
.7	.8	1.2	1.6	.9	Debt/Worth	.9	.7	.8	.8	.9
1.6	1.7	2.2	2.6	1.7		1.6	1.5	1.6	1.7	1.7
5.6	3.1	3.1	3.3	3.2		3.1	3.0	3.0	3.3	3.2
(81) 93.5	(449) 34.5	32.4	19.6	(641) 36.7	% Profit Before Taxes/ Tangible Net Worth	(648) 36.6	(665) 30.6	(592) 25.1	(546) 33.4	(641) 36.7
26.7	15.8	14.6	11.4	15.9		15.4	11.7	11.6	14.2	15.9
4.5	4.5	3.1	1.5	4.5		2.2	.3	.5	3.5	4.5
23.0	11.9	10.5	7.5	12.5	% Profit Before Taxes/ Total Assets	13.4	11.5	10.2	11.9	12.5
9.0	5.6	4.6	3.1	5.6		5.6	4.2	4.0	5.4	5.6
1.4	1.6	1.1	.3	1.5		.5	-.7	-.1	1.0	1.5
(75) 1.0	(444) .8	(95) .5		(623) .7	% Depr., Dep., Amort./ Revenues	(635) .7	(663) .7	(593) .7	(544) .7	(623) .7
1.8	1.3	.7		1.2		1.2	1.2	1.2	1.2	1.2
3.6	1.8	1.1		1.8		1.9	1.9	1.8	1.9	1.8
(50) 6.1	(295) 2.3	(43) 1.2		(391) 2.2	% Officers', Directors', Owners' Comp/Revenues	(364) 2.6	(394) 2.3	(353) 2.2	(325) 2.4	(391) 2.2
9.3	4.0	1.8		4.1		4.5	4.6	4.3	4.5	4.1
12.6	6.7	3.6		7.4		7.3	7.1	7.4	7.4	7.4
52794M	1767397M	2009876M	5794464M	9624531M	Contract Revenues ($)	9041515M	4580046M	8021039M	5065597M	9624531M
24526M	598730M	673415M	2011615M	3308286M	Total Assets ($)	2591705M	1528793M	2650918M	1637907M	3308286M

M = $ thousand   MM = $ million
See Pages 1 through 15 for Explanation of Ratios and Data

Current Data Sorted By Revenue						Comparative Historical Data				

Postretirement Benefits / Type of Statement

0-1MM	1-10MM	10-50MM	50 & OVER	ALL				3	9	20
3	15	2		20	**# Postretirement Benefits** / **Type of Statement**					
	16	11		27	Unqualified	46	33	27	34	27
8	111	5		124	Reviewed	148	118	121	119	124
14	31			45	Compiled	47	38	45	36	45
3				3	Tax Returns	3	3	3	7	3
6	23	3		32	Other	29	25	20	24	32

61 (4/1-9/30/94)   170 (10/1/94-3/31/95)

0-1MM	1-10MM	10-50MM	50 & OVER	ALL		4/1/90-3/31/91 ALL	4/1/91-3/31/92 ALL	4/1/92-3/31/93 ALL	4/1/93-3/31/94 ALL	4/1/94-3/31/95 ALL
31	181	19		231	**NUMBER OF STATEMENTS**	273	217	216	220	231
%	%	%	%	%	**ASSETS**	%	%	%	%	%
16.9	10.7	5.6		11.1	Cash & Equivalents	11.3	12.6	10.5	11.7	11.1
32.4	45.3	49.0		43.9	A/R - Progress Billings	38.4	35.6	39.6	40.9	43.9
1.6	3.8	5.9		3.7	A/R - Current Retention	4.6	4.8	4.5	4.5	3.7
8.2	8.4	6.1		8.2	Inventory	11.2	10.0	10.5	9.0	8.2
2.0	4.4	4.2		4.1	Cost & Est. Earnings In Excess of Billings	3.9	3.6	3.8	4.8	4.1
1.6	3.0	3.7		2.9	All Other Current	4.0	3.8	3.7	2.8	2.9
62.8	75.7	74.5		73.9	Total Current	73.4	70.4	72.6	73.8	73.9
26.4	16.6	12.8		17.6	Fixed Assets (net)	18.8	19.6	19.6	16.8	17.6
.2	1.2	.0		1.0	Joint Ventures & Investments	.4	1.7	.6	1.1	1.0
2.9	.6	.0		.9	Intangibles (net)	.7	.5	1.2	1.1	.9
7.8	5.8	12.6		6.7	All Other Non-Current	6.7	7.8	6.1	7.1	6.7
100.0	100.0	100.0		100.0	Total	100.0	100.0	100.0	100.0	100.0
					LIABILITIES					
13.7	10.0	10.7		10.5	Notes Payable - Short Term	8.1	11.3	11.1	11.3	10.5
21.9	21.6	20.2		21.6	A/P - Trade	21.6	21.5	20.4	22.0	21.6
.0	.1	.1		.1	A/P - Retention	.1	.1	.1	.3	.1
1.1	2.3	4.1		2.3	Billings in Excess of Costs & Est. Earnings	2.1	2.1	2.4	3.3	2.3
.5	.9	.3		.8	Income Taxes Payable	.8	.6	.6	.7	.8
2.5	3.1	2.2		2.9	Cur. Mat.- L/T/D	4.2	3.7	3.6	3.0	2.9
8.7	10.5	11.5		10.4	All Other Current	7.8	8.2	8.2	8.2	10.4
48.4	48.5	49.1		48.5	Total Current	44.7	47.6	46.4	48.9	48.5
14.0	7.7	5.2		8.3	Long Term Debt	9.1	9.5	9.3	8.4	8.3
.2	1.3	.2		1.1	Deferred Taxes	1.0	.5	1.0	.9	1.1
1.1	1.4	1.0		1.3	All Other Non-Current	1.1	1.4	1.0	.9	1.3
36.2	41.1	44.6		40.8	Net Worth	44.1	41.0	42.3	41.0	40.8
100.0	100.0	100.0		100.0	Total Liabilities & Net Worth	100.0	100.0	100.0	100.0	100.0
					INCOME DATA					
100.0	100.0	100.0		100.0	Contract Revenues	100.0	100.0	100.0	100.0	100.0
36.6	24.3	20.3		25.7	Gross Profit	26.3	25.1	24.6	24.2	25.7
31.1	21.0	19.0		22.2	Operating Expenses	23.4	23.4	23.2	21.6	22.2
5.5	3.3	1.4		3.4	Operating Profit	2.8	1.7	1.4	2.6	3.4
.2	.3	.4		.3	All Other Expenses (net)	.4	.2	.3	.1	.3
5.2	3.0	1.0		3.1	Profit Before Taxes	2.4	1.5	1.1	2.5	3.1
					RATIOS					
2.0	2.3	1.9		2.2	Current	2.5	2.2	2.4	2.2	2.2
1.4	1.6	1.5		1.6		1.7	1.5	1.6	1.6	1.6
.9	1.2	1.3		1.2		1.2	1.1	1.2	1.2	1.2
3.8	3.7	4.0		3.8	Receivables/Payables	3.8	3.5	4.1	3.9	3.8
(27) 2.1	(179) 2.4	2.9	(225) 2.4	2.4		(213) 2.1	(213) 2.1	(217) 2.4	(225) 2.3	2.4
.9	1.6	2.1		1.6		1.4	1.3	1.6	1.5	1.6
25 14.5	37 9.8	50 7.3	36 10.1	10.1	Revenues/Receivables	35 10.3	33 11.1	34 10.6	35 10.4	36 10.1
37 10.0	56 6.5	69 5.3	55 6.6	6.6		53 6.9	50 7.3	53 6.9	54 6.7	55 6.6
65 5.6	79 4.6	78 4.7	78 4.7	4.7		74 4.9	70 5.2	73 5.0	74 4.9	78 4.7
7 50.2	18 20.0	19 19.7	17 21.2	21.2	Cost of Revenues/Payables	18 20.6	16 23.2	16 22.5	18 20.2	17 21.2
27 13.3	31 11.8	31 11.6	31 11.9	11.9		28 12.9	31 11.9	27 13.5	29 12.4	31 11.9
46 7.9	44 8.3	46 7.9	45 8.1	8.1		47 7.7	47 7.7	41 8.9	46 8.0	45 8.1
7.2	6.9	9.8		7.2	Revenues/Working Capital	6.3	7.0	6.7	7.1	7.2
21.1	11.1	13.1		11.8		10.9	11.9	11.5	11.5	11.8
-125.6	24.0	17.7		25.6		27.0	44.5	30.2	30.1	25.6
15.6	13.8	13.4		14.2	EBIT/Interest	7.2	6.0	6.9	10.5	14.2
(25) 7.4	(163) 4.6	2.4	(207) 4.5	4.5		(244) 3.1	(194) 2.4	(196) 2.3	(193) 3.8	(207) 4.5
.3	1.9	1.1		1.6		1.3	.8	-.2	1.6	1.6
	8.4			8.0	Net Profit + Depr., Dep., Amort./Cur. Mat. L/T/D	5.6	4.8	4.4	5.4	8.0
	(81) 3.3		(95) 3.5	3.5		(136) 2.7	(89) 1.8	(96) 2.3	(109) 2.8	(95) 3.5
	1.1			1.1		.8	.6	.6	1.1	1.1
.3	.2	.2		.2	Fixed/Worth	.2	.2	.2	.2	.2
.7	.4	.3		.4		.4	.5	.4	.4	.4
1.9	.7	.4		.8		.7	.9	.8	.7	.8
.5	.8	.7		.8	Debt/Worth	.7	.7	.7	.7	.8
1.5	1.4	1.3		1.4		1.3	1.5	1.4	1.4	1.4
4.6	2.7	1.9		2.7		2.5	3.0	2.6	2.7	2.7
71.4	44.5	27.2		46.1	% Profit Before Taxes/ Tangible Net Worth	33.9	30.9	29.0	40.2	46.1
(27) 43.0	(174) 18.1	5.8	(220) 18.9	18.9		(264) 15.4	(204) 8.1	(209) 9.6	(209) 18.1	(220) 18.9
4.3	6.0	.7		5.1		3.8	-.7	-5.4	3.1	5.1
47.3	15.6	10.3		16.6	% Profit Before Taxes/ Total Assets	13.6	12.6	11.4	15.0	16.6
16.3	6.8	2.6		6.9		5.8	3.3	3.4	6.3	6.9
-2.2	2.2	.3		1.8		.7	-.6	-2.0	1.0	1.8
1.3	.8	.8		.8	% Depr., Dep., Amort./ Revenues	.9	.9	.9	.7	.8
(27) 1.8	(174) 1.2	(18) 1.0	(219) 1.3	1.3		(250) 1.4	(200) 1.5	(202) 1.4	(200) 1.2	(219) 1.3
3.4	1.9	1.6		2.0		2.1	2.2	2.1	1.9	2.0
4.3	2.5			2.7	% Officers', Directors', Owners' Comp/Revenues	2.6	2.6	2.5	2.3	2.7
(22) 6.3	(101) 4.0		(129) 4.4	4.4		(137) 4.3	(103) 4.6	(124) 4.2	(121) 3.8	(129) 4.4
9.4	6.7			7.2		7.7	8.1	6.9	6.3	7.2
21140M	656125M	338816M		1016081M	Contract Revenues ($)	1211661M	878196M	862521M	885989M	1016081M
6797M	244103M	122113M		373013M	Total Assets ($)	442976M	322553M	296934M	308927M	373013M

M = $ thousand   MM = $ million
See Pages 1 through 15 for Explanation of Ratios and Data

Current Data Sorted By Revenue | Comparative Historical Data

Postretirement Benefits — Type of Statement

Type of Statement	1	4	3		8		1	4		8
Unqualified		10	11		21		25	41	29	16	21
Reviewed	3	39	3		45		36	39	33	38	45
Compiled	7	15	1		23		18	19	22	17	23
Tax Returns	1				1					1	1
Other	3	8	4	1	16		13	10	13	7	16

48 (4/1-9/30/94)   58 (10/1/94-3/31/95)

	0-1MM	1-10MM	10-50MM	50 & OVER	ALL		4/1/90-3/31/91	4/1/91-3/31/92	4/1/92-3/31/93	4/1/93-3/31/94	4/1/94-3/31/95
							ALL	ALL	ALL	ALL	ALL
NUMBER OF STATEMENTS	14	72	19	1	106		92	109	97	79	106
ASSETS	%	%	%	%	%		%	%	%	%	%
Cash & Equivalents	16.8	7.7	12.1		9.6		9.7	10.7	9.4	9.8	9.6
A/R - Progress Billings	39.1	47.1	39.2		44.9		36.8	40.7	41.1	38.2	44.9
A/R - Current Retention	1.1	4.0	4.4		3.6		6.6	5.3	5.4	3.5	3.6
Inventory	2.2	3.3	6.7		3.8		4.6	4.7	5.5	5.4	3.8
Cost & Est. Earnings In Excess of Billings	1.2	5.6	6.7		5.2		5.6	4.0	4.6	3.8	5.2
All Other Current	2.2	2.8	7.6		3.6		2.1	3.7	2.6	5.6	3.6
Total Current	62.7	70.5	76.6		70.6		65.4	69.1	68.7	66.3	70.6
Fixed Assets (net)	30.8	20.7	18.3		21.6		25.8	21.1	22.8	23.8	21.6
Joint Ventures & Investments	.0	.4	.3		.3		.7	.9	1.1	1.0	.3
Intangibles (net)	2.9	2.9	.1		2.4		.3	.4	.4	1.3	2.4
All Other Non-Current	3.6	5.6	4.6		5.1		7.7	8.5	7.0	7.6	5.1
Total	100.0	100.0	100.0		100.0		100.0	100.0	100.0	100.0	100.0
LIABILITIES											
Notes Payable - Short Term	12.1	12.1	9.0		11.5		7.8	9.9	10.7	10.9	11.5
A/P - Trade	16.3	18.8	21.9		18.9		17.0	15.9	16.6	19.3	18.9
A/P - Retention	.0	.1	.8		.2		.6	.0	.5	.2	.2
Billings in Excess of Costs & Est. Earnings	.9	3.0	3.1		2.7		4.3	2.6	3.0	2.6	2.7
Income Taxes Payable	1.4	.8	1.2		1.0		1.2	1.0	1.0	.4	1.0
Cur. Mat. - L/T/D	3.3	3.2	2.3		3.0		4.9	4.3	4.2	4.6	3.0
All Other Current	8.8	9.1	8.6		8.9		8.5	9.3	8.1	9.3	8.9
Total Current	42.8	47.2	46.8		46.3		44.2	43.1	44.2	47.2	46.3
Long Term Debt	21.1	10.9	10.1		12.0		14.3	9.1	9.5	12.3	12.0
Deferred Taxes	1.8	1.4	1.0		1.3		1.7	1.4	.9	.9	1.3
All Other Non-Current	.2	1.4	3.6		1.6		.6	2.4	1.4	1.8	1.6
Net Worth	34.1	39.1	38.4		38.7		39.1	44.0	44.1	37.9	38.7
Total Liabilities & Net Worth	100.0	100.0	100.0		100.0		100.0	100.0	100.0	100.0	100.0
INCOME DATA											
Contract Revenues	100.0	100.0	100.0		100.0		100.0	100.0	100.0	100.0	100.0
Gross Profit	36.6	19.0	16.6		21.2		22.2	22.5	22.7	21.3	21.2
Operating Expenses	29.6	17.4	12.6		18.4		18.8	18.7	20.8	20.1	18.4
Operating Profit	7.1	1.6	4.0		2.8		3.4	3.8	1.9	1.2	2.8
All Other Expenses (net)	.4	.5	1.1		.6		.9	.9	.4	.4	.6
Profit Before Taxes	6.7	1.1	2.9		2.2		2.5	3.0	1.6	.8	2.2

RATIOS

Ratio	0-1MM	1-10MM	10-50MM	50 & OVER	ALL	4/1/90-3/31/91	4/1/91-3/31/92	4/1/92-3/31/93	4/1/93-3/31/94	4/1/94-3/31/95
Current	2.3	2.1	3.0		2.3	2.2	2.5	2.5	1.9	2.3
	1.6	1.5	1.3		1.5	1.5	1.7	1.5	1.5	1.5
	.9	1.1	1.2		1.1	1.1	1.2	1.2	1.1	1.1
Receivables/Payables	UND	5.5	3.3		5.7	6.7	6.5	7.3	4.4	5.7
	(13) 2.4	3.1	2.6	(105)	2.9	2.5 (107)	3.3	3.1 (78)	2.2 (105)	2.9
	1.5	1.7	1.2		1.6	1.7	2.0	1.8	1.6	1.6
Revenues/Receivables	30 12.2	52 7.0	48 7.6	50	7.3	38 9.5	43 8.5	44 8.3	38 9.6	50 7.3
	54 6.8	74 4.9	66 5.5	69	5.3	61 6.0	63 5.8	62 5.9	52 7.0	69 5.3
	87 4.2	94 3.9	91 4.0	94	3.9	85 4.3	85 4.3	81 4.5	74 4.9	94 3.9
Cost of Revenues/Payables	0 UND	19 19.6	18 20.7	17	21.1	14 25.5	8 47.6	11 34.6	14 25.3	17 21.1
	28 13.2	31 11.8	38 9.7	31	11.6	26 13.8	24 15.3	27 13.5	30 12.3	31 11.6
	53 6.9	45 8.1	61 6.0	50	7.3	46 8.0	41 8.8	47 7.8	47 7.8	50 7.3
Revenues/Working Capital	6.2	6.7	4.7		6.3	7.4	5.9	6.0	7.1	6.3
	13.4	10.4	10.9		10.8	12.3	10.6	12.7	15.4	10.8
	-47.9	31.2	22.3		27.7	46.8	33.3	33.5	51.6	27.7
EBIT/Interest	17.8	16.5	11.4		15.9	5.3	13.9	10.8	7.9	15.9
	(10) 7.2	(63) 3.5	(18) 2.5	(92)	4.0	(86) 2.8	(97) 2.4	(87) 4.0	(72) 2.2	(92) 4.0
	4.3	1.0	1.3		1.4	1.2	1.3	.5	-.8	1.4
Net Profit + Depr., Dep., Amort./Cur. Mat. L./T/D		6.4	4.8		6.6	5.1	5.6	5.5	3.9	6.6
		(34) 2.2	(11) 2.7	(52)	3.0	(59) 2.3	(51) 2.2	(44) 2.0	(44) 1.3	(52) 3.0
		.8	1.5		.9	.9	1.0	.1	-.2	.9
Fixed/Worth	.2	.2	.2		.2	.3	.1	.2	.2	.2
	.9	.5	.4		.5	.6	.4	.4	.5	.5
	2.2	1.4	.8		1.3	1.3	1.2	1.0	2.1	1.3
Debt/Worth	1.2	.7	.7		.7	.9	.6	.6	.9	.7
	2.3	1.6	2.3		1.8	1.8	1.4	1.5	1.5	1.8
	6.5	5.2	3.3		4.1	3.1	2.8	2.6	4.0	4.1
% Profit Before Taxes/Tangible Net Worth	100.9	47.9	24.1		46.3	39.7	31.6	34.1	24.5	46.3
	39.5 (64)	14.5	8.3	(98)	16.2	(90) 14.8	(106) 15.3	(94) 11.4	(69) 7.1	(98) 16.2
	24.5	1.4	5.0		4.1	3.0	2.7	-2.7	-10.7	4.1
% Profit Before Taxes/Total Assets	22.2	12.7	8.6		15.8	14.7	12.9	14.9	10.5	15.8
	13.4	4.7	3.2		5.0	5.7	4.5	5.3	3.2	5.0
	7.4	.1	.7		1.0	.8	.9	-1.9	-4.7	1.0
% Depr., Dep., Amort./Revenues	1.3	.9	.7		.9	.7	.8	.7	.9	.9
	(12) 2.2	(69) 1.5	(18) 1.4	(99)	1.5	(89) 2.0	(99) 1.4	(92) 1.5	(76) 1.4	(99) 1.5
	6.7	2.9	2.5		2.7	3.5	2.5	2.8	3.3	2.7
% Officers', Directors', Owners' Comp/Revenues		2.6	1.7		2.4	1.5	2.3	2.1	3.0	2.4
	(42)	3.6	(10) 2.3	(60)	3.6	(50) 3.9	(49) 3.9	(46) 3.8	(42) 4.3	(60) 3.6
		2.9	3.6		6.7	8.2	7.9	6.6	5.7	6.7
Contract Revenues ($)	8147M	285058M	415647M	1020231M	1729083M	787025M	1031179M	624532M	446823M	1729083M
Total Assets ($)	3726M	134078M	188326M	537463M	863593M	377882M	470023M	275642M	187544M	863593M

M = $ thousand   MM = $ million
See Pages 1 through 15 for Explanation of Ratios and Data

Current Data Sorted By Revenue   Comparative Historical Data

Postretirement Benefits / Type of Statement

Type of Statement	0-1MM	1-10MM	10-50MM	50 & OVER	ALL		4/1/90-3/31/91	4/1/91-3/31/92	4/1/92-3/31/93	4/1/93-3/31/94	4/1/94-3/31/95
# Postretirement Benefits	2	5		1	8					2	8
Unqualified	3	9	4	2	18		14	7	15	6	18
Reviewed	4	28	4	1	37		30	21	41	14	37
Compiled	4	16			20		24	17	15	4	20
Tax Returns	2	1			3		1	2	1	2	3
Other	4	23	3		30		9	6	16	9	30

Current: 20 (4/1-9/30/94)   88 (10/1/94-3/31/95)

	0-1MM	1-10MM	10-50MM	50 & OVER	ALL		4/1/90-3/31/91 ALL	4/1/91-3/31/92 ALL	4/1/92-3/31/93 ALL	4/1/93-3/31/94 ALL	4/1/94-3/31/95 ALL
NUMBER OF STATEMENTS	17	77	11	3	108		78	53	88	35	108
ASSETS	%	%	%	%	%		%	%	%	%	%
Cash & Equivalents	19.8	8.3	7.9		10.5		12.3	14.2	10.1	10.5	10.5
A/R - Progress Billings	33.4	42.5	38.1		40.7		33.1	33.8	36.7	34.8	40.7
A/R - Current Retention	.1	2.6	1.3		2.0		3.5	1.8	2.8	1.6	2.0
Inventory	16.0	12.8	11.8		12.9		13.6	13.2	11.1	13.9	12.9
Cost & Est. Earnings In Excess of Billings	.3	2.6	9.7		2.9		2.7	4.2	4.1	4.9	2.9
All Other Current	2.6	3.2	1.3		3.0		2.4	2.3	2.6	3.8	3.0
Total Current	72.2	72.1	70.0		72.1		67.5	69.4	67.4	69.6	72.1
Fixed Assets (net)	20.8	20.3	23.9		20.6		21.9	22.3	22.7	20.2	20.6
Joint Ventures & Investments	.0	.1	.3		.1		.5	.6	.6	.2	.1
Intangibles (net)	1.5	2.2	.4		1.8		.5	.4	.9	1.1	1.8
All Other Non-Current	5.6	5.3	5.4		5.4		9.7	7.3	8.4	9.0	5.4
Total	100.0	100.0	100.0		100.0		100.0	100.0	100.0	100.0	100.0
LIABILITIES											
Notes Payable - Short Term	12.4	9.8	7.4		10.0		11.6	11.3	11.3	14.0	10.0
A/P - Trade	4.1	20.2	18.8		17.7		19.6	19.0	17.0	20.7	17.7
A/P - Retention	.0	.1	.0		.2		1.0	.4	.0	.0	.2
Billings in Excess of Costs & Est. Earnings	.1	3.1	1.1		2.3		1.0	1.5	1.7	2.6	2.3
Income Taxes Payable	.4	.9	2.0		.9		1.4	.5	.7	.6	.9
Cur. Mat. - L/T/D	3.0	3.1	3.8		3.1		5.1	3.4	4.0	5.7	3.1
All Other Current	18.5	10.4	8.2		11.8		7.6	8.0	5.5	9.3	11.8
Total Current	38.6	47.6	41.3		46.0		47.4	44.2	40.1	52.8	46.0
Long Term Debt	7.5	10.8	9.4		9.9		9.6	8.0	11.3	9.2	9.9
Deferred Taxes	.1	1.0	.7		.8		1.2	1.1	1.1	1.8	.8
All Other Non-Current	7.4	3.4	1.1		4.2		2.3	2.7	1.4	3.3	4.2
Net Worth	46.5	37.3	47.5		39.2		39.5	43.9	46.2	33.0	39.2
Total Liabilities & Net Worth	100.0	100.0	100.0		100.0		100.0	100.0	100.0	100.0	100.0
INCOME DATA											
Contract Revenues	100.0	100.0	100.0		100.0		100.0	100.0	100.0	100.0	100.0
Gross Profit	37.5	26.6	21.4		27.6		29.7	28.0	30.3	28.7	27.6
Operating Expenses	28.7	22.6	17.6		22.7		26.0	26.1	27.3	28.3	22.7
Operating Profit	8.8	4.0	3.7		4.9		3.6	1.9	3.0	.4	4.9
All Other Expenses (net)	.4	.9	.5		.8		.6	.2	1.1	.8	.8
Profit Before Taxes	8.4	3.1	3.2		4.1		3.1	1.7	1.9	-.4	4.1

RATIOS

Ratio	0-1MM	1-10MM	10-50MM	50 & OVER	ALL		4/1/90-3/31/91	4/1/91-3/31/92	4/1/92-3/31/93	4/1/93-3/31/94	4/1/94-3/31/95
Current	2.7 / 2.0 / 1.0	2.6 / 1.5 / 1.1	2.0 / 1.7 / 1.3		2.5 / 1.5 / 1.1		2.2 / 1.7 / 1.1	2.8 / 1.7 / 1.2	2.7 / 1.7 / 1.1	1.6 / 1.4 / 1.1	2.5 / 1.5 / 1.1
Receivables/Payables	(14) UND / UND / 2.8	5.8 / 2.3 / 1.3	3.5 / 2.0 / 1.4	(105)	8.4 / 2.5 / 1.4		(76) 4.1 / 2.1 / 1.6	(52) 3.5 / 2.1 / 1.6	7.4 / 2.8 / 1.6	3.8 / 2.2 / .8	(105) 8.4 / 2.5 / 1.4
Revenues/Receivables	(0) UND / (41) 9.0 / (89) 4.1	(29) 12.8 / (55) 6.6 / (79) 4.6	(25) 14.7 / (61) 6.0 / (70) 5.2		(25) 14.6 / (53) 6.9 / (78) 4.7		(25) 14.4 / (46) 8.0 / (74) 4.9	(17) 21.9 / (46) 8.0 / (73) 5.0	(33) 11.0 / (52) 7.0 / (68) 5.4	(17) 21.0 / (54) 6.8 / (76) 4.8	(25) 14.6 / (53) 6.9 / (78) 4.7
Cost of Revenues/Payables	(0) UND / (0) UND / (14) 26.4	(10) 35.1 / (29) 12.6 / (42) 8.6	(12) 29.7 / (32) 11.4 / (46) 7.9		(4) 102.7 / (25) 14.8 / (40) 9.2		(10) 37.5 / (30) 12.2 / (50) 7.3	(15) 24.8 / (28) 13.0 / (49) 7.5	(11) 32.6 / (27) 13.6 / (49) 7.5	(24) 15.3 / (30) 12.1 / (63) 5.8	(4) 102.7 / (25) 14.8 / (40) 9.2
Revenues/Working Capital	2.9 / 6.6 / NM	7.6 / 15.0 / 46.4	7.6 / 10.3 / 21.1		7.0 / 13.7 / 47.1		6.7 / 15.0 / 142.6	6.4 / 11.6 / 48.1	5.7 / 9.9 / 38.8	8.6 / 16.0 / 39.4	7.0 / 13.7 / 47.1
EBIT/Interest	(12) 54.8 / 4.4 / .7	(73) 15.9 / 6.1 / 1.9	10.0 / 3.9 / 2.1	(98)	16.0 / 5.4 / 2.0		(69) 5.6 / 2.9 / 1.5	(48) 8.1 / 2.4 / .7	(77) 8.4 / 2.8 / .4	(32) 11.7 / 1.4 / -1.6	(98) 16.0 / 5.4 / 2.0
Net Profit + Depr., Dep., Amort./Cur. Mat. L/T/D		(33) 6.5 / 2.7 / 1.6		(46)	6.0 / 2.5 / 1.3		(40) 4.6 / 2.2 / 1.1	(19) 4.7 / 1.8 / .8	(37) 3.9 / 2.1 / 1.3	(16) 4.9 / .5 / -1.1	(46) 6.0 / 2.5 / 1.3
Fixed/Worth	.1 / .4 / 1.2	.2 / .5 / 1.2	.2 / .4 / 1.3		.2 / .4 / 1.2		.2 / .6 / 1.4	.2 / .4 / .8	.2 / .4 / 1.2	.2 / .5 / 1.9	.2 / .4 / 1.2
Debt/Worth	.6 / 1.3 / 2.5	.8 / 1.8 / 4.2	.8 / 1.2 / 2.0		.8 / 1.6 / 3.5		.7 / 1.6 / 3.8	.5 / 1.1 / 2.7	.6 / 1.4 / 2.6	.9 / 2.1 / 7.0	.8 / 1.6 / 3.5
% Profit Before Taxes/Tangible Net Worth	62.1 / 27.0 / .6	(71) 52.8 / 26.4 / 6.6	27.5 / 13.7 / 2.7	(101)	55.1 / 25.8 / 3.2		(73) 34.7 / 13.5 / 5.5	(48) 28.2 / 12.9 / 4.2	(83) 22.7 / 9.2 / -5.7	(32) 30.9 / 7.5 / -20.5	(101) 55.1 / 25.8 / 3.2
% Profit Before Taxes/Total Assets	28.3 / 14.0 / .2	19.3 / 9.8 / 1.3	11.3 / 7.0 / 1.3		22.1 / 9.6 / 1.2		10.2 / 5.7 / 2.2	9.0 / 5.4 / 1.3	11.2 / 4.2 / -2.0	8.1 / 2.8 / -5.8	22.1 / 9.6 / 1.2
% Depr., Dep., Amort./Revenues	(12) 1.5 / 2.0 / 4.5	(67) .6 / 1.1 / 2.2	.4 / 2.1 / 3.1	(92)	.6 / 1.5 / 2.4		(72) .8 / 1.7 / 3.2	(48) .8 / 1.8 / 2.7	(81) 1.0 / 1.7 / 3.0	(31) .8 / 1.5 / 2.6	(92) .6 / 1.5 / 2.4
% Officers', Directors', Owners' Comp/Revenues		(38) 3.2 / 4.3 / 6.4		(49)	3.2 / 4.4 / 6.6		(46) 2.7 / 5.5 / 8.4	(23) 2.4 / 4.6 / 7.9	(49) 3.1 / 5.7 / 9.6	(14) 2.8 / 3.4 / 5.9	(49) 3.2 / 4.4 / 6.6
Contract Revenues ($)	10145M	254686M	215208M	1572054M	2052093M		553214M	209893M	1166516M	105586M	2052093M
Total Assets ($)	8461M	91460M	95914M	426592M	622427M		228956M	80490M	318920M	40930M	622427M

© Robert Morris Associates 1995

M = $ thousand   MM = $ million

See Pages 1 through 15 for Explanation of Ratios and Data

Current Data Sorted By Revenue | **Comparative Historical Data**

0-1MM	1-10MM	10-50MM	50 & OVER	ALL	Type of Statement	4/1/90-3/31/91	4/1/91-3/31/92	4/1/92-3/31/93	4/1/93-3/31/94	4/1/94-3/31/95
1	17	5	1	24	# Postretirement Benefits			7	12	24
2	73	50	11	136	Unqualified	146	139	132	116	136
8	90	10	1	109	Reviewed	92	126	103	108	109
23	10	1		34	Compiled	28	24	34	27	34
	1			1	Tax Returns		1	2	4	1
2	24	7	1	34	Other	28	23	22	26	34

102 (4/1-9/30/94)   212 (10/1/94-3/31/95)

0-1MM 35	1-10MM 198	10-50MM 68	50 & OVER 13	ALL 314	NUMBER OF STATEMENTS	ALL 294	ALL 313	ALL 293	ALL 281	ALL 314
%	%	%	%	%	ASSETS	%	%	%	%	%
14.7	13.3	12.1	10.3	13.1	Cash & Equivalents	14.1	14.9	15.9	13.7	13.1
28.2	36.0	35.3	29.1	34.7	A/R - Progress Billings	32.2	30.7	30.3	30.6	34.7
.6	3.8	4.9	3.1	3.7	A/R - Current Retention	4.5	3.6	4.7	5.2	3.7
3.5	1.5	1.9	1.7	1.8	Inventory	2.1	2.5	3.2	1.8	1.8
1.5	4.3	2.9	3.6	3.7	Cost & Est. Earnings In Excess of Billings	3.7	3.1	3.8	3.4	3.7
3.6	2.4	3.3	2.9	2.8	All Other Current	3.4	3.7	3.9	3.3	2.8
52.0	61.4	60.5	50.7	59.7	Total Current	60.0	58.4	61.9	58.0	59.7
38.2	31.9	30.0	38.8	32.5	Fixed Assets (net)	32.5	32.2	29.5	33.4	32.5
1.3	.9	2.4	.2	1.2	Joint Ventures & Investments	.9	2.0	1.4	1.4	1.2
1.1	.8	1.5	1.3	1.0	Intangibles (net)	.3	.5	.6	.6	1.0
7.4	5.1	5.6	9.0	5.6	All Other Non-Current	6.3	7.0	6.7	6.7	5.6
100.0	100.0	100.0	100.0	100.0	Total	100.0	100.0	100.0	100.0	100.0
					LIABILITIES					
12.7	6.2	5.0	6.5	6.7	Notes Payable - Short Term	6.0	6.2	7.3	6.5	6.7
10.3	18.0	20.3	14.7	17.5	A/P - Trade	16.5	15.7	17.0	17.0	17.5
.1	.3	1.5	.0	.5	A/P - Retention	.6	.7	.4	.4	.5
.3	2.1	3.2	4.6	2.2	Billings in Excess of Costs & Est. Earnings	2.4	2.0	2.3	2.3	2.2
1.0	.7	.7	.9	.8	Income Taxes Payable	1.0	1.2	.9	.6	.8
5.7	5.7	5.9	6.9	5.8	Cur. Mat. - L/T/D	6.4	5.6	5.3	5.8	5.8
10.8	6.2	8.8	7.3	7.3	All Other Current	6.5	5.7	6.2	5.9	7.3
40.8	39.1	45.5	40.8	40.8	Total Current	39.3	37.0	39.5	38.4	40.8
10.3	10.5	10.7	16.0	10.8	Long Term Debt	11.4	11.4	10.0	11.1	10.8
.7	2.3	2.0	2.5	2.1	Deferred Taxes	2.1	1.7	1.6	1.7	2.1
1.7	.9	1.4	2.3	1.2	All Other Non-Current	1.0	.8	1.4	1.7	1.2
46.5	47.1	40.5	38.4	45.2	Net Worth	46.2	49.0	47.5	47.0	45.2
100.0	100.0	100.0	100.0	100.0	Total Liabilities & Net Worth	100.0	100.0	100.0	100.0	100.0
					INCOME DATA					
100.0	100.0	100.0	100.0	100.0	Contract Revenues	100.0	100.0	100.0	100.0	100.0
37.8	21.8	13.5	18.9	21.7	Gross Profit	21.5	21.8	20.2	21.4	21.7
33.8	17.8	10.9	12.7	17.9	Operating Expenses	18.2	19.6	18.4	18.6	17.9
4.1	4.0	2.6	6.2	3.8	Operating Profit	3.3	2.2	1.8	2.9	3.8
.4	.3	.1	1.6	.3	All Other Expenses (net)	.2	.1	−.1	.3	.3
3.6	3.7	2.5	4.6	3.5	Profit Before Taxes	3.2	2.1	1.9	2.6	3.5
					RATIOS					
2.8	2.4	1.8	1.5	2.2	Current	2.4	2.4	2.6	2.2	2.2
1.2	1.6	1.3	1.1	1.4		1.5	1.6	1.6	1.5	1.4
.7	1.1	1.0	1.0	1.1		1.2	1.2	1.2	1.2	1.1
8.1	4.2	3.0	4.0	3.7	Receivables/Payables	3.9	4.4	3.9	4.3	3.7
(32) 2.2	2.3	1.9	1.9	(311) 2.1		(289) 2.4	(309) 2.4	(288) 2.1	(277) 2.2	(311) 2.1
1.5	1.5	1.5	1.3	1.5		1.5	1.4	1.4	1.4	1.5
17 21.4	41 8.8	43 8.4	50 7.3	41 8.9	Revenues/Receivables	41 9.0	38 9.7	37 9.8	40 9.2	41 8.9
37 10.0	62 5.9	57 6.4	74 4.9	61 6.0		58 6.3	51 7.1	54 6.7	54 6.8	61 6.0
79 4.6	79 4.6	74 4.9	85 4.3	79 4.6		74 4.9	74 4.9	73 5.0	78 4.7	79 4.6
3 132.0	17 21.4	21 17.7	17 21.4	16 22.2	Cost of Revenues/Payables	16 23.0	13 27.1	15 24.2	14 25.7	16 22.2
17 21.7	29 12.7	37 9.9	37 9.9	29 12.4		30 12.0	28 12.9	29 12.4	29 12.6	29 12.4
50 7.3	55 6.6	51 7.2	69 5.3	54 6.8		49 7.5	47 7.8	48 7.6	47 7.7	54 6.8
5.5		9.4	5.9	6.4	Revenues/Working Capital	6.2	6.0	5.7	7.1	6.4
31.7	12.2	15.5	41.2	13.5		11.8	12.0	10.7	12.4	13.5
−20.6	37.3	125.5	104.1	71.5		26.2	26.3	24.6	39.0	71.5
13.1	17.8	19.8	17.2	17.5	EBIT/Interest	9.7	10.0	9.2	10.0	17.5
(30) 2.8	(177) 6.0	(65) 4.1	3.0	(285) 4.5		(260) 3.2	(288) 3.1	(271) 3.2	(261) 3.9	(285) 4.5
1.1	1.7	1.3	1.9	1.5		1.3	1.2	1.0	1.7	1.5
7.9	5.2	3.2		4.1	Net Profit + Depr., Dep., Amort./Cur. Mat. L/T/D	4.8	4.1	4.3	3.7	4.1
(14) 1.6	(97) 2.2	(33) 1.8	(149) 2.1			(190) 2.2	(188) 2.0	(150) 2.0	(170) 2.0	(149) 2.1
−.1	1.1	1.0		1.1		1.1	.8	.8	1.1	1.1
.4	.4	.5	.5	.4	Fixed/Worth	.4	.4	.4	.4	.4
1.1	.7	.8	1.0	.8		.7	.7	.6	.7	.8
2.0	1.2	1.3	2.1	1.3		1.1	1.1	1.0	1.2	1.3
.5	.6	.9	.8	.6	Debt/Worth	.6	.6	.5	.6	.6
1.2	1.2	1.6	2.3	1.3		1.2	1.1	1.2	1.1	1.3
2.9	2.4	3.2	3.1	2.4		2.0	2.1	2.1	2.1	2.4
38.8	38.3	29.3	38.5	35.6	% Profit Before Taxes/Tangible Net Worth	31.1	26.2	26.8	30.7	35.6
(34) 21.3	(194) 20.4	(67) 13.9	11.2	(308) 18.6		(291) 13.5	(309) 12.9	(288) 11.7	(273) 14.0	(308) 18.6
6.2	6.1	2.1	6.9	5.3		3.5	1.2	.5	2.7	5.3
16.2	17.7	10.8	11.9	15.5	% Profit Before Taxes/Total Assets	14.9	13.1	11.0	13.9	15.5
8.6	8.9	4.9	4.9	7.1		6.0	5.4	4.6	6.1	7.1
.0	2.2	.7	2.9	1.8		1.4	.4	.1	1.4	1.8
2.1	1.7	1.9	1.8	1.8	% Depr., Dep., Amort./Revenues	1.8	2.1	1.8	1.9	1.8
(31) 6.6	(186) 3.4	(65) 2.7	(10) 2.7	(292) 3.2		(272) 3.7	(293) 3.9	(277) 3.4	(264) 3.5	(292) 3.2
11.1	5.0	4.0	5.3	5.2		6.0	6.3	5.5	5.5	5.2
7.2	2.0	1.3		1.9	% Officers', Directors', Owners' Comp/Revenues	1.7	2.2	1.8	2.0	1.9
(15) 9.2	(98) 3.8	(30) 2.5	(146) 3.7			(142) 3.2	(156) 4.3	(152) 3.3	(149) 3.7	(146) 3.7
14.4	4.3	4.3		6.2		5.8	5.8			6.2
21134M	844333M	1326579M	1471506M	3663552M	Contract Revenues ($)	2807448M	2545024M	2811979M	3862759M	3663552M
12465M	398666M	685376M	936827M	2033334M	Total Assets ($)	1310647M	1260438M	1301815M	2017173M	2033334M

M = $ thousand   MM = $ million
See Pages 1 through 15 for Explanation of Ratios and Data

PART V

CONSTRUCTION FINANCIAL MANAGEMENT ASSOCIATION DATA

Interpretation of
Construction Financial Management Association (CFMA) Data

CFMA's data should only be regarded as general information. It cannot be used to establish industry norms for a number of reasons, including the following:

(1) The financial statements used in the composite are not selected by any random or statistically reliable method. CFMA members voluntarily submitted financial data pertaining to themselves. Note that contractors' statements have no upper asset/sales limits.

(2) Many companies provide varied services; CFMA includes a contractor in a classification if at least one third of its annual contract revenue was completed within that classification.

(3) Some of the SIC group samples may be rather small in relation to the total number of firms in a given industry category. A relatively small sample can increase the chances that some of our composites do not fully represent an industry group.

(4) There is the chance that an extreme statement can be present in a sample, causing a disproportionate influence on the industry composite. This is particularly true in a relatively small sample.

(5) Companies within the same industry may differ in their method of operations which in turn can directly influence their financial statements. Since such differences affect financial data included in our sample, our composite calculations could be significantly affected.

(6) Other considerations that can result in variations among different companies engaged in the same general line of business are: different labor markets; geographical location; different accounting methods; quality of service rendered; sources and methods of financing; and terms of sale.

The use of CFMA's data may be helpful when considered with other methods of financial analysis. Nevertheless, RMA and CFMA do not recommend the use of CFMA's data to establish norms or parameters for a given industry or grouping, or the industry as a whole. Although CFMA believes that its data is accurate and representative within the confines of the aforementioned reasons, RMA and CFMA specifically make no representations regarding the accuracy or representativeness of the figures printed in this supplement of the RMA Annual Statement Studies.

CAUTION

ABOUT THE CONSTRUCTION FINANCIAL MANAGEMENT ASSOCIATION (CFMA) DATA

Once again, we are delighted to include excerpts from CFMA's *Seventh Annual Construction Industry Financial Survey*. CFMA is the construction industry's professional association of financial managers and has more than 5,800 members in 74 chapters throughout the U.S.

The data presented here are based on a survey sent to approximately 3,200 general members employed within construction firms. In addition, surveys were also sent to approximately 4,000 companies from the *Engineering News Record's* list of U.S. contractors with revenue greater than one million dollars. Of the 975 total survey participants, 65% or 633 companies participated in the CFMA survey in 1994 and 88% or 855 companies provided detailed financial statement information. The data submitted were compiled and analyzed by KPMG Peat Marwick LLP, in cooperation with CFMA. Almost all companies (95%) included in the survey recognize contract revenue and profit in accordance with the percentage of completion method of accounting. Likewise, our *Statement Studies* contractor data primarily reflects only this method of accounting. It is entirely possible that some of the same contractor companies are included in both the CFMA and *Statement Studies* data presentations. The inclusion of the CFMA data has not affected our *Statement Studies* contractor composite data.

Fiscal year-end closing dates reflected in the CFMA survey data range from 6/30/94 through 3/31/95. The CFMA data are most comparable to the RMA contractor data from 4/1/94 through 3/31/95 appearing in this edition.

The survey respondents were classified into five categories of construction based on the type of work performed. Classification was based on the level of contract volume completed for various SIC codes. A contractor was included in a classification if at least one third of its annual contract revenue was completed within that classification. CFMA categories certain SIC codes together. The classifications and SIC codes included in each are as follows:

INDUSTRIAL AND NONRESIDENTIAL CONTRACTORS

1531	Operative builders
1541	Industrial buildings and warehouses
1542	Nonresidential construction

HEAVY AND HIGHWAY CONTRACTORS

1611	Highway and street construction
1622	Bridge, tunnel, & elevated highway
1623	Water, sewer, and utility lines
1629	Heavy construction, other

SPECIALTY TRADES CONTRACTORS

1711	Plumbing, heating, air conditioning
1721	Painting, paper hanging, decorating
1731	Electrical work
1741	Masonry and other stonework
1742	Plastering, drywall, and insulation
1743	Terrazzo, tile, marble, mosaic work
1751	Carpentry
1752	Floor laying and floor work
1761	Roofing and sheet metal work
1771	Concrete work
1781	Water well drilling
1791	Structural steel erection
1793	Glass and glazing work
1794	Excavating and foundation work
1795	Wrecking and demolition work
1796	Installing building equipment
1799	Special trade contractors

The CFMA financial data includes balance sheets, statements of earnings, and financial ratios. The balance sheets and statements of earnings represent a weighted average of all companies included in each classification. Percentages are presented for each dollar amount in the financial statements. Due to rounding, the totals may not agree to the sum of various accounts. Such variations are few and insignificant.

The financial ratios are calculated from the composite balance sheets and statements of earnings data. They are not averages of ratios for all companies included in the classification, except where specifically indicated.

Certain financial ratios are included in the survey that represent the simple average of those ratios for each company reporting financial information in the survey. These ratios are not calculated from the composite (weighted average) financial information because the elements needed to calculate the ratio were not compiled on a composite basis. These ratios are labeled "average" and include Backlog to Equity, Backlog to Working Capital, and Months in Backlog.

If you wish to purchase CFMA's financial survey report or have questions about their data, contact Paula Wristen, Editor and Communications Manager, Construction Financial Management Association, 707 State Road, Suite 223, Princeton, NJ 08540-1413. Phone: 609/683-5000; Fax: 609/683-4821.

CFMA COMPARATIVE FINANCIAL DATA

BALANCE SHEET
Most Recent Year-End

	All Companies Composite		Ind & Non-Res Composite		Heavy & Highway Composite		Specialty Trades Composite	
	Amount	Percent	Amount	Percent	Amount	Percent	Amount	Percent
Current Assets:								
Cash and cash equivalents	$2,392,959	11.9%	$3,275,965	13.3%	$2,574,438	11.1%	$955,262	7.9%
Marketable securities and short-term investments	1,243,299	6.2	2,012,895	8.2	1,096,077	4.7	269,262	2.2
Receivables:								
Contract receivables currently due	7,015,876	34.9	9,113,554	37.1	5,904,227	25.4	5,083,254	41.8
Retainages on contracts	2,277,602	11.3	3,249,581	13.2	1,858,802	8.0	1,270,623	10.5
Unbilled work	212,269	1.1	327,850	1.3	155,331	0.7	84,502	0.7
Other receivables	353,466	1.8	415,486	1.7	566,102	2.4	129,363	1.1
Less allowance for doubtful accounts	(49,878)	0.2	(39,025)	0.2	(49,668)	0.2	(60,425)	0.5
Total Receivables, net	9,809,335	48.8	13,067,446	53.2	8,434,794	36.2	6,507,317	53.5
Inventories	390,040	1.9	261,393	1.1	518,746	2.2	428,319	3.5
Costs and recognized earnings in excess of billings on uncompleted contracts	1,115,369	5.6	961,730	3.9	1,562,299	6.7	1,113,113	9.2
Investments in construction joint ventures	219,204	1.1	349,682	1.4	226,426	1.0	25,268	0.2
Other current assets	492,868	2.5	602,489	2.5	586,932	2.5	390,095	3.2
Total Current Assets	15,663,074	78.0	20,531,600	83.6	14,999,712	64.4	9,688,636	79.7
Property, plant and equipment	7,272,184	36.2	4,084,851	16.6	17,177,053	73.8	4,201,542	34.6
Less accumulated depreciation	(4,393,223)	21.9	(2,299,610)	9.4	(10,535,349)	45.3	(2,533,296)	20.8
Property, Plant and Equipment, net	2,878,961	14.3	1,785,241	7.3	6,641,704	28.5	1,668,246	13.7
Other assets	1,402,346	7.0	2,017,357	8.2	1,509,601	6.5	563,166	4.6
Intangible assets	146,110	0.7	238,073	1.0	128,255	0.6	234,367	1.9
Total Assets	$20,090,491	100.0%	$24,572,271	100.0%	$23,279,272	100.0%	$12,154,415	100.0%
Number of Participants	855		384		220		292	

CFMA COMPARATIVE FINANCIAL DATA

	All Companies Composite		Ind & Non-Res Composite		Heavy & Highway Composite		Specialty Trades Composite	
	Amount	Percent	Amount	Percent	Amount	Percent	Amount	Percent
Current Liabilities:								
Current maturity on long-term debt	$394,495	2.0%	$397,571	1.6%	$670,245	2.9%	$183,935	1.5%
Notes payable and lines of credit	604,818	3.0	682,373	2.8	538,467	2.3	543,261	4.5
Accounts payable:								
Trade, including currently due subcontractors	4,887,247	24.3	7,536,329	30.7	3,721,755	16.0	2,356,506	19.4
Subcontractor retainages	1,773,330	8.8	3,076,945	12.5	1,012,833	4.4	415,859	3.4
Other	306,173	1.5	609,397	2.5	74,300	0.3	49,067	0.4
Total Accounts Payable	**6,966,750**	**34.7**	**11,222,671**	**45.7**	**4,808,888**	**20.7**	**2,821,432**	**23.2**
Accrued expenses	1,117,329	5.6	1,083,061	4.4	1,214,931	5.2	1,122,235	9.2
Billings in excess of costs and recognized earnings on uncompleted contracts	1,967,071	9.8	2,505,561	10.2	1,891,631	8.1	1,485,246	12.2
Income taxes:								
Current	82,149	0.4	78,411	0.3	82,548	0.4	79,155	0.7
Deferred	55,376	0.3	55,878	0.2	76,650	0.3	34,450	0.3
Total income taxes	137,525	0.7	134,289	0.5	159,198	0.7	113,605	0.9
Other current liabilities	273,335	1.4	348,193	1.4	279,952	1.2	140,118	1.2
Total Current Liabilities	**11,461,323**	**57.0**	**16,373,719**	**66.6**	**9,563,312**	**41.1**	**6,409,832**	**52.7**
Long-term debt, excluding current maturities	1,389,331	6.9	925,852	3.8	3,002,336	12.9	897,446	7.4
Deferred income taxes	218,282	1.1	167,229	0.7	506,098	2.2	79,301	0.7
Other	302,168	1.5	489,014	2.0	228,409	1.0	113,894	0.9
Minority interests	77,175	0.4	117,079	0.5	65,340	0.3	37,418	0.3
Total Liabilities	**13,448,279**	**66.9**	**18,072,893**	**73.5**	**13,365,495**	**57.4**	**7,537,891**	**62.0**
Net Worth:								
Stock, par value	528,890	2.6	435,020	1.8	658,770	2.8	536,442	4.4
Additional paid-in capital	902,842	4.5	942,746	3.8	1,204,743	5.2	799,199	6.6
Retained earnings	5,428,782	27.0	5,271,669	21.5	8,391,584	36.0	3,511,520	28.9
Treasury stock	(218,302)	1.1	(150,057)	0.6	(341,320)	1.5	(230,637)	1.9
Total Net Worth	**6,642,212**	**33.1**	**6,499,378**	**26.5**	**9,913,777**	**42.6**	**4,616,524**	**38.0**
Total Liabilities and Net Worth	**$20,090,491**	**100.0%**	**$24,572,271**	**100.0%**	**$23,279,272**	**100.0%**	**$12,154,415**	**100.0%**
Number of Participants	855		384		220		292	

CFMA COMPARATIVE FINANCIAL DATA

STATEMENT OF EARNINGS
Most Recent Year-End

	All Companies Composite		Ind & Non-Res Composite		Heavy & Highway Composite		Specialty Trades Composite	
	Amount	Percent	Amount	Percent	Amount	Percent	Amount	Percent
Contract revenue	$53,100,596	98.6%	$71,057,702	99.4%	$50,337,119	97.7%	$31,814,987	97.8%
Other revenue	734,793	1.4	428,351	0.6	1,191,800	2.3	715,600	2.2
Total Revenue	53,835,389	100.0	71,486,053	100.0	51,528,919	100.0	32,530,587	100.0
Contract cost	(48,773,473)	90.6	(66,948,523)	93.7	(45,234,772)	87.8	(27,779,299)	85.4
Other cost	(584,542)	1.1	(287,944)	0.4	(871,183)	1.7	(691,773)	2.1
Total Cost	(49,358,015)	91.7	(67,236,467)	94.1	(46,105,955)	89.5	(28,471,072)	87.5
Gross Profit	4,477,374	8.3	4,249,586	5.9	5,422,964	10.5	4,059,515	12.5
Selling, general and administrative expenses	(3,499,576)	6.5	(3,295,906)	4.6	(4,045,759)	7.9	(3,321,721)	10.2
Income from Operations	977,798	1.8	953,680	1.3	1,377,205	2.7	737,794	2.3
Interest income	137,169	0.3	186,741	0.3	159,597	0.3	47,951	0.1
Interest expense	(152,321)	0.3	(102,867)	0.1	(298,682)	0.6	(121,481)	0.4
Other income (expense), net	66,211	0.1	80,832	0.1	109,007	0.2	12,702	0.0
Net Earnings (Loss) before Taxes	1,028,857	1.9	1,118,386	1.6	1,347,127	2.6	676,966	2.1
Income tax (expense) benefit	(195,340)	0.4	(220,063)	0.3	(286,295)	0.6	(117,897)	0.4
Net Earnings (Loss)	$833,517	1.5%	$898,323	1.3%	$1,060,832	2.1%	$559,069	1.7%
Number of Participants	855		384		220		292	

CFMA COMPARATIVE FINANCIAL DATA

KEY FINANCIAL RATIOS
Most Recent Year-End

Liquidity Ratios	All Companies Composite	Ind & Non-Res Composite	Heavy & Highway Composite	Specialty Trades Composite
Current Ratio	1.4	1.3	1.6	1.5
Quick Ratio	1.2	1.1	1.3	1.2
Days of Cash	16.0	16.5	18.0	10.6
Working Capital Turnover	12.8	17.2	9.5	9.9
Profitability Ratios				
Return on Assets	4.1%	3.7%	4.6%	4.6%
Return on Equity	12.5%	13.8%	10.7%	12.1%
Times Interest Earned	7.8	11.9	5.5	6.6
Leverage Ratios				
Debt to Equity	2.0	2.8	1.3	1.6
Revenue to Equity	8.1	11.0	5.2	7.0
Asset Turnover	2.7	2.9	2.2	2.7
Fixed Asset Ratio	43.3%	27.5%	67.0%	36.1%
Equity to G & A Expenses	1.9	2.0	2.5	1.4
Underbillings to Equity	20.0%	19.8%	17.3%	25.9%
Average Backlog to Equity	6.6	10.2	3.9	3.8
Average Backlog to Working Capital	10.4	15.9	7.1	5.4
Average Months in Backlog	9.6	11.1	8.8	6.4
Efficiency Ratios				
Days in Accounts Receivable	48.9	47.8	44.9	57.0
Days in Inventory	2.8	1.4	4.1	5.4
Days in Accounts Payable	37.9	43.6	29.6	30.4
Operating Cycle	29.9	22.1	37.4	42.6

CFMA Industrial and Non-Residential Contractors Composite

BALANCE SHEET

Current Assets:	1995 Participants Amount	Percent	1994 Participants Amount	Percent
Cash and cash equivalents	$3,275,965	13.3 %	$3,004,438	13.6 %
Marketable securities and short-term investments	2,012,895	8.2	2,142,783	9.7
Receivables:				
Contract receivables currently due	9,113,554	37.1	8,269,596	37.3
Retainages on contracts	3,249,581	13.2	2,649,338	12.0
Unbilled work	327,850	1.3	749,623	3.4
Other receivables	415,486	1.7	421,930	1.9
Less allowance for doubtful accounts	(39,025)	0.2	(28,055)	0.1
Total Receivables, net	**13,067,446**	**53.2**	**12,062,432**	**54.5**
Inventories	261,393	1.1	130,328	0.6
Costs and recognized earnings in excess of billings on uncompleted contracts	961,730	3.9	661,531	3.0
Investments in construction joint ventures	349,682	1.4	335,723	1.5
Other current assets	602,489	2.5	852,482	3.8
Total Current Assets	**20,531,600**	**83.6**	**19,189,717**	**86.7**
Property, plant and equipment	4,084,851	16.6	3,302,427	14.9
Less accumulated depreciation	(2,299,610)	9.4	(1,902,405)	8.6
Property, Plant and Equipment, net	**1,785,241**	**7.3**	**1,400,022**	**6.3**
Other assets	2,017,357	8.2	1,501,605	6.8
Intangible assets	238,073	1.0	54,447	0.2
Total Assets	**$24,572,271**	**100.0 %**	**$22,145,791**	**100.0 %**

Current Liabilities:	1995 Participants Amount	Percent	1994 Participants Amount	Percent
Current maturity on long-term debt	$397,571	1.6 %	$249,701	1.1 %
Notes payable and lines of credit	682,373	2.8	272,400	1.2
Accounts payable:				
Trade, including currently due subcontractors	7,536,329	30.7	7,829,284	35.4
Subcontractor retainages	3,076,945	12.5	2,454,274	11.1
Other	609,397	2.5	319,087	1.4
Total Accounts Payable	**11,222,671**	**45.7**	**10,602,645**	**47.9**
Accrued expenses	1,083,061	4.4	863,907	3.9
Billings in excess of costs and recognized earnings on uncompleted contracts	2,505,561	10.2	2,507,410	11.3
Income taxes:				
Current	78,411	0.3	85,446	0.4
Deferred	55,878	0.2	40,931	0.2
Total income taxes	134,289	0.5	126,377	0.6
Other current liabilities	348,193	1.4	328,994	1.5
Total Current Liabilities	**16,373,719**	**66.6**	**14,951,434**	**67.5**
Long-term debt, excluding current maturities	925,852	3.8	781,017	3.5
Deferred income taxes	167,229	0.7	171,748	0.8
Other	489,014	2.0	582,667	2.6
Minority interests	117,079	0.5	72,754	-0.3
Total Liabilities	**18,072,893**	**73.5**	**16,559,620**	**74.8**
Net Worth:				
Stock, par value	435,020	1.8	380,633	1.7
Additional paid-in capital	942,746	3.8	624,989	2.8
Retained earnings	5,271,669	21.5	4,783,512	21.6
Treasury stock	(150,057)	0.6	(202,963)	0.9
Total Net Worth	**6,499,378**	**26.5**	**5,586,171**	**25.2**
Total Liabilities and Net Worth	**$24,572,271**	**100.0 %**	**$22,145,791**	**100.0 %**

Composite

FINANCIAL RATIOS

	1995 Participants	1994 Participants
Liquidity Ratios		
Current Ratio	1.3	1.3
Quick Ratio	1.1	1.2
Days of Cash	16.5	16.0
Working Capital Turnover	17.2	15.9
Profitability Ratios		
Return on Assets	3.7 %	1.9 %
Return on Equity	13.8 %	7.5 %
Times Interest Earned	11.9	12.7
Leverage Ratios		
Debt to Equity	2.8	3.0
Revenue to Equity	11.0	12.1
Asset Turnover	2.9	3.0
Fixed Asset Ratio	27.5 %	25.1 %
Equity to G & A Expenses	2.0	1.9
Underbillings to Equity	19.8 %	25.3 %
Average Backlog to Equity	10.2	10.9
Average Backlog to Working Capital	15.9	14.3
Average Months in Backlog	11.1	10.8
Efficiency Ratios		
Days in Accounts Receivable	47.8	46.2
Days in Inventory	1.4	0.7
Days in Accounts Payable	43.6	45.8
Operating Cycle	22.1	17.1

STATEMENT OF EARNINGS

	1995 Participants Amount	Percent	1994 Participants Amount	Percent
Contract revenue	$71,057,702	99.4 %	$66,940,678	99.1 %
Other revenue	428,351	0.6	598,105	0.9
Total Revenue	71,486,053	100.0	67,538,783	100.0
Contract cost	(66,948,523)	93.7	(63,683,501)	94.3
Other cost	(287,944)	0.4	(396,072)	0.6
Total Cost	(67,236,467)	94.1	(64,079,573)	94.9
Gross Profit	4,249,586	5.9	3,459,210	5.1
Selling, general and administrative expenses	(3,295,906)	4.6	(2,993,930)	4.4
Income from Operations	953,680	1.3	465,280	0.7
Interest income	186,741	0.3	190,138	0.3
Interest expense	(102,867)	0.1	(50,366)	0.1
Other income (expense), net	80,832	0.1	(13,623)	0.0
Net Earnings (Loss) before Taxes	1,118,386	1.6	591,429	0.9
Income tax (expense) benefit	(220,063)	0.3	(172,865)	0.3
Net Earnings (Loss)	$898,323	1.3 %	$418,564	0.6 %

NUMBER OF PARTICIPANTS

Survey Year	Number
1995	384
1994	316

CFMA Heavy & Highway Contractors
Composite

BALANCE SHEET

Assets

	1995 Participants		1994 Participants	
	Amount	Percent	Amount	Percent
Current Assets:				
Cash and cash equivalents	$2,574,438	11.1 %	$2,887,148	11.2 %
Marketable securities and short-term investments	1,096,077	4.7	1,130,624	4.4
Receivables:				
Contract receivables currently due	5,904,227	25.4	6,256,997	24.2
Retainages on contracts	1,858,802	8.0	1,614,294	6.2
Unbilled work	155,331	0.7	160,417	0.6
Other receivables	566,102	2.4	826,223	3.2
Less allowance for doubtful accounts	(49,668)	0.2	(125,980)	0.5
Total Receivables, net	8,434,794	36.2	8,731,951	33.7
Inventories	518,746	2.2	659,576	2.5
Costs and recognized earnings in excess of billings on uncompleted contracts	1,562,299	6.7	1,760,761	6.8
Investments in construction joint ventures	226,426	1.0	315,370	1.2
Other current assets	586,932	2.5	822,244	3.2
Total Current Assets	14,999,712	64.4	16,307,674	63.0
Property, plant and equipment	17,177,053	73.8	17,016,923	65.7
Less accumulated depreciation	(10,535,349)	45.3	(9,428,515)	36.4
Property, Plant and Equipment, net	6,641,704	28.5	7,588,408	29.3
Other assets	1,509,601	6.5	1,815,046	7.0
Intangible assets	128,255	0.6	170,990	0.7
Total Assets	$23,279,272	100.0 %	$25,882,118	100.0 %

Liabilities and Net Worth

	1995 Participants		1994 Participants	
	Amount	Percent	Amount	Percent
Current Liabilities:				
Current maturity on long-term debt	$670,245	2.9 %	$712,235	2.8 %
Notes payable and lines of credit	538,467	2.3	542,881	2.1
Accounts payable:				
Trade, including currently due subcontractors	3,721,755	16.0	4,210,014	16.3
Subcontractor retainages	1,012,833	4.4	684,648	2.6
Other	74,300	0.3	119,415	0.5
Total Accounts Payable	4,808,888	20.7	5,014,077	19.4
Accrued expenses	1,214,931	5.2	1,225,661	4.7
Billings in excess of costs and recognized earnings on uncompleted contracts	1,891,631	8.1	1,922,530	7.4
Income taxes:				
Current	82,548	0.4	164,643	0.6
Deferred	76,650	0.3	40,458	0.2
Total income taxes	159,198	0.7	205,101	0.8
Other current liabilities	279,952	1.2	468,583	1.8
Total Current Liabilities	9,563,312	41.1	10,091,068	39.0
Long-term debt, excluding current maturities	3,002,336	12.9	3,645,503	14.1
Deferred income taxes	506,098	2.2	530,330	2.0
Other	228,409	1.0	347,863	1.3
Minority interests	65,340	0.3	46,598	0.2
Total Liabilities	13,365,495	57.4	14,661,362	56.6
Net Worth:				
Stock, par value	658,770	2.8	676,437	2.6
Additional paid-in capital	1,204,743	5.2	873,142	3.4
Retained earnings	8,391,584	36.0	9,998,248	38.6
Treasury stock	(341,320)	1.5	(327,071)	1.3
Total Net Worth	9,913,777	42.6	11,220,756	43.4
Total Liabilities and Net Worth	$23,279,272	100.0 %	$25,882,118	100.0 %

STATEMENT OF EARNINGS

	1995 Participants Amount	Percent	1994 Participants Amount	Percent
Contract revenue	$50,337,119	97.7 %	$52,874,208	94.8 %
Other revenue	1,191,800	2.3	2,922,479	5.2
Total Revenue	**51,528,919**	**100.0**	**55,796,687**	**100.0**
Contract cost	(45,234,772)	87.8	(47,640,594)	85.4
Other cost	(871,183)	1.7	(2,437,498)	4.4
Total Cost	**(46,105,955)**	**89.5**	**(50,078,092)**	**89.8**
Gross Profit	**5,422,964**	**10.5**	**5,718,595**	**10.2**
Selling, general and administrative expenses	(4,045,759)	7.9	(4,145,593)	7.4
Income from Operations	**1,377,205**	**2.7**	**1,573,002**	**2.8**
Interest income	159,597	0.3	209,591	0.4
Interest expense	(298,682)	0.6	(323,281)	0.6
Other income (expense), net	109,007	0.2	118,430	0.2
Net Earnings (Loss) before Taxes	**1,347,127**	**2.6**	**1,577,742**	**2.8**
Income tax (expense) benefit	(286,295)	0.6	(266,060)	0.5
Net Earnings (Loss)	**$1,060,832**	**2.1 %**	**$1,311,682**	**2.4 %**

FINANCIAL RATIOS

	1995 Participants	1994 Participants
Liquidity Ratios		
Current Ratio	1.6	1.6
Quick Ratio	1.3	1.3
Days of Cash	18.0	18.6
Working Capital Turnover	9.5	9.0
Profitability Ratios		
Return on Assets	4.6 %	5.1 %
Return on Equity	10.7 %	11.7 %
Times Interest Earned	5.5	5.9
Leverage Ratios		
Debt to Equity	1.3	1.3
Revenue to Equity	5.2	5.0
Asset Turnover	2.2	2.2
Fixed Asset Ratio	67.0 %	67.6 %
Equity to G & A Expenses	2.5	2.7
Underbillings to Equity	17.3 %	17.1 %
Average Backlog to Equity	3.9	3.7
Average Backlog to Working Capital	7.1	6.6
Average Months in Backlog	8.8	8.9
Efficiency Ratios		
Days in Accounts Receivable	44.9	44.9
Days in Inventory	4.1	4.7
Days in Accounts Payable	29.6	31.1
Operating Cycle	37.4	37.1

NUMBER OF PARTICIPANTS

Survey Year	Number
1995	220
1994	164

CFMA Specialty Trade Contractors
Composite

BALANCE SHEET

Assets

	1995 Participants Amount	Percent	1994 Participants Amount	Percent
Current Assets:				
Cash and cash equivalents	$955,262	7.9 %	$712,426	6.8 %
Marketable securities and short-term investments	269,262	2.2	136,546	1.3
Receivables:				
Contract receivables currently due	5,083,254	41.8	5,155,926	49.1
Retainages on contracts	1,270,623	10.5	964,429	9.2
Unbilled work	84,502	0.7	56,013	0.5
Other receivables	129,363	1.1	161,141	1.5
Less allowance for doubtful accounts	(60,425)	0.5	(58,982)	0.6
Total Receivables, net	6,507,317	53.5	6,278,527	59.8
Inventories	428,319	3.5	328,428	3.1
Costs and recognized earnings in excess of billings on uncompleted contracts	1,113,113	9.2	963,604	9.2
Investments in construction joint ventures	25,268	0.2	30,266	0.3
Other current assets	390,095	3.2	338,952	3.2
Total Current Assets	9,688,636	79.7	8,788,749	83.7
Property, plant and equipment	4,201,542	34.6	3,249,713	30.9
Less accumulated depreciation	(2,533,296)	20.8	(2,032,161)	19.3
Property, Plant and Equipment, net	1,668,246	13.7	1,217,552	11.6
Other assets	563,166	4.6	437,493	4.2
Intangible assets	234,367	1.9	58,728	0.6
Total Assets	$12,154,415	100.0 %	$10,502,522	100.0 %

Liabilities and Net Worth

	1995 Participants Amount	Percent	1994 Participants Amount	Percent
Current Liabilities:				
Current maturity on long-term debt	$183,935	1.5 %	$199,045	1.9 %
Notes payable and lines of credit	543,261	4.5	491,287	4.7
Accounts payable:				
Trade, including currently due subcontractors	2,356,506	19.4	2,386,910	22.7
Subcontractor retainages	415,859	3.4	128,446	1.2
Other	49,067	0.4	59,410	0.6
Total Accounts Payable	2,821,432	23.2	2,574,766	24.5
Accrued expenses	1,122,235	9.2	1,067,804	10.2
Billings in excess of costs and recognized earnings on uncompleted contracts	1,485,246	12.2	1,154,226	11.0
Income taxes:				
Current	79,155	0.7	37,098	0.4
Deferred	34,450	0.3	27,917	0.3
Total income taxes	113,605	0.9	65,015	0.6
Other current liabilities	140,118	1.2	159,261	1.5
Total Current Liabilities	6,409,832	52.7	5,711,404	54.4
Long-term debt, excluding current maturities	897,446	7.4	1,569,558	14.9
Deferred income taxes	79,301	0.7	34,034	0.3
Other	113,894	0.9	241,025	2.3
Minority interests	37,418	0.3	(66,686)	0.6
Total Liabilities	7,537,891	62.0	7,489,335	71.3
Net Worth:				
Stock, par value	536,442	4.4	253,112	2.4
Additional paid-in capital	799,199	6.6	822,043	7.8
Retained earnings	3,511,520	28.9	2,201,178	21.0
Treasury stock	(230,637)	1.9	(263,146)	2.5
Total Net Worth	4,616,524	38.0	3,013,187	28.7
Total Liabilities and Net Worth	$12,154,415	100.0 %	$10,502,522	100.0 %

Composite

STATEMENT OF EARNINGS

	1995 Participants Amount	Percent	1994 Participants Amount	Percent
Contract revenue	$31,814,987	97.8 %	$30,115,297	97.4 %
Other revenue	715,600	2.2	814,441	2.6
Total Revenue	32,530,587	100.0	30,929,738	100.0
Contract cost	(27,779,299)	85.4	(26,420,526)	85.4
Other cost	(691,773)	2.1	(596,366)	1.9
Total Cost	(28,471,072)	87.5	(27,016,892)	87.3
Gross Profit	4,059,515	12.5	3,912,846	12.7
Selling, general and administrative expenses	(3,321,721)	10.2	(3,433,964)	11.1
Income from Operations	737,794	2.3	478,882	1.5
Interest income	47,951	0.1	55,272	0.2
Interest expense	(121,481)	0.4	(132,921)	0.4
Other income (expense), net	12,702	0.0	(86,494)	0.3
Net Earnings (Loss) before Taxes	676,966	2.1	314,739	1.0
Income tax (expense) benefit	(117,897)	0.4	(85,224)	0.3
Net Earnings (Loss)	$559,069	1.7 %	$229,515	0.7 %

FINANCIAL RATIOS

	1995 Participants	1994 Participants
Liquidity Ratios		
Current Ratio	1.5	1.5
Quick Ratio	1.2	1.2
Days of Cash	10.6	8.3
Working Capital Turnover	9.9	10.1
Profitability Ratios		
Return on Assets	4.6 %	2.2 %
Return on Equity	12.1 %	7.6 %
Times Interest Earned	6.6	3.4
Leverage Ratios		
Debt to Equity	1.6	2.5
Revenue to Equity	7.0	10.3
Asset Turnover	2.7	2.9
Fixed Asset Ratio	36.1 %	40.4 %
Equity to G & A Expenses	1.4	0.9
Underbillings to Equity	25.9 %	33.8 %
Average Backlog to Equity	3.8	5.8
Average Backlog to Working Capital	5.4	5.6
Average Months in Backlog	6.4	6.7
Efficiency Ratios		
Days in Accounts Receivable	57.0	61.2
Days in Inventory	5.4	4.4
Days in Accounts Payable	30.4	32.6
Operating Cycle	42.6	41.3

NUMBER OF PARTICIPANTS

Survey Year	Number
1995	292
1994	266

PART VI

THE FIRST NATIONAL BANK OF CHICAGO CONSUMER AND DIVERSIFIED FINANCE COMPANY RATIOS

THE FIRST NATIONAL BANK OF CHICAGO
CONSUMER FINANCE (DIRECT CASH LENDING) COMPANY RATIOS

STATEMENT DATE		12-31-92	12-31-93	12-31-94
ASSETS				
Volume for Period (Millions)	1	23,013	26,097	31,469
Total Outstanding (Millions)	2	37,699	41,275	45,701
Average Net Receivables (Millions)	3	4,101	4,370	5,877
% Direct Cash Loans (Real Estate Collateral) to Total Receivables	4	43.3	41.6	33.0
% Direct Cash Loans (Unsecured or Collateral other than Real Estate) to Total Receivables	5	36.9	33.7	38.0
% Retail Contracts to Total Receivables	6	18.6	22.9	21.6
Average Amount of Individual Loan Balances	7	3,290	3,759	3,080
% Loans to Present Borrowers	8	63.1	N/A	N/A
% Loans Written for Longer than 60 Months	9	12.3	12.2	N/A
ASSET QUALITY				
Past Due and Delinquent Accounts (Recency Basis) % Total Recency Delinquency	10	1.6	1.4	N/A
% Total Contractual Delinquency	11	2.8	2.8	2.3
% Reserve for Losses to Net Receivables	12	2.5	2.7	2.8
Ratio—Reserve for Losses to Total Charge-Offs Net of Recoveries	13	1.6	1.9	2.0
% Net Charge-Offs to Liquidations	14	3.3	3.3	3.3
% Net Charge-Offs to Average Net Receivables	15	2.2	1.8	2.1
% Recoveries on Loans Charged Off	16	22.7	21.7	21.9

STATEMENT DATE		12-31-92	12-31-93	12-31-94
LIQUIDITY				
% Average Monthly Cash Principal Collections to Average Net Monthly Outstandings	17	5.1	4.1	4.6
Number of Months' Collections Required to Pay Total Non-Subordinated Debt (Net of Cash) applying % in Ratio #17 to Fiscal Date Net Outstandings	18	18.9	21.1	19.9
% Open Market Borrowings to Total Non-Subordinated Debt	19	29.0	30.2	31.5
% Unused Credit Facilities to Open Market Borrowings	20	125.4	116.4	123.4
LEVERAGE/CAPITAL STRUCTURE				
Ratio—Total Non-Subordinated Debt to Working Capital	21	4.6	6.2	8.3
Ratio—Total Liabilities to Tangible Net Worth	22	6.2	6.6	7.2
Ratio—Total Debt to Net Worth Plus Reserve for Loan Losses	23	4.7	5.1	5.4
% Subordinated Term Debt to Capital Funds	24	26.0	20.6	17.5
% Capital and Earned Surplus to Capital Funds	25	79.8	84.0	85.0
EARNINGS				
% Gross Finance Revenue to Average Net Receivables	26	19.6	17.8	18.6
% Interest Expense to Average Net Receivables	27	6.4	5.4	5.7
% Operating Expenses (Excluding Loss Provision) to Average Net Receivables	28	7.3	7.4	7.5
% Loss Provision to Average Net Receivables	29	2.1	2.1	2.4
% Net Finance Profit to Average Net Receivables	30	3.6	3.8	4.2
% Consolidated Net Income to Average Net Worth	31	19.1	20.0	21.6
% Consolidated Net Income to Average Total Assets	32	3.4	3.3	3.5
% Dividends to Consolidated Net Income	33	50.5	45.8	42.6
% Interest and Debt Expenses to Average Total Borrowings	34	7.3	6.2	6.2
Ratio—Times Interest Earned	35	2.0	2.2	2.3

Reprinted with permission from The First National Bank of Chicago. Inquiries on the data appearing on this and the next page should be directed to Raymond Neihengen, Managing Director, First Chicago Capital Markets Inc., 312/732-2968.

THE FIRST NATIONAL BANK OF CHICAGO
DIVERSIFIED FINANCE COMPANY RATIOS

STATEMENT DATE		12-31-92	12-31-93	12-31-94
ASSETS				
Volume for Period (Millions)	1	405,377	455,883	561,362
Total Outstandings (Millions)	2	314,308	329,680	375,284
Average Net Receivables (Millions)	3	15,331	15,647	17,749
% Retail Receivables to Total Receivables	4	44.7	31.7	34.6
% Direct Consumer Loans to Total Receivables	5	11.5	19.5	15.7
% Commercial Loans to Total Receivables	6	43.8	48.8	49.7
ASSET QUALITY				
% Commercial Loan Balances with Installments Delinquent 60 Days or Over (Contractual Basis) to Total Related Receivables	7	1.8	1.2	0.7
% Consumer Loan Balances with Installments Delinquent 60 Days or Over (Contractual Basis) to Total Related Receivables	8	2.0	1.9	2.0
% Consumer Losses (Charge-Offs Net of Recoveries) to Consumer Receivables Liquidated	9	4.0	3.0	3.5
% Commercial Loan Losses (Charge-Offs Net of Recoveries) to Commercial Loans Liquidated	10	2.5	1.8	1.6
% Reserve for Losses to Net Receivables	11	2.3	2.3	2.0
Ratio—Reserve for Losses to Total Charge-offs Net of Recoveries	12	1.8	2.1	2.5
% Net Charge-offs to Average Net Receivables	13	1.4	1.3	0.9
Repossessions to Net Worth	14	11.5	10.1	5.5

STATEMENT DATE		12-31-92	12-31-93	12-31-94
LIQUIDITY				
% Receivables Maturing over 12 Months	15	61.3	58.0	53.3
% Cash, Wholesale, Fast Turning Commercial Loans and Installment Receivables Maturing in 12 Months to Total Non-Subordinated Debt	16	39.6	37.9	39.2
Number of Months' Collections Required to Pay Total Non-Subordinated Debt (Net of Cash, Wholesale, and Fast Turning Commercial Loans)	17	19.2	18.5	21.49
% Commercial Paper Borrowings to Total Non-Subordinated Debt	18	39.0	35.2	33.2
% Unused Credit Facilities to Commercial Paper Borrowings	19	117.9	116.7	114.5
LEVERAGE/CAPITAL STRUCTURE				
Ratio—Total Non-Subordinated Debt to Working Capital	20	7.9	8.3	9.6
Ratio—Total Liabilities to Tangible Net Worth	21	7.4	7.2	7.6
Ratio—Total Debt to Net Worth Plus Reserve for Loan Losses	22	5.4	5.2	5.4
% Subordinated Term Debt to Capital Funds	23	18.4	15.5	16.6
% Capital and Earned Surplus to Capital Funds	24	87.4	88.6	90.8
EARNINGS				
% Gross Finance Revenue to Average Net Receivables	25	14.7	15.1	14.9
% Interest Expense to Average Net Receivables	26	5.9	5.3	5.1
% Operating Expenses (Excluding Loss Provision) to Average Net Receivables	27	3.3	4.0	3.7
% Loss Provision to Average Net Receivables	28	1.4	1.3	1.0
% Net Profit From Finance Operations to Average Net Receivables	29	2.0	1.7	2.0
% Consolidated Net Income to Average Net Worth	30	12.4	11.5	13.4
% Consolidated Net Income to Average Total Assets	31	1.7	1.4	1.8
% Dividends to Consolidated Net Income	32	56.9	52.6	61.2
% Interest and Debt Expenses to Average Total Borrowings	33	6.6	5.9	6.0
Ratio—Times Interest Earned	34	1.5	1.6	1.7

PART VII

SOURCES OF COMPOSITE FINANCIAL DATA—A BIBLIOGRAPHY

SOURCES OF COMPOSITE FINANCIAL DATA—A BIBLIOGRAPHY

This *Annual Statement Studies* edition covers 425 different industries. However, we often receive requests for information on industries not covered or for supplemental data on some of the ones that we include in the book. To answer such requests, we publish this separate bibliography of other sources of composite financial data.

The information contained in this section is divided into two parts:

1) A subject index which enables you to determine which entry or entries cover a particular line of business. For example, if you need data on drug stores, the index indicates the entry numbers (not page numbers) of the listed sources that provide it.

2) The actual list of sources of information, citing title, publisher, price and a brief explanation of the data available.

This year we have again expanded the listing of sources for agricultural data, which was introduced two years ago. The data cited primarily concentrates on costs and operating performance of agricultural economies throughout the U.S. Some sources also include production data.

A word of caution is in order. Robert Morris Associates does not endorse, approve, recommend, or in any way attempt to judge the validity of any non-RMA statistics provided by the sources cited in this section. Our purpose is merely to advise you of the availability of this additional material.

NOTICE

The source and availability of data are shown for each item. Requests for publications should be made to the source indicated and NOT to the Philadelphia Office of Robert Morris Associates.

SOURCES SUBJECT INDEX

Please refer to the "Introduction" on page 909 for instructions on how to use this Bibliography. A key point to remember is that the numbers given after each topic below are not page but source numbers. A listing of the sources starts on the opposite page.

MANUFACTURING

ORDER PUBLICATIONS DIRECTLY FROM PUBLISHER

1 Statistics of Paper, Paperboard & Wood Pulp. American Forest & Paper Association, 1111 19th Street, NW, Suite 800, Washington, DC 20036. Tel: 202/463-2700. Fax: 202/463-5180. Annual. Price: $365 in U.S.; $380 overseas.

Financial data based on Federal Trade Commission Reports (now Dept. of Commerce) Covers sales, taxes and profits going back to 1950. Also includes cash flow information, production, capacity, consumption, and import/export data.

2 Special Statistical Report on Profit, Sales and Production Trends of the Men's and Boys' Clothing Industry. Clothing Manufacturers Association of the U.S.A., 1290 Avenue of the Americas, New York, NY 10104. Tel: 212/757-6664. Annual. Price: Free to members; $25 to nonmembers; $20 each for more than one copy.

Report includes net profits on sales and on net worth for past 20 years, plus statistics on domestic production and sales, imports, industry size, employment and earnings. A survey of consumer purchases by price categories and population projections are also included.

3 Aerospace Facts and Figures. Compiled by Aerospace Industries Association of America, Inc., 1250 Eye Street, NW, #1200, Washington, D.C. 20005-3924. Tel: 202/371-8561. Annual. Price: $29 prepaid per copy. Discounts available for purchases exceeding 10 books.

Aerospace industry composite income statement, balance sheet, and profit ratios.

4 Printing Industries of America, Inc., Annual Financial Ratio Studies. Printing Industries of America, Inc., Financial Services Department, 100 Daingerfield Road, Alexandria, VA 22314-2888. Tel: 703/519-8138 or 800/742-2666. Annual. Price (for those not in the database): Members, $100/book plus $6.50 postage & handling; $650/complete set plus $10 p&h; Nonmembers, $155/book, plus $6.50 p&h, $995/complete set plus $10 p&h. Full set volume discounts available.

The printing industry's only benchmark tool to measure individual company financial performance, published in 14 volumes. Covers ratio information on liquidity, operating expenses, leverage and profitability.

5 Key Business Ratios Survey of Rigid and Folding Carton Companies. National Paperbox Association, 1201 East Abingdon Drive, Suite 203, Alexandria, VA 22314. Tel: 703/684-2212. Biennial. Price: $75 to members; $95 to nonmembers.

Features financial and operating ratios which indicate the range and average for the industry.

6 Industry Operating Ratio Study. National Association of Quick Printers, 401 North Michigan Avenue, Chicago, IL 60611-4267. Tel: 312/644-6610. Fax: 312/245-1084. Published as developed. Price: $75 to members; $145 to nonmembers. Call for volume discounts.

Provides information on balance sheet, profit and loss, net owner's compensation, payroll costs, sales per employee, sales per square foot, growth analysis, credit sales, aging of accounts receivable, and inventory turnover. Also includes a section on profit leaders. Study is based on survey responses from both members and nonmembers.

7 Quick Printing Industry Wage & Benefit Survey. National Association of Quick Printers, 401 North Michigan Avenue, Chicago, IL 60611-4267. Tel: 312/644-6610. Fax: 312/245-1084. Published as developed. Price: $75 to members; $145 to nonmembers. Call for volume discounts.

Compilation of data received from nearly 1,000 quick printers on employee compensation and benefits. Also includes personnel policies and types of training.

8 Metal Treating Institute Operational Cost Survey. Metal Treating Institute, 302 Third Street, #1, Neptune Beach, FL 32266-5138. Tel: 904/249-0448. Annual. Price: Free to participants; $100 prepaid to nonparticipating members; $150 prepaid to nonmembers.

Includes operating expenses as a percentage of sales. Expenses include labor, supervision, factory supplies, utilities, maintenance, rent, shipping, equipment rental, etc.

9 Wage, Salary and Benefits Survey. Metal Treating Institute, 302 Third Street, #1, Neptune Beach, FL 32266-5138. Tel: 904/249-0448. Annual. Price: Free to participants; $45 prepaid to nonmembers.

Includes data for 26 labor classifications and executive levels divided by regions in the U.S.

10 Manufacturer Employee Compensation Survey Report. National Truck Equipment Association 37400 Hills Tech Drive, Farmington Hills, MI 48331-3414 Tel: 810/489-7090. Published every few years. Price: $100 to nonparticipants.

Survey results of NTEA manufacturer members on wages/compensation, hospitalization plans, benefits plans, vacation policies, sick leave policies, personal leave, paid holidays and shop production incentives. Data presented regionally and nationally with union/non-union comparisons.

WHOLESALING

ORDER PUBLICATIONS DIRECTLY FROM PUBLISHER

11 Operating Performance Report. American Supply Association, 222 Merchandise Mart Plaza, Suite 1360, Chicago, IL 60654. Tel: 312/464-0090. Annual. Price: $45 to members; $150 per copy prepaid to nonmembers. Volume discounts negotiable.

Operating ratios for wholesalers of plumbing, heating, cooling, and piping products grouped according to sales volume and product category, with twelve-year trend comparisons.

12 NWDA Fact Book. National Wholesale Druggists' Association, 1821 Michael Faraday Drive, Suite 400, Reston, VA 22090. Tel: 703/787-0000. Annual. Price: $30 to members; $295 to nonmembers. Volume discounts considered for larger orders.

Provides a statistical overview of the wholesale drug industry along with its customer and supplier industries and health care environment. 48 pp.

13 NWDA Operating Survey. National Wholesale Druggists' Association, 1821 Michael Faraday Drive, Suite 400, Reston, VA 22090. Tel: 703/787-0000. Annual. Price: $30 to members; $295 to nonmembers. Volume discounts considered for larger orders.

Extensive survey of income and expenses in the wholesale drug business. Analyzes expenses as a percent of sales by profit groupings, volume of sales, and geographic area, with special historical treatment of certain expense items. Balance sheet data are also given by profit and volume groups.

14 **Profitability Analysis Report.** The Industrial Distribution Association, Three Corporate Square, Suite 201, Atlanta, GA 30329. Tel: 404/325-2776. Fax: 404/325-2784. Annual. Price: $100 to members; $250 to nonmembers.

Financial and statistical information presented by sales volume, region, general or specialty lines, and return on total assets.

15 **Annual Distributor Productivity Report.** Fluid Power Distributors Association, 201 Barclay Pavilion West, Rt. 70 East, Cherry Hill, NJ 08034. Tel: 609/795-6113. Annual. Price: Free to participating members; $250 to members; $500 to nonmembers. All orders must be prepaid.

Financial analysis of typical fluid power distributor performance in terms of sales growth, ROI, gross margin, etc.

16 **Paper Annual Report.** The National Paper Trade Association 111 Great Neck Road, Great Neck, NY 11021. Tel: 516/829-3070. Annual. Price: Free to participating members; $350 to nonparticipating members & nonmembers. Volume discounts available.

Yearly study of financial and operating profitability of wholesale paper and plastics distributors; includes analysis of 843 financial ratios by region, size and type of distributor.

17 **Annual Profitability Report.** The National Paper Trade Association, 111 Great Neck Road, Great Neck, NY 11021. Tel: 516/829-3070. Annual. Price: Free to participating members; $250 to nonparticipating members and nonmembers. Volume discounts available.

Analysis of significant financial statistics and trends in financial performance in the paper and plastics distribution.

18 **Quarterly Business Report.** The National Paper Trade Association, 111 Great Neck Road, Great Neck, NY 11021. Tel: 516/829-3070. Quarterly. Price: Free to participating members; $100 to nonparticipating members and nonmembers. Volume discounts available.

A quarterly report on sales, inventory, and receivables collected from paper and plastics wholesalers.

RETAILING

ORDER PUBLICATIONS DIRECTLY FROM PUBLISHER

19 **The Dealer Compensation Survey Report/1991.** National Office Products Association, 301 N. Fairfax Street, Alexandria, VA 22314-2696. Tel: 703/549-9040. Triennial. Price: $50 to members; $200 to nonmembers.

Based on data furnished by nearly 1,000 NOPA dealers. Presents benchmark information detailing dealer compensation methods and benefit packages, as well as actual salary levels, for outside and inside sales forces, management and administrative personnel, and hourly employees.

20 **Dealer Financial Comparison and Performance Benchmarking Guide.** National Office Products Association, 301 N. Fairfax Street, Alexandria, VA 22314-2696. Tel: 703/549-9040. Annual. Price: $70 to members; $210 to nonmembers. Volume discounts available.

Discusses the principles & goals of financial management; presents financial & operating performance benchmarks; includes a

process designed to help dealers evaluate their performance compared to others in the industry, to determine their particular strengths and weaknesses.

21 **Cost and Profit Ratios for Vending Operators.** National Automatic Merchandising Association, 20 North Wacker Drive, Suite 3500, Chicago, IL 60606. Tel: 312/346-0370. Annual. Price: $100 to members; $250 to nonmembers.

Summary statistics of profits and operating expenses given as a percentage of sales, along with product line figures such as sales per machine, total sales volume per line, etc.

22 **Cost of Doing Business—Farm and Power Equipment Dealers, Industrial Dealers, and Outdoor Power Equipment (O.P.E.) Dealers.** North American Equipment Dealers Association, 10877 Watson Road, St. Louis, MO 63127-1081. Tel: 314/821-7220. Annual. Price: Free to participating members; $50 per copy.

Sales, margin, expenses and balance sheet data along with Employee Productivity Analysis for each of the three industries covered. The agricultural study includes seven volume size groups and ten regions.

23 **NHFA Operating Experiences Report.** National Home Furnishings Association, P.O. Box 2396, High Point, NC 27261. Tel: 910/883-1650. Annual. Price: $50 to members; $300 to nonmembers.

The information contained within this report is designed to identify a businesses strengths and weaknesses. This information will enable home furnishings retailers to better manage their businesses, and allow them to measure their business in relation to industry statistics. The operating report includes comparative financial ratios and statistics by dealer: sales volume size, geographic region, product emphasis, and special analysis which focuses on high profit firms.

24 **Cost of Doing Business Survey for Retail Sporting Goods Stores.** National Sporting Goods Association, 1699 Wall Street, Mt. Prospect, IL 60056-5780. Tel: 708/439-4000. Fax: 708/439-0111. Biennial. Price: Free to members; $95 per copy to nonmembers.

Based on responses of more than 300 sporting goods stores and specialty sport shops, the survey contains income statements, balance sheets, and productivity ratios by retail sales volume, number of stores, full line vs. specialty, profitability, and team business. Productivity ratios included are: sales per employee, profit per employee, sales per total selling square foot, profit per total selling square foot and inventory turnovers. 70 pp.

25 **Cost of Doing Business Survey.** Photo Marketing Association International, 3000 Picture Place, Jackson, MI 49201. Tel: 517/788-8100. Biennial. Price: Free to industry participants; $195 to members; $225 to nonmembers.

Summary financial statements, plus extensive expense and other data and comparative analysis by each of several photographic industry segments: specialty photo/video store without and with on-site processing; retail one-hour photo labs; wholesale/captive photo labs; professional, commercial, "people," and general services labs; school portrait firms; photo/video repair firms; and portrait studios.

26 **Cost of Doing Business & Financial Position Survey of the Retail Lumber & Building Material Dealers of the Northeastern States.** Northeastern Retail Lumber Association, 339 East Avenue, Rochester, NY 14607. Tel: 716/325-1626. Annual. Price: $75 to participating members; $175 to nonparticipating members; $300 to nonmembers.

Data include sales trends, sales per dollar of investment, gross margins, inventory pricing methods, operating expenses, profit margins, and rates of return. Operating data are presented by sales volume, population concentration, customer type, and inventory method.

27 **Food Marketing Industry Speaks.** Food Marketing Institute, 800 Connecticut Avenue, N.W., Washington, D.C. 20006. Tel: 202/452-8444. (Publications Sales). Annual. Price: $40 per copy for nonmembers; $60 for both the Executive Report & Companion Report. Volume discounts available.

Based on a survey of retailers and wholesalers, the report reviews the general economic setting and overall food industry performance, such as retail distribution center and store operations. Each year it highlights a different section of the supermarket industry.

28 **Facts About Store Development.** Food Marketing Institute, 800 Connecticut Avenue, N.W., Washington, D.C. 20006. Tel: 202/452-8444. (Publications Sales). Annual. Price: $40 per copy for nonmembers. Volume discounts available.

Reports data on store development, including new store size, investment, rental and remodeling costs, types of stores constructed and changes in service and specialty departments. Complements Food Marketing Industry Speaks.

29 **Annual Financial Review.** Food Marketing Institute, 800 Connecticut Avenue, N.W., Washington, D.C. 20006. Tel: 202/452-8444. (Publications Sales). Price: $40 per copy for nonmembers. Volume discounts available.

Presents a financial picture of the supermarket industry, including data on profits, return on investment, capital structure, debt, and equity. Also included is an annual balance sheet and income statement for the entire supermarket industry.

30 **Management Compensation Study for Wholesalers and Large Retailers.** Food Marketing Institute, 800 Connecticut Avenue, N.W., Washington, D.C. 20006. Tel: 202/452-8444 (Publications Sales). Annual. Price: $300 to members; $900 to nonmembers. Volume discounts available.

Contains compensation levels for over 40 positions, many by region and metropolitan regions. Positions including senior executives, headquarters staff, top merchandise executives and store operations positions. Also included is information on compensation programs.

31 **Operations Review.** Food Marketing Institute, 800 Connecticut Ave., N.W., Washington, D.C. 20006. Tel: 202/452-8444. (Publications Sales). Quarterly. Price: $25 to members; $50 to nonmembers. Volume discounts available

Current year available to participants only. A 17-page report of company operating ratios.

32 **Operating Results of Independent Supermarkets.** Food Marketing Institute, 800 Connecticut Avenue, N.W., Washington, D.C. 20006. Tel: 202/452-8444. (Publications Sales). Annual. Price: $25 to members; $50 to nonmembers. Volume discounts available.

Report on store level productivity measures, expenses, inventory turns, gross margins, and other income items. Store figures are presented by region, store type and other important categories.

33 **Supermarket Pharmacies.** Food Marketing Institute, 800 Connecticut Avenue, N.W., Washington, D.C. 20006. Tel: 202/452-8444. (Publications Sales). Price: $10 to members; $20 to nonmembers. Volume discounts available.

A special 18-page research report providing a complete profile of in-store pharmacies. Topics covered include the organization of the pharmacy department, pharmacy products and services, sales/profits, comments on pharmacies and future pharmacy development.

34 **Survey of Wage Rates for Hourly Employees.** National Restaurant Association, 1200 17th Street, N.W., Washington, DC 20036. Tel: 202/331-5900. Biennial. Price: $20 to members; $40 to nonmembers.

Data on hourly wage rates by type of employee for the entire U.S., for certain geographical regions, and by individual state, and for various substate/city areas.

35 **Restaurant Industry Operations Report.** Published by the National Restaurant Association, 1200 17th Street, N.W., Washington, D.C. 20036. Tel: 202/331-5900. Based on information prepared by Deloitte & Touche. Annual. NRA price per copy: Members $39; nonmembers $78. Copies available from NRA upon request.

Study of the financial performance of restaurants. Analysis of income and expenses are based on dollar amounts per seat and ratio to total sales.

36 **Compensation for Salaried Personnel in Food Service.** Published by the National Restaurant Association, 1200 17th Street, N.W., Washington, D.C. 20036. Tel: 202/331-5900. Based on information prepared by the Hay Group. Triennial. NRA price per copy: Members $30; nonmembers $55. Copies available from NRA upon request.

Breaks down total compensation in relation to sales volume and other parameters for all corporate or top executive positions. Includes statistics on executive fringe benefits, leave policies, and other industry perquisites.

37 **The NARD-Lilly Digest.** NARD, 205 Daingerfield Road, Alexandria, VA 22314. Tel: 703/683-8200 or Fax: 703/683-3619. Annual. Price: $30 per copy. 20% discount on 100+ copies.

Comprehensive study of community pharmacies showing a detailed breakdown of expenses with stores grouped according to sales volume and prescription activity. Also gives balance sheet data and selected financial ratios.

38 **Lilly Hospital Pharmacy Survey.** Eli Lilly and Company, Lilly Corporate Center, Drop Code 1057 Indianapolis, IN 46285. Tel: 317/276-3641 or Fax: 317/276-5985. Annual. Price: $30 per copy. 20% discount on 100+ copies.

Presents the most recent and detailed information available on the operational statistics of hospital pharmacies in the United States.

39 **Automotive Executive Magazine: August 1995 Issue.** National Automobile Dealers Association, 8400 Westpark Drive, McLean, VA 22102. Tel: 703/821-7208. Annual. Price: $10 per copy.

Provides statistics relevant to the economic impact of franchised new car and truck dealers. Both current year and historical data are included.

40 **Business Performance Report.** National Shoe Retailers Association, 9861 Broken Land Parkway, Suite 255, Columbia, MD 21046-1151. Tel: 800/673-8446. Fax: 410/381-1167. Biennial. Price: $45 to members; $75 to nonmembers.

Based on financial data compiled from over 1700 independent shoe retail companies, the BPR includes statistical data and a complete analysis of operational expenses and profit/loss. Covers men's, women's, children's, and family shoe companies. Complete with charts, graphs, and performance ratios.

41 **Distributor Profit Survey Report.** National Truck Equipment Association, 37400 Hills Tech Drive, Farmington Hills, MI 48331-3414. Tel: 810/489-7090. Annual. Price: $75 to nonmembers.

Contains a strategic profit model, a composite balance sheet and income statement, financial ratio analysis, a product profile, and an employee productivity profile of commercial truck body and equipment distributors.

42 **Distributor Employee Compensation Survey Report.** National Truck Equipment Association, 37400 Hills Tech Drive, Farmington Hills, MI 48331-3414. Tel: 810/489-7090. Annual. Price: $100 to nonparticipants.

Survey report on employee compensation practices of NTEA distributor members. Includes detailed analyses of base salary and bonus levels for executive or management positions, as well as compensation levels for employee positions by sales volume, regional differentials and line of business category. Also includes extensive cross-industry data from 9 other distributor organizations.

43 **The Cost-of-Doing Business Study.** National Retail Hardware Association/Home Center Institute, 5822 West 74th Street, Indianapolis, IN 46278. Tel: 1-800/772-4424. Fax: 317/328-4354. Annual. Price: $34.95 to members; $62.95 to nonmembers. Volume discounts available.

Detailed financial information about hardware stores, home centers, lumber outlets ... includes composite income statements, balance sheets and profitability ratios. Reported in categories such as store profitability, sales volume, salesfloor size, and location.

44 **The Merchandising Report.** National Retail Hardware Association/Home Center Institute, 5822 West 74th Street, Indianapolis, IN 46278. Tel: 1-800/772-4424. Fax: 317/328-4354. Annual. Price: $29.95 to members; $54.95 to nonmembers. Volume discounts available.

Profiles 23 major product categories in hardware stores, home centers, lumber outlets ... provides average performance ratios including sales, inventory and gross margin per square foot, sales to inventory ratio, gross margin percentage, and GMROI for each department by type of store.

45 **The Compensation Report.** National Retail Hardware Association/Home Center Institute, 5822 West 74th Street, Indianapolis, IN 46278. Tel: 1-800/772-4424. Fax: 317/328-4354. Annual. Price: $19.95 to members; $35.95 to nonmembers. Volume discounts available.

Outlines employment and salary practices in hardware stores, home centers, lumber outlets. Summarizes the number and type of employees in each type of store and their salary ranges. Broken out into categories such as store profitability, sales volume, salesfloor size and location.

46 **Ski Cost of Doing Business Survey.** National Ski Retailers Association, 1699 Wall Street, Mt. Prospect, IL 60056-5780. Tel: 708/439-4293. Fax: 708/439-0111. Biennial. Price: Free to members; $95 to nonmembers.

Prepared for the National Ski Retailers Association by Industry Insights, Inc., the survey contains income statements, balance sheets and productivity ratios by shop type (non-area ski shop, area ski shop and sporting goods store with ski department), by dollar volume and by single vs. multi-store operations. Key performance measures are included for profitability (net profit before tax to total revenues, net profit before tax to total assets, net profit before tax to net worth and owners' compensation and profits to revenues), productivity (gross margin on merchandise sales, total revenues per selling square foot, operating margins per selling square foot, revenues per employee and payroll as a percent of operating margin) and financial management (total net debt to total assets, current ratio and quick ratio). (56 pages)

SERVICE AND CONSTRUCTION

ORDER PUBLICATIONS DIRECTLY FROM PUBLISHER

47 **IRSA Report.** International Health, Racquet & Sportsclub Association, 263 Summer Street, Boston, MA 02210. Tel: 617/951-0055. Annual. Price: $100 to members; $400 to nonmembers.

This publication provides information on key club operating figures including revenue and expense ratios, sales and marketing figures, capital investment, compensation, and general industry growth data.

48 **1993 Compensation & Benefits Survey.** Building Service Contractors Association International, 10201 Lee Highway, Suite 225, Fairfax, VA 22030. Tel: 800/368-3414. Fax: 703/352-0493. Biennial. Price: $25 to members; $50 to nonmembers; Volume discounts available.

Presents compensation and benefits data from a national cross-section of building service contractors. Section I contains compensation and salary structure for management personnel. Section II contains compensation and wage structure for hourly production personnel. Section III reports on employee benefits. Separate calculations based on size of company, union/non-union personnel, and type of company ownership. 1993, 32 pp. BSCAI gratefully acknowledges HOST/RACINE's sponsorship of this publication. Order# RP60.

49 **1994 Financial & Operating Ratios Study.** Building Service Contractors Association International, 10201 Lee Highway, Suite 225, Fairfax, VA 22030. Tel: 800/368-3414. Fax: 703/352-0493. Biennial. Price: $25 to members; $50 to nonmembers; Volume discounts available.

Presents financial and operating ratios from a national cross-section of building service contractors. Presents operating ratios for categories of income, direct expense, administrative, sales and promotion, office expense, facility expense, and taxes. Also presents six financial ratios: receivables to sales, current, acid-test, equity, return on stockholders' investment, and return on permanent investment. Separate calculations based on size of company and type of ownership. 1995, 50 pp. Order# RP 76.

50 **1993 Gas Facts, 1991 and 1992 Data, A Statistical Record of the Gas Utility Industry.** American Gas Association, 1515 Wilson Boulevard, Arlington, VA 22209. Tel: 703/841-8559. Annual. Price: $27.50 to members; $55 to nonmembers.

A detailed collection of charts and tables that provides current and historical data on reserves, supply, storage, pipeline mileage, sales, revenues, customers, prices, consumption, appliance and housing, financial, construction and personnel. It includes a glossary of terms and conversion table. Previous editions of Gas Facts are also available.

51 **1993 Gas Data Book, 1992 Data.** American Gas Association, 1515 Wilson Boulevard, Arlington, VA 22209. Tel: 703/841-8559. Annual. Price: $1 to members; $2 to nonmembers.

An abbreviated version of Gas Facts. It covers reserves, supply, sales, revenues, prices, consumption, financial data and personnel.

52 **Handbook of Investor Owned A.G.A. Member Companies.** American Gas Association, 1515 Wilson Boulevard, Arlington, VA 22209. Tel: 703/841-8559. Annual. Price: $20 to members; $35 to nonmembers.

Provides up-to-date annual financial data on 110 investor owned members of the American Gas Association.

53 **Historical Statistics of the Gas Utility Industry: 1976-1985.** American Gas Association, 1515 Wilson Boulevard, Arlington, VA 22209. Tel: 703/841-8559. Annual. Price: $25 to members; $50 to nonmembers.

Contains 10 years of tabular data on reserves, supply, storage pipeline mileage, sales, revenues, customers, prices, consumption, appliance and housing, financial, construction and personnel.

54 **Financial Performance Report.** National Electrical Contractors Association, 3 Bethseda Metro Center, Suite 1100, Bethseda, MD 20814. Tel: 301/657-3110. Biennial. Price: $20 to members; $50 prepaid to nonmembers.

A statistical review of the impact of financial ratios, operating costs and capital investment in the electrical contracting business. With several classes of business as established on the basis of annual productive payroll, analysis is made of expense items as a percent of sales, percent of prime cost, and percent of direct labor cost. Also shown is the detailed breakdown of operating overhead expenses by the foregoing percentages. Each class includes selected financial ratios.

55 **The Cost Study: Income & Cost for Origination and Servicing of 1-4 Unit Residential Loans.** Mortgage Bankers Association of America, 1125 15th Street, N.W., Washington, D.C. 20005-2766. Tel: 202/861-6574 (Publications Dept.). Annual. Price: $100 to members; $200 prepaid to nonmembers. Add 10% for handling.

An analysis of income and costs for origination, warehousing, marketing, and servicing of 1-4 unit residential mortgage loans.

56 **MBA National Delinquency Survey.** Mortgage Bankers Association of America, 1125 15th Street, N.W., Washington, D.C. 20005-2766. Tel: 202/861-6574 (Publications Dept.). Quarterly. Price: $30 per year. Single copies are $10 per issue. Add 10% of total for handling.

Delinquency and foreclosure rates for the nation, various regions, and all states for conventional and government single-family loans.

57 **MBA Mortgage Banking Performance Report.** Mortgage Bankers Association of America, 1125 15th Street, N.W., Washington, DC 20005-2766. Tel: 202/861-6574 (Publications Dept.). Quarterly & Annual. Price: $300 to members; $400 to nonmembers for three quarterly editions, plus the annual summary. $125 to members; $175 to nonmembers for the annual summary only. $75 to members; $100 to nonmembers for the quarterly editions only.

Provides a wide array of information on mortgage banking companies, including balance sheet and income statement data, and operational and performance ratios.

58 **MBA Weekly Survey of Mortgage Interest Rates & Application Volume.** Mortgage Bankers Association of America, 1125 15th Street, N.W., Washington, DC 20005-2766. Tel: 202/861-6574 (Publications Dept.). Weekly. Price: $150 to members; $300 to nonmembers.

Available every Thursday via fax, this report provides percentage change in retail applications (number and dollar, volume refinances and purchases, total conventional, and FHA/VA) from the preceding week and the same week last year; average contract rate and points on six, popular mortgage products; refinancing and ARM's as a percent of applications; average loan sizes; and updated application volume indexes for convenient comparisons since March 1990.

59 **1995 BOMA Experience Exchange Report.** Building Owners and Managers Association International, 1201 New York Avenue, N.W., Suite 300, Washington, D.C. 20005. Tel: 202/408-2662. Annual. Price: $155 to members; $275 to nonmembers.

Detailed analysis of office building operating expenses and rental income reported in dollars per square foot. Data tables include North American cities as well as U.S./Canadian national averages by age, height and size of building. Special analyses of all electric, medical, single purpose, agency managed, corporate facility, and government buildings.

60 **Statistics of the Local Exchange Carriers.** United States Telephone Association, 1401 H Street, NW, Suite 600, Washington, D.C. 20005. Tel: 202/326-7300. Annual. Price: $250 to members; $350 to nonmembers. Member rates to nonmembers for multiple copies.

Statistical summary of the telephone industry including composite balance sheets and income statements, as well as financial and operating ratios. Contains operating results submitted by individual companies.

61 **Phonefacts.** United States Telephone Association, 1401 H Street, NW, Suite 600, Washington, D.C. 20006. Tel: 202/326-7300. Annual. Price: $1.50 to members; $3 to nonmembers.

Presents financial summary of the year and preview for the coming year. Trends or operating revenues, total number of telephones, and total plant capacity. Also highlights patterns of growth over the last decade and a half.

62 **Statistical Yearbook of the Electric Utility Industry.** Edison Electric Institute, 701 Pennsylvania Avenue, N.W., Washington, D.C. 20004-2696. Tel: 202/508-5000. Annual. Price: $36 per copy prepaid to members; $45 per copy prepaid to nonmembers, plus shipping and handling. Item #01-93-05.

Data compiled from company reports, and other appropriate sources, on operational and financial aspects of the total electric utility industry. Categories include national and state statistics on installed capacity; electric generation and supply; sales, revenue, and customers by class of service; investor-owned data are presented for operating and related ratios; fuel use; financial; and general economics series. Published annually in the fall.

63 **Statistical Yearbook of the Electric Utility Industry—Disk Version.** Edison Electric Institute, 701 Pennsylvania Avenue, N.W., Washington, D.C. 20004-2696. Tel: 202/508-5424. Fax: 202/508-5030. Annual. Price: $36 to members; $45 to nonmembers. Item #01-93-06 3.5.

All the same valuable information found in the Statistical Yearbook. The design of the Yearbook as a Lotus 123 worksheet eases the handling of tables and allows the production of graphics without re-keying information.

64 **EEI's EEI-EZstat-Database of Electric Utility Financial and Operating Data.** Edison Electric Institute, 701 Pennsylvania Avenue, N.W., Washington, D.C. 20004-2696. Tel: 202/508-5424. Fax: 202/508-5030. Annual. Price: Single Year Database # 01-94-13 (First Copy)-$525; Multiple Year Database 1991-1993 #01-94-12 (First Copy)-$975. Detailed information on

EEI-EZstat; contact EEI's Statistics Dept. at 202/508-5579; Fax: 202/508-5380.

65 **Digest of Electric Utility Financial Ratios.** Edison Electric Institute, 701 Pennsylvania Avenue, N.W., Washington, D.C. 20004-2696. Tel: 202/508-5000. Price: $8 to members; $10 to nonmembers, plus shipping and handling. Item #04-88-10.

Analyze industry financial reports with the method of calculations outlined in this digest. Numerous indicators used by the industry are provided-earnings and return, dividends, revenue and sales, expense, tax, plant, depreciation, and others. With this publication, you can be assured that all your necessary analysis has been completed.

66 **EEI Pocketbook of Electric Utility Industry Statistics.** Edison Electric Institute, 701 Pennsylvania Avenue, N.W., Washington, D.C. 20004-2696. Tel: 202/508-5000. Annual. Price: $2.40 per copy prepaid to members (minimum order is ten copies); $3 per copy prepaid to nonmembers (minimum order is ten copies), plus shipping and handling. #01-93-09.

A pocket-sized quick reference of national electric industry data; some dating from 1902 to the present. Categories include data on installed capacity and generation; capital and finance; sales, revenue and customers; fuels; private and public ownership. Published annually in the fall.

67 **Income and Fees of Accountants in Public Practice.** National Society of Public Accountants, 1010 North Fairfax Street, Alexandria, VA 22314. Tel: 703/549-6400. Fax: 703/549-2984. Triennial. Price: $40 to members; $60 to non-members.

Report covers six general areas of interest: (1) tax return fees and policies, (2) number of clients, (3) income by type of service, (4) hourly billing fees of principals, employees, and type of service performed, (5) office facilities and data processing use, and (6) gross and net income, together with employee cost and expense levels, as well as some general characteristics of the sample.

68 **Cost of Doing Business Survey.** American Rental Association, 1900 19th Street, Moline, IL 61265. Tel: 309/764-2475. Annual. Price: One free copy to all members; additional member copies $10; $30 to nonmembers.

Includes detailed income and expense breakdowns for all rental firms responding in their survey, as well as balance sheet data for the same companies. Then the data are broken down by size of firm, source of revenues, type of equipment rented, and geographic region.

69 **Advertising Age.** Crain Communications, Inc., 220 East 42nd Street, New York, NY 10017. Tel: 212/210-0100. Fax: 212/210-0200. Weekly. Price: $3.00 per copy; $99 annually. Volume discounts available.

Periodically publishes financial data on the advertising and marketing field.

70 **Economic Analysis of United States Ski Areas.** National Ski Areas Association, 133 South Van Gordan Street, Suite 300, Lakewood, CO 80228. Tel: 303/987-1111. Annual. Price: $100 to members; $175 to nonmembers. Current edition shipped, unless otherwise specified.

An in-depth review of critical ski area financial data. This analysis uses basic ski area characteristics (size, location, days of operation, capacity, skier visits, lift ticket prices etc.); critical economic ratios, profitability, regional variations, and other measures. This analysis paints a picture of the industry and is widely used by appraisers and financial institutions.

71 **Air Transport.** Air Transport Association of America, 1301 Pennsylvania Avenue, N.W., Washington, D.C. 20004. Tel: 202/626-4000. Annual. Price: Free to members; $10 to nonmembers. Volume discounts available.

Operating revenues and expenses in dollar amounts compared over a period of years. Also includes balance sheet data for various types of airlines and other related airline industry statistics.

72 **Railroad Revenues, Expenses, and Income.** Association of American Railroads, 50 F Street, N.W.—Room 5900, Washington, D.C. 20001-1564. Tel: 202/639-2311. Quarterly. Price: $25 to members; $75 to nonmembers for annual subscription.

A quarterly publication showing detailed financial data for Class I railroad industry by quarter. Compiled for most recent quarter and year-to-date with comparisons to prior year. Includes data by railroad and district. (4 pages)

73 **Rail Cost Adjustment Factor.** Association of American Railroads, 50 F Street, N.W.—Room 5900, Washington, D.C. 20001-1564. Tel: 202/639-2311. Quarterly. Price: Free to members; $75 to nonmembers. Annual subscription includes quarterly filings. (EF 253)

A quarterly publication of the filing submitted to the Interstate Commerce Commission (ICC) under Ex Parte No. 290 (Sub. No. 2) procedures. Includes composite forecast indexes of railroad prices for the U.S., covering labor, fuel, materials and supplies, equipment rents, depreciation, and other expenses. Available 25 days before the end of a quarter.

74 **Railroad Ten-Year Trends.** Association of American Railroads, 50 F Street, N.W., Room 5900, Washington, D.C. 20001. Tel: 202/639-2309. Annual. Price: $50 to members; $100 nonmember.

Contemporary railroad economics, including an overview of the U.S. freight railroad industry; Class I industry performance, traffic, revenue and rates, financial statistics, employment, plant and equipment, and operations; a list of U.S. freight railroads; and profiles of railroad-related organizations. Each edition includes the ten most recent years' information, when available. (172 pages)

75 **Railroad Facts.** Association of American Railroads, 50 F Street, N.W.—Room 5900, Washington, D.C. 20001. Tel: 202/639-2309. Annual. Price: $4 to members; $8 to nonmembers. Volume discounts available. (80 pages).

Financial and operating statistics for Class I railroads for the most recent year and selected prior years. Data include financial results, traffic, operating averages, plant and equipment, employment and wages, and fuel consumption and cost. Includes a two year comparative table of statistical highlights and a one-page profile of each Class I railroad. (80 pages)

76 **Railroads and States.** Association of American Railroads, 50 F Street, N.W.—Room 5900, Washington, D.C. 20001. Tel: 202/639-2309. Periodic. Price: $8 to members; $15 to nonmembers. The nonmember price for this publication applies to non-railroads and the member price applies to all railroads, not just full AAR members.

Provides state-by-state statistics and rankings for the number of railroads, total rail miles, rail carloads handled, total tons carried by rail, total railroad employment, total wages of rail employees, average wages per rail employee, average fringe benefits per rail employee, number of railroad retirement beneficiaries, and payments to railroad retirement beneficiaries. The volumes of the most important commodities handled within each state are shown along with a map of each state's rail network. A list of each railroad operating in each state, and two pages of information covering Amtrak are also included. (135 pages)

77 **Analysis of Class I Railroads.** Association of American Railroads, 50 F Street, N.W.—Room 5900, Washington, D.C. 20001. Tel: 202/639-2302. Annual. Price: $75 each for 1978-1985 editions; $100 each for the 1986 edition; $200 each for the 1987-94 edition. Full member railroads should call for price information.

An annual publication showing about 750 financial and operating statistics and ratios for each Class I railroad, summarized by district and for the U.S. Extremely comprehensive, including financial results, resources, operations and rankings. Includes index and references. (Latest version-122 pages/spiral bound)

78 **Cost of Operations Survey.** American Collectors Association, Inc., 4040 West 70th Street, Minneapolis, Minnesota 55435. Tel: 612/926-6547. Annual. Price: $50 to members; $100 prepaid to nonmembers. Volume discounts negotiable.

Income and expense averages based on a national survey of approximately 250 collection agencies. Regional breakdowns provided.

79 **Factbook and Directory.** Mortgage Insurance Companies of America, 727 15th Street, N.W., Suite 1200, Washington, D.C. 20005. Tel: 202/393-5566. Annual. Free of charge.

Includes a review and description of the industry's financial statements.

80 **Summary Annual Report.** National Marine Bankers Association, 200 East Randolph Drive, #5100, Chicago, IL 60601-6528. Tel: 312/946-6250. Annual. Free of charge. Members receive complete data; nonmembers receive brief summaries.

Includes statistics on terms, turnover, charge-offs, and delinquencies for recreational marine lending.

81 **MGMA Annual Cost Survey Report.** Medical Group Management Association, 104 Inverness Terrace East, Englewood, CO 80112-5306. Tel: 303/799-1111. Annual. Price: $100 to members; $215 prepaid to nonmembers; $167 to affiliates. Volume discounts available on more than 10 orders.

Provides revenue and expense data on the operation of medical group practices. Separate statistics are reported by geographic region, size of practice, and specialty medical group.

82 **Statistical Report of Defense Credit Unions.** Defense Credit Union Council, 805 15th Street, N.W., Suite 300, Washington, D.C. 20005-2207. Tel: 202/682-5993. Annual. Price: Free to members; $50 to nonmembers.

Provides detailed information on the services and operations of the individual defense credit unions. This 111-page report includes a section on operating ratios by common bond group.

83 **Dollars & Cents of Shopping Centers: 1995.** The Urban Land Institute, 625 Indiana Avenue, N.W., Washington, D.C. 20004-2930. Tel: 800/321-5011. Price: $219.95 prepaid to members, plus shipping and handling; $269.95 prepaid to nonmembers, plus shipping and handling. ULI publication code number: D 66.

Includes comprehensive data on shopping centers in the U.S. and Canada. Contains statistics on the type and age of center, geographic locations and types of tenants. It also offers special reports on high and low sales tenants, department stores, food courts, parking ratios, changes in operational results, and data on new leases.

84 **Dollars & Cents of Convenience Centers: 1995.** The Urban Land Institute, 625 Indiana Avenue, N.W., Washington, D.C. 20004-2930. Available September 1995. Tel: 800/321-5011. Call for prices.

Nine major and 50 total categories of operational data are presented for the shopping center as a whole, along with figures for sales, total rent, percentage rent, common area charges as a percent of sales, as well as other facts about individual tenants.

85 **Dollars & Cents of Power Centers: 1995.** The Urban Land Institute, 625 Indiana Avenue, N.W., Washington, D.C. 20004-2930. Tel: 800/321-5011. Available September 1995. Call for prices.

This report compares the performance of approximately 50 power centers (shopping centers owned by 3 or more big box or category killer stores as compared to more traditional community and super community shopping centers.) The operational study contains a full range of comparative tables on 129 individual tenants including tenant mix, sales, rents, percentage rents, common area charges, taxes, insurance, total charges, and other related facts. Fifty categories of operating expenses, operating income, and the net operating.

86 **Dollars & Cents of Downtown/Intown Shopping Centers: 1995.** The Urban Land Institute, 625 Indiana Avenue, N.W., Washington, D.C. 20004-2930. Tel: 800/321-5011. Call for prices.

This study is based on data collected from 601 super regional, regional community, and neighborhood shopping centers and broken down according to location into three subsets: downtown/intown centers, inner suburban centers, and outer suburban centers. You'll find nine major and 50 total categories of operational data for the shopping center as whole and a full range of tables comparing tenant mix, sales, total rents, percentage rents, property taxes, insurance, total charges, total charges as a percent of sales, and other related information.

87 **Dollars & Cents of Small Town/Nonmetropolitan Shopping Centers: 1995.** The Urban Land Institute, 625 Indiana Avenue, N.W., Washington, D.C. 20004-2930. Tel: 800/321-5011. Call for prices.

Based on data collected from 171 super regional, regional, community, and neighborhood shopping centers, the operational analysis in this report is presented in the same format as the basic Dollars & Cents of Shopping Centers: 1993 publication. Contains tables on 150 tenant types comparing tenant sales, total rents, percentage rents, common area charges, taxes, insurance, total charges, total charges as a percent of sales, and other related information. Centerwide data are provided for 50 categories of operating income, operating expenses, net operating balance and tenant mix.

88 **Dollars & Cents of Renovated/Expanded Shopping Centers: 1995.** The Urban Land Institute, 625 Indiana Avenue, N.W., Washington, D.C. 20004-2930. Tel: 800/321-5011. Price: Call for prices.

Data are provided for renovated centers; centers that were expanded; & centers that were both renovated and expanded. Tenant data are provided for 150 tenant types comparing sales, rents, percentage rents, common area charges, taxes, insurance, total charges, and total charges as a percentage of sales. Centerwide data are provided for 50 categories of operating income, operating expenses, net operating balance and tenant mix.

89 **Dollars & Cents of Shopping Centers In the Top 20 Metropolitan Areas: 1995.** The Urban Land Institute, 625 Indiana Avenue, N.W., Washington, D.C. 20004-2930. Tel: 800/321-5011. Call for prices.

This report is the first comprehensive study of the performance of shopping centers in America's largest cities. It is presented with sections on super regional, regional, community, and neighborhood centers. The report also includes tenant sales, rents, percentage rents, common area charges, taxes insurance, total charges and total charges as a percent of sales for 150 different tenant types. Further, this study features centerwide data comparing 50 different categories of operating expenses, operating income, net operating balance and tenant mix. Centerwide data are also presented for all shopping centers by region and age of centers.

90 **ULI Market Profiles: 1995.** The Urban Land Institute, 625 Indiana Avenue, N.W., Washington, D.C. 20004-2930. Tel: 800/321-5011. Price: Volume I: North America (M#47); $249.95 to members; $299.95 to nonmembers. Volume II: Europe (#M48); $49.95 to members; $99.95 to nonmembers. Volume III: Pacific Rim (#M49); $24.95 to members; $49.95 to nonmembers. Three-Volume Set (#M50); $299.95 to members; $399.95 to nonmembers.

This three volume set provides profiles of numerous metropolitan areas including descriptions of the development climate, public policy issues, economic evaluations, and demographics. It also presents tables for land prices, lease rates, sales prices and rents. Maps of recent development activities and planned projects are also featured.

91 **Dollars & Cents of Super Community Shopping Centers: 1995.** The Urban Land Institute, 625 Indiana Avenue. N.W., Washington, D.C. 20004-2930. Tel: 800/321-5011. Call for prices.

This study presents a comparison of the centers broken down by size—those that are 25,000 square feet or smaller and those that are larger. A new type of entity, known as a "power center," is found within the larger group. As in other Dollars & Cents reports, you'll find information ranging from 50 categories of centerwide operational data to facts about 100 individual tenants ranging from sales data to rents, percentage rents, common area charges, taxes, insurance, and total charges as a percent of sales.

92 **Construction Industry Annual Financial Survey.** Construction Financial Management Association, Princeton Gateway Corporate Campus, 707 State Road, Suite 223, Princeton, NJ 08540-1413. Tel: 609/683-5000. Annual. Price: $20 to survey respondents; $119 to members and $149 to nonmembers who did not complete the survey. Volume discounts available.

Comparative financial data on construction contractors with key ratios and analysis by type of construction, size, and region. Survey includes sections on general organizational and industry issues, plus accounting policies and methods, and a five year comparative analysis. New benchmarking data on MIS, professional consultants, and organizational issues. (300 pp.)

93 **American Trucking Trends, 1994-95 Edition.** American Trucking Associations, Trucking Information Services, Inc., 2200 Mill Road, Alexandria, VA 22314. Tel: 703/838-1978. Annual. Price: $35 to members; $45 to nonmembers. Volume discounts based on individual quotes. A comprehensive publication of trucking statistics and industry trends, designed to provide a general profile of industry characteristics and operations.

94 **Financial and Operating Statistics Series: Motor Carrier Annual Report.** American Trucking Associations, Trucking Information Services, Inc., 2200 Mill Road, Alexandria, VA 22314. Tel: 703/838-1978. Annual. Price: $400; Annual Summary Tables $50; $495 in combination with Motor Carrier Quarterly Report.

Annual financial and operating statistics for individual Class I and II federally regulated motor carriers of property. Includes balance sheet, income statement, number of trucks, tractors and trailers owned or rented, detailed operating expenses and physical operating statistics, financial ratios and operating derivations. Also contains detailed summary tables.

95 **Trucking Activity Report.** American Trucking Associations, Trucking Information Services, Inc., 2200 Mill Road, Alexandria, VA 22314. Tel: 703/838-1978. Monthly. Price: $450/yr. for participating motor carriers; $695/yr. for all other subscribers.

Monthly newsletter providing detailed information on fleet operations based on an on-going survey of a broad spectrum of motor carriers. Information includes traffic levels, revenue per loan by trailer type, revenue per ton, revenue per mile, equipment utilization, driver turnover, fuel costs, insurance costs, and many other bench marking concepts for different segments of the industry.

96 **Financial and Operating Statistics Series: Motor Carrier Quarterly Report.** American Trucking Associations, Trucking Information Services, Inc., 2200 Mill Road, Alexandria, VA 22314. Tel: 703/838-1978. Quarterly. Price: $400/ yr., $150/qtr., $495 in combination with Motor Carrier Annual Report.

Quarterly financial and operating statistics including detailed income statement, as well as tonnage and mileage figures, for all individual Class I and II federally regulated motor carriers of property contained in the report. Also contains summary tables.

97 **Nursing Home Reporting System: Financial Data.** Agency for Health Care Administration, Center for Health Statistics, 2727 Mahan Drive, Tallahassee, FL 32308-5403. Tel: 904/922-5861. Annual. Price: $8.

Contains financial data on licensed nursing homes in Florida, including number of beds, occupancy rates, and revenue statistics.

98 **Hospital Financial Data.** Agency for Health Care Administration, Center for Health Statistics, 2727 Mahan Drive, Tallahassee, FL 32308-5403. Tel: 904/922-5861. Annual. Price: $6.

Contains hospital data on patient days, payers, revenue and expenses.

99 **Clubs in Town and Country.** Pannell Kerr Forster, P.C., 5845 Richmond Highway, Alexandria, VA 22303. Tel: 703/329-1952. Annual. Price: $50 prepaid. Available on written request.

Dollar and percentage figures on income and expenses of city clubs and country clubs with geographic and membership size breakdowns for each group.

100 **International Hotel Trends: A Statistical Summary.** PKF Consulting, 425 California Street, San Francisco, CA 94104. Tel: 415/421-5378. Annual. Price: $125 prepaid. Available on written request.

Presents operating ratios for international hotels compared with those in the U.S. based on total sales and income. Also includes detailed analysis of operations on a regional basis for hotels throughout the world.

101 **Trends in the Hotel Industry—U.S. Edition.** PKF Consulting, 425 California Street, San Francisco, CA 94104. Tel: 415/421-5378. Annual. Price: $195 prepaid. Available on written request.

Extensive study of operating costs for hotels and motels with figures reported in percentages and dollar amounts. Various breakdowns of data include type of facility, geographic area, number of rooms, and rates charged.

102 **Trends in the Hotel Industry.** PKF Consulting, 425 California Street, San Francisco, CA 94104. Tel: 415/421-5378. Monthly. (Contact local office for information).

Report of occupancy and average daily rate for U.S. hotels by city and region.

103 **Federal Taxes and the Private Club.** Pannell Kerr Forster, PC, 5845 Richmond Highway, Alexandria, VA 22303. Tel: 703/329-1952 Annual. Free of charge. Available on written request.

Composite tax information relevant to the private club industry.

104 **U.K. Trends: Outlook in the Hotel & Tourism Industries.** Pannell Kerr Forster Associates, New Garden House, 78 Hatton Garden, London EC1N 8JA, England, UK. Tel: (71)831-7393. Annual. Available on written request.

Extensive study of hotel & tourism industry in U.K. Figures are reported in percentages and dollar amounts. Various breakdowns of data include geographic area, number of rooms, and rates charged.

105 **Eurotrends: Outlook in the Hotel & Tourism Industries.** Pannell Kerr Forster Associates, New Garden House, 78 Hatton Garden, London EC1N 8JA, England, UK. Tel: (71)831-7393. Annual. Available on written request.

Extensive study of hotel & tourism industry across Europe. Figures are reported in percentages and dollar amounts. Various breakdowns of data include geographic area, number of rooms, and rates charged.

106 **Trends in the Mexican Hotel Industry.** PKF Consulting, 425 California Street, Suite 1650, San Francisco, CA 94104. Tel: 415/421-5378. Annual. Available upon written request.

Extensive study of Mexican hotel industry. Figures are reported in percentages and dollar amounts. Various breakdowns of data include geographic area, number of rooms, and rates charged.

107 **1995 Television Employee Compensation and Fringe Benefits Report.** National Association of Broadcasters, 1771 N Street, N.W., Washington, D.C. 20036-2891. Tel: 800/368-5644. Biennial. Price: $100 to members; $200 to nonmembers.

This report provides information on average and median compensation for over 20 staff positions. Also includes data on average number of paid holidays, sick days and vacation days and information on the various types of fringe benefits offered by different television stations.

108 **Radio Station Salaries.** National Association of Broadcasters, 1771 N Street, N.W., Washington, D.C. 20036-2891. Tel: 800/368-5644. Annual. Price $100 to members; $200 to nonmembers.

Provides information on average and median compensation for over 35 staff positions, information on the high and low salaries paid for each position, and information on the total compensation paid for each position.

109 **Television Financial Report.** National Association of Broadcasters, 1771 N Street, N.W., Washington, D.C. 20036-2891. Tel: 800/368-5644. Annual. Price $160 to members; $300 to nonmembers.

Presents statistical information on revenues, expenses, and profit margins of television stations for the previous year by station type, DMA market and revenue size groupings.

110 **Television Market Analysis.** National Association of Broadcasters, 1771 N Street, N.W., Washington, D.C. 20036-2891. Tel: 800/368-5644. Annual. Price: $250 to members; $450 to nonmembers.

Presents television financial data, including revenue and expense data for more than 100 markets. Includes 5-year history for most of these markets.

111 **Advertising Revenues Per Television Household: A Market By Market Analysis.** National Association of Broadcasters, 1771 N Street, N.W., Washington D.C. 20036-2891. Tel: 800/368-5644. Annual. Price: $75 to members; $150 to nonmembers.

Analyzes the revenue history of local television markets on a per television household basis; demonstrates how markets are faring without the influence of fluctuations in population.

112 **Trends in Radio Station Sales.** National Association of Broadcasters, 1771 N Street, N.W., Washington D.C. 20036-2891. Tel: 800/368-5644. Annual. Price: $140 to members; $290 to nonmembers.

This guide provides the open market selling prices, and reviews the evolving patterns in radio station values. Information on each transaction includes call letters, station type, market rank, frequency, date sale announced, sale price of station, and previous sale year. Also included is an analysis of appreciation in values for station type groupings, market size groupings and region groupings.

113 **The Television Industry: 1995 Market-by-Market Review.** National Association of Broadcasters, 1771 N Street, N.W., Washington D.C. 20036-2891. Tel: 800/368-5644. Annual. Price: $400 to members; $600 to nonmembers.

This publication provides detailed financial and market data on an DMA basis. Information includes: Actual television market revenues; enhanced revenue projections to assist in budgeting and forecasting; cable penetration: ratings history and station sales.

114 **Regional Differences in Television Station Financial Performance.** National Association of Broadcasters, 1771 N Street, N.W., Washington D.C. 20036-2891. Tel: 800/368-5644. Annual. Price: $75 to members; $150 to nonmembers.

Compares data on station and market financial performance in four major regions of the country: east, south, midwest, and west. The test examines regional differences in net revenue, local/national regional advertising, revenues per TV household delivered, expenses, employee compensation, projectability and cash flow. The text also analyzes the performance of stations separately for both affiliates and independents.

115 **A Financial Profile of Television Stations by Network Affiliations.** National Association of Broadcasters, 1771 N Street, N.W., Washington D.C. 20036-2891. Tel: 800/368-5644. Annual. Price: $100 to members; $200 to nonmembers.

In this publication you will find ABC, CBS, NBC, and FOX comparisons for affiliate prime-time ratings, pre-tax profits, total expenses, advertising revenues and cash flow figures and financial performance. It provides both national and market size level historical reviews. The text also includes a summary of tables for the different affiliate groups, nationwide and by market size, for the four years examined.

116 **The Almanac of Hospital Financial and Operating Indicators.** The Center for Healthcare Industry Performance Studies, 1550 Old Henderson Road, Suite S-277, Columbus, OH 43220. Tel: 800/859-2447. Annual. Price: $95 to members; $350 to nonmembers. Call for information and a brochure.

This annual report, published each fall, analyzes the financial and operating performance of the U.S. hospital industry. Using 77 key financial and operating ratios, the report examines such areas as profitability, liquidity, capital structure, asset activity, length of stay, intensity of service, utilization, pricing, and productivity. Five years of data are presented for national, regional, bedsize, rural, urban, revenue, teaching, and other comparison groups. Additional group data and custom analysis reports are available upon request at any time. Database is updated weekly.

117 **Survey of Industry Activity.** Equipment Leasing Association of America, 1300 North 17th Street, Suite 1010, Arlington, VA 22209. Tel: 703/527-8655. Fax: 703/527-2649. Semiannual. Price: $35 to members; $395 to nonmembers.

Based on a survey of ELA members, this report provides statistical and financial information on the $125 billion U.S. equipment leasing industry.

118 **Leasing Buyer's Guide.** Equipment Leasing Association of America, 1300 North 17th Street, Suite 1010, Arlington, VA 22209. Tel: 703/527-8655. Fax: 703/527-2649. Semiannual. Price: $35 to survey respondents, $395 for members not responding, $70 for members not eligible to respond. Previous year data available for $35.

Contains nationwide listings of key resources for the leasing industry including funding sources, accountants, appraisers, remarketers, insurance specialists, executive recruiters, and attorneys.

AGRICULTURE

ORDER PUBLICATIONS DIRECTLY FROM PUBLISHER

119 **Enterprise Budgets.** Auburn University, 203 Comer Hall, Auburn, AL 36849-5406. Tel: 205/844-5602. Periodic. Price: Free of charge.

Current estimated costs and returns for producing major crop and livestock enterprises in Alabama.

120 **Farm Business Analysis Association—Annual Report.** Auburn University, 203 Comer Hall, Auburn, AL 36849-5406. Tel: 205/844-5602. Annual. Price: Free of charge. Annual report summarizing financial performance and characteristics of Alabama farms enrolled in the association.

121 **Maryland Agricultural Statistics—Summary for 1993.** Agricultural Statistics Service, 50 Harry S. Truman Parkway, Annapolis, MD 21401. Tel: 410/841-5740. Annual. Price: Free of charge.

This is a summary of the major series of agricultural statistics. These series include crop production data, livestock and poultry numbers, production, prices, income and data describing many other facets of agriculture. This publication provides two years of county data for selected data series.

122 **Agricultural Statistics—Annual Report.** Economic Research Service, National Agricultural Statistics Service, U.S. Dept. of Agriculture, 341 Victory Drive, Herndon, VA 22070. Tel: 800/999-6779. Annual. Price: $20. 600 pp. Stock #ZAG-95.

A comprehensive statistical report containing current and historical agricultural data, revised annually.

123 **Agricultural and Nonagricultural Banking Statistics, 1980-1991.** Economic Research Service, National Agricultural Statistics Service, U.S. Dept. of Agriculture, 341 Victory Drive, Herndon, VA 22070. Tel: 800/999-6779. June 1994. Price: $12. 62 pp. Stock #SB-883.

Statistical Bulletin. Operating statistics for 1980-1991 illustrate important differences between agricultural and nonagricultural banks.

124 **Nonmetro, Metro, and U.S. Bank-Operating Statistics, 1987-1989.** Economic Research Service, National Agricultural Statistics Service, U.S. Dept. of Agriculture, 341 Victory Drive, Herndon, VA 22070. Tel: 800/999-6779. March 1991. Price $15. 145 pp. Stock #SB-823.

Statistical Bulletin. Presents and analyzes weighted and unweighted mean-operating statistics for nonmetro, metro, and all U.S. banks for 1987-89.

125 **Farm Credit System Bank and Association Operating Statistics, 1986-1991.** Economic Research Service, National Agricultural Statistics Service, U.S. Dept. of Agriculture, 341 Victory Drive, Herndon, VA 22070. Tel: 800/999-6779. May 1994. Price: $12. 75 pp. Stock #SB-882.

Statistical Bulletin. Describes operating statistics for and structural changes in the Farm Credit System (FCS) banks and associations for 1986-91, including statistics on FCS district loan portfolios.

126 **An Analysis of Financial Performance of Federal Land Banks, Federal Intermediate Credit Bank Farm Credit Bank and Related Associates, 1986-89.** Economic Research Service, National Agricultural Statistics Service, U.S. Dept. of Agriculture, 341 Victory Drive, Herndon, VA 22070. Tel: 800/999-6779. April 1991. Price $9. 24 pp. Stock #AGES 9117.

Staff Report.

127 **Profit Efficiency of Farm Credit System Associations.** Economic Research Service, National Agricultural Statistics Service, U.S. Dept. of Agriculture, 341 Victory Drive, Herndon, VA 22070. Tel: 800/999-6779. November 1991. Price $7.50. 15 pp. Stock #AGES 9155.

Staff report.

128 **Bank Operating Statistics.** Economic Research Service, National Agricultural Statistics Service, U.S. Dept. of Agriculture, 341 Victory Drive, Herndon, VA 22070. Tel: 800/999-6779. May 1994. Price: $25. 3.5" disk. Stock #94014. (George Wallace, ERS, 202/501-6751.)

U.S. data on characteristics of agricultural and nonagricultural banks, 1980-91, including measures of profitability, liquidity, solvency, and efficiency. Also includes State data on return on assets for agricultural and nonagricultural banks.

129 **Farm Credit System Operating Statistics.** Economic Research Service, National Agricultural Statistics Service, U.S. Dept. of Agriculture, 341 Victory Drive, Herndon, VA 22070. Tel: 800/999-6779. Annual. Price $35. Two 3.5" disks. Stock #94011. (Robert Collender, ERS, 202/501-6746)

Data by Farm Credit System association, on mean and weighted mean asset and liability items and income and expense items. Also includes selected lending statistics, 1986-91.

130 **Costs of Production, PKG-15.** Economic Research Service, National Agricultural Statistics Service, U.S. Dept. of Agriculture, 341 Victory Drive, Herndon, VA 22070. Tel: 800/999-6779. Price $24. Stock #PKG-15.

Includes Peanuts: State-Level costs of Production, 1986-88; Cotton: State-Level Costs of Production, 1986-88; Corn: State-Level Costs of Production, 1986-88; Barley: State-Level Costs of Production, 1986-88.

131 **Major Statistical Series of the U.S. Department of Agriculture, Volume 12: Costs of Production.** Economic Research Service, National Agricultural Statistics Service, U.S. Dept. of Agriculture, 341 Victory Drive, Herndon, VA 22070. Tel: 800/999-6779. March 1992. Price: $9. Stock #AH-671-12.

The updated volume describes the estimation procedures and data sources for making estimates of annual costs of production for major crop and livestock enterprises. Each budget assesses cash receipts, itemized cash expenses, economic costs, yields, prices, and net returns.

132 **State-Level Costs of Production, 1987.** Economic Research Service, National Agricultural Statistics Service, U.S. Dept. of Agriculture, 341 Victory Drive, Herndon, VA 22070. Tel: 800/999-6779. March 1989. 88 pp. Price: $12. Stock # AGES 8913.

Staff report.

133 **Barley: State-Level Costs of Production, 1986-88.** Economic Research Service, National Agricultural Statistics Service, U.S. Dept. of Agriculture, 341 Victory Drive, Herndon, VA 22070. Tel: 800/999-6779. June 1990. 26 pp. Price: $9. Stock # AGES 9046.

Staff report.

134 **Costs of Production.** Economic Research Service, National Agricultural Statistics Service, U.S. Dept. of Agriculture, 341 Victory Drive, Herndon, VA 22070. Tel: 800/999-6779. July 1994. Price: $35. Stock # 94010 (Two 3.5" disks) Mitch Morehart, ERS, 202/219-0100.

U.S. and regional data, 1982-92, on corn, grain sorghum, oats barley, wheat soybeans, rice, peanuts, cotton, sugarbeets sugar cane, milk, cow-calf, hog farrow-to-finish, hog farrow-to-feeder, and hog pig-to-finish production costs.

135 **U.S. and State Farm Sector Financial Ratios, 1960-91.** Economic Research Service, National Agricultural Statistics Service, U.S. Dept. of Agriculture, 341 Victory Drive, Herndon, VA 22070. Tel: 800/999-6779. June 1993. Price: $15. Stock # SB-857.

Presents national and state level estimates of liquidity, efficiency, solvency, and profitability ratios.

136 **Profitability of Farm Businesses: A Regional, Farm Type, and Size Analysis.** Economic Research Service, National Agricultural Statistics Service, U.S. Dept. of Agriculture, 341 Victory Drive, Herndon, VA 22070. Tel: 800/999-6779. June 1994. Price: $9. Stock # SB-884.

This report uses recent data to show the wide income variance among farms, a third of which are not profitable, and shows the major part played by larger and more specialized farms in the total production of U.S. agricultural.

137 **Farming Operations and Households in Farm Areas: A Closer Look.** Economic Research Service, National Agricultural Statistics Service, U.S. Dept. of Agriculture, 341 Victory Drive, Herndon, VA 22070. Tel: 800/999-6779. May 1994. Price: $9. Stock # AER-685.

This report examines characteristics of farm business and farm operator households in three groups of counties: farming-dependent, major farming, and residual.

138 **Farm Operating and Financial Characteristics, 1990.** Economic Research Service, National Agricultural Statistics Service, U.S. Dept. of Agriculture, 341 Victory Drive, Hern-

don, VA 22070. Tel: 800/999-6779. August 1993. Price: $15. Stock # SB-860.

Presents operating and financial characteristics, including farm business income, expenses, assets, and liabilities.

139 **Farm Sector Balance Sheet, Including Operator Households, 1960-1989: United States and by State.** Economic Research Service, National Agricultural Statistics Service, U.S. Dept. of Agriculture, 341 Victory Drive, Herndon, VA 22070. Tel: 800/999-6779. August 1991. 211 pp. Price: $15. Stock # SB-826.

Furnishes the latest farm sector balance sheet estimates developed by ERS, incorporating numerous revisions in estimating procedures and changes in data in national and state-level estimates of assets, debt, and equity.

140 **Farm Sector Balance Sheet, Including Operator Households, 1960-1989, and Excluding Operator Households, 1974-89: By Sales Class.** Economic Research Service, National Agricultural Statistics Service, U.S. Dept. of Agriculture, 341 Victory Drive, Herndon, VA 22070. Tel: 800/999-6779. November 1991. 48 pp. Price: $9. Stock # SB-831.

Furnishes the latest farm sector balance sheet estimates developed by ERS. The distribution of farm assets, debt and equity has shifted over time.

141 **Financial Characteristics of U.S. Farms, January 1, 1989: A Summary.** Economic Research Service, National Agricultural Statistics Service, U.S. Dept. of Agriculture, 341 Victory Drive, Herndon, VA 22070. Tel: 800/999-6779. July 1989. 16 pp. Price: $7.50. Stock # AIB-569.

Summarizes information on the financial performance of farmers from the January 1, 1989, Farm Costs and Returns Survey.

142 **Forecasting Farm Income: Documenting USDA's Economic Model.** Economic Research Service, National Agricultural Statistics Service, U.S. Dept. of Agriculture, 341 Victory Drive, Herndon, VA 22070. Tel: 800/999-6779. August 1993. 48 pp. Price: $9. Stock # TB-1825.

Describes the components and equations in USDA's farm income forecasting model, an accounting model for forecasting crop and livestock receipts for 32 individual commodities, government program payments for each program commodity, and expenses for 21 inputs, such as feed, seed, fertilizer, interest, and labor.

143 **Aspects of Farm Finances: Distribution of Income, Family Income, and Direct Payments, 1986.** Economic Research Service, National Agricultural Statistics Service, U.S. Dept. of Agriculture, 341 Victory Drive, Herndon, VA 22070. Tel: 800/999-6779. April 1990. 28 pp. Price $9. Stock # AER-630.

Cross-classifies 1986 Farm Costs and Returns Survey data to more clearly show the diverse nature of farms and their greatly varying financial conditions.

144 **Cash Receipts.** Economic Research Service, National Agricultural Statistics Service, U.S. Dept. of Agriculture, 341 Victory Drive, Herndon, VA 22070. Tel: 800/999-6779. March 1993. Price: $25, includes 3.5" disk. Stock # 89014. (Roger Strickland, ERS, 202/219-0806.)

State data on cash receipts for 25 leading commodities, 1960-91. Includes state rankings by commodity.

145 **Monthly Cash Receipts.** Economic Research Service, National Agricultural Statistics Service, U.S. Dept. of Agriculture, 341 Victory Drive, Herndon, VA 22070. Tel: 800/999-6779.

December 1992. Price: $35, includes two 3.5" disks. Stock # 93008. (Roger Strickland, ERS, 202/219-0806.)

The U.S. data cover 12 major agricultural commodity groups; State data covers three commodity groups.

146 U.S. Farm Income. Economic Research Service, National Agricultural Statistics Service, U.S. Dept. of Agriculture, 341 Victory Drive, Herndon, VA 22070. Tel: 800/999-6779. May 1990. Price: $25, includes 3.5" disk. Stock # 90022. (Cheryl Steele, ERS, 202/219-0793.)

Historical farm income statistics, 1910-1989. Reports gross and net farm income, net cash income, cash receipts, and related data.

147 Structural and Financial Characteristics of U.S. Farms, 1990: 15th Annual Family Farm Report to Congress. Economic Research Service, National Agricultural Statistics Service, U.S. Dept. of Agriculture, 341 Victory Drive, Herndon, VA 22070. Tel: 800/999-6779. March 1994. 64 pp. Price $12. Stock # AIB-690.

About 1.8 million farms operated 1 billion acres of land in the contiguous U.S. in 1990. The average acreage operated was 588 acres per reporting farm, and gross farm sales averaged $63,200.

148 Characteristics of Large-Scale Farms, 1987. Economic Research Service, National Agricultural Statistics Service, U.S. Dept. of Agriculture, 341 Victory Drive, Herndon, VA 22070. Tel: 800/999-6779. April 1993. Price: $9. 24 pp. Stock # AIB-668.

Uses 1987 data and earlier Census of Agriculture data to summarize the major structural and financial characteristics of large-scale farms.

149 Financial Performance of Specialized Corn-Soybean Farms, 1987. Economic Research Service, National Agricultural Statistics Service, U.S. Dept. of Agriculture, 341 Victory Drive, Herndon, VA 22070. Tel: 800/999-6779. January 1990. 12 pp. Price: $7.50. Stock # AIB-583.

Finds that specialized corn-soybean farms fared better financially in 1987 than most other specialized commodity farms.

150 Characteristics and Production Costs of U.S. Wheat Farms, 1989. Economic Research Service, National Agricultural Statistics Service, U.S. Dept. of Agriculture, 341 Victory Drive, Herndon, VA 22070. Tel: 800/999-6779. October 1993. 22 pp. Price $9. Stock # AIB-683.

This research report finds that producing a bushel of wheat cost U.S. farmers an average $2.07 in variable cash expenses in 1989, as individual farms costs ranged from less than $1.37 to more than $3.49 per bushel.

151 Food Cost Review, 1993. Economic Research Service, National Agricultural Statistics Service, U.S. Dept. of Agriculture, 341 Victory Drive, Herndon, VA 22070. Tel: 800/999-6779. Annual. 46 pp. Price $9. Stock # AER-696.

This report presents USDA's findings on the 1993 farm-to-retail rice spread. Food prices increased 2.2 percent in 1993, less than the overall increase in the CPI for the third consecutive year.

152 Costs of Producing U.S. Livestock, 1972-1987: Estimating and Methodology Update. Economic Research Service, National Agricultural Statistics Service, U.S. Dept. of Agriculture, 341 Victory Drive, Herndon, VA 22070. Tel: 800/999-6779. April 1990. 98 pp. Price: $12. Stock # AER-632.

Presents a way to make a consistent set of cost and returns estimates of U.S. livestock production in 1972-87, a period in which there were data gaps and in which many estimating methods and formats were used.

153 Price Spreads for Beef and Pork. Economic Research Service, National Agricultural Statistics Service, U.S. Dept. of Agriculture, 341 Victory Drive, Herndon, VA 22070. Tel: 800/999-6779. February 1994. Price: $25, included 3.5" disk. Stock # 90006. (Lawrence Duewer, ERS, 202/219-1269.)

Monthly data, 1970-93, on farm-to-retail price spreads for beef and pork. Includes farm-to-carcass and carcass-to-retail spreads and retail prices.

154 Costs and Structure of U.S. Hog Production, 1988-91. Economic Research Service, National Agricultural Statistics Service, U.S. Dept. of Agriculture, 341 Victory Drive, Herndon, VA 22070. Tel: 800/999-6779. March 1994. 22 pp. Price: $9. Stock # AIB-692.

Shows that hog producers' receipts and costs from 1988-91 peaked in 1990.

155 Financial Performance of Specialized Hog Farms. Economic Research Service, National Agricultural Statistics Service, U.S. Dept. of Agriculture, 341 Victory Drive, Herndon, VA 22070. Tel: 800/999-6779. December 1989. 12 pp. Price: $7.50. Stock # AIB-578.

Research report finds that specialized hog farms had more favorable financial conditions in 1987 than most other commodity specialty farms.

156 Costs of Producing Oranges in California and Florida, 1988-89. Economic Research Service, National Agricultural Statistics Service, U.S. Dept. of Agriculture, 341 Victory Drive, Herndon, VA 22070. Tel: 800/999-6779. June 1991. 8 pp. Price $7.50.

Research report based on a March 1990 survey.

157 Financial Performance of U.S. Floriculture and Environmental Horticulture Farm Businesses, 1987-91. Economic Research Service, National Agricultural Statistics Service, U.S. Dept. of Agriculture, 341 Victory Drive, Herndon, VA 22070. Tel: 800/999-6779. September 1993. 150 pp. Price: $15. Stock # SB-862.

Statistical bulletin finds that the U.S. green industry is the fastest growing agricultural sector in grower cash receipts, with an average annual growth rate of 9 percent since 1982.

158 Financial Characteristics of Horticultural Farms. Economic Research Service, National Agricultural Statistics Service, U.S. Dept. of Agriculture, 341 Victory Drive, Herndon, VA 22070. Tel: 800/999-6779. September 1993. Price: $25, includes 3.5" disk. Stock # 93019. (Doyle Johnson, ERS, 202/501-7949.

Reports income statements, balance sheets, and financial ratios estimated through the Farm Costs and Returns Survey for all growers of nonedible, horticultural crops, 1987-91. Income and balance sheet data are reported by size of farm and by region. Includes income and sales data form special tabulations of the 1987 Census of Agriculture.

159 Rural Conditions and Trends. Economic Research Service, National Agricultural Statistics Service, U.S. Dept. of Agriculture, 341 Victory Drive, Herndon, VA 22070. Tel: 800/999-6779. Quarterly. Price: 1 yr., $13; 2 yrs., $24; 3 yrs., $35. Stock # RCA.

Track rural events on a variety of subjects: national economic trends, employment and under-employment, industrial structure, earnings and income, poverty, and population. Occasional special articles look at topics such as national economic links to rural America and the farm labor force. Quick-read text and sharp graphics will help you get the information you need.

160 **Crop Values.** Economic Research Service, National Agricultural Statistics Service, U.S. Dept. of Agriculture, 341 Victory Drive, Herndon, VA 22070. Tel: 800/999-6779. Annual. Price: $9. Stock # ZCV-95.

Marketing year average prices and value of production of principal crops, preliminary 1994 and revised 1992 and 1993. Note: State estimates for fruits and nuts included in "Non-citrus Fruits and Nuts, Preliminary."

161 **U.S. Average Costs of Production for Major Field Crops.** Economic Research Service, National Agricultural Statistics Service, U.S. Dept. of Agriculture, 341 Victory Drive, Herndon, VA 22070. Tel: 800/999-6779. December 1991, 15 pp. Price: $7.50 Stock #AIB-639.

Finds that costs of production for most commodities increased only modestly from 1989 to 1990. Cotton rose the most, at 6 percent, while wheat, oats, and barley were relatively stable.

162 **Cotton Production Costs Vary Widely by Region, Yield, and Operation Size.** Economic Research Service, National Agricultural Statistics Service, U.S. Dept. of Agriculture, 341 Victory Drive, Herndon, VA 22070. Tel: 800/999-6779. January 1991, 11 pp. Price: $7.50. Stock #AIB-617.

Describes the cost of producing cotton in 1987 to see how yield, size, irrigation and other inputs, land tenure, and producer age and education affected cotton production costs among and within regions.

163 **Cow-Calf Costs of Production, 1990-91.** Economic Research Service, National Agricultural Statistics Service, U.S. Dept. of Agriculture, 341 Victory Drive, Herndon, VA 22070. Tel: 800/999-6779. May 1993, 24 pp. Price: $9. Stock #AIB-670.

Finds that net returns after both cash and economic costs improved for cow/calf producers in 1990 and 1991.

164 **Farm Business Balance Sheet, 1960-91: United States and by State.** Economic Research Service, National Agricultural Statistics Service, U.S. Dept. of Agriculture, 341 Victory Drive, Herndon, VA 22070. Tel: 800/999-6779. May 1993, 228 pp. Price: $15 Stock #SB-856.

This report furnishes the latest farm business balance sheet estimates developed by ERS.

165 **Loan Repayment Problems of Farmers in the Mid-1980's.** Economic Research Service, National Agricultural Statistics Service, U.S. Dept. of Agriculture, 341 Victory Drive, Herndon, VA 22070. Tel: 800/999-6779. September 1991, 29 pp. Price: $9. Stock #AER-649.

Reviews the bottom line of the 1980's farm financial crisis: farmers' loan defaults and subsequent loan losses. The financial squeeze subsided during the late 1980's, mainly through a combination of debt repayment and loan write-offs.

166 **Farm Production Expenditures.** Economic Research Service, National Agricultural Statistics Service, U.S. Dept. of Agriculture, 341 Victory Drive, Herndon, VA 22070. Tel: 800/999-6779. Annual. Price: $9. Stock #ZPE-95.

Revised 1993 and preliminary, 1994: Estimates of farm production expenditures, by U.S. farm production regions and economic class for major expenses.

167 **Costs of Producing Milk, 1989 & 1990.** Economic Research Service, National Agricultural Statistics Service, U.S. Dept. of Agriculture, 341 Victory Drive, Herndon, VA 22070. Tel: 800/999-6779. Price: $7.50 per copy. Order # AIB-653.

A look at the economic costs of U.S. milk production. Covers average U.S. milk prices, as well as cash receipts per cwt. of milk sold for 1989 and 1990.

168 **Costs of Producing Grapefruit in California & Florida/1988-89.** Economic Research Service, National Agricultural Statistics Service, U.S. Dept. of Agriculture, 341 Victory Drive, Herndon, VA 22070. Tel: 800/999-6779. Price: $7.50 per copy. Order # AER-652.

Based on a March 1990 survey, total costs were $6.82 for producing a 64-pound box of grapefruit in California and $5.00 for an 85-pound box in Florida. 7 pp.

169 **Characteristics & Production Costs of U.S. Soybean Farms, 1990.** Economic Research Service, National Agricultural Statistics Service, U.S. Dept. of Agriculture, 341 Victory Drive, Herndon, VA 22070. Tel: 800/999-6779. Price: $7.50 per copy. Order # AIB-658.

Compares selected farm characteristics and production costs among soybean growers grouped by variable costs, enterprise size, and production region.

170 **Farm Businesses End the Decade with Strong Financial Performance.** Economic Research Service, National Agricultural Statistics Service, U.S. Dept. of Agriculture, 341 Victory Drive, Herndon, VA 22070. Tel: 800/999-6779. Price: $9 per copy. Order # AIB-616.

Presents findings (as of January 1, 1990) on the financial performance of U.S. farms. 21 pp.

171 **Financial Performance of U.S. Farm Business, 1987-90.** Economic Research Service, National Agricultural Statistics Service, U.S. Dept. of Agriculture, 341 Victory Drive, Herndon, VA 22070. Tel: 800/999-6779. Price: $14 per copy. Order # AER-661.

Describes the financial situation of U.S. farms in 1990, when farm businesses continued recovery from the early to mid-1980's. Farm businesses in 1990 were in the strongest financial condition since 1984, based on their overall financial performance.

172 **State-Level Costs of Production: Major Field Crops, 1987-1989.** Economic Research Service, National Agricultural Statistics Service, U.S. Dept. of Agriculture, 341 Victory Drive, Herndon, VA 22070. Tel: 800/999-6779. Price: $11 per copy. Order # SB-838.

Includes data on production cash costs and returns per planted acre, production economic costs and returns per planted acre; and average machinery use per planted acre, by State, for barley, corn, cotton, oats, peanuts, rice, grain sorghum, soybeans, and wheat.

173 **Structural Change in the U.S. Farm Sector, 1974-1987.** Economic Research Service, National Agricultural Statistics Service, U.S. Dept. of Agriculture, 341 Victory Drive, Herndon, VA 22070. Tel: 800/999-6779. Price: $8 per copy. Order # AIB-647.

Summarizes the structure of the U.S. farm sector, and the trend toward fewer but larger farms. Includes data on farm household income vs. nonfarm households.

174 Characteristics & Production Costs of U.S. Rice Farms, 1988. Economic Research Service, National Agricultural Statistics Service, U.S. Dept. of Agriculture, 341 Victory Drive, Herndon, VA 22070. Tel: 800/999-6779. Price: $7.50 per copy. Order # AIB-657.

Compares selected farm characteristics and production costs among rice producers grouped by variable costs, enterprise size, and production region.

175 The Economic Well-Being of Farm Operator Households, 1988-90. Economic Research Service, National Agricultural Statistics Service, U.S. Dept. of Agriculture, 341 Victory Drive, Herndon, VA 22070. Tel: 800/999-6779. Price: $15 per copy. Order # AER-666.

This report, based on household data from the Farm Costs and Returns Survey, describes the characteristics of farm operator households, their farm businesses, and their sources of off-farm income. The average farm household now has an income comparable to that for all households, although well-being varies significantly. About 90 percent of farm operator households received income from off-farm sources.

176 Characteristics & Production Costs of U.S. Grain Sorghum Farms, 1990. Economic Research Service, National Agricultural Statistics Service, U.S. Dept. of Agriculture, 341 Victory Drive, Herndon, VA 22070. Tel: 800/999-6779. Price: $9 per copy. Order # AIB-661.

Covers data on grain sorghum bushels produced, acres planted, location, production costs, variable cash expenses per acre, and average costs.

177 Food Costs . . . From Farm to Retail, 1993. Economic Research Service, National Agricultural Statistics Service, U.S. Dept. of Agriculture, 341 Victory Drive, Herndon, VA 22070. Tel: 800/999-6779. Annual. Price: $7.50 per copy. Order # AIB-698.

This report reviews how much food costs are changing and why. Also examines how much of the consumer food dollar goes to the farmer and how much to food processors and marketers.

178 Agricultural Outlook. Economic Research Service, National Agricultural Statistics Service, U.S. Dept. of Agriculture, 341 Victory Drive, Herndon, VA 22070. Tel: 800/999-6779. Monthly. Price: $9 per issue, $42 for a one-year subscription of 11 issues. Order # AGO.

This publication is the main source for USDA's farm income and food price forecasts. Emphasizes the short-term outlook for all major areas of the agricultural economy. Also presents long-term analyses of such issues as U. S. ag policy, trade forecasts, food safety, the environment, and farm financial institutions.

179 How Costs of Production Vary. Economic Research Service, National Agricultural Statistics Service, U.S. Dept. of Agriculture, 341 Victory Drive, Herndon, VA 22070. Tel: 800/999-6779. Price: $7.50 per copy. Order # AIB-599.

Analyzes groups of producers at various cost levels and shows that costs of producing crops per unit of output vary considerably by farm. 22 pp.

180 U.S. Farm & Farm Related Employment, 1989. Economic Research Service, National Agricultural Statistics Service, U.S. Dept. of Agriculture, 341 Victory Drive, Herndon, VA 22070. Tel: 800/999-6779. Price: $6 per copy. Order # AIB-654.

Examines farm and farm-related employment in industries ranging from farm operations to grocery stores that sell farm products. Also looks at nonmetro reliance on farm jobs and share of total state employment by farm and farm related industries.

181 Agricultural Income & Finance: Situation & Outlook Report. Economic Research Service, National Agricultural Statistics Service, U.S. Dept. of Agriculture, 341 Victory Drive, Herndon, VA 22070. Tel: 800/999-6779. Annual. Price: $9 per copy, $18 for one-year subscription of 4 issues. Order # AIS.

This periodical looks at farm income, profitability, government payments, production expenses, debts and assets, and other areas of farm finance.

182 Agricultural Finance Data Book. Federal Reserve Board, Publications Services, MS 138, Washington, DC 20551. Tel: 202/452-3245. Quarterly. Price: $5 per year. Complimentary for colleges, public libraries and government agencies.

This is a compilation of various data on current developments in agricultural finance. Large portions of the data come from regular surveys conducted by the Board of Governors or Federal Reserve Banks. Other portions come from the quarterly call report data of commercial banks or from the reports of other financial institutions involved in agricultural lending.

183 Missouri Farm Business Summary. Department of Agricultural Economics, University of Missouri, 216 Mumford Hall, Columbia, MO 65211. Tel: 314/882-0136. Annual. Price: Free of charge.

This report summarizes the profit and loss statement, assets used in the farm business, selected production and efficiency factors, and enterprise data, for farmers enrolled in the University sponsored Management Information Record (MIR) Program.

184 Selected Practices and the Financial Indicators of Sustainable Versus Conventional Farms in North Dakota. Department of Agricultural Economics, Agricultural Experiment Station, North Dakota State University, Fargo, ND 58105-5636. Tel: 701/237-7444. Price: $2.50 per report. Order # AEM No. 134.

Farm and financial characteristics of farm operations that use sustainable, mixed-type, or conventional practices were compared. The specific objective was to determine the differences in farm practices and farm finances among conventional, mixed-type, and sustainable practices.

185 Financial and Operating Performance of Cooperative Unit-Train Shippers in North Dakota. Department of Agricultural Economics, Agricultural Experiment Station, North Dakota State University, Fargo, ND 58105-5636. Tel: 701/237-7444. Price: $2.50 per report. Order # AER No. 234.

This study analyzes performance of unit-train shipping cooperative elevators in North Dakota. Financial data from 1978-1986 were used to derive measures of performance, and comparisons are made between single-and-multiple-plant firms. Results indicate that financial and operating performance varies between firm type and geographic location. Further return on equity has declined since 1981.

186 North Dakota Crop Production Economics in 1991. Department of Agricultural Economics, Agricultural Experiment Station, North Dakota State University, Fargo, ND 58105-5636. Tel: 701/237-7444. Price: $2.50 per report. Order # AER No. 268.

Estimates the financial impact and, using a panel of farm operators as a proxy for a typical North Dakota cash grain farm, examines the implication of changes in net farm income on the debt-servicing capacity of grain producers.

187 **Financing North Dakota's Agriculture.** Department of Agricultural Economics, Agricultural Experiment Station, North Dakota State University, Fargo, ND 58105-5636. Tel: 701/237-7444. Price: $2.50 per report. Order # AER No. 228.

This report describes agricultural financial markets in North Dakota. The first section summarizes North Dakota farmers use of debt capital. The second section describes lenders that have extended credit to North Dakota farmers. The final section reviews various public programs of agricultural credit that are available to farmers in the state.

188 **Performance Factors and Management Practices Related to Earnings of East Central North Dakota Crop Farms.** Department of Agricultural Economics, Agricultural Experiment Station, North Dakota State University, Fargo, ND 58105-5636. Tel: 701/237-7444. Price: $2.50 per report. Order # AER No. 224.

The objective of this study was to identify farm management measures that explain variation in returns to operator labor and management. Farm record summary data were used to identify factors related to returns. Interview data from farmers with record summaries were used to determine management practices related to factors associated with returns.

189 **Financial, Managerial, and Attitudinal Characteristics of North Dakota Farm Families: Results of the 1986 Farm Survey.** Department of Agricultural Economics, Agricultural Experiment Station, North Dakota State University, Fargo, ND 58105-5636. Tel: 701/237-7444. Price: $2.50 per report. Order # AER No. 222.

This report is organized into four parts: (1) the financial situation of the farm operators making up the sample; (2) the changes in management practices brought about by the present economic environment; (3) the attitudes and opinions of these operators concerning the causes of the present situation, perceptions of farming and farmers in general, and views on financial assistance policies; and (4) the effects of economic stress on the personal lives of farm and ranch families.

190 **Selected Characteristics of Business Operators in North Dakota Agricultural Trade Centers.** Department of Agricultural Economics, Agricultural Experiment Station, North Dakota State University, Fargo, ND 58105-5636. Tel: 701/237-7444. Price: $2.50 per copy. Order # AER No. 217.

This report examines selected characteristics of business operators and former business operators in six North Dakota communities: Carrington, Casselton, Grafton, Hettinger, Jamestown, and Stanley. Specific characteristics examined include: business characteristics, business financial characteristics, business management characteristics, demographic characteristics, personal financial characteristics, trade patterns, participation in community organizations and activities, and attitudes and perceptions concerning local business condition.

191 **Financial Benchmarks of North Dakota Farm Operators 1992 Update.** Department of Agricultural Economics, Agricultural Experiment Station, North Dakota State University, Fargo, ND 58105-5636. Tel: 701/237-7444. Price: $2.50 per report. Order # AER No. 311.

The purpose of this study was to develop financial benchmarks for North Dakota farm operators. Objectives were to identify financial measures and describe procedures to estimate measures to include as financial benchmarks. Benchmarks were used to determine the financial position and performance of North Dakota farm operators.

192 **Alaska Agricultural Statistics 1994.** Alaska Agricultural Statistics Service, U.S. Department of Agriculture, P.O. Box 799, Palmer, AK 99645. Tel: 907/745-4272. Annual. Price: $5.

Crop and livestock information and statistics for Alaska.

193 **Analysis of Operating Statements of Local Farm Supply and Marketing Cooperatives.** Cooperative Services Program of USDA's RBCDS, Ag Box 3255, Washington, DC 20250-3255. Tel: 202/690-0357. Fax: 202/720-4641. Annual. Price: $4. (RR 134. 11/94)

Operating expenses by cooperative size and type, common size operating statements for 1983-1990.

194 **Corn Belt Grain Cooperatives Adjust to Challenges of 1980s, Poised for 1990s.** Cooperative Services Program of USDA's RBCDS, Ag Box 3255, Washington, DC 20250-3255. Tel: 202/690-0357. Fax: 202/720-4641. Annual. Price: $4. (RR 117. 8/93)

Analysis of operating statement, balance sheet, and structure data for local grain-handling (corn-soybeans) cooperatives in the Corn Belt for 1983-91. Two size groups, and detailed operating expenses for 1989.

195 **Wheat Grain Cooperatives Adjust to Challenges of 1980s, Poised for 1990s.** Cooperative Services Program of USDA's RBCDS, Ag Box 3255, Washington, DC 20250-3255. Tel: 202/690-0357. Fax: 202/720-4641. Annual. Price: $3. (RR 132. 6/94.)

Analysis of operating statement, balance sheet, and structure data for local grain-handling (wheat, grain sorghum, barley, oats) cooperatives in the Southern Plains, Northern Plains, and Pacific Northwest for 1983-91. Two size groups, and detailed operating expenses for 1989.

196 **Farmer Cooperatives Magazine (Monthly).** Cooperative Services Program of USDA's RBCDS, Ag Box 3255, Washington, DC 20250-3255. Tel: 202/690-0357. Fax: 202/720-4641. Annual. Price: $21 Annual Subscription (Via GPO); $2.25 per copy.

Carries news and research reports relating to the issues and challenges facing farmers and their cooperatives. Occasional issues feature common size income statement data for farm cooperatives based on size. Only national publication devoted exclusively to agribusiness cooperatives.

197 **Working with Financial Statements.** Cooperative Services Program of USDA's RBCDS, Ag Box 3255, Washington, DC 20250-3255. Tel: 202/690-0357. Fax: 202/720-4641. Annual. Price: $2. (CIR 43. 1995)

Designed to help members understand and analyze their cooperative's financial statements. This report is oriented to grain marketing and farm supply cooperatives.

198 **Cooperative Financing and Taxation.** Cooperative Services Program of USDA's RBCDS, Ag Box 3255, Washington, DC 20250-3255. Tel: 202/690-0357. Fax: 202/720-4641. Annual. Price: $2. (CIR 1 Section 9. 1991)

Provides an overview of cooperative finance and the characteristics of agricultural cooperatives that make their financial and taxation requirements unique.

199 **Leasing as an Alternative Method of Financing for Agricultural Cooperatives.** Cooperative Services Program of USDA's RBCDS, Ag Box 3255, Washington, DC 20250-

3255. Tel: 202/690-0357. Fax: 202/720-4641. Annual. Price: $3. (RR 89. 1989)

This publication discusses lease contracting from a pre-and post-1986 tax reform standpoint.

200 **Equity Redemption and Member Equity Allocations of Agricultural Cooperatives.** Cooperative Services Program of USDA's RBCDS, Ag Box 3255, Washington, DC 20250-3255. Tel: 202/690-0357. Fax: 202/720-4641. Annual. Price: $4. (RR124.)

This 1991-92 survey of farmer cooperatives shows current equity redemption practices including how equity is distributed between allocated and unallocated accounts. The report updates a 20 year-old study and reflects many changes in the financial, operational, and structural makeup of cooperatives. Equity redemption practices are at the center of all cooperative financial considerations.

201 **Farmer Cooperative Statistics, 1993.** Cooperative Services Program of USDA's RBCDS, Ag Box 3255, Washington, DC 20250-3255. Tel: 202/690-0357. Fax: 202/720-4641. Annual. Price: $3. (SR 43.)

This annual report provides aggregate statistical information about farmer cooperatives which are classified by principal product marketed and major function. Information collected from 4,222 cooperatives. Trends in number of cooperatives, membership, sales volume, liabilities and net worth were reported.

202 **Top 100 Cooperatives, 1993 Financial Profile.** Cooperative Services Program of USDA's RBCDS, Ag Box 3255, Washington, DC 20250-3255. Tel: 202/690-0357. Fax: 202/720-4641. Annual. Price: $1. (Misc. Report)

This is a reprint of articles and charts from "Farmer Cooperatives" magazine. They present a financial snapshot of the nation's 100 largest agricultural cooperatives—from gross profit and net operating margins to return on total assets, debt to asset ratios, and liquidity measures. Some cooperatives use this data as a barometer to measure their own financial status. Earlier annual reports available. Individual cooperatives not identified.

203 **Production Costs for Selected Florida Vegetables, 1991-1992.** University of Florida, Food & Resource Economics Department, PO Box 110240, Gainesville, FL 32611-0240. Tel: 904/392-1826. Annual. Price: Free of charge.

Costs of production are reported for thirteen vegetables crops produced in one or more of ten production areas in Florida. In all, twenty-seven crop area combinations are presented along with net return analyses. Labor and machinery cost breakdowns by operation are detailed in appendix tables.

204 **Contribution of the Turfgrass Industry to Florida's Economy, 1991/92: A Value Added Approach.** University of Florida, Food & Resource Economics Department, PO Box 110240, Gainesville, FL 32611-0240. Tel: 904/392-1826. Annual. Price: $15.00.

This survey shows sales, cash costs, assets purchased, depreciation and profit margin for Florida's turfgrass industry, 1991-92.

205 **Cost and Returns for Rice Production on Muck Soils in Florida, 1992.** University of Florida, Food & Resource Economics Department, PO Box 110240, Gainesville, FL 32611-0240. Tel: 904/392-1826. Annual. Free of charge.

Costs and returns for rice production on muck soils in Florida during the 1992 season were estimated from previously published data and additional updated information provided by local producers and dealers servicing them. An efficient 560-acre farm, growing a main crop and a ratoon crop in rotation with sugarcane or vegetables, was assumed. (Report EI 92-2).

206 **An Economic and Agronomic Profile of Florida's Turfgrass Sod Industry.** University of Florida, Food & Resource Economics Dept., PO Box 110240, Gainesville, FL 32611-0240. Tel: 904/392-1826. Annual. Free of charge.

The report consists of two parts; In the first part, key findings from the 1987 study are discussed. Variables are examined within the context of firm size and soil type and include sod production, sod harvesting, irrigation practices, and industry problems. Part two attempts to uncover important changes in the industry which have transpired over the 25 years from 1963 to 1987. (Report ER92-1)

207 **Budgeting Costs and Returns for Central Florida Citrus Production, 1991-92.** University of Florida, Food & Resource Economics Department, PO Box 110240, Gainesville, FL 32611-0240. Tel: 904/392-1826. Annual. Free of charge.

Estimated costs and returns of growing round oranges in the Central Florida citrus area are presented. Central Florida production area refers to Polk and Highlands counties. The format presented may be used by individual growers to budget costs and returns, utilizing individual data on specific groves. (Report EI 92-4)

208 **Budgeting Costs and Returns for Indian River Citrus Production, 1991-92.** University of Florida, Food & Resource Economics Department, PO Box 110240, Gainesville, FL 32611-0240. Tel: 904/392-1826. Annual. Free of charge.

Estimated costs and returns of growing seedless grapefruit in the Indian River area of Florida. The format presented may be used by individual growers to budget costs and returns, utilizing individual data on specific groves. (Report EI 92-6)

209 **Budgeting Costs and Returns for Southwest Florida Citrus Production, 1991-92.** University of Florida, Food & Resource Economics Department, PO Box 110240, Gainesville, FL 32611-0240. Tel: 904/392-1826. Annual. Free of charge.

Estimated costs and returns of growing processed-market round oranges and fresh-market seedless grapefruit in the Southwest area of Florida. This report presents two budgets constructed from current data and provides a format for growers to analyze costs and returns from their individual records. (Report EI 92-5)

210 **Estimated Cost of Packing Florida Citrus, 1990-91 Season.** University of Florida, Food & Resource Economics Department, PO Box 110240, Gainesville, FL 32611-0240. Tel: 904/392-1826. Annual. Free of charge.

A summary of the estimated weighted average with comparative packing costs per 4/5 bushel carton for Interior and Indian River region for each type of fruit is presented. (Report EI 92-7)

211 **Estimated Average Picking, Roadsiding, and Hauling Charges for Florida Citrus, 1990-91 Season.** University of Florida, Food & Resource Economics Department, PO Box 110240, Gainesville, FL 32611-0240. Tel: 904/392-1826. Annual. Free of charge.

A summary of the 1990-91 season picking, roadsiding, and hauling charges for various citrus fruit varieties is presented in this report. Comparative charges for the 1987-88 and 1988-89 seasons are also presented. (Report EN-28)

212 **1994 Enterprise Budgets for Agronomic Crops.** University of Florida, Food & Resource Economics Department, PO Box 110240, Gainesville, FL 32611-0240. Tel: 904/392-1826. Annual. Free of charge.

Estimated budgets for various agronomic crops.

213 **Crop Enterprise Cost Analysis.** University of Georgia, College of Agricultural & Environmental Sciences, Coliseum, Room 2301, Athens, GA 30602-4356. Tel: 706/542-2632. Annual. Price: Free of charge.

Includes budgets that are designed to assist in estimating potential costs and returns for major field crops in the Coastal Plains and adjoining areas of South Georgia.

214 **Georgia Agriculture at a Glance.** University of Georgia, College of Agricultural & Environmental Sciences, Coliseum, Room 2301, Athens, GA 30602-4356. Tel: 706/542-2632. Annual. Price: Free of charge.

The purpose of this report is to provide an overview of Georgia agriculture, and how the industry is a part of today's economy. Includes the top ten commodities and their ranking in Georgia and the United States, and also includes expenditures by item for Georgia farms.

215 **1994 Farm Machinery Custom Rates.** University of Georgia, College of Agricultural & Environmental Sciences, Coliseum, Room 2301, Athens, GA 30602-4356. Tel: 706/542-2632. Annual. Price: Free of charge.

Provides rates commonly charged by custom operator for farm machinery operations.

216 **Enterprise Budget Worksheet Program and Data Diskette.** University of Idaho, Department of Agricultural Economics & Rural Sociology, Moscow, ID 83843. Tel: 208/885-7635. Biennial. Price: $25.

This Program calculates the cost of producing livestock and crops. A data diskette for each district requires the Enterprise Budget Worksheet Computer Program and are available for $5.

217 **Crop and Livestock Cost and Return Estimates Notebook (Includes 3-ring binder).** University of Idaho, Department of Agricultural Economics & Rural Sociology, Moscow, ID 83843. Tel: 208/885-7635. Biennial. Price: $50.

Cost and return estimates show the typical cost of producing livestock and crops in four districts in Idaho.

218 **District I Crop Cost and Return Estimates-Northern Idaho: 17 Budgets.** University of Idaho, Department of Agricultural Economics & Rural Sociology, Moscow, ID 83843. Tel: 208/885-7635. Biennial. Price: $9.40.

These cost and return estimates show typical cost of producing crops commonly grown in Northern Idaho.

219 **District II Crop Cost and Return Estimates-Southwestern Idaho: 17 Budgets.** University of Idaho, Department of Agricultural Economics & Rural Sociology, Moscow, ID 83843. Tel: 208/885-7635. Biennial. Price: $9.40.

These cost and return estimates show typical cost of producing crops commonly grown in Southwestern Idaho.

220 **District III Crop Cost and Return Estimates-Southcentral Idaho: 30 Budgets.** University of Idaho, Department of Agricultural Economics & Rural Sociology, Moscow, ID 83843. Tel: 208/885-7635. Biennial. Price: $15.80.

These cost and return estimates show typical cost of producing crops commonly grown in Southcentral Idaho.

221 **District IV Crop Cost and Return Estimates-Southeastern Idaho: 18 Budgets.** University of Idaho, Department of Agricultural Economics & Rural Sociology, Moscow, ID 83843. Tel: 208/885-7635. Biennial. Price: $9.70.

These cost and return estimates show typical cost of producing crops commonly grown in Southeastern Idaho.

222 **Idaho Livestock Budgets: 26 Budgets (Includes 3-ring binder).** University of Idaho, Department of Agricultural Economics & Rural Sociology, Moscow, ID 83843. Tel: 208/885-7635. Biennial. Price: $17.15.

These cost and return estimates show typical cost of producing livestock under alternative management systems.

223 **Dairy Farm Management.** Cornell University, Agricultural Experiment Station, College of Agriculture & Life Sciences, 155 Warren Hall, Ithaca, NY 14853. Tel: 607/255-4534. Annual. Price: One free copy, thereafter $3. each.

Provides complete market value financial data plus physical, economic, and financial management performance indicators.

224 **Financial Characteristics of Illinois Farms 1992-93.** University of Illinois at Urbana-Champaign, Agricultural Finance Program, Department of Ag Economics, Urbana, IL 61801. Tel: 217/333-1827. Annual. Price: $5.

The data contains financial performance measures and characteristics of a sample of Illinois farms enrolled in the Illinois Farm Business Farm Management Association. The data is grouped into categories based on size, type, tenure, age and financial structure of the farm business. The format and procedures used to calculate the data resemble those used by Robert Morris Associates.

225 **Summary of Illinois Farm Business Records 1993.** University of Illinois at Urbana-Champaign, Department of Ag Economics, Urbana, IL 61801. Tel: 217/333-0754. Annual. Price: $5.

The data presents 1993 income and expenses reported by over 7,000 participating Illinois farmers-including nearly 20 percent of all farms of 500 acres or more. Includes an analysis of recent changes in farm income for grain and livestock enterprises throughout Illinois. Comprehensive tables show average 1993 results by farm size, region, type of operation, and soil fertility rating.

226 **Crop and Livestock Budgets, Examples for Illinois, 1993-94.** University of Illinois at Urbana-Champaign, Department of Ag Economics, Urbana, IL 61801. Tel: 217/333-1811. Biennial. Price: $5.

Presented in this report are cost and return estimates for the major crop and livestock enterprises in Illinois. Crop data is presented for different areas of the state and utilizing different tillage systems and different crop rotations.

227 **New Mexico Crop Cost and Return Estimates.** New Mexico State University, Cooperative Extension Service, Box 30003, Dept. 3169, Las Cruces, NM 88003-8003. Tel: 505/646-3215. Annual. Price: Free of charge.

Presented in this report are cost and return estimates for irrigated and dryland crops in New Mexico. A total of 59 representative farm budgets covering all major water types, land types, farm sizes, and producing areas are released annually. Cost and

928

returns for traditional and nontraditional crops and for commercial and part-time farms are estimated.

228 **Understanding and Using NMSU Crop and Livestock Enterprise Budgets.** New Mexico State University, Cooperative Extension Service, Box 30003, Dept. 3169, Las Cruces, NM 88003-8003. Tel: 505/646-3215. Updated as needed. Price: Free of charge.

This publication will describe how to read and interpret a New Mexico State University crop or livestock enterprise budget.

229 **Range Livestock Cost and Return Estimates for New Mexico.** New Mexico State University, Agricultural Experiment Station, Box 30003, Dept. 3169, Las Cruces, NM 88003-8003. Tel: 505/646-3215. Annual. Price: Free of charge.

This report gives cost and return estimates for range livestock ranches in all areas of New Mexico. Cost and return estimates are given for different sizes of cow/calf operations, for five different ranching areas in New Mexico, for yearling stocker operations in the northeast corner of the state, and for sheep ranches in southwest and central New Mexico.

230 **Enterprise Budgets.** Oregon State University, Ballard Extension Hall 213, Corvallis, OR 97331-3601. Tel: 503/737-1409. Published as developed. Price: Call for enterprise listing and charge (if any).

Estimated costs and returns for producing agricultural commodities on a per unit basis. Information is collected from panels that include farmers, researchers, field representatives, lenders, and agency personnel.

231 **Executive Summary 1994 Kansas Farm Records Analysis.** Kansas State University, Cooperative Extension Service, Extension Agricultural Economics, Waters Hall, Manhattan, KS 66506-4026. Tel: 913/532-1503. Annual. Price: Free of Charge.

This annual report of whole farm and enterprise cost-of-production analysis information is the result of the efforts of many farm families throughout Kansas keeping detailed farm business and financial records. The tables will provide you with a glimpse of the information on a state-wide basis.

232 **The Enterprise Analysis Report 1994 Management Information.** Kansas State University, Kansas Farm Management Associations, Department of Agricultural Economics, Cooperative Extension Service, Manhattan, KS 66506. Tel: 913/532-1503. Annual. Price: $5.00.

This study uses empirical data from Kansas Farm Management Association member farms. This data is on a calendar year basis and may include cost of production information from parts of two fiscal years; for example, wheat and feeder cattle.

233 **The Annual Report 1994 Management Information.** Kansas State University, Kansas Farm Management Associations, Department of Agricultural Economics, Cooperative Extension Service, Manhattan, KS 66506. Tel: 913/532-1503. Annual. Price: $5.00.

This report provides detailed information for understanding agricultural production and economic conditions affecting the profitability of agriculture and farming operations. The information is summarized by association, county, income categories, type of farm, etc., to allow comparison with records or association computer analysis summaries.

234 **The County Report—1994 Farm Records Analysis Summary.** Kansas State University, Kansas Farm Management Associations, Department of Agricultural Economics, Cooperative Extension Service, Manhattan, KS 66506. Tel: 913/532-1503. Annual. Price: $5.00.

This analysis report represents an aggregate analysis of farms grouped into the following two categories: a) Net Farm Income, and b) Farm Type. This report is for persons that have need for Farm Management Association farm summaries that have been localized by counties.

235 **Agricultural Economics Report.** Michigan State University East Lansing, Department of Agricultural Resources, Agriculture Hall, East Lansing, MI 48824-1039. Tel: 517/355-2153. Annual. Price: Free of charge. Number 580.

This report provides statistical information about the financial results on crop farms during 1994, information on the trends in resource use, income and costs during the last four years, and production costs for comparative analysis and forward planning.

236 **Pennsylvania Dairy Farm Business Analysis.** Pennsylvania State University, College of Agricultural Sciences, Cooperative Extension, University Park, PA 16802. Tel: 814/865-5461. Annual. Price: Free of charge. Extension Circular 403.

Includes information from 1,060 Pennsylvania dairy farms which are owner-operator units for which wholesale milk sales and sale of dairy stock account for most of the gross income produced. Contains dairy farms business financial analysis, balance sheet data, cast receipts, expenses, and net farm income. Also includes information on debt carrying capacity.

237 **Farm Economics.** Pennsylvania State University, College of Agricultural Sciences, Cooperative Extension, University Park, PA 16802. Tel: 814/865-5461. Bimonthly. Price: Free of charge.

Periodically includes data, such as hourly wages paid for hired labor, regarding farm operations in Pennsylvania.

238 **Financial Performance Measures for Iowa Farms.** Publications Distribution, Iowa State University, Ames, IA 50011. Tel: 515/294-5247. Annual. Price: $.50 per copy. (Fm 1845)

Provides financial measures by farm size and type to help judge an operation's performance. Includes worksheets to analyze liquidity, profitability, solvency and liquidity, and historical comparative data.

239 **Estimated Costs of Crop Production in Iowa.** Publications Distribution, Iowa State University, Ames, IA 50011. Tel: 515/294-5247. Annual. Price: $.75 per copy. (Fm 1712)

Includes estimated costs of production for corn, corn silage, soybeans, oats, and alfalfa hay.

240 **Livestock Enterprise Budgets for Iowa.** Publications Distribution, Iowa State University, Ames, IA 50011. Tel: 515/294-5247. Annual. Price: $1.00 per copy. (Fm 1815)

Includes estimated costs of production for swine, beef cattle, dairy cattle, and sheep.

241 **Iowa Farm Custom Rate Survey.** Publications Distribution, Iowa State University, Ames, IA 50011. Tel: 515/294-5247. Annual. Price: Free of charge. (Fm 1698)

Provides average rates charged for custom machinery operations based on a survey of custom operators and farmers.

242 **Iowa Farm Costs and Returns.** Publications Distribution, Iowa State University, Ames, IA 50011. Tel: 515/294-5247. Annual. Price: $1.75. (Fm 1789)

Summarizes costs and returns, production efficiencies, and financial position of commercial farming operations, by farm size. Data is from records of Iowa Farm Business Association members.

243 **Iowa Land Value Survey.** Publications Distribution, Iowa State University, Ames, IA 50011. Tel: 515/294-5247. Annual. Price: Free of charge. (Fm 1825)

Summarizes current Iowa farmland market values. Based on a survey of real estate brokers, appraisers, and lenders.

244 **1993 Iowa Farm Finance Survey.** Publications Distribution, Iowa State University, Ames, IA 50011. Tel: 515/294-5247. Annual. Price: $.25. (Fm 1843)

Summarizes the financial condition of a random sample of Iowa farmers, and classifies them by solvency and cash flow coverage.

245 **Colorado Agricultural Statistics 1994.** Colorado Ag Statistics Service, 645 Parfet Street, Rm. W201, Lakewood, CO 80215. Tel: 303/236-2300. Annual. Price: $10.

Statistics include: Farm income and cash receipts; Marketing year average prices by commodity; Monthly prices received by commodity.

246 **Financial Characteristics of Record-keeping and Average Farms in North Dakota.** Department of Agricultural Economics, North Dakota State University, Fargo, ND 58105. Tel: 701/237-7444. Price: $2.50 per copy. AER No. 245.

This study compares the economic performance and financial characteristics of North Dakota farmers belonging to the Farm Business Management Education recordkeeping program and those randomly surveyed in the U.S. Department of Agriculture's Farm Costs and Returns Survey. Measures of FCRS and FBME firm profitability are shown.

247 **Entering the 1990s: An Update of the Financial Status of North Dakota Farm and Ranch Operators.** Department of Agricultural Economics, North Dakota State University, Fargo, ND 58105. Tel: 701/237-7444. Price: $2.50 per copy. AER No. 260.

This report addresses how the drought conditions in North Dakota in the late 1980s, plus the farm financial situation, affected the financial status of farmers and ranchers. Selected financial items for farm and ranch operators are shown in one of the eight tables included in the publication.

248 **Revitalizing the Retail Trade Sector in Rural Communities: Experiences of 13 North Dakota Towns.** Department of Agricultural Economics, North Dakota State University, Fargo, ND 58105. Tel: 701/237-7444. Price: $2.50 per copy. AER No. 250.

Provides information and insights that will enhance informational programs developed to meet the needs of rural business persons and community leaders. Shows balance sheet and income statement characteristics of businesses surveyed in twelve North Dakota towns.

STATEMENT STUDIES INDEX
FOR
PARTS I-IV

STATEMENT STUDIES INDEX FOR PARTS I-IV

A complete description of each industry category listed below begins on page 19.

STATEMENT STUDIES INDEX FOR PARTS I-IV

A complete description of each industry category listed below begins on page 19.

STATEMENT STUDIES INDEX FOR PARTS I-IV

A complete description of each industry category listed below begins on page 19.

STATEMENT STUDIES INDEX FOR PARTS I-IV

A complete description of each industry category listed below begins on page 19.

RMA INDUSTRY COMPARISON-C-139

FOR USE WITH RMA ANNUAL STATEMENT STUDIES

INDUSTRY: _____

Name: _____ Address: _____ SIC#: _____

	Date		Date		Date	
	RMA	Customer	RMA	Customer	RMA	Customer
ASSETS						
Cash & Equivalents						
Trade Receivables–(net)						
Inventory						
All Other Current						
Total Current						
Fixed Assets (net)						
Intangibles (net)						
All Other Non-Current						
Total Assets	100.0%	100.0%	100.0%	100.0%	100.0%	100.0%
LIABILITIES						
Notes Payable-Short Term						
Cur. Mat.-L/T/D						
Trade Payables						
Income Taxes Payable						
All Other Current						
Total Current						
Long Term Debt						
Deferred Taxes						
All Other Non-Current						
Net Worth						
Total Liabilities & Net Worth	100.0%	100.0%	100.0%	100.0%	100.0%	100.0%
INCOME DATA						
Net Sales	100.0%	100.0%	100.0%	100.0%	100.0%	100.0%
Cost Of Sales						
Gross Profit						
Operating Expenses						
Operating Profit						
All Other Expenses (net)						
Profit Before Taxes						
RATIOS						
Current						
Quick						
Sales/Receivables						
Cost of Sales/Inventory						
Cost of Sales/Payables						
Sales/Working Capital						
EBIT/Interest						
Net Profit + Depr., Dep., Amort./Cur. Mat. L/T/D						
Fixed/Worth						
Debt/Worth						
% Profit Before Taxes/Tangible Net Worth						
% Profit Before Taxes/Total Assets						
Sales/Net Fixed Assets						
Sales/Total Assets						
% Depr., Dep., Amort./Sales						
% Officers', Directors', Owners' Comp/Sales						
Net Sales ($)						
Total Assets ($)						

SAMPLE

THIS FORM MAY BE PURCHASED FROM:
BANKERS SYSTEMS INC.
Box 1457
ST. CLOUD, MN 56302-1457 • (612) 251-3060

936

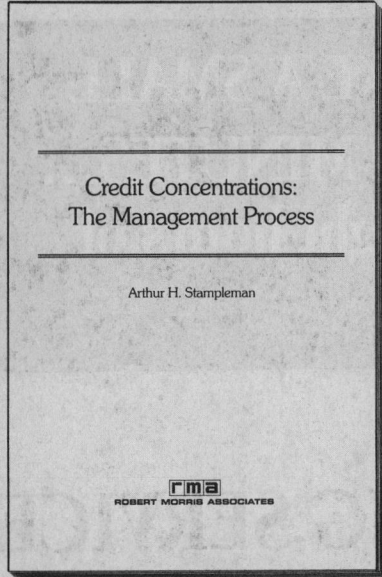

What Every Lender Should Know About Bankruptcy

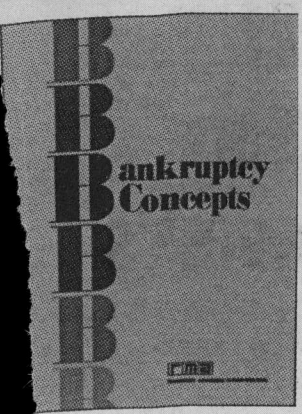

Not so long ago, troubled loans were often resolved by a workout, by filing a lawsuit against the borrower, or by a foreclosure on collateral securing the loan. Today, debtors are more creative twisting the bankruptcy laws to delay and even completely avoid their obligations to you, the loan officer.

How to Level the Playing Field

Clearly, lenders need help—the kind of help this comprehensive, yet jargon-free, book provides. *Bankruptcy Concepts: A Desk Reference for Lenders* will:

Familiarize you with the provisions of the Bankruptcy Code and how these provisions relate to one another

Alert you to the serious and inflexible deadlines often present in bankruptcy cases

Suggest courses of action to take in troubled loan cases to minimize the effects of bankruptcy

Act as a general reference to enhance communications between loan officers and your legal staff and outside bankruptcy counsel

This last goal, by itself, will pay for this book many times over by maximizing the results obtained in a bankruptcy case while minimizing costs to the lender.

A Practical Approach Explained in Lay Terms

Bankruptcy Concepts serves as a practical guide to the Bankruptcy Code and bankruptcy courts. It presents information in lay language and assists you in understanding unfamiliar terms and concepts by providing

A commonsense discussion of the Code presented in a logical format with a discussion of general bankruptcy concepts followed by a chapter-by-chapter review of the various forms of bankruptcy relief, including liquidation, reorganization, and plans of individuals with regular incomes

Extensive cross-referencing

A glossary of bankruptcy terms with concise definitions of key terms

A detailed index of terms and concepts providing a quick reference to relevant sections in the book

What's in It for You?

A Brief History of Bankruptcy Law
• Early Bankruptcy Acts • Organization of the Bankruptcy Code • Additional Bankruptcy Authorities

Workout Agreements
• Workouts Without Bankruptcy • Treatment of Workout Agreements • Prepackaged Bankruptcies

Basic Bankruptcy Principles
• Role of Players in a Bankruptcy Case • The Automatic Stay • Proofs of Claim

Transfer Avoidance
• Fraudulent Conveyances in Upstream Guaranties • Preferences • Equitable Subordination

Liquidation
• Eligibility for Relief • Chapter 7 Players • Proofs of Claim or Interest • Objections to Claims • Effect of the Automatic Stay • Dismissal • Discharge of Indebtedness • Reaffirmation of Indebtedness and Redemption of Personal Property

Reorganization
• Eligibility of Relief • Chapter 11 Players • Proofs of Claim or Interest • Objections to Claims • Reorganization • Adequate Protection • Debtor-in-Possession Financing • Automatic Stay Issues • Conversion or Dismissal • Choice of Conversation or Dismissal • Likelihood of Success • Dismissal for Lack of Good Faith • Plan and Disclosure Statement

Adjustments of Debts of a Family Farmer
• Eligibility for Relief • Chapter 12 Trustees • Proofs of Claim or Interest • Discharge

Adjustments of Debts
• Eligibility for Relief • Chapter 13 Trustees • Proofs of Claim or Interest • Discharge • Objections to Plan

Price: $55.00
DISCOUNT PRICE FOR RMA MEMBER INSTITUTIONS: $38.00

You can order three ways: Send payment to ROBERT MORRIS ASSOCIATES Customer Service Department, P.O. Box 8500 S-1140, Philadelphia, PA 19178 Or call (800) 677-7621 and charge it to your VISA® or MasterCard®. Or fax your order to (215) 851-9205.

Please send me ___ copies of *Bankruptcy Concepts* (32651) at _____ per copy.

❑ Check enclosed
❑ Charge to my credit card
  ❑ VISA ❑ MasterCard

VISA *MasterCard*

TOTAL_____

Credit Card Account Number _____ Expiration Date _____ Signature _____

Name _____ Title _____

Shipping Address _____

City _____ State _____ Zip _____

Calif., Ga., Ill., and Pa. residents please include applicable sales tax. Price subject to change without notice. All payments must be made in U.S. dollars, and all checks must be drawn on U.S. banks. Please allow 3 to 4 weeks for delivery. When returning materials to RMA, please ship via UPS or any other method that is traceable and insured.

SSB/95

CREDIT CONSIDERATIONS
VOLUME III

- **Other Industries**
  - Film Makers
  - Hazardous Waste Handlers
  - Hotel/Casinos
  - Mining Companies
  - Environmental Waste Management

- **Real Estate/Contractors**
  - Asbestos Removal Firms
  - Adult Congregate Living Facilities
  - Golf Course Communities
  - Small Hotels, Motels, Inns

- **Retailers**
  - Floral Shops
  - Independent Grocers
  - Mobile Home Dealers
  - Video Stores

- **Wholesalers**
  - Beer Distributors

- **Service Companies**
  - Accounting Firms
  - Car Rental Agencies
  - Car Washes
  - Cleaning and Janitorial Services
  - Community Associations
  - Local Exchange Telephone Companies
  - Motion Picture Theaters
  - Travel Agencies

The more you know about your customer's business the better your lending decision is going to be. Therefore, it follows that the more industries with which you are familiar, the better your loan portfolio can be. With this need in mind, RMA published *Credit Considerations,* Volumes I and II—overviews of more than 80 industries.

RMA's *Credit Considerations: Financial and Credit Characteristics of Selected Industries,* Volume III, brings you the same reliable information on 27 more industries and three forms of financing: government contract receivables, fund accounting, and community development corporations.

Each article gives you a description of the industry; its financial information; an analysis of potential credit risk; typical financing needs; and collateral unique to the particular industry.

Credit Considerations, Volume III, comes in a convenient three-ring binder with dividers that separate the major sections of the book:

- **Agricultural Credits**
  - Vineyards

- **Manufacturers**
  - Food Processors
  - Generic Pharmaceuticals
  - Sawmills
  - Specialty Chemical Manufacturers

Each of the contributors to *Credit Considerations,* Volume III, is an experienced commercial banker who specializes in the subject he or she covers. Their experience can help you make better informed lending decisions in each of these industries.

This book is written primarily for commercial lenders, analysts, and loan review personnel. However, if you have a need to understand a credit from any perspective—senior management, correspondent banking, training—you'll want this book on your desk for constant reference.

Price: $130.00

DISCOUNT PRICE FOR RMA MEMBER INSTITUTIONS: $89.00